W9-AQE-182

MODERN
CONCORDANCE
TO THE
NEW TESTAMENT

MODERN
CONCORDANCE
TO THE
NEW TESTAMENT

Based on the French *Concordance de la Bible, Nouveau
Testament* produced under the aegis of the *Association
de la Concordance française de la Bible*

Edited and revised following all current English
translations of the New Testament by

MICHAEL DARTON

Theodore Lownik Library
Illinois Benedictine College
Lisle, Illinois 60532

DOUBLEDAY & COMPANY, INC.
Garden City, New York

© 1976 by Darton Longman & Todd Ltd and Doubleday & Company Inc.

Texts from the *Jerusalem Bible*, © 1966, 1967 and 1968 by Darton Longman
& Todd Ltd and Doubleday & Company Inc.

Arrangement in Themes and by Greek roots based on the French *Concordance de la Bible, Nouveau Testament*, edited by Sr Jeanne d'Arc O.P.,
published under the aegis of the *Association de la Concordance française de
la Bible* by Editions du Cerf and Editions Desclee De Brouwer, 1970

All Rights Reserved
Printed in the United States of America
First Edition

225.45
D226m

WITHDRAWN

CONTENTS

A Card on which is printed:
List of signs and symbols used as marginal references
List of signs and symbols used within the texts
List of abbreviated names of books of the New Testament
List of abbreviated names of books of the Old Testament

The publishers of this Concordance gratefully acknowledge the debt that this work, though completely revised and edited in English, owes to the groundwork and research of the French editors.

INTRODUCTION

THE CONCORDANCE

In English-speaking countries, a Concordance to the Bible has for many years been an essential instrument for the student, and almost as necessary a reference book for the minister of religion. It consists (in the words of the Shorter Oxford Dictionary) of *an alphabetical arrangement of the principal words contained* in the Bible, *with citations of the passages in which they occur*.

The most common uses for such a book have been two:

To find any given text in the Bible and learn its context even if only one of the principal words in that text is remembered;

To make a survey of all that was written in the Bible on a given subject – or all that was written or said on a given subject by one writer or speaker – by looking up the texts collected under a key word on that subject.

Till now, the typical Concordance has been based on the Authorised (or 'King James') Version, and a Concordance on such a plan is comparatively easy to compile. It remains of great value as long as every student of the Bible uses only the one version of the text for all purposes, and as long as that version is accepted as invariably and precisely true to the original text which lie behind it.

A Concordance based on the Authorised Version

In the centuries during which 'the Bible' was, for the average English-speaking reader, the Authorised Version, and the older texts in Hebrew and Greek were tacitly assumed simply to be more primitive stages in the development of the scriptures, a Concordance to the Authorised Version was a valuable and adequate tool for the student and scholar. As such, it was efficient in many ways – though not in all.

For instance, if the student was looking for a New Testament text in which the original writer had written the Greek word for 'flesh' (*sarx*), he would find every instance except one listed under the English word FLESH. The one exception appeared some distance away: it was under CARNAL. In the main, an index of the English words used had many correspondences with an index of the Greek words in the New Testament. But there were enough differences to ensure that the Concordance, though perfect as an index to the words in the English Authorised Version, could not be used as an authoritative guide to the thinking of the original writers in their own languages.

The requirements of a modern Concordance

In the nineteen-seventies, when there are no less than five accepted versions of the Bible very widely used in English-speaking countries for public worship and for study, and many more versions used for reading in less formal circumstances; when, inside a single parish church or in a single classroom, different texts may be successively used or compared – then a Concordance which relies solely on the actual words used in the Authorised Version is no longer going to serve the main purposes of its compilation. It is well known that it is no longer possible to translate the ancient languages into English by substituting a literal equivalent for each word; the unit of translation is often the phrase and sometimes the sentence, rather than the word.

So, whereas in the Authorised Version, every occurrence of 'flesh' in Greek (except one) is represented by *flesh* in English, modern Bibles are found to make use of all the following alternatives:

flesh	natural
carnal	human standards
body	worldly standards
bodily	unspiritual self
nature	lower nature
sensual	outward appearance
physical being	mankind
mortal	every one
human beings	race
self-indulgence	people

and in addition, 'no flesh' in Greek can appear in English as:

no one   no man
no living thing   no human

It will be noticed that there are words in these lists which must occur elsewhere in the New Testament with quite different meanings or in different senses: the most obvious example is perhaps *race* ('ethnic group' but also 'contest'). A purely verbal Concordance to modern texts would bring together into one list all instances of the use of 'race' without any reference to differences in meaning or sense whatever. Such a Concordance would also entirely fail to bring together all the instances in which the original Greek text used the idea *flesh*.

Again, we should consider the old type of Concordance and examine how accurate it was as a guide to what the original writers of the Bible wrote, and therefore how they thought. As far as the English and Greek words were in a one-for-one relation (as in the Revised Version of 1880), each Greek word being represented invariably by the same English word, we can safely use an English verbal Concordance as an index to the original Greek words.

But suppose the writer was a stylist who varied his phrases and his words; or suppose that two writers dealing with the same subject habitually used different words and expressions to convey the same meaning – but we need not merely suppose it: it happened.

To express the idea 'light, give light to, lighten', writers in the New Testament use not only a group of related words:

phōs   *phōstēr*   *epi-phainō*
phōtizō   *phōtismos*   *epi-phōskō*
phōteinos   *phanos*   *epi-phauskō*
                phainō

but also words which have no relation at sight:

lampō   *lychnos*   *augazō*   *phengos*
lampas   *lychnia*   *augē*
lampros   *ap-augasma*
lamprōs   *di-augazō*
lamprotēs   *di-augēs*
ek-lampō   *tel-augōs*
peri-lampō

So even if it were possible to base the arrangement of a New Testament Concordance on the Greek words used, it would not serve the student or the scholar as a true index and guide to the theme, subjects and ideas of the books of the New Testament.

A Concordance must be thematic as well as verbal; it must be both English and Greek.

About this Concordance

The work has been brilliantly done in the French language by a group under the direction of Sr Joan of Arc, O.P., as a first stage in the provision of a Concordance to the whole Bible. This English Concordance is based on that groundwork, though a very great number of revisions and changes in order have been made in the transference from a modern French Testament to modern English Testaments.

The Concordance is English *and* Greek. The headings, or key-words, and the related words serving as headings or subdivisions, are in English – so the Concordance can be used to find any text, with its reference, when any one of its principal words, in English, is known. The Greek words are also given at the head of each subdivision, grouped according to their roots, and annotated to show their respective frequency; these Greek words are all transliterated into the English alphabet, though there are Greek indexes at the end in the original Greek characters. A marginal sign against each text indicates which of the Greek words is represented by the English key-word of the text.

The Concordance is thematic *and* verbal. The presentation is by subject matter: 341 themes subdivided under their Greek roots according to sense. In these themes, all the 5,600-odd Greek words (apart from definite and indefinite articles and the most common prepositions) of the New Testament, and the many more words in the vocabulary of English New Testaments, are conveniently grouped so that the Concordance succeeds on the one hand in avoiding the scattering of the texts into as many separate articles or headings as there are distinguishable words, and on the other hand in marking the close connection between words which, though slightly different in form, are similar in derivation or meaning.

So, for instance, a number of words which by the accident of their English forms would be separated in the old style of Concordance, are here grouped together (under BELIEVE – FAITH):

Belief, Believe   Doubt
Believer   Entrust (to)
Commission (to)   Faith, Faithful
Conviction   Faithless

Fidelity	Reliable
Good faith	Sceptical
Hesitate	Sure
Incredible	Trust (with)
Lack of faith	Trustworthy
Little faith	Truth
Not to believe	Unbeliever
Refuse to believe	Unfaithful

A parallel grouping of Greek words, according to their related meanings, will also be found, although this does not influence the order of the entries for the English user. For instance, under the same heading (GATHERING) are:

ek-klēsia

syn-eimi

syn-erchomai

ap-antaō, ap-antēsis, hyp-antaō, hyp-antēsis, syn-antaō

sym-ballō

a-throizō, syn-a-throizō, ep-a-throizomai

sy-strephō, sy-strophē

epi-stasis, syn-eph-istēmi

*syn-agō, syn-agōgē, apo-syn-agōgos, archi-syn-agōgos,
    epi-syn-agō, epi-syn-agōgē*

logeia, syl-legō

sōreuō, epi-sōreuō

syn-airō

The English index lists the words used in the New Testaments of *all* the English-language Bibles in wide use, and refers the user to the key-words which form the heading under which each of the words will be found in its brief context.

The index of Greek words similarly refers the user to the English headings under which texts containing each word are found in translation. While the Greek index allows this work to be used as an analytical Concordance to the Greek Testament with all the textual quotations given in English translation, it is also possible to use the book as a complete and accurate Concordance to the New Testament in any English translation without reference to any Greek words at all.

Its use, then, for many readers will be as a Concordance to the English New Testament which gives invaluable insights into subtle connections between words and themes in the Bible, and at times to differences and distinctions between them, by immediate and easy reference to the words of the original Greek lying behind the English texts.

LAY-OUT

This Concordance is divided into Themes. Each Theme begins with a heading of one, two or three key-words in large type between rules.

Beneath this heading appears a list of all the headings within the Theme, accompanied, where appropriate, by the major Greek root forms. In this list of headings, the main headings – usually, though not always, introducing a single Greek root – are in **bold type**. All other headings are in ordinary (medium) type. For example, in the Theme HEAVEN, the list of headings is:

1. Heaven – the Heavens: *ouranos* 　1: Heaven, Heavenly – Sky – Air 　2: Heaven, Heavenly – Earth, 　　Earthly	**2. Heaven – Sky:** *dio-petēs*

(Following this, and before the first main heading introducing all its various subdivisions and texts, may come one or more Notes, mostly concerning special marginal references, but all denoting points of particular interest and importance within the framework of the Theme. Notes may be of this kind (in MAN – PEOPLE – WOMAN):

For Son of Man *see* **SON – DAUGHTER 1. d)**

or of this kind (in EARTH – LAND – COUNTRY):

For Heaven and Earth *see* **HEAVEN 1.2:**

or concerning marginal references:

A = Angel　　　　J = the Jews

in texts where it may be of importance to students to be able to pick out at once those in which Angels or the Jews feature.)

Then appears the first main heading—unless the entire Theme is based upon one single Greek root and its derivatives, in which case there are no main headings at all. A main heading introducing a section based upon a single Greek root is followed immediately by an alphabetical list of the Greek root and its secondary and derivative forms. Each form is numbered consecutively according to the total number of times—the frequency with which—it was used by the writers of the New Testament. With that number to the left of each form, the frequency itself appears to the right, in italics. The numbers on the left then act as marginal references to the texts, so that any Greek form at all can immediately be linked to its appropriate texts. It has, however, occasionally been necessary to split up a single Greek form over two Themes in this Concordance, because of widely divergent senses in English which were nevertheless comparable in Greek thought. Where this has occurred, the proportions—the number of times the form is used in the section compared with the total number of times used in the New Testament—are shown as the frequency. For example:

1. FREE, SET FREE, RELEASE – RANSOME, REDEEM: *LUŌ*

2	*luō*	*30/42*	7 *lytrōtēs*	*1*
6	*lytron*	*2*	8 *anti-lytron*	*1*
4	*lytroō*	*3*	1 *apo-luō*	*52/67*
5	*lytrōsis*	*3*	3 *apo-lytrōsis*	*10*

and the figures 2 to 8 will appear as marginal references to the text within the section; the figure 1, as the basic form of the section, is omitted. (Note that the basic form of the section is not necessarily the form in the heading!) Though in this example there are eight different Greek forms, there are many cases in the Concordance where the list comprises just one.

(It is possible that below this list of Greek forms, a Note such as the ones in parenthesis above may appear. If there is a Note at this point, its scope is obviously limited to influence within this one section only.)

Where, during compilation, it was found that there were very few examples of some Greek words of very similar meaning, a main heading may introduce more than one

Greek form, using subheadings to do so. For instance (in the Theme HOUSE):

4. Room – Storey
  1: Private room – Hiding place – Storehouse: *tameion*
  2: Upper room, Room upstairs: *hyper-ōon*
  3: Upper room, Room upstairs: *ana-gaion*
  4: Storey, Floor: *(tri)-stegos*

Otherwise, and generally, subheadings and sub-subheadings are used either to indicate distinctions in the English meanings although translating one Greek root and derivatives, or to separate one or two Greek derivative forms that may be of particular importance to students and scholars.

There are a very few Themes that have no headings at all, just a list of Greek forms leading on to the texts. (For example, INHERIT – HEIR – HERITAGE.)

The Texts

The references to the left of each text quoted are abbreviated according to the usage of the *Jerusalem Bible*: see the List of Abbreviated Names of the Books of the New Testament. It is hoped that the abbreviations will be readily comprehensible to everyone.

Immediately following any reference there may appear a *marginal* reference: either one of the signs and symbols used as marginal references throughout the Concordance (see the List of Signs and Symbols Used as Marginal References), or a marginal reference applying only within the Theme or section and indicating some point of particular importance to students and scholars – a Note to this effect will preface the Theme or section in this case.

Between these marginal references and the texts themselves, there may also be a number which (as outlined above) indicates which of the secondary and derivative Greek forms is being translated on that line of text; if no number appears, it is the basic Greek form that is being translated.

The texts as they are printed are taken, for the most part, directly from the *Jerusalem Bible* – here to be regarded as a representative modern translation. (It should be remembered at all times that the headings and the indexes are based upon, and drawn from, *all* the most used modern translations in the English-speaking world.) In each text, the Greek word specifically translated into English is printed in *italics*; the rest of the text, in ordinary (Roman) type, comprises usually just enough for the reader to grasp the immediate context, or enough to support the sense. The translation of the Greek word may not always be a single word in English; translation of verbs in particular may call upon the use of a phrase. Past, future and passive verbs do not usually have their auxiliaries italicised, though some active Greek verbs normally translated as passive English verbs cannot be treated in that way: *thaumazō*, which the Authorised Version translates as 'to marvel', in this Concordance appears mostly as 'to *be astonished*', for example. Where the text used has for one reason or another become less than literal in translation, each text with such a passage in it has the literal translation quoted within brackets. Brackets are also reserved for Greek textual variants and editorial additions either to complete the sense or to impart useful information to scholar or student. See also the List of Signs and Symbols Used Within the Texts. When an Old Testament text is quoted (from the New Testament), an additional reference is given within parentheses.

HOW TO USE THIS BOOK

A person will be able to use this Concordance

to recall to his mind a quotation from the New Testament of which he can remember only a word or two, or perhaps only the main idea;

to see what the New Testament has to say on a particular theme – more particularly, what Jesus or God or St Paul (for example) had to say;

and for these two purposes, the *English Index* is invaluable;

to study the original Greek words and their use by the original writers, so understanding more fully exactly what those writers had in mind and wanted to say;

to understand why there may be differences – and divisive differences – between modern English translations, by seeing clearly the underlying unity of ideas and expression in the Greek train of thought;

and for these two purposes, the *Greek Index* is essential.

The English Index

Entries in the English Index, while most frequently single nouns, adjectives or verbs (though pronouns and prepositions are by no means excluded), may also represent the expression more of an idea, and thus comprise two or even three related forms. For example:

> Dawn
> but: Employ, Employment
> and: Have, Had, Has

with either the most obvious or the most used form first – often the same thing.

However, to avoid errors, all forms are cross-indexed so that even in cases where two forms would normally have been separated into individual entries because of alphabetical order (e.g. Get, Got; or Easier, Easy), the reader is directed to the right place.

The richness and wide use of English idiom within all modern translations has also necessitated the inclusion of many entries consisting of phrases and clauses; for example:

> Have a child
> Have (a thing) done
> Have on, Wear
> Have to

so that a reader researching a Theme, for instance, should not be afraid to think in terms of such natural and idiomatic forms of expression.

Directly beneath each entry appears an exact reference to where the word, words, phrase or clause in question is to be found in the main body of the text, indicated by the (title of the) Theme under which it has been classified, and the section number or numbers within that Theme. The title of the Theme is given in full so that in the case of English homonyms there can be no question of which sense is meant by any reference.

Very frequently there is more than one reference beneath an entry. To help the student or scholar, various simple typographic devices have been used to distinguish the relative importance of each reference.

Important references are printed in **bold type**; such a reference means that the word or words of the entry appear in the main heading of the section indicated by the reference.

Slightly less important references appear in ordinary (medium) type, and mean that the word or words of the entry appear in the subheading or sub-subheading of the section indicated by the reference.

References preceded by a + and printed in *italic type* show that the word or words of the entry do not appear in any

heading but may nevertheless be of sufficient importance to be able to be looked up in the section indicated.

When a reference includes two or more sections from the same Theme, the title of the Theme is not repeated unless a later reference is of the third kind above.

The Greek Index

The Greek Index is much more like a normal index. Entries are of one word each; the total number of times each word is used in the New Testament is also shown. Where one Greek word has had to be split over more than one English Theme, the titles of the Themes are given, together with the proportion of times the word is used under each classification, so obviating the need for any typographic distinctions over relative importance.

For further details see the Introductory explanation at the beginning of the Index itself, and the Note on Greek Transliteration below.

There is also an *Index to Proper Names*, of people and places.

A Note on the Transliteration of the Greek

In this Concordance, the process of transliterating the original Greek has been carried out not with the overall design of producing a letter-for-letter form instantly recognisable by those who already have a reasonable vocabulary in Greek, but with the intention of producing a form that is firstly legible to those who are not at all familiar with the Greek alphabet, and secondly *pronounceable* by them according to the fashion generally accepted in schools and universities and by scholars.

This does unfortunately mean, however, that those who do have a fair knowledge of Greek may occasionally find a transliteration that at first seems anomalous although immediately recognisable.

Perhaps the most disturbing of these apparent anomalies will be in the Greek combinations

$$\gamma\gamma, \gamma\kappa, \gamma\xi, \text{ and } \gamma\chi,$$

where the (first) γ has in this Concordance been changed to an *n*, so that these combinations become

$$ng, nk, nx, \text{ and } nch.$$

As might be expected, θ, $\dot{\rho}$, ϕ and ψ become *th, rh, ph* and *ps* (and those not familiar with the Greek alphabet should remember the last two in particular should they wish to consult the Greek Index at the correct point). The Greek χ has been made *ch* rather than *kh* because it was thought that readers would be quite familiar with the Scottish or German pronunciation. As for vowels, η and ω have been rendered $\bar{e}$ and $\bar{o}$. The Greek υ has been made both *u* and *y* depending where in the word it comes: the idea behind this is to try to prevent readers' unwittingly making it the English *u* or *y*, but to recall to them the fact that it represents a sound we do not have, a sound like the French *u*, the German *ü* and the Swedish *y*.

CONCORDANCE OF THEMES
AND WORDS

A

ABOMINATION

1: Abomination = Sacrilege
2: Abomination = (What is) Detest- | able, Loathsome, Obscene, Outrageous

3 *bdelyktos* 1   2 *bdelyssō* 2
1 *bdelygma* 6

1: ABOMINATION = SACRILEGE

Mt 24 15   you see the disastrous *abomination* . . . set up in the Holy Place (Dn 9 27)
Mk 13 14   you see the disastrous *abomination* set up where it ought not to be (Dn 9 27)

2: ABOMINATION = (WHAT IS) DETESTABLE, LOATHSOME, OBSCENE, OUTRAGEOUS

Lk 16 15   *what* is thought highly of by men *is loathsome* in the sight of God.
Rm 2 22   2 you *despise* idols, yet you rob their temples.
Tt 1 16   3 they are *outrageously* rebellious and quite incapable of doing good.
Rv 17 4   The woman . . . was holding a gold winecup filled with ⌈the *disgusting* (or: *abominations* and the) filth of her fornication;
5   Babylon the Great, the mother of all the prostitutes and all the *filthy practices* on the earth.
21 8   the legacy . . . for those who break their word, or worship 2 *obscenities*, for murderers and fornicators . . . is the second death
27   Nothing unclean may come into [the city]: no one who does *what is loathsome* or false,

ABOVE – OVER

1. Above, Up, Over: *anō*
1: From above, Up(ward), Above = Heaven(ly)
2: High, Up(wards), Above – the Top, Brim
3: Over, (Directly) Above

4: Jesus (Far) Above all, Higher than all
2. God and Christ Above all, Over all: *epi*
3. Above, Superior to, Over: *hyper*

1. ABOVE, UP, OVER: *ANŌ*

1 *anō*   *11*   3 *ep-anō* (5)
5 *anōterikos*   *1*   4 *hyper-anō* 3
2 *anōthen*   (10)

1: FROM ABOVE, UP(WARD), ABOVE = HEAVEN(LY)

E = Height, Heaven // Earth, Below

Jn 3 3   2 unless a man is born ⌈*from above* (or: again), he cannot see the kingdom of God.
7   2 You must be born ⌈*from above* (or: again).
31 E   2 He who comes *from above* is above all others;
8 23 E   You are from below; I am *from above*.
11 41   Then Jesus lifted *up* his eyes and said:
Jn 19 11   You would have no power over me . . . if it had not been 2 given you *from above*;
Ac 2 19 E   I will display portents in heaven *above*
Ga 4 26 E   The Jerusalem *above*, however, is free
Ph 3 14   I am racing for . . . the prize to which God calls us *upwards* to receive
Col 3 1   you must look for the things that are in *heaven*, where Christ is . . . ² Let your thoughts be on *heavenly* things, 2 E   not on the things that are on the earth,

Jm 1 17   2 all that is good . . . is given us *from above*; it comes down from the Father of all light;
3 15 E   principles of this kind are not the wisdom that comes down 17   2 *from above*: they are only earthly, animal . . . ¹⁷whereas 2 the wisdom that comes down *from above* is . . . pure;

2: HIGH, UP(WARDS), ABOVE – THE TOP, BRIM

Mt 27 51   2 the veil of the Temple was torn in two from *top* to bottom;
Mk 15 38   2 the veil of the Temple was torn in two from *top* to bottom.
Lk 14 10   My friend, move up *higher*.
Jn 2 7   'Fill the jars with water', and they filled them to the *brim*.
19 23   [Jesus's] undergarment was . . . woven in one piece from 2 ⌈*neck* to hem (lit. the *top*);
Ac 19 1   5 Paul made his way ⌈*overland* (lit. through the *upper* country) as far as Ephesus,
Heb 10 8   [Jesus] says ⌈*first* (lit. *above*): You did not want . . . the sacrifices, the oblations,
12 15   Be careful that . . . no root of bitterness should begin to grow (G *upwards*) and make trouble;

3: OVER, (DIRECTLY) ABOVE

Mt 2 9   3 [the star] went forward and halted *over* the place where the child was.
27 37   3 *Above* [Jesus's] head was placed the charge against him;
Heb 9 5   4 outspread *over* [the throne of mercy] were the glorious cherubs.
Rv 20 3 ⓓ   [The angel] threw him into the Abyss, and shut the entrance 3 and sealed it *over* him,

4: JESUS (FAR) ABOVE ALL, HIGHER THAN ALL

Jn 3 31   3 He who comes from above is *above* all others . . . He who 3 comes from heaven (§ is *above* all others)
Ep 1 21   [God used his power to make Christ sit at his right hand, in 4 heaven,] *far above* every Sovereignty, Authority, Power,
4 10   4 The one who rose *higher* than all the heavens . . . is none other than the one who descended.

2. GOD AND CHRIST ABOVE ALL, OVER ALL: *EPI*

epi (+ gen.) (2)

Rm 9 5   Christ . . . is *above* all, God for ever blessed!
Ep 4 6   one God who is Father of all, *over* all, through all and within all.

3. ABOVE, SUPERIOR TO, OVER: *HYPER*

hyper (+ acc.) (5)

Mt 10 24 <   The disciple is not *superior to* his teacher, nor the slave *superior to* his master.
Lk 6 40 <   The disciple is not *superior to* his teacher;
Ep 1 22 X   [God] made [Christ], ⌈as the ruler of (lit. *above*) everything, the head of the Church;
Ph 2 9 X   God . . . gave [Christ] the name which is *above* all other names

ABRAHAM – ISAAC – JACOB

Abraham 73 E	*Esau*	*3*	*Hamor** [*Emmor*]	*1* (Ac 7 16)
I *Isaac* 20	*Hagar* [*Agar*]	*2* (Ga 4)	*Lazarus**	*4* (Lk 16)
J *Jacob* 25	(*Ishmael*)	(Ga 4)		
	Rachel	*1* (Mt 2)		
	Rebecca [*Rebekah*]	*1* (Rm 9)	*Ramah** [*Rama*]	*1* (Mt 2)
S *Sarah* [*Sara*]	*4*		*Shechem** [*Sychem*]	2 (Ac 7 16

A = *Abraham – Isaac – Jacob*
P = *Jacob* = the People of Israel
Note: Jacob is called Israel in Rm 9 6

Mt	1 1	A genealogy of Jesus Christ, son of David, son of *Abraham*:
	2 A	*Abraham* was the father of *Isaac*, *Isaac* the father of *Jacob*, *Jacob* the father of Judah and his brothers,
	17	The sum of generations is therefore: fourteen from *Abraham* to David;
	2 18	(Jr 31 15) A voice was heard in Ramah*, sobbing ... it was *Rachel* weeping for her children,
	3 9	do not presume to tell yourselves, 'We have *Abraham* for our father', because ... God can raise children for *Abraham* from these stones.
	8 11 A	many will come ... to take their places with *Abraham* and *Isaac* and *Jacob* at the feast in the kingdom of heaven;
	22 32 A	(Ex 3 6) I am the God of *Abraham*, the God of *Isaac* and the God of *Jacob*. God is God, not of the dead, but of the living.
Mk	12 26 A	(Ex 3 6) I am the God of *Abraham*, the God of *Isaac* and the God of *Jacob*.
Lk	1 33 P	[Jesus] will rule over the House of *Jacob* for ever
	55	[God] has come to the help of Israel ... mindful of his mercy ... to *Abraham* and to his descendants
	73	[the Lord remembers] the oath he swore to our father *Abraham*
	3 8	do not think of telling yourselves, 'We have *Abraham* for our father' because ... God can raise children for *Abraham* from these stones.
	34 A	[Jesus was as it was thought] son of *Jacob*, son of *Isaac*, son of *Abraham*,
	13 16	this woman, a daughter of *Abraham* whom Satan has held bound these eighteen years – was it not right to untie her bonds on the sabbath day?
	28 A	you see *Abraham* and *Isaac* and *Jacob* and all the prophets in the kingdom of God, and yourselves turned outside.
	16 20	[There was a rich man] and at his gate there lay a poor man called Lazarus* ... [22] Now the poor man died and was carried away ... to the bosom of *Abraham*.
	22	
	23	The rich man also died ... [23] ... in Hades he looked up and saw *Abraham* a long way off with Lazarus* in his bosom. [24] So he cried out, 'Father *Abraham*, pity me and send Lazarus* to ... cool my tongue',
	24	
	25	'My son,' *Abraham* replied [to the rich man] ' ... during your life good things came your way, just as bad things came the way of Lazarus* ... [27] The rich man replied, ' ... send Lazarus* to my ... [28] ... five brothers, to give them warning ... ' [29] 'They have Moses and the prophets,' said *Abraham* 'let them listen to them.' [30] 'Ah no, father *Abraham*,' said the rich man
	29	
	30	
	19 9	[Zacchaeus] too is a son of *Abraham*;
	20 37 A	Moses ... calls the Lord (Ex 3 6) the God of *Abraham*, the God of *Isaac* and the God of *Jacob*.
Jn	4 5 J	Sychar, near the land that *Jacob* gave to his son Joseph.
	6 J	[6] *Jacob*'s well is there
	12 J	Are you a greater man than our father *Jacob* ... ?
	8 33	[The Jews answered Jesus,] We are descended from *Abraham* and we have never been the slaves of anyone;
	37	you are descended from *Abraham*; but in spite of that you want to kill me
	39	'Our father is *Abraham*'. Jesus said to them: 'If you were *Abraham*'s children, you would do as *Abraham* did. [40] As it is, you want to kill me ... that is not what *Abraham* did.'
	40	
	52	*Abraham* is dead ... [53] Are you greater than our father *Abraham* ... ?
	53	
	56	Your father *Abraham* rejoiced to think that he would see my Day; he saw it and was glad. [57] The Jews then said, 'You are not fifty yet, and you have seen *Abraham*!' [58] Jesus replied: ' ... before *Abraham* ever was, I Am'.
	57	
	58	
Ac	3 13 A	(Ex 3 6, 15) the God of *Abraham*, *Isaac* and *Jacob*, the God of our ancestors ... has glorified his servant Jesus,
	25	You are ... the heirs of the covenant God made with our ancestors when he told *Abraham* (Gn 22 18):
	7 2	The God of glory appeared to our ancestor *Abraham*,
	8 A	when his son *Isaac* was born [Abraham] circumcised him on the eighth day. *Isaac* did the same for *Jacob*, and *Jacob* for the twelve patriarchs.
	12 J	(Gn 42 2) When *Jacob* heard that there was grain for sale in Egypt, he sent our ancestors there on a first visit,
	14 J	(Gn 45 9–11) Joseph then sent for his father *Jacob* and his whole family, a total of seventy-five people. [15] (Gn 46 3f) *Jacob* went down into Egypt and (Gn 49 33) after he and our ancestors had died there, [16] (cf. Gn 33 19; 50 13) their bodies were brought back to Shechem* and buried in the tomb that *Abraham* had bought and paid for from the sons of Hamor*, the father of Shechem*.
	15 J	
	16	
	17	the time drew near for God to fulfil the promise he had solemnly made to *Abraham*,
	32 A	(Ex 3 6) I am the God of your ancestors, the God of *Abraham*, *Isaac* and *Jacob*.
	46 P	(cf. 2 S 7 2) [David] asked permission to have a temple built for the 「House (▽God) of *Jacob*,
	13 26	My brothers, sons of *Abraham*'s race,

Rm	4 1	Apply this to *Abraham*, the ancestor from whom we are all descended.
	2	If *Abraham* was justified as a reward for doing something, he would really have had something to boast about.
	3	(Gn 15 6) *Abraham* put his faith in God, and this faith was considered as justifying him.
	4 9	Think of *Abraham* ... his faith ... was considered as justifying him,
	12	follow our ancestor *Abraham* along the path of faith he trod before he had been circumcised.
	13	The promise ... was not made to *Abraham* ... on account of any law
	16	those who belong to the faith of *Abraham* who is the father of all of us.
	19 S	Even the thought that his body was past fatherhood ... and *Sarah* too old to become a mother, did not shake his belief.
	9 6	Not all those who descend from Israel (= Jacob) are Israel; [7] not all the descendants of *Abraham* are his true children. Remember (Gn 21 12): It is through *Isaac* that your name will be carried on,
	7 I	
	9 S	(Gn 18 10) I shall visit you ... and *Sarah* will have a son.
	10 I	*Rebecca* ... was pregnant by our ancestor *Isaac*,
	13 J E	(Ml 1 2,3) I showed my love for *Jacob* and my hatred for *Esau*.
	11 1	I, an Israelite, descended from *Abraham*
	26 P	(Is 59 20) The liberator will come from Zion, he will banish godlessness from *Jacob*.
2 Co	11 22	Israelites? So am I. Descendants of *Abraham*? So am I.
Ga	3 6	Take *Abraham* for example (Gn 15 6): he put his faith in God, and this faith was considered as justifying him. [7] ... it is those who rely on faith who are the sons of *Abraham*. [8] Scripture ... proclaimed the Good News long ago when *Abraham* was told (Gn 12 3): In you all the pagans will be blessed.
	7	
	8	
	9	Those ... who rely on faith receive the same blessing as *Abraham*, the man of faith.
	14	This was done so that in Christ Jesus the blessing of *Abraham* might include the pagans,
	16	the promises were addressed to *Abraham* and to his descendants
	18	it was precisely in the form of a promise that God made his gift to *Abraham*.
	29	Merely by belonging to Christ you are the posterity of *Abraham*,
	4 22	*Abraham* had two sons, one (= Ishmael) by the slave-girl, and one (= Isaac) by his free-born wife.
	24	the women stand for the two covenants. The first who comes from Mount Sinai, and whose children are slaves, is *Hagar* – [25] since Sinai (§*Hagar*) is in Arabia
	25 I	
	28 I	you ... like *Isaac*, are children of the promise,
Heb	2 16	(cf. Is 41 8–9) [Jesus] took to himself descent from *Abraham*.
	6 13	When God made the promise to *Abraham*, he swore by his own self,
	7 1	*Melchizedek* ... went to meet *Abraham* ... [2] ... it was to him that *Abraham* gave a tenth of all that he had.
	2	
	4	how great this man [Melchizedek] must have been, if the patriarch *Abraham* paid him a tenth of the treasure ...
	5	[5] ... the descendants of Levi who are admitted to the priesthood are obliged ... to take tithes ... from their own brothers although they too are descended from *Abraham*. [6] But this man, who was not of the same descent, took his tenth from *Abraham*, and he gave his blessing to the holder of the promises.
	6	
	9	Levi himself, who received tithes, actually paid them, in the person of *Abraham*,
	11 8 A	It was by faith that (cf. Gn 12 1–4) *Abraham* obeyed the call to set out ... [9] ... (cf. Gn 26 3; 35 12) he arrived ... in the Promised Land, and lived there ... with *Isaac* and *Jacob*, who were heirs with him of the same promise.
	9	
	11 S	It was equally by faith that *Sarah* ... was made able to conceive,
	17 I	It was by faith that (cf. Gn 22) *Abraham*, when put to the test, offered up *Isaac*. He offered to sacrifice his only son even though the promises had been made to him [18] (Gn 21 12) It is through *Isaac* that your name will be carried on.
	18 I	
	20 I J	It was by faith that this same *Isaac* gave his blessing to *Jacob* and *Esau* for the still distant future. [21] By faith *Jacob*, when he was dying, blessed each of Joseph's sons,
	21 E J	
	12 16 E	be careful that there is no immorality, or that any of you does not degrade religion like *Esau* (cf. Gn 25 33), who sold his birthright for one single meal.
Jm	2 21	*Abraham* our father was justified by his deed (Gn 22 9), because he offered his son *Isaac* on the altar ... [23] ... (Gn 15 6) *Abraham* put his faith in God ... that is why he was called (Is 41 8) 'the friend of God'.
	23 I	
1 P	3 6 S	[wives should be obedient to their husbands] like *Sarah*, who was obedient to *Abraham*, and called him (Gn 18 12 G) her lord.

ABYSS – HADES – HELL

1. **Gulf:** *chasma*
2. **Abyss – the Underworld – Pit, Underground cave**
   1: Abyss – the Underworld: *a-byssos*
      a) the Sea
      b) Place of the dead, Sheol, the Underworld

   c) Place of demons
   2: Consign to the Underworld, Send to Hell – Pit, Underground cave: *siros* and *tartaroō*
3. **Hades – the Underworld – Hell:** *hadēs*
4. **Hell:** *geenna*

1. GULF: *CHASMA*

chasma 1

Lk 16 26 [Abraham replied to the rich man:] between us and you a great *gulf* has been fixed,

2. ABYSS – THE UNDERGROUND – PIT, UNDERGROUND CAVE

1: ABYSS – THE UNDERWORLD: *A-BYSSOS*

2 *bythos* 1   1 *a-byssos* 9

a) the Sea

2 Co 11 25 2 I have been ... once adrift in the *open sea* for a night and a day.

b) Place of the dead, Sheol, the Underworld

Rm 10 7 to bring Christ back from the dead ... (Dt 30 13) Who will go down to the *underworld*?

c) Place of demons

Lk 8 31 [the demons] pleaded with [Jesus] not to order them to depart into the *Abyss*.
Rv 9 1 a star ... was given the key to the shaft leading down to the *Abyss*. 2 ... he unlocked the shaft of the *Abyss*,
   11 As their leader [the locusts] had their emperor, the angel of the *Abyss*,
11 7 the beast that comes out of the *Abyss* is going to make war on [the two witnesses]
17 8 The beast ... is yet to come up from the *Abyss*, but only to go to his destruction.
20 1 I saw an angel come down from heaven with the key of the *Abyss* in his hand
   3 He threw [the dragon] into the *Abyss*,

2: CONSIGN TO THE UNDERWORLD, SEND TO HELL – PIT, UNDERGROUND CAVE: *SIROS* and *TARTAROŌ*

1 *siros* 1   2 *tartaroō* 1

2 P 2 4 2 When angels sinned, God ... *sent them down to* ⌜the underworld (or: *hell*) and consigned them to ⌜the dark underground caves (▽chains of darkness)

3. HADES – THE UNDERWORLD – HELL: *HADĒS*

hadēs 11

Mt 11 23 (Is 14 15) as for you, Capernaum, did you want to be exalted as high as heaven? You shall be thrown down to *hell*.
16 18 the gates of the *underworld* can never hold out against [my Church].
Lk 10 15 (Is 14 15) Capernaum ... ? You shall be thrown down to *hell*.
16 23 In his torment in *Hades* [the rich man] ... saw Abraham a long way off with Lazarus in his bosom.
Ac 2 24 God raised [Jesus] to life, freeing him from the pangs of *Hades*;
   27 (Ps 16 10) you will not abandon my soul to *Hades* nor allow your holy one to experience corruption.
   31 the Christ ... is the one who was not abandoned to *Hades*,
Rv 1 18 I am to live for ever and ever, and I hold the keys of death and of the *underworld*.
6 8 another horse appeared, deathly pale, and its rider was called Plague, and *Hades* followed at his heels.
20 13 Death and *Hades* were emptied of the dead that were in them;
   14 Death and *Hades* were thrown into the burning lake.

4. HELL: *GEENNA*

geenna 12

Mt 5 22 if a man calls [his brother] 'Renegade' he will answer for it in *hell* fire.
   29 it will do you less harm to lose one part of you than to have your whole body thrown into *hell*.
   30 it will do you less harm to lose one part of you than to have your whole body go to *hell*.
10 28 fear him rather who can destroy both body and soul in *hell*.
18 9 it is better for you to enter into life with one eye, than to have two eyes and be thrown into the *hell* of fire.
23 15 when you have [a proselyte] you make him twice as fit for *hell* as you are.
   33 how can you escape being condemned to *hell*?
Mk 9 43 it is better for you to enter into life crippled, than to have two hands and go to *hell*, into the fire that cannot be put out.
   45 it is better for you to enter into life lame, than to have two feet and be thrown into *hell*.
9 47 it is better for you to enter into the kingdom ... with one eye, than to have two eyes and be thrown into *hell*
Lk 12 5 fear him who, after he has killed, has the power to cast into *hell*.
Jm 3 6 the tongue ... catching fire itself from *hell* ... sets fire to the whole wheel of creation.

ACCOMPANY – FOLLOW – AFTER

1. **Accompany:** *syn-(h)epomai*
2. **Accompany – Follow – Next:** *erchomai*
   1: Accompany, Come with – Follow
   2: Following, Next
3. **Following, Next:** *metaxu*
4. **Follow:** *akoloutheō*
   1: Follow (Jesus) – Accompany (Jesus)
   2: Follow (a person, an angel)

3: Follow (figuratively) – Accompany
5. **Next (day):** *echomenos*
6. **After, Afterwards – Next, Following (day):** *hexēs*
7. **After, Afterwards, Later:** *hysteron*
8. **After – Behind – Back:** *opiso*
   1: (Come, Follow, Go) After
   2: Behind – Back
   3: After (in time or place)
9. **(Be) Succeeded (by):** *dia-dochos*

1. ACCOMPANY: *SYN-(H)EPOMAI*

syn-(h)epomai 1

Ac 20 4 [Paul] was *accompanied* by Sopater, ... Aristarchus and Secundus

2. ACCOMPANY – FOLLOW – NEXT: *ERCHOMAI*

3 *erchomai* 1/635   2 *ep-eimi* 5
1 *syn-erchomai* 10/32

1: ACCOMPANY, COME WITH – FOLLOW

Lk 23 55 the women ... had *come* from Galilee *with* Jesus
Jn 11 33 the Jews ... ⌜*followed* (or: *came with*) [Mary],
Ac 1 21 We must ... choose someone who has *been with* us the whole time that the Lord Jesus was travelling round with us,
9 39 Peter ⌜*went back with* (lit. got up and *accompanied*) [the two men to Dorcas]
10 23 [Peter was] *accompanied* by some of the brothers from Jaffa.
   45 Jewish believers who had *accompanied* Peter were all astonished
11 12 the Spirit told me to have no hesitation about *going* [back] *with* [the three men from Caesarea].
15 38 [John Mark] had ⌜refused to share (lit. not *accompanied* them) in their work.
21 16 Some of the disciples from Caesarea *accompanied* us
25 17 [the Jews] *came* here *with* me,

2: FOLLOWING, NEXT

Ac 7 26 2 The *next* day ... [Moses] came across some of them fighting,
13 44 3 The *next* sabbath almost the whole town assembled
16 11 2 we made a straight run for Samothrace; the *next* day for Neapolis,

Ac 20 15   2 The *next* day we . . . arrived opposite Chios.
   21 18   2 The *next* day Paul went with us to visit James,
   23 11   2 *Next* night, the Lord appeared to [Paul]

3. FOLLOWING, NEXT: *METAXU*

metaxu (*1*)

Ac 13 42   [Paul and his friends] were asked to preach on the same theme the *following* sabbath.

4. FOLLOW: *AKOLOUTHEŌ*

   1   *akoloutheō 91*   4   *ex-akoloutheō 3*
   6   *kat-akoloutheō 2*   3   *par-akoloutheō 4*
   2   *ep-akoloutheō 4*   5   *syn-akoloutheō 3*

1: FOLLOW (JESUS) – ACCOMPANY (JESUS)

Mt 4 20   [Simon and Andrew] left their nets at once and *followed* him.
     22   leaving the boat and their father, [James and John] *followed* him.
     25   Large crowds *followed* him.
   8 1   large crowds *followed* him.
     10   Jesus . . . said to those *following* him,
     19   Master, I will *follow* you wherever you go.
     22   *Follow* me, and leave the dead to bury their dead.
     23   he got into the boat *followed* by his disciples.
   9 9   Jesus . . . saw a man named Matthew sitting by the customs house and he said to him, '*Follow* me'. And he got up and *followed* him.
     27   As Jesus went on his way two blind men *followed* him
  10 38   Anyone who does not take his cross and *follow* in my footsteps is not worthy of me.
  12 15   Many *followed* him and he cured them all,
  14 13   the people . . . *went after* him on foot.
  16 24   If anyone wants to ⌜be a follower of mine (lit. come after me), let him . . . take up his cross and *follow* me.
  19 2   Large crowds *followed* him and he healed them there.
     21   go and sell what you own . . . then come, *follow* me.
     27   We have left everything and *followed* you. What are we to have . . . ?
     28   you who have *followed* me will yourselves sit on twelve thrones to judge the twelve tribes of Israel.
  20 29   As they left Jericho a large crowd *followed* him.
  20 34   their sight returned and they *followed* him.
  21 9   The crowds who went in front of him and those who *followed* were all shouting: Hosanna
  26 58   Peter *followed* him at a distance, and . . . reached the high priest's palace,
  27 55   many women were there . . . who had *followed* Jesus from Galilee
Mk 1 18   at once [Simon and Andrew] left their nets and *followed* him.
   2 14   he said to [Levi], '*Follow* me'. And he got up and *followed* him.
     15   there were many [tax collectors and sinners] among his *followers*.
   3 7   great crowds from Galilee *followed* him.
   5 24   a large crowd *followed* him; they were pressing all round him.
     37   5 he allowed no one to *go with* him except Peter and James and John
   6 1   his disciples ⌜*accompanied* (or: *followed*) him.
   8 34   If anyone wants to ⌜be a follower (G come) ⌜of mine (lit. after me), let him . . . take up his cross and *follow* me.
   9 38   Master, we saw a man who ⌜is not one of (lit. does not *follow*) us casting out devils in your name; and because he ⌜was not one of (lit. did not *follow*) us we tried to stop him.
  10 21   Go and sell everything you own . . . then come, *follow* me.
     28   We have left everything and *followed* you.
     32   those who *followed* were apprehensive.
     52   immediately his sight returned and he *followed* him along the road.
  11 9   those who *followed* were all shouting, 'Hosanna'.
  14 51   5 A young man who *followed* him had nothing on but a linen cloth.
     54   Peter had *followed* him at a distance,
  15 41   These [women] used to *follow* him and look after him when he was in Galilee.
Lk 5 11   [Simon, James and John] left everything and *followed* him.
     27   [Jesus] said to [Levi], '*Follow* me'. 28 And leaving everything he got up and *followed* him.
     28
   7 9   Jesus . . . said to the crowd *following* him,

Lk 9 11   the crowds got to know [where Jesus was] and they *went after* him.
     23   If anyone wants to ⌜be a follower of mine (lit. come after me), let him . . . take up his cross every day and *follow* me.
     49   we saw a man casting out devils in your name, and because he ⌜is not with (lit. does not *follow*) us we tried to stop him.
     57   I will *follow* you wherever you go.
     59   Another to whom he said, '*Follow* me', replied,
     61   I will *follow* you, sir, but first let me go and say good-bye to my people at home.
  18 22   Sell all that you own . . . then come, *follow* me.
     28   We left all we had to *follow* you.
     43   [the blind man] *followed* him praising God,
  22 39   He then left . . . with the disciples *following*.
     54   Peter *followed* at a distance.
  23 27   Large numbers of people *followed* him,
     49   5 the women who had *accompanied* him from Galilee . . . saw all this happen.
Jn 1 37   the two disciples [of John the Baptist] *followed* Jesus. 38 Jesus turned round, saw them *following* . . . 40 One of these two who became *followers* of Jesus . . . was Andrew,
     38
     40
     43   he met Philip and said, '*Follow* me'.
   6 2   a large crowd *followed* him,
   8 12   anyone who *follows* me will not be walking in the dark;
  10 27   The sheep that belong to me . . . *follow* me.
  12 26   If a man serves me, he must *follow* me,
  13 36   Where I am going you cannot *follow* me now; you will *follow* me later.
     37   Why can't I *follow* you now?
  18 15   Simon Peter, with another disciple, *followed* Jesus.
  21 19   After this he said, '*Follow* me'.
     20   Peter . . . saw the disciple Jesus loved *following* them
     22   I want him to stay behind till I come . . . You are to *follow* me.
1 P 2 21   2 Christ . . . left an example for you to *follow*
Rv 14 4   the ones who have kept their virginity . . . *follow* the Lamb wherever he goes;
  19 14   ⌜Behind (lit. *Following*) [the Word of God], dressed in linen of dazzling white, [rode] the armies of heaven

2: FOLLOW (A PERSON, AN ANGEL)

Mt 9 19 X   Jesus rose and, with his disciples, *followed* [the official].
Mk 14 13   you will meet a man carring a pitcher of water. *Follow* him,
Lk 22 10   you will meet a man carrying a pitcher of water. *Follow* him
  23 55   6 the women who had come from Galilee with Jesus were *following behind*.
Jn 10 4 <   the sheep *follow* [the shepherd] because they know his voice.
     5 <   5 They never *follow* a stranger
  11 31   the Jews . . . *followed* [Mary], thinking that she was going to the tomb
  20 6   Simon Peter who was *following* [the other disciple] now came up,
Ac 12 8   the angel . . . said [to Peter], ' . . . *follow* me'.
     9   Peter *followed* [the angel],
  13 43   many Jews . . . ⌜joined (lit. *followed*) Paul and Barnabas,
  16 17   6 This girl [who was a soothsayer] started *following* Paul and the rest of us
  21 36   the whole mob *was after* [Paul], shouting, 'Kill him!'
1 Co 10 4 X   they all drank from the spiritual rock that *followed* them as they went, and that rock was Christ.
Rv 6 8   another horse appeared . . . and its rider was called Plague, and Hades *followed* at his heels.
  14 8   A second angel *followed* [the first one], calling,
     9   A third angel *followed*, shouting aloud,

3: FOLLOW (FIGURATIVELY) – ACCOMPANY

Mk 16 17   3 These are the signs that will ⌜be associated with (or: *accompany*) believers:
     20   [the Lord worked with them] confirming the word by the 2 signs that *accompanied* it.
Lk 1 3   3 I in my turn, after carefully ⌜going over (lit. *following*) the whole story . . . have decided to write an ordered account
1 Tm 4 6   show that you have really digested . . . the good doctrine 3 which you have [always] *followed*.
   5 10   2 [a widow must have] ⌜been active in (lit. *gone after*) all kinds of good work.
     24   2 others have faults that are not discovered until *afterwards*.
2 Tm 3 10   3 You ⌜know (lit. have *followed*) . . . what I have taught,
2 P 1 16   It was not ⌜any cleverly invented myths that we were 4 repeating when (lit. *following* any cleverly invented myths that) we brought you the knowledge of the power . . . of our Lord Jesus Christ;

2 P 2 2   4 there will be many who *copy* their shameful behaviour
        15   4 They have . . . wandered off to *follow* the path of Balaam
Rv 14 13   Happy are those who die in the Lord . . . since their good
                 deeds ⌐go with (or: *follow*) them.

5. NEXT (DAY): *ECHOMENOS*

echomenos 3/5

Lk 13 33   But for today and tomorrow and the *next* [day] I must go on,
Ac 20 15   we . . . made Miletus the *next* [day].
   21 26   So the *next* day Paul took the men along and was purified
                 with them,

6. AFTER, AFTERWARDS – NEXT, FOLLOWING (DAY): *HEXĒS*

2 (*hē*) *hexēs 5*   1 *kath-exēs 5*

Lk 1 3   I *in my turn* . . . have decided to write an ordered account
                 for you,
    7 11   2 *soon afterwards* [Jesus] went to a town called Nain,
    8 1   *after* [this Jesus] made his way through towns and villages
    9 37   2 on the *following* day . . . a large crowd came to meet [Jesus].
Ac 3 24   all the prophets . . . from Samuel *onwards*, have predicted
                 these days.
   11 4   Peter in reply gave [the Jews] the details ⌐point by point
                 (lit. *successively*):
   18 23   [Paul continued] his journey through the Galatian country
                 and *then* through Phrygia,
   21 1   2 the *next* [day] we reached Rhodes,
   25 17   2 I . . . took my seat on the tribunal the *very next* [day]
   27 18   2 the *next* [day] they began to jettison the cargo,

7. AFTER, AFTERWARDS, LATER: *HYSTERON*

hysteron 6/11

Mt 4 2   [Jesus] fasted for forty days . . . *after* [which] he was very
                 hungry,
   21 29   <   [My boy, you go and work in the vineyard today.] He
                 answered, 'I will not go', but *afterwards* thought better
                 of it and went.
      32   Even *after* seeing that, you refused to . . . believe in [John
                 the Baptist].
   25 11   <   The other bridesmaids arrived *later*.
Jn 13 36   Where I am going you cannot follow me now; you will
                 follow me *later*.
Heb 12 11   *later*, . . . [the punishment] bears fruit in peace and goodness.

8. AFTER – BEHIND – BACK: *OPISŌ*

X = after, (from) behind Jesus
Ⓓ = after Satan

1 *opisō 35*   2 *opisthen 7*

1: (COME, FOLLOW, GO) AFTER

Mt 4 19 X   ⌐Follow (lit. Come *after*) me and I will make you fishers
                 of men.
   10 38 X   Anyone who does not take his cross and follow *in my foot-
                 steps* is not worthy of me.
   15 23 X   2 Give her what she wants . . . because she is shouting *after* us.
   16 24 X   If anyone wants to ⌐be a follower of mine (lit. come *after*
                 me), let him renounce himself
Mk 1 17 X   ⌐Follow (lit. Come *after*) me and I will make you into
                 fishers of men.
      20 X   [James and John] went *after* [Jesus].
    8 34 X   If anyone wants to ⌐be a follower (G come) ⌐of mine (lit.
                 after me), let him renounce himself
Lk 9 23 X   If anyone wants to ⌐be a follower of mine (lit. come *after*
                 me), let him renounce himself
   14 27 X   Anyone who does not . . . come *after* me cannot be my
                 disciple.
   19 14   his compatriots . . . sent a delegation ⌐to follow (lit. *after*)
                 him
   21 8   many will come using my name . . . ⌐Refuse to join (lit. Do
                 not go *after*) them.
Jn 12 19 X   the whole world is running *after* him!
Ac 5 37   Judas the Galilean . . . attracted ⌐crowds of supporters (lit.
                 the world *after* him);

Ac 20 30   there will be men coming forward . . . to induce the disciples
                 ⌐to follow (lit. *after*) them.
1 Tm 5 15 Ⓓ   there are already some who have left us ⌐to follow (lit.
                 after) Satan.
2 P 2 10⌐   [the Lord can hold the wicked for their punishment,]
                 especially those who ⌐are governed by (lit. run *after*)
                 their . . . bodily desires
Jude   7   The fornication of Sodom and Gomorrah and the other
                 nearby towns ⌐was equally unnatural, and it (lit. in
                 running *after* their unnatural desires) is a warning to us
Rv 12 15   the serpent vomited water from his mouth . . . *after* the
                 woman,
   13 3   the whole world had marvelled and ⌐followed (lit. gone *after*)
                 the beast.

2: BEHIND – BACK

Mt 9 20 X   2 Then *from behind* him came a woman . . . and she touched
                 the fringe of his cloak,
   16 23 X   Get *behind* me, Satan!
   24 18   if a man is in the fields, he must not turn *back* to fetch his
                 cloak.
Mk 5 27 X   2 [a woman] came up *behind* him . . . and touched his cloak.
    8 33 X   Get *behind* me, Satan!
   13 16   if a man is in the fields, he must not turn *back* to fetch his
                 cloak.
Lk 7 38 X   [The woman] waited *behind* him at his feet, weeping, and
                 her tears fell on his feet,
    8 44 X   2 [A woman] came up *behind* him and touched the fringe of
                 his cloak,
    9 62   Once the hand is laid on the plough, no one who looks *back*
                 is fit for the kingdom of God.
   17 31   nor must anyone in the fields turn *back* either.
   23 26   they seized on a man, Simon from Cyrene . . . and made
         X   2 him shoulder the cross and carry it *behind* Jesus.
Jn 6 66   many of his disciples ⌐left him (lit. went *back*)
   18 6   When Jesus said, 'I am he', they moved *back*
   20 14   [Mary of Magdala] turned ⌐round (lit. *back*) and saw Jesus
                 standing there,
Ph 3 13 O   I forget the *past* and I strain ahead for what is still to come;
Rv 1 10   I heard a voice *behind* me, shouting like a trumpet,
    4 6   In the centre . . . were four animals with many eyes, in front
           2   and *behind*.
    5 1   2 (Ezk 2 10) there was a scroll that had writing on *back* and
                 front

3: AFTER (IN TIME OR PLACE)

Mt 3 11   the one who ⌐follows (lit. comes *after*) me is more powerful
                 than I am,
Mk 1 7   Someone is ⌐following (lit. coming *after*) me, someone who
                 is more powerful than I am,
Jn 1 15   He who comes *after* me ranks before me because he existed
                 before me.
      27   [there stands among you] the one who is coming *after* me;
                 and I am not fit to undo his sandal-strap.
      30   A man is coming *after* me who ranks before me because he
                 existed before me.

9. (BE) SUCCEEDED (BY): *DIA-DOCHOS*

dia-dochos 1

Ac 24 27   Felix was *succeeded* by Porcius Festus

ACCUSE – CHARGE – DEFEND

1. Accuse – Charge
  1: Accuse, Charge, Accusation –
     Take to court: *en-kaleō*
  2: Accuse, Prosecute – Bring a
     Charge against, Make an
     Accusation: *kat-ēgoreō*
**2. Answer for, (Be) Liable – Guilty –
   Deserve:** *en-ochos*
3. In the Act: *auto-phoros*
4. Case – Charge – Reason: *aitia*

  a) (Legal) Case, Grounds –
     Charge, Accusation
  b) Reason – Case, Pretext –
     Source
5. Defence – Answer – Excuse
  1: Defence – Answer, Explain –
     Excuse: *apo-logia*
  2: Excuse: *pro-phasis*
  3: Go to (a person's) defence:
     amynō

1. ACCUSE – CHARGE

1: ACCUSE, CHARGE, ACCUSATION – TAKE TO COURT: *EN-KALEŌ*

1 *en-kaleō* 7   2 *en-klēma* 2

Ac 19 38		If Demetrius and the craftsmen . . . want to complain about anyone . . . let them *take the case to court*.
	40	We could easily be *charged* with rioting
23 28		Wanting to find out ⌐what *charge* they were *making* (or: why they were *making a charge*) against [Paul] . . . ²⁹⌐
	29	found that the *accusation* concerned disputed points of their
	2	Law, but that there was no *charge* deserving death or imprisonment.
25 16		the accused . . . is given an opportunity to defend himself
	2	against the *charge*.
26 2		I consider myself fortunate . . . in that . . . I am to answer today all the *charges made* against me by the Jews,
	7	I am actually *put on trial* by Jews!
Rm 8 33		Could anyone *accuse* those that God has chosen?

2: ACCUSE, PROSECUTE – BRING A CHARGE AGAINST, MAKE AN ACCUSATION: *KAT-ĒGOREŌ*

4 *kat-ēgōr*   1   3 *kat-ēgoria* 3
1 *kat-ēgoreō* 23   2 *kat-ēgoros* 5

X = Jesus accused

Mt 12 10	X		[the Pharisees] asked [Jesus] . . . hoping for something to use ⌐against (lit. to *accuse*) him.
27 12	X		he was *accused* by the chief priests and the elders
Mk 3 2	X		they were watching [Jesus] . . . hoping for something to use ⌐against (lit. to *accuse*) him.
15 3	X		the chief priests *brought* many *accusations against* him.
4	X		See how many *accusations* they are *bringing against* you!
Lk 6 7			The scribes and the Pharisees were watching him . . . hoping
	X		to find something to use ⌐against (lit. to *accuse*) him.
23 2	X		[the elders] began their *accusation*
10			the chief priests and the scribes were there, violently *pressing*
	X		their *accusations*.
14	X		I have . . . found no case against the man in respect of all
	X		the *charges* you *bring against* him.
Jn 5 45			Do not imagine that I am going to *accuse* you before the Father: . . . Moses will *be* your *accuser*.
8 6			[the scribes and the Pharisees] asked him this as a test,
	X		looking for something to use ⌐against (lit. to *accuse*) him.
18 29	X	3	What *charge* do you bring against this man?
Ac 22 30			[the tribune] wanted to know what precise *charge* the Jews were *bringing* [against Paul].
23 30		2	I . . . have notified his *accusers* that they must state their case against [Paul] in your presence.
35		2	I will hear your case as soon as your *accusers* are here too.
24 2			Paul was called, and Tertullus opened for the *prosecution*,
8		2	(ᵛ Since [Lysias] ordered [Paul's] *accusers* to appear before you) . . . you can find out for yourself the truth of all ⌐our accusations against (lit. of which we *accuse*) this man.
13			neither can they prove any of the *accusations* they are *making against* me now.
19			some Jews from Asia . . . these are the ones who should have . . . *accused* me of whatever they had against me.
25 5			if there is anything wrong about the man, they can *bring a charge against* him.
11			if there is no substance in the *accusations* these persons *bring against* me . . . I appeal to Caesar.
16			Romans are not in the habit of surrendering any man,
/2			until the *accused* confronts his *accusers* and is given an opportunity to defend himself against the charge.
18		2	[Paul's] *accusers* did not ⌐charge (lit. indict) him with any accusation of the crimes I had expected;
28 19			not that I had any *accusation to make against* my own nation.
Rm 2 15			[pagans] have *accusation* and defence, that is, their own inner mental dialogue.
1 Tm 5 19		3	Never accept any *accusation* brought against an elder unless it is supported by two or three witnesses.
Tt 1 6			his children must be believers and not uncontrollable or
		3	liable to be *charged* with disorderly conduct.
Rv 12 10 ①		4/	the ⌐persecutor (or: *accuser*), who *accused* our brothers day and night before our God, has been brought down.

2. ANSWER FOR, (BE) LIABLE – GUILTY – DESERVE: *EN-OCHOS*

en-ochos 9/10

Mt 5 21		if anyone does kill he must ⌐*answer for* (or: be *liable* for) it before the court.
22		anyone who is angry with his brother will ⌐*answer for* (or: be *liable* for) it before the court; if a man calls his brother "Fool" he will ⌐*answer for* (or: be *liable* for) it before the Sanhedrin; and if a man calls him "Renegade" he will ⌐*answer for* (or: be *liable* for) it in hell fire.
26 66	X	They answered, 'He *deserves* to die'.
Mk 3 29		but let anyone blaspheme against the Holy Spirit and he will never have forgiveness: he is *guilty* of an eternal sin.
14 64	X	they all gave their verdict: he *deserved* to die.
1 Co 11 27		anyone who eats the bread . . . unworthily will ⌐be *behaving unworthily* towards (or: *answer for* it to) the body . . . of the Lord.
Jm 2 10		if a man keeps the whole of the Law, except for one small point . . . he is still *guilty* of breaking it all.

3. IN THE ACT: *AUTO-PHŌROS*

auto-phōros 1

Jn 8 4		this woman was caught *in the very act* of committing adultery,

4. CASE – CHARGE – REASON: *AITIA*

1 *aitia*   20   5 *aitios*   1
4 *aitiōma* 1   3 *an-aitios* 2
2 *aition*   4   6 *pro-aitiaomai* 1

a) (Legal) Case, Grounds – Charge, Accusation

Mt 12 5		on the sabbath day the Temple priests break the sabbath
	3	*without being blamed* for it
7	3	you would not have condemned the *blameless*.
27 37		Above [Jesus's] head was placed the *charge* against him;
Mk 15 26		The inscription giving the *charge* against [Jesus] read:
Lk 23 4	2	I find no *case* against this man.
14	2	I have . . . found no *case* against the man in respect of all the charges you bring against him.
22	2	I have found no *case* against [Jesus] that deserves death,
Jn 18 38		I find no *case* against [Jesus].
19 4		I find no *case*.
6		I can find no *case* against [Jesus].
Ac 13 28		they found ⌐nothing to justify (lit. no *case* for) [Jesus's] death,
19 40	2	there was no *ground* for it all, and we can give no reason for this gathering.
23 28		Wanting to find out what *charge* they were making against [Paul],
25 7		the Jews . . . surrounded [Paul], making many serious
	4	*accusations*
18		[Paul's] accusers did not indict him with any *accusation* of the crimes I had expected.
27		It seems . . . pointless to send a prisoner without indicating the *charges* against him.
28 18		they found me guilty of ⌐nothing involving (lit. no *case* meriting) the death penalty;
Rm 3 9	6	as we ⌐said before (lit. have already *made out the case*), Jews and Greeks are all under sin's dominion.

b) Reason – Case, Pretext – Source

Mt 19 3		Is it against the Law for a man to divorce his wife on any *pretext* whatever?
10 ○		If that is ⌐how things are (or: the *case*) between husband and wife, it is not advisable to marry.
Lk 8 47		the woman . . . explained . . . ⌐why (lit. for what *reason*) she had touched [Jesus]
Ac 10 21		⌐why (lit. for what *reason*) have you come?
22 24		to find out the *reason* for the outcry against [Paul].
28 20		That is ⌐why (lit. the *reason*) I have asked to see you
2 Tm 1 6		That is ⌐why (lit. the *reason*) I am reminding you now to fan into a flame the gift that God gave you
12		It is only ⌐on account of this (lit. for this *reason*) that I am experiencing fresh hardships
Tt 1 13		that is a true statement. ⌐*So* (or: For this *reason*) you will have to be severe in correcting them,
Heb 2 11		that is ⌐why (lit. the *reason*) he openly calls them brothers
5 9 ●	5	[Christ] became for all who obey him the *source* of eternal salvation

5. DEFENCE – ANSWER – EXCUSE

1: DEFENCE – ANSWER, EXPLAIN – EXCUSE: *APO-LOGIA*

1 *apo-logeomai* 10   3 *an-apo-logētos* 2
2 *apo-logia*   8

Lk 12 11		do not worry about how to *defend yourselves*
21 14		you are not to prepare your *defence*,
Ac 19 33		Alexander . . . raised his hand for silence in the hope of being able to *explain things* to the people.
22 1	2	listen to what I have to say to you in my *defence*.
24 10		I can therefore *speak* with confidence *in my defence*.
25 8		Paul's *defence* was this, 'I have committed no offence . . .'
16		Romans are not in the habit of surrendering any man,
2		until the accused . . . is given an opportunity to *defend* himself against the charge.
26 1		Paul held up his hand and began ⌐his defence (lit. to *defend himself*)¬:
2		I consider myself fortunate . . . that . . . I am to *answer* today all the charges
24		[Paul] had reached this point in ⌐his defence (lit. *defending himself*)¬ when Festus shouted out,
Rm 1 20	3	such people are *without excuse*: ²¹ they knew God and yet refused to honour him as God or to thank him;
2 1	3	So no matter who you are, if you pass judgement you *have no excuse*.
15		[pagans] have accusation and *defence*, that is, their own inner mental dialogue.
1 Co 9 3	2	My *answer* to those who want to interrogate me is this:
2 Co 7 11	2	what keenness, what *explanations*, what indignation . . !
12 19		you have been thinking that our *defence* is addressed to you,
Ph 1 7	2	my work *defending* and establishing the gospel.
16		this is my invariable way of *defending* the gospel.
2 Tm 4 16	2	The first time I had to present my *defence*, there was not a single witness to support me.
1 P 3 15	2	always have your *answer* ready for people who ask you the reason for the hope that you all have.

2: EXCUSE: *PRO-PHASIS*

pro-phasis 1/6

Jn 15 22	but as it is they have no *excuse* for their sin.

3: GO TO (A PERSON'S) DEFENCE: *AMYNŌ*

amynō 1

Ac 7 24	When [Moses] saw one of [his countrymen] being ill-treated he ⌐*went to* his *defence* (or: went to his aid)¬

ADD – AGAIN

---

1. Add – Again, Also: *pros-tithēmi*
   1: Add – Increase – (Be) Given (extra)

2: Again – Also – As well
2. Again, A second time: *palin*
3. Again: *anōthen*

1. ADD – AGAIN, ALSO: *PROS-TITHĒMI*

1 *pros-tithēmi 18*   2 *pros-ana-tithemai 1/2*

1: ADD – INCREASE – (BE) GIVEN (EXTRA)

Mt 6 27		Can any of you . . . *add* one single cubit to his span of life?
33		Set your hearts on his kingdom first, and on his righteousness, and all these other things will be *given* you *as well*.
Mk 4 24		The amount you measure out is the amount you will be given – and ⌐more besides (lit. some *added*)¬;
Lk 3 20		[Herod] *added* a further crime to all the rest by shutting John up in prison.
12 25		Can any of you . . . *add* a single cubit to his span of life?
31		set your hearts on his kingdom, and these other things will be *given* you *as well*.
17 5 X		The apostles said to the Lord, '*Increase* our faith'.
Ac 2 41		That very day about three thousand were *added* to their number.
47 X		Day by day the Lord *added* to their community those destined to be saved.
5 14		the numbers of men and women who came to believe in the Lord *increased* steadily.
11 24		a large number of people were ⌐won over (lit. *added*)¬ to the Lord.
13 36		David . . . was ⌐*buried* with (lit. *added* to)¬ his ancestors
Ga 2 6	2	these leaders . . . had nothing to *add* to the Good News as I preach it.

Ga 3 19		the purpose of *adding* the Law . . . was . . . to specify crimes,
Heb 12 19		the great voice speaking . . . made everyone that heard it beg that ⌐no more should be said to them (lit. not a word should be *added*)¬.

2: AGAIN – ALSO – AS WELL

Lk 19 11		[Jesus] ⌐*went on* to tell (lit. *also* told)¬ a parable,
20 11		[the landlord] persevered and sent a second servant *also*;
12		He ⌐*still* (lit. *again*)¬ persevered and sent a third;
Ac 12 3		[Herod] decided to arrest Peter *as well*.

2. AGAIN, A SECOND TIME: *PALIN*

palin (14)

Mt 21 36 <		⌐*Next* (lit. *Again*)¬ [the landowner] sent some more servants,
22 4 <		⌐*Next* (lit. *Again*)¬ [the king] sent some more servants.
26 72		And *again*, with an oath, [Peter] denied it,
Mk 12 4 <		⌐*Next* (lit. *Again*)¬ he sent another servant to them;
14 70		But *again* [Peter] denied it.
Jn 4 13		Whoever drinks this water will get thirsty *again*;
10 17		I lay down my life in order to take it up *again*. ¹⁸ . . . it is
18		in my power to take it up *again*;
12 28		I have glorified [my name], and I will glorify it *again*.
14 3		I shall ⌐*return* (lit. come *again*)¬ to take you with me;
16 22		I shall see you *again*, and your hearts will be full of joy,
18 27		*Again* Peter denied it;
Rm 11 23		God is perfectly able to graft [the Jews] *back again*;
Heb 6 6		[people who once received a share of the Holy Spirit] and yet in spite of this have fallen away – it is impossible for them to be renewed *a second time*.

3. AGAIN: *ANŌTHEN*

anōthen (2)

Jn 3 3		unless a man is born ⌐*from above* (or: *again*)¬, he cannot see the kingdom of God.
7		You must be born ⌐*from above* (or: *again*)¬.

ADORN – CROWN

---

1. Adorn, Adornment, Decorate – Tidy, Courteous – Trim (a lamp): *kosmeō*
2. a Ring: *daktylios*
3. Coronet, Diadem: *dia-dēma*

4. Crown: *stephanos*
   1: Crown, Wreath – (Be) Crowned
   2: (Be) Garlanded

1. ADORN, ADORNMENT, DECORATE – TIDY, COURTEOUS – TRIM (A LAMP): *KOSMEŌ*

1 *kosmeō 10*   3 *kosmos 1/186*
2 *kosmios 2*

Mt 12 44 O		finding [its home] unoccupied, swept and *tidied*, [the unclean spirit collects seven other spirits]
23 29		Alas for you, scribes and Pharisees, . . . who . . . *decorate* the tombs of holy men,
25 7		all those bridesmaids woke up and *trimmed* their lamps,
Lk 11 25 O		finding [its home] swept and *tidied*, [the unclean spirit brings seven other spirits]
21 5		remarking how [the Temple] was *adorned* with fine stone-work and votive offerings.
1 Tm 2 9	2	women are to wear ⌐suitable (lit. *tidy*)¬ clothes . . ; their *adornment* is [to do good works]
3 2 O	2	the president must . . . be temperate, discreet and *courteous*,
Tt 2 10		[the slaves] must show complete honesty at all times, so that they ⌐are in every way a credit to (lit. in every way *adorn*)¬ the teaching of God
1 P 3 3 O		[Wives,] Do no ⌐*dress up* for show (lit. go in for outward *adornment*)¬: . . . ⁴ all this should be inside, . . . ⁵ That
5	3	was how the holy women of the past ⌐*dressed* themselves attractively (lit. *adorned* themselves)¬
Rv 21 2		I saw the holy city, . . . as beautiful as a bride ⌐all *dressed* (lit. *adorned*)¬ for her husband.
19		The foundations of the city wall were ⌐*faced* (lit. *adorned*)¬ with all kinds of precious stone:

2. A RING: *DAKTYLIOS*

1 *daktylios 1*   2 *(chryso-)daktylios 1*

Lk 15 22 <   the father said . . ., '. . . put a *ring* on his finger'
Jm 2 2   suppose a man comes into your synagogue, beautifully
          2   dressed and with a gold *ring* on,

3. CORONET, DIADEM: *DIA-DĒMA*

dia-dēma 3

Rv 12 3   a huge red dragon which had seven heads and ten horns,
                 and each of the seven heads crowned with a *coronet*.
   13 1   I saw a beast emerge from the sea; it had seven heads and
                 ten horns, with a *coronet* on each of its ten horns,
   19 12   [the rider of the white horse was called Faithful and True]
                 his head was crowned with many *coronets*;

4. CROWN: *STEPHANOS*

3 *stemma* *1*   1 *stephanos 18*
2 *stephanoō 3*

1: CROWN, WREATH – (BE) CROWNED

Mt 27 29 X   having twisted some thorns into a *crown* [the soldiers
                 put this on his head
Mk 15 17 X   They . . . twisted some thorns into a *crown* and put it on
                 him.
Jn 19 2 X   the soldiers twisted some thorns into a *crown* and put it
                 on his head,
       5 X   Jesus then came out wearing the *crown* of thorns
1 Co 9 25   All the fighters at the games go into strict training . . .
                 just to win a *wreath* that will wither away,
Ph 4 1   dear friends; you are my joy and my *crown*.
1 Th 2 19   you will be the *crown* of which we shall be proudest in the
                 presence of our Lord Jesus
2 Tm 2 5   2 an athlete . . . cannot *win* any *crown* unless he has kept
                 all the rules of the contest;
       4 8   all there is to come now is the *crown* of righteousness re-
                 served for me,
Heb 2 7 X   2 (Ps 8 5) you *crowned* him with glory and splendour.
       9   . . . ⁹ Jesus . . . was for a short while made lower than
          X   2 the angels and is now *crowned* with glory and splendour
                 because he submitted to death.
Jm 1 12   the man who stands firm . . . will win the prize of life,
                 the *crown* that the Lord has promised to those who love
                 him.
1 P 5 4   When the chief shepherd appears, you will be given the
                 crown of unfading glory.
Rv 2 10   Even if you have to die, keep faithful, and I will give you
                 the *crown* of life for your prize.
    3 11   hold firmly to what you already have, and let nobody take
                 your ᴵprize (lit. *crown*) away from you.
    4 4   twenty-four elders sitting, dressed in white robes with
                 golden *crowns* on their heads,
      10   the twenty-four elders . . . threw down their *crowns* in
                 front of the throne,
    6 2   the rider on [the white horse] . . . was given the victor's
                 crown
    9 7   [the locusts] had things that looked like gold *crowns* on
                 their heads,
   12 1   a woman, adorned with the sun, was standing on the moon,
                 and with the twelve stars on her head for a *crown*.
   14 14 X   one like a son of man with a gold *crown* on his head

2: GARLANDED

Ac 14 13   3 The priests of Zeus-outside-the-gate . . . brought *garlanded*
                 oxen to the gates.

AGREEMENT – CONSENT

1. **Agree(ment) – Harmony – Unity:**
   homo-phrōn
2. **Common consent – One accord –
   Together, United:** *homo-thymadon*
3. **Approve – Consent to, Content to:**
   syn-eu-dokeō
4. **Acknowledge – Agree:** *sym-phēmi*
5. **Accept – Agree:** *ex-(h)omo-logeō*

6. **Agree(ment) – Match:** *sym-phōneō*
7. **Agreement – Consent – Plan:**
   syn-tithemai
   a) to a course of action
   b) Honour – Keep faith
8. **Make a sign (of assent):** *epi-neuō*
9. **Vote:** *psēphos*

1. AGREE(MENT) – HARMONY – UNITY: *HOMO-PHRŌN*

              2   *phroneō 1/26*   3 *homo-phrōn 1*
1 *to auto phroneō*   *5*

Rm 12 16   *Treat* everyone with *equal* kindness;
   15 5   may he who helps us . . . help you all to ᴵ*be tolerant* (or:
                 live in harmony) with each other,
2 Co 13 11   *Be united*; live in peace,
Ph 2 2   then *be united* in your convictions and [united] in your love,
          2   with a *common* [purpose and a common] *mind*.
       4 2   I appeal to Evodia and I appeal to Syntyche to *come to
                 agreement with each other*, in the Lord;
1 P 3 8   3 you should all *agree* among yourselves . . . love the brothers,

2. COMMON CONSENT – ONE ACCORD – TOGETHER, UNITED: *HOMO-THYMADON*

homo-thymadon 11

Ac 1 14   All these *joined together* in continuous prayer,
    2 46   [The faithful] went *as a body* to the Temple every day but
                 met in their houses for the breaking of bread;
    4 24   they lifted up their voice to God *all together*.
    5 12   [The faithful] all used to meet *by common consent* in the
                 Portico of Solomon.
    7 57   [the members of the council] ᴵ*all* (or: *with one accord*) rushed
                 at [Stephen],
    8 6   The people *united* in welcoming the message Philip preached,
   12 20   [the Tyrians and Sidonians] sent a *joint* deputation [to
                 Herod] . . . and . . . negotiated a treaty,
   15 25   so we have decided *unanimously* to elect delegates
   18 12   [while Gallio was proconsul] the Jews made a *concerted*
                 attack on Paul
   19 29   The whole town was in an uproar ᴵand the mob (lit. and
                 with one accord) rushed to the theatre
Rm 15 6   so that *united in mind* and voice you may give glory to the
                 God and Father of our Lord Jesus Christ.

3. APPROVE – CONSENT TO, CONTENT TO: *SYN-EU-DOKEŌ*

syn-eu-dokeō 6

Lk 11 48   In this way you both witness what your ancestors did and
                 approve it;
Ac 8 1   Saul entirely *approved* of the killing [of Stephen].
   22 20   I was standing by in *full agreement* with [Stephen's] mur-
                 derers,
Rm 1 32   those who behave like this . . . ᴵ*encourage* others to do (or:
                 approve of others' doing) the same.
1 Co 7 12   If a brother has a wife who is an unbeliever, and she ᴵ*is
                 content* (or: *consents*) *to* live with him . . . ¹³ and if a
       13   woman has an unbeliever for her husband, and he ᴵ*is
                 content* (or: *consents*) *to* live with her, she must not leave
                 him.

4. ACKNOWLEDGE – AGREE: *SYM-PHĒMI*

sym-phēmi 1

Rm 7 16   When I act against my own will, that means I ᴵ*have a self
                 that acknowledges that* (or: *agree*) the Law is good,

5. ACCEPT – AGREE: *EX-(H)OMO-LOGEŌ*

ex-(h)omo-logeō 1/10

Lk 22 6   [They agreed to give him money. Judas] ᴵ*accepted* (or: *agreed*),
                 and looked for an opportunity to betray [Jesus]

6. AGREE(MENT) – MATCH: *SYM-PHŌNEŌ*

1 *sym-phōneō 6*   3 *sym-phōnos 1*
2 *sym-phōnēsis 1*   4 *a-sym-phōnos 1*

Mt 18 19   if two of you . . . *agree* to ask anything at all,
   20 2   [The landowner] *made an agreement* with the workers for
                 one denarius a day,
      13   did we not *agree* on one denarius?
Lk 5 36   the piece taken from the new [cloak] will not *match* the old.
Ac 5 9   So you and your husband have *agreed* to put the Spirit of
                 the Lord to the test!

Ac 15	15	[God first arranged to enlist a people for his name out of the pagans.] This is entirely *in harmony* with the words of the prophets,
28	25 4	[Paul and the Jews of Rome] *disagreed* among themselves
1 Co 7	5 3	[husband and wife,] do not refuse each other except by *mutual consent* . . . to leave yourselves free for prayer;
2 Co 6	15 X ⓓ 2	Christ ⌐is not the ally of (lit. cannot *agree* with) Beliar, nor has a believer anything to share with an unbeliever.

7. AGREEMENT – CONSENT – PLAN: *SYN-TITHEMAI*

1	*syn-tithemai 3*	3	*syn-kata-tithemai 1*
2	*syn-kata-thesis 1*	4	*a-syn-thetos 1*

a) to a course of action

Lk 22	5	[the chief priests] *agreed* to give [Judas] money.
23	51 3	[Joseph] had not *consented* to what the others had planned and carried out.
Jn 9	22	the Jews . . . had already *agreed* to expel from the synagogue anyone who should acknowledge Jesus as the Christ.
Ac 23	20	The Jews have *made a plan* to ask you to take Paul down to the Sanhedrin
2 Co 6	16 2	The temple of God has no ⌐*common ground* (or: *agreement*) with idols,

b) Honour – Keep faith

Rm 1	31 4	*without brains, honour, love or pity.*

8. MAKE A SIGN (OF ASSENT): *EPI-NEUŌ*

epi-neuō 1

Ac 18	20	They asked [Paul] to stay longer but he ⌐declined (lit. did not *make a sign of assent*),

9. VOTE: *PSĒPHOS*

psēphos 1/3

Ac 26	10	when [the saints] were sentenced to death I cast my *vote* against them.

ALLOW

1. Let, Allow – Give leave (to), Give permission: *epi-trepō*	**3. Allow, Let – Leave, Left:** *eaō*
2. Be allowed, Be permitted – Have a right (to): *ex-estin*	**4. Concession, Suggestion:** *syn-gnōmē*

1. LET, ALLOW – GIVE LEAVE (TO), GIVE PERMISSION: *EPI-TREPŌ*

epi-trepō 18

Mt 8	21 X	Sir, *let* me go and bury my father first.
19	8	Moses *allowed* you to divorce your wives,
Mk 5	13 X	[Send us to the pigs, let us go into them.] So he *gave* them *leave.*
10	4	Moses *allowed* us . . . to divorce.
Lk 8	32 X	the devils pleaded with him to *let* them go into [the pigs].
	X	So he *gave* them *leave.*
9	59 X	*Let* me go and bury my father first.
61	X	first *let* me go and say good-bye to my people
Jn 19	38	Joseph . . . asked Pilate to let him remove the body of Jesus. Pilate *gave permission*,
Ac 21	39	Paul [said to the tribune,] '. . . . Please *give* me *permission* to speak to the people.' ⁴⁰ The man *gave* his *consent.*
40	
26	1	Agrippa said to Paul, 'You have *leave* to speak on your own behalf'.
27	3	Julius was considerate enough to *allow* Paul to go to his friends
28	16	Paul was *allowed* to stay in lodgings of his own
1 Co 14	34	women are to remain quiet at meetings since they have no *permission* to speak;
16	7 ⊝	I hope to spend some time with you, the Lord *permitting.*

1 Tm 2	12	I am not *giving permission* for a woman to teach or to tell a man what to do.
Heb 6	3 ⊝	This, God ⌐willing (lit. *permitting*), is what we propose to do.

2. BE ALLOWED, BE PERMITTED – HAVE A RIGHT (TO): *EX-ESTIN*

1	*ex-estin 32*	2	*ex-ousia 13/103*

Mt 12	2	Look, your disciples are doing something [picking ears of corn] that ⌐is forbidden (lit. *is not permitted*) on the sabbath.
4	[David] ate the loaves of offering which neither he nor his followers *were allowed* to eat,
10	⌐Is it against the Law (lit. *Is it permitted*) to cure a man on the sabbath day?
12	it *is permitted* to go good on the sabbath day.
14	4	It ⌐is against the Law (lit. *is not allowed*) for you to have [your brother's wife].
19	3	⌐Is it against the Law (lit. *Is it permitted*) for a man to divorce his wife . . .?
20	15	*Have I no right* to do what I like with my own?
22	17	*Is it permissible* to pay taxes to Caesar or not?
27	6	It ⌐is against the Law (lit. *is not allowed*) to put this into the treasury; it is blood-money.
Mk 2	24	Look, why are [your disciples] doing something [picking ears of corn] on the sabbath day that ⌐is forbidden (lit. *is not permitted*)?
26	[David] ate the loaves of offering which only the priests *are allowed* to eat,
3	4	⌐Is it against the law (lit. *Is it permitted*) on the sabbath day to do good . . .?
6	18	It ⌐is against the law (lit. *is not allowed*) for you to have your brother's wife.
10	2	⌐Is it against the law (lit. *Is it permitted*) for a man to divorce his wife?
12	14	*Is it permissible* to pay taxes to Caesar or not?
Lk 6	2	Why are you doing something [picking ears of corn] that ⌐is forbidden (lit. *is not permitted*) on the sabbath day?
4	[David] took the loaves of offering . . . which only the priests *are allowed* to eat?
9	⌐is it against the law (lit. *is it permitted*) on the sabbath to do good . . .?
14	3	⌐Is it against the law (lit. *Is it permitted*) . . . to cure a man on the sabbath or not?
20	22	*Is it permissible* for us to pay taxes to Caesar or not?
Jn 5	10	It is the sabbath; you *are not allowed* to carry your sleeping-mat.
18	31	We *are not allowed* to put a man to death.
Ac 2	29	⌐no one can deny (lit. I *may* confidently state; or: I *may* state plainly) that the patriarch David himself is dead
8	37	[Is there anything to stop me being baptised?] (ᵛ. . . . If you believe with all your heart, it *is allowed*.)
16	21	practices which it ⌐is unlawful (lit. *is not permitted*) for us as Romans to accept
21	37	Paul . . . asked the tribune if he *could* have a word with him.
22	25	⌐Is it legal (lit. *Is it permitted*) for you to flog a . . . Roman citizen . . .?
1 Co 6	12	'For me there are no ⌐forbidden things (lit. things which *are* not *permitted*)'; maybe, but not everything does good. I agree there are no ⌐forbidden things (lit. things which *are* not *permitted*) for me, but I am not going to let anything dominate me.
8	9 2	Only be careful that you do not make use of this ⌐freedom (lit. *right*) in a way that proves a pitfall for the weak.
9	4 2/2	Have we not every *right* to eat and drink? ⁵ And the *right* to take a Christian woman round with us, like all the other apostles . . . and Cephas? ⁶ Are Barnabas and I the only ones who are not *allowed* to stop working?
5	
6	2
12	2/2	Others are allowed these *rights* over you and our *right* is surely greater?
18	2	the *rights* which the gospel gives me.
10	23	'For me there are no ⌐forbidden things (lit. things which *are* not *allowed*)', but not everything does good. True, there are no ⌐forbidden things (lit. things which *are* not *allowed*), but it is not everything that helps the buildings to grow.
2 Co 12	4	things which must not and *cannot* be put into human language.
2 Th 3	9 2	not because we had no *right* to be [a burden to you],
Heb 13	10	our own altar from which those who serve the tabernacle have no *right* to eat.
Rv 9	10 2	[The locusts'] tails were like scorpions' . . . and it was with them that they ⌐were *able* (or: had the power) to injure people for five months.
11	6 2	[The two witnesses] ⌐are *able* (or: have the power) to lock up the sky so that it does not rain . . .; they ⌐are *able* (or: have the power) to turn water into blood
2	

Rv 22 14   Happy are those who will have washed their robes clean,
         2   so that they will have the *right* to feed on the tree of life

3. ALLOW, LET – LEAVE, LEFT: *EAŌ*

1 *eaō* 11   2 *(pros-)eaō* 1

Mt 24 43   the householder . . . would not have *allowed* anyone to
            break through the wall of his house.
Lk 4 41 X he would not *allow* [the devils] to speak
   22 51   at this Jesus spoke. '*Leave off*! . . . That will do!'
Ac 14 16 Θ In the past [God] *allowed* each nation to go its own way;
   16 7 Ⓢ the Spirit of Jesus would not *allow* [Paul and Timothy to
            cross the frontier into Bithynia],
   19 30   Paul wanted to make an appeal to the people, but the
            disciples refused to *let* him;
   23 32   [the soldiers] *left* the mounted escort to go on with [Paul]
   27 7 2 The wind would not *allow* us to touch [at Cnidus],
      32   the soldiers cut the boat's ropes and *let* it drop away.
      40 ○ They slipped the anchors and *left* them to the sea,
   28 4   divine vengeance would not *let* him live.
1 Co 10 13 Θ You can trust God not to *let* you be tried beyond your
            strength,

4. CONCESSION, SUGGESTION: *SYN-GNŌMĒ*

syn-gnōmē 1

1 Co 7 6   This is a ⌐suggestion (or: *concession*), not a rule [for
            husbands and wives]:

ALONE – ONLY

1: Alone – Only
   a). (God) Alone – Only (God)
   b) (Jesus is) Alone – Only (Jesus)
   c) (A person is) Alone – Only (a
      person)

   d) Alone, Only (generally)
      Merely, Just
2: Only-begotten, Only (son, daughter, child)
   a) of God
   b) of others

    1 *monon* 66   2   *monos* 46 ⎫48   4 *mono-genēs*   9
    6 *monoō* 1   3 *kata monas* 2 ⎭   5 *mon(-ophthalmos)* 2

1: ALONE – ONLY

a) (God) Aone – Only (God)

Mt 4 10 2 (Dt 6 13 G) worship the Lord your God, and serve him
            alone.
   24 36 2 nobody knows [that day and hour] . . . no one but the
            Father *only*.
Lk 4 8 2 (Dt 6 13 G) worship the Lord your God, and serve him
            alone.
    5 21 2 Who can forgive sins but God *alone*?
Jn 5 44   you . . . are not concerned with the approval that comes
         2 from the *one* God
   17 3 2 eternal life is this: to know you, the *only* true God,
Rm 16 27 2 He *alone* is wisdom; give glory therefore to him through
            Jesus Christ
1 Tm 1 17 2 To the eternal King, the undying . . . and *only* God, be
            honour and glory
    6 15 2 God, the blessed and *only* Ruler of all,
      16 2 [God] *alone* is immortal,
Jude 25 2 To God, the *only* God . . . be the glory,
Rv 15 4 2 [Lord,] you *alone* are holy,

b) (Jesus is) Alone – Only (Jesus)

Mt 14 23 2 When evening came, he was there *alone*,
   17 8 2 [Peter, James and John] saw no one but *only* Jesus.
Mk 4 10 3 When he was *alone*, the Twelve . . . asked what the parables
            meant.
    6 47 2 the boat was far out on the lake, and he was *alone* on the land.
    9 8 2 [Peter, James and John] saw no one with them any more but
            only Jesus.
Lk 9 18 3 Now one day . . . he was praying *alone*
      36 2 after the voice had spoken, Jesus was found *alone*.
Jn 6 15 2 Jesus . . . escaped back to the hills *by himself*.
    8 9 2 Jesus was left *alone* with the woman,
      16 2 I am not *alone*: the one who sent me is with me;
      29 2 he who sent me is with me, and has not left me *to myself*,

---

Jn 16 32 2 you will be scattered . . . and leaving me *alone*. And yet I
         2 am not *alone*, because the Father is with me.
Jude 4   Certain people . . . were condemned for . . . rejecting our
         2 *only* Master and Lord, Jesus Christ.

c) (A person is) Alone – Only (a person)

Mt 5 47   if you ⌐save your greetings for (lit. greet *only*) your brothers,
            are you doing anything exceptional?
   12 4   [David] ate the loaves of offering . . . which were for the
         2 priests *only*
   18 15   If your brother does something wrong, go and have it out
         2 with him *alone*,
Mk 9 2 2 Jesus . . . led [Peter, James and John] . . . where they could
            be *alone* by themselves.
Lk 6 4 2 [David] took the loaves . . . which *only* the priests were
            allowed to eat
   10 40 2 my sister is leaving me to do the serving *all by myself*
   24 18 2 You must be the *only* [person] . . . in Jerusalem who does
            not know the things that have been happening there
Jn 6 22 2 the disciples had set off *by themselves*.
   11 52   [Jesus was to die for the nation –] and not for the nation
            only, but to gather together the scattered children of God.
   17 20   I pray not *only* for these, but for those also who . . . believe
            in me.
Ac 11 19   they usually proclaimed the message *only* to Jews.
   26 29   I wish . . . that not *only* you but all who have heard me today
            would come to be as I am
Rm 3 29   Is God the God of Jews *alone* and not of the pagans too?
    4 23   Scripture however does not refer *only* to [Abraham] but to
            us as well when it says that his faith was thus considered;
    9 24   we are those people; ⌐whether we were Jews or pagans (lit.
            not *only* Jews but pagans too –) we are the ones he has
            called.
   11 3   (1 K 19 10) they have killed your prophets . . . I, [Elijah,]
         2 and I *only*, remain,
   16 4 2 I am not the *only* [one] to owe [Prisca and Aquila] a debt of
            gratitude, all the churches among the pagans do as well.
1 Co 9 6 2 Are Barnabas and I the *only* [ones] who are not allowed to
            stop working?
   14 36 2 Do you think . . . that [the word of God] has come *only*
            to you?
Ga 6 4   if you find anything to boast about, it will at least be some-
         2 thing of ⌐your own (lit. you *alone*),
Ph 2 27   God took pity on [Epaphroditus], and ⌐on me as well as him
            (lit. not on him *alone* but on me as well),
    4 15 2 no other church helped me . . . You were the *only* [ones];
Col 4 11 2 [Aristarchus, Mark and] Justus . . . are the *only* [ones]
            actually working with me
1 Th 3 1 2 we decided it would be best to be left *without a companion*
            at Athens,
1 Tm 5 5 6 a woman who is really widowed and *left without anybody* can
            give herself up to God
2 Tm 4 8   the Lord . . . will give [the crown of righteousness] . . . not
            only to me but to all those who have longed for his Appear-
            ing.
      11 2 *only* Luke is with me.
Heb 9 7 2 the second tent is entered . . . *only* by the high priest
2 Jn   1   my greetings to the Lady . . . whom I love in the truth – and
         2 I am not the *only* [one], for so do all who . . . know the
            truth –

d) Alone, Only (generally)– Merely, Just

Mt 4 4 2 (Dt 8 3) Man does not live on bread *alone* but on every word
            that comes from the mouth of God.
    8 8   *just* give the word and my servant will be cured.
    9 21   If I can *only* touch his cloak I shall be well again.
   10 42   If anyone gives *so much as* a cup of cold water to one of these
            little ones . . . he will . . . not lose his reward.
   14 36   [People were] begging [Jesus] *just* to let [the sick] touch the
            fringe of his cloak.
   18 9 5 it is better for you to enter into life with *one* eye,
   21 19   ]Jesus] found *nothing* on [the fig tree] *but* leaves.
      21   not *only* will you do what I have done to the fig tree, but even
            if you say to this mountain, 'Get up . . .', it will be done.
Mk 5 36   Do not be afraid; *only* have faith.
    6 8   take nothing for the journey *except* a staff –
    9 47   it is better for you to enter into the kingdom of God with
         5 *one* eye,
Lk 4 4 2 (Dt 8 3) Man does not live on bread *alone*.
    8 50   Do not be afraid, *only* have faith and [your daughter] will be
            safe.
   24 12 2 ᵛ Peter . . . saw the binding cloths *but nothing else*;¹
Jn 5 18   not ⌐content with (lit. *only* was he) breaking the sabbath, he
            spoke of God as his own Father,
   12 9   a large number of Jews . . . came not *only* on account of
            Jesus but also to see Lazarus
      24 2 unless a wheat grain . . . dies, it remains *only* [a single grain];
   13 9   [Lord, wash] not *only* my feet, but my hands and my head as
            well!

Ac 8 16 [the Samaritans] had *only* been baptised in the name of the Lord Jesus.
18 25 [Apollos] had *only* experienced the baptism of John.
19 26 not *just* in Ephesus but nearly everywhere in Asia, this man Paul has . . . converted a great number of people
27 This threatens not *only* to discredit our trade, but also to reduce the sanctuary of . . . Diana to unimportance.
21 13 I am ready not *only* to be tied up but even to die in Jerusalem
27 10 we run the risk of losing not *only* the cargo . . . but also our lives
Rm 1 32 yet they do it; and ⌜what is worse, (lit. not *only* do they do it, they) encourage others to do the same.
4 12 [Abraham became the] ancestor, also, of those who though circumcised ⌜do not rely on that fact alone (lit. are not *only* circumcised),
16 [the promise is] available to all of Abraham's descendants, not *only* those who belong to the Law
5 3 that is not ⌜all (lit. [the] *only* [thing we can boast about]);
11 Not *merely* [because we have been reconciled] but because we are filled with joyful trust in God,
8 23 not *only* creation, but . . . we too groan inwardly
9 10 ⌜Even more to the point is (lit. Not *only* that but) what was said to Rebecca when she was pregnant
13 5 obey, therefore, not *only* because you are afraid of being punished but also for conscience' sake.
1 Co 7 39 [A widow] is free to marry anybody she likes, *only* it must be in the Lord.
15 19 If our hope in Christ has been for this life *only*, we are the most unfortunate of all people.
2 Co 7 7 [God comforted us] not *only* by [Titus's] arrival but also by the comfort which he had gained from you.
8 10 you were the first . . . not *only* in taking action but even in deciding to.
19 ⌜More than (lit. Not *only*) that, he happens to be the same brother who has been elected . . . to be our companion
21 we are trying to do right not *only* in the sight of God but also in the sight of men.
9 12 doing this holy service is not *only* supplying all the needs of the saints, but it is also increasing the amount of thanksgiving
Ga 1 23 [the churches of Judaea] had heard *nothing except* that their one-time persecutor was now preaching the faith
2 10 The *only* [thing] they insisted on was that we should remember to help the poor,
3 2 Let me ask you *one* question:
4 18 It is always a good thing to win people over – and ⌜I do not have to be (lit. not *only* when I am) there with you –
5 13 you were called . . . to liberty; *but* be careful, or this liberty will provide an opening for self-indulgence.
6 12 [these people who] want to force circumcision on you . . . *only* want to escape persecution
Ep 1 21 [Christ is] far above every Sovereignty . . . not *only* in this age but also in the age to come.
Ph 1 27 ⌜Avoid anything in your everyday lives that could (lit. In your everyday lives associate yourselves *only* with what would not) be unworthy of the gospel of Christ,
29 [God] has given you the privilege not *only* of believing in Christ, but of suffering for him as well.
2 12 continue to do as I tell you, as you always have; not *only* . . . when I was there . . . but even more now
1 Th 1 5 the Good News . . . came to you not *only* as words, but as power
8 the word of the Lord started to spread – and not *only* throughout Macedonia
2 8 we were eager to hand over to you not *only* the Good News but our whole lives as well.
2 Th 2 7 Rebellion is at its work already, but *in secret*,
1 Tm 5 13 [young widows] learn how to be idle . . . and then, not *merely* idle, they learn to be gossips
2 Tm 2 20 Not the *only* [dishes of all the] dishes in a large house are made of gold and silver;
Heb 9 10 they are rules about the outward life, connected *only* with foods
12 26 (Hg 2 6) I shall make the earth shake . . . and not *only* the earth but heaven as well.
Jm 1 22 you must do what the word tells you, and not *just* listen to it
2 24 it is . . . not *only* by believing that a man is justified.
1 P 2 18 Slaves must be . . . obedient to their masters, not *only* when they are kind . . . but also when they are unfair.
1 Jn 2 2 [Christ] is the sacrifice that takes our sins away, and not *only* ours, but the whole world's.
5 6 Christ . . . came . . . not with water *only*, but with water and blood;

2: ONLY-BEGOTTEN, ONLY (SON, DAUGHTER, CHILD)

a) of God

Jn 1 14 4 we saw his glory . . . that is his as the *only* [Son] of the Father,
Jn 1 18 4 it is (G God) the *only* Son, who is nearest to the Father's heart,
3 16 4 God . . . gave his *only* Son,
18 whoever refuses to believe is condemned already, because he 4 has refused to believe in the name of God's *only* Son.
1 Jn 4 9 4 God sent into the world his *only* Son

b) of others

Lk 7 12 4 [at Nain] a dead man was being carried out for burial, the *only* son of his mother,
8 42 4 [Jairus] had an *only* daughter about twelve years old,
9 38 4 I implore you to look at my son: he is my *only* [child].
Heb 11 17 4 Abraham . . . offered to sacrifice his *only* [son]

ANGEL

1: Angel of the Lord
2: The Archangel Gabriel
3: Particular Archangels or Angels
4: Angels (generally)
5: the Angels of the seven churches

1 *angelos 170/176* 2 *arch-angelos 2*
3 *(is-)angelos 1*

1: ANGEL OF THE LORD

Mt 1 20 the *angel* of the Lord appeared to [Joseph] in a dream
24 Joseph . . . did what the *angel* of the Lord had told him to do:
2 13 the *angel* of the Lord appeared to Joseph in a dream
19 the *angel* of the Lord appeared in a dream to Joseph
28 2 the *angel* of the Lord, descending from heaven, came and rolled away the stone
5 the *angel* spoke: and he said to the women,
Lk 2 9 The *angel* of the Lord appeared to [the shepherds]
10 the *angel* said, '. . . I bring you news of great joy'
13 suddenly with the *angel* there was a great throng of the heavenly host,
Jn 5 4 v for at intervals the *angel* of the Lord came down into the pool . . . ⌝
Ac 5 19 the *angel* of the Lord opened the prison gates
7 30 in the wilderness near Mount Sinai, an *angel* appeared to [Moses]
35 [Moses] was now sent to be both leader and redeemer through the *angel* who had appeared to him in the bush.
38 through Moses . . . our ancestors could communicate with the *angel* who had spoken to him on Mount Sinai;
8 26 The *angel* of the Lord spoke to Philip
12 7 suddenly the *angel* of the Lord stood there, and the cell was
8 filled with light . . . [8] The *angel* then said [to Peter],
9 'Put on your belt and sandals' . . . [9] Peter followed him, but had no idea that what the *angel* did was all happening
10 in reality . . . [10]. . . they went through [the iron gate]
11 and . . . suddenly the *angel* left him. [11] It was only then that Peter came to himself . . . he said, 'The Lord really did send his *angel*'
23 the *angel* of the Lord struck [Herod] down,

2: THE ARCHANGEL GABRIEL

G: *Gabriel 2*

Lk 1 11 Then there appeared to [Zechariah] the *angel* of the Lord,
13 the *angel* said to him, 'Zechariah, do not be afraid'
18 Zechariah said to the *angel*, 'How can I be sure of this?'
19 G The *angel* replied, 'I am *Gabriel* who stand in God's presence'
G In the sixth month the *angel Gabriel* was sent by God [to Mary]
30 the *angel* said to her, 'Mary, do not be afraid'
34 Mary said to the *angel*, 'But how can this come about . . .?'
35 'The Holy Spirit will come upon you' the *angel* answered
38 And the *angel* left [Mary].
2 21 they gave him the name Jesus, the name the *angel* had given him before his conception.

3: PARTICULAR ARCHANGELS OR ANGELS

M: *Michael 2*

Lk 22 43 an *angel* appeared to [Jesus] . . . to give him strength.
Jn 12 29 It was an *angel* speaking to [Jesus].
20 12 [Mary] saw two *angels* . . . sitting where the body of Jesus had been,

Ac	6	15	[Stephen's] face appeared to them like the face of an *angel*.
	10	3	[Cornelius] saw the *angel* of God come into his house
		7	When the *angel* . . . had gone, Cornelius called two of the slaves
		22	Cornelius . . . was directed by a holy *angel* to send for you
	11	13	[Cornelius] had seen an *angel* standing in his house
	12	15	[Rhoda insisted that Peter was standing outside.] They said to her, 'You are out of your mind . . . It must be his *angel*!'
	23	9	Suppose a spirit has spoken to [Paul], or an *angel*?
	27	23	Last night there was standing beside me an *angel* of the God to whom I belong
2 Co	11	14 ⓓ	Satan himself goes disguised as an *angel* of light,
	12	7 ⓓ	I was given a thorn in the flesh, an *angel* of Satan
Ga	1	8	if anyone preaches a version of the Good News different . . . whether it be ourselves or an *angel* . . . he is to be condemned.
	4	14	you welcomed me as an *angel* of God,
1 Th	4	16 2	the voice of the *archangel* will call out the command
Heb	13	2	some people have entertained *angels* without knowing it.
Jude		9 M 2	the *archangel Michael* . . . was engaged in argument with the devil
Rv	1	1	God . . . sent his *angel* . . . to his servant John,
	5	2	I saw a powerful *angel* who called with a loud voice,
	7	1	I saw four *angels*, standing at the four corners of the earth,
		2	I saw another *angel* rising where the sun rises . . . he called in a powerful voice to the four *angels*
	8	2	I saw . . . the seven *angels* who stand in the presence of God.
		3	Another *angel*, who had a golden censer, came and stood at the altar.
		4	from the *angel*'s hand the smoke of the incense went up in the presence of God
		5	the *angel* took the censer
		6	The seven *angels* that had the seven trumpets now made ready to sound.
		8	The second *angel* blew his trumpet,
	8	10	The third *angel* blew his trumpet,
		12	the fourth *angel* blew his trumpet,
		13	trouble for all the people . . . at the sound of the other three trumpets which the three *angels* are going to blow.
	9	1	Then the fifth *angel* blew his trumpet,
		11 ⓓ	As their leader [the locusts] had their emperor, the *angel* of the Abyss,
		13	The sixth *angel* blew his trumpet,
		14	[The voice] spoke to the sixth *angel* . . . and said, 'Release the four *angels* that are chained up at the great river'
		15	These four *angels* . . . were released
	10	1	I saw another powerful *angel* . . . wrapped in a cloud,
		5	the *angel* that I had seen, standing on the sea . . . raised his right hand
		7	at the time when the seventh *angel* is heard . . . God's secret intention will be fulfilled,
		8	take that open scroll out of the hand of the *angel*
		9	I went to the *angel* and asked him to give me the small scroll,
		10	I took [the scroll] out of the *angel*'s hand,
	11	15	Then the seventh *angel* blew his trumpet,
	12	7 M	*Michael* with his [angels] attacked the dragon.
	14	6	I saw another *angel*, flying high overhead,
		8	A second *angel* followed him, calling, 'Babylon has fallen'
		9	A third *angel* followed, shouting aloud,
		15	another *angel* came out of the sanctuary,
		17	Another *angel* . . . came out of the temple in heaven,
		18	the *angel* in charge of the fire left the altar
		19	the *angel* set his sickle to work on the earth
	15	1	I saw next, in heaven . . . seven *angels* . . . bringing the seven plagues
		6	out [of the Tent] came the seven *angels* with the seven plagues,
		7	One of the four animals gave the seven *angels* seven golden bowls
		8	no one could go into [the temple] until the seven plagues of the seven *angels* were completed.
	16	1	I heard a voice . . . shouting to the seven *angels*,
		5	I heard the *angel* of water say,
	17	1	One of the seven *angels* that had the seven bowls came to speak to me,
		7	The *angel* said to me, 'Don't you understand?'
	18	1	I saw another *angel* come down from heaven,
		21	a powerful *angel* picked up a boulder like a great millstone,
	19	17	I saw an *angel* standing in the sun,
	20	1	Then I saw an *angel* come down from heaven
	21	9	One of the seven *angels* that had the seven bowls . . . came to speak to me,
		12	at each of the twelve gates there was an *angel*.
		17	the *angel* was using the ordinary cubit.
	22	6	the Lord God . . . has sent his *angel* . . . to his servants
		8	I knelt at the feet of the *angel* who had shown [these things] to me,
		16	I, Jesus, have sent my *angel* to make these revelations

4: ANGELS (GENERALLY)

Mt	4	6	(Ps 91 11) He will put you in his *angels*' charge,
		11	*angels* appeared and looked after [Jesus].
	13	39	the harvest is the end of the world; the reapers are the *angels*.
		41	The Son of Man will send his *angels* and they will gather out of his kingdom all things that provoke offences
		49	at the end of time the *angels* will . . . separate the wicked from the just
	16	27	the Son of Man is going to come in the glory of his Father with his *angels*,
	18	10	[the] *angels* [of these little ones] in heaven are continually in the presence of my Father
	22	30	at the resurrection men and women do not marry; no, they are like the *angels* (ᵛ of God) in heaven.
	24	31	[the Son of Man] will send his *angels* . . . to gather his chosen
		36	as for that day and hour, nobody knows it, neither the *angels* of heaven, nor the Son,
	25	31	the Son of Man comes in his glory, escorted by all the *angels*,
		41 ⓓ	Go . . . to the eternal fire prepared for the devil and his *angels*.
	26	53	my Father . . . would promptly send more than twelve legions of *angels*
Mk	1	13	[Jesus] remained [in the wilderness] for forty days . . . and the *angels* looked after him.
	8	38	the Son of Man . . . comes in the glory of his Father with the holy *angels*.
	12	25	when they rise from the dead . . . they are like the *angels* in heaven.
	13	27	[the Son of Man] will send the *angels* to gather his chosen
		32	as for that day or hour, nobody knows it, neither the *angels* of heaven, nor the Son;
Lk	2	15	when the *angels* had gone from them into heaven, the shepherds said . . . 'Let us go to Bethlehem'
	4	10	(Ps 91 11) He will put his *angels* in charge of you to guard you,
	9	26	the Son of Man . . . comes in his own glory and in the glory of the Father and the holy *angels*.
	12	8	if anyone openly declares himself for me in the presence of men, the Son of Man will declare himself for him in the presence of God's *angels*. ⁹ But the man who disowns me in the presence of men will be disowned in the presence of God's *angels*.
		9	
	15	10	there is rejoicing among the *angels* of God over one repentant sinner.
	16	22	the poor man died and was carried away by the *angels* to the bosom of Abraham.
	20	36 3	they can no longer die, for they are the same as the *angels*,
	24	23	[the women] had seen a vision of *angels* who declared [Jesus] was alive.
Jn	1	51	you will see heaven laid open and, above the Son of Man, the *angels* of God ascending and descending.
Ac	7	53	You . . . had the Law brought to you by *angels*
	23	8	the Sadducees say there is neither resurrection, nor *angel*, nor spirit,
Rm	8	38	no *angel*, no prince, nothing that exists . . . can ever come between us and the love of God
1 Co	4	9	we have been put on show in front of the whole universe, *angels* as well as men.
	6	3	we are also to judge *angels*,
	11	10	That is the argument for women's covering their heads with a symbol of the authority over them, out of respect for the *angels*.
	13	1	If I have all the eloquence of men or of *angels*, but speak without love, I am simply a gong booming
Ga	3	19	The Law was promulgated by *angels*, assisted by an intermediary.
Col	2	18	Do not be taken in by people who like grovelling to *angels*
2 Th	1	7	the Lord Jesus appears from heaven with the *angels* of his power.
1 Tm	3	16	He was made visible in the flesh . . . seen by *angels*,
	5	21	Before God, and before Jesus Christ and the *angels* he has chosen, I put it to you as a duty to keep these rules
Heb	1	4	[the Son] is now as far above the *angels* as the title which he has inherited is higher than their own name. ⁵ God has never said to any *angel*: . . . today I have become your father;
		5	
		6	when [God] brings the First-born into the world, he says (Ps 97 7): Let all the *angels* of God worship him. ⁷ About the *angels*, he says (Ps 104 4): He makes his *angels* winds and his servants flames of fire,
		7	
		13	God has never said to any *angel*: Sit at my right hand
	2	2	a promise that was made through *angels* proved to be so true
		5	[God] did not appoint *angels* to be rulers of the world to come,
		7	(Ps 8 6) For a short while you made him lower than the *angels*;
		9	Jesus . . . was for a short while made lower than the *angels*

Heb	2 16		it was not the *angels* that [Jesus] took to himself; he took to himself descent from Abraham.
	12 22		what you have come to is . . . the heavenly Jerusalem where the millions of *angels* have gathered
1 P	1 12		Even the *angels* long to catch a glimpse of these things.
	3 22		[Jesus Christ] has made the *angels* and Dominations and Powers his subjects.
2 P	2 4	Ⓓ	When *angels* sinned, God did not spare them:
	11		the *angels* . . . make no . . . accusation against [the glorious ones] in front of the Lord.
Jude	6	Ⓓ	let me remind you of the *angels* who had supreme authority but did not keep it
Rv	3 5		I shall . . . acknowledge [the] names [of those who prove victorious] in the presence of my Father and his *angels*.
	5 11		I heard the sound of an immense number of *angels* gathered round the throne
	7 11		all the *angels* who were standing in a circle round the throne . . . prostrated themselves
	12 7	Ⓓ	Michael with his *angels* attacked the dragon. The dragon fought back with his *angels*,
	9	Ⓓ	The great dragon . . . were hurled down to the earth and his *angels* were hurled down with him.
	14 10		[All those who worship the beast] will be tortured in the presence of the holy *angels* and the Lamb

5: THE ANGELS OF THE SEVEN CHURCHES

Rv	1 20	the seven stars are the *angels* of the seven churches,
	2 1	Write to the *angel* of the church in Ephesus
	8	Write to the *angel* of the church in Smyrna
	12	Write to the *angel* of the church in Pergamum
	18	Write to the *angel* of the church in Thyatira
	3 1	Write to the *angel* of the church in Sardis
	7	Write to the *angel* of the church in Philadelphia
	14	Write to the *angel* of the church in Laodicea

ANGER

1. Anger: *orgē*
  1: (God's) Anger, Wrath – (Divine) Retribution – Judgement
  2: Anger, Hot temper, Rage (generally)

2. Anger – Fury – Rage: *thymos*
  1: (God's) Fury, Fierce anger, Wrath
  2: Fury, Rage, Bad temper (generally)

3. Angry, Angered: *pros-ochthizō*
4. Be angry: *cholaō*
5. Indignant – Angry: *agan-akteō*
6. Infuriated – Stung to fury: *dia-priō*
7. Be furious with – Have a grudge against – Assail: *en-echō*
8. Fury: *em-mainomai*
9. Fury: *a-noia*
10. Rage: *phruassō*

1. ANGER: *ORGĒ*

1 *orgē*	36	5 *par-orgismos*	1
4 *orgilos*	1	3 *par-orgizō*	2
2 *orgizō*	9		

1: (GOD'S) ANGER, WRATH – (DIVINE) RETRIBUTION – JUDGEMENT

Mt	3 7	who warned you to fly from the *retribution* that is coming?
Lk	3 7	who warned you to fly from the *retribution* that is coming?
	21 23	great misery will descend on the land and ᴦwrath (or: *judgement*) on this people.
Jn	3 36	the *anger* of God stays on [anyone who refuses to believe in the Son].
Rm	1 18	The *anger* of God is being revealed . . . against all . . . impiety
	2 5	Your stubborn refusal to repent is only adding to the *anger* God will have towards you on that day of *anger* . . .
	8	⁸ for the unsubmissive . . . there will be *anger* and fury.
	3 5	how can we say God is unjust when . . . he gets *angry* with us in return?
	4 15	Law involves ᴦ*the possibility of punishment* (or: *retribution*)
	5 9	is it likely that [Christ] would now fail to save us from God's *anger*?
	9 22	although God is ready to show his *anger* . . . he patiently puts up with the people who make him *angry*,
	12 19	Never try to get revenge; leave that . . . to God's *anger*.
Ep	2 3	by nature we were as much under God's *anger* as the rest of the world.
	5 6	God's *anger* comes down on those who rebel against him.
Col	3 6	this is the sort of behaviour that makes God *angry*.

1 Th

1 Th	1 10	you are now waiting for Jesus . . . to come from heaven to save us from the *retribution* which is coming.
	2 16	[The Jews put the Lord Jesus to death,] but *retribution* is overtaking them at last.
	5 9	God never meant us to experience the *Retribution*, but to win salvation
Heb	3 11	(Ps 95 11) [How unreliable these people . . .!] in my *anger*, I swore that not one would reach the place of rest
	4 3	(Ps 95 11) in *anger*, I swore that not one would reach the place of rest
Rv	6 16	hide us away from the One who sits on the throne and from the *anger* of the Lamb. ¹⁷ For the Great Day of ᴦhis (ᵛ their) *anger* has come,
	11 18	The nations were seething with rage and now the time has come for your *anger*,
	14 10	the wine of God's fury . . . is ready, undiluted, in his cup of *anger*;
	16 19	God made [Babylon] drink the full winecup of his *anger*.
	19 15	[The Word] is the one who will . . . tread out the wine of Almighty God's fierce *anger*.

2: ANGER, HOT TEMPER, RAGE (GENERALLY)

Mt	5 22		2 anyone who is *angry* with his brother will answer for it before the court;
	18 34	<	2 in his *anger* the master handed [the wicked servant] over to the torturers
	22 7	<	2 The king was *furious*. He despatched his troops, destroyed those murderers
Mk	1 41	X	2 ᴦFeeling sorry for him (ᵛ In *anger*), Jesus . . . touched [the leper].
	3 5	X	grieved to find them so obstinate, he looked *angrily* round [the synagogue]
Lk	14 21	<	2 the householder, in a *rage*, said to his servant, 'Go . . . and bring in here the poor'
	15 28	<	2 [The elder son] was *angry* then and refused to go in.
Rm	10 19		3 I will make you *angry* with an irreligious people.
	13 4		The authorities are there to . . . carry out God's ᴦrevenge (lit. *anger*) by punishing wrongdoers. ⁵ You must obey, therefore, not only because you are afraid of ᴦbeing punished (lit. *retribution*), but also for conscience' sake.
Ep	4 26		2 (Ps 4 4 G) Even if you are *angry*, you must not sin: never let the sun set on your *anger*
	31		Never . . . lose your temper, or *raise your voice to* anybody,
	6 4		3 parents, never drive your children to *resentment*
Col	3 8		you . . . must give all these things up: getting *angry*, being bad-tempered, spitefulness,
1 Tm	2 8		I want the men to lift their hands up reverently in prayer, with no *anger* or argument.
Tt	1 7		[an elder] must be irreproachable: never an arrogant or *hot-tempered* man,
Jm	1 19		be . . . slow to speak and slow to [rouse your] *temper*;
	20		²⁰ God's righteousness is never served by man's *anger*;
Rv	11 18		2 The nations were seething with *rage*,
	12 17	Ⓓ	2 the dragon was *enraged* with the woman and went away to make war on the rest of her children,

2. ANGER – FURY – RAGE: *THYMOS*

1 *thymos*	18	3 *thymo*(-*macheō*)	1
2 *thymoomai*	1		

1: (GOD'S) FURY, FIERCE ANGER, WRATH

Rm	2 8	for the unsubmissive . . . there will be anger and *fury*.
Rv	14 8	Babylon . . . gave the whole world the wine of God's *anger* (§ for her prostitution) to drink.
	10	[All those who worship the beast] will be made to drink the wine of God's *fury* which is ready . . . in his cup of anger;
	19	the angel . . . harvested the whole vintage of the earth and put it into . . . the winepress of God's *anger*,
	15 1	the seven plagues . . . are the last of all, because they exhaust the ᴦ*anger* (or: *wrath*) of God.
	7	seven golden bowls filled with the *anger* of God
	16 1	empty the seven bowls of God's *anger* over the earth.
	19	God made [Babylon] drink the full winecup of his ᴦ*fierce* (or: *furious*) anger.
	18 3	All the nations have been intoxicated by the wine (§ of the *fury*) of [Babylon's] prostitution;
	19 15	[The Word] will . . . tread out the wine of Almighty God's ᴦ*fierce* (or: *furious*) anger.

2: FURY, RAGE, BAD TEMPER (GENERALLY)

Mt	2 16	2 Herod was *furious* . . . and . . . had all the male children killed
Lk	4 28	everyone in the [Nazareth] synagogue was *enraged*.

Ac 12 20	3	Herod was *on bad terms* with the Tyrians
19 28		[Paul's] speech roused [the Ephesians] to *fury*,
2 Co 12 20		I am afraid . . . that . . . there will be wrangling, jealousy, and *tempers roused*,
Ga 5 20		the results [of self-indulgence] are obvious: . . . feuds and wrangling, jealousy, *bad temper* and quarrels;
Ep 4 31		Never have grudges against others, or *lose your temper*, or raise your voice to anybody,
Col 3 8		you . . . must give all these things up; getting angry, being *bad-tempered*, spitefulness,
Heb 11 27	Θ	[Moses] left Egypt and was not afraid of the king's *anger*;
Rv 12 12	⑩	the devil has gone down to you in a *rage*,

3. ANGRY, ANGERED: *PROS-OCHTHIZŌ*

pros-ochthizō 2

Heb 3 10	Θ	(Ps 95 10 G) That was why I was *angry* with that generation
17	Θ	those who made God *angry* for forty years were the ones who sinned

4. BE ANGRY: *CHOLAŌ*

cholaō 1

Jn 7 23	why *are* you *angry* with me for making a man whole . . . on a sabbath?

5. INDIGNANT – ANGRY: *AGAN-AKTEŌ*

1 *agan-akteō 7*   2 *agan-aktēsis 1*

Mt 20 24	the other ten . . . were ⌐indignant (or: *angry*) with [James and John].
21 15	At the sight of . . . the children shouting, 'Hosanna . . .', the chief priests and the scribes were *indignant*.
26 8	When they saw [the expensive ointment poured out], the disciples were *indignant*;
Mk 10 14 X	Jesus . . . was *indignant* and said . . , 'Let the little children come to me'
41	the other ten . . . began to feel ⌐indignant (or: *angry*) with James and John,
14 4	Some who were there said to one another *indignantly*, 'Why this waste of ointment?'
Lk 13 14	the synagogue official was *indignant* because Jesus had healed on the sabbath,
2 Co 7 11	2 what keenness, what explanations, what *indignation*, what alarm!

6. INFURIATED – STUNG TO FURY: *DIA-PRIŌ*

dia-priō 2

Ac 5 33	[The apostles' words] so *infuriated* [the Sanhedrin] that they wanted to put them to death.
7 54	[The Jews] were *infuriated* when they heard [Stephen's words],

7. BE FURIOUS WITH – HAVE A GRUDGE AGAINST – ASSAIL: *EN-ECHŌ*

en-echō 2/3

Mk 6 19	Herodias . . . ⌐was *furious with* (or: *had a grudge against*) [John the Baptist]
Lk 11 53	the scribes and the Pharisees began ⌐a *furious attack* on [Jesus] (or: to *assail* [Jesus] *fiercely*)

8. FURY: *EM-MAINOMAI*

em-mainomai 1

Ac 26 11	my *fury* against [Christians in Jerusalem] was so extreme that I even pursued them

9. FURY: *A-NOIA*

a-noia 1/2

Lk 6 11	[the scribes and the Pharisees] were ⌐furious (lit. filled with *fury*),

10. RAGE: *PHRUASSŌ*

phruassō 1

Ac 4 25	(Ps 2 1) Why this ⌐arrogance (or: *rage*) among the nations . . .?

ANIMALS

---

1. **Animal(s) – Beast**
   - 1: Animals: *zōon*
   - 2: (Wild) Beast(s) – Animal: *thērion*
     - a) Wild beasts, Wild animals – Creature
     - b) (the two) Beasts (of Revelation)
   - 3: (fourfooted) Animals, Quadrupeds: *tetra-pous*
   - 4: Animal, Beast – Mount – Cattle: *ktēnos*
2. **Specific animals**
   - 1: Lion – Leopard – Bear: *leōn, pardalis* and *arkos*
   - 2: Fox: *alōpēx*
   - 3: Wolf: *lykos*
   - 4: Camel: *kamēlos*
   - 5: Horse – Horseman, Cavalry: *hippos*
   - 6: Donkey, Ass
     - a) Beast of burden, Ass: *hypozygion*
     - b) Donkey, Ass: *onos*
     - c) Colt, Foal: *pōlos*
   - 7: Ox, Bull – Calf, Heifer – Cattle
     - a) Ox – Cattle: *bous*
     - b) Bulls, Oxen – Fattened cattle: *tauros* and *sitistos*
     - c) Fatted calf – Bull-calf: *moschos*
     - d) Heifer: *damalis*
     - e) Cattle: *thremma*
   - 8: Lamb – Sheep
     - a) Lamb: *amnos*
     - b) Lamb: *arnion*
     - c) Sheep: *probaton*
   - 9: Goat, Kid
     - a) Goat, Kid: *eriphos*
     - b) Goat: *tragos*
   - 10: Pig – Sow
     - a) Pigs, Swine: *choiros*
     - b) Sow: *hus*
   - 11: Dog: *kuōn*
3. **Horn(s) – Tail**
   - 1: Horn: *keras*
     - a) Horn, Horns (of an animal)
     - b) Horn (figuratively)
   - 2: Tail: *oura*

1. ANIMAL(S) – BEAST

1: ANIMALS: *ZŌON*

zōon 3/23

Heb 13 11	The bodies of the *animals* whose blood is brought into the sanctuary . . . are burnt outside the camp,
2 P 2 12	people who only insult anything that they do not understand are not reasoning beings, but simply *animals*
Jude 10	these people abuse anything they do not understand . . . just by nature like unreasoning *animals*

2: (WILD) BEAST(S) – ANIMAL: *THĒRION*

1 *thērion 45*   2 *thērio(-macheō) 1*

a) Wild beasts, Wild animals – Creature

V = Viper

Mk 1 13		[Jesus] remained [in the wilderness] . . . with the *wild beasts*,
Ac 11 6		I saw all sorts of animals and *wild beasts*
28 4	V	the natives [of Malta] saw the *creature* suspended from [Paul's] hand
5	V	[Paul] shook the *creature* off into the fire
1 Co 15 32	Δ	2 what good would it do me to fight the *wild animals* at Ephesus?
Tt 1 12		Cretans were never anything but liars, dangerous *animals* and lazy:
Heb 12 20		If even an *animal* touches the mountain, it must be stoned.
Jm 3 7		*Wild animals* and birds, reptiles and fish can all be tamed by man,
Rv 6 8		[Plague and Hades] were given authority . . . to kill by the sword, by famine, by plague and *wild beasts*.

b) (the two) Beasts (of Revelation)

Rv 11 7		the *beast* that comes out of the Abyss is going to make war on [the two witnesses]
13 1		I saw a *beast* emerge from the sea; it had seven heads and ten horns . . . ² . . . the *beast* was like a leopard . . . the dragon had handed over to it his own power . . . ³ . . . the whole world had marvelled and followed the *beast*.
2		
3		
4		⁴ They prostrated themselves in front of the dragon because he had given the *beast* his authority; and they prostrated themselves in front of the *beast*, saying, 'Who can compare with the *beast*?'

Rv 13	11	a second *beast* . . . had two horns like a lamb, but made a
	12	noise like a dragon. [12] This second *beast* . . . extended its authority everywhere, making the world . . . worship the first *beast*,
	14	Through the miracles which it was allowed to do on behalf of the first *beast*, it was able to . . . persuade [people] to
	15	put up a statue in honour of the *beast* . . . [15] It was allowed to breathe life into [this] statue of the *beast*, so that the [statue of the] *beast* was able to speak and to have anyone who refused to worship the statue of the *beast* put to death.
	17	[the second beast] made it illegal for anyone to buy or sell anything unless he had been branded with the name of the *beast*
	18	the number of the *beast* . . . is the number of a man, the number 666.
14	9	All those who worship the *beast* [will be made to drink the wine of God's fury]
	11	There will be no respite . . . for those who worshipped the *beast*
15	2	[I saw] those who had fought against the *beast* and won,
16	2	on all the people who had been branded with the mark of the *beast* . . . there came disgusting and virulent sores.
	10	The fifth angel emptied his bowl over the throne of the *beast*
	13	from the jaws of dragon and *beast* . . . I saw three foul spirits come;
17	3	I saw a woman riding a scarlet *beast*
	7	I will tell you the meaning of this woman, and of the *beast* she is riding,
	8	The *beast* . . . once was and now is not . . . and the people of the world . . . will think it miraculous when they see how the *beast* once was and now is not
	11	The *beast*, who once was and now is not, is at the same time the eighth [emperor]
	12	The ten horns are ten kings who . . . will have royal authority only . . . in association with the *beast*.
	13	[The ten kings] are all of one mind in putting their strength . . . at the *beast*'s disposal,
	16	the ten horns and the *beast* will turn against the prostitute,
	17	Gold influenced their minds to . . . agree together to put their royal powers at the *beast*'s disposal
19	19	Then I saw the *beast*, with all the kings of the earth
	20	the *beast* was taken prisoner together with the false prophet who had . . . deceived all who had been branded with the mark of the *beast*
20	4	I saw . . . those who refused to worship the *beast* or his statue
	10	Then the devil . . . will be thrown into the lake of fire and sulphur, where the *beast* and the false prophet are,

3: (FOURFOOTED) ANIMALS, QUADRUPEDS: *TETRA-POUS*

tetra-pous 3

Ac 10	12	[the sheet] contained every possible sort of *animal* and bird,
11	6	I . . . saw all sorts of *animals* and wild beasts
Rm 1	23	they exchanged the glory of . . . God for a worthless imitation, for the image . . . of birds, of *quadrupeds* and reptiles.

4: ANIMAL, BEAST – MOUNT – CATTLE: *KTĒNOS*

ktēnos 4

Lk 10	34	[the Samaritan] lifted him on to his own ⌐mount (lit. *animal*),
Ac 23	24	provide ⌐horses (lit. *animals*) for Paul,
1 Co 15	39	there is human flesh, *animals*' flesh,
Rv 18	13	[there is nobody left to buy] their stocks of *cattle*, sheep, horses

2. SPECIFIC ANIMALS

1: LION – LEOPARD – BEAR: *LEŌN, PARDALIS* and *ARKOS*

1 leōn 9   2 arkos 1   3 pardalis 1

2 Tm 4	17	(cf. Ps 22 22) I was rescued from the *lion*'s mouth.
Heb 11	33	through faith [Gideon, Barak . . . and the prophets] could keep a *lion*'s mouth shut,
1 P 5	8	the devil is prowling round like a roaring *lion*,
Rv 4	7	The first animal was like a *lion*,
5	5 X	the *Lion* of the tribe of Judah . . . has triumphed,
9	8	[these locusts had] teeth like *lions*' teeth.
	17	the horses had *lions*' heads,
10	3	he shouted so loud, it was like a *lion* roaring.
13	2	3/2 the beast was like a *leopard*, with paws like a *bear* and a mouth like a *lion*;

2: FOX: *ALŌPĒX*

alōpēx 3

Mt 8	20	*Foxes* have holes and the birds of the air have nests,
Lk 9	58	*Foxes* have holes and the birds of the air have nests,
13	32	You may go and give that *fox* [Herod] this message: . . . I cast out devils

3: WOLF: *LYKOS*

lykos 6

Mt 7	15	false prophets . . . come to you disguised as sheep but underneath are ravenous *wolves*.
10	16	I am sending you out like sheep among *wolves*;
Lk 10	3	I am sending you out like lambs among *wolves*;
Jn 10	12	The hired man . . . abandons the sheep and runs away as soon as he sees a *wolf* coming, and then the *wolf* attacks
Ac 20	29	fierce *wolves* will invade you and will have no mercy on the flock.

4: CAMEL: *KAMĒLOS*

kamēlos 6

Mt 3	4	John wore a garmet made of *camel*-hair
19	24	it is easier for a *camel* to pass through the eye of a needle
23	24	You blind guides! Straining out gnats and swallowing *camels*!
Mk 1	6	John wore a garment of ⌐camel-skin (G *camel*-hair),
10	25	It is easier for a *camel* to pass through the eye of a needle
Lk 18	25	it is easier for a *camel* to pass through the eye of a needle

5: HORSE – HORSEMEN, CAVALRY: *HIPPOS*

2 hippeus 2   1 hippos 17
3 hippikos 1

Ac 23	23 2	Get two hundred soldiers ready to leave for Caesarea by the third hour of the night with seventy *cavalry*
	32 2	[the soldiers] left the *mounted* escort to go on with [Paul]
Jm 3	3	Once we put a bit into the *horse*'s mouth . . . we have the whole animal under our control.
Rv 6	2	a white *horse* appeared, and the rider on it was holding a bow;
	4	out came another *horse*, bright red, and its rider . . . was given a huge sword.
	5	a black *horse* appeared, and its rider was holding a pair of scales;
	8	another *horse* appeared . . . and its rider was called Plague,
9	7	these locusts were like *horses* armoured for battle;
	9	the noise of [the locusts'] wings sounded like a great charge of *horses* and chariots into battle.
	16 3	there were in [the four angels'] army twice ten thousand times ten thousand *mounted* men.
	17	In my vision I saw the *horses*, and the riders . . . the *horses* had lions' heads,
	19	All the *horses*' power was in their mouths and their tails:
14	20	the blood . . . was up to the *horses*' bridles
18	13	[there is nobody left to buy] their stocks of cattle, sheep, *horses*
19	11	I saw . . . a white *horse* appear; its rider was called Faithful and True;
	14	Behind [The Word of God] . . . rode the armies of heaven on white *horses*.
	18	There will be [at God's feast] . . . the flesh of *horses* and their riders
	19	the beast, with all the kings of the earth . . . gathered together to fight the ⌐rider (lit. [warrior for justice] on his *horse*)
	21	All the rest were killed by the sword of the [rider] on the *horse*,

6: DONKEY, ASS

a) Beast of burden, Ass: hypo-zygion

hypo-zygion 2

Mt 21	5	(Zc 9 9) he rides on a donkey and on a colt, the foal of ⌐a *beast of burden* (or: an *ass*).
2 P 2	16	(cf. Nb 22 28–33) The dumb *donkey* put a stop to that prophet's madness

b) Donkey, Ass: onos

2 onarion 1   1 onos 6

Mt 21	2	you will . . . find a tethered *donkey* and a colt with her.
	5	(Zc 9 9) he is humble, he rides on a *donkey* and on a colt, the foal of ⌐a *beast of burden* (or: an *ass*).

Mt 21	7	[The disciples] brought the *donkey* and the colt,
Lk 13	15	Is there one of you who does not untie his ox or his *donkey* from the manger on the sabbath and take it out for watering?
14	5	Which of you here, if his ᵣson (ᵛ*donkey*) falls into a well . . . will not pull him out on a sabbath day . . .?
Jn 12	14	2 Jesus found a *young donkey* and mounted it – as scripture says: ¹⁵ (Zc 9 9) . . . see, your king is coming, mounted on the colt of a *donkey*.
	15	

c) Colt, Foal: pōlos

pōlos 12

Mt 21	2	you will . . . find a tethered donkey and a *colt* with her.
	5	(Zc 9 9) your king . . . rides on a donkey and on a *colt*, the foal of ᵣa beast of burden (or: an ass).
	7	[The disciples] brought the donkey and the *colt*,
Mk 11	2	you will find a tethered *colt*
	4	[The disciples] went off and found a *colt*
	5	What are you doing, untying that *colt*?
	7	they took the *colt* to Jesus
Lk 19	30	you will find a tethered *colt*
	33	As they were untying the *colt*, its owner said, 'Why are you untying that *colt*?'
	35	throwing their garments over the *colt*'s back they helped Jesus on to it.
Jn 12	15	(Zc 9 9) see, your king is coming, mounted on the *colt* of a donkey.

7: OX, BULL – CALF, HEIFER – CATTLE

a) Ox – Cattle: bous

bous 8

Lk 13	15	Is there one of you who does not untie his *ox* or his donkey from the manger on the sabbath . . .?
14	5	Which of you here, if his ᵣson (ᵛ donkey) falls into a well, or his *ox*, will not pull him out on a sabbath day . . .?
	19	I have bought five yoke of *oxen*
Jn 2	14	in the Temple [Jesus] found people selling *cattle* and sheep
	15	. . . ¹⁵ . . . he drove them all out . . . *cattle* and sheep as well,
1 Co 9	9	(Dt 25 4) You must not put a muzzle on the *ox* when it is treading out the corn. Is it about *oxen* that God is concerned . . .?
1 Tm 5	18	(Dt 25 4) You must not muzzle an *ox* when it is treading out the corn;

b) Bulls, Oxen – Fattened cattle: tauros *and* sitistos

    1 tauros 4   *2 sitistos 1*

Mt 22	4	/2 my *oxen* and *fattened cattle* have been slaughtered,
Ac 14	13	The priests of Zeus . . . brought garlanded *oxen* to the gates.
Heb 9	13	The blood of goats and *bulls* and the ashes of a heifer . . . restore the holiness [of those who are defiled]
10	4	*Bulls*' blood and goats' blood are useless for taking away sins,

c) Fatted calf – Bull-calf: moschos

    1 moschos   3⎫   *6*   *3 moscho(-poieō) 1*
    2 moschos siteutos 3⎭

I = Idol

Lk 15	23	2 Bring the *calf we have been fattening*, and kill it;
	27	2 your father has killed the *calf we had fattened*
	30	2 for this son of yours . . . you kill the *calf we had been fattening*.
Ac 7	41 I	3 [the Israelites] made a *bull calf*
Heb 9	12	[Christ] has entered the sanctuary . . . taking with him not the blood of goats and *bull calves*, but his own blood,
	19	Moses . . . took the *calves*' blood, the goats' blood and some water,
Rv 4	7	the second [animal was] like a *bull*,

d) Heifer: damalis

damalis 1

Heb 9	13	The blood of goats . . . and the ashes of a *heifer* . . . restore the holiness [of those who are defiled]

e) Cattle: thremma

thremma 1

Jn 4	12	our father Jacob . . . drank from [this well] himself with his sons and his *cattle*

8: LAMB – SHEEP

a) Lamb: amnos

amnos 4

Jn 1	29 X	Look, there is the *lamb* of God that takes away the sin of the world.
	36 X	John . . . said, 'Look, there is the *lamb* of God'.
Ac 8	32 X	(Is 53 7) like a *lamb* that is dumb in front of its shearers . . . he never opens his mouth.
1 P 1	19 X	[the ransom was paid] in the precious blood of a *lamb* without spot or stain,

b) Lamb: arnion

    2 arēn 1   *1 arnion 30*

Lk 10	3	2 I am sending you out like *lambs* among wolves.
Jn 21	15	Jesus said to Simon Peter . . ., 'Feed my *lambs*'.
Rv 5	6 X	Then I saw . . . a *Lamb* that seemed to have been sacrificed;
	8 X	the four animals prostrated themselves before the *Lamb*
	12 X	The *Lamb* that was sacrificed is worthy to be given power,
	13 X	To the One who is sitting on the throne and to the *Lamb*, be all praise;
6	1 X	Then I saw the *Lamb* break one of the seven seals,
	16 X	hide us away from the One who sits on the throne and from the anger of the *Lamb*.
7	9 X	[a huge number of people] were standing in front of the throne and in front of the *Lamb*,
	10 X	Victory to our God, who sits on the throne, and to the *Lamb*!
	14 X	These are the people who . . . have washed their robes white . . . in the blood of the *Lamb*.
	17 X	the *Lamb* . . . will be their shepherd and will lead them to springs of living water;
12	11 X	They have triumphed over [the dragon] by the blood of the *Lamb*
13	8 X	everybody whose name has not been written down . . . in the book of the sacrificial *Lamb* [will worship the beast]
	11	a second beast . . . had two horns like a *lamb*,
14	1 X	Next in my vision I saw Mount Zion, and standing on it a *Lamb*
	4 X	[those who have kept their virginity] follow the *Lamb* wherever he goes; they have been redeemed . . . to be the first-fruits for God and the *Lamb*.
	10 X	[those who worship the beast] will be tortured in the presence of the holy angels and the *Lamb*
15	3 X	[those who had fought against the beast] were singing the hymn . . . of the *Lamb*:
17	14 X	[the ten kings] will go to war against the *Lamb*; but the *Lamb* . . . will defeat them
	X	
19	7 X	this is the time for the marriage of the *Lamb*
	9	Happy are those who are invited to the wedding feast of the *Lamb*,
21	9 X	Come here and I will show you the bride that the *Lamb* has married.
	14	each one of [the twelve foundation stones] bore the name of one of the twelve apostles of the *Lamb*.
	X	
	22 X	the Lord God Almighty and the *Lamb* were themselves the temple,
	23 X	the *Lamb* was a lighted torch for [the city].
	27 X	only those who are listed in the *Lamb*'s book of life [may come into the city].
22	1	the angel showed me the river of life rising from the throne of God and of the *Lamb*
	X	
	3 X	The throne of God and of the *Lamb* will be in its place in the city;

c) Sheep: probaton

    3 probatikos 1   *1 probaton 37*
    2 probation 2

Mt 7	15	Beware of false prophets . . . disguised as *sheep*
9	36	the crowds . . . were . . . like *sheep* without a shepherd.
10	6	go rather to the lost *sheep* of the House of Israel.
	16	I am sending you out like *sheep* among wolves;
12	11	If any one of you here had only one *sheep* and it fell down a hole on the sabbath day, would he not . . . lift it out?
	12	Now a man is far more important than a *sheep*,
15	24	I was sent only to the lost *sheep* of the House of Israel.
18	12	Suppose a man has a hundred *sheep* and one of them strays;
25	32	the shepherd separates *sheep* from goats.
	33	[The Son of Man] will place the *sheep* on his right hand and the goats on his left.
26	31	(Zc 13 7) I shall strike the shepherd and the *sheep* of the flock will be scattered,
Mk 6	34	they were like *sheep* without a shepherd.
14	27	(Zc 13 7) I shall strike the shepherd and the *sheep* will be scattered,
Lk 15	4	What man among you with a hundred *sheep*, losing one would not . . . go after the missing one . . .?

Lk 15	6	I have found my *sheep* that was lost.
Jn 2	14	in the Temple [Jesus] found people selling cattle and *sheep*
	15	. . . [15] . . . he drove them all out . . . cattle and *sheep* as well,
5	2	3 Now at the *Sheep* Pool in Jerusalem there is a ᵛ building (G pool), called Bethzatha in Hebrew,
10	1	anyone who does not enter the *sheep*fold through the gate
	2	. . . is a thief; [2] The one who enters through the gate is the shepherd of the *flock*; [3] . . . the *sheep* hear his voice,
	3	
	4	one by one he calls his own *sheep* . . . [4] . . . he goes ahead of them and the *sheep* follow
	7	I am the gate of the *sheep*[fold]. [8] All others who have come are thieves . . . but the *sheep* took no notice of them.
	8	
	11	the good shepherd is one who lays down his life for his *sheep*. [12] The hired man, since . . . the *sheep* do not belong to him, abandons the *sheep* . . . as soon as he sees a wolf coming . . . [13] . . . he is only a hired man and has no concern for the *sheep*.
	12	
	13	
	15	I lay down my life for my *sheep*.
	16	there are other *sheep* I have that are not of this fold,
	26	you do not believe, because you are no *sheep* of mine.
	27	The *sheep* that belong to me listen to my voice;
21	16	2 Jesus said to [Simon Peter], 'Look after my *sheep*'.
	17	2 Jesus said to [Simon Peter], 'Feed my *sheep*'.
Ac 8	32	(Is 53 7) Like a *sheep* that is led to the slaughter-house . . . he never opens his mouth.
Rm 8	36	(Ps 44 23) we are . . . reckoned as *sheep* for the slaughter.
Heb 13	20	our Lord Jesus . . . the great Shepherd of the *sheep*
1 P 2	25	(Is 53 6) You had gone astray like *sheep*
Rv 18	13	[there is nobody left to buy] their stocks of cattle, *sheep*, horses and chariots,

9: GOAT, KID

a) Goat, Kid: eriphos

2 eriphion 1   1 eriphos 2

Mt 25	32	[the Son of Man] will separate men one from another as the shepherd separates sheep from *goats*. [33] He will place the sheep on his right hand and the *goats* on his left.
	33	
Lk 15	29	[the elder son] answered his father, '. . . you never offered me so much as a *kid*

b) Goat: tragos

tragos 4

Heb 9	12	[Christ] has entered the sanctuary . . . taking with him not the blood of *goats* . . . but his own blood . . . [13] The blood of *goats* and bulls and the ashes of a heifer . . . restore the holiness of their outward lives;
	13	
	19	Moses . . . took the calves' blood, the *goats*' blood and some water,
10	4	Bulls' blood and *goats*' blood are useless for taking away sins,

10: PIG – SOW

a) Pigs, Swine: choiros

choiros 12

Mt 7	6	○	do not throw your pearls in front of *pigs*,
8	30		there was a large herd of *pigs* feeding, [31] and the devils pleaded with Jesus, 'If you cast us out, send us into the herd of *pigs*'. [32] . . . they came out and made for the *pigs*; and at that the whole herd charged down the cliff into the lake
	31		
	32		
Mk 5	11		there was on the mountainside a great herd of *pigs* feeding, [12] and the unclean spirits begged [Jesus], 'Send us to the *pigs*, let us go into them'. [13] So . . . the unclean spirits . . . went into the *pigs*.
	12		
	13		
	16		those who had witnessed it reported . . . what had become of the *pigs*.
Lk 8	32		there was a large herd of *pigs* feeding there . . . [33] The devils came out of the man and went into the *pigs*,
	33		
15	15		one of the local inhabitants . . . put him . . . to feed the *pigs*.
	16		[the prodigal son] would willingly have filled his belly with the husks the *pigs* were eating

b) Sow: hus

hus 1

| 2 P 2 | 22 | When the *sow* has been washed, it wallows in the mud. |

11: DOG: KUŌN

1 kuōn 5   2 kynarion 4

Mt 7	6		Do not give *dogs* what is holy;
15	26		It is not fair to take the children's food and throw it to the *house-dogs*. [27] . . . but even the *house-dogs* can eat scraps that fall from their master's table.
	27	2/2	
Mk 7	27		it is not fair to take the children's food and throw it to the *house-dogs*. [28] . . . but the *house-dogs* . . . can eat the children's scraps.
	28	2/2	
Lk 16	21		*Dogs* even came and licked [Lazarus's] sores.
Ph 3	2		Beware of *dogs*! Watch out for the people who are making mischief.
2 P 2	22		(Pr 26 11) The *dog* goes back to his own vomit
Rv 22	15		These others must stay outside [the city]: *dogs*, fortune-tellers, and fornicators, and murderers,

3. HORN(S) – TAIL

1: HORN: KERAS

keras 11

a) Horn, Horns (of an animal)

Rv 5	6	[the Lamb] had seven *horns*, and it had seven eyes,
12	3	a huge red dragon which had seven heads and ten *horns* [appeared]
13	1	I saw a beast emerge from the sea: it had seven heads and ten *horns*, with a coronet on each of its ten *horns*,
	11	I saw a second beast . . . it had two *horns* like a lamb,
17	3	I saw . . . a scarlet beast which had seven heads and ten *horns*
	7	I will tell you the meaning . . . of the beast . . . with the seven heads and the ten *horns*.
	12	The ten *horns* are ten kings
	16	the ten *horns* . . . will turn against the prostitute,

b) Horn (figuratively)

| Lk 1 | 69 | [Blessed be the Lord, for] he has raised up for us a ᵣpower (lit. *horn*) for salvation |
| Rv 9 | 13 | I heard a voice come out of the four *horns* of the golden altar |

2: TAIL: OURA

oura 5

Rv 9	10	[These locusts'] *tails* were like scorpions' *tails*, with stings,
	19	All the horses' power was in . . . their *tails*: their *tails* were like snakes,
12	4	[The dragon's] *tail* dragged a third of the stars from the sky

---

ANOINT – OIL

| **1. Anoint:** *chriō*
  1: (Christ, a Christian, is) An-
    ointed – (the) Anointing
  2: Anoint = Daub, Smear | **2. Anoint (with oil, with ointment):** *a-leiphō*
3. Oil: *elaion* |

1. ANOINT: CHRIŌ

**1 chriō 5   4 en-chriō 1
2 chrisma 3   3 epi-chriō 2**

For other Greek forms, especially *christos*, see **JESUS CHRIST 1.**

1: (CHRIST, A CHRISTIAN, IS) ANOINTED – (THE) ANOINTING

Lk 4	18		(Is 61 1) The spirit of the Lord has been given to me, for he has *anointed* me.
Ac 4	27		your holy servant Jesus whom you *anointed*,
10	38		God had *anointed* [Jesus] with the Holy Spirit
2 Co 1	21		it is God himself who . . . has *anointed* us,
Heb 1	9		(Ps 45 8) God, your God, has *anointed* you with the oil of gladness,
1 Jn 2	20	2	you have been *anointed* by the Holy One, and have all received the knowledge.
	27	2	you have not lost the *anointing* that he gave you, . . . the *anointing* he gave teaches you everything;

2: ANOINT = DAUB, SMEAR

Jn	9 6 X		3	[Jesus] made a paste with the spittle, ˅anointed (G put this over) the eyes of the blind man,
	11 X		3	Jesus . . . made a paste, *daubed* my eyes with it
Rv	3 18		4	[Laodicea,] buy from me . . . eye ointment to ⌐put (lit. *smear*) on your eyes

2. ANOINT (WITH OIL, WITH OINTMENT): A-LEIPHŌ

a-leiphō 9

Mt	6 17	when you fast, ⌐put oil on your head (lit. *anoint* your head with oil) and wash your face,
Mk	6 13	[the Twelve] *anointed* many sick people with oil and cured them.
	16 1	Mary . . . and Salome, bought spices with which to go and *anoint* him.
Lk	7 38	[the women] covered his feet with kisses and *anointed* them with the ointment.
	46	You did not *anoint* my head with oil, but she has *anointed* my feet with ointment.
Jn	11 2	It was the same Mary . . . who *anointed* the Lord with ointment
	12 3	Mary brought in a pound of very costly ointment . . . and with it *anointed* the feet of Jesus,
Jm	5 14	[the elders] must *anoint* [the sick man] with oil in the name of the Lord

3. OIL: ELAION

elaion 11

Mt	25 3	the foolish [bridesmaids] did take their lamps, but they
	4 <	brought no *oil*, 4 whereas the sensible ones took flasks of *oil* as well as their lamps
	8 <	the foolish ones said to the sensible ones, 'Give us some of your *oil*: our lamps are going out'.
Mk	6 13	[the Twelve] anointed many sick people with *oil* and cured them.
Lk	7 46	[Simon,] You did not anoint my head with *oil*,
	10 34	[The Samaritan] bandaged his wounds, poured *oil* and wine on them.
	16 6	['How much do you owe my master?'] 'One hundred measures of *oil*'
Heb	1 9	(Ps 45 8) God, your God, has anointed you with the *oil* of gladness.
Jm	5 14	[the elders] must anoint [the sick man] with *oil* in the name of the Lord
Rv	6 6	do not tamper with the *oil* or the wine.
	18 13	[there is nobody left in Babylon to buy] wine, *oil*, flour and corn;

AS MANY AS – AS MUCH AS

1: All who, Those who – As many as	Whenever
2: Everything that, All that – Whatever – How much	4: As long as
3: Every time that – As often as –	5: As much as, As far as, In so far as – Just as, Equal

1	*hosos* (83)	3	*hosakis* 3
2	*eph' hoson* (2)		

1: ALL WHO, THOSE WHO – AS MANY AS

Mt	14 36	*all those who* touched [the fringe of Jesus's cloak] were completely cured.
	22 9 ●	invite ⌐everyone (lit. *as many as*) you can find to the wedding.
Mk	3 10	*all who* were afflicted . . . were crowding forward to touch [Jesus]
	6 56	*all those who* touched [Jesus] were cured.
Lk	9 5	As for *those who* do not welcome you . . . leave their town
Jn	1 12 ●	to *all who* did accept him he gave power to become children of God,
Ac	2 39 ●	The promise that was made is for . . . *all those who* are far away,
	4 6	[the rulers, elders and scribes had a meeting with] ⌐all the members (lit. *all who* were) of the high-priestly families.
	34	*all those who* owned land or houses would sell them,
	10 45	Jewish believers *who* had accompanied Peter were *all* astonished
	13 48	*all who* were destined for eternal life became believers.

Rm	2 12 ●	⌐Sinners (lit. *All those who* were sinners) who were not subject to the Law will perish all the same, without that Law; ⌐sinners (lit. *all those who* were sinners) who were under the Law will have that Law to judge them.
	6 3 ●	⌐when we (lit. *all of us who*) were baptised in Christ Jesus . . . were baptised in his death;
	8 14 ●	⌐Everyone (lit. *As many a person as* is) moved by the Spirit is a son of God.
Ga	3 10 ●	*those who* rely on the keeping of the Law are under a curse,
	27 ●	⌐All (lit. *As many of you as* have been) baptised in Christ, you have all clothed yourselves in Christ,
	6 12	It is ⌐only self-interest that makes them (lit. It is all [with the intention of] making a good showing for *those who*) want to force circumcision on you –
	16	Peace and mercy to *all who* follow this rule,
Ph	3 15	⌐We who (lit. *All of us who*) are called perfect must all think in this way.
Col	2 1	I do have to struggle . . . for *so many* others who have never seen me face to face.
1 Tm	6 1 ●	⌐All slaves (lit. *As many as* are slaves) under the yoke must have unqualified respect for their masters,
Heb	2 15 ●	[Christ could] set free *all those who* had been held in slavery
Rv	2 24	on . . . *all of you* who have not accepted this teaching . . . I am not laying any special duty;
	3 19	I am the one who reproves and disciplines *all those* he loves
	13 15	[The second beast] was allowed . . . to have ⌐anyone who (lit. *all those who*) refused to worship the statue of the beast put to death.
	18 17	*all those who* make a living from the sea will be keeping a safe distance,

2: EVERYTHING THAT, ALL THAT – WHATEVER – HOW MUCH

Mt	17 12	they treated [Elijah[as they pleased (lit. did *whatever* they pleased to [Elijah])
	18 18 ●	*whatever* you bind on earth shall be considered bound in heaven; *whatever* you loose on earth shall be considered loosed in heaven.
Mk	3 8	great numbers who had heard of *all* [Jesus] was doing came to him.
	5 19	tell [your people] *all that* the Lord in his mercy has done for you.
	20	the man . . . spread throughout the Decapolis *all that* Jesus had done for him.
	6 30	The apostles . . . told [Jesus] *all* they had done and *all* they had taught.
	9 13	they have ⌐treated [Elijah] as they pleased (lit. done *whatever* they pleased to [Elijah])
	10 21 ●	Go and sell *everything* you own
Lk	4 23	We have heard *all that* happened in Capernaum, do the same here
	8 39	'Go back home . . . and report *all that* God has done for you.' So the man . . . spread throughout the town *all that* Jesus had done for him.
	9 10	the apostles gave [Jesus] an account of *all* they had done.
	11 8	persistence will be enough to make him . . . give his friend *all* he wants.
	12 3	*whatever* you have said in the dark will be heard in the daylight,
Jn	11 22 ●	*whatever* you ask of God, he will grant you
	16 13	[the Spirit of truth] will say only *what* he has learnt;
Ac	4 23 ●	[the apostles] told [the community] *everything* the chief priests and elders had said to them.
	28 ●	[Herod and Pontius Pilate made an alliance] only to bring about *the very thing that* you had predetermined
	9 13	people have told me about . . . *all* the harm [Saul] has been doing to your saints in Jerusalem.
	16	I myself will show him *how much* he himself must suffer for my name.
	39	[They showed Peter] tunics and ⌐other clothes (G *all that*) Dorcas had made
	14 27	[Paul and Barnabas] gave an account of *all that* God had done with them.
	15 4	[Paul and Barnabas] gave an account of *all that* God had done with them.
	12	they listened to Paul and Barnabas describing *all* the signs . . . God had worked through them
Rm	3 19	Now *all* this *that* the Law says is said . . . for the benefit of those who are subject to the Law,
	15 4	*everything that* was written long ago . . . was meant to teach us something about hope
1 Co	2 9	(Is 64 3) we teach . . . things beyond the mind of man, *all that* God has prepared for those who love him.
2 Co	1 20 ●	*however many* the promises God made, the Yes to them all is in him.
Ph	4 8	fill your minds with *everything that* is true, *everything that* is noble, *everything that* is good and ⌐pure (lit. *everything that* is pure), *everything that* we love and ⌐honour (lit. *everything that* we honour),

2 Tm 1 18	You know ... *how much* [Onesiphorus] helped me at Ephesus.
Jude 10	these people abuse *anything* they do not understand; and *the* [*only*] *things* they do understand ... will turn out to be fatal to them.
Rv 1 2	John has written down *everything* he saw

3: EVERY TIME THAT – AS OFTEN AS – WHENEVER

1 Co 11 25	3 *Whenever* you drink [this cup], do this as a memorial of me.
26	3 *every time* you eat this bread and drink this cup, you are proclaiming his death,
Rv 11 6	3 [My two witnesses] are able to lock up the sky ... *as often as* they like.

4: AS LONG AS

Mt 9 15	the bridegroom's attendants would never think of mourning 2 *as long as* the bridegroom is still with them.
Mk 2 19	*As long as* they have the bridegroom with them, they could not think of fasting.
Rm 7 1	laws affect a person only ᴾduring (lit. for *as long as*) his lifetime.
1 Co 7 39	A wife is tied *as long as* her husband is alive.
Ga 4 1	an heir ... is no different from a slave for *as long as* he remains a child.
Heb 10 37	(Hab 2 3) Only a little while now, ᴾa very little while (lit. just *as long as* that, only *as long as* that), and the one that is coming will have come;
2 P 1 13	2 it is my duty, *as long as* I am in this tent, to keep stirring you up with reminders,

5: AS MUCH AS, AS FAR AS, IN SO FAR AS – JUST AS, EQUAL

Mt 25 40	*in so far as* you did this to one of the least of these brothers of mine, you did it to me.
45	*in so far as* you neglected to do this to one of the least of these, you neglected to do it to me.
Mk 3 28	all men's sins will be forgiven, and ᴾall their blasphemies (lit. *however much* they blaspheme);
7 36	ᴾthe more (lit *as much as*) [Jesus] insisted, the more widely they published [the healing of the deaf man],
Jn 6 11	Jesus took ... the fish, giving out *as much as* was wanted.
Heb 3 3	he has been found to deserve ᴾa greater glory than Moses. It (lit. *as much* a greater glory than Moses *as*) is the difference between the honour given to the man that built the house and the house itself.
7 20	ᴾWhat is more (lit. And *for all that*), this was not done without the taking of an oath.
8 6	[Christ] has been given a ministry of a far higher order, and *to the same degree* it is a better covenant of which he is the mediator,
9 27	ᴾSince (lit. *In so far as*) men only die once, [so Christ too offers himself only once]
Rv 18 7	ᴾEvery one of her shows and orgies is to be matched by a (lit. For *as much as* she put on her shows and orgies, she should receive a similar amount of) torture or ... grief,
21 16	the city ... was twelve thousand furlongs in length ... and *equal* in height.

ASIA

1. **Asia**
   1: The province of Asia
   2: Ephesus, the capital of the province
2. **Cappadocia, Pontus and Bithynia**
3. **Caria**
4. **Cilicia**
5. **Galatia**
6. Lycaonia
7. Lycia
8. Lydia
9. Mysia
10. Pamphylia
11. Phrygia
12. Pisidia

1. ASIA

1: THE PROVINCE OF ASIA
Asia 20   Asiarch 1 (Ac 19 31)

Ac 2 9	people from ... Judaea and Cappadocia, Pontus and *Asia*, ... ¹¹ we hear [these Galilean men] preaching in our own language about the marvels of God.

Ac 6 9	certain people came forward to debate with Stephen, ... others from Cilicia and *Asia*.
16 6	[Paul and Timothy] travelled through Phrygia ... having been told by the Holy Spirit not to preach the word in *Asia*.
19 10	people from all over *Asia*, both Jews and Greeks, were able to hear the word of the Lord.
22	[Paul] remained for a time in *Asia*.
26	nearly everywhere in *Asia*, this man Paul has persuaded and converted a great number of people
27	Diana ... venerated all over *Asia*, yes, and everywhere in the civilised world.
31	some of the *Asiarchs*, who were friends of [Paul's],
20 4	[Paul] was accompanied (ᵛ as far as *Asia*) by Sopater ... as well as Tychicus and Trophimus who were from *Asia*.
16	Paul had decided to pass wide of Ephesus so as to avoid spending time in *Asia*,
18	ever since the first day I set foot among you in *Asia*,
21 27	some Jews from *Asia* caught sight of [Paul] in the Temple and stirred up the crowd and seized him,
24 19	some Jews from *Asia* ... – these are the ones who should have appeared before you and accused me
27 2	a vessel from Adramyttium bound for ports on the *Asiatic* coast,
Rm 16 5	Greetings to my friend Epaenetus, the first of *Asia*'s gifts to Christ;
1 Co 16 19	All the churches of *Asia* send you greetings.
2 Co 1 8	the things we had to undergo in *Asia* were more of a burden then we could carry,
2 Tm 1 15	Phygelus and Hermogenes and all the others from *Asia* refuse to have anything more to do with me.
1 P 1 1	Peter ... to all those living among foreigners in the Dispersion of Pontus, Galatia, Cappadocia, *Asia* and Bithynia,
Rv 1 4	John, to the seven churches of *Asia*:

2: EPHESUS, THE CAPITAL OF THE PROVINCE
Ephesus 16   A Alexander 2   1 polis 2/164
Ephesians 5   D Demetrius 2
Tyrannus 1 (Ac 19 9)

Ac 18 19	[Paul, Priscilla and Aquila] reached *Ephesus* ... [Paul]
21	went alone to the synagogue ... ²¹ Then he sailed from *Ephesus*.
24	An Alexandrian Jew named Apollos now arrived in *Ephesus*.
19 1	While Apollos was in Corinth, Paul made his way overland as far as *Ephesus*,
9	[Paul] took his disciples apart ... in the lecture room of *Tyrannus*.
17	Everybody in *Ephesus*, both Jews and Greeks, heard about this episode;
24 D	A silversmith called *Demetrius*, who employed a large number of craftsmen making silver shrines of Diana,
26	not just in *Ephesus* but nearly everywhere in Asia, this man Paul has ... converted a great number of people
28	[the silversmiths] started to shout, 'Great is Diana of the *Ephesians*!'
29 1	The whole *town* was in an uproar
33 A	The Jews pushed *Alexander* to the front, and when some of the crowd shouted encouragement (ᵛ made him stand
A	away from the crowd) [*Alexander*] raised his hand for silence in the hope of being able to explain things to the people.
34	When they realised he was a Jew, they all started shouting ... 'Great is Diana of the *Ephesians*!'
35	When the town clerk eventually succeeded in calming the crowd, he said, 'Citizens of *Ephesus*! Is there anybody
1	alive who does not know that the *city* of the *Ephesians* is the guardian of the temple of great Diana ...
38 D	If *Demetrius* and the craftsmen ... want to complain
20 16	Paul had decided to pass wide of *Ephesus*
17	From Miletus [Paul] sent for the elders of the church at *Ephesus*.
21 29	[Jews from Asia] had, in fact, previously seen Trophimus the *Ephesian* in the city with [Paul]
1 Co 15 32	what good would it do me to fight the wild animals at *Ephesus*?
16 8	shall be staying at *Ephesus* until Pentecost ⁹ because a big and important door has opened for my work
Ep 1 1	From Paul ... to the saints [who are at *Ephesus*]
1 Tm 1 3	As I asked you when I was leaving for Macedonia, please stay at *Ephesus*,
2 Tm 1 18	You know ... how much [Onesiphorus] helped me at *Ephesus*.
4 12	I have sent Tychicus to *Ephesus*.
Rv 1 11	Write down all that you see in a book, and send it to the seven churches of *Ephesus*, Smyrna, Pergamum, Thyatira, Sardis, Philadelphia and Laodicea.

Rv 2 1   Write to the angel of the church in *Ephesus* . . . ² I know . . . how hard you work and how much you put up with.

2. CAPPADOCIA, PONTUS AND BITHYNIA

Bithynia 2   *Pontus 3*
Cappadocia 2

Ac 2 9   Parthians, Medes and Elamites; people from . . . *Cappadocia, Pontus* and Asia,

16 7   When [Paul and Timothy] reached the frontier of Mysia they thought to cross it into *Bithynia,*

18 2   a Jew called Aquila whose family came from *Pontus.*

1 P 1 1   Peter . . . to all those living among foreigners in the Dispersion of *Pontus*, Galatia, *Cappadocia*, Asia and *Bithynia,*

3. CARIA

Cnidus 1   *Miletus 3*   *Trogyllium 1*

Ac 20 15   we touched at Samos and, after stopping at *Trogyllium*, made *Miletus* the next day.

17   From *Miletus* [Paul] sent for the elders of the church of Ephesus.

27 7   we had difficulty in making *Cnidus.*

2 Tm 4 20   I left Trophimus ill at *Miletus.*

4. CILICIA

Cilicia 8   *Tarsus 5*   1 *polis* 1/164

Ac 6 9   certain people came forward to debate with Stephen . . . others from *Cilicia* and Asia,

9 11   ask . . . for someone called Saul, who comes from *Tarsus.*

30   the brothers [at Damascus] . . . sent [Saul] off from there to *Tarsus.*

11 25   Barnabas then left for *Tarsus* to look for Saul,

15 23   to the brothers of pagan birth in . . . Syria and *Cilicia.*

41   [Paul] travelled through Syria and *Cilicia,*

21 39   1 I am a Jew and a citizen of the well-known *city of Tarsus* in *Cilicia.*

22 3   I am a Jew and was born at *Tarsus* in *Cilicia.*

23 34   The governor . . . learning that [Paul] was from *Cilicia* . . .

27 5   [we sailed] across the open sea off *Cilicia* and Pamphylia . . . to reach Myra

Ga 1 21   After that I went to Syria and *Cilicia,*

5. GALATIA

Galatia 5   *Galatian 2*   *Gaul* 1*

Ac 16 6   [Paul and Timothy] travelled through Phrygia and the *Galatian* country,

18 23   [Paul] continuing his journey through the *Galatian* country and then through Phrygia,

1 Co 16 1   you are to do as I told the churches in *Galatia* to do.

Ga 1 2   From Paul to the churches of *Galatia*, and from all the brothers who are here with me,

3 1   Are you people in *Galatia* mad? Has someone put a spell on you,

2 Tm 4 10 △   Crescens has gone to *Galatia* (ᵛ *Gaul**) and Titus to Dalmatia;

1 P 1 1   Peter . . . to all those living among foreigners in the Dispersion of Pontus, *Galatia*, Cappadocia,

6. LYCAONIA

Lycaonia 2   *Derbe 4*   1 *polis* 6/164
          Iconium 6
    L *Lystra 6*

Ac 13 51   [The Jews of Antioch expelled Paul and Barnabas] so they . . . went off to *Iconium*;

14 1   At *Iconium* they went to the Jewish synagogue,

4   1 The people in the *city* were divided,

6   [Paul and Barnabas] went off for safety to *Lycaonia* where,

L 1   in the *towns* of *Lystra* and *Derbe* and in the surrounding country,

8 L   A man sat there [in *Lystra*] who had never walked in his life,

11   When the crowd saw what Paul had done they shouted in the language of *Lycaonia*, 'These people are gods who have come down to us . . .' ¹³ The priests of ˹Zeus-outside-the-Gate (lit. Zeus-outside-the-*town*) proposing that all the

L 1   people should offer sacrifice with them,

Ac 14 19   Then some Jews arrived from Antioch and *Iconium* . . .

L 1   They stoned Paul and dragged him outside the *town*, thinking he was dead.

20 L 1   but . . . [Paul] stood up and went back to the *town*. The next day he and Barnabas went off to *Derbe.*

21   1 Having preached the Good News in that *town* . . . they went
L   back through *Lystra* and *Iconium* to Antioch.

16 1 L   From there [Paul] went to *Derbe*, and then on to *Lystra*. Here there was a disciple called Timothy . . .

2 L   The brothers at *Lystra* and *Iconium* spoke well of Timothy,

20 4   [Paul] was accompanied by . . . Gaius ᵛ from Doberus (G from *Derbe*) and Timothy,

2 Tm 3 11   persecutions . . . that came to me in places like Antioch,
L   *Iconium* and *Lystra*

7. LYCIA

Lycia 1   *Myra 2*
Patara 1

Ac 21 1   we reached Rhodes, and from there went on to *Patara* (ᵛ and *Myra*)

27 5   then across the open sea off Cilicia . . . to reach *Myra* in *Lycia.*

8. LYDIA

Philadelphia 2   *Smyrna 2*   1 *polis* 1/164
Sardis 3   *Thyatira 4*

Ac 16 14   1 Lydia . . . from the *town* of *Thyatira* who was in the purple-dye trade.

Rv 1 11   Write . . . to the seven churches of Ephesus, *Smyrna*, Pergamum, *Thyatira*, *Sardis*, *Philadelphia* and Laodicea.

2 8   Write to the angel of the church in *Smyrna* . . . ⁹ I know the trials you have had,

18   Write to the angel of the church in *Thyatira* . . . ²⁰ you are encouraging the woman Jezebel

24   But on the rest of you in *Thyatira* . . . who have not accepted this teaching

3 1   Write to the angel of the church in *Sardis* . . . you are reputed to be alive and yet are dead.

4   There are a few in *Sardis* . . . who have kept their robes from being dirtied,

7   Write to the angel of the church in *Philadelphia* and say, 'Here is the message of the holy and faithful one

9. MYSIA

Mysia 2   *Adramyttium 1*   *Antipas 1* (Rv 2)
          Assos 2
          Pergamum 2
          Troas 6

Ac 16 7   When [Paul and Timothy] reached the frontier of *Mysia* they thought to cross it into Bithynia . . . ⁸ they went

8   through *Mysia* and came down to *Troas.*

11   Sailing from *Troas* we made a straight run for Samothrace;

20 5   [Sopater . . . Trophimus] went on to *Troas* where they waited for us.

6   We ourselves left Philippi . . . and met them . . . at *Troas,*

13   we set sail for *Assos*, where we were to take Paul on board;

Rv 20 14   When [Paul] rejoined us at *Assos* we . . . went on to Mitylene.

27 2   We boarded a vessel from *Adramyttium*

2 Co 2 12   When I went up to *Troas* to preach the Good News of Christ,

2 Tm 4 13   bring the cloak I left with Carpus in *Troas,*

Rv 1 11   Write . . . to the seven churches of Ephesus . . . *Pergamum,*

2 12   Write to the angel of the church in *Pergamum* . . . ¹³ I

13   know where you live, in the place where Satan is enthroned . . . and that you . . . did not disown your faith in me even when my faithful witness, *Antipas*, was killed

10. PAMPHYLIA

Pamphylia 5   *Attalia 1*
Perga 3

Ac 2 10   [There were . . . men living in Jerusalem from every nation . . . people from] Phrygia and *Pamphylia,*

13 13   Paul and his friends went by sea from Paphos to *Perga* in *Pamphylia*

14   The others carried on from *Perga* till they reached Antioch in Pisidia.

Ac 14 24	They passed through Pisidia and reached *Pamphylia*. ²⁵ Then
25	after proclaiming the word at *Perga* they went down to *Attalia*
15 38	[Mark] who had deserted them in *Pamphylia*
27 5	then across the open sea off Cilicia and *Pamphylia*, to reach Myra

11. PHRYGIA

Phrygia 3   Colossae 1   Laodicea 6
Hierapolis 1   Laodicean 1

Ac 2 10	[There were . . . men living in Jerusalem from every nation . . . people from] *Phrygia* and Pamphylia,
16 6	[Paul and Timothy] travelled through *Phrygia* and the Galatian country,
18 23	[Paul] spent a short time [in Antioch] before continuing his journey through the Galatian country and then through *Phrygia*,
Col 1 2	From Paul . . . to the saints in *Colossae*,
2 1	I do have to struggle hard for . . . those in *Laodicea*,
4 13	[Epaphras] works hard for . . . those at *Laodicea* and *Hierapolis*,
15	Please give my greetings to the brothers at *Laodicea* and to Nympha and the church which meets in her house.
16	send [this letter] on to be read in the church of the *Laodiceans*; and get the letter from *Laodicea* for you to read yourselves.
Rv 1 11	Write . . . to the seven churches of Ephesus . . . and *Laodicea*.
3 14	Write to the angel of the church in *Laodicea* . . . ¹⁵ . . . you are neither cold nor hot

12. PISIDIA

Pisidia 2   Antioch 4   1 polis 2/164

Ac 13 14		[Paul and Barnabas] reached *Antioch* in *Pisidia*.
44	1	almost the whole *town* assembled to hear the word of God.
50		the Jews worked upon some of the devout women of the
	1	upper classes and the leading men of the *city*
14 19		some Jews arrived from *Antioch* and Iconium, and turned the people against the apostles.
21		[Paul and Barnabas] went back through Lystra and Iconium to *Antioch*.
24		[Paul and Barnabas] passed through *Pisidia* and reached Pamphylia.
2 Tm 3 11		the persecutions . . . that came to me in places like *Antioch*, Iconium and Lystra

---

ASK – PRAY

1. Question – Examine: *ana-krinō*
  1: Question – Examine – Study
  2: Question (judicially) – Examine
2. Ask – Examine: *etazō*
  1: Ask – Find out – Inquire
  2: Examine
3. Ask – Inquire, Enquire – Interrogate: *pynthanomai*
4. Ask: *erōtaō*
  1: Ask – Put a question – Question
  2: Ask (judicially) – Put a question – Question
  3: Ask for, Beg – Ask to, Urge, Invite – Ask that, Request
  4: Ask (God) – Pray (to)
5. Ask – Plead, Beg – Advocate: *para-kaleō*
  1: Ask, Invite, Appeal to – Beg, Beseech – Plead, Implore

  2: the Advocate – Counsellor (*para-klētos*)
6. Ask – Pray – Beg: *aiteō*
  1: Ask (God) – Pray
  2: Ask – Demand, Call for – Beg
  3: Beggar – Beg
7. Ask – Pray – Beg: *deomai*
  1: Ask (God) – Pray, Prayer – Supplication, Petition
  2: Ask (Jesus) – Beg – Implore
  3: Ask – Beg, Beseech – Appeal
8. Pray – Prayer: *euchomai*
  1: Jesus prays to God
  2 Pray – Say prayers
9. Intercession – Plead: *en-tynchanō*
  1: Intercede – Plead for
  2: "Plead against" = Petition (against) – Complain about (to a third party)

1. QUESTION – EXAMINE: *ANA-KRINŌ*

1 ana-krinō 9/16   2 ana-krisis 1

1: QUESTION – EXAMINE – STUDY

Ac 17 11	every day [the Jews of Beroea] *studied* the scriptures

1 Co 10 25	Do not hesitate to eat anything that is sold in butchers' shops: there is no need to *raise questions* of conscience;
27	eat whatever is put in front of you, without *asking questions*

2: QUESTION (JUDICIALLY) – EXAMINE

Lk 23 14	Now I have *gone into the matter* [of Jesus] myself in your presence
Ac 4 9	you are *questioning* us today about an act of kindness to a cripple,
12 19	Herod . . . had the guards *questioned*, and . . . gave orders for their execution.
24 8	if you *ask* [Lysias] you can find out for yourself the truth of all our accusations
25 26	2 after the *examination* [of Paul] I may have something to write [to his Imperial Majesty].
28 18	[The Romans] *examined* me and would have set me free,
1 Co 9 3	to those who want to *interrogate* me [I say]: Have we not every right to eat and drink?

2. ASK – EXAMINE: *ETAZŌ*

2 an-etazō 2   1 ex-etazō 3

1: ASK – FIND OUT – INQUIRE

Mt 2 8	Go and *find out* all about the child,
10 11	*ask* for someone trustworthy and stay with him
Jn 21 12	None of the disciples was bold enough to *ask* [Jesus], 'Who are you?'

2: EXAMINE

Ac 22 24	2 the tribune . . . ordered [Paul] to be *examined* under the lash,
29	2 those who were about to *examine* [Paul] hurriedly withdrew,

3. ASK – INQUIRE, ENQUIRE – INTERROGATE: *PYNTHANOMAI*

pynthanomai 11

Mt 2 4	[Herod] *enquired* of them where the Christ was to be born.
Lk 15 26	[Hearing music the elder son] *asked* what it was all about.
18 36	When [the blind man] heard the crowd going past he *asked* what it was all about.
Jn 4 52	[The court official] *asked* them when the boy had begun to recover.
Ac 4 7	[The Sanhedrin] began to *interrogate* [the prisoners],
10 18	[The men sent by Cornelius were] calling out to ˹know (lit. *ask*)˺ if . . . Peter was lodging there.
29	[Peter said,] I ˹should like to know exactly (lit. am *enquiring*)˺ why you sent for me.
21 33	the tribune . . . *enquired* who [Paul] was and what he had done.
23 19	the tribune . . . *asked*, 'What is it you have to tell me?'
20	²⁰ . . . The Jews have made a plan to ask you to take Paul down to the Sanhedrin tomorrow, as though they meant to *inquire* more closely into his case.
34	˹Learning (lit. Having *learnt by enquiry*)˺ that [Paul] was from Cilicia [the governor] said,

4. ASK: *ERŌTAŌ*

1 erōtaō 63   2 ep-erōtaō 56
3 di-erōtaō 1   4 ep-erōtēma 1

X = Question put to Jesus

1: ASK – PUT A QUESTION – QUESTION

Mt 12 10	X	2	[The Pharisees] *asked* him, 'Is it against the law to cure a man on the sabbath day?'
16 13			Jesus . . . *put this question* to his disciples, 'Who do people say the Son of Man is?'
17 10	X	2	the disciples *put this question* to him, 'Why do the scribes say . . .?'
19 17	X	2	Why do you *ask* me about what is good?
21 24			'And I' replied Jesus 'will *ask* you a question, only one: ²⁵ John's baptism . . .?'
22 23	X	2	Sadducees . . . *put this question* to him, ²⁸ 'Now at the resurrection . . .?'
35	X	2	one of [the Pharisees] *put a question*, ³⁶ 'Master, which is the greatest commandment'. . .?

Mt 22	41		2	Jesus *put* to [the Pharisees] *this question,* [42] 'What is your opinion about the Christ?'
	46	X	2	no one dared to *ask* him any further questions.
Mk 4	10	X		the Twelve, together with the others who formed his company, *asked* what the parables meant.
	5	9	2	'What is your name?' Jesus *asked* [the unclean spirit].
7	5	X	2	So these Pharisees and scribes *asked* him, 'Why do your disciples not respect the tradition of the elders . . .?'
	17	X	2	his disciples *questioned* him about the parable.
8	5			[Jesus] *asked* them, 'How many loaves have you?'
	23		2	he *asked* [the blind man], 'Can you see anything?'
	27		2	he *put this question* to his disciples, 'Who do people say I am?'
	29		2	'But you', he *asked* 'who do you say I am?'
9	11	X	2	[Peter, James and John] *put this question* to him, 'Why do the scribes say that Elijah has to come first?'
	16		2	'What are you arguing about with [the scribes]?' he *asked.*
	21		2	Jesus *asked* the father, 'How long has this been happening to him?'
	28	X	2	his disciples *asked* him privately, 'Why were we unable to cast [the unclean spirit] out?'
	32	X	2	[the disciples] were afraid to *ask* him.
	33		2	[Jesus] *asked* them, 'What were you arguing about on the road?'
10	2	X	2	Some Pharisees . . . *asked,* 'Is it against the law for a man to divorce his wife?'
	10	X	2	the disciples *questioned* him again about this,
	17	X	2	a man . . . *put this question* to him, '. . . what must I do to inherit eternal life?'
11	29		2	Jesus said to them, 'I will *ask* you a question, only one . . . [30] John's baptism . . .?'
12	18	X	2	Sadducees *put this question* to him, [23] 'Now at the resurrection . . .?'
	28	X	2	One of the scribes . . . *put a question* to him, 'Which is the first of all the commandments?'
	34	X	2	no one dared to *question* him any more.
13	3	X	2	Peter, James, John and Andrew *questioned* him privately, [4] 'Tell us, when is this going to happen . . .?'
15	44			Pilate . . . summoned the centurion and *enquired,* if [Jesus] was already dead.
Lk 2	46		2	[Jesus' parents] found him . . . sitting among the doctors and *asking* them questions;
3	10		2	all the people *asked* [John the Baptist], 'What must we do, then?'
	14		2	Some soldiers *asked* him in their turn, 'What about us . . .'
6	9		2	I *put it* to you: is it against the law on the sabbath to do good,
8	9	X	2	His disciples *asked* him what this parable might mean,
	30		2	'What is your name?' Jesus *asked* [the unclean spirit].
9	18		2	in the presence of his disciples he *put this question* to them, 'Who do the crowds say I am?'
	45	X		[The Son of Man is going to be handed over into the power of men:] they were afraid to *ask* him about what he had just said.
17	20	X	2	*Asked* by the Pharisees when the kingdom of God was to come,
18	18	X	2	A member of one of the leading families *put this question* to him, 'what have I to do to inherit eternal life?'
	40		2	Jesus . . . *asked* [the blind man], [41] 'What do you want me to do for you?'
19	31			If anyone *asks* you, 'Why are you untying [the colt]?'
20	3			'And I' replied Jesus 'will *ask* you a question.'
	21	X	2	They *put* to him *this question,* [22] 'Is it permissible for us to pay taxes to Caesar or not?'
	27	X	2	Some Sadducees . . . *put this question* to him, [33] 'Now, at the resurrection . . .?'
	40	X	2	[the scribes] would not dare to *ask* him any more questions.
21	7	X	2	[some people] *put* to him *this question:* 'Master . . . when will this [destruction of the Temple] happen . . .?'
22	64	X	2	[the guards] blindfolded him and *questioned* him . . . 'Who hit you then?'
	68			if I *question* you, you will not answer.
Jn 1	19			the Jews sent priests and Levites . . . to *ask* [John], 'Who are you?'
	21			'Well then,' they *asked* 'are you Elijah?'
	25			they *put* this further *question* to him, 'Why are you baptising . . .?'
5	12			[the Jews] *asked,* 'Who is the man who said to you, "Pick up your mat and walk".'
8	7	X		As they persisted with their *question* . . . [Jesus] said, 'If there is one of you who has not sinned . . .'
9	2	X		His disciples *asked* him, 'Rabbi, who sinned . . .'
	15			the Pharisees *asked* him how he had come to see,
	19			*asking* [the parents] . . . 'how is it that he is now able to see?'
16	5	X		Not one of you has *asked,* 'Where are you going?'
	19	X		Jesus knew that they wanted to *question* him,
	23	X		you will not *ask* me any questions.
	30	X		Now we see that you know everything, and do not have to wait for *questions to be put* into words;
18	7		2	[Jesus] *asked* [the soldiers] a second time, 'Who are you looking for?'
Ac 1	6	X		they *asked* him, 'Lord, has the time come? Are you going to restore the kingdom to Israel?'
Ac 10	17		3	the men sent by Cornelius . . . had *asked* where Simon's house was and they were now standing at the door,
Rm 10	20		2	(Is 65 1) I have revealed myself to those who did not consult (lit. *ask for*) me;
1 Co 14	35		2	If [women] have any questions [to ask], they should *ask* their husbands

2: ASK (JUDICIALLY) – PUT A QUESTION – QUESTION

Mt 27	11	X	2	the governor *put* to him *this question,* 'Are you the king of the Jews?'
Mk 14	60	X	2	the high priest . . . *put this question* to Jesus, 'Have you no answer to that?'
	61	X	2	The high priest *put a* second *question* to him, 'Are you the Christ . . .?'
15	2	X	2	Pilate *questioned* him, 'Are you the king of the Jews?'
	4	X	2	Pilate *questioned* him again, 'Have you no reply at all?'
Lk 23	3	X	2	Pilate *put* to him *this question,* 'Are you the king of the Jews?'
	6		2	Pilate . . . *asked* if the man were a Galilean?
	9	X	2	[Herod] *questioned* [Jesus] at some length;
Jn 9	21			He is old enough: ⌐let him speak for himself (lit. *ask* him).
	23			the parents [of the man who was born blind] said, 'He is old enough; *ask* him.'
18	19	X		The high priest *questioned* Jesus about . . . his teaching.
	21	X		why *ask* me? *Ask* my hearers what I taught:
Ac 5	27		2	the high priest ⌐demanded an explanation (lit. *questioned* them).
	23 34		2	The governor . . . *asked* [Paul] what province he came from.

3: ASK FOR, BEG – ASK TO, URGE, INVITE – ASK THAT, REQUEST

Mt 15	23	X		his disciples . . . *pleaded* with him, 'Give her what she wants
16	1	X	2	The Pharisees and Sadducees . . . *asked* if he would show them a sign
Mk 7	26	X		the woman . . . *begged* him to cast the devil out of her daughter.
Lk 4	38	X		Simon's mother-in-law was suffering from a high fever and they *asked* him to do something for her.
5	3			[Jesus] *asked* [Simon] to put out a little from the shore.
7	3	X		[A centurion] sent some Jewish elders to him to *ask* him to come and heal his servant
	36	X		One of the Pharisees *invited* him to a meal.
8	37	X		The entire population of the Gerasene territory . . . *asked* Jesus to leave them.
11	37	X		a Pharisee *invited* him to dine at his house.
14	18	<		The first [who had been invited] said, '. . . ⌐Please (lit. I *beg* you,) accept my apologies.'
	19	X		Another said, '. . . ⌐Please (lit. I *beg* you,) accept my apologies.'
	32	X		[The less strong king] would send envoys to ⌐sue (lit. *beg*) for peace.
16	27			The rich man replied, 'Father, I *beg* you then to send Lazarus
Jn 4	31	X		the disciples were *urging* him, 'Rabbi, do have something to eat.'
	40	X		the Samaritans . . . *begged* him to stay with them.
	47	X		[A court official] *asked* him to come and cure his son
12	21			[Some Greeks] *put* this *request* to [Philip], 'Sir, we should like to see Jesus.'
19	31			the Jews *asked* Pilate to have the legs [of the crucified] broken
	38			Joseph of Arimathaea . . . *asked* Pilate to let him remove the body of Jesus.
Ac 3	3			When [the cripple] saw Peter and John . . . he *begged* from them.
10	48			[The converted pagans in Caesarea] *begged* [Peter] to stay on for some days.
16	39			[The magistrates] *begged* [Paul and Silas] to leave the town.
18	20			[The Jews at Ephesus] *asked* [Paul] to stay longer
23	18			The prisoner Paul . . . *requested* me to bring this young man to you;
	20			The Jews have made a plan to *ask* you to take Paul down to the Sanhedrin tomorrow.
Ph 4	3			I *ask* you, Syzygus . . . to help [Evodia and Syntyche]
1 Th 4	1			brothers, we *urge* you . . . to make more and more progress
5	12			We *appeal* to you, my brothers, to be considerate to those who are working amongst you
2 Th 2	1			⌐please (lit. I *beg* you,) [2] do not get excited too soon
2 Jn	5			I am writing . . . to *plead:* let us love one another.

4: ASK (GOD) – PRAY (TO)

Jn 14	16	X		I shall *ask* the Father, and he will give you another Advocate
16	26	X		I do not say that I shall *pray* to the Father for you,
17	9	X		I *pray* for them; I am not *praying* for the world but for those you have given me,
	15	X		I am not *asking* you to remove them from the world,
	20	X		I *pray* not only for these,

| 1 P | 3 | 21 | 4 | the baptism . . . ʳa pledge (or: a *request*) made to God from a good conscience, |
| 1 Jn | 5 | 16 | | there is a sin that is death, and I will not say that you must *pray* about that. |

5. ASK – PLEAD, BEG – ADVOCATE: *PARA-KALEŌ*

1 *para-kaleō* 60/109   2 *para-klētos* 5
3 *para-klēsis* 2

1: ASK, INVITE, APPEAL TO – BEG, BESEECH – PLEAD, IMPLORE

Θ = Asked from God;   X = Asked from Jesus

Mt	8	5	X	a centurion came up and *pleaded* with him.
		31	X	and the devils *pleaded* with Jesus, '. . . send us into the herd of pigs'.
		34	X	[the Gadarenes] *implored* him to leave the neighbourhood.
	14	36	X	*begging* him just to let [the sick] touch the fringe of his cloak.
	18	29	<	His fellow servant fell at his feet and *implored* him,
		32	<	I cancelled all that debt of yours when you *appealed to* me.
	26	53	Θ	Or do you think that I cannot *appeal to* my Father
Mk	1	40	X	A leper came to him and *pleaded* on his knees:
	5	10	X	[the unclean spirit] *begged* him earnestly not to send them out of the district.
		12	X	and the unclean spirits *begged* him,
		17	X	[the Gerasenes] began to *implore* Jesus to leave the neighbourhood.
		18	X	the man who had been possessed *begged* to be allowed to stay with him.
		23	X	[Jairus] *pleaded* with him earnestly, saying, 'My little daughter is desperately sick.'
	6	56	X	*begging* him to let [the sick] touch even the fringe of his cloak.
	7	32	X	they brought him a deaf man . . . and they *asked* him to lay his hand on him.
	8	22	X	some people brought to him a blind man whom they *begged* him to touch.
Lk	7	4	X	[the elders of Capernaum] *pleaded* earnestly with him. '[The centurion] deserves this of you'
	8	31	X	[the devils] *pleaded* with him not to order them to depart into the Abyss. ³² . . . the devils *pleaded* with him to let them go into [pigs].
		32	X	
		41	X	Jairus . . . fell at Jesus' feet and *pleaded* with him to come to his house,
	15	28	<	[the elder son] refused to go in, and his father came out to *plead* with him;
Ac	8	31		[the eunuch] *invited* Philip to get in and sit by his side.
	9	38		the disciples . . . sent two men ʳwith an urgent message for [Peter] (lit. to *appeal to* [Peter]), 'Come . . . as soon as possible'.
	13	42		As [Paul and his companions] left they were *asked* to preach on the same theme the following sabbath.
	16	9		a Macedonian . . . *appealed to* [Paul] in these words, 'Come across to Macedonia'
		15		[Lydia] *sent* us an *invitation*: '. . . come and stay with us';
		39		[the magistrates] came and *begged* [Paul and Silas] (§ when they had taken them out they asked them) to leave the town.
	19	31		some of the Asiarchs . . . sent messages *imploring* [Paul] not to take the risk of going into the theatre.
	21	12		we and everybody there *implored* Paul not to go on to Jerusalem.
	24	4		I *beg* you to give us a brief hearing.
	25	2		The chief priests and leaders of the Jews informed [Festus] of of the case against Paul, urgently ³ *asking* him . . . to have [Paul] transferred to Jerusalem.
	28	14		[at Puteoli] we found some brothers and ʳwere much rewarded by staying (or: were *asked* to stay) a week with them.
		20		That is why I have *asked* to see you
Rm	12	1		I *beg* you . . . by offering your living bodies as a holy sacrifice,
	15	30		But I *beg* you, brothers, by our Lord Jesus Christ and the love of the Spirit, to help me
	16	17		I *implore* you, brothers, be on your guard against anybody who encourages trouble
1 Co	1	10		I do *appeal to* you, brothers . . . to be united again in your belief
	4	16		That is why I *beg* you to copy me
	16	12		As for our brother Apollos, I *begged* him to come to you
		15		There is something else to *ask* you, brothers, ¹⁶ . . . put yourselves at the service of people like this,
2 Co	2	8		So I am *asking* you to give some definite proof of your love for him.
	5	20		it is as though God were *appealing* through us,
	6	1		we *beg* you once again not to neglect the grace of God
	8	4		3 [the Macedonians begging and] *begging* us for the favour of sharing in this service to the saints . . . ⁶ Because of this, we have *asked* Titus . . . to bring this work of mercy to the same point of success
		6		

2 Co	8	17		3 [Titus] did what we *asked* him;
	9	5		I have thought it necessary to *ask* these brothers to go on to you ahead of us,
	10	1		this is Paul himself *appealing to* you by the gentleness . . . of Christ
	12	8	X	I have *pleaded* with the Lord three times for [the angel of Satan] to leave me,
Ep	4	1		I . . . *implore* you therefore to lead a life worthy of your vocation.
Ph	4	2		I *appeal to* Evodia and I *appeal to* Syntyche to come to agreement with each other, in the Lord;
1 Th	4	1		we urge you and *appeal to* you in the Lord Jesus to make more and more progress
	5	14		And this is what we *ask* you to do, brothers: warn the idlers, give courage to those who are apprehensive,
1 Tm	1	3		ʳplease (lit. I *beg* you to) stay at Ephesus,
Phm		9		I am *appealing to* your love instead,
		10		I am *appealing to* you for a child of mine . . . Onesimus.
Heb	13	19		I *ask* you very particularly to pray
		22		I do *ask* you, brothers, to take these words of advice kindly;
Jude		3		I have been forced to write to you now and *appeal to* you to fight hard for the faith

2: THE ADVOCATE – COUNSELLOR (*PARA-KLĒTOS*)

Jn	14	16		2 [the Father] will give you another *Advocate* to be with you for ever, ¹⁷ that Spirit of truth
		26		2 the *Advocate*, the Holy Spirit, whom the Father will send in my name, will teach you everything and remind you of all I have said to you.
	15	26		2 When the *Advocate* comes . . . the Spirit of truth who issues from the Father, he will be my witness.
	16	7		2 because unless I go, the *Advocate* will not come to you;
1 Jn	2	1	X	2 we have our *advocate* with the Father, Jesus Christ, who is just;

6. ASK – PRAY – BEG: *AITEO*

2	*aitēma*	3	7	*ex-aiteomai*	1
1	*aiteō*	70	5	*par-aiteomai*	2/12
3	*ap-aiteō*	2	8	*pros-aiteō*	1
4	*ep-aiteō*	2	6	*pros-aitēs*	2

A = Ask – Pray // Give – Receive

1: ASK (GOD) – PRAY

Mt	6	8		your Father knows what you need before you *ask* him.
	7	7	A	*Ask*, and it will be given to you . . . ⁸ For the one who *asks* always receives . . . ⁹ Is there a man among you who would hand his son a stone when he *asked* for bread? ¹⁰ Or would hand him a snake when he *asked* for a fish? ¹¹ . . . how much more will your Father in heaven give good things to those who *ask* him!
		8		
		9	A	
		10	A	
		11		
			A	
	18	19	A	if two of you on earth agree to *ask* anything at all, it will be granted
	21	22	A	if you have faith, everything you *ask* for in prayer you will receive.
Mk	11	24	A	everything you *ask* and pray for, believe that you have it already,
Lk	11	9	A	*Ask*, and it will be given to you . . . ¹⁰ For the one who *asks* always receives . . . ¹¹ What father among you would hand his son a stone when he *asked* for bread? . . . ¹² Or hand him a scorpion if he *asked* for an egg? ¹³ . . . how much more will the heavenly Father give the Holy Spirit to those who *ask* him!
		10		
		11	A	
		12	A	
		13		
Jn	11	22	A	[Martha said to Jesus,] Whatever you *ask* of God, he will grant you.
	14	13	A	Whatever you *ask* for in my name I will do,
		14	A	If you *ask* for anything in my name, I will do it.
	15	7	A	you may *ask* what you will and you shall get it.
		16	A	the Father will give you anything you *ask* in my name.
	16	23	A	anything you *ask* for from the Father he will grant in my name.
		24	A	Until now you have not *asked* for anything in my name. *Ask* and you will receive,
		26		you will *ask* in my name; and I do not say that I shall pray to the Father for you,
Ac	7	46		[David] *asked* permission to have a temple built for ʳthe House (ᵛ the God) of Jacob,
Ep	3	20		Glory be to him whose power, working in us, can do infinitely more than we can *ask*
Ph	4	6		2 if there is anything you need, pray for it, *asking* God for it with prayer and thanksgiving,
Col	1	9		we have never failed to pray for you, and what we *ask* God is that . . you should reach the fullest knowledge of his will.

Jm	1	5 A	If there is any one of you who needs wisdom, he must *ask*
		6 A	God . . . it will be given to him. [6] But he must *ask* with faith,
	4	2	Why you don't have what you want is because you don't *pray* for it;
		3	When you do *pray* and don't get it, it is because you have not *prayed* properly,
1 Jn	3	22 A	whatever we *ask* him, we shall receive,
	5	14 A	if we *ask* him for anything, and it is in accordance with his will, he will hear us; [15] and, knowing that whatever we
		15 A	may *ask*, he hears us, we know that we have already been
		2/	granted ⌜what (lit. the things *asked* for that) we *asked* of him.
		16 A	If anybody sees his brother commit a sin . . . he has only to *pray*, and God will give life to the sinner

2: ASK – DEMAND, CALL FOR – BEG
X = Question put to Jesus

Mt	5	42 A	Give to anyone who *asks*, and if anyone wants to borrow, do not turn away.
	14	7	[Herod] promised on oath to give [the daughter of Herodias]
		A	anything she *asked*.
	20	20 X	the mother of Zebedee's sons came . . . to *make a request* of [Jesus]
		22	You do not know what you are *asking*
	27	20	The chief priests . . . had persuaded the crowd to *demand* the release of Barabbas
		58 A	[Joseph of Arimathaea] *asked* for the body of Jesus.
Mk	6	22 A	*Ask* me anything you like and I will give it you.
		23 A	I will give you anything you *ask*,
		24 A	[The daughter of Herodias] said to her mother, 'What shall
		25	I *ask* for?' . . . 'The head of John the Baptist'. [25] The
		A	girl . . . *made her request*,
	10	35 X A	we want you to do ⌜us a favour (lit. something we *ask* you for us).
		38 X A	You do not know what you are *asking*
	15	6	5 Pilate used to release a prisoner for them, anyone they *asked* for.
		8	the crowd . . . began to *ask* Pilate the customary favour,
		43 A	Joseph of Arimathaea . . . *asked* for the body of Jesus.
Lk	1	63	[Zechariah] *asked* for a writing-tablet and wrote, 'His name is John'.
	6	30 A /3	Give to everyone who *asks* you, and do not *ask* for your property *back* from the man who robs you.
	12	20	3 Fool! This very night the *demand* will be made for your soul;
		48	when a man has had a great deal given him on trust, even
		A	more will be ⌜expected (lit. *demanded*) of him.
	22	31 Ⓓ	7 Satan . . . has got his ⌜wish (lit. *demand*) to sift you all
	23	23	they kept on shouting . . , *demanding* that he should be crucified.
		24 A	2 Pilate then gave his verdict: their *demand* was to be granted.
		25	[Pilate] released the man they *asked* for.
		52 (A)	[Joseph of Arimathaea] *asked* for the body of Jesus.
Jn	4	9	You are a Jew and you *ask* me, a Samaritan, for a drink?
		10 X A	you would have been the one to *ask*, and he would have given you living water.
Ac	3	14	It was . . . you who *demanded* the reprieve of a murderer
	9	2	[Saul] *asked* [the high priest] for letters addressed to the synagogues
	12	20	the Tyrians and Sidonians . . . negotiated (lit. *asked* for) a treaty,
	13	21 A	[men of Israel] *demanded* a king, and God gave them Saul
		28	[the people of Jerusalem] *asked* Pilate to have [Jesus] executed.
	16	29	The gaoler *called for* lights,
	25	3	[The chief priests and leaders of the Jews informed Festus] *asking* him to support them rather than Paul, and to have him transferred to Jerusalem.
		15	the chief priests and elders of the Jews . . . *demanding* [Paul's] condemnation.
1 Co	1	22	while the Jews *demand* miracles
Ep	3	13	I *beg* you, never lose confidence
Heb	12	19	5 the great voice speaking which made everyone that heard it *beg* that no more should be said to them.
1 P	3	15	and always have your answer ready for people who *ask* you the reason for the hope that you all have.

3: BEGGAR – BEG

Mk	10	46	6 Bartimaeus . . . a blind *beggar*, was sitting at the side of the road.
Lk	16	3	4 what am I to do? . . . Go *begging*? I should be too ashamed.
	18	35	4 there was a blind man sitting at the side of the road *begging*.
Jn	9	8	6 His neighbours and people who earlier had seen him *begging*
		8	said, 'Isn't this the man who used to sit and *beg*?'
Ac	3	2	and they used to put [the cripple] down every day near the Temple entrance . . . so that he could *beg*

7. ASK – PRAY – BEG: *DEOMAI*

2 *deēsis* 18   1 *deomai* 22

1: ASK (GOD) – PRAY, PRAYER – SUPPLICATION, PETITION
3 *hiketēria* 1

X = the Prayer of Jesus

Mt	9	38	so *ask* the Lord of the harvest to send labourers to his harvest.
Lk	1	13	2 your *prayer* has been heard. Your wife Elizabeth is to bear you a son
	2	37	[Anna] never left the Temple, serving God night and day with
		2	fasting and *prayer*.
	5	33	2 John's disciples are always fasting and saying *prayers*, and the disciples of the Pharisees too,
	10	2	so *ask* the Lord of the harvest to send labourers to his harvest.
	21	36	Stay awake, *praying* at all times
	22	32 X	but I have *prayed* for you, Simon, that your faith may not fail,
Ac	4	31	As they *prayed*, the house . . . rocked;
	8	22	Repent of this wickedness of yours, and *pray* to the Lord
		24	*Pray* to the Lord for me yourselves
	10	2	[Cornelius] *prayed* constantly to God.
Rm	1	10	[I never fail] to *ask* to be allowed at long last the opportunity to visit you.
	10	1	2 and I *pray* to God for [Israel] to be saved.
2 Co	1	11	2 You must all join in the *prayers* for us:
	9	14	2 And [the saints'] *prayers* for you, too, show how they are drawn to
Ep	6	18	2 Pray all the time, *asking* for what you need, praying in the
		2	Spirit on every possible occasion. . . . *pray* for all the saints;
Ph	1	4	2/2 every time I *pray* for all of you, I *pray* with joy,
		19	2 I know this will help to save me, thanks to your *prayers*
	4	6	2 if there is anything you need, *pray* for it, asking God for it with prayer and thanksgiving
1 Th	3	10	We are earnestly *praying* night and day to be able to see you
1 Tm	2	1	2 there should be *prayers* offered for everyone –
	5	5	a woman who is really widowed . . . can . . . consecrate all
		2	her days and nights to *petitions* and prayer.
2 Tm	1	3	Night and day . . . I remember you in my *prayers*;
Heb	5	7 X 2/3	[Christ] offered up *prayer* and *entreaty* . . . to the one who had the power to save him out of death,
Jm	5	16	2 The heartfelt *prayer* of a good man works very powerfully.
1 P	3	12	(Ps 34 16) the eyes of the Lord are turned towards the virtuous
		2	(§ his ears to their *cry*.)

2: ASK (JESUS) – BEG – IMPLORE

Lk	5	12	[The leper] *implored* him. 'Sir, . . . you can cure me.'
	8	28 Ⓓ	Jesus, . . . I *implore* you, do not torture me.
		38	The man . . . *asked* to be allowed to stay with him,
	9	38	Master, . . . I *implore* you to look at my son:

3: ASK – BEG, BESEECH – APPEAL

Lk	9	40	I *begged* your disciples to cast [the spirit] out,
Ac	8	34	[The eunuch said to Philip,] ⌜Tell me (lit. I *beseech* you), is the prophet referring to himself or someone else?
	21	39	⌜Please (lit. I *beg* you,) give me permission to speak to the people.
	26	3	[Paul said to King Agrippa,] I *beg* you to listen to me patiently
2 Co	5	20	the *appeal* that we make in Christ's name is: be reconciled to God,
	8	4	[The churches in Macedonia are] *begging* and begging us for the favour of sharing in this service to the saints
	10	2	[I, Paul,] only *ask* that I do not have to bully you when I come,
Ga	4	12	Brothers, all I *ask* is that you should copy me as I copied you.

8. PRAY – PRAYER: *EUCHOMAI*

4 *euchē*	1/3	2 *pros-euchē*	37
3 *euchomai*	2/6	1 *pros-euchomai*	87

1: JESUS PRAYS TO GOD

Mt	14	23	he went up into the hills by himself to *pray*.
	19	13	People brought little children to him, for him to lay his hands on them and say a *prayer*.
	26	36	Stay here while I go over there to *pray*.
		39	he fell on his face and *prayed*. 'My Father,' he said 'if it is possible, let this cup pass me by.

Mt 26	42	Again, a second time, he went away and *prayed*: '. . . your will be done!'
	44	he went away again and *prayed* for the third time, repeating the same words.
Mk 1	35	[Jesus] went off to a lonely place and *prayed* there.
6	46	he went off into the hills to *pray*.
14	32	Stay here while I *pray*.
	35	[Jesus] *prayed* that . . . this hour might pass him by.
	39	Again he went away and *prayed*, saying the same words.
Lk 3	21	Jesus after his own baptism was at *prayer*,
5	16	he would always go off to some place where he could . . . *pray*.
6	12	he went out into the hills to *pray*; and he spent the whole
	2	night in *prayer* to God.
9	18	Now one day when he was *praying* alone in the presence of his disciples
	28	he took with him Peter and John and James and went up the mountain to *pray*. ²⁹ As he *prayed*, the aspect of his face
	29	was changed
11	1	he was . . . *praying*, and when he had finished one of his disciples said, 'Lord, teach us to pray,
22	41	Then he withdrew from them . . . and knelt down and *prayed*. ⁴² 'Father,'
	44	In his anguish he *prayed* even more earnestly,
	45	2 When he rose from *prayer* he went to the disciples

2: PRAY – SAY PRAYERS

Mt 5	44	love your enemies and *pray* for those who persecute you;
6	5	And when you *pray*, do not imitate the hypocrites: they love to *say* their *prayers* standing up in the synagogues
	6	But when you *pray*, go to your private room and . . . *pray* to your Father who is in that secret place,
	7	In your *prayers* do not babble as the pagans do,
	9	So you should *pray* like this: Our Father in heaven,
17	21	2 (ᵛAs for this kind [of devil], it is cast out only by *prayer* and fasting)
21	13	2 (Is 56 7) my house will be called a house of *prayer*; but you are turning it into a robbers' den.
	22	And if you have faith, everything you ask for in *prayer* you will receive.
24	20	*Pray* that you will not have to escape in winter or on a sabbath.
26	41	You should be awake, and *praying* not to be put to the test.
Mk 9	29	This is the kind [of unclean spirit] . . . that can only be driven out by *prayer*.
11	17	2 (Is 56 7) My house will be called a house of *prayer* for all the peoples?
	24	everything you ask and *pray* for, believe that you have it already, and it will be yours.
	25	And when you stand in *prayer*, forgive whatever you have against anybody,
12	40	[the scribes] are the men who swallow the property of widows, while making a show of lengthy *prayers*.
13	18	*Pray* that this may not be in winter.
	33	stay awake (ᵛ and *pray*), because you never know when the time will come.
14	38	You should be awake, and *praying* not to be put to the test.
Lk 1	10	And at the hour of incense the whole congregation was outside, *praying*.
6	28	*pray* for those who treat you badly.
11	1	Lord, teach us to *pray*, just as John taught his disciples. ² He said to them, 'Say this when you *pray*: Father, may your
	2	name be held holy,
18	1	Then he told them a parable about the need to *pray* continually and never lose heart.
	10	Two men went up to the Temple to *pray*, one a Pharisee, the other a tax collector. ¹¹ The Pharisee stood there and *said*
	11	this *prayer* to himself.
19	46	2 (Is 56 7) my house will be a house of *prayer*.
20	47	[the scribes] who swallow the property of widows, while making a show of lengthy *prayers*.
22	40	*Pray* not to be put to the test.
	46	Get up and *pray* not to be put to the test.
Ac 1	14	2 All these joined in continuous *prayer*, together with several women, including Mary the mother of Jesus,
	24	they *prayed*, 'Lord . . . show us therefore which of these two you have chosen
2	42	These remained faithful . . . to the breaking of bread and to
	2	the *prayers*.
3	1	2 Peter and John were going up to the Temple for the *prayers* at the ninth hour,
6	4	2 [we will] continue to devote ourselves to *prayer* and to the service of the word.
	6	They presented [the seven deacons] to the apostles, who *prayed* and laid their hands on them.
8	15	[Peter and John] *prayed* for the Samaritans to receive the Holy Spirit,
9	11	ask for . . . Saul, who comes from Tarsus. At this moment he is *praying*,

Ac 9	40	Peter . . . knelt down and *prayed*. Then he . . . said, 'Tabitha, stand up'.
10	4	2 Your offering of *prayers* and alms . . . has been accepted by God.
	9	Peter went to the housetop at about the sixth hour to *pray*.
	30	Cornelius replied, '. . . I was *praying* in my house at the ninth hour,
	31	2 Cornelius, your *prayer* has been heard and your alms have been accepted as a sacrifice in the sight of God;
11	5	'One day, when I was in the town of Jaffa, [Peter] began 'I fell into a trance as I was *praying* and had a vision . . .'
12	5	2 the Church *prayed* to God for [Peter] unremittingly.
	12	the house of Mary the mother of John Mark, where a number of people had assembled and were *praying*.
13	3	after fasting and *prayer* [the apostles] laid their hands on [Barnabas and Saul]
14	23	with *prayer* and fasting [Paul and Barnabas] commended [the disciples at Lystra] to the Lord
16	13	we went along the river . . . this was a customary place for
	2	*prayer*.
	16	2 One day as we were going to *prayer*,
	25	Late that night Paul and Silas were *praying* and singing God's praises,
20	36	[Paul] knelt down with all [the disciples at Ephesus] and *prayed*.
21	5	we were out of the town [of Tyre]. When we reached the beach, we knelt down and *prayed*;
22	17	when I was *praying* in the Temple, I fell into a trance
28	8	Paul went in to see [Publius's father], and after a *prayer* he laid his hands on the man and healed him.
Rm 1	10	2 I never fail to mention you in my *prayers*,
8	26	when we cannot choose words in order to *pray* properly, the Spirit himself expresses our plea in a way that could never be put into words,
12	12	2 Do not give up if trials come; and keep on *praying*.
15	30	2 help me through my dangers by *praying* to God for me.
1Co 7	5	Do not refuse each other except . . . to leave yourselves free
	2	for *prayer*;
11	4	For a man to *pray* or prophesy with his head covered is a sign of disrespect to his head. ⁵ For a woman, however, it
	5	is a sign of disrespect to her head if she *prays* or prophesies unveiled;
	13	Ask yourselves if it is fitting for a woman to *pray* to God without a veil;
14	13	anybody who has the gift of tongues must *pray* for the power of interpreting them.
	14	if I use this gift in my *prayers*, my spirit may be *praying* but
	15	my mind is left barren. ¹⁵ . . . Surely I should *pray* not only with the spirit but *pray* with the mind as well?
2Co 13	7	3 We *pray* to God that you will do nothing wrong;
	9	3 What we ask in our *prayers* is for you to be made perfect.
Ep 1	16	2 [I] have never failed to remember you in my *prayers*
6	18	2/ *Pray* all the time, asking for what you need, *praying* in the Spirit on every possible occasion.
Ph 1	9	My *prayer* is that your love for each other may . . . never stop improving your knowledge
4	6	if there is anything you need, pray for it, asking God for it
	2	with *prayer* and thanksgiving,
Col 1	3	We have never failed to remember you in our *prayers* and to give thanks for you to God,
	9	we have never failed to *pray* for you, and what we ask God is that . . . you should reach the fullest knowledge of his will.
4	2	2 Be persevering in your *prayers* and be thankful as you stay awake to pray.
	3	*Pray* for us especially, asking God to show us opportunities for announcing the message
	12	2 Epaphras . . . never stops battling for you, *praying* that you will never lapse
1Th 1	2	2 We always mention you in our *prayers* and thank God for you all,
5	17	*pray* constantly; ¹⁸ and for all things give thanks to God,
	25	*Pray* for us, my brothers.
2Th 1	11	we *pray* continually that our God will make you worthy of his call,
3	1	*pray* for us; pray that the Lord's message may spread quickly,
1Tm 2	1	2 there should be prayers offered for everyone – *petitions*, intercessions and thanksgiving –
	8	In every place, then, I want the men to lift their hands up reverently in *prayer*,
5	5	But a woman who is really widowed . . . can . . . consecrate
	2	all her days and nights to petitions and *prayer*.
Phm	4	2 I always mention you in my *prayers* and thank God for you,
	22	2 I am hoping through your *prayers* to be restored to you.
Heb 13	18	We are sure that your own conscience is clear . . . *pray* for us.
	19	I ask you very particularly to *pray* that I may come back to you all the sooner.
Jm 5	13	If any one of you is in trouble, he should *pray*; . . . ¹⁴ If one
	14	of you is ill, he should send for the elders of the church, and they must anoint him with oil in the name of the Lord and *pray* over him.

Jm	5 15	4	The *prayer* of faith will save the sick man
	16		*pray* for one another, and this will cure you;
	17	/2	Elijah . . . *prayed* ⌐*hard* (lit. a *prayer*) for it not to rain, and no rain fell . . . [18] then he *prayed* again and the sky gave rain
	18		
1 P	3 7		husbands must always treat their wives with consideration in their life together . . . This will stop anything from coming in the way of your *prayers*.
		2	
	4 7	2	to *pray* better, keep a calm and sober mind.
Jude	20		use your most holy faith as your foundation . . , *praying* in the Holy Spirit;
Rv	5 8		each one of them . . . had a golden bowl full of incense made of the *prayers* of the saints.
		2	
	8 3		A large quantity of incense was given to [the angel] to offer with the *prayers* of all the saints
		2	
	4		the smoke of the incense went up in the presence of God and with it the *prayers* of the saints.
		2	

9. INTERCESSION – PLEAD: *EN-TYNCHANŌ*

2 en-teuxis   2   3 *hyper-en-tynchanō 1*
1 en-tynchanō 5

1: INTERCEDE – PLEAD FOR

Rm	8 26	Ⓢ	the Spirit himself ⌐*expresses our plea* (or: *intercedes*) in a way that could never be put into words,
	27	Ⓢ	3 the *pleas* of the saints *expressed* by the Spirit are according to the mind of God.
	34	X	could anyone condemn? Could Christ Jesus? No! He . . . *pleads* for us.
1 Tm	2 1	2	there should be prayers offered for everyone . . . *intercessions* and thanksgiving
	4 5	2	the word of God and the *prayer* make [all food] holy.
Heb	7 25	X	[Jesus] is living for ever to *intercede* for all who come to God through him.

2: "PLEAD AGAINST" = PETITION (AGAINST) – COMPLAIN ABOUT (TO A THIRD PARTY)

Ac	25 24		the whole Jewish community has *petitioned* me [about Paul],
Rm	11 2		Do you remember . . . how [Elijah] *complained* to God *about* Israel's behaviour?

ASTONISHED – WONDER

1. Be astonished, Be amazed, Take by surprise – Marvel (at), Amazement, Wonder – Wonderful: *thaumazō*	dumbfounded
	2: Trance
2. (Be) Astonished, Amazed, Spellbound – Make a deep impression on – Awestruck: *ek-plēssō*	**4. Be astonished, Be astounded, Be struck with amazement – Excitement, Alarm – Daze:** *thambos*
3. Be astounded, Astonishment – Be dumbfounded – Trance: *ex-(h)istēmi*	**5. a Wonder, Marvel, Strange thing:** *en-doxos*
1: Be astounded, Be amazed, Be astonished – Astonishment – Be	**6. Overcome (with astonishment):** *peri-echō*

1. BE ASTONISHED, BE AMAZED, TAKE BY SURPRISE – MARVEL (AT), AMAZEMENT, WONDER – WONDERFUL: *THAUMAZŌ*

3 *thauma*   2   1   *thaumazō 42/43*
4 *thaumasios 1*   5 *ek-thaumazō*   *1*
2 *thaumastos 6*

Mt	8 10	X	When Jesus heard [what the centurion said] he *was astonished*
	27		The men *were astounded* and said, 'Whatever kind of man is this?'
	9 33		the people *were amazed*. 'Nothing like this has ever been seen in Israel' they said.
	15 31		The crowds *were astonished* to see the dumb speaking,
	21 15	4	At the sight of the *wonderful things* [Jesus] did . . . the chief priests . . . were indignant.
	20		The disciples *were amazed* when they saw [the fig tree wither].
	42	2	(Ps 118 23) the Lord's doing . . . is *wonderful* to see
	22 22		[Give back to Caesar what belongs to Caesar.] This reply *took* them *by surprise*,
	27 14		to the governor's complete *amazement*, [Jesus] offered no reply

Mk	5 20		[the Gerasene demoniac told] all that Jesus had done for him. And everyone *was amazed*.
	6 6	X	[Jesus] *was amazed* at their lack of faith.
	12 11	2	(Ps 118 23) the Lord's doing . . . is *wonderful* to see
	17	5	This reply [of Jesus] *took* them completely *by surprise*.
	15 5		to Pilate's *amazement*, Jesus made no further reply.
	44		Pilate, *astonished* that [Jesus] should have died so soon,
Lk	1 21		the people . . . *were surprised* that [Zechariah] stayed in the sanctuary so long.
	63		[Zechariah] wrote, 'His name is John'. And they *were* all *astonished*.
	2 18		everyone . . . *was astonished* at what the shepherds had to say.
	33		the child's father and mother stood there *wondering* at the things that were being said about [Jesus],
	4 22		they *were astonished* by the gracious words that came from [Jesus's] lips.
	7 9	X	Jesus . . . *was astonished* at [the centurion]
	8 25		They *were* awestruck and *marvelled* . . . 'Who can this be . . .?'
	9 43		everyone *was full of* ⌐*admiration* for (or: *amazement* at) all [Jesus] did,
	11 14		the dumb man spoke, and the people *were amazed*.
	38		The Pharisee . . . *was surprised* that [Jesus] had not first washed before the meal.
	20 26		[Jesus's] answer *took* them *by surprise* and they were silenced.
	24 12		⌐Peter . . . went back home, *amazed* at what had happened⌐.
	41		[the disciples] still could not believe it, and they stood there *dumbfounded*;
Jn	3 7		Do not *be surprised* when I say: You must be born from above.
	4 27		his disciples . . . *were surprised* to find [Jesus] speaking to a woman,
	5 20		even greater things than these, works that will *astonish* you.
	28		Do not *be surprised* at this, for the hour is coming when the dead will leave their graves
	7 15		The Jews *were astonished* and said, 'How did he learn to read? He has not been taught.'
	21		One work I did, and you *are* all *surprised* by it.
	9 30	2	Now here is an *astonishing thing*! [Jesus] has opened my eyes, and you don't know where he comes from!
Ac	2 7		They *were* amazed and *astonished*. 'Surely' they said 'all these men speaking are Galileans?'
	3 12		Why *are* you so *surprised* at this? Why are you staring at us as though we had made this man walk by our own power . . .?
	4 13		[The members of the Sanhedrin] *were astonished* at the assurance shown by Peter and John,
	7 31		Moses *was amazed* by what he saw [in the flames of a bush].
	13 41		(Hab 1 5) mockers; *be amazed*, and perish!
2 Co	11 14	3	There *is* nothing *unexpected* about that; . . . Satan himself goes disguised as an angel of light,
Ga	1 6		I *am astonished* at the promptness with which you have turned away from the one who called you
2 Th	1 10		[our Lord Jesus,] ⌐seen in his glory by (lit. the *wonder* of) all who believe in him;
1 P	2 9	2	God . . . called you out of the darkness into his *wonderful* light.
1 Jn	3 13		You must not *be surprised*, brothers, when the world hates you;
Rv	13 3		the whole world had *marvelled* and followed the beast.
	15 1	2	What I saw next, in heaven, was a great and *wonderful* sign:
	3	2	How great and *wonderful* are all your works, Lord God Almighty;
	17 6		when I saw [the woman], I ⌐was completely mystified (lit.
	7	/3	*marvelled* in great *amazement*). [7] The angel said to me, ⌐'Don't you understand (lit. What *are* you *amazed at*)?' . . . [8] The beast . . . once was and now is not . . .
	8		And the people of the world . . . will *think* it *miraculous* when they see how the beast once was and now is not and is still to come.

2. (BE) ASTONISHED, AMAZED, SPELLBOUND – MAKE A DEEP IMPRESSION ON – AWESTRUCK: *EK-PLĒSSŌ*

ek-plēssō 13

Mt	7 28		Jesus had now finished what he wanted to say, and his teaching *made a deep impression on* the people
	13 54		they were *astonished* and said, 'Where did the man get this wisdom . . .?'
	19 25		When the disciples heard this they were *astonished*.
	22 33		his teaching *made a deep impression on* the people who heard it.
Mk	1 22		his teaching *made a deep impression on* them because, unlike the ⌐scribes, he taught them with authority.

Mk 6 2   most of them were *astonished* . . . They said, 'Where did the man get all this?'

7 37   Their ⌐*admiration* (or: *astonishment*) was unbounded. 'He has done all things well,' they said

10 26   They were more *astonished* than ever . . . 'who can be saved?'

11 18   the people were ⌐carried away (lit. *spellbound*) by his teaching.

Lk 2 48   [Jesus's parents] were ⌐*overcome* (or: *astonished*) when they saw [Jesus],

4 32   his teaching *made a deep impression on* them because he spoke with authority.

9 43   everyone was *awestruck* by the greatness of God.

Ac 13 12   The proconsul . . . became a believer, being *astonished* by what he had learnt about the Lord.

3. BE ASTOUNDED, ASTONISHMENT – BE DUMBFOUNDED – TRANCE: *EX-(H)ISTĒMI*

1 *ex-(h)istēmi 15/17*   2 *ek-stasis 7*

1: BE ASTOUNDED, BE AMAZED, BE ASTONISHED – ASTONISHMENT – BE DUMBFOUNDED

Mt 12 23   All the people *were astounded* and said, 'Can this be the son of David?'

Mk 2 12   [the paralytic] walked out in front of everyone, so that they *were all astounded*

5 42   2 The little girl got up . . . they were *overcome with astonishment,*

6 51   the wind dropped. [The disciples] *were* utterly and completely *dumbfounded,*

16 8   the women . . . ran away from the tomb because they were 2 frightened ⌐*out of their wits* (or: and *amazed*);

Lk 2 47   all those who heard [Jesus] *were astounded* at his intelligence and his replies.

5 26   2 [the paralytic got up.] They *were* all *astounded*

8 56   [the child got up.] Her parents *were astonished,*

24 22   some women from our group have *astounded* us:

Ac 2 7   They *were amazed* and astonished. 'Surely' they said 'all these men speaking are Galileans?'

12   Everyone *was amazed* and . . . they asked one another what it all meant.

3 10   2 They *were* all astonished and ⌐unable to explain (lit. *dumbfounded* at) what had happened to [the lame man].

8 9   Simon . . . *astounded* the Samaritan people.

11   They had only been won over to [Simon] because of the long time he had spent ⌐*working* on them (lit. *astounding* them by working) with his magic.

13   Simon . . . *was astonished* when he saw the wonders and great miracles that took place.

9 21   All [Saul's] hearers *were amazed.*

10 45   Jewish believers . . . *were* all *astonished* that the gift of the Holy Spirit should be poured out on the pagans too,

12 16   they . . . *were amazed* to see that it really was Peter himself.

2: TRANCE

Ac 10 10   2 [Peter] fell into a *trance*

11 5   2 [Peter said:] I fell into a *trance* as I was praying and had a vision

22 17   2 when I was praying in the Temple, I fell into a *trance*

4. BE ASTONISHED, BE ASTOUNDED, BE STRUCK WITH AMAZEMENT – EXCITEMENT, ALARM – DAZE: *THAMBOS*

2 *thambeō 3*   1 *ek-thambeō 4*
3 *thambos 3*   4 *ek-thambos 1*

Mk 1 27   2 [the unclean spirit went out of the man.] The people were . . . *astonished*

9 15   The moment they saw [Jesus] the whole crowd *were struck with amazement*

10 24   2 The disciples *were astounded* by these words.

32   2 Jesus was walking on ahead of [the disciples]; they were *in a daze*

14 33 X   [at Gethsemane] a sudden *fear came over* [Jesus], and great distress.

16 5   On entering the tomb [the women] saw a young man in a white robe . . . and they *were struck with amazement.*

6   There is no need for *alarm* . . . Jesus . . . has risen,

Lk 4 36   3 *Astonishment* seized [the people] and they were all saying to one another, 'What teaching!'

5 9   Simon . . . and his companions were completely 3 overcome with *astonishment* at the catch they had made.

Ac 3 10   [Everyone could see the paralysed beggar walking.] They 3 *were* all *astonished* . . . [11] Everyone came running towards

11   4 [Peter and John] *in great excitement,*

5. A WONDER, MARVEL, STRANGE THING: *EN-DOXOS*

1 *en-doxos 1/4*   2 *para-doxos 1*

Lk 5 26   2 We have seen *strange things* today.

13 17   all the people were overjoyed at all the *wonders* [Jesus] worked.

6. OVERCOME (WITH ASTONISHMENT): *PERI-ECHŌ*

peri-echō 1

Lk 5 9   Simon Peter . . . and all his companions were completely *overcome* with astonishment at the catch they had made.

B

BALAAM

BALAAM – NICOLAITANS

Balaam 3   Beor [Bosor] 1   Nicolaitans 2
Balak 1   Korah [Core] 1

2 P	2 15	[the unbelievers] have left the right path and wandered off to follow the path of *Balaam* son of *Beor*
Jude	11	they have rushed to make the same mistake as *Balaam* (cf. Nb 22–24) . . . they have rebelled just as *Korah* did (cf. Nb 16) – and share the same fate
Rv	2 6	[To the angel of the church of Ephesus] you loathe as I do what the *Nicolaitans* are doing
	14	[To the angel of the church in Pergamum] some of you are followers of *Balaam,* who taught *Balak* to set a trap for the Israelites . . .
	15	among you too, there are some as bad who accept what the *Nicolaitans* teach

BE

1. Be: *eimi*
  1: (God) Is
    a) (absolute sense:) God is, was – God exists
    b) (+ predicate:) I am, will be, (the) God . . .
  2: (Jesus) Is, Was
    a) The Word was
    b) (absolute in Greek:) I Am – I am He
    c) (+ compl. or attrib.) – It is I, I am he
    d) (who Jesus) is – (who, what) is (Jesus?)
  3: (Men, Things) Are (alive) – There is, are – Exist, Live, Have being (absolute sense)
  4: (A person) Is, Was (+ compl. or attrib.) – Who is, are? (senses with predicate)
  5: Real, True, Genuine – Indeed, Certainly
  6: to Mean, Be the equivalent of, Be all about – That is (to say)
  7: Happen, Come about, Be
  8: Be (somewhere, there, here), Stay – (where) is (?)
2. Be – Become – Come to be: *ginomai*

  1: Be (alive), Live – Appear, Come – There was, were
  2: Be
    a) Be (at, in), Reach, Arrive – Come (to), Go (to) – Rank
    b) Be, Be done – Happen, Take place, Come (to be) – Done, Worked, Made
    c) Be (a time, a day) – the Coming (of a time), Came
  3: Become, Make oneself into – Turn into, Be made – Prove to be
  4: Come into being, Become (for the first time) – Made new, Rebirth – Finished (for the first time)
  5: Existence – Birth, Nature
3. Being, Nature – (Give) Substance (to): *hypo-stasis*
4. (How People) Are – Are doing: *echō*
5. It is, There are: *agō*
6. Be (Was, Were, Is): *hyp-archō*
7. Nature – Birth – Being: *physis*
  1: Natural, Physical – By nature, By birth – a Nature, a Kind
  2: Being united – Being for the first time

1. BE: *EIMI*

1		*eimi* (242)	3 *ontōs* 10
2	*egō*	*eimi* 40	
4	*eni* (= *en-esti*)	6	

1: (GOD) IS

a) (absolute sense:) God is, was – God exists

Heb	11 6	anyone who comes to [God] must believe that he *exists*
Rv	1 4	grace and peace to you from him who *is*, who *was*, and who is to come,
	8	the Lord God, who *is*, who *was*, and who is to come,
	4 8	he *was*, he *is* and he is to come.

Rv	11 17	Almighty Lord God, He-*Is*-and-He-*Was*,
	16 5	You are the holy He-*Is*-and-He-*Was*, the Just One,

b) (+ predicate:) I am, will be, (the) God . . .

Mt	22 32	(Ex 3 6) I *am* the God of Abraham, the God of Isaac and the God of Jacob
2 Co	6 16	(Lv 26 12) I *will be* their God and they shall be my people.
	18	(cf. 2 S 7 14) [I will welcome you] and *be* your father,
Heb	1 5	(2 S 7 14) I *will be* a father to him
	8 10	(Lv 26 12) I *will be* their God and they shall be my people.
Rv	1 8	I *am* the Alpha and the Omega
	21 7	(2 S 7 14) I *will be* his God and he a son to me.

2: (JESUS) IS, WAS

a) The Word was

Jn	1 1	In the beginning *was* the Word: the Word *was* with God and the Word *was* God. ² He *was* with God in the beginning.
	9	The Word *was* the true light
	10	He *was* in the world
	15	John appears as his witness. He proclaims: . . . he *existed* before me.
Col	1 17	Before anything was created, [the Son] *existed*,
1 Jn	1 1	Something which has *existed* since the beginning,
	2	the eternal life which *was* with the Father

b) (absolute in Greek:) I Am – I am He

Jn	8 24	2 if you do not believe that *I am He*, you will die in your sins.
	28	2 When you have lifted up the Son of Man, then you will know that *I am He*
	58	2 before Abraham ever was, *I Am*.
	13 19	2 so that when it does happen you may believe that *I am He*.

c) (+ predicate in Greek:) I am (+ compl. or attrib.) – It is I, I am he

Mt	11 29	learn from me, for I *am* gentle and humble in heart,
	14 27	2 Courage! *It is I!* Do not be afraid!
	27 43	he did say, 'I *am* the son of God'.
Mk	6 50	2 Courage! *It is I!* Do not be afraid.
	14 62	2 [Are you the Christ, the Son of the Blessed one?] *I am*,
Lk	22 70	'So you are the Son of God then?' He answered, 'It is you who say *I am*.'
	24 39	2 Look at my hands and feet; yes, *it is I* indeed.
Jn	4 26	[I know that Messiah, Christ is coming.] I who am speaking to you, . . . *I am he*.
	6 20	2 *It is I*. Do not be afraid.
	35	2 *I am* the bread of life.
	41	2 *I am* the bread that came down from heaven.
	48	2 *I am* the bread of life.
	51	2 *I am* the living bread which has come down from heaven.
	8 12	2 *I am* the light of the world;
	9 5	As long as I am in the world I *am* the light of the world.
	10 7	2 *I am* the gate of the sheepfold;
	9	2 *I am* the gate. Anyone who enters through me will be safe:
	11	2 *I am* the good shepherd: the good shepherd . . . lays down his life
	14	2 *I am* the good shepherd; I know my own
	36	you say . . . 'You are blaspheming', because he says, 'I *am* the Son of God'.
	11 25	2 *I am* the resurrection (ᵛ and the life).
	13 13	You call me Master and Lord, and rightly; so I *am*.
	14 6	2 *I am* the Way, the Truth and the Life.
	15 1	2 *I am* the true vine, and my Father is the vinedresser.
	5	2 *I am* the vine, you are the branches.
	18 5	2 'Who are you looking for?' . . . 'Jesus the Nazarene' . . .
	6	2 '*I am he*.' . . . ⁶ When Jesus said, '*I am he*,' they . . . fell to the ground. ⁷ He asked them a second time, 'Who are
	8	2 you looking for?' . . . ⁸ 'I have told you that I *am he*.'
	37	'So you are a king then?' 'It is you who say it . . . Yes, I *am* a king.'
	19 21	This man said 'ᵛ am King of the Jews.
Ac	9 5	2 'Who are you, Lord?' . . . '*I am* Jesus, and you are persecuting me.'
	22 8	2 *I am* Jesus the Nazarene, and you are persecuting me.
	26 15	2 *I am* Jesus, and you are persecuting me.
Rv	1 17	2 (Is 44 6) *it is I*, the First and the Last; [I am] the Living One.
	2 23	2 *it is I* who search heart and loins

Rv 22 16   2 *I am* of David's line, the root of David

             d) (who Jesus) is – (who, what) is (Jesus?)

Mt 8 27   Whatever kind of man *is* this? Even the winds and the sea obey him.
14 28   Lord, . . . if it is you, tell me to come to you across the water.
16 13   Who do people say the Son of Man *is*?
15   But you, . . . who do you say I *am*?
21 10   the whole city was in turmoil. Who *is* this?
Mk 4 41   Who can this *be*? Even the wind and the sea obey him.
6 3   This *is* the carpenter, surely, the son of Mary . . .?
8 27   Who do people say I *am*?
29   But you, . . . who do you say I *am*?
Lk 5 21   Who *is* this man talking blasphemy?
7 49   Who *is* this man, that he even forgives sins?
8 25   Who can this *be*, that gives orders even to winds and waves . . .?
9 9   who *is* this I hear such reports about?
18   Who do the crowds say I *am*?
20   But you, . . . who do you say I *am*?
19 3   Zacchaeus was anxious to see what kind of man Jesus *was*,
Jn 4 10   If you only knew . . . who it *is* that is saying to you: Give me a drink,
5 12   Who *is* the man who said to you, 'Pick up your mat and walk?'
13   The man had no idea who it *was*,
8 25   Who *are* you? . . . What I have told you from the outset.
9 36   'Sir, . . . tell me who [the Son of Man] *is* so that I may believe in him. ³⁷ Jesus said, '. . . he *is* (§ who is) speaking to you.'
37
12 34   Who *is* this Son of Man?
21 12   None of the disciples was bold enough to ask, 'Who *are* you?'
Ac 9 5   'Who *are* you, Lord?' . . . 'I am Jesus, and you are persecuting me.'
22 8   'Who *are* you, Lord?' . , . 'I am Jesus the Nazarene, and you are persecuting me.'
26 15   'Who *are* you, Lord?' . . . 'I am Jesus, and you are persecuting me.'

3: (MEN, THINGS) ARE (ALIVE) – THERE IS, ARE – EXIST, LIVE, HAVE BEING (Absolute sense)

Mt 2 18   (Jr 31 15 G) Rachel . . ., refusing to be comforted because [her children] *were* no more.
6 30   the grass in the field . . . *is there* today
23 30   had we *lived* in our fathers' day.
Lk 12 28   the grass in the field . . . *is there* today
Jn 1 4   All that came to be *had life* in him and that life was the light of men,
17 5   that glory I had with you before ever the world *was*.
Ac 17 28   it is in [God] that we live, and move, and *exist*,
Rm 4 17   God . . . calls into *being* what does not exist.
13 1   the ᴿcivil authorities (lit. the *existing* authorities) were appointed by God.
1 Co 1 28   the ones that God has chosen – those who *are* nothing at all to show up those who *are* everything.
6 5   4 *is there* really not one reliable man among you . . .?
Ga 3 28   4 there *are* no more [distinctions between] Jew and Greek, there *are* no more slave and free, there *are* no more male and female, but all of you are one in Christ Jesus.
4/4
Col 3 11   4 there *is* no [room for distinction between] Greek and Jew, between the circumcised or the uncircumcised, or between barbarian and Scythian, slave and free man. There is only Christ: he is everything
Jm 1 17   4 with [the Father] there *is* no such thing as alteration, no shadow of a change.
Rv 4 11   it was only by your will that everything was made and *exists*.
17 8   The beast you have seen once *was* and now *is* not, . . . the people of the world . . . will think it miraculous when they see how the beast once *was* and now *is* not and is still to come.
10   Five of [the emperors] have already gone, one *is here* now, and one is yet to come;
11   The beast . . . once *was* and now *is* not,
21 1   there *was* no longer any sea.
4   there will *be* no more death, and there will *be* no more mourning
22 3   The ban will *be* lifted.
5   It will never *be* night again

4: (A PERSON) IS, WAS (+ Compl. or Attrib.) – WHO IS, ARE? (Senses with predicate)

Mt 24 5   2 many will come using my name and saying, 'I *am* the Christ,
26 22   2 [The disciples] started asking him in turn, 'It *is* not I, Lord, surely?'
25   2 Judas . . . asked in his turn, 'It *is* not I, Lord, surely?'

Mk 13 6   2 Many will come using my name and saying, 'I *am* he,
14 19   [The disciples] asked him, one after another, '[It *is*] not I surely?'
Lk 1 66   What will this child [John the Baptist] *turn out to be*?
21 8   2 many will come using my name and saying, 'I *am* he,
Jn 1 19   the Jews sent priests . . . to ask [John], 'Who *are* you?'
22   Well then, . . . *are* you Elijah?
9 8   '*Isn't* this the man who used to sit and beg?' . . . ⁹ 'Yes, it *is* the same one.' . . . [The man born blind] said, 'I *am* the man.'
9
13 24   Ask who it *is* [Jesus] means,
25   [the disciple Jesus loved] said, 'Who *is* it, Lord?'
Ac 5 36   Theudas . . . claimed to *be* someone [important],
8 9   Simon . . . had given it out that he *was* someone [momentous],
11 17   who *was* I to stand in God's way?
13 25   2/ I *am* not the one you imagine me to *be*;
19 15   Jesus I recognise, and I know who Paul is, but who *are* you?
21 23   the tribune . . . arrested Paul . . . and enquired who he *was*
1 Co 3 7   Neither the planter nor the waterer ᴿmatters (lit. *is* anything): only God,
10 19   Does this mean that the food sacrificed to idols ᴿhas a real value (lit. *is* anything), or that the idol itself *is* ᴿreal (lit. anything)?
13 2   if I have faith . . . but without love, then I *am* nothing at all.
15 10   by God's grace ᴿthat is (lit. I *am*) what I *am*,
2 Co 12 11   Though I *am* a nobody, there is not a thing these arch-apostles have that I do not have as well.
Ga 2 6   these people . . . are acknowledged ᴿleaders (lit. to *be* something) – not that their ᴿimportance (lit. *being* something) would matter to me,
6 3   It is the people who *are* not important who often make the mistake of thinking that they *are*
Jm 1 24   [It is like looking at your own features in a mirror and then] immediately forgetting what you ᴿlooked like (lit. *were*).
1 Jn 3 2   what we are to *be* in the future has not yet been revealed;
Rv 7 13   Do you know who these people *are*, dressed in white robes . . .?

5: REAL, TRUE, GENUINE – INDEED, CERTAINLY

Mk 11 32   3 everyone held that John was a *real* prophet.
Lk 23 47   3 the centurion . . . said, 'This was *certainly* a great and good man.
24 34   3 Yes, *it is true*. The Lord has risen
Jn 8 36   3 if the Son makes you free, you will be free *indeed*.
1 Co 14 25   3 [if an unbeliever came in] he would . . . worship God, declaring that God is among you *indeed*.
Ga 3 21   3 We could *certainly* have been justified by the Law, if the Law . . . had been capable of giving life.
1 Tm 5 3   3 Be considerate to widows; I mean those who are *truly* widows.
5   3 a woman who is *really* widowed and left without anybody can give herself up to God
16   3 enable [the Church] to support those who are *genuinely* widows.
6 19   this is the way they can save up a good capital sum for the future if they want to make sure of the only life that is *real*.
3

6: TO MEAN, BE THE EQUIVALENT OF, BE ALL ABOUT – THAT IS (TO SAY)

Mt 1 23   Immanuel, a name which *means* God-is-with-us.
9 13   Go and learn the *meaning* of the words (Ho 6 6): What I want is mercy, not sacrifice.
12 7   if you had understood the *meaning* of the words (Ho 6 6): What I want is mercy, not sacrifice.
27 33   Golgotha, *that is*, the place of the skull,
46   Eli, Eli, . . . *that is*, My God, my God,
Mk 1 27 O   The people . . . started asking each other what it all *meant*. Here is a teaching that is new . . . and with authority behind it:
3 17   Boanerges *or* Sons of Thunder;
5 41   Talitha kum! which *means*, Little girl, . . . get up.
7 2   with unclean hands, *that is*, without washing them.
11   Corban (*that is*, dedicated to God),
34   Ephphatha, *that is*, Be opened.
9 10   among themselves they discussed what rising from the dead could *mean*.
12 42   two small coins, *the equivalent of* a penny.
15 16   the inner part of the palace, *that is*, the Praetorium,
22   Golgotha, which *means* the place of the skull,
34   Eloi, Eloi, . . . which *means*, My God, my God,
Lk 8 11   This, then, is what the parable [of the sower] *means*:
12 1   Be on your guard against the yeast of the Pharisees – *that is*, their hypocrisy.
15 26   [the elder son] asked what it *was all about*.
18 36   When [the blind man] heard the crowd going past he asked what it *was all about*,

Lk 20 17		Then what does this text in the scriptures *mean* (Ps 118 22) . . .?
Jn 1 41		the Messiah – which *means* the Christ –
7 36		What does he *mean* when he says: You will look for me and not find me . . .?
16 17		What does he *mean*, 'In a short time you will no longer see me . . .?
18		What *is* this short time?
Ac 1 19		the field came to be called in their language Hakeldama, *that is*, the Bloody Acre.
2 12		Everyone . . . asked one another what it all *meant*.
4 36		the apostles surnamed [Joseph] Barnabas (which *means* 'son of encouragement').
10 17		Peter was still worrying over the *meaning* of the vision he had seen,
17 20		Some of the things you said seemed startling to us and we would like to find out what they *mean*.
19 4		the one who was to come after [John] – *in other words* Jesus.
Rm 7 18		I know of nothing good living in me – living, *that is*, in my unspiritual self –
9 8		[It is through Isaac that your name will be carried on,] which *means* that it is not physical descent that decides who are the children of God;
10 6		Do not tell yourself ⌐you have to bring Christ down – as in the text: Who will go up to heaven? (lit. Who will go up to
7		heaven? – *that is*, to bring Christ down;) ⌐or ⌐that you have to bring Christ back from the dead – as in the text: Who will go down to the underworld? (lit. Who will go down to the underworld? – *that is*, to bring Christ up.)
8		The word, *that is* the faith we proclaim, is very near to you,
Ep 4 9		When it says, he ascended, what can it *mean* if not that he descended . . .?
5 5		fornication or . . . promiscuity – which *is* worshipping a false God –
6 17		you must . . . receive the ⌐word of God from the Spirit to use as a sword (lit. sword of the Spirit, *that is*, the word of God).
Phm 12		I am sending [Onesimus] back to you, and with him – ⌐I could say (lit. to me *the equivalent of*) – a part of my own self.
Heb 2 14		⌐the devil, who had power over death (lit. he who had power over death, *that is*, the devil).
7 2		king of Salem, *that is*, king of peace;
5		the descendants of Levi . . . are obliged by the Law to take tithes from the people, and *this is* taking them from their own brothers
9 11		the more perfect tent . . . is better than the one made by men's hands ⌐because (lit. *that is*,) it is not of this created order;
10 20		a living opening through the [sanctuary] curtain, *that is to say*, [Christ's] body.
11 16		they are longing for a better homestead, *that is*, their heavenly homeland.
13 15		an unending sacrifice of praise, a verbal sacrifice *that is*,
1 P 3 20		that ark . . . saved only a small ⌐group of (lit. group, *that is*,) eight people
Rv 21 17		a hundred and forty-four cubits high ⌐ – the angel was using the ordinary cubit (lit. of the ordinary human measure – *that is*, of the angel's).

7: HAPPEN, COME ABOUT, BE

Mt 24 3		when is this going to *happen* . . .?
Mk 13 4		when is this going to *happen* . . .?
Lk 1 34		Mary said to the angel, 'But how can this *come about* . . .?'
21 7		Master, . . . when will this *happen* . . .?
Rv 1 19		write down all [that you see of] present *happenings*

8: BE (SOMEWHERE, THERE, HERE), STAY – (WHERE) IS (?)

Mt 2 2 X		Where *is* the infant king of the Jews . . .?
13		escape into Egypt, and *stay* there until I tell you,
15		[Joseph] *stayed* [in Egypt] until Herod was dead.
6 21		where your treasure *is*, there will your heart *be* also.
12 6 X		here, I tell you, *is* something greater than the Temple.
41 X		there *is* something greater than Jonah here.
42 X		there *is* something greater than Solomon here.
17 4		Lord, . . . it is wonderful for us to *be* here;
18 20		where two or three ⌐meet (lit. *are* [gathered]) in my name, I
X ●		shall *be there* with them.
24 23		'Look, here [is] the Christ' or, 'He [is] there',
26		If, then, they say to you, 'Look, he *is* in the desert', do not go there;
28 6 X		[Jesus] *is* not here, for he has risen,
Mk 2 1 X		word went round that [Jesus] *was* back; . . . ⁴ . . . they
4 X		stripped the roof over the place where Jesus *was*;
4 38 X		he *was* in the stern,
6 55 X		[people brought the sick] to wherever they heard he *was*.

Mk 9 5 X		it is wonderful for us to *be* here;
13 21 X		'Look, here [is] the Christ' or, 'Look, he [is] there',
14 3 X		Jesus *was* at Bethany
14		Where *is* my dining room . . .?
15 41 X		These [women] used to . . . look after him when he *was* in Galilee.
16 6 X		he has risen, he *is* not here.
Lk 2 6		[Mary and Joseph] *were* [in Bethlehem]
44 X		[Mary and Joseph] assumed he *was* with the caravan,
5 12 X		Jesus *was* in one of the towns when [a leper] appeared,
7 25		those who go in for fine clothes . . . *are to be found* at court!
9 12 X		we *are* in a lonely place here;
33 X		it is wonderful for us to *be* here;
10 6		if a man of peace *lives* there, your peace will . . . rest on him;
11 1 X		he *was* in a certain place praying,
31 X		and [there is] something greater than Solomon here.
32 X		and [there is] something greater than Jonah here.
12 34		where your treasure *is*, there will your heart *be* also.
17 17		The [other] nine, where [are they]?
21		there will be no one to say, 'Look [the kingdom is] here! Look [the kingdom is] there!'
23 X		They will say to you, 'Look [the Son of Man is] there!' or, 'Look [the Son of Man is] here!'
31		anyone who *is* on the housetop . . . must not come down
34		two will *be* in one bed: one will be taken,
35		two women will *be* grinding corn together: one will be taken,
22 11		Where *is* the dining room in which I can eat . . .?
23 7		Herod . . . *was* also in Jerusalem at that time.
24 6 X		He *is* not here; he has risen.
53		[the apostles] *were* continually in the Temple praising God
Jn 1 48		I saw you when you *were* under the fig tree.
4 6		Jacob's well *is* there
6 24 X		the people saw that neither Jesus nor his disciples *were* there,
7 11 X		'Where *is* he?' they said.
34 X ●		where I *am*, you cannot come.
36 X		where I *am*, you cannot come?
8 10		Woman, where *are* they? Has no one condemned you?
19 Θ		Where *is* your Father?
9 12 X		They asked [the man born blind], 'Where *is* he?'
11 15 X		for your sake I am glad I *was* not there
21 X		If you had *been* there, my brother would not have died,
30 X		he *was* still at the place where Martha had met him.
32 X		as soon as [Mary] ⌐saw [Jesus] (lit. came to where Jesus *was*) she threw herself at his feet.
57 X		anyone who knew where he *was* must inform [the chief priests]
12 9 X		a large number of Jews heard that he *was* there
26 X ●		wherever I *am*, my servant will *be* there too.
14 3 X ●		I shall return to take you with me; so that where I *am* you may *be* too.
17 24		Father, I want those you have given me to be with me where
X ●		I *am*,
Ac 2 29		David himself is dead . . .: his tomb *is* still with us.
11 5		I *was* in the town of Jaffa,
11		three men stopped outside the house where we *were* staying;
16 3		[Timothy was circumcised] on account of the Jews who *were* in the locality
28		Don't do yourself any harm; we *are* all here.
19 1		Apollos *was* in Corinth,
22 5		[I had] letters to their brothers who *were* in Damascus.
Rm 1 7		To you all . . . who *are* God's beloved in Rome,
1 Co 1 2		to the church of God that *is* in Corinth
20		Where [are] the philosophers now? Where [are] the scribes? Where [are] any of our thinkers today?
15 55		Death, where [is] your victory? Death, where [is] your sting?
2 Co 1 1		Paul . . . to the church of God that *is* at Corinth, and to all the saints who *are* in the whole of Achaia.
Ep 1 1		Paul . . . to the saints who are faithful to Christ Jesus (§ who *are* at Ephesus)
Ph 1 1		to all the saints in Christ Jesus [who *are* at Philippi],
Heb 7 10		[Levi] *was* still in the loins of his ancestor
8 4 X		if [Jesus] *were* on earth, he would not be a priest at all,
2 P 3 4		Well, where *is* this coming?

2. BE – BECOME – COME TO BE: *GINOMAI*

3	*genesis* 1/5	2 *palin-genesia* 2
1	*ginomai* (234)	5 *pro-ginomai* 1
4	*epi-ginomai* 1	

1: BE (ALIVE), LIVE – APPEAR, COME – THERE WAS, WERE

Mk 1 4		John the Baptist *appeared* in the wilderness,
Lk 1 5		In the days of King Herod of Judaea *there lived* a priest called Zechariah
Jn 1 6		A man *came*, sent by God. His name was John.
8 58		before Abraham ever *was*, I Am.

Ac 20 18 You know ʳwhat my way of life has been (lit. how I have *lived*)
1 Th 1 5 you observed ʳthe sort of life (lit. how) we *lived*
2 P 2 1 *there were* false prophets in the past history of our people,
1 Jn 2 18 you were told that an Antichrist must *come*,
Rv 16 18 since *there have been* men on the earth

2: BE

a) Be (at, in), Reach, Arrive – Come (to), Go (to) – Rank

Mt 26 6 X Jesus *was* at Bethany
Mk 4 11 to those who *are* outside everything comes in parables,
9 33 X when he *was* in the house he asked them,
Lk 19 9 Today salvation has *come* to this house,
22 40 X they *reached* [the Mount of Olives]
24 22 some women . . . *went* to the tomb
Jn 1 15 X He who comes after me *ranks* before me
17 grace and truth have *come* through Jesus Christ
30 X A man is coming after me who *ranks* before me
6 21 in no time [the boat] *reached* the shore
25 X Rabbi, when did you *come* here?
Ac 13 5 [Paul and Barnabas] ʳlanded at (lit. *reached*) Salamis
19 21 After I have *been* there . . . I must go on to see Rome
20 16 Paul . . . *was* anxious to *be* in Jerusalem . . . for the day of Pentecost.
21 17 ʳOn our arrival (lit. When we *arrived*) in Jerusalem the brothers gave us a very warm welcome.
35 When Paul *reached* the steps . . . he had to be carried by the soldiers;
27 7 we had difficulty in *making* Cnidus.
28 13 4 a south wind *sprang up*
1 Co 2 3 I *came* among you in great fear and trembling
Ga 3 14 This was done so that in Christ Jesus the blessing of Abraham might ʳinclude (lit. *come to*) the pagans,
17 no law that *came* 430 years later could cancel that
2 Tm 1 17 as soon as [Onesimus] *reached* Rome, he really searched hard for me
Heb 9 11 now Christ has come, as the high priest of all the blessings which ᵛ *were* to come (G have *come*)
2 Jn 12 I hope instead to *visit* you and talk to you personally,
Rv 1 9 I *was* on the island of Patmos

b) Be, Be done – Happen, Take place, Come (to be) – Done, Worked, Made

Mt 1 22 all this *took place* to fulfil the words spoken by the Lord through the prophet:
5 18 not one dot . . . shall disappear from the Law until its purpose is *achieved*.
6 10 your will be *done*,
8 13 you have believed, so let this *be done* for you.
9 29 Your faith deserves it, so let this *be done* for you.
11 20 [Jesus reproached] the towns in which most of his miracles had been *worked*.
21 if the miracles *done* in you had been *done* in Tyre and Sidon, they would have repented
23 if the miracles *done* in you had been *done* in Sodom, it would have been standing yet.
15 28 Let your wish ʳbe granted (lit. *be done*).
18 19 it will ʳbe granted (lit. *be done*) to you by my Father in heaven.
31 when they saw what had *happened* . . . [his fellow servants] went to their master and reported ʳthe whole affair (lit. all that had *happened*) to him.
21 4 This *took place* to fulfil the prophecy.
21 if you say to this mountain,' Get up and throw yourself into the sea', it will *be done*.
42 (Ps 118 23) This was the Lord's *doing*
24 6 (Dn 2 28) this is something that must *happen*,
20 Pray that ʳyou will not have to escape (lit. your flight will not *happen*) in winter
21 (cf. Dn 12 1) there will be great distress such as . . . since the world began, there never has *been*, nor ever will *be* again.
34 before this generation has passed away all these things will have *taken place*.
26 42 your will be *done*!
54 how would the scriptures be fulfilled that say this is the way it must *be*?
56 all this *happened* to fulfil the prophecies in scripture
27 54 the centurion . . . had seen the earthquake and all that was *taking place*,
28 11 some of the guard went off . . . to tell the chief priests all that had *happened*.
Mk 2 27 The sabbath was *made* for man,
5 14 the people came to see what had really *happened*.
16 All those who had witnessed it reported what had *happened*
33 the woman . . . knew what had *happened* to her,
6 2 What . . . [are] these miracles that are *worked* through him?
9 21 How long has this been *happening* to him?

Mk 11 23 if anyone says to this mountain, 'Get up . . .', believing that what he says will *happen*, it will be done for him.
12 11 (Ps 118 23) This was the Lord's *doing*
13 7 (Dn 2 28) this is something that must *happen*,
18 Pray that this may not *be* in winter
19 (cf. Dn 12 1) there will be such distress as, until now, has not ʳbeen equalled (lit. *been*) since the beginning . . . nor ever will *be* again.
29 So with you when you see these things *happening*:
30 before this generation has passed away all these things will have *taken place*.
14 4 Why *is there* this waste of ointment?
Lk 1 20 you will be silenced . . . until this has *happened*.
38 let what you have said *be done* to me.
2 15 Let us go . . . and see this thing that has *happened* which the Lord has made known to us.
4 23 We have heard all that *happened* in Capernaum, do the same here
8 34 When the swineherds saw what had *happened* they ran off
35 the people went out to see what had *happened*.
56 [Jesus] ordered them not to tell anyone what had *happened*.
9 7 Herod . . . had heard about all that was *going on*;
10 13 if the miracles *done* in you had been *done* in Tyre and Sidon, they would have repented
12 54 you say at once that rain is coming, and ʳso it does (lit. it *is*)
55 you say it will be hot, and it *is*.
13 17 all the people were overjoyed at the wonders he *worked*.
14 22 your orders have been *carried out*
17 26 As it *was* in Noah's day so will it also be in the days of the Son of Man.
28 It will be the same as it *was* in Lot's day:
21 7 when will this *happen*, then, and what sign will there be . . .?
9 (Dn 2 28) this is something that must *happen*
28 When these things begin to *take place*, stand erect,
31 So with you when you see these things *happening*:
32 before this generation has passed away all will have *taken place*.
36 [pray] for the strength to survive all that is going to *happen*,
22 42 let your will *be done*, not mine.
23 8 [Herod] was hoping to see some miracle *worked* by [Jesus]
24 Pilate then gave his verdict: their demand was to *be* [granted].
31 what will *happen* when [the wood] is dry?
47 When the centurion saw what had *taken place*, he gave praise to God
48 when all the people . . . saw what had *happened*, they went home beating their breasts.
24 12 ᵛ Peter . . . went back home, amazed at what had *happened*ʳ
18 You must be the only person . . . in Jerusalem who does not know the things that have been *happening* there,
21 two whole days have gone by since it all *happened*;
Jn 1 28 This *happened* at Bethany,
3 9 How can that *be* [possible]?
5 14 something worse may *happen* to you.
13 19 I tell you this now before it *happens*, so that when it does *happen* you may believe
14 22 ʳDo you (lit. *Is it that you*) intend to show yourself to us and not to the world?
29 I have told you this now before it *happens*, so that when it does *happen* you may believe.
15 7 you may ask what you will and ʳyou shall get it (lit. it will *be done*).
19 36 all this *happened* to fulfil the words of scripture:
Ac 2 43 The many miracles . . . *worked* through the apostles made a deep impression on everyone.
4 16 a miracle was *worked* through [these men]
21 all the people were giving glory to God for what had *happened*.
28 [Herod and Pilate made an alliance] to bring about the very thing that you . . . had predetermined should *happen*.
30 [Lord, help your servants] ʳto work miracles (lit. that miracles might be *worked*) . . . through the name of . . . Jesus.
5 7 [Sapphira] came in, not knowing what had *taken place*.
12 So many signs and wonders were *worked*
24 Δ the chief priests . . . wondered what this could ʳmean (lit. *be*).
7 40 (Ex 32 1) we do not know what has *come over* this Moses
8 13 wonders and great miracles . . . *took place*.
10 16 This ʳwas repeated (lit. *happened*) three times
37 You must have heard ʳabout the recent happenings (lit. what has *happened*) in Judaea;
11 10 This ʳwas repeated (lit. *happened*) three times,
12 5 ʳthe Church prayed (lit. prayer was *made*) to God for [Peter]
9 Peter . . . had no idea that what the angel did was all *happening* in reality;
13 12 The proconsul who had watched everything that had *happened*, became a believer.
32 ʳGod made the promise (lit. the promise was *made* by God)
14 3 the Lord supported all they said . . , allowing signs and wonders to be *performed* by them.
19 10 This *went on* for two years,
26 ○ gods *made* by [human] hands are not gods at all.
20 3 a plot ʳorganised (lit. *made*) against [Paul] by the Jews

Ac 21 14 The Lord's will *be done*.
   24 2 the reforms ᶠthis nation owes (lit. that have *taken place* for this nation owing) to your foresight [we accept]
   26 6 it is for my hope in the promise *made* by God to our ancestors that I am on trial,
       22 I have stood firm . . ., saying nothing more than what the prophets . . . said would *happen*:
   28 6 [the inhabitants of Malta] had waited a long time without seeing anything out of the ordinary *happen* to [Paul],
       9 When this *happened*, the other sick people on the island came
Rm 3 25 5 the past, when ᶠsins (lit. evil *done*) went unpunished
1 Co 4 5 Then will be the time for each one to *have* whatever praise he deserves,
    7 36 [if anyone] feels that it would not be fair to his daughter . . . and that ᶠhe should do something about it (lit. something should *be done*), he is free to do as he likes:
    9 15 I am not writing all this ᶠto secure this treatment (lit. so that all should *happen* like this) for myself.
  10 6 These things all *happened* as warnings for us,
  14 26 it must always *be* for the common good.
      40 let everything *be done* with propriety
  15 54 then the words of scripture will ᶠcome true (lit. *happen*):
  16 2 collections need not *be made* after I have come.
      14 Let everything you do *be done* in love.
Ep 5 12 The things which are *done* in secret are things that people are ashamed even to speak of;
1 Th 3 4 that is what has *happened* now,
2 Tm 2 18 [Hymenaeus and Philetus] claim that the resurrection has already *taken place*.
Heb 9 11 Christ has come, as the high priest of all the blessings which ᵛ were to come (G have *come*).
Jm 3 10 the blessing and the curse come out of the same mouth . . . My brothers, this must *be* wrong –
Rv 1 1 This is the revelation . . . about the things which are now to *take place* very soon;
      19 write down all that you see of . . . things that are still to *come*.
   4 1 I will show you what is to *come* in the future.
  16 17 a voice shouted from the sanctuary, 'The end has *come*'.
  21 6 [I am making the whole of creation new.] It is already *done*.
  22 6 God . . . has sent his angel to reveal . . . what is soon to *take place*.

        c) Be (a time, a day) – the Coming (of a time), Came

Mt 8 16 ᶠThat evening (lit. When evening *came*) they brought him many who were possessed by devils.
  14 6 ᶠduring the celebrations for Herod's birthday (lit. when the celebrations for Herod's birthday *came*),
      15 When evening *came*, the disciples went to him
      23 When evening *came*, he was there alone,
  16 2 ᶠIn the evening (lit. When evening has *come*) you say, 'It will be fine; there is a red sky'
  20 8 ᶠIn the evening (lit. When evening *came*), the owner of the vineyard said to his bailiff, 'Call the workers,
  26 2 It will *be* Passover . . . in two days' time,
      20 When evening *came* [Jesus] was at table
  27 1 When morning *came*, all the chief priests and the elders . . . met in council
      57 When it *was* evening, there came a rich man of Arimathaea,
Mk 1 32 ᶠThat evening (lit. When evening *came*) . . . they brought to [Jesus] all who were sick
   4 35 With the *coming* of evening that same day, [Jesus] said to them, 'Let us cross over
   6 2 With the *coming* of evening [Jesus] began teaching
      21 An opportunity *came* on Herod's birthday [for Herodias to have John killed]
      35 By now it *was* [getting] very late,
      47 When evening *came* the boat was far out on the lake,
  11 19 when evening *came* ᵛ he (G they) went out of the city.
  14 17 When evening *came* [Jesus] arrived with the Twelve.
  15 33 When the sixth hour *came* there was darkness over the whole land
      42 It *was* now evening, and . . . it was Preparation Day
Lk 4 42 When daylight *came* [Jesus] left the house
   6 13 When day *came* he summoned his disciples
  22 14 When the hour *came* he took his place at table,
      66 When day ᶠbroke (lit. *came*) there was a meeting of the elders of the people
Jn 6 16 ᶠThat evening (lit. When evening *came*) the disciples went down to the shore of the lake
  10 22 It *was* the time when the feast of Dedication was being celebrated in Jerusalem.
  21 4 It *was* light by now, and there stood Jesus on the shore,
Ac 12 18 When daylight *came* there was a great commotion among the soldiers,
  16 35 When it *was* daylight the magistrates sent the officers
  23 12 When it *was* day, the Jews held a secret meeting
  27 27 ᶠOn the fourteenth night (lit. When the fourteenth night *came*) we were being driven one way and another
      29 they prayed for ᶠdaylight (lit. the *coming* of day)

Ac 27 33 Just before ᶠdaybreak (lit. the *coming* of day) Paul urged them all . . . to eat.
      39 When day *came* they did not recognise the land,

3: BECOME, MAKE ONESELF INTO – TURN INTO – BE MADE – PROVE TO BE

Mt 4 3 tell these stones to *turn into* loaves.
  13 32 when [the mustard seed] has grown it . . . *becomes* a tree
  21 42 X (Ps 118 22) It was the stone rejected by the builders that *became* the keystone.
Mk 12 10 X (Ps 118 22) It was the stone rejected by the builders that *became* the keystone.
Lk 4 3 tell this stone to *turn into* a loaf.
  13 19 like a mustard seed which . . . *became* a tree,
  20 17 X (Ps 118 22) It was the stone rejected by the builders that *became* the keystone?
Jn 1 14 X The Word *was made* flesh,
   2 9 the steward tasted the water, and it had *turned into* wine.
   4 14 the water that I shall give will *turn into* a spring . . . welling up to eternal life.
  16 20 your sorrow will *turn to* joy.
Ac 4 11 (Ps 118 22) This is the stone rejected by you the builders, but which has *proved to be* the keystone.
  12 18 O the soldiers . . . could not imagine what had *become* of Peter.
Rm 2 25 ᶠyou might as well have stayed uncircumcised (lit. your circumcision *becomes* uncircumcision).
   6 5 ᶠIf in union (lit. If we *are* united) with Christ we have imitated his death,
   7 13 Does that mean that something good ᶠkilled me (lit. *became* death to me)? Of course not.
1 Co 1 30 X Christ Jesus . . . has *become* our wisdom, and our virtue, and our holiness, and our freedom.
   8 9 Do not make use of this freedom in a way that *proves* a pitfall
   9 20 I *made myself* a Jew to the Jews . . . ²² For the weak I *made myself* weak. I *made myself* all things to all men
  13 1 I ᶠam simply (lit. I have *become*) a gong booming
  15 37 the thing that you sow is not what is going to *come*;
2 Co 5 21 God made the sinless one into sin, so that in him we might *become* the goodness of God.
   6 14 Do not ᶠharness yourselves (lit. *become*) in an uneven team with unbelievers.
Ga 3 13 X Christ redeemed us from the curse of the Law by ᶠbeing (lit. *becoming*) cursed for our sake,
1 P 2 7 X (Ps 118 22) the stone rejected by the builders has *proved to be* the keystone.
Rv 8 8 a third of the sea *turned into* blood,
      11 a third of all water *turned to* bitter wormwood,
  18 2 Babylon . . . has *become* the haunt of devils

4: COME INTO BEING, BECOME (FOR THE FIRST TIME) – MADE NEW, REBIRTH – FINISHED (FOR THE FIRST TIME)

Mt 19 28 2 when all is *made new* . . . the Son of Man sits on his throne
Jn 1 3 Through him all things *came to be*, not one thing *had its being* but through him.ᵛ ⁴ All that *came to be* had life in him (G of all that *came to be*. ⁴ In him was life)
      10 He was in the world that *had its being* through him
1 Co 15 45 (Gn 2 7) The first man, Adam, . . . *became* a living soul;
Tt 3 5 2 [God] saved us, by means of the cleansing water of *rebirth* and by renewing us with the Holy Spirit
Heb 4 3 God's work was undoubtedly all *finished* at the beginning of the world;
  11 3 ᶠno apparent cause can account for (lit. what is not seen *goes to make up*) the things we can see.
Jm 3 6 3 the tongue . . . sets fire to the whole wheel of *creation* (or: *existence*).
      9 men . . . are *made* in God's image:

5: EXISTENCE – BIRTH, NATURE

Jm 3 6 the tongue . . . sets fire to the whole wheel of creation (or: *existence*).

3. BEING, NATURE – (GIVE) SUBSTANCE (TO): *HYPO-STASIS*
hypo-stasis 2/5

Heb 1 3 ⊖ [the Son] is . . . the perfect copy of [God's] *nature*, sustaining the universe
  11 1 Only faith can ᶠguarantee (or: *give substance to*) the blessings that we hope for.

4. (HOW PEOPLE) ARE – ARE DOING: ECHŌ

echō (1)

Ac 15 36		Paul said to Barnabas, 'Let us go back . . . so that we can see how the brothers *are doing*'.

5. IT IS, THERE ARE: AGŌ

agō 2/67

Lk 24 21		⌐two whole days have gone by (lit. *it is* the third day) since it all happened;
Ac 19 38		*there are* the assizes and the proconsuls; let them take the case to court.

6. BE (WAS, WERE, IS): HYP:ARCHŌ

hyp-archō (3)

Lk 16 23		⌐In his (lit. *Being* in) torment in Hades, [the rich man] looked up
Ac 10 12		[Peter saw something like a huge sheet being let down from heaven;] ⌐it contained (lit. in it *there was*) every possible sort of animal and bird,
Ph 3 20		our homeland *is* in heaven

7. NATURE – BIRTH – BEING: PHYSIS

2	*physikos*	3	4	(neo-)*phytos* 1
3	*physikōs*	1	5	*sym-phytos* 1
1	*physis*	14		

1: NATURAL, PHYSICAL – BY NATURE, BY BIRTH – A NATURE, A KIND

Rm	1 26	2	their women have turned from *natural* intercourse to
	27	2	un*natural* practices [27] and . . . their menfolk have given up *natural* intercourse
	2 14		pagans are led by ⌐reason (lit. *nature*) to do what the Law commands,
	27		the man who keeps the Law, even though he has not been *physically* circumcised,
	11 21		God did not spare the *natural* branches,
	24		if you were cut from your *natural* wild olive to be grafted un*naturally* on to a cultivated olive, it will be much easier for them, the *natural* branches,
1 Co 11 14			[Ask yourselves if] *nature* itself does not tell you that long hair on a man is nothing to be admired;
Ga	2 15		we ⌐were born Jews (lit. are Jews *by birth*)
	4 8		gods who are not ⌐really gods (lit. gods *by nature*) at all.
Ep	2 3		*by nature* we were as much under God's anger as the rest of the world.
Jm	3 7		reptiles and fish of every *kind* can all be tamed by ⌐man (lit. human *kind*),
2 P	1 4 Θ		you will be able to share the divine *nature*
	2 12	2	these people . . . are . . . ⌐born (lit. *by nature*) to be caught and killed
Jude	10	3	the only things they do understand – just *by nature* like unreasoning animals –

2: BEING UNITED – BEING FOR THE FIRST TIME

Rm	6 5	5	if ⌐in union with (lit. we *are united* with, or: we are the same plant as) Christ we have imitated his death
1 Tm 3 6		4	[The elder-in-charge] should not be a *new* ⌐convert (lit. *being*, or: *plant*),

---

BEAR – BIRTH – CHILD

---

1. Conceive – (Be) With child, Pregnant
  1: Conceive: *syl-lambanō*
  2: (Be) With child, Pregnant: *en gastri echō*
  3: (Be) With child: *en-kuos*
2. Have a child, Bring to birth – Make one's child: *apo-kueō*

3. Beget, Be the father of – Bear, Give birth to – Born: *gennaō*
  1: Beget, Be the father of – Bear, Give birth to
  a) God begets, is the father of, gives new birth
  b) A man is the father of

(with lists from Mt and Lk)
  c) A woman Bears, Gives birth to
  d) Beget, Become the father of, figuratively
  2: (Be) Born
  a) Jesus is Born, Descended from, Begotten
  b) Born of the Spirit – Begotten by God
  c) Born, Birth, Origin – Race, Native – Family, Brood, Offspring
  d) an animal is Born
  3: Grandchildren
  4: Well-born, Noble – Low-born, Common
  5: Genealogy – Ancestry – Descent
4. Bear, Born, Give birth to – Child: *tiktō*
  1: Bear, Give birth to – Have a child – Mother
  2: (Be) Born
  3: First-born, Eldest – Birthright
  4: Child, Children
  a) Child, Children, of God, of Wisdom

  b) Child, Children – Son – Childless
  c) Children, in a wider sense: "My child", "My son"
  d) (Little) Children (*teknion*)
  5: Give birth to, figuratively: Yield, Give
  6: (Hebraism:) Children of wrath, of light, of a curse
5. Descendants, Descended – Children, Offspring – Issue, Seed: *sperma*
6. Root – Scion: *rhiza*
7. Baby – Child – Boy
  1: Baby, Infant – Little Children, Child: *brephos*
  2: Child, Children – Baby – the Unlearned, the Simple: *nēpios*
  3: Child – Boy: *pais*
  a) Jesus as a child – the Boy Jesus
  b) Little Child, Children, Childhood – Boy(s)
8. Little girl, Girl: *korasion*
9. Born unexpectedly – (of) Untimely birth: *ek-trōma*
10. Babes, Babies at the breast – Suckle, Suck: *thēlazō*
11. Barren: *steiros*

1. CONCEIVE – (BE) WITH CHILD, PREGNANT

1: CONCEIVE: SYL-LAMBANŌ

syl-lambanō 5/16

Lk	1 24	his wife Elizabeth *conceived*,
	31	[Mary,] You are to *conceive* and bear a son,
	36	Elizabeth has, in her old age, herself *conceived* a son,
	2 21	Jesus, the name the angel had given him before his *conception*.
Jm	1 15 ○	the desire *conceives* and gives birth to sin,

2: (BE) WITH CHILD, PREGNANT: EN GASTRI ECHŌ

en gastri echō 7

Mt	1 18	Mary . . . was found to be *with child* through the Holy Spirit.
	23	(Is 7 14) The virgin will *conceive* and give birth to a son
	24 19	Alas for those *with child*, or with babies at the breast, *Repeated* in Mk 13 17 *and* Lk 21 23
1 Th 5 3		the worst suddenly happens, as suddenly as labour pains come on a *pregnant* woman;
Rv 12 2		She was *pregnant*, and in labour,

3: (BE) WITH CHILD: EN-KUOS

en-kuos 1

Lk	2 5	Mary, [Joseph's] betrothed . . . was *with child*.

2. HAVE A CHILD, BRING TO BIRTH – MAKE ONE'S CHILD: APO-KUEŌ

apo-kueō 2

Jm	1 15 ○	when sin is fully grown, it too *has a child*, and the child is death.
	18 Θ	By his own choice [the Father of all light] *made* us *his children* by the message of the truth

3. BEGET, BE THE FATHER OF – BEAR, GIVE BIRTH TO – BORN: GENNAŌ

11	*genea-logeō*	1	5	*ginomai*	(4)
7	*genea-logia*	2	13	*a-genēs*	1
8	*genesia (ta)*	2	14	*a-genea-logētos*	1
3	*genesis*	4/5	10	*ana-gennaō*	1

12	*genetē*	*1*	15	*arti-gennētos*	*1*
1	*gennaō*	99	16	*ek-gonos*	*1*
4	*gennēma*	4	6	*eu-genēs*	*3*
9	*gennētos*	2	17	*tekno-goneō*	*1*
2	*genos*	*15/21*	18	*tekno-gonia*	*1*

These lists are to be
read as synopses

1 Genealogy of
Jesus Christ,
son of David,
son of Abraham:

Read this column
from bottom to
top and from
left to right

1: BEGET, BE THE FATHER OF – BEAR, GIVE BIRTH TO

a) God begets, is the father of, gives new birth

Ac 13 33   (Ps 2 7) You are my son: today I have *become* your *father*.
             Repeated in Heb 1 5; 5 5

1 P 1 3   10 God . . . has *given* us a *new birth as* his *sons*, by raising Jesus
             Christ from the dead,

1 Jn 5 1   whoever loves the Father that *begot* him loves the child
             whom he begets.

b) A man is the father of

Kings of Judah:

*Abijah** (1)	2
*Ahaz** [*Achaz*]	2
*Amon** [*Amos**] (2)	2
*Asa** [*Asaph**]	2
*Azariah** [*Uzziah, Ozias*]	2
*Hezekiah** [*Ezekias*]	2
*Jechoniah**	2
*Jehoshaphat** [*Josaphat*]	2
*Joram**	2
*Josiah**	2
*Jotham** [*Joatham*]	2
*Manasseh** (2)	2
*Rehoboam** [*Roboam*]	2

Others:

*Abiud**	2
*Achim**	2
*Addi**	1
*Admin**	1
*Amminadab** [*Aminadab*]	3
*Amos** (3)	1
*Arni** [*Aram*] (2)	3
*Arphaxad**	1
*Azor**	2
*Boaz** [*Booz*]	2
*Cainan** (1)	1
*Cainan** (2)	1
*Cosam**	1
*Eber** [*Heber*]	1
*Eleazar**	2
*Eliakim** (1)	2
*Eliakim** (2)	1
*Eliezer**	1
*Eliud**	2
*Elmadam**	1
*Enos**	1
*Er**	1
*Esli**	1
*Heli**	1
*Hezron** [*Esrom**]	3
*Jacob** (2)	2
*Jannai**	1
*Jared**	1
*Joanan** [*Joanna*]	1
*Joda** [*Juda*]	1
*Jonam**	1
*Jorim**	1
*Josech** [*Joseph*]	1
*Joseph** (2)	1

*Joseph** (3)	1
*Joshuah** [*Jose, Jesus**] (2)	1
*Judah** (2)	1
*Lamech**	1
*Levi** (3)	1
*Levi** (4)	1
*Maath**	1
*Mahalaleel** [*Maleleel*]	1
*Mattatha**	1
*Mattathias** (1)	1
*Mattathias** (2)	1
*Matthan**	2
*Matthat**	1
*Melchi** (1)	1
*Melchi** (2)	1
*Melea**	1
*Menna**	1
*Methuselah** [*Mathusala*]	1
*Naggai**	1
*Nahor** [*Nachor*]	3
*Nahshon** [*Naasson*]	1
*Nahum**	1
*Nathan**	1
*Neri**	1
*Obed**	3
*Peleg** [*Phalec*]	1
*Perez** [*Phares*]	3
*Ram** [*Aram*] (2)	2
*Rhesa**	1
*Reu** [*Ragau*]	1
*Sala** [*Salmon*] (1)	1
*Salmon**	2
*Semein**	1
*Serug** [*Saruch*]	1
*Seth**	1
*Shealtiel** [*Salathiel*]	3
*Shelah** [*Sala*] (2)	1
*Shem** [*Sem*]	1
*Symeon** [*Simeon*] (2)	1
*Terah** [*Thara*]	1
*Zadok** [*Sadoc*]	2
*Zerah** [*Zara*]	1
*Zerubbabel** [*Zorobabel*]	3

Women:

[*Bathsheba*] = (the wife of) *Uriah**	1
[*Rahab* → *Judaea* 6]	
*Ruth**	1
*Tamar** [*Thamar*]	1

N.B. Names occurring once only, except for Zerah and those of the women, may
be found in Luke; names occurring twice, plus Zerah and the women, may be
found in Matthew; names occurring three times are to be found in both Matthew
and Luke. All names except for Zerah are given as those of ancestors of Jesus
Christ. The figures in parentheses beside names is a distinguishing mark
between people of the same name included in the Index to Proper Names.

Mt 1 1–16

2 Abraham
   begot Isaac, Isaac
   begot Jacob, Jacob
3 *begot* Judah and his brothers,
   ³ Judah
   begot Perez* and Zerah*, of
      Tamar*, Peleg*
   begot Hezron*, Hezron*
4 *begot* Ram*, Ram*
   begot Amminadab*, Amminadab*
   begot Nahshon*, Nahshon*
5 *begot* Salmon*, ⁵ Salmon*
   begot Boaz*, of Rahab*; Boaz*
   begot Obed*, of Ruth*; Obed*
6 *begot* Jesse, ⁶ Jesse
   begot King David, David
7 *begot* Solomon, of the wife of
      Uriah*, ⁷ Solomon
   begot Rehoboam*, Rehoboam*
   begot Abijah*, Abijah*
8 *begot* ᵛ Asa* (G Asaph), ᵛ Asa*
      (G Asaph)
   begot Jehoshaphat*, Jehoshaphat*
   begot Joram*, Joram*
9 *begot* Azariah*, ⁹ Azariah*
   begot Jotham*, Jotham*
   begot Ahaz*, Ahaz*
10 *begot* Hezekiah*, ¹⁰ Hezekiah*
   begot Manasseh*, Manasseh*
   begot ᵛ Amon* (G Amos*),
      ᵛ Amon* (G Amos*)
11 *begot* Josiah*, ¹¹ Josiah*
   begot Jechoniah* and his
      brothers . . .
12 After the deportation to Babylon,
   Jechoniah*

   begot Shealtiel*, Shealtiel*
13 *begot* Zerubbabel*, ¹⁶ Zerubbabel*
   begot Abiud*, Abiud*
   begot Eliakim*, Eliakim*
14 *begot* Azor*, ¹⁴ Azor*
   begot Zadok*, Zadok*
   begot Achim*, Achim*
15 *begot* Eliud*, ¹⁵ Eliud*
   begot Eleazar*, Eleazar*
   begot Matthan*, Matthan*

16 *begot* Jacob*, ¹⁶ Jacob*

   begot Joseph the husband of Mary
      of whom was born Jesus
      who is called Christ.

Lk 3 23–38

of Adam, of God
38 of Mahalaleel*, of Cainan, ³⁸ of
      Enos*, of Seth*,
37 of Methuselah*, of Enoch, of
      Jared*,
   of Arphaxad*, of Shem*, of
      Noah, of Lamech*,
36 of Peleg*, of Eber*, of Shelah*,
      ³⁶ of Cainan*,
35 of Terah*, of Nahor*, ³⁵ of
      Serug*, of Reu*,
   of Abraham,
   of Isaac,
34 of Jacob*,
   of Judah*,

   of Perez*,

   of ᵛ Hezron* (G Esrom),
   of Arni*,
33 of Amminadab*, of Admin*
   of Nahshon*,
   of Sala* (ᵛ Salmon),
   of Boaz*,
   of Obed*,
32 of Jesse,
   of David,

31 of Melea*, of Menna*, of
      Mattatha*, of Nathan*,
   of Judah*, of Joseph*, of Jonam*,
      of Eliakim*,
30 of Jorim*, of Matthat*, of Levi*,
      ³⁰ of Symeon*,
29 of Elmadam*, of Er*, of Joshua*,
      of Eliezer*,
28 of Neri*, ²⁸ of Melchi*, of Addi*
      of Cosam*,
   of Shealtiel*,
   of Zerubbabel*,

27 of Semein*, of Josech*, of Joda*,
      ²⁷ of Joanan*, of Rhesa*,
26 of Esli*, of Naggai*, ²⁶ of
      Maath*, of Mattathias*,
25 of Joseph*, ²⁵ of Mattathias*, of
      Amos*, of Nahum*,
24 of Matthat*, of Levi*, of Melchi*,
      of Jannai*,

   of Heli*,
   of Joseph,
23 And Jesus, . . . being the son, as
      it was thought,

Ac 7 8   when ⌐his son Isaac was born (or: he *became the father of Isaac*) he circumcised him on the eighth day.

29   [Moses] went to stay in the land of Midian, where he *became the father of* two sons.

c) A woman Bears, Gives birth to

Lk 1 13   Your wife Elizabeth is to *bear* you a son

57   Elizabeth . . . *gave birth to* a son;

23 29   Happy are . . . the wombs that have never *borne*,

Jn 16 21   A woman in childbirth suffers . . . but when she has *given birth to* the child she forgets the suffering

Ga 4 24   The first [woman] . . . ⌐whose children are slaves (lit. who *bears* children into slavery), is Hagar

1 Tm 2 15   18 [a woman] will be saved by *childbearing*,

5 14   17 ⌐*have* (or: *bear*) *children*

d) Beget, Become the father of, figuratively

1 Co 4 15   it was I who *begot* you in Christ Jesus

2 Tm 2 23   these futile and silly speculations . . . only ⌐*give rise to* (or: *breed*) quarrels;

Phm 10   a child of mine, whose *father* I *became* while wearing these chains: I mean Onesimus.

2: (BE) BORN

a) Jesus is Born, Descended from, Begotten

Mt 1 16   of [Mary] *was born* Jesus

18   3 This is how Jesus Christ came to *be born*.

20   she has *conceived* what is in her by the Holy Spirit.

2 1   After Jesus has *been born* at Bethlehem in Judaea

4   [Herod] enquired of [the chief priests and scribes] where the Christ was to *be born*.

Lk 1 35   And so the child *to be born* will be holy

Jn 1 13   ≠ who *was* (G were) *born* not out of human stock or urge of the flesh or will of man but of God himself.

18 37   Yes, I am a king. I *was born* for this . . .: to bear witness to the truth;

Rm 1 3   the Son of God who, according to the human nature he
5   took, *was a descendant of* the family of David:

Ga 4 4 5/5 God sent his Son, *born* of a woman, *born* a subject of the Law,

1 Jn 5 18   We know that anyone who has been begotten by God does not sin, because the *begotten* [Son] of God protects him,

b) Born of the Spirit – Begotten by God

Jn 1 13   ≠ who was (G were) *born* not out of human stock nor urge of the flesh or will of man but of God himself.

3 3   unless a man is *born* from above, he cannot see the kingdom
4   of God. 4 Nicodemus said, How can a grown man be *born*? Can he go back into his mother's womb and be
5   *born* again? 5 Jesus replied: . . . unless a man is *born* through water and the Spirit, he cannot enter the kingdom
6   of God: 6 what is *born* of the flesh is flesh; what is *born*
7   of the Spirit is spirit. 7 Do not be surprised when I say:
8   You must be *born* from above. 8 The wind blows wherever it pleases . . . That is how it is with all who are *born* of the Spirit.

8 41   We were not *born* of prostitution, . . . we have one father: God.

P 1 23 10 your ⌐new birth (lit. being *born anew*) was not from any mortal seed but from the everlasting word of the living and eternal God.

1 Jn 2 29   everyone whose life is righteous has been *begotten* by [God].

3 9   No one who has been *begotten* by God sins; . . . he cannot sin when he has been *begotten* by God.

4 7   everyone who loves is *begotten* by God

5 1   Whoever believes that Jesus is the Christ has been *begotten* by God; and whoever loves the Father that begot him loves the child ⌐whom he begets (lit. who is *begotten*).

4   anyone who has been *begotten* by God has already overcome the world;

18   anyone who has been *begotten* by God does not sin, because the begotten Son of God ⌐protects him (ᵛ protects himself)

c) Born, Birth, Origin – Race, Native – Family, Brood, Offspring

Mt 3 7   4 *Brood* of vipers, who warned you to fly from the retribution . . .?

11 11   9 of all the [children] *born* of women, a greater than John the Baptist has never been seen;

12 34   4 *Brood* of vipers, how can your speech be good when you are evil?

Mt 14 6   8 during the celebrations for Herod's *birthday* the daughter of Herodias danced

19 12   There are eunuchs *born* that way from their mother's womb.

23 33   4 Serpents, *brood* of vipers, how can you escape being condemned to hell?

26 24   Better for that man if he had never been *born*!

Mk 6 21   8 An opportunity came on Herod's *birthday* when he gave a banquet

7 26   2 the woman was a pagan, by *birth* a Syrophoenician,

14 21   Better for that man if he had never been *born*!

Lk 1 14   [Elizabeth is to bear you a son] and many will rejoice at his *birth*,

3 7   4 *Brood* of vipers, who warned you to fly from the retribution . . .?

7 28   9 of all the [children] *born* of women, there is no one greater than John;

Jn 3 4   Can [a grown man] go back into his mother's womb and be *born* again?

6   what is *born* of the flesh is flesh;

9 1 12 [Jesus] saw a man who had been blind from *birth*.

2   who sinned, this man or his parents, for him to have been *born* blind?

19   Is this man really your son who you say was *born* blind?

20   We know he is our son and we know he was *born* blind,

32   it is unheard of for anyone to open the eyes of a man who was *born* blind;

34   Are you trying to teach us . . . and you a sinner through and through, since you were *born*!

16 21   [a woman] forgets the suffering in her joy that a man has been *born* into the world.

Ac 2 8   How does it happen that each of us hears them in his own *native* language?

4 6   2 [The elders and scribes had a meeting with] all the members of the high-priestly *families*.

36   2 There was a Levite of Cypriot *origin* called Joseph

7 8   2 when his son Isaac was *born* [Abraham] circumcised him

13   2 Joseph . . . told Pharaoh about his *family*.

19   2 [The king of Egypt] exploited our *race*, and ill-treated our ancestors,

20   2 It was at this period that Moses was *born*,

13 26   2 My brothers, sons of Abraham's *race*,

17 28 Θ 2/2 We are all his *children*. 29 Since we are the *children* of God,
29   we have no excuse

18 2   2 [Paul] met . . . Aquila whose *family* came from Pontus.

24   2 ⌐An Alexandrian Jew (lit. A Jew, Alexandrian by *birth*), named Apollos now arrived in Ephesus.

22 3   I am a Jew . . . and was *born* at Tarsus in Cilicia.

28   'It cost me a large sum to acquire this citizenship'. 'But I was *born* to it' said Paul.

Rm 9 11   more to the point is what was said to Rebecca . . . before her twin children were *born*

2 Co 11 26 2 I have been in danger . . . from my [own] *people*

Ga 1 14   2 I stood out among ⌐other Jews (lit. others of my *race* and) of my generation,

4 23   The child of the slave-girl was *born* in the ordinary way; the child of the free woman was born as the result of a promise.

29   the child *born* in the ordinary way persecuted the child born in the Spirit's way,

Ph 3 5   2 I was born of the *race* of Israel and of the tribe of Benjamin,

Heb 11 12 5 there *came from* one man . . . more descendants than could be counted,

23   Moses, when he was *born*, was hidden by his parents

Jm 1 23   like looking at ⌐your own features (lit. the features you were
3   *born* with) in a mirror

1 P 2 2 15 You are *new born*, and, like babies, you should be hungry for nothing but milk

9 ● 2 (cf. Is 43 20) you are a chosen *race* . . . a consecrated nation,

Rv 22 16 X 2 I am ⌐of David's line (lit. David's *offspring*), the root of David and the bright star of the morning.

d) an animal is born

2 P 2 12   these people . . . are not reasoning beings, but simply animals *born* to be caught and killed,

3: GRANDCHILDREN

1 Tm 5 4 16 If a widow has children or *grandchildren*, they are to learn . . . to do their duty to their own families

4: WELL-BORN, NOBLE – LOW-BORN, COMMON

Lk 19 12   6 A man *of noble birth* went to a distant country

Ac 17	11	6	[At Beroea] the Jews were more ⌐open-minded (lit. *noble-minded*) than those in Thessalonika.
1 Co 1	26	6	how many [of you] were influential people, or came *from noble families*?
	28	13	those whom [the world thinks] *common* . . . are the ones that God has chosen

5: GENEALOGY – ANCESTRY – DESCENT

Mt 1	1	3	A *genealogy* of Jesus Christ,
1 Tm 1	4	7	[stop] taking notice of myths and endless *genealogies*;
Tt 3	9	7	avoid pointless speculations, and those *genealogies*,
Heb 7	3	14	[Melchizedek] *has no father, mother or ancestry*,
	6	11	[Melchizedek] who *was not of the same descent*, took his tenth from Abraham,

4. BEAR, BORN, GIVE BIRTH TO – CHILD: *TIKTŌ*

3	*teknion*	9	6	(*philo-*)*teknos*	1
1	*teknon*	100	7	*prōto-tokia* (ta)	1
2	*tiktō*	18	4	*prōto-tokos*	8
5	*a-teknos*	2	8	*tekno*(*-tropheō*)	1

1: BEAR, GIVE BIRTH TO – HAVE A CHILD – MOTHER

Mt 1	21	2	[Mary] will *give birth to* a son and you must name him Jesus,
	23	2	(Is 7 14) The virgin will conceive and *give birth to* a son
	25	2	[Mary] *gave birth to* a son; and [Joseph] named him Jesus.
Lk 1	31	2	You are to conceive and *bear* a son,
	57	2	the time came for Elizabeth to *have her child*, and she gave birth to a son;
2	6	2/2	the time came for [Mary] to *have her child*, ⁷ and she *gave birth to* a son, her first-born.
	7		
Jn 16	21	2	A woman in *childbirth* suffers, because her time has come;
Ga 4	27	2	(Is 54 1) Shout for joy, you barren women who *bore no children*!
Rv 12	2	2	[The woman was] crying aloud in the pangs of *childbirth*.
	4	2	the dragon stopped in front of the woman as she was *having the child*, so that he could eat it as soon as it was *born* from its mother.
	2		
	5	2	The woman *brought* a male child *into the world*,
	13	2	the devil . . . sprang in pursuit of . . . the *mother* of the male child,

2: (BE) BORN

Mt 2	2 X	2	Where is the *new-born* king of the Jews?
Lk 2	11 X	2	Today in the town of David a saviour has been *born* to you;

3: FIRST-BORN, ELDEST – BIRTHRIGHT

Lk 2	7 X	4	[Mary] gave birth to a son, her *first-born*.
Rm 8	29 X	4	so that his Son might be the *eldest* of many brothers.
Col 1	15 X	4	[Christ] is the image of the unseen God and the *first-born* of all creation,
	18 X	4	he was the *first* to be *born* from the dead,
Heb 1	6 X	4	[God] brings the *First-born* into the world,
11	28	4	[Moses] sprinkled the blood to prevent the Destroyer from touching any of the *first-born* sons of Israel.
12	16	7	Esau . . . sold his *birthright* for one single meal.
	23	4	[You have come to the city of the living God] with the whole Church in which everyone is a *first-born* son
Rv 1	5 X	4	Jesus Christ, the faithful witness, the *First-born* from the dead,

4: CHILD, CHILDREN

a) Child, Children, of God, Wisdom

Mt 11	19		wisdom has been proved right by her ⌐actions (ᵛ *children*).
Lk 7	35		Wisdom has been proved right by all her *children*.
Jn 1	12		to all who did accept him he gave power to become *children* of God.
11	52		Jesus was to die . . . to gather together in unity the scattered *children* of God.
Rm 8	16		The Spirit himself and our spirit bear united witness that we are *children* of God. ¹⁷ And if we are *children* we are heirs as well:
	17		

Rm 8	21		[creation still retains the hope] to enjoy the same freedom and glory as the *children* of God.
9	8		it is not physical descent that decides who are the *children* of God; it is only the children of the promise who will count as the true descendants.
Ep 5	1		Try, then, to imitate God, as *children* of his that he loves,
Ph 2	15		perfect *children* of God among a deceitful and underhand brood,
1 P 1	14		Do not behave in the way that you liked to before you learnt the truth; make a habit of ⌐obedience (lit. *being obedient children*):
1 Jn 3	1		Think of the love that the Father has lavished on us by letting us be called God's *children*; and that is what we are. . . . ² My dear people, we are already the *children* of God
	2		
	10		In this way we distinguish the *children* of God from the children of the devil:
5	2		We can be sure that we love God's *children* if we love God himself

b) Child, Children – Son – Childless

Mt 7	11		If you . . . know how to give your *children* what is good,
10	21		Brother will betray brother . . . and the father his *child*; *children* will rise against their parents
15	26		It is not fair to take the *children's* food and throw it to the house-dogs.
18	25		his master gave orders that he should be sold, together with his wife and *children*
19	29		everyone who has left houses, brothers, sisters, father, mother, *children*
21	28		A man had two *sons*. He went and said to the first, My boy, you go and work in the vineyard today.
22	24		(Dt 25 5) if a man dies *child*less,
27	25		His blood be on us and on our *children*!
Mk 7	27		The children should be fed first, because it is not fair to take the *children's* food and throw it to the house-dogs.
10	29		there is no one who has left . . . father, *children* or land for my sake . . . ³⁰ who will not be repaid a hundred times over . . . mothers, *children* and land
	30		
12	19		(Dt 25 5) if a man's brother dies leaving a wife but no *child*,
13	12		Brother will betray brother . . . and the father his *child*; *children* will rise against their parents
Lk 1	7		[Zechariah and Elizabeth] were *child*less:
	17		[John] will go before [the Lord] to turn the hearts of fathers towards their *children*
2	48 X		his mother said to [Jesus], My *child*, why have you done this to us?
11	13		If you . . . know how to give your *children* what is good,
14	26		If any man comes to me without hating his . . . wife, *children*, . . . he cannot be my disciple.
15	31		My *son*, you are with me always
18	29		there is no one who has left . . . parents or *children* for the sake of the kingdom of God ³⁰ who will not be given repayment
	30		
20	28	5	if a man's married brother dies *child*less,
	29	5	The first, having married a wife, died *child*less.
	31		all seven . . . died leaving no *children*.
23	28		Daughters of Jerusalem, . . . weep rather for yourselves and for your *children*.
Ac 2	39		The promise that was made is for you and your *children*,
7	5		God . . . promised to give [this land] to [Abraham] and after him to his descendants, *child*less though he was.
13	33		[It was to our ancestors that God made the promise but] it is to us, their *children*, that he has fulfilled it.
21	5		Together with the women and *children* they all escorted us on our way
	21		you [authorise] all Jews living among the pagans . . . not to circumcise their *children*
Rm 9	8		it is not *physical descent* that decides who are the children of God; it is only the children of the promise who will count as the true descendants.
1 Co 7	14		If this were not so, your *children* would be unclean.
2 Co 12	14		*Children* are not expected to save up for their parents, but parents for *children*.
Ga 4	31		we are the *children*, not of the slave-girl, but of the free-born wife.
Ep 6	1		*Children*, be obedient to your parents
	4		parents, never drive your *children* to resentment
Col 3	20		*Children*, be obedient to your parents always,
	21		parents, never drive your *children* to resentment
1 Th 2	7		Like a mother feeding and looking after her own *children*,
	11		we treated every one of you as a father treats his *children*,
1 Tm 3	4		[A presiding elder] must be a man who . . . brings his *children* up to obey him
	12		Deacons . . . must be men who manage their *children* and families well.
5	4		If a widow has *children* or grandchildren,
	10	8	[The widow] must be a woman known for . . . the way in which she has brought up her *children*,

Tt	1	6		[an elder's] *children* must be believers
	2	4		[the older women should] show the younger women how
		6		they should . . . love their *children*,

c) Children, in a wider sense: "My child", "My son"

A = Children of Abraham (or Sarah)

Mt	2	18		(Jr 31 15) it was Rachel weeping for her *children*,
	3	9	A	God can raise *children* for Abraham from these stones.
	9	2		Jesus said to the paralytic, 'Courage, my *child*,
	23	37		Jerusalem, . . . How often have I longed to gather your *children*,
Mk	2	5		Jesus said to the paralytic, 'My *child*, your sins are forgiven.
	10	24		The disciples were astounded by these words, but Jesus insisted, 'My *children*, . . . how hard it is to enter the kingdom of God!
Lk	3	8	A	God can raise *children* for Abraham from these stones.
	13	34		Jerusalem, . . . How often have I longed to gather your *children*,
	16	25		My *son*, Abraham replied, remember that during your life good things came your way,
	19	44		[Jerusalem,] they will dash you and the *children* inside your walls to the ground;
Jn	8	39	A	If you were Abraham's *children*, you would do as Abraham did.
Rm	9	7	A	not all the descendants of Abraham are his true *children*.
		8		. . . [8] . . . it is not physical descent that decides who are
			A	the children of God; it is only the *children* of the promise who will count as the true descendants.
1 Co	4	14		I am saying this . . . to bring you, as my dearest *children*, to your senses.
		17		I have sent you Timothy, my dear and faithful *son* in the Lord:
2 Co	6	13		I speak as if to *children* of mine:
Ga	4	19		my ᵛ little children (G *children*)! I must go through the pain of giving birth to you all over again,
		25		the present Jerusalem . . . is a slave like her *children*.
		27		(Is 54 1) there are more *sons* of the forsaken one than sons of the wedded wife.
		28	A	you, my brothers, like Isaac, are *children* of the promise,
Ph	2	22		[Timothy] has proved himself by working with me . . . like a *son* helping his father.
1 Tm	1	2		to Timothy, true *child* of mine in the faith;
		18		Timothy, my *son*, these are the instructions that I am giving you:
2 Tm	1	2		to Timothy, dear *child* of mine,
	2	1		Accept the strength, my dear *son*, that comes from the grace of Christ Jesus.
Tt	1	4		To Titus, true *child* of mine in the faith that we share,
Phm		10		a *child* of mine, whose father I became while wearing these chains: I mean Onesimus.
1 P	3	6	A	You are now [Sarah's] *children*, as long as you live good lives
1 Jn	3	10		In this way we distinguish the children of God from the *children* of the devil:
2 Jn		1		From the Elder: my greetings to the Lady, the chosen one, and to her *children*,
		4		It has given me great joy to find that your *children* have been living the life of truth
		13		Greetings to you from the *children* of your sister, the chosen one.
3 Jn		4		It is always my greatest joy to hear that my *children* are living according to the truth.
Rv	2	23		I will see that [Jezebel's] *children* die,
	12	4		so that he could eat ᶜit (lit. the *child*) as soon as it was born from its mother.
		5		and the *child* was taken straight up to God

d) (Little) children (teknion)

Jn	13	33		3 My *little children*, I shall not be with you much longer.
Ga	4	19		3 my ᵛ *little children* (G children), I must go through the pain of giving birth to you all over again,
1 Jn	2	1		3 I am writing this, my [little] *children*, to stop you sinning;
		12		3 I am writing to you, my own [little] *children*, whose sins have already been forgiven
		28		3 Live in Christ, then, my [little] *children*,
	3	7		3 My [little] *children*, do not let anyone lead you astray:
		18		3 My [little] *children*, our love is not to be just words
	4	4		3 [little] *Children*, . . . you are from God
	5	21		3 [little] *Children*, be on your guard against false gods.

5: GIVE BIRTH TO (FIGURATIVELY) – YIELD, GIVE

| Heb | 6 | 7 | | 2 A field that has been well watered . . . and *gives* the crops that are wanted |

| Jm | 1 | 15 | | 2 the desire conceives and *gives birth to* sin, |

6: (HEBRAISM:) CHILDREN OF WRATH, OF LIGHT, OF A CURSE

Ep	2	3		by nature we were as much ᶜunder (lit. *children* of) God's anger as the rest of the world.
		5 8		be like *children* of light,
2 P	2	14		with their eyes always looking for adultery, . . . They are ᶜunder (lit. *children* of) a curse.

5. DESCENDANTS, DESCENDED – CHILDREN, OFFSPRING – ISSUE, SEED: *SPERMA*

sperma 36/44

A = Descendants of Abraham; D = Descendants of David

Mt	22	24		(cf. Dt 25 5) his brother is to marry the widow, to raise *children* for his brother.
		25		the first married and then died without *children*,
Mk	12	19		(cf. Dt 25 5) the man must marry the widow to raise up *children* for his brother.
		20		there were seven brothers. The first married a wife and then
		21		died leaving no *children*. [21] The second married the widow,
		22		and . . . died leaving no *children* . . . [22] . . . none of the seven left any *children*.
Lk	1	55	A	his mercy to Abraham and to his *descendants* for ever.
	20	28		(cf. Dt 25 5) the man must marry the widow to raise up *children* for his brother.
Jn	7	42	D	the Christ must be *descended* from David
	8	33	D	We are *descended* from Abraham
		37	A	I know that you are *descended* from Abraham;
Ac	3	25	A	(Gn 22 18) God . . . told Abraham: in your *offspring* all the families of the earth will be blessed.
	7	5		God . . . promised to give [this land] to [Abraham] and after him to his *descendants*, . . . [6] . . . his *descendants*
		6	A	(Gn 15 13) would be exiles in a foreign land,
	13	23	D	God has raised up for Israel one of David's *descendants*, Jesus
Rm	1	3	D	the Son of God . . . was a *descendant* of David:
	4	13		The promise of inheriting the world wa not made to Abraham and his *descendants* on account of any law
		16	A	so that [the promise] may be . . . available to all of Abraham's *descendants*,
		18	A	exactly as [Abraham] had been promised (Gn 15 5): Your *descendants* will be as many as the stars.
	9	7	A	not all the *descendants* of Abraham are his true children. Remember (Gn 21 12): It is through Isaac that your
		8	A	name will ᶜbe carried on (lit. *descend*), [8] . . . it is only the children of the promise who will count as the true
			A	*descendants*.
		29	A	(Is 1 9) Had the Lord of hosts not left us some *descendants* we should now be like Sodom,
	11	1	A	I, an Israelite, *descended* from Abraham
2 Co	11	22	A	Hebrews, are they? So am I. . . . *Descendants* of Abraham? So am I.
Ga	3	16		the promises were addressed to Abraham and to his *descendants* – notice . . . that scripture does not use a plural word as if there were several *descendants*, it uses the singular: to his *posterity*, which is Christ.
		19	A	until the *posterity* came to whom the promise was addressed.
		29	A	you are the *posterity* of Abraham,
2 Tm	2	8	D	Jesus Christ . . , sprung from the *race* of David;
Heb	2	16	A	Christ took to himself *descent* from Abraham.
	11	11		It was equally by faith that Sarah . . . was made able to
			A	ᶜconceive (lit. found a *posterity*),
		18	A	(Gn 21 12) It is through Isaac that your name will ᶜbe carried on (lit. *descend*).
1 Jn	3	9	Δ	No one who has been begotten by God sins; because God's ᶜ*seed* (or: *posterity*) remains inside him, he cannot sin
Rv	12	17		[the dragon] went away to make war on the rest of [the woman's] *children*,

6. ROOT – SCION: *RHIZA*

rhiza 3/17

| Rm | 15 | 12 | X | (Is 11 10) The *root* of Jesse will appear, |
| Rv | 5 | 5 | X | the *Root* of David has triumphed, |

Rv 22 16 X   I am of David's line, the *root* of David

7. BABY – CHILD – BOY

1: BABY, INFANT – LITTLE CHILDREN, CHILD: *BREPHOS*

brephos 8

Lk 1 41   as soon as Elizabeth heard Mary's greeting, the *child* leapt in her womb
    44   the *child* in my womb leapt for joy.
 2 12 X   you will find a *baby* wrapped in swaddling clothes
    16 X   [the shepherds] found Mary and Joseph, and the *baby* lying in a manger.
 18 15   People even brought *little children* to [Jesus], for him to touch them;
Ac 7 19   [Pharaoh] ill-treated our ancestors, forcing them to expose their *babies*
2 Tm 3 15   ever since you were a *child*, you have known the holy scriptures
1 P 2 2   You are new born, and, like *babies*, you should be hungry for nothing but milk

2: CHILD, CHILDREN – BABY – THE UNLEARNED, THE SIMPLE: *NĒPIOS*

2 nēpiazō 1   1 nēpios 14

Mt 11 25   I bless you, Father, . . . for . . . revealing [these things] to mere *children*.
 21 16   (Ps 8 2) By the mouths of *children*, babies in arms, you have made sure of praise.
Lk 10 21   I bless you, Father, . . . for . . . revealing [these things] to mere *children*.
Rm 2 20   if you can teach the ignorant and instruct the *unlearned*
1 Co 3 1   I treated you as sensual men, still *infants* in Christ.
 13 11   When I was a *child*, I used to talk like a *child*, and think like a *child*, and argue like a *child*, but now I am a man, all *childish* ways are put behind me.
 14 20   2 You can be *babies* as far as wickedness is concerned, but mentally you must be adult.
Ga 4 1   an heir . . . is no different from a slave for as long as he remains a *child*.
    3   ⌐before we came *of age* (or: while we were *children*) we were as good as slaves to the elemental principles of this world,
Ep 4 14   Then we shall not be *children* any longer, . . . ¹⁵ we shall grow in all ways into Christ,
Heb 5 13   anyone who is still living on milk cannot digest the doctrine of righteousness because he is still a *baby*.

3: CHILD – BOY: *PAIS*

3 paidarion 1   4 paidiothen 1
1 paidion 52   2 pais 9/24

a) Jesus as a child – the Boy Jesus

Mt 2 8   Go and find out all about the *child*,
    9   the star . . . halted over the place where the *child* was.
    11   [the wise men] saw the *child* with his mother
    13   take the *child* and his mother . . . and escape into Egypt, . . . because Herod intends to search for the *child*
    14   Joseph . . , taking the *child* and his mother . . , left that night
    20   take the *child* and his mother . . . and go back . . . for those who wanted to kill the *child* are dead.
    21   Joseph . . , taking the *child* and his mother . . , went back to the land of Israel.
Lk 2 17   [the shepherds] saw the *child*
    27   the parents brought . . . the *child* Jesus [into the Temple]
    40   the *child* grew to maturity,
    43   2 the *boy* Jesus stayed behind in Jerusalem

b) Little child, Children, Childhood – Boy(s)

Mt 2 16   2 Herod . . . had all the *male children* killed who were two years old or under,
 11 16   like *children* shouting to each other
 14 21   Those who ate numbered about 5,000 men, to say nothing of women and *children*.
 15 38   4,000 men had eaten, to say nothing of women and *children*.
 17 18   2 the devil came out of the *boy*

Mt 18 2   [Jesus] called a *little child* to him and . . . ³ said . . . unless
    3   you . . . become like *little children* you will never enter
    4   the kingdom of heaven. ⁴ . . . the one who makes himself as little as this *little child* is the greatest in the kingdom of
    5   heaven. ⁵ Anyone who welcomes a *little child* . . . in my name welcomes me.
 19 13   People brought *little children* to him,
    14   Let the *little children* alone,
 21 15   2 the *children* shouting 'Hosanna to the Son of David'
Mk 5 39   The *child* is not dead, but asleep.
    40   taking with him the *child's* father and mother . . . he went into the place where the *child* lay. ⁴¹ And taking the *child*
    41   by the hand he said to her, 'Talitha, . . . Little girl, . . . get up.'
 7 28   the house-dogs under the table can eat the *children's* scraps.
    30   she went . . . home and found the *child* lying on the bed
 9 21   4 How long has this been happening to him? *From childhood*,
    24   the father of the *boy* cried out, 'I do have faith.'
    36   [Jesus] then took a *little child*, . . . and said to them,
    37   ³⁷ Anyone who welcomes one of these *little children* in my name, welcomes me;
 10 13   People were bringing *little children* to him, for him to touch them.
    14   Let the *little children* come to me;
    15   anyone who does not welcome the kingdom of God like a *little child* will never enter it.
Lk 1 59   on the eighth day they came to circumcise the *child* [= John the Baptist];
    66   What will this *child* turn out to be? they wondered.
    76   And you, *little child*, you shall be called Prophet of the Most High;
    80   Meanwhile the *child* grew up
 7 32   They are like *children* shouting to one another
 8 51   [Jesus] allowed no one to go in with him except . . . the
    2   *child's* father and mother.
    54   2 *Child*, get up.
 9 42   2 Jesus rebuked the unclean spirit and cured the *boy*
    47   Jesus . . . took a *little child*
    48   Anyone who welcomes this *little child* in my name welcomes me;
 11 7   my *children* and I are in bed;
 18 16   Let the *little children* come to me,
    17   anyone who does not welcome the kingdom of God like a *little child* will never enter it.
Jn 4 49   come down before my *child* dies.
    51   2 his servants met him with the news that his *boy* was alive.
 6 9   3 There is a *small boy* here with two barley loaves and two fish;
 16 21   when she has given birth to the *child* she forgets the suffering
 21 5   Jesus called out, 'Have you caught anything, ⌐friends (lit. *children*)?
Ac 20 12   2 They took the *boy* [= Eutychus] away alive,
1 Co 14 20   you are not to be *childish* in your outlook.
Heb 2 13   (Is 8 18) Here I am with the *children* whom God has given me.
    14   all the *children* share the same blood and flesh,
 11 23   Moses . . . was hidden by his parents for three months; they . . . saw he was such a fine *child*.
1 Jn 2 14   I have written to you, *children*,
    18   *Children*, these are the last days;

8. LITTLE GIRL, GIRL: *KORASION*

1 korasion 8   2 talitha 1

Mt 9 24   [Jesus] said, 'Get out of here; the *little girl* is not dead, she is asleep.
    25   he went inside and took the *little girl* by the hand;
 14 11   The head [of John the Baptist] was brought in . . . and given to the *girl* who took it to her mother.
Mk 5 41   2 [Jesus] said to her, 'Talitha, kum!' which means, *Little girl, . . . get up.*
    42   The *little girl* got up at once and began to walk about,
 6 22   [Herod] said to the *girl*, 'Ask me anything you like'
    28   [the guard] brought the head [of John the Baptist] . . . and gave it to the *girl*, and the *girl* gave it to her mother.

9. BORN UNEXPECTEDLY – (OF) UNTIMELY BIRTH: *EK-TRŌMA*

ek-trōma 1

1 Co 15 8   last of all [Christ] appeared to me too; it was as though I was *born when no one expected it.*

10. BABES, BABIES AT THE BREAST – SUCKLE, SUCK: *THĒLAZŌ*

thēlazō 6

Mt 21	16	(Ps 8 3) By the mouths of children, *babes in arms*, you have made sure of praise.
24	19	Alas for those with child, or *with babies at the breast*, *Repeated in Mk 13 17 and Lk 21 23*
Lk 11	27	Happy . . . the breasts you have *sucked*!
23	29	Happy are . . . the breasts that never ᴦ*suckled* (or: fed) [a baby]

11. BARREN: *STEIROS*

steiros 4

Lk 1	7	Elizabeth was *barren*
	36	[Elizabeth] whom people called *barren* is now in her sixth month,
23	29	people will say, 'Happy are those who are *barren*'
Ga 4	27	(Is 54 1) Shout for joy, you *barren* women

BEAR WITH – PATIENCE

---

1. **Bear (with), Endure, Put up with:** *pherō*
2. **Bear, Put up with, Stand:** *stegō*
3. **Bear (with), Put up with, Tolerate – Forbearance, Tolerance, Endure:** *an-echomai*
4. **Patience – Forbearance, Tolerance:** *epi-eikeia*
5. **Patience – Perseverance, Endurance Fortitude:** *hypo-monē*
6. **Patience, Be patient:** *makro-thymia*
   1: Patience (of God, of our Lord)
   2: Patience, (Be) Patient

1. BEAR (WITH), ENDURE, PUT UP WITH: *PHERŌ*

2 pherō 2/68   *1 hypo-pherō 3*
3 tropo-phoreō 1

Ac 13 18 ⊖	3	for about forty years [God] ᵛ took care of (G *bore with*) [our ancestors] in the wilderness.
Rm 9 22 ⊖	2	God . . . patiently *puts up with* the people who make him angry,
1 Co 10 13		with any trial [God] will give you a way out of it and the strength to *bear* it.
2 Tm 3 11		[you know] all the persecutions I have *endured*;
Heb 12 20	2	[The Israelites] ᴦwere appalled at (lit. could not *bear*) the order that was given:
1 P 2 19		there is some merit in *putting up with* the pains of unearned punishment if it is done for the sake of God

2. BEAR, PUT UP WITH, STAND: *STEGŌ*

stegō 4

1 Co 9 12		we have *put up with* anything rather than obstruct the Good News
13 7		[love] is always ready to ᴦexcuse (lit. *bear*) . . . whatever comes.
1 Th 3 1		we could not *bear* the waiting any longer,
5		when I could not *stand* waiting any longer, I sent to assure myself of your faith:

3. BEAR (WITH), PUT UP WITH, TOLERATE – FORBEARANCE, TOLERANCE, ENDURE: *AN-ECHOMAI*

1 an-echomai 15	*4 an-exi(-kakos) 1*
2 an-ektos 5	*3 an-ochē 2*

Mt 10 15	2	on the day of Judgement it will ᴦnot go as hard with (lit. be more *bearable* for) the land of Sodom and Gomorrah ᴦas with (lit. than for) that town.
11 22	2	it will ᴦnot go as hard on Judgement day with (lit. be more *bearable* on Judgement day for) Tyre and Sidon ᴦas with (lit. than for) that town.
24	2	it will ᴦnot go as hard with (lit. be more *bearable* for) the land of Sodom on Judgement day ᴦas with (lit. than for) you.
17 17 X		Faithless and perverse generation! . . . How much longer must I *put up with* you?

Mk 9 19 X		You faithless generation! . . . How much longer must I *put up with* you?
Lk 9 41 X		Faithless and perverse generation! . . . How much longer must I . . . *put up with* you?
10 12	2	on that day it will ᴦnot go as hard with (lit. be more *bearable* for) Sodom ᴦas with (lit. than for) that town.
14	2	it will ᴦnot go as hard with (lit. be more *bearable* for) Tyre and Sidon at the Judgement ᴦas with (lit. than for) you.
Ac 18 14		Listen, you Jews. If this were a misdemeanour or a crime, I would ᴦnot hesitate to attend to (lit. have reason to *put up with*) you;
Rm 2 4 ⊖	3	are you abusing his abundant goodness, *patience* and *toleration* . . .?
3 25 ⊖	3	[in the past] sins went unpunished because ᴦhe held his hand (lit. of his *forbearance*),
1 Co 4 12		when we are hounded, we *put up with* it;
2 Co 11 1		I only wish you were able to *tolerate* a little foolishness from me. But of course: you *are tolerant towards* me.
4		you have only to receive a new spirit, different from the one you have already received . . . and you ᴦwelcome it with open arms (lit. *bear with* it as much as possible).
19		You are all wise men and can cheerfully *tolerate* fools, ²⁰ yes,
20		even to *tolerating* somebody who makes slaves of you,
Ep 4 2		*Bear with* one another charitably,
Col 3 13		*Bear with* one another;
2 Th 1 4		we can take special pride in you for your constancy and faith under all the persecutions . . . you *have to bear*.
2 Tm 2 24	4	a servant of the Lord . . . has to be kind to everyone . . . and *patient*.
4 3		The time is sure to come when, far from *being content with* sound teaching, people will be avid for the latest novelty
Heb 13 22		I do ask you, brothers, to *take* these words of advice *kindly*;

4. PATIENCE – FORBEARANCE, TOLERANCE: *EPI-EIKEIA*

2 epi-eikeia 2   *1 epi-eikēs 2/5*

Ac 24 4	2	[Felix,] I beg you to have *patience* enough to give us a brief hearing.
2 Co 10 1 X		this is Paul himself appealing to you by the gentleness and *patience* of Christ
Ph 4 5	2	Let your *tolerance* be evident to everyone:
1 Tm 3 3		[the elder-in-charge must be temperate,] ᴦkind (or: *forbearing*) and peaceable.

5. PATIENCE – PERSEVERANCE, ENDURANCE, FORTITUDE: *HYPO-MONĒ*

2 hypo-menō 10/17   *1 hypo-monē 32*   *Job* 1 (Jm 5)*

Lk 8 15		As for the [seed] in the rich soil, this is people . . . who . . . yield a harvest through their ᴦ*perseverance* (or: *patience*).
21 19		Your *endurance* will win you your lives.
Rm 2 7		For those who sought renown . . . by ᴦalways (lit. *patiently*) doing good there will be eternal life;
5 3		These sufferings bring *patience*, as we know, ⁴ and *patience*
4		brings perseverance,
8 25		we must hope to be saved . . . it is something we must wait for with *patience*.
12 12	2	ᴦDo not give up if (lit. *Be patient* when) trials come; and keep on praying.
15 4		the scriptures . . . teach us something about hope from ᴦthe examples scripture gives of how people who did not give up were helped by God (lit. the encouragement of scripture and through *endurance*).
5		may he who helps us ᴦwhen we refuse to give up (lit. to be *patient*), help you all to be tolerant with each other,
1 Co 13 7	2	[love] is always ready to ᴦexcuse (lit. *bear*), to trust, to hope, and to *endure* whatever comes.
2 Co 1 6		this should be a consolation to you, supporting you in *patiently bearing* the same sufferings as we bear.
6 4		we prove we are servants of God by great *fortitude* in times of . . . distress;
12 12		You have seen . . . the things that mark the true apostle, ᴦunfailingly (lit. *patiently*) produced: the signs, the marvels,
Col 1 11		You will have in you the strength . . . ᴦnever to give in, but (lit. to *endure*, and) to bear anything joyfully,
1 Th 1 3		[we] constantly remember . . . how you have . . . *persevered* through hope,
2 Th 1 4		we can take special pride in you for your *constancy* and faith under all the persecutions . . . you have to bear.
3 5		May the Lord turn your hearts towards . . . the *fortitude* of Christ.
1 Tm 6 11		You must aim to be saintly . ., *patient* and gentle.
2 Tm 2 10	2	I *bear* it all for the sake of those who are chosen.

2 Tm 3	10	you know my faith, my patience and my love; my *constancy* [11] and the persecutions . . . that came to me
Tt 2	2	The older men should be . . . sound in faith and love and *constancy*.
Heb 10	32	Remember all the sufferings that you had to ⌐meet (lit. *endure*)
	2 36	You will need *endurance* to do God's will
12	1	we . . . should . . . keep running *steadily* in the race we have started.
	2 X 2/2	Jesus . . . *endured* the cross . . . [3] Think of the way he *stood*
	3	such opposition from sinners
	7 2	*Suffering* is part of your training;
Jm 1	3	your faith is only put to the test to make you *patient*, [4] but
	4	*patience* too is to have its practical results
5	11 2	it is *those who had endurance* that we say are the blessed ones. You have heard of the *patience* of Job*,
1 P 2	20	2 there is nothing meritorious in *taking* a beating *patiently*, if you have done something wrong to deserve it. The merit,
	2	in the sight of God, is in *bearing* it *patiently* . . . after doing your duty.
2 P 1	6	[add] *patience* to your self-control, true devotion to your *patience*
Rv 1	9	My name is John, and . . . I . . . share your sufferings, your kingdom, and all you *endure*.
2	2	I know . . . how much you *put up with* . . . [3] I know, too,
	3	that you have *patience*, and have suffered for my name without growing tired.
	19	I know your faith and devotion and how much you *put up with*,
3	10	Because you have kept my commandment to *endure* [trials], I will keep you safe in the time of trial
13	10	This is why the saints must have *constancy* and faith.
14	12	This is why there must be *constancy* in the saints

6. PATIENCE, BE PATIENT: *MAKRO-THYMIA*

2 *makro-thymeō* 10   3 *makro-thymōs* 1
1 *makro-thymia* 14

1: PATIENCE (OF GOD, OF OUR LORD)

Lk 18	7	will not God see justice done to his chosen who cry to him
	2	day and night even when he ⌐delays to help (lit. *is patient* with) them?
Rm 2	4	are you abusing his abundant goodness, patience and *toleration* . . .?
9	22	God . . . *patiently* puts up with the people who make him angry,
1 Tm 1	16	Christ meant to make me the greatest evidence of his . . . *patience*
1 P 3	20	it was long ago . . . when God was still waiting *patiently* that these spirits refused to believe.
2 P 3	9	2 The Lord . . . is *being patient* with you . . . wanting nobody to be lost
	15	Think of our Lord's *patience* as your opportunity to be saved:

2: PATIENCE, (BE) PATIENT

Mt 18	26 <	2 ⌐Give me time (lit. *Be patient* with me) . . . and I will pay
	29 <	2 ⌐Give me time (lit. *Be patient* with me) and I will pay you.
Ac 26	3	3 [King Agrippa], I beg you to listen to me *patiently*.
1 Co 13	4	2 Love is always *patient* and kind;
2 Co 6	6	We prove we are God's servants by our . . . *patience* and kindness;
Ga 5	22	the Spirit brings . . . love, joy, peace, *patience*,
Ep 4	2	Bear with one another . . . in complete selflessness, gentleness and *patience*.
Col 1	11	You will have in you the strength . . . to ⌐bear anything (lit. *be patient*) joyfully,
3	12	you should be clothed in . . . gentleness and *patience*.
1 Th 5	14	2 care for the weak and *be patient* with everyone.
2 Tm 3	10	you know my faith, my *patience* and my love;
4	2	proclaim the message . . . correct error, call to obedience – but do all with *patience*
Heb 6	12	[imitate] those who have the faith and the *perseverance* to inherit the promises.
	15	2 Abraham *persevered* and saw the promise fulfilled.
Jm 5	7	2 Now *be patient*, brothers, until the Lord's coming. Think of
	2	the farmer: how *patiently* he *waits* for the precious fruit
	8 2	of the ground . . . [8] You too have to *be patient* . . .
	10	[10] For your example, brothers, in submitting with *patience*, take the prophets

BEAT – STRIKE – WOUND

1. **Knock**: *krouō*
2. **Beat, Strike, Slap – Thrash, Flog – Receive strokes (of the lash)**: *derō*
3. **Beat, Strike, Slap – Wound, Injure – Torture**: *typtō*
4. **Strike (out at), Smite, Strike down – Tap**: *patassō*
5. **Strike (out at), Hit, Wound – Sting**: *paiō*
6. **Beat,   Strike – Wound – Plague**: *plēssō*
    1: Beat, a Beating, Brawler – Flogged, Whipped – Lashes, Stripes
    2: Wound – Injury
    3: Struck, Blasted, by a Plague
7. **Strike, Beat against – Slaughter, Defeat**: *koptō*
    1: Strike – Beat upon, Lash against

    2: Slaughter – Defeat, Rout
8. **Strike, Hit – Slap, Blow**: *rhapizō*
9. **Beat, Strike, Hit with the fists – Buffeted, Roughly handled – a Beating**: *kolaphizō*
10. **Beat about the head, Wound in the head**: *kephalaioō*
11. **Treat hard, Bruise, Discipline, *therefore* (metaphorically): Wear (a person) out, Worry to death**: *hyp-ōpiazō*
12. **Scourge, Flog, Punish severely – the Lash**: *mastigoō*
13. **Scourge, Flog – a Whip**: *phra-gelloō*
14. **Wounds – Mauled, Battered, Bruised**: *traumatizō*
15. **Wounds**: *mōlōps*

X = Jesus Beaten, Struck, Scourged

1. KNOCK: *KROUŌ*

krouō 9

Mt 7	7	*knock*, and the door will be opened to you. [8] . . . the one
	8	who *knocks* will always have the door opened to him.
Lk 11	9	*knock*, and the door will be opened to you. [10] . . . the one
	10	who *knocks* will always have the door opened to him.
12	36	men . . . ready to open the door as soon as [the master] comes and *knocks*.
13	25	you may find yourself *knocking* on the door,
Ac 12	13	[Peter] *knocked* at the outside door
	16	Peter, meanwhile, was still *knocking*,
Rv 3	20	Look, I am standing at the door, *knocking*.

2. BEAT, STRIKE, SLAP – THRASH, FLOG – RECEIVE STROKES (OF THE LASH): *DERŌ*

derō 15

Mt 21	35 <	the tenants . . . *thrashed* one [servant], killed another
Mk 12	3 <	[The owner of the vineyard sent a servant to the tenants:] they . . . *thrashed* him . . . [5] And he sent . . . a number
	5 <	of others, and they *thrashed* some and killed the rest.
13	9	they will hand you over to sanhedrins; you will be *beaten*
Lk 12	47 <	The servant who knows what his master wants, but has not
	<	even started . . . will *receive* very many *strokes* of the lash. [48] The one who did not know, but deserves to be
	48	beaten . . . will *receive* fewer *strokes*.
20	10 <	the tenants *thrashed* [the servant], and sent him away empty-handed. [11] But [the owner] . . . sent a second servant;
	11 <	they *thrashed* him too
22	63 X	the men who guarded Jesus were mocking and *beating* him.
Jn 18	23 X	if there is no offence in [what I said], why do you *strike* me?
Ac 5	40	they . . . gave orders for [the apostles] to be *flogged*, warned them not to speak in the name of Jesus
16	37	[The magistrates] *flog* Roman citizens in public
22	19	[Paul said:] I used to go . . . *flogging* those who believed in you;
1 Co 9	26	that is how I fight, not *beating* the air.
2 Co 11	20	even to tolerating somebody who . . . *slaps* you in the face.

3. BEAT, STRIKE, SLAP – WOUND, INJURE – TORTURE: *TYPTŌ*

2 *tympanizō* 1   1 *typtō* 13

B = Beat one's breast

Mt 24	49	[the dishonest servant] sets about *beating* his fellow servants
27	30 X	[the soldiers] took the reed and *struck* him on the head
Mk 15	19 X	They *struck* his head with a reed
Lk 6	29	To the man who *slaps* you on one cheek, present the other cheek too;
12	45	[the dishonest servant] sets about *beating* the menservants and the maids,
18	13 B	The tax collector . . . *beat* his breast
23	48 B	all the people . . . went home *beating* their breasts.
Ac 18	17	they all turned on Sosthenes . . . and *beat* him

Ac 21 32	the crowd . . . stopped *beating* Paul when they saw the tribune
23 2	Ananias ordered his attendants to *strike* [Paul] on the mouth.
3 ⊖	³ Then Paul said to him, 'God will surely *strike* you . . . How can you sit there to judge me . . . and then break the Law by ordering a man to *strike* me?'
1 Co 8 12 ○	By . . . *injuring* [your brothers'] weak consciences, it would be Christ against whom you sinned.
Heb 11 35	2 others submitted to *torture* . . . so that they would rise again to a better life.

4. STRIKE (OUT AT), SMITE, STRIKE DOWN – TAP: *PATASSŌ*

patassō 10

Mt 26 31 X	(Zc 13 7) the scripture says: I shall *strike* the shepherd
51	one of the followers of Jesus . . . *struck* out at the high priest's servant and cut off his ear.
Mk 14 27 X	(Zc 13 7) I shall *strike* the shepherd and the sheep will be scattered.
Lk 22 49	Lord, shall we *strike* with our swords? ⁵⁰ And one of them
50	*struck* out at the high priest's servant, and cut off his right ear.
Ac 7 24	[Moses] rescued the man by *striking down* the Egyptian.
12 7	the angel . . . *tapped* Peter on the side and woke him.
23	the angel of the Lord *struck* [Herod] *down* . . . He was eaten away with worms and died.
Rv 11 6	[the two witnesses] are able to . . . *strike* the whole world with any plague
19 15	From [the] mouth [of The Word of God] came a sharp sword to *strike* the pagans with;

5. STRIKE (OUT AT), HIT, WOUND – STING: *PAIŌ*

paiō 5

Mt 26 68 X	Play the prophet, Christ! Who *hit* you then?
Mk 14 47 X	one of the bystanders drew his sword and *struck* out at the high priest's servant,
Lk 22 64 X	Play the prophet . . . Who *hit* you then?
Jn 18 10	Simon Peter, who carried a sword . . . *wounded* the high priest's servant,
Rv 9 5	the pain was to be the pain of a scorpion's *sting*.

6. BEAT, STRIKE – WOUND – PLAGUE: *PLĒSSŌ*

2 *plēktēs 2*   3 *plēssō 1*
1 *plēgē 22*

1: BEAT, A BEATING, BRAWLER – FLOGGED, WHIPPED – LASHES, STRIPES

Lk 10 30	brigands . . . *beat* [the man] and then made off,
12 48	The one who did not know [his master's wishes], but deserves to be *beaten* . . . will receive fewer strokes.
Ac 16 23	[Paul and Silas] were given many *lashes*
2 Co 6 5	[we prove we are servants of God] when we are *flogged*,
11 23	The servants of Christ? . . . so am I, and more than they: more, because . . . I have been *whipped* so many times more . . . ²⁴ Five times I had the thirty-nine lashes from the Jews (cf. ⌐ : 25 3); ²⁵ three times I have been beaten with sticks;
1 Tm 3 3	2 [the elder-in-charge must not be] ⌐hot-tempered (lit. a *brawler*), but kind and peaceable.
Tt 1 7	[the elder] must be irreproachable: never . . . ⌐violent (lit. 2 a *brawler*),

2: WOUND – INJURY

Ac 16 33	[the gaoler] took [Paul and Silas] to wash their *wounds*,
Rv 13 3	this deadly *injury* [of the beast] had healed
12	the first beast, which had had the fatal *wound* and had been healed.
14	the beast that had been *wounded* by the sword and still lived.

3: STRUCK, BLASTED, BY A PLAGUE

| Rv 8 12 | 3 a third of the sun and a third of the moon . . . were *blasted*, |
| 9 18 | It was by these three *plagues*, the fire, the smoke and the sulphur coming out of [the] mouths [of the horses], that the one third of the human race was killed. |

Rv 9 20	the rest of the human race, who escaped these *plagues*, refused . . . to abandon . . . the idols
11 6	[the two witnesses] are able to . . . *strike* the whole world with any *plague* as often as they like.
15 1	seven angels were bringing the seven *plagues* that are the last of all,
6	[the Tent of the Testimony opened in heaven] and out came the seven angels with the seven *plagues*,
8	no one could go into [the temple] until the seven *plagues* of the seven angels were completed.
16 9	[people] cursed the name of God who had the power to cause such *plagues*,
21	the people . . . cursed God for sending a *plague* of hail; it was the most terrible *plague*.
18 4	Come out . . . away from [Babylon], so that you do not share in her crimes and have the same *plagues* to bear.
8	within a single day, the *plagues* will fall on her; disease and mourning and famine.
21 9	One of the seven angels that had the seven bowls full of the seven last *plagues* came to speak to me,
22 18	if anyone adds anything to [the prophecies], God will add to him every *plague* mentioned in the book;

7. STRIKE, BEAT AGAINST – SLAUGHTER, DEFEAT: *KOPTŌ*

2 *kopē 1*   1 *pros-koptō 3/8*

1: STRIKE – BEAT UPON, LASH AGAINST

Mt 4 6	(Ps 91 12) his angels . . . will support you . . . in case you *strike* your foot against a stone.
7 27 <	floods rose, gales blew and *struck* that house,
Lk 4 11	(Ps 91 12) [the angels] will hold you up . . . in case you *strike* your foot against a stone.

2: SLAUGHTER – DEFEAT, ROUT

| Heb 7 1 | 2 Abraham . . . was on his way back after *defeating* the kings, |

8. STRIKE, HIT – SLAP, BLOW: *RHAPIZŌ*

2 *rhapizō 2*   1 *rhapisma 3*

Mt 5 39	2 if anyone *hits* you on the right cheek, offer him the other as well;
26 67 X	2 they spat in his face . . . others . . . *struck* him,
Mk 14 65 X	the attendants rained *blows* on him.
Jn 18 22 X	one of the guards . . . gave Jesus a *slap* in the face,
19 3 X	they *slapped* him in the face.

9. BEAT, STRIKE, HIT WITH THE FISTS – BUFFETED, ROUGHLY HANDLED – A BEATING: *KOLAPHIZŌ*

kolaphizō 5

Mt 26 67 X	they spat in his face and *hit* him with their fists;
Mk 14 65 X	Some of them . . . began *hitting* him with their fists
1 Co 4 11	To this day . . . we are *beaten* and have no homes;
2 Co 12 7	I was given a thorn in the flesh, an angel of Satan to *beat* me
1 P 2 20	there is nothing meritorious in taking a *beating* patiently if you have done something wrong to deserve it.

10. BEAT ABOUT THE HEAD, WOUND IN THE HEAD: *KEPHALAIOŌ*

kephalaioō 1

| Mk 12 4 < | [the other servant] they *beat about the head* |

11. TREAT HARD, BRUISE, DISCIPLINE, therefore (metaphorically): WEAR (A PERSON) OUT, WORRY TO DEATH: *HYP-ŌPIAZŌ*

hyp-ōpiazō 2

| Lk 18 5 < | [this widow] will persist in coming and *worry* me *to death*. |
| 1 Co 9 27 | I *treat* my body *hard* and make it obey me, |

12. SCOURGE, FLOG, PUNISH SEVERELY – THE LASH: *MASTIGOŌ*

1 *mastigoō* 7   3 *mastizō 1*
2 *mastix*   2/6

Mt 10 17		they will . . . *scourge* you in their synagogues.
20 19 X		they will hand [the Son of Man] over . . . to be mocked and *scourged* and crucified;
23 34		[some prophets and wise men] you will *scourge* in your synagogues
Mk 10 34 X		they will . . . *scourge* [the Son of Man] and put him to death;
Lk 18 33 X		when they have *scourged* him they will put him to death;
Jn 19 1 X		Pilate then had Jesus taken away and *scourged*;
Ac 22 24		the tribune . . . ordered [Paul] to be examined under the 2 *lash*,
25		3 Is it legal for you to *flog* a man who is a Roman citizen . . .?
Heb 11 36		2 Some [prophets] had to bear being pilloried and *flogged*,
12 6 ○		(Pr 3 12 G) the Lord . . . *punishes* all those that he acknowledges as his sons.

13. SCOURGE, FLOG – A WHIP: *PHRAGELLOŌ*

1 *phragelloō 2*   2 *phragellion 1*

Mt 27 26 X		[Pilate] ordered Jesus to be first *scourged* and then handed over to be crucified.
Mk 15 15 X		having ordered Jesus to be *scourged*, [Pilate] handed him over to be crucified.
Jn 2 15		2 Making a *whip* out of some cord, [Jesus] drove them all out of the Temple, cattle and sheep as well,

14. WOUNDS – MAULED, BATTERED, BRUISED: *TRAUMATIZŌ*

2 *trauma 1*   1 *traumatizō 2*

Lk 10 34		2 [the Samaritan] bandaged [the] *wounds* [of the man who had fallen into the hands of brigands],
20 12 <		[the tenants] *wounded* [the third servant] also, and threw him out.
Ac 19 16		[the seven sons of Sceva fled from that house naked and] badly *mauled*.

15. WOUNDS: *MŌLŌPS*

mōlōps 1

1 P 2 24 X		(Is 53 5) through [Christ's] *wounds* you have been healed.

BEFORE

1. Before – Formerly, Previously, Long ago – the Past
1: Before, Earlier – (of) Old, Former – First: *pro*
2: Before, Previously: *pro-(h)yp-archō*
3: Beforehand: *pro-lambanō*
4: Forestall: *pro-phthanō*
5: Once, Formerly, Previously – Past, Long ago: *pote*
6: Long ago, (in the) Past: *palai*
7: For a long time (past): *anōthen*
8: the Past: *par-oichomai*

2. Before – In front of – Opposite
1: Before – In front of: *en-ōpion*
a) Before, In the sight of (God) – In the presence of (angels) – In front of, Ahead of (Jesus)
b) Before, In front of, In the sight of (generally) – Publicly – To, For, On behalf of
2: Before – In front of: *em-prosthen*
a) Before (God), In front of (Christ), In the presence of (angels) – At (the feet of), To
b) Before, In the presence of (generally) – In front of, Ahead (of)
3: Before – In front of – Opposite: *en-anti*
a) Before, In the sight of (God) – In front of, Facing, Opposite (Jesus)
b) Opposite, Facing, In front of (generally) – In public
4: Opposite: *anti-pera*

---

1. BEFORE – FORMERLY, PREVIOUSLY, LONG AGO – THE PAST

1: BEFORE, EARLIER – (OF) OLD, FORMER – FIRST: *PRO*

2 *pro*   (3)   3 *proteros 1*
1 *proteron 10*

Mt 5 12		2 this is how they persecuted the prophets *before* you.
Jn 6 62		What if you should see the Son of Man ascend to where he was *before*?
7 50		Nicodemus – the same man who had come to Jesus *earlier*
9 8		people who *earlier* had seen [the blind man] begging said,
Rm 16 7		2 Andronicus and Junias . . . became Christians *before* me,
2 Co 1 15		I had meant to come to you *first*, so that you would benefit doubly;
Ga 4 13		⌐at the beginning (or: *earlier*) . . . that illness gave me the opportunity to preach the Good News to you,
Ep 4 22		3 You must give up your *old* way of life;
Col 1 17 X		2 *Before* anything was created, he existed,
1 Tm 1 13		[Christ called me into his service] even though *formerly* I used to be a blasphemer
Heb 4 6		those who *first* heard the Good News failed to reach [the place of rest] through their disobedience,
7 27		the other high priests [offer sacrifices] *first* for their own sins and then for those of the people,
10 32		Remember all the sufferings that you had to meet after you received the light, in *earlier* days;
1 P 1 14		Do not behave in the way that you liked to *before* you learnt the truth;

2: BEFORE, PREVIOUSLY: *PRO-(H)YP-ARCHŌ*

pro-(h)yp-archō 2

Lk 23 12		though Herod and Pilate had been enemies *before*, they were reconciled that same day.
Ac 8 9		a man called Simon had ⌐already (lit. *previously*) practised magic arts in the town

3: BEFOREHAND: *PRO-LAMBANŌ*

pro-lambanō 1/3

Mk 14 8		she has anointed my body *beforehand* for its burial.

4: FORESTALL: *PRO-PHTHANŌ*

pro-phthanō 1

Mt 17 25 X		⌐before [Peter could speak] (or: *forestalling* [Peter]), Jesus said, 'Simon, what is your opinion?

5: ONCE, FORMERLY, PREVIOUSLY – PAST, LONG AGO: *POTE*

pote (18)

N = Once, Formerly, Long ago // Now

Jn 9 13		They brought the man who had *formerly* been blind to the Pharisees.
Rm 7 9		*Once*, when there was no Law, I was alive;
11 30 N		Just as you ⌐changed from being (lit. were *once*) disobedient to God [so those who are disobedient now will enjoy mercy]
Ga 1 13		You must have heard of my *former* career as a practising Jew,
23 N		[the churches in Judaea] had heard nothing except that their *one-time* persecutor was now preaching the faith he had *previously* tried to destroy;
Ep 2 2 N		[you were dead through the sins] in which you *once* used to live
3		We all were among them too *in the past*, living sensual lives,
11		Do not forget, then, that *there was a time when* you . . . were pagans physically,
13 N		now in Christ Jesus, you that used to be *once* so far apart from us have been brought very close,
5 8 N		You were darkness *once*, but now you are light in the Lord;
Col 1 21 N		[Not] *long ago*, you were foreigners and enemies,
3 7 N		it is the way in which you *once* used to live
Tt 3 3		*there was a time when* we too were ignorant, disobedient and misled
Phm 11 N		[Onesimus] was of no use to you *before*,
1 P 2 10 N		*Once* you were not a people at all
3 5		That was how the holy women *of the past* dressed themselves
20		Now it Nwas *long ago* when . . . these spirits refused to believe.

6: LONG AGO, (IN THE) PAST: *PALAI*

1 *palai* 6   **2** *ek-palai* 2

Mt	11 21	Tyre and Sidon . . . would have repented *long ago*
Lk	10 13	Tyre and Sidon . . . would have repented *long ago,*
2 Co	12 19	*All this time* you have been thinking that our defence is addressed to you,
Heb	1 1	At various times *in the past* . . . God spoke to our ancestors through the prophets;
2 P	1 9	he has forgotten how his *past* sins were washed away.
	2 3	2 for [false teachers] the Condemnation, [pronounced] *so long ago,* is at its work already,
	3 5	2 there were heavens *at the beginning (lit. long ago),* and . . . the earth was formed by the word of God
Jude	4	Certain people have infiltrated among you, and they are the ones you had a warning about, in writing, *long ago,*

7: FOR A LONG TIME (PAST): *ANŌTHEN*

anōthen (1)

Ac	26 5	[The Jews] have known me *for a long time*

8: THE PAST: *PAR-OICHOMAI*

par-oichomai 1

Ac	14 16	In the *past* [God] allowed each nation to go its own way;

2. BEFORE – IN FRONT OF – OPPOSITE

1: BEFORE – IN FRONT OF: *EN-ŌPION*

1   *en-ōpion* 94   **2**   *pros-ōpon* 12/76
4   *kat-en-ōpion* 2/3   **3**   *pro pros-ōpou*   5

a) Before, In the sight of (God) – In the presence of (angels) – In front of, Ahead of (Jesus)

Mt	11 10 X	3 (Ml 3 1) I am going to send my messenger *before* you;
	18 10	2 their angels in heaven are continually *in the presence of* my Father
Mk	1 2 X	3 (Ml 3 1) I am going to send my messenger *before* you;
Lk	1 15	[John] will be great *in the sight of* the Lord;
	17 X	With the spirit . . . of Elijah, he will go *before* [the Lord]
	19	I am Gabriel who stand *in God's presence,*
	75	[God granted us] to serve him in holiness and virtue *in his presence,*
	76 X	And you, little child . . . you will go *before* the Lord
	5 18 X	some men appeared, carrying . . . a paralysed man whom they were trying to . . . lay down *in front of* [Jesus].
	7 27 X	3 (Ml 3 1) I am going to send my messenger *before* you;
	9 52 X	3 [Jesus] sent messengers *ahead of* him.
	10 1 X	3 the Lord . . . sent them out *ahead of* him, in pairs,
	12 6	not one [sparrow] is forgotten *in God's sight.*
	9	the man who disowns me in the presence of men will be disowned *in the presence of* God's angels.
	13 26 X	We once ate and drank in *your company;*
	15 10	there is rejoicing ʳamong (lit. *in the presence of*) the angels of God over one repentant sinner.
	16 15	what is thought highly of by men is loathsome *in the sight of* God.
Ac	2 28	(Ps 16 11) you will fill me with gladness through your *presence.*
	3 20	2 so that the Lord may send the time of comfort from *within* his *presence.*
	4 19	You must judge whether *in God's eyes* it is right to listen to you and not to God.
	7 46	[David] won ʳGod's favour (lit. favour *in the sight of* God)
	10 31	your alms have been accepted as a sacrifice *in the sight of* God;
	33	Here we all are, assembled *in front of* ᵛ you (G God) to hear what message God has given you for us.
Rm	3 20	no one can be justified *in the sight of* God by keeping the Law:
	14 22	Hold on to your own belief, ʳas between yourself and God (lit. for when you are *in the presence of* God)
1 Co	1 29	The human race has nothing to boast about ʳto (lit. *before*) God,
2 Co	2 10 X	2 I have forgiven it for your sake *in the presence of* Christ.
	4 2	the way we commend ourselves to every human being with a conscience is by stating the truth openly *in the sight of* God.
	7 12	[I wrote the letter] to make you realise, *in the sight of* God, your own concern for us.
	8 21	we are trying to do right not only *in the sight of* God but also in the sight of men.

Ga	1 20	I swear *before* God that what I have just written is the literal truth.
Ep	1 4	4 he chose us . . . to be holy and spotless . . . *in his presence,*
Col	1 22	4 Now you are able to appear *before* him holy . . . and blameless
2 Th	1 9 X	It will be their punishment to be . . . excluded from the *presence* of the Lord
1 Tm	2 3	To do this . . . will ʳplease (lit. be pleasing *in the sight of*) God our saviour:
	5 4	this is what ʳpleases (lit. is pleasing *in the sight of*) God.
	21	*Before* God, and *before* Jesus Christ and the angels . . . I put it to you as a duty to keep these rules
	6 13	*before* God . . . and *before* Jesus Christ . . . I put to you the duty [14] of doing all that you have been told,
2 Tm	2 14	tell them ʳin the name of (lit. *before*) God that there is to be no wrangling about words:
	4 1 X	*Before* God and *before* Christ Jesus . . . I put this duty to you . . . [2] proclaim the message
Heb	4 13	No created thing can hide ʳfrom (lit. *before*) [God]; everything is uncovered
	9 24	Christ . . . entered . . . heaven itself, so that he could appear *in the* actual *presence* of God
	13 21	[I pray that God may] turn us all into whatever is acceptable ʳto himself (G *in his own sight*)
Jm	4 10	Humble yourselves *before* the Lord
1 P	3 4	this is what is precious *in the sight of* God.
1 Jn	3 22	we . . . live the kind of life that ʳhe wants (lit. is pleasing *in his sight*).
Rv	3 2	I have failed to notice anything in the way you live that ʳmy God could possibly call perfect (lit. could possibly be called perfect *in the sight of* God),
	5	I shall . . . acknowledge [the] names [of those who prove victorious] *in the presence of* my Father and *in the presence of* his angels.
	4 10	the twenty-four elders prostrated themselves *before* him . . . and threw down their crowns *in front of* the throne,
	5 8 X	the four animals prostrated themselves *before* [the Lamb]
	7 9 X	a huge number . . . of people . . . *in front of* the throne and *in front of* the Lamb,
	11	all . . . prostrated themselves *before* the throne,
	8 2	I saw . . . the seven angels who stand *in the presence of* God.
	4	the smoke of the incense went up *in the presence of* God
	9 13	I heard a voice come out of . . . the golden altar *in front of* God.
	11 4	the two lamps that stand *before* the Lord of the world.
	16	The twenty-four elders, enthroned *in the presence of* God,
	12 10	the persecutor, who accused our brothers day and night *before* our God.
	14 10 X	in fire and brimstone they will be tortured *in the presence of* the holy angels and *in the presence of* the Lamb
	15 4	(Ps 86 9) the pagans will come and ʳadore (lit. prostrate themselves *before*) you
	16 19	Babylon the Great was not forgotten ʳby (lit. *in the sight of* God:
	20 11	2 *In his presence,* earth and sky vanished,

b) Before, In front of, In the sight of (generally) – Publicly – To, For, On behalf of

Lk	2 31	2 [the salvation] which you have prepared *for* all the nations
	4 7 ⑩	ʳWorship (lit. Prostrate yourself *before*) me, then,
	5 25	*before* their very *eyes* [the paralytic] got up . . . and went home
	8 47	the woman . . . explained *in front of* all the people . . . how she had been cured
	12 9	the man who disowns me *in the presence of* men will be disowned in the presence of God's angels.
	14 10	everyone with you at the table will see you honoured *before* them.
	15 18	Father, I have sinned against heaven and ʳagainst you (or: *in your sight*);
	21	Father, I have sinned against heaven and ʳagainst you (or: *in your sight*).
	16 15	You are the very ones who pass yourselves off as virtuous *in* people's *sight,*
	23 14	[Pilate] said, '. . . I have gone into the matter myself *in your presence* . . .'
	24 11	this story of theirs seemed pure nonsense ʳto (lit. *before*) them,
	43	[Jesus took a piece of grilled fish] and ate *before their eyes.*
Jn	20 30	There were many other signs that Jesus worked ʳand the disciples saw (lit. *in the sight of* the disciples),
Ac	2 25 X	(Ps 16 8) I saw the Lord *before* me always,
	3 13	2 the same Jesus you . . . disowned *in the presence of* Pilate
	4 10	by this name . . . this man is able to stand up perfectly healthy, here *in your presence,* today.
	6 5	The whole assembly approved of ʳthis proposal (lit. the proposal put *before* them)
	6	[the assembly] presented these ʳto (or: *before*) the apostles,

Ac 7 45   the nations . . . were driven out by God ⌐as we advanced (lit.
    2   *before* us as we advanced).
  9 15   this man is my chosen instrument to bring my name *before*
      pagans
  10 30   I suddenly saw a man *in front of* me in shining robes.
    33   Here we all are, asembled *in front of* ᵛ you (G God) to hear
      what message God has given you for us.
  13 24   2 [Jesus's] coming was ⌐heralded (lit. announced *beforehand*) by
      John when he proclaimed a baptism of repentance
  19 9   some of the congregation . . . began attacking the Way *in
      front of* the others,
    19   a number of [the believers] who had practised magic . . .
      made a bonfire of [their books] *in public.*
  27 35   [Paul] took some bread, gave thanks to God *in front of*
      them all,
Rm 12 17   you are interested only in ⌐the highest ideals (lit. what is
      noble *in the sight of* all).
2Co 8 21   we are trying to do right . . . also *in the sight of* men.
    24   2 So then, *in front of* all the churches, give them a proof of
      your love,
1Tm 5 20   If any of [the elders] are at fault; reprimand them *publicly,*
  6 12   you made your profession and spoke up for the truth *in
      front of* many witnesses.
3 Jn 6   They are a proof ⌐to (or: *before*) the whole Church of your
      charity
Rv 1 4   grace and peace . . . from the seven spirits in [God's]
      presence *before* his throne,
  2 14   Balaam . . . taught Balak to set a trap ⌐for (or: *in front of*)
      the Israelites
  3 8   I have opened *in front of* you a door
    9   I will make them come and fall ⌐at (lit. *before*) your feet
  4 5   *in front of* the throne there were seven flaming lamps burning,
    6   ⌐Between the throne and myself (lit. *In front of* the throne)
      was a sea
  7 15   [the persecuted] now stand *in front of* God's throne
  8 3   the golden altar . . . stood *in front of* the throne;
  12 4   the dragon stopped *in front of* the woman as she was having
      the child,
  13 12   This second beast was ⌐servant to (lit. *in the presence of*) the
      first beast, and extended its authority everywhere,
    13   even to calling down fire from heaven on to the earth ⌐while
      people watched (lit. *in front of* people who watched).
    14   the miracles which it was allowed to do *on behalf of* the
      first beast,
  14 3   There *in front of* the throne they were singing a new hymn
      in the presence of the four animals
  19 20   the false prophet who had worked miracles *on the beast's
      behalf*
  20 12   I saw the dead . . . standing *in front of* his throne,

2: BEFORE – IN FRONT OF: *EM-PROSTHEN*

em-prosthen 48

a) *Before (God), In front of (Christ), In the presence of (angels) –
At (the feet of), To*

Mt 10 32   I will declare myself for him *in the presence of* my Father
    33   I will disown [the one who disowns me] *in the presence of*
      my Father
  11 10 X   (Ml 3 1) I am going to send my messenger . . . he will
      prepare your way *before* you.
    26   Yes, Father, for that is what ⌐it pleased (lit. was pleasing *to*)
      you to do.
  18 14   it is never the will ⌐of (lit. *before*) your Father in heaven
      that one of these little ones should be lost.
  25 32 X   All the nations will be assembled *before* [the Son of Man]
  27 29 X   To make fun of [Jesus] they knelt ⌐to (or: *before*) him
Lk 5 19 X   they . . . lowered [the paralytic] and his stretcher down
      . . . *in front of* Jesus.
  7 27 X   (Ml 3 1) I am going to send my messenger . . . he will
      prepare the way *before* you.
  10 21   Yes, Father, for that is what ⌐it pleased (lit. was pleasing *to*)
      you to do.
  12 8   the Son of Man will declare himself for him *in the presence
      of* God's angels.
  14 2 X   There *in front of* [Jesus] was a man with dropsy,
  19 27 <   as for my enemies . . . execute them *in my presence.*
  21 36 X   praying . . . for the strength . . . to stand with confidence
      before the Son of Man.
Jn 3 28 X   I myself am not the Christ; I am the one who has been sent
      in front of him.
Ac 10 4   Your offering of prayers and alms . . . ⌐has been accepted by
      God (lit. has ascended as a memorial *before* God).
2Co 5 10 X   all the truth about us will be brought out ⌐in (lit. *before*) the
      law court of Christ,
1Th 1 3   [we] constantly remember *before* God . . . your faith in
      action,
  2 19 X   the crown of which we shall be proudest *in the presence of*
      our Lord Jesus

1Th 3 9   all the joy we feel *before* our God on your account
    13   may [the Lord] so confirm your hearts in holiness that you
      may be blameless *in the sight of* our God and Father
1Jn 3 19   [we will] be able to quieten our conscience *in his presence,*
Rv 19 10   I knelt *at* [the angel's] feet to worship him,
  22 8   I knelt *at the feet of* the angel . . . to worship him;

b) *Before, In the presence of (generally) – In front of, Ahead (of)*

Mt 5 16   In the same way your light must shine *in the sight of* men,
    24   leave your offering there *before* the altar,
  6 1   Be careful not to parade your good deeds *before* men
    2   when you give alms, do not have it trumpeted *before* you;
  7 6   do not throw your pearls *in front of* pigs,
  10 32   if anyone declares himself for me *in the presence of* men, I
      will declare myself for him
    33   But the one who disowns me *in the presence of* men, I will
      disown
  17 2   There *in their presence* [Jesus] was transfigured:
  23 13   Pharisees . . . shut up the kingdom of heaven *in men's
      faces,*
  26 70   [Peter] denied it *in front of* them all.
  27 11   Jesus, then, was brought *before* the governor,
Mk 2 12   [the paralytic] walked out *in front of* everyone,
  9 2   There *in their presence* [Jesus] was transfigured:
Lk 12 8   if anyone openly declares himself for me *in the presence of*
      men, the Son of Man will declare himself for him
  19 4   [Zacchaeus] ran *ahead* and climbed a sycamore tree
    28   [Jesus] went on *ahead*, going up to Jerusalem.
Jn 1 15   He who comes after me ranks *before* me because he existed
      [before] me.
    30   A man is coming after me who ranks *before* me because he
      existed [before] me.
  10 4 <   [The good shepherd] goes *ahead of* [the sheep],
  12 37   ⌐Though they had been present when [Jesus] gave so many
      signs (lit. Though Jesus had given so many signs *in front
      of* them).
Ac 18 17   they . . . beat [Sosthenes] *in front of* the court house.
Ga 2 14   I said to Cephas *in front of* everyone,
Ph 3 13 ●   I forget the past and I strain *ahead* for what is still to come;
      ¹⁴ I am racing for the finish,
Rv 4 6   four animals with many eyes, *in front* and behind.

3: BEFORE – IN FRONT OF – OPPOSITE: *EN-ANTI*

5	anti-krys 1	6	en-antios 1/8
4	en-anti 2	1	ap-en-anti 3/4
2	en-antion (5)	1	kat-en-anti 9

a) *Before, In the sight of (God) – In front of, Facing, Opposite (Jesus)*

Mk 15 39 X   6 The centurion . . . was standing *in front of* him,
Lk 1 6   2 [Zechariah and Elizabeth] were worthy *in the sight of* God,
    8   4 [Zechariah] was exercising his priestly office *before* God
  24 19   2 Jesus . . . was a great prophet . . . *in the sight of* God and
      of the whole people;
Ac 8 21   4 [Simon,] ⌐God can see how (lit. *in the sight of* God) your
      heart is warped.
Rm 4 17   Abraham is our father *in the eyes of* God, in whom he put
      his faith,
2Co 2 17   we speak as men of sincerity, as envoys of God and *in God's
      presence.*
  12 19   it is *before* God that we, in Christ, are speaking;

b) *Opposite, Facing, In front of (generally) – In public*

Mt 21 2   Go to the village *facing* you,
  27 24   Pilate . . . washed his hands *in front of* the crowd
    61   Mary of Magdala and the other Mary were there, sitting
      3 *opposite* the sepulchre.
Mk 11 2   Go off to the village *facing* you,
  12 41   [Jesus] sat down *opposite* the treasury and watched the people
  13 3   [Jesus] was sitting *facing* the Temple, on the Mount of
      Olives,
Lk 19 30   Go off to the village *opposite*,
  20 26   2 they were unable to find fault with anything [Jesus] had to
      say *in public;*
Ac 3 16   It is faith in that name that has restored this man to health,
    3   ⌐as you can all see (lit. *in front of* you all)
  7 10   [God] rescued [Joseph] . . . by making him wise enough
    2   ⌐to attract the attention of (lit. *in the sight of*) Pharaoh
  8 32   2 (Is 53 7) like a lamb that is dumb *in front of* its shearers,
  20 15   5 The next day we . . . arrived *opposite* Chios.
Rm 3 18   3 (Ps 36 1) there is no fear of God *before* their eyes.

4: OPPOSITE: *ANTI-PERA*

anti-pera 1

Lk 8 26   They came to land in the country of the Gerasenes, which
      is *opposite* Galilee.

BEGINNING

1. Begin, Beginning: *archomai*
1: Begin to – Start – Set about
2: Beginning of the world – Creation
3: Beginning – Source (= God or Christ)
4: Beginning (of a thing) – Outset

(of a project) – From the first
5: First-fruits
2. Begin (to cry) – Burst into (tears): *epi-ballō*
3. Alpha and Omega

1. BEGIN, BEGINNING: *ARCHOMAI*

2	*archē*	42|56
1	*archomai*	84|86
3	*ap-archē*	9

4	*en-archomai*	2
5	*pro-en-archomai*	2

1: BEGIN TO – START – SET ABOUT

Mt	4	17 X	Jesus *began* his preaching
	11	7 X	Jesus *began* to talk to the people about John:
		20 X	he *began* to reproach the towns
	12	1	His disciples were hungry and *began* to pick ears of corn
	14	30	[Peter] took fright and *began* to sink.
	16	21 X	Jesus *began* to make it clear to his disciples that he was destined to . . . suffer
		22	taking [Jesus] aside, Peter *started* to remonstrate with him.
	18	24	When the reckoning *began*, they brought [the king] a man who owed ten thousand talents;
	20	8	Call the workers . . , *starting* with the last arrivals
	24	49	[the dishonest servant] *sets about* beating his fellow servants
	26	22	[the disciples] *started* asking him in turn, 'Not I, Lord, surely?'
		37 X	sadness ⌐came (lit. *began* to come) over him, and great distress.
		74	[Peter] *started* calling down curses on himself
Mk	1	45	[the leper] *started* talking about [his cure] freely
	2	23	his disciples *began* to pick ears of corn
	4	1 X	[Jesus] *started* to teach by the lakeside
	5	17	[the Gerasenes] *began* to implore Jesus to leave the neighbourhood
		20	the man . . . ⌐proceeded (lit. *started*) to spread . . . all that Jesus had done for him.
	6	2 X	he *began* teaching in the synagogue
		7 X	[Jesus] *began* to send [the Twelve] out in pairs
		34 X	he *set himself* to teach them at some length.
		55	[people] *started* hurrying all through the countryside
	8	11	The Pharisees came up and *started* a discussion with [Jesus];
		31 X	he *began* to teach [the disciples] that the Son of Man was destined to suffer
		32	Peter *started* to remonstrate with [Jesus].
	10	28	Peter ⌐took this up (lit. *began*). 'What about us?' he asked
		32 X	taking the Twelve aside he *began* to tell them what was going to happen to him.
		41	the other ten . . . *began* to feel indignant with James and John.
		47	[the blind man] *began* to shout and to say, '. . . Jesus, have pity on me'.
	11	15 X	he went into the Temple and *began* driving out those who were selling and buying there;
	12	1 X	He ⌐went on (lit. *began*) to speak to [the scribes and elders] in parables.
	13	5 X	Jesus *began* to tell [Peter, James, John and Andrew], 'Take care that no one deceives you.
	14	19	[The Twelve] ⌐were (lit. *began* to be) distressed and asked him, one after another, 'Not I, surely?'
		33 X	a sudden fear ⌐came (lit. *began* to come) over him
		65	Some of [the Sanhedrin] *started* spitting at [Jesus]
		69	The servant-girl . . . again *started* telling the bystanders, 'This fellow is one of them'.
		71	[Peter] *started* calling down curses on himself
	15	8	the crowd . . . *began* to ask Pilate the customary favour.
		18	[the soldiers] *began* saluting him, 'Hail, king of the Jews!'
Lk	3	8	do not ⌐think of (lit. *begin*) telling yourselves, 'We have Abraham for our father
		23 X	When he *started* to teach, Jesus was about thirty years old,
	4	21 X	he *began* to speak to [the people in the synagogue], 'This text is being fulfilled today
	5	21	The scribes and the Pharisees *began* to think this over . . . 'Who can forgive sins but God alone?'
	7	15	the dead man sat up and *began* to talk,
		24 X	he *began* to talk to the people about John,
		38	[the woman's] tears ⌐fell on (lit. *began* to wet) his feet
		49	Those who were with him at table *began* to say to themselves, 'Who is this man . . .?'
Lk	9	12	⌐It was (lit. It was *beginning* to be) late afternoon when the Twelve came to [Jesus]
	11	29 X	he ⌐addressed (lit. *began* to address) [the crowds], 'This is a wicked generation;
		53	the scribes and the Pharisees *began* a furious attack on [Jesus]
	12	1 X	he *began* to speak, . . . 'Be on your guard against the yeast of the Pharisees
		45	[the unjust servant] *sets about* beating the menservants
	13	25	you may ⌐find yourself (lit. *begin*) knocking on the door
		26	then you will ⌐find yourself (lit. *begin*) saying, 'We once ate and drank in your company;
	14	9	then, to your embarrassment, you ⌐would have to go and (lit. will *begin* to) take the lowest place
		18	all alike *started* to make excuses.
		29	the onlookers would all *start* making fun of him and saying,
		30	³⁰'Here is a man who *started* to build and was unable to finish'.
	15	14	[the prodigal son] *began* to feel the pinch,
		24	[the prodigal son's family] *began* to celebrate.
	19	37	the whole group of disciples joyfully *began* to praise God
		45 X	[Jesus] went into the Temple and *began* driving out those who were selling.
	20	9 X	he ⌐went on (lit. *began*) to tell the people this parable:
	21	28	When these things *begin* to take place, stand erect,
	22	23	[the Twelve] *began* to ask one another which of them it could be who was to [betray Jesus]
	23	2	[The chief priests and scribes] *began* their accusation
		5 X	[Jesus's teaching] has come all the way from Galilee, where he *started*, down to here.
		30	they will *begin* to say to the mountains, 'Fall on us!
	24	27 X	*starting* with Moses and going through all the prophets, [Jesus] explained . . . the passages . . . about himself.
		47	repentance . . . ʷould be preached to all the nations, *beginning* from Jeᵣusalem,
Jn	8	9	[the scribes and Pharisees] went away one by one, *beginning* with the eldest,
	13	5 X	[Jesus] *began* to wash the disciples' feet
Ac	1	1 X	In my earlier work . . . I dealt with everything Jesus had done and taught from the *beginning*
		22	[We must choose] someone who was with us ⌐right (lit. *starting*) from the time when John was baptising
	2	4	[The apostles] *began* to speak foreign languages
	8	35	*Starting* . . . with this text of scripture, Philip proceeded to explain the Good News
	10	37	You must have heard . . . about Jesus of Nazareth and how he *began* in Galilee,
	11	4	Peter in reply ⌐gave (lit. *began* to give) them the details
		15	I had scarcely *begun* to speak when the Holy Spirit came down on them
	18	26	Priscilla and Aquila heard [Apollos] ⌐speak (lit. *begin* to speak) boldly in the synagogue,
	24	2	Tertullus ⌐opened for (lit. *began*) the prosecution,
	27	35	[Paul] took some bread . . . and *began* to eat.
2Co	3	1	⌐Does this sound like a new attempt (lit. Are we *beginning* again) to commend ourselves to you?
	8	6	5 we have asked Titus, since he has already *made a beginning*, to bring this work of mercy to the . . . point of success among you.
		10	5 you *were the first*, . . . not only in taking action but even in deciding to.
Ga	3	3	Are you foolish enough to end in outward observances what
		4	you *began* in the Spirit?
Ph	1	6 θ	4 the One who *began* this good work . . . will see that it is finished
1P	4	17	The time has come for the judgement to *begin* at the household of God;

2: BEGINNING OF THE WORLD – CREATION

Mt	19	4	2 the creator from the *beginning* made them male and female
		8	Moses allowed you to divorce your wives, but it was not 2 like this from the *beginning*.
	24	21	there will be great distress such as, until now, since the world 2 *began*, there never has been.
Mk	10	6	2 from the *beginning* of creation God made them male and female.
	13	19	there will be such distress as, until now, has not been equalled 2 since the *beginning* when God created the world,
Jn	1	1	2 In the *beginning* was the Word:
		2	2 [The Word] was with God in the *beginning*.
	8	44	2 [The devil] was a murderer from the *start*;
2Th	2	13	2 God chose you ᵛ from the *beginning* (G as the first-fruits) to be saved by the sanctifying Spirit
Heb	1	10	(Ps 102 25 G) It was you, Lord, who laid earth's foundations 2 in the *beginning*,
2P	3	4	2 Everything goes on as it has . . . since it *began* at the creation.
1Jn	1	1	2 Something which has existed since the *beginning* . . . this is our subject.

1 Jn 2 13   you, fathers, . . . have come to know the one who has existed
      2   since the *beginning*;
      14   you have come to know the one who has existed since the
      2   *beginning*;
  3 8   2 the devil was a sinner from the *beginning*.

3: BEGINNING – SOURCE (= GOD or CHRIST)

Col 1 18   2 As [Christ] is the *Beginning*, he was first to be born from the
              dead,
Rv   3 14   2 Here is the message of the Amen, . . . the ultimate *source*
              of God's creation:
    21 6 Θ 2 I am the Alpha and the Omega, the *Beginning* and the End.
    22 13   2 I am the Alpha and the Omega . . . the *Beginning* and the
              End.

4: BEGINNING (OF A THING) – OUTSET (OF A PROJECT) – FROM THE FIRST

Mt 24 8   2 All this is only the *beginning* of the birthpangs.
Mk 1 1   2 The *beginning* of the Good News about Jesus Christ,
   13 8   2 This is the *beginning* of the birthpangs.
Lk 1 2   2 these were handed down to us by those who from the *outset*
              were eyewitnesses
Jn 2 11   2 This was the *first* of the signs given by Jesus:
    6 64   2 Jesus knew from the *outset* those who did not believe,
    8 25 Δ 'Who are you?' Jesus answered: 'What I have told you from
      2   the *outset* (or: Exactly what I have told you)'.
   15 27   2 you have been with me from the *outset*.
   16 4   2 I did not tell you this from the *outset*,
Ac 11 15   the Holy Spirit came down on them in the same way as it
      2   came on us at the *beginning*,
   26 4   2 My manner of life . . , a life spent from the *beginning*
              among my own people . . . is common knowledge among
              the Jews.
Ph 4 15   2 In the *early* days of the Good News . . no other church
              helped me
Heb 2 3   2 The promise was *first* announced by the Lord himself
    3 14   we shall remain co-heirs with Christ only if we keep a grasp
      2   on our *first* confidence right to the end.
    5 12   you need someone to teach you all over again ⌜the elementary
      2   principles of interpreting (lit. from the *outset* the elementary
              principles of) God's oracles.
    6 1   2 Let us leave behind us then all the ⌜elementary (lit. *beginning*
              of the) teaching about Christ
    7 3   2 [Melchizedek's] life has no *beginning* or ending;
1 Jn 2 7   this is . . . an old commandment that you were given from the
      2   *beginning*,
      24   Keep alive in yourselves what you were taught in the
      2/2   *beginning*: as long as what you were taught in the *beginning*
              is alive in you, you will live in the Son
    3 11   2 This is the message as you heard it from the *beginning*:
2 Jn   5   I am writing now . . . to give you . . . the [old command-
      2   ment] which we were given at the *beginning*,
       6   this is . . . the commandment which you have heard since the
      2   *beginning*, to live a life of love.

5: FIRST-FRUITS

Rm 8 23 Ⓢ 3 all of us . . . possess the *first-fruits* of the Spirit,
   11 16   3 A whole batch of bread is made holy if the *first* handful of
              dough is made holy.
   16 5   3 Epaenetus, the *first* of Asia's gifts to Christ;
1 Co 15 20   3 Christ has in fact been raised from the dead, the *first-fruits*
              of all who have fallen asleep.
      23   [All men will be brought to life in Christ;] but all of them in
      3   their proper order: Christ as the *first-fruits* and then . . .
              those who belong to him.
   16 15   3 the Stephanas family . . . were the *first-fruits* of Achaia
2 Th 2 13   3 God chose you ⱽ from the beginning (G as the *first-fruits*) to
              be saved by the sanctifying Spirit
Jm 1 18   [God] made us his children . . . so that we should be a sort of
      3   *first-fruits* of all that he had created.
Rv 14 4   they have been redeemed from amongst men to be the
      3   *first-fruits* of God

2. BEGIN (TO CRY) – BURST INTO (TEARS): *EPI-BALLŌ*

epi-ballō 1/18

Mk 14 72 Δ   [Peter] ⌜*burst into* tears (or: *began to weep*).

---

3. ALPHA and OMEGA

1 *alpha* 3   2 *ō* 3

Rv 1 8 Θ /2 I am the *Alpha* and the *Omega*, says the Lord God,
   21 6 Θ /2 I am the *Alpha* and the *Omega*, the Beginning and the End.
   22 13 X /2 I am the *Alpha* and the *Omega*, the First and the Last,

---

BELIEVE – FAITH

1. Believe, Faith – Unbelief, Faithless – Trust: *pisteuō*
1: Believing, Faith – Unbelieving, Faithless
a) Believe, Become a Believer – (the) Faith, the Faithful
b) Faith//Little Faith, Lack of Faith, Faithless – Believing// Unbelieving, (Not to, Refusing to) believe
c) Believe//Not to believe, in falsehood, false prophets
d) Believe (generally) – Incredible, Sceptical – Doubt, Conviction

2: Faithful, Trust(ed), Reliable – Unfaithful
a) Faithful(ness), Fidelity, Truth, of God or of Christ
b) Faithful(ness), Sure, Good faith – Trust, Trustworthy, Reliable – Unfaithful, Lack of fidelity
3: Entrust to, Trust with – Commission (a person) to

2. Doubt – Hesitate
1: *di-stazō*
2: *dia-krinō*

1. BELIEVE, FAITH – UNBELIEF, FAITHLESS – TRUST: *PISTEUŌ*

1	*pisteuō*	243	7	*a-pisteō*	8
2	*pistis*	240/242	5	*a-pistia*	12
9	*pistoō*	1	4	*a-pistos*	23
3	*pistos*	67	10	*oligo-pistia*	1
6	*a-peitheō*	9/14	8	*oligo-pistos*	5

1: BELIEVING, FAITH – UNBELIEVING, FAITHLESS

H = Faith // Hope; L = Faith // Love, 'Charity'

a) Believe, Become a Believer – (the) Faith, the Faithful

Mt 8 10   2 nowhere in Israel have I found *faith* like this.
      13   [Jesus to the centurion:] you have *believed*, so let this be done
              for you.
    9 2   2 Seeing their *faith*, Jesus said to the paralytic, 'Courage, . . .'
      22   [Jesus said to [the woman who suffered from a haemorrhage],
      2   'Courage, . . . your *faith* has restored you to health'
      28   [Jesus] said to [the two blind men], 'Do you *believe* I can do
              this?' They said, 'Sir, we do'. ²⁹ Then he touched their
      2   eyes saying, 'Your *faith* deserves it, so let this be done
              for you'.
   15 28   Jesus answered [the Canaanite woman], 'Woman, you have
      2   great *faith*.'
   18 6   anyone who is an obstacle to bring down one of these
              little ones who *have faith* in me would be better drowned.
   21 21   2 if you have *faith* and do not doubt at all . . .²² And if you
      22   *have faith*, everything you ask for in prayer you will
              receive.
   27 42   let him come down from the cross now, and we will *believe*
              in him.
Mk 1 15   Repent, and *believe* the Good News.
    2 5   2 Seeing their *faith*, Jesus said to the paralytic,
    5 34   [Jesus to the woman who suffered from a haemorrhage:]
      2   My daughter . . . your *faith* has restored you to health;
      36   [Jesus] said to the official [Jairus], 'Do not be afraid; only
              have faith'.
    9 42   anyone who is an obstacle to bring down one of these little
              ones who *have faith*,
   10 52   2 'Go; your *faith* has saved you'. And immediately his sight
              returned
   11 22   2 Have *faith* in God. ²³ . . . if anyone says to this mountain,
      23   'Get up . . .' *believing* that what he says will happen, it
      24   will be done for him. ²⁴ . . . everything you ask and pray
              for, *believe* that you have it already, and it will be yours.
   15 32   Let the Christ . . . come down from the cross now, for us to
              see it and *believe*.
   16 17   These are the signs that will be associated with *believers*:
Lk 1 45   blessed is she who *believed* that the promise made her by the
              Lord would be fulfilled.
    5 20   2 Seeing their *faith* [Jesus] said, '. . . your sins are forgiven
              you'.
    7 9   2 not even in Israel have I found *faith* like this.

Lk　7　50　2　[Jesus] said to the woman [who was a sinner], 'Your *faith* has saved you;'

　　8　12　　the devil . . . carries away the word from their hearts in case they should *believe* and be saved.

　　　13　　these have no root; they *believe* for a while,

　　　48　　[Jesus to the woman suffering from a haemorrhage:] your
　　　　2　*faith* has restored you to health;

　　　50　　[Jesus to Jairus:] Do not be afraid, only *have faith* and [your daughter] will be safe.

　17　5　2　The apostles said to the Lord, 'Increase our *faith*'. ⁶ The
　　　6　2　Lord replied, 'Were your *faith* the size of a mustard seed . . .'

　　　19　2　[Jesus to one of the ten lepers:] Stand up . . . Your *faith* has saved you.

　18　8　2　when the Son of Man comes, will he find any *faith* on earth?

　　　42　　[Jesus to the blind man of Jericho:] Receive your sight.
　　　　2　Your *faith* has saved you.

　22　32　2　I have prayed for you, Simon, that your *faith* may not fail,

　24　25　　You foolish men! So slow to *believe* the full message of the prophets!

Jn　1　7　　[John] came as a witness . . . so that everyone might *believe* through him.

　　　12　　he gave power to become children of God to all who *believe* in the name of him

　　　50　　You *believe* that just because I said: I saw you under the fig tree.

　　2　11　　[at Cana Jesus] let his glory be seen, and his disciples *believed* in him.

　　　22　　when Jesus rose from the dead, his disciples . . . *believed* the scripture and the words he had said.

　　　23　　many *believed* in his name when they saw the signs that he gave,

　　3　15　　so that everyone who *believes* may have eternal life in [the Son]

　　　16　　so that everyone who *believes* in [the Son] may not be lost

　　4　39　　Many Samaritans . . . had *believed* in [Jesus] on the strength
　　　41　　of the woman's testimony . . . ⁴¹ when he spoke to them
　　　42　　many more came to *believe*; ⁴² and they said to the woman, 'Now we no longer *believe* because of what you told us . . .'

　　　50　　The man *believed* what Jesus had said
　　　53　　The father . . . and all his household *believed*.

　　5　24　　whoever . . . *believes* in the one who sent me, has eternal life;

　　6　29　　This is working for God: you must *believe* in the one he has sent.

　　　30　　What sign will you give to show us that we should *believe* in you?

　　　35　　he who *believes* in me will never thirst.

　　　40　　it is my Father's will that whoever sees the Son and *believes* in him shall have eternal life,

　　　47　　everybody who *believes* has eternal life.

　　　69　　[Simon Peter answered:] we *believe* . . . that you are the Holy One of God.

　　7　31　　There were many people in the crowds . . . who *believed* in [Jesus]

　　　38　　[Let the man come and drink] who *believes* in me! . . .
　　　39　　From his breast shall flow fountains of living water. ³⁹ He was speaking of the Spirit which those who *believed* in him were to receive;

　　　48　　Have any of the authorities *believed* in him?

　　8　30　　many came to *believe* in him
　　　31　　To the Jews who *believed* in him Jesus said:

　　9　35　　[Jesus to the man born blind:] Do you *believe* in the Son of
　　　36　　Man? ³⁶ . . . the man replied 'tell me who he is so that
　　　38　　I may *believe* in him' . . . ³⁸ The man said, 'Lord, I *believe*', and worshipped him.

　10　42　　many of them *believed* in him.

　11　15　　[Lazarus is dead;] and . . . I am glad . . . because now you will *believe*.

　　　25　　Jesus said: . . . If anyone *believes* in me, even though he
　　　26　　dies he will live, ²⁶ and whoever lives and *believes* in me will
　　　27　　never die. Do you *believe* this? ²⁷ 'Yes, Lord,' [Martha] said 'I *believe* that you are the Christ,'

　　　40　　Jesus replied [to Martha], 'Have I not told you that if you *believe* you will see the glory of God?'

　　　42　　I speak . . . so that they may *believe* it was you who sent me.

　　　45　　Many of the Jews . . . *believed* in him,

　　　48　　If we let him go on in this way everybody will *believe* in him,

　12　11　　many of the Jews were leaving [the chief priests] and *believing* in Jesus.

　　　36　　*believe* in the light and you will become sons of light.

　　　42　　there were many who did *believe* in him, even among the leading men,

　　　44　　Whoever *believes* in me *believes* not in me but in the one who sent me.

　　　46　　whoever *believes* in me need not stay in the dark any more.

　13　19　　so that . . . you may *believe* that I am He.

Jn　14　11　　*believe* me when I say that I am in the Father and the Father is in me; *believe* it on the evidence of this work,

　　　12　　whoever *believes* in me will perform the same works as I do myself,

　　　29　　I have told you this now before it happens, so that . . you may *believe*.

　16　27　　the Father himself loves you for . . . *believing* that I came from God.

　　　30　　because of this we *believe* that you came from God.
　　　31　　Do you *believe* at last?

　17　8　　they . . . have *believed* that it was you who sent me.

　　　20　　I pray not only for these, but for those also who through their words will *believe* in me.

　　　21　　May they all be one . . . so that the world may *believe* it was you who sent me.

　19　35　　This is the evidence of one who saw it . . . and he gives it so that you may *believe* as well.

　20　8　　Then the other disciple . . . also went in; he saw and he *believed*

　　　29　　You *believe* because you can see me. Happy are those who have not seen and yet *believe*.

　　　31　　These [signs] are recorded so that you may *believe* that Jesus is the Christ . . . and that *believing* this you may have life through his name.

Ac　2　24　　The *faithful* all lived together and owned everything in common;

　　3　16　2　it is the name of Jesus which, through our *faith* in it, has
　　　　2　brought back the strength of this man . . . It is *faith* in that name that has restored this man to health,

　　4　4　　many of those who had listened to [Peter's and John's] message *became believers*,

　　　32　　The whole group of *believers* was united, heart and soul;

　　5　14　　the numbers of men and women who came to *believe* in the Lord increased steadily.

　　6　5　2　Stephen, a man full of *faith* and of the Holy Spirit,
　　　7　2　a large group of priests made their submission to the *faith*.

　　8　12　　when they *believed* Philip's preaching . . . they were baptised,
　　　13　　even Simon himself *became a believer*.
　　　37　　(ᵛ Philip said, 'If you *believe* with all your heart, you may [be baptised].' [The eunuch] replied, 'I *believe* . . .')

　　9　42　　The whole of Jaffa heard about it and many *believed* in the Lord.

　10　43　3　all who *believe* in Jesus will have their sins forgiven
　　　45　　Jewish *believers* . . . were all astonished

　11　17　　God was giving [the uncircumcised] the identical thing he gave to us when we *believed* in the Lord Jesus Christ;

　　　21　　a great number *believed* and were converted to the Lord.

　　　24　　[Barnabas] was a good man, filled with the Holy Spirit and
　　　　2　with *faith*.

　13　8　　Elymas . . . tried . . . to prevent the proconsul's conversion
　　　　2　to the *faith*.

　　　12　　The proconsul . . . *became a believer*, being astonished by what he had learnt about the Lord.

　　　39　　[Through him justification from all sins] is offered to every *believer*.

　　　48　　all who were destined for eternal life *became believers*.

　14　9　2　Seeing that the man had the *faith* to be cured, [Paul said to the cripple,]

　　　22　　[Paul and Barnabas] put fresh heart into the disciples,
　　　　2　encouraging them to persevere in the *faith*.

　　　23　　[Paul and Barnabas] commended [their disciples] to the Lord in whom they had come to *believe*.

　　　27　2　[God] had opened the door of *faith* to the pagans.

　15　5　　certain members of the Pharisees' party who had *become believers* objected,

　　　7　　God made his choice among you: the pagans were to learn the Good News from me and so *become believers* . . .

　　　9　2　⁹ God made no distinction between them and us since he purified their hearts by *faith*.

　　　11　　we *believe* that we are saved in the same way as they are: through the grace of the Lord Jesus.

　16　1　　Timothy, whose mother was a Jewess who had become a
　　　3　*believer*;

　　　5　2　So the churches grew strong in the *faith*,

　　　15　3　[Lydia:] If you really think me a true *believer* in the Lord,

　　　31　　*Become a believer* in the Lord Jesus, and you will be saved, and your household too.

　　　34　　the whole family [of the gaoler] celebrated their conversion to *belief* in God.

　17　12　　Many Jews [at Beroea] *became believers*,
　　　34　　some [Athenians] . . . attached themselves to [Paul] and *became believers*,

　18　8　　Crispus . . . and his whole household, all *became believers* in the Lord. A great many Corinthians who had heard [Paul] *became believers*

　　　27　　[Apollos] was able . . . to help the *believers* considerably

　19　2　　Did you receive the Holy Spirit when you *became believers*?
　　　4　　[John] insisted that the people should *believe* in . . . Jesus.

Ac 19	18		Some *believers*, too, came forward to admit in detail how they had used spells
20	21	2	[Paul,] urging both Jews and Greeks . . . to *believe* in our Lord Jesus.
21	20		you see . . . how thousands of Jews have now *become believers*,
	25		The pagans who have *become believers* . . . must abstain from things offered to idols.
22	19		I used to go from synagogue to synagogue, imprisoning . . . those who *believed* in you;
24	14 H		retaining my *belief* in all points of the Law and . . . in the prophets;
	24	2	Felix . . . gave [Paul] a hearing on the subject of *faith* in Christ Jesus.
26	18	2	so that [the pagans] may . . . receive, through *faith* in me, forgiveness of their sins
	27		King Agrippa, do you *believe* in the prophets? I know you ʳdo (lit. *believe*).
Rm 1	5	2	our apostolic mission to preach the obedience of *faith* to all pagan nations
	8	2	your *faith* is spoken of all over the world.
	12	2	[I am longing] to find encouragement among you from our common *faith*.
	16		the Good News . . . is the power of God saving all who *have faith*
	17	2/2	[the Good News] reveals the justice of God to us: it shows how *faith* leads to *faith*, or as scripture says (Hab 2 4):
		2	The upright man finds life through *faith*.
3	22	2	the same justice of God . . . comes through *faith* to everyone . . . who *believes* in Jesus Christ.
	25		[Jesus] was appointed by God to sacrifice his life so as to
		2	win reconciliation through *faith*. In this way God makes
	26	2	his justice known . . . ²⁶ . . . for the present age, by
		2	showing . . . that he justifies everyone who *believes* in Jesus.
	27	2	What sort of law excludes [boasts]? . . . it is the law of *faith*,
	28	2	as we see it, a man is justified by *faith*
	30	2	God . . . will justify the circumcised because of their *faith*
	31	2	and justify the uncircumcised through their *faith*. ³¹ Do we mean that *faith* makes the Law pointless? Not at all:
4	3		(Gn 15 6) Abraham *put* his *faith* in God,
	5	2	when a man has nothing to *show* except *faith* in the one who justifies sinners, then his *faith* is considered as justifying him.
	9	2	Think of Abraham again: his *faith* . . . was considered as justifying him,
	11	2	when [Abraham] was circumcised later it was only as a sign and guarantee that the *faith* . . . justified him. In this way Abraham became the ancestor of all uncircumcised *believers*. ¹² and ancestor, also, of those who . . .
	12	2	follow our ancestor Abraham along the path of *faith* he trod before he had been circumcised.
	13	2	The promise . . . [was made] on account of the righteousness which consists in *faith*.
	14	2	If the world is only to be inherited by those who submit to the Law, then *faith* is pointless
	16	2	the promise depends on *faith*, so that it may be a free gift and be available to all of Abraham's descendants, not only those who belong to the Law but also those who
		2	belong to the *faith* of Abraham who is the father of all of us. ¹⁷ . . . in the eyes of God, in whom he *put* his *faith*,
	17		
	18 H		[Abraham] *believed*, and . . . so he did become the father of many nations
	19	2	Even the thought that his body was past fatherhood . . . did not shake his *belief*.
	24		we *believe* in him who raised Jesus our Lord from the dead,
5	1	2	through our Lord Jesus Christ, by *faith* we are judged
	2 H	2	righteous, and at peace with God, ² since it is by *faith* and through Jesus that we have entered this state of grace
6	8		we *believe* that having died with Christ we shall return to life with him:
9	30		the pagans . . . found . . . a righteousness that comes of
		2	*faith*, ³¹ while Israel, looking for a righteousness derived from law failed to do what that law required. ³² Why did
	32	2	they fail? Because they relied on good deeds instead of trusting in *faith*.
	33		(Is 28 16) only those who *believe* in him will have no cause for shame.
10	4		now the Law has come to an end with Christ, and everyone who *has faith* may be justified,
	6	2	the righteousness that comes from *faith* says this:
	8	2	The word, that is the *faith* we proclaim, is very near to you, if you *believe* in your heart that God raised [Jesus] from the dead, then you will be saved.
	10		By *believing* from the heart you are made righteous;
	11		(Is 28 16) those who *believe* in him will have no cause for shame.
	14		[Israelites] will not ask his help unless they *believe* in him, and they will not *believe* in him unless they have heard of him,

Rm 10	16		(Is 53 1) Lord, how many *believed* what we proclaimed?
	17	2	*faith* comes from what is preached,
12	3	2	Each of you must judge himself soberly by the standard of the *faith* God has given him.
	6	2	If your gift is prophecy, then use it as your *faith* suggests;
13	11	2	our salvation is even nearer than it was when we *were converted*.
14	1	2	If a person's *faith* is not strong enough, welcome him all the same
	22	2	Hold on to your own *belief*, as between yourself and God
	23	2	anybody who eats in a state of doubt is condemned, because he is not in ʳgood faith (or: *faith*); and every act done ʳin
		2	bad faith (or: not in *faith*) is a sin.
15	13 H		May the God of hope bring you such joy and peace in your *faith*
16	26	2	[the revelation of a mystery] must be broadcast to pagans everywhere to bring them to the obedience of *faith*.
1 Co 1	21		God wanted to save those who *have faith* through the foolishness of the message
2	5	2	so that your *faith* should . . . depend . . . on the power of God.
3	5		Apollos . . . Paul? They are servants who brought the *faith* to you.
12	9	2	another [may have] the gift of *faith* given by the same Spirit
13	2 L	2	if I have *faith* in all its fulness, to move mountains,
	7		[Love] is always ready to excuse, to ʳtrust (or: *believe*), to hope,
	13 H L	2	there are three things that last: *faith*, hope and love;
15	2		*believing* anything else will not lead to anything.
	11		I preach what they preach, and this is what you all *believed*.
	14	2	if Christ has not been raised then . . . your *believing* [our preaching] is useless;
	17 H		if Christ has not been raised, ʳyou are still in your sins (lit.
		2	your *faith* is useless).
16	13	2	Be awake to all the dangers; stay firm in the *faith*;
2 Co 1	24	2/2	We are not dictators over your *faith* . . . in the *faith* you are steady enough.
4	13	2	we have the same spirit of *faith* that is mentioned in scripture (Ps 116 10) – I *believed*, and therefore I spoke – we too *believe* and therefore we too speak,
5	7	2	going as we do by *faith* and not by sight
8	7	2	You always have the most of everything – of *faith*, of eloquence, of understanding,
10	15	2	we trust that, as your *faith* grows, we shall get taller and taller,
13	5	2	Examine yourselves to make sure you are in the *faith*; test yourselves.
Ga 1	23	2	their one-time persecutor was now preaching the *faith* he had previously tried to destroy;
2	16	2/	we acknowledge that what makes a man righteous is . . . *faith* in Jesus Christ. We had to *become believers* in Christ Jesus
		2	. . . and now we hold that *faith* in Christ . . . is what justifies us,
	20	2	The life I now live . . . I live in *faith* . . . in the Son of God
3	2	2	was it because you practised the Law that you received the Spirit, or because you *believed* what ʳwas preached to you (lit. you heard)?
	5	2	Does God give you the Spirit . . . because you practise the Law, or because you *believed* what ʳwas preached to you (lit. you heard)?
	6		(Gn 15 6) [Abraham] *put* his *faith* in God . . . ⁷ Don't you
	7	2	see that it is those who rely on *faith* who are the sons of Abraham?
	8	2	Scripture foresaw that God was going to use *faith* to justify the pagans,
	9	2	Those therefore who rely on *faith* receive the same blessing
		3	as Abraham, the *man of faith*.
	11	2	(Hab 2 4) the righteous man finds life through *faith*. ¹² The
	12	2	Law is not even based on *faith*
	14	2	so that through *faith* we might receive the promised Spirit.
	22	2	the promise can only be given through *faith* in Jesus Christ and can only be given to those who *have* this *faith*.
	23	2	Before *faith* came, we were allowed no freedom by the Law;
	24	2	we were being looked after till *faith* was revealed. ²⁴ The Law was to be our guardian until the Christ came and we
	25	2	could be justified by *faith*. ²⁵ Now that ʳthat time (lit.
		2	*faith*) has come we are no longer under that guardian,
	26	2	²⁶ and you are, all of you, sons of God through *faith* in Christ Jesus.
5	5 H	2	Christians are told by the Spirit to look to *faith* for those
	6 L		rewards that righteousness hopes for, ⁶ since in Christ
		2	. . . what matters is *faith* that makes it powers felt through love.
6	10		we must do good to all, and especially to our brothers in the
		2	*faith*.
Ep 1	1		From Paul . . . to the saints ʳwho are faithful to (lit. and the *faithful* in) Christ Jesus:

Ep 1 13   you too . . . have heard the message . . . and have *believed* it;
   15   2   having once heard about your *faith* in the Lord Jesus . . .
   19   how infinitely great is the power that [God] has exercised for us *believers*.
  2   8   2   it is by grace that you have been saved, through *faith*;
  3 12   we are bold enough to approach God in complete confidence,
    2   through our *faith* in [Christ];
   17   2   so that Christ may live in your hearts through *faith*,
  4   5 H 2   [one hope,] one Lord, one *faith*, one baptism,
   13   2   we are all to come to unity in our *faith*
  6 16   2   always carrying the shield of *faith*
   23 L   May God the Father and the Lord Jesus Christ grant peace,
    2   love and *faith* to all the brothers.
Ph 1 25   I feel sure I shall survive . . . and help you to progress in
    2   the *faith*
   27   you are unanimous in meeting the attack with firm resistance,
    2   united by your love for the *faith* of the gospel
   29   [God] has given you the privilege . . . of *believing* in Christ,
  2 17   2   if my blood has to be shed as part of your own sacrifice and
    2   offering – which is your *faith* – I shall still be happy
  3   9   2   I want only the perfection that comes through *faith* in Christ,
    2   and is from God and based on *faith*.
Col 1   4 H L 2 we heard about your *faith* in Christ Jesus and the love that you show towards all the saints
   23 H   as long as you persevere and stand firm on the solid base
    2   of the *faith*,
  2   5   2   delighted to . . . see how firm your *faith* in Christ is.
    7   2   you must be . . . held firm by the *faith* you have been taught,
   12   2   you have been raised up with [Christ] through your *belief* in the power of God who raised him from the dead.
1 Th 1   3 H L 2 [we] remember . . . how you have shown your *faith* in action, worked for love and persevered through hope,
    7   This has made you the great example to all *believers*
    8   2   the news of your *faith* in God has spread everywhere.
  2 10   our treatment of you, since you *became believers*, has been impeccably right
   13   [the message] is still a living power among you who *believe* it.
  3   2   [we sent] Timothy . . . to keep you firm and strong in the
    2   *faith*
    5   2   I sent to assure myself of your *faith*:
    6 L 2   Timothy . . . has given us good news of your *faith*
    7   2   your *faith* has been a great comfort to us
   10   We are earnestly praying night and day to be able to . . .
    2   make up any shortcomings in your *faith*.
  4 14   We *believe* that Jesus died and rose again,
  5   8 H L 2 let us put on *faith* and love for a breastplate, and the hope of salvation for a helmet.
2 Th 1   3 L 2   your *faith* is growing so wonderfully
    4   2   your constancy and *faith* under all the persecutions
   10   [the Lord Jesus] comes to be . . . seen in his glory by all who *believe* in him; and you are *believers*, through our witness.
   11   we pray . . . that our God will . . . complete all that you
    2   have been doing through *faith*;
  3   2   2   *faith* is not given to everyone.
1 Tm 1   2   2   Timothy, true child of mine in the *faith*;
    4   instead of furthering the designs of God which are revealed
    2   in *faith*.
    5 L 2   there should be love, coming out of . . . a sincere *faith*.
   13   5   ᵣuntil I *became a believer* I had been acting (or: I had
   14 L   been acting in unbelief and) in ignorance; ¹⁴ and the
    2   grace . . . filled me with *faith* and with the love
   16   all the other people who would later ᵣhave to trust (or:
    2   *have faith*) in him to come to eternal life.
   19   2   [I ask you to fight] with *faith* and a good conscience for your weapons. Some people have put conscience aside and
    2   wrecked their *faith* in consequence.
  2   7   2   I have been named . . . a teacher of the *faith* and the truth to the pagans,
   15 L   [a woman] will be saved . . . provided she . . . is constant
    2   in *faith* and love and holiness.
  3   9   [Deacons] must be conscientious believers in the mystery of
    2   the *faith*.
   13   Those . . . who carry out their duties well as deacons will . . . be rewarded with great assurance in their work for
    2   the *faith* in Christ Jesus.
   16   [Jesus Christ] was . . . proclaimed to the pagans, *believed* in by the world,
  4   1   during the last times there will be some who will desert the
    2   *faith*
    3   rules about abstaining from foods which God created to be
    3   accepted with thanksgiving by all *who believe* and who know the truth.
    6   show that you have really digested the teaching of the *faith* and the good doctrine
   10 H 3   we have put our trust in . . . the saviour of . . . all *believers*.
   12 L 3   be an example to all the *believers* in . . . your love, your
    2   *faith*
  5 16   3   If a *Christian woman* has widowed relatives,

1 Tm 6   2   3   Slaves whose masters are *believers* . . . should serve them all the better, since those who have the benefit of their
    3   services are *believers*
   10   [For the love of money] some . . . have wandered away
    2   from the *faith*,
   11 L 2   You must aim to be saintly and religious, filled with *faith* and love, patient and gentle.
   12   2   Fight the good fight of the *faith* and win for yourself the eternal life
   21   by adopting [the 'knowledge' which is not knowledge at
    2   all], some have gone right away from the *faith*.
2 Tm 1   5   2   I am reminded of the sincere *faith* which you have; it came first to live in your grandmother Lois,
   13 L 2   Keep as your pattern the sound teaching . . . in the *faith* and love that are in Christ Jesus.
  2 18   [Hymenaeus and Philetus] claim that the resurrection has
    2   already taken place. Some people's *faith* cannot stand up to them.
   22 L 2   fasten your attention on holiness, *faith*, love and peace,
  3   8   2   Men like this defy the truth . . . their minds are corrupt and
    2   their *faith* spurious.
   10 L 2   you know my *faith*, my patience and my love;
   15   2   the wisdom that leads to salvation through *faith* in Christ Jesus.
  4   7   2   I have run the race to the finish; I have kept the *faith*;
Tt   1   1 H   From Paul . . . an apostle of Jesus Christ to bring those
    2   whom God has chosen to *faith*
    4   2   To Titus, true child of mine in the *faith* that we share, wishing you grace and peace
    6   3   [the elder's] children must be *believers*
   13   be severe in correcting them, and make them sound in the
    2   *faith*
  2   2 L 2   The older men should be . . . sound in *faith* and love and constancy.
    3   8   so that those who now *believe* in God may keep their minds constantly occupied in doing good works.
   15 L 2   Greetings to those who love us in the *faith*.
Phm   5 L 2   I hear of the love and the *faith* which you have
    6   2   I pray that this *faith* will give rise to a sense cf fellowship
Heb 4   2   2   they did not share the *faith* of those who listened.
    3   We . . . who *have faith*, shall reach a place of rest,
  6   1   the fundamental doctrines . . .: the turning away from dead
    2   actions and towards *faith* in God;
   12 H 2   imitating those who have the *faith* and the perseverance to inherit the promises.
10 22 H L 2 let us be sincere in heart and filled with *faith*,
   38   2   (Hab 2 4) The righteous man will live by *faith*,
   39   You and I are not the sort of people who draw back . . .
    2   we . . . keep *faithful*
11   1 H 2   Only *faith* can guarantee the blessings that we hope for, or prove the existence of the realities that at present remain unseen.
    3   2   It is by *faith* that we understand that the world was created by one word from God,
    4   2   It was because of his *faith* that Abel offered God a better sacrifice than Cain,
    5   2   It was because of his *faith* that Enoch was taken up
    7   2   It was through his *faith* that Noah . . . built an ark . . . By [his faith] . . . he was able to claim the righteousness
    2   which is the reward of *faith*.
    8   2   It was by *faith* that Abraham obeyed the call to set out . . .
    9   2   ⁹ By *faith* he arrived . . . in the Promised Land,
   11   2   It was . . . by *faith* that Sarah . . . was made able to conceive,
   13   2   All these died in *faith*, before receiving any of the things that had been promised,
   17   2   It was by *faith* that Abraham, when put to the test, offered up Isaac. He offered to sacrifice his only son
   20   2   It was by *faith* that . . . Isaac gave his blessing
   21   2   By *faith* Jacob . . . blessed each of Joseph's sons,
   22   2   It was by *faith* that . . . Joseph recalled the Exodus of the Israelites
   23   2   It was by *faith* that Moses, when he was born, was hidden by his parents
   24   2   It was by *faith* that . . . Moses refused to be known as the
   27   2   son of Pharaoh's daughter . . . ²⁷ It was by *faith* that he left Egypt . . . he held to his purpose like a man who
   28   2   could see the Invisible. ²⁸ It was by *faith* that he kept the Passover
   29   2   It was by *faith* they crossed the Red Sea
   30   2   It was through *faith* that the walls of Jericho fell down
   31   2   It was by *faith* that Rahab the prostitute . . . was not killed with the unbelievers.
   33   [Gideon . . . and the prophets] were men who through
    2   *faith* conquered kingdoms,
   39   2   These are all heroes of *faith*,
12   2   2   Jesus, who leads us in our *faith* and brings it to perfection:
13   7   2   Remember your leaders . . . imitate their *faith*.
Jm   1   3   2   your *faith* is only put to the test to make you patient.
    6   2   But he must ask with *faith*, and no trace of doubt,

Jm	2 1	2	do not try to combine *faith* in Jesus Christ, our glorified Lord, with the making of distinctions between classes of people.
	5	2	it was those who are poor . . . that God chose, to be rich in *faith*
	14	2/2	Take the case . . . of someone who has never done a single good act but claims that he has *faith*. Will that *faith* save him?
	17	2	*Faith* is like that: if good works do not go with it, it is quite dead. [18] This is the way to talk to people of that kind:
	18	2	'You say you have *faith* and I have good deeds; I will
		2	prove to you that I have *faith* by showing you my good
		2	deeds – now you prove to me that you have *faith* without any good deeds to show.'
	19		You *believe* in the one God – that is creditable enough, but the demons *have the same belief*, and they tremble with
	20	2	fear. [20] Do realise . . . that *faith* without good deeds is useless.
	22	2/2	*faith* and deeds were working together; [Abraham's] *faith*
	23		became perfect by what he did. [23] . . . (Gn 15 6) Abraham
	24		*put* his *faith* in God . . . [24] You see now that it is by doing something good, and not only by *believing*, that a man is
	26	2	justified . . . [26] A body dies when it is separated from the spirit, and in the same way *faith* is dead if it is separated from good deeds.
	5 15	2	The prayer of *faith* will save the sick man
1 P	1 5 H	2	Through your *faith*, God's power will guard you until the salvation
	7		so that, when Jesus Christ is revealed, your *faith* will have . . . praise . . . [8] You did not see him, yet you love him;
	8		and still without seeing him, you are already filled with a joy so glorious that it cannot be described, because you
	9	2	*believe*; [9] and you are sure of the end to which [v] your (G the) *faith* looks forward, that is, the salvation of your souls.
	21	3	Through him you now have *faith* in God, who raised him
	H	2	. . . so that you would have *faith* and hope in God.
	5 9	2	Stand up to [the devil], strong in *faith*
2 P	1 1	2	From Simeon Peter . . . to all who treasure the same *faith* as ourselves,
	5 L		to attain this, you will have to do your utmost yourselves,
		2	adding goodness to the *faith* that you have,
1 Jn	3 23		His commandments are these: that we *believe* in the name of his Son Jesus Christ and that we love one another
	4 16		We ourselves have known and *put* our *faith* in God's love towards ourselves.
	5 1		Whoever *believes* that Jesus is the Christ has been begotten by God;
	4	2	this is the victory over the world – our *faith*. [5] Who can
	5		overcome the world? Only the man who *believes* that Jesus is the Son of God:
	13		you who *believe* in the name of the Son of God may be sure that you have eternal life.
Jude	3	2	fight hard for the *faith* which has been once and for all entrusted to the saints.
	20 L	2	use your most holy *faith* as your foundation and build on that . . . [21] keep yourselves within the love of God
Rv	2 13		you still hold firmly to my name, and did not disown your *faith* in me
	19 L	2	I know all about you and how charitable you are; I know your *faith* and devotion
	13 10	2	This is why the saints must have constancy and *faith*.
	14 12	2	This is why there must be constancy in the saints who keep . . . *faith* in Jesus.

b) Faith||Little Faith, Lack of Faith, Faithless – Believing||Unbelieving, (Not to, Refusing to) believe

Mt	6 30	8	will [God] not much more look after you, you men *of little faith*?
	8 26	8	Why are you so frightened, you men *of little faith*?
	13 58	5	[Jesus] did not work many miracles there because of their *lack of faith*
	14 31	8	Man *of little faith* . . . why did you doubt?
	16 8	8	Men *of little faith*, why are you talking among yourselves about having no bread?
	17 17	4	*Faithless* and perverse generation! . . . How much longer must I be with you?
	20	10/5	Because [v] you have *little faith* ([v] of your *lack of faith*)
		2	. . . if your *faith* were the size of a mustard seed . . . nothing would be impossible for you.
	21 25		Then why did you refuse to *believe* [John]?
	32		John came to you . . . but you did not *believe* him, and yet the tax collectors and prostitutes [r] did (lit. *believed*) . . . you refused to think better of it and *believe* in him.
Mk	4 40	2	Why are you so frightened? How is it that you have no *faith*?
	6 6	5	[Jesus] was amazed at their *lack of faith*.
	9 19	4	You *faithless* generation . . . How much longer must I be with you?

Mk	9 23		Everything is possible for anyone who *has faith*. [24] . . .
	24		the father of the boy cried out, 'I do *have faith*. Help the
	5		*little faith* I have!'
	11 31		Then why did you refuse to *believe* [John]?
	16 11	7	But they *did not believe* [Mary] when they heard her say that [Jesus] was alive and that she had seen him.
	13		[two of Jesus's former companions] told the others, who did not *believe* them either.
	14	5	[Christ] reproached [the Eleven] for their *incredulity* and obstinacy, because they had refused to *believe* those who had seen him after he had risen.
	16	/7	He who *believes* and is baptised will be saved; he who *does not believe* will be condemned.
Lk	1 20		Since you have not *believed* my words . . . you will be silenced
	8 25	2	[the wind and the waves subsided.] He said to [the disciples], 'Where is your *faith*?'
	9 41	4	*Faithless* and perverse generation . . . How much longer must I be among you . . .?
	12 28	8	how much more will [God] look after you, you men *of little faith*!
	20 5		Why did you refuse to *believe* [John]?
	22 67		'If you are the Christ, tell us.' 'If I tell you . . . you will not *believe* me,
	24 11	7	[the women told all this to the Eleven] but . . . they *did not believe* them.
	41	7	Their joy was so great that [the apostles] still *could not believe* it,
Jn	3 12		If you do not *believe* me when I speak about things in this world, how are you going to *believe* me when I speak to you about heavenly things?
	18		No one who *believes* in him will be condemned; but whoever refuses to *believe* is condemned already, because he has refused to *believe* in the name of God's only Son.
	36	6	Anyone who *believes* in the Son has eternal life, but anyone who *refuses to believe* in the Son will never see life:
	4 48		So you will not *believe* unless you see signs and portents!
	5 38		because you do not *believe* in the one he has sent.
	44 H		How can you *believe* . . . [45] . . . you place your hopes on
	46		Moses, and Moses will be your accuser. [46] If you really *believed* him you would *believe* me too, since it was I that he was writing about; [47] but if you refuse to *believe*
	47		what he wrote, how can you *believe* what I say?
	6 36		you can see me and still you do not *believe*.
	64		there are some of you who do not *believe*. For Jesus knew . . . those who did not *believe*,
	7 5		Not even his brothers . . . *had faith* in him.
	8 24		You will die in your sins . . . if you do not *believe* that I am He,
	45		I speak the truth and for that very reason, you do not *believe* me.
	46		why do you not *believe* me?
	10 25		I have told you, but you do not *believe*.
	26		you do not *believe*, because you are no sheep of mine.
	37		If I am not doing my Father's work, there is no need to
	38		*believe* me; [38] but if I am doing it, then even if you refuse to *believe* in me, at least *believe* in the work I do;
	12 37		Though . . . he gave so many signs, they did not *believe* in him.
	38		(Is 53 1) Lord, who could *believe* what we have heard said . . .?
	39		Indeed, they were unable to *believe*
	14 10		Do you not *believe* that I am in the Father and the Father is in me?
	16 9		[the Advocate will show the world how wrong it was] about sin: proved by their refusal to *believe* in me;
	20 25		unless I can put my hand into his side, I refuse to *believe*
	27	4	Give me your hand; put it into my side. [r] Doubt (or: be
		3	*faithless*) no longer but *believe*.
Ac	13 41		(Hab 1 5) I am doing something . . . that you would not *believe* if you were to be told of it.
	14 1		At Iconium . . . a great many Jews and Greeks *became*
	2	6	*believers*. [2] Some of the Jews, however, *refused to believe*, and they poisoned the minds of the pagans
	19 9	6	the attitude of some of the congregation hardened into *unbelief* . . . they began attacking the Way
Rm	11 20		[the branches of the olive tree] were cut off, but through
		5	their *unbelief*; if you still hold firm, it is only thanks
		2	to your *faith*.
	23	5	the Jews, if they give up their *unbelief*, [will be] grafted back
	15 31	6	Pray that I may escape the *unbelievers* in Judaea,
1 Co	6 6		so one brother brings a court case against another in front
		4	of *unbelievers*?
	7 12	4	If a brother has a wife who is an *unbeliever* . . . he must not
	13	4	send her away; [13] and if a woman has an *unbeliever*
	14		for her husband . . . she must not leave him. [14] This is
		4	because the *unbelieving* husband is made one with the
		4	saints through his wife, and the *unbelieving* wife is made one with the saints through her husband . . .

1 Co 7 15   4 However, if the *unbelieving* partner does not consent, they may separate;

10 27   4 If an *unbeliever* invites you to his house . . . eat whatever is put in front of you,

14 22   the strange languages are meant to be a sign not for *believers*

     4 but for *unbelievers*, while on the other hand, prophecy is

   4/ a sign not for *unbelievers* but for *believers*.

23   4 any uninitiated people or *unbelievers*, coming into a meeting . . . where everybody was speaking in tongues, would say you were all mad; ²⁴ but if you were all prophesying

24   4 and an *unbeliever* . . . came in, he would find himself analysed

2 Co 4 4   4 the *unbelievers* whose minds the god of this world has blinded,

6 14   4 Do not harness yourselves in an uneven team with *unbelievers*. ¹⁵ . . . nor has a *believer* anything to share with an *unbeliever*.

15   3

     4

2 Th 2 12   4 to condemn all who refused to *believe* in the truth . . .

13   ¹³ . . . we must be continually thanking God . . . because

   2 God chose you . . . to be saved . . . by *faith* in the truth.

1 Tm 1 13   ˹until I became a *believer* I had been acting (or: I had been acting in *unbelief* and) in ignorance;

   5

5 8   Anyone who does not look after his own relations . . .

   2/4 has rejected the *faith* and is worse than an *unbeliever*.

Tt 1 15   4 to those who have been corrupted and *lack faith*, nothing can be pure

Heb 3 12   5 a wicked mind, so *unbelieving* as to turn away from the living God.

19   ˹because they were unfaithful (or: because of their *unbelief*) . . . they were not able to reach [the place of rest].

   5

11 6   2 it is impossible to please God without *faith*, since anyone who comes to him must *believe* that he exists

31   2 It was by *faith* that Rahab the prostitute . . . was not killed with the *unbelievers*.

   6

1 P 2 6   (Is 28 16) I lay in Zion a precious cornerstone . . . and the man who ˹rests his trust on (or: has faith in) it will not be disappointed. ⁷ That means that for you who are

7   /7 *believers*, it is precious; but for *unbelievers*, the stone . . . has proved to be the keystone, ⁸ . . . They stumble

8   6 over it because they *do not believe* in the word;

3 1   if there are some husbands who have ˹not yet obeyed

   6 (lit. *refused to believe*) the word,

20   6 it was long ago . . . that these spirits [in prison] *refused to believe*.

4 17   what will [the judgement] be when it comes down to those

   6 who *refuse to believe* God's Good News?

1 Jn 5 10   Everybody who *believes* in the Son of God has this testimony inside him; and anyone who will not *believe* God is making God out to be a liar, because he has not ˹trusted (or: *believed*) the testimony God has given about his Son.

Jude 5   the Lord . . . destroyed the men who did not ˹trust (or: *believe*) him.

Rv 21 8   the legacy . . . for ˹those who break their word (or: *faithless*) . . . is the second death in the burning lake of sulphur.

   4

c) Believe||Not to believe, in falsehood, false prophets

Mt 24 23   If anyone says to you then, 'Look, here is the Christ' . . . do not *believe* it;

26   If, then, they say to you . . . 'Look, he is in some hiding place', do not *believe* it;

Mk 13 21   if anyone says to you then, 'Look, here is the Christ' . . . do not *believe* it;

Th 2 11   God is sending a power to delude them and make them *believe* what is untrue

d) Believe (generally) – Incredible, Sceptical – Doubt, Conviction

Jn 4 21   *Believe* me, woman, the hour is coming

9 18   the Jews would not *believe* that the man had been blind

20 27   4 put [your hand] into my side. ˹*Doubt* (or: be faithless)

   3 no longer but *believe*.

Ac 9 26   [the disciples] were all afraid of [Saul]: they could not *believe* he was really a disciple.

26 8   4 Why does it seem *incredible* to you that God should raise the dead?

28 24   some were convinced by what [Paul] said, while the rest

   7 *were sceptical*.

Rm 4 20   Abraham refused either to deny [the promise] or even to

   5/2 *doubt* it, but drew strength from *faith*

14 2   those who *believe* they may eat any sort of meat

1 Co 11 18   I hear that . . . there are separate factions among you, and I half *believe* it

---

2: FAITHFUL, TRUST(ED), RELIABLE – UNFAITHFUL

a) Faithful(ness), Fidelity, Truth, of God or of Christ

Rm 3 3   What if some of them were *unfaithful*? Will their lack of

   2 fidelity cancel God's *fidelity*?

1 Co 1 9   God by calling you has joined you to his Son . . . and

   3 God is *faithful*.

10 13   3 ˹You can trust God not to (lit. God is *faithful*; he will not) let you be tried beyond your strength,

2 Co 1 18   3 I swear by God's *truth*, there is no Yes and No about what we say to you.

1 Th 5 24   God has called you and he ˹will not fail you (lit. is

   3 *faithful*)

2 Th 3 3   3 the Lord is *faithful*, and he will give you strength

2 Tm 2 13   3 We may be unfaithful, but he is always *faithful*,

Heb 2 17   3 so that he could be a compassionate and *trustworthy* high priest of God's religion,

3 2   3 [Jesus] was *faithful* to the one who appointed him,

10 23   3 the one who made the promise is *faithful*.

11 11   by faith . . . Sarah . . . believed that he who had made the

   3 promise would be *faithful* to it.

1 P 4 19   even those whom God allows to suffer must trust themselves

   3 to the *constancy* of the creator

1 Jn 1 9   3 God who is *faithful* and just will forgive our sins

Rv 1 5   3 [grace and peace] from Jesus Christ, the *faithful* witness,

3 14   3 Here is the message of the Amen, the *faithful*, the true witness,

19 11   3 I saw . . . a white horse appear; its rider was called *Faithful and True*;

b) Faithful(ness), Sure, Good faith – Trust, Trustworthy, Reliable – Unfaithful, Lack of fidelity

Mt 23 23   2 justice, mercy, *good faith*! These you should have practised,

24 45   < 3 What sort of servant, then, is *faithful* and wise

25 21   < 3/3 Well done, good and *faithful* servant . . . you can be *faithful* in small things,

23   < 3 Well done, good and *faithful* servant . . . you can be *faithful* in small things,

Lk 12 42   < 3 What sort of steward, then, is *faithful* and wise enough for the master to place him over his household . . .?

46   The master [of the bad servant] will . . . send him to the

   4 same fate as the *unfaithful*.

16 10   < 3/3 The man who can be *trusted* in little things can be *trusted* in great;

11   3 If then you cannot be *trusted* with money, that tainted thing,

12   3 if you cannot be *trusted* with what is not yours,

19 17   < 3 my good servant . . . you have proved yourself *faithful* in a very small thing,

Jn 14 1   *Trust* in God still, and *trust* in me.

Ac 13 34   3 (Is 55 3) the *sure* and holy things promised to David.

27 25   I *trust* in God that things will turn out just as I was told;

Rm 3 3   7/5 What if some of them *were unfaithful*? Will their *lack of fidelity* cancel God's fidelity?

14 23   anybody who eats in a state of doubt is condemned, because

   2 he is not in ˹*good faith* (or: faith); and every act ˹done

   2 in bad faith (lit. not done in *good faith*) is a sin.

1 Co 4 2   What is expected of stewards is that each one should be

   3 found *worthy of* his *trust*.

17   3 Timothy, my dear and *faithful* son in the Lord:

7 25   About remaining celibate, I . . . give my own opinion as

   3 one who . . . has stayed *faithful*.

13 7   [Love] is always ready to excuse, to ˹*trust* (or: believe), to hope,

Ga 5 22   2 What the Spirit brings is . . . ˹*trustfulness* (or: *faithfulness*)

Ep 6 21   3 Tychicus, my *loyal* helper in the Lord,

Col 1 2   3 [From Paul] to the saints in Colossae, our *faithful* brothers in Christ;

7   3 [Epaphras] is . . . a *faithful* deputy for ˹us (ᵛ you) as Christ's servant,

4 7   3 Tychicus . . . is . . . a *loyal* helper . . . in the service of the Lord.

9   3 Onesimus, that dear and *faithful* brother

1 Tm 1 12   3 Christ . . . judged me *faithful* enough to call me

15   3 Here is a saying that you can *rely* on and nobody should doubt:

16   all the other people who would later ˹have to *trust* (or: have faith) in him to come to eternal life.

3 1   3 Here is a saying that you can *rely* on:

11   3 the women must be . . . quite *reliable*.

4 9   3 that is a saying that you can *rely* on and nobody should doubt it.

2 Tm 1 12   I know who it is that I have *put my trust* in,

2 2   You have heard everything that I teach . . . hand it on to

   3 *reliable* people

11   3 Here is a saying that you can *rely* on:

13   7 We may *be unfaithful*, but he is always faithful,

3 14   9 You must keep to what you have been taught and *know to be true*;

Tt	1	9	3 [an elder] must have a firm grasp of the *unchanging* message of the tradition,
	2	10	2 [the slaves] must show complete ⸢honesty (lit. *fidelity*) at all times,
	3	8	3 This is doctrine that you can *rely* on.
Heb	3	5	3 Moses was *faithful* in the house of God,
		19	5 it was ⸢because they were *unfaithful* (or: because of their unbelief) that they were not able to reach [the place of rest]
1 P	2	6	(Is 28 16) I lay in Zion a precious cornerstone . . . and the man who ⸢*rests his trust* on (or: has faith in) it will not be disappointed.
	5	12	3 Silvanus, who is a brother I know I can *trust*,
1 Jn	4	1	It is not every spirit . . . that you can *trust*;
	5	10	Everybody who *believes* in the Son of God has this testimony inside him; and anyone who will not *believe* God is making God out to be a liar, because he has not ⸢*trusted* (or: believed) the testimony God has given about his Son.
3 Jn		5	3 you have done *faithful* work in looking after these brothers,
Jude		5	the Lord . . . destroyed the men who did not ⸢*trust* (or: believe) him.
Rv	2	10	3 Even if you have to die, keep *faithful*,
		13	3 my *faithful* witness, Antipas,
	17	14	[the ten kings] will be defeated by [the Lamb's] followers, the called . . . the *faithful*.
	21	5	3 what I am saying is *sure* and will come true.
		8	4 the legacy . . . for ⸢*those who break their word* (or: those who are faithless) . . . is the second death in the burning lake of sulphur.
	22	6	3 All that you have written is *sure* and will come true:

3: ENTRUST TO, TRUST WITH – COMMISSION (A PERSON) TO

Lk	16	11	who will *trust* you with genuine riches?
Jn	2	24	Jesus . . . did not *trust himself* to them;
Rm	3	2	the Jews are the people to whom God's message was *entrusted*.
1 Co	9	17	[preaching] is a responsibility which has been ⸢put into my hands (lit. *entrusted* to me).
Ga	2	7	I had been *commissioned* to preach the Good News to the uncircumcised just as Peter had been commissioned to preach it to the circumcised.
1 Th	2	4	God . . . decided that we were fit to be *entrusted* with the Good News,
1 Tm	1	11	[the sound teaching] that goes with . . . the gospel that was *entrusted* to me.
Tt	1	3	by the command of God . . . I have been *commissioned* to proclaim [his message].

2. DOUBT – HESITATE

1: DOUBT – HESITATE: *DI-STAZŌ*

di-stazō 2

Mt	14	31	Man of little faith . . . why did you *doubt*?
	28	17	[the disciples] fell down before him, though some *hesitated*.

2: DOUBT – HESITATE : *DIA-KRINŌ*

dia-krinō 9/19

Mt	21	21	if you have faith and do not *doubt* at all,
Mk	11	23	if anyone says to this mountain . . . with no *hesitation* in his heart but believing that what he says will happen, it will be done for him.
Ac	10	20	do not *hesitate* about going back with them;
	11	12	the Spirit told me to have no *hesitation* about going back with them.
Rm	4	20	Since God had promised it, Abraham refused either to deny it or even to *doubt* it,
	14	23	anybody who eats in [a state of] *doubt* is condemned,
Jm	1	6	he must ask with faith, and no trace of *doubt*, because a person who *has doubts* is like . . . waves
Jude		22	When there are some who *have doubts*, ⱽ reassure (G pity) them;

BELONG TO

1. BELONG TO – BE OF (A PERSON, GOD): *GINOMAI*

ginomai (7)

Mt	18	12	Suppose ⸢a man has a hundred sheep (lit. a hundred sheep *are* a man's)
Lk	20	14	let us kill him so that the inheritance will *be* ours.
Rm	7	3	if [a married woman] ⸢*gives herself* (lit. *belongs*) to another man while her husband is still alive, she is legally an adulteress; but after her husband is dead . . . she can ⸢*marry* (lit. *belong to*) someone else without becoming an adulteress. ⁴ That is why you . . . who . . . are now dead to the Law, can now ⸢*give yourselves* (lit. *belong*) to another . . . to him who rose from the dead
Rv	11	15	The kingdom of the world has *become* the kingdom *of* our Lord and his Christ,
	12	10	Victory and power . . . ⸢*have been won* by (lit. *are of*) God,

2. BELONG TO – BE OF (A PERSON), BE FOR (A PERSON)

1 belonging expressed by genitive or dative cases	*(63)*	
2 *emos*	*(10)*	with *eimi* (54)
3 *sos*	*(10)*	or without
4 *hymeteros*	*(2)*	
5 *peri-ousios*	*1*	

1: BELONG TO (GOD, CHRIST)

Mt	6	13	(ⱽ For yours *is* the kingdom, the power and the glory . . .)
	20	15	2 Have I no right to do what I want with *my own*?
		23	2 as for seats at my right hand and my left, these *are* not *mine* to grant;
	22	21	give back to Caesar what belongs to Caesar – and to God what *belongs to* God.
	25	27	2 I would have recovered *my* capital with interest
Mk	9	41	because you *belong to* Christ
	10	40	2 seats at my right hand or my left . . . *are* not *mine* to grant;
	12	17	Give back to Caesar what belongs to Caesar – and to God what *belongs to* God.
Lk	2	49	Did you not know that I must be busy with my *Father's* affairs?
	4	7	3 [this power] shall all *be yours*.
	20	25	give back to Caesar what belongs to Caesar – and to God what *belongs to* God.
Jn	7	16	2 My teaching *is* not *from myself*: it comes from the one who sent me;
	14	24	2 My word *is* not *my own*: it is the word of the one who sent me.
	16	15	2 Everything the Father has *is mine*;
	17	6	3 the men you took . . . to give me . . . They *were yours*
		9	I . . . pray . . . for those you have given me because they *belong to you*:
		10	2/3 all ⸢I have (lit. *mine*) *is yours*
			3/2 and all ⸢you have (lit. *yours*) [is] *mine*,
Ac	17	28	We *are* all his children.
	18	10	⸢I have (lit. There *are*) so many people on my side in this city
	27	23	an angel of the God *to* whom I *belong* and whom I serve,
Rm	8	9	unless you possessed the Spirit of Christ you would not *belong to* him.
	14	8	alive or dead we *belong to* the Lord.
1 Co	1	12	'I am for Paul,' . . . 'I [am] *for* Christ.'
	3	23	you *belong to* Christ and Christ *belongs to* God.
2 Co	4	7	such an overwhelming power *comes from* God and not from us.
	10	7	Anybody who is convinced that he *belongs to* Christ must . . . reflect that we all *belong to* Christ no less than he does.
Ga	5	24	You cannot *belong to* Christ Jesus unless you crucify all self-indulgent passions and desires
Col	2	17	the ⸢reality (lit. body) is ⸢Christ (lit. *of* Christ; or: *for* Christ),
2 Tm	2	19	The Lord knows those who *are* his own
Tt	2	14	He sacrificed himself . . . to purify a people so that it could 5 *be his very own*
1 P	4	11	Jesus Christ . . . *to* him alone *belong* all glory and power for ever and ever.

2: BE OF, BE FOR (A PERSON)

Mt	5	3	the poor in spirit; theirs *is* the kingdom of heaven.
		10	those who are persecuted in the cause of right: theirs *is* the kingdom of heaven.
	16	22	this must not ⸢*happen to you* (lit. *be* your [fate]).
	19	14	little children . . . it is *to* such as these that the kingdom of heaven *belongs*.
		27	We have . . . followed you. ⸢What are we to have (lit. What is to *be* ours), then?
	20	14	3 Take *your* earnings and go.

Mt 25 25   3 Here . . . is [your talent]; it was *yours*, you have it back.
Mk 5 19   3 Go home to *your* [people]
     10 14   little children . . . it is *to* such as these that the kingdom of heaven *belongs*.
     11 23   if anyone says [and believes it] will happen, it will *be* [done] *for* him.
       24   everything that you ask and pray for . . . will *be* yours.
     12 7   let us kill him, and the inheritance will *be* ours.
Lk 5 3   [Jesus] got into one of the boats – it *was* Simon's
     6 20   4 happy are you who are poor: *yours* is the kingdom of God.
       30   3 do not ask for *your* property back from the man who robs you.
     9 13   ⌐We have no more than five loaves (lit. There *are* no more than five loaves *for* us) and two fish,
       55   But [Jesus] turned and rebuked [James and John], (ᵛ 'You do not know what kind of spirit you *are of* . . .'),
     12 20   this hoard of yours, whose will it *be* then?
       24   the ravens . . . ⌐they have (lit. *for* them there *are*) no store-houses and no barns;
     15 31   2/3 all ⌐I have (lit. *mine*) is yours.
     16 12   if you cannot be trusted with what is not yours, who will
           4 give you [what is] *your very own*?
     18 16   little children . . . it is *to* such as these that the kingdom of God *belongs*.
Jn 10 12   the hired man . . . the sheep do not *belong to* him,
     19 24   let's throw dice to decide ⌐who is to have (lit. whose will *be*) [Jesus's] undergarment,
Ac 1 7   It *is not for* you to know the times or dates that the Father has decided
     2 39   The promise that was made *is for* you and your children,
     7 44   ⌐our ancestors possessed the Tent of Testimony (lit. the Tent of Testimony *was* our ancestors')
     9 2   [Saul asked for authorisation to arrest] any ⌐followers of (lit. people who *were of*) the Way,
     10 6   Simon the tanner whose house *is* by the sea.
     19 14   Among those who [pronounced the name of the Lord Jesus over people who were possessed] *were* seven sons *of* Sceva,
     21 9   ⌐[Philip] had four virgin daughters (lit. There *were* four virgin daughters *of* his) who were prophets.
       11   The man this girdle *belongs to* will be bound . . . by the Jews
Rm 9 4   ⌐[The Israelites] were adopted (lit. *To* the Israelites *was* [given] adoption) as sons, . . . the glory and the covenants;
       5   . . . ⁵ ⌐They are descended from (lit. *Of* them also *were*) the patriarchs
1Co 1 12   all these slogans that you have, like: 'I *am for* Paul,' 'I [am] *for* Apollos,' 'I [am] *for* Cephas,' 'I [am] *for* Christ.'
     3 4   What could be more unspiritual than your slogans, 'I *am for* Paul' and 'I [am] *for* Apollos'
       22   Paul, Apollos, Cephas, the world . . . *are* all your servants; ²³ but you belong to Christ and Christ belongs to God.
     6 19   Your body, you know, is the temple of the Holy Spirit . . . You *are* not your own property;
2Co 12 14   it is you I want, not ⌐your possessions (lit. things *of* yours).
1Th 5 5   we do not *belong to* the night or *to* darkness,
       8   we *belong to* the day and we should be sober;
Heb 5 14   Solid food *is for* mature men

BIRDS – INSECTS

1. **Fly, Flying – Wing:** *petomai*
2. **Birds**
   1: Birds: *peteinon*
   2: Bird – Hen: *orneon*
   3: Chicks – Brood: *nossos*
   4: Dove, Pigeon – Turtledove: *peristera* and *trygōn*
   5: Sparrow: *strouthion*

   6: Raven: *korax*
   7: Eagle – Vulture: *aetos*
3. **Insects**
   1: Gnat, Midge: *kōnōps*
   2: Bees': *melissios*
   3: Locust: *akris*
   4: Moth – Woodworm: *sēs* and *brōsis*
   5: Worm: *skōlēx*

1. FLY, FLYING – WING: *PETOMAI*

1 *petomai* 5   2 *pteryx* 5

Mt 23 37   2 a hen gathers her chicks under her *wings*,
Lk 13 34   2 a hen gathers her brood under her *wings*,
Rv 4 7   the fourth animal was like a *flying* eagle.
     8   2 Each of the four animals had six *wings*
   8 13   I heard an eagle, calling aloud *as it flew* high overhead, 'Trouble,
   9 9   2 the noise of [the locusts'] *wings* sounded like a great charge of horses and chariots

Rv 12 14   2/ [the woman] was given a huge pair of eagle's *wings* to *fly* [away] . . . into the desert,
   14 6   I saw another angel, *flying* high overhead,
   19 17   an angel . . . shouted aloud to all the birds that were *flying* high overhead in the sky.

2. BIRDS

1: BIRDS: *PETEINON*

1 *peteinon* 14   2 *ptēnos* 1

Mt 6 26   Look at the *birds* in the sky . . . your heavenly Father feeds them.
   8 20   Foxes have holes and the *birds* of the air have nests,
   13 4   some seeds fell on the edge of the path, and the *birds* came and ate them up.
     32   the *birds* of the air come and shelter in its branches.
Mk 4 4   some of the seed fell on the edge of the path, and the *birds* came and ate it up.
     32   the *birds* of the air can shelter in its shade.
Lk 8 5   some [seed] fell on the edge of the path . . . and the *birds* of the air ate it up.
   9 58   Foxes have holes and the *birds* of the air have nests,
   12 24   God feeds [the ravens]. And how much more are you worth than the *birds*!
   13 19   the *birds* of the air sheltered in its branches.
Ac 10 12   [the sheet] contained every possible sort of animal and ⌐bird, walking, crawling or flying ones (lit. *bird* and reptile).
   11 6   I . . . saw all sorts of animals . . . ⌐everything possible that could walk, crawl or fly (lit. and reptiles and *birds* of the air).
Rm 1 23   they exchanged the glory of . . . God for . . . the image of mortal man, of *birds*, of quadrupeds and reptiles.
1Co 15 39   2 there is human flesh, animals' flesh, the flesh of *birds*
Jm 3 7   Wild animals and *birds*, reptiles and fish can all be tamed by man,

2: BIRD – HEN: *ORNEON*

1 *orneon* 3   2 *ornis* 2

Mt 23 37   2 I longed to gather your children as a *hen* gathers her chicks under her wings,
Lk 13 34   2 I longed to gather your children, as a *hen* gathers her brood under her wings,
Rv 18 2   Babylon . . . has become . . . a lodging for every . . . loathsome *bird*.
   19 17   an angel . . . shouted aloud to all the *birds* that were flying high overhead in the sky,
     21   all the *birds* were gorged with their flesh.

3: CHICKS – BROOD: *NOSSOS*

1 *nossia* 1   3 *nossos* 1
2 *nossion* 1

Mt 23 37   2 a hen gathers her *chicks* under her wings,
Lk 2 24   (Lv 12 8) offer in sacrifice . . . a pair of turtledoves or two
          3 ⌐young pigeons (lit. pigeon *chicks*).
   13 34   a hen gathers her *brood* under her wings.

4: DOVE, PIGEON – TURTLEDOVE: *PERISTERA* and *TRYGŌN*

1 *peristera* 10   2 *trygōn* 1

Mt 3 16 Ⓢ   Jesus . . . saw the Spirit of God descending like a *dove* and coming down on him.
   10 16   be cunning as serpents and yet as harmless as *doves*.
   21 12   Jesus . . . upset . . . the chairs of those who were selling *pigeons*.
Mk 1 10 Ⓢ   [Jesus] saw . . . the Spirit, like a *dove*, descending on him.
   11 15   [Jesus] upset . . . the chairs of those who were selling *pigeons*.
Lk 2 24   2 (Lv 12 8) offer in sacrifice . . . a pair of *turtledoves* or two ⌐young pigeons (lit. *pigeon* chicks).
   3 22 Ⓢ   the Holy Spirit descended on [Jesus] . . . like a *dove*.
Jn 1 32 Ⓢ   I saw the Spirit coming down on [Jesus] from heaven like a *dove*
   2 14   in the Temple [Jesus] found people selling cattle . . . and *pigeons* . . . ¹⁶ and said to the *pigeon*-sellers, 'Take all this out of here

5: SPARROW: *STROUTHION*

strouthion 4

Mt 10	29	Can you not buy two *sparrows* for a penny?
	31	there is no need to be afraid; you are worth more than hundreds of *sparrows*.
Lk 12	6	Can you not buy five *sparrows* for two pennies?
	7	There is no need to be afraid: you are worth more than hundreds of *sparrows*.

6: RAVEN: *KORAX*

korax 1

Lk 12 24   Think of the *ravens* . . . God feeds them.

7: EAGLE – VULTURE: *AETOS*

aetos 5

Mt 24	28	<	Wherever the corpse is, there will the *vultures* gather.
Lk 17	37	<	Where the body is, there too will the *vultures* gather.
Rv 4	7		the fourth creature was like a flying eagle.
	8 13		I heard an *eagle*, calling aloud as it flew high overhead,
	12 14		[the woman] was given a huge pair of *eagle*'s wings to fly away . . . into the desert,

3. INSECTS

1: GNAT, MIDGE: *KŌNŌPS*

kōnōps 1

Mt 23 24   You blind guides! Straining out *gnats* and swallowing camels!

2: BEES': *MELISSIOS*

melissios 1

Lk 24 42   they offered [Jesus] a piece of grilled fish (ᵛ and a *bees'* honeycomb),

3: LOCUST: *AKRIS*

akris 4

Mt 3	4	[John's] food was *locusts* and wild honey.
Mk 1	6	John . . . lived on *locusts* and wild honey.
Rv 9	3	out of the smoke dropped *locusts*
	7	these *locusts* were like horses armoured for battle;

4: MOTH – WOODWORM: *SĒS* AND *BRŌSIS*

1 *sēs*	*3*	3 *brōsis* 2/11	
2 *sēto*(-*brōtos*) 1			

Mt 6	19 /3	Do not store up treasures for yourselves on earth, where *moths* and ʳ*woodworms* (or: rust) destroy them
	20 /3	store up treasures for yourselves in heaven, where neither *moth* nor ʳ*woodworms* (or: rust) destroy them
Lk 12	33	Get yourselves . . . treasure . . . in heaven where no thief can reach it and no *moth* destroy it.
Jm 5	2	2 [an answer for the rich,] your clothes are all eaten up by *moths*.

5: WORM: *SKŌLĒX*

1 *skōlēx* 1	2 *skōlēko*(-*brōtos*) 1	

Mk 9	48	[in hell] their *worm* does not die nor their fire go out.
Ac 12	23	2 [Herod] was eaten away with *worms* and died.

BITTER – SEVERE

---

1. BITTER(NESS) – SOUR – VENOM

1: BITTER(NESS) – (TURN) SOUR, BRACKISH – (BE) HARSH: *PIKROS*

1 *pikrainō* 4	3 *pikros* 2	
2 *pikria* 4	4 *pikrōs* 2	

Mt 26	75	4 [Peter] went outside and wept *bitterly*.
Lk 22	62	4 [Peter] went outside and wept *bitterly*.
Ac 8	23	2 [Simon the magician,] you are trapped in the *bitterness* of gall and the chains of sin.
Rm 3	14	2 (Ps 10 7 G) *bitter* curses fill their mouths.
Ep 4	31	2 Never have grudges (lit. *bitternesses*) against others, or lose your temper, or raise your voice to anybody,
Col 3	19	Husbands, love your wives and ʳtreat them with gentleness (lit. do not *be harsh* to them).
Heb 12	15	2 Be careful . . . that no root of *bitterness* should begin to grow and make trouble;
Jm 3	11	does any water supply give a flow of fresh water and salt (lit. *brackish*) water out of the same pipe?
	14	3 if at heart you have the *bitterness* of jealousy, or a self-seeking ambition,
Rv 8	11	a third of all water *turned* to *bitter* wormwood, so that many people died from drinking it.
	10 9	(Ezk 3 3) the small scroll . . . will *turn* your stomach *sour*,
	10	when I had eaten [the scroll] my stomach *turned sour*.

2: WORMWOOD – VINEGAR – GALL – VENOM

a) Wormwood: *apsinthos*

apsinthos 2

Rv 8 11   this was the star called *Wormwood*, and a third of all water turned to bitter *wormwood*, so that many people died from drinking it.

b) Vinegar – Sour wine: *oxos*

oxos 6

Mt 27	48	a sponge which he dipped in *vinegar* and . . . gave it [Jesus] to drink.
Mk 15	36	Someone ran and soaked a sponge in *vinegar*
Lk 23	36	The soldiers . . . approached to offer him *vinegar*
Jn 19	29	A jar full of *vinegar* stood there, so putting a sponge soaked in the *vinegar* on a hyssop stick they held it up to his mouth.
	30	After Jesus had taken the *vinegar* he said, 'It is accomplished';

c) Gall: *cholē*

cholē 2

Mt 27	34	they gave [Jesus] wine to drink mixed with *gall*,
Ac 8	23	it is plain to me that you are trapped in the bitterness of *gall* and the chains of sin.

d) Venom, Poison: *ios*

ios 2/3

Rm 3	13	their tongues are full of deceit. Vipers' *venom* is on their lips.
Jm 3	8	the tongue – it is a pest that will not keep still, full of deadly *poison*.

2. SEVERE – SHARP – AUSTERE

a) Severe, Severity, Strict – Sharp: *apo-tomos*

1 *apo-tomia* 2	2 *apo-tomōs* 2	

Rm 11	22 Θ	Do not forget that God can be *severe* as well as kind: he is *severe* to those who fell,
2 Co 13	10	I am writing this from a distance, so that when I am with you I shall not need to be *strict*,
Tt 1	13	2 you will have to be *severe* in correcting them, and make them sound in the faith

b) Severe, Austere – Exacting, Hard: *austēros*

austēros 2

Lk 19	21	I was afraid of you; for you are an *exacting* man;
	22	So you knew I was an *exacting* man,

BLACK – WHITE – RED

---

1. WHITE – WHITEWASHED

1: WHITE: *LEUKOS*

2 *leukainō* 2   1 *leukos* 25

Mt	5 36	you cannot turn a single hair *white* or black.
	17 2	[Jesus] was transfigured: . . . his clothes became as *white* as light.
	28 3	[the angel's] robe [was] *white* as snow.
Mk	9 3	[Jesus was transfigured:] his clothes became dazzlingly *white* (ᵛ like snow), ˹whiter than any bleacher could make them (lit. more than any bleacher could *wash* them *white*).
	16 5	On entering the tomb [the women] saw a young man in a *white* robe
Lk	9 29	the aspect of [Jesus's] face was changed and his clothing became ˹brilliant as lightning (lit. dazzling *white*).
Jn	4 35	look at the fields; already they are *white*, ready for harvest.
	20 12	[Mary] saw two angels in *white* sitting where the body of Jesus had been,
Ac	1 10	suddenly two men in *white* were standing near [the apostles]
Rv	1 14	[I saw a figure like a Son of man.] His head and his hair were *white* as *white* wool or as snow,
	2 17	to those who prove victorious I will give the hidden manna and a *white* stone
	3 4	There are a few in Sardis . . . who . . . are fit to come with me, dressed in *white*. ⁵ Those who prove victorious will be dressed, like these, in *white* robes
	18	I warn you, buy from me . . . *white* robes to clothe you
	4 4	[on the thrones] I saw twenty-four elders sitting, dressed in *white* robes
	6 2	Immediately a *white* horse appeared,
	11	Each of [the martyrs] was given a *white* robe
	7 9	a huge number . . . of people from every nation . . . standing in front of . . . the Lamb, dressed in *white* robes
	13	Do you know who these people are, dressed in *white* robes . . .?
	14	2 they have *washed* their robes *white* again in the blood of the Lamb,
	14 14	I saw a *white* cloud and, sitting on it, one like a son of man
	19 11	I saw . . . a *white* horse appear; its rider was called Faithful and True;
	14	Behind [the horseman], dressed in linen of dazzling *white*, rode the armies of heaven on *white* horses.
	20 11	I saw a great *white* throne and the One who was sitting on it.

2: WHITEWASHED: *KONIAŌ*

koniaō 2

Mt	23 27	Alas for you, scribes and Pharisees, you hypocrites! You who are like *whitewashed* tombs
Ac	23 3	Paul said to [the high priest Ananias], 'God will surely strike you, you *whitewashed* wall!

2. BLACK: *MELAS*

melas 3

Mt	5 36	you cannot turn a single hair white or *black*.
Rv	6 5	a *black* horse appeared, and its rider was holding a pair of scales;
	12	the sun went as *black* as coarse sackcloth;

3. RED – FIERY RED – FLAME COLOUR: *PYRROS*

3 *pyrinos* 1   2 *pyrros* 2
1 *pyrrazō* 2

Mt	16 2	In the evening you say, 'It will be fine; there is a *red* sky,'
	3	³ and in the morning, 'Stormy weather today; the sky is *red* and overcast.'
Rv	6 4	2 out came another horse, bright *red*, and its rider was . . . given a huge sword.
	9 17	I saw the horses, and the riders with their breastplates of
		3 *flame colour*, hyacinth-blue and sulphur-yellow;
	12 3	2 a second sign appeared in the sky, a huge *red* dragon

4. GREEN – SICKLY – PALE: *CHLŌROS*

chlōros 3/4

Mk	6 39	[Jesus] ordered [the disciples] to get all the people together in groups on the *green* grass,
Rv	6 8	another horse appeared, deathly *pale*, and its rider was called Plague;
	8 7	every blade of (§ *green*) grass was burnt.

BLAME – REBUKE – WARN NOT TO

1. **Discredit – Criticism – Blame:** *mōmaomai*
2. **Complain – (Find) Fault – Blame:** *memphomai*
3. **Reprove, Rebuke, Reprimand – Convict (of) – Expose (as wrong), Refute:** *elenchō*
4. **Rebuke, Reprove, Scold – Remonstrate with – Order (not to):** *epi-timaō*
5. **Speak harshly to:** *epi-plēssō*
6. **Have a complaint against (a person):** *echō kata, pros*
7. **Complain – Murmur (against), Grumble (at):** *gongysmos*
8. **Threaten – Warn (never to) – Caution (not to):** *ap-eileō*
9. **Sternly warn – Angrily express indignation with:** *em-brimaomai*

1. DISCREDIT – CRITICISM – BLAME: *MŌMAOMAI*

mōmaomai 2

2 Co	6 3	We do nothing that people might object to, so as not to ˹bring *discredit* on (or: find *blame* in) our function as God's servants
	8 20	We hope that in this way there will be no ˹accusations (lit. *criticism*) made about our administering such a large fund;

2. COMPLAIN – (FIND) FAULT – BLAME: *MEMPHOMAI*

1 *memphomai* 2   3 *momphē* 1
2 *mempsi(-moiros)* 1

Rm	9 19	In that case, how can God ever *blame* anyone . . .?
Col	3 13	3 forgive each other as soon as a ˹quarrel begins (or: *complaint* arises)
Heb	8 8 Θ	God does *find fault* with them; he says: . . . I will establish a new covenant [but not like the one I made with their ancestors]
Jude	16	2 [irreligious] ˹grumblers (or: *complainers*) governed only by their own desires,

3. REPROVE, REBUKE, REPRIMAND – CONVICT (OF) – EXPOSE (AS WRONG), REFUTE: *ELENCHŌ*

1 *elenchō* 18   4 *ap-elegmos* 1
2 *elegmos* 1   5 *dia-kat-elenchomai* 1
3 *elenxis* 1

Mt	18 15	If your brother does something wrong, go and *have it out* with him alone,
Lk	3 19	[John] *criticised* [Herod] for his relations with his brother's wife Herodias
Jn	3 20	everybody who does wrong hates the light . . . for fear his actions should be ˹*exposed* (or: *reproved*);
	8 46 ⑤	Can one of you *convict* me of sin?
	16 8 ⑤	[the Advocate] will *show* the world *how wrong* it was about sin, and about who was in the right, and about judgement:
Ac	18 28	5 by the energetic way [Apollos] *refuted* the Jews in public
	19 27	4 This threatens . . . to *discredit* our trade,
1 Co	14 24	if you were all prophesying and an unbeliever or uninitiated person came in, he would find himself ˹*analysed* (lit. *reproved*) and judged by everyone
Ep	5 11	having nothing to do with the futile works of darkness but [*exposing* (or: *reproving*) them by contrast.
	13	anything *exposed* by the light will be illuminated
1 Tm	5 20	If any of them are at fault, *reprimand* them publicly,
2 Tm	3 16	All scripture . . . can profitably be used for teaching, for
		2 *refuting* [error],
	4 2	*Refute* [falsehood], ˹correct (lit. *reprove*) [error], call to obedience –
Tt	1 9	[the elder] can be counted on for . . . *refuting* those who argue against [the sound doctrine].
	13	you will have to be severe in ˹*correcting* (lit. *refuting*) them, and make them sound in the faith
	2 15	Now this is what you are to say, whether you are giving instruction or ˹*correcting* (lit. *refuting*) errors;
Heb	12 5 Θ	(Pr 3 11) when the Lord corrects you, do not treat it lightly; but do not get discouraged when he *reprimands* you.
Jm	2 9	as soon as you make distinctions between classes of people, you are . . . *under condemnation* for breaking the Law.
2 P	2 16	Balaam . . . thought he could profit best by sinning, until
		3 he was *called to order* for his faults.
Jude	15 Θ	[the Lord will come] to pronounce judgement on all mankind and to *sentence* the wicked
	22	When there are some who have doubts, ᵛ *reassure* them (G take pity on them);

Rv 3 19 X (Pr 3 12) I am the one who *reproves* and disciplines all those he loves:

4. REBUKE, REPROVE, SCOLD – REMONSTRATE WITH – ORDER (NOT TO): *EPI-TIMAŌ*

epi-timaō 30

Mt 8 26 X [Jesus] *rebuked* the winds and the sea; and all was calm again.
   12 16 X [Jesus cured them all,] but *warned* them not to make him known.
   16 20 X [Jesus] *gave* the disciples strict *orders* not to tell anyone that he was the Christ.
      22   Peter started to *remonstrate with* [Jesus] . . . 'this must not happen to you'.
   17 18 X when Jesus *rebuked* it the devil came out of the boy
   19 13   People brought little children to [Jesus] . . . The disciples ⌜*turned* them *away* (or: *remonstrated with* them),
   20 31   the crowd *scolded* [the two blind men] and told them to keep quiet,
Mk 1 25 X Jesus *said sharply* [to the unclean spirit], 'Be quiet! Come out of him!'
    3 12 X [Jesus] *warned* [the unclean spirits] strongly not to make him known.
    4 39 X [Jesus] woke up and *rebuked* the wind and said to the sea, 'Quiet now!'
    8 30 X [Peter said to him, 'You are the Christ.'] And he *gave* them strict *orders* not to tell anyone about him.
      32   taking [Jesus] aside, Peter started to *remonstrate with* him.
      33 X [33] But . . . he *rebuked* Peter and said to him, 'Get behind me, Satan!'
    9 25 X Jesus . . . *rebuked* the unclean spirit . . . 'I command you: come out of him and never enter him again.'
   10 13   People were bringing little children to [Jesus] . . . The disciples ⌜*turned* them *away* (or: *remonstrated with* them),
      48   [people] *scolded* [the blind man] and told him to keep quiet,
Lk 4 35 X Jesus *said sharply*, 'Be quiet! Come out of him!'
      39 X Leaning over [Simon's mother-in-law Jesus] *rebuked* the fever
      41 X he *rebuked* [the devils] and would not allow them to speak
    8 24 X [Jesus] woke up and *rebuked* the wind and the rough water;
    9 21 X he *gave* [the disciples] strict *orders* not to tell anyone
      42 X Jesus *rebuked* the unclean spirit and cured the boy
      55 X he turned and *rebuked* [James and John],
   17 3   If your brother does something wrong, *reprove* him
   18 15   People even brought little children to [Jesus] . . . but when the disciples saw this they ⌜*turned* them *away* (or: *remonstrated with* them).
      39   The people in front *scolded* [the blind man] and told him to keep quiet,
   19 39 X Some Pharisees . . . said . . . , 'Master, *check* your disciples'
   23 40   [One of the criminals abused Jesus,] but the other spoke up and *rebuked* him. 'Have you no fear of God at all?'
2 Tm 4 2   proclaim the message . . . refute [falsehood], ⌜*correct* (lit. *reprove*) [error], call to obedience –
Jude   9 Θ the archangel Michael [said to the devil], 'Let the Lord ⌜*correct* (lit. *rebuke*) you'.

5. SPEAK HARSHLY TO: *EPI-PLĒSSŌ*

epi-plēssō 1

1 Tm 5 1   Do not *speak harshly to* a man older than yourself,

6. HAVE A COMPLAINT AGAINST (A PERSON): *ECHŌ KATA, PROS*

1 *echō kata* (+ gen.) 5   2 *echō pros* (+ acc.) 2

Mt 5 23   if you . . . remember that your brother *has something against* you [go and be reconciled with him first]
Mk 11 25   when you stand in prayer, forgive whatever you *have against* anybody,
Ac 19 38 2 If Demetrius and the craftsmen . . . want to *complain* about anyone, there are the assizes
   24 19   [the] Jews from Asia . . . should have . . . accused me of
          2 whatever they *had against* me.
Rv 2 4   I *have* this *complaint* [to make] (§ *against* you): you have less love now than you used to
      14   I *have* one or two *complaints* [to make]:
      20   I *have* a *complaint* [to make]: you are encouraging the woman Jezebel

7. COMPLAIN – MURMUR (AGAINST), GRUMBLE (AT): *GONGYSMOS*

2 *gongysmos* 4   1 *gongyzō* 8
4 *gongystēs* 1   3 *dia-gongyzō* 2

Mt 20 11 < [the vineyard labourers] *grumbled* at the landowner.
Lk 5 30   The Pharisees and their scribes *complained* to his disciples . . . 'Why do you eat and drink with tax collectors . . .?'
   15 2 3 the Pharisees and the scribes *complained*. 'This man . . . welcomes sinners
   19 7 3 They all *complained* . . . 'He has gone to stay at a sinner's house'
Jn 6 41   the Jews were *complaining* to each other about [Jesus] –
      43   [43] Jesus said in reply, 'Stop *complaining* to each other.'
      61   Jesus was aware that his followers were *complaining* . . . and said, 'Does this upset you?'
    7 12 2 People stood in groups ⌜*whispering* (lit. *murmuring*) about [Jesus].
      32   Hearing that ⌜*rumours* (lit. *murmurings*) like this about [Jesus] were spreading among the people, the Pharisees sent the Temple police to arrest him.
Ac 6 1 2 the Hellenists made a *complaint* against the Hebrews:
1 Co 10 10   You must never *complain*: some of [our fathers] ⌜*did* (lit. *complained*), and they were killed
Ph 2 14 2 Do all that has to be done without *complaining* or arguing
1 P 4 9 2 Welcome each other into your houses without *grumbling*.
Jude 16 4 They are ⌜*mischief-makers* (lit. *murmurers*), grumblers

8. THREATEN – WARN (NEVER TO) – CAUTION (NOT TO): *AP-EILEŌ*

1 *ap-eilē* 3   3 *pros-ap-eileō* 1
2 *ap-eileō* 2

Ac 4 17 2 let us *caution* them never to speak to anyone in this name again.
      21 3 The court repeated the *warnings* and then released [Peter and John];
      29   And now, Lord, take note of their *threats*
    9 1   Saul was still breathing *threats* to slaughter the Lord's disciples.
Ep 6 9   those of you who are employers, . . . do without *threats*,
1 P 2 23 X 2 [Christ] was insulted and . . . he *made no threats*

9. STERNLY WARN – ANGRILY EXPRESS INDIGNATION WITH: *EM-BRIMAOMAI*

em-brimaomai 3/5

Mt 9 30 X Jesus *sternly warned* [the two blind men], 'Take care that no one learns about this'.
Mk 1 43 X Jesus . . . sent [the leper] away and *sternly-ordered* him, 'Mind you say nothing to anyone'
   14 5   Ointment like this could have been sold . . . and the money given to the poor; and they *were angry with* [the woman].

BLESS – PRAISE – GLORY

1. Bless – Praise
1: Bless – Praise: *eu-logeō*
 a) Blessed (by God) – Blessing
 b) Blessed (by Jesus, by a person) – Praise (to God)
 c) Praise falsely – Flatter
2: Praise: *aineō*
 a) Praise (God)
 b) Praise (a person), Congratulate, Commend
3: Speak well of (a person): *kalōs legō*
4: Praise, Honour, of good repute: *eu-phēmia*
5: Commend – Recommendation: *syn-(h)istēmi*

6: Flattery: *kolakeia*
2. Glory, Splendour – Praise, Honour: *doxa*
 a) Glory, Praise, Honour (given) to God – God and the Son Glorified – the Glory of God
 b) Splendour, Brightness, Glory – Honour, Admiration – Proud of, Approval
 c) the Glorious Ones – Celestial Angels
3. Alleluia (Hallelujah)
4. Meritorious – Credit – Glory: *kleos*

B = Bless, Praise // Curse or Insult
C = Curse or Insult // Bless, Praise

1. BLESS – PRAISE

1: BLESS – PRAISE: *EU-LOGEŌ*

1	*eu-logeō*	41	5 *kat-eu-logeō* 1
3	*eu-logētos*	8	4 *en-eu-logeō* 2
2	*eu-logia*	12/26	

a) Blessed (by God) – Blessing

Mt 25 34 C Come, you whom my Father has *blessed*, take . . . the kingdom prepared for you

Ac 3 25 (Gn 22 18) in your offspring all the families of the earth will be *blessed*.
4

Rm 15 29 2 I shall arrive with rich *blessings* from Christ.

Ga 3 8 4 (Gn 12 3) In you all the pagans will be *blessed*.
9 C Those . . . who rely on faith receive the same *blessing* as Abraham.
14 C 2 in Christ Jesus the *blessing* of Abraham might include the pagans,

Ep 1 3 /2 God . . . who has *blessed* us with all the spiritual *blessings* of heaven in Christ.

Heb 6 7 C a field that . . gives the crops that are wanted . . . is
2 given God's *blessing*.
14 (Gn 22 17) I will ˹shower (lit. surely *bless* you with) *blessings* [on you] and give you many descendants.

1 P 3 9 instead, pay back with a blessing . . . so that you inherit
2 a *blessing* yourself.

b) Blessed (by Jesus, by a person) – Praise (to God)

Mt 14 19 he took the 5 loaves and the 2 fish . . . and *said the blessing*.
21 9 (Ps 118 26) *Blessings* on him who comes in the name of the Lord!
23 39 (Ps 118 26) *Blessings* on him who comes in the name of the Lord!
26 26 Jesus took some bread, and when he had *said the blessing* he broke it and gave it to the disciples.

Mk 6 41 Then [Jesus] took the 5 loaves and the 2 fish . . . and *said the blessing*;
8 7 over these [small fish] he *said a blessing* and ordered them to be distributed also.
10 16 5 [Jesus] laid his hands on [the little children] and *gave* them his *blessing*.
11 9 (Ps 118 26) *Blessings* on him who comes in the name of the Lord!
10 *Blessings* on the coming kingdom of our father David!
14 22 [Jesus] took some bread, and when he had *said the blessing* he broke it and gave it to them.
61 ● 3 Are you the Christ . . . the Son of the *Blessed One*?

Lk 1 42 [Elizabeth said:] Of all women you are the most *blessed*, and *blessed* is the fruit of your womb.
64 [Zechariah's] power of speech returned and he spoke and *praised* God.
68 3 (Ps 41 14) *Blessed* be the Lord . . . for he has . . . come to [his people's] rescue
2 28 [Simeon] took [the child Jesus] into his arms and *blessed* God; and he said:
34 Simeon *blessed* them and said to Mary his mother '. . . this child . . is destined . . . to be a sign that is rejected
6 28 C *bless* those who curse you, pray for those who treat you badly.
9 16 Then he took the 5 loaves and the 2 fish . . . and *said the blessing* over them; then he broke them and handed them to his disciples
13 35 (Ps 118 26) *Blessings* on him who comes in the name of the Lord!
19 38 (Ps 118 26) *Blessings* on the King who comes, in the name of the Lord!
24 30 [Jesus] took the bread and *said the blessing*; then he broke it and handed it to them.
50 [Jesus] took them out as far as the outskirts of Bethany, and lifting up his hands he *blessed* them.
51 as he *blessed* them, he . . . was carried up to heaven.
53 they were continually in the Temple ᵛ praising (G *blessing*) God.

Jn 12 13 (Ps 118 26) *Blessings* on the King of Israel, who comes in the name of the Lord.

Ac 3 26 God raised up his servant and sent him to *bless* you

Rm 1 25 3 instead of the creator, who is *blessed* for ever!
9 5 3 Christ who is above all, God for ever *blessed*!
12 14 C *Bless* those who persecute you: never curse them, *bless* them.

1 Co 4 12 C When we are cursed, we answer with a *blessing*;
10 16 2/ The *blessing*-cup that we *bless* is a communion with the blood of Christ,
14 16 Any uninitiated person will never be able to say Amen . . . if you only *bless* God with the spirit,

2 Co 1 3 3 *Blessed* be the God and Father of our Lord Jesus Christ,
11 31 3 The God and Father of the Lord Jesus – *bless* him for ever –

Ep 1 3 3 *Blessed* be God the Father of our Lord Jesus Christ, who has blessed us with all the spiritual blessings of heaven

Heb 7 1 Melchizedek . . . went to meet Abraham . . . and *blessed*
6 him . . . ⁶ But this man . . . *gave* his *blessing* to the
7 holder of the promises. ⁷ Now . . . a *blessing is given* by a superior to an inferior.
11 20 It was by faith that this same Isaac gave his *blessing* to Jacob and Esau
21 By faith Jacob, when he was dying, *blessed* each of Joseph's sons.
12 17 2 when [Esau] wanted to obtain the *blessing* . . . he was rejected

Jm 3 9 C We use [the tongue] to *bless* the Lord and Father, but we also use it to curse men who are made in God's image:
10 C 2 the *blessing* and the curse come out of the same mouth.

1 P 1 3 3 *Blessed* be God the Father of our Lord Jesus Christ, who . . . has given us a new birth
3 9 C Never pay back one wrong with another . . . instead, pay back with a *blessing*. That is what you are called to do, so that you inherit a blessing yourself.

Rv 5 12 2 The Lamb . . . is worthy to be given . . . *blessing*.
13 To the One who is sitting on the throne and to the Lamb,
2 be all *praise*,
7 12 2 with these words, 'Amen. *Praise* . . . to our God . . .'

c) Praise falsely – Flatter

Rm 16 18 People like that . . . confusing the simple-minded with their
2 ˹pious and *persuasive arguments* (or: kind and *flattering* words).

2: PRAISE: *AINEŌ*

2	*aineō*	9	3 *ep-aineō* 6
5	*ainesis*	1	1 *ep-ainos* 11
4	*ainos*	2	

a) Praise (God)

Mt 21 16 (Ps 8 3) By the mouths of children . . . you have made sure
4 of *praise*

Lk 2 13 2 there was a great throng of the heavenly host, *praising* God
20 2 the shepherds went back glorifying and *praising* God for all they had heard and seen;
18 43 4 and all the people . . . gave *praise* to God
19 37 2 the whole group of disciples joyfully began to *praise* God
24 53 2 [the apostles] were continually in the Temple ᵛ *praising* (G blessing) God.

Ac 2 47 2 [The early Christians] *praised* God
3 8 [after his cure the lame man] went with [Peter and John]
2 into the Temple . . . *praising* God. ⁹ Everyone could see
9 2 him walking and *praising* God,

Rm 15 11 2 (Ps 117 1) Let all the pagans *praise* the Lord, let all the
3 peoples *sing* his *praises*.

Ep 1 6 [God chose us] to make us *praise* the glory of his grace,
12 [we were] chosen to be, for ˹his greater (lit. the *praise* of his) glory, the people who would put their hopes in Christ
14 those whom God has taken for his own, to make his glory *praised*.

Ph 1 11 you will reach the perfect goodness . . . for the glory and *praise* of God.

Heb 13 15 5 let us offer God an unending sacrifice of *praise*,

Rv 19 5 2 (Ps 135 1) *Praise* our God, you servants of his

b) Praise (a person), Congratulate, Commend

Lk 16 8 < 3 The master *praised* the dishonest steward for his astuteness.

Rm 2 29 The real Jew . . . may not be *praised* by man, but he will be [praised] by God.
13 3 you must live honestly and authority may even *honour* you.

1 Co 4 5 Leave [judgement] until the Lord comes . . . Then will be the time for each one to have whatever *praise* he deserves,
11 2 3 ˹You have done well in (lit. I *commend* you for) . . . maintaining the traditions
17 3 I cannot ˹say that you have done well in (lit. *commend* you for) holding meetings that do you more harm than good.
22 3 What am I to say to you? *Congratulate* you? I cannot
3 *congratulate* you on this.

2 Co 8 18 the brother who is ˹famous for (lit. has been *commended* by) spreading the gospel.

Ph 4 8 fill your minds with . . . everything that can be thought virtuous or worthy of *praise*.

1 P 1 7 when . . . your faith will have been tested and proved like gold . . . you will have *praise*
2 14 [Accept] the governors as commissioned by [the Lord] to . . . *praise* good citizenship.

3: SPEAK WELL OF (A PERSON): *KALŌS LEGŌ*

kalōs legō 1

Lk 6 26 C   Alas for you when the world *speaks well of* you!

4: PRAISE, HONOUR, OF GOOD REPUTE: *EU-PHĒMIA*

1 *eu-phēmia 1*   2 *eu-phēmos 1*

2Co 6 8 C   [We are God's servants,] prepared for . . . blame or *praise*;
Ph 4 8   2 fill your minds with everything that . . . we love and *honour*,

5: COMMEND – RECOMMENDATION: *SYN-(H)ISTĒMI*

1 *syn-(h)istēmi, -anō 9/16*   2 *sy-statikos 1*

Rm 16 1   I *commend* to you our sister Phoebe.
2Co 3 1   Does this sound like a new attempt to *commend* ourselves
            2 to you? . . . we need no letters of *recommendation*
    4 2   the way we *commend* ourselves to every human being with
            a conscience is by stating the truth
    5 12   This is not another attempt to *commend* ourselves to you:
    6 4   we ⌜prove we are (or: *commend* ourselves as) servants of
            God
  10 12   We are not being so bold as to . . . invite comparison with
            certain people who ⌜write their own references (lit.
            recommend themselves.
    18 ●   It is not the man who *commends* himself that can be accepted,
            but the man who is *commended* by the Lord.
  12 11   you are the ones who should have been *commending* me.

6: FLATTERY: *KOLAKEIA*

kolakeia 1

1 Th 2 5   never . . . have our speeches been simply *flattery*,

2. GLORY, SPLENDOUR – PRAISE, HONOUR: *DOXA*

1 *doxa 167*   4 *en-doxazō 2*
2 *doxazō 61*   3 *en-doxos 3/4*
                 5 *syn-doxazō 1*

P = Glory, Splendour //Power

a) Glory, Praise, Honour (given) to God – God and the Son Glorified – the Glory of God

Mt 5 16   2 so that, seeing your good works, they may *give the praise*
            to your Father
    6 13 P   (ᵛ yours is the kingdom, the power and the *glory*, for ever)
    9 8   2 the crowd . . . *praised* God for giving such power to men.
  15 31   2 The crowds were astonished . . . and they *praised* the God
            of Israel.
  16 27   the Son of Man is going to come in the *glory* of his Father
            with his angels,
  19 28   when . . . the Son of Man sits on his throne of *glory*,
  24 30 P   they will see the Son of Man coming . . . with power and
            great *glory*.
  25 31   When the Son of Man comes in his *glory* . . . he will take
            his seat on his throne of *glory*.
Mk 2 12   2 they . . . all . . . *praised* God saying, 'We have never seen
            anything like this'.
    8 38   the Son of Man . . . when he comes in the *glory* of his Father
            with the holy angels.
  10 37   Allow us to sit . . . in your *glory*.
  13 26 P   they will see the Son of Man coming . . . with great power
            and *glory*;
Lk 2 9   the *glory* of the Lord shone round [the shepherds].
    14   *Glory* to God in the highest heaven,
    20   2 the shepherds went back *glorifying* and praising God
    32   [my eyes have seen the salvation] and the *glory* of your
            people Israel.
    4 15   2 [Jesus] taught in their synagogues and everyone *praised*
            him.
    5 25   2 [the paralytic] went home *praising* God.
    26   2 They were all astounded and *praised* God,
    7 16   2 Everyone was filled with awe and *praised* God
    9 26   when [the Son of Man] comes in his own *glory* and in that
            of the Father and the holy angels.
    31   [they were Moses and Elijah] appearing in *glory*, and they
            were speaking of his passing
    32   Peter and his companions . . . saw his *glory*
  13 13   2 [the crippled woman] straightened up, and she *glorified*
            God.

Lk 17 15   2 one of [the ten lepers] turned back *praising* God
    18   It seems that no one has come back to give *praise* to God,
            except this foreigner.
  18 43   [the blind man's] sight returned and he followed him
         2 *praising* God,
  19 38   *glory* in the highest heavens!
  21 27 P   they will see the Son of Man . . . with power and great
            glory.
  23 47   2 the centurion . . . *gave praise* to God and said, 'This was a
            great and good man'.
  24 26   Was it not ordained that the Christ should suffer and so
            enter into his *glory*?
Jn 1 14   [The Word,] we saw his *glory*, the *glory* that is his as the
            only Son of the Father,
    2 11   Jesus . . . at Cana . . . let his *glory* be seen,
    5 44   you . . . are not concerned with the *approval* that comes
            from the one God
    7 18   when [a man] is working for the *honour* of one who sent him,
            then he is sincere
    39   2 because Jesus had not yet been *glorified*.
    8 54   2/ If I were to *seek* my own *glory* that would be no *glory* at all;
         2 my *glory* is conferred by the Father,
    9 24   Give *glory* to God! . . . this man is a sinner.
  11 4   This sickness will end . . . in God's *glory* and through it
         2 the Son of God will be *glorified*.
    40   if you believe you will see the *glory* of God
  12 16   2 after Jesus had been *glorified*, [his disciples] remembered
    23   2 Now the hour has come for the Son of Man to be *glorified*.
    28 2/2 Father, *glorify* your name! A voice came from heaven, 'I
         have *glorified* it, and I will *glorify* it again'.
    41   Isaiah . . . saw his *glory*,
    43   they put *honour* from men before the *honour* that comes
            from God.
  13 31   2 Now has the Son of Man been *glorified*, and in him God has
    32 2/2 been *glorified*. ³² If God has been *glorified* in him, God
       2/2 will in turn *glorify* him in himself, and will *glorify* him
         very soon.
  14 13   Whatever you ask . . . I will do, so that the Father may be
         2 *glorified* in the Son.
  15 8   2 It *is to the glory of* my Father that you should bear much
            fruit,
  16 14 Ⓢ 2 [the Spirit of truth] will *glorify* me,
  17 1 2/2 Father . . . *glorify* your Son so that your Son may *glorify*
            you;
    4   2 I have *glorified* you on earth
    5   2/ Father . . . *glorify* me with that *glory* I had with you
    10   2 [they belong to you] and in them I am *glorified*.
    22   I have given them the *glory* you gave to me,
    24   so that they may always see the *glory* you have given me
  21 19   2 the kind of death by which Peter would *give glory* to
            God.
Ac 3 13   2 the God of our ancestors . . . has *glorified* his servant Jesus,
    4 21   2 all the people were *giving glory* to God for what had
            happened.
    7 2   The God of *glory* appeared to our ancestor Abraham,
    55   Stephen . . . saw the *glory* of God,
  11 18   2 and they *gave glory* to God. 'God' they said 'can evidently
            grant even the pagans the repentance . . .'
  12 23   because [Herod] had not given the *glory* to God.
  13 48   2 the pagans . . . *thanked* the Lord for his message
  21 20   2 They *gave glory* to God when they heard this.
Rm 1 21   2 they knew God and yet refused to *honour* him as God or to
            thank him;
    23   they exchanged the *glory* of the immortal God
    2 7   For those who sought *glory* and honour and immortality . . .
    10   *glory*, honour and peace will come to everyone who does good
    3 7   since my untruthfulness makes God demonstrate his truth-
            fulness and thus gives him *glory*,
    23   Both Jew and pagan sinned and forfeited God's *glory*,
    4 20   Abraham . . . *gave glory* to God,
    5 2   we can boast about looking forward to God's *glory*.
    6 4   as Christ was raised from the dead by the Father's *glory*,
    8 17   we are . . . coheirs with Christ, sharing his sufferings so as
        5 to *share* his *glory*.
    18   what we suffer in this life can never be compared to the
            glory, as yet unrevealed, which is waiting for us.
    21   to enjoy the same freedom and *glory* as the children of God.
    30   2 with those [God] justified he shared his *glory*.
    9 4   [Israelites] were adopted as sons, they were given the *glory*
            and the covenants;
    23   to whom he wants to reveal the richness of his *glory*, people
            he had prepared for this *glory* long ago.
  11 36   To him be *glory* for ever! Amen.
  15 6   2 so that . . . you may *give glory* to the God and Father of
            our Lord Jesus Christ.
    7   It can only be to God's *glory* then, for you to treat each other
            . . . as Christ treated you.
    9   2 it was also to get the pagans to *give glory* to God for his
            mercy,
  16 27   give *glory* therefore to him . . . for ever and ever.

1 Co 2 7 The hidden wisdom of God . . . is the wisdom that God predestined to be for our *glory* before the ages began.

8 they would not have crucified the Lord of *Glory*;

6 20 2 you should use your body for the *glory* of God.

10 31 Whatever you eat . . . do it for the *glory* of God.

11 7 A man . . . is the image of God and reflects God's *glory*; but woman is the reflection of man's glory.

15 43 the thing that is sown is contemptible but what is raised is *glorious*;

2 Co 1 20 we answer Amen to the *praise* of God.

4 4 to stop them seeing the light shed by the Good News of the *glory* of Christ, who is the image of God.

6 to radiate the light of the knowledge of God's *glory*, the glory on the face of Christ.

15 so that the more grace is multiplied among people, the more thanksgiving there will be, to the *glory* of God.

17 the troubles . . . though they weigh little, train us for the carrying of a weight of eternal *glory*

8 19 this errand of mercy that, for the *glory* of God, we have undertaken

23 the other two brothers, who are delegates of the churches, are a real *glory* to Christ.

9 13 2 that makes them *give glory* to God for the way you accept and profess the gospel

Ga 1 5 [God our Father], to whom be *glory* for ever and ever.

24 2 [the churches in Judaea] *gave glory* to God for me.

Ep 1 6 [God chose us] to make us praise the *glory* of his grace,

12 [we were chosen from the beginning] for his greater *glory*,

14 those whom God has taken for his own, to make his *glory* praised.

17 May . . . the Father of *glory*, give you a spirit of wisdom

18 P so that you can see . . . what rich *glories* he has promised the saints will inherit

3 13 the trials that I go through . . . are your *glory*.

16 Out of his infinite *glory*, may [God] give you the power

21 *glory* be to him . . . in the Church and in Christ Jesus

5 27 3 so that when [Christ] took [the Church] to himself she would be *glorious*,

Ph 1 11 for the *glory* and praise of God.

2 11 [every tongue should acclaim] Jesus Christ as Lord, to the *glory* of God the Father.

3 21 [Jesus Christ] will transfigure these wretched bodies of ours into copies of his *glorious* body.

4 19 God will fulfil all your needs . . . as lavishly and *gloriously* as only God can.

20 *Glory* to God, our Father, for ever and ever.

Col 1 11 P You will have in you the strength, based on his own *glorious* power, to give in,

27 It was God's purpose . . . to show all the rich *glory* of this mystery to pagans. The mystery is Christ among you, your hope of *glory*:

3 4 you too will be revealed in all your *glory* with [Christ].

1 Th 2 12 God, who is calling you to share the *glory* of his kingdom.

2 Th 1 9 It will be their punishment to be . . . excluded from the presence of the Lord and from the *glory* of his strength

10 P 4 10 . . . when he comes to be *glorified* among his saints

12 4 the name of our Lord Jesus Christ will be *glorified* in you and you in him,

2 14 so that you should share the *glory* of our Lord Jesus Christ.

3 1 4 pray that the Lord's message may . . . be *received with honour*

1 Tm 1 11 [the sound teaching] that goes with the Good News of the *glory* of the blessed God,

17 To the eternal King . . . *glory* for ever and ever.

3 16 [Christ] was made visible in the flesh . . . taken up in *glory*.

2 Tm 2 10 so that . . . [the chosen] may have the salvation . . . and the eternal *glory*

4 18 To him be *glory* for ever and ever.

Tt 2 13 the Appearing of the *glory* of our great God and saviour Christ Jesus.

Heb 1 3 [the Son] is the radiant light of God's *glory* . . . gone to take his place . . . at the right hand

2 7 (Ps 8 6) you crowned [the Son of Man] with *glory* and splendour.

9 we do see in Jesus one who . . . is now crowned with *glory* and splendour

10 it was his purpose to bring a great many of his sons into *glory*,

3 3 [Jesus] has been found to deserve a greater *glory* than Moses.

5 5 2 Nor did Christ *give* himself *the glory* of becoming high priest,

9 5 outspread over [the throne of mercy] were the *glorious* cherubs.

13 21 through Jesus Christ, to whom be *glory* for ever and ever.

Jm 2 1 do not try to combine faith in Jesus Christ, our *glorified* Lord, with the making of distinctions

1 P 1 7 your faith will have been tested . . . and then you will have praise and *glory* and honour.

8 2 you are already filled with a joy so *glorious* that it cannot be described,

1 P 1 11 The Spirit of Christ . . . foretold the sufferings of Christ and the *glories* that would come after them,

21 Through [Christ] you now have faith in God, who . . . gave him *glory*

2 12 so that [pagans] can see your good works for themselves and . . . 2 ⌐give thanks to (or: *glorify*) God

4 11 P 2 so that in everything God may *receive the glory*, through Jesus Christ, since to him alone belong all *glory* and power

13 you will enjoy a much greater gladness when [Christ's] *glory* is revealed.

14 Ⓢ you have the Spirit of *glory* . . . resting on you.

16 if anyone of you should suffer for being a Christian . . . he 2 should *thank* God that he has been called one.

5 1 I have a share in the *glory* that is to be revealed.

4 you will be given the crown of unfading *glory*.

10 P God . . . who called you to eternal *glory*

2 P 1 3 P God himself, who has called us by his own *glory* and goodness.

17 [Jesus] was honoured and *glorified* by God the Father, when the Sublime *Glory* itself spoke to him

3 18 To him be *glory*, in time and in eternity.

Jude 24 Glory be to him who can . . . bring you safe to his *glorious* presence.

25 P To God, the only God . . . be the *glory*, majesty,

Rv 1 6 P to him, then, be *glory* and power for ever and ever

4 9 the animals *glorified* and honoured . . . the One sitting on the throne,

11 P our God, you are worthy of *glory* and honour

5 12 P The Lamb that was sacrificed is worthy to be given power . . . *glory*

13 P To the One who is sitting on the throne . . . be . . . honour, *glory* and power,

7 12 P Amen. Praise and *glory* . . . and strength to our God

11 13 the survivors . . . could only *praise* the God of heaven.

14 7 Fear God and *praise* him,

15 4 2 Who would not revere and *praise* your name, O Lord?

8 P The smoke from the *glory* and the power of God filled the temple

16 9 people . . . cursed the name of God . . . and they would not repent and *praise* him.

18 1 I saw another angel . . . the earth was lit up with his *glory*.

19 1 P Victory and *glory* and power to our God!

7 give *praise* to God, because this is the time for the marriage of the Lamb.

21 11 [Jerusalem coming down from God out of heaven] had all the radiant *glory* of God

23 [the city] was lit by the radiant *glory* of God

b) Splendour, Brightness, Glory – Honour, Admiration – Proud of, Approval

Mt 4 8 all the kingdoms of the world and their *splendour*.

6 2 2 this is what the hypocrites do . . . to win men's *admiration*.

29 Solomon in all his ⌐*regalia* (or: *glory*)

Lk 4 6 P I will give you all this power and the *glory* of these kingdoms, for it has been committed to me

7 25 3 those who go in for *fine* clothes

12 27 Solomon in all his ⌐*regalia* (or: *glory*)

14 10 everyone with you at the table will see you *honoured*.

Jn 5 41 As for human *approval*, this means nothing to me.

44 you look to one another for *approval*

7 18 When a man's doctrine is his own he is hoping to get *honour* for himself;

8 50 X Not that I care for my own *glory*,

54 X 2/ If I were to *seek* my own *glory* that would be no *glory* at all;

12 43 they put *honour* from men before the honour that comes from God.

Ac 22 11 The light had been so *dazzling* that I was blind

Rm 11 13 I have been sent to the pagans as their apostle, and I am 2 *proud* of being sent,

1 Co 4 10 3 you are *celebrities*, we are nobodies.

11 7 O but woman is the *reflection of the glory* of man.

15 a woman . . . thinks long hair her *glory*

12 26 2 If one part [of the body] is *given* special *honour*, all parts enjoy it.

15 40 the heavenly bodies have a ⌐beauty (lit. *splendour*) of their own and the earthly bodies a different one. 41 The sun has its *brightness*, the moon a different *brightness*, and the stars a different *brightness*, and the stars differ from each other in *brightness*.

2 Co 3 7 if the administering of death . . . was accompanied by such a *brightness* that the Israelites could not bear looking at the face of Moses, though it was a *brightness* that faded, 8 then how much greater will be the *brightness* that surrounds the administering of the Spirit! 9 For if there was any *splendour* in administering condemnation, there must be very much greater *splendour* in administering justification. 10 compared with this greater *splendour*, the

10 2 thing that used to have such *splendour* now seems to have no *splendour*; 11 and if what was so temporary had

11 2 any *splendour*, there must be much more *splendour* in what is going to last for ever.

2 Co	3 18	our unveiled faces reflecting like mirrors the *brightness of the Lord*, [we] all grow *brighter* and *brighter* as we are turned into the image that we reflect;
	6 8	[we are God's servants] prepared for *honour* or disgrace,
Ph	3 19	they are *proudest of* something they ought to think shameful;
1 Th	2 6	nor have we ever looked for any special *honour* from men,
	20	you are our *pride* and our joy.
1 P	1 24	(Is 40 6 G) All flesh is grass and its *glory* like the wild flower's.
Rv	18 7	2 Every one of [Babylon's] *shows* and orgies
	21 24	the kings of the earth will bring it their ʳ*treasures* (lit. *glory*).
	26	the nations will come, bringing their ʳ*treasure* (lit. *glory*) and their wealth.

c) the Glorious Ones – Celestial Angels

2 P	2 10	people with no reverence are not afraid of offending against *the glorious ones*,
Jude	8	these people . . . not only . . . disregard authority, but abuse *the glorious angels* as well.

3. ALLELUIA (HALLELUJAH)

hallēlouia 4

Rv	19 1	the great sound of a huge crowd in heaven, singing, '*Alleluia!*
	3	Victory . . . to our God . . .' ³ They sang again, '*Alleluia!*'
	4	the twenty-four elders and the four animals prostrated themselves . . . and they cried, 'Amen, *Alleluia*'.
	6	I seemed to hear the voices of a huge crowd . . . answering, '*Alleluia!* The reign of the Lord . . . has begun;'

4. MERITORIOUS – CREDIT – GLORY: *KLEOS*

kleos 1

1 P	2 20	there is nothing *meritorious* (or: what *credit* is there) in taking a beating patiently if you have done something wrong to deserve it.

BOAST – PROUD – ARROGANT

1. (Something to) Boast about, Make oneself superior to – (Be) Proud of, Take pride in – Rejoice in, Glory, in: *kauchaomai*

2. Boastful
1: Boastful, Proud – Pride: *alazoneia*
2: Boastful – Put on airs: *perpereuomai*
3: Boastful, High flown – Big (of words): *hyper-onkos*

3. Arrogance, Arrogant
1: Arrogant – Wilful, Headstrong: *auth-adēs*
2: Arrogance: *phruassō*

3: Arrogance, Pride – Proud, Haughty, Arrogant: *hyper-ēphania*
4. **(Be) Conceited, Self-important, Puffed up – Inflate with Pride – Arrogance, Obstinacy:** *physioō*
5. **Demented by Pride, Swollen with Self-importance, Full of Self-conceit – Conceited, Pompous:** *typhoō*
6. **Proudly claim to do – Boasts, Claims:** *aucheō*
7. **Conceit, Vanity – Vainglory:** *keno-doxia*
8. **Exaggerate one's importance, Think highly of oneself:** *hyper-phroneō*

1. (SOMETHING TO) BOAST ABOUT, MAKE ONESELF SUPERIOR TO – (BE) PROUD OF, TAKE PRIDE IN – REJOICE IN, GLORY IN: *KAUCHAOMAI*

1	*kauchaomai 36*	4 *kata-kauchaomai 4*
2	*kauchēma 11*	5 *en-kauchaomai 1*
3	*kauchēsis 11*	

Rm	2 17	you call yourself a Jew . . . and *are proud of* your God,
	23	By *boasting* about the Law and then disobeying it, you bring God into contempt.
	3 27	3 So what becomes of our *boasts*? There is no room for them.
	4 2	If Abraham was justified as a reward for doing something,
	2	he would really have had *something to boast about*,
	5 2	we can *boast* about looking forward to God's glory.
	3	we can *boast* about our sufferings.
	11	we are *filled with joyful trust* in God, through our Lord Jesus Christ,
	11 18	4 but still, do not *make* yourself *superior* to the branches; if
	4	you do *make* yourself *superior*, remember that you do not support the root;

Rm	15 17	3 I have some reason to be *proud of* what I, in union with Christ Jesus, have been able to do for God.
1 Co	1 29	The human race has nothing to *boast* about to God,
	31	(Jr 9 23) if anyone wants to *boast*, let him *boast* about the Lord.
	3 21	there is nothing to *boast* about in anything human:
	4 7	if [some special right] was given, how can you *boast* as though it were not?
	5 6	2 The *pride* that you take in yourselves is hardly to your credit.
	9 15	2 I would rather die than let anyone take away *something* that
	16	2 *I* can *boast of*. ¹⁶ Not that I do *boast* of preaching the gospel, since it is a duty
	15 31	3 I can swear it by the *pride* that I take in you in Christ Jesus
2 Co	1 12	3 There is one *thing we are proud of*, and our conscience tells us it is true:
	14	2 you can be as *proud of* us as we are of you.
	5 12	2 we are simply giving you reasons to be *proud of* us, so that you will have an answer ready for the people who can *boast* more about what they seem than what they are.
	7 4	3 I am so *proud of* you that . . . my joy is overflowing.
	14	I had rather *boasted* to [Titus] about you . . . in fact, our
	3	*boasting* to Titus has proved to be . . . true.
	8 24	3 prove to [all the churches] that we are right to be *proud of* you.
	9 2	I know how anxious you are to help; in fact, I *boast* about you to the Macedonians,
	3	2 I am sending the brothers . . . to make sure that our *boasting* about you does not prove to have been empty this time,
	10 8	Maybe I do *boast* rather too much about our authority,
	13	We, on the other hand, are not going to *boast* without a standard to measure against:
	15	So we are not *boasting* without any measure,
	16	not *boasting* of the work already done.
	17	(Jr 9 23) If anyone wants to *boast*, let him *boast* of the Lord.
	11 10	3 this *cause of boasting* will never be taken from me in the regions of Achaia.
	12	leaving no opportunity for those people who are looking for an opportunity to claim equality with us in what they *boast of*.
	16	let me *do a little boasting* of my own.
	17	What I am going to say now is . . . said . . . in the certainty
	3	that I have *something to boast about*.
	18	So many others have been *boasting* of their worldly achievements, that I will *boast* myself.
	30	If I am to *boast*, then let me *boast* of my own feebleness.
	12 1	Must I go on *boasting*, though there is nothing to be gained by it?
	5	I will *boast* about a man like that, but I will not *boast* about
	6	anything of my own except my weaknesses. ⁶ If I should decide to *boast*, I should not be made to look foolish,
	9	I shall be very happy to make my weaknesses my special *boast*
Ga	6 4	Let each of you examine his own conduct; if you find
	2	*anything to boast about*, it will at least be something of your own,
	13	they only want you to be circumcised so that they can *boast* of the fact.
	14	the only thing I can *boast* about is the cross of our Lord
Ep	2 9	[you have been saved through faith;] not by anything that you have done, so that nobody can *claim the credit*.
Ph	1 26	2 so you will have another *reason to* ʳ*give praise* to (lit. *rejoice in*) Christ Jesus on my account
	2 16	2 This would give me *something to be proud of* for the Day of Christ,
	3 3	We are the real people of the circumcision, we who . . . *have our own glory* from Christ Jesus
1 Th	2 19	3 you will be the crown of which we shall be *proudest* in the presence of our Lord Jesus
2 Th	1 4	5 among the churches of God we can *take* special *pride in* you
Heb	3 6	we are his house, as long as we cling to our hope with the
	2	confidence that we *glory* in.
Jm	1 9	It is right for the poor brother to *be proud of* his high rank, ¹⁰ and the rich one to be thankful that he has been humbled,
	2 13	4 the merciful ʳ*need have no fear* of (lit. *may glory in*) judgement.
	3 14	if at heart you have the bitterness of jealousy . . . never
	4	*make* any *claims* for yourself
	4 16	/3 how *proud* and sure of yourselves you are now! *Pride* of this kind is always wicked.

2. BOASTFUL

1: BOASTFUL, PROUD – PRIDE: *ALAZONEIA*

1	*alazoneia 2*	2 *alazōn 2*

Rm	1 30	2 arrogant and *boastful*, enterprising in sin,
2 Tm	3 2	2 People will be self-centred and grasping; *boastful*, arrogant
Jm	4 16	how proud and ʳsure (lit. *boastful*) of yourselves you are now!

1 Jn 2 16   nothing the world has to offer – . . . the lustful eye, *pride* in possessions – could ever come from the Father but only from the world;

2: BOASTFUL – PUT ON AIRS: *PERPEREUOMAI*

perpereuomai 1

1 Co 13 4   love is never *boastful* or conceited;

3: BOASTFUL, HIGH-FLOWN – BIG (OF WORDS): *HYPER-ONKOS*

hyper-onkos 2

2 P 2 18   With their *high-flown* talk, which is all hollow, they tempt
Jude 16   with mouths full of *boastful* talk,

3. ARROGANCE, ARROGANT

1: ARROGANT – WILFUL, HEADSTRONG: *AUTH-ADĒS*

auth-adēs 2

Tt 1 7   [the elder] must be irreproachable: never an *arrogant* or hot-tempered man, nor a heavy drinker
2 P 2 10   ⌜people with no reverence (lit. *wilful* or *headstrong* people) are not afraid of offending against the glorious ones,

2: ARROGANCE: *PHRUASSŌ*

phruassō 1

Ac 4 25   (Ps 2 1) Why this ⌜*arrogance* (or: rage) among the nations,

3: ARROGANCE, PRIDE – PROUD, HAUGHTY, ARROGANT: *HYPER-ĒPHANIA*

2 hyper-ēphania 1   *1 hyper-ēphanos 5*

Mk 7 22   2 fornication . . . envy, slander, *pride*, folly.
Lk 1 51   [God] has routed the *proud* of heart.
Rm 1 30   rude, *arrogant* and boastful,
2 Tm 3 2   People will be . . . boastful, *arrogant* and rude;
Jm 4 6   (Pr 3 34 G) God opposes the *proud*
1 P 5 5   (Pr 3 34 G) God refuses the *proud*

4. (BE) CONCEITED, SELF-IMPORTANT, PUFFED UP – INFLATE WITH PRIDE – ARROGANCE, OBSTINACY: *PHYSIOŌ*

1 physioō 7   *2 physiōsis 1*

1 Co 4 6   it is not for you, so full of your own *importance*, to go taking sides for one man against another.
    18   some of you became *self-important*, ¹⁹ but . . . I shall want
    19   to know not what these *self-important* people have to say, but what they can do,
  5 2   How can you be so *proud* of yourselves?
  8 1   knowledge gives *self-importance* – it is love that makes the building grow.
  13 4   love *is* never boastful or *conceited*;
2 Co 12 20   2 I am afraid of . . . *obstinacies* and disorder.
Col 2 18   people like that are . . . *inflating* themselves to a false importance with their worldly outlook.

5. DEMENTED BY PRIDE, SWOLLEN WITH SELF-IMPORTANCE, FULL OF SELF-CONCEIT – CONCEITED, POMPOUS: *TYPHOŌ*

typhoō 3

1 Tm 3 6   [The elder] should not be a new convert, in case *pride* might turn his head and then he might be condemned as the devil
  6 4   [Anyone who teaches anything different] is simply ignorant and must be *full of self-conceit*
2 Tm 3 4   [people] will be treacherous . . . and *demented by pride*,

6. PROUDLY CLAIM TO DO – BOASTS, CLAIMS: *AUCHEŌ*

aucheō 1

Jm 3 5   the tongue . . . can *proudly claim that it does* great things.

7. CONCEIT, VANITY – VAINGLORY: *KENO-DOXIA*

1 keno-doxia 1   *2 keno-doxos 1*

Ga 5 26   2 We must stop being *conceited*, provocative and envious.
Ph 2 3   There must be no competition among you, no *conceit*;

8. EXAGGERATE ONE'S IMPORTANCE, THINK HIGHLY OF ONESELF: *HYPER-PHRONEŌ*

hyper-phroneō 1

Rm 12 3   I want to urge each one among you not to *exaggerate his real importance*.

BODY

1. **Body:** *sōma*
  a) Body, Bodily – Self – Corpse
  b) the Body (of Christ) – Reality
2. **Corpse – Dead body**
  1: *kōlon*
  2: *ptōma*
3. **Skin – the Touch of the body:** *chrōs*
4. **Part of the body – Member, Limb – Organ:** *melos*
5. **The body externally**
  1: Breast(s), Chest: *stēthos*
  2: Breast(s), Chest: *mastos*
  3: Chest: *thōrax*
  4: the Side: *pleura*
  5: Shoulder(s): *ōmos*
  6: the Back: *nōtos*
  7: Bosom – Lap: *kolpos*
  8: Waist – Loins: *osphys*
6. **The body internally**
  1: Stomach – Digestion: *stomachos*
  2: Stomach – Womb: *gastēr*
    a) Stomach
    b) Womb
  3: Stomach – Womb – Breast, Heart: *koilia*
    a) Stomach, Belly
    b) Womb
    c) Breast, Heart
  4: Womb: *mētra*
  5: Loins: *nephros*
  6: Entrails – (Inner) Feeling, Self – Affection, Tender: *splanchna*
    a) Entrails, Bowels
    b) (Inner) Feeling, Self – Affection, Tender(ness)

1. BODY: *SŌMA*

1 sōma   141/142   *3 sōmatikōs 1*
2 sōmatikos   2   *4 sys-sōmos*   1

C = Corpse

a) Body Bodily – Self – Corpse

B = Body that is not human   S = Body // Spirit, Soul

Mt 5 29   it will do you less harm to lose one part of you than to have your whole *body* thrown into hell. ³⁰ . . . to lose one part of you than to have your whole *body* go to hell.
  6 22   The lamp of the *body* is the eye . . . if your eye is sound,
    23   your whole *body* will be filled with light. ²³ But if your eye is diseased, your whole *body* will be all darkness.
    25   I am telling you not to worry about . . . your *body* and how you are to clothe it. Surely . . . the *body* [means] more than clothing!
  10 28 S   Do not be afraid of those who kill the *body* . . . fear him rather who can destroy both *body* and soul in hell.
  27 52 C   the *bodies* of many holy men rose from the dead,
Mk 5 29   [the woman with a haemorrhage] felt in her*self* that she was cured of her complaint.
Lk 3 22 B   2 the Holy Spirit descended on [Jesus] in *bodily* shape, like a dove.
  11 34   The lamp of your *body* is your eye. When your eye is sound, your whole *body* too is filled with light; but when it is diseased your *body* too will be all darkness . . . ³⁶ If, therefore, your whole *body* is filled with light . . . it will be light entirely,
  12 4   Do not be afraid of those who kill the *body*
    22   I am telling you not to worry about . . . your *body* and how you are to clothe it. ²³ For . . . the *body* [means] more than clothing.
  17 37 C   Where the *body* is, there too will the vultures gather.
Jn 19 31 C   to prevent the *bodies* remaining on the cross during the sabbath
Ac 9 40 C   [Peter] turned to the ⌜dead woman (lit. *corpse*) and said, 'Tabitha, stand up'.
Rm 1 24   God left [the wicked] to . . . the practices with which they dishonour their own *bodies*,
  4 19   Even the thought that his *body* was past fatherhood . . did not shake [Abraham's] belief.

Rm 6 6   our former selves have been crucified with [Christ] to destroy this sinful *body*

12   you must not let sin reign in your mortal *bodies*

7 24   Who will rescue me from this *body* doomed to death?

8 10 S   Though your *body* may be dead it is because of sin, but if

11 S   Christ is in you then your spirit is life itself . . . [11] . . . he who raised Jesus from the dead will give life to your own mortal *bodies* through his Spirit

13 S ○   if by the Spirit you put an end to the misdeeds of the *body* you will live.

23   we . . . groan inwardly as we wait for our *bodies* to be set free.

12 1   worship [God], I beg you, . . . by offering your living *bodies* as a holy sacrifice.

1 Co 5 3 S   Though I am far away in *body*, I am with you in spirit,

6 13   the *body* . . . is not meant for fornication; it is for the Lord, and the Lord for the *body*.

15   You know, surely, that your *bodies* are members making up the body of Christ;

16   a man who goes with a prostitute is one *body* with her,

18   Keep away from fornication. All the other sins are committed outside the *body*; but to fornicate is to sin against your own *body*.

19 S   Your *body*, you know, is the temple of the Holy Spirit . . .

20   [20] . . . use your *body* for the glory of God.

7 4   The wife has no rights over her own *body*; it is the husband who has them. In the same way, the husband has no rights over his *body*;

34 S   all [an unmarried woman] need worry about is being holy in *body* and spirit.

9 27   I treat my *body* hard and make it obey me,

13 3   if I even let them take my *body* to burn it, but am without love, it will do me no good whatever.

15 35   what sort of *body* do [dead people] have when they come

37 B   back? . . . [37] . . . the thing that you sow is not ⌐what (lit. the *body* that) is going to come; you sow a bare grain, of wheat . . . [38] and then God gives it the sort of *body*

38 B   that he has chosen: each sort of seed gets its own sort of *body*.

40 B   there are heavenly *bodies* and there are earthly *bodies*;

44 S   when it is sown it *embodies* the soul, when it is raised it *embodies* the spirit. If the soul has its own *embodiment*, so does the spirit have its own [embodiment].

2 Co 4 10   we carry with us in our *body* the death of Jesus, so that the life of Jesus, too, may always be seen in our *body*.

5 6   to live in the *body* means to be exiled from the Lord,

8   we . . . actually want to be exiled from the *body* and make our home with the Lord.

10   each of us will get what he deserves for the things he did in the *body*, good or bad.

10 10   when [Paul] is with you you see only ⌐half a man (lit. a weak *bodily* presence [of a man]) and no preacher at all.

12 2   I know a man in Christ who . . . was caught up – whether still in the *body* or out of the *body*, I do not know . . . –

3   right into the third heaven . . . [3] . . . this same person – whether in the *body* or out of the *body*, I do not know . . . – [4] was caught up into paradise

Ga 6 17   the marks on my *body* are those of Jesus.

Ep 5 28   husbands must love their wives as they love their own *bodies*;

Ph 1 20   My one hope . . . is that . . . I shall have the courage for Christ to be glorified in my *body*, whether by my life or by my death.

3 21   [Jesus Christ] will transfigure these wretched *bodies* of ours into copies of his glorious body.

Col 2 11 ○   you have been circumcised with a circumcision . . . performed . . . by the complete stripping of your *body* of flesh.

23   It may be argued that true wisdom is to be found in these [false ascetics], with their . . . severe treatment of the *body*;

1 Th 5 23 S   may you all be kept safe and blameless, spirit, soul and *body*, for the coming of our Lord Jesus Christ.

1 Tm 4 8   [2] *Physical* exercises are useful enough, but the usefulness of spirituality is unlimited,

Heb 10 22   as we go in, let us be sincere in heart . . . and our *bodies* washed with pure water.

13 3   Keep in mind those who are . . . being badly treated, since you too are in the *body*.

11 B C   The *bodies* of the [sacrificial] animals . . . are burnt outside the camp,

Jm 2 16   without giving them these bare necessities of ⌐life (lit. the *body*),

26 S   A *body* dies when it is separated from the spirit, and in the same way faith is dead if it is separated from good deeds.

3 2   the only man who could reach perfection would be someone . . . able to control every part of him*self*. [3] Once we

3   put a bit into the horse's mouth . . . we have the ⌐whole animal (lit. animal's whole *body*) under our control.

B

6   the tongue is a whole wicked world in itself: it infects the whole *body*;

Jude 9 C   the archangel Michael . . . was engaged in argument with the devil about the *corpse* of Moses,

b) the Body (of Christ) – Reality
M = Mystic body

Mt 26 12   When [this woman] poured this ointment on my *body*, she did it to prepare me for burial.

26   Take [this bread] and eat, . . . this is my *body*.

27 58 C   [Joseph of Arimathaea] went to Pilate and asked for the *body* of Jesus.

59 C   Joseph took the *body*, wrapped it in a clean shroud

Mk 14 8   [this woman] has anointed my *body* beforehand for its burial.

22   Take [this bread] . . . this is my *body*.

15 43 C   Joseph of Arimathaea . . . asked for the *body* of Jesus.

Lk 22 19   This is my *body* which will be given for you;

23 52 C   [Joseph of Arimathaea] went to Pilate and asked for the *body* of Jesus.

55 C   the women . . . took note of the tomb and of the position of the *body*.

24 3 C   on entering [the tomb the women] discovered that the *body* of the Lord Jesus was not there.

23 C   when [the women] did not find the *body*, they came back to tell us

Jn 2 21   [Jesus] was speaking of the sanctuary that was his *body*,

19 38 C   Joseph of Arimathaea . . . asked Pilate to let him remove the *body* of Jesus . . . so they came and took ⌐it (lit. the *body*) away.
C

40 C   They took the *body* of Jesus and wrapped it . . . in linen cloths,

20 12 C   [Mary] saw two angels . . . sitting where the *body* of Jesus had been,

Rm 7 4   you, my brothers, . . . through the *body* of Christ are now dead to the Law,

12 4   Just as each of our *bodies* has several parts . . . [5] so all of

5 M   us, in union with Christ, form one *body*,

1 Co 10 16   the bread that we break is a communion with the *body* of

17 M   Christ. [17] . . . though there are many of us, we form a single *body*

11 24   This is my *body*, which is for you;

27   anyone who eats the bread or drinks the cup of the Lord unworthily will be behaving unworthily towards the *body*

29   and blood of the Lord . . . [29] . . . a person who eats and drinks without recognising the *Body* is eating and drinking his own condemnation.

12 12   Just as a human *body*, though it is made up of many parts, is a single unit because all these parts (§ of the *body*),

13 M   though many, make one *body*, so it is with Christ. [13] In the one Spirit we were all baptised (§ to make only one *body*),

14   Nor is the *body* to be identified with any one of its many

15   parts. [15] If the foot were to say, 'I am not a hand and so I do not belong to the *body*', would that mean that it stopped being part of the *body*? [16] If the ear were to say,

16   '. . . I do not belong to the *body*', would that mean that it was not a part of the *body*? [17] If your whole *body* was

17   just one eye, how would you hear anything? . . . [18] . . .

18   God put all the separate parts into the *body* on purpose. [19] If all the parts were the same, how could it be a *body*?

19   [20] As it is, the parts are many but the *body* is one.

20

22   What is more, it is precisely the parts of the *body* that seem to be the weakest which are the indispensable ones;

23   [23] and it is the least honourable parts of the *body* that we clothe with the greatest care . . . [24] . . . God has arranged

24   the *body* so that more dignity is given to the parts which are without it, [25] and so that there may not be disagree-

25   ments inside the *body*,

27 M   you together are Christ's *body*;

Ep 1 23 M   [God has made Christ the head of the Church] which is his *body*,

2 16 M   [this was] to unite [Jews and pagans] in a single *Body* and reconcile them with God.

3 6 M   pagans now share the same inheritance, . . . they are [parts

4   of] the *same body*, in Christ Jesus

4 4 M   There is one *Body*, one Spirit,

12 M   the saints together make a unity in the work of service, building up the *body* of Christ.

16 M   by [Christ] the whole *body* is . . . joined together . . . So the *body* grows

5 23 M   Christ is head of the Church and saves the whole *body*,

30 M   [the Church] is his *body* – and we are its living parts.

Ph 3 21   [Jesus Christ] will transfigure these wretched bodies of ours into copies of his glorious *body*.

Col 1 18 M   the Church is his *body*, he is its head.

22   he has reconciled you, by his death and in that mortal *body*.

24 M   It makes me happy to suffer for you . . . to make up all that has still to be undergone by Christ for the sake of his *body*, the Church.

Col	2	9	3 In his *body* lives the fullness of divinity,
		17 M	[Festivals and sabbaths] were only pale reflections of what was coming: ⌈the *reality* is (or: the *body* is [that] of) Christ.
		19 M	it is the head that adds strength and holds the whole *body* together,
	3	15 M	it is for [the peace of Christ] that you were called together as parts of one *body*.
Heb	10	5	(Ps 40 7 G) You who wanted no sacrifice or oblation, prepared a *body* for me.
		10	[God's] will was for us to be made holy by the offering of his *body* made once and for all by Jesus Christ.
1 P	2	24	He was bearing our faults in his own *body* on the cross,

2. CORPSE – DEAD BODY

1: CORPSE – DEAD BODY: *KŌLON*

kōlon 1

Heb	3	17	those who made God angry . . . were the ones who sinned and whose *dead bodies* were left lying in the wilderness.

2: CORPSE – DEAD BODY: *PTŌMA*

ptōma 7

Mt	14	12	John's disciples came and took the *body* and buried it;
	24	28	Wherever the *corpse* is, there will the vultures gather.
Mk	6	29	John's disciples . . . came and took his *body* and laid it in a tomb.
	15	45 X	[Pilate] granted the *corpse* to Joseph [of Arimathaea]
Rv	11	8	[The] *corpses* [of the two witnesses] will lie in the main street of the Great City . . . ⁹ Men out of every . . .
		9	nation will stare at their *corpses*, for three-and-a-half days, not letting ⌈them (lit. their *corpses*) be buried,

3. SKIN – THE TOUCH OF THE BODY: *CHRŌS*

chrōs 1

Ac	19	12	handkerchiefs or aprons ⌈which had touched [Paul] (lit. from [contact with] his *skin*) were taken to the sick, and they were cured

4. PART OF THE BODY – MEMBER, LIMB – ORGAN: *MELOS*

melos 35

X = parts of Christ's body

Mt	5	29	it will do you less harm to lose one *part* of you than to have your whole body thrown into hell. ³⁰ . . . it will do you less harm to lose one *part* of you
		30	
Rm	6	13	you must not let any *part of your body* turn into an unholy weapon fighting on the side of sin . . . you should make every *part of your body* into a weapon fighting on the side of God.
		19	as once you put ⌈your bodies (lit. the *parts of your bodies*) at the service of vice . . . so now you must put ⌈them (lit. the *parts of your bodies*) at the service of righteousness.
	7	5	Before our conversion our sinful passions . . . fertilised our ⌈bodies (lit. *members*) to make them give birth to death.
		23	I can see that ⌈my body follows (lit. the *parts of my body* follow) a different law that . . . makes me a prisoner of that law of sin which lives inside my ⌈body (lit. *parts*).
	12	4	each of our bodies has several *limbs* and each *organ* has a separate function, ⁵ so all of us, in union with Christ, form one body, and as *parts* of it we belong to each other.
		5 X	
1 Co	6	15 X	your bodies are *members* making up the body of Christ; do you think I can take *parts* of Christ's *body* and join them to the ⌈body (lit. *members*) of a prostitute?
		X	
	12	12	Just as a human body, though it is made up of many *parts*, is a single unit because all these *parts*, though many, make one body, so it is with Christ.
		14	Nor is the body to be identified with any one of its many *parts*.
		18	God put all the separate *parts* into the body on purpose.
		19	¹⁹ If all the *parts* were the same, how could it be a body?
		20	²⁰ As it is, the *parts* are many but the body is one.
		22	What is more, it is precisely the *parts* of the body that seem to be the weakest which are the indispensable ones.
		25	[God has arranged the body] so that there may not be disagreements inside the body, but that each *part* may be equally concerned for all the others. ²⁶ If one *part* is hurt,
		26	

1 Co	12	26	all *parts* are hurt with it. If one *part* is given special honour, all *parts* enjoy it.
		27 X	you together are Christ's body; but each of you is a different *part* of it.
Ep	4	16	by [Christ] the whole body is . . . joined together, every joint adding its own strength, for each separate *part* to work according to its function.
		25 X	You must speak the truth to one another, since we are all *parts* of one another.
	5	30	[A man looks after his own body, and that is the way Christ treats the Church,] because it is his body – and we are its living *parts*.
Col	3	5	you must kill ⌈everything in (lit. the *part* of) you that belongs only to earthly life: fornication, impurity,
Jm	3	5	So is the tongue only a tiny *part* of the body, but it can proudly claim that it does great things . . . ⁶ . . . Among all the *parts of the body*, the tongue is a whole wicked world in itself;
		6	
	4	1	Where do these . . . battles between yourselves first start? Isn't it precisely in the desires fighting inside your own ⌈selves (lit. *members*)?

5. THE BODY EXTERNALLY

1: BREAST(S), CHEST: *STĒTHOS*

stēthos 5

Lk	18	13	The tax collector . . . beat his *breast* and said, 'God, be merciful'
	23	48	all the people . . . went home beating their *breasts*.
Jn	13	25 X	leaning back on Jesus' *breast* [John] said, 'Who is it, Lord?'
	21	20 X	Peter . . . saw the disciple Jesus loved following them – the one who had leaned on his *breast* at the supper
Rv	15	6	out came the seven angels . . . wearing pure white linen, fastened round their ⌈waists (lit. *chests*) with golden girdles.

2: BREAST(S), CHEST: *MASTOS*

mastos 3

Lk	11	27	Happy the womb that bore you and the *breasts* you sucked!
	23	29	Happy . . . the wombs that have never borne, the *breasts* that have never suckled!
Rv	1	13 X	a Son of man, dressed in a long robe tied at the ⌈waist (lit. *chest*) with a golden girdle.

3: CHEST: *THŌRAX*

thōrax 1/5

Rv	9	9	[The locusts] had ⌈body-armour (or: *chests*) like iron breast-plates,

4: THE SIDE: *PLEURA*

pleura 5

Jn	19	34 X	one of the soldiers pierced his *side* with a lance;
	20	20 X	[Jesus] showed them his hands and his *side*.
		25 X	unless I can put my hand into his *side*, I refuse to believe.
		27 X	[Jesus spoke to Thomas,] Give me your hand; put it into my *side*.
Ac	12	7	the angel . . . tapped Peter on the *side* and woke him.

5: SHOULDER(S): *ŌMOS*

ōmos 2

Mt	23	4	[scribes and Pharisees] tie up heavy burdens and lay them on men's *shoulders*,
Lk	15	5	would he not joyfully take [the sheep] on his *shoulders* . . .?

6: THE BACK: *NŌTOS*

nōtos 1

Rm	11	10	(Ps 69 24) may . . . their *backs* bend for ever.

7: BOSOM – LAP: *KOLPOS*

kolpos 5/6

Lk	6	38	Give, and there will be gifts for you: a full measure . . . will be poured into your ⌈lap (or: *bosom*);

Lk 16 22	the poor man died and was carried away by the angles to the *bosom* of Abraham. The rich man also died and was buried. [23] In his torment in Hades he . . . saw Abraham a long way off with Lazarus in his *bosom*.
23	
Jn 1 18 Θ	it is the only Son, who is ⌐nearest to the Father's heart (lit. in the Father's *bosom*), who has made him known.
13 23 X	The disciple Jesus loved was reclining ⌐next to (lit. on the *bosom* of) Jesus;

8: WAIST – LOINS: *OSPHYS*

osphys 8

Mt 3 4	This man John wore a garment made of camel-hair with a leather belt round his *waist*,
Mk 1 6	John wore a garment of camel-skin (§ and a leather girdle round his *waist*)
Lk 12 35	See that you ⌐are dressed for action (lit. have girded your *loins*)
Ac 2 30	God had sworn [David] an oath to make one of ⌐his descendants (lit. [the descendants of] his *loins*) succeed him on the throne,
Ep 6 14	So stand your ground, with truth buckled round your *waist*,
Heb 7 5	the descendants of Levi . . . are obliged by the Law to take tithes . . . from their own brothers although they too are descended from (§ the *loins* of) Abraham.
10	[Levi] was still in the *loins* of his ancestor
1 P 1 13	⌐Free your minds, then, of encumbrances; control them (lit. Gird up the *loins* of your mind, then; control yourself)

6. THE BODY INTERNALLY

1: STOMACH – DIGESTION: *STOMACHOS*

stomachos 1

1 Tm 5 23	have a little wine for the sake of your *digestion*

2: STOMACH – WOMB: *GASTĒR*

gastēr 2/9

a) Stomach

Tt 1 12	Cretans were never anything but . . . dangerous animals and lazy ⌐gluttons (lit. *stomachs*);

b) Womb

Lk 1 31	You are to conceive in your *womb* and bear a son,

3: STOMACH – WOMB – BREAST, HEART: *KOILIA*

koilia 23

a) Stomach, Belly

Mt 12 40	Jonah was in the *belly* of the sea-monster for three days and three nights,
15 17	whatever goes into the mouth passes through the *stomach* and is discharged into the sewer
Mk 7 19	[whatever goes into a man from outside] does not go into his heart but through his *stomach*
Lk 15 16	[the prodigal son] would willingly have filled his *belly* with the husks the pigs were eating
Rm 16 18	People like that . . . are slaves of their own ⌐appetites (lit. *stomachs*),
1 Co 6 13	Food is only meant for the *stomach*, and the *stomach* for food: yes, and God is going to do away with both of them.
Ph 3 19	[These people] make ⌐foods (lit. the *stomach*) into their god and are proudest of something they ought to think shameful;
Rv 10 9	[the angel said,] Take [the small scroll] and eat it; it will turn your *stomach* sour . . . [10] . . . when I had eaten it my *stomach* turned sour.
10	

b) Womb

Mt 19 12	There are eunuchs born that way from their mother's *womb*,
Lk 1 15	Even from his mother's *womb* [John the Baptist] will be filled with the Holy Spirit,
41	as soon as Elizabeth heard Mary's greeting, the child leapt in her *womb*
42	Of all women you are the most blessed, and blessed is the fruit of your *womb*.
44	the child in my *womb* leapt for joy.
2 21	they gave him the name Jesus, the name the angel had given him ⌐before his conception (lit. while in the *womb*).
11 27	Happy the *womb* that bore you
23 29	people will say, 'Happy are . . . the *wombs* that have never borne'

Jn 3 4	Can [a man] go back into his mother's *womb* and be born again?
Ac 3 2	there was a man being carried past. He was a cripple from ⌐birth (lit. his mother's *womb*);
14 8	A man sat there . . . [whose] feet were crippled from ⌐birth (lit. his mother's *womb*);
Ga 1 15	God . . . had specially chosen me while I was still in my mother's *womb*.

c) Breast, Heart

Jn 7 38	[Let the man come and drink] who believes in me! . . . From his *breast* shall flow fountains of living water.

4: WOMB *MĒTRA*

mētra 2

Lk 2 23	(Ex 13 2) Every ⌐first-born male (lit. male [child] that opens the *womb*) must be consecrated to the Lord
Rm 4 19	Even the thought that . . . ⌐Sarah [was] too old to become a mother (lit. Sarah's *womb* [was] dead too), did not shake [Abraham's] belief.

5: LOINS: *NEPHROS*

nephros 1

Rv 2 23	it is I who search heart and *loins*

6: ENTRAILS – (INNER) FEELING, SELF – AFFECTION, TENDER: *SPLANCHNA*

1	*splanchna* 11	3	*poly-splanchnos* 1
2	*eu-splanchnos* 2		

a) Entrails, Bowels

Ac 1 18	[Judas] burst open, and all his *entrails* poured out.

b) (Inner) Feeling, Self – Affection, Tender(ness)

Lk 1 78 Θ	by the *tender* mercy of our God
2 Co 6 12	the constraint is in your own ⌐selves (or: *affections*).
7 15	[Titus's] own personal *affection* for you is all the greater
Ep 4 32	2 Be friends with one another, and ⌐kind (or: *tender-hearted*),
Ph 1 8 X	God knows how much I miss you all, *loving* you as Christ Jesus loves you.
2 1 X	if love can persuade at all, . . . or any *tenderness* and sympathy, [2] then be united
Col 3 12	you should be clothed in ⌐sincere compassion, in (lit. *feelings* of compassion, of) kindness and humility,
Phm 7	you have ⌐put new heart into (lit. refreshed the *feelings* of) the saints.
12	I am sending [Onesimus] back to you, and with him – I could say – [a part of] my own *self*.
20	⌐put new heart into me (lit. refresh my *feelings*), in Christ.
Jm 5 11 Θ	3 the Lord is ⌐kind (or: *tender-hearted*) and compassionate.
1 P 3 8	be sympathetic; love the brothers, ⌐have compassion (lit. be *tender-hearted*) and be self-effacing.
1 Jn 3 17	If a man . . . saw that one of his brothers was in need, but closed his ⌐heart (lit. *feelings*) to him, how could the love of God be living in him?

BORROW – LEND

1. Borrow – Lend – Creditor: *daneizō* | **2. Lend:** *kichrēmi*

1. BORROW – LEND – CREDITOR: *DANEIZŌ*

2	*daneion* 1	1	*daneizō* 4
3	*daneistēs* 1		

Mt 5 42	if anyone wants to *borrow*, do not turn away,
18 27 <	2 the servant's master . . . cancelled the *debt*.
Lk 6 34	you *lend* to those from whom you hope to receive . . . Even sinners *lend* to sinners to get back the same amount.
35	*lend* without any hope of return.
7 41 <	3 There was once a *creditor* who had two men in his debt;

2. LEND: *KICHRĒMI*

kichrēmi 1

Lk 11 5   My friend, *lend* me three loaves,

BREAK – GRIND – TEAR

1. Break – Crush
  1: Break: *kat-agnymi*
  2: Break – Crush – Shatter: *syn-tribō*
  3: Break up – Dash to pieces: *syn-thlaō*; Crush, Grind, to powder: *likmaō*
  4: Crushed – Oppressed: *thrauō*
  5: Break: *klaō*
    a) Break (bread) – Pieces, Scraps
    b) Break off – Lop off
  6: Break (a person's heart): *syn-thryptō*
2. Mill – Grind – Rub
  1: Millstone – Mill: *mylos*
  2: Millstone: *onikos*
  3: Grinding: *alēthō*
  4: Rub: *psōchō*

3. Tear – Burst – Split
  1: Tear – Break: *rhēgnymi*
    a) Tear (one's clothes)
    b) Tear to pieces – Burst – Break
    c) Break into (shouts of) joy
  2: Tear – Split: *schizō*
    a) Tear – Split
    b) Moral split – Division (of opinion)
  3: Snap apart – Tear to pieces: *dia-spaō*
  4: Burst open: *lakeō*
4. Pluck – Tear off
  1: Pluck, Pick (ears of corn): *tillō*
  2: Pluck out – Tear out: *ex-oryssō*
  3: Tear off (a person's clothes): *peri-rhēgnymi*

---

1. BREAK – CRUSH

1: BREAK: *KAT-AGNYMI*

kat-agnymi 4

Mt 12 20 X   (Is 42 3) He will not *break* the crushed reed
Jn 19 31   the Jews asked Pilate to have the legs *broken*
     32   the soldiers . . . *broke* the legs of the first man . . . and then of the other.
     33   When they came to Jesus, . . . instead of *breaking* his legs [34] one of the soldiers pierced his side

2: BREAK – CRUSH – SHATTER: *SYN-TRIBŌ*

1 *syn-tribō 7*   2 *syn-trimma 1*

Mt 12 20   (Is 42 3) He will not break the *crushed* reed
Mk 5 4   [the madman] had snapped the chains and *broken* the fetters,
   14 3   She *broke* the jar and poured the ointment on [Jesus's] head.
Lk 9 39   [the spirit] is slow to leave him, but when it does it leaves the boy *worn out*.
Jn 19 36   (Ps 34 20) Not one bone of his will be *broken*;
Rm 3 16   2 (Is 59 7) wherever [the sinners] go there is havoc and *ruin*.
   16 20 Θ   The God of peace will soon *crush* Satan beneath your feet.
Rv 2 27   (Ps 2 9) [I will give those who prove victorious the authority over the pagans] to rule them with an iron sceptre and *shatter* them like earthenware.

3: BREAK UP – DASH TO PIECES and CRUSH, GRIND, TO POWDER: *SYN-THLAŌ* and *LIKMAŌ*

1 *likmaō 2*   2 *syn-thlaō 2*

Mt 21 44   2 (§ Anyone who falls on that stone will be *dashed to pieces*; anyone it falls on will be *crushed*.)
Lk 20 18   2 Anyone who falls on that stone will be *dashed to pieces*; anyone it falls on will be *crushed*.

4: CRUSHED – OPPRESSED: *THRAUŌ*

thrauō 1

Lk 4 18   (Is 58 6) The spirit of the Lord has been given to me . . . to set the *downtrodden* free,

5: BREAK: *KLAŌ*

1 *klaō* 14   5 *kata-klaō* 2
4 *klasis* 2   3 *ek-klaō* 3
2 *klasma* 9

a) *Break (bread) – Pieces, Scraps*

Mt 14 19 X   *breaking* the loaves he handed them to his disciples
     20   2 they collected the *scraps* remaining, twelve baskets full.

Mt 15 36 X   he took the seven loaves and the fish, and he gave thanks and *broke* them
     37   2 they collected what was left of the *scraps*, seven baskets full.
   26 26 X   when he had said the blessing he *broke* [the bread] and gave it to the disciples.
Mk 6 41 X   5 [Jesus] said the blessing; then he *broke* the loaves and handed them to his disciples
     43   2 They collected twelve basketfuls of *scraps* of bread and pieces of fish.
    8 6 X   he took the seven loaves, and after giving thanks he *broke* them
      8   2 they collected seven basketfuls of the *scraps* left over.
     19 X   When I *broke* the five loaves . . . how many baskets full of *scraps* did you collect?
     20   when [I broke] the seven loaves . . . how many baskets full of *scraps* did you collect?
   14 22 X   he took some bread, and when he had said the blessing he *broke* it and gave it to them.
Lk 9 16 X   he took the five loaves and the two fish . . . and said the blessing over them; then he *broke* them
     17   2 when the *scraps* remaining were collected they filled twelve baskets.
   22 19 X   Then he took some bread, and when he had given thanks, *broke* it and gave it to them;
   24 30 X   he took the bread and said the blessing; then he *broke* it and handed it to them.
     35 X   4 they told . . . how they had recognised him at the *breaking* of bread.
Jn 6 12   2 Pick up the *pieces* left over,
     13   2 [the disciples] filled twelve hampers with *scraps* left over
Ac 2 42   These remained faithful . . . to the brotherhood, to the *breaking* of bread and to the prayers.
     46   [the faithful] met in their houses for the *breaking* of bread;
   20 7   we met to *break* bread.
     11   [Paul] went back upstairs where he *broke* bread and ate
   27 35   [Paul] took some bread, gave thanks to God in front of them all, *broke* it and began to eat.
1 Co 10 16   the bread that we *break* is a communion with the body of Christ.
    11 24 X   [the Lord Jesus took some bread,] and thanked God for it and *broke* it,

b) *Break off – Lop off*

Rm 11 17   3 some of the branches have been *cut off*,
     19   3 Those branches were *cut off* on purpose to let me be grafted
     20   3 in! . . . [20] they were *cut off*, but through their unbelief;

6: BREAK (A PERSON'S HEART): *SYN-THRYPTŌ*

syn-thryptō 1

Ac 21 13   What are you trying to do – ⌐weaken my resolution (or: *break* my heart) by your tears?

2. MILL – GRIND – RUB

1: MILLSTONE – MILL: *MYLOS*

2 *mylikos 1*   1 *mylos 4*
3 *mylinos 1*

Mt 18 6   anyone who is an obstacle . . . would be better drowned . . . with a great *millstone* round his neck.
   24 41   of two women at the *millstone* grinding, one is taken, one left.
Mk 9 42   anyone who is an obstacle . . . would be better thrown into the sea with a great *millstone* round his neck.
Lk 17 2   It would be better for him to be thrown into the sea with a 2 *millstone* put round his neck
Rv 18 21   3 a powerful angel picked up a boulder like a great *millstone*,
     22   (Jr 25 10) never again will . . . the sound of the *mill* be heard;

2: MILLSTONE: *ONIKOS*

onikos 2

Mt 18 6   anyone who is an obstacle . . . would be better drowned . . . with a great mill*stone* round his neck.
Mk 9 42   anyone who is an obstacle . . . would be better thrown into the sea with a great mill*stone* round his neck.

3: GRINDING: *ALĒTHŌ*

alēthō 2

Mt 24 41   of two women at the millstone *grinding*, one is taken, one left.
Lk 17 35   two women will be *grinding* corn together:

4: RUB: *PSŌCHŌ*

psōchō 1

Lk	6 1	his disciples were picking ears of corn, *rubbing* them in their hands and eating them.

3. TEAR – BURST – SPLIT

1: TEAK – BREAK: *RHĒGNYMI*

4 *rhēgma*	1	2 *dia-(r)rhēssō 5*
1 *rhēgnymi, rhēssō 5|7*		3 *pros-rhēgnymi 2*

a) Tear (one's clothes)

Mt	26 65	2 the high priest *tore* his clothes and said, 'He has blasphemed'.
Mk	14 63	2 The high priest *tore* his robes . . .[64] 'You heard the blasphemy.
Ac	14 14	2 Barnabas and Paul . . . *tore* their clothes

b) Tear to pieces – Burst – Break

Mt	7 6	dogs . . . and . . . pigs . . . may . . . *tear* you *to pieces*.
	9 17	the skins *burst*, the wine runs out, and the skins are lost.
Mk	2 22	the [new] wine will *burst* the skins,
Lk	5 6	2 their nets began to *tear*,
	37	the new wine will *burst* the skins
	6 48	3 when the river was in flood it ⌐bore down on (lit. *broke* upon) that house
	49	3 the river ⌐bore down on (lit. *broke* upon) it, . . . and what a
	4	*ruin* that house became!
Lk	8 29	2 [the madman] would always *break* the fastenings,

c) Break into (shouts of) joy

Ga	4 27	(Is 54 1) Shout for joy, you barren women . . . *Break into* shouts of *joy* and gladness,

2: TEAR – SPLIT: *SCHIZŌ*

2 *schisma 8*	1 *schizō 11*

a) Tear – Split

Mt	9 16	2 the patch pulls away from the cloak and the *tear* gets worse.
	27 51	the veil of the Temple was *torn* in two from top to bottom; the earth quaked; the rocks *split*
Mk	1 10 ○	[Jesus baptised by John] saw the heavens *torn* apart
	2 21	2 the patch pulls away from it . . . and the *tear* gets worse.
	15 38	[Jesus breathed his last.] And the veil of the Temple was *torn* in two
Lk	5 36	No one *tears* a piece from a new cloak to put it on an old cloak; if he does, not only will he have *torn* the new one, but the piece . . . will not match the old.
	23 45	The veil of the Temple was *torn* right down the middle
Jn	19 24	Instead of *tearing* [the seamless garment], let's throw dice
	21 11	in spite of there being so many [fish] the net was not *broken*.

b) Moral split – Division (of opinion)

Jn	7 43	2 the people *could not agree* about [Jesus].
	9 16	2 there was *disagreement* among [the Pharisees]
	10 19	2 These words [of Jesus's] caused *disagreement* among the Jews.
Ac	14 4	The people in the city were *divided*, some supported the Jews, others the apostles,
	23 7	a dispute broke out between the Pharisees and Sadducees, and the assembly was *split*
1 Co	1 10	2 instead of *disagreeing* among yourselves . . . be united again in your belief and practice.
	11 18	when you all come together as a community, there are separate
		2 *factions* among you,
	12 25	[God has arranged the body] so that there may not be
		2 *disagreements* inside the body,

3: SNAP APART – TEAR TO PIECES: *DIA-SPAŌ*

dia-spaō 2

Mk	5 4	[the madman] had *snapped* the chains and broken the fetters,
Ac	23 10	the tribune, afraid that they would *tear* Paul *to pieces*, ordered his troops to go down and haul him out

4: BURST OPEN: *LAKEŌ*

lakeō 1

Ac	1 18	[Judas, having been one of our number,] fell headlong and *burst open*,

4. PLUCK – TEAR OFF

1: PLUCK, PICK (EARS OF CORN): *TILLŌ*

tillō 3

Mt	12 1	His disciples were hungry and began to *pick* ears of corn
Mk	2 23	his disciples began to *pick* ears of corn as they went along.
Lk	6 1	his disciples were *picking* ears of corn,

2: PLUCK OUT – TEAR OUT: *EX-ORYSSŌ*

ex-oryssō 1|2

Ga	4 15	you would have gone so far as to *pluck out* your eyes and give them to me.

3: TEAR OFF (A PERSON'S CLOTHES): *PERI-RHĒGNYMI*

peri-rhēgnymi 1

Ac	16 22	the magistrates had ⌐them stripped (or: their clothes *torn off*) and ordered them to be flogged.

BROTHER

---

1. Brother – Sister: *adelphos*
  1: Brother – Sister (literally), unnamed
  2: Brothers and Sisters of particular people
    a) Cain and Abel
    b) Lazarus, Martha and Mary
    c) Various
  3: Brothers and Sisters of Jesus
  4: 'Brothers' and 'Sisters' = Christians

  a) the Brothers – the Sister(s) – the Brotherhood
  b) "(My) Brothers"
  c) 'Brother' or 'Sister' (said) of named persons
  5: 'Brother' (in a wide sense) = Neighbour, Friend, Countryman
2. Cousin: *anepsios*
3. Relations, Relatives, Family – Kin, Kinsfolk, Kindred – Compatriots, Countryman: *syn-genēs*

1. BROTHER – SISTER: *ADELPHOS*

2 *adelphē*	26	3 *(phil-)adelphia 6*
1 *adelphos*	345	6 *(phil-)adelphos 1*
4 *adelphotēs*	2	5 *(pseud-)adelphos 2*

1: BROTHER – SISTER (literally), UNNAMED

Mt	10 21	*Brother* will betray *brother* to death, and the father his child;
	19 29	/2 everyone who has left . . . *brothers*, *sisters*, father, mother . . . for the sake of my name will be repaid
	22 24	(Dt 25 5) if a man dies childless, his *brother* is to marry the widow . . . to raise children for his *brother*. [25] Now we
	25	had a case involving seven *brothers*; the first . . . died . . . leaving his wife to his *brother*; [26] the same thing happened with the second and third and so on to the seventh,
Mk	10 29	/2 there is no one who has left . . . *brothers*, *sisters*, father
	30	. . . for my sake . . . [30] who will not be repaid a hundred
		/2 times over . . . *brothers*, *sisters*, mothers,
	12 19	(Dt 25 5) if a man's *brother* dies leaving a wife but no child, ⌐the man [the surviving] *brother*) must marry the widow to raise up children for his *brother*. [20] Now there
	20	were seven *brothers*.
	13 12	*Brother* will betray *brother* to death, and the father his child;
Lk	12 13	Master, tell my *brother* to give me a share of our inheritance.
	14 12	When you give a lunch . . . do not ask your . . . *brothers*, relations or rich neighbours.
	26	If any man comes to me without hating his father . . .
		/2 *brothers*, *sisters* . . . he cannot be my disciple.
	15 27 <	[The servant said to the elder son:] Your *brother* has come
	32 <	it was only right we should celebrate . . . because your *brother* . . . was lost and is found.
	16 28	[send Lazarus,] since I have five *brothers*, to give them warning
	18 29	there is no one who has left house, wife, *brothers* . . . for the sake of the kingdom of God [30] who will not be given repayment
	20 28	(Dt 25 5) if a man's married *brother* dies childless, ⌐the man (lit. the [surviving] *brother*) must marry the widow
	29	to raise up children for his *brother*. [29] Well then, there were seven *brothers*.
	21 16	You will be betrayed even by parents and *brothers*,

Rm 12 10	3	Love each other as much as *brothers* should,
1 Th 4 9	3	As for ⌐loving our brothers (or: *brotherly* love), there is no need for anyone to write to you about that,
1 Tm 5 1		treat the younger men as *brothers* [2] . . . Always treat young
2	2	women with propriety, as if they were *sisters*.
Heb 13 1	3	Continue to love each other like *brothers*,
1 P 1 22		You have been obedient to the truth and purified your souls
3	3	until you can love like *brothers*,
3 8	6	be sympathetic; ⌐love the brothers (or: in *brotherly* love), have compassion ·

2: BROTHERS AND SISTERS OF PARTICULAR PEOPLE

a) Cain and Abel

Cain 3   Abel 4

Mt 23 35	you will draw down on yourselves the blood of every holy man that has been shed on earth, from the blood of *Abel* the Holy to the blood of Zechariah son of Barachiah
Lk 11 51	from the blood of *Abel* to the blood of Zechariah,
Heb 11 4	It was because of his faith that *Abel* offered God a better sacrifice than *Cain*, and for that he was declared to be righteous
12 24	Jesus, the mediator who brings . . . a blood for purification which pleads more insistently than *Abel*'s.
1 Jn 3 12	[we are to love one another;] not to be like *Cain*, who belonged to the Evil One and cut his *brother*'s throat . . . simply for this reason, that his own life was evil and his *brother* lived a good life.
Jude 11	[these people] have followed *Cain*;

b) Lazarus, Martha and Mary

Lazarus 11   Mary 11   Martha 13

Lk 10 38		a woman named *Martha* welcomed [Jesus] into her house.
39	2	[39] She had a *sister* called *Mary*, who . . . listened to [Jesus] speaking. [40] Now *Martha* who was distracted with
40	2	all the serving said, 'Lord, do you not care that my *sister* is leaving me to do the serving all by myself?' . . .
41		[41] . . . '*Martha*, *Martha*,' [Jesus] said 'you worry and fret
42		about so many things, [42] . . . It is *Mary* who has chosen the better part'
Jn 11 1		There was a man named *Lazarus* who lived in the village of
2		Bethany with the two *sisters*, *Mary* and *Martha*, and he was ill. [2] . . . *Mary*, ⌐the sister of the sick man *Lazarus* (lit. whose *brother* *Lazarus* was ill) . . . [had] anointed
3	2	the Lord with ointment . . . [3] The *sisters* sent this message to Jesus, 'Lord, the man you love is ill'.
5	2	Jesus loved *Martha* and her *sister* and *Lazarus*,
11		Our friend *Lazarus* is resting, I am going to wake him.
14		Jesus put it plainly, '*Lazarus* is dead'
19		many Jews had come to *Martha* and *Mary* to sympathise
20		with them over their *brother*. [20] When *Martha* heard that Jesus had come she went to meet him. *Mary* remained
21		sitting in the house. [21] *Martha* said to Jesus, 'If you had been here, my *brother* would not have died,'
23		'Your *brother*' said Jesus to her 'will rise again.' [24] *Martha*
24		said, 'I know he will rise again . . . on the last day.'
28	2	she went and called her *sister* *Mary*, saying . . . 'The Master is here'
30		Jesus . . . was still at the place where *Martha* had met him.
31		the Jews . . . were in the house sympathising with *Mary*
32		*Mary* went to Jesus . . . saying, 'Lord, if you had been here, my *brother* would not have died'
39	2	*Martha*, the dead man's *sister*, said to him, 'Lord, by now he will smell'
43		[Jesus] cried in a loud voice, '*Lazarus*, here! Come out!'
45		Many of the Jews who had come to visit *Mary* . . . believed in him,
12 1		Jesus went to Bethany, where *Lazarus* was, whom he had
2		raised from the dead. [2] They gave a dinner for him there; *Martha* waited on them and *Lazarus* was among those at table. [3] *Mary* brought in a pound of very costly ointment
3		. . . and with it anointed the feet of Jesus,
9		a large number of Jews . . . came not only on account of Jesus but also to see *Lazarus* whom he had raised from the dead. [10] Then the chief priests decided to kill *Lazarus*
10		as well,
17		when [Jesus] called *Lazarus* out of the tomb

c) Various

Mt 1 2	Jacob the father of Judah and his *brothers*,
11	Josiah was the father of Jechoniah and his *brothers*,
4 18	[Jesus] saw two *brothers*, Simon, who was called Peter, and
21	his *brother* Andrew . . . [21] Going on from there he saw

Mt 4 21		another pair of *brothers*, James son of Zebedee and his *brother* John;
10 2		These are the names of the twelve apostles: first, Simon who is called Peter, and his *brother* Andrew; James the son of Zebedee, and his *brother* John;
14 3		Herod . . . had arrested John . . . because of Herodias, his *brother* Philip's wife.
17 1		James and his *brother* John
20 24		the other ten [apostles] . . . were indignant with the two *brothers* [James and John].
Mk 1 16		[Jesus] saw Simon and his *brother* Andrew . . . [19] . . . he
19		saw James son of Zebedee and his *brother* John;
3 17		James the son of Zebedee and John the *brother* of James,
5 37		James and John the *brother* of James.
6 17		Herod . . . had . . . John arrested . . . because of Herodias,
18		his *brother* Philip's wife whom he had married. [18] For John had told Herod, 'It is against the law for you to have your *brother*'s wife'.
Lk 3 1		Herod . . , his *brother* Philip tetrarch of the lands of Ituraea
19		Herod . . . whom [John] criticised for his relations with his *brother*'s wife
6 14		[Jesus picked out twelve:] Simon whom he called Peter, and his *brother* Andrew;
Jn 1 40		One of these two who became followers of Jesus . . . was Andrew, the *brother* of Simon Peter. [41] Early next morning,
41		Andrew met his *brother*
6 8		Andrew, Simon Peter's *brother*, said, [9] 'There is a small boy here'
19 25		Near the cross of Jesus stood his mother and his mother's
2		*sister*, Mary the wife of Clopas,
Ac 7 13		(Gn 45 1) it was on the second [visit] that Joseph made himself known to his *brothers*,
12 2		[Herod] beheaded James the *brother* of John,
23 16	2	the son of Paul's *sister* heard of the ambush
Rm 61 15	2	[Greetings to] Nereus and his *sister*,
Jude 1		From Jude . . . *brother* of James;

3: BROTHERS AND SISTERS OF JESUS

H = Human relationship to Jesus

Mt 12 46 H		He was still speaking . . . when his mother and his *brothers* appeared; they were . . . anxious to have a word with him.
47 H		[47] (§ Someone said to him, 'Your mother and *brothers* are
48		here . . .') [48] . . . Jesus replied, 'Who is my mother? Who
49		are my *brothers*?' [49] And stretching out his hand towards his disciples he said, 'Here are my mother and my
50		*brothers*. [50] Anyone who does the will of my Father . . .
13 55 H	/2	is my *brother* and *sister* and mother.'
56 H	2	Is not his mother the woman called Mary, and his *brothers* James and Joseph and Simon and Jude? [56] His *sisters*, too, are they not all here with us?
25 40		in so far as you did this to one of the least of these *brothers* of mine, you did it to me.
28 10		go and tell my *brothers* that they must leave for Galilee;
Mk 3 31 H		His mother and *brothers* now arrived and . . . sent in a
32 H		message asking for him. [32] . . . 'Your mother and *brothers*
33 H	2	and *sisters* are outside asking for you'. [33] He replied, 'Who
34		are my mother and my *brothers*?' [34] And looking round
35		. . . he said, 'Here are my mother and my *brothers*. [35] Anyone who does the will of God, that person is my
6 3 H	/2	*brother* and *sister* and mother.'
H	2	This is . . . surely the son of Mary, the *brother* of James and Joset and Jude and Simon? His *sisters*, too, are they not here with us?
Lk 8 19 H		His mother and his *brothers* came looking for him . . .
20 H		[20] . . . 'Your mother and *brothers* . . . want to see you.
21		[21] . . . 'My mother and my *brothers* are those who hear the word of God and put it into practice'.
Jn 2 12		he went down to Capernaum with his mother and ⌐the (ᵛ his)
(H)		*brothers*,
7 3 H		[the feast of Tabernacles drew near.] His *brothers* said to
5 H		him, 'Why not . . . go to Judaea . . .' [5] Not even his
10 H		*brothers*, in fact, had faith in him . . . [10] However, after his *brothers* had left for the festival, he went up as well,
20 17 (H)		go and find ᵛ the (G my) *brothers* and tell them: I am ascending to my Father and your Father,
Ac 1 14		[the apostles] joined in continuous prayer, together with
H		. . . Mary the mother of Jesus, and with his *brothers*.
Rm 8 29		so that his Son might be the eldest of many *brothers*.
1 Co 9 5 Δ		like all the other apostles and the *brothers* of the Lord and Cephas?
Ga 1 19 H		[in Jerusalem] I only saw James, the *brother* of the Lord,
Heb 2 11		[the Son] openly calls them *brothers* [12] in the text (Ps 22 23):
12		I shall announce your name to my *brothers*,
17		It was essential that he should . . . become completely like his *brothers*

4: 'BROTHERS' AND 'SISTERS' = CHRISTIANS

a) the Brothers – the Sister(s) – the Brotherhood

Mt 23	8	you have only one Master, and you are all *brothers*.
Lk 22	32	I have prayed for you, Simon . . . and once you have recovered, you in your turn must strengthen your *brothers*.
Jn 2	12	[Jesus] went down to Capernaum with his mother and ʳthe (ᵛ his) *brothers*,
20	17	go and find ᵛ the (G my) *brothers* and tell them: I am ascending to my Father and your Father,
21	23	The rumour then went out among the *brothers* that this disciple would not die.
Ac 1	15	Peter stood up to speak to the *brothers* – there were about a hundred and twenty personsˈ
9	30	[the Hellenists became determined to kill Saul.] When the *brothers* knew, they took him to Caesarea,
10	23	[Peter] was . . . accompanied by some of the *brothers* from Jaffa.
11	1	The apostles and the *brothers* in Judaea heard that the pagans too had accepted the word of God,
12	[Peter said:] The six *brothers* here came with me as well,
29	The disciples decided to send relief . . . to the *brothers* living in Judaea.
12	17	[Peter] described to them how the Lord had led him out of prison. He added, 'Tell James and the *brothers*'.
14	2	Some of the Jews [at Iconium] . . . poisoned the minds of the pagans against the *brothers*
15	1	some men came down from Judaea and taught the *brothers*,
3	this news was received with the greatest satisfaction by the *brothers*.
22	Judas known as Barsabbas and Silas, both leading men in the *brotherhood*,
23	The apostles and elders, your *brothers*, send greetings to the *brothers* of pagan birth
32	Judas and Silas . . . spoke . . . encouraging . . . the *brothers*.
33	These two spent some time there, and then the *brothers* wished them peace and they went back
36	Let us go back . . . so that we can see how the *brothers* are doing.
40	Before Paul left, he . . . was commended by the *brothers* to the grace of God.
16	2	The *brothers* at Lystra . . . spoke well of Timothy,
40	[Paul and Silas] went to Lydia's house where they saw all the *brothers* and gave them some encouragement;
17	6	[the Jews in Thessalonika] only found Jason and some of the *brothers*,
10	When it was dark the *brothers* immediately sent Paul and Silas away to Beroea,
14	the *brothers* [in Beroea] arranged for Paul to go immediately
18	18	Paul took leave of the *brothers* and sailed for Syria,
27	When Apollos thought of crossing over to Achaia, the *brothers* encouraged him
21	7	at Ptolemais . . . we greeted the *brothers* and stayed one day with them.
17	On our arrival in Jerusalem the *brothers* gave us a very warm welcome.
22	5	[the elders] even sent me with letters to their *brothers* in Damascus.
28	14	[at Puteoli] we found some *brothers* and were much rewarded by staying a week with them.
15	When the *brothers* [in Rome] heard of our arrival they came to meet us,
Rm 14	10	never pass judgement on a *brother* or treat a *brother* with contempt,
13	make up your mind never to be the cause of your *brother* tripping
15	if your attitude to food is upsetting your *brother*, then you are hardly being guided by charity.
21	abstain from . . . anything . . . that would make your *brother* trip
16	14	Greetings to Asyncritus . . . Hermas, and all the *brothers* who are with them;
1 Co 5	11	you should not associate with a *brother* Christian who is leading an immoral life,
6	5	is there really not one reliable man among you to settle differences between *brothers* ⁶ and so one *brother* brings a court case against another *brother* in front of unbelievers?
8	you are doing . . . the cheating, and to your own *brothers*.
7	12	If a *brother* has a wife who is an unbeliever, and she is content to live with him, he must not send her away . . .
14	¹⁴ . . . the unbelieving wife is made one with the saints through her ʳhusband (lit. *brother*) . . . ¹⁵ However,
15	if the unbelieving partner does not consent, they may
/2	separate; in these circumstances, the *brother* or *sister* is not tied:
8	11	your knowledge could become the ruin of someone weak, of a *brother* for whom Christ died. ¹² By sinning in this way against your *brothers* . . . it would be Christ against whom you sinned. ¹³ That is why, since food can be the

1 Co 8	13	occasion of my *brother's* downfall, I shall never eat meat . . . in case I am the cause of a *brother's* downfall.
9	5	[Have we not] the right to take a ʳChristian woman (lit. *sister*) round with us . . .?
15	6	[Christ] appeared to more than five hundred of the *brothers* at the same time,
16	11	the *brothers* and I are waiting for [Timothy].
12	I begged [Apollos] to come to you with the *brothers*
20	[All the churches of Asia send you greetings.] All the *brothers* send you their greetings.
2 Co 8	22	To accompany [Titus and Luke], we are sending a third *brother*, of whose keenness we have often had proof
23	the other two *brothers* . . . are delegates of the churches,
9	3	I am sending the *brothers* all the same,
5	I have thought it necessary to ask these *brothers* to go on to you ahead of us,
11	9	the *brothers* who came from Macedonia provided me with everything I wanted.
Ga 1	2	[From Paul] and from all the *brothers* who are here with me [to the churches of Galatia]
Ep 6	23	May God the Father and the Lord Jesus Christ grant peace . . . to all the *brothers*.
Ph 1	14	most of the *brothers* have taken courage in the Lord
4	21	The *brothers* who are with me send their greetings.
Col 1	2	[From Paul and Timothy] to the saints in Colossae, our faithful *brothers* in Christ:
4	15	Please give my greetings to the *brothers* at Laodicea
1 Th 4	6	[God] wants nobody . . . to sin by taking advantage of a *brother* in these matters;
10	[loving one another,] this is what you are doing with all the *brothers* throughout the whole of Macedonia.
5	26	Greet all the *brothers* with the holy kiss.
27	this letter is to be read to all the *brothers*.
2 Th 3	6	keep away from any of the *brothers* who refuses to work
15	you are not to regard him as an enemy but as a *brother* in need of correction.
1 Tm 4	6	If you put all this to the *brothers*, you will be a good servant of Christ Jesus
6	2	Slaves whose masters are believers are not to think any the less of them because they are *brothers*;
2 Tm 4	21	Greetings to you from Eubulus . . . and all the *brothers*.
Phm	16	[so that you could have Onesimus back,] not as a slave any more, but . . . a dear *brother*;
Jm 1	9	It is right for the poor *brother* to be proud of his high rank,
2	15	/2 If one of the *brothers* or one of the *sisters* is in need of clothes
4	11	Anyone who slanders a *brother*, or condemns a *brother*, is speaking against the Law and condemning the Law.
1 P 2	17	Have respect for everyone and love for our ʳcommunity (lit.
4	*brotherhood*);
5	9	4 ʳyour *brothers* (lit. the *brotherhood*) all over the world [is] suffering the same things.
2 Jn	13	2 Greetings to you from the children of your *sister*, the chosen one.
3 Jn	3	It was a great joy to me when some *brothers* came
5	My friend, you have done faithful work in looking after these *brothers*, even though they were complete strangers to you.
10	[Diotrephes] refuses to welcome our *brothers*,
Rv 6	11	their fellow servants and *brothers* had been killed just as they had been.
12	10	now that the persecutor, who accused our *brothers* . . . has been brought down.
19	10	I am a servant just like you and all your *brothers* who are witnesses to Jesus.
22	9	I am a servant just like you and like your *brothers* the prophets

b) "(My) Brothers"

Ac 1	16	[Peter said:] *Brothers*, the passage of scripture had to be fulfilled
6	3	you, *brothers*, must select from among yourselves seven men of good reputation,
15	7	'My *brothers*,' [Peter] said 'you know perfectly well that . . . God made his choice among you: the pagans were to learn the Good News from me'
13	it was James who spoke. 'My *brothers*,' he said 'listen to me . . .'
Rm 1	13	*brothers* . . . I have often planned to visit you
7	1	*Brothers*, those of you who have studied law will know that laws affect a person only during his lifetime.
4	you, my *brothers*, who through the body of Christ are now dead to the Law,
8	12	my *brothers*, there is no necessity for us to obey our unspiritual selves
10	1	*Brothers*, . . . I pray to God for [the Jews] to be saved.
11	25	There is a hidden reason for all this, *brothers*, of which I do not want you to be ignorant,
12	1	my *brothers*, . . . worship [God] . . . by offering your living bodies as a holy sacrifice,
15	14	my *brothers* . . . I am quite certain that you are full of good intentions,

Rm 15 30   I beg you, *brothers* . . . to help me through my dangers by praying to God for me.

16 17   I implore you, *brothers*, be on your guard against anybody who encourages trouble

1 Co 1 10   I do appeal to you, *brothers* . . . to make up the differences between you,

11   my dear *brothers*, it is clear that there are serious differences among you.

26   Take yourselves for instance, *brothers*, at the time when you were called:

2 1   As for me, *brothers*, when I came to you,

3 1   *Brothers*, I myself was unable to speak to you as people of the Spirit:

4 6   in everything I have said here, *brothers*, I have taken . . . myself as an example

7 24   Each one of you, my *brothers*, should stay as he was . . . at the time of his call.

29   *Brothers*, . . . our time is growing short.

10 1   *brothers*, . . . our fathers were all guided by a cloud

11 33   my dear *brothers*, when you meet for the Meal, wait for one another.

12 1   Now my dear *brothers*, I want to clear up a wrong impression about spiritual gifts.

14 6   Now suppose, my dear *brothers*, I am someone with the gift of tongues,

20   *Brothers*, you are not to be childish in your outlook.

26   So, my dear *brothers*, what conclusion is to be drawn?

39   my dear *brothers*, by all means be ambitious to prophesy,

15 1   *Brothers*, I want to remind you of the gospel I preached to to you,

31   I face death every day, *brothers*, and I can swear it by the pride that I take in you in Christ Jesus our Lord.

50   Or else, *brothers*, put it this way: flesh and blood cannot inherit the kingdom of God:

58   Never give in then, my dear *brothers*,

16 15   There is something else to ask you, *brothers*.

2 Co 1 8   we should like you to realise, *brothers*, that . . . we despaired of coming through alive.

8 1   Now here, *brothers*, is the news of the grace of God

13 11   In the meantime, *brothers*, we wish you happiness;

Ga 1 11   The fact is, *brothers* . . . the Good News I preached is not a human message

3 15   Compare this, *brothers*, with what happens in ordinary life.

4 12   *Brothers*, all I ask is that you should copy me

28   you, my *brothers* . . . are children of the promise,

31   So, my *brothers*, we are the children, not of the slave-girl, but of the free-born wife.

5 11   As for me, my *brothers*, if I still preach circumcision, why am I still persecuted?

13   My *brothers*, you were called, as you know, to liberty;

6 1   *Brothers*, if one of you misbehaves . . . you . . . should [set him right] in a spirit of gentleness,

18   The grace of our Lord Jesus Christ be with your spirit, my *brothers*.

Ph 1 12   I am glad to tell you, *brothers*, that the things that happened to me have actually been a help to the Good News.

3 1   Finally, my *brothers*, rejoice in the Lord.

13   I can assure you my *brothers*, I am far from thinking that I have already won.

17   My *brothers*, be united in following my rule of life.

4 1   my *brothers* and dear friends . . . you are my joy and my crown.

8   Finally, *brothers*, fill your minds with everything that is true,

1 Th 1 4   We know, *brothers*, that God loves you and that you have been chosen,

2 1   You know yourselves, my *brothers*, that our visit to you has not proved ineffectual.

9   Let me remind you, *brothers*, how hard we used to work,

14   you, my *brothers*, have been like the churches of God . . . in Judaea.

17   we had been separated from you – in body but never in thought, *brothers*

3 7   *brothers*, your faith has been a great comfort to us

4 1   Finally, *brothers*, we urge you . . . to make more and more progress

10   we do urge you, *brothers*, to go on making even greater progress

13   We want you to be quite certain, *brothers*, about those who have died,

5 1   You will not be expecting us to write anything to you, *brothers*, about 'times and seasons',

4   But it is not as if you live in the dark, my *brothers*,

12   We appeal to you, my *brothers*, to be considerate to those who . . . are above you

14   this is what we ask you to do, *brothers*: warn the idlers,

25   Pray for us, my *brothers*.

2 Th 1 3   we must be continually thanking God for you, *brothers*;

2 1   To turn now, *brothers*, to the coming of our Lord Jesus Christ

2 13   we must be continually thanking God for you, *brothers* whom the Lord loves,

15   Stand firm, then, *brothers*,

3 1   Finally, *brothers*, pray for us;

6   we urge you, *brothers*, to keep away from any of the brothers who refuses to work

13   My *brothers*, never grow tired of doing what is right.

Heb 3 1   you who are holy *brothers* and have had the same heavenly call

12   Take care, *brothers*, that there is not in any one of your community a wicked mind,

10 19   *brothers*, through the blood of Jesus we have the right to enter the sanctuary,

13 22   I do ask you, *brothers*, to take these words of advice kindly;

Jm 1 2   My *brothers*, you will always have your trials but . . . try to treat them as a happy privilege;

16   Make no mistake about this, my dear *brothers*:

19   Remember this, my dear *brothers*: be quick to listen

2 1   My *brothers*, do not try to combine faith in Jesus Christ . . . with the making of distinctions between classes of people.

5   my dear *brothers*: it was those who are poor . . . that God chose,

14   Take the case, my *brothers*, of someone who has never done a single good act but claims that he has faith.

3 1   Only a few of you, my *brothers*, should be teachers,

10   My *brothers*, this must be wrong

12   Can a fig tree give you olives, my *brothers* . . .?

4 11   *Brothers*, do not slander one another.

5 7   be patient, *brothers*, until the Lord's coming.

9   Do not make complaints against one another, *brothers*,

10   For your example, *brothers*, . . . take the prophets

12   Above all, my *brothers*, do not swear by heaven

19   My *brothers*, if one of you strays away from the truth,

2 P 1 10   *Brothers*, you have been called and chosen: work all the harder to justify it.

1 Jn 3 13   You must not be surprised, *brothers*, when the world hates you;

c) 'Brother' or 'Sister' (said) of named persons

Ac 9 17   *Brother* Saul, I have been sent by the Lord Jesus

21 20   [The elders to Paul:] But you see, *brother*, . . . how thousands of Jews have now become believers,

22 13   [Ananias] stood beside me and said, "*Brother* Saul, receive your sight!"

Rm 16 1   2 our *sister* Phoebe, a deaconess of the church at Cenchreae.

23   Erastus . . . sends his greetings; so does our *brother* Quartus.

1 Co 1 1   I, Paul, . . . together with *brother* Sosthenes, send greetings ² to the church of God in Corinth,

16 12   As for our *brother* Apollos, I begged him to come to you

2 Co 1 1   From Paul . . . and from Timothy, one of the *brothers*, to the church of God at Corinth

2 13   I was . . . uneasy in mind at not meeting *brother* Titus [at Troas]

8 18   As [Titus's] companion we are sending the *brother* [Luke?] who is famous in all the churches

12 18   Titus went at my urging, and I sent the *brother* that came with him.

Ep 6 21   my dear *brother* Tychicus, my loyal helper in the Lord,

Ph 2 25   *brother* Epaphroditus . . . my companion in working

Col 1 1   From Paul , . . and from our *brother* Timothy ² to the saints in Colossae,

4 7   Tychicus will tell you all the news . . . He is a *brother* I love very much,

9   I am sending Onesimus, that dear and faithful *brother*

1 Th 3 2   [we] sent our *brother* Timothy, who is God's helper

Phm 1   From Paul . . . and from our *brother* Timothy; to our dear

2   2 fellow worker Philemon, ² our *sister* Apphia,

7   they tell me, *brother*, how you have put new heart into the saints.

20   Well then, *brother*, I am counting on you,

Heb 13 23   I want you to know that our *brother* Timothy has been set free.

1 P 5 12   Silvanus . . . is a *brother* I know I can trust,

2 P 3 15   our *brother* Paul, who is so dear to us, told you this when he wrote to you

Rv 1 9   My name is John, and . . . I am your *brother* and share your sufferings,

5: 'BROTHER' (in a wide sense) = NEIGHBOUR, FRIEND, COUNTRYMAN

Mt 5 22   anyone who is angry with his *brother* will answer for it before the court; if a man calls his *brother* "Fool" he will answer for it before the Sanhedrin;

23   if you . . . remember that your *brother* has something against you, ²⁴ leave your offering there before the altar, go and be reconciled with your *brother* first,

Mt	5 47	if you save your greetings for your *brothers*, are you doing anything exceptional?
	7 3	Why do you observe the splinter in your *brother*'s eye . . . ?
	4	How dare you say to your *brother*, "Let me take the splinter out of your eye" . . . ?
	5	then you will see clearly enough to take the splinter out of your *brother*'s eye.
	18 15	If your *brother* does something wrong, go and have it out with him alone . . . If he listens to you, you have won back your *brother*.
	21	how often must I forgive my *brother* if he wrongs me?
	35	unless you each forgive your *brother* from your heart.
Lk	6 41	Why do you observe the splinter in your *brother*'s eye . . . ?
	42	How can you say to your *brother*, "*Brother*, let me take out the splinter that is in your eye" . . . ? Take the plank out of your own eye first, and then you will see clearly enough to take out the splinter that is in your *brother*'s eye.
	17 3	If your *brother* does something wrong, reprove him
Ac	2 29	[Men of Israel,] *brothers*, . . . David himself is dead
	37	[the Jews] said to Peter and the apostles, 'What must we do, *brothers*?'
	3 17	Now I know, *brothers* [men of Israel], that neither you nor your leaders had any idea what you were really doing;
	22	(Dt 18 15) The Lord God will raise up a prophet . . . from among your own *brothers*;
	7 2	My *brothers*, my fathers, listen to what I have to say.
	23	[Moses] decided to visit his *countrymen*, the sons of Israel.
	25	[Moses] thought his *brothers* realised that through him God would liberate them,
	26	Friends, . . . you are *brothers*;
	37	(Dt 18 15) God will raise up a prophet . . . from among your own *brothers*.
	13 15	the presidents of the synagogue sent [Paul and Barnabas] a message: '*Brothers*, if you would like to address some words of encouragement . . .'
	26	My *brothers*, sons of Abraham's race,
	38	My *brothers*, . . . it is through [Jesus] that forgiveness of your sins is proclaimed.
	22 1	[Paul to the Jews of Jerusalem:] My *brothers*, my fathers, listen
	23 1	[Paul to the Sanhedrin:] My *brothers*, to this day I have conducted myself . . . with a perfectly clear conscience.
	5	*Brothers*, I did not realise it was the high priest,
	6	*Brothers*, I am a Pharisee and the son of Pharisees.
	28 17	[Paul] called together the leading Jews . . . '*Brothers*, . . . I was arrested in Jerusalem . . .'
	21	We have received no letters . . . nor has any *countryman* of yours arrived here with any report . . . of anything to your discredit.
Rm	9 3	I would willingly . . . be cut off from Christ if it could help my *brothers* of Israel,
2 Co	11 26	5 I have been in danger . . . from *so-called brothers*.
Ga	2 4	⌐some who do not really belong to the brotherhood (lit. *so-called brothers*) have furtively crept in to spy
	5	
1 Th	4 9	3 As for ⌐loving our *brothers* (or: brotherly love), there is no need for anyone to write to you about that,
Heb	7 5	the descendants of Levi . . . are obliged by the Law to take tithes . . . from their own *brothers*
	8 11	(Jr 31 34) There will be no further need . . . to say to *brother*
1 P	3 8	6 be sympathetic; ⌐love the *brothers* (or: in brotherly love), have compassion
2 P	1 7	3 [add] kindness towards your *fellow men* to your devotion, 3 and, to this kindness towards your *fellow men*, love.
1 Jn	2 9	Anyone who claims to be in the light but hates his *brother* is still in the dark.
	10	anyone who loves his *brother* is living in the light
	11	the man who hates his *brother* . . . is in the darkness,
	3 10	anybody . . . not loving his *brother* is no child of God's.
	14	[we have passed out of death and into life,] because we love our *brothers*.
	15	to hate your *brothers* is to be a murderer,
	16	we, too, ought to give up our lives for our *brothers*.
	17	If a man who was rich . . . saw that one of his *brothers* was in need,
	4 20	Anyone who says, 'I love God', and hates his *brother*, is a liar, since a man who does not love the *brother* . . . cannot love God.
	21	anyone who loves God must also love his *brother*.
	5 16	If anybody sees his *brother* commit a sin . . . he has only to pray, and God will give life to the sinner

2. COUSIN: *ANEPSIOS*

anepsios 1

Col	4 10	Aristarchus . . . sends his greetings, and so does Mark, the *cousin* of Barnabas

3. RELATIONS, RELATIVES, FAMILY – KIN, KINSFOLK, KINDRED – COMPATRIOTS, COUNTRYMEN: *SYN-GENĒS*

2 *syn-geneia* 3	3 *syn-geneus* 2
1 *syn-genēs* 9	4 *syn-genis* 1

Mk	6 4	A prophet is only despised in his own country, among his 3 own *relations*
Lk	1 36	4 your *kinswoman* Elizabeth has . . . herself conceived a son,
	58	when [Elizabeth's] neighbours and *relations* heard that the Lord had shown her so great a kindness, they shared her joy.
	61	2 [Elizabeth,] no one in your *family* has that name,
	2 44	[Joseph and Mary] went to look for [Jesus] among their 3 *relations* and acquaintances.
	14 12	When you give a lunch . . . do not ask your friends, brothers, *relations*
	21 16	You will be betrayed even by . . . brothers, *relations* and friends;
Jn	18 26	On of the high priest's servants, a *relation* of the man whose ear Peter had cut off, said,
Ac	7 3	(Gn 12 1) [God said to Abraham:] Leave your country and 2 your *family*
	14	2 Joseph then sent for his father Jacob and his whole *family*,
	10 24	Cornelius . . . had asked his *relations* and close friends to be [at Caesarea],
Rm	9 3	I would willingly be condemned . . . if it could help my brothers of Israel, my ⌐own flesh and blood (lit. *relations*)
	16 7	[Greetings to] Andronicus and Junias, my *compatriots*
	11	[Greetings] to my *compatriot* Herodion;
	21	my *compatriots*, Jason and Sosipater [send their greetings].

BUILDING

1. Build
  1 : Build – Rebuild – Edification: *oiko-domeō*
    a) the Temple (of Jerusalem *and* of the Body of Christ)
    b) Build (generally)
    c) Build (figuratively): Edify – Benefit, Improve, Do (some) Good – Encourage
  2 : Build: *kata-skeuazō*
  3 : Built: *en-dōmēsis*
2. Foundations – Foundation stones: *themelios*
    a) Founded, Foundation (generally)
    b) Foundation, Base (figuratively)
3. Pillar – Portico
  1 : Pillar: *stylos*
  2 : Portico – Colonnade: *stoa*
4. Palace – Court – Fold: *aulē*
    a) Palace – Courtyard – Forecourt
    b) Court (of the temple)
    c) Sheepfold – Fold
5. Roof – Housetops
  1 : Roof: *stegē*
  2 : Housetops – Flat roof: *dōma*
6. Gate – Door – Window
  1 : Gate: *pylē*
    a) Gate (generally)
    b) (figuratively)
  2 : Door – Entrance – Window: *thyra*
    a) Door – Entrance (generally)
    b) Door – Gate – Doorkeeper (figuratively)
    c) Window

1. BUILD

1: BUILD – REBUILD – EDIFICATION: *OIKO-DOMEŌ*

2 *oiko-domē* 18	4 *an-oiko-domeō* 2
1 *oiko-domeō* 40	3 *ep-oiko-domeō* 7
5 *oiko-domos* 1	6 *syn-oiko-domeō* 1

D = Build // Destroy

a) The Temple (of Jerusalem and *of the Body of Christ)*

Mt	24 1 D	[Jesus'] disciples came up to draw his attention to the 2 Temple *buildings*.
	26 61 D ●	I have power to destroy the Temple of God and in three days *build* it up.
	27 40 D ●	So you would destroy the Temple and *rebuild* it in three days!
Mk	13 1	Look at the size of those stones, Master! Look at the size 2 of those *buildings*! ² And Jesus said to him, 'You see
	D 2	these great *buildings*? Not a single stone will be left on another: everything will be destroyed.'
	14 58 D ●	I am going to destroy this Temple . . . and in three days *build* another,
	15 29 D ●	Aha! So you would destroy the Temple and *rebuild* it in three days!
Jn	2 20 D	It has taken forty-six years to *build* this sanctuary: are you going to raise it up in three days?
Ac	7 47	it was Solomon who actually *built* God's house for him.

Ac 7 49   (Is 66 1) With heaven my throne . . . what house could you *build* me . . .?

b) Build (generally)

Mt 7 24   like a sensible man who *built* his house on rock.
    26 D   like a stupid man who *built* his house on sand.
  21 33   a landowner . . . planted a vineyard; he fenced it round . . . and *built* a tower;
  23 29   scribes and Pharisees . . . who *build* the sepulchres of the prophets
Mk 12 1   A man planted a vineyard; he fenced it round . . . and *built* a tower;
Lk 4 29   [the crowd] took [Jesus] up to the brow of the hill their town was *built* on,
  6 48   like the man who when he *built* his house . . . laid the foundations on rock; when the river was in flood it . . . could not shake it, it was so well *built*.
  49 D   like the man who *built* his house on soil, with no foundations:
  7 5   [the centurion] is the one who *built* the synagogue.
  11 47   Alas for you who *build* the tombs of the prophets,
  48   [your ancestors] did the killing, you do the *building*.
  12 18 D   I will pull down my barns and *build* bigger ones,
  14 28   which of you here, intending to *build* a tower,
  30   Here is a man who started to *build* and was unable to finish.
  17 28   It will be the same as it was in Lot's day: people were . . . planting and *building*,

c) Build (figuratively): Edify – Benefit, Improve, Do (some) Good – Encourage

Mt 16 18   You are Peter and on this rock I will *build* my Church.
  21 42   (Ps 118 22) It was the stone rejected by the *builders*
  Repeated in Mk 12 10; Lk 20 17
Ac 4 11   5 [Jesus Christ] is the stone rejected by you the *builders*,
  9 31   ᵛ The churches (G the Church) . . . were now left in peace, *building* themselves up,
  15 16 D   4 (Am 9 11) I shall return and *rebuild* the fallen House of 4 David; I shall *rebuild* it from its ruins and restore it.
  20 32   the word of [God's] grace that has power to *build* you up
Rm 14 19 D   let us adopt any custom that leads to peace and our mutual 2 *improvement*,
  15 2   2 Each of us should thing of his neighbours and *help* them *to become stronger* [Christians].
  20   I had no wish to *build* on other men's foundations;
1 Co 3 9   2 you are God's farm, God's *building*. ¹⁰ . . . I . . . laid the 10 3 foundations, on which someone else is doing the *building*.
  3 Everyone doing the *building* must work carefully . . .
  12 3   ¹² On this foundation you can *build* in gold,
  14 3   if [each man's] *structure* stands up to [the fire],
  8 1   knowledge gives self-importance – it is love that makes the *building* grow.
  10   his own conscience, even if it is weak, may *encourage* him to eat food which has been offered to idols.
  10 23   For me there are no forbidden things, but not everything *does good*.
  14 3   the man who prophesies does talk to other people, to their 2 *improvement*, their encouragement and their consolation.
  4   ⁴ The one with the gift of tongues talks for his own *benefit*, but the man who prophesies does so for the *benefit* of the community.
  5   unless of course [the man with the gift of tongues] offers 2 an interpretation so that the church may get some *benefit*.
  12   concentrate on those [spiritual gifts] which will grow to 2 *benefit* the community.
  17   However well you make your thanksgiving, the [uninitiated person] gets no *benefit* from it.
  26   At all your meetings . . . [all that is done] must always be 2 for the common *good*.
2 Co 5 1 D   2 there is a *house* built by God for us, an everlasting home . . . in the heavens.
  10 8 D   2 the Lord gave [authority] to me for *building* you up and not for pulling you down,
  12 19   it is before God that we . . are speaking; and it is all 2 . . . for your *benefit*.
  13 10 D   2 the authority which the Lord gave me for *building* up and not for destroying.
Ga 2 18   If I were to ʳreturn to a position I had already abandoned (lit. *rebuild* something I had destroyed), I should be admitting I had done something wrong.
Ep 2 20   3 You are part of a *building* that has the apostles and prophets for its foundations, and Christ Jesus himself for its main 21 2 cornerstone. ²¹ As every *structure* is aligned on him, all 22 grow into one holy temple in the Lord; ²² and you too, in 6 him, are being *built into* a house where God lives,
  4 12   the saints together make a unity in the work of service, *building* up the body of Christ.
  16 2   So the body grows until it has *built* itself up, in love.
  29 2   let your words be for the *improvement* of others,
Col 2 7   3 you must be rooted in [Jesus Christ] and *built* on him
1 Th 5 11   So give *encouragement* to each other,

1 P 2 5   so that you . . . may be living stones *making* a spiritual house.
  7   (Ps 118 22) the stone rejected by the *builders*
Jude 20   3 use your most holy faith as your foundation and *build* on that,

2: BUILD: *KATA-SKEUAZŌ*

kata-skeuazō 5/11

Heb 3 3   It is the difference between the honour given to the man that *built* the house and to the house itself. ⁴ Every house is 4 Θ *built* by someone, of course; but God *built* everything that exists.
  11 7   Noah . . . *built* an ark to save his family.
1 P 3 20   when Noah was still *building* that ark

3: BUILT: *EN-DŌMĒSIS*

en-dōmēsis 1

Rv 21 18   The wall was *built* of diamond,

2. FOUNDATIONS – FOUNDATION STONES: *THEMELIOS*

3 *themelion 1*   1 *themelios 15*
2 *themelioō 3*

a) Founded, Foundation (generally)

Mt 7 25   2 [the house] was *founded* on rock.
Lk 6 48   the man who when he built his house . . . laid the *foundations* 49 on rock . . . ⁴⁹ . . . the man who built his house . . . with no *foundations*:
  14 29   if he laid the *foundation* and then found himself unable to finish the work,
Ac 16 26   there was an earthquake that shook the prison to its 3 *foundations*.
Heb 1 10 X   2 (Ps 102 25) It is you, Lord, who laid earth's *foundations* in the beginning,
  11 10   [Abraham] looked forward to a city *founded*, designed and built by God.
Rv 21 14   The city walls stood on twelve *foundation stones*,
  19   The *foundations* of the city wall were faced with all kinds of precious stone: the first (§ *foundation*) with diamond, the second lapis lazuli . . . ²⁰ . . . the twelfth amethyst.

b) Foundation, Base (figuratively)

Rm 15 20   I had no wish to build on other men's *foundations*;
1 Co 3 10   I succeeded as an architect and laid the *foundations*,
  11   For the *foundation*, nobody can lay any other than the one which has already been laid, that is Jesus Christ. ¹² On 12 this *foundation* you can build in gold . . . or in wood,
Ep 2 20   You are part of a building that has the apostles and prophets for its *foundations*,
  3 17   2 planted in love, and *built on* love,
Col 1 23   2 as long as you persevere and stand firm on the solid *base* of the faith,
1 Tm 6 19   [Tell the rich to be willing to share –] this is the way they can save up a good ʳcapital sum (lit. *foundation*) for the future
2 Tm 2 19   God's solid *foundation stone* is still in position,
Heb 6 1   Let us leave behind . . . all the elementary teaching about Christ and concentrate on its completion, without going over the *fundamental* doctrines again:
1 P 5 10   the God of all grace . . . will confirm, strengthen and 2 *support* you.

3. PILLAR – PORTICO

1: PILLAR: *STYLOS*

stylos 4

Ga 2 9   James, Cephas and John, these leaders, these *pillars*,
1 Tm 3 15   the Church of the living God, ʳwhich upholds (lit. *pillar* and support of) the truth
Rv 3 12   Those who prove victorious I will make into *pillars* in the sanctuary of my God,
  10 1   I saw another powerful angel . . . his legs were *pillars* of fire.

2: PORTICO – COLONNADE: *STOA*

stoa 4

Jn	5 2	at the Sheep Pool in Jerusalem there is a building . . . consisting of five *colonnades*;
	10 23	Jesus was in the Temple walking up and down in the *Portico of Solomon*,
Ac	3 11	Everyone came running towards [Peter and John and the cripple] . . . to the *Portico of Solomon*,
	5 12	[The believers] all used to meet by common consent in the *Portico of Solomon*.

4. PALACE – COURT – FOLD: *AULĒ*

1 *aulē 12*   2 *pro-aulion 1*

a) Palace – Courtyard – Forecourt

Mt	26 3	the chief priests . . . assembled in the *palace* of the high priest,
	58	Peter followed [Jesus] at a distance, and . . . reached the high priest's *palace*,
	69	Peter was sitting outside in the *courtyard*,
Mk	14 54	Peter had followed [Jesus] at a distance, right into the high priest's *palace*,
	66	Peter was down below in the *courtyard*,
	68	2 [Peter] went out into the *forecourt*.
	15 16	The soldiers led [Jesus] away to the inner part of the *palace*,
Lk	11 21	So long as a strong man fully armed guards his own *palace*,
	22 55	They had lit a fire in the middle of the *courtyard*
Jn	18 15	This disciple . . . went with Jesus into the high priest's *palace*

b) Court (of the temple)

Rv	11 2	leave out the outer *court* and do not measure it,

c) Sheepfold – Fold

Jn	10 1	anyone who does not enter the *sheepfold* through the gate . . . is a thief
	16	there are other sheep I have that are not of this *fold*,

5. ROOF – HOUSETOPS

1: ROOF: *STEGĒ*

1 *stegē 3*   2 *apo-stegazō 1*

Mt	8 8	Sir, I am not worthy to have you under my *roof*;
Mk	2 4	2/ [the four men] stripped the *roof* over the place where Jesus was;
Lk	7 6	Sir . . . I am not worthy to have you under my *roof*;

2: HOUSETOPS – FLAT ROOF: *DŌMA*

dōma 7

Mt	10 27	what you hear in whispers, proclaim from the *housetops*.
	24 17	if a man is on the *housetop*, he must not come down to collect his belongings;
Mk	13 15	if a man is on the *housetop*, he must not come down . . . to collect any of his belongings;
Lk	5 19	[the men carrying the paralytic] went up on to the *flat roof*
	12 3	what you have whispered in hidden places will be proclaimed on the *housetops*.
	7 31	anyone on the *housetops*, with his possessions in the house, must not come down to collect them,
Ac	10 9	Peter went to the *housetop* . . . to pray.

6. GATE – DOOR – WINDOW

1: GATE: *PYLĒ*

2 *pylē 10*   1 *pylōn 18*

a) Gate (generally)

Mt	26 71	When [Peter] went out to the *gateway* another servant-girl saw him
Lk	7 12	2 When [Jesus] was near the *gate* of the town [Nain]
	16 20	at [the rich man's] *gate* there lay a poor man called Lazarus,
Ac	3 10	[everyone] recognised him as the man who used to sit begging 2 at the Beautiful *Gate* of the Temple.
	9 24	2 [the Jews] kept watch on the *gates* [of Damascus] day and night,

Ac	10 17	the men sent by Cornelius . . . were now standing at the *door*,
	12 10	2 [Peter and the angel] reached the iron *gate* leading to the city.
	13	[Peter] knocked at the outside door (§ of the *entrance*)
	14	instead of opening the *door*, [Rhoda] ran inside with the news that Peter was standing at the main *entrance*.
	14 13	The priests of Zeus-outside-the-Gate . . . brought garlanded oxen to the *gates*.
	16 13	2 [at Philippi] we went along the river outside the *gates* as . . . this was a customary place for prayer.
Heb	13 12 ●	2 Jesus too suffered outside the *gate* [of Jerusalem]

b) Gate (figuratively)

Mt	7 13	2 Enter by the narrow *gate*, since ⌜the road that leads to 2 perdition is wide and spacious (§ the *gate* is wide and the road spacious that leads to perdition) . . . ¹⁴ but it is a 2 narrow *gate* and a hard road that leads to life,
	14	
	16 18 ○	2 the *gates* of the underworld can never hold out against [my Church].
Rv	21 12	The walls of [the holy city] . . . had twelve *gates*; at each of the twelve *gates* there was an angel . . . ¹³ on the east there were three *gates*, on the north three *gates*, on the south three *gates*, and on the west three *gates*.
	13	
	15	a gold measuring rod to measure the city and its *gates*
	21	The twelve *gates* were twelve pearls, each *gate* being made of a single pearl,
	25	The *gates* of [the holy city] will never be shut by day – and there will be no night there –
	22 14	those who will have washed their robes clean . . . can come through the *gates* into the city.

2: DOOR – ENTRANCE – WINDOW: *THYRA*

1 *thyra 39*   2 *thyr-ōros 4*
3 *thyris 2*

a) Door – Entrance (generally)

Mt	6 6	when you pray, go to your private room and . . . shut your *door*,
	27 60	[Joseph of Arimathaea] rolled a large stone across the *entrance* of [Jesus'] tomb
Mk	1 33	The whole town came crowding round the *door*,
	2 2	so many people collected [at the house where Jesus was] that there was no room left, even in front of the *door*.
	11 4	a colt tethered near a *door* in the open street.
	15 46	[Joseph of Arimathaea] rolled a stone against the *entrance* to [Jesus'] tomb,
	16 3	Who will roll away the stone for us from the *entrance* to the tomb?
Lk	11 7	The *door* is bolted now . . . I cannot get up
Jn	18 16	Peter stayed outside the *door*. So the other disciple . . . 2 spoke to the woman who was *keeping the door* and brought 2 Peter in. ¹⁷ The maid *on duty at the door* said to Peter,
	17	
	20 19	the *doors* were closed in the room where the disciples were . . . Jesus came and stood among them.
	26	Eight days later the disciples were in the house again . . . The *doors* were closed, but Jesus came in
Ac	3 2	they used to put [the cripple] down every day near the Temple *entrance* called the Beautiful Gate
	5 9	You hear those footsteps (§ at the *door*)? They have just been to bury your husband.
	19	the angel of the Lord opened the prison *gates*
	23	We found the gaol securely locked and the warders on duty at the *gates*,
	12 6	guards kept watch at the main *entrance* to the prison.
	13	[Peter] knocked at the *outside door* (§ of the entrance)
	16 26	All the *doors* [of the prison] flew open . . . ²⁷ When the gaoler woke and saw the *doors* wide open,
	27	
	21 30	[the people] dragged [Paul] out of the Temple, and the *gates* were closed behind them.

b) Door – Gate – Doorkeeper (figuratively)

Mt	24 33	know that [the Son of Man] is near, at the very *gates*.
	25 10 <	the *door* [of the wedding hall] was closed.
Mk	13 29	know that [the Son of Man] is near, at the very *gates*.
	34 <	2 [the master] has told the *doorkeeper* to stay awake.
Lk	13 24 <	Try your best to enter by the narrow *door*,
	25 <	Once the master of the house has . . . locked the *door*, you may find yourself knocking on the *door*,
Jn	10 1 <	anyone who does not enter the sheepfold through the *gate* . . . 2 < is a thief . . . ² The one who enters through the *gate* is 3 < 2 the shepherd of the flock; ³ the *gatekeeper* lets him in,
	2 <	
	3 < 2	
	7 X	I am the *gate* of the sheepfold . . . ⁹ I am the *gate*. Anyone 9 who enters through me will be safe.
	9	
Ac	14 27	[God] had opened the *door* of faith to the pagans.
1 Co	16 9	[at Ephesus] a big and important *door* has opened for my work

2 Co	2 12	I went up to Troas . . . and the *door* was wide open for my work there in the Lord,
Col	4 3	asking God to ⌐show us opportunities (lit. open a *door*) for announcing the message
Jm	5 9	the Judge is already . . . waiting at the *gates*.
Rv	3 8	I have opened in front of you a *door* that nobody will be able to close
	20	I am standing at the *door*, knocking. If one of you . . . opens the *door*, I will come in to share his meal.
	4 1	in my vision, I saw a *door* open in heaven

c) Window

Ac	20 9	3	Eutychus who was sitting on the *window*-sill . . . fell to the ground three floors below.
2 Co	11 33	3	I had to be let down over the wall in a hamper, through a *window*,

---

BURY – TOMB

---

1. Bier: *soros*	**3. Bury, Burial – Sepulchre, Tomb,**
2. (Be) Carried out for burial – Bury:	**Grave:** *thaptō*
komizō	**4. Tomb:** *mnēmeion*

X = Tomb, Sepulchre, of Jesus

1. BIER: *SOROS*

soros 1

Lk	7 14	[the Lord] put his hand on the *bier* and the bearers stood still,

2. (BE) CARRIED OUT FOR BURIAL – BURY: *KOMIZŌ*

1 ek-komizō 1   2 syn-komizō 1

Lk	7 12		a dead man was being *carried out for burial*, the only son of his mother,
Ac	8 2	2	some devout people . . . *buried* Stephen

3. BURY, BURIAL – SEPULCHRE, TOMB, GRAVE: *THAPTŌ*

6	*taphē*	1	3	*en-taphiasmos 2*
2	*taphos*	7	4	*en-taphiazō 2*
1	*thaptō*	11	5	*syn-thaptō 2*

Mt	8 21		Sir, let me go and *bury* my father first.
	22		Follow me, and leave the dead to *bury* their dead.
	14 12		John's disciples came and took the body [of John] and *buried* it;
	23 27	2	you hypocrites . . . are like whitewashed *tombs*
	29	2	you hypocrites . . . build the *sepulchres* of the prophets
	26 12 X		When [this woman] poured this ointment on my body, she
	4		did it [to prepare me] for *burial*.
	27 7		[the chief priests] bought the potter's field with [the silver
	6		pieces] as a ⌐*graveyard* (or: *cemetery*) for foreigners,
	61 X	2	Mary of Magdala and the other Mary were there, sitting
	2		opposite the *sepulchre*.
	64 X	2	give the order to have the *sepulchre* kept secure until the third day,
	66 X	2	they . . . made the *sepulchre* secure, putting seals on the stone
	28 1	2	Mary of Magdala and the other Mary went to visit the *sepulchre*.
Mk	14 8 X	3	[this woman] has anointed my body beforehand for its *burial*.
Lk	9 59		Let me go and *bury* my father first.
	60		Leave the dead to *bury* their dead;
	16 22		the rich man also died and was *buried*.
Jn	12 7 X	3	she had to keep this scent for the day of my *burial*.
	19 40		They took the body of Jesus and wrapped it . . . in linen
	4		cloths, following the Jewish *burial* custom.
Ac	2 29		David himself is dead and *buried*: his tomb is still with us.
	5 6		The younger men . . . carried [Ananias's body] out and
			buried it.
	9		They have just been to *bury* your husband; they will carry you out, too.
	10		the young men . . . *buried* [Sapphira] by the side of her husband.
Rm	3 13 ○		Their throats are yawning *graves*;
	6 4 X	5	when we were baptised we *went into the tomb* with [Christ]

1 Co	15 4 X		[Christ] was *buried*; and . . . he was raised to life
Col	2 12 X	5	You have been *buried with* [Christ], when you were baptised; and by baptism, too, you have been raised up with him

4. TOMB: *MNĒMEION*

2 mnēma 10   1 mnēmeion 38

Mt	8 28		two demoniacs came towards [Jesus] out of the *tombs*
	23 29		you hypocrites . . . who build the sepulchres of the prophets and decorate the *tombs* of holy men,
	27 52		the *tombs* opened and the bodies of many holy men rose from
	53		the dead, [53] and these, after [Christ's] resurrection, came out of the *tombs*,
	60 X		[Joseph] put [the body of Jesus] in his own new *tomb* . . .
	X		He then rolled a large stone across the entrance of the *tomb*
	28 8 X		the women came quickly away from the *tomb* and ran to tell the disciples.
Mk	5 2		a man with an unclean spirit came out from the *tombs*
	3	2	towards [Jesus]. [3] The man lived in the *tombs* . . . [5] All
	5	2	night and day, among the *tombs* . . . he would howl
	6 29		John's disciples . . . came and took [John's] body and laid it in a *tomb*.
	15 46 X	2	[Joseph] laid [the body of Jesus] in a *tomb* . . . He then rolled
	X		a stone against the entrance of the *tomb*.
	16 2 X	2	on the first day of the week [the women] went to the *tomb*
	3		. . . [3] They had been saying to one another, 'Who will roll away the stone for us from the entrance to the *tomb*?'
	5 X		On entering the *tomb* [the women] saw a young man
	8 X		the women . . . ran away from the *tomb*
Lk	8 27	2	nor did [the demoniac] live in a house, but in the *tombs*.
	11 44		Alas for you [Pharisees], because you are like the unmarked *tombs* that men walk on without know it!
	47		Alas for you who build the *tombs* of the prophets,
	23 53 X	2	[Joseph] put [the body of Jesus] in a *tomb* which was hewn in stone
	55 X		the women . . . took note of the *tomb* and of the position of the body.
	24 1 X	2	[the women] went to the *tomb* with the spices . . . [2] They
	2 X		found that the stone had been rolled away from the *tomb*,
	9 X		When the women returned from the *tomb* they told all this to the Eleven
	12 X		ᵛ Peter, however, went running to the *tomb*.⌐
	22 X		some women . . . went to the *tomb* in the early morning,
	24 X		Some of our friends went to the *tomb*
Jn	5 28		the hour is coming when the dead will leave their *graves* at the sound of his voice:
	11 17		Jesus found that Lazarus had been in the *tomb* for four days
	31		the Jews . . . followed [Mary] . . . thinking that she was going to the *tomb* to weep there.
	38		Still sighing, Jesus reached the *tomb*:
	12 17		All who had been with [Jesus] when he called Lazarus out of the *tomb* . . . were telling how they had witnessed it;
	19 41 X		in this garden [there was] a new *tomb* . . . [42] Since . . . the
	42		*tomb* was near at hand, they laid Jesus there.
	20 1 X		Mary of Magdala came to the *tomb*. She saw that the stone
	2 X		had been moved away from the *tomb* [2] and came running
	X		to Simon Peter . . . 'They have taken the Lord out of the
	3		*tomb*' she said . . . [3] So Peter set out with the other disciple
	4 X		to go to the *tomb*. [4] . . . the other disciple, running faster
	6 X		than Peter, reached the *tomb* first . . . [6] Simon Peter . . .
	8 X		went right into the *tomb* . . . [8] Then the other disciple who
	X		had reached the *tomb* first also went in;
	11 X		Mary stayed outside near the *tomb* . . . she stooped to look
	X		inside the *tomb*, [12] and saw two angels
Ac	2 29	2	David himself is dead and buried: his *tomb* is still with us.
	7 16		[our ancestors'] bodies were brought back to Shechem and
	2		buried in the *tomb* that Abraham had bought
	13 29 X		[the Jews] took [Jesus] down from the tree and buried him in a *tomb*.
Rv	11 9		Men out of every people . . . will stare at [the] corpses [of the two witnesses] . . . not letting them be ⌐buried (lit.
	2		placed in a *tomb*),

BUY – SELL – TRADE

---

1. Buy	1: *pipraskō*
1: *ōneomai*	2: *pōleō*
2: *agorazō*	3: *apo-didōmi*
a) Buy – Spend money on	**3. Offer for sale – Peddle – Hawk:**
b) Buy back – Ransom –	*kapēleuō*
Redeem	**4. Meat Market:** *makellon*
2. Sell – Trade – Market, Merchant	

1. BUY

1: BUY: ŌNEOMAI

ōneomai 1

Ac 7 16   our ancestors'] bodies were . . . buried in the tomb that Abraham had *bought* and paid for

2: BUY: AGORAZŌ

1 *agorazō* 30   2 *ex-agorazō* 3/4

a) Buy – Spend money on

Mt 13 44 <   he . . . sells everything he owns and *buys* the field.
    46 <   he goes and sells everything he owns and *buys* [the pearl of great value].
 14 15   send the people away . . . to *buy* themselves some food.
 21 12   Jesus . . . went into the Temple and drove out all those who were selling and *buying* there;
 25 9   you had better go to those who sell [oil] and *buy* some for yourselves.
    10   [The foolish bridesmaids] had gone off to *buy* [oil] when the bridegroom arrived.
 27 7   [the chief priests] *bought* the potter's field
Mk 6 36   send them away, and they can go . . . to *buy* themselves something to eat
    37   Are we to go and *spend* two hundred denarii *on* bread . . .?
 11 15   [Jesus] began driving out those who were selling and *buying* [in the Temple];
 15 46   [Joseph] *bought* a shroud, took Jesus down from the cross,
 16 1   Mary of Magdala . . . and Salome *bought* spices
Lk 9 13   unless we are to go . . . and *buy* food for all these people.
 14 18   I have *bought* a piece of land and must go and see it.
    19   I have *bought* five yoke of oxen
 17 28   in Lot's day people were eating . . . *buying* and selling,
 22 36   if you have no sword, sell your cloak and *buy* one,
Jn 4 8   His disciples had gone into the town to *buy* food.
  6 5   Where can we *buy* some bread for these people to eat?
 13 29   *Buy* what we need for the festival,
1 Co 7 30 those whose life is *buying* things should live as though they had nothing of their own;
Rv 3 18 < I warn you, *buy* from me the gold that has been tested in the fire
 13 17   [the second beast] made it illegal for anyone to *buy* or sell anything unless he had been branded with the name of the beast
 18 11   there is nobody left to *buy* their cargoes of goods;

b) Buy back – Ransom – Redeem

1 Co 6 20 you have been *bought* and paid for. That is why you should use your body for the glory of God.
  7 23   You have all been *bought* and paid for; do not be slaves of other men.
Ga 3 13   2 Christ *redeemed* us from the curse of the Law
  4 5   2 [God sent his Son] to *redeem* the subjects of the Law
Ep 5 16   2 your lives should ʳ*redeem* (or: make the most of) [this wicked age].
2 P 2 1 false teachers . . . disown the Master who *purchased* their freedom.
Rv 5 9   with your blood you *bought* men for God of every race,
 14 3   they were singing a new hymn . . . that could only be learnt by the hundred and forty-four thousand who had been *redeemed* from the world. [4] These are the ones who . . .
    4   have been *redeemed* from amongst men to be the first-fruits for God

2. SELL – TRADE – MARKET, MERCHANT

1: SELL – TRADE – MARKET, MERCHANT: PIPRASKŌ

1 *pipraskō* 9   5 *em-porion* 1
3 *em-poreuomai* 2   2 *em-poros* 5
4 *em-poria*   1

Mt 13 45 < 2 the kingdom of heaven is like a *merchant* looking for fine pearls; [46] . . . he goes and *sells* everything he owns and buys [the pearl of great value].
 18 25   he had no means of paying, so his master gave orders that he should be *sold*,
 22 5   4 one went off to his farm, another to his *business*,
 26 9   [This ointment] could have been *sold* at a high price and the money given to the poor.

Mk 14 5   Ointment like this could have been *sold* for over three hundred denarii
Jn 2 16   5 stop turning my Father's house into a *market*-place.
 12 5   Why wasn't this ointment *sold* for three hundred denarii . . .?
Ac 2 45   [the faithful] *sold* their goods . . . and shared out the proceeds
  4 34   all those who owned land . . . would sell them, and bring the money from ʳthem (lit. the *sale*),
  5 4   after you had *sold* [your land] wasn't the money yours to do with as you liked?
Rm 7 14 ○ I have been *sold* as a slave to sin.
Jm 4 13   3 we are going to spend a year there, *trading*, and make some money.
2 P 2 3 ○ 3 [The false teachers] will eagerly ʳtry to buy (lit. *trade* on) you for themselves with insidious speeches,
Rv 18 3   2 every *merchant* [has] grown rich through [Babylon's] debauchery. There will be weeping and distress over
    11   2 [Babylon] among all the *traders* of the earth,
    15   2 The *traders* who had made a fortune out of [Babylon] will be standing at a safe distance
    23   2 Your *traders* were the princes of the earth,

2: SELL – TRADE – MARKET, MERCHANT: PŌLEŌ

1 *pōleō* 22   2 (porphyro-)*pōlis* 1

Mt 10 29   ʳCan you not buy two sparrows (lit. Are not two sparrows *sold*) for a penny?
 13 44 <   he . . . *sells* everything he owns and buys the field.
 19 21   *sell* what you own and give the money to the poor,
 21 12   Jesus then went into the Temple and drove out all those who were *selling* and buying there; he upset . . . the chairs of those who were *selling* pigeons.
 25 9   you had better go to those who *sell* [oil] and buy some for yourselves.
Mk 10 21   Go and *sell* everything you own and give the money to the poor,
 11 15   [Jesus] began driving out those who were *selling* and buying [in the Temple]; he upset . . . the chairs of those who were *selling* pigeons.
Lk 12 6   ʳCan you not buy five sparrows (lit. Are not five sparrows *sold*) for two pennies?
    33   *Sell* your possessions and give alms.
 17 28   in Lot's day people were . . . drinking, buying and *selling*,
 18 22   *Sell* all that you own
 19 45   [Jesus] went into the Temple and began driving out those who were *selling*.
 22 36   if you have no sword, *sell* your cloak and buy one,
Jn 2 14   in the Temple [Jesus] found people *selling* cattle and sheep and pigeons,
    16   [Jesus] said to the pigeon-*sellers*, '. . . stop turning my Father's house into a market-place'.
Ac 4 34   all those who owned land or houses would *sell* them,
    37   [Barnabas] *sold* [his land] and brought the money,
  5 1   Ananias . . . and his wife, Sapphira, agreed to *sell* property;
 16 14   2 Lydia . . . was in the purple-dye *trade*.
1 Co 10 25 Do not hesitate to eat anything that is *sold* in butchers' shops:
Rv 13 17   [the second beast] made it illegal for anyone to buy or *sell* anything unless he had been branded with the name of the beast

3: SELL – TRADE – MARKET, MERCHANT: APO-DIDŌMI

apo-didōmi 3/48

Ac 5 8   Peter challenged [Sapphira], 'Tell me, was this the price you *sold* the land for?'
  7 9   (Gn 37 28) The patriarchs were jealous of Joseph and *sold* him into slavery in Egypt.
Heb 12 16 (Gn 25 33) Esau . . . *sold* his birthright for one single meal.

3. OFFER FOR SALE – PEDDLE – HAWK: KAPĒLEUŌ

kapēleuō 1

2 Co 2 17 At least we do not go round *offering* the word of God *for sale*,

4. MEAT MARKET: MAKELLON

makellon 1

1 Co 10 25 Do not hesitate to eat anything that is sold in *butchers' shops*:

C

CAESAR

Augustus (= *Augoustos*)	*1* (Lk 2)	*Caesar* 29	august: 1 *sebastos* 3
Claudius	*2* (Ac 11; 18)		
Tiberius	*1* (Lk 3)		

Note: In Ac 25 – 28 *Caesar* refers to *Nero*

Mt 22	17	Is it permissible to pay taxes to *Caesar* or not?
	21	[Whose head is this?] *Caesar's . . .* give back to *Caesar* what belongs to *Caesar* – and to God what belongs to God.
Mk 12	14	Is it permissible to pay taxes to *Caesar* or not?
	16	Whose head is this? Whose name? *Caesar's . . .* ¹⁷ *. . .* Give back to *Caesar* what belongs to *Caesar*
	17	
Lk 2	1	*Caesar Augustus* issued a decree for a census of the whole world to be taken.
	3	In the fifteenth year of *Tiberius Caesar's* reign . . . the word of God came to John
20	22	Is it permissible for us to pay taxes to *Caesar* or not?
	24	Show me a denarius. Whose head and name are on it?
	25	*Caesar's . . .* ²⁵ *. . .* give back to *Caesar* what belongs to *Caesar*
23	2	We found this man [Jesus] . . . opposing payment of the tribute to *Caesar*
Jn 19	12	If you set [Jesus] free you are no friend of *Caesar's*; anyone who makes himself king is defying *Caesar.*
	15	The chief priests answered, 'We have no king except *Caesar.*'
Ac 11	28	a famine . . . happened before the reign of *Claudius* came to an end.
17	7	[The people who have been turning the world upside down] have broken every one of *Caesar's* edicts by claiming that there is another emperor, Jesus.
18	2	*Claudius* had expelled all the Jews from Rome.
25	8	Paul's defence was this, 'I have committed no offence whatever against either Jewish law, or the Temple, or *Caesar.*
	10	I am standing before the tribunal of *Caesar*, and this is where I should be tried.
	11	I appeal to *Caesar.*
	12	Festus . . . replied, 'You have appealed to *Caesar*; to *Caesar* you shall go.'
	21	Paul put in an appeal for his case to be reserved for the judgement of the *august* [emperor], so I ordered him to be remanded until I could send him to *Caesar.*
	25	when [Paul] himself appealed to the *august* [emperor], I decided to send him.
26	32	[Paul] could have been set free if he had not appealed to *Caesar.*
27	1	Paul and some other prisoners were handed over to a centurion called Julius, of the *Augustan* cohort.
	24	Do not be afraid, Paul. You are destined to appear before *Caesar,*
28	19	I was forced to appeal to *Caesar,*
Ph 4	22	All the saints send their greetings, especially those of the *imperial* household.

CAESAREA – JOPPA

Caesarea (in Palestine)	*15*	*Antipatris*	*1* (Ac 23)	*1 polis 3/164*
J *Joppa* [*Jaffa*]	*10*	*Azotus*	*1* (Ac 8)	
Lydda	*3* (Ac 9)	*Gaza*	*1* (Ac 8)	
		Sharon [*Saron*]	*1* (Ac 9 35)	

Ac 8	26	[Philip,] set out at noon along the road that goes from Jerusalem down to *Gaza,*
	40	Philip found that he had reached *Azotus* and continued his journey proclaiming the Good News in every town as far as *Caesarea.*
9	30	the brothers . . . took [Saul] to *Caesarea,*
	32	Peter . . . came to the saints living down in *Lydda.*
	35	everybody who lived in *Lydda* and *Sharon* saw [the paralytic get up]

Ac 9	36 J	At *Jaffa* there was a woman disciple called Tabitha, ³⁷ . . .
	38 J	she . . . died . . . ³⁸ *Lydda* is not far from *Jaffa*, so . . . they sent two men . . . for [Peter],
	42 J	The whole of *Jaffa* heard about it and many believed in the Lord.
	43 J	Peter stayed on some time in *Jaffa*, lodging with a leather-tanner called Simon.
10	1	One of the centurions of the Italica cohort stationed in *Caesarea* was called Cornelius.
	5 J	Now you must send someone to *Jaffa* and fetch a man . . . known as Peter.
	8 J	[Cornelius called two of the slaves] and sent them off to *Jaffa*
	9	while [the men sent by Cornelius] . . . had only a short
	J 1	distance to go before reaching ⌐*Jaffa* (lit. the *city*), Peter went to the housetop . . . to pray.
	23	Next day [Peter] was ready to go off with them, accompanied by some of the brothers from *Jaffa*. ²⁴ They reached *Caesarea*
	24 J	the following day and Cornelius was waiting for them.
	32 J	you must send to *Jaffa* and fetch Simon known as Peter
11	5 J 1	'When I was in the *town* of *Jaffa*,' [Peter] began, 'I fell into a trance while I was praying
	11	three men . . . had been sent from *Caesarea* to fetch me,
	13 J	Send to *Jaffa* and fetch Simon known as Peter,
12	19	before leaving Judaea to take up residence in *Caesarea* [Herod] gave orders for [the guards'] execution.
18	22	[Paul] landed at *Caesarea*, and went up to greet the church.
21	8	we left and came to *Caesarea.*
	16	Some of the disciples from *Caesarea* accompanied us [to Jerusalem]
23	23	Get two hundred soldiers ready to leave for *Caesarea*
	31	The soldiers . . . escorted [Paul] by night to *Antipatris.*
	33	On arriving at *Caesarea* the escort delivered the letter to the governor
25	1	Three days after his arrival . . . Festus went up to Jerusalem from *Caesarea.*
	4	Festus replied that Paul would remain in custody in *Caesarea,*
	6	After staying [in Jerusalem] for eight or ten days at the most, [Festus] went down to *Caesarea.*
	13	Agrippa and Bernice arrived in *Caesarea* and paid their respects to Festus
	23	Agrippa and Bernice . . . entered the audience chamber
	1	attended by the tribunes and the *city* notables;

CARE – CONCERN – DEVOTION

1. **Care (for), Look after, (Be) Concerned – Prepare for – Neglect:** *melō*
2. **Care (Be) Concerned – Worry, Anxiety, Anxious**
  1: Care, (Be) Concerned, Anxious – Worry, Anxiety: *merimna*
  2: Worry, Be anxious: *met-eōrizō*
3. **Do one's best to, Take pains to, Strive to:** *askeō*
4. **Do all one can to, (Be) Anxious to, Concern – Keen(ness), Eager, Earnest – Effort, Care, Zeal:** *spoudē*
5. **Anxious to, Eager to – Readiness – Willing(ly), Readily:** *pro-thymia*
6. **Undertake to, Determine to, Try to:**

7. **In = Busy with, Absorbed in – Take care:** *en*
8. **Devoted to, Occupied with, Absorbed in:** *syn-echō*
9. **Devote oneself to:** *scholazō*
10. **Occupy oneself in, Engage in:** *pro-(h)istēmi*
11. **Care for, Look after – Cherish:** *thalpō*
12. **Look after, Provide for, Make provision for – Foresight – (Be) Interested in:** *pro-noia*
13. **Busybody – Interfere, Meddle:** *peri-ergos*

1. CARE (FOR), LOOK AFTER, (BE) CONCERNED – PREPARE FOR – NEGLECT: *MELŌ*

4	*meletaō* 2	5 *epi-meleia*	*1*
1	*melō* 10	3 *epi-meleomai*	*3*
2	*a-meleō* 4	6 *epi-melōs*	*1*
		7 *pro-meletaō*	*1*

Mt 22	5 2	[Come to the wedding.] But they *were not interested*:
	16 X	you . . . teach the way of God . . . a man's rank *means nothing* to you.
Mk 4	38 X	Master, do you not *care*? We are going down!

Mk 12 14 X	you are an honest man . . . rank *means* no*thing* to you,
Lk 10 34	3 [the Samaritan] carried him to the inn and *looked after*
35	him. ³⁵ . . . he took out two denarii and handed them to the innkeeper. '*Look after* him,'
40 X	Lord, do you not *care* that my sister is leaving me to do the serving all by myself?
15 8	6 what woman . . . would not . . . search *thoroughly* till she found [the lost drachma]?
21 14	7 Keep this carefully in mind: you are not to *prepare* your defence.
Jn 10 13	he is only a hired man and *has no concern* for the sheep.
12 6	[Judas] said this, not because he *cared about* the poor,
Ac 4 25 ○	4 (Ps 2 1) Why . . . these futile *plots* among the peoples?
18 17	Gallio refused to *take* any *notice* at all.
27 3	Julius was considerate enough to allow Paul to go to his
5	friends to *be looked after*.
1 Co 7 21	If, when you were called, you were a slave, do not *let this bother you*;
9 9 Θ	Is it about oxen that God *is concerned*,
1 Tm 3 5	how can any man who does not understand how to manage
3	his own family *have responsibility for* the church of God?
4 14	2 You have in you a spiritual gift . . . do not *let it lie unused.*
15	4 ¹⁵ *Think hard* about all this,
Heb 2 3	2 we shall certainly not go unpunished if we *neglect* this salvation
8 9	(Jr 31 32 G) They abandoned that covenant of mine, and so
Θ 2	I on my side *deserted* them. It is the Lord who speaks.
1 P 5 7 Θ	unload all your worries on to [God], since he is *looking after* you.

2. CARE, (BE) CONCERNED – WORRY, ANXIETY, ANXIOUS

1: CARE, (BE) CONCERNED, ANXIOUS – WORRY, ANXIETY: *MERIMNA*

2 *merimna* 6	3 *a-merimnos* 2
1 *merimnaō* 19	4 *pro-merimnaō* 1

Mt 6 25	I am telling you not to *worry* about life
27	Can any of you, for all his *worrying*, add one single cubit to his span of life?
28	And why *worry* about clothing?
31	So do not *worry*; do not say, 'What are we to eat?'
34	So do not *worry* about tomorrow: tomorrow will *take care* of itself.
10 19	when they hand you over, do not *worry* about how to speak or what to say;
13 22	2 the *worries* of this world and the lure of riches choke the word
28 14	we undertake to put things right with him ourselves and to
3	see ʳthat you do not get into trouble (lit. you *free from anxiety*).
Mk 4 19	2 the *worries* of this world . . . choke the word
13 11	4 when they lead you away to hand you over, do not *worry beforehand* about what to say;
Lk 8 14	2 as they go on their way they are choked by the *worries* and riches
10 41	Martha, . . . you *worry* and fret about so many things,
12 11	do not *worry* about now to defend yourselves
22	I am telling you not to *worry* about your life . . . ²⁵ Can
25	any of you, for all his *worrying*, add a single cubit to his
26	span of life? ²⁶ If the smallest things, therefore, are outside your control, why *worry* about the rest?
21 34	Watch yourselves, or your hearts will be coarsened with
2	debauchery and drunkenness and the *cares* of life,
1 Co 7 32	3 I would like to see you *free from* all *worry*. An unmarried
33	man can *devote* himself *to* the Lord's affairs . . . ³³ but a married man has to *bother* about the world's affairs . . .
34	³⁴ . . . In the same way an unmarried woman . . . can *devote* herself *to* the Lord's affairs . . . The married woman has to *worry* about the world's affairs
12 25	[God has arranged the body so] that each part may *be equally concerned* for all the others.
2 Co 11 28	2 my daily preoccupation: my *anxiety* for all the churches.
Ph 2 20	I have nobody else like [Timothy] here, as whole-heartedly *concerned* for your welfare:
4 6	There is no need to *worry*; but if there is anything you need, pray for it,
1 P 5 7	2 unload all your *worries* on to [God], since he is looking after you.

2: WORRY, BE ANXIOUS: *MET-EŌRIZŌ*

met-eōrizō 1

Lk 12 29	you must not set your hearts on things to eat and things to drink; nor must you *worry*.

3. DO ONE'S BEST TO, TAKE PAINS TO, STRIVE TO: *ASKEŌ*

askeō 1

Ac 24 16	I . . . *do my best to* keep a clear conscience

4. DO ALL ONE CAN TO, (BE) ANXIOUS TO, CONCERN – KEEN(NESS), EAGER, EARNEST – EFFORT, CARE, ZEAL: *SPOUDĒ*

3 *speudō* 2	2 *spoudazō* 10	5 *spoudaios* 3
4 *spoudaiōs* 4	1 *spoudē* 10	

Lk 7 4	4 When [the Jewish elders] came to Jesus they pleaded *earnestly* with him.
Ac 20 16	3 [Paul] *was anxious* to be in Jerusalem . . . for the day of Pentecost.
Rm 12 8	Let . . . the officials be *diligent*,
11	Work for the Lord with untiring *effort* and with great earnestness
2 Co 7 11	Just look at what suffering in God's way has brought you: what *keenness*,
12	it was to make you realise, in the sight of God, your own *concern* for us.
8 7	You always have the most of everything . . . of understanding, of *keenness* for any cause,
8	I am just testing the genuineness of your love against the *keenness* of others.
16	I thank God for putting into Titus' heart the same *concern* for you
17	5 [Titus] is *more concerned* than ever, and is visiting you on his own initiative.
22	5 a third brother, of whose *keenness* we have often had proof
5	. . . and who is particularly *keen* about this,
Ga 2 10	2 we should remember to help the poor, as indeed I *was anxious* to do.
Ep 4 3	2 *Do all you can to* preserve the unity of the Spirit
Ph 2 28	4 I shall send [Epaphroditus] back as promptly as (or: *eagerly as*) I can;
1 Th 2 17	2 we had an especially strong desire and *longing* to see you face to face again,
2 Tm 1 17	4 [Onesiphorus] searched ʳhard (lit. *eagerly*) for me and found out where I was.
2 15	2 *Do all you can to* present yourself in front of God as a man who has come through his trials,
4 9	2 *Do your best to* come and see me as soon as you can.
21	2 *Do your best to* come before the winter.
Tt 3 13	4 *Do all you can to* see to all the travelling arrangements for Zenas
Heb 4 11	2 We must therefore *do everything we can to* reach this place of rest,
6 11	Our one desire is that . . . you should go on showing the same *earnestness*
2 P 1 5	you will have to *do your utmost* yourselves, adding goodness to the faith that you have,
10	2 work all the harder (lit. be all the more *zealous*) to justify [your calling].
15	2 I shall *take* great *care* that . . . you will still have a means to recall these things to memory.
3 12	3 while you wait and *long for* (or: work to hasten) the Day of God to come,
14	2 *do your best to* live lives without spot or stain
Jude 3	I was *eagerly* looking forward to writing to you

5. ANXIOUS TO, EAGER TO – READINESS – WILLING(LY), READILY: *PRO-THYMIA*

1 *pro-thymia* 5	3 *pro-thymōs* 1
2 *pro-thymos* 3	

Mt 26 41	2 The spirit is *willing*, but the flesh is weak.
Mk 14 38	2 The spirit is *willing*, but the flesh is weak.
Ac 17 11	[the Jews at Beroea] welcomed the word very *readily*;
Rm 1 15	2 it is this that makes me ʳwant (lit. *eager*) to bring the Good News to you
2 Co 8 11	let the results be worthy, as far as you can afford it, of the ʳdecision you made (lit. *readiness* with which you made the decision)
12	As long as the *readiness* is there, a man is acceptable with whatever he can afford;
19	for the glory of God, we have undertaken to satisfy our ʳimpatience (lit. *eagerness*) to help.
9 2	I know how *anxious* you are to help; in fact, I boast about you to the Macedonians,
1 P 5 2	watch over [the flock of God] . . . not for sordid money,
3	but because you are *eager* to do it.

6. UNDERTAKE TO, DETERMINE TO, TRY TO: *EPI-CHEIREŌ*

epi-cheireō 3

Lk	1 1	many others have *undertaken to* draw up accounts of the events
Ac	9 29	after [Saul] had spoken to the Hellenists . . . they *became determined to* kill him.
	19 13	some itinerant Jewish exorcists *tried* pronouncing the name of the Lord

7. IN = BUSY WITH, ABSORBED IN – TAKE CARE: *EN*

en (+ dat.) (2)

Lk	2 49	Did you not know that I must be *busy with* my Father's affairs?
1 Tm	4 15	Think hard about all this, and ʳput it into practice (lit. be *absorbed in* it),

8. DEVOTED TO, OCCUPIED WITH, ABSORBED IN: *SYN-ECHŌ*

syn-echō 1/12

Ac	18 5	Paul ʳ*devoted* all *his time to* (or: was totally *absorbed in*) preaching,

9. DEVOTE ONESELF TO: *SCHOLAZŌ*

scholazō 1/2

1 Co	7 5	Do not refuse each other except . . . for an agreed time, to ʳleave yourselves free for (or: *devote yourselves to*) prayer;

10. OCCUPY ONESELF IN, ENGAGE IN: *PRO-(H)ISTĒMI*

pro-(h)istēmi 2/8

Tt	3 8	so that those who now believe in God may *keep* their minds constantly *occupied in* doing good works.
	14	All our people are to learn to *occupy themselves in* doing good works for their practical needs as well,

11. CARE FOR, LOOK AFTER – CHERISH: *THALPŌ*

thalpō 2

Ep	5 29	A man . . . feeds [his own body] and *looks after* it;
1 Th	2 7	like a mother feeding and *looking after* her own children,

12. LOOK AFTER, PROVIDE FOR, MAKE PROVISION FOR – FORE-SIGHT – (BE) INTERESTED IN: *PRO-NOIA*

1 pro-noeō 3   2 pro-noia 2

Ac	24 2	2 the reforms this nation owes to your *foresight*
Rm	12 17	(Pr 3 4 G) you *are interested* only *in* the highest ideals.
	13 14	2 ʳforget about (lit. do not only *be interested in*) satisfying your bodies with all their cravings.
2 Co	8 21	(Pr 3 4 G) we are *trying* to do right not only in the sight of God but also in the sight of men.
1 Tm	5 8	Anyone who does not *look after* his own relations . . . has rejected the faith

13. BUSYBODY – INTERFERE, MEDDLE: *PERI-ERGOS*

1 peri-ergazomai 1   2 peri-ergos 1/2

2 Th	3 11	there are some of you who are living in idleness, doing no work themselves but *interfering* with everyone else's.
1 Tm	5 13	2 [young widows] learn to be gossips and *meddlers in* other people's *affairs*,

CAREFUL – ACCURATE – STRICT

Careful, Ask carefully, (in) Detail – Accurate, Exact, Ascertain – Strict

3 *akribeia 1*	2 *akriboō 2*
4 *akribēs 1*	1 *akribōs 9*

Mt	2 7	2 Herod . . . *asked* [the wise men] *the exact* date on which the star had appeared.
	8	Go and find out ʳall about (lit. *carefully* about) the child,
	16	2 reckoning by the date he had *been careful to ask* the wise men.
Lk	1 3	I in my turn, after *carefully* going over the whole story . . , have decided to write an ordered account
Ac	18 25	[Apollos] . . . was *accurate in* all the *details* he taught about Jesus, . . . ²⁶ . . . Priscilla and Aquila . . . gave him ʳfurther (lit. more *accurate*) instruction about the Way.
	26	
	22 3	3 I was taught the *exact observance* of the Law of our ancestors.
	23 15	as though you meant to examine [Paul's] case more *closely*;
	20	as though they meant to inquire more *closely* into [Paul's] case.
	24 22	Felix, who knew more *accurately* about the Way than most people,
	26 5	4 I followed the *strictest* party in our religion
Ep	5 15	ʳbe very careful (lit. take *strict* care) about the sort of lives you lead,
1 Th	5 2	you know *very well* that the Day of the Lord is going to come like a thief in the night.

CATCH – SEIZE – STEAL

1. **Catch:** *agreuō*
2. **(Be) Caught:** *halōsis*
3. **Catch, Trap:** *drassomai*
4. **Snare, Trap – Catch out:** *thēreuō*
5. **Trap, Snare:** *pagideuō*
6. **Lie in wait for, Ambush – Set traps (for):** *en-(h)edra*
7. **Catch – Seize:** *krateō*
   1: Arrest, Take in charge – (the authorities) Seize, Lay hands on
   2: Take (by the hand), Catch hold of – Seize (generally) – Cling to
8. **Catch – Seize, Arrest – Take:** *piazō*
   1: Arrest, Apprehend – Seize, Catch, Take prisoner
   2: Catch (fish)
   3: Take (by the hand)
9. **Take by force, Snatch, Seize – Burgle, Rob – to Exact, Extortion**
   1: Take by force, Snatch, Seize – Burgle, Plunder, Rob – Grasping, Extortion: *harpazō*

2: to Exact, Collect, Draw out – Bailiff: *prassō*
10. **Spoil(s)**
    1: *skylon*
    2: *(akro-)thinion*
11. **Robber – Brigand, Bandit:** *lēstēs*
12. **Rob – Capture:** *sylaō*
    1: Rob
    2: Capture
13. **Steal, Theft – Thief, Burglar:** *kleptō*
14. **Petty thieving, Pilfering, Stealing – Keep back (what is due):** *nosphizomai*
15. **Defraud, Cheat – Take advantage of, Exploit**
    1: Cheat, Defraud: *syko-phanteō*
    2: Defraud, Cheat – Not to give, Refuse, Deny: *apo-stereō*
    3: Exploit, Take advantage of, Defraud: *pleon-ekteō*
16. **Kidnappers:** *andra-podistēs*

1. CATCH: *AGREUŌ*

1 agra 2   2 zō-greō 2
3 agreuō 1

Mk	12 13 X	[the Jews] sent to [Jesus] some Pharisees and some Herodians 3 to *catch* him *out* in what he said.
Lk	5 4	pay out your nets for a *catch*.
	9	[Simon Peter] and all his companions were completely
	10	overcome by the *catch* they had made; ¹⁰ . . . Jesus said
	2	to Simon, '. . . from now on it is men you will *catch*'.
2 Tm	2 26 ⑩	2 once out of the trap where the devil *caught* them

2. (BE) CAUGHT: *HALŌSIS*

halōsis 1

2 P	2 12	these people . . . are . . . simply animals born to be *caught* and killed,

3. CATCH, TRAP: *DRASSOMAI*

drassomai 1

1 Co 3 19 Θ	(Jb 5 13) God ⌐is not convinced by the arguments of the wise (lit. *catches* the wise in their own arguments).

4. SNARE, TRAP – CATCH OUT: *THĒREUŌ*

1 *thēra 1*   2 *thēreuō 1*

Lk 11 54 X 2	[the scribes and Pharisees tried to force answers from him,] setting traps to *catch* him *out* in something he might say.
Rm 11 9	May their own table prove a trap for them, a *snare*

5. TRAP, SNARE: *PAGIDEUŌ*

2 *pagideuō 1*   1 *pagis 5*

Mt 22 15 X 2	the Pharisees went away to work out . . . how to *trap* him in what he said.
Lk 21 35	[that day will be sprung on you suddenly,] like a *trap*.
Rm 11 9	(Ps 69 22) May their own table prove a *trap* for them, a snare
1Tm 3 7 ⅅ	so that [the elder] never . . . falls into the devil's *trap*.
6 9	People who long to be rich . . . get *trapped* into all sorts of . . . dangerous ambitions
2 Tm 2 26 ⅅ	once out of the *trap* where the devil caught them

6. LIE IN WAIT FOR, AMBUSH – SET TRAPS (FOR): *EN-(H)EDRA*

1 *en-(h)edra 2*   2 *en-(h)edreuō 2*

Lk 11 54 X 2	[the scribes and Pharisees tried to force answers from him,] *setting traps* to catch him out in something he might say.
Ac 23 16	the son of Paul's sister heard of the *ambush* [they were laying]
21 2	There are more than forty of them *lying in wait for* [Paul]
25 3	[The chief priests and leaders of the Jews] were . . . preparing an *ambush* to murder [Paul] on the way.

7. CATCH – SEIZE: *KRATEŌ*

krateō 30/47

1: ARREST, TAKE IN CHARGE – (THE AUTHORITIES) SEIZE, LAY HANDS ON

Mt 14 3	it was Herod who had *arrested* John,
21 46 X	though [the chief priests and scribes] would have liked to *arrest* him they were afraid of the crowds,
26 4 X	[the chief priests and elders] made plans to *arrest* Jesus
48 X	The one I kiss, . . . he is the man. *Take* him *in charge*.
50 X	Then they . . . seized Jesus and *took* him *in charge*.
55 X	I sat teaching in the Temple day after day and you never *laid hands on* me.
57 X	The men who had *arrested* Jesus led him off to Caiaphas
Mk 6 17	it was this same Herod who had sent to have John *arrested*,
12 12 X	they would have liked to *arrest* him,
14 1	the chief priests and the scribes were looking for a way to *arrest* Jesus by some trick
44 X	The one I kiss, . . . he is the man. *Take* him *in charge*,
46 X	The others seized him and *took* him *in charge*.
49 X	I was among you . . . day after day and you never *laid hands on* me.
Ac 24 6	We *placed* [Paul] under arrest,

2: TAKE (BY THE HAND), CATCH HOLD OF – SEIZE (GENERALLY) – CLING TO

Mt 9 25	[Jesus] *took* the little girl by the hand
12 11	would [you] not *get hold of* [the sheep] and lift it out [of the hole]?
18 28	this servant . . . *seized* [his fellow servant] by the throat
22 6	the rest *seized* [the king's] servants, maltreated them and killed them.
28 9	the women . . , falling down before [Jesus], *clasped* his feet.
Mk 1 31	[Jesus] *took* Simon's mother-in-law by the hand and helped her up.
3 21 X	his relatives . . . set out to *take charge of* him,
5 41	*taking* the child by the hand [Jesus] said to [Jairus's daughter],
9 27	Jesus *took* the boy by the hand and helped him up,
14 51	They *caught hold of* [the young man who followed Jesus].

Lk 8 54	*taking* her by the hand [Jesus] called to [Jairus's daughter],
Ac 2 24	it was impossible for [Jesus] to be *held in* [the pangs of Hades];
3 11	the [lame] man was still *clinging to* Peter and John.
Heb 6 18	we . . . should have a strong encouragement to *take a firm grip* on the hope that is held out to us.
Rv 2 15	there are some . . . who ⌐accept (lit. *cling to*) what the Nicolaitans teach.
20 2	[an angel] ⌐overpowered (lit. *seized*) the dragon,

8. CATCH – SEIZE, ARREST – TAKE: *PIAZŌ*

piazō 12

1: ARREST, APPREHEND – SEIZE, CATCH, TAKE PRISONER

Jn 7 30 X	They would have *arrested* him then,
32 X	the Pharisees sent the Temple police to *arrest* him.
44 X	Some would have liked to *arrest* him,
8 20 X	No one *arrested* him,
10 39 X	They wanted to *arrest* him then, but he eluded them.
11 57 X	anyone who knew where he was must inform them so that they could *arrest* him.
Ac 12 4	[Herod] *apprehended* and put Peter in prison,
2 Co 11 32	the ethnarch . . . put guards round the city to *catch* me,
Rv 19 20	the Beast was *taken prisoner*,

2: CATCH (FISH)

Jn 21 3	they . . . *caught* nothing that night.
10	Bring some of the fish you have just *caught*.

3: TAKE (BY THE HAND)

Ac 3 7	Peter then *took* [the lame man] by the hand and helped him to stand up.

9. TAKE BY FORCE, SNATCH, SEIZE – BURGLE, ROB – TO EXACT, EXTORTION

1: TAKE BY FORCE, SNATCH, SEIZE – BURGLE, PLUNDER, ROB – GRASPING, EXTORTION: *HARPAZŌ*

4 *harpagē*	3	1 *harpazō*	14
6 *harpagmos*	1	5 *di-harpazō*	2
2 *harpax*	5	3 *syn-harpazō*	4

Mt 7 15 2	false prophets . . . come to you disguised as sheep but underneath are *ravenous* wolves.
11 12	the violent are *taking* [the kingdom of heaven] *by storm*.
12 29 < 5	can anyone make his way into a strong man's house and *burgle* his property unless he has tied up the strong man first? Only then can he *burgle* his house.
13 19 ⅅ	the evil one comes and *carries off* what was sown in his heart;
23 25 4	You . . . clean the outside of cup and dish and leave the inside full of *extortion* and intemperance.
Mk 3 27 < 5	no one can make his way into a strong man's house and *burgle* his property unless he has tied up the strong man first. Only then can he *burgle* his house.
Lk 8 29 ⅅ 3	It was a devil that had *seized* [on] him a great many times.
11 39 4	inside yourselves you are filled with *extortion* and wickedness.
18 11 2	I am not *grasping* . . . like the rest of mankind,
Jn 6 15	Jesus . . . could see they were about to come and take him *by force* and make him king,
10 12 <	the wolf ⌐attacks (lit. *plunders*) and scatters the sheep;
28	no one will ever ⌐*steal* (or: *snatch*) [my sheep] from me.
29	no one can ⌐*steal* (or: *snatch*) from the Father.
Ac 6 12 3	they took Stephen *by surprise*, and . . . brought him before the Sanhedrin.
8 39 Ⓢ	Philip was *taken away* by the Spirit of the Lord,
19 29 3	the mob rushed to the theatre *dragging along* two of Paul's Macedonian travelling companions, Gaius and Aristarchus.
23 10	the tribune . . . ordered his troops to . . . *haul* [Paul] *out* [of the Sanhedrin] and bring him to the fortress.
27 15 3	The ship was *caught* and could not be turned head-on to the wind.
1 Co 5 10 2	I was not meaning to include . . . all ⌐*swindlers* (or: *robbers*) . . . [11] . . . you should not associate with a
11 2	brother Christian who is . . . ⌐*dishonest* (lit. a *robber*);
6 10 2	thieves, usurers . . . and ⌐*swindlers* (or: *robbers*) will never inherit the kingdom of God.
2 Co 12 2	I know a man . . . who . . . was *caught up* . . . into the third heaven.

2 Co	12	4	[this same person] was *caught up* into paradise
Ph	2	6	6 [Christ Jesus] did not *cling to* [his] equality with God
1 Th	4	17	[we] will be *taken up* into the clouds . . . to meet the Lord
Heb	10	34	4 you happily accepted ꜓being stripped (or: the *seizure*) of your belongings,
Jude		23	when there are some to be saved from the fire, *pull* them *out*;
Rv	12	5	the child was *taken* [straight] *up* to God

2: TO EXACT, COLLECT, DRAW OUT – BAILIFF: *PRASSŌ*

1 *praktōr* 2   2 *prassō* 2/39

Lk	3	13	2 *Exact* no more than your rate.
	12	58	the judge [may] hand you over to the *bailiff* and the *bailiff* have you thrown into prison.
	19	23	2 On my return I could have *drawn* [my money] *out* with interest.

10. SPOIL(S)

1: SPOIL(S): *SKYLON*

skylon 1

Lk	11	22	when someone stronger than he is . . . defeats him, the stronger man . . . shares out his *spoil*.

2: SPOIL(S): *(AKRO-)THINION*

(akro-)thinion 1

Heb	7	4	Abraham paid a tenth of the *treasure* he had *captured*.

11. ROBBER – BRIGAND, BANDIT: *LĒSTĒS*

lēstēs 15

Mt	21	13	(Jr 7 11) my house will be called a house of prayer; but you are turning it into a *robbers'* den.
	26	55 X	Am I a *brigand*, that you had to . . . capture me with swords . . .?
	27	38	two *robbers* were crucified with him,
		44	Even the *robbers* who were crucified with him taunted him
Mk	11	17	(Jr 7 11) My house will be called a house of prayer . . . But you have turned it into a *robbers'* den.
	14	48 X	Am I a *brigand* . . . that you had to . . . capture me with swords and clubs?
	15	27	they crucified two *robbers* with him,
Lk	10	30	A man . . . fell into the hands of ꜓brigands (or: *bandits*);
		36	Which of these three . . . proved himself a neighbour to the man who fell into the *brigands'* hands?
	19	46	(Jr 7 11) my house will be a house of prayer. But you have turned it into a *robbers'* den.
	22	52 X	Am I a *brigand* . . . that you had to set out with swords and clubs?
Jn	10	1	anyone who does not enter the sheepfold through the gate, but gets in some other way is a thief and a *brigand*.
		8 <	All others who have come are thieves and *brigands*;
	18	40	Barabbas was a *brigand*.
2 Co	11	26	I have been in danger from . . . *brigands*,

12. ROB – CAPTURE: *SYLAŌ*

1 *sylaō*   1   3 *(hiero-)syleō* 1
2 *syl-agōgeō* 1

1: ROB

Rm	2	22	3 you despise idols, yet you *rob* their temples.
2 Co	11	8	I was *robbing* other churches, living on them so that I could serve you.

2: CAPTURE

Col	2	8	2 Make sure that no one [traps you and] *deprives* you *of your freedom* by some secondhand . . . philosophy

13. STEAL, THEFT – THIEF, BURGLAR: *KLEPTŌ*

4 *klemma 1*   2 *kleptō 13*
1 *kleptēs 16*   3 *klopē 2*

Mt	6	19	Do not store up treasures for yourselves on earth, where
		20 /2	. . . *thieves* can break in and *steal*. [20] But . . . in heaven,
		/2	where . . . *thieves* cannot break in and *steal*.
	15	19 3	From the heart come evil intentions: murder, . . . *theft*,
	19	18 2	(Ex 20 15) You must not kill. . . . You must not *steal*.
	24	43 <	if the householder had known at what time of night the *burglar* would come,
	27	64 2	for fear his disciples come and *steal* him [away]
	28	13 2	His disciples came during the night and *stole* him [away] while we were asleep.
Mk	7	21	it is from within . . . that evil intentions emerge: fornication,
		3	*theft*,
	10	19 2	(Ex 20 15) You must not kill; . . . You must not *steal*;
Lk	12	33	Get yourselves . . . treasure. . . in heaven where no *thief* can reach it
		39 <	if the householder had known at what hour the *burglar* would come,
	18	20	(Ex 20 15) You must not commit adultery; . . . You must
		2	not *steal*;
Jn	10	1	anyone who does not enter the sheepfold through the gate,
		<	but gets in some other way is a *thief* and a brigand.
		8 <	All others who have come are *thieves* and brigands;
		10 < /2	The *thief* comes only to *steal* and kill and destroy.
	12	6	[Judas] was a *thief*; he was in charge of the common fund and used to help himself to the contributions.
Rm	2	21 2/2	You preach against *stealing*, yet you *steal*;
	13	9 2	(Ex 20 15) you shall not *steal*, you shall not covet,
1 Co	6	10	*thieves*, usurers, . . . will never inherit the kingdom of God.
Ep	4	28 2/2	Anyone who *was a thief* must stop *stealing*.
1 Th	5	2 ●	the Day of the Lord is going to come like a *thief* in the
			night. . . . [4] But it is not as if you live in the dark, . . .
		4 ●	for that Day to overtake you like a *thief*.
1 P	4	15	None of you should ever deserve to suffer for being a murderer, a *thief*,
2 P	3	10 ●	The Day of the Lord will come like a *thief*,
Rv	3	3 ●	If you do not wake up, I shall come to you like a *thief*,
	9	21 4	Nor did they give up their murdering, or . . . *stealing*.
	16	15 ●	I shall come like a *thief*. Happy is the man who has stayed awake

14. PETTY THIEVING, PILFERING, STEALING – KEEP BACK (WHAT IS DUE): *NOSPHIZOMAI*

nosphizomai 3

Ac	5	2	[Ananias agreed to sell a property;] but . . . he *kept back* part of the proceeds,
		3	how can Satan have so possessed you that you should . . . *keep back* part of the money from the land?
Tt	2	10	[Tell the slaves that] there must be no *petty thieving*

15. DEFRAUD, CHEAT – TAKE ADVANTAGE OF, EXPLOIT

1: CHEAT, DEFRAUD: *SYKO-PHANTEŌ*

syko-phanteō 2

Lk	3	14	꜓No [extortion by] false accusation (or: No *cheating*)!
	19	8	if I have *cheated* anybody I will pay him back four times the amount.

2: DEFRAUD, CHEAT – NOT TO GIVE, REFUSE, DENY: *APO-STEREŌ*

apo-stereō 5

Mk	10	19	You must not bring false witness; You must not *defraud*;
1 Co	6	7	oughtn't you to let yourselves . . . be *cheated*? [8] But you are
		8	doing the wronging and the *cheating*, and to your own brothers.
	7	5 ○	[Husband and wife,] do not *refuse* each other
1 Tm	6	5	people who are ꜓neither rational nor informed (lit. not rational and have been *denied* the truth) . . . imagine that religion is a way of making a profit.

3: EXPLOIT, TAKE ADVANTAGE OF, DEFRAUD: *PLEON-EKTEŌ*

pleon-ekteō 5

2 Co	2	11 Ⓓ	so we will not be ꜓outwitted (or: *taken advantage of*) by Satan –
	7	2	We have not injured anyone, or ruined anyone, or *exploited* anyone.
	12	17	So we *exploited* you, did we, through one of the men that I
		18	have sent to you? [18] . . . Can Titus have *exploited* you?
1 Th	4	6	[God] wants nobody at all ever to ꜓sin by *taking* (or: sin against or *take*) advantage of a brother

16. KIDNAPPERS: *ANDRA-PODISTĒS*

andra-podistēs 1

1 Tm 1 10	[laws are framed] for those who are immoral with women or with boys, for *kidnappers*, for liars and for perjurers –

CHANGE

1. **Change – Turn into – Unalterable, Unchangeable:** *meta-tithēmi*
2. **Change – Turn into, Be turned into:** *meta-strephō*
3. **Change – Turn into, Be turned to:** *meta-trepō*
4. **Change – Alter, Vary – Exchange for:** *allassō*
5. **One thing for another – For:** *anti*
6. **Repay (good deeds):** *amoibē*

1. CHANGE – TURN INTO – UNALTERABLE, UNCHANGEABLE: *META-TITHĒMI*

1 *meta-thesis* 2/3   3 *a-meta-thetos* 2
2 *meta-tithēmi* 2/6

Heb 6 17		God wanted to make the heirs to the promise thoroughly realise that his purpose was *unalterable*,
18	Θ 3	there would be two *unalterable* things in which it was impossible for God to be lying,
7 12	2/	any *change* in the priesthood must mean a *change* in the Law as well.
12 27		The words 'once more' show that . . . the things being shaken . . . are going to be *changed*,
Jude 4	2	Certain people . . . were condemned for *turning* the grace of our God *into* immorality,

2. CHANGE – TURN INTO, BE TURNED INTO: *META-STREPHŌ*

1 *strephō* 2/21   2 *meta-strephō* 2

Mt 18 3 ●		unless you *change* and become like little children you will never enter the kingdom of heaven.
Ac 2 20	2	(Jl 3 4) The sun will *be turned into* darkness and the moon into blood
Ga 1 7	2	some troublemakers among you want to *change* the Good News
Rv 11 6		[the two witnesses] are able to *turn* water *into* blood

3. CHANGE – TURN INTO, BE TURNED TO: *META-TREPŌ*

1 *tropē* 1   2 *meta-trepō* 1

Jm 1 17		with [the Father of all light] there is no . . . alteration, no shadow of a *change*.
4 9	Θ 2	be miserable ⌐instead of (lit. and *change* from) laughing,

4. CHANGE – ALTER, VARY – EXCHANGE FOR: *ALLASSŌ*

1 *allassō* 6   3 *met-allassō* 2
2 *ant-allagma* 2   4 *par-allagē* 1

Mt 16 26	2	what has a man to offer *in exchange for* his life?
Mk 8 37	2	what can a man offer *in exchange for* his life?
Ac 6 14 X		Jesus . . . is going to *alter* the traditions that Moses handed down to us.
Rm 1 23		[the pagans] *exchanged* the glory of the immortal God *for* . . . the image of mortal man,
25	3	[the pagans] have ⌐given up (lit. *exchanged*) divine truth *for* a lie
26	3	their women have ⌐*turned* from natural intercourse *to* (or: *exchanged* natural intercourse *for*) unnatural practices
1 Co 15 51 ●		we are not all going to die, but we shall all be *changed*.
52		⁵² This will be instantaneous, . . . we shall be *changed*
Ga 4 20		I wish I were with you now so that I could ⌐know exactly what to say (lit. *vary* the way that I am saying this to you);
Heb 1 12		(Ps 102 26) you will roll them up like a cloak, and like a garment they will be *changed*.
Jm 1 17	Θ 4	with [the Father of all light] there is no . . . *alteration*, no shadow of a change.

5. ONE THING FOR ANOTHER – FOR: *ANTI*

anti (6)

Mt 5 38		(Ex 21 24) Eye *for* eye and tooth *for* tooth.
Rm 12 17		Never repay evil ⌐with (lit. *for*) evil
1 Th 5 15		Make sure that people do not try to ⌐take revenge (lit. repay evil *for* evil);
1 P 3 9		Never pay back one wrong ⌐with (lit. *for*) another, nor an angry word ⌐with (lit. *for*) another one;

6. REPAY (GOOD DEEDS): *AMOIBĒ*

amoibē 1

1 Tm 5 4	children . . . are to learn first of all to . . . *repay* [their debt to] their parents,

---

CHARIOT

1. **Chariot – Carriage:** *harma*
2. **Chariot:** *rhedē*

1. CHARIOT – CARRIAGE: *HARMA*

harma 4

Ac 8 28		as [the Ethiopian] sat in his *chariot* he was reading the prophet Isaiah. ²⁹ The Spirit said to Philip, Go up and meet that *chariot*.
29		
38		[The eunuch] ordered the *chariot* to stop, . . . and Philip baptised him.
Rv 9 9		the noise of [the locusts'] wings sounded like a great charge of horses and *chariots* into battle.

2. CHARIOT: *RHEDĒ*

rhedē 1

Rv 18 13	[There will be weeping . . . among all the traders of the earth when there is nobody left to buy their] horses and *chariots*,

---

CHOOSE

1. **Choose – Chosen – Elect:** *ek-legomai*
2. **Choose, Elect:** *cheiro-toneō*
3. **Choose (to):** *haireomai*

X = Jesus, chosen by God

1. CHOOSE – CHOSEN – ELECT: *EK-LEGOMAI*

1 *ek-lektos* 24   4 *syn-ek-lektos* 1
2 *ek-legomai* 22   5 *epi-legomai* 1
3 *ek-logē* 7

Mt 20 16		(ᵛ for many are called, but few are *chosen*.)
22 14		For many are called, but few are *chosen*.
24 22		but shortened that time shall be, for the sake of those who are *chosen*.
24		false Christs . . . will arise . . . to deceive even the *chosen*,
31		[the Son of Man] will send his angels . . . to gather his *chosen*
Mk 13 20	2	the Lord . . . did shorten the time, for the sake of the *elect* whom he *chose*.
22		false Christs . . . will arise . . . to deceive the *elect*,
27		[the Son of Man] will send the angels to gather his *chosen*
Lk 6 13	2	[Jesus] summoned his disciples and ⌐picked out (lit. *chose*) twelve of them;
9 35 X	2	This is my Son, ⌐the *Chosen* [One] (ᵛ the beloved). Listen to him.
10 42	2	It is Mary who has *chosen* the better part;
14 7	2	[Jesus] had noticed how [the guests] ⌐picked (lit. *chose*) the places of honour.

Lk 18	7		will not God see justice done to his *chosen* . . .?
23	35	X	let him save himself if he is the Christ of God, the *Chosen* [One].
Jn 1	34	X	I am the witness that he is the ᵛ *Chosen* [One] ⟨G the Son⟩ of God.
6	70	2	Have I not *chosen* you, you Twelve?
13	18	2	I know the ones I have *chosen*;
15	16	2/2	You did not *choose* me, no, I *chose* you;
19		2	my *choice* withdrew you from the world,
Ac 1	2	2	[Jesus] gave his instructions to the apostles he had *chosen*
24		2	Lord, . . . show us . . . which of these two you have *chosen*
6	5	2	The whole assembly . . . *elected* Stephen . . . Philip . . . and Nicolaus
9	15	3	[Saul] is my *chosen* instrument to bring my name before pagans . . . and before the people of Israel;
13	17	2	The God of our nation Israel *chose* our ancestors,
15	7	2	Peter . . . said, '. . . God *made his choice* among you:
22		2	the apostles and elders decided to *choose* delegates
25		2	we have decided unanimously to *elect* delegates
40		5	Before Paul left, he *chose* Silas to accompany him
Rm 8	33		Could anyone accuse those that God has *chosen*?
9	11	3	In order ᶠto stress that God's choice is free (lit. that God's *selective* purpose might stand) [Rebecca was told]
11	5		there is a remnant, *chosen* by grace.
7		3	It was not Israel as a whole that found what it was seeking, but only the *chosen* [few].
28		3	as the *chosen* [people the Jews] are still loved by God,
16	13		[Greetings] to Rufus, a *chosen* servant of the Lord,
1 Co 1	27	2	it was to shame the wise that God *chose* what is foolish by human reckoning, and to shame what is strong that he *chose* what is weak by human reckoning;
		2	
28		2	those whom the world thinks . . . contemptible are the ones that God has *chosen*
Ep 1	4	2	Before the world was made, he [chose us,] *chose* us in Christ.
Col 3	12		You are God's *chosen* race, his saints;
1 Th 1	4	3	We know, brothers, that God loves you and that you have *been chosen*,
1 Tm 5	21		Before God, and before Jesus Christ and the angels he has *chosen*, I put it to you as a duty to keep these rules
2 Tm 2	10		I bear it all for the sake of [those who are] *chosen*,
Tt 1	1		Paul, . . . an apostle of Jesus Christ to bring those whom God has *chosen* to faith
Jm 2	5	2	it was those who are poor according to the world that God *chose*, to be rich in faith
1 P 1	1		Peter, apostle of Jesus Christ, sends greetings to all those . . . who have been *chosen*, ² by the provident purpose of God
2	4	X	[Jesus] is the living stone, rejected by men but *chosen* by God
6		X	(Is 28 16) I lay in Zion a precious cornerstone that I have *chosen*
9			(Is 43 20) you are a *chosen* race, . . . a consecrated nation,
5	13	4	Your sister in Babylon, who is *with* you *among the chosen*, sends you greetings;
2 P 1	10	3	Brothers, you have been called and *chosen*: work all the harder to justify it.
2 Jn	1		From the Elder: my greetings to the Lady, the *chosen* [one],
13			Greetings to you from the children of your sister, the *chosen* [one].
Rv 17	14		the Lamb . . . will defeat them and they will be defeated by his followers, the called, the *chosen*, the faithful.

2. CHOOSE, ELECT: *CHEIRO-TONEŌ*

2 *cheiro-toneō* 1/2   1 *pro-cheiro-toneō* 1

Ac 10	41	Θ	God allowed [Jesus raised to life] to be seen . . . by certain witnesses God had *chosen beforehand*.
2 Co 8	19	2	the same brother . . . has been *elected* by the churches to be our companion

3. CHOOSE (TO) : *HAIREOMAI*

1 *haireomai* 3   3 *pro-(h)aireomai* 1
2 *hairetizō* 1

Mt 12	18	X	2 (Is 42 1) Here is my servant whom I have *chosen*, my beloved,
9	7		3 Each one should give what he has *decided* in his own mind, not . . . because he is made to,
Ph 1	22		[death or] living in this body . . . doing work which is having good results – I do not know what I should *choose*.
2 Th 2	13		God *chose* you from the beginning to be saved
Heb 11	25		[Moses] *chose* to be ill-treated in company with God's people

CIRCUMCISION

CIRCUMCISION – UNCIRCUMCISED

3	*kata-tomē*	1	5 *akro-bystia* 20
2	*peri-temnō*	17	
1	*peri-tomē*	36	
4	*a-peri-tmētos*	1	

Lk 1	59	2	on the eighth day they came to *circumcise* the child;
2	21	2	When the eighth day came . . . the child was to be *circumcised*,
Jn 7	22		Moses ordered you to practise *circumcision* . . . and you *circumcise* on the sabbath. ²³ Now if a man can be *circumcised* on the sabbath . . . why are you angry with me for making a man whole . . . on a sabbath?
23		2/	
Ac 7	8	2	[Abraham] made the covenant of *circumcision*: so when his son Isaac was born he *circumcised* him on the eighth day. Isaac did the same for Jacob, and Jacob for the twelve patriarchs.
51		4	You stubborn people with your ᶠpagan (lit. *uncircumcised*) hearts and [pagan] ears. You are always resisting the Holy Spirit.
10	45		ᶠJewish (lit. *Circumcised*) believers . . . were all astonished that the gift of the Holy Spirit should be poured out on the pagans too,
11	2		the ᶠJews (lit. *circumcised*) criticised [Peter] ³ and said, 'So you have been visiting the *uncircumcised*
3		5	
15	1	2	some men . . . taught the brothers, 'Unless you have yourselves *circumcised* in the tradition of Moses you cannot be saved.'
5		2	certain . . . believers objected, insisting that the pagans should be *circumcised*
16	3	2	Paul . . . had [Timothy] *circumcised*.
21	21	2	[you are] authorising [all Jewish believers living among pagans] not to *circumcise* their children
Rm 2	25		It is a good thing to be *circumcised* if you keep the Law; but if you break the Law, you might as well have stayed *uncircumcised*. ²⁶ If a man who is *not circumcised* obeys the commandments of the Law, surely that makes up for *not being circumcised* and counts as *circumcision*? ²⁷ More than that, the man who keeps the Law, even though he has *not been physically circumcised*, is a living condemnation of the way you disobey the Law in spite of *being circumcised* . . . ²⁸ . . . *circumcision* is more than a physical operation. ²⁹ . . . the real *circumcision* is in the heart
26		5/5	
27		5/	
		5	
28			
29			
3	1		Is there any advantage in *being circumcised*?
30		/5	there is only one God, and he is the one who will justify the *circumcised* because of their faith and [justify] the *uncircumcised* through their faith.
4	9	5	Is this happiness meant only for the *circumcised*, or is it meant for ᶠothers (lit. the *uncircumcised*) as well? . . . [Abraham's] faith, we say, was considered as justifying him, ¹⁰ but when was this done? When he was already *circumcised* or ᶠbefore he had been (lit. while he was still *not*) *circumcised*? It was ᶠbefore he had been (lit. while he still was *not*) *circumcised*, not ᶠafter (lit. when he had had *circumcision*).
10			
		5	
		5	
11			when he was *circumcised* later it was only as a sign and guarantee that the faith he had ᶠbefore his (lit. while he had still *not had*) *circumcision* justified him. In this way Abraham became the ancestor of all *uncircumcised* believers
		5	
		5	
12			[Abraham became] ancestor, also, of those who though *circumcised* do not rely on ᶠthat fact (lit. *circumcision*) alone, but follow . . . Abraham along the path of faith he trod ᶠbefore he had been (lit. while he was still *not*) *circumcised*.
		5	
15	8		Christ became the servant of ᶠcircumcised Jews (lit. *circumcision*) . . . so that God could . . . carry out the promises made to the patriarchs,
1 Co 7	18	2	If anyone had already been *circumcised* at the time of his call, he need not disguise it, and anyone who was *uncircumcised* . . . need not be *circumcised*; ¹⁹ because to be *circumcised* or *uncircumcised* means nothing: what does matter is to keep the commandments of God.
		5	
19		2	
		/5	
Ga 2	3	2	though Titus . . . is a Greek, he was not obliged to be *circumcised*.
7		5	I had been commissioned to preach the Good News to the *uncircumcised* just as Peter had been commissioned to preach it to the *circumcised*. ⁸ The same person whose action had made Peter the apostle of the *circumcised* had given me a similar mission to the pagans. ⁹ So, James, Cephas and John . . . shook hands with Barnabas and me . . . we were to go to the pagans and they to the *circumcised*.
8			
9			
12			[Peter] stopped [eating with the pagans] for fear of the group that insisted on *circumcision*.
5	2	2	if you allow yourselves to be *circumcised*, Christ will be of no

Ga	5	3	2 benefit to you at all. ³ . . . Everyone who accepts *circumcision* is obliged to keep the whole Law . . .⁶ . . . in Christ
		6	Jesus whether you are *circumcised* or ┌not (lit. *uncircumcised*) makes no difference – what matters is faith
		/5	
		11	if I still preach *circumcision*, why am I still persecuted?
	6	12	2 It is only self-interest that makes them want to force *circumcision* on you . . . ¹³ They accept *circumcision*, but do not keep the Law themselves; they only want you to be *circumcised* so that they can boast of the fact.
		13	2
			2
		15	It does not matter if a person is *circumcised* or ┌not (lit. *uncircumcised*); what matters is . . . to become an altogether new creature.
		5	
Ep	2	11	5 you . . . were pagans physically, termed the *Uncircumcised* by those who speak of themselves as the *Circumcision* by reason of a physical operation,
Ph	3	2	3 Watch out for the *cutters*. ³ We are the real people of the *circumcision*,
		3	
		5	I was *circumcised* when I was eight days old.
Col	2	11	2/ In [Christ] you have been *circumcised*, with a *circumcision* not performed by human hand but by the complete stripping of your body of flesh. This is *circumcision* according to Christ.
		13	5 You were dead, because you were sinners and had *not been circumcised*:
	3	11	in that image there is no room for distinction between Greek and Jew, between the *circumcised* and the *uncircumcised* . . . There is only Christ:
		/5	
	4	11	Of all those who have come over from the *Circumcision*, [Aristarchus, Mark and Justus] are the only ones actually working with me for the kingdom of God.
Tt	1	10	you have there a great many people who need to be disciplined, . . . particularly among those of the *Circumcision*.

CITY – TOWN – VILLAGE

1. Town – City – Citizen: *polis*
1: Town – City
2: Citizen, Local inhabitant –

Citizenship – Fellow-citizen
2. Village(s): *kōmē*
3. List of towns and cities

1. TOWN – CITY – CITIZEN: *POLIS*

1 *polis*	47/164	4	*politeuma* 1
3 *politeia*	2	5	*sym-politēs* 1
2 *politēs*	4		

1: TOWN – CITY

Mt	5	14	A *city* built on a hill-top cannot be hidden.
	9	35	Jesus made a tour through all the *towns* and villages,
	10	11	Whatever *town* or village you go into, ask for someone trustworthy
		14	if anyone does not welcome you . . . walk out of the . . . *town* . . . ¹⁵ . . . on the day of Judgement it will not go as hard with the land of Sodom . . . as with that *town*.
		15	
		23	If they persecute you in one *town*, take refuge in the next; . . . you will not have gone the round of the *towns* of Israel before the Son of Man comes.
	11	1	Jesus . . . moved on . . . to teach and preach in their *towns*.
	12	25	no *town* . . . divided against itself can stand.
	14	13	the people . . , leaving the *towns*, went after [Jesus] on foot.
	22	7	The king . . destroyed those murderers and burnt their *town*
	23	34	you will . . . hunt [prophets] from *town* to *town*;
Mk	1	45	Jesus could no longer go openly into any *town*,
	6	33	from every *town* they all hurried to the place on foot
		56	wherever [Jesus] went, to village, or *town*, or farm, they laid down the sick in the open spaces,
Lk	1	39	Mary . . . went . . . to a *town* in the hill country of Judah.
	2	3	everyone went to his own *town* to be registered,
	4	43	I must proclaim the Good News of the kingdom of God to the other *towns* too,
	5	12	Jesus was in one of the *towns* when a man appeared, covered with leprosy.
	7	37	a woman came in, who had a bad name in the *town*.
	8	1	[Jesus] made his way through *towns* and villages preaching,
		4	people from every *town* [were] finding their way to [Jesus],
	9	5	As for those who do not welcome you . . . leave their *town*
	10	1	the Lord . . . sent [the seventy-two] . . . to all the *towns* and places he himself was to visit.
		8	Whenever you go into a *town* where they make you welcome, eat what is set before you.

Lk	10	10	whenever you enter a *town* and they do not make you welcome, go out . . . and say, ¹¹ 'We wipe off the very dust of your *town* that clings to our feet . . .' ¹² . . . on that day it will not go as hard with Sodom as with that *town*.
		11	
		12	
	13	22	Through *towns* and villages [Jesus] went teaching,
	14	21	Go out quickly into the streets . . . of the *town* and bring in here the poor,
	18	2	There was a judge in a certain *town* . . . who had neither fear of God not respect for man. ³ In the same *town* there was a widow
		3	
	19	17	my good servant, . . . you shall have the government of ten *cities*.
		19	you shall be in charge of five *cities*.
Ac	5	16	People even came crowding in from the *towns* round about Jerusalem
	8	40	[Philip proclaimed] the Good News in every *town*
	15	21	Moses has always had his preachers in every *town*,
		36	Let us go back and visit all the *towns* where we preached the word of the Lord,
	16	4	As [Paul and Timothy] visited one *town* after another, they passed on the decisions reached by the apostles
	20	23	the Holy Spirit, in *town* [after town], has made it clear enough that imprisonment and persecution await me.
	26	11	I even pursued [the saints] into foreign *cities*.
2 Co	11	26	I have been . . . in danger in the *towns*,
Tt	1	5	I left you behind . . . to get everything organised . . . and appoint elders in every *town*,
Heb	13	14 ○	there is no eternal *city* for us in this life but we look for one in the life to come.
Jm	4	13	Today or tomorrow, we are off to this or that *town*;
Rv	16	19	the *cities* of the world collapsed;

2: CITIZEN, LOCAL INHABITANT – CITIZENSHIP – FELLOW-CITIZEN

Lk	15	15	2 [the prodigal] hired himself out to one of the local *inhabitants*
	19	14 <	2 his *compatriots* detested [the man of noble birth]
Ac	21	39	2 I am . . . a *citizen* of the well-known city of Tarsus in Cilicia.
	22	28	3 It cost me a large sum to acquire this *citizenship*.
Ep	2	12 ●	3 you . . . were excluded from *membership* of Israel, aliens with no part in the covenants with their Promise;
		19 ●	5 you are *citizens like* all the saints,
Ph	3	20 ●	4 our *homeland* is in heaven,
Heb	8	11	(Jr 31 34 G) There will be no further need for ┌neighbour to try to teach neighbour (lit. anybody to try to teach his *fellow-citizen*),
			2

2. VILLAGE(S): *KŌMĒ*

1 *kōmē* 27   2 *kōmo-polis* 1

Mt	9	35	Jesus made a tour through all the towns and *villages*,
	10	11	Whatever town or *village* you go into, ask for someone trustworthy
	14	15	they can go to the *villages* to buy themselves some food.
	21	2	Go to the *village* [Bethphage] facing you,
Mk	1	38	2 Let us go elsewhere, to the neighbouring *country towns*, so that I can preach there too,
	6	6	[Jesus] made a tour round the *villages*, teaching.
		36	they can go to the . . . *villages* round about, to buy themselves something to eat.
		56	wherever [Jesus] went, to *village*, or town, or farm, they laid down the sick in the open spaces,
	8	23	[Jesus] led [the blind man] outside the *village* [Bethsaida].
		26	[Jesus said to the blind man,] Do not even go into the *village* [Bethsaida].
		27	Jesus . . . left for the *villages* round Caesarea Philippi.
	11	2	Go off to the *village* [Bethphage, or Bethany] facing you,
Lk	5	17	Pharisees . . . had come from every *village* in Galilee, from Judaea and from Jerusalem.
	8	1	[Jesus] made his way through towns and *villages* preaching,
	9	6	[the Twelve] went from *village* [to village] proclaiming the Good News
		12	they can go to the *villages* and farms round about to find lodging and food;
		52	[Jesus's messengers] went into a Samaritan *village*
		56	[Jesus and his disciples] went off to another *village*.
	10	38	[Jesus] came to a *village* [Bethany], and a woman named Martha welcomed him into her house.
	13	22	Through towns and *villages* [Jesus] went teaching,
	17	12	As [Jesus] entered one of the *villages*, ten lepers came to meet him.
	19	30	Go off to the *village* [Bethphage, or Bethany] opposite,
	24	13	two of [the disciples] were on their way to a *village* called Emmaus,
		28	When they drew near to the *village* [Emmaus] . . . [Jesus] made as if to go on;

Jn 7 42	Does not scripture say that the Christ must . . . come from the *town* of Bethlehem?
11 1	Lazarus . . . lived in the *village* of Bethany with the two sisters, Mary and Martha,
30	Jesus had not yet come into the *village* [Bethany];
Ac 8 25	[the apostles] went back to Jerusalem, preaching the Good News to a number of Samaritan *villages*.

3. LIST OF TOWNS AND CITIES

NB. The name of a town or city may be followed by the number of times the Greek word *polis* is applied to it, e.g. *Babylon p10.*
The heading under which the towns and cities are to be found is printed beneath each.

Adramyttium
Asia 9.
Aenon
River – Flow – Fountain 1.3:
Alexandria
Egypt
Antioch in Pisidia p 2
Asia 12.
Antioch (in Syria)
Syria
Antipatris
Caesarea – Joppa
Apollonia
Greece 4.
Arimathaea p 1
Judaea 2.
Assos
Asia 9.
Athens p 1
Greece 2.
Attalia
Asia 10.
Azotus
Caesarea – Joppa
Babylon p 10
Mesopotamia 2.
Beroea
Greece 4.
Bethany (1)
Judaea 3.
Bethany (2)
River – Flow – Fountain 1.3:
Bethlehem p 2
Judaea 4.
Bethphage
Judaea 3.
Bethsaida p 2
Galilee 3.
Cana
Galilee 1.
Capernaum p 3
Galilee 3.
Cenchreae
Greece 3.
Caesarea (in Palestine) p 1
Caesarea – Joppa
Caesarea Philippi
Peter and the Twelve
Chorazin
Galilee 3.
Cnidus
Asia 3.
Colossae
Asia 11.
Corinth p 2
Greece 3.
Cyrene
Cyrene
Dalmanutha
Galilee 3.
Damascus p 2
Damascus
Derbe p 1
Asia 6.
Doberus
Greece 4.
Emmaus
Judaea 5.
Ephesus p 2
Asia 1.2:
Ephraim p 1
Judaea 1.

Gadara p 2
Decapolis
Gaza
Caesarea – Joppa
Gennesaret
Galilee 3.
Gerasa p 4
Decapolis
Gomorrah (p 1)
Sodom
Haran
Mesopotamia 1.
Hierapolis
Asia 11.
Iconium p 1
Asia 6.
Jericho
Judaea 6.
Jerusalem p 44
Jerusalem
Joppa p 2
Caesarea – Joppa
Laodicea
Asia 11.
Lasea p 1
Island 3:
Lydda
Caesarea – Joppa
Lystra p 3
Asia 6.
Magdala
Galilee 3.
Miletus
Asia 3.
Mitylene
Island 5:
Myra
Asia 7.
Nain p 3
Galilee 4.
Nazareth p 6
Galilee 2.
Neapolis
Greece 4.
Nicopolis
Greece 3.
Nineveh
Mesopotamia 3.
Paphos
Island 2:
Patara
Asia 7.
Pergamum
Asia 9.
Perga
Asia 10.
Phoenix
Island 3:
Philadelphia
Asia 8.
Philippi p 4
Greece 4.
Ptolemais
Tyre and Sidon
Puteoli
Rome
Ramah
Abraham
Rhegium
Rome
Rome
Rome

Salamis
Island 2:
Salem
King 4:g)
Salim
River – Flow – Fountain 1.3:
Sardis
Asia 8.
Seleucia
Syria
Shechem
Abraham
Sidon
Tyre and Sidon
Smyrna
Asia 8.
Sodom p 1
Sodom
Sychar p 5
Samaria
Syracuse
Rome
Tarsus p 1
Asia 4.

Thessalonika p 1
Greece 4.
Thyatira p 1
Asia 8.
Tiberias
Galilee 3.
Troas
Asia 9.
Tyre p 1
Tyre and Sidon
Zarephath
Tyre and Sidon

towns (round the lake) *p 1*
Galilee 3.
towns (of Lycaonia) *p 1*
Asia 6.
towns (of Samaria) *p 4*
Samaria
towns (near Sodom) *p 1*
Sodom

CLOTH

1. Cloth, Fabric
1: Linen – Fine linen: *byssinos*
2: Linen – Flax, Wick: *linon*
  a) Linen
  b) Wick (Flax)
3: Wool: *erion*
4: Silk(s): *sērikos*
5: Purple (cloth, dye and colour): *porphyra*
6: Scarlet (cloth and colour): *kokkinos*
7: Cloth: *rhakos*
2. Cloths, Pieces of cloth
1: Veil – Curtain: *kata-petasma*
2: Sheet – Linen wrapping: *othonē*
  a) Sheet
  b) Binding cloths – Linen wrappings

3: Bands – Linen strips: *keiria*
4: Shroud – a Linen cloth: *sindōn*
5: Piece of linen, a Cloth – Handkerchief, Napkin: *soudarion*
6: Towel: *lention*
7: Scarves – Aprons: *simikinthion*
3. Spin – Weave – Needle, Sew
1: Spin: *nēthō*
2: Weave, Woven: *hyphainō*
3: Needle – Sew
  a) Needle – Sew, Seamless: *rhaphis*
  b) Needle: *belonē*

1. CLOTH, FABRIC

1: LINEN – FINE LINEN: *BYSSINOS*
1 *byssinos* 5   2 *byssos* 1

Lk 16 19	2 a rich man who used to dress in purple and *fine linen*
Rv 18 12	stocks of . . . *linen* and purple and silks and scarlet;
16	mourn for [Babylon]; for all the *linen* and purple and scarlet that you wore,
19 8	[the Lamb's] bride . . . has been able to dress herself in dazzling white *linen*, because her *linen* is made of the good deeds of the saints
14	Behind him, dressed in *linen* of dazzling white, rode the armies of heaven

2: LINEN – FLAX, WICK: *LINON*
linon 2

a) Linen

Rv 15 6	seven angels . . . wearing pure white *linen*,

b) Wick (Flax)

Mt 12 20 <	(Is 42 3) [My servant] will not . . . put out the smouldering *wick*

3: WOOL: *ERION*
erion 2

Heb 9 19	Moses . . . took the . . . blood and some water, and with these he sprinkled the book itself and all the people, using scarlet *wool* and hyssop;

Rv 1 14 (Dn 7 9) [The Son of man's] head and his hair were white as white *wool* or as snow,

4: SILK(S): *SĒRIKOS*
sērikos 1

Rv 18 12 stocks of . . . linen and purple and *silks* and scarlet;

5: PURPLE (CLOTH, DYE AND COLOUR): *PORPHYRA*
1 *porphyra* 4 3 *porphyro(pōlis)* 1
2 *porphyreos* 4

Mk 15 17 [The soldiers] dressed [Jesus] up in *purple*,
20 they took off the *purple* and dressed him in his own clothes.
Lk 16 19 a rich man who used to dress in *purple* and fine linen
Jn 19 2 2 the soldiers . . . dressed [Jesus] in a *purple* robe.
5 Jesus then came out wearing the crown of thorns and the 2 *purple* robe.
Ac 16 14 3 Lydia . . . who was in the *purple-dye* trade.
Rv 17 4 2 The woman was dressed in *purple* and scarlet, and glittered with gold and jewels and pearls,
18 12 stocks of . . . linen and *purple* and silks and scarlet;
16 2 mourn for [Babylon]; for all the linen and *purple* and scarlet that you wore,

6: SCARLET (CLOTH AND COLOUR): *KOKKINOS*
kokkinos 6

Mt 27 28 [the soldiers] stripped [Jesus] and made him wear a *scarlet* cloak,
Heb 9 19 Moses . . . took the . . . blood and some water, and with these he sprinkled . . . all the people, using *scarlet* wool and hyssop,
Rv 17 3 ○ I saw a woman riding a *scarlet* beast
4 The woman was dressed in purple and *scarlet*,
18 12 stocks of . . . linen and purple and silks and *scarlet*;
16 mourn for [Babylon]; for all the linen and purple and *scarlet* that you wore,

7: CLOTH: *RHAKOS*
rhakos 2

Mt 9 16 No one puts a piece of unshrunken *cloth* on to an old cloak,
Mk 2 21 No one sews a piece of unshrunken *cloth* on an old cloak;

2. CLOTHS, PIECES OF CLOTH

1: VEIL – CURTAIN: *KATA-PETASMA*
kata-petasma 6

Mt 27 51 [Jesus yielded up his spirit.] At that, the *veil* of the Temple was torn in two
Mk 15 38 And the *veil* of the Temple was torn in two from top to bottom;
Lk 23 45 The *veil* of the Temple was torn right down the middle;
Heb 6 19 [In this hope] we have an anchor for our soul, . . . reaching
○ right through beyond the *veil* 20 where Jesus has entered
9 3 beyond the second *veil*, an innermost part which was called the Holy of Holies
10 20 [we have a right to enter the sanctuary] by a new way which
○ [Jesus] has opened for us, a living opening through the *curtain*, that is to say, his body.

2: SHEET – LINEN WRAPPING: *OTHONĒ*
2 *othonē* 2 1 *othonion* 5

a) Sheet

Ac 10 11 2 [Peter] saw . . . something like a big *sheet* being let down to earth
11 5 2 I . . . had a vision of something like a big *sheet* being let down from heaven

b) Binding cloths – Linen wrappings

Lk 24 12 ᵛ Peter . . . saw the *binding cloths* but nothing else¹
Jn 19 40 [Joseph and Nicodemus] took the body of Jesus and wrapped it with the spices in *linen cloths*,
20 5 [John] bent down and saw the *linen cloths* lying on the ground,
6 . . . ⁶ Simon Peter . . . went right into the tomb, saw the

Jn 20 7 *linen cloths* on the ground, ⁷ and also the cloth that had been over [Jesus's] head; this was not with the *linen cloths*

3: BANDS – LINEN STRIPS: *KEIRIA*
keiria 1

Jn 11 44 The dead man [Lazarus] came out, his feet and hands bound with *bands of stuff*

4: SHROUD – A LINEN CLOTH: *SINDŌN*
sindōn 6

Mt 27 59 Joseph took the body [of Jesus], wrapped it in a clean *shroud*
Mk 14 51 A young man who followed [Jesus] had nothing on but a *linen cloth*. They caught hold of him, ⁵² but he left the
52 *cloth* in their hands and ran away naked.
15 46 [Joseph] bought a *shroud*, took Jesus down from the cross, wrapped him in the *shroud* and laid him in a tomb
Lk 23 53 [Joseph] asked for the body of Jesus. He . . . wrapped it in a *shroud* and put him in a tomb

5: PIECE OF LINEN, A CLOTH – HANDKERCHIEF, NAPKIN: *SOUDARION*
soudarion 4

Lk 19 20 Sir, here is your pound. I put it away safely in a *piece of linen*
Jn 11 44 The dead man [Lazarus] came out, his feet and hands bound with bands of stuff and a *cloth* round his face.
20 7 [Simon Peter saw] the *cloth* that had been over [Jesus'] head;
Ac 19 12 *handkerchiefs* or aprons which had touched [Paul] were taken to the sick, and they were cured

6: TOWEL: *LENTION*
lention 2

Jn 13 4 taking a *towel*, [Jesus] wrapped it round his waist; ⁵ he . . .
5 began to wash the disciples' feet and to wipe them with the *towel*

7: SCARVES – APRONS: *SIMIKINTHION*
simikinthion 1

Ac 19 12 handkerchiefs or *aprons* which had touched [Paul] were taken to the sick, and they were cured

3. SPIN – WEAVE – NEEDLE, SEW

1: SPIN: *NĒTHŌ*
nēthō 2

Mt 6 28 Think of the flowers growing in the fields; they never have to work or *spin*;
Lk 12 27 Think of the flowers; they never have to *spin* or weave;

2: WEAVE, WOVEN: *HYPHAINŌ*
1 *hyphainō* 1 2 *hyphantos* 1

Lk 12 27 Think of the flowers; they never have to spin or *weave*;
Jn 19 23 2 [Jesus's] undergarment was seamless, *woven* in one piece from neck to hem;

3: NEEDLE – SEW

a) Needle – Sew, Seamless: rhaphis
1 *rhaphis* 2 2 *a-rrhaphos* 1
3 *epi-rhaptō* 1

Mt 19 24 it is easier for a camel to pass through the eye of a *needle*
Mk 2 21 3 No one *sews* a piece of unshrunken cloth on an old cloak;
10 25 It is easier for a camel to pass through the eye of a *needle*
Jn 19 23 2 [Jesus's] undergarment was *seamless*, woven in one piece from neck to hem;

b) Needle: belonē
belonē 1

Lk 18 25 it is easier for a camel to pass through the eye of a *needle*

CLOTHING

1. Clothe, Clothing, Dress – Wear – Wrap (in, up)
1: Clothe(d), Dress(ed) – Wear: *en-duō*
   a) Clothe(d), Dress(ed) – Wear – Clothing, Garment
   b) Clothe, Dress (figuratively) – Put on, Wear – Clothing (figuratively)
2: Clothe(d), Dress(ed), Arrayed – Wear – Robe: *peri-ballō*
3: Clothe(d), Dress(ed) – Wear: *amphiazo*
4: Clothing: *skepasma*
5: Wrap oneself (in), Clothe oneself (with): *en-komboomai*
6: Wrap in swaddling clothes: *sparganoō*
7: Wrap: *en-tylissō*
8: Wrap: *en-eileō*

2. Cloak – Robe – Tunic
1: Cloak, Robe – Clothes, Clothing, Garments: *himation*
2: Cloak, Robe, Mantle: *chlamus*
3: Cloak: *phailonēs*
4: Robe: *stolē*
5: Long robe, Ankle-length garment: *pod-ērēs*
6: Fringe, Tassel: *kras-pedon*
7: Tunic: *chitōn*
8: Belt, Girdle – Put on a belt, Fasten round the waist, Gird: *zōnē*

3. Shoes, Footwear – Sandals: *hypo-dēma* and *sandalion*

4. Skin, Leather – Sackcloth
1: Skin, Leather: *derma* and *mēlōtē*
2: Sackcloth: *sakkos*

5. Strip (off) – Naked
1: Strip (off): *ek-duō*
   a) Strip, Take off
   b) Strip, Strip off, Not to wear clothes (figuratively)
2: Naked: *gymnos*
   a) Naked
   b) Uncovered
   c) Bare

A = Angel

1. CLOTHE, CLOTHING, DRESS – WEAR – WRAP (IN, UP)

1: CLOTHE(D), DRESS(ED) – WEAR: *EN-DUŌ*

3 *en-didyskō*	2	5 *en-dysis*	1
2 *en-dyma*	8	4 *ep-en-duomai*	2
1 *en-duō*	28	6 *ep-en-dytēs*	1

a) Clothe(d), Dress(ed) – Wear – Clothing, Garment

Mt 3 4	2	This man John wore a *garment* made of camel-hair (cf. 2 K 1 8; Zc 13 4)
6 25		I am telling you not to worry . . . about your body and how you are to *clothe* it. Surely . . . the body [means] more than *clothing*!
28	2	why worry about *clothing*?
22 11	< /2	the king . . . noticed one man who was not ꜛ*wearing* (or: *dressed* in) a wedding *garment*,
12	<	2 How did you get in here . . . without a wedding *garment*?
27 31	X	they took off the cloak and *dressed* [Jesus] in his own clothes
28 3	A	2 [the angel's] *robe* [was] white as snow.
Mk 1 6		John wore a *garment* of camel-ꜜskin (G hair),
6 9		Do not ꜛ*take* a spare (lit. *wear* a second) tunic.
15 17	X	3 [The soldiers] *dressed* him *up* in purple,
20	X	they took off the purple and *dressed* [Jesus] in his own clothes
Lk 8 27		for a long time [the demoniac] had *worn* no clothes,
12 22		I am telling you not to worry . . . about your body and how you are to *clothe* it.
23	2	the body [means] more than *clothing*.
15 22	<	Bring out the best robe and *put* it *on* [the prodigal son];
16 19	3	There was a rich man who used to *dress* in purple and fine linen
Jn 21 7	6	Simon Peter, who had practically nothing on, wrapped his *cloak* round him
Ac 12 21		Herod, *wearing* his robes of state . . . made a speech
1 P 3 3	5	Do not *dress* up for show: . . . *wearing* gold bracelets and fine clothes;
Rv 1 13	X	[I saw] a figure like a Son of man, *dressed* in a long robe
15 6	A	out came the seven angels . . . *wearing* pure white linen,
19 14	A	Behind [The Word of God], *dressed* in linen of dazzling white, rode the armies of heaven

b) Clothe, Dress (figuratively) – Put on, Wear – Clothing (figuratively)

Mt 7 15	2	Beware of false prophets who come to you ꜛ*disguised as sheep* (lit. in sheep's *clothing*)
Lk 24 49		Stay in the city . . . until you are *clothed* with the power from on high.
Rm 13 12		let us ꜛ*arm* ourselves and appear in (lit. *dress* ourselves in the armour of) the light.
14		Let your ꜛ*armour* (lit. *clothing*) be the Lord Jesus Christ;
1 Co 15 53		our present perishable nature must *put on* imperishability and this mortal nature must *put on* immortality.
54		When this perishable nature has *put on* imperishability, and

1 Co 15 54		when this mortal nature has *put on* immortality, then the words of scripture will come true:
2 Co 5 2		4 we groan as we wait with longing to *put on* our heavenly home
3		*over* the other; [3] we should like to be found *wearing clothes* and not without them. [4] Yes, we . . . find it a burden being
4		still in this tent, not that we want to strip it off, but to
4		*put the* [second] *garment over* it and to have what must die taken up into life.
Ga 3 27		All baptised in Christ, you have all *clothed* yourselves in Christ
Ep 4 24		[You must put aside your old self] so that you can *put on* the new self
6 11		*Put* God's armour *on*
14		stand your ground . . . *wearing* integrity for a breastplate,
Col 3 10		[You have stripped off your old behaviour with your old self] and you have *put on* a new self
12		you should *be clothed* in sincere compassion, . . . gentleness and patience. [14] Over all these clothes . . . put on love.
1 Th 5 8		let us *put on* faith and love for a breastplate,

2: CLOTHE(D), DRESS(ED), ARRAYED – WEAR – ROBE: *PERI-BALLŌ*

1 *peri-ballō* 23   2 *peri-bolaion* 2

Mt 6 29		not even Solomon . . . was ꜛ*robed* (or: *arrayed*) like one of these [flowers].
31		How are we to be *clothed*?
25 36	X	[I was] naked and you *clothed* me . . . [38] When did we see
38	X	you . . . naked and *clothe* you . . .?
43	X	I was . . . naked and you never *clothed* me,
Mk 14 51		A young man . . . had nothing *on* but a linen cloth.
16 5	A	On entering the tomb they saw a young man *dressed* in a white robe
Lk 12 27		not even Solomon . . . was ꜛ*robed* (or: *arrayed*) like one of these [flowers].
23 11	X	Herod . . . *put* a rich cloak *on* [Jesus]
Jn 19 2	X	the soldiers . . . *dressed* him in a purple robe.
Ac 12 8		*Wrap* your cloak *round* you and follow me.
1 Co 11 15	2	a woman . . . was given her hair as a *covering*,
Heb 1 12	2	you will roll [the earth and the heavens] up like a *cloak*, and like a garment they will be changed.
Rv 3 5		Those who prove victorious will be *dressed* . . . in white robes;
18		[Laodicea,] buy from me . . . white robes to *clothe* you
4 4		Round the throne . . . I saw twenty-four elders sitting *dressed* in white robes
7 9		I saw a huge number . . . of people . . . *dressed* in white robes
13		Do you know who these people are, *dressed* in white robes . . .?
10 1	A	I saw another angel . . . *wrapped* in a cloud,
11 3		I shall send my two witnesses to prophesy . . , *wearing* sackcloth.
12 1		a great sign appeared . . .: a woman, *adorned with* the sun,
17 4		The woman was *dressed* in purple and scarlet,
18 16		all the linen and purple and scarlet that [Babylon] *wore* . . . are all destroyed
19 8		His bride . . . has been able to *dress* herself in dazzling white linen,
13	X	ꜛhis cloak (lit. the cloak he was *wearing*) was soaked in blood.

3: CLOTHE(D), DRESS(ED) – WEAR: *AMPHIAZŌ*

2 *amphiazō* 1   1 *amphi-(h)ennymi* 3

Mt 6 30		if that is how God *clothes* the grass . . . will he not much more look after you . . .?
11 8		what did you go out to see? A man *wearing* fine [clothes]?
Lk 7 25		what did you go out to see? A man *dressed* in fine clothes?
12 28	2	if that is how God *clothes* the grass . . . how much more will he look after you,

4: CLOTHING: *SKEPASMA*

skepasma 1

1 Tm 6 8		as long as we have food and *clothing*, let us be content with that.

5: WRAP ONESELF (IN), CLOTHE ONESELF (WITH): *EN-KOMBOOMAI*

en-komboomai 1

1 P 5 5	○	*wrap yourselves* in humility to be servants of each other,

6: WRAP IN SWADDLING CLOTHES: *SPARGANOŌ*

sparganoō 2

Lk	2	7	X	[Mary] *wrapped* [her son] *in swaddling clothes*,
		12	X	you will find a baby *wrapped in swaddling clothes*

7: WRAP: *EN-TYLISSŌ*

en-tylissō 2/3

Mt	27	59	Joseph took the body, *wrapped* it in a clean shroud
Lk	23	53	[Joseph] took [the body of Jesus] down, *wrapped* it in a shroud and put him in a tomb

8: WRAP: *EN-EILEŌ*

en-eileō 1

Mk	15	46	[Joseph] took Jesus down from the cross, *wrapped* him in the shroud and laid him in a tomb

2. CLOAK – ROBE – TUNIC

1: CLOAK, ROBE – CLOTHES, CLOTHING, GARMENTS: *HIMATION*

2 *esthēs* 7	1 *himation* 60
5 *esthēsis* 1	3 *himatismos* 5
	4 *himatizō* 2

Mt	5	40		if a man . . . would have your tunic, let him have your *cloak* as well.
	9	16	<	No one puts a piece of unshrunken cloth on to an old *cloak*, because the patch pulls away from the *cloak*
		20		a woman who had suffered from a haemorrhage for twelve
		21	X	years . . . touched the fringe of his *cloak*, [21] for she said to
			X	herself, 'If I can only touch his *cloak* I shall be well again'.
	14	36		[people were] begging him just to let them touch the fringe of
			X	his *cloak*.
	17	2	X	his *clothes* became as white as the light.
	21	7		[The disciples] brought the donkey and the colt, then laid their
		8		*cloaks* on their backs and [Jesus] sat on them. [8] Great crowds of people spread their *cloaks* on the road,
	24	18		if a man is in the fields, he must not turn back to fetch his *cloak*.
	26	65		the high priest tore his *clothes*
	27	31	X	[the soldiers] dressed [Jesus] in his own *clothes*
		35	X	[the soldiers] shared out his *clothing* by casting lots,
Mk	2	21	<	No one sews a piece of unshrunken cloth on an old *cloak*;
	5	15	4	[the people] saw the demoniac sitting there, *clothed* and in his full senses
		27	X	[the woman] touched his *cloak*. [28] 'If I can touch even his
		28	X	*clothes*,' she had told herself 'I shall be well again.'
		30	X	Who touched my *clothes*?
	6	56	X	[people were] begging him to let them touch even the fringe of his *cloak*.
	9	3	X	his *clothes* became dazzlingly white,
	10	50		throwing off his *cloak*, [the blind man] jumped up and went to Jesus.
	11	7		[the disciples] threw their *cloaks* on [the colt's] back, and
		8		[Jesus] sat on it. [8] Many people spread their *cloaks* on the road,
	13	16		if a man is in the fields, he must not turn back to fetch his *cloak*.
	15	20	X	[the soldiers] dressed [Jesus] in his own *clothes*.
		24	X	[the soldiers] shared out his *clothing*,
Lk	5	36	<	No one tears a piece from a new *cloak* to put it on an old *cloak*;
	6	29		to the man who takes your *cloak* . . . do not refuse your tunic.
	7	25		what did you go out to see? A man dressed in fine *clothes*? . . .
			3	those who go in for fine *clothes* . . . are to be found at court!
	8	27		for a long time [the demoniac] had worn no *clothes*,
		35	4	the people . . . found the man . . . *clothed* and in his full senses;
		44	X	[the woman] touched the fringe of his *cloak*; and the haemorrhage stopped at that instant.
	9	29	X	3 his *clothing* became brilliant as lightning.
	19	35		throwing their *garments* over [the colt's] back [the disciples]
		36		helped Jesus on to it. [36] . . . people spread their *cloaks* in the road,
	22	36		if you have no sword, sell your *cloak* and buy one,
	23	11	X	2 Herod . . . put a rich *cloak* on [Jesus]
		34	X	[the soldiers] cast lots to share out his *clothing*.

Lk	24	4	A	2 two men in brilliant *clothes* suddenly appeared at their side.
Jn	13	4	X	[Jesus] removed his *outer garment* and, taking a towel, wrapped it round his waist;
		12	X	When [Jesus] had . . . put on his *clothes* again he went back to the table.
	19	2	X	the soldiers . . . dressed him in a purple *robe*.
		5	X	Jesus then came out wearing . . . the purple *robe*.
		23	X	the soldiers . . . took his *clothing* and divided it into four shares,
		24	X	(Ps 22 19) They shared out my *clothing* among them. They
			X 3	cast lots for my *clothes*.
Ac	1	10	A	5 suddenly two men in white *garments* were standing near them
	7	58		The witnesses [to the stoning of Stephen] put down their *clothes* at the feet of a young man called Saul.
	9	39		the widows stood round [Peter] in tears, showing him tunics and other *clothes* Dorcas had made.
	10	30	A	2 I suddenly saw a man in front of me in shining *robes*.
	12	8		[Peter,] wrap your *cloak* round you and follow me.
		21		2 Herod, wearing his *robes* of state . . . made a speech
	14	14		Barnabas and Paul . . . tore their *clothes*,
	16	22		the magistrates had ⌈them stripped (lit. their *clothes* torn off) and ordered [Paul and Silas] to be flogged.
	18	6		[Paul] took his *cloak* and shook it out in front of them,
	20	33		3 I have never asked anyone for money or *clothes*;
	22	20		when the blood of your witness Stephen was being shed, I was . . . minding their *clothes*.
		23		They were yelling, waving their *cloaks*
1 Tm	2	9		women are . . . to be dressed quietly and modestly, without
			3	. . . jewellery or expensive *clothes*;
Heb	1	11		(Ps 102 27) [the earth and the heavens will] wear out like a *garment*; [12] you will roll them up like a cloak, and like a
		12		*garment* they will be changed.
Jm	2	2		suppose a man comes into your synagogue, beautifully
			2	*dressed* . . . and at the same time a poor man comes in, in
		3	2/2	shabby *clothes*, [3] . . . you take notice of the well-*dressed* man,
	5	2		[the rich,] your *clothes* are all eaten up by moths.
1 P	3	3		Do not dress up for show: . . . wearing . . . fine *clothes*;
Rv	3	4		There are a few . . . who have kept their *robes* from being dirtied;
		5		Those who prove victorious will be dressed . . . in white *robes*;
		18		[Laodicea,] buy from me . . . white *robes* to clothe you
	4	4		Round the throne . . . I saw twenty-four elders sitting, dressed in white *robes*
	16	15		Happy is the man who has . . . not taken off his *clothes*
	19	13	X	⌈his *cloak* (lit. the *cloak* he was wearing) was soaked in blood.
		16	X	On his *cloak* . . . there was a name written: The King of kings

2: CLOAK, ROBE, MANTLE: *CHLAMUS*

chlamus 2

Mt	27	28	X	[the soldiers] stripped [Jesus] and made him wear a scarlet *cloak*,
		31	X	[the soldiers] took off the *cloak* and dressed [Jesus] in his own clothes

3: CLOAK: *PHAILONĒS*

phailonēs 1

2 Tm	4	13	When you come, bring the *cloak* I left with Carpus in Troas

4: ROBE: *STOLĒ*

1 *stolē* 9	2 *kata-stolē* 1
3 *sy-stellō* 1/2	

Mk	12	38		Beware of the scribes who like to walk about in *long robes*,
	16	5	A	[the women] saw a young man in a white *robe*
Lk	15	22	<	Bring out the best *robe* and put it on him;
	20	46		Beware of the scribes who like to walk about in *long robes*
Ac	5	6		3 The younger men . . . *wrapped* the body [of Ananias] *in a sheet*.
1 Tm	2	9		2 I direct that women are to *wear* suitable *clothes*
Rv	6	11		Each of them was given a white *robe*,
	7	9		I saw a huge number . . . of people . . . dressed in white *robes*
		13		Do you know who these people are, dressed in white *robes*
		14		. . .? [14] . . . These are the people who . . . have washed their *robes* white again in the blood of the Lamb,
	22	14		Happy are those who will have washed their *robes* clean, so that they will have the right to feed on the tree of life

5: LONG ROBE, ANKLE-LENGTH GARMENT: *POD-ĒRĒS*

pod-ērēs 1

Rv	1 13 X	[I saw] a figure like a Son of man, dressed in a *long robe* tied at the waist with a golden girdle.

6: FRINGE, TASSEL: *KRAS-PEDON*

kras-pedon 5

Mt	9 20 X	a woman, who had suffered from a haemorrhage for twelve years . . . touched the *fringe* of his cloak.
	14 36 X	[people were] begging [Jesus] just to let them touch the *fringe* of his cloak.
	23 5	Everything [the scribes and the Pharisees] do is done to attract attention, like wearing . . . longer *tassels*,
Mk	6 56 X	[people were] begging [Jesus] to let them touch even the *fringe* of his cloak.
Lk	8 44 X	[a woman suffering from a haemorrhage] came up behind [Jesus] and touched the *fringe* of his cloak;

7: TUNIC: *CHITŌN*

chitōn 11

Mt	5 40	if a man . . . would have your *tunic*, let him have your cloak as well.
	10 10	[Provide yourselves] with no haversack for the journey or spare *tunic* or footwear
Mk	6 9	[The Twelve] were to wear sandals but, he added, 'Do not ˹take a spare (lit. wear a second) *tunic*'.
	14 63	The high priest tore his *robes*,
Lk	3 11	If anyone has two *tunics* he must share with the man who has none,
	6 29	to the man who takes your cloak . . . do not refuse your *tunic*'
	9 3	Take nothing for the journey: . . . and let none of you take a spare *tunic*.
Jn	19 23 X	the soldiers . . . took [Jesus's] clothing and divided it into four shares, one for each soldier; then his ˹*undergarment* (or: *tunic*). His ˹*undergarment* (or: *tunic*) was seamless, woven in one piece from neck to hem;
	X	
Ac	9 39	the widows stood round [Peter] in tears, showing him *tunics* and other clothes Dorcas had made
Jude	23	there are others to whom you must be kind with great caution, keeping your distance even from [outside] *clothing* which is contaminated by ˹vice (lit. the flesh).

8: BELT, GIRDLE – PUT ON A BELT, FASTEN ROUND THE WAIST, GIRD: *ZŌNĒ*

1	*zōnē*	8	4	*dia-zōnnymi*	3
3	*zōnnymi*	3	2	*peri-zonnymai*	6
5	*ana-zōnnymai 1*				

Mt	3 4	John wore a garment . . . with a leather *belt* round his waist,
	10 9	Provide yourselves with no gold . . , not even with a few coppers for your ˹purses (lit. *belts*),
Mk	1 6	John wore a garment of camel-˹skin (G hair), and (§ had a leather *belt* round his waist, and) he lived on locusts
	6 8	[Jesus] instructed them to take nothing for the journey . . . no coppers for their ˹purses (lit. *belts*).
Lk	12 35 < 2	See that you ˹are dressed for action (lit. have your *belts* round your waists) and have your lamps lit.
	37 < 2	the master . . . will ˹put on an apron (lit. *put on his belt*) . . . and wait on them.
	17 8 < 2	˹make yourself tidy (lit. *put on your belt*) and wait on me
Jn	13 4 X 4	taking a towel, [Jesus] wrapped it *round his waist*; ⁵ he then . . . began to wash the disciples' feet and to wipe them with
	5 X 4	the towel he ˹was wearing (lit. had *fastened round his waist*).
	21 7 4	Peter, who had practically nothing on, wrapped his cloak *round* him
	18 3	when you were young you *put on* your own *belt* . . . but when you grow old . . . somebody else will *put a belt round* you
Ac	12 8 3	*Put on* your *belt* and sandals.
	21 11	[Agabus] took Paul's *girdle*, and tied up his own feet and hands, and said, '. . . The man this *girdle* belongs to will be bound like this by the Jews in Jerusalem
Ep	6 14 ○ 2	stand your ground, with truth *buckled round* your waist,
1 P	1 13 ○ 5	˹Free your minds, then, of encumbrances (lit. *Fasten the belts round* your minds, then):
Rv	1 13 X 2	[I saw] a Son of man, dressed in a long robe *tied at the waist* with a golden *girdle*.
	15 6 A	out came the seven angels . . . wearing pure white linen,
	2/	*fastened round their waists* with golden *girdles*.

3. SHOES, FOOTWEAR – SANDALS: *HYPO-DĒMA* and *SANDALION*

1	*hypo-dēma*	10	3	*sandalion 2*
2	*hypo-deō*	3		

Mt	3 11 X	I am not fit to ˹carry (or: take off) his *sandals*;
	10 10	[Provide yourselves] with no haversack for the journey or spare tunic or *footwear* or a staff,
Mk	1 7 X	I am not fit to kneel down and undo the strap of his *sandals*.
	6 9 3/2	They were to ˹wear sandals (lit. have *sandals* as *footwear*) but, [Jesus] added, 'Do not wear a spare tunic'.
Lk	3 16 X	I am not fit to undo the strap of his *sandals*;
	10 4	Carry no purse, no haversack, no *sandals*.
	15 22 <	put a ring on his finger and *sandals* on his feet.
	22 35	I sent you out without purse or haversack or *sandals*,
Jn	1 27 X	I am not fit to undo his *sandal*-strap
Ac	7 33	(Ex 3 5) Take off your *shoes*; the place where you are standing is holy ground.
	12 8 2/3	Put on your belt and *put shoes on*, your *sandals*.
	13 25 X	I am not fit to undo his *sandal*.
Ep	6 15 ○ 2	[stand your ground,] wearing for *shoes* on your feet the eagerness to spread the gospel of peace

4. SKIN, LEATHER – SACKCLOTH

1: SKIN, LEATHER: *DERMA* and *MĒLŌTĒ*

2	*derma*	1	4	*mēlōtē 1*	5	*aigeios 1*
1	*dermatinos 2*					
3	*derris*	1				

Mt	3 4	John wore a garment . . . with a *leather* belt round his waist,
Mk	1 6 3	John wore a garment of camel-˹*skin* (G hair), and (§ had a *leather* belt round his waist, and) he lived on locusts and wild honey.
Heb	11 37 4	they were homeless, and dressed in the *skins of sheep* and (§ the *skins of*) goats;
	2/5	

2: SACKCLOTH: *SAKKOS*

sakkos 4

Mt	11 21	Tyre and Sidon . . . would have repented long ago in *sackcloth* and ashes.
Lk	10 13	Tyre and Sidon . . . would have repented long ago . . . in *sackcloth* and ashes.
Rv	6 12	the sun went as black as coarse *sackcloth*;
	11 3	I shall send my two witnesses to prophesy . . . wearing *sackcloth*.

5. STRIP (OFF) – NAKED

1: STRIP (OFF): *EK-DUŌ*

1	*ek-duō 5*		3	*ap-ek-dysis 1*
2	*ap-ek-duō 2*			

a) Strip, Take off

Mt	27 28 X	[the soldiers] *stripped* him and made him wear a scarlet cloak,
	31 X	[the soldiers] *took off* the cloak
Mk	15 20 X	[the soldiers] *took off* the purple
Lk	10 30	[the brigands] *took all he had* (lit. *stripped* him), beat him . . . leaving him half dead.

b) Strip, Strip off, Not to wear clothes (*figuratively*)

2Co	5 4	we groan and find it a burden being still in this tent, not that we want to *strip* it *off*, but to put the second garment over it
Col	2 11 3	you have been circumcised . . . by the *complete stripping* of your body of flesh.
	15 2	[God] ˹*got rid of* (lit. *stripped off*) the Sovereignties and the Powers,
	3 9 2	You have *stripped off* your old behaviour with your old self,

2: NAKED: *GYMNOS*

3	*gymniteuō 1*		2	*gymnotēs 3*
1	*gymnos*	15		

a) Naked

Mt	25 36 X	[I was] *naked* and you clothed me,
	38 X	When did we see you . . . *naked* and clothe you . . . ?
	43 X	I was . . . *naked* and you never clothed me,

Mt 25 44 X   when did we see you . . . *naked* . . . and did not come to your help?

Mk 14 51   A young man who followed [Jesus] had nothing on but a linen cloth (G over [his] *naked* [body]). They caught hold

      52   of him, [52] but he left the cloth in their hands and ran away *naked*.

Jn 21 7   Simon Peter, who ˹had practically nothing on (lit. was *naked*), wrapped his cloak round him

Ac 19 16   [the sons of Sceva] fled from that house *naked* and badly mauled.

Rm 8 35   Nothing therefore can come between us and the love of Christ,

      2   even if we are . . . *lacking* food or *clothes*,

1 Co 4 11   3 we *go without* food and drink and *clothes*;

2 Co 5 3   we should like to be found wearing clothes and not ˹without them (lit. *naked*).

    11 27   2 I have been in the cold *without clothes*.

Jm 2 15   If one of the brothers or one of the sisters is *in need of clothes* . . . [16] and one of you says to them, '. . . keep yourself warm . . .', then what good is that?

Rv 3 17   you are . . . poor, and blind and *naked* too. [18] I warn you,

      18   buy from me . . . robes to clothe you and cover your

       2   shameful *nakedness*,

    16 15   Happy is the man who has . . . not taken off his clothes so that he does not go out *naked* and expose his shame.

    17 16   the ten horns . . . will turn against the prostitute, and strip off her clothes and leave her *naked*;

b) Uncovered

Heb 4 13   everything is *uncovered* and open to the eyes of the one to whom we must give account of ourselves.

c) Bare

1 Co 15 37   you sow a *bare* grain, say of wheat . . . and then God gives it the sort of body that he has chosen:

COME – ARRIVE

1. Come: *erchomai*
- 1: (God, the Spirit) Comes
  - a) (God) Comes, (is to) Come
  - b) (the Spirit) Comes
- 2: (an angel, Satan) Comes
  - a) (an angel) Came
  - b) (Satan) Comes, Came – (Satan's) Arrival
- 3: (Jesus) Comes
  - a) (Jesus) Comes (as the Messiah) – (Jesus's eschatological) Coming
  - b) (Jesus) Comes to(wards), Goes to, Went to – (Jesus) Comes into, Reaches, Rejoins: *erchomai eis* and *erchomai pros*
  - c) (Jesus) Comes, Goes (generally)
- 4: (a person) Comes, Came
  - a) Come to (Jesus): *erchomai pros*
  - b) Come to (Jesus)
  - c) Come to, Go to, Reach – Visit, Go into: *erchomai pros* and *erchomai eis*

- d) Come (generally) – Arrive
- e) Come (figuratively)
  - 5: Come (to the Father)
  - 6: (a time) Comes
  - 7: (things, animals) Come

2. (the Lord) Comes: *atha*

3. Come: *hēkō*
  - a) (a person) Comes
  - b) (a thing) Comes

4. "Come!": *deuro*

5. Come – Be here, Be present: *par-eimi*
  - a) (the Lord's) Coming – (the Rebel's) Coming
  - b) Be here, Present – (Have) Arrived, Come

6. Come (to), Attain – Come (upon), Overtake: *phthanō*

7. Arrive (at), Come (to), Reach: *para-ginomai*

8. Arrive (in, at), Reach, Come (to): *kat-antaō*

9. Reach, Come (to) – Pass (into), Penetrate: *chōreō*

10. Reach: *hikneomai*

---

1. COME: *ERCHOMAI*

5	*eleusis*	1	4	*ep-an-erchomai*	2
1	*erchomai 634/635*		6	*ep-eis-erchomai*	1
2	*ep-erchomai*	9	3	*kat-erchomai 5/15*	

1: (GOD, THE SPIRIT) COMES

a) (God) Comes, (is to) Come

Mt 21 40 <   Now when the owner of the vineyard *comes*, what will he do to those tenants?

Mk 12 9 <   Now what will the owner of the vineyard do? He will *come* and make an end of the tenants

Lk 13 6 <   he *came* looking for fruit on [the fig tree] but found none

      7 <   for three years now I have been *coming* to look for fruit on this fig tree and finding none.

Lk 20 16 <   He will *come* and make an end of these tenants

Jn 14 23   If anyone loves me . . . my Father will love him, and we shall *come* to him

Rm 9 9   (Gn 18 10) I shall *visit* you . . . and Sarah will have a son.

Rv 1 4   grace and peace to you from him who is, who was, and who is to *come*,

      8   the Lord God, who is, who was, and who is to *come*, the Almighty;

     4 8   Holy is the Lord God, the Almighty; he was, he is and he is to *come*.

b) (the Spirit) Comes

Mt 3 16   Jesus . . . saw the Spirit of God descending like a dove and *coming* [down] on him.

Lk 1 35   2 The Holy Spirit will *come upon* you

Jn 15 26   When the Advocate *comes* . . . he will be my witness.

   16 7   unless I go, the Advocate will not *come* to you;

      8   when [the Advocate] *comes*, he will show the world how wrong it was,

     13   when the Spirit of truth *comes* he will lead you to the complete truth.

Ac 1 8   2 you will receive power when the Holy Spirit *comes on* you,

   19 6   the Holy Spirit *came* [down] on [the disciples of John the Baptist],

2: (AN ANGEL, SATAN) COMES

a) (an angel) Came

Ac 12 10   [the angel and Peter] ˹reached (lit. *came* to) the iron gate

Rv 8 3   Another angel . . . *came* and stood at the altar.

   17 1   One of the seven angels . . . *came* to speak to me,

   21 9   One of the seven angels . . . *came* to speak to me,

b) (Satan) Comes, Came – (Satan's) Arrival

Mt 12 44   'I will return to the home I came from' . . . on *arrival*, finding it unoccupied [the spirit collects seven other spirits and they set up house there]

   13 19   the evil one *comes* and carries off what was sown in his heart,

     25 <   While everybody was asleep his enemy *came*,

Mk 4 15   Satan *comes* and carries away the word that was sown in them.

Lk 8 12   the devil *comes* and carries away the word from their hearts

   11 25   on *arrival*, [the unclean spirit finds his former home] swept

Jn 14 30   the prince of this world is *on his way*.

3: (JESUS) COMES

P = Jesus comes with other people

a) (Jesus) Comes (as the Messiah) – (Jesus's eschatological) Coming

E = eschatological coming

Mt 3 11   the one who ˹follows (lit. is *coming* after) me is more powerful than I am,

    5 17   Do not imagine that I have *come* to abolish the Law . . . I have *come* not to abolish but to complete them.

    9 13   I did not *come* to call the virtuous, but sinners.

   10 35 E?   you will not have gone the round of the towns of Israel before the Son of Man *comes*.

     34   Do not suppose that I have *come* to bring peace to the earth: it is not peace I have *come* to bring, but a sword. [35] For I have *come* to set a man against his father,

   11 3   Are you the one who is to *come* . . .?

     19   The Son of Man *came*, eating and drinking,

   16 27 E   the Son of Man is going to *come* in the glory of his Father

     28 E   there are some . . . here who will not taste death before they see the Son of Man *coming* with his kingdom.

   18 11   (ᵛ . . . for the Son of Man has *come* to save those who were lost.)

   20 28   the Son of Man *came* not to be served but to serve,

   21 5   (Zc 9 9) Look, your king *comes* to you;

     9   The crowds . . . were all shouting: . . . (Ps 118 26) Blessings on him who *comes* in the name of the Lord!

   23 39 E?   you shall not see me any more until you say: (Ps 118 26) Blessings on him who *comes* in the name of the Lord!

   24 30 E   all the peoples . . . will see the Son of Man *coming* on the clouds

     42 E   stay awake, because you do not know . . . when your master is *coming*.

     44 E   the Son of Man is *coming* at an hour you do not expect.

     46 <   Happy that servant if his master's *arrival* finds him at this employment.

   25 10 <   They had gone off to buy [oil] when the bridegroom *arrived*.

     19 <   the master of those servants *came* [back] and went through his accounts

     27 <   on my *return* I would have recovered my capital with interest.

     31 E   When the Son of Man *comes* in his glory . . . he will take his seat on his throne

Mt	26	64	E

Mt 26 64 E   you will see the Son of Man . . . *coming* on the clouds of heaven.

Mk 1 7   Someone is ⌐following (lit. *coming* after) me, someone who is more powerful than I am,

    24   Have you *come* to destroy us?

2 17   I did not *come* to call the virtuous, but sinners.

8 38 E   the Son of Man . . . *comes* in the glory of his Father

10 45   the Son of Man himself did not *come* to be served but to serve,

11 9   (Ps 118 26) Blessings on him who *comes* in the name of the Lord!

13 26 E   they will see the Son of Man *coming* in the clouds with great power

    35 <   stay awake, because you do not know when the master . . .

    36 <   is *coming* . . . ³⁶ if he *comes* unexpectedly, he must not find you asleep.

14 62 E   you will see the Son of Man . . . *coming* with the clouds of heaven.

Lk 3 16   someone is *coming*, someone who is more powerful than I am,

4 34   Have you *come* to destroy us?

5 32   I have not *come* to call the virtuous, but sinners to repentance.

7 19   Are you the one who is to *come* . . .?

    20   Are you the one who is to *come* . . .?

    34   The Son of Man *comes*, eating and drinking,

9 26 E   if anyone is ashamed of me . . . of him the Son of Man will be ashamed when he *comes* in his . . . glory

    56   (ᵛ for the Son of Man did not *come* to destroy men's lives but to save them.)

12 36 <   Be . . . ready to open the door as soon as [the master] *comes*

    37   and knocks. ³⁷ Happy those servants whom the master

    38 <   finds awake when he *comes* . . . ³⁸ It may be in the second watch he *comes*,

    40 E   the Son of Man is *coming* at an hour you do not expect.

    43 <   Happy that servant if his master's *arrival* finds him at this employment.

    45 <   My master is taking his time *coming*.

    49   I have *come* to bring fire to the earth.

13 35 E?   (Ps 118 26) Blessings on him who *comes* in the name of the Lord!

18 8 E   when the Son of Man *comes*, will he find any faith on earth?

19 10   the Son of Man has *come* to seek out and save what was lost.

    13 <   Do business . . . until I ⌐get back (lit. *come*).

    15 <   4 on his *return* . . . he sent for those servants

    23 <   On my *return* I could have drawn [the money] out with interest.

    38   (Ps 118 26) Blessings on the King who *comes*, in the name of the Lord!

21 27 E   they will see the Son of Man *coming* in a cloud with power

23 42 E?   Jesus, . . . remember me when you *come* into your kingdom.

Jn 1 9   The Word was the true light that enlightens all men; and he was *coming* into the world.

    11   [The Word] *came* to his own domain and his own people did not accept him

    15   He who *comes* after me ranks before me

    27   [there stands among you] the one who is *coming* after me;

    30   A man is *coming* after me who ranks before me

3 2   you are a teacher who *comes* from God;

    19   the light has *come* into the world

    31   He who *comes* from above is above all others . . . He who *comes* from heaven [bears witness to the things he has seen]

4 25   Messiah – that is, Christ – is *coming*; and when he *comes* he will tell us everything.

5 43   I have *come* in the name of my Father

6 14   This really is the prophet who is to *come* into the world.

7 27   when the Christ *appears* no one will know where he comes from.

    28   I have not *come* of myself:

    31   When the Christ *comes*, will he give more signs than this man?

    41   Would the Christ ⌐be (lit. *come*) from Galilee? ⁴² Does not

    42   scripture say that the Christ must be descended from David and *come* from the town of Bethlehem?

8 14   I know where I *came* from and where I am going; but you do not know where I *come* from or where I am going.

    42   I have come here from God; yes I have *come* from him; not that I *came* because I chose,

9 39   It is for judgement that I have *come* into this world,

10 10   I have *come* so that [the sheep] may have life

11 27   you are the Christ, the Son of God, the one who was to *come* into this world.

12 13   (Ps 118 26) Blessings on the King . . . who *comes* in the name of the Lord.

    15   (Zc 9 9) daughter of Zion; see, your king is *coming*,

    27   it was for this very reason that I have *come* to this hour.

    46   I, the light, here come into the world . . . ⁴⁷ . . . I have

    47   *come* not to condemn the world, but to save the world:

14 3 E   I shall ⌐return (lit. *come* back) to take you with me;

    18 O   I will not leave you orphans; I will *come* [back] to you.

    23 O   If anyone loves me . . . my Father will love him, and we shall *come* to him

    28 E?   I am going away, and shall *return*.

Jn 15 22   If I had not *come* . . . they would have been blameless;

16 28   I came from the Father and have *come* into the world

18 37   I *came* into the world for this: to bear witness to the truth;

21 22 E   If I want him to stay behind till I *come*, what does it matter to you?

    23 E   Jesus had . . . said . . , 'If I want him to stay behind till I *come*'.

Ac 1 11 E   this same Jesus will *come* [back] in the same way as you have seen him go

7 52   5 your ancestors . . . killed those who foretold the *coming* of the Just One,

13 25   that one is *coming* after me and I am not fit to undo his sandal.

19 4   [John] insisted that the people should believe in the one who was to *come* after him –

1 Co 4 5 E   Leave that until the Lord *comes*:

11 26 E   Until the Lord *comes* . . . you are proclaiming his death,

Ep 2 17   he *came* to bring the good news of peace,

2 Th 1 10 E   he *comes* to be glorified among his saints

1 Tm 1 15   Christ Jesus *came* into the world to save sinners.

Heb 10 37 E   (Hab 2 3 G) the one that is *coming* will have come; he will not delay.

1 Jn 4 2   every spirit which acknowledges that Jesus the Christ has *come* in the flesh is from God;

    5 6   Jesus Christ . . . *came* by water and blood,

2 Jn 7   There are many deceivers . . . refusing to admit that Jesus Christ has *come* in the flesh.

Jude 14 E   the Lord will *come* with his saints in their tens of thousands,

Rv 1 7 E   (Dn 7 13) It is he who is *coming* in the clouds;

2 5   if you will not repent, I shall *come* to you and take your lampstand from its place.

    16   You must repent, or I shall soon *come* to you and attack these people

3 11   Soon I shall ⌐be with (lit. *come* to) you:

16 15 E   I shall *come* like a thief.

22 7 E   Very soon now, I shall ⌐be with (lit. *come* to) you again.

    12 E   Very soon now, I shall ⌐be with (lit. *come* to) you again,

    17 E   The Spirit and the Bride say, 'Come'. Let everyone who listens

        E   answer, 'Come'.

    20 E   I shall indeed ⌐be with (lit. *come* to) you soon. Amen; come, Lord Jesus.

b) (Jesus) *Comes to(wards)*, *Goes to*, *Went to* – (Jesus) *Comes into*, *Reaches*, *Rejoins*: erchomai eis and erchomai pros

Mt 3 14   It is I who need baptism from you . . . and yet you *come to* me!

8 14   *going into* Peter's house Jesus found Peter's mother-in-law in bed

    28   [Jesus] *reached* the country of the Gadarenes on the other side

9 1   [Jesus] crossed the water and *came to* his own town [= Capernaum].

    23   Jesus *reached* the official's house and saw the flute-players,

    28   when Jesus *reached* the house the blind men came up with him

12 9   [Jesus] *went to* their synagogue,

13 36   leaving the crowds, [Jesus] *went to* the house;

    54   *coming to* his home town, [Jesus] taught the people

14 25   [Jesus] *went towards* [the disciples], walking on the lake,

    34 P   Having made the crossing, they *came to* land at Gennesaret.

15 39   [Jesus] *went to* the district of Magadan.

16 13   Jesus *came to* the region of Caesarea Philippi

17 14 P   As [Jesus and the disciples] were *rejoining* the crowd a man came up to him

    24 P   When they *reached* Capernaum, the collectors of the half-shekel came to Peter

19 1   Jesus . . . left Galilee and *came into* the part of Judaea which is on the far side of the Jordan.

21 1 P   they were near Jerusalem and had *come in* sight of Bethphage

    23   [Jesus] had *gone into* the Temple and was teaching,

26 36 P   Jesus *came* with them *to* a small estate called Gethsemane;

    40   [Jesus] *came* [back] *to* the disciples and found them sleeping,

    45   [Jesus] *came* [back] *to* the disciples and said to them,

Mk 1 14   After John had been arrested, Jesus *went into* Galilee.

    29 (P)   On leaving the synagogue, ᵛ he (G they) *went* with James and John straight *to* the house of Simon and Andrew.

3 20   [Jesus] *went* home again,

5 1 P   They *reached* the country of the Gerasenes on the other side of the lake,

    38 P   they *came to* the official's house

6 1   Going from that district, [Jesus] *went to* his home town

    48   [Jesus] *came towards* [the disciples], walking on the lake,

    53 P   Having made the crossing, they *came to* land at Gennesaret

7 31   [Jesus] *went* by way of Sidon *towards* the Sea of Galilee,

8 10   [Jesus] *went to* the region of Dalmanutha.

    22 P   They *came to* Bethsaida, and some people brought . . . a blind man

9 14 P   When they *rejoined* the disciples they saw a large crowd

    33 P   They *came to* Capernaum,

10 1   [Jesus] *came to* the district of Judaea and the far side of the Jordan.

    46 P   They *reached* Jericho;

Mk 11 15 P   they *reached* Jerusalem
      27 P   They *came to* Jerusalem again,
  14 32 P   They *came to* a small estate called Gethsemane,
Lk 2 51   [Jesus] then went down with [his parents] and *came to* Nazareth
  4 16   [Jesus] *came to* Nazara, where he had been brought up,
  8 51   When [Jesus] *came to* the house he allowed no one to go in with him
  14 1   [Jesus] had *gone* for a meal *to* the house of one of the leading Pharisees
  22 45   [Jesus] *went to* the disciples and found them sleeping
Jn 1 29   seeing Jesus *coming towards* him, John said, 'Look, there is the lamb of God
  3 22 P   Jesus *went* with his disciples *into* the Judaean countryside
  4 5   [Jesus] *came to* the Samaritan town called Sychar,
    45   on his arrival the Galileans received [Jesus] well,
    46   [Jesus] *went* again *to* Cana in Galilee,
    54   This was the second sign given by Jesus, on his *return* from Judaea to Galilee.
  6 17   It was getting dark by now and Jesus had still not *rejoined* them.
  11 30   Jesus had not yet *come into* the village;
    38   Jesus *reached* the tomb:
  12 1   Six days before the Passover, Jesus *went to* Bethany,
    12   the crowds . . . heard that Jesus was *on his way to* Jerusalem.
  13 6   He *came to* Simon Peter, who said to him, 'Lord, are you going to wash my feet?'

c) (Jesus) Comes, Goes (generally)

Mt 4 13   leaving Nazareth [Jesus] *went* and settled in Capernaum,
  8 7   'I will *come* myself and cure him' said Jesus.
    29   Have you *come* here to torture us before the time?
  9 18   My daughter has just died, but *come* and lay your hand on her
  15 29   Jesus . . . *reached* the shores of the Sea of Galilee,
  21 19   Seeing a fig tree by the road, [Jesus] *went* up to it
  26 43   [Jesus] *came* [back] again and found [the disciples] sleeping,
Mk 1 9   It was at this time that Jesus *came* from Nazareth in Galilee
    39   [Jesus] *went* all through Galilee, preaching in their synagogues
  5 23   My little daughter is desperately sick. [Do] *come* and lay your hands on her
  11 13   Seeing a fig tree . . . [Jesus] *went* to see if he could find any fruit on it, but when he *came* [up] to it he found nothing
  14 17   When evening came [Jesus] *arrived* with the Twelve.
    37   [Jesus] *came* [back] and found [the disciples] *sleeping*,
    40   once more [Jesus] *came* [back] and found them sleeping,
    41   [Jesus] *came* [back] a third time
Lk 7 3   [the centurion] sent some Jewish elders . . . to ask [Jesus] to *come* and heal his servant.
  10 1   the Lord . . . sent them out . . . to all the towns . . . he himself was to *visit*.
  19 5   When Jesus *reached* the spot he looked up
Jn 11 17   On *arriving*, Jesus found that Lazarus had been in the tomb for four days already.
    20   Martha heard that Jesus had *come*
    34   Lord, *come* and see.
    56   Will he *come* to the festival or not?
  20 19   Jesus *came* and stood among [the disciples].
    24   Thomas . . . was not with them when Jesus *came*.
    26   The doors were closed, but Jesus *came* [in]
  21 13   Jesus then *stepped* [forward], took the bread and gave it to them
Rv 5 7   The Lamb *came* [forward] to take the scroll from the right hand of the One sitting on the throne,

4: (A PERSON) COMES, CAME

a) Come to (Jesus): erchomai pros

Mt 14 28   'Lord, . . . tell me to *come to* you across the water.' ²⁹ 'Come'
    29   said Jesus . . . Peter . . . started walking towards Jesus *coming to* him across the water,
  19 14   Let the little children alone, and do not stop them *coming to* me;
  25 36   [I was] in prison and you *came to* [see] me.
    39   [When did we see you] in prison and *go to* [see] you?
Mk 1 40   A leper *came to* [Jesus]
    45   people from all around would *come to* [Jesus].
  2 13   all the people *came to* [Jesus],
  3 8   great numbers . . . *came to* [Jesus].
  5 15   They *came to* Jesus and saw the demoniac sitting there,
  10 14   Let the little children *come to* me;
    50   [the blind man] jumped up and *went to* Jesus.
  11 27   the chief priests and the scribes and the elders *came to* [Jesus],
  12 18   some Sadducees . . . *came to* [Jesus]
Lk 6 47   Everyone who *comes to* me and listens to my words [is like the man who laid the foundations on rock]
  7 7   I did not presume to *come to* you myself;
  8 35   When they *came to* Jesus they found the man from whom the devils had gone out sitting at the feet of Jesus,

Lk 14 26   If any man *comes to* me without hating his father . . . he cannot be my disciple.
  18 16   Let the little children *come to* me,
Jn 1 47   Jesus saw Nathanael *coming*
  3 2   [Nicodemus] *came* to Jesus by night
    26   [Jesus] is baptising now; and everyone is *going to* him.
  4 30   people . . . started *walking towards* [Jesus].
    40   when the Samaritans *came up to* [Jesus], they begged him to stay
  5 40   you refuse to *come to* me for life!
  6 5   Looking up, Jesus saw the crowds *approaching*
    35   He who *comes to* me will never be hungry;
    37   All that the Father gives me will come to me, and whoever *comes to* me I shall not turn him away;
    44   No one can *come to* me unless he is drawn by the Father
    45   to hear the teaching of the Father . . . is to *come to* me.
    65   no one could *come to* me unless the Father allows him.
  7 37   If any man is thirsty, let him *come to* me!
    50   Nicodemus – the same man who had *come to* Jesus earlier –
  8 2   as all the people *came to* [Jesus], he . . . began to teach them.
  10 41   Many people . . . *came to* [Jesus]
  11 29   Mary got up quickly and *went to* [Jesus].
  19 3   [The soldiers] kept *coming up to* him and saying, 'Hail, king of the Jews!'
    39   Nicodemus came as well – the same one who had first *come to* Jesus at night-time –

b) Come (to Jesus)

Mt 2 2   We . . . have *come* to do [Jesus] homage.
    8   when you have found him, let me know, so that I too may *go* and do him homage.
  9 10   a number of tax collectors and sinners *came* to sit at the table with Jesus
  14 12   John's disciples . . . *went off* to tell Jesus.
    29   'Come' said Jesus. Then Peter . . . started walking . . . across the water,
  15 25   the woman had *come up* and was kneeling at [Jesus's] feet.
  16 24   If anyone wants to ᵛbe a follower of mine (lit. *come* following me), let him renounce himself
Mk 2 3   some people *came* bringing [Jesus] a paralytic
    18   people *came* and said to him, 'Why is it that John's disciples . . . fast, but your disciples do not?'
  3 31   His mother and brothers now *arrived*
  5 14   the people *came* to see what had really happened.
    22   one of the synagogue officials *came up*, Jairus by name,
    27   [the woman with a haemorrhage] *came up* behind [Jesus] through the crowd and touched his cloak.
    33   the woman *came* [forward] . . . and she fell at his feet
    35   some people *arrived* from the house of the synagogue official
  6 31   there were so many *coming* and going that the apostles had no time even to eat.
  7 1   The Pharisees and some of the scribes who had *come* from Jerusalem gathered round [Jesus],
    25   A woman . . . *came* and fell at [Jesus's] feet.
  8 34   If anyone wants to ᵛbe a follower of mine (G *come* following me), let him renounce himself
  12 14   These *came* and said to him, 'Master, . . . Is it permissible to pay taxes to Caesar or not?'
  14 3   a woman *came* [in] with an alabaster jar of very costly ointment,
    45   when the traitor *came*, he went straight up to Jesus
Lk 2 16   [the shepherds] ⌐hurried away and found (lit. *came* hurriedly to find) Mary and Joseph,
  4 42   The crowds went to look for [Jesus], and when they had caught up (lit. *come up*) with him they wanted to prevent him leaving
  5 17   there were Pharisees and doctors of the Law who had *come* from every village in Galilee
  6 18   [his disciples with a great crowd of people] had *come* to hear [Jesus] and to be cured
  8 41   now there *came* a man named Jairus,
    47   Seeing herself discovered, the woman *came* [forward] trembling,
  9 23   If anyone wants to ⌐be a follower of mine (lit. *come* following me), let him renounce himself
  13 14   *Come* and be healed on one of those days and not on the sabbath.
  14 27   Anyone who does not . . . *come* after me cannot be my disciple.
Jn 1 39   'Come and see' [Jesus] replied; so they *went* and saw where he lived,
    46   'Come and see' replied Philip.
  6 15   Jesus . . . could see they were about to *come* and take him by force and make him king,
  12 9   a large number of Jews heard that [Jesus] was there and *came*
    22   Andrew and Philip together *went* to tell Jesus.
  19 33   When they *came* to Jesus, they found he was already dead.
    38   Joseph of Arimathaea . . . asked Pilate to let him remove the body of Jesus . . . so ⌐they (ᵛ he) *came* and took it away.

Jn 19	39	Nicodemus *came* as well –
Rv 22	17	let all who are thirsty *come*:

c) Come to, Go to, Reach – Visit, Go into: erchomai pros *and* erchomai eis

Mt 2	11	*going into* the house [the wise men] saw the child
7	15	Beware of false prophets who *come to* you disguised as sheep
16	5	The disciples, having ⌐crossed to (lit. *come to*) the other shore, had forgotten to take any food.
17	25	[Peter] *went into* the house.
21	32	John *came to* you, a pattern of true righteousness,
27	33	they had *reached* a place called Golgotha
28	11	some of the guard *went off into* the city to tell the chief priests all that had happened.
Mk 14	16	The disciples set out and *went to* the city
Lk 1	43	Why should I be honoured with a *visit* from the mother of my Lord?
3	3	[John] *went through* the whole Jordan district
15	6	[Would he not,] when he *got home*, call together his friends and neighbours?
20	<	[the prodigal son] *went* [back] *to* his father.
16	28	give [my brothers] warning so that they do not *come to* this place of torment
18	3 <	there was a widow who kept on *coming to* him
Jn 3	26	[John's disciples] *went to* John and said,
4	45	the Galileans . . . too had *attended* [the festival].
6	17	[the disciples] got into a boat to *make for* Capernaum
24		the people . . . ⌐crossed to (lit. *came to*) Capernaum to look for Jesus.
7	45	The police *went* [back] *to* the chief priests
11	19	many Jews had *come to* Martha and Mary to sympathise with them
45		Many of the Jews who had *come to* visit Mary . . . believed in [Jesus],
20	1	It was very early . . . when Mary of Magdala *came to* the tomb.
2		[Mary of Magdala] *came* running *to* Simon Peter and the other disciple,
3		Peter set out with the other disciple to *go to* the tomb.
4		the other disciple . . . *reached* the tomb first;
8		the other disciple who had *reached* the tomb first also went in;
Ac 4	23	[the apostles] *went to* the community and told them everything
8	27	an Ethiopian had *been* on pilgrimage *to* Jerusalem
40		Philip . . . continued his journey . . . ⌐as far as (lit. until he *came to*) Caesarea.
11	20	some of them . . . who came from Cyprus and Cyrene, *went to* Antioch where they started preaching to the Greeks.
13	13	Paul and his friends *went* by sea from Paphos *to* Perga
14		[At Antioch the apostles] *went to* synagogue
51		[Paul and Barnabas] *went off to* Iconium;
14	24	[Paul and Barnabas] *reached* Pamphylia.
17	1	[Paul and Silas] eventually *reached* Thessalonika,
15		Paul's escort . . . went back with instructions for Silas and Timothy to *rejoin* Paul as soon as they could.
18	1	Paul left Athens and *went to* Corinth.
7		[Paul] *moved to* the house next door that belonged to . . . Justus.
19	1	Paul *made his way* overland *as far as* Ephesus,
20	2	[Paul] *made his way into* Greece,
6		We ourselves . . . *met* them five days later at Troas,
14		we . . . *went on to* Mitylene.
15		we . . . *made* Miletus the next day.
21	1	we set a straight course and *arrived at* Cos;
8		The next day we left and *came to* Caesarea.
11		[Agabus arrived from Judaea] ⌐to see (lit. and *came to*) us.
22	11	I *came to* Damascus.
13		[Ananias] *came to* [see] me;
27	8	we *came to* a place called Fair Havens,
28	13	on the second day we *made* Puteoli,
14		we *came to* Rome.
23		a large number of [Romans Jews] *visited* [Paul] *at* his lodgings.
Rm 1	10	[I never fail in my prayers] to ask to be allowed . . . to *visit* you,
13		I have often planned to *visit* you –
15	22	That is the reason why I have been kept from *visiting* you
23		I have been longing to *pay* you *a visit*.
29		when I *reach* you I shall arrive with rich blessings from Christ.
32		I shall be feeling very happy when I *come to* enjoy a period of rest among you.
1Co 2	1	when I *came to* you, ⌐it was not (lit. I did not *come*) with any show of oratory or philosophy,
4	18	it seemed that I was not [coming to] *visit* you,
19		I will be *visiting* you soon,
21		It is for you to decide: do I *come* with a stick in my hand . . .?
14	6	Now suppose . . . I am someone with the gift of tongues, and I [come to] *visit* you,
16	5	I shall be *coming to* you after I have passed through Macedonia–
11		Send [Timothy] happily on his way to *come* [back] *to* me;
12		As for our brother Apollos, I begged him to *come to* you
2Co 1	15	I had mean to *come to* you first . . . [16] staying with you before going to Macedonia and *coming* [back] *to* you again

2Co 1	23	I did not *come to* Corinth after all
2	1	I made up my mind not to *pay* you *a* second distressing *visit*.
12		I *went up to* Troas
7	5	Even after we had *come to* Macedonia . . . there was no rest
12	14	I am all prepared now to *come to* you for the third time,
13	1	This will be the third time I have *come to* you.
Ga 1	21	After that I *went to* Syria and Cilicia,
2	11	Cephas *came to* Antioch,
Col 4	10	if [Mark] *comes to* you, give him a warm welcome –
1Th 2	18	we tried hard to [come and] *visit* you;
3	6	Timothy ⌐is now back (lit. has just *come to* us) from you
1Tm 3	14	I am hoping that I may ⌐be with (lit. *visit*) you soon;
2Tm 4	9	Do your best to *come* [and see me] as soon as you can.
Tt 3	12	lose no time in *joining* me at Nicopolis,
2Jn	10	If anyone *comes to* you bringing a different doctrine, you must not receive him

d) Come (generally) – Arrive

Mt 2	23	[Joseph] ⌐settled (lit. *came* to settle) in a town called Nazareth.
3	7	[John the Baptist] saw a number of Pharisees . . . *coming* for baptism
5	24	go and be reconciled with your brother first, and then *come* [back] and present your offering.
8	9	I say to one man: Go, and he goes; to another: *Come* [here], and he *comes*;
11	14	[John] is the Elijah who was to ⌐return (lit. *come*).
18		John *came*, neither eating nor drinking,
12	42	the Queen of the South . . . *came* from the ends of the earth
17	10	Why do the scribes say then that Elijah has to *come* first?
11		Elijah is to *come* to see that everything is . . . as it should be;
12		Elijah has *come* already and they did not recognise him
18	31 <	His fellow servants . . . *went* to their master and reported the whole affair to him.
20	9 <	those who were hired at about the eleventh hour *came* [forward] and received one denarius each.
10 <		When the first *came*, they expected to get more,
22	3 <	He sent his servants to call those who had been invited, but they would not *come*.
24	5	many will *come* using my name
43 <		if the householder had known at what time . . . the burglar would *come*, he would have stayed awake
25	11 <	The other bridesmaids *arrived* later.
26	47	[Jesus] was still speaking when Judas . . . *appeared*,
27	49	Wait . . . and see if Elijah will *come* to save him.
57		When it was evening, there *came* a rich man of Arimathaea,
64		give the order to have the sepulchre kept secure . . . for fear his disciples *come* and steal him away
28	1	Mary of Magdala and the other Mary *went* to visit the sepulchre.
13		His disciples *came* during the night and stole him away
Mk 6	29	John's disciples . . . *came* and took [John's] body
9	11	Why do the scribes say that Elijah has to *come* first?
12		Elijah is to *come* first . . . to see that everything is as it should be;
13		Elijah has *come* and they have treated him as they pleased,
12	42	A poor widow *came* and put in two small coins,
13	6	Many will *come* using my name
14	66	While Peter was . . . in the courtyard, one of the high priest's servant-girls *came* [up].
15	21	Simon of Cyrene . . . was *coming* [in] from the country,
36		Wait and see if Elijah will *come* to take him down.
43		there *came* Joseph of Arimathaea,
16	1	Mary of Magdala, Mary the mother of James, and Salome, bought spices with which to *go* and anoint [the body of Jesus]
2		. . . [2] . . . they *went* to the tomb, just as the sun was rising.
Lk 1	59	on the eighth day they *came* to circumcise [John];
2	44	[Joseph and Mary] *went* to look for [Jesus] among their relations
3	12	There were tax collectors too who *came* for baptism,
5	7	they signalled to their companions . . . to *come* and help them; when these *came*, they filled the two boats to sinking point.
7	8	I say to one man: Go, and he goes; to another: *Come* [here], and he *comes*;
33		John the Baptist *comes*, not eating bread, not drinking wine,
8	49	someone *arrived* from the house of the synagogue official
10	32 <	a Levite who *came* to the place saw [the wounded man],
33 <		a Samaritan traveller . . . *came* upon [the wounded man]
35 <		[4] on my *way back* I will make good any extra expense you have.
11	22 <	[2] someone stronger than he is ⌐attacks (lit. *comes* up) and . . . takes away all the weapons he relied on
31 <		the Queen of the South . . . *came* from the ends of the earth
12	39 <	if the householder had known at what hour the burglar would *come*, he would not have let anyone break through the wall
14	9 <	the person who invited you both may *come* and say, 'Give up your place to this man'.
10 <		when your host *comes*, he may say, 'My friend, move up higher'.
17 <		he sent his servants to say to those who had been invited, '*Come* [along]: everything is ready now'.

Lk 14	20	<	I have just got married and so am unable to *come*.
	31		what king . . . would not first . . . consider whether . . . he could stand up to the other who *advanced* against him . . .?
15	25	<	on his *way* [back] . . . [the elder son] could hear music
	30	<	this son of yours . . . *comes* [back] after swallowing up your property –
18	5	<	this widow . . . will persist in *coming* and worry me to death.
19	18	<	Then *came* the second [servant] and said, 'Sir, your one pound has made *five*'.
	20	<	Next *came* the other and said, 'Sir, here is your pound. I put it away safely
21	8		many will *come* using my name
23	26		Simon from Cyrene . . . was *coming* [in] from the country,
	33		they *reached* the place called The Skull.
24	1		[the women] *went* to the tomb with the spices they had prepared.
	23		when [the women] did not find the body, they *came* [back]
Jn 1	7		[John] *came* as a witness,
	31		I *came* baptising with water.
4	7		a Samaritan woman *came* to draw water,
	16		'Go and call your husband' said Jesus to her 'and *come* [back] here.'
	27		At this point his disciples ᴿreturned (lit. *came* [back]),
5	7		while I am *still on the way*, someone else gets [into the pool] before me.
	43		if someone else *comes* in his own name you will accept him.
9	7		the blind man . . . washed himself, and *came* [away] with his sight restored.
10	8	<	All others who have *come* are thieves and brigands;
	10	<	The thief *comes* only to steal
11	32		as soon as [Mary] ᴿsaw (lit. *came* [up] to) [Jesus] she threw herself at his feet,
	48		the Romans will *come* and destroy the Holy Place
12	12		the crowds . . . had *come* [up] for the festival
	22		Philip *went* to tell Andrew, and Andrew and Philip together *went* to tell Jesus.
18	3		[Judas] ᴿbrought (lit. *came* with) the cohort to this place
19	32		the soldiers *came* and broke the legs of the first man
20	6		Simon Peter who was following now *came* [up],
	18		Mary of Magdala *went* and told the disciples that she had seen the Lord
21	3		They replied [to Simon Peter], 'We'll *come* with you'.
	8		The other disciples *came* [on] in the boat,
Ac 5	15		the sick were even taken out into the streets . . . in the hope that at least the shadow of Peter might fall across some of them as he *went* [past].
8	36		[Philip and the eunuch] *came* to some water,
9	17		the Lord Jesus . . . appeared to you *on your way* here
	21		[Saul] *came* here for the sole purpose of arresting [the people who invoke this name]
10	29		I made no objection to *coming* when I was sent for;
11	12		The six brothers here *came* with me as well,
12	10		[Peter and the angel] *reached* the iron gate
	12		[Peter] *went* [straight] to the house of Mary
14	19	2	some Jews *arrived* . . . and turned the people against the apostles.
16	7		[Paul and Timothy] *reached* the frontier of Mysia
	37		[The magistrates] *come* and escort us out themselves.
	39		[The magistrates] *came* and begged [Paul and Silas] to leave the town.
17	13		the Jews of Thessalonika . . . *went* [to Beroea] to make trouble and stir up the people.
18	2		Aquila . . . and his wife Priscilla had recently ᴿleft (lit. *come* from) Italy
	5	3	Silas and Timothy had ᴿarrived (or: come down) from Macedonia,
	22	3	[Paul] *landed* at Caesarea, and went up to greet the church.
19	18		Some believers, too, *came* [forward] to admit . . . how they had used spells
21	3	3	we sailed to Syria and *put in* at Tyre,
	10	3	a prophet called Agabus ᴿarrived (or: came down) from Judaea
	22		they are bound to hear that you have *come*.
24	8		(ᵛ Lysias intervened . . . ordering his accusers to *appear* before you;)
25	23		Agrippa and Bernice *arrived* in great state
27	5	3	[we sailed] across the open sea . . . taking a fortnight to *reach* Myra in Lycia.
28	15		the brothers [in Rome] . . . *came* to meet us, as far as the Forum of Appius
1 Co 11	34		The other matters I shall adjust when I *come*.
15	35	○	what sort of body do [dead people] have when they *come* [back]?
16	2		collections need not be made after I have *come*.
	10		If Timothy *comes*, show him that he has nothing to be afraid of
	12		Apollos . . . was quite firm that he did not want to *go* yet and he will *come* as soon as he can.
2 Co 2	3		I wrote as I did to make sure that, when I *come*, I should not be distressed
9	4		some of the Macedonians . . . are *coming* with me

2 Co 11	4		any new*comer* has only to proclaim a new Jesus . . . and you welcome it with open arms.
	9		the brothers who *came* from Macedonia provided me with everything I wanted.
12	20		What I am afraid of is that when I *come* I may find you different
	21		I am afraid that on my next *visit*, my God may make me ashamed on your account
13	2		when I *come* again, I shall have no mercy.
Ga 2	12		[Cephas's] custom had been to eat with the pagans [before] certain friends of James *arrived*; but after [they] *arrived* he stopped
	3	19	This was done to specify crimes, until the posterity *came* to whom the promise was addressed.
Ph 1	27		whether I *come* to you . . . or stay at a distance . . . I shall know that you are unanimous
	2	24	I shall be *coming* soon myself.
1Tm 4	13		Make use of the time until I *arrive*
2Tm 4	13		When you *come*, bring the cloak I left with Carpus
	21		Do your best to *come* before the winter.
Heb 11	8		[Abraham] set out without knowing where he was *going*.
13	23		Timothy . . . will be with me when I *come* and see you.
2 P 3	3		during the last days there are bound to ᴿbe (lit. *come*) people who will be scornful,
1 Jn 2	18		an Antichrist must *come*,
4	3		any spirit which will not say this of Jesus . . . is the spirit of Antichrist, whose *coming* you were warned about.
3 Jn	3		some brothers *came* and told of your faithfulness to the truth,
	10		if I *come*, I shall tell everyone how [Diotrephes] has behaved
Rv 7	13		Do you know who these people are . . . and where they have *come* from?
	14		These are the people who have ᴿbeen (lit. *come*) through the great persecution,
17	10		one [emperor] is yet to *come*; once ᴿhere (lit. *come*), he must stay for a short while.

e) Come (figuratively)

Mk 5	26	[the woman with a haemorrhage] had spent all she had without being any better for it, in fact, she was *getting* worse.
14	38	You should be . . . praying not to ᴿbe put (lit. *come*) to the test.
Lk 15	17	[the prodigal son] *came* to his senses
Jn 3	20	everybody who does wrong hates the light and avoids *coming* into it,
	21	the man who lives by the truth *comes* [out] into the light,
5	24	without ᴿbeing brought (lit. *coming*) to judgement, he has passed from death to life.
2 Co 12	1	I will *move on* to the visions . . . I have had from the Lord.
1 Tm 2	4	[God] wants everyone to . . . *reach* full knowledge of the truth.
2 Tm 3	7	[They are silly women who] can never *come* to knowledge of the truth.

5: COME (TO THE FATHER)

Jn 7	34	where I am you cannot *come*.
	36	where I am, you cannot *come*
8	21	Where I am going, you cannot *come*.
	22	Where I am going, you cannot *come*
13	33	where I am going, you cannot *come*.
14	6	No one can *come* to the Father except through me.
17	11	I am *coming* to you.
	13	now I am *coming* to you

6: (A TIME) COMES

Mt 9	15	the time will *come* for the bridegroom to be taken away
Mk 2	20	the time will *come* for the bridegroom to be taken away
14	41	The hour has *come*. Now the Son of Man is to be betrayed
Lk 5	35	the time will *come* . . . for the bridegroom to be taken away
17	22	A time will *come* when you will long to see one of the days of the Son of Man
21	6	the time will *come* when not a single stone will be left on another:
	35	6 [that day] will *come down* on every living man on the face of the earth.
22	7	The day of Unleavened Bread *came* [round],
23	29	the days will surely *come* when people will say, 'Happy are those who are barren,
Jn 4	21	the hour is *coming* when you will worship the Father neither on this mountain nor in Jerusalem.
	23	the hour will *come* . . . when true worshippers will worship the Father in spirit and truth:
5	25	the hour will *come* . . . when the dead will hear the voice of the Son of God,
	28	the hour is *coming* when the dead will leave their graves
7	30	because his time had not yet *come* no one laid a hand on him.
8	20	his time had not yet *come*.
9	4	the night will soon ᴿbe here (lit. *come*) when no one can work

Jn	12 23	Now the hour has *come* for the Son of Man to be glorified.
	13 1	the hour had *come* for him to pass from this world to the Father.
	16 2	the hour is *coming* when anyone who kills you will think he is doing a holy duty for God.
	4	when the time for it *comes* you may remember that I told you.
	21	A woman in childbirth suffers, because her time has *come*;
	25	the hour is *coming* when I shall no longer speak . . . in metaphors;
	32	the time will *come* – in fact it has *come* already – when you will be scattered.
	17 1	Father, the hour has *come*: glorify your Son
Ac	2 20	(Jl 3 4) The sun will be turned into darkness . . . before the great Day of the Lord ʳdawns (lit. *comes*).
	3 20	[Repent,] so that the Lord may ʳsend the time of comfort (lit. let the time of comfort *come*).
	18 21	(ᵛ It is essential that I celebrate the *coming* festival in Jerusalem.)
Ga	4 4	when the appointed time *came*, God sent his Son.
Ep	2 7	2 This was to show for all ages to *come* . . . how infinitely rich he is in grace.
1 Th	5 2	the Day of the Lord is [going] to *come* like a thief in the night
Heb	8 8	(Jr 31 31) See, the days are *coming*
Rv	3 10	I will keep you safe in the time of trial which is going to *come*
	6 17	the Great Day of his anger has *come*,
	14 7	the time has *come* for him to sit in judgement;
	15	harvest time has *come*

7: (THINGS, ANIMALS) COME

Mt	2 9	the star . . . ʳhalted (lit. *came* to a halt) over the place where the child was.
	6 10	[may] your kingdom *come*,
	7 25	Rain came down, floods ʳrose (lit. *came*),
	27	Rain came down, floods ʳrose (lit. *came*),
	10 13	if the house deserves it, let your peace ʳdescend (lit. *come*) upon it;
	13 4	some seeds fell on the edge of the path, and the birds *came* and ate them up.
	32	the birds of the air *come* and shelter in its branches.
	18 7	Obstacles indeed ʳthere must be (lit. have to *come*), but alas for the man ʳwho provides them (lit. through whom they *come*)!
	23 35	you will ʳdraw (lit. make to *come*) down on yourselves the blood of every holy man
	24 39	they suspected nothing till the Flood *came*
Mk	4 4	the birds *came* and ate (the seed] up.
	21	Would ʳyou bring in a lamp to put it (lit. a lamp *come* [in] only to be put) under a tub . . .?
	22	there is . . . nothing kept secret except to ʳbe brought (lit. *come*) to light.
	9 1	there are some . . . here who will not taste death before they see the kingdom of God *come* with power.
	10 30	[there is no one who has left house . . .] who will not be repaid . . . in the world to *come*, eternal life.
	11 10	Blessings on the *coming* kingdom of our father David!
Lk	8 17	nothing is . . . secret but it will be known and ʳbrought (lit. *come*) to light.
	11 2	may . . . your kingdom *come*;
	12 54	When you see a cloud . . . you say at once that rain is *coming*,
	16 21	Dogs even *came* and licked his sores.
	17 1	Obstacles are sure to *come*, but alas for the one ʳwho provides them (lit. through whom they *come*)!
	20	Asked by the Pharisees when the kingdom of God was to *come*, he gave them this answer, 'The *coming* of the kingdom of God does not admit of observation
	27	the Flood *came* and destroyed them all.
	18 30	[there is no one who has left house . . .] who will not be given repayment . . . and, in the world to *come*, eternal life.
	21 26	[There will be] men dying of fear as they await what ʳmenaces (lit. is *coming* to) the world,
	22 18	I shall not drink wine until the kingdom of God *comes*.
Jn	3 8	you cannot tell where [the wind] *comes* from or where it is going.
	4 35	Four months and then *comes* the harvest
	6 23	Other boats . . . had *put in* from Tiberias,
	10 12	The hired man . . . abandons the sheep . . . as soon as he sees a wolf *coming*,
	12 28	A voice *came* from heaven,
	16 13	the Spirit of truth . . . will tell you of [the things to] *come*.
	18 4	Knowing everything that was ʳgoing to happen to him (lit. to *come*), Jesus then came forward
Ac	7 11	Then a famine *came* that caused much suffering
	8 24	Pray to the Lord . . . so that none of the things you have 2 spoken about may ʳhappen (lit. *come*) to me.
	11 5	This sheet *reached* the ground quite close to me.
	13 40	2 be careful – or what the prophets say will ʳhappen (lit. *come*) to you.

Ac	19 27	This threatens . . . ʳto discredit our trade (lit. our trade's *coming* into discredit),
Rm	3 8	That would be the same thing as saying: Do evil ʳas a means to good (lit. so that good may *come* of it).
	7 9	when the commandment *came*, sin came to life
1 Co	13 10	once perfection *comes*, all imperfect things will disappear.
Ga	3 23	Before faith *came*, we were allowed no freedom by the Law;
	25	Now that ʳthat time (lit. faith) has *come* we are no longer under that guardian,
Ep	5 6	God's anger *comes* [down] on those who rebel against him.
Ph	1 12	the things that happened to me have actually ʳbeen (lit. *come* as) a help to the Good News.
Col	3 6	this is the sort of behaviour ʳthat makes God angry (lit. upon which God's anger *comes* [down]).
1 Th	1 10	you are now waiting for Jesus . . . to save us from the retribution which is *coming*.
2 Th	2 3	It cannot happen until . . . the Rebel . . . has *appeared*.
Heb	6 7	A field that has been well watered by the *coming* of frequent rain . . . gives the crops that are wanted
Jm	5 1	2 weep for the miseries that are *coming* to you.
Rv	6 1	I heard one of the four animals shout . . ., '*Come*'.
	3	I heard the second animal shout, '*Come*'.
	5	I heard the third animal shout, '*Come*'.
	7	I heard the voice of the fourth animal shout, '*Come*'.
	9 12	That was the first of the troubles; there are still two more to *come*.
	11 14	That was the second of the troubles; the third is to *come* quickly after it.
	18	now ʳthe time has come for your own anger, and (lit. your anger has *come*, as has the time) for the dead to be judged,
	18 10	mourn for . . . Babylon, . . . ʳdoomed as you are (lit. your doom *coming*) within a single hour.
	19 7	let us be glad . . . because . . . the marriage of the Lamb has *come*.

2. (THE LORD) COMES: *ATHA*

(Maran) atha 1   *(Marana) tha 1*

1 Co	16 22	ᵛMaran *atha* (= The Lord is *coming*; G Marana *tha* = Our Lord, *come*!)

3. COME: *HĒKŌ*

hēkō 26

Mt	8 11	many will *come* from east and west to take their places . . . at the feast in the kingdom of heaven;
	24 50 <	his master will *come* on a day he does not expect
Mk	8 3	some ᵛ have *come* (G are) a great distance,
Lk	12 46 <	his master will *come* on a day he does not expect
	13 29	men from east and west, from north and south, will *come* to take their places at the feast
	15 27 <	Your brother has *come*
Jn	4 47 X	hearing that Jesus had *arrived* in Galilee from Judaea, [the court official] went and asked him to come
	6 37	All that the Father gives me will *come* to me,
	8 42 X	I have come here from God; yes, I have *come* from him; not that I came because I chose,
Rm	11 26 X	(cf. Is 59 20) The liberator will *come* from Zion,
Heb	10 7 X	(Ps 40 8) God, here I am! I am *coming* to obey your will.
	9 X	(Ps 40 8) Here I am! I am *coming* to obey your will.
	37 X	(Hab 2 3) Only a little while . . . and the one that is coming will not delay; he will not delay.
1 Jn	5 20 X	We know, too, that the Son of God has *come*,
Rv	2 25 X	hold firmly on to what you already have until I *come*.
	3 3 X	If you do not wake up, I shall *come* to you like a thief, without telling you at what hour to expect ʳme (lit. my *coming*).
	X	
	9	I will make [the synagogue of Satan] *come* and fall at your feet
	15 4	(Ps 86 9) all the pagans will *come* and adore you

b) (a thing) Comes

Mt	23 36	all of this will ʳrecoil on (lit. *come* upon) this generation.
	24 14	then the end will *come*.
Lk	13 35	you shall not see me till the time *comes*
	19 43	a time is *coming* when your enemies will raise fortifications all round you,
Jn	2 4	My hour has not *come* yet.
2 P	3 10	The Day of the Lord will *come* like a thief,
Rv	18 8	within a single day, the plagues will ʳfall (lit. *come*) on her:

4. "COME!": *DEURO*

2 deuro 8/9   *1 deute 12*

Mt	4 19	ʳFollow (lit. *Come* and follow) me and I will make you fishers of men.

Mt	11	28	*Come* to me, all you who labour
	19	21	2 go and sell what you own . . . then *come*, follow me.
	21	38	< This is the heir. *Come on*, let us kill him
	22	4	< *Come* to the wedding.
	25	34	*Come*, you whom my Father has blessed,
	28	6	*Come* and see the place where [Jesus] lay,
Mk	1	17	⌐Follow (lit. *Come* and follow) me and I will make you into fishers of men.
	6	31	You must *come away* to some lonely place . . . and rest for a while;
	10	21	2 Go and sell everything you own . . . then *come*, follow me.
	12	7	< This is the heir. *Come on*, let us kill him,
Lk	18	22	2 Sell all that you own . . . then *come*, follow me.
Jn	4	29	*Come* and see a man who has told me everything I ever did;
	11	43	2 Lazarus, here! *Come out!*
	21	12	Jesus said to [the disciples], '*Come* and have breakfast'.
Ac	7	3	2 (Gn 12 1) Leave your country . . . and *go* to the land I will show you.
		34	2 (Ex 3 10) *come here* and let me send you into Egypt.
Rv	17	1	2 *Come here* and I will show you the punishment given to the famous prostitute
	19	17	*Come here*. Gather together at the great feast that God is giving.
	21	9	2 *Come here* and I will show you the bride that the Lamb has married.

5. COME – BE HERE, BE PRESENT: *PAR-EIMI*

1 *par-eimi* 24   3 *sym-par-eimi* 1
2 *par-ousia* 24

a) (*the Lord's*) Coming – (*the Rebel's*) Coming

Mt	24	3	2 what will be the sign of your *coming* and of the end of the world?
		27	2 the *coming* of the Son of Man will be like lightning striking
		37	2 As it was in Noah's day, so will it be when the Son of Man *comes*.
		39	2 It will be like this when the Son of Man *comes*.
1 Co	15	23	2 after the *coming* of Christ, those who belong to him [will be brought to life]
1 Th	2	19	you will be the crown of which we shall be proudest . . . 2 when [our Lord Jesus] *comes*;
	3	13	may he so confirm your hearts in holiness that you may be 2 blameless . . . when our Lord Jesus Christ *comes*
	4	15	2 any of us who are left alive until the Lord's *coming* will not have any advantage
	5	23	2 may you all be kept safe . . . for the *coming* of our Lord Jesus Christ.
2 Th	2	1	2 To turn now, brothers, to the *coming* of our Lord Jesus Christ
		8	2 The Lord will . . . annihilate [the Rebel] with his glorious
		9	2/2 appearance at his *coming*. 9 But when the Rebel *comes*, Satan will set to work:
Jm	5	7	2 Now be patient, brothers, until the Lord's *coming*.
		8	2 the Lord's *coming* will be soon.
2 P	1	16	2 we brought you the knowledge of the power and the *coming* of our Lord Jesus Christ;
	3	4	2 Well, where is this *coming*?
		12	2 you wait and long for the Day of God to *come*,
1 Jn	2	28	Live in Christ . . . so that . . . we may have full confidence, 2 and not turn from him in shame at his *coming*.

b) Be here, Present – (Have) Arrived, Come

A = Be absent // Be present

Mt	26	50	My friend, do what you *are here* for.
Lk	13	1	It was just about this time that some people *arrived*
Jn	7	6	The right time for me has not *come* yet,
	11	28	X The Master *is here* and wants to see you.
Ac	10	21	why *have* you *come*?
		33	*Here* we all *are*, assembled in front of ⌐ you (G God)
	12	20	the Tyrians and Sidonians . . . ⌐sent (lit. *came in*) a joint deputation [to Herod]
	17	6	The people who have been turning the whole world upside down *have come here* now;
	24	19	these are the ones who should have *appeared* before you
	25	24	3 King Agrippa, and all here *present with* us,
1 Co	5	3	A Though I am far away in body, I ⌐am with you (lit. am *present*) in spirit and have already condemned the man . . . as if I were actually *present*.
	16	17	A 2 I am delighted that Stephanas, . . . and Achaicus *have arrived*.
2 Co	7	6	2 God . . . comforted us by the *arrival* of Titus, 7 and not only
		7	2 by his *arrival* but also by the comfort which he had gained from you.
	10	2	A I only ask that I do not have to bully you when I *come*,
		10	A 2 when he is (§ *present*) with you you see only half a man . . .
	11		A ¹¹ . . . whatever we are like . . . when we are absent, that is what we shall be like . . . when we are *present*.

2 Co	11	9	When I was (§ *present*) with you . . . I was no burden to anyone;
	13	2	A I gave warning when I was (§ *present*) with you the second time
		10	A I am writing this . . . so that when I am (§ *present*) with you I shall not need to be strict,
Ga	4	18	I do not have to *be there* with you –
		20	I wish I were (§ *present*) with you now
Ph	1	26	A you will have another reason to give praise to Christ . . . 2 when I ⌐am with you again (lit. return and am *present* with you).
	2	12	A 2 continue to do . . . as you did when I *was there* with you,
Col	1	6	[The Good News] *has reached* you
Heb	12	11	any punishment is most painful *at the time*,
	13	5	be content with whatever you have *at present*;
2 P	1	9	⌐without them (lit. if [these qualities] are not *present* in him) a man is blind
		12	I am continually recalling the same truths to you, even though you *already* know them
Rv	17	8	The beast . . . is yet to *come* [up] from the Abyss,

6. COME (TO), ATTAIN – COME (UPON), OVERTAKE: *PHTHANŌ*

phthanō 7

Mt	12	28	the kingdom of God has ⌐*overtaken* (or: *come upon*) you.
Lk	11	20	the kingdom of God has ⌐*overtaken* (or: *come upon*) you.
Rm	9	31	Israel, looking for a righteousness derived from law ⌐*failed* to do what the law required (lit. never *attained* to that law).
2 Co	10	14	we did *come* all the way to you with the gospel of Christ.
Ph	3	16	let us go forward on the road that has brought us to where we ⌐*are* (lit. have *come* to).
1 Th	2	16	retribution is ⌐*overtaking* (or: *coming upon*) them at last.
	4	15	any of us who are left alive until the Lord's coming will not ⌐have any advantage over (lit. *overtake*) those who have died.

7. ARRIVE (AT), COME (TO), REACH: *PARA-GINOMAI*

1 *para-ginomai* 37/38   2 *sym-para-ginomai* 1

Mt	2	1	some wise men *came* to Jerusalem from the east.
	3	1	In due course John the Baptist *appeared*;
		13	X Then Jesus *appeared*: he came from Galilee
Mk	14	43	Judas, one of the Twelve, *came up* with a number of men
Lk	7	4	When [the Jewish elders] *came* to Jesus they pleaded . . . with him.
		20	When the men *reached* Jesus they said, 'John the Baptist has sent us to you,
	8	19	[Jesus's] mother and his brothers *came* looking for him,
	11	6	a friend of mine on his travels has just *arrived* at my house
	12	51	X Do you suppose that I ⌐*am here* (lit. have *come*) to bring peace on earth?
	14	21	< The servant *returned* and reported this to his master.
	19	16	< The first [servant] *came in* and said, 'Sir, your one pound has brought in ten'.
	22	52	Jesus spoke to the chief priests . . . and elders who had *come* for him.
	23	48	2 all the people who had *gathered* for the spectacle saw what had happened,
Jn	3	23	John was baptising at Aenon . . . and people were *going* there to be baptised.
	8	2	X At daybreak [Jesus] *appeared* in the Temple again;
Ac	5	21	When the high priest *arrived*, he and his supporters convened the Sanhedrin
		22	the officials *arrived* at the prison
		25	Then a man *arrived* with fresh news.
	9	26	When [Paul] *got* to Jerusalem he tried to join the disciples,
		39	on [Peter's] *arrival* they took him to the upstairs room,
	10	33	you have been kind enough to *come*.
	11	23	⌐There (lit. Having *arrived*) [Barnabas] could see for himself that God had given grace,
	13	14	[Paul and his friends] *reached* Antioch in Pisidia.
	14	27	On their *arrival* [Paul and Barnabas] assembled the church
	15	4	When they *arrived* in Jerusalem they were welcomed by the church
	17	10	Paul and Silas . . . visited the Jewish synagogue [at Beroea] as soon as they *arrived*.
	18	27	When [Apollos] *arrived* [at Achaia] he was able . . . to help the believers considerably
	20	18	When [the elders of the church of Ephesus] *arrived* [Paul] addressed these words to them:
	21	18	Paul went with us to visit James, and all the elders ⌐*were present* (lit. *arrived*).
	23	16	the son of Paul's sister . . . *came* and made his way into the fortress

Ac 23 35   I will hear your case as soon as your accusers ˹are here too (lit. *arrive*).
   24 17   I *came* to bring alms to my nation
       24   Felix *came* with his wife Drusilla
   25 7   As soon as Paul *appeared*, the Jews . . . surrounded him,
       15   ˹while I was (lit. when I *arrived*) in Jerusalem the chief priests and elders . . . laid information against [Paul],
   28 21   nor has any countryman of yours *arrived* here with any report
1 Co 16 3   When I ˹am with (lit. *reach*) you, I will send your offering to Jerusalem
Heb 9 11 X   now Christ has *come*, as the high priest of all the blessings which were to come.

8. ARRIVE (IN, AT), REACH, COME (TO): *KAT-ANTAŌ*

kat-antaō 13

Ac 16 1   [Paul] ˹went (lit. *came*) to Derbe, and then on to Lystra.
   18 19   [Paul, Priscilla and Aquila] *reached* Ephesus.
       24   An Alexandrian Jew named Apollos now *arrived* in Ephesus.
   20 15   The next day we . . . *arrived* opposite Chios.
   21 7   The end of our voyage from Tyre came when we *landed* at Ptolemais,
   25 13   King Agrippa and Bernice *arrived* in Caesarea.
   26 7   [It is] the promise that our twelve tribes . . . hope to *attain*.
   27 12   the majority were for putting out . . . in the hope of *reaching* and even wintering at Phoenix –
   28 13   we followed the coast up to where we *reached* Rhegium.
1 Co 10 11   it was . . . a lesson for us ˹who are living at (lit. for whom has *come*) the end of the age.
   14 36   Do you think . . . that [the word of God] has *come* only to you?
Ep 4 13   In this way we are all to *come* to unity in our faith
Ph 3 11   I can hope to *take my place* in the resurrection of the dead.

9. REACH, COME (TO) – PASS (INTO), PENETRATE: *CHŌREŌ*

chōreō 3/10

Mt 15 17   whatever goes into the mouth *passes* through the stomach
Jn 8 37   nothing I say has *penetrated* into you.
2 P 3 9   [The Lord wants] everybody to ˹be brought to change his ways (lit. *come* to change his ways; or: *reach* repentance).

10. REACH: *HIKNEOMAI*

2 aph-ikneomai 1   *1 eph-ikneomai 2*

Rm 16 19   ˹Your fidelity to Christ, anyway, is famous (lit. The fame of
     2   your fidelity to Christ, anyway, has *reached*) everywhere,
2 Co 10 13   the yardstick which God gave . . . is long enough to *reach* to you.
      14   We are not stretching further than we ought; otherwise we should not have *reached* you,

---

COME DOWN – LET DOWN

1. Descend, Come down, Go down: *kata-bainō*
  a) Descend, Come down (from heaven, from the sky)
  b) Descend, Go down, (Be) Thrown down (to the underworld)
  c) Go down, Come down, Travel down (a road, to or from a place)
  d) Get out (of), Step down (from, a boat)

  e) Come down, Go down (from being higher) – Fall
2. Come down, Go down: *kat-erchomai*
3. Take down (Jesus from the cross): *kath-aireō*
4. Let down, Lower
  1: *kath-iēmi*
  2: *chalaō*

1. DESCEND, COME DOWN, GO DOWN: *KATA-BAINŌ*

1 kata-bainō 82   *4 syn-kata-bainō 1*
3 kata-basis 1   *2 kata-bibazō 2*

a) Descend, Come down (from heaven, from the sky)

Mt 3 16 Ⓢ   Jesus . . . saw the Spirit of God *descending* like a dove
    7 25   Rain *came down*, floods rose,
      27   Rain *came down*, floods rose,
   28 2   the angel of the Lord, *descending* from heaven,
Mk 1 10 Ⓢ   [Jesus] saw . . . the Spirit, like a dove, *descending* on him.

Lk 3 22 Ⓢ   the Holy Spirit *descended* on [Jesus] in bodily shape, like a dove.
    8 23   a squall *came down* on the lake
    9 54   Lord, do you want us to ˹call down fire (lit. call on fire to *come down*) from heaven to burn them up?
Jn 1 32 Ⓢ   I saw the Spirit *coming down* on [Jesus] from heaven like a dove
      33 Ⓢ   The man on whom you see the Spirit *come down* and rest
      51   you will see heaven laid open and, above the Son of Man, the angels of God ascending and *descending*.
    3 13 X   No one has gone up to heaven except the one who *came down* from heaven,
    5 4   ᵛ the angel of the Lord *came down* into the pool, . . .˺
    6 33 X   the bread of God is that which *comes down* from heaven
      38 X   I have *come down* from heaven . . . to do the will of the one who sent me.
      41 X   I am the bread that *came down* from heaven.
      42 X   How can he now say, "I have *come down* from heaven"?
      50 X   this is the bread that *comes down* from heaven,
      51 X   I am the living bread which has *come down* from heaven.
      58 X   This is the bread *come down* from heaven;
Ac 7 34 Θ   (Ex 3 8) I have *come down* to liberate [my people].
   10 11   [Peter] saw . . . something like a big sheet ˹being let down to earth (lit. *coming down* to earth being let down) by its four corners;
   11 5   I . . . had a vision of something like a big sheet ˹being let down from heaven (lit. *coming down* from heaven being let down) by its four corners.
   14 11   These people are gods who have *come down* to us disguised as men.
Ep 4 9 X Δ   When it says, 'he ascended', what can it mean if not that he *descended right down* to the lower regions of the earth?
      10   ¹⁰ The one who rose higher than all the heavens . . . is none other than the one who *descended*.
1 Th 4 16   the Lord himself will *come down* from heaven;
Jm 1 17   it is all that is good . . . which is given us from above; it *comes down* from the Father of all light;
Rv 3 12   the new Jerusalem which *comes down* from my God in heaven,
   10 1   I saw another powerful angel *coming down* from heaven,
   12 12 Ⓓ   but for you, earth and sea, trouble is coming – because the devil has *gone down* to you in a rage,
   13 13   it worked great miracles, even to ˹calling down fire (lit. making fire *come down*) from heaven on to the earth
   16 21   hail, with great hailstones weighing a talent each, *fell* from the sky
   18 1   I saw another angel *come down* from heaven,
   20 1   I saw an angel *come down* from heaven
      9   fire will *come down* on them from heaven and consume them.
   21 2   I saw the holy city, and the new Jerusalem, *coming down* from God out of heaven,
      10   [an angel] showed me Jerusalem, the holy city, *coming down* from God out of heaven.

b) Descend, Go down, (Be) Thrown down (to the underworld)

Mt 11 23   2 (Is 14 15) Capernaum, . . . You shall ˹be *thrown* (or: be *brought*; G go) *down* to hell.
Lk 10 15   2 (Is 14 15) Capernaum, . . . You shall ˹be *thrown* (or: be *brought*; G go) *down* to hell.
Rm 10 7   as in the text: Who will *go down* to the underworld?
Ep 4 9 X Δ   When it says, 'he ascended', what can it mean if not that he *descended right down* to the lower regions of the earth?
      10   ¹⁰ The one who rose higher than all the heavens . . . is none other than the one who *descended*.

c) Go down, Come down, Travel down (a road, to or from a place)

Mk 3 22   The scribes who had *come down* from Jerusalem
Lk 2 51 X   [Jesus] then *went down* with [his parents] and came to Nazareth
   10 30   A man was once ˹on his way (lit. *going*) *down* from Jerusalem to Jericho
      31   a priest happened to be *travelling down* the same road,
   18 14   [The tax collector] ˹went home (lit. *went down* to his home) again at rights with God;
Jn 2 12 X   he *went down* to Capernaum with his mother and the brothers.
    4 47 X   [the official] went and asked [Jesus] to *come down* and cure his son
      49 X   Sir, . . . *come down* before my child dies.
      51   while he was still ˹on the journey back (lit. *travelling down*) his servants met him
    6 16   the disciples *went down* to the shore of the lake
Ac 7 15   Jacob *went down* into Egypt
    8 15   [Peter and John] *went down* [to Samaria from Jerusalem]
      26   along the road that *goes* from Jerusalem *down* to Gaza,
   14 25   after proclaiming the word at Perga [Paul and Barnabas] *went down* to Attalia
   16 8   [Paul and Timothy] *came down* to Troas.
   18 22   [Paul] landed at Caesarea, and went up to greet the church. Then he *came down* to Antioch

Ac 24	1	the high priest Ananias *came down* with some of the elders
	22	When Lysius the tribune has *come down* I will go into your case.
25	5	4 Let your authorities *come down* with me
	6	[Festus] *went down* to Caesarea and . . . had Paul brought in,
	7	the Jews who had *come down* from Jerusalem surrounded [Paul],

d) Get out (of), Step down (from, a boat)

Mt 14	29	Peter *got out* of the boat and started walking . . . across the water,

e) Come down, Go down (from being higher) – Fall

Mt 8	1 X	After he had *come down* from the mountain
17	9 X	As they *came down* from the mountain Jesus gave them this order,
24	17	if a man is on the housetop, he must not *come down* to collect his belongings;
27	40 X	If you are God's son, *come down* from the cross!
	42 X	let him *come down* from the cross now,
Mk 9	9 X	As they *came down* from the mountain he warned them
13	15	if a man is on the housetop, he must not *come down* . . . to collect any of his belongings;
15	30 X	Then save yourself: *come down* from the cross now,
	32 X	Let the Christ, the king of Israel, *come down* from the cross now.
Lk 6	17 X	He then *came down* [from the hills] with [the Twelve]
17	31	anyone on the housetop, with his possessions in the house, must not *come down* to collect them,
19	5	Zacchaeus, *come down*.
	6	And he ⌐hurried *down* (lit. *came down* quickly)
	37	3 as [Jesus] was approaching the ⌐*downward slope* (or: *descent*) of the Mount of Olives,
22	44	[Jesus's] sweat *fell* to the ground like great drops of blood.
Jn 5	7	while I am still on the way, someone *gets down* there before me.
Ac 8	38	Philip and the eunuch both *went down* into the water
10	20	⌐Hurry (lit. Get up and *go*) *down*, and do not hesitate about going back with them;
	21	Peter *went down* [to the men]
20	10	Paul *went down* and stooped to clasp the boy to him.
23	10	the tribune . . . ordered his troops to *go down*

2. COME DOWN, GO DOWN: *KAT-ERCHOMAI*

kat-erchomai 12/15

Lk 4	31 X	He *went down* to Capernaum
9	37 X	when they were *coming down* from the mountain a large crowd came to meet him
Ac 8	5	Philip . . . *went down* to a Samaritan town
9	32	Peter . . . eventually *came down* to the saints living *down* in Lydda.
11	27	some prophets *came down* to Antioch from Jerusalem,
12	19	before leaving Judaea to *go down* and take up residence in Caesarea
13	4	[Barnabas and Saul], sent on their mission . . , *went down* to Seleucia
15	1	some men *came down* from Judaea and taught the brothers,
	30	The [delegates] left [Jerusalem] and *went down* to Antioch,
18	5	After Silas and Timothy had ⌐*come down* (or: *arrived*) from Macedonia,
21	10	a prophet called Agabus ⌐*came down* (or: *arrived*) from Judaea
Jm 3	15	principles of this kind are not the wisdom that *comes down* from above:

3. TAKE DOWN (JESUS FROM THE CROSS): *KATH-AIREŌ*

kath-aireō 4/9

Mk 15	36	Wait and see if Elijah will come to *take* him *down*.
	46	[Joseph] *took* Jesus *down* from the cross,
Lk 23	53	[Joseph] *took* [Jesus's body] *down*,
Ac 13	29	they *took* him *down* from the tree and buried him in a tomb.

4. LET DOWN, LOWER

1: LET DOWN, LOWER: *KATH-IĒMI*

kath-iēmi 4

Lk 5	19	they . . . *lowered* [the paralytic] and his stretcher down through the tiles
Ac 9	25	the disciples . . . *let* [Saul] *down* from the top of the wall, lowering him in a basket.
10	11	[Peter] saw . . . something like a big sheet ⌐being let down to earth (lit. coming down to earth being *let down*) by its four corners;

Ac 11	5	a vision of something like a big sheet ⌐being let down from heaven (lit. coming down from heaven being *let down*) by its four corners.

2: LET DOWN, LOWER: *CHALAŌ*

chalaō 7

Mk 2	4	when they had made an opening [in the roof], they *lowered* the stretcher on which the paralytic lay.
Lk 5	4	⌐*pay out* (or: *let down*) your nets for a catch.
	5	Master, . . . if you say so, I will ⌐*pay out* (or: *let down*) the nets.
Ac 9	25	the disciples . . . *let* [Saul] *down* from the top of the wall, *lowering* him in a basket.
27	17	they ⌐*floated out* (lit. *lowered*) the sea-anchor
	30	some of the crew . . . *lowered* the ship's boat into the sea
2 Co 11	33	I had to be *let down* over the wall in a hamper,

CONFUSION – DISTURB

1. Unsettle (the mind of a person): *ana-skeuazō*	1: (Be) Disturbed, Troubled (in mind) – (Be) Agitated, Shaken
2. Be perplexed, Be bewildered, Wonder – Worry – Despair: *a-poreō*	2: (civil) Disturbance, Commotion – Make trouble
3. Bewilder, Confound – Confusion – Stir up: *syn-cheō*	3: (the surface of a pool is) Disturbed
4. Disorder, Confusion– (Be) Mobbed: *a-kata-stasia*	**6. Riot, Uprising–Trouble, Dissension, Revolt – Disturb:** *stasis*
5. (Be) Disturbed, Trouble(d) – Disturbance: *tarassō*	**7. Riot – Commotion, Uproar, Disturbance – Worry, Fret:** *thorybos*

1. UNSETTLE (THE MIND OF A PERSON): *ANA-SKEUAZŌ*

ana-skeuazō 1

Ac 15	24	some of our members . . . have *unsettled* your minds.

2. BE PERPLEXED, BE BEWILDERED, WONDER – WORRY – DESPAIR: *A-POREŌ*

1 *a-poreō* 6		2 *di-a-poreō* 4	
4 *a-poria* 1		3 *ex-a-poreō* 2	

Mk 6	20	When [Herod] had heard [John] speak he *was* greatly *perplexed*,
Lk 9	7	2 Herod the tetrarch . . . *was puzzled*,
21	25	4 nations [will be] in agony, *bewildered* by the clamour of the ocean and its waves;
24	4	[the women] stood there *not knowing what to think*,
Jn 13	22	The disciples looked at one another, *wondering* which [Jesus] meant.
Ac 2	12	2 Everyone was amazed and *unable to explain it*;
5	24	2 the chief priests . . . *wondered* what this could mean.
10	17	2 Peter was still *worrying* over the meaning of the vision
25	20	⌐Not feeling qualified (lit. *Perplexed* as to how) to deal with questions of this sort, I asked [Paul] if he would be willing to go to Jerusalem to be tried there
2 Co 1	8	the things we had to undergo in Asia were more of a burden
	3	than we could carry, so that we *despaired* of coming through alive.
4	8	/3 we *see no answer to our problems*, but never *despair*;
Ga 4	20	I *have no idea what to do* for ⌐the best (lit. you).

3. BEWILDER, CONFOUND – CONFUSION – STIR UP: *SYN-CHEŌ*

2 *syn-cheō* 1		3 *syn-chysis* 1	
1 *syn-chynnō* 4			

Ac 2	6	they all assembled, each one *bewildered* to hear these men speaking his own language.
9	22	[Saul] was able to *throw* the Jewish colony at Damascus *into complete confusion*
19	29	3 The whole town was in an *uproar*
	32	the assembly itself ⌐had no idea what was going on (lit. was *in utter confusion*):
21	27	2 some Jews from Asia . . . *stirred up* the crowd and seized [Paul],
	31	there was ⌐*rioting* (or: *confusion*) all over Jerusalem.

4. DISORDER, CONFUSION – (BE) MOBBED: *A-KATA-STASIA*

a-kata-stasia 5

Lk 21	9	when you hear of wars and *revolutions*, do not be frightened,
1 Co 14	33 Θ	God is not a God of *disorder* but of peace.
2 Co 6	5	[We prove we are servants of God by great fortitude] when we are flogged, or sent to prison, or *mobbed*;
12	20	What I am afraid of is that . . . there will be wrangling, . . . obstinacies and *disorder*.
Jm 3	16	Wherever you find jealousy . . . you find *disharmony*, and wicked things of every kind being done;

5. (BE) DISTURBED, TROUBLE(D) – DISTURBANCE: *TARASSŌ*

3	*tarachē*	*1*	4 *dia-tarassō 1*	
2	*tarachos*	*2*	5 *ek-tarassō 1*	
1	*tarassō*	*18*		

1: (BE) DISTURBED, TROUBLED (IN MIND) – (BE) AGITATED, SHAKEN

Mt 2	3	When King Herod heard this he was ⌐perturbed (or: *disturbed*),
14	26	when the disciples saw [Jesus] walking on the lake they were ⌐terrified (lit. *shaken*).
Mk 6	50	[the disciples] had all seen [Jesus walking on the lake] and were ⌐terrified (lit. *shaken*).
Lk 1	12	The sight *disturbed* Zechariah and he was overcome with fear.
	29	4 [Mary] was *deeply disturbed* by these words
24	38	Why are you so *agitated*, and why are these doubts rising in your hearts?
Jn 11	33 X	At the sight of [Mary's] tears . . . Jesus said ⌐in great distress (lit. *greatly troubled*),
12	27 X	Now my soul is *troubled*.
13	21 X	Jesus was *troubled* in spirit
14	1	Do not let your hearts be *troubled*.
	27	Do not let your hearts be *troubled* or afraid.
Ac 15	24	some of our members have *disturbed* you with their demands and have unsettled your minds.
17	8	This accusation *alarmed* the citizens and the city councillors
Ga 5	10	anybody who *troubles* you in the future will be condemned,
1 P 3	14	(Is 8 12) There is no need to be afraid or to *worry* about them.

2: (CIVIL) DISTURBANCE, COMMOTION – MAKE TROUBLE

Ac 12	18	2 When daylight came there was a great *commotion* among the soldiers,
16	20	5 These people are *causing a disturbance* in our city. They are Jews
17	13	the Jews of Thessalonika . . . went [to Beroea] to *make trouble* and stir up the people.
19	23	2 a rather serious *disturbance* broke out in connection with the Way.
Ga 1	7	some *troublemakers* among you want to change the Good News

3: (THE SURFACE OF A POOL IS) DISTURBED

Jn 5	4	ᵛ the angel of the Lord came down into the pool, and the water was *disturbed*, and the first person to enter the water
	3	after this *disturbance* was cured⌐
	7	I have no one to put me into the pool when the water is *disturbed*;

6. RIOT, UPRISING – TROUBLE, DISSENSION, REVOLT – DISTURB: *STASIS*

3	*stasiastēs*	*1*	2 *ana-statoō 3*	
1	*stasis*	*8/9*		

Mk 15	7	3 Barabbas was then in prison with the *rioters* who had committed murder during the *uprising*.
Lk 23	19	[Barabbas] had been thrown into prison for *causing a riot*
	25	[Pilate] released the man . . . who had been imprisoned for *rioting*
Ac 15	2	This led to ⌐disagreement (or: *dissension*),
17	6	2 The people who have been *turning* the whole world *upside down* have come here now;
19	40	We could easily be charged with *rioting* for today's happenings;
21	38	2 So you are not the Egyptian who *started the* recent *revolt* . . .?
23	7	a *dispute* broke out between the Pharisees and Sadducees,
	10	⌐Feeling was running high (lit. The *dissension* was becoming violent),
24	5	[Paul] stirs up *trouble* among Jews the world over,

Ga 5	12	2 Tell those who are *disturbing* you I would like to see the knife slip.

7. RIOT – COMMOTION, UPROAR, DISTURBANCE – WORRY, FRET: *THORYBOS*

3	*thorybazō*	*1*	1 *thorybos 7*	
2	*thorybeō*	*4*		

Mt 9	23	2 Jesus . . . saw the fluteplayers, with the crowd *making a commotion*
26	5	there must be no *disturbance* among the people.
27	24	Pilate saw . . . that in fact a *riot* was imminent.
Mk 5	38	Jesus noticed all the *commotion*,
	39	2 Why all this *commotion* and crying?
14	2	there will be a *disturbance* among the people.
Lk 10	41	3 Martha, . . . you *worry* and *fret* about so many things,
Ac 17	5	2 The Jews . . . soon had the whole city *in an uproar*.
20	1	When the *disturbance* was over, Paul sent for the disciples
	10	2 'There is no need to *worry*,' [Paul] said 'there is still life in [Eutychus].'
21	34	the *noise* made it impossible for [the tribune] to get any positive information,
24	18	there was no crowd involved, and no *disturbance*.

CORNER – SQUARE

1. Corner	*b)* Cornerstone, Keystone
1: Corner: *gōnia*	2: Corner: *archē*
a) Corner – Square	**2. Square – Groups, Rows, Ranks:** *prasia*

1. CORNER

1: CORNER: *GŌNIA*

1	*gōnia*	*9*	2 *(akro-)gōniaios 2*	
3	*tetra- gōnos*	*1*		

a) Corner – Square

Mt 6	5	the hypocrites . . . love . . . to say their prayers standing . . . at the street *corners*
Ac 26	26	after all, these things were not done in a *corner*.
Rv 7	1	I saw four angels, standing at the four *corners* of the earth,
20	8	Satan will . . . come out to deceive all the nations in the four *corners* of the earth,
21	16	3 The plan of the city is perfectly *square*,

b) Cornerstone, Keystone

4 *kephalē 5/75*

Mt 21	42	(Ps 118 22) It was the stone rejected by the builders that 4/ became the *keystone*.
		Repeated in Mk 12 10; Lk 20 17
Ac 4	11	4/ [Jesus] is the stone . . . which has proved to be the *keystone*.
Ep 2	20	You are part of a building that has . . . Christ Jesus himself 2 for its main *cornerstone*.
1 P 2	6	2 (Is 28 16) See how I lay in Zion a precious *cornerstone* that I have chosen
	7	for unbelievers, (Ps 118 22) the stone rejected by the builders 4/ has proved to be the *keystone*

2: CORNER: *ARCHĒ*

archē 2/56

Ac 10	11	[Peter saw] something like a big sheet being let down to earth by its four *corners*;
11	5	[Peter saw] something like a big sheet being let down from heaven by its four *corners*.

2. SQUARE – GROUPS, ROWS, RANKS: *PRASIA*

prasia 2

Mk 6	40	they sat down on the ground in ⌐squares (lit. *square groups*) of hundreds and fifties.

COVENANT – WILL

1: Covenant – Make a Covenant | 3: Will, Testament – Testator
2: Ark of the covenant |

1 *dia-thēkē 33*   2 *dia-tithemai 7*

1: COVENANT – MAKE A COVENANT

Mt	26 28	(cf. Ex 24 8) this is my blood, the blood of the *covenant*, which is to be poured out for many
Mk	14 24	(cf. Ex 24 8) This is my blood, the blood of the *covenant*, which is to be poured out for many.
Lk	1 72	[God] remembers his holy *covenant*, [73] the oath he swore to our father Abraham
	22 20	(cf. Jr 31 31) This cup is the new *covenant* in my blood
Ac	3 25	You are the heirs of the prophets, the heirs of the *covenant* God *made* with our ancestors
	7 8	[God] made the *covenant* of circumcision [with Abraham]:
Rm	9 4	[my brothers of Israel] were given the glory and the *covenants*;
	11 27	(Is 59 21) this is the *covenant* I will make with them when I take their sins away.
1 Co	11 25	(cf. Jr 31 31) This cup is the new *covenant* in my blood.
2 Co	3 6	[God] has given us the qualifications to be the administrators of this new *covenant*,
	14 ○	that same veil is still there when the old *covenant* is being read,
Ga	4 24	[Hagar and Sarah] stand for the two *covenants*.
Ep	2 12	you had no Christ and were . . . aliens with no part in the *covenants* with their Promise;
Heb	7 22	it is a greater *covenant* for which Jesus has become our guarantee.
	8 6	it is a better *covenant* of which [Christ] is the mediator,
	8	(Jr 31 31–32) I will establish a new *covenant* with the House of Israel and the House of Judah, [9] but not a *covenant* like the one I made with their ancestors . . . They abandoned that *covenant* of mine, and so I on my side deserted them.
	10	/2 (Jr 31 33) this is the *covenant* I will *make* with the House of Israel
	9 15	[Christ] brings a new *covenant*, as the mediator . . . his death took place to cancel the sins that infringed the earliest *covenant*.
	20	(Ex 24 8) This is the blood of the *covenant* that God has laid down for you.
	10 16	/2 (Jr 31 33) This is the *covenant* I will *make* with them
	29	anyone who . . . treats the blood of the *covenant* . . . as if it were not holy . . . will be condemned
	12 24	[you have come] to Jesus, the mediator who brings a new *covenant*
	13 20	our Lord Jesus [has] . . . become the great Shepherd . . . by the blood that sealed an eternal *covenant*,

2: ARK OF THE COVENANT

3 *kibōtos 2/6*

Heb	9 4 3/	to [the tent called the Holy of Holies] belonged . . . the *ark* of the *covenant* . . . In this were kept . . . the stone tablets of the *covenant*.
Rv	11 19	3 the sanctuary of God in heaven opened, and the *ark* of the *covenant* could be seen inside it.

3: WILL, TESTAMENT – TESTATOR

Lk	22 29	2/2 now I *confer* a kingdom on you, just as my Father *conferred* one on me:
Ga	3 15	If a *will* has been drawn up in due form, no one is allowed to disregard it
	17	once God had expressed his *will* in due form, no law . . . could cancel that
Heb	9 16	/2 wherever a *will* is in question, the death of the *testator* must be established; [17] indeed, [it] (lit. a *will*) only becomes valid with that death, since it is not meant to have any effect while the *testator* is still alive.
	17 2	

COVER – VEIL

1: Cover – Veil – Blindfold | 3: Plated (with gold) – Overlaid,
2: Cover (up) sins | Covered

2	*kalymma 4*	6	*epi-kalyptō 1*
1	*kalyptō 8*	4	*peri-kalyptō 3*
3	*kata-kalyptō 3*	7	*syn-kalyptō 1*
5	*epi-kalymma 1*	8	*para-kalyptō 1*

1: COVER – VEIL – BLINDFOLD

H = Cover the head, the face

Mt	8 24		[the waves were breaking right over the boat (lit. the boat was *covered* by the waves).
	10 26		everything that is now *covered* will be uncovered, and everything now hidden will be made clear.
Mk	14 65 H	4	Some of them . . . *blindfolding* [Jesus], began hitting him
Lk	8 16		No one lights a lamp to *cover* it with a bowl
	9 45		[the disciples] did not understand him when he said this; it
	8		was *hidden* from them so that they should not see the meaning of it,
	12 2	7	Everything that is now *covered* will be uncovered,
	22 64 H	4	They *blindfolded* [Jesus] and questioned him. 'Play the prophet' they said.
	23 30		(Ho 10 8) Then they will begin to say . . . to the hills, 'Cover us!'
1 Co	11 6 H	3	a woman who will not *wear a veil* ought to have her hair cut off. If a woman is ashamed to have her hair cut off . . . she ought to *wear a veil*.
	7 H	3	A man should certainly not *cover* his head, since he is the image of God
2 Co	3 13 H	2	(Ex 34 33) Moses . . . put a *veil* over his face . . . [14] . . . to
	14	2	this very day, that same *veil* is still there when the old
	15	2	covenant is being read . . . [15] Yes, even today, whenever
	16	2	Moses is read, the *veil* is over their minds. [16] 'It (lit. The *veil*) will not be removed until they turn to the Lord.
	4 3		If our gospel does not penetrate the *veil*, then the *veil* is on those who are not on the way to salvation;
1 P	2 16	5	never use your freedom as [an excuse (lit. a *veil*) for wickedness.

2: COVER (UP) SINS

Rm	4 7	6	(Ps 32 1) Happy those whose crimes are forgiven, whose sins are [blotted out (lit. *covered*);
Jm	5 20		(Pr 10 12) anyone who can bring back a sinner from the wrong way . . . will be . . . *covering up* a great number of sins.
1 P	4 8		(Pr 10 12) never let your love for each other grow insincere, since love *covers over* many a sin.

3: PLATED (WITH GOLD) – OVERLAID, COVERED

Heb	9 4	4 the ark of the covenant, *plated* all over with gold.

CRUCIFY – HANG

1. Crucify
   1: Crucify – Cross: *stauros*
   2: the Tree = Cross – Gibbet: *xylon*
   3: Fasten (to the cross)
     a) Nail: *hēlos*
     b) Crucify: *pros-pēgnymi*

2. Hang
   1: Hang: *kremazō*
     a) Hang on the cross
     b) Hang
   2: Hanged: *ap-anchomai*

1. CRUCIFY

1: CRUCIFY – CROSS: *STAUROS*

1 *stauroō 46*	4 *ana-stauroō 1*
2 *stauros 27*	3 *sy-stauroō 5*

Mt	10 38	2	Anyone who does not take his *cross* and follow in my footsteps is not worthy of me.
	16 24	2	If anyone wants to be a follower of mine, let him . . . take up his *cross*
	20 19		[the chief priests and scribes] will hand [the Son of Man] over to the pagans to be . . . *crucified*;
	23 24		I am sending you prophets . . .: some you will slaughter and *crucify*,
	26 2		the Son of Man will be handed over to be *crucified*.
	27 22		They all said, 'Let him be *crucified*!'
	23		they shouted all the louder, 'Let him be *crucified*!'
	26		[Pilate] ordered Jesus to be . . . handed over to be *crucified*.

Mt 27	31	[the soldiers] led him away to *crucify* him.
	32	they came across a man from Cyrene, Simon by name, and 2 enlisted him to carry his *cross*.
	35	When [the soldiers] had finished *crucifying* him they shared out his clothing
	38	At the same time two robbers were *crucified* with him,
	40	save yourself! If you are God's son, come down from the 2 *cross*!
	42	2 let him come down from the *cross* now, and we will believe in him.
	44	3 Even the robbers who were *crucified with* him taunted him in the same way.
28	5	I know you are looking for Jesus, who was *crucified*.
Mk 8	34	If anyone wants to be a follower of mine, let him . . . take up 2 his *cross*
15	13	They shouted back, '*Crucify* him!'
	14	But they shouted all the louder, '*Crucify* him!'
	15	Pilate, . . . having ordered Jesus to be scourged, handed him over to be *crucified*.
	20	[The soldiers] led him out to *crucify* him.
	21	They enlisted a passer-by, Simon of Cyrene, . . . to carry 2 his *cross*.
	24	Then they *crucified* him, and shared out his clothing,
	25	It was the third hour when they *crucified* him,
	27	they *crucified* two robbers with him,
	30	2 save yourself: come down from the *cross*!
	32	2 Let the Christ . . . come down from the *cross* now, for us to 3 see it and believe. Even those who were *crucified with* him taunted him.
16	6	You are looking for Jesus of Nazareth, who was *crucified*: he has risen,
Lk 9	23	If anyone wants to be a follower of mine, let him . . . take 2 up his *cross*
14	27	2 Anyone who does not carry his *cross* . . . cannot be my disciple.
23	21	but they shouted back, '*Crucify* him! *Crucify* him!'
	23	But they kept on shouting at the top of their voices, demanding that he should be *crucified*.
	26	they seized on a man, Simon from Cyrene, . . . and made 2 him shoulder the *cross*
	33	When they reached the place called The Skull, they *crucified* him there and the two criminals also,
24	7	the Son of Man had to be . . . *crucified*,
	20	our chief priests and our leaders . . . had him *crucified*.
Jn 19	6	the chief priests and the guards shouted, '*Crucify* him! *Crucify* him!' Pilate said, 'Take him yourselves and *crucify* him:'
	10	Surely you know I have power to release you and I have power to *crucify* you?
	15	'*Crucify* him!' 'Do you want me to *crucify* your king?' said Pilate.
	16	in the end Pilate handed him over to them to be *crucified*.
	17	2 carrying his own *cross* he went out of the city to the place of 18 the skull . . . [18] where they *crucified* him with two others,
	19	2 Pilate wrote out a notice and had it fixed to the *cross*;
	20	the place where Jesus was *crucified* was not far from the city,
	23	When the soldiers had finished *crucifying* Jesus they took his clothing
	25	2 Near the *cross* of Jesus stood his mother and his mother's sister.
	31	2 to prevent the bodies remaining on the *cross* during the sabbath
	32	the soldiers came and broke the legs of the first man who had 3 been *crucified with* him and then of the other.
	41	At the place where he had been *crucified* there was a garden,
Ac 2	36	God has made this Jesus whom you *crucified* both Lord and Christ.
4	10	Jesus Christ, the Nazarene, the one you *crucified*,
Rm 6	6	3 our former selves have been *crucified with* him
1 Co 1	13	Was it Paul that was *crucified* for you?
	17	2 the terms of philosophy in which the *crucifixion* of Christ cannot be expressed.
	18	2 The language of the *cross* may be illogical to those who are not on the way to salvation,
	23	here are we preaching a *crucified* Christ; to the Jews an obstacle . . , to the pagans madness,
2	2	the only knowledge I claimed to have was about Jesus, and only about him as the *crucified* Christ.
	8	It is a wisdom that none of the masters of this age have ever known, or they would not have *crucified* the Lord of Glory;
2 Co 13	4	he was *crucified* through weakness, and still he lives now through the power of God.
Ga 2	19	3 I have been *crucified with* Christ,
3	1	the plain explanation you have had of the *crucifixion* of Jesus Christ
5	11	if I still [preached circumcision], would there still be any 2 scandal of the *cross*?
	24	You cannot belong to Christ Jesus unless you *crucify* all self-indulgent passions
6	12	2 they want to escape persecution for the *cross* of Christ

Ga 6	14	2 the only thing I can boast about is the *cross* of our Lord Jesus Christ, through whom the world is *crucified* to me,
Ep 2	16	2 [by restoring peace] through the *cross* to unite [Jews and pagans] in a single Body
Ph 2	8	he was humbler yet, even to accepting death, death on a 2 *cross*.
3	18	2 there are many who are behaving as the enemies of the *cross* of Christ
Col 1	20	2 when he made peace by his death on the *cross*.
2	14	He has . . . cancelled every record of the debt we had to 2 pay . . . by nailing it to the *cross*;
Heb 6	6	4 They cannot be repentant if they have wilfully *crucified* the Son of God
12	2	for the sake of the joy which was still in the future, he endured 2 the *cross*,
Rv 11	8	the main street of the Great City . . . in which their Lord was *crucified*.

2: THE TREE = CROSS – GIBBET: *XYLON*

xylon 5/20

Ac 5	30	it was you who had [Jesus] executed by hanging on a *tree*.
10	39	they killed him by hanging him on a *tree*,
13	29	[the people of Jerusalem] took him down from the *tree* and buried him in a tomb.
Ga 3	13	(Dt 21 23) Cursed be everyone who is hanged on a *tree*.
1 P 2	24	He was bearing our faults in his own body on the *cross*,

3: FASTEN (TO THE CROSS)

a) Nail: *hēlos*

1 hēlos 2   2 pros-(h)ēloō 1

Jn 20	25	Unless I see the holes that the *nails* made in his hands and can put my finger into the holes ⌐they (lit. the *nails*) made . . . I refuse to believe.
Col 2	14	He has . . . cancelled every record of the debt we had to 2 pay . . . by *nailing* it to the cross;

b) Crucify: *pros-pēgnymi*

pros-pēgnymi 1

Ac 2	23	This man . . . you took and had *crucified*

2. HANG

1: HANG: *KREMAZŌ*

2 kremamai 3   2 ek-kremamai 1
1 kremazō 4

a) Hang on the cross

Lk 23	39	One of the criminals *hanging* there abused him.
Ac 5	30	it was you who had him executed by *hanging* on a tree.
10	39	they killed him by *hanging* him on a tree,
Ga 3	13	2 (Dt 21 23) Cursed be everyone who is *hanged* on a tree.

b) Hang

Mt 18	6	anyone who is an obstacle to bring down one of these little ones . . . would be better drowned in the depths of the sea with a great millstone (§ *hung*) round his neck.
22	40	On these two commandments [to love God and your neigh- 2 bour] *hang* the whole Law, and the Prophets also.
Lk 19	48	3 the people . . . *hung* on [Jesus's] words.
Ac 28	4	2 When the natives saw the creature *hanging* from Paul's hand

2: HANGED: *AP-ANCHOMAI*

ap-anchomai 1

Mt 27	5	flinging down the silver pieces . . . [Judas] went and *hanged* himself.

CURSE – ABUSE – SLANDER

1. Curse – Accursed
  1: Curse(d), Accursed: *ara*
  2: Curse – Speak evil of: *kako-logeō*

  a) Curse
  b) Speak evil of
  3: Curse – Accursed, Condemned – Ban: *ana-thema*

2. Abuse, Insult – Slander – Blaspheme

1: Blaspheme – Insult, Abuse, Curse – Slander, Speak evil of: *blas-phēmeō*
2: Insult, Abuse, Revile – Slander: *loidoreō*
3: Insult, Abuse – Reproach – Humiliation, Stigma: *oneidizō*
4: Slander, Speak against, Disparage – Backbiting: *kata-laleō*
5: Slander – Denounce, Complain of: *dia-ballō*
6: Gossip – Whispering libeller: *psithyrismos*
7: Malign, Revile – Treat spitefully: *ep-ēreazō*
8: Insult, (Be) Insolent – Maltreat – Attack, Damage: *hubris*
  a) Insult, (Be) Insolent – Maltreat, Treat shamefully – Attack
  b) Damage, Injury
9: False accusation – Extortion: *syko-phanteō*
10: Blame – Bad reputation: *dys-phēmeō*

1. CURSE – ACCURSED

1: CURSE(D), ACCURSED: *ARA*

4	*ara*	1	5	*ep-aratos*	1
1	*kat-ara*	6	3	*epi-kat-aratos*	2
2	*kat-araomai*	5			

B = Bless, Praise // Curse or Insult
C = Curse or Insult // Bless, Praise

Mt	25	41	B	2	Go away from me, *with your curse upon you*, to the eternal fire
Mk	11	21		2	Look, Rabbi . . . the fig tree you *cursed* has withered away.
Lk	6	28	B	2	bless those who *curse* you,
Jn	7	49		5	This rabble knows nothing about the Law – they are *damned*.
Rm	3	14		4	(Ps 10 7) bitter *curses* fill their mouths.
	12	14	B	2	Bless those who persecute you: never *curse* them, bless them.
Ga	3	10			those who rely on the keeping of the Law are under a *curse*
				3	. . . (Dt 27 26) *Cursed* be everyone who does not persevere in observing everything prescribed
		13	B	/3	Christ redeemed us from the *curse* of the Law by being *cursed* for our sake . . . (Dt 21 23) *Cursed* be everyone who is hanged on a tree.
Heb	6	8	B		[a field] that grows brambles and thistles is . . . practically *cursed*.
Jm	3	9	B	2	We use [the tongue] to bless the Lord and Father, but we also use it to *curse* men who are made in God's image:
		10	B		the blessing and the *curse* come out of the same mouth.
2 P	2	14			Greed is the one lesson their minds have learnt. They are under a *curse*.

2: CURSE – SPEAK EVIL OF: *KAKO-LOGEŌ*

| 2 *kakōs legō* | 1 | 1 *kako-logeō* | 4 |

a) Curse

Mt	15	4		(Ex 12 17) Anyone who *curses* father or mother must be put to death.
Mk	7	10		(Ex 12 17) Anyone who *curses* father or mother must be put to death.
Ac	23	5	2	(Ex 22 27) You must not *curse* a ruler of your people.

b) Speak evil of

| Mk | 9 | 39 | | no one who works a miracle in my name is likely to *speak evil of* me. |
| Ac | 19 | 9 | | some of the congregation . . . began ⌐attacking (lit. *speaking evil of*) the Way |

3: CURSE – ACCURSED, CONDEMNED – BAN: *ANA-THEMA*

| 1 *ana-thema* | 5/6 | 3 *kata-thema* | 1 |
| 2 *ana-thematizō* | 1/4 | 4 *kata-thematizō* | 1 |

Mt	26	74	4	[Peter] started *calling down curses* on himself and swearing, 'I do not know the man'.
Mk	14	71	2	[Peter] started *calling down curses* on himself and swearing,
Rm	9	3		I would willingly be ⌐*condemned* (or: *accursed*) and be cut off from Christ if it would help my brothers of Israel.
1 Co	12	3		no one can be speaking under the influence of the Holy Spirit and say, '*Curse* Jesus',
	16	22		If anyone does not love the Lord, a *curse* on him.
Ga	1	8		if anyone preaches a version of the Good News different from the one we have already preached . . . he is to be ⌐*condemned* (or: *accursed*).
		9		if anyone preaches a version of the Good News different from the one you have already heard, he is to be ⌐*condemned* (or: *accursed*).
Rv	22	3	3	(Zc 14 11) The *ban* will be lifted.

2. ABUSE, INSULT – SLANDER – BLASPHEME

1: BLASPHEME – INSULT, ABUSE, CURSE – SLANDER, SPEAK EVIL OF: *BLAS-PHĒMEŌ*

| 1 *blas-phēmeō* | 34 | 3 *blas-phēmos* | 4 |
| 2 *blas-phēmia* | 18 | | |

Ⓢ = Blasphemy against the Spirit

Mt	9	3		some scribes said to themselves, 'This man is *blaspheming*'.
	12	31	2	every one of men's sins and *blasphemies* will be forgiven, but
			Ⓢ 2	*blasphemy* against the Spirit will not be forgiven.
	15	19	2	from the heart come evil intentions: . . . perjury, *slander*.
	26	65		the high priest tore his clothes and said, 'He has *blasphemed*
			2	. . . You have just heard the *blasphemy*'.
	27	39		The passers-by *jeered* at him . . . [40] . . . save yourself!
Mk	2	7		He is *blaspheming*. Who can forgive sins but God?
	3	28		all men's sins will be forgiven, and ⌐all their blasphemies
		29	2/	(lit. as many *blasphemies* as they have *blasphemed*); [29] but
			Ⓢ	let anyone *blaspheme* against the Holy Spirit and he will never have forgiveness:
	7	22	2	[it is from within that evil intentions emerge:] . . . *slander*, pride,
	14	64	2	[the high priest said,] You heard the *blasphemy*.
	15	29		The passers-by *jeered* at him . . . [30] . . . save yourself!
Lk	5	21	2	Who is this man talking *blasphemy*? Who can forgive sins but God alone?
	12	10	Ⓢ	he who *blasphemes* against the Holy Spirit will not be forgiven.
	22	65		they continued *heaping insults* on him.
	23	39		One of the criminals hanging there *abused* him.
Jn	10	33	2	We are . . . stoning you . . . for *blasphemy* . . . you claim to be God.
		36		you say to someone the Father has . . . sent into the world, 'You are *blaspheming*',
Ac	6	11	3	We heard [Stephen] using *blasphemous* language
	13	45		the Jews . . . used *blasphemies* and contradicted everything Paul said.
	18	6		When [the Jews] . . . started to *insult* him, [Paul] took his cloak and shook it out in front of them,
	19	37		[Paul and his companions] are not *guilty of* any . . . *blasphemy* against our goddess [Diana].
	26	11		[I tried] in this way to force [the saints] to *renounce* their *faith*;
Rm	2	24		(Is 52 5) It is your fault that the name of God is *blasphemed* among the pagans.
	3	8		Some *slanderers* have accused us of teaching this,
	14	16		you must not ⌐compromise your privilege (lit. allow your privilege to be *insulted*),
1 Co	10	30		why should I be *blamed* for food for which I have thanked God?
Ep	4	31	2	Never . . . lose your temper, or raise your voice to anybody, or *call* each other *names*,
Col	3	8	2	you . . . must give all these things up: . . . spitefulness, *abusive language* and dirty talk;
1 Tm	1	13	3	I [Paul] used to be a *blasphemer* and did all I could to injure . . . the faith.
		20		I have handed [Hymenaeus and Alexander] over to Satan to teach them not to be *blasphemous*.
	6	1		the name of God and our teaching are not *brought into disrepute*.
		4	2	All that can come of [self-conceit] is jealousy, . . . *abuse*
2 Tm	3	2	3	[in the last days] people will be self-centred . . . *irreligious*;
Tt	2	5		the message of God is never *disgraced*.
	3	2		[Remind them] not to go *slandering* other people or picking quarrels,
Jm	2	7		Aren't [the rich] the ones who *insult* the honourable name to which you have been dedicated?
1 P	4	4		[the pagans] begin to *spread libels about* you.
2 P	2	2		the Way of Truth will be *brought into disrepute* on [the false teachers'] account.
		10		people with no reverence are not afraid of *offending against*
		11	3	the glorious ones, [11] but the angels . . . make no . . . *accusation* against them in front of the Lord. [12] . . . these people who only *insult* anything that they do not understand are . . . simply animals
Jude		8		[the false teachers] disregard authority, . . . *abuse* the glorious angels
		9	2	Not even the archangel Michael . . . dared to denounce [the devil] in the language of *abuse*.
		10		these people *abuse* anything they do not understand;
Rv	2	9	2	I know . . . the *slanderous accusations* that have been made by the people who profess to be Jews
	13	1	2	[the beast's] heads were marked with *blasphemous* titles.
		5	2	For forty-two months the beast was allowed to mouth its boasts and *blasphemies*
		6	2/	[the beast] mouthed its *blasphemies* against God, (§ *blasphemies*) against his name, his heavenly Tent
	16	9		[People] *cursed* the name of God . . . and they would not repent

Rv 16 11   instead of repenting . . . they *cursed* the God of heaven
    21   They *cursed* God for sending a plague of hail;
    17 3   2 I saw . . . a scarlet beast which had . . . *blasphemous* titles written all over it.

2: INSULT, ABUSE, REVILE – SLANDER: *LOIDOREŌ*

1 *loidoreō* 4	3		*loidoros* 2
2 *loidoria* 3	4	*anti-loidoreō* 1	

Jn 9 28   [the Jews] *hurled abuse at* [the blind man]:
Ac 23 4   It is God's high priest you are *insulting*!
1 Co 4 12 B   When we are *cursed*, we answer with a blessing;
    5 11   you should not associate with a brother Christian who is . . .
     3   idolatrous, or a *slanderer*,
    6 10   3 *slanderers* and swindlers will never inherit the kingdom of God.
1 Tm 5 14   it is best for young widows to marry . . . and not give the
     2   enemy any chance to *raise a scandal* about them;
1 P 2 23   /4 [Christ] was *insulted* and did not *retaliate with insults*;
    3 9 B 2/2 Never pay back . . . an *angry word* with another *angry word*;

3: INSULT, ABUSE – REPROACH – HUMILIATION, STIGMA: *ONEIDIZŌ*

2 *oneidismos* 5	3 *oneidos* 1	
1 *oneidizō*	9	

R = Reproach

Mt 5 11   Happy are you when people *abuse* you . . . on my account.
   11 20 R   [Jesus] began to *reproach* the towns . . . because they refused to repent.
   27 44   Even the robbers who were crucified with [Jesus] *taunted* him.
Mk 15 32   Even those who were crucified with him *taunted* him.
   16 14 R   [Jesus] showed himself to the Eleven . . . He *reproached* them for their incredulity
Lk 1 25   3 it has pleased [the Lord] to take away the *humiliation* I suffered among men.
   6 22 B   Happy are you when people . . . *abuse* you, denounce your name as criminal, on account of the Son of Man.
Rm 15 3   /2 (Ps 69 10) the *insults* of those who *insult* you fall on me
1 Tm 3 7   people outside the Church should speak well of [the elder],
     2   so that he never gets a *bad reputation*
Heb 10 33   [Remember all the sufferings that you had] by being yourselves
     2   publicly exposed to *insults* and violence,
   11 26   2 [Moses] considered that the *insults* offered to the Anointed were something more precious than all the treasures of Egypt
   13 13   2 Let us go to [Jesus] . . . and share his *degradation*.
Jm 1 5 R   God . . . gives to all freely and *ungrudgingly*;
1 P 4 14   It is a blessing for you when they *insult* you for bearing the name of Christ.

4: SLANDER, SPEAK AGAINST, DISPARAGE – BACKBITING: *KATA-LALEŌ*

3	*laleō* (kata) 1/299	2 *kata-lalia* 2	
1 *kata-laleō*	5	4 *kata-lalos* 1	

Ac 6 13   3 This man is always *making speeches against* this Holy Place
Rm 1 30   4 *slanderers*, enemies of God, rude, arrogant, [deserve to die]
2 Co 12 20   2 there will be . . . intrigues and *backbiting* and gossip,
Jm 4 11   do not *slander* one another. Anyone who *slanders* a brother . . . is *speaking against* the Law
1 P 2 1   Be sure, then, you are never spiteful . . . or envious and
     2   *disparaging* of each other.
    12   behave honourably among pagans so that they can . . . give thanks . . . for the things which now make them *denounce* you as criminals
    3 16   give [your answer] with courtesy . . . so that those who malign you . . . may be proved wrong in ⌐the accusations that they bring (lit. *speaking against* you).

5: SLANDER – DENOUNCE, COMPLAIN OF: *DIA-BALLŌ*

2 *dia-ballō* 1   1 *dia-bolos* 3/39

Lk 16 1   2 a steward . . . was *denounced* . . . for being wasteful with his property.
1 Tm 3 11   the women must be respectable, not *gossips*
2 Tm 3 3   [in the last days people] will be *slanderers*
Tt 2 3   the older women should behave as though they were religious, with no *scandalmongering*

6: GOSSIP – WHISPERING LIBELLER: *PSITHYRISMOS*

1 *psithyrismos* 1   2 *psithyristēs* 1

Rm 1 30   2 [the pagans are addicted to envy, murder; they are] *libellers*,
2 Co 12 20   What I am afraid of is that . . . there will be . . . intrigues and backbiting and *gossip*,

7: MALIGN, REVILE – TREAT SPITEFULLY: *EP-ĒREAZŌ*

ep-ēreazō 2

Lk 6 28 Δ   bless those who curse you, pray for those who *treat* you *badly*.
1 P 3 16   give [your answer] with courtesy . . . so that those who *malign* you when you are living a good life . . . may be proved wrong

8: INSULT, (BE) INSOLENT – MALTREAT – ATTACK, DAMAGE: *HUBRIS*

2 *hubris*	3	1 *hubrizō* 5	
3 *hubristēs* 2	4	*en-hubrizō* 1	

a) Insult, (Be) Insolent – Maltreat, Treat shamefully – Attack

Ⓢ, X = Insult, Maltreat the Spirit, Jesus

Mt 22 6   the rest [of those who had been invited to the wedding] seized his servants, *maltreated* them and killed them.
Lk 11 45   Master, . . . when you speak like this you *insult* us too.
   18 32 X   he will be handed over to the pagans and will be . . . *maltreated* and spat on,
Ac 14 5   a move was made by pagans as well as Jews to *make attacks on* [the apostles]
Rm 1 30   3 enemies of God, ⌐rude (or: *insolent*), arrogant and boastful,
2 Co 12 10   2 I am quite content with my weaknesses, and with *insults*,
1 Th 2 2   We had . . . been *grossly insulted* at Philippi,
1 Tm 1 13   I used to be a blasphemer and did all I could to injure and
     3   *discredit* the faith.
Heb 10 29 Ⓢ 4 anyone who . . . *insults* the Spirit of grace, will be condemned to a far severer punishment.

b) Damage, Injury

Ac 27 10   I can see this voyage will ⌐be dangerous and that we run the
     2   risk of (lit. end in serious *damage* and in) losing . . . our lives
    21   if you had listened to me . . . you would have spared your-
     2   selves all this *damage* and loss.

9: FALSE ACCUSATION – EXTORTION: *SYKO-PHANTEŌ*

syko-phanteō 1/2

Lk 3 14   No intimidation! ⌐No [*extortion by*] *false accusation* (or: No cheating)!

10: BLAME – BAD REPUTATION: *DYS-PHĒMEŌ*

1 *dys-phēmeō* 1   2 *dys-phēmia* 1

1 Co 4 13   we *are insulted* and we answer politely.
2 Co 6 8 B   2 [We are servants of God] prepared for . . . *blame* or praise;

CUSTOM – PRACTICE

1. Custom, Customary – Practice – Manners: *ethos*
    a) Custom = (ritual or legal) Practice, (Mosaic) Tradition – Customary, Usual
    b) Custom = (personal) Habit, (Be) Used to – Usual
    c) Manners, Morals
2. Practice: *hexis*
3. Customary: *nomizomai*

1. CUSTOM, CUSTOMARY – PRACTICE – MANNERS: *ETHOS*

2 *eiōtha* 4	1	*ethos* 12	
4 *ethizō* 1	5	*ēthos* 1	
	3 *syn-ētheia* 3		

a) Custom = (ritual or legal) Practice, (Mosaic) Tradition – Customary, Usual
Lk 1 9   it fell to [Zechariah] by lot, as the ritual *custom* was, to enter the Lord's sanctuary
   2 27   the parents brought in the child Jesus to do for him ⌐what
     4   the Law required (lit. *what was customary* under the Law),
Jn 18 39   3 according to a *custom* of yours I should release one prisoner at the Passover;

Jn 19 40		They . . . wrapped [the body of Jesus] with the spices in linen cloths, following the Jewish burial *custom*.
Ac 6 14		Jesus the Nazarene is going to . . . alter the ʳtraditions (or: *customs*) that Moses handed down to us.
15 1		Unless you have yourselves circumcised in the *tradition* of Moses you cannot be saved.
16 21		[Jews] are advocating *practices* which it is unlawful . . . to accept or follow.
21 21		you instruct all Jews . . . to break away from Moses, authorising them not . . . to follow the *customary practices*.
25 16		Romans are not in the *habit* of surrendering any man, until the accused . . . is given an opportunity to defend himself
26 3		you are an expert in matters of *custom* and controversy among the Jews.
28 17		I have done nothing against . . . the *customs* of our ancestors,
1 Co 11 16	3	it is not the *custom* with us, nor in the churches of God.

b) Custom = (personal) Habit, (Be) Used to – Usual

Mt 27 15	2	At festival time it *was* the governor's *practice* to release a prisoner for the people,
Mk 10 1 X	2	again he taught them, as his *custom* was.
Lk 2 42		When [Jesus] was twelve years old, they went up [to Jerusalem] for the feast as *usual*.
4 16		[Jesus] went into the synagogue on the sabbath day as he *usually* did.
X	2	
22 39 X		He then left to make his way as *usual* to the Mount of Olives,
Ac 17 2	2	Paul as *usual* introduced himself [in the Jewish synagogue in Thessalonika]
1 Co 8 7	3	There are some who have been so long *used to* idols that they eat this food
Heb 10 25		Do not stay away from the meetings of the community, as some ʳdo (lit. have the *habit* of doing),

c) Manners, Morals

1 Co 15 33	5	Bad friends ruin the ʳnoblest people (lit. good *manners*).

2. PRACTICE: *HEXIS*

hexis 1

Heb 5 14	Solid food is for mature men with minds trained by *practice* to distinguish between good and bad.

3. CUSTOMARY: *NOMIZOMAI*

nomizomai 1/15

Ac 16 13	we went along the river outside the gates as . . . ᵛ this was a *customary* (G there we thought might be a) place for prayer.

CUT – DIVISION

1. Cut – Hew – Saw
  1: Cut: *koptō*
    a) Cut off (from a person) – Gash
    b) Cut, Cut down
  2: Cut keenly: *temnō*
    a) Sharp-cutting, Finely-cutting
    b) Cut off – Cut in pieces
  3: Hewn out of rock: *la-tomeō*
  4: Edge of a sword – Double-edged, Two-edged: *stoma*
  5: Sharp: *oxys*
  6: Sawn in half – Sawn in two: *prizō*
  7: Axe: *axinē*
2. Division – Definition – Separate, Distinct
  1: Division – Variety – Party: *di-(h)aireō*
    a) Divide – Distribute – Variety
    b) Party, Faction – Sect – Heresy
  2: Separate – Exclude: *ek-kleiō*
  3: Set one person against another: *dichazō*
  4: Division of the priesthood – Section, Class: *eph-ēmeria*
  5: Set apart – Set limits to: *horizō*
    a) Set apart, Separate – Specially chosen
    b) Appointed – Predestined – Determined, Determined the boundaries
  6: "Cut straight" = Keep on a straight course: *temnō*
  7: Distinction: *dia-stolē*
3. Division – Share – Lot, Allot
  1: Share – Part – Divide: *merizō*
    a) Share, Give out – Portion, Lot – Divide
    b) Part, Partly, Partial
    c) Divided (figuratively)
    d) Parts of a country, Region, District
    e) Party – Section, Group of people
    f) For one's part – Trade
    g) In turn – Times
  2: Share – Lot, Allotted: *klēros*
  3: Allotted, Fall by lot – Cast lots: *lanchanō*
  4: Fall to, Come to: *epi-ballō*

---

1. CUT – HEW – SAW

1: CUT: *KOPTŌ*

3	*koptō* 2/8	1	*ek-koptō* 10
2	*apo-koptō* 6	4	*kata-koptō* 1

a) Cut off (from a person) – Gash

Mt 5 30		if your right hand should cause you to sin, *cut* it *off*
18 8		If your hand or your foot should cause you to sin, *cut* it *off*
Mk 5 5	4	[the demoniac] would . . . *gash* himself with stones.
9 43	2	if your hand should cause you to sin, *cut* it *off*;
45	2	if your foot should cause you to sin, *cut* it *off*,
Jn 18 10	2	Simon Peter . . . wounded the high priest's servant, *cutting off* his right ear.
26	2	a relation of the man whose ear Peter had *cut off*,
Ga 5 12 ○	2	Tell those who are disturbing you I would like to see ʳthe knife slip (lit. them *cut*).

b) Cut, Cut down

Mt 3 10		any tree which fails to produce good fruit will be *cut down*
7 19		Any tree that does not produce good fruit is *cut down*
21 8	3	others were *cutting* branches from the trees
Mk 11 8	3	others [spread] greenery which they had *cut* in the fields.
Lk 3 9		any tree which fails to produce good fruit will be *cut down*
13 7		for three years now I have been coming to look for fruit on this fig tree and finding none. *Cut* it *down*:
9		it may bear fruit next year; if not, then you can *cut* it *down*.
Ac 27 32	2	the soldiers *cut* the boat's ropes
Rm 11 22		you will find yourself *cut off* too,
24		if you were *cut* from your natural wild olive to be grafted
2 Co 11 12		ʳleaving no opportunity (lit. *cutting off* every opportunity) for those people who are looking for an opportunity to claim equality with us

2: CUT KEENLY: *TEMNŌ*

2 *tomos* 1		1 *dicho-tomeō* 2	

a) Sharp-cutting, Finely-cutting

Heb 4 12	2	The word of God . . . *cuts* like any double-edged sword but more *finely*:

b) Cut off – Cut in pieces

Mt 24 51		The master [of the dishonest servant] will *cut* him *off* and send him to the same fate as the hypocrites,
Lk 12 46		The master [of the dishonest servant] will *cut* him *off* and send him to the same fate as the unfaithful.

3: HEWN OUT OF ROCK: *LA-TOMEŌ*

1 *la-tomeō* 2		2 *la-xeutos* 1	

Mt 27 60		[Joseph of Arimathaea put Jesus' body] in his own new tomb which he had *hewn out* of the rock.
Mk 15 46		a tomb which had been *hewn out* of the rock.
Lk 23 53	2	[Joseph of Arimathaea] put [Jesus' body] in a tomb which was *hewn* in stone

4: EDGE OF A SWORD – DOUBLE-EDGED, TWO-EDGED: *STOMA*

2 *stoma* 2/78		1 *di-stomos* 3	

Lk 21 24	2	[This people] will fall by the *edge* of the sword
Heb 4 12		The word of God . . . *cuts* like any *double-edged* sword but more finely:
11 34	2	[Gideon and the prophets could] . . . ʳemerge unscathed from battle (lit. escape the *edge* of the sword).
Rv 1 16		out of his mouth came a sharp sword, *double-edged*,
2 12		Here is the message of the one who has the sharp sword, *double-edged*:

5: SHARP: *OXYS*

oxys 7/8

Rv 1 16		[a figure like a Son of man,] out of his mouth came a *sharp* sword, double-edged,
2 12		Here is the message of the one who has the *sharp* sword, double-edged:
14 14		one like a son of man with . . . a *sharp* sickle in his hand.
17		Another angel, who also carried a *sharp* sickle,
18		the angel in charge of the fire . . . shouted aloud to the one with the *sharp* sickle, 'Put your *sharp* sickle in and reap:'

Rv 19 15   From [the] mouth [of the Word of God] came a *sharp*
            sword to strike the pagans with;

6: SAWN IN HALF – SAWN IN TWO: *PRIZŌ*
prizō, priō 1

Heb 11 37   They were stoned, or *sawn in half*, or beheaded;

7: AXE: *AXINĒ*
axinē 2

Mt 3 10   Even now the *axe* is laid to the roots of the trees,
Lk 3 9   even now the *axe* is laid to the roots of the trees,

2. DIVISION – DEFINITION – SEPARATE, DISTINCT

1: DIVISION – VARIETY – PARTY: *DI-(H)AIREŌ*

| 1 *hairesis* | 9 | 3 *di-(h)aireō* | 2 |
| 4 *hairetikos* | 1 | 2 *di-(h)airesis* | 3 |

a) Divide – Distribute – Variety

Lk 15 12   3 the father *divided* the property between [his two sons].
1 Co 12 4   2 There is a *variety* of gifts but always the same Spirit; 5 there
       5   2 are *all sorts* of service to be done, but always to the same
       6   2 Lord; 6 working in *all sorts* of different ways in different
                people, it is the same God who is working in all of them.
       11 Ⓢ All these [gifts] are the work of one and the same Spirit,
       3   who *distributes* different gifts to different people just as
                he chooses.

b) Party, Faction – Sect – Heresy

C = "sect", signifying Christians

Ac 5 17   Then the high priest intervened with all his supporters from
                the *party* of the Sadducees.
   15 5   certain members of the Pharisees' *party* who had become
                believers objected,
   24 5 C   this man [Paul] . . . is a ringleader of the Nazarene *sect*.
      14 C   it is according to the Way which they describe as a *sect*
                that I worship the God of my ancestors,
   26 5   I followed the strictest *party* in our religion and lived as a
                Pharisee.
   28 22 C   all we know about this *sect* is that opinion everywhere
                condemns it.
1 Co 11 19   there must no doubt be *separate groups* among you,
Ga 5 20   [the results of self-indulgence are obvious:] quarrels;
                disagreements, *factions*,
Tt 3 10   ᴦIf a man disputes what you teach . . . have no more to do
       4   with him (lit. Avoid any *heretical* man):
2 P 2 1   false teachers, who will insinuate their own *disruptive views*

2: SEPARATE – EXCLUDE: *EK-KLEIŌ*
ek-kleiō 2

Rm 3 27   So what becomes of our boasts? ᴦThere is no room for them
                (lit. They should be *excluded*).
Ga 4 17   by *separating* you from me, they want to win you over

3: SET ONE PERSON AGAINST ANOTHER: *DICHAZŌ*
dichazō 1

Mt 10 35   I have come to *set* a man *against* his father . . . a daughter-
                in-law against her mother-in-law.

4: DIVISION OF THE PRIESTHOOD – SECTION, CLASS: *EPH-ĒMERIA*
eph-ēmeria 2

Lk 1 5   a priest called Zechariah who belonged to the Abijah *section
                of the priesthood*,
     8   it was the turn of Zechariah's *section* to serve,

5: SET APART – SET LIMITS TO: *HORIZŌ*

2 *horizō*	8	5 *apo-di-(h)orizō*	1
4 *horo-thesia*	1	3 *pro-(h)orizō*	6
1 *aph-orizō*	10		

---

a) Set apart, Separate – Specially chosen

Mt 13 49   the angels will . . . *separate* the wicked from the just
   25 32   [the Son of Man] will *separate* men one from another as the
                shepherd *separates* sheep from goats.
Lk 6 22   Happy are you when people . . . *drive* you out,
Ac 13 2   the Holy Spirit said, 'I want Barnabas and Saul *set apart*
                for the work to which I have called them'.
   19 9   [Paul] broke with [those who attacked the Way] and *took*
                his disciples *apart*
Rm 1 1   From Paul . . . who has been . . . *specially chosen* to preach
                the Good News
2 Co 6 17   (Is 52 11) come away from [unbelievers] and *keep aloof*,
                says the Lord.
Ga 1 15   God, who had *specially chosen* me while I was still in my
                mother's womb, called me
   2 12   [Cephas stopped eating with pagans] and *kept away from*
                them altogether for fear of the group that insisted on
                circumcision.
Jude 19   These unspiritual . . . people ᴦare nothing but mischief-
     5   makers (lit. *cause division*).

b) Appointed – Predestined – Determined, Determined the boundaries

Lk 22 22 Θ The Son of Man does indeed go to his fate even as it has
     2   been *decreed*,
Ac 2 23   This man [Jesus], who was put into your power by the
          Θ 2 *deliberate* intention and foreknowledge of God,
   4 28 Θ   [Pilate made an alliance against your holy servant Jesus,]
                but only to bring about the very thing that you . . . had
     3   *predetermined* should happen.
   10 42 Θ 2 God has *appointed* [Jesus] to judge everyone, alive or dead.
   11 29   2 The disciples *decided* to send relief . . . to the brothers
                living in Judaea.
   17 26 Θ 2 [God] *decreed* how long each nation should flourish and
     4   what the *boundaries* of its territory should be.
      31 Θ [God] has fixed a day when the whole world will be judged
     2   . . . and he has *appointed* a man to be the judge.
Rm 1 4 Θ   2 Jesus . . . was ᴦ*proclaimed* (lit. the *predestined*) Son of God
   8 29 Θ   3 They are the ones [God] *chose specially* long ago and intended
      30 Θ to become true images of his Son . . . 30 He called those
     3   he *intended* for this;
1 Co 2 7 Θ 3 the wisdom that God *predestined* to be for our glory before
                the ages began.
Ep 1 5 Θ   3 [God chose us,] *determining* that we should become his
                adopted sons, through Jesus Christ
      11 Θ 3 it is in [Christ] that we were . . . *chosen from the beginning*,
                under the predetermined plan of the one who guides all
                things
Heb 4 7 Θ   2 God *fixed* another day when, much later, he said 'today'

6: "CUT STRAIGHT" = KEEP ON A STRAIGHT COURSE: *TEMNŌ*
(*ortho-*)*tomeō 1*

2 Tm 2 15   present yourself in front of God as a man who . . . has *kept
                a straight course* with the message of the truth.

7: DISTINCTION: *DIA-STOLĒ*
dia-stolē 3

Rm 3 22   it is the same justice of God that comes through faith to
                everyone, Jew and pagan ᴦalike (lit. without *distinction*),
   10 12   scripture . . . makes no *distinction* between Jew and Greek.
1 Co 14 7   if one note on [a musical instrument] cannot be *distinguished*
                from another, how can you tell what tune is being played?

3. DIVISION – SHARE – LOT, ALLOT

1: SHARE – PART – DIVIDE: *MERIZŌ*

4 *meris*	5	7 *dia-merismos*	1
5 *merismos*	2	3 *dia-merizō*	11
6 *meristēs*	1	8 (*mempsi-*)*moiros*	1
2 *merizō*	14	9 (*poly-*)*merōs*	1
1 *meros*	42	10 *sym-merizomai*	1

a) Share, Give out – Portion, Lot – Divide

Mt 24 51   The master [of the dishonest servant] will cut him off and
                send him to the same *fate* as the hypocrites.
   27 35   3 [the soldiers] *shared out* his clothing by casting lots,
Mk 6 41   2 [Jesus] also *shared out* the two fish among them all.
   15 24   3 they crucified him, and *shared out* his clothing, casting lots
Lk 10 42   4 It is Mary who has chosen the better *part*;
   12 13   2 Master, tell my brother to give me a *share* of our inheritance
      14   who appointed me . . . ᴦthe arbitrator of your claims (lit. to
       6   *apportion*)?

Lk 12 46		The master [of the dishonest servant] will cut him off and send him to the same *fate* as the unfaithful.
15 12		Father, let me have the *share* of the estate that would come to me.
22 17	3	Take this [cup] and *share* it among you,
23 34	3	they cast lots to *share out* his clothing.
24 42		they offered him a *piece* of grilled fish,
Jn 13 8		If I do not wash you, you can have ⌐nothing in common (lit. no *part*) with me.
19 23		the soldiers . . . took his clothing and divided it into four *shares*, one *share* for each soldier.
24	3	(Ps 22 18) They *shared out* my clothing among them.
Ac 2 3	3	tongues of fire . . . *separated* and came to rest on the head of each of them.
45	3	[the faithful] sold their goods . . . and *shared out* the proceeds among themselves
8 21	4	You have no *share*, no rights, in this [money]: God can see how your heart is warped.
Rm 12 3	2	Each of you must judge himself soberly by the standard of the faith God has *given* him.
1 Co 7 17	2	what each one has is what the Lord has *given* him
9 13	10	those serving at the altar can claim their *share* [of food] from the altar
2 Co 6 15	4	nor has a believer anything to *share* with an unbeliever.
10 13	2	taking for our measure the yardstick which God ⌐gave (or: *apportioned*) us
Col 1 12	4	thanking the Father who has made it possible for you to ⌐join (lit. *share* the lot of) the saints
Heb 2 4 Ⓢ	5	God himself confirmed [the apostles'] witness . . . by freely *giving* the *gifts* of the Holy Spirit.
7 2	2	it was to [Melchizedek] that Abraham *gave* a tenth of all that he had.
Jude 16	8	They are mischief-makers, ⌐grumblers (lit. who complain of their *lot*)
Rv 20 6		blessed are those who *share* in the first resurrection;
21 8		the ⌐legacy for (lit. *lot* of) . . . idolators or any other sort of liars, is . . . the burning lake of sulphur.
22 19		God will cut off his *share* of the tree of life

b) Part, Partly, Partial

Lk 11 36		If . . . your whole body is filled with light, and no ⌐trace of (lit. *part*) darkness,
Jn 21 6		Throw the net out to ⌐starboard (lit. the right *side* of the boat)
Ac 5 2		[Ananias] brought ⌐the rest (lit. a *part*) [of the proceeds] and presented it to the apostles.
Rm 11 15		One *section* of Israel has become blind,
15 15		The reason why I have written to you, and put some ⌐things (lit. *parts*) rather strongly,
24		after enjoying a *little* of your company,
1 Co 11 18		I hear . . . there are separate factions among you, and I *half* (or: *partly*) believe it
13 9		For our knowledge is ⌐imperfect (lit. *partial*) and our prophesying is ⌐imperfect (lit. *partial*); ¹⁰ but once perfection comes, all ⌐imperfect (lit. *partial*) things will disappear . . . ¹² . . . The knowledge that I have now is ⌐imperfect (lit. *partial*);
10		
12		
2 Co 1 14		you ⌐do not know us very well yet (lit. know us only *partly*)
3 10		⌐In fact (lit. On this *point*) . . . the thing that used to have such splendour now seems to have none;
9 3		to make sure that our boasting about you does not prove to have been empty ⌐this time (lit. on this *point*),
Ep 4 16		for each separate *part* [of the body] to work according to its function.
Col 2 16		never let anyone else decide . . . ⌐whether (lit. on the *point* of whether or not) you are to observe annual festivals,
Heb 4 12	5	The word of God . . . can slip through *the place where* the soul *is divided* from the spirit,
9 5		This is not the time to ⌐go into greater detail about this (lit. talk about things *in particular*).
Rv 16 19		The Great City ⌐was split into (lit. became) three *parts*

c) Divided (figuratively)

Mt 12 25	2	Every kingdom *divided* against itself is heading for ruin; and no town, no household *divided* against itself can stand.
2		
26 Ⓓ	2	²⁶ Now if Satan casts out Satan, he is *divided* against himself;
Mk 3 24	2	If a kingdom is *divided* against itself, that kingdom cannot last. ²⁵ And if a household is *divided* against itself, that household can never stand. ²⁶ Now if Satan has rebelled against himself and is *divided*, he cannot stand either
25	2	
26 Ⓓ	2	
Lk 11 17	3	Every kingdom *divided* against itself is heading for ruin . . .
18 Ⓓ	3	¹⁸ So too with Satan: if he is *divided* against himself, how can his kingdom stand?
12 51		Do you suppose that I am here to bring peace on earth? No, I tell you, but rather *division*. ⁵² For from now on a household of five will be *divided*: three against two and two against three; ⁵³ the father *divided* against the son, son against father,
52	7	
3		
53	3	
1 Co 1 13 X	2	Has Christ been *parcelled out*?
7 34	2	[a married man has to bother about the world's affairs:] he is *torn two ways*.

d) Parts of a country, Region, District

Mt 2 22		[Joseph] left for [Nazareth, in] the *region* of Galilee.
15 21		Jesus . . . withdrew to the *region* of Tyre and Sidon,
Mk 8 10		Jesus came to the *region* of Caesarea Philippi [Jesus] went to the *region* of Dalmanutha.
Ac 2 10		Egypt and the *parts* of Libya round Cyrene;
16 13	4	Philippi . . . the principal city of that particular *district* of Macedonia.
19 1		Paul made his way ⌐overland (lit. through the upper *parts*) as far as Ephesus,
20 2		[Paul set out for Macedonia.] On his way through those ⌐areas (or: *parts*) he said many words of encouragement
Ep 4 9 Δ		what can it mean if not that [Christ] descended right down to the lower *regions* of the earth?

e) Party – Section, Group of people

Ac 23 6		one ⌐section [of the Sanhedrin] was made up of Sadducees and the other of Pharisees,
9		some of the scribes from the Pharisees' *party* stood up

f) For one's part – Trade

Ac 19 27		This threatens . . . to discredit our *trade*,
1 Co 12 27		you together are Christ's body; but each of you is a ⌐different (lit. *particular*) part of it.

g) In turn – Times

1 Co 14 27		If there are people present with the gift of tongues, let only two or three, at the most, be allowed to use it, and only one at a time,
Heb 1 1	9	At various *times* in the past and in various different ways, God spoke to our ancestors

2: SHARE – LOT, ALLOTTED: *KLĒROS*

1 *klēros* 10/11   2 *pros-klēroō* 1

Mt 27 35		[the soldiers] shared out his clothing by casting *lots*,
Mk 15 24		they crucified him, and shared out his clothing, casting *lots*
Lk 23 34		they cast *lots* to share out his clothing.
Jn 19 24		(Ps 22 18) They shared out my clothing among them. They cast *lots* for my clothes.
Ac 1 17		[Judas] actually ⌐sharing (lit. being allotted a *share* of) this ministry of ours.
26		They then drew *lots* for [Joseph and Matthias], and as the *lot* fell to Matthias, he was listed as one of the twelve apostles.
8 21		[Simon,] You have no share, no ⌐rights (lit. *lot*), in this:
17 4 ○	2	Some of [the Jews] . . . ⌐joined (lit. threw in their *lot* with) Paul and Silas,
26 18		so that [the pagans] may . . . receive . . . a ⌐share in the inheritance (or: *share*) of the sanctified.
1 P 5 3		Never be a dictator over any ⌐group that is put in your charge (lit. that are *allotted* to you),

3: ALLOTTED, FALL BY LOT – CAST LOTS: *LANCHANŌ*

lanchanō 4

Lk 1 9		it *fell* to [Zechariah] *by lot* . . . to enter the Lord's sanctuary
Jn 19 24		let's *throw dice* to decide who is to have [the seamless undergarment].
Ac 1 17		[Judas] actually ⌐sharing (lit. *being allotted* a share of) this ministry of ours.
2 P 1 1		From Simeon Peter . . . to all who ⌐treasure (lit. have been *allotted*) the same faith as ourselves,

4: FALL TO, COME TO: *EPI-BALLŌ*

epi-ballō 1/18

Lk 15 12		Father, let me have the share of the estate that would ⌐come (or: *fall*) to me.

CYRENE – LIBYA

Cyrene	*1*	Libya	*1*	Alexander	*1*
Cyrenian	⎫	Syrtis (banks, shallows)	*1*	Rufus	*1*
from/of Cyrene	⎬6			Simon	*3*

Mt 27 32	they came across a man *from Cyrene*, Simon by name, and enlisted him to carry [Jesus'] cross.

Mk 15 21	They enlisted a passer-by, *Simon of Cyrene*, father of *Alexander* and *Rufus*, . . . to carry his cross.	
Lk 23 26	they seized on a man, *Simon from Cyrene*, . . . and made him shoulder the cross	
Ac 2 10	[devout men living in Jerusalem from every nation,] people from . . . the parts of *Libya* round *Cyrene*;	

Ac 6 9	people came forward to debate with Stephen, some from *Cyrene* and Alexandria
11 20	Some of them, . . . who came from Cyprus and *Cyrene*, went to Antioch where they started preaching to the Greeks,
13 1	In the church at Antioch the following were prophets and teachers: Barnabas, . . . Lucius *of Cyrene*,
27 17	afraid of running aground on the *Syrtis* banks,

D

DAMASCUS

Damascus 15	A Ananias 6	1 polis 2/164
(the people) of Damascus 1 (2 Co)	Judas 1 (Ac 9 11)	

Ac 9	2	[Saul had gone to the high priest] and asked for letters addressed to the synagogues in *Damascus* . . . ³ Suddenly, while he was travelling to *Damascus* . . . there came a light from heaven all round him.
	3	
	6 1	Get up now and go into the *city*,
	8	and they had to lead [Saul] into *Damascus* by the hand.
	10 A	A disciple called *Ananias* who lived in *Damascus* had a vision in which he heard the Lord say to him, '*Ananias*!'
	11 A	. . . ¹¹ . . . You must go to Straight Street and ask at the house of *Judas* for someone called Saul, who comes from Tarsus. ¹² . . . he is praying, having had a vision of a man called *Ananias* . . . laying hands on him . . .
	12 A	
	13 A	*Ananias* said, 'Lord, several people have told me about . . .
	17 A	all the harm he has been doing . . .' ¹⁷ Then *Ananias* went. He entered the house,
	19	After [Saul] had spent only a few days with the disciples in *Damascus*,
	22	[Saul] was able to throw the Jewish colony at *Damascus* into complete confusion
	27	how [Saul] had preached boldly at *Damascus* in the name of Jesus.
22	5	[the high priest and the whole council of elders] even sent me with letters to their brothers in *Damascus*.
	6	I was on that journey and nearly at *Damascus* when about midday a bright light . . . shone round me.
	10	The Lord answered, 'Stand up and go into *Damascus* . . .'
	11	and so I came to *Damascus*.
	12 A	Someone called *Ananias* . . . highly thought of by all the Jews living there, ¹³ came to see me;
26	12	I was going to *Damascus*, armed with full powers . . . from the chief priests,
	20	I started preaching, first to the people of *Damascus*,
2 Co 11	32	When I was in *Damascus*, the ethnarch of King Aretas put guards round the *city* [of *the people of Damascus*]
	1	
Ga 1	17	I went off to Arabia at once and later went straight back from there to *Damascus*.

DAVID

David 59	Saul 1	⎫	1 basileus 2/115
J Jesse 5	Kish 1	⎬(Ac 13 21)	

X = Jesus, the Christ, son of David or of his line

Mt 1	1 X	A genealogy of Jesus Christ, son of *David*, son of Abraham:
	5 J	Obed was the father of *Jesse*; ⁶ and *Jesse* was the father of
	6 1	*King David. David* was the father of Solomon, whose mother had been Uriah's wife,
	17	The sum of generations is therefore: fourteen from Abraham to *David*: fourteen from *David* to the Babylonian deportation;
	20	Joseph son of *David*, do not be afraid to take Mary home as your wife,
9	27 X	two blind men followed him shouting, 'Take pity on us, Son of *David*'.
12	3	Have you not read what *David* did when he and his followers were hungry (cf. 1 S 21 1–7)
	23 X	Can this be the Son of *David*?
15	22 X	a Canaanite woman . . . started shouting, 'Sir, Son of *David*, take pity on me.
20	30 X	two blind men . . . shouted, 'Lord! Have pity on us, Son of *David*.'
	31 X	Lord! Have pity on us, Son of *David*.
21	9 X	The crowds . . . were all shouting: Hosanna to the Son of *David*!
	15 X	the children shouting, 'Hosanna to the Son of *David*'
22	42	What is your opinion about the Christ? Whose son is he?

Mt 22	43 X	'*David's*' they told him. ⁴³ 'Then how is it' he said 'that *David* . . . calls him Lord, where he says: (Ps 110 1) . . .
	45	⁴⁵ If *David* can call him Lord, then how can he be his son?
Mk 2	25	Did you never read what *David* did . . . when he and his followers were hungry (cf. 1 S 21 1–7)
10	47 X	[a blind beggar began to shout] Son of *David*, Jesus, have pity on me.
	48 X	Son of *David*, have pity on me.
11	10	Blessings on the coming kingdom of our father *David*!
12	35 X	How can the scribes maintain that the Christ is the son of *David*?
	36	*David* himself . . . said: (Ps 110 1) The Lord said to my Lord . . .
	37	*David* himself calls him Lord, in what way then can he be his son?
Lk 1	27	a virgin betrothed to a man named Joseph, of the House of *David*;
	32 X	The Lord God will give him the throne of his ancestor *David*;
	69	and [God] has raised up for us a power for salvation in the House of his servant *David*,
2	4	Joseph . . . travelled up to Judaea, to the town of *David* called Bethlehem, since he was of *David's* House and line;
	11	Today in the town of *David* a saviour has been born to you;
3	31 J	[Jesus] son of *David*, ³² son of *Jesse*, son of Obed,
6	3	So you have not read what *David* did when he and his followers were hungry (cf. 1 S 21 1–7)
18	38 X	[a blind man called out] Jesus, Son of *David*, have pity on me.
	39 X	Son of *David*, have pity on me.
20	41 X	How can people maintain that the Christ is son of *David*? ⁴² Why, *David* himself says . . . (Ps 110 1) . . . ⁴⁴ *David* here calls him Lord; how then can he be his son?
	42	
	44	
Jn 7	42 X	the Christ must be descended from *David* and come from the town of Bethlehem [where *David* was]
Ac 1	16	the Holy Spirit, speaking through *David*, foretells the fate of Judas, (cf. Ps 41 10)
2	25	as *David* says of [Jesus]: (Ps 16 8–11) I saw the Lord before me always,
	29	the patriarch *David* himself is dead . . . his tomb is still with us.
	34	For *David* himself never went up to heaven;
4	25	you it is who said . . . speaking through our ancestor *David*, your servant (Ps 2 1–2): Why this arrogance . . .?
7	45	Here it stayed until the time of *David*.
13	21	God gave them *Saul* son of *Kish*, a man of the tribe of Benjamin.
	22 J	1 he deposed him and made *David* their *king*, of whom he approved in these words (cf. Ps 89 21): I have selected *David* son of *Jesse*, a man after my own heart,
	34	(Is 55 3) To you I shall give the sure and holy things promised to *David*.
	36	Now when *David* . . . died . . . he has certainly experienced corruption.
15	16	(Am 9 11) I shall return and rebuild the fallen House of *David*;
Rm 1	3 X	the Son of God who, according to the human nature he took, was a descendant of *David*:
4	6	And *David* says the same: a man is happy . . . (Ps 32 1–2)
11	9	And *David* says (Ps 69 23–24): May their own table prove a trap . . .
15	12 X J	(Is 11 10) The root of *Jesse* will appear,
2 Tm 2	8 X	Remember . . . Jesus Christ . . , sprung from the race of *David*;
Heb 4	7	God fixed another day when . . . he said 'today' through *David* . . . (cf. Ps 95 7)
11	32	There is not time for me to give an account of . . . Jephthah, or of *David*,
Rv 3	7	Here is the message of the holy and faithful one who has the key of *David*,
5	5 X	the Root of *David*, has triumphed,
22	16 X	I am of *David's* line, the root of *David*

DEAF – DUMB – BLIND

1. **Deaf and Dumb**: *kōphos*
2. **Dumb**: *a-lalos*
3. **Speechless (in amazement)**: *eneos*
4. **Blind, Blind man**: *typhlos*

1. DEAF and DUMB: *KŌPHOS*

kōphos 14

Mt	9 32	[The two blind men] had only just left when a man was brought
	33	to [Jesus], a *dumb* demoniac. [33] . . . when the devil was cast out, the *dumb* [man] spoke
	11 5	lepers are cleansed, and the *deaf* hear,
	12 22	they brought to [Jesus] a blind and *dumb* demoniac; and he cured him, so that the *dumb* [man] could speak
	15 30	large crowds came to [Jesus] bringing . . . the blind, the *dumb*
	31	The crowds were astonished to see the *dumb* speaking,
Mk	7 32	they brought [Jesus] a *deaf* [man] who had an impediment in his speech;
	37	[Jesus] makes the *deaf* hear and the dumb speak.
	9 25	Jesus . . . rebuked the unclean spirit. '*Deaf* and dumb spirit . . . come out'
Lk	1 22	[Zechariah] could only make signs to them, and remained *dumb*.
	7 22	the blind see again . . . and the *deaf* hear,
	11 14	[Jesus] was casting out a devil and it was *dumb*; but when the devil had gone out the *dumb* [man] spoke,

2. DUMB: *A-LALOS*

a-lalos 3

Mk	7 37	[Jesus] makes the deaf hear and the *dumb* speak.
	9 17	Master, I have brought my son to you; there is a spirit of *dumbness* in him,
	25	Deaf and *dumb* spirit . . . I command you: come out of him

3. SPEECHLESS (IN AMAZEMENT): *ENEOS*

eneos 1

Ac	9 7	The men travelling with Saul stood there *speechless*,

4. BLIND, BLIND MAN: *TYPHLOS*

2 typhloō 3   1 typhlos 50

M = Metaphorically

Mt	9 27		As Jesus went on his way two *blind men* followed him
	28		when Jesus reached the house the *blind men* came up with him
	11 5		(cf. Is 35 5) the *blind* see again, and the lame walk,
	12 22		they brought to [Jesus] a *blind* and dumb demoniac;
	15 14	M	[The Pharisees] are *blind men* leading *blind men*; and if one *blind man* leads another (§ *blind man*), both will fall into a pit.
	30		large crowds came to [Jesus] bringing . . . the *blind*, the dumb,
	31		The crowds were astonished to see the dumb speaking . . and the *blind* with their sight,
	20 30		there were two *blind men* sitting at the side of the road.
	21 14		There were also *blind* and lame [people] who came to [Jesus] in the Temple,
	23 16	M	Alas for you, *blind* guides! You who say, 'If a man swears by the Temple, it has no force . . .' [17] Fools and *blind*! For
	17	M	which is of greater worth, the gold or the Temple . . .?
	19	M	[19] You *blind men*! For which is of greater worth, the offering or the altar that makes the offering sacred? . . .
	24	M	[24] You *blind* guides! Straining out gnats and swallowing camels!
	26	M	*Blind* Pharisee! Clean the inside of cup . . . first so that the outside may become clean as well.
Mk	8 22		some people brought to [Jesus] a *blind man* whom they begged him to touch.
	23		[Jesus] took the *blind man* by the hand and led him outside the village.
	10 46		Bartimaeus . . . a *blind* beggar, was sitting at the side of the road.
	49		they called the *blind man*. '. . . get up; he is calling you.'
	51		What do you want . . .? 'Rabbuni,' the *blind man* said to him 'Master, let me see again.'
Lk	4 18		(Is 61 1 G) the Lord . . . has sent me . . . to proclaim . . . to the *blind* new sight,
	6 39		Can one *blind man* guide another (§ *blind man*)?
	7 21		It was just then that [Jesus] . . . gave the gift of sight to many who were *blind*.
	22		(cf. Is 35 5) the *blind* see again, the lame walk,
	14 13		when you have a party, invite the poor . . . the lame, the *blind*;
	21		bring in here the poor . . . the *blind* and the lame.

Lk	18 35		there was a *blind man* sitting at the side of the road begging.
Jn	5 3		under these [porticos] were crowds of sick people – blind, lame, paralysed
	9 1		[Jesus] saw a man who had been *blind* from birth.
	2		Rabbi, who sinned . . . for him to have been born *blind*?
	13		They brought the man who had been *blind* to the Pharisees.
	17		[the Pharisees] spoke to the *blind man* again, 'What have you to say about him yourself, now that he has opened your eyes?'
	18		the Jews would not believe that the man had been *blind*
	19		Is this man really your son who you say was born *blind*? . . .
	20		[20] . . . We know he is our son and we know he was born *blind*,
	24		So the Jews again sent for the man who had been *blind*
	25		I was *blind* and now I can see.
	32		it is unheard of for anyone to open the eyes of a man who was born *blind*;
	39	M	I have come . . . so that . . . those with sight [may] turn *blind*.
	40	M	some Pharisees . . . said to him, 'We are not *blind*, surely?'
	41	M	[41] Jesus replied: '*Blind*? If you were, you would not be guilty,
	10 21		could a devil open the eyes of the *blind*?
	11 37		He opened the eyes of the *blind man*, could he not have prevented this man's death?
	12 40	M 2	(Is 6 10) [The Lord] has *blinded* their eyes . . . for fear they should see with their eyes
Ac	13 11		the hand of the Lord will strike you: you will be *blind*,
Rm	2 19	M	you are convinced you can guide the *blind* and be a beacon to those in the dark,
2 Co	4 4	M 2	the unbelievers whose minds the god of this world has *blinded*,
2 P	1 9	M	without [these virtues] a man is *blind* or else short-sighted;
1 Jn	2 11	M	the man who hates his brother . . . is in the darkness, not knowing where he is going, because ⌐it is too dark to see
	2		(lit. darkness has *blinded* his eyes).
Rv	3 17	M	you are wretchedly and pitiably poor, and *blind* and naked too.

DECAPOLIS

D (The) Decapolis 3	Gadarenes 1	1 polis 6/164
(= 'ten towns')	Gerasenes 3	

Mt	4 25	D	Large crowds followed him, coming from Galilee, *the Decapolis*,
	8 28		When he reached the country of the *Gadarenes* on the other side, two demoniacs came towards him
	33	1	The swineherds ran off and made for the *town*, where they told the whole story,
	34	1	At this the whole *town* set out to meet Jesus;
Mk	5 1		They reached the country of the *Gerasenes* on the other side of the lake
	14	1	The swineherds ran off and told their story in the *town* and in the country round about;
	20	D	So the man went off and proceeded to spread throughout *the Decapolis* all that Jesus had done for him.
	7 31	D	[Jesus] went . . . towards the Sea of Galilee, right through *the Decapolis* region.
Lk	8 26		They came to land in the country of the *Gerasenes*, which is opposite Galilee. [27] . . . a man from the *town* who was possessed by devils came towards [Jesus];
	27	1	
	34	1	the swineherds . . . told their story in the *town* and in the country round about; [37] The entire population of the *Gerasene* territory . . . asked Jesus to leave them.
	37		
	39	1	So the man went off and spread throughout the *town* all that Jesus had done for him.

DECEIVE – TRICK – PRETENCE

1. Deceive – Trick – Lure astray
1: Deceive, Mislead, Impostor – Mistake, Error, Wrong – Wander, Lead astray: *planaō*
2: Wiles – Devices, Tactics: *methodeia*
3: Deceive, Seduce – Lure, Mislead – Delusive, Illusory, Mistake: *apataō*

4: Seduce–Entice, Lure: *deleazō*
5: Deceiving in speech: *paralogizomai*
  a) Deceive, Mislead
  b) Double-talking
6: Trick – Deceit, Treachery – Fraud: *dolos*
7: Cunning, Crafty, Deceitful: *pan-ourgia*

8: **False, Insidious – Fabrication:** *plastos*
9: **Impostors – Charlatans:** *goēs*
10: **Tricks:** *kybeia*
2. **Lie – False:** *pseudomai*
   a) Lie, Liar – False, Pretence – So-called
   b) False, Counterfeit (prophet, Christ, Apostle, doctor)

c) False (witness), Lying (evidence) – Perjury
3. **Hypocrisy – Pretence, Appearrance**
   1: Hypocrite, Hypocrisy – Pose, Pretence, Insincerity: *hypokrisis*
   2: Pretence, Appearance, Show – Cloak, Cover: *pro-phasis*
4. **Make as if to:** *pros-poieomai*

1. DECEIVE – TRICK – LURE ASTRAY

1: DECEIVE, MISLEAD, IMPOSTOR – MISTAKE, ERROR, WRONG – WANDER, LEAD ASTRAY: *PLANAŌ*

1	*planaō*	39	3	*planos* 5
2	*planē*	10	4	*apo-planaō* 2
5	*planētēs*	1		

Mt 18 12 Suppose a man has a hundred sheep and one of them *strays*;
13 will he not . . . go in search of the *stray*? ¹³ . . . it gives him more joy than do the ninety-nine that did not *stray*
22 29 You *are wrong*, because you understand neither the scriptures nor the power of God.
24 4 Take care that no one *deceives* you; ⁵ because many will
5 come using my name . . . and they will *deceive* many.
11 Many false prophets will arise; they will *deceive* many,
24 false Christs and false prophets will . . . produce great signs . . , enough to *deceive* even the chosen,
27 63 X 3 this *impostor* said, while he was still alive, After three days I
64 shall rise again. ⁶⁴ Therefore give the order to have the sepulchre kept secure . . . for fear his disciples come and steal him away and tell the people, He has risen from the
2 dead. This last *piece of fraud* would be worse than what went before.
Mk 12 24 Is not the reason why you *go wrong*, that you understand neither the scriptures nor the power of God?
27 He is God, not of the dead, but of the living. You *are* very much *mistaken*.
13 5 Take care that no one *deceives* you. ⁶ Many will come using
6 my name . . . and they will *deceive* many,
22 false Christs and false prophets will . . . produce signs
4 . . . to *deceive* the elect, if that were possible.
Lk 21 8 Take care not to be *deceived*,
Jn 7 12 X Some said, he is a good man; others, No, he is *leading* the people *astray*.
47 'So' the Pharisees answered [the police] 'you have been *led astray* as well?
Rm 1 27 2 getting an appropriate reward for their *perversion*.
1 Co 6 9 ⌐You know perfectly well that (lit. *Make no mistake:*) people who do wrong will not inherit the kingdom of God.
15 33 You must stop *being led astray*: Bad friends ruin the noblest people.
2 Co 6 8 3 taken for *impostors* while we were genuine;
Ga 6 7 Don't *delude* yourself into thinking God can be cheated:
Ep 4 14 at the mercy of all the tricks men play and their cleverness in
2 practising *deceit*.
1 Th 2 3 2 We have not taken to preaching because we are *deluded*, or immoral,
2 Th 2 11 2 God is sending a power to *delude* them
1 Tm 4 1 some . . . will desert the faith and choose to listen to
3 *deceitful* spirits
6 10 there are some who, pursuing [the love of money] have
4 *wandered away* from the faith,
2 Tm 3 13 these wicked impostors will go from bad to worse, *deceiving* others and *deceived* themselves.
Tt 3 3 there was a time when we too were ignorant, disobedient and *misled*
Heb 3 10 (Ps 95 10) How *unreliable* these people
5 2 [the high priest] can sympathise with those who are ignorant or ⌐*uncertain* (or: *straying*)
11 38 ○ [Gideon . . . and the prophets] ⌐went out to live (lit. *wandered*) in deserts
Jm 1 16 *Make* no *mistake* about this, my dear brothers:
5 19 if one of you *strays* away from the truth, and another brings him back to it, ²⁰ he may be sure that anyone who can
20 2 bring back a sinner from the *wrong* way will be saving a soul
1 P 2 24 You had *gone astray* like sheep
2 P 2 15 They have left the right path and *wandered* off to follow the path of Balaam
18 they tempt back the ones who have only just escaped from
2 ⌐*paganism* (lit. *deception*)
3 17 2 be careful not to get carried away by the *errors* of unprincipled people,
1 Jn 1 8 If we say we have no sin in us, we *are deceiving* ourselves

1 Jn 2 26 This is all that I am writing to you about the people who are trying to *lead* you *astray*.
3 7 My children, do not let anyone *lead* you *astray*:
4 6 those who know God listen to us; . . . This is how we can
2 tell the spirit of truth from the spirit of *falsehood*.
2 Jn 7 3 There are many *deceivers* about in the world, refusing to admit that Jesus Christ has come . . . They are the
● 3 *Deceiver*; they are the Antichrist.
Jude 11 May [the wicked] get what they deserve . . . they have
2 rushed to make the same *mistake* as Balaam . . . ¹³ [They
13 5 are] like ⌐*shooting* (lit. *wandering*) stars
Rv 2 20 by her teaching [Jezebel] is *luring* my servants away to commit . . . adultery
12 9 Ⓓ the devil . . . had *deceived* all the world,
13 14 Through the miracles . . . [the second beast] was able to *win over* the people of the world
18 23 [Babylon,] all the nations were *under your spell*.
19 20 the false prophet . . . had *deceived* all who had been branded with the mark of the beast
20 3 Ⓓ [The angel] threw [the devil] into the Abyss . . . to make sure he would not *deceive* the nations again
8 Ⓓ [When the thousand years are over, Satan] will come out to *deceive* all the nations
10 Ⓓ the devil, who *misled* them, will be thrown into the lake of fire and sulphur,

2: WILES – DEVICES, TACTICS: *METH-ODEIA*

meth-odeia 2

Ep 4 14 Then we shall not be . . . at the mercy of all the tricks men play and their cleverness at ⌐*practising deceit* (lit. deceitful *wiles*).
6 11 Ⓓ Put God's armour on so as to resist the devil's *tactics*.

3: DECEIVE, SEDUCE – LURE, MISLEAD – DELUSIVE, ILLUSORY, MISTAKE: *APATAŌ*

3	*apataō* 3	4	(*phren-*)*apataō* 1
1	*apatē* 7	5	(*phren-*)*apatēs* 1
2	*ex-apataō* 6		

Mt 13 22 the worries of this world and the *lure* of riches choke the word
Mk 4 19 the worries of this world, the *lure* of riches . . . choke the word,
Rm 7 11 2 sin took advantage of the commandment to *mislead* me,
16 18 2 *confusing* the simple-minded with their pious and persuasive arguments.
1 Co 3 18 2 *Make* no *mistake* about it:
2 Co 11 3 Ⓓ 2 the serpent, with his cunning, *seduced* Eve,
Ga 6 3 4 It is the people who are not important who often *make* the *mistake* of thinking that they are.
Ep 4 22 your old self, which gets corrupted by following *illusory* desires.
5 6 3 Do not let anyone *deceive* you with empty arguments:
Col 2 8 Make sure that no one *traps* you . . . by some ⌐*secondhand* (lit. *delusive*), empty, rational philosophy
2 Th 2 3 2 Never let anyone *deceive* you in this way.
10 [when the Rebel comes there will be a show of portents] and everything evil that can *deceive* those who are bound for destruction
1 Tm 2 14 Ⓓ 3 it was not Adam who was *led astray* but the woman who was
2 *led astray* and fell into sin.
Tt 1 10 5 a great many people . . . *try to make others believe* [nonsense], particularly those of the Circumcision.
Heb 3 13 keep encouraging one another so that none of you is hardened by the *lure* of sin.
Jm 1 26 Nobody must imagine that he is religious while he still
3 goes on *deceiving* himself
2 P 2 13 [the wicked] amuse themselves *deceiving* you even when they are your guests at a meal.

4: SEDUCE – ENTICE, LURE: *DELEAZŌ*

deleazō 3

Jm 1 14 Everyone who is tempted is attracted and *seduced* by his own wrong desire.
2 P 2 14 [the wicked] will *seduce* any soul which is at all unstable.
18 [the wicked] tempt back the ones who have only just escaped from paganism, ⌐*playing on* (lit. *enticing*) their bodily desires

5: DECEIVING IN SPEECH: *PARA-LOGIZOMAI*

2 *di-logos* 1   1 *para-logizomai* 2

a) *Deceive, Mislead*

Col 2 4 to make sure that no one *deceives* you with specious arguments.

Jm 1 22   you must do what the word tells you, and not just listen to it and *deceive* yourselves.

b) Double-talking

1 Tm 3 8   deacons must be respectable men ⌐whose¬ word can be 2 trusted (lit. who do no *double-talking*),

6: TRICK – DECEIT, TREACHERY – FRAUD: *DOLOS*

2 *dolioō 1*	4	*doloō 1*	
3 *dolios 1*	1	*dolos 11*	
	5	*a-dolos 1*	

Mt 26 4   [the chief priests and elders] made plans to arrest Jesus by some *trick*

Mk 7 22   [from men's hearts emerge] avarice, malice, *deceit,*
14 1   the chief priests and the scribes were looking for a way to arrest Jesus by some *trick*

Jn 1 47   When Jesus saw Nathanael coming he said . . . 'There is an Israelite . . . incapable of *deceit.*

Ac 13 10   [Paul said to Elymas,] You utter *fraud,*

Rm 1 29   [pagans] are . . . addicted to . . . wrangling, *treachery* and spite.
3 13   2 (Ps 5 9) their tongues are full of *deceit.*

2 Co 4 2   we will have . . . no deceitfulness or ⌐watering down (lit. 4 *falsifying*) the word of God;
11 13   3 These people are . . . *dishonest* workmen disguised as apostles of Christ.
12 16   like the cunning fellow that I am, I took you in by a *trick.*

1 Th 2 3   We have not taken to preaching because we are . . . trying to *deceive* anyone;

1 P 2 1   Be sure, then, you are never spiteful, or *deceitful,*
2   like babies, you should be hungry for nothing but milk – 5 the spiritual ⌐honesty (or: *lack of deceitfulness*) which will help you to grow up
22 X   (Is 53 9) there had been no *perjury* in his mouth.
3 10   (Ps 34 14) Anyone who wants to have a happy life . . . must banish . . . *deceitful* conversation from his lips;

7: CUNNING, CRAFTY, DECEITFUL: *PAN-OURGIA*

1 *pan-ourgia 5*	2 *pan-ourgos 1*	

Lk 20 23   he was aware of their *cunning* and said,

1 Co 3 19   (Jb 5 13) The Lord knows wise men's thoughts: he ⌐knows how useless they are (lit. traps the wise in their own *cunning*).

2 Co 4 2   we will have . . . no *deceitfulness* or watering down the word of God;
11 3 Ⓓ   the serpent, with his *cunning,* seduced Eve,
12 16   2 like the *cunning* fellow that I am, I took you in by a trick.

Ep 4 14   at the mercy of all the tricks men play and their ⌐cleverness (or: *cunning*) in ⌐practising deceit (lit. deceitful wiles)

8: FALSE, INSIDIOUS – FABRICATION: *PLASTOS*

plastos 1

2 P 2 3   [false prophets] will eagerly try to buy you for themselves with *insidious* speeches,

9: IMPOSTORS – CHARLATANS: *GOĒS*

goēs 1

2 Tm 3 13   these wicked *impostors* will go from bad to worse

10: TRICKS: *KYBEIA*

kybeia 1

Ep 4 14   at the mercy of all the *tricks* men play and their cleverness in practising deceit

2. LIE – FALSE: *PSEUDOMAI*

6	*pseudēs*	*3*	13	*pseudo(-didaskalos)*	*1*	
1	*pseudomai*	*12*	14	*pseudo-logos*	*1*	
3	*pseudos*	*10*	5	*pseudo(-martyreō)*	*5*	
11	*pseusma*	*1*	9	*pseudo(-martyria)*	*2*	
4	*pseustēs*	*10*	10	*pseudo(-martys)*	*2*	
7	*pseud(-adelphos)*	*2*	15	*pseud(-ōnymos)*	*1*	
12	*pseud(-apo-stolos)*	*1*	2	*pseudo(-pro-phētes)*	*11*	
8	*pseudo(-christos)*	*2*	16	*a-pseudēs*	*1*	

a) Lie, Liar – False, Pretence – So-called

Mt 5 11   Happy are you when people . . . speak all kinds of *false* calumny against you on my account.

Jn 8 44 Ⓓ   The devil is your father, . . . there is no truth in him at all: 3 when he *lies* he is drawing on his own store, because he is 4 a *liar* and the father of lies.

Ac 5 3 55 X   4 if I were to say: I do not know [God], I should be a *liar,*
4   how can Satan have so possessed you that you should *lie* to the Holy Spirit . . .? [4] . . . It is not to men that you have *lied,* but to God.

Rm 1 25   3 [the pagans] have given up divine truth for a *lie,*
3 4   (Ps 116 11) God will always be true, even though everyone 4 proves to be *false,*
7   11 my *untruthfulness* makes God demonstrate his truthfulness
9 1   What I want to say now is no *pretence;* . . . it is the truth

2 Co 11 26   7 I have been in danger from . . . *so-called* brothers.
31   The God and Father of the Lord Jesus . . . . knows that I am not *lying.*

Ga 1 20   I swear before God that what I have just written is ⌐the literal truth (lit. by no means a *falsehood*).
2 4   7 some who ⌐do not really (lit. are only *pretending* to) belong to the brotherhood have furtively crept in to spy

Ep 4 25   3 there must be no more *lies:* You must speak the truth to one another,

Col 3 9   never tell each other *lies.*

2 Th 2 9   3 when the Rebel comes . . . there will be . . . a *deceptive show* of signs and portents,
11   3 God is sending a power to . . . make them believe *what is untrue*

1 Tm 1 10   4 [laws are] for *liars* and for perjurers
2 7   I am telling the truth and no *lie*
4 2   14 the cause of this is the *lies* told by hypocrites
6 20   15 Have nothing to do with . . . the knowledge *which is not* [knowledge] *at all;*

Tt 1 2 Θ   hope of the eternal life that was promised . . . by God. 16 He does *not lie*
12   4 Cretans were never anything but *liars,*

Heb 6 18 Θ   there would be two unalterable things in which it was impossible for God to be *lying,*

Jm 3 14   never . . . cover up the truth with *lies*
  we are *lying* because we are not living the truth.

1 Jn 1 6   4 To say that we have never sinned is to call God a *liar*
10 Θ
2 4   Anyone who says, I know him, and does not keep his 4 commandments, is a *liar,*
21   3 no *lie* can come from the truth.
22   The man who denies that Jesus is the Christ – he is the 4 *liar,*
27 X   3 the anointing he gave you teaches you everything; you are anointed with truth, not with a *lie,*
4 20   Anyone who says, I love God, and hates his brother is a 4 *liar,*
5 10 Θ   anyone who will not believe God is making God out to be 4 a *liar,*

Rv 3 9   those who profess to be Jews, but are *liars,*
14 5   3 (Is 53 9; Zp 3 13) They never allowed a *lie* to pass their lips
21 8   6 fortune-tellers, idolaters or any other sort of *liars,*
27   no one who does *what is* loathsome or *false,*
22 15   3 everyone of *false* speech and [false] life.

b) False, Counterfeit (prophet, Christ, Apostle, doctor)

Mt 7 15   2 Beware of *false* prophets
24 11   2 Many *false* prophets will arise;
24   8/2 *false* Christs and *false* prophets will arise

Mk 13 22   8/2 *false* Christs and *false* prophets will arise

Lk 6 26   2 This was the way their ancestors treated the *false* prophets.

Ac 13 7   2 [a Jewish magician called Bar-jesus.] This *false* prophet

2 Co 11 13   12 These people are *counterfeit* apostles, they are dishonest workmen

2 P 2 1   2 As there were *false* prophets in the past history of our people, 13 so you too will have your *false* teachers,

1 Jn 4 1   2 there are many *false* prophets, now, in the world.

Rv 2 2   you tested the impostors who called themselves apostles 6 and proved they were *liars,*
16 13   2 from the jaws of dragon and beast and *false* prophet I saw three foul spirits come;
19 20   2 the beast was taken prisoner, together with the *false* prophet
20 10   2 the lake of fire and sulphur, where the beast and the *false* prophet are,

c) False (witness), Lying (evidence) – Perjury

Mt 15 19   9 from the heart come evil intentions: murder . . . *perjury,* slander.
19 18   5 (Ex 20 16) You must not bring *false* witness.
26 59   The chief priests . . . were looking for evidence against Jesus, 9 however *false,*
60   10 several *lying* witnesses came forward,

Mk 10 19   5 (Ex 20 16) You must not bring *false* witness;
14 56   5 Several . . . brought *false* evidence against [Jesus], but their evidence was conflicting.

Mk 14 57   5 Some stood up and submitted this *false* evidence against [Jesus],
Lk 18 20   5 (Ex 20 16) You must not bring *false* witness;
Ac 6 13   6 [the elders and scribes] put up *false* witnesses
1 Co 15 15 10 we are shown up as witnesses who have committed *perjury* before God,

3. HYPOCRISY – PRETENCE, APPEARANCE

1: HYPOCRITE, HYPOCRISY – POSE, PRETENCE, INSINCERITY: *HYPO-KRISIS*

3 *hypo-krinomai* 1	1 *hypo-kritēs* 17
2 *hypo-krisis* 6	4 *syn-hypo-krinomai* 1

Mt 6 2   when you give alms, do not have it trumpeted before you; this is what the *hypocrites* do
     5   when you pray, do not imitate the *hypocrites*:
    16   When you fast do not put on a gloomy look as the *hypocrites* do:
    7 5   *Hypocrite*! Take the plank out of your own eye first,
   15 7   *Hypocrites*! It was you Isaiah meant when he so rightly prophesied:
   22 18   You *hypocrites*! Why do you set this trap for me?
   23 13   Alas for you, scribes and Pharisees, you *hypocrites*!
          Repeated in 23 15, 23, 25, 27, 29
    28   2 you appear to people from the outside like good honest men, but inside you are full of *hypocrisy* and lawlessness.
   24 51   The [servant's] master will . . . send him to the same fate as the *hypocrites*,
Mk 7 6   It was of you *hypocrites* that Isaiah so rightly prophesied
   12 15   2 Seeing through their *hypocrisy* he said to them, 'Why do you set this trap for me?
Lk 6 42   *Hypocrite*! Take the plank out of your own eye first,
   12 1   2 Be on your guard against the yeast of the Pharisees – that is, their *hypocrisy*.
    56   *Hypocrites*! You know how to interpret the face of the earth and the sky.
   13 15   *Hypocrites*! . . . Is there one of you who does not [water] his ox . . . on the sabbath . . . ?
   20 20   3 [the scribes and chief priests] sent agents to *pose* as men devoted to the Law,
Ga 2 13   4 The other Jews *joined* [Cephas] *in this pretence* and even
         2 Barnabas ˹felt himself obliged to *copy their behaviour* (or:
         2 got carried away with their *insincerity*).
1 Tm 4 2   [Some will desert the faith] and the cause of this is the lies
         2 told by *hypocrites*
1 P 2 1   2 Be sure, then, you are never spiteful . . . or *hypocritical*,

2: PRETENCE, APPEARANCE, SHOW – CLOAK, COVER: *PRO-PHASIS*

pro-phasis 5/6

Mk 12 40   [scribes] are the men who swallow the property of widows, while *making a show of* lengthy prayers.
Lk 20 47   [Beware of the scribes] who swallow the property of widows while *making a show of* lengthy prayers.
Ac 27 30   some of the crew . . . lowered the ship's boat into the sea ˹as though (or: *pretending*) to lay out anchors
Ph 1 18   Whether ˹from dishonest motives (lit. in *pretence*) or in sincerity, Christ is proclaimed;
1 Th 2 5   never at any time have our speeches been . . . a *cover* for trying to get money;

4. MAKE AS IF TO: *PROS-POIEOMAI*

pros-poieomai 1

Lk 24 28 X   he *made as if* to go on;

DEFILE – FILTH

1. Defile – Pollution
  1: Defile, Taint, Corrupt – Pollution: *miainō*
  2: Defile, Soil, Dirty – Pollute: *molynō*
  3: Pollution: *alisgēma*
2. Make unclean, Defile – Profane, Unclean: *koinos*
3. Unclean – Filth: *a-kathartos*
  a) Unclean (spirits)
  b) Unclean – Filth(y) Impurity – Offal, Refuse
4. Rubbish, Filth: *skybalon*

5. Filth(y), Dirt(y), Unclean – Impurity – Shabby: *rhypos*
6. Mud, Mire: *borboros*
7. Manure, Manure heap, Dung-hill: *kopria*
8. Sewer – Drain: *aph-edrōn*
9. Scum, Offscouring: *peri-psēma*
10. Stain, Speck, Spot – Contaminate: *spilos*
11. Blemish, Blot
  1: *spilas*
  2: *mōmos*
12. Wrinkle: *rhytis*

---

1. DEFILE – POLLUTION

1: DEFILE, TAINT, CORRUPT – POLLUTION: *MIAINŌ*

1 *miainō* 5	3 *miasmos* 1
2 *miasma* 1	

Jn 18 28   [The Jews] did not go into the Praetorium themselves or they would be *defiled* and unable to eat the passover.
Tt 1 15   to those who have been *corrupted* and lack faith, nothing can be pure – the *corruption* is both in their minds and in their consciences.
Heb 12 15   no root of bitterness should begin to grow . . ; this can ˹poison (lit. *taint*) a whole community.
2 P 2 10   3 those who are governed by their *corrupt* bodily desires
     20   2 anyone who has escaped the *pollution* of the world . . . by coming to know our Lord
Jude 8   in their delusions [the false teachers] not only *defile* their bodies . . . but abuse the glorious angels as well.

2: DEFILE, SOIL, DIRTY – POLLUTE: *MOLYNŌ*

1 *molynō* 3	2 *molysmos* 1

1 Co 8 7   some . . . eat this food as though it really had been sacrificed to the idol, and their conscience . . . is *defiled* by it.
2 Co 7 1   2 let us wash off all that can *soil* either body or spirit,
Rv 3 4   There are a few in Sardis . . . who have kept their robes from being *dirtied*,

3: POLLUTION: *ALISGĒMA*

alisgēma 1

Ac 15 20   a letter telling them merely to abstain from anything *polluted* by idols,

2. MAKE UNCLEAN, DEFILE – PROFANE, UNCLEAN: *KOINOS*

1 *koinoō* 14	2 *koinos* 10/14

Mt 15 11   What goes into the mouth does not *make* a man *unclean*; it is what comes out of the mouth that *makes* him *unclean*.
    18   the things that come out of the mouth come from the heart, and it is these that *make* a man *unclean*. [19] For from the heart come evil intentions; . . . [20] These are the things that *make* a man *unclean*. But to eat with unwashed hands does not *make* a man *unclean*.
Mk 7 2   2 some of his disciples were eating with *unclean* hands, that is, without washing them.
     5   2 Why do your disciples . . . eat their food with *unclean* hands?
    15   Nothing that goes into a man from outside can *make* him *unclean*; it is the things that come out of a man that *make* him *unclean*. . . . [18] . . . whatever goes into a man from outside cannot *make* him *unclean*, . . . [20] . . . It is what comes out of a man that *makes* him *unclean*. [21] For it is from within . . . that evil intentions emerge: . . . [23] All these evil things come from within and *make* a man *unclean*.
Ac 10 14   2 Peter answered, '. . . I have never yet eaten anything *profane* or unclean'.
    15   What God has made clean, you have no right to call *profane*.
    28   2 I must not call anyone *profane* or unclean.
   11 8   2 nothing *profane* or unclean has ever crossed my lips.
     9   What God has made clean, you have no right to call *profane*.
   21 28   [Paul] has *profaned* this Holy Place by bringing Greeks into the Temple.
Rm 14 14   2 no food is *unclean* in itself; however, if someone thinks that
        2/2 a particular food is *unclean*, then it is *unclean* for him.
Heb 9 13   The blood of goats and bulls and the ashes of a heifer are sprinkled on those who have incurred *defilement* and they restore the holiness of their outward lives;
   10 29   2 anyone who . . . treats the blood of the covenant . . . as if it were ˹not holy (lit. *unclean*), . . . will be condemned
Rv 21 27   2 Nothing *unclean* may come into [the new Jerusalem]: no one who does what is loathsome

3. UNCLEAN – FILTH: *A-KATHARTOS*

2 *a-katharsia* 10	3 *peri-katharma* 1
1 *a-kathartos* 31	

a) Unclean (spirits)

Mt 10 1   [Jesus] gave [his twelve disciples] authority over *unclean* spirits

Mt	12 43	When an *unclean* spirit goes out of a man it wanders
Mk	1 23	a man possessed by an *unclean* spirit,
	26	the *unclean* spirit threw the man into convulsions
	27	he gives orders even to *unclean* spirits and they obey him.
	3 11	the *unclean* spirits . . . would fall down before him and shout, 'You are the Son of God?'
	30	An *unclean* spirit is in [Jesus].
	5 2	a man with an *unclean* spirit came out from the tombs towards him.
	8	Come out of the man, *unclean* spirit!
	13	the *unclean* spirits came out and went into the pigs,
	6 7	he . . . began to send [the Twelve] out in pairs giving them authority over the *unclean* spirits.
	7 25	A woman whose little daughter had an *unclean* spirit heard about him
	9 25	he rebuked the *unclean* spirit. 'Deaf and dumb spirit, . . . I command you: come out of him'
Lk	4 33	a man who was possessed by the spirit of an *unclean* devil,
	36	He gives orders to *unclean* spirits . . . and they come out.
	6 18	People tormented by *unclean* spirits were also cured,
	8 29	Jesus had been telling the *unclean* spirits to come out
	9 42	Jesus rebuked the *unclean* spirit and cured the boy
	11 24	When an *unclean* spirit goes out of a man it wanders
Ac	5 16	People . . . [brought] with them their sick and those tormented by *unclean* spirits.
	8 7	*unclean* spirits . . . came shrieking out of many who were possessed,
Rv	16 13	from the jaws of dragon and beast . . . I saw three *foul* spirits come;
	18 2	Babylon . . . has become . . . a lodging for every *foul* spirit

b) Unclean – Filth(y), Impurity – Offal, Refuse

Mt	23 27	You who are like whitewashed tombs that look handsome on the outside but inside are full of . . . every kind of ⌐corruption (lit. *filth*).
Ac	10 14	I have never yet eaten anything profane or *unclean*.
	28	I must not call anyone profane or *unclean*.
	11 8	nothing profane or *unclean* has ever crossed my lips.
Rm	1 24	2 God left [the pagans] to their *filthy* enjoyments
	6 19	as once you put your bodies at the service of ⌐vice (lit. *impurity*).
1 Co	4 13	3 We are treated as the *offal* of the world,
	7 14	If this were not so, your children would be *unclean*, whereas in fact they are holy.
2 Co	6 17	(Is 52 11) Touch nothing that is *unclean*,
	12 21	2 those who . . . have still not repented of the *impurities* . . . they committed.
Ga	5 19	2 When self-indulgence is at work the results are obvious: fornication, ⌐gross indecency (lit. *filthiness*) and sexual irresponsibility;
Ep	4 19	2 they . . . eagerly pursue a career of ⌐indecency (lit. *impurity*) of every kind.
	5 3	Among you there must be not even a mention of fornication
	5	2 or *impurity* in any of its forms, . . . ⁵ For . . . nobody who actually indulges in fornication or *impurity*. . . can inherit anything of the kingdom of God.
Col	3 5	2 you must kill everything in you that belongs only to earthly life: fornication, *impurity*, guilty passion,
1 Th	2 3	2 We have not taken to preaching because we are deluded, or *immoral*,
	4 7	2 We have been called by God to be holy, not to be *immoral*;
Rv	17 4	a gold winecup filled with the disgusting *filth* of her fornication;
	18 2	Babylon has . . . become a lodging for every . . . *dirty*, loathsome bird.

4. RUBBISH, FILTH: *SKYBALON*

skybalon 1

Ph	3 8	I look on everything as so much *rubbish* if only I can have Christ

5. FILTH(Y), DIRT(Y), UNCLEAN – IMPURITY – SHABBY: *RHYPOS*

2 rhypainō 1   1 rhyparos 2
3 rhyparia 1   4 rhypos 1

Jm	1 21	3 do away with all the *impurities* and bad habits that are still left in you
	2 2	a poor man comes in, in *shabby* clothes,
1 P	3 21	4 baptism . . . is not the washing off of physical *dirt* but a pledge made to God from a good conscience,
Rv	22 11	/2 let the . . . *unclean* continue to be *unclean*;

6. MUD, MIRE: *BORBOROS*

borboros 1

2 P	2 22	When the sow has been washed, it wallows in the *mud*.

7. MANURE, MANURE HEAP, DUNG-HILL: *KOPRIA*

1 kopria 1   2 koprion 1

Lk	13 8 <	2 give me time to dig round [the fig tree] and *manure* it:
	14 35	[if the salt loses its taste] It is good for neither soil nor *manure heap*.

8. SEWER – DRAIN: *APH-EDRŌN*

aph-edrōn 2

Mt	15 17	whatever goes into the mouth . . . is discharged into the *sewer*?
Mk	7 19	it does not go into his heart but through his stomach and passes out into the *sewer*?

9. SCUM, OFFSCOURING: *PERI-PSĒMA*

peri-psēma 1

1 Co	4 13	We are treated as . . . the *scum* of the earth.

10. STAIN, SPECK, SPOT – CONTAMINATE: *SPILOS*

1 spiloō 2   2 spilos 2

Ep	5 27	2 so that when [Christ] took [the Church] to himself she would be glorious, with no *speck* or wrinkle
Jm	3 6	the tongue . . . *infects* the whole body;
2 P	2 13	2 They are ⌐unsightly (lit. *stains*) and blots on your society:
Jude	23	keeping your distance even from outside clothing which is *contaminated* by vice.

11. BLEMISH, BLOT

1: BLEMISH, BLOT: *SPILAS*

spilas 1

Jude	12	They are ⌐a dangerous obstacle to (or: *blemishes* on your) community meals,

2: BLEMISH, BLOT: *MŌMOS*

mōmos 1

2 P	2 13	They are ⌐unsightly (lit. stains and) *blots* on your society:

12. WRINKLE: *RHYTIS*

rhytis 1

Ep	5 27	so that when [Christ] took [the Church] to himself she would be glorious, with no speck or *wrinkle*

DESERT

1: Desert (of Sinai) – Wilderness (of the Exodus)	Desolate
2: Wilderness, Desert – Lonely (place),	3: Forsaken (woman) – Deserted (wife)

2 erēmia 4   1 erēmos 48

1: DESERT (OF SINAI) – WILDERNESS (OF THE EXODUS)

Jn	3 14	Moses lifted up the serpent in the *desert*,
	6 31	our fathers had manna to eat in the *desert*;
	49	Your fathers ate the manna in the *desert* and they are dead;
Ac	7 30	in the *wilderness* near Mount Sinai, an angel appeared to [Moses]

Ac 7 36   It was Moses who . . . led them . . . through the *wilderness*
    38   When they held the assembly in the *wilderness* it was only through Moses that our ancestors could communicate with the angel
    42   (Am 5 25) Did you bring me . . . sacrifices in the *wilderness* . . . ?
    44   While they were in the *desert* our ancestors possessed the Tent of Testimony
  13 18   for about forty years [God] took care of them in the *wilderness*.
1 Co 10 5   the corpses [of our fathers] littered the *desert*.
Heb 3 8   (Ps 95 8) the Day of Temptation in the *wilderness*,
    17   [the] dead bodies [of those who sinned] were left lying in the *wilderness*.

2: WILDERNESS, DESERT – LONELY (PLACE), DESOLATE

Mt 3 1   John the Baptist . . . preached in the *wilderness* of Judaea
   3   (Is 40 3) A voice cries in the *wilderness*: Prepare a way for the Lord,
  4 1   Jesus was led by the Spirit out into the *wilderness*
  11 7   What did you go out into the *wilderness* to see?
  14 13   Jesus . . . withdrew by boat to a *lonely* place
    15   This is a *lonely* place . . . so send the people away,
  15 33 2 Where could we get enough bread in this *deserted place* . . . ?
  23 38   Your house will be left to you ᵛ *desolate*,
  24 26   they say to you, 'Look, [the Christ] is in the *desert*,
Mk 1 3   (Is 40 3) A voice cries in the *wilderness*: Prepare a way for the Lord,
   4   John the Baptist appeared in the *wilderness*,
   12   the Spirit drove [Jesus] out into the *wilderness*
   13   [Jesus] remained in the *wilderness* for forty days,
   35   [Jesus] went off to a *lonely* place
   45   [Jesus] had to stay outside in places *where nobody lived*.
  6 31   You must come away to some *lonely* place all by yourselves
   32   they went off in a boat to a *lonely* place where they could be by themselves.
   35   This is a *lonely* place
  8 4 2 Where could anyone get bread . . . in a *deserted place* like this?
Lk 1 80   [John the Baptist] lived out in the *wilderness* until the day he appeared openly to Israel.
  3 2   the word of God came to John son of Zechariah, in the *wilderness*.
   4   (Is 40 3) A voice cries in the *wilderness*: Prepare a way for the Lord,
  4 1   Jesus . . . was led by the Spirit through the *wilderness*,
   42   [Jesus] made his way to a *lonely* place.
  5 16   [Jesus] would always go off to *some place where he could be alone*
  7 24   What did you go out into the *wilderness* to see?
  8 29   the devil would drive [the demoniac] out into the *wilds*.
  9 12   we are in a *lonely* place here.
  15 4   What man among you . . . would not leave the ninety-nine [sheep] in the *wilderness* and go after the missing one . . . ?
Jn 1 23   (Is 40 3) I am . . . a voice that cries in the *wilderness*:
  11 54   Jesus . . . left the district for a town called Ephraim, in the country bordering on the *desert*.
Ac 1 20   (Ps 69 26) Let his camp be ᵣreduced to ruin (lit. *desolate*), let there be no one to live in it.
  8 26   the road that goes from Jerusalem down to Gaza, the *desert* road.
  21 38   So you are not the Egyptian who . . . led those four thousand cut-throats out into the *desert*?
2 Co 11 26 2 [I have been] in danger in the towns, . . . in the *open country*,
Heb 11 38 2 [people] went out to live in *deserts* and mountains and in caves
Rv 12 6   the woman escaped into the *desert*,
   14   [the woman] was given a huge pair of eagle's wings to fly away from the serpent into the *desert*,
  17 3   [the angel] took me in spirit to a *desert*,

3: FORSAKEN (WOMAN) – DESERTED (WIFE)

Ga 4 27   (Is 54 1) there are more sons of the *forsaken* one than sons of the wedded wife.

DESIRE – LONGING

1. Desire: *epi-thymia*
  1: Covet, Evil desires – Lust, Passions
  2: Desire to – Long to, Long for
2. Long for (a person's presence) – Want to be with – Miss: *epi-potheō*

3. Feel devoted towards – Yearn (in love) for: *homeiromai*
4. Passion, Lust – Want to, Long for: *oregomai*
5. Passions: *pathos*
6. Wish – Pray for (a thing) – Hope: *euchomai*

1. DESIRE: *EPI-THYMIA*

  2 *epi-thymeō* 16   1 *epi-thymia* 38
  3 *epi-thymētēs* 1

1: COVET, EVIL DESIRES – LUST, PASSIONS

Mt 5 28 2 if a man looks at a woman *lustfully*, he has already committed adultery with her
Mk 4 19   the worries of this world, the lure of riches and all the other *passions* come in to choke the word,
Jn 8 44 ⓓ you prefer to do what your father *wants*.
Ac 20 33 2 I have never ᵣasked anyone for (lit. *coveted*) money or clothes;
Rm 1 24   God left them to ᵣtheir filthy enjoyments (lit. the *lusts* in their minds)
  6 12   you must not let sin reign . . . or command your obedience to bodily *passions*,
  7 7   I should not . . . have known what it means to *covet* if the
    2 Law had not said (Ex 20 17) You shall not *covet*.
   8   sin took advantage of [this commandment] to produce all kinds of *covetousness* in me,
  13 9 2 (Ex 20 17) you shall not *covet*,
   14   forget about satisfying your bodies with all their *cravings*.
1 Co 10 6   These things all happened as warnings for us, not to have the
   3/2 wicked *lusts* for forbidden things that they ᵣhad (lit. *lusted* for).
Ga 5 16   you will be in no danger of yielding to *self-indulgence*,
   17 2 *self-indulgence* is the opposite of the Spirit,
   24   You cannot belong to Christ Jesus unless you crucify all *self-indulgent* passions and *desires*.
Ep 2 3   We all were among them too in the past . . . ruled entirely by our own physical *desires*
  4 22   you must put aside your old self, which gets corrupted by following illusory *desires*.
Col 3 5   fornication, impurity . . . evil *desires* . . .⁶ all this . . . makes God angry.
1 Th 4 5   [use the body in a way that is holy,] not giving way to ᵣselfish (lit. passions of) *lust* like the pagans
1 Tm 6 9   they get trapped into all sorts of . . . dangerous ᵣambitions (or: *desires*)
2 Tm 2 22   Instead of giving in to your *impulses* . . . fasten your attention on holiness,
  3 6   [they are] silly women who . . . follow one *craze* after another
  4 3   people will . . . collect themselves a whole series of teachers according to their own *tastes*;
Tt 2 12   [God's grace] taught us . . . to give up . . . all our worldly *ambitions*;
  3 3   we too were . . . enslaved by different *passions* and luxuries;
Jm 1 14   Everyone who is tempted is attracted and seduced by his own wrong *desire*. ¹⁵ Then the *desire* conceives and gives birth to sin,
   15
  4 2 2 You *want* something and you haven't got it;
1 P 1 14   Do not behave in the way that you ᵣliked to (lit. *desired* to) before
  2 11   I urge you . . . to keep yourselves free from the selfish *passions*
  4 2   for the rest of his life on earth [the person who has had bodily suffering] is not ruled by human *passions* . . .³ You spent quite long enough in the past . . . behaving indecently, giving way to your *passions*,
   3
2 P 1 4   you will be able . . . to escape corruption in a world that is sunk in ᵣvice (lit. *lusts*).
  2 10   [the Lord can hold the wicked for their punishment until the day of Judgement,] especially those who are governed by their . . . bodily *desires*
   18   they tempt back the ones who have only just escaped from paganism, playing on their bodily *desires* with debaucheries.
  3 3   there are bound to be people who will be scornful, the kind who ᵣalways please themselves what they do (lit. indulge their own *desires*),
1 Jn 2 16   the ᵣsensual body (lit. *desires* of the flesh), the *lustful* eye, pride in possessions – could never come from the Father, but only from the world; ¹⁷ and the world, with all it *craves for*, is coming to an end;
   17
Jude 16   They are . . . grumblers governed only by their own *desires*,
   18   there are going to be people who sneer at religion and follow nothing but their own *desires* for wickedness.

2: DESIRE TO – LONG TO, LONG FOR

Mt 13 17 2 many prophets and holy men *longed* to see what you see,
Lk 15 16 2 he ᵣwould willingly have filled (lit. *longed* to fill) his belly with the husks
  16 21 2 [Lazarus] *longed* to fill himself with the scraps that fell from the rich man's table.
  17 22 2 you will *long* to see one of the days of the Son of Man
  22 15 X 2/ I have *longed* (§ with a great *longing*) to eat this passover with you

Ph	1 23	I *want* to be gone and be with Christ,
1 Th	2 17	we had an especially strong [desire and] *longing* to see you face to face again,
1 Tm	3 1	2 To *want* to be a presiding elder is to *want* to do a noble work.
Heb	6 11	2 Our one *desire* is that every one of you should go on showing the same earnestness to the end,
1 P	1 12	2 Even the angels *long* to catch a glimpse of these things.
Rv	9 6	2 men will *long for* death and not find it anywhere;
	18 14	All the fruits you had *set your hearts on* have failed you;

2. LONG FOR (A PERSON'S PRESENCE) – WANT TO BE WITH – MISS: *EPI-POTHEŌ*

1 epi-potheō 9   3 epi-pothētos 1
2 epi-pothēsis 2   4 epi-pothia 1

Rm	1 11	I am *longing* to see you
	15 23	4 for many years I have been *longing* to pay you a visit.
2 Co	5 2	we wait with *longing* to put on our heavenly home over the other;
	7 7	2 [Titus] has told us all about how you *want* to see me,
	11	Just look at what suffering in God's way has brought you: 2 what keenness, . . . what *aching* to see me, what concern for me,
	9 14	they are *drawn to* you on account of all the grace that God has given you.
Ph	1 8	God knows how much I *miss* you all,
	2 26	[Epaphroditus] *misses* you all,
	4 1	3 I *miss* you very much, dear friends; you are my joy and my crown.
1 Th	3 6	[Timothy was] telling us that you . . . *want* to see us quite as much as we want to see you.
2 Tm	1 4	[I] *long* to see you again to complete my happiness.
Jm	4 5 Δ	Surely you don't think scripture is wrong when it says: the spirit which he sent to live in us *wants* us for himself alone?
1 P	2 2	like babies, you should *be hungry for* nothing but milk – the spiritual honesty

3. FEEL DEVOTED TOWARDS – YEARN (IN LOVE) FOR: *HOMEIROMAI*

homeiromai 1

1 Th	2 8	we *felt so devoted* and protective *towards* you . . . that we were eager to hand over to you . . . our whole lives

4. PASSION, LUST – WANT TO, LONG FOR: *OREGOMAI*

1 oregomai 3   2 orexis 1

Rm	1 27	2 their menfolk . . . consumed with *passion* for each other,
1 Tm	3 1	To *want* to be a presiding elder is to want to do a noble work.
	6 10	'The love of money is the root of all evils' and there are some who, *pursuing* it, have wandered away from the faith,
Heb	11 16	they were *longing* for a better homeland, their heavenly homeland.

5. PASSIONS: *PATHOS*

2 pathēma 2/16   1 pathos 3

Rm	1 26	God has abandoned them to degrading *passions*:
	7 5	2 Before our conversion our sinful *passions*, quite unsubdued by the Law, fertilised our bodies
Ga	5 24	You cannot belong to Christ Jesus unless you crucify all 2 self-indulgent *passions* and desires.
Col	3 5	you must kill everything in you that belongs only to earthly life: fornication, impurity, guilty *passion*, evil desires
1 Th	4 5	[use the body in a way that is holy,] not giving way to ⌜selfish (lit. *passions* of) lust like the pagans

6. WISH – PRAY FOR (A THING) – HOPE: *EUCHOMAI*

euchomai 4/6

Ac	26 29	I *wish* before God that . . . you . . . would come to be as I am
	27 29	afraid that we might run aground . . . they . . . *prayed for* daylight.
Rm	9 3	I *would willingly* be condemned . . . if it could help my brothers
3 Jn	2	My dear friend [Gaius], I *hope* everything is going happily with you

DESPISE – DISREGARD

1. Despise, Scorn, Contempt – Disregard, Treat lightly
  1: Treat with scorn, Despise, Think the less of – Disregard, Have no respect for – Mocker: *kata-phroneō*
  2: Treat with contempt, Despised, Contemptible – Be scornful of, Reject: *ex-ou-th-eneō*
  3: Treat lightly, Disdain: *olig-ōreō*
2. Overlook(ed), Neglect(ed)
  1: *para-the-ōreō*
  2: *par-erchomai*

1. DESPISE, SCORN, CONTEMPT – DISREGARD, TREAT LIGHTLY

1: TREAT WITH SCORN, DESPISE, THINK THE LESS OF – DISREGARD, HAVE NO RESPECT FOR – MOCKER: *KATA-PHRONEŌ*

1 kata-phroneō 9   3 peri-phroneō 1
2 kata-phronētēs 1

Mt	6 24	No one can be the slave of two masters: . . . or [he will] *treat* the first with respect and the second *with scorn*.
	18 10	See that you never *despise* any of these little ones.
Lk	16 13	No servant can be the slave of two masters; . . . or [he will] *treat* the first with respect and the second *with scorn*.
Ac	13 41	2 (Hab 1 5 G) Cast your eyes around you, *mockers*; be amazed, and perish!
Rm	2 4	are you [who judge others] *abusing* [God's] abundant goodness, patience and toleration . . . ?
1 Co	11 22	Surely you ⌜have enough respect for the community of God not to (lit. will not *treat* the community of God *with scorn* and) make poor people embarrassed?
1 Tm	4 12	Do not let people *disregard* you because you are young,
	6 2	Slaves whose masters are believers are not to *think* any the *less of* them because they are brothers.
Tt	2 15	this is what you are to say . . ; you can do so with full 3 authority, and no one is to ⌜question (lit. *disregard*) it.
Heb	12 2 X	Jesus . . . endured the cross, *disregarding* the shamefulness of it,
2 P	2 10	those who are governed by their corrupt bodily desires and *have no respect for* authority.

2: TREAT WITH CONTEMPT, DESPISED, CONTEMPTIBLE – BE SCORNFUL OF, REJECT: *EX-OU-TH-ENEŌ*

1 ex-ou-th-eneō 11   2 ex-ou-d-eneō 1

Mk	9 12	how is it that the scriptures say about the Son of Man that 2 he is to suffer grievously and be *treated with contempt*?
Lk	18 9	[Jesus] spoke the following parable to some people who . . . *despised* everyone else.
	23 11	Herod . . . *treated* Jesus *with contempt* and made fun of him;
Ac	4 11	(Ps 118 22) This [Jesus] is the stone *rejected* by you the builders,
Rm	14 3	Meat-eaters must not *despise* the scrupulous.
	10	you should never pass judgement on a brother or *treat* him *with contempt*,
1 Co	1 28	those whom the world thinks common and *contemptible* are the ones that God has chosen
	6 4	the people you appointed to try [such cases] were *not* even *respected* in the Church.
	16 11	nobody is to *be scornful of* [Timothy].
2 Co	10 10	when [Paul] is with you you see . . . ⌜no preacher at all (lit a *contemptible* preacher).
Ga	4 14	you never showed the least sign of *being* ⌜revolted (lit. *scornful of*) or disgusted by my disease . . ; instead you welcomed me
1 Th	5 20	[Never] *treat* the gift of prophecy *with contempt*;

3: TREAT LIGHTLY, DISDAIN: *OLIG-ŌREŌ*

olig-ōreō 1

Heb	12 5	(Pr 3 11) My son, when the Lord corrects you, do not *treat* it *lightly*;

2. OVERLOOK(ED), NEGLECT(ED)

1: OVERLOOK(ED), NEGLECT(ED): *PARA-THE-ŌREŌ*

para-the-ōreō 1

Ac	6 1	the Hellenists made a complaint against the Hebrews: in the daily distribution their own widows were being *overlooked*.

2: OVERLOOK(ED), NEGLECT(ED): *PAR-ERCHOMAI*

par-erchomai 1/30

Lk 11 42   alas for you Pharisees! You who . . . *overlook* justice and the love of God!

DESTROY

1. Destroy, Break (up) – Abolish – Fall apart: *luō*
2. Destroy, Pull down – Demolish: *kath-aireō*
3. Destroy – Burn, Consume (by fire): *an-(h)aliskō*
4. Destroyed – Destructive: *erēmoō*
  a) Destroyed, Ruin(ed) – Desolate – Laid waste
  b) Disastrous – Creating Desolation
5. Destroy – Corrode, Disappear – Distort: *a-phanizō*
6. Rust – Corrosion
  1: *brōsis*
  2: *ios*
7. Rotted, Rotting: *sēpō*
8. Destroy – Corrupt, Incorruptible, Mortal – Perish, Imperishable, Immortal: *phtheirō*
9. Work for the destruction of – Harry: *lymainomai*
10. Try to destroy – Damage – Attack: *portheō*
11. Do away with, Break – Disregard – Thwart: *a-theteō*
12. Destroy – Use up, Come to an end, Fade – Do away with: *kat-argeō*
13. Destroy, Be destroyed – Perish, Ruin – Lose: *ap-ollymi*
  a) Perish, Die – Be destroyed – Get killed
  b) Destroy (a person), Do away with – Make an end of (a person)
  c) Ruin, Perdition, Destruction – (a thing) Destroys, Is destroyed
  d) Lose, Be lost (in all senses) – Waste
  e) the Destroyer
  f) Abaddon, Apollyon
14. Ruin – Upset: *ana-trepō*
15. Destruction – Ruin: *kata-strephō*
16. Lose, Loss – Ruin: *zēmia*
17. Lose, Be lost: *apo-bolē*
18. Razed – Broken down: *kata-skaptō*
19. Dash to the ground: *edaphizō*

1. DESTROY, BREAK (UP) – ABOLISH – FALL APART: *LUŌ*

2 *luō* 13/42   1   *kata-luō* 15/17
3 *a-kata-lytos*   1

Mt 5 17 X   Do not imagine that I have come to *abolish* the Law or the Prophets. I have come not to *abolish* but to complete them.
    19   2 the man who ⌐*infringes* (or: *breaks*) even one of the least of these commandments . . . will be considered the least
  24 2   not a single stone here will be left on another: everything will be *destroyed*.
  26 61 X   I have power to *destroy* the Temple of God and in three days built it up.
  27 40 X   So you would *destroy* the Temple and rebuild it in three days! Then save yourself!
Mk 13 2   Not a single stone will be left on another: everything will be *destroyed*.
  14 58 X   I am going to *destroy* this Temple made by human hands,
  15 29 X   Aha! So you would *destroy* the Temple and rebuild it in three days!
Lk 21 6   All these things you are staring at now . . . everything will be *destroyed*.
Jn 2 19   2 *Destroy* this sanctuary, and in three days I will raise it up.
  5 18 X   2 not content with *breaking* the sabbath, [Jesus] spoke of God as his own Father,
  7 23   2 so that the Law of Moses is not *broken*,
  10 35   2 scripture cannot be ⌐*rejected* (lit. *broken*).
Ac 5 38   If this enterprise, this movement of theirs, is of human origin it will *break up* of its own accord; [39] but if it does . . .
  39   come from God you will . . . be unable to *destroy* them
  6 14 X   Jesus the Nazarene is going to *destroy* this Place
  13 43   2 When the meeting *broke up* many Jews . . . joined Paul
  27 41   2 the stern began to *break up* with the pounding of the waves.
Rm 14 20   do not ⌐*wreck* (lit. *destroy*) God's work over a question of food.
2 Co 5 1   when the tent . . . is ⌐*folded up* (or: *destroyed*), there is a house built by God . . . in the heavens.
Ga 2 18   If I were to ⌐*return* to a position I had already abandoned (lit. rebuild something I had already *broken up*), I should be admitting I had done something wrong.
Ep 2 14 X   2 [Christ] has made the two into one and *broken down* the barrier which used to keep them apart,
Heb 7 16   3 [a priest who has become one] by the power of an *indestructible* life.
2 P 3 10   The Day of the Lord will come . . . the elements will catch fire and *fall apart*,
  11   2 everything is *coming to an end* like this,

2 P 3 12   2 the sky will ⌐*dissolve* (lit. be *destroyed*) in flames.
1 Jn 3 8 X   2 It was to ⌐*undo* (or: *abolish* all that the devil has done that the Son of God appeared.
Rv 5 2 X   2 Is there anyone worthy to open the scroll and *break* the seals of it?

2. DESTROY, PULL DOWN – DEMOLISH: *KATH-AIREŌ*

1 *kath-aireō* 4/9   2 *kath-airesis* 3

Lk 1 52   He has *pulled down* princes from their thrones and exalted the lowly.
  12 18   I will *pull down* my barns and build bigger ones,
Ac 13 19 ⊖   [the God of this people] had *destroyed* seven nations in Canaan,
2 Co 10 4   [our weapons] are strong enough, in God's cause, to *demolish*
    2/   fortresses. We *demolish* sophistries, [5] and . . . arrogance . . .
  8   2 the Lord gave [the authority] to me for building you up and not for *pulling* you *down*,
  13 10   2 the authority which the Lord gave me for building up and not for *destroying*.

3. DESTROY – BURN, CONSUME (BY FIRE): *AN-(H)ALISKŌ*

1 *an-(h)aliskō* 2   2 *kat-an-(h)aliskō* 1

Lk 9 54   (cf. 2 K 1 10) do you want us to call down fire from heaven to *burn* [the Samaritans] *up* (ᵛ as Elijah did)?
Ga 5 15   you had better watch or you will *destroy* the whole community.
Heb 12 29 ⊖   2 (Dt 4 24) For our God is a *consuming* fire.

4. DESTROYED – DESTRUCTIVE: *ERĒMOŌ*

1 *erēmoō* 5   2 *erēmōsis* 3

a) Destroyed, Ruin(ed) – Desolate – Laid waste

Mt 12 25   Every kingdom divided against itself is ⌐*heading for ruin* (or: *laid waste*);
Lk 11 17   Every kingdom divided against itself is ⌐*heading for ruin* (or: *laid waste*),
  21 20   2 Jerusalem . . . will soon *be laid desolate*,
Rv 17 16   the ten horns and the beast will turn against the prostitute, ⌐*strip off her clothes* and leave her (lit. leaving her *desolate* and) *naked*;
  18 17   your riches are all *destroyed* within a single hour.
  19   [Babylon], *ruined* within a single hour.

b) Disastrous – Creating Desolation

Mt 24 15   2 (Dn 9 27) So when you see the *disastrous* abomination,
Mk 13 14   2 (Dn 9 27) When you see the *disastrous* abomination

5. DESTROY – CORRODE, DISAPPEAR – DISTORT: *A-PHANIZŌ*

1 *a-phanizō* 5   2 *a-phanismos* 1

Mt 6 16   the hypocrites . . . ⌐*pull long* (lit. *distort* their) faces
  19   on earth . . . moths and woodworms *destroy* [the treasures]
  20   in heaven . . . neither moth nor woodworms *destroy* them
Ac 13 41   (Hab 1 5 G) mockers; be amazed, and ⌐*perish* (or: *disappear*)!
Heb 8 13   2 anything old only gets more antiquated until . . . it *disappears*.
Jm 4 14   you are no more than a mist that is here for a little while and then *disappears*.

6. RUST – CORROSION

1: RUST – CORROSION: *BRŌSIS*

brōsis 2/11

Mt 6 19   on earth . . . moths and ⌐*woodworms* (or: *rust*) destroy
  20   in heaven . . . neither moth nor ⌐*woodworms* (or: *rust*) destroy

2: RUST – CORROSION: *IOS*

1 *ios* 1/3   2 *kat-ioō* 1

Jm 5 3   2 All your gold and your silver are *corroding away*, and the same *corrosion* will be your own sentence,

7. ROTTED, ROTTING: *SĒPŌ*
sēpō 1

Jm 5 2		Your wealth is all *rotting*, your clothes are all eaten up by moths.

8. DESTROY – CORRUPT, INCORRUPTIBLE, MORTAL – PERISH, IMPERISHABLE, IMMORTAL: *PHTHEIRŌ*

5	*phthartos 6*	8	*a-phthoria 1*
1	*phtheirō 9*	9	*kata-phtheirō 1*
2	*phthora 9*	6	*dia-phtheirō 6*
3	*a-phtharsia 7*	7	*dia-phthora 6*
4	*a-phthartos 7*		

Lk 12 33 — in heaven . . . no thief can reach [the treasure] and no moth *destroy* it. `6`

Ac 2 27 X 7 (Ps 16 10) nor allow your holy one to experience *corruption*.
   31 X 7 [Christ's] body did not experience *corruption*.
   13 34 — The fact that God raised [Jesus] from the dead, never to return to *corruption*, is no more than what he had declared
   X 7
   35 . . . ³⁵ (Ps 16 10) You will not allow your holy one to experience *corruption*. ³⁶ . . . David . . . certainly experienced *corruption*. ³⁷ The one whom God has raised up, has not experienced *corruption*.
   36 X 7
   37 X 7
   X 7

Rm 1 23 Θ 4 [the pagans] exchanged the glory of the *immortal* God . . .
   5 for the image of *mortal* man,
   2 7 3 For those who sought renown and honour and *immortality* by always doing good there will be eternal life:
   8 21 — [creation retains the hope] of being freed . . . from its slavery
   2 to ʳ*decadence* (or: *corruption*),

1 Co 3 17 — If anybody should *destroy* the temple of God, God will *destroy* him,
   9 25 — All the fighters . . . go into strict training; they do this just
   5 to win a wreath that will ʳ*wither away* (lit. *perish*), but we
   4 do it for a wreath that will *never* ʳ*wither* (lit. *perish*).
   15 33 — Bad friends *ruin* the noblest people.
   42 — It is the same with the resurrection of the dead: the thing
   2/3 that is sown is *perishable* but what is raised is *imperishable*;
   50 — flesh and blood cannot inherit the kingdom of God: and
   2/3 the *perishable* cannot inherit ʳ*what lasts for ever* (or: the
   3 *imperishable*).
   52 4 the dead will be raised, *imperishable*, and we shall be changed
   53 5 as well, ⁵³ because our present *perishable* nature must put
   3 on *imperishability* and this *mortal* nature must put on
   5 *immortality*. ⁵⁴ When this *perishable* nature has put on
   54 3 *imperishability* . . . scripture will come true:

2 Co 4 16 6 though this outer man of ours may be *falling into decay*, the inner man is renewed day by day.
   7 2 — We have not injured anyone, or *ruined* anyone,
   11 3 — I am afraid that . . . your ideas may get *corrupted*
Ga 6 8 — if he sows in the field of self-indulgence he will get a harvest
   2 of *corruption* out of it;

Ep 4 22 — you must put aside your old self, which gets *corrupted* by following illusory desires.
   6 24 3 ʳMay grace and *eternal* life be with all who love our Lord Jesus Christ (or: May grace be with all who love our Lord
   3 Jesus Christ in *eternal* life).

Col 2 22 — these prohibitions are only concerned with things that
   2 *perish* by their very use –

1 Tm 1 17 Θ 4 To the eternal King, the *undying* . . . God, be honour and glory
   6 5 — unending disputes by people who ʳare neither rational nor
   6 (lit. have allowed their minds to be *corrupted* and are not) informed

2 Tm 1 10 — Christ Jesus . . . *abolished* death, and he has proclaimed life
   3 and *immortality* through the Good News;
   3 8 9 Men like this defy the truth . . . their minds are *corrupt* and their faith spurious.

Tt 2 7 8 be an example to them in your ʳ*sincerity* (or: *incorruptibility*) and earnestness

1 P 1 4 4 the promise of an inheritance that ʳ*can never be spoilt* (or:
   4 is *imperishable*) or soiled and never fade away,
   18 5 the ransom . . . was not paid in anything *corruptible*, neither in silver nor gold,
   23 5 your new birth was not from any *mortal* seed but from the
   4 *everlasting* word of the living and eternal God.
   3 4 4 all this should be inside, in a person's heart, *imperishable*: the ornament of a sweet and gentle disposition

2 P 1 4 2 you will be able to . . . escape *corruption* in a world that is sunk in vice.
   2 12 — these people who only insult anything that they do not understand are . . . simply animals born to be caught and
   /2 ʳ*killed* (lit. *destroyed*), and they will quite certainly *destroy*
   2 themselves by their own work of *destruction*,
   19 2 [false teachers] themselves are slaves . . . to *corruption*;
Jude 10 — the only things [false teachers] do understand . . . will turn out to ʳ*be fatal to* (or: *destroy*) them.

Rv 8 9 6 a third of all ships were *destroyed*.
   11 18 6/6 The time has come to *destroy* those who are *destroying* the earth.
   19 2 — the famous prostitute . . . *corrupted* the earth with her fornication;

9. WORK FOR THE DESTRUCTION OF – HARRY: *LYMAINOMAI*
lymainomai 1

Ac 8 3 — Saul then *worked for the* total *destruction of* the Church:

10. TRY TO DESTROY – DAMAGE – ATTACK: *PORTHEŌ*
portheō 3

Ac 9 21 — [Saul] *organised the attack* in Jerusalem *against* the people who invoke [Jesus's] name,
Ga 1 13 — how merciless I was in persecuting the Church of God, how much *damage* I did to it,
   23 — their one-time persecutor was now preaching the faith he had previously *tried to destroy*;

11. DO AWAY WITH, BREAK – DISREGARD – THWART: *A-THETEŌ*
1 *a-theteō 6/16*   2 *a-thetēsis 2*

Mk 7 9 — How ingeniously you ʳ*get round* (lit. *break*) the commandment of God in order to preserve your own tradition!
Lk 7 30 — the Pharisees and the lawyers had *thwarted* what God had in mind for them.
1 Co 1 19 Θ (Is 29 14) I shall *destroy* the wisdom of the wise and ʳ*bring to nothing* (or: *do away with*) all the learning of the learned.
Ga 2 21 — I cannot ʳ*bring myself to give up* (lit. *do away with*) God's gift:
   3 15 — If a will has been drawn up in due form, no one is allowed to *disregard* it or add to it.
1 Tm 5 12 — [young widows want to marry again] and then people condemn them for ʳ*being unfaithful to* (lit. *breaking*) their original promise.
Heb 7 18 2 The earlier commandment is thus *abolished*,
   9 26 X 2 [Christ] has made his appearance . . . to *do away with* sin
   10 28 — Anyone who ʳ*disregards* (or: *breaks*) the Law of Moses is ruthlessly put to death

12. DESTROY – USE UP, COME TO AN END, FADE – DO AWAY WITH: *KAT-ARGEŌ*
kat-argeō 23/27

Lk 13 7 — Cut [the fig tree] down: why should it be *taking up* the ground?
Rm 3 3 — Will their lack of fidelity ʳ*cancel* (or: *put an end to*) God's fidelity?
   31 — Do we mean that faith ʳ*makes the Law pointless* (lit. *does away with* the Law)?
   4 14 — If the world is only to be inherited by those who submit to the Law . . . the promise [is] ʳ*worth nothing* (lit. *destroyed*).
   6 6 — our former selves have been crucified with [Christ] to *destroy* this sinful body
1 Co 1 28 — God has chosen those who are nothing at all to ʳ*show up* Θ (lit. *do away with*) those who are everything.
   2 6 — a wisdom . . . of the masters of our age, which are *coming to their end*.
   6 13 — the stomach [is meant] for food . . . and God is going to Θ *do away with* both of them.
   13 8 — gifts of prophecy . . . ʳ*must fail* (lit. will *come to an end*) . . Θ and knowledge . . . ʳ*must fail* (lit. will *come to an end*).
   10 — once perfection comes, all imperfect things will *disappear*.
   15 24 X [Christ] hands over the kingdom to God the Father, having *done away with* every sovereignty, authority and power
   26 X . . . ²⁶ and the last of the enemies to be *destroyed* is death,
2 Co 3 7 — the Israelites could not bear looking at the face of Moses, though it was a brightness that ʳ*faded* (or: *came to an end*)
   11 — if what ʳ*was so temporary* (lit. could *come to an end*) had any splendour,
   13 — so that the Israelites would not notice the ending of what had to *fade*.
   14 X a veil never lifted, since ʳChrist alone can remove it (lit. it can only be *destroyed* by Christ).
Ga 3 17 X once God had expressed his will . . . no law . . . could cancel that and ʳ*make the promise meaningless* (lit. *do away with* the promise).
   5 11 — ʳwould there be (lit. wouldn't this *do away with*) any scandal of the cross?

Ep	2 14 X	[Christ] actually *destroying* in his own person the hostility
2 Th	2 8	the Rebel appears openly. The Lord will kill him . . .
	X	*annihilate* him with his glorious appearance at his coming.
2 Tm	1 10 X	[Christ Jesus] *abolished* death, and he has proclaimed life
Heb	2 14 X	by his death [Christ] could *take away all the power of* the devil, who had power over death,

13. DESTROY, BE DESTROYED – PERISH, RUIN – LOSE: *AP-OLLYMI*

4	*olethreuō*	1	2	*ap-ōleia*	18
5	*olethreutēs*	1	1	*ap-olluō,* *ap-ollymi,*	92
3	*olethros*	4	7	*ap-ollyōn*	1
6	*ex-olethreuō*	1	8	*syn-ap-ollymi*	1

S = Destroy(ed)//Save(d)

a) Perish, Die – Be destroyed – Get killed

Mt	8 25 S	Save us, Lord, we are ⌐going down (lit. *perishing*)!
	26 52	all who draw the sword will *die* by the sword.
Mk	4 38	Master, do you not care? We are ⌐going down (lit. *perishing*)!
Lk	8 24	Master! We are ⌐going down (lit. *perishing*)!
	11 51	Zechariah, who *was murdered* between the altar and the sanctuary.
	13 3	unless you repent you will all *perish* as [the Galileans] did [at the hands of Pilate].
	5	unless you repent you will all *perish* as they did.
	33	it would not be right for a prophet to *die* outside Jerusalem.
	15 17 <	and here am I *dying* of hunger!
Jn	3 16	so that everyone who believes in him may not ⌐be lost (lit. *perish*)
	10 28	[my sheep] will never ⌐be lost (lit. *perish*)
	11 50	it is better . . . than for the whole nation to *be destroyed*.
Ac	5 37	Judas the Galilean . . . *got killed* too,
Rm	2 12	Sinners who were not subject to the Law will *perish* all the same,
	9 22	God . . . patiently puts up with the people who make him angry, however much they deserve to *be destroyed*.
1 Co	10 9	some of [the Israelites] . . . *were killed* by snakes.
	10	some of them . . . *were killed* by the Destroyer.
	15 18	[if Christ has not been raised,] all who have died in Christ have *perished*.
2 Co	2 15 S	We are Christ's incense to God for those who are being saved and for those who are ⌐not (lit. to *be destroyed*);
	4 9	we have been persecuted, but never deserted; knocked down, but never *killed*;
Ph	1 28 S 2	the sure sign that [your enemies] will ⌐lose (or: *be destroyed*) and you will be saved.
Heb	10 39 2	You and I are not the sort of people who draw back, and ⌐are lost (or: *are destroyed*) by it;
	11 31 8	Rahab the prostitute . . . *was not killed* with the unbelievers.
2 P	3 6	the world of that time *was destroyed* by being flooded by water. ⁷ But . . . the present sky and earth are . . . being reserved until Judgement day so that all sinners may *be destroyed*.
	7 2	
Jude	11	[the false teachers] have rebelled just as Korah did – and ⌐share the same fate (lit. *perish* just as he did).

b) Destroy (a person), Do away with – Make an end of (a person)

X = Do away with, Destroy, Jesus

Mt	2 13 X	Herod intends to search for the child and *do away with* him.
	12 14	the Pharisees . . . began to plot against [Jesus], discussing how to *destroy* him.
	X	
	21 41 <	He will *bring those wretches to a wretched end*
	22 7 <	The king . . . *destroyed* those murderers
	27 20 X	the elders . . . had persuaded the crowd to demand . . . the *execution* of Jesus.
Mk	1 24	Have you come to *destroy* us?
	3 6 X	The Pharisees . . . began to plot . . . against [Jesus], discussing how to *destroy* him.
	9 22	[the spirit] has often thrown [the boy] into the fire and into the water, in order to *destroy* him.
	11 18 X	they tried to find some way of *doing away with* him;
	12 9 <	the owner of the vineyard . . . will come and *make an end of* the tenants
Lk	4 34	Have you come to *destroy* us?
	17 27	[in Noah's day] the Flood came and *destroyed* them all.
	29	God rained fire and brimstone from heaven and it *destroyed* them all.
	19 47 X	The chief priests and the scribes . . . tried to *do away with* him,
	20 16 <	the owner of the vineyard . . . will come and *make an end of* these tenants
Jn	10 10 S	The thief comes only to steal and kill and *destroy*.
Jm	4 12 S	he is the only judge and has the power to acquit or to ⌐*sentence* (lit. *destroy*).
Jude	5	the Lord . . . *destroyed* the men who did not trust him.

c) Ruin, Perdition, Destruction – (a thing) Destroys, Is Destroyed

Mt	7 13 2	the road that leads to *perdition* is wide
	10 28	fear him rather who can *destroy* both body and soul in hell.
Lk	6 9	is it against the law on the sabbath to . . . save life, or to *destroy* it?
	S	
	9 56	[Jesus] . . . rebuked [James and John], (ᵛ saying, 'The Son of Man did not come to *destroy* men's lives but to save them';)
	S	
Jn	6 27	Do not work for food *that cannot last*,
	17 12	not one is lost except the ⌐one who chose to be lost (or: son of *perdition*),
	2	
Ac	8 20 Δ 2	May your silver ⌐be lost (or: *be destroyed*) forever, and you with it,
Rm	14 15	You are certainly not free to eat what you like if that means the *downfall* of someone for whom Christ died.
1 Co	1 18 S	The language of the cross may be illogical to those who ⌐are not on the way to salvation (lit. *are on the way to ruin*),
	19	(Is 29 14) I shall *destroy* the wisdom of the wise
	5 5 S 3	so that his sensual body may *be destroyed*
	8 11	your knowledge could *become the ruin of* someone weak,
2 Co	4 3	the veil is on those who ⌐are not on the way to salvation (lit. *are on the way to ruin*);
Ph	3 19	[the enemies of Christ's cross] are destined ⌐to be lost (or: for *ruin*).
	S 2	
1 Th	5 3 3	It is when people are saying, How quiet and peaceful it is, that the *worst* suddenly happens,
2 Th	1 9 3	It will be their punishment ⌐to be lost (or: *be ruined*) eternally,
	2 3 2	It cannot happen until . . . the Rebel, the ⌐*Lost One* (or: Man of *Perdition*), has appeared.
	10 S	those who are *bound for destruction* because they would not grasp the love of truth
1 Tm	6 9 3	ambitions which eventually plunge them into *ruin* and *destruction*.
	2	
Heb	1 11	(Ps 102 26) all will *vanish*, though you remain,
Jm	1 11	what looked so beautiful now *disappears*. It is the same with the rich man:
1 P	1 7 2	your faith . . . is more precious than gold, which is *corruptible*
2 P	2 1	false teachers, who will insinuate their own *disruptive* views 2 . . . ⌐They will destroy themselves (lit. Their *destruction* will come upon them)
	2	for them . . . *Destruction* is not asleep.
	3 16	points that uneducated . . . people distort, . . . – ⌐a fatal thing for them to do (lit. bringing them to their own *ruin*).
	2	
Rv	17 8 2	The beast you have seen . . . is yet to come up from the Abyss, but only to go to his *destruction*. . . . ¹¹ The
	11 2	beast . . . is going to his *destruction*.

d) Lose, Be lost (in all senses) – Waste

Mt	5 29	it will do you less harm to *lose* one part of you
	30	it will do you less harm to *lose* one part of you
	9 17	the skins burst . . . and . . . are *lost*.
	10 6	go rather to the *lost* sheep of the House of Israel.
	39	Anyone who finds his life will *lose* it; anyone who *loses* his life for my sake will find it.
	42	If anyone gives . . . water to one of these little ones because he is a disciple, . . . he will . . . not *lose* his reward.
	15 24	I was sent only to the *lost* sheep of the House of Israel.
	16 25	anyone who wants to save his life will *lose* it; but anyone who *loses* his life for my sake will find it.
	18 11 S	(ᵛ For the Son of Man came to save the *lost*)
	14	it is never the will of your Father in heaven that one of these little ones should be *lost*.
	26 8 2	Why this *waste* [of ointment]?
Mk	2 22	the wine is *lost* and the skins too.
	8 35 S	anyone who wants to save his life will *lose* it; but anyone who *loses* his life for my sake . . . will save it.
	S	
	9 41	If anyone gives you . . . water . . . because you belong to Christ, . . . he will . . . not *lose* his reward.
	14 4 2	Why this *waste* of ointment?
Lk	5 37	and the skins will be *lost*.
	9 24 S	anyone who wants to save his life will *lose* it; but anyone who *loses* his life for my sake, that man will save it.
	S	
	25	What gain is it . . . for a man to have won the whole world and to have *lost* . . . his very self?
	15 4 <	What man . . . with a hundred sheep, *losing* one, would not . . . go after the *missing* one . . . ?
	<	
	6 <	I have found my sheep that was *lost*.
	8 <	what woman with ten drachmas would not, if she *lost* one, . . . search . . . ?
	9 <	I have found the drachma I *lost*.
	24 <	this son of mine was . . . *lost* and is found.
	32 <	your brother . . . was *lost* and is found.
	17 33	Anyone who tries to preserve his life will *lose* it; and anyone who *loses* it will keep it safe.
	19 10	the Son of Man has come to seek out and save what was *lost*.
	S	
	21 18	not a hair of your head will *be lost*.
Jn	3 16 S	so that everyone who believes in him may not ⌐be lost (or: perish).

Jn	6 12	Pick up the pieces left over, so that nothing gets *wasted*.
	39	the will of him who sent me is that I should *lose* nothing of all that he has given to me,
	10 28	[my sheep] will never ʳ*be lost* (or: perish)
	12 25	Anyone who loves his life *loses* it;
	17 12	I have watched over [those you gave me] and not one is
	/2	*lost* except the ʳone who chose to *be lost* (or: son of perdition),
	18 9	Not one of those you gave me have I *lost*.
Ac	3 23	(Lv 23 29) The man who does not listen to that prophet is
	6	to be *cut off* from the people.
	8 20 Δ	2 May your silver ʳ*be lost* (or: be destroyed) forever, and you with it,
	27 34	Not a hair of your heads will be *lost*.
Ph	1 28 S	2 This would be a sure sign that [your enemies] will ʳ*lose* (or: be destroyed) and you will be saved.
	3 19 S	2 [The enemies of the cross of Christ] are destined ʳ*to be lost* (or: for ruin).
2 Th	1 9	3 It will be their punishment to ʳ*be lost* (or: be ruined) eternally,
	2 3	2 It cannot happen until . . . the Rebel, the ʳ*Lost One* (or: Man of Perdition), has appeared.
Heb	10 39	You and I are not the sort of people who draw back, and
	2	ʳ*are lost* (or: are destroyed) by it;
2 P	3 9	The Lord . . . is being patient with you all, wanting nobody to *be lost*
2 Jn	8	Watch yourselves, or all our work will *be lost*
Rv	18 14	ʳgone (lit. *lost*) for ever . . . is your life of magnificence and ease.

e) the Destroyer

1 Co	10 10	5 some of [the Israelites] . . . were killed by the *Destroyer*.
Heb	11 28	4 to prevent the *Destroyer* from touching any of the first-born sons of Israel.

f) Abaddon, Apollyon

9 abbadōn 1

Rv	9 11	9 the angel of the Abyss, whose name in Hebrew is *Abaddon*,
	7	or *Apollyon* in Greek.

14. RUIN – UPSET: *ANA-TREPŌ*

ana-trepō 2/3

2 Tm	2 18	the men who have gone right away from the truth . . . ʳSome people's faith cannot stand up to them (lit. *upsetting* the faith of some people).
Tt	1 11	men of this kind *ruin* whole families,

15. DESTRUCTION – RUIN: *KATA-STREPHŌ*

2 kata-strephō 1/3   1 kata-strophē 2

Ac	15 16	(Am 9 11 G) I shall rebuild [the fallen House of David]
	2	from its *ruins*
2 Tm	2 14	wrangling about words: all that this ever achieves is the *destruction* of those who are listening.
2 P	2 6	The cities of Sodom and Gomorrah, these too [God] condemned and . . . *destroyed*

16. LOSE, LOSS – RUIN: *ZĒMIA*

2 zēmia 4   1 zemioō 6

Mt	16 26	What . . . will a man gain if he wins the whole world and *ruins* his life?
Mk	8 36	What gain . . . is it for a man to win the whole world and *ruin* his life?
Lk	9 25	What gain . . . is it for a man to have won the whole world and to have lost or *ruined* his very self?
Ac	27 10	2 we run the risk of *losing* not only . . . the ship but also our lives
	21	2 you would have spared yourselves all this damage and *loss*.
1 Co	3 15	if [a man's building] is burnt down, he will *be the loser*,
2 Co	7 9	you have ʳcome to no kind of harm from (lit. *lost* nothing through) us.
Ph	3 7	because of Christ, I have come to consider all of these advantages that I had as ʳ*disadvantages* (or: loss). 8 . . . I ʳbelieve
	8	2 nothing can happen that will outweigh the supreme advantage of knowing
	2	as *loss* because of) the supreme advantage of knowing
	2	Christ Jesus my Lord. For him I have accepted the *loss* of everything,

17. LOSS, BE LOST: *APO-BOLĒ*

apo-bolē 1/2

Ac	27 22	There will be no *loss* of life at all, only of the ship.

18. RAZED – BROKEN DOWN: *KATA-SKAPTŌ*

kata-skaptō 1

Rm	11 3	(1 K 19 10) Lord, they have killed your prophets and *broken down* your altars.

19. DASH TO THE GROUND: *EDAPHIZŌ*

edaphizō 1

Lk	19 44	[Jerusalem, your enemies] will *dash* you . . . *to the ground*;

DEVIL

1. Devils, Demons – Demoniac – Possessed: *daimōn*	3. Satan
2. Devil: *dia-bolos*	4. Beliar, Belial

1. DEVILS, DEMONS – DEMONIAC – POSSESSED: *DAIMŌN*

4 *daimōn*	1	3 *daimonion echō*	8
5 *daimoniōdēs*	1	2 *daimonizomai*	13
1 *daimonion*	54/63		

B = *Beelzebul* 7

Mt	4 24	2 the *possessed*, epileptics, the paralysed, were all brought to [Jesus],
	7 22	did we not . . . cast out *demons* in your name.
	8 16	2 they brought [Jesus] many who were *possessed by devils*. He cast out the spirits
	28	2 two *demoniacs* came towards [Jesus] out of the tombs
	31	4 the *devils* pleaded with Jesus, 'If you cast us out . . .'
	33	The swineherds . . . told the whole story, including what had
	2	happened to the *demoniacs*.
	9 32	2 a man was brought to [Jesus], a dumb *demoniac*. 33 And when
	33	the *devil* was cast out, the dumb man spoke
	34	It is through the prince of *devils* that he casts out *devils*.
	10 8	cleanse the lepers, cast out *devils*.
	25 B X	If they have called the master of the house *Beelzebul*,
	11 18	John came, neither eating nor drinking, and they say, 'He
	3	is *possessed*'.
	12 22	2 Then they brought to [Jesus] a blind and dumb *demoniac*;
	24	the Pharisees . . . said, 'The man casts out *devils* only through
	B	*Beelzebul*, the prince of *devils*'.
	27 B	And if it is through *Beelzebul* that I cast out *devils*,
	28	But if it is through the Spirit of God that I cast *devils* out, then know that the kingdom of God has overtaken you.
	15 22	2 Sir . . . My daughter is *tormented by a devil*.
	17 18	And when Jesus rebuked it the *devil* came out of the boy
Mk	1 32	they brought to [Jesus] all who were sick and those who were
	2	*possessed by devils*.
	34	[Jesus] also cast out many *devils*, but he would not allow [the *devils*] to speak;
	39	And [Jesus] went all through Galilee, preaching . . . and casting out *devils*.
	3 15	[Jesus appointed twelve] with power to cast out *devils*.
	22 B X	The scribes . . . were saying, '*Beelzebul* is in him' and, 'It is through the prince of *devils* that he casts *devils* out'.
	5 15	2 They . . . saw the *demoniac* sitting there . . . who had had
	16	the legion in him before . . . 16 And those who had witnessed it reported what had happened to the *demoniac*
	2	
	18	2 the man who had been *possessed* begged to be allowed to stay with [Jesus]
	6 13	[the Twelve] cast out many *devils*,
	7 26	Now the woman was a pagan . . . and she begged him to cast the *devil* out of her daughter.
	29	the *devil* has gone out of your daughter. 30 . . . she found the
	30	child lying on the bed and the *devil* gone.
	9 38	Master, we saw a man who is not one of us casting out *devils* in your name;
	16 9	Mary of Magdala from whom [Jesus] had cast out seven *devils*.

Mk 16 17 — believers: in my name they will cast out *devils*;

Lk 4 33 — there was a man who was possessed by the spirit of an unclean *devil*,

35 — But Jesus said sharply, 'Be quiet! Come out of him!' And the *devil*, throwing the man down . . . went out of him

41 — *Devils* too came out of many people,

7 33 3 — For John the Baptist comes . . . and you say, 'He is *possessed*'.

8 2 — Mary surnamed the Magdalene, from whom seven *demons* had gone out,

27 3 — a man from the town who was *possessed by devils* came towards [Jesus];

29 — the *devil* would drive him out into the wilds. 30 'What is your

30 — name?' Jesus asked. 'Legion' he said – because many *devils* had gone into him.

33 — The *devils* came out of the man and went into the pigs,

35 — the people . . . found the man from whom the *devils* had gone out

36 2 — Those who had witnessed it told them how *the man who had been possessed* came to be healed.

38 — The man from whom the *devils* had gone out asked to be allowed to stay with [Jesus]

9 1 — [Jesus] gave [the Twelve] power and authority over all *devils*

42 — the *devil* threw [the boy] to the ground in convulsions.

49 — we saw a man casting out *devils* in your name.

10 17 — Lord . . . even the *devils* submit to us when we use your name.

11 14 — [Jesus] was casting out a *devil* and it was dumb; but when the *devil* had gone out the dumb man spoke,

15 B — It is through *Beelzebul*, the prince of *devils*, that he casts out *devils* . . . 18 So too with Satan: if he is divided against himself, how can his kingdom stand? – Since you assert that it is through *Beelzebul* that I cast out *devils*.

19 B — Now if it is through *Beelzebul* that I cast out *devils*, through whom do your own experts cast them out?

20 — But if it is through the finger of God that I cast out *devils*,

13 32 — You may go and give that fox [Herod] this message: Learn that today and tomorrow I cast out *devils*

Jn 7 20 X 3 — The crowd replied, 'You are mad (lit. You are possessed of a *devil*)!

8 48 X 3 — you are a Samaritan and *possessed by a devil*? 49 Jesus

49 X 3 — answered: 'I am not *posssessed*; no, I honour my Father,

52 X 3 — Now we know for certain that you are *possessed*.

10 20 X 3 — Many said, 'He is *possessed*, he is raving.'

21 X 2 — Others said, 'These are not the words of a man *possessed by a devil*: could a *devil* open the eyes of the blind?'

1 Co 10 20 — the sacrifices that they offer they sacrifice to *demons* who are not God. I have no desire to see you in communion with *demons*.

21 — You cannot drink the cup of the Lord and the cup of *demons*. You cannot take your share at the table of the Lord and at the table of *demons*.

1 Tm 4 1 — there will be some who will desert the faith and choose to listen to deceitful spirits and doctrines that come from the *devils*;

Jm 2 19 — You believe in the one God . . . but the *demons* have the same belief, and they tremble with fear.

3 15 5 — principles of this kind are not the wisdom that comes down from above: they are only earthly, animal and *devilish*.

Rv 9 20 — But the rest of the human race . . . refused . . . to stop worshipping *devils*.

16 14 — [three foul spirits like frogs] were *demon* spirits, able to work miracles,

18 2 — Babylon . . . has become the haunt of *devils* and a lodging for every foul spirit

2. DEVIL: *DIA-BOLOS*

dia-bolos 36/39

J = 'Devil' applied to Judas

Mt 4 1 — Then Jesus was led . . . out into the wilderness to be tempted by the *devil*.

5 — The *devil* then took him to the holy city

8 — Next, taking him to a very high mountain, the *devil* showed him all the kingdoms of the world

11 — Then the *devil* left him,

13 39 — the enemy who sowed [the darnel], the *devil*;

25 41 — the eternal fire prepared for the *devil* and his angels.

Lk 4 2 — [Jesus] being tempted [in the wilderness] by the *devil*

3 — Then the *devil* said to him, 'If you are the Son of God . . .'

5 — the *devil* showed him . . . all the kingdoms of the world

6 — 6 and [the *devil*] said to him, 'I will give you all this power . . .'

13 — the *devil* left [Jesus], to return at the appointed time.

8 12 — and then the *devil* comes and carries away the word from their hearts

Jn 6 70 J — Yet one of you [Twelve] is a *devil*.

8 44 — The *devil* is your father . . . he is a liar, and the father of lies.

Jn 13 2 — the *devil* had already put it into the mind of Judas . . . to betray [Jesus],

Ac 10 38 — Jesus went about . . . curing all who had fallen into the power of the *devil*,

13 10 — [Paul said to the magician Elymas] you son of the *devil*,

Ep 4 27 — you will give the *devil* a foothold.

6 11 — Put God's armour on so as to be able to resist the *devil's* tactics.

1 Tm 3 6 — [the elder-in-charge] might be condemned as the *devil* was condemned.

7 — so that he never . . . falls into the *devil's* trap.

2 Tm 2 26 — once out of the trap where the *devil* caught them and kept them enslaved.

Heb 2 14 — [Christ] could take away all the power of the *devil*, who had power over death,

Jm 4 7 — resist the *devil*, and he will run away from you.

1 P 5 8 — your enemy the *devil* is prowling round like a roaring lion,

1 Jn 3 8 — to lead a sinful life is to belong to the *devil*, since the *devil* was a sinner from the beginning. It was to undo all that the *devil* has done that the Son of God appeared.

10 — In this way we distinguish the children of God from the children of the *devil*:

Jude 9 — the archangel Michael, when he was engaged in argument with the *devil*

Rv 2 10 — the *devil* is going to send some of you to prison to test you,

12 9 — The great dragon, the primeval serpent, known as the *devil* or Satan,

12 — the *devil* has gone down to you in a rage,

20 2 — the dragon, that primeval serpent which is the *devil* and Satan,

10 — Then the *devil*, who misled them, will be thrown into the lake of fire and sulphur,

3. SATAN

satanas 36

P = 'Satan' applied to Peter

Mt 4 10 — Then Jesus replied, 'Be off, *Satan*!'

12 26 — Now if *Satan* casts out *Satan*, he is divided against himself;

16 23 P — [Jesus] turned and said to Peter, 'Get behind me, *Satan*! You are an obstacle in my path,

Mk 1 13 — [Jesus] remained [in the wilderness] for forty days, and was tempted by *Satan*.

3 23 — How can *Satan* cast out *Satan*? . . . 26 Now if *Satan* . . . is divided, he cannot stand either – it is the end of him.

26

4 15 — *Satan* comes and carries away the word that was sown in them.

8 33 P — [Jesus] rebuked Peter and said to him, 'Get behind me, *Satan*!'

Lk 10 18 — [Jesus] said to [the 72], 'I watched *Satan* fall like lightning from heaven'.

11 18 — So too with *Satan*: if he is divided against himself, how can his kingdom stand?

13 16 — a daughter of Abraham who *Satan* has held bound these eighteen years

22 3 — Then *Satan* entered into Judas, surnamed Iscariot,

31 — Simon, Simon! *Satan*, you must know, has got his wish to sift you all

Jn 13 27 — after Judas had taken the bread, *Satan* entered him.

Ac 5 3 — Ananias . . . how can *Satan* have so possessed you

26 18 — so that [the pagans] may turn . . . from the domination of *Satan* to God,

Rm 16 20 — The God of peace will soon crush *Satan* beneath your feet.

1 Co 5 5 — [the man who is living with his father's wife] is to be handed over to *Satan* so that his sensual body may be destroyed

7 5 — then come together again in case *Satan* should take advantage of your weakness to tempt you.

2 Co 2 11 — And so we will not be outwitted by *Satan* – we know well enough what his intentions are.

11 14 — if *Satan* himself goes disguised as an angel of light,

12 7 — I was given a thorn in the flesh, an angel of *Satan* to beat me

1 Th 2 18 — and we tried hard to come and visit you . . . but *Satan* prevented us.

2 Th 2 9 — But when the Rebel comes, *Satan* will set to work: there will be all kinds of miracles and a deceptive show of signs

1 Tm 2 10 — [men who have wrecked their faith] like Hymenaeus and Alexander, whom I have handed over to *Satan*

5 15 — there are already some who have left us to follow *Satan*.

Rv 2 9 — the people who profess to be Jews but are really members of the synagogue of *Satan*.

13 — [Pergamum] the place where *Satan* is enthroned, and that you . . . did not disown your faith in me even when . . . Antipas, was killed in your own town, where *Satan* lives.

24 — the rest of you in Thyatira, all of you who have not . . . learnt the secrets of *Satan*,

3 9 — Now I am going to make the synagogue of *Satan* – those who profess to be Jews . . . fall at your feet

12 9 — The great dragon, the primeval serpent, known as the devil or *Satan* who had deceived all the world,

Rv 20	2		the dragon, that primeval serpent which is the devil and *Satan*,
	7		*Satan* will be released from his prison and will come out to deceive all the nations

4. BELIAR, BELIAL

beliar 1

2 Co 6 15   Christ is not the ally of *Beliar* (ᵛ *Belial*),

DIE – KILL

---

1. Die, Death, Dead

1: Die, Death, Be dead – Immortality: *thnēskō*
 a) Die, Death, Be dead – Mortal
 b) Immortality
 c) Half dead
2: Die, Death, Be dead: *teleutaō*
3: Die (to faults, to sin): *apo-ginomai*
4: (Jesus) Breathed his last, Died: *ek-pneō*
5: Died, Dead: *ek-psychō*
6: Dead, the Dead: *nekros*
 a) Dead, Dead men – Corpse
 b) Dead, the Dead (contrasted with Resurrection, the Living, Birth)
7: Be gone, Depart – Let go (to death): *ana-luō*

2. Kill – Put to death, Execute – Murder

1: Kill, Put to death – Murderer: *apo-kteinō*

2: Kill, Put to death, Execute – Dispose of, Do away with, Murder: *an-(h)aireō*
3: Execute, Kill, Do away with: *dia-cheirizomai*
4: Kill, Slaughter (an animal): *thuō*
5: Slaughter, Cut the throat (of): *sphazō*
 a) Cut the throat (of), Slaughter, Kill
 b) Victim Sacrificed, Sacrificial Slaughter – (Be) Slain
6: Cut-throats, Assassins: *sikarios*
7: People who kill, Murderers: *-loēs*
8: Murder, Murderer, Kill: *phoneuō*
9: Have (a person) put to death, Pass the death-sentence, Put an end to – Be put to death, Deadly: *thanatoō*
10: Behead(ed), Cut the head off: *apo-kephalizō*
11: Behead(ed): *pelekizō*

R = Dead, Death//Resurrection or in the context of Resurrection,
L = Dead, Death//Living, Life

1. DIE, DEATH, DEAD

1: DIE, DEATH, BE DEAD – IMMORTALITY: *THNĒSKŌ*

1	*thanatos* 120	2	*apo-thnēskō* 112
3	*thnēskō* 9	6	*syn-apo-thnēskō* 3
4	*thnētos* 6	7	*epi-thanatios* 1
5	*a-thanasia* 3	8	*hēmi-thanēs* 1

a) Die,ᵛ Death, Be dead – Mortal

P = Plague

Mt	2 20	3	those who wanted to kill the child *are dead*.
	4 16		(Is 9 1) those who dwell in the land and shadow of *death*
	8 32	2	the whole herd [of pigs] . . . *perished* in the water.
	9 24 R	2	the little girl *is not dead*, she is asleep.
	10 21		Brother will betray brother to *death*, and the father his child;
	15 4		(Ex 21 17) Anyone who curses father or mother must ʳbe put to (lit. die the) *death*.
	16 28		there are some . . . who will not taste *death* before they see the Son of Man
	20 18 X R		They will condemn [the Son of Man] to *death*
	22 24	2	(Dt 25 5) if a man *dies* childless,
	27 6 R	2	last of all the woman herself *died*.
	26 35	2	Even if I have to *die* with you, I will never disown you.
	38 X		My soul is sorrowful to the point of *death*.
	66 X		What is your opinion? They answered, 'He deserves to *die*.'
Mk	5 35	2	Your daughter *is dead*: why put the Master to any further trouble?
	39 R	2	The child *is not dead*, but asleep.
	7 10		(Ex 21 17) Anyone who curses father or mother must ʳbe put to (lit. die the) *death*.
	9 1		there are some . . . who will not taste *death* before they see the kingdom of God come with power.
	26		the boy lay there so like a corpse that most of [the people]
		2	said, 'He *is dead*'.

	10 33 X R		They will condemn [the Son of Man] to *death*
	12 19 R	2	if a man's brother *dies* leaving a wife but no child,
	20		there were seven brothers. The first married a wife and then
	21 R 2/2		*died* leaving no children. ²¹ The second . . . too *died*
	22		. . .; with the third it was the same . . . ²² Last of all
	R	2	the woman herself *died*.
	13 12		Brother will betray brother to *death*, and the father his child;
	14 31	6	If I have to *die with* you, I will never disown you.
	34 X		My soul is sorrowful to the point of *death*.
	64 X		they all gave their verdict: he deserved to *die*.
	15 44 X	3	Pilate, astonished that he should have *died* so soon, . .
	X	2	enquired if he *was already dead*.
Lk	1 79		(Is 9 1) those who live in darkness and the shadow of *death*,
	2 26		[Simeon] would not see *death* until he had set eyes on the Christ
	7 12 R	3	[at Nain] a *dead man* was being carried out for burial,
	8 42 R	2	[Jairus] had an only daughter . . . who was *dying*.
	49 R	3	Your daughter has *died*. Do not trouble the Master any further.
	52 R	2	she *is not dead*, but asleep. ⁵³ But they laughed at him, know-
	53 R	2	ing she *was dead*.
	9 27		there are some . . . who will not taste *death* before they see the kingdom of God.
	16 22	2	the poor man *died* and was carried away . . . to the bosom
		2	of Abraham. The rich man also *died* and was buried.
	20 28 R	2	(Dt 25 5) if a man's married brother *dies* childless,
	29		there were seven brothers. The first, having married a wife,
	31 R	2	*died* childless. ³⁰ The second ³¹ and then the third . . .
	32 R	2	. . . all seven . . . *died* leaving no children. ³² Finally
	R	2	the woman herself *died*.
	36 R	2	they can no longer *die*, for they are . . . children of the resurrection
	22 33		I would be ready to go to prison with you, and to *death*.
	23 15 X		the man has done nothing that deserves *death*,
			I have found no case against him that deserves *death*,
	24 20 X		our leaders handed him over to be sentenced to *death*,
Jn	4 47		[the court official] asked [Jesus] to come and cure his son
	49	2	as he was at the point of *death*, . . . ⁴⁹ . . come down before my child *dies*.
	5 24 L		whoever listens to my words . . . has passed from *death* to life.
	6 49	2	Your fathers ate the manna in the desert and they *are dead*;
	50 L	2	⁵⁰ but . . . a man may eat [this bread] and not *die*.
	58 L	2	This is . . . not like the bread our ancestors ate: they *are dead*,
	8 21	2	I am going away; . . . and you will *die* in your sin.
	24		You will *die* in your sins. Yes, if you do not believe that I
		2	am He, you will *die* in your sins.
	51 L		whoever keeps my word will never see *death*. ⁵² The Jews
	52 L	2	said, '. . . Abraham *is dead*, and the prophets . . . and yet you say, Whoever keeps my word will never know the
	53		taste of *death*. ⁵³ Are you greater than . . . Abraham,
		2/2	who *is dead*? The prophets *are dead* too.
	11 4		This sickness will end not in *death* but in God's glory,
	13		Jesus . . . referred to the *death* of Lazarus, but they thought
	14		that by rest he meant sleep, so ¹⁴ Jesus put it plainly,
		2	Lazarus *is dead*;
	16	2	Let us go too, and *die* with him.
	21	2	If you had been here, my brother would not have *died*,
	25		I am the resurrection. If anyone believes in me, even though
	26 R L 2		he *dies* he will live, ²⁶ and whoever lives and believes in
	L	2	me will never *die*.
	32	2	if you had been here, my brother would not have *died*.
	37	2	could he not have prevented this man's *death*?
	44	3	[Jesus cried, 'Lazarus, come out!'] The *dead man* came out.
	50 X	2	it is better for one man to *die* for the people, than for the
	51		whole nation to be destroyed. ⁵¹ . . . [Caiaphas] made
	X	2	this prophecy that Jesus was to *die* for the nation
	12 24	2	unless a wheat grain falls on the ground and *dies*, it remains
		2	only a single grain; but if it *dies*, it yields a rich harvest.
	33 X		By these words [Jesus] indicated the kind of *death* he would
	X	2	*die*.
	18 14 X	2	It is better for one man to *die* for the people.
	32		to fulfil the words Jesus had spoken indicating the way (lit.
	X /2		kind of *death*) he was going to *die*.
	19 7		We have a Law . . . and according to that Law he ought
	X	2	to *die*,
	33		When [the soldiers] came to Jesus, they found he was already
	X	3	*dead*,
	21 19		In these words [Jesus] indicated the kind of *death* by which Peter would give glory to God
	23		The rumour then went out among the brothers that this
		2	disciple [John] would not *die*. Yet Jesus had not said to
		2	Peter, 'He will not *die*,
Ac	2 24		You killed him, but God raised him to life, freeing him from
	X R		the pangs of ᵛ Hades (G *death*);
	7 4	2	after his father *died* God made [Abraham] leave Haran and come to this land
	9 37 R L 2		[Tabitha] got ill and *died*,

Ac 13 28 X   Though they found nothing to justify his *death*,

14 19   They stoned Paul and dragged him outside the town, thinking
     3   he was *dead*.

21 13   2 I am ready . . . to *die* in Jerusalem for the name of the
       Lord Jesus.

22   4   I even persecuted this Way to the *death*,

23 29   there was no charge [against Paul] deserving *death*

25 11   If I am guilty of committing any ᶠcapital crime (lit. crime
     /2   meriting *death*), I do not ask to be spared the *death* penalty.

19 X L 3 about a *dead man* called Jesus whom Paul alleged to be alive.

25   I am satisfied that [Paul] has ᶠcommitted no capital crime (lit.
       done nothing to deserve *death*),

26 31   This man is doing nothing that deserves *death*

28 18   they found me guilty of nothing involving the *death* penalty;

Rm 1 32   They know what God's verdict is: that those who behave like
       this deserve to *die*

5   6 X 2/2 Christ *died* for sinful men. ⁷ It is not easy to *die* even for a
     7   good man – though of course for someone really worthy,

8 X 2/2 a man might be prepared to *die* – ⁸ but . . . Christ *died* for
       us while we were still sinners.

10 X L   When we were reconciled to God by the *death* of his Son,

12   sin entered the world through one man, and through sin
       death, and thus *death* has spread through the whole human
       race

14   *death* reigned over all from Adam to Moses,

15   2 If it is certain that through one man's fall so many *died*,

17 L   If it is certain that *death* reigned over everyone

21 L   just as sin reigned wherever there was *death*,

6   2 L   2 We *are dead* to sin, so how can we continue to live in it?
     3   ³ . . . when we were baptised in Christ Jesus we were

4 X   baptised to his *death*; ⁴ . . . when we were baptised we
   X R L   joined him in *death*,

5   R   If in union with Christ we have imitated his *death*,

7   2 When a man *dies* . . . he has finished with sin. ⁸ But we

8 X L 2 believe that having *died* with Christ we shall return to life
     9   with him; ⁹ Christ . . . having been raised from the
   X R 2/   *dead* will never *die* again. *Death* has no power over him

10 XL 2/2 any more. ¹⁰ When he *died*, he *died*, once for all, to sin,

12   4 That is why you must not let sin reign in your *mortal* bodies

16   You cannot be slaves to sin that leads to *death* and at the
       same time slaves of obedience

21 L   that sort of behaviour ends in *death*.

23 L   the wage paid by sin is *death*;

7   2   [a woman's legal] obligations [to her husband] come to an

3 L   2 end if the husband *dies*. ³ So . . . after her husband is
     L   2 *dead* . . . she can marry someone else
     5   to make [our bodies] give birth to *death*.

6   2 now we are . . . freed by *death* from our imprisonment,

10 L   2 [sin came to life] and I *died*: the commandment was meant to
     L   lead me to life but it turned out to mean *death* for me,

13   Does that mean that something good ᶠkilled (lit. brought
       death to) me? Of course not. But sin . . . used that good
       thing to ᶠkill (lit. bring *death* to) me;

24   Who will rescue me from this body doomed to *death*?

8   2 the law of the spirit of life . . . has set you free from the law
     L   of sin and *death*.

6 L   It is *death* to limit oneself to what is unspiritual;

11   he who raised Jesus from the dead will give life to your own
     L   4 *mortal* bodies

13   If you do live in that [unspiritual] way, you are doomed to
     L   2 *die*;

34 X R 2 Christ Jesus not only *died* for us – he rose from the dead,

38 L   neither *death* nor life . . . ³⁹ . . . can ever come between us
       and the love of God

14   7   2 The life and *death* of each of us has its influence on others;
     8 L 2/2 ⁸ . . . if we *die*, we *die* for the Lord, so that alive or
       2/2 *dead* we belong to the Lord. ⁹ . . . Christ both *died* and came

9 X R 2 to life . . . so that he might be Lord both of the dead and
       of the living.

15   You are certainly not free to eat what you like if that means
     X 2 the downfall of someone for whom Christ *died*.

1 Co 3 22 L   the world, life and *death* . . . are all your servants;

4   9   God has put us apostles at the end of his parade, with the
     7   men *sentenced to death*;

8 11 X   2 someone weak, . . . for whom Christ *died*.

9 15   2 I would rather *die* than let anyone take away something . . .

11 26   every time you eat this bread . . . you are proclaiming [the
     X   Lord's] *death*,

15   3 X R 2 Christ *died* for our sins, in accordance with the scriptures;
   21 R   *Death* came through one man and . . the resurrection of the
   22 L   2 dead has come through one man. ²² Just as all men *die*
       in Adam, so all men will be brought to life in Christ.

26   the last of the enemies to be destroyed is *death*,

31   2 I ᶠface death (lit. *die*) every day,

32 R   (Is 22 13) If the dead are not raised, you say, Let us eat and
       drink today; tomorrow we shall be *dead*.

53   4 this *mortal* nature must put on immortality. ⁵⁴ When . . .

54   4 this *mortal* nature has put on immortality then the words of
       scripture will come true (Is 25 8): *Death* is swallowed up in
       victory. ⁵⁵ (Ho 13 14): *Death*, where is your victory?

1 Co 15 56   *Death*, where is your sting? ⁵⁶ Now the sting of *death* is sin,

2 Co 1   9   we were carrying our own *death* warrant with us,
     10   he saved us from *dying*,

2 16   for [those who are not being saved] the smell of *death* that
     L   leads to *death*,

3   7   if the administering of *death*, in the written letters engraved on
       stones, was accompanied by such a brightness . . . ⁸ how
       much greater will be the brightness that surrounds the
       administering of the Spirit!

4 11   we are consigned to our *death* every day, . . . so that in our
     4   *mortal* flesh the life of Jesus . . . may be openly shown.

12 L   ¹² So *death* is at work in us, but life in you.

5   4 L   4 to have what *must die* taken up into life.

14 X 2/2 if one man has *died* for all, then all men should *be dead*;

15 X L 2 ¹⁵ and the reason he *died* for all was so that living men
       should live no longer for themselves, but for him who
   X R 2 *died* and was raised to life for them.

6   9 L   2 [we are] said to be *dying* and here we are alive;

7   3 L   6 you are in our hearts – together we live or *together we die*.

10   to suffer as the world knows suffering brings *death*.

11 23   I have been . . . whipped . . . almost to *death*,

Ga 2 19 L   2 through the Law I *am dead* to the Law, so that now I can live
       for God.

21 X   2 if the Law can justify us, there is no point in the *death* of
       Christ,

Ph 1 20   My one hope . . . is that . . . I shall have the courage for
       Christ to be glorified in my body, whether by my life or
     L   by my *death*.

21 L   2 Life to me . . . is Christ, but then *death* would bring me some-
       thing more;

2   8 X   [Jesus] was humbler yet, even to accepting *death*, *death* on a
       cross.

27   [Epaphroditus] has been ill, and almost *died*, . . . ³⁰ It was

30   for Christ's work that he came so near to *dying*,

3 10   I want . . . to share [Christ's] sufferings by reproducing the

11 X R   pattern of his *death*. ¹¹ That is the way I can hope to take
       my place in the resurrection of the dead.

Col 1 22 X   [Jesus] has reconciled you, by his *death* and in that mortal
       body.

2 20 X L 2 If you have really *died* with Christ to the principles of this
       world,

3   3 L   2 you have *died*, and now the life you have is hidden with
       Christ in God.

1 Th 4 14 X R 2 Jesus *died* and rose again, and . . . it will be the same for
       those who have died in Jesus;

5 10 X L 2 [our Lord Jesus Christ] who *died* for us so that, alive or dead,
       we should still live united to him.

1 Tm 5   6 L   3 [The widow] who thinks only of pleasure *is already dead*
       while she is still alive:

2 Tm 1 10 L   our saviour Christ Jesus . . . abolished *death*,

2 11 X L 6 If we have *died with* him, then we shall live with him.

Heb 2   9   Jesus . . . is now crowned with glory . . . because he sub-
     X   mitted to *death*; . . . he had to experience *death* for all
       mankind.

14 X   so that by his *death* he could take away all the power of the
   15 ⑩   devil, who had power over *death*, ¹⁵ and set free all those
       who had been held in slavery all their lives by the fear of
     L   *death*.

5   7 X   the one who had the power to save [Christ] out of *death*,

7   8 L   2 in the one case it is ordinary *mortal* men . . . and in the other,
       someone . . . still alive.

23   there used to be a great number of those other priests, because
       death put an end to each one

9 15 X   his *death* took place to cancel the sins that infringed the earlier
       covenant.

16 X   the *death* of the testator must be established;

27   2 men only *die* once, and after that comes judgement,

10 28   Anyone who disregards the Law of Moses ᶠis ruthlessly put
       2 to death (lit. *dies* ruthlessly)

11   4   2 Abel offered God a . . . sacrifice . . . Though [he *is*] *dead*,
       he still speaks by faith.

5   because of his faith . . . Enoch was taken up and did not
       have to experience *death*:

13   2 All these *died* in faith,

21   2 By faith Jacob, [when he was] *dying*, blessed each of Joseph's
       sons.

37   They were stoned, or sawn in half, ᶠor beheaded (lit. they
       2 *died* by being killed with a sword);

Jm 1 15   when sin is fully grown, it . . . has a child, and the child is
       death.

5 20   anyone who can bring back a sinner from the wrong way . . .
       will be saving a soul from *death*

1 P 3 18 X L 2 Christ . . . *died* once for sins, (ᵛ suffering) for the guilty,

1 Jn 3 14 L   we have passed out of *death* and into life, . . . ¹⁵ If you
   15   refuse to love, you must remain *dead*;

5 16   If anybody sees his brother commit a sin that is not a *deadly*
       sin, he has only to pray, and God will give life to the sinner
       – not those who commit a *deadly* sin; for there is a sin

17   that is *death*, ... ¹⁷ Every kind of wrong-doing is sin, but
       not all sin is *deadly*.

Jude	12		[The wicked] are like . . . barren trees which are then uprooted in the winter and so are twice *dead*;
		2	
Rv	1	18	I was dead and now I am to live for ever . . . and I hold the keys of *death* and of the underworld.
	2	10 L	Even if you have to *die*, keep faithful, and I will give you the crown of life
		11	for those who prove victorious there is nothing to be afraid of in the second *death*.
		23	I will ⌐see that [Jezebel's] children die (lit. kill her children *dead*),
	3	2	2 revive what little you have left: it is *dying* fast.
	6	8 P	its rider was called ⌐Plague (lit. *Death*), and Hades followed at his heels. They were given authority . . . to kill by the sword, . . . by ⌐plague (lit. *death*)
		P	
		9	a third of all the living things in the sea ⌐were killed (lit. *died*),
		2	
		11	2 many people *died* from drinking [the bitter water].
	9	6	men will long for *death* and not find it anywhere; they will want to *die* and *death* will evade them.
		2/	
	12	11 L	even in the face of *death* they would not cling to life.
	13	3	one of [the beast's] ⌐heads seemed to have had ⌐a fatal wound (lit. its throat cut *fatally*) but . . . this *deadly* injury had healed
		12	the first beast, which had had the *fatal* wound
	14	13	2 Happy are ⌐those (lit. the dead) who *die* in the Lord!
	16	3	the sea . . . turned to blood, like the blood of a corpse, and every living creature in the sea *died*.
		2	
	18	8 P	plagues will fall on [Babylon]; ⌐disease (lit. *death*) and mourning and famine.
	20	6	the second *death* cannot affect them
		14	*Death* and Hades were emptied of the dead that were in them; . . . Then *Death* and Hades were thrown into the burning lake. This burning lake is the second *death*;
	21	4	there will be no more *death*, . . . The world of the past has gone.
		8	the legacy for cowards . . . is the second *death* in the burning lake of sulphur.

b) Immortality

1 Co	15	53	5 this mortal nature must put on *immortality*.
		54	5 when this mortal nature has put on *immortality*.
1 Tm	6	16 Θ	5 the Lord of lords, who alone ⌐is immortal (lit. has *immortality*),

c) Half dead

Lk	10	30	8 [the] brigands . . . made off, leaving [the man] *half dead*.

2: DIE, DEATH, BE DEAD: *TELEUTAŌ*

1 *teleutaō* 11   2 *teleutē* 1

Mt	2	15	2 [Joseph] stayed [in Egypt] until Herod *was dead*.
		19	After Herod's *death*, the angel of the Lord appeared in a dream to Joseph
	9	18 L	My daughter has just *died*,
	15	4	(Ex 21 17) Anyone who curses father or mother must ⌐be put to (lit. *die* the) death.
	22	25	the first [of seven brothers] married and then *died* without children,
Mk	7	10	(Ex 21 17) Anyone who curses father or mother must ⌐be put to (lit. *die* the) death.
	9	48	(Is 66 24) [thrown into hell] where their worm does not *die*
Lk	7	2	A centurion there had a servant . . . who was sick and near *death*.
Jn	11	39	Martha, the sister of [the man] who had *died*, said, 'Lord, by now he will smell;'
Ac	2	29	the patriarch David himself *is dead* and buried:
	7	15	Jacob went down into Egypt and . . . *died* there,
Heb	11	22	when he was ⌐about to die (lit. *dying*) Joseph recalled the Exodus of the Israelites

3: DIE (TO FAULTS, TO SIN): *APO-GINOMAI*

apo-ginomai 1

1 P	2	24 L	so that we might *die* to our faults and live for holiness;

4: (JESUS) BREATHED HIS LAST, DIED: *EK-PNEŌ*

ek-pneō 3

Mk	15	37 X	Jesus gave a loud cry and *breathed his last*.
		39 X	The centurion . . . had seen how he had *died*,
Lk	23	46 X	'Father, into your hands I commit my spirit.' With these words he *breathed his last*.

5: DIE, DEAD: *EK-PSYCHŌ*

2 *apo-psychō* 1   1 *ek-psychō* 3

Lk	21	26	2 men *dying* of fear
Ac	5	5	Ananias fell down *dead*.
		10	[Sapphira] dropped *dead* at [Peter's] feet.
	12	23	[Herod] was eaten away with worms and *died*.

6: DEAD, THE DEAD: *NEKROS*

2 *nekroō*   3   3 *nekrōsis* 2
1 *nekros* 53/130

For Rise, Raise from the Dead *see* RISE – RAISE – HIGH 1.3: *and* 2.3:

a) Dead, Dead men – Corpse

Mt	8	22	Follow me, and leave the *dead* to bury their *dead*.
	23	27	whitewashed tombs that inside . . . are full of *dead* [men's] bones
	28	4	The guards were so . . . frightened of [the angel], that they were like *dead* men.
Mk	9	26	the boy lay there so like a *corpse* that most of [the crowd] said, 'He is dead.'
Lk	9	60	Leave the *dead* to bury their *dead*; . . . go and spread the news of the kingdom
Ac	5	10	the young men . . . found [Sapphira] was *dead*,
	28	6	[the Maltese] were expecting [Paul] at any moment to . . . drop *dead*
Rm	7	8	when there is no Law, sin is *dead*.
Heb	6	1	the fundamental doctrines . . : the turning away from *dead* actions
	9	17	[a will] only becomes valid ⌐with that death (lit. when [the testator] is *dead*),
	11	12	there came from one man, . . . who was already [as good as] *dead* himself, more descendants than could be counted,
		2	
Jm	2	17	if good works do not go with it, [faith] is quite *dead*.
		26	A body ⌐dies (lit. is *dead*) when it is separated from the spirit, and . . . faith is [dead] if it is separated from good deeds.
Rv	1	17	When I saw [the Son of man], I fell in a *dead* faint at his feet,
	11	18	the time has come . . . for the *dead* to be judged,
	14	13	Happy are ⌐those (lit. the *dead*) who die in the Lord!
	16	3	the sea . . . turned to blood, like the blood of a *corpse*,

b) Dead, the Dead (contrasted with Resurrection, the Living, Birth)

Mt	22	32	God is God, not of the *dead*, but of the living.
Mk	12	27	He is God, not of the *dead*, but of the living.
Lk	15	24 <	this son of mine was *dead*, and has come back to life;
		32 <	your brother here was *dead*, and has come to life;
	16	30 <	if someone comes to them from the *dead*, they will repent.
	20	38	he is God, not of the *dead*, but of the living;
	24	5	Why look among the *dead* for someone who is alive?
Jn	5	25	the *dead* will hear the voice of the Son of God, and . . . live.
Ac	10	42	God has appointed [Jesus] to judge everyone, alive or *dead*.
	20	9	[Eutychus] was picked up *dead*.
Rm	4	17	God . . . who brings the *dead* to life and calls into being what does not exist.
		19	Even the thought that his body was ⌐past fatherhood (lit. [as good as] *dead*) . . . and ⌐Sarah too old to become a mother (lit. Sarah's womb *dead* too), did not shake [Abraham's] belief.
		2	
		3	
	6	11	consider yourselves to be *dead* to sin but alive for God
		13	consider yourselves *dead* men brought back to life;
	8	10	Though your body may be *dead* . . , if Christ is in you then your spirit is life itself
	10	7	[Do not tell yourself] you have to bring Christ back from the *dead*
	11	15	do you know what [the Jews'] admission will mean? Nothing less than ⌐a resurrection (lit. *life*) from the *dead*!
	14	9	Christ both died and came to life . . . so that he might be Lord both of the *dead* and of the living.
2 Co	4	10 X	3 we carry . . . in our body the *death* of Jesus,
Ep	2	1	you were *dead*, through . . . the sins [in which you used to live]
		5	when we were *dead* through our sins, he brought us to life
Col	1	18 X	[Christ] was first to be born from the *dead*,
	2	13	You were *dead* . . : he has brought you to life with him,
	3	5	[you have died, and now the life you have is hidden with Christ in God.] That is why you must ⌐kill (lit. *make* [as good as] *dead*) everything in you that belongs only to earthly life: . . . especially greed, which is the same thing as worshipping a false god;
		2	
2 Tm	4	1	Christ Jesus, who is to be judge of the living and the *dead*,
Heb	9	14	the blood of Christ . . . can purify our inner self from *dead* actions
	13	20	the God of peace, who brought our Lord Jesus back from the *dead*
		X	
1 P	4	5	the judge who is ready to judge the living and the *dead*.
		6	the *dead* had to be told the Good News as well,
Rv	1	5 X	Jesus Christ, . . . the First-born from the *dead*,
		18 X	I was *dead* and now I am to live for ever and ever, and I hold the keys of death and of the underworld.

Rv	2	8	say, "Here is the message of the First and the Last, who was
		X	*dead* and has come to life again:
	3	1	you are reputed to be alive and yet are *dead*.
	20	12	I saw the *dead*, both great and small, standing in front of
		13	his throne, . . and . . . the *dead* were judged. ¹³ The
			sea gave up all the *dead* who were in it; Death and Hades
			were emptied of the *dead* that were in them;

7: BE GONE, DEPART – LET GO (TO DEATH): *ANA-LUŌ*

1 *ana-luō* 1/2   3 *apo-luō* 1/67
2 *ana-lysis* 1

Lk	2	29	3 you can *let* your servant *go* in peace,
Ph	1	23	I want to be *gone* and be with Christ,
2 Tm	4	6	2 the time has come for me to *be gone*.

2. KILL – PUT TO DEATH, EXECUTE – MURDER

X = Kill, Murder, Jesus – Put Jesus to death

1: KILL, PUT TO DEATH – MURDERER: *APO-KTEINŌ*

2 (*anthrōpo-*)*ktonos* 3   1 *apo-kteinō* 74

Mt	10	28	Do not be afraid of those who *kill* the body but cannot *kill*
			the soul: fear him rather who can destroy both body and
			soul in hell.
	14	5	[Herod] had wanted to *kill* [John]
	16	21 X R	he was destined . . . to be *put to death* and to be raised up on
			the third day.
	17	23 X R	they will *put* [the Son of Man] *to death*, and on the third day
			he will be raised again.
	12	35	the tenants [of the vineyard] seized [the owner's] servants,
		<	thrashed one, *killed* another and stoned a third.
		38 <	'This is the heir. Come on, let us *kill* him and take over his
		39 <	inheritance.' ³⁹ So they . . . *killed* him.
	22	6	[those invited to the wedding] seized [the king's] servants
		<	. . . and *killed* them.
	23	34	I am sending you prophets . . : some you will *slaughter* and
			crucify,
		37	Jerusalem, you that *kill* the prophets and stone those who are
			sent to you!
	24	9	they will hand you over to be tortured and *put to death*;
	26	4	[the chief priests] made plans to arrest Jesus by some trick
		X	and have him *put to death*.
Mk	3	4	Is it against the law on the sabbath day to . . . save life, or to
			kill?
	6	19	Herodias . . . was furious with [John] and wanted to *kill* him;
	8	31 X R	the Son of Man was destined to . . . be *put to death*, and
			after three days to rise again;
	9	31 X R	they will *put* [the Son of Man] *to death*; and three days after
			he has been *put to death* he will rise again.
	10	34 X R	[pagans] will . . . *put* him *to death*; and after three days he
			will rise again.
	12	5 <	[the owner of the vineyard] sent another [servant] and him
			[the tenants] *killed*; then a number of others, and they
			thrashed some and *killed* the rest. ⁶ . . . He sent his son
		7	. . . last of all. . . . ⁷ . . . [They] said to each other, 'This
			is the heir. Come on, let us *kill* him, and the inheritance will
		8 <	be ours.' ⁸ So they seized him and *killed* him
	14	1 X	a way to arrest Jesus by some trick and have him *put to death*.
Lk	9	22 X	The Son of Man . . . is destined to . . . be *put to death*,
			and to be raised up on the third day.
	11	47	Alas for you who build the tombs of the prophets, the men
		48	your ancestors *killed*! ⁴⁸ . . . they *did the killing*, you do
		49	the building. ⁴⁹ . . . I will send them prophets and apostles;
			some they will *slaughter*
	12	4	Do not be afraid of those who *kill* the body . . . ⁵ . . . fear
		5	him who, after he has *killed*, has the power to cast into hell.
	13	4	those eighteen [people] on whom the tower at Siloam fell and
			killed them?
		31	'Go away' [some Pharisees] said. 'Leave this place, because
		X	Herod means to *kill* you.'
		34	Jerusalem, you that *kill* the prophets
	18	33 X R	they will *put* [the Son of Man] *to death*; and on the third day
			he will rise again.
	20	14 <	'This is the heir,' [the tenants] said, 'let us *kill* him so that the
		15 <	inheritance will be ours.' ¹⁵ So they threw him out of the
		<	vineyard and *killed* him.
Jn	5	18 X	that only made the Jews even more intent on *killing* him,
			because . . . he spoke of God as his own Father,
	7	1	he ᵛ could (G would) not stay in Judaea, because the Jews
		X	were out to *kill* him.
		19 X	'Why do you want to *kill* me?' ²⁰ The crowd replied, 'You
		20 X	are mad! Who wants to *kill* you?'

Jn	7	25	some of the people of Jerusalem were saying, 'Isn't this the
		X	man they want to *kill*?'
	8	22 X	Will he *kill* himself? Is that what he means by saying, Where
			I am going, you cannot come?
		37 X	in spite of that you want to *kill* me
		40 X	you want to *kill* me
		44 Ⓓ	2 The devil . . . was a *murderer* from the start;
	11	53 X	they were determined to *kill* him.
	12	10	The chief priests decided to *kill* Lazarus as well,
	16	2	the hour is coming when anyone who *kills* you will think
			he is doing a holy duty for God.
	18	31 X	We are not allowed to *put* a man *to death*.
Ac	3	15 X L R	while you *killed* the prince of life.
	7	52	[your ancestors] *killed* those who foretold the coming of the
			Just One,
	21	31	[The crowd] would have *killed* [Paul]
	23	12	the Jews . . . made a vow not to eat or drink until they had
			killed Paul.
		14	We have made a solemn vow to let nothing pass our lips
			until we have *killed* Paul.
	27	42	The soldiers planned to *kill* the prisoners
Rm	7	11	sin, through that commandment, *killed* me.
	11	3	(1 K 19 10) Lord, they have *killed* your prophets
2 Co	3	6 L	the written letters *bring death*, but the Spirit gives life.
Ep	2	16	In his own person Christ *killed* the hostility [between Jew
			and pagan].
1 Th	2	15 X	[the Jews] *put* the Lord Jesus *to death*, and the prophets too.
1 Jn	3	15	2/2 to hate your brother is to be a *murderer*, and *murderers* . . .
			do not have eternal life in them.
Rv	2	13	my faithful witness, Antipas, was *killed* in your town,
		23 .	I will ʳsee that [Jezebel's] children die (lit. *kill* her children
			dead),
	6	8	[Plague and Hades] were given authority . . . to *kill* by the
			sword,
		11	until . . . their fellow servants . . . had been *killed* just as
			they had been.
	9	5	[The locusts] were not to *kill* them, but to give them pain
		15	These four angels . . . were released to *destroy* a third of
			the human race.
		18	It was by these three plagues . . . that the one third of the
			human race was *killed*.
		20	the rest of the human race, who ʳescaped (lit. had not been
			killed by) these plagues,
	11	5	if anyone does try to harm them he will certainly be *killed*
			in this way,
		7	the beast . . . is going to make war on them and . . . *kill*
			them.
		13	seven thousand persons were *killed* in the earthquake,
	13	10	being *killed* by the sword for those who ʳare to be *killed* (G
			kill) by the sword.
		15	the statue of the beast was able . . . to have anyone who
			refused to worship the statue of the beast *put to death*.
	19	21	All the rest were *killed* by the sword of the rider,

2: KILL, PUT TO DEATH, EXECUTE – DISPOSE OF, DO AWAY WITH, MURDER: *AN-(H)AIREŌ*

1 *an-(h)aireō* 22/24   2 *an-(h)airesis* 1

Mt	2	16	[Herod] had all the male children *killed*
Lk	22	2 X	the chief priests . . . were looking for some way of *doing*
			away with [Jesus],
	23	32	with [Jesus] they were also leading out two other criminals to
			be *executed*.
Ac	2	23 X	you . . . had [Jesus the Nazarene] crucified and *killed* by
			men outside the Law.
	5	33	This so infuriated [the Sanhedrin] that they wanted to *put*
			[the apostles] *to death*.
		36	when [Theudas] was *killed*, all his followers scattered
	7	28	Do you intend to *kill* me as you *killed* the Egyptian yesterday?
	8	1	2 Saul entirely approved of the *killing* [of Stephen].
	9	23	the Jews worked out a plot to *kill* [Saul] . . . ²⁴ . . . To
		24	make sure of *killing* him they kept watch on the gates
			[of Damascus] day and night,
		29	after [Saul] had . . . argued with [the Hellenists], they became
			determined to *kill* him.
	10	39 X	they *killed* [Jesus] by hanging him on a tree,
	12	2	[Herod] ʳbeheaded (lit. *put to death* by the sword) James the
			brother of John,
	13	28 X	[the chief priests] asked Pilate to have [Jesus] *executed*.
	16	27	the gaoler . . . drew his sword and was about to ʳcommit
			suicide (lit. *kill* himself),
	22	20	I was standing by in full agreement with ʳhis murderers
			(lit. those *putting* [Stephen] *to death*),
	23	15	we . . . are prepared to ʳ*dispose of* (or: *kill*) [Paul] before
			he reaches you.
		21	more than forty [Jews] . . . have vowed not to eat or drink
			until they have ʳ*got rid of* (or: *killed*) [Paul].
		27	This man had been seized by the Jews and would have been
			murdered by them

Ac	25	3	[The chief priests] were . . . preparing an ambush to *murder* [Paul]
	26	10	when [the saints] were ʳsentenced (or: *put*) *to death* I cast my vote against them.
2 Th	2	8	(Is 11 4) The Lord will *kill* [the Rebel] with the breath of his mouth

3: EXECUTE, KILL, DO AWAY WITH: *DIA-CHEIRIZOMAI*

dia-cheirizomai 2

Ac	5	30 X R	it was you who had [Jesus] *executed* by hanging on a tree.
	26	21	the Jews . . . tried to *do away with* me.

4: KILL, SLAUGHTER (AN ANIMAL): *THUŌ*

thuō 7/14

Mt	22	4 <	my oxen and fattened cattle have been *slaughtered*,
Lk	15	23 <	Bring the calf we have been fattening, and *kill* it; we are going to have a feast,
		27 <	Your brother has come . . . and your father has *killed* the calf we had fattened . . . ²⁹ . . . you never offered me so much as a kid . . . to celebrate with my friends. ³⁰ But,
		30 <	for this son of yours, . . you *kill* the calf we had been fattening.
Jn	10	10 <	The thief comes only to steal and *kill* and destroy.
Ac	10	13	Now, Peter; *kill* and eat!
	11	7	Now, Peter; *kill* and eat!

5: SLAUGHTER, CUT THE THROAT (OF): *SPHAZŌ*

2	*sphagē*	3	1	*sphazō*	10
3	*sphagion*	1	4	*kata-sphazō*	1

a) Cut the throat (of), Slaughter, Kill

Lk	19	27 <	4 *execute* [my enemies] in my presence.
Jm	5	5	2 in the time of *slaughter* you went on eating to your heart's content.
1 Jn	3	12	Cain, who belonged to the Evil One and *cut* his brother's *throat*; *cut* his brother's *throat* simply for this reason,
Rv	6	4	its rider was given this duty: to take away peace from the earth ʳand set people killing (lit. so that people *killed*) each other.
		9	the souls of all the people who had been *killed* on account of the word of God,
	13	3	one of [the beast's] heads seemed to have had ʳa fatal wound (lit. its *throat cut* fatally).
	18	24	the blood of prophets . . . and ʳall the blood that was ever shed (lit. of all those who were ever *killed*) on earth.

b) Victim Sacrificed, Sacrificial Slaughter – (Be) Slain

Ac	7	42	3 (Am 5 25) Did you bring me *victims* and sacrifices in the wilderness for all those forty years . . .?
	8	32 X	2 (Is 53 7) Like a sheep that is led to the *slaughter*[-house],
Rm	8	36	(Ps 44 22) For your sake we are being . . . reckoned as 2 sheep for the *slaughter*.
Rv	5	6 X	I saw . . . a Lamb that seemed to have been *sacrificed*;
		9 X	you were *sacrificed*, and with your blood bought men for God of every race, language,
		12 X	The Lamb that was *sacrificed* is worthy to be given power,
	13	8 X	the book of life of the *sacrificial* Lamb.

6: CUT-THROATS, ASSASSINS: *SIKARIOS*

sikarios 1

Ac	21	38	the Egyptian who . . led those four thousand *cut-throats* out into the desert?

7: PEOPLE WHO KILL, MURDERERS: *-LŌĒS*

2 (*mētro-*)*lōēs 1*   1 (*patro-*)*lōēs 1*

1 Tm	1	9	/2 laws . . . are for *people who kill* their fathers, *people who kill* their mothers and for murderers,

8: MURDER, MURDERER, KILL: *PHONEUŌ*

1	*phoneuō 12*	2	*phonos 9*
3	*phoneus 7*	4	(*andro-*)*phonos 1*

Mt	5	21	(Ex 20 13) it was said to our ancestors: You must not *kill*; and if anyone does *kill* he must answer for it before the court.
	15	19	2 From the heart come evil intentions: *murder*, adultery,

Mt	19	18	[keep the commandments.] (Ex 20 13): You must not *kill*.
	22	7 <	3 [The king] despatched his troops, destroyed those *murderers*
	23	31	You are the sons of those who *murdered* the prophets!
		35	Zechariah . . . whom you *murdered* between the sanctuary and the altar.
Mk	7	21	it is from within . . . that evil intentions emerge: fornication, 2 theft, *murder*,
	10	19	You know the commandments (Ex 20 13): You must not *kill*; . . . You must not steal;
	15	7	a man called Barabbas was then in prison with the rioters 2 who had committed *murder* during the uprising.
Lk	18	20	You know the commandments (Ex 20 13): . . . You must not *kill*;
	23	19	[Barabbas] had been thrown into prison for causing a riot 2 . . . and for *murder*.
		25	[Pilate] released the man . . . who had been imprisoned 2 for . . . *murder*,
Ac	3	14	you . . . accused . . . the Just One, you . . . demanded the 3 reprieve of a *murderer*
	7	52 X	3 you have become [the Just One's] betrayers, his *murderers*.
	9	1	Saul was still breathing threats to *slaughter* the Lord's disciples.
	28	4	3 The man must be a *murderer*,
Rm	1	29	2 they are . . . addicted to envy, *murder*, wrangling,
	13	9	(Ex 20 13) You shall not commit adultery, you shall not *kill*,
1 Tm	1	9	[laws] are for people who kill their fathers or mothers and for 4 *murderers*,
Heb	11	37	They were stoned, or sawn in half, ʳor beheaded (lit. they 2 died by being *killed* with a sword);
Jm	2	11	It was the same person who said, You must not commit adultery and (Ex 20 13) You must not *kill*. Now if you *commit murder*, you do not have to commit adultery as well to become a breaker of the Law.
	4	2	You want something and you haven't got it; so you are prepared to *kill*.
	5	6	It was you who condemned the innocent and *killed* them; they offered you no resistance.
1 P	4	15	None of you should ever deserve to suffer for being a 3 *murderer*, a thief,
Rv	9	21	Nor did [those who escaped these plagues] give up the 2 *murdering* . . . or stealing.
	21	8	3 But the legacy for . . . *murderers* . . . is the second death in the burning lake of sulphur.
	22	15	3 These others must stay outside: . . . *murderers*, and . . . everyone of false speech and false life.

9: HAVE (A PERSON) PUT TO DEATH, PASS THE DEATH-SENTENCE, PUT AN END TO – BE PUT TO DEATH, DEADLY: *THANATOŌ*

2 *thanasimos 1*   3 *thanatē-phoros 1*
1 *thanatoō*   11

Mt	10	21	children will rise against their parents and *have them put to death*.
	26	59 X	The chief priests . . . were looking for evidence against Jesus . . . on which they might *pass the death-sentence*.
	27	1 X	the chief priests . . . met in council to *bring about the death* of Jesus.
Mk	13	12	children will rise against their parents and *have them put to death*.
	14	55 X	The chief priests . . . were looking for evidence against Jesus on which they might *pass the death-sentence*.
	16	18	[believers in my name] will . . . be unharmed should they 2 drink *deadly* poison.
Lk	21	16	some of you will *be put to death*.
Rm	7	4	you . . . who through the body of Christ are now *dead* to the Law,
	8	13 L	if by the Spirit you *put an end to* the misdeeds of the body you will live.
		36	(Ps 44 22) For your sake we are *being massacred* daily,
2 Co	6	9	[we are] rumoured to *be executed* before we are sentenced;
Jm	3	8	3 the tongue . . . is . . . full of *deadly* poison.
1 P	3	18 X L	In the body [Christ] *was put to death*, in the spirit he was raised to life,

10: BEHEAD(ED), CUT THE HEAD OFF: *APO-KEPHALIZŌ*

apo-kephalizō 4

Mt	14	10	[Herod] had John *beheaded* in the prison.
Mk	6	16	[Herod] said [of Jesus], 'It is John whose *head I cut off*';
		28	The man went off and *beheaded* [John] in prison;
Lk	9	9	Herod said, 'John? I *beheaded* him.'

11: BEHEAD(ED): *PELEKIZŌ*

pelekizō 1

Rv	20	4	all who had been *beheaded* for having witnessed for Jesus

DIG – PIERCE – HOLE

1. Dig – Break through – Pit
1: Dig: *skaptō*
2: Dig a hole – Make an opening –
   Break through into: *oryssō*
3: Pit – Ditch – Hole: *bothynos*
2. Pierce
1: Pierce
   a) Pierce: *ek-kenteō*
   b) Pierce – Cut (to the heart) –

Stab: *nyssō*
   c) Pierce: *peri-peirō*
2: Eye (of a needle): *trēma*
3. Opening – Hole in the ground: *opē*
   a) Opening – Outlet
   b) Hole – Cave – Ravine
4. Hole – Fox's hole: *phōleos*
5. Den – Cave: *spēlaion*

1. DIG – BREAK THROUGH – PIT

1: DIG: *SKAPTŌ*

skaptō 3

Lk	6 48	the man who when he built his house *dug*, and ┌*dug deep* (lit. went very deep),
	13 8	leave [the fig tree] one more year and give me time to *dig* round it
	16 3	what am I to do? *Dig*? I am not strong enough.

2: DIG A HOLE – MAKE AN OPENING – BREAK THROUGH INTO: *ORYSSŌ*

2 *oryssō 3*   1 *di-oryssō 4*
3 *ex-oryssō 1/2*

Mt	6 19	Do not store up treasures . . . on earth, where . . . thieves can *break in* and steal, ²⁰ But . . . in heaven, where . . . thieves cannot *break in* and steal.
	20	
	21 33	2 a man . . . planted a vineyard; he fenced it round, *dug* a winepress in it and built a tower;
	24 43	if the householder had known at what time of the night the burglar would come, he . . . would not have allowed anyone to *break through* the wall of his house.
	25 18	2 the man who had received one [talent] . . . *dug a hole* in the ground and hid his master's money.
Mk	2 4	3 when [the four men] had *made an opening* [in the roof], they lowered the stretcher on which the paralytic lay.
	12 1	2 A man planted a vineyard; he fenced it round, *dug* out a trough for the winepress and built a tower;
Lk	12 39	if the householder had known at what hour the burglar would come, he would not have let anyone *break through* the wall of his house.

3: PIT – DITCH – HOLE: *BOTHYNOS*

bothynos 3

Mt	12 11	If . . . [a] sheep . . . fell down a *hole* on the sabbath
	15 14	if one blind man leads another, both will fall into a *pit*.
Lk	6 39	Can one blind man guide another? Surely both will fall into a *pit*?

2. PIERCE

1: PIERCE

a) Pierce: ek-kenteō

ek-kenteō 2

Jn	19 37	(Zc 12 10) They will look on the one whom they have *pierced*.
Rv	1 7	everyone will see him, even those who *pierced* him,

b) Pierce – Cut (to the heart) – Stab: nyssō

1 *nyssō 1*   2 *kata-nyssō 1*

Jn	19 34	one of the soldiers *pierced* his side
Ac	2 37	2 Hearing this [the Jews] were *cut* to the heart

c) Pierce: peri-peirō

peri-peirō 1

1 Tm	6 10	there are some who, pursuing [money], have wandered away from the faith and so ┌given their souls (lit. *pierced* themselves with) any number of fatal wounds.

2: EYE (OF A NEEDLE): *TRĒMA*

1 *trēma 2*   2 *trymalia 1*

Mt	19 24	it is easier for a camel to pass through the *eye* of a needle than for a rich man to enter the kingdom of heaven.
Mk	10 25	2 it is easier for a camel to pass through the *eye* of a needle than for a rich man to enter the kingdom of God.
Lk	18 25	it is easier for a camel to pass through the *eye* of a needle than for a rich man to enter the kingdom of God.

3. OPENING – HOLE IN THE GROUND: *OPĒ*

opē 2

a) Opening – Outlet

Jm	3 11	does any water supply give a flow of fresh water and salt water out of the same ┌pipe (lit. *outlet*)?

b) Hole – Cave – Ravine

Heb	11 38	[the prophets] went out to live in deserts and mountains and in caves and *ravines*.

4. HOLE – FOX'S HOLE: *PHŌLEOS*

phōleos 2

Mt	8 20	Foxes have *holes* . . . but the Son of Man has nowhere to lay his head.
Lk	9 58	Foxes have *holes* . . . but the Son of Man has nowhere to lay his head.

5. DEN – CAVE: *SPĒLAION*

spēlaion 6

Mt	21 13	(Jr 7 11) According to scripture . . . my house will be called a house of prayer, but you are turning it into a robbers' *den*.
Mk	11 17	(Jr 7 11) Does not scripture say: My house will be called a house of prayer . . .? But you have turned it into a robbers' *den*.
Lk	19 46	(Jr 7 11) According to scripture, . . . my house will be a house of prayer. But you have turned it into a robbers' *den*.
Jn	11 38	Jesus reached the tomb [of Lazarus]; it was a *cave* with a stone to close the opening.
Heb	11 38	[the prophets] went out to live in deserts and mountains and in *caves* and ravines.
Rv	6 15	the whole population . . . took to the mountains to hide in *caves* and among the rocks.

DISHONOUR – SHAME

1. Dishonour, Treat shamefully, Degrade – Disgrace, Humiliate – Contemptible, Ordinary: *a-timazō*
2. Be Ashamed, Put to Shame, Embarrass – Shame(ful), Disgrace(ful) –

Dirty, Squalid, Coarse: *aischyn*
3. (Be) Ashamed, Put to Shame – Feel in the wrong, Be at a loss: *en-tropē*

1. DISHONOUR, TREAT SHAMEFULLY, DEGRADE – DISGRACE, HUMILIATE – CONTEMPTIBLE, ORDINARY: *A-TIMAZŌ*

1 *a-timazō 7*   3 *a-timos 4*
2 *a-timia 7*

Mt	13 57	3 A prophet is only *despised* in his own country and in his own house,
Mk	6 4	3 A prophet is only *despised* in his own country, among his own relations and in his own house;
	12 4	[the owner of the vineyard] sent another servant to [the tenants]; him they . . . *treated shamefully*.
Lk	20 11	[the owner of the vineyard] sent a second servant . . . [the tenants] *treated* him *shamefully*
Jn	8 49	you want to *dishonour* me.
Ac	5 41	[the apostles were] glad to have had the honour of *suffering humiliation* for the sake of the name.

Rm	1 24	God left them to . . . the practices with which they *dishonour* their own bodies,
	26 2	God has abandoned them to *degrading* passions:
	2 23 ⊖	By boasting about the Law and then disobeying it, you *bring* God *into contempt*.
	9 21 2	It is surely for [the potter] to decide whether . . . to make a special pot or an *ordinary* one?
1 Co	4 10 3	you are celebrities, we are ⌐nobodies (lit. *ordinary* people).
	11 14 2	long hair on a man is *nothing to be admired*,
	12 23 3	it is the *least honourable* parts of the body that we clothe with the greatest care.
	15 43 2	[at the resurrection of the dead] the thing that is sown is *contemptible* but what is raised is glorious;
2 Co	6 8	[We prove we are God's servants,] prepared for honour or *disgrace*,
	11 21 2	I hope ⌐you are ashamed of us (lit. we are *in disgrace* with you) for being weak with you
2 Tm	2 20 2	Not all the dishes . . . are made of gold and silver . . . some are kept for special occasions and others are for *ordinary* purposes.
Jm	2 6	you *have no respect for* anybody who is poor.

2. BE ASHAMED, PUT TO SHAME, EMBARRASS – SHAME(FUL), DISGRACE(FUL) – DIRTY, SQUALID, COARSE: *AISCHYNĒ*

5	*aischros*	4	6	*aischro(-kerdēs)* 2
7	*aischrotēs*	1	8	*aischro(-kerdōs)* 1
3	*aischynē*	6	9	*aischro(-logia)* 1
4	*aischynomai*	5	1	*kat-aischynō* 13
			2	*ep-aischynomai* 11
			10	*an-ep-aischyntos* 1

Mk	8 38 2	if anyone . . . *is ashamed* of me . . . the Son of Man will
	X 2	also *be ashamed* of him
Lk	9 26 2	if anyone *is ashamed* of me . . . of him the Son of Man will
	X 2	*be ashamed*
	13 17	all [Jesus's] adversaries were *covered with confusion*,
	14 9 3	then, to your *embarrassment*, you would have to . . . take the lowest place
	16 3 4	Go begging? I should *be too ashamed*.
Rm	1 16 2	I *am* not *ashamed* of the Good News:
	5 5	this hope ⌐is not deceptive (lit. will not *put us to shame*), because the love of God has been poured into our hearts
	6 21 2	what did you get from this? Nothing but experiences that now *make you blush*,
	9 33	(Is 28 16 G) See how I lay in Zion a stone to stumble over . . . only those who believe in him will have no *cause for shame*.
	10 11	(Is 28 16 G) those who believe in him will have no *cause for shame*,
1 Co	1 27	it was to *shame* the wise the God chose what is foolish . . . and to *shame* what is strong that he chose what is weak
	11 4	For a man to pray . . . with his head covered *is a sign of disrespect* to his head.
	5	For a woman, however, it *is a sign of disrespect* to her head if she prays . . . unveiled
	6 5	a woman *is ashamed* to have her hair cut off
	22	Surely you have enough respect for the community of God not to *make* poor people *embarrassed*?
	14 35 5	it ⌐*does not seem right* (lit. is *embarrassing*) for a woman to raise her voice at meetings.
2 Co	4 2 3	we will have none of the reticence of those who *are ashamed*,
	7 14	I had rather boasted to [Titus] about you, and now I have not been *made to look foolish*;
	9 4	If some of the Macedonians . . . found you unprepared, we should be *humiliated* . . . after being so confident.
	10 8 4	Maybe I do boast rather too much about our authority, but . . . I shall not *be ashamed* of it.
Ep	5 4 7	There must be no *coarseness*, or salacious talk . . . all this is wrong for you;
	12 5	The things which are done in secret are things that people *are ashamed* even to speak of;
Ph	1 20 4	My one hope and trust is that I shall never ⌐have to admit defeat (lit. *be put to shame*),
	3 19 3	they are proudest of something they ought to think *shameful*;
Col	3 8 9	you . . . must give all these things up: getting angry . . . abusive language and *dirty* talk;
1 Tm	3 8 6	deacons must be respectable men . . . with no *squalid* greed for money.
2 Tm	1 8 2	you are never to *be ashamed* of witnessing to the Lord,
	12 2	I am experiencing fresh hardships . . . but I ⌐have not lost confidence (lit. shall not be *put to shame*),
	16 2	Onesiphorus . . . has never *been ashamed* of my chains.
	2 15 10	Do all you can to present yourself in front of God as a man . . . who has no *cause to be ashamed*
Tt	1 7 6	[the elder] must be irreproachable: never an arrogant . . . man . . . nor out to make ⌐money (lit. *squalid* profits);

Tt	1 11 5	men of this kind ruin whole families, by teaching . . . with the *vile* motive of making money.
Heb	2 11 2	the one who sanctifies, and the ones who are sanctified, are of the same stock; that is why he ⌐openly calls (lit. *is not ashamed* to call) them brothers
	11 16 ⊖ 2 X	God *is* not *ashamed* to be called [our fathers'] God,
	12 2 X 3	Jesus . . . endured the cross, disregarding the *shamefulness* of it,
1 P	2 6	(Is 28 16 G) See how I lay in Zion a precious cornerstone . . . and the man who rests his trust on it will not be ⌐disappointed (lit. *put to shame*).
	3 16	those who slander you . . . may be ⌐proved wrong (lit. *put to shame*)
	4 16 4	if anyone of you should suffer for being a Christian, then he is not to *be ashamed* of it;
	5 2 8	Be the shepherds of the flock of God . . . not for *sordid* money, but because you are eager to do it.
1 Jn	2 28 4	Live in Christ . . . so that . . . we may have full confidence, and not turn from him *in shame* at his coming.
Jude	13 3	[false teachers are] like wild sea waves capped with *shame* as if with foam;
Rv	3 18 3	buy . . . white robes to . . . cover your *shameful* nakedness,

3. (BE) ASHAMED, PUT TO SHAME – FEEL IN THE WRONG, BE AT A LOSS: *EN-TROPĒ*

1 *en-trepō* 3/9   2 *en-tropē* 2

1 Co	1 14	I am saying all this not just to *make* you *ashamed* but to bring you . . . to your senses.
	6 5 2	You should be *ashamed*: is there really not one reliable man among you . . . ?
	15 34 2	there are some of you who seem not to know God at all; you should be *ashamed*.
2 Th	3 14	If anyone refuses to obey what I have written . . . have nothing to do with him, so that he will *feel* that he is *in the wrong*:
Tt	2 8	any opponent will *be at a loss*, with no accusation to make against us.

DISPERSE – SCATTER

---

1. **(The) Dispersion, Dispersed – Scattered**: *dia-spora*	3. **Scattered – Dispersed – Broken up**: *dia-luō*
2. **Scatter**: *skorpizō*	4. **Spread**: *dia-nemō*
1: Scatter – Rout	5. **Spread – Strew**: *strōnnymi*
2: Scatter (possessions) wastefully – Squander	1: Spread (a cloak)
3: Scatter (seed) – Give (out) alms	2: Be strewn over, Litter
	3: Strew = Make a bed, Furnish with a couch

1. (THE) DISPERSION, DISPERSED – SCATTERED: *DIA-SPORA*

1 *dia-speirō* 3   2 *dia-spora* 3

Jn	7 35 2	Is [Jesus] going abroad to the [people who are] *dispersed* among the Greeks . . . ?
Ac	8 1	everyone [in the church of Jerusalem] except the apostles ⌐fled to (lit. *scattered* into) the country districts
	4	Those who had ⌐escaped (lit. *scattered*) went from place to place
	11 19	Those who had ⌐escaped (lit. *scattered*) during the persecution that happened because of Stephen travelled as far as Phoenicia
Jm	1 1 2	From James . . . greetings to the twelve tribes of the *Dispersion*.
1 P	1 1 2	Peter . . . sends greetings to all those living among foreigners in the *Dispersion*

2. SCATTER: *SKORPIZŌ*

2 *skorpizō* 5   1 *dia-skorpizō* 9

1: SCATTER – ROUT

Mt	26 31	(Zc 13 7) I shall strike the shepherd and the sheep of the flock will be *scattered*,
Mk	14 27	(Zc 13 7) I shall strike the shepherd and the sheep will be *scattered*,
Lk	1 51 ⊖	he has *routed* the proud of heart.

Jn 10 12 < 2   the wolf attacks and *scatters* the sheep;
   11 52   to gather together in unity the *scattered* children of God.
   16 32   2   you will be *scattered*, each going his own way
Ac 5 37   [Judas the Galilean] all his followers *dispersed*.

2: SCATTER (POSSESSIONS) WASTEFULLY – SQUANDER

Mt 12 30   2   he who does not gather with me *scatters*.
Lk 11 23   2   he who does not gather with me *scatters*.
   15 13   the younger son . . . *squandered* his money on a life of
                debauchery.
   16 1   a steward . . . was denounced to him for *being wasteful*
                with his property.

3: SCATTER (SEED) – GIVE (OUT) ALMS

Mt 25 24 <   you were a hard man . . . gathering where you have not
               scattered;
      26 <   I . . . gather where I have not *scattered*
2 Co 9 9 ⊖   (Ps 112 9) He was free in *almsgiving*, and gave to the poor:

3. SCATTERED – DISPERSED – BROKEN UP: *DIA-LUŌ*
dia-luō 1

Ac 5 36   all [Theudas'] followers *scattered*

4. SPREAD: *DIA-NEMŌ*
dia-nemō 1

Ac 4 17   to stop the whole thing *spreading* any further among the
               people, let us caution them

5. SPREAD – STREW: *STRŌNNYMI*

    1   *strōnnymi, strōnnuō 6*
    2   *kata-strōnnymi, kata-strōnnuō 1*
    3   *hypo-strōnnuō 1*

1: SPREAD (A CLOAK)

Mt 21 8   people *spread* their cloaks on the road, while others were
               cutting branches . . . and *spreading* them in his path
Mk 11 8   Many people *spread* their cloaks on the road, others greenery
               which they had cut in the fields.
Lk 19 36   3   people *spread* their cloaks in the road,

2: BE STREWN OVER, LITTER

1 Co 10 5   2 ⌐their [corpses] *littered* (or: they *were strewn over*) the desert.

3: STREW = MAKE A BED, FURNISH WITH A COUCH

Mk 14 15   [the owner of the house] will show you a . . . room *furnished*
               with couches,
Lk 22 12   The man will show you a large upper room *furnished with*
               couches.
Ac 9 34   Peter said to him, 'Aeneas, Jesus Christ cures you: get up
               and ⌐*fold up your sleeping mat* (or: *make your bed*).'

DISTANCE – AWAY – FROM

1. Far – Distance – Way off
  1: Far – Distance – Way off: *makros*
  2: Far, Further – Distance – Way off: *porrō*
2. Be absent – Away, Far away – Distance: *ap-eimi*

3. (Be away) From: ap-echō
4. Distance – Interval – Later, Further: di-(h)istēmi
5. Past – Over – Later: dia-ginomai
6. Beyond, Further than: ep-ekeina

1. FAR – DISTANCE – WAY OFF

1: FAR – DISTANCE – WAY OFF: *MAKROS*

        2 *makran 10*   1 *makrothen 14*
        3 *makros 2/4*

Mt 8 30   2   Now *at a distance* there was a large herd of pigs
   26 58   Peter followed [Jesus] *at a distance*,
   27 55   many women were there, watching *from a distance*,
Mk 5 6   Catching sight of Jesus *from a distance*, [the maniac] ran up
    8 3   some have come *a great distance*.
   11 13   Seeing a fig tree in leaf *some distance away*,
   12 34 ● 2 You are not *far* from the kingdom of God.
   14 54   Peter had followed [Jesus] *at a distance*, right into the high
               priest's palace,
   15 40   There were some women watching *from a distance*
Lk 7 6   2   [Jesus] was not very *far* from the house when the centurion
               sent word
   15 13 < 3 the younger son . . . left for a *distant* country
   20 20 < 2 While [the prodigal son] was still *a long way off*,
   16 23 <   in Hades [the rich man] saw Abraham *a long way off* with
               Lazarus
   18 13 <   The tax collector stood *some distance away*, not daring even
               to raise his eyes to heaven;
   19 12 < 3 A man of noble birth went to a *distant* country
   22 54   Peter followed *at a distance*.
   23 49   All [Jesus's] friends stood *at a distance*;
Jn 21 8   2   [the disciples] were only about a hundred yards *from* land.
Ac 2 39   the promise . . . is for you . . . and for all those who are
         ●   *far away*,
   17 27 ● 2 [the deity] is not *far* from any of us,
   22 21 ● 2 I am sending you out to the pagans *far away*.
Ep 2 13 ● 2 you that used to be so *far apart* from us have been brought
               very close, by the blood of Christ.
      17 ● 2 (Is 57 19) peace to you who were *far away* and peace to those
               who were near at hand.
Rv 18 10   [the kings of the earth] keep *at a* [safe] *distance* [from Babylon]
               from fear of her agony.
      15   The traders who had made a fortune out of [Babylon] will be
               standing *at a* [safe] *distance* from fear of her agony.
      17   all those who make a living from the sea will be keeping *a*
               [safe] *distance*,

2: FAR, FURTHER – DISTANCE – WAY OFF: *PORRŌ*

        1 *porrō 4*   2 *porrōthen 2*

Mt 15 8   (Is 29 13) This people honours me only with lip-service, while
         ●   their hearts are *far* from me.
Mk 7 6   (Is 29 13) This people honours me only with lip-service, while
         ●   their hearts are *far* from me.
Lk 14 32   while the other king was still *a long way off*,
   17 12   2   [the ten lepers] stood *some way off* [13] and called to him,
   24 28   [Jesus] made as if to go ⌐on (lit. *further*);
Heb 11 13 ● 2 All these died . . . before receiving any of the things that had
               been promised, but they saw them *in the far distance*

2. BE ABSENT – AWAY, FAR AWAY – DISTANCE: *AP-EIMI*

        1 *ap-eimi 7*   2 *ap-ousia 1*

1 Co 5 3   Though I *am far away* in body, I am with you in spirit,
2 Co 10 1   I, the man who is so humble when he is facing you, but bullies
               you when he *is at a distance*.
      11   whatever we are like in the words of our letters when we *are*
               absent,
   13 2   I give warning . . . ⌐before I come (lit. though as yet I *am not*
               there),
      10   That is why I am writing this *from a distance*,
Ph 1 27   whether I come . . . or *stay at a distance*
    2 12   2   do as I tell you . . . now that I *am no longer there*;
Col 2 5   I may *be absent* in body, but in spirit I am there

3. (BE AWAY) FROM: *AP-ECHŌ*
ap-echō 2/15

Mt 14 24   the boat, ᵛ by now far out on the lake (G *was* several hundred
               yards *from* the shore),
Lk 24 13   a village called Emmaus, seven miles *away from* Jerusalem,

4. DISTANCE – INTERVAL – LATER, FURTHER: *DI-(H)ISTĒMI*
        1 *di-(h)istēmi 2/3*   2 *dia-stēma 1*

Lk 22 59   About an hour *later* another man insisted,
Ac 5 7   2 About three hours *later* [Ananias's] wife came in,
  27 28   after a short *interval* they sounded again

5. PAST – OVER – LATER: *DIA-GINOMAI*

dia-ginomai 3

Mk 16 1   When the sabbath was *over*, [Mary, Mary and Salome] bought spices
Ac 25 13   Some days *later* King Agrippa and Bernice arrived
  27 9   A great deal of time had ⌐been lost (lit. gone *past*),

6. BEYOND, FURTHER THAN: *EP-EKEINA*

1 *ep-ekeina 1*   2 *hyper-ekeina 1*

Ac 7 43   (Am 5 27) I will exile you even *further than* Babylon.
2 Co 10 16   2 we shall be carrying the gospel to places far *beyond* you.

DO – MAKE – BEHAVE

1. **Creation – Institution:** *ktizō*
   1: (God the) Creator – Creation, Creature, Living things – Made (by God)
   2: Institution
2. **Do – Work – Make:** *ergazomai*
   1: (God) Makes, Works, Builds– Actions, Works, Deeds (of Christ) – What is Done (by God or Jesus)
   2: Work(s) of the devil – What (a sinner, the devil) does, did
   3: Do – Work – Behave
      a) (Do) Work, Earn a living, Industry – Worker, Labourer – Idle
      b) Do, Doer, Behave, Perform, Practise – What (a person) does, did, Things done, made – Way (a person) lives, Works, Actions, Deeds
   4: Produce, Cause – Gain, Profit, Bring (in), Make – Trade with, Involve
   5: Work (together) with, Help, Co-operate – Fellow-worker, Colleague – Join in, Share work
   6: Be at work in, Effectual in, Function – Energy, Power, Make one's power felt – Guide, Drive, Inspire
3. **Make – Do – Behave – Keep:** *poieō*
   1: Make (= Create), Maker, Put up – a Work, Things made
   2: Produce, Bear (fruit) – Bring forth, Put out – Make (a profit)
   3: Celebrate – Give, Hold a feast for – Keep (a festival)
   4: Do (marvellous things), Work (miracles), Perform (wonders) – Show, Produce (power) – Give (signs)
   5: Make (a person, a thing) + noun or adjective or verb
      a) Make (something) of (a person, oneself, a place), Claim to be, Appoint – Turn (a thing, a person) into

   b) Make (a person, a thing) + adjective or verb – Force to be, Have (a thing) done
   6: Do (right), Live (a good) life – Give (alms), Acts of charity – Show (mercy, pity)
   7: Do (evil, what is forbidden), Lead (a sinful) life, Commit (sin, crime) – Behave (improperly)
   8: Do (as asked, required, sentenced), Treat (as one pleases) – Keep (the law, commandments), Act upon (instructions), Put into Practice
   9: Do (the same, as much), Copy – Treat as (the same), Deal with (similarly)
   10: Do (generally), Act, Behave – Work, Execute – Make, Provide, Cause
   11: Writers, Poets
4. **Made, Built, by hand – Hands (at work) – (Operation) Performed by hand:** *cheiro-poiētos*
5. **Do, Act, Behave – Commit, Practise, Keep – Use, Deal with:** *prassō*
6. **Behave – Live**
   1: Manner of life, Live – Conduct: *agōgē*
   2: Conduct oneself, Live – Manner of life: *politeuomai*
   3: Behave, Treat – Way of life, Career: *ana-strephō*
   4: Treat, Deal with: *pros-pherō*
   5: Behave, Behaviour – Bearing: *kata-stēma*
   6: Live – Way, Manner: *tropos*
      a) Live, Life
      b) Way – (the same) Manner, As, Just as – Equally
7. **Produce, Show – Perform, Do – Form (a conspiracy):** *didōmi*
8. **Craftsmen, Trade – Art, Skill, Craft – Architect, Builder, Carpenter:** *technitēs*
9. **Tanner of leather:** *byrseus*

1. CREATION – INSTITUTION: *KTIZŌ*

1 *ktisis 19*   4 *ktistēs 1*
3 *ktisma 4*   2 *ktizō 15*

1: (GOD THE) CREATOR – CREATION, CREATURE, LIVING THINGS – MADE (BY GOD)

Mt 19 4   2 the *creator* . . . made them male and female
Mk 10 6   from the beginning of *creation* God made them male and female.

Mk 13 19   /2 since the beginning of *creation* when God *created* the world,
  16 15   proclaim the Good News to all *creation*
Rm 1 20   Ever since God *created* the world his everlasting power and deity – however invisible – have been there for the mind to see in the things he has made.
  25   /2 they have . . . served *creatures* instead of the *creator*,
 8 19   The whole *creation* is eagerly waiting for God to reveal his sons. [20] It was not for any fault on the part of *creation* that it was made unable to attain its purpose, it was made so by God; but *creation* still retains the hope [21] of being freed . . . [22] . . . the entire *creation* . . . has been groaning in one great act of giving birth;
  22
  39   nor any *created thing*, can ever come between us and the love of God
1 Co 11 9   2 man was not *created* for the sake of woman, but woman for the sake of man.
2 Co 5 17   And for anyone who is in Christ, there is a new *creation*;
Ga 6 15   what matters is for him to become an altogether new *creature*.
Ep 2 10   2 We are God's work of art, *created* in Christ Jesus
  15   2 This was to *create* one single New Man in himself out of the two of them
 3 9   2 the mystery . . . has been kept hidden in God, the *creator* of everything.
 4 24   2 put on the new self that has been *created* in God's way,
Col 1 15   [Christ is] the first-born of all *creation*, [16] for in him were
  16   2 *created* all things in heaven and on earth . all things
     2 were *created* through him and for him.
  23   the Good News . . . which has been preached ⌐to the whole human race (lit. to all *creation* under heaven),
 3 10   2 a new self which . . . is renewed in the image of its *creator*;
1 Tm 4 3   2 foods which God *created* to be accepted with thanksgiving
  4   3 Every*thing* God has *created* is good,
Heb 4 13   No *created thing* can hide from him;
 9 11   the more perfect tent, which is better than the one made by men's hands because it is not of this *created order*;
Jm 1 18   so that we should be a sort of first-fruits of all that he had *created*.
    3
1 P 4 19   those whom God allows to suffer must trust themselves to the constancy of the *creator*
    4
2 P 3 4   Everything goes on as it has since the fathers died, as it has since it began at the *creation*.
Rv 3 14   Here is the message of . . . the ultimate source of God's *creation*:
 4 11   2 you *made* all the universe and it was only by your will that
    2 everything was *made* and exists.
 5 13   3 Then I heard all the living *things in creation* . . . crying,
 8 9   3 a third of all the ⌐living things (lit. *creatures*) in the sea were killed,
 10 6   2 [the angel] swore by the One who . . . *made* heaven . . . earth . . . and the sea

2: INSTITUTION

1 P 2 13   accept the authority of every social *institution*:

2. DO – WORK – MAKE: *ERGAZOMAI*

7 *en-ergeia*	8	1	*ergon*	168
11 *en-ergēma*	2	12	*dēmi-ourgos*	1
4 *en-ergeō*	21	3	*kat-ergazomai*	22
10 *en-ergēs*	3	13	*pros-ergazomai*	1
8 *ergasia*	6	9	*syn-ergeō*	5
5 *ergatēs*	16	6	*syn-ergos*	13
2 *ergazomai*	40	14	*syn-(h)yp-ourgeō*	1

1: (GOD) MAKES, WORKS, BUILDS – ACTIONS, WORKS, DEEDS (OF CHRIST) – WHAT IS DONE (BY GOD OR JESUS)

Mt 11 2   John . . . had heard *what* Christ *was doing*
  19   wisdom has been proved right by her *actions* (ᵛ children).
Lk 24 19   Jesus . . . a great prophet by the *things he* said and *did*
Jn 4 34   My food is to do the will of the one who sent me, and to complete his *work*.
 5 17   2/2 My Father goes on *working*, and so do I go on *working*.
  20   the Father . . . will show him even greater things than these, *works* that will astonish you.
  36   the *works* my Father has given me to carry out, these same *works* of mine testify that the Father has sent me.
 6 30   So they said, 'What sign will you give . . . that we should
    2 believe in you? What *work* will you do?
 7 3   let your disciples see the *works* you are doing;
  21   One *work* I did, and you are all surprised by it.
 9 3   he was born blind so that the *works* of God might be displayed in him.
  4   2/ I must *carry òut* the *work* of the one who sent me;
 10 25   The *works* I do in my Father's name are my witness;

Jn	10	32	I have done many good *works* for you to see, *works* from my
		33	Father; for which of these are you stoning me? ³³ The Jews answered him, 'We are not stoning you for [doing] good *work* . . .'
		37	If I am not doing my Father's *work*, there is no need to believe
		38	me; ³⁸ but if I am doing it . . . believe in the *work* I do;
	14	10	it is the Father, living in me, who is doing this *work*.
		11	believe it on the evidence of this *work*,
		12	whoever believes in me will perform the same *works* as I do myself,
	15	24	If I had not performed such *works* among them as no one else has ever done,
	17	4	I have . . . finished the *work* that you gave me to do.
Ac	13	41	2/ (Hab 1 5) I am *doing* ┌something (lit. a *work*, indeed a *work*) . . . that you would not believe if you were to be told of it.
Rm	14	20	do not wreck God's *work* over a question of food.
	15	18	3 What I am presuming to speak of . . . is only *what* Christ himself *has done*
1 Co	12	11 Ⓢ	4 All these are the *work* of one and the same Spirit,
2 Co	5	5	3 This is the purpose for which God *made* us,
Ga	2	8 X	4 The same person whose *action* had made Peter the apostle of
		X	4 the circumcised had ┌given me a similar mission to (lit. *acted* towards me similarly on behalf of) the pagans.
	3	5 Θ ?	4 Does God . . . *work* miracles among you because you practise the Law . . .?
Ep	1	19 Θ	how infinitely great is the power that he has exercised for us
		7	. . . This you can tell from the *strength* of his power
	3	7 Θ	7 a gift of grace from God who gave it to me by (§ the *working* of) his own power.
Ph	1	6	the One who began this good *work* in you will see that it is finished
Heb	1	10	(Ps 102 26) the heavens are the *work* of your hands;
	3	9	(Ps 95 9) your ancestors challenged me . . . though they had seen *what* I *could do*
	4	3	God's *work* was undoubtedly all finished at the beginning of the world;
		4	(Gn 2 2) After all his *work* God rested on the seventh day.
	12 Θ	10	The word of God is something alive and *active*: it cuts like any double-edged sword but more finely:
	11	10	12 a city founded, designed and *built* by God.
Rv	15	3	How great and wonderful are all your *works*, Lord

2: WORK(S) OF THE DEVIL – WHAT (A SINNER, THE DEVIL) DOES, DID

Jn	8	41	What you are doing is *what* your father *does*.
1 Jn	3	8	It was to undo *all that* the devil *has done* that the Son of God appeared.

3: DO – WORK – BEHAVE

a) (Do) Work, Earn a living, Industry – Worker, Labourer

Mt	9	37	5 The harvest is rich but the *labourers* are few, so ask the Lord
		5	of the harvest to send *labourers* to his harvest.
	10	10	[proclaim that the kingdom of heaven is close at hand . . . Provide yourselves with no gold . . .] for the *workman* deserves his keep.
	20	1 <	5 a landowner going out . . . to hire *workers* for his vineyard.
		2 <	5 ² He made an agreement with the *workers* for one denarius a day,
		8 <	5 Call the *workers* and pay them their wages,
	21	28 <	2 My boy, you go and *work* in the vineyard today.
Mk	13	34 <	a man travelling abroad . . . left . . . each [servant] with his own *task*.
Lk	10	2	5 The harvest is rich but the *labourers* are few, so ask the Lord
		5	of the harvest to send *labourers* to his harvest.
		7	Stay in the same house, taking what food and drink they have to offer, for the *labourer* deserves his wages.
	13	14	2 There are six days . . when *work* is to be done.
Jn	6	27	2 Do not *work* for food that cannot last;
	9	4	2 the night will soon be here when no one can *work*.
Ac	13	2	I want Barnabas and Saul set apart for the *work* to which I have called them.
	14	26	[Barnabas and Paul] commended to the grace of God for the *work* they had now completed.
	15	38	[John Mark] who . . . had refused to share in their *work*.
	18	3	when [Paul] found [Aquila and Priscilla] were tentmakers
		2	. . . he lodged with them and ┴*worked* there (G they
		2	*worked* together).
	19	24	8 Demetrius, who ┌employed (lit. provided *work* for) a large number of craftsmen
	25	5	[Demetrius] called a general meeting of his own ┌men (lit.
		5	*workers*) with others in the same trade . . . he said 'it is
		8	on this *industry* that we depend for our prosperity.'
Rm	4	4	2 If a man has *work* to show, his wages are not considered as a
		5	favour but as his due; ⁵ but when a man has ┌nothing (lit. no *work*) to show except faith . . . his faith is considered as justifying him.

1 Co	3	13	the *work* of each builder is going to be clearly revealed . . .
		14	the fire will test the quality of each man's *work*. ¹⁴ If the structure of his *work* stands up to it, he will get his wages;
		15	¹⁵ if ┌it (lit his *work*) is burnt down, he will be the loser,
	4	12	2 we *work* for our living with our own hands.
	9	1	You are all my *work* in the Lord.
		6	Are Barnabas and I the only ones who are not allowed to stop
		2	*working*?
		13	2 the ministers *serving* in the Temple get their food from the Temple
	15	58	keep on working at the Lord's *work* always,
	16	9	[at Ephesus] a big and important door has opened for my
		10	*work*
		10	2/ like me, [Timothy] is *doing* the Lord's *work*,
2 Co	11	13	These people are counterfeit apostles, they are dishonest
		5	*workmen*
Ep	4	12	the saints together make a unity in the *work* of service,
		28	Anyone who was a thief . . . should try to find some useful
		2	manual *work* instead, and be able to do some good
Ph	1	22	if living in this body means doing *work* which is having good results
	2	12	3 *work* for your salvation 'in fear and trembling'.
		30	It was for Christ's *work* that [Epaphroditus] came so near to dying,
Col	3	23	2 [slaves,] whatever your work is, *work* wholeheartedly
1 Th	2	9	2 Let me remind you . . . how hard we used to *work*, slaving night and day so as not to be a burden on any one of you while we were proclaiming God's Good News to you.
	4	11	2 make a point of living quietly . . . and *earning* your *living*,
	5	13	Have the greatest respect and affection for them because of their *work*.
2 Th	3	8	2 we *worked* night and day, slaving and straining, so as not to be a burden on any of you.
		10	We gave you a rule . . : not to let anyone have any food if he
		11	refused to do any *work*.
		12	there are some of you who are living in idleness, doing no
		2	*work* themselves . . . ¹² . . we order . . . people of this
		2	kind to go on quietly *working*
1 Tm	3	1	To want to be a presiding elder is to want to do a noble *work*.
	5	10	[a widow must have] been active in all kinds of good *work*
		18	5 As scripture says . . . and again: The *worker* deserves his pay.
2 Tm	2	15	Do all you can to present yourself . . . as a man . . . who has
		5	no cause to be ashamed of his *work*,
Tt	2	7	make the preaching of the Good News your life's *work*,
Heb	4	10	make yourself an example to them of *working* for good: to reach the place of rest is to rest after your *work*, as God did after his.
Jm	1	4	but patience too is to have its ┌practical results (lit. *work* perfected)
	5	4	5 *Labourers* mowed your fields, and you cheated them – listen to the wages that you kept back, calling out:
2 Jn		8	2 Watch yourselves, or all our (ᵛ your) *work* will be lost
		11	To greet him would make you a partner in his wicked *work*.
3 Jn		5	2 you have done faithful *work* in looking after these brothers,
Rv	2	26	those who prove victorious, and keep ┌working for me (lit. my *works*) until the end,
	18	17	2 sailors and all those who *make a living* from the sea

b) Do, Doer, Behave, Perform, Practise – What (a person) does, did, Things done, made – Way (a person) lives, Works, Actions, Deeds

Mt	5	16	so that, seeing your good *works*, they may give the praise to your Father
	7	23	2 (Ps 6 9) away from me, you ┌evil men (lit. who *do* evil)!
	23	3	do not be guided by what they *do*: since they do not practise what they preach.
		5	Everything they *do* is done to attract attention,
	26	10	2/ What she has *done* for me is one of the good *works* indeed!
Mk	14	6	2/ What she has *done* for me is one of the good *works*.
Lk	11	48	you both witness *what* your ancestors *did* and approve it; they did the killing, you do the building.
	12	58	8 when you go to court with your opponent, ┌try (lit. *do what you can*) to settle with him on the way,
	13	27	5 (Ps 6 9) Away from me, all you ┌wicked men (lit. *workers* of wickedness)!
Jn	3	19	because their *deeds* were evil.
		20	for fear his *actions* should be exposed;
		/2	so that it may be plainly seen that *what* he *does* is done in God.
	6	28	2/ What must we do it we are to *do* the *works* that God wants?
		29	²⁹ Jesus gave them this answer, 'This is *working* for God: you must believe in the one he has sent'.
	7	7	The world . . . I give evidence that its ┌ways (lit. *works*) are evil.
	8	39	If you were Abraham's children, you would do as Abraham *did*.
Ac	5	38	If this enterprise, this ┌movement (lit. *work*) of theirs, is of human origin . . . ³⁹ but if it does in fact come from God . . .
	7	22	Moses . . . became a man with power both in his speech and his *actions*.

Ac 7 41 [the sons of Israel] were perfectly happy with *something* they had *made* for themselves.

9 36 Tabitha . . . never tired of *doing* good or giving in charity.

10 35 2 anybody . . . who fears God and *does* what is right is acceptable to him.

26 20 urging [the pagans] to . . . turn to God, proving their change of heart by their *deeds*.

Rm 1 27 3 their menfolk . . . consumed with passion . . . men *doing* shameless things with men

2 6 (Ps 62 13) [God] will repay each one as his *works* deserve.

7 ⁷ For those who sought renown . . . by always *doing* good there will be eternal life . . . ⁹ Pain and suffering will

9 come to every human being who *employs himself in* evil

3 . . . ¹⁰ renown . . . and peace will come to everyone

10 who *does* good

2

15 They can point to the ⸢substance (lit. *practice*) of the Law engraved on their hearts

3 20 no one can be justified . . . by ⸢keeping (lit. *practising*) the Law:

27 So what becomes of our boasts? . . . What sort of law excludes them? The sort of law that tells us what to *do*?

28 On the contrary . . . ²⁸ since . . . a man is justified by faith and not by doing something the Law tells him to *do*.

4 2 If Abraham was justified as a reward for *doing something*,

6 a man is happy if God considers him righteous, irrespective of good *deeds*:

7 15 3 I cannot understand my own *behaviour* . . . ¹⁶ When I act

17 3 against my own will . . . ¹⁷ . . . the thing *behaving* in that

18 way is not my self but sin living in me. ¹⁸ . . . though the

3 will to do what is good is in me, the *performance* is not

20 . . . ²⁰ When I act against my will, then, it is not my true

3 self *doing* it, but sin

9 12 [God's choice is free] since it depends on the one who calls, not on human ⸢merit (lit. *deeds*),

32 [the Israelites] relied on good *deeds* instead of trusting in faith.

11 6 By grace . . . nothing therefore to do with good *deeds*,

13 3 Good *behaviour* is not afraid of magistrates;

10 2 Love is the one thing that cannot ⸢hurt (lit. *do* harm to) your neighbour;

12 let us give up all the *things* we prefer to *do* under cover of the dark;

15 18 to win the allegiance of the pagans, using *what* I have said and *done*

1 Co 5 2 A man who *does a thing* like that ought to have been expelled from the community.

3 3 I . . . have already condemned the man who *did* this thing.

2 Co 9 8 you will always . . . have something to spare for all sorts of good *works*.

10 11 whatever we are like in the words of our letters . . . that is what we shall be like in our *actions*

11 15 They will come to the end that ⸢they deserve (lit. corresponds to their *actions*).

12 12 3 You have seen *done* among you all the things that mark the true apostle,

Ga 2 16 we acknowledge that what makes a man righteous is not ⸢obedience to (lit. *practising*) the Law . . . we hold that faith in Christ rather than ⸢fidelity to (lit. *practising*) the Law is what justifies us, and that no one can be justified by ⸢keeping (lit. *practising*) the Law.

3 2 was it because you *practised* the Law that you received the Spirit . . .?

5 Does God give you the Spirit . . . because you *practise* the Law . . .?

10 those who rely on the ⸢keeping (lit. *practice*) of the Law are under a curse,

6 4 Let each of you examine his own *conduct*;

10 2 we must *do* good to all,

Ep 2 9 [you have been saved] not by anything you have *done*

10 created in Christ Jesus to ⸢live the good life (lit. *do* good) as from the beginning he had meant us to [live it].

4 19 8 they . . . eagerly ⸢pursue (lit. *practise*) a career of indecency

5 11 having nothing to do with the futile *works* of darkness

6 13 or you will not be able to put up any resistance when the worst happens, or ⸢have enough resources (lit. having

3 *done* everything possible) to hold your ground.

Ph 2 13 ⊖ 4 It is God . . . who puts both the will and the *action* into you.

Col 1 10 showing the results in all the good *actions* you do

21 Not long ago . . . enemies, in the way that you used to think and the evil *things* that you *did*;

3 17 and never say or *do* anything except in the name of the Lord Jesus,

1 Th 1 3 we . . . constantly remember . . . how you have shown your faith in *action*, worked for love

2 Th 1 11 fulfil all your desires for goodness and complete *all that* you *have been doing* through faith;

2 17 [May God] comfort you and strengthen you in everything good that you *do* or say.

1 Tm 2 10 [women's adornment is] to do the sort of good *works* that are proper

1 Tm 5 10 [a widow] must be a woman known for her good *works*

25 the good that people *do* can be obvious;

6 18 [the rich] are to do good, and be rich in good *works*,

2 Tm 1 9 [God] who has saved us . . . not because of anything we ourselves have *done*

2 21 the way for anyone to become a vessel for special occasions . . . kept ready for any good *work*.

3 17 This is how the man who is dedicated to God becomes fully equipped and ready for any good *work*.

4 14 (Ps 62 13) the Lord will repay him for *what he has done*.

18 The Lord will rescue me from all evil ⸢attempts (lit. *actions*)

Tt 1 16 They claim to have knowledge of God but the *things they do* are nothing but a denial of him; they are . . . quite incapable of *doing* good.

2 14 to purify a people so that it . . . would have no ambition except to *do* good.

3 1 Remind them that it is their duty . . . to be ready to *do* good at every opportunity;

5 not because [God] was concerned with any righteous *actions* we might have done ourselves;

8 so that those who now believe in God may keep their minds constantly occupied in doing good *works*.

14 All our people are to learn to occupy themselves in doing good *works*

Heb 6 1 without going over the fundamental doctrines again: the turning away from dead *actions*

10 God would not be so unjust as to forget all you have *done*,

9 14 how much more effectively the blood of Christ . . . can purify our inner self from dead *actions*

10 24 Let us . . . stir a response in love and good *works*.

11 33 2 [Gideon . . . David] who through faith . . . *did* what is right

13 21 [I pray that God] may make you ready to do his will in any kind of good *action*;

Jm 1 20 2 God's righteousness is never ⸢served (lit. *performed*) by man's anger;

25 not listening and then forgetting, but *actively* putting [the perfect law of freedom] into practice

2 9 as soon as you make distinctions between classes of people, you are *committing* sin,

2

14 Take the case . . . of someone who has never done a single good *act* but claims that he has faith . . . ¹⁷ . . . if good

17 *works* do not go with [faith], it is quite dead. ¹⁸ This is the

18 way to talk to people of that kind: 'You say you have faith and I have good *deeds*; I will prove to you that I have faith by showing you my good *deeds* – now you prove to me that you have faith without any good *deeds* to show.

20 Do realise, you senseless man, that faith without good *deeds*

21 is useless. ²¹ You surely know that Abraham our father was justified by his *deed*, because he offered his son Isaac on the altar? ²² There you see it: faith and *deeds* were working

22 together; his faith became perfect by *what he did* . . . ²⁴ You

24 see now that it is by *doing something* [good], and not only by believing, that a man is justified. ²⁵ There is another

25 example . . . Rahab the prostitute, justified by her *deeds* . . . ²⁶ A body dies when it is separated from the spirit,

26 and in the same way faith is dead if it is separated from good *deeds*.

3 13 If there are any wise or learned men . . . let them show it by their good lives, with humility and wisdom in their *actions*.

1 P 1 17 If you are acknowledging as your Father one who . . . judges everyone according to *what he has done*,

2 12 so that they can see your good *works* for themselves and . . . give thanks to God

4 3 3 You spent quite long enough in the past ⸢living (lit. *practising*) the sort of life that pagans live,

2 P 2 8 [Lot] was outraged in his good soul by the ⸢crimes (lit. *evil being done*) that he saw

3 10 the earth and all the *works* that it contains will be burnt up.

1 Jn 3 12 [Cain] cut his brother's throat simply for this reason, that his own ⸢life was (lit. *actions* were) evil and his brother lived a good life.

18 our love is not to be just words or mere talk, but something real and *active*;

3 Jn 10 I shall tell everyone how [Diotrephes] has *behaved*,

Jude 15 to sentence the wicked for all the wicked *things* they *have done*,

Rv 2 2 [Ephesus,] I know ⸢all about you (lit. *what you have been doing*): how hard you work and how much you put up with.

5 repent, and *do* as you used to at first,

6 you loathe as I do *what the Nicolaitans are doing*.

19 [Thyatira,] I know ⸢all about you (lit. *what you have been doing*) and how charitable you are; I know your faith and devotion . . . and I know how you are still ⸢making progress (lit. *doing* more and more).

22 [I will test them severely] unless they repent of their *practices*,

23 (Ps 62 13) I . . . give each one of you what your *behaviour* deserves.

3 1 [Sardis,] I know ⸢all about you (lit. *what you have been doing*) . . . ² . . . I have failed to notice anything in the *way* you

2 *live* that my God could possibly call perfect,

Rv 3 8 [Philadelphia,] I know ʳall about you (lit. *what* you *have been doing*) . . . you have kept my commandments

15 [Laodicea,] I know ʳall about you (lit. *what* you *have been doing*): how you are neither cold nor hot.

9 20 the rest of the human race . . . refused either to abandon the *things* they *had made* with their own hands . . . or to stop worshipping devils.

14 13 now they can rest for ever after their work, since their good *deeds* go with them.

16 11 instead of repenting for *what* they *had done*, they cursed the God of heaven

18 6 [Babylon] must be paid double the amount ʳshe exacted (lit. *that she herself did*).

20 12 the record of *what* they *had done* in their lives, by which the dead were judged.

13 every one was judged according to the *way* in which he *had lived.*

22 12 (Ps 62 13) bringing the reward to be given to every man according to what he ʳdeserves (lit. has *done*).

4: PRODUCE, CAUSE – GAIN, PROFIT, BRING (IN), MAKE – TRADE WITH, INVOLVE

Mt 25 16 The man who had received the five talents promptly went and
2 *traded with* them and made five more.

Lk 19 16 13 your one pound has *brought in* ten.

Ac 16 16 8 a slave-girl who . . . made a lot of ʳmoney (lit. *profit*) for her masters . . . ¹⁹ When her masters saw that there was no
19 8 hope of making any more ʳmoney out of her (lit. *profit* from her),

Rm 4 15 3 Law *involves* the possibility of punishment for breaking the law

5 3 3 These sufferings *bring* patience, as we know,

7 8 3 sin took advantage of [this commandment] to *produce* all kinds of covetousness in me,

13 3 sin . . . used that good thing to ʳkill me (lit. *cause* my death);

2 Co 4 17 3 the troubles which are soon over, though they weigh little, ʳtrain us for (lit. *produce* for us) the carrying of ʳan eternal weight of glory (ᵛ a weight of eternal glory)

7 10 2 To suffer in God's way ʳmeans (lit. *brings* a) changing for the better . . . but to suffer as the world knows suffering
11 3 *brings* death. ¹¹ Just look at what suffering in God's way
3 has *brought* you:

9 11 3 all the generous things which . . . are the *cause* of thanks-giving to God.

Jm 1 3 3 your faith is only put to the test to *make* you patient,

5: WORK (TOGETHER) WITH, HELP, CO-OPERATE – FELLOW-WORKER, COLLEAGUE – JOIN IN, SHARE WORK

Mk 16 20 ⊖ [the Eleven] going out, preached everywhere, the Lord
9 *working with* them

Rm 8 28 ⊖ 9 ʳby turning everything to their good God *co-operates* with all those who love him [ᵛ for those who love God everything
9 *conspires* for good)

16 3 6 My greetings to Prisca and Aquila, my *fellow workers* in Christ Jesus;

9 6 [Greetings] to Urban, my *fellow worker* in Christ;

21 6 Timothy, who is *working with* me, sends his greetings;

1 Co 3 9 6 [I did the planting, Apollos did the watering] We are *fellow workers* with God;

16 16 6 put yourselves at the service of people like this, and anyone who helps and *works with* them.

2 Co 1 11 14 You must all *join in* the prayers for us:

24 6 We are . . . *fellow workers* with you for your happiness;

6 1 9 As [God's] *fellow workers*, we beg you

8 23 6 Titus . . . is my own colleague and *fellow worker* in your interests;

Ph 2 25 brother Epaphroditus . . . was sent as your representative
6 to help me when I needed someone to be my *companion in working*, and battling,

4 3 6 [Evodia, Syntyche . . .] Clement and the others who *worked with* me. Their names are written in the book of life.

Col 4 11 Of all those who have come over from the Circumcision, these
6 are the only ones actually *working with* me for the kingdom of God.

1 Th 3 2 6 Timothy, who is God's *helper* (ᵛ slave) in spreading the Good News

Phm 1 6 From Paul . . . to our dear *fellow worker* Philemon,

24 6 my *colleagues* Mark, Aristarchus, Demas and Luke.

Jm 2 22 9 [Abraham offered Isaac:] faith and deeds were *working together*; his faith became perfect by what he did.

3 Jn 8 6 it is our duty to welcome men of this sort and contribute our *share* to their work for the truth.

6: BE AT WORK IN, EFFECTUAL IN, FUNCTION – ENERGY, POWER, MAKE ONE'S POWER FELT – GUIDE, DRIVE, INSPIRE

Mt 14 2 4 that is why miraculous powers *are at work in* [Jesus].

Mk 6 14 4 that is why miraculous powers *are at work in* him.

Rm 7 5 4 our sinful passions . . . ʳfertilised (lit. *were at work in*) our bodies

1 Co 12 6 ⊖ 11 *working* in all sorts of different ways in different people, it is
4 the same God who is *working* in all of them.

10 11 one [gift], the *power* of miracles; another, prophecy;

2 Co 1 6 4 this should *be* a consolation *to* you, supporting you in patiently bearing the same sufferings as we bear.

4 12 4 So death *is at work in* us, but life in you.

Ga 5 6 4 faith . . . *makes its power felt* through love.

19 4 When self-indulgence *is at work* the results are obvious: fornication, gross indecency

Ep 1 11 ⊖ 4 the one who *guides* all things as he decides by his own will;

20 ⊖ 4 [God's power] *at work in* Christ,

2 2 Ⓓ 4 the ruler who governs the air, the spirit who *is at work in* the rebellious.

3 20 ⊖ 4 Glory be to him whose power, *working in* us, can do infinitely more than we can ask or imagine;

4 16 by [Christ] the whole body is fitted and joined together . . .
7 for each separate part to work according to its *function*.

Ph 3 21 X 7 by the same *power* with which he can subdue the whole universe.

Col 1 29 X 7/4 I struggle wearily on, helped only by his *power driving* me irresistibly.

2 12 ⊖ 7 through your belief in the *power* of God who raised [Christ]

1 Th 2 13 ⊖ 4 [God's message] is still a living *power* among you who believe it.

2 Th 2 7 4 Rebellion *is at its work* already, but in secret,

9 Ⓓ 7 when the Rebel comes, Satan will set to *work*: there will be all kinds of miracles

11 ⊖ 7 God is sending a *power* to delude them

Phm 6 ʳthat this faith will give rise to a sense of fellowship that will show you all the good things that we are able to do (lit.
10 that the fellowship of your faith may *become effectual in* a full knowledge of every good thing in us)

Jm 5 16 4 the ʳheartfelt (lit. *active*) prayer of a good man works very powerfully.

3. MAKE – DO – BEHAVE – KEEP: *POIEŌ*

3 poiēma	2	2	poiētēs	6
1 poieō	520/567	5	(moscho-)poieō	1
4 poiēsis	1	6	(skēno-)poios	1

1: MAKE (= CREATE), MAKER, PUT UP – A WORK, THINGS MADE

Mt 17 4 I will *make* three tents here,

19 4 ⊖ (Gn 1 27) the creator . . . *made* them male and female

Mk 9 5 let us *make* three tents;

10 6 ⊖ (Gn 1 27) God *made* them male and female.

Lk 9 33 let us *make* three tents,

11 40 ⊖ Did not he who *made* the outside *make* the inside too?

Jn 2 15 X *Making* a whip out of some cord,

9 6 X he . . . *made* a paste with the spittle,

11 X The man called Jesus . . . *made* a paste,

14 X when Jesus *made* the paste

18 18 the servants and guards had ʳlit (lit. *made*) a charcoal fire

Ac 1 1 In my earlier work . . . I ʳdealt with (lit. *set out*) everything Jesus had done

4 24 ⊖ Master . . . it is you who *made* heaven and earth and sea,

7 40 (Ex 32 1) [they] said to Aaron, '*Make* some gods to be our
41 5 leaders' ⁴¹ . . . they *made* a bull calf and offered sacrifice to the idol.

43 (Am 5 26) those idols that you had *made* to adore.

44 God . . . telling [Moses] to *make* an exact copy of the pattern

50 ⊖ (Is 62 2) [heaven, earth . . .] Was not all this *made* by my hand?

9 39 tunics and other clothes Dorcas had *made*

14 15 ⊖ the living God who *made* heaven

15 17 ⊖ (Am 9 12) ʳsays the Lord who *made* this ¹⁸ known so long ago (ᵛ says the Lord who *does* these things. From of old the Lord knows his work)

17 24 ⊖ the God who *made* the world and everything in it

26 ⊖ [God] *created* the whole human race so that they could occupy the entire earth,

18 3 6 [Aquila and Priscilla] were tent*makers*,

19 24 A silversmith called Demetrius, who employed a large number of craftsmen *making* silver shrines of Diana,

Rm 1 20 [God's] power and deity – however invisible – have been
⊖ 3 there for the mind to see in the *things* he has *made*.

9 20 The pot has no right to say to the potter: Why did you *make*

Rm	9	21	me this shape? 21 Surely a potter can . . . use a particular lump of clay to *make* a special pot
Ep	2	10 Θ	3 We are God's *work* of art, created in Christ Jesus
		14 X	he . . . has *made* the two [people] into one
Heb	1	2 Θ	the Son . . . through whom he *made* everything there is.
	8	5	(Ex 25 40) See that you *make* everything according to the pattern
	12	27 Θ	the things being shaken are *created* things, they are going to be changed,
Rv	13	14	[the beast] was able to . . . persuade them to *put up* a statue in honour of the beast
	14	7 Θ	worship the *maker* of heaven and earth and sea and every waterspring.

2: PRODUCE, BEAR (FRUIT) – BRING FORTH, PUT OUT – MAKE (A PROFIT)

Mt	3	8	if you are repentant, *produce* the appropriate fruit,
		10	any tree which fails to *produce* good fruit will be cut down
	7	17	a sound tree *produces* good fruit but a rotten tree *produces* bad fruit.
		19	Any tree that does not *produce* good fruit is cut down
	13	23	the one who yields a harvest and *produces* now a hundredfold, now sixty, now thirty.
		26	When the new wheat sprouted and ⌜ripened (lit. *produced* grain),
	21	43	the kingdom of God will be . . . given to a people who will *produce* its fruit.
	25	16	The man who had received the five talents . . . *made* five more.
Mk	4	32	[a mustard seed] grows . . . and *puts out* big branches
Lk	3	8	if you are repentant, *produce* the appropriate fruits,
		9	any tree which fails to *produce* good fruit will be cut down
	6	43	There is no sound tree that *produces* rotten fruit, nor again a rotten tree that *produces* sound fruit.
	8	8	some seed . . . grew and *produced* its crop a hundredfold.
	13	9	it may *bear* fruit next year;
	19	18	your one pound has *made* five.
Jm	3	12	Can a fig tree ⌜give you (lit. *produce*) olives . . . or a vine ⌜give (lit. *bear*) figs? No more can sea water ⌜give you (lit. *produce*) fresh water.
Rv	22	2	the trees of life, which *bear* twelve crops of fruit in a year,

3: CELEBRATE – GIVE, HOLD A FEAST FOR – KEEP (A FESTIVAL)

Mt	22	2 <	a king who *gave a feast for* his son's wedding.
	26	18 X	It is at your house that I am *keeping* Passover with my disciples.
Mk	6	21	[Herod] *gave* a banquet for the nobles
Lk	5	29	[In Jesus's] honour Levi *held* a great reception
	14	12	When you *give* a lunch or a dinner, do not ask your friends
		13	. . . 13 when you *have* a party, invite the poor,
		16 <	There was a man who *gave* a great banquet.
Jn	12	2	[at Bethany] they *gave* a dinner for [Jesus]
Heb	11	28	by faith . . . [Moses] *kept* the Passover and sprinkled the blood

4: DO (MARVELLOUS THINGS), WORK (MIRACLES), PERFORM (WONDERS) – SHOW, PRODUCE (POWER) – GIVE (SIGNS)

Mt	7	22	did we not . . . *work* many miracles in your name?
	9	28 X	Do you believe I can *do* this [= restore your sight]?
	13	58 X	[at Nazareth, Jesus] did not *work* many miracles
	20	32 X	What do you want me to *do* for you? 33 . . . let us have our sight back.
	21	15 X	At the sight of the wonderful things he *did* . . . the chief priests and the scribes were indignant.
		21	if you have faith . . . not only will you *do* [that] to the fig tree,
Mk	3	8 X	great numbers who had heard of all he was *doing* came to him.
	5	19 X	[Jesus] said to [the demoniac], 'Go home to your people and tell them all that the Lord in his mercy has *done* for you'.
		20 X	20 So the man went off and proceeded to spread . . . all that Jesus had *done* for him.
	6	5 X	[at Nazareth, Jesus] could *work* no miracle
	9	39	no one who *works* a miracle . . . is likely to speak evil of [Jesus]
	10	51 X	What do you want me to *do* for you?
	13	22	false prophets will arise and *produce* signs and portents
Lk	1	25 Θ	[Elizabeth conceived . . .] 'The Lord has *done* this for me' she said
		49 Θ	the Almighty has *done* great things for me . . . 51 He has *shown* the power of his arm.
		51 Θ	
	4	23 X	We have heard all that happened in Capernaum, *do* the same here
	8	39 Θ	'report all that God has *done* for you.' So the man went off
		X	and spread . . . all that Jesus had *done* for him.

Lk	9	43 X	everyone was full of admiration for all he *did*,
	18	41 X	What do you want me to *do* for you?
Jn	2	11 X	This was the first of the signs [given by] Jesus: it was *given* at Cana in Galilee.
		23 X	when they saw the signs that he *gave*,
	3	2 X	no one could *perform* the signs that you *do*
	4	45 X	the Galileans received him well, having seen all that he had *done* at Jerusalem
		54 X	This was the second sign *given* by Jesus, on his return from Judaea
	5	16 X	he *did* things like this on the sabbath
		36 X	these same works ⌜of mine (lit. that I have been *doing*) testify that the Father has sent me.
	6	2 X	a large crowd . . . impressed by the signs he *gave* by curing the sick.
		6 X	he himself knew exactly what he was going to *do*.
		14 X	The people, seeing this sign that he had *given*, said,
		30 X	What sign will you *give* . . . ? What work will you *do*?
	7	3 X	let your disciples see the works you are *doing*;
		4 X	since you are *doing* all this, you should let the whole world see.
		21 X	One work I *did*, and you are all surprised by it.
		31 X	the Christ . . . will he *give* more signs than this man has *given*?
	9	16	How could a sinner *produce* signs like this?
	10	25 X	The works I *do* . . . are my witness;
		37 X	If I am not *doing* my Father's work, there is no need to believe me; 38 but if I am *doing* it . . . believe in the work
		38 X	
		41	John *gave* no signs,
	11	37 X	could he not have ⌜prevented this man's death (lit. *worked* it so that this man did not die)?
		45 X	Many of the Jews who . . . had seen what he *did* believed in him, 46 but some of them went to tell the Pharisees what Jesus had *done*.
		46 X	
		47 X	Here is this man *working* all these signs
	12	18 X	they had heard that [Jesus] had *given* this sign.
		37 X	they had been present when he *gave* so many signs,
	14	10 Θ	it is the Father, living in me, who is *doing* this work.
		12 X	whoever believes in me will *perform* the same works as I *do* myself, he will *perform* even greater works,
	15	24 X	If I had not *performed* such works among them as no one else has ever *done*,
	20	30 X	There were many other signs that Jesus *worked*
	21	25 X ∆	There were many other things that Jesus *did*;
Ac	2	22 Θ	Jesus . . . commended to you by God by the . . . signs that God *worked* through him
	4	7	By what power . . . have you men *done* this?
	6	8	Stephen . . . began to *work* miracles and great signs
	7	36	It was Moses who, after *performing* miracles and signs . . . led them
	8	6	they had heard of the miracles [Philip] *worked*
	14	11	[Paul healed a cripple.] When the crowd saw what Paul had *done*
	15	12 Θ	all the signs and wonders God had *worked* through [Barnabas and Paul]
	19	11 X	the miracles *worked* by God at Paul's hands
Rv	13	13	[the beast] *worked* great miracles, even to calling down fire from heaven
		14	the miracles which [the beast] was allowed to *do*
	16	14 ⓓ	[three foul spirits like frogs] in fact were demon spirits, able to *work* miracles,
	19	20	the false prophet who had *worked* miracles on the beast's behalf

5: MAKE (A PERSON, A THING) + noun or adjective or verb

a) Make (something) of (a person, oneself, a place), Claim to be, Appoint – Turn (a thing, a person) into

Mt	4	19 X	I will *make* you fishers of men.
	5	32 X	everyone who divorces his wife . . . *makes* her an adulteress;
	21	13	you are *turning* [my house] *into* a robber's den.
	23	15	You who travel over sea . . . to *make* a single proselyte, and . . . *make* him twice as fit for hell as you are.
Mk	1	17 X	I will *make* you *into* fishers of men.
	3	14 X	he *appointed* twelve; they were to be his companions
		16 X	so he *appointed* the Twelve:
	11	17 X	you have *turned* [my house] *into* a robbers' den.
Lk	16	9	use money, tainted as it is, to ⌜win (lit. *make*) you friends,
	19	46 X	you have *turned* [my house] *into* a robbers' den.
Jn	2	16	stop *turning* my Father's house *into* a market.
	4	1 X	Jesus . . . was *making* . . . more disciples than John
		46 X	He went again to Cana . . . where he had *changed* the water *into* wine.
	6	15	they were about to come and . . . *make* [Jesus] king,
	8	53 X	Are you greater than our father Abraham . . .? . . . Who are you *claiming to be*?
	10	33 X	you are only a man and you *claim to be* God.
	19	7 X	he ought to die, because he has *claimed to be* the Son of God.
		12 X	anyone who *makes* himself king is defying Caesar.

Ac	2 36	Θ	God has *made* this Jesus . . . both Lord and Christ.
	26 28		A little more, and your arguments would *make* a Christian *of* me.
1 Co	6 15		do you think I can take parts of Christ's body and ʳjoin them to (lit. *make* them part of) the body of a prostitute?
2 Co	5 21	Θ	For our sake God *made* the sinless one into sin,
Heb	1 7	Θ	(Ps 104 4) He *makes* his angels winds
	3 2	Δ	[Jesus] was faithful to the one who *appointed* him,
Rv	1 6	X	[Jesus Christ who] *made* us a line of kings, priests
	3 12	X	Those who prove victorious I will *make into* pillars in the sanctuary of my God,
	5 10	X	you . . . *made* them a line of kings and priests,

b) Make (a person, a thing) + adjective or verb – Force to be, Have (a thing) done

Mt	3 3		(Is 40 3) *make* [the Lord's] paths straight.
	5 36		you cannot *turn* a single hair white or black.
	12 16		[Jesus] warned them not to *make* him known.
	33		*Make* a tree sound . . . *make* a tree rotten
	20 12	<	The men who came last . . . have done only one hour, and you have ʳtreated (lit. *made*) them the same as us,
	26 73		your accent ʳgives you away (lit. *makes* it obvious).
	28 14		we undertake . . . to *see that* you do not get into trouble.
Mk	1 3		(Is 40 3) Prepare a way for the Lord, *make* his paths straight,
	3 12		[Jesus] warned them strongly not to *make* him known.
	7 37	X	he *makes* the deaf hear
Lk	3 4		(Is 40 3) Prepare a way for the Lord, *make* his paths straight.
	5 34		Surely you cannot *make* the bridegroom's attendants fast . . .?
	18 7	Θ	Now will not God see justice *done* to his chosen . . .? ⁸ I
	8	Θ	promise you, he will see justice *done* to them . . . speedily.
Jn	5 11	X	the man who ʳcured me (G *made* me cured)
	15	X	it was Jesus who had ʳcured him (G *made* him cured)
	18	X	[Jesus] *made* himself God's equal.
	6 10		*Make* the people sit down.
	7 23	X	why are you angry with me for *making* a man whole . . . on a sabbath?
	16 2		They will ʳexpel you (lit. *force* you *to be* expelled) from the synagogues,
Ac	3 12		as though we had *made* this man walk by our own power
	5 34		Gamaliel . . . asked to *have* the men taken outside
	7 19		[the new king of Egypt ill-treated our ancestors] *forcing* them to expose their babies
	15 17	Θ	(Am 9 12) says the Lord who *made* this ¹⁸ known so long ago (ᵛ says the Lord who does these things. From of old the Lord knows his work)
Col	4 16		send [this letter] on to ʳbe (lit. *have*) read in the church of the Laodiceans,
Heb	12 13		(Pr 4 26) ʳsmooth out (lit. *make* smooth) the path you tread;
2 P	1 10		you have been . . . chosen: work all the harder to ʳjustify it (lit. *make* [the choice] justified)
1 Jn	1 10		To say that we have never sinned is to ʳcall (lit. *make*) God a liar
	5 10		anyone who will not believe God is *making* God out to be a liar,
Rv	3 9	X	I will *make* them come and fall at your feet
	12 15		like a river . . . ʳto sweep [the woman] away (G to *have* her swept away) in the current,
	13 12		This second beast . . . extended its authority . . . *making* the world and all its people worship the first beast,
	13		even to ʳcalling down (lit. *making* come down) fire from heaven
	15		It was allowed . . . to *have* anyone who refused to worship the statue of the beast put to death.
	16		He *compelled* everyone . . . to be branded
	17 16		the beast will turn against the prostitute, and ʳstrip off her clothes (lit. *have* her *stripped*) and leave her naked;
	21 5	Θ	Now I am *making* the whole of creation new

6: DO (RIGHT), LIVE (A GOOD) LIFE – GIVE (ALMS), ACTS OF CHARITY – SHOW (MERCY, PITY)

Mt	6 1		Be careful not to *parade* your good deeds before men
	2		So when you *give* alms, do not have it trumpeted before you
	3		. . . ³ But when you *give* alms, your left hand must not know
Lk	1 72	Θ	Thus he *shows* mercy to our ancestors,
	10 37		[a neighbour is] the one who *took* pity on him . . . Jesus said to him, 'Go, and do the same yourself'.
Jn	3 21		the man who *lives* by the truth comes out into the light,
Ac	9 36		Tabitha . . . who never tired of doing good or *giving* in charity.
	10 2		Cornelius . . . *gave* generously to Jewish causes
	24 17		I came to *bring* alms to my nation
Rm	3 12		(Ps 14 3) there is not one ʳgood man (lit. man who *does* good) left,
	10 5		(Lv 18 5) those who ʳkeep (lit. *practise* righteousness within) the Law will draw life from it.
Tt	3 5		it was not because [God] was concerned with any righteous actions we might have *done* ourselves;

Jm	2 13		there will be judgement without mercy for those who have ʳbeen merciful (lit. *exercised* mercy) themselves;
1 Jn	1 6		we are lying because we are not *living* the truth.
	2 29		everyone whose *life is* righteous has been begotten by [God].
	3 7		to *live* a holy *life* is to be holy just as [God] is holy;
	10		anybody not *living* a holy *life* . . . is no child of God's.
Rv	2 5		repent, and *do* as you used to at first,
	22 11		let those who *do* good go on, and those who are holy continue to be holy,

7: DO (EVIL, WHAT IS FORBIDDEN), LEAD (A SINFUL) LIFE, COMMIT (SIN, CRIME) – BEHAVE (IMPROPERLY)

Mt	12 2		[by picking corn] your disciples are *doing* something that is forbidden to *do* on the sabbath.
	13 41		his angels . . . will gather . . . all who *do* evil,
Mk	2 24		why are they *doing* something on the sabbath day that is forbidden?
	15 7		the rioters who had *committed* murder during the uprising.
Lk	3 19		for all the other crimes Herod had *committed*,
	6 2		Why are you *doing* something that is forbidden (ᵛ to *do*) on the sabbath day?
Jn	8 34		everyone who *commits* sin is a slave (G of sin)
Ac	28 17		I have *done* nothing against our people or the customs
Rm	1 28		God has left them . . . to their monstrous *behaviour*.
	32		and yet they *do* it; and what is worse, encourage others to do the same.
	2 3		you judge those who behave like this while you are *doing* exactly the same,
1 Co	6 18		All the other sins are *committed* outside the body;
2 Co	11 7		Or ʳwas I (lit. have I *done*) wrong . . . by preaching the gospel of God to you and taking no fee for it?
Jm	5 15		if [the sick man] has *committed* any sins, he will be forgiven.
1 P	2 22	X	[Christ suffered . . .] He had not *done* anything wrong,
1 Jn	3 4		Anyone who ʳsins (lit. *commits* a sin) at all ʳbreaks (lit. *does* break) the law,
	8		to *lead a* sinful *life* is to belong to the devil,
	9		No one who has been begotten by God ʳsins (lit. *commits* sins);
Rv	21 27		Nothing unclean may come into it: no one who *does* what is loathsome
	22 15		These others must stay outside . . . everyone of false speech and false ʳlife (lit. *deeds*).

8: DO (AS ASKED, REQUIRED, SENTENCED), TREAT (AS ONE PLEASES) – KEEP (THE LAW, COMMANDMENTS), ACT UPON (INSTRUCTIONS), PUT INTO PRACTICE

Mt	1 24		[Joseph] *did* what the angel of the Lord had told him to do: he took his wife to his home
	5 19		the man who infringes even one of the least of these commandments and teaches others to *do* the same
	7 12		So always *treat* others as you would like them to *treat* you;
	21		but the person who *does* the will of my Father
	24		everyone who listens to these words of mine and *acts on* them
	26		everyone who listens to these words of mine and does not *act on* them
	8 9		I say . . . to my servant: *Do* this, and he *does* it.
	12 50		Anyone who *does* the will of my Father in heaven,
	17 12		Elijah has come already and they . . . *treated* him as they pleased;
	20 15	<	Have I no right to *do* what I like with my own?
	21 6		the disciples . . . *did* as Jesus had told them. ⁷ They brought the donkey and the colt,
	31	<	Which of the two *did* the father's will?
	23 3		*do* what [the scribes] tell you and listen to what they say; but do not be guided by what they do: since they do not *practise* what they preach.
	23		You who pay your tithe of mint . . . and have neglected . . . justice, mercy . . . These you should have *practised*, without neglecting the others.
	24 46	<	Happy that servant if his master's arrival finds him at this *employment*.
	26 19		The disciples *did* what Jesus told them and prepared the Passover.
	28 15		The soldiers . . . *carried out* their instructions,
Mk	3 35		Anyone who does the will of God . . . is my brother
	9 13		Elijah has come and they have *treated* him as they pleased,
	10 17		what must I *do* to inherit eternal life?
	35	X	we want you to *do* us a favour.
	36	X	What is it you want me to *do* for you?
Lk	2 27		the parents brought in the child Jesus to *do* for him what the Law required,
	5 6		[pay out your nets . . .] when they had *done* this they netted . . . a huge number of fish
	6 10		'Stretch out your hand'. He *did* so,
	31		*Treat* others as you would like them to *treat* you.

Lk	6	46	Why do you call me, 'Lord, Lord' and not *do* what I say?
		47	Everyone who . . . listens to my words and *acts on* them
		49	But the one who listens and *does* nothing
	7	8	I say . . . to my servant: *Do* this, and he *does* it.
	8	21	those who hear the word of God and *put* it *into practice*.
	9	15	[Get them to sit down . . .] They *did* so and made them all sit down.
	10	25	what must I *do* to inherit eternal life?
		28	*do* this and life is yours.
	11	42	These you should have *practised*, without leaving the others undone.
	12	43 <	Happy that servant if his master's arrival finds him at this *employment*.
		47 <	The servant who . . . has not even started to *carry out* those wishes [of his master's], will receive very many strokes of the lash.
	17	9	Must he be grateful to the servant for *doing* what he was
		10	told? [10] So with you: when you have *done* all you have been told to do, say . . . we have *done* no more than it is our duty to *do*.
	18	18	what have I to *do* to inherit eternal life?
Jn	2	5	*Do* whatever he tells you.
	4	34 X	My food is to *do* the will of the one who sent me,
	6	38 X	I have come from heaven, not to *do* my own will, but the will of the one who sent me.
	7	17	if anyone is prepared to *do* [God's] will, he will know whether my teaching is from God
		19	yet not one of you *keeps* the Law!
	8	28 X	I *do* nothing of myself: what the Father has taught me is what I preach;
		29 X	I always *do* what pleases him.
		38	you *put into action* the lessons learnt from your father.
		44	The devil is your father, and you prefer to *do* what your father wants.
	9	31	God does listen to men who are devout and *do* his will.
	13	17	Now that you know this, happiness will be yours if you *behave* accordingly.
	14	13 X	Whatever you ask for in my name I will *do*,
		14 X	If you ask for anything in my name, I will *do* it.
		31 X	I am *doing* exactly what the Father told me.
	15	14	if you *do* what I command you.
	17	4 X	I have . . . finished the work that you gave me to *do*.
Ac	4	28	[Herod and Pilate made an alliance] only to *bring about* the very thing that you in your strength and your wisdom had predetermined
	11	30	[the disciples decided to send relief.] They *did* this and delivered their contributions to the elders in the care of Barnabas and Saul.
	12	8	The angel then said [to Peter], 'Put on your belt and sandals'. After he had *done* this,
	13	22	David . . . will *carry out* my whole purpose.
	16	21	practices which it is unlawful for us . . . to accept or ⌐follow (lit. *perform*).
		30	what must I *do* to be saved?
	21	23	So do as we suggest.
	22	10	What am I to *do*, Lord? . . . you will be told what you have been appointed to *do*.
Rm	2	13	2 It is not listening to the Law but *keeping* it that will make people holy
		14	pagans . . . are led by reason to *do* what the Law commands,
	4	21 Θ	God had power to *do* what he had promised.
	7	15	I cannot understand my own behaviour I fail to carry out the things I want to do, and I find myself *doing* the very things I hate.
		16	When I *act* against my own will,
		20	When I *act* against my will,
	9	28 Θ	(Is 10 23) the Lord will *execute* his sentence on the earth.
1 Co	7	36	he is free to *do* as he likes: he is not sinning
	16	1	about the collection made for the saints: you are to *do* as I told
Ga	3	10	(Dt 27 16) Cursed be everyone who does not persevere in *observing* everything prescribed in the book of the Law.
		12	(Lv 18 5) The man who *practises* these precepts finds life through [practising] them.
	5	3	Everyone who accepts circumcision is obliged to *keep* the whole Law.
		17	you do not always *carry out* your good intentions.
Ep	2	3	We all were among them . . . living sensual lives, ⌐ruled entirely by (lit. *acting* entirely *upon*) our own physical desires
	3	20 Θ	Glory be to him whose power, working in us, can *do* infinitely more than we can ask or imagine;
	6	6	you are slaves of Christ and wholeheartedly *do* the will of God.
2 Th	3	4	you are *doing* and will go on *doing* all that we tell you.
Phm		21	I am . . . sure that you will *do* even more than I ask.
Heb	10	7 X	(Ps 40 8f) God . . . I am coming to ⌐obey (lit. *act upon*) your will.
		9 X	(Ps 40 8f) I am coming to ⌐obey (lit. *act upon*) your will.
		36	You will need endurance to *do* God's will and gain what he has promised.
	13	21	may [God] make you ready to *do* his will in any kind of good

Heb	13	21 Θ	action; and *turn* ⌐us all into (lit. in us all) whatever is acceptable *to* himself
Jm	1	22	2 you must *do* what the word tells you,
		23	2 To listen to the word and not ⌐obey (lit. *act upon* it)
		25	the man who looks steadily at the perfect law of freedom . . .
		2	actively *putting* it *into practice* – will be happy in all that
		4	he *does*.
	4	11	2 if you condemn the Law, you have stopped *keeping* it and become a judge over it.
1 Jn	2	17	anyone who *does* the will of God remains for ever.
	3	22	we . . . *live* the kind of life that he wants.
	5	2	if we love God himself and *do* what he has commanded us;
Rv	17	17	God influenced their minds to *do* what he intended,

9: DO (THE SAME, AS MUCH), COPY – TREAT AS (THE SAME), DEAL WITH (SIMILARLY)

Mt	5	46	if you love those who love you . . . Even the tax collectors *do* as much, do they not?
		47	Even the pagans *do* as much, do they not?
	7	12	So always *treat* others as you would like them to treat you;
	18	35 Θ	[the master handed him over to the torturers . . .] And that is how my heavenly Father will *deal with* you
	20	5 <	At about the sixth hour and again at about the ninth hour, he went out and *did* the same.
	21	36 <	he sent some more servants . . . and [the tenants] *dealt with* them in the same way.
	23	3	do not ⌐be guided by (lit. *do*) what [the scribes] do;
Lk	3	11	If anyone has two tunics he must share . . . and the one with something to eat must *do* the same.
	6	23	This was the way their ancestors *treated* the prophets.
		26	This was the way their ancestors *treated* the false prophets.
		31	*Treat* others as you would like them to treat you.
		33	if you do good to those who do good to you . . . ? For even sinners *do* that much.
	9	54	do you want us to call down fire from heaven . . . (ᵛ as Elijah *did*)
	10	37	[a neighbour is] The one who took pity on him . . . *do* the same
	15	19	*treat* me as one of your paid servants.
Jn	5	19 X	the Son can *do* nothing by himself: he can do only what he
		Θ Θ	sees the Father *doing*: and whatever the Father *does* the
		20 X	Son *does* too. [20] For the Father . . . shows him everything
		Θ	he *does* himself.
	13	15 X	so that you may *copy* what I have *done* to you.
Ep	6	9	employers, *treat* your slaves in the same spirit;

10: DO (GENERALLY), ACT, BEHAVE – WORK, EXECUTE – MAKE, PROVIDE, CAUSE

Mt	5	47	if you save your greetings for your brothers, are you *doing* anything exceptional?
	6	2	do not have [your alms] trumpeted before you: this is what the hypocrites *do*
		3	your left hand must not know what your right is *doing*;
	12	3	Have you not read what David *did* when he and his followers were hungry – [4] . . . how they ate the loaves of offering
	13	28 <	[where does the darnel come from?] Some enemy has *done* this
	20	12 <	The men who came last . . . have *done* only one hour,
	21	23 X	What authority have you for *acting* like this?
		24 X	I will then tell you my authority for *acting* like this.
		27 X	Nor will I tell you my authority for *acting* like this.
		40 <	what will he *do* to those tenants?
	23	5	Everything they *do* is to attract attention,
	25	40	in so far as you *did* this to one . . . of these brothers of mine, you *did* it to me.
		45	in so far as you neglected to *do* this to one of the least of these, you neglected to *do* it to me.
	26	12	When she poured this ointment on my body, [this woman] *did* it to prepare me for burial. [13] I tell you solemnly,
		13	wherever . . . the Good News is proclaimed, what she has *done* will be told also, in remembrance of her.
	27	22	what am I to *do* with Jesus . . .?
Mk	2	23	his disciples began to pick ears of corn as they ⌐went along (lit. *made* their way along).
		25	Did you never read what David *did* . . .?
	3	6	The Pharisees . . . began to ⌐plot (lit. *make* a plot) with the Herodians against him,
	5	32	[Who touched me?] Jesus continued to look all round to see who had *done* it.
	6	30	[the apostles] told [Jesus] all they had *done*
	7	12	he is forbidden from that moment to *do* anything for his father or mother.
		13	[you make God's word null and void;] you *do* many other things like this.
	11	3	If anyone says to you, 'What are you *doing*?'

Mk 11	5	X	What are you *doing*, untying that colt?
	28	X	What authority have you for *acting* like this? Or who gave you authority to *do* these things?
	29	X	I will tell you my authority for *acting* like this.
	33	X	Nor will I tell you my authority for *acting* like this.
12	9	<	Now what will the owner of the vineyard *do*?
14	8		[this woman] has *done* what was in her power
	9		what she has *done* will be told also,
15	1		the chief priests together with the elders . . . had their plan ⌐ready (ᵛ *made*),
	8		the crowd . . . began to ask Pilate ⌐the customary favour (lit. for what it was Pilate's custom to *do*),
	12		what am I to *do* with the man you call king of the Jews?
	15		Pilate, anxious to ⌐placate the crowd (lit. *cause* the crowd to be placated),
Lk 1	68	Θ	the Lord . . . has ⌐come to (lit. *provided*) [his people's] rescue
2	48	X	My child, why have you *done* this to us?
3	10		all the people asked [John the Baptist] 'What must we *do* then?
	12		tax collectors . . . said to [John the Baptist], 'Master, what must we *do*?'
	14		Some soldiers asked . . . 'What about us? What must we *do*?'
5	33		John's disciples are always . . . ⌐saying (lit. *making*) prayers,
6	3		So you have not read what David *did*
	11		[the scribes] began to discuss the best way of *dealing with* Jesus.
9	10		the apostles gave . . . an account of all they had *done*.
12	4		those who kill the body and after that can *do* no more.
	17		What am I to *do*? I have not enough room to store my crops.
	18		This is what I will *do*: I will pull down my barns
	33		⌐Get (lit. *Make*) yourselves purses that do not wear out,
	48		[the servant who] deserves to be beaten for what he has *done*,
13	22	X	[Jesus] went teaching, *making* his way to Jerusalem.
16	3	<	what am I to *do*? . . . ⁴ Ah, I know what I will *do*
	8	<	The master praised the dishonest steward for his ⌐astuteness (lit. having *acted* so astutely).
19	48		[the chief priests tried to do away with Jesus] but they did not see how they could *carry* this *out*
20	2	X	Tell us . . . what authority have you for *acting* like this?
	8	X	Nor will I tell you my authority for *acting* like this.
	13	<	the owner of the vineyard said, 'What am I to *do*? I will send them my dear son.'
	15	<	Now what will the owner of the vineyard *do* to them?
22	19		*do* this as a memorial of me.
23	31		if men *use* the green wood like this,
	34		they do not know what they are *doing*.
Jn 2	18	X	What sign can you show us to justify what you have *done*?
4	29		a man who has told me everything I ever *did*;
	39		He told me all I have ever *done*,
5	27	X	[the Father] has appointed [the Son] ⌐supreme judge (lit. to *execute* judgement);
	30	X	I can *do* nothing by myself;
6	28		What must we *do* if we are to do the works that God wants?
7	4		if a man wants to be known he does not *do* things in secret;
	51		surely the Law does not allow us to pass judgement on a man without . . . discovering what he is ⌐about (lit. *doing*)?
8	39		If you were Abraham's children, you would *do* as Abraham did. ⁴⁰ As it is, you want to kill me . . . that is not what Abraham *did*.
	40		
	41		What you are *doing* is what your father [the devil] does.
9	26	X	What did he *do* to you? How did he open your eyes?
	33	X	if this man were not from God, he couldn't *do* a thing.
11	47		the chief priests and Pharisees called a meeting . . . what *action* are we taking?
12	16		this was in fact ⌐how they had received (lit. what they had *done* to receive) [Jesus].
13	7	X	At the moment you do not know what I am *doing*, but later you will understand.
	12	X	Do you understand . . . what I have *done* to you?
	27		[Judas,] what you are going to *do*, *do* quickly.
14	23	Θ X	If anyone loves me . . . we shall . . . *make* our home with him.
15	5		cut off from me you can *do* nothing.
	15		a servant does not know his master's *business*;
	21		[they will persecute you;] it will be on my account that they will *do* all this,
16	3		They will *do* these things because they have never known either the Father or myself.
18	35	X	Pilate answered [Jesus] '. . . what have you *done*?
19	23		the soldiers . . . took his clothing and ⌐divided it into four shares (lit. *made* four shares of it),
	24		This is exactly what the soldiers *did*.
Ac 1	1	X	I dealt with everything Jesus had *done* and taught
2	37		What must we *do*, brothers? ³⁸ 'You must repent,' Peter answered
4	16		What are we going to *do* with these men?
7	24		[Moses] ⌐went to (lit. *acted* in) [his countryman's] defence and rescued the man by killing the Egyptian.

Ac 8	2		some devout people . . . *made* great mourning for [Stephen].
9	6		go into the city, and you will be told what you have to *do*.
10	39	X	everything [Jesus] *did* throughout the countryside of Judaea and in Jerusalem itself:
14	15		Friends, what do you think you are *doing*? We are only human beings
	27	Θ	[Paul and Barnabas] gave an account of all that God had *done* with them,
15	3		this news ⌐was received with the greatest satisfaction by (lit. *caused* the greatest satisfaction to) the brothers.
	4	Θ	[Paul and Barnabas] gave an account of all that God had *done* with them,
16	18		[the slave-girl] *did* this every day afterwards
19	14		Among those who *did* this were seven sons of Sceva,
20	24		life to me is not a thing to ⌐waste words on (lit. *make* speeches about),
21	13		What are you trying to *do* – weaken my resolution by your tears?
	19	Θ	[Paul] gave a detailed account of all that God had *done* among the pagans through his ministry.
	33		the tribune . . . enquired . . . what [Paul] had *done*.
22	26		Do you realise what you are *doing*? . . . This man is a Roman citizen.
23	12		the Jews ⌐held (lit. *formed*) a secret meeting
	13		There were more than forty who *took part* in this conspiracy,
24	12		it is not true that they ever found me . . . ⌐stirring up (lit. *causing* trouble with) the mob,
25	3		They were, in fact, *preparing* an ambush to murder [Paul]
	17		I ⌐wasted no time (lit. *made* no delay) but took my seat on the tribunal
26	10		[. . . to oppose the name of Jesus.] This I *did* in Jerusalem;
27	18		they began to ⌐jettison (lit. *see to* the jettisoning of) the cargo
Rm 12	20		(Pr 25 22) let [your enemy] drink. ⌐Thus (lit. By *doing* so) you heap red-hot coals on his head.
13	14		⌐forget (lit. do not *do* anything) about satisfying your bodies
15	26		Macedonia and Achaia have decided to ⌐send a generous contribution to (lit. *make* a generous collection for) the poor
16	17		be on your guard against anybody who ⌐encourages (lit. *causes*) trouble or puts difficulties in the way of the doctrine
1 Co 9	23		I still *do* this, for the sake of the gospel,
10	13	Θ	with any trial [God] will ⌐give you (lit. *provide*) a way out of it
	31		whatever you *do* at all, *do* it for the glory of God.
11	24		This is my body . . . *do* this as a memorial of me.
	25		Whenever you drink it, *do* this as a memorial of me.
15	29		what do people hope to ⌐gain (lit. *do*) by being baptised for the dead?
2 Co 8	10		it is only fair to you, since you were the first . . . not only in *taking action* but even in deciding to. ¹¹ So now finish the work
	11		
	12		I intend to go on *doing* what I am *doing* now
Ga 2	10		we should remember to help the poor, as indeed I was anxious to *do*.
Ep 3	11	Θ	according to the plan which he had ⌐had (lit. *made*) from all eternity
4	16		So the body ⌐grows (lit. goes on *working*) until it has built itself up,
Ph 1	4		every time I pray . . . I ⌐pray (lit. *do* it) with joy,
2	14		*Do* all that has to be done without complaining
Col 3	17		never say or *do* anything except in the name of the Lord Jesus,
	23		[Slaves, . . .] Whatever your *work* is, put your heart into it
1 Th 4	10		[love one another . . .] in fact this is what you are *doing* with all the brothers
5	11		So give encouragement to each other, and keep strengthening one another, as you *do* already.
	24	Θ ?	God has called you and he will ⌐not fail you (lit. *provide*).
1 Tm 1	13		I used to be a blasphemer . . . I had been *acting* in ignorance;
2	1		there should be prayers ⌐offered (lit. *made*) for everyone
4	16		[be an example to all:] always *do* this, and in this way you will save . . . yourself
5	21		a duty to keep these rules . . . and never to ⌐be influenced (lit. *do* anything) by favouritism.
2 Tm 4	5		*make* the preaching of the Good News your life's work,
Phm	14		I did not want to *do* anything without your consent;
Heb 1	3	X	now that [the Son] has ⌐destroyed the defilement (lit. *caused* the purification) of sin,
6	3		This, God willing, is what we propose to *do*.
7	27	X	to offer sacrifices . . . [Jesus] has *done* this once and for all
8	9	Θ	(Jr 31 32) not a covenant like the one I *made* with their ancestors
13	6		(Ps 118 6) With the Lord to help me . . . what can man *do* to me?
	17		your leaders . . . must give an account of the way they look after your souls; make this a joy for them to *do*,
	19		[pray for us.] I ask you very particularly to ⌐pray (lit. *do* that)
Jm 2	12		Talk and *behave* like people who are going to be judged by the law of freedom
4	15		If it is the Lord's will, we shall still be alive to *do* this or that.
2 P 1	10		If you *do* all these things there is no danger that you will ever fall away.

3 Jn	5	you have *done* faithful work in looking after these brothers,
	10	I shall tell everyone how [Diotrephes] has *behaved*,
Jude	3	⌐I was eagerly looking forward to writing (lit. I was *making* a great effort to write) to you
	15 Θ	[the Lord will come] to ⌐pronounce (lit. *execute*) judgement on all mankind
Rv 13	5	For forty-two months the beast was allowed . . . to *do* whatever it wanted,
	12	This second beast . . . *extended* [the first beast's] *authority* everywhere,
17	17	God influenced their minds to *do* what he intended, to ⌐agree together (lit. *work* to the single plan) to put their royal powers at the beast's disposal

11: WRITERS, POETS

| Ac 17 28 | 2 indeed some of your own *writers* have said: |

4. MADE, BUILT, BY HAND – HANDS (AT WORK) – (OPERATION) PERFORMED BY HAND: *CHEIRO-POIĒTOS*

2 *cheir* 7/178 1 *cheiro-poiētos* 6
3 *a-cheiro-poiētos* 3

Mk 14 58	I am going to destroy this Temple *made by* human *hands*, and in three days build another, *not made by* human *hands*.
Ac 7 41	[Our ancestors] were perfectly happy with [the bull calf] they had made ⌐for themselves (lit. with their own *hands*).
48	the Most High does not live in a house that human *hands* have built;
50 Θ	2 (Is 66 2) Was not all this made by my *hand*?
17 24	God . . . does not make his home in shrines *made by* human *hands*.
19 26	2 gods made by *hand* are not gods at all.
2 Co 5 1	there is a house built by God for us, an everlasting home *not made by* human *hands*,
Ep 2 11	those who speak of themselves as the Circumcision by reason of ⌐a physical operation (lit. an operation *performed by* hand),
4 28	2 a thief . . . shall try to find some useful *manual* work . . . and be able to do some good
Col 2 11	3 you have been circumcised, with a circumcision *not performed by* human *hand*,
1 Th 4 11	we do urge you, brothers . . . to make a point of . . . ⌐earning your living (lit. working with your *hands*)
Heb 1 10 X	(Ps 102 26) Lord . . . the heavens are the work of your *hands*;
9 11	Christ . . . has passed through . . . the more perfect tent, which is better than the one *made by* men's *hands* because it is not of this created order;
24	It is not as though Christ had entered a ⌐man-made sanctuary (lit. sanctuary *made by* men's *hands*) . . . but it was heaven itself,
Rv 9 20	the rest of the human race . . . refused either to abandon the things they had made with their own *hands* . . . or to stop worshipping devils.

5. DO, ACT, BEHAVE – COMMIT, PRACTISE, KEEP – USE, DEAL WITH: *PRASSŌ*

3 *pragma* 1/11   2 *praxis* 6
1 *prassō* 36/39

Mt 16 27	the Son of Man . . . will reward each one according to his *behaviour*.
Lk 22 23	which of them it could be who was to *do* this thing.
23 15 X	the man has *done* nothing that deserves death,
41	we deserved [the sentence]: we are paying for what we *did*.
X	But this man has *done* nothing wrong.
51	[Joseph of Arimathaea] had not consented to what the others had planned and *carried out*.
Jn 3 20	everybody who *does* wrong hates the light
5 29	those who did good will rise again to life; and those who *did* evil, to condemnation.
Ac 3 17	[you handed over Jesus . . .] neither you nor your leaders had any idea what you were really *doing*;
5 35	[the Sanhedrin wanted to put the apostles to death:] be careful how you *deal with* these people.
15 29	Avoid these, and you will *do* what is right.
16 28	Don't *do* yourself any harm; we are all here.
17 7	They have ⌐broken (lit. *acted* against) every one of Caesar's edicts
19 18	Some believers, too, came forward to admit in detail how they had *used* spells

Ac 19 19	a number of them who had *practised* magic collected their books
36	there is no need for you to . . . *do* anything rash.
25 11	If I am guilty of *committing* any capital crime,
25	I am satisfied that he has *committed* no capital crime,
26 9	it was my duty to *use* every means to oppose the name of Jesus
20	urging them to repent and turn to God, proving their change of heart by ⌐their deeds (lit. the deeds they then *did*).
31	This man is *doing* nothing that deserves death
Rm 1 32	[impiety, perversion, depravity:] those who *behave* like this deserve to die – and yet they do it; and what is worse, encourage others to *do* the same.
2 1	since you *behave* no differently from those you judge. [2] We know that God condemns that sort of *behaviour* . . . [3] and
2	
3	when you judge those who *behave* like this while you are doing exactly the same, do you think you will escape God's judgement?
25	It is a good thing to be circumcised if you *keep* the Law;
7 15	I fail to carry out the things I want to *do*, and I find myself doing the very things I hate.
19	instead of doing the good things I want to do, I *carry out* the sinful things I do not want.
8 13	2 if by the Spirit you put an end to the *misdeeds* of the body you will live.
9 11	before [Esau and Jacob] had *done* good or evil.
12 4	2 each part [of the body] has a separate *function*,
13 4	The authorities are there to serve God: they carry out God's revenge by punishing wrong*doers*.
1 Co 5 2	A man who *does* a thing like that ought to have been expelled from the community.
9 17	If I had chosen this *work* myself, I might have been paid for it,
2 Co 5 10	each of us will get what he deserves for the things he *did* . . . good or bad.
12 21	the impurities, fornication and debauchery they *committed*.
Ga 5 21	[fornication, gross indecency . . .] envy . . . those who *behave* like this will not inherit the kingdom of God.
Ep 6 21	I should like you to know . . . what I am *doing*;
Ph 4 9	Keep *doing* all the things that you learnt from me
Col 3 9	2 You have stripped off your old *behaviour* with your old self,
1 Th 4 11	⌐attending to (lit. *carrying out*) your own business
Jm 3 16	Wherever you find jealousy and ambition, you find . . . 3 wicked *things* of every kind being *done*;

6. BEHAVE – LIVE

1: MANNER OF LIFE, LIVE – CONDUCT: *AGŌGĒ*

agōgē 1

| 2 Tm 3 10 | You know . . . what I have taught, how I *have lived*, what I have aimed at; |

2: CONDUCT ONESELF, LIVE – MANNER OF LIFE: *POLITEUOMAI*

politeuomai 2

| Ac 23 1 | to this day I have *conducted myself* before God with a perfectly clear conscience. |
| Ph 1 27 | ⌐Avoid anything in your everyday lives (lit. *Do in your everyday lives* nothing) that would be unworthy of the gospel of Christ. |

3: BEHAVE, TREAT – WAY OF LIFE, CAREER: *ANA-STREPHŌ*

2 *ana-strephō* 7/10   1 *ana-strophē* 13

2 Co 1 12	2 we have always *treated* everybody . . . with the reverence and sincerity which comes from God,
Ga 1 13	my *career* as a practising Jew,
Ep 2 3	2 We all were . . . living sensual *lives*,
4 22	You must give up your old *way of life*;
1 Tm 3 15	2 I wanted you to know how people ought to *behave* in God's family
4 12	be an example to all the believers in the way you speak and *behave*,
Heb 10 33	[Remember the sufferings you had to meet,] sometimes . . . as associates of others who were *treated* in the same way,
13 7	as you reflect on the outcome of [your leaders'] *lives*, imitate their faith.
18	2 we are certainly determined to *behave* honourably in everything we do;
Jm 3 13	If there are any wise . . . men among you, let them show it by their good *lives*,
1 P 1 15	be holy in all you do
17	2 you must ⌐be scrupulously careful (lit. *behave* scrupulously properly) as long as you are living away from your home

1 P	1 18	the ransom that was paid to free you from the useless *way of life* your ancestors handed down
	2 12	Always *behave* honourably among pagans
	3 1	some husbands . . . may find themselves won over . . . by the way their wives *behave,*
	2	when they see how faithful and conscientious ⌐they are (lit. their *behaviour* is).
	16	those who slander you when you are living a good *life* in Christ
2 P	2 7	Lot . . . had been sickened by the shameless way in which these vile people *behaved*
	18	the ones who have only just escaped ⌐from paganism (lit.
	2	from those who *live* in error),
	3 11	you should be living holy and saintly *lives*

4: TREAT, DEAL WITH: *PROS-PHERŌ*

pros-pherō 1/46

Heb 12	7 Θ	God is *treating* you as his sons.

5: BEHAVE, BEHAVIOUR – BEARING: *KATA-STĒMA*

kata-stēma 1

Tt	2 3	the older women should *behave* as though they were religious,

6: LIVE – WAY, MANNER: *TROPOS*

1 tropos 13   2 (poly-)tropos 1

a) Live, Life

Heb 13	5	Put greed out of your *lives*

b) Way – (the same) Manner, As, Just as – Equally

Mt 23	37	I longed to gather your children, *as* a hen gathers her chicks
Lk 13	34	*as* a hen gathers her brood under her wings,
Ac	1 11	this same Jesus will come back in the same *way* as you have seen him go
	7 28	(Ex 2 14) Do you intend to kill me *as* you killed the Egyptian yesterday?
	15 11	we believe that we are saved in the same *way* as they are:
	27 25	I trust in God that things will turn out *just as* I was told;
Rm	3 2	[Is a Jew better off? Is there any advantage in being circumcised?] A great advantage in every *way.*
Ph	1 18	Whether from dishonest *motives* or in sincerity Christ is proclaimed;
2 Th	2 3	Never let anyone deceive you in this *way.*
	3 16	May the Lord of peace himself give you peace . . . in every *way.*
2 Tm	3 8	Men like this defy the truth *just as* Jannes and Jambres defied Moses.
Heb	1 1	2 At various times in the past and in various *ways,* God spoke to our ancestors
Jude	7	The fornication of Sodom and Gomorrah and the other nearby towns was *equally* unnatural,

7. PRODUCE, SHOW – PERFORM, DO – FORM (A CONSPIRACY): *DIDŌMI*

didōmi 4/415

Mt 24	24	false Christs . . . will . . . *produce* great signs and portents,
Mk	3 6	The Pharisees . . . began to ⌐*form* a plot) . . . against [Jesus],
Ac	2 19 Θ	(Jl 3 3) I will *display* portents in heaven above
	14 3 Θ?	the Lord supported all [Paul and Barnabas] said . . . allowing signs and wonders to be *performed* by them.

8. CRAFTSMEN, TRADE – ART, SKILL, CRAFT – ARCHITECT, BUILDER, CARPENTER: *TECHNITĒS*

2 technē	3	3	tektōn 2
1 technitēs 4		4	archi-tektōn 1
		5	homo-technos 1

Mt 13	55	3 This is the *carpenter's* son, surely?
Mk	6 3 X	3 This is the *carpenter,* surely, the son of Mary . . .?
Ac 17	29	anything in gold, silver . . . that has been ⌐carved and designed by (lit. created by the *craft* and imagination of) a man.
	18 3	[Paul visited Aquila and Priscilla,] and when he found they
	2/5	were in the *trade* of tentmakers, *of the same trade* as himself,

Ac 19	24	A silversmith called Demetrius . . . employed a large number of *craftsmen*
	38	If Demetrius and the *craftsmen* he has with him want to complain
1 Co	3 10	4 I succeeded as an *architect* and laid the foundations,
Heb 11	10 Θ	a city ⌐founded, designed and built by God (lit. with God as founder, *architect* and builder)
Rv 18	22	/2 never again will *craftsmen* of every *skill* be found [in Babylon]

9. TANNER OF LEATHER: *BYRSEUS*

byrseus 3

Ac	9 43	Peter stayed . . . in Jaffa, lodging with a *leather-tanner* called Simon.
	10 6	[Peter,] who is lodging with Simon the *tanner*
	32	Peter who is lodging in the house of Simon the *tanner,*

DOWN – BELOW – UNDER

1: Down, Below, the Bottom	3: Under (the Earth) – Down – Lower (regions)
2: Below = on (the) Earth	4: Under, in age

1 katō   (10)   2 hypo-katō (2)
3 katōteros   1

1: DOWN, BELOW, THE BOTTOM

Mt	4 6	If you are the Son of God . . . throw yourself *down;*
	27 51	the veil of the Temple was torn in two from top to *bottom;*
Mk 14	66	Peter was *down below* in the courtyard,
	15 38	the veil of the Temple was torn in two from top to *bottom.*
Lk	4 9	If you are the Son of God . . . throw yourself *down* from here
Ac 20	9	Eutychus . . . fell to the ground three floors *below.*

2: BELOW = ON (THE) EARTH

Jn	8 23	You are from *below;* I am from above.
Ac	2 19	I will display portents in heaven above and signs on earth *below.*

3: UNDER (THE EARTH) – DOWN – LOWER (REGIONS)

Jn 12	31	the prince of this world is to be ⌐overthrown (lit. thrown *down;* G driven out).
Ep	4 9	3 [Christ] descended right down to the *lower* regions ⌐of the earth (= under the earth, or: where the earth is)
Rv	5 3	2 there was no one, in heaven or on the earth or *under* the earth, who was able to open the scroll
	13	I heard all the living things in creation – everything that
	2	lives in the air, and on the ground, and *under* the ground . . . crying,

4: UNDER, IN AGE

Mt	2 16	Herod . . . had all the male children killed who were two years old or *under,*

DRAG – DRAW

1. Drag: *syrō*	**3. Draw – Pull:** *spaomai*
2. Drag – Draw: *helkō*	1: Draw (a sword)
1: Drag – Draw (a sword) – Haul in (a net)	2: Pull out – Draw(n) up
2: Draw (figuratively) – Attract	3: Pull on, Draw out
	4: (Be) Distracted, Distraction
	5: Draw away – Withdraw – Induce

1. DRAG: *SYRŌ*

1 syrō 5   2 kata-syrō 1

Lk 12	58	2 your opponent . . . may *drag* you before the judge

Jn 21	8	The other disciples came on in the boat, *towing* the net and the fish;
Ac 8	3	Saul . . . went from house to house ⌈arresting (lit. *dragging off*) both men and women and sending them to prison.
14	19	the people . . . *stoned* Paul and *dragged* him outside the town,
17	6	[the Jews] only found Jason and some of the brothers, and these they *dragged* before the city council,
Rv 12	4	[The dragon's] tail *dragged* a third of the stars from the sky

2. DRAG – DRAW: *HELKŌ*

1 *helkuō, helkō* 8   2 *ex-(h)elkō* 1

1: DRAG – DRAW (A SWORD) – HAUL IN (A NET)

Jn 18	10	Simon Peter, who carried a sword, *drew* it
21	6	there were so many fish that [the disciples] could not *haul* [the net] in.
	11	Simon Peter went aboard and *dragged* the net to the shore,
Ac 16	19	[the slave-girl's] masters . . . seized Paul and Silas and *dragged* them to the law courts in the market place
21	30	people . . . seized Paul and *dragged* him out of the Temple,
Jm 2	6	Isn't it always the rich who are against you? Isn't it always their doing when you are *dragged* before the court?

2: DRAW (FIGURATIVELY) – ATTACT

Jn 6	44 ⊖	No one can come to me unless he is *drawn* by the Father
12	32 X	I shall *draw* all (ᵛ men) to myself.
Jm 1	14	2 Everyone who is tempted is *attracted* and seduced by his own wrong desire.

3. DRAW – PULL: *SPAOMAI*

2	*spaomai* 2	4	*epi-spaomai* 1
3	*ana-spaō* 2	5	*peri-spaō* 1
1	*apo-spaō* 4	6	*a-peri-spastōs* 1

1: DRAW (A SWORD)

Mt 26	51	one of the followers of Jesus grasped his sword and *drew* it;
Mk 14	47	2 one of the bystanders *drew* his sword and struck out at the high priest's servant,
Ac 16	27	2 the gaoler . . . *drew* his sword and was about to commit suicide,

2: PULL OUT – DRAW(N) UP

Lk 14	5	3 Which of you here, if his son falls into a well . . . will not *pull* him *out* . . . without hesitation?
Ac 11	10	3 [the sheet] was *drawn up* to heaven again.

3: PULL ON, DRAW OUT

Co 7	18	If anyone had already been circumcised at the time of his call, he need not ⌈disguise it (lit. *pull on* [himself]), 4

4: (BE) DISTRACTED, DISTRACTION

Lk 10	40	5 Martha . . . was *distracted* with all the serving
Co 7	35	I say this . . . to make sure that . . . you give your ⌈undivided attention (lit. attention *without distraction*) to the Lord. 6

5: DRAW AWAY – WITHDRAW – INDUCE

Lk 22	41 X	[Jesus] *withdrew* from them, about a stone's throw away,
Ac 20	30	there will be men coming forward . . . to *induce* the disciples to follow them.
21	1	When we had at last ⌈torn ourselves (lit. *drawn*) *away* from [the elders of Ephesus] and put to sea, we . . . arrived at Cos;

DRIVE – SEND OUT – PUSH

1. Drive out – Send out – Take out: *ek-ballō*
  a) Cast out (demons) – Drive out (devils)
  b) Drive out, Throw out, Expel – Tear out, Turn out, Push out – Discharge
  c) Take out, Send out, Bring out – Draw (out)
2. Send out, Dismiss – Drive out: *ap-elaunō*
3. Drive out – Expel: *ex-airō*

4. Drive – Row – Push
  1: Drive – Row a boat: *elaunō*
    a) Drive
    b) Row a boat
  2: Drive (out) – Run aground: *ex-ōtheō*
  3: Push forward, to the front: *pro-ballō*
  4: Push, Prompt, Encourage (a person): *pro-bibazō*
5. Drive back: *klinō*

1. DRIVE OUT – SEND OUT – TAKE OUT: *EK-BALLŌ*

2 *ballō* 1/122   1 *ek-ballō* 78/81

a) Cast out (demons) – Drive out (devils)

Mt 7	22	did we not . . . *cast out* demons in your name . . .?
8	16 X	he *drove out* the spirits with a word
31 X	If you *cast* us *out*, send us into the herd of pigs.
9	33 X	when the devil was *cast out*, the dumb man spoke . . .
34	³⁴ But the Pharisees said, 'It is through the prince of devils that he *casts out* devils'.
X	
10	1	[Jesus] gave authority [to his twelve disciples] over unclean spirits with power to *cast* them *out* . . . ⁸ Cure the sick . . . *cast out* devils.
8	
12	24 X	the Pharisees . . . said, 'The man *casts out* devils only through Beelzebul . . .' ²⁵ . . . he said to them, . . . ²⁶ 'Now if Satan *casts out* Satan, he is divided against himself . . .
26 ⒟	
27 X	²⁷ And if it is through Beelzebul that I *cast out* devils, through whom do your own experts *cast* them *out*? . . .
28 X	²⁸ But if it is through the Spirit of God that I *cast* devils *out* . . .'
17	19	the disciples [said], 'Why were we unable to *cast* it *out*?'
Mk 1	34 X	he also *cast out* many devils,
39 X	he went all through Galilee, preaching in their synagogues and *casting out* devils.
3	15	[Jesus appointed twelve to be sent out to preach] with power to *cast out* devils.
22 X	It is through the prince of devils that he *casts* devils *out*.
23 ⒟	How can Satan *cast out* Satan?
6	13	[the Twelve] *cast out* many devils,
7	26 X	the woman . . . begged him to *cast* the devil *out* of her daughter.
9	18	I asked your disciples to *cast* [the spirit of dumbness] *out*
28	Why were we unable to *cast* it *out*?
38	we saw a man who is not one of us *casting out* devils in your name.
16	9 X	he appeared first to Mary of Magdala from whom he had *cast out* seven devils.
17	in my name they will *cast out* devils;
Lk 9	40	I begged your disciples to *cast* [the spirit] *out*,
49	we saw a man *casting out* devils in your name,
11	14 X	He was *casting out* a devil and it was dumb . . . ¹⁵ But some of [the people] said, 'It is through Beelzebul, the prince of devils, that he *casts out* devils'.
15 X	
18 X	you assert that it is through Beelzebul that I *cast out* devils.
19 X	¹⁹ Now if it is through Beelzebul that I *cast out* devils, through whom do your own experts *cast* them *out*? . . .
20 X	²⁰ But if it is through the finger of God that I *cast out* devils,
13	32	You may go and give that fox this message: Learn that today and tomorrow I *cast out* devils
X	
Jn 12	31 ●	now the prince of this world is to be ᵛ overthrown (G *driven out*).

b) Drive out, Throw out, Expel – Tear out, Turn out, Push out – Discharge

Mt 8	12	the subjects of the kingdom will be *turned out* into the dark,
9	25	when the people had been *turned out*
15	17	Can you not see that whatever . . . passes through the stomach . . . is *discharged* into the sewer?
21	12 X	Jesus then went into the Temple and *drove out* all those who were selling and buying there;
39	they seized [the heir] and *threw* him *out* of the vineyard
22	13	Bind [the man without a wedding garment] hand and foot and *throw* him *out* into the dark,
25	30	As for this good-for-nothing servant, *throw* him *out* into the dark,
Mk 1	12 ⒮	the Spirit *drove* [Jesus] *out* into the wilderness
5	40 X	he *turned* them all *out* and . . . went into the place where the child lay.

Mk 9 47   if your eye should cause you to sin, *tear* it *out*;
   11 15 X   he went into the Temple and began *driving out* those who were selling and buying there;
   12 8   they seized [the heir] and killed him and *threw* him *out* of the vineyard.
Lk 4 29   [everyone in the synagogue] sprang to their feet and *hustled* [Jesus] *out* of the town;
   13 28   there will be weeping . . . when you see . . . yourselves *turned outside.*
   19 45 X   he . . . began *driving out* those who were selling.
   20 12   they wounded [the third servant] also, and *threw* him *out.*
       15   they *threw* [the heir] *out* of the vineyard and killed him.
Jn 2 15 X   he *drove* [the cattle-sellers] all *out* of the Temple,
    6 37 X   whoever comes to me I shall not *turn* him *away*;
    9 34   [the Jews] *drove* [the man born blind] *away.*
       35   Jesus heard they had *driven* him *away*,
Ac 7 58   they ⌐sent (or: *drove*) [Stephen] *out* of the city and stoned him.
   13 50   the Jews . . . persuaded [the leading men of the city] to . . . *expel* [Paul and Barnabas] from their territory.
Ga 4 30   [Gn 21 10] *Drive away* that slave-girl and her son;
1 Jn 4 18   2 fear is *driven out* by perfect love:
3 Jn   10   [Diotrephes] *expels* [those who would have liked to welcome our brothers] from the church.

c) Take out, Send out, Bring out – Draw (out)

Mt 7 4   How dare you say to your brother, 'Let me *take* the splinter
        5   *out* of your eye' . . .? ⁵ Hypocrite! *Take* the plank *out* of your own eye first, and then you will see clearly enough to *take* the splinter *out* of your brother's eye.
    9 37   ask the Lord of the harvest to *send* labourers *out* to his harvest.
   12 20   [Is 42 3] He will not break the crushed reed . . . till he has *led* the truth to victory:
       35   A good man *draws* good things from his store of goodness; a bad man *draws* bad things from his store of badness.
   13 52   a householder . . . *brings out* from his storeroom things both new and old.
Mk 1 43 X   Jesus immediately *sent* [the leper] *away*
Lk 6 42   How can you say to your brother, 'Brother, let me *take out* the splinter that is in your eye' . . .? Hypocrite! *Take* the plank *out* of your own eye first, and then you will see clearly enough to *take out* the splinter that is in your brother's eye.
   10 2   ask the Lord of the harvest to *send* labourers *out* to his harvest.
       35   [the Samaritan] *took out* two denarii and handed them to the innkeeper.
Jn 10 4   When [the shepherd] has *brought out* his flock, he goes ahead of them,
Ac 7 58   they ⌐sent (or: *drove*) [Stephen] *out* of the city and stoned him.
    9 40   Peter *sent* them all *out* of the room
   16 37   They . . . think they can *push* us *out* on the quiet!
Jm 2 25   Rahab . . . welcomed the messengers and showed them a different way to *leave.*

2. SEND OUT, DISMISS – DRIVE OUT: *AP-ELAUNŌ*
ap-elaunō 1

Ac 18 16   [Gallio] *sent* the Jews *out* of the court.

3. DRIVE OUT – EXPEL: *EX-AIRŌ*
ex-airō 1

1 Co 5 13   [Dt 24 7] You must *drive out* this evil-doer from among you.

4. DRIVE – ROW – PUSH

1: DRIVE – ROW A BOAT: *ELAUNŌ*
elaunō 5

a) Drive

Lk 8 29 Ⓓ   the devil would *drive* [the madman] out into the wilds.
Jm 3 4   no matter how big [ships] are, even if a gale is *driving* them, the man at the helm can steer them
2 P 2 17   People like this are . . . fogs ⌐swirling in the wind (lit. *driven* by a whirlwind),

b) Row a boat

Mk 6 48   [Jesus] could see [the disciples] were worn out with *rowing*,

Jn 6 19   [The disciples] had *rowed* three or four miles when they saw Jesus walking on the lake

2: DRIVE (OUT) – RUN AGROUND: *EX-ŌTHEŌ*
ex-ōtheō 2

Ac 7 45 Θ   the nations . . . were *driven out* by God as we advanced.
   27 39   [the sailors] planned to *run* the ship *aground* on [the beach] if they could.

3: PUSH FORWARD, TO THE FRONT: *PRO-BALLŌ*
pro-ballō 1/2

Ac 19 33   The Jews *pushed* Alexander *to the front*,

4: PUSH, PROMPT, ENCOURAGE (A PERSON): *PRO-BIBAZŌ*
pro-bibazō 2

Mt 14 8   *Prompted* by her mother, [Salome] said,
Ac 19 33   The Jews pushed Alexander to the front, and . . . some of the crowd *shouted encouragement*

5. DRIVE BACK: *KLINŌ*
klinō 1/7

Heb 11 34   weak people . . . were given strength [to] *drive back* foreign invaders.

DRY – WITHER

1: Dry (land)	4: (Trees, Plants) Wither, Wither away
2: Dry up, (Be) Dry	
3: Dried = Ripe	5: (Part of the body is) Withered – (Be) Paralysed, (Go) Rigid

1 *xērainō 15*   2 *xēros 8*

1: DRY (LAND)

Mt 23 15   2 Pharisees . . . who travel over sea and *dry* [land] to make a single proselyte,
Heb 11 29   2 [the Israelites] crossed the Red Sea as easily as *dry* land,

2: DRY UP, (BE) DRY

Mk 5 29   the source of the [woman's] bleeding *dried up* instantly,
Lk 23 31   if men use the green wood like this, what will happen when
     < 2   it is *dry*?
Rv 16 12   all the water of the river [Euphrates] *dried up* so that a way was made for the kings of the East to come in.

3: DRIED = RIPE

Rv 14 15   harvest time has come and the harvest of the earth is *ripe*.

4: (TREES, PLANTS) WITHER, WITHER AWAY

Mt 13 6   as soon as the sun came up [the seeds] were scorched and,
     <   not having any roots, they *withered away.*
   21 19   at that instant the fig tree *withered.*
       20   What happened to the fig tree . . . that it *withered* there and then?
Mk 4 6   when the sun came up [the seed] was scorched and, not having
     <   any roots, it *withered away.*
   11 20   they saw the fig tree *withered* to the roots.
       21   the fig tree you cursed has *withered away.*
Lk 8 6 <   when [the seed] came up it *withered away*, having no moisture
Jn 15 6   Anyone who does not remain in me is like a branch that has been thrown away – he *withers*;
Jm 1 11   the scorching sun comes up, and the grass *withers*,
1 P 1 24   [Is 40 7] The grass *withers*, the flower falls,

5: (PART OF THE BODY IS) WITHERED – (BE) PARALYSED, (GO) RIGID

Mt	12	10	2 a man was there . . . who had a *withered* hand.
Mk	3	1	there was a man there who had a *withered* hand.
		3	2 [Jesus] said to the man with the *withered* hand, 'Stand up'

Mk	9	18	he foams at the mouth and grinds his teeth and goes *rigid*.
Lk	6	6	2 a man was there whose right hand was *withered*.
		8	2 [Jesus] said to the man with the *withered* hand, 'Stand up!'
Jn	5	3	2 crowds of sick people – blind, lame, *paralysed* – waiting for the water to move;

E

EARTH – LAND – COUNTRY

1. the Ground – the Earth
 1: the Ground: *edaphos*
 2: the Ground – Under the earth: *chamai*
  a) the Ground
  b) Under the earth
2. Dust – Earthly, On earth
 1: Dust: *koni-ortos*
 2: Earthly, On earth – Dust: *choikos*
3. Earth – Land – the Ground: *gē*
  a) the Earth – Earthly
  b) the Land – the Ground – Soil, Earth
  c) (under) Ground – (in the heart of the) Earth
  d) the Land (of Israel) – the Countryside
  e) the Land (of Sodom, of Midian)
4. Field(s) – Land, the Countryside: *agros*

  a) a Field, (piece of) Land – Farm
  b) the Field(s), the Country (side)
  c) Wild
5. Land – Country, District – Field, Estate: *chōra*
  a) (cultivated) Land, Field, Estate
  b) Country, Land – Countryside – District
6. Region(s), District, Neighbourhood
  1: Region(s): *klima*
  2: District, Neighbourhood, Region – Territory: *horion*
7. Arabia – Illyricum, Dalmatia – Spain
  1: Arabia, Arabs
  2: Illyricum = Dalmatia
  3: Spain

1. THE GROUND – THE EARTH

1: THE GROUND: *EDAPHOS*

edaphos 1

Ac 22 7   I fell to the *ground* and heard a voice saying, 'Saul, Saul, why are you persecuting me?'

2: THE GROUND – UNDER THE EARTH: *CHAMAI*

1 *chamai* 2   2 *kata-chthonios* 1

a) the Ground

Jn 9 6   [Jesus] spat on the *ground*, made a paste with the spittle,
  18 6   [the cohort and the guards] moved back and fell to the *ground*.

b) Under the earth

Ph 2 10   [God raised him high] so that all beings in the heavens, on
  2   earth and ⌐in the underworld (or: under the earth), should bend the knee at the name of Jesus

2. DUST – EARTHLY, ON EARTH

1: DUST: *KONI-ORTOS*

koni-ortos 5

Mt 10 14   as you walk out of the . . . town shake the *dust* from your feet.
Lk 9 5   when you leave their town shake the *dust* from your feet
  10 11   We wipe off the very *dust* of your town that clings to our feet, and leave it with you.
Ac 13 51   [Paul and Barnabas] shook the *dust* from their feet in defiance
  22 23   [The Jews] were yelling . . . and throwing *dust* into the air,

2: EARTHLY, ON EARTH – DUST: *CHOIKOS*

1 *choikos* 4   2 *chous* 2

Mk 6 11   2 as you walk away shake off the *dust* from under your feet
1 Co 15 47   The first man, being from the earth, is *earthly* by nature; the second man is from heaven. [48] As this *earthly* man was, so are [we] *on earth*; and as the heavenly man is, so are we in heaven. [49] And we, who have been modelled on the *earthly* man, will be modelled on the heavenly man.
  48
  49
Rv 18 19   2 [The captains and seafaring men] will throw *dust* on their heads,

3. EARTH – LAND – THE GROUND: *GĒ*

1 *gē* 174/252   2 *epi-geios* 1/7

a) the Earth – Earthly

see also Heaven and Earth *under* **HEAVEN 1.2:**

Mt 5 4   Happy the gentle: they shall have the *earth* for their heritage.
  13   You are the salt of the *earth*.
  9 6   the Son of Man has authority on *earth* to forgive sins,
  10 34   Do not suppose that I have come to bring peace to the *earth*:
  12 42   the Queen of the South . . . came from the ends of the *earth*
  17 25   From whom do the kings of the *earth* take toll or tribute?
  23 35   you will draw down on yourselves the blood of every holy man that has been shed on *earth*,
  24 30   all the peoples of the *earth* will beat their breasts;
Mk 2 10   the Son of Man has authority on *earth* to forgive sins,
  4 31   a mustard seed . . . is the smallest of all the seeds on *earth*;
  9 3   [Jesus's] clothes became . . . whiter than any *earthly* bleacher could make them.
Lk 2 14   peace on *earth* to men who enjoy [God's] favour.
  5 24   the Son of Man has authority on *earth* to forgive sins,
  11 31   the Queen of the South . . . came from the ends of the *earth*
  12 49   I have come to bring fire to the *earth*,
  51   Do you suppose that I am here to bring peace on *earth*?
  18 8   when the Son of Man comes, will he find any faith on *earth*?
  21 35   [that day] will come down on every living man on the face of the *earth*.
Jn 12 32   when I am lifted up from the *earth*, I shall draw all men to myself.
  17 4   I have glorified you on *earth*
Ac 1 8   you will be my witnesses not only in Jerusalem but . . . to the ends of the *earth*.
  3 25   (Gn 22 18) in your offspring all the families of the *earth* will be blessed.
  4 26   (Ps 2 2) Kings on *earth* setting out to war,
  8 33   (Is 53 8) his life on *earth* has been cut short!
  10 11   [Peter] saw . . . something like a big sheet being let down to ⌐earth (or: the ground)
  13 47   (Is 49 6) I have made you a light for the nations, so that my salvation may reach the ends of the *earth*.
  17 26   [God] created the whole human race so that they could occupy the entire *earth*
  22 22   Rid the *earth* of the man!
Rm 9 17   (Ex 9 16) I raised you up . . . to make my name known throughout the *world*.
  28   (Is 10 23) the Lord will execute his sentence on the *earth*.
  10 18   (Ps 19 4) their voice has gone out through all the *earth*, and their message to the ends of the world.
1 Co 10 26   (Ps 24 1) the *earth* and everything that is in it belong to the Lord.
Ep 4 9   [Christ] descended right down to the lower regions ⌐of the earth (= under the earth, or: where the *earth* is).
  Δ
  6 3   (Ex 20 12) you will prosper and have a long life ⌐in the land (or: on the *earth*).
Col 3 2   Let your thoughts be on heavenly things, not on the things that are on the *earth*,
  5   kill everything in you that belongs only to *earthly* life:
Jm 3 15   principles of this kind are not the wisdom that comes down
  2   from above: they are only *earthly*,
  5 5   On *earth* you have had a life of comfort and luxury;
Rv 1 5   Jesus Christ, . . . the Ruler of the kings of the *earth*.
  7   all the races of the *earth* will mourn over [Jesus Christ].
  3 10   I will keep you safe in the time of trial which is going to come . . . to test the people of the *earth*.
  5 6   God has sent [the seven Spirits] out all over the *world*.
  10   [the Lamb] made [every people and nation] a line of kings and priests, to serve our God and to rule the *world*.
  6 4   out came another horse . . . and its rider was given this duty: to take away peace from the *earth*
  8   [Plague and Hades] were given authority over a quarter of the *earth*, to kill . . . by plague and wild beasts of the *earth*.
  10   how much longer will you wait before you pass sentence . . . on the inhabitants of the *earth*?
  15   the *earthly* rulers . . . took to the mountains to hide in caves
  7 1   I saw four angels, standing at the four corners of the *earth*, holding the four winds of the *earth* back
  8 5   the angel . . . filled [the censer] with the fire from the altar, which he then threw down on to the *earth*,
  7   hail and fire, mixed with blood, were dropped on the *earth*; a third of the *earth* was burnt up,

Rv	8 13	Trouble, trouble, trouble, for all the people on *earth*
	9 3	out of the smoke dropped locusts onto the *earth* which were given the powers that scorpions have on the *earth*:
	4	[the locusts] were forbidden to harm any ʳfields (lit. grass of the *earth*)
	11 4	These are the two olive trees . . . that stand before the Lord of the *world*.
	10	the people of the *earth* will be glad . . . because these two prophets have been a plague to the people of the *earth*.
	18	The time has come to destroy those who are destroying the *earth*.
	12 16	the *earth* came to [the woman's] rescue; ʳit (lit. the *earth*) opened its mouth and swallowed the river
	13 3	the whole *world* had marvelled and followed the beast.
	8	all people of the *earth* will worship [the beast].
	12	This second beast was . . . making the *earth* and all its people worship the first beast,
	14	[the second beast] was able to win over the people of the *earth* and persuade ʳthem (lit. the people of the *earth*) to put up a statue in honour of the beast
	14 3	they were singing a new hymn . . . that could only be learnt by the hundred and forty-four thousand who had been redeemed from the *earth*.
	6	I saw another angel . . . sent to announce the Good News . . . to all who live on the *earth*,
	15	the harvest of the *earth* is ripe.
	16	the [angel] sitting on the cloud set his sickle to work on the *earth*, and the *earth*'s harvest was reaped.
	18	cut all the bunches off the vine of the *earth*;
	19	So the angel set his sickle to work on the *earth* and harvested the whole vintage of the *earth*
	16 1	I heard a voice . . . shouting to the seven angels, 'Go, and empty the seven bowls of God's anger over the *earth*'.
	2	²The first angel went and emptied his bowl over the *earth*;
	18	[there was] the most violent earthquake that anyone has ever seen since there have been men on the *earth*.
	17 2	[I will show you the punishment given to] the one with whom all the kings of the *earth* have committed fornication, and who has made all the population of the *earth* drunk with the wine of her adultery.
	5	Babylon . ., the mother of all the prostitutes . . . on the *earth*.
	8	the people of the *earth* . . . will think [the beast] miraculous
	18	The woman . . . is the great city which has authority over all the rulers on *earth*.
	18 3	every king in the *earth* has committed fornication with her, and every merchant in the *earth* grown rich through her debauchery.
	9	There will be mourning . . . for her by the kings of the *earth*
	11	There will be weeping . . . over her among all the traders of the *earth*
	23	Your traders were the princes of the *earth*,
	24	In her you will find . . . all the blood that was ever shed on *earth*.
	19 2	[God] has condemned the famous prostitute who corrupted the *earth*
	19	I saw the beast, with all the kings of the *earth*
	20 8	Satan . . . will come out to deceive all the nations in the four corners of the *earth*,
	21 24	the kings of the *earth* will bring [Jerusalem] their treasures.

b) the Land – the Ground – Soil, Earth

Mt	10 29	not one [sparrow] falls to the *ground* without your Father knowing.
	13 5 <	Others fell on patches of rock where they found little *soil* and sprang up straight away, because there was no depth of *earth* . . . ⁸ Others fell on rich *soil* and produced their crop,
	8 <	
	23 <	the one who received the seed in rich *soil* is the man who hears the word and understands it;
	14 24	the boat, by now far out ᵛ on the lake (G from the *land*), was battling with a heavy sea,
	34	Having made the crossing, they came to *land* at Gennesaret.
	15 35	[Jesus] instructed the crowd to sit down on the *ground*
	25 18	the man who had received one [talent] went off and dug a hole in the *ground* and hid his master's money.
	25	I was afraid, and I went off and hid your talent in the *ground*.
	27 51	[Jesus yielded up his spirit;] the *earth* quaked;
Mk	4 1	The people were all along the *shore*, at the water's edge.
	5 <	Some seed fell on rocky ground where it found little *soil* and sprang up straightaway, because there was no depth of *earth* . . . ⁸ And some seeds fell into rich *soil* and . . . produced a crop;
	8 <	
	20 <	those who have received the seed in rich *soil* . . . hear the word and accept it
	26 <	This is what the kingdom of God is like. A man throws seed on the *land*.

Mk	4 28 <	Of its own accord the *land* produces first the shoot, then the ear,
	31	a mustard seed . . . at the time of its sowing in the *soil* is the smallest of all the seeds
	6 47	the boat was far out on the lake, and [Jesus] was alone on the *land*.
	53	Having made the crossing, they came to *land* at Gennesaret
	8 6	[Jesus] instructed the crowd to sit down on the *ground*,
	9 20	the spirit . . . threw the boy into convulsions, and he fell to the *ground*
	14 35	going on a little further [Jesus] threw himself on the *ground*
Lk	5 3	[Jesus] asked [Simon] to put out a little from the *shore*.
	11	bringing their boats back to *land*, [Simon, James and John] left everything and followed [Jesus].
	6 49	the one who listens and does nothing is like the man who built his house on *soil*, with no foundations;
	8 8 <	some seed fell into rich *soil* and . . . produced its crop
	15 <	As for the part in the rich *soil*, this is people . . . who . . . take [the word] to themselves and yield a harvest
	27	[Jesus] was stepping ʳashore (lit. onto the *land*) when a man . . . who was possessed by devils came towards him;
	13 7	why should [this fig tree] be taking up the *ground*?
	14 35	[The salt that loses its taste] is good for neither *soil* nor manure heap.
	22 44	[Jesus's] sweat fell to the *ground* like great drops of blood.
	24 5	Terrified, the women ʳlowered their eyes (lit. turned their faces to the *ground*).
Jn	6 21	in no time [the boat] reached the *shore* at the place they were making for.
	8 6	Jesus bent down and started writing on the *ground* with his finger.
	8	[Jesus] bent down and wrote on the *ground* again.
	12 24	unless a wheat grain falls on the *ground* and dies, it remains only a single grain;
	21 8	[the disciples] were only about a hundred yards from *land*.
	9	As soon as [the disciples] came ʳashore (lit. onto the *land*) they saw . . . a charcoal fire with fish cooking on it.
	11	Simon Peter went aboard and dragged the net to the *shore*,
Ac	7 33	(Ex 3 5) the place where you are standing is holy *ground*.
	9 4	He fell to the *ground*, and then he heard a voice saying, 'Saul, Saul got up from the *ground*,
	10 11	[Peter] saw . . . something like a big sheet being let down to ʳearth (or: the *ground*)
	26 14	We all fell to the *ground*, and I heard a voice . . , 'Saul, Saul,
	27 39	When day came [the crew] did not recognise the *land*,
	43	the centurion . . . gave orders that those who could swim should jump overboard first and so get ʳashore (lit. onto the *land*),
	44	In this way all came safe and sound to *land*.
Ep	6 3	(Ex 20 12) you will prosper and have a long life ʳin the *land* (or: on the earth).
Heb	6 7	ʳA field (lit. *Land*) that has been well watered . . . gives the crops that are wanted
	11 29	It was by faith they crossed the Red Sea as easily as dry *land*,
	38	[Gideon, Barak . . and the prophets] went out to live in deserts . . . and ravines in the *earth*.
Jm	5 7	Think of a farmer: how patiently he waits for the precious fruit of the *ground*
Rv	7 1	I saw four angels . . . holding the four winds . . . back to keep them from blowing over the *land* or the sea
	2	another angel . . . called . . . to the four angels whose duty was to devastate *land* and sea,
	3	Wait before you do any damage on *land* or at sea or to the trees,
	13 11	I saw a second beast; it emerged from the *ground*;

c) (under) Ground – (in the heart of the) Earth

Mt	12 40	the Son of Man [will] be in the heart of the *earth* for three days and three nights.
Ep	4 9 Δ	[Christ] descended right down to the lower regions ʳof the earth (= under the *earth*, or: where the earth is)
Rv	5 3 Δ	there was no one, in heaven or on the earth or under the *earth* who was able to open the scroll
	13	I heard all the living things . . . in the air, and on the ground, and under the *ground* and in the sea, crying,

d) the Land (of Israel) – the Countryside

C Canaan 2

Mt	2 6	(Mi 5 1) Bethlehem, in the *land* of Judah,
	20	take the child and his mother with you and go back to the *land* of Israel.
	21	Joseph got up and . . . went back to the *land* of Israel.
	4 15	(Is 8 23) *Land* of Zebulun! *Land* of Naphtali!
	9 26	the news spread all round the *countryside*.
	31	they talked about [Jesus] all over the *countryside*.
	27 45	From the sixth hour there was darkness over all the *land*
Mk	15 33	When the sixth hour came there was darkness over the whole *land*

Lk	4 25	in Elijah's day . . . a great famine raged throughout the *land*,
	21 23	great misery will descend on the *land*
	23 44	a darkness came over the whole *land* until the ninth hour.
Jn	3 22	Jesus went . . . into the Judaean *countryside* and . . . baptised.
Ac	7 3	(Gn 12 1) Leave your country . . . and go to the *land* I will show you.
	4	God made [Abraham] leave Haran and come to this *land* where you are living today.
	11 C	(Gn 41 54) Then a famine . . . caused much suffering throughout Egypt and *Canaan*,
	13 19 C	(Dt 7 1) When [God] had destroyed seven nations in the *land* of *Canaan*, he put [our ancestors] in possession of their *land*
Heb	11 9	By faith [Abraham] arrived . . . in the Promised *Land*, and lived there as if in a strange country,
Rv	20 9	[Gog and Magog] will come swarming over the entire *country*

e) the Land (of Sodom, of Midian)

Midian 1

Mt	10 15	it will not go as hard with the *land* of Sodom and Gomorrah as with that town.
	11 24	it will not go as hard with the *land* of Sodom on Judgement day as with you.
Ac	7 29	(Ex 2 15) Moses . . . went to stay in the *land* of *Midian*,

4. FIELD(S) – LAND, THE COUNTRYSIDE: *AGROS*

2 *agrios* 3   3 *agr(-auleō)* 1
1 *agros* 37

a) a Field, (piece of) Land – Farm

Mt	13 24 <	The kingdom of heaven may be compared to a man who sowed good seed in his *field*.
	27 <	Sir, was it not good seed that you sowed in your *field*?
	31 <	The kingdom of heaven is like a mustard seed which a man took and sowed in his *field*.
	36 <	Explain the parable about the darnel in the *field* to us.
	38 <	The *field* is the world;
	44 <	The kingdom of heaven is like treasure hidden in a *field* which someone has found; . . . he sells everything he owns and buys the *field*.
	19 29	everyone who has left houses . . . or *land* for the sake of my name will be repaid
	22 5	one went off to his ᴿ*farm* (or: *land*), another to his business,
	27 7	[the chief priests] bought the potter's *field* [with the thirty silver pieces]
	8	the *field* is called the *Field* of Blood today.
	10	(Zc 11 13) they gave [the thirty silver pieces] for the potter's *field*,
Mk	6 36	they can go to the *farms* and villages round about,
	56	wherever [Jesus] went, to village . . . or *farm*, they laid down the sick in the open spaces,
	10 29	there is no one who has left house . . . or *land* for my sake
	30	. . . ³⁰ who will not be repaid a hundred times over, houses . . . *land*
	11 8	Many people spread their cloaks on the road, others greenery which they had cut in the *fields*.
Lk	9 12	they can go to the villages and *farms* round about
	14 18	I have bought a *piece of land* and must go and see it.
	15 15	one of the local inhabitants . . . put [the prodigal son] on his ᴿ*farm* (or: *field*) to feed the pigs.
	25	the elder son was out in the *fields*,
	17 7	Which of you, with a servant . . . would say to him when he returned from the *fields*,
Ac	4 37	[Barnabas] owned a *piece of land* and he sold it and . . . presented [the money] to the apostles.

b) the Field(s), the Country(side)

Mt	6 28	Think of the flowers growing in the *fields*;
	30	that is how God clothes the grass in the *field* which is here today and thrown into the furnace tomorrow,
	24 18	if a man is in the *fields*, he must not turn back
	40	Then of two men in the *fields* one is taken, one left;
Mk	5 14	The swineherds . . . told their story in the town and in the *country* round about;
	13 16	if a man is in the *fields*, he must not turn back
	15 21	They enlisted . . . Simon of Cyrene . . . who was coming in from the *country*, to carry [Jesus's] cross.
	16 12	[Jesus] showed himself . . . to two of them as they were on their way into the *country*.
Lk	2 8	In the countryside close by there were shepherds who lived in the *fields*
	8 34	the swineherds . . . told their story in the town and in the *country* round about;

Lk	12 28	that is how God clothes the grass in the *field* which is there today and thrown into the furnace tomorrow,
	17 31	nor must anyone in the *fields* turn back either.
	36	(ᵛ Then of two men in the *fields* one is taken, one left;)
	23 26	they seized on a man, Simon from Cyrene, who was coming in from the *country*, and made him shoulder the cross

c) Wild

Mt	3 4	2 [John's] food was locusts and *wild* honey.
Mk	1 6	2 John . . . lived on locusts and *wild* honey.
Jude	13	2 [these people are] like *wild* sea waves capped with shame as if with foam;

5. LAND – COUNTRY, DISTRICT – FIELD, ESTATE: *CHŌRA*

1 *chōra* 28   3 *peri-chōros* 9
2 *chōrion* 10

a) (cultivated) Land, Field, Estate

Hakel-dama 1 (Ac 1)   *Gethsemane* 2 (Mt; Mk)

Mt	26 36	2 Jesus came with them to a *small estate* called *Gethsemane*;
Mk	14 32	2 They came to a *small estate* called *Gethsemane*,
Lk	12 16	There was once a rich man who . . . had a good harvest from his *land*,
Jn	4 35	look at the *fields*; already they are white, ready for harvest!
Ac	1 18	2 [Judas] bought a *field* with the money he was paid for his crime . . . ¹⁹ . . . the *field* came to be called the Bloody
	19	2 ᴿ*Acre* (or: *field*) in their language *Hakeldama*.
	4 34	2 all those who owned *land* or houses would sell them,
	5 3	how can Satan have so possessed you that you should . . . keep back part of the money from the *land*?
	8	2 Tell me, was this the price you sold the *land* for?
	28 7	2 In that neighbourhood there were *estates* belonging to the prefect of the island, whose name was Publius.
Jm	5 4	Labourers mowed your *fields*, and you cheated them

b) Country, Land – Countryside – District

Mt	2 12	[the wise men] returned to their own *country* by a different way
	3 5	3 the whole Jordan *district* made their way to [John the Baptist],
	4 16	(Is 9 1) on those who dwell in the *land* and shadow of death, a light has dawned.
	8 28	When [Jesus] reached the *country* of the Gadarenes . . . two demoniacs came towards him
	14 35	3 When the local people recognised [Jesus] they spread the news through the whole *neighbourhood*
Mk	1 5	ᴿAll (lit. The entire *country* of) Judaea and all the people of Jerusalem made their way to [John the Baptist],
	28	3 [Jesus's] reputation rapidly spread . . . through all the surrounding Galilean *countryside*.
	5 1	They reached the *country* of the Gerasenes
	10	[the unclean spirit] begged [Jesus] earnestly not to send them out of the *district*.
	6 55	[people] started hurrying all through the *countryside*
Lk	2 8	In the *countryside* close by there were shepherds
	3 1	Philip, tetrarch of the *lands* of Ituraea and Trachonitis,
	3	3 [John] went through the whole Jordan *district* proclaiming a baptism
	4 14	3 [Jesus's] reputation spread throughout the *countryside*.
	37	3 reports of [Jesus] went all through the surrounding *countryside*.
	7 17	this opinion of [Jesus] spread throughout Judaea and all over the *countryside*.
	8 26	They came to land in the *country* of the Gerasenes,
	37	3 The entire population of the Gerasene *territory* was in a state of panic
	15 13	the younger son . . . left for a distant *country*
	14	that *country* experienced a severe famine,
	15	[the prodigal son] hired himself out to one of the *local* inhabitants
	19 12 <	A man of noble birth went to a distant *country* to be appointed king
	21 21	those in *country* districts must not take refuge in [Jerusalem].
Jn	4 5	2 Sychar, near the *land* that Jacob gave to his son Joseph.
	11 54	Jesus . . . left . . . for a town called Ephraim, in the *country* bordering on the desert,
	55	many of the *country* people . . . had gone up to Jerusalem
Ac	8 1	everyone . . . fled to the *country* districts of Judaea and Samaria.
	10 39	I . . . can witness to everything [Jesus] did throughout the *countryside* of Judaea
	12 20	[the] *country* [of the Tyrians and Sidonians] depend for its food supply on King Herod's territory.
	13 49	the word of the Lord spread through the whole *countryside*.
	14 6	the apostles . . . went off for safety to Lycaonia where, in the towns of Lystra and Derbe and in the *surrounding country* [they preached the Good News].

Ac 16	6	[Paul and Timothy] travelled through Phrygia and the Galatian *country*,
18	23	[Paul continued] his journey through the Galatian *country* and then through Phrygia,
26	20	I started preaching . . . to . . . all the *countryside* of Judaea,
27	27	the crew sensed that *land* of some sort was near.

6. REGION(S), DISTRICT, NEIGHBOURHOOD

1: REGIONS: *KLIMA*

klima 3

Rm 15	23	Now, however, having no more work to do ⌐here (lit. in these *regions*), [I hope to see you]
2 Co 11	10	this cause of boasting will never be taken from me in the *regions* of Achaia,
Ga 1	21	After that I went to the *regions* of Syria and Cilicia,

2: DISTRICT, NEIGHBOURHOOD, REGION – TERRITORY: *HORION*

horion 12

Mt 2	16	in Bethlehem and its surrounding *district* [Herod] had all the male children killed
4	13	Capernaum, a lakeside town ⌐on the borders (lit. in the *territory*) of Zebulun and Naphtali.
8	34	[the Gadarenes] implored [Jesus] to leave the *neighbourhood*.
15	22	Then out came a Canaanite woman from [the] *district* [of Tyre and Sidon]
	39	[Jesus] went to the *district* of Magadan.
19	1	Jesus . . . came into the ⌐*part* (or: *region*) of Judaea which is on the far side of the Jordan.
Mk 5	17	[the Gerasenes] began to implore Jesus to leave the *neighbourhood*.
7	24	[Jesus] set out for the *territory* of Tyre.
	31	Returning from the *district* of Tyre, [Jesus] went by way of Sidon . . . right through the Decapolis *region*.
10	1	[Jesus] came to the *district* of Judaea and the far side of the Jordan.
Ac 13	50	the Jews . . . persuaded them to turn against Paul and Barnabas and expel them from their *territory*.

7. ARABIA – ILLYRICUM, DALMATIA – SPAIN

1: ARABIA, ARABS

Arabs 1   Arabia 2

Ac 2	11	Cretans and *Arabs*; we hear them preaching in our own language about the marvels of God.
Ga 1	17	I went off to *Arabia* at once and later . . . to Damascus.
4	25	since (§ Hagar, Mount) Sinai is in *Arabia*

2: ILLYRICUM = DALMATIA

Dalmatia 1   Illyricum 1

Rm 15	19	from Jerusalem to *Illyricum*, I have preached Christ's Good News
2 Tm 4	10	Titus [has gone] to *Dalmatia*;

3: SPAIN

Spain 2

Rm 15	24	I hope to see you on my way to *Spain*
	28	when I have done this . . . I shall set out for *Spain*

EASIER – DIFFICULT

1. Easier: *eu-kopos*	**3:** Difficult (to face), (causing) Trouble – Fierce, Violent: *chalepos*
2. Difficult, Hard – Fierce	
1: Hard: *dys-kolos*	**4:** Fierce – Savage(s): *an-(h)ēmeros*
2: Hard, With Difficulty – Hardly, Scarcely – Struggle, (Be) Slow to: *molis*	

1. EASIER: *EU-KOPOS*

eu-kopos 7

Mt 9	5	which of these is *easier*: to say, 'Your sins are forgiven . . .'
19	24	it is *easier* for a camel to pass through the eye of a needle
Mk 2	9	Which of these is *easier*: to say to the paralytic, 'Your sins are forgiven'
10	25	It is *easier* for a camel to pass through the eye of a needle
Lk 5	23	Which of these is *easier*: to say, 'Your sins are forgiven you'
16	17	It is *easier* for heaven and earth to disappear
18	25	it is *easier* for a camel to pass through the eye of a needle

2. DIFFICULT, HARD – FIERCE

1: HARD: *DYS-KOLOS*

2 dys-kolos 1   1 dys-kolōs 3

Mt 19	23		it will be *hard* for a rich man to enter the kingdom of heaven.
Mk 10	23		How *hard* it is for those who have riches to enter the kingdom of God! ²⁴ . . . how *hard* it is to enter the kingdom of God!
	24	2	
Lk 18	24		How *hard* it is for those who have riches to make their way into the kingdom of God!

2: HARD, WITH DIFFICULTY – HARDLY, SCARCELY – STRUGGLE, (BE) SLOW TO: *MOLIS*

molis 7

Lk 9	39	[the spirit] *is slow to* leave [my son] but when it does it leaves the boy worn out.
Ac 14	18	Even this speech . . . was *scarcely* enough to stop the crowd offering [Barnabas and Paul] sacrifice.
27	7	we had *difficulty* in making Cnidus.
	8	[we] *struggled* along the coast [of Crete]
	16	We . . . managed *with* some *difficulty* to bring the ship's boat under control.
Rm 5	7 ●	[Christ died for sinful men.] It is *not easy* to die even for a good man
1 P 4	18 ●	If it is *hard* for a good man to be saved, what will happen to the wicked . . .?

3: DIFFICULT (TO FACE), (CAUSING) TROUBLE – FIERCE, VIOLENT: *CHALEPOS*

chalepos 2

Mt 8	28	two demoniacs . . . creatures so *fierce* that no one could pass that way.
2 Tm 3	1	in the last days there are going to be some *difficult* times.

4: FIERCE – SAVAGE(S): *AN-(H)ĒMEROS*

an-(h)ēmeros 1

2 Tm 3	3	[people will be] profligates, ⌐*savages* and (or: *fierce*) enemies of everything that is good;

EAST – WEST

1. East: *ana-tolē*	**4. South**
2. West: *dysmē*	1: *notos*
3. North: *borras*	2: *mes-(h)ēmbria*
	5. South-west and North-west: *lips* and *chōros*

1. EAST: *ANA-TOLĒ*

ana-tolē 9/10

Mt 2	1	some wise men came to Jerusalem from the *east*.
	2	We saw his star ⌐as it rose (or: in the *east*)
	9	there in front of them was the star they had seen ⌐rising (or: in the *east*);
8	11	many will come from *east* and west to take their places with Abraham . . . at the feast in the kingdom of heaven;
24	27	like lightning striking in the *east*
Lk 13	29	men from *east* and west, from north and south, will come to take their places at the feast in the kingdom of God.
Rv 7	2	I saw another angel rising ⌐where the sun rises (or: in the *east*),

Rv 16 12	a way was made for the kings of ʳthe *East* (or: where the sun rises) to come in.	
21 13	[The city had twelve gates;] on the *east* there were three gates,	

2. WEST: *DYSMĒ*

dysmē 5

Mt 8 11	many will come from east and *west*
24 27	like lightning striking in the east and flashing far into the *west*.
Lk 12 54	When you see a cloud looming up in the *west*
13 29	men from east and *west*, from north and south, will come
Rv 21 13	[The city had twelve gates;] on the *west* three gates.

3. NORTH: *BORRAS*

borras 2

Lk 13 29	men from east and west, from *north* and south, will come
Rv 21 13	[The city had twelve gates;] on the *north* three gates,

4. SOUTH

1: SOUTH: *NOTOS*

notos 4/7

Mt 12 42	○	On Judgement day the Queen of the *South* will rise up
Lk 11 31	○	On Judgement day the Queen of the *South* will rise up
13 29		men from east and west, from north and *south*, will come
Rv 21 13		[The city had twelve gates;] on the *south* three gates,

2: SOUTH: *MES-(H)ĒMBRIA*

mes-(h)ēmbria 1/2

Ac 8 26	Be ready to set out ʳat noon (or: *south*) along the road that goes from Jerusalem down to Gaza,

5. SOUTH-WEST and NORTH-WEST: *LIPS* and *CHŌROS*

1 chōros 1   2 lips 1

Ac 27 12	2/ Phoenix – a harbour in Crete, facing *south-west* and *north-west*.

EAT – FOOD – DRINK

1. Famine – Hunger, Hungry, Starving – to Fast
1: Famine – Hunger, Hungry: *limos*
2: Be hungry, to Hunger – Feel, Go hungry: *peinaō*
3: to Fast – Hungry, Starving: *nēsteia*
4: Go hungry, Be without food: *a-sitia*

2. Eat
1: Eat, Ate: *trōgō*
2: Eat, Ate: *esthiō*
  a) (People) Eat, Ate
  b) (Birds and animals) Eat (up), Ate (up)
  c) Eat (figuratively) – Swallow (up), Devour, Consume

3. Food – Feed
1: Food – Feed (on), Eat: *brōma*
2: Food – Feed: *trephō*
  a) Food – Feed
  b) Feed (figuratively) = Bring (a child) up – Look after, Take care of, Nurse
3: Food (made of) Grain: *sition*
4: Food, Sustenance: *chortasma*
5: Feed – Crumb, Scrap, Morsel: *psōmizō*

  a) Feed, Give food
  b) Piece of bread, Crumb – Scrap, Morsel
6: Feed (pigs, lambs, sheep): *boskō*
7: Pasture: *nomē*

4. Foodstuffs
1: Bread – Loaf, Loaves: *artos*
2: Dough: *phyrama*
3: Flour
  a) Flour – Meal: *aleuron*
  b) (Fine) Flour: *semidalis*
4: Manna: *manna*
5: Honey – Honeycomb
  a) Honey: *meli*
  b) Honeycomb: *kērion*
6: Egg: *ōon*
7: Salt, Salty, Salted – Become tasteless, Lose taste: *halas*, *mōrainō*

5. to Taste
1: to Taste: *geuomai*
  a) to Taste
  b) to Taste = Eat, Ate
  c) to Taste (spiritually)
  d) to Taste (death)
2: to Season: *artuō*

6. Something good to eat – Glutton: *phagos*

  a) Something good to eat
  b) Glutton
7. Dinner, Supper – Banquet, Feast
1: Dine – Dinner, Lunch, Banquet – Have breakfast: *ariston*
2: Supper, Dinner – Banquet, Feast: *deipnon*
3: Love feast – Community meal: *agapē*
8. Manger: *phatnē*
9. Thirsty – Be thirsty: *dipsos*
10. Drink – Cup – Swallow: *pinō*
  a) Drink, Drinker – Cup
  b) Drink (from) the Cup (of the eucharist, of heaven)
  c) Drink the Cup (of Christ)
  d) Drink (figuratively) – Cup (of anger, of evil)
  e) Give (a person something)

  to Drink, to Water (animals, plants) – Cup
  f) Swallow – (Be) Swallowed up, Drowned
11. Milk: *gala*
12. Wine – Strong drink – Drunk
1: Wine: *oinos*
  a) Wine
  b) Wine (figuratively)
2: New wine: *gleukos*
3: Strong drink: *sikera*
4: Drunk, Drunkard, Drunkenness: *methē*
13. Carousing – Orgy, Wild party
1: Feast with, Carouse with: *syn-eu-ōcheomai*
2: Orgy, Revel, Wild party – Carousing: *kōmos*

1. FAMINE – HUNGER, HUNGRY, STARVING – TO FAST

1: FAMINE – HUNGER, HUNGRY: *LIMOS*

limos 12

T = Hunger//Thirst

Mt 24 7		There will be *famines* and earthquakes here and there.
Mk 13 8		There will be earthquakes here and there; there will be *famines*.
Lk 4 25		in Elijah's day . . . a great *famine* raged throughout the land,
15 14		When [the prodigal son] had spent it all, that country experienced a severe *famine*,
17		and here am I dying of *hunger*!
21 11		There will be great earthquakes and plagues and *famines* here and there;
Ac 7 11		(Gn 41 54) Then a *famine* came that caused much suffering throughout Egypt and Canaan,
11 28		a *famine* would spread over the whole empire.
Rm 8 35		Nothing . . . can come between us and the love of Christ, even if we are . . . *lacking food* or clothes;
2 Co 11 27	T	I have been *hungry* and thirsty and often starving;
Rv 6 8		(Ezk 14 21) to kill by the sword, by *famine*, by plague and wild beasts.
18 8		the plagues will fall on [Babylon]: disease and mourning and *famine*.

2: BE HUNGRY, TO HUNGER – FEEL HUNGRY, GO HUNGRY: *PEINAŌ*

1 peinaō 23   2 pros-peinos 1

T = Hunger//Thirst   F = Be hungry//Be filled

Mt 4 2	X	He fasted for forty days and forty nights, after which he was very *hungry*,
5 6	F T	Happy those who *hunger* and thirst for what is right: they shall be satisfied.
12 1		His disciples *were hungry* and began to pick ears of corn
3		what David did when he and his followers *were hungry*
21 18	X	As he was returning to the city in the early morning, he *felt hungry*.
25 35	X T	[take for your heritage the kingdom prepared for you.] For I *was hungry* and you gave me food; I was thirsty
37	X T	Lord, when did we see you *hungry* and feed you; or thirsty . . .?
42	X T	[Go . . . to the eternal fire.] For I *was hungry* and you never gave me food; I was thirsty . . .
44	X T	Lord, when did we see you *hungry* or thirsty . . .?
Mk 2 25		what David did in his time of need when he and his followers *were hungry*
11 12	X	Next day as they were leaving Bethany, he *felt hungry*
Lk 1 53	F	The *hungry* he has filled with good things,
4 2	X	During [his forty days in the wilderness] he ate nothing and at the end he *was hungry*.
6 3		what David did when he and his followers *were hungry*
21	F	Happy you who *are hungry* now: you shall be satisfied.
25	F	Alas for you who have your fill now: you shall *go hungry*.
Jn 6 35	T	He who comes to me will never *be hungry*; he who believes in me will never thirst.
Ac 10 10		2 [Peter] felt *hungry* and was looking forward to his meal,
Rm 12 20	T	(Pr 25 21) If your enemy *is hungry* you should give him food, and if he is thirsty
1 Co 4 11	T	we *go without food* and drink and clothes;
11 21		one person *goes hungry* while another is getting drunk.
34		Anyone who *is hungry* should eat at home,

Ph 4 12 F I am ready for anything anywhere: ʳfull stomach (lit. being full) or ʳempty stomach (lit. *being hungry*),
Rv 7 16 T They will never *hunger* or thirst again;

3: TO FAST – HUNGRY, STARVING: *NĒSTEIA*

2 nēsteia 7 3 nēstis 2
1 nēsteuō 20

P = Fasting//Prayer

Mt 4 2 X He *fasted* for forty days and forty nights, after which he was very hungry,
6 16 P When you *fast* do not put on a gloomy look as the hypocrites
17 do . . . to let men know they are *fasting*. . . . ¹⁷ But when
18 you *fast*, put oil on your head . . . ¹⁸ so that no one will know you are *fasting* except your Father
9 14 Why is it that we and the Pharisees *fast* (ᵛ so much), but your
15 disciples do not *fast* [at all]? ¹⁵ Jesus replied, '. . . the time will come for the bridegroom to be taken away . . . and then they will *fast*.
15 32 3 I do not want to send [these people] off *hungry*,
17 21 (ᵛ This is the kind [of devil] that can only be driven out by
P 2 prayer and *fasting*.)
Mk 2 18 One day when John's disciples . . . were *fasting*, . . . some people came and said to him, 'Why is it that John's disciples and the disciples of the Pharisees *fast*, but your disciples do not *fast* [at all]? ¹⁹ Jesus replied, 'Surely the bridegroom's
19 attendants would never think of *fasting* while the bridegroom is still with them? As long as they have the bridegroom with them, they could not think of *fasting*. ²⁰ But
20 the time will come for the bridegroom to be taken away from them, and then . . . they will *fast*.
8 3 3 If I send them off home *hungry* they will collapse on the way:
9 29 This is the kind [of devil] . . . that can only be driven out by
P 2 prayer and *fasting*).
Lk 2 37 P 2 [Anna] serving God night and day with *fasting* and prayer.
5 33 'John's disciples are always *fasting* and saying prayers, . . .
34 but yours go on eating and drinking.' ³⁴ Jesus replied, 'Surely you cannot make the bridegroom's attendants
35 *fast* while the bridegroom is still with them? ³⁵ But the time will come . . . for the bridegroom to be taken away from them . . . [and] they will *fast*.'
18 12 [The Pharisee's prayer:] I *fast* twice a week;
Ac 13 2 P while they were offering worship to the Lord and *keeping a fast*,
3 P after *fasting* and prayer they laid hands on [Saul and Barnabas]
14 23 [Paul and Barnabas] appointed elders, and with prayer and
2 *fasting* they commended them to the Lord
27 9 navigation was already hazardous since it was now well
O 2 after the time of the *Fast*,
2 Co 6 5 [we prove we are servants of God] when we are . . . sleepless,
2 *starving*,
11 27 I have worked and laboured, . . . I have been hungry and
2 thirsty and often *starving*;

4: GO HUNGRY, BE WITHOUT FOOD: *A-SITIA*

1 a-sitia 1 2 a-sitos 1

Ac 27 21 they had *been without food* for a long time,
33 2 For fourteen days . . . you have been in suspense, *going hungry* and eating nothing.

2. EAT

D = Eat//Drink

1: EAT, ATE: *TRŌGŌ*

trōgō 6

Mt 24 38 D in those days before the Flood people were *eating*, drinking,
Jn 6 54 D Anyone who does *eat* my flesh and drink my blood has eternal life,
56 D He who *eats* my flesh and drinks my blood lives in me
57 whoever *eats* me will draw life from me.
58 anyone who *eats* this bread will live for ever.
13 18 (Ps 41 9) Someone who ʳshares my table rebels (lit. *eats* bread with me) raises his heel) against me.

2: EAT, ATE: *ESTHIŌ*

1 esthiō 157 3 syn-esthiō 5
2 kat-esthiō 14

a) (People) Eat, Ate

Mt 6 25 I am telling you not to worry about your life and what you are to *eat*,
31 D do not say, 'What are we to *eat*? What are we to drink?'
9 11 X Why does your master *eat* with tax collectors and sinners?
11 18 D John came, neither *eating* nor drinking, and they say, 'He is
19 X D possessed'. ¹⁹ The Son of Man came, *eating* and drinking, and they say, 'Look, a glutton'
12 1 His disciples . . . began to pick ears of corn and *eat* them.
4 [David and his followers] *ate* the loaves of offering which neither he nor his followers were allowed to *eat*,
14 16 give them something to *eat* yourselves.
20 They all *ate* as much as they wanted, . . . ²¹ Those who
21 *ate* numbered about five thousand
15 2 your disciples . . . do not wash their hands when they *eat* ʳfood (lit. bread).
20 to *eat* with unwashed hands does not make a man unclean.
32 these people . . . have nothing to *eat*.
37 They all *ate* as much as they wanted, . . . ³⁸ Now four
38 thousand men had *eaten*,
24 49 D [the dishonest servant] sets about beating his fellow servants and *eating* and drinking with drunkards,
25 35 X D I was hungry and you gave me ʳfood (lit. [something] to *eat*);
42 X D I was hungry and you never gave me ʳfood (lit. [something] to *eat*);
26 17 X Where do you want us to make the preparations for you to *eat* the passover?
21 X while they were *eating* he said, '. . . one of you is about to betray me'.
26 X as they were *eating*, Jesus took some bread and gave it to the the disciples. 'Take it and *eat*,' he said this is my body.'
Mk 1 6 ● D John . . . ʳlived on (lit. *ate*) locusts and wild honey.
2 16 X When the scribes . . . saw him *eating* with sinners and tax
X collectors, they said . . , 'Why does he *eat* with tax collectors and sinners?'
26 [David] *ate* the loaves of offering which only the priests are allowed to *eat*,
3 20 such a crowd collected that they could not even ʳhave a meal (lit. *eat* bread).
5 43 [Jesus] told them to give [the little girl] something to *eat*.
6 31 the apostles had no time even to *eat*.
36 'send them away . . . to buy themselves something to *eat*.'
37 ³⁷ [Jesus] replied, 'Give them something to *eat* yourselves'.
42 They all *ate* as much as they wanted . . . ⁴⁴ Those who had
44 *eaten* the loaves numbered five thousand men.
7 2 some of his disciples were *eating* [their] bread with unclean
3 hands. . . . ³ . . . the Pharisees, and the Jews in general,
4 . . . never *eat* without washing their arms . . . ⁴ and . . . they never *eat* without first sprinkling themselves,
5 ⁵ . . . 'Why do your disciples . . . *eat* their ʳfood (lit. bread) with unclean hands?
8 1 they had nothing to *eat*.
2 for three days now . . . [they] have had nothing to *eat*.
8 They *ate* as much as they wanted, . . . ⁹ . . . there had been about four thousand people.
11 14 [Jesus to the fig tree:] May no one ever *eat* fruit from you again
14 12 X Where do you want us to . . . make the preparations for you to *eat* the passover?
14 X Where is the dining room in which I can *eat* the passover with my disciples?
18 X while they were at table *eating*, Jesus said, '. . . one of you is about to betray me, one of you *eating* with me'.
22 X D as they were *eating* he took some bread,
Lk 4 2 X During that time he *ate* nothing
5 30 X D Why do you *eat* and drink with tax collectors and sinners?
33 D John's disciples are always fasting . . . but yours go on *eating* and drinking.
6 1 his disciples were picking ears of corn . . . and *eating* them.
4 how [David] . . . took the loaves of offering and *ate* them . . , loaves which only the priests are allowed to *eat*?
7 33 D John the Baptist comes, not *eating* bread, not drinking wine, and you say, 'He is possessed'. ³⁴ The Son of Man comes,
34 X D *eating* and drinking, and you say, 'Look, a glutton'
36 X One of the Pharisees invited him to ʳa meal (lit. *eat* with him).
8 55 [Jesus] told them to give [the little girl] something to *eat*.
9 13 Give them something to *eat* yourselves.
17 They all *ate* as much as they wanted,
10 7 D Stay in the same house, *taking* what *food* and drink they have
8 to offer, . . . ⁸ [Wherever] they make you welcome, *eat* what is set before you.
12 19 D take things easy, *eat*, drink, have a good time.

Lk 12 22   [do not] worry about your life and what you are to *eat*,
     29 D you must not set your hearts on things to *eat* and things to drink;
     45 D the servant who . . . sets about . . . *eating* and drinking and getting drunk,
  13 26 D We once *ate* and drank in your company;
  14 1 X he had gone ⸢for a meal to (lit. to *eat* bread in) the house of one of the leading Pharisees;
     15   Happy the man who will ⸢be at the feast (lit. *eat* bread) in the kingdom of God!
  15 2 X 3 This man . . . welcomes sinners and *eats with* them.
     23   Bring the calf we have been fattening, and kill it; we are going to ⸢have a feast, (lit. *eat* and have) a celebration,
  17 8 D wait on me while I *eat* and drink. You can *eat* and drink yourself afterwards
     27 D People were *eating* and drinking, marrying . . . right up to the day Noah went into the ark,
     28 D in Lot's day: people were *eating* and drinking, buying and selling,
  22 8 X Go and make the preparations for us to *eat* the passover.
     11 X Where is the dining room in which I can *eat* the passover with my disciples?
     15 X I have longed to *eat* this passover with you before I suffer;
     16 X D ¹⁶ because . . . I shall not *eat* it again until it is fulfilled in the kingdom of God.
     30 ● D you will *eat* and drink at my table in my kingdom,
  24 43 X [a piece of grilled fish] which he took and *ate* before their eyes.
Jn 4 31 X the disciples were urging him, 'Rabbi, [do have something to] *eat*';
     32 X ○ I have food to *eat* that you do not know about.
     33 X Has someone been bringing him ⸢food (lit. [something] to *eat*)?
  6 5   Where can we buy some bread for these people to *eat*?
     23   Other boats . . . had put in from Tiberias, near the place where the bread had been *eaten*.
     26   you are . . . looking for me because . . . you had all the bread you wanted to *eat*.
     31   Our fathers had manna to *eat* in the desert; as scripture says (Ps 78 24): He gave them bread from heaven to *eat*.
     49   Your fathers *ate* the manna in the desert and they are dead;
     50 ● ⁵⁰ but this is the bread that comes down from heaven,
     51 ● so that a man may *eat* it and not die. ⁵¹ . . . Anyone who *eats* this bread will live for ever.
     52 ● How can this man give us his flesh to *eat*?
     53 ● D if you do not *eat* the flesh of the Son of Man and drink his blood, you will not have life in you.
     58   This is . . . not like the bread our ancestors *ate*:
  18 28   they would be defiled and unable to *eat* the passover.
Ac 9 9 D For three days [Saul] was without his sight, and *took* neither *food* nor drink.
  10 13   Now, Peter; kill and *eat*!
     14   I have never yet *eaten* anything profane or unclean.
     41 D3 we have *eaten* and drunk *with* him after his resurrection
  11 3 3 So you have been visiting the uncircumcised and *eating with* them, have you?
     7   Now, Peter; kill and *eat*!
  23 12 D the Jews . . . made a vow not to *eat* or drink until they had killed Paul.
     21 D they have vowed not to *eat* or drink until they have got rid of him.
  27 35   [Paul] took some bread, gave thanks to God . . . broke it and began to *eat*.
Rm 14 2   People range from those who believe they may *eat* any sort of meat to those whose faith is so weak they dare not *eat* anything except vegetables. ³ Meat-*eaters* must not despise the ⸢scrupulous (lit. those who will not *eat*). On the other hand, the ⸢scrupulous (lit. those who will not *eat*) must not condemn those who feel free to *eat* anything they choose,
     6   The one who *eats* meat ⸢also does so (lit. *eats*) in honour of the Lord, since he gives thanks to God; but then the man who ⸢abstains does that too (lit. will not *eat* does not *eat*) in honour of the Lord, and so he also gives God thanks.
     20   food . . . becomes evil if by *eating* it you make somebody else fall away. ²¹ In such cases the best course is ⸢to abstain from (lit. not to *eat*) meat and wine and anything else that would make your brother . . . fall
     21 D
     23   anybody who *eats* in a state of doubt is condemned
1 Co 5 11 3 you should not even *eat* [a meal] *with* people like that.
  8 7   some . . . *eat* this food as though it really had been sacrificed to the idol, . . . ⁸ . . . we lose nothing if we refuse to *eat*, we gain nothing if we *eat*.
     8
     10   his own conscience . . . may encourage him to *eat* food which has been offered to idols.
     13   I shall never *eat* meat again in case I am the cause of a brother's downfall.
  9 4 D Have we not every right to *eat* and drink?
     7   nobody ever planted a vineyard and refused to *eat* the fruit of it. Who has there ever been that kept a flock and did not *feed on* the milk from his flock?

1 Co 9 13   the ministers serving in the Temple ⸢get their (lit. *eat*) [food] from the Temple
  10 3 D all [our fathers] *ate* the same spiritual food; ⁴ and all drank the same spiritual drink.
     7 D (Ex 32 6) After sitting down to *eat* and drink, the people got up to amuse themselves.
     18   those who *eat* the sacrifices are in communion with the altar.
     25   Do not hesitate to *eat* anything that is sold in butcher's shops:
     27   If an unbeliever invites you to his house, . . . *eat* whatever is put in front of you . . . ²⁸ But if someone says to you "This food was offered in sacrifice", then . . . you should not *eat* it,
     28
     31 D Whatever you *eat*, whatever you drink, whatever you do at all, do it for the glory of God.
  11 20   it is not the Lord's Supper that you are *eating*, ²¹ since when the time comes to *eat*, everyone is in . . . a hurry to start his own supper . . . ²² Surely you have homes for *eating* and drinking in?
     21
     22 D
     26 ● D every time you *eat* this bread and drink this cup, you are proclaiming his death, ²⁷ and so anyone who *eats* the bread or drinks the cup of the Lord unworthily will be behaving unworthily . . . ²⁸ Everyone is to recollect himself before *eating* this bread and drinking this cup; ²⁹ because a person who *eats* and drinks without recognising the Body is *eating* and drinking his own condemnation.
     27 ● D
     28 ●
     29 ● D
       ● D
       ●
     33 ● when you meet for the *Meal*, wait for one another. ³⁴ Anyone who is hungry should *eat* at home,
     34 ●
  15 32 D (Is 22 13) Let us *eat* and drink today; tomorrow we shall be dead.
Ga 2 12 3 [Peter's] custom had been to *eat with* the pagans,
2 Th 3 8   nor did we ever ⸢have our meals (lit. *eat* our bread) at anyone's table without paying for them;
     10   We gave you a rule . . . not to let anyone have ⸢any food (lit. anything to *eat*) if he refused to do any work.
     12   we order . . . people of this kind to go on . . . earning the food that they *eat*.
Heb 13 10   We have our own altar from which those who serve the tabernacle have no right to *eat*.
Rv 2 7   those who prove victorious I will ⸢feed (lit. allow to *eat*) from the tree of life
     14   the Israelites . . . committed adultery by *eating* food that had been sacrificed to idols.
     20   Jezebel . . . is luring my servants away to commit the adultery of *eating* food which has been sacrificed to idols.
  10 9 2 the angel . . . said, 'Take [the scroll] and *eat* it;' . . . ¹⁰ So I . . . *swallowed* it; . . . but when I had *eaten* it my stomach turned sour.
     10 2
  17 16 2 they will *eat* [the prostitute's] flesh
  19 18 2 There will be the flesh of kings for you to *eat*, and the flesh of great generals

b) (Birds and animals) Eat (up), Ate (up)

Mt 13 4 2 some seeds fell . . . and the birds came and *ate* them *up*.
  15 27   even house-dogs can *eat* the scraps that fall from their master's table.
Mk 4 4 2 some of the seed fell . . . and the birds came and *ate* it *up*.
   7 28   but the house-dogs under the table can *eat* the children's scraps.
Lk 8 5 2 some [seed] fell . . . and the birds of the air *ate* it *up*.
  15 16   the husks the pigs were *eating*
Rv 12 4 ⒟ the dragon stopped in front of the woman . . . so that he could *eat* [the child] as soon as it was born
      2

c) Eat (figuratively) – Swallow (up), Devour, Consume

Mk 12 40 2 [Beware of the scribes] who *swallow* the property of widows,
Lk 15 30 2 this son of yours . . . comes back after *swallowing up* your property
  20 47 2 [Beware of the scribes] who *swallow* the property of widows,
Jn 2 17 2 (Ps 69 9) Zeal for your house will *devour* me.
2 Co 11 20 2 tolerating somebody who . . . ⸢makes you feed him (lit. *devours* you),
Ga 5 15 2 If you go . . . ⸢tearing each other to pieces (lit. *devouring* each other),
Heb 10 27 2 (Is 26 11) the raging fire that is to ⸢burn (lit. *consume*) rebels.
Jm 5 3   the same corrosion will . . . *eat* into your body.
Rv 11 5 2 Fire can come from their mouths and *consume* their enemies
  20 9 2 fire will come down on them from heaven and *consume* them.

3. FOOD – FEED

D = Food//Drink

1: FOOD – FEED (ON), EAT: *BRŌMA*

3 *bibrōskō*	1	2	*brōsis*	9/11
1 *brōma*	17	5	(*skōlēko-*)*brōtos*	1
4 *brōsimos*	1	6	(*sēto-*)*brōtos*	1

Mt	14	15	send the people away, and they can . . . buy themselves some *food*.
Mk	7	19	Thus [Jesus] pronounced all *foods* clean.
Lk	3	11	the one with *something to eat* must [share it].
	9	13	unless we are to go . . . and buy *food* for all these people.
	24	41 X	4 Have you anything here *to eat*?
Jn	4	32 X ○	2 I have *food* to eat that you do not know about.
		34 X ○	My *food* is to do the will of the one who sent me,
	6	13	they . . . filled twelve hampers with scraps ⌐over from
			3 the meal of (lit. by those who had *fed on*) five barley loaves.
		27	2/2 Do not work for *food* that cannot last, but work for *food* that endures to eternal life,
		55	D 2 my flesh is real *food*
Ac	12	23	5 [Herod] was *eaten away* with worms and died.
Rm	14	15	if your attitude to *food* is upsetting your brother, . . . You are certainly not free to ⌐*eat* what (lit. choose whatever *food*) you like if that means the downfall of someone for whom Christ died.
		17	D 2 the kingdom of God does not mean the *eating* or drinking of this or that,
		20	do not wreck God's work over a question of *food*.
1 Co	3	2	D What I fed you with was milk, not [solid] *food*,
	6	13	*Food* is only meant for the stomach, and the stomach for *food*;
	8	4	2 about the *eating* of food sacrificed to idols:
		8	*Food* . . . cannot bring us in touch with God:
		13	since *food* can be the occasion of my brother's downfall,
	10	3	D all [our fathers] ate the same spiritual *food* 4 and all drank the same spiritual drink,
2 Co	9	10	The one who provides seed for the sower and bread for 2 *food*
Col	2	16	never let anyone else decide what ⌐you should eat (lit. should D 2 be your *food*) or drink,
1 Tm	4	3	they will . . . lay down rules about abstaining from *foods* which God created
Heb	9	10	D they are rules about the outward life, connected with *foods* and drinks
	12	16	2 Esau, who sold his birthright for one single *meal*.
	13	9	it is better to rely on grace for inner strength than on *dietary* laws
Jm	5	2	6 Your wealth is all rotting, your clothes are all *eaten up* by moths.

2: FOOD – FEED: *TREPHŌ*

2	*trephō*	9	7	*dia-trophē 1*
1	*trophē*	16	4	*ek-trephō 2*
5	*tropho-phoreō 1*		8	*en- trephō 1*
6	*trophos 1*		9	*syn-trophos 1*
3	*ana-trephō 3*		10	*(tekno-)tropheō 1*

a) Food – Feed

Mt	3	4	[John's] *food* was locusts and wild honey.
	6	25	Surely life means more than *food*,
		26	Look at the birds in the sky . . . your heavenly Father Θ 2 *feeds* them.
	10	10	the workman deserves his ⌐keep (lit. *food*).
	24	45	What sort of servant . . . is . . . wise enough for the master to place him over his household to give them their *food* . . .?
	25	37	D 2 Lord, when did we see you hungry and *feed* you . . .?
Lk	12	23	life means more than *food*
		24	Θ 2 Think of the ravens. . . . God *feeds* them.
	23	29	Happy are . . . the breasts that have never ⌐suckled (or: 2 *fed*) [a baby]!
Jn	4	8	His disciples had gone . . . to buy *food*.
Ac	2	46	They . . . met in their houses for the breaking of bread; they shared their *food* gladly and generously;
	9	19	after taking some *food* [Saul] regained his strength.
	12	20	[the Tyrians' and Sidonians'] country depended for its 2 *food* [supply] on King Herod's territory.
	14	17	[God] gives you *food* and makes you happy.
	27	33	Paul urged them all to have *something to eat*.
		34	Let me persuade you to have *something to eat*;
		36	they all . . . took *something to eat*
		38	When they had ⌐eaten what (lit. had all the *food*) they wanted they lightened the ship
Ep	5	29	4 A man never hates his own body, but he *feeds* it
1 Th	2	7	6 Like a mother *feeding* . . . her own children,
1 Tm	4	6	you will be a good servant of Christ Jesus and show that ○ 8 you have really *digested* the teaching of the faith
	6	8	7 as long as we have *food* and clothing, let us be content with that.
Heb	5	12	○ you have gone back to needing milk, and not solid *food*.
		14	○ Solid *food* is for mature men
Jm	2	15	If one of the brothers or . . . sisters . . . has not enough *food* to live on,
	5	5	in the time of slaughter you went on ⌐eating to your heart's 2 content (lit. *feeding* yourselves).

Rv	12	6	God made a place of safety ready, for her to be ⌐looked after 2 (or: *fed*)
		14	to fly away . . . to the place where she was to be ⌐looked 2 after (or: *fed*)

b) Feed *(figuratively)* = Bring (a child) up – Look after, Take care of, Nurse

Lk	4	16 X	2 He came to Nazareth, where he had been *brought up*,
Ac	7	20	3 Moses was . . . *looked after* for three months in his father's house,
		21	3 Pharaoh's daughter . . . *brought* [Moses] *up* as her own son.
	13	1	9 Manaen, who had been *brought up with* Herod the tetrarch,
		18	5 for about forty years [God] *took care of* them in the desert.
	22	3	3 I was *brought up* in this city.
Ep	6	4	4 in *bringing* [your children] *up* correct them . . . as the Lord does.
1 Tm	5	10	She must be a woman known for . . . the way in which she 10 has *brought up* her children,
Rv	12	6	God made a place of safety ready, where she was to be 2 ⌐*looked after* (or: fed)
		14	to fly away . . . to the place where she was to be ⌐looked 2 *after* (or: fed)

3: FOOD (MADE OF) GRAIN: *SITION*

1 *sition 1*	2 *epi-sitismos 1*

Lk	9	12	the people . . . can go to the villages . . . to find lodging 2 and *food*;
Ac	7	12	(Gn 42 2) When Jacob heard that there was *grain* for sale in Egypt, he sent our ancestors there

4: FOOD, SUSTENANCE: *CHORTASMA*

chortasma 1

Ac	7	11	a famine came . . . and our ancestors could find ⌐nothing to eat (lit. no *food*).

5: FEED – CRUMB, SCRAP, MORSEL: *PSŌMIZŌ*

2 *psichion 2*	3 *psōmizō 1/2*
1 *psōmion 4*	

a) Feed, Give food

Rm	12	20	D 3 (Pr 25 21) If your enemy is hungry, you should *give* him *food*,

b) Piece of bread, Crumb – Scrap, Morsel

Mt	15	27	2 but even house-dogs can eat the ⌐*scraps* (or: *crumbs*) that fall from their master's table.
Mk	7	28	but the house-dogs under the table can eat the children's 2 ⌐*scraps* (or: *crumbs*).
Jn	13	26	'It is the one' replied Jesus 'to whom I give the *piece of bread* that I shall dip in the dish.' He dipped the *piece of bread*
		27	and gave it to Judas . . . 27 . . . after Judas had taken the *bread* Satan entered him.
		30	As soon as Judas had taken the *piece of bread* he went out.

6: FEED (PIGS, LAMBS, SHEEP): *BOSKŌ*

boskō 9

Mt	8	30	there was a large herd of pigs *feeding*,
		33	⌐The swineherds (lit. Those who *fed* them) ran off
Mk	5	11	there was . . . a great herd of pigs *feeding*,
		14	⌐The swineherds (lit. Those who *fed* them) ran off
Lk	8	32	there was a large herd of pigs *feeding*
		34	⌐the swineherds (lit. those who *fed* them) . . . ran off
	15	15	one of the local inhabitants . . . put [the prodigal son] on his farm to *feed* the pigs.
Jn	21	15 ○	Jesus said to [Peter], '*Feed* my lambs'.
		17 ○	Jesus said to him, '*Feed* my sheep.'

7: PASTURE: *NŌMĒ*

nomē 2

Jn	10	9	I am the gate. Anyone who enters through me will be safe: he will . . . be sure of finding *pasture*.
2 Tm	2	17	<	Talk of this kind ⌐corrodes (lit. finds its *pasture* [eating its way]) like gangrene,

4. FOODSTUFFS

1: BREAD – LOAF, LOAVES: *ARTOS*

artos 98

F = Loaves//Fish

Mt	4	3		'If you are the Son of God, tell these stones to turn into *loaves*'. ⁴ But he replied, '. . . (Dt 8 3): Man does not live on *bread* alone'
		4		
	6	11		Give us today our daily *bread*.
	7	9	F	Is there a man among you who would hand his son a stone when he asked for *bread*?
	12	4		[David and his followers] ate the *loaves* of offering
	14	17	F	All we have with us is five *loaves* and two fish.
		19	F	[Jesus] took the five *loaves* and the two fish, raised his eyes to heaven and said the blessing. And breaking the *loaves* he handed them to his disciples who gave them to the crowds.
	15	2		your disciples . . . do not wash their hands when they eat ꜛfood (lit. *bread*).
		26		It is not fair to take the children's ꜛfood (lit. *bread*) and throw it to the house-dogs.
		33		'Where could we get enough *bread* in this deserted place to feed such a crowd?' ³⁴ Jesus said to them, 'How many *loaves* have you?' 'Seven' they said
		34		
		36	F	he took the seven *loaves* and the fish, . . . broke them and handed them to the disciples
	16	5		the disciples . . . had forgotten to take any ꜛfood (lit. *loaves*).
		7		'we have not brought any *bread*.' ⁸ Jesus . . . said, '. . . why are you talking . . . about having no *bread*? ⁹ . . . Do you not remember the five *loaves* for the five thousand . . .? ¹⁰ Or the seven *loaves* for the four thousand? . . . ¹¹ . . . I was not talking about *bread*?' . . . ¹² Then they understood that he was telling them to be on their guard, not against the yeast for making *bread*,
		8		
		9		
		10		
		11		
		12		
	26	26	●	Jesus took some *bread* . . . 'Take it . . . this is my body.'
Mk	2	26		[David] ate the *loaves* of offering
	3	20		such a crowd collected that they could not even ꜛhave a meal (lit. eat *bread*).
	6	8		[Jesus] instructed them to take nothing – no *bread*, no haversack,
		37		Are we to go and spend two hundred denarii on *bread* for them to eat?
		38	F	'How many *loaves* have you?' [Jesus] asked
		41	F	he took the five *loaves* and the two fish . . . then he broke the *loaves*
		44		Those who had eaten the *loaves* numbered five thousand men.
		52		[The disciples] had not seen what the miracle of the *loaves* meant;
	7	2		his disciples were eating [their] *bread* with unclean hands,
		5		Why do your disciples . . . eat their ꜛfood (lit. *bread*) with unclean hands?
		27		it is not fair to take the children's ꜛfood (lit. *bread*) and throw it to the house-dogs.
	8	4		'Where can anyone get *bread* to feed these people . . .? ⁵ He asked them, 'How many *loaves* have you?' 'Seven' they said. ⁶ . . . he took the seven *loaves*
		5	F	
		6	F	
		14		The disciples had forgotten to take ꜛany food (lit. *loaves*)
		16		'It is because we have no *bread*.' ¹⁷ And Jesus . . . said to them, 'Why are you talking about having no *bread*?'
		17		
		19		When I broke the five *loaves* among the five thousand, . . . ²⁰ And when I broke the seven [loaves] for the four thousand,
	14	22	●	[Jesus] took some *bread* . . . 'Take it . . . this is my body.'
Lk	4	3		'tell this stone to turn into a *loaf*.' ⁴ But Jesus replied, '. . . (Dt 8 3): Man does not live on *bread* alone.'
		4		
	6	4		[David] took the *loaves* of offering and ate them
	7	33		John the Baptist comes, not eating *bread*, . . . and you say, 'He is possessed'.
	9	3		Take nothing for the journey: neither staff, . . . nor *bread*.
		13	F	We have no more than five *loaves* and two fish,
		16	F	he took the five *loaves* and the two fish, . . . broke them and handed them to his disciples
	11	3		give us each day our daily *bread*,
		5		My friend, lend me three *loaves*,
		11	F	What father among you would ᵛ hand his son a stone when he asked for *bread*?
	14	1		[Jesus] had gone ꜛfor a meal to (lit. to eat *bread* in) the house of one of the leading Pharisees;
		15		Happy the man who will ꜛbe at the feast (lit. eat *bread*) in the kingdom of God!
	15	17		How many of my father's paid servants have more ꜛfood (lit. *bread*) than they want,
	22	19	●	he took some *bread*, . . . broke it and gave it to them, saying, 'This is my body'
	24	20	●	while he was with [the two disciples at Emmaus] . . . he took the *bread* and said the blessing; then he broke it and handed it to them.

Lk	24	35	●	they had recognised him at the breaking of *bread*.
Jn	6	5		'Where can we buy some *bread* . . .?' . . . ⁷ Philip answered, 'Two hundred denarii would only buy enough *bread* to give them a small piece each.'
		7		
		9	F	There is a small boy here with five barley *loaves* and two fish;
		11	F	Jesus took the *loaves*, gave thanks, and gave them out
		13		they . . . filled twelve hampers with scraps left over from the meal of five barley *loaves*.
		23		near the place where the *bread* had been eaten.
		26		you are . . . looking for me because . . . you had all the *bread* you wanted to eat.
		31		'(Ps 78 24) He gave them *bread* from heaven to eat.' ³² Jesus answered, '. . . it was not Moses who gave you *bread* from heaven, it is my Father who gives you [the bread] from heaven, the true *bread*; ³³ for the *bread* of God is that which comes down from heaven and gives life to the world. ³⁴ 'Sir,' they said 'give us that *bread* always.' ³⁵ Jesus answered: 'I am the *bread* of life.'
		32		
		33	X	
		34	X	
		35	X	
		41	X	because he had said, 'I am the *bread* that came down from heaven'.
		48	X	I am the *bread* of life. ⁴⁹ Your fathers ate the manna . . . and they are dead; ⁵⁰ but this is the *bread* that comes down from heaven, so that a man may eat it and not die. ⁵¹ I am the living *bread* which has come down from heaven. Anyone who eats this *bread* will live for ever; and the *bread* that I shall give is my flesh, for the life of the world.
		50	X	
		51		
			X	
			X	
		58	X	This is the *bread* come down from heaven; not like [the bread] our ancestors ate: they are dead, but anyone who eats this *bread* will live for ever.
			X	
	13	18		(Ps 41 9) Someone who ꜛshares my table rebels (lit. eats *bread*) with me raises his heel) against me.
	21	9	F	[the disciples] saw that there was some *bread* there, and a charcoal fire with fish cooking on it.
		13	F	Jesus . . . took the *bread* and gave it to them, and the same with the fish.
Ac	2	42		These remained faithful to . . . the breaking of *bread*
		46		they . . . met in their houses for the breaking of *bread*;
	20	7		On the first day of the week we met to break *bread*.
		11		[Paul] went back upstairs where he broke *bread* and ate
	27	35		[Paul] took some *bread*, gave thanks to God . . , broke it and began to eat.
1 Co	10	16	●	the *bread* that we break is a communion with the body of Christ. ¹⁷ The fact that there is only one *loaf* means that . . . we form a single body because we all have a share in this one *loaf*.
		17	●	
			●	
	11	23	●	on the same night that he was betrayed, the Lord Jesus took some *bread*
		26	●	every time you eat this *bread* . . . you are proclaiming his death, ²⁷ and so anyone who eats the *bread* . . . unworthily will be behaving unworthily towards the body . . . of the Lord. ²⁸ Everyone is to recollect himself before eating this *bread*
		27	●	
		28	●	
2 Co	9	10		(Is 55 10) The one who provides . . . *bread* for food
2 Th	3	8		nor did we ever ꜛhave our meals (lit. eat our *bread*) at anyone's table without paying for them;
		12		we order . . . people of this kind to go on . . . earning the ꜛfood (lit. *bread*) that they eat.
Heb	9	2		the first [compartment of the tent], in which . . . the presentation *loaves* were kept,

2: DOUGH: *PHYRAMA*

phyrama 4/5

Rm	11	16	A whole batch [of bread] is made holy if the first handful of *dough* is made holy;
1 Co	5	6	a small amount of yeast is enough to leaven all the *dough*, ⁷ so get rid of all the old yeast, and make yourselves into a completely new batch of ꜛbread (lit. *dough*).
		7	
Ga	5	9	The yeast seems to be ꜛspreading through the whole batch of of you (lit. leavening all the *dough*).

3: FLOUR

a) *Flour – Meal:* aleuron

aleuron 2

Mt	13	33	like the yeast a woman took and mixed in with three measures of *flour*
Lk	13	21	like the yeast a woman took and mixed in with three measures of *flour*

b) *(Fine) Flour:* semidalis

semidalis 1

Rv	18	13	[when there is nobody left in Babylon to buy] wine, oil, *flour* and corn;

4: MANNA: *MANNA*

manna 4

Jn	6 31	Our fathers had *manna* to eat in the desert; . . . bread from heaven
	49	Your fathers ate the *manna* in the desert and they are dead;
Heb	9 4	In [the ark of the covenant was] kept the gold jar containing the *manna*,
Rv	2 17 ○	to those who prove victorious I will give the hidden *manna*

5: HONEY – HONEYCOMB

a) Honey: meli

meli 4

Mt	3 4	[John's] food was locusts and wild *honey*.
Mk	1 6	John . . . lived on locusts and wild *honey*.
Rv	10 9	(Ezk 3 3) in your mouth [the scroll] will taste as sweet as
	10	*honey*. [10] So I . . . swallowed it; it was as sweet as *honey* in my mouth,

b) Honeycomb: kērion

kērion 1

Lk	24 42	[the apostles] offered [Jesus] a piece of grilled fish (ᵛ and a bees' *honeycomb*),

6: EGG: *ŌON*

ōon 1

Lk	11 12	[What father among you would] hand [his son] a scorpion if he asked for an *egg*?

7: SALT, SALTY, SALTED – BECOME TASTELESS, LOSE TASTE: *HALAS, MŌRAINŌ*

1	*halas*	8	4 *an-(h)alos*	1	6 *mōrainō* 2/4
2	*halizō*	2	5 *syn-(h)alizomai* 1		
3	*halukos*	1			

Mt	5 13	You are the *salt* of the earth. But if the *salt*
	6/2	*becomes tasteless*, what can *make* it *salty* again?
Mk	9 49	2 everyone will be *salted* with fire.
	50	*Salt* is a good thing, but if *salt* has become ⌐insipid (lit.
	4/	*unsalty*), how can you season it again? Have *salt* in yourselves
Lk	14 34	*Salt* is a useful thing. But if the *salt* itself
	6	*loses* its *taste*, how can it be seasoned again?
Ac	1 4 ○	5 When [Jesus] had been ⌐at table (lit. *taking salt*) with [the apostles],
Col	4 6	Talk to [those who are not Christians] agreeably and with a
	○	⌐flavour of wit (lit. seasoning of *salt*),
Jm	3 12	3 No more can ⌐sea (lit. *salty*) water give you fresh water.

5. TO TASTE

1: TO TASTE: *GEUOMAI*

geuomai 15

a) to Taste

Mt	27 34 X	[Jesus] *tasted* [the wine mixed with gall] but refused to drink.
Jn	2 9	the steward *tasted* the water, and it had turned into wine.

b) to Taste = Eat, Ate

Lk	14 24	not one of those who were invited shall *have a taste of* my banquet.
Ac	10 10	[Peter] felt hungry and was looking forward to ⌐his meal (lit. *eating*),
	20 11	[Paul] went back upstairs where he broke bread and *ate*
	23 14	We have made a solemn vow ⌐to let nothing pass our lips (lit. not to *taste* anything)
Col	2 21	[Why do you still let rules dictate to you?] It is forbidden to pick up this, it is forbidden to *taste* that,

c) to Taste (spiritually)

Heb	6 4	those people who . . . once . . . *tasted* the gift from heaven
	5	. . . [5] and ⌐appreciated (lit. *tasted*) the good message of
	6	God . . . [6] and yet have fallen away [shall not] be renewed a second time.
1 P	2 3	(Ps 34 8) now . . . you have *tasted* the goodness of the Lord.

d) to Taste (death)

Mt	16 28	there are some of these standing here who will not *taste* death before they see the Son of Man coming with his kingdom.
Mk	9 1	there are some standing here who will not *taste* death
Lk	9 27	there are some standing here who will not *taste* death
Jn	8 52	Whoever keeps my word will never [know the] *taste* [of] death.
Heb	2 9 X	he had to ⌐experience (lit. *taste*) death for all mankind.

2: TO SEASON: *ARTUŌ*

artuō 3

Mk	9 50	if salt has become insipid, how can you *season* it again?
Lk	14 34	if the salt itself loses its taste, how can it be *seasoned* again?
Col	4 6	Talk to [those who are not Christians] agreeably and with a ⌐flavour of wit (lit. *seasoning* of salt),

6. SOMETHING GOOD TO EAT – GLUTTON: *PHAGOS*

1	*phagos* 2	2	*pros-phagion* 1

a) Something good to eat

Jn	21 5	2 Jesus called out, 'Have you caught *anything good to eat*, friends?'

b) Glutton

Mt	11 19 X	The Son of Man came, eating and drinking, and they say, 'Look, a *glutton*'
Lk	7 34 X	The Son of Man comes, eating and drinking, and you say, 'Look, a *glutton*'

7. DINNER, SUPPER – BANQUET, FEAST

1: DINE – DINNER, LUNCH, BANQUET – HAVE BREAKFAST: *ARISTON*

1	*aristaō* 3	2	*ariston* 3

Mt	22 4 <	2 I have my *banquet* all prepared, . . . everything is ready. Come to the wedding.
Lk	11 37 X	a Pharisee invited him to *dine* at his house.
	38	The Pharisee . . . was surprised that [Jesus] had not washed
	2	before ⌐the meal (lit. *dinner*).
	14 12	2 When you give a *lunch* or a dinner, do not ask your friends,
Jn	21 12 X	Jesus said to [the disciples], 'Come and *have breakfast*'.
	15 X	After ⌐the meal (lit. *breakfast*) Jesus said to Simon Peter,

2: SUPPER, DINNER – BANQUET, FEAST: *DEIPNON*

1	*deipneō* 4	2	*deipnon* 16

Mt	23 6	[The scribes and Pharisees want] to take the place of honour at *banquets*
Mk	6 21	on Herod's birthday when he gave a *banquet*
	12 39	[the scribes like] to take . . . the places of honour at *banquets*;
Lk	14 12	When you give a lunch or a *dinner*, do not ask your friends
	16 <	a man . . . gave a great *banquet*,
	17 <	When the time for the *banquet* came, he sent his servant to . . . those who had been invited,
	24 <	not one of those who were invited shall have a taste of my *banquet*.
	17 8	2 Get my *supper* laid;
	20 46	the scribes who like to . . . take the . . . places of honour at *banquets*,
	22 20	2 He did the same with the cup after *supper*
Jn	12 2	[Jesus went to Bethany, where Lazarus was.] They gave a *dinner* for him there;
	13 2	They were at *supper* . . . [4] [Jesus] got up from the ⌐table
	4	(lit. *supper*), removed his outer garment
	21 20	the disciple . . . who had leaned on [Jesus'] breast at the *supper*
1 Co	11 20 ●	when you hold these meetings, it is not the Lord's *Supper*
	21	that you are eating, [21] since . . . everyone is in such a hurry to start his own *supper*
	25	2 In the same way he took the cup after *supper*,
Rv	3 20 X	2 I will come in to share his ⌐meal (lit. *supper*), side by side with him.
	19 9 ●	Happy are those who are invited to the wedding *feast* of the Lamb.
	17 ●	Gather together at the great *feast* that God is giving.

3: LOVE FEAST – COMMUNITY MEAL: *AGAPĒ*

agapē 2/117

2 P	2 13	they amuse themselves ⌐deceiving you even when (ᵛ in their *love-feasts* even though) they ⌐are your guests at a meal (lit. feast with you);
Jude	12	They are a dangerous obstacle to your ⌐*community meals* (or: *love-feasts*),

8. MANGER: *PHATNĒ*

phatnē 4

Lk	2 7	she gave birth to a son . . . and laid him in a *manger*
	12	you will find a baby . . . lying in the *manger*.
	16	they . . . found . . . the baby lying in the *manger*.
	13 15	Is there one of you who does not untie his ox. . . from the *manger* on the sabbath and take it out for watering?

9. THIRST – BE THIRSTY: *DIPSOS*

1 *dipsaō 16*   2 *dipsos 1*

H = Thirst//Hunger

Mt	5 6	H	Happy those who hunger and *thirst* for what is right:
	25 35	X H	I was hungry . . . I *was thirsty* and you gave me drink;
	37	X H	Lord, when did we see you hungry . . . or *thirsty* and give you drink?
	42	X H	I *was thirsty* and you never gave me anything to drink;
	44	X H	when did we see you . . . *thirsty* . . . and did not come to your help?
Jn	4 13		Whoever drinks this water will *get thirsty* again; ¹⁴ but
	14		anyone who drinks the water that I shall give will never *be thirsty* again: . . . ¹⁵ 'Sir,' said the woman 'give me some of that water, so that I may never *get thirsty*'
	15		
	6 35	H	he who believes in me will never *thirst*.
	7 37		If any man *is thirsty*, let him come to me!
	19 28	X	Jesus knew that everything had now been completed, and . . . he said: 'I *am thirsty*'.
Rm	12 20	H	(Pr 25 21) If your enemy . . . *is thirsty*, let him drink
1 Co	4 11	H	we *go without* food and drink and clothes;
2 Co	11 27	H 2	I have been hungry and *thirsty* and often starving;
Rv	7 16	H	They will never hunger or *thirst* again;
	21 6		I will give water from the well of life free to anybody who *is thirsty*;
	22 17		let all who *are thirsty* come: all who want it may have the water of life,

10. DRINK – CUP – SWALLOW: *PINŌ*

1	*pinō*	74	4	*kata-pinō*	7
6	*poma*	2	10	*(hydro-)poteō*	1
5	*posis*	3	7	*(oino-)potēs*	2
2	*potērion*	32	11	*sym-pinō*	1
3	*potizō*	15	8	*sym-posion*	2
9	*potos*	1			

E = Drink//Eat

a) Drink, Drinker – Cup

Mt	6 25	E	[do not] worry about your life and what you are to eat (§ or what you are to *drink*),
	31	E	What are we to eat? What are we to *drink*?
	11 18	E	John came, neither eating nor *drinking*, and they say, 'He is possessed'. ¹⁹ The Son of Man came, eating and *drinking*, and they say, 'Look, a glutton and a ⌐*drunkard* (lit. *drinker* of wine),'
	19	X E	
	23 25	2	you hypocrites! You who clean the outside of *cup* and dish ²⁶ . . . Clean the inside of *cup* and dish first
	26	2	
	24 38	E	in those days before the Flood people were eating, *drinking*, taking wives
	49	E	[the dishonest servant] sets about . . . eating and *drinking* with drunkards,
	27 34	X	[the soldiers] gave [Jesus] wine to *drink* mixed with gall, which he tasted but refused to *drink*.
		X	
Mk	2 16	X E	Why does he eat (ᵛ and *drink*) with tax collectors and sinners?
	6 39		[Jesus] ordered [the disciples] to get all the people ⌐together
		8/8	in groups on (lit. *drinking-group* by *drinking-group* over) the green grass,
	7 4		There are also many other observances which have been handed down to [the Jews] concerning the washing of
		2	*cups* and pots
	16 18		[believers] will . . . be unharmed should they *drink* deadly poison;
Lk	1 15		[John] must *drink* no wine,

Lk	5 30	E	Why do you eat and *drink* with tax collectors and sinners?
	33	E	John's disciples are always fasting . . . but yours go on eating and *drinking*.
	39		nobody who has been *drinking* old wine wants new.
	7 33	E	John the Baptist comes, not eating bread not *drinking* wine, . . .
	34	X E	³⁴ The Son of Man comes, eating and *drinking*, and you say, 'Look, a glutton and a ⌐*drunkard* (lit. *drinker* of wine),'
	7		
	10 7	E	Stay in the same house, *taking* what food and drink they have to offer,
	11 39	2	You clean the outside of *cup* and plate,
	12 19	E	take things easy, eat, *drink*, have a good time.
	29		you must not set your hearts on things to eat and things to *drink*;
	45	E	[the servant] sets about . . . eating and *drinking* and getting drunk,
	13 26	E	We once ate and *drank* in your company;
	17 8	E	wait on me while I eat and *drink*. You can eat and *drink* yourself afterwards
	27	E	People were eating and *drinking*, marrying wives and husbands, right up to the day Noah went into the ark,
	28	E	in Lot's day: people were eating and *drinking*, buying and selling,
Jn	4 7	X	Jesus said to [the Samaritan woman], 'Give me a *drink*'.
	9	X	you ask me, a Samaritan, for a *drink*?
	10		If you only knew . . . who it is that is saying to you: Give me a *drink*, you would have been the one to ask, and he would have given you living water.
		X	
	12		our father Jacob who gave us this well and *drank* from it himself with his sons and his cattle?
	13		Whoever *drinks* this water will get thirsty again; ¹⁴ but
	14	●	anyone who *drinks* the water that I shall give will never be thirsty again:
	7 37	●	If any man is thirsty, let him come to me! Let the man come and *drink* ³⁸ who believes in me!
Ac	9 9	E	For three days [Saul] was without his sight, and *took* neither food nor *drink*.
	10 41	X E 11	Now we are . . . witnesses – we have eaten and *drunk with* [Jesus] after his resurrection from the dead
	23 12		the Jews . . . made a vow not to eat or *drink* until they had killed Paul.
	21	E	more than forty of them . . . have vowed not to eat or *drink* until they have got rid of him.
Rm	14 17	E 5	the kingdom of God does not mean eating or *drinking* this or that,
	21	E	the best course is ⌐to abstain from meat and wine and (lit. not to eat meat or *drink* wine or) anything else that would make your brother trip
1 Co	9 4	E	Have we not every right to eat and *drink*?
	10 7	E	(Ex 32 6) After sitting down to eat and *drink*, the people got up to amuse themselves.
	31	E	Whatever you eat, whatever you *drink*,
	11 22	E	Surely you have homes for eating and *drinking* in?
	15 32	E	(Is 22 13) Let us eat and *drink* today; tomorrow we shall be dead.
Col	2 16	E 5	never let anyone else decide what you should eat or *drink*,
1 Tm	5 23	10	You should give up *drinking* only water and have a little wine
Heb	9 10	E 6	they are rules . . . connected with foods and *drinks*
1 P	4 3		You spent quite long enough in the past . . . having wild parties and *drunken* [orgies]
		9	

b) Drink (from) the Cup (of the eucharist, of heaven)

Mt	26 27	2	[Jesus] took a *cup*, and when he had returned thanks he gave it to them. '*Drink* all of you from this, . . . ²⁹ . . . I shall not *drink* wine until the day I *drink* the new wine with you in the kingdom of my Father.'
	29	X	
Mk	14 23	2	[Jesus] took a *cup*, and when he had returned thanks he gave it to them, and all *drank* from it, . . . ²⁵ . . . 'I shall not *drink* any more wine until the day I *drink* the new wine in the kingdom of God.'
	25	X	
Lk	22 17	2	taking a *cup*, [Jesus] gave thanks and said, 'Take this and share it among you, ¹⁸ because from now on . . . I shall not *drink* wine until the kingdom of God comes.
	18	X	
	20	2	He did the same with the *cup* after supper, and said, 'This *cup* is the new covenant in my blood'
	30	E	you will eat and *drink* at my table in my kingdom,
Jn	6 53	E	if you do not eat the flesh of the Son of Man and *drink* his blood, you will not have life in you. ⁵⁴ Anyone who does eat my flesh and *drink* my blood has eternal life, . . .
	54	E	
	55	E 5	⁵⁵ For . . . my blood is real *drink*. ⁵⁶ He who eats my flesh and *drinks* my blood lives in me
	56		
1 Co	10 4	E /6	all *drank* the same spiritual *drink*, since they all *drank* from the spiritual rock . . . and that rock was Christ.
	16	E 2	The blessing-*cup* that we bless is a communion with the blood of Christ,
	21	E /2	You cannot *drink* the *cup* of the Lord and the *cup* of demons.
	11 25	2/2	[Jesus] took the *cup* after supper, and said, 'This *cup* is the new covenant in my blood.' ²⁶ . . . every time you . . .
	26	E /2	*drink* this *cup*, you are proclaiming his death, ²⁷ and so

1 Co 11 27   E /2   anyone who . . . *drinks* the *cup* of the Lord unworthily
will be behaving unworthily towards the . . . blood of the
     28   Lord. [28] Everyone is to recollect himself before . . .
     29   E /2   *drinking* this *cup*; [29] because a person who eats and
         E   *drinks* without recognising the Body is eating and *drinking*
         E   his own condemnation.

c) Drink the Cup (of Christ)

Mt 20 22   /2   'Can you *drink* the *cup* that I am going to
                drink?' . . . 'We can.'
     23   /2   'Very well,' he said 'you shall *drink* my *cup*.'
   26 39   2   My father, . . . if it is possible, let this *cup* pass me by.
     42   2   My father, . . . if this (ᵛ *cup*) cannot pass by without my
               drinking it, your will be done!
Mk 10 38   /2   Can you *drink* the *cup*
               that I must *drink* . . .?
     39   /2   The *cup* that I must *drink*
               you shall *drink*,
   14 36   Abba (Father)! . . . Everything is possible for you. Take
        2   this *cup* away from me.
Lk 22 42   2   Father, . . . if you are willing, take this *cup* away from me.
Jn 18 11   /2   am I not to *drink* the *cup* that the Father has given me?

d) Drink (figuratively) – Cup (of anger, of evil)

Rv 14 8   3   Babylon which *gave* the whole world the wine of God's
               anger *to drink*.
     10   [All those who worship the beast] will be made to *drink* the
        2   wine of God's fury which is ready, undiluted, in his *cup*
               of anger;
   16 6   blood is what you have given them to *drink*;
     19   Babylon the Great was not forgotten: God ʳmade her
        2   *drink* (lit. *gave her*) the full wine*cup* of his anger.
   17 4   2   The woman . . . was holding a gold [wine]*cup* filled with the
               disgusting filth of her fornication;
   18 3   All the nations have ʳbeen intoxicated by (lit. *drunk*) the wine
               of (§ the anger of) her prostitution;
     6   2   She is to have a doubly strong *cup* of her own mixture.

e) Give (a person something) to Drink, to Water (animals, plants) – Cup

Mt 10 42   3/2   If anyone *gives* [to *drink*] so much as a *cup* of cold water to
               one of these little ones
   25 35   X E 3   I was thirsty and you *gave* me *drink*;
     37   X E 3   when did we see you . . . thirsty and *give* you *drink*?
     42   X E 3   I was thirsty and you never *gave* me [anything] *to drink*;
   27 48   X   3   he dipped [the sponge] in vinegar and . . . *gave* it him *to
               drink*.
Mk 9 41   3/2   If anyone *gives* you a *cup* of water *to drink*
   15 36   X   3   Someone . . . soaked a sponge in vinegar and . . . *gave*
               it him *to drink*
Lk 13 15   Is there one of you who does not untie his ox . . . on the
        3   sabbath and take it out for *watering*?
Rm 12 20   E 3   (Pr 25 21) If your enemy is . . . thirsty, ʳ*let* (or: *give*) him
               drink.
1 Co 3 2   E 3   What I ʳfed you with (lit. *gave you to drink*) was milk,
     6   3   I did the planting, Apollos did the *watering*, . . . [7] Neither
     7   3   the planter nor the *waterer* matters: . . . [8] It is all one who
     8   3   does the planting and who does the *watering*,
   12 13   ●   3   one Spirit was *given* to us all *to drink*.
Heb 6 7   A field that has been well *watered* by frequent rain,

f) Swallow – (Be) Swallowed up, Drowned

Mt 23 24   4   You blind guides! Straining out gnats and *swallowing* camels!
1 Co 15 54   4   (Is 25 8) Death is *swallowed up* in victory.
2 Co 2 7   give him your forgiveness . . , or he might ʳbreak down
        4   from so (lit. be *swallowed up* in too) much misery.
     5 4   we want . . . to have what must die ʳtaken up into (lit.
        4   *swallowed up* by) life.
Heb 11 29   4   while the Egyptians . . . were *drowned*.
1 P 5 8   the devil is prowling round like a roaring lion, looking for
   Ⓓ   4   someone to ʳeat (lit. *swallow up*).
Rv 12 16   4   the earth . . . opened its mouth and *swallowed* the river
               thrown up by the [dragon].

11. MILK: GALA
gala 5

1 Co 3 2   What I fed you with was *milk*, not solid food,
   9 7   Who has there ever been that kept a flock and did not feed
               on *milk* from his flock?
Heb 5 12   you have gone back to needing *milk*, and not solid food.
     13   [13] Truly, anyone who is still living on *milk* cannot digest
               the doctrine of righteousness
1 P 2 2   You are new born, and, like babies, you should be hungry
               for nothing but *milk*

12. WINE – STRONG DRINK – DRUNK
1: WINE: OINOS

| 1 oinos | 35 | 4 | oino-phlygia | 1 |
| 2 oino(-potēs) | 2 | 3 | par-oinos | 2 |

a) Wine

Mt 9 17   Nor do people put new *wine* into old wineskins; if they do, the
               skins burst, the *wine* runs out, and the skins are lost. No;
               they put new *wine* into fresh skins and both are preserved.
   11 19   The Son of Man came . . . and they say, 'Look, a glutton
        2   and a ʳdrunkard (lit. drinker of *wine*).'
   27 34   [the soldiers] gave [Jesus] *wine* to drink mixed with gall,
Mk 2 22   nobody puts new *wine* into old wineskins; if he does, the
               wine will burst the skins, and the *wine* is lost and the skins
               too. No! New *wine*, fresh skins!
   15 23   [The soldiers] offered [Jesus] *wine* mixed with myrrh
Lk 1 15   [John] must drink no *wine*, no strong drink.
   5 37   nobody puts new *wine* into old skins; if he does, the new
     38   *wine* will burst the skins . . . [38] No; new *wine* must be
               put into fresh skins.
   7 33   John the Baptist comes, not eating bread, not drinking *wine*,
     34   The Son of Man comes, . . . and you say, 'Look, a glutton
        2   and a ʳdrunkard (lit. drinker of *wine*),'
   10 34   [The Samaritan] bandaged his wounds, pouring oil and
               wine on them.
Jn 2 3   ᵛ When they ran out of *wine*, since the *wine* provided for the
               wedding was all finished (G When the *wine* was running
               out), the mother of Jesus said to him, 'They have no *wine*'.
     9   the steward tasted the water, and it had turned into *wine*.
     10   . . . the steward called the bridegroom [10] and said, 'People
               generally serve the best *wine* first . . . but you have kept
               the best *wine* till now'.
   4 46   [Jesus] went again to Cana . . . where he had changed the
               water into *wine*
Rm 14 21   the best course is to abstain from meat and *wine*
Ep 5 18   (Pr 23 31 G) Do not drug yourselves with *wine*, this is simply
               dissipation;
1 Tm 3 3   [a presiding elder must be] not ʳa heavy drinker (lit. too
       3   *fond of wine*);
     8   deacons must be . . . moderate in the amount of *wine* they
               drink
   5 23   You should . . . have a little *wine* for the sake of your
               digestion
Tt 1 7   as president, . . . he must be irreproachable: not . . . ʳa
       3   heavy drinker (lit. too *fond of wine*)
   2 3   the older women should behave as though they were religious,
               with no . . . habitual *wine*-drinking
1 P 4 3   4   You spent long enough in the past . . . *drinking all
               the time*, having wild parties and drunken orgies
Rv 6 6   do not tamper with the oil or the *wine*.
   18 13   [there is nobody left in Babylon to buy] *wine*, oil, flour and
               corn;

b) Wine (figuratively)

Rv 14 8   Babylon which gave the whole world the *wine* of Gods'
               anger to drink.
     10   [All those who worship the beast] will be made to drink the
               wine of God's fury which is ready, undiluted, in his cup of
               anger;
   16 19   God made [Babylon] drink the full *wine*cup of his anger.
   17 2   [the prostitute] who has made all the population of the world
               drunk with the *wine* of her adultery.
   18 3   All the nations have ʳbeen intoxicated by (lit. drunk) the
               wine of (§ the anger of) her prostitution;
   19 15   [The Word of God] is the one who will . . . tread out the
               wine of Almighty God's fierce anger.

2: NEW WINE: GLEUKOS
gleukos 1

Ac 2 13   They have been drinking too much *new wine*

3: STRONG DRINK: SIKERA
sikera 1

Lk 1 15   [John] must drink no wine, no *strong drink*.

4: DRUNK, DRUNKARD, DRUNKENNESS: METHĒ

| 3 methē | 3 | 2 methyskō | 5 |
| 1 methuō | 5 | 4 methysos | 2 |

Mt 24 49   [the dishonest servant] sets about . . . eating and drinking
               with *drunkards*,

Lk 12 45	2	[the servant] sets about . . . eating and drinking and *getting drunk,*
21 34		Watch yourselves, or your hearts will be coarsened with
	3	debauchery and *drunkenness*
Jn 2 10		People generally serve the best wine first, and keep the
	2	cheaper sort till the guests *have had plenty to drink;*
Ac 2 15		[Peter said,] These men *are* not *drunk,*
Rm 13 13	3	no *carousing* or *drunken orgies,* no promiscuity
1 Co 5 11		you should not associate with a brother Christian who is
	4	. . . a *drunkard,* or is dishonest;
6 10		[people who do wrong will not inherit the kingdom of God:]
	4	thieves, usurers, *drunkards,*
11 21		one person goes hungry while another is *getting drunk.*
Ga 5 21	3	[The results of self-indulgence:] envy; *drunkenness,* orgies
Ep 5 18	2	Do not ⌈drug yourselves (lit. *get drunk)* with wine, this is simply dissipation;
1 Th 5 7	2/	Night is the time for sleepers to sleep and *drunkards to be drunk,*
Rv 17 2		[the prostitute] who has made all the population of the
	2	world *drunk* with the wine of her adultery.
6		[the woman] *was drunk,* [drunk] with the blood of the martyrs

13. CAROUSING – ORGY, WILD PARTY

1: FEAST WITH, CAROUSE WITH: *SYN-EU-ŌCHEOMAI*

syn-eu-ōcheomai 2

2 P 2 13		they amuse themselves ⌈deceiving you even when (ᵛ in their love-feasts even though) they ⌈are your guests at a meal (lit. *feast with* you);
Jude 12		They are a dangerous obstacle to your community meals, coming ⌈for the food (lit. to *feast with* you)

2: ORGY, REVEL, WILD PARTY – CAROUSING: *KŌMOS*

kōmos 3

Rm 13 13		no *carousing* or drunken orgies, no promiscuity
Ga 5 21		[The results of self-indulgence:] envy; drunkenness, *orgies*
1 P 4 3		You spent quite long enough in the past . . . drinking all the time, having ⌈*wild parties* (or: *revels*) and drunken orgies

EGYPT

Egypt	25	(from) *Alexandria*	2	P *Pharaoh*		5
Egyptian	5	*Alexandrian*	2	1 *basileus*		4/115
				2 *gē*		6/252

In Revelation, Egypt = Rome

Mt 2 13		the angel . . . [said] to Joseph '. . . escape into *Egypt*,'
14		. . . ¹⁴ So Joseph . . . left that night for *Egypt*, . . .
15		¹⁵ This was to fulfil what the Lord had spoken . . . (Ho 11 1): I called my son out of *Egypt*.
19		the angel of the Lord appeared in a dream to Joseph in *Egypt*
Ac 2 10		[devout men living in Jerusalem from every nation,] people from . . . *Egypt*
6 9		certain people came forward to debate with Stephen, some from Cyrene and *Alexandria*
7 6		(Gn 15 13) God [told Abraham] that his descendants would
	2	be exiles in a foreign *land,*
9		(cf. Gn 37 13) The patriarchs . . . sold [Joseph] into slavery
10 P 1		in *Egypt.* But (Gn 41 38–45) God . . . ¹⁰ [made] him wise enough to attract the attention of *Pharaoh king* of *Egypt,*
11		who made him governor of *Egypt* . . . ¹¹ (Gn 41 54) Then a famine came that caused much suffering throughout *Egypt*
12		(Gn 42 2) When Jacob heard that there was grain for sale in *Egypt,* he sent our ancestors there . . .
13 P		(cf. Gn 45 2) Joseph told *Pharaoh* about his family.
15		(Gn 46 6) Jacob went down into *Egypt* and . . . died there
17		(Ex 1 7–8) our nation in *Egypt* grew larger and larger, until
	1	a new *king* came to power in *Egypt* who knew nothing of Joseph.
21 P		(cf. Ex 2 5–10) *Pharaoh's* daughter adopted [Moses] and
22		brought him up as her own son. ²² So Moses was taught all the wisdom of the *Egyptians*
24		(Ex 2 12) [Moses] rescued the man by killing the *Egyptian.*
28		(Ex 2 14) Do you intend to kill me as you killed the *Egyptian* yesterday?

Ac 7 34		(Ex 3 7) I have seen the way my people are ill-treated in *Egypt*, . . . let me send you into *Egypt*.
36		(Ex 7 3) Moses . . ., after performing miracles and signs
	2	in (§ the *land* of) *Egypt*, led them out
39		(cf. Nb 14 3) our ancestors . . . turned back to *Egypt* in
40		their thoughts, ⁴⁰ and said to Aaron (Ex 32 1), . . . we do
	2	not understand what has come over this Moses who led us out of (§ the *land* of) *Egypt*.
13 17		God . . . made our people great when they were living as
	2	foreigners in (§ the *land* of) *Egypt*;
18 24		An *Alexandrian* Jew named Apollos now arrived in Ephesus.
21 38		[The tribune said to Paul:] So you are not the *Egyptian* who . . . led those 4,000 cut-throats out into the desert?
27 6		[At Myra] the centurion found an *Alexandrian* ship leaving for Italy
28 11		we set sail in a ship that . . . came from *Alexandria*
Rm 9 17 P		in scripture [God] says to *Pharaoh* (Ex 9 16): It was for this I raised you up,
Heb 3 16		the people who were brought out of *Egypt* by Moses.
8 9		(Jr 31 32) I took them by the hand to bring them out of the
	2	*land* of *Egypt*.
11 23 P 1		(cf. Ex 2 2) [Moses' parents] defied the *royal* edict
24 P		Moses refused to be known as the son of *Pharaoh's* daughter
26		. . . ²⁶ He considered that the insults offered to the Anointed were something more precious than all the treasures of
27		*Egypt* . . . ²⁷ . . . (Ex 2 15) he left *Egypt* and was not
P 1		afraid of the *king's* anger;
29		[the Israelites] crossed the Red Sea . . . while the *Egyptians* . . . were drowned.
Jude 5	2	the Lord rescued the nation from (§ the *land* of) *Egypt*,
Rv 11 8		the Great City known by the symbolic names Sodom and *Egypt*,

ELEMENT

1: Elemental spirits, Elemental principles	3: Elementary principles, First principles
2: the Elements	

stoicheion 7

1: ELEMENTAL SPIRITS, ELEMENTAL PRINCIPLES

Ga 4 3		before we came of age we were as good as slaves to the
9		*elemental principles* of this world, ⁹ . . . how can you want to go back to *elemental things* like these . . .?
Col 2 8		some . . . empty, rational philosophy based on the *principles* of this world instead of on Christ.
20		If you have really died with Christ to the *principles* of this world, why do you let rules dictate to you . . .?

2: THE ELEMENTS

2 P 3 10		[When] the Day of the Lord [comes] . . . the *elements* will catch fire and fall apart,
12		when . . . the *elements* melt in the heat.

3: ELEMENTARY PRINCIPLES, FIRST PRINCIPLES

Heb 5 12	you need someone to teach you all over again, the *elementary principles* of interpreting God's oracles;

ELIJAH – ELISHA

Elijah 30   *Elisha 1* (Lk 4)   *Naaman 1* (Lk 4)

M = Moses//Elijah

Mt 11 14		(cf. Ml 3 23) [John] is the *Elijah* who was to return.
16 14		Some say [the Son of Man] is John the Baptist, some *Elijah.*
17 3 M		Suddenly Moses and *Elijah* appeared to them; . . . ⁴ '. . .
4 M		I will make three tents here, one for you, one for Moses and one for *Elijah.*

Mt 17	10	(cf. Ml 3 23) 'Why do the scribes say then that *Elijah* has to come first?' [11] 'True,' [Jesus] replied, '*Elijah* is to come to see that everything is once more as it should be; [12] however, I tell you that *Elijah* has come already and they did not recognise him . . .' [13] The disciples understood then that he had been speaking of John the Baptist.
	11	
	12	
27	47	[Jesus cried out, 'Eli, Eli . . .'] some . . . said, 'The man is calling on *Elijah*,'
	49	Wait . . . and see if *Elijah* will come to save him.
Mk 6	15	Others said [of Jesus], 'He is *Elijah*;'
8	28	[Some say you are] John the Baptist, . . . others *Elijah*.
9	4 M	*Elijah* appeared to them with Moses . . . [5] . . . let us make three tents, one for you, one for Moses and one for *Elijah*.
	5 M	
	11	(cf. Ml 3 23) 'Why do the scribes say then that *Elijah* has to come first?' [12] 'True,' he said, '*Elijah* is to come first . . . [13] However, I tell you that *Elijah* has come and they have treated him as they pleased,'
	12	
	13	
15	35	[Jesus cried out, 'Eloi, Eloi . . .'] some . . . said, 'Listen, he is calling on *Elijah*. [36] . . . Wait and see if *Elijah* will come to take him down.'
	36	
Lk 1	17	With the spirit and power of *Elijah*, [John] will go before [the Lord]
4	25	There were many widows in Israel . . . in *Elijah*'s day, . . . [26] but *Elijah* was not sent to any one of these: (cf 1 K 17 9) he was sent to a widow at Zarephath, . . . [27] And in the prophet *Elisha*'s time there were many lepers in Israel, (cf. 2 K 5 14) but none of these was cured, except the Syrian, *Naaman*.
	26	
	27	
9	8	others [said of Jesus] that *Elijah* had reappeared,
	19	[Some say you are] John the Baptist; others *Elijah*;
	30	Suddenly there were two men talking to [Jesus]; they were Moses and *Elijah* [31] . . . and they were speaking of his passing
		M
	33	let us make three tents, one for you, one for Moses and one for *Elijah*.
		M
	54	do you want us to call down fire from heaven to burn them up (cf. 2 K 1 10f) [v] as *Elijah* did?
Jn 1	21	'are you *Elijah*?' 'I am not,' [John] said.
	25	Why are you baptising if you are not the Christ, and not *Elijah* . . .?
Rm 11	2	Do you remember what scripture says of *Elijah* – how he complained to God about Israel's behaviour? (cf. 1 K 19 10)
Jm 5	17	*Elijah* was a human being like ourselves – (cf. 1 K 17 1; 18 1) he prayed hard for it not to rain,

EMPTY – WORTHLESS – IN VAIN

1. Empty: *kenos*
  1: Empty(-handed)
  2: Empty oneself
  3: Empty = Pointless, Make void
    – Useless, In vain
2. Empty, Worthless – Useless, In vain

  – Nonsense: *mataios*
3. Worthless: *rhaka*
4. In vain, Wasted – For Nothing, Without cause: *eikē*
5. For no reason, Without cause, To no purpose: *dōrean*

1. EMPTY: *KENOS*

2 *kenoō* 5		4 *kenōs*	1
1 *kenos* 18		3 *keno(-phōnia)*	2

1: EMPTY(-HANDED)

Mk 12	3	[the tenants] seized the man, thrashed him and sent him away *empty*[-handed].
Lk 1	53	The hungry [God] has filled with good things, the rich sent *empty* away.
20	10	the tenants thrashed [the servant], and sent him away *empty*[-handed].
	11	[the tenants] thrashed [the second servant] too and . . . sent him away *empty*[-handed].

2: EMPTY ONESELF

| Ph 2 | 7 X | 2 [Christ] *emptied* himself to assume the condition of a slave. |

3: EMPTY = POINTLESS, MAKE VOID – USELESS, IN VAIN

Ac 4	25	(Ps 2 1) Why . . . these *futile* plots among the peoples?
Rm 4	14	If the world is only to be inherited by those who submit to the Law, then faith is *pointless*
	2	

1 Co 1	17	in the terms of philosophy . . . the crucifixion of Christ [2] *cannot be expressed* (lit. would be *made pointless*).
	2	
9	15	2 I would rather die than let anyone *take away* (lit. *make void*) something that I can boast of.
15	10	the grace that [God] gave me has not been *fruitless*.
	14	if Christ has not been raised then our preaching is *useless* and your believing it is *useless*;
	58	in the Lord, you cannot be labouring *in vain*.
2 Co 6	1	we beg you once again not to *neglect* (lit. make *void*) the grace of God that you have received.
9	3	I am sending the brothers . . . to make sure that our boasting about you does not prove to have been *empty* this time,
	2	
Ga 2	2	I did so for fear the course I was adopting . . . would *not be allowed* (lit. be *in vain*).
Ep 5	6	Do not let anyone deceive you with *empty* arguments:
Ph 2	16	[This] would mean that I had not run in the race (§ *for nothing*) and exhausted myself *for nothing*.
Col 2	8	Make sure that no one traps you . . . by some secondhand, *empty*, rational philosophy
1 Th 2	1	our visit to you has not proved *ineffectual*.
3	5	I was afraid . . . all our work might have been *wasted*.
1 Tm 6	20	3 Have nothing to do with . . . *pointless* philosophical discussions
2 Tm 2	16	3 Have nothing to do with *pointless* philosophical discussions
Jm 2	20	Do realise, you *senseless* man, that faith without good deeds is useless.
4	5	4 Surely you don't think scripture is *wrong* . . .?

2. EMPTY, WORTHLESS – USELESS, IN VAIN – NONSENSE: *MATAIOS*

4 *mataioō* 1		5 *mataio(-logia)* 1	
1 *mataios* 6		6 *mataio(-logos)* 1	
2 *mataiotēs* 3		3 *matēn* 2	

Mt 15	9	3 (Is 29 13 G) The worship they offer me is *worthless*;
Mk 7	7	3 (Is 29 13 G) The worship they offer me is *worthless*,
Ac 14	15	We have come . . . to make you turn from these *empty* [idols] to the living God
Rm 1	21	4 [the pagans] made *nonsense* out of logic
8	20	It was not for any fault on the part of creation that it was [2] made *unable to attain its purpose*,
	2	
1 Co 3	20	(Ps 94 11) The Lord knows wise men's thoughts: he knows how *useless* they are;
15	17	if Christ has not been raised, your faith is *worthless* and you are still in your sins.
Ep 4	17	I want to urge you . . . not to go on living [the aimless kind of life (lit. with *empty* minds in the way) that pagans live.
	2	
1 Tm 1	6	There are some people who have . . . taken a road that leads [5] to *empty* speculation;
	5	
Tt 1	10	6 you have there a great many people . . . who talk *nonsense* and try to make others believe it,
3	9	disputes about the Law . . . are useless and *can do no good to anyone*.
Jm 1	26	Nobody . . . is religious while he still goes on deceiving himself and not keeping control over his tongue: anyone who does this has [the wrong idea of (lit. a *worthless*) religion.
1 P 1	18	the ransom . . . was paid to free you from the *useless* way of life your ancestors handed down
2 P 1	18	2 With their high-flown talk, which is all *hollow*, they tempt back the ones who have only just escaped from paganism,

3. WORTHLESS: *RHAKA*

rhaka 1

| Mt 5 | 22 | if a man calls his brother "*Fool*" he will answer for it before the Sanhedrin; |

4. IN VAIN, WASTED – FOR NOTHING, WITHOUT CAUSE: *EIKĒ*

eikē 7

Mt 5	22	anyone who is angry with his brother ([v] *without a cause*) will answer for it before the court;
Rm 13	4	the bearing of the sword [has its significance (lit. is not *for nothing*).
1 Co 15	2	believing anything else [will *not lead to anything* (or: is *in vain*).
Ga 3	4	Have all the [favours (or: sufferings) you received been *wasted*? And if this were so, they would most certainly have been *wasted*.

Ga	4 11	You make me ˹feel (lit. fear) I have *wasted* my ˹time (lit. efforts).
Col	2 18	people like that are always . . . inflating themselves to a *false* importance

5. FOR NO REASON, WITHOUT CAUSE, TO NO PURPOSE: *DŌREAN*

dōrean 2/9

Jn	15 25	(Ps 35 19) They hated me *for no reason.*
Ga	2 21	if the Law can justify us, there is *no point in* the death of Christ.

ENCOURAGE – BOLD – PERSUADE

1. **Courage, Take heart – Be brave, Full of confidence, Rely (on) – Bully:** *tharseō*
2. **Courage, Confidence – Take courage, Take heart – Cheerful:** *eu-thymeō*
3. **Confidence, Certainty:** *hypo-stasis*
4. **Boldness, Confidence, Assurance – Preach fearlessly, Speak out boldly:** *par-rhēsia*
5. **Dare, Be bold enough (to):** *tolmaō*
6. **Encourage, Give support to:** *pro-trepomai*
7. **Comfort:** *par-ēgoria*
8. **Encourage – Urge, Advise – Console:** *para-kaleō*
 1: Encourage(ment) – Urge, Exhort – Preach, Advise

 2: Console, Comfort, Reassure – Consolation – Help
9. **Console, Sympathise with – Encourage, Persuade:** *para-mytheomai*
10. **Persuade, Convince – (Be) Persuaded, Trust (in):** *peithō*
 1: Persuade, Convince, Win over – (Be) Persuaded, Certain, Sure – Urge
 2: Trust (in) – Rely (on) – Confidence (in)
11. **Teach, Encourage, Convince – (Be) Convinced, Conclude:** *sym-bibazō*
12. **Urge, Ask – Advise, Warn:** *par-aineō*
13. **Intimidate, Bully:** *dia-seiō*

1. COURAGE, TAKE HEART – BE BRAVE, FULL OF CONFIDENCE, RELY (ON) – BULLY: *THARSEŌ*

2 *tharreō* 6	1 *tharseō* 7	
	3 *tharsos* 1	

Mt	9 2	*Courage,* my child, your sins are forgiven.
	22	*Courage,* my daughter, your faith has restored you to health.
	14 27	*Courage!* It is I! Do not be afraid.
Mk	6 50	*Courage!* It is I! Do not be afraid.
	10 49	they called the blind man, '*Courage*,' they said 'get up; he is calling you.'
Jn	16 33	*be brave*: I have conquered the world.
Ac	23 11	the Lord appeared to [Paul] and said, '*Courage!* You have borne witness for me in Jerusalem'
	28 15	When Paul saw [the brothers in Rome] he thanked God and took ˹*courage* (or: *heart*).
2 Co	5 6	2 We are always *full of confidence,*
	8	2 we are *full of confidence* . . . and actually want to be exiled from the body
	7 16	2 I am very happy knowing that I can *rely* on you so completely.
	10 1	2 I, the man who . . . *bullies* you when he is at a distance.
	2	2 I only ask that I do not have to *bully* you when I come, with all the confident assurance I mean to show
Heb	13 6	2 we can say *with confidence*: With the Lord to help me, I fear nothing:

2. COURAGE, CONFIDENCE – TAKE COURAGE, TAKE HEART – CHEERFUL: *EU-THYMEŌ*

2 *a-thymeō* 1	3 *eu-thymos* 1	
1 *eu-thymeō* 3	4 *eu-thymōs* 1	

Ac	24 10	4 I can therefore speak *with confidence* in my defence.
	27 22	I ask you ˹not to give way to despair (lit. *to take heart*).
	25	So *take courage,* friends;
	36	3 they all plucked up *courage* and took something to eat themselves.
Col	3 21	Parents, never drive your children to resentment or you will 2 make them *feel* ˹*frustrated* (or: *discouraged*).
Jm	5 13	if anyone is ˹*feeling happy* (or: *cheerful*), he should sing a psalm.

3. CONFIDENCE, CERTAINTY: *HYPO-STASIS*

hypo-stasis 3/5

2 Co	9 4	If some of the Macedonians . . . found you unprepared, we should be humiliated . . . after *being so confident.*
	11 17	What I am going to say now is . . . said . . . in the *certainty* that I have something to boast about.
Heb	3 14	we shall remain co-heirs with Christ only if we keep a grasp on our first *confidence* right to the end.

4. BOLDNESS, CONFIDENCE, ASSURANCE – PREACH FEARLESSLY, SPEAK OUT BOLDLY: *PAR-RHĒSIA*

1 *par-rhēsia* 20/31 2 *par-rhēsiazomai* 9

Ac	2 29	Brothers, ˹no one can deny (lit. I may *confidently* state; or: I may state plainly) that . . . David . . . [31] . . . foresaw and spoke about . . . the resurrection of the Christ:
	4 13	They were astonished at the *assurance* shown by Peter and John,
	29	Lord, . . . help your servants to proclaim your message with all *boldness,*
	31	[the apostles] began to proclaim the word of God *boldly.*
	9 27	2 [Saul] had *preached boldly* at Damascus in the name of Jesus.
	28	2 Saul now started to go round . . . *preaching fearlessly* in the name of the Lord.
	13 46	2 Then Paul and Barnabas *spoke out boldly.*
	14 3	2 Paul and Barnabas stayed on for some time, *preaching fearlessly* for the Lord;
	18 26	2 Priscilla and Aquila heard [Apollos] *speak boldly* in the synagogue.
	19 8	2 [Paul] began by going to the synagogue, where he *spoke out boldly*
	26 26	2 to [the king] I now *speak with assurance,*
	28 31	2 [Paul spent two years in Rome,] teaching . . . with complete ˹*freedom* (or: *confidence*) and without hindrance from anyone.
2 Co	3 12	Having this hope, we can be quite *confident;*
	7 4	I have the very greatest *confidence* in you,
Ep	3 12	[in Christ Jesus] we are *bold* enough to approach God
	6 19	pray for me to be given an opportunity to . . . speak *without fear*
	20	2 pray that . . . I may *speak* as *boldly* as I ought to.
Ph	1 20	My one hope and trust is that . . . I shall have the *courage* for Christ to be glorified in my body,
1 Th	2 2	2 it was our God who gave us the *courage* to proclaim his Good News
1 Tm	3 13	Those . . . who carry out their duties well as deacons will . . . be rewarded with great *assurance*
Phm	8	in Christ I can ˹have no diffidence about telling (lit. *confidently* tell) you . . . to do whatever is your duty,
Heb	3 6	we cling to our hope with the *confidence* that we glory in.
	4 16	Let us be *confident,* then, in approaching the throne of grace,
	10 19	through the blood of Jesus we have the ˹*right* (lit. *confidence*) to enter the sanctuary,
	35	Be as *confident* now, then, since the reward is so great.
1 Jn	2 28	Live in Christ . . . so that if he appears, we may have full *confidence,*
	3 21	we ˹need not be afraid (lit. may be *confident*) in God's presence,
	4 17	we can face the day of Judgement ˹without fear (lit. *confidently*);
	5 14	We are quite *confident* that if we ask [God] for anything . . . he will hear us;

5. DARE, BE BOLD ENOUGH (TO): *TOLMAŌ*

1 *tolmaō* 16	3 *tolmētēs* 1	
2 *tolmērōs* 1	4 *apo-tolmaō* 1	

Mt	22 46	no one *dared* to ask [Jesus] any further questions.
Mk	12 34	no one *dared* to question [Jesus] any more.
	15 43	Joseph of Arimathaea . . . *boldly* went to Pilate
Lk	20 40	[the scribes] would not *dare* to ask [Jesus] any more questions.
Jn	21 12	None of the disciples *was bold enough* to ask, 'Who are you?'
Ac	5 13	No one else ever *dared* to join [the believers].
	7 32	Moses trembled and did not *dare* to look any more.
Rm	5 7	for someone really worthy a man might *be prepared* to die
	10 20	4 Isaiah said more ˹clearly (lit. *boldly*): I have been found by those who did not seek me,
	15 15	The reason why I have written to you, and put some things 2 rather *strongly,* is to refresh your memories,
	18	What I am *presuming* to speak of . . . is only what Christ himself has done
1 Co	6 1	How *dare* one of your members take up a complaint against another in the lawcourts of the unjust . . . ?

2 Co 10	2	I only ask that I do not have to bully you when I come, with all the confident *assurance* I mean to show
	12	We are not *being so bold* as to rank ourselves . . . with certain people
	11 21	if anyone ʳwants some brazen speaking (lit. *dares* to speak brazenly) . . . then I ʳcan (lit. *dare*) be as brazen as any of them,
Ph	1 14	most of the brothers . . . are getting more and more *daring* in announcing the Message without any fear.
2 P	2 10	3 Such *self-willed* people with no reverence are not afraid of offending against the glorious ones,
Jude	9	Not even the archangel Michael . . . *dared* to denounce [the devil] in the language of abuse;

6. ENCOURAGE, GIVE SUPPORT TO: *PRO-TREPOMAI*

pro-trepomai 1

Ac 18 27		When Apollos thought of crossing over to Achaia, the brothers *encouraged* him

7. COMFORT: *PAR-ĒGORIA*

par-ēgoria 1

Co 4 11		[Aristarchus, Mark and Jesus Justus] have been a [great] *comfort* to me.

8. ENCOURAGE – URGE, ADVISE – CONSOLE: *PARA-KALEŌ*

1 *para-kaleō 50/109* 3 *sym-para-kaleō 1*
2 *para-klēsis 27*

1: ENCOURAGE(MENT) – URGE, EXHORT – PREACH, ADVISE

Lk	3 18	there were many other things [John] said to *exhort* the people and to announce the Good News to them.
Ac	2 40	[Paul] spoke to them for a long time . . . and . . . *urged* them,
	4 36	Joseph whom the apostles surnamed Barnabas (which means 'son of *encouragement*').
	13 15	2 if you would like to address some words of *encouragement* to the congregation, please do so.
	14 22	[Paul and Barnabas] put fresh heart into the disciples, *encouraging* them to persevere in the faith.
	15 31	2 The community . . . were delighted with the *encouragement* [the letter] gave them.
	32	Judas and Silas . . . spoke for a long time, *encouraging* and strengthening the brothers.
	16 40	[Paul and Silas] went to Lydia's house where they . . . *gave* [the brothers] some *encouragement*;
	20 1	after *speaking words of encouragement* to [the disciples, Paul] . . . set out for Macedonia. ² On his way through those areas he *said* many *words of encouragement* to them
	2	
	27 33	Paul *urged* them all to have something to eat.
	34	*Let me persuade* you to have something to eat;
Rm	1 12	3 [I am longing] to find *encouragement* among you from our common faith.
	12 8	[Our gifts differ according to the grace given us.] Let the /2 *preachers* deliver sermons, the almsgivers give
1 Co 14	3	the man who prophesies does talk to other people, to their 2 . . . *encouragement* and their consolation.
	31	you can all prophesy in turn, so that everybody will learn something and . . . be *encouraged*.
2 Co 2	7	the best thing now is to *give* [the man in question] your forgiveness and *encouragement*,
	7 13	That is what we have found so *encouraging*. With this 2 *encouragement*, too, we had the even greater happiness of finding Titus so happy;
	12 18	Titus went at my *urging*,
Ph	2 1	2 If our life in Christ ʳmeans anything to (lit. can *urge*) you [then be united]
Col	2 2	It is all to . . . *stir* your minds,
1 Th 2	3	2 We have not taken to *preaching* because we are deluded, *teaching* you *what is right*, encouraging you . . . to live a life worthy of God,
	12	
	3 2	[we] sent our brother Timothy . . . to *keep* you firm and *strong* in the faith
	4 10	we do *urge* you, brothers, to go on making even greater progress
	5 11	*give encouragement* to each other, . . . as you do already.
2 Th 3 12		we order and *call on* people of this kind to go on quietly working
1 Tm 2 1		My *advice is* that . . . there should be prayers offered for everyone

1 Tm 4 13		Make use of the time until I arrive by reading to the people, 2 *preaching* and teaching.
5 1		Do not speak harshly to a man older than yourself, but *advise* him as you would your own father;
6 2		This is what you are to teach them to believe and *persuade* them to do.
2 Tm 4 2		Refute falsehood, correct error, *call to obedience*
Tt 1 9		[an elder] must have a firm grasp of . . . the tradition, so that he can be counted on for . . . *expounding* the sound doctrine
2 6		you have got to *persuade* the younger men to be moderate
15		this is what you are to say, whether you are *giving instruction* or correcting errors;
Heb 3 13		Every day, . . . *keep encouraging* one another
6 18		2 so that we . . . should have a strong *encouragement* to take a firm grip on the hope that is held out to us.
10 25		*encourage* each other to go [to the meetings of the community];
12 5		2 Have you forgotten that *encouraging* [text] in which you are addressed as sons (Pr 3 11f)?
13 22		2 I do ask you, brothers, to take these words of *advice* kindly;
1 P 2 11		I *urge* you . . . to keep yourselves free from . . . selfish passions
5 1		I have something to *tell* your elders:
12		I write these few words . . . to *encourage* you

2: CONSOLE, COMFORT, REASSURE – CONSOLATION – HELP

Mt	2 18	(Jr 31 15) it was Rachel . . . refusing to be *comforted*
	5 5	Happy those who mourn: they shall be *comforted*.
Lk	2 25	2 [Simeon] looked forward to Israel's *comforting*
	6 24	2 alas for you who are rich: you are having your *consolation* now.
	16 25	Now [Lazarus] is being *comforted* here while you are in agony.
Ac	9 31	The ᵛ churches (G Church) . . . left in peace . . . filled with 2 the *consolation* of the Holy Spirit.
	20 12	They took [Eutychus] away alive, and were greatly *encouraged*.
	28 14	we found some brothers [at Puteoli] and ʳwere *much rewarded* by staying (or: were asked to stay) a week with them.
Rm 15	4	scripture gives [examples] of how people who did not give 2 up were *helped* by God.
	5	2 may he who *helps* us when we refuse to give up, help you all
1 Co 4 13		we are insulted and we ʳ*answer politely* (or: *are helpful*).
2 Co 1	3	2/ Blessed be . . . the God of all *consolation*, ⁴ who *comforts* us in all our sorrows, so that we can ʳoffer consolation /2 *console* others with) . . . the *consolation* that ʳwe have received (lit. *consoles* us) from God. ⁵ Indeed, as the sufferings of Christ overflow to us, so, through Christ, does our *consolation* overflow. ⁶ When we are made to suffer, it is for your 2/ *consolation* and salvation. When, instead, we are *comforted*, this should be a *consolation* to you . . . ⁷ . . . sharing our sufferings, you will also share our *consolations*.
	4	
	5	
	6	
	7	2
	7 4	I am so proud of you that in all our trouble I am filled with 2 *consolation*
	6	God *comforts* the miserable, and he *comforted* us, by the 7 2 arrival of Titus, ⁷ and . . . also by the *comfort* ʳwhich he had gained from (lit. by which he had been *consoled* by) you.
	13 11	try to grow perfect; *help* one another.
Ep 6 22		I am sending [Tychicus] to you . . . to give you news about us and *reassure* you.
Col 4 8		I am sending [Tychicus] to you . . . to give you news about us and to *reassure* you
1 Th 3 7		your faith has *been a* great *comfort* to us in the middle of our own troubles
	4 18	With such thoughts as these you should *comfort* one another
2 Th 2 16		May our Lord Jesus Christ himself, and God our Father who 17 2/ has given us . . . such inexhaustible *comfort* . . . ¹⁷ *comfort* you and strengthen you
Phm 7		2 I am so delighted, and *comforted*, to know of your love;

9. CONSOLE, SYMPATHISE WITH – ENCOURAGE, PERSUADE: *PARA-MYTHEOMAI*

1 *para-mytheomai 4* 3 *para-mythion 1*
2 *para-mythia 1*

Jn 11 19		many Jews had come to Martha and Mary to *sympathise with* them over their brother.
	31	the Jews . . . were in the house *sympathising with* Mary
1 Co 14 3		the man who prophesies does talk to other people, to their 2 . . . *encouragement* and their *consolation*.
Ph 2 1		3 If our life in Christ means anything to you, if love can *persuade* at all [then be united]
1 Th 2 12		teaching you what was right, *encouraging* you and appealing to you to live a life worthy of God, who is calling you
5 14		*give courage to* those who are apprehensive, care for the weak

10. PERSUADE, CONVINCE – (BE) PERSUADED, TRUST (IN): *PEITHŌ*

4	*peismonē*	*1*	6	*pithano(-logia)*	*1*
1	*peithō*	*26|*	7	*ana-peithō*	*1*
2	*peithō* (pft)	*19|⁵³*	8	*eu-peithēs*	*1*
5	*peithos*	*1*			
3	*pepoithēsis*	*6*			

1: PERSUADE, CONVINCE, WIN OVER – (BE) PERSUADED, CERTAIN, SURE – URGE

Mt 27 20		The chief priests and the elders . . . had *persuaded* the crowd to demand the release of Barabbas
28 14		should the governor come to hear of this, we undertake to *put things right with* him ourselves
Lk 16 31		they will not be *convinced* even if someone should rise from the dead.
18 9	2	[The Lord] spoke the following parable to some people who *prided themselves* on being virtuous
20 6		the people . . . are *convinced* that John was a prophet.
Ac 12 20		a joint deputation . . . managed to *enlist the support of* Blastus, the king's chamberlain,
13 43		Paul and Barnabas *urged* [the Jews] to remain faithful to the grace God had given them.
14 19		some Jews arrived from Antioch . . . and ⌐turned the people against the apostles (lit. *persuaded* the people).
17 4		Some of [the Jews in Thessalonika] were *convinced* and joined Paul
18 4		[Paul] used to hold debates in the synagogues, trying to *convert* Jews as well as Greeks.
13	7	We accuse this man . . . of *persuading* people to worship God in a way that breaks the Law.
19 8		[Paul] argued *persuasively* about the kingdom of God [in Ephesus].
26		this man Paul has *persuaded* and converted a great number of people
21 14		[Paul] would not be *persuaded* [not to go on to Jerusalem],
23 21		Do not ⌐let them *persuade* you (or: listen to them).
26 26		[I am] *confident* that nothing of all this is lost on [the king];
28		A little more, and your ⌐arguments (lit. *persuasion*) would make a Christian of me.
28 23		[Paul] put his case to [the Roman Jews] . . . trying to *persuade* them about Jesus,
24		some were *convinced* by what he said, while the rest were sceptical.
Rm 2 19	2	if you [who call yourself a Jew] are *convinced* you can guide the blind . . . ²¹ then why not teach yourself as well as the others?
8 38		I am *certain* of this: neither death nor life . . . ³⁹ . . . can ever come between us and the love of God
14 14		I ⌐am perfectly well aware (lit. know and am *certain*) . . . that no food is unclean in itself;
15 14		I am quite *certain* that you are full of good intentions,
1 Co 2 4	5	in my speeches . . . there were none of the *persuasive* arguments that belong to philosophy;
2 Co 1 15	3	Because I was so *sure* of this, I had meant to come to you first,
2 3	2	I am *sure* you all know that I could never be happy unless you were.
3 4	3	Before God, we are *confident* of this through Christ:
5 11		we try to *win* people *over*.
10 7	2	Anybody who is *convinced* that he belongs to Christ must go on to reflect that we all belong to Christ
Ga 1 10 ○		whom am I trying to ⌐please (lit. *convince*) – man, or God?
5 8	4	You were not *prompted* by him who called you!
10		I feel *sure* that, united in the Lord, you will agree with me,
Ph 1 6	2	I am quite *certain* that the One who began this good work in you will see that it is finished
25	2	This *weighs* with me *so much* that I feel sure I shall survive and stay with you all,
Col 2 4		I say this to make sure that no one deceives you with
6		⌐specious (lit. *persuasive*) arguments.
2 Tm 1 5		I ⌐have no doubt (lit. am *convinced*) that it is the same faith in you as well.
12		I ⌐have no doubt at all (lit. am *persuaded*) that [Christ Jesus] is able to take care of all that I have entrusted to him
Heb 6 9		we are *sure* you are in a better state and on the way to salvation.
13 18		We are *sure* that our own conscience is clear
Jm 3 17		the wisdom that comes down from above is . . . ⌐considerate
8		(lit. easily *won over*);
1 Jn 3 19		only by this can we be *certain* that we are children of the truth

2: TRUST (IN) – RELY (ON) – CONFIDENCE (IN)

Mt 27 43 X	2	He *puts his trust* in God . . . For he did say, 'I am the son of God'.

Mk 10 24	2	how hard it is (ᵛ for those who *trust* in wealth) to enter the kingdom of God!
Lk 11 22	2	the stronger man takes away all the weapons he *relied* on
2 Co 1 9	2	it has taught us not to *rely* on ourselves but only on God,
8 22	3	we are sending a third brother . . . who . . . has great *confidence* in you.
10 2	3	I only ask that I do not have to bully you when I come, with all the *confident* assurance I mean to show
Ep 3 12	3	This is why we are bold enough to approach God in complete *confidence*, through our faith in [Christ Jesus];
Ph 1 14	2	most of the brothers have *taken* ⌐courage (lit. *confidence*) in the Lord from these chains of mine
2 24	2	I continue to *trust*, in the Lord, that I shall be coming soon myself.
3 3		we have our own glory from Christ Jesus without having to
4	2/3	*rely* on a physical operation. ⁴ If it came to *relying* on physical evidence, I should be fully qualified myself. Take
2		any man who thinks he can *rely* on what is physical: I am even better qualified.
2 Th 3 4	2	we, in the Lord, *have* every *confidence* that you are doing . . . all that we tell you.
Phm 21	2	I am writing with [complete] *confidence* in your compliance,
Heb 2 13	2	(Is 8 17) In him I ⌐*hope* (lit. *trust*);

11. TEACH, ENCOURAGE, CONVINCE – (BE) CONVINCED, CONCLUDE: *SYM-BIBAZŌ*

sym-bibazō 4/7

Ac 9 22 ○		[Saul] *demonstrated* that Jesus was the Christ.
16 10		[we were] *convinced* that God had called us to bring [the Macedonians] the Good News.
19 33		The Jews pushed Alexander to the front, and . . . some of the crowd *shouted encouragement*
1 Co 2 16		(Is 40 13) Who can know the mind of the Lord, so who can *teach* him?

12. URGE, ASK – ADVISE, WARN: *PAR-AINEŌ*

par-aineō 2

Ac 27 9	navigation was already hazardous . . . so Paul *gave* them this ⌐*warning* (or: *advice*),
22	I ⌐*ask* (or: *urge*) you not to give way to despair.

13. INTIMIDATE, BULLY: *DIA-SEIŌ*

dia-seiō 1

Lk 3 14	No *intimidation*! ⌐No [extortion by] false accusation (or: No cheating)!

END – LAST

1. **End – Complete, Perfect(ly) – Purpose, Fulfil:** *telos*
   a) End(ing), Finish, Complete, Over – Fulfil, Accomplish, Do, Purpose – Finally, Completely, Certainly
   b) Perfect, Perfection – Full-grown, Mature, Adult
2. **Perfect:** *kat-artizō*
   a) Perfect = Fully trained, Equipped, Ready – Fit (for), Deserving (to) – Set right
   b) Perfect = Complete, End – Make sure (of) – Prepare, Mend
3. **End, Finish:** *di-anuō*
4. **End, Tip – Top, Chief – Ripe:** *akmazō*
   a) End(s), Bounds, Tip – Top, Chief
   b) "Top of the heap" = Treasure, Spoil(s)
   c) Grow old – Ripe

5. **End(s), Bounds – Endless, Interminable:** *peras*
6. **the Finish, Goal:** *skopos*
7. **Unceasing, Endless – Cease, Stop**
   1: Unceasing, Endless – Constant(ly), Continual, Always – Cease, End: *dia-leipō*
   2: Cease, Finish, Subside – Over, Stop – Fail to: *pauō*
8. **Cease – (a wind) Drops:** *kopazō*
9. **the Last – End(s):** *eschatos*
   a) Last day(s), Last trumpet, Last Adam, Last enemy
   b) Last, Latest, Lowest – End up (by), At the end
   c) Ends, Bounds, Uttermost parts
   d) (Breathing one's) Last – the point of Death, Death's door – Desperately sick
10. **Last, Lastly, Finally – Eventually:** *hysteron*

1. END – COMPLETE, PERFECT(LY) – PURPOSE, FULFIL: *TELOS*

3	*teleioō*	23	15	*teles-phoreō*	1
4	*teleios*	19	10	*apo-teleō*	2
13	*teleiōs*	1	11	*ek-teleō*	2
8	*teleiōsis*	2	5	*epi-teleō*	10
9	*teleiotēs*	2	12	*pan-teleś*	2
14	*teleiōtēs*	1	7	*syn-teleia*	6
2	*teleō*	26/28	6	*syn-teleō*	7
1	*telos*	38/41			

a) End(ing), Finish, Complete, Over – Fulfil, Accomplish, Do, Purpose – Finally, Completely, Certainly

S = Fulfilment of the Scripture

Mt 7 28 2 Jesus had now *finished* what he wanted to say,
10 22 the man who stands firm to the *end* will be saved.
23 2 you will not have ⌐gone (lit. *finished*) the round of the towns of Israel before the Son of Man comes.
11 1 2 When Jesus had *finished* instructing his twelve disciples
13 39 7 the harvest is the *end* of the world;
40 7 so it will be at the *end* of time.
49 7 at the *end* of time: the angels will . . . separate the wicked from the just
53 2 When Jesus had *finished* these parables
19 1 2 Jesus had now *finished* what he wanted to say,
24 3 7 what will be the sign of your coming and of the *end* of the world?
6 do not be alarmed . . . the *end* will not be yet.
13 the man who stands firm to the *end* will be saved.
14 This Good News . . . will be proclaimed to the whole world . . . And then the *end* will come.
26 1 2 Jesus had now *finished* all he wanted to say,
58 Peter . . . sat down with the attendants to see what the *end* would be.
28 20 7 I am with you always; yes, to the *end* of time.
Mk 3 26 ⓓ if Satan has rebelled against himself and is divided . . . it is the *end* of him.
13 4 6 what sign will there be that all this is about to be *fulfilled*?
7 When you hear of wars . . . do not be alarmed . . . the *end* will not be yet.
13 the man who stands firm to the *end* will be saved.
Lk 1 33 [Jesus] will rule . . . for ever and his reign will have no *end*.
45 blessed is she who believed that the promise made her by the Lord would be *fulfilled*.
2 39 2 When [Joseph and Mary] had *done* everything the Law of the Lord required, they went back to Galilee,
43 3 after ⌐the feast (lit. the *end* of the feast)
4 2 6 at the *end* [of the forty days Jesus] was hungry.
13 6 Having *exhausted* all these [ways of] tempting [Jesus], the devil left him,
12 50 2 There is a baptism I must still receive, and how great is my distress till it is *over*!
13 11 12 [the woman] was bent double and ⌐quite unable to stand upright (or: unable to stand *quite* upright).
12
32 X 10 today and tomorrow I *finish* casting out devils and on the third day *attain* my end.
14 29 < 11 if he . . . found himself unable to *finish* the work, the on-lookers would all start making fun of him
30 < 11 Here is a man who started to build and was unable to *finish*.
18 5 I must give this widow her just rights, or she will *end*lessly be coming and worry me to death.
31 S we are going up to Jerusalem, and everything that is written
2 . . . is to ⌐come true (or: be *accomplished*).
21 9 do not be frightened, for . . . the *end* is not so soon.
22 37 S 2 these words of scripture have to be *fulfilled* in me . . . what scripture says about me is even now reaching its *fulfilment*.
Jn 2 3 they ran out of wine, since the wine provided for the wedding
6 was all *finished*.
4 34 X 3 My food is . . . to *complete* [the] work [of the one who sent me]
5 36 X 3 the works my Father has given me to *carry out*,
13 1 [Jesus] had always loved those who were his . . . but now he showed ⌐how to love them to the *end* (or: how perfect his love was).
17 4 X 3 I have . . . *finished* the work that you gave me to do.
23 With me in them and you in me, may they be . . . ⌐perfectly
3 (or: *completely*) one
19 28 2 Jesus knew that everything had now been *completed*, and to
S 3 *fulfil* the scripture perfectly he said: 'I am thirsty'.
30 2 [Jesus] said, '[It is] *accomplished*'; and . . . gave up his spirit.
Ac 13 29 S 2 When they had *carried out* everything that scripture foretells about him they took him down from the tree
20 24 3 provided that when I *finish* my race I have carried out the mission the Lord Jesus gave me
21 27 6 The seven days were nearly *over*

Rm 2 27 2 the man who ⌐keeps (lit. *fulfils*) the Law, even though he has not been physically circumcised, is a living condemnation of the way you disobey the Law
6 21 that sort of behaviour *ends* in death.
22 you get a reward leading to your sanctification and *ending* in eternal life.
9 28 6 (Is 10 22) ⌐without hesitation (lit. with *finality*) . . . the Lord will execute his sentence on the earth.
10 4 the Law has come to an *end* with Christ.
15 28 5 So when I have *done* this and officially handed over what has been raised, I shall set out for Spain
1 Co 1 8 [God] will keep you steady . . . until the ⌐last day (lit. *end*)
10 11 All this . . . was . . . to be a lesson for us who are living at the *end* of the age.
15 24 After that will come the *end*, when [the Christ] hands over the kingdom to God
2 Co 1 13 There are no hidden meanings in our letters besides what you can ⌐read for yourselves and (lit. *certainly*) understand.
3 13 Moses . . . put a veil over his face so that the Israelites would not notice the *ending* of what had to fade.
7 1 5 let us . . . in the fear of God ⌐*complete* our consecration (or: reach perfection)
8 6 5 we have asked Titus . . . to bring this work of mercy *to the same point* of success among you.
11 5/5 So now *finish* the work and let the *results* be worthy . . . of the decision you made
11 15 [The servants of Satan] will come to the *end* that they deserve.
Ga 3 3 5 Are you foolish enough to *end* in outward observances what you began in the Spirit?
5 16 2 you will be in no danger of ⌐yielding to (lit. *fulfilling*) self-indulgence,
Ph 1 6 the One who began this good work in you will see that it is
5 *finished*
3 19 5 [the enemies of the cross of Christ] ⌐are destined to be (lit. will end by being) lost.
1 Th 2 16 They never stop trying to finish off the sins they have begun, but retribution is overtaking them ⌐at last (lit. *finally*).
1 Tm 1 5 The only *purpose* of this instruction is that there should be love,
2 Tm 4 7 2 I have run the race to the *finish*; I have kept the faith;
Heb 3 6 as long as we cling to our hope with the confidence that we glory in (§ unwavering right till the end)
14 we shall remain co-heirs with Christ only if we keep a grasp on our first confidence right to the *end*.
6 1 Let us leave behind us then all the elementary teaching about Christ and concentrate on its ⌐perfection (or: *completion*).
8 [the field] that grows brambles . . . will *end* by being burnt.
11 you should go on showing the same earnestness to the *end*,
7 3 [Melchizedek's] life has no beginning or *ending* . . . He remains a priest for ever.
25 12 [Christ's] power to save is *utterly certain*.
8 5 5 Moses, when he had the Tent to build, was warned by God
8 6 (Jr 31 31) I will *establish* a new covenant with . . . Israel
9 6 5 priests are constantly going into the outer tent to *carry out* their acts of worship,
26 7 [Christ] has made his appearance . . . now at the *end* of the last age,
Jm 1 4 4 you will become fully-developed, *complete*
2 8 2 the right thing to do is to *keep* the supreme law of scripture:
5 11 You have heard of the patience of Job, and understood the Lord's *purpose*,
1 P 1 9 you are sure of the *end* to which ᵛ your (G the) faith looks forward, that is, the salvation of your souls.
13 13 put your trust ⌐in nothing but (lit. *completely* in) . . . grace
3 8 *Finally*: you should all agree among yourselves
4 7 Everything will soon come to an *end*,
17 what will ⌐[the judgement] be when it comes down to (lit. be the *end* of) those who refuse to believe God's Good News?
5 9 ⌐your brothers all over the world are suffering the same things
5 (lit. the same things are being *done* to your brothers all over the world).
1 Jn 4 12 as long as we love one another . . . [God's] love will be
3 ⌐brought to perfection (or: *complete*) in us.
Rv 2 26 To those who . . . keep working for me until the *end* . . . authority
10 7 2 God's secret intention will be *fulfilled*,
11 7 2 When [my two witnesses] have *completed* their witnessing, the beast . . . is going to . . . kill them.
15 1 2 the seven plagues that are the last of all, because they *exhaust* the anger of God.
8 2 no one could go into [the temple] until the seven plagues of the seven angels were *completed*.
17 17 2 until the time when God's words should be *fulfilled*.
20 3 2 to make sure [Satan] would not deceive the nations again until the thousand years had *passed*.
5 2 the rest of the dead did not come to life until the thousand years were *over*.
7 2 When the thousand years are *over*, Satan will be released
21 6 Θ I am the Alpha and the Omega, the Beginning and the *End*.
22 13 X I am the Alpha and the Omega, the First and the Last, the Beginning and the *End*.

b) Perfect, Perfection – Full-grown, Mature, Adult

Mt	5 48 Θ	4	You must therefore be *perfect* just as your heavenly Father
		4	is *perfect*.
	19 21	4	If you wish to be *perfect*, go and sell what you own
Lk	8 14		the part that fell into thorns, this is people who . . . do not
		15	reach *maturity*.
Jn	13 1		[Jesus] had always loved those who were his . . . but now he showed ⌐how *perfect* his love was (or: how to love them to the end).
	17 23	3	With me in them and you in me, may they be . . . ⌐*perfectly* (or: *completely*) one
Rm	12 2		This is the only way to discover the will of God . . . what is
		4	the *perfect* thing to do.
1 Co	2 6	4	we have a wisdom to offer those who have reached *maturity*:
	13 10	4	once *perfection* comes, all imperfect things will disappear.
	14 20	4	Brothers . . . mentally you must be *adult*.
2 Co	7 1	5	let us . . . ⌐reach *perfection* (or: *complete our consecration*) in the fear of God
	12 9	2	my power *is at its best* in weakness.
Ep	4 13	4	until we become the *perfect* Man . . . with the fullness of Christ himself.
Ph	3 12	3	Not that I have *become perfect* yet: I have not yet won,
	15	4	We who are called 'perfect' must all think in this way.
Col	1 28	4	we . . . instruct everyone, to make them all *perfect* in Christ.
	3 14	9	Over all these clothes, to keep them together and *complete* them, put on love.
	4 12	4	praying that you will never lapse but always hold *perfectly* and securely to the will of God.
Heb	2 10		it was appropriate that God, for whom everything exists and
		3	through whom everything exists, should *make perfect*
	X		. . . the leader who would take them to their salvation.
	5 9 X	3	having been *made perfect*, he became . . . the source of eternal salvation
	14	4	Solid food is for *mature* men
	6 1		Let us leave behind us then all the elementary teaching about
		9	Christ and concentrate on its ⌐*perfection* (or: *completion*),
	7 11	8	if *perfection* had been reached through the levitical priesthood
	19	3	the Law could not *make* anyone *perfect*;
	28 X	3	the promise on oath . . . appointed the Son who is *made perfect* for ever.
	9 9	3	None of the gifts . . . can possible *bring* any worshipper *to perfection*
	11	4	Christ . . . has passed through the greater, the more *perfect* tent,
	10 1	3	the Law . . . is quite incapable of *bringing* the worshippers *to perfection*,
	14	3	By virtue of that one single offering, [Christ] has *achieved* the eternal *perfection* of all whom he is sanctifying.
	11 40	3	[the prophets] were not to *reach perfection* except with us.
	12 2	14	Jesus . . . leads us in our faith and *brings* it *to perfection*:
	23	3	You have . . . been placed with the spirits of the saints who have been *made perfect*;
Jm	1 4	4	patience too is to ⌐have its practical results (lit. *come to perfection*) so that you will become fully-developed,
		4	*complete*
	15	10	when sin is *fully grown*, it too has a child, and the child is death.
	17	4	it is all that is good, everything that is *perfect*, which is given us from above;
	25	4	the man who looks steadily at the *perfect* law of freedom
	2 22	3	[Abraham's] faith *became perfect* by what he did.
	3 2	4	the only man who could reach *perfection* would be someone who never said anything wrong
1 Jn	2 5	3	when anyone does obey what he has said, God's love *comes to perfection* in him.
	4 12		as long as we love one another . . . [God's] love will be
		3	⌐*brought to perfection* (or: *complete*) in us.
	17	3	Love will *come* to its *perfection* in us
	18	4	fear is driven out by *perfect* love . . . anyone who is afraid
		3	is still im*perfect* in love.

2. PERFECT: *KAT-ARTIZŌ*

3	*artios*	1	1	*kat-artizō* 13
4	*ap-artismos*	1	7	*pro-kat-artizō* 1
5	*kat-artisis*	1	2	*ex-artizō* 2
6	*kat-artismos* 1			

a) Perfect = Fully trained, Equipped, Ready – Fit (for), Deserving (to) – Set right

Lk	6 40		the *fully trained* disciple will always be like his teacher.
Rm	9 22		God . . . patiently puts up with the people who make him angry, however much they ⌐*deserve* (or: *are due*) to be destroyed.
1 Co	1 10		be ⌐*united* (lit. *perfect*) again in your belief
2 Co	13 9	5	What we ask in our prayers is for you to be *made perfect*.
	11		we wish you happiness; try to *grow perfect*;
Ga	6 1		if one of you misbehaves . . . *set* him *right* . . . in a spirit of gentleness,

Ep	4 12	6	the saints together ⌐*make a unity* in (or: are *equipped* for) the work of service,
2 Tm	3 17	3	the man who is dedicated to God becomes *fully equipped* and
		2	*ready* for any good work.
Heb	13 21 Θ		may [God] *make* you *ready* to do his will in any kind of good action;
1 P	5 10 Θ		the God of all grace . . . will *see that all is well* again:

b) Perfect = Complete, End – Make sure (of) – Prepare, Mend

Mt	4 21		James . . . and his brother John . . . were . . . *mending* their nets.
	21 16 X		(Ps 8 3 G) By the mouths of children, babes in arms, you have *made sure* of praise
Mk	1 19		James . . . and . . . John . . . were in their boat, *mending* their nets.
Lk	14 28		which of you here, intending to build a tower, would not first . . . work out the cost to see if he had enough to
		4	*complete* it?
Ac	21 5	2	when our time was ⌐*up* (or: *ended*) we set off.
2 Co	9 5		I have thought it necessary to ask these brothers to . . .
		7	*make sure in advance* that the gift you promised is all ready,
1 Th	3 10		We are earnestly praying . . . to be able to . . . *make up* any shortcomings in your faith
Heb	10 5 Θ		(Ps 40 7 G) You who wanted no sacrifice . . . *prepared* a body for me
	11 3 Θ		the world was *created* by one word from God

END, FINISH: *DI-ANUŌ*

di-anuō 1

Ac	21 7	The *end* of our voyage from Tyre came when we landed at Ptolemais,

4. END, TIP – TOP, CHIEF – RIPE: *AKMAZŌ*

3	*akmazō* 1	2	*akro(-gōniaios)* 2
1	*akron* 6	4	*akro(-thinion)* 1
		5	*hyper-akmos* 1

a) End(s), Bounds, Tip – Top, Chief

Mt	24 31		[the Son of Man] will send his angels . . . to gather his chosen . . . from one *end* of heaven to the other (§ *end*).
Mk	13 27		[the Son of Man] will send the angels to gather his chosen . . . from the *ends* of the world to the *ends* of heaven.
Lk	16 24		Father Abraham, . . . send Lazarus to dip the *tip* of his finger in water
Ep	2 20 X		You are part of a building that has . . . Christ Jesus himself
		2	for its ⌐*main* (lit. *top*; or: *chief*) cornerstone.
Heb	11 21		(Gn 47 31 G) Jacob, . . . leaning on the *end* of his stick
1 P	2 6 X	2	(Is 28 16) I lay in Zion a precious (§ *top*; or: *chief*) cornerstone

b) "Top of the heap" = Treasure, Spoil(s)

Heb	7 4	4	Abraham paid [Melchizedek] a tenth of the *treasure* he had captured.

c) Grow old – Ripe

1 Co	7 36		if there is anyone who feels that it would not be fair to his
		5	daughter to let her *grow too old* for marriage,
Rv	14 18		cut all the bunches off the vine of the earth; all its grapes are
		3	*ripe*.

5. END(S), BOUNDS – ENDLESS, INTERMINABLE: *PERAS*

1	*peras* 4	2	*a-perantos* 1

Mt	12 42		the Queen of the South . . . came from the *ends* of the earth
Lk	11 31		the Queen of the South . . . came from the *ends* of the earth
Rm	10 18		(Ps 19 4) their message [has gone] to the *ends* of the world.
1 Tm	1 4		[insist that certain people stop] taking notice of myths and
		2	*endless* genealogies;
Heb	6 16		confirmation by an oath puts an *end* to all dispute.

6. THE FINISH, GOAL: *SKOPOS*

skopos 1

Ph	3 14	I am racing for the *finish*, for the prize

7. UNCEASING, ENDLESS – CEASE, STOP

1: UNCEASING, ENDLESS – CONSTANT(LY), CONTINUAL, ALWAYS – CEASE, END: *DIA-LEIPŌ*

3	*dia-leipō* 1	1	*a-dia-leiptōs* 4
2	*a-dia-leiptos* 2	4	*ek-leipō* 1/4

Lk	7 45	3 [this woman] ᶠhas been covering (lit. has not *ceased* covering) my feet with kisses
Rm	1 9	I ᶠnever fail to (lit. *always*) mention you in my prayers,
	9 2	2 my sorrow is so great, my mental anguish so *endless*,
1 Th	1 2	[we] *constantly* remember . . . how you have shown your faith
	2 13	we *constantly* thank God for you
	5 17	pray *constantly*;
2 Tm	1 3	2 *always* I remember you in my prayers;
Heb	1 12	4 (Ps 102 27) [Lord], your years are *unending*.

2: CEASE, FINISH, SUBSIDE – OVER, STOP – FAIL TO: *PAUŌ*

1 *pauō* 14/15		2 *kata-pauō* 1/4	
		3 *a-kata-paustos* 1	

Lk	5 4	[Jesus] had *finished* speaking
	8 24	[Jesus] rebuked the wind and the rough water; and they *subsided*
	11 1	when [Jesus] had *finished* [praying] one of his disciples said,
Ac	5 42	[the apostles] never *stopped* . . . their proclamation of the Good News of Christ Jesus
	6 13	[Stephen] never *stops* making speeches against this Holy Place
	13 10	[Elymas,] why don't you *stop* twisting the . . . ways of the Lord?
	14 18	2 Even this speech . . . was scarcely enough to *stop* the crowd offering [Paul and Barnabas] sacrifice.
	20 1	When the disturbance was *over*, Paul . . . set out for Macedonia.
	31	for three years I never *ceased* to keep you right,
	21 32	the crowd . . . *stopped* beating Paul when they saw the tribune
1 Co	13 8	the gift of languages . . . will ᶠnot continue for ever (lit. *cease*);
Ep	1 16	[I] have never *ceased* to remember you in my prayers
Col	1 9	That will explain why . . . we have never *ceased* to pray for you,
Heb	10 2	Otherwise, the offering of [sacrifices] would have *stopped*,
1 P	4 1	anyone who . . . has bodily suffering has *finished* with sin,
2 P	2 14	3 with their eyes ᶠalways looking for (lit. never *ceasing* from) adultery,

8. CEASE – (A WIND) DROPS: *KOPAZŌ*

kopazō 3

Mt	14 32	as [Jesus and Peter] got into the boat the wind *dropped*.
Mk	4 39	the wind *dropped*, and all was calm again.
	6 51	[Jesus] got into the boat with them, and the wind *dropped*.

9. THE LAST – END(S): *ESCHATOS*

1 *eschatos* 53   2 *eschatōs echō* 1

a) Last day(s), Last trumpet, Last Adam, Last enemy

Jn	6 39	I should raise [all that my Father has given to me] up on the *last* day.
	40	it is my Father's will that whoever . . . believes in [the Son] . . . I shall raise him up on the *last* day.
	44	I will raise him up at the *last* day.
	54	Anyone who does eat my flesh . . . I shall raise . . . up on the *last* day.
	11 24	he will rise again at the resurrection on the *last* day.
	12 48	the word itself . . . will be his judge on the *last* day.
Ac	2 17	(Jl 3 1) In the ᶠdays to come (lit. *last* days) . . . I will pour out my spirit
1 Co	15 26	the *last* of the enemies to be destroyed is death,
	45 X	the *last* Adam has become a life-giving spirit.
	52	when the *last* trumpet sounds . . . the dead will be raised,
2 Tm	3 1	in the *last* days there are going to be some difficult times.
Heb	1 2	in our own time, the *last* days, [God] has spoken to us through his Son,
Jm	5 3	It was a burning fire that you stored up as your treasure for the *last* days.

1 P	1 5	the salvation . . . is revealed at the *last* time.
	20	[Christ] has been revealed only in our time, the *last* ages,
2 P	3 3	during the *last* days there are bound to be people who will be scornful,
1 Jn	2 18	these are the *last* days . . . several antichrists have already appeared; we know from this that these are the *last* days.
Jude	18	At the *last* time . . . there are going to be people who sneer at religion

b) Last, Latest, Lowest – End up (by), At the end

Mt	5 26	you will not get out till you have paid the *last* penny.
	12 45	the man *ends up by* being worse than he was before.
	19 30	Many who are first will be *last*, and the *last*, first.
	20 8 <	pay them their wages, starting with the *last* arrivals and ending with the first.
	12 <	The men who came *last* . . . have done only one hour,
	14 <	I choose to pay the *last*-comer as much as I pay you.
	16 <	Thus the *last* will be first, and the first, *last*.
	27 64	This *last* piece of fraud would be worse than what went before.
Mk	9 35	If anyone wants to be first, he must make himself *last* of all
	10 31	Many who are first will be *last*, and the *last*, first.
	12 6	He had still someone left: his beloved son. He sent him to them *last* of all.
	22	*Last* of all the woman herself died.
Lk	11 26	the man *ends up by* being worse than he was before.
	12 59	you will not get out till you have paid the very *last* penny.
	13 30	there are those now *last* who will be first, and those now first who will be *last*.
	14 9 <	then, to your embarrassment, you would have to go and take the *lowest* place.
	10 <	when you are a guest, make your way to the *lowest* place
Jn	7 37	On the *last* day . . . of the festival, Jesus . . . cried out: 'If any man is thirsty,
	8 9	[the scribes and the Pharisees] went away one by one, beginning with the eldest (ᵛ to the *last*)
1 Co	4 9	God has put us apostles *at the end* of his parade,
	15 8	*last* of all [Christ] appeared to me too;
2 P	2 20	anyone who . . . allows himself to be entangled by [the pollution] a second time . . . will *end up* in a worse state than he began in.
Rv	1 17 X	Do not be afraid; it is I, the First and the *Last*; I am the Living One,
	2 8 X	Here is the message of the First and the *Last*, who was dead and has come to life again:
	19	I know ᶠhow you are still making progress (lit. your *latest* good works exceed the first).
	15 1	the seven plagues that are the *last* of all, because they exhaust the anger of God.
	21 9	the seven bowls full of the seven *last* plagues
	22 13 X	I am the Alpha . . . the First and the *Last*, the Beginning and the End.

c) Ends, Bounds, Uttermost parts

Ac	1 8	you will be my witnesses . . . to the *ends* of the earth.
	13 47	(Is 49 6) so that my salvation may reach the *ends* of the earth.

d) (Breathing one's) Last – the Point of Death, Death's door – Desperately sick

Mk	5 23	2 My little daughter is *desperately sick*. Do come and lay your hands on her

10. LAST, LASTLY, FINALLY – EVENTUALLY: *HYSTERON*

1 *hysteron* 5/11   2 *hysteros* 1

Mt	21 37 <	*Finally* [the landowner] sent his son to [the tenants].
	22 27	then *last* of all the woman herself died.
	26 60	*Eventually* two [lying witnesses] stepped forward
Mk	16 14	*Lastly*, [Jesus] showed himself to the Eleven themselves
Lk	20 32	*Finally* the woman herself died.
1 Tm	4 1	2 during the *last* times there will be some who will desert the faith

---

ENEMY – OPPOSE – AGAINST

---

1. Enemy – Enmity, Hostility: *echthros*

2. Opponent, Adversary, Enemy: *anti-dikos*

3. Enemy, Adversary, Opponent – Oppose, (Be) Contrary to: *anti-keimai*

4. Against – Oppose – Opponent, Enemy: *en-antios*

5. Oppose – Resist: *anti-tassomai*

6. Resist – Withstand – Oppose: *anth-istēmi*

7. Resist: *anti-piptō*

8. Against, Opposed to: *kata* + gen.

9. Against, Contrary to: *para* + acc.

1. ENEMY – ENMITY, HOSTILITY: *ECHTHROS*
2 echthra 6   1 echthros 32

Mt	5 43	it was said: You must love your neighbour and hate your *enemy*.
	44	But I say this to you: love your *enemies* and pray for those who persecute you;
	10 36	(Mi 7 6) A man's *enemies* will be those of his own household.
	13 25 <	While everybody was asleep his *enemy* came, sowed darnel all among the wheat,
	28 <	Some *enemy* has done this
	39 ⒟ <	the *enemy* who sowed [the darnel is] the devil;
	22 44	(Ps 110 1) I will put your *enemies* under your feet
Mk	12 36	(Ps 110 1) I will put your *enemies* under your feet
Lk	1 71	[God proclaimed] that he would save us from our *enemies*
	74	[God swore] that he would grant us . . . to be delivered from the hands of our *enemies*, to serve him
	6 27	Love your *enemies*, do good to those who hate you,
	35	Instead, love your *enemies* and do good,
	10 19 ⒟	I have given you power to tread underfoot serpents and scorpions and the whole strength of the *enemy*;
	19 27 <	as for my *enemies* who did not want me for their king . . . execute them
	43	a time is coming [Jerusalem] when your *enemies* . . . will encircle you
	20 43	(Ps 110 1) I will make your *enemies* a footstool for you.
	23 12 2	though Herod and Pilate had been *enemies* before, they were reconciled
Ac	2 35	(Ps 110 1) I make your *enemies* a footstool for you.
	13 10	[Elymas,] you son of the devil, you *enemy* of all true religion,
Rm	5 10	when we were reconciled to God . . . we were still *enemies*;
	8 7 2	to limit oneself to what is unspiritual is to be *at enmity* with God:
	11 28	The Jews are *enemies* of God only with regard to the Good News, and [enemies] only for your sake;
	12 20	(Pr 25 21) If your *enemy* is hungry, you should give him food,
1 Co	15 25	(Ps 110 1) until he has put all his *enemies* under his feet
	26	the last of the *enemies* to be destroyed is death,
Ga	4 16	Is it telling you the truth that has made me your *enemy*?
	5 20 2	[the results of self-indulgence:] . . . *feuds* and wrangling,
Ep	2 14 2	[Christ has destroyed] in his own person the *hostility* [between Jews and pagans]
	16 2	In his own person [Christ] killed the *hostility*.
Ph	3 18	there are many who are behaving as the *enemies* of the cross of Christ.
Col	1 21	you were foreigners and *enemies*, in the way that you used to think . . . [but now Christ has reconciled you]
2 Th	3 15	[If anyone refuses to obey what I have written] you are not to regard him as an *enemy* but as a brother in need of correction.
Heb	1 13	(Ps 110 1) I will make your *enemies* a footstool for you.
	10 13	(Ps 110 1) [Christ's] *enemies* are made into a footstool for him.
Jm	4 4 2	don't you realise that making the world your friend is making God your *enemy*? Anyone who chooses the world for his friend turns himself into God's *enemy*.
Rv	11 5	Fire can come from [the two witnesses'] mouths and consume their *enemies*
	12	While their *enemies* were watching, [the two witnesses] went up to heaven in a cloud.

2. OPPONENT, ADVERSARY, ENEMY: *ANTI-DIKOS*
anti-dikos 5

Mt	5 25	Come to terms with your *opponent* in good time . . . or ꜛhe (lit. the *adversary*) may hand you over to the judge
Lk	12 58	when you go to court with your *opponent*, try to settle with him on the way,
	18 3	I want justice from you against my *enemy*!
1 P	5 8 ⒟	your *enemy* the devil is prowling round like a roaring lion,

3. ENEMY, ADVERSARY, OPPONENT – OPPOSE, (BE) CONTRARY TO: *ANTI-KEIMAI*
anti-keimai 8

Lk	13 17	all [Jesus's] *adversaries* were covered with confusion,
	21 15	a wisdom that none of your *opponents* will be able to resist or contradict.
1 Co	16 9	there is a great deal of *opposition*.
Ga	5 17	it is precisely because [self-indulgence and the Spirit] are so *opposed* that you do not always carry out your good intentions.
Ph	1 28	[you are] quite unshaken by your *enemies*.

2 Th	2 4	This is the *Enemy*, the one who claims to be so much greater than all that men call god,
1 Tm	1 10	[laws are framed for] perjurers – and for everything else that is *contrary to* the sound teaching
	5 14 ⒟?	it is best for young widows to marry again and . . . not give the *enemy* any chance to raise a scandal about them;

4. AGAINST – OPPOSE – OPPONENT, ENEMY: *EN-ANTIOS*
1 en-antios 7/8   2 hyp-en-antios 2
3 ap-en-anti 1/4

Mt	14 24	the boat . . . was battling with a heavy sea, for there was a ꜛhead-wind (lit. wind *against* it).
Mk	6 48	[the disciples] were worn out with rowing, for the wind was *against* them;
Ac	17 7 3	They have ꜛbroken (lit. acted *against*) every one of Caesar's edicts
	26 9	I once thought it was my duty to use every means to *oppose* the name of Jesus the Nazarene.
	27 4	as the winds were *against* us we sailed under the lee of Cyprus
	28 17	I have done nothing *against* our people
Col	2 14 2	[God has] cancelled every record of the debt ꜛthat we had to pay (lit. *against* us);
1 Th	2 15	[the Jews] have been . . . acting in a way that . . . makes them the *enemies* of the whole human race.
Tt	2 8 ⒟?	any *opponent* will be at a loss,
Heb	10 27 2	(Is 26 11) the raging fire . . . is to burn ꜛ*rebels* (or: *enemies*).

5. OPPOSE – RESIST: *ANTI-TASSOMAI*
anti-tassomai 5

Ac	18 6	[the Jews] ꜛturned against (or: *opposed*) [Paul] and started to insult him,
Rm	13 2	anyone who ꜛ*opposes* (or: *resists*) authority is resisting God's decision, and such resisting is bound to be punished.
Jm	4 6	(Pr 3 34 G) God *opposes* the proud but he gives generously to the humble.
	5 6	It was you who condemned the innocent and killed them; they *offered* you no *resistance*.
1 P	5 5	(Pr 3 34 G) God *opposes* the proud

6. RESIST – WITHSTAND – OPPOSE: *ANTH-ISTĒMI*
1 anth-istēmi 14   2 anti-kath-istēmi 1

Mt	5 39	I say this to you: *offer* the wicked man no *resistance*.
Lk	21 15	a wisdom that none of your opponents will be able to *resist* or contradict.
Ac	6 10	they could not ꜛ*get the better of* (or: *withstand*) [Stephen] because of his wisdom,
	13 8	Elymas Magos . . . *tried to stop* [Barnabas and Saul]
Rm	9 19 ⊖	no one can *oppose* his will
	13 2	anyone who *opposes* (or: *resists*) authority is *resisting* God's decision, and such *resisting* is bound to be punished.
Ga	2 11	When Cephas came to Antioch . . . I *opposed* him to his face,
Ep	6 13 ⒟	rely on God's armour, or you will not be able to *put up* any *resistance* when the worst happens,
2 Tm	3 8	Men like this *defy* the truth just as Jannes and Jambres *defied* Moses.
	4 15	[Alexander] has been bitterly *contesting* everything that we say.
Heb	12 4 2	In the fight against sin, you have not yet had to *keep fighting* to the point of death.
Jm	4 7 ⒟	Give in to God, then; *resist* the devil,
1 P	5 9 ⒟	*Stand up to* [the devil], strong in faith

7. RESIST: *ANTI-PIPTŌ*
anti-piptō 1

Ac	7 51 Ⓢ	You are always *resisting* the Holy Spirit,

8. AGAINST, OPPOSED TO: *KATA* + genitive
kata (+ gen.) (20)

Mt	12 14	the Pharisees . . . began to plot *against* [Jesus],
	30	He who is not with me is *against* me,
	26 59	The chief priests . . . were looking for evidence *against* Jesus, however false

Mt 27	1	all the chief priests . . . ʳmet in council to bring about the death of (lit. took counsel *against*) Jesus.
Mk 3	6	The Pharisees . . . began to plot with the Herodians *against* [Jesus].
	9 40	Anyone who is not *against* us is for us.
	14 55	The chief priests . . . were looking for evidence *against* Jesus,
	56	Several . . . brought false evidence *against* [Jesus],
	57	Some stood up and submitted this false evidence *against* [Jesus],
Lk 9	50	anyone who is not *against* you is for you.
	11 23	He who is not with me is *against* me;
Jn 19	11	'You would have no power ʳover (lit. *against*) me' replied Jesus
Ac 4	26	princes making an alliance, *against* the Lord and *against* his Anointed.
	21 28	This is the man who preaches . . . *against* our people, . . . the Law and . . . this place.
Rm 8	31	With God on our side who can be *against* us?
1 Co 15	15	we swore in evidence ʳbefore (lit. *against*) God that he had raised Christ to life.
2 Co 13	8	We have no power to ʳresist (lit. fight *against*) the truth;
Ga 3	21	Does this mean that there is *opposition between* the Law and the promises of God?
Col 2	14	[God has] cancelled every record of the debt *against* us that we had to pay;

9. AGAINST, CONTRARY TO: *PARA* + accusative

para (+ acc.) (5)

Ac 18	13	We accuse this man . . . of persuading people to worship God *in a way that* ʳbreaks (lit. *is contrary to*) the Law.
Rm 1	26	their women have turned from natural intercourse to ʳun-natural practices (lit. practices *against* nature)
4	18	ʳThough . . . Abraham's hope could not be fulfilled, he hoped (lit. Abraham was hoping *against* hope) and believed,
11	24	you were cut from your natural wild olive to be grafted ʳun-naturally (lit. *contrary to* nature) on to a cultivated olive,
16	17	be on your guard against anybody who . . . puts difficulties ʳin the way of (lit. *against*) the doctrine you have been taught.

ENTER – GO IN – COME IN

1. Enter – Go in – Come in: *eis-erchomai*
  1: (angels, unclean spirits) Enter, Go in, Come in
  a) (angels) Go in, Come in
  b) (devils) Go in(to), Enter
  2: (Jesus) Enters, Goes in (to), Comes in
  3: (a person) Enters, Goes in(to), Comes in(to)
  a) Go into, Go back, Go to – Enter – Come in, Come to, Reach
  b) Enter, Go into (the Kingdom) – Come into, Reach (life everlasting)
  c) Come in for (reward, temptation)
  4: Go through into, Enter through – Come in by, Arise, Start – Reach

2. Go in(to), Come in, Enter: *eis-poreuomai*
  a) (a person) Enters
  b) (a thing) Enters
3. Go in(to) – Go on: *em-bainō*
  a) Get into (a boat)
  b) Enter – Arrive – Set foot in
  c) Go on(about) – Take a stand on
4. Enter, Entrance – Coming – Visit: *eis-(h)odos*
5. Visit, Visitation – Come to the help of: *epi-skeptomai*
  1: (God) Visits – (God's) Visitation
  2: (a person) Visits, Comes to the help of
6. Infiltrate – Insinuate oneself, Worm one's way in: *en-dynō*

1. ENTER – GO IN – COME IN: *EIS-ERCHOMAI*

2 *eis-eimi*	4	3 *par-eis-erchomai*	2
1 *eis-erchomai*	196	4 *syn-eis-erchomai*	2

1: (ANGELS, UNCLEAN SPIRITS) ENTER, GO IN, COME IN

a) (angels) Go in, Come in

Lk 1	28	[The angel Gabriel] *went in* and said to [Mary],
Ac 10	3	[Cornelius] had a vision in which he distinctly saw the angel of God *come into* his house

b) (devils) Go in(to), Enter

Mt 12	45	[the unclean spirit] collects seven other spirits more evil than itself, and they *go in* and set up house there,
Mk 5	12	Sends us to the pigs, let us *go into* them.
	13	the unclean spirits came out and *went into* the pigs,
9	25	Deaf and dumb spirit, . . . I command you: come out of him and never *enter* him again.
Lk 8	30	many devils had *gone into* [the Gerasene demoniac].
	32	the devils pleaded with [Jesus] to let them *go into* these [pigs]
	33	. . . ³³ The devils came out of the man and *went into* the pigs,
11	26	[the unclean spirit] brings seven other spirits more wicked than itself, and they *go in* and set up house there,
22	3	Then Satan *entered* [into] Judas,
Jn 13	27	Satan *entered* [Judas].

2: (JESUS) ENTERS, GOES IN (TO), COMES IN

P = Jesus enters with other people

Mt 8	5	When he *went into* Capernaum a centurion came up
	8	Sir, I am not worthy ʳto have you (lit. that you should *come in*) under my roof;
9	25	he *went in*[side] and took the little girl by the hand;
21	10	when he *entered* Jerusalem, the whole city was in turmoil.
	12	Jesus then *went into* the Temple and drove out all those who were selling and buying there;
Mk 1	21	he ʳwent to (lit. *entered*) the synagogue and began to teach.
	45	Jesus could no longer *go* openly *into* any town,
2	1	he ʳreturned to Capernaum (lit. *entered* Capernaum again)
3	1	He *went* again *into* a synagogue,
5	39	He *went in* and said to them, '. . . The child is not dead,
7	17	When he had *gone* back *into* the house . . . his disciples questioned him about the parable.
	24	he *went into* a house and did not want anyone to know he was there,
9	28	When he had ʳgone indoors (lit. *entered* the house) his disciples asked him privately,
11	11	He *entered* Jerusalem [and went] into the Temple.
	15	he *went into* the Temple and began driving out those who were selling and buying there;
Lk 4	16	He . . . *went into* the synagogue
	38	Leaving the synagogue he ʳwent to (lit. *entered*) Simon's house.
6	6	he *went into* the synagogue and began to teach,
7	1	he *went into* Capernaum.
	6	I am not worthy ʳto have you (lit. that you should *come in*) under my roof;
	36	he ʳarrived at (lit. *entered*) the Pharisee's house and took his place at table,
	44	I *came into* your house . . . ⁴⁵ You gave me no kiss, but she
	45	has been covering my feet with kisses ever since I *came in*.
8	41	Jairus . . . pleaded with him to ʳcome (lit. *enter*) his house,
	51 P	he allowed no one to *go in* with him except Peter and John and James
10	38	he ʳcame to (lit. *entered*) a village,
11	37	He *went in* and sat down at the table.
17	12	as he *entered* one of the villages, ten lepers came to meet him.
19	1	He *entered* Jericho
	7	He has *gone* (§ *in*) to stay at a sinner's house
	45	he *went into* the Temple and began driving out those who were selling.
24	26	Was it not ordained that the Christ should suffer and so *enter* into his glory?
	29	he *went in* to stay with them.
Jn 6	22 P	4 the crowd . . . saw . . . that Jesus had not ʳgot into (lit. *entered*) the boat with his disciples,
18	1 P	he *went into* [the garden] with his disciples.
Ac 1	21 O	the Lord Jesus was ʳtravelling round (lit. *coming in* and going out) with us,
Heb 6	20	Jesus has *entered* [beyond the veil] before us and on our behalf,
9	12	he has *entered* the sanctuary once and for all,
	24	It is not as though Christ had *entered* a man-made sanctuary . . . it was heaven itself,
10	5	this is what he said, on *coming into* the world . . . ⁷ . . . 'God . . . I am coming to obey your will.'
Rv 3	20	If one of you . . . opens the door, I will *come in* to share his meal,

3: (A PERSON) ENTERS, GOES IN(TO), COMES IN(TO)

a) Go into, Go back, Go to – Enter – Come in, Come to, Reach

Mt 2	21	Joseph got up and . . . *went back* to the land of Israel.
6	6	when you pray, *go to* your private room
10	5	do not *enter* any Samaritan town;
	11	Whatever town or village you *go into*, ask for someone trustworthy,

Mt 10 12   As you *enter* his house, salute it,
   12 4   [David] *went into* the house of God
       29   how can anyone ᶠ*make his way into* (or: *enter*) a strong man's house . . . ?
   17 25   [Peter] *went into* the house,
   22 11 < the king *came in* to look at the guests
       12 < How did you *get in* here . . . without a wedding garment?
   24 38   people were eating, drinking . . . right up to the day Noah *went into* the ark,
   25 10 < Those who were ready *went in* with [the bridegroom]
   26 58   Peter . . . *went in* [to the high priest's palace] and sat down with the attendants
   27 53   [the bodies of many holy men rose from the dead,] and . . . *entered* the Holy City
Mk 2 26   [David] *went into* the house of God
    3 27   no one can ᶠ*make his way into* (or: *enter*) a strong man's house
    6 10   If you *enter* a house anywhere, stay there
       22   the daughter of . . . Herodias *came in* and danced,
       25   The girl ᶠ*hurried* (lit. *went* hurriedly) straight *back* to the king and made her request,
    7 25   A woman . . . ᵛ*came in*) and fell at his feet.
    8 26   Do not even *go into* the village.
   13 15   if a man is on the housetop, he must not come down to *go into* the house to collect any of his belongings;
   14 14   say to the owner of the house which [the man] *enters*, 'The Master says: Where is my dining room . . . ?'
   15 43   Joseph of Arimathaea . . . boldly *went to* Pilate
   16 5   On *entering* the tomb [the women] saw a young man
Lk 1 9   it fell to [Zechariah] by lot . . . to *enter* the Lord's sanctuary
       40   [Mary] *went into* Zechariah's house and greeted Elizabeth.
    6 4   [David] *went into* the house of God,
    9 4   Whatever house you *enter*, stay there;
       34   when they *went into* the cloud the disciples were afraid.
       52   These [messengers] . . . *went into* a Samaritan village
   10 5   Whatever house you *go into*, let your first words be, 'Peace to this house!'
        8   Whenever you *go into* a town where they make you welcome, eat what is set before you.
       10   whenever you *enter* a town and they do not make you welcome, go out
   14 23 < force people to *come in* to make sure my house is full;
   15 28 < [The elder son] was angry then and refused to *go in*,
   17 7   Which of you . . . would say to [your servant] when he *returned* from the fields,
       27   People were eating and drinking . . . right up to the day Noah *went into* the ark,
   21 21   those in country districts must not ᶠ*take refuge* (lit. *go*) *in* [the city].
   22 10   as you *go into* the city you will meet a man
   24 3   on *entering* [the tomb the women] discovered that the body of the Lord Jesus was not there.
Jn 3 4   Can he *go back* into his mother's womb and be born again?
   10 1 < anyone who does not *enter* the sheepfold through the gate . . . is a thief
        2 < The one who *enters* through the gate is the shepherd
        9 < Anyone who *enters* through me will be safe: he will *go* freely *in* and out
   18 15   4 This disciple . . . *went* with Jesus *into* the high priest's palace,
       28   [The Jews] did not *go into* the Praetorium themselves
       33   Pilate *went back* into the Praetorium
   19 9   Re-*entering* the Praetorium, [Pilate] said to Jesus,
   20 5   [the other disciple reached the tomb first] but did not *go in*.
        6   Simon Peter . . . *went* right *into* the tomb,
        8   Then the other disciple . . . also *went in*;
Ac 1 13   when [the apostles] *reached* the city they went to the upper room
    3 3   this man saw Peter and John ᶠon their way into (lit. about to 2 *enter*) the Temple
        8   [the lame man] *went* with them *into* the Temple,
    5 7   [Ananias's] wife [Sapphira] *came in*,
       10   When the young men *came in* they found she was dead,
       21   [the apostles] *went into* the Temple at dawn
    9 6   *go into* the city, and you will be told what you have to do.
       12   [Saul] had a vision of a man called Ananias *coming in*
       17   Then Ananias went. He *entered* the house,
   10 24   [Peter] *reached* Caesarea the following day,
       25   as Peter *reached* the house Cornelius went out to meet him,
       27   Talking together [Cornelius and Peter] *went in* to meet all the people assembled there,
   11 3   So you have been ᶠ*visiting* (lit. *entering* the houses of) the uncircumcised
       12   we *entered* the man's house.
   14 1   At Iconium [Paul and Barnabas] *went to* the Jewish synagogue,
       20   [Paul] stood up and *went back* to the town.
   16 15   ᶠ*come* (lit. *come in*) and stay with us.
       40   [Paul and Silas] *went to* Lydia's house
   17 2   [They reached Thessalonika, where there was a Jewish synagogue.] Paul as usual ᶠintroduced himself (lit. *went in*)

Ac 18 7   [At Corinth Paul] left the synagogue and ᶠmoved to (lit. *entered*) the house next door that belonged to . . . Justus.
       19   [At Ephesus Paul] *went* alone *to* the synagogue
   19 8   [At Ephesus Paul] began by *going to* the synagogue,
       30   Paul wanted to ᶠ*make an appeal to* (lit. *enter* the assembly of) the people,
   20 29   when I have gone fierce wolves will *invade* you
   21 8   [At Caesarea] we ᶠcalled on (lit. *entered* the house of) Philip the evangelist,
       18   2 Paul *went* with us to [visit] James,
       26   2 Paul . . . ᶠ*visited* (lit. *entered*) the Temple
   23 16   the son of Paul's sister . . . ᶠ*made his way* (or: *went*) *into* the fortress
       33   On *arriving at* Caesarea the escort delivered the letter
   25 23   Agrippa and Bernice . . . *entered* the audience chamber
   28 8   Paul *went in* to see [Publius's father], and . . . healed him.
       16   On our *arrival* in Rome Paul was allowed to stay in lodgings
1 Co 14 23   any . . . unbelievers, *coming into* a meeting of the whole church, . . . would say you were all mad;
       24   if . . . an unbeliever . . . *came in*, he would find himself analysed
Ga 2 4   3 some who do not really belong to the brotherhood have . . . *crept in* to spy on the liberty we enjoy
Heb 9 6   2 priests are constantly *going into* the outer tent to carry out their acts of worship, ⁷ but the second tent [is entered] only once a year,
       25   the high priest *going into* the sanctuary year after year [has to offer himself again and again]
Jm 2 2   suppose a man *comes into* your synagogue, beautifully dressed . ., and at the same time a poor man *comes in*,
Rv 15 8   The smoke . . . filled the temple so that no one could *go into* it
   21 27   Nothing unclean may *come into* [the holy city] . . . but only those who are listed in the Lamb's book of life.
   22 14   Happy are those who will have washed their robes . . . so that they . . . can *come* through the gates *into* the city.

b) Enter, Go into (the Kingdom) – Come in, Reach (life everlasting)

Mt 5 20   if your virtue goes no deeper than that of the scribes . . . you will never *get into* the kingdom of heaven.
    7 13   *Enter* by the narrow gate, since the road that leads to perdition is wide . . . and many ᶠtake (lit. *enter* by) it;
       21   It is not those who say to me, 'Lord, Lord', who will *enter* the kingdom of heaven,
   18 3   unless you change and become like little children you will never *enter* the kingdom of heaven.
        8   it is better for you to *enter* [into] life crippled
        9   it is better for you to *enter* [into] life with one eye,
   19 17   if you wish to *enter* [into] life, keep the commandments.
       23   it will be hard for a rich man to *enter* the kingdom of heaven.
       24   it is easier for a camel to pass through the eye of a needle than for a rich man to *enter* the kingdom of heaven.
   23 13   You . . . shut up the kingdom of heaven in men's faces, neither *going in* yourselves nor allowing others to *go in* who want to (§ *go in*).
   25 21 < ᶠcome and join in (lit. *enter* [into]) your master's happiness.
       23 < ᶠcome and join in (lit. *enter* [into]) your master's happiness.
Mk 9 43   it is better for you to *enter* [into] life crippled,
       45   it is better for you to *enter* [into] life lame,
       47   it is better for you to *enter* [into] the kingdom of God with one eye,
   10 15   anyone who does not welcome the kingdom of God like a little child will never *enter* it.
       23   How hard it is for those who have riches to *enter* the kingdom of God! ²⁴ . . . My children, how hard it is to *enter* the kingdom of God! ²⁵ It is easier for a camel to pass through the eye of a needle than for a rich man to *enter* the kingdom of God.
Lk 11 52   You have not *gone in* yourselves, and have prevented others *going in*
   13 24   Try your best to *enter* by the narrow door, because . . . many will try to *enter* and will not succeed.
   18 17   anyone who does not welcome the kingdom of God like a little child will never *enter* it.
       25   it is easier for a camel to pass through the eye of a needle than for a rich man to *enter* the kingdom of God.
Jn 3 5   unless a man is born through water and the Spirit, he cannot *enter* the kingdom of God:
Ac 14 22   We all have to experience many hardships . . . before we *enter* the kingdom of God.
Rm 11 25   this will last only until the whole pagan world has *entered*,
Heb 3 11   (Ps 95 11) I swore that not one would *reach* the place of rest
       18   Those that he swore would never *reach* the place of rest . . . were those who had been disobedient.
       19   it was because they were unfaithful that they were not able to *reach* [the place of rest].
    4 1   the promise of *reaching* the place of rest . . . still holds good,

Heb 4	3	We . . . who have faith, shall *reach* a place of rest, as in the text (Ps 95 11): . . . I swore that not one would *reach* the place of rest
	5	(Ps 95 11) They shall not *reach* the place of rest
	6	It is established . . . that there would be some people who would *reach* it, and . . . those who first heard the Good News failed to *reach* it through their disobedience,
	10	to *reach* the place of rest is to rest after your work,
	11	We must . . . do everything we can to *reach* this place of rest,

c) Come in for (reward, temptation)

Mt 26	41	You should be . . . praying not to ⌐be put to the test (lit. *come in for* temptation).
Lk 22	40	Pray not to ⌐be put to the test (lit. *come in for* temptation).
	46	pray not to ⌐be put to the test (lit. *come in for* temptation).
Jn 4	38	Others worked for [the harvest]; and you have *come into* the rewards of their trouble.

4: GO THROUGH INTO, ENTER THROUGH – COME IN BY, ARISE, START – REACH

Mt 15	11	What *goes into* the mouth does not make a man unclean;
	19 24	it is easier for a camel to *pass through* the eye of a needle
Lk 9	46	Jesus knew what thoughts were *going through* their minds,
	18 25	it is easier for a camel to *pass through* the eye of a needle
Ac 11	8	nothing profane or unclean has ever ⌐crossed my lips (lit. *gone through* my mouth).
Rm 5	12	sin *entered* the world through one man, and through sin death,
	20	3 When law *came*, it was to multiply the opportunities of falling
Heb 6	19	[Take a firm grip on the hope that is held out to us.] Here we have an anchor for our soul . . . *reaching* right through beyond the veil
Jm 5	4	the cries of the reapers have *reached* the ears of the Lord
Rv 11	11	⌐God breathed life into [the two witnesses] (lit. a breath of life coming from God *entered* them) and they stood up,

2. GO IN(TO), COME IN, ENTER: *EIS-POREUOMAI*
eis-poreuomai 18

a) (a person) Enters

Mk 1	21	They ⌐went as far as (lit. *entered*) Capernaum,
	5 40 X	he turned them all out and . . . *went into* the place where the child lay.
	6 56 X	wherever he *went* . . . they laid down the sick in the open spaces,
	11 2	as soon as you *enter* [the village] you will find a tethered colt
Lk 8	16	he puts [the lamp] on a lamp-stand so that people may see the light when they *come in*.
	11 33	[They put the lamp] on the lamp-stand so that people may see the light when they *come in*.
	18 24 ●	How hard it is for those who have riches to ⌐*make their way into* (or: *enter*) the kingdom of God!
	19 30	Go off to the village . . . and as you *enter* it you will find a tethered colt
	22 10	Follow [the man] into the house he *enters*
Ac 3	2	they used to put [the cripple] down every day near the Temple entrance . . . so that he could beg from the people *going in*.
	8 3	[Saul] *went* from house to house arresting both men and women
	9 28 ○	Saul now started to ⌐*go round* (lit. *go in* and come out) with [the disciples] in Jerusalem,
	28 30	Paul . . . welcomed all who *came* to [visit] him,

b) (a thing) Enters

Mt 15	17	whatever *goes into* the mouth passes through the stomach
Mk 4	19	the worries of this world . . . *come in* to choke the word,
	7 15	Nothing that *goes into* a man from outside can make him unclean . . . [18] . . . whatever *goes into* a man from outside
	18	
	19	cannot make him unclean, [19] because it does not *go into* his heart but through his stomach

3. GO IN(TO) – GO ON: *EM-BAINŌ*

1 em-bainō 18   4 em-bibazō 1
3 em-bateuō 1   2 epi-bainō 2/6

a) Get into (a boat)

Mt 8	23 X	he *got into* the boat followed by his disciples.
	9 1 X	He *got* [back] *into* the boat, crossed the water
	13 2 X	he *got into* a boat and sat there.

Mt 14	22	[Jesus] made the disciples *get into* the boat
	15 39 X	he *got into* the boat and went to the district of Magadan.
Mk 4	1 X	he *got into* a boat on the lake and sat down.
	5 18 X	As he was *getting into* the boat, the man who had been possessed begged to be allowed to stay with him.
	6 45	[Jesus] made his disciples *get into* the boat
	8 10 X	*getting into* the boat with his disciples, [Jesus] went to the region of Dalmanutha.
	13 X	leaving [the Pharisees] again and re-*embarking* [Jesus] went away to the opposite shore.
Lk 5	3 X	He *got into* one of the boats – it was Simon's
	8 22 X	he *got into* a boat with his disciples
	37 X	he *got into* the boat and went back.
Jn 6	17	[the disciples] *got into* a boat to make for Capernaum
	24	the people . . . *got into* those boats and crossed to Capernaum
	21 3	[Simon Peter and six of the disciples] went out and *got into* the boat
Ac 21	6	we *went aboard* and they returned home.
	27 6	4 the centurion found an Alexandrian ship . . . and *put us aboard*.

b) Enter – Arrive – Set foot in

Jn 5	4	ᵛ . . . the first person to *enter* [the water] . . . ⌐
Ac 20	18	2 ever since the first day I *set foot* among you *in* Asia,
	25 1	2 Three days after his *arrival* . . . Festus went up to Jerusalem

c) Go on (about) – Take a stand on

Col 2	18	3 people like that are always *going on* about some vision they ⌐*have* (ᵛ have not) had,

4. ENTER, ENTRANCE – COMING – VISIT: *EIS-(H)ODOS*
eis-(h)odos 5

Ac 13	24 X	[Jesus's] *coming* was heralded by John when he proclaimed a baptism of repentance
1 Th 1	9	other people tell us ⌐how we started the work among you (lit. what our *coming* to you was like),
	2 1	You know yourselves, my brothers, that our *visit* to you has not proved ineffectual.
Heb 10	19	we have the right to *enter* the sanctuary,
2 P 1	11	In this way you will be granted *admittance* into the eternal kingdom of our Lord

5. VISIT, VISITATION – COME TO THE HELP OF: *EPI-SKEPTOMAI*

1 epi-skeptomai 10/11   2 epi-skopē 2/4

1: (GOD) VISITS – (GOD'S) VISITATION

Lk 1	68	Blessed be the Lord . . . for he has *visited* his people,
	78 X	our God . . . will bring the rising Sun to *visit* us,
	7 16	A great prophet has appeared among us; God has *visited* his people.
	19 44	[Jerusalem,] you did not recognise ⌐your opportunity when 2 God offered it (lit. the time of your *visitation*)!
Ac 15	14	God . . . ⌐arranged (lit. *made a visitation*) to enlist a people for his name out of the pagans.
Heb 2	6 X	(Ps 8 5) What is . . . the son of man that you should *care for* him?
1 P 2	12	behave honourably among pagans so that they can . . , 2 when the day of ⌐reckoning (lit. his *visitation*) comes, give thanks to God

2: (A PERSON) VISITS, COMES TO THE HELP OF

Mt 25	36	[I was] sick and you *visited* me,
	43	I was . . . sick and in prison and you never *visited* me.
Ac 7	23	[Moses] decided to *visit* his countrymen,
	15 36	Let us go back and *visit* all the towns where we preached . . . so that we can see how the brothers are doing.
Jm 1	27	Pure, unspoilt religion . . . is this: *coming to the help of* orphans and widows when they need it,

6. INFILTRATE – INSINUATE ONESELF, WORM ONE'S WAY IN: *EN-DYNŌ*

1 en-dynō 1   2 par-eis-dyō 1

2 Tm 3	6	those men . . . *insinuate themselves* into families
Jude	4	2 Certain people have *infiltrated* among you,

EUNUCH

1: Eunuch, Made a eunuch	2: Eunuch (as an Ethiopian official)
2 *eun-ouchizō* 2	1 *eun-ouchos* 8

1: EUNUCH, MADE A EUNUCH

Mt 19 12 There are *eunuchs* born that way from their mother's womb,
/2 there are *eunuchs* ⌐made that way (lit. who are *made*
/2 *eunuchs*) by men and there are *eunuchs* who have *made*
themselves ⌐that way (lit. *eunuchs*) for the sake of the
kingdom of heaven.

2: EUNUCH (AS AN ETHIOPIAN OFFICIAL)

Ac 8 27 he was a *eunuch* and an officer at the court of the kandake,
or queen, of Ethiopia,
34 the *eunuch* turned to Philip and said, '. . . is the prophet
referring to himself . . .?
36 the *eunuch* said, 'Look, there is some water here; is there
38 anything to stop me being baptised?' . . . ³⁸ Philip and
the *eunuch* both went down into the water and Philip
39 baptised him. ³⁹ . . . Philip was taken away by the Spirit
of the Lord, and the *eunuch* never saw him again

EVER – ETERNAL – AGE

1. (for) Ever – Eternal, Eternity – Age: *aiōn* 1: (God, Christ, the Kingdom are for) Ever, Eternity 2: Eternal, Everlasting (life, salvation, glory) 3: Eternal, Everlasting (fire, punishment) 4: Ever (= a lifetime) – Always – Continually	5: Age (past), Long ago, (ancient) Times – Ever (since creation) 6: (this) Age, Age (to come) – World **2. For ever, For all time – Continually, Repeatedly:** *di-ēnekēs* **3. Always, For ever – Continually, At all times, Constantly:** *pantote*

1. (FOR) EVER – ETERNAL, ETERNITY – AGE: *AIŌN*

3 *aei*	7	1 *aiōn*	126
4 *aidios*	2	2 *aiōnios*	70

1: (GOD, CHRIST, THE KINGDOM ARE FOR) EVER, ETERNITY

Mt 6 13 (ᵛ For yours is the kingdom, the power and the glory, for
ever. Amen.)
Lk 1 33 [Jesus] will rule over the House of Jacob for *ever*
55 [God is mindful] of his mercy to Abraham and to his descendants for *ever*.
Jn 12 34 The Law has taught us that the Christ will remain for *ever*.
Rm 1 20 4 Ever since God created the world his *everlasting* power and
deity . . . have been there for the mind to see
25 [pagans] served creatures instead of the creator, who is
blessed for *ever*. Amen!
9 5 Christ . . . is above all, God for *ever* blessed! Amen.
11 36 To [God] be glory for *ever*! Amen.
16 26 2 it is all part of the way the *eternal* God wants things to be.
27 give glory therefore to [God] through Jesus Christ for *ever*
and *ever*. Amen.
2 Co 9 9 (Ps 112 9) his good deeds ⌐will never be forgotten (lit. remain
for *ever*).
11 31 The God and Father of the Lord Jesus . . . bless him for
ever –
Ga 1 5 to [God] be glory for *ever* and *ever*. Amen.
Ep 3 11 the Sovereignties . . . should learn . . . according to the
plan which [God] had had from *all eternity* in Christ
Jesus
Ph 4 20 Glory to God, our Father, for *ever* and *ever*. Amen.
1 Tm 1 17 To the ⌐eternal King (lit. King for *ever*), . . . be honour and
glory for *ever* and *ever*. Amen.
6 16 2 to [God] be honour and *everlasting* power. Amen.
2 Tm 4 18 To [the Lord] be glory for *ever* and *ever*. Amen.
Heb 1 8 (Ps 45 7) God, your throne shall last for *ever* and *ever*;
5 6 (Ps 110 4) You are a priest of the order of Melchizedek, and
for *ever*.

Heb 6 20 Jesus has . . . become a high priest of the order of Melchizedek,
and for *ever*.
7 17 (Ps 110 4) You are a priest of the order of Melchizedek, and
for *ever*.
21 (Ps 110 4) you are a priest, and for *ever*.
24 this one, because he remains for *ever*, can never lose his
priesthood.
28 the Son . . . is made perfect for *ever*.
9 14 Christ . . . offered himself as the perfect sacrifice . . . through
2 the *eternal* Spirit,
13 8 Jesus Christ is the same today as he was yesterday and as he
will be for *ever*.
20 God . . . brought . . . Jesus back from the dead to become
2 the great Shepherd . . . by the blood that sealed an *eternal*
covenant,
21 to [Jesus Christ] be glory for *ever* and *ever*, Amen.
1 P 1 25 (Is 40 8) the word of the Lord remains for *ever*.
4 11 to [God] alone belong all glory and power for *ever* and *ever*.
5 10 2 the God of all grace . . . called you to *eternal* glory . . .
11 ¹¹ His power lasts for *ever* and *ever*. Amen.
2 P 1 11 2 you will be granted admittance into the *eternal* kingdom of
our Lord and saviour Jesus Christ.
3 18 To [Jesus Christ] be glory, in time and in *eternity*. Amen.
Jude 25 To God . . . be . . . authority and power . . . now and for
ever. Amen.
Rv 1 6 to [God], then, be glory and power for *ever* and *ever*. Amen.
18 I was dead and now I am to live for *ever* and *ever*,
4 9 the One sitting on the throne . . . lives for *ever* and *ever*,
10 the twenty-four elders prostrated themselves . . . to worship
the One who lives for *ever* and *ever*,
5 13 To the One who is sitting on the throne and to the Lamb,
be all . . . glory and power, for *ever* and *ever*.
7 12 Praise and glory . . . to our God for *ever* and *ever*. Amen.
10 6 [the angel] swore by the One who lives for *ever* and *ever*,
11 15 our Lord . . . will reign for *ever* and *ever*.
15 3 just and true are all your ways, King of ⌐nations (ᵛ *eternity*),
7 God . . . lives for *ever* and *ever*.

2: ETERNAL, EVERLASTING (LIFE, SALVATION, GLORY)

Mt 19 16 2 what good deed must I do to possess *eternal* life?
29 everyone who has left houses . . . will be repaid a hundred
2 times over, and also inherit *eternal* life.
25 46 2 the virtuous [will go] to *eternal* life.
Mk 10 17 2 what must I do to inherit *eternal* life?
30 [there is no one who has left house, brothers,] who will
2 not be repaid . . . and, in the world to come, *eternal* life.
Lk 10 25 2 what must I do to inherit *eternal* life?
16 9 use money . . . to win you friends, and . . . they will welcome
2 you into the tents *of eternity*.
18 18 2 what have I to do to inherit *eternal* life?
30 [there is no one who has left house, wife,] who will not be
2 given repayment . . . and, in the world to come, *eternal*
life.
Jn 3 15 [the Son of Man must be lifted up,] so that everyone who
2 believes may have *eternal* life in him.
16 God . . . gave his only Son, so that everyone who believes
2 . . . may have *eternal* life.
36 2 Anyone who believes in the Son has *eternal* life,
4 14 anyone who drinks the water that I shall give will ⌐never (lit.
not *ever*) be thirsty again: the water that I shall give will
2 turn into a spring inside him, welling up to *eternal* life.
36 2 already [the reaper] is bringing in the grain for *eternal* life,
5 24 2 whoever listens to my words . . . has *eternal* life;
39 2 You study the scriptures, believing that in them you have
eternal life;
6 27 2 work for food that endures to *eternal* life,
40 2 whoever sees the Son and believes in him shall have *eternal*
life,
47 2 everybody who believes has *eternal* life.
51 Anyone who eats this bread will live for *ever*;
54 2 Anyone who does eat my flesh and drink my blood has
2 *eternal* life,
58 anyone who eats this bread will live for *ever*.
68 2 You have the message of *eternal* life.
8 51 whoever keeps my word will ⌐never (lit. not *ever*) see death.
52 Whoever keeps my word will ⌐never (lit. not *ever*) know the
taste of death.
10 28 2/ I give [my sheep] *eternal* life; they will ⌐never (lit. not *ever*)
be lost
11 26 whoever lives and believes in me will ⌐never (lit. not *ever*) die.
12 25 Anyone who loves his life loses it; anyone who hates his life
2 in this world will keep it for the *eternal* life.
50 2 I know that his commands mean *eternal* life.
17 2 2 let [your Son] give *eternal* life to all those you have entrusted
3 2 to him. ³ And *eternal* life is this: to know you . . . and
Jesus Christ whom you have sent.
Ac 13 46 2 since you do not think yourselves worthy of *eternal* life, we
must turn to the pagans.

Ac 13	48	2 all who were destined for *eternal* life became believers.
Rm 2	7	For those who sought renown . . . by always doing good
		2 there will be *eternal* life;
5	21	2 grace will reign to bring *eternal* life thanks to the righteousness that comes through Jesus Christ our Lord.
6	22	Now . . . you get a reward leading to your sanctification
	23	2 and ending in *eternal* life. ²³ For . . . the present given by
		2 God is *eternal* life in Christ Jesus our Lord.
2 Co 4	17	the troubles which are soon over . . . train us for the carrying
		2 of a weight of *eternal* glory
	18	visible things last only for a time, and the invisible things are
		2 *eternal*.
5	1	2 there is . . . an *everlasting* home . . . in the heavens.
Ga 6	8	if [a man] sows in the field of the Spirit he will get from it a
		2 harvest of *eternal* life.
2 Th 2	16	2 God . . . has given us . . . such ⌐inexhaustible (lit. *everlasting*) comfort and such sure hope,
1 Tm 1	16	all the other people . . . would later have to trust in [Christ]
		2 to come to *eternal* life.
6	12	2 win for yourself the *eternal* life to which you were called
2 Tm 2	10	I bear it all for the sake of those who are chosen, so that
		2 . . . they may have the salvation . . . and the *eternal* glory
Tt 1	2	2 [Paul, an apostle] to give them the hope of the *eternal* life that was promised
3	7	[Christ] did this so that we should . . . become heirs looking
		2 forward to inheriting *eternal* life.
Heb 5	9	having been made perfect, [Christ] became for all who obey
		2 him the source of *eternal* salvation
6	2	[Let us leave behind us then all the elementary teaching]
		2 about the resurrection of the dead and *eternal* judgement.
9	12	2 [Christ has] won an *eternal* redemption for us.
	15	2 people . . . were called to an *eternal* inheritance
1 Jn 1	2	2 we are . . . telling you of that *eternal* life
2	17	anyone who does the will of God remains for *ever*.
	25	2 what is promised to you by his own promise is *eternal* life.
3	15	2 murderers . . . do not have *eternal* life in them.
5	11	2 God has given us *eternal* life
	13	I have written all this to you so that you . . . may be sure
		2 that you have *eternal* life.
	20	2 This is the true God, this is *eternal* life.
2 Jn	2	the truth . . . lives in us and will be with us for *ever*.
Jude	21	wait for the mercy of our Lord Jesus Christ to give you
		2 *eternal* life.
Rv 14	6	another angel [was] . . . sent to announce the Good News
		2 of *eternity*
22	5	[the servants of God] will reign for *ever* and *ever*.

3: ETERNAL, EVERLASTING (FIRE, PUNISHMENT)

Mt 18	8	it is better for you to enter into life crippled or lame, than to
		2 have two hands or two feet and be thrown into *eternal* fire.
Mt 25	41	2 Go away from me, with your curse upon you, to the *eternal* fire
	46	2 they will go away to *eternal* punishment, and the virtuous to eternal life.
Mk 3	29	let anyone blaspheme against the Holy Spirit and he will
		⌐never (lit. not *ever*) have forgiveness: he is guilty of an
		2 *eternal* sin.
2 Th 1	9	2 It will be their punishment to be lost *eternally*,
Jude	6	[God] has kept [the angels who left their appointed sphere]
		4 down in the dark, in ⌐spiritual (lit. *everlasting*) chains,
	7	Sodom and Gomorrah . . . are paying for their crimes in
		2 *eternal* fire.
	13	[false teachers are] like shooting stars bound for an *eternity* of black darkness.
Rv 14	11	the smoke of their torture will go up for *ever* and *ever*.
19	3	The smoke of [Babylon] will go up for *ever* and *ever*.
20	10	the devil . . . will be thrown into the lake of fire and sulphur, where the beast and the false prophet are, and their torture will not stop, day or night, for *ever* and *ever*.

4: EVER (= A LIFETIME) – ALWAYS – CONTINUALLY

Mt 21	19	May you ⌐never (lit. not *ever*) bear fruit again;
Mk 11	14	May no one *ever* eat fruit from you again
Jn 8	35	Now the slave's place in the house is not ⌐assured (lit. for *ever*), but the son's place is ⌐assured (lit. for *ever*).
13	8	'[Never!]' said Peter 'You shall ⌐never (lit. not *ever*) wash my feet.'
14	16	the Father . . . will give you another Advocate to be with you for *ever*,
Ac 7	51	3 You stubborn people . . . are *always* resisting the Holy Spirit,
1 Co 8	13	I shall ⌐never (lit. not *ever*) eat meat again in case I am the cause of a brother's downfall.
2 Co 4	11	while we are still alive, we are consigned to our death ⌐every
		3 day (lit. *continually*), for the sake of Jesus,

2 Co 6	10	3 [we are] thought most miserable and yet we are *always* rejoicing;
Ep 3	21	glory be to him from generation to generation in the Church and in Christ Jesus for *ever* and *ever*. Amen.
Tt 1	12	3 Cretans were ⌐never anything but (lit. *always*) liars,
Phm	15	you have been deprived of Onesimus for a time, but it was
		2 only so that you could have him back for *ever*,
Heb 3	10	3 (Ps 95 10 G) How unreliable these people *always* are who refuse to grasp my ways!
1 P 3	15	3 *always* have your answer ready for people who ask you the reason for the hope that you all have.
2 P 1	12	3 That is why I am *continually* recalling the same truths to you, even though you already know them

5: AGE (PAST), LONG AGO, (ANCIENT) TIMES – EVER (SINCE CREATION)

Lk 1	70	[God] proclaimed, by the mouth of his holy prophets from [ancient] *times*, that he would save us
Jn 9	32	*Ever* [since the world began] it is unheard of for anyone to open the eyes of a man who was born blind;
Ac 3	21	God proclaimed [the universal restoration], speaking through his holy prophets (§ through the *ages*).
15	18	[the Lord made this] known so *long ago*.
Rm 16	25	I proclaim Jesus Christ, the revelation of a mystery kept
		2 secret for *endless* ages,
1 Co 2	7	The hidden wisdom of God . . . is the wisdom that God predestined to be for our glory before the *ages* [began].
10	11	it was written down to be a lesson for us who are living at the end of the *age*.
Ep 3	9	Through all the *ages*, this [mystery] has been kept hidden in God,
Col 1	26	the message . . . was a mystery hidden for . . . *centuries*
2 Tm 1	9	This grace had already been granted to us . . . ⌐before the
		2 beginning of time (lit. from *eternity*).
Tt 1	2	2 the eternal life . . . was promised so *long ago* by God.
Heb 9	26	[Christ] has made his appearance . . . now at the end of the [last] *age*,
Jude	25	To God . . . be the glory , . . which he had before ⌐time (lit. the *ages*) [began], now and for ever. Amen.

6: (THIS) AGE, AGE (TO COME) – WORLD

Mt 12	32	let anyone speak against the Holy Spirit and he will not be forgiven either in this ⌐world (or: *age*) or in the next.
13	22	the worries of this *world* and the lure of riches choke the word
	39	the harvest is the end of the *world*;
	40	so it will be at the end of ⌐time (lit. the *age*).
	49	This is how it will be at the end of ⌐time (lit. the *age*):
24	3	what will be the sign of your coming and of the end of the *world*?
28	20	I am with you always; yes, to the end of ⌐time (lit. the *age*).
Mk 4	19	the worries of this *world* . . . come in to choke the word,
10	30	[there is no one who has left house, brothers,] who will not be repaid . . . now in this present time and, in the *world* to come, eternal life.
Lk 16	8	the children of this *world* are more astute in dealing with their own kind than are the children of light.
18	30	[there is no one who has left house, wife,] who will not be given repayment . . . and, in the *world* to come, eternal life.
20	34	The children of this *world* take wives and husbands, ³⁵ but
	35	those who are judged worthy of a place in the other *world* and in the resurrection from the dead do not marry
Rm 12	2	Do not model yourselves on the behaviour of the *world* around you,
1 Co 1	20	Where are any of our thinkers ⌐today (lit. of this *age*)?
2	6	we have a wisdom to offer . . : not a philosophy of our *age* . . , still less of the masters of our *age*;
	8	It is a wisdom that none of the masters of this *age* have ever known,
3	18	if any one of you thinks of himself as wise, ⌐in the ordinary sense of the word (lit. according to the wisdom of the *age*), then he must learn to be a fool
2 Co 4	4	the god of this *world* has blinded [the minds of unbelievers],
Ga 1	4	[Christ,] in order to rescue us from this present wicked *world* sacrificed himself for our sins,
Ep 1	21	[Christ is] far above every Sovereignty . . . not only in this *age* but also in the [age] to come.
2	2 Δ	you were following the ⌐way (lit. *age*) of this world,
	7	This was to show for all *ages* to come . . . how infinitely rich [God] is in grace.
1 Tm 6	17	those who are rich in this *world*'s goods . . . are not to look down on other people;
2 Tm 4	10	Demas has deserted me for love of this ⌐life (lit. *age*)
Tt 2	12	we have to . . . give up . . . all our *world*ly ambitions;
Heb 1	2	through [the Son] he made ⌐everything there is (lit. the *ages*)

| Heb | 6 | 5 | [those who were brought into the light,] appreciated the good message of God and the powers of the *world* to come |
| | 11 | 3 | we understand that the *world* was created by one word from God, |

2. FOR EVER, FOR ALL TIME – CONTINUALLY, REPEATEDLY: *DI-ĒNEKĒS*

di-ēnekēs 4

Heb	7	3	[Melchizedek] remains a priest *for ever*.
	10	1	the same sacrifices [are] *repeatedly* offered year after year.
		12	[Christ has] taken his place *for ever*, at the right hand of God,
		14	[Christ] has achieved the *eternal* perfection of all whom he is sanctifying.

3. ALWAYS, FOR EVER – CONTINUALLY, AT ALL TIMES, CONSTANTLY: *PANTOTE*

2 *dia pantos 10*   1 *pantote 41*

Mt	18	10	2	their angels . . . are *continually* in the presence of my Father
	26	11		You have the poor with you *always* but you will not *always* have me.
Mk	5	5	2	*All* night and [all] day, among the tombs . . , [the demoniac] would howl
	14	7		You have the poor with you *always* . . . but you will not *always* have me.
Lk	15	31		My son, you are with me *always* and all I have is yours.
	18	1		[Jesus] told them . . . about the need to pray *continually*
	24	53	2	[the apostles] were *continually* in the Temple praising God.
Jn	6	34		Sir, . . . give us that bread *always*.
	7	6		*any time* is the right time for you.
	8	29		I *always* do what pleases [my Father].
	11	42		I knew indeed that you *always* hear me,
	12	8		You have the poor with you *always*, you will not *always* have me.
	18	20		I have *always* taught in the synagogue and in the Temple
Ac	2	25	2	(Ps 16 8) I saw the Lord before me *always*,
	10	2	2	[Cornelius] prayed *constantly* to God.
	24	16	2	I . . . do my best to keep a clear conscience *at all times* before God and man.
Rm	1	10		[I never fail to mention you in my prayers,] and ⌐to (lit. *always*) ask to be allowed . . . to visit you,
	11	10	2	(Ps 69 24) may . . . their backs bend *for ever*.
1 Co	1	4		I ⌐never stop (lit. am *always*) thanking God for all the graces you have received
	15	58		keep on working at the Lord's work *always*,
2 Co	2	14		Thanks be to God who, ⌐wherever he goes (lit. *continually*), makes us, in Christ, partners of his triumph,
	4	10		*always*, wherever we may be, we carry with us in our body the death of Jesus,
	5	6		We are *always* full of confidence, [going as we do by faith]
	9	8		God . . . will make sure that you will *always* have all you need
Ga	4	18		It is *always* a good thing to win people over –
Ep	5	20		[Sing hymns when you are together,] so that *always* and everywhere you are giving thanks to God
Ph	1	4		*every time* I pray for all of you, I pray with joy,
		20		My one hope . . . is that . . . now as *always* I shall have the courage for Christ to be glorified in my body,
	2	12		continue to do as I tell you, as you *always* have;
	4	4		I want you to be happy, *always* happy in the Lord;
Col	1	3		We ⌐have never failed to (lit. *always*) . . . give thanks for you to God,
	4	6		*Always* talk to [those who are not Christians] agreeably
		12		Epaphras . . . ⌐never stops (lit. is *always*) battling for you,
1 Th	1	2		We *always* mention you in our prayers
	2	16		They ⌐never stop (lit. are *always*) trying to finish off the sins they have begun,
	3	6		you *always* remember us with pleasure and want to see us
	4	17		So we shall stay with the Lord *for ever*.
	5	15		you must all *always* think of what is best for each other
		16		Be happy *at all times*;
2 Th	1	3		We feel we must be *continually* thanking God for you, brothers;
		11		Knowing this, we pray *continually*
	2	13		we feel that we must be *continually* thanking God for you,
	3	16	2	May the Lord . . . give you peace *all the time* and in every way.
2 Tm	3	7		[these silly women follow one craze after another] ⌐in the attempt (lit. *always*) attempting) to educate themselves,
Phm		4		I *always* mention you in my prayers and thank God for you,
Heb	7	25		[Christ's] power to save is utterly certain, since he is living *for ever*
	9	6	2	priests are *constantly* going into the outer tent
	13	15	2	let us offer God an *unending* sacrifice of praise,

EVIL – WRONG – HARM

1. Evil – Wicked, Wrong – Harm: *kakos*
  1: Evil, Wicked, Bad – Malice, Spite(fulness) – Wrong, Wickedness
  2: Do evil, Do harm, Do wrong – Criminal
  3: Oppress, Ill-treat, Treat badly

2. Evil, Wicked, Bad – Crime – Malice: *ponēros*
  1: the Evil One
  2: Evil (spirits)
  3: Evil, Wicked(ness), Bad – Bad men, Criminal – Malice, Crime(s)

3. (Do) Wrong, Wicked(ness), Harm – Crime, Evil, Sin – Dishonest, Unjust, Unfair: *a-dikia*

4. Lawless, Evil, Wickedness – Break the law, Sin – Criminal: *a-nomia*

5. Lawless, Unprincipled – Unlawful, Forbidden: *a-thesmos*
  1: Unprincipled men, Vile people – (the) Wicked, Lawless – Degrading
  2: Forbidden, Unlawful

6. Godless(ness), Wicked(ness), Sinful – Profane

7.   1: Godless(ness) – Wicked, Irreligious, Sinful – Impiety *a-sebeia*
  2: Profane – Godless, Irreverent *bebēloō*

7. Sin – (Do) Wrong
  1: Sin(s) – Sinner(s) – Sinful, Wrong: *hamartia*
  2: Sin (against), Do wrong (to): *hyper-bainō*

8. Evil, Bad, Wicked – Wrong: *phaulos*

9. Wrong, Wrong-headed: *a-topos*

10. Bad, Rotten – Evil: *sapros*

**11. Bad, Worse – (Become) Inferior, (Be) Dominated, Mastered, by: *hēsson*

12. Worse: *cheirōn*

13. Harm(ful), Hurt, Do harm: *blaptō*

14. villain, Impostor, Fraud – Crime: *rhadi-ourgēma*

15. Break (the Law) – Disobey
  1: Break (the Law) – Infringe, Disobey – Sin, Do wrong: *para-basis*
  2: Disobey: *par-erchomai*

16. Tainted, Debased: *a-chreoō*

G = Evil, Wrong, Harm // Good, Holy, Right

1. EVIL – WICKED, WRONG – HARM: *KAKOS*

2	*kakia*	11		6		*kak-ourgos*	4
4	*kakoō*	6		7		*kako-poieō*	4
1	*kakos*	41/50		8		*kako-poios*	3
5	*kakōs*	4/16		3		*kakon poieō*	9
10	*kakōsis*	1		12	(*an-exi-*)*kakos*		1
9	*kak-oucheō*	2		13		*syn-kak-oucheō*	1
11	*kako-ētheia*	1					

1: EVIL, WICKED, BAD – MALICE, SPITE(FULNESS) – WRONG, WICKEDNESS

Mt	6	34		2	Each day has enough ⌐trouble (lit. *evil*) of its own.
	15	22	5		a Canaanite woman started shouting, . . . 'My daughter is *badly* tormented by a devil.
	21	41	<		[The owner of the vineyard] will bring those ⌐wretches (lit. *bad men*) to a ⌐wretched (lit. *bad*) end
	24	48	< /5		the ⌐*dishonest* (or: *wicked*) servant who says to himself, My master is taking his time.
Mk	7	21			it is from within . . . that *evil* intentions emerge:
Lk	16	25	G		during your life good things came your way, just as *bad things* came the way of Lazarus.
Jn	18	23	X G5/		If there is something *wrong* in what I said, point the *wrong* out;
Ac	8	22		2	[Simon the magician,] Repent of this *wickedness* of yours,
	23	9			We find nothing ⌐*wrong* with (or: *evil* in) this man.
	28	5			[Paul] came to no *harm* [from the viper].
Rm	1	29		2	[pagans] are steeped in all sorts of . . . *malice*, and addicted
		30	11		to . . . *spite*. ³⁰ Libellers, . . . enemies of God, . . . enterprising in *sin* (or: *evil*), . . . ³¹ without brains, honour, love; (ᵛ implacable and) without pity.
	7	21	G		every single time I want to do good it is [something] *evil* that comes to hand.
	12	17	G		Never repay *evil* with *evil*
		21	G		Resist *evil* and conquer *evil* with good.
	14	20			all food is clean, but it becomes *evil* if by eating it you make somebody else fall away.
	16	19	G		I only hope that you are also wise in what is good, and innocent of [what is] *bad*.
1 Co	5	8		2	getting rid of all the old yeast of ⌐*evil* (or: *malice*) and wickedness,
	10	6			not to have the *wicked* lusts . . . that they had.
	13	5			[love] ⌐is not resentful (lit. does not think *evil*).
	14	20		2	You can be babies as far as *wickedness* is concerned, but mentally you must be adult.
	15	33	G		*Bad* friends ruin the noblest people.
Ep	4	31		2	Never . . . allow any sort of *spitefulness*.
Col	3	5			kill everything in you that belongs only to earthly life: guilty passion, *evil* desires

Col	3	8		2 you . . . must give all these things up: . . . *spitefulness*, abusive language
1 Th	5	15	G	Make sure that people do not try to ⌐take revenge (lit. repay *evil* with *evil*);
1 Tm	6	10		The love of money is the root of all *evils*
2 Tm	2	24	12	a servant of the Lord . . . has to be . . . patient (§ amid *evils*).
	4	14		Alexander the coppersmith has ⌐done me a lot of harm (or: displayed a lot of *spitefulness* towards me).
Tt	1	12		Cretans were never anything but liars, ⌐dangerous (lit. *evil*) animals and lazy.
	3	3		2 we lived then in *wickedness* and ill-will,
Heb	5	14	G	men with minds trained by practice to distinguish between good and *bad*.
Jm	1	13	θ	God cannot be tempted ⌐to do anything wrong (lit. with anything *evil*),
		21		2 do away with all the . . . *bad* habits that are still left in you
	3	8		the tongue . . . is ⌐a pest (lit. an *evil*) that will not keep still,
	4	3		when you do pray [for what you want] and don't get it is
		5		because you have ⌐not prayed properly (lit. prayed *wrongly*),
1 P	2	1		2 Be sure . . . you are never *spiteful*,
		16		2 never use your freedom as an excuse for *wickedness*.
	3	9	G	Never pay back one *wrong* with another *wrong*,
		10		(Ps 34 13) Anyone who wants to have a ⌐happy (lit. *good*)
		11	G	life . . . must banish *malice* from his tongue . . ; [11] he must never yield to *evil* but must practise good;
3 Jn		11	G	My dear friend, never follow such a *bad* example, but keep following the good one;
Rv	2	2		I know you cannot stand *wicked* men,
	16	2		there came ⌐disgusting (lit. *evil*) and virulent sores.

2: DO EVIL, DO HARM, DO WRONG – CRIMINAL

Mt	27	23	X	3 [Pilate] asked, 'What ⌐harm (or: *evil*) has he *done*?'
Mk	3	4	G 7	Is it against the law on the sabbath day to do good, or to do *evil* . . ?
	15	14	X	3 Pilate asked them, 'What ⌐harm (or: *evil*) has he *done*?'
Lk	6	9	G	7 is it against the law on the sabbath to do good, or to do *evil* . . .?
	23	22	X	3 [Pilate said,] What ⌐harm (or: *evil*) has this man *done*?
		32		6 with them they were also leading out two other *criminals* to be executed.
		33		6 they crucified him there and the two *criminals* also,
		39		6 One of the *criminals* hanging there abused him.
Jn	18	30	X	3 If he were not ⌐a criminal (lit. *doing evil*), we should not be handing him over to you.
Ac	9	13		3 all the ⌐harm (or: *evil*) [Saul] has been *doing* to your saints
	16	28		Don't do yourself any *harm*;
	18	10		4 no one will even attempt to ⌐hurt you (or: *do you harm*).
Rm	2	9	G	Pain and suffering will come to every human being who employs himself in *evil*
	3	8	G	3 That would be the same as saying: Do *evil* as a means to good.
	7	19	G	I carry out the *sinful things* I do not want.
	13	3		Good behaviour is not afraid of magistrates; only ⌐criminals (lit. those who do *evil*) have anything to fear. . . . [4] . . .
		4	G	3 If you ⌐break the law (lit. *do wrong*) . . . you may well have fear: . . . The authorities . . . carry out God's revenge by punishing *wrong*doers.
		10		Love is the one thing that cannot ⌐hurt (lit. do *harm* to) your neighbour;
2 Co	13	7	G	3 We pray to God that you will *do nothing wrong*:
Ph	3	2		Watch out for the people who are ⌐making mischief (lit. workers of *evil*).
2 Tm	2	9	6	I have . . . hardships to bear [for Jesus Christ], even to being chained like a *criminal*
	4	14		Alexander the coppersmith has ⌐done me a lot of *harm* (or: displayed a lot of spitefulness towards me)
1 P	2	12	G 8	the things which now make [the pagans] denounce you as *criminals*.
		14	G 8	[accept the authority of] the governors as commissioned by [God] to punish ⌐criminals (lit. those who *do wrong*) and praise good citizenship.
	3	12	G 3	Because the face of the Lord frowns on ⌐evil men (lit. men who *do evil*),
		13	G	4 No one can ⌐hurt you (or: *do you harm*) if you are determined to do only what is right:
		17	G	7 it is better to suffer for doing right than for *doing wrong*
	4	15	8	None of you should ever deserve to suffer for being . . . a *criminal*
3 Jn		11	G	7 the person who *does* [what is] *wrong* has never seen God.

3: OPPRESS, ILL-TREAT, TREAT BADLY

Ac	7	6		4 (Gn 15 13) [Abraham's] descendants would be . . . *oppressed* for four hundred years,
		19		4 [the king] *ill-treated* our ancestors,
		34	10	(Ex 3 7) I have seen ⌐the way my people are ill-treated (lit. the *ill-treatment* of my people) in Egypt,

Ac	12	1		Herod started ⌐persecuting certain members of the Church (lit. laying hands violently on certain members of the Church in order to *oppress* them).
	14	2	4	Some of the Jews . . . *poisoned* the minds of the pagans against the brothers.
Heb	11	25	13	[Moses] chose to *be ill-treated* in company *with* God's people
		37	9	they were penniless and were *given* [nothing but] *ill-treatment*.
	13	3	9	Keep in mind . . . those who are being *badly treated*,

2. EVIL, WICKED, BAD – CRIME – MALICE: *PONĒROS*

2 ponēria 7   1 ponēros 78

1: THE EVIL ONE

Mt	5	37		All you need say is Yes if you mean yes, No if you mean no: anything more than this comes from the *evil one*.
	6	13		but save us from ⌐the *Evil One* (or: evil).
	13	19		the *evil one* comes and carries off what was sown in his heart:
		38		the darnel [is] the subjects of the *evil one*;
Jn	17	15		I am not asking you to remove them from the world, but to protect them from the *evil one*.
Ep	6	16		always carrying the shield of faith so that you can use it to put out the burning arrows of the *evil one*.
2 Th	3	3		the Lord . . . will give you strength and guard you from the *evil one*.
1 Jn	2	13		you, young men, who have already overcome the *Evil One*;
		14		you, young men, because you have overcome the *Evil One*.
	3	12		not to be like Cain, who belonged to the *Evil One* and cut his brother's throat; . . . simply for this reason, that his own life was evil and his brother lived a good life.
	5	18		anyone who has been begotten by God does not sin, . . . the *Evil One* does not touch him.
		19		the whole world lies in the power of the *Evil One*.

2: EVIL (SPIRITS)

Mt	12	45		it then goes off and collects seven other spirits more *evil* than itself,
Lk	7	21		[Jesus] cured many people of diseases and of *evil* spirits,
	8	2		certain women who had been cured of *evil* spirits and ailments:
	11	26		it then goes off and brings seven other spirits more *wicked* than itself,
Ac	19	12		they were cured of their illnesses, and the *evil* spirits came out of them.
		13		pronouncing the name of the Lord Jesus over people who were possessed by *evil* spirits;
		15		The *evil* spirit replied, 'Jesus I recognise,
		16		the man with the *evil* spirit hurled himself at them
Ep	6	12	2	we have to struggle . . against . . . the spiritual army of *evil* in the heavens.

3: EVIL, WICKED(NESS), BAD – BAD MEN, CRIMINAL – MALICE, CRIME(S)

Mt	5	11		Happy are you when people . . . speak all kinds of ⌐calumny (lit. *evil*) against you
		39		offer the *wicked man* no resistance.
		45	G	your Father in heaven . . . causes his sun to rise on *bad men* as well as good,
	6	13		save us from ⌐the *Evil One* (or: evil).
		23		if your eye is ⌐diseased (lit. *bad*).
	7	11	G	If you, then, who are *evil*, know how to give your children what is good,
		17	G	a rotten tree [produces] *bad* fruit. [18] A sound tree cannot
		18	G	bear *bad* fruit.
	9	4		Why do you have such *wicked* thoughts in your hearts?
	12	34	G	how can your speech be good when you are *evil*?
		35	G	a *bad* man draws *bad* things from his store of *badness*.
		39		It is an *evil* and unfaithful generation that asks for a sign!
		45		That is what will happen to this *evil* generation.
	13	49		the angels will . . . separate the *wicked* from the just
	15	19		from the heart come *evil* intentions: murder, adultery, . . . slander.
	16	4		It is an *evil* and unfaithful generation that asks for a sign!
	18	32		You *wicked* servant, . . . [33] Were you not bound . . . to have pity . . ?
	20	15	G	⌐Why be envious (lit. Is your eye *evil*) because I am generous?
	22	10		these servants . . . collected together everyone they could find, *bad* and good alike;
		18	2	Jesus was aware of their *malice* and replied,
	25	26	G	You *wicked* and lazy servant!
Mk	7	22	2	[from within emerge] avarice, *malice*, . . . ⌐envy (lit. an *evil* eye), . . . [23] All these *evil* things come from within
		23		
Lk	3	19		Herod . . . whom [John] criticised for . . . all the other *crimes* Herod had committed,

Lk	6	22		Happy are you when people . . . denounce your name as *criminal*,
		35	G	the Most High . . . is kind to the ungrateful and the *wicked*.
		45	G	a *bad* man draws what is *bad* from the store of *badness*.
	11	13	G	If you then, who are *evil*, know how to give your children what is *good*,
		29		This is a *wicked* generation, it is asking for a sign.
		34		When your eye is . . . ᵣdiseased (lit. *bad*) your body too will be all darkness.
		39	2	inside yourselves you are filled with extortion and *wickedness*.
	19	22	G	You *wicked* servant! . . . Out of your own mouth I condemn you.
Jn	3	19		their deeds were *evil*.
	7	7		The world . . . does hate me, because I give evidence that its ways are *evil*.
Ac	3	26	2	God . . . sent [his servant] to bless you by turning every one of you from your *wicked ways*.
	17	5		The Jews . . . enlisted the help of ᵣa gang from the market place (lit. some *evil* men of the lowest kind),
	18	14		If this were a misdemeanour or a *bad crime*,
	25	18		his accusers did not charge him with any of the *crimes* I had expected;
	28	21		nor has any countryman of yours arrived here with any report . . . of anything ᵣto your discredit (lit. *bad* about you).
Rm	1	29	2	[the pagans] are steeped in all sorts of depravity, *rottenness*, greed
	12	9	G	sincerely prefer good to *evil*.
1 Co	5	8	2	getting rid of all the old yeast of evil and *wickedness*
Ga	1	4		in order to rescue us from this present *wicked* world [Jesus Christ] sacrificed himself
Ep	5	16		This may be a *wicked* age, but your lives should redeem it.
	6	13		That is why you must rely on God's armour, or you will not be able to put up any resistance when the ᵣworst happens (lit. *evil* day comes),
Col	1	21		you were . . . enemies [of God], in the way that you used to think and the *evil* things that you did;
1 Th	5	22	G	avoid every form of *evil*.
2 Th	3	2		pray that we may be preserved from the interference of bigoted and *evil* people,
1 Tm	6	4		All that can come of this is . . . abuse and *wicked* mistrust of one another;
2 Tm	3	13		while these *wicked* impostors will go from bad to worse,
	4	18		The Lord will rescue me from all *evil* attempts on me,
Heb	3	12		Take care . . . that there is not in any one of your community a *wicked* mind,
	10	22		our minds . . . free from any trace of *bad* conscience
Jm	2	4		you have . . . turned yourselves into judges, ᵣand corrupt judges at that (lit. open to *evil* thoughts)?
	4	16		Pride of this kind is always *wicked*.
1 Jn	3	12		[Cain's] life was *evil* and his brother lived a good life.
2 Jn		11		To greet him would make you a partner in his *wicked* work
3 Jn		10		the *wicked* accusations [Diotrephes] has been circulating against us.
Rv	16	2		there came disgusting and ᵣvirulent (lit. *malignant*) sores.

3. (DO) WRONG, WICKED(NESS), HARM – CRIME, EVIL, SIN – DISHONEST, UNJUST, UNFAIR: *A-DIKIA*

4 *a-dikēma* 3	3 *a-dikos* 12
1 *a-dikeō* 28	5 *a-dikōs* 1
2 *a-dikia* 25	

Mt	5	45		your Father in heaven . . . causes . . . his rain to fall on
			G 3	honest and *dishonest* men alike.
	20	13		I am not *being unjust* to you; did we not agree on one denarius?
Lk	10	19		nothing shall ever *hurt* you.
	13	27	2	(Ps 6 8) Away from me, all you ᵣwicked men (lit. workers of *evil*)!
	16	8	< 2	The master praised the *dishonest* steward
		9	2	use money, tainted (lit. *dishonest*) as it is, to win you friends,
		10	3/3	the man who is *dishonest* in little things will be *dishonest* in great.
		11	3	If then you cannot be trusted with money, that tainted (lit. *dishonest*) thing,
	18	6	< 2	You notice what the *unjust* judge has to say?
		11	G 3	I am not grasping, *unjust*, adulterous like the rest of mankind,
Jn	7	18		when [a man] is working for the honour of one who sent him,
			X 2	then he is . . . by no means ᵣdishonest (lit. *dishonest*).
Ac	1	18	2	[Judas] bought a field with the money he was paid for his *crime*.
	7	24		When [Moses] saw one of [his countrymen] *being ill-treated* he went to his defence
		26		Friends, . . . why are you *hurting* each other?
		27		the man who was ᵣattacking (lit. *hurting*) his fellow-country-man
	8	23	2	[Peter to Simon:] you are trapped in the . . . chains of *sin*.
	18	14	4	If this were a *misdemeanour* or a bad crime,

Ac	24	15	G 2	there will be a resurrection of good men and *bad men* alike.
		20	4	let those who are present say what *crime* they found (ᵛ me guilty of)
	25	10		I have *done* the Jews no *wrong*, . . . ¹¹ If I am guilty of
		11		committing any capital *crime*,
Rm	1	18		The anger of God is being revealed . . . against all the
			2	impiety and ᵣdepravity (lit. *wickedness*) of men who keep
			2	truth imprisoned in their *wickedness*.
		29	2	[the pagans] are steeped in all sorts of ᵣdepravity (lit. *wickedness*), rottenness, greed
	2	8	2	for the unsubmissive who . . . took ᵣdepravity (lit. *wickedness*) [for their guide]
	3	5	Θ 2	if our *lack of holiness* makes God demonstrate his integrity,
			Θ G 3	how can we say God is *unjust* when . . . he gets angry with us in return?
	6	13	G 2	you must not let any part of your body turn into an *unholy* weapon
	9	14	Θ 2	Does it follow that God is *unjust*?
1 Co	6	1		How dare one of your members take up a complaint against
			G 3	another in the lawcourts of the *unjust* instead of before
		7		the saints? . . . ⁷. . . oughtn't you to let yourselves
		8	G	*be wronged* . . . ? ⁸ But you are *doing the wronging* . . .
		9	G 3	⁹ . . . people who *do wrong* will not inherit the kingdom of God:
	13	6	2	Love takes no pleasure in other people's *sins*
2 Co	7	2		We have not *injured* anyone,
		12		the letter . . . was not written for the sake either of the *offender* or of the [one] *offended*;
	12	13	2	For this *unfairness*, please forgive me.
Ga	4	12		You have never ᵣtreated me in an unfriendly way (lit. *done me any wrong*) before;
Col	3	25		anyone who *does wrong* will be repaid ᵣin kind (lit. for the *wrong done*)
2 Th	2	10	2	everything *evil* that can deceive those who are bound for destruction
		12	2	all who refused to believe in the truth and chose *wickedness* instead.
2 Tm	2	19	2	All who call on the name of the Lord must avoid *sin*.
Phm		18		if [Onesimus] has *wronged* you in any way or owes you anything,
Heb	6	10	Θ 3	God would not be so *unjust* as to forget all you have done,
	8	12	2	(Jr 31 34) I will forgive their *iniquities*
Jm	3	6	2	the tongue is a whole *wicked* world in itself:
1 P	2	19		there is some merit in putting up with the pains of ᵣunearned
			5	(lit. *unjust*) punishment
	3	18	3	Christ himself . . . had . . . died for the ᵣguilty (lit. *un-*
			X G	*righteous*),
2 P	2	9	G 3	the Lord can . . . hold the *wicked* for their punishment until the day of Judgement,
		13	G /2	[Self-willed people will] *get their reward of evil for the evil* that they do. . . . ¹⁵ They have . . . wandered off to follow
		15		the path of Balaam . . . who thought he could profit best
			2	by *sinning*.
1 Jn	1	9		God . . . will forgive our sins and purify us from everything
			Θ G 2	that is *wrong*.
	5	17	2	Every kind of *wrongdoing* is sin,
Rv	2	11		for those who prove victorious ᵣthere is nothing to be afraid of (lit. will not be *harmed*) in the second death.
	6	6	○	do not ᵣtamper with (lit. *harm*) the oil or the wine.
	7	2		another angel . . . called . . . to the four angels whose duty was to *devastate* land and sea,
		3		Wait before you *do any damage* on land or at sea
	9	4		[the locusts] were forbidden to *harm* any fields or crops or trees
		10		[the locusts] were able to *injure* people for five months.
		19		[the horses'] tails were like snakes, and had heads that were able to *wound*.
	11	5		Fire can . . . consume their enemies if anyone tries to *harm* [my two witnesses]; and if anybody does try to *harm* them he will certainly be killed in this way.
	18	5	4	God has [Babylon's] *crimes* in mind:
	22	11	G	Meanwhile let the *sinner* go on *sinning*,

4. LAWLESS, EVIL, WICKEDNESS – BREAK THE LAW, SIN – CRIMINAL: *A-NOMIA*

| 1 *a-nomia* 15 | 3 *para-nomia* 1 |
| 2 *a-nomos* 5/10 | |

F = Forgive, Wash away, Remit, Cover, Free from, sin

Mt	7	23		(Ps 6 9) away from me, you *evil* men!
	13	41		his angels . . . will gather out of his kingdom all things that provoke offences and all who do *evil*,
	23	28		inside you are full of hypocrisy and *lawlessness*.
	24	12		with the increase of *lawlessness*, love in most men will grow cold.
Mk	15	28	X 2	(ᵛ . . . (Is 53 12) He let himself be taken for a *criminal*.)

Lk 22 37 X 2 (Is 53 12) He let himself be taken for a *criminal*.
Rm 4 7 F (Ps 32 1) Happy those whose *crimes* are forgiven,
  6 19 once you put your bodies at the service of vice ⌐and immorality (lit. from *evil* to *evil*),
2 Co 6 14 Virtue is no companion for *crime*.
2 Th 2 3 ● It cannot happen until . . . the ⌐Rebel (lit. Man of ⌐*lawlessness*: ᵛ *sin*), the Lost One, has appeared.
  7 ● ⌐Rebellion (lit. *Lawlessness*) is at its work already,
  8 ● 2 when the ⌐Rebel (lit. *Lawless One*) comes, Satan will set to work:
1 Tm 1 9 laws are not framed for people who are good . . . they are for
  2 *criminals* and revolutionaries, for the irreligious and the wicked,
Tt 2 14 F (cf. Ps 130 8) [Christ Jesus] sacrificed himself for us in order to set us free from all *wickedness*
Heb 1 9 (Ps 45 8) virtue you love as much as you hate *wickedness*.
  10 17 F I will never call their sins to mind, or their *offences*.
2 P 2 8 2 [Lot] was outraged . . . by the ⌐crimes (lit. *evil* deeds) that he saw and heard of every day.
  16 3 [Balaam] was called to order for his *faults*.
1 Jn 3 4 Anyone who sins at all *breaks the law*, because to sin is to *break the law*.

5. LAWLESS, UNPRINCIPLED – UNLAWFUL, FORBIDDEN: *A-THESMOS*

1 *a-themitos* 2   2 *a-thesmos* 2

1: UNPRINCIPLED MEN, VILE PEOPLE – (THE) WICKED, LAWLESS – DEGRADING

1 P 4 3 You spent quite long enough in the past . . . ⌐*degrading yourselves* by following (or: following forbidden) false gods.
2 P 2 7 Lot . . . had been sickened by the shameless way these
  2 ⌐*vile* (or: *lawless*) *people* behaved
  3 17 2 be careful not to get carried away by the errors of ⌐*unprincipled* (or: *wicked*) *people*,

2: FORBIDDEN, UNLAWFUL

Ac 10 28 it is ⌐*forbidden* (or: *unlawful*) for Jews to mix with people of another race
1 P 4 3 You spent quite long enough in the past . . . ⌐*degrading yourselves* by following (or: following *forbidden*) false gods.

6. GODLESS(NESS), WICKED(NESS), SINFUL – PROFANE

1: GODLESS(NESS) – WICKED, IRRELIGIOUS, SINFUL – IMPIETY: *A-SEBEIA*

2 *a-sebeia* 6   1 *a-sebēs* 9
3 *a-sebeō* 2

Rm 1 18 2 The anger of God is being revealed . . . against all the *impiety* and depravity of men
  4 5 when a man has nothing to show except faith in the one who justifies *sinners*, then his faith is considered as justifying him.
  5 6 Christ died for *sinful men*.
  11 26 (Is 59 20) The liberator will come from Zion, he will banish
  2 *godlessness* from Jacob.
1 Tm 1 9 [laws are framed] for the *irreligious* and the wicked,
2 Tm 2 16 philosophical discussions . . . only lead further and further
  2 ⌐away from true religion (lit. *toward godlessness*).
Tt 2 12 give up ⌐everything that does not lead to God (lit. every
  2 *impiety*)
1 P 4 18 (Pr 11 31) If it is hard for a good man to be saved, what will happen to the *wicked* and to sinners?
2 P 2 5 [God] sent the Flood over a *disobedient* world.
  6 [God] destroyed [Sodom and Gomorrah] completely, as a
  3 warning to *anybody lacking reverence* in the future;
  3 7 the present sky and earth . . . are only being reserved until Judgement day so that all ⌐*sinners* (lit. *sinful* men) may be destroyed.
Jude 4 Certain people have infiltrated among you . . . *denying all religion*, turning the grace of our God into immorality,
  15 /2 [the Lord will come] to sentence the *wicked* for all the *wicked* things ⌐they have done (lit. in which they have done
  3 *wicked*), and for all the defiant things said against him by *irreligious* sinners.
  18 there are going to be people who sneer at religion and follow
  2 nothing but their own desires for *wickedness*.

2: PROFANE – GODLESS, IRREVERENT: *BEBĒLOŌ*

2 *bebēloō* 2   1 *bebēlos* 5

Mt 12 5 2 the Temple priests ⌐break (lit. *profane*) the sabbath without being blamed for it
Ac 24 6 2 [Paul] has even attempted to *profane* the Temple.
1 Tm 1 9 [laws are framed] for the sacrilegious and the *irreverent*;
  4 7 Have nothing to do with *godless* myths and old wives' tales.
  6 20 Have nothing to do with . . . pointless and *profane* philosophical discussions
2 Tm 2 16 Have nothing to do with . . . *profane* philosophical discussions
Heb 12 16 be careful . . . that any of you does not *degrade religion*

7. SIN – (DO) WRONG

1: SIN(S) – SINNER(S) – SINFUL, WRONG: *HAMARTIA*

3 *hamartanō*   43   2 *hamartōlos* 47
4 *hamartēma*   4   6 *an-(h)amartētos* 1
1 *hamartia*   171/174   5 *pro-(h)amartanō* 2

F = Forgive, Wash away, Remit, Cover, Free from, sin

Mt 1 21 F [Jesus] is the one who is to save his people from their *sins*.
  3 6 as they were baptised by [John] . . . they confessed their *sins*.
  9 2 F Jesus said to the paralytic, 'Courage, . . . your *sins* are forgiven'.
  5 F which of these is easier: to say, 'Your *sins* are forgiven', or to say, 'Get up and walk'?
  6 F the Son of Man has authority on earth to forgive *sins*,
  10 2 a number of tax collectors and *sinners* came to sit at the table with Jesus and his disciples. ¹¹ . . . Why does your master
  11 eat with tax collectors and *sinners*? . . . ¹³ . . . I did not
  13 2 come to call the virtuous, but *sinners*.
  11 19 Look, a glutton and . . . a friend of tax collectors and
  2 *sinners*.
  12 31 F every one of men's *sins* and blasphemies will be forgiven, but blasphemy against the Spirit will not be forgiven.
  18 15 3 If your brother *does something wrong* . . . have it out with him alone,
  21 F 3 how often must I forgive my brother if he *wrongs* me?
  26 28 F this is my blood . . . which is to be poured out for many for the forgiveness of *sins*.
  45 2 the Son of Man is to be betrayed into the hands of *sinners*.
  27 4 3 I have *sinned*; . . . I have betrayed innocent blood.
Mk 1 4 F John the Baptist appeared . . . proclaiming a baptism of repentance for the forgiveness of *sins*.
  5 as they were baptised by [John] . . . they confessed their *sins*.
  2 5 F Jesus said to the paralytic, 'My child, your *sins* are forgiven'.
  7 F Who can forgive *sins* but God?
  9 F Which of these is easier: to say . . , 'Your *sins* are forgiven' or to say, 'Get up . . . and walk'?
  10 F the Son of Man has authority on earth to forgive *sins*,
  15 2 a number of tax collectors and *sinners* were also sitting at the table with Jesus and his disciples . . . ¹⁶ When the scribes
  16 2 saw him eating with *sinners* . . . they said to his disciples,
  17 2 'Why does he eat with tax collectors and *sinners*?' ¹⁷ . . . Jesus . . . said to them, '. . . I did not come to call the
  2 virtuous, but *sinners*.'
  3 28 F 4 all men's *sins* will be forgiven, and all their blasphemies;
  29 F ²⁹ but let anyone blaspheme against the Holy Spirit and
  4 . . . he is guilty of an eternal *sin*.
  8 38 2 if anyone in this adulterous and *sinful* generation is ashamed of me . . . the Son of Man will also be ashamed of him
  14 41 2 the Son of Man is to be betrayed into the hands of *sinners*.
Lk 1 77 F [you will go before the Lord] to give his people knowledge of salvation through the forgiveness of their *sins*;
  3 3 F [John proclaimed] a baptism of repentance for the forgiveness of *sins*,
  5 8 Simon Peter . . . fell at the knees of Jesus saying, 'Leave me,
  2 Lord; I am a *sinful man*'.
  20 F [Jesus said to the paralytic,] My friend, your *sins* are forgiven you.
  21 F Who can forgive *sins* but God alone?
  23 F Which of these is easier: to say, 'Your *sins* are forgiven you' or to say, 'Get up and walk'?
  24 F the Son of Man has authority on earth to forgive *sins*,
  30 2 Why do you eat . . . with tax collectors and *sinners*?
  32 2 I have not come to call the virtuous, but *sinners* to repentance.
  6 32 2 Even *sinners* love those who love them.
  33 if you do good to those who do good to you, what thanks can
  2 you expect? For even *sinners* do that much.
  34 2/2 Even *sinners* lend to *sinners* to get back the same amount.
  7 34 2 [the Son of Man is] a friend of tax collectors and *sinners*.

Lk 7 37   2 a woman came in, who ʳhad a bad name (lit. was a *sinner*) in the town.

39   If this man were a prophet, he would know . . . what ʳa bad
  2 name she has (lit. sort of woman she is – a *sinner*).

47 F   her *sins*, her many [sins], must have been forgiven her,

48 F   [Jesus] said to her, 'Your *sins* are forgiven'.

49 F   Who is this man, that he even forgives *sins*?

11 4 F   [Say this when you pray: Father . . .] forgive us our *sins*,

13 2   2 Do you suppose these Galileans . . . were greater *sinners* than any other Galileans?

15 1   2 The tax collectors and the *sinners*, meanwhile, were all seeking his company

2   2 This man [Jesus] . . . welcomes *sinners* and eats with them.

7   there will be more rejoicing in heaven over one repentant
  2 *sinner* than over ninety-nine virtuous men

10   there is rejoicing among the angels of God over one repentant
  2 *sinner*.

18   3 [the prodigal son is to say:] Father, I have *sinned* against heaven and against you;

21   3 Father, I have *sinned* against heaven and against you.

17 3 F   3 If your brother *does something wrong* . . . and . . . is sorry,

4 F   3 forgive him. ⁴ And if he *wrongs* you seven times a day . . . you must forgive him.

18 13 F   2 The tax collector . . . said, 'God, be merciful to me, a *sinner*'.

19 7   2 [Jesus] has gone to stay at a *sinner*[= Zacchaeus]'s house

24 7   2 the Son of Man had to be handed over into the power of *sinful men*

47 F   [it is written] that, in his name, repentance for the forgiveness of *sins* would be preached to all the nations.

Jn 1 29 F   Look, there is the lamb of God that takes away the *sin* of the world.

5 14   [Jesus said to the sick man,] Now you are well again, be sure
  3 not to *sin* any more,

8 7   6 If there is one of you who ʳhas not sinned (lit. is *sinless*), let him be the first to throw a stone at her.

11   3 go away, and don't *sin* any more.

21   you will die in your *sin*.

24   You will die in your *sins*. Yes, if you do not believe that I am He, you will die in your *sins*.

34   everyone who commits *sin* is a slave to *sin*.

46 X   Can one of you convict me of *sin*?

9 2   3 who *sinned* . . . for him to have been born blind?

3   3 Neither he nor his parents *sinned*,

16 X   2 How could a *sinner* produce signs like this?

24 X   2 For our part, we know that this man is a *sinner*.

25 X   2 I don't know if he is a *sinner*;

31   2 We know that God doesn't listen to *sinners*,

34   Are you trying to teach us, . . . and you a *sinner* through and through, since you were born!

41   Blind? If you were, you would not be *guilty*, but since you say, 'We see', your *guilt* remains.

15 22   if I had not spoken to them, they would have ʳbeen blameless (lit. had no *sin*); but as it is they have no excuse for their *sin*.

24   If I had not performed such works among them as no one else has ever done, they would be ʳblameless (lit. without *sin*).

16 8   [the Advocate] will show the world how wrong it was, about
9   *sin* . . . ⁹ about *sin*: proved by their refusal to believe in me;

19 11   the one who handed me over to you has the greater *guilt*.

20 23 F   For those whose *sins* you forgive, they are forgiven;

Ac 2 38 F   every one of you must be baptised in the name of Jesus Christ for the forgiveness of your *sins*,

3 19 F   you must repent . . . so that your *sins* may be wiped out,

5 31 F   God has now raised [Jesus] up . . . to give repentance and forgiveness of *sin* through him to Israel.

7 60   Lord, do not hold this *sin* against them;

10 34 F   all who believe in Jesus will have their *sins* forgiven through his name.

13 38 F   it is through [Jesus] that forgiveness of your *sins* is proclaimed.

22 16 F   It is time you . . . had your *sins* washed away while invoking his name.

25 8   Paul's defence was this, 'I have ʳcommitted no offence what-
  3 ever (lit. not *sinned* at all) against either Jewish law, or the Temple, or Caesar'.

26 18 F   [I am sending you to the pagans,] so that they may . . . receive, through faith in me, forgiveness of their *sins*

Rm 2 12   3 *Sinners* who were not subject to the Law will perish all the
  3 same, without that Law; *sinners* who were under the Law have that Law to judge them.

3 7   You might as well say that . . . I should not be judged to be
  2 a *sinner* at all.

9   Jews and Greeks are all under *sin*'s dominion.

20   all that law does is to tell us what is *sinful*.

23   3 Both Jew and pagan *sinned* and forfeited God's glory,

25   4 [in the past] *sins* went unpunished because [God] held his hand,

4 7 F   (Ps 32 1–2) Happy those whose crimes are forgiven, whose
8   *sins* are blotted out; ⁸ happy the man ʳwhom the Lord considers sinless (lit. against whom the Lord holds no *sin*).

Rm 5 8   2 Christ died for us while we were still *sinners*.

12   *sin* entered the world through one man, and through *sin* death, and thus death has spread through the whole human
13   3/ race because everyone has *sinned*. ¹³ *Sin* existed in the world long before the Law was given. There was now and so no one could be accused of the *sin* of 'law-breaking',
14   ¹⁴ yet death reigned over all from Adam to Moses, even
  3 though their *sin*, unlike that of Adam, was not a matter of breaking a law.

16   The results of the gift also outweigh the results of one man's
  3 *sin*:

19   2 by one man's disobedience many were made *sinners*,

20   however great the number of *sins* committed, grace was even greater;

21   just as *sin* reigned wherever there was death, so grace will reign

6 1   Does it follow that we should remain in *sin* so as to let grace
2   have greater scope? ² Of course not, We are dead to *sin*, so how can we continue to live in it?

6   our former selves have been crucified with [Christ] to destroy this *sinful* body and to free us from the slavery of *sin*.

7 F   ⁷ When a man dies, of course, he has finished with *sin*.

10   [Christ] died, once for all, to *sin* . . . ¹¹ and in that way, you
11   too must consider yourselves to be dead to *sin*

12   you must not let *sin* reign in your mortal bodies . . . ¹³ . . .
13   you must not let any part of your body turn into an unholy weapon fighting on the side of *sin*;

14   *sin* will no longer dominate your life, since you are living by grace

15   Does the fact that we are living by grace . . . mean that we
  3 are free to *sin*?

16   You cannot be slaves of *sin* that leads to death and at the same time slaves of obedience

17   You were once slaves of *sin*, but . . . you submitted . . . to
18 F   the creed you were taught. ¹⁸ You may have been freed from the slavery of *sin*, but only to become 'slaves' of righteousness.

20   When you were slaves of *sin*, you felt no obligation to right-
22 F   eousness, . . . ²² Now, however, you have been set free from *sin*, you have been made slaves of God.

23   the wage paid by *sin* is death;

7 5   Before our conversion our *sinful* passions . . . fertilised our bodies

7   Does it follow that the Law itself is *sin*? Of course not. What I mean is that I should not have known what *sin* was except for the Law.

8   it was this commandment that *sin* took advantage of to produce all kinds of covetousness in me, for when there is no Law, *sin* is dead.

9   when the commandment came, *sin* came to life

11   *sin* took advantage of the commandment to mislead me, and so . . . killed me.

13   *sin*, to show itself ʳin its true colours (lit. as a *sin*), used that good thing to kill me; and thus *sin*, thanks to the command-
  2 ment, was able to exercise all its *sinful* power.

14   I am unspiritual; I have been sold as a slave to *sin*

17   the thing behaving in that way is not my self but *sin* living in me.

20   When I act against my will . . . it is not my true self doing it, but *sin* which lives in me.

23   my body follows a different law that . . . makes me a prisoner of that law of *sin* which lives inside my body.

25   it is I who . . . serve in my unspiritual self the law of *sin*.

8 2   the law of the spirit . . . has set you free from the law of *sin*
3   God dealt with *sin* by sending his own Son in a body as physical as any *sinful* body, and in that body God con-demned *sin*.

10   Though your body may be dead it is because of *sin*, but if Christ is in you then your spirit is life itself

11 27 F   (Is 27 9) I take their *sins* away.

14 23   every act done in bad faith is a *sin*.

1 Co 6 18   4 All the other *sins* are committed outside the body; but to
  3 fornicate is to *sin* against your own body.

7 28   3/3 if you marry, it is no *sin*, and it is not a *sin* for a young girl to get married.

36   3 he is free to do as he likes: he is not *sinning* if there is a marriage.

8 12   3 By *sinning* in this way against your brothers . . . it would be
  3 Christ against whom you *sinned*.

15 3   Christ died for our *sins*, in accordance with the scriptures;

17   if Christ has not been raised, you are still in your *sins*.

34   3 Come to your senses . . . and leave *sin* alone;

56   Now the sting of death is *sin*, and *sin* gets its power from the Law.

2 Co 5 21 X   ● For our sake God made the ʳsinless one (lit. one who had not known *sin*) into sin,

11 7   Or was I *wrong*, lowering myself so as to lift you high, by preaching the gospel of God to you and taking no fee for it?

12 21   5 I shall be grieving over all those who *sinned before*

13 2   5 I gave warning . . . to those who *sinned before*

Ga 1 4　in order to rescue us from this present wicked world [Christ]
　　　　sacrificed himself for our *sins*,
　2 15　2 we were born Jews and not pagan *sinners*,
　　17　if we were to admit that the result of looking to Christ to
　　　2 justify us is to make us *sinners* like the rest, it would follow
　　　　that Christ had induced us to *sin*, which would be absurd,
　3 22　scripture makes no exceptions when it says that *sin* is master
　　　　everywhere.
Ep 2 1　you were dead, through the crimes and the *sins* [2] in which
　　　　you used to live
　4 26　3 (Ps 4 5) Even if you are angry, you must not *sin*:
Col 1 14 F　in [the Son] we gain . . . the forgiveness of our *sins*.
1 Th 2 16　(Gn 15 16) [The Jews] never stop trying to finish off the *sins*
　　　　they have begun,
2 Th 2 3　It cannot happen until . . . ˹the Rebel (ᵛ the Man of *sin*)
　　　　. . . has appeared.
1 Tm 1 9　2 laws are . . . framed . . . for the irreligious and the *wicked*,
　　　　for the sacrilegious and the irreverent;
　　15　2 Christ Jesus came into the world to save *sinners*.
　5 20　3 If any of [the elders] *are at fault*, reprimand them publicly;
　　22　never make yourself an accomplice in anybody else's *sin*;
　　24　The ˹faults (lit. *sins*) of some people are obvious long before
　　　　anyone makes any complaint about them,
2 Tm 3 6　[Have nothing to do with] men who insinuate themselves into
　　　　families in order to get influence over silly women who are
　　　　obsessed with their *sins*
Tt 3 11　any man of that sort has already . . . condemned himself as
　　　3 a *sinner*.
Heb 1 3 F　[the Son] has destroyed the defilement of *sin*,
　2 17 F　[Christ], a compassionate and trustworthy high priest . . .
　　　　able to atone for human *sins*.
　3 13　keep encouraging one another so that none of you is hardened
　　　　by the lure of *sin*,
　　17　those who made God angry for forty years were the ones
　　　3 who *sinned*
　4 15 X　[Jesus] has been tempted in every way that we are, though he
　　　　is without *sin*.
　5 1 F　Every high priest . . . is appointed . . . to offer gifts and
　　　　sacrifices for *sins*;
　7 26 X　the ideal high priest would have to be . . . beyond the
　　27 F　2 influence of *sinners* . . . [27] one who would not need to
　　　　offer sacrifices every day, as the other high priests do for
　　　　their own *sins*
　8 12 F　(Jr 31 34) I will . . . never call their *sins* to mind.
　9 26 F　[Christ] has made his appearance once and for all . . . to do
　　　　away with *sin* by sacrificing himself.
　　28 F　(Is 53 12) Christ . . . offers himself only once to take the
　　　　˹faults (lit. *sins*) of many on himself, and when he appears
　　　　a second time, it will not be to deal with *sin*
　10 2　the worshippers, when they had been purified once, would
　　3　have no awareness of *sins*. [3] Instead of that, the *sins* are
　　4 F　recalled year after year in the sacrifices. [4] Bulls' blood and
　　　　goats' blood are useless for taking away *sins*,
　　11 F　sacrifices . . . are quite incapable of taking *sins* away.
　　12 F　[Christ] has offered one single sacrifice for *sins*,
　　17 F　(Jr 31 34) I will never call their *sins* to mind, or their offences.
　　18 F　[18] When all [*sins*] have been forgiven, there can be no more
　　　　sin offerings.
　　26 F　3 If . . . we should deliberately *commit* any *sins*, then there is no
　　　　longer any sacrifice for ˹them (lit. the *sins*).
　11 25　[Moses] chose to be ill-treated . . . rather than to enjoy for a
　　　　time the pleasures of *sin*.
　12 1　we . . . should throw off . . . the *sin* that clings so easily,
　　3　2 Think of the way [Christ] stood such opposition from *sinners*
　　4　In the fight against *sin*, you have not yet had to keep fighting
　　　　to the point of death.
　13 11 F　the animals whose blood is brought into the sanctuary by the
　　　　high priest for the atonement of *sin* are burnt outside the
　　　　camp,
Jm 1 15　the desire . . . gives birth to *sin*, and . . . *sin* . . . too has a
　　　　child, and the child is death.
　2 9　as soon as you make distinctions between classes of people,
　　　　you are committing *sin*, and under condemnation for
　　　　breaking the Law.
　4 8　2 Clean your hands, you *sinners*, and clear your minds,
　　17　Everyone who knows what is the right thing to do and
　　　　doesn't do it commits a *sin*.
　5 15 F　if [the sick man] has committed any *sins*, he will be forgiven;
　　16　confess your *sins* to one another . . . and this will cure you;
　　20 F　2 (Pr 10 12) anyone who can bring back a *sinner* from the
　　　　wrong way . . . will be saving a soul from death and
　　　　covering up a great number of *sins*.
1 P 2 20　there is nothing meritorious in taking a beating patiently if
　　　3 you have *done something wrong* to deserve it.
　　22 X　[Christ] had not done anything *wrong*,
　　24　[Christ] was bearing our ˹faults (lit. *sins*) in his own body on
　　　　the cross, so that we might die to our ˹faults (lit. *sins*) and
　　　　live for holiness;
　3 18　Christ himself, innocent though he was, had died once for
　　　　sins.

1 P 4 1　anyone who in this life has bodily suffering has broken with
　　　　sin,
　8 F　(Pr 10 12) love covers over many a *sin*.
　18　(Pr 11 31) If it is hard for a good man to be saved, what will
　　　　happen to the wicked and to *sinners*?
2 P 1 9 F　[a man] has forgotten how his past *sins* were washed away.
　2 4　3 When angels *sinned*, God did not spare them:
　　14　men with an infinite capacity for *sinning*,
1 Jn 1 7 F　the blood of Jesus . . . purifies us from all *sin*.
　8　If we say we have no *sin* in us, we are deceiving ourselves
　9 F　. . . [9] but if we acknowledge our *sins*, then God . . . will
　10　3 forgive our *sins* . . . [10] To say that we have never *sinned* is
　　　　to call God a liar
　2 1　3 I am writing this . . . to stop you *sinning*; but if anyone
　　　3 should *sin*, we have our advocate . . . Jesus Christ, who is
　2 F　just; [2] he is the sacrifice that takes our *sins* away,
　12 F　I am writing to you . . . whose *sins* have already been forgiven
　　　　through his name;
　3 4　Anyone who *sins* at all breaks the law, because to *sin* is to
　5 F　break the law. [5] Now you know that he appeared in order
　6 X　to abolish *sin*, and that in him there is no *sin*; [6] anyone who
　　3/3　lives in God does not *sin*, and anyone who *sins* has never
　　　　seen him or known him.
　8 Ⓓ　to lead a *sinful* life is to belong to the devil, since the devil
　9　3 *was a sinner* from the beginning . . . [9] No one who has
　　/3　been begotten by God *sins*; . . . he cannot *sin* when he has
　　　　been begotten by God.
　4 10 F　[God] sent his Son to be the sacrifice that takes our *sins* away.
　5 16　3 If anybody sees his brother ˹commit (lit. *sin* [by committing])
　　　　a *sin* that is not [a] deadly [sin], he has only to pray, and
　　　3 God will give life to the sinner – not those who *commit* a
　17　deadly *sin*; for there is a *sin* that is death . . . [17] Every
　18　kind of wrong-doing is *sin*, but not all *sin* is deadly. [18] . . .
　　　3 anyone who has been begotten by God does not *sin*,
Jude 15　2 all the defiant things said against [the Lord] by irreligious
　　　　sinners
Rv 1 5 F　[Jesus Christ] has ˹washed (G taken) away our *sins* with his
　　　　blood,
　18 4　you do not share in [Babylon's] *crimes* and have the same
　5　plagues to bear. [5] Her *sins* have reached up to heaven,

2: SIN (AGAINST) – (DO) WRONG: *HYPER-BAINŌ*

hyper-bainō 1

1 Th 4 6　[God] wants nobody at all ever to ˹*sin* by taking (or: *sin
　　　　against* or take) advantage of a brother

8. EVIL, BAD, WICKED – WRONG: *PHAULOS*

phaulos 6

Jn 3 20　everybody who does *wrong* hates the light
　5 29 G　those who did *evil* [will rise again] to condemnation.
Rm 9 11 G　before either [Esau or Jacob] had done good or *evil*
2 Co 5 10 G　each of us will get what he deserves for the things he did in
　　　　the body, good or *bad*.
Tt 2 8　then any opponent will be at a loss, with ˹no accusation to
　　　　make (lit. nothing *bad* to say) against us.
Jm 3 16　Wherever you find jealousy and ambition, you find . . .
　　　　wicked things of every kind being done;

9. WRONG, WRONG-HEADED: *A-TOPOS*

a-topos 4

Lk 23 41 X　we are paying for what we did. But this man has done nothing
　　　　wrong.
Ac 25 5　if there is anything *wrong* about the man [Paul], they can
　　　　bring a charge against him.
　28 6　[the inhabitants of Malta] waited a long time without seeing
　　　　anything ˹out of the ordinary (lit. *wrong*) happen to [Paul],
2 Th 3 2　pray that we may be preserved from the interference of
　　　　˹bigoted (lit. *wrong-headed*) and evil people,

10. BAD, ROTTEN – EVIL: *SAPROS*

sapros 8

Mt 7 17 G　a *rotten* tree [produces] bad fruit.
　18 G　a *rotten* tree [cannot] bear good fruit.
　12 33 G　make a tree *rotten* and its fruit will be *rotten*.
　13 48 G　the fishermen . . . collect the good [fish] . . . and throw
　　　　away those that are ˹no use (lit. *bad*).
Lk 6 43 G　There is no sound tree that produces *rotten* fruit, nor again a
　　 G　*rotten* tree that produces sound fruit.

Ep 4 29 G   Guard against ˹foul talk (lit. *evil* talk passing your lips);

11. BAD, WORSE – (BECOME) INFERIOR, (BE) DOMINATED, MASTERED, BY: *HĒSSON*

2 *hēsson*   1/2   3 *hēttēma* 2
1 *hēttaomai, hēssaomai* 2/3

Rm 11 12   Think of the extent to which . . . the pagan world has
     3   benefited from [the Jews'] fall and ˹defection (lit. *becoming inferior*)
1 Co 6 7   3 It is *bad* [enough] for you to have lawsuits at all
    11 17   2 holding meetings that ˹do you more *harm* than (or: are more for the *worse* than for your) good.
2 P 2 19   if anyone lets himself be *dominated* by anything, then he is a
     20   slave to it; 20 and anyone who has escaped the pollution of the world once . . . and who then allows himself to be . . . *mastered*, will end up in a worse state than he began in.

12. WORSE: *CHEIRŌN*

cheirōn 11

Mt 9 16   the patch pulls away from the cloak and the tear gets *worse*.
   12 45   the man ends up by being *worse* than he was before.
   27 64   This last piece of fraud would be *worse* than what went before.
Mk 2 21   the patch pulls away from [the cloak], . . . and the tear gets *worse*.
   5 26   after long and painful treatment under various doctors, . . . [the woman] was getting *worse*.
Lk 11 26   the man ends up by being *worse* than he was before.
Jn 5 14   be sure not to sin any more, or something *worse* may happen to you.
1 Tm 5 8   Anyone who does not look after his own relations . . . is *worse* than an unbeliever.
2 Tm 3 13   these wicked impostors will go from bad to *worse*,

13. HARM(FUL), HURT, DO HARM: *BLAPTŌ*

2 *blaberos* 1   1 *blaptō* 2

Mk 16 18   [believers will] be un*harmed* should they drink deadly poison;
Lk 4 35   the devil . . . went out of [the man] without *hurting* him at all.
1 Tm 6 9   People who long to be rich . . . get trapped into all sorts of
     2   foolish and ˹dangerous (lit. *harmful*) ambitions

14. VILLAIN, IMPOSTOR, FRAUD – CRIME: *RHADI-OURGĒMA*

1 *rhadi-ourgēma* 1   2 *rhadi-ourgia* 1

Ac 13 10   2 [Paul said to Elymas:] You utter fraud, you ˹impostor (or: *villain*),
   18 14   If this were a misdemeanour or a *crime*, I would not hesitate to attend to you;

15. BREAK (THE LAW) – DISOBEY

1: BREAK (THE LAW) – INFRINGE, DISOBEY – SIN, DO WRONG: *PARA-BASIS*

3 *para-bainō* 2/3   2 *para-batēs* 5
1 *para-basis* 7

Mt 15 2   3 Why do your disciples ˹break away from (or: *break*) the tradition of the elders?
     3   3 And why do you . . . ˹break away from (or: *break*) the commandment of God . . .?
Rm 2 23   By boasting about the Law and then *disobeying* it, you bring God into contempt.
     25   2 if you *break* the Law, you might as well have stayed uncircumcised.
     27   the man who keeps the Law . . . is a living condemnation of
       2   the way you *disobey* the Law in spite of being circumcised
   4 15   Law involves the possibility of punishment for *breaking* the law
   5 14   death reigned over all from Adam to Moses, even though their sin, unlike that of Adam, was not a matter of *breaking* a law.
Ga 2 18   2 I should be admitting I had *done something wrong*.
   3 19   What then was the purpose of adding the Law? This was done to specify *crimes*,
1 Tm 2 14   the woman . . . was led astray and fell into *sin*.
Heb 2 2   every *infringement* and disobedience brought its own proper punishment,
   9 15   his death took place to cancel the *sins* that infringed the earlier covenant.
Jm 2 9   as soon as you make distinctions between classes of people,
     2   you are . . . under condemnation for *breaking* the Law.
     11   if you commit murder, you do not have to commit adultery as
     2   well to become a *breaker* of the Law.

2: DISOBEY: *PAR-ERCHOMAI*

par-erchomai 1/30

Lk 15 29   I have slaved for you and never once *disobeyed* your orders,

16. TAINTED, DEBASED: *A-CHREOŌ*

a-chreoō 1

Rm 3 12   (Ps 14 3) All have turned aside, *tainted* all alike;

F

FACE

1: FACE – PRESENCE – APPEARANCE

a) Face (of God) – the Presence (of God)

1 Co 13	12	Now we are seeing a dim reflection . . . but then we shall be seeing *face* to *face*.
1 P 3	12	(Ps 34 16) the *face* of the Lord frowns on evil men,
Jude	24	Glory be to him who can . . . bring you safe to his glorious *presence*,
Rv 6	16	hide us away from (G the *face* of) the One who sits on the throne
22	4	[God's servants] will see his *face*, and his name will be written on their foreheads.

b) Face (of Jesus) – (Jesus sets his) Face (toward)

Mt 17	2	his *face* shone like the sun
26	39	he fell on his *face* and prayed. 'My Father,' he said
	67	they spat in his *face*
Mk 14	65	Some of them . . . blindfolding him (lit. covering his *face* with a cloth), began hitting him with their fists
Lk 9	29	As he prayed, the aspect of his *face* was changed
	51	he resolutely took the road for (lit. set his *face* toward) Jerusalem
	53	the people would not receive him because he was making for (lit. had set his *face* toward) Jerusalem.
2 Co 4	6	God's glory, the glory on the *face* of Christ.
Rv 1	16	his *face* was like the sun shining with all its force.

c) Face, Features – (Fall) on one's Face
A = Angel

Mt 6	16	the hypocrites . . . pull long *faces* to let men know they are fasting.
	17	when you fast, put oil on your head and wash your *face*,
17	6	the disciples fell on their *faces*,
Lk 5	12	Seeing Jesus [the leper] fell on his *face*
17	16	[one of the ten lepers] threw himself (lit. fell on his *face*) at the feet of Jesus
24	5	Terrified, the women lowered their eyes (lit. turned their *faces* to the ground).
Jn 11	44	The dead man [Lazarus] came out . . . with . . . a cloth round his *face*.
Ac 5	41	[the apostles] left the *presence* of the Sanhedrin
6 15 A		[Stephen's] *face* appeared to them like the *face* of an angel.
20	25	I now feel sure that none of you . . . will ever see my *face* again.
	38	they would never see [Paul's] *face* again.
25	16	until the accused confronts (lit. *faces*) his accusers
1 Co 13	12	Now we are seeing a dim reflection . . . but then we shall be seeing *face* to *face*.
14	25	[an unbeliever or uninitiated person] would . . . fall on his *face* and worship God,
2 Co 3	7	the Israelites could not bear looking at the *face* of Moses because of the brightness of his *face*
	13	Moses . . . put a veil over his *face*
	18	we, with our unveiled *faces* reflecting . . . the brightness of the Lord,
10	1	I, the man who is so humbled when he is *facing* you, but bullies you when he is at a distance.
	7	*Face* plain facts (or: You see only what is superficial).
11	20	[you tolerate] somebody who . . . slaps you in the *face*.
Ga 1	22	[I, Paul] was still not known by sight (lit. by my *face*) to the churches of Christ in Judaea,
2	11	When Cephas came to Antioch, however, I opposed him to his *face*,
Col 2	1	many others who have never seen my *face*.
1 Th 2	17	after we had been separated from you – in body (lit. in *presence*) but never in thought, brothers – we had an especially strong desire and longing to see your *face* again,
3	10	We are earnestly praying . . . to be able to see your *face* again
Jm 1	23	To listen to the word and not obey is like looking at your own *features* in a mirror
Rv 4	7	the third animal had a human *face*,
7 11 A		all the angels . . . *touched the ground with their foreheads*,
9	7	[the locusts] had . . . *faces* that seemed to be human *faces*,
10 1 A		I saw another . . . angel . . . his *face* was like the sun,
11	16	The twenty-four elders . . . *touched the ground with their foreheads* worshipping God
12 14 ⒟		away from (G the *face* of) the serpent

d) Face (of the earth) – Appearance (of the sky)

Mt 16	3	You know how to read the *face* of the sky,
Lk 12	56	You know how to interpret the *face* of the earth and the sky.
21	35	every living man on the *face* of the earth.
Ac 17	26	[God] created the whole human race so that they could occupy the entire (lit. the whole *face* of the) earth,

2: FOREHEAD (*MET-ŌPON*)

Rv 7	3	2 Wait . . . until we have put the seal on the *foreheads* of the servants of our God.
9	4	[the locusts] were . . . told only to attack any men who were 2 without God's seal on their *foreheads*.
13	16	[the beast] compelled everyone . . . to be branded on the 2 right hand or on the *forehead*,
14	1	144 000 people, all with [the Lamb's] name and his Father's 2 name written on their *foreheads*.
	9	All those who worship the beast . . . or have had themselves 2 branded on the hand or *forehead*,
17	5	2 on her *forehead* was written a name . . . Babylon the Great,
20	4	I saw . . . those who refused to . . . have the brand-mark on 2 their *foreheads*
22	4	2 [God's] name will be written on their *foreheads*.

FARM

1. TENANT-FARMER – VINEDRESSER, VINEYARD, VINE

1: TENANT-FARMER – FARM, CULTIVATE: *GE-ŌRGOS*

    2 *ge-ōrgeō* 1   1 *ge-ōrgos* 19
    3 *ge-ōrgion* 1

Mt 21	33	There was a man . . . who planted a vineyard . . . then he
	34 <	leased it to *tenants* . . .³⁴ . . . he sent his servants to

Mt 21	35 <	*tenants* to collect his produce. ³⁵ But the *tenants* seized his servants,
	38 <	when the *tenants* saw the son, they said . . . 'let us kill him'
	40 <	what will [the owner] do to those *tenants*?
	41 <	He will . . . lease the vineyard to other *tenants*
Mk 12	1 <	A man planted a vineyard . . . then he leased it to *tenants* and went abroad. ² When the time came, he sent a servant
	2 <	to the *tenants* to collect from ⌐them (lit. the *tenants*) his share of the produce from the vineyard.
	7 <	those *tenants* said to each other, 'This is the heir . . . let us kill him'
	9 <	the owner of the vineyard . . . will come and make an end of the *tenants* and give the vineyard to others.
Lk 20	9 <	A man planted a vineyard and leased it to *tenants*, and went
	10 <	abroad . . . ¹⁰ . . . he sent a servant to the *tenants* to get his share of the produce of the vineyard from them. But
	<	the *tenants* . . . sent him away empty-handed.
	14 <	when the *tenants* saw him they put their heads together. 'This is the heir,'
	16 <	[The owner of the vineyard] will come and make an end of these *tenants* and give the vineyard to others.
Jn 15	1 Θ	I am the true vine, and my Father is the *vinedresser*.
1 Co 3	9	3 you are God's *farm*, God's building.
2 Tm 2	6	the working *farmer* . . . has the first claim on any crop that is harvested.
Heb 6	7	A field . . . gives the crops that are wanted by the owners
	2	who ⌐grew (lit. *cultivated*) them,
Jm 5	7	Think of the *farmer*: how patiently he waits for the precious fruit of the ground

2: VINEDRESSER: *AMPEL-OURGOS*

ampel-ourgos 1

Lk 13	7 <	[The owner] said to the ⌐*man who looked after the vineyard* (or: *vinedresser*), 'Look here, for three years now I have been coming to look for fruit on this fig tree and finding none.'

3: VINEYARD, VINE: *AMPELOS*

2 ampelos 9   *1 ampelōn 23*

Mt 20	1	the kingdom of heaven is like a landowner going out at day-break to hire workers for his *vineyard*. ² He made an
	2	agreement with the workers for one denarius a day, and sent them to his *vineyard*.
	4	You go to my *vineyard* too
	7	You go into my *vineyard* too.
	8	In the evening, the owner of the *vineyard* said to his bailiff,
21	28	My boy, you go and work in the *vineyard* today.
	33	There was a man, a landowner, who planted a *vineyard*
	39	[the tenants] threw [the son] out of the *vineyard* and killed him.
	40	Now when the owner of the *vineyard* comes, what will he
	41	do to those tenants? ⁴¹ . . . he will lease the *vineyard* to other tenants who will deliver the produce to him
26	29	2 I shall not drink new ⌐wine (lit. the fruit of the *vine*) until the day I drink the new [wine] with you
Mk 12	1	A man planted a *vineyard* . . . he leased it to tenants and
	2	went abroad. ² When the time came, he sent a servant to the tenants to collect . . . his share of the produce from the *vineyard*.
	8	they killed [the son] and threw him out of the *vineyard*.
	9	Now what will the owner of the *vineyard* do? He will . . . make an end of the tenants and give the *vineyard* to others.
14	25	2 I shall not drink any more ⌐wine (lit. of the fruit of the *vine*) until the day I drink the new [wine]
Lk 13	6	A man had a fig tree planted in his *vineyard*,
20	9	A man planted a *vineyard* and leased it to tenants,
	10	he sent a servant to the tenants to get his share of the produce of the *vineyard*
	13	the owner of the *vineyard* said, '. . . I will send them my dear son.'
	15	they threw [the son] out of the *vineyard* and killed him. Now
	16	what will the owner of the *vineyard* do to them? ¹⁶ He will make an end of these tenants and give the *vineyard* to others.
22	18	2 I shall not drink ⌐wine (lit. the fruit of the *vine*) until the day I drink the new [wine]
Jn 15	1 X	2 I am the true *vine* and my Father is the vinedresser,
	4	As a branch cannot bear fruit all by itself, but must remain
	2	part of the *vine*, neither can you unless you remain in me.
	5 X	2 ⁵ I am the *vine*, you are the branches.
1 Co 9	7	nobody ever planted a *vineyard* and refused to eat the fruit of it.
Jm 3	12	2 Can a fig tree give you olives . . . or a *vine* give figs?
Rv 14	18	2 Cut all the bunches off the *vine* of the earth; all its grapes
	19	are ripe. ¹⁹ So the angel set his sickle to work on the earth
	2	and harvested the whole *vintage* of the earth,

2. CROPS – GRASS

1: CROPS – VEGETATION: *BOTANĒ*

botanē 1

Heb 6	7	A field . . . gives the *crops* that are wanted by the owners who grew them,

2: CROPS – GREEN GROWTH: *CHLŌROS*

chlōros 1/4

Rv 9	4	[the locusts] were forbidden to harm any fields or *crops* or trees.

3: GRASS, BLADE, HAY – FIELD: *CHORTOS*

chortos 15

Mt 6	30	Now if that is how God clothes the *grass* in the field which is there today and thrown into the furnace tomorrow,
13	26	the new ⌐wheat (lit. *grass*) sprouted and ripened,
14	19	[Jesus] gave orders that the people were to sit down on the *grass*.
Mk 4	28	Of its own accord the land produces first the ⌐*shoot* (or: *blade*) then the ear,
6	39	The [Jesus] ordered them to get all the people together in groups on the green *grass*.
Lk 12	28	God clothes the *grass* in the field which is there today and thrown into the furnace tomorrow,
Jn 6	10	There was plenty of *grass* there.
1 Co 3	12	On this foundation you can build . . . in wood, *grass* and straw.
Jm 1	10	[it is right for] the rich one to be thankful that he has been humbled, because riches last no longer than the flowers in
	11	the *grass*; ¹¹ the scorching sun comes up, and the *grass* withers, the flower falls.
1 P 1	24	(Is 40 6–7) All flesh is *grass* and its glory like the ⌐wild flower's (lit. flower's in the *field*). The *grass* withers, the flower falls.
Rv 8	7	every blade of *grass* was burnt.
9	4	[the locusts] were forbidden to harm any *fields* or crops

3. SOW, SEED – CORN, WHEAT, BARLEY – DARNEL

1: SEED – GRAIN: *KOKKOS*

kokkos 7

Mt 13	31 <	The kingdom of heaven is like a mustard *seed*
17	20 <	if your faith were the size of a mustard *seed*
Mk 4	31 <	[The kingdom of God] is like a mustard *seed*
Lk 13	19 <	[The kingdom of God] is like a mustard *seed*
17	6 <	Were your faith the size of a mustard *seed*
Jn 12	24 <	unless a wheat *grain* falls on the ground and dies, it remains only a single grain;
1 Co 15	37	the thing that you sow is not what is going to come; you sow a bare *grain*,

2: SOW, SEED and EARS OF CORN: *SPEIRŌ* and *STACHYS*

1	speirō	52	3 sporos	5
2	sperma	9/44	6 epi-speirō	1
5	spora	1	7 spermo(-logos)	1
4	sporimos	3		

a) Sow, Sower – Seed

Mt 6	26	Look at the birds in the sky. They do not *sow* or reap
13	3 <	Imagine a *sower* going out to *sow*. ⁴ As he *sowed*, some [seeds]
	4	fell on the edge of the path.
	18 <	You . . . are to hear the parable of the *sower*.
	19 <	the evil one comes and carries off what was *sown* in his heart: this is the man who *received the seed* on the edge of the path.
	20 <	The one who *received the seed* on patches of rock is the man who hears the word . . . ²¹ but he has no root in him,
	22 <	The one who *received the seed* in thorns is the man who hears the word, but the worries of this world . . . choke the word,
	23 <	the one who *received the seed* in rich soil is the man who hears the word and understands it;
	24 <	The kingdom of heaven may be compared to a man who
	25 < 2/	*sowed* good seed in his field. ²⁵ . . . his enemy . . .
	< 6	*sowed* darnel all *among* the wheat,
	27 < 2/	Sir, was it not good seed that you *sowed* in your field?
	31	The kingdom of heaven is like a mustard seed which a man
	32 < 2/	. . . *sowed* in his field. ³² It is the smallest of all the *seeds*,

Mt 13 37 X /2 The *sower* of the good *seed* is the Son of Man. [38] . . . the
38　　2　good *seed* is the subjects of the kingdom; the darnel, the
39 Ⓓ　subjects of the evil one; [39] the enemy who *sowed* them, the devil;
25 24 <　[You are a hard man] reaping where you have not *sown* and gathering where you have not scattered;
26 <　So you knew that I reap where I have not *sown*

Mk 4 3 <　Imagine a *sower* going out to sow. [4] . . . as he *sowed* some
4　[of the seed] fell on the edge of the path,
14 <　What the *sower* is *sowing* is the word. [15] Those on the edge of
15 <　the path where the word is *sown* . . . Satan comes and
16 <　carries away the word that was *sown* in them. [16] . . . those
<　who *receive the seed* on patches of rock are people who . . . welcome [the word] . . . [17] but they have no root in them,
18 <　there are others who *receive the seed* in thorns.
20 <　there are those who have *received the seed* in rich soil: they hear the word and accept it
26 <　This is what the kingdom of God is like. A man throws
27　3　*seed* on the land. [27] . . . while he sleeps, when he is awake,
< 3　the *seed* is sprouting and growing;
31　[The kingdom of God] is like a mustard seed which at the
<　time of its *sowing* in the soil is the smallest of all the
32 < 2/　*seeds* . . . [32] yet once it is *sown* it grows into the biggest shrub of them all

Lk 8 5 <//3| A *sower* went out to sow his *seed*. As he *sowed*, some fell on the edge of the path
11 < 3　the *seed* is the word of God.
12 24　Think of the ravens. They do not *sow* or reap;
19 21 <　I was afraid of you; for you . . . reap what you have not *sown*.
22　So you knew I was an exacting man . . . reaping what I
<　have not *sown*?

Jn 4 36　thus *sower* and reaper rejoice together. [37] For here the
37　proverb holds good: one *sows*, another reaps;

Ac 17 18　7 Does this ⌈parrot (lit. *seed*-collector) know what he's talking about?

1 Co 9 11　we have *sown* spiritual things for you,
15 36　They are stupid questions. Whatever you *sow* in the ground
37　has to die before it is given new life [37] and the thing that you *sow* is not what is going to come; you *sow* a bare grain
38　. . . [38] and then God gives it the sort of body that he
2　has chosen: each sort of *seed* gets its own sort of body.
42　the thing that is *sown* is perishable but what is raised is
43　imperishable; [43] the thing that is *sown* is contemptible but what is raised is glorious; the thing that is *sown* is
44　weak but what is raised is powerful; [44] when it is *sown* it embodies the soul, when it is raised it embodies the spirit.

2 Co 9 6　thin *sowing* means thin reaping; the more you *sow*, the more you reap.
10　2/ The one who provides *seed* for the *sower* . . . will provide
3　you with all the *seed* you want

Ga 6 7　where a man *sows*, there he reaps: [8] if he *sows* in the field of self-indulgence he will get a harvest of corruption out of it; if he *sows* in the field of the Spirit he will get from it a harvest of eternal life.

Jm 3 18　Peacemakers, when they work for peace, *sow* the seeds which will bear fruit in holiness.

1 P 1 23　5 your new birth was not from any mortal *seed* but from the everlasting word of the living . . . God.

1 Jn 3 9　No one who has been begotten by God sins; because God's
Δ 2　*seed* remains inside him,

b) Ears of corn, Cornfields (= Fields sown with corn seed)

8 stachys 5

Mt 12 1　4 Jesus took a walk . . . through the *cornfields*. His disciples
8　. . . began to pick *ears of corn* and eat them.

Mk 2 23　4 [Jesus] happened to be taking a walk through the *cornfields*,
8　and his disciples began to pick *ears of corn*
4 28　8 the land produces first the shoot, then the *ear*, then the full
8　grain in the *ear*.

Lk 6 1　4 [Jesus] happened to be taking a walk through the *cornfields*,
8　and his disciples were picking *ears of corn*,

3: WHEAT – CORN: SITOS

1 sitos 14　　2 sito(-metrion) 1

Mt 3 12　[Jesus will] gather his *wheat* into the barn;
13 25　his enemy . . . sowed darnel all among the *wheat*, and made off. [26] . . . the new ⌈wheat (lit. grass) sprouted and ripened
29　when you weed out the darnel you might pull up the *wheat* with it.
30　First collect the darnel . . . then gather the *wheat* into my barn.

Mk 4 28　the land produces first the shoot, then the ear, then the full ⌈grain (lit. *corn*) in the ear.

Lk 3 17　[Christ's] winnowing-fan is in his hand . . . to gather the *wheat* into his barn;

Lk 12 18　[The rich man thought to himself,] I will . . . store all my ⌈grain (lit. *corn*) and my goods [in the new barns],
42　What sort of steward [is good enough] for the master to place him over his household to give them their allowance
2　of ⌈food (lit. *corn*) . . . ?
16 7　how much do you owe? One hundred measures of *wheat*
22 31　Satan . . . has got his wish to sift you all like *wheat*.

Jn 12 24　unless a *wheat* grain falls on the ground and dies, it remains only a single grain.

Ac 27 38　they lightened the ship by throwing the *corn* overboard

1 Co 15 37　you sow a bare grain, say of *wheat* or something like that,

Rv 6 6　A ration of *corn* for a day's wages, and three rations of barley for a day's wages,
18 13　[nobody left to buy their] wine, oil, flour and *corn*.

4: BARLEY: KRITHĒ

2 krithē 1　　1 krithinos 2

Jn 6 9　There is a small boy here with five *barley* loaves and two fish.
13　[the disciples] filled twelve hampers with scraps left over from the meal of five *barley* loaves.

Rv 6 6　2 A ration of corn for a day's wages, and three rations of *barley* for a day's wages

5: DARNEL – WEEDS: ZIZANION

zizanion 8

Mt 13 25　his enemy came, sowed *darnel* all among the wheat, and made off.
26　When the new wheat sprouted . . . the *darnel* appeared as well.
27　Was it not good seed that you sowed . . .? If so, where does the *darnel* come from?
29　when you weed out the *darnel* you might pull up the wheat with it.
30　First collect the *darnel* . . . then gather the wheat
36　Explain the parable about the *darnel* in the field to us.
38　the *darnel* is the subjects of the evil one.
40　the *darnel* is gathered up and burnt in the fire

4. STRAW, STUBBLE – CHAFF

1: STRAW, STUBBLE: KALAMĒ

kalamē 1

1 Co 3 12　On this foundation you can build . . . in wood, grass and *straw*,

2: CHAFF: ACHYRON

achyron 2

Mt 3 12　But the *chaff* he will burn in a fire that will never go out.
Lk 3 17　but the *chaff* he will burn in a fire that will never go out.

5. OLIVE: ELAIA

1 elaia 4/13　　2 agri-elaios 2
　　　　　　　3 kalli-elaios 1

Rm 11 17　some of the branches have been cut off, and, like shoots of
2　*wild olive*, you have been grafted among the rest to share with them (§ the root and) the rich sap provided by the *olive tree* itself,
24　2 if you were cut from your natural *wild olive* to be grafted
3　unnaturally on to a *cultivated olive*, it will be much easier for them, the natural branches, to be grafted back on the *olive tree*

Jm 3 12　Can a fig tree give you *olives* . . . or a vine give figs?
Rv 11 4　[my two witnesses] are the two *olive trees* and the two lamps

6. BARN – WINEPRESS

1: BARN, GRANARY: APO-THĒKĒ

apo-thēkē 6

Mt 3 12　[the one who follows me] will . . . gather his wheat into the *barn*;

Mt 6 26   Look at the birds in the sky. They do not . . . gather into barns;
    13 30 <   gather the wheat into my *barn*.
Lk 3 17   [the one who is more powerful than I am will] gather the wheat into his *barn*;
    12 18 <   I will pull down my *barns* and build bigger ones,
    24   the ravens . . . have no storehouses and no *barns*;

2: WINEPRESS: *LĒNOS*

1 *lēnos* 5   2 *hypo-lēnion* 1

Mt 21 33   a landowner who planted a vineyard . . . dug a *winepress* in it
Mk 12 1   A man planted a vineyard; he . . . dug out a trough for the
    2   *winepress*
Rv 14 19   the angel . . . harvested the whole vintage . . . and put it
    20   into . . . the *winepress* of God's anger, [20] a huge *winepress* outside the city, where it was trodden until the blood . . . came out of the *winepress*
    19 15   [The Word of God] is the one who will . . . tread ˹out the wine (lit. the *winepress*) of Almighty God's fierce anger.

7. (TO) PLANT: *PHYTEUŌ*

2 *phyteia* 1	3 *em-phytos* 1
1 *phyteuō* 11	4 (*neo-*)*phytos* 1
	5 *sym-phytos* 1

Mt 15 13 Θ 2/   Any *plant* my heavenly Father has not *planted* will be pulled up by the roots.
    21 33 <   a man . . . *planted* a vineyard . . . then he leased it to tenants
Mk 12 1 <   A man *planted* a vineyard . . . then he leased it to tenants
Lk 13 6 <   A man had a fig tree *planted* in his vineyard,
    17 6   Be uprooted and *planted* in the sea,
    28   in Lot's day people were . . . *planting* and building.
    20 9 <   A man *planted* a vineyard and leased it to tenants,
Rm 6 5 ●   5   ˹in union (or: being part of the same *plant*) with Christ we have imitated his death,
1 Co 3 6   I did the *planting*, Apollos did the watering, but God made
    7   things grow. [7] Neither the *planter* nor the waterer matters:
    8   only God who makes things grow. [8] It is all one who does the *planting* and who does the watering,
    9 7   nobody ever *planted* a vineyard and refused to eat the fruit of it.
1 Tm 3 6   4   [The elder] should not be a new ˹convert (or: *plant*),
Jm 1 21   3   accept and submit to the word which has been *planted* in you

8. (TO) GRAFT: *EN-KENTRIZŌ*

en-kentrizō 6

Rm 11 17   like shoots of wild olive, you have been *grafted* among the rest to share with them the rich sap provided by the olive tree itself,
    19   You will say, 'Those branches were cut off on purpose to let me be *grafted* in!'
    23   if they give up their unbelief, [the Jews will be] *grafted*
     Θ   back in your place. God is perfectly able to *graft* them back
    24   again; [24] after all, if you were cut . . . to be *grafted* unnaturally on to a cultivated olive, it will be much easier for them, the natural branches, to be *grafted* back on the tree they came from.

9. PLOUGH: *AROTRIAŌ*

1 *arotriaō* 3   2 *arotron* 1

Lk 9 62 <   2   Once the hand is laid on the *plough*, no one who looks back is fit for the kingdom of God.
    17 7   Which of you, with a servant *ploughing* or minding sheep . . .?
1 Co 9 10   the *plough*man ought to *plough* in expectation,

10. REAP – HARVEST – GATHER

1: HARVEST – REAP, MOW

a) Reap – Harvest: therismos

2 therismos 13	1 therizō 21
3 theristēs 2	

Mt 6 26   the birds in the sky . . . do not sow or *reap*

Mt 9 37 <   2   The *harvest* is rich but the labourers are few, [38] so ask the
    38 <2/2   Lord of the *harvest* to send labourers to his *harvest*.
    13 30 <2/2   Let them both grow till the *harvest*; and at *harvest* time I
    <   3   shall say to the *reapers*: First collect the darnel . . . to be burnt, then gather the wheat
    39 <2/3   the *harvest* is the end of the world; the *reapers* are the angels.
    25 24 <   I had heard you were a hard man, *reaping* where you have not sown
    26 <   I *reap* where I have not sown
Mk 4 29   when the crop is ready, he loses no time: he ˹starts to reap
    <   2   (lit. puts in his sickle) because the *harvest* has come.
Lk 10 2 <   2   The *harvest* is rich but the labourers are few, so ask the Lord
    <2/2   of the *harvest* to send labourers to his *harvest*.
    12 24   the ravens . . . do not sow or *reap*;
    19 21 <   you are an exacting man: you . . . *reap* what you have not sown.
    22 <   So you knew I was an exacting man . . . *reaping* what I have not sown?
Jn 4 35   Have you not got a saying: Four months and then the
    2   *harvest*? Well . . . look at the fields; already they are white,
    36 2/   ready for *harvest*! Already [36] the *reaper* is being paid his wages, already he is bringing in the grain for eternal life,
    37   and thus sower and *reaper* rejoice together. [37] . . . one
    38   sows, another *reaps*; [38] I sent you to *reap* a harvest you had not worked for.
1 Co 9 11   If we have sown spiritual things for you, why should you be surprised if we *harvest* your material things?
2 Co 9 6   thin sowing means thin *reaping*; the more you sow, the more you *reap*.
Ga 6 7   where a man sows, there he *reaps*: [8] if he sows in the field
    8   of self-indulgence he will *get a harvest of* corruption out of it; if he sows in the field of the Spirit he will *get* from it
    9   *a harvest of* eternal life. [9] We must never get tired of doing good . . . we shall *get our harvest* at the proper time.
Jm 5 4   the cries of the *reapers* have reached the ears of the Lord
Rv 14 15   Put your sickle in and *reap*: *harvest* time has come and the
    16   2   *harvest* of the earth is ripe. [16] Then . . . the earth's harvest was *reaped*.

b) Mow: amaō

amaō 1

Jm 5 4   Labourers *mowed* your fields, and you cheated them

2: SICKLE: *DREPANON*

drepanon 8

Mk 4 29   he ˹starts to reap (lit. puts in his *sickle*) because the harvest has come.
Rv 14 14   a son of man with . . . a sharp *sickle* in his hand.
    15   another angel . . . shouted . . . 'Put your *sickle* in and reap'
    16   the one sitting . . . set his *sickle* to work on the earth,
    17   Another angel . . . also carried a sharp *sickle*.
    18   the angel . . . shouted aloud to the one with the sharp *sickle* 'Put your *sickle* in and cut all the bunches off the vine'
    19   So the angel set his *sickle* to work on the earth and harvested the whole vintage of the earth

3: GATHER – HARVEST: *TRYGAŌ*

trygaō 3

Lk 6 44   people do not . . . *gather* grapes from brambles.
Rv 14 18   *cut* all the bunches *off* the vine of the earth; all its grapes are
    19   ripe. [19] So the angel set his sickle to work on the earth and *harvested* the whole vintage

11. WINNOWING – THRESHING – SIFTING

1: WINNOWING-FAN – THRESHING-FLOOR: *PTUON* and *HALŌN*

1 *halōn* 2   2 *ptuon* 2

Mt 3 12 X 2/   His *winnowing-fan* is in his hand; he will clear his *threshing-floor*
Lk 3 17 X 2/   His *winnowing-fan* is in his hand to clear his *threshing-floor*

2: THRESH – TREAD OUT: *ALOAŌ*

aloaō 3

1 Co 9 9   (Dt 25 4) You must not put a muzzle on the ox when it is *treading out* the corn.
    10   the *thresher* [ought to thresh] in the expectation of getting his share.

1 Tm 5 18 (Dt 25 4) You must not muzzle an ox when it is *treading out* the corn;

3: SIFT: *SINIAZŌ*
siniazō 1

Lk 22 31 Simon, . . . Satan . . . has got his wish to *sift* you all

FATHER – MOTHER

1. Father: *patēr*
  1: God the Father
    a) (Jesus's) Father – (God the) Father
    b) (Man's heavenly) Father – (Our) Father
    c) Father (of mercies, glory, spirits, light)
  2: The Devil as Father
  3: Human Fathers
    a) Father
    b) Father and Mother
    c) Parents
    d) Father = Ancestor, Patriarch
  4: Family – Lineage, Line (of descent)
  5: "Fatherland" = Home town, Own country
2. Mother: *mētēr*
  1: Mother
  2: (Jesus's) Mother
3. Grandmother: *mammē*
4. Parents: *goneis*
5. Orphans – Bereft: *orphanos*

1. FATHER: *PATĒR*

1	*patēr*	415	3	*patri-archēs*	4
4	*patria*	3	7	*patro(-lōēs)*	1
6	*patrikos*	1	8	*patro(-para-dotos)*	1
2	*patris*	8	9	*a-patōr*	1
5	*patrōos*	3	10	*pro-patōr*	1

1: GOD THE FATHER
11 *Abba* 3

a) (*Jesus's*) *Father* – (*God the*) *Father*

Mt 7 21 the person who does the will of my *Father* in heaven.
  10 32 I will declare myself for him in the presence of my *Father* in heaven.
    33 I will disown [him] in the presence of my *Father* in heaven.
  11 25 I bless you, *Father*, Lord of heaven and of earth,
    26 Yes, *Father*, for that is what it pleased you to do.
    27 Everything has been entrusted to me by my *Father*; and no one knows the Son except the *Father*, just as no one knows the *Father* except the Son
  12 50 Anyone who does the will of my *Father* in heaven,
  15 13 Any plant my heavenly *Father* has not planted will be pulled up by the roots.
  16 17 it was not flesh and blood that revealed this to you but my *Father* in heaven.
    27 the Son of Man is going to come in the glory of his *Father*
  18 10 their angels . . . are continually in the presence of my *Father* in heaven.
    19 if two of you on earth agree to ask anything . . . it will be granted . . . by my *Father* in heaven.
    35 that is how my heavenly *Father* will deal with you
  20 23 they belong to those to whom they have been allotted by my *Father*.
  24 36 as for that day and hour, nobody knows it, . . . but the *Father* only.
  25 34 Come, you whom my *Father* has blessed, take for your heritage the kingdom prepared for you
  26 29 From now on . . . I shall not drink wine until the day I drink the new wine with you in the kingdom of my *Father*.
    39 My *Father*, . . . if it is possible, let this cup pass me by.
    42 My *Father*, . . . your will be done!
    53 do you think that I cannot appeal to my *Father* . . .?
  28 19 baptise them in the name of the *Father* and of the Son and of the Holy Spirit,
Mk 8 38 when [the Son of Man] comes in the glory of his *Father*
  13 32 as for that day or hour, nobody knows it, . . . but the *Father*.
  14 36 11/ '*Abba* (*Father*)!' [Jesus] said '. . . Take this cup away from me.'
Lk 2 49 Did you not know that I must be busy with my *Father's* affairs?
  9 26 when [the Son of Man] comes in his own glory and in the glory of the *Father*
  10 21 I bless you, *Father*, . . . for hiding these things from the learned . . . Yes, *Father*, for that is what it pleased you to do.

Lk 10 22 Everything has been entrusted to me by my *Father*; and no one knows who the Son is except the *Father*, and who the *Father* is except the Son
  22 29 I confer a kingdom on you, just as my *Father* conferred one on me:
    42 *Father*, . . . if you are willing, take this cup away from me.
  →23 34 *Father*, forgive them; they do not know what they are doing.
    46 *Father*, into your hands I commit my spirit.
  24 49 And now I am sending down to you what the *Father* has promised.
Jn 1 14 the glory that is his as the only Son of the *Father*,
    18 the only Son who is nearest to the *Father's* heart,
  2 16 stop turning my *Father's* house into a market.
  3 35 The *Father* loves the Son and has entrusted everything to him.
  4 21 the hour is coming when you will worship the *Father* neither on this mountain nor in Jerusalem. . . . 23 . . . true worshippers will worship the *Father* in spirit and truth: that is the kind of worshipper the *Father* wants.
  5 17 My *Father* goes on working,
    18 he spoke of God as his own *Father*,
    19 the Son can do nothing by himself; he can do only what he sees the *Father* doing:
    20 For the *Father* loves the Son and shows him everything he does himself,
    21 as the *Father* raises the dead and gives them life, so the Son gives life
    22 for the *Father* judges no one;
    23 so that all may honour the Son as they honour the *Father*. Whoever refuses to honour the Son refuses honour to the *Father* who sent him.
    26 the *Father*, who is the source of life, has made the Son the source of life;
    36 the works my *Father* has given me to carry out . . . testify
    37 that the *Father* has sent me. 37 Besides, the *Father* who sent me bears witness to me himself.
    43 I have come in the name of my *Father*
    45 Do not imagine that I am going to accuse you before the *Father*:
  6 27 for on [the Son of Man] the *Father*, God himself, has set his seal.
    32 it was not Moses who gave you bread from heaven, it is my *Father*
    37 All that the *Father* gives me will come to me,
    40 it is my *Father's* will that whoever sees the Son and believes in him shall have eternal life,
    44 No one can come to me unless he is drawn by the *Father* who sent me,
    45 to hear the teaching of the *Father*, and learn from it, is to come to me.
    46 Not that anybody has seen the *Father*, except the one who comes from God: he has seen the *Father*.
    57 I, who am sent by the living *Father*,
    65 I told you that no one could come to me unless the *Father* allows him.
  8 16 the one who sent me (ᵛ – the *Father* –) is with me;
    18 the *Father* who sent me is my witness too.
    19 'Where is your *Father*?' Jesus answered: 'You do not know me, nor do you know my *Father*; if you did know me, you would know my *Father* as well'.
    27 [The Jews] failed to understand that he was talking to them about the *Father*.
    28 what the *Father* has taught me is what I preach;
    38 What I . . . speak of is what I have seen with my *Father*;
    49 I am not possessed; no, I honour my *Father*,
    54 my glory is conferred by the *Father*,
  10 15 just as the *Father* knows me and I know the *Father*;
    17 The *Father* loves me, because I lay down my life
    18 this is the command I have been given by my *Father*.
    25 The works I do in my *Father's* name
    29 The *Father* who gave [the sheep] to me is greater than anyone, and no one can steal from the *Father*.
    30 The *Father* and I are one.
    32 I have done many good works for you to see, works from my *Father*;
    36 someone the *Father* has consecrated and sent into the world,
    37 If I am not doing my *Father's* work, there is no need to believe me;
    38 the *Father* is in me and I am in the *Father*.
  11 41 *Father*, I thank you for hearing my prayer.
  12 26 If anyone serves me, my *Father* will honour him.
    27 What shall I say: *Father*, save me from this hour?
    28 *Father*, glorify your name!
    49 what I was to say . . . was commanded by the *Father* who sent me, 50 . . . what the *Father* has told me is what I speak.
  13 1 Jesus knew that the hour had come for him to pass from this world to the *Father*.
    3 Jesus knew that the *Father* had put everything into his hands,
  14 2 There are many rooms in my *Father's* house;
    6 I am the Way . . . No one can come to the *Father* except through me. 7 If you know me, you know my *Father* too.

Jn 14	8	... 8 Philip said, 'Lord, let us see the *Father* ...'....
	9	9 ... 'To have seen me is to have seen the *Father*, so how
	10	can you say, "Let us see the *Father*?" 10 Do you not believe that I am in the *Father* and the *Father* is in me? ... it is the *Father*, living in me, who is doing this work.
	11	11 You must believe me when I say that I am in the *Father* and the *Father* is in me;'
	12	because I am going to the *Father*.
	13	so that the *Father* may be glorified in the Son.
	16	I shall ask the *Father*, and he will give you another Advocate
	20	I am in my *Father* and you in me and I in you.
	21	anybody who loves me will be loved by my *Father*,
	23	if anyone loves me he will keep my word, and my *Father* will love him,
	24	my word is not my own: it is the word of the ᵛ one (G *Father*) who sent me.
	26	the Advocate, the Holy Spirit, whom the *Father* will send in my name,
	28	If you loved me you would have been glad to know that I am going to the *Father*, for the *Father* is greater than I.
	31	the world must be brought to know that I love the *Father* and that I am doing exactly what the *Father* told me.
15	1	I am the true vine, and my *Father* is the vinedresser.
	8	It is to the glory of my *Father* that you should bear much fruit,
	9	As the *Father* has loved me, so I have loved you.
	10	as I have kept my *Father*'s commandments
	15	I have made known to you everything I have learnt from my *Father*.
	16	the *Father* will give you anything you ask him in my name.
	23	Anyone who hates me hates my *Father*.
	24	they have seen all this, and still they hate both me and my *Father*.
	26	When the Advocate comes, whom I shall send you from the *Father*,
16	3	They will do these things because they have never known either the *Father* or myself.
	10	proved by my going to the *Father* and your seeing me no more;
	15	Everything the *Father* has is mine;
	17	What does he mean, ... 'I am going to the *Father*?'
	23	anything you ask for from the *Father* he will grant in my name.
	25	the hour is coming when I shall ... tell you about the *Father* in plain words.
	26	I do not say that I shall pray to the *Father* for you, 27 because
	27	the *Father* himself loves you for loving me and believing that I came from ⌐God (ᵛ the *Father*).
	28	I came from the *Father* and have come into the world and now I leave the world to go to the *Father*.
	32	I am not alone, because the *Father* is with me.
17	1	*Father*, the hour has come: glorify your Son
	5	Now, *Father*, it is time for you to glorify me
	11	Holy *Father*, keep those you have given me true to your name,
	21	*Father*, may they be one in us,
	24	*Father*, I want those you have given me to be with me where I am,
	25	*Father*, Righteous One, the world has not known you,
18	11	am I not to drink the cup that the *Father* has given me?
20	17	I have not yet ascended to the *Father*.... I am ascending to my *Father* and your father, to my God and your God.
	21	As the *Father* sent me, so am I sending you.
Ac 1	4	[Jesus] had told [the Twelve] ... to wait [at Jerusalem] for what the *Father* had promised.
	7	It is not for you to know times or dates that the *Father* has decided by his own authority,
2	33	[Jesus] has received from the *Father* the Holy Spirit,
Rm 6	4	as Christ was raised from the dead by the *Father*'s glory,
15	6	so that ... you may give glory to the God and *Father* of our Lord Jesus Christ.
1 Co 8	6	there is one God, the *Father*, ... and there is one Lord, Jesus Christ,
15	24	the end, when he hands over the kingdom to God the *Father*,
2 Co 1	3	Blessed be the God and *Father* of our Lord Jesus Christ,
11	31	The God and *Father* of the Lord Jesus ... knows that I am not lying.
Ga 1	1	Paul ... an apostle, ... appointed by Jesus Christ and by God the *Father*
Ep 1	3	Blessed be God the *Father* of our Lord Jesus Christ,
2	18	both of us have in the one Spirit our way to come to the *Father*.
3	14	This, then, is what I pray, kneeling before the *Father*, 15 from whom every family, whether spiritual or natural, takes its name:
6	23	May God the *Father* and the Lord Jesus Christ grant peace, love and faith to all the brothers.
Ph 2	11	every tongue should acclaim Jesus Christ as Lord, to the glory of God the *Father*.
Col 1	3	We have never failed to ... give thanks for you to God, the *Father* of our Lord Jesus Christ,

Col 1	12	thanking the *Father* who has made it possible for you to join the saints
3	17	in the name of the Lord Jesus, giving thanks to God the *Father* through him.
1 Th 1	1	to the Church in Thessalonika which is in God the *Father* and the Lord Jesus Christ;
2 Th 1	2	wishing you grace and peace from God the *Father* and the Lord Jesus Christ.
1 Tm 1	2	wishing you grace, mercy and peace from God the *Father* and from Christ Jesus our Lord.
2 Tm 1	2	wishing you grace, mercy and peace from God the *Father* and from Christ Jesus our Lord.
Tt 1	4	wishing you grace and peace from God the *Father* and from Christ Jesus our saviour.
Heb 1	5	(2 S 7 14) I will be a *father* to him
1 P 1	2	[to all those .., who have been chosen,] by the provident purpose of God the *Father*, to be made holy by the Spirit, obedient to Jesus Christ
	3	Blessed be God the *Father* of our Lord Jesus Christ,
2 P 1	17	[our Lord Jesus Christ] was honoured and glorified by God the *Father*,
1 Jn 1	2	the eternal life which was with the *Father* and has been made visible to us.
	3	we are in union with the *Father* and with his Son Jesus Christ.
2	1	if anyone sin, we have an advocate with the *Father*, Jesus Christ, who is just;
	14	children, ... you already know the *Father*;
	15	The love of the *Father* cannot be in any man who loves the world,
	16	nothing the world has to offer ... could ever come from the *Father*
	22	the Antichrist ... is denying the *Father* as well as the Son,
	23	23 because no one who has the *Father* can deny the Son, and to acknowledge the Son is to have the *Father* as well.
	24	you will live in the Son and in the *Father*
3	1	Think of the love that the *Father* has lavished on us, by letting us be called God's children;
4	14	the *Father* sent his Son as saviour of the world.
2 Jn	3	we shall have grace, mercy and peace from God the *Father* and from Jesus Christ, the Son of the *Father*.
	4	as we were commanded by the *Father*.
	9	only those who keep to what he taught can have the *Father* and the Son with them.
Jude	1	to those who are dear to God the *Father* and kept safe for Jesus Christ,
Rv 1	6	[Jesus Christ has] made us a line of kings, priests to serve his God and *Father*;
2	28	[the authority over the pagans] which I myself have been given by my *Father*,
3	5	I shall ... acknowledge their names in the presence of my *Father* and his angels.
	21	I ... took my place with my *Father* on his throne.
14	1	I saw ... a Lamb who had with him a hundred and forty-four thousand people, all with his name and his *Father*'s name written on their foreheads.

b) (*Man's heavenly*) *Father* – (*Our*) *Father*

Mt 5	16	so that ... they may give the praise to your *Father* in heaven.
	45	in this way you will be sons of your *Father* in heaven,
	48	You must ... be perfect just as your heavenly *Father* is perfect.
6	1	you will lose all reward from your *Father* in heaven.
	4	your *Father* who sees all that is done in secret will reward you.
	6	pray to your *Father* who is in that secret place, and your *Father* who sees all that is done in secret will reward you.
	8	your *Father* knows what you need before you ask him.
	9	Our *Father* in heaven, may your name be held holy,
	14	if you forgive others their failings, your heavenly *Father* will forgive you yours;
	15	if you do not forgive others, your *Father* will not forgive your failings either.
	18	so that no one will know you are fasting except your *Father* who sees all that is done in secret; and your *Father* who sees all that is done in secret will reward you.
	26	the birds ... do not sow or reap ... yet your heavenly *Father* feeds them.
	32	Your heavenly *Father* knows you need them all.
7	11	how much more will your *Father* in heaven give good things to those who ask him!
10	20	the Spirit of your *Father* will be speaking in you.
	29	not one [sparrow] falls to the ground without your *Father* knowing.
13	43	the virtuous will shine like the sun in the kingdom of their *Father*.
18	14	it is never the will of your *Father* in heaven that one of these little ones should be lost.
23	9	You must call no one on earth your father, since you have only one *Father*, and he is in heaven.
Mk 11	25	so that your *Father* in heaven may forgive your failings too.

Mk 11 26	(ᵛ But if you do not forgive, neither will your *Father* in heaven forgive your failings.)
Lk 6 36	Be compassionate as your *Father* is compassionate.
11 2	*Father*, may your name be held holy,
13	how much more will the heavenly *Father* give the Holy Spirit to those who ask him!
12 30	Your *Father* well knows you need them.
32	it has pleased your *Father* to give you the kingdom.
Jn 8 41	'we have one *father*: God.' ⁴² Jesus answered: 'If God were your *father*, you would love me,'
42	
20 17	I am ascending to my Father and your *Father*, to my God and your God.
Rm 1 7	may God our *Father* and the Lord Jesus Christ send grace and peace.
8 15	The spirit you received . . . is the spirit of sons, and it makes us cry out, '*Abba, Father*!'
11/	
1 Co 1 3	May God our *Father* and the Lord Jesus Christ send you grace and peace.
2 Co 1 2	Grace and peace to you from God our *Father* and the Lord Jesus Christ.
3	Blessed be the God and Father of our Lord Jesus Christ, ʳa gentle *Father* (or: the Father of mercies) and the God of all consolation,
6 18	(2 S 7 14) I will . . . be your *father*,
Ga 1 3	We wish you the grace and peace of God our *Father* and of the Lord Jesus Christ, ⁴ who . . . sacrificed himself for our sins, in accordance with the will of God our *Father*,
4	
4 6	God has sent the Spirit of his Son into our hearts: the Spirit that cries, '*Abba, Father*',
11/	
Ep 1 2	Grace and peace to you from God our *Father* and from the Lord Jesus Christ,
4 6	[There is one Lord, one faith, one baptism,] and one God who is *Father* of all, over all, through all and within all.
5 20	so that always and everywhere you are giving thanks to God who is our *Father* in the name of our Lord Jesus Christ.
Ph 1 2	We wish you the grace and peace of God our *Father* and of the Lord Jesus Christ.
4 20	Glory to God, our *Father*, for ever and ever.
Col 1 2	Grace and peace to you from God our *Father*.
1 Th 1 3	[We] constantly remember before God our *Father* how you have shown your faith in action,
3 11	May God our *Father* himself, and our Lord Jesus Christ, make it easy for us to come to you.
13	that you may be blameless in the sight of our God and *Father*
2 Th 1 1	to the Church in Thessalonika which is in God our *Father* and the Lord Jesus Christ;
2 16	May our Lord Jesus Christ himself, and God our *Father* who has given us his love
Phm 3	wishing you the grace and the peace of God our *Father* and the Lord Jesus Christ.
Heb 12 9	we ought to be even more willing to submit ourselves to ʳour spiritual *Father* (or: the Father of spirits)
Jm 1 27	Pure, unspoilt religion, in the eyes of God our *Father* is this:
3 9	We use [the tongue] to bless the Lord and *Father*,
1 P 1 17	If you are acknowledging as your *Father* one who . . . judges everyone according to what he has done,

c) Father (of mercies, glory, spirits, light)

2 Co 1 3	the God and Father of our Lord Jesus Christ, ʳa gentle *Father* (or: the *Father* of mercies)
Ep 1 17	the God of our Lord Jesus Christ, the *Father* of glory,
Heb 12 9	we ought to be even more willing to submit ourselves to ʳour spiritual Father (or: the *Father* of spirits)
Jm 1 17	all that is good . . . comes down from the *Father* of all light;

2: THE DEVIL AS FATHER

Jn 8 38	What I . . . speak of is what I have seen with my Father; but you, you put into action the lessons learnt from your *father*.
41	What you are doing is what your *father* does.
44	The devil is your *father*, and you prefer to do what your *father* wants. . . . he is a liar, and the *father* of lies.

3: HUMAN FATHERS

a) Father

Mt 2 22	Archelaus had succeeded his *father* Herod as ruler of Judaea
4 21	[Jesus] saw another pair of brothers, James . . . and . . . John; they were in their boat with their *father* Zebedee, . . . and he called them. ²² At once, leaving the boat and their *father*, they followed him.
22	
8 21	Sir, let me go and bury my *father* first.
10 21	Brother will betray brother to death, and the *father* his child;
21 31 <	Which of the two [sons] did the *father*'s will?
23 9	You must call no one on earth your *father*, since you have only one Father, and he is in heaven.

Mk 1 20	leaving their *father* Zebedee in the boat . . ., they went after [Jesus].
9 21	Jesus asked the *father* [of the epileptic boy],
24	the *father* of the boy cried out, 'I do have faith.'
13 12	Brother will betray brother to death, and the *father* his child;
15 21	Simon of Cyrene, *father* of Alexander and Rufus,
Lk 1 17 ○	(Ml 3 24) to turn the hearts of *fathers* towards their children
67	[John's] *father* Zechariah was filled with the Holy Spirit
9 42	Jesus . . . cured the boy and gave him back to his *father*,
59	Let me go and bury my *father* first.
11 11	What *father* among you would hand your son a stone when he asked for bread?
15 12 <	The younger [son] said to his *father*, '*Father*, let me have the share of the estate that would come to me.'
17 <	How many of my *father*'s paid servants have more food than they want,
18 <	I will . . . go to my *father* and say: '*Father*, I have sinned'
20 <	So he . . . went back to his *father*. While he was still a long way off, his *father* saw him
<	
21 <	*Father*, I have sinned against heaven and against you.
22 <	the *father* said to his servants, 'Quick! Bring out the best robe'
27 <	your *father* has killed the calf we had fattened because he has got [your brother] back safe and sound.
28 <	his *father* came out to plead with [the elder son]; ²⁹ but he answered his *father*, 'Look, all these years I have slaved for you'
29 <	
16 27	Father, I beg you to send Lazarus to my *father*'s house,
Jn 4 53	The *father* realised that this was exactly the time when Jesus had said, 'Your son lives'.
Ac 7 2	[Stephen said to the Sanhedrin:] My brothers, my *fathers*, listen to what I have to say.
4	after his *father* died God made [Abraham] leave Haran and come to this land;
14	Joseph then sent for his *father* Jacob
20	[Moses] was looked after for three months in his *father*'s house.
16 1	a disciple called Timothy, whose mother was a Jewess who had become a believer; but his *father* was a Greek.
3	everyone knew his *father* was a Greek.
22 1 ○	[Paul said to the Jews of Jerusalem:] My brothers, my *fathers*, listen to what I have to say to you in my defence
28 8	Publius's *father* was in bed,
1 Co 4 15 ○	You . . . have . . . not more than one *father* and it was I who begot you in Christ Jesus
5 1	one of you is living with his *father*'s wife.
Ga 4 2	[an heir] is under the control of guardians . . . until he reaches the age fixed by his *father*.
Ep 6 4	And ʳparents (lit. *fathers*), never drive your children to resentment
Ph 2 22	[Timothy] has proved himself by working with me . . . like a son helping his *father*.
Col 3 21	ʳParents (lit. *Fathers*), never drive your children to resentment
1 Th 2 11	we treated every one of you as a *father* treats his children,
Heb 12 7	Has there ever been any son whose *father* did not train him?
9	we have all had our human *fathers* who punished us,
1 Jn 2 13	I am writing to you, *fathers*,
14	I have written to you, *fathers*,

b) Father and Mother

	12 *mētēr* 30/84	14 *mētro(-lōēs)* 1
	13 *a-mētōr* 1	

Mt 10 35	(Mi 7 6) I have come to set a man against his *father*, a daughter against her *mother*,
12	
37 /12	Anyone who prefers *father* or *mother* to me is not worthy of me.
15 4	God said (Ex 20 12): Do your duty to your *father* and *mother* and (Ex 21 17) Anyone who curses *father* or *mother* must be put to death ⁵ But you say, 'If anyone says to his *father* or *mother*, "Anything I have that I might have used to help you is dedicated to God", ⁶ he is rid of his duty to *father* or *mother*'.
12/	
5 12	
/12	
6 /12	
19 5 /12	(Gn 2 24) a man must leave *father* and *mother*, and cling to his wife.
19 /12	(Ex 20 12) Honour your *father* and *mother*,
29 /12	everyone who has left . . . *father*, *mother*, children or land for the sake of my name
Mk 5 40 /12	taking with him the child's *father* and *mother* and his own companions,
7 10	Moses said (Ex 20 12): Do your duty to your *father* and your *mother*, and (Ex 12 17), Anyone who curses *father* or *mother* must be put to death. ¹¹ But you say, 'If a man says to his *father* or *mother*: "Anything I have that I might have used to help you is Corban . . .", ¹² then he is forbidden from that moment to do anything for his *father* or *mother*'.
12/	
11 12	
/12	
12	
12	
10 7 /12	(Gn 2 24) a man must leave *father* and *mother*,
19 /12	(Ex 20 12) Honour your *father* and *mother*.

Mk 10 29 12/ there is no one who has left . . . sisters, *mother*, *father*,
    30 children or land for my sake . . . ³⁰ who will not be repaid
    12 a hundred times over, . . . sisters, *mothers*, children and land

Lk 1 59 they were going to call [the child] Zechariah after his *father*,
    60 12 ⁶⁰ but his *mother* spoke up. 'No,' she said 'he is to be
    62 called John'. . . . ⁶² [They] made signs to his *father* to find out what he wanted him called.

  2 33 X /12 the child's *father* and *mother* stood there wondering at the things that were being said about him,
    48 X 12/ his *mother* said to him, '. . . See how worried your *father* and I have been, looking for you.'
  8 51 [Jesus] allowed no one to go in with him except Peter and
    /12 . . . the child's *father* and *mother*.
  12 53 the *father* divided against the son, son against *father*,
    12/12 *mother* against daughter, daughter against *mother*,
  14 26 /12 If any man comes to me without hating his *father*, *mother*, wife,
  18 20 /12 (Ex 20 12) Honour your *father* and *mother*.
Jn 6 42 Surely this is Jesus son of Joseph . . . We know his *father*
    X 12 and *mother*.
Ep 5 31 /12 (Gn 2 24) a man must leave his *father* and *mother* and be joined to his wife,
  6 2 /12 (Ex 20 12) Honour your *father* and *mother*,
1 Tm 1 9 7/14 laws . . . are for people who kill their *fathers* or *mothers*
  5 1 Do not speak harshly to a man older than yourself, but advise
    2 him as you would your own *father*; treat . . . ² . . . older
    12 women as you would your *mother*.
Heb 7 3 9/13 [Melchizedek] has *no father*, *no mother* or ancestry,

c) parents

Heb 11 23 Moses . . . hidden by his *parents* for three months;

d) Father = Ancestor, Patriarch

A = Abraham; D = David

Mt 3 9 A We have Abraham for our *father*,
  23 30 had we lived in our *fathers*' day.
    32 finish off the work that your *fathers* began.
Mk 11 10 D Blessings on the coming kingdom of our *father* David!
Lk 1 32 D The Lord God will give [Jesus] the throne of his *ancestor* David.
    55 according to the promise he made to our *ancestors*
    72 Thus he shows mercy to our *ancestors*,
    73 A the oath he swore to our *father* Abraham
  3 8 A We have Abraham for our *father*
  6 23 This was the way their *ancestors* treated the prophets.
    26 This was the way their *ancestors* treated the false prophets.
  11 47 Alas for you who build the tombs of the prophets, the men
    48 your *ancestors* killed. ⁴⁸ In this way you both witness what your *ancestors* did and approve it;
  16 24 A [The rich man] cried out, '*Father* Abraham, pity me and send Lazarus'
    27 A *Father*, I beg you then to send Lazarus to my father's house,
    30 A Ah no, *father* Abraham, . . . but if someone comes to them from the dead,
Jn 4 12 Are you a greater man than our *father* Jacob . . . ?
    20 Our *fathers* worshipped on this mountain,
  6 31 Our *fathers* had manna to eat in the desert;
    49 Your *fathers* ate the manna in the desert
    58 not like the bread our *ancestors* ate:
  7 22 not that [circumcision] began with [Moses], it goes back to the *patriarchs*
  8 39 A Our *father* is Abraham
    53 A Are you greater than our *father* Abraham . . . ?
    56 A Your *father* Abraham rejoiced to think that he would see my Day;
Ac 2 29 D 3 the *patriarch* David himself is dead
  3 13 A the God of Abraham, Isaac and Jacob, the God of our *ancestors*,
    25 You are the heirs of . . . the covenant God made with our *ancestors*
  4 25 D speaking through our *ancestor* David,
  5 30 it was the God of our *ancestors* who raised up Jesus,
  7 2 A The God of glory appeared to our *ancestor* Abraham,
    8 3 Jacob [circumcised] the twelve *patriarchs*.
    9 3 The *patriarchs* were jealous of Joseph
    11 Then a famine came . . . and our *ancestors* could find nothing to eat.
    12 Jacob . . . sent our *ancestors* [to Egypt] on a first visit,
    15 after [Jacob] and our *ancestors* had died there,
    19 [a new king of Egypt] ill-treated our *ancestors*,
    32 A (Ex 3 6) I am the God of your *ancestors*, the God of Abraham,
    38 it was only through Moses that our *ancestors* could communicate with the angel
    39 This is the man that our *ancestors* refused to listen to:
    44 While they were in the desert our *ancestors* possessed the Tent of Testimony . . . ⁴⁵ It was handed down from one *ancestor* of ours to another until Joshua brought it into

Ac 7 45 the country we had conquered from the nations which were driven out by God as ⌜we (lit. our *ancestors*) advanced.
    51 just as your *ancestors* used to do.
    52 Can you name a single prophet your *ancestors* never persecuted?
  13 17 The God of our nation Israel chose our *ancestors*,
    32 It was to our *ancestors* that God made the promise but ³³ it is to us, the children, that he has fulfilled it,
    36 David . . . died; he was buried with his *ancestors*
  15 10 the very burden that neither we nor our *ancestors* were strong enough to support?
  22 3 5 I . . . was taught the exact observance of the Law *of our ancestors*,
    14 The God of our *ancestors* has chosen you to . . . see the Just One
  24 14 5 it is according to the Way . . . that I worship the God *of my ancestors*,
  26 6 it is for my hope in the promise made by God to our *ancestors* that I am on trial,
  28 17 5 although I have done nothing against our people or the customs *of our ancestors*,
    25 the Holy Spirit . . . told your *ancestors* through the prophet Isaiah:
Rm 4 1 A 10 Abraham, the *ancestor* from whom we are all descended.
    11 A In this way [Abraham] became the *ancestor* of all uncircumcised believers, . . . ¹² and *ancestor*, also, of those who
    12 A though circumcised . . . follow our *ancestor* Abraham
    A along the path of faith he trod before he had been circumcised.
    16 so that [the promise] may be . . . available to . . . those who
    A belong to the faith of Abraham who is the *father* of all of
    17 A us. ¹⁷ As scripture says (Gn 17 5): I have made you the *ancestor* of many nations
    18 A [Abraham] did become the *father* of many nations
  9 5 [The Israelites] are descended from the *patriarchs*
    10 Rebecca when she was pregnant by our *ancestor* Isaac,
  11 28 [the Jews] are still loved by God, loved for the sake of their *ancestors*.
  15 8 so that God could faithfully carry out the promises made to the *patriarchs*,
1 Co 10 1 our *fathers* were all guided by a cloud
Ga 1 14 6 how enthusiastic I was for the traditions *of my ancestors*,
Heb 1 1 God spoke to our *ancestors* through the prophets;
  3 9 (Ps 95 9) when your *ancestors* challenged me and tested me,
  7 4 A 3 if the *patriarch* Abraham paid him a tenth of the treasure
    10 A [Levi] was still in the loins of his *ancestor*
  8 9 (Jr 31 32) not a covenant like the one I made with their *ancestors*
Jm 2 21 A Abraham our *father* was justified by his deed,
1 P 1 18 8 to free you from the useless way of life your *ancestors* handed down
2 P 3 4 Everything goes on as it has since the *Fathers* died,

4: FAMILY – LINEAGE, LINE (OF DESCENT)

Lk 2 4 4 Joseph . . . was of David's House and *line*,
Ac 3 25 4 in your offspring all the *families* of the earth will be blessed.
Ep 3 15 4 [the Father,] from whom every *family*, whether spiritual or natural, takes its name:

5: "FATHERLAND" = HOME TOWN, OWN COUNTRY

Mt 13 54 X 2 coming to his *home town*, [Jesus] taught the people in their synagogue
    57 2 A prophet is only despised in his *own country* and in his own house,
Mk 6 1 X 2 [Jesus] went to his *home town*
    4 2 A prophet is only despised in his *own country*, among his own relations
Lk 4 23 X 2 do the same here in your *own countryside*.
    24 2 no prophet is ever accepted in his *own country*.
Jn 4 44 2 there is no respect for a prophet in his *own country*,
Heb 11 14 ● 2 they are in search of their real *homeland*. . . . ¹⁶ . . . they were longing for a better homeland, their heavenly homeland.

2. MOTHER: *MĒTĒR*

mētēr 55/84

For Father and Mother see 1.3:b)

1: MOTHER

Mt 14 8 Prompted by her *mother* [the daughter of Herodias] said,
    11 'Give me John the Baptist's head' . . . ¹¹ The head was . . . given to the girl who took it to her *mother*.
  19 12 There are eunuchs born that way from their *mother*'s womb,

Mt 20	20	the *mother* of Zebedee's sons came . . . to make a request of [Jesus],
	27 56	[many women were there . . .] Among them were Mary of Magdala, Mary the *mother* of James and Joseph, and the *mother* of Zebedee's sons.
Mk 6	24	[The daughter of Herodias] said to her *mother*, 'What shall I ask for?' She replied, 'The head of John the Baptist'.
	28	. . . ²⁸ The man . . . brought the head . . . and the girl gave it to her *mother*.
	15 40	There were some women watching . . . Among them were Mary of Magdala, Mary who was the *mother* of James
Lk 1	15	Even from his *mother*'s womb [John] will be filled with the Holy Spirit,
	7 12	a dead man was being carried out for burial, the only son of his *mother*, and she was a widow. . . . ¹⁵ And the dead man
	15	sat up and . . . Jesus gave him to his *mother*.
Jn 3	4	Can he go back into his *mother*'s womb and be born again?
Ac 3	2	He was a cripple from ⌐birth (lit. his *mother*'s womb);
	12 12	the house of Mary the *mother* of John Mark,
	14 8	his feet were crippled from ⌐birth (lit. his *mother*'s womb);
Rm 16	13	[Greetings] to Rufus . . . and to his *mother* who has been [a mother] to me too.
Ga 1	15	(Is 49 1) God, who had specially chosen me while I was still in my *mother*'s womb,
	4 26 ○	The Jerusalem above, however, is free and is our *mother*,
2 Tm 1	5	the sincere faith which you have . . . came first to live in your grandmother Lois, and your *mother* Eunice,
Rv 17	5 ○	Babylon the Great, the *mother* of all the prostitutes and all the filthy practices on the earth.

2: (JESUS'S) MOTHER

Mt 1	18	This is how Jesus Christ came to be born. His *mother* Mary was betrothed to Joseph;
2	11	[the wise men] saw the child with his *mother* Mary,
	13	'Get up, [Joseph,] take the child and his *mother* with you, and escape into Egypt, . . .' ¹⁴ So Joseph got up and, taking
	14	the child and his *mother* with him, left that night for Egypt,
	20	'Get up, take the child and his *mother* with you and go back to the land of Israel, . . .' ²¹ So Joseph got up and, taking
	21	the child and his *mother* with him, went back
12	46	his *mother* and his brothers appeared; . . . ⁴⁷ (ᵛ Someone
	47	said to him, 'Your *mother* and brothers are here and
	48	would like to speak to you'.) ⁴⁸ . . . Jesus replied, 'Who is
	49	my *mother*? Who are my brothers?' ⁴⁹ And stretching out
	○	his hand towards his disciples he said, 'Here are my *mother*
	50	and my brothers. ⁵⁰ Anyone who does the will of my Father
	○	in heaven, he is my brother and sister and *mother*.'
13	55	This is the carpenter's son, surely? Is not his *mother* the woman called Mary . . .?
Mk 3	31	His *mother* and brothers now arrived . . . asking for him.
	32	³² . . . 'Your *mother* and brothers and sisters are outside
	33	asking for you'. ³³ He replied, 'Who are my *mother* and
	34 ○	my brothers?' ³⁴ And . . . he said, 'Here are my *mother*
	35	and my brothers. ³⁵ Anyone who does the will of God,
	○	that person is my brother and sister and *mother*.'
Lk 1	43	Why should I be honoured with a visit from the *mother* of my Lord?
2	34	Simeon . . . said to Mary his *mother*, 'You see this child:'
	48	[when they found Jesus] his *mother* said to him, 'My child, why have you done this to us?'
	51	His *mother* stored up all these things in her heart.
8	19	His *mother* and his brothers came looking for him, . . .
	20	²⁰ He was told, 'Your *mother* and brothers . . . want
	21 ○	to see you'. ²¹ But he said in answer, 'My *mother* and my brothers are those who hear the word of God and put it into practice'.
Jn 2	1	there was a wedding at Cana in Galilee. The *mother* of Jesus was there,
	3	the *mother* of Jesus said to him, 'They have no wine'. ⁴ Jesus
	5	said, 'Woman, why turn to me? . . .' ⁵ His *mother* said to the servants, 'Do whatever he tells you'.
	12	he went down to Capernaum with his *mother* and the brothers,
19	25	Near the cross of Jesus stood his *mother* and his *mother*'s sister, Mary the wife of Clopas, and Mary of Magdala.
	26	²⁶ Seeing his *mother* and the disciple he loved standing near her, Jesus said to his *mother*, 'Woman, this is your son'. ²⁷ Then to the disciple he said, 'This is your *mother*'.
	27 ○	
Ac 1	14	All these joined in continuous prayer, together with several women, including Mary the *mother* of Jesus,

3. GRANDMOTHER: *MAMMĒ*

mammē 1

2 Tm 1	5	the sincere faith which you have . . . came first to live in your grandmother Lois, and your mother Eunice,

4. PARENTS: *GONEIS*

1 *goneis* 20 2 *pro-gonos* 2

Mt 10	21	children will rise against their *parents*
Mk 13	12	children will rise against their *parents*
Lk 2	27 X	when the *parents* brought in the child Jesus
	41 X	Every year his *parents* used to go to Jerusalem
	43 X	the boy Jesus stayed behind in Jerusalem without his *parents* knowing it.
8	56	[The] *parents* [of Jairus's daughter] were astonished,
18	29	there is no one who has left . . . brothers, *parents* or children for the sake of the kingdom of God ³⁰ who will not be given repayment
21	16	You will be betrayed even by *parents* and brothers,
Jn 9	2	'Rabbi, who sinned, this man or his *parents*, for him to have been born blind?' ³ 'Neither he nor his *parents* sinned,'
	3	Jesus answered
	18	the Jews would not believe . . . without first sending for his *parents*
	20	His *parents* answered, 'We know he is our son'
	22	His *parents* spoke like this out of fear of the Jews, . . .
	23	²³ This was why his *parents* said, '. . . ask him'.
Rm 1	30	enterprising in sin, rebellious to *parents*,
2 Co 12	14	Children are not expected to save up for their *parents*, but *parents* for children.
Ep 6	1	Children, be obedient to your *parents*
Col 3	20	Children, be obedient to your *parents* always
1 Tm 5	4	children . . . are to learn first of all to . . . repay their debt
	2	to their *parents*,
2 Tm 1	3 2	remembering my duty to [God] as my *ancestors* did,
3	2	People will be . . . rude; disobedient to their *parents*, ungrateful, irreligious;

5. ORPHANS – BEREFT: *ORPHANOS*

orphanos 2

Jn 14	18	I will not leave you *orphans*; I will come back to you.
Jm 1	27	Pure, unspoilt religion . . is this: coming to the help of *orphans* and widows

FAVOURITISM – PARTIALITY

Favour, (Have) Favourites, (Make) Distinctions – Partiality, Respecter of persons – Flatter

2	*pros-ōpon lambanō* 2	6	*eis pros-ōpon blepō* 2
1	*pros-ōpo-lēmpsia* 4	7	*pros-ōpon thaumazō* 1
3	*pros-ōpo-lēmpteō* 1		
4	*pros-ōpo-lēmptēs* 1		
5	*a-pros-ōpo-lēmptōs* 1		

Mt 22	16	Master, we know that you are an honest man and teach the way of God in an honest way, and that you are not afraid
	X 6	of anyone, because ⌐a man's rank means nothing to you (lit. you do not *look* at a man's *outward appearance*).
Mk 12	14	Master, we know you are an honest man, that you are not afraid of anyone, because ⌐a man's rank means nothing to
	X 6	you (lit. you do not *look* at a man's *outward appearance*),
Lk 20	21 X	Master, we know . . . you ⌐*favour* no one (or: are no
	2	*respecter of persons*),
Ac 10	34 Θ	Peter addressed them:'. . . I have now come to realise . . .
	4	that God does not *have favourites*, ³⁵ but that anybody of any nationality who fears God . . . is acceptable to him.
Rm 2	11	[Pain and suffering . . . honour and peace . . . Jews first,
	Θ	but Greeks as well.] God *has no favourites*.
Ga 2	6	As a result, these people who are acknowledged leaders
	Θ 2	not that their importance matters to me, since God *has no favourites* –
Ep 6	9	employers, . . . your slaves . . . and you have the same
	X	Master in heaven and he is not *impressed* by one person more than by another.
Col 3	25	anyone who does wrong will be repaid in kind and he does
	X	not *favour* one person more than another.
Jm 2	1	do not try to combine faith in Jesus Christ, our glorified Lord, with the *making* of *distinctions* between classes of people. ² Now suppose a man comes into your synagogue, beautifully dressed and . . . a poor man comes in, in shabby clothes, ³ and you take notice of the well-dressed man . . . ⁴ . . . you have used two different standards in
	9	your mind . . . ⁹ but as soon as you *make distinctions*
	3	between classes of people, you are committing sin,

1 P 1 17 Θ 5 If you are acknowledging as your Father one who *has* no *favourites* and judges everyone according to what he has done,

Jude 16 7 [irreligious sinners are] ready with *flattery* for other people when they see some advantage in it.

FEAR – AWE

1. Be afraid of, Fear: *phobos*
a) Be afraid (of), Fear (in religious senses) – Fright, Terror, Make a deep impression on – Awe, Respect, Reverence
b) Be afraid (of), Fear (generally) – Misgiving, Caution – Fearless

2. Devout – Reverence, Holy fear: *eu-labeia*

3. Religious – Fear, Awe, Frighten: *deos*

a) Religious, Religion – Fear, Awe
b) Frighten(ed), Fearful, Afraid – Coward

4. Frighthearted – Apprehensive: *oligo-psychos*

5. Frightened, Shaken – Worry, Alarm, Fear: *ptoēsis*

6. Be alarmed: *throeō*

7. Tremble
1: *phrissō*
2: *tremō*

1. BE AFRAID OF, FEAR: *PHOBOS*

1	*phobeomai* 95	4	*a-phobōs* 4
5	*phoberos* 3	8	*ek-phobeō* 1
7	*phobētron* 1	6	*ek-phobos* 2
2	*phobos* 47	3	*em-phobos* 5

a) Be afraid (of), Fear (in religious senses) – Fright, Terror, Make a deep impression on – Awe, Respect, Reverence

Mt 1 20 Joseph . . , do not *be afraid* to take Mary home as your wife,

9 8 [The paralytic got up and went home.] A *feeling of awe came over* the crowd when they saw this,

10 28 Do not *be afraid* of those who kill the body . . . *fear* him rather who can destroy both body and soul in hell.

17 6 the disciples fell on their faces, [overcome] with *fear.* ⁷ But
7 Jesus . . . said 'do not *be afraid.*'

27 54 the centurion, together with the others guarding Jesus . . . *were terrified*

28 4 2 The guards were . . . so *frightened* of [the angel] that they
5 were like dead men. ⁵ But the angel . . . said to the women, 'There is no need for you to *be afraid.*'

8 2 Filled with *awe* and great joy the women . . . ran to tell the disciples.

10 Jesus said to [the women], 'Do not *be afraid*;'

Mk 4 41 /2 [The disciples] were ᵣfilled (lit. *awestruck*) with great *terror,* and said to one another, 'Who can this be?'

5 15 [The Gerasenes] saw the demoniac sitting there . . . and they *were afraid.*

6 20 Herod *was afraid of* John, knowing him to be a good and holy man,

50 [Jesus] spoke to [the disciples], and said, 'Courage! It is I! Do not *be afraid.*'

9 6 6 [Peter] did not know what to say; they were so *frightened.*

16 8 the women . . . ran away from the tomb because . . . they *were afraid.*

Lk 1 12 2 Zechariah . . . was overcome with *fear.*

13 the angel said to him, 'Zechariah, do not *be afraid,*'

30 the angel said to her, 'Mary, do not *be afraid*; you have won God's favour.'

50 [God's] mercy reaches from age to age for those who *fear* him.

65 [Zechariah's power of speech returned.] All their neighbours
2 were filled with *awe*

2 9 the glory of the Lord shone round [the shepherds]. They
10 /2 ᵣwere terrified (lit. *frightened* and in great *fear*), ¹⁰ but the angel said, 'Do not *be afraid* . . . I bring you news of great joy,'

5 10 Jesus said to Simon, 'Do not *be afraid*'

26 [The paralytic got up and went home.] They were all . . .
2 filled with *awe,* saying, 'We have seen strange things today'.

7 16 2 [The dead man sat up.] Everyone was filled with *awe*

8 25 [It was calm again. The disciples] were *awestruck* and astonished

35 [the Gerasenes] found [the demoniac] sitting at the feet of Jesus . . . and they *were afraid.*

37 The entire population of the Gerasene territory was in a
2 state of *panic*

9 34 when they went into the cloud the disciples *were afraid.*

Lk 12 5 [Do not be afraid of those who kill the body.] I will tell you whom to *fear: fear* him who, after he has killed, has the power to cast into hell. Yes, I tell you, *fear* him.

18 2 < There was a judge in a certain town . . . who *had* neither *fear of* God nor respect for man.

4 < Maybe I *have* neither *fear of* God nor respect for man,

19 21 < [Sir, I put your pound away safely] because I *was afraid of* you;

21 11 7 there will be *fearful sights* and great signs from heaven.

26 2 men dying of *fear* as they await what menaces the world,

23 40 *Have* you no *fear of* God at all? . . . You got the same sentence as he did,

24 5 3 *Terrified*, the women lowered their eyes.

37 3 In a state of alarm and *fright*, [the disciples] thought they were seeing a ghost.

Jn 6 19 [the disciples] saw Jesus walking on the lake . . . This
20 *frightened* them, ²⁰ but he said, 'It is I. Do not *be afraid.*'

12 15 (cf. Zc 9 9) Do not *be afraid*, daughter of Zion; see, your king is coming,

19 8 [He has claimed to be the Son of God.] When Pilate heard them say this his *fear* increased.

Ac 2 43 The many miracles and signs worked through the apostles
2 *made a deep impression on* everyone.

5 5 2 Ananias fell down dead. This *made a profound impression on* everyone present.

11 2 [Sapphira dropped dead at Peter's feet.] This *made a profound impression on* the whole Church

9 31 The churches throughout Judaea, Galilee and Samaria were
2 . . . living in the *fear* of the Lord,

10 2 [The centurion Cornelius] and the whole of his household were devout and God-*fearing.*

4 3 [Cornelius] stared at the vision in *terror*

22 The centurion Cornelius . . . is an upright and God-*fearing* man,

35 anybody of any nationality who *fears* God . . . is acceptable to him.

13 16 Men of Israel, and *fearers* of God, listen!

26 My brothers, sons of Abraham's race, and all you who *fear* God,

19 17 Everybody in Ephesus . . . heard about [the evil spirit and
2 the exorcists]; ᵣthey *were* all greatly *impressed* (or: *fear* seized them all),

24 25 when [Paul] began to treat of . . . the coming Judgement,
3 Felix *took fright*

Rm 3 18 2 there is no *fear* of God before their eyes.

8 15 The spirit you received is not the spirit of slaves bringing
2 *fear* into your lives again;

11 20 Rather than making you proud, that should make you *afraid.*

2 Co 5 11 2 it is with the *fear* of the Lord in mind that we try to win people over.

7 1 2 to reach perfection of holiness in the *fear* of God.

11 2 Just look at what suffering in God's way has brought you:
2 what keenness, . . . what *alarm!*

Ep 5 21 2 Give way to one another in ᵣobedience to (lit. *respect* for) Christ,

33 let every wife *respect* her husband.

Ph 2 12 2 work for your salvation in *fear* and trembling.

Heb 10 27 If, after we have been given knowledge of the truth, we . . .
5 commit any sins, then there . . . will be left only the *dreadful* prospect of judgement

31 5 It is [a] *dreadful* [thing] to fall into the hands of the living God.

12 21 (Dt 9 19) The whole scene [on the mountain] was so
5/6 *terrible* that Moses said: I am *afraid*, and was trembling [with fright].

1 P 1 17 2 you must be ᵣscrupulously careful (lit. behave with *respect*) as long as you are living away from your home.

2 17 *fear* God and honour the emperor.

3 2 [their husbands] see how faithful and ᵣconscientious (lit. full
2 of *respect*) they are.

16 [always have your answer ready for people who ask you the reason for your hope.] But give it with courtesy and
2 *respect*

1 Jn 4 18 2/2 In love there can be no *fear*, but *fear* is driven out by perfect love: because to *fear* is to expect punishment, and anyone who *is afraid* is still imperfect in love.

Jude 12 4 coming for the food and quite ᵣshamelessly (lit. *fearlessly*) looking after themselves.

23 2 there are others to whom you must be kind with *great caution,*

Rv 1 17 Do not *be afraid*; it is I, the First and the Last; I am the Living One,

11 11 God breathed life into [the two witnesses] . . . and everybody
2 who saw it happen was *terrified*;

13 3 the survivors [of the earthquake], *overcome with fear*, could only praise the God of heaven.

18 the time has come for . . . all who ᵣworship (lit. *fear*) you . . . to be rewarded.

14 7 *Fear* God and praise him, because the time has come for him to sit in judgement;

Rv 15	4	Who would not *revere* and praise your name, O Lord?
19	5	Praise our God, . . . all who . . . *revere* him.

b) Be afraid (of), Fear (generally) – Misgiving, Caution – Fearless

Mt 2	22	[Joseph] *was afraid* to go [to Judaea],
10	26	Do not *be afraid of* [men] therefore.
	28	Do not *be afraid of* those who kill the body but cannot kill the soul;
	31	there is no need to *be afraid*; you are worth more than hundreds of sparrows.
14	5	[Herod] had wanted to kill [John] but *was afraid of* the people,
	26	2 the disciples . . . *were terrified* . . . ²⁷ . . . Jesus called out to them, saying, 'Courage! It is I! Do not *be afraid*.'
	27	
	30	as soon as [Peter] felt the force of the wind, he *took fright*
21	26	if we say [John's baptism came] from man, we have the people to *fear*, for they all hold that John was a prophet.
	46	though [the chief priests and Pharisees] would have liked to arrest [Jesus] they *were afraid of* the crowds, who looked on him as a prophet.
25	25	I *was afraid*, and went off and hid your talent in the ground.
Mk 5	33	the woman [cured of a haemorrhage] came forward, *frightened* and trembling because she knew what had happened to her,
	36	Jesus . . . said to [Jairus], 'Do not *be afraid;* only have faith'.
9	32	[the disciples] did not understand what [Jesus] said and *were afraid* to ask him.
10	32	going up to Jerusalem . . . [the disciples] were in a daze, and those who followed were *apprehensive*.
11	18	the chief priests and the scribes . . . *were afraid of* [Jesus] because the people were carried away by his teaching.
	32	[the chief priests] had the people to *fear*, for everyone held that John was a real prophet.
12	12	[the chief priests] would have liked to arrest [Jesus] . . . but they *were afraid of* the crowds.
Lk 1	74	the oath [God] swore to our father Abraham that he would grant us, *free from fear*, to be delivered from . . . our enemies,
	4	
8	50	Jesus . . . spoke to [Jairus], 'Do not *be afraid*, only have faith and she will be safe'.
9	45	[the disciples] *were afraid* to ask [Jesus] about what he had just said.
12	4	Do not *be afraid of* those who kill the body
	7	There is no need to *be afraid*: you are worth more than hundreds of sparrows.
	32	There is no need to *be afraid*, little flock, for it has pleased your Father to give you the kingdom.
20	19	But for their *fear* of the people, the scribes and the chief priests would have liked to lay hands on [Jesus]
22	2	the chief priests and the scribes were looking for some way of doing away with [Jesus], because they ⌐*mistrusted* (or: *feared*) the people.
Jn 7	13	2 no one spoke about [Jesus] openly, for *fear* of the Jews.
9	22	[The blind man's] parents spoke like this out of *fear* of the Jews,
19	38	Joseph of Arimathaea . . . was a disciple of Jesus – though a secret one because he *was afraid of* the Jews –
	2	
20	19	the doors were closed in the room where the disciples were, for *fear* of the Jews.
	2	
Ac 5	26	[The guards escorting the apostles] *were afraid* to use force in case the people stoned them.
9	26	they *were* all *afraid of* [Saul]: they could not believe he was really a disciple.
16	38	the magistrates . . . were *horrified* to hear that [Paul and Silas] were Roman citizens.
18	9	the Lord spoke to Paul in a vision, 'Do not *be afraid* to speak out, nor allow yourself to be silenced'
22	29	the tribune himself *was alarmed* when he realised that he had put a Roman citizen in chains.
23	10	the tribune, *afraid* that [the crowd] would tear Paul to pieces, ordered his troops to . . . bring him into the fortress.
27	17	*afraid of* running aground on the Syrtis banks,
	24	Do not *be afraid*, Paul. You are destined to appear before Caesar.
	29	Then, *afraid* that we might run aground . . . they dropped four anchors
Rm 13	3	2 Good behaviour *is not afraid* of magistrates . . . If you want to live without *being afraid of* authority, you must live honestly . . . ⁴ . . . If you break the law . . . you may well *have fear*:
	4	
	7	Pay every government official what he has a right to ask – ⌐*whether it be* . . . fear or honour (lit. if it be *respect*, *respect*; if honour, *honour*).
	2	
	2	
1 Co 2	3	2 I came among you in great *fear* and trembling
16	10	4 If Timothy comes, show him that he *has nothing to be afraid of* in you:
2 Co 7	5	2 quarrels outside, *misgivings* inside.

2 Co 7	15	2 with what ⌐*deep respect* (lit. *fear* and trembling) you welcomed [Titus].
10	9	8 I do not want you to think of me only as someone who *frightens* you by letter.
11	3	I *am afraid* that . . . your ideas may get corrupted and turned away from simple devotion to Christ.
12	20	What I *am afraid of* is that when I come I may find you different from what I want you to be,
Ga 2	12	[Cephas stopped eating with the pagans] and kept away from them altogether for *fear* of the group that insisted on circumcision.
4	11	You make me ⌐*feel* (lit. *fear*) I have wasted my time with you.
Ep 6	5	2 Slaves, be obedient . . . with ⌐*deep respect* (lit. *fear* and trembling) . . . as you are obedient to Christ.
Ph 1	14	most of the brothers . . . are getting more and more daring in announcing the Message *without any fear*.
	4	
Col 3	22	Slaves, be obedient . . . out of *respect* for the Master.
1 Tm 5	20	If any of them are at fault, reprimand them publicly, ⌐*as a warning to the rest* (lit. so that the rest may feel *afraid*).
	2	
Heb 2	15	all those who had been held in slavery all their lives by the *fear* of death.
	2	
4	1	*Be careful*, then: the promise . . . still holds good
11	23	[Moses'] parents . . . ⌐*defied* (lit. did not *fear*) the royal edict when they saw he was such a fine child.
	27	It was by faith that [Moses] left Egypt and *was not afraid of* the king's anger;
13	6	With the Lord to help me, I *fear* nothing:
1 P 2	18	2 Slaves must be respectful and obedient to their masters,
3	6	You are now [Sarah's] children, as long as you live good lives and do not give way to *fear* or worry.
	14	/2 There is no need to *be afraid* with any *fear*, or to worry about them.
Rv 2	10	[Smyrna,] Do not *be afraid of* the sufferings that are coming to you:
18	10	[the kings of the earth will] keep at a safe distance from *fear* of [Babylon's] agony.
	2	
	15	The traders . . . will be standing at a safe distance from *fear* of her agony,
	2	

2. DEVOUT – REVERENCE, HOLY FEAR: *EU-LABEIA*

	2 *eu-labeia*	2	1 *eu-labēs* 4
	3 *eu-labeomai* 1		

Lk 2	25	Simeon . . . was an upright and *devout* man;
Ac 2	5	there were *devout* men living in Jerusalem
8	2	There were some *devout* people . . . who buried Stephen
22	12	Ananias, a *devout* follower of the Law
Heb 5	7 X	2 [Christ] *submitted* so *humbly* that his prayer was heard.
11	7	3 Noah . . . felt a *holy fear* and built an ark
12	28	Let us . . . worship God in the way that he finds acceptable,
	2	in *reverence* and fear.

3. RELIGIOUS – FEAR, AWE, FRIGHTEN: *DEOS*

	3 *deilia* 1	5 *deisi-daimōn*	1
	4 *deiliaō* 1	6 *deisi-daimonia*	1
	1 *deilos* 3	7 *deos*	1
	2 *deinōs* 2		

a) Religious, Religion – Fear, Awe

Ac 17	22	5 Men of Athens, I have seen . . . how extremely *scrupulous* you are *in all religious matters*,
25	19	[the Jews' elders] had some argument or other with [Paul] about their own *religion*
	6	
Heb 12	28	Let us . . . worship God in the way that he finds acceptable, in reverence and ⌐*fear* (or: *awe*).
	7	

b) Frighten(ed), Fearful, Afraid – Coward

Mt 8	6	my servant is lying at home paralysed, and in ⌐*great* (lit. *fearful*) pain.
	2	
	26	Why are you so *frightened*, you men of little faith?
Mk 4	40	Why are you so *frightened*? How is it that you have no faith?
Lk 11	53	2 the scribes and the Pharisees began a ⌐*furious* (lit. *frightening*) attack on [Jesus]
Jn 14	27	4 Do not let your hearts *be troubled* or *afraid*.
2 Tm 1	7	3 God's gift was not a spirit of *timidity*, but the Spirit of power,
Rv 21	8	the legacy for *cowards* . . . is the second death in the burning lake of sulphur.

4. FAINTHEARTED – APPREHENSIVE: *OLIGO-PSYCHOS*

oligo-psychos 1

1 Th 5 14	give courage to ⌐those who are apprehensive (or: the *fainthearted*), care for the weak

5. FRIGHTENED, SHAKEN – WORRY, ALARM, FEAR: *PTOĒSIS*

1 *ptoeō 2* 3 *ptyrō 1*
2 *ptoēsis 1*

Lk 21 9	when you hear of wars and revolutions, do not be *frightened*,
24 37	In a state of *alarm* and fright, [the disciples] thought they were seeing a ghost.
Ph 1 28	3 [meeting the attack with firm resistance,] quite un*shaken* by your enemies.
1 P 3 6	You are now [Sarah's] children, as long as you live good 2 lives and do not give way to fear or *worry*.

6. BE ALARMED: *THROEŌ*

throeō 3

Mt 24 6	do not *be alarmed*, for this is something that must happen,
Mk 13 7	When you hear of wars and rumours of wars, do not *be alarmed*,
2 Th 2 2	do not *get excited* too soon or *alarmed* by any prediction

7. TREMBLE

1: TREMBLE: *PHRISSŌ*

phrissō 1

Jm 2 19 ⑤	the demons [believe in God too], and they *tremble with fear*.

2: TREMBLE; *TREMŌ*

2 *tremō 3* 3 *en-tromos 3*
1 *tromos 5*

Mk 5 33	the woman [cured of a haemorrhage] came forward, fright-2 ened and *trembling* . . . and she fell at [Jesus'] feet
16 8	the women came out and ran away from the tomb because they were ⌐frightened out of their wits (lit. *trembling* and out of their wits [with fright]);
Lk 8 47	2 the woman [cured of a haemorrhage] came forward *trembling*, and . . . explained
Ac 7 32	3 Moses *trembled* and did not dare to look any more.
16 29	3 The gaoler . . . threw himself *trembling* at the feet of Paul and Silas,
1 Co 2 3	I came among you in great fear and *trembling*
2 Co 7 15	with what ⌐deep respect (lit. fear and *trembling*) you welcomed [Titus].
Ep 6 5	Slaves, be obedient to . . . your masters . . . with ⌐deep respect (lit. fear and *trembling*) . . . as you are obedient to Christ.
Ph 2 12	work for your salvation in fear and *trembling*.
Heb 12 21	The whole scene [on the mountain] was so terrible that 3 Moses said: I am afraid, and was *trembling* with fright.
2 P 2 10	Such self-willed people . . . ⌐are not afraid of offending (lit. 2 do not *tremble* to offend) against the glorious ones,

FERVENT – HOT – COLD

1. Fervent(ly), Earnest(ly), Energetically – Unremitting – Sincere: *ek-tenōs*	3. Warm oneself, Keep warm – Heat: *thermainō*
	4. Lukewarm: *chliaros*
2. Hot = Ardent, Fervent, Earnest: *zeō*	5. Cool – Cold: *psychos*

1. FERVENT(LY), EARNEST(LY), ENERGETICALLY – UNREMITTING – SINCERE: *EK-TENŌS*

3 *ek-teneia 1* 1 *ek-tenōs 3*
4 *ek-tenēs 1* 2 *eu-tonōs 2*

Lk 22 44	In his anguish [Jesus] prayed even more *earnestly*,
23 10	2 the chief priests and the scribes were there, *violently pressing* their accusations.
Ac 12 5	All the time Peter was under guard the Church prayed to God for him ⌐*unremittingly* (or: *fervently*).
18 28	2 [Apollos was able to help the believers] by the *energetic way* he refuted the Jews in public
26 7	[it is for my hope in the promise that I am on trial,] the 3 promise that our twelve tribes, ⌐*constant* (lit. *fervent*) in worship night and day, hope to attain.
1 P 1 22	let your love for each other be ⌐*real* (lit. *sincere*) and from the heart
4 8	4 never let your love for each other grow in*sincere*,

2. HOT = ARDENT, FERVENT, EARNEST: *ZEŌ*

2 *zeō 2* 1 *zestos 3*

Ac 18 25	2 [Apollos] preached [about Jesus] with great spiritual *earnestness*
Rm 12 11	2 Work for the Lord . . . with great *earnestness* of spirit.
Rv 3 15	[Laodicea,] you are neither cold nor *hot*. I wish you 16 were ⌐one or the other (lit. cold or *hot*), [16] but since you are neither (§ *hot* nor cold), but only lukewarm, I will spit you out of my mouth.

3. WARM ONESELF, KEEP WARM – HEAT: *THERMAINŌ*

1 *thermainō 6* 2 *thermē 1*

Mk 14 54	Peter . . . was sitting with the attendants *warming himself* at the fire.
67	[A servant-girl] saw Peter *warming himself* there,
Jn 18 18	the servants and guards . . . were standing there *warming themselves*; so Peter stood there too, *warming himself* with the others.
25	Simon Peter stood there *warming himself*,
Ac 28 3	2 a viper brought out by the *heat* attached itself to [Paul's hand.
Jm 2 16	I wish you well; *keep yourself warm* and eat plenty.

4. LUKEWARM: *CHLIAROS*

chliaros 1

Rv 3 16	since you are . . . only *lukewarm*, I will spit you out of my mouth.

5. COOL – COLD: *PSYCHOS*

3 *psychō 1* 1 *psychros 4*
2 *psychos 3* 4 *kata-psychō 1*

Mt 10 42	If anyone gives . . . a cup of *cold* water to one of these little ones, . . . he will . . . not lose his reward.
24 12	3 with the increase of lawlessness, love in most men will *grow cold*;
Lk 16 24	4 Father Abraham, . . . send Lazarus to . . . *cool* my tongue.
Jn 18 18	2 Now it was *cold*, and the servants and guards had lit a charcoal fire
Ac 28 2	The inhabitants . . . lit a huge fire because . . . the weather 2 was *cold*.
2 Co 11 27	2 I have worked and laboured . . . I have been in the *cold* without clothes.
Rv 3 15	[Laodicea,] you are neither *cold* nor hot. I wish you were 16 ⌐one or the other (lit. *cold* or hot), [16] but since you are neither (§ hot nor *cold*), but only lukewarm, I will spit you out of my mouth.

FESTIVAL

1. Festival (time), Festivities – Celebrate a Feast: *heortē*	2. Gather for a Festival – Festal Assembly: *pan-ēgyris*

1. FESTIVAL (TIME), FESTIVITIES – CELEBRATE A FEAST: *HEORTĒ*

2 *heortazō 1* 1 *heortē 27*

Mt 26	5	[Jesus' arrest] must not be during the *festivities*; there must be no disturbance among the people.
27	15	At *festival time* it was the governor's practice to release a prisoner
Mk 14	2	[to arrest Jesus . . .] It must not be during the *festivities*,
15	6	At *festival time* Pilate used to release a prisoner
Lk 2	41	[Jesus'] parents used to go to Jerusalem for the *feast* of the Passover. ⁴² When he was twelve years old, they went up for the *feast*
42		
22	1	The *feast* of Unleavened Bread, called the Passover, was now drawing near,
23	17	(ᵛ [Pilate] was under obligation to release one man for them every *feast* day)
Jn 2	23	During [Jesus'] stay in Jerusalem for the *feast* of the Passover
4	45	the Galileans received [Jesus] well, having seen all that he had done at Jerusalem during the *festival* ʳwhich they too had attended the *festival*
5	1	there was a (ᵛ the) Jewish *festival*, and Jesus went up to Jerusalem.
6	4	It was shortly before the Jewish *feast* of Passover.
7	2	the Jewish *feast* of Tabernacles drew near,
8	Go up to the *festival* yourselves: I am ʳnot going (ᵛ not going yet) to this *festival*, because for me the time is not ripe yet . . . ¹⁰ However, after his brothers had left for the *festival*, [Jesus] went up as well, but quite privately,
10	
11	At the *festival* the Jews were on the look-out for [Jesus]:
14	When the *festival* was half over, Jesus went to the Temple
37	On the last day and greatest day of the *festival*, Jesus stood there and cried out:
11	56	Will [Jesus] come to the *festival* or not?
12	12	the crowds who had come up for the *festival* heard that Jesus was on his way to Jerusalem.
20	Among those who went up to worship at the *festival* were some Greeks.
13	1	before the *festival* of the Passover . . . Jesus knew that the hour had come for him to pass from this world to the Father.
29	Buy what we need for the *festival*,
Ac 18	21	(ᵛ It is absolutely essential for me to celebrate the next *festival* in Jerusalem)
1 Co 5	8	2 let us *celebrate the feast* . . . having only the unleavened bread of sincerity and truth.
Col 2	16	never let anyone else decide . . . whether you are to observe annual *festivals*, New Moons or sabbaths.

2. GATHER FOR A FESTIVAL – FESTAL ASSEMBLY: *PAN-ĒGYRIS*

pan-ēgyris 1

Heb 12	22	you have come to . . . Mount Zion . . . where the millions of angels have *gathered for the festival*,

FIGHT – STRUGGLE

1. **Fight, Wrestle, Struggle:** *palē*
2. **Fight, Box:** *pykteuō*
3. **Fight, Battle – Struggle, Strive:** *agōnizomai*
   1: Fight (competitively or figuratively), Race – Strive (to),

    Struggle (to)
    2: Fight (literally) – Conquer
4. **Strive, Struggle, Compete:** *athleō*
5. **Train, Training, Exercise:** *gymnazō*
6. **Yield:** *eikō*

1. FIGHT, WRESTLE, STRUGGLE: *PALĒ*

palē 1

Ep 6	12	it is not against human enemies that we have to *struggle*,

2. FIGHT, BOX: *PYKTEUŌ*

pykteuō 1

1 Co 9	26	that is how I *fight*, not beating the air.

3. FIGHT, BATTLE – STRUGGLE, STRIVE: *AGŌNIZOMAI*

2	*agōn* 6	4 *kat-agōnizomai 1*
1	*agōnizomai 8*	5 *ep-agōnizomai 1*
3	*ant-agōnizomai 1*	6 *syn-agōnizomai 1*

1: FIGHT (COMPETITIVELY OR FIGURATIVELY), RACE – STRIVE (TO), STRUGGLE (TO)

Lk 13	24	*Try your best* to enter by the narrow door,
Rm 15	30	6 ʳhelp me through my dangers (lit. *strive with* me) by praying to God for me.
1 Co 9	25	All the *fighters* at the games go into strict training;
Ph 1	30	2 You and I are together in the same *fight* as you saw me fighting before
Col 1	29	It is for this I *struggle* wearily on,
2	1	I want you to know that I do have to *struggle* for you,
4	12	Epaphras . . . never stops *battling* for you, praying that you will never lapse
1 Th 2	2	God . . . gave us the courage to proclaim his Good News for you in the face of great *opposition*.
1 Tm 4	10	the point of all our toiling and ʳbattling (or: *striving*) is that we have put our trust in the living God
6	12	/2 *Fight* the good *fight* of the faith
2 Tm 4	7	/2 I have *fought* the good *fight* to the end;
Heb 12	1	we too, then, should . . . keep running steadily in the *race* we have started.
2	
4	3 In the *fight* against sin, you have not yet had to keep fighting to the point of death.
Jude	3	5 I . . . appeal to you to *fight hard* for the faith

2: FIGHT (LITERALLY) – CONQUER

Jn 18	36	my men would have *fought* to prevent my being surrendered to the Jews.
Heb 11	33	4 These were men who through faith *conquered* kingdoms,

4. STRIVE, STRUGGLE, COMPETE: *ATHLEŌ*

1 *athleō* 2	2 *syn-athleō* 2	
3 *athlēsis* 1		

Ph 1	27	so that . . . I shall know that you are unanimous in meeting the attack ʳwith firm resistance, united by (lit. *striving in unity* through) your love for the faith
2	
4	3	[Evodia and Syntyche] ʳwere a help to me when I was fighting (lit. *struggled with* me) to defend the Good News
2	
2 Tm 2	5	or ʳtake an athlete – he (lit. a person who *competes*) cannot win any crown unless he has ʳkept (lit. *competed* according to) all the rules of the contest;
Heb 10	32	3 Remember all the sufferings that you had to ʳmeet (lit. *struggle with endurance* through)

5. TRAIN, TRAINING, EXERCISE: *GYMNAZŌ*

2 *gymnasia* 1	1 *gymnazō* 4	

1 Tm 4	7	/2 *Train* yourself spiritually. ⁸ Physical *exercises* are useful enough,
8	
Heb 5	14	men with minds *trained* by practice to distinguish between good and bad.
12	11	any punishment is most painful at the time, . . . but later, in those ʳon whom it has been used (lit. who have been *trained* by it), it bears fruit
2 P 2	14	Greed is the one lesson their minds ʳhave learnt (lit. are *trained* in).

6. YIELD: *EIKŌ*

eikō 1

Ga 2	5	to safeguard for you the true meaning of the Good News . . . I refused . . . to *yield* to . . . people [who do not really belong to the brotherhood]

FILL – FULL – FULFIL

1. **Fill – Full – Cargo:** *gemō*
   1: Fill – Full
   2: Cargo
2. **Full:** *mestos*
3. **Fill – Full – Fulfil:** *pimplēmi*
   1: Fill, Full, Fullness – Complete, Make up
     a) Fill – Full, Filled
     b) Fullness (of God, or Christ) – (God is) Full, (God) Fills
     c) (A person is) Filled (with)

  d) Full, Fill (figuratively) Complete, Finish – Supply, Provide, Make up
  2: Fulfil
    a) Fulfil (words of prophecy)
    b) Fulfil (the law, righteousness)
    c) (the time is) Fulfilled, Come
    d) Fulfil = Accomplish – Take place, Happen
  3: (Be) Convinced, Fully assured – Complete conviction

1. FILL – FULL – CARGO: *GEMŌ*

2 *gemizō* 9   3 *gomos* 3
1 *gemō*   11

1: FILL – FULL

Mt 23	25		You who clean the outside . . . and leave the inside *full* of extortion and intemperance.
	27		whitewashed tombs that . . . inside are *full* of dead men's bones
Mk 4	37	2	the waves were breaking into the boat so that it was almost ˹swamped (lit. *filled*).
15	36	2	Someone ran and ˹soaked a sponge in (lit. *filled* a sponge with) vinegar
Lk 11	39		inside yourselves you are *filled* with extortion and wickedness.
14	23	< 2	force people to come in to make sure my house is *full*;
15	16	2	[the prodigal] would willingly have *filled* his belly with the husks the pigs were eating
Jn 2	7	2/2	'Fill the jars with water', and they *filled* them to the brim.
6	13	2	they . . . *filled* twelve hampers with scraps
Rm 3	14		(Ps 10 7) bitter curses *fill* their mouths.
Rv 4	6		four animals ˹with many (lit. *full* of) eyes,
	8		Each of the four animals ˹had (lit. was *full* of) eyes all the way round
5	8		a golden bowl *full* of incense
8	5	2	the angel took the censer and *filled* it with the fire from the altar,
15	7		seven golden bowls *filled* with the anger of God
	8	2	The smoke from the glory and the power of God *filled* the temple
17	3		a scarlet beast which . . . ˹had blasphemous titles written all over it (lit. was *full* of blasphemous titles).
	4		a golden winecup *filled* with the disgusting filth of her fornication;
21	9		the seven bowls *full* of the seven last plagues

2: CARGO

Ac 21	3	3	the ship was to unload her *cargo* [at Tyre].
Rv 18	11	3	when there is nobody left to buy [the traders'] *cargoes* of goods;
	12	3	their *stocks* of gold and silver, jewels and pearls,

2. FULL: *MESTOS*

1 *mestos* 9   2 *mestoō* 1

Mt 23	28		inside you are *full* of hypocrisy and lawlessness.
Jn 19	29		A jar *full* of vinegar stood there, so putting a sponge ˹soaked in (lit. *full* of) vinegar on a hyssop stick
21	11		Simon Peter . . . dragged the net to the shore, *full* of big fish.
Ac 2	13	2	They ˹have been drinking too much (lit. are *full* of) new wine
Rm 1	29		[the pagans] are . . . ˹addicted to (lit. *full* of) envy, murder, wrangling,
15	14		I am quite certain that you are *full* of good intentions,
Jm 3	8		the tongue . . . is . . . *full* of deadly poison.
	17	Θ	the wisdom that comes down from above . . . is *full* of compassion
2 P 2	14		with their eyes ˹always looking for (lit. *full* of) adultery;

3. FILL – FULL – FULFIL: *PIMPLĒMI*

2	*pimplēmi*	24	6	*ana-pleroō*	6
4	*plērēs*	16	12	*ant-ana-pleroō*	1
3	*plērōma*	17	10	*pros-ana-plēroō*	2
1	*plēroō*	87	13	*ek-plēroō*	1
11	*plēsmonē*	1	14	*ek-plērōsis*	1
5	*plēro-phoreō*	6	8	*em-pimplēmi*	4
7	*plēro-phoria*	4	15	*em-piplaō*	1
			9	*sym-plēroō*	3

1: FILL, FULL, FULLNESS – COMPLETE, MAKE UP

a) Fill – Full, Filled

Mt 13	48		When [the net] is *full*, the fishermen haul it ashore;
14	20	4	they collected the scraps remaining, twelve baskets *full*.
15	37	4	they collected what was left of the scraps, seven baskets *full*.
22	10	2	the wedding hall was *filled* with guests.
27	48	2	one of them quickly ran to get a sponge which he ˹dipped in (lit. *filled* with) vinegar

Mk 4	28	< 4	the land produces first the shoot, then the ear, then the *full* grain in the ear.
6	43	3	They collected twelve ˹basketfuls (lit. baskets *full*) of scraps
8	19	4	how many baskets *full* of scraps did you collect?
	20	3	how many baskets *full* of scraps did you collect?
Lk 3	5		(Is 40 4) Every valley will be *filled* [in],
5	7	2	they *filled* the two boats to sinking point.
	12	4	a man appeared, ˹covered with (lit. *full* of) leprosy.
8	23	9	When a squall came down on the lake the boat started ˹taking in (lit. *filling* with) water
Jn 12	3		the house was *full* of the scent of the ointment.
Ac 2	2		the noise of [the wind] *filled* the entire house
1 Co 10	26	3	(Ps 24 1) the earth and ˹everything that is in (lit. *what fills*) it belong to the Lord.

b) Fullness (of God, of Christ) – (God is) Full, (God) Fills

Lk 1	53	8	(Ps 107 9) The hungry he has *filled* with good things,
Jn 1	14	4	the only Son of the Father, *full* of grace and truth. . .
	16	3	[16] Indeed, from his *fullness* we have . . . received grace
Ac 2	28		(Ps 16 11) you will *fill* me with gladness through your presence.
14	17	15	he gives you food and ˹makes you happy (lit. *fills* your heart with happiness).
Rm 15	13		May the God of hope ˹bring you (lit. *fill* you with) such joy and peace in your faith
Ep 1	23	3	[the Church] is his body, the *fullness* of him who *fills* the whole creation.
3	19	3	until . . . you are filled with the utter *fullness* of God.
4	10		The one who rose higher than all the heavens to *fill* all things
	13	3	until we become the perfect Man, fully mature with the *fullness* of Christ himself.
Col 1	19	3	God wanted all ˹perfection (lit. *fullness*) to be found in [Christ]
2	9	3	In [Christ's] body lies the *fullness* of divinity

c) (A person is) Filled (with)

Ⓢ = Filled with the Holy Spirit

Lk 1	15	Ⓢ	2	from his mother's womb [John] will be *filled* with the Holy Spirit,
	41	Ⓢ	2	Elizabeth was *filled* with the Holy Spirit.
	67	Ⓢ	2	Zechariah was *filled* with the Holy Spirit
2	40			the child [Jesus] grew to maturity, and he was *filled* with wisdom;
4	1	Ⓢ	4	*Filled* with the Holy Spirit, Jesus left the Jordan and was led by the Spirit through the wilderness,
	28		2	everyone in the synagogue was ˹enraged (lit. *filled* with rage)
5	26		2	They were all . . . *filled* with awe, saying, 'We have seen strange things today'.
6	11		2	But they were ˹furious (lit. *filled* with rage),
Jn 16	6			you are ˹sad (lit. *filled* with sadness) at heart because I have told you this.
Ac 2	4	Ⓢ	2	They were all *filled* with the Holy Spirit, and began to speak foreign languages
3	10		2	They were all ˹astonished (lit. *filled* with astonishment) and unable to explain what had happened
4	8	Ⓢ	2	Peter, *filled* with the Holy Spirit, addressed [the rulers, elders and scribes],
	31	Ⓢ	2	the house where they were assembled rocked; they were all *filled* with the Holy Spirit
5	3	Ⓓ	2	Ananias, . . . how can Satan have so ˹possessed you (lit. *filled* your heart) that you should lie to the Holy Spirit
	17		2	˹Prompted by (lit. *Filled* with) jealousy, [18] [the high priest and his supporters] arrested the apostles
6	3			you . . . must select from among yourselves seven men . . . ,
	5	Ⓢ	4	*filled* with the Spirit and with wisdom; . . . [5] The whole
		Ⓢ	4	assembly . . . elected Stephen, a man *full* of faith and of the Holy Spirit,
	8		4	Stephen was *filled* with grace and power and began to work miracles
7	55	Ⓢ	4	Stephen, *filled* with the Holy Spirit, gazed into heaven
9	17			Saul, I have been sent by the Lord Jesus . . . so that you may recover your sight and be *filled* with the Holy Spirit.
	36		2	Tabitha, . . . who ˹never tired of doing good or (lit. was *full* of good works and) giving in charity.
11	24	Ⓢ	4	[Barnabas] was a good man, *filled* with the Holy Spirit and with faith.
13	9	Ⓢ	2	Paul, *filled* with the Holy Spirit, looked [Elymas] full in the face [10] and said, 'You ˹utter fraud, you impostor (lit.
	10		4	[are] *filled* with deceit and deception),'
	45		2	When they saw the crowds, the Jews, ˹prompted by (lit. *filled* with) jealousy, . . . contradicted everything Paul said,
	52	Ⓢ		the disciples were *filled* with joy and the Holy Spirit.
19	28		4	This speech ˹roused them to (lit. *filled* them with) fury,
	29		2	The whole town was ˹in an uproar (lit. *full* of confusion)
Rm 1	29			[men] are ˹steeped in (lit. *full* of) all sorts of depravity,
15	14			I am quite certain that you are full of good intentions, ˹perfectly well (lit. *fully*) instructed and able
	29		3	when I reach you I shall arrive with ˹rich (lit. the *fullness* of) blessings from Christ.

| 2 Co | 7 | 4 | | I am *filled* with consolation and my joy is overflowing. |

2 Co 7 4   I am *filled* with consolation and my joy is overflowing.
Ep 3 19 ●   until . . . you are *filled* with the utter fullness of God.
   5 18 Ⓢ   Do not drug yourselves with wine . . ; be *filled* with the Spirit.
Ph 1 11   [the Day of Christ,] when you will ⌐reach the perfect (lit. be *filled* with) goodness which Jesus Christ produces in us
Col 1 9   we ask God . . . that through perfect wisdom . . . you should ⌐reach the fullest (lit. be *filled* with the) knowledge of his will.
   2 10 ●   in [Christ] you too find your own *fulfilment*.
2 Tm 1 4   [I] long to see you again to ⌐complete my (or: be *filled* with) happiness.
Heb 10 22   7 let us be sincere in heart and *filled* with faith,

d) Full, Fill (figuratively) = Complete, Finish – Supply, Provide, Make up

P = Full, Fill, Supply, in physical senses

Mt 5 17   Do not imagine that I have come to abolish the Law or the Prophets. I have come not to abolish but to ⌐complete (or: fulfil) them.
   9 16 P   3 because the ⌐patch (lit. [bit] *supplied* [later]) pulls away from the cloak
   23 32   *finish off* the work that your fathers began.
Mk 2 21 P   3 the ⌐patch (lit. [bit] *supplied* [later]) pulls away from [the cloak]
Lk 1 23   2 When [Zechariah's] time of service *came to an end* he returned home.
   6 25 P   8 Alas for you who have your *fill* now: you shall go hungry.
   7 1 X   When he had *come to the end* of all he wanted the people to hear,
   21 24   until the age of the pagans is *completely over*.
Jn 3 29   This same joy I feel, and now it is *complete*.
   6 12 P   8 When they had ⌐eaten enough (lit. were *full*), he said to the disciples, 'Pick up the pieces left over,'
   15 11   I have told you this so that . . . your joy [may be] *complete*.
   16 24   Ask and you will receive, and so your joy will be *complete*.
   17 13   I say these things to share my joy with them to the *full*.
Ac 5 28   You have *filled* Jerusalem with your teaching.
   7 30   Forty years *later* . . . an angel appeared to him
   9 23   Some time *passed*,
   12 25   Barnabas and Saul *completed* their task
   13 25   Before John *ended* his career he said, 'I am not the one'
   14 26   [Paul and Barnabas had] . . . been commended to the grace of God for the work they had now *completed*.
   19 21   When all this was *over* Paul made up his mind to go back to Jerusalem
   21 26   [Paul gave] notice of the time when the period of purification 14 would be *over*
   24 27   When the two years *came to an end*, Felix was succeeded by Porcius Festus
Rm 11 12   think how much more [the pagan world] will ⌐benefit from 3 (lit. be *completed* by) the conversion of [the Jews]
   25   One section of Israel has become blind, but this will last 3 only until the *whole* pagan world has entered,
   15 19   I have preached Christ's Good News ⌐to the utmost of my capacity (lit. *fully*).
   24   8 I hope . . , after *enjoying* a little of your company, to complete the rest of the journey
1 Co 14 16   6 Anyone *filling* the position of an uninitiated person will never be able to say Amen
   16 17   6 Stephanus, Fortunatus and Achaicus . . . *make up* for your absence.
2 Co 9 12   10 doing this holy service is not only *supplying* all the needs of the saints,
   10 6   Once you have given your *complete* obedience,
   11 9   10 the brothers who came from Macedonia *provided* me with everything I wanted.
Ga 4 4   3 when the appointed time ⌐came (or: *came to an end*), God sent his Son,
   5 14   the whole of the Law is *summarised* in a single command (Lv 19 18): Love your neighbour as yourself.
Ep 1 10   3 when the times had *run* [their course] *to the end*:
Ph 2 2   That is the one thing which would make me *completely* happy.
   30   6 [Epaphroditus] risked his life to *give* me the help that you were not able to give me
   4 18   I am *fully provided* now that I have received from Epaphroditus 19 the offering that you sent, . . . ¹⁹ In return my God will *fulfil* all your needs,
Col 1 24   It makes me happy . . . in my own body to do what I can 12 to *make up* all that still has to be undergone by Christ
   2 23 P   11 ⌐once the flesh starts to protest (lit. in controlling the *satiating* of the flesh), [these prohibitions] are no use at all.
   4 12   praying that you will never lapse but always hold perfectly 5 and ⌐securely (lit. *fully*) to the will of God.
1 Th 2 16   6 They never stop trying to *finish off* the sins they have begun,
2 Th 1 11   we pray continually that our God will . . . *fulfil* all your
Θ   desires for goodness and *complete* all that you have been doing through faith;
2 Tm 1 4   [I] long to see you again to ⌐complete my (or: be *filled* with) happiness.

2 Tm 4 5   make the preaching of the Good News your life's work, in 5 *thoroughgoing* service.
   17   5 so that through me the *whole* message might be proclaimed
1 Jn 1 4   We are writing this to you to make ⌐our own (ᵛ your) joy *complete*.
2 Jn 8   4 Watch yourselves, or all our work will be lost and not get the ⌐reward it deserves (lit. *full* reward).
   12   I hope . . . to visit you . . . so that ⌐our (ᵛ your) joy may be *complete*.
Rv 3 2   So far I have failed to notice anything in the way you live that my God could possibly call *perfect*,
   6 11   until the roll was *complete* and their . . . brothers had been killed

2: FULFIL

a) Fulfil (words of prophecy)

Mt 1 22   all this took place to *fulfil* the words spoken by the Lord through the prophet (Is 7 14):
   2 15   This was to *fulfil* what the Lord had spoken through the prophet (Ho 11 1):
   17   It was then that the words spoken through the prophet were *fulfilled* (Jr 31 15):
   23   In this way the words spoken through the prophets were to be *fulfilled*: He will be called a Nazarene.
   4 14   In this way the prophecy of Isaiah was to be *fulfilled* (Is 8 23 – 9 1)
   5 17   Do not imagine that I have come to abolish the Law or the Prophets. I have come not to abolish but to ⌐complete (or: *fulfil*) them.
   8 17   This was to *fulfil* the prophecy of Isaiah (Is 53 4):
   12 17   This was to *fulfil* the prophecy of Isaiah (Is 42 1–4):
   13 14   6 So in their case this prophecy of Isaiah is being *fulfilled* (Is 6 9):
   35   This was to *fulfil* the prophecy (Ps 78 2):
   21 4   This took place to *fulfil* the prophecy (Zc 9 9):
   26 54   how would the scriptures be *fulfilled* . . .?
   56   all this happened to *fulfil* the prophecies in scripture
   27 9   The words of the prophet Jeremiah were then *fulfilled* (Zc 11 12–13; cf. Jr 19 1; 32 7–9):
Mk 14 49   But this is to *fulfil* the scriptures.
      (ᵛ And the scriptures were *fulfilled* . . . (Is 53 12) . . .)
Lk 1 20   you have not believed my words, which will ⌐come true (lit be *fulfilled*) at their appointed time,
   4 21   This text is being *fulfilled* today even as you listen (Is 61 1–2)
   21 22   this is the time of vengeance when all that scripture says 2 must be *fulfilled*.
   24 44   everything written about me in the Law of Moses, in the Prophets and in the Psalms, has to be *fulfilled*.
Jn 12 38   this was to *fulfil* the words of the prophet Isaiah (Is 53 1):
   13 18   what the scripture says must be *fulfilled* (Ps 41 9):
   17 12   not one is lost except the one who chose to be lost, and this was to *fulfil* the scriptures.
   18 9   This was to *fulfil* the words [Jesus] had spoken (cf. Jn 6 39; 17 12), 'Not one of those you gave me have I lost'.
   32   This was to *fulfil* the words Jesus had spoken (cf. Jn 3 14; 12 32–33) indicating the way he was going to die.
   19 24   In this way the words of scripture were *fulfilled* (Ps 22 18): They shared out my clothing
   36   all this happened to *fulfil* the words of scripture (Ex 12 46): Not one bone of his will be broken
Ac 1 16   the passage of scripture had to be *fulfilled* in which the Holy Spirit, speaking through David, foretells the fate of Judas,
   3 18   this was the way God *carried out* what he had foretold,
   13 27   What the people of Jerusalem and the rulers did . . . was in fact to *fulfil* the prophecies read on every sabbath.
   33   13 it is to us . . . that [God] has *fulfilled* [the promise made to our ancestors], by raising Jesus from the dead.
Jm 2 23   This is ⌐what scripture really means (lit. how scripture was *fulfilled*) when it says (Gn 15 6): Abraham put his faith in God,

b) Fulfil (the law, righteousness)

Mt 3 15   it is fitting that we should, in this way, *do all that righteousness demands*.
Jn 15 25   all this was only to *fulfil* the words written in their Law (Ps 35 19):
Rm 8 4   He did this in order that the Law's just demands might be *satisfied* in us,
   13 8   If you love your fellow men you have *carried out* ⌐your obligations (lit. what the law requires). . . . ¹⁰ Love . .
   10   3 is the ⌐answer to (lit. *fulfilment* of) every one of the commandments.
Ga 6 2   6 You should carry each other's troubles and *fulfil* the law of Christ.

c) (the time is) Fulfilled, Come

Mk 1 15   'The time has *come*' [Jesus] said 'and the kingdom of God is close at hand.'

Lk 1 57 2 the time *came* for Elizabeth to have her child, and she gave birth to a son;
  2 6 2 the time *came* for [Mary] to have her child,
  21 2 When the eighth day *came* and the child [Jesus] was to be circumcised,
  22 2 when the day *came* for them to be purified
  9 51 9 as the time *drew near* for [Jesus] to be taken up to heaven,
Jn 7 8 for me the time is not ʳripe (lit. *fulfilled*) yet.
Ac 2 1 9 When Pentecost day *came* [round],
  7 23 ʳAt (lit. *Came*) the age of forty [Moses] decided to visit his countrymen,
Ga 4 4 3 when the appointed time ʳ*came* (or: came to an end), God sent his Son,

d) Fulfil = Accomplish – Take place, Happen

Lk 1 1 5 accounts of the events that have *taken place* among us,
  9 31 his passing which he was to *accomplish* in Jerusalem.
  22 16 I shall not eat [the passover] again until it is *fulfilled* in the kingdom of God.
Col 1 25 God made me responsible for ʳdelivering (lit. *accomplishing*) God's message to you,
  4 17 Reemmber the service that the Lord wants you to do, and try to *carry it out.*
2 Th 1 11 Θ we pray continually that our God will . . . *fulfil* all your desires for goodness and complete all that you have been doing through faith;
Heb 6 11 go on showing the same earnestness to the end, to the
  7 *perfect fulfilment* of our hopes,

3: (BE) CONVINCED, FULLY ASSURED – COMPLETE CONVICTION

Rm 4 21 5 [Abraham gave glory to God,] *convinced* that God had power to do what he had promised.
  14 5 5 each must be left free to ʳhold (lit. be *convinced* of) his own opinion.
Col 2 2 7 so that your understanding may come to ʳ*full development*
  7 (or: *complete conviction*),
  4 12 praying that you will never lapse but always hold perfectly
  5 and ʳsecurely (lit. *fully assured*) to the will of God.
1 Th 1 5 7 the Good News . . . came to you . . . as *utter conviction.*

FIND – HAPPEN

1. Find, Find (oneself to be) – Find (a person), Meet: *heuriskō*	**2:** Rarely found = Unusual, Remarkable – Perhaps
2. Find – Get to, Attain – Chance: *tynchanō*	**3. Chance – Happen by chance:** *synkyria*
1: Attain – Earn, Obtain	**4. Happen:** *sym-bainō*

1. FIND, FIND (ONESELF TO BE) – FIND (A PERSON), MEET: *HEURISKŌ*

1	*heuriskō*	175	3	*eph-euretēs*	1
2	*an-(h)euriskō*	2			

Θ = Find God; X = Find Jesus

Mt 1 18 Mary . . . ʳwas found to be (lit. *found* herself to be) with child through the Holy Spirit.
  2 8 X when you have *found* [the child], let me know,
  7 7 search, and you will *find* . . . ⁸ For . . . the one who searches
  8 always *finds*;
  14 it is a narrow gate . . . that leads to life, and only a few *find* it.
  8 10 nowhere in Israel have I *found* faith like this.
  10 39 Anyone who *finds* his life will lose it; anyone who loses his life for my sake will *find* it.
  11 29 Shoulder my yoke . . . and you will *find* rest for your souls!
  12 43 Ⓓ an unclean spirit . . . wanders . . . looking for a place to rest, and cannot *find* one. ⁴⁴ . . . *finding* [the house it came from] unoccupied [it collects seven other spirits and they go in]
  13 44 < The kingdom of heaven is like treasure hidden in a field which someone has *found*;
  46 < when [a merchant looking for fine pearls] *finds* one of great value he . . . sells everything . . . and buys it.
  16 25 anyone who loses his life for my sake will *find* it.
  17 27 take the first fish that bites, open its mouth and there you will *find* a shekel;

Mt 18 13 < if he *finds* [the one stray sheep], it gives him more joy than do the ninety-nine who did not stray at all.
  28 < as this servant went out, he happened to *meet* a fellow servant
  20 6 < [the landowner] *found* more men standing round,
  21 2 you will immediately *find* a tethered donkey
  19 [Jesus] went up to [the fig tree] and *found* nothing . . . but leaves.
  22 9 < invite everyone you can *find* to the wedding.
  10 < So these servants . . . collected together everyone they could *find*,
  24 46 Happy that servant if his master's arrival *finds* him at this employment.
  26 40 [Jesus] came back to the disciples and *found* them sleeping,
  43 he came back again and *found* them sleeping,
  60 [The chief priests were looking for evidence against Jesus.] But they could not *find* any,
  27 32 On their way out, they *came across* a man from Cyrene,
Mk 1 37 X when [Simon and his companions] *found* [Jesus] they said, 'Everybody is looking for you'.
  7 30 [the Syrophoenician woman] *found* the child lying on the bed and the devil gone.
  11 2 as soon as you enter [the village] you will *find* a tethered colt
  4 [The disciples] went off and *found* a colt tethered
  13 [Jesus] went to see if he could *find* any fruit on [the fig tree] but . . . he *found* nothing but leaves;
  13 36 if [the master] comes unexpectedly, he must not *find* you asleep.
  14 16 The disciples . . . *found* everything as [Jesus] had told them,
  37 [Jesus] came back and *found* them sleeping,
  40 once more he came back and *found* them sleeping,
  55 The chief priests . . . were looking for evidence against Jesus . . . but they could not *find* any.
Lk 1 30 Mary, do not be afraid; you have ʳwon (lit. *found*) God's favour.
  2 12 X you will *find* a baby . . . lying in a manger.
  16 X 2 [the shepherds] *found* Mary and Joseph, and the baby lying in a manger.
  45 X When [Jesus's parents] failed to *find* him they went back to Jerusalem . . . ⁴⁶ . . . they *found* him in the Temple,
  46 X
  4 17 [Jesus] *found* the place where it is written: (Is 61 1–2)
  5 19 the crowd made it impossible to *find* a way of getting [the paralytic] in,
  6 7 The scribes . . . were watching [Jesus] . . . hoping to *find* something to use against him.
  7 9 not even in Israel have I *found* faith like this.
  10 the messengers . . . *found* the servant in perfect health.
  8 35 the people . . . *found* the man from whom the devils had gone out sitting at the feet of Jesus,
  9 12 the people . . . can go to the villages and farms round about to *find* lodging and food;
  36 after the voice had spoken, Jesus was *found* alone.
  11 9 search, and you will *find* . . . ¹⁰ For . . . the one who searches always *finds*;
  10
  24 Ⓓ an unclean spirit . . . wanders . . . looking for a place to rest, and not *finding* one . . . ²⁵ But . . . *finding* [the home it came from] swept and tidied, ²⁶ it . . . brings seven other spirits
  25
  12 37 Happy those servants whom the master *finds* awake
  38 happy those servants if he *finds* them ready.
  43 Happy that servant if his master's arrival *finds* him at this employment.
  13 6 < A man had a fig tree . . . and he came looking for fruit on it but *found* none. ⁷ . . . for three years now I have been coming to look for fruit on this fig tree and *finding* none.
  7 <
  15 4 < What man among you . . . would not leave the ninety-nine [sheep] . . . and go after the missing one till he *found* it? ⁵ And when he *found* it, would he not . . . call together his friends ⁶ and . . . say, 'I have *found* my sheep that was lost.'
  5 <
  6 <
  8 < what woman . . . would not . . . search thoroughly till she *found* [the lost drachma]? ⁹ And then, when she had *found* it, call together her friends and . . . say, 'I have *found* the drachma I lost'?
  9 <
  24 < this son of mine . . . was lost and is *found*.
  32 < rejoice, because your brother . . . was lost and is *found*.
  17 18 no one ʳhas come back (lit. *may be found* to come back) to give praise to God, except this foreigner.
  18 8 when the Son of Man comes, will he *find* any faith on earth?
  19 30 as you enter [the village] you will *find* a tethered colt
  32 The messengers went off and *found* everything just as [Jesus] had told them.
  48 [the high priests] ʳdid not see (lit. could not *find*) how they could [do away with Jesus]
  22 13 [Peter and John] set off and *found* everything as [Jesus] had told them,
  45 [Jesus] went to the disciples and *found* them sleeping
  23 2 X We *found* this man inciting our people to revolt,
  4 I *find* no case against this man.
  14 I have . . . *found* no case against the man

Lk 23	22	I have *found* no case against him that deserves death,
24	2	[The women] *found* that the stone had been rolled away from the tomb, but [3] on entering discovered that the body of the Lord Jesus was not ⌜there (lit. to be *found* anywhere).
	3 X	
	23 X	when [the women] did not *find* the body, they came back to tell us
	24	Some of our friends went to the tomb and *found* everything exactly as the women had reported,
	33	[the two disciples from Emmaus] *found* the Eleven assembled
Jn 1	41 X	Andrew *met* his brother and said to him, 'We have *found* the Messiah'
	43	Jesus . . . *met* Philip and said, 'Follow me'.
	45 X	Philip *found* Nathanael and said to him, 'We have *found* the one Moses wrote about
2	14	in the Temple [Jesus] *found* people selling cattle
5	14	After a while Jesus *met* [the paralytic whom he had c*ured*] in the Temple
6	25 X	When [the people] *found* him on the other side [of the lake], they said to him, 'Rabbi, when did you come here?'
7	34 X	You will look for me and will not *find* me:
	35 X	Where is he going that we shan't be able to *find* him?
	36 X	What does he mean when he says: You will look for me and will not *find* me:
9	35	when [Jesus] *found* [the blind man] he said to him, 'Do you believe in the Son of Man?'
10	9	Anyone who enters through me will be . . . sure of *finding* pasture.
11	17	Jesus *found* that Lazarus had been in the tomb for four days
12	14	Jesus *found* a young donkey and mounted it
18	38	I *find* no case against him.
19	4	Pilate . . . said to them, '. . . I *find* no case'.
	6	I can *find* no case against him.
21	6	Throw the net out to starboard and you'll *find* something.
Ac 4	21	The court . . . released [Peter and John]; they could not ⌜think of (lit. *find*) any way to punish them,
5	10	When the young men came in they *found* [Sapphira] was dead,
	22	when the officials arrived at the prison they *found* [Peter and John] were not inside,
	23	We *found* the gaol securely locked . . . but . . . we *found* no one inside.
	39	if [this movement] does in fact come from God . . . you might *find* yourselves fighting against God.
7	11	Then a famine came . . . and our ancestors could *find* nothing to eat.
	46	[David] ⌜won (lit. *found*) God's favour and asked (Ps 132 5) permission to ⌜have a temple built (lit. *find* a site) for the ⌜House (ᵛ God) of Jacob,
8	40	Philip *found* that he had reached Azotus
9	2	[Saul] asked for letters . . . that would authorise him to arrest . . . any followers of the Way . . . that he could *find*.
	33	[In Lydda Peter] *found* a man called Aeneas, a paralytic
10	27	[At Caesarea Peter] went in to *meet* all the people assembled there,
11	26	when [Barnabas] *found* [Saul at Tarsus] he brought him to Antioch.
12	19	Herod put out ⌜an unsuccessful search for [Peter] (lit. a search for [Peter] which did not *find* him);
13	6	at Paphos [Saul and Barnabas] ⌜came in contact with (lit. *met*) a Jewish magician called Bar-jesus,
	22	(Ps 89 20) I have ⌜selected (lit. *found*) David . . . a man after my own heart,
	28	Though they *found* nothing to justify [Jesus's] death, they condemned him
17	6	[The Jews, searching for Paul and Silas] only *found* Jason
	23	I ⌜noticed (lit. *found*) . . . an altar inscribed: To An Unknown God.
	27	so that all nations might seek ᵛ the deity (G God) and . . . succeed in *finding* him.
18	2	[in Corinth Paul] *met* a Jew called Aquila
19	1	[in Ephesus Paul] *found* a number of disciples.
	19	The value of [the burnt books] was calculated ⌜to be (lit. and *found* to be) fifty thousand silver pieces.
21	2	[At Patara] we *found* a ship bound for Phoenicia,
	4	2 We ⌜sought out (lit. *found*) the disciples [at Tyre] and stayed there a week.
23	9	We *find* nothing wrong with this man.
	29	I *found* that the accusation concerned disputed points of their Law,
24	5	we *find* this man a perfect pest; he stirs up trouble among Jews
	12	it is not true that they ever *found* me arguing with anyone
	18	it was in connection with [alms and offerings] that they *found* me in the Temple;
	20	let those who are present say what crime they *found* me guilty of
27	6	[At Myra] the centurion *found* an Alexandrian ship leaving for Italy

Ac 27	28	They took soundings and *found* twenty fathoms; after a short interval they . . . *found* fifteen fathoms.
28	14	[at Puteoli] we *found* some brothers
Rm 1	30	Libellers, slanderers, enemies of God, . . . ⌜enterprising in (lit. [good at] *finding*) sin, [deserve to die]
4	1	Apply this to (§ what was *found* by) Abraham, the ancestor from whom we are all descended.
7	10	the commandment was meant to lead me to life but it ⌜turned out (lit. was *found*) to mean death for me,
	21	⌜this seems to be (lit. I *find* it) the rule, that every single time I want to do good it is something evil that comes to hand.
10	20 ⊖	(Is 65 1) I have been *found* by those who did not seek me,
1 Co 4	2	What is expected of stewards is that each one should be *found* worthy
15	15	we ⌜are shown up as (lit. *find* ourselves to be) witnesses who have committed perjury before God,
2 Co 2	13	I was . . . uneasy in mind at not *meeting* brother Titus [at Troas],
5	3	we should like to be *found* wearing clothes
9	4	If some of the Macedonians . . . *found* you unprepared, we should be humiliated
11	12	those people . . . are looking for an opportunity ⌜to claim equality (lit. to be *found* equal) with us in what they boast of.
12	20	I am afraid . . . that . . . I may *find* you different from what I want you to be, and you may *find* that I am not as you would like me to be;
Ga 2	17	if we were to admit that the result of looking to Christ to justify us is ⌜to make us (lit. that we *find* ourselves to be) sinners
Ph 2	7	[Christ] emptied himself . . . and ⌜became as men are (lit. was *found* in the form of a man),
3	9	[if only I can have Christ] and be ⌜given a place (lit. *found*) in him.
2 Tm	117	[in Rome Onesiphorus] searched hard for me and *found* out where I was.
	18	May it be the Lord's will that [Onesiphorus] shall *find* the Lord's mercy on that Day.
Heb 4	16	Let us be confident, then, in approaching the throne of grace, that we shall . . . *find* grace
9	12	[Christ] has entered the sanctuary, . . . having ⌜won (lit. *found*) eternal redemption for us.
11	5	(Gn 5 24 G) Enoch was taken up and . . . was not to be *found*
12	17	when [Esau] wanted to obtain [his father's] blessing afterwards . . . he ⌜was unable to elicit (lit. could not *find* [a way to]) a change of heart.
1 P 1	7	your faith will have been tested . . . and then you will ⌜have (lit. *find*) praise
2	22	(Is 53 9) there ⌜had been (lit. was *found*) no perjury in his mouth.
2 P 3	10	the earth and all that it contains will be ᵛ burnt up (G *found*).
	14	do your best to live lives without spot or stain so that he will *find* you at peace.
2 Jn	4	It has given me great joy to *find* that your children have been living the life of truth
Rv 2	2	you tested the impostors who called themselves apostles and ⌜proved (lit. *found*) they were liars.
3	2	I have failed to ⌜notice (lit. *find*) anything in the way you live that my God could possibly call pefect,
5	4	⌜there was nobody (lit. nobody had been *found*) fit to open the scroll and read it,
9	6	When this happens, men will long for death and not *find* it anywhere;
12	8	[the dragon and his angels] were defeated and ⌜driven out of (lit. no place was *found* for them in) heaven.
14	5	They never allowed a lie ⌜to pass (lit. to be *found* on) their lips
16	20	Every island vanished and the mountains ⌜disappeared (lit. were *found* no more);
18	14	gone for ever, never to ⌜return (lit. be *found*), is your life of magnificence and ease.
	21	Babylon is going to be hurled down, never to be ⌜seen (lit. *found*) again.
	22	never again will craftsmen of every skill be *found*
	24	In [Babylon] you will *find* the blood of prophets and saints,
20	11	earth and sky vanished, leaving ⌜no trace (lit. nothing to be *found*).
	15	anybody whose name could not be *found* written in the book of life was thrown into the burning lake.

2. FIND – GET TO, ATTAIN – CHANCE: *TYNCHANŌ*

1	*tynchanō* 12	3 *para-tynchanō* 1
2	*epi-tynchanō* 5	4 *syn-tynchanō* 1

1: ATTAIN – EARN, OBTAIN

Lk 8	19	4 His mother and his brothers . . . could not *get to* [Jesus] because of the crowd.

Lk 20 35	those who are judged worthy ⌐of (lit. to *attain*) a place in the other world . . . do not marry
Ac 24 2	the unbroken peace ⌐we enjoy (lit. *obtained* for us)
26 22	I ⌐was blessed with (lit. *obtained*) God's help,
27 3	Julius was considerate enough to allow Paul to go to his friends to ⌐be looked after (lit. *obtain* some attention).
Rm 11 7	2 It was not Israel as a whole that *found* what it was seeking, 2 but only the chosen few (§ *found* it).
2 Tm 2 10	I bear it all for the sake of those who are chosen, so that in the end they may ⌐have (lit. *obtain*) . . . salvation
Heb 6 15	Abraham persevered and ⌐saw the promise fulfilled (lit. 2 *obtained* the promise).
8 6 X	[Christ] has ⌐been given (lit. *obtained*) a ministry of a far higher order,
11 33	2 These were men who through faith . . . *earned* the promises.
35	others submitted to torture . . . so that they would rise again to (§ *attain*) a better life.
Jm 4 2	2 You want something and you haven't ⌐got (lit. *obtained*) it; so you are prepared to kill.

2: RARELY FOUND = UNUSUAL, REMARKABLE – PERHAPS

Ac 17 17	in the market place [in Athens Paul] had debates . . . with 3 anyone who ⌐would face him (lit. *chanced* to be there).
19 11	So *remarkable* were the miracles worked by God at Paul's hands
28 2	The inhabitants [of Malta] treated us with *unusual* kindness.
1 Co 14 10	There are ⌐any (lit. an *extraordinary*) [number of] different languages in the world,
15 37	you sow a bare grain, say of wheat ⌐or something like that (lit. *perhaps*),
16 6	I may be staying with you, *perhaps*

3. CHANCE – HAPPEN BY CHANCE: *SYN-KYRIA*

syn-kyria 1

Lk 10 31	a priest *happened* to be travelling down the same road,

4. HAPPEN: *SYM-BAINŌ*

sym-bainō 8

Mk 10 32	[Jesus] began to tell [the Twelve] what was going to *happen* to him.
Lk 24 14	[the two disciples on their way to Emmaus] were talking together about all that had *happened*.
Ac 3 10	They were . . . unable to explain what had *happened* to [the lame man].
20 19	all the . . . trials that ⌐came (lit. *happened*) to me through the plots of the Jews.
21 35	the crowd became so violent that (§ it eventually *happened* that) [Paul] had to be carried by the soldiers;
1 Co 10 11	All this *happened* to [our ancestors] as a warning,
1 P 4 12	There is nothing extraordinary in what has *happened* to you.
2 P 2 22	What ⌐he has done (lit. has *happened* to him) is exactly as the proverb rightly says:

FIRE – BURN

1. Fire, Flame – Burn – to Light
1: Fire, Flame – Burn(ing), Blazing – Test by fire, (Be) Tortured: *pyr*
2: Burn, Brand – Scorch – to Light: *kaiō*
 a) Burn, Catch fire – Blazing, (in) Flames – (Be) Burnt
 b) Light a lamp – Alight, Lit, Burning
 c) Scorching Heat of the sun – Scorch, Blaze, Hot
 d) Burn, (metaphorically) – (Be) Consumed with, On fire
 e) Branded with a red-hot iron – Seared
3: Flame, Flaming – Set fire to, Catch fire from: *phlox*

4: to Light, Kindle – Set fire to, Set ablaze: *haptō*
5: Burnt, Set on fire: *em-piprēmi*
6: Fire, Blaze – Firelight: *phōs*
2. Furnace, Oven, Stove – Fire
1: Furnace, Oven, Stove – Fire: *klibanos*
2: Furnace: *kaminos*
3. Charcoal fire – Fire of coals: *anthrakia*
4. Reduce to ashes, Turn to ashes, Burn: *tephroō*
5. Smoke – Smoulder
1: Smoke: *kapnos*
2: Smouldering: *typhō*
6. Put out, Quench – Go out – Never to go out, Unquenchable: *sbennymi*
 a) Put out, Quench, Extinguish – Stifle – Go out

b) Never to go out – Unquench-able, Not to be put out
7. Refined by fire: *pyroō*
8. Grilled – Broiled – Cooked: *optos*

9. Sulphur, Brimstone – Sulphur-yellow: *theion*
10. Ashes: *spodos*

1. FIRE, FLAME – BURN – TO LIGHT

1: FIRE, FLAME – BURN(ING), BLAZING – TEST BY FIRE, (BE) TORTURED: *PYR*

1	*pyr*	71	2	*pyroō* 5/6
4	*pyra*	2	3	*pyrōsis* 3
5	*pyrinos* 1		6	*ana-zō-pyreō* 1

Mt 3 10	any tree which fails to produce good fruit will be cut down and thrown on the *fire*.
11	the one who follows me . . . will baptise you with the Holy Spirit and *fire*. [12] . . . the chaff he will burn in a *fire* that will never go out.
12	
5 22	if a man calls [his brother] 'Renegade' he will answer for it in hell *fire*.
7 19	Any tree that does not produce good fruit is . . . thrown on the *fire*.
13 40	just as the darnel is gathered up and burnt in the *fire*, so it will be at the end of time.
42	[his angels will] throw [all who do evil] into the *blazing* furnace.
50	[the angels will] throw [the wicked] into the *blazing* furnace
17 15	[my son] is always falling into the *fire* or into the water.
18 8	it is better for you to enter into life crippled . . . than to 9 . . . be thrown into eternal *fire*. [9] . . . it is better for you to enter into life with one eye, than to . . . be thrown into the hell of *fire*.
25 41	Go away from me, with your curse upon you, to the eternal *fire*
Mk 9 22	[the spirit] has often thrown him into the *fire* and into the water.
43	it is better . . . to enter into life crippled, than to . . . go to hell, into the *fire* that cannot be put out.
48	(Is 66 24) [hell] where their worm does not die nor their *fire* go out.
49	everyone will be salted with *fire*.
Lk 3 9	any tree which fails to produce good fruit will be . . . thrown on the *fire*.
16	someone who is more powerful than I am . . . will baptise you with the Holy Spirit and *fire*.
17	the chaff he will burn in a *fire* that will never go out.
9 54	do you want us to call down *fire* from heaven to burn them up (ᵛ as Elijah did)?
12 49	I have come to bring *fire* to the earth, and how I wish it were blazing already!
17 29	(Gn 19 24) [in Sodom,] God rained *fire* and brimstone from heaven
22 55	They had lit a *fire* in the middle of the courtyard
Jn 15 6	these [dry] branches are collected and thrown on the *fire*, and they are burnt.
Ac 2 3	something appeared to them that seemed like tongues of *fire*;
19	(Jl 3 3) I will display . . . signs on earth . . . (§ blood and *fire* and a cloud of smoke)
7 30	an angel appeared to [Moses] in the flames of a bush that was on *fire*.
28 2	[The inhabitants of Malta] made us all welcome, and they 4 lit a huge *fire*
3	Paul had collected a bundle of sticks and was putting them 4 on the *fire*
5	[Paul] shook the creature off into the *fire*
Rm 12 20	(Pr 25 22) you heap *red-hot* coals on his head.
1 Co 3 13	That day will begin with *fire*, and the *fire* will test the quality of each man's work . . . [15] if it is burnt down, he will be 15 the loser, and though he is saved himself, it will be as one who has gone through *fire*.
7 9	2 it is better to be married than to *be tortured*.
2 Co 11 29	2 when any man is made to fall, I am *tortured*.
Ep 6 16	2 always carrying the shield of faith . . . to put out the *burning* arrows of the evil one.
2 Th 1 8	[Jesus] will come in flaming *fire*
2 Tm 1 6	6 I am reminding you now to *fan into a flame* the gift that God gave you
Heb 1 7	(Ps 104 4) [God] makes . . . his servants flames of *fire*,
10 27	the dreadful prospect of judgement and of the raging *fire* than is to burn rebels.
11 34	[the prophets could] put out blazing *fires*
12 18	What you have come to is nothing known to the senses: not a blazing *fire*,
29 Θ	(Dt 4 24) our God is a consuming *fire*.

Jm 3	5	Think how small a *flame* can set fire to a huge forest; [6] the
	6	tongue is a *flame* like that . . . it sets fire to the whole wheel of creation.
5	3	your gold and your silver are corroding away, and the same corrosion will . . . eat into your body. ⌈It was a burning *fire* (or: Like a *fire*) that you stored up as your treasure for the last days.
1 P 1	7	gold . . . is corruptible even though it bears testing by *fire*
4	12	you must not think it unaccountable that you should be tested by *fire*.
2 P 3	7	by the same word, the present sky and earth are destined for *fire*,
	12	2 the sky will dissolve in *flames*
Jude	7	Sodom and Gomorrah . . . are paying for their crimes in eternal *fire*.
	23	when there are some [who have doubts] to be saved from the *fire*, pull them out;
Rv 1	14	[a Son of man:] his eyes like a *burning* flame,
2	18	the Son of God who has eyes like a *burning* flame
3	18	2 buy from me the gold that has been ⌈tested (or: refined) by *fire*
4	5	in front of the throne there were seven *flaming* lamps burning,
8	5	the angel took the censer and filled it with the *fire* from the altar,
	7	hail and *fire*, mixed with blood, were dropped on the earth;
	8	it was as though a great mountain, all on *fire*, had been dropped into the sea:
9	17	5 the riders with their breastplates *of flame* colour . . . and sulphur-yellow; the horses had lions' heads, and *fire*, smoke and sulphur were coming out of their mouths.
	18	by these three plagues, the *fire*, the smoke and the sulphur
10	1	I saw another powerful angel . . . his legs were pillars of *fire*.
11	5	*Fire* can come from [my two witnesses'] mouths and consume their enemies
13	13	[the beast] worked great miracles, even to calling down *fire* from heaven on to the earth
14	10	in *fire* and brimstone [those who worshipped the beast] will be tortured
	18	the angle in charge of the *fire* . . . shouted aloud
15	2	I seemed to see a glass lake suffused with *fire*,
16	8	the sun . . . was made to scorch people with its *flames*;
17	16	the ten horns and the beast will . . . burn the remains [of the prostitute] in the *fire*.
18	8	[Babylon] will be burnt right up in the *fire*.
	9	3 [the kings of the earth] see the smoke as she *burns*,
	18	3 [the seafaring men,] watching the smoke as she *burns*,
19	12	[Faithful and True:] His eyes were flames of *fire*,
	20	[the beast and the false prophet] were thrown alive into the *fiery* lake of burning sulphur.
20	9	*fire* will come down on [Gog and Magog] from heaven and consume them.
	10	the devil . . . will be thrown into the lake of *fire* and sulphur,
	14	Death and Hades were thrown into the *burning* lake. This *burning* lake is the second death;
	15	anybody whose name could not be found written in the book of life was thrown into the *burning* lake.
21	8	the legacy . . . for murderers and fornicators . . . is the second death in the burning lake of *fire* and sulphur.

2: BURN, BRAND – SCORCH – TO LIGHT: *KAIŌ*

2	*kaiō*	12	6	*kausoomai* 2
5	*kauma*	2	8	*kaustēriazō* 1
3	*kaumatizō*	4	1	*kata-kaiō* 13
7	*kausis*	1	9	*ek-kaiō* 1
4	*kausōn*	3		

a) Burn, Catch fire – Blazing, (in) Flames – (Be) Burnt

Mt 3	12 X	but the chaff he will *burn* in a fire that will never go out.
13	30	collect the darnel and tie it in bundles to *be burnt*,
	40	just as the darnel *is* gathered up and *burnt* in the fire,
Lk 3	17 X	but the chaff he will *burn* in a fire that will never go out.
Jn 15	6	these [dry] branches are collected and thrown on the fire, 2 and they *are burnt*.
Ac 19	19	a number of them who had practised magic collected their books and *made a bonfire* of them in public.
1 Co 3	15	if [his structure] *is burnt* down, he will be the loser,
13	3	2 if I even let them take my body to *burn* it,
Heb 6	8	7 [the field] that grows brambles . . . will end by *being burnt*.
12	18	2 What you have come to is . . . not a *blazing* fire, or a gloom
13	11	The bodies of the animals . . . *are burnt* outside the camp,
2 P 3	10	The Day of the Lord will come . . . and then . . . the elements will *catch fire* and fall apart, the earth and all that it contains will be ⌄ *burnt* up (G uncovered).
	12	6 the elements [will] melt in the *heat*.
Rv 8	7	a third of the earth *was burnt* up, and a third of all trees *was burnt*, and every blade of grass *was burnt*.
	8	2 it was as though a great mountain, ⌈all on fire (lit. *blazing* with fire), had been dropped into the sea:

Rv 8	10	2 a huge star fell from the sky, *burning* like a ball of fire,
17	16	the ten horns and the beast will . . . *burn* the remains [of the prostitute] in the fire.
18	8	[Babylon] will be *burnt* right up.
19	20	[the beast and the false prophet] were thrown alive into the 2 fiery lake of *burning* sulphur.
21	8	the legacy . . . for murderers and fornicators . . . is the 2 second death in the *burning* lake of sulphur.

b) Light a lamp – Alight, Lit, Burning

Mt 5	15	2 No one *lights* a lamp to put in under a tub;
Lk 12	35	2 See that you are dressed for action and have your lamps *lit*.
Jn 5	35	2 John was a lamp *alight* and shining
Rv 4	5	2 in front of the throne there were seven flaming lamps *burning*, the seven Spirits of God.

c) Scorching Heat of the sun – Scorch, Blaze, Hot

Mt 13	6	3 as soon as the sun came up [the seeds] were *scorched*
20	12	4 we have done a heavy day's work in all the *heat*.
Mk 4	6	3 when the sun came up [the seed] was *scorched*
Lk 12	55	4 when the wind is from the south you say it will be *hot*,
Jm 1	11	4 the *scorching* sun comes up, and the grass withers,
Rv 7	16	5 neither the sun nor *scorching* wind will ever plague them,
16	8	3 the sun . . . was made to *scorch* people with its flames;
	9	3/5 [9] but though people were *scorched* by the fierce *heat* of it, they cursed the name of God

d) Burn (metaphorically) – (Be) Consumed with, On fire

Lk 24	32	2 Did not our hearts *burn* within us . . .?
Rm 1	27	9 their menfolk have given up natural intercourse to be *consumed with* passion for each other,

e) Branded with a red-hot iron – Seared

1 Tm 4	2	the cause of this is the lies told by hypocrites whose con-8 sciences are *branded* as though *with a red-hot iron*:

3: FLAME, FLAMING – SET FIRE TO, CATCH FIRE FROM: *PHLOX*

2 *phlogizō* 2   1 *phlox* 7

Lk 16	24	I am in agony in these *flames*.
Ac 7	30	(Ex 3 2) an angel appeared to [Moses] in the *flames* of a bush that was on fire.
2 Th 1	8	[Jesus] will come in *flaming* fire
Heb 1	7	(Ps 104 4) [God] makes . . . his servants *flames* of fire,
Jm 3	6	2/2 *catching* fire itself *from* hell, [the tongue] *sets fire to* the whole wheel of creation.
Rv 1	14	[a Son of man:] his eyes like a burning *flame*,
2	18	the Son of God who has eyes like a burning *flame*
19	12	His eyes were *flames* of fire,

4: TO LIGHT, KINDLE – SET FIRE TO, SET ABLAZE: *HAPTŌ*

1 *haptō* 4   2 *an-(h)aptō* 2
3 *peri-(h)aptō* 1

Lk 8	16	No one *lights* a lamp to cover it with a bowl
11	33	No one *lights* a lamp and puts it . . . under a tub,
12	49 ○	2 I have come to bring fire . . . how I wish it were *blazing* already!
15	8	what woman . . . would not, if she lost one [drachma], *light* a lamp
22	55	3 they had *lit* a fire in the middle of the courtyard
Ac 28	2	[the inhabitants of Malta] made us all welcome, and t hey *lit* a huge fire because it had started to rain
Jm 3	5	2 Think how small a flame can *set fire to* a huge forest;

5: BURNT, SET ON FIRE: *EM-PIPRĒMI*

em-piprēmi, *em-prēthō* 1

Mt 22	7	his troops . . . *burnt* their town.

6: FIRE, BLAZE – FIRELIGHT: *PHŌS*

phōs 2/71

Mk 14	54	Peter had followed [Jesus] . . . right into the high priest's palace, and was sitting with the attendants warming himself at the *fire*.
Lk 22	56	as [Peter] was sitting there by the *blaze* a servant-girl saw him,

2. FURNACE, OVEN, STOVE – FIRE

1: FURNACE, OVEN, STOVE – FIRE: *KLIBANOS*

klibanos 2

Mt	6 30	the grass in the field which is . . . thrown into the *furnace* tomorrow,
Lk	12 28	the grass in the field which is . . . thrown into the *furnace* tomorrow,

2: FURNACE: *KAMINOS*

kaminos 4

Mt	13 42	[his angels] throw them into the blazing *furnace*,
	50	[the angels will] throw them into the blazing *furnace*
Rv	1 15	like burnished bronze when it has been refined in a *furnace*,
	9 2	smoke poured up out of the Abyss like the smoke from a huge *furnace*

3. CHARCOAL FIRE – FIRE OF COALS: *ANTHRAKIA*

1 *anthrakia 2*   2 *anthrax 1*

Jn	18 18	the servants and guards had lit a *charcoal fire*
	21 9	[the disciples] saw . . . a *charcoal fire*
Rm	12 20	2 (Pr 25 22) you heap red-hot *coals* on his head.

4. REDUCE TO ASHES, TURN TO ASHES, BURN: *TEPHROŌ*

tephroō 1

2 P	2 6	The cities of Sodom and Gomorrah, these too [God] condemned and *reduced to ashes*;

5. SMOKE – SMOULDER

1: SMOKE: *KAPNOS*

kapnos 13

Ac	2 19	(Jl 3 3) (§ blood and fire and a cloud of *smoke*)
Rv	8 4	from the angel's hand the *smoke* of the incense went up in the presence of God
	9 2	*smoke* poured up out of the Abyss like the *smoke* from a huge furnace so that the sun and the sky were darkened by the *smoke*, ³ and out of the *smoke* dropped locusts
	17	fire, *smoke* and sulphur were coming out of [the] mouths [of the horses].
	18	by these three plagues, the fire, the *smoke* and the sulphur . . . one third of the human race was killed.
	14 11	the *smoke* of their torture will go up for ever and ever.
	15 8	The *smoke* from the glory . . . of God filled the temple
	18 9	There will be . . . weeping for [Babylon] by the kings of the earth who . . . see the *smoke* as she burns,
	18	[the seafaring men,] watching the *smoke* as [Babylon] burns,
	19 3	Alleluia! The *smoke* of her will go up for ever and ever.

2: SMOULDERING: *TYPHŌ*

typhō 1

Mt	12 20	(Is 42 3) He will not . . . put out the *smouldering* wick

6. PUT OUT, QUENCH – GO OUT – NEVER TO GO OUT, UNQUENCHABLE: *SBENNYMI*

1 *sbennymi 6*   2 *a-sbestos 3*

a) Put out, Quench, Extinguish – Stifle – Go out

Mt	12 20 X	(Is 42 3) He will not . . . *put out* the smouldering wick
	25 8	Give us some of your oil: our lamps are *going out*.
Ep	6 16	always carrying the shield of faith so that you can use it to *put out* the burning arrows of the evil one.
1 Th	5 19	Never try to *suppress* the Spirit
Heb	11 34	[Gideon . . . the prophets could] *put out* blazing fires

b) Never to go out – Unquenchable, Not to be put out

Mt	3 12	2 but the chaff he will burn in a fire that will *never go out*.
Mk	9 43	2 go to hell, into the fire that *cannot be put out*.
	48	(Is 66 24) [in hell] where their worm does not die nor their fire *go out*.
Lk	3 17	2 but the chaff he will burn in a fire that will *never go out*.

7. REFINED BY FIRE: *PYROŌ*

pyroō 2/6

Rv	1 15	like burnished bronze when it has been *refined* in a furnace,
	3 18	buy from me the gold that has been ⌐tested (or: *refined*) by fire

8. GRILLED – BROILED – COOKED: *OPTOS*

optos 1

Lk	24 42	[the apostles] offered [Jesus] a piece of *grilled* fish,

9. SULPHUR, BRIMSTONE – SULPHUR-YELLOW: *THEION*

1 *theion 7*   2 *theiōdēs 1*

Lk	17 29	(Gn 19 24) [in Sodom] God rained fire and *brimstone*
Rv	9 17	I saw . . . the riders with their breastplates of flame colour, 2 hyacinth-blue and *sulphur-yellow*; the horses had lions' heads, and fire, smoke and *sulphur* were coming out of their mouths.
	18	these three plagues, the fire, the smoke and the *sulphur*
	14 10	in fire and *brimstone* they will be tortured
	19 20	[the beast and the false prophet] were thrown alive into the fiery lake of burning *sulphur*.
	20 10	the devil . . . will be thrown into the lake of fire and *sulphur*.
	21 8	the legacy . . . for murderers and fornicators . . . is the second death in the burning lake of *sulphur*.

10. ASHES: *SPODOS*

spodos 3

Mt	11 21	Tyre and Sidon . . . would have repented long ago in sackcloth and *ashes*.
Lk	10 13	Tyre and Sidon . . . would have repented long ago, sitting in sackcloth and *ashes*.
Heb	9 13	the *ashes* of a heifer are sprinkled on those who have incurred defilement

FIRM – CONFIRM – GUARANTEE

1. **Firm(ly), Steadfast:** *hedraios*
2. **Firm – Strengthen**
   1: Firm, Solid – Become firm, Grow strong, Strengthen: *stereos*
   2: Strengthen – Firm: *stērizō*
      a) Strengthen – Firm
      b) Fixed (firmly) – Resolutely set
      c) Unstable, Unbalanced
3. **Secure, Safe, Sure – Make secure – Certain, Definite:** *a-sphaleia*
4. **Give assurance (of), Endorse:** *pistis*
5. **Affirm, Reaffirm, Validate – Nullify, Make void:** *kyroō*
6. **Confirm, Establish – (Make) Valid, True, Firm – Guarantee:** *bebaios*
7. **Guarantee – Assurance:** *hypo-stasis*
8. **Guarantee:** *mesiteuō*
9. **Guarantee, Guarantor – Surety:** *en-guos*
10. **Pledge, Guarantee:** *arrabōn*
11. **Pledge:** *ep-erōtēma*

1. FIRM(LY), STEADFAST: *HEDRAIOS*

1 *hedraios 3*   2 *hedraiōma 1*

1 Co	7 37	if someone has *firmly* made his mind up, without any compulsion . . . to keep his daughter as she is, he will be doing a good thing.
	15 58	⌐Never give in (lit. Be *steadfast*) then, . . . never admit defeat;
Col	1 23	persevere [and stand] *firm* on the solid base of the faith,
1 Tm	3 15	the Church . . . upholds the truth and ⌐keeps it safe (lit. 2 makes it *firm*, or: is the bulwark of it).

2. FIRM – STRENGTHEN

1: FIRM, SOLID – BECOME FIRM, GROW STRONG, STRENGTHEN: *STEREOS*

3 *stereōma 1*   1 *stereos 4*
2 *stereoō 3*

Ac	3	7	2 Instantly [the lame man's] feet and ankles *became firm*,
		16	2 the name of Jesus . . . has *brought back the strength* of this man
	16	5	2 So the churches *grew strong* in the faith,
Col	2	5	3 I am . . . delighted to . . . see how *firm* your faith in Christ is.
2 Tm	2	19	God's *solid* foundation stone is still in position,
Heb	5	12	you have gone back to needing milk, and not *solid* food . . .
		14	[14] *Solid* food is for mature men
1 P	5	9	Stand up to [the devil], ⌐*strong* (or: *firm*) in faith

2: STRENGTHEN – FIRM: *STĒRIZŌ*

4	*stērigmos*	1	3	*a-stēriktos*	2
1	*stērizō*	14	2	*epi-stērizō*	3

a) Strengthen – Firm

Lk	22	32	Simon, . . . once you have recovered, you in turn must *strengthen* your brothers.
Ac	14	22	2 [Paul and Barnabas] ⌐*put fresh heart into* (lit. *strengthened the resolve of*) the disciples, encouraging them to persevere in the faith.
	15	32	2 Judas and Silas . . . spoke for a long time . . . *strengthening* the brothers.
		41	2 [Paul] travelled through Syria and Cilicia, *consolidating* the churches.
	18	23	[Paul continued] his journey . . . through Phrygia, ⌐*encouraging* (or: *strengthening*) all the followers.
Rm	1	11	I am longing to see you . . . to *strengthen* you by sharing a spiritual gift with you,
	16	25 Θ	Glory to him who is able to *give* you *the strength* to live according to the Good News
1 Th	3	2	[we] sent our brother Timothy . . . to *keep* you *firm* and strong in the faith
		13 X	may he so *confirm* your hearts in holiness that you may be blameless in the sight of our God
2 Th	2	17 X Θ	[May Jesus Christ and God] comfort you and *strengthen* you in everything good that you do or say.
	3	3 X	he will *give* you *strength* and guard you from the evil one,
Jm	5	8	⌐*do not lose* (lit. *strengthen* your) heart, because the Lord's coming will be soon.
1 P	5	10 Θ	the God of all grace . . . will *confirm*, strengthen and support you.
2 P	1	12	I am continually recalling the same truths to you, even though you already know them [and] *firmly* [hold them].
	3	17	4 be careful not to get carried away . . . from the ⌐*firm ground* that you are standing on (or: *stability* that you are standing with).
Rv	3	2	*revive* what little you have left; it is dying fast.

b) Fixed (firmly) – Resolutely set

Lk	9	51 X	[Jesus] ⌐*resolutely took* the road (lit. *resolutely set* his sights on leaving) for Jerusalem
	16	26	between us and you a great gulf has been *fixed*,

c) Unstable, Unbalanced

2 P	2	14	3 [false teachers] will seduce any soul which is at all *unstable*.
	3	16	3 these are the points that uneducated and *unbalanced* people distort,

3. SECURE, SAFE, SURE – MAKE SECURE – CERTAIN, DEFINITE: *A-SPHALEIA*

3	*a-sphaleia*	3	2	*a-sphalizō*	4
1	*a-sphalēs*	5	4	*a-sphalōs*	3

Mt	27	64	2 give the order to have the sepulchre *kept secure* until the third day . . . [65] 'You may have your guard' said Pilate
		65	2 to them. 'Go and *make* all as *secure* as you know how.'
		66	2 [66] So they went and *made* the sepulchre *secure*, putting seals on the stone
Mk	14	44	Take [the one I kiss] in charge, and see he is ⌐*well guarded* (lit. *kept secure*)
Lk	1	4	3 your Excellency may learn how *well founded* the teaching is that you have received.
Ac	2	36	4 the whole House of Israel can ⌐*be* (lit. *know as*) *certain* that God has made this Jesus . . . both Lord and Christ.
	5	23	3 We found the gaol *securely* locked
	16	23	the gaoler was told to keep ⌐*a close watch* on them (lit. them under *secure guard*).
		24	2 [the gaoler] threw [Paul and Silas] into the inner prison and *fastened* their feet in the stocks.
	21	34	the noise made it impossible for [the tribune] to get any *positive* information,

Ac	22	30	[the tribune] wanted to know what *precise* charge the Jews were bringing,
	25	26	I have nothing *definite* that I can write to his Imperial Majesty about [Paul];
Ph	3	1	It is no trouble to me to repeat what I have already written . . . and . . . it will make for *safety*.
1 Th	5	3	It is when people are saying, 'How quiet and peaceful it is (lit. What peace and *security*)' that the worst suddenly happens
Heb	6	19	Here we have an anchor for our soul, as *sure* as it is firm,

4. GIVE ASSURANCE (OF), ENDORSE: *PISTIS*

pistis 1/242

Ac	17	31	God has ⌐*publicly proved* (or: *given assurance* of) this by raising [Jesus] from the dead.

5. AFFIRM, REAFFIRM, VALIDATE – NULLIFY, MAKE VOID: *KYROŌ*

2	*kyroō*	2	1	*a-kyroō*	3
			3	*pro-kyroō*	1

Mt	15	6	you have *made* God's word *null and void* by means of your tradition.
Mk	7	13	you *make* God's word *null and void* for the sake of your tradition.
2 Co	2	8	2 I am asking you to ⌐*give some definite proof of* (or: *reaffirm*) your love for [the man in question].
Ga	3	15	2 If a will has been *drawn up* in due form (lit. *validated*), no one is allowed to disregard it
		17	3 once God has ⌐*expressed his will* in due form (lit. *validated* his will), no law . . . could . . . *make* the promise *meaningless*.

6. CONFIRM, ESTABLISH – (MAKE) VALID, TRUE, FIRM – GUARANTEE: *BEBAIOS*

2	*bebaioō*	8	3	*bebaiōsis*	2
1	*bebaios*	9	4	*dia-bebaioomai*	2

Mk	16	20 X	2 [the Eleven] preached everywhere, the Lord . . . *confirming* the word by the signs that accompanied it.
Rm	4	16	the promise depends on faith, so that it may . . . ⌐*be available to* (lit. be made *valid* for) all of Abraham's descendants,
	15	8 X	2 Christ became the servant of circumcised Jews . . . so that God could faithfully ⌐*carry out* (lit. *make good*) the promises
1 Co	1	6	2 the witness to Christ has . . . ⌐*been strong* (or: been *confirmed*) among you
		8 X	2 [Jesus Christ] will *keep* you *steady* . . . until the last day,
2 Co	1	7	our hope for you is ⌐*confident* (lit. *firm*)
		21 Θ	2 it is God himself who ⌐*assures* (or: *guarantees*) us all . . . of our standing in Christ,
Ph	1	7	3 you have shared . . . my work defending and *establishing* the gospel
Col	2	7	2 you must be rooted in [Christ] and . . . *held firm* by the faith
T 1m	1	7	[some] doctors of the Law . . . understand neither the arguments they are using nor the opinions they are *upholding*.
Tt	3	8	4 I want you to *be quite uncompromising* in teaching all this,
Heb	2	2	a promise that was made through angels proved to be so *true* that every infringement . . . brought its own proper punishment.
		3	2 The promise . . . is *guaranteed* to us by those who heard [the Lord]
	3	6	we are [Christ's] house, as long as (§ *firm* to the end) we cling to our hope
		14	we shall remain co-heirs with Christ only if we keep a *firm* grasp on our first confidence right to the end.
	6	16	3 between men, *confirmation* by an oath puts an end to all dispute.
		19	Here we have an anchor for our soul, as sure as it is *firm*,
	9	17	[a will] only becomes *valid* with that death,
	13	9	2 it is better to rely on grace for [inner] *strength* than on dietary laws
2 P	1	10	you have been called and chosen: work all the harder to ⌐*justify* (lit. *confirm*) it.
		19	So we have *confirmation* of what was said in prophecies;

7. GUARANTEE – ASSURANCE: *HYPO-STASIS*

hypo-stasis 1/5

Heb 11 1   Only faith can ⌈*guarantee* (or: give substance to) the blessings that we hope for,

8. GUARANTEE: *MESITEUŌ*

mesiteuō 1

Heb 6 17   when God wanted to make the heirs to the promise thoroughly realise that his purpose was unalterable, he ⌈conveyed (or: *guaranteed*) this by an oath;

9. GUARANTEE, GUARANTOR – SURETY: *EN-GUOS*

en-guos 1

Heb 7 22 X   it is a greater covenant for which Jesus has become our *guarantee*.

10. PLEDGE, GUARANTEE: *ARRABŌN*

arrabōn 3

2 Co 1 22   [God has anointed us,] giving us the *pledge*, the Spirit, that we carry in our hearts.
    5 5   God . . . has given us the *pledge* of the Spirit.
Ep 1 14   [the Holy Spirit is] the *pledge* of our inheritance

11. PLEDGE: *EP-ERŌTĒMA*

ep-erōtēma 1

1 P 3 21   the baptism . . . is . . . ⌈a *pledge* (or: an appeal) made to God from a good conscience,

FISH

1. **Fish:** *ichthys*
2. **Fish:** *opsarion*
3. **Fish – Sea creatures:** *en-(h)alios*
4. **Sea monster – Whale:** *kētos*
5. **Fisher, Fishermen – to Fish:** *halieuō*

6. **Net – Dragnet – Hook**
   1: (Fishing-)Net: *diktuon*
   2: Dragnet, Net: *sagēnē*
   3: (Fishing-)Hook: *ankistron*

1. FISH: *ICHTHYS*

2 ichthydion 2   1 ichthys 20

Mt 7 10   [Who] would hand [his son] a snake when he asked for a *fish*?
14 17   All we have with us is five loaves and two *fish*.
    19   [Jesus] took the five loaves and the two *fish* . . . and said the blessing.
15 34   2 How many loaves have you? Seven . . . and a few *small fish* . . . ³⁶ . . . [Jesus] took the seven loaves and the *fish*, and he gave thanks
    36
17 27   take the first *fish* that bites, open its mouth
Mk 6 38   How many loaves have you? . . . they said, 'Five, and two *fish*'.
    41   [Jesus] took the five loaves and the two *fish* . . . he also shared out the two *fish* among them all. ⁴² They all ate as much as they wanted. ⁴³ They collected twelve basketfuls of scraps of bread and pieces of *fish*.
    43
    8 7   2 They had a few *small fish* as well,
Lk 5 6   they netted . . . a huge number of *fish*
    9   [Simon Peter was] completely overcome by the catch of *fish* they had made;
9 13   We have no more than five loaves and two *fish*,
    16   [Jesus] took the five loaves and two *fish* . . . and said the blessing over them;
11 11   [What father would] hand [his son] a snake instead of a *fish* (§ when he asked for a *fish*)?
24 42   [the apostles] offered [Jesus] a piece of grilled *fish*,
Jn 21 6   there were so many *fish* that they could not haul [the net] in.
    8   The other disciples came on in the boat, towing the net and the *fish*;

Jn 21 11   the net [was] full of big *fish*, one hundred and fifty-three of them;
1 Co 15 39   there is . . . the flesh of birds and the flesh of *fish*.

2. FISH: *OPSARION*

opsarion 5

Jn 6 9   There is a small boy here with five barley loaves and two *fish*;
    11   Jesus took the loaves . . . and gave them out . . . he then did the same with the *fish*,
21 9   [the disciples] saw that there was some bread there, and a charcoal fire with *fish* cooking on it. ¹⁰ Jesus said, 'Bring some of the *fish* you have just caught' . . . ¹³Jesus . . . took the bread and gave it to them, and the same with the *fish*.
    10
    13

3. FISH – SEA CREATURES: *EN-(H)ALIOS*

en-(h)alios 1

Jm 3 7   Wild animals . . . and *fish* can all be tamed by man,

4. SEA MONSTER – WHALE: *KĒTOS*

kētos 1

Mt 12 40   (Jon 2 1) Jonah was in the belly of the *sea-monster* for three days and three nights,

5. FISHER, FISHERMEN – TO FISH: *HALIEUŌ*

1 haleeus 5   2 halieuō 1

Mt 4 18   Simon . . . and Andrew . . . were making a cast in the lake with their net, for they were *fishermen*. ¹⁹ [Jesus] said to them, 'Follow me and I will make you *fishers* of men'.
    19
Mk 1 16   [Jesus] saw Simon and . . . Andrew casting a net in the lake – for they were *fishermen*. ¹⁷ And Jesus said to them, 'Follow me and I will make you into *fishers* of men'.
    17
Lk 5 2   The *fishermen* . . . were washing their nets.
Jn 21 3   2 Simon Peter said, 'I'm going *fishing*'.

6. NET – DRAGNET – HOOK

1: (FISHING-)NET: *DIKTUON*

diktuon 12

Mt 4 20   [Simon and Andrew] left their *nets* at once and followed [Jesus] . . .
    21   James . . . and John . . . were . . . mending their *nets*.
Mk 1 18   at once [Simon and Andrew] left their *nets* and followed [Jesus].
    19   James . . . and John . . . were . . . mending their *nets*.
Lk 5 2   The fishermen . . . were washing their *nets*.
    4   [Jesus] said to Simon, '. . . pay out your *nets* for a catch'.
    5   ⁵ . . . Simon replied, '. . . if you say so, I will pay out the *nets*.' ⁶ And . . . they netted such a huge number of fish that their *nets* began to tear,
    6
Jn 21 6   Throw the *net* out to starboard and you'll find something.
    8   The other disciples came on in the boat, towing the *net* and the fish . . . ¹¹ Simon Peter went aboard and dragged the *net* to the shore, full of big fish, one hundred and fifty-three of them; and in spite of there being so many the *net* was not broken.
    11

2: DRAGNET, NET: *SAGĒNĒ*

sagēnē 1

Mt 13 47   the kingdom of heaven is like a *dragnet* cast into the sea

3: (FISHING-)HOOK: *ANKISTRON*

ankistron 1

Mt 17 27   [Jesus said to Peter:] go to the lake and cast a *hook;* take the first fish that bites,

FITTING – WORTHY

1. Fitting – Proper
  1: Fitting, Fit to – (Im)Proper – Duty: *an-(h)ēkō*
  2: Befit, Fitting – Become – Proper: *prepō*
2. Decency, Respectability: *eu-schēmōn*
  a) Decent, Respectable – Proper
  b) Respected – Upper class – Honourable
3. Modestly – Shamelessly: *aidōs*
4. Worthy

1: Worthy – Deserving – Judged worthy: *axios*
  a) Fit to – Worthy, Judged worthy – Appropriate
  b) Deserving – Worthy of, Judged worthy
2: Respectable – Principled – Noble: *semnos*
3: (Be) Worthy, Fit to – Qualified: *hikanos*
4: Fit, Suitable: *eu-thetos*

1. FITTING – PROPER

1: FITTING, FIT TO – (IM)PROPER – DUTY: *AN-(H)ĒKŌ*

1 *an-(h)ēkō* 3   2 *kath-ēkō* 2

Ac 22 22	2	Rid the earth of [Paul]! He is not *fit* to live!
Rm 1 28		God has left [the unbelievers] to their own irrational ideas and to ʳtheir monstrous behaviour (lit. behaviour which is not *proper*).
	2	
Ep 5 4		There must be no coarseness, or salacious talk and jokes – all this is ʳwrong (lit. im*proper*) for you;
Col 3 18		give way to your husbands, as ʳyou should (lit. is *fitting*) in the Lord.
Phm 8		in Christ I can have no diffidence about telling you to do . . . your *duty*,

2: BEFIT, FITTING – BECOME – PROPER: *PREPŌ*

1 *prepō* 7   2 *(hiero-)prepēs* 1

Mt 3 15		it is *fitting* that we should . . . do all that righteousness demands.
1 Co 11 13		Ask yourselves if it is *fitting* for a woman to pray to God without a veil;
Ep 5 3		Among you there must not be even a mention of fornication or impurity . . . this would hardly *become* the saints!
1 Tm 2 10		[women's] adornment is to do the sort of good works that are *proper* for women who profess to be religious.
Tt 2 1		preach the behaviour which ʳgoes with (or: *befits*) healthy doctrine.
3		the older women should ʳbehave as though they were religious (lit. display the behaviour that *befits* saints)
	2	
Heb 2 10		it was *appropriate* that God . . . should make perfect . . . the leader who would take them to their salvation.
7 26		To *suit* us, the ideal high priest would have to be holy

2. DECENCY, RESPECTABILITY: *EU-SCHĒMŌN*

1 *eu-schēmōn* 5   3 *eu-schēmosynē* 1
2 *eu-schēmonōs* 3

a) Decent, Respectable – Proper

Rm 13 13	2	Let us live *decently*
1 Co 7 35		I say this . . . simply to make sure that everything is *as it should be*,
12 23		it is the least honourable parts of the body that we clothe with the greatest ʳcare (lit. *honour*; or: *propriety*). So our
	3	
24		more improper parts get decorated ²⁴ in a way that our more proper parts do not need.
14 40	2	let everything be done *with propriety* and in order.
1 Th 4 12	2	so . . . you are seen to be *respectable* by those outside the Church,

b) Respected – Upper class – Honourable

Mk 15 43		Joseph of Arimathaea, a ʳprominent (lit. *respected*) member of the Council,
Ac 13 50		the Jews worked upon some of the devout women *of the upper classes*
17 12		many Greek women *from the upper classes* [became believers]

3. MODESTLY – SHAMELESSLY: *AIDŌS*

1 *aidōs* 1   2 *an-aideia* 1

Lk 11 8	2	if . . . not . . . for friendship's sake, ʳpersistence (lit. *shamelessness*) will be enough to make [the man] get up

1 Tm 2 9		I direct that women are . . . to be dressed ʳquietly (lit. *modestly*) and soberly

4. WORTHY

1: WORTHY – DESERVING – JUDGED WORTHY: *AXIOS*

2 *axioō* 7	5 *an-axios* 1	
1 *axios* 41	6 *an-axiōs* 1	
3 *axiōs* 6	4 *kat-axioō* 3	

a) Fit to – Worthy, Judged worthy – Appropriate

Mt 3 8		if you are repentant, produce the *appropriate* fruit,
10 37		Anyone who prefers father or mother to me is not *worthy* of me. Anyone who prefers son or daughter to me is not *worthy* of me. ³⁸ Anyone who does not take his cross and follow in my footsteps is not *worthy* of me.
38		
Lk 3 8		if you are repentant, produce the *appropriate* fruits,
23 41		we are paying *appropriately* for what we did.
Jn 1 27		I am not *fit* to undo his sandal-strap.
Ac 5 41		[the apostles] left . . . the Sanhedrin glad to have ʳhad the honour (lit. been *judged worthy*) of suffering humiliation for the sake of the name.
4		
13 25		I am not *fit* to undo his sandal.
46		since you do not think yourselves *worthy* of eternal life,
15 38		Paul ʳwas not in favour of taking along the very man who had deserted them (lit. did not *judge* the man who had deserted them *worthy* to be taken along)
2		
26 20		ʳproving their change of heart by their deeds (lit. performing deeds *appropriate* to penitents)
28 22	2	We *think* it would be as well to hear your own account
Rm 16 2	3	Give [Phoebe] . . . a welcome *worthy* of saints,
1 Co 6 2	5	if the world is to be judged by you, how can you be *unfit* to judge trifling cases?
11 27	6	anyone who . . . drinks the cup of the Lord *unworthily* will be behaving unworthily towards . . . the Lord.
16 4		if it seems *worth* while for me to go [to Jerusalem] too, they can travel with me.
Ep 4 1	3	lead a life *worthy* of your vocation.
Ph 1 27	3	Avoid anything . . . that would be un*worthy* of the gospel
Col 1 10		you will be able to lead the kind of life ʳwhich the Lord expects of you (lit. *worthy* of the Lord)
3		
1 Th 2 12	3	appealing to you to live a life *worthy* of God, who is calling you
2 Th 1 3	2	We feel we must be continually thanking God for you, brothers; *quite rightly*,
11		we pray continually that our God will make you *worthy* of his call,
3 Jn 6		help them on their journey in a way ʳthat God would approve (lit. *worthy* of God)
3		

b) Deserving – Worthy of, Judged worthy

Mt 10 10		the workman *deserves* his keep.
11		ask for someone trust*worthy* and stay with him
13		if the house *deserves* it, let your peace descend upon it; if it does not *deserve* it, let your peace come back to you.
22 8		those who were invited [to the wedding] proved to be un*worthy*,
Lk 7 4		[The centurion] *deserves* this of you, they said [to Jesus]
7	2	I am not *worthy* to have you under my roof;
10 7		the labourer *deserves* his wages.
12 48		The [servant] who . . . *deserves* to be beaten
15 19		I no longer *deserve* to be called your son;
21		I no longer *deserve* to be called your son
20 35	4	those who are *judged worthy* of a place in the other world
23 15		[Jesus] has done nothing that *deserves* death,
Ac 23 29		I found that . . . there was no charge [against Paul] *deserving* death or imprisonment.
25 11		If I am guilty of committing any ʳcapital crime (lit. crime *worthy* of death), I do not ask to be spared the death penalty.
25		I am satisfied that [Paul] has committed no ʳcapital crime (lit. crime *worthy* of death),
26 31		[Paul] is doing nothing that *deserves* death or imprisonment.
Rm 1 32		They know what God's verdict is: that those who behave like this *deserve* to die
8 18 ○		what we suffer in this life can never ʳbe compared to (lit. *merit*) the glory . . . which is waiting for us.
2 Th 1 5	4	the purpose of [this persecution] is that you may be *found worthy* of the kingdom of God;
1 Tm 1 15		Here is a saying that you can rely on and ʳnobody should doubt (lit. *worthy* of complete belief): that Christ Jesus came into the world to save sinners.
4 9		that is a saying that you can rely on and ʳnobody should doubt it (lit. *worthy* of complete belief).
5 17		The elders who do their work well . . . ʳare to be given (lit. *deserve*) double consideration,
2		

1 Tm	5 18	The worker *deserves* his pay.
	6 1	All slaves . . . ˹must have unqualified respect for their masters (lit. ought to consider their masters *worthy* of unqualified respect),
Heb	3 3	2 [Jesus] has been found to *deserve* a greater glory than Moses.
	10 29	anyone who tramples on the Son of God . . . will be ˹con- 2 demned to (lit. *judged worthy* of) a far severer punishment.
	11 38	[the prophets] ˹were too good for the world (lit. of whom the world was not *worthy*)
Rv	3 4	they are *fit* to come with me, dressed in white.
	4 11	You are . . . our God, you are *worthy* of glory and honour
	5 2	Is there anyone *worthy* to open the scroll and break the seals of it?
	4	there was nobody *fit* to open the scroll and read it,
	9	You are *worthy* to take the scroll and break the seals of it,
	12	The Lamb that was sacrificed is *worthy* to be given power,
	16 6	blood is what you have given them to drink; it is what they *deserve*.

2: RESPECTABLE – PRINCIPLED – NOBLE: *SEMNOS*

1 *semnos* 4   2 *semnotēs* 3

Ph	4 8	fill your minds with everything that is true, everything that is *noble*,
1 Tm	2 2	2 so that we may be able to live religious and *reverent* lives
	3 4	[The elder-in-charge] must be a man who . . . brings his 2 children up to obey him and be ˹well-behaved (or: of high principles):
	3 8	deacons must be *respectable* men
	11	In the same way, the women must be *respectable*,
Tt	2 2	The older men should be reserved, *dignified*, moderate,
	7	when you are teaching, be an example . . . in your sincerity 2 and *earnestness*

3: (BE) WORTHY, FIT TO – QUALIFIED: *HIKANOS*

2 *hikanoō*   2   3 *hikanotēs* 1
1 *hikanos (eimi)* 9/40

Mt	3 11	I *am* not *fit* to carry his sandals;
	8 8	The centurion replied, 'Sir, I *am* not *worthy* to have you under my roof . . .'
Mk	1 7	I *am* not *fit* to kneel down and undo the strap of his sandals.
Lk	3 16	I *am* not *fit* to undo the strap of his sandals.
	7 6	I *am* not *worthy* to have you under my roof;
1 Co	15 9	I am the least of the apostles; in fact . . . I hardly *deserve* the name apostle;
2 Co	2 16	who could *be qualified* for work like this?
	3 5	not that we *are qualified* in ourselves to claim anything as 6 3 our own work; all our *qualifications* come from God. ⁶ He 2 is the one who has given us the *qualifications* to be the administrators of this new covenant,
Col	1 12	2 the Father who has made ˹it possible for you (lit. you *fit*) to join the saints
2 Tm	2 2	hand [my teaching] on to reliable people so that they in turn will be ˹able (lit. *qualified*) to teach others.

4: FIT, SUITABLE: *EU-THETOS*

1 *eu-thetos* 3   2 *an-eu-thetos* 1

Lk	9 62	no one who looks back is *fit* for the kingdom of God.
	14 35	[The salt that loses its taste] is ˹good (or: *fit*) for neither soil nor manure heap.
Ac	27 12	2 the harbour was *unsuitable* for wintering,
Heb	6 7	A field that has been well watered . . . gives the crops [that are] *wanted*

FLESH – BLOOD – BONE

1. Flesh
  1: Flesh : *sarx*
    a) Flesh, Body – Human nature, Worldly standards – Physical, Unspiritual
    b) Flesh, Body – Unspiritual, Natural (contrasted with Spirit, Ghost, Spiritual)
    c) Flesh and Blood

    d) All flesh – Mankind, Human beings – No one
  2: Meat: *kreas*
2. Blood
  1: Blood: *haima*
  2: Drops (of blood) – Clots: *thrombos*
3. Bone
  1: Bone: *osteon*
  2: Marrow: *myelos*

1. FLESH

1: FLESH: *SARX*

3 *sarkikos* 7   1   *sarx* 137 ⎤
4 *sarkinos* 4   2 *pasa sarx*   9 ⎦ 146

a) Flesh, Body – Human nature, Worldly standards – Physical, Unspiritual

Mt	19 5	(Gn 2 24) a man must . . . cling to his wife, and the two become one *body*. ⁶ They are no longer two, therefore, but one *body*.
Mk	10 8	(Gn 2 24) the two become one *body*. They are no longer two . . . but one *body*.
Jn	1 14 X	The Word was made *flesh*,
	8 15	You judge by *human standards*; I judge no one,
Ac	2 26 X	(Ps 16 9) my *body* too will rest in hope
	31 X	Christ: he is the one . . . whose *body* did not experience corruption.
Rm	2 28	circumcision is more than a *physical* operation.
	4 1	Abraham, ˹from whom we are all descended (lit. our ancestor according to the *flesh*).
	6 19	If I may use human terms to help your ˹natural (lit. *physical*) weakness
	7 5	˹Before our conversion (lit. While we were in the *flesh*) our sinful passions . . . fertilised our bodies
	18	I know of nothing good living in me – living, that is, in my *unspiritual self* –
	25	I who serve in my *unspiritual self* the law of sin.
	9 3	my brothers of Israel. ⁴ my own *flesh* [and blood].
	5 X	from their *flesh* [and blood] came Christ.
	8	it is not *physcial* descent that decides who are the children of God;
	11 14	I have been sent to the pagans . . . to make my own ˹people (lit. *flesh*) envious of you,
	13 14	forget about satisfying your *bodies* with all their cravings.
1 Co	1 26	how many of you were wise ˹in the ordinary sense of the world (lit. according to the *flesh*)?
	7 28	[those who marry] will have their troubles . . . in ˹their married life (lit. the *flesh*)
	10 18	Look at the other Israel, the ˹race (lit. *physical*),
	15 39	Everything that is *flesh* is not the same *flesh*: there is human [flesh], animals' *flesh*, the *flesh* of birds and [the flesh] of fish.
2 Co	1 12	by the grace of God we have done this without ˹ulterior (lit. 3 *worldly*) motives.
	17	Do you really think . . . my motives are ordinary *human* ones . . . ?
	3 3	not on stone tablets but on the tablets of ˹your living (lit. 4 *human*) hearts.
	4 11	so that in our mortal *flesh* the life of Jesus, too, may be openly shown.
	5 16	we do not judge anyone by the standards of the *flesh*. Even X if we did once know Christ in the *flesh*, that is not how we know him now.
	7 5	there was no rest for this *body* of ours.
	10 2	people . . . think we go by ordinary *human* motives. ³ We 3 live in the *flesh*, of course, but the muscles that we fight 4 with are not *flesh*. ⁴ Our war is not fought with weapons 3 *of flesh*
	11 18	So many others have been boasting of their *worldly* achievements,
	12 7	I was given a thorn in the *flesh*,
Ga	2 20	I live now not ˹with my own life (lit. in the *flesh*) but with the life of Christ who lives in me.
	4 13	even at the beginning, when that ˹illness (lit. *bodily* weakness) gave me the opportunity to preach the Good News to you,
	14	¹⁴ you never showed the slightest sign of being revolted or disgusted by my ˹disease (lit. *body*)
	5 13	be careful, or this liberty will provide an opening for ˹self-indulgence (lit. *human nature*).
	24	You cannot belong to Christ Jesus unless you crucify all ˹self-indulgent (lit. *physical*) passions and desires.
	6 12	It is only ˹self-interest (lit. wanting to put up a good show *to the world*) that makes them want to force circumcision on you.
	13	they only want you to be circumcised so that they can boast of ˹the fact (lit. your *body*).
Ep	2 3	We all were among them too in the past, living *sensual* lives, ruled entirely by our own *physical* desires
	11	you who were pagans *physically*, termed the Uncircumcised by those who speak of themselves as the Circumcised by reason of a *physical* operation,
	14 X	[Christ] is the peace between us . . . destroying in his own *person* the hostility
	5 29	a man never hates his own *body*, but he feeds it
	31	(Gn 2 24) the two will become one *body*.
	6 5	be obedient to the men who are called your masters ˹in this world (lit. by *worldly standards*)

Ph 1 22 if living in this *body* means doing work which is having good results – I do not know what I should choose.
24 for me to stay alive in this *body* is a more urgent need for your sake.
Col 1 22 X [God] has reconciled you, by his death and in [his] *mortal* body.
24 in my own *body* to do what I can to make up all that has still to be undergone by Christ
2 1 many others who have never seen me ʳface to face (lit. in the *flesh*).
11 In [Jesus] you have been circumcised . . . by the complete stripping of your body of *flesh*.
13 You were dead, because you were sinners and (§ your *body*) had not been circumcised;
18 inflating themselves to a false importance with their *worldly* outlook.
23 ʳonce the flesh starts to protest (lit. in controlling the satiating of the *flesh*) [human doctrines and regulations] are no use
3 22 Slaves, be obedient to the men who are called your masters ʳin this world (lit. by *worldly standards*)
Phm 16 [Onesimus will return to you] as a ʳblood brother (lit. brother in the *flesh*) as well as a brother in the Lord.
Heb 5 7 X During his life ʳon earth (lit. in the *flesh*) [Jesus] offered up prayer and entreaty
7 16 [a priest] not by virtue of a law about *physical* descent,
9 10 rules about the *outward life*, connected with foods and drinks
10 20 a new way which [Jesus] has opened for us, . . . through the
X curtain, that is to say his *body*.
Jm 5 3 the same corrosion . . . will eat into your *body*.
1 P 2 11 3 keep yourselves free from the ʳselfish (lit. *physical*) passions that attack the soul.
3 21 a type of the baptism which . . . is not the washing off of *physical* dirt
4 1 X Think what Christ suffered in ʳthis life (lit. the *flesh*), and then arm yourselves with the same resolution that he had: anyone who in this life has *bodily* suffering has broken with sin, ² because for the rest of his life ʳon earth (lit. in the *flesh*) he is . . . ruled . . . only by the will of God.
2 P 2 10 those who are governed by their corrupt *bodily* desires
18 playing on their *bodily* desires with debaucheries.
1 Jn 2 16 nothing the ʳworld (lit. *flesh*) has to offer . . . could ever come from the Father.
4 2 every spirit which acknowledges that Jesus the Christ has come
X in the *flesh* is from God;
2 Jn 7 X many deceivers . . . refusing to admit that Jesus Christ has come in the *flesh*.
Jude 7 The fornication of Sodom and Gomorrah . . . was ʳequally unnatural (lit. the same; they perverted *human nature*),
8 in their delusions they . . . defile their *bodies*
23 keeping your distance even from outside clothing which is contaminated by ʳvice (lit. the *flesh*).
Rv 17 16 they will eat [the prostitute's] *flesh* and burn the remains
19 18 There will be the *flesh* of kings for you, and the *flesh* of great generals and (§ the *flesh* of) heroes, the *flesh* of horses and their riders and (§ the *flesh*) of all kinds of men,
21 all the birds were gorged with their *flesh*.

b) **Flesh, Body – Unspiritual, Natural (contrasted with Spirit, Ghost, Spiritual)**
Mt 26 41 The spirit is willing, but the *flesh* is weak
Mk 14 38 The spirit is willing, but the *flesh* is weak
Lk 24 39 X a ghost has no *flesh* and bones as you can see I have.
Jn 3 6 what is born of the *flesh* is *flesh*; what is born of the spirit is spirit.
6 63 It is the spirit that gives life, the *flesh* has nothing to offer.
Rm 1 3 X the Son of God . . . according to the *human nature* he took, was a descendant of David:
7 14 4 The Law . . . is spiritual; but I am *unspiritual*;
8 3 God has done what the Law, because of our *unspiritual* nature, was unable to do. God dealt with sin by sending his own
X Son in a *body* as physical as any sinful body, and in that *body* God condemned sin.
4 [we] behave not as our *unspiritual* nature but as the spirit dictates.
5 The *unspiritual* are interested only in what is *unspiritual*,
6 It is death to limit oneself to what is *unspiritual*; life and peace can come only with concern for the spiritual.
7 to limit oneself to what is *unspiritual* is to be at enmity with God:
8 People who are interested only in *unspiritual* things can never be pleasing to God. ⁹ Your interests, however, are not in the *unspiritual*, but in the spiritual,
12 there is no necessity for us to obey our *unspiritual* selves or to live *unspiritual* lives. ¹³ If you do live ʳthat way (lit. *unspiritual* lives) you are doomed to die; but if by the Spirit you put an end to the misdeeds of the body you will live.
15 27 the pagans who share the spiritual possessions of these poor
O 3 people have a duty to help them with *temporal* [possessions].
1 Co 3 1 4 I treated you as *sensual* men,

1 Co 3 3 3 you are still *unspiritual*. Isn't that obvious from . . . the way
3 that you go on behaving like ʳordinary (lit. *unspiritual*) people?
5 5 he is to be handed over to Satan so that his *sensual body* may be destroyed and his spirit saved on the day of the Lord.
6 16 a man who goes with a prostitute is one body with her, since the two, as it is said (Gn 2 24), become one *flesh*. ¹⁷ But anyone who is joined to the Lord is one spirit with him.
9 11 If we have sown spiritual things for you, why should you be
O 3 surprised if we harvest your *material things*?
2 Co 7 1 let us wash off all that can soil either *body* or spirit,
Ga 3 3 Are you foolish enough to end in *outward observances* what you began in the Spirit?
4 23 The child of the slave-girl was born in the ʳordinary (lit. *natural*) way;
29 the child born in the ʳordinary (lit. *natural*) way persecuted the child born in the Spirit's way,
5 16 if you are guided by the Spirit you will be in no danger of yielding to ʳself-indulgence (lit. the desires of the *body*), ¹⁷ since ʳself-indulgence (lit. the desires of the *body* are) the opposite of the Spirit, the Spirit is totally against ʳsuch a thing (lit. the desires of the *body*) . . . ¹⁸ If you are led by the Spirit, no law can touch you. ¹⁹ ʳWhen self-indulgence is at work the results (lit. The results of being *unspiritual*) are obvious: fornication, gross indecency . . . ²² What the Spirit brings is very different: love, joy,
6 8 if he sows in the ʳfield of self-indulgence (lit. *flesh*) he will get a harvest of corruption out of ʳit (lit. the *flesh*);
Ep 6 12 it is not against *human* enemies that we have to struggle, but against . . . the spiritual army of evil
Ph 3 3 we have our own glory from Christ Jesus without having to rely on a *physical* [operation]. ⁴ If it came to relying on
4 *physical* evidence, I should be fully qualified myself. Take any man who thinks he can rely on what is *physical*: I am even better qualified [circumcised from the 8th day; Hebrew; Pharisee].
Col 2 5 I may be absent in *body*, but in spirit I am there among you,
1 Tm 3 16 X He was made visible in the *flesh*, attested by the Spirit,
Heb 9 13 The blood of goats . . . and the ashes of a heifer are sprinkled on those who have incurred defilement and they restore the holiness of their *outward lives*; ¹⁴ how much more effectively the blood of Christ . . . ?
12 9 we have all had our *human* fathers who punished us,
1 P 3 18 X In the *body* [Christ] was put to death, in the spirit he was raised to life,
4 6 the dead had to be told the Good News as well, so that though, in ʳtheir life on earth (lit. the *flesh*) they had been through the judgement that comes to all humanity, they might come to God's life in the spirit.

c) *Flesh and Blood*
5 haima 10/97

Mt 16 17 /5 Simon, . . . it was not *flesh* and *blood* that revealed this to you but my Father in heaven;
Jn 1 13 5 ≠ him (G they) who was (G were) born not out of *human stock* or urge of the *flesh* or will of man but of God himself ≠.
6 51 X the bread that I shall give is my *flesh*, for the life of the
52 X world. ⁵² . . . How can this man give us his *flesh* to eat?
53 X ⁵³ . . . if you do not eat the *flesh* of the Son of Man and
54 X drink his *blood*, you will not have life in you. ⁵⁴ Anyone
X /5 who does eat my *flesh* and drink my *blood* has eternal life
55 X /5 . . . ⁵⁵ For my *flesh* is real food and my *blood* is real drink.
56 X /5 ⁵⁶ He who eats my *flesh* and drinks my *blood* lives in me and I live in him
1 Co 15 50 /5 *flesh* and *blood* cannot inherit the kingdom of God:
Ga 1 16 I did not stop to discuss this with ʳany human being (lit.
/5 anyone of *flesh* and *blood*), . . . ¹⁷ But I sent off to Arabia
Ep 6 12 it is not against ʳhuman enemies (lit. enemies of *flesh* and
5 *blood*) that we have to struggle but against . . . the spiritual army of evil
Heb 2 14 X 5/ Since all the children share the same *blood* and *flesh*, he too shared equally in it,

d) *All flesh – Mankind, Human beings – No one*
(*pasa sarx* + negative = *no flesh*, hence: *no, no one*)

Mt 24 22 2 if that time had not been shortened, *no one* would have survived;
Mk 13 20 2 if the Lord had not shortened that time, *no one* would have survived;
Lk 3 6 2 (Is 40 5 G) all *mankind* shall see the salvation of God.
Jn 17 2 2 [Father,] through the power over all *mankind* that you have given [your Son], let him give eternal life to all
Ac 2 17 2 (Jl 3 1) In the days to come . . . I will pour out my spirit on
2 all *mankind*.
Rm 3 20 2 (Ps 143 2) *no one* can be justified in the sight of God by keeping the Law:

2: MEAT: *KREAS*

kreas 2

Rm 14 21	the best course is to abstain from *meat* and wine
1 Co 8 13	since food can be the occasion of my brother's downfall, I shall never eat *meat* again,

2. BLOOD

1: BLOOD: *HAIMA*

1	*haima*	87/97	3	*haimo(-rrhoeō) 1*
2	*haimat(-ek-chysia)*	*1*		

A = Blood of animals

Mt 9 20	a woman . . . had suffered from a ⌐haemorrhage (lit. flow of blood) for twelve years,
23 30	We would never have joined [our fathers] in shedding the *blood* of the prophets.
35	you will draw down on yourselves the *blood* of every holy man that has been shed on earth, from the *blood* of Abel the Holy to the *blood* of Zechariah
26 28 X	this is my *blood*, [the blood] of the covenant, which is to be poured out for many
27 4 X	'I have sinned,' [Judas] said, 'I have betrayed innocent *blood*.'
6 X	It is against the Law to put this into the treasury; it is *blood*-money.
8	this is why the field is called the Field of *Blood* today.
24 X	Pilate . . . said, 'I am innocent of this man's *blood* (ᵛ the *blood* of this just man) . . .' 25 And the people, to a man,
25 X	shouted back, 'His *blood* be on us and on our children.'
Mk 5 25	a woman . . . had suffered from a ⌐haemorrhage (lit. flow of *blood*) for twelve years;
29	the source of the *bleeding* dried up instantly,
14 24 X	This is my *blood*, [the blood] of the covenant, which is to be poured out for many.
Lk 8 43	there was a woman suffering from a ⌐haemorrhage (lit. flow of *blood*) for twelve years,
44	the ⌐haemorrhage (lit. flow of *blood*) stopped at that instant.
11 50	this generation will have to answer for every prophet's *blood*
51	. . . 51 from the *blood* of Abel to the *blood* of Zechariah,
13 1	some people . . . told [Jesus] about the Galileans whose *blood* Pilate had mingled with that of their sacrifices.
22 20 X	This cup is the new covenant in my *blood* which will be poured out for you.
44 X	his sweat fell to the ground like great drops of *blood*.
Jn 19 34 X	immediately there came out [from his pierced side] *blood* and water.
Ac 1 19	the field came to be called the *Bloody* Acre, in their language Hakeldama.
2 19	(Jl 3 3) (§ *blood* and fire and columns of smoke)
20	(Jl 3 4) The sun will be turned into darkness and the moon into *blood*
5 28 X	You . . . seem determined to fix the guilt of this man's ⌐death (lit. *blood*) on us.
15 20 A	we send them a letter telling them merely to abstain from . . . the meat of strangled animals and from *blood*.
29 A	you are to abstain from . . . *blood*, from the meat of strangled animals
18 6	[Paul shook his cloak, saying,] 'Your *blood* be on your own heads';
20 26	I swear that ⌐my conscience is clear as far as all of you are concerned (lit. I am innocent of the *blood* of all of you),
28 X	he bought with ⌐his own *blood* (or: the *blood* of his Own) [the Church of God]
21 25 A	The pagans who have become believers . . . must abstain from . . . *blood*, from the meat of strangled animals
22 20	when the *blood* of your witness Stephen was being shed, I was standing by
Rm 3 15	Their feet are swift when *blood* is to be shed,
25 X	Christ Jesus . . . was appointed by God ⌐to sacrifice his life so as (lit. through his own *blood*) to win reconciliation
5 9 X	Having ⌐died (lit. shed his *blood*) to make us righteous, is it likely that he would now fail to save us from God's anger?
1 Co 10 16 X	The blessing-cup that we bless is a communion with the *blood* of Christ,
11 25 X	This cup is the new covenant in my *blood*,
27 X	anyone who . . . drinks the cup of the Lord unworthily will be behaving unworthily towards the . . . *blood* of the Lord.
Ep 1 7 X	in [Jesus], through his *blood*, we gain our freedom,
2 13 X	you . . . have been brought very close, by the *blood* of Christ.
Col 1 20	[God wanted] all things to be reconciled through him . . .
X	when he made peace ⌐by his death on the (lit. by the *blood* of his) cross.
Heb 9 7	the second tent is entered . . . only by the high priest who must . . . take the *blood* to offer

Heb 9 12 A	[Christ] has entered the sanctuary once and for all, taking with him not the *blood* of goats and bull calves, but his own
X	*blood*,
13 A	The *blood* of goats . . . and the ashes of a heifer are sprinkled on those who have incurred defilement and they restore the holiness of their outward lives; 14 how much more effectively
14 X	the *blood* of Christ, . . . can purify our inner self
18 A	even the earlier covenant needed ⌐something to be killed (lit. *blood*) in order to take effect,
19 A	Moses . . . took the calves' [blood], the goats' *blood* and some water,
20 A	This is the *blood* of the covenant that God has laid down for you.
21 A	[Moses] sprinkled the tent and all the liturgical vessels with *blood*
22 A 12	according to the Law almost everything has to be purified with *blood*; and if there is no shedding of *blood*, there is no remission.
25 A	the high priest . . . with the *blood* that is not his own.
10 4 A	Bulls' [blood] and goats' *blood* are useless for taking away sins,
19 X	through the *blood* of Jesus we have the right to enter the sanctuary,
29 X	anyone who . . . treats the *blood* of the covenant which sanctified him as if it were not holy,
11 28 A	It was by faith that [Moses] kept the Passover and sprinkled the *blood*
12 4	In the fight against sin, you have not yet had to keep fighting to the point of ⌐death (lit. *blood*).
24 X	a *blood* for purification which pleads more insistently than Abel's.
13 11 A	The bodies of the animals whose *blood* is brought into the sanctuary by the high priest
12 X	Jesus too suffered . . . to sanctify the people with his own *blood*.
20 X	to become the great Shepherd of the sheep by the *blood* that sealed an eternal covenant,
1 P 1 2 X	obedient to Jesus Christ and sprinkled with his *blood*.
19 X	[the ransom that was paid to free you was paid] in the precious *blood* of a lamb without spot or stain,
1 Jn 1 7 X	the *blood* of Jesus, his Son, purifies us from all sin.
5 6 X	Jesus Christ who came by water and *blood*, not with water only, but with water and *blood*;
8 X	[there are three witnesses], the Spirit, the water and the *blood*,
Rv 1 5 X	[Jesus Christ] has washed away our sins with his *blood*,
5 9 X	with your *blood* you bought men for God of every race,
6 10	how much longer will you wait before you . . . take vengeance for our ⌐death (lit. *blood*)
12	the moon turned red as *blood* all over,
7 14 X	they have washed their robes white again in the *blood* of the Lamb,
8 7	hail and fire, mixed with *blood*, were dropped on the earth;
8	a third of the sea turned into *blood*,
11 6	[the two witnesses] are able to turn water into *blood*
12 11	[Michael and his angels] have triumphed over [the dragon]
X	by the *blood* of the Lamb
14 20	[the whole vintage of the earth] was trodden until the *blood* that came out of the winepress was up to the horses' bridles
16 3	the second angel emptied his bowl over the sea, and it turned to *blood*, like [the blood of] a corpse,
4	the third angel emptied his bowl into the rivers . . . and they turned into *blood*.
6	they spilt the *blood* of the saints and prophets, and *blood* is what you have given them to drink;
17 6	[the woman] was drunk . . . with the *blood* of the saints, and the *blood* of the martyrs of Jesus;
18 24	In [Babylon] you will find the *blood* of prophets and saints,
19 2	[our God] has avenged ⌐his servants that [the famous prostitute] killed (lit. the *blood* of his servants killed by her).
13 X	[the cloak of the rider, the Word of God,] was soaked in *blood*,

2: DROPS (OF BLOOD) – CLOTS: *THROMBOS*

thrombos 1

Lk 22 44 X	his sweat fell to the ground like great *drops* of blood.

3. BONE

1: BONE: *OSTEON*

osteon 4

Mt 23 27	whitewashed tombs that . . . inside are full of dead men's *bones*
Lk 24 39	a ghost has no flesh and *bones* as you can see I have.
Jn 19 36	(Ex 12 46) Not one *bone* of his will be broken;

Heb 11 22   It was by faith that . . . Joseph . . . made the arrangements for his ʳown burial (lit. *bones*).

2: MARROW: *MYELOS*
myelos 1

Heb 4 12   The word of God . . . can slip through the place where the . . . joints [are divided] from the *marrow*;

FOOLISH – MAD

---

1. **Senseless (people), Fools:** *a-sophos*
2. **Foolish, Senseless – Not understanding:** *a-syn-(h)etos*
3. **Fool, Folly, Foolish – Mad:** *a-phrōn*
4. **Fool, Foolish, Stupid – Madness, Folly:** *mōria*
5. **Foolish – Mad – Ignorant:** *a-noētos*
6. **(Be) Mad, Raving, Out of one's mind:** *mania*
7. **Be out of one's mind, Be beside oneself – Seem out of one's senses:** *ex-(h)istēmi*
8. **Rash, Reckless:** *pro-petēs*

S = Foolish, Mad//Sensible, Wise

1. SENSELESS (PEOPLE), FOOLS: *A-SOPHOS*
a-sophos 1

Ep 5 15 S   be . . . like intelligent and not like *senseless* [people].

2. FOOLISH, SENSELESS – NOT UNDERSTANDING: *A-SYN-(H)ETOS*
a-syn-(h)etos 5

Mt 15 16   [Jesus to Peter:] 'Do even you *not* yet *understand*?'
Mk 7 18   [Jesus to the disciples:] 'Do you *not understand* either?'
Rm 1 21   [such people] knew God and yet refused to honour him . . .; instead, they made nonsense out of logic and their ʳempty (lit. *senseless*; or: *uncomprehending*) minds were darkened.
     S
     31   [God has left them to their own irrational ideas,] *without brains*, honour, love or pity.
Rm 10 19   (Dt 32 21) Moses [said]: 'I will make you . . . angry with ʳan irreligious (lit. *a foolish*) people.'

3. FOOL, FOLLY, FOOLISH – MAD: *A-PHRŌN*

| 1 *a-phrōn* | 11 | 3 *para-phroneō* | 1 |
| 2 *a-phrosynē* | 4 | 4 *para-phronia* | 1 |

Mk 7 22   [it is from within . . . that evil intentions emerge:] avarice,
       2   . . . pride, *folly*.
Lk 11 40   *Fools*! Did not he who made the outside make the inside too?
   12 20   *Fool*! This very night the demand will be made for your soul;
Rm 2 20   If you can teach the ʳignorant (lit. *foolish*) . . . ²¹ then why not teach yourself . . . ?
1 Co 15 36   ['How are dead people raised and what sort of body do they have . . . ?'] They are *stupid* questions.
2 Co 11 1   2 I only wish you were able to tolerate a little *foolishness* from me.
       16   let no one take me for a *fool*; but if you must, then treat me as a *fool* . . . ¹⁷ What I am going to say now is . . . said
       17
       19   2 as if in [a fit of] *folly*, . . . ¹⁹ You are all wise men and can cheerfully tolerate *fools*,
     S
       21   2 I am still talking as a *fool*
       23   3 The servants of Christ [are they]? I must be *mad* to say this, but so am I,
   12 6   If I should decide to boast, I should not be [made to look] *foolish*,
       11   I have been [talking like] a *fool*,
Ep 5 17   do not be *thoughtless* but recognise what is the will of the Lord.
1 P 2 15   God wants you to be good citizens, so as to silence what *fools* are saying in their ignorance.
2 P 2 16   4 A dumb donkey put a stop to that prophet's *madness*

4. FOOL, FOOLISH, STUPID – MADNESS, FOLLY: *MŌRIA*

| 3 *mōrainō* | 2/4 | 1 *mōros* | 12 |
| 2 *mōria* | 5 | 4 *mōro(-logia)* | 1 |

Mt 5 22   if a man calls his brother '*Fool*' he will answer for it before the Sanhedrin;
    7 26   everyone who listens to these words of mine and does not act on them will be like a *stupid* man who built his house on sand.
     S
   23 17   *Fools* and blind! For which is of greater worth, the gold or the Temple . . . ?
   25 2 S   Five of [the bridesmaids] were *foolish* and five were sensible:
      3 S   ³ the *foolish* [ones] did take their lamps, but they brought no oil, . . . ⁸ and the *foolish* [ones] said to the sensible [ones], 'Give us some of your oil;
      8 S
Rm 1 22   The more they called themselves philosophers, the more *stupid* they *grew*,
      3 S
1Co 1 18 S   2 The language of the cross may be ʳillogical (or: *folly*) to those who are not on the way to salvation,
     20 S   3 Do you see now how God has ʳshown up the (lit. *made*) *foolishness* of human wisdom? ²¹ . . . God wanted to
     21
      S   2 save those who have faith through the *foolishness* of the message that we preach.
     23   here are we preaching a crucified Christ; to the . . . pagans
     25 2/   *madness*, . . . ²⁵ For God's *foolishness* is wiser than human wisdom,
     27   it was to shame the wise that God chose what is *foolish* by human reckoning,
      S
    2 14   An unspiritual person . . . sees [the spiritual things we
      S   2 teach] as *nonsense*;
    3 18   if any one of you thinks of himself as wise, in the ordinary sense . . ., then he must learn to be a *fool* before he really can be wise. ¹⁹ . . . Because the wisdom of the world is
     19
      S   2 *foolishness* to God.
    4 10 S   Here we are, *fools* for the sake of Christ,
Ep 5 4   4 There must be no coarseness, or ʳsalacious (lit. *foolish*) talk and jokes
2 Tm 2 23   Avoid these *futile* and silly speculations,
Tt 3 9   avoid *pointless* speculations,

5. FOOLISH – MAD – IGNORANT: *A-NOĒTOS*
1 *a-noētos* 6   2 *a-noia* 1/2

Lk 24 25   You *foolish* men! So slow to believe the full message of the prophets!
Rm 1 14   I owe a duty to . . . the educated just as much as to the *uneducated*,
      S
Ga 3 1   Are you people in Galatia *mad*?
      3   Are you *foolish* enough to end in outward observances what you began in the Spirit?
1Tm 6 9   People who long to be rich . . . get trapped into all sorts of *foolish* . . . ambitions
2Tm 3 9   2 their *foolishness* . . . must become obvious to everybody.
Tt 3 3   there was a time when we too were *ignorant*, disobedient and . . . enslaved by . . . luxuries;

6. (BE) MAD, RAVING, OUT OF ONE'S MIND: *MANIA*
1 *mainomai* 5   2 *mania* 1

Jn 10 20   Many said [of Jesus], 'He is possessed, he *is raving*';
Ac 12 15   They said to [Rhoda], 'You *are out of your mind*',
   26 24   Festus shouted out, 'Paul, you *are out of your mind*; all that
     25 S   2 learning of yours is driving you *mad*'. ²⁵ 'Festus . .,' answered Paul 'I *am* not *mad*:'
1 Co 14 23   any uninitiated people . . . would say you *were* all *mad*;

7. BE OUT OF ONE'S MIND, BE BESIDE ONESELF – SEEM OUT OF ONE'S SENSES: *EX-(H)ISTĒMI*
ex-(h)istēmi 2/17

Mk 3 21   [Jesus's] relatives . . . [were] convinced he *was out of his mind*.
2Co 5 13 S   If we *seemed out of our senses*, it was for God;

8. RASH, RECKLESS: *PRO-PETĒS*
pro-petēs 2

Ac 19 36   there is no need for you to get excited or do anything *rash*.
2Tm 3 4   [in the last days people] will be treacherous and *reckless* and demented by pride,

FOOT – LEG

1. Foot – Ankle – Heel
  1: Foot – Footstool – On foot: *pous*
  a) Foot, Feet
  b) Footstool – Between the feet
      and the ground
  c) On foot – Go by road, by
      land
  2: Feet and Ankles: *basis* and
     sphydron
  3: Heel: *pterna*

2. Trample (on), Tread (on): *pateō*
  a) Trample (on), Tread underfoot
  b) Tread (the winepress) – Tread
      out (wine)
3. Leg(s) – Knee(s) – Thigh
  1: Leg(s): *skelos*
  2: Knee(s): *gonu*
  3: Thigh: *mēros*
4. Foot's length, Square foot: *bēma*
5. Kick: *laktizō*

---

1. FOOT – ANKLE – HEEL

1: FOOT – FOOTSTOOL – ON FOOT: *POUS*

3 *pezē* 2   1   *pous*   94
4 *pezeuō* 1   2 *hypo-podion* 8

a) Foot, Feet

Mt	4	6 X	(Ps 91 12) in case you hurt your *foot* against a stone.
	10	14	as you walk out of the house . . . shake the dust from your *feet*.
	15	30	large crowds came to him bringing the lame . . . and many
		X	others; these they put down at his *feet*,
	18	8	if your hand or your *foot* should cause you to sin, cut it off . . : it is better for you to enter into life crippled . . . than to have two hands or two *feet* and be thrown into eternal fire.
	22	13	Bind him hand and *foot* and throw him out into the dark,
	28	9	the women came up to him and, falling down before him,
		X	clasped his *feet*.
Mk	5	22 X	Jairus . . . fell at his *feet* [23] and pleaded with him
	6	11	shake off the dust from under your *feet* as a sign to them.
	7	25 X	A woman . . . came and fell at his *feet*.
	9	45	if your *foot* should cause you to sin, cut it off; it is better . . . than to have two *feet* and be thrown into hell.
Lk	1	79	to guide our *feet* into the way of peace.
	4	11	(Ps 91 12) in case you hurt your *foot* against a stone.
	7	38 X	She waited behind him at his *feet*, weeping, and her tears
		X	fell on his *feet* . . .; then she covered his *feet* with kisses and anointed him with the ointment.
		44	Simon, . . . I came into your house, and you poured no
		X	water over my *feet*, but she has poured out her tears over
		45 X	my *feet* . . . [45] You gave me no kiss, but she has been
		46 X	covering my *feet* with kisses . . . [46] You did not anoint
		X	my head with oil, but she has anointed my *feet* with ointment.
	8	35	the people . . . found the man from whom the devils had
		X	gone out sitting at the *feet* of Jesus,
		41 X	Jairus . . . fell at Jesus's *feet* and pleaded with him
	9	5	shake the dust from your *feet* as a sign to them
	10	11	We wipe off the very dust of your town that clings to our *feet*,
		39	[Martha] had a sister called Mary, who sat down at the Lord's
		X	*feet* and listened to him
	15	22	put a ring on his finger and sandals on his *feet*.
	17	16 X	[one of the lepers] threw himself at the *feet* of Jesus and thanked him.
	24	39 X	Look at my hands and *feet*; yes, it is I indeed,
		40 X	˅ . . . he showed them his hands and *feet*.[1]
Jn	11	2	the same Mary . . . who anointed the Lord with ointment and wiped his *feet* with her hair.
		32 X	Mary . . . threw herself at his *feet*,
		44	The dead man came out, his *feet* and hands bound with bands of stuff
	12	3 X	Mary . . . anointed the *feet* of Jesus, wiping ʳthem (lit his
		X	*feet*) with her hair.
	13	5	[Jesus] began to wash the disciples' *feet*
		6	Lord, are you going to wash my *feet*?
		8	You shall never wash my *feet*.
		9	Then, Lord, . . . [wash] not only my *feet*, but my hands and my head as well!
		10	No one who has taken a bath needs washing (§ more than his *feet*), he is clean all over.
		12	When he had washed their *feet* . . . he went back to the table. 'Do you understand . . . what I have done to you?'
		14	If I, . . . the Lord and Master, have washed your *feet*, you should wash each other's *feet*.
	20	12	[Mary] saw two angels . . . sitting where the body of Jesus had been, one at the head, the other at the *feet*.
Ac	4	35	[all those who owned houses would sell them and bring the money] to present it ʳto (lit. at the *feet* of) the apostles;

Ac	4	37	[Barnabas] brought the money, and presented it ʳto (lit. at the *feet* of) the apostles.
	5	2	[Ananias] brought the rest and presented it ʳto (lit. at the *feet* of) the apostles.
		9	You hear those *footsteps*? They have just been to bury your
		10	husband. . . . [10] Instantly [Sapphira] dropped dead at his *feet*.
	7	5	God did not give [Abraham] a single square foot (§ to put his *foot* on) of this land
		33	(Ex 3 5) Take off your shoes from your *feet*; the place where you are standing is holy ground.
		58	The witnesses [of the stoning of Stephen] put down their clothes at the *feet* of a young man called Saul.
	10	25	Cornelius went out to meet [Peter], knelt at his *feet* and prostrated himself.
	13	25 X	I am not fit to undo his sandal on his *foot*.
		51	[Paul and Barnabas] shook the dust [of Antioch] from their *feet* in defiance and went off to Iconium;
	14	8	a man [in Lystra] . . . [whose] *feet* were crippled from birth;
		10	Get to your *feet* – stand up,
	16	24	[the gaoler] threw [Paul and Silas] into the inner prison and fastened their *feet* in the stocks.
	21	11	[Agabus] took Paul's girdle, and tied up his own *feet* and hands,
	22	3	I studied ʳunder (lit. at the *feet* of) Gamaliel
	26	16	[The Lord to Saul:] get up and stand on your *feet*,
Rm	3	15	(Is 59 7) Their *feet* are swift when blood is to be shed,
	10	15	(Is 52 7) The *footsteps* of those who bring good news is a welcome sound.
1Co	12	15 <	If the *foot* were to say, 'I am not a hand and so I do not belong to the body',
		21 <	nor can the head say to the *feet*, 'I do not need you'.
Ep	6	15	wearing for shoes on your *feet* the eagerness to spread the gospel of peace
1Tm	5	10	[The widow] must be a woman known for . . . the way in which she has . . . shown hospitality to strangers and washed the saints' *feet*,
Heb	12	13	(Pr 4 26) smooth out the path ʳyou tread (lit. for your *feet*)
Rv	1	15 X	[a figure like a Son of man,] his *feet* like burnished bronze
		17 X	I fell in a dead faint at his *feet*,
	2	18 X	the Son of God who has . . . *feet* like burnished bronze:
	3	9	I will make them come and fall at your *feet*
	10	1	[the angel's] ʳlegs (lit. *feet*) were pillars of fire.
		2	he put his right *foot* in the sea and his left [foot] on the land
	11	11	God breathed life into them and they stood up on their *feet*,
	13	2	the beast was like a leopard, with *paws* like a bear
	19	10	Then I knelt at his *feet* to worship him,
	22	8	I knelt at the *feet* of the angel who had shown [these things] to me,

b) Footstool – Between the feet and the ground

Mt	5	35	(Is 66 1) [do not swear] by the earth, since that is [God's]
		Θ /2	*footstool*;
	7	6	do not throw your pearls in front of pigs, or they may trample them under their *feet* and then turn on you
	22	44 X	(Ps 110 1) Sit at my right hand and I will put your enemies under your *feet*?
Mk	12	36	(Ps 110 1) Sit at my right hand and I will put your enemies
		X 2/	(˅ as a *stool*) under your *feet*.
Lk	20	43	(Ps 110 1) Sit at my right hand and I will make your enemies
		X /2	a *footstool* for you.
Ac	2	35	(Ps 110 1) Sit at my right hand until I make your enemies
		X /2	a *footstool* for you.
	7	49 /2	(Is 66 1) With heaven my throne and earth my *footstool*,
Rm	16	20	The God of peace will soon crush Satan beneath your *feet*.
1Co	15	25	(Ps 110 1) until he has put all his enemies under his *feet*
		27 X?	(Ps 8 6) everything is to be put under his *feet*.
Ep	1	22 X	(Ps 8 6) [God] has put all things under his *feet*,
Heb	1	13	(Ps 110 1) Sit at my right hand and I will make your enemies
		X /2	a *footstool* for you.
	2	8	(Ps 8 6) You have put ʳhim in command of everything (lit.
		X	everything under his *feet*).
	10	13	(Ps 110 1) where [Christ] is now waiting until his enemies
		X /2	are made into a *footstool* for him.
Jm	2	3	2 You can sit on the floor by my *foot-rest*.
Rv	12	1	a woman, . . . ʳstanding on the moon (lit. the moon beneath her *feet*),

c) On foot – Go by road, By land

Mt	14	13	3 the people . . . went after [Jesus] *on foot*.
Mk	6	33	3 they all hurried to the place *on foot*
Ac	20	13	4 Paul . . . wanted to *go by road*.

2: FEET and ANKLES: *BASIS* and *SPHYDRON*

1 *basis* 1   2 *sphydron* 1

Ac	3	7	/2 Instantly his *feet* and *ankles* became firm,

3: HEEL: *PTERNA*

pterna 1

Jn 13 18   (Ps 41 9) Someone who shares my table ʳrebels (lit. has lifted his *heel*) against me.

2. TRAMPLE (ON), TREAD (ON): *PATEŌ*

1 *pateō 5*   2 *kata-pateō 5*

a) Trample (on), Tread underfoot

Mt 5 13   2   if salt becomes tasteless . . . [it] can only be thrown out to be *trampled underfoot* by men.

   7 6   2   do not throw your pearls in front of pigs, or they may *trample* them under their feet and then turn on you

Lk 8 5   2   some [seed] fell on the edge of the path and was *trampled on*;

   10 19   I have given you power to *tread underfoot* serpents and scorpions

   12 1   2   people had gathered in their thousands so that they were *treading on* one another.

   21 24   Jerusalem will be *trampled down* by the pagans

Heb 10 29   2   you may be sure that anyone who *tramples on* the Son of God . . . will be condemned to a far severer punishment.

Rv 11 2   [the pagans] will *trample on* the holy city for forty-two months.

b) Tread (the winepress) – Tread out (wine)

Rv 14 20   [the winepress of God's anger,] outside the city, where it was *trodden*

   19 15   X   he is the one who will . . . *tread out* the wine of Almighty God's fierce anger.

3. LEG(S) – KNEE(S) – THIGH

1: LEG(S): *SKELOS*

skelos 3

Jn 19 31   the Jews asked Pilate to have the *legs* [of the crucified men]
     32   broken . . . ³² . . . the soldiers came and broke the *legs*
     33   of the first . . . and then of the other. ³³ When they came to
      X   Jesus, . . . instead of breaking his *legs* ³⁴ one of the soldiers pierced his side

2: KNEE(S): *GONU*

gonu 2/12

Lk 5 8   Simon Peter . . . fell at the *knees* of Jesus
Heb 12 12   (Is 35 3) So hold up your limp arms and steady your trembling *knees*

3: THIGH: *MĒROS*

mēros 1

Rv 19 16 X   On his cloak and on his *thigh* there was a name written: The King of kings

4. FOOT'S LENGTH, SQUARE FOOT: *BĒMA*

bēma 1/12

Ac 7 5   God did not give [Abraham] a single *square foot* of this land

5. KICK: *LAKTIZŌ*

laktizō 1

Ac 26 14   [Saul,] . . . It is hard for you, *kicking* like this against the goad.

FOR

1. **For:** *hyper*
   1: For = On behalf of, For the sake of
   2: For = On the side of
2. **For (= On behalf of):** *anti*

3. **For (= To, In):** *eis*
4. **On account of, For the sake of – About, For:** *dia*
5. **For the sake of, On account of:** *heneka*

1. FOR: *HYPER*

hyper + genitive (74)

1: FOR = ON BEHALF OF, FOR THE SAKE OF

X = Christ is, acts, for

Mk 14 24 X   This is my blood . . . which is to be poured out *for* many.
Lk 22 19 X   This is my body which will be given *for* you;
     20   This cup is the new covenant in my blood which will be
      X   poured out *for* you.
Jn 6 51 X   the bread that I shall give is my flesh, *for* the life of the world.
   10 11 X   the good shepherd is one who lays down his life *for* his sheep.
     15 X   I lay down my life *for* my sheep.
   11 4   This sickness will end . . . ʳin (lit. *for*) God's glory,
     50 X   [Caiaphas said,] it is better for one man to die *for* the people,
     51   . . . ⁵¹ . . . he made this prophecy that Jesus was to die
     52 X   *for* the nation – ⁵² and not *for* the nation only, but to gather together in unity the scattered children of God.
   13 37   Peter said to him, . . . I will lay down my life *for* you'
     38   'Lay down your life *for* me?' answered Jesus.
   15 13   A man can have no greater love than to lay down his life
     (X)   *for* his friends.
   17 19 X   *for* their sake I consecrate myself
   18 14 X   It is better for one man to die *for* the people.
Ac 5 41   glad to have had the honour of suffering humiliation *for* [the sake of] the name.
   9 16   how much he himself must suffer *for* my name.
   15 26   [Paul and Barnabas] have dedicated their lives ʳto (lit. *for*) the name of our Lord Jesus Christ.
   21 13   I [Paul] am ready . . . to die in Jerusalem *for* the name of the Lord Jesus Christ.
Rm 1 5   to teach the obedience of faith to all pagan nations ʳin honour of (lit. *for*) his name.
   5 6 X   Christ died *for* sinful men.
     7 X   It is not easy to die even *for* a good man – though of course *for* someone really worthy, a man might be prepared to
     8 X   die – ⁸ but . . . Christ died *for* us while we were still sinners.
   8 32 X   God . . . gave [his own Son] up ʳto benefit (lit. *for*) us all.
   9 3   I would willingly be condemned . . . ʳif it could help (lit.
     X   *for*) my brothers of Israel,
   14 15   the downfall of someone *for* whom Christ died.
   15 8   Christ became the servant of circumcised Jews . . . not only
     X   ʳso that God could faithfully carry (lit. *for* the faithfulness of God in carrying) out the promises made to the patriarchs,
   16 4 X   [Christ Jesus] who risked death ʳto save (lit. *for*) my life:
1Co 1 13   Was it Paul that was crucified *for* you?
   11 24 X   This is my body, which is *for* you;
   15 3 X   Christ died *for* our sins,
     29   what do people hope to gain by being baptised *for* the dead? . . . why be baptised *on their behalf*?
2Co 5 14 X   if one man has died *for* all, then all men should be dead;
     15 X   ¹⁵ and the reason he died *for* all was so that living men should live . . . for him who died and was raised to life
     X   *for* them.
     20   we are ambassadors *for* Christ; . . . the appeal that we make ʳin Christ's name (lit. *for* Christ's *sake*) is: be reconciled to God.
     21   *For* our *sake* God made the sinless one into sin,
   12 10   the agonies I go through *for* Christ's *sake*.
     15   I am perfectly willing to spend what I have . . . ʳin the interests of (lit. *for*) your souls.
Ga 1 4 X   [the Lord Jesus Christ] sacrificed himself *for* our sins,
   2 20   the Son of God who loved me and who sacrificed himself
     X   *for* my sake.
   3 13 X   Christ redeemed us . . . by being cursed *for* our *sake*,
Ep 3 1   I, Paul, a prisoner of Christ Jesus *for* [the sake of] you pagans.
     13   the trials that I go through *on your account*
   5 2   as [Christ] loved you, giving himself up ʳin our place (lit.
     X   *for* us) as a fragrant offering
     25 X   just as Christ loved the Church and sacrificed himself *for* her
   6 20   [the mystery of the gospel] ʳof (lit. *for*) which I am an ambassador in chains;
Ph 1 29   [God] has given you the privilege . . . of suffering *for* [Christ]
Col 1 24   It makes me happy to suffer *for* you, and in my own body to do what I can to make up all that has still to be undergone by Christ *for* [the sake of] his body, the Church.
   2 1   I want you to know that I do have to struggle hard *for* you,
   4 12   Epaphras . . . never stops battling *for* you, praying that you
     13   will never lapse . . . ¹³ . . . he works hard *for* you,
1Th 5 10 X   [our Lord Jesus Christ] died *for* us
2Th 1 5   it is *for* [the sake of] this that you are suffering now
1Tm 2 6 X   [Christ Jesus] sacrificed himself as a ransom *for* them all.
Tt 2 14 X   [Christ Jesus] sacrificed himself *for* us
Heb 2 9 X   Jesus . . . had to experience death *for* all mankind.
   6 20 X   [beyond the veil] where Jesus has entered before us and on our *behalf*,

Heb	9 24	so that [Christ] could appear in the actual presence of God on our *behalf*.
1 P	2 21 X	because Christ suffered *for* you
	3 18 X	Christ . . . died *for* the guilty,
1 Jn	3 16 X	he gave up his life *for* us; and we, too, ought to give up our our lives *for* our brothers.
3 Jn	7	It was entirely *for* [the sake of] the name that they set out,

2: FOR = ON THE SIDE OF

Mk	9 40	Anyone who is not against us is *for* us
Lk	9 50	anyone who is not against you is *for* you.
Rm	8 31	With God ⌜on our side (lit. *for* us) who can be against us?

2. FOR (= ON BEHALF OF): ANTI

anti (3)

Mt	17 27	take [the shekel] and give it to them *for* me and [for] you.
	20 28	the Son of Man came . . . to give his life as a ransom *for* many,
Mk	10 45	the Son of man . . . [came] to give his life as a ransom *for* many.

3. FOR (= TO, IN): EIS

eis (8)

Mt	26 10	What she has done *for* me is one of the good works indeed!
Rm	11 36	All that exists . . . is by him and *for* him.
	16 5	Greetings ⌜to (or: *for*) my friend Epaenetus, the first of Asia's gifts to Christ;
1 Co	8 6	there is one God, the Father, from whom all things come and *for* whom we exist;
2 Co	11 3	your ideas may get . . . turned away from simple devotion ⌜to (or: *for*) Christ.
Col	1 16	all things were created through him and *for* him.
	20	[God wanted] all things to be reconciled through [Christ] and *for* [Christ],
Phm	6	all the good things that we are able to do *for* Christ.

4. ON ACCOUNT OF, FOR THE SAKE OF, BECAUSE OF, – ABOUT, FOR: DIA

dia + accusative (15)

Mt	27 19	I have been upset all day by a dream I had *about* him.
Mk	13 13	You will be hated by all men *on account of* my name;
Lk	21 17	You will be hated by all men *on account of* my name,
Jn	7 43	So the people could not agree *about* him.
	12 9	a large number of Jews . . . came not only *on account of* Jesus but also to see Lazarus
	30	It was not *for* my *sake* that this voice came, but for yours.
	15 21	it will be *on* my *account* that they will do all this,
1 Co	4 10	Here we are, fools *for the sake of* Christ,
2 Co	4 5	we are preaching . . . Christ Jesus as the Lord, and ourselves as your servants *for Jesus' sake*.
	11	we are consigned to our death every day, *for the sake of* Jesus,
Ph	3 7	*because of* Christ, I have come to consider all these advantages that I had as disadvantages. [8] Not only that, but I believe nothing can happen that will outweigh the supreme advantage ⌜of knowing (lit. gained *on account of* the knowledge of) Christ Jesus my Lord. *For* him I have accepted the loss of everything.
Heb	2 10	God, *for* whom everything exists and through whom everything exists,
1 P	2 13	*For the sake of* the Lord, accept the authority of every social institution;

5. FOR THE SAKE OF, ON ACCOUNT OF: HENEKA

2 *heineken* (2)   3 *heneka* (1)   1 *heneken* (12)

Mt	5 11	Happy are you when people abuse you . . . *on* my *account*.
	10 18	You will be dragged before . . . kings *for* my *sake*.
	39	anyone who loses his life *for* my *sake* will find it.
	16 25	anyone who loses his life *for* my *sake* will find it.
	19 29	everyone who has left houses . . . *for the sake of* my name
Mk	8 35	anyone who loses his life *for* my *sake*, and for the sake of the gospel, will save it.
	10 29	no one who has left house, brothers, sisters, . . . *for my sake* and *for the sake of* the gospel
	13 9	you will stand before . . . kings *for* my *sake*,
Lk	6 22	3 Happy are you when people hate you . . . *on account of* the Son of Man.

Lk	9 24	anyone who loses his life *for* my *sake*, that man will save it.
	18 29	2 no one who has left house, wife, brothers, . . . *for the sake of* the kingdom of God
	21 12	men will . . . bring you before kings . . . *because of* my name
Ac	28 20	2 it is *on account of* the hope of Israel that I wear this chain.
Rm	8 36	(Ps 44 22) *For* your *sake* we are being massacred daily

FOREIGN – ALIEN

1. Foreign, Strange – Hospitality: *xenos*
  1: Foreigner, Stranger – Alien, Outlandish
  2: Entertain, Lodge – Show hospitality, Welcome – Lodging
  3: (Seem) Strange, (Think) Startling, Unaccountable
	2. Barbarian, Savage – Native: *barbaros*
	3. Foreigners, Strangers – Estranged, Alien: *allotrios*
	4. Exiled, Live among foreigners – Nomads: *ek-dēmeō*
	5. Stay, Live as a foreigner – Visitors: *par-oikos*
	6. Deportation, Exile: *met-oikizō*

1. FOREIGN, STRANGE – HOSPITALITY: XENOS

4 *xenia*	2	6	*xeno-docheō*	1
2 *xenizō*	10	5	*philo-xenia*	2
1 *xenos*	14	3	*philo-xenos*	3

1: FOREIGNER, STRANGER – ALIEN, OUTLANDISH

Mt	25 35 X	I was a *stranger* and you made me welcome;
	38 X	When did we see you a *stranger* and make you welcome . . .?
	43 X	I was a *stranger* and you never made me welcome;
	44 X	when did we see you . . . a *stranger* or naked . . .?
	27 7	bought the potter's field . . . as a graveyard for *foreigners*,
Ac	17 18	[Paul] sounds like a propagandist for some *outlandish* gods.
	21	The one amusement the Athenians and the *foreigners* living there seem to have,
Ep	2 12 ●	[you were] *aliens* with no part in the covenants with their Promise;
	19 ●	So you are no longer *aliens* or foreign visitors:
Heb	11 13 ●	recognising that they were only *strangers* and nomads on earth.
	13 9	Do not let yourselves be led astray by all sorts of *strange* doctrines:
3 Jn	5	looking after these brothers, even though they were complete *strangers* to you.

2: ENTERTAIN, LODGE – SHOW HOSPITALITY, WELCOME – LODGING

Ac	10 6	2 [Peter] *is lodging* with Simon the tanner
	18	2 to know if . . . Peter *was lodging* there.
	23	2 Peter asked them in and *gave* them *lodging*.
	32	2 [Peter] *is lodging* in the house of Simon the tanner,
	21 16	2 the house of a Cypriot with whom we were to *lodge*;
	28 7	2 Publius . . . *entertained* us hospitably for three days.
	23	4 a large number of [the Roman Jews] visited [Paul] at his *lodgings*.
Rm	12 13	5 you should make *hospitality* your special care.
	16 23	Greetings from Gaius who *is entertaining* me
1 Tm	3 2	3 the president must be . . . temperate, . . . courteous, *hospitable*
	5 10	6 [A widow] must be a woman known for . . . the way in which she has . . . *shown hospitality* to strangers
Tt	1 8	3 [an elder must be] a man who *is hospitable* and a friend of all that is good;
Phm	22	4 will you get a place *ready* for me *to stay in*?
Heb	13 2	5 remember always to *welcome strangers*, for by doing this, 2 some people have *entertained* angels without knowing it.
1 P	4 9	3 *Welcome* each other *into your houses* without grumbling.

3: (SEEM) STRANGE, (THINK) STARTLING, UNACCOUNTABLE

Ac	17 20	2 Some of the things you said *seemed startling* to us
1 P	4 4	2 people *cannot understand* why you no longer hurry off with them
	12	2 you must not *think it* ⌜*unaccountable* (or: *strange*) that you should be tested by fire. There is nothing *extraordinary* in what has happened to you.

2. BARBARIAN, SAVAGE – NATIVE: *BARBAROS*

barbaros 6   *Scythia(n)**

Ac 28	2	The *inhabitants* treated us with unusual kindness.
	4	When the *natives* saw the creature hanging from [Paul's] hand
Rm 1	14	I owe a duty to Greeks just as much as to *barbarians*,
1 Co 14	11	if I am ignorant of what the sounds mean, I am a *savage* to the man who is speaking, and he is a *savage* to me.
Col 3	11	there is no room for distinction between Greek and Jew, . . . or between *barbarian* and Scythian*

3. FOREIGNER, STRANGERS – ESTRANGED, ALIEN: *ALLOTRIOS*

1	*allotrios* 7/14	3 *allo-genēs* 1
2	*ap-allotrioō* 3	4 *allo-phylos* 1

Mt 17	25	From whom do . . . kings . . . take . . . tribute? From their sons or from *foreigners*? ²⁶ . . . From *foreigners*,
	26	
Lk 17	18	no one has come back to give praise to God, except this 3 *foreigner*.
Jn 10	5 <	[The sheep] never follow a *stranger* . . : they do not recognise the voice of *strangers*.
Ac 7	6	(Gn 15 13) that [Abraham's] descendants would be exiles in a *foreign* land,
	10 28	4 it is forbidden for Jews to mix with *people of another race*
Ep 2	12 ●	2 you . . . were *excluded* from membership of Israel,
4	18 ●	2 they are *estranged* from the life of God,
Col 1	21 ●	2 Not long ago, you were *foreigners* and enemies,
Heb 11	9	[Abraham] arrived, as a foreigner, in the Promised Land, and lived there as if in a *strange* country,
	34	[Samson, Jephtha and David] were given strength, to . . . drive back *foreign* invaders.

4. EXILED, LIVE AMONG FOREIGNERS – NOMADS: *EK-DĒMEŌ*

1 *ek-dēmeō* 3	3 *epi-dēmeō* 2	
2 *par-epi-dēmos* 3		

Ac 2	10	3 ⌐*visitors* (or: *exiles*) from Rome – ¹¹ . . . we hear them preaching in our own language
	17 21	3 the Athenians and the foreigners *living* there
2 Co 5	6 ●	to live in the body means to *be exiled* from the Lord,
	8 ○	we . . . want to *be exiled* from the body and make our home with the Lord.
	9 ○	Whether we are living in the body or *exiled* from it,
Heb 11	13 ●	2 recognising that they were only strangers and *nomads* on earth.
1 P 1	1	2 Peter . . . sends greetings to all *those living among foreigners* in the Dispersion
	2 11 ●	2 I urge you . . . while you are visitors and *pilgrims* to keep yourselves free from the selfish passions

5. STAY, LIVE AS A FOREIGNER – VISITORS: *PAR-OIKOS*

2 *par-oikeō* 2	3 *par-oikia* 2	
1 *par-oikos* 4		

Lk 24	18 X	2 You must be the only person *staying* in Jerusalem who does not know the things that have been happening there these last few days.
Ac 7	6	(Gn 15 13) that [Abraham's] descendants would *be exiles* in a foreign land,
	29	Moses fled . . . and he went to *stay* in the land of Midian,
	13 17	The God of our nation Israel chose our ancestors, and made 3 our people great when they were *living as foreigners* in Egypt;
Ep 2	19 ●	So you are no longer aliens or *foreign visitors*:
Heb 11	9	2 [Abraham] arrived, *as a foreigner*, in the Promised Land, and lived there as if in a strange country,
1 P 1	17 ●	3 you must be scrupulously careful as long as you are *living away from* your home.
	2 11 ●	I urge you . . . while you are *visitors* and pilgrims

6. DEPORTATION, EXILE: *MET-OIKIZŌ*

1 *met-oikesia* 4	2 *met-oikizō* 2	

Mt 1	11	Then the *deportation* to Babylon took place.
	12	After the *deportation* to Babylon: Jechoniah was the father of Shealtiel,

Mt 1	17	The sum of generations is therefore: . . . fourteen from David to the Babylonian *deportation*; and fourteen from the Babylonian *deportation* to Christ.
Ac 7	4	2 God *made* [Abraham] *leave* Haran *and come to* this land
	43	2 (Am 5 27) now I will *exile* you even further than Babylon.

FORT – WALL – TOWER

1. Fortress, Stronghold – Camp, Barracks – Fortification	3: Fortification, Siege-works, Rampart: *charax*
1: Fortress, Camp, Barracks, therefore Army: *par-em-bolē*	**2. Wall – Barrier, Dividing Wall:** *teichos*
2: Stronghold, Fortress: *ochyrōma*	**3. Tower:** *pyrgo*

1. FORTRESS, STRONGHOLD – CAMP, BARRACKS – FORTIFICATION

1: FORTRESS, CAMP, BARRACKS, therefore ARMY: *PAR-EM-BOLĒ*

2 *par-em-ballō* 1   1 *par-em-bolē* 10

Lk 19	43	2 your enemies will raise (lit. *camp* with) fortifications all round you,
Ac 21	34	the tribune ordered Paul to be taken into the *fortress*.
	37	Just as Paul was being taken into the *fortress*, he asked the tribune if he could have a word with him.
22	24	the tribune had [Paul] brought into the *fortress*
23	10	the tribune . . . ordered his troops to go down and . . . bring [Paul] into the *fortress*.
	16	the son of Paul's sister . . . made his way into the *fortress*
	32	[the soldiers] returned to the *fortress*.
Heb 11	34 ○	[Gideon, Barak, Samson] were given strength to . . . drive back foreign ⌐invaders (lit. *armies*; or: *encampments*).
13	11	(Lv 16 27) The bodies of the animals . . . are burnt outside the *camp*,
	13	Let us go to [Jesus], then, outside the *camp*,
Rv 20	9	[the nations] will . . . besiege the *camp* of the saints, which is the city that God loves.

2: STRONGHOLD, FORTRESS: *OCHYRŌMA*

ochyrōma 1

2 Co 10	4	Our war is not fought with weapons of flesh, yet they are strong enough . . . to demolish *fortresses*.

3: FORTIFICATION, SIEGE-WORKS, RAMPART: *CHARAX*

charax 1

Lk 19	43	[Jerusalem,] your enemies will raise *fortifications* all round you,

2. WALL – BARRIER, DIVIDING WALL: *TEICHOS*

1 *teichos* 9	3 *meso-toichon* 1	
2 *toichos* 1		

Ac 9	25	the disciples . . . let [Saul] down from the top of the *wall*, lowering him in a basket.
23	3 ○	2 God will surely strike you, you whitewashed *wall*!
2 Co 11	33	I had to be let down over the *wall* in a hamper,
Ep 2	14 ●	3 [Christ has] broken down the *barrier* which used to keep them apart, actually destroying in his own person the hostility
Heb 11	30	It was through faith that the *walls* of Jericho fell down
Rv 21	12	The *walls* of [the messianic Jerusalem] were of a great height,
	14	The city *walls* stood on twelve foundation stones,
	15	The angel . . . was carrying a gold measuring rod to measure the city and its gates and *wall*.
	17	He measured its *wall*,
	18	The *wall* was built of diamond,
	19	The foundations of the city *wall* were faced with all kinds of precious stone:

3. TOWER: *PYRGOS*

pyrgos 4

Mt 21	33 <	a landowner . . . planted a vineyard; he fenced it round . . . and built a *tower*;

Mk 12	1	<	A man planted a vineyard . . . and built a *tower*;
Lk 13	4		those eighteen on whom the *tower* at Siloam fell and killed them
	14 28		which of you here, intending to build a *tower*, would not first . . . work out the cost . . .?

FREE – SET FREE

1. Free, Set free, Release – Ransom, Redeem: *luō*
  1: Free, Loose, Untie
    a) Untie, Undo, Unbind – Take off, Loose
    b) Release, Free, from chains
    c) Free, Loose(n), figuratively – Untie, Undo
  2: Release, Free, Let go – Dismiss – Pardon
    a) Send away, Send off, Dismiss
    b) Release, Let (a prisoner) go, Set free
    c) Free = Rid (of an infirmity)
    d) (Grant) Pardon, Forgive

3: Release, Set free = Redeem, Ransom, Liberate – Redemption, Freedom, Deliverance
2. Unfasten, Loosen – Freedom, Liberty: *an-(h)iēmi*
  1: Unfasten, Loosen
  2: Liberty, Freedom, Release
3. Free, Make free, Set free – Exempt – Freedom, Liberty: *eleutheria*
4. Freedmen: *libertinos*
5. Set free, Deliver (from): *ap-allassō*
6. Discharged – Separate (oneself from), Sever (with): *kat-argeō*
7. Unoccupied, Empty – Leave (oneself) free: *scholazō*

1. FREE, SET FREE, RELEASE – RANSOM, REDEEM: *LUŌ*

2	*luō*	30/42	6	*lytron*	2	
1	*apo-luō*	52/67	4	*lytroō*	3	
9	*lysis*	1	5	*lytrōsis*	3	(in 3: only)
			7	*lytrōtēs*	1	
			8	*anti-lytron*	1	
			3	*apo-lytrōsis*	10	

1: FREE, LOOSE, UNTIE

a) Untie, Undo, Unbind – Take off, Loose

Mt 21	2		you will . . . find a tethered donkey and a colt with her.
		2	*Untie* them
Mk 1	7	2	I am not fit to . . . *undo* the strap of his sandals.
	11 2	2	you will find a tethered colt . . . *Untie* it
	4	2	They . . . found a colt . . . they *untied* it,
	5	2	What are you doing, *untying* that colt?
Lk 3	16	2	I am not fit to *undo* the strap of his sandals;
	13 15	2	Is there one of you who does not *untie* his ox . . . on the sabbath . . .?
	19 30	2	you will find a tethered colt . . . *Untie* it
	31	2	If anyone asks you, 'Why are you *untying* it?' you are to say,
	33	2	As they were *untying* the colt, its owner said, 'Why are you
		2	*untying* that colt?'
Jn 1	27	2	I am not fit to *undo* his sandal-strap.
	11 44		The dead man [Lazarus] came out, his feet and hands bound
		2	with bands of stuff . . . Jesus said to them, '*Unbind* him,'
Ac 7	33	2	(Ex 3 5) *Take off* your shoes.
	13 25	2	I am not fit to *undo* his sandal.

b) Release, Free, from chains

Ac 22	30	2	[The tribune had put Paul in chains;] he *freed* Paul
Rv 9	14	2	*Release* the four angels that are chained up at the great river Euphrates.
	15	2	These four angels . . . were *released*
20	3	2	[Satan] must be *released*, but only for a short while.
	7	2	Satan will be *released* from his prison [8] and will come out to deceive all the nations

c) Free, Loose(n), figuratively – Untie, Undo

Mt 16	19	●2/2	whatever you *loose* on earth shall be considered *loosed* in heaven.
18	18	●2/2	whatever you *loose* on earth shall be considered *loosed* in heaven.
Mk 7	35	2	the ligament of his tongue was *loosened* and he spoke clearly.
Lk 13	16		this woman . . . whom Satan has held bound these eighteen
		2	years – was it not right to *untie* her bonds on the sabbath day?
Ac 2	24	2	God raised [Jesus] to life, *freeing* him from the pangs of Hades;
1 Co 7	27	9	If you are tied to a wife, do not look for *freedom*; if you
		2	are *free* of a wife, then do not look for one.

| 1 Jn 3 | 8 | X | 2 | It was to *undo* all that the devil has done that the Son of God appeared. |
| Rv 1 | 5 | ● | 2 | [Jesus] has [v] washed away (G *released* us from) our sins with his blood, |

2: RELEASE, FREE, LET GO – DISMISS – PARDON

a) Send away, Send off, Dismiss

Mt 14	15	X	*send* the people *away*, and they can go go the villages to buy themselves some food.
	22	X	he made the disciples . . . go on ahead . . . while he would *send* the crowds *away*.
	23	X	After *sending* the crowds *away* he went up into the hills
15	23	X	⌐Give [this Canaanite woman] what she wants (lit. *Send her away*) . . . because she is shouting after us.
	32	X	I do not want to *send* them *off* hungry,
	39	X	when he had *sent* the crowds *away* he got into the boat
Mk 6	36	X	*send* them *away*, and they can go to . . . buy themselves something to eat.
	45	X	he made his disciples get into the boat . . . while he himself *sent* the crowd *away*.
8	3	X	If I *send* them *off* home hungry they will collapse on the way;
	9	X	[They ate . . .] He *sent* them *away*
Lk 8	38	X	he *sent* [the man from whom the devils had gone out] *away*.
9	12	X	*Send* the people *away*, and they can go to the villages . . . round about to find . . . food;
	14 4	X	he took the man and cured him and *sent* him *away*.
Ac 13	3		they laid their hands on [Barnabas and Paul] and *sent* them *off*.
	15 30		⌐The party left and (lit. Having been *dismissed*, the party) went down to Antioch,
	33		the brothers wished [Judas and Silas] peace and ⌐they went (lit. *sent them off*) back to those who had sent them.
	19 41		When [the town clerk in Ephesus] had finished this speech he *dismissed* the assembly.
	23 22		The tribune ⌐*let* the young man *go* (or: *sent* the young man *away*)
	28 25		[the Roman Jews] disagreed among themselves and . . . ⌐went away (lit. were being *dismissed*),

b) Release, Let (a prisoner) go, Set free

Mt 18	27		the servant's master . . . *let* him *go* and cancelled the debt.
27	15		At festival time . . . it was the governor's practice to *release* a prisoner . . . [17] . . . Pilate said to them, 'Which do you want me to *release* for you: Barabbas, or Jesus . . .?'
	17		
	21		Which of the two do you want me to *release* for you?
	26		he *released* Barabbas for them.
Mk 15	6		At festival time Pilate used to *release* a prisoner for them,
	9		Do you want me to *release* for you the king of the Jews?
	11		The chief priests . . . had incited the crowd to demand that [Pilate] should *release* Barabbas
	15		So Pilate . . . *released* Barabbas for them
Lk 23	16		[Pilate said:] I shall have him flogged and then *let* him *go*.
	17		[17] (ᵛ For at the time of the festival he was obliged to *release* one prisoner to them.) [18] But as one man they
	18		howled . . . '⌐Give us Barabbas (lit. *Release* Barabbas to us)!'
	20		Pilate was anxious to *set* Jesus *free*
	22		I shall have him punished and then *let* him *go*.
	25		[Pilate] *released* the man they asked for, who had been imprisoned for rioting
Jn 18	39		according to a custom of yours I should *release* one prisoner . . . would you like me, then, to *release* the king of the Jews?
19	10		I have power to *release* you and I have power to crucify you
	12		Pilate was anxious to *set* him *free*, but the Jews shouted, 'If you *set* him *free* you are no friend of Caesar's';
Ac 3	13		Pilate had decided to *release* him.
4	21		The court . . . *released* [Peter and John];
	23		As soon as [Peter and John] were *released* they went to the community
5	40		[the Sanhedrin] gave orders for [the apostles] to be flogged . . . and *released* them.
16	35		*Release* those men [Paul and Silas].
	36		The magistrates have sent an order for your *release*;
17	9		[the city councillors] made Jason and the rest give security before *setting* them *free*.
26	32		The man [Paul] could have been *set free* if he had not appealed to Caesar.
28	18		[the Romans] would have *set* me *free*,
Heb 13	23		I want you to know that our brother Timothy has been *set free*.

c) Free = Rid (of an infirmity)

| Lk 13 | 12 | | Woman, you are *rid* of your infirmity |

d) (Grant) Pardon, Forgive

Lk	6 37	grant *pardon*, and you will be *pardoned*.

3: RELEASE, SET FREE = REDEEM, RANSOM, LIBERATE – REDEMPTION, FREEDOM, DELIVERANCE

Mt	20 28	6	the Son of Man came . . . to give his life as a *ransom* for many.
Mk	10 45	6	the Son of Man [came] . . . to give his life as a *ransom* for many.
Lk	1 68	5	the Lord . . . has visited his people, he has come to their *rescue*
	2 38	5	[Anna] spoke of the child to all who looked forward to the *deliverance* of Jerusalem.
	21 28	3	your *liberation* is near at hand.
	24 21	4	Our own hope had been that he would be the one to *set* Israel *free*.
Ac	7 35	7	[Moses] was now sent to be both leader and *redeemer*
Rm	3 24	3	both [Jew and pagan] are justified . . . by *being redeemed* in Christ Jesus
	8 23	3	we wait (§ for adoption as sons and) for our bodies to *be set free*.
1 Co	1 30	3	Christ Jesus . . . has become . . . our virtue, and our holiness, and out *freedom*.
Ep	1 7	3	in [Christ], through his blood, we gain our *freedom*,
	14	3	the pledge of our inheritance which brings *freedom* for those whom God has taken for his own,
	4 30	3	the Holy Spirit of God . . . has marked you with his seal for you to *be set free* when the day comes.
Col	1 14	3	in [Jesus], we gain our *freedom*, the forgiveness of our sins.
1 Tm	2 6	8	[Christ Jesus] sacrificed himself as a *ransom* for them all.
Tt	2 14	4	(cf. Ps 130 8) [Christ Jesus] sacrificed himself for us in order to *set* us *free* from all wickedness
Heb	9 12	5	[Christ] has entered the sanctuary . . . having won an eternal *redemption* for us.
	15	3	his death took place to ⌐cancel (lit. *redeem*) the sins that infringed the earlier covenant.
	11 35	3	others submitted to torture, refusing *release* so that they would rise again to a better life.
1 P	1 18	4	the *ransom that was paid to free* you from the useless way of life . . . was not paid in anything corruptible,

2. UNFASTEN, LOOSEN – FREEDOM, LIBERTY: *AN-(H)IĒMI*

3 an-(h)esis 1/5   2 aph-esis 2/17
1 an-(h)iēmi 2/4

1: UNFASTEN, LOOSEN

Ac	16 26	the chains ⌐fell (lit. were *unfastened*) from all the prisoners.
	27 40	at the same time [the crew] *loosened* the lashings of the rudders;

2: LIBERTY, FREEDOM, RELEASE

Lk	4 18 ●	2 2	(Is 61 2) The spirit of the Lord . . . has sent me . . . to proclaim *liberty* to captives . . . (Is 58 6) to set the downtrodden ⌐*free* (lit. at *liberty*),
Ac	24 23	3	[Felix] gave orders to the centurion that Paul should be kept under arrest but *free* from restriction,

3. FREE, MAKE FREE, SET FREE – EXEMPT – FREEDOM, LIBERTY: *ELEUTHERIA*

2 eleutheria 11   1   eleutheros 23
3 eleutheroō 7   4   ap-eleutheros 1

S = Free man // Slave, Servant

Mt	17 26		Well then, the sons are *exempt* [from toll or tribute].
Jn	8 32		[Jesus said to the Jews who believed in him:] the truth will
	33	3	*make* you *free*. 33 They answered . . . 'what do you mean,
	36 S	3/	"You will be made *free*"'? 34 Jesus replied: . . . 36 So if the Son *makes* you *free*, you will be *free* indeed.
Rm	6 18 S	3	You may have been *freed* from the slavery of sin, but only to become 'slaves' of righteousness . . . 20 When you were
	20	S	slaves of sin, you ⌐felt no obligation to (lit. were *free* with regard to) righteousness . . . 22 Now, however, you
	22	S	3	have been *set free* from sin, you have been made slaves of God, and you get a reward leading to your sanctification
	7 3		after her husband is dead ⌐[the wife's] legal obligations come to an end (lit. she is *exempt* from that law), and she can marry someone else without becoming an adulteress.

Rm	8 2	3	the law of the spirit . . . has *set* you *free* from the law of sin and death.
	21 S	3	[creation still retains the hope] of being *freed*, like us, from
	S	2	its slavery to decadence, to enjoy the same *freedom* and glory as the children of God.
1 Co	7 21 S		if you should have the chance of being *free* [from slavery], accept it. 22 A slave, when he is called in the Lord, be-
	22	S	4/	comes the Lord's *freedman*, and a *freeman* called in the Lord becomes Christ's slave.
	39		if the husband dies, [the wife] is *free* to marry anybody she likes,
	9 1		I, personally, am *free*:
	19 S		though I am ⌐not a slave of (lit. as *free* as) any man I have made myself the slave of everyone
	10 29	2	Why should my *freedom* depend on somebody else's con- science?
	12 13		In the one Spirit we were all baptised . . . slaves as well
	S		as ⌐citizens (lit. *free* [men]),
2 Co	3 17	2	where the Spirit of the Lord is, there is *freedom*.
Ga	2 4 S	2	some . . . have furtively crept in to spy on the *liberty* we enjoy in Christ Jesus,
	3 28		there are no more distinctions between Jew and Greek,
	S		slave and *free* [man],
	4 22		Abraham had two sons, one by the slave-girl, and one by
	S		his *free-born* wife.
	23 S		the child of the *free* woman was born as the result of a promise.
	26 S		The Jerusalem above, however, is *free* and is our mother,
	30		(Gn 21 10) this slave-girl's son is not to share the inherit-
	S		ance with the son of the *free* woman. 31 So . . . we are
	31 S		the children, not of the slave-girl, but of the *free-born*
	S		wife.
	5 1 S	3/2	When Christ *freed* us, he meant us to *remain free*.
	13	2	My brothers, you were called . . . to *liberty*; but be careful,
		2	or this *liberty* will provide an opening for self-indulgence.
Ep	6 8 S		everyone, whether a slave or [a] *free* [man], will be properly rewarded by the Lord for whatever work he has done well.
Col	3 11		in that image there is no room for distinction between . . . slave and *free* [man].
Jm	1 25	2	the man who looks steadily at the perfect law of *freedom* and makes that his habit . . . will be happy in all that he does.
	2 12	2	Talk and behave like people who are going to be judged by the law of *freedom*,
1 P	2 16 S		You are slaves of . . . God, so behave like *free* [men], and
		2	never use your *freedom* as an excuse for wickedness.
2 P	2 19	2	[False teachers] may promise *freedom* but they themselves are slaves, slaves to corruption;
Rv	6 15 S		Then all . . . slaves and ⌐citizens (lit. *free* [men]), took to the mountains to hide in caves
	13 16		[The second beast] compelled everyone . . . slave and
	S		⌐citizen (lit. *free* [man]) to be branded on the right hand
	19 18		There will be the flesh of kings for you, and the flesh . . .
	S		of all kinds of men, ⌐citizens (lit. *free* [men]) and slaves,

4. FREEDMEN: *LIBERTINOS*

libertinos 1

Ac	6 9	some . . . members of the synagogue called the Synagogue of *Freedmen*,

5. SET FREE, DELIVER (FROM): *AP-ALLASSŌ*

ap-allassō 2/3

Lk	12 58	when you go to court with your opponent, try to ⌐settle with (lit. *set* yourself *free* from) him on the way,
Heb	2 15 ●	[Christ] *set free* all those who had been held in slavery . . by the fear of death.

6. DISCHARGED – SEPARATE (ONESELF FROM), SEVER (WITH): *KAT-ARGEŌ*

kat-argeō (apo) 4/27

Rm	7 2	all these obligations [of a wife] *come to an end* if the hus- band dies.
	6	now we *are rid* of the Law, *freed* by death from our im- prisonment,
1 Co	13 11	now I am a man, all childish ways *are put behind* me.
Ga	5 4	if you do look to the Law to make you justified, then you have *separated* yourselves from Christ,

7. UNOCCUPIED, EMPTY – LEAVE (ONESELF) FREE: *SCHOLAZŌ*

scholazō 2

Mt 12 44		on arrival, finding [the home] *unoccupied*, swept and tidied, [45] it . . . collects seven other spirits
1 Co 7 5		Do not refuse each other except by mutual consent, and then only . . . to ⌐*leave*¬ yourselves *free* for (or: devote yourselves to) prayer;

FRUIT

1. Fruit – Bear, Produce, Harvest – Come (out) of, Grow: *genēma*	Crop, Harvest, Grain – Fruitful, Unfruitful, Barren: *karpos*
a) (literally:) Fruit – Bear – Grow, Come from	2: Fruit(s): *opōra*
b) (figuratively:) Harvest, Produce, Give rise to – Come of	**3. Grapes – Bunches, Clusters**
2. Fruit, Grain, Crop – Results – Unfruitful, Barren	1: Grapes – Bunches, Clusters: *botrys*
1: Fruit(s), Produce, Results –	2: Grapes – Clusters: *staphylē*
	4. Winter Figs: *olynthos*
	5. Husks, Pods: *keration*

1. FRUIT – BEAR, PRODUCE, HARVEST – COME (OUT) OF, GROW: *GENĒMA*

1 *genēma* 5   2 *ginomai* (2)

a) (literally:) Fruit – Bear – Grow, Come from

Mt 21 19	2	May you never *bear* fruit again
26 29		I shall not drink ⌐wine (lit. *fruit* of the vine) until the day I drink the new wine with you in the kingdom of my Father.
Mk 14 25		I shall not drink any more ⌐wine (lit. *fruit* of the vine) until the day I drink . . . in the kingdom of God.
Lk 12 18		I will . . . store all my ⌐grain (ᵛ *fruits*) and my goods in [the new barns],
22 18		I shall not drink ⌐wine (lit. *fruit* of the vine) until the kingdom of God comes.

b) (figuratively:) Harvest, Produce, Give rise to – Come of

2 Co 9 10		The one who provides seed . . . will . . . make the *harvest* of your good deeds a larger one,
1 Tm 6 4	2	All that can *come of* this is jealousy, contention, abuse

2. FRUIT, GRAIN, CROP – RESULTS – UNFRUITFUL, BARREN

1: FRUIT(S), PRODUCE, RESULTS – CROP, HARVEST, GRAIN – FRUITFUL, UNFRUITFUL, BARREN: *KARPOS*

1 *karpos*	66	4 *karpo(-phoros)*	1
2 *karpo(-phoreō)*	8	3 *a-karpos*	7

Mt 3 8		if you are repentant, produce the appropriate *fruit*,
10		any tree which fails to produce good *fruit* will be cut down and thrown on the fire.
7 16		You will be able to tell [the false prophets] by their *fruits*
17		. . . [17] In the same way, a sound tree produces good
18		*fruit* but a rotten tree bad *fruit*. [18] A sound tree cannot
19		bear bad *fruit*, nor a rotten tree bear good *fruit*. [19] Any tree that does not produce good *fruit* is cut down and
20		thrown on the fire. [20] I repeat, you will be able to tell them by their *fruits*.
12 33		Make a tree sound and its *fruit* will be sound; make a tree rotten and its *fruit* will be rotten. For the tree can be told by its *fruit*.
13 8		Others [seeds] fell on rich soil and produced their *crop*, some a hundredfold, some sixty, some thirty.
22		the worries . . . and the lure of riches choke the word and
	3	so he ⌐*produces* nothing (lit. remains *unfruitful*).
23		the man who hears the word and understands it . . . is the
	2	one who yields a *harvest* and produces now a hundredfold, now sixty, now thirty.
26		When the new wheat sprouted and ⌐*ripened* (lit. bore *fruit*), the darnel appeared as well.
21 19		May you never bear *fruit* again

Mt 21 34		When ⌐vintage time (lit. the time of the *fruit*) drew near he sent his servants to the tenants to collect his *produce*.
41		He will . . . lease the vineyard to other tenants who will deliver the *produce* to him when the season arrives.
43		the kingdom of God will be . . . given to a people who will produce its *fruit*.
Mk 4 7		the thorns . . . choked [the seed], and it produced no *crop*;
8		some seeds . . . produced *crop*; and yielded thirty, sixty, even a hundredfold.
19		the worries of this world . . . come in to choke the word.
	3	and so it ⌐*produces* nothing (lit. remains *unfruitful*).
20	2	they hear the word and accept it and yield a *harvest*, thirty and sixty and a hundredfold.
28	2	the land produces *crop*, first the shoot, then the ear,
29		And when the *crop* is ready, he loses no time: he starts to reap
11 14		[Jesus] addressed the fig tree. 'May no one ever eat *fruit* from you again'
12 2		he sent a servant . . . to collect . . . his share of the *produce* from the vineyard.
Lk 1 42		Of all women you are the most blessed, and blessed is the *fruit* of your womb.
3 8		if you are repentant, produce the appropriate *fruits*,
9		any tree which fails to produce good *fruit* will be cut down
6 43		There is no sound tree that produces rotten *fruit*, nor again
44		a rotten tree that produces sound *fruit*. [44] For every tree can be told by its own *fruit*:
8 8		some seed . . . produced its *crop* a hundredfold.
15		people . . . who have heard the word and take it to themselves and yield a *harvest* through their perseverance.
12 17		What am I to do? I have not enough room to store my *crops*.
13 6		A man had a fig tree . . . and he came looking for *fruit* on it but found none.
7		for three years now I have been coming to look for *fruit* on this fig tree and finding none.
9		it may bear *fruit* next year;
20 10		he sent a servant . . . to get his share of the *produce* of the vineyard
Jn 4 36		the reaper . . . is bringing in the *grain* for eternal life,
12 24		if [a wheat grain] dies, it yields a rich *harvest*.
15 2		Every branch in me that bears no *fruit* [my Father] cuts away, and every branch that does bear *fruit* he prunes to make it bear even more *fruit*.
4		a branch cannot bear *fruit* all by itself,
5		Whoever remains in me, with me in him, bears *fruit* in plenty;
8		It is to the glory of my Father that you should bear much *fruit*,
16		I commissioned you to go out and to bear *fruit*, *fruit* that will last;
Ac 2 30		God had sworn [David] an oath to make one of ⌐his descendants (lit. the *fruits* of his loins) succeed him on the throne,
14 17	4	[God] makes your *crops* grow when they should,
Rm 1 13		in the hope that I might work as *fruitfully* among you as I have done among the other pagans,
6 21		⌐what (lit. what *fruit*) did you get from this? Nothing but experiences that now make you blush,
22		set free from sin . . . you get a ⌐*reward* (lit. *fruit*) leading to your sanctification
7 4		[Christ] rose from the dead to make us ⌐*productive* (lit.
	2	productive of *fruit*) for God.
5	2	our sinful passions . . . fertilised our bodies to make them ⌐*give birth* to (lit. give birth to *fruit* for) death.
15 28		when I have . . . officially handed over ⌐what has been raised (lit. the *fruits*), I shall set out for Spain
1 Co 9 7		nobody ever planted a vineyard and refused to eat the *fruit* of it.
14 14		if I use this gift [of tongues] in my prayers, my spirit may
	3	be praying but my mind is left *barren*.
Ga 5 22		⌐What the Spirit brings (lit. The *harvest* of the Spirit) is . . . love, joy, peace,
Ep 5 9		the *effects* of the light are seen in complete goodness and right living and truth.
11	3	having nothing to do with the *futile* works of darkness
Ph 1 11		you will reach the perfect goodness which is the *fruit* Jesus Christ produces in us
22		if living in this body means doing work which is having good *results* – I do not know what I should choose.
4 17		what is valuable to me is the ⌐*interest* (lit. *fruit*) that is mounting up in your account.
Col 1 6		[The Good News] is spreading . . . and producing the same
	2	*results* as it has among you
10	2	you will be able to lead . . . a life acceptable to [the Lord] . . . showing the *results* in all the good actions you do
2 Tm 2 6		it is the working farmer who has the first claim on any *crop* that is harvested.
Tt 3 14		people are to . . . occupy themselves in doing good works
	3	. . . and not to be entirely *unproductive*.
Heb 12 11		later, in those on whom [the punishment] has been used, it bears *fruit* in peace and goodness.

Heb 13 15	a verbal sacrifice that is offered every time ⸢we acknowledge (lit. as the *fruit* of our lips giving thanks to) his name.
Jm 3 17	the wisdom that comes down from above . . . shows itself by ⸢doing good (lit. good *results*);
18	Peacemakers, when they work for peace, sow the seeds which will bear *fruit* in holiness.
5 7	how patiently [a farmer] waits for the precious *fruit* of the ground
18	the sky gave rain and the earth gave *crops*.
2 P 1 8	If you have a generous supply of these, they will not leave you ineffectual or *unproductive*:
Jude 12 3	[The false teachers are] like *barren* trees which are then uprooted in the winter and so are twice dead;
Rv 22 2	the trees of life, which bear twelve crops of *fruit* in a year, one crop of *fruit* in each month,

2: FRUIT(S): *OPŌRA*

opōra 1

Rv 18 14	All the *fruits* you had set your hearts on have failed you;

3. GRAPES – BUNCHES, CLUSTERS

1: GRAPES – BUNCHES, CLUSTERS: *BOTRYS*

botrys 1

Rv 14 18	cut all the *bunches* off the vine of the earth;

2: GRAPES – CLUSTERS: *STAPHYLĒ*

staphylē 3

Mt 7 16	Can people pick *grapes* from thorns . . .?
Lk 6 44	people do not . . . gather *grapes* from brambles.
Rv 14 18	cut all the bunches off the vine of the earth; all its *grapes* are ripe.

4. WINTER FIGS: *OLYNTHOS*

olynthos 1

Rv 6 13	the stars of the sky fell . . . like *figs* dropping from a *fig* tree when a high wind shakes it;

5. HUSKS, PODS: *KERATION*

keration 1

Lk 15 16	he would willingly have filled his belly with the *husks* the pigs were eating but no one offered him anything.

G

GAIN – PROFIT

1. **Win (over), Gain – Make money, Make more, Greed(y) for money – Assets, Advantages:** *kerdos*
2. **Way to make a profit, Means of gain – Yield dividends, Bring profits:** *porismos*
3. **Make the most of, Make good use of, Use to the full:** *ex-agorazō*
4. **Interest:** *tokos*
5. **Make a profit, Gain by trading – Do business, Trade:** *pragmateuomai*
6. **Gain (favour), Curry (favour):** *kata-tithemai*
7. **Benefit by, Have the benefit of:** *anti-lambanomai*
8. **Derive benefit (from):** *oninamai*

1. WIN (OVER), GAIN – MAKE MONEY, MAKE MORE, GREED(Y) FOR MONEY – ASSETS, ADVANTAGES: *KERDOS*

| 1 *kerdainō* 17 | 3 (aischro-)*kerdēs* 2 |
| 2 *kerdos* 3 | 4 (aischro-)*kerdōs* 1 |

P = to win a person

Mt 16 26		What, then, will a man gain if he *wins* the whole world and ruins his life?
18 15	P	If your brother does something wrong, go and have it out with him . . . If he listens to you, you have *won* back your brother.
25 16	<	The man who had received the five talents . . . *made* five more.
17	<	The man who had received two *made* two more
20	<	you entrusted me with five talents; here are five more that I have *made*.
22	<	you entrusted me with two talents; here are two more that I have *made*.
Mk 8 36		What gain, then, is it for a man to *win* the whole world and ruin his life?
Lk 9 25		What gain, then, is it for a man to have *won* the whole world and to have . . . ruined his very self?
Ac 27 21		you would have ⌐*spared* (lit. not *gained*) yourselves all this damage and loss.
1 Co 9 19	P	I have made myself the slave of everyone so as to *win* as many as I could. [20] I made myself a Jew to the Jews, to
20	P	*win* the Jews; that is, I . . . made myself a subject of the
	P	Law . . . to *win* those who are subject to the Law.
21	P	[21] . . . I was free of the Law myself . . . to *win* those who
22	P	have no Law. [22] ⌐For (lit. To *win*) the weak I made myself weak.
Ph 1 12	2	Life to me . . . is Christ, but then death would *bring* me *something more*;
3 7	2	because of Christ, I have come to consider all these *advantages* that I had as disadvantages. [8] . . . I have accepted the
8		loss of everything . . . if only I can ⌐*have* (lit. *gain*) Christ
1 Tm 3 8		deacons must be . . . moderate in the amount of wine they
3		drink and with no squalid *greed for money*.
Tt 1 7		[the elder] must be irreproachable: never . . . violent, nor
3		out to *make money*;
11		men of this kind ruin whole families, by teaching . . . with
2		the vile motive of *making money*.
Jm 4 13		we are going to spend a year there, trading, and *make* some *money*.
1 P 3 1	P	husbands who have not yet obeyed the word . . . may find themselves *won* over . . . by the way their wives behave,
5 2		4 Be the shepherds of the flock of God . . . not *for* sordid *money*,

2. WAY TO MAKE A PROFIT, MEANS OF GAIN – YIELD DIVIDENDS, BRING PROFITS: *PORISMOS*

porismos 2

| 1 Tm 6 5 | | people who . . . imagine that religion is a *way of making a profit*. |
| 6 | | Religion . . . does *bring* large *profits*, but only to those who are content with what they have. |

3. MAKE THE MOST OF, MAKE GOOD USE OF, USE TO THE FULL: *EX-AGORAZŌ*

ex-agorazō 2/4

| Ep 5 16 | | your lives should ⌐*make the most of* (or: redeem) [this wicked age] |
| Col 4 5 | | be sure you *make the best use of* your time |

4. INTEREST: *TOKOS*

tokos 2

| Mt 25 27 | < | on my return I would have recovered my capital with *interest* |
| Lk 19 23 | < | On my return I could have drawn [my money] out with *interest*. |

5. MAKE A PROFIT, GAIN BY TRADING – DO BUSINESS, TRADE: *PRAGMATEUOMAI*

| 1 *pragmateuomai* 1 | 2 *dia-pragmateuomai* 1 |

| Lk 19 13 | < | *Do business* with these [ten pounds] . . . until I get back. |
| 15 | < | 2 he sent for those servants . . to find out what *profit* each had *made*. |

6. GAIN (FAVOUR), CURRY (FAVOUR): *KATA-TITHEMAI*

kata-tithemai 2/3

| Ac 24 27 | | being anxious to *gain* favour with the Jews, Felix left Paul in custody. |
| 25 9 | | Festus was anxious to *gain* favour with the Jews, so he said to Paul, |

7. BENEFIT BY, HAVE THE BENEFIT OF: *ANTI-LAMBANOMAI*

anti-lambanomai 1/3

| 1 Tm 6 2 | | those who *have the benefit of* their services are believers |

8. DERIVE BENEFIT (FROM): *ONINAMAI*

oninamai 1

| Phm 20 | | ⌐I am counting on you (lit. let me *derive* some *benefit* from you), in the Lord; |

GALILEE

1. **Galilee – Cana**
2. **Nazareth, Nazarene**
3. **Capernaum and the other towns round the lake**
4. **Nain**

1. GALILEE – CANA

Galilee	62	C *Cana* 4 (Jn)
Galilean	} 11	
from/of Galilee		

Mt 2 22	[Joseph] left for the region of *Galilee*.
3 13	Jesus . . . came from *Galilee* to the Jordan to be baptised by John.
4 12	Hearing that John had been arrested [Jesus] went back to *Galilee*,
15	(Is 8 23) Land of Zebulun . . . *Galilee* of the nations!
18	As [Jesus] was walking by the Sea of *Galilee* he saw . . . Simon . . . and his brother Andrew;

Mt 4 23 [Jesus] went round the whole of *Galilee* . . . proclaiming the Good News . . . and curing . . . 25 Large crowds followed him, coming from *Galilee*, the Decapolis,

15 29 Jesus . . . reached the shores of the Sea of *Galilee*,

17 22 One day when they were together in *Galilee*, Jesus said to them, 'The Son of Man is going to be handed over . . .'

19 1 Jesus . . . left *Galilee* and came into the part of Judaea which is on the far side of the Jordan.

21 11 This is the prophet Jesus from Nazareth in *Galilee*.

26 32 after my resurrection I shall go before you to *Galilee*.

69 You too were with Jesus the *Galilean*.

27 55 many women . . . had followed Jesus from *Galilee* and looked after him.

28 7 he is going before you to *Galilee*; it is there you will see him.

10 my brothers . . . must leave for *Galilee*; they will see me there.

16 the eleven disciples set out for *Galilee*, to the mountain

Mk 1 9 Jesus came from Nazareth in *Galilee* and was baptised

14 After John had been arrested, Jesus went into *Galilee*.

16 As [Jesus] was walking along by the Sea of *Galilee* he saw Simon and his brother Andrew

28 his reputation rapidly spread . . . through all the surrounding *Galilean* countryside.

39 [Jesus] went all through *Galilee*, preaching . . . and casting out devils.

3 7 great crowds from *Galilee* followed him.

6 21 [Herod] gave a banquet for . . . the leading figures in *Galilee*.

7 31 [Jesus] went by way of Sidon towards the Sea of *Galilee*, right through the Decapolis region.

9 30 they made their way through *Galilee*; and [Jesus] did not want anyone to know,

14 28 after my resurrection I shall go before you to *Galilee*.

70 You are one of them for sure! Why, you are a *Galilean*.

15 41 These [women] used to follow [Jesus] and look after him when he was in *Galilee*.

16 7 go and tell . . . Peter, "He is going before you to *Galilee*; it is there you will see him",

Lk 1 26 the angel Gabriel was sent . . . to a town in *Galilee* called Nazareth,

2 4 Joseph set out from the town of Nazareth in *Galilee* and travelled up to Judaea,

39 [Jesus and his parents] went back to *Galilee*, to their own town of Nazareth.

3 1 when Pontius Pilate was governor of Judaea, Herod tetrarch of *Galilee*,

4 14 Jesus . . . returned to *Galilee*; and his reputation spread throughout the countryside.

31 [Jesus] went down to Capernaum, a town in *Galilee*,

44 he continued his preaching in the synagogues of ⌜Judaea (ᵛ *Galilee*).

5 17 among the audience there were . . . doctors of the Law who had come from every village in *Galilee*, from Judaea

8 26 They came to land in the country of the Gerasenes, which is opposite *Galilee*.

13 1 some people . . . told [Jesus] about the *Galileans* whose blood Pilate had mingled with that of their sacrifices.

2 ² . . . he said to them, 'Do you suppose these *Galileans* . . . were greater sinners than any other *Galileans*?'

17 11 on the way to Jerusalem [Jesus] travelled along the border between Samaria and *Galilee*.

22 59 This fellow [Peter] was certainly with him. Why, he is a *Galilean*.

23 5 He is inflaming the people with his teaching . . . all the way from *Galilee*, where he started, down to here. ⁶ Pilate . . . asked if the man were a *Galilean*;

49 the women who had accompanied him from *Galilee*,

55 the women who had come from *Galilee* with Jesus were following [Joseph]

24 6 Remember what he told you when he was still in *Galilee*:

Jn 1 43 The next day, after Jesus had decided to leave for *Galilee*, he met Philip

2 1 C Three days later there was a wedding at *Cana* in *Galilee*.

11 C This was the first of the signs given by Jesus: it was given at *Cana* in *Galilee*.

4 3 [Jesus] left Judaea and went back to *Galilee*.

43 Jesus left [Samaria] for *Galilee*.

45 on his arrival in *Galilee* the *Galileans* received him well . . .

46 C ⁴⁶ He went again to *Cana* in *Galilee* . . . there was a court official there . . . ⁴⁷ and, hearing that Jesus had arrived

47 in *Galilee* from Judaea, he . . . asked him to . . . cure his son . . . ⁵⁴ This was the second sign given by Jesus, on

54 his return from Judaea to *Galilee*.

6 1 Jesus went off to the other side of the Sea of *Galilee* – or of Tiberias –

7 1 Jesus stayed in *Galilee*; he could not stay in Judaea,

9 Having said that, [Jesus] stayed behind in *Galilee*.

41 Would the Christ be from *Galilee*?

52 Are you a *Galilean* too? Go into the matter, and see for ourself: prophets do not come out of *Galilee*.

12 21 These [Greeks] approached Philip, who came from Bethsaida in *Galilee*,

21 2 C Nathanael from *Cana* in *Galilee*,

Ac 1 11 Why are you men *from Galilee* . . . looking into the sky?

2 7 Surely . . . all these men speaking are *Galileans*?

5 37 Judas the *Galilean* . . . who attracted crowds of supporters;

9 31 The churches throughout Judaea, *Galilee* and Samaria were now left in peace,

10 37 You must have heard about the recent happenings in Judaea; about Jesus of Nazareth and how he began in *Galilee*,

13 31 he appeared to those who had accompanied him from *Galilee* to Jerusalem:

2. NAZARETH, NAZARENE

Nazareth 11 Nazarene [Nazorean] (=Nazōraios) 13 1 polis 6/164
Nazara 1 from/of Nazareth (=Nazarēnos) 6

Mt 2 23 1 [Joseph] settled in a *town* called *Nazareth*. In this way the words spoken through the prophets were to be fulfilled: He will be called a *Nazarene*.

4 13 leaving *Nazareth* [Jesus] went and settled in Capernaum,

21 11 This is the prophet Jesus from *Nazareth* in Galilee.

26 71 This man [Peter] was with Jesus the *Nazarene*.

Mk 1 9 It was at this time that Jesus came from *Nazareth* in Galilee

24 What do you want with us, Jesus *of Nazareth*?

10 47 When [the blind man] heard that it was Jesus *of Nazareth*, he began to shout

14 67 You too were with Jesus, the man *from Nazareth*.

16 6 You are looking for Jesus *of Nazareth*, who was crucified: he has risen,

Lk 1 26 1 the angel Gabriel was sent . . . to a *town* in Galilee called *Nazareth*, ²⁷ to a virgin betrothed to . . . Joseph,

2 4 1 Joseph set out from the *town* of *Nazareth* in Galilee and travelled up to Judaea,

39 1 [Jesus and his parents] went back to Galilee, to their own *town* of *Nazareth*.

51 [Jesus] came to *Nazareth* and lived under [his parents'] authority.

4 16 [Jesus] came to *Nazara*, where he had been brought up,

29 1 They . . . hustled [Jesus] out of the *town*; and they took him 1 up to the brow of the hill their *town* was built on,

34 What do you want with us, Jesus *of Nazareth*?

18 37 they told [the blind man in Jericho] that Jesus the *Nazarene* was passing by.

24 19 All about Jesus *of Nazareth* . . . who proved he was a great prophet

Jn 1 45 [the Messiah] is Jesus son of Joseph, from *Nazareth*.

46 From *Nazareth*? . . . Can anything good come from that place?

18 5 [Who are you looking for?] They answered, 'Jesus the *Nazarene*'.

7 'Who are you looking for?' They said, 'Jesus the *Nazarene*'.

19 19 a notice . . . fixed to the cross . . . ran: 'Jesus the *Nazarene*, King of the Jews'.

Ac 2 22 Jesus the *Nazarene* was a man commended to you by God

3 6 Peter said, '. . . in the name of Jesus Christ the *Nazarene*, walk!'

4 10 by the name of Jesus Christ the *Nazarene* . . . this man is able to stand up perfectly healthy,

6 14 We have heard [Stephen] say that Jesus the *Nazarene* is going to destroy this Place

10 38 [Peter said, You know . .] Jesus *of Nazareth*. God had anointed him with the Holy Spirit

22 8 I am Jesus the *Nazarene*, and you are persecuting me.

24 5 [Paul] is a ringleader of the *Nazarene* sect.

26 9 I once thought it was my duty to use every means to oppose the name of Jesus the *Nazarene*.

3. CAPERNAUM and THE OTHER TOWNS ROUND THE LAKE

B *Bethsaida* 7   M {*Magadan* 1 / *Magdala* 1}   1 polis 6/164
Capernaum 16
C *Chorazin* 2   T *Tiberias* 3
Dalmanutha 1
G *Gennesaret* 3

Mt 4 13 leaving Nazareth [Jesus] went and settled in *Capernaum*.

8 5 When [Jesus] went into *Capernaum* a centurion came up

9 1 1 [Jesus] got back in the boat . . . and came to his own *town*.

11 20 1 [Jesus] began to reproach the *towns* in which . . . his miracles had been worked, because they refused to repent. ²¹ Alas

21 for you, *Chorazin*! Alas for you, *Bethsaida*! . . . ²³ And as

23 C B for you, *Capernaum*, did you want to be exalted as high as heaven?

14 34 G they came to land at *Gennesaret*.

Mt 15 39	M	[Jesus] went to the district of ⌐Magadan (ˇ Magdala).
17 24		When they reached Capernaum, the collectors of the half-shekel came to Peter
Mk 1 21		They went as far as Capernaum, and . . . [Jesus] went to the synagogue and began to teach.
33	1	The whole town came crowding round the door,
2 1		When [Jesus] returned to Capernaum . . . word went round that he was back;
6 45	B	he made his disciples . . . go on ahead to Bethsaida,
53	G	they came to land at Gennesaret
8 10		[Jesus] went to the region of Dalmanutha.
22	B	They came to Bethsaida, and some people brought to him a blind man
9 33		They came to Capernaum, and when [Jesus] was in the house, he asked them,
Lk 4 23		We have heard all that happened in Capernaum, do the same here
31	1	[Jesus] went down to Capernaum, a town in Galilee, and taught them on the sabbath.
5 1	G	[Jesus] was standing one day by the Lake of Gennesaret,
7 1		[Jesus] went into Capernaum. ² A centurion there had a servant . . . who was . . . near death.
9 10	B 1	[Jesus] withdrew to a town called Bethsaida
10 13	C B	Alas for you, Chorazin! Alas for you, Bethsaida! . . . ¹⁵ And
15		as for you, Capernaum, did you want to be exalted high as heaven?
Jn 1 44	B 1	Philip came from the same town, Bethsaida, as Andrew and Peter.
2 12		After [the wedding at Cana] he went down to Capernaum with his mother and the brothers,
4 46		there was a court official there whose son was ill at Capernaum
6 1	T	Jesus went off to the other side of the Sea of Galilee – or of Tiberias –
17		[the disciples] got into a boat to make for Capernaum on the other side of the lake.
23	T	Other boats, however, had put in from Tiberias,
24		the people . . . crossed to Capernaum to look for Jesus.
59		He taught this doctrine [about the bread of life] at Capernaum, in the synagogue.
12 21	B	Philip, who came from Bethsaida in Galilee,
21 1	T	Jesus showed himself again to the disciples. It was by the Sea of Tiberias,

4. NAIN

Nain 1   1 polis 3/164

Lk 7 11	1	[Jesus] went to a town called Nain . . . ¹² When he was near
12	1	the gate of the town it happened that a dead man was being carried out for burial, the only son of his mother
	1	. . . And a considerable number of the townspeople were with her.

GARDEN

1. **Garden – Paradise**
   1: Garden, Gardener: *kēpos*
   2: Paradise (Garden): *paradeisos*
2. **Garden plants – Herbs**
   1: Vegetables – Herbs – Garden plants: *lachanon*

3. **Flower – Lily**
   1: Flower: *anthos*
   2: Flower – Lily: *krinon*

2: Mint – Dill – Cummin – Rue
3: Mustard: *sinapi*
4: Hyssop – Marjoram: *hyssōpos*

1. GARDEN – PARADISE

1: GARDEN, GARDENER: *KĒPOS*

1 kēpos 5   2 kēp-ouros 1

Lk 13 19		a mustard seed which a man took and threw into his garden.
Jn 18 1		[Jesus] crossed the Kedron valley. There was a garden there.
26		Didn't I see you in the garden with him?
19 41		At the place where [Jesus] had been crucified there was a garden, and in this garden a new tomb.
20 15	2	Supposing [Jesus] to be the gardener, [Mary] said, 'Sir, . . .'

2: PARADISE (GARDEN): *PARADEISOS*

paradeisos 3

Lk 23 43		today you will be with me in paradise.
2 Co 12 4		[this man in Christ] was caught up into paradise.
Rv 2 7		the tree of life set in God's paradise.

2. GARDEN PLANTS – HERBS

1: VEGETABLES – HERBS – GARDEN PLANTS: *LACHANON*

lachanon 4

Mt 13 32	<	when [the mustard seed] has grown it is the biggest ⌐shrub (or: garden plant) of all,
Mk 4 32	<	[the mustard seed] grows into the biggest ⌐shrub (or: garden plant) of them all,
Lk 11 42		alas for you Pharisees! You who pay your tithe of mint and rue and all sorts of garden herbs
Rm 14 2		[people] dare not eat anything except vegetables

2: MINT – DILL – CUMMIN – RUE

1 anēthon 2	2 hēdy-osmon 2	
3 kyminon 1	4 pēganon 1	

Mt 23 23	2 / 3/	Alas for you, scribes . . . who pay your tithe of mint and dill and cummin and have neglected the weightier matters of the Law,
Lk 11 42	2 / 4/	But alas for you Pharisees! You who pay your tithe of mint and ⌐rue (ˇ dill) and all sorts of garden herbs and overlook justice

3: MUSTARD: *SINAPI*

sinapi 5

Mt 13 31		The kingdom of heaven is like a mustard seed
17 20		if your faith were the size of a mustard seed
Mk 4 31		[the kingdom of God] is like a mustard seed . . . the smallest of all the seeds
Lk 13 19		[the kingdom of God] is like a mustard seed
17 6		Were your faith the size of a mustard seed

4: HYSSOP – MARJORAM: *HYSSŌPOS*

hyssōpos 2

Jn 19 29		putting a sponge soaked in the vinegar on a hyssop stick
Heb 9 19		Moses . . . took blood and some water, and with these he sprinkled the book . ., using scarlet wool and hyssop.

3. FLOWER – LILY

1: FLOWER: *ANTHOS*

anthos 4

Jm 1 10		(Is 40 6) riches last no longer than the flowers in the grass.
11		the scorching sun comes up, and . . . the flower falls.
1 P 1 24		(Is 40 6–7) All flesh is grass and its glory like the wild flower's. The grass withers, the flower falls.

2: FLOWER – LILY: *KRINON*

krinon 2

Mt 6 28		Think of the flowers growing in the field.
Lk 12 27		Think of the flowers; they never have to spin or weave.

GATHERING

1. **Church – Assembly:** *ek-klēsia*
   1: Church – Community – Congregation
   2: Assembly (generally)
2. **Assemble, Meet together, Gather – Meeting:** *syn-erchomai*
3. **Meet – Come towards:** *ap-antaō*
4. **Join, Rejoin – Meet:** *sym-ballō*
5. **Assemble – Call together – Gather:** *a-throizō*
6. **Go together – Gather:** *sy-strephō*
7. **Stir up – Collect:** *syn-eph-istēmi*
8. **Gathering:** *syn-agō*

1: Gather, Collect, Assemble (people) – Meet
2: the Synagogue
  a) Synagogue
  b) Synagogue official, President – Ruler
3: Gather, Collect, Pick up (things) – Store
9. **Pick – Collect – Gather:** *syl-legō*
10. **Heap (up) – Burden:** *sōreuō*
11. **Put together, therefore Settle (an account):** *syn-airō*

1. CHURCH – ASSEMBLY: *EK-KLĒSIA*

ek-klēsia 114

1: CHURCH – COMMUNITY – CONGREGATION

Mt	16 18	You are Peter and on this rock I will build my *Church*.
	18 17	[If your brother does something wrong and] refuses to listen to [the witnesses], report it to [the] *community*; and if he refuses to listen to the *community*, treat him like a pagan
Ac	5 11	This made a profound impression on the whole *Church*
	8 1	a bitter persecution started against the *church* in Jerusalem,
	3	Saul then worked for the total destruction of the *Church*;
	9 31	˅ The *churches* (G The *church*) throughout Judaea, Galilee and Samaria were now left in peace, building themselves up,
	11 22	The *church* in Jerusalem heard [that a great number were converted to the Lord in Antioch]
	26	[Barnabas and Saul] were to live together in that *church* a whole year,
	12 1	King Herod started persecuting certain members of the *Church*.
	5	All the time Peter was under guard the *Church* prayed to God for him
	13 1	In the *church* at Antioch the following were prophets and teachers:
	14 23	[Paul and Barnabas] appointed elders in each of these *churches*,
	27	On their arrival [in Antioch, Paul and Barnabas] assembled the *church*
	15 3	All the members of the *church* saw [Paul and Barnabas] off, and . . . they passed through Phoenicia . . . ⁴ When they arrived in Jerusalem they were welcomed by the *church* and by the apostles and elders,
	22	the apostles . . . decided to choose delegates to send to Antioch with Paul and Barnabas; the whole *church* concurred with this.
	41	[Paul] travelled through . . . Cilicia, consolidating the *churches*.
	16 5	the *churches* grew strong in the faith, as well as growing daily in numbers.
	18 22	[Paul] landed at Caesarea, and went up to greet the *church*.
	20 17	[Paul] sent for the elders of the *church* of Ephesus. ¹⁸ . . . he addressed these words to them: . . . ²⁸ . . . feed the *Church* of God which he bought with his own blood.
	28	
Rm	16 1	I commend to you . . . Phoebe, a deaconess of the *church* at Cenchreae.
	4	[My greetings to Prisca and Aquila;] all the *churches* among the pagans [owe them a debt of gratitude]. ⁵ My greetings also to the *church* that meets at their house.
	5	
	16	All the *churches* of Christ send greetings.
	23	Greetings from Gaius . . . and from the whole *church* that meets in his house.
1 Co	1 2	[I, Paul, send greetings] to the *church* of God in Corinth,
	4 17	I teach [the way I live in Christ] everywhere in all the *churches*.
	6 4	the people you appointed to try [cases like that] were not even respected in the *Church*.
	7 17	This is the ruling I give in all the *churches*.
	10 32	Never do anything offensive to anyone – to Jews or Greeks or to the *Church* of God.
	11 16	[arguing] is not the custom with us, not in the *churches* of God.
	18	when you all come together as a *community*, there are separate factions among you,
	22	Surely you have enough respect for the *community* of God . . . ?
	12 28	In the *Church*, God has given the first place to apostles,
	14 4	the man who prophesies does so for the benefit of the *community*.
	5	[the man with the gift of tongues should offer] an interpretation so that the *church* may get some benefit.
	12	concentrate on those [gifts] which will . . . benefit the *community*.
	19	when I am in the presence of the *community* I would rather say five words that mean something than ten thousand words in a tongue.
	23	unbelievers, coming into a meeting of the whole *church* where everybody was speaking in tongues, would say you were all mad!
	28	If there is no interpreter present, [people with the gift of tongues] must keep quiet in *church*
	33	As in all the *churches* of the saints, ³⁴ women are to remain quiet at *meetings* since . . . ³⁵ . . . it does not seem right for a woman to raise her voice at *meetings*.
	34	
	35	
	15 9	I persecuted the *Church* of God,
	16 1	you are to do as I told the *churches* in Galatia to do.
	19	All the *churches* of Asia send you greetings. [So do] Aquila and Prisca, with the *church* that meets at their house,
2 Co	1 1	From Paul . . . to the *church* of God at Corinth
	8 1	here . . is the news of the grace of God which was given in the *churches* in Macedonia;

2 Co	8 18	we are sending the brother who is famous in all the *churches* for spreading the gospel. ¹⁹ . . . the same brother who has been elected by the *churches* to be our companion
	19	
	23	the other two brothers . . . are delegates of the *churches* . . .
	24	²⁴ So then, in front of all the *churches*, give them a proof of your love,
	11 8	I was robbing other *churches* living on them so that I could serve you.
	28	there is my daily preoccupation: my anxiety for all the *churches*.
	12 13	Is there anything of which you have had less than the other *churches*?
Ga	1 2	From Paul to the *churches* of Galatia,
	13	how merciless I was in persecuting the *Church* of God,
	22	[I] was still not known by sight to the *churches* of Christ in Judaea,
Ep	1 22	[Christ is] the head of the *Church*; ²³ which is his body,
	3 10	the Sovereignties and Powers should learn . . . through the *Church*, how comprehensive God's wisdom really is,
	21	glory be to him . . . in the *Church* and in Christ Jesus for ever
	5 23	as Christ is head of the *Church* . . . so is a husband the head of his wife; ²⁴ and as the *Church* submits to Christ, so should wives to their husbands,
	24	
	25	Husbands should love their wives just as Christ loved the *Church*
	27	[Christ made the Church clean] so that when he took ⸢her (lit. the *Church*) to himself she would be glorious,
	29	A man . . . looks after [his own body]; and that is the way Christ treats the *Church*,
	32	This mystery . . . applies to Christ and the *Church*.
Ph	3 6	as for working for religion, I was a persecutor of the *Church*;
	4 15	In the early days . . . no other *church* helped me with gifts of money.
Col	1 18	Now the *Church* is his body, he is its head.
	24	It makes me happy . . . to do what I can to make up all that has still to be undergone by Christ for the sake of his body, the *Church*.
	4 15	Please give my greetings to the brothers at Laodicea and to Nympha and the *church* which meets in her house
	16	send [this letter] on to be read in the *church* of the Laodiceans;
1 Th	1 1	From Paul . . . to the *Church* of Thessalonika
	2 14	you . . . have been like the *churches* of God . . . which are in Judaea,
2 Th	1 1	From Paul . . . to the *Church* in Thessalonika
	4	among the *churches* of God we can take special pride in you
1 Tm	3 5	how can any man who does not understand how to manage his own family have responsibility for the *church* of God;
	15	God's family – that is, . . . the *Church* of the living God,
	5 16	a Christian woman . . . should support [her widowed relatives] and not make the *Church* bear the expense
Phm	2	[From Paul to Philemon,] and the *church* that meets in your house;
Heb	2 12	(Ps 22 23) I shall . . . praise you in ⸢full *assembly* (or: the *congregation*)
	12 23	[you have come for the festival,] with the whole *Church* in which everyone is a first-born son
Jm	5 14	If one of you is ill, he should send for the elders of the *church*,
3 Jn	6	[These brothers] are a proof to the whole *Church* of your charity
	9	I have written a note for the members of the *church*,
	10	[Diotrephes] expels [people who would have liked to welcome our brothers] from the *church*.
Rv	1 4	From John, to the seven *churches* of Asia:
	11	Write down all that you see in a book, and send it to the seven *churches*
	20	the seven stars are the angels of the seven *churches*, and the seven lamp-stands are the seven *churches* themselves.
	2 1	Write to the angel of the *church* in Ephesus
	7	If anyone has ears to hear, let him listen to what the Spirit is saying to the *churches*:

Repeated in 2 11, 17, 29; 3 6, 13, 22.

	8	Write to the angel of the *church* in Smyrna
	12	Write to the angel of the *church* in Pergamum
	18	Write to the angel of the *church* in Thyatira
	23	all the *churches* realise that it is I who search heart and loins
	3 1	Write to the angel of the *church* in Sardis
	7	Write to the angel of the *church* in Philadelphia
	14	Write to the angel of the *church* in Laodicea
	22 16	I, Jesus, have sent . . . these revelations to you for the sake of the *churches*.

2: ASSEMBLY (GENERALLY)

Ac	7 38	[our ancestors] held the *assembly* in the wilderness
	19 32	[in Ephesus] the *assembly* itself had no idea what was going on;
	39	If you want to ask any more questions you must raise them in the regular *assembly* . . . ⁴¹ When [the town clerk] had finished this speech he dismissed the *assembly*.
	41	

2. ASSEMBLE, MEET TOGETHER, GATHER – MEETING: *SYN-ERCHOMAI*

2 *syn-eimi* 1   1 *syn-erchomai* 21/32

Mk	3 20	once more . . . a crowd *collected*
	14 53	all the chief priests and the elders and the scribes *assembled*
Lk	5 15	large crowds *assembled*
	8 4	2 With a large crowd *gathering*, . . . [Jesus] used this parable:
Jn	18 20	I have always taught in the synagogue and in the Temple where all the Jews *meet together*:
Ac	1 6	Now having *met together*, [the apostles] asked [Jesus],
	2 6	at this sound [devout men living in Jerusalem] *assembled*,
	5 16	People even ⌜came crowding in (lit. *gathered*) from the towns round about Jerusalem, bringing with them their sick
	10 27	[Peter] went in to meet all the people *assembled* there,
	16 13	We . . . preached to the women who had come to the *meeting*.
	19 32	most of them did not even know why they had been ⌜summoned (lit. *assembled*).
	21 22	ᵛ Inevitably there will be a *meeting* of the whole body⌝, since they are bound to hear that you have come.
	22 30	[the tribune] gave orders for a *meeting* of . . . the entire Sanhedrin;
	28 17	When [the leading Jews in Rome] had *assembled*, [Paul] said to them,
1 Co	11 17	I cannot say that you have done well in holding *meetings* that do you more harm than good.
	18	when you all *come together* . . . there are separate factions among you,
	20	when you *hold these meetings*, it is not the Lord's Supper that you are eating,
	33	when you *meet* for the Meal, wait for one another.
	34	then your *meeting* will not bring your condemnation.
	14 23	unbelievers, coming into a *meeting* of the whole church where everybody was speaking in tongues, would say you were all mad;
	26	At all your *meetings*, let everyone be ready with a psalm

3. MEET – COME TOWARDS: *AP-ANTAŌ*

5 *ap-antaō* 2   1 *hyp-antaō* 10
3 *ap-antēsis* 3   4 *hyp-antēsis* 3
                    2 *syn-antaō* 7

X = Meet Jesus

Mt	8 28 X	two demoniacs *came towards* [Jesus]
	34 X	4 the whole town set out to *meet* Jesus;
	25 1 <	4 Ten bridesmaids . . . went to *meet* the bridegroom.
	6 <	3 The bridegroom is here! Go out and *meet* him.
	28 9	And there, coming to *meet* [the women], was Jesus.
Mk	5 2 X	a man with an unclean spirit *came out* from the tombs *towards* him.
	14 13	5 you will *meet* a man carrying a pitcher of water.
Lk	8 27 X	He was stepping ashore when a man . . . who was possessed by devils *came towards* him;
	9 18 X	one day when he was praying alone ⌜in the presence of his 2 disciples (ᵛ his disciples *came towards* him)
	37 X	2 a large crowd came to *meet* him.
	14 31	what king marching to war . . . would not first . . . consider whether . . . he could ⌜stand up to (lit. *meet*) the other who advanced against him . . . ?
	17 12 X	5 ten lepers came to *meet* him.
	22 10	2 you will *meet* a man carrying a pitcher of water.
Jn	4 51	[the court official's] servants *met* him with the news that his boy was alive.
	11 20 X	When Martha heard that Jesus had come she went to *meet* him.
	30 X	Jesus . . . was still at the place where Martha had *met* him.
	12 13 X	4 They took branches of palm and went out to *meet* him,
	18 X	it was because of this, too, that the crowd came out to *meet* him:
Ac	10 25	2 Cornelius went out to *meet* [Peter],
	16 16	we *met* a slave-girl who was a soothsayer
	20 22	I am on my way to Jerusalem, but have no idea what will 2 ⌜happen to (lit. *meet*) me there.
	28 15	3 the brothers . . . came to *meet* us, as far as the Forum of Appius
1 Th	4 17 X ●	3 [we] will be taken up in the clouds . . . to *meet* the Lord
Heb	7 1	2 Melchizedek . . . went to *meet* Abraham
	10	2 Melchizedek came to *meet* [Abraham].

4. JOIN, REJOIN – MEET: *SYM-BALLŌ*

sym-ballō 3/7

Lk	14 31	what king marching to war ⌜against (lit. to *meet*) another king would not first . . . consider

Ac	17 18	a few Epicurean and Stoic philosophers ⌜argued with (or: *met*) [Paul].
	20 14	When [Paul] *rejoined* us at Assos we took him aboard

5. ASSEMBLE – CALL TOGETHER – GATHER: *A-THROIZŌ*

2 *a-throizō* 1   1 *syn-a-throizō* 2
3 *ep-a-throizomai* 1

Lk	11 29	3 The crowds ⌜got even bigger (lit. *gathered around*) and [Jesus] addressed them,
	24 33	2 [In Jerusalem] they found the Eleven *assembled together* with their companions,
Ac	12 12	a number of people had *assembled* [in the house of Mary the mother of John Mark]
	19 25	[Demetrius] *called a* general *meeting* of his own men with others in the same trade,

6. GO TOGETHER – GATHER: *SY-STREPHŌ*

1 *sy-strephō* 2   2 *sy-strophē* 2

Mt	17 22	One day [Jesus and his disciples] *were together* in Galilee,
Ac	19 40	2 we can give no reason for this *gathering*.
	23 12	2 the Jews held a [secret] *meeting* at which they made a vow not to eat . . . until they had killed Paul.
	28 3	Paul had *collected* a bundle of sticks

7. STIR UP – COLLECT: *SYN-EPH-ISTĒMI*

1 *epi-stasis* 1/2   2 *syn-eph-istēmi* 1

Ac	16 22	2 The crowd ⌜joined in and showed (lit. *moved up together showing*) its hostility to [Paul and Silas]
	24 12	it is not true that they ever found me . . . ⌜stirring up (or: *collecting*) the mob,

8. GATHERING: *SYN-AGŌ*

1 *syn-agō* 56/59   3 *archi-syn-agōgos* 9
2 *syn-agōgē* 56   4 *epi-syn-agō* 8
5 *apo-syn-agōgos* 3 6 *epi-syn-agōgē* 2

1: GATHER, COLLECT, ASSEMBLE (PEOPLE) – MEET

Mt	2 4	[Herod] *called together* all the chief priests and the scribes of the people,
	13 2	such crowds *gathered* round [Jesus] that he got into a boat
	18 20	where two or three *meet* in my name, I shall be there with them.
	22 10 <	these servants . . . *collected together* everyone they could find,
	34	the Pharisees . . . *got together*
	41	While the Pharisees were *gathered* round, Jesus put to them this question,
	23 37 X	4 Jerusalem, . . . how often have I longed to *gather* your 4 children, as a hen *gathers* her chicks under her wings,
	24 28	Wherever the corpse is, there will the vultures *gather*.
	31	4 [the Son of Man] will send his angels . . . to *gather* his chosen from the four winds,
	25 32	All the nations will be *assembled* before [the Son of Man]
	26 3	the chief priests and the elders of the people *assembled* in the place of the high priest,
	57	Jesus [was] led . . . off to Caiaphas . . . where the scribes and the elders were *assembled*.
	27 17	when the crowd *gathered*, Pilate said to them,
	27	The governor's soldiers . . . *collected* the whole cohort round [Jesus].
	62	the chief priests and the Pharisees ⌜went in a body to (lit. *assembled* before) Pilate
	28 12	[the chief priests] *held a meeting* with the elders
Mk	1 33	4 The whole town ⌜came crowding (lit. *gathered*) round the door,
	2 2	so many people *collected* that there was no room left,
	4 1	a huge crowd *gathered* round [Jesus]
	5 21	a large crowd *gathered* round [Jesus]
	6 30	The apostles *rejoined* Jesus
	7 1	The Pharisees and some of the scribes . . *gathered* round [Jesus],
	13 27	4 [the Son of Man] will send the angels to *gather* his chosen
Lk	12 1	4 the people had *gathered* in their thousands
	13 34 X	4 How often have I longed to *gather* your children, as a hen [*gathers*] her brood under her wings,

Lk 17 37   4 Where the body is, there too will the vultures *gather*.
    22 66   there was a *meeting* of the elders of the people,
Jn 11 47   the chief priests and the Pharisees ⌐called a meeting (lit. *assembled* the council).
      52 X   [Caiaphas made this prophecy that Jesus was] to *gather together* in unity the scattered children of God.
    18 2   Jesus had often *met* his disciples [in Gethsemane],
Ac 4 5   the rulers, elders and scribes *had a meeting* in Jerusalem
      26   (Ps 2 2) Kings . . . and princes ⌐making an alliance (lit. *assembling*) against the Lord and against his Anointed. ²⁷ This is what has come true: . . . Herod and Pontius Pilate ⌐made an alliance (lit. *met*) . . . against your holy servant Jesus
      31   the house where [the apostles] were *assembled* rocked;
   11 26   [Barnabas and Saul] were to ⌐live together (lit. *meet*) in that church a whole year,
   13 43   2 When the *meeting* broke up many Jews . . . joined Paul and Barnabas,
      44   almost the whole town *assembled* to hear the word of God.
   14 27   On their arrival [in Antioch, Paul and Barnabas] *assembled* the church
   15 6   The apostles and elders *met* to look into the matter,
      30   [the delegates] *summoned* the whole community
   20 7   we met to break bread . . . ⁸ A number of lamps were lit in the upstairs room where we were *assembled*,
1Co 5 4   When you are *assembled* together . . . I am spiritually present
2Th 2 1   To turn now . . . to the coming of . . . Jesus Christ and how
      6   we shall all be *gathered* round him;
Heb 10 25   6 Do not stay away from the *meetings* of the community,
Jm 2 2   2 suppose a man comes into your ⌐synagogue (or: *assembly*), beautifully dressed
Rv 16 14 ⒟   demon spirits, . . . going out to all the kings of the world to *call* them *together* for the war
      16 ⒟   They *called* the kings *together* at the place called, in Hebrew, Armageddon.
   19 17   *Gather together* at the great feast that God is giving.
      19   I saw . . . all the kings . . . and their armies, *gathered together* to fight
Rv 20 8 ⒟   [Satan] will come out to deceive all the nations . . . and ⌐*mobilise* (lit. *assemble*) them for war.

2: THE SYNAGOGUE

a) Synagogue

Mt 4 23   2 [Jesus] went round the whole of Galilee teaching in their *synagogues*,
    6 2   2 This is what the hypocrites do in the *synagogues*
      5   the hypocrites . . . love to say their prayers standing up in the
       2 *synagogues*
    9 35   Jesus made a tour through all the towns and villages, teaching
       2 in their *synagogues*
   10 17   2 they will . . . scourge you in their *synagogues*.
   12 9   2 [Jesus] moved on from there and went to their *synagogue*,
   13 54   coming to his home town [Nazareth, Jesus] taught the people
       2 in their *synagogue*
   23 6   [Everything the Pharisees do is done to attract attention,]
       2 like wanting to take . . . the front seats in the *synagogues*,
      34   2 some [prophets] you will scourge in your *synagogues*
Mk 1 21   2 in Capernaum . . . [Jesus] went to the *synagogue* and began to teach,
      23   2 In their *synagogue* . . . there was a man possessed by an unclean spirit,
      29   2 On leaving the *synagogue*, [Jesus] went . . . to the house of Simon
      39   2 [Jesus] went all through Galilee, preaching in their *synagogues*
    3 1   2 [Jesus] went again into a *synagogue*,
    6 2   With the coming of the sabbath he began teaching in the
       2 *synagogue*
   12 39   the scribes . . . like . . . to take the front seats in the
       2 *synagogues*
   13 9   2 you will be beaten in *synagogues*;
Lk 4 15   2 [in Galilee Jesus] taught in their *synagogues*
      16   2 [Jesus] came to Nazara . . . and went into the *synagogue*
      20   2 all eyes in the *synagogue* were fixed on him.
      28   2 When they heard this everyone in the *synagogue* was enraged.
      33   2 [Jesus went to Capernaum.] In the *synagogue* there was a man who was possessed by the spirit of an unclean devil,
      38   2 Leaving the *synagogue* [Jesus] went to Simon's house.
      44   2 [Jesus] continued his preaching in the *synagogues* of Judaea.
    6 6   2 on another sabbath [Jesus] went into the *synagogue* and began to teach,
    7 5   2 he is [the centurion] who built the *synagogue* [of Capernaum]
   11 43   2 Pharisees . . . like taking the seats of honour in the *synagogues*
   12 11   2 When they take you before *synagogues* . . . do not worry about how to defend yourselves
   13 10   2 One sabbath day [Jesus] was teaching in one of the *synagogues*,
   20 46   2 Beware of the scribes . . . who love . . . to take the front
       2 seats in the *synagogues*
   21 12   2 they will hand you over to the *synagogues* and to imprisonment,

Jn 6 59   2 [Jesus] taught this doctrine at Capernaum, in the *synagogue*.
    9 22   5 [the Jews] agreed to *expel from the synagogue* anyone who should acknowledge Jesus as the Christ.
   12 42   there were many who did believe in [Jesus] . . . but they did
       5 not admit it, through fear . . . of being *expelled from the synagogue*:
   16 2   5 They will *expel* you *from the synagogues*,
   18 20   2 I have always taught in the *synagogue* and in the Temple where all the Jews meet together:
Ac 6 9   2 people came forward . . . who were members of the *synagogue* called the Synagogue of Freedmen,
    9 2   2 [Saul] asked for letters addressed to the *synagogues* in Damascus,
      20   2 [Saul] began preaching in the *synagogues*, 'Jesus is the Son of God'.
   13 5   at Salamis [Barnabas and Saul] proclaimed the word of God
       2 in the *synagogues* of the Jews;
      14   2 [at Antioch in Pisidia Paul] went to *synagogue* on the sabbath
   14 1   2 At Iconium [Paul and Barnabas] went to the Jewish *synagogue*,
   15 21   2 Moses . . . is read aloud in the *synagogues*
   17 1   2 [Paul and Silas] reached Thessalonika, where there was a
       2 Jewish *synagogue*.
      10   2 [in Beroea] Paul and Silas . . . visited the Jewish *synagogue*
      17   2 In the *synagogue* [in Athens Paul] held debates with the Jews
   18 4   2 Every sabbath [Paul] used to hold debates in the *synagogues* [in Corinth],
      7   2 [Paul] left the *synagogue* and moved to the house next door that belonged to . . . Justus.
      19   2 in Ephesus . . . [Paul] went alone to the *synagogue*
      26   2 [in Ephesus Apollos spoke] boldly in the *synagogue*,
   19 8   2 [Paul] began by going to the *synagogue* [in Ephesus] where he spoke out boldly
   22 19   I used to go ⌐from synagogue to synagogue (lit. to every
       2 *synagogue*) imprisoning and flogging those who believed in you;
   24 12   it is not true that they ever found me . . . stirring up the mob,
       2 either in the Temple, in the *synagogues*, or about the town;
   26 11   2 I often went round the *synagogues* . . . trying . . . to force them to renounce their faith;
Jm 2 2   2 suppose a man comes into your ⌐*synagogue* (or: assembly), beautifully dressed and with a gold ring on,
Rv 2 9 ⒟   the people who profess to be Jews but are really members of
       2 the *synagogue* of Satan
    3 9 ⒟   2 I am going to make the *synagogue* of Satan – those who profess to be Jews, but are liars . . . fall at your feet

b) Synagogue official, President – Ruler

      7 *archōn* 3/37   J *Jairus*   2
          Sosthenes 1 (Ac 18)

Mt 9 18   7 up came one of the *officials* . . . and said, 'My daughter has just died'
      23   7 Jesus reached the *official*'s house
Mk 5 22 J   3 one of the *synagogue officials* came up, *Jairus* by name,
      35   3 people arrived from the house of the *synagogue official*
      36   3 Jesus . . . said to the *official*, 'Do not be afraid; only have faith'.
      38   3 they came to the *official*'s house
Lk 8 41 J   7 now there came a man named *Jairus*, who was an *official*
       2 of the *synagogue*.
      49   3 someone arrived from the house of the *synagogue official*
   13 14   3 the *synagogue official* was indignant because Jesus had healed on the sabbath,
Ac 13 15   3 [at Antioch in Pisidia] the *presidents of the synagogue* sent [Paul and his companions] a message:
   18 8   3 Crispus, *president of the synagogue* [in Corinth], and his whole household, all became believers in the Lord.
      17   3 they all turned on *Sosthenes*, the *synagogue president*, and beat him

3: GATHER, COLLECT, PICK UP (THINGS) – STORE

Mt 3 12 X   he will . . . *gather* his wheat into the barn;
    6 26   the birds in the sky . . . do not sow . . . or *gather* into barns;
   12 30   he who does not *gather* with me scatters.
   13 30 <   then *gather* the wheat into my barn.
      47 <   a dragnet cast into the sea . . . brings in [a haul of] all kinds.
   25 24 <   you were . . . *gathering* where you have not scattered;
      26 <   So you knew that I . . . *gather* where I have not scattered?
Lk 3 17 X   [the Messiah's] winnowing-fan is in his hand . . . to *gather* the wheat into his barn;
   11 23   he who does not *gather* with me scatters.
   12 17 <   I have not enough room to *store* my crops. ¹⁸ I will . . . build
      18 <   bigger [barns], and *store* all my grain . . . in them,
   15 13   the younger son *got together* everything he had and left
Jn 4 36   the reaper . . . is *bringing in* the grain for eternal life,
    6 12   *Pick up* the pieces left over . . . ¹³ So they *picked* them *up*,
      13   and filled twelve hampers
   15 6   [withered branches] are *collected* and thrown on the fire,

9. PICK – COLLECT – GATHER: *SYL-LEGŌ*

2　　　　*logeia 2*　　1 *syl-legō 8*
3 *(spermo-)logos 1*

Mt 7 16	Can people *pick* grapes from thorns?
13 28 <	Do you want us to go and ⌐weed (lit. *gather*) [the darnel]
29 <	. . .? ²⁹ No, because when you ⌐weed out (lit. *gather*) the
30 <	darnel you might pull up the wheat with it. ³⁰ Let them both grow . . . at harvest time I shall say . . : First *collect* the darnel
40 <	as the darnel is *gathered* up and burnt in the fire, so it will be
41 <	at the end of time. ⁴¹ . . . angels . . . will *gather* out of his kingdom all things that provoke offences
48 <	the fishermen . . . *collect* the good ones in a basket
Lk 6 44	people do not *pick* figs from thorns,
Ac 17 18	⌐Does this parrot know what he's talking about? (lit. What
3	does this seed-*picker* want to say?)
1 Co 16 1	2 Now about the *collection* made for the saints:
2	each one of you must put aside what he can afford, so that
2	*collections* need not be made after I have come

10. HEAP (UP) – BURDEN: *SŌREUŌ*

1 *sōreuō 2*　　2 *epi-sōreuō 1*

Rm 12 20	(Pr 25 22) you should give [your enemy] food . . . thus you *heap* red-hot coals on his head.
2 Tm 3 6	Of the same kind, too, are those men who . . . get influence over silly women who are ⌐obsessed (lit. *burdened*) with their sins
4 3	2 The time is sure to come when people . . . *collect* themselves a whole series of teachers

11. PUT TOGETHER, therefore SETTLE (AN ACCOUNT): *SYN-AIRŌ*

syn-airō 3

Mt 18 23	a king . . . decided to *settle* his accounts with his servants.
24	²⁴ . . . the *reckoning* began,
25 19	the master of those servants came back and ⌐went through (lit. *settled*) his accounts with them.

GENERATION

genea 43

Mt 1 17	The sum of *generations* is therefore: fourteen *generations* from Abraham to David; fourteen *generations* from David to the Babylonian deportation; and fourteen *generations* from the Babylonian deportation to Christ.
11 16	What description can I find for this *generation*? It is like children shouting to each other
12 39	It is an evil and unfaithful *generation* that asks for a sign!
41	On Judgement day the men of Nineveh will stand up with
42	this *generation* and condemn it . . . ⁴² . . . the Queen of the South will rise up with this *generation* and condemn it,
45	That is what will happen to this evil *generation*.
16 4	It is an evil and unfaithful *generation* that asks for a sign!
17 17	Faithless and perverse *generation*!
23 36	all of this will recoil on this *generation*.
24 34	before this *generation* has passed away all these things will have taken place.
Mk 8 12	Why does this *generation* demand a sign? . . . no sign shall be given to this *generation*.
38	if anyone in this adulterous and sinful *generation* is ashamed of me . . . the Son of Man will also be ashamed of him
9 19	You faithless *generation* . . . How much longer must I be with you?
13 30	before this *generation* has passed away all these things will have taken place.
Lk 1 48	all *generations* will call me blessed.
50	his mercy reaches from ⌐age (lit. *generation*) to ⌐age (lit. *generation*)
7 31	What description, then, can I find for the men of this *generation*?
9 41	Faithless and perverse *generation*!
11 29	This *generation* is a wicked *generation*;
30	just as Jonah became a sign to the Ninevites, so will the Son of Man be to this *generation*.
31	the Queen of the South will rise up with the men of this *generation* and condemn them,

Lk 11 32	the men of Nineveh will stand up with this *generation* and condemn it,
50	this *generation* will have to answer for every prophet's blood
51	that has been shed . . . ⁵¹ Yes, I tell you, this *generation* will have to answer for it all.
16 8	the children of this world are more astute in dealing with their own ⌐kind (lit. *generation*) than are the children of light.
17 25	[the Son of Man] must . . . be rejected by this *generation*.
21 32	before this *generation* has passed away all will have taken place.
Ac 2 40	Save yourselves from this perverse *generation*.
8 33	(Is 53 8) Who will ever talk about his ⌐descendants (lit. *generation*)
13 36	when David in his own ⌐time (lit. *generation*) had served God's purposes he died;
14 16	In past *generations* [God] allowed each nation to go its own way;
15 21	Moses has ⌐always (lit. from early *generations*) had his preachers in every town,
Ep 3 5	This mystery . . . was unknown to any men in past *generations*;
21	glory be to him from one *generation* to the next in the Church
Ph 2 15	(Dt 32 5) perfect children of God among a deceitful and underhand *generation*,
Col 1 26	the message . . . was a mystery hidden for *generations* and centuries
Heb 3 10	(Ps 95 10) That was why I was angry with that *generation*

GIVE

1. Give, Offer, Hand over – Grant, Allow – Share (out): *didōmi*
　1: God Gives, Grants – God's Gift – Gift of the Spirit
　2: Christ Gives, Grants – Christ's Gift
　3: Gift to God – Offer, Offering – Dedicated to God
　4: Give, Grant, Allow – Entrust, Deliver – Share, Offer, Hand (over) to
　5: Lease – Let (a property) out to
　6: Free, Without paying – As a Gift
　7: Jesus Given, Sacrificed, Betrayed
　　a) Jesus Sacrificed himself, Gave himself up
　　b) Betrayed, Handed over, Delivered – the Traitor
　8: Betray (others), Arrest, Hand over – Consign to, Commit to, Abandon to

　9: Hand down, Pass on – Tradition
　10: Produce (a crop) – Yield, Bear (fruit)
　11: Give (in non-literal senses)
2. Gift – Bounty, Bountifully: *eu-logia*
3. Give away – Bestow: *psōmizō*
4. Provide – Afford – Cause: *par-echō*
5. Give, Provide, Supply – Add (strength), Support: *chor-ēgeō*
6. Give, Treat with, Bestow: *apo-nemō*
7. Offer Proffer: *ep-echō*
8. Offer, Present (to)
　1: Offer, Offering – Present: *pros-pherō*
　　a) Offer, Offering – Present (an offering) – Oblation (according to the old testament)
　　b) Offering (of Christ, of Christians)
　　c) Offer (generally)
　2: (Loaves of) Offering, Presentation: *pro-thesis*
　3: Offer (sacrifice): *an-agō*

1. GIVE, OFFER, HAND OVER – GRANT, ALLOW – SHARE (OUT): *DIDŌMI*

1	*didōmi*	389/415	11		*dia-didōmi*	4
10	*doma*	4	12		*ek-didomai*	4
6	*dōrea*	11	20		*ek-dotos*	1
8	*dōrean*	7/9	7		*epi-didōmi*	10
15	*dōrēma*	2	9		*meta-didōmi*	5
13	*dōreomai*	3	21		*eu-meta-dotos*	1
4	*dōron*	19	2		*para-didōmi*	118/119
16	*dosis*	2	5		*para-dosis*	13
18	*dotēs*	1	22	*(patro-)para-dotos*	1
19	*ana-didōmi*	1	23		*pro-didōmi*	1
17	*ant-apo-didōmi*	2/7	14		*pro-dotēs*	3
3	*apo-didōmi*	20/48				

Ⓢ = Gift of the Spirit

1: GOD GIVES, GRANTS – GOD'S GIFT – GIFT OF THE SPIRIT

Mt 6 11	*Give* us today our daily bread.
7 11	If you . . . *give* your children what is good, how much more will your Father . . . *give* good things to those who ask him!
9 8	the crowd . . . praised God for *giving* such power to men.

Lk	1	32	The Lord God will *give* [Jesus] the throne of his ancestor David;
		74	[God swore the oath] that he would *grant* us . . . to serve him
	11	3	*give* us each day our daily bread,
		13 Ⓢ	the heavenly Father [will] *give* the Holy Spirit to those who ask him
	12	32	it has pleased your Father to *give* you the kingdom.
Jn	3	27	A man can lay claim only to what is *given* him from heaven.
		34 Ⓢ	he whom God has sent speaks God's own words: God *gives* him the Spirit without reserve.
	4	10 6	If you only knew ⌐what God is offering (lit. *God's gift*) and who it is that is saying to you: Give me a drink . . . he would have *given* you living water.
	5	22	the Father . . . has *entrusted* all judgement to the Son,
		26	the Father . . . has ⌐made the Son (lit. *allowed* the Son to be) the source of life; ²⁷ and . . . has ⌐appointed him supreme judge (lit. *given* him the power to exercise judgement).
		27	
		36	the works my Father has *given* me to carry out,
	6	31	(Ps 78 24) He *gave* them bread from heaven to eat.
		32	it is my Father who *gives* you the bread from heaven,
		37	All that the Father *gives* me will come to me,
		39	the will of him who sent me is that I should lose nothing of all that he has *given* to me,
		65	no one could come to me unless the Father *allows* him.
	10	29	ⱽ The Father who *gave* them to me is greater than anyone (G As for my Father, what he has *given* me is greater than all)
	11	22	whatever you ask of God, he will *grant* you.
	12	49	what I had to speak, was ⌐commanded (lit. *given* me as a commandment) by the Father
	14	16 Ⓢ	I shall ask the Father, and he will *give* you another Advocate
	15	16	the Father will *give* you anything you ask in my name.
	16	23	anything you ask for from the Father he will *grant* in my name.
	17	2	through the power . . . you have *given* him, let him give eternal life to all those you have ⌐*entrusted* (or: *given*) to him.
		4	I have . . . finished the work that you *gave* me to do.
		6	I have made your name known to the men you took from the world to *give* me. They were yours and you *gave* them to me;
		7	they know that all you have *given* me comes indeed from you;
		8	I have given them the teaching you *gave* to me,
		9	I pray . . . for those you have *given* me, ¹¹ Holy Father,
		11	ⱽ keep those you have *given* me true to your name (G keep those in your name which you have *given* me)
		12	While I was with them, ⱽ I kept those you had *given* me true to your name (G I kept those true to your name which you had *given* me)
		22	I have given them the glory you *gave* to me,
		24	I want those you have *given* me to be with me . . . so that they may always see the glory you have *given* me
	18	9	Not one of those you *gave* me have I lost.
		11	am I not to drink the cup that the Father has *given* me?
Ac	2	4	the Spirit *gave* them the gift of speech.
		27 Θ	(Ps 16 10) you will not . . . *allow* your holy one to experience corruption.
		38 Ⓢ 6	you will receive the *gift* of the Holy Spirit.
	4	29	⌐*help* (lit. *grant*) your servants to proclaim your message
	5	31	God has now raised [Jesus] up . . . to *give* . . . forgiveness of sins through him to Israel.
		32 Ⓢ	God has *given* [the Holy Spirit] to those who obey him.
	7	5	God did not *give* [Abraham] . . . this land to call his own, yet he promised to *give* it to him
		8	Then he ⌐*made* (lit. *gave*) the covenant of circumcision:
		10	[God] rescued [Joseph] . . . by ⌐making him wise (lit. *giving* him wisdom) enough to attract the attention of Pharaoh
		25	through [Moses] God would ⌐liberate them (lit. *grant* them deliverance),
	8	20 Ⓢ 6	thinking that money could buy *what* God has *given* for nothing!
	10	40	God . . . *allowed* [Jesus] to be seen ⁴¹ . . . by certain witnesses
		45 Ⓢ 6	the *gift* of the Holy Spirit should be poured out on the pagans too
	11	17 Ⓢ /6	God was *giving* [the pagans] the identical *thing* he *gave* to us
		18	God . . . can evidently *grant* even the pagans the repentance that leads to life.
	13	20	[God] *gave* [the men of Israel] judges, down to the prophet Samuel. ²¹ Then . . . God *gave* them Saul
		21	
		34	(cf. Is 55 3) To you I shall *give* the sure and holy things promised to David.
		35 Θ	(Ps 16 10) You will not *allow* your holy one to experience corruption.
	14	17	[God] ⌐*sends* (lit. *gives*) you rain from heaven,
	15	8 Ⓢ	God . . . showed his approval of [pagans] by *giving* the Holy Spirit to them just as he had to us.
	17	25	God] *gives* everything – including life and breath – to everyone.

Ac	20	32	the word of his grace . . . has power . . . to *give* you your inheritance
Rm	5	15	divine grace, coming through the one man, Jesus Christ, came to so many as an abundant free *gift*.
		6	
		16 15	The results of the *gift* also outweigh the results of one man's sin:
		17 6	Jesus Christ will cause everyone to reign in life who receives the free *gift* . . . of being made righteous.
	11	8	(Is 29 10) God has *given* [the rest] a sluggish spirit,
		35	How could anyone receiving anything from God think it was a loan *returned*?
	15	5 17	may [God] . . . ⌐help you all to (lit. *grant* that you all may) be tolerant with each other,
		15	God has *given* me this special position. ¹⁶ He has appointed me as a priest of Jesus Christ.
1 Co	1	4	thanking God for all the graces you have ⌐received (lit. been *given*) through Jesus Christ.
	3	5 Δ	the different ways [of Apollos and Paul] . . . were ⌐assigned (lit. *given*) to them by the Lord.
		10	By the grace God *gave* me, I . . . laid the foundations,
	12	7 Ⓢ	The particular way in which the Spirit is *given* to each person is for a good purpose. ⁸ One may have the gift of preaching with wisdom *given* him by the Spirit;
		8	
		24	God has arranged the body so that more dignity is *given* to the parts which are without it,
	15	38	God *gives* . . . each sort of seed . . . its own sort of body.
		57	let us thank God for *giving* us the victory through our Lord Jesus Christ.
2 Co	1	22 Ⓢ	[God] has anointed us . . . *giving* us the pledge, the Spirit [that we carry] in our hearts.
	5	5 Ⓢ	God . . . has *given* us the pledge of the Spirit.
		18	It is all God's work. It was God who . . . *gave* us the work of handing on this reconciliation
	8	1	the grace of God . . . was *given* in the churches in Macedonia;
	9	9	(Ps 112 9) He was free in almsgiving, and *gave* to the poor:
		15 6	Thanks be to God for his inexpressible *gift*!
	12	7	to stop me from getting too proud I was *given* a thorn in the flesh,
Ep	1	17	May . . . God . . . *give* you a spirit of wisdom and perception of what is revealed,
		22	[God] ⌐*made* (lit. *appointed*) [Christ] . . . the head of the Church;
	2	8 4	it is by grace that you have been saved . . . by a *gift* from God;
	3	2	I have been *entrusted* by God with the grace he meant for you,
		7 6	I have been made the servant of that gospel by a *gift* of grace from God who *gave* it to me
		8	I . . . have been *entrusted* with this special grace . . . of proclaiming to the pagans the infinite treasure of Christ
		16	may [the Father] *give* you the power through his Spirit for your hidden self to grow strong,
Col	1	25	I became the servant of the Church when God *made* me *responsible for* delivering God's message
1 Th	4	8 Ⓢ	God, who *gives* you his Holy Spirit.
2 Th	2	16	God . . . has *given* us his love and, through his grace, such inexhaustible comfort and such sure hope,
	3	16	May the Lord of peace himself *give* you peace
2 Tm	1	7	God's *gift* was not a spirit of timidity, but the Spirit of power,
		16	I hope the Lord will ⌐be kind (lit. *grant* mercy) to all the family of Onesiphorus,
		18	May it be the Lord's will that he shall ⌐find (lit. be *given*) the Lord's mercy
	2	7	the Lord will ⌐show (lit. *grant*) you how to understand it all.
		25	people who dispute what he says . . . God may *give* them a change of mind
Heb	2	13	(Is 8 18) Here I am with the children whom God has *given* me.
	6	4 6	people who . . . tasted the *gift* from heaven,
Jm	1	5	If there is any one of you who needs wisdom, he must ask God, who *gives* to all freely . . . it will be *given* to him.
		17 16/15	All good *giving*, every perfect *gift* is from above; it comes down from the Father of all light;
	4	6	But he has ⌐been even more generous (lit. *given* even more grace) to us, as scripture says (Pr 3 34): God . . . *gives* generously to the humble.
1 P	1	21	God, who raised [Jesus] from the dead and *gave* him glory
	5	5	(Pr 3 34) God . . . will always ⌐favour (lit. *give* generously) to the humble.
2 P	1	3 13	By his divine power, he has *given* us all the things that we need
		4 13	he has *given* us the guarantee of something very great
1 Jn	3	1	Think of the love that the Father has ⌐lavished on (lit. *given*) us,
		24 Ⓢ	We know that he lives in us by the Spirit that he has *given* us.
	4	13 Ⓢ	he ⌐lets us share (lit. *gives* us a share in) his Spirit.
	5	11	God has *given* us eternal life
		16	he has only to pray, and God will *give* life to the sinner
Rv	1	1	This is the revelation *given* by God to Jesus Christ . . . about the things which are now to take place very soon;

Rv 2 23 it is I who . . . *give* each one of you what your behaviour deserves.
11 18 now the time has come . . . for your servants . . . to be ʳrewarded (lit. *given* their reward)
16 6 blood is what you have *given* them to drink;
19 God ʳmade [Babylon] (lit. *gave* [Babylon] to) drink the full winecup of his anger.

2: CHRIST GIVES, GRANTS – CHRIST'S GIFT

Mt 10 1 [Jesus] summoned his twelve disciples, and *gave* them authority over unclean spirits
14 19 breaking the loaves he ʳhanded (lit. *gave*) them to his disciples who gave them to the crowds.
15 36 he . . . broke [the seven loaves] and ʳhanded (lit. *gave*) them to the disciples who gave them to the crowds.
16 19 [You are Peter . . .] I will *give* you the keys of the kingdom of heaven;
20 23 as for seats at my right hand . . . these are not mine to *grant*;
26 26 Jesus took some bread . . . and *gave* it to the disciples.
27 Then he took a cup . . . and *gave* it to them.
Mk 6 7 he summoned the Twelve and began to send them out in pairs *giving* them authority over the unclean spirits.
41 [Jesus] . . . ʳhanded (lit. *gave*) [the five loaves] to his disciples to distribute
8 6 [Jesus] . . . ʳhanded (lit. *gave*) [the seven loaves] to his disciples to distribute;
10 37 *Allow* us to sit one at your right hand and the other at your left
40 as for seats at my right hand . . . these are not mine to *grant*;
14 22 [Jesus] took some bread . . . and *gave* it to them. 'Take it,' he said
23 Then [Jesus] took a cup, and . . . he *gave* it to them,
Lk 7 15 the dead man sat up . . . and Jesus *gave* him to his mother.
9 1 [Jesus] called the Twelve together and *gave* them power and authority over all devils
16 [Jesus] ʳhanded (lit. *gave*) [the five loaves] to his disciples to distribute
10 19 I have *given* you power to tread underfoot . . . the whole strength of the enemy;
21 15 I myself shall *give* you an eloquence and a wisdom
22 19 he took some bread . . . broke it and *gave* it to them, saying,
24 30 7 [Jesus] took the bread . . . broke it and ʳhanded (lit. *gave*) it to them.
Jn 1 12 to all who did accept him he *gave* power to become children of God,
4 10 If you only knew what God is offering and who it is that is saying to you: Give me a drink . . . he would have *given* you living water . . . ¹⁴ anyone who drinks the water that I shall *give* will never be thirsty again: the water that I shall *give* will turn into a spring inside him . . . ¹⁵ 'Sir,' said the woman 'give me some of that water . . .'
6 27 the kind of food the Son of Man is ʳoffering (or: *giving*) (G will *offer*) you,
33 for the bread of God . . . *gives* life to the world.
34 Sir . . . *give* us that bread always.
51 the bread that I shall *give* is my flesh, for the life of the world.
52 How can this man *give* us his flesh to eat?
10 28 I *give* [my sheep] eternal life;
13 15 I have *given* you an example
26 [One of you will betray me.] It is the one . . . to whom I *give* the piece of bread . . . He dipped the piece of bread and *gave* it to Judas
34 I *give* you a new commandment: love one another;
14 27 Peace I bequeath to you, my own peace I *give* you, a peace the world cannot [give], this *is* my *gift* to you.
17 2 through the power over all mankind that you have given [Christ], let him *give* eternal life to all
22 I have *given* them the glory you gave to me,
19 30 Δ 2 bowing his head [Jesus] *gave* up his spirit.
21 13 Jesus . . . took the bread and *gave* it to them, and the same with the fish.
1 Co 15 24 2 After that will come the end, when he ʳhands (lit. *gives*) over the kingdom to God the Father,
2 Co 10 8 the Lord *gave* [authority] to me for building you up
13 10 [I am writing] with the authority which the Lord *gave* me for building you up
Ep 4 7 Each one of us, however, has been *given* his own share of grace, *given* as Christ allotted it.
6 8 (cf. Ps 68 19) When he ascended to the height . . . he *gave* gifts to men.
10 11 to some, his *gift* was that they should be apostles;
2 Tm 4 8 all there is to come now is the crown of righteousness . . . which the Lord . . . will *give* to me on that Day;
3 which the Lord . . . will *give* to me on that Day;
1 Jn 3 23 His commandments are . . . that we love one another as he ʳtold us (lit. *gave* us the commandment) to.

1 Jn 5 20 the Son of God has come, and has *given* us the power to know the true God.
Rv 2 7 those who prove victorious I will ʳfeed (lit. *allow* to eat) from the tree of life
10 Even if you have to die, keep faithful, and I will *give* you the crown of life
17 to those who prove victorious I will *give* the hidden manna and I will *give* them a white stone
21 I have *given* [Jezebel] time to reform
26 To those who . . . keep working for me . . . I will *give* the authority over the pagans
28 I will *give* him the Morning Star.
3 21 Those who prove victorious I will *allow* to share my throne,
11 3 I shall ʳsend (lit. *allow*) my two witnesses to prophesy
21 6 I will *give* water from the well of life free to anybody who is thirsty;

3: GIFT TO GOD – OFFER, OFFERING – DEDICATED TO GOD
24 *korban* [*Corban*] 1

Mt 5 23 4 if you are bringing your *offering* to the altar and there remember that your brother has something against you,
24 4 ²⁴ leave your *offering* there . . . go and be reconciled
4 with your brother first, and then . . . present your *offering*.
8 4 4 go and show yourself to the priest and make the *offering* prescribed by Moses,
15 5 Anything I have that I might have used to help you is
4 *dedicated* [to God],
23 18 4 [You say] if a man swears by the *offering* that is on the altar,
19 4/4 he is bound. ¹⁹ You blind men! For which is of greater worth, the *offering* or the altar that makes the *offering* sacred?
Mk 7 11 Anything I have that I might have used to help you is
24/4 *Corban* (that is, *dedicated* [to God]),
Lk 2 24 4 [Jesus's parents took him up to Jerusalem] to *offer* in sacrifice . . . a pair of turtledoves
21 1 4 rich people [were] putting their *offerings* into the treasury;
4 these have all contributed money into the ʳtreasury (lit.
4 *offerings*) that they had over,
Rm 11 35 (Jb 41 3) How could anyone receiving anything from God
23 think it was a ʳloan (lit. *gift*) returned?
2 Co 8 5 [The Macedonians] *offered* their own selves first to God and, under God, to us.
Heb 5 1 4 Every high priest . . . is appointed . . . to offer *gifts* and sacrifices for sins;
8 3 4 It is the duty of every high priest to offer *gifts* and sacrifices,
4 4 there are others who make the *offerings* laid down by the Law
9 9 4 None of the *gifts* and sacrifices offered . . . can possibly bring any worshipper to perfection
11 4 Abel . . . was declared to be righteous when God made
4 acknowledgement of his *offerings*.
Rv 8 3 A large quantity of incense was given to [the angel] to *offer* with the prayers of all the saints on the golden altar

4: GIVE, GRANT, ALLOW – ENTRUST, DELIVER – SHARE, OFFER, HAND (OVER) TO

X = Give to Jesus   Θ = Give to God

Mt 2 11 X 4 [the wise men] offered [Jesus] *gifts* of gold and frankincense and myrrh.
4 9 Ⓓ X I will *give* you all these . . . if you . . . worship me.
5 31 (Dt 24 1) Anyone who divorces his wife must *give* her a writ of dismissal.
42 *Give* to anyone who asks,
7 6 Do not *give* dogs what is holy;
7 Ask, and it will be *given* to you;
9 7 Is there a man among you who would *hand* his son a stone
10 7 when he asked for bread? ¹⁰ Or would *hand* him a snake
11 when he asked for a fish? ¹¹ If you . . . know how to *give*
10 your children ʳwhat is good (lit. *good gifts*), how much more will your Father in heaven [give]
10 8 You received without charge, *give* without charge.
19 what you are to say will be *given* to you when the time comes;
11 27 X 2 Everything has been *entrusted* to me by my Father;
12 39 an evil . . . generation . . . ! The only sign it will be *given* is the sign of the prophet Jonah.
13 11 the mysteries of the kingdom of heaven are ʳrevealed to you (lit. *granted* for you to know), but they are not ʳrevealed
12 to them (lit. *granted* for them to know). ¹² For anyone who has will be *given* more,
14 7 [Herod] promised on oath to *give* her anything she asked.
8 ⁸ . . . she said, 'Give me John the Baptist's head.'
9 ⁹ The king . . . ordered it to be *given* her, ¹⁰ . . . and had
11 John beheaded . . . ¹¹ The head was . . . *given* to the girl
16 Jesus replied, '. . . *give* them something to eat yourselves'

Mt 16 4   an evil . . . generation . . ! The only sign it will be *given* is the sign of Jonah.

26   what has a man to *offer* in exchange for his life?

17 27   take [the shekel] and *give* it to them for me and for you.

19 7   why did Moses command that a writ of dismissal should be *given* . . ?

11   It is not everyone who can accept what I have said, but only those to whom it is *granted*.

21   sell what you own and *give* the money to the poor,

21 23 X   who *gave* you this authority?

41 ⊖ 3   He will . . . lease the vineyard to other tenants who will *deliver* the produce to him

43   the kingdom of God will be taken from you and *given* to a people who will produce its fruit.

22 21 3   *give back* to Caesar what belongs to Caesar

24 29   the moon will ⌐lose (lit. not *give* out) its brightness,

45   What sort of servant . . . is . . . wise enough for the master to place him over his household to *give* them their food

25 8 <   *Give* us some of your oil:

14 < 2   a man . . . summoned his servants and *entrusted* his property

15 <   to them. 15 To one he *gave* five talents, to another two, to a third one;

20 < 2   you *entrusted* me with five talents; here are five more that I have made.

22 < 2   you *entrusted* me with two talents; here are two more that I have made.

28 <   take the talent from him and *give* it to the man who has the five talents.

29   to everyone who has will be *given* more,

35 X   I was hungry and you *gave* me food;

42 X   I was hungry and you never *gave* me food;

26 9   This could have been sold . . . and the money *given* to the poor.

15   What are you prepared to *give* me if I hand him over to you?

27 34 X   they *gave* him wine to drink mixed with gall,

58 3   Pilate thereupon ordered [the body of Jesus] to be *handed over*.

28 12   [the chief priests] *handed* a considerable sum of money to the soldiers

18 X   All authority in heaven and on earth has been *given* to me.

Mk 2 26   [David] ate the loaves of offering . . . he also *gave* some to the men with him

4 11   The secret of the kingdom of God is *given* to you,

25   the man who has will be *given* more;

5 43   [Jesus] told them to *give* [Jairus's daughter] something to eat.

6 2 X   What is this wisdom that has been *granted* him . . ?

22   the king said . . , 'Ask me anything you like and I will *give* it you'. 23 And he swore her an oath, 'I will *give* you anything you ask'

25   I want you to *give* me John the Baptist's head . . . on a dish.

28   [the guard] *gave* [the head] to the girl, and the girl *gave* it to her mother.

37   '*Give* them something to eat' . . . 'Are we to . . . spend two hundred denarii on bread ⌐for them to eat (lit. to *give* them as food)?'

8 12   no sign shall be *given* to this generation.

37   what can a man *offer* in exchange for his life?

10 21   sell everything you own and *give* the money to the poor,

11 28 X   who *gave* you authority to do these things?

12 9 <   the owner . . . will . . . *give* the vineyard to others.

17 3   *Give back* to Caesar what belongs to Caesar

13 11   say whatever is *given* to you when the time comes,

24   the moon will ⌐lose (lit. not *give* out) its brightness,

34 <   a man travelling abroad . . . has . . . ⌐left his servants in charge (lit. *given* his servants authority),

14 5   Ointment like this could have been sold . . . and the money *given* to the poor;

15 23 X   They *offered* him wine mixed with myrrh,

45 13   [Pilate] *granted* the corpse to Joseph

Lk 1 77   [you will go before the Lord] to *give* his people knowledge of salvation

3 11 9   If anyone has two tunics he must *share with* the man who has none,

4 6 ⒟ X   I will *give* you . . . the glory of these kingdoms, for it has ⒟ 2/   been *committed* to me and I *give* it to anyone I choose.

17 X 7   they *handed* him the scroll of the prophet Isaiah.

20 3   [Jesus] *gave* [the scroll] *back* to the assistant and sat down.

6 4   [David] took the loaves of offering and ate them and *gave* them to his followers,

30   *Give* to everyone who asks you,

38   *Give*, and there will be *gifts* for you:

7 44   I came into your house, and you ⌐poured no water over (or: *gave* me no water for) my feet,

8 10   The mysteries of the kingdom of God are ⌐revealed to you (lit. *granted* for you to know);

18   anyone who has will be *given* more;

55   [Jesus] told them to *give* [Jairus's daughter] something to eat.

9 13   *Give* them something to eat yourselves.

10 22 X 2   Everything has been *entrusted* to me by my Father;

Lk 10 35 <   [the Samaritan] *handed* [two denarii] to the innkeeper.

11 7   I cannot get up to *give* [bread to] you. 8 . . . if the man does

8 <   not get up and *give* it him for friendship's sake, persistence will . . . make him . . . *give* his friend all he wants.

9   Ask, and it will be *given* to you;

11 7   What father . . . would *hand* his son a stone when he asked

12 7   for bread? Or *hand* him a snake instead of a fish? 12 Or

13 7   *hand* him a scorpion if he asked for an egg? 13 If you . . . know how to *give* your children ⌐what is good (lit.

10   good *gifts*), how much more will the heavenly Father [*give*]

22 11   the stronger man . . . *shares* out his spoil.

29   This is a wicked generation . . . The only sign it will be *given* is the sign of Jonah.

41   Instead, *give* alms from what you have

12 33   Sell your possessions and *give* alms.

42   What sort of steward . . . is . . . wise enough for the master to place him over his household to *give* them . . . food . . ?

48   When a man has had a great deal *given* him, a great deal will be demanded of him;

14 9   *Give* up your place to this man.

15 12 <   ⌐let me have (lit. *give* me) the share . . . that would come to me.

16 <   [the prodigal son] would willingly have filled his belly with the husks . . . but no one *offered* him anything.

29 <   you never *offered* me so much as a kid

16 12   if you cannot be trusted with what is not yours, who will *give* you what is your very own?

18 22 11   Sell all that you own and *distribute* the money to the poor,

19 8   [Zacchaeus said,] I am going to *give* half my property to the 3   poor, and if I have cheated anybody I will ⌐pay (or: *give*) him *back* four times the amount.

13 <   He summoned ten of his servants and *gave* them ten pounds.

15 <   he sent for those servants to whom he had *given* the money,

24 <   Take the pound from him and *give* it to the man who has ten pounds.

26   to everyone who has will be *given* more;

20 2 X   who is it that *gave* you this authority?

10 <   he sent a servant to the tenants ⌐to get (lit. to be *given*) his share of the produce of the vineyard from them.

16 <   He will come and . . . *give* the vineyard to others.

25 3   *give back* to Caesar what belongs to Caesar

24 42 X 7   [the apostles] *offered* him a piece of grilled fish,

Jn 1 17   the Law was *given* through Moses, grace and truth come through Jesus Christ.

3 35 X   The Father loves the Son and has *entrusted* everything to him.

4 5   Sychar, near the land that Jacob *gave* to his son Joseph.

7 X   Jesus said to [the Samaritan woman], '*Give* me a drink'

10 X   . . . 10 . . . If you only knew what God is offering and who it is that is saying to you: *Give* me a drink . . . he would have given you living water.

12   our father Jacob . . . *gave* us this well

6 11 11   Jesus . . . *gave* [the loaves] out to all who were sitting ready;

32   it was not Moses who *gave* you bread from heaven, it is my Father

7 19   Did not Moses *give* you the Law?

22   Moses ⌐ordered you to practise (lit. *gave* you) circumcision

39 ⑤   ⌐there was no Spirit as yet (ᵛ the Spirit had not yet been *given*)

12 5   Why wasn't this ointment sold . . . and the money *given* to the poor?

13 3 X   Jesus knew that the Father had ⌐put (lit. *given*) everything into his hands,

29   some of them thought Jesus was . . . telling [Judas] to *give* something to the poor.

14 27   my own peace I give you, a peace the world cannot *give*,

19 11   You would have no power over me . . . if it had not been *given* you from above;

Ac 3 6   [Peter to the cripple:] I will *give* you what I have . . . walk!

16   our faith in [Jesus] has ⌐brought (lit. *given*) back the strength of this man

4 12   of all the names in the world *given* to men, this is the only one by which we can be saved.

35 11   [the money] was then *distributed* to any members who might be in need.

8 18 ⑤   Simon saw that the Spirit was *given* through the imposition of hands

19   *Give* me the same power

12 4 2   [Herod] put Peter in prison, *assigning* four squads of four soldiers each to guard him in turns.

14 26 ⊖   Antioch, where they had originally been ⌐commended (lit. 2   *entrusted*) to the grace of God

15 30   The party left and went down to Antioch, where they . . . 7   *delivered* the letter.

40 ⊖ 2   Before Paul left, he . . . was ⌐commended (lit. *entrusted*) by the brothers to the grace of God.

20 35   There is more happiness in *giving* than in receiving.

Ac 23	33	19 the escort *delivered* the letter to the governor
24	26	[Felix] had hopes of ʳreceiving (lit. being *given*) money from Paul,
27	1	2 Paul and some other prisoners were *handed over* to a centurion
Rm 1	11	9 I am longing to see you . . . to strengthen you by *sharing* a spiritual gift with you,
5	5 Ⓢ	the love of God has been poured into our hearts by the Holy Spirit which has been *given* us.
6	17	you submitted without reservation to the creed you were ʳtaught (lit. *entrusted* with).
12	3	In the light of the grace I have ʳreceived (lit. been *given*)
	6	Our gifts differ according to the grace *given* us.
	8	9 Let . . . the alms*givers* ʳgive (lit. do so) freely,
1 Co 11	15	woman . . . was *given* her hair as a covering,
2 Co 9	7	18 (cf. Pr 22 8 G) God loves a cheerful *giver*.
Ga 2	9	James, Cephas and John . . . shook hands with . . . me, recognising the grace thus *given* me:
3	21	if the Law we were *given* had been capable of giving life,
	22	the promise . . . through faith in Jesus Christ . . . can only be *given* to those who have this faith.
4	15	you would even have gone so far as to pluck out your eyes and *give* them to me.
Ep 4	28	a thief . . . should try to find some useful manual work instead, and be able to do some good by ʳhelping (lit. *giving* to) others that are in need.
	29	let your words be for the improvement of others . . . and ʳdo good (lit. *give* grace) to your listeners,
6	19	pray for me to be *given* an opportunity to open my mouth . . . and give out the mystery of the gospel
Ph 4	15	16 no other church helped me with *gifts* of money.
	17	10 It is not your *gift* that I value;
1 Th 2	8	9 we were eager to *hand over* to you not only the Good News but our whole lives as well.
2 Th 3	9	This was . . . in order to ʳmake ourselves an example (lit. *give* an example in ourselves) for you to follow.
1 Tm 4	14	You have in you a spiritual gift which was *given* to you when the prophets spoke
6	18	21 [the rich] are . . . to ʳbe generous and (lit. *give* generously and be) willing to share
2 Tm 1	9	This grace had . . . been *granted* to us, in Christ Jesus, before the beginning of time,
Jm 2	16	If . . . one of you says to [brothers in need], 'I wish you well . . .' without *giving* them these bare necessities of life, then what good is that?
5	18	[Elijah] prayed again and the sky *gave* rain and the earth *gave* crops.
1 P 2	23 Ⓔ	2 when he was tortured . . . he ʳput his trust in (lit. *entrusted* himself to) the righteous judge
2 P 3	15	Paul . . . wrote to you with the wisdom that is his special *gift*.
Rv 6	2	the rider on [the white horse] . . . was *given* the victor's crown
	4	[the bright red horse's] rider was *given* this duty: to take away peace from the earth . . . He was *given* a huge sword.
	8	Plague and Hades . . . . were *given* authority over a quarter of the earth,
	11	Each of [the martyrs] was *given* a white robe,
7	2	another angel . . . called . . . to the four angels ʳwhose duty was (lit. to whom it was *given*) to devastate land and sea,
8	2	I saw seven trumpets being *given* to the seven angels
	3	A large quantity of incense was *given* to [another angel]
9	1	a star . . . was *given* the key to the shaft leading down to the Abyss.
	3	locusts . . . were *given* the powers that scorpions have
	5	[The locusts] were . . . to *give* [people] pain
10	9	I went to the angel and asked him to *give* me the small scroll,
11	1	I was *given* a long cane as a measuring rod,
	2	the outer court [of the Temple] . . . has been *handed* over to pagans
	10	the people of the world will . . . celebrate . . . by [giving] *presents* to each other,
12	14	[the woman] was *given* a huge pair of eagle's wings
13	2 Ⓓ	the dragon had *handed* over to [the beast] his own power
	4 Ⓓ	They prostrated themselves in front of the dragon because he had *given* the beast his authority;
	5	the beast was *allowed* to mouth its boasts . . . and it was *allowed* to do whatever it wanted for forty-two months;
	7	It was *allowed* to make war against the saints . . . and *given* power over every race,
	14	Through the miracles which [the second beast] was *allowed* to do . . . it was able to win over the people
	15	It was *allowed* to ʳbreathe (lit. *give* the breath of) life into this statue [of the first beast],
15	7	One of the four animals *gave* the seven angels seven golden bowls
16	8	The fourth angel . . . was ʳmade (lit. *allowed*) to scorch people
17	13	The ten kings] are all of one mind in *putting* their strength . . . at the beast's disposal,

Rv 17	17	God influenced their minds . . . to agree together to *put* their royal powers at the beast's disposal
18	7	Every one of [Babylon's] shows and orgies is to ʳbe matched by a (lit. cause to be *given* an equal) torture or a grief.
19	8	[the bride of the Lamb] has been ʳable (lit. *allowed*) to dress herself in dazzling white linen,
20	4	I saw those who are *given* the power to be judges take their seats on [thrones].
	13	The sea *gave* up all the dead who were in it; ¹⁴ Death and
	14	Hades ʳwere emptied of (lit. *gave* up) the dead that were in them;
22	12	3 the reward to be *given* to every man according to what he deserves.

5: LEASE – LET (A PROPERTY) OUT TO

Mt 21	33	12 a man . . . planted a vineyard . . . then he *leased* it
	41	12 He will . . . *lease* the vineyard to other tenants
Mk 12	1	12 A man planted a vineyard . . . then he *leased* it to tenants
Lk 20	9	12 A man planted a vineyard and *leased* it

6: FREE, WITHOUT PAYING – AS A GIFT

Mt 10	8	8/8 You received *without charge*, give *without charge*.
Rm 3	24	8 both [Jew and pagan] are justified through the *free gift* of his grace
2 Co 11	7	8 *taking no fee* for [preaching] . . . ⁹ . . . I was no burden to anyone;
2 Th 3	8	8 nor did we ever have our meals at anyone's table *without paying*
Rv 21	6	8 I will give water from the well of life *free* to anybody who is thirsty;
22	17	8 all who want it may have the water of life, and have it *free*.

7: JESUS GIVEN, SACRIFICED, BETRAYED

a) Jesus Sacrificed himself, Gave himself up

Mt 20	28	the Son of Man came . . . to *give* his life as a ransom
Mk 10	45	the Son of Man . . . did . . . come . . . to *give* his life as a ransom
Lk 22	19	This is my body which will be *given* for you;
Ga 1	4	[Jesus Christ] *sacrificed* himself for our sins,
2	20	2 the son of God . . . loved me and . . . *sacrificed* himself for my sake.
Ep 5	2	2 Christ . . . loved you, *giving* himself up in our place
	25	2 just as Christ loved the Church and *sacrificed* himself for her
1 Tm 2	6	[Christ Jesus] who *sacrificed* himself as a ransom for them all.
Tt 2	14	[Christ Jesus] *sacrificed* himself for us in order to set us free

b) Betrayed, Handed over, Delivered – the Traitor

Mt 10	4	2 Judas Iscariot, the one who was to *betray* him.
17	22	2 The Son of Man is going to be *handed over* into the power of men;
20	18	2 the Son of Man is about to be *handed over* to the chief priests and scribes.
	19	2 they will *hand him over* to the pagans to be mocked
26	2	2 the Son of Man will be *handed over* to be crucified.
	15	2 What are you prepared to give me if I *hand him over* to you?
	16	2 he looked for an opportunity to *betray* him.
	21	2 one of you is about to *betray* me.
	23	Someone who has dipped his hand into the dish with me,
		2 will *betray* me.
	24	2 alas for that man by whom the Son of Man is *betrayed*!
	25	2 Judas, who was to *betray* him, asked in his turn, 'Not I . . .?'
	45	Now the hour has come when the Son of Man is to be
	46	2/2 *betrayed* into the hands of sinners. ⁴⁶ . . . My *betrayer* is already close at hand.
	48	2 the *traitor* had arranged a sign with them. 'The one I kiss,'
27	2	2 They . . . led him away to *hand him over* to Pilate.
	3	2 Judas his *betrayer* was filled with remorse . . . ⁴ 'I have
	4	2 sinned;' he said 'I have *betrayed* innocent blood.'
	18	2 Pilate knew it was out of jealousy that they had *handed* him over.
	26	2 [Pilate] ordered Jesus to be . . . *handed over* to be crucified.
Mk 3	19	2 Judas Iscariot, the man who was to *betray* him.
9	31	2 The Son of Man is *delivered* into the hands of men;
10	33	2 the Son of Man is about to be *handed over* to the chief priests
	2	2 . . . They will . . . *hand him over* to the pagans,
14	10	2 Judas . . . approached the chief priests with an offer to *hand* Jesus over to them.
	11	2 he looked for a way of *betraying* him when the opportunity should occur.
	18	2 one of you is about to *betray* me,
	21	2 alas for that man by whom the Son of Man is *betrayed*!
	41	2 Now the Son of Man is to be *betrayed* into the hands of sinners.

Mk 14	42	2	My *betrayer* is close at hand already.
	44	2	the *traitor* had arranged a signal with them.
15	1	2	the chief priests . . . *handed* him *over* to Pilate.
	10	2	it was out of jealousy that the chief priests had *handed* Jesus *over*.
	15	2	Pilate . . . *handed* him *over* to be crucified.
Lk 6	16	14	Judas Iscariot who became a *traitor*.
9	44	2	The Son of Man is going to be *handed over* into the power of men.
18	32	2	he will be *handed over* to the pagans
20	20		they . . . sent agents to pose as men devoted to the Law
		2	. . . to *hand* him *over* . . . authority of the governor.
22	4		[Judas] went to the chief priests . . . to discuss a scheme
		2	for *handing* Jesus *over* to them.
	6	2	He . . . looked for an opportunity to *betray* him to them
	21	2	here with me on the table is the hand of the man who *betrays* me. [22] The Son of Man does indeed go to his fate . . . but
	22	2	alas for that man by whom he is *betrayed*! [23] And they began to ask . . . which of them . . . was to do this thing.
	48	2	Judas, are you *betraying* the Son of Man with a kiss?
23	25	2	[Pilate] *handed* Jesus *over* to them to deal with as they pleased.
24	7	2	the Son of Man had to be *handed over* into the power of sinful men
	20	2	our chief priests and our leaders *handed* him *over* to be sentenced to death,
Jn 3	16	Θ	God loved the world so much that he *gave* his only Son,
6	64	2	Jesus knew . . . who it was that would *betray* him.
	71	2	Judas . . . was the man . . . who was going to *betray* him.
12	4	2	Judas . . . the man who was to *betray* him – said,
13	2	2	the devil had already put it into the mind of Judas . . . to *betray* him.
	11	2	He knew who was going to *betray* him,
	21	2	I tell you most solemnly, one of you will *betray* me.
18	2	2	Judas the *traitor* knew the place well,
	5	2	Judas the *traitor* was standing among [the soldiers]
	30	2	If he were not a criminal, we should not be *handing* him *over* to you.
	35	2	It is your own people and the chief priests who have *handed* you *over* to me;
	36	2	my men would have fought to prevent my being *surrendered* to the Jews.
19	11	2	the one who *handed* me *over* to you has the greater guilt.
	16	2	Pilate *handed* him *over* to them to be crucified.
21	20	2	the disciple . . . who . . . had said to him, 'Lord, who is it that will *betray* you?'
Ac 2	23	20	This man, who was *put into your power* by the deliberate intention . . . of God,
3	13	2	God . . . has glorified . . . the same Jesus you *handed over* and then disowned in the presence of Pilate . . . [17] . . . I know . . . that neither you nor your leaders had any idea what you were really doing;
7	52	14	the Just One, and now you have become his *betrayers*, his murderers,
Rm 4	25	2	Jesus . . . was ˥put to death (lit. *handed over*) for our sins
8	32	Θ 2	God did not spare his own Son, but *gave* him up to benefit us all,
1 Co 11	23	2	on the same night that he was *betrayed*, the Lord Jesus took some bread,

8: BETRAY (OTHERS), ARREST, HAND OVER – CONSIGN TO, COMMIT TO, ABANDON TO

Ⓓ = Hand over to Satan

Mt 4	12	2	Hearing that John had been *arrested* [Jesus] went back to Galilee,
5	25	2	[your opponent] may *hand* you *over* to the judge and the judge to the officer,
10	17	2	Beware of men: they will *hand* you *over* to sanhedrins
	19	2	when they *hand* you *over*, do not worry about how to speak
	21	2	Brother will *betray* brother to death,
18	34	2	the master [of the unforgiving debtor] *handed* him *over* to the torturers
24	9	2	they will *hand* you *over* to be tortured and put to death;
	10	2	men will *betray* one another and hate one another.
Mk 1	14	2	After John had been *arrested*, Jesus went into Galilee,
13	9	2	they will *hand* you *over* to sanhedrins;
	11	2	when they lead you away to *hand* you *over*, do not worry beforehand about what to say;
	12	2	Brother will *betray* brother to death,
Lk 9	42	3	[Jesus] cured the boy and *gave* him *back* to his father,
12	58	2	the judge [may] *hand* you *over* to the bailiff
21	12	2	they will *hand* you *over* to the synagogues and to imprisonment,
	16	2	You will be *betrayed* even by parents
Ac 7	42	2	God turned away from them and *abandoned* them to the worship of the army of heaven,
8	3	2	[Saul] went from house to house arresting both men and women and ˥sending (lit. *consigning*) them to prison.

Ac 15	26	2	[Barnabas and Paul] have ˥dedicated (lit. *committed*) their lives to the name of our Lord Jesus Christ.
21	11		The man [Paul] . . . will be bound . . . by the Jews . . . and
		2	*handed over* to the pagans.
22	4		I even persecuted this Way to the death, and ˥sent (lit. *consigned*) women as well as men to prison
27	15 ○		The ship . . . could not be turned head-on to the wind, so we
		7	had to ˥give way (lit. *abandon* ourselves) to it and let ourselves be driven.
28	17	2	I was arrested in Jerusalem and *handed over* to the Romans.
Rm 1	24	2	God ˥left them to (lit. *gave* them up to) their filthy enjoyments
	26	2	God has *abandoned* them to degrading passions:
	28	2	God has ˥left them to (lit. *given* them up to) their own irrational ideas
1 Co 5	5 Ⓓ	2	[the guilty man] is to be *handed over* to Satan
13	3	2	if I even ˥let them take (lit. *give* them) my body to burn it, but am without love,
2 Co 4	11	2	we are *consigned* to our death every day, for the sake of Jesus,
Ep 4	19	2	[the pagans] have *abandoned* themselves to sexuality
1 Tm 1	20 Ⓓ	2	Hymenaeus and Alexander, whom I have *handed over* to Satan
2 Tm 3	4	14	[in the last days people] will be *treacherous* and reckless
2 P 2	4	2	God did not spare [the angels]: he . . . *consiged* them to the dark underground caves
Rv 3	9 X		I am going to ˥make (lit. *consign*) the synagogue of Satan . . . I will make them come and fall at your feet

9: HAND DOWN, PASS ON – TRADITION

Mt 15	2	5	Why do your disciples break away from the *tradition* of the elders?
	3		why do you . . . break away from the commandment of God
	6	5	for the sake of your *tradition*? . . . [6] . . . you have made
		5	God's word null and void by means of your *tradition*.
Mk 7	3	5	the Pharisees . . . follow the *tradition* of the elders and never eat without washing their arms
	5	5	Why do your disciples not respect the *tradition* of the elders
	8	5	You put aside the commandment of God to cling to human
	9	5	*traditions*. [9] . . . you get round the commandment of
	13	5	God in order to preserve your own *tradition* . . . [13] . . .
		5/2	you make God's word null and void for the sake of your *tradition* which you have *handed down*.
Lk 1	2	2	[accounts of the events] exactly as these were *handed down* to us by those who from the outset were eyewitnesses
Jn 17	8		I have *given* them the teaching you gave to me,
	14		I *passed* your word on to them,
Ac 6	14	2	Jesus . . . is going to . . . alter the traditions that Moses *handed down* to us.
7	38		[Moses] was entrusted with words of life to *hand on* to us.
16	4	2	[Paul and Timothy] *passed on* the decisions reached by the apostles
1 Co 11	2	5	You have done well . . . in maintaining the *traditions* just as I *passed* them *on* to you.
	23	2	this is what I received from the Lord, and in turn *passed on* to you:
15	3	2	I ˥taught (lit. *handed on* to) you what I had been taught myself, namely that Christ died for our sins,
Ga 1	14	5	how enthusiastic I was for the *traditions* of my ancestors
Col 2	8	5	philosophy [is] based on the ˥principles (lit. *traditions*) of this world instead of on Christ.
2 Th 2	15	5	Stand firm . . . and keep the *traditions* that we taught you,
3	6	5	keep away from any of the brothers who refuses to work or to live according to the *tradition* we passed on to you.
1 P 1	18		the ransom . . . was paid to free you from the useless way of
		22	life your ancestors *handed down*
2 P 2	21		It would even have been better for him never to have learnt the way of holiness, than to . . . desert the holy rule that
		2	was ˥entrusted (lit. *passed on*) to him.
Jude	3		I . . . appeal to you to fight hard for the faith which has
		2	been once and for all ˥entrusted (lit. *handed on*) to the saints.

10: PRODUCE (A CROP) – YIELD, BEAR (FRUIT)

Mt 13	8 <		Other [seeds] . . . *produced* their crop,
Mk 4	7 <		Some seed fell into thorns . . . and it *produced* no crop.
	8 <		[8] And some seeds fell into rich soil and . . . *produced* crop;
Heb 12	11	3	any punishment . . . *bears* fruit in peace and goodness.
Rv 22	2		the trees of life . . . bear twelve crops of fruit in a year,
		3	*producing* one in each month,

11: GIVE (in non-literal senses)

Mt 5	33	3	You . . . must *fulfil* your oaths to the Lord.
12	36		for every unfounded word . . . they will ˥answer (lit. have
		3	to *give* an answer) on Judgement day,
26	48		the traitor had *arranged* a sign with them.
Mk 14	44		the traitor had *arranged* a signal with them.

Lk 7 45   You *gave* me no kiss,
   12 58   ⌐try to settle (lit. *give* yourself the task of settling) with [your opponent] on the way,
   16 2 < 3 *Draw* me *up* an account of your stewardship
   17 18   no one has come back to *give* praise to God,
   18 43   all the people . . . *gave* praise to God
Jn 1 22   We must ⌐take back (lit. *give*) an answer to those who sent us.
    9 24   the Jews . . . said to [the blind man], '*Give* glory to God!'
   11 57   The chief priests . . . had by now *given* their orders:
   18 22   one of the guards standing by *gave* Jesus a slap
   19 3   they ⌐slapped him (lit. *gave* him a slap) in the face.
        9   Jesus ⌐made (lit. *gave*) no answer.
Ac 1 26   [The apostles] then ⌐drew (lit. *gave*) lots for [Barsabbas and Matthias],
    4 33   The apostles . . . were all *given* great respect.
    9 41   Peter *gave* her his hand and helped [Tabitha] to her feet,
   12 23   [Herod] had not *given* the glory to God.
   19 31 ○ imploring [Paul] not to ⌐take the risk of (lit. *betray* himself potentially by) going into the theatre,
       40 3 we can *give* no reason for this gathering.
Rm 4 20   Abraham . . . *gave* glory to God,
   12 19   ⌐leave (lit. *give* way for) that . . . to God's anger
   14 12   each of us must *give* an account of himself.
1 Co 7 3 3 The husband must *give* his wife what she has the right to expect, and so too the wife to the husband.
       25   About remaining celibate, I . . . *give* my own opinion
    9 12   we have to put up with anything rather than ⌐obstruct (lit. *provide* an obstruction to) the Good News of Christ
   14 7   Think of a ⌐musical instrument (lit. lifeless thing that *gives* out sound) . . . if one note on it cannot be ⌐distinguished (lit. *given* a distinguishing difference) from another, how can you tell what tune is being played?
        8   if no one can be sure which call the trumpet has ⌐sounded (lit. *given*), who will be ready for the attack?
        9   if your tongue does not *produce* intelligible speech, how can anyone know what you are saying?
2 Co 5 12   we are simply *giving* you reasons to be proud of us,
    6 3   We ⌐do nothing (lit. *give* no cause for scandal) that people might object to,
    8 10   I am only ⌐making (lit. *giving*) a suggestion;
Ga 2 9   James, Cephas . . . ⌐shook hands with (lit. *gave* their right hands to) Barnabas and me as a sign of partnership;
Ep 4 27   or else you will *give* the devil a foothold.
1 Th 3 9 17 How can we ⌐thank (lit. *give* thanks to) God enough for you . . .?
    4 2   You have not forgotten the instructions we *gave* you
2 Th 1 8   [Christ] will come . . . to *impose* the penalty on all who do not acknowledge God
1 Tm 5 14   [young widows should] not *give* the enemy any chance to raise a scandal about them;
Heb 13 17 3 your leaders . . . must *give* an account of the way they look after your souls;
1 P 4 5 3 [the pagans] will have to ⌐answer (lit. *give* an answer) for [their indecent behaviour] in front of the judge
Rv 4 9   the animals ⌐glorified (lit. *gave* glory) and honoured and gave thanks to the One sitting on the throne,
   11 13   the survivors . . . could only ⌐praise (lit. *give* praise to) the God of heaven.
   14 7   Fear God and ⌐praise (lit. *give* praise to) him,
   16 9   they would not repent and ⌐praise (lit. *give* praise to) him.
   19 7   let us . . . *give* praise to God, because this is the time for the marriage of the Lamb.

2. GIFT – BOUNTY, BOUNTIFULLY: *EU-LOGIA*

eu-logia 4/16

2 Co 9 5   I have thought it necessary to ask these brothers to . . . make sure . . . that the *gift* you promised is all ready, and that it all comes as a *gift* . . . and not by being extorted from you.
        6   the more *bountifully* you sow, the more *bountifully* you reap.

3. GIVE AWAY – BESTOW: *PSŌMIZŌ*

psōmizō 1/2

1 Co 13 3   If I *give away* all that I possess . . . but am without love,

4. PROVIDE – AFFORD – CAUSE: *PAR-ECHŌ*

par-echō 16

Mt 26 10   Why are you ⌐upsetting the woman (lit. *causing* the woman to be upset)?

Mk 14 6   Leave her alone. Why are you ⌐upsetting her (lit. *causing* her to be upset)?
Lk 6 29   To the man who slaps you on one cheek, *present* the other cheek too;
    7 4 X [the centurion] deserves ⌐this of you (lit. your *providing* this)
   11 7   Do not ⌐bother me (lit. *cause* me bother). The door is bolted
   18 5   since she keeps ⌐pestering me (lit. *causing* me such bother) I must give this widow her just rights,
Ac 16 16   a slave-girl . . . ⌐made (lit. *provided*) a lot of money for her masters
   17 31 ⊖ [God] has fixed a day when the whole world will be judged, and . . . has publicly ⌐proved (lit. *provided* proof of) this by raising this man from the dead.
   19 24   Demetrius . . . ⌐employed (or: *provided* employment for) a large number of craftsmen
   22 2   the silence they *afforded* him was even greater than before.
   28 2   The inhabitants ⌐treated us with (lit. *afforded* us) unusual kindness.
Ga 6 17   I want to be *given* no more trouble from anybody after this;
Col 4 1   Masters, *make sure that* your slaves *are given* what is just and fair,
1 Tm 1 4   myths . . . are only likely to ⌐raise (lit. *give* rise to) irrelevant doubts instead of furthering the designs of God
    6 17 ⊖ God who, out of his riches, *gives* us all that we need
Tt 2 7   ⌐make yourself (lit. *provide* yourself as) an example to them of working for good:

5. GIVE, PROVIDE, SUPPLY – ADD (STRENGTH), SUPPORT: *CHOR-ĒGEŌ*

	2 *chor-ēgeō 2*	1 *epi-chor-ēgeō 5*
		3 *epi-chor-ēgia 2*

2 Co 9 10 ⊖ /2 The one who *provides* seed for the sower . . . will *provide* you with all the seed you want
Ga 3 5 ⊖ Does God *give* you the Spirit so freely . . . because you practise the Law . . .?
Ep 4 16   by [the head, Christ] the whole body is fitted and joined together, every joint *adding* its own strength,
Ph 1 19 3 this will help to save me, thanks to your prayers and to the help which will be *given* to me by the Spirit of Jesus.
Col 2 19   the head . . . *adds* strength and holds the whole body together, with all its joints and sinews
1 P 4 11 ⊖ if you are a helper, help as though every action was done ⌐at God's orders (lit. with strength *supplied* by God);
2 P 1 5 2 do your utmost yourselves, *adding* goodness to the faith that you have
       11   In this way you will be *granted* admittance into the eternal kingdom

6. GIVE, TREAT WITH, BESTOW: *APO-NEMŌ*

apo-nemō 1

1 P 3 7   husbands must always ⌐treat their wives *with* (or: *give* their wives) consideration

7. OFFER, PROFFER: *EP-ECHŌ*

ep-echō 1/5

Ph 2 16   [you will shine in the world] because you are ⌐offering it (or: holding fast) the word of life.

8. OFFER, PRESENT (TO)

1: OFFER, OFFERING – PRESENT: *PROS-PHERŌ*

	3 *ana-pherō 5/10*	1 *pros-pherō 30/46*
		2 *pros-phora 9*

a) Offer, Offering – Present (an offering) – Oblation (according to the Old Testament)
Mt 5 23   if you are ⌐bringing your offering to (or: *presenting* your offering at) the altar and there remember that your brother has something against you, 24 . . . be reconciled with your brother first, and then come back and *present* your offering.
        8 4   go and show yourself to the priest and ⌐make the offering (lit. *offer* the gift) prescribed by Moses
Mk 1 44   ⌐make the offering (lit. *offer* the gift) for your healing prescribed by Moses
Lk 5 14   ⌐make the offering (lit. *offer* the gift) for your healing as Moses prescribed it,
Ac 7 42   (Am 5 25) Did you ⌐bring (or: *offer*) me victims and sacrifices in the wilderness . . .?

Ac 21 26	2/	Paul . . . visited the Temple to give notice of the time when . . . the *offering* would have to be *presented* on behalf of of each of them.
24 17	2	I came to bring alms to my nation and to make *offerings*;
Heb 5 1		Every high priest . . . is appointed . . . to *offer* gifts and sacrifices for sins;
3		he has to ⌜make sin offerings (lit. *offer* sacrifices for sin) for himself as well as the people.
7 27	3	[the ideal high priest] would not need to *offer* sacrifices every day, as the other high priests do for their own sins and then for those of the people,
8 3		It is the duty of every high priest to *offer* gifts and sacrifices, and so this one too must have something to *offer*.
4		there are others who ⌜make the offerings (lit. *offer* the gifts) laid down by the Law
9 7		the high priest . . . must . . . take the blood to *offer* for his own faults and the people's.
9		None of the gifts and sacrifices *offered* under these regulations can possibly bring any worshipper to perfection
10 1		the Law . . . is quite incapable of bringing the worshippers to perfection, with the same sacrifices repeatedly *offered* year after year. ² Otherwise, the *offering* of them would have stopped,
5	2	(Ps 40 7) You . . . wanted no sacrifice or *oblation*,
8	/2	(Ps 40 7) You did not want what the Law lays down as the things to be *offered*, that is: the sacrifices, the *oblations*,
11		All the priests stand at their duties . . . *offering* over and over again the same sacrifices
18	2	When all sins have been forgiven, there can be no more sin *offerings*.
11 4		Abel *offered* God a better sacrifice than Cain,
17		It was by faith that Abraham, when put to the test, *offered* up Isaac. He *offered* to sacrifice his only son
Jm 2 21	3	Abraham . . . *offered* his son Isaac on the altar

b) Offering (of Christ, of Christians)

Rm 15 16		I am to . . . make [the pagans] acceptable as an *offering*,
Ep 5 2 X	2	Christ . . . loved you, giving himself up in our place as a fragrant *offering* and a sacrifice to God.
Heb 7 27 X		[the ideal high priest] would not need to offer sacrifices every day . . . because he has done this once . . . by
3		*offering* himself.
9 14 X		Christ . . . *offered* himself as the perfect sacrifice to God
25 X		he does not have to *offer* himself again and again,
28 X		Christ . . . *offers* himself only once to take the faults of many on himself,
10 10 X	2	this will was for us to be made holy by the *offering* of his body made once and for all by Jesus Christ.
12 X		[Christ] has *offered* one single sacrifice for sins,
14 X	2	By virtue of that one single *offering*, he has achieved the eternal perfection of all whom he is sanctifying.
13 15	3	Through [Christ], let us *offer* God an unending sacrifice of praise
1 P 2 5	3	you . . , the holy priesthood that *offers* the spiritual sacrifices

c) Offer (generally)

Mt 2 11	[the wise men] *offered* [the child] gifts of gold and frankincense and myrrh.
Lk 23 36	The soldiers . . . approached to *offer* [Jesus] vinegar
Jn 16 2	anyone who kills you will think he is ⌜doing a holy duty for (lit. *offering* a holy service to) God.
Ac 8 18	When Simon saw that the Spirit was given through the imposition of hands by the apostles, he *offered* them some money.
Heb 5 7	During his life on earth, [Jesus] *offered* [up] prayer and entreaty,

2: (LOAVES OF) OFFERING, PRESENTATION: *PRO-THESIS*

pro-thesis 4/12

Mt 12 4	[David and his followers] ate the loaves of *offering*
Mk 2 26	[David] ate the loaves of *offering*
Lk 6 4	[David] took the loaves of *offering* and ate them
Heb 9 2	There was a tent which comprised two compartments: the first, in which . . . the table and the *presentation* loaves were kept, was called the Holy Place;

3: OFFER (SACRIFICES): *AN-AGŌ*

an-agō 1/23

Ac 7 41	(Ex 32 6) [our ancestors] *offered* sacrifice to the idol.

GO – PASS

1. **Walk – Go about**
  1: Walk – Go about, Went about: *peri-pateō*
    a) literally
    b) figuratively: Walk, Be guided by – Live – Behave
  2: Go about, Went about – Itinerant: *peri-erchomai*
  3: Go about together: *ana-strephō*
  4: Go round, Go about – Tour: *peri-agō*
    a) Go round – Tour
    b) Go around – Grope
  5: Walk uprightly, straight: (*ortho-*)*podeō*
2. **Go:** *poreuomai*
  1: Go
    a) Go towards – Make one's way to, Make for: *poreuomai eis*
    b) Go to – Gather round (a person): *poreuomai pros*
    c) various: *poreuomai* only
  2: (Jesus) Goes (from the world)
  3: Go (figuratively) – Follow – Live, Behave
  4: Going = Pursuits, Business
3. **Go:** *hyp-agō*
  1: Go
  2: (Jesus) Goes (to the Father)
4. **Go – Set out for:** *ap-erchomai*
  1: (Jesus) Goes, Leaves (for), Sets out (for)
    a) towards: *ap-erchomai eis*
    b) various: *ap-erchomai* only
  2: (A person) Goes, Makes for, Sets out (for)
    a) towards: *ap-erchomai eis*
    b) to a person (or his home): *ap-erchomai pros*
    c) Go away, after – Make off: *ap-erchomai* only
  3: Gone, Left, Passed (figuratively)
5. **Go – Depart:** *aph-ixis*
6. **Go abroad – Journey – Travel:** *apo-dēmeō*
7. **Be gone, Depart – Return:** *ana-luō*
8. **Get out – Go:** *apo-* and *ek-bainō*
  1: Come ashore – Go out (of a boat)
  2: Escape, Way out – Outcome
  3: Go = Turn, Opportunity, Time – Go towards, Help to
9. **Go before, Go on ahead**
  1: Go before: *pro-agō*
    a) Go before (a person) – Ahead, In front of
    b) Go before (in time) – Earlier
  2: Go before, Lead – Go on ahead: *pro-erchomai*
  3: Go before, Lead: *pro-poreuomai*
10. **Go – Pass:** *di-* and *par-erchomai*
  1: Go through, Pass through – Spread
    a) Go through, Pass through, Cross – Travel, Journey – Come, Intervene
    b) Pierce – Spread
  2: Pass by
  3: Pass away – Past, Gone – Disappear
11. **Go past – Cross – Across:** *dia-* and *para-poreuomai*
  1: Pass by, Go (past) – Visit – Make one's way, Walk
  2: Cross over (water) – Make a crossing
  3: the Other side, Far shore – Across, Beyond, Trans-
12. **Sail, Go, along the coast – Cross to**
  1: Sail along the coast: *para-legomai*
  2: Cross to: *para-ballō*
13. **Slip through – Pierce, Penetrate:** *di-*(*h*)*ikneomai*
14. **Go on, Go further – Advance**
  1: Go on, Go further – Advance: *pro-erchomai*
  2: Go on: *pro-bainō*
    a) Go on, Go further
    b) Advance in age – Be well on
  3: Go further, Go on: *pros*(*-eaō*)
  4: Advance – Progress: *pro-koptō*
  5: Go too far, Go beyond – Go ahead: *pro-agō*
15. **Pass:** *di-* and *par-agō*
  1: Pass one's days – Lead one's life, Live
  2: Pass on – Pass by – Pass away
    a) Pass on, by – Walk on, Go along
    b) Pass away – Come to an end – Over
16. **Pass over – Pass away:** *dia-* and *para-bainō*
  1: Pass over = Cross – Come across, Come over
  2: Never passing away = Permanent, Perpetual
17. **Pass through – Make one's way Go journeying:** *di-* and *para-*(*h*)*odeuō*

1. WALK – GO ABOUT

1: WALK – GO ABOUT, WENT ABOUT: *PERI-PATEŌ*

1 *peri-pateō* 95   2 *em-peri-pateō* 1

a) literally

Mt 4 18 X	[Jesus] was *walking* by the Sea of Galilee
9 5	[Jesus said to the paralytic,] Get up and *walk*
11 5	the blind see again, and the lame *walk*,
14 25 X	he went towards [the disciples], *walking* on the lake,
26 X	the disciples saw him *walking* on the lake
29	Peter . . . started *walking* towards Jesus across the water,
15 31	The crowds were astonished to see . . . the lame *walking* . . . and they praised the God of Israel.
Mk 2 9	Get up, pick up your stretcher and *walk*
5 42	The little girl got up at once and began to *walk about*,
6 48 X	he came towards [the disciples], *walking* on the lake,
49 X	when they saw him *walking* on the lake they thought it was a ghost
8 24	people . . . look like trees to me, but they are *walking about*.
11 27 X	as Jesus was *walking* in the Temple, the chief priests . . . came to him,

Mk	12 38	Beware of the scribes who like to *walk about* in long robes,
	16 12	[Jesus] showed himself . . . to two of [the disciples] as they were *walking* on their way into the country.
Lk	5 23	Get up and *walk*
	7 22	the blind see again, the lame *walk*
	11 44	you are like the unmarked tombs that men *walk* on without knowing it!
	20 46	Beware of the scribes who like to *walk about* in long robes
	24 17	What matters are you discussing as you *walk* along?
Jn	1 36 X	Jesus *passed*, and John stared hard at him
	5 8	Get up, pick up your sleeping-mat and *walk*,
	9	The man . . . picked up his mat and *walked* away.
	11	the man who cured me told me, 'Pick up your mat and *walk*'.
	12	Who is the man who said to you, 'Pick up your mat and *walk*'?
	6 19 X	[the disciples] saw Jesus *walking* on the lake
	66	many of his disciples left [Jesus] and stopped *going* with him.
	7 1 X	Jesus ⌐stayed (lit. *went about*) in Galilee; he could not ⌐stay
	X	(lit. *go about*) in Judaea,
	10 23 X	Jesus was in the Temple *walking* up and down in the Portico
	11 54 X	Jesus no longer *went about* openly among the Jews,
	21 18	when you were young and . . . *walked* where you liked;
Ac	3 6	in the name of Jesus Christ the Nazarene, *walk*!
	8	[the lame man] began to *walk*, and he went . . . into the Temple, *walking* and jumping and praising God. [9] Everyone could see him *walking*
	9	
	12	Why are you staring at us as though we had made this man *walk* by our own power . . .?
	14 8	A man sat there who had never *walked* in his life,
	10	the cripple jumped up and began to *walk*.
1 P	5 8 ⓓ	the devil is *prowling round* . . . looking for someone to eat.
Rv	3 4	a few . . . are fit to ⌐come (lit. *walk*) with me, dressed in white.
	9 20	idols . . . can neither see nor hear nor ⌐move (or: *walk*)
	16 15	Happy is the man who has . . . not taken off his clothes so that he does not *go* ⌐out (lit. *about*) naked

b) figuratively: Walk, Be guided by – Live – Behave

Mk	7 5	Why ⌐do your disciples not respect (lit. *are* your disciples not *guided by*) the tradition of the elders . . .?
Jn	8 12	anyone who follows me will not be *walking* in the dark;
	11 9	A man can *walk* in the daytime without stumbling . . . [10] but if he *walks* at night he stumbles,
	10	
	12 35	*Walk* while you have the light . . .; he who *walks* in the dark does not know where he is going.
Ac	21 21	you instruct all Jews living among the pagans . . . not to . . . *follow* the customary practices.
Rm	6 4	we joined him in death, so that . . . we too might *live* a new life.
	8 4	us, who *behave* not as our unspiritual nature but as the spirit dictates.
	13 13	Let us *live* decently as people do in the daytime:
	14 15	you are hardly *being guided by* charity.
1 Co	3 3	Isn't it obvious . . . from the way that you go on *behaving* like ordinary people?
	7 17	[each one] should continue to *live* as he was when God's call reached him.
2 Co	4 2	we will have . . . no *behaving* with deceitfulness or watering down the word of God;
	5 7	*going* as we do by faith and not by sight
	6 16 ⊖	2 (Lv 26 12) I will make my home among them and *live* with them;
	10 2	people . . . think we *go* by ordinary human motives.
	3	We *live* in the flesh, of course,
	12 18	[Titus] and I have always *been guided by* the same spirit and trodden in the same tracks.
Ga	5 16	if you *are guided by* the Spirit you will be in no danger of yielding to self-indulgence,
Ep	2 2	[you were dead through the sins] in which you used to *live*
	10	We are . . . created in Christ Jesus to *live* the good life as from the beginning [God] had meant us to live it.
	4 1	I . . . implore you . . . to *lead a life* worthy of your vocation.
	17	I want to urge you . . . not to *go on living* the aimless kind of life that pagans *live*.
	5 2	*follow* Christ by loving as he loved you,
	8	⌐be (lit. *behave*) like children of light,
	15	be very careful about the ⌐sort of lives you lead (lit. *way you live*),
Ph	3 17	Take as your models everybody who is already ⌐doing (lit. *living* like) this . . . [18] . . . there are many who are *behaving* as the enemies of the cross of Christ.
	18	
Col	1 10	you will be able to ⌐lead the kind of life (lit. *live* in a way) which the Lord expects of you,
	2 6	*live* your whole life according to the Christ you have received
	3 7	it is the way in which you used to *live*
	4 5	⌐Be tactful (lit. *Go* tactfully) with those who are not Christians
1 Th	1 12	[we are] appealing to you to *live* a life worthy of God,
	4 1	make . . . progress in the kind of life that you are meant to *live*: the life that God wants, . . . as you are already *living* it.

1 Th	4 12	so . . . you are seen to ⌐be respectable (lit. *behave* with dignity) by those outside the Church
2 Th	3 6	keep away from any of the brothers who ⌐refuses to work (lit. *lives* in idleness)
	11	there are some of you who are *living* in idleness,
Heb	13 9	it is better to rely on grace . . . than on dietary laws which have done no good to those who ⌐kept (lit. *were guided by*) them.
1 Jn	1 6	If we say that we are in union with God while we are *living* in darkness, we are lying . . . [7] But if we *live* our lives in the light . . . we are in union with one another,
	7	
	2 6	[we are in God] only when the one who claims to be living in [God] is *living* the same kind of life as Christ *lived*.
	X	
	11	the man who hates his brother . . . ⌐is (lit. *walks*) in darkness
2 Jn	4	your children have been *living* the life of truth
	6	To love is to *live* according to his commandments: this is the commandment . . ., to *live* a life of love.
3 Jn	3	some brothers . . . told . . . ⌐of your life (lit. how you *lived*) in the truth.
	4	my children are *living* according to the truth.
Rv	2 1 X	the one who *lives* surrounded by the seven golden lamp-stands;
	21 24	(Is 60 3) The pagan nations will *live* by its light

2: GO ABOUT, WENT ABOUT – ITINERANT: *PERI-ERCHOMAI*

peri-erchomai 2/4

Ac	19 13	some *itinerant* Jewish exorcists tried pronouncing the name of the Lord Jesus over people who were possessed
Heb	11 37	[the prophets] ⌐were homeless (lit. *went about*) and . . . they were penniless

3: GO ABOUT TOGETHER: *ANA-STREPHŌ*

ana-strephō 1/10

Mt	17 22	One day . . . they ⌐were together (ᵛ were *going about together*) in Galilee,

4: GO ROUND, GO ABOUT – TOUR: *PERI-AGŌ*

peri-agō 5/6

a) Go round – Tour

Mt	4 23 X	He *went round* the whole of Galilee teaching
	9 35 X	Jesus *made a tour* through all the towns and villages, teaching
	23 15	You [scribes and Pharisees] who *travel over* sea and land to make a single proselyte,
Mk	6 6 X	He *made a tour* round the villages, teaching.

b) Go around – Grope

Ac	13 11	[Elymas] *groped about* to find someone to lead him by the hand.

5: WALK UPRIGHTLY, STRAIGHT: *(ORTHO-)PODEŌ*

(ortho-)podeō 1

Ga	2 14	they were not ⌐respecting the true meaning of (lit. *walking uprightly* according to) the Good News,

2. GO: *POREUOMAI*

3 *poreia*	2	4 *epi-poreuomai* 1
1 *poreuomai* 151		2 *sym-poreuomai* 4

1: GO

a) Go towards – Make one's way to, Make for: poreuomai eis

Mt	2 20	[Joseph,] *go* [back] *to* the land of Israel,
	17 27	*go to* the lake and cast a hook;
	21 2	*Go to* the village facing you;
	25 41	*Go away* from me, with your curse upon you, *to* the eternal fire
	28 16	the eleven disciples *set out for* Galilee, *to* the mountain
Mk	16 12	[Jesus] showed himself . . . *to* two of [the disciples] as they were *on their way into* the country.
	15	*Go* [out] *to* the whole world; proclaim the Good News
Lk	1 39	Mary *set out* . . . and *went* as quickly as she could *to* a town in the hill country of Judah.
	2 41	Every year [Jesus's] parents used to *go to* Jerusalem
	4 42 X	he left the house and *made his way to* a lonely place
	5 24	get up, and pick up your stretcher and *go* home

Lk	7	11 X	he *went to* a town called Nain, accompanied by his disciples
	9	12	Send the people away, and they can *go to* the villages and farms
		51 X	he resolutely *took the road for* Jerusalem
		53 X	but the people would not receive him because he was *making for* Jerusalem . . . ⁵⁶ and they *went off to* another village.
		56	
	13	22 X	Through towns and villages he went teaching, making his *way to* Jerusalem.
		3	
	17	11 X	*on the way to* Jerusalem he travelled along the border between Samaria and Galilee.
	19	12 <	A man of noble birth *went to* a distant country
	22	33	I would be ready to *go to* prison with you, and *to* death.
		39 X	He then left to *make his way* as usual *to* the Mount of Olives,
	24	13	two of [the disciples] were *on their way to* . . . Emmaus,
Jn	7	35 X	Where is he going . . .? Is he *going* abroad *to* the people who are dispersed . . .?
		53	[The chief priests and Pharisees] all *went* home.
	8	1 X	Jesus *went* to the Mount of Olives.
Ac	1	25	Judas abandoned [this ministry] to *go to* his proper place.
	12	17	[Peter] left [Mary's house] and *went to* another place.
	16	7	[Paul and Timothy] thought to *cross* [the frontier] *into* Bithynia,
		16	One day . . . we were *going to* prayer,
	18	6	from now on I can *go to* the pagans with a clear conscience.
	19	21	Paul made up his mind to *go* [back] *to* Jerusalem through Macedonia
	20	1	Paul . . . *set out for* Macedonia.
		22	I am *on my way to* Jerusalem, but have no idea what will happen to me there,
	22	5	they even ⌐sent me with letters to (lit. gave me letters when I *went to*) their brothers in Damascus.
		10	Stand up and *go into* Damascus,
	25	20	I asked [Paul] if he would be willing to *go to* Jerusalem to be tried there
	26	12	I was *going to* Damascus,
Rm	15	24	I hope to see you *on my way to* Spain
		25	I ⌐must take (lit. am *going* with) a present [of money] *to* the saints in Jerusalem,
1 Tm	1	3	As I asked you when I was *leaving for* Macedonia, please stay at Ephesus,
2 Tm	4	10	Demas has . . . *gone to* Thessalonika,
Jm	4	13	we *are off to* this or that town;

b) Go to – Gather round (a person): poreuomai pros

Mt	10	6	*go* rather *to* the lost sheep of . . . Israel.
	25	9	you had better *go to* those who sell [oil] and buy some
	26	14	Judas Iscariot *went to* the chief priests
Mk	10	1	² again crowds *gathered round* [Jesus],
Lk	8	4	⁴ With . . . people from every town *finding their way to* [Jesus],
	11	5	Suppose one of you . . . *goes to* [his friend] in the middle of the night
	15	18 <	I will leave this place and *go to* my father
	16	30	if someone *comes to* [my brothers] from the dead, they will repent.
Jn	20	17	*go and find* ⌄ the (G my) brothers, and tell them: I am ascending to my Father
Ac	27	3	Julius was considerate enough to allow Paul to *go to* his friends
	28	26	(Is 6 9) *Go to* this nation and say:

c) various: poreuomai only

Mt	2	8	*Go* and find out all about the child,
		9	[the wise men] *set out*.
	8	9	I say to one man: *Go*, and he *goes*;
	9	13	*Go* and learn the meaning of the words:
	10	7	As you *go*, proclaim that the kingdom of heaven is close at hand.
	11	4	*Go* back and tell John what you hear and see;
		7	[John's] messengers were *leaving*,
	12	1 X	Jesus *took a walk* one sabbath day through the cornfields.
		45 ⓓ	[the unclean spirit] *goes off* and collects seven other spirits
	18	12 <	will he not leave the ninety-nine . . . and *go* in search of the stray?
	19	15 X	he laid his hands on [the children] and *went* on his way.
	21	6	So the disciples *went* [out]
	22	9 <	*go to* the crossroads in the town and invite everyone you can find
		15	the Pharisees *went* [away] to work out between them how to trap [Jesus]
	24	1 X	Jesus left the Temple, and as he was *going* [away] his disciples came up
	25	16	The man who had received the five talents promptly *went* and traded with them
	27	66	So [the chief priests and the Pharisees] *went* and made the sepulchre secure,
	28	7	*go* quickly and tell his disciples, 'He has risen from the dead'
		11	[the women] were *on their way* [from the sepulchre],
		19	*Go*, therefore, make disciples of all the nations;

Mk	16	10	[Mary of Magdala] *went* to those who had been [Jesus's] companions,
Lk	2	3	everyone *went* to his own town to be registered.
	4	30 X	he slipped through the crowd and *walked away*.
		42 X	The crowds . . . wanted to prevent him *leaving* them,
	7	6 X	Jesus *went* with them,
		8	I say to one man: *Go*, and he *goes*;
		11 X	² he went to a town called Nain, *accompanied by* his disciples
		22	*Go* [back] and tell John what you have seen and heard:
		50	Your faith has saved you; *go in peace*.
	8	48	your faith has restored you to health; *go in peace*.
	9	13	We have no more . . . unless we are to *go* ourselves and buy food for all these people.
		52	[Jesus's messengers] *set out*, and they went into a Samaritan village
		57 X	As [Jesus and his disciples] *travelled along* they met a man who said to him, 'I will follow you'
	10	37	*Go*, and do the same yourself.
		38 X	In the *course of their journey* he came to a village,
	11	26 ⓓ	[the unclean spirit] then *goes off* and brings seven other spirits.
	13	31 X	some Pharisees came up. 'Go away' they said. 'Leave this place, because Herod means to kill you.' ³² He replied, 'You may *go* and give that fox this message: . . .
		32	
		33 X	³³ But for today and tomorrow . . . I must *go* [on],
	14	10	when you are a guest, *make your way* to the lowest place
		19	I have bought five yoke of oxen and am *on my way* to try them out.
		25 X	² Great crowds *accompanied* him *on his way* and he . . . spoke to them.
		31 <	what king *marching* to war against another king would not first . . . consider . . .?
	15	4 <	What man . . . would not leave the ninety-nine [sheep] . . . and *go* after the missing one . . .?
		15	[the prodigal son] *went* and hired himself out to one of the local inhabitants
	17	14	*Go* and show yourselves to the priests.
		19	Stand up and *go on your way*. Your faith has saved you.
	19	29 X	he *went* on ahead, going up to Jerusalem.
		36 X	As he *moved off*, people spread their cloaks in the road,
	22	8	*Go* and make the preparations for us to eat the passover.
	24	15 X	² Jesus himself came up and *walked by their side*;
		28	When they drew near to the village to which they were *going*,
		X	he made as if to *go on*.
Jn	4	50	'*Go* home, . . . your son will live.' The man believed what Jesus had said and *started on his way*;
	7	35 X	Where is he *going* . . .? Is he going abroad to the people who are dispersed . . .?
	8	11	[Jesus said to the adulterous woman:] *go* [away], and don't sin any more.
	10	4 <	[the shepherd] *goes* ahead of them, and the sheep follow
	11	11 X	Lazarus is resting, I am *going* to wake him.
Ac	5	20	*Go* and stand in the Temple, and tell the people all about this new Life.
		41	[the apostles] *left* [the presence of] the Sanhedrin
	8	26	[Philip,] be ready to set out at noon to *go* along the road that goes from Jerusalem down to Gaza,
		27	[Philip] set off and *went on his journey*,
		36	⌐Further (lit. As they *went*) along the road they came to some water,
		39	the eunuch . . . *went* on his way rejoicing.
	9	3	[Saul] was *travelling* to Damascus and just before he reached the city, there came a light from heaven
		11	[Ananias,] you must [set out and] *go* to Straight Street
		15	You must *go* . . . because this man is my chosen instrument
	10	20	Hurry down, and do not hesitate about *going* [back] with them;
	16	36	you can go now and *be on your way* (§ in peace).
	17	14	the brothers arranged for Paul to *go* immediately as far as the coast,
	21	5	we *set off* . . . and . . . they all escorted us on our way
	22	6	I was *on that journey* and nearly at Damascus
		21	*Go!* I am sending you out to the pagans far away.
	23	23	[the tribune] said, 'Get two hundred soldiers ready to *leave* for Caesarea'
	24	25	Felix . . . said [to Paul], 'You may *go* for the present'
	25	12	You have appealed to Caesar; to Caesar you shall *go*.
	26	13	a light . . . shone brilliantly round me and ⌐my fellow travellers (lit. those who *travelled* with me).
1 Co	10	27	If an unbeliever invites you to his house, *go* if you want to,
	16	4	if it seems worth while for me to *go* [to Jerusalem] too, they can *travel* with me.
		6	make sure that it is you who send me on my way wherever ⌐my travels take me (lit. I *go*).

2: (JESUS) GOES (FROM THE WORLD)

Lk	22	22	The Son of Man does indeed *go* to his fate

Jn 14	2	I am *going* now to prepare a place for you, ³ and after I have *gone* and prepared you a place, I shall return
	12	I am *going* to the Father.
	28	If you loved me you would have been glad to know that I am *going* to the Father,
16	7	if I do *go*, I will send [the Advocate] to you.
	28	now I leave the world to *go* to the Father.
Ac 1	10	[The apostles] were still staring into the sky where he had *gone*
	11	Jesus will come back in the same way as you have seen him *go* [to heaven].
1 P 3	19	in the spirit, [Christ] *went* to preach to the spirits in prison.
	22	[Jesus Christ] has *entered* heaven and is at God's right hand,

3: GO (FIGURATIVELY) – FOLLOW – LIVE, BEHAVE

Lk 1	6	[Zechariah and Elizabeth] scrupulously ⌐observed (lit. *followed*) all the commandments . . . of the Lord.
21	8	many will come using my name . . . ⌐Refuse to (lit. Do not *go* and) join them.
Ac 9	31	The churches . . . were now left in peace, . . . *living* in the fear of the Lord,
14	16	In the past [God] allowed each nation to *go* its own way;
1 P 4	3	living the sort of life that pagans live, *behaving* indecently,
2 P 2	10	those who ⌐are governed by (lit. *follow*) their corrupt bodily desires
3	3	there are bound to be people who will be scornful, the kind who always ⌐please themselves what they do (lit. *follow* their own desires),
Jude	11	they have *followed* Cain;
	16	They are . . . grumblers ⌐governed only by (lit. who *follow*) their own desires,
	18	there are going to be people who . . . *follow* nothing but their own desires

4: GOING = PURSUITS, BUSINESS

Lk 8	14	as they *go on their way* they are choked by the worries and riches and pleasures of life
Jm 1	11	3 It is the same with the rich man: his *business* goes on; he himself perishes.

3. GO: *HYP-AGŌ*

2 agō 7/67   1 hyp-agō 79

1: GO

Mt 4	10	ⓐ	*Be off*, Satan!
5	24		*go* and be reconciled with your brother first,
	41		if anyone orders you to go one mile, *go* two miles with him.
8	4		*go* and show yourself to the priest
	13		*Go* [back], then; you have believed, so let this be done for you.
	32	ⓐ	[Jesus] said to [the devils], '*Go* then', and they came out and made for the pigs;
9	6		[Jesus] said to the paralytic, '. . . *go off* home'.
13	44		[the man who has found treasure] *goes off* happy,
16	23		[Jesus] said to Peter, ⌐Get (lit. *Go*) behind me, Satan!'
18	15		If your brother does something wrong, *go* and have it out with him alone,
19	21		If you wish to be perfect, *go* and sell what you own
20	4	<	'You *go* to my vineyard too' . . . ⁵ So they went.
	7	<	You *go* into my vineyard too.
	14	<	Take your earnings and *go*.
21	28	<	My boy, you *go* and work in the vineyard today.
26	18		*Go* to so-and-so in the city
	24	X	The Son of Man is *going* to his fate, as the scriptures say he will,
	46		2 Get up! Let us *go*! My betrayer is already close at hand.
27	65		*Go* and make all as secure as you know how.
28	10		*go* and tell my brothers that they must leave for Galilee;
Mk 1	38		2 Let us *go* elsewhere, to the neighbouring country towns,
	44		*go* and show yourself to the priest,
2	11		get up, pick up your stretcher, and *go off* home.
5	19		*Go* home to your people
	34		My daughter, . . . *go* in peace and be free from your complaint.
6	31		there were so many coming and *going*
	33		people saw them *going*, and many could guess where;
	38		How many loaves have you? . . . *Go* and see.
7	29		you may *go* home happy; the devil has gone out of your daughter.
8	33		[Jesus said to Peter:] ⌐Get (lit. *Go*) behind me, Satan!
10	21		*Go* and sell everything you own and . . . follow me.
	52		*Go*; your faith has saved you.
11	2		*Go off* to the village facing you,

Mk 14	13		*Go* into the city and you will meet a man
	21	X	the Son of Man is *going* to his fate, as the scriptures say he will,
	42		2 Get up! Let us *go*! My betrayer is close at hand already.
16	7		you must *go* and tell his disciples . . , 'He is going before you to Galilee'
Lk 8	42	X	the crowds were almost stifling Jesus as he *went* [to Jairus's house].
10	3		*Start off* now, but remember, I am sending you out like lambs among wolves.
12	58		when you *go* to court with your opponent, try to settle with him on the way,
17	14		'Go and show yourselves to the priests'. Now as they were *going* [away] they were cleansed.
19	30		*Go off* to the village opposite,
Jn 3	8		you cannot tell where [the wind] comes from or where it is *going*. That is how it is with all who are born of the Spirit.
4	16		*Go* and call your husband . . . and come back here.
6	21		the boat . . . reached the shore at the place they were *making* for.
	67	○	do you want to *go* away too?
7	3	X	his brothers said to [Jesus], 'Why not leave this place and *go* to Judaea . . . ?'
9	7		*Go* and wash in the Pool of Siloam
	11		[Jesus] said to me, '*Go* and wash at Siloam';
11	7	X	2 [Jesus said] to the disciples, 'Let us *go* to Judaea'.
	8	X	the Jews wanted to stone you; are you *going* back again?
	15	X	2 [Lazarus is dead;] let us *go* to him.
	16		2 Thomas . . . said to the other disciples, 'Let us *go* too, and die with him'.
	31		[the Jews] followed [Mary], thinking that she was *going* to the tomb
	44		Unbind [Lazarus], let him *go* [free].
12	11	○	many of the Jews were *leaving* [the chief priests] and believing in Jesus.
	35	<	he who walks in the dark does not know where he is *going*.
14	31	X	2 Come now, let us *go*,
15	16	○	I commissioned you to *go* out and to bear fruit,
	18		If I am the one you are looking for, let these others *go*.
21	3		Simon Peter said, 'I'm *going* fishing'.
Jm 2	16		⌐I wish you well (lit. *Go* in peace); keep yourself warm and eat plenty,
1 Jn 2	11	<	the man who hates his brother . . . is in the darkness, not knowing where he is *going*,
Rv 10	8		*Go* . . . and take that open scroll out of the hand of the angel
13	10		Captivity for those who are destined ⌐for (lit. to *go* into) captivity;
14	4	X	they follow the Lamb wherever he *goes*;
16	1		*Go*, and empty the seven bowls of God's anger over the earth.
17	8		The beast . . . is yet to come up from the Abyss, but only to *go* to his destruction.
	11		the eighth [emperor] is *going* to his destruction.

2: (JESUS) GOES (TO THE FATHER)

Jn 7	33	then I shall *go* [back] to the one who sent me.
8	14	I know where I came from and where I am *going*; but you do not know where I come from or where I am *going*.
	21	I am *going* [away]; . . . Where I am *going*, you cannot come.
	22	Will he kill himself? Is that what he means by saying, 'Where I am *going*, you cannot come'?
13	3	Jesus knew that . . . he had come from God and was ⌐returning (lit. *going*) to God,
	33	where I am *going*, you cannot come.
	36	Simon Peter said, 'Lord, where are you *going*?' Jesus replied, 'Where I am *going* you cannot follow me now'
14	4	You know the way to the place where I am *going*.
	5	Lord, we do not know where you are *going*,
	28	I am *going* [away], and shall return.
16	5	now I am *going* to the one who sent me. Not one of you has asked, 'Where are you *going*?'
	10	[The Advocate will show the world how wrong it was] about who was in the right: . . . proved by my *going* to the Father and your seeing me no more;
	17	What does he mean, '. . . I am *going* to the Father'?

4. GO – SET OUT FOR: *AP-ERCHOMAI*

2 ap-eimi 1   1 ap-erchomai 118

1: (JESUS) GOES, LEAVES (FOR), SETS OUT (FOR)

a) towards: ap-erchomai eis

Mt 8	18	Jesus . . . gave orders to *leave for* the other side.
16	21	Jesus . . . was destined to *go to* Jerusalem and suffer grievously

Mk 1 35 [Jesus] *went off to* a lonely place and prayed there.
6 32 [Jesus and the disciples] *went off* in a boat *to* a lonely place
46 he *went off into* the hills to pray.
7 24 He left that place and *set out for* the territory of Tyre.
8 13 re-embarking he *went away to* the opposite shore.
Jn 4 3 he left Judaea and *went back to* Galilee.
10 40 He *went back* again *to* the far side of the Jordan to stay in the district where John had once been baptising.
11 54 Jesus . . . *left* . . . *for* the country bordering on the desert,

b) various: ap-erchomai only

Mt 8 19 One of the scribes . . . said to [Jesus], 'Master, I will follow you wherever you *go*'.
16 4 leaving [the Pharisees] standing there, [Jesus] *went away*.
26 36 Stay here while I *go* over there to pray.
42 Again, a second time, [Jesus] *went away* and prayed:
44 Leaving [the disciples sleeping] he *went away* again and prayed
Mk 5 17 [the Gerasenes] began to implore Jesus to *leave* the neighbourhood.
24 Jesus *went* with [the synagogue official] and a large crowd followed him;
14 39 Again [Jesus] *went away* and prayed,
Lk 8 37 The entire population of the Gerasene territory . . . asked Jesus to *leave* them.
9 57 I will follow you wherever you *go*.
Jn 6 1 Jesus *went off to* the other side of the Sea of Galilee
12 36 Having said this, Jesus *left* them and kept himself hidden.
16 7 it is for your own good that I am *going* because unless I *go* the Advocate will not come to you;

2: (A PERSON) GOES, MAKES FOR, SETS OUT (FOR)

a) towards: ap-erchomai eis

Mt 5 30 it will do you less harm to lose one part of you than to have your whole body *go to* hell.
8 32 ⓓ [the devils] came out and *made for* the pigs;
33 The swineherds ran off and *made for* the town,
9 7 [the paralytic] got up and *went* home.
10 5 Do not *turn your steps to* pagan territory,
14 15 the people . . . can *go to* the villages to buy themselves some food.
22 5 one *went off to* his farm, another to his business,
25 46 they will *go away to* eternal punishment, and the virtuous to eternal life.
28 10 go and tell my brothers that they must *leave for* Galilee;
Mk 6 36 send [the people] away, and they can *go to* the farms
7 30 [the Syrophoenician woman] *went off to* her home
9 43 it is better for you to enter into life crippled, than to have two hands and *go to* hell,
Lk 1 23 When his time of service came to an end [Zechariah] *returned* home.
5 25 [the paralysed man] got up . . . and *went* home praising God.
8 31 ⓓ [the devils] pleaded with [Jesus] not to order them to *depart into* the Abyss.
Jn 4 8 His disciples had *gone into* the town to buy food.
28 The woman put down her water jar and *hurried* [back] *to* the town
6 66 many of his disciples *left* [Jesus] and stopped going with him.
18 6 [the soldiers] *moved back* and fell to the ground.
Ac 17 10 2 [Paul and Silas] ʳ*visited* (or: *went to*) the Jewish synagogue as soon as they arrived [at Beroea].
Rm 15 28 I shall *set out for* Spain and visit you on the way.
Ga 1 17 nor did I go up to Jerusalem . . . I *went off to* Arabia

b) to a person (or his home): ap-erchomai pros

Mk 3 13 [Jesus] summoned those he wanted. So they *came to* him
14 10 Judas Iscariot . . . *approached* the chief priests with an offer to hand Jesus over to them.
Lk 24 12 ᵛ Peter . . . *went back* [home], amazed at what had happened.ˡ
Jn 4 47 [the court official] *went* and asked [Jesus] to come and cure his son
6 68 Lord, who shall we *go to*? You have the message of eternal life,
11 46 some of [the Jews] *went to* [tell] the Pharisees
20 10 The disciples then *went* [home again].
Rv 10 9 I *went to* the angel and asked him to give me the small scroll,

c) Go away, after – Make off: ap-erchomai only

Mt 2 22 [Joseph] was afraid to *go* [to Judaea],
8 21 Sir, let me *go* and bury my father first.
13 25 his enemy came, sowed darnel . . . and *made off*.
28 Do you want us to *go* and weed it out?
46 [the merchant] *goes* and sells everything he owns
14 16 There is no need for them to *go*: give them something to eat
18 30 [the debtor] *went* and had [his fellow servant] thrown into prison

Mt 19 22 when the young man heard these words he *went away* sad, for he was a man of great wealth.
20 5 < [You go to my vineyard too . . .] So they *went*.
21 29 (30) < afterwards [the first son] thought better of it and *went* [to the vineyard].
30 (29) < the second [son] answered, 'Certainly, sir', but did not *go*.
22 22 [the Pharisees] left [Jesus] alone and *went away*.
25 10 [The five bridesmaids] had *gone off* to buy [oil]
18 the man who had received one [talent] *went off* and dug a hole in the ground and hid his master's money.
25 I *went off* and hid your talent in the ground.
27 5 [Judas] *made off*, and *went* and hanged himself.
60 [Joseph] rolled a large stone across the entrance of the tomb and *went away*.
28 8 the women *came* quickly *away* from the tomb and ran to tell the disciples.
Mk 1 20 leaving their father Zebedee . . . [James and John] *went after* him.
5 20 [the cured demoniac] *went off* and proceeded to spread throughout the Decapolis all that Jesus had done for him.
6 27 The man *went off* and beheaded [John the Baptist] in prison;
37 Are we to *go* and spend two hundred denarii on bread . . .?
10 22 he *went away* sad, for he was a man of great wealth.
11 4 [The disciples] *went off* and found a colt tethered
12 12 [the elders] left [Jesus] alone and *went away*.
14 12 Where do you want us to *go* and make the preparations for you to eat the passover?
16 13 These [two disciples] *went back* and told the others [that Jesus had appeared to them],
Lk 1 38 the angel *left* [Mary].
2 15 when the angels had *gone* . . . the shepherds said to one another, 'Let us go to Bethlehem'
5 14 *go* and show yourself to the priest
7 24 When John's messengers had *gone* [Jesus] began to talk
8 39 [the cured demoniac] *went off* and spread throughout the town all that Jesus had done for him.
9 59 Let me *go* and bury my father first.
60 your duty is to *go* and spread the news of the kingdom of God.
10 30 [the brigands] then *made off*, leaving him half dead.
17 23 They will say to you, 'Look [the Son of Man]!' . . . *Make no move*; do not set off in pursuit;
19 32 The messengers *went off* and found everything just as he had told them.
22 4 [Judas] *went to* the chief priests
13 [The disciples] *set off* and found everything as he had told them,
24 24 Some of our friends *went to* the tomb
Jn 5 15 The man *went back* and told the Jews that it was Jesus who had cured him.
6 22 the disciples had *set off* by themselves.
9 7 the blind man *went off* and washed himself [in the Pool of Siloam] and came away with his sight restored.
11 I *went*, and when I washed I could see.
11 28 [Martha] *went* and called her sister Mary,
12 19 ○ look, the whole world is *running after* him!
Ac 4 15 [the Sanhedrin] ordered [Peter and John] to ʳstand outside (lit. *go* [out])
5 26 The captain *went* with his men and fetched [the apostles].
9 17 Ananias *went* . . . and . . . laid his hands on Saul
10 7 When the angel . . . had *gone*, Cornelius called two of the slaves
16 39 [The magistrates] came and begged [Paul and Silas] to *leave* the town.
23 32 [The soldiers] left the mounted escort to *go on* with [Paul]
28 29 (ᵛ When he said this, the Jews *went away* arguing among themselves.)
Jm 1 24 [To listen to the word and not obey is like looking at your own features in a mirror,] *going off* and immediately forgetting what you looked like.
Rv 12 17 ⓓ the dragon . . . *went away* to make war on the rest of [the woman's] children,
16 2 The first angel *went* and emptied his bowl over the earth;

3: GONE, LEFT, PASSED (FIGURATIVELY)

Mt 4 24 [Jesus's] fame *spread* throughout Syria,
Mk 1 42 the leprosy *left* him at once and he was cured.
Lk 5 13 the leprosy *left* him at once.
Jude 7 Sodom and Gomorrah . . . are ʳpaying for their crimes (lit. being punished for having *gone after* such immoral practices) in eternal fire.
Rv 9 12 That was how the first of the troubles *passed*; there are still two more to come.
11 14 That was how the second of the troubles *passed*; the third is to come quickly after it.
18 14 All the fruits . . . *gone* for ever, never to return,
21 1 the first heaven and the first earth had *disappeared* now,
4 The world of the past has *gone*.

5. GO – DEPART: *APH-IXIS*

aph-ixis 1

Ac 20 29   when I have ⌐gone (or: *departed*) fierce wolves will invade you

6. GO ABROAD – JOURNEY – TRAVEL: *APO-DĒMEŌ*

1 *apo-dēmeō 6*   2 *syn-ek-dēmos 2*
3 *apo-dēmos 1*

Mt 21 33   a man . . . leased [his vineyard] to tenants and *went abroad.*
   25 14   a man *on his way abroad* . . . summoned his servants and
      15   entrusted his property to them. ¹⁵ . . . Then he *set out.*
Mk 12 1   A man . . . leased [his vineyard] to tenants and *went abroad.*
   13 34   3 It is like a man *travelling abroad:*
Lk 15 13   the younger son . . . *left* for a distant country
   20 9   A man . . . leased [his vineyard] to tenants, and *went abroad*
Ac 19 29   the mob [was] dragging along two of Paul's Macedonian
      2   *travelling companions,* Gaius and Aristarchus.
2 Co 8 19   the same brother . . . has been elected by the churches to
     2   be our *companion on* [this] *errand*

7. BE GONE, DEPART – RETURN: *ANA-LUŌ*

ana-luō 2

Lk 12 36 <   Be like men waiting for their master to *return* from the
        wedding feast,
Ph 1 23   I want to *be gone* and be with Christ,

8. GET OUT – GO: *APO-* and *EK-BAINŌ*

1 *apo-bainō 4*   3 *ek-bainō 1*
2 *ek-basis 2*

1: COME ASHORE – GO OUT (OF A BOAT)

Lk 5 2   [Jesus] caught sight of two boats . . . The fishermen had
        gone out of them
Jn 21 9   As soon as [the disciples] *came* ashore they saw . . . a
        charcoal fire

2: ESCAPE, WAY OUT – OUTCOME

1 Co 10 13   2 with any trial [God] will give you ⌐a *way out* of (or: an *es-*
        cape from) it
Heb 11 15   3 They can hardly have meant the country they *came* from,
   13 7   2 as you reflect on the *outcome* of [your leaders'] lives, imitate
        their faith.

3: GO = TURN, OPPORTUNITY, TIME – GO TOWARDS, HELP TO

Lk 21 13   that will *be* your *opportunity* to bear witness.
Ph 1 19   I know this will *help* to save me.

9. GO BEFORE, GO ON AHEAD

1: GO BEFORE: *PRO-AGŌ*

pro-agō 15/20

a) Go before (a person) – Ahead, In front of

Mt 2 9   there *in front of* [the wise men] was the star . . . it *went*
        forward and halted
  14 22   [Jesus] made the disciples . . . *go on ahead* to the other side
        [of the lake]
  21 9   The crowds who *went in front of* him and those who followed
        were all shouting: Hosanna
    31   tax collectors and prostitutes are *making their way* into the
        kingdom of God *before* you.
  26 32 X   after my resurrection I shall *go before* you to Galilee.
  28 7 X   tell his disciples, 'He has risen from the dead and now he is
        going before you to Galilee'
Mk 6 45   [Jesus] made his disciples . . . *go on ahead* to Bethsaida,
  10 32 X   Jesus was *walking on ahead* of [the disciples] . . . those who
        followed were apprehensive.
  11 9   those who *went in front* and those who followed were all
        shouting, 'Hosanna!'
  14 28 X   after my resurrection I shall *go before* you to Galilee.

Mk 16 7 X   tell his disciples and Peter, 'He is *going before* you to Galilee'
Lk 18 39   The people *in front* scolded [the blind man]

b) Go before (in time) – Earlier

1 Tm 1 18   I ask you to remember the words ⌐once (lit. *earlier*) spoken
        over you by the prophets,
  5 24   The faults of some people are obvious long *before* anyone
        makes any complaint about them,
Heb 7 18   The *earlier* commandment is thus abolished because it was
        neither effective nor useful,

2: GO BEFORE, LEAD – GO ON AHEAD: *PRO-ERCHOMAI*

pro-erchomai 6/9

Mk 6 33   from every town they all hurried to the place on foot and
        reached it *before* [the apostles].
Lk 1 17   With the spirit and power of Elijah, [John] will *go before*
        [the Lord]
  22 47   a number of men appeared, and *at the head of them* [went]
        the man called Judas,
Ac 20 5   [Paul's companions] all *went on* to Troas where they waited
        for us.
    13   We were now to *go on ahead* by sea, so we set sail for Assos,
2 Co 9 5   I have thought it necessary to ask these brothers to *go on*
        to you *ahead* of us,

3: GO BEFORE, LEAD: *PRO-POREUOMAI*

pro-poreuomai 2

Lk 1 76   you will *go before* the Lord to prepare the way for him.
Ac 7 40   [our ancestors] said to Aaron, 'Make some gods to ⌐be our
        leaders (lit. *lead us*)'

10. GO – PASS: *DI-* and *PAR-ERCHOMAI*

1 *di-erchomai 41*   2   *par-erchomai 28/30*
3 *anti-par-erchomai*   2

1: GO THROUGH, PASS THROUGH – SPREAD

a) Go over, through, Pass through, Cross – Travel, Journey – Come, Intervene

Mt 12 43 ⓓ   When an unclean spirit goes out of a man it *wanders through*
        waterless country
Mk 4 35 X   Let us *cross over* to the other side.
  10 25   It is easier for a camel to *pass through* the eye of a needle
        than for a rich man to enter the kingdom of God.
Lk 2 15   Let us *go* to Bethlehem
  4 30 X   he *slipped through* the crowd and walked away.
  8 22 X   Let us *cross over* to the other side of the lake.
  9 6   So [the Twelve] set out and *went* from village to village
  11 24 ⓓ   [the unclean spirit] *wanders through* waterless country
  12 37   [the master] will . . . sit [the servants] down at table and
      2   [*going from one to another*] wait on them.
  17 7   2 *Come* and have your meal immediately
    11 X   he *travelled* along the border between Samaria and Galilee.
  19 1 X   He entered Jericho and was *going through* the town
Jn 4 4 X   he had to *cross* Samaria.
   15   give me some of that water, so that I may never . . . have to
        come here again to draw water.
Ac 8 4   Those who had escaped [the persecution in Jerusalem]
        went from place to place preaching the Good News.
  40   Philip . . . *continued his journey* proclaiming the Good News
        in every town as far as Caesarea.
  9 32   Peter *visited* one place after another and eventually came to
        the saints living down in Lydda.
  38   *Come* and visit us [at Jaffa] as soon as possible.
  10 38 X   Jesus *went about* doing good
  11 19   Those who had escaped during the persecution . . . *travelled*
        as far as Phoenicia
  12 10   [Peter and the angel] *passed through* two guard posts
  13 6   [Paul and Barnabas] *travelled* the whole length of the island
        [of Cyprus],
  14   The others *carried on* from Perga till they reached Antioch
  14 24   [Paul and Barnabas] *passed through* Pisidia
  15 3   [Paul and Barnabas] *passed through* Phoenicia and Samaria
  41   [Paul] *travelled through* Syria and Cilicia
  16 6   [Paul and Timothy] *travelled through* Phrygia and the Galatian
        country,
  8   2 they *went through* Mysia
  17 23   [Paul said, 'Men of Athens,] I *strolled round* admiring your
        sacred monuments'
  18 23   [Paul] spent a short time [at Antioch] before *continuing his*
        journey through the Galatian country and then [through]
        Phrygia,

Ac 18 27	Apollos thought of *crossing over* to Achaia,
19 1	Paul *made his way over*land as far as Ephesus,
21	Paul made up his mind to *go* [back] to Jerusalem *through* Macedonia and Achaia.
20 2	*On his way through* those areas [Paul] said many words of encouragement to them
25	none of you among whom I have *gone about* proclaiming the kingdom will ever see my face again.
24 7	2 (ᵛ the tribune Lysias *intervened* . . .)
1 Co 10 1	our fathers . . . all *passed through* the sea.
16 5	I shall be coming to you after I have *passed through* Macedonia – and I am doing no more than *pass through* Macedonia –
2 Co 1 16	[I had meant to stay] with you before *going* to Macedonia
Heb 4 14 X	in Jesus, the Son of God, we have the supreme high priest who has *gone through* to the highest heaven,

b) Pierce – Spread

Lk 2 35	a sword will *pierce* your own soul too
5 15	[Jesus's] reputation continued to ⌐grow (lit. *spread*),
Rm 5 12	death has *spread* through the whole human race

2: PASS BY

Mt 8 28	2 [the two demoniacs were] so fierce that no one could *pass* that way.
26 39	2 if it is possible, let this cup *pass* me *by*.
42	2 if this (ᵛ cup) cannot *pass by* without my drinking it, your will be done!
Mk 6 48	[Jesus] came towards [the disciples], walking on the lake.
X	2 He was going to *pass* them *by*,
14 35	2 [Jesus] prayed that . . . this hour might *pass* him *by*.
Lk 10 31	3 a priest . . . *passed by on the other side.*
32	3 a Levite . . *passed by on the other side.*
18 37 X	2 they told [the blind man] that Jesus the Nazarene was *passing by.*
19 4 X	2 Jesus . . . was to *pass* that way.

3: PASS AWAY – PAST, GONE – DISAPPEAR

Mt 5 18	2 till heaven and earth *disappear*, not one dot . . . shall
	2 *disappear* from the Law
14 15	2 the time has *slipped by*;
24 34	2 before this generation has *passed away* all these things will have taken place.
35	2 Heaven and earth will *pass away*, but my words will never
	2 *pass away*
Mk 13 30	2 before this generation has *passed away* all these things will have taken place.
31	2 Heaven and earth will *pass away*, but my words will never
	2 *pass away*.
Lk 16 17	2 It is easier for heaven and earth to *disappear* than for one little stroke to drop out of the Law
21 32	2 before this generation has *passed away* all will have taken place.
33	2 Heaven and earth will *pass away*, but my words will never
	2 *pass away*.
Ac 27 9	2 it was now well ⌐after (lit. *past*) the time of the Fast,
2 Co 5 17	2 the old creation has *gone*,
Jm 1 10	2 riches ⌐last no longer than (lit. will *pass away* like) the flowers in the grass;
1 P 4 3	2 You spent quite long enough in the *past* living the sort of life that pagans live,
2 P 3 10	2 with a roar the sky will *vanish*,

11. GO PAST – CROSS – ACROSS: *DIA-* and *PARA-POREUOMAI*

$$1 \begin{cases} peran \\ eis\ to\ peran \end{cases} 23 \qquad 3 \quad dia\text{-}poreuomai\ 5$$
2 *dia-peraō* 6   4 *para-poreuomai* 5

1: PASS BY, GO (PAST) – VISIT – MAKE ONE'S WAY, WALK

Mt 27 39	4 The *passers-by* jeered at [Jesus];
Mk 2 23 X	4 he happened to be *taking a walk* through the cornfields,
9 30 X	4 [Jesus and the disciples] *made their way* through Galilee;
11 20 X	4 Next morning, as [Jesus and the disciples] *passed by*, they saw the fig tree withered to the roots.
15 29	4 The *passers-by* jeered at [Jesus];
Lk 6 1 X	4 he happened to be *taking a walk* through the cornfields,
13 22 X	3 Through towns and villages he *went* teaching,
18 36	3 When [the blind man] heard the crowd *going past* he asked what it was all about,
Ac 16 4	3 [Paul and Timothy] *visited* one town after another,
Rm 15 24	3 I hope to see you *on my way* to Spain

2: CROSS OVER (WATER) – MAKE A CROSSING

Mt 9 1 X	2 He got back in the boat, *crossed* the water and came to his own town.
14 34 X	2 Having *made the crossing*, [Jesus and the disciples] came to land at Gennesaret.
Mk 5 21 X	2 Jesus had *crossed* again in the boat to the other side,
6 53 X	2 Having *made the crossing*, [Jesus and the disciples] came to land at Gennesaret.
Lk 16 26	between us and you a great gulf has been fixed, to stop . . .
	● 2 any *crossing* from your side to ours.
Ac 21 2	2 [At Patara] we found a ship ⌐bound for (lit. which *made the crossing* to) Phoenicia,

3: THE OTHER SIDE, FAR SHORE – ACROSS, BEYOND, TRANS-

J = beyond the Jordan

Mt 4 15 J	(Is 8 23) Way of the sea *on the far side* of Jordan,
25 J	Large crowds followed [Jesus], coming from . . . Judaea and *Trans*jordania.
8 18	Jesus . . . gave orders to leave for *the other side*.
28	[Jesus] reached the country of the Gadarenes *on the other side*,
14 22	[Jesus] made the disciples . . . go on ahead to *the other side*
16 5	The disciples, having crossed to *the other shore*, had forgotten to take any food.
19 1 J	Jesus . . . came into the part of Judaea which is *on the far side* of the Jordan.
Mk 3 8 J	[From] *Trans*jordania and the region of Tyre and Sidon, great numbers . . . came to [Jesus],
4 35	With the coming of evening . . . [Jesus] said to them, 'Let us cross over to *the other side*'.
5 1	They reached the country of the Gerasenes *on the other side* of the lake,
21	Jesus had crossed again in the boat to *the other side*,
6 45	[Jesus] made his disciples get into the boat and go on ahead ᵛ to *the other side*⌐ to Bethsaida,
8 13	leaving [the Pharisees] . . . [Jesus] went away to *the opposite shore*.
10 1 J	[Jesus] came to the district of Judaea and *the far side* of the Jordan.
Lk 8 22	[Jesus] said to [the disciples], 'Let us cross over to *the other side* of the lake'.
Jn 1 28 J	This happened at Bethany, *on the far side* of the Jordan,
3 26 J	the man who was with you *on the far side* of the Jordan . . . is baptising now;
6 1	Jesus went off to *the other side* of the Sea of Galilee
17	[the disciples] got into a boat to make for Capernaum *on the other side* of the lake.
22	the crowd . . . had stayed *on the other side*
25	[the disciples] found [Jesus] *on the other side*,
10 40 J	[Jesus] went back again to *the far side* of the Jordan
18 1	Jesus left with his disciples and crossed ⌐the Kedron valley (lit. to *the other side* of the river).

12. SAIL, GO, ALONG THE COAST – CROSS TO

1: SAIL ALONG THE COAST: *PARA-LEGOMAI*
para-legomai 2

| Ac 27 8 | [we] ⌐struggled along the coast (lit. *went along the coast* with difficulty) |
| 13 | they . . . began to *sail past* Crete, close inshore. |

2: CROSS TO: *PARA-BALLŌ*
para-ballō 1

| Ac 20 15 | The second day we ⌐touched at (or: *crossed to*) Samos |

13. SLIP THROUGH – PIERCE, PENETRATE: *DI-(H)IKNEOMAI*
di-(h)ikneomai 1

| Heb 4 12 ● | The word of God . . . can ⌐*slip through* (or: *pierce*) the place where the soul is divided from the spirit, |

14. GO ON, GO FURTHER – ADVANCE

1: GO ON, GO FURTHER – ADVANCE: *PRO-ERCHOMAI*
pro-erchomai 3/9

Mt	26	39	X	*going* on a little *further* [Jesus] fell on his face and prayed.
Mk	14	35	X	*going* on a little *further* [Jesus] threw himself on the ground and prayed
Ac	12	10		[Peter and the angel] *walked the whole length* of one street

2: GO ON: *PRO-BAINŌ*
pro-bainō 5

a) Go on, Go further

Mt 4 21 X   *Going on* from there he saw another pair of brothers, James . . . and . . . John;

Mk 1 19 X   *Going on* a little further, he saw James . . . and his brother John;

b) Advance in age – Be well on

Lk 1 7   [Zechariah and Elizabeth] were both ⌐*getting on* (or: *advanced*) in years.

18   I am an old man and my wife is *getting on* in years.

2 36   Anna . . . was *well on* in years . . . [37] . . . She was now eighty-four

3: GO FURTHER, GO ON: *PROS(-EAŌ)*
pros(-eaō) 1

Ac 27 27   The wind would not allow us to ⌐*touch there* (or: *go on further*)

4: ADVANCE – PROGRESS: *PRO-KOPTŌ*
2 pro-kopē 3   1 pro-koptō 6

Lk 2 52 X   Jesus *increased* in wisdom . . . and in favour with God and men.

Rm 13 12   The night is *almost over*,

Ga 1 14   [You must have heard] ⌐how I stood out (lit. *of my progress*) among other Jews of my generation.

Ph 1 12   the things that happened to me have actually ⌐been a help to 2 (lit. *served to advance*) the Good News.

25   2 I shall . . . stay with you all, and help you to *progress* in the faith

1 Tm 4 15   2 everyone will be able to see how you are *advancing*.

2 Tm 2 16   pointless philosophical discussions . . . *lead further and further* away from true religion.

3 9   they will not be able to *go on* any longer: their foolishness . . . must become obvious to everybody.

13   these wicked impostors will *go* from bad to worse,

5: GO TOO FAR, GO BEYOND – GO AHEAD: *PRO-AGŌ*
pro-agō 1/20

2 Jn 9   If anybody does not keep within the teaching of Christ but *goes beyond* it, he cannot have God with him:

15. PASS: *DI-* and *PAR-AGŌ*
2 di-agō 2   1 par-agō 10

1: PASS ONE'S DAYS – LEAD ONE'S LIFE, LIVE

1 Tm 2 2   [there should be prayers offered for everyone] so that we 2 may be able to *live* religious . . . lives in peace and quiet.

Tt 3 3   2 we *lived* then in wickedness and ill-will,

2: PASS ON – PASS BY – PASS AWAY

a) Pass on, by – Walk on, Go along

Mt 9 9 X   As Jesus was *walking on* from there he saw a man named Matthew

27 X   As Jesus *went on his way* two blind men followed him

20 30 X   [the two blind men] heard that it was Jesus who was *passing by*,

Mk 1 16 X   As he was *walking along* by the Sea of Galilee he saw Simon

Mk	2	14	X	As he was *walking on* he saw Levi
	15	21		They enlisted a *passer-by*, Simon of Cyrene . . . to carry his cross
Jn	9	1	X	As he *went along* he saw a man who had been blind from birth.

b) Pass away – Come to an end – Over

1 Co 7 31   the world as we know it is *passing away*.

1 Jn 2 8   the night is *over*,

17   the world, with all it craves for, is *coming to an end*;

16. PASS OVER – PASS AWAY: *DIA-* and *PARA-BAINŌ*
1 dia-bainō 3   2 a-para-batos 1

1: PASS OVER = CROSS – COME ACROSS, COME OVER

Lk 16 26 ●   between us and you a great gulf has been fixed, to stop anyone . . . *crossing* from our side to yours,

Ac 16 9   *Come across* to Macedonia and help us.

Heb 11 29   It was by faith they *crossed* the Red Sea as easily as dry land,

2: NEVER PASSING AWAY = PERMANENT, PERPETUAL

Heb 7 24   2 [Jesus] ⌐can never lose his (lit. has a *perpetual*) priesthood.

17. PASS THROUGH – MAKE ONE'S WAY – GO JOURNEYING:
DI- and *PARA-(H)ODEUŌ*
1 di-(h)odeuō 2   2 par-(h)odos 1

Lk 8 1 X   he *made his way* through towns and villages preaching,

Ac 17 1   *Passing through* Amphipolis and Apollonia, [Paul and Silas] eventually reached Thessalonika,

1 Co 16 7   2 I do not want to make it only a *passing* visit to you

---

GOD

1. God: *theos*
1: God
2: God and the gods
3: The gods
    a) Diana, Artemis
    b) Baal
    c) the (Heavenly) Twins – Castor and Pollux
    d) Moloch – Rephan
    e) Zeus, Jupiter – Hermes, Mercury

2. Gods – Deities – Divinities: *daimonion*

1. GOD: *THEOS*

4	*thea*	*1* (3:a))	8	*theo(-didaktos)*	*1* (1 Th)
2	*(to) theion*	*2* (2:)	9	*theo(-machos)*	*1* (Ac)
3	*theios*	*2/4*	10	*theo(-pneustos)*	*1* (2 Tm)
5	*theiotēs*	*1* (Rm)	11	*theo(-sebēs)*	*1* (Jn)
1	*theos*	*1206/1324*	12	*theo(-stygēs)*	*1* (Rm)
6	*(hē) theos*	*1* (3:a))	13	*a-theos*	*1* (Ep)
7	*theotēs*	*1* (Col)	14	*(philo-)theos*	*1* (2 Tm)

M = God//Man

For Son of God *see* SON – DAUGHTER 1.1:a)

1: GOD

Eli *2* (Mt 27 46)   Emmanuel [Immanuel] *1* (Mt 1 23)
Eloi *2* (Mk 15 34)

Mt 1 23 X   (Is 7 14) *Immanuel*, a name which means '*God*-is-with-us'.

3 9   *God* can raise children for Abraham from these stones.

16   Jesus . . . saw the Spirit of *God* descending like a dove

4 4 M   (Dt 8 3) Man does not live on bread alone but on every word that comes from the mouth of *God*.

7   (Dt 6 16) You must not put the Lord your *God* to the test.

10   (Dt 6 13) You must worship the Lord your *God*,

5 8   Happy the pure in heart: they shall see *God*.

34   do not swear at all, either by heaven, since that is *God's* throne . . .

6 24   No one can be the slave of two masters . . . both of *God* and of money.

Mt 6 30 Now if that is how *God* clothes the grass in the field . . .
9 8 M the crowd . . . praised *God* for giving such power to men.
12 4 how [David] went into the house of *God*
28 if it is through the Spirit of *God* that I cast devils out,
15 3 (M) And why do you . . . break away from the commandment of
4 *God* for the sake of your tradition? ⁴ For *God* said: Do your
duty to your father and mother . . . ⁶ . . . you have made
6 *God's* word null and void by means of your tradition.
31 The crowds . . . praised the *God* of Israel.
16 16 You are the Christ . . . the Son of the living *God*.
23 M the way you think is not *God's* way but man's.
19 6 M what *God* has united, man must not divide.
26 M For men . . . this is impossible; for *God* everything is
possible.
21 12 Jesus then went into the Temple (ᵛ of *God*)
22 16 Master, we know that you . . . teach the way of *God* in an
honest way,
21 give back to Caesar what belongs to Caesar – and to *God*
what belongs to *God*.
29 you understand neither the scriptures nor the power of *God*.
30 For at the resurrection men and women . . . are like the
angels (ᵛ of *God*) in heaven.
31 have you never read what *God* himself said to you: ³² (Ex 3 6)
32 I am the *God* of Abraham, the *God* of Isaac and the *God*
of Jacob? God is God, not of the dead, but of the living.
37 (Dt 6 5) You must love the Lord your *God* with all your heart,
23 22 when a man swears by heaven he is swearing by the throne of
God
26 61 This man said, 'I have power to destroy the Temple of *God*
. . .'
63 I put you on oath by the living *God* to tell us if you are the
Christ,
27 43 He puts his trust in *God*; now let God rescue him if he wants
him.
46 Jesus cried out . ., 'Eli, Eli, lama sabachthani?' that is
(Ps 22 2), 'My *God*, my *God*, why have you deserted me?'
Mk 1 14 Jesus . . . proclaimed the Good News from *God*.
24 I know who you are: the Holy One of *God*.
2 7 (X) Who can forgive sins but *God*?
12 they were all astounded and praised *God*
26 how [David] went into the house of *God*
3 35 Anyone who does the will of *God*, that person is my brother
5 7 What do you want with me, Jesus, son of the Most High
God? Swear by *God* you will not torture me!
7 8 M You put aside the commandment of *God* to cling to human
traditions.
9 How ingeniously you get round the commandment of *God* in
order to preserve your own tradition!
13 you make *God's* word null and void for the sake of your
tradition which you have handed down.
8 33 M the way you think is not *God's* way but man's.
10 9 M what *God* has united, man must not divide.
18 No one is good but *God* alone.
27 M For men . . . it is impossible, but not for *God*: because
everything is possible for *God*.
11 22 Have faith in *God*.
12 14 you teach the way of *God* in all honesty.
17 Give back to Caesar what belongs to Caesar – and to *God*
what belongs to *God*.
24 you understand neither the scriptures nor the power of *God*?
26 how *God* spoke to [Moses] and said: (Ex 3 6) I am the *God* of
27 Abraham, the *God* of Isaac and the *God* of Jacob? ²⁷ He
is *God*, not of the dead, but of the living.
29 (Dt 6 4) the Lord our *God* is the one Lord, ³⁰ (Dt 6 5) and you
30 must love the Lord your *God* with all your heart,
13 19 since the beginning when *God* created the world,
15 34 Jesus cried out . ., 'Eloi, Eloi, lama sabachthani?' which
means, (Ps 22 2) 'My *God*, my *God*, why have you deserted
me?'
16 19 at the right hand of *God* [the Lord Jesus] took his place,
Lk 1 6 [Zechariah and Elizabeth] were worthy in the sight of *God*,
8 [Zechariah] was exercising his priestly office before *God*
16 [John] will bring back many of the sons of Israel to the Lord
their *God*
19 I am Gabriel who stand in *God's* presence,
26 the angel Gabriel was sent by *God* to a town . . . called
Nazareth,
30 Mary, do not be afraid; you have won *God's* favour.
32 The Lord *God* will give [Jesus] the throne of his ancestor
David;
37 for nothing is impossible to *God*.
47 my spirit exults in *God* my saviour;
64 [Zechariah] spoke and praised *God*.
68 Blessed be the Lord, the *God* of Israel,
78 this by the tender mercy of our *God*
2 13 there was a great throng of the heavenly host, praising *God*
14 M Glory to *God* in the highest heaven,
20 the shepherds went back glorifying and praising *God*
28 [Simeon] blessed *God*;
38 [Anna] began to praise *God*;

Lk 2 40 *God's* favour was with [the child Jesus].
52 M Jesus increased . . . in favour with *God* and men.
3 2 M the word of *God* came to John
6 (Is 40 5 G) And all mankind shall see the salvation of *God*.
8 *God* can raise children for Abraham from these stones.
38 [Jesus] son of Adam, son of *God*.
4 8 (Dt 6 13) You must worship the Lord your *God*,
12 (Dt 6 16) You must not put the Lord your *God* to the test.
34 I know who you are: the Holy One of *God*.
5 1 the crowd . . . listening to the word of *God*,
21 (X) Who can forgive sins but *God* alone?
25 [the paralysed man] got up . . . and went home praising *God*
26 They were all astounded and praised *God*,
6 4 how [David] went into the house of *God*
12 [Jesus] spent the whole night in prayer to *God*.
7 16 Everyone . . . praised *God* saying, 'A great prophet has
appeared . . . *God* has visited his people'.
29 the tax collectors too, acknowledged *God's* plan by accepting
baptism from John;
30 the Pharisees . . . had thwarted what *God* had in mind for
them.
8 11 the seed is the word of *God*.
21 My mother and my brothers are those who hear the word of
God
28 What do you want with me, Jesus, son of the Most High *God*?
39 Go back home . . . and report all that *God* has done for you.
9 20 'who do you say I am?' . . . 'The Christ of *God*' [Peter] said.
43 everyone was awestruck by the greatness of *God*.
10 27 (Dt 6 5) You must love the Lord your *God* with all your heart,
11 20 if it is through the finger of *God* that I cast out devils,
28 Still happier those who hear the word of *God* and keep it!
42 But alas for you Pharisees! You who . . . overlook justice and
the love of *God*!
49 the Wisdom of *God* said, 'I will send them prophets . . .'
12 6 And yet not one [sparrow] is forgotten in *God's* sight.
8 the Son of Man will declare himself for him in the presence of
God's angels.
9 the man who disowns me . . . will be disowned in the presence
of *God's* angels.
20 *God* said to him, 'Fool . . . the demand will be made for your
soul'
21 So it is when a man stores up treasure for himself in place of
making himself rich in the sight of *God*.
24 yet *God* feeds [the ravens].
28 if that is how *God* clothes the grass in the field
13 13 [the crippled woman] straightened up, and she glorified *God*.
15 10 there is rejoicing among the angels of *God* over one repentant
sinner.
16 13 No servant can be the slave of two masters . . . of *God* and
of money.
15 M *God* knows your hearts. For what is thought highly of by
men is loathsome in the sight of *God*.
17 15 one of [the lepers] turned back praising *God*
18 no one has come back to give praise to *God*, except this
foreigner.
18 2 M a judge . . . who had neither fear of *God* nor respect for man.
4 M Maybe I have neither fear of *God* nor respect for man,
7 Now will not *God* see justice done to his chosen who cry to
him . . .?
11 I thank you, *God*, that I am not . . . like the rest of mankind,
13 *God*, be merciful to me, a sinner.
19 No one is good but *God* alone.
27 M Things that are impossible for men . . . are possible for *God*.
43 [the cured blind man in Jericho] followed him praising *God*,
and all the people who saw it gave praise to *God*
19 37 the whole group of disciples joyfully began to praise *God*
20 21 Master . . . you . . . teach the way of *God* in all honesty.
25 give back to Caesar what belongs to Caesar – and to *God*
what belongs to *God*.
37 (Ex 3 6) Moses . . . calls the Lord the *God* of Abraham, the
38 *God* of Isaac and the *God* of Jacob. ³⁸ Now he is *God*, not
of the dead, but of the living;
22 69 the Son of Man will be seated at the right hand of the Power
of *God*.
23 35 let him save himself if he is the Christ of *God*, the Chosen One.
40 Have you no fear of *God* at all?
47 the centurion . . . gave praise to *God*
24 19 Jesus . . . was a great prophet . . . in the sight of *God* and
of the whole people;
53 they were continually in the Temple praising *God*.
Jn 1 1 X the Word was with *God* and the Word was *God*. ² He was
2 with *God* in the beginning.
6 A man came, sent by *God*.
12 he gave power to become children of *God*, to all who believe
13 in the name of him ¹³ ≠ who was born (G those who are
born) not out of human stock or urge of the flesh or will of
man but of *God* himself.
18 No one has ever seen *God*; it is ᵛ the only Son (G *God*, the only-
begotten), who is nearest to the Father's heart, who has
made him known.

Jn	1	29	John said, 'Look, there is the lamb of *God* that takes away the sin of the world.'
		36	[John] said, 'Look, there is the lamb of *God*'.
		51	you will see . . . above the Son of Man, the angels of *God* ascending and descending.
	3	2	Rabbi . . . you are a teacher who comes from *God*; for no one could perform the signs that you do unless *God* were with him.
		16	*God* loved the world so much that he gave his only Son . . .
		17	¹⁷ For *God* sent his Son into the world not to condemn
		21	it may be plainly seen that what he does is done in *God*.
		33	all who do accept his testimony are attesting the truthfulness
		34	of *God*, ³⁴ since he whom *God* has sent speaks *God*'s own words: *God* gives him the Spirit without reserve . . .
		36	³⁶ . . . anyone who refuses to believe in the Son . . . the anger of *God* stays on him.
	4	10	If you only knew what *God* is offering
		24	*God* is spirit,
	5	18 X	[Jesus] spoke of *God* as his own Father, and so made himself *God*'s equal.
		42	you have no love of *God* in you.
		44	you . . . are not concerned with the approval that comes from the one *God*?
	6	27	the Son of Man . . . on him the Father, *God* himself, has set his seal.
		28	What must we do if we are to do the works that *God* wants?
		29	²⁹ . . . This is working for *God*: you must believe in the one he has sent.
		33	the bread of *God* is that which comes down from heaven
		45	(Is 54 13) They will all be taught by *God*,
		46	the one who comes from *God*: he has seen the Father.
		69	we know that you are the Holy One of *God*.
	7	17	if anyone is prepared . . . he will know whether my teaching is from *God*
	8	40	I tell you the truth as I have learnt it from *God*;
		41	we have one father: *God*. ⁴² Jesus answered: 'If *God* were your
		42	father, you would love me, since I have come here from *God*;'
		47	A child of *God* listens to the words of *God*; if you refuse to listen, it is because you are not *God*'s children.
		54	my glory is conferred by the Father, by the one of whom you say, 'He is our *God*'
	9	3	so that the works of *God* might be displayed in him.
		16	This man cannot be from *God*: he does not keep the sabbath.
		24	Give glory to *God*!
		29	we know that *God* spoke to Moses,
		31	/11 We know that *God* doesn't listen to sinners, but *God* does listen to men who are devout
		33	if this man were not from *God*, he couldn't do a thing.
	11	4	This sickness will end . . . in *God*'s glory
		22	whatever you ask of *God*, [God] will grant you.
		40	if you believe you will see the glory of *God*?
		52	to gather together in unity the scattered children of *God*.
	12	43 M	they put honour from men before the honour that comes from *God*.
	13	3	Jesus knew . . . that he had come from *God* and was returning to *God*,
		31	Now has the Son of Man been glorified, and in him *God* has been glorified.
		32	If *God* has been glorified in him, *God* will in turn glorify him in himself,
	14	1	Trust in *God* still, and trust in me.
	16	2	anyone who kills you will think he is doing a holy duty for *God*.
		27	believing that I came from *God*.
		30	because of this we believe that you came from *God*.
	17	3	And eternal life is this: to know you, the only true *God*, and Jesus Christ whom you have sent.
	20	17	I am ascending to my Father . . . to my *God* and your *God*.
		28 X	Thomas replied [to Jesus], 'My Lord and my *God*!'
	21	19	the kind of death by which Peter would give glory to *God*.
Ac	2	11	we hear them preaching . . . about the marvels of *God*.
		17	In the days to come – it is ʳthe Lord (lit. *God*) who speaks – I will pour out my spirit on all mankind.
		22	Jesus . . . was a man commended to you by *God* by the miracles . . . and signs that *God* worked through him . . .
		23	²³ This man, who was put into your power by the deliberate intention and foreknowledge of *God* . . . ²⁴ . . . *God*
		24	raised him to life,
		30	[David] knew that *God* had sworn him an oath to make one of his descendants succeed him on the throne,
		32	*God* raised this man Jesus to life . . . ³³ Now raised to the
		33	heights by *God*'s right hand, he has received from the Father
		36	the Holy Spirit . . . ³⁶ . . . *God* has made this Jesus . . . both Lord and Christ.
		39	The promise that was made is . . . for all those whom the Lord our *God* will call to himself.
		47	[the faithful] praised *God*
	3	8	[the lame man] went with them into the Temple . . . praising *God*.

Ac	3	9	Everyone could see him walking and praising *God*.
		13	the *God* of Abraham, Isaac and Jacob, the *God* of our ancestors, who has glorified his servant Jesus,
		15	*God*, however, raised him from the dead,
		18	this was the way *God* carried out what he had foretold,
		21	the universal restoration comes which *God* proclaimed,
		22	(Dt 18 15) The Lord *God* will raise up a prophet
		25	You are the heirs of the prophets, the heirs of the covenant *God* made with our ancestors
		26	It was for you in the first place that *God* raised up his servant
	4	10	Jesus Christ . . . whom *God* raised from the dead,
		19 (M)	You must judge whether in *God*'s eyes it is right to listen to you and not to *God*.
		21	all the people were giving glory to *God* for what had happened.
		24	[the apostles] lifted up their voice to *God*
		31	they . . . began to proclaim the word of *God* boldly.
	5	4 M	It is not to men that you have lied, but to *God*.
		29 M	Obedience to *God* comes before obedience to men;
		30	it was the *God* of our ancestors who raised up Jesus . . .
		31	³¹ . . . *God* has now raised him up to be leader and saviour
		32	. . . ³² We are witnesses to all this, we and the Holy Spirit whom *God* has given
		39 M	if it does in fact come from *God* . . . you might find yourselves
	9		fighting against *God*.
	6	2	It would not be right for us to neglect the word of *God*
		7	The word of ʳthe (lit. *God*) continued to spread:
		11	We heard [Stephen] using blasphemous language against Moses and against *God*.
	7	2	The *God* of glory appeared to our ancestor Abraham,
		6	The actual words *God* used . . . are that his descendants would be exiles in a foreign land,
		7	(Gn 15 14) 'But I will pass judgement on the nation . . .' *God* said
		9	But *God* was with [Joseph],
		17	the time drew near for *God* to fulfil the promise he had solemnly made to Abraham,
		20	Moses . . . favoured by *God*.
		25	through [Moses] *God* would liberate them,
		32	(Ex 3 6) I am the *God* of your ancestors, the *God* of Abraham, Isaac and Jacob.
		35	the same Moses . . . was now sent (§ by *God*) to be both leader and redeemer
		37	(Dt 18 15) God will raise up a prophet . . . from among your own brothers.
		45	the country we had conquered from the nations which were driven out by *God* as we advanced.
		46	[David] won *God*'s favour and asked permission to have a temple built for ʳthe House (ᵛ the *God*) of Jacob,
		55	Stephen . . . saw the glory of *God*, and Jesus standing at
		56	*God*'s right hand. ⁵⁶ 'I can see '. . . the Son of Man standing at the right hand of *God*.'
	8	10	[Simon the magician] is the *divine* power
		14	Samaria had accepted the word of *God*,
		20	thinking that money could buy what *God* has given for nothing!
		21	*God* can see how your heart is warped.
	10	2	devout and *God*-fearing . . . [Cornelius] prayed constantly to *God*.
		3	[Cornelius] distinctly saw the angel of *God* come into his house
		4	Your offering of prayers and alms . . . has been accepted by *God*.
		15	What *God* has made clean, you have no right to call profane.
		22	Cornelius . . . is an upright and *God*-fearing man,
		28	*God* has made it clear to me that I must not call anyone profane
		31	Cornelius . . . your alms have been accepted as a sacrifice in the sight of *God*;
		33	Here we all are, assembled in front of ʳyou (G *God*) to hear what message *God* has given you for us.
		34	*God* does not have favourites.
		38	*God* had anointed [Jesus] with the Holy Spirit . . . because
		40	*God* was with him . . . ⁴⁰ yet . . . *God* raised him to life
		41	and allowed him to be seen, ⁴¹ . . . by certain witnesses
		42	*God* had chosen beforehand . . . ⁴² . . . *God* has appointed him to judge everyone, alive or dead.
		46	[Jewish believers] could hear [the pagans] . . . proclaiming the greatness of *God*.
	11	1	the pagans too had accepted the word of *God*,
		9	What *God* has made clean, you have no right to call profane.
		17	I realised then that *God* was giving them the identical thing he gave to us . . . who was I to stand in *God*'s way?
		18	[the Jews in Jerusalem] gave glory to *God*. '*God*' they said 'can evidently grant even the pagans the repentance . . .'
		22	[at Antioch Barnabas] could see for himself that *God* had given grace,
	12	5	the Church prayed to *God* for [Peter] unremittingly.
		23	because [Herod] had not given the glory to *God*.
		24	The word of *God* continued to spread and to gain followers.
	13	5	[Barnabas and Saul] proclaimed the word of *God*.
		7	Sergius Paulus . . . asked to hear the word of *God*,

Ac 13	16	Men of Israel, and fearers of *God*, listen!
	17	The *God* of our nation Israel chose our ancestors,
	21	they demanded a king, and *God* gave them Saul
	23	*God* has raised up for Israel . . . Jesus, as Saviour,
	26	all you who fear *God*,
	30	*God* raised [Jesus] from the dead,
	32	It was to our ancestors that *God* made the promise but [33] it is to us . . . that he has fulfilled it,
	36	Now when David . . . had served *God*'s purposes he died;
	37	The one whom *God* has raised up, however, has not experienced corruption.
	43	Paul and Barnabas urged them to remain faithful to the grace *God* had given them.
	44	to hear the word of ˹the Lord (ᵛ the Lord)
	46	We had to proclaim the word of *God*
14	26	[Paul and Barnabas] sailed for Antioch, where they had originally been commended to the grace of *God* for the work they had now completed.
	27	[Paul and Barnabas] gave an account of all that *God* had done with them,
15	4	[Paul and Barnabas] gave an account of all that *God* had done with them.
	7	[Peter said] *God* made his choice among you: the pagans were to learn the Good News from me . . . [8] In fact *God* . . .
	8	showed his approval of them by giving the Holy Spirit to them . . . [10] It would only provoke *God*'s anger now . . .
	10	
	12	[the assembly] listened to Barnabas and Paul describing all the signs and wonders *God* had worked through them
	14	Simeon has described how *God* first arranged to enlist a people for his name out of the pagans.
	19	pagans who turn to *God*,
	40	Paul . . . was commended by the brothers to the grace of ˹*God* (G the Lord)
16	10	*God* had called us to bring [to Macedonia] the Good News.
	14	Lydia, a ˹devout woman (lit. worshipper of *God*) . . . the Lord opened her heart
	17	Here are the servants of the Most High *God*;
	25	Paul and Silas were praying and singing *God*'s praises,
	32	[Paul and Silas] preached the word ˹of the Lord (G or *God*) to [the gaoler] . . . [34] . . . the whole family celebrated their conversion to belief in *God*.
	34	
17	13	the word of *God* was being preached by Paul in Beroea as well,
18	7	a worshipper of *God* called Justus.
	11	Paul stayed there preaching the word of *God* among them
	13	We accuse this man . . . of persuading people to worship *God*
	21	I will come back . . . *God* willing.
	26	Priscilla and Aquila . . . gave [Apollos] further instruction about the Way (§ of *God*).
19	11	So remarkable were the miracles worked by *God* at Paul's hands
20	21	[Paul] urging both Jews and Greeks to turn to *God* and to believe in our Lord Jesus.
	24	the mission . . . was to bear witness to the Good News of *God*'s grace.
	27	I have without faltering put before you the whole of *God*'s purpose.
	28	the Holy Spirit has made you the overseers, to feed the Church ˹of *God* (ᵛ of the Lord) which he bought with his own blood.
	32	And now I commend you ˹to *God* (G to the Lord),
21	19	[Paul] gave a detailed account of all that *God* had done
	20	They gave glory to *God* when they heard this.
22	3	I was as full of duty towards *God* as you are today.
	14	The *God* of our ancestors has chosen you to know his will,
23	1	I have conducted myself before *God* with a perfectly clear conscience.
	3	*God* will surely strike you,
	4	It is *God*'s high priest you are insulting!
24	14	I worship the *God* of my ancestors,
	15	I hold the same hope in *God* . . . that there will be a resurrection
	16 M	I . . . do my best to keep a clear conscience at all times before *God* and man.
26	6	the promise made by *God* to our ancestors
	8	Why does it seem incredible to you that *God* should raise the dead?
	18	so that [the pagans] may turn . . . from the dominion of Satan to *God*,
	20	I started preaching . . . urging them to repent and turn to *God*,
	22	I was blessed with *God*'s help, and so I have stood firm to this day,
	29	I wish before *God* that . . . you . . . would come to be as I am
27	23	Last night there was standing beside me an angel of the *God*
	24	*God* grants you the safety of all who are sailing with you.
	25	I trust in *God* that things will turn out just as I was told;
	35	[Paul] took some bread, gave thanks to *God*
28	15	[Paul] thanked *God*
	28	this salvation of *God* has been sent to the pagans;

Rm 1	1	Paul . . . specially chosen to preach the Good News that *God* [2] promised long ago
	7	To you all, then, who are *God*'s beloved in Rome . . . may *God* our Father and the Lord Jesus Christ send grace
	8	First I thank my *God* . . . for all of you
	9	*God* . . . knows that I never fail to mention you in my prayers,
	10	the opportunity to visit you, if [*God*] so wills.
	16	the Good News . . . is the power of *God* saving all who have faith . . . [17] since this is what reveals the justice of *God* . . . [18] The anger of *God* is being revealed from heaven against all the impiety . . . [19] For what can be known about *God* is perfectly plain to them since *God* himself has made it plain. [20] Ever since God created the world his everlasting power and *deity* – however invisible – have been there for the mind to see in the things he has made . . . [21] they knew *God* and yet refused to honour him as *God* or to thank him . . . [23] they exchanged the glory of the immortal *God* . . . for the image of mortal man . . . [24] That is why *God* left them to their filthy enjoyments . . . [25] since they have given up *divine* truth for a lie . . . [26] That is why *God* has abandoned them to degrading passions . . . [28] . . . since they refused to see it was rational to acknowledge *God*, *God* has left them to their own irrational ideas . . . [30] Libellers, slanderers, enemies of *God* . . . [32] They know what *God*'s verdict is . . .
	17	
	18	
	19	
	20 5	
	21	
	23 M	
	24	
	25	
	26	
	28	
	30 12	
	32	
2	2 M	*God* condemns that sort of behaviour impartially . . . [3] . . . do you think you will escape *God*'s judgement? [4] Or are you abusing his abundant goodness . . . not realising that this goodness of *God* is meant to lead you to repentance? [5] Your stubborn refusal to repent is only adding to the anger *God* will have towards you
	3 M	
	4	
	5	
	11	*God* has no favourites.
	13	It is not listening to the Law but keeping it that will make people holy in the sight of *God*.
	16	on the day when . . . *God* . . . judges the secrets of mankind.
	17	If you call yourself a Jew . . . and are proud of your *God*,
	23	disobeying [the Law], you bring *God* into contempt.
	24	the name of *God* is blasphemed among the pagans.
	29 M	A Jew like that may not be praised by man, but he will be praised by *God*.
3	2	the Jews are the people to whom *God*'s message was entrusted.
	3	[3] . . . Will their lack of fidelity cancel *God*'s fidelity? [4] That would be absurd. *God* will always be true even though everyone proves to be false . . . [5] But if our lack of holiness makes *God* demonstrate his integrity, how can we say *God* is unjust . . . ? [6] That would be absurd, it would mean *God* could never judge the world. [7] You might as well say that since my untruthfulness makes *God* demonstrate his truthfulness and thus gives him glory, I should not be judged
	4 M	
	5	
	6	
	7	
	11	(Ps 14 2) there is . . . not one who looks for *God*.
	18	(Ps 36 1) there is no fear of *God* before their eyes.
	19	[the Law is meant] to lay the whole world open to *God*'s judgement;
	21	*God*'s justice . . . has now been revealed outside the Law, [22] since it is the same justice of *God* that comes through faith to everyone . . . who believes in Jesus Christ.
	22	
	23	Both Jew and pagan sinned and forfeited *God*'s glory,
	25	[Jesus] was appointed by *God* to sacrifice his life so as to win reconciliation through faith. In this way *God* makes his justice known;
	29	Is God the *God* of Jews alone . . . ? Of the pagans too, most certainly, [30] since there is only one *God*,
	30	
4	2	Abraham . . . would really have had something to boast about, though not in *God*'s sight [3] . . . (Gn 15 6) Abraham put his faith in *God*,
	3	
	6	And David says the same: a man is happy if *God* considers him righteous,
	17	*God* . . . who brings the dead to life and calls into being what does not exist.
	20	Since *God* had promised it, Abraham . . . gave glory to *God*,
5	1	through our Lord Jesus Christ . . . we are . . . at peace with *God*,
	2	we can boast about looking forward to *God*'s glory.
	5	the love of *God* has been poured into our hearts
	8	what proves that *God* loves us is that Christ died for us
	10	we were reconciled to *God* by the death of his Son,
	11	we are filled with joyful trust in *God*, through our Lord Jesus Christ,
	15	it is even more certain that *divine* grace,
6	10	so [Christ's] life now is life with *God*;
	11	you too must consider yourselves to be dead to sin but alive for *God*
	13	offer yourselves to *God* . . . make every part of your body into a weapon fighting on the side of *God*;
	17	thank *God* you submitted . . . to the creed you were taught.
	22	you have been set free from sin, you have been made slaves of *God*,
	23	the present given by *God* is eternal life in Christ Jesus our Lord.

Rm 7 4 you . . . can now give yourselves . . . to him who rose from the dead to make us productive for *God*.
 22 In my inmost self I dearly love *God*'s Law,
 25 Thanks be to *God* through Jesus Christ our Lord! In short, it is I who with my reason serve the Law of *God*,
 8 3 and in that body *God* condemned sin.
 7 to limit oneself to what is unspiritual is to be at enmity with *God*: such a limitation never could . . . submit to *God*'s law. [8] People who are interested only in unspiritual things can never be pleasing to *God*. [9] Your interests, however, are . . . in the spiritual, since the Spirit of *God* has made his home in you.
 8
 9
 14 Everyone moved by the Spirit is a son of *God*.
 16 The Spirit himself and our spirit bear united witness that we are children of *God*. [17] . . . heirs of *God* and coheirs with Christ,
 17
 21 to enjoy the same freedom and glory as the children of *God*.
 27 the pleas of the saints expressed by the Spirit are according to the mind of *God*.
 28 by turning everything to their good *God* co-operates with all those who love [*God*],
 31 With *God* on our side . . . [33] Could anyone accuse those that *God* has chosen? When *God* acquits, [34] could anyone condemn? Could Christ Jesus . . . at *God*'s right hand . . .
 33
 34
 39 [nothing] can ever come between us and the love of *God* made visible in Christ Jesus our Lord.
 9 5 X Christ who is above all, *God* for ever blessed!
 6 Does this mean that *God* has failed to keep his promise?
 8 it is not physical descent that decides who are the children of *God*; it is only the children of the promise
 11 In order ᶠto stress that God's choice is free (lit. that *God*'s selective purpose might stand),
 14 Does it follow that *God* is unjust?
 16 the only thing that counts is not what human beings want or try to do, but the mercy of *God*.
 20 M what right have you, a human being, to cross-examine *God*?
 22 *God* . . . patiently puts up with the people who make him angry,
 26 (Ho 2 1) they will now be called the sons of the living *God*.
 10 1 I pray to *God* for [the Jews] to be saved. [2] I can swear to their fervour for *God* . . . [3] Failing to recognise the righteousness that comes from *God*, they try to promote their own idea of it, instead of submitting to the righteousness of *God*.
 2
 3
 9 if you believe in your heart that *God* raised [Jesus] from the dead, then you will be saved.
 11 1 is it possible that *God* has rejected his people? . . . [2] (Ps 94 14 G) [I] could never agree that *God* had rejected his people . . . Do you remember what scripture says of Elijah – how he complained to *God* about Israel's behaviour?
 2
 8 (Is 29 10) *God* has given them a sluggish spirit,
 21 *God* did not spare the natural branches,
 22 Do not forget that *God* can be severe as well as kind: he is severe to those who fell, and ᶠhe (lit. *God*) is kind to you, but only for as long as he chooses to be,
 23 *God* is perfectly able to graft them back again;
 29 *God* never takes back his gifts or revokes his choice.
 30 you changed from being disobedient to *God*,
 32 *God* has imprisoned all men in their own disobedience
 33 How rich are the depths of *God* – how deep his wisdom and knowledge –
 12 1 Think of *God*'s mercy . . . I beg you . . . by offering your living bodies as a holy sacrifice, truly pleasing to *God*.
 2 discover the will of *God*
 3 Each one of you must judge himself soberly by the standard of the faith *God* has given him.
 13 1 Since all government comes from *God*, the civil authorities were appointed by *God*, [2] and so anyone who resists authority is rebelling against *God*'s decision . . . [4] The state is there to serve *God* for your benefit . . . they carry out *God*'s revenge by punishing wrongdoers.
 2
 4
 6 all government officials are *God*'s officers. [They serve God] by collecting taxes.
 14 3 [people whose faith is not strong,] *God* has welcomed them.
 6 The one who eats meat also does so in honour of the Lord, since he gives thanks to *God*; but then the man who abstains does that too in honour of the Lord, and so he also gives *God* thanks.
 10 We shall all have to stand before the judgement seat of ᶠ*God* (ᵛ Christ);
 11 (Is 45 23 G) By my life – it is the Lord who speaks – . . . every tongue shall praise *God*.
 12 It is to *God*, therefore, that each of us must give an account of himself.
 18 M If you serve Christ in this way you will please *God*
 20 do not wreck *God*'s work over a question of food.
 22 Hold on to your own belief, as between yourself and *God*
 15 4 people who did not give up were helped by *God*. [5] And may he . . . help you all to be tolerant
 6 so that . . . you may give glory to the *God* and Father of our Lord Jesus Christ.

Rm 15 7 It can only be to *God*'s glory . . . for you to treat each other . . . as Christ treated you.
 8 The reason Christ became the servant . . . was not only so that *God* could faithfully carry out the promises . . . [9] it was also to get the pagans to give glory to *God* for his mercy,
 9
 13 May the *God* of hope bring you such joy
 15 since *God* has given me this special position. [16] He has appointed me as a priest . . . bringing the Good News from *God*
 16
 17 I have some reason to be proud of what I, in union with Christ Jesus, have been able to do for *God*.
 19 by the power of the Holy Spirit ᵛ of *God*.
 30 help me through my dangers by praying to *God* for me.
 32 if *God* wills, I shall . . . come to enjoy a period of rest
 33 May the *God* of peace be with you all!
 16 20 The *God* of peace will soon crush Satan beneath your feet.
 26 [the revelation of the mystery] must be broadcast . . . it is all part of the way the eternal *God* wants things to be.
 27 give glory therefore to [*God*] through Jesus Christ
 1 Co 1 1 I, Paul, appointed by *God* to be an apostle . . . [2] to the church of *God* in Corinth . . . [3] May *God* our Father and the Lord Jesus Christ send you grace and peace.
 2
 3
 4 I never stop thanking *God* for all the graces [of *God*] you have received
 9 *God* by calling you has joined you to his Son, Jesus Christ,
 14 I am thankful (ᵛ to *God*) that I never baptised any of you after Crispus and Gaius
 18 those of us who are on the way [to salvation] see [the language of the cross] as *God*'s power to save.
 20 Do you see now how *God* has shown up the foolishness of human wisdom?
 21 If it was *God*'s wisdom that human wisdom should not know *God*, it was because *God* wanted to save those who have faith through the foolishness of the message that we preach.
 24 Christ who is the power and the wisdom of *God*. [25] For *God*'s foolishness is wiser than human wisdom, and *God*'s weakness is stronger than human strength.
 25 M
 27 *God* chose what is foolish by human reckoning . . . [*God*] chose what is weak by human reckoning; [28] those whom the world thinks . . . contemptible are the ones that *God* has chosen . . . [29] The human race has nothing to boast about to *God*,
 28
 29
 30 by *God*'s doing [Christ Jesus] has become our wisdom,
 2 1 I came . . . simply to tell you what *God* had guaranteed.
 5 M your faith should not depend on human philosophy but on the power of *God*.
 7 The hidden wisdom of *God* which we teach . . . is the wisdom that *God* predestined to be for our glory
 9 M we teach . . . all that *God* has prepared for those who love him.
 10 These are the very things that *God* has revealed to us through the Spirit, for the Spirit reaches . . . even the depths of *God*. [11] . . . the depths of *God* can only be known by the Spirit of *God*, [12] . . . we have received the Spirit that comes from *God*, to teach us to understand the gifts that [*God*] has given us . . . [14] An unspiritual person is one who does not accept anything of the Spirit of *God*:
 11 M
 12
 14
 3 6 I did the planting . . . but *God* made things grow.
 7 only *God*, who makes things grow [matters].
 9 We are fellow workers with *God*; you are *God*'s farm, *God*'s building.
 10 By the grace *God* gave me, I . . . laid the foundations,
 16 you were *God*'s temple and . . . the Spirit of *God* was living among you? [17] If anybody should destroy the temple of *God*, *God* will destroy him, because the temple of *God* is sacred;
 17
 19 the wisdom of this world is foolishness to *God*.
 23 but you belong to Christ and Christ belongs to *God*.
 4 1 as . . . stewards entrusted with the mysteries of *God*.
 5 Then will be the time for each one to have whatever praise he deserves, from *God*.
 9 *God* has put us apostles at the end of his parade,
 5 13 But of those who are outside, *God* is the judge.
 6 11 justified through the name of the Lord Jesus Christ and through the Spirit of our *God*.
 13 Food is only meant for the stomach . . . *God* is going to do away with both of them. But the body . . . is for the Lord,
 14 *God*, who raised the Lord from the dead, will . . . raise us up too.
 19 Your body . . . is the temple of the Holy Spirit, who is in you since you received him from *God* . . . [20] . . . you should use your body for the glory of *God*.
 20
 7 7 everybody has his own particular gifts from *God*,
 15 *God* has called you to a life of peace.
 17 each one . . . should continue as he was when *God*'s call reached him.
 19 what does matter is to keep the commandments of *God*.
 24 Each one of you . . . should stay as he was before *God* at the time of his call.

1 Co	7 40	I too have the Spirit of *God*, I think.
	8 3	any man who loves *God* is known by him.
	8	Food, of course, cannot bring us in touch with *God*:
	9 9	Is it about oxen that *God* is concerned . . . ?
	21	I was . . . not free from *God*'s law,
	10 5	most of them failed to please *God*
	13	You can trust *God* not to let you be tried beyond your strength,
	31	whatever you do at all, do it for the glory of *God*.
	32	Never do anything offensive to anyone – to Jews . . . or to the Church of *God*;
	11 3	*God* is the head of Christ.
	7	A man . . . is the image of *God* and reflects God's glory;
	12	both [man and woman] come from *God*.
	13	Ask yourselves if it is fitting for a woman to pray to *God* without a veil;
	16	it is not the custom with us, not in the churches of *God*.
	22	Surely you have enough respect for the community of *God* . . .
	12 3	no one can be speaking under the influence of the Holy Spirit (§ of *God*) and say, 'Curse Jesus',
	6	it is the same *God* who is working in all of them.
	18	*God* put all the separate parts into the body on purpose.
	24	*God* has arranged the body
	28	In the Church, *God* has given the first place to apostles,
	14 2 M	Anybody with the gift of tongues speaks to *God*, but not to other people;
	18	I thank *God* that I have a greater gift of tongues than all of you,
	25	[an unbeliever] would . . . worship *God*, declaring that *God* is among you indeed.
	28	they must . . . speak only to themselves and to *God*.
	33	*God* is not a God of disorder but of peace.
	36	Do you think the word of *God* came out of yourselves?
	15 9	I persecuted the Church of *God*,
	10	but by *God*'s grace that is what I am . . . I, or rather the grace of *God* that is with me, have worked
	15	we are shown up as witnesses who have committed perjury before *God*, because we swore in evidence before *God* that he had raised Christ to life.
	24	After that will come the end, when [Christ] hands over the kingdom to *God*
	28	so that *God* may be all in all.
	34	there are some of you who seem not to know *God* at all;
	38	*God* gives [a grain] the sort of body that he has chosen;
	57	So let us thank *God* for giving us the victory through our Lord Jesus Christ.
2 Co	1 1	From Paul, appointed by *God* to be an apostle . . . to the church of *God* at Corinth . . . ² Grace and peace to you
	2	from *God* our Father and the Lord Jesus Christ.
	3	Blessed be the *God* and Father of our Lord Jesus Christ, a gentle Father and the *God* of all consolation, ⁴ who comforts us . . . so that we can offer others . . . the consolation that we have received from *God* ourselves.
	4	
	9	not to rely on ourselves but only on *God*,
	12	with the reverence and sincerity which come from *God*, and by the grace of *God* we have done this without ulterior motives.
	18	I swear by *God*'s truth,
	20	however many the promises *God* made, the Yes to them all is in [Christ] . . . 'through him' . . . we answer Amen to the praise of *God*. ²¹ Remember it is *God* himself who assures us all,
	21	
	23	By my life, I call *God* to witness
	2 14	Thanks be to *God* who . . . makes us, in Christ, partners of his triumph,
	15	We are Christ's incense to *God*
	17	we do not go round offering the word of *God* for sale, as many other people do. In Christ, we speak . . . as envoys of *God* and in *God*'s presence.
	3 3	you are a letter from Christ . . . written . . . with the Spirit of the living *God*,
	4	Before *God*, we are confident of this through Christ: ⁵ . . . all our qualifications come from *God*.
	5	
	4 2	we will have . . . no deceitfulness or watering down the word of *God* . . . we commend ourselves to every human being with a conscience . . . by stating the truth openly in the sight of *God*.
	6	the same *God* . . . has shone in our minds to radiate the light of the knowledge of *God*'s glory, the glory on the face of Christ.
	7	such an overwhelming power comes from *God*
	15	the more grace is multiplied among people, the more thanksgiving there will be, to the glory of *God*.
	5 1	there is a house built by *God* for us,
	5	This is the purpose for which *God* made us,
	11	*God* knows us for what we really are,
	13	If we seemed out of our senses, it was for *God*;
	18	It is all *God*'s work.
	19	*God* in Christ was reconciling the world to himself,
	20	it is as though *God* were appealing through us . . . be reconciled to *God*.

2 Co	5 21	so that in [Christ] we might become the goodness of *God*.
	6 1	we beg you . . . not to neglect the grace of *God*
	4	we prove we are servants of *God* . . . ⁷ by the power of *God*;
	16	The temple of *God* has no common ground with idols, and that is what we are – the temple of the living *God*. We have *God*'s word for it: (Lv 26 12) . . . I will be their *God* and they shall be my people.
	7 1	let us . . . reach perfection of holiness in the fear of *God*.
	6	But *God* comforts the miserable, and he comforted us,
	9	Yours has been a kind of suffering that *God* approves . . .
	10	¹⁰ To suffer in *God*'s way means changing for the better
	11	. . . ¹¹ Just look at what suffering in *God*'s way has brought you:
	12	[the letter] was to make you realise, in the sight of *God*, your own concern for us.
	8 1	the grace of *God* which was given in the churches in Macedonia;
	5	they offered their own selves first to ʳGod (lit. the Lord) and, under *God*, to us.
	16	I thank *God* for putting into Titus' heart the same concern for you
	9 7	(Pr 22 9 G) *God* loves a cheerful giver.
	8	there is no limit to the blessings which *God* can send you
	11	generous things . . . are the cause of thanksgiving to *God*.
	12	¹² For doing this holy service . . . is also increasing the amount of thanksgiving that *God* receives. ¹³ . . . offering this service . . . makes them give glory to *God*
	13	
	14	all the grace that *God* has given you.
	15	Thanks be to *God* for his inexpressible gift!
	10 4	Our . . . weapons . . . are strong enough, in *God*'s cause, to demolish fortresses.
	5	the arrogance that tries to resist the knowledge of *God*;
	13	taking for our measure the yardstick which *God* gave us
	11 2	the jealousy that I feel for you is *God*'s own jealousy:
	7	by preaching the gospel of *God* to you and taking no fee for it?
	11	Would I do that if I did not love you? *God* knows I do.
	31	The *God* and Father of the Lord Jesus . . . knows that I am not lying.
	12 2	whether still in the body or out of the body . . . *God* knows
	3	whether in the body or out of the body . . . *God* knows
	19	it is before *God* that we, in Christ, are speaking;
	21	I am afraid that . . . my *God* may make me ashamed on your account
	13 4	[Christ] lives now through the power of *God* . . . we shall live with him, through the power of *God*,
	7	We pray to *God* that you will do nothing wrong:
	11	the *God* of love and peace will be with you.
	13	The grace of the Lord Jesus Christ, the love of *God* and the fellowship of the Holy Spirit be with you all.
Ga	1 2 M	[Paul] appointed by Jesus Christ and by *God* the Father who raised Jesus from the dead.
	3	peace of *God* our Father and of the Lord Jesus Christ, ⁴ who . . . sacrificed himself . . . in accordance with the will of *God*
	4	
	10 M	So now whom am I trying to please – man, or *God*?
	13	how merciless I was in persecuting the Church of *God*,
	15	Then ᵛ *God*, who had specially chosen me while I was still in my mother's womb,
	20	I swear before *God* that what I have just written is the literal truth.
	24	[the churches in Judaea] gave glory to *God* for me.
	2 6	*God* has no favourites
	19	I am dead to the Law, so that now I can live for *God*.
	21	I cannot bring myself to give up *God*'s gift:
	3 6	Take Abraham for example: he put his faith in *God*,
	8	Scripture foresaw that *God* was going to use faith to justify the pagans,
	11	The Law will not justify anyone in the sight of *God*,
	17	*God* had expressed his will in due form,
	18	it was precisely in the form of a promise that *God* made his gift to Abraham.
	20	Now there can only be an intermediary between two parties, yet *God* is one.
	21	Does this mean that there is opposition between the Law and the promises of *God*?
	4 4	*God* sent his Son, born of a woman,
	6	*God* has sent the Spirit of his Son into our hearts: the Spirit that cries, 'Abba, Father',
	7	you are not a slave any more; and if *God* has made you son, then he has made you heir.
	14	you welcomed me as an angel of *God*,
	6 7	Don't delude yourself into thinking *God* can be cheated:
	16	Peace and mercy to all . . . who form the Israel of *God*.
Ep	1 1	Paul, appointed by *God* to be an apostle of Christ Jesus,
	2	Grace and peace to you from *God* our Father and from the Lord Jesus Christ.
	3	Blessed be *God* the Father of our Lord Jesus Christ, who has blessed us
	17	the *God* of our Lord Jesus Christ, the Father of glory,
	2 4	*God* . . . was generous with his mercy:

Ep	2	8	you have been saved . . . by a gift from *God*;
		10	We are *God*'s work of art, created in Christ Jesus to live the good life
		12	you had no Christ . . . you were immersed in this world,
		13	without hope and *without God*.
		16	through the cross . . . reconcile them with *God*.
		19	you are . . . part of *God*'s household.
		22	you too . . . are being built into a house where *God* lives, in the Spirit.
	3	2	how I have been entrusted by *God* with the grace
		7	by a gift of grace from *God* who gave it to me
		9	Through all the ages, [the mystery] has been kept hidden in *God*,
		10	how comprehensive *God*'s wisdom really is,
		19	you are filled with the utter fullness of *God*.
	4	6	[one Lord,] one *God* who is Father of all, over all, through all and within all.
		18	[the pagans] are estranged from the life of *God*,
		24	the new self that has been created in *God*'s way,
		30	otherwise you will only be grieving the Holy Spirit of *God*
		32	*God* forgave you in Christ.
	5	1	Try, then, to imitate *God*, as children of his that he loves,
		2	² and follow Christ by loving as he loved you, giving himself up in our place as a fragrant offering and a sacrifice to *God*.
		6	it is for this loose living that *God*'s anger comes down on those who rebel against him.
		20	you are giving thanks to *God* who is our Father in the name of our Lord Jesus Christ.
	6	6 M	because you are slaves of Christ and wholeheartedly do the will of *God*.
		11	Put *God*'s armour on
		13	you must rely on *God*'s armour,
		17	receive the word of *God* from the Spirit to use as a sword.
		23	May *God* the Father and the Lord Jesus Christ grant peace, love and faith
Ph	1	2	peace of *God* our Father and of the Lord Jesus Christ.
		3	I thank my *God*
		8	*God* knows how much I miss you all,
		11	for the glory and praise of *God*.
		14	brothers . . . are getting more and more daring in announcing the Message (§ of *God*) without any fear.
		28	It would be a sign from *God* ²⁹ that he has given you the privilege . . . of suffering for [Christ] as well.
	2	6 X M	[Christ's] state was *divine*, yet he did not cling to his equality with *God*
		9	But *God* raised [Christ] high
		11	every tongue should acclaim Jesus Christ as Lord, to the glory of *God* the Father.
		13	It is *God* . . . who puts both the will and the action into you.
		15	perfect children of *God* among a deceitful and underhand brood,
		27	[Epaphroditus] has been ill . . . but *God* took pity on him,
	3	3	we who worship in accordance with the Spirit of *God*;
		9	the perfection that comes through faith in Christ, and is from *God*
		14	I am racing . . . for the prize to which *God* calls us upwards to receive
		15	If there is some point on which you see things differently, *God* will make it clear to you;
	4	6	if there is anything you need, pray for it, asking *God* for it
		7	that peace of *God*, which is so much greater than we can understand,
		9	Then the *God* of peace will be with you.
		18	the offering that you sent . . . the sacrifice that *God* accepts
		19	In return my *God* will fulfil all your needs,
		20	Glory to *God*, our Father,
Col	1	1	From Paul, appointed by *God* to be an apostle of Christ Jesus,
		2	Grace and peace to you from *God* our Father.
		3	We . . . give thanks for you to *God*, the Father of our Lord Jesus Christ,
		6	you heard about *God*'s grace and understood what this really is.
		10	increasing your knowledge of *God*.
		15 X	[Christ] is the image of the unseen *God*
		25	*God* made me responsible for delivering *God*'s message to you,
		27	It was *God*'s purpose . . . to show all the rich glory of this mystery to pagans.
	2	2	until you really know *God*'s secret (ᵛ the mystery of Christ) ³ in which all the jewels of wisdom and knowledge are hidden.
		9 X 7	In [Christ's] body lives the fullness of *divinity*,
		12	you have been raised up . . . through your belief in the power of *God*
		19	the body . . . can reach its full growth in *God*.
	3	1	Christ . . . sitting at *God*'s right hand.
		3	now the life you have is hidden with Christ in *God*.
		6	all this is the sort of behaviour that makes *God* angry.
		12	You are *God*'s chosen race,
		16	With gratitude in your hearts sing psalms . . . to *God*;

Col	3	17	in the name of the Lord Jesus, giving thanks to *God* the Father through him.
	4	3	Pray . . . asking *God* to show us opportunities for announcing the message
		12	praying that you will . . . always hold . . . to the will of *God*.
1 Th	1	1	the Church in Thessalonika which is in *God* the Father and the Lord Jesus Christ;
		2	We always . . . thank *God* for you all,
		3	before *God* our Father
		4	We know, brothers, that *God* loves you and that you have been chosen,
		8	the word of the Lord started to spread . . . for the news of your faith in *God* has spread everywhere.
		9	people tell us . . . how you broke with idolatry when you were converted to *God* and became servants of the real, living *God*:
	2	2	it was our *God* who gave us the courage to proclaim [*God*'s] Good News to you
		4 M	*God* . . . entrusted [us] with the Good News, and when we are speaking, we are not trying to please men but *God*,
		5	we can swear it before *God*, that never at any time have our speeches been simply flattery,
		8	we were eager to hand over to you . . . ʳthe (lit. *God*'s) Good News
		9	slaving . . . while we were proclaiming *God*'s Good News to you.
		10	You are witnesses, and so is *God*,
		12	appealing to you to live a life worthy of *God*, who is calling you
		13	Another reason why we constantly thank *God* for you is that as soon as you heard . . . *God*'s message, you accepted it for what it really is, *God*'s message
		14 M	you, my brothers, have been like the churches of *God* . . . in Judaea,
		15 M	[the Jews] who put the Lord Jesus to death . . . cannot please *God*
	3	2	our brother Timothy, who is *God*'s helper
		9	How can we thank *God* enough for you, for all the joy we feel before our *God* on your account?
		11	*God* our Father himself, and our Lord Jesus Christ,
		13	may he so confirm your hearts in holiness that you may be blameless in the sight of our *God* and Father
	4	1	make more and more progress in . . . the life that *God* wants, as you learnt from us,
		3	What *God* wants is for you all to be holy.
		5	like the pagans who do not know *God*.
		7	We have been called by *God* to be holy . . . ⁸ . . . anyone
		8 M	who objects is not objecting to a human authority, but to *God*,
		9 8	you have learnt from *God* yourselves to love one another,
		14	those who have died in Jesus: *God* will bring them with him.
		16	At the trumpet of *God* . . . the Lord himself will come down from heaven;
	5	9	*God* never meant us to experience the Retribution,
		18	this is what *God* expects you to do in Christ Jesus.
		23	May the *God* of peace make you perfect and holy;
2 Th	1	1	the Church in Thessalonika which is in *God* our Father and the Lord Jesus Christ;
		2	peace from *God* the Father and the Lord Jesus Christ.
		3	we must be continually thanking *God*
		4	among the churches of *God* we can take special pride in you
		5	It all shows that *God*'s judgement is just, and the purpose of it is that you may be found worthy of the kingdom of *God* . . . ⁶ *God* will very rightly repay with injury those who are injuring you,
		8	all who do not acknowledge *God* and refuse to accept the Good News of our Lord Jesus.
		11	we pray . . . that our *God* will make you worthy of his call,
		12	Christ will be glorified in you . . . by the grace of our *God* and the Lord Jesus Christ.
	2	11	*God* is sending a power to delude them
		13	we must be continually thanking *God* for you, brothers whom the Lord loves, because *God* chose you
		16	May our Lord Jesus Christ himself, and *God* our Father [comfort you]
	3	5	May the Lord turn your hearts towards the love of *God* and the fortitude of Christ.
1 Tm	1	1	From Paul, apostle of Christ Jesus appointed by the command of *God* our saviour and of Christ Jesus
		2	to Timothy . . . peace from *God* the Father and from Christ Jesus
		4	the designs of *God* which are revealed in faith.
		11	the Good News of the glory of the blessed *God*,
		17	To the eternal King, the undying, invisible and only *God*,
	2	3	*God* our saviour: ⁴ he wants everyone to be saved
		5 M	there is only one *God*, and there is only one mediator between *God* and mankind . . . Christ Jesus,
	3	5	how can any man who does not understand how to manage his own family have responsibility for the church of *God*?

1 Tm 3 15 I wanted you to know how people ought to behave in *God*'s family – that is, in the Church of the living *God*,
4 3 rules about abstaining from foods which *God* created
4 Everything *God* has created is good . . . ⁵ the word of *God* and the prayer make it holy.
5 the living *God* . . . is the saviour of the whole human race but particularly of all believers.
10 this is what pleases *God*.
5 4 a woman who is really widowed . . . can give herself up to *God*
5 Before *God*, and before Jesus Christ and the angels he has chosen, I put it to you as a duty
21 so that the name of *God* and our teaching are not brought into disrepute.
6 1 as a man dedicated to *God*, you must avoid all that.
11 before *God* . . . and before Jesus Christ . . . I put to you the duty
13 Warn those who are rich . . . not to set their hopes on money . . . but on *God*
17

2 Tm 1 1 From Paul, appointed by *God* to be an apostle of Christ Jesus
2 to Timothy . . . peace from *God* the Father and from Christ Jesus
3 Night and day I thank *God*,
6 I am reminding you now to fan into a flame the gift that *God* gave you
7 *God*'s gift was not a spirit of timidity,
8 bear the hardships . . . relying on the power of *God*
2 9 they cannot chain up *God*'s news.
14 tell them in the name of *God* that there is to be no wrangling about words:
15 Do all you can to present yourself in front of *God* as a man who has come through his trials,
19 *God*'s solid foundation stone is still in position,
25 *God* may give them a change of mind
3 4 14 [people will be] preferring their own pleasure to *God*.
16 10 All scripture is inspired by *God* and can profitably be used
17 This is how the man who is dedicated to *God* becomes fully equipped
4 1 Before *God* and before Christ Jesus . . . I put this duty to you . . . ² proclaim the message

Tt 1 1 From Paul, servant of *God*, an apostle of Jesus Christ to bring those whom *God* has chosen to faith . . . ² and to give them the hope of the eternal life that was promised so long ago by *God*. He does not lie ³ and so . . . he revealed his decision, and, by the command of *God* our saviour, I have been commissioned to proclaim it.
3
4 To Titus . . . peace from *God* the Father and from Christ Jesus
7 as president, he will be *God*'s representative,
16 [those who have been corrupted] claim to have knowledge of *God*
2 5 so that the message of *God* is never disgraced.
10 they are . . . a credit to the teaching of *God* our saviour.
11 *God*'s grace has been revealed,
13 X the glory of our great *God* and saviour Christ Jesus.
3 4 the kindness and love of *God* our saviour for mankind were revealed,
8 those who now believe in *God*

Phm 3 the peace of *God* our Father and the Lord Jesus Christ.
4 I always mention you in my prayers and thank *God* for you,

Heb 1 1 *God* . . . ² . . . has spoken to us through his Son,
6 (Ps 97 7 G) Let all the angels of *God* worship him.
8 X (Ps 45 7) *God*, your throne shall last for ever and ever;
9 (Ps 45 8) *God*, your *God*, has anointed you with the oil of gladness,
2 4 *God* himself confirmed their witness with signs
9 by *God*'s grace [Jesus] had to experience death
13 (Is 8 18) Here I am with the children whom *God* has given me.
17 so that [Christ] could be a compassionate and trustworthy high priest of *God*'s religion.
3 4 *God* built everything that exists.
12 a wicked mind, so unbelieving as to turn away from the living *God*.
4 4 (Gn 2 2) *God* rested on the seventh day.
9 a place of rest reserved for *God*'s people, the seventh-day rest,
10 rest after your work, as *God* did after his.
12 The word of *God* is something alive and active:
5 1 M Every high priest . . . is appointed to act for men in their relations with *God*,
4 No one takes this honour on himself, but each one is called by *God*,
10 [Jesus] was acclaimed by *God* with the title of high priest
12 you need someone to teach you . . . the elementary principles of interpreting *God*'s oracles;
6 1 without going over the fundamental doctrine again: the turning . . . towards faith in *God*;
3 This, *God* willing, is what we propose to do.
5 [those who] appreciated the good message of *God*
7 A field . . . is given *God*'s blessing.
10 *God* would not be so unjust as to forget

Heb 6 13 M *God* . . . swore by his own self,
17 In the same way . . . *God* . . . conveyed this by an oath,
18 ¹⁸ so that there would be two unalterable things in which it was impossible for *God* to be lying,
7 1 Melchizedek . . . a priest of *God* Most High,
19 something better – the hope that brings us nearer to *God*.
25 [Jesus] is living for ever to intercede for all who come to *God*
8 10 (Jr 31 33) I will be their *God* and they shall be my people.
9 14 how much more effectively the blood of Christ, who offered himself . . . to *God* . . . so that we do our service to the living *God*.
20 (Ex 24 8) This is the blood of the covenant that *God* has laid down for you.
24 Christ had entered . . . heaven itself, so that he could appear in the actual presence of *God*
10 7 (Ps 40 9) *God*, here I am! I am coming to obey your will.
12 [Jesus] has taken his place for ever, at the right hand of *God*,
21 we have the supreme high priest over all the house of *God*.
31 It is a dreadful thing to fall into the hands of the living *God*.
36 You will need endurance to do *God*'s will
11 3 the world was created by one word from *God*,
4 Abel offered *God* a better sacrifice . . . he was declared to be righteous when *God* made acknowledgement of his offerings.
5 (Gn 5 24) Enoch . . . *God* had taken him . . . he had pleased *God*.
6 it is impossible to please *God* without faith, since anyone who comes to him must believe that he exists
10 [Abraham] looked forward to a city . . . built by *God*.
16 *God* is not ashamed to be called their *God*,
19 *God* had the power even to raise the dead;
25 [Moses] chose to be ill-treated in company with *God*'s people
40 *God* had made provision for us to have something better,
12 2 Jesus . . . from now on has taken his place at the right of *God*'s throne.
7 *God* is treating you as his sons.
15 Be careful that no one is deprived of the grace of *God*
22 you have come to . . . the city of the living *God* . . . ²³ . . .
23 to *God* himself, the supreme Judge,
28 Let us . . . worship *God* . . . in reverence and fear. ²⁹ For
29 (Dt 4 24) our *God* is a consuming fire.
13 4 fornicators and adulterers will come under *God*'s judgement.
7 your leaders, who preached the word of *God* to you,
15 Through [Jesus], let us offer *God* an unending sacrifice of praise,
16 these are sacrifices that please *God*.
20 the *God* of peace, who brought our Lord Jesus back from the dead

Jm 1 1 From James, servant of *God* and of the Lord Jesus Christ.
5 If there is any one of you who needs wisdom, he must ask *God*,
13 Never . . . say, '*God* sent the temptation'; *God* cannot be tempted to do anything wrong, and he does not tempt anybody.
20 *God*'s righteousness is never served by man's anger;
27 Pure, unspoilt religion, in the eyes of *God* our Father is this:
2 5 it was those who are poor . . . that *God* chose.
19 You believe in the one *God* . . . the demons have the same belief,
23 (Gn 15 6) Abraham put his faith in *God* . . . he was called 'the friend of *God*'.
3 9 M We use [the tongue] to bless the Lord and Father, but we also use it to curse men who are made in *God*'s image:
4 4 making the world your friend is making *God* your enemy? Anyone who chooses the world for his friend turns himself into *God*'s enemy.
6 (Pr 3 34 G) *God* opposes the proud
7 Give in to *God*, then; resist the devil,
8 The nearer you go to *God*, the nearer he will come to you.

1 P 1 2 [to those living among foreigners, who have been chosen] by the provident purpose of *God* the Father,
3 Blessed be *God* the Father of our Lord Jesus Christ,
5 *God*'s power will guard you until the salvation
21 Through [Christ] you now have faith in *God* . . . and hope in *God*.
23 your new birth was . . . from the everlasting word of the living and eternal *God*.
2 4 M [Jesus] is the living stone . . . chosen by *God* . . . set yourselves close to him ⁵ so that you too, the holy priesthood
5 that offers the spiritual sacrifices which Jesus Christ has made acceptable to *God*, may be living stones
10 now you are the People of *God*;
12 so that [the pagans] can see your good works for themselves and . . . give thanks to *God*
15 *God* wants you to be good citizens,
16 You are slaves of no one except *God*,
17 Have . . . love for our community; fear *God*
19 there is some merit in putting up with the pains . . . for the sake of *God*
20 The merit, in the sight of *God*, is in bearing [the pain] patiently
3 4 this is what is precious in the sight of *God*. ⁵ . . . the holy women . . . hoped in *God* and were tender and obedient

1 P	3	17	if it is the will of *God* that you should suffer, it is better to suffer for doing right
		18	Christ himself . . . died . . . to lead us to *God*.
		20	*God* was still waiting patiently,
		21	the baptism . . . a pledge made to *God* from a good conscience,
		22	[Jesus Christ] has entered heaven and is at *God*'s right hand,
	4	2 M	for the rest of his life . . . he is not ruled by human passions but only by the will of *God*.
		6 M	so that though . . . they had been through the judgement that comes to all humanity, they might come to *God*'s life in the spirit.
		10	like good stewards responsible for all those different graces of *God*,
		11	If you are a speaker, speak in words which seem to come from *God*; . . . help as though every action was done at *God*'s orders; so that in everything *God* may receive the glory,
		14	the Spirit of glory, the Spirit of *God* resting on you.
		16	if anyone of you should suffer for being a Christian . . . he should thank *God* that he has been called one.
		17	The time has come for the judgement to begin at the household of *God* . . . what will it be when it comes down to those who refuse to believe *God*'s Good News?
		19	So even those whom *God* allows to suffer must trust themselves to the constancy of the creator
	5	2	Be the shepherds of the flock of *God* . . . *God* wants it;
		5	(Pr 3 34 G) *God* refuses the proud
		6	Bow down, then, before the power of *God*
		10	the *God* of all grace . . . will see that all is well again:
		12	this true grace of *God*
2 P	1	1 X	through the righteousness of our *God* and saviour Jesus Christ.
		2	as you come to know (§ *God* and Jesus) our Lord
		3 X 3	By his *divine* power, he has given us all the things that we need
		4	for life . . . [4] . . . through [the glory and goodness of
		3	Christ] you will be able to share the *divine* nature
		17	[Jesus] was honoured and glorified by *God* the Father,
		21	When men spoke for *God* it was the Holy Spirit that moved them.
	2	4	When angels sinned, *God* did not spare them:
	3	5	the earth was formed by the word of *God*
		12	you wait and long for the Day of *God* to come,
1 Jn	1	5	*God* is light; there is no darkness in him at all.
	2	5	*God*'s love comes to perfection in him.
		14	*God*'s word has made its home in you,
		17	anyone who does the will of *God* remains for ever.
	3	1	by letting us be called *God*'s children;
		2	we are already the children of *God*
		9	No one who has been begotten by *God* sins . . . he cannot sin when he has been begotten by *God*.
		10	In this way we distinguish the children of *God* from the children of the devil: anybody not living a holy life . . . is no child of *God*'s.
		17	how could the love of *God* be living in him?
		20	*God* is greater than our conscience . . . [21] . . . if we cannot be condemned by our own conscience, we need not be afraid in *God*'s presence,
		21	
	4	1	test [the spirits], to see if they come from *God* . . . [2] You can
		2	tell the spirits that come from *God* by this: every spirit which acknowledges that Jesus the Christ has come in the
		3	flesh is from *God*; [3] but any spirit which will not say this
		4	of Jesus is not from *God* . . . [4] . . . you are from *God*
		6	. . . [6] . . . But we are children of *God*, and those who know *God* listen to us; those who are not of *God* refuse to listen to us.
		7	let us love one another since love comes from *God* and everyone who loves is begotten by *God* and knows *God*. [8] Anyone who fails to love can never have known *God*, because *God* is love.
		8	
		9	*God*'s love for us was revealed when *God* sent into the world his only Son
		10	this is the love I mean: not our love for *God*, but God's love for us
		11	since *God* has loved us so much, we too should love one another.
		12	No one has ever seen *God*; but as long as we love one another *God* will live in us
		15	If anyone acknowledges that Jesus is the Son of God, *God*
		16	lives in him, and he in *God*. [16] We ourselves have known . . . *God*'s love towards ourselves. *God* is love and anyone who lives in love lives in *God*, and *God* lives in him.
		20	Anyone who says, 'I love *God*', and hates his brother, is a liar, since a man who does not love the brother that he can see cannot love *God*, whom he has never seen. [21] . . .
		21	anyone who loves *God* must also love his brother.
	5	1	Whoever believes that Jesus is the Christ has been begotten by *God*;
		2	We can be sure that we love *God*'s children if we love *God*
		3	himself and do what he has commanded us; [3] this is what loving *God* is – keeping his commandments;

1 Jn	5	4	anyone who has been begotten by *God* has already overcome the world;
		9 M	*God*'s testimony is much greater, and this is *God*'s testimony, given as evidence for his Son.
		10	anyone who will not believe *God* is making God out to be a liar, because he has not trusted the testimony *God* has given about his Son.
		11	*God* has given us eternal life
		18	anyone who has been begotten by *God* does not sin, because the begotten Son of *God* protects him,
		19	We know that we belong to *God*,
		20 X	This [Jesus Christ] is the true *God*, this is eternal life.
2 Jn		3	grace . . . from *God* the Father and from Jesus Christ, the Son of the Father.
		9	If anybody does not keep within the teaching of Christ . . . he cannot have *God* with him:
3 Jn		6	you could help them on their journey in a way that *God* would approve.
		11	anyone who does what is right is a child of *God*, but the person who does what is wrong has never seen *God*.
Jude		1	to those who are called, to those who are dear to *God* the Father and kept safe for Jesus Christ,
		4	[certain people infiltrated among you] turning the grace of our *God* into immorality, and rejecting our only Master and Lord, Jesus Christ.
		21	keep yourselves within the love of *God* and wait for the mercy of our Lord Jesus Christ
		25	To [God,] the only *God*, who saves us through Jesus Christ
Rv	1	1	This is the revelation given by *God* to Jesus Christ
		2	[John] swears it is the word of *God* guaranteed by Jesus Christ.
		6	[Jesus] made us a line of kings, priests to serve his *God* and Father;
		8	'I am the Alpha and the Omega' says the Lord *God*, who is, who was, and who is to come, the Almighty.
		9	having preached *God*'s word and witnessed for Jesus;
	2	7	the tree of life set in *God*'s paradise.
	3	1	Here is the message of the one who holds the seven spirits of *God*
		2	I have failed to notice anything in the way you live that my *God* could possibly call perfect,
		12	Those who prove victorious I will make into pillars in the sanctuary of my *God* . . . I will inscribe on them the name of my *God* and the name of the city of my *God*, the new Jerusalem which comes down from my *God*
		14	Here is the message of the Amen . . . the ultimate source of *God*'s creation:
	4	5	in front of the throne there were seven flaming lamps burning, the seven Spirits of *God*.
		8	Holy, Holy, Holy is the Lord *God*, the Almighty;
		11	You are our Lord and our *God*, you are worthy of glory
	5	6	[the Lamb] had seven eyes, which are the seven Spirits *God* has sent
		9	you were sacrificed, and with your blood you bought men for *God* . . . [10] and made them a line of kings and priests, to serve our *God*
		10	
	6	9	the souls of all the people who had been killed on account of the word of *God*.
	7	2	another angel . . . carrying the seal of the living *God*;
		3	until we have put the seal on the foreheads of the servants of our *God*.
		10	Victory to our *God* . . . and to the Lamb!
		11	all the angels . . . prostrated themselves . . . worshipping *God*
		12	Praise . . . power and strength to our *God*
		15	they now stand in front of *God*'s throne
		17	the Lamb . . . will be their shepherd . . . and *God* will wipe away all tears
	8	2	the seven angels who stand in the presence of *God*.
		4	the smoke of the incense went up in the presence of *God*
	9	4	men who were without *God*'s seal on their foreheads.
		13	the golden altar in front of *God*.
	10	7	*God*'s secret intention will be fulfilled,
	11	1	Go and measure *God*'s sanctuary,
		11	*God* breathed life into them
		13	the survivors . . . could only praise the *God* of heaven.
		16	The twenty-four elders, enthroned in the presence of *God*, prostrated themselves . . . worshipping *God*
		17	We give thanks to you, Almighty Lord *God*,
		19	Then the sanctuary of *God* in heaven opened,
	12	5	the child was taken straight up to *God* . . . [6] while the woman
		6	escaped into the desert, where *God* had made a place of safety ready,
		10	Victory . . . won by our *God*, and all authority for his Christ, now that the persecutor, who accused our brothers . . . before our *God*, has been brought down.
		17	all who obey *God*'s commandments and bear witness for Jesus
	13	6	[the beast] mouthed its blasphemies against *God*,
	14	4	they have been redeemed from amongst men to be the first-fruits for *God* and for the Lamb.

Rv 14	7	Fear *God* and praise him,
	10	[those who worship the beast] will be made to drink the wine of *God*'s fury
	12	the saints who keep the commandments of *God* and faith in Jesus.
	19	the angel . . . put [the vintage of the earth] into a huge winepress, the winepress of *God*'s anger.
15	1	the seven plagues that . . . exhaust the anger of *God*.
	2	They all had harps from *God*, ³ and they were singing the hymn of Moses, the servant of *God* . . .: How great . . . are all your works, Lord *God* Almighty.
	3	
	7	seven golden bowls filled with the anger of *God*
	8	The smoke from the glory and the power of *God* filled the temple
16	1	empty the seven bowls of *God*'s anger over the earth.
	7	Truly, Lord *God* Almighty.
	9	they cursed the name of *God* who had the power to cause such plagues,
	11	they cursed the *God* of heaven
	14	the Great Day of *God* the Almighty.
	19	Babylon . . . was not forgotten: *God* made her drink the full winecup of his anger.
	21	they cursed *God* for sending a plague of hail;
17	17	*God* influenced their minds to do what he intended . . . until the time when *God*'s words should be fulfilled.
18	5	*God* has [Babylon's] crimes in mind:
	8	The Lord *God* . . . has great power.
	20	*God* has given judgement for you against her.
19	1	Alleluia! Victory and glory and power to our *God*!
	4	Then the twenty-four elders . . . worshipped *God* . . . 'Amen, Alleluia'.
	5	a voice came from the throne . . . 'Praise our *God* . . .'
	6	Alleluia! The reign of the Lord our *God* Almighty has begun;
	9	All the things you have written are true messages from *God*.
	10	It is *God* that you must worship.
	13	[the rider] is known by the name, The Word of *God*.
	15	the wine of Almighty *God*'s fierce anger.
	17	Come here. Gather together at the great feast that *God* is giving.
20	4	beheaded for having witnessed for Jesus and for having preached *God*'s word,
	6	they will be priests of *God* and of Christ
21	2	the holy city . . . coming down from *God* out of heaven,
	3 M	Here *God* lives among men . . . ᶠand he will be their *God*; his name is *God*-with-them (lit. and he, *God* with them, will be their *God*) (ᵛ G and *God* himself will be with them.)
	7	I will be his *God* and he a son to me.
	10	the holy city, coming down from *God* out of heaven. ¹¹ It had all the radiant glory of *God*
	11	
	22	the Lord *God* Almighty and the Lamb were themselves the temple,
	23	[the city] was lit by the radiant glory of *God* and the Lamb was a lighted torch for it.
22	1	the river of life, rising from the throne of *God* and of the Lamb
	3	The throne of *God* and of the Lamb will be in its place in the city;
	5	the Lord *God* will be shining on them.
	6	the Lord *God* who gives the spirit to the prophets
	9	It is *God* that you must worship.
	18	*God* will add to him every plague mentioned in the book;
	19	*God* will cut off his share of the tree of life

2: GOD and THE GODS

Jn 10	33 X M	you are only a man and you claim to be *God*. ³⁴ Jesus answered: . . . (Ps 82 6) I said, you are *gods*? ³⁵ So the Law uses the word *gods* of those to whom the word of *God* was addressed,
	34	
	35	
Ac 7	40	[the sons of Israel] said to Aaron (Ex 32 1), 'Make some *gods* to be our leaders . . .' ⁴² *God* turned away from them
	42	
12	22 M	The people acclaimed [Herod] with, 'It is a *god* speaking, not a man!'
14	15	We are only human beings . . . We have come with good news to make you turn from these empty idols to the living *God* who made heaven and earth and the sea and all that these hold.
17	23	[men of Athens,] I noticed . . . an altar inscribed: To An Unknown *God*. Well . . . ²⁴ . . . the *God* who made the world . . . Lord of heaven and earth . . . ²⁶ . . . created the whole human race . . . ²⁷ . . . so that all nations might seek ᵛ the *deity* (G *God*)
	24	
	27	
	M 2/	
	29	Since we are the children of *God*, we have no excuse for thinking that the *deity* looks like anything in gold,
	2	
	30	*God* . . . is telling everyone everywhere that they must repent,
28	6	[the inhabitants of Malta] began to say [Paul] was a *god*.
1 Co 8	4	we know . . . that there is no *god* but the One. ⁵ And even if there were things called *gods* . . . there certainly seem to be '*gods*' and 'lords' in plenty – ⁶ still for us there is one
	5	
	6	

1 Co 8	6	*God*, the Father, from whom all things come and for whom we exist; and there is one Lord, Jesus Christ,
	10 20	they sacrifice to demons who are not *God*.
2 Co 4	4 Ⓓ	the unbelievers whose minds the *god* of this world has blinded, to stop them seeing the light shed by the Good News of the glory of Christ, who is the image of *God*.
	X	
Ga 4	8	Once you were ignorant of *God*, and enslaved to '*gods*' who are not really gods at all; ⁹ but now that you have come to acknowledge *God* – or rather, now that *God* has acknowledged you – how can you want to go back to elemental things like these . . .?
	9	
Ph 3	19	[there are many who] make foods into their *god*
2 Th 2	4	the Enemy, the one who claims to be so much greater than all that men call '*god*' . . . that he enthrones himself in *God*'s sanctuary and claims that he is *God*.
	Ⓓ	

3: THE GODS

a) Diana, Artemis

Artemis 5

Ac 19	24	Demetrius . . . making silver shrines of *Diana*,
	26	ᶠgods (lit. things) made by hand are not *gods* at all.
	27	This threatens . . . to reduce the sanctuary of the great goddess *Diana* to unimportance . . . ²⁸ . . . they started to shout, 'Great is *Diana* of the Ephesians!'
	28 4	
	34	they all started shouting . . . 'Great is *Diana* of the Ephesians!'
	35	the city of the Ephesians is the guardian of the temple of great *Diana* and of her statue that fell from heaven?
	37 6	These men . . . are not guilty of any sacrilege or blasphemy against our *goddess*.

b) Baal

Baal 1

Rm 11	4	(1 K 19 18) seven thousand men who have not bent the knee to *Baal*.

c) the (Heavenly) Twins – Castor and Pollux

Dioskouroi 1

Ac 28	11	[the ship] came from Alexandria and her figurehead was the *Twins*.

d) Moloch – Rephan

Moloch 1   Rephan (ᵛRompha) 1

Ac 7	43	(Am 5 26) you carried the tent of *Moloch* on your shoulders and the star of the god ᵛ*Rephan* (G *Rompha*),

e) Zeus, Jupiter – Hermes, Mercury

Hermes 1   Zeus 2

Ac 14	11	These people are *gods* who have come down to us disguised as men.
	12	They addressed Barnabas as *Zeus*, and since Paul was the principal speaker they called him *Hermes*. ¹³ The priests of *Zeus*-outside-the-Gate . . . brought garlanded oxen
	13	

2. GODS – DEITIES – DIVINITIES: *DAIMONION*

daimonion 1/63

Ac 17	18	others said [about Paul], 'He sounds like a propagandist for some outlandish *gods*'.

GOOD – BETTER

1. Good: *agathos*	**3. Good – Kind: *chrēstos***
a) Good (applied to God or Jesus)	a) Goodness, Kindness, of God
b) Good – Good things – Goodness	b) Good(ness), Kind(ness), generally
c) Good works – Do good	**4. Good – Well – Kind: *eu***
d) Better – Superior – Greater	a) Do good – Do well – Show kindness
2. Good – Well – Right: *kalos*	b) Goodwill – (Be) On good terms (with a person)
a) Good – Well – Right, Honourable	c) Go well for (a person, a purpose) – Succeed – Thrive
b) Good works – Do well – Do right	**5. Good, Sound – Generously – Liberally, Freely**
c) It is good – It is right	
d) It is better – Rather	
e) (speak) Rightly –(speak) Well	

1: Good, Sound – Generous, Generosity – Liberally, Freely: *ha-plotēs*
2: Generous: *a-phelotēs*
6. Be better (for a person), Be good (for) – Be helpful (to): *sym-pherō*
7. (Be) Better (for) – (Be) Of no advantage (to), – (Be) the loser: *lysi-teleō*
8. Be better: *pro-echomai*
9. Be useful (to), Do (a person) good, Be the better (for) – Gain (from), Profit (by), Advantage: *ōpheleō*

10. Use, Useful – Exercise, Practice – Of no use: *chraomai*
  a) Use, Exercise – Practice
  b) Useful – Of (no) use, Good-for-nothing
11. Arch- (ironically), Super-, Superlative: *hyper-lian*
12. Beautiful – Handsome
  1: Well-favoured – Fine – Beautiful: *asteios*
  2: Beautiful – Handsome: *hōraios*
  3: Beautiful – Lovely: *eu-prepeia*

B = Good, Well // Bad, Wicked

1. GOOD: *AGATHOS*

1	*agathos*	96/103	11	(*phil-*)*agathos*	1	
5	*agathōsynē*	4	12	(*a-phil-*)*agathos*	1	
6	*agatho-ergeō*	1				
7	*agath-ourgeō*	1				
3	*agatho-poieō*	9				
8	*agatho-poiia*	1				
9	*agatho-poios*	1	13	*beltion*	1	
4	*to agathon poieō*	6	2	*kreissōn*	18/19	
10	*ta agatha poieō*	1	14	*kreissōn poieō*	1	

a) Good (applied to God or Jesus)

Mt 19 17 Θ — Why do you ask me about what is good? There is one alone who is *good*.
Mk 10 17 — *Good* master, what must I do . . . ? ¹⁸ Jesus said to him, 18 Θ — 'Why do you call me *good*? No one is *good* but God alone.'
Lk 18 18 — *Good* Master, what have I to do . . . ? ¹⁹ Jesus said to him, 19 Θ — 'Why do you call me *good*? No one is *good* but God alone.'
Jn 1 46 — From Nazareth? . . . Can anything *good* come from that place?
7 12 — Some said [about Jesus], 'He is a *good* man

b) Good – Good things – Goodness

Mt 5 45 B — your Father . . . causes his sun to rise on bad men as well as *good*, and his rain to fall on honest and dishonest men alike.
7 11 B — If you . . . know how to give your children what is *good*, how much more will your Father . . . give *good things* to those who ask him!
17 B — In the same way, a *sound* tree produces good fruit
18 B — A *sound* tree cannot bear bad fruit,
12 34 B — how can your speech be *good* when you are evil?
35 B — A *good* man draws *good things* from his store of *goodness*;
19 17 — Why do you ask me about what is *good*?
20 15 B < — Why be envious because I am ˹generous (lit. *good*)?
22 10 B < — these servants . . . collected together everyone they could find, bad and good alike;
25 21 B < — Well done, *good* and faithful servant;
23 B < — Well done, *good* and faithful servant;
Mk 10 18 — No one is *good* but God alone.
Lk 1 53 — (Ps 107 9) The hungry [God] has filled with *good things*,
6 45 B — A *good* man draws what is *good* from the store of *goodness* in his heart.
8 8 < — some seed fell into ˹rich (lit. *good*) soil
15 < — As for the part in the rich soil, this is people with a noble and ˹generous (lit. *good*) heart who have heard the word and take it to themselves
10 42 — It is Mary who has chosen the ˹better (lit. *good*) part;
11 13 B — If you then, who are evil, know how to give your children what is *good*,
12 18 < — I will . . . store all my grain and my *goods* in [my new barns],
19 < — My soul, you have plenty of *good things* laid by
16 25 B < — during your life *good things* came your way, just as bad things came the way of Lazarus.
18 19 — No one is *good* but God alone.
19 17 B < — Well done, my *good* servant!
23 50 — Then . . . an *upright* and virtuous man named Joseph [arrived].
Jn 1 46 — From Nazareth? . . . Can anything *good* come from that place?
Ac 11 24 — [Barnabas] was a *good* man,
23 1 — Paul . . . began to speak, '. . . I have conducted myself . . . with a perfectly ˹clear (lit. *good*) conscience'.
Rm 3 8 B — Do evil as a means to *good*.
5 7 B — for *someone really worthy*, a man might be prepared to die
7 12 — what [the Law] commands is sacred, just and *good*. ¹³ Does
13 — that mean that *something good* killed me? Of course not. But sin . . . used that *good thing* to kill me;
18 — I know of nothing *good* living in me
8 28 — by turning everything to their *good* God co-operates with all those who love him,

Rm 10 15 — (Is 52 7) The footsteps of those who bring *good* [news] is a welcome sound.
12 2 — discover the will of God and know what is *good* . . . what is the perfect thing to do.
9 B — sincerely prefer *good* to evil.
21 B — conquer [evil] with *good*.
14 16 — you must not compromise your ˹privilege (lit. *good*),
15 2 — Each of us should think of his neighbours ˹and help (lit. for their *good*, helping) them
14 5 — I am quite certain that you are full of *good intentions*,
16 19 B — I only hope that you are also wise in what is *good*, and innocent of what is bad.
Ga 5 22 5 — What the Spirit brings is . . . patience, kindness, *goodness*,
6 6 — People under instruction should always ˹contribute something to the support of (lit. share their *goods* with) the man who is instructing them.
Ep 4 28 — Anyone who was a thief . . . should try to find some useful manual work instead, and be able to ˹do some good by helping (or: work *honestly* to help) others
29 B — let your words be ˹for the improvement (lit. such as is *good* for the edifying) of others,
5 9 5 — the effects of the light are seen in complete *goodness* and right living and truth.
1 Th 3 6 — telling us that you always remember us with *pleasure*
5 15 B — you must all think of what is ˹best (lit. *good*)
2 Th 1 11 5 — God will . . . fulfil all your desires for *goodness*
2 16 — God our Father who has given us . . . such ˹sure (lit. *good*) hope,
1 Tm 1 5 — there should be love, coming out of . . . a ˹clear (lit. *good*) conscience
19 — [fight like a good soldier] with faith and a *good* conscience
2 Tm 3 3 12 — [People will be] unappeasable , . . and enemies of everything that is *good*;
Tt 1 8 11 — [an elder,] a man who is hospitable and a friend of all that is *good*;
2 5 — [the older women should show the younger women] how they are to be . . . *good*
10 — [the slaves] must show ˹complete (lit. *good*) honesty
Heb 9 11 — Christ . . . the high priest of all the ˹blessings (lit. *good things*) which were to come.
10 1 — since the Law has no more than a reflection of the *good things* to come . . . it is quite incapable
13 21 — [I pray that God] may make you ready to do his will in any kind of ˹good (ᵛ *good action*);
Jm 1 17 — it is all that is *good* (ᵛ *good*), everything that is perfect, which is given us from above;
3 17 — the wisdom that comes down from above is . . . full of compassion and shows itself by ˹doing good (lit. *good* fruits);
1 P 2 18 — Slaves must be respectful . . . to their masters, not only when they are *kind*
3 10 — (Ps 34 13 G) Anyone who wants to have a ˹happy (lit. *good*) life . . . must banish malice from his tongue,
13 B — No one can hurt you if you are determined to do only what is ˹right (lit. *good*);
16 — [have your answer ready but] give it with courtesy . . . and with a ˹clear (lit. *good*) conscience, so that those who slander you when you are living a *good* life. . . . may be proved wrong
21 — the baptism . . . is . . . a pledge made to God from a *good* conscience,

c) Good works – Do good

Mt 19 16 4 — Master, what *good deed* must I *do* to possess eternal life?
Mk 3 4 B 4 — Is it against the law on the sabbath day to *do good*, or to do evil;
Lk 6 9 B 3 — is it against the law on the sabbath to *do good*, or to do evil?
33 3/3 — if you *do good* to those who *do good* to you, what thanks can you expect?
35 3 — *do good*, and lend without any hope of return.
Jn 5 29 B 10 — those who *did good* will rise again to life;
Ac 9 36 — Tabitha . . . never tired of doing *good* or giving in charity.
14 17 Θ 7 — [God] did not leave you without evidence of himself in the *good things* he does for you;
Rm 2 7 — For those who sought renown . . . by always doing *good* there will be eternal life;
10 B — renown, honour and peace will come to everyone who does *good*
7 19 B 4 — instead of *doing the good things* I want to do,
9 11 B — before her twin children [= Esau and Jacob] were born and before either had done *good* or evil.
13 3 B — *Good* behaviour is not afraid of magistrates . . . If you want to live without being afraid of authority, you must ˹live honestly (lit. *do good*) . . . ⁴ The state is there to serve
4 4 — God ˹for your benefit (lit. to lead you to [do] *good*)
1 Co 7 38 — the man who sees that his daughter is married has done a good thing but the man who keeps his daughter unmarried has *done* something even *better*.
2 Co 5 10 B 14 — each of us will get what he deserves for the things he did . . . *good* or bad.

2 Co 9 8   you will . . . still have something to spare for all sorts of *good* works.

Ga 6 10   we must do *good* to all, and especially to our brothers in the faith.

Ep 2 10   created in Christ Jesus to live the *good* life as from the beginning he had meant us to live it.

4 28   he should try to find some useful manual work instead, and be able to ꜰdo some *good* by helping (or: work honestly to help) others

6 8   everyone . . . will be properly rewarded by the Lord for
4   whatever ꜰwork he has done well (or: *good work* he has *done*)

Ph 1 6   the One who began this *good* work in you will see that it is finished

Col 1 10   showing the results in all the *good* actions you do

2 Th 2 17   [May Jesus Christ and God] strengthen you in everything *good* that you do or say.

1 Tm 2 10   [women's adornment is] to do the sort of *good* works that are proper

5 10   [a widow must have] been active in all kinds of *good* work.

6 18 6   [the rich] are to do *good*, and be rich in *good* works,

2 Tm 2 21   to avoid these faults . . . is the way for anyone to become a vessel . . . kept ready for any *good* work.

3 17   the man who is dedicated to God becomes fully equipped and ready for any *good* work.

Tt 1 16   they are outrageously rebellious and quite incapable of doing *good*

3 1   Remind them that it is their duty . . . to be ready to do *good*

Phm 6   all the *good things* that we are able to do for Christ.

14   it would have been forcing ꜰyour act of kindness (lit. a *good deed* from you), which should be spontaneous.

Heb 13 21   may [God] make you ready to do his will in any kind of *good* action;

1 P 2 14 B   [accept the authority of] the governors as commissioned by [God] . . . to praise ꜰgood citizenship (lit. those who
15 9/3   do *good*). 15 God wants you to ꜰbe good citizens (lit. *do good*), so as to silence what fools are saying in their ignorance.

20   The merit . . . is in bearing [the beating] patiently when you
3   are punished after doing ꜰyour duty (lit. *good*).

3 6 3   You are now [Sarah's] children, as long as you *live good lives*

11 B   (Ps 34 15) [Anyone who wants to have a happy life] must
4   never yield to evil but must *practise good*;

17 B 3   it is better to suffer for *doing* ꜰright (lit. *good*) than for doing wrong.

4 19   even those whom God allows to suffer must trust themselves
8   to the constancy of the creator and go on *doing good*.

3 Jn 11 B   never follow such a bad example, but keep following the
/3   *good* one; anyone who *does* what is ꜰright (lit. *good*) is a child of God,

d) Better – Superior – Greater

1 Co 7 9 2   it is *better* to be married than to be tortured.

11 17   I cannot say that you have done well in holding meetings
2   that do you *more* harm than *good*.

Ph 1 23   I want to . . . be with Christ, which would be very much the
2   *better*,

2 Tm 1 18 13   You know *better* than anyone else how much [Onesiphorus] helped me at Ephesus.

Heb 1 4 X 2   [the Son] is now as far ꜰabove (or: *superior* to) the angels

6 9 2   you are in a *better* state and on the way to salvation.

7 7 2   it is indisputable that a blessing is given by a *superior* to an inferior.

19 2   this commandment is replaced by something *better* – the hope that brings us nearer to God.

22 2   it is a *greater* covenant for which Jesus has become our guarantee.

8 6 2   it is a *better* covenant of which [Christ] is the mediator,
2   founded on *better* promises.

9 23   the heavenly things themselves have to be purified by a
2   ꜰhigher (or: *better*) sort of sacrifice than this.

10 34 2   you owned something that was *better* and lasting.

11 16 2   [those who had faith] were longing for a *better* homeland, their heavenly homeland.

35 2   refusing release so that they would rise again to a *better* life.

40 2   God had made provision for us to have something *better*,

12 24 2   a blood for purification which pleads *more* insistently than Abel's.

1 P 3 17 2   it is *better* to suffer for doing right

2 P 2 21 2   It would even have been *better* for him never to have learnt the way of holiness,

2. GOOD – WELL – RIGHT: *KALOS*

1 *kalos*	97/102	6	*kalo-poieō*	1	
2 *kalōs*	24/37	4	*to kalon poieō*	4	
5 *kalo(-didaskalos)*	1	3	*kalōs poieō*	11	
		7	*poieō*	1	

a) Good – Well – Right, Honourable

Mt 3 10   any tree which fails to produce *good* fruit will be cut down

7 17 B   a sound tree produces *good* fruit . . . [18] A sound tree cannot
18 B   bear bad fruit, nor a rotten tree bear *good* fruit. [19] Any
19   tree that does not produce *good* fruit is cut down

12 33 B   Make a tree ꜰsound (lit. *good*) and its fruit be ꜰsound (lit. *good*);

13 8 <   Others fell on ꜰrich (lit. *good*) soil and produced their crop,
23 <   the one who received the seed in ꜰrich (lit. *good*) soil

24 <   The kingdom of heaven . . . a man who sowed *good* seed
27 <   was it not *good* seed that you sowed in your field?

37 <   The sower of the *good* seed is the Son of Man. [38] . . . the
38 <   *good* seed is the subjects of the kingdom;

45 <   the kingdom of heaven is like a merchant looking for *fine* pearls;

48 B <   [the fishermen] collect the *good* ones in a basket

15 7 2   Hypocrites! It was you Isaiah meant when he so *rightly* prophesied:

Mk 4 8 <   some seeds fell into ꜰrich (lit. *good*) soil

20 <   there are those who have received the seed in ꜰrich (lit. *good*) soil:

7 6 2   It was of you hypocrites that Isaiah so *rightly* prophesied

9 2   How ꜰingeniously (lit. *well*) you get round the commandment of God in order to preserve your own tradition!

9 50   Salt is a *good* thing, but if salt has become insipid,

Lk 3 9   any tree which fails to produce *good* fruit will be cut down

6 38   a ꜰfull (lit. *good*) measure . . . will be poured into your lap;

43 B   There is no ꜰsound (lit. *good*) tree that produces rotten fruit,
B   nor again a rotten tree that produces ꜰsound (lit. *good*) fruit.

48   when the river was in flood it . . . could not shake [that house],
2   as it was *well* built.

8 15 <   As for the part in the ꜰrich (lit. *good*) soil, this is people with a ꜰnoble (lit. *good*) and generous heart who have heard the word and take it to themselves

14 34   Salt is a ꜰuseful (lit. *good*) thing. But if the salt itself loses its taste,

21 5   some were talking about the Temple, remarking how it was adorned with *fine* stonework

Jn 2 10   People generally serve the ꜰbest (lit. *good*) wine first . . . but you have kept the ꜰbest (lit. *good*) wine till now.

10 11 X   I am the *good* shepherd: the *good* shepherd is one who lays
14 X   down his life for his sheep . . . [14] I am the *good* shepherd;

Ac 25 10 2   I have done the Jews no wrong, as you *very well* know.

Rm 7 16   I have a self that acknowledges that the Law is *good*,

12 17   let everyone see that you are interested only in ꜰthe highest ideals (lit. *good*).

1 Co 5 6   The pride that you take in yourselves is hardly ꜰto your credit (lit. *good*; or: *right*).

14 17 2   However *well* you make your thanksgiving, the other gets no benefit from it.

2 Co 8 21   (Pr 3 4 G) we are trying to do *right*

11 4   you have only to receive . . . a new gospel . . . and you
2   ꜰwelcome it with open arms (lit. give it a *good* reception).

Ga 4 17 2   ꜰThe blame lies in the way (lit. It is for no *good* purpose that) they have tried to win you over:

18   It is always a good thing to win people over . . . for a *good* purpose

5 7 2   You began your race *well*: who made you less anxious . . . ?

1 Th 5 21 B   think before you do anything – hold on to what is *good*

1 Tm 1 8   the Law is *good*, but only provided it is treated like any law,

18   remember the words . . . taking them to heart to fight like a *good* soldier

3 1   To want to be a presiding elder is to want to do ꜰa noble (lit. an *honourable*) work.

4   [the presiding elder] must be a man who manages his own
2   family *well*

7   It is also necessary that people outside the Church should speak *well* of him,

12   Deacons . . . must be men who manage their children and
2   families *well*.

13 2   Those of them who carry out their duties *well* as deacons will earn a high (lit. an *honourable*) standing for themselves

4 4   Everything God has created is *good*,

6   you will be a *good* servant of Christ Jesus and show that you have really digested . . . the *good* doctrine

5 17 2   The elders who do their work *well* while they are in charge

6 12   Fight the *good* fight of the faith . . . you made ꜰyour (lit. the *good*) profession and spoke up for the truth in front of many witnesses

13 X   Jesus Christ, who ꜰspoke up as a witness for the truth (lit. made the *good* profession [for the truth] as a witness) in front of Pontius Pilate,

19   this is the way they can save up a *good* capital sum

2 Tm 1 14   You have been trusted to look after something *precious*,

2 3   Put up with your share of difficulties, like a *good* soldier of Christ Jesus.

4 7   I have fought the *good* fight to the end;

Tt 2 3 5   the older women . . . are to be the teachers of [the] *right* [behaviour]

Heb	5 14 B	mature men with minds trained by practice to distinguish between *good* and bad.
	13 18	We are sure that our own conscience is ⌐clear (lit. *good*) and
	2	we are certainly determined to behave *honourably* in everything we do;
Jm	2 3	you take notice of the well-dressed man, and say, 'Come this
	2	way to the ⌐best (lit. *good*) seats';
	7 X	Aren't [the rich] the ones who insult the *honourable* name to which you have been dedicated?
	3 13	If there are any wise . . . men . . . let them show it by their *good* lives, with humility and wisdom in their actions.
1 P	2 12	Always behave *honourably* among pagans
	4 10	like *good* stewards responsible for all these different graces of God,

b) Good works – Do well – Do right

Mt	5 16	so that, seeing your *good* works, [men] may give praise to your Father
	12 12	3 it is permitted to *do good* on the sabbath day.
	26 10	What she has done for me is one of the *good* works indeed!
Mk	7 37 X	3 [Jesus] has *done* all things *well* . . . he makes the deaf hear and the dumb speak.
	14 6	What she has done for me is one of the *good* works.
Lk	6 27	3 *do good* to those who hate you,
Jn	10 32 X	I have done many *good* works for you to see, [works] from my Father
	33 X	We are not stoning you for doing a *good* work
Ac	10 33	[Cornelius said to Peter:] ⌐you have been kind enough to (lit.
	3	it is *good* of you to have) come.
Rm	7 18	the will to do what is *good* is in me, the performance is not,
	21 B	4 every single time I want to *do good* it is something evil that comes to hand.
1 Co	7 37	if someone has firmly made his mind up . . . in complete freedom of choice, to keep his daughter as she is, he will be *doing a good thing*. [38] . . . the man who sees that his
	38	3
	3	daughter is married has *done a good thing* but the man who keeps his daughter unmarried has done something even better.
2 Co	13 7 B	4 we would rather that you *did well* even though we failed.
Ga	6 9	4 We must never get tired of *doing good* because . . . we shall get our harvest at the proper time.
Ph	4 14	3 it was *good* of you to share with me in my hardships.
2 Th	3 13	6 never grow tired of *doing* what is *right*.
1 Tm	5 10	[a widow] must be a woman known for her *good* works
	25	the *good* that people do can be obvious;
	6 18	[the rich] are to *do good*, and be rich in *good* works,
Tt	2 7	make yourself an example to them of working for *good*:
	14	[Jesus] sacrificed himself . . . to purify a people so that it . . . would have no ambition except to do *good*.
	3 8	so that those who now believe in God may keep their minds constantly occupied in doing *good* works.
	14	All our people are to learn to occupy themselves in doing *good* works
Heb	10 24	to stir a response in love and *good* works.
Jm	2 8	3 *the right thing to do* is to keep the supreme law of scripture: you must love your neighbour
	19	You believe in the one God – that is ⌐creditable enough (lit.
	3	*doing right*),
	4 17	4 Everyone who knows what is *the right thing to do* and
	7	doesn't *do* it commits a sin.
1 P	2 12	so that they can see your *good* works for themselves and . . . give thanks to God
2 P	1 19	3 you will be *right* to depend on prophecy and take it as a lamp
3 Jn	6	3 ⌐it would be (lit. you would be *doing*) *a very good thing* if you could help [the brothers] on their journey

c) It is good – It is right

Mt	15 26	It is not ⌐fair (lit. *right*) to take the children's food and throw it to the house-dogs.
	17 4	Lord , . . it is ⌐wonderful (lit. *good*) for us to be here.
Mk	7 27	it is not ⌐fair (lit. *right*) to take the children's food
	9 5	Rabbi . . . it is ⌐wonderful (lit. *good*) for us to be here;
Lk	9 33	Master, it is ⌐wonderful (lit. *good*) for us to be here.
Rm	14 21	⌐the best course is (lit. it is *right*) to abstain from . . . anything . . . that would make your brother trip
1 Co	7 1	it is [a] *good* [thing] for a man not to touch a woman;
	8	widows and those who are not married: it is [a] *good* [thing] for them to stay as they are, like me,
	26	in these present times of stress this is *right*: that it is *good* for a man to stay as he is.
Ga	4 18	It is always [a] *good* [thing] to win people over . . . for a good purpose
1 Tm	2 3	[There should be prayers offered for everyone.] To do this is *right*, and will please God
Tt	3 8	doing good works. All this is *good*, and will do nothing but good to everybody.
Heb	13 9	it is ⌐better (lit. *good*) to rely on grace for inner strength

d) It is better – Rather

Mt	18 8	it is *better* for you to enter into life crippled
	9	it is *better* for you to enter into life with one eye,
	26 24	*Better* for that man if he had never been born!
Mk	9 42	But anyone who is an obstacle . . . would be *better* thrown into the sea
	43	it is *better* for you to enter into life crippled,
	45	it is *better* for you to enter into life lame,
	47	it is *better* for you to enter into the kingdom of God with one eye,
	14 21	*Better* for that man if he had never been born!
1 Co	9 15	I would *rather* die than let anyone take away something that I can boast of.

e) (Speak) Rightly – (Speak) Well

Mk	12 28 X	2 One of the scribes who . . . had observed how *well* Jesus had answered them . . . put a question to him,
	32 X	2 *Well* spoken, Master; what you have said is true: that [God] is one and there is no other.
Lk	20 39 X	2 *Well* put, Master
Jn	4 17	2 You are *right* to say, 'I have no husband'
	8 48	2 Are we not *right* in saying that you are a Samaritan . . .?
	13 13	2 You call me Master . . . and *rightly*;
	18 23 X B	2 if ⌐there is no offence in it (lit. I have spoken *rightly*), why do you strike me?
Ac	28 25 Ⓢ	2 How ⌐aptly (lit. *rightly*) the Holy Spirit spoke when he told your ancestors through the prophet Isaiah:
Rm	11 19	You will say, 'Those branches were cut off . . ., ⌐True (lit.
	2	Quite *right*),
Heb	6 5 ⊖	[those who] appreciated the *good* message of God

3. GOOD – KIND: *CHRĒSTOS*

3	*chrēsteuomai*	1	1 *chrēstotēs*	10
2	*chrēstos*	7	4 *chrēsto(-logia)*	1

a) Goodness, Kindness, of God

Lk	6 35 B	2 for [the Most High] himself is *kind* to the ungrateful and the wicked.
Rm	2 4	are you abusing his abundant *goodness*, patience and tolera-
	2	tion, not realising that this *goodness* of God is meant to lead you to repentance?
	11 22	Do not forget that God can be severe as well as *kind*: . . . he is *kind* to you, but only for as long as ⌐he chooses to be (lit. you continue in his *kindness*),
Ep	2 7	This was to show . . . through his *goodness* towards us in Christ Jesus, how infinitely rich [God] is in grace.
Tt	3 4	when the *kindness* and love of God our saviour for mankind were revealed,
1 P	2 3	2 (Ps 34 9) now that you have tasted the *goodness* of the Lord.

b) Good(ness), Kind(ness), generally

Mt	11 30 X	2 my yoke is ⌐easy (lit. *kind*) and my burden light.
Lk	5 39	2 'The old [wine] is *good*' he says.
Rm	3 12	(Ps 14 3) All have turned aside . . . there is not one ⌐good man (lit. *man who does good*) left
	16 18	confusing the simple-minded with their pious and persua-
	4	sive arguments (lit. *kind* and flattering words).
1 Co	13 4	3 Love is always patient and *kind*;
	15 33 B	2 Bad friends ruin ⌐the noblest people (lit. *good* manners).
2 Co	6 6	2 we are God's servants by our . . . patience and *kindness* . . . by a love free from affection;
Ga	5 22	What the Spirit brings is . . . love . . . patience, *kindness*, goodness
Ep	4 32	2 Be friends with one another, and *kind*,
Col	3 12	you should be clothed in sincere compassion, in *kindness* and humility,

4. GOOD – WELL – KIND: *EU*

a) Do good – Do well – Show kindness

1	*eu*	5/6	5 *eu poieō*	1
2	*eu-ergesia*	2	6 *eu-poiia*	1
3	*eu-ergeteō*	1		
4	*eu-ergetēs*	1		

D = Do good

Mt	25 21	*Well* done, good and faithful servant;
	23	*Well* done, good and faithful servant;
Mk	14 7 D	5 you can *be kind* to [the poor] whenever you wish,
Lk	19 17	*Well* done, my good servant!
	22 25 D	4 those who have authority over them are given the title *Benefactor*.

Ac 4 9 D 2 you are questioning us today about an *act of kindness* to a cripple,
10 38 D X 3 Jesus went about *doing good* and curing
15 29 you are to abstain from food sacrificed to idols, from blood . . . Avoid these, and you will do what is *right*
Ep 6 3 (Dt 5 16) [Honour your father . . .] and ⌐you will prosper (lit. it will be to your own *good*)
1 Tm 6 2 D 2 those who have the benefit of ⌐their services (lit. the *good* they do) are . . . dear to God.
Heb 13 16 D 6 Keep *doing good works* and sharing your resources,

b) Goodwill – (Be) On good terms (with a person)

1 *eu-noeō 1*   2 *eu-noia 1*

Mt 5 25 Come to *terms* with your opponent
Ep 6 7 2 Work hard and *willingly*, but do it for the sake of the Lord

c) Go well for (a person, a purpose) – Succeed – Thrive

eu-(h)odoō 4

Rm 1 10 [I never fail] to ask to be allowed at long last ⌐the opportunity to visit (lit. to *succeed* in visiting) you, if [God] so wills.
1 Co 16 2 each one of you must put aside what he can afford (lit. *succeeds* in affording),
3 Jn 2 I hope everything is *going happily with* you and that you are ⌐as well (lit. *thriving*) physically as you are spiritually.

5. GOOD, SOUND – GENEROUSLY – LIBERALLY, FREELY

1: GOOD, SOUND – GENEROUS, GENEROSITY – LIBERALLY, FREELY: *HA-PLOTĒS*

3 *ha-plōs 1*   1 *ha-plotēs 4|8*
2 *ha-plous 2*

Mt 6 22 2 if your eye is ⌐*sound* (or: *good*), your whole body will be filled with light
Lk 11 34 2 When your eye is ⌐*sound* (or: *good*), your whole body too is filled with light
Rm 12 8 Let . . . the almsgivers give *freely*,
2 Co 8 2 [the] constant cheerfulness and [the] intense poverty [of the churches in Macedonia] have overflowed in a wealth of *generosity*.
9 11 made richer in every way, you will be able to do all the *generous things* which . . . are the cause of thanksgiving to God.
13 [the saints] give glory to God . . . for your sympathetic *generosity* to them
Jm 1 5 Θ 3 God . . . gives to all *freely*

2: GENEROUS: *A-PHELOTĒS*

a-phelotēs 1

Ac 2 46 The faithful . . . shared their food gladly and ⌐*generously* (or: sincerely).

6. BE BETTER (FOR A PERSON), BE GOOD (FOR) – BE HELPFUL (TO): *SYM-PHERŌ*

1 *sym-pherō 14|15*   2 *sym-phoros 2*

Mt 5 29 it will ⌐*do you less harm* (lit. *be better* for you) to lose one part of you than to have your whole body thrown into hell.
30 it will ⌐*do you less harm* (lit. *be better* for you) to lose one part of you than to have your whole body go to hell.
18 6 anyone who is an obstacle to bring down one of these little ones . . . would *be better* drowned
19 10 If that is how things are between husband and wife, it ⌐is not advisable (lit. would *be better* not) to marry.
Jn 11 50 it *is better* for one man to die for the people,
16 7 it *is for* your own *good* that I am going
18 14 It is *better* for one man to die for the people.
Ac 20 20 I have not hesitated to do anything that would *be helpful* to you; I have preached to you, and instructed you both in public and in your homes,
1 Co 6 12 For me there are no forbidden things; maybe, but not everything *does good*.
7 35 2 I say this only to *help* you,
10 23 For me there are no forbidden things, but not everything *does good*.
33 2 I try to be helpful . . , not anxious for my own *advantage* but for [the advantage] of everybody else,

1 Co 12 7 The particular way in which the Spirit is given to each person *is for* [a] *good* [purpose].
2 Co 8 10 I am only making a suggestion; it ⌐is only fair to (lit. would *be good* for) you,
12 1 Must I go on boasting, though there is nothing to *be gained* by it?
Heb 12 10 [our spiritual Father punishes us] *for our own good*, so that we may share his own holiness.

7. (BE) BETTER (FOR) – (BE) OF NO ADVANTAGE (TO), (BE) THE LOSER: *LYSI-TELEŌ*

1 *lysi-teleō 1*   2 *a-lysi-telēs 1*

Lk 17 2 It would be *better* for him to be thrown into the sea with a millstone put round his neck
Heb 13 17 your leaders . . . must give an account of the way they look after your souls; make this a joy for them to do, and not a grief – you yourselves would be the *losers*.

8. BE BETTER: *PRO-ECHOMAI*

pro-echomai 1

Rm 3 9 Δ *are* we any *better* off? Not at all:

9. BE USEFUL (TO), DO (A PERSON) GOOD, BE THE BETTER (FOR) – GAIN (FROM), PROFIT (BY), ADVANTAGE: *ŌPHELEŌ*

4 *ōpheleia 2*   3 *ophelos 3*
1 *ōpheleō 15*   5 *an-ōphelēs 2*
2 *ōphelimos 4*

Mt 15 5 Anything I have that I might have *used to help* you is dedicated to God
16 26 What, then, will a man *gain* if he wins the whole world and ruins his life?
27 24 Then Pilate saw that he was ⌐*making no impression* (lit. *gaining* nothing) . . . So he . . . washed his hands
Mk 5 26 [the woman with a haemorrhage] had spent all she had without *being* any the *better* for it,
7 11 Anything I have that I might have *used to help* you is Corban
8 36 What *gain*, then, is it for a man to win the whole world . . . ?
Lk 9 25 What *gain*, then, is it for a man to have won the whole world . . . ?
Jn 6 63 It is the spirit that gives life, the flesh ⌐has nothing to offer (lit. *is of* no *help*).
12 19 You see, there is ⌐nothing you can do (lit. nothing to *be gained*);
Rm 2 25 It *is a good thing* to be circumcised if you keep the Law;
3 1 4 Is there any *advantage* in being circumcised?
1 Co 13 3 if I even let them take my body to burn it, but am without love, it will *do* me no *good* whatever.
14 6 what *use* shall I *be* if all my talking reveals nothing new . . . ?
15 32 3 If my motives were only human ones, what *good* would it *do* me . . . ?
Ga 5 2 X if you allow yourselves to be circumcised, Christ will *be of* no *benefit* to you at all.
1 Tm 4 8 2/2 Physical exercises are *useful* enough, but the *usefulness* of spirituality is unlimited,
2 Tm 3 16 2 All scripture . . . can *profitably be used* for teaching,
Tt 3 8 2 good works . . . *do* nothing but *good* to everybody. [9] But
9 5 . . . pointless speculations . . . and disputes . . . are *useless*
Heb 4 2 hearing the message *did* them no *good* because they did not share the faith
7 18 5 The earlier commandment is thus abolished, because it was neither effective *nor useful*,
13 9 dietary laws . . . have *done* no *good* to those who kept them.
Jm 2 14 3 ⌐Take (lit. Of what *good* is it [in]) the case of someone who has never done a single good act . . . ? [15] If one of the brothers or of the sisters is in need of clothes . . . [16] and
16 one of you says to them, '. . . keep yourself warm . . .'
3 then what *good* is that?
Jude 16 They are mischief-makers . . . ready with flattery . . .
4 when they see some *advantage* in it.

10. USE, USEFUL – EXERCISE, PRACTICE – OF NO USE: *CHRAOMAI*

1 *chraomai 11*   7 *a-chrēstos 1*
6 *chrēsimos 1*   8 *apo-chrēsis 1*
3 *chrēsis 2*   5 *kata-chraomai 2*
4 *a-chreios 2*   2 *eu-chrēstos 3*

a) Use, Exercise – Practice

Ac 27 3		Julius ⌐was considerate (lit. *exercised* benevolence) enough to allow Paul to go to his friends
17		⌐*with the help of* (or: *using*) tackle [the crew] bound cables round the ship;
Rm 1 26		their women have turned from natural [intercourse] to
27	3	unnatural *practices* 27 and . . . their menfolk have given
1 Co 7 21	3	up natural ⌐intercourse (lit. *practices* with women)
		if you should have the chance of being free, ⌐accept (lit. *make use of*) it.
31		those who have to *deal with* the world should not ⌐become engrossed (lit. *make use of*) it.
9 12	5	In fact we have never *exercised* this right.
15		I have not *exercised* any of these rights,
18		my reward is . . . to be able to offer the Good News free,
	5	and not ⌐insist on (lit. *exercise*) the rights which the gospel gives me.
2 Co 1 17		Do you think I was ⌐not sure of my own intentions (lit. *engaging in* lightheartedness) when I planned this?
3 12		Having this hope, we can ⌐be quite confident (lit. *exercise* great confidence);
13 10		I am writing this . . . so that when I am with you I shall not need to ⌐be strict (lit. *exercise* severity),
Col 2 22		all these prohibitions are only concerned with things that
	8	perish by their very *use*
1 Tm 1 8		the Law is good, but only provided it is *treated* like any law,
5 23		⌐have (lit. *use*) a little wine for the sake of your digestion

b) Useful – Of (no) use, Good-for-nothing

Mt 25 30	4	As for this *good-for-nothing* servant, throw him out into the dark,
Lk 17 10	4	We are ⌐merely (lit. *useless*) servants:
2 Tm 2 14		there is to be no wrangling about words: ⌐all that this ever
	6	achieves is (lit. that is *of no use* at all, except for) the destruction of those who are listening.
21		I am speaking about . . . the way for anyone to become a
	2	vessel for special occasions, *fit* for the Master himself *to use*,
4 11	2	I find [Mark] a *useful* helper in my work.
Phm 11	7/2	[Onesimus] was *of no use* to you before, but he will be *useful* to you now,

11. ARCH- (IRONICALLY), SUPER-, SUPERLATIVE: *HYPER-LIAN*

hyper-lian 2

2 Co 11 5	As far as I can tell, these ⌐*arch-* (or: *super-*)apostles have nothing more than I have.
12 11	there is not a thing these ⌐*arch-* (or: *super-*)apostles have that I do not have as well.

12. BEAUTIFUL – HANDSOME

1: WELL-FAVOURED – FINE – BEAUTIFUL: *ASTEIOS*

asteios 2

Ac 7 20	(Ex 2 2) It was at this period that Moses was born, a [fine] child [and] *favoured* by God.
Heb 11 23	(Ex 2 2) [Moses] was such a *fine* child.

2: BEAUTIFUL – HANDSOME: *HŌRAIOS*

hōraios 4

Mt 23 27	whitewashed tombs . . . look *handsome* on the outside,
Ac 3 2	the Temple entrance [was] called the *Beautiful* Gate
10	the man . . . used to sit begging at the *Beautiful* Gate of the Temple.
Rm 10 15	(Is 52 7) ⌐The footsteps of those who bring good news is a welcome sound (lit. How *beautiful* the feet of those who bring good news)!

3: BEAUTIFUL – LOVELY: *EU-PREPEIA*

eu-prepeia 1

Jm 1 11	the scorching sun comes up, and the grass withers . . . what looked so *beautiful* now disappears.

GRACE – THANKS

1: Grace, Favour – Gift – Work of Mercy
  a) Grace, Favour(ed) of God, of Christ – God's Free Gift, the Gift of Grace
  b) Favour, Respect – Gracious – Merit, (Be) Approved
  c) Work of Charity, Errand of Mercy – Generous – Gift
2: Give, Bestow, Hand over – Forgive
  a) God Gives as a Gift, Jesus Bestows – Grant as a Privilege
  b) Forgive, Pardon – Forgiveness
  c) Hand over, Surrender, Give up, a person
3: to Thank, Give thanks
  a) Give thanks to God, to Jesus – Thanksgiving, Thankful
  b) Thank(s), Grateful, Gratitude – Credit – Ungrateful

1 *charis*	156	7 *a-charistos*	2
4 *charisma*	17	2 *eu-charisteō*	38
6 *charitoō*	2	5 *eu-charistia*	15
3 *charizomai*	23	8 *eu-charistos*	1

1: GRACE, FAVOUR – GIFT – WORK OF MERCY

a) Grace, Favour(ed) of God, of Christ – God's Free Gift, the Gift of Grace

Lk 1 28	6	Rejoice, so highly *favoured*! The Lord is with you.
30		Mary, do not be afraid; you have won God's *favour*.
2 40		the child [Jesus] grew . . . and God's *favour* was with him.
52		Jesus increased in wisdom . . . and in *favour* with God and men.
Jn 1 14		The Word . . . the only Son of the Father, full of *grace* and truth.
16		from his fulness we have . . . received . . . *grace* in return for *grace*,
17		*grace* and truth have come through Jesus Christ.
Ac 6 8		Stephen was filled with *grace* . . . and began to work miracles
7 46		[David] won God's *favour*
11 23		[Barnabas] could see for himself that God had given *grace*, and this pleased him,
13 43		Paul and Barnabas urged [the converts] to remain faithful to the *grace* God had given them.
14 3		the Lord supported all [Paul and Barnabas] said about his gift of *grace*, allowing signs
26		Antioch, where [Paul and Barnabas] had originally been commended to the *grace* of God
15 11		we believe that we are saved . . . through the *grace* of the Lord Jesus.
40		Before Paul left, he . . . was commended by the brothers to the *grace* of God
18 27		Apollos . . . was able by God's *grace* to help the believers considerably
20 24		the mission . . . that was to bear witness to the Good News of God's *grace*.
32		I commend you to God, and to the word of his *grace*
Rm 1 5		Through [Jesus Christ] we received *grace* and our apostolic mission
7		To you all . . . may God our Father and the Lord Jesus Christ send *grace* and peace.
11		I am longing to see you . . . to strengthen you by sharing a
	4	spiritual *gift* with you,
3 24		[all who believe] are justified through the free gift of his *grace* by being redeemed in Christ Jesus
4 16		the promise [of inheriting the world] depends on faith, so that it may be a ⌐*free gift* (or: *gift of grace*)
5 2		it is by faith and through Jesus that we have entered this state of *grace*
15	4	but the *gift* itself considerably outweighed the fall. If it is certain that through one man's fall so many died, it is even more certain that divine *grace*, coming through the one man, Jesus Christ, came to so many as an abundant ⌐*free gift*
16		(or: *gift of grace*). 16 The results of the gift also outweigh the results of one man's sin: for . . . now after many falls
17	4	comes *grace* with its verdict of acquittal. 17 . . . it is even more certain that one man, Jesus Christ, will cause everyone to reign in life who receives the ⌐*free gift* (or: *gift of grace*) . . . of being made righteous.
20		however great the number of sins committed, *grace* was even
21		greater; 21 and so, just as sin reigned wherever there was death, so *grace* will reign to bring eternal life
6 1		Does it follow that we should remain in sin so as to let *grace* have greater scope?
14		you are living by *grace* and not by law. 15 Does the fact that
15		we are living by *grace* and not by law mean that we are free to sin?
23	4	the *present* given by God is eternal life in Christ Jesus our Lord.
11 5		Today the same thing has happened: there is a remnant,
6		chosen by *grace*. 6 By *grace*, you notice, nothing therefore to do with good deeds, or *grace* would not be *grace* at all!

Rm 11 29 4 God never takes back his *gifts* or revokes his choice.
   12 3   In the light of the *grace* I have received I want to urge each one among you not to exaggerate his real importance.
   6 4/ Our *gifts* differ according to the *grace* given us.
   15 15   God has given me this ⌐special position (lit. *grace*). ¹⁶ He has appointed me as a priest of Jesus Christ,
   16 20   The *grace* of our Lord Jesus Christ be with you.
   24   (ᵛ The *grace* of our Lord Jesus Christ be with you all. Amen.)
1 Co 1 3   May God our Father and the Lord Jesus Christ send you *grace* and peace.
   4   I never stop thanking God for all the *graces* you have received through Jesus Christ.
   7 4 so that you will not be without any of the *gifts* of the Spirit
   3 10   By the *grace* God gave me, I . . . laid the foundations,
   7 7 4 everybody has his own particular *gifts* from God,
   12 4 4 There is a variety of *gifts* but always the same Spirit;
   9 4 another again [may have] the *gift* of healing, through this one Spirit;
   28   In the Church, God has given the first place to apostles . . .
   30 4 after them, miracles, and after them the *gift* of healing;
   30 4 or [do] all have the *gift* of healing?
   31 4 Be ambitious for the higher *gifts*.
   15 10   by God's *grace* that is what I am, and the *grace* that he gave me has not been fruitless . . . I, or rather the *grace* of God that is with me, have worked harder than any of the others;
   16 23   The *grace* of the Lord Jesus be with you.
2 Co 1 2   *Grace* and peace to you from God our Father and the Lord Jesus Christ.
   11   the more people there are asking for help for us, the more
   4 will be giving thanks when the *gift* is granted to us.
   12   by the *grace* of God we have [treated everybody with sincerity] without ulterior motives.
   4 15   the more *grace* is multiplied among people, the more thanksgiving there will be,
   6 1   we beg you . . . not to neglect the *grace* of God
   8 1   here . . . is the news of the *grace* of God which was given in the churches of Macedonia.
   9 8   there is no limit to the ⌐blessings (lit. *grace*; or: *gifts*) which God can send you
   14   they are drawn to you on account of all the *grace* that God has given you. ¹⁵ Thanks be to God for his inexpressible gift!
   12 9   My *grace* is enough for you: my power is at its best in weakness.
   13 13   The *grace* of the Lord Jesus Christ, the love of God and the fellowship of the Holy Spirit be with you all.
Ga 1 3   We wish you the *grace* and peace of God our Father and of the Lord Jesus Christ,
   6   you have turned away from the one who called you by the *grace* of Christ
   15   God, who had specially chosen me . . . called me through his *grace*
   2 9   [James, Cephas and John] shook hands with . . . me, recognising the *grace* thus given me
   21   I cannot bring myself to give up God's ⌐*gift* (or: *grace*):
   5 4   if you do look to the Law to make you justified, then you . . . have fallen from *grace*.
   6 18   The *grace* of our Lord Jesus Christ be with your spirit,
Ep 1 2   *Grace* and peace to you from God our Father and from the Lord Jesus Christ.
   6   [God chose us] to make us praise the glory of his *grace*, his
   7 6 *free gift* to us in the Beloved, ⁷ in whom . . . we gain . . . the forgiveness of our sins. Such is the richness of the *grace*
   2 5   it is through *grace* that you have been saved
   7   This was to show . . . how infinitely rich he is in *grace*
   8   Because it is by *grace* that you have been saved, through faith;
   3 2   I have been entrusted by God with the *grace* he meant for you,
   7   I have been made the servant of that gospel by a gift of *grace* from God who gave it to me . . . ⁸ I . . . have been
   8   entrusted with this special *grace* . . . of proclaiming to the pagans the infinite treasure of Christ
   4 7   Each one of us . . . has been given his own share of *grace*, given as Christ allotted it.
   29   let your words be for the improvement of others . . . and ⌐do good (lit. give *grace*) to your listeners,
   6 24   May *grace* and eternal life be with all who love our Lord Jesus Christ.
Ph 1 2   We wish you the *grace* and peace of God our Father and of the Lord Jesus Christ.
   7   you have shared the ⌐privileges which have been mine (lit. *grace* which is my responsibility):
   4 23   May the *grace* of the Lord Jesus Christ be with your spirit.
Col 1 2   *Grace* and peace to you from God our Father.
   6   you heard about God's *grace* and understood what this really is.
   4 18   *Grace* be with you.
1 Th 1 1   wishing you *grace* and peace.

1 Th 5 28   The *grace* of our Lord Jesus Christ be with you.
2 Th 1 2   wishing you *grace* and peace from God the Father and the Lord Jesus Christ.
   12   the name of our Lord . . . will be glorified . . . by the *grace* of our God and the Lord Jesus Christ.
   2 16   God . . . who has given us his love and, through his *grace*, such inexhaustible comfort and such sure hope,
   3 18   May the *grace* of our Lord Jesus Christ be with you all.
1 Tm 1 2   to Timothy . . . wishing you *grace*, mercy and peace from God . . . and from Christ Jesus our Lord.
   14   the *grace* of our Lord filled me with faith
   4 14 4 You have in you a *spiritual gift* which was given to you when the prophets spoke . . . do not let it lie unused.
   6 21   *Grace* be with you.
2 Tm 1 2   to Timothy . . . wishing you *grace*, mercy and peace from God the Father and from Christ Jesus our Lord.
   6 4 fan into a flame the *gift* that God gave you when I laid my hand on you.
   9   [God] has saved us . . . for his own purpose and by his own *grace* . . . granted to us, in Christ Jesus, before the beginning of time, ¹⁰ . . . revealed by the Appearing of our saviour
   2 1   Accept the strength . . . that comes from the *grace* of Christ Jesus.
   4 22   *Grace* be with you.
Tt 1 4   To Titus . . . wishing you *grace* and peace from God the Father and from Christ Jesus our saviour.
   2 11   God's *grace* has been revealed,
   3 7   [God] did this so that we should be justified by his *grace*, to become heirs
   15   *Grace* be with you all.
Phm 3   wishing you the *grace* and the peace of God our Father and the Lord Jesus Christ.
   25   May the *grace* of our Lord Jesus Christ be with your spirit.
Heb 2 9   by God's *grace* [Christ] had to experience death for all mankind.
   4 16   Let us be confident, then, in approaching the throne of *grace*, that we shall have mercy from him and find *grace*
   10 29   anyone . . . who insults the Spirit of *grace*, will be condemned
   12 15   Be careful that no one is deprived of the *grace* of God
   28   Let us . . . hold on to the *grace*
   13 9   it is better to rely on *grace* for inner strength than on dietary laws
   25   *Grace* be with you all.
Jm 4 6   he has ⌐been even more generous (or: given even more *grace*) to us . . . (Pr 3 34): God . . . gives ⌐generously (or: his *grace*) to the humble.
1 P 1 2   *Grace* and peace be with you more and more.
   10   their prophecies were about the *grace* which was to come to you.
   13   the *grace* that will be given you when Jesus Christ is revealed.
   3 7   a woman . . . is equally an heir to the life of *grace*.
   4 10 4 Each one of you has received a special ⌐*grace* (or: *gift*), so, like good stewards responsible for all these different *graces* of God, put yourselves at the service of others.
   5 5   (Pr 3 34) God . . . will always *favour* the humble.
   10   You will have to suffer only for a little while: the God of all *grace* . . . will see that all is well again:
1 P 5 12   I write . . . to encourage you never to let go this true *grace* of God
2 P 1 2   May you have more and more *grace* and peace as you come to know our Lord more and more.
   3 18   go on growing in the *grace* and in the knowledge of our Lord and saviour Jesus Christ.
2 Jn 3   we shall have *grace*, mercy and peace from God the Father and from Jesus Christ,
Jude 4   Certain people have infiltrated among you . . . turning the *grace* of our God into immorality,
Rv 1 4   *grace* and peace to you from him who is, who was, and who is to come, from the seven spirits . . . ⁵ and from Jesus Christ,
   22 21   May the *grace* of the Lord Jesus be with you all.

b) Favour, Respect – Gracious – Merit, (Be) Approved

Lk 2 52 X   Jesus increased in wisdom . . . and in *favour* with God and men.
   4 22 X   [Jesus] won the approval of all . . . by the *gracious* words that came from his lips.
Ac 2 47   [the faithful] were *looked up to* by everyone.
   4 33   The apostles . . . were all given great *respect*.
   7 10   [God] rescued [Joseph] . . . by giving him *grace* and wisdom . . . to attract the attention of Pharaoh
   24 27   being anxious to gain *favour* with the Jews, Felix left Paul in custody.
   25 3   [The chief priests informed Festus of the case against Paul] asking him to ⌐support (lit. *favour*) them rather than Paul,
   25 9   Festus was anxious to gain *favour* with the Jews,
Rm 4 4   If a man has work to show, his wages are not considered as a *favour* but as his due;

2 Co	1 15		I had meant to come to you first, so that you would ⸢benefit doubly (lit. be doubly *favoured*);
	8 4		[the churches in Macedonia have been] begging us for the *favour* of sharing in this service to the saints
Col	4 6		Talk to [those who are not Christians] ⸢agreeably (lit. *graciously*)
1 P	2 19		there is some *merit* in putting up with the pains of unearned punishment if it is done for the sake of God ²⁰ . . . The
	20		*merit*, in the sight of God, is in bearing [the beating] patiently when you are punished after doing your duty.

c) Work of Charity, Errand of Mercy – Generous – Gift

1 Co	16 3		I will send your *offering* to Jerusalem by the hand of whatever men you give letters of reference to;
2 Co	8 6		we have asked Titus . . . to bring this *work of mercy* to the same point of success among you.
	7		we expect you to put the most into this *work of mercy*
	9	X	Remember how *generous* the Lord Jesus was:
	19		[Titus] happens to be the same brother who has been elected by the churches to be our companion on this *errand of mercy*
Jm	4 6		he has ⸢been even more *generous* (or: given even more grace) to us . . . (Pr 3 34): God . . . gives ⸢*generously* (or: his grace) to the humble.

2: GIVE, BESTOW, HAND OVER – FORGIVE

a) God Gives as a Gift, Jesus Bestows – Grant as a Privilege

Lk	7 21	3	[Jesus] *gave* the gift of sight to many who were blind.
Ac	27 24	3	God *grants* you the safety of all who are sailing with you.
Rm	8 32	3	after such a gift . . . [God] will not refuse anything he can *give*.
1 Co	2 12	3	we have received the Spirit . . . from God, to teach us to understand the gifts that he has *given* us.
Ga	3 18	3	as the result of a promise . . . God *made his gift* to Abraham.
Ph	1 29	3	[God] has *given* you the privilege not only of believing in Christ, but of suffering for him as well.
	2 9	3	God . . . *gave* [Jesus] the name which is above all other names

b) Forgive, Pardon – Forgiveness

Lk	7 42	<	3	[the creditor] *pardoned* them both. Which of them will love
	43	<	3	him more? ⁴³ The one who was *pardoned* more,
2 Co	2 7		3	[Someone has been the cause of pain;] the best thing now is to *give* him your *forgiveness* and encouragement,
	10		3/3	Anybody that you *forgive*, I [forgive]; and as for my *forgiving* anything – if there has been anything to be *forgiven*, I have [forgiven] it for your sake
	12 13		3	I have not myself been a burden on you? For this unfairness, please *forgive* me.
Ep	4 32		3	Be friends . . . *forgiving* each other as readily as God
		⊖	3	*forgave* you in Christ.
Col	2 13	⊖	3	he has brought ⸢you (ᵛ us) to life with [Christ], he has *forgiven* us all our sins.
	3 13	X	3/3	*forgive* each other . . . The Lord has *forgiven* you; now you must do the same.

c) Hand over, Surrender, Give up, a person

Ac	3 14	3	It was you . . . who demanded the *reprieve* of a murderer
	25 11	3	no one has a right to *surrender* me to them.
	16	3	Romans are not in the habit of *surrendering* any man, until the accused . . . is given an opportunity to defend himself
Phm	22	3	I am hoping through your prayers to be *restored* to you.

3: TO THANK, GIVE THANKS

a) Give thanks to God, to Jesus – Thanksgiving, Thankful

Mt	15 36	X	2	he took the seven loaves and the fish, and he *gave thanks* and broke them
	26 27	X	2	he took a cup, and when he had *returned thanks* he gave it to them.
Mk	8 6	X	2	he took the seven loaves, and after *giving thanks* he broke them
	14 23	X	2	he took a cup, and when he had *returned thanks* he gave it to them,
Lk	6 35		7	the Most High . . . himself is kind to the *ungrateful* and the wicked.
	17 16		2	[one of the ten cured lepers] threw himself at the feet of Jesus and *thanked* him. The man was a Samaritan.
	18 11		2	The Pharisee . . . said this prayer to himself, 'I *thank* you, God, that I am not . . . like the rest of mankind,'
	22 17	X	2	Then, taking a cup, he *gave thanks* and said, 'Take this . . .'
	19	X	2	Then he took some bread, and when he had *given thanks*, broke it and gave it to them,
Jn	6 11	X	2	Jesus took the loaves, *gave thanks*, and gave them out to all who were sitting ready; he then did the same with the fish,

Jn	6 23	X		the place where the bread had been eaten (§ after the Lord had *given thanks*).
	11 41	X	2	Jesus . . . said: 'Father, I *thank* you for hearing my prayer.'
Ac	27 35		2	[Paul] took some bread, *gave thanks* to God . . . broke it
	28 15		2	When Paul saw [the brothers in Rome] he *thanked* God
Rm	1 8		2	I *thank* my God . . . for the way in which your faith is spoken of all over the world.
	21		2	[the pagans] knew God and yet refused to honour him as God or to *thank* him;
	6 17		2	*thank* God you submitted without reservation to the creed you were taught.
	7 25			*Thanks* be to God through Jesus Christ our Lord!
	14 6		2	The one who eats meat also does so in honour of the Lord, since he *gives thanks* to God; but then the man who abstains does that too in honour of the Lord, and so he also *gives God thanks*.
1 Co	1 4		2	I never stop *thanking* God for all the graces you have received
	14		2	I am *thankful* that I never baptised any of you after Crispus and Gaius
	10 30		2	If I take my share with *thankfulness*, why should I be blamed for food for which I have *thanked* God?
	11 24	X	2	[Jesus] *thanked* God for [the bread] and broke it, and he said, 'This is my body . . .'
	14 16		5	Any uninitiated person will never be able to say Amen to your *thanksgiving*, if you only bless God with the spirit, for he will have no idea what you are saying. ¹⁷ However
	17		2	well you *make* your *thanksgiving*, the other gets no benefit from it. ¹⁸ I *thank* God that I have a greater gift of tongues than all of you,
	18		2	
	15 57			let us *thank* God for giving us the victory through our Lord Jesus Christ.
2 Co	1 11			the more people there are asking for help for us, the more will be *giving thanks* when it is granted to us.
	2 14			*Thanks* be to God who . . . makes us, in Christ, partners of his triumph,
	4 15		5	the more grace is multiplied among people, the more *thanksgiving* there will be,
	8 16		2	I *thank* God for putting into Titus' heart the same concern for you that I have myself.
	9 11			you will be able to do all the generous things which . . . are
	12		5	the cause of *thanksgiving* to God. ¹² For doing this holy
			5	service . . . is also increasing the amount of *thanksgiving* that God receives.
	15			*Thanks* be to God for his inexpressible gift!
Ep	1 16		2	[having heard about your faith, I] have never failed to . . . *thank* God for you.
	5 4		5	raise your voices in *thanksgiving* instead.
	20		2	so that always and everywhere you are *giving thanks* to God . . . in the name of our Lord Jesus Christ.
Ph	1 3		2	I *thank* my God whenever I think of you;
	4 6			if there is anything you need, pray for it, asking God for it
			5	with prayer and *thanksgiving*,
Col	1 3		2	We have never failed to . . . *give thanks* for you to God . . .
				⁴ ever since we heard about your faith
	12		2	*thanking* the Father who has made it possible for you to join the saints
	2 7			you must be rooted in [Christ] and built on him . . . and full
			5	of *thanksgiving*.
	3 15		8	Always be *thankful*.
	16			With *gratitude* in your hearts sing psalms and hymns and inspired songs to God;
	17			never say or do anything except in the name of the Lord
			2	Jesus, *giving to thanks* God the Father through him.
	4 2		5	Be persevering in your prayers and be *thankful* as you stay awake to pray.
1 Th	1 2		2	We always . . . *thank* God for you all,
	2 13		2	Another reason why we constantly *thank* God for you is that as soon as you heard the message . . . you accepted it
	3 9		5	How can we *thank* God enough for you . . .?
	5 18		2	for all things *give thanks* to God,
2 Th	1 3		2	we must be continually *thanking* God for you . . . because your faith is growing so wonderfully
	2 13		2	we must be continually *thanking* God for you . . . because God chose you
1 Tm	1 12			I *thank* Christ Jesus our Lord, who has given me strength,
	2 1		5	there should be prayers offered for everyone – petitions, intercessions and *thanksgiving*
	4 3			abstaining from foods which God created to be accepted
	4		5	with *thanksgiving* by all who believe . . . ⁴ . . . no food
			5	is to be rejected, provided *grace* is said for it:
2 Tm	1 3			I *thank* God . . . remembering my duty to him . . . and I always remember you in my prayers;
Phm	4		2	I always . . . *thank* God for you, ⁵ because I hear of the love and the faith which you have
Rv	4 9		5	the animals glorified and honoured and gave *thanks* to the One sitting on the throne,
	7 12		5	[all the angels said:] Amen. Praise . . . and *thanksgiving* . . . to our God
	11 17		2	We *give thanks* to you, Almighty Lord God,

b) Thank(s), Grateful, Gratitude – Credit – Ungrateful

Lk	6 32	Δ	If you love those who love you, what *thanks* can you expect?
	33		. . .[33] And if you do good to those who do good to you, what
	34	Δ	*thanks* can you expect? . . .[34] And if you lend to those
		Δ	from whom you hope to receive, what *thanks* can you expect?
	17 9	Δ	Must he be *grateful* to the servant for doing what he was told?
Ac	24 3		[the unbroken peace and the reforms] are matters we accept
	5		. . . with all *gratitude*.
Rm	16 4		[My greetings to Prisca and Aquila:] I am not the only one
	2		to *owe* them *a debt of gratitude*,
2 Tm	3 2		7 [in the last days] people will be . . . *ungrateful*,

---

GREAT – MANY – MORE

---

1. Great, Big – Loud – Important: *megas*
- a) Great (applied to God, Christ, of the works of God), Greatness, Majesty – Proclaim the greatness of, 'Magnify', Glorify the Lord – Great things
- b) Great (applied to a person, angels), Great men – (Man) of great importance, Held in great honour – Tall, Grown up
- c) Great (applied to Babylon), the Great City, the Famous Prostitute
- d) Loud (voice) – At the top of (one's voice) – Aloud
- e) Big (applied to plants, animals, things, etc.), Large, Great – Huge, Enormous
- f) Great (qualitatively), Profound – (a Matter) of great worth, of great solemnity – Important

2. Such – So great, So much, So many
- 1: Such – So great – Stature: *hēlikos*
  - a) Such, So great, How great – Big, Large, Huge
  - b) Stature
- 2: So much, So many – Such, This – Like this: *tosoutos*

3. (Be) Greater than, Supreme, Better – (in) Authority, (of) High Office: *hyper-echō*

4. Large, Considerable (quantity), a Number (of) – Long (time), Some (time), Many: *hikanos*

5. Many – More – Much, Great: *polys*
- 1: Multiply, Increase – Abundant, Many times over, Overflow
- 2: Many – Much – Large, Great, Long
  - a) Many, Much (as pronouns) – (the) Majority, Most
  - b) Many (as adjective qualifying people) – Large (crowds), Great (crowds) – A number of (people)

- c) Many, Much (as adjectives qualifying time) – Long (time), Very (late)
- d) Many, Much (as adjectives generally) – Several, Plenty of – Great
- 3: Much, More (as adverbs) – Further – Freely, Earnestly, Strongly
- 4: More than (in contexts of particular interest) – Greater than
- 5: Much more, All the more, Even more

6. Number(s), Crowd, Many – Increase, Multiply: *plēthos*
- 1: Crowd(s), Number(s), Multitude (of people) – Assembly, Group, Community – Increase (in number), Multiply
- 2: Many (things), Number, Multitude – Increase, Be more and more, Multiply – Bundle

7. Not a few, No little: *ouk oligos*
- a) Not a few (people) = a Number of
- b) No little = Great, Long, Serious

8. More, Rather – Better, Greater – Especially: *mallon*
- 1: More, Rather (than), Instead (of) – Better (to), Greater
- 2: Especially, Particularly, Most

9. More
- 1: More, Further: *peraiterō*
- 2: More than, Over: *ep-anō*

10. More (than), Abundance, Overflow – Increase, Greater, Have too much – Be left over, Remain: *perisseuō*

11. Be worth more, Be more important, Be of more value – Be superior, Be higher, Be best: *dia-pherō*

12. Surpass, Exceed, Excessive – Be better, Greater – Transcendent, Immeasurable: *hyper-ballō*

13. (Be a) Burden, Weighty matter – Heavy, Press (on) – Be weighed down, Dull: *baros*

14. Be a burden (on): *kata-narkaō*

---

1. GREAT, BIG – LOUD – IMPORTANT: *MEGAS*

6	*megaleios*	1	2 *megalynō*	8
3	*megaleiotēs*	3	1 *megas*	245
7	*megalōs*	1	8 *megethos*	1
4	*megalōsynē*	3	5 *megistan*	3
			9 *megalo-prepēs*	1

L = Great // Little, Small, Least (*mikros*, *elachistos*)

a) Great (applied to God, Christ, or the works of God), Greatness, Majesty – Proclaim the greatness of, 'Magnify', Glorify the Lord – Great things

Mt	4 16	(Is 9 1) The people . . . has seen a *great* light;

Mt	5 35		Jerusalem . . . is the city of the *great* king.
	12 6	X	Now here . . . is something *greater* than the Temple.
Lk	1 32	X	[Jesus] will be *great* and will be called Son of the Most High.
	46		2 My soul *proclaims the greatness of* the Lord
	49		the Almighty has done *great things* for me.
	58		2 the Lord had *shown* [Elizabeth] so *great* a kindness,
	7 16	X	A *great* prophet has appeared among us;
	9 43		3 everyone was awestruck by the *greatness* of God.
Jn	1 50		You will see *greater* things than that.
	4 12	X	Are you a *greater* man than our father Jacob . . .?
	5 20		[the Father] will show [the Son] even *greater* things than these,
	36		my testimony is *greater* than John's:
	8 53	X	Are you *greater* than our father Abraham . . .?
	10 29		The Father ⱽ who gave them (G in what he gave) to me is *greater* than anyone,
	14 12		he will perform even *greater* works, because I am going to the Father.
	28		the Father is *greater* than I.
Ac	2 11		6 we hear them preaching . . . about the ⌐marvels (lit. *great things*) of God.
	20		(Jl 3 4) the *great* Day of the Lord dawns.
	6 8		Stephen . . . began to work miracles and *great* signs among the people.
	8 10	O	He is the divine power that is called *Great*.
	13		[Simon the magician] was astonished when he saw the wonders and *great* miracles that took place.
	10 46		2 they could hear them . . . *proclaiming the greatness of* God.
	19 17	X	2 the name of the Lord Jesus came to be *held in great honour*.
Ep	1 19		8 how infinitely *great* is the power that he has exercised for us believers.
	5 32		This mystery ⌐has many implications (lit. is a *great* one); but I am saying it applies to Christ and the Church.
Ph	1 20	X	now as always I shall have the courage for Christ to be
	2		*glorified* in my body,
1 Tm	3 16		the mystery of our religion is very *deep* indeed:
Tt	2 13	X	our *great* God and saviour Christ Jesus.
Heb	1 3		[the Son] has gone to take his place . . . at the right hand
	4		of divine *Majesty*.
	4 14	X	in Jesus . . . we have the *supreme* high priest
	6 13		God . . . swore by his own self, since it was impossible for him to swear by anyone *greater*:
	16		Men . . . swear an oath by something *greater* than themselves,
	8 1		[Our high priest] has his place at the right of the throne
			4 of divine *Majesty* in the heavens,
	9 11		Christ . . . has passed through the *greater*, the more perfect tent,
	10 21	X	we have the *supreme* high priest over all the house of God.
	13 20	X	our Lord Jesus . . . the *great* Shepherd of the sheep
2 P	1 4		[God] has given us the guarantee of something very *great* and wonderful to come:
	16	X	3 we had seen his *majesty* for ourselves.
	17		9 the *Sublime* Glory itself spoke to [Jesus]
1 Jn	3 20		God is *greater* than our conscience
	4 4		you have in you one who is *greater* than anyone in this world;
	5 9		God's testimony is much *greater*,
Jude	6		[God] has kept [the angels] down in the dark . . . to be judged on the *great* day.
	25		4 To God, the only God . . . be the glory, *majesty*, authority and power,
Rv	6 17		(Jl 2 11) the *Great* Day of his anger has come,
	11 17		We give thanks to you, Almighty Lord God . . . for using your *great* power
	15 3		How *great* and wonderful are all your works, Lord God Almighty;
	16 14		the *Great* Day of God the Almighty.
	19 17		Gather together at the *great* feast that God is giving.

b) Great (applied to a person, angels), Great men – (Man) of great importance, Held in great honour – Tall, Grown up

Mt	5 19	L	the man who keeps [the commandments] and teaches them will be considered *great* in the kingdom of heaven.
	11 11	L	of all the children born of women, a *greater* than John the Baptist has never been seen; yet the least in the kingdom of heaven is *greater* than he is.
	18 1		Who is the *greatest* in the kingdom of heaven? . . .[4] . . .
	4		the one who makes himself as little as this little child is the *greatest* in the kingdom of heaven.
	20 25		among the pagans the rulers lord it over them, and their *great men* make their authority felt. [26] . . . anyone who wants to be *great* among you must be your servant,
	23 11		The *greatest* among you must be your servant.
Mk	6 21		5 Herod . . . gave a banquet for the ⌐nobles (lit. *great men*) of his court,
	9 34		[the Twelve] had been arguing which of them was the *greatest*.
	10 42		among the pagans . . . their *great men* make their authority felt. [43] . . . anyone who wants to become *great* among you must be your servant,
Lk	1 15		[John] will be *great* in the sight of the Lord;

Lk 7 28 L　of all the children born of women, there is no one *greater* than John; yet the least in the kingdom of God is *greater* than he is.

9 46　An argument started . . . about which of them was the *greatest*.

48 L　the least among you all, that is the one who is *great*.

22 24　A dispute arose . . . about which should be reckoned the *greatest*,

26　the *greatest* among you must behave as if he were the youngest

27　. . . ²⁷ For who is the *greater*: the one at table or the one who serves?

Jn 13 16　no servant is *greater* than his master, no messenger is *greater* than the man who sent him.

15 20　A servant is not *greater* than his master.

Ac 5 13　2 the people ⸢were loud in their praise (lit. *held them in great honour*)

8 9　Simon [the magician] . . . had given it out that he was someone *momentous*, ¹⁰ and everyone believed what he said; *eminent* citizens and ordinary people alike

10 L

26 22 L　I have stood firm . . . testifying to *great* and small alike,

Rm 9 12 L　(Gn 25 23) the *elder* shall serve the younger,

1 Co 14 5　the man who prophesies is *of greater importance* than the man with the gift of tongues,

2 Co 10 15　2 we trust that . . . we shall *get taller* ⸢and taller (lit. more and more), when judged by our own standard.

Heb 8 11 L　(Jr 31 34) they will all know me, the least no less than the *greatest*,

11 24　when he *grew to manhood*, Moses refused to be known as the son of Pharaoh's daughter

2 P 2 11　the angels in their *greater* strength . . . make no complaint

Rv 6 15　5 all the earthly rulers, the ⸢governors (lit. *great men*) . . . took to the mountains to hide in caves

11 18 L　all who worship you, small or *great*

13 16 L　[The second beast] compelled everyone – small and *great* . . . – to be branded

18 23　5 Your traders were the ⸢princes (lit. *great men*) of the earth,

19 5 L　all who, *great* or small, revere [God].

18 L　There will be the flesh of kings for you . . . and of all kinds of men, citizens and slaves, small and *great*.

20 12 L　I saw the dead, both *great* and small, standing in front of his throne,

c) Great (applied to Babylon), the Great City, the Famous Prostitute

Rv 11 8　the *Great* City known by the symbolic names Sodom and Egypt,

14 8　Babylon the *Great* has fallen,

16 19　The *Great* City was split into three parts . . . Babylon the *Great* was not forgotten:

17 1　I will show you the punishment given to the *famous* prostitute

5　Babylon the *Great*, the mother of all the prostitutes . . . on the earth.

18　The woman you saw is the *great* city

18 2　Babylon the *Great* has fallen,

10　mourn for this *great* city, Babylon,

16　mourn for this *great* city; for all the linen . . . that you wore,

18　Has there ever been a city as *great* as this!

19　mourn for this *great* city

21　That is how the *great* city of Babylon is going to be hurled down,

19 2　[God] has condemned the *famous* prostitute

d) Loud (voice) – At the top of (one's voice) – Aloud

Mt 20 31　they only shouted more *loudly*, 'Lord! Have pity on us,'

24 31　[the Son of Man] will send his angels with a *loud* trumpet

27 46　about the ninth hour, Jesus cried out in a *loud* voice, 'Eli, Eli, lama sabachthani?'

50　Jesus, again crying out in a *loud* voice, yielded up his spirit.

Mk 1 26　the unclean spirit threw the man into convulsions and with a *loud* cry went out of him.

5 7　[the demoniac] shouted *at the top of* his voice, 'What do you want with me, Jesus'

15 34　at the ninth hour Jesus cried out in a *loud* voice, 'Eloi, Eloi'

37　Jesus gave a *loud* cry and breathed his last.

Lk 1 42　[Elizabeth] gave a *loud* cry and said, 'Of all women you are the most blessed'

4 33　there was a man who was possessed by the spirit of an unclean devil, and it shouted *at the top of* its voice,

8 28　[the demoniac] cried out *at the top of* his voice,

17 15　one of [the ten cured lepers] turned back praising God *at the top of* his voice

19 37　the whole group of disciples joyfully began to praise God *at the top of* their voices

23 23　they kept on shouting *at the top of* their voices,

46　when Jesus had cried out in a *loud* voice, he said, 'Father'

Jn 11 43　[Jesus] cried in a *loud* voice, 'Lazarus, here! Come out!'

Ac 5 13　2 the people ⸢were loud in their praises (or: held them in great honour)

Ac 7 57　the members of the council shouted out *at the top of* their voices and stopped their ears with their hands;

60　[Stephen] said *aloud*, 'Lord, do not hold this sin against them';

8 7　unclean spirits . . . came shrieking with a *loud* voice out of many who were possessed,

14 10　Paul said in a *loud* voice, 'Get to your feet – stand up',

16 28　Paul shouted *at the top of* his voice, 'Don't do yourself any harm; we are all here'.

23 9　The shouting grew *louder*.

26 24　Festus shouted out *at the top of* his voice, 'Paul, you are out of your mind'

Rv 1 10　I heard a voice . . . ⸢shouting like (lit. as *loud* as) a trumpet,

5 2　I saw a powerful angel who called with a *loud* voice, 'Is there anyone worthy to open the scroll . . .?'

12　[an immense number of angels] ⸢shouting (lit. saying in a *loud* voice), 'The Lamb that was sacrificed is worthy'

6 10　[the souls of all the people who had been killed on account of the word of God] shouted *aloud*, 'Holy, faithful Master, how much longer will you wait . . .?'

7 2　another angel . . . called in a *powerful* voice to the four angels

10　[a huge number of people] shouted *aloud*, 'Victory to our God'

8 13　I heard an eagle, calling *aloud* . . , 'Trouble, trouble, trouble'

10 3　[another angel] shouted so *loud*, it was like a lion roaring.

11 12　[the two witnesses] heard a *loud* voice from heaven say to them, 'Come up here',

15　⸢voices could be heard shouting (lit. *loud* voices could be heard) in heaven,

12 10　I heard a ⸢voice shout (lit. *loud* voice crying) from heaven, 'Victory and power . . . have been won by our God'

14 7　[another angel] was calling in a *loud* voice, 'Fear God'

9　A third angel followed, shouting *aloud*,

15　another angel . . . shouted *aloud* . . . 'Put your sickle in and reap'

18　the angel . . . shouted *aloud* . . . 'Put your sickle in . . .'

16 1　I heard a *loud* voice from the sanctuary

17　a *loud* voice shouted from the sanctuary, 'The end has come'.

19 1　I seemed to hear the *great* sound of a huge crowd . . . singing, 'Alleluia!'

17　an angel . . . shouted *aloud* . . . 'Come here.'

21 3　I heard a *loud* voice call from the throne, 'You see this city? Here God lives among men.'

e) Big (applied to plants, animals, things, etc.), Large, Great – Huge, Enormous

Mt 13 32 L <　when [a mustard seed] has grown it is the *biggest* shrub of all

23 5　[the scribes and the Pharisees,] ⸢wearing . . . longer (lit. *enlarging*) their) tassels,

2

27 60　[Joseph] rolled a *large* stone across the entrance of the tomb

Mk 4 32 L <　[a mustard seed] grows into the *biggest* shrub of them all and puts out *big* branches

5 11　there was . . . a *great* herd of pigs

13 2　You see these *great* buildings?

14 15　He will show you a *large* upper room furnished with couches,

16 4　the stone – which was very *big* – had already been rolled back.

Lk 12 18 <　I will pull down my barns and build *bigger* ones,

16 26　between us and you a *great* gulf has been fixed,

22 12　The man will show you a *large* upper room furnished with couches.

Jn 21 11　Simon Peter . . . dragged the net to the shore, full of *big* fish,

Ac 10 11　[Peter] saw . . . something like a *big* sheet being let down to earth

11 5　I . . . had a vision of something like a *big* sheet being let down from heaven

1 Co 16 9　a *big* and important door has opened for my work

2 Tm 2 20　Not all the dishes in a *large* house are made of gold

Rv 6 4　[The rider] was given a *huge* sword,

8 8　it was as though a *great* mountain, all on fire, had been dropped into the sea:

10　a *huge* star fell from the sky,

9 2　smoke poured up out of the Abyss like the smoke from a *huge* furnace

14　Release the four angels that are chained up at the *great* river Euphrates.

12 3 ⓓ　a second sign appeared . . . a *huge* red dragon

9 ⓓ　The *great* dragon . . . was hurled down to the earth

14　she was given a *huge* pair of eagle's wings

14 19　a *huge* winepress, the winepress of God's anger,

16 12　The sixth angel emptied his bowl over the *great* river Euphrates;

21　hail, with *great* hailstones weighing a talent each, fell from the sky

18 21　a boulder like a *great* millstone,

20 1　an angel . . . with . . . an *enormous* chain.

11　I saw a *great* white throne

21 10　In the spirit, [the angel] took me to the top of an *enormous* high mountain,

12　The walls of [the holy city] were of a *great* height,

f) Great (qualitatively), Profound – (a Matter) of great worth, of great solemnity – Important

A = Diana [Artemis]

Mt	2	10	The sight of the star filled [the Magi] with *great* delight,
	7	27	and ⌜what a (lit. *great* was the) fall it had!
	8	24	a storm broke over the lake, so ⌜violent (lit. *great*) that the waves were breaking right over the boat.
		26	⌜all was (lit. there was a *great*) calm again.
	15	28	Woman, you have *great* faith.
	22	36	which is the *greatest* commandment of the Law?
		38	This is the *greatest* and the first commandment.
	23	17	which is *of greater worth*, the gold or the Temple . . .?
		19	which is *of greater worth*, the offering or the altar . . .?
	24	21	then there will be *great* distress
		24	false prophets will . . . produce *great* signs and portents,
	28	2	there was a ⌜violent (lit. *great*) earthquake,
		8	Filled with awe and *great* joy the women came quickly away from the tomb
Mk	4	37	Then ⌜it began to blow a gale (lit. a *great* wind began to blow)
		39	the wind dropped, and ⌜all was (lit. there was a *great*) calm again.
		41	[The disciples] were filled with *great* awe
	5	42	they were overcome with *great* astonishment,
	12	31	There is no commandment *greater* than these [you must love God and your neighbour].
Lk	2	9	[The shepherds] were ⌜terrified (lit. *greatly* afraid),
		10	I bring you news of *great* joy,
	4	25	a *great* famine raged throughout the land,
		38	Simon's mother-in-law was suffering from a *high* fever
	5	29	In his honour Levi held a *great* reception in his house,
	6	49	⌜what a (lit. was the *great*) ruin that house became!
	8	37	The entire population of the Gerasene territory was in a state of *great* panic
	14	16	There was a man who gave a *great* banquet,
	21	11	There will be *great* earthquakes . . . there will be . . . *great* signs from heaven.
		23	*great* misery will descend on the land and wrath on this people.
	24	52	[the apostles] went back to Jerusalem full of *great* joy;
Jn	6	18	The wind was ⌜strong (lit. *great*), and the sea was getting rough.
	7	37	On the last day and *greatest* day of the festival, Jesus . . . cried out:
	15	13 X	A man can have no *greater* love than to lay down his life for his friends.
	19	11	the one who handed me over to you has the *greater* guilt.
		31	that sabbath was a day *of special solemnity*
Ac	4	33	The apostles continued to testify . . . with *great* power, and they were all given *great* respect.
	5	5	Ananias fell down dead. This made a *profound* impression on everyone present.
		11	This made a *profound* impression on the whole Church
	7	11	Then a famine came that caused ⌜much (lit *great*) suffering
	8	1	a ⌜bitter (lit. *great*) persecution started against the church in Jerusalem,
		2	some devout people . . . buried Stephen and made *great* mourning for him.
	11	28	Agabus . . . predicted that a *great* famine would spread
	15	3	this news was received with the *greatest* satisfaction by the brothers.
	16	26	Suddenly there was a *great* earthquake
	19	27 A	This threatens . . . to reduce the sanctuary of the *great* goddess Diana [Artemis] to unimportance. It could end up
		A 3	by taking away all the *prestige* of a goddess venerated all over Asia, yes, and everywhere in the civilised world.
		28 A	*Great* is Diana [Artemis] of the Ephesians!
		34 A	*Great* is Diana [Artemis] of the Ephesians!
		35 A	the city of the Ephesians is the guardian of the temple of great Diana [Artemis]
	26	29	'Little or ⌜more (lit. *great*),' Paul replied 'I wish before God that . . . you . . . would come to be as I am'
Rm	9	2	my sorrow is so *great*,
1 Co	9	11	If we have sown spiritual things for you, why should ⌜you be surprised (lit. it be so *great* a surprise to you) if we harvest your material things?
	12	31	Be ambitious for the *higher* gifts.
	13	13	there are three things that last: faith, hope and love; and the *greatest* of these is love.
2 Co	11	15	⌜there is no need to be surprised when (lit. it is no *great* thing if) [Satan's] servants, too, disguise themselves as the servants of righteousness.
Ph	4	10	7 It is a *great* joy to me, in the Lord, that . . . you have shown some concern for me
1 Tm	6	6	Religion . . . does bring *large* profits, but only to those who are content with what they have.
Heb	10	35	Be as confident now, then, since the reward is so *great*.
	11	26	the insults offered to the Anointed were something more *precious* than all the treasures of Egypt,

Jm	3	1	those of us who teach can expect ⌜a stricter judgement (lit. a *greater* reward or penalty).
		5 L	So is the tongue only a tiny part of the body, but it can proudly claim that it does *great things*.
	4	6	[God] has ⌜been even more generous (lit. given an even *greater amount* of grace) to us,
3 Jn		4	It is always my *greatest* joy to hear that my children are living according to the truth.
Rv	2	22	I am consigning her . . . and all her partners . . . to troubles that will test them ⌜severely (lit. *greatly*),
	6	12	there was a ⌜violent (lit. *great*) earthquake
		13	the stars . . . fell . . . like figs dropping from a fig tree when a *high* wind shakes it;
	7	14	These are the people who have been through the *great* persecution,
	11	11	everybody who saw it happen was ⌜terrified (lit. *greatly* afraid),
		13	there was a ⌜violent (lit. *great*) earthquake,
		19	Then came flashes of lightning . . . and ⌜violent (lit. *great*) hail.
	12	1	a *great* sign appeared in heaven:
		12	the devil has gone down to you in a *great* rage,
	13	2	the dragon had handed over to [the beast] his own *great* power and his throne
		5	(Dn 7 8) the beast was allowed to mouth its ⌜boasts (lit. *great* words)
		13	[the second beast] worked *great* miracles,
	14	2	I heard a sound . . . like the sound of the ocean or a *great* roar of thunder;
	15	1	What I saw next, in heaven, was a *great* and wonderful sign:
	16	9	people were scorched by the ⌜fierce (lit. *great*) heat
		18	there were flashes of lightning . . . and a ⌜violent (lit. *great*) earthquake, *greater* than anyone has ever seen
		21	They cursed God for sending a plague of hail; it was the ⌜most terrible (lit. *greatest*) plague.
	17	6	I was ⌜completely (lit. *greatly*) mystified.
	18	1	I saw another angel come down from heaven, with *great* authority given to him;

2. SUCH – SO GREAT, SO MUCH, SO MANY

1: SUCH – SO GREAT – STATURE: *HĒLIKOS*

1	*hēlikia* 5/8		4	*pēlikos* 2
3	*hēlikos* 2		2	*tēlikoutos* 4

L = Great // Little, Small, Least (*mikros, elachistos*)

a) Such, So great, How great – Big, Large, Huge

2 Co	1	10	2 [God] saved us from ⌜dying again (lit. *such* a death),
Ga	6	11	4 Take good note of what I am adding . . . in *large* letters.
Col	2	1	3 I want you to know that I do have to struggle ⌜hard (lit. *so greatly*) for you
Heb	2	3	we shall . . . not go unpunished, if we neglect ⌜this salvation
		2	that is (lit. *such* a salvation) promised to us.
	7	4	4 think *how great* [Melchizedek] must have been, if . . . Abraham paid him a tenth of the treasure
Jm	3	4 L	2 no matter *how big* [ships] are . . . the man at the helm can steer them . . . by controlling a tiny rudder.
		5	3 Think how small a flame can set fire to a *huge* forest;
Rv	16	18	2 [no one] has ever seen such or *so great* [an earthquake] since there have been men on earth

b) Stature

Mt	6	27	Can any of you . . . add one single cubit to his ⌜span of life (or: *stature*)?
Lk	2	52 X	Jesus increased in wisdom, in *stature*, and in favour
	12	25	Can any of you . . . add a single cubit to his ⌜span of life (or: *stature*)?
	19	3	[Zacchaeus] was too ⌜short (lit. small of *stature*)
Ep	4	13 X ●	we become the perfect Man, ⌜fully mature with (lit. of the full *stature* of) the fullness of Christ himself.

2: SO MUCH, SO MANY – SUCH, THIS – LIKE THIS: *TOSOUTOS*

tosoutos 20

Mt	8	10	nowhere in Israel have I found ⌜faith *like this* (or: *such* faith)
	15	33	Where could we get ⌜enough (or: *so much*) bread in this deserted place to feed *such* a crowd?
Lk	7	9	not even in Israel have I found ⌜faith *like this* (or: *such* faith)
	15	29	*all these* years I have slaved for you
Jn	6	9	what is that between *so many*?

Jn 12 37	Though [Jesus] gave *so many* signs, they did not believe in him;	
14 9	Have I been with you *all this* time, Philip, . . . and you still do not know me?	
21 11	in spite of there being *so many* [fishes] the net was not broken.	
Ac 5 8	'Tell me, was *this* the price you sold the land for?' 'Yes,' [Sapphira] said '*that* was the price.'	
1 Co 14 10	There are *any number of* different languages in the world,	
Ga 3 4	Have ⌐all the⌐ (lit. *so many*) ⌐favours⌐ (or: *sufferings*) you received been wasted?	
Heb 1 4	[the Son] is now *as* far above the angels as the title which he has inherited is higher than their own name.	
4 7	*much* later, [God] said 'today'	
7 22	⌐And it follows (lit. *So much* so) that it is a greater covenant	
10 25	*so much* more so as you see the Day drawing near.	
12 1	With *so many* witnesses in a great cloud on every side of us,	
Rv 18 7	For every one of [Babylon's] shows and orgies is to be matched *just so much* torture and grief.	
17	⌐your (lit. *so many*) riches are all destroyed within a single hour.

3. (BE) GREATER THAN, SUPREME, BETTER – (IN) AUTHORITY, (OF) HIGH OFFICE: *HYPER-ECHŌ*

3 (*hoi*) *kat' ex-ochēn* 1	1 *hyper-echō* 5
	2 *hyper-ochē* 2

Ac 25 23	Agrippa and Bernice arrived . . . attended by the tribunes and the city *notables*;	3
Rm 13 1	You must all obey the ⌐governing (lit. *supreme*) authorities.	
1 Co 2 1	when I came to you, it was not with any ⌐show of oratory (lit. *lofty* words) or philosophy,	2
Ph 2 3	Always consider the other person to be *better* than yourself,	
3 8	nothing can happen that will outweigh the *supreme advantage* of knowing Christ	
4 7	that peace of God, which is so much *greater* than we can understand, will guard your hearts	
1 Tm 2 2	[there should be prayers offered] especially for kings and others in *authority*,	2
1 P 2 13	accept the authority of every social institution: the emperor, as the *supreme authority*,	

4. LARGE, CONSIDERABLE (QUANTITY), A NUMBER (OF) – LONG (TIME), SOME (TIME), MANY: *HIKANOS*

hikanos 27/40

Mt 28 12	[the chief priests] handed a *considerable* sum of money to the soldiers
Mk 10 46	[Jesus] left Jericho with his disciples and a *large* crowd,
Lk 7 12	a *considerable* number of the townspeople were with [the widow of Nain].
8 27	for a *long* time [the demoniac] had worn no clothes,
32	there was a *large* herd of pigs feeding there
20 9	A man . . . went abroad for a *long* while.
23 8	Herod . . . had been wanting for a *long* time to set eyes on [Jesus];
9	[Herod] questioned [Jesus] *at some length*;
Ac 8 11	They had only been won over to [Simon] because of the *long* time he had spent working on them with his magic.
9 23	*Some* time passed, and the Jews worked out a plot to kill [Saul].
43	Peter stayed on *some* time in Jaffa,
11 24	a *large* number of people were won over to the Lord.
26	[Barnabas and Saul] were to live together [at Antioch] a whole year, instructing a *large* number of people.
12 12	[Peter] went straight to the house of Mary . . . where *a number* [of people] had assembled
14 3	Paul and Barnabas stayed on [at Iconium] for *some* time . . .
21	²¹ Having . . . made a *considerable* number of disciples [at Derbe], they went back . . . to Antioch.
18 18	After staying on [in Corinth] for *some* time, Paul . . . sailed for Syria,
19 19	a *number* of [believers] who had practised magic collected their books and made a bonfire of them
26	this man Paul has persuaded and converted *a great number* of people
20 8	A *number* of lamps were lit in the upstairs room
11	[Paul] ⌐carried on talking (lit. talked for *some* time)
37	[the elders of Ephesus] were all ⌐in (lit. shedding *many*) tears;
22 6	a ⌐bright (lit. *great*) light from heaven suddenly shone round me.
Ac 27 7	For *some* days we made little headway,
9	A *great deal* of time had been lost,
Rm 15 23	for *many* years I have been longing to pay you a visit.
1 Co 11 30	*many* of you are weak . . . and *some* of you have died.

5. MANY – MORE – MUCH, GREAT: *POLYS*

2	*pleiōn*	55	3	*pollō mallon*	12
5	*pleistos*	4	6	*poly mallon*	2
4	*pleonazō*	9	8	*poly(-logia)*	1
1	*polys*	358	9	*poly(-merōs)*	1
7	*polla-plasiōn*	2	10	*poly(-tropōs)*	1
			11	*hyper-pleonazō*	1

F = Many // Few

1: MULTIPLY, INCREASE – ABUNDANT, MANY TIMES OVER, OVERFLOW

Mt 19 29	everyone who has left houses, brothers . . . will be repaid ⌐a hundred (G *many*) times over,	7
Lk 18 30	[there is no one who has left house, wife . . .] who will not be given repayment *many times over*	
Rm 5 20	When law came, it was to *multiply* the opportunities of falling, but however ⌐great the number of sins committed (lit. the number of sins committed *multiplied*), grace was even greater;	4
6 1	Does it follow that we should remain in sin so as to let grace ⌐have greater scope (lit. *increase*)?	4
2 Co 4 15	the more grace *is multiplied* among people, the more thanksgiving there will be,	4
8 15	(Ex 16 18) The man who gathered much *had* none *too much*,	4
Ph 4 17	what is valuable . . . is the interest that *is mounting up* in your account.	4
1 Th 3 12	May the Lord ⌐be generous in increasing (lit. *abundantly* increase) your love	4
2 Th 1 3	your faith is growing so wonderfully and the love you have for one another never stops *increasing*;	4
1 Tm 1 14	the grace of our Lord ⌐filled (lit. *overflowed* for) me	11
2 P 1 8	If you have ⌐a generous supply (lit. an *abundance*) of these [virtues], they will not leave you ineffectual	4
Rv 17 1	the famous prostitute . . . rules enthroned beside ⌐abundant (or: *many*) waters,	

2: MANY – MUCH – LARGE, GREAT, LONG

a) Many, Much (as pronouns) – (the) Majority, Most

Mt 5 12	Rejoice . . . for your reward will be ⌐great (or: *much*) in heaven;	
7 13 F	the road that leads to perdition is wide . . . and *many* take it;	
22	When the day comes *many* will say to me, 'Lord, . . .'	
8 11	*many* will come from east and west to take their places with Abraham . . . at the feast in the kingdom of heaven; ¹² but the subjects of the kingdom will be turned out into the dark.	
16	they brought [Jesus] *many* who were possessed by devils.	
11 20	[Jesus] began to reproach the towns in which *most* of his miracles had been worked,	5
12 15	*Many* followed [Jesus] and he cured them all,	
19 30	*Many* who are first will be last, and the last, first.	
20 16 F	(ᵛ for *many* are called but few are chosen)	
28 ●	the Son of Man came . . . to give his life as a ransom for *many*.	
21 36	Next [the landowner] sent some more servants, this time *a larger number*,	2
22 14 F	For *many* are called, but few are chosen.	
24 5	*many* will come using my name . . . and they will deceive *many*.	
10	then *many* will fall away;	
11	Many false prophets will arise; they will deceive *many*,	
12	with the increase of lawlessness, love in *most* [men] will grow cold;	
25 21 F	you can be faithful in ⌐small (lit. *few*) [things], I will trust you with ⌐greater (lit. *many*);	
23 F	you can be faithful in ⌐small (lit. *few*) [things], I will trust you with ⌐greater (lit. *many*);	
26 28 ●	this is my blood . . . which is to be poured out for *many* for the forgiveness of sins.	
27 53	[the bodies of many holy men] came out of the tombs . . . and appeared to ⌐a number of people (lit. *many*).	
Mk 2 2	*many* [people] collected [in the house in Capernaum]	
15	there were *many* [of the tax collectors and sinners] among his followers.	
3 10	[Jesus] had cured . . . *many*	
5 9 ⓓ	My name is legion . . . for there are *many* of us.	
6 2	*most* [of them] were astonished when they heard [Jesus].	
31	there were so *many* coming and going that the apostles had no time even to eat.	
33	people saw them going, and *many* could guess where;	
9 26	the boy lay there so like a corpse that *most* [of them] said, 'He is dead'.	
10 31	*Many* who are first will be last,	

Mk 10	45 ●	the Son of Man . . . [came] to give his life as a ransom for *many.*
	48	*many* [of them] scolded [the blind man] and told him to keep quiet,
11	8	*Many* [people] spread their cloaks on the road,
12	37	the *great majority* of the people heard this with delight.
	41	*many* of the rich put in *a great deal* [of money]
13	6	*Many* will come using my name . . . and they will deceive *many.*
14	24 ●	This is my blood, the blood of the covenant, which is to be poured out for *many.*
	56	*Several* . . . brought false evidence against [Jesus],
Lk 1	1	*many* [others] have undertaken to draw up accounts of the events that have taken place among us,
	14	*many* will rejoice at [John's] birth,
	16	[John] will bring back *many* of the sons of Israel to the Lord
2	34	this child [Jesus] . . . is destined for the fall and for the rising of *many* in Israel,
	35	a sword will pierce your own soul too – so that the secret thoughts of *many* may be laid bare.
4	41	Devils too came out of *many* [people],
7	21	[Jesus] cured *many* [people] of diseases . . . and gave the gift of sight to *many* who were blind.
10	41 F	Martha, . . . you worry and fret about so *many things,*
11	53	the scribes and the Pharisees . . . tried to force answers from 2 [Jesus] on ⌐innumerable (lit. *a great number* [of]) [questions].
12	48	When a man has had ⌐*a great deal* (or: much) given him, ⌐*a great deal* (or: much) will be demanded of him; when a man has had ⌐*a great deal* (or: much) given him on trust, even more will be expected of him.
13	24	*many* will try to enter and will not succeed.
14	16	a man . . . gave a great banquet, and he invited ⌐a large number of people (lit. *many*).
16	10 F	The man who can be trusted in ⌐little (lit. few) [things] can be trusted in ⌐great (lit. *many*); the man who is dishonest in ⌐little (lit. few) [things] will be dishonest in ⌐great (lit. *many*).
21	8	*many* will come using my name and saying, 'I am he'
Jn 2	23	*many* believed in his name
4	41	2 when [Jesus] spoke to [the Samaritans] *many more* came to believe;
6	60	*many* of his followers said, 'This is intolerable language'.
	66	*many* of his disciples left [Jesus] and stopped going with him.
7	31	*many* [people] in the crowds . . . believed in [Jesus];
8	26	About you I have *much* to say and [much] to condemn;
	30	As [Jesus] was saying this, *many* came to believe in him.
10	20	*Many* said, 'He is possessed, he is raving';
	41	*Many* [people] . . . came to [Jesus]
	42	*many* of them believed in him.
11	45	*Many* of the Jews who had come to visit Mary . . . believed in [Jesus],
	55	*many* of the country people . . . had gone up to Jerusalem
12	11	*many* of the Jews were leaving [the chief priests] and believing in Jesus.
	42	there were *many* who did believe in [Jesus], even among the leading men,
16	12	I still have *many things* to say to you
Ac 4	4	*many* of those who had listened to their message became believers,
8	7	unclean spirits . . . came shrieking out of *many* who were possessed,
9	13	*several* [people] have told me about this man [Saul]
	42	The whole of Jaffa heard about it and *many* believed in the Lord.
10	27	[in Caesarea Cornelius and Peter] went in to meet ⌐all the (lit. *many*) [people] assembled there.
17	12	*Many* of the Jews [at Beroea] became believers, and so did ⌐many (lit. not a few) Greeks
19	18	*Some* of those who had become believers came forward to admit in detail how they had used spells
	32	2 *most* of them did not even know why they had been summoned.
26	10	I myself threw *many* of the saints into prison,
27	12	2 the *majority* were for . . . wintering at Phoenix
Rm 5	15 ●	If it is certain that through one man's fall [so] *many* died, it is even more certain that divine grace, coming through the one man, Jesus Christ, came to [so] *many* as an abundant free gift.
	19 ●	As by one man's disobedience *many* were made sinners, so by one man's obedience *many* will be made righteous.
12	5	⌐all of us (lit. we, though *many*), in union with Christ, form one body,
16	2	[Phoebe] has looked after *a great many* [people], myself included.
1 Co 1	26	how *many* of you were wise . . . how *many* were influential people, how *many* came from noble families?
9	19	I have made myself the slave of everyone so as to win ⌐as 2 many as I could (lit. *most*).
10	5	2 *most* of [our fathers] failed to please God

1 Co 10	17 ●	The fact that there is only one loaf means that, though there are *many* of us, we form a single body
	33	not anxious for my own advantage but for the advantage of ⌐everybody else (lit. *many*),
11	30	that is why *many* of you are weak and ill
12	12 ●	Just as a human body, though it is made up of many parts, is a single unit because all these parts, though *many*, make one body, so it is with Christ.
	14 ●	Nor is the body to be identified with any one part of its *many*
	20 ●	the parts are *many* but the body is one.
15	6	2 *most* of [the brothers] are still alive,
2 Co 1	11	the *more* [people] there are asking for help for us, the *more* will be giving thanks when it is granted to us.
2	6	2 The punishment already imposed by the *majority* . . . is enough;
	17	we do not go round offering the word of God for sale, as *many* [other people] do.
4	15	the more grace is multiplied among people, the more thanks-giving there will be from *a greater number*, to the glory of 2 God.
6	10	taken for paupers though we make ⌐others (lit. *many*) rich,
8	15	[Ex 16 18] The man who gathered *much* had none too much,
	22	we are sending a third brother, of those keenness we have often had proof in *many* [different ways],
9	2	2 your zeal has been a spur to *many more.*
11	18	*many* [others] have been boasting of their worldly achieve-ments,
12	21	I shall be grieving over ⌐all (lit. *many of*) those who sinned
Ga 3	16	scripture does not use a plural word as if there were *several* [descendants], it uses the singular . . . which is Christ.
Ph 1	14	2 *most* of the brothers have taken courage in the Lord from these chains of mine
3	18	*many* . . . are behaving as the enemies of the cross of Christ.
Heb 2	10	it was [God's] purpose to bring *a great many* of his sons into glory,
9	28 ●	(Is 53 12) Christ . . . offers himself only once to take the faults of *many* on himself,
12	15	bitterness . . . can poison ⌐a whole community (lit. *many*).
Jm 3	1	⌐Only a few (lit. Not too *many*) of you . . . should be teachers,
2 P 2	2	there will be *many* who copy [the] shameful behaviour [of the false teachers]
2 Jn	12	There are *several things* I have to tell you,
3 Jn	13	There were *several things* I had to tell you

b) *Many (as adjective qualifying people) – Large (crowds), Great (crowds) – A number of (people)*

Mt 3	7	*a number of* Pharisees and Sadducees
4	25	*large* crowds
8	1	*large* crowds
	18	*great* crowds
9	10	*a number of* tax collectors
13	2	⌐such (lit. so *great*) crowds
	17	*many* prophets and holy men
14	14	*large* crowd
15	30	*large* crowds . . . *many* others
19	2	*large* crowds
20	29	*large* crowd
21	8	5 *Great* crowds
24	11	*Many* false prophets
26	47	*large* ⌐number of men (or: crowd)
	60	*several* lying witnesses
27	52	*many* holy men
	55	*many* women
Mk 1	34	*many* devils
2	15	*a number of* tax collectors and sinners
3	7	*great* crowds
	8	*great* numbers
4	1	5 such a *huge* crowd
5	21	*large* crowd
	24	*large* crowd
	26	⌐various (lit. *many*) doctors
6	13	*many* devils . . . *many* sick people
	34	*large* crowd
8	1	*great* crowd
9	14	*large* crowd
12	5	*a number of* others
	41	*many* [of the] rich [people]
15	41	*many* other women
Lk 1	16	*many* [of the] sons of Israel
4	25	*many* widows
	27	*many* lepers
5	15	*large* crowds
	29	*large* gathering
6	17	*large* gathering . . . *great* crowd
7	11	*great* ⌐number of people (or: crowd)
	21	*many* [who were] blind [people]
8	3	*several* others

Lk	8	4	*large* crowd
		30	*many* devils
	9	37	*large* crowd
	10	24	*many* prophets and kings
	14	25	*Great* crowds
	23	27	*Large* numbers of people
Jn	4	1	2 *more* disciples
		39	*Many* Samaritans
	6	2	*Large* crowd
		5	*large* crowds
	11	19	*many* Jews
		45	*many* [of the] Jews
	12	9	*large* number of Jews
		11	*many* [of the] Jews
		12	*great* crowds
	19	20	*many* [of the] Jews
Ac	6	7	*large* group of priests
	8	7	*several* paralytics and cripples
	11	21	*great* number [of people]
	13	43	*many* Jews and devout converts
	14	1	a *great* many Jews and Greeks
	15	35	*many* others
	17	4	a *great* many God-fearing people
	18	8	[a great] *many* Corinthians
		10	*many* people on my side
	23	13	2 *more than* forty
		21	2 *more than* forty
	28	23	2 *a large number of* [Jews]
Rm	4	17	*many* nations
		18	*many* nations
	8	29	*many* brothers
1 Co	4	15	*more than* one father
	8	5	*many* "gods" and "lords" *plenty*
	14	27	5 three, *at the most*
Ga	1	14	*many* other Jews
	4	27	*many more* sons of the forsaken
Ph	1	14	2 *most* [of the] brothers
1 Tm	6	12	*many* witnesses
2 Tm	2	2	in public (lit. before *many* witnesses)
Tt	1	10	[a great] *many* people
Heb	2	10	[a great] *many* sons [of God]
	7	23	2 *a great number of* . . . priests
1 Jn	2	18	*several* antichrists
	4	1	*many* false prophets
2 Jn		7	*many* deceivers
Rv	5	11	*an immense number of* angels
	7	9	*huge* number of people (or: crowd)
	8	11	*many* people
	10	11	*many* different nations
	19	1	*huge* crowd
		6	*huge* crowd

c) Many, Much (as adjectives qualifying time) – Long (time), Very (late)

Mt	25	19	a *long* time
Mk	6	35	getting *very* late . . . getting *very* late
Lk	2	36	well on in (lit. of *many*) years
	12	19	*many* years
	15	13	A few (lit. Not *many*) days
Jn	2	12	only a few (lit. not *many*) days
	5	6	a *long* time
Ac	1	5	*many* days
	4	22	2 over (lit. *more than*) forty years
	13	31	2 *many* days
	16	18	every day (lit. *many* days)
	21	10	2 *several* days
	24	10	*many* years
		11	2 *more than* twelve days
		17	2 *several* years
	25	6	2 ten days, *at the most*
		14	2 *several* days
	27	14	not *long* before
		20	*a number of* days
		21	a *long* time
	28	6	a *long* time

d) Many, Much (as adjectives generally) – Several, Plenty of – Great

Mt	2	18	loud (or: *great*) lamenting
	5	12	reward will be *great* (or: *much*)
	6	7 8	*many* words
	7	22	*many* miracles
	8	30	*large* herd of pigs
	9	37 F	harvest is rich (lit. *great*)
	10	31	hundreds of (lit. *many*) sparrows
	11	20 5	*most* [of his] miracles
	13	5	little (lit. not *much*) soil
		58	*many* miracles
	14	24	(G *several* furlongs) out
	19	22	*great* wealth (or: *many* possessions)
	26	53	2 *more than* twelve legions

Mk	4	5	little (lit. not *much*) soil
		33	*many* parables
	7	4	*many* other observances
		13	*many* other things
	10	22	*great* wealth (or: *many* possessions)
	13	26	*great* power and glory
	15	3	*many* accusations
Lk	3	18	*many* other things he said
	5	6	*huge* number of fish
	6	23	reward will be *great*
		35	*great* reward
	7	47 F	*many* sins
	8	29	[a great] *many* times
	10	2 F	harvest is rich (lit. *great*)
		40	all the serving (lit. *many* tasks)
	12	7	hundreds of (lit. *many*) sparrows
		19	*plenty of* good things
		47 F	*many* strokes of the lash
	21	27	*great* glory
	22	65	continued (lit. said *many* other things)
Jn	3	23	*plenty of* water
	6	10	*plenty of* grass
	7	12	*much* whispering about [Jesus]
		31	2 *more* signs
	10	32	*many* good works
	11	47	all these (lit. *many*) signs
	12	24	a rich (lit. *great*) harvest
	14	2	*many* rooms
	15	2	2 even *more* [fruit]
		5	fruit *in plenty*
		8	*much* fruit
	20	30	*many* other signs
	21	25	*many* other things
Ac	1	3	*many* demonstrations
	2	40	2 *many* arguments
		43	*many* miracles and signs
	5	12a	*many* signs and wonders
	8	8	*great* rejoicing
		25	*a number of* villages
	10	2	generously (lit. *much* alms)
	14	22	*many* hardships
	15	7	*long* discussion
		28	2 beyond (or: *more than*) essentials
		32	spoke for a long time (lit. *many* words)
	16	16	*a lot of* money
		23	*many* lashes
	20	2	*many* words
	21	40	all was quiet (lit. there was a *great* silence)
	22	28	*large* sum
	23	10	Feeling was running high (lit. A *great* dispute arose)
	24	2	unbroken (lit. *great*) peace
		7ᵛ	by (ᵛ with *great*) force
	25	7	*many* serious accusations
		23	in *great* state
	26	9	every (lit. *many*) means
		24	all that (lit. the *great*) learning
	27	10	losing (lit. *much* damage to) the cargo and ship
	28	10	*many* marks of respect
Rm	3	2	*great* advantage
	5	16	*many* falls
	9	22	patiently (lit. with *much* patience)
	12	4	*several* parts [of the body]
1 Co	12	3	*great* fear and trembling
	12	12	*many* parts [of the body]
	16	9	a *great* deal of opposition
2 Co	2	4	*great* fortitude
	3	12	deep (lit. *great*) distress
	6	4	be quite confident (lit. have *great* confidence)
	7	4	*great* confidence . . . *great* pride
	8	2	*great* trials
		4	begging with *great* persistence
	9	12 22	*great* confidence
			amount of thanksgiving (lit. *many* thanksgivings)
Ep	2	4	[so] *much* love
1 Th	1	5	utter (lit. *great*) conviction
		6	*great* opposition
	2	2	*great* opposition
		17	strong (lit. *great*) desire
1 Tm	3	8	the amount of (lit. how *much*) wine
		13	*great* assurance
	6	9	all sorts of (lit. *many*) foolish ambitions
		10	any number of (lit. *many*) fatal wounds
2 Tm	4	14	*a lot of* harm
Tt	2	3	no habitual (lit. not *much*) wine-drinking
Phm		7	I am so delighted (lit. It gives me *great* delight)
		8	no diffidence (lit. *much* confidence)
Heb	1	1	10 At various (lit. *Many*) times in the past
		9	*various different* ways
	3	3	2/2 *greater* glory . . . *more* honour
	5	11	*many* things to say

Heb 10 32		⌐all the (lit. the *great*) sufferings
11 4	2	⌐better (lit. *greater*) sacrifice
1 P 1 3		*great* mercy
Rv 1 15		⌐the ocean (lit. *many* waters)
8 3		*A great quantity of* incense
9 9		⌐a *great* charge of (or: *many* charging) horses
14 2		⌐the ocean (lit. *many* waters)
17 1		⌐abundant (or: *many*) waters
19 6		⌐the ocean (lit. *many* waters)
12		*many* coronets

3: MUCH, MORE (as adverbs) – FURTHER – FREELY, EARNESTLY, STRONGLY

Mt 5 20	2	virtue goes no *more* deeply
9 14ᵛ		Pharisees fast ⌐*much* (or: *often*)
13 3		told them ⌐*many things* (lit. *much*)
16 21		suffer ⌐*grievously* (lit. *much*)
20 10	2	get *more*
26 9		sold ⌐at a high price (lit. *for much*)
27 19		I have been [*much*] upset
Mk 1 45		talking about it ⌐*freely* (or: *much*)
3 12		he warned them *strongly*
4 2		taught them ⌐*many things* (lit. *much*)
5 10		he begged him *earnestly*
23		[he] pleaded with him *earnestly*
26		⌐*painful treatment* (lit. suffering *much*)
38		wailing *unrestrainedly*
43		he ordered them *strictly*
6 20		he was *greatly* perplexed
34		teach them *at some length*
8 31		suffer ⌐*grievously* (lit. *much*)
9 12		suffer ⌐*grievously* (lit. *much*)
26		(G shaking the boy *violently*)
12 27		You are *very much* mistaken.
Lk 3 13	2	Exact no *more than* your rate.
7 42	2	Which . . . will love him *more*?
43	2	who was pardoned *more*
47		⌐shown such great love (lit. loved [so] *much*)
9 13	2	have no *more than* five
22		suffer ⌐*grievously* (lit. *much*)
17 25		suffer ⌐*grievously* (lit. *much*)
Jn 14 30		talk . . . any *longer*
21 15	2	love me *more than* these
Ac 4 17	2	spreading any *further*
18 20	2	stay *longer*
27		help the believers *considerably*
20 9	2	Paul went *on and on*
24 4	2	take up [too] *much* . . . time
28 29ᵛ		arguing *hotly*
Rm 16 6		worked so *hard*
12		done so much
1 Co 16 12		I ⌐begged (lit. *strongly* urged)
19		*warmly* send you [best] wishes
2 Co 8 22		is *particularly* keen
Col 4 13		works *hard*
2 Tm 2 16	2	lead *further* away
3 9	2	go on any *longer*
Jm 5 16		prayer . . . works *very powerfully*
Rv 2 19	2	⌐making progress (lit. doing *more*)
5 4		I wept ⌐*bitterly* (lit. *much*)

4: MORE THAN (in contexts of particular interest) – GREATER THAN

Mt 6 25	2	Surely life means *more than* food,
12 41 X	2	there is something *greater than* Jonah here.
42 X	2	there is something *greater than* Solomon here.
Mk 12 43	2	this poor widow has put *more* in *than* all who have contributed to the treasury;
Lk 11 31 X	2	there is something *greater than* Solomon here.
32 X	2	there is something *greater than* Jonah here.
12 23	2	life means *more than* food,
21 3	2	this poor widow has put in *more than* any of them;

5: MUCH MORE, ALL THE MORE, EVEN MORE

Mt 6 30 3		if that is how God clothes the grass in the field . . . will he not *much more* look after you, you men of little faith?
Mk 10 48	3	[Bartimaeus] only shouted *all the* ⌐louder (lit. *more*),
Lk 18 39	3	[the blind man] shouted *all the* ⌐louder (lit. *more*),
Rm 5 9 3		Having died to make us righteous, ⌐is it likely that he would now fail to (lit. *much more* will he now [be likely to]) save us
10 3		now that we have been reconciled, surely ⌐we may count on being (lit. *much more* we are) saved
15 3		it is *even more* [certain] that divine grace . . . came to so many as an abundant free gift.

Rm 5 17	3	it is *even more* [certain] that . . . Jesus Christ will cause everyone to reign in life who receives the free gift
1 Co 12 22	3	⌐What is (lit. *Much*) more, it is precisely the parts of the body that seem to be the weakest which are the indispensable ones;
2 Co 3 9	3	there must be *very much greater* [splendour] in administering justification.
11	3	there must be *much more* [splendour] in what is going to last for ever.
Ph 1 23	3	I want to . . . be with Christ, which would be *very much* the better
2 12	3	*even more* now . . . work for your salvation
Heb 12 9	6	we ought [to be] *even more* [willing] to submit ourselves to our spiritual Father,
25	6	⌐how shall we (lit. by *how much more* shall we not) escape [our punishment] . . .?

6. NUMBER(S), CROWD, MANY – INCREASE, MULTIPLY: *PLĒTHOS*

1	*plēthos* 32	3	*pam-plēthei* 1
2	*plēthynō* 12		

1: CROWD(S), NUMBER(S), MULTITUDE (OF PEOPLE) – ASSEMBLY GROUP, COMMUNITY – INCREASE (IN NUMBER), MULTIPLY

Mk 3 7		great *crowds* from Galilee followed [Jesus].
8		[from] Jerusalem, Idumaea . . . great *numbers* . . . came to [Jesus]
Lk 1 10		the whole *congregation* was outside, praying.
2 13		suddenly with the angel there was a *great throng* of the heavenly host,
6 17		there was a large gathering of his disciples with a great *crowd* of people
8 37		The entire *population* of the Gerasene territory . . . asked Jesus to leave them.
19 37		the whole *group* of disciples joyfully began to praise God
23 1		The whole *assembly* then rose,
18	3	⌐as one man (lit. *as a crowd together*) they howled,
27		Large *numbers* of people followed [Jesus]
Jn 5 3		under these [five porticoes] were *crowds* of sick people
Ac 2 6		at this sound ⌐they all (lit. the *multitude*) assembled,
4 32		The *whole group* of believers was united, heart and soul;
5 14		the *numbers* of men and women who came to believe in the Lord increased . . . ¹⁶ *People* even came *crowding* in from
16		the towns round about Jerusalem,
6 1	2	About this time . . . the number of disciples was *increasing*,
2		the Twelve called a *full meeting* of the disciples
5		The whole *assembly* approved of this proposal
7	2	the number of disciples in Jerusalem *was greatly increased*,
7 17	2	our nation in Egypt grew larger and ⌐larger (lit. *multiplied*),
9 31	ᵛ	The churches (G The Church) . . . were left in peace
2		and ⌐filled with (lit. *increasing* themselves in) the consolation of the Holy Spirit.
14 1		a great *many* Jews and Greeks became believers.
4		The *people* in the city were divided,
15 12		This silenced the entire *assembly*,
30		The party . . . went down to Antioch, where they summoned the [whole] *community*
17 4		a great *many* God-fearing (ᵛ people and) Greeks, as well as a number of rich women [joined Paul and Silas].
19 9		some of the *congregation* . . . began attacking the Way
21 22	ᵛ	there will be a meeting of the *whole body*]
36		the whole *mob* of the people were after them, shouting, 'Kill him!'
23 7		the *assembly* was split between the two parties.
25 24		the whole Jewish *community* has petitioned me,
Heb 6 14	2	(Gn 22 17) I will . . . ⌐give you many descendants (lit. *increasingly multiply* you).
11 12		more descendants than could be counted, as many in *numbers* as the stars of heaven

2: MANY (THINGS), NUMBER, MULTITUDE – INCREASE, BE MORE AND MORE, MULTIPLY – BUNDLE

Mt 24 12	2	with the *increase* of lawlessness, love in most men will grow cold;
Lk 5 6		they netted . . . a huge *number* of fish
Jn 21 6		there were so *many* fish that they could not haul [the net] in.
Ac 12 24		The word of God continued to spread and to ⌐gain followers (lit. *increase*).
28 3		Paul had collected a *bundle* of sticks
2 Co 9 10		The one who provides seed for the sower . . . will provide you with ⌐all the seed you want and (lit. the seed and *multiply* it to) make the harvest of your good deeds a larger one,

Jm	5 20	(Pr 10 12) anyone who can bring back a sinner . . . will be . . . covering up a *great number* of sins.
1 P	1 2	2 Grace and peace *be with you more and more.*
	4 8	(Pr 10 12) love covers over *many a* sin.
2 P	1 2	2 May you *have more and more* grace and peace
Jude	2	⌐wishing you all mercy and peace and love (lit. mercy, 2 peace and love *be with you more and more*).

7. NOT A FEW, NO LITTLE: *OUK OLIGOS*

ouk oligos 8

a) Not a few (people) = a Number of

Ac	17 4	Some . . . joined Paul and Silas, and so did . . . *a number of* rich women.
	12	Many Jews became believers, and so did many Greek women . . . and *a number of* the men.

b) No little = Great, Long, Serious

Ac	12 18	there was a *great* commotion among the soldiers,
	14 28	[Paul and Barnabas] stayed [in Antioch] . . . for *some* time.
	15 2	Paul and Barnabas had had a *long* argument with these men
	19 23	a *rather serious* disturbance broke out
	24	Demetrius . . . ⌐employed (lit. brought *a lot of* work to) a large number of craftsmen
	27 20	the storm ⌐raged unabated (lit. was *not* raging *any the less*)

8. MORE, RATHER – BETTER, GREATER – ESPECIALLY: *MALLON*

2 *malista 12*   1 *mallon 67/81*

1: MORE, RATHER (THAN), INSTEAD (OF) – BETTER (TO), GREATER

Mt	6 26	Are you not ⌐worth *much more* (ᵛ *better*) than [birds] are ?
	7 11	how much *more* will your Father in heaven give good things
	10 6	go *rather* to the lost sheep of the House of Israel.
	25	If they have called the master of the house Beelzebul, ⌐what will they not (lit. how much *more* will they) say of his household ?
	28	fear him *rather* who can destroy both body and soul in hell.
	18 13	[the lost sheep] gives him *more* joy than do the ninety-nine
	25 9	you had *better* go to those who sell [oil]
	27 24	Pilate saw . . . ⌐that in fact (lit. *rather* that) a riot was imminent
Mk	5 26	⌐in fact (lit. *rather*), she was getting worse.
	7 36	the more [Jesus] insisted, the *more* ⌐widely (or: abundantly) they published it.
	9 42	anyone who is an obstacle . . . would be *better* thrown into the sea with a great millstone round his neck.
	15 11	The chief priests . . . had incited the crowd to demand that he should release Barabbas for them *instead.*
Lk	5 15	His reputation continued to ⌐grow (lit. spread *more and more*),
	11 13	how much *more* will the heavenly Father give the Holy Spirit
	12 24	how much *more* are you worth than the birds !
	28	if . . . God clothes the grass . . . how much *more* will he look after you,
Jn	3 19	men . . . prefer darkness ⌐to (lit. *rather* than) the light
	5 18	that only made the Jews even *more* intent on killing [Jesus],
	12 43	they ⌐put honour from men before (lit. liked honour from men *more* than) the honour that comes from God.
	19 8	When Pilate heard them say this ⌐his fears increased (lit. he was even *more* afraid).
Ac	4 19	You must judge whether in God's eyes it is right to listen to you ⌐and not (lit. *rather* than) to God.
	5 14	the number of men and women who came to believe . . . increased ⌐steadily (lit. *more and more*).
	29	Obedience to God ⌐comes before (lit. *rather* than) obedience to men ;
	9 22	Saul's power increased ⌐steadily (lit. *more and more*),
	20 35	There is *more* happiness in giving than in receiving.
	22 2	the silence was *even greater* than before.
	27 11	the centurion took *more* notice of the captain and the ship's owner
Rm	8 34	Jesus . . . not only died for us – *more*, he rose from the dead,
	11 12	how much *more* [the pagan world] will benefit from the conversion of them all.
	24	⌐it will be much easier (lit. how much *more* easy will it be) for them, the natural branches, to be grafted back
	14 13	you should *instead* make up your mind never to be the cause of your brother tripping
1 Co	5 2	*Instead* you should be in mourning.
	6 7	oughtn't you *rather* to let yourselves be wronged, and *rather* let yourselves be cheated ?
	7 21	If you should have the chance of being free, accept it *instead.*

1 Co	9 12	Others are allowed these rights . . . our right is surely *greater* ?
	15	I would *rather* die
	14 5	I would much *rather* you could prophesy,
	18	I have a *greater* gift of tongues than all of you,
2 Co	2 7	⌐the best thing now is to (lit. now you should *rather*) give him your forgiveness
	3 8	how much *greater* will be the brightness that surrounds the administering of the Spirit !
	5 8	we . . . want *more* to be exiled from the body
	7 7	I am ⌐happier (lit. *more* happy) now than I was before.
	13	we had the *even* greater happiness of finding Titus so happy ;
Ga	4 9	you have come to acknowledge God – or *rather* . . . God has acknowledged you
	27	(Is 54 1) there are many *more* sons of the forsaken one than sons of the wedded wife.
Ep	4 28	Anyone who was a thief . . . should try to find some useful manual work *instead.*
	5 4	raise your voices in thanksgiving *instead.*
Ph	1 9	exposing [the futile works of darkness] *by contrast.* My prayer is that your love for each other may increase *more and more*
	12	the things that happened to me have *actually* been a help to the Good News.
	3 4	I am even *better* qualified.
1 Th	4 1	make *more and more* progress in the kind of life that you are meant to live :
	10	we do urge you . . . to go on making *even greater* progress
1 Tm	1 4	these things are ⌐only (lit. *more*) likely to raise irrelevant doubts
	6 2	[slaves] should serve [their masters] *all the better*, since those who have the benefit of their services are believers
2 Tm	3 4	[in the last days people will be] preferring their own pleasure ⌐to (lit. *more than*) God.
Phm	9	I am appealing to your love *instead,*
	16	a dear brother ; especially dear to me, but how much *more* to you,
Heb	9 14	how much *more* [effectively] the blood of Christ . . . can purify our inner self
	10 25	encourage each other . . . the *more* so as you see the Day drawing near.
	11 25	[Moses] chose to be ill-treated in company with God's people *rather* than to enjoy for a time the pleasures of sin.
	12 13	then the injured limb will not be wrenched, ⌐it will (lit. but will *rather*) grow strong again.
2 P	1 10	you have been called and chosen : work all the ⌐harder (lit. *more*) to justify it.

2: ESPECIALLY, PARTICULARLY, MOST

Ac	20 38	2 what saddened them ⌐most (or: *especially*) was his saying they would never see his face again.
	25 26	I have produced [Paul] before you all, and before you 2 *in particular*, King Agrippa,
	26 3	2 [I consider myself fortunate,] ⌐the more so (lit. *especially*) because you are an expert
1 Co	14 1	hope for the spiritual gifts as well, *especially* prophecy.
2 Co	12 9	I shall . . . make my weaknesses my *special* boast
Ga	6 10	2 we must do good . . . *especially* to our brothers in the faith.
Ph	4 22	2 All the saints send their greetings, *especially* those of the imperial household.
1 Tm	4 10	the living God . . . is the saviour of the whole human race 2 but *particularly* of all believers.
	5 8	2 Anyone who does not look after his own relations, *especially* if they are living with him, has rejected the faith
	17	2 The elders . . . are to be given double consideration, *especially* those who are assiduous in preaching and teaching.
2 Tm	4 13	2 bring . . . the scrolls, *especially* the parchment ones.
Tt	1 10	you have there a great many people who need to be disciplined 2 . . . *particularly* among those of the Circumcision.
Phm	16	2 a dear brother ; *especially* dear to me,
2 P	2 10	2 [the Lord can hold the wicked for their punishment,] *especially* those who are governed by their corrupt bodily desires

9. MORE

1: MORE, FURTHER: *PERAITERŌ*

peraiterō 1

Ac	19 39	if you want to ask any *more* questions

2: MORE THAN, OVER: *EP-ANŌ*

ep-anō (2)

Mk	14 5	Ointment like this could have been sold for *over* three hundred denarii

| 1 Co 15 | 6 | | Next [Christ] appeared to *more than* five hundred of the brothers |

10. MORE (THAN), ABUNDANCE, OVERFLOW – INCREASE, GREATER, HAVE TOO MUCH – BE LEFT OVER, REMAIN: *PERISSEUŌ*

6	perisseia	4	3	perisseterōs	12
5	perisseuma	5	10	ek-perissōs	1
1	perisseuō	39	11	hyper-ek-perissōs	1
4	perissos	6	8	hyper-ek-perissou	2
7	perissōs	4	9	hyper-perisseuō	2
2	perissoteros	16	12	hyper-perissōs	1

Mt 5	20		if your virtue *goes no deeper* than that of the scribes and Pharisees, you will never get into the kingdom of heaven.
	37		[Do not swear . . .] All you need say is 'Yes' if you mean
		4	yes, 'No' if you mean no; anything *more than* this comes from the evil one.
	47		if you save your greetings for your brothers, are you doing
		4	anything ⌐*exceptional* (or: *more*)?
11 9		2	[John,] a prophet? Yes . . . and *much more* than a prophet:
12 34		5	a man's words flow out of ⌐what fills (lit. the *overflowing* of) his heart.
13 12			anyone who has will be given more, and he will *have more than enough*;
14 20			they collected the scraps *remaining*,
15 37			they collected what *was left* [*over*] of the scraps, seven baskets full.
25 29			to everyone who has will be given more, and he will *have more than enough*;
27 23		7	they shouted *all the* ⌐louder (lit. *more*),
Mk 6 51		4	[The disciples] were utterly and *completely* dumbfounded,
7 36		2	the more [Jesus] insisted, the more ⌐widely (or: *abundantly*) they published it.
	37	12	Their admiration was *unbounded*.
8 8		5	they collected seven basketfuls of the scraps *left over*.
10 26		7	[The disciples] were *more* astonished *than ever*.
12 33			To love [God] . . . and to love your neighbour as yourself,
		2	this is *far more* important than any holocaust
	40	2	The *more* [severe] will be the sentence they receive
	44		they have all put in money they *had over*, but she . . . put in everything she possessed,
14 31		10	[Peter] repeated still *more* [earnestly], 'If I have to die with you, I will never disown you'.
15 14		7	they shouted *all the* ⌐louder (lit. *more*),
Lk 6 45		5	a man's words flow out of ⌐what fills (lit. the *overflowing* of) his heart.
7 26		2	[John,] a prophet? Yes . . . and *much more* than a prophet:
9 17			the scraps *remaining* were collected
12 4		2	after [killing the body they] can do no *more*.
	15		a man's life is not made secure by what he owns, even when he *has more than he needs*.
	48	2	when a man has had a great deal given him on trust, *even more* will be expected of him.
15 17			How many of my father's paid servants have *more food than they want*,
20 47		2	The *more* [severe] will be the sentence they receive
21 4			these have all contributed money they *had over*,
Jn 6 12			Pick up the pieces *left over*,
	13		they . . . filled twelve hampers with scraps *left over* from the meal
10 10		4	I have come so that they may have life and have it ⌐*to the full* (or: *abundantly*).
Ac 16 5			the churches grew strong in the faith, as well as *growing* daily in numbers.
26 11		7	my fury against them was so *extreme* that I even pursued them into foreign cities.
Rm 3 1		4	Well then, is a Jew any *better off*?
	7		my untruthfulness makes God ⌐demonstrate (lit. *give an abundance* of) his truthfulness
5 15			it is even more certain that divine grace . . . came to so many as an *abundant* free gift.
	17		it is even more certain that . . . Jesus Christ will cause
		6	everyone to reign in life who receives the *abundant* free gift
	20	9	however great the number of sins committed, grace *was even greater*;
15 13			the power of the Holy Spirit will ⌐remove all bounds to (lit. *give* you *an abundance* of) hope.
1 Co 8 8			we lose nothing if we refuse to eat, we gain nothing *more* if we eat.
12 23			it is the least honourable parts of the body that we clothe
		2	with the *greatest* care. So our more improper parts get
		2	decorated with *more modesty*
	24	2	*more* dignity is given to the parts which are without it,
14 12			since you aspire to spiritual gifts, concentrate on *excelling* in those which will grow to benefit the community.
15 10		2	I . . . have worked ⌐harder (lit. *more*) than any of the others;

1 Co 15	58		⌐keep on working at (lit. *abound* in) the Lord's work always,
2 Co 1	5		as the sufferings of Christ *overflow* to us, so through Christ, does our consolation *overflow*.
	12	3	we have always treated everybody, and *more* especially you, with the reverence and sincerity which come from God,
2 4		3	I wrote . . . to let you know *how much* love I have for you.
7		2	he might break down from ⌐so (or: *too*) much misery.
3 9			there must be an *abundance* of very much greater [splendour] in administering justification.
4 15			all this is for your benefit, so that [as the *more*] grace is multiplied among people, the *more* thanksgiving there will be,
7 4		9	I am filled with consolation and my joy *is overflowing*.
	13	3	With this encouragement . . . we had the *even greater* happiness of finding Titus so happy;
	15	3	His own personal affection for you is *all the greater* when he remembers how willing you have all been,
8 2		6	their *constant* cheerfulness and their intense poverty have *overflowed* in a wealth of generosity.
7			You always *have the most* of everything – of faith, of eloquence . . . – so we expect you to *put the most* into this work of mercy too.
14		5	[it is a question of balancing] what happens to be your *surplus* now against their present need, and one day they
		5	may have *something to spare* that will supply your own need.
9 1		4	⌐There is really no need for (lit. It would *be too much* of) me to write to you on the subject of offering your services
8			[God] will make sure that you will always *have all you need* . . . and still *have something to spare* for all sorts of good works.
12			doing this holy service is . . . ⌐increasing the amount of thanksgiving (lit. an *abundant* source of the many thanks-givings)
10 8		2	Maybe I do boast rather *too much* about our authority,
15		6	we trust that . . . we shall get taller ⌐and taller (lit. *more and more*)
11 23		3	The servants of Christ? . . . so am I, and . . . *more*, because
		3	I have worked harder, I have been sent to prison *more* often,
12 15		3	Because I love you *more*, must I be loved the less?
Ga 1 14		3	how ⌐enthusiastic (lit. *excessive*) I was for the traditions of my ancestors.
Ep 1 8			Such is the richness of the grace which he has ⌐showered (or: *lavished*) on us
3 20		8	[God's] power . . . can do *infinitely more* than we can ask
Ph 1 9			My prayer is that your love . . . may increase more and more and never stop *improving* your knowledge
14		3	most of the brothers . . . are getting *more and more* daring in announcing the Message
26			you will have ⌐another (or: *more*) reason to give praise to Christ Jesus on my account when I am with you again.
4 12			I know how to be poor and I know how to ⌐be rich (lit. *have more than enough*) . . . now I am ready for . . . poverty or *plenty*.
18			I have everything that I need and *more*:
Col 2 7			you must be . . . ⌐full of (lit. *overflowing* with) thanks-giving.
1 Th 2 18		3	we tried *hard* to come and visit you;
3 10		8	We are *earnestly* praying . . . to be able to see you face to face again
12			May the Lord be generous in *increasing* your love
4 1			make more and more *progress* in the kind of life that you are meant to live:
10			we do urge you . . . to go on *making* even greater *progress*
5 13		11	Have the *greatest* respect and affection for them
Heb 2 1		3	We ought . . . to turn our minds *more* attentively than before to what we have been taught,
6 17		2	God wanted to make the heirs to the promise *more* [thoroughly] realise that his purpose was unalterable,
7 15		2	This becomes even *more* [clearly] evident
13 19		3	I ask you *very* particularly to pray
Jm 1 21		6	do away with all the impurities . . . that are still *left* in you

11. BE WORTH MORE, BE MORE IMPORTANT, BE OF MORE VALUE – BE HIGHER, BE BEST: *DIA-PHERŌ*

| | 1 | dia-pherō | 8/13 | 2 | dia-phoros | 2/4 |

Mt 6 26			*Are* you not *worth* (G much) *more* than [birds] are?
10 31			you *are worth more* than hundreds of sparrows.
12 12			a man *is far more important* than a sheep,
Lk 12 7			you *are worth more* than hundreds of sparrows.
24			how much *more* are you *worth* than the birds!
Rm 2 18			if you . . . can tell *what is* ⌐right (lit. *more important*), [why not teach yourself as well as the others?]
Ga 2 6			not that ⌐their importance matters to me (lit. they *are more important* to me, whatever they might be),

Ph	1 10	[never stop improving your knowledge] so that you can always recognise *what is best*.
Heb	1 4	[Jesus] is now as far above the angels as the title which he
	2	has inherited *is higher* than their own name.
	8 6	2 [Christ] has been given a ministry *of a far higher order*,

12. SURPASS, EXCEED, EXCESSIVE – BE BETTER, GREATER – TRANSCENDENT, IMMEASURABLE: *HYPER-BALLŌ*

2 *hyper-ballō*	5	1 *hyper-bolē*	8
3 *hyper-ballontōs*	1		

Rm	7 13	thus sin . . . was able to ⌐exercise all (lit. *exceed*) its sinful power.
1 Co	12 31	I am going to show you a way that *is better than* any of them.
2 Co	1 8	the things we had to undergo in Asia were ⌐more of a burden (lit. an *excessive* burden, more) than we could carry,
	3 10	2 compared with this ⌐greater (or: *surpassing*) splendour, the thing that used to have such splendour now seems to have none;
	4 7	such ⌐an overwhelming (or: a *transcendent*) power comes from God and not from us.
	17	the troubles . . . though they weigh little, train us for the carrying of a weight of eternal glory which is ⌐out of all proportion to them (lit. *excessively greater*).
	9 14	2 the *surpassing* grace that God has given you.
	11 23	The servants of Christ? . . . so am I, and . . . more, because
	3	I have been . . . whipped *so many times more*,
	12 7	In view of the *extraordinary nature* of these revelations, to stop me from getting too proud I was given a thorn in the flesh.
Ga	1 13	You must have heard . . . how ⌐merciless (lit *excessive*) I was in persecuting the Church of God,
Ep	1 19	2 how *exceedingly* great is the power that [God] has exercised
	2 7	2 This was to show . . . how *immeasurably* rich [God] is in grace.
	3 19	2 knowing the love of Christ, which ⌐is beyond (or: *surpasses*) all knowledge,

13. (BE A) BURDEN, WEIGHTY MATTER – HEAVY, PRESS (ON) – BE WEIGHED DOWN, DULL: *BAROS*

1 *bareomai*	6	7 *a-barēs*	1
5 *bareōs*	2	8 *kata-bareō*	1
2 *baros*	6	9 *kata-barynō*	1
6 *barynō*	1	4 *epi-bareō*	3
3 *barys*	6		

Mt	13 15	5 (Is 6 10 G) their ears are *dull* of hearing,
	20 12	2 we have ⌐done a *heavy* day's work (or: borne the *burden* of the day) in all the heat.
	23 4	3 [The Pharisees] tie up *heavy* burdens and lay them on men's shoulders,
	23	3 Alas for . . . you who . . . have neglected the *weightier matters* of the Law
	26 43	[Jesus] found them sleeping, their eyes were so *heavy*.
Mk	14 40	9 [the disciples'] eyes were so *heavy*;
Lk	9 32	Peter and his companions were *heavy* with sleep,
	21 34	Watch yourselves, or your hearts will ⌐be coarsened (lit. *be weighed down*) with debauchery and drunkenness
Ac	3 14	6 It was you who ⌐accused (lit. *put the burden on*; G repudiated) the Holy One, the Just One,
	15 28	It has been decided by the Holy Spirit and by ourselves not
	2	to saddle you with any *burden* beyond these essentials:
	20 29	3 ⌐fierce (lit. *burdensome*) wolves will invade you and will have no mercy on the flock.
	25 7	the Jews . . . surrounded [Paul], making many ⌐serious (lit.
	3	*weighty*) accusations
	28 27	5 (Is 6 10 G) their ears are *dull* of hearing
2 Co	1 8	the things we had to undergo in Asia were ⌐more of a burden (lit. an excessive *burden*, more) than we could carry,
	2 5	Someone has been the cause of pain . . . to some degree –
	4	not to ⌐overstate it (lit. *press* it too heavily) – to all of you.
	4 17	the troubles . . . though they ⌐weigh little (lit. *are light*),
	2	train us for the carrying of a *weight* of eternal glory
	5 4	we groan and find it a *burden* being still in this tent,
	10 10	3 [Paul] writes ⌐powerful (lit. *weighty*) and strongly-worded letters
	11 9	I was no burden to anyone . . . I was very careful . . .
	7	*not to be a burden* to you in any way,
	12 16	8 I personally ⌐put no *pressure* on (or: *was no burden* to) you,
Ga	6 2	2 You should carry each other's ⌐troubles (lit. *burdens*)
1 Th	2 7	2 we could have imposed ourselves on you with full *weight*, as apostles of Christ.

1 Th	2 9	4 we used to work . . . so as not to *be a burden* on any one of you
2 Th	3 8	4 we worked . . . so as not to *be a burden* on any of you.
1 Tm	5 16	a Christian woman . . . should support [her widowed relatives] and not ⌐make the Church bear the expense (lit. *burden* the Church)
1 Jn	5 3	3 [God's] commandments are not ⌐difficult (lit. *burdensome*),
Rv	2 24	2 I am not laying any special ⌐duty (lit. *burden*);

14. BE A BURDEN (ON): *KATA-NARKAŌ*

kata-narkaō 3

2 Co	11 9	I *was* no burden to anyone:
	12 13	I have not myself *been a burden* on you
	14	I am not going to *be a burden* on you:

GREECE

1. Greece, Greek – Hellenists	3. Achaia, Corinth, Cenchreae, Nicopolis
2. Athens – Areopagus	4. Macedonia

1. GREECE, GREEK – HELLENISTS

6 *Hellas*	1	3 *Hellēnis*	2
1 *Hellēn*	26	4 *Hellēnistēs*	2
2 *Hellēnikos*	2	5 *Hellēnisti*	2

J = Greek // Jew

Mk	7 26	3 the woman was a ⌐pagan (lit. *Greek*), by birth a Syrophoenician.
Lk	23 38	2 Above [Jesus] there was an inscription (▽ in *Greek*, Latin and Hebrew writing)
Jn	7 35 J	The Jews then said . . . 'Is he going abroad to the people who are dispersed among the *Greeks* and will he teach the *Greeks*?'
	12 20	Among those who went up to worship at the festival were some *Greeks*. 21 These . . . put this request to [Philip], 'Sir, we should like to see Jesus'.
	19 20	5 the writing was in Hebrew, Latin and *Greek*.
Ac	6 1	4 the *Hellenists* made a complaint against the Hebrews:
	9 29	4 after [Saul] had spoken to the *Hellenists* . . . they became determined to kill him.
	11 20	Some . . . who came from Cyprus and Cyrene, went to Antioch where they started preaching to the *Greeks*.
	14 1 J	At Iconium . . . many Jews and *Greeks* became believers.
	16 1 J	[Timothy's] mother was a Jewess who had become a believer;
	3 J	but his father was a *Greek* . . . 3 . . . [Paul] had [Timothy] circumcised. This was on account of the Jews in the locality where everyone knew his father was a *Greek*.
	17 4 J	Some of [the Jews] were convinced . . . and so [were] . . . many God-fearing (▽ people and) *Greeks*,
	12 J	3 Many Jews became believers, and so did many *Greek* women from the upper classes
	18 4 J	Every sabbath [Paul] used to hold debates . . . trying to convert Jews as well as *Greeks*.
	19 10 J	people from all over Asia, both Jews and *Greeks*, were able to hear the word of the Lord.
	17 J	Everybody in Ephesus, both Jews and *Greeks*, heard about this episode;
	20 2	On his way through [Macedonia Paul] said many words of
	6	encouragement . . . and then made his way into *Greece*,
	21 J	[I have preached] urging both Jews and *Greeks* to turn to God
	21 28	[Paul] has profaned this Holy Place by bringing *Greeks* into the Temple.
	37	5 The tribune said [to Paul], 'You speak *Greek*, then?'
Rm	1 14	I owe a duty to *Greeks* just as much as to barbarians,
	16 J	the Good News . . . is the power of God saving all who have faith – Jews first, but *Greeks* as well.
	2 9 J	Pain and suffering will come to . . . Jews first, but *Greeks*
	10 J	as well; 10 renown, honour and peace will come to . . . Jews first, but *Greeks* as well.
	3 9 J	Jews and *Greeks* are all under sin's dominion.
	10 12 J	[scripture] makes no distinction between Jew and *Greek*: all belong to the same Lord

1Co	1 22 J	the Jews demand miracles and the *Greeks* look for wisdom, [23] here are we preaching a crucified Christ . . . to the pagans madness, [24] but to those who have been called, whether they are Jews or *Greeks*, a Christ who is . . . the wisdom of God.	
	24 J		
	10 32 J	Never do anything offensive to anyone – to Jews or *Greeks* or to the Church of God;	
	12 13 J	In the one Spirit we were all baptised, Jews as well as *Greeks*,	
Ga	2 3 J	Titus . . . is a *Greek*, he was not obliged to be circumcised.	
	3 28 J	there are no more distinctions between Jew and *Greek* . . . but all of you are one in Christ Jesus.	
Col	3 11 J	there is no room for distinction between *Greek* and Jew . . . There is only Christ:	
Rv	9 11	As their leader they had . . . the angel of the Abyss, whose name in Hebrew is Abaddon, or Apollyon in *Greek*.	
	2		

2. ATHENS – AREOPAGUS

Athens	4	(Council, Court, of the) *Areopagus*	2
Athenians ⎫		*Areopagite* (Member of the Council)	1
Men of *Athens* ⎭	2	*Damaris*	1
1 *polis*	1/164	*Dionysius*	1

Ac 17 15		Paul's escort took him as far as *Athens*, and went back with instructions for Silas and Timothy to rejoin Paul . . . [16] Paul waited for them in *Athens* and there his whole soul was revolted at the sight of a *city* given over to idolatry.
16		
	1	
19		They invited [Paul] to accompany them to the Council of the *Areopagus*,
21		The one amusement the *Athenians* . . . seem to have, apart from discussing the latest ideas, is listening to lectures about them. [22] So Paul stood before the whole Council of the *Areopagus* and made this speech: Men of *Athens*, I have seen . . . how extremely scrupulous you are in all religious matters,
22		
34		some . . . became believers, among them *Dionysius* the *Areopagite* and a woman called *Damaris*, and others besides.
18 1		After this Paul left *Athens* and went to Corinth,
1 Th 3 1		When we could not bear the waiting any longer, we decided it would be best to be left without a companion at *Athens*,

3. ACHAIA, CORINTH, CENCHREAE, NICOPOLIS

Achaia	10	⎧ *Corinth*	6	1 *polis* 2/164
Nicopolis	1	C ⎨ *Corinthians* ⎫ 2	
Cenchreae	2	⎩ Men of *Corinth* ⎭	

Ac 18 1 C		Paul left Athens and went to *Corinth*, [2] where he met . . . Aquila
8 C		A great many *Corinthians* who had heard [Paul] became believers and were baptised.
10 C	1	I have so many people on my side in this *city*
12		while Gallio was proconsul of *Achaia*, the Jews made a concerted attack on Paul
18		At *Cenchreae* [Paul] had his hair cut off, because of a vow he had made.
27		When Apollos thought of crossing over to *Achaia*, the brothers encouraged him
19 1 C		While Apollos was in *Corinth*, Paul made his way overland as far as Ephesus,
21		Paul made up his mind to go back to Jerusalem through Macedonia and *Achaia*.
Rm 15 26		Macedonia and *Achaia* have decided to send a generous contribution to the poor among the saints at Jerusalem.
16 1		Phoebe, a deaconess of the church at *Cenchreae*.
23 C	1	Erastus, the *city* treasurer, sends his greetings;
1 Co 1 2 C		[I, Paul . . . send greetings] to the church of God in *Corinth*,
16 15		the Stephanas family . . . were the first-fruits of *Achaia*,
2 Co 1 1 C		From Paul . . . to the church of God at *Corinth* and to all the saints in the whole of *Achaia*.
23 C		the reason why I did not come to *Corinth* after all was to spare your feelings.
6 11 C		*Corinthians*, we have spoken to you very frankly;
9 2		I boast about you to the Macedonians, telling them, '*Achaia* has been ready since last year'.
11 10		this cause of boasting will never be taken from me in the regions of *Achaia*.
1 Th 1 7		This has made you the great example to all believers in Macedonia and *Achaia* [8] since it was from you that the word . . . started to spread – and not only throughout Macedonia and *Achaia*,
8		
2 Tm 4 20 C		Erastus remained at *Corinth*,
Tt 3 12		lose no time in joining me at *Nicopolis*,

4. MACEDONIA

Macedonia	22	*Neapolis*	1 (Ac 16)
Macedonian ⎫	5	P ⎧ *Philippi*	4
of *Macedonia* ⎭		⎨ *Philippians*	
Amphipolis	1 (Ac 17)	⎩ (people) of *Philippi* ⎭	1
Apollonia	1 (Ac 17)	⎧ *Thessalonika* [*Thessalonica*]	5
B ⎧ *Beroea*	2	T ⎨ *Thessalonian*	
⎨ from *Beroea*	1	⎩ (people) from, of, *Thessalonika* ⎭	4
⎩ from *Doberus*	1 (Ac 20)	1 *polis*	5/164

Ac 16 9		Paul had a vision: a *Macedonian* . . . appealed to him in these words, 'Come across to *Macedonia* . . .' [10] Once he had seen this vision we lost no time in arranging a passage to *Macedonia*, convinced that God had called us to bring them the Good News. [11] . . . we made a straight run for . . . *Neapolis*, [12] and from there for *Philippi*, a Roman colony and the principal *city* of that particular district of *Macedonia*. After a few days in this *city* [13] we went . . . outside the gates
10		
11		
12 P		
P	1	
P	1	
20 P	1	[Paul and Silas] are causing a disturbance in our *city*.
39 P	1	[the magistrates] begged them to leave the *town*.
17 1		Passing through *Amphipolis* and *Apollonia*, [Paul and Silas] eventually reached *Thessalonika*, where there was a Jewish synagogue.
T		
5 T	1	The Jews . . . soon had the whole *city* in an uproar.
10		When it was dark the brothers . . . sent Paul and Silas away to *Beroea*, where they visited the Jewish synagogue as soon as they arrived. [11] Here the Jews were more open-minded than those in *Thessalonika*,
B		
11		
T		
13 T		When the Jews of *Thessalonika* heard that the word of God was being preached by Paul in *Beroea* . . . they went there to make trouble
B		
18 5		After Silas and Timothy had arrived from *Macedonia*, Paul devoted all his time to preaching.
19 21		Paul made up his mind to go back to Jerusalem through *Macedonia* and Achaia . . . [22] So he sent . . . Timothy and Erastus ahead of him to *Macedonia*,
22		
29		the mob rushed to the theatre [of Ephesus] dragging along two of Paul's *Macedonian* travelling companions, Gaius and Aristarchus.
20 1		When the disturbance was over, Paul . . . set out for *Macedonia*.
3		a plot organised against [Paul] . . . made him decide to go back by way of *Macedonia*. [4] He was accompanied by Sopater, son of Pyrrhus, who came from *Beroea*; Aristarchus and Secundus who came from *Thessalonika*; Gaius ᵛ from *Doberus* (G from Derbe),
4		
B		
T		
6 P		We ourselves left *Philippi* . . . and met them . . . at Troas,
27 2 T		we had Aristarchus with us, a *Macedonian* of *Thessalonika*.
Rm 15 26		*Macedonia* and Achaia have decided to send a generous contribution to the poor among the saints at Jerusalem.
1 Co 16 5		I shall be coming to you after I have passed through *Macedonia* – and I am doing no more than pass through *Macedonia* –
2 Co 1 16		[I had meant to come to you first] staying with you before going to *Macedonia* and coming back to you again on the way back from *Macedonia*,
2 13		I . . . went on to *Macedonia*.
7 5		Even after we had come to *Macedonia* . . . there was no rest for this body of ours.
8 1		here . . . is the news of the grace of God which was given in the churches of *Macedonia*;
9 2		I know how anxious you are to help; in fact, I boast about you to the *Macedonians*,
4		If some of the *Macedonians* who are coming with me found you unprepared, we should be humiliated
11 9		the brothers who came from *Macedonia* provided me with everything I wanted.
Ph 1 1		From Paul and Timothy . . . to all the saints . . . who are at *Philippi*
P		
4 15 P		as you people of *Philippi* well know, when I left *Macedonia*, no other church helped me with gifts of money. You were the only ones; [16] and twice since my stay in *Thessalonika* you have sent me what I needed.
16 T		
1 Th 1 1		From Paul, Silvanus and Timothy, to the Church in *Thessalonika*
T		
7		This has made you the great example to all believers in *Macedonia* and Achaia [8] since it was from you that the word . . . started to spread – and not only throughout *Macedonia* and Achaia, for the news of your faith in God has spread everywhere.
8		
2 2		We had . . . been given rough treatment and been grossly insulted at *Philippi*,
P		
4 10		[love one another,] this is what you are doing with all the brothers throughout the whole of *Macedonia*.
2 Th 1 1		From Paul, Silvanus and Timothy, to the Church in *Thessalonika*
T		
1 Tm 1 3		As I asked you when I was leaving for *Macedonia*, please stay at Ephesus,

2 Tm 4 10 T Demas has deserted me . . . and gone to *Thessalonika,*

GREETINGS – FAREWELL

1. Greet, Salute – (Send) Greetings to | **2. Hail, Greetings – Farewell:** *chairō*
– Say goodbye to: *aspazomai* | **3. Farewell:** *rhōnnymai*

1. GREET, SALUTE – (SEND) GREETINGS TO – SAY GOODBYE TO: *ASPAZOMAI*

2 *aspasmos* 10   3 *ap-aspazomai* 1
1 *aspazomai* 59

Mt 5 47   if you save your *greetings* for your brothers, are you doing anything exceptional?
10 12   As you enter his house, *salute* it,
23 7   2 [Everything the scribes and Pharisees do is done to attract attention, like] *being greeted* obsequiously in the market squares
Mk 9 15   The moment they saw [Jesus] the whole crowd . . . ran to *greet* him.
12 38   2 Beware of the scribes who like to . . . *be greeted* obsequiously in the market squares,
15 18   [the soldiers] began *saluting* [Jesus], 'Hail, king of the Jews!'
Lk 1 29   2 [Mary] asked herself what [the angel Gabriel's] *greeting* could mean,
40   [Mary] went into Zechariah's house and *greeted* Elizabeth.
41   2 as soon as Elizabeth heard Mary's *greeting,* the child leapt in her womb
44   2 the moment your *greeting* reached my ears,
10 4   Carry no purse, . . . *Salute* no one on the road.
11 43   2 Alas for you Pharisees who like . . . *being greeted* obsequiously in the market squares!
20 46   2 Beware of the scribes who . . . love to *be greeted* obsequiously in the market squares,
Ac 18 22 [Paul] landed at Caesarea, and went up to *greet* the church.
20 1   [at Ephesus] Paul sent for the disciples . . , *said goodbye* and set out for Macedonia.
21 6   3 after *saying goodbye to* each other, we went aboard and they returned home.
7   we landed at Ptolemais, where we *greeted* the brothers
19   After *greeting* [the elders in Jerusalem Paul] gave a detailed account of all that God had done among the pagans
25 13   King Agrippa and Bernice arrived in Caesarea and *paid* their *respects* to Festus.
Rm 16 3   My *greetings* to Prisca and Aquila . . . [5] My [greetings] also
5   to the church that meets at their house. *Greetings to* my
6   friend Epaenetus . . .; [6] *greetings to* Mary . . .; [7] *greetings*
7   *to* those outstanding apostles Andronicus and Junias . . .;
8   [8] *greetings to* Ampliatus . . .; [9] *greetings to* Urban . . .
10   Stachys . . .; [10] *greetings to* Apelles . . .; *greetings to*
          everyone who belongs to the household of Aristobulus;
11   [11] *greetings to* my compatriot Herodion; *greetings to*
          those in the household of Narcissus who belong to the
12   Lord; [12] *greetings to* Tryphaena and Tryphosa . . .;
13   *greetings to* my friend Persis . . .; [13] *greetings to* Rufus . . .
15   [14] *Greetings to* Asyncritus, Phlegon, . . .; [15] *greetings to*
16   Philologus and Julia, Nereus . . . [16] *Greet* each other with
          a holy kiss. All the churches of Christ *send greetings.*
21   Timothy, who is working with me, *sends* his *greetings;* . . .
22   [22] I, Tertius, who wrote out this letter, *greet* you in the
23   Lord. [23] *Greetings* from Gaius, . . . Erastus, the city
          treasurer, *sends* his *greetings;* so does our brother Quartus.
1 Co 16 19 All the churches of Asia *send* you *greetings.* Aquila and Prisca,
            with the church that meets at their house, *send* you their
20   *warmest wishes,* in the Lord. [20] All the brothers *send* you
            their *greetings. Greet* one another with a holy kiss.
21   2 This *greeting* is in my own hand – Paul.
2 Co 13 12 *Greet* one another with the holy kiss. All the saints *send* you
            greetings.
Ph 4 21   My *greetings to* every one of the saints in Christ Jesus. The
22   brothers who are with me *send* their *greetings.* [22] All the
            saints *send* their *greetings.*
Col 4 10   Aristarchus, who is here in prison with me, *sends* his *greetings,*
            and so does Mark, . . . [11] Jesus Justus adds his . . .
12   [12] Epaphras, your fellow citizen, *sends* his *greetings;* . . .
14   [14] *Greetings* from my dear friend Luke, the doctor, and
15   also from Demas. [15] Please *give* my *greetings to* the brothers
            at Laodicea.
18   2 Here is a *greeting* in my own handwriting – PAUL.
1 Th 5 26   *Greet* all the brothers with the holy kiss.
2 Th 3 17   2 From me, PAUL, these *greetings* in my own handwriting,
2 Tm 4 19   *Greetings to* Prisca and Aquila, and the family of Onesiphorus.
21   *Greetings to* you from Eubulus, Pudens, Linus, Claudia and
            all the brothers.

Tt 3 15   All those who are with me *send* their *greetings. Greetings to*
          those who love us in the faith.
Phm 23   Epaphras, a prisoner with me in Christ Jesus, *sends* his
          greetings;
Heb 11 13 All these died in faith, before receiving any of the things that
          had been promised, but they saw them in the far distance
          and *welcomed* them,
13 24   *Greetings to* all your leaders and to all the saints. The saints
          of Italy *send* you *greetings.*
1 P 5 13 Your sister in Babylon, who is with you among the chosen,
14   *sends* you *greetings;* so does my son, Mark. [14] *Greet* one
          another with a kiss of love.
2 Jn 13   *Greetings to* you from the children of your sister, the chosen
          one.
3 Jn 15   Peace be with you; *greetings* from your friends; *greet* each
          of our friends by name.

2. HAIL, GREETINGS – FAREWELL: *CHAIRŌ*

chairō 12/74

Mt 26 49 [Judas] went straight up to Jesus and said, '*Greetings,*
          Rabbi', and kissed him.
27 29   [the soldiers] knelt to [Jesus] saying, '*Hail,* king of the Jews!'
28 9   And there, coming to meet [Mary of Magdala and the other
          Mary] was Jesus. '*Greetings*' he said.
Mk 15 18 [the soldiers] began saluting [Jesus], '*Hail,* king of the Jews!'
Lk 1 28   [The angel Gabriel] went in and said to her, '*Rejoice* (or:
          Hail) so highly favoured!'
Jn 19 3   [The soldiers] kept coming up to [Jesus] and saying, '*Hail,*
          king of the Jews!'
Ac 15 23 The apostles and elders, your brothers, *send greetings to*
          the brothers of pagan birth
23 26   Claudius Lysias to his Excellency the governor Felix,
          greetings.
2 Co 13 11 In the meantime, brothers, [we wish you] happiness (or:
          farewell);
Jm 1 1   From James . . . *Greetings to* the twelve tribes of the Dis-
          persion.
2 Jn 10   If anyone comes to you bringing a different doctrine, you must
11   not . . . even *give* him *a greeting.* [11] To *greet* him would
          make you a partner in his wicked work.

3. FAREWELL: *RHŌNNYMAI*

rhōnnymai 2

Ac 15 29 Avoid these and you will do what is right. *Farewell.*
23 30   I hasten to send [this man, Paul] to you, . . . ([v] *Farewell.*)

GROW – SPROUT – BUD

1. Grow – Spread: *auxanō* | **Produce Crops:** *blastanō*
  a) Grow (of plants), Grow strong | **5. Grow (up,) Come up, Spring up –**
  b) Grow (of people), Grow up | **Sprout, Come out, Put forth:**
  c) Grow (greater, larger), Spread | *phuō*
     (widely), Increase – Make to | **6. Spring up – Sprout:** *ex-ana-tellō*
     grow – Continue to spread | **7. to Bud – Come out in leaf:**
2. Grow, (Be) Growing: *mēkynō* | *pro-ballō*
3. Grow up (of plants): *ana-bainō* | **8. Blossom afresh, Flourish again:**
4. Sprout, Grow Buds – Bear (fruit), | *ana-thallō*

1. GROW – SPREAD: *AUXANŌ*

1 *auxō, auxanō* 23   3 *hyper-auxanō* 1
2 *auxēsis*   2 4 *syn-auxanō* 1

  a) Grow (of plants), Grow strong

Mt 6 28   Think of the flowers *growing* in the fields;
13 30   4 Let [the wheat and the darnel] *both grow* till the harvest;
32   when [a mustard seed] has *grown* it is the biggest shrub of all
Mk 4 8   some seeds . . . *growing* tall and *strong,* produced crop;
Lk 12 27 Think of the flowers ([v] *growing* in the fields); they never
          have to spin or weave;
13 19   a mustard seed . . . *grew* and became a tree,

  b) Grow (of people), Grow up

Lk 1 80   the child [John the Baptist] *grew up* and his spirit matured.
2 40 X   the child [Jesus] *grew* to maturity, and he was filled with
          wisdom;

c) *Grow (greater, larger), Spread (widely), Increase – Make to grow – Continue to spread*

Jn	3 30	X	He must *grow* greater, I must grow smaller.
Ac	6 7		The word of the Lord *continued to spread*: the number of disciples in Jerusalem was greatly increased,
	7 17		our nation in Egypt *grew* larger and larger,
	12 24		The word of God *continued to spread* and to gain followers.
	19 20		the word of the Lord *spread* more and more widely and successfully
1 Co	3 6	Θ	I did the planting . . . but God *made* things *grow*.
	7	Θ	only God . . . *makes* things *grow*.
2 Co	9 10	Θ	The one who provides seed . . . will . . . *make* the harvest of your good deeds *a larger one*,
	10 15		we trust that, as your faith *grows*, we shall get taller
Ep	2 21		As every structure is aligned on [Christ], all *grow* into one holy temple in the Lord;
	4 15		If we live . . . in love, we shall *grow* in all ways into Christ,
	16	2	who is the head [16] . . . So the body *grows* until it has built itself up,
Col	1 6		[the Good News] is *spreading* all over the world and producing the same results as it has among you
	10		you will be able to lead the kind of life which the Lord expects of you . . . *increasing* your knowledge of God.
	2 19		the head . . . holds the whole body together . . . and this is the only way in which it can ʳreach (lit. *grow* to) its full
		2	*growth* in God.
2 Th	1 3	3	your faith is *growing* so wonderfully and the love that you have for one another never stops increasing;
1 P	2 2		like babies, you should be hungry for nothing but milk – the spiritual honesty which will help you to *grow* up to salvation –
2 P	3 18		go on *growing* in the grace and in the knowledge of our Lord

2. GROW, (BE) GROWING: *MĒKYNŌ*

mēkynō 1

Mk	4 27	the seed is sprouting and *growing*; how, [the sower] does not know.

3. GROW UP (OF PLANTS): *ANA-BAINŌ*

ana-bainō 4/81

Mt	13 7	the thorns *grew up* and choked them.
Mk	4 7	the thorns *grew up* and choked it,
	8	some seeds . . . *growing tall* and strong, produced crop;
	32	[a mustard seed] *grows* into the biggest shrub of them all

4. SPROUT, GROW BUDS – BEAR (FRUIT), PRODUCE CROPS: *BLASTANŌ*

blastanō 4

Mt	13 26	<	When the new wheat *sprouted* . . . the darnel appeared as well.

Mk	4 27	<	while [the sower] sleeps, when he is awake, the seed is *sprouting* and growing;
Heb	9 4		In [the ark of the covenant] were kept . . . Aaron's branch that *grew* the *buds*, and the stone tablets of the covenant.
Jm	5 18		the sky gave rain and the earth ʳgave (lit. *produced*) crops.

5. GROW (UP), COME UP, SPRING UP – SPROUT, COME OUT, PUT FORTH: *PHUŌ*

1 *phuō* 3	2 *ek-phuō* 2
	3 *sym-phuomai* 1

Mt	24 32	2	Take the fig tree as a parable: as soon as . . . its leaves *come out*, you know that summer is near.
Mk	13 28	2	Take the fig tree as a parable: as soon as . . . its leaves *come out*, you know that summer is near.
Lk	8 6	<	Some seed fell on rock, and when it *came up* it withered away . . . [7] Some seed fell amongst thorns and the thorns
	7	<	
	8	< 3/	*grew with* it and choked it. [8] And some seed . . . *grew* and produced its crop a hundredfold.
Heb	12 15		Be careful . . . that no root of bitterness should begin to *grow*

6. SPRING UP – SPROUT: *EX-ANA-TELLŌ*

ex-ana-tellō 2

Mt	13 5	<	[some seeds] *sprang up* straight away, because there was no depth of earth;
Mk	4 5	<	Some seed . . . *sprang up* straightaway, because there was no depth of earth;

7. TO BUD – COME OUT IN LEAF: *PRO-BALLŌ*

pro-ballō 1/2

Lk	21 30	As soon as you see [the fig tree and indeed every tree] *bud*, you know that summer is now near.

8. BLOSSOM AFRESH, FLOURISH AGAIN: *ANA-THALLŌ*

ana-thallō 1

Ph	4 10	It is a great joy to me . . . that at last ʳyou have shown some concern for me again (lit. your concern for me has *blossomed afresh*);

H

HAND – ARM

1. Hand, Hands: *cheir*
 1: Hand (generally)
 2: Lay one's hands (on a person) –
    the Imposition, Laying-on, of
    hands
 3: (Lay) Hands (upon – Seize,
    Arrest)
 4: the Hands (of God, of a person)
    = the Power – Strength

 5: (By, At) the hand of (=
    through)
2. Finger: *daktylos*
3. Arm(s)
 1: *ankalē*
 2: *brachiōn*
4. As far as, Up to, the Elbow:
    pygmē

For Work done by hand, Manual work *see* DO – MAKE – BEHAVE 4.
For Stretch out one's hand (*tēn cheira ek-teinō*) *see* STRETCH OUT 3.1:

1. HAND, HANDS: *CHEIR*

1 *cheir*	159/178	3 *cheir*(-*agōgos*)	1
2 *cheir*(-*agōgeō*)	2	4 *auto-cheir*	1

1: HAND (GENERALLY)

Mt 3 12 [the one who follows me, his] winnowing-fan is in his *hand*;
 4 6 (Ps 91 12) [his angels] will support you on their *hands*
 5 30 if your right *hand* should cause you to sin, cut it off
 8 15 [Jesus] touched her *hand* and the fever left her,
 9 25 [Jesus] took the little girl by the *hand*; and she stood up.
 12 10 a man was [in the synagogue] . . . who had a withered *hand*.
 15 2 [Your disciples] do not wash their *hands* when they eat food.
 20 to eat with unwashed *hands* does not make a man unclean.
 18 8 If your *hand* or your foot should cause you to sin, cut it off . . . : it is better . . . than to have two *hands* . . . and be thrown into eternal fire.
 22 13 Bind him *hand* and foot and throw him out into the dark,
 26 23 Someone who has dipped his *hand* into the dish with me,
 27 24 Pilate . . . took some water, washed his *hands* in front of the crowd
Mk 1 31 [Jesus] took her by the *hand* and helped her up.
 3 1 there was a man [in the synagogue] who had a withered *hand*.
 3 He said to the man with the withered *hand*, 'Stand up'
 5 he . . . said to the man, ['Stretch out your hand'.] He stretched it out and his *hand* was better.
 5 41 taking the child by the *hand* he said to her, '. . . get up'.
 7 2 [the Pharisees] noticed that some of his disciples were eating with unclean *hands*,
 3 the Pharisees, and the Jews in general, . . . never eat without washing their ⌐arms (lit. *hands*) ⌐as far as the elbow (ᵛ frequently);
 5 Why do your disciples . . . eat with unclean *hands*?
 8 23 [Jesus] took the blind man by the *hand* and led him outside the village.
 9 27 Jesus took [the boy] by the *hand* and helped him up,
 43 if your *hand* should cause you to sin, cut it off; it is better . . . than to have two *hands* and go to hell,
 16 18 they will pick up snakes ᵛ in their *hands*⌐,
Lk 3 17 X His winnowing-fan is in his *hand*
 4 11 (Ps 91 12) [His angels] will hold you up on their *hands*
 6 1 his disciples were picking ears of corn, rubbing them in their *hands*
 6 a man was [in the synagogue] whose right *hand* was withered.
 8 [Jesus] said to the man with the withered *hand*, 'Stand up!'
 10 ['Stretch out your hand'.] He did so, and his *hand* was better.
 8 54 taking [the child] by the *hand* [Jesus] called to her, 'Child, get up',
 9 62 Once the *hand* is laid on the plough, no one who looks back is fit for the kingdom of God.
 15 22 put a ring on his ⌐finger (lit. *hand*)
 22 21 here with me on the table is the *hand* of the man who betrays me.
 24 39 X Look at my *hands* and feet;

Lk 24 40 X ⌐And as he said this he showed them his *hands* and feet.⌐
 50 X lifting up his *hands* he blessed them.
Jn 11 44 The dead man came out, his feet and *hands* bound with bands of stuff
 13 9 Then, Lord, . . . [wash] not only my feet, by my *hands* and my head as well!
 20 20 X [Jesus] showed them his *hands* and his side.
 25 X Unless I see the holes that the nails made in his *hands* . . .
 X and unless I can put my *hand* into his side,
 27 X Put your finger here; look, here are my *hands*. Give me your *hand*; put it into my side.
Ac 3 7 Peter then took him by the *hand* and helped him to stand up.
 9 8 2 they had to lead [Saul] into Damascus by the *hand*.
 41 Peter gave her his *hand* and helped her to her feet,
 12 7 the chains fell from [Peter's] *hands*.
 17 With a gesture of his *hand* [Peter] stopped them talking,
 13 16 Paul . . . held up a *hand* for silence
 17 25 Nor is [God] dependent on anything that human *hands* can do for him,
 19 33 Alexander . . . raised his *hand* for silence
 20 34 the work these *hands* did earned enough to meet my needs
 21 11 [Agabus] took Paul's girdle, and tied up his own feet and *hands*,
 40 Paul . . . gestured to the people with his *hand*.
 22 11 2 my companions had to take me by the *hand*; and so I came to Damascus.
 23 19 the tribune took [the young man] by the *hand* and drew him aside
 27 19 4 they threw the ship's gear overboard *with their own hands*.
 28 3 a viper . . . attached itself to [Paul's] *hand*.
 4 When the natives saw the creature hanging from his *hand*
Rm 10 21 Θ (Is 65 2) Each day I stretched out my *hand* to a disobedient . . . people.
1 Co 4 12 we work for our living with our own *hands*.
 12 15 If the foot were to say, 'I am not a *hand*'
 21 The eye cannot say to the *hand*, 'I do not need you',
 16 21 This greeting is ⌐in (or: from) my own *hand* – Paul.
Ga 6 11 Take good note of what I am adding in my own *hand*[writing]
Col 4 18 Here is a greeting in my own *hand*[writing] – Paul.
2 Th 3 17 From me, Paul, these greetings in my own *hand*[writing],
1 Tm 2 8 I want the men to lift their *hands* up reverently in prayer,
Phm 19 I am writing this in my own *hand*[writing]: I, Paul,
Heb 8 9 (Jr 31 32) on the day I took them by the *hand* to bring them out of . . . Egypt.
 12 12 (Is 35 3) hold up your limp ⌐arms (lit. *hands*) and steady your trembling knees
Jm 4 8 Clean your *hands*, you sinners,
1 Jn 1 1 Something . . . that we have . . . touched with our *hands*: the Word, who is life
Rv 1 16 In his right *hand* he was holding seven stars,
 6 5 [the] rider ⌐was holding (lit. had in his *hand*) a pair of scales,
 7 9 standing in front of the throne . . . holding palms in their *hands*.
 8 4 from the angel's *hand* the smoke of the incense went up
 10 2 In his *hand* [the angel] had a small scroll, unrolled;
 5 the angel . . . raised his right *hand* to heaven,
 8 Go . . . and take that open scroll out of the *hand* of the angel
 10 I took [the scroll] out of the angel's *hand*,
 13 16 [The beast] compelled everyone . . . to be branded on the right *hand* or on the forehead,
 14 9 All those who . . . have had themselves branded on the *hand* or forehead,
 14 X I saw . . . one like a son of man with . . . a sharp sickle in his *hand*.
 17 4 the woman ⌐was holding (lit. had in her *hand*) a gold winecup
 20 1 I saw an angel come down from heaven with the key of the Abyss in his *hand*
 4 those who . . . would not have the brand-mark on their foreheads or *hands*;

2: LAY ONE'S HANDS (ON A PERSON) – THE IMPOSITION, LAYING-ON, OF HANDS

7 *tithēmi*	1/99	6 *epi-thesis*	4
		5 *epi-tithēmi*	20/40

Mt 9 18 X 5/ My daughter has just died, but come and *lay your hand* on her and her life will be saved.

Mt 19	13	X	5	People brought little children to him, for him to *lay his hands* on them
	15	X	5/	he *laid his hands* on them and went on his way.
Mk 5	23	X	5	My little daughter is desperately sick. Do come and *lay your hands* on her to make her better
6	5	X	5/	he cured a few sick people by *laying his hands* on them.
7	32			they brought him a deaf man . . . and they asked him to
		X	5/	*lay his hands* on him.
8	23	X	5/	*laying his hands* on [the blind man,] he asked, 'Can you see
	25	X	5/	anything?' . . . ²⁵ Then he *laid his hands* on the man's eyes again and he saw clearly;
10	16	X	7/	he put his arms round [the children], *laid his hands* on them and gave them his blessing.
16	18		5/	[believers] will *lay their hands* on the sick, who will recover.
Lk 4	40	X	5/	*Laying his hands* on each [of the sick] he cured them.
13	13	X	5/	he *laid his hands* on [the crippled woman]. And at once she straightened up,
Ac 6	6			They presented [the seven deacons] to the apostles, who
			5/	prayed and *laid their hands* on them.
8	17		5/	[Peter and John] *laid hands* on [the Samaritans],
	18		6/	When Simon saw that the Spirit was given through the *imposition of hands* by the apostles, he offered them some
	19		5/	money. ¹⁹ 'Give me the same power,' he said 'so that anyone I *lay my hands* on will receive the Holy Spirit.'
9	12		5/	[Saul] is praying, having had a vision of a man called Ananias . . . *laying hands* on him to give him back his sight.
	17		5/	Ananias . . . *laid his hands* on Saul and said, '. . . I have been sent by the Lord . . . so that you may recover your sight and be filled with the Holy Spirit'.
13	3		5/	after fasting and praying [the prophets and teachers of Antioch] *laid their hands* on [Barnabas and Saul] and sent them off.
19	6		5/	the moment Paul *laid hands* on [John's disciples] the Holy Spirit came down on them,
28	8		5/	Paul went to see [Publius's father], and after a prayer he *laid his hands* on the man and healed him.
1 Tm 4	14		6/	a spiritual gift which was given to you when . . . the body of elders *laid their hands* on you;
5	22		6/	Do not be too quick to *lay hands* on any man,
2 Tm 1	6		6/	the gift that God gave you when I *laid my hands* on you.
Heb 6	2		6/	[the fundamental doctrines:] the teaching about baptisms and the *laying-on of hands*;

3: (LAY) HANDS (UPON = SEIZE, ARREST)

Mt 26	50		they . . . ᵣseized (lit. laid *hands* on) Jesus and took him in charge.
Mk 14	46		The others ᵣseized (lit. laid *hands* on) [Jesus] and took him in charge.
Lk 20	19		the scribes and the chief priests would have liked to lay *hands* on [Jesus]
21	12		men will ᵣseize (lit. lay *hands* on) you and persecute you;
22	53		When I was among you in the Temple day after day you never moved to lay *hands* on me.
Jn 7	30		because his time had not yet come no one laid a *hand* on [Jesus].
	44		Some would have liked to arrest [Jesus], but no one actually laid *hands* on him.
Ac 4	3		[The Sadducees] ᵣarrested (lit. laid *hands* on) [Peter and John]
5	18		[the high priest and the Sadducees] ᵣarrested (lit. laid *hands* on) the apostles and had them put in the common goal.
12	1		Herod started ᵣpersecuting (lit. laying *hands* violently on) certain members of the Church.
21	27		some Jews from Asia caught sight of [Paul] in the Temple, and stirred up the crowd and ᵣseized (lit. laid *hands* on) him,

4: THE HANDS (OF GOD, OF A PERSON) = THE POWER – STRENGTH

Mt 17	22		The Son of Man is going to be handed over into the *power* of men;
26	45		the Son of Man is to be betrayed into the *hands* of sinners.
Mk 9	31		The Son of Man will be delivered into the *hands* of men;
14	41		the Son of Man is to be betrayed into the *hands* of sinners.
Lk 1	66 Θ		And indeed the *hand* of the Lord was with [John the Baptist].
	71		that [God] would save us from . . . the *hands* of all who hate us.
	74		that [God] would grant us . . . to be delivered from the *hands* of our enemies,
9	44		The Son of Man is going to be handed over into the *power* of men.
23	46 Θ		Father, into your *hands* I commit my spirit.
24	7		the Son of Man had to be handed over into the *power* of sinful men.
Jn 3	25		The Father loves the Son and has entrusted everything to
		X	ᵣhim (lit. his *hand*).
10	28		[my sheep] will never be lost and no one will ever steal them
		X	from ᵣme (lit. my *hand*).

Jn 10	29 Θ		no one can steal from the *hand* of the Father.
	39		They wanted to arrest [Jesus] then, but he eluded ᵣthem (lit. their *hands*).
13	3		Jesus knew that the Father had put everything into his
		X	*hands*,
Ac 4	28		but only to bring about the very thing that you ᵣin your
		●	*strength* (or: by your *hand*) and your wisdom had pre-determined should happen.
11	21	X	The *hand* of the Lord helped them
12	11		The Lord . . . has saved me from Herod's *hands*
13	11 Θ?		'Now watch how the *hand* of the Lord will strike you: . . .' [Elymas] groped about to find someone to lead him by
		3	the *hand*.
21	11		[Paul] will be . . . handed over to the *hands* of the pagans.
24	7		(ᵛ the tribune Lysias . . . took him out of our *hands* by force,)
28	17		I was arrested in Jerusalem and handed over into the *hands* of the Romans.
2 Co 11	33		I had to be let down over the wall in a hamper . . . in order to escape from [King Aretas's] *hands*.
Heb 10	31 Θ		It is a dreadful thing to fall into the *hands* of the living God.
1 P 5	6 Θ		Bow down . . . before the ᵣpower (lit. powerful *hand*) of God
Rv 19	2		[our God] has avenged his ᵣservants that she killed (lit.
	Θ		servants' blood at her *hand*).

5: (BY, AT) THE HAND OF (= THROUGH)

Mk 6	2		What . . . [are] the miracles that are worked ᵣthrough
		X	him (lit. by his *hands*)?
Ac 2	23		you . . . had [this man] crucified by the *hands* of men outside the Law.
5	12		many signs and wonders were worked among the people at the *hands* of the apostles
7	25		his brothers realised that at [Moses'] *hands* God would liberate them,
	35		Moses . . . was now sent to be both leader and redeemer ᵣthrough (lit. by the *hand* of) the angel
11	30		They . . . delivered their contributions to the elders ᵣin the care (lit. by the *hand*) of Barnabas and Saul.
14	3		the Lord . . . [allowed] signs and wonders to be performed ᵣby them (lit. at their *hands*).
15	23		[The apostles and elders chose Barsabbas and Silas] and ᵣgave them this letter to take with them (lit. wrote this [letter] through their *hands*):
19	11		So remarkable were the miracles worked by God at Paul's *hands*
Ga 3	19		The Law was promulgated by angels, ᵣassisted by (lit. by the *hand* of) an intermediary,

2. FINGER: *DAKTYLOS*

daktylos 8

Mt 23	4		[The scribes and Pharisees] tie up heavy burdens and lay them on men's shoulders, but will they lift a *finger* to move them? Not they!
Mk 7	33 X		[Jesus] put his *fingers* into the [deaf man's] ears
Lk 11	20 Θ		if it is through the *finger* of God that I cast out devils,
	46		burdens that you yourselves do not move a *finger* to lift.
16	24		Father Abraham, . . . send Lazarus to dip the tip of his *finger* in water and cool my tongue,
Jn 8	6		Jesus bent down and started writing on the ground with his
		X	*finger*.
20	25		Unless I . . . can put my *finger* into the holes [the nails] made,
	27		[Jesus] spoke to Thomas, 'Put your *finger* here; look, here are my hands.'

3. ARM(S)

1: ARM(S): *ANKALĒ*

ankalē 1

Lk 2	28		[Simeon] took [the child Jesus] into his *arms* and blessed God;

2: ARM: *BRACHIŌN*

brachiōn 3

Lk 1	51 Θ		[The Lord] has shown the power of his *arm*,
Jn 12	38 Θ		(Is 53 1) to whom has the ᵣpower (lit. *arm*) of the Lord been revealed?
Ac 13	17 Θ		(Ex 6 1) ᵣby divine power (lit. with *arm* [raised] high) [God] led [our ancestors] out [of Egypt],

4. AS FAR AS, UP TO, THE ELBOW: *PYGMĒ*

pygmē 1

Mk 7 3   the Pharisees . . . never eat without washing their arms
⌈*as far as the elbow* (ᵛ frequently);

HARDNESS – HARD HEART – SOFT

1. Hardness: *sklēros*
  a) Hard, Harden – Hardness (of heart) – Stubborn, Obstinate, Defiant
  b) Strong (winds) – Fierce (gale)
2. Hardened, Hardness (of heart) – Closed, Dull (minds) – Blind (to truth): *pōrōsis*

3. Coarse(n) – Gross – Dull: *pachynō*
4. (With) Sense dulled, (Be) Dead to feeling: *ap-algeō*
5. Implacable, Unappeasable: *a-spondos*
6. Soft, Fine – Effeminate: *malakos*
7. Supple, Tender: *hapalos*

See also **HEART**

1. HARDNESS: *SKLĒROS*

2 *sklēros   5*   3 *sklēro(-kardia)   3*
4 *sklērotēs 1*   5 *sklēro(-trachēlos) 1*
1 *sklērynō 6*

a) *Hard, Harden – Hardness (of heart) – Stubborn, Obstinate, Defiant*

Mt 19 8   3 It was because you were so *unteachable* . . . that Moses allowed you to divorce your wives,
    25 24 < 2 I had heard you were a *hard* man,
Mk 10 5   3 It was because you were so *unteachable* that [Moses] wrote this commandment for you.
    16 14   3 [Jesus] reproached [the Eleven] for their incredulity and *obstinacy*.
Jn 6 60   2 his followers said, 'This is *intolerable* language.'
Ac 7 51   5 You *stubborn* people, with your pagan hearts and pagan ears. You are always resisting the Holy Spirit,
    19 9   some . . . *hardened* into unbelief . . . began attacking the Way
    26 14   2 Saul, . . . it is *hard* for you, kicking like this against the goad.
Rm 2 5   4 Your *stubborn* refusal to repent is only adding to the anger God will have towards you
    9 18 Θ   when God wants to show mercy he does, and when he wants to *harden* someone's heart he does so.
Heb 3 8   (Ps 95 8) [If only you would listen to him today;] do not *harden* your hearts,
    13   so that none of you is *hardened* by the lure of sin.
    15   (Ps 95 8) If only you would listen to him today; do not *harden* your hearts,
    4 7   (Ps 95 8) If only you would listen to him today; do not *harden* your hearts.
Jude 15   2 all the *defiant* things said against [the Lord] by irreligious sinners.

b) *Strong (winds) – Fierce (gale)*

Jm 3 4   2 even if a ⌈*gale* (lit. *hard* wind) is driving [ships], the man at the helm can steer them

2. HARDENED, HARDNESS (OF HEART) – CLOSED, DULL (MINDS) – BLIND (TO TRUTH): *PŌRŌSIS*

1 *pōroō 5*   2 *pōrōsis 3*

Mk 3 5   2 grieved to find them so *obstinate*, [Jesus] . . . said to the man,
    6 52   they had not seen what the miracle of the loaves meant; their minds were *closed*.
    8 17   Are your minds *closed*?
Jn 12 40   (cf. Is 6 10) He has blinded their eyes, he has *hardened* their heart,
Rm 11 7   The rest were ⌈not allowed to see (lit. *blind* to) the truth;
    25   2 One section of Israel has become *blind*,
2 Co 3 14   their minds had been *dulled*; indeed . . . that same veil is still there when the old covenant is being read,
Ep 4 18   [the pagans] are . . . without knowledge because they have
    2   ⌈*shut* their hearts to (lit. *hardened* their hearts against) it

---

3. COARSE(N) – GROSS – DULL: *PACHYNŌ*

pachynō 2

Mt 13 15   (cf. Is 6 10) For the heart of this nation has *grown coarse*,
Ac 28 27   (cf. Is 6 10) For the heart of this nation has *grown coarse*,

4. (WITH) SENSE DULLED, (BE) DEAD TO FEELING: *AP-ALGEŌ*

ap-algeō 1

Ep 4 19   Their *sense* [of right and wrong] once *dulled*, [the pagans] eagerly pursue a career of indecency

5. IMPLACABLE, UNAPPEASABLE: *A-SPONDOS*

a-spondos 2

Rm 1 31   without brains, honour, love; (ᵛ *implacable* and without pity.
2 Tm 3 3   [In the last days people will be] heartless and *unappeasable*;

6. SOFT, FINE – EFFEMINATE: *MALAKOS*

malakos 4

Mt 11 8   what did you go out to see? A man wearing ⌈*fine* (or: *soft*) clothes? Oh no, those who wear ⌈*fine* (or: *soft*) clothes are to be found in palaces.
Lk 7 25   what did you go out to see? A man dressed in ⌈*fine* (or: *soft*) clothes?
1 Co 6 9   adulterers, ⌈*catamites* (lit. *effeminate* [men]), sodomites
    10   . . . will never inherit the kingdom of God.

7. SUPPLE, TENDER: *HAPALOS*

hapalos 2

Mt 24 32   Take the fig tree as a parable: as soon as its twigs grow ⌈*supple* (or: *tender*) . . . you know that summer is near.
Mk 13 28   Take the fig tree as a parable: as soon as its twigs grow ⌈*supple* (or: *tender*) . . . you know that summer is near.

HATE

1. Hate – Loathe, Loathsome: *miseō* | **2. Hate, Hateful:** *apo-stygeō*

For Love // Hate see **LOVE**, under the sign H

1. HATE – LOATHE, LOATHSOME: *MISEŌ*

miseō 40

Mt 5 43 ○   it was said: You must love your neighbour and *hate* your enemy.
    6 24 ○ < No one can be the slave of two masters: he will either *hate* the first and love the second,
    10 22   You will be *hated* by all men on account of my name;
    24 9   you will be *hated* by all the nations on account of my name.
    10   men will betray one another and *hate* one another.
Mk 13 13   You will be *hated* by all men on account of my name;
Lk 1 71   [God proclaimed] that he would save us from our enemies and from the hands of all who *hate* us.
    6 22   Happy are you when people *hate* you . . . on account of the Son of Man.
    27   Love your enemies, do good to those who *hate* you,
    14 26 ○   If any man comes to me without *hating* his father . . . he cannot be my disciple.
    16 13 ○ < No servant can be the slave of two masters: he will either *hate* the first and love the second,
    19 14 <   his compatriots *detested* [the man of noble birth]
Lk 21 17   You will be *hated* by all men on account of my name,
Jn 3 20   everybody who does wrong *hates* the light and avoids it,
    7 7   The world cannot *hate* you, but it does *hate* me,
    12 25 ○   anyone who *hates* his life in this world will keep it for the eternal life.

Jn 15	18	If the world *hates* you, remember that it *hated* me before you. [19] . . . because you do not belong to the world . . . the world *hates* you.
	23	Anyone who *hates* me *hates* my Father.
	24	they have seen all this, and still they *hate* both me and my Father.
	25	(Ps 69 4) They *hated* me for no reason.
	17 14	I passed your word on to them, and the world *hated* them,
Rm 7	15	I fail to carry out the things I want to do, and I find myself doing the very things I *hate*.
	9 13 O	(Ml 1 3) I *showed* my love for Jacob and my *hatred* for Esau.
Ep 5	29	A man never *hates* his own body,
Tt 3	3	we lived then in wickedness . . , *hating* each other and hateful ourselves.
Heb 1	9	(Ps 45 7) virtue you love as much as you *hate* wickedness.
1 Jn 2	9	Anyone who claims to be in the light but *hates* his brother is still in the dark.
	11	the man who *hates* his brother . . . is in the darkness,
	3 13	You must not be surprised, brothers, when the world *hates* you;
	15	to *hate* your brother is to be a murderer,
	4 20	Anyone who says, 'I love God', and *hates* his brother, is a liar,
Jude	23	there are others to whom you must be kind with great caution, ⸢keeping your distance even from (lit. *regarding as loathsome* even) outside clothing which is contaminated by vice.
Rv 2	6	you *loathe* as I ⸢do (lit. *loathe*) what the Nicolaitans are doing
	17 16	the time will come when the ten horns and the beast will ⸢turn against (lit. *come to loathe*) the prostitute,
	18 2	Babylon the Great . . . has become . . . a lodging for every foul spirit and dirty, *loathsome* bird.

2. HATE, HATEFUL: *APO-STYGEŌ*

1	*stygētos 1*	3 (theo-)*stygēs 1*
2	*apo-stygeō 1*	

Rm 1	30	3 Libellers, slanderers, ⸢enemies of (lit. *hateful* to) God,
	12 9	Do not let your love be a pretence, but sincerely prefer good and *hate* evil.
Tt 3	3	We lived then in wickedness and ill-will, hating each other and *hateful* ourselves.

HAVE – OWN – POSSESS

1. Have: *echō*
1: Have on, Wear – Carry – Hold
2: Have (a relationship with or to a person)
3: Have, Be possessed by (a spirit)
4: Have (generally) – Own, Possess
2. Own: *idios*
1: (A thing, an animal, is a person's) Own
2: (A person is another's) Own

3: On (a person's) own, By oneself, Alone – Privately
3. Win, Gain – Obtain – Make (a person's) own: *peri-poieomai*
4. Acquire, Get, Win – Possess, Own – Goods, Wealth, Property: *ktaomai*
5. Property – Money – Estate: *ousia*
6. Own – Possessions, Property – Goods: *hyp-archō*
7. Prosperity – Wealth – Means: *eu-poreomai*

1. HAVE: *ECHŌ*

1	*echō (307)*	3 *kat-echō 3/18*
2	*ap-echō 6/15*	4 *kata-schesis 2*

1: HAVE ON, WEAR – CARRY – HOLD

Mt 3	4	This man John *wore* a garment made of camel-hair
	22 12	How did you get in here, my friend, without *wearing* a wedding garment?
	26 7	a woman came to [Jesus] ⸢with (lit. *carrying*) an alabaster jar
Mk 14	3	a woman came in ⸢with (lit. *carrying*) an alabaster jar
Jn 12	6	[Judas] ⸢was in charge of (lit. used to *carry*) the common fund and used to help himself to the contributions.
	13 29	Judas *had* [charge of] the common fund,
	18 10	Simon Peter, who *carried* a sword, drew it
1 Co 11	4	For a man to pray or prophesy ⸢with his head covered (lit. *wearing* something to cover his head) is a sign of disrespect

1 Co 11	10	That is the argument for women's ⸢covering (lit. *wearing* on) their heads . . . a symbol of the authority over them,
2 Co 1	9	Yes, we were *carrying* our own death warrant with us,
	4 7	We are only the earthenware jars that *hold* this treasure,
2 Tm 2	19	God's solid foundation stone is still in position, and this is the inscription it *has on* it:
Heb 12	28	Let us . . . *hold* [on] to the grace that we have been given
Rv 1	16 X	In his right hand he was *holding* seven stars,
	18 X	now I am to live for ever . . . and I *hold* the keys of death
	2 12 X	the one who *has* the sharp sword, double-edged:
	3 1 X	the one who *holds* the seven spirits of God and the seven stars:
	7 X	the holy and faithful one who *has* the key of David,
	5 8	each one of [the twenty-four elders] was *holding* a harp
	6 2	the rider on [the white horse] was *holding* a bow;
	5	[the black horse's] rider was *holding* a pair of scales;
	7 2	I saw another angel . . . *carrying* the seal of the living God;
	8 3	Another angel, who *had* a golden censer, came and stood at the altar.
	6	The seven angels that *had* the seven trumpets now made ready to sound them.
	9 4	[the locusts were] told only to attack any men who ⸢were without (lit. did not *have*) God's seal on their foreheads.
	14	[A voice] spoke to the sixth angel ⸢with (lit. who *had*) the trumpet,
	17	I saw . . . the riders ⸢with (lit. who *had*) their breastplates of flame colour,
	10 2	In his hand [the angel] *had* a small scroll, unrolled;
	13 17	[the beast] made it illegal for anyone to buy . . . anything unless he *had* been branded with (lit. the brand-mark of) the name of the beast
	14 1	I saw . . . a hundred and forty-four thousand people, all ⸢with (lit. *had*) [the Lamb's] name and his Father's name written on their foreheads.
	14	I saw . . . a son of man ⸢with (lit. who *had*) a gold crown on his head
	17	Another angel, who also *carried* a sharp sickle, came out of the temple in heaven,
	18	the angel . . . shouted aloud to the one ⸢with (lit. who was *carrying*) the sharp sickle,
	15 1	seven angels were *bringing* the seven plagues that are the last of all,
	2	those who had fought against the beast and won . . . *had* harps from God,
	6	out came the seven angels ⸢with (lit. who *had*) the seven plagues, wearing pure white linen,
	16 2	[the angel emptied his bowl] on all the people who *had* ⸢been branded with (lit. the brand of) the mark of the beast
	17 1	One of the seven angels that *had* the seven bowls came to speak to me,
	4	The woman . . . was *holding* a gold winecup
	19 12 X	the name [the rider] *had* written on him was known only to himself,
	16 X	On his cloak and on his thigh ⸢there was (lit. he *had*) a name written: The King of kings
	20 1	I saw an angel . . . ⸢with (lit. who *had*) the key of the Abyss in his hand
	21 9	One of the seven angels that *had* the seven bowls . . . came to speak to me,
	15	The angel that was speaking to me was *carrying* a gold measuring rod

2: HAVE (A RELATIONSHIP WITH OR TO A PERSON)

Mt 3	9	We *have* Abraham for our father,
	8 9	I . . . *have* soldiers under me;
	9 36	the crowds . . . were . . . like sheep ⸢without (lit. who did not *have*) a shepherd.
	21 28	A man *had* two sons.
	22 24	(Dt 25 5) if a man dies ⸢childless (lit. without *having* any children), his brother is to marry the widow,
	25	the first [brother] married and then died without *having* any children,
	26 11	You *have* the poor with you always, but you will not always *have* me.
	27 16	Now ⸢there was (lit. [the governor] *had*) at that time a notorious prisoner whose name was Barabbas.
	65	'You may *have* your guard' said Pilate to [the chief priests].
Mk 2	19	As long as [the bridegroom's attendants] *have* the bridegroom with them, they could not think of fasting.
	6 34	they were like sheep ⸢without (lit. who did not *have*) a shepherd,
	12 6 <	[The owner of the vineyard] *had* still someone left: his beloved son.
	14 7	You *have* the poor with you always . . . but you will not always *have* me.
Lk 3	8	We *have* Abraham for our father
	4 40	all those who *had* friends suffering from diseases . . . brought them to [Jesus],

Lk 7 8 I . . . *have* soldiers under me;
  11 5 Suppose one of you *has* a friend and goes to him . . . to say,
  15 11 < [Jesus] also said, 'A man *had* two sons.'
  16 1 < There was a rich man and he *had* a steward
    28 send Lazarus to my father's house, since I *have* five brothers, to give them warning
    29 O They *have* Moses and the prophets . . . let them listen to them.
  17 7 Which of you, ⌐with (lit. if he *had*) a servant ploughing . . . would say to him . . . ?
Jn 5 7 Sir, . . . I *have* no one to put me into the pool
  8 41 we *have* one father: God.
  12 8 You *have* the poor with you always, you will not always *have* me.
    48 he who rejects me and refuses my words *has* his judge already:
  19 15 We *have* no king except Caesar.
Ac 13 5 ⌐John acted (lit. [Barnabas and Saul] *had* John) as their assistant.
  15 21 Moses has always *had* his preachers in every town,
  25 16 Romans are not in the habit of surrendering any man, until the accused ⌐confronts his accusers (lit. has *had* his accusers before him)
Rm 1 28 [the pagans] refused to see it was rational to ⌐acknowledge God (lit. *have* God in [the forefront of] their minds),
1 Co 4 15 You might *have* thousands of guardians in Christ,
Ga 4 22 [The Law] says . . . that Abraham *had* two sons,
Ep 2 12 you [had no] Christ . . . you were immersed in this world, ⌐without (lit. not *having* any) hope and without God.
Ph 1 7 You *have* a permanent place in my heart,
  2 20 I *have* nobody else like [Timothy] here, as wholeheartedly concerned for your welfare:
Col 4 1 Masters, . . . you too *have* a Master in heaven.
1 Tm 3 4 [a presiding elder] ⌐brings his children up (lit. *has* his children) to obey him
  5 4 If a widow *has* children or grandchildren, they are to learn first of all to do their duty to their own families
    16 If a Christian woman *has* widowed relatives, she should support them
  6 2 Slaves ⌐whose masters are (lit. who *have* masters who are) believers are not to think any the less of them because they are brothers;
Tt 1 6 [each elder] must *have* children [who are] believers
Heb 4 14 in Jesus . . . we *have* the supreme high priest
    15 it is not as if we *had* a high priest who was incapable of feeling our weaknesses with us;
  8 1 The great point . . . is that we *have* a high priest of exactly this kind.
  12 1 ⌐With (lit. *Having*) so many witnesses in a great cloud on every side of us,
    9 we have all *had* our human fathers who punished us,
1 Jn 2 1 we *have* our advocate with the Father, Jesus Christ,
    23 no one who *has* the Father can deny the Son, and to acknowledge the Son is to *have* the Father as well.
  5 12 anyone who *has* the Son has life, anyone who does not *have* the Son does not have life.
2 Jn 9 If anybody does not keep within the teaching of Christ . . . he cannot *have* God with him: only those who keep to what he taught can *have* the Father and the Son with them.
Rv 2 14 ⌐some of you are (lit. you *have* with you some) followers of Balaam,
    15 among you, too, ⌐there are (lit. you *have*) some . . . who accept what the Nicolaitans teach.
  3 4 ⌐There are (lit. You *have*) a few of Sardis . . . who have kept their robes from being dirtied,
  9 11 As their leader [the locusts] *had* their emperor, the angel of the Abyss,

3: HAVE, BE POSSESSED BY (A SPIRIT)

Mk 3 22 X The scribes . . . were saying, ⌐'Beelzebul is in him' (lit. 'He *has* [been possessed by] Beelzebul')
    30 X they were saying, ⌐'An unclean spirit is in him' (lit. 'He *has* an unclean spirit').
  5 15 They . . . saw the demoniac . . . in his full senses – the very man who had *had* the legion in him before –
  7 25 A woman whose little daughter *had* an unclean spirit heard about [Jesus]
  9 17 Master, I have brought my son to you; ⌐there is (lit. he *has*) a spirit of dumbness in him,
Lk 4 33 there was a man who *was possessed by* the spirit of an unclean devil,
  13 11 a woman was there who for eighteen years had *been possessed by* a spirit that left her enfeebled;
Ac 8 7 There were . . . unclean spirits that came shrieking out of many who *were possessed*,
  16 16 we met a slave-girl who ⌐was a soothsayer (lit. *was possessed by* an oracular spirit)
  19 13 Jewish exorcists tried pronouncing the name of the Lord Jesus over people who *were possessed by* evil spirits;

4: HAVE (GENERALLY) – OWN, POSSESS

Mt 5 46 if you love those who love you, ⌐what right have you to claim (lit. how can you *have*) any credit?
  6 1 by doing this you will ⌐lose all (lit. not *have* any) reward from your Father in heaven.
    2 2 I tell you solemnly, they have *had* their reward.
    5 2 I tell you solemnly, they have *had* their reward.
    16 2 I tell you solemnly, they have *had* their reward.
  8 20 X Foxes *have* holes and the birds of the air have nests, but the Son of Man *has* nowhere to lay his head.
  12 11 If any one of you here *had* only one sheep and it fell down a hole on the sabbath day, would he not . . . lift it out?
  13 12 anyone who *has* will be given more, and he will have more than enough; but from anyone who *has* not, even what he *has* will be taken away.
    44 he hides [the treasure] again, goes off happy, sells everything he *owns* and buys the field.
    46 he goes and sells everything he *owns* and buys [the pearl of great value].
  14 17 All we *have* with us is five loaves and two fish.
  15 30 large crowds came to [Jesus] *bringing* the lame,
    32 I feel sorry for all these people; they . . . *have* nothing to eat.
    34 How many loaves *have* you?
  16 8 why are you talking among yourselves about *having* no bread?
  18 25 his master gave orders that he should be sold, together with . . . all his *possessions*,
  19 16 Master, what good deed must I do to *possess* eternal life?
    21 sell what you own and give the money to the poor, and you will *have* treasure in heaven;
    22 the young man . . . went away sad, for he ⌐was a man of (lit. *had*) great wealth.
  21 38 This is the heir . . . let us kill him and ⌐take over (lit. *have*) his inheritance.
  25 25 I went off and hid your talent . . . Here it is; it was yours, you *have* it back.
    28 take the talent . . . and give it to the man who *has* the ten talents.
    29 to everyone who *has* will be given more, and he will have more than enough; but from the man who *has* not, even what he *has* will be taken away.
Mk 4 25 the man who *has* will be given more; from the man who *has* not, even what he *has* will be taken away.
  6 38 How many loaves *have* you?
  8 1 they *had* nothing to eat.
    2 I feel sorry for all these people; they . . . *have* nothing to eat.
    5 How many loaves *have* you?
    7 They *had* a few small fish as well,
    14 they *had* only one loaf with them in the boat.
    16 [the disciples] said to one another, 'It is because we *have* no bread'.
    17 Why are you talking about *having* no bread?
  9 50 *Have* salt in yourselves
  10 21 sell everything you *own* and give the money to the poor, and you will *have* treasure in heaven;
    22 he went away sad, for he ⌐was a man of (lit. *had*) great wealth.
    23 How hard it is for those who *have* riches to enter the kingdom of God!
  12 44 [this poor widow] from the little she had has put in everything she *possessed*,
Lk 3 11 If anyone *has* two tunics he must share with the man who *has* none, and the one ⌐with (lit. who *has*) something to eat must do the same.
  6 24 2 alas for you who are rich: you are *having* your consolation now.
  7 40 Simon, I *have* something to say to you.
    42 They ⌐were unable (lit. *had* nothing with which) to pay,
  8 18 anyone who *has* will be given more; from anyone who *has* not, even what he thinks he *has* will be taken away.
  9 3 let none of you ⌐take (lit. *have*) a spare tunic.
    58 X Foxes *have* holes and the birds of the air have nests, but the Son of Man *has* nowhere to lay his head.
  11 6 a friend of mine . . . has just arrived at my house and I ⌐have nothing to offer him;
  12 17 What am I to do? I *have* not enough room to store my crops.
    19 I will say to my soul: . . . you *have* plenty of good things laid by for many years to come;
  13 6 A man *had* a fig tree planted in his vineyard,
  14 28 which of you here, intending to build a tower, would not first . . . work out the cost to see if he *had* enough to complete it?
  15 4 What man among you ⌐with (lit. if he *had*) a hundred sheep, losing one, would not . . . go after the missing one . . . ?
    8 what woman ⌐with (lit. if she *had*) ten drachmas would not, if she lost one . . . search thoroughly till she found it?
  18 22 Sell all that you own . . . and you will *have* treasure in heaven;

Lk 18	24		How hard it is for those who *have* riches to make their way into the kingdom of God!
19	20		Sir, here is your pound. I ᵀput it away safely (lit. *had* it safely put away) in a piece of linen
	24		Take the pound from him and give it to the man who *has* ten pounds.
	25		But, sir, he *has* ten pounds.
	26		to everyone who *has* will be given more; but from the man who *has* not, even what he *has* will be taken away.
21	4		[this poor widow] from the little she had has put in all she *had* to live on.
22	36		if you *have* a purse, take it; if you have a haversack, do the same; if you *have* no sword, sell your cloak and buy one,
24	41		*Have* you anything here to eat?
Jn 2	3		ᵛ When they ᵀran out of (lit. *had* no more) wine, since the wine provided for the wedding was all finished (G When the wine was running out), the mother of Jesus said to him, 'They *have* no wine'.
3	15		everyone who believes may *have* eternal life in him.
	16		everyone who believes in him . . . may *have* eternal life.
	36		Anyone who believes in the Son *has* eternal life,
4	11	X	You *have* no bucket, sir, . . . and the well is deep; how could you ᵀget (lit. *have*) this living water?
	32	X	I *have* food to eat that you do not know about.
5	4		ᵛ the first person to enter the water . . . was cured of any ailment he ᵀsuffered from (lit. *had*).
	24	X	whoever listens to my words . . . *has* eternal life;
	26	Θ	the Father, who ᵀis the source of (lit. *has*) life, has made the Son ᵀthe source of (lit. *have*) life;
		X	
	36	X	ᵀmy testimony (lit. the testimony I *have*) is greater than John's:
	38		ᵀhis word finds no home (lit. you do not *have* his word living) in you
	39		You study the scriptures, believing that in them you *have* eternal life;
	40		yet you refuse to come to me ᵀfor (lit. to *have*) life!
6	9		There is a small boy here ᵀwith (lit. who *has*) five barley loaves and two fish;
	40		whoever sees the Son and believes in him shall *have* eternal life,
	47		everybody who believes *has* eternal life.
	53		if you do not eat the flesh of the Son of Man . . . you will not *have* life in you.
	54		Anyone who does eat my flesh and drink my blood *has* eternal life,
	68	X	You *have* the message of eternal life,
8	12		anyone who follows me . . . will *have* the light of life.
	26		About you I *have* much to say
10	10		I have come so that [the sheep] may *have* life and have it to the full.
	16	X	there are other sheep I *have* that are not of this fold,
12	35		Walk while you *have* the light,
	36		While you still *have* the light, believe in the light
14	21		Anybody who ᵀreceives (lit. *has*) my commandments and keeps them will be one who loves me;
16	12		I still *have* many things to say to you
	15	Θ	Everything the Father *has* is mine;
19	7		'We *have* a Law,' the Jews replied
20	31		believing [that Jesus is the Christ] you may *have* life through his name.
21	5		*Have* you [caught] anything, friends?
Ac 2	44		The faithful all lived together and *owned* everything in common;
3	6		I have neither silver nor gold, but I will give you what I *have*: in the name of Jesus Christ . . . walk!
7	5	O 4	God . . . promised to give *possession* of [the land to Abraham]
	45	O 4	Joshua brought [the Tent of Testimony] into the ᵀcountry we had conquered from (lit. *possession* of) the nations
23	17		this young man . . . *has* something to tell [the tribune].
	18		this young man . . . *has* something to tell you.
	19		What is it you *have* to tell me?
28	19		not that I *had* any accusation to make against my own nation.
Rm 1	13		I have often planned to visit you . . . in the hope that I might ᵀwork . . . fruitfully (lit. *have* fruit) among you
2	14		pagans who never ᵀheard of (lit. *had*) the Law . . . may not actually 'possess' the Law,
	20		your Law ᵀembodies (lit. *has* in it) all knowledge and truth,
4	2		If Abraham was justified as a reward for doing something, he would really have *had* something to boast about,
6	21		what did you ᵀget (lit. *have*) from this?
	22		Now . . . you ᵀget (lit. *have*) a reward leading to your sanctification
8	9		unless you *possessed* the Spirit of Christ you would not belong to him.
	23		all of us . . . *possess* the first-fruits of the Spirit,
12	6		ᵀOur gifts (lit. The gifts we *have*) differ according to the grace given us.
1Co 2	16		we are those who *have* the mind of Christ.

1Co 4	7		What do you *have* that was not given to you?
6	19		Your body . . . is the temple of the Holy Spirit, who is in you since you ᵀreceived (lit. *had*) him from God.
7	7		everybody *has* his own particular gifts from God,
	30	3	those whose life is buying things should live as though they *had* nothing of their own;
	40		I too *have* the Spirit of God, I think.
8	1		'We all *have* knowledge'; yes, that is so,
	10		you, a man who ᵀunderstands (lit. *has* the knowledge),
9	17		I might have ᵀbeen paid (lit. *had* some sort of reward) for [this work],
11	22		Surely you *have* homes for eating and drinking in? Surely [you have] enough respect for the community of God not to make ᵀpoor people (lit. people who *have* nothing) embarrassed?
12	30		[do] all *have* the gift of healing?
13	2		If I *have* the gift of prophecy . . . and if I *have* faith in all its fullness . . . but ᵀwithout (lit. I do not *have*) love, then I am nothing at all.
14	26		At all your meetings, let everyone ᵀbe ready with (lit. *have* ready) a psalm or (§ *have*) a sermon or (§ *have*) a revelation, or ᵀready to use (lit. *have* ready) his gift of tongues or ᵀto give (lit. *have*) an interpretation;
2Co 4	13		we *have* the same spirit of faith . . . we too believe
5	1		ᵀthere is (lit. we *have*) a house built by God for us, an everlasting home . . . in the heavens.
	12		you will *have* an answer ready for the people who can boast more about what they seem than what they are.
6	10	/3	[we are taken] for people *having* nothing though we *have* everything.
7	1		ᵀWith (lit. *Having*) promises like these made to us . . . let us wash off all that can soil
8	11		let the results be worthy, as far as you ᵀcan afford it (lit. *have* the ability), of the decision you made so promptly.
	12		¹² As long as the readiness is there, a man is acceptable with whatever he ᵀcan afford (lit. *has*); never mind what ᵀis beyond his means (lit. he does not *have*).
9	8		you will always *have* all you need for yourselves . . . and still have something to spare for all sorts of good works.
Ep 1	7		in [Jesus Christ], through his blood, we *gain* . . . the forgiveness of our sins.
5	5		nobody who . . . indulges in fornication . . . can ᵀinherit (lit. *possess* the heritage of) anything of the kingdom of God.
Ph 4	18	2	I *have* everything that I need and more:
Col 1	14		in [the Son], we *gain* our freedom,
1Tm 3	9		[Deacons] must ᵀbe conscientious believers (lit. *have* a conscientious belief) in the mystery of the faith.
6	8		as long as we *have* food and clothing, let us be content with that.
	16	Θ	[God] alone ᵀis immortal (lit. *has* immortality),
Phm	15	2	you could *have* [Onesimus] back for ever,
Heb 5	14		Solid food is for mature men ᵀwith (lit. who *have*) minds trained by practice to distinguish between good and bad.
6	19		[In this hope] we *have* an anchor for our soul,
7	6		[Melchizedek] took his tenth from Abraham, and gave his blessing to the *holder* of the promises.
	24	X	this one . . . ᵀcan never lose (lit. will always *possess*) his priesthood.
8	3		It is the duty of every high priest to offer gifts . . . so this one too must *have* something to offer.
10	34		you happily accepted being stripped of your belongings, knowing that you *owned* something that was better
13	14		ᵀthere is (lit. we *have*) no eternal city [for us] in this life
Jm 4	2		You want something and you haven't ᵀgot it; . . . Why you don't *have* what you want is because you don't pray for it;
2P 1	19		So we *have* confirmation of what was said in prophecies;
1Jn 2	7		this is not a new commandment . . . but an old commandment that you ᵀwere given (lit. have *had*) from the beginning,
	20		you have ᵀbeen anointed (lit. *had* your anointing) by the Holy One,
3	15		murderers . . . do not *have* eternal life in them.
4	21		this is the commandment that ᵀhe has given us (lit. we have *had* from him),
5	10		Everybody who believes in the Son of God *has* this testimony inside him;
	12		anyone who has the Son *has* life, anyone who does not have the Son does not *have* life.
	13		you who believe in the name of the Son of God may be sure that you *have* eternal life.
	15		we know that we *have* already [been granted] what we asked of him.
2Jn	5		I am writing now . . . to give you . . . the [commandment] which we ᵀwere given at (lit. have *had* from) the beginning,
	12		There are several things I *have* to tell you,
3Jn	13		There were several things I *had* to tell you
Jude	19		These ᵀunspiritual and selfish people (lit. worldly people who do not *have* the spirit) are nothing but mischief-makers.
Rv 2	6		ᵀIt is (lit. You *have* it) in your favour . . . that you loathe . . . what the Nicolaitans are doing.

Rv 2 24		on the rest of you in Thyatira . . . who *have* not [accepted] this teaching . . . I am not laying any special duty;
	25	hold firmly on to what you already *have* until I come.
3 11		hold firmly to what you already *have*,
6 9		I saw . . . the souls of all the people who had been killed on account of the word of God, for ˹witnessing to it (lit. the witness they *had*).
12 6		the woman escaped into the desert, where ˹God had made (lit. she *had*) a place of safety ready,
	17	the dragon . . . went away to make war on . . . all who . . . *bear* witness for Jesus.
14 6		I saw another angel . . . ˹sent to announce (lit. who *had*) the Good News of eternity
18 19		this great city . . . has made a fortune for every *owner* of a sea-going ship;
19 10		I am a servant just like . . . all your brothers who ˹are witnesses (lit. *bear* witness) to Jesus.
21 11		[Jerusalem] *had* all the radiant glory of God

2. OWN: *IDIOS*

```
1    idios   98 ⎫
3    idia     1 ⎬ 116
2    kat'idian 17 ⎭
```

1: (A THING, AN ANIMAL, IS A PERSON'S) OWN

Mt 9 1	X	He . . . crossed the water and came to his *own* town.
13 57	(X)	A prophet is only despised in his (ˇ *own*) country
22 5	<	one went off to his *own* farm, another to his business,
25 15	<	To one he gave five talents, to another two . . . each in proportion to his *own* ability.
Mk 15 20	X	when [the soldiers] had finished making fun of him, they . . . dressed him in his *own* clothes.
Lk 6 41		Why do you observe the splinter in your brother's eye and never notice the plank in your *own*?
	44	every tree can be told by its *own* fruit:
10 34	<	[The good Samaritan] then lifted him on to his *own* mount,
18 28		We left ˹all we had (lit. our *own*) to follow you.
Jn 1 11	X	He came to his *own* [domain] and his own [people] did not accept him.
4 44	(X)	there is no respect for a prophet in his *own* country,
5 43		if someone else comes in his *own* name you will accept him.
7 18		When a man's doctrine is ˹his own (lit. from himself) he is hoping to get ˹honour for himself (lit. his *own* honour);
8 44	⒟	when he lies he is drawing on his *own* [store],
10 3	<	one by one [the good shepherd] calls his *own* sheep
4	<	When he has brought out his *own* flock, he goes ahead of them,
12	<	The hired man, since . . . the sheep ˹do not belong to him (lit. are not his *own*), abandons the sheep
16 32		you will be scattered, each [going] his *own* [way]
19 27		the disciple took [Mary] in his *own* [home].
Ac 1 7	Θ	It is not for you to know times or dates that the Father has decided by his *own* authority,
19		the field came to be called the Bloody Acre, in their *own* language Hakeldama.
25		Judas abandoned [this ministry] to go to his *proper* place.
2 6		they all assembled, each one bewildered to hear these men speaking his *own* language.
8		How does it happen that each of us hears them in his *own* native language?
3 12		Why are you staring at us as though we had made this man walk by our *own* power . . .?
4 32		no one claimed ˹for his own use (lit. as his *own*) anything that he had, as everything they owned was held in common.
13 36		David in his *own* time had served God's purposes
20 28	X	feed the Church of God which he bought with ˹his *own* blood (or: the blood of his Own).
21 6		[the disciples at Tyre] returned to their *own* [home].
25 19		[the Jews] had some argument or other with [Paul] about their *own* religion
28 30		Paul spent the whole of the two years in his *own* rented lodging.
Rm 10 3		Failing to recognise the righteousness that comes from God, they try to promote their *own* idea of it,
11 24		it will be much easier for . . . the natural branches to be grafted back on ˹the tree they came from (lit. their *own* tree).
14 5		each must be left free to hold his *own* opinion.
1 Co 3 8		each will duly ˹be paid (lit. receive his *own* reward) according to his *own* share in the work.
4 12		we work for our living with our *own* hands.
6 18		to fornicate is to sin against your *own* body.
7 4		The wife has no rights over her *own* body . . . In the same way, the husband has no rights over his *own* body;
7		everybody has his *own particular* gifts from God,

1 Co 7 37		if someone has firmly made his *own* mind up . . . in complete freedom of his *own* choice, to keep his daughter as she is, he will be doing a good thing.
9 7		Nobody ever paid his *own* money to stay in the army,
11 21		everyone is in such a hurry to start his *own* supper
15 23		all . . . in their *proper* order: Christ as the first-fruits
38		each sort of seed gets its *own* [sort of] body.
Ga 6 5		Everyone will get his *own* burden to carry.
9		we shall get our harvest at the *proper* time.
Ep 4 28		Anyone who was a thief . . . should try to find some useful ˹manual work (lit. work to do with his *own* hands) instead,
1 Th 4 11		make a point of living quietly, attending to your *own* [business] and ˹earning your living (lit. working with your *own* hands),
1 Tm 2 6		[Christ Jesus] is the evidence of this, sent at the ˹appointed (lit. *proper*) time,
3 4		[The elder] must be a man who manages his *own* family well
5		how can any man who does not . . . manage his *own* family have responsibility for the church of God?
12		Deacons . . . must be men who manage their *own* children and families well.
4 2		hypocrites whose *own* consciences are branded as though with a red-hot iron:
5 4		children . . . are to learn first of all to do their duty to their *own* families
6 15		at the *due* time [Jesus Christ] will be revealed . . . the King of kings
2 Tm 1 9	Θ	[God] has saved us . . . for his *own* purpose
4 3		people will . . . collect themselves a whole series of teachers according to their *own* tastes;
Tt 1 3		at the ˹appointed (lit. *proper*) time, [God] revealed his decision,
Heb 4 10	Θ	rest after your work, as God did after his *own*.
7 27	X	[To suit us, the ideal high priest] would not need to offer sacrifices every day, as the other high priests do for their *own* sins
9 12	X	[Christ] has entered the sanctuary . . . taking with him . . . his *own* blood,
13 12	X	Jesus too suffered . . . to sanctify the people with his *own* blood.
Jm 1 14		Everyone who is tempted is . . . seduced by his *own* wrong desire.
2 P 1 3	Θ	God . . . has called us by his *own* glory and goodness.
20		the interpretation of scriptural prophecy ˹is never a matter for the individual (lit. should never be one's *own*).
2 16		[Balaam] was called to order for his *own* faults.
22		(Pr 26 11) The dog goes back to his *own* vomit
3 3		there are bound to be people . . . who always ˹please themselves (lit. pursue their *own* pleasure in) what they do,
16		these are the points that uneducated . . . people distort . . . ˹a fatal thing for them to do (lit. bringing them to their *own* ruin).
17		be careful not to get carried away . . . from ˹the (lit. your *own*) firm ground that you are standing on.
Jude 6		let me remind you of the angels who . . . left their ˹appointed (lit. *own*) sphere;

2: (A PERSON IS ANOTHER'S) OWN

Mt 25 14	<	a man on his way abroad . . . summoned his *own* servants
Mk 4 34	X	he explained everything to his *own* disciples when they were alone.
Jn 1 11	X	He came to his *own* [domain] and his *own* [people] did not accept him.
41		Andrew met his *own* brother [Simon]
5 18	X	he spoke of God as his *own* Father,
13 1	X	He had always loved [those who were] his *own* in the world,
15 19		If you belonged to the world, the world would love [you as] its *own*:
Ac 4 23		they went to ˹the community (lit. their *own* [people])
20 28	Θ	feed the Church of God which he bought with ˹his *own* blood (or: the blood of his *Own*).
24 23		[Felix] gave orders . . . that none of [Paul's] *own* [people] should be prevented from seeing to his needs.
24		Felix came with his (§ *own*) wife Drusilla
Rm 8 32	Θ	God did not spare his *own* Son,
14 4		It is not for you to condemn someone else's servant . . . it is his *own* master's business;
1 Co 7 2		let each man have his [own] wife and each woman her *own* husband.
14 35		If [women] have any questions to ask, they should ask their *own* husbands at home:
Ep 5 22		Wives should regard their *own* husbands as they regard the Lord,
1 Th 2 14		you . . . have been like the churches . . . in Judaea, suffering the same treatment from your *own* countrymen
1 Tm 5 8		Anyone who does not look after his *own* [relations] . . . has rejected the faith
6 1		All slaves . . . must have unqualified respect for their *own* masters,

Tt	1	12		one of their *own* prophets . . . said, 'Cretans were never anything but liars'
	2	5		[the younger women] are to . . . do as their *own* husbands tell them,
		9		the slaves . . . are to be obedient to their *own* masters
1 P	3	1		wives should be obedient to their *own* husbands.
		5		the holy women . . . were tender and obedient to their *own* husbands;

3: ON (A PERSON'S) OWN, BY ONESELF, ALONE – PRIVATELY

Mt	14	13		Jesus . . . withdrew by boat to a lonely place where they could be *by themselves*.
		23	2	[Jesus] went up into the hills *by himself* to pray.
	17	1	2	Jesus . . . led them up a high mountain where they could be *alone*.
		19	2	the disciples came *privately* to Jesus.
	20	17	2	Jesus . . . took the Twelve ⌐to one side (lit. *on their own*)
	24	3	2	the disciples . . . asked [Jesus] *privately*,
Mk	4	34	2	[Jesus] explained everything to his disciples when they were *alone*.
	6	31	2	come away to some lonely place all *by yourselves* and rest
		32	2	they went off in a boat to a lonely place where they could be *by themselves*.
	7	33	2	[Jesus] took [the deaf man] aside *in private*, away from the crowd,
	9	2	2	Jesus took with him Peter and James and John and led them up a high mountain where they could be alone *by themselves*.
		28	2	When [Jesus] had gone indoors his disciples asked him *privately*,
	13	3	2	Peter, James, John and Andrew questioned [Jesus] *privately*,
Lk	9	10	2	[Jesus] took them with him and withdrew to a town called Bethsaida where they could be *by themselves*.
	10	23	2	turning to his disciples [Jesus] spoke to them *in private*,
Ac	23	19	2	the tribune . . . drew [the son of Paul's sister] aside *alone*
1 Co	12	11	3	the same Spirit . . . distributes [different] gifts to *separate* people
Ga	2	2	2	*privately* I laid before the leading men the Good News

3. WIN, GAIN – OBTAIN – MAKE (A PERSON'S) OWN: *PERI-POIEOMAI*

2 *peri-poieomai* 3   1 *peri-poiēsis* 5

Lk	17	33	2	Anyone who tries to ⌐preserve (or: *gain*) his life will lose it;
Ac	20	28	2	feed the Church of God which he ⌐obtained (or: *won*) with ⌐his own blood (or: the blood of his Own).
Ep	1	14		the pledge of our inheritance . . . brings freedom for those whom God has *taken for his own*,
1 Th	5	9		God . . . meant us . . . to *win* salvation
2 Th	2	14		[God] called you to this so that you should ⌐share (lit. *obtain*) the glory of our Lord Jesus Christ.
1 Tm	3	13	2	Those . . . who carry out their duties well as deacons will ⌐earn (or: *gain*) a high standing for themselves
Heb	10	39		we are the sort who keep faithful until our ⌐souls are saved (lit. life is *made our own*).
1 P	2	9		(cf. Is 43 21 G) you are a chosen race . . . a people ⌐set apart (lit. *made [God's] own*)

4. ACQUIRE, GET, WIN – POSSESS, OWN – GOODS, WEALTH, PROPERTY: *KTAOMAI*

**1 *ktaomai* 7   3 *ktētōr* 1
2 *ktēma* 4**

Mt	10	9		*Provide yourselves with* no gold or silver,
	19	22	2	the young man . . . went away sad, for he was a man of great *wealth*.
Mk	10	22	2	he went away sad, for he was a man of great *wealth*.
Lk	18	12		I pay tithes on all I *get*.
	21	19		Your endurance will *win* you your lives.
Ac	1	18		[Judas] ⌐bought (lit. *acquired*) a field with the money he was paid for his crime.
	2	45	2	[the faithful] sold their *goods* and possessions
	4	34	3	all *those who owned* land or houses would sell them,
	5	1	2	[Ananias] agreed to sell a *property*;
	8	20		thinking that money could ⌐buy (lit. *get*) what God has given for nothing!
	22	28		It cost me a large sum to *acquire* this citizenship.
1 Th	4	4	○	[God wants] you to know how to ⌐use (lit. *possess*) the body that belongs to him in a way that is holy and honourable,

5. PROPERTY – MONEY – ESTATE: *OUSIA*

1 *ousia* 2   2 (*ta*) *en-onta* 1

Lk	11	41	2	Instead, give alms from *what you have*
	15	12		Father, let me have the share of the ⌐estate (or: *property*) that would come to me.
		13		the younger son . . . squandered his *money* on a life of debauchery.

6. OWN – POSSESSIONS, PROPERTY – GOODS: *HYP-ARCHŌ*

**2 *hyp-archō* (3)   3 *hyp-arxis* 2
1 (*ta*) *hyp-archonta* 14**

Mt	19	21		If you wish to be perfect, go and sell *what you own*.
	24	47		[the master] will place him over every*thing* he *owns*.
	25	14		a man . . . summoned his servants and entrusted his *property* to them.
Lk	8	3		Joanna . . . Susanna, and several others . . . provided for [Jesus and the Twelve] out of their own *resources*.
	11	21		So long as a strong man . . . guards his own palace, his *goods* are undisturbed;
	12	15		a man's life is not made secure by *what he owns*,
		33		Sell your *possessions* and give alms.
		44		[the master] will place him over every*thing* he *owns*.
	14	33		none of you can be my disciple unless he gives up all his *possessions*.
	16	1		a rich man . . . had a steward who was denounced to him for being wasteful with his *property*.
	19	8		[Zacchaeus said,] I am going to give half my *property* to the poor,
Ac	2	45	3	[the faithful] sold their goods and *possessions*
	3	6	2	I *have* neither silver nor gold,
	4	32		no one claimed for his own use anything that he *had*,
		37	2	[Barnabas] *owned* a piece of land
1 Co	13	3		If I give away all that I *possess* . . . but am without love, it will do me no good whatever.
Heb	10	34		you happily accepted being stripped of your *belongings*, knowing that you ⌐owned something (lit. had a *possession*) that was better and lasting.
2 P	1	8	2	If you *have* a generous supply of these [virtues], they will not leave you ineffectual or unproductive:

7. PROSPERITY – WEALTH – MEANS: *EU-POREOMAI*

1 *eu-poreomai* 1   2 *eu-poria* 1

| Ac | 11 | 29 | | The disciples decided to send relief, each to contribute ⌐what he *could afford* (or: according to his *means*), to the brothers living in Judaea. |
| | 19 | 25 | 2 | it is on this industry that we depend for our ⌐prosperity (or: *wealth*). |

HEAD – HAIR

1. Head: *kephalē*	**3. Hair**
a) Head	1: Hair: *thrix*
b) Head (figuratively)	a) (human) Hair
c) Come under the heading (of) – the Point (of)	b) (camel-)Hair, Hairy
2. Skull – Cheek – Neck	2: Have long hair: *komē*
1: Skull: *kranion*	**4. Shave (the head) – Shear, Shorn**
2: Cheek: *siagōn*	1: Shear, (Be) Shorn, Shaved – Have the hair cut off: *keirō*
3: Neck: *trachēlos*	2: Shave (the head): *xyraō*

1. HEAD: *KEPHALĒ*

**3 *kephalaion* 1/2   2 *ana-kephalaioomai* 2
1 *kephalē* 70/75**

a) Head

Mt	5	36		Do not swear by your own *head* . . . since you cannot turn a single hair white or black.
	6	17		when you fast, put oil on your *head* and wash your face,
	8	20	X	the Son of Man has nowhere to lay his *head*.
	10	30		every hair on your *head* has been counted.
	14	8		Give me John the Baptist's *head*, here, on a dish.

Mt 14	11		The *head* was brought in on a dish and given to the girl
26	7		a woman came to [Jesus] with an alabaster jar of the most
		X	expensive ointment, and poured it on his *head*
27	29		having twisted some thorns into a crown [the soldiers] put
		X	this on [Jesus's] *head*
	30	X	[the soldiers] took the reed and struck [Jesus] on the *head*
			with it
	37	X	Above [Jesus's] *head* was placed the charge against him;
	39		The passers-by jeered at [Jesus]; they shook their *heads*
Mk 6	24		What shall I ask for? . . . The *head* of John the Baptist.
	25		I want you to give me John the Baptist's *head*.
	27		the king . . . sent one of the bodyguard with orders to
	28		bring John's *head*. ²⁸ The man . . . brought the *head* on
			a dish
14	3	X	[the woman] poured the ointment on [Jesus's] *head*.
15	19	X	[The soldiers] struck [Jesus's] *head* with a reed
	29		The passers-by jeered at [Jesus]; they shook their *heads*
Lk 7	38		[the woman's] tears fell on [Jesus's] feet, and she wiped them
			away with ˹her hair (lit. the hair from her *head*);
	46	X	You did not anoint my *head* with oil,
9	58	X	the Son of Man has nowhere to lay his *head*.
12	7		every hair on your *head* has been counted.
21	18		not a hair of your *head* will be lost.
	28		stand erect, hold your *heads* high, because your liberation is
			near
Jn 13	9		'Lord,' said Simon Peter , '[wash] not only my feet, but
			my hands and my *head* as well!'
19	2	X	the soldiers twisted some thorns into a crown and put it
			on [Jesus's] *head*,
	30	X	Jesus . . . said, 'It is accomplished'; and bowing his *head*
			he gave up his spirit.
20	7	X	the cloth that had been over [Jesus's] *head* . . . was . . .
			rolled up
	12		two angels [were] sitting where the body of Jesus had been,
			one at the *head*, the other at the feet.
Ac 18	6		Your blood be on your own *heads*;
	18		At Cenchreae [Paul] had his ˹hair cut off (lit. *head* shaved),
21	24		pay all the expenses connected with the shaving of their
			heads.
27	34		Not a hair of your *heads* will be lost.
Rm 12	20		(Pr 25 22) Thus you heap red-hot coals on [your enemy's]
			head.
1Co 11	4		For a man to pray . . . with his *head* covered is a sign of
			disrespect to his *head*.
	5		For a woman . . . it is a sign of disrespect to her head if
			she prays . . . ˹unveiled (lit. with her *head* uncovered);
	7		A man should certainly not cover his *head*,
	10		That is the argument for women's covering their *heads* with
			a symbol of the authority over them,
12	21		nor can the *head* say to the feet, 'I do not need you'.
Rv 1	14	X	His *head* and his hair were white as white wool
4	4		I saw twenty-four elders . . . with golden crowns on their
			heads.
9	7		these locusts . . . had . . . gold crowns on their *heads*,
	17		the ˹horses had (lit. horses' *heads* were) lions' *heads*.
	19		[the horses'] tails . . . had *heads* that were able to wound.
10	1		I saw another powerful angel . . . with a rainbow over his
			head;
12	1		a woman [appeared] . . . with the twelve stars on her *head*
			for a crown
	3	Ⓓ	a huge red dragon . . . had seven *heads* . . . each of the
			seven *heads* crowned with a coronet.
13	1		[the beast] had seven *heads* . . . and its *heads* were marked
			with blasphemous titles.
	3		one of its *heads* seemed to have had a fatal wound
14	14	X	I saw . . . one like a son of man with a gold crown on his
			head
17	3		I saw a woman riding a scarlet beast which had seven *heads*
	7		I will tell you the meaning . . . of the beast . . . with the
			seven *heads*
	9		the seven *heads* are the seven hills,
18	19		[captains and seafaring men] will throw dust on their *heads*
19	12	X	his *head* was crowned with many coronets;

b) Head (*figuratively*)

1Co 11	3	X	Christ is the *head* of every man, man is the *head* of woman,
			and God is the *head* of Christ.
	4		For a man to pray . . . with his head covered is a sign
		X	of disrespect to his *head*.
	5		For a woman . . . it is a sign of disrespect to her *head* if
			she prays or prophesies unveiled;
Ep 1	10		2 [God has let us know] that he would *bring* everything
			together *under* Christ, *as head*,
	22	X	[God] made [Christ], as the ruler of everything, the *head*
			of the Church.
4	15	X	we shall grow in all ways into Christ, who is the *head*
5	23	X	as Christ is *head* of the Church . . . so is a husband the
			head of his wife;
Col 1	18	X	Now the Church is his body, he is its *head*.

Col 2	10	X	[you will find your own fulfilment] in the one who is the
			head of every Sovereignty and Power.
	19	X	A man of this sort is not united to the *head*, and it is the
			[head] that adds strength and holds the whole body
			together,

c) Come under the heading (*of*) – the Point (*of*)

Rm 13	9		2 All the commandments . . . ˹are summed up in (or: *come*
			under the heading of) this single commandment: . . . love
			your neighbour.
Heb 8	1		3 The ˹*great point* (or: *sum*) of all that we have said is that
			we have a high priest of exactly this kind.

2. SKULL – CHEEK – NECK

1: SKULL: *KRANION*

1 *kranion* 4   2 *Golgotha* 3

Mt 27	33		2 they . . . reached a place called *Golgotha*, that is, the place
			of the *skull*,
Mk 15	22		2 They brought Jesus to the place called *Golgotha*, which
			means the place of the *skull*.
Lk 23	33		When they reached the place called The *Skull*, they crucified
			[Jesus]
Jn 19	17		[Jesus] went . . . to the place of the *skull* or, as it was called
			2 in Hebrew, *Golgotha*,

2: CHEEK: *SIAGŌN*

siagōn 2

Mt 5	39		if anyone hits you on the right *cheek*, offer him the other
			as well;
Lk 6	29		To the man who slaps you on one *cheek*, present the other
			[cheek] too;

3: NECK: *TRACHĒLOS*

1 *trachēlos* 7   2 (*sklēro*-)*trachēlos* 1

Mt 18	6		anyone who is an obstacle . . . would be better drowned
			. . . with a great millstone round his *neck*.
Mk 9	42		anyone who is an obstacle . . . would be better thrown into
			the sea with a great millstone round his *neck*.
Lk 15	20		[His father] ˹clasped him in his arms (lit. fell on his *neck*)
			and kissed him tenderly.
17	2		It would be better for him to be thrown into the sea with a
			millstone put round his *neck*
Ac 7	51		2 You ˹stubborn (lit. stiff-*necked*) people, with your pagan
			hearts
15	10		It would only provoke God's anger . . . if you ˹imposed
			on the disciples the very burden (lit. put on the disciples'
			necks the very yoke) that neither we nor our ancestors
			were strong enough to support
20	37		[the elders of Ephesus] put their arms round Paul's *neck*
			and kissed him;
Rm 16	4		[Prisca and Aquila] risked ˹death (lit. their *necks*) to save
			my life:

3. HAIR

1: HAIR: *THRIX*

1 *thrix* 15   2 *trichinos* 1

a) (*human*) Hair

Mt 5	36		you cannot turn a single *hair* white or black.
10	30		every *hair* on your head has been counted.
Lk 7	38		[the woman's] tears fell on [Jesus's] feet, and she wiped
			them away with ˹her hair (lit. the *hair* from her head);
	44		this woman . . . wiped [my feet] with her *hair*.
12	7		every *hair* on your head has been counted.
21	18		not a *hair* of your head will be lost.
Jn 11	2		It was the same Mary . . . who . . . wiped [Jesus's] feet with
			her *hair*.
12	3		Mary . . . anointed the feet of Jesus, wiping them with her
			hair;
Ac 27	34		Not a *hair* of your heads will be lost.
1 P 3	3		Do not dress up for show; doing up your *hair*, wearing gold
Rv 1	14	X	His head and his *hair* were white as white wool
9	8		[the locusts'] *hair* [was] like women's *hair*.

b) (*camel*-)Hair, Hairy

Mt 3	4		John wore a garment made of camel-*hair*

Mk 1 6   John wore a garment of ^v camel-skin (G camel-*hair*),
Rv 6 12   2 the sun went as black as ⌐coarse (lit. *hairy*) sackcloth;

2: HAVE LONG HAIR: *KOMĒ*

1 komaō 2   2 komē 1

1 Co 11 14   [Ask yourselves] whether nature itself does not tell you that
       15   *long hair* on a man is nothing to be admired, ¹⁵ while a
       2/   woman, who was given her *hair* as a covering, thinks *long
              hair* her glory?

4. SHAVE (THE HEAD) – SHEAR, SHORN

1: SHEAR, (BE) SHORN, SHAVED – HAVE THE HAIR CUT OFF: *KEIRŌ*

keirō 4

Ac 8 32   (Is 53 8) like a lamb that is dumb in front of its *shearers* . . .
            he never opens his mouth.
   18 18   At Cenchreae [Paul] had his ⌐hair cut off (lit. head *shaved*),
            because of a vow he had made.
1 Co 11 6 a woman who will not wear a veil ought to *have her hair cut
            off*. If a woman is ashamed to *have her hair cut off* or
            shaved, she ought to wear a veil.

2: SHAVE (THE HEAD): *XYRAŌ*

1 xyraō 2   2 xyraō, xyrō 1

Ac 21 24   pay all the expenses connected with the *shaving* of [these
            men's] heads.
1 Co 11 5 [a woman] might as well have [her hair] *shaved* [off].
        6 2 if a woman is ashamed to have her hair cut off or *shaved*, she
            ought to wear a veil.

HEAR – LISTEN – LEARN

1. Ear: *ous*
1: the Ear cut off by Simon Peter
2: Ears – Whisper, Come to the ears of – Give ear to
2. Hear – Listen to – Learn: *akouō*
1: Ears – Hear, Hearing
2: (God) Hears – (God) Listens to
3: Hear (God) – Listen to (God) – Learn (from God)
4: Hear (Scripture) – Listen to, Learn from, Taught by (Scripture)
5: Hear, Hear of (Jesus) – Listen to (Jesus)
6: Hear, Seem to hear (in Revelation)
7: Hear, Listen to, Be told – Understand, Learn, Take notice of – Refuse to listen

3. Listen (to), Hear – Audience chamber: *akroatēs*
4. Heed, Take notice of – Attend to, Listen to – Hold to, Be devoted to: *pros-echō*
1: Attend (to), Pay attention to – Listen to – Heed, Take notice of
2: Treat with respect, Be devoted to – Hold to
5. Learn, Be taught – Disciple: *manthanō*
1: Learn, Be taught – Educated
2: Disciples
  a) of Jesus, of the kingdom
  b) of John the Baptist, of Moses, of the Pharisees

1. EAR: *OUS*

3 ōtarion 2   1   ous   37
2 ōtion   3   4 en-ōtizomai 1

1: THE EAR CUT OFF BY SIMON PETER

Mt 26 51   one of the followers of Jesus . . . struck out at the high
        2 priest's servant, and cut off his *ear*.
Mk 14 47   one of the bystanders . . . struck out at the high priest's
        3 servant, and cut off his *ear*.
Lk 22 50   one of [Jesus's followers] struck out at the high priest's
        51 servant, and cut off his right *ear*. ⁵¹ . . . touching the
        2 man's *ear* [Jesus] healed him.
Jn 18 10   Simon Peter . . . wounded the high priest's servant, cutting
        3 off his right *ear*.
      26   One of the high priest's servants, a relation of the man
        2 whose *ear* Peter had cut off, said,

2: EARS – WHISPER, COME TO THE EARS OF – GIVE EAR TO

Mt 10 27   what you hear in *whispers*, proclaim from the housetops.
   11 15   If anyone has *ears* to hear, let him listen!
   13 9   Listen, anyone who has *ears*!
      15   (Is 6 10) their *ears* are dull of hearing, and they have shut
            their eyes, for fear they should see with their eyes, hear
            with their *ears*,
      16   happy are your eyes because they see, your *ears* because they
            hear!
      43   Listen, anyone who has *ears*!
Mk 4 9   Listen, anyone who has *ears* to hear!
     23   If anyone has *ears* to hear, let him listen to this.
   7 16   ^v If anyone has *ears* to hear, let him listen to this.⌐
     33   [Jesus] put his fingers into the [deaf] man's *ears*
   8 18   Have you eyes that do not see, *ears* that do not hear?
Lk 1 44   the moment your greeting reached my *ears*, the child in my
            womb leapt for joy.
   4 21   This text is being fulfilled today ¡even ⌐as you listen (lit.
            within your *hearing*).
   8 8   Listen, anyone who has *ears* to hear!
   9 44   you must have these words constantly in your ⌐mind (lit.
            ears):
   12 3   what you have *whispered* in hidden places will be proclaimed
            on the housetops.
   14 35   Listen, anyone who has *ears* to hear!
Ac 2 14   4 Men of Judaea, . . . ⌐listen carefully to (lit. *give ear to*)
            what I say.
   7 51   You stubborn people, with your pagan hearts and pagan
            ears.
     57   all the members of the council . . . stopped their *ears* with
            their hands; then they all rushed at [Stephen].
   11 22   This came to the *ears* of the church in Jerusalem and they
            sent Barnabas to Antioch.
   28 27   (Is 6 10) their *ears* are dull of hearing and they have shut
            their eyes, for fear they should see with their eyes, hear
            with their *ears*,
Rm 11 8   (Is 29 10) God has given them . . . unseeing eyes and in-
            attentive *ears*, and they are still like that today.
1 Co 2 9   (Is 64 3) we teach what . . . no *ear* has heard.
   12 16   If the *ear* were to say, 'I am not an eye. . .' would that mean
            that it was not a part of the body?
Jm 5 4   the cries of the reapers have reached the *ears* of the Lord
1 P 3 12   (Ps 34 16) the eyes of the Lord are turned towards the
            righteous, his *ears* are open to their prayers.
Rv 2 7   If anyone has *ears* to hear, let him listen to what the Spirit
            is saying to the churches:
         Repeated in 2 11, 17, 29; 3 6, 13, 22.
   13 9   If anyone has *ears* to hear, let him listen:

2. HEAR – LISTEN TO – LEARN: *AKOUŌ*

2   akoē   24   6 ep-akouō 1
1   akouō   431   4 par-akouō 3
5   di-akouō   1   7 pro-akouō 1
3   eis-akouō   5

1: EARS – HEAR, HEARING

Mt 13 15   (Is 6 10) the heart of this nation has grown coarse, their
            ears are dull of *hearing*,
Mk 7 35   2 [the deaf man's] *ears* were opened,
Lk 7 1   [Jesus] had come to the end of all he wanted ⌐the people to
        2 hear (lit. to say in the people's *hearing*),
Ac 17 20   2 Some of the things you said within our *hearing* seemed
            startling to us
   28 27   (Is 6 10) the heart of this nation has grown coarse, their
            ears are dull of *hearing*
1 Co 12 17 2 If your whole body was just one eye, how would you *hear*
        2 anything? If it was just one *ear*, how would you smell
            anything?
2 Tm 4 3   people will be ⌐avid for the latest novelty (lit. seized with
        4 2 itching *ears*) . . . ⁴ and then, instead of ⌐listening to (lit.
        2 using those *ears* for) the truth, they will turn to myths.
Heb 5 11   you have grown so ⌐slow at understanding (lit. dull of
        2 *hearing*)

2: (GOD) HEARS – (GOD) LISTENS TO

Mt 6 7   the pagans . . . think that by using many words they will
        3 make themselves *heard*.
Lk 1 13   3 Zechariah, do not be afraid, your prayer has been *heard*.
Jn 9 31   We know that God doesn't *listen to* sinners, but God does
            listen to men who are devout and do his will.
   11 41   Father, I thank you for *hearing* my prayer. ⁴² I knew indeed
      42   that you always *hear* me,

Ac 7 34   (Ex 3 7) I have *heard* [my people's] groans,
10 31   3 Cornelius, your prayer has been *heard*
2Co 6 2   6 (Is 49 8) At the favourable time, I have *listened to* you; on the day of salvation I came to your help.
Heb 5 7   3 [Christ] submitted so humbly that his prayer was *heard*.
1 Jn 5 14   if we ask [God] for anything . . . in accordance with his will, he will *hear* us; ¹⁵ and, knowing that whatever we may ask, he *hears* us, we know that we have already been granted what we asked of him.
15

3: HEAR (GOD) – LISTEN TO (GOD) – LEARN (FROM GOD)

Mt 17 6   When they *heard* [the voice from the cloud], the disciples fell on their faces,
Jn 3 32 X   [He who comes from heaven] bears witness to the things he has seen and *heard*,
5 30 X   I can only judge as I ʳam told (lit. have *heard* [from God how]) to judge,
37   You have never *heard* [the Father's] voice,
6 45   to *hear* the teaching of the Father . . . is to come to me.
8 26 X   what I have *learnt* from [the one who sent me] I declare to the world.
40 X   I tell you the truth as I have *learnt* it from God;
47   A child of God *listens to* the words of God; if you refuse to *listen*, it is because you are not God's children.
12 29   People standing by, who *heard* [the voice from heaven], said it was a clap of thunder;
15 15 X   I have made known to you everything I have *learnt* from my Father.
16 13 Ⓢ   the Spirit of truth . . . will say only what he has *learnt*;
Ac 11 7 Δ   I *heard* a voice that said to me, 'Now, Peter; kill and eat!'
1Co 14 21   (Is 28 12) through the lips of foreigners I shall talk to the nation, and still they will not *listen to* me, says the Lord.
3
2Co 12 4   [this man] was caught up into paradise and *heard* things which . . . cannot be put into human language.
Heb 3 7   (Ps 95 7) If only you would *listen to* him today; ⁸ do not harden your hearts,
15   (Ps 95 7) If only you would *listen to* him today;
16   those who rebelled after they had *listened* were all the people who were brought out of Egypt
4 2   2 *hearing* the message did them no good because they did not share the faith of those who *listened*.
7   (Ps 95 7) If only you would *listen to* him today;
12 19   the great voice . . . made everyone that *heard* it beg that no more should be said to them.
2 P 1 18   We *heard* this ourselves, spoken from heaven,

4: HEAR (SCRIPTURE) – LISTEN TO, LEARN FROM, TAUGHT BY (SCRIPTURE)

Mt 5 21   You have *learnt* how it was said to our ancestors: You must not kill;
27   You have *learnt* how it was said: You must not commit adultery.
33   Again, you have *learnt* how it was said . . .: You must not break your oath,
38   You have *learnt* how it was said: Eye for eye
43   You have *learnt* how it was said: You must love your neighbour
Mk 12 29   (Dt 6 4) *Listen*, Israel, the Lord our God is the one Lord,
Lk 16 29   They have Moses and the prophets . . . let them *listen to* them.
31   If they will not *listen* either *to* Moses or [to] the prophets, they will not be convinced
Jn 12 34   The Law has *taught* us that the Christ will remain for ever.
Ga 4 21   *listen to* what the Law says.
Jm 5 11   You have *heard of* the patience of Job,

5: HEAR, HEAR OF (JESUS) – LISTEN TO (JESUS)

Mt 2 3   When King Herod *heard* [of the infant Jesus] he was perturbed,
9   Having *listened to* what the king had to say, [the wise men] set out.
4 24   2 [Jesus's] *fame* spread throughout Syria,
7 24   everyone who *listens to* these words of mine and acts on them will be like a sensible man
26   everyone who *listens to* these words of mine and does not act on them will be like a stupid man
10 27   what you *hear* in whispers, proclaim from the housetops.
11 2   John in his prison had *heard* what Christ was doing
4   Go back and tell John what you *hear* and see;
15   If anyone has ears [to hear], let him *listen*!
12 19   (Is 42 2) nor will anyone *hear* [my servant's] voice in the streets.
24   [Can this be the Son of David?] the Pharisees *heard* this
13 9   *Listen*, anyone who has ears!

Mt 13 13   they . . . *listen* without *hearing* or understanding.
14   2/ (Is 6 9) You will *listen* and ʳ*listen* again (lit. *hear*), but not understand,
15   (Is 6 10) the heart of this nation has grown coarse . . . for fear they should . . . *hear* with their ears,
16   happy are . . . your ears because they *hear*!
17   many prophets and holy men longed . . . to *hear* what you *hear*, and never *heard* it.
18   You, therefore, are to *hear* the parable of the sower.
19   When anyone *hears* the word of the kingdom without understanding, the evil one . . . carries off what was sown in his heart:
20   The one who received [the seed] on patches of rock is the man who *hears* the word and welcomes it at once with joy.
22   The one who received the seed in thorns is the man who *hears* the word, but the worries of this world . . . choke [it].
23   the one who received the seed in rich soil is the man who *hears* the word and understands it;
43   *Listen*, anyone who has ears!
14 1   /2 Herod the tetrarch *heard* about the *reputation* of Jesus,
13   the people *heard* of [Jesus's departure] and . . . went after him
15 10   *Listen* and understand. ¹¹ What goes into the mouth does not make a man unclean;
12   the Pharisees were shocked when they *heard* what you said
17 5   This is my Son, the Beloved . . . *Listen to* him.
19 22   when the young man *heard* these words he went away sad,
25   [It will be hard for a rich man to enter the kingdom.] When the disciples *heard* this they were astonished.
20 30   [the two blind men] *heard* that it was Jesus who was passing by,
21 16   Do you *hear* what [the children] are saying?
33   *Listen to* another parable.
45   When they *heard* his parables, the chief priests and the scribes realised he was speaking about them;
22 22   [Give back to Caesar what belongs to Caesar.] ʳThis reply (lit. When they *heard* this, it) took [the Pharisees] by surprise,
33   his teaching made a deep impression on the people who *heard* it.
34   the Pharisees *heard* that [Jesus] had silenced the Sadducees
26 65   There! You have just *heard* the blasphemy.
27 47   When some of those who stood there *heard* this, they said, 'The man is calling on Elijah',
28 14   should the governor *come to hear of* this,
Mk 1 28   2 [Jesus's] *reputation* rapidly spread everywhere,
2 1   ʳword went round (lit. it was *heard*) that [Jesus] was back;
3 8   great numbers who had *heard of* all [Jesus] was doing came to him.
21   When his relatives *heard* of this, they set out to take charge of [Jesus],
4 3   *Listen*! Imagine a sower going out to sow.
9   *Listen*, anyone who has ears to *hear*!
12   (cf. Is 6 9) they . . . may *hear* and *hear* again, but not understand;
15   people . . . have no sooner *heard* [the word] than Satan . . . carries [it] away
16   those who receive the seed on patches of rock are people who, when first they *hear* the word, welcome it at once with joy.
18   These have *heard* the word, ¹⁹ but the worries . . . choke [it]
20   they *hear* the word and accept it and yield a harvest,
23   If anyone has ears to *hear*, let him *listen to* this.
24   Take notice of what you are *hearing*.
33   he spoke the word to them, so far as they were capable of ʳunderstanding (lit. *hearing*) it.
5 27   [A woman] had *heard* about Jesus,
6 2   he began teaching in the synagogue [at Nazareth] and most of them were astonished when they *heard* him.
14   King Herod had *heard* about [Jesus],
16   when Herod *heard* this he said, 'It is John'
55   [people] brought the sick . . . to wherever they *heard* he was.
7 14   *Listen to* me, all of you, and understand.
16   ᵛ If anyone has ears to *hear*, let him *listen to* this.ʳ
25   A woman . . . *heard* about [Jesus] straightaway
8 18   Have you . . . ears that do not *hear*?
9 7   This is my Son, the Beloved. *Listen to* him.
10 47   [the blind man] *heard* that it was Jesus of Nazareth,
11 14   'May no one ever eat fruit from you' . . . his disciples *heard* him say this.
18   [Jesus drove out the sellers and buyers.] This *came to the ears of* the chief priests and scribes,
12 37   the great majority of the people *heard* this with delight.
14 11   [Judas approached the chief priests with an offer to hand Jesus over.] They were delighted to *hear* it,
58   We *heard* him say, 'I am going to destroy this Temple'
64   You *heard* the blasphemy.

Mk 15	35	When some of those who stood by *heard* this, they said, '[Listen,] he is calling on Elijah.'
16	11	they did not believe [Mary of Magdala] when they *heard* her say that [Jesus] was alive
Lk 2	18	everyone who *heard* it was astonished at what the shepherds had to say.
	20	the shepherds went back . . . praising God for all they had *heard*
	47	all those who *heard* [Jesus] were astounded at his intelligence and his replies.
4	23	We have *heard* all that happened in Capernaum,
	28	[There were many widows in Israel . . .] When they *heard* this everyone in the synagogue was enraged.
5	1	the crowd [was] pressing round him *listening to* the word of God.
	15	large crowds would gather to *hear* him
6	18	[a great crowd of people] who had come to *hear* him
	27	I say this to you who are *listening*: Love your enemies,
	47	Everyone who comes to me and *listens to* my words and acts on them
	49	But the one who *listens* and does nothing
7	1	When [Jesus] had come to the end of all he wanted the 2 people to *hear*,
	3	Having *heard* about Jesus [the centurion] sent some Jewish elders to him
	22	Go back and tell John what you have seen and *heard*:
8	8	*Listen*, anyone who has ears to *hear*!
	10	(cf. Is 6 10) so that they may . . . *listen* but not understand.
	12	Those on the edge of the path are those who have *heard* [the word], and then the devil comes
	13	people who, when they first *hear* it, welcome the word with joy.
	14	people who have *heard*, but as they go on their way they are choked by . . . worries
	15	people . . . who have *heard* the word and take it to themselves and yield a harvest
	18	So take care how you *hear*;
	21	My mother and my brothers are those who *hear* the word of God
9	7	Herod the tetrarch had *heard* all about what was going on;
	9	who is this I *hear* such reports about?
	35	This is my Son, the Chosen One. *Listen to* him.
10	16	Anyone who *listens to* you *listens to* me; anyone who rejects you rejects me
	24	many prophets . . . wanted . . . to *hear* what you *hear*, and never *heard* it.
	39	Mary . . . sat down at the Lord's feet and *listened to* him speaking.
11	28	Still happier those who *hear* the word of God and keep it!
14	15	[When you give a lunch . . .] On *hearing* this, one of those gathered round the table said to him,
	35	*Listen*, anyone who has ears to *hear*!
15	1	The tax collectors and the sinners . . . were all seeking his company to *hear* what he had to say.
16	14	The Pharisees, who loved money, *heard* all this
18	23	[Sell all that you own] But when [the rich man] *heard* this he was filled with sadness,
	26	[It is difficult for a rich man] 'In that case' said the *listeners* 'who can be saved?'
19	11	[the Son of Man has come to save what was lost.] While the people were *listening to* this he went on to tell a parable,
	48	[the chief priests could not do away with him] because the people *listening* as a whole hung on his words.
20	16	[The vineyard will be given to others.] *Hearing* this [the people] said, 'God forbid!'
	45	While all the people were *listening*, he said to the disciples, [Beware of the scribes]
21	38	from early morning the people would gather round him in the Temple to *listen to* him.
22	71	We have *heard* it for ourselves from his own lips.
23	6	[He is inflaming the people . . .] When Pilate *heard* this, he asked
	8	Herod was delighted to see Jesus; he had *heard* about him
Jn 1	37	[There is the Lamb of God.] *Hearing* this, the two disciples [of John] followed Jesus.
	40	One of these two who became followers of Jesus after *hearing* what John had said was Andrew,
3	29	the bridegroom's friend . . . stands there and *listens*,
4	1	the Pharisees had *found out* that [Jesus] was making . . . more disciples than John
	42	[the people of Sychar said,] we have *heard* him ourselves and we know that he really is the saviour of the world.
	47	*hearing* that Jesus had arrived in Galilee from Judaea, [the court official] . . . asked him to come and cure his son
5	24	whoever *listens to* my words . . . has eternal life;
	25	the hour will come . . . when the dead will *hear* the voice of the Son of God, and all who *hear* will live.
	28	the hour is coming when the dead will leave their graves ᶠat the sound of (lit. *hearing*) his voice:

Jn 6	60	[My flesh is real food and my blood is real drink.] After *hearing* it, many of his followers said, '. . . How could anyone ᶠaccept (or: *listen to*) it?'
7	32	*Hearing* . . . rumours like this . . the Pharisees sent the Temple police to arrest [Jesus].
	40	Several people who had been *listening* said, 'Surely he must be the prophet',
	51	the Law does not allow us to pass judgement on a man without *giving* him a *hearing*
8	9	[If there is one of you who has not sinned . . .] When [the scribes] *heard* this they went away one by one,
	43	you are unable to ᶠunderstand (lit. *hear*) my language.
9	32	it is un*heard of* for anyone to open the eys of [the blind];
	40	[I have come into this world, so that those without sight may see.] *Hearing* this, some Pharisees . . . said . . 'We are not blind'
10	3	the sheep *hear* [the shepherd's] voice,
	16	there are other sheep I have . . . They too will *listen to* my voice,
	20	He is possessed . . .; why bother to *listen to* him?
	27	The sheep that belong to me *listen to* my voice;
11	20	Martha *heard* that Jesus had come
	29	[The Master wants to see you.] *Hearing* this, Mary got up quickly
12	12	the crowds . . . *heard* that Jesus was on his way to Jerusalem.
	18	they had *heard* that [Jesus] had given this sign.
	38	2 (Is 53 1 G) Lord, who could believe what we have *heard* said . . .?
	47	If anyone *hears* my words and does not keep them . . . it is not I who shall condemn him,
14	24	ᵛ my (G the) *word* (§ that you are *listening to*) is not my own:
	28	You *heard* me say: I am going away,
16	13	the Spirit of truth . . . will say only what he has ᶠlearnt (or: *heard*);
18	21	Ask my *hearers* what I taught:
	37	all who are on the side of truth *listen to* my voice.
19	8	[He has claimed to be the Son of God.] When Pilate *heard* them say this his fears increased.
	13	[If you set him free . . .] *Hearing* these words, Pilate had Jesus brought out,
21	7	ᶠAt these words (lit. *Hearing*) 'It is the Lord', Simon Peter . . . jumped into the water.
Ac 1	4	It is . . . what you have *heard* me speak about:
2	22	Men of Israel, *listen to* what I am going to say: Jesus [lives]
	33	what you see and *hear* is the outpouring of that Spirit.
	37	*Hearing* this, [the Jews] were cut to the heart
3	22	(Dt 18 15) God will raise up a prophet . . . for you . . .; you must *listen to* whatever he tells you. ²³ The man who
	23	does not *listen to* that prophet is to be cut off from the people.
4	4	many of those who had *listened to* [the apostles'] message became believers,
	20	We cannot promise to stop proclaiming what we have seen and *heard*.
5	33	*Hearing* this so infuriated [the Sanhedrin] that they wanted to put [the apostles] to death.
6	14	We have *heard* [Stephen] say that Jesus . . . is going to destroy this Place
7	2	[Stephen] replied, My brothers, my fathers, *listen to* what I have to say. The God of glory appeared to our ancestor Abraham,
	54	[You have murdered the Just One.] They were infuriated when they *heard* this,
9	4	he *heard* a voice saying, 'Saul, Saul,'
	7	though [Saul's companions] *heard* the voice they could see no one.
	21	[Saul began preaching: Jesus is the Son of God.] All his *hearers* were amazed.
10	22	Cornelius . . . was directed by a holy angel . . . to *listen to* what you have to say.
	33	Here we all are, assembled . . . to *hear* what message God has given you for us.
	44	While Peter was still speaking the Holy Spirit came down on all the *listeners*.
13	7	the proconsul Sergius Paulus . . . summoned Barnabas and Paul and asked to *hear* the word of God,
	16	Men of Israel, and fearers of God, *listen*!
	44	almost the whole town assembled to *hear* the word of God.
	48	[we must turn to the pagans.] It made the pagans very happy to *hear* this
14	9	as [the cripple] *listened to* Paul preaching, he managed to catch his eye.
15	7	[Peter said, '. . . the pagans were to ᶠlearn (or: *hear*) the Good News from me'
16	14	Lydia, a devout woman . . . *listened to* us, and the Lord opened her heart to accept what Paul was saying.
17	32	ᶠAt this mention of (lit. *Hearing of*) rising from the dead, some . . . burst out laughing; others said, 'We would like to *hear* you talk about this again'.
18	8	many Corinthians who had *heard* [Paul] became believers

Ac 18 26   Priscilla and Aquila *heard* [Apollos] speak boldly
    19 5   [John insisted that people should believe in Jesus.] When they *heard* this, they were baptised in the name of the Lord Jesus.
        10   people from all over Asia . . . were able to *hear* the word of the Lord.
    22 1   *listen to* what I have to say to you in my defence.
         2   When they ˹realised (lit. *heard*) [Paul] was speaking in Hebrew, the silence was even greater
         7   I . . . *heard* a voice saying, 'Saul, Saul,
         9   The people with me . . . did not *hear* his voice
       14   The God of our ancestors has chosen you . . . to see the Just One and *hear* his own voice speaking, [15] because you are to be his witness . . . testifying to what you have seen and *heard*.
       22   [I am sending you out to the pagans.] So far they had *listened to* him, but at these words they began to shout,
    24 24   Felix . . . sent for Paul and *gave him a hearing* on the subject of faith in Christ Jesus.
    25 22   Agrippa said to Festus, 'I should like to *hear* the man myself'. 'Tomorrow' he answered 'you shall *hear* him.'
    26 3   [Paul said to Agrippa,] I beg you to *listen to* me patiently.
       14   I *heard* a voice saying to me . . . 'Saul, Saul,
       29   I wish . . . that not only you but all who have *heard* me today would come to be as I am
    28 22   We think it would be as well to *hear* your own account
       26 2/ (Is 6 9) You will *hear* and *hear* again but not understand,
       27   their ears are dull . . . for fear they should . . . *hear* with their ears,
       28   this salvation of God has been sent to the pagans; they will *listen to* it.
Rm 10 14   they will not believe in him unless they have *heard of* him, and they will not *hear of* him unless they get a preacher,
       16   (Is 53 1 G) Lord, how many believed what ˹we proclaimed (lit. they *heard* from us)?
       17 2 So faith comes from what is ˹preached (lit. *heard*), and what
         2 is ˹preached (lit. *heard*) comes from the word of Christ.
       18   Let me put the question: is it possible that they did not *hear*?
    11 8   (cf. Dt 29 3) God has given them . . . ˹inattentive ears (lit. ears that do not *hear*),
    15 21   (Is 52 15 G) those who have never *heard* about him will understand.
1 Co 2 9   we teach . . . the things that . . . no ear has *heard*,
Ga 3 2   was it because you practised the Law that you received the Spirit, or because you believed what was ˹preached to (lit. 2 *heard* by) you?
        5   Does God give you the Spirit . . . because you practise the Law, or because you believed what was ˹preached to (lit. 2 *heard* by) you?
Ep 1 13   Now you too, in [Christ], have *heard* the message of the truth
     4 21   [that is hardly the way you have learnt from Christ,] unless you failed to *hear* him properly
Col 1 5 7 It is only recently that you *heard of* [the hope stored up for you in heaven], when it was announced in the message of the truth.
        6   [The Good News is] producing the same results as it has among you ever since . . . you *heard* about God's grace and understood what that really is.
       23   [never let] yourselves drift away from the hope promised by the Good News, which you have *heard*,
1 Th 2 13 2 as soon as you *heard* the message that we brought you as God's message, you accepted it
Heb 2 1   We ought . . . to turn our minds more attentively . . . to what we have ˹been taught (lit. *heard*),
        3   The promise [of salvation] was first announced by the Lord himself, and is guaranteed to us by those who have *heard* him;
1 Jn 1 1   Something . . . that we have *heard*, . . . the Word, who is life – this is our subject . . . [3] What we have seen and *heard* we are telling you
        5   This is what we have *heard* from him, . . . God is light;
     2 24   Keep alive in yourselves what you ˹were taught (lit. *heard*) in the beginning: as long as what you ˹were taught (lit. *heard*) in the beginning is alive in you, you will live in the Son
Rv 3 20   If one of you *hears* me calling and opens the door, I will come in to share his meal

6: HEAR, SEEM TO HEAR (IN REVELATION)

Rv 1 10   I *heard* a voice behind me, shouting like a trumpet,
     4 1   I *heard* the same voice speaking to me, . . . saying, 'Come up here:
     5 11   I *heard* the sound of an immense number of angels
       13   I *heard* all the living things in creation . . . crying, 'To the One who is sitting on the throne . . . be all praise',
     6 1   I *heard* one of the four animals shout . . . 'Come',
        3   I *heard* the second animal shout, 'Come'.
        5   I *heard* the third animal shout, 'Come'.

Rv 6 6   I *seemed to hear* a voice shout from among the four animals and say, 'A ration of corn for a day's wages,
        7   I *heard* the voice of the fourth animal shout, 'Come'.
     7 4   I *heard* how many [servants of God] were sealed [on the forehead]:
     8 13   I *heard* an eagle, calling aloud . . , 'Trouble,
     9 13   I *heard* a voice come out of the four horns of the golden altar
       16   I ˹learnt (lit. *heard*) how many there were in [the angels'] army:
    10 4   I was preparing to write, when I *heard* a voice from heaven say to me,
        8   the voice I had *heard* from heaven
    11 12   [the two witnesses stood up;] then ˅ I *heard* (G they *heard*) a loud voice from heaven say to them, 'Come up here',
    12 10   I *heard* a voice shout from heaven, 'Victory
    14 2   I *heard* a sound coming out of the sky . . .; ˹it seemed to be (lit. the voice I *heard* was like) the sound of harpists
       13   I *heard* a voice from heaven say to me: 'Write down: Happy are those who die in the Lord!
    16 1   I *heard* a voice from the sanctuary shouting to the seven angels, 'Go,
        5   I *heard* the angel of water say, 'You are . . . the Just One,
        7   I *heard* the altar itself say, '. . . the punishments you give are . . . just.'
    18 4   A new voice spoke from heaven; I *heard* it say, 'Come out, my people,
    19 1   After this I *seemed to hear* the great sound of a huge crowd in heaven,
        6   I *seemed to hear* the voices of a huge crowd,
    21 3   I *heard* a loud voice call from the throne, '. . . Here God lives among men.
    22 8   I, John, am the one who *heard* and saw these things. When I had *heard* and seen them all, I knelt

7: HEAR, LISTEN TO, BE TOLD – UNDERSTAND, LEARN TAKE NOTICE OF – REFUSE TO LISTEN

Mt 2 18   (Jr 31 15) A voice was *heard* in Ramah . . . it was Rachel weeping
       22   [Joseph] *learnt* that Archelaus had succeeded his father Herod as ruler of Judaea
     4 12 X *Hearing* that John had been arrested he went back to Galilee,
     8 10 X [Just give the word and my servant will be cured.] When Jesus *heard* this he was astonished
     9 12 X [Why does your master eat with sinners?] When he *heard* this he replied, 'It is not the healthy who need the doctor,
    10 14   if anyone does not . . . *listen to* what you have to say . . . walk out
    11 5   lepers are cleansed, and the deaf *hear*.
    12 42   the Queen of the South . . . came . . . to *hear* the wisdom of Solomon;
    14 13 X When Jesus *received* (lit. *heard*) [the news of John's murder] he withdrew . . . to a lonely place
    18 15   have it out with [your brother] alone . . . If he *listens to* you, you have won back your brother. [16] If he does not
       16   *listen*, take two or three others along with you . . . [17] But
       17 4 if he *refuses to listen to* these, report it to the community;
         4 and if he *refuses to listen to* the community, treat him like a pagan
    20 24   When the other ten *heard* this they were indignant with the two brothers.
    24 6 /2 You will *hear of* wars and *rumours* of wars;
    27 13 X Do you not *hear* how many charges they have brought against you?
Mk 2 17 X [Why does he eat with sinners?] When Jesus *heard* this he said to them 'It is not the healthy who need the doctor,
     5 36 X 4 [Your daughter is dead.] Jesus had *overheard* this remark
     6 11   if . . . people refuse to *listen to* you . . . walk away
       20   When [Herod] had *heard* [John] speak he was greatly perplexed, and yet he liked to *listen to* him.
       29   When John's disciples *heard* about [his death], they came and took his body
     7 37   [Jesus] makes the deaf *hear* and the dumb speak.
    10 41   When the other ten *heard* this they began to feel indignant with James and John,
    12 28   One of the scribes . . . had *listened to* them debating
    13 7 /2 When you *hear of* wars and *rumours* of wars, do not be alarmed,
Lk 1 41   as soon as Elizabeth *heard* Mary's greeting, the child leapt in her womb
       58   [Elizabeth's] relations *heard* that the Lord had shown her so great a kindness,
       66   All those who *heard of* [John's birth] treasured it in their hearts
     2 46 X they found him in the Temple, sitting among the doctors, *listening to* them, and asking them questions;
     7 9 X When Jesus *heard* these words he was astonished at [the centurion]
       22   the blind see again . . . and the deaf *hear*,

Lk	7 29	All the people who *heard* [John, accepted] baptism
	8 50 X	[Your daughter has died.] Jesus had *heard* this, and he spoke to the man, 'Do not be afraid,
	11 31	the Queen of the South . . . came . . . to *hear* the wisdom of Solomon;
	12 3	whatever you have said in the dark will be *heard* in the daylight,
	15 25	as [the elder son] drew near the house, he could *hear* music
	16 2	[The rich man said to his steward,] What is this I *hear* about you?
	18 6	You *notice* what the unjust judge has to say?
	22 X	[I have kept all these from my earliest days.] When Jesus *heard* this he said, '. . . Sell all that you own
	36	When [the blind beggar] *heard* the crowd going past he asked what it was all about,
	21 9	when you *hear of* wars and revolutions, do not be frightened,
Jn	3 8	The wind blows wherever it pleases; you *hear* its sound,
	8 38	you put into action the lessons *learnt* from your father.
	9 27	I have told you once and you wouldn't *listen*. Why do you want to *hear* it all again?
	35 X	Jesus *heard* [the Pharisees] had driven [the blind man] away,
	10 8	All others who have come [to the sheepfold] are thieves . . . but the sheep *took no notice* of them.
	11 4 X	[Lord, the man you love is ill.] On ʳreceiving (lit. *hearing*) [the message] Jesus said, 'This sickness will end not in death
	6 X	yet when he *heard* that Lazarus was ill he stayed where he was
Ac	2 6	they all assembled, each one bewildered to *hear* these men speaking each his own language.
	8	How does it happen that each of us *hears* them in his own native language? ⁹ Parthians . . . ¹¹ . . . Cretans, and
	11	Arabs; we *hear* them preaching in our own language about the marvels of God.
	4 19	You must judge whether in God's eyes it is right to *listen to* you and not to God.
	24	When [the community] *heard* [what the Sanhedrin had said to Peter and John] they lifted up their voice to God all together.
	5 5	[You have lied to God.] When he *heard* this Ananias fell down ʳdead. This made a profound impression on everyone ʳpresent (lit. who was *listening*).
	11	[Sapphira's death] made a profound impression on . . . all who *heard* it.
	21	[Go and tell the people all about this new Life. The apostles] did as they *were told*; they . . . began to preach.
	24	[When we unlocked the door we found no one inside.] When . . . the chief priests *heard* this news they wondered what this could mean.
	6 11	We *heard* [Stephen] using blasphemous language
	7 12	(Gn 42 2) Jacob *heard* that there was grain for sale in Egypt,
	8 6	The people . . . had *heard of* the miracles [Philip] worked
	14	the apostles in Jerusalem *heard* that Samaria had accepted the word of God,
	30	Philip . . . *heard* [the eunuch] reading Isaiah the prophet
	9 13	Ananias said, 'Lord, ʳseveral people have told me (lit. I have *heard* from several people) about . . . all the harm [Saul] has been doing
	38	the disciples *heard* that Peter was [at Lydda],
	10 46	[The Jewish believers] could *hear* [the pagans] speaking strange languages and proclaiming the greatness of God.
	11 1	The apostles and the brothers in Judaea *heard* that the pagans too had accepted the word of God,
	18	[Who was I to stand in God's way?] *Hearing* this account satisfied [the apostles in Judaea].
	22	[A great number at Antioch were converted.] The church in Jerusalem *heard* about this
	14 14	Barnabas and Paul *heard* [that the people of Lystra were going to sacrifice oxen to them]
	15 12	the entire assembly . . . *listened to* Barnabas and Paul describing all the signs . . . God had worked . . . among the pagans.
	13	'My brothers,' [James] said '*listen to* me.
	24	We *hear* that some of our members have disturbed you with their demands
	16 38	the magistrates . . . were horrified to *hear* [Paul and Silas] were Roman citizens.
	17 8	*Hearing* this accusation alarmed . . . the city councillors,
	21	The one amusement the Athenians . . . seem to have . . . is *listening to* lectures about [the latest ideas].
	19 2	we *were* never even *told* there was such a thing as a Holy Spirit.
	26	you must have . . . *heard* how . . . this man Paul has . . . converted a great number of people
	28	*Hearing* this speech roused [the Ephesians] to fury
	21 12	When we *heard* [the prophet Agabus], we . . . implored Paul not to go on to Jerusalem.
	20	[Paul told of all that God had done among the pagans through his ministry. The brothers] gave glory to God when they *heard* this

Ac	21 22	[The Jewish believers] are bound to *hear* that you have come.
	22 26	When he *heard* [Paul's claim to be a Roman citizen] the centurion went and told the tribune;
	23 16	the son of Paul's sister *heard of* the ambush
	35	5 [the governor] said [to Paul], 'I will *hear* your [case] as soon as your accusers are here too'.
	24 4	[Tertullus said to Felix,] I beg you to *give* us *a* brief *hearing*.
	28 15	When the brothers [in Rome] *heard of* our arrival they came to meet us,
1 Co	5 1	I have *been told* as an undoubted fact that one of you is living with his father's wife.
	11 18	I *hear* that . . . there are separate factions among you,
	14 2 ○	Anybody with the gift of tongues speaks to God, but not to other people; because nobody *understands* him
2 Co	12 6	I am not going to [boast], in case anyone should begin to think I am better than he can actually see and *hear* me to be.
Ga	1 13	You must have *heard of* my career as a practising Jew,
	23	[The churches in Judaea] had *heard* nothing except that their one-time persecutor was now preaching the faith
Ep	1 15	I, having once *heard* about your faith in the Lord Jesus . . . ¹⁶ have never failed to remember you in my prayers
	3 2	You have probably *heard* how I have been entrusted by God with . . . grace
	4 29	Guard against foul talk; . . . do good to your *listeners*,
Ph	1 27	so that, whether I come . . . or stay at a distance and only *hear* about you, I shall know that you are . . . united
	30	You and I are together in the same fight as you saw me fighting before and, as you will have *heard*, I am fighting still.
	2 26	[Epaphroditus] is worried because you *heard* about his illness.
	4 9	Keep doing all the things that you learnt from me and have been taught by me and have *heard* or seen that I do.
Col	1 4	we *heard* about your faith in Christ Jesus
	9	ever since the day [Epaphras] *told* us [of your faith] we have never failed to pray for you,
2 Th	3 11	we *hear* that there are some of you who are living in idleness,
1 Tm	4 16	Take great care about what you do and . . . teach; . . . in this way you will save both yourself and those who *listen to* you.
2 Tm	1 13	Keep as your pattern the sound teaching you have *heard* from me,
	2 2	You have *heard* everything that I teach in public;
	14	all that [wrangling about words] ever achieves is the destruction of those who are *listening*.
	4 4	2 instead of *listening to* the truth, [people] will turn to myths.
	17	the Lord . . . gave me power, so that through me the whole message might be proclaimed for all the pagans to *hear*;
Phm	5	I *hear* of the love and the faith which you have for the Lord Jesus
Heb	5 11	2 you have grown so slow at *understanding*.
Jm	1 19	be quick to *listen* but slow to speak
	2 5	*Listen*, my dear brothers: it was those who are poor . . . that God chose,
2 P	2 8	[Lot] was outraged in his good soul by the crimes that he 2 saw and *heard of* every day.
1 Jn	2 7	this is . . . the original commandment which was the message ʳbrought to you (lit. you were to *hear*).
	18	you *were told* that an Antichrist must come,
	3 11	This is the message as you *heard* it from the beginning: that we are to love one another;
	4 3	any spirit which will not say this of Jesus . . . is the spirit of Antichrist, whose coming you *were warned about*.
	5	they are of the world . . . and the world *listens to* them.
	6	those who know God *listen to* us; those who are not of God refuse to *listen to* us.
2 Jn	6	this is the commandment which you have *heard* since the beginning, to live a life of love.
3 Jn	4	It is always my greatest joy to *hear* that my children are living according to the truth.
Rv	1 3	Happy the man who reads this prophecy, and happy those who *listen to* it.
	2 7	If anyone has ears [to hear], let him *listen to* what the Spirit is saying to the churches:
		Repeated in 2 11, 17, 29; 3 6, 13, 22.
	3 3	do you remember how eager you were when you first *heard* the message?
	9 20	idols made of gold . . . can neither see nor *hear* nor move
	13 9	If anyone has ears [to hear], let him *listen*:
	18 22	Never again . . . will be *heard* the song of harpists . . .; never again will . . . the sound of the mill be *heard* . . .
	23	²³ never again will be *heard* the voices of bridegroom and bride.
	22 17	Let everyone who *listens* answer, 'Come'.
	18	This is my solemn warning to all who *hear* the prophecies in this book:

3. LISTEN (TO), HEAR – AUDIENCE CHAMBER: *AKROATĒS*

      2 akroatērion 1   3 ep-akroaomai 1
      1 akroatēs   4

Ac	16 25	Paul and Silas were praying and singing God's praises, 3 while the other prisoners *listened*.
	25 23	2 Agrippa and Bernice . . . entered the *audience chamber*
Rm	2 13	It is not *listening to* the Law but keeping it that will make people holy
Jm	1 22	you must do what the word tells you, and not just *listen to* it and deceive yourselves. ²³ To *listen to* the word and not obey is like looking . . . in a mirror
	23	
	25	not *listening* then forgetting, but actively putting [the law] into practice.

4. HEED, TAKE NOTICE OF – ATTEND TO, LISTEN TO – HOLD TO, BE DEVOTED TO: *PROS-ECHŌ*

      2 ant-echomai 3/4   1 pros-echō 12/24

1: ATTEND (TO), PAY ATTENTION TO – LISTEN TO – HEED, TAKE NOTICE OF

Ac	8 6	The people united in ⌐welcoming (lit. *listening carefully to*) the message Philip preached,
	10	everyone ⌐believed (lit. *paid attention to*) what [Simon] said;
	11	They had only *been won over to* [Simon] because of the long time he had spent working on them with his magic.
	16 14	the Lord opened [Lydia's] heart to accept what Paul was saying.
1Tm	1 4	[stop] *taking notice of* myths and endless genealogies;
	3 8	deacons must be . . . ⌐moderate in the amount of wine they drink (lit. not only *interested in* drinking wine)
	4 1	there will be some who will desert the faith and choose to *listen to* deceitful spirits
	13	⌐*Make use of the time* until I arrive by (or: *Attend to*) . . . preaching and teaching.
Tt	1 14	[make them sound in the faith] so that they stop *taking notice of* Jewish myths
Heb	2 1	We ought, then, to *turn our minds* more *attentively* than before *to* what we have been taught,
	7 13	[Judah,] a different tribe, the members of which have never ⌐*done service at* (or: *attended to*) the altar
2 P	1 19	you will be right to ⌐*depend on* (or: *heed*) prophecy

2: TREAT WITH RESPECT, BE DEVOTED TO – HOLD TO

Mt	6 24	2 No one can be the slave of two masters . . . or *treat* the first *with respect* and the second with scorn.
Lk	16 13	2 No servant can be the slave of two masters . . . or *treat* the first *with respect* and the second with scorn.
Tt	1 9	2 [the elder] must ⌐*have a firm grasp of* (or: *be devoted to*) the unchanging message

5. LEARN, BE TAUGHT – DISCIPLE: *MANTHANŌ*

      2 manthanō   25   4 mathētria 1
      1 mathētēs 261   5 a-mathēs   1
      3 mathēteuō   4   6 sym-mathētēs 1

1: LEARN, BE TAUGHT – EDUCATED

Mt	9 13	2 Go and *learn* the meaning of the words (Ho 6 6): What I want is mercy, not sacrifice.
	11 29	2 *learn* from me, for I am gentle and humble in heart
	24 32	2 ⌐Take the fig tree as a parable (lit. *Learn* from this parable about the fig tree):
Mk	13 28	2 ⌐Take the fig tree as a parable (lit. *Learn* from this parable about the fig tree):
Jn	6 45	2 to hear the teaching of the Father, and *learn* from it, is to come to me.
	7 15 X	2 How did he learn to read? He has not *been taught*.
Ac	23 27	2 I . . . got [Paul] away, having *discovered* that he was a Roman citizen.
Rm	16 17	be on your guard against anybody who . . . puts difficulties 2 in the way of the doctrine you have *been taught*.
1 Co	4 6	I have taken Apollos and myself as an example for you to 2 *learn* from (remember the maxim: Keep to what is written):
	14 31	2 you can all prophesy in turn, so that everybody will *learn* something
	35	If [women] have ⌐any questions to ask (lit. anything they 2 want to *learn*), they should ask their husbands at home:
Ga	3 2	2 Let me ⌐ask you one question (lit. *learn* one thing from you): was it because you practised the Law . . .?

Ep	4 20	2 that is hardly the way you have *learnt* from Christ,
Ph	4 9	2 Keep doing all the things that you *learnt* from me
	11	2 I have *learnt* to manage on whatever I have,
Col	1 7	2 Epaphras, ⌐who taught you (lit. from whom you *learnt*) [the Good News], is one of our closest fellow workers
1Tm	2 11	2 During *instruction*, a woman should be quiet
	5 4	2 children . . . are to *learn* first of all to do their duty to their own families
	13	2 [young widows] *learn* how to be idle and go round from house to house;
2Tm	3 7	[silly women follow one craze after another] in the attempt 2 to *educate themselves*,
	14	2 You must keep to what you have *been taught* . . .; remember 2 who ⌐your teachers were (lit. you have *been taught* by),
Tt	3 14	2 All our people are to *learn* to occupy themselves in doing good
Heb	5 8 X	2 [Christ] *learnt* to obey through suffering;
2 P	3 16	5 these are the points that *uneducated* . . . people distort,
Rv	14 3	2 they were singing . . . a hymn that could only be *learnt* by the hundred and forty-four thousand

2: DISCIPLES

a) *of Jesus, of the kingdom*

      J = (John) the disciple whom Jesus loved

Mt	5 1	[Jesus] sat down and was joined by his *disciples*.
	8 21	one of his *disciples* said to him, 'Sir, let me go and bury my father first'.
	23	[Jesus] got into the boat followed by his *disciples*.
	9 10	a number of tax collectors and sinners came to sit at the table with Jesus and his *disciples*. ¹¹ . . . the Pharisees . . . said to his *disciples*, 'Why does your master eat with . . . sinners?'
	11	
	14	Why is it that . . . your *disciples* do not [fast]?
	19	Jesus rose and, with his *disciples*, followed [the official].
	37	He said to his *disciples*, 'The harvest is rich
	10 1	He summoned his twelve *disciples*, and gave them authority
	24 <	The *disciple* is not superior to his teacher, . . . ²⁵ It is
	25 <	enough for the *disciple* that he should grow to be like his teacher,
	42	If anyone gives so much as a cup of cold water to one of these little ones because he is a *disciple*,
	11 1	When Jesus had finished instructing his twelve *disciples*
	12 1	His *disciples* were hungry and began to pick ears of corn
	2	your *disciples* are doing something that is forbidden on the sabbath.
	49	stretching out his hand towards his *disciples* he said, 'Here are my mother and my brothers.
	13 10	the *disciples* . . . asked, 'Why do you talk to them in parables?'
	36	his *disciples* . . . said, 'Explain the parable about the darnel in the field to us.'
	52	3 every scribe who becomes a *disciple* of the kingdom of heaven is like a householder
	14 15	When evening came the *disciples* . . . said, '. . . send the people away,
	19	breaking the loaves he handed them to his *disciples* ⌐who (lit. and the *disciples*) gave them to the crowds.
	22	Directly after this he made the *disciples* get into the boat
	26	when the *disciples* saw him walking on the lake they were terrified.
	15 2	Why do your *disciples* break away from the tradition of the elders?
	12	the *disciples* . . . said, 'Do you know that the Pharisees were shocked . . .?'
	23	his *disciples* . . . pleaded with him. 'Give her what she wants,'
	32	Jesus called his *disciples* to him and said, 'I feel sorry for all these people;
	33	The *disciples* said to him, 'Where could we get enough bread . . .?'
	36	he took the seven loaves and the fish, and . . . handed them to the *disciples* ⌐who (lit. and the *disciples*) gave them to the crowds.
	16 5	The *disciples* . . . had forgotten to take any food.
	13	he put this question to his *disciples*, 'Who do people say the Son of Man is?'
	20	he gave the *disciples* strict orders not to tell anyone that he was the Christ.
	21	Jesus began to make it clear to his *disciples* that he was destined to . . . suffer grievously
	24	Jesus said to his *disciples*, 'If anyone wants to be a follower of mine,
	17 6	When they heard this, the *disciples* fell on their faces,
	10	the *disciples* put this question to him, 'Why do the scribes say then that Elijah has to come first?'
	13	The *disciples* understood then that he had been speaking of John the Baptist.

Mt 17	16	I took [my lunatic son] to your *disciples* and they were unable to cure him.
	19	the *disciples* came privately to Jesus. 'Why were we unable to cast [the devil] out?'
18	1	the *disciples* came to Jesus and said, 'Who is the greatest . . .?'
19	10	The *disciples* said to him, '. . . it is not advisable to marry.'
	13	People brought little children to him, . . . The *disciples* turned them away.
	23	Jesus said to his *disciples*, '. . . it will be hard for a rich man to enter the kingdom of heaven.'
	25	the *disciples* . . . were astonished. 'Who can be saved, then?'
20	17	Jesus . . . took the Twelve (ᵛ *disciples*) to one side
21	1	When they . . . had come in sight of Bethphage . . . Jesus sent two *disciples*,
	6	So the *disciples* went out
	20	The *disciples* were amazed . . . 'What happened to the tree . . . that it withered?'
23	1	addressing the people and his *disciples*, Jesus said, 'The scribes
24	1	his *disciples* came up to draw his attention to the Temple buildings.
	3	the *disciples* came and asked him privately, '. . . when is this going to happen?
26	1	Jesus . . . told his *disciples*, 'It will be Passover . . . in two days' time,
	8	When they saw [the expensive ointment poured out] the *disciples* were indignant;
	17	the *disciples* came to Jesus to say, 'Where do you want us to make the preparations for . . . the passover?'
	18	It is at your house that I am keeping Passover with my *disciples*.
	19	The *disciples* did what Jesus told them
	20	When evening came he was at table with the twelve (§ *disciples*).
	26	Jesus took some bread, and . . . gave it to the *disciples*
	35	Peter said '. . . . I will never disown you.' And all the *disciples* said the same.
	36	[at] Gethsemane . . . he said to his *disciples*, 'Stay here
	40	He came back to the *disciples* and found them sleeping,
	45	he came back to the *disciples* and said to them, 'You can sleep on now
	56	all the *disciples* deserted him and ran away.
27	57	a rich man of Aramathaea, called Joseph, who had himself
	3	become a *disciple* of Jesus.
	64	have the sepulchre kept secure . . . for fear his *disciples* come and steal him away
28	7	go quickly and tell his *disciples*, He has risen
	8	the women . . . ran to tell the *disciples*.
	13	you must say, His *disciples* came . . . and stole him away
	16	Meanwhile the eleven *disciples* set out for Galilee,
	19	3 make *disciples* of all the nations;
Mk 2	15	a number of tax collectors and sinners were also sitting at the table with Jesus and his *disciples*;
	16	the scribes . . . said to his *disciples*, 'Why does he eat with . . . sinners?'
	18	Why is it that . . . your *disciples* do not [fast]?
	23	his *disciples* began to pick ears of corn
3	7	Jesus withdrew with his *disciples* to the lakeside,
	9	he asked his *disciples* to have a boat ready for him
4	34	he explained everything to his *disciples* when they were alone.
5	31	His *disciples* said to him, 'You see how the crowd is pressing round you
6	1	he went to his home town and his *disciples* accompanied him.
	35	his *disciples* came up to him and said, '. . . ³⁶ send them away
	41	he took the five loaves and the two fish . . . then he . . . handed them to his *disciples* to distribute
	45	he made his *disciples* get into the boat
7	2	[The Pharisees] noticed that some of his *disciples* were eating with unclean hands . . . ⁵ So [they] asked him, 'Why do your *disciples* not respect the tradition of the elders . . .?'
	17	his *disciples* questioned him about the parable.
8	1	he called his *disciples* to him and said '. . . ² I feel sorry for all these people;
	4	His *disciples* replied, 'Where could anyone get bread to feed these people . . .?'
	6	he took the seven loaves, and . . . handed them to his *disciples* to distribute;
	10	getting into the boat with his *disciples*, [he] went to the region of Dalmanutha.
	27	Jesus and his *disciples* left for the villages round Caesarea Phillippi. On the way he put this question to his *disciples*, 'Who do people say I am?'
	33	turning and seeing his *disciples*, he rebuked Peter . . . 'Get behind me, Satan!'
	34	He called the people and his *disciples* to him and said, 'If anyone wants to be a follower of mine,

Mk 9	14	When they rejoined the *disciples* they saw a large crowd round them
	18	I asked your *disciples* to cast [the spirit of dumbness] out and they were unable to.
	28	his *disciples* asked him privately, 'Why were we unable to cast it out?'
	31	he was instructing his *disciples*; '. . . The Son of Man will be delivered into the hands of men;
10	10	the *disciples* questioned him again about [divorce],
	13	People were bringing little children to him, . . . The *disciples* turned them away,
	23	Jesus . . . said to his *disciples*, 'How hard it is for those who
	24	have riches to enter the kingdom of God!' ²⁴ The *disciples* were astounded
	46	as he left Jericho with his *disciples* and a large crowd,
11	1	When they were approaching Jerusalem . . . he sent two of his *disciples*
	14	he addressed the fig tree. . . . And his *disciples* heard him
12	43	he called his *disciples* and said to them, '. . . this poor widow has put more in than all
13	1	one of his *disciples* said to him, 'Look at the size of those stones, Master!'
14	12	his *disciples* said to him, 'Where do you want us to . . . make the preparations for . . . the passover?'
	13	he sent two of his *disciples*, saying to them, 'Go into the city
	14	Where is my dining room in which I can eat the passover with my *disciples*?
	16	The *disciples* set out and . . . prepared the Passover.
	32	Jesus said to his *disciples*, 'Stay here while I pray.'
16	7	you must go and tell his *disciples* and Peter, He is going before you to Galilee; it is there you will see him,
Lk 5	30	The Pharisees and their scribes complained to his *disciples* . . . 'Why do you eat and drink with . . . sinners?'
6	1	one sabbath . . . his *disciples* were picking ears of corn
	13	When day came he summoned his *disciples* and picked out twelve of them; he called them apostles:
	17	there was a large gathering of his *disciples*
	20	fixing his eyes on his *disciples* he said: 'How happy are you who are poor:
40	<	The *disciple* is not superior to his teacher; the fully trained disciple will always be like his teacher.
7	11	he went to a town called Nain, accompanied by his *disciples* and a great number of people.
8	9	His *disciples* asked him what this parable might mean,
	22	he got into a boat with his *disciples*
9	14	he said to his *disciples*, 'Get them to sit down in parties of about fifty.
	16	he took the five loaves and . . . handed them to his *disciples* to distribute
	18	one day when he was praying alone in the presence of his *disciples* he put this question to them, 'Who do the crowds say I am?'
	40	I begged your *disciples* to cast [the spirit] out, and they could not.
	43	he said to his *disciples*, ⁴⁴ '. . . The Son of Man is going to be handed over
	54	the *disciples* James and John said, 'Lord, do you want us to call down fire . . .?'
10	23	turning to his *disciples* he spoke to them in private, 'Happy the eyes that see what you see,
11	1	one of his *disciples* said, 'Lord, teach us to pray,
12	1	he began to speak, first of all to his *disciples*. 'Be on your guard against the yeast of the Pharisees
	22	he said to his *disciples*, '. . . [do not] worry about your life
14	26	If any man comes to me without hating his father, . . . he cannot be my *disciple*.
	27	Anyone who does not carry his cross . . . cannot be my *disciple*.
	33	none of you can be my *disciple* unless he gives up all his possessions.
16	1	He also said to his *disciples*, 'There was a rich man
17	1	He said to his *disciples*, 'Obstacles are sure to come,
	22	He said to his *disciples*, '. . . you will long to see one of the days of the Son of Man
18	15	People even brought little children to him, . . . but . . . the *disciples* . . . turned them away.
19	29	he sent two of his *disciples*, telling them, ³⁰ '. . . you will find a tethered colt
	37	the whole group of *disciples* joyfully began to praise God
	39	Some Pharisees . . . said to him, 'Master, check your *disciples*',
20	45	he said to the *disciples*, 'Beware of the scribes
22	11	Where is the dining room in which I can eat the passover with my *disciples*?
	39	He then left to make his way . . . to the Mount of Olives, with the *disciples* following.
	45	he went to the *disciples* and found them sleeping for sheer grief.
Jn 2	2	Jesus and his *disciples* had also been invited [to the wedding at Cana].

Jn 2 11 He let his glory be seen, and his *disciples* believed in him.

12 he went down to Capernaum with his mother and the brothers (§ and his *disciples*),

17 Then his *disciples* remembered the words of scripture: Zeal for your house will devour me.

22 when Jesus rose from the dead, his *disciples* . . . believed the scripture and the words he had said.

3 22 Jesus went with his *disciples* into the Judaean countryside

4 1 the Pharisees had found out that he was making and baptising more *disciples* than John – 2 though in fact it was his *disciples* who baptised.

8 His *disciples* had gone into the town to buy food.

27 his *disciples* returned, and were surprised to find him speaking to a woman,

31 Meanwhile, the *disciples* were urging him, 'Rabbi, do have something to eat;

33 the *disciples* asked one another, 'Has someone been bringing him food?'

6 3 Jesus climbed the hillside, and sat down there with his *disciples*.

8 One of his *disciples*, Andrew, . . . said, 9 'There is a small boy here

12 he said to the *disciples*, 'Pick up the pieces left over,

16 the *disciples* went down to the shore of the lake

22 the crowd . . . saw that . . . Jesus had not got into the boat with his *disciples*, but that the *disciples* had set off by themselves.

24 neither Jesus nor his *disciples* were there,

60 many of his *followers* said, 'This is intolerable language.

61 Jesus was aware that his *followers* were complaining about it and said, 'Does this upset you?'

66 After this, many of his *disciples* left him and stopped going with him.

7 3 Why not . . . go to Judaea, and let your *disciples* see the works you are doing;

8 31 If you make my word your home you will indeed be my *disciples*,

9 2 His *disciples* asked him, 'Rabbi, who sinned . . .?

27 [The man born blind] replied, '. . . Do you want to become his *disciples* too?'

28 You can be his *disciple*, . . . we are disciples of Moses:

11 7 saying to the *disciples*, 'Let us go to Judaea.

8 The *disciples* said, 'Rabbi, . . . the Jews wanted to stone you.

12 The *disciples* said . . , 'Lord, if [Lazarus] is able to rest he is sure to get better.

16 6 Thomas . . . said to the other *disciples*, 'Let us go too, and die with him.

54 Jesus . . . left the district for a town called Ephraim . . . and stayed there with his *disciples*.

12 4 Judas Iscariot – one of his *disciples*, the man who was to betray him –

16 At the time his *disciples* did not understand this,

13 5 he . . . began to wash the *disciples*' feet

22 The *disciples* looked at one another,

23 J The *disciple* Jesus loved was reclining next to Jesus;

35 By this love you have for one another, everyone will know that you are my *disciples*.

15 8 It is to the glory of my Father that you should bear much fruit, and then you will be my *disciples*.

16 17 some of his *disciples* said to one another, 'What does he mean . . .?'

29 His *disciples* said, 'Now you are speaking plainly

18 1 Jesus left wth his *disciples* and crossed the Kedron valley. There was a garden there, and he went into it with his *disciples*. 2 . . . Jesus had often met his *disciples* there,

15 J Simon Peter, with another *disciple*, followed Jesus. This *disciple* . . . was known to the high priest,

16 J the other *disciple* . . . went out . . . and brought Peter in.

17 Aren't you another of that man's *disciples*?

19 The high priest questioned Jesus about his *disciples* and his teaching.

25 Aren't you another of his *disciples*?

19 26 J Seeing his mother and the *disciple* he loved standing near her, Jesus said '. . . this is your son.' 27 Then to the *disciple*

J he said, 'This is your mother.' And from that moment the *disciple* made a place for her in his home.

38 Joseph of Arimathaea, who was a *disciple* of Jesus – though a secret one

20 2 [Mary of Magdala] came running to Simon Peter and the other *disciple*, the one Jesus loved. . . . 3 . . . Peter set

3 J

4 J out with the other *disciple* to go to the tomb. 4 They ran together, but the other *disciple*, running faster than Peter, reached the tomb first; 5 he bent down . . . but

8 J did not go in. . . . 8 Then the other *disciple* who had

10 J reached the tomb first also went in; . . . 10 The *disciples* then went home again.

18 Mary of Magdala went and told the *disciples* that she had seen the Lord

Jn 20 19 the doors were closed in the room where the *disciples* were,

20 . . . Jesus came . . . 20 . . . The *disciples* were filled with

25 joy when they saw the Lord, . . . 25 When the *disciples* said, 'We have seen the Lord,' [Thomas] answered, . . .

26 26 Eight days later the *disciples* were in the house again

30 There were many other signs that Jesus worked and the *disciples* saw,

21 1 Jesus showed himself again to the *disciples*. . . . 2 Simon Peter, Thomas . . . and two more of the *disciples* were

2 together.

4 there stood Jesus on the shore, though the *disciples* did not realise that it was Jesus.

7 J The *disciple* Jesus loved said to Peter, 'It is the Lord.' . . .

8 8 The other *disciples* came on in the boat,

12 None of the *disciples* was bold enough to ask, 'Who are you?'

14 This was the third time that Jesus showed himself to the *disciples*

20 J Peter . . . saw the *disciple* Jesus loved following them

23 J The rumour then went out among the brothers that this *disciple* would not die.

24 J This *disciple* is the one who vouches for these things

Ac 6 1 when the number of *disciples* was increasing, the Hellenists made a complaint against the Hebrews:

2 So the Twelve called a full meeting of the *disciples*

7 the number of *disciples* in Jerusalem was greatly increased,

9 1 Saul was still breathing threats to slaughter the Lord's *disciples*.

10 A *disciple* called Ananias who lived in Damascus

19 [Saul] spent only a few days with the *disciples* in Damascus,

25 the *disciples* took him and let him down from the top of a wall . . . in a basket.

26 [at] Jerusalem [Saul] tried to join the *disciples*, but they were all afraid of him: they could not believe he was really a *disciple*.

36 4 At Jaffa there was a woman *disciple* called Tabitha,

38 the *disciples* . . . sent two men [to Peter]

11 26 It was at Antioch that the *disciples* were first called Christians.

29 The *disciples* decided to send relief [to Judaea],

13 52 the *disciples* were filled with joy and the Holy Spirit.

14 20 The *disciples* came crowding round [Paul] but . . . he stood up and went back to the town.

21 3 Having . . . made a considerable number of *disciples*,

22 [Paul and Barnabas] went back . . . to Antioch. 22 They put fresh heart into the *disciples*

28 They stayed [at Antioch] with the *disciples* for some time.

15 10 if you imposed on the *disciples* the very burden that neither we nor our ancestors were strong enough to support?

16 1 [At Lystra] there was a *disciple* called Timothy,

18 23 [Paul continued] his journey through . . . Phrygia, encouraging all the *followers*.

27 the brothers . . . wrote asking the *disciples* [in Achaia] to welcome [Apollos].

19 1 Paul [arrived in] Ephesus, where he found a number of *disciples*.

9 [Paul] took his *disciples* apart to hold daily discussions in the lecture room of Tyrannus.

30 Paul wanted to make an appeal to the people, but the *disciples* refused to let him;

20 1 When the disturbance [in Ephesus] was over, Paul sent for the *disciples*

30 there will be men coming forward . . . to induce the *disciples* to follow them.

21 4 We sought out the *disciples* [in Tyre] and stayed there a week.

16 Some of the *disciples* from Caesarea . . . took us to the house of a Cypriot . . . he was called Mnason and had been one of the earliest *disciples*.

b) *of John the Baptist, of Moses, of the Pharisees*

Mt 9 14 John's *disciples* came to [Jesus] and said, 'Why is it that . . . your disciples do not [fast]?'

11 2 John . . . sent his *disciples* to ask [Jesus], 3 'Are you the one who is to come . . .?'

14 12 John's *disciples* came and took the body

22 16 [the Pharisees] sent their *disciples* to [Jesus], together with the Herodians,

Mk 2 18 One day when John's *disciples* and the Pharisees were fasting, some people . . . said to [Jesus], 'Why is it that John's *disciples* and the *disciples* of the Pharisees fast, but your disciples do not?'

6 29 When John's *disciples* heard about [his death], they came and took his body.

Lk 5 33 John's *disciples* are always fasting . . . and [the disciples] of the Pharisees too, but yours go on eating and drinking.

7 18 The *disciples* of John gave him all this news, and John, summoning two of his *disciples*, sent them to the Lord

11 1 Lord, teach us to pray, just as John taught his *disciples*.

Jn 1 35 as John stood there again with two of his *disciples*, Jesus passed,

Jn	1 37	Hearing this, the two *disciples* followed Jesus.
	3 25	Some of John's *disciples* had opened a discussion with a Jew about purification,
	9 28	You can be his disciple, . . . we are *disciples* of Moses:

HEART

1: Heart of a person	2: the Heart of God
a) Heart – Mind	3: the Heart of the earth
b) (hardness of) Heart – (closed) Minds – Obstinacy	

1 kardia	157	2 (sklēro-)kardia 3
3 kardio(-gnōstēs)	2	

1: HEART OF A PERSON

a) Heart – Mind

Mt	5 8	Happy the pure in *heart*: they shall see God.
	28	if a man looks at a woman lustfully, he has already committed adultery with her in his *heart*.
	6 21	where your treasure is there will your *heart* be also.
	9 4	Why do you have such wicked thoughts in your *hearts*?
	11 29 X	Shoulder my yoke and learn from me, for I am gentle and humble in *heart*,
	12 34	a man's words flow out of what fills his *heart*.
	13 19	When anyone hears the word of the kingdom without understanding, the evil one comes and carries off what was sown in his *heart*:
	15 8	(Is 29 13) This people honours me only with lip-service, while their *hearts* are far from me.
	18	the things that come out of the mouth come from the *heart*,
	19	from the *heart* come evil intentions: murder, adultery,
	18 35	unless you each forgive your brother from your *heart*,
	22 37	(Dt 6 5) You must love the Lord your God with all your *heart*,
	24 48	as for the dishonest servant who says ᵊto himself (lit. in his *heart*), My master is taking his time,
Mk	2 6	some scribes were sitting there, and they thought ᵊto themselves (lit. in their *hearts*),
	8	Why do you have these thoughts in your *hearts*?
	7 6	(Is 29 13) This people honours me only with lip-service, while their *hearts* are far from me.
	19	[whatever goes into a man from outside cannot make him unclean,] because it does not go into his *heart* but through his stomach
	21	it is from within, from men's *hearts*, that evil intentions emerge:
	11 23	if anyone says to this mountain, Get up and throw yourself into the sea, with no hesitation in his *heart*
	12 30	(Dt 6 5) you must love the Lord your God with all your *heart*,
	33	To love [God] with all your *heart* . . . is far more important than any . . . sacrifice.
Lk	1 17	(Ml 3 24) [John] will go before [the Lord] to turn the *hearts* of fathers towards their children
	51	[God] has routed the proud of *heart*.
	66	All those who heard of it treasured it in their *hearts*.
	2 19	Mary . . . treasured all these things and pondered them in her *heart*.
	35	so that ᵊthe secret thoughts (lit. the thoughts in the *hearts*) of many may be laid bare.
	51	[Jesus's] mother stored up all these things in her *heart*.
	3 15	the people . . . were beginning to ᵊthink that John might be (lit. wonder in their *hearts* if John was) the Christ,
	5 22	What are these thoughts you have in your *hearts*?
	6 45	A good man draws what is good from the store of goodness in his *heart*; a bad man draws what is bad from the store of badness. For a man's words flow out of what fills his *heart*.
	8 12	the devil comes and carries away the word from their *hearts*
	15	As for the [seed] in the rich soil, this is people with a noble and generous *heart* who have heard the word and take it to themselves
	9 47	Jesus knew what thoughts were going through [his disciples'] *minds*, and he took a little child
	10 27	(Dt 6 5) You must love the Lord your God with all your *heart*,
	12 34	where your treasure is, there will your *heart* be also.
	45	the servant who says ᵊto himself (lit. in his *heart*), My master is taking his time coming,
	16 15	God knows your *hearts*.

Lk	21 14	Keep this carefully in *mind*: you are not to prepare your defence,
	24 25	You foolish men! So ᵊslow (lit. slow of *heart*) to believe the full message of the prophets!
	32	Did not our *hearts* burn within us as he talked to us . . . ?
	38	why are these doubts rising in your *hearts*?
Jn	13 2	the devil had already put it into the *mind* of Judas Iscariot . . . to betray him.
	14 1	Do not let your *hearts* be troubled.
	27	Do not let your *hearts* be troubled or afraid.
	16 6	you are sad at *heart* because I have told you this.
	22	but I shall see you again, and your *hearts* will be full of joy,
Ac	1 24 3	Lord, you can read everyone's *heart*;
	2 26	(Ps 16 9) So my *heart* was glad and my tongue cried out with joy;
	37	Hearing this, [the Jews] were cut to the *heart*
	46	[the faithful] shared their food gladly and ᵊgenerously (lit. with serenity of *mind*)
	4 32	The whole group of believers was united, *heart* and soul;
	5 3	Ananias, . . . how can Satan have so ᵊpossessed you (lit. filled your *heart*) that you should lie to the Holy Spirit . . . ? ⁴ . . . What put this scheme into your *mind*?
	7 23	ᵊ[Moses] decided (lit. it came into [Moses'] *mind*) to visit his countrymen,
	39	[Moses' followers] turned back to Egypt in their *thoughts*,
	54	ᵊThey were infuriated (lit. Their *hearts* shook with fury) when they heard [Stephen's words]
	8 21	God can see how your *heart* is warped.
	22	you may still be forgiven for ᵊthinking as you did (lit. that thought of your *heart*)
	37	(ᵛ Philip said: 'If you believe with all your *heart*, it is allowed.')
	11 23	[Barnabas] urged them all to remain faithful to the Lord with *heart*felt devotion;
	14 17	[the living God] ᵊgives you food and makes you happy (lit. satisfies your *hearts* with food and happiness).
	15 8 3	God, who can read everyone's *heart*, shows his approval of [the pagans] by giving the Holy Spirit to them . . . ⁹ . . . he purified their *hearts* by faith.
	16 14	the Lord opened [Lydia's] *heart* to accept what Paul was saying.
	21 13	are you trying to . . . weaken my ᵊresolution (lit. *mind*) by your tears?
Rm	1 24	That is why God left them to ᵊtheir filthy enjoyments (lit. the desires of their *hearts*)
	2 15	[The pagans] can point to the substance of the Law engraved on their *hearts*
	29	the real circumcision is in the *heart*
	5 5	the love of God has been poured into our *hearts* by the Holy Spirit
	6 17	you submitted ᵊwithout reservation (lit. with all your *heart*) to the creed you were taught.
	8 27	God who knows everything in our *hearts* knows perfectly well what [the Holy Spirit] means,
	9 2	my sorrow is so great, my *mental* anguish so endless,
	10 1	I have ᵊthe very warmest (lit. the most *heart*felt) love for the Jews, and I pray to God for them
	6	Do not ᵊtell yourself (lit. say in your *heart*) you have to bring Christ down
	8	(Dt 30 14) The word . . . is very near to you, it is on your lips and in your *heart*.
	9	if you believe in your *heart* that God raised [Jesus] from the dead, then you will be saved. ¹⁰ By believing from the *heart* you are made righteous;
	16 18	People like that . . . are slaves of their own appetites, confusing the simple-*minded* with their pious and persuasive arguments.
1Co	2 9	(Is 64 3) we teach . . . things beyond the *mind* of man,
	4 5	the Lord . . . will . . . reveal the secret intentions of men's *hearts*.
	7 37	if someone has firmly made his *mind* up . . . to keep his daughter as she is, he will be doing a good thing.
	14 25	[if an unbeliever came in while you were all prophesying] he would have ᵊhis secret thoughts (lit. the secrets of his *heart*) laid bare.
2Co	1 22	[God has given us] the pledge, the Spirit, that we carry in our *hearts*.
	2 4	When I wrote to you, in deep distress and anguish of *mind*,
	3 2	you are yourselves our letter, written on our *hearts*,
	3	you are a letter from Christ, . . . written . . . not on stone tablets but on the tablets of your living *hearts*.
	15	even today, whenever Moses is read, the veil is over [the] *minds* [of the Israelites].
	4 6	It is the same God who said, 'Let there be light . . . ' who has shone in our *minds*
	5 12	the people who can boast more about what they seem than what ᵊthey are (lit. is in their *hearts*).
	6 11	Corinthians, we have spoken to you very frankly; our *mind* has been opened in front of you.
	7 3	you are in our *hearts* – together we live or together we die

2 Co	8 16	I thank God for putting into Titus' *heart* the same concern for you that I have myself.
	9 7	Each one should give what he has decided in his own *mind*,
Ga	4 6	God has sent the Spirit of his Son into our *hearts*:
Ep	1 18	May [God] enlighten the eyes of your *mind*
	3 17	so that Christ may live in your *hearts* through faith,
	5 19	go on singing and chanting to the Lord in your *hearts*,
	6 5	Slaves, be obedient to . . . your masters . . . ʳwith deep respect (lit. in serenity of *heart*)
	22	I am sending [Tychicus] to you . . . to . . . reassure ʳyou (lit. your *minds*).
Ph	1 7	You have a permanent place in my *heart*,
	4 7	that peace of God . . . will guard your *hearts*
Col	2 2	[I have to struggle hard] to bind you together in love and to stir your *minds*,
	3 15	may the peace of Christ reign in your *hearts*,
	16	With gratitude in your *hearts* sing psalms . . . to God.
	22	Slaves, be obedient to . . . your masters . . . whole-*heartedly*, out of respect to the Master.
	4 8	I am sending [Tychicus] to you . . . to reassure ʳyou (lit. your *minds*).
1 Th	2 4	we are not trying to please men but God, who ʳcan read our inmost thoughts (lit. knows our *hearts*).
	17	A short time after we had been separated from you – in body but never in ʳthought (lit. *mind*), brothers –
	3 13	may [the Lord] so confirm your *hearts* in holiness that you may be blameless
2 Th	2 17	[May Jesus Christ and God] comfort ʳyou (lit. your *hearts*) and strengthen ʳyou (lit. them)
	3 5	May the Lord turn your *hearts* towards the love of God
1 Tm	1 5	love, coming out of a pure *heart*, a clear conscience and a sincere faith.
2 Tm	2 22	in union with all those who call on the Lord with pure *minds*.
Heb	4 12	The word of God . . . can judge the ʳsecret emotions and thoughts (lit. emotions and thoughts of the *heart*).
	8 10	(Jr 31 33) I will put my laws into their *minds* and write them on their *hearts*.
	10 16	(Jr 31 33) I will put my laws into their *hearts* and write them on their minds
	22	let us be sincere in *heart* and filled with faith, our *minds* sprinkled and free from any trace of bad conscience
	13 9	it is better to rely on grace ʳfor inner strength (lit. to strengthen the *heart*)
Jm	1 26	Nobody must imagine that he is religious while he still goes on deceiving ʳhimself (lit. his own *heart*)
	3 14	if at *heart* you have the bitterness of jealousy . . . never make any claims for yourself
	4 8	clear your *minds*, you waverers
	5 5	in the time of slaughter you went on eating to your *heart's* content.
	8	do not lose *heart*, because the Lord's coming will be soon.
1 P	1 22	let your love for each other be real and from the *heart*
	3 4	[beauty] should be inside, in a person's *heart*, imperishable: the ornament of a sweet and gentle disposition
	15	Simply reverence the Lord Christ in your *hearts*,
2 P	1 19	until the dawn comes and the morning star rises in your *minds*.
	2 14	Greed is the one lesson their *minds* have learnt.
1 Jn	3 19	we are . . . able to quieten our ʳconscience (lit. *heart*) in [God's] presence, ²⁰whatever accusations ʳit (lit. our *heart*) may raise against us, because God is greater than our ʳconscience (lit. *heart*) and he knows everything.
	21	²¹ . . . if we cannot be condemned by our own ʳconscience (lit. *heart*) we need not be afraid in God's presence.
Rv	2 23	it is I who search *heart* and loins
	17 17	God influenced their *minds* to do what he intended,
	18 7	I am the queen on my throne, [Babylon] says ʳto herself (lit. in her *heart*),

b) (Hardness of) Heart – (Closed) Minds – Obstinacy

Mt	13 15	(Is 6 10) the *heart* of this nation has grown coarse, . . . and they have shut their eyes, for fear they should see with their eyes, . . . understand with their *heart*,
	19 8	it was because ʳyou were so unteachable (lit. of the hardness of your *heart*) . . . that Moses allowed you to divorce your wives,
Mk	3 5	grieved to find them so *obstinate*, [Jesus] looked angrily round [the synagogue]
	6 52	[the disciples] had not seen what the miracle of the loaves meant; their *minds* were closed.
	8 17	Why are you talking about having no bread? . . . Are your *minds* closed?
	10 5	It was because ʳyou were so unteachable (lit. of the hardness of your *heart*) that [Moses] wrote this commandment for you.
	16 14	[Jesus] reproached [the Eleven] for their incredulity and *obstinacy*,
Lk	21 34	Watch yourselves, or your *hearts* will be coarsened with debauchery

Jn	12 40	(Is 6 9–10) [God] has blinded their eyes, he has hardened their *heart*, for fear they should see with their eyes and understand with their *heart*,
Ac	7 51	You stubborn people, with your pagan *hearts* and pagan ears. You are always resisting the Holy Spirit,
	28 27	(Is 6 10) the *heart* of this nation has grown coarse, . . . and they have shut their eyes, for fear they should see with their eyes, . . . understand with their *heart*,
Rm	1 21	[men] made nonsense out of logic and their empty *minds* were darkened.
	2 5	ʳYour stubborn refusal to repent (lit. The obstinacy of your *hearts* in not repenting) is only adding to [God's] anger
Ep	4 18	intellectually [pagans] are in the dark, . . . without knowledge because they have shut their *hearts* to it.
Heb	3 8	(Ps 95 8) do not harden your *hearts*, as happened in the Rebellion,
	10	(Ps 95 10) How ʳunreliable (lit. unstable in their *hearts*) these people who refuse to grasp my ways!
	12	Take care, brothers, that there is not in any one of your community a wicked *mind*,
	15	(Ps 95 8) do not harden your *hearts*, as happened in the Rebellion,
	4 7	(Ps 95 8) do not harden your *hearts*,

2: THE HEART OF GOD

Ac	13 22	(cf 1 S 13 14) I have selected David son of Jesse, a man after my own *heart*,

3: THE HEART OF THE EARTH

Mt	12 40	so will the Son of Man be in the *heart* of the earth for three days and three nights.

HEAVEN

1. Heaven – the Heavens: *ouranos*	**2. Heaven – Sky:** *dio(-petēs)*
1: Heaven, Heavenly – Sky – Air	
2: Heaven, Heavenly, and Earth, Earthly	

1. HEAVEN – THE HEAVENS: *OURANOS*

3	*ouranios*	9	2	*ep-ouranios*	18/19
1	*ouranos*	243/276	4	*(mes-)ouranēma*	3
5	*ouranothen*	2			

1: HEAVEN, HEAVENLY – SKY – AIR

Mt	3 16	As soon as Jesus was baptised he came up from the water, and suddenly the *heavens* opened . . . ¹⁷And a voice
	17	spoke from *heaven*, 'This is my Son,
	5 12	be glad, for your reward will be great in *heaven*;
	16	seeing your good works, [men] may give the praise to your Father in *heaven*.
	45	3 in this way you will be the sons of your Father in *heaven*,
	48	3 You must therefore be perfect just as your *heavenly* Father is perfect.
	6 1	by [parading your good deeds] you will lose all reward from your Father in *heaven*.
	9	Our Father in *heaven*, may your name be held holy,
	14	3 if you forgive others their failings, your *heavenly* Father will forgive you yours;
	26	Look at the birds in the *sky*. They do not sow or reap . . . 3 yet your *heavenly* Father feeds them.
	32	3 Your *heavenly* Father knows you need [food, drink and clothing].
	7 11	how much more will your Father in *heaven* give good things to those who ask him?
	21	the person who does the will of my Father in *heaven*.
	8 20	Foxes have holes and the birds of the *air* have nests,
	10 32	I will declare myself for him in the presence of my Father in *heaven*.
	33	But the one who disowns me in the presence of men, I will disown in the presence of my Father in *heaven*.
	11 23	as for you, Capernaum, did you want to be exalted as high as *heaven*?
	12 50	Anyone who does the will of my Father in *heaven*,

Mt	13	32	the birds of the *air* come and shelter in its branches.
	14	19	[Jesus] took the five loaves . . . raised his eyes to *heaven* and said the blessing
	15	13	3 Any plant my *heavenly* Father has not planted will be pulled up by the roots.
	16	1	The Pharisees . . . asked if he would show them a sign from *heaven*. ² He replied, 'In the evening you will say,
		2	It will be fine; there is a red *sky*, ³ and in the morning,
		3	Stormy weather today; the *sky* is red and overcast. You know how to read the face of the *sky*,
		17	it was not flesh and blood that revealed this to you but my Father in *heaven*.
	18	10	never despise any of these little ones, for . . . their angels in *heaven* are continually in the presence of my Father in *heaven*.
		14	it is never the will of your Father in *heaven* that one of these little ones should be lost.
		35	3 that is how my Father *in heaven* will deal with you
	19	21	sell what you own and give the money to the poor, and you will have treasure in *heaven*;
	21	25 ○	John's baptism: where did it come from: *heaven* or man? . . . If we say from *heaven* he will retort,
	22	30	at the resurrection men and women do not marry; no, they are like the angels in *heaven*.
	23	22	when a man swears by *heaven* he is swearing by the throne of God
	24	29	the stars will fall from the *sky* and the powers of *heaven* will be shaken.
		30	the sign of the Son of Man will appear in *heaven*; then too all the peoples of the earth will . . . see the Son of Man coming on the clouds of *heaven*
		31	he will send his angels . . . to gather his chosen . . . from one end of *heaven* to the other.
		36	as for that day and hour, nobody knows it, neither the angels of *heaven*, nor the Son,
	26	64	you will see the Son of Man . . . coming on the clouds of *heaven*.
	28	2	the angel of the Lord, descending from *heaven*, came and rolled away the stone
Mk	1	10	No sooner had [Jesus] come up out of the water than he saw the *heavens* torn apart and . . . ¹¹ a voice came from *heaven*, 'You are my Son,
		11	
	4	32	the birds of the *air* can shelter in its shade.
	6	41	[Jesus] took the five loaves and . . . raised his eyes to *heaven* and said the blessing;
	7	34	looking up to *heaven* [Jesus] sighed; and he said to [the blind man] . . . 'Be opened'.
	8	11	The Pharisees . . . demanded of him a sign from *heaven*,
	10	21	sell everything you own and . . . you will have treasure in *heaven*;
	11	25	forgive what you have against anybody, so that your Father in *heaven* may forgive your failings too.
		26	(ᵛ . . . your Father who is in *heaven* will forgive you no more . . .)
		30 ○	John's baptism: did it come from *heaven*, or from man? . . . ³¹ If we say from *heaven*, he will say,
		31	
	12	25	when they rise from the dead, men and women do not marry; no, they are like the angels in *heaven*.
	13	25	the stars will come falling from *heaven* and the powers in the *heavens* will be shaken.
		32	as for that day or hour, nobody knows it, neither the angels of *heaven*, nor the Son;
	14	62	you will see the Son of Man . . . coming with the clouds of *heaven*.
	16	19	the Lord Jesus . . . was taken up into *heaven*:
Lk	2	13	suddenly with the angel there was a great throng of the *heavenly* host,
		15	3 when the angels had gone from them into *heaven*, the shepherds said
	3	21	while Jesus after his own baptism was at prayer, *heaven* opened ²² and . . . a voice came from *heaven*, 'You are my Son,
		22	
	4	25	*heaven* remained shut for three years and six months and a great famine raged
	6	23	your reward will be great in *heaven*.
	8	5	some [seed] fell on . . . the path and . . . the birds of the *air* ate it up.
	9	16	[Jesus] took the five loaves . . . raised his eyes to *heaven*, and said the blessing
		54	do you want us to call down fire from *heaven* . . . ?
		58	Foxes have holes and the birds of the *air* have nests,
	10	15	Capernaum, did you want to be exalted high as *heaven*?
		18	I watched Satan fall like lightning from *heaven*.
		20	your names are written in *heaven*.
	11	13	how much more will the *heavenly* Father give the Holy Spirit to those who ask him!
		16	Others asked him . . . for a sign from *heaven*;
	12	33	Get yourselves . . . treasure that will not fail you, in *heaven*
	13	19	the birds of the *air* sheltered in its branches.
	15	7	there will be more rejoicing in *heaven* over one repented sinner

Lk	15	18 ○	Father, I have sinned against *heaven* and against you;
		21 ○	Father, I have sinned against *heaven* and against you;
	17	24	as the lightning flashing from one part of *heaven* lights up the other part of *heaven*,
		29	the day Lot left Sodom, God rained fire and brimstone from *heaven*
	18	13	The tax collector stood . . . not daring even to raise his eyes to *heaven*;
		22	sell all that you own . . . and you will have treasure in *heaven*;
	19	38	Peace in *heaven* and glory in the highest [heavens]!
	20	4 ○	John's baptism: did it come from *heaven*, or from man? ⁵ . . . If we say from *heaven*, he will say,
		5	
	21	11	there will be fearful sights and great signs from *heaven*.
	22	43	an angel appeared to [Jesus], coming from *heaven* to give him strength.
	24	51	as [Jesus] blessed [the apostles], he . . . ᵛ was carried up to *heaven*ᵛ.
Jn	1	32	I saw the Spirit coming down on him from *heaven* like a dove
		51	you will see *heaven* laid open and . . . the angels of God ascending and descending.
	3	13	No one has gone up to *heaven* except the one who came down from *heaven*, the Son of Man ᵛ who is in *heaven*ᵛ;
		27	A man can lay claim only to what is given him from *heaven*.
	6	31	(Ps 78 24) He gave them bread from *heaven* to eat.
		32	it was not Moses who gave you bread from *heaven*, it is my Father who gives you the bread from *heaven*, the true bread; ³³ for the bread of God is that which comes down from *heaven*
		33	
		38	because I have come from *heaven* . . . to do the will of the one who sent me.
		41	he had said, I am the bread that came down from *heaven*.
		42	How can he now say, I have come down from *heaven*?
		50	this is the bread that comes down from *heaven*, so that a man may eat it and not die. ⁵¹ I am the living bread which has come down from *heaven*.
		51	
		58	This is the bread come down from *heaven*;
	12	28	A voice came from *heaven*, 'I have glorified [my name],
	17	1	Jesus raised his eyes to *heaven* and said: 'Father, the hour has come:
Ac	1	10	[The apostles] were still staring into the *sky*
		11	Why are you . . . looking into the *sky*? Jesus who has been taken up from you (§ into *heaven*) . . . will come back in the same way as you have seen him go ʳthere (lit. into *heaven*).
	2	2	[When Pentecost day came round the apostles] heard what sounded like a powerful wind from *heaven*,
		5	there were devout men living in Jerusalem from every nation under *heaven*,
		34	David himself never went up to *heaven*:
	3	21	[Jesus] whom *heaven* must keep till the universal restoration comes
	4	12	of all the names ʳin the world (lit. under *heaven*) given to men, this is the only one by which we can be saved.
	7	42	God . . . abandoned them to the worship of the army of *heaven*,
		55	Stephen, filled with the Holy Spirit, gazed into *heaven*
		56	I can see *heaven* thrown open
	9	3	there came a light from *heaven* all round [Saul].
	10	11	[Peter] saw *heaven* thrown open and something like a big sheet being let down
		16	suddenly the container was drawn up to *heaven* again.
	11	5	I . . . had a vision of something like a big sheet being let down from *heaven*
		9	the voice spoke from *heaven*, 'What God has made clean
		10	the whole of it was drawn up to *heaven* again.
	14	17	5 [God] sends you rain from *heaven*, he makes your crops grow
	22	6	I was . . . nearly at Damascus when about midday a bright light from *heaven* suddenly shone round me.
	26	13	5 I saw a light brighter than the sun come down from *heaven*.
		19	3 I could not disobey the *heavenly* vision.
Rm	1	18	The anger of God is being revealed from *heaven*
	10	6	(Dt 30 12) Who will go up to *heaven*?
2 Co	12	2 ○	a man . . . who . . . was caught up . . . right into the third *heaven*.
Ga	1	8	if anyone preaches a version of the Good News different from [ours], whether it be ourselves or an angel from *heaven*,
Ep	1	3	2 God the Father . . . who has blessed us with all the spiritual blessings of *heaven* in Christ.
		20	2 [God] used [his power] to raise [Christ] from the dead and 2 to make him sit at his right hand, in *heaven*,
	2	6	2 [God] gave us a place with him in *heaven*, in Christ Jesus
	3	10	2 so that the Sovereignties and Powers (§ of *heaven*) should learn . . . how comprehensive God's wisdom really is,
	4	10	The one who rose higher than all the *heavens*
	6	9	[Employers,] do without threats, remembering that [your slaves] and you have the same Master in *heaven*
		12	it is not against human enemies that we have to struggle, 2 but against . . . the spiritual army of evil in the *heavens*.

Col 1 5   the hope which is stored up for you in *heaven*.
     23   the Good News, which . . . has been preached to ʳthe whole human race (lit. every creature under *heaven*),
   4 1   Masters, . . . you too have a Master in *heaven*.

1 Th 1 10   you are now waiting for Jesus . . . to come from *heaven*
   4 16   the Lord himself will come down from *heaven*;

2 Th 1 7   when the Lord Jesus appears from *heaven* with the angels of his power.

Heb 3 1   2 all you who . . . have had the same *heavenly* call
   4 14   the supreme high priest who has gone through to the highest *heaven*,
   6 4   2 those people who . . . tasted the gift from *heaven*,
   7 26   the ideal high priest would have to be . . . raised up above the *heavens*;
   8 5   [earthly priests] only maintain the service of a . . . reflection 2 of the *heavenly* realities.
   9 23   only the copies of *heavenly* [things] can be purified [by 2 shedding the blood of animals], and the *heavenly* [things] themselves have to be purified by a higher sort of sacrifice
     24   it was *heaven* itself [that Christ entered] on our behalf.
  11 12   descendants . . . as many as the stars of *heaven*
  12 22   2 what you have come to is . . . the *heavenly* Jerusalem
     23   where the . . . angels have gathered . . . ²³ with the whole Church in which everyone is . . . a citizen of *heaven*.

1 P 1 4   an inheritance that . . . is being kept for you in the *heavens*.
     12   the Holy Spirit sent from *heaven*,
   3 22   Jesus Christ, who has entered *heaven* and is at God's right hand,

2 P 1 18   [This is my Son.] We heard this ourselves, spoken from *heaven*,

Rv 3 12   the new Jerusalem which comes down from my God in *heaven*,
   4 1   I saw a door open in *heaven*
     2   I saw a throne standing in *heaven*,
   8 1   there was silence in *heaven*
     10   a huge star fell from the *sky*, burning like a ball of fire,
     13   I heard an eagle, calling aloud as it flew ʳoverhead (lit. in 4 the middle of the *sky*),
  11 12   [the two witnesses] heard a loud voice from *heaven* say to them, 'Come up here,' and . . . they went up to *heaven* in a cloud.
     13   the survivors . . . could only praise the God of *heaven*.
     15   voices could be heard shouting in *heaven*.
     19   the sanctuary of God in *heaven* opened,
  12 1   a great sign appeared in *heaven*: a woman,
     3   a second sign appeared in the *sky*, a huge red dragon
  13 6   [the beast] mouthed its blasphemies against . . . [God's] *heavenly* Tent
  14 2   I heard a sound coming out of the *sky*
     6   I saw another angel flying high ʳoverhead (lit. in the middle 4 of the *sky*)
     13   I heard a voice from *heaven* say to me,
     17   Another angel . . . came out of the temple in *heaven*,
  15 1   What I saw next, in *heaven*, was a great and wonderful sign:
     5   the sanctuary, the Tent of the Testimony, opened in *heaven*,
  16 11   [those stricken with plague] cursed the God of *heaven*,
     21   great hailstones . . . fell from the *sky* on the people.
  18 4   A new voice spoke from *heaven*;
     5   [Babylon's] sins have reached up to *heaven*,
     20   Now *heaven*, celebrate [Babylon's] downfall,
  19 1   I seemed to hear the great sound of a huge crowd in *heaven*,
     11   I saw *heaven* open, and a white horse appear;
     14   Behind [The Word of God] . . . rode the armies of *heaven*
     17   4 all the birds that were flying high overhead in the *sky*,
  20 1   I saw an angel come down from *heaven*
     9   fire will come down on [Satan's people] from *heaven*
  21 2   I saw . . . the new Jerusalem, coming down from God out of *heaven*,
     10   Jerusalem, the holy city, coming down from God out of *heaven*.

2: HEAVEN, HEAVENLY, and EARTH, EARTHLY
6 gē 70/252   7 epi-geios 6/7

Mt 5 18   /6 till *heaven* and *earth* disappear, not one dot . . . shall disappear from the Law
     34   do not swear at all, either by *heaven*, since that is God's
     35   6 throne; ³⁵ or by the *earth*, since that is his footstool;
   6 10   6/ your will be done, on *earth* as in *heaven*.
     19   6 Do not store up treasures for yourselves on *earth*, . . .
     20   ²⁰ But store up treasures for yourselves in *heaven*,
  11 25   /6 I bless you, Father, Lord of *heaven* and of *earth*,
  16 19   I will give you the keys of the kingdom of *heaven*: whatever
     6/   you bind on *earth* shall be considered bound in *heaven*;
     6   whatever you loose on *earth* shall be considered loosed in *heaven*.
  18 18   6 whatever you bind on *earth* shall be considered bound in
     /6   *heaven*; whatever you loose on *earth* shall be considered loosed in *heaven*.

Mt 18 19   6 if two of you on *earth* agree to ask anything at all, it will be granted to you by my Father in *heaven*.
  23 9   6 You must call no one on *earth* your father, since you have 3 only one father, and he is in *heaven*.
  24 35   /6 *Heaven* and *earth* will pass away, but my words will never pass away.
  28 18   /6 All authority in *heaven* and on *earth* has been given to me.

Mk 13 27   he will send the angels to gather his chosen from . . . the 6/ ends of the *world* to the ends of *heaven*.
     31   /6 *Heaven* and *earth* will pass away, but my words will not pass away.

Lk 10 21   /6 I bless you, Father, Lord of *heaven* and of *earth*,
  12 56   6 Hypocrites! You know how to interpret the face of the *earth* and the *sky*.
  16 17   /6 It is easier for *heaven* and *earth* to disappear than for one little stroke to drop out of the Law.
  21 25   6 on *earth* [there will be] nations in agony . . . ²⁶ . . . for
     26   the powers of *heaven* will be shaken.
     33   /6 *Heaven* and *earth* will pass away, but my words will never pass away.

Jn 3 12   7 If you do not believe me when I speak about things *in this world*, how are you going to believe me when I speak to 2 you about *heavenly* things?
     31   6/6 he who is born of the *earth* is *earthly* himself and speaks in 6/ an *earthly* way. He who comes from *heaven* ³² bears witness to the things he has seen

Ac 2 19   (Jl 3 3) I will display portents in *heaven* above and signs on 6 *earth* below.
   4 24   /6 Master . . . it is you who made *heaven* and *earth* and sea, and everything in them;
   7 49   /6 (Is 66 1) With *heaven* my throne, and *earth* my footstool,
  10 12   6 every possible animal that walked or crawled on the *earth*, and every bird that flew in the *sky*.
  11 6   [Peter] saw all sorts of animals and wild beasts – everything 6 possible that could walk or crawl on the *earth*, every bird that could fly in the *sky*.
  14 15   /6 the living God who made *heaven* and *earth* and the sea and all that these hold.
  17 24   /6 [God] is himself Lord of *heaven* and *earth*, he does not make his home in shrines

1 Co 8 5   even if there were things called gods, either in the *sky* or 6 on *earth*
  15 40   2/7 there are *heavenly* bodies and there are *earthly* bodies;
     2   but the *heavenly* bodies have a beauty of their own and 2 the *earthly* bodies a different one.
     47   6 The first man, being from the *earth*, is earthly by nature;
     48   the second man is from *heaven*. ⁴⁸ As this earthly man 2 was, so are we on earth; and as the *heavenly* man is, so
     49   2 are we *in heaven*. ⁴⁹ And we, who have been modelled on 2 the earthly man, will be modelled on the *heavenly* man.

2 Co 5 1   7 we know that when the tent that we live in *on earth* is folded up, there is a house built by God for us . . . in the *heavens*.
     2   ² . . . we groan as we wait with longing to put on our *heavenly* home

Ep 1 10   bring everything together under Christ, as head, everything 6 in the *heavens* and everything on *earth*.
   3 15   [the Father,] from whom every family, whether ʳspiritual or 6 natural (lit. in *heaven* or *earth*), takes its name:

Ph 2 10   2/7 all beings *in the heavens*, on *earth* and in the underworld, should bend the knee at the name of Jesus
   3 19   7 the things they think important are *earthly* things. ²⁰ For
     20   us, our homeland is in *heaven*, and from [heaven] comes the saviour we are waiting for,

Col 1 16   /6 in him were created all things in *heaven* and on *earth*: [God wanted all things to be reconciled through Christ,] every-
     20   /6 thing in *heaven* and everything on *earth*,

Heb 1 10   6 It is just, Lord, who laid *earth's* foundations in the beginning, the *heavens* are the work of your hands;
   8 1   we have a high priest [who] . . . has his place . . . in the *heavens*, . . . ⁴ In fact, if he were on *earth*, he would not
     4   /6 be a priest at all,
  11 13   [our ancestors recognised] that they were only strangers and 6 nomads on *earth*. ¹⁶ . . . they were longing for
     16   2 . . . their *heavenly* homeland.
  12 25   6 The people who refuse to listen to . . . a voice on *earth* could not escape their punishment, and how shall we escape if we turn away from a voice . . . from *heaven*?
     26   6 That time he made the *earth* shake, but now he has given us this promise: I shall make [the earth] shake once 6/ more and not only the *earth* but *heaven* as well.

Jm 5 12   /6 my brothers, do not swear by *heaven* or by the *earth*,
     17   6 no rain fell (§ on the *earth*) for three-and-a-half years;
     18   ¹⁸ then [Elijah] prayed again and the *sky* gave rain and 6 the *earth* gave crops.

2 P 3 5   They are choosing to forget that there were *heavens* at the 6 beginning, and that the *earth* was formed by the word of God
     7   /6 by the same word, the present *sky* and *earth* are destined for fire,

2 P	3 10	/6 with a roar the *sky* will vanish, . . . the *earth* and all that it contains will be burnt up.
	12	the Day of God . . . when the *sky* will dissolve in flames,
	13 ●	. . . ¹³ What we are waiting for is what he promised: /6 the new *heavens* and new *earth*,
Rv	5 3	/6 there was no one, in *heaven* or on the *earth* or under the 6 *earth*, who was able to open the scroll
	13	/6 everything that lives in the *air*, and on the *ground* 6 and under the *ground*, and in the sea,
	6 13	/6 the stars of the *sky* fell on to the *earth*
	14	the *sky* disappeared like a scroll rolling up
	9 1	/6 I saw a star that had fallen from *heaven* on to the *earth*,
	10 1	I saw another powerful angel coming down from *heaven*,
	2	. . . ² . . . he put his right foot in the sea and his left
	4	6/ foot on the *land* . . . ⁴ . . . I heard a voice from *heaven*
	5	say to me, 'Keep the words . . . secret . . .' ⁵ Then the 6 angel that I had seen standing on the sea and the *land*, raised
	6	his right hand to *heaven*, ⁶ and swore by the One who /6 . . . made *heaven* and all that is in it, and *earth* and all it bears,
	8	I heard the voice I had heard from *heaven* speaking to me again, . . . 'Go . . . and take the open scroll out of the 6 hand of the angel that is standing on sea and *land*.
	11 6	[my two witnesses] are able to lock up the *sky* . . . and 6 strike the whole *world* with any plague
	12 4	[The dragon's] tail dragged a third of the stars from the /6 the *sky* and dropped them to the *earth*.
	7	war broke out in *heaven* . . . The dragon [and] . . . his
	8	angels . . . . ⁸ . . . were defeated and driven out of *heaven*.
	9 6	⁹ The great dragon . . . was hurled down to the *earth* and his angels were hurled down with him.
	10	Then I heard a voice shout from *heaven* . . . ¹² 'Let the
	12	*heavens* rejoice and all who live there; but for you, 6 *earth* and sea, trouble is coming –
	13	As soon as the devil found himself thrown down to the 6 *earth*, he sprang in pursuit of the woman,
	13 13	/6 calling down fire from *heaven* on to the *earth*
	14 7	/6 worship the maker of *heaven* and *earth* and sea and every water-spring.
	18 1	I saw another angel coming down from *heaven*, . . . the 6 *earth* was lit up with his glory.
	20 11	6/ *earth* and *sky* vanished, leaving no trace.
	21 1 ●	/6 Then I saw a new *heaven* and a new *earth*; /6 the first *heaven* and the first *earth* had disappeared now, and there was no longer any sea.

2. HEAVEN – SKY: *DIO*(-*PETĒS*)

dio(-*petēs*) 1

Ac	19 35	the city of the Ephesians is the guardian of the temple of great Diana and of her statue that fell from *heaven*

HEBREW

1: a Hebrew, Hebrews	2: the Hebrew language, in Hebrew

4 *Hebraikos* 1	3 *Hebrais* 3
2 *Hebraios* 4	1 *Hebraisti* 7

1: A HEBREW, HEBREWS

Ac	6 1	2 the Hellenists made a complaint against the *Hebrews*;
2 Co	11 22	2 *Hebrews*, are they? So am I. Israelites? So am I. Descendants of Abraham? So am I.
Ph	3 5	I was born of the race of Israel and of the tribe of Benjamin, 2/2 a *Hebrew* born of *Hebrew* parents,

2: THE HEBREW LANGUAGE, IN HEBREW

Lk	23 38	Above [Jesus] there was an inscription (ᵛ in Greek, Latin 4 and *Hebrew* writing)
Jn	5 2	at the Sheep Pool in Jerusalem there is a building, called Bethzatha in *Hebrew*,
	19 13	a place called the Pavement, in *Hebrew* Gabbatha.
	17	the place of the skull or, as it was called in *Hebrew*, Golgotha,
	20	the writing was in *Hebrew*, Latin and Greek.
	20 16	[Mary] said to [Jesus] in *Hebrew*, 'Rabbuni!' – which means Master.
Ac	21 40	3 [Paul] spoke to [the people of Jerusalem] in *Hebrew*.

Ac	22 2	3 When they realised [Paul] was speaking *in Hebrew*, the silence was even greater than before.
	26 14	3 I heard a voice saying to me *in Hebrew*, 'Saul, Saul'
Rv	9 11	the angel of the Abyss, whose name *in Hebrew* is Abaddon, or Apollyon in Greek.
	16 16	[The demon spirits] called the kings together at the place called, *in Hebrew*, Armageddon.

HELP – SUPPORT

1. Go to the aid of: *amynō*	**6.** Help – Stand by: *par-(h)istēmi*
2. Help: *boē-theō*	**7.** Help, Assist – Support: *ep-arkeō*
3. Help: *epi-kouria*	**8.** Support, Take the part of, Help: *para-ginomai*
4. Help: *sym-ballō*	**9.** Support, Care for: *ant-echomai*
5. Help, Come to the help of: *anti-lambanomai*	**10.** Support: *syn-epi-tithemai*

1. GO TO THE AID OF: *AMYNŌ*

amynō 1

Ac	7 24	When [Moses] saw one of [his countrymen] being ill-treated he ʳwent to his defence (or: *went to* his *aid*)

2: HELP: *BOĒ-THEŌ*

2 *boē-theia* 2	3 *boē-thos* 1
1 *boē-theō* 8	

Mt	15 25 X	'Lord,' [the Canaanite woman] said '*help* me.'
Mk	9 22 X	[the father of the epileptic demoniac said,] '. . . have pity on us and *help* us.
	24 X	I do have faith. *Help* the little faith I have!
Ac	16 9	Come across to Macedonia and *help* us.
	21 28	Men of Israel, *help*! This is the man who preaches . . . against our people,
	27 17	2 They hoisted [the ship's boat] aboard and with the *help* [of tackle] bound cables round the ship;
2 Co	6 2 Θ	[God] says (Is 49 8): . . . on the day of salvation I *came to* your *help*.
Heb	2 18 X	[Jesus] is able to *help* others who are tempted.
	4 16 Θ 2	Let us be confident . . . that we shall . . . find grace when we are in need of *help*.
	13 6 Θ 3	(Ps 118 6) With the Lord to *help* me, I fear nothing: the earth *came to* [the woman's] *rescue*;
Rv	12 16	

3. HELP: *EPI-KOURIA*

epi-kouria 1

Ac	26 22 Θ	I was blessed with God's *help*, and so I have stood firm to this day,

4. HELP: *SYM-BALLŌ*

sym-ballō 1/7

Ac	18 27	When [Apollos] arrived [in Achaia] he was able by God's grace to *help* the believers considerably

5. HELP, COME TO THE HELP OF: *ANTI-LAMBANOMAI*

1 *anti-lambanomai* 2/3	2 *syn-anti-lambanomai* 2
4 *anti-lēmpsis* 1	3 *syl-lambano* 2/16

Lk	1 54 Θ	[God] has *come to the help of* Israel his servant,
	5 7	they signalled to their companions in the other boat to come and *help* them;
	10 40	Martha . . . said, 'Lord, do you not care that my sister is leaving me to do the serving all by myself? Please tell her 2 to *help* me.'
Ac	20 35	we must exert ourselves to ʳsupport (or: *help*) the weak,
Rm	8 26 Ⓢ	2 The Spirit too *comes to help* us in our weakness,
1 Co	12 28	4 after [miracles] the gift of healing, *helpers*, good leaders,
Ph	4 3	3 I ask you, Syzygus . . . to *help* [Evodia and Syntyche] in this.

6. HELP – STAND BY: *PAR-(H)ISTĒMI*

1 *par-(h)istēmi* 2/41   2 *pro-statis* 1

Rm 16 2   /2 *help* [Phoebe] with anything she needs: she has ⸢*looked after*
2   (or: *helped*) a great many people, myself included.
2 Tm 4 17 X   the Lord *stood by* me and gave me power,

7. HELP, ASSIST – SUPPORT: *EP-ARKEŌ*

ep-arkeō 3

1 Tm 5 10   [a widow] must be a woman known . . . for the way in
which she has . . . *helped* people who are in trouble
16   If a Christian woman has widowed relatives, she should
support them and not make the Church bear the expense
but enable it to *support* those who are genuinely widows.

8. SUPPORT, TAKE THE PART OF, HELP: *PARA-GINOMAI*

para-ginomai 1/38

2 Tm 4 16   The first time I had to present my defence, there was not a
single witness to *support* me.

9. SUPPORT, CARE FOR: *ANT-ECHOMAI*

ant-echomai 1/4

1 Th 5 14   give courage to those who are apprehensive, *care for* the
weak

10. SUPPORT: *SYN-EPI-TITHEMAI*

syn-epi-tithemai 1

Ac 24 9   The Jews *supported* [Tertullus], asserting that these were the
facts.

HOLY

1. Holy, Sacred – Sanctify, Conse-crate – Saint: *hagios*
  1: (God is) Holy, Held holy,
    Hallowed – Holiness
  2: (Jesus is) Holy, Consecrated –
    Sanctify
  3: (the spirit of) Holiness – (the)
    Sanctifying (Spirit)
  4: Holy (angels)
  5: (A person is) Holy, Conse-
    crated, Sanctified – Holiness
  6: the Saints
    a) of the early Church
    b) of the resurrection
  7: Holy (place), Sanctuary – Holy
    of Holies

  8: (the) Holy (City)
  9: (A thing is) Holy, Sacred –
    Make holy, Sanctify
2. Holy – Reverent, Devout – Irre-ligious: *hosios*
  1: (God, Christ is) Holy
  2: (A person is) Holy, Reverent,
    Devout – Holiness
  3: Sacrilegious – Irreligious
3. Holy, Sacred – Religious, Rever-ent – Sacrilege: *hieros*
  1: Holy, Sacred – Religious,
    Reverent
  2: Sacrilege – Rob a temple

For Holy Spirit see SPIRIT – SOUL – PERSON 1.1:a)

1. HOLY, SACRED – SANCTIFY, CONSECRATE – SAINT: *HAGIOS*

  3 *hagiasmos* 10   4 *(ta) hagia* 10 ⎫   5 *hagiōsynē* 3
  2 *hagiazō* 28   7 *(to) hagion* 1 ⎬145/235   6 *hagiotēs* 2
             1   *hagios* 134 ⎭

For pneuma hagion see SPIRIT – SOUL – PERSON 1.1:a)

1: (GOD IS) HOLY, HELD HOLY, HALLOWED – HOLINESS

Mt 6 9   2 Our Father in heaven, may your name be *held holy*,
Lk 1 49   (Ps 111 9) *Holy* is his name,
11 2   2 Father, may your name be *held holy*,
Jn 17 11   *Holy* Father, keep those you have given me true to your
name,
2 Co 1 12   we have always treated everybody, and especially you, with
6   the *reverence* and sincerity which come from God,

Heb 12 10   [God punishes us] all for our own good, so that we may
6   share his own *holiness*.
1 P 1 15   be holy in all you do, since it is the *Holy* [One] who
16   called you, ¹⁶ and scripture says (Lv 11 44): Be holy, for
I am *holy*.
Rv 4 8   day and night [the four animals] never stopped singing: *Holy,*
holy, holy is the Lord God, the Almighty;
6 10   *Holy*, faithful Master, how much longer will you wait before
you pass sentence . . . ?

2: (JESUS IS) HOLY, CONSECRATED – SANCTIFY

Mk 1 24   Jesus . . . I know who you are: the *Holy* [One] of God.
Lk 1 35   [Gabriel to Mary:] The Holy Spirit will come upon you . . .
And so the child will be *holy* and will be called Son of God.
4 34   Jesus . . . I know who you are: the *Holy* [One] of God.
Jn 6 69   we know that you are the *Holy* [One] of God.
10 36   2 you say to someone the Father has *consecrated* and sent
into the world, 'You are blaspheming',
17 19   2 for their sake I *consecrate* myself so that they too may be
consecrated in truth.
Ac 3 14   It was you who ⱽaccused (G disowned) the *Holy* [One].
4 27   an alliance . . . against your *holy* servant Jesus whom you
anointed,
30   by stretching out your hand to heal and to work miracles . . .
through the name of your *holy* servant Jesus.
1 Co 1 30   Christ Jesus . . . has become our wisdom, and our virtue,
3   and our *holiness*,
Heb 2 11   2 the one who *sanctifies*, and the ones who are sanctified, are
of the same stock;
1 P 3 15   2 Simply *reverence* the Lord Christ in your hearts,
1 Jn 2 20   you have been anointed by the *Holy* [One],
Rv 3 7   Here is the message of the *holy* and faithful one who has the
key of David,

3: (THE SPIRIT OF) HOLINESS – (THE) SANCTIFYING (SPIRIT)

Rm 1 4   Jesus Christ our Lord who, in the order of the spirit, the
5   spirit of *holiness* that was in him, was proclaimed Son of
God
2 Co 6 6   We prove we are God's servants by . . . a spirit *of holiness*,
2 Th 2 13   3 God chose you . . . to be saved by the *sanctifying* Spirit

4: HOLY (ANGELS)

Mk 8 38   when [the Son of Man] comes in the glory of his Father with
the *holy* angels.
Lk 9 26   when [the Son of Man] comes in his own glory and in the
glory of the Father and the *holy* angels.
Ac 10 22   The centurion Cornelius . . . was directed by a *holy* angel
to send for you
Jude 14   the Lord will come with his ⸢*saints* (or: *holy* [ones]) in their
tens of thousands,
Rv 14 10   [those who worship the beast] will be tortured in the presence
of the *holy* angels and the Lamb

5: (A PERSON IS) HOLY, CONSECRATED, SANCTIFIED – HOLINESS

Mt 27 52   the tombs opened and the bodies of many *holy men* rose from
the dead,
Mk 6 20   Herod was afraid of John, knowing him to be a good and
holy man,
Lk 1 70   even as he proclaimed, by the mouth of his *holy* prophets
2 23   (Ex 13 2) Every first-born male must be *consecrated* to the
Lord
Jn 17 17   2 *Consecrate* them in the truth;
19   for their sake I consecrate myself so that they too may be
2   *consecrated* in truth.
Ac 3 21   the universal restoration . . . which God proclaimed, speaking
through his *holy* prophets.
20 32   the word of [God's] grace that has power to . . . give you
2   your inheritance among all the *sanctified*.
26 18   so that [the pagans] may . . . receive . . . a share in the
2   inheritance of the *sanctified*.
Rm 6 19   now you must put [your bodies] at the service of . . .
3   *sanctification*.
22   3 you get a reward leading to your *sanctification*.
11 16   A whole batch of bread is [made holy] if the first handful of
dough is [made] *holy*; all the branches are [holy] if the root
is *holy*.
1 Co 1 2   2 [I, Paul], to the *holy* people of Jesus Christ,
6 11   2 now you have been washed clean, and *sanctified*,
7 14   2 the unbelieving husband is *made one with the saints* through
2   his wife, and the unbelieving wife is *made one with the*
saints through her husband. If this were not so, your
children would be unclean, whereas in fact they are *holy*.

1 Co 7 34 all [an unmarried woman] need worry about is being *holy* in body and spirit.

2 Co 7 1 let us wash off all that can soil either body or spirit, to reach
5 perfection of *holiness*

Ep 1 4 he chose us . . . in Christ, to be *holy* and spotless,
3 5 This mystery [of Christ] that has now been revealed through the Spirit to his *holy* apostles and prophets
5 26 [Christ loved the Church and sacrificed himself for her]
2 to *make her holy.* He made her clean . . . ²⁷ so that . . .
27 she would be . . . *holy* and faultless.

Col 1 22 now he has reconciled you, by his death . . . Now you are able to appear before him *holy,* pure and blameless

1 Th 3 13 5 may he so confirm your hearts in *holiness* that you may be blameless in the sight of God our Father
4 3 3 What God wants is for you all to *be holy.* He wants . . .
4 ⁴ . . . each one of you to know how to use the body . . .
7 3 . . . in a way that is *holy* and honourable, . . . ⁷ We have
3 been called by God to *be holy,* not to be immoral.
5 23 2 May the God of peace *make* you perfect and *holy;*

1 Tm 2 15 [A] woman will be saved by childbearing, provided she
3 . . . is constant in faith and love and *holiness.*

2 Tm 1 9 [God] has saved us and called us ʳto be *holy* (or: with a holy call)
2 21 to avoid these faults . . . is the way for anyone to become
2 a vessel for special occasions, *consecrated* and fit for the Master himself to use,

Heb 2 11 2 the one who sanctifies, and the [ones who are] *sanctified,* are of the same stock;
3 1 all you who are *holy* brothers . . . should turn your minds to Jesus,
9 13 The blood of goats and bulls and the ashes of a heifer . . .
2 restore the *holiness* of their outward lives;
10 10 2 [God's] will was for us to be *made holy* by the offering of his body made once and for all by Jesus Christ.
14 By virtue of that one single offering, he has achieved the
2 eternal perfection of all whom he is *sanctifying.*
29 anyone who . . . treats the blood of the covenant which
2 *sanctified* him as if it were not holy . . . will be condemned
12 14 3 Always be wanting . . . the *holiness* without which no one can ever see the Lord.
13 12 2 Jesus too suffered outside the gate to *sanctify* the people with his own blood.

1 P 1 2 [to all those living among foreigners in the Dispersion . . ,
who have been chosen] by . . . God the Father, to be
3 *made holy* by the Spirit,
15 be *holy* in all you do, since it is the Holy One who has called
16 you, ¹⁶ and scripture says (Lv 11 44): Be *holy,* for I am holy.
2 9 you are . . . a royal priesthood, a *consecrated* nation,
3 5 That was how the *holy* women of the past dressed themselves attractively — they hoped in God

2 P 3 2 recalling to you what was said in the past by the *holy* prophets
11 you should be living *holy* and saintly lives

Rv 20 6 Happy and *blessed* are those who share in the first resurrection;
22 11 /2 let those who . . . are *holy* continue to *be holy.*

6: THE SAINTS

a) of the early Church

Ac 9 13 all the harm [Saul] has been doing to your *saints* in Jerusalem
32 Peter . . . eventually came to the *saints* living down in Lydda.
41 Peter helped [Tabitha] to her feet, then he called in the *saints* and widows,
26 10 I myself threw many of the *saints* into prison,

Rm 1 7 To you all . . . who are God's beloved in Rome, called to be *saints,*
8 27 the pleas of the *saints* expressed by the Spirit are according to the mind of God.
12 13 If any of the *saints* are in need you must share with them;
15 25 I must take a present of money to the *saints* in Jerusalem,
26 Macedonia and Achaia have decided to send a generous contribution to the poor among the *saints* at Jerusalem.
31 Pray that . . . the aid I carry to Jerusalem may be accepted by the *saints.*
16 2 Give [Phoebe] . . . a welcome worthy of *saints,*
15 [Greetings] to Philologus and . . . Olympas and all the *saints* who are with them.

1 Co 1 2 to the holy people of Jesus Christ, who are called to take their place among all the *saints* everywhere
6 1 How dare one of your members take up a complaint against another in the lawcourts of the unjust instead of before the *saints?*
2 it is the *saints* who are to 'judge the world';
14 33 As in all the churches of the *saints,* ³⁴ women are to remain quiet at meetings
16 1 Now about the collection made for the *saints:*
15 the Stephanas family . . . have really worked hard to help the *saints.*

2 Co 1 1 to all the *saints* in the whole of Achaia.
8 4 the favour of sharing in this service to the *saints*

2 Co 9 1 on the subject of offering your services to the *saints,*
12 doing this holy service is not only supplying all the needs of the *saints,*
13 12 All the *saints* send you greetings.

Ep 1 1 to the *saints* who are faithful to Christ Jesus,
15 the love that you show towards all the *saints,*
3 8 I, who am less than the least of all the *saints,*
18 you will with all the *saints* have strength to grasp the breadth and the length . . . [of the love of Christ]
4 12 so that the *saints* together make a unity in the work of service,
5 3 even a mention of fornication . . . would hardly become the *saints!*
6 18 Never get tired of staying awake to pray for all the *saints;*

Ph 1 1 to all the *saints* in Christ Jesus,
4 21 My greetings to every one of the *saints* in Christ Jesus.
22 All the *saints* send their greetings,

Col 1 2 to the *saints* in Colossae,
4 the love that you show towards all the *saints*
26 the message which was a mystery hidden for generations . . . and has now been revealed to the *saints.*
3 12 You are God's chosen race, his *saints;*

1 Tm 5 10 [The widow] must be a woman known for . . . the way in which she has . . . washed the *saints'* feet,

Phm 5 the love and the faith which you have for the Lord Jesus and for all the *saints.*
7 they tell me . . . how you have put new heart into the *saints.*

Heb 6 10 the services you have done, and are still doing, for the *saints.*
13 24 Greetings to all your leaders and to all the *saints.*

Jude 3 the faith which has been once and for all entrusted to the *saints.*

Rv 5 8 each one of [the twenty-four elders] . . . had a golden bowl full of incense made of the prayers of the *saints.*
8 3 incense was given to [the angel] to offer with the prayers of all the *saints* . . . ⁴ . . . the smoke of the incense went
4 up in the presence of God and with it the prayers of the *saints.*
11 18 the time has come . . . for the *saints* . . . to be rewarded.
13 7 [The beast] was allowed to make war against the *saints*
10 the *saints* must have constancy and faith.
14 12 there must be constancy in the *saints* who keep . . . faith in Jesus.
16 6 they spilt the blood of the *saints* and the prophets,
17 6 [the woman] was drunk, drunk with the blood of the *saints,* and the blood of the martyrs of Jesus;
18 20 Now heaven, celebrate [Babylon's] downfall, and all you *saints,* apostles and prophets!
24 In [Babylon] you will find the blood of prophets and *saints.*
19 8 her linen is made of the good deeds of the *saints.*
20 9 they will . . . besiege the camp of the *saints,*
22 21 May the grace of the Lord Jesus be with ʳyou all (ᵛ all the *saints*).

b) of the resurrection

Ep 1 18 what rich glories [God] has promised the *saints* will inherit
2 19 you are citizens like all the *saints,*

Col 1 12 thanking the Father who has made it possible for you to join the *saints*

1 Th 3 13 when our Lord Jesus Christ comes with all his *saints.*

2 Th 1 10 when he comes to be glorified among his *saints*

7: HOLY (PLACE), SANCTUARY – HOLY OF HOLIES

Mt 24 15 (Dn 9 27) the disastrous abomination, . . . set up in the *Holy* Place

Ac 6 13 This man is always making speeches against this *Holy* Place
21 28 he has profaned this *Holy* Place by bringing Greeks into the Temple.

1 Co 3 17 the temple of God is *sacred;*

Ep 2 21 all grow into one *holy* temple in the Lord;

Heb 8 2 4 he is the minister of the *sanctuary*
9 1 The first covenant also had its laws governing worship,
7 and its *sanctuary,* [a sanctuary] on this earth.
2 4 the first [compartment of the tent] was called the *Holy* [Place];
3 beyond the second veil, an innermost part which was called
4/4 the *Holy* of *Holies*
8 4 no one has the right to go into the *sanctuary* so long as the outer tent remains standing;
12 4 [Christ] has entered the *sanctuary* once and for all, taking with him . . . his own blood,
24 4 It is not as though Christ had entered a man-made *sanctuary* . . . ; but it was heaven itself
25 4 the high priest [goes] into the *sanctuary* year after year with the blood that is not his
10 19 through the blood of Jesus we have the right to enter the
4 *sanctuary,*
13 11 The bodies of the animals whose blood is brought into the
4 *sanctuary* for the atonement of sin

8: (THE) HOLY (CITY)

Mt	4 5	The devil then took [Jesus] to the *holy* city and made him stand on the parapet of the Temple.
	27 53	[the bodies of many holy men] came out of the tombs, entered the *Holy* City and appeared to a number of people.
Rv	11 2	[the pagans] will trample on the *holy* city for forty-two months.
	21 2	I saw the *holy* city, and the new Jerusalem, coming down . . . out of heaven,
	10	[the angel] showed me Jerusalem, the *holy* city, coming down . . . out of heaven.
	22 19	God will cut off his share of . . . the *holy* city,

9: (A THING IS) HOLY, SACRED – MAKE HOLY, SANCTIFY

Mt	7 6	Do not give dogs what is *holy*;
	23 17	which is of greater worth, the gold or the Temple that
	19	2 *makes* the gold *sacred*? . . . ¹⁹ . . . the offering or the 2 altar that *makes* the offering *sacred*?
Lk	1 72	[God] remembers his *holy* covenant.
Ac	7 33	(Ex 3 5) Take off your shoes; the place where you are standing is *holy* ground.
Rm	1 2	[the Good News that God] promised long ago . . . in the *holy* scriptures
	7 12	The Law is *sacred*, and what it commands is *sacred*,
	12 1	by offering your living bodies as a *holy* sacrifice, truly pleasing to God.
	15 16	2 and so make [the pagans] acceptable as an offering, *made holy* by the Holy Spirit.
	16 16	Greet each other with a *holy* kiss.
1 Co	16 20	Greet one another with a *holy* kiss.
2 Co	13 12	Greet one another with the *holy* kiss.
1 Th	5 26	Greet all the brothers with the *holy* kiss.
1 Tm	4 5	2 the word of God and the prayer *make* [any food] *holy*.
2 Tm	1 9	[God] who has saved us and called us ⌜to be holy (or: with a *holy* call)
1 P	2 5	you too, the *holy* priesthood that offers the spiritual sacrifices which Jesus Christ has made acceptable to God,
2 P	1 18	when we were with him on the *holy* mountain.
	2 21	better . . . than to know [the way of holiness] and afterwards desert the *holy* rule
Jude	20	you . . . must use your most *holy* faith as your foundation

2. HOLY – REVERENT, DEVOUT – IRRELIGIOUS: *HOSIOS*

1 *hosios* 8		2 *hosiotēs* 2	
4 *hosiōs* 1		3 *an-hosios* 2	

1: (GOD, CHRIST IS) HOLY

Ac	2 27	[David says of Jesus] (Ps 16 10): you will not . . . allow your *holy* [one] to experience corruption.
	13 34	that God raised [Jesus] from the dead, never to [see] corruption, is no more than what he had declared (Is 55 3): To you I shall give the sure and *holy* things promised to David.
	35	³⁵ This is explained by another text (Ps 16 10): You will not allow your *holy* [one] to experience corruption.
Heb	7 26	To suit us, the ideal high priest would have to be *holy*, innocent and uncontaminated, beyond the influence of sinners.
Rv	15 4 Θ	O Lord . . . You alone are *holy*,
	16 5 Θ	You are the *holy* He-Is-and-He-Was,

2: (A PERSON IS) REVERENT, DEVOUT – HOLINESS

Lk	1 75	2 to serve him in *holiness* and virtue
Ep	4 24	the new self that has been created in God's way, in the 2 goodness and *holiness* of the truth.
1 Th	2 10	our treatment of you . . . has been impeccably ⌜right (lit. 4 *holy*) and fair.
1 Tm	2 8	I want the men to lift their hands up *reverently* in prayer,
Tt	1 8	[an elder must be] sensible, moral, *devout* and self-controlled;

3: SACRILEGIOUS – IRRELIGIOUS

1 Tm	1 9	3 laws are . . . framed for . . . the *sacrilegious* and the irreverent;
2 Tm	3 2	3 People [in the last days] will be . . . ungrateful, *irreligious*;

3. HOLY, SACRED – RELIGIOUS, REVERENT – SACRILEGE: *HIEROS*

1 *hieros*	1/2	3 *hiero-syleō* 1	
2 *hiero(-prepēs)*	1	4 *hiero-sylos* 1	

1: HOLY, SACRED – RELIGIOUS, REVERENT

2 Tm	3 15	ever since you were a child, you have known the *holy* scriptures
Tt	2 3	2 the older women should behave as though they were *religious*,

2: SACRILEGE – ROB A TEMPLE

Ac	19 37	4 These men you have brought here are not *guilty of* any *sacrilege* or blasphemy
Rm	2 22	3 you despise idols, yet you *rob* their *temples*.

HONOUR – RESPECT

1. Honour, Respect – Ambition: *timē* 1: Honour, Consideration, Respect – Duty, Hold in high regard, Distinguished – Favourite, Dear	2: Make (it) a point of (honour to), a Rule to, an Ambition to – (Be) Intent on **2. Respect:** *en-trepō* **3. Standing:** *bathmos*

Θ = Honour God; X = Honour Jesus Christ

P = Honour one's Parents

1. HONOUR, RESPECT – AMBITION: *TIMĒ*

2 *timaō*	19/21	3 *en-timos*	3/5
1 *timē*	27/41	4 *philo-timeomai*	3
5 *timios*	2/13		

1: HONOUR, CONSIDERATION, RESPECT – DUTY, HOLD IN HIGH REGARD, DISTINGUISHED – FAVOURITE, DEAR

Mt	15 4 P	2 (Ex 20 12) God said: *Do your duty to* your father and mother . . . ⁵ But you say, 'If anyone says to his father or mother: Anything . . . that I might have used to help
	6 P	2 you is dedicated to God', ⁶ he is rid of his *duty* to father or mother.
	8 Θ	2 (Is 29 13) This people *honours* me only with lip-service, while their hearts are far from me.
	19 19 P	2 (Ex 20 12) *Honour* your father and mother,
Mk	7 6 Θ	2 (Is 29 13) This people *honours* me only with lip-service, while their hearts are far from me.
	10 P	2 (Ex 20 12) Moses said: *Do your duty to* your father and your mother,
	10 19 P	2 (Ex 20 12) You know the commandments: . . . *Honour* your father and mother.
Lk	7 2	3 A centurion . . . had a servant, a *favourite* of his,
	14 8	3 A more *distinguished* person than you may have been invited,
	18 20 P	2 (Ex 20 12) You know the commandments: . . . *Honour* your father and mother.
Jn	4 44	[Jesus] himself had declared that there is no *respect* for a prophet in his own country,
	5 23 X Θ 2/2 X Θ 2/2	[the Father has entrusted all judgement to the Son,] so that all may *honour* the Son as they *honour* the Father. Whoever refuses *honour* to the Son refuses *honour* to the Father who sent him.
	8 49 Θ	2 I am not possessed; no, I *honour* my Father,
	12 26	2 If anyone serves me, my Father will *honour* him.
Ac	5 34	5 Gamaliel . . . was a doctor of the Law and *respected* by the whole people,
	28 10	2/ [the inhabitants of Malta] *honoured* us with many *marks of respect*,
Rm	2 7	For those who sought renown and *honour* . . . by always doing good there will be eternal life;
	10	renown, *honour* and peace will come to everyone who does good
	12 10	have a profound *respect* for each other.
	13 7	Pay every government official what he has a right to ask – [if it be] *honour* [give] *honour*
1 Co	12 23	[the least honourable parts of the body] we clothe with the greatest ⌜care (lit. *honour*) . . . ²⁴ . . . God has arranged the body so that more *dignity* is given to the parts which are without it,

Ep	6 2 P	2 (Ex 20 12) The first commandment . . . is: *Honour* your father and mother,
Ph	2 29	3 people like [Epaphroditus] are to be *honoured*.
1 Th	4 4	use the body that belongs to [God] in a way that is holy and *honourable*,
1 Tm	1 17 Θ	To the eternal King, the undying . . . God, be *honour* and glory
	5 3	2 *Be considerate* to widows; I mean those who are truly widows.
	17	The elders who do their work well . . . are to be given double ⌈*consideration* (or: remuneration), especially those who are assiduous in preaching and teaching.
	6 1	All slaves 'under the yoke' must have unqualified *respect* for their masters,
Heb	16 Θ	to him be *honour* and everlasting power.
	2 7	(Ps 8 6) you crowned him with glory and ⌈*splendour* (lit. *honour*).
	X	
	9	we do see in Jesus one who was for a short while made lower than the angels and is now crowned with glory
	X	and ⌈*splendour* (lit. *honour*)
	3 3	It is the difference between the *honour* given to the man that built the house and to the house itself.
	5 4	No [high priest] takes this *honour* on himself,
	13 4	5 Marriage is to be *honoured* by all, and marriages are to be kept undefiled,
1 P	1 7	you will have praise and glory and *honour*.
	2 17	2 *Have respect for* everyone and love for our community; fear
	2	God and *honour* the emperor.
	3 7	[husbands must treat their wives with consideration,] *respecting* a woman as one who . . . is equally an heir to the life of grace.
2 P	1 17 X	[Jesus] was *honoured* and glorified by God the Father,
Rv	4 9 Θ	the animals glorified and *honoured* and gave thanks to the
	11	One sitting on the throne . . . [11] . . . our God, you are
	Θ	worthy of glory and *honour* and power,
	5 12	The Lamb that was sacrificed is worthy to be given power
	X	. . . *honour*, glory and blessing.
	13	To the One who is sitting on the throne and to the Lamb, be
	Θ X	all praise, *honour*, glory and power,
	7 12 Θ	Amen. Praise and . . . *honour* and power and strength to our God
	21 26	the nations will come [to Jerusalem], bringing their treasure and their ⌈*wealth* (or: *honour*).

2: MAKE (IT) A POINT OF (HONOUR TO), A RULE TO, AN AMBITION TO – (BE) INTENT ON

Rm	15 20	4 I have always . . . *made it an unbroken rule* never to preach where Christ's name has already been heard.
2 Co	5 9	4 we *are intent on* pleasing [the Lord].
1 Th	4 11	4 [we urge you, brothers,] to *make a point of* living quietly . . . and earning your living,

2. RESPECT: *EN-TREPŌ*

en-trepō 6/9

Mt	21 37 <	They will *respect* my son
Mk	12 6 <	They will *respect* my son
Lk	18 2 <	There was a judge . . . who had neither fear of God nor
	4 <	*respect* for man . . . [4] . . . Maybe I have neither fear of God nor *respect* for man,
	20 13 <	I will send them my dear son. Perhaps they will *respect* him.
Heb	12 9	we have all had our human fathers who punished us, and we *respected* them for it;

3. STANDING: *BATHMOS*

bathmos 1

1 Tm	3 13	Those . . . who carry out their duties well as deacons will earn a high *standing* for themselves

HOPE – EXPECT – WAIT FOR

1. Hope – Trust – Expect: *elpizō*
  a) (Religious) Hope, Trust – Put one's hope in, Set one's hopes on – Look forward to
  b) Hope – Trust – Expect (generally)
2. Wait for – Expect
	1: Wait for – Expect: *ek-dechomai*
	  a) (Religious) Expectation – Wait for, Look forward to – Live in the hope of
	  b) Wait for – Expect – Suspense (generally)
	2: Wait for, Await: *menō*

1. HOPE – TRUST – EXPECT: *ELPIZŌ*

1 *elpis 53*	3 *ap-elpizō 1*
2 *elpizō 31*	4 *pro-elpizō 1*

a) (Religious) Hope, Trust – Put one's hope in, Set one's hopes on – Look forward to

L = Hope//Love   F = Hope//Faith

Mt	12 21	2 (Is 42 4 G) in [my servant's] name the nations will *put their hope*.
Lk	24 21	2 Our own *hope* had been that he would be the one to set Israel free.
Jn	5 45 F	2 you *place* your *hopes* on Moses, and Moses will be your accuser.
Ac	2 26	(Ps 16 9) my body, too, will rest in the *hope* that you will not abandon my soul to Hades
	23 6	It is for our *hope* in the resurrection of the dead that I am on trial.
	24 15 F	I hold the same *hope* in God as they do that there will be a resurrection
	26 6	it is for my *hope* in the promise . . . that I am on trial,
	7	2 [7] the promise that our twelve tribes . . . *hope* to attain. For that *hope* . . . I am actually put on trial by the Jews!
	28 20	it is on account of the *hope* of Israel that I wear this chain.
Rm	4 18	Though it seemed Abraham's *hope* could not be fulfilled,
	F	⌈he hoped and he believed (lit. he believed with *hope*),
	5 2 F	we can boast about *looking forward* to God's glory.
	4	patience brings perseverance, and perseverance brings *hope*,
	5 L	[5] and this *hope* is not deceptive,
	8 20	creation still retains the *hope* [21] of being freed . . . from its slavery to decadence,
	24	In *hope* we have salvation; in *hope*, not for what we can see,
	/2	or we should not be *hoping* – nobody *hopes* for something
	25 2	which he can already see. [25] But *having this hope for* what we cannot yet see, we are able to go on waiting for it with steady confidence.
	12 12 L	If you have *hope*, this will make you cheerful. Do not give up if trials come;
	15 4	everything . . . written . . . in the scriptures was meant to teach us something about *hope*
	12	2 (Is 42 4 G) in him the pagans will *put their hope*.
	13	May the God of *hope* bring you such joy and peace in your faith that the power of the Holy Spirit will remove all
	F	bounds to *hope*.
1 Co	13 13 F L	there are three things that last: faith, *hope* and love;
	15 19 F	2 If our *hope* in Christ has been for this life only, we are the most unfortunate of all people.
2 Co	1 10	2 it is our firm *hope* in [God], that . . . he will save us again.
	3 12	Having this *hope*, we can be quite confident;
Ga	5 5	Christians are told by the Spirit to look to faith for ⌈those
	F L	rewards that righteousness *hopes* for (lit. the *hope* of righteousness),
Ep	1 12	4 chosen to be . . . the people who would *put their hopes* in Christ before he came.
	18	so that you can see what *hope* [God's] call holds for you,
	2 12	[pagans,] you were immersed in this world, without *hope* and without God.
	4 4 F	you were all called into one and the same *hope* when you were called.
Ph	1 20	My one hope and *trust* is that I shall never have to admit defeat,
Col	1 5 F L	because of the *hope* which is stored up for you in heaven.
	23	stand firm on the solid base of the faith, never letting your-
	F	selves drift away from the *hope* promised by the Good News,
	27	The mystery is Christ among you, your *hope* of glory:
1 Th	1 3	[We] constantly remember . . . how you have shown your faith in action, worked for love and persevered through
	F L	*hope*,
	2 19	What do you think is our ⌈pride (lit. *hope*) and our joy? You are;
	4 13	make sure that you do not grieve about [those who have died], like the other people who have no *hope*.
	5 8 F L	let us put on . . . the *hope* of salvation for a helmet.
2 Th	2 16	God our Father who has given us . . . such inexhaustible comfort and such sure *hope*,
1 Tm	1 1	Christ Jesus our *hope*,
	4 10 F	2 we have *put our trust* in the living God
	5 5	a woman who is really widowed . . . can ⌈give herself up to
	2	(lit. *set her hopes on*) God
	6 17	2 Warn those who are rich . . . not to *set their hopes* on money,
Tt	1 2 F	to give [the chosen] the *hope* of the eternal life that was promised
	2 13	while we are waiting in *hope* for the blessing which will come with the Appearing of the glory of our great God and saviour Christ Jesus.
	3 7	He did this so that we should be justified by his grace, to become heirs *looking forward* to inheriting eternal life.
Heb	3 6	as long as we cling (§ fast to the very end) to our *hope* with the confidence that we glory in.

Heb	6	11		Our one desire is that . . . you should go on showing the same earnestness to the end, to the perfect fulfilment of our *hopes*,
		18	F	encouragement to take a firm grip on the *hope* that is held out to us. [19] Here we have an anchor for our soul, as sure as it is firm,
	7	19		now this commandment is replaced by something better – the *hope* that brings us nearer to God.
	10	23	F L	Let us keep firm in the *hope* we profess, because the one who made the promise is faithful.
	11	1	F	2 Only faith can guarantee the blessings that we *hope* for,
1 P	1	3		God the Father . . . has given us a new birth as his sons, by raising Jesus Christ from the dead, so that we have a sure *hope*
			F	
		13		2 *put* your *trust* in nothing but the grace that will be given you when Jesus Christ is revealed.
		21	F	so that you would have faith and *hope* in God.
	3	5		That was how the holy women of the past dressed themselves
			2	attractively – they *hoped* in God
		15		people who ask you for the reason for the *hope* that you all have.
1 Jn	3	3		Surely everyone who entertains this *hope* must purify himself,

b) Hope – Trust – Expect (generally)

Lk	6	34		2 if you lend to those from whom you *hope* to receive,
		35		3 lend without any *hope* of return.
	23	8		2 Herod . . . was *hoping* to see some miracle worked by [Jesus].
Ac	16	19		When her masters saw that there was no *hope* of making any more money out of her,
	24	26		2 at the same time [Felix] had *hopes* of receiving money from Paul,
	27	20		we gave up all *hope* of surviving,
Rm	15	24		2 I *hope* to see you on my way to Spain,
1 Co	9	10		the ploughman ought to plough in *expectation*, and the thresher to thresh in the *expectation* of getting his share.
	13	7	●	2 [love] is always ready to excuse, to trust, to *hope*, and to endure whatever comes.
	16	7		2 I *hope* to spend some time with you,
2 Co	1	7		our *hope* for you is confident,
		14		2 I *hope* that . . . you can be as proud of us as we are of you.
	5	11		2 I *hope* that in your consciences you know us too.
	8	5		and, what was quite un*expected* [the Christians in Macedonia] offered their own selves . . . to God
	10	15		we *trust* that, as your faith grows, we shall get taller and taller.
	13	6		2 but we, as I *hope* you will come to see, have not failed [the test].
Ph	2	19		2 I *hope*, in the Lord Jesus, to send Timothy to you soon.
		23		2 That is why [Timothy] is the one I am *hoping* to send you,
1 Tm	3	14		2 I am *hoping* that I may be with you soon;
Phm		22		2 I am *hoping* through your prayers to be restored to you.
2 Jn		12		2 I *hope* . . . to visit you and talk to you personally,
3 Jn		14		2 I *hope* to see you soon

2. WAIT FOR – EXPECT

1: WAIT FOR – EXPECT: *EK-DECHOMAI*

4	*ek-dechomai* 7	2 *pros-dechomai* 8/14
7	*ek-doche* 1	1 *pros-dokao* 16
3	*ap-ek-dekomai* 8	6 *pros-dokia* 2
5	*apo-kara-dokia* 2	

a) (Religious) Expectation – Wait for, Look forward to – Live in the hope of

Mt	11	3		[John sent to ask Jesus,] Are you the one who is to come, or have we got to *wait* for someone else?
Mk	15	43		2 Joseph of Arimathaea . . . who himself *lived in the hope of* seeing the kingdom of God,
Lk	2	25		2 Simeon . . . *looked forward to* Israel's comforting
		38		2 Anna . . . spoke of the child [Jesus] to all who *looked forward to* the deliverance of Jerusalem.
	3	15		A feeling of *expectancy* had grown among the people, who were beginning to think that John might be the Christ,
	7	19		[John] sent [two of his disciples] to the Lord to ask, Are you the one who is to come, or must we *wait for* someone else?
		20		[20] . . . John the Baptist has sent us to you, to ask, Are you the one . . . or have we to *wait for* someone else?
	23	51		2 [Joseph of Arimathaea] *lived in the hope of* seeing the kingdom of God.
Rm	8	19		5/3 The whole creation is *eagerly waiting for* God to reveal his sons.
		23		3 we too groan inwardly as we *wait for* our bodies to be set free.
		25		3 we are able to go on *waiting for* [what we cannot yet see] with steady confidence.
1 Co	1	7		3 while you are *waiting for* our Lord Jesus Christ to be revealed;
Ga	5	5		3 Christians are told by the Spirit to *look to* faith for those rewards that righteousness hopes for,

Ph	1	20		5 My one *hope* and trust is that I shall never have to admit defeat.
	3	20		3 from heaven comes the saviour we are *waiting for*, the Lord Jesus Christ,
Tt	2	13		2 while we are *waiting* in hope *for* the blessing which will come with the Appearing of the glory of . . . Christ Jesus.
Heb	9	28		3 when Christ appears a second time it will . . . be to . . . reward with salvation those who are *waiting for* him.
	10	13		4 where [Christ] is now *waiting* until his enemies are made into a footstool for him.
		27		7 There will be left only the dreadful *prospect* of judgement
	11	10		4 [Abraham] *looked forward to* a city founded, designed and built by God.
1 P	3	20	○	3 God was still *waiting* patiently,
2 P	3	12		while you *wait* and long *for* the Day of God to come,
		13		What we are *waiting for* is what he promised: the new heavens and new earth,
		14		while you are *waiting*, do your best to live lives without spot or stain
Jude		21		2 keep yourselves within the love of God and *wait for* the mercy of our Lord Jesus Christ.

b) Wait for – Expect – Suspense (generally)

Mt	24	50	<	his master will come on a day he does not *expect*
Lk	1	21		Meanwhile the people were *waiting for* Zechariah
	8	40		Jesus was welcomed by the crowd, for they were all there *waiting* for him.
	12	36	<	2 Be like men *waiting for* their master to return from the wedding feast,
		46	<	his master will come on a day he does not *expect*
	21	26	●	6 men dying of fear while they *await* what menaces the world,
Jn	5	3		4 crowds of sick people . . . [v]*waiting for* the water to move;
Ac	3	5		[The lame man] turned to Peter and John] *expectantly hoping* to get something from them,
	10	24		Cornelius was *waiting for* [Peter and his companions].
	12	11		The Lord really did send his angel and has saved me
			6	from . . . all that the Jewish people were so *certain would happen* to me.
	17	16		4 Paul *waited for* [Silas and Timothy] in Athens
	23	21		2 [The Jews] are ready now and only *waiting for* your order to be given.
	27	33		For fourteen days . . . you have been in *suspense*,
	28	6		although [the inhabitants of Malta] were *expecting* [Paul] at any moment to swell up or drop dead . . . After they had *waited* a long time . . . they . . . began to say he was a god.
1 Co	11	33		4 when you meet for the Meal, *wait for* one another.
	16	11		4 the brothers and I are *waiting for* [Timothy].
Jm	5	7	<	4 how patiently [a farmer] *waits for* the precious fruit of the ground

2: WAIT FOR, AWAIT: *MENO*

| 1 | *meno* 2/120 | 2 *ana-meno* 1 |
| | | 3 *peri-meno* 1 |

Ac	1	4	●	[Jesus] had told [the apostles] not to leave Jerusalem,
			3	but to *wait* there *for* what the Father had promised.
	20	5		[Sopater . . . and Trophimus] went on to Troas where they *waited for* us.
		23		[Paul to the elders of Ephesus:] the Holy Spirit . . . has made it clear enough that imprisonment and persecution *await* me.
1 Th	1	10	●	2 you are now *waiting for* Jesus, his son, . . . to come from heaven

HOUSE

1. House, Home – Household: *oikos*	*b)* Nest – (Birds) Shelter
a) a House, Home	**3. Praetorium:** *praitorion*
b) the House, Household, of God	**4. Room – Storey**
c) House, Home, figuratively	1: Private room – Hiding place – Storehouse: *tamieion*
d) Household, Family	2: Upper room, Room upstairs: *hyper-oon*
e) the House of Judah, of Israel, of David	3: Upper room, Room upstairs: *ana-gaion*
2. Tent, Tabernacle – Nest – Live (in): *skene*	4: Storey, Floor: *(tri-)stegos*
a) Tent, Tabernacle, Booth – Dwelling, Habitation – Live (in), Rest	**5. Have no home, Be homeless:** *a-stateo*

1. HOUSE, HOME – HOUSEHOLD: *OIKOS*

3	oikeios	*3*	
6	oikēma	*1*	
7	oiketeia	*1*	
4	oikētērion	*2*	
2	oikia	*93*	

5	oikiakos	*2*
1	oikos	*116*
8	oik(-ourgos)	*1*
9	pan-oikei	*1*

a) a House, Home

Mt 2 11   2 going into the *house* [the Magi] saw the child with his mother Mary,

5 15   they put [the lamp] on the lamp-stand where it shines for
2   everyone in the *house*.

7 24   2 a sensible man who built his *house* on rock.
25   2 gales blew and hurled themselves against that *house*,
26   2 a stupid man who built his *house* on sand.
27   2 gales blew and struck that *house*,

8 6   2 Sir . . . my servant is lying at *home* paralysed,
14   2 going into Peter's *house* Jesus found Peter's mother-in-law in bed with fever.

9 6   pick up your bed and go off *home*.
7   the man got up and went *home*,
10   2 [Jesus] was at dinner in the *house*
23   2 When Jesus reached the official's *house* . . . he said,
28   2 when Jesus reached the *house* the blind men came up with him

10 12   2/2 As you enter his *house*, salute it, [13] and if the *house* deserves
13   it, let your peace descend upon it;
14   2 if anyone does not welcome you . . . walk out of the *house*

11 8   those who wear fine clothes are to be found in ⌐palaces (lit. kings' *houses*).

12 29   2 how can anyone make his way into a strong man's *house* . . . unless he has tied up the strong man first? Only
2   then can he burgle his *house*.

13 1   2 Jesus left the *house* and sat by the lakeside,
36   2 leaving the crowds, [Jesus] went to the *house*;

17 25   2 [Peter] went into the *house*. But before he could speak, Jesus said,

19 29   2 everyone who has left *houses* . . . for the sake of my name will be repaid

23 38   Your *house* will be left to you desolate,

24 17   if a man is on the housetop, he must not come down into
2   the *house* to collect his belongings;
43   the householder . . . would not have allowed anyone to
2   break through the wall of his *house*.

26 6   2 Jesus was at Bethany in the *house* of Simon the leper,

Mk 1 29   2 [Jesus] went . . . straight to the *house* of Simon and Andrew.

2 1   When [Jesus] returned to Capernaum some time later, word went round that he was ⌐back (lit. at *home*);
11   get up, pick up your stretcher, and go off *home*.
15   2 When Jesus was at dinner at [Levi's] *house*,

3 20   [Jesus] went *home* again, and once more . . . a crowd collected
27   2 no one can make his way into a strong man's *house* . . . unless he has tied up the strong man first. Only then can
2   he burgle his *house*.

5 19   Go *home* to your people and tell them
38   So they came to the official's *house*

6 10   2 If you enter a *house* anywhere, stay there

7 17   When [Jesus] had gone back into the *house* . . . his disciples questioned him about the parable.
24   2 [at Tyre, Jesus] went into a *house* . . . he could not pass unrecognised.
30   [the Syrophoenician woman] went off to her *home*

8 3   If I send them off *home* hungry they will collapse on the way;
26   Jesus sent [the blind man who was cured] *home*,

9 28   When [Jesus] had gone ⌐indoors (lit. back into the *house*) his disciples asked him privately,
33   2 when [Jesus] was in the *house* he asked [his disciples],

10 10   2 Back in the *house* the disciples questioned him again
29   2 there is no one who has left *house*, brothers . . . for the
30   sake of the gospel [30] who will not be repaid a hundred
2   times over, *houses*, brothers

12 40 ○   2 [the scribes] who swallow the ⌐property (lit. *homes*) of widows,

13 15   if a man is on the housetop, he must not . . . go into the
2   *house* to collect any of his belongings;
34   2 a man travelling abroad . . . has gone from *home*, and left his servants in charge,

14 3   2 Jesus was at Bethany in the *house* of Simon the leper;

Lk 1 23   [Zechariah] returned *home*.
40   [Mary] went into Zechariah's *house* and greeted Elizabeth.
56   Mary . . . went back *home*.

4 38   2 Leaving the synagogue [Jesus] went to Simon's *house*.

5 24   get up, and pick up your stretcher and go *home*.
25   And immediately [the paralytic] . . . went *home*
29   2 In [Jesus's] honour Levi held a great reception in his *house*,

6 48   2 the man . . . built his *house* . . . on rock . . . the river
2   . . . bore down on that *house* but could not shake it,

Lk 6 49   2 the man . . . built his *house* on soil . . . and what a ruin
2   that *house* became!

7 6   2 [Jesus] was not very far from the *house* [of the centurion]
10   when the messengers got back to the *house* they found the servant in perfect health.
36   When [Jesus] arrived at the Pharisee's *house* and took his
37   place at table, [37] a woman came in, who had a bad name in the town. She had heard he was dining ⌐with the Pharisee
2   (lit. at the Pharisee's *house*).
44   2 I came into your *house*, and you poured no water over my feet,

8 27   2 nor did [the man who was possessed by devils] live in a *house*,
39   Go back *home* . . . and report all that God has done for you.
41   Jairus . . . pleaded with [Jesus] to come to his *house*,
51   2 When [Jesus] came to the *house* he allowed no one to go in

9 4   2 Whatever *house* you enter, stay there;
61   let me go and say good-bye to my people at *home*.

10 5   2 Whatever *house* you go into, let your first words be, 'Peace to this *house*!'
7   2/2 Stay in the same *house* . . . do not move from *house* to
2   *house*.
38   2 a woman named Martha welcomed [Jesus] into her *house*.

12 39   the householder . . . would not have let anyone break through the wall of his *house*.

13 35   So be it! Your *house* will be left to you.

14 1   on a sabbath day [Jesus] had gone . . . to the *house* of one of the leading Pharisees;
23   force people to come in to make sure my *house* is full;

15 6   [would the man who found the lost sheep not,] when he got *home*, call together his friends and neighbours?
8   what woman . . . would not, if she lost one [drachma] . . .
2   sweep out the *house* . . . ?
25   2 as [the elder son] drew near the *house*, he could hear music

16 4   I will . . . make sure that . . . there will be some to welcome me into their *homes*.
27   I beg you . . . to send Lazarus to my father's *house*,

17 31   2 anyone on the housetop, with his possessions in the *house*, must not come down to collect them,

18 14   [the publican] went *home* again at rights with God;
29   2 there is no one who has left *house* [who will not be given repayment]

19 5   Zacchaeus . . . I must stay at your *house* today.

20 47 ○   [Beware of the scribes] who swallow the ⌐property (lit.
2   *homes*) of widows,

22 10   2 Follow [the man] into the *house* he enters [11] and tell the
11   owner of the *house*,
54   2 they took [Jesus] to the high priest's *house*.

Jn 2 16   stop turning my Father's house into a ⌐market (lit. *house* of trade).

7 53   They all went *home*,

8 35   2 the slave's place in the *house* is not assured, but the son's place is assured.

11 20   Mary remained sitting in the *house*.
31   2 the Jews who were in the *house* sympathising with Mary

12 3   2 the *house* was full of the scent of the ointment.

Ac 2 2   they heard what sounded like a powerful wind from heaven, the noise of which filled the entire *house*
46   [The faithful] met in their *houses* for the breaking of bread;

4 34   2 all those who owned land or *houses* would sell them,

5 42   [The apostles] preached every day . . . in private *houses*,

8 3   Saul . . . went ⌐from house to house (lit. to many *houses*) arresting both men and women

9 11   2 ask at the *house* of Judas for someone called Saul,
17   2 Ananias . . . entered the *house*,

10 6   2 Simon the tanner whose *house* is by the sea.
17   2 the men sent by Cornelius . . . had asked where Simon's *house* was
22   Cornelius . . . was directed . . . to send for you and bring you to his *house*
30   I was praying in my *house*
32   2 Peter who is lodging in the *house* of Simon the tanner,

11 11   2 three men stopped outside the *house*
12   we entered the man's [= Cornelius's] *house*.
13   he had seen an angel standing in his *house*

12 7   6 the *cell* was filled with light.
12   2 [Peter] went straight to the *house* of Mary

16 15   [Lydia] sent us an invitation: . . . come and stay ⌐with us (lit. at my *house*).
32   they preached the word of the Lord to [the gaoler] and to
2   all ⌐his family (lit. the people in his *house*).
34   Afterwards [the gaoler] took them *home*

17 5   2 The Jews . . . made for Jason's *house*,

18 7   2/2 [Paul] moved to the *house* next door, the *house* that belonged to . . . Justus.

19 16   [the sons of Sceva] fled from that *house*

20 20   I have . . . instructed you both in public and in your *homes*,

21 8   we ⌐called on (lit. went to the *house* of) Philip . . . and stayed with him.

Rm 16 5   the church that meets at [Prisca and Aquila's] *house*.
1 Co 11 22 2 Surely you have *homes* for eating and drinking in?
      34   Anyone who is hungry should eat at *home*,
   14 35   If [women] have any questions to ask, they should ask their
              husbands at *home*:
   16 19   Aquila and Prisca, with the church that meets at their *house*,
              send you their warmest wishes,
Col 4 15   greetings . . . to Nympha and the church which meets in
              her *house*.
1 Tm 5 13   [young widows] learn how to be idle and go round ˹from
      2   house to house (lit. the *houses*);
2 Tm 2 20   2 Not all the dishes in a large *house* are made of gold
Tt 2 5   [the older women should show the younger women] how to
       8   ˹work in their homes (lit. do the *house*work),
Phm   2   the church that meets in your *house*;
Heb 3 3   It is the difference between the honour given to the man
       4   that built [the house] and to the *house* itself. [4] Every
              house is built by someone, [it collects, of course;]
2 Jn   10   If anyone comes to you bringing a different doctrine, you
       2   must not receive him in your *house*

              b) the House, Household, of God

Mt 12 4   how [David] went into the *house* of God
   21 13   (Is 56 7) my *house* will be called a *house* of prayer;
Mk 2 26   how [David] went into the *house* of God
   11 17   (Is 56 7) My *house* will be called a *house* of prayer for all
              the peoples
Lk 6 4   how [David] went into the *house* of God,
   11 51 ○ Zechariah, who was murdered between the altar and the
              sanctuary.
   19 46   (Is 56 7) my *house* will be a *house* of prayer.
Jn 2 16   stop turning my Father's *house* into a market.
      17   (Ps 69 10) Zeal for your *house* will devour me.
   14 2   2 There are many rooms in my Father's *house*;
Ac 7 47   it was Solomon who actually built God's *house* for him.
      49   (Is 66 1) what *house* could you build me . . . ?
Ga 6 10   we must do good to all, and especially to ˹our brothers (lit.
       3   those *of the household*) in the faith.
Ep 2 19   3 you are citizens like all the saints, and part *of* God's *house-
              hold*.
1 Tm 3 15   God's ˹family (lit. *household*) – that is . . . the Church of
              the living God,
Heb 3 2   [Jesus] was faithful . . . just like Moses, who stayed faithful
              in all his *house*;
       5   Moses was faithful in the *house* of God, as a servant . . .
       6   [6] but Christ was faithful as a son, and as the master in
              the *house*. And we are his *house*,
   10 21   we have the supreme high priest over all the *house* of God.
1 P 2 5   so that you too . . . may be living stones making a spiritual
              house.
    4 17   The time has come for the judgement to begin at the *house-
              hold* of God;

              c) House, Home, figuratively

Mt 12 44 ⓘ 'I will return to the *home* I came from'. But on arrival,
              finding it unoccupied, [it collects seven other spirits]
Lk 11 24 ⓘ I will go back to the *home* I came from.
2 Co 5 1   2 when the tent that ˹we live in (lit. is our *house*) on earth is
              folded up, there is a [house built] by God for us, an ever-
              lasting *home* not made by [human] hands, in the heavens.
       2   [2] In this present state . . . we wait with longing to put
       4   on our heavenly *home* over the other;
Jude   6   let me remind you of the angels who . . . left their appointed
       4   ˹sphere (lit. *home*);

              d) Household, Family

Mt 10 25   If they have called the master of the house Beelzebul, what
       5   will they not say of his *household*?
      36   5 A man's enemies will be [those of] his own *household*.
   12 25   2 no *household* divided against itself can stand.
   13 57   A prophet is only despised in his own country and in his
       2   own *house*,
   24 25   What sort of servant, then, is faithful and wise enough for
       7   the master to place him over his *household* . . . ?
Mk 3 25 2/2 if a *household* is divided against itself, that *household* can
              never stand.
    6 4   2 A prophet is only despised . . . in his own *house*;
   13 35   2 you do not know when the master of the *house* is coming,
Lk 11 17 △ a *household* divided against ˹itself (lit. the *household*) col-
              lapses.
   12 52   from now on a *household* of five will be divided:
   19 9   Today salvation has come to this *house*,
Jn 4 53   2 [the court official] and all his *household* believed.
Ac 7 10   Pharaoh . . . put [Joseph] in charge of the royal *household*,
      20   Moses . . . was looked after for three months in his father's
              house,
   10 2   [Cornelius] and the whole of his *household* were devout and
              God-fearing,
   11 14   [Cornelius, Peter] has a message for you that will save you
              and your entire *household*.

Ac 16 15   After [Lydia] and her *household* had been baptised she sent
              us an invitation:
      31   [Paul and Silas] told [the gaoler], 'Become a believer in the
              Lord Jesus, and you will be saved, and your *household*
      34   9 too' . . . [34] Afterwards he . . . and the *whole family*
              celebrated their conversion to belief in God.
   18 8   Crispus . . . and his whole *household*, all became believers
              in the Lord.
1 Co 1 16   there is also the *family* of Stephanas . . . that I baptised too.
   16 15   2 the Stephanas *family* . . . were the first-fruits of Achaia,
Ph 4 22   All the saints send their greetings, especially those of the
              imperial *household*.
1 Tm 3 4   [The elder-in-charge] must be a man who manages his own
              family well
       5   how can any man who does not understand how to manage
              his own *family* have responsibility . . . ?
      12   Deacons . . . must be men who manage their . . . *families*
              well.
    5 4   children . . . are to learn first of all to do their duty to their
              own *families*
       8   Anyone who does not look after his own relations, especially
       3   if they are ˹living with him (lit. *of his* own *household*), has
              rejected the faith
2 Tm 1 16   I hope the Lord will be kind to all the *family* of Onesiphorus.
    3 6   2 men who insinuate themselves into *families* in order to get
              influence over silly women
    4 19   Greetings to Prisca and Aquila, and the *family* of Onesi-
              phorus.
Tt 1 11   men of this kind ruin whole *families*,
Heb 11 7   It was through his faith that Noah . . . built an ark to save
              his *family*.

              e) the House of Judah, of Israel, of David

Mt 10 6   go rather to the lost sheep of the *House* of Israel.
   15 24   I was sent only to the lost sheep of the *House* of Israel.
Lk 1 27   a virgin betrothed to a man named Joseph, of the *House* of
              David;
      33   he will rule over the *House* of Jacob for ever
      69   [God] has raised up for us a power for salvation in the
              House of his servant David,
    2 4   Joseph . . . was of David's *House* and line,
Ac 2 36   the whole *House* of Israel can be certain that God has made
              this Jesus . . . both Lord and Christ.
    7 42   (Am 5 25) Did you bring me victims and sacrifices . . . you
              House of Israel?
      46   [David] asked permission to have a temple built for the
            ˹*House* (˅ God) of Jacob,
Heb 8 8   (Jr 31 31) I will establish a new covenant with the *House*
              of Israel and the *House* of Judah,
      10   (Jr 31 33) this is the covenant I will make with the *House*
              of Israel

              2. TENT, TABERNACLE – NEST – LIVE (IN): *SKĒNĒ*

1 *skēnē*	20	8	*skēno(-poios)*	1
4 *skēnōma*	3	3	*kata-skēnoō*	4
2 *skēnoō*	5	6	*kata-skēnōsis*	2
5 *skēnos*	2	9	*epi-skēnoō*	1
7 *skēno-pēgia*	1			

              a) Tent, Tabernacle, Booth – Dwelling, Habitation – Live (in), Rest

              B = Human body; T = Liturgical tent

Mt 17 4   Peter spoke to Jesus. 'Lord . . . if you wish, I will make
              three *tents* here,'
Mk 9 5   let us make three *tents*,
Lk 9 33   let us make three *tents*,
   16 9   use money . . . to win you friends, and thus make sure that
              . . . they will welcome you into the *tents* of eternity.
Jn 1 14 X 2 The Word was made flesh, he *lived* among us,
    7 2   7 the Jewish feast *of Tabernacles* drew near,
Ac 2 26 X 3 (Ps 16 9) my body, too, will *rest* in the hope
    7 43   (Am 5 26 G) you carried the *tent* of Moloch
      44 T While they were in the desert our ancestors possessed the
              Tent of Testimony
      46 (Θ) 4 [David] asked permission to have a ˹temple (lit. *dwelling-
              place*) built for the ˹*House* (˅ God) of Jacob,
   15 16   (Am 9 11) I shall . . . rebuild the fallen ˹*House* (lit. *dwelling*)
              of David;
   18 3   8 [Aquila and Priscilla] were *tent*makers,
2 Co 5 1 B 5 when the *tent* that we live in on earth is folded up, there is
              . . . an everlasting *home* . . . in the heavens.
       4 B 5 we groan and find it a burden being still in this *tent*,
   12 9   9 so that the power of Christ may ˹*stay* over (or: *rest* upon)
              me,
Heb 8 2 T [Jesus, the high priest] is the minister of the sanctuary and
              of the true *Tent* of Meeting which the Lord, and not any
              man, set up.

Heb	8	5	T		Moses, when he had the *Tent* to build,
	9	2	T		There was a *tent* which comprised two compartments: the first . . . was called the Holy Place; ³ then beyond the
		3	T		second veil, ˩an innermost part (lit. a *tent*) which was called the Holy of Holies
		6	T		priests are constantly going into the outer *tent*
		8	T		no one has the right to go into the sanctuary as long as the outer *tent* remains standing;
		11	T		Christ . . . has passed through the greater, the more perfect *tent* . . . ¹² and he has entered the sanctuary
		21	T		[Moses] sprinkled the *tent* and all the liturgical vessels with blood
	11	10			[Abraham] lived there in *tents* while he looked forward to a city . . . built by God.
	13	10	T		We have our own altar from which those who serve the *tabernacle* have no right to eat.
2 P	1	13	B	4	I am sure it is my duty, as long as I am in this *tent*, to keep stirring you up with reminders,
		14	T	4	I know the time for taking off this *tent* is coming soon,
Rv	7	15		2	the One who sits on the throne will *spread his tent* over them
	12	12		2	Let the heavens rejoice and all who *live* there;
	13	6	Θ		[the beast] mouthed its blasphemies against God . . . his
			/2		heavenly *Tent* and all those who *are sheltered* there.
	15	5	T		the sanctuary, the *Tent* of the Testimony, opened in heaven,
	21	3	Θ	/2	Here God *lives* among men. He will *make his home* among them;

b) Nest – (Birds) Shelter

Mt	8	20		6	Foxes have holes and the birds of the air have *nests*,
	13	32	<	3	the birds of the air come and ˩*shelter* (or: *make nests*) in its branches.
Mk	4	32	<	3	the birds of the air can ˩*shelter* (or: *make nests*) in its shade.
Lk	9	58		6	the birds of the air have *nests*,
	13	19	<	3	the birds of the air ˩*sheltered* (or: *made nests*) in its branches.

3. PRAETORIUM: *PRAITŌRION*

praitōrion 8

Mt	27	27		The governor's soldiers took Jesus with them into the *Praetorium*
Mk	15	16		The soldiers led [Jesus] away to the inner part of the palace, that is, the *Praetorium*,
Jn	18	28		They then led Jesus from the house of Caiaphas to the *Praetorium* . . . they did not go into the *Praetorium* themselves
		33		Pilate went back into the *Praetorium*
	19	9		Re-entering the *Praetorium*, [Pilate] said to Jesus,

| Ac | 23 | 35 | | [the governor] ordered [Paul] to be held in Herod's *praetorium*. |
| Ph | 1 | 13 | | My chains, in Christ, have become famous . . . all over the *Praetorium* |

4. ROOM – STOREY

1: PRIVATE ROOM – HIDING PLACE – STOREHOUSE: *TAMIEION*

tamieion 4

Mt	6	6		when you pray, go to your *private room*
	24	26		If, then, they say to you, '. . . Look, [the Christ] is in some *hiding place*', do not believe it;
Lk	12	3		what you have whispered in *hidden places* will be proclaimed on the housetops.
		24		the ravens . . . have no *storehouse* and no barns; yet God feeds them.

2: UPPER ROOM, ROOM UPSTAIRS: *HYPER-ŌON*

hyper-ōon 4

Ac	1	13		[in Jerusalem the apostles] went to the *upper room*
	9	37		they washed [Tabitha] and laid her out in a *room upstairs*.
		39		on [Peter's] arrival they took him to the *upstairs room*,
	20	8		[in Troas,] in the *upstairs room* where we were assembled,

3: UPPER ROOM, ROOM UPSTAIRS: *ANA-GAION*

ana-gaion 2

| Mk | 14 | 15 | | [The owner of the house] will show you a large *upper room* |
| Lk | 22 | 12 | | The man will show you a large *upper room* |

4: STOREY, FLOOR: *(TRI-)STEGOS*

(tri-)stegos 1

| Ac | 20 | 9 | | Eutychus . . . fell to the ground three *floors* below. |

5. HAVE NO HOME, BE HOMELESS: *A-STATEŌ*

a-stateō 1

| 1 Co | 4 | 11 | | we are beaten and *have no homes*; |

IDLE – DELAY

1. Idle, Idler, (in) Idleness: *a-takteō*
2. Idle, Useless, Ineffectual – Lazy: *argos*
3. Lazy – to Flag – Delay: *okneō*
  1: Lazy – to Flag – (Be no) Trouble (to)
  2: Delay

4. Slow, Lazy, Dull: *nōthros*
5. Slow, Be slow – Be delayed: *bradys*
6. Delay: *mellō*
7. Delay, Take (one's) time – (Be) Late: *chronizō*
8. Come too late: *hystereō*
9. Adjourn – Waste time, Delay: *ana-ballomai*

1. IDLE, IDLER, (IN) IDLENESS: *A-TAKTEŌ*

2 *a-takteō* 1   1 *a-taktōs* 2
3 *a-taktos* 1

1 Th 5 14	3	warn the *idlers*, give courage to those who are apprehensive, keep away from any of the brothers who *refuses to work*
2 Th 3 6	2	we were not *idle* when we were with you, [8] . . . no, we worked night and day,
7		
11		we hear that there are some of you who are living *in idleness*,

2. IDLE, USELESS, INEFFECTUAL – LAZY: *ARGOS*

2 *argeō* 1   1 *argos* 8

Mt 12 36		for every ⌐unfounded⌐ (or: *idle*) word men utter they will answer on Judgement day,
20 3	<	[A landowner hired workers for his vineyard.] Going out at about the third hour he saw others standing *idle* in the market place
6	<	at about the eleventh hour he went out and found more men standing round, . . . 'Why have you been standing here *idle* all day?'
1 Tm 5 13		[young widows] learn how to be *idle* and go round from house to house;
Tt 1 12		Cretans were never anything but . . . dangerous . . . and *lazy*.
Jm 2 20		faith without good deeds is *useless*.
2 P 1 8		If you have a generous supply of [devotion, kindness and love], they will not leave you *ineffectual* or unproductive;
2 3	2	for [your false teachers] the Condemnation . . . is ⌐at its work already⌐ (lit. by no means *idle*),

3. LAZY – TO FLAG – DELAY: *OKNEŌ*

2 *okneō* 1   1 *oknēros* 3

1: LAZY – TO FLAG – (BE NO) TROUBLE (TO)

Mt 25 26		You wicked and *lazy* servant! . . . [27] . . . you should have deposited my money with the bankers,
Rm 12 11		Work for the Lord with ⌐untiring⌐ (lit. no *flagging* in) effort and with great earnestness of spirit.
Ph 3 1		It is no *trouble* to me to repeat what I have already written to you,

2: DELAY

Ac 9 38	2	the disciples . . . sent two men with an urgent message for [Peter], 'Come and visit us ⌐as soon as possible⌐ (lit. without *delay*).'

4. SLOW, LAZY, DULL: *NŌTHROS*

nōthros 2

Heb 5 11	you have grown so *slow* at understanding.
6 12	[every one of you should go on showing the same earnestness to the end,] never growing ⌐careless⌐ (lit. *lazy*),

5. SLOW, BE SLOW – BE DELAYED: *BRADYS*

2 *bradynō* 2   3 *bradytēs*   1
1 *bradys* 3   4 *brady(-ploeō)* 1

Lk 24 25		You foolish men! So *slow* to believe
Ac 27 7	4	For some days we made ⌐little⌐ (lit. *slow*) headway,
1 Tm 3 15	2	in case I should *be delayed*,
Jm 1 19		be quick to listen but *slow* to speak and *slow* to rouse your temper.
2 P 3 9 Θ	2	The Lord *is* not *being slow* to carry out his promises, as
3		anybody else might be called *slow*;

6. DELAY: *MELLŌ*

mellō (1)

Ac 22 16	And now why *delay*? It is time you were baptised

7. DELAY, TAKE (ONE'S) TIME – (BE) LATE: *CHRONIZŌ*

chronizō 5

Mt 24 48	<	My master is *taking* his *time*,
25 5	<	The bridegroom was *late*,
Lk 1 21		the people . . . were surprised that [Zechariah] ⌐stayed in the sanctuary so long⌐ (lit. *delayed* in the sanctuary).
12 45	<	My master is *taking* his *time* coming,
Heb 10 37	X	(Hab 2 3) Only a little while now . . . and the one that is coming will have come; he will not *delay*.

8. COME TOO LATE: *HYSTEREŌ*

hystereō 1/16

Heb 4 1	none of you must think he has ⌐come too late⌐ for (or: failed to reach) it.

9. ADJOURN – WASTE TIME, DELAY: *ANA-BALLOMAI*

1 *ana-ballomai* 1   2 *ana-bolē* 1

Ac 24 22		Felix . . . *adjourned* the case,
25 17	2	I *wasted* no *time* but took my seat on the tribunal

---

IDOL

1: Idol, Idolatry, Idolater – False gods
2: Food sacrificed to idols, Meat offered to heathen deities
3: the Temple of an Idol, Heathen temple

5 *eidōleion*   1   4 *eidōlo-latria* 4
1 *eidōlon*   11   2 *eidōlo-thytos* 9
3 *eidōlo-latrēs* 7   6 *kat-eidōlos*   1

1: IDOL, IDOLATRY, IDOLATER – FALSE GODS

Ac 7 41		[The Israelites] made a bull calf and offered sacrifice to the *idol*.
15 20		telling them merely to abstain from anything polluted by *idols*,
17 16	6	[Athens] a city ⌐given over to idolatry⌐ (or: *full of idols*).
Rm 2 22		you despise *idols*, yet you rob their temples.
1 Co 5 10	3	I was not meaning to include . . . all usurers . . . or *idol-worshippers*. [11] . . . you should not associate with a brother
11	3	Christian who *is* . . . a usurer, or *idolatrous*,
6 9	3	*idolaters*, adulterers, . . . will never inherit the kingdom of God.

1 Co	8	4		we know that *idols* do not really exist in the world
		7		There are some who have been so long used to *idols* that they eat this food as though it really had been sacrificed to the idol,
	10	7	3	Do not become *idolaters* as some of [the Israelites] did,
		14	4	you must keep clear of *idolatry*.
		19		Does this mean that the food sacrificed to idols has a real value, or that the *idol* itself is real?
	12	2		when you were pagans, whenever you were irresistibly drawn, it was towards dumb *idols*.
2 Co	6	16		The temple of God has no common ground with *idols*,
Ga	5	20	4	[the results of self-indulgence:] *idolatry* and sorcery; feuds
Ep	5	5		nobody who actually indulges in fornication or impurity or
			3	promiscuity – which is *worshipping a false god* – can inherit anything of the kingdom of God.
Col	3	5		fornication, . . . evil desires and especially greed, which is the
			4	same thing as *worshipping a false god*;
1 Th	1	9		you broke with ⌐idolatry (lit. *idols*) when you were converted to God
1 P	4	3		having . . . drunken orgies and degrading yourselves by
			4	*following false gods*.
1 Jn	5	21		Children, be on your guard against *false gods*.
Rv	9	20		the rest . . . refused . . . to abandon . . . the *idols* made of gold, silver, . . . and wood
	21	8	3	But the legacy for cowards, for . . . *idolaters* or any other sort of liars, is the second death in the burning lake
	22	15	3	These others must stay outside: . . . *idolaters*, and everyone of false speech and false life.

2: FOOD SACRIFICED TO IDOLS, MEAT OFFERED TO HEATHEN DEITIES

Ac	15	29	2	you are to abstain from *food sacrificed to idols*, from blood,
	21	25	2	The pagans . . . must abstain from *things sacrificed to idols*, from blood,
1 Co	8	1	2	Now about *food sacrificed to idols*. We all have knowledge; yes, . . . but . . .
		4	2	Well then, about *food sacrificed to idols*: we know that idols do not really exist
		7		There are some who have been so long used to idols that
			2	they eat this *food* as though it really had been *sacrificed to the idol*,
		10		his own conscience, even if it is weak, may encourage him
			2	to eat *food which has been offered to idols*.
	10	19	2	Does this mean that the *food sacrificed to idols* has a real value . . .?
Rv	2	14		Balaam . . . taught Balak to set a trap for the Israelites so
			2	that they committed adultery by eating *food that had been sacrificed to idols*;
		20		Jezebel . . . is luring my servants away to commit the adultery
			2	of eating *food which has been sacrificed to idols*.

3: THE TEMPLE OF AN IDOL, HEATHEN TEMPLE

| 1 Co | 8 | 10 | 5 | Suppose someone sees you . . . eating in some *temple of an idol*; |

IMAGE – FORM – EXAMPLE

1. Image, Likeness: *eikōn*
  1: Image, Likeness – Statue
  2: Image, Likeness (of God, of Christ, of Adam)
  3: Be like
  4: Image, Picture (of good things to come)
2. Carved Representation – Stamp, Imprint, Mark: *charagma*
3. Mark(s): *stigma*
4. Engraved Form – Type, Pattern: *typos*
  1: Engrave(d), Print, Mark – Form, Figure
  2: 'Types' = Events or persons prefiguring the messianic age – Symbolic Warnings

  3: Pattern, Example – (Be) Modelled on, Model
5. Form(ed) – Transform(ed): *morphē*
  1: Form, Be formed – Pattern, Shape, Appearance
  2: (Be) Transfigured, Transformed, Turned (into)
6. Form – Conform – Transform: *schēma*
  1: Form
  2: Model (oneself on), Take as an example, Conform to
  3: Disguise, Masquerade – Transfigure, Transform
7. Example, Model, Copy: *deigma*
8. Follow an example, Imitate, Copy – Be like, Imitator: *mimeomai*

d = Idol

1. IMAGE, LIKENESS: *EIKŌN*

1 *eikōn* 23   2 *eoika* 2

1: IMAGE, LIKENESS – STATUE

Mt	22	20		Whose ⌐head (lit. *likeness*) is this? . . . ²¹ Caesar's
Mk	12	16		Whose ⌐head (lit. *likeness*) is this?
Lk	20	24		Whose ⌐head (lit. *likeness*) and name are on it?
Rm	1	23		[men] exchanged the glory of the immortal God for a
			d	worthless imitation, for the *image* of mortal man, of birds,
Rv	13	14		[the second beast] was able to . . . persuade [the people]
			d	to put up a *statue* in honour of the beast that had been wounded
		15	d	It was allowed to breathe life into this *statue*, so that the
			d	*statue* of the beast was able to speak, and to have anyone
			d	who refused to worship the *statue* of the beast put to death.
	14	9	d	All those who worship the beast and his *statue*,
		11		There will be no respite for those who worshipped the beast
			d	or its *statue*
	15	2		I seemed to see . . . those who had fought against the beast
			d	. . . and against his *statue*
	16	2		on all the people who had been branded with the mark of the
			d	beast and had worshipped its *statue*, there came . . . virulent sores.
	19	20		all who had been branded with the mark of the beast and
			d	worshipped his *statue*.
	20	4	d	those who refused to worship the beast or his *statue*

2: IMAGE, LIKENESS (OF GOD, OF CHRIST, OF ADAM)

A = Image of Adam

Rm	8	29		They are the ones [God] chose specially long ago and intended to become true *images* of his Son,
1 Co	11	7		A man . . . is the *image* of God
	15	49		[The first man is earthly by nature; the second is from heaven.]
			A	And we, who have ⌐been modelled on (lit. *worn the likeness of*) the earthly man, will ⌐be modelled on (lit. *wear the likeness of*) the heavenly man.
2 Co	3	18		we, with our unveiled faces reflecting like mirrors the brightness of the Lord, . . . are turned into the *image* that we reflect;
	4	4		the glory of Christ, who is the *image* of God
Col	1	15		[Christ] is the *image* of the unseen God
	3	10		the more [the new self] is renewed in the *image* of its creator;

3: BE LIKE

| Jm | 1 | 6 | 2 | a person who doubts *is like* the waves thrown up in the sea when the wind drives. |
| | | 23 | 2 | To listen to the word and not obey *is like* looking at your own features in a mirror |

4: IMAGE, PICTURE (OF GOOD THINGS TO COME)

| Heb | 10 | 1 | | since the Law has no more than a reflection of these realities, and no finished *picture* of them, it is quite incapable of bringing the worshippers to perfection, |

2. CARVED REPRESENTATION – STAMP, IMPRINT, MARK: *CHARAGMA*

1 *charagma* 8   2 *charaktēr* 1

Ac	17	29		we have no excuse for thinking that the deity looks like anything . . . that has been *carved* and designed by a man.
Heb	1	3 X		He is the radiant light of God's glory and the perfect ⌐copy
			2	(lit. *stamp*) of his nature,
Rv	13	16		[The beast] compelled everyone . . . to ⌐be branded (lit. have a *mark* put) on the right hand or on the forehead,
		17		¹⁷ and made it illegal for anyone to buy or sell anything unless he had been ⌐branded (lit. *marked*) with the name of the beast or with the number of its name.
	14	9		All those who worship the beast and his statue, and have had ⌐themselves branded (lit. the *mark* put) on the hand or forehead,
		11		There will be no respite . . . for those who worshipped the beast . . . or accepted ⌐branding with (lit. the *mark* of) its name.
	16	2		on all the people who had been branded with the *mark* of the beast . . . there came . . . virulent sores.
	19	20		the false prophet who . . . deceived all who had been branded with the *mark* of the beast
	20	4		those who . . . would not have the brand-*mark* on their foreheads or hands;

3. MARK(S): *STIGMA*

stigma 1

Ga 6 17   the *marks* on my body are those of Jesus.

4. ENGRAVED FORM – TYPE, PATTERN: *TYPOS*

4	*typikōs 1*	5	*en-typoō 1*
1	*typos 15*	3	*hypo-typōsis 2*
2	*anti-typos 2*		

1: ENGRAVE(D), PRINT, MARK – FORM, FIGURE

Jn 20 25   Thomas answered, 'Unless I can see the ⌐holes (lit. *prints*)
               that the nails made in his hands and can put my finger into
               the ⌐holes (lit. *marks*; G *places*) they made, . . . I refuse
               to believe.'
Ac 7 43   (Am 5 26) you carried the tent of Moloch on your shoulders
     d   and the star of the god Rephan, those ⌐idols (or: *figures*)
               that you had made to adore.
    23 25   [Lysias] wrote a letter ⌐in these terms (lit. of this *form*):
2 Co 3 7   5 the administering of death, in the written letters *engraved*
               on stones,

2: 'TYPES' = EVENTS OR PERSONS PREFIGURING THE MESSIANIC AGE – SYMBOLIC WARNINGS

Rm 5 14   Adam ⌐*prefigured* (or: was a *type* of) the One to come,
1 Co 10 6   These things all happened as *warnings* for us,
    11   4 All this happened to them *as a warning*,
Heb 9 .24   It is not as though Christ had entered a man-made sanctuary
     2   which ⌐was only modelled on (or: is only *symbolic* of)
               the real one; but it was heaven itself,
1 P 3 21   2 That water [of the Flood] ⌐is a *type* of (or: *prefigured*) the
               baptism which saves you now,

3: PATTERN, EXAMPLE – (BE) MODELLED ON, MODEL

Ac 7 44   the Tent of Testimony . . . had been constructed according
               to the instructions God gave Moses, telling him to make an
               exact copy of the *pattern* he had been shown.
Rm 6 17   you submitted without reservation to the ⌐creed (lit. *pattern*
               of teaching) you were taught.
Ph 3 17   Take as your *models* everybody who is already doing this
               and study them as you used to study us.
1 Th 1 7   This has made you the great *example* to all believers
2 Th 3 9   in order to make ourselves an *example* for you to follow.
1 Tm 1 16   Jesus Christ meant to make me the greatest ⌐evidence (lit.
     3   *example*) of his inexhaustible patience
     4 12   be an *example* to all the believers in the way you speak and
               behave,
2 Tm 1 13   3 Keep as your *pattern* the sound teaching you have heard from
               me,
Tt 2 7   in everything you do make yourself an *example* to them of
               working for good;
Heb 8 5   (Ex 25 40) See that you make everything according to the
               pattern shown you
    9 24   It is not as though Christ had entered a man-made sanctuary
               which ⌐was only *modelled on* (or: is only symbolic of) the
               real one;
1 P 5 3   Never be a dictator over any group that is put in your charge,
               but be an *example* that the whole flock can follow.

5. FORM(ED) – TRANSFORM(ED): *MORPHĒ*

2	*morphē 3*	1	*meta-morphoō 4*
5	*morphoō 1*	6	*sym-morphizō 1*
3	*morphōsis 2*	4	*sym-morphos 2*

1: FORM, BE FORMED – PATTERN, SHAPE, APPEARANCE

Mk 16 12 X   2 [Jesus] showed himself under another *form* to two of them
Rm 2 20   3 your Law ⌐embodies (lit. is the very *pattern* of) all knowledge
               and truth,
    8 29   They are the ones he chose specially long ago and intended
     4   to ⌐become (lit. *be formed as*) true images of his Son,
Ga 4 19   I must go through the pain of giving birth to you all over
     5   again, until Christ is *formed* in you.
Ph 2 6 X   2 His ⌐state (lit. *form*) was divine, yet he did not cling to his
     7   equality with God ⌐but emptied himself to assume the
     2   ⌐condition (lit. *form*) of a slave, and became as men are;
               and being as all men are, he was humbler yet,

Ph 3 10   6 All I want is to . . . share [Christ's] sufferings by *reproducing
               the pattern* of his death.
    21   [Jesus Christ] will transfigure these wretched bodies of ours
     4   ⌐into copies (lit. *following the pattern*) of his glorious body.
2 Tm 3 5   3 [In the last days people] will keep up the *outward appearance*
               of religion but will have rejected the inner power of it.

6. (BE) TRANSFIGURED, TRANSFORMED, TURNED (INTO)

Mt 17 2 X   There in their presence he was *transfigured*:
Mk 9 2 X   There in their presence he was *transfigured*:
Rm 12 2   Do not model yourselves on the behaviour of the world
               around you, but let your behaviour ⌐change, modelled
               (lit. *be transformed*) by your new mind.
2 Co 3 18   we, with our unveiled faces reflecting like mirrors the bright-
               ness of the Lord, all grow brighter . . . as we are *turned
               into* the image that we reflect;

6. FORM – CONFORM – TRANSFORM: *SCHĒMA*

2	*schēma 2*	3	*sy-schēmatizomai 2*
1	*meta-schēmatizō 5*		

1: FORM

1 Co 7 31   2 the world ⌐as we know it (lit. in its [present] *form*) is passing
               away.
Ph 2 7 X   2 ⌐being as all men are (lit. revealed in human *form*), he was
               humbler yet,

2: MODEL (ONESELF ON), TAKE AS AN EXAMPLE, CONFORM TO

Rm 12 2   3 Do not *model* yourselves on the behaviour of the world
               around you,
1 Co 4 6   in everything I have said here . . . I have *taken* Apollos and
               myself *as an example*
1 P 1 14   3 Do not ⌐behave in the way that (lit. *model* your behaviour
               on what) you liked to before you learnt the truth;

3: DISGUISE, MASQUERADE – TRANSFIGURE, TRANSFORM

2 Co 11 13   Those people are . . . dishonest workmen *disguised* as
    14 ⓓ   apostles of Christ. [14] . . . Satan himself goes *disguised*
    15   as an angel of light, [15] . . . his servants, too, *disguise*
               themselves as the servants of righteousness.
Ph 3 21   [Jesus Christ] will *transfigure* these wretched bodies of ours
               into copies of his glorious body.

7. EXAMPLE, MODEL, COPY: *DEIGMA*

2 *deigma 1*   1 *hypo-deigma 6*

Jn 13 15 X   I have given you an *example* so that you may copy what I
               have done to you.
Heb 4 11   or some of you might copy this *example* of disobedience
               and be lost.
     8 5   these [high priests] only maintain the service of a *model*
               or a reflection of the heavenly realities.
     9 23   only the *copies* of heavenly things can be purified in this way,
Jm 5 10   For your *example* . . . in submitting with patience take
               the prophets
2 P 2 6   he destroyed [Sodom and Gomorrah] completely, as ⌐a
               warning (lit. an *example*) to anyone lacking reverence
               in the future:
Jude 7   2 it is ⌐a warning (lit. an *example*) to us that [Sodom and
               Gomorrah] are paying for their crimes in eternal fire.

8. FOLLOW AN EXAMPLE, IMITATE, COPY – BE LIKE, IMITATOR: *MIMEOMAI*

2	*mimeomai 4*	3	*sym-mimētēs 1*
1	*mimētēs 6*		

Θ = Imitate God   X = Imitate Christ

1 Co 4 16   That is why I beg you to *copy* me
    11 1 X   Take me *for your model*, as I take Christ.
Ep 5 1 Θ   Try . . . to *imitate* God, as children of his that he loves,
Ph 3 17   3 be ⌐united in following my rule (lit. *united in copying* my
               way) of life.
1 Th 1 6 X   you were led to become *imitators* of us, and of the Lord;
     2 14   you . . . have *been like* the churches of God . . . in Judaea,
2 Th 3 7   2 You know how you are supposed to *imitate* us:
     9   2 in order to make ourselves an example for you to *follow*.

Heb	6 12	*imitating* those who have the faith and the perseverance to inherit the promises.
	13 7	2 Remember your leaders, . . . *imitate* their faith.
3 Jn	11	2 never *follow* such *a* bad *example*, but keep following the good one;

IMMORALITY

1. Fornication – Prostitute – Immorality: *porneia*	**3. Debauchery – Indecency – Dissipation**
1: Fornication, Sexual immorality – Prostitute – Immoral (people)	1: Licentiousness, Debauchery – Indecency – Shameless: *aselgeia*
2: Fornication – Prostitute (in figurative senses)	2: Dissipation, Loose living – Debauchery: *a-sōtia*
2. Adultery: *moicheia*	3: Debauchery, Dissipation: *kraipalē*
1: Adultery, Commit adultery	4: Shame, Shameless – Indecent – (Be) Rude: *a-schēmoneō*
2: Adultery, Adulterous (in figurative senses) – Unfaithful	

1. FORNICATION – PROSTITUTE – IMMORALITY: *PORNEIA*

2 *pornē*	12	3 *pornos*	10
1 *porneia*	25	5 *ek-porneuō*	1
4 *porneuō*	8		

1: FORNICATION, SEXUAL IMMORALITY – PROSTITUTE – IMMORAL (PEOPLE)

Mt	5 32	everyone who divorces his wife, except for the case of *fornication*, makes her an adulteress;
	15 19	from the heart come . . . adultery, *fornication*, theft,
	19 9	the man who divorces his wife – I am not speaking of *fornication* – and marries another, is guilty of adultery.
	21 31	2 tax collectors and *prostitutes* are making their way into the kingdom of God before you. ³² For . . . the tax collectors
	32	2 and *prostitutes* [believed John].
Mk	7 21	from men's hearts . . . evil intentions emerge: *fornication*, theft, murder,
Lk	15 30	for this son of yours, when he comes back after swallowing
		2 up your property – he and his ʳwomen (lit. *prostitutes*) – you kill the calf we had been fattening.
Ac	15 20	we send [the pagans] a letter telling them merely to abstain from . . . *fornication*,
	29	you are to abstain from . . . *fornication*.
	21 25	The pagans . . . , as we wrote . . . , must abstain from . . . *fornication*.
1 Co	5 1	This is [a case of] *sexual immorality* among you that must be unparalleled even in [cases of] *fornication* among pagans.
	9	When I wrote in my letter to you not to associate with
	10	3 *people living immoral lives*, ¹⁰ I was not meaning . . . all
		3 the *people* in the world *who are sexually immoral* . . .
	11	¹¹ . . . [but] a brother Christian who is [leading an]
		3 *immoral* [life],
	6 9	3 *people of immoral lives*, idolaters, adulterers, . . . ¹⁰ . . . will never inherit the kingdom of God.
	13	the body . . . is not meant for *fornication*;
	15	do you think I can take parts of Christ's body and join
	16	2 them to the body of a *prostitute*? Never! ¹⁶ . . . a man
		2 who goes with a *prostitute* is one body with her.
	18	/4 Keep away from *fornication*. . . . to *fornicate* is to sin against your own body.
	7 2	since ʳsex (lit. *sexual immorality*) is always a danger, let each man have his own wife
	10 8	4 We must never *fall into sexual immorality*: some of [our
		4 fathers] ʳdid (lit. became *sexually immoral*),
2 Co	12 21	those who . . . have not repented of the impurities, *fornication* and debauchery they committed.
Ga	5 19	When self-indulgence is at work the results are obvious: *fornication*, gross indecency and sexual irresponsibility;
Ep	5 3	Among you there must not be even a mention of *fornication*
	5	3 or impurity in any of its forms, . . . ⁵ . . . nobody *who* actually *indulges in fornication* or impurity . . . can inherit anything of the kingdom of God.
Col	3 5	you must kill everything in you that belongs only to earthly life: *fornication*, impurity, guilty passion,
1 Th	4 3	[God] wants you to keep away from *fornication*,
1 Tm	1 10	3 [laws are framed for] those *who are immoral with women* or with boys or with men, for liars
Heb	11 31	2 It was by faith that Rahab the *prostitute* welcomed the spies
	12 16	3 be careful that there is no *immorality*,
	13 4	3 *fornicators* and adulterers will come under God's judgement.

Jm	2 25	2 Rahab the *prostitute*, justified by her deeds
Jude	7	5 The *fornication* of Sodom and Gomorrah and the other nearby towns was equally unnatural,
Rv	2 14	the Israelites . . . ʳcommitted adultery by (lit. started being
		4 *immoral* and) eating food that had been sacrificed to idols;
	20	Jezebel . . . is luring my servants away to ʳcommit the
		4 adultery of (lit. *fornication* and) eating food which has been sacrificed to idols. ²¹ . . . she is not willing to change
	21	her ʳadulterous life (lit. *fornication*).
	9 21	Nor did [those who escaped these plagues] give up their . . . *fornication* or stealing.
	21 8	3 the legacy for . . . murderers and *fornicators* . . . is the second death in the burning lake
	22 15	These others must stay outside: dogs, fortune-tellers, and
		3 *fornicators*.

2: FORNICATION, PROSTITUTE (IN FIGURATIVE SENSES)

Jn	8 41	[the Jews said to Jesus,] 'We were not born of *prostitution*, . . . we have one father: God.'
Jude	7	5 The *fornication* of Sodom and Gomorrah and the other nearby towns was equally unnatural,
Rv	14 8	Babylon . . . gave the whole world the wine of God's anger to drink (§ through her *fornication*).
	17 1	I will show §you the punishment given to the famous
		2 *prostitute*
	2	[Babylon,] the one with whom all the kings of the earth
		4 have *committed fornication*, and who has made all the population of the world drunk with the wine of her ʳadultery (lit. *prostitution*).
	4	she was holding a gold winecup filled with the disgusting filth of her *fornication*;
	5	2 Babylon the Great, the mother of all the *prostitutes* and all the filthy practices on the earth. . . . ⁹ the seven heads are the seven hills, and the woman is sitting on them. . . .
	15	2 ¹⁵ . . . The waters you saw, beside which the *prostitute* was sitting, are all the peoples,
	16	2 the ten horns and the beast will turn against the *prostitute*,
	18 3	All the nations have been intoxicated by the wine of her
		/4 *prostitution*; every king in the earth has *committed fornication* with her.
	9	4 the kings of the earth who have *fornicated* with her
	19 2	2 He . . . has condemned the famous *prostitute* who corrupted the earth with her fornication;

2. ADULTERY: *MOICHEIA*

2 *moichalis*	7	1 *moicheuō*	15
3 *moichaomai*	4	5 *moichos*	3
4 *moicheia*	3		

1: ADULTERY, COMMIT ADULTERY

Mt	5 27	It was said (Ex 20 14); You must not *commit adultery*.
	28	²⁸ But I say to you: if a man looks at a woman lustfully, he has already committed *adultery* with her in his heart.
	32	everyone who divorces his wife, except for the case of fornication, *makes her an adulteress*; and anyone who marries
		3 a divorced woman *commits adultery*.
	15 19	4 From the heart come evil intentions: . . *adultery*, fornication,
	19 9	the man who divorces his wife – I am not speaking of forni-
		3 cation – and marries another, is guilty of *adultery*.
	18	(Ex 20 14) You must not kill. You must not *commit adultery*.
Mk	7 22	[from men's hearts emerge] fornication, murder, theft,
		4 *adultery*,
	10 11	The man who divorces his wife and marries another is guilty
	12	3 of *adultery* against her. . . . ¹² And if a woman divorces her husband and marries another she is guilty of
		3 *adultery* too.
	19	(Ex 20 14) You must not kill; You must not *commit adultery*;
Lk	16 18	Everyone who divorces his wife and marries another is guilty of *adultery*, and the man who marries a woman divorced by her husband *commits adultery*.
	18 11	5 I am not . . . *adulterous* like the rest of mankind,
	20	(Ex 20 14) You must not *commit adultery*; You must not kill;
Jn	8 3	The scribes and Pharisees brought a woman along [to Jesus]
		4 who had been caught *committing adultery*;
	4	Master, this woman has been caught in the very act of *committing adultery*;
Rm	2 22	you forbid *adultery*, yet you *commit adultery*;
	7 3	if [a woman] gives herself to another man while her hus-
		2 band is still alive, she is legally an *adulteress*; but after her husband is dead . . . she can marry someone else
		2 without becoming an *adulteress*.

Rm 13	9	All the commandments: You shall not *commit adultery*, . . . and so on, are summed up in this single command: You must love your neighbour as yourself.
1 Co 6	9	people who do wrong will not inherit the kingdom of God:
	5	. . . idolaters, *adulterers*,
Heb 13	4	Marriage is to be honoured by all, and marriages are to be
	5	kept undefiled, because fornicators and *adulterers* will come under God's judgement.
Jm 2	11	It was the same person who said (Ex 20 14), 'You must not *commit adultery*' and 'You must not kill'. Now if you commit murder, you do not have to *commit adultery* as well to become a breaker of the Law.
2 P 2	14	2 with their eyes always looking for *adultery*;

2: ADULTERY, ADULTEROUS (IN FIGURATIVE SENSES) – UNFAITHFUL

Mt 12	39	2 It is an evil and *unfaithful* generation
16	4	2 It is an evil and *unfaithful* generation
Mk 8	38	2 this *adulterous* and sinful generation
Jm 4	4	2 You [are as unfaithful as] *adulterous* [wives];
Rv 2	22	I am consigning [Jezebel] to bed, and all her partners in *adultery* to troubles that will test them severely.

3. DEBAUCHERY – INDECENCY – DISSIPATION

1: LICENTIOUSNESS, DEBAUCHERY – INDECENCY – SHAMELESS: *ASELGEIA*

aselgeia 10

Mk 7	22	[from men's hearts emerge . . . adultery,] avarice, . . . *indecency*,
Rm 13	13	Let us live decently . . .: no drunken orgies . . . or *licentiousness*,
2 Co 12	21	those who . . . have still not repented of the impurities, fornication and *debauchery* they committed.
Ga 5	19	When self-indulgence is at work the results are obvious: fornication, gross indecency and *sexual irresponsibility*;
Ep 4	19	they have abandoned themselves to *sexuality* and eagerly pursue a career of indecency of every kind.
1 P 4	3	You spent quite long enough in the past living the sort of life that pagans live, behaving *indecently*,
2 P 2	2	there will be many who copy [the] *shameful behaviour* [of false teachers]
	7	Lot, . . . a holy man who had been sickened by the *shameless* way these vile people behaved
	18	playing on their bodily desires with *debaucheries*.
Jude	4	turning the grace of our God into *immorality*,

2: DISSIPATION, LOOSE LIVING – DEBAUCHERY: *A-SŌTIA*

1 a-sōtia 3   2 a-sōtōs 1

Lk 15	13	the younger son . . . squandered his money on a life of
	2	*debauchery.*
Ep 5	18	Do not drug yourselves with wine, this is simply *dissipation.*
Tt 1	6	[an elder's] children must be believers and not . . . liable to be charged with ˹disorderly conduct (lit. *loose living*).
1 P 4	4	people cannot understand why you no longer hurry off with them to join this ˹flood which is rushing down to ruin (lit. reckless *dissipation*),

3: DEBAUCHERY, DISSIPATION: *KRAIPALĒ*

kraipalē 1

Lk 21	34	Watch yourselves, or your hearts will be coarsened with *debauchery* and drunkenness

4: SHAME, SHAMELESS – INDECENT – (BE) RUDE: *A-SCHĒMONEŌ*

*3 a-schēmōn   1   2 a-schēmosynē 2
1 a-schēmoneō 2*

Rm 1	27	2 men doing *shameless things* with men
1 Co 7	36	anyone who feels that it would ˹not be fair (lit. *not be behaving properly*) to his daughter to let her grow too old for marriage, . . . is free to do as he likes:
12 23	○	3 it is the *least honourable* parts of the body that we clothe with the greatest care.
13	5	[love] *is never rude*
Rv 16 15	○	Happy is the man who has . . . not taken off his clothes so
	2	that he does not . . . expose his *shame*.

INHERIT – HEIR – HERITAGE

6 *klēroō*	*1*		2 *klēro-nomos 15*	
4 *klēros*	*2/11*		7 *kata-klēro-nomeō 1*	
1 *klēro-nomeō*	*18*		5 *syn-klēro-nomos 4*	
3 *klēro-nomia*	*14*			

Mt 5	4		Happy the gentle: they shall *have* the earth *for* their *heritage*.
19	29		everyone who has left houses, brothers . . . for the sake of my name will . . . *inherit* eternal life.
21	38	< 2	This is the *heir*. Come on, let us kill him and take over his
		3	*inheritance.*
25	34		Come, you whom my Father has blessed, *take for* your *heritage* the kingdom
Mk 10	17		what must I do to *inherit* eternal life?
12	7	< 2/3	This is the *heir*. Come on, let us kill him, and the *inheritance* will be ours.
Lk 10	25		what must I do to *inherit* eternal life?
12	13	3	Master, tell my brother to give me a share of our *inheritance*.
18	18		what have I to do to *inherit* eternal life?
20	14	< 2/3	This is the *heir* . . . let us kill him so that the *inheritance* will be ours.
Ac 7	5		God did not give [Abraham] a single square foot of this
		3	land ˹to call his own (lit. as an *inheritance*),
13	19		When [God] had destroyed seven nations in Canaan, he
		7	˹put [our ancestors] in possession of their land (lit. *gave them their land as an inheritance*)
20	32	3	God . . . has power to . . . give you your *inheritance* among all the sanctified.
26	18		[I am sending you to the pagans] so that they may . . .
		4	receive . . . a ˹*share in the inheritance* of (or: place among) the sanctified.
Rm 4	13	2	The promise of *inheriting* the world was not made to Abraham and his descendants on account of any law but on
	14		account of the righteousness which consists in faith. [14] If
		2	the world is only to be *inherited* by those who submit to the Law, then faith is pointless
8	17	2/2	if we are children we are *heirs* as well: *heirs* of God and
	X	5	*coheirs with Christ*,
1 Co 6	9		people who do wrong will not *inherit* the kingdom of God:
	10		thieves, usurers . . . will never *inherit* the kingdom of God.
15	50		flesh and blood cannot *inherit* the kingdom of God: and the perishable cannot *inherit* what lasts for ever.
Ga 3	18	3	If you *inherit* something as a legal right, it does not come to you as the result of a promise,
	29		Merely by belonging to Christ you are the posterity of
		2	Abraham, the *heirs* he was promised.
4	1	2	an *heir* . . . is no different from a slave for as long as he remains a child.
	7	2	if God has made you son, then he has made you *heir*.
	30		(Gn 21 10) this slave-girl's son is not to *share the inheritance* with the son of the free woman
5	21		those who behave like this will not *inherit* the Kingdom of God.
Ep 1	11	6	it is in [Christ] that we were ˹*claimed as God's own* (or: *given our share in the heritage*) . . . [12] chosen to be, for his greater glory, the people who would put their hopes in Christ before he came.
	14	3	the pledge of our *inheritance* . . . brings freedom for those whom God has taken for his own,
	18		you can see . . . what rich glories [God] has promised the
		3	saints will *inherit*
3	6	5	pagans now *share the same inheritance* . . . they are parts of the same body,
5	5		nobody who actually indulges in fornication or impurity
		3	. . . can *inherit* anything of the kingdom of God.
Col 1	12		the Father . . . has made it possible for you to join the saints
		4	and with them to ˹*inherit* (lit. share the *inheritance* of) the light.
3	24	3	the Lord will repay you by making you his *heirs*.
Tt 3	7	2	[God] did this so that we should . . . become *heirs* looking forward to [inheriting] eternal life.
Heb 1	2 X		[God] has spoken to us through his Son, the Son that he has appointed to *inherit* everything
	4 X		the title which [the Son] has *inherited* is higher than [the angels'] own name.
	14		[the angels] are all spirits whose work is service, sent to help those who will *be the heirs of* salvation.
6	12		imitating those who have the faith and the perseverance to *inherit* the promises.
	17	2	God wanted to make the *heirs* to the promise thoroughly realise that his purpose was unalterable,
9	15		[Christ] brings a new covenant . . . so that the people who
		3	were called to an eternal *inheritance* may actually receive what was promised.
11	7	2	Noah . . . was able to ˹claim (lit. *inherit*) the righteousness which is the reward of faith.

Heb 11	8	Abraham obeyed the call to set out for a country that was
	9	3 the *inheritance* given to him . . . ⁹ . . . he arrived . . . in the Promised Land, and lived there . . . with Isaac
	5	and Jacob, who were *heirs with* him of the same promise.
12	17	when [Esau] wanted to ˹obtain (lit. *inherit*) the blessing afterwards, he was rejected
Jm 2	5	it was those who are poor according to the world that God
	2	chose, to be rich in faith and to be the *heirs* to the kingdom
1 P 1	4	3 [God has given us] the promise of an *inheritance* that can never be spoilt
3	7	husbands must always treat their wives with consideration
	5	. . . respecting a woman as one who . . . is *equally an heir* to the life of grace.
	9	pay back with a blessing. That is what you are called to do, so that you *inherit* a blessing yourself.
Rv 21	7	it is the rightful *inheritance* of the one who proves victorious; and I will be his God and he a son to me.

INSIDE – OUTSIDE

1. Inside, In: *en*
1: In, Into, Inside (a place)
2: Those who are inside (the community)
3: In, Inside, Within (a man, a thing)
4: Among
5: In (God), In (Jesus Christ), In (the Spirit)

2. Outside, Outer, Out: *exō*
1: Out, Outer – Outside (a place) – Foreign
2: Out (into darkness), Outside (the kingdom of heaven)
3: Those who are outside (the community)
4: Outside (a man, a thing) – Outward, Outer

1. INSIDE, IN: *EN*

6	*eis*	(1)	3 *esō* 8/9
1	*en*	(70)	7 *hoi esō* 1
4	*entos*	3	5 *esōteros* 2
		2	*esōthen* 12

1: IN, INTO, INSIDE (A PLACE)

Mt 26	58	Peter followed [Jesus] . . . and when he reached the high
	3	priest's palace, he went *in*
Mk 14	54	3 Peter had followed [Jesus] . . . right *into* the high priest's palace,
15	16	3 The soldiers led [Jesus] away to the ˹inner part (or: *inside*) of the palace,
Lk 11	7	2 the man answers *from inside* the house, '. . . my children and I are in bed.'
Jn 20	26	3 the disciples were *in* the house again
Ac 5	23	We found the gaol securely locked . . . but . . . no one
	3	*inside.*
16	24	5 [the gaoler] threw [Paul and Silas] into the *inner* prison
Heb 6	19 ●	we have an anchor for our soul, . . . reaching right ˹through
	5	*beyond* (lit. *to the inside of*) the veil

2: THOSE WHO ARE INSIDE (THE COMMUNITY)

1 Co 5	12	7 Of *those inside* you can surely be the judges. But of those who are outside, God is the judge.

3: IN, INSIDE, WITHIN (A MAN, A THING)

Mt 7	15	2 false prophets who . . . ˹underneath (lit. *inside*) are ravenous wolves.
23	25	You who clean the outside of cup and dish and leave the
	2	*inside* full of extortion and intemperance. ²⁶ Clean the
	4	*inside* of cup and dish first
	27	You who are like whitewashed tombs that look handsome
	2	on the outside, but *inside* are full of dead men's bones and every kind of corruption. ²⁸ In the same way you
	28	appear . . . from the outside like good honest men,
	2	but *inside* you are full of hypocrisy and lawlessness.
Mk 7	21	2 it is *from within*, from men's hearts, that evil intentions
	23	2 emerge: . . . ²³ All these evil things come *from within*
Lk 11	39	2 You clean the outside of cup and plate, while *inside* yourselves
	40	2 you are filled with . . . wickedness. ⁴⁰ Fools! Did not
	2	he who made the outside make the *inside* too?
17	21	4 the kingdom of God is ˹among (or: *within*) you.

Rm 7	22	3 In my *inmost* self I dearly love God's Law,
2 Co 4	16	though this outer man of ours may be falling into decay,
	3	the *inner* man is renewed day by day.
7	5	we found trouble on all sides: quarrels outside, misgivings
	2	*inside.*
Ep 3	16	may he give you the power through his Spirit for your
	3	˹hidden (lit. *inner*) self to grow strong,
Rv 4	8	Each of the four animals had . . . eyes all the way round
	2	as well as *inside*;
5	1	(Ezk 2 10) a scroll that had writing on back and ˹front
	2	(lit. *inside*)

4: AMONG

Lk 17	21	4 the kingdom of God is ˹among (or: within) you.
Rm 12	3	I want to urge each one *among* you not to exaggerate his real importance.
1 Co 14	25	declaring that God is *among* you indeed.

5: IN (GOD), IN (JESUS CHRIST), IN (THE SPIRIT)

Lk 22	20	This cup is the new covenant *in* my blood
	37	these words of scripture have to be fulfilled *in* me:
Jn 1	3	not one thing had its being but through him^v. All that
	4	came to be ⁴ had life *in* him (G of all that came to be. ⁴ *In* him was life)
	18	6 the only Son, who is ˹nearest to (or: *in*) the Father's heart,
3	12	so that it may be plainly seen that what he does is done *in* God.
5	26	the Father, who ˹is the source of life (lit. *has life in him*) has made the Son ˹the source of life (lit. *have life in him*);
10	38	the Father is *in* me and I am *in* the Father.
14	10	I am *in* the Father and the Father is *in* me?
	11	I am *in* the Father and the Father is *in* me;
	20	I am *in* my Father and you *in* me and I *in* you.
	30	the prince of this world . . . has no ˹power over me (lit. [foothold] *in* me),
15	2	Every branch *in* me that bears no fruit
16	33	so that you may find peace *in* me.
17	21	Father, may they be (^v one) *in* me, may they be . . . completely one
	23	With me in them and you *in* me, may they be . . . one
Ac 4	12	Of all the names . . . given to men, this is the only one ˹by (lit. *in*) which we can be saved.
17	28	it is *in* [God] that we live, and move, and exist,
Rm 5	9	˹Having died to make us righteous (lit. Since it is *in* his blood that we are made righteous),
1 Co 1	5	I thank [God] that you have been enriched *in* [Christ] in so many ways,
2 Co 1	19	˹with (lit. *in*) Christ [Jesus] it was always Yes, ²⁰ and however
	20	many the promises God made, the Yes to them all is *in* him.
5	21	so that *in* him we might become the goodness of God.
13	4	we are ˹weak, as he was (or: weak *in* him),
Ga 1	6	you have turned away from the one who called you *in* the grace of Christ and have decided to follow a different version of the Good News.
Ep 1	4	[God] chose us *in* Christ, . . . ⁶ to make us praise the glory
	6	of his grace, his free gift to us *in* the Beloved, ⁷ *in* whom,
	7	through his blood, we gain our freedom,
	9	the hidden plan he so kindly made *in* Christ from the beginning
	11	it is *in* him that we are claimed as God's own,
	13	you too, *in* him, . . . have been stamped with the seal of the Holy Spirit
2	15	destroying *in* his own person the hostility caused by the rules and decrees of the Law. This was to create one single New Man *in* himself out of the two of them . . . ¹⁶ . . . *In*
	16	his own person he killed the hostility.
	21	As every structure is aligned on him, all grow into one holy temple *in* the Lord;
	22	you too, *in* him, are being built into a house
3	9	the mystery . . . has been kept hidden *in* God,
	12	˹This is why (lit. *In* [Christ]) we are bold enough to approach God
4	30	The Holy Spirit of God ˹who has marked you (lit. *in* whom you have been marked) with his seal
Ph 3	9	I want only the perfection that comes through faith *in* Christ,
4	13	There is nothing I cannot master ˹with the help of (lit. *in*) the One who gives me strength.
Col 1	14	[the Son that he loves,] and *in* him, we gain our freedom,
	16	*in* him were created all things
	17	˹he holds all things (lit. *in* him all things are held) in unity.
	19	God wanted all perfection to be found *in* him
2	3	[until you really know God's secret, Christ,] *in* whom all the jewels of wisdom and knowledge are hidden.
	6	You must live your whole life ˹according to (lit. *in*) the Christ you have received . . . ⁷ you must be rooted *in* him

Col	2	9		*In* his body lives the fullness of divinity and in him you too
		10		find your own fulfilment, [10] *in* the one who is the head of every . . . Power.
		11		*In* him you have been circumcised,
		15	Δ	he got rid of the . . . Powers, and paraded them . . . ⌐behind (lit. leading them *in*) him in his triumphal procession.
	3	3		now the life you have is hidden with Christ *in* God.
1 Th	1	1		to the Church in Thessalonika which is *in* God the Father and the Lord Jesus Christ;
2 Th	1	1		to the Church in Thessalonika which is *in* God our Father and the Lord Jesus Christ;
1 P	1	2		[chosen] by the provident purpose of God the Father, ⌐to be (lit. *in* being) made holy by the Spirit,
	3	19	Δ	and, *in* the spirit, [Christ] went to preach to the spirits in prison.
1 Jn	1	5		God is light; there is no darkness *in* him at all.
	2	5		We can be sure that we are *in* God
	3	5		*in* him there is no sin;
	5	20		We are *in* the true God, we we are in his Son, Jesus Christ.
Jude		1		to those who are ⌐dear to (or: beloved *in*) God the Father

2. OUTSIDE, OUTER, OUT: *EXŌ*

4	ektos	(3)	5	exōteros	3
1	exō	(23)	2	exōthen	11 } 12
3	hoi exō	5	6	hoi exōthen	1

1: OUT, OUTER – OUTSIDE (A PLACE) – FOREIGN

Mt	12	46		his mother and his brothers . . . were standing *outside* and were anxious to have a word with him.
		47		(§ Your mother and your brothers are standing *outside* here.)
	26	69		Peter was sitting *outside* in the courtyard.
Mk	1	45		Jesus could no longer go openly into any town, but had to stay *outside* in places where nobody lived.
	3	31		His mother and brothers . . . , standing *outside*, sent in a message asking for him.
		32		Your mother and brothers and sisters are *outside* asking for you.
	11	4		They . . . found a colt tethered near a door *out* in the open street.
Lk	1	10		the whole congregation was *outside*, praying.
	8	20		Your mother and brothers are standing *outside* and want to see you.
Jn	11	43		Lazarus, here! Come *out*!
	18	16		Peter stayed *outside* the door.
	19	4		Pilate . . . said to them, 'Look I am going to bring him *out* to you.'
		13		Pilate had Jesus brought *out*,
	20	11		Mary stayed *outside* near the tomb, weeping.
Ac	5	34		Gamaliel . . . asked to have the men taken *outside* for a time.
	16	30		[the gaoler] escorted [Paul and Silas] *out*, saying, 'Sirs, what must I do to be saved?'
	26	11		I even pursued [the saints] into *foreign* cities.
Heb	13	11		The bodies of the animals whose blood is brought into the sanctuary by the high priest for the atonement of sin are burnt *outside* the camp, [12] and so Jesus too suffered
		12		*outside* the gate to sanctify the people with his own blood.
		13		[13] Let us go to him, then, *outside* the camp, and share his degradation.
Rv	11	2	2	but leave out the *outer* court and do not measure it,

2: OUT (INTO DARKNESS), OUTSIDE (THE KINGDOM OF HEAVEN)

Mt	8	12	5	the subjects of the kingdom will be turned *out* into the dark,
	22	13	5	Bind him hand and foot and throw him *out* into the dark,
	25	30	5	throw him *out* into the dark,
Lk	13	25		you may find yourself *outside* knocking on the door,
Rv	14	20	2	[the whole vintage of the earth was put into a huge winepress] *outside* the city, where it was trodden
	12	15		These others must stay *outside*: dogs, fortune-tellers, . . . and everyone of false speech

3: THOSE WHO ARE OUTSIDE (THE COMMUNITY)

Mk	4	11	3	to *those who are outside* everything comes in parables,
1 Co	5	12	3	It is not my business to pass judgement on *those outside*. Of
		13	3	those who are inside, you can surely be the judges. [13] But of *those who are outside*, God is the judge.
Col	4	5	3	Be tactful with *those who are* ⌐not Christians (lit. *outside*)
1 Th	4	12	3	so that you are seen to be respectable by *those outside* the Church,
1 Tm	3	7	6	It is also necessary that *people outside* the Church should speak well of him,

4: OUTSIDE (A MAN, A THING) – OUTWARD, OUTER

Mt	23	25	2	You who clean the *outside* of cup and dish
		26	4	Clean the inside of cup and dish first so that the *outside* may become clean as well.
		27	2	You who are like whitewashed tombs that look handsome on the *outside*,
		28	2	In the same way you appear to people from the *outside* like good honest men,
Mk	7	15	2	Nothing that goes into a man from *outside* can make him unclean; . . . [18] . . . whatever goes into a man *from outside* cannot make him unclean,
		18	2	
Lk	11	39	2	You clean the *outside* of cup and plate,
		40	2	Did not he who make the *outside* make the inside too?
1 Co	6	18	4	Keep away from fornication. All the other sins are committed *outside* the body;
2 Co	4	16	2	though this *outer* man of ours may be falling into decay,
	7	5	2	we found trouble on all sides: quarrels *outside*, misgivings inside.
	12	2	4	whether [this man was] still in the body or *out* of the body, I do not know;
1 P	3	3	2	[Women,] Do not dress up ⌐for show (lit. *outwardly*):

INTERPRET – EXPLAIN

1. Interpret – Explain – Translate: *hermēneuō*	2. Interpret *syn-krinō*
1: Interpret, Interpretation – Explain, Difficult to explain	3. Interpretation – Explain, Settle: *epi-luō*
2: (Be) Translated, Interpreted (as) – Mean	4. Explain – Report, Tell: *dia-sapheō*
	5. Explain: *phrazō*

1. INTERPRET – EXPLAIN – TRANSLATE: *HERMĒNEUŌ*

4	hermēneia	2	5	di-(h)ermēneutēs	1
3	hermēneuō	3	6	dys-(h)ermēneutos	1
2	di-(h)ermēneuō	6	1	meth-ermēneuō	8

1: INTERPRET, INTERPRETATION – EXPLAIN, DIFFICULT TO EXPLAIN

Lk	24	27	X	2	he *explained* to [the two disciples] the passages throughout the scriptures that were about himself.
1 Co	12	10		4	another [is given] the gift of tongues and another the *ability to interpret* them.
		30		2	Do all speak strange languages, and all *interpret* them?
	14	5		2	unless . . . [the man with the gift of tongues] *offers an interpretation* so that the church may get some benefit.
		13		2	anybody who has the gift of tongues must pray for the power of *interpreting* them.
		26			At all your meetings, let everyone be ready . . . to use his gift of tongues or to give an *interpretation*; . . . [27] If there are people present with the gift of tongues, . . . there must
		27		4	
		28		2/5	be someone to *interpret*. [28] If there is no *interpreter* present, they must keep quiet
Heb	5	11		6	we have many things to say, and they are *difficult to explain*

2: (BE) TRANSLATED, INTERPRETED (AS) – MEAN

Mt	1	23		Immanuel, a name which *translated* means 'God-is-with-us'.
Mk	5	41		'Talitha, kum!' which *translated* means 'Little girl, I tell you to get up'.
	15	22		Golgotha, which *translated* means the place of the skull.
		34		'Eloi, Eloi, lama sabachthani?' which *translated* means 'My God, my God, why have you deserted me?'
Jn	1	38		Rabbi, – which *means* Teacher –
		41		the Messiah – which *translated* means the Christ –
		42	3	Cephas – *meaning* Rock.
	9	7	3	Siloam (a name that *translated* means 'sent').
Ac	4	36		Barnabas (which *translated* means 'son of encouragement').
	9	36	2	Tabitha, or Dorcas when *translated* into Greek,
	13	8		Elymas Magos – as he was called when *translated* into Greek –
Heb	7	2	3	*By* the *interpretation* of his name, [Melchizedek] is, first. 'king of righteousness'

2. INTERPRET: *SYN-KRINŌ*

syn-krinō 1/3

1 Co	2	13		we ⌐teach (lit. *interpret*) spiritual things ⌐spiritually (or: to those who have the spirit).

3. INTERPRETATION – EXPLAIN, SETTLE: *EPI-LUŌ*

1 *epi-luō* 2   2 *epi-lysis* 1

Mk 4 34 X he *explained* everything to his disciples when they were alone.
Ac 19 39 if you want to ask any more questions ⌐you must raise them (lit. *explain* them; or: you may *have* them *settled*) in the regular assembly.
2 P 1 20 2 the *interpretation* of scriptural prophecy is never a matter for the individual.

4. EXPLAIN – REPORT, TELL: *DIA-SAPHEŌ*

dia-sapheō 2

Mt 13 36 X *Explain* the parable about the darnel in the field to us.
18 31 His fellow servants . . . went to their master and *reported* the whole affair to him.

5. EXPLAIN: *PIIRAZŌ*

phrazō 1

Mt 15 15 X *Explain* the parable [on clean and unclean] for us.

IRON

2 *sidēros* 1   1 *sidēreos* 5

Ac 12 10 [Peter and the angel] reached the *iron* gate leading to the city.
Rv 2 27 (Ps 2 9) I will give [those who prove victorious] the authority over the pagans . . , to rule them with an *iron* sceptre
9 9 [The locusts] had body-armour like *iron* breastplates,
12 5 (Ps 2 9) the son who was to rule all nations with an *iron* sceptre,
18 12 2 [when there is nobody left in Babylon to buy] pieces in ivory, . . . or *iron* or marble;
19 15 (Ps 2 9) [The Word of God] is the one who will rule [the pagans] with an *iron* sceptre,

---

ISLAND

1: Island
2: Cyprus, Cypriot
3: Crete, Cretan

4: Malta
5: Islands in the Aegean

2 *nēsion* 1   1 *nēsos* 9

1: ISLAND

Rv 6 14 1 all the mountains and *islands* were shaken from their places.
16 20 1 every *island* vanished and the mountains disappeared;

2: CYPRUS, CYPRIOT

Cyprus 5	Paphos 2
Cypriot 3	Salamis 1

Ac 4 36 There was a Levite of *Cypriot* origin . . . whom the apostles surnamed Barnabas
11 19 Those who had escaped . . . travelled as far as Phoenicia and *Cyprus* and Antioch, . . . 20 Some of them, . . . who
20 came *from Cyprus* and Cyrene, went preaching to the Greeks,
13 4 [Barnabas and Paul] went down to Seleucia and from there
5 sailed to *Cyprus*. 5 They landed at *Salamis* and proclaimed the word of God . . . 6 They travelled the whole length of
6 1 the *island*, and at *Paphos* they came in contact with a Jewish magician
13 Paul and his friends went by sea from *Paphos* to Perga
15 39 Barnabas sailed off with Mark to *Cyprus*.
21 3 After sighting *Cyprus* . . . we sailed to Syria

Ac 21 16 to the house of a *Cypriot* with whom we were to lodge; he was called Mnason and had been one of the earliest disciples.
27 4 From [Sidon] we . . . sailed under the lee of *Cyprus*,

3: CRETE, CRETAN

Cauda ⎫ 1	Fair Havens 1	3 polis 1/164
Clauda ⎭	(= kaloi limenes)	
Crete 5	Lasea 1	
Cretan 2	Phoenix 1	
	[Cape] Salmone 1	

Ac 2 11 Jews and proselytes alike – *Cretans* and Arabs; we hear them preaching in our own language about the marvels of God.
27 7 we sailed under the lee of *Crete* off *Cape Salmone* 8 . . .
8 3 until we came to a place called *Fair Havens*, near the *town* of *Lasea*.
12 the majority were for putting out from there in the hope of wintering at *Phoenix* – a harbour in *Crete*,
13 they weighed anchor and began to sail past *Crete*, close inshore.
16 2 We ran under the lee of a *small island* called ⌐*Cauda* (G *Clauda*)
21 if you had listened to me and not put out from *Crete*,
Tt 1 5 I left you behind in *Crete* . . . to get everything organised there
12 *Cretans* were never anything but liars, dangerous animals and lazy:

4: MALTA

Malta 1   *Publius** 2

Ac 27 26 1 we are to be stranded on some *island*.
28 1 Once we had come safely through, we discovered that the
1 *island* was called *Malta*.
7 1 there were estates belonging to the prefect of the *island*, whose name was Publius*. He received us and entertained
8 us hospitably . . . 8 . . . Publius'* father was in bed,
9 1 . . . 9 . . . the other sick people on the *island* came as well
11 1 we set sail in a ship that had wintered in the *island*;

5: ISLANDS IN THE AEGEAN

Chios 1	Rhodes 1	Mitylene 1
Cos 1	Samos 1	
Patmos 1	Samothrace 1	

Ac 16 11 Sailing from Troas we made a straight run for *Samothrace*;
20 14 When he rejoined us at Assos we . . . went on to *Mitylene*.
15 The next day we . . . arrived opposite *Chios*. The second day we touched at *Samos*
21 1 we . . . arrived at *Cos*; the next day we reached *Rhodes*, and from there went on to Patara.
Rv 1 9 1 I [John] was on the *island* of *Patmos*

ISRAEL

Israel 68   *Israelite* ⎫ 9
               of Israel ⎭

Mt 2 6 (Mi 5 1) And you, Bethlehem, . . . out of you will come a leader who will shepherd my people *Israel*.
20 take the child and his mother . . . and go back to the land of *Israel*,
21 Joseph got up and . . . went back to the land of *Israel*.
8 10 nowhere in *Israel* have I found faith like this.
9 33 Nothing like this has ever been seen in *Israel*
10 6 go rather to the lost sheep of the House of *Israel*.
23 you will not have gone the round of the towns of *Israel* before the Son of Man comes.
15 24 I was sent only to the lost sheep of the House of *Israel*.
31 and they praised the God of *Israel*.
19 28 you will yourselves sit on twelve thrones to judge the twelve tribes of *Israel*.
27 9 (Zc 11 13) they took the thirty silver pieces, the sum at which the precious One was priced by children of *Israel*,
42 He is the king of *Israel*; let him come down from the cross
Mk 12 29 (Dt 6 4f) Listen, *Israel*, the Lord our God is the one Lord,

Mk 15	32	Let the Christ, the king of *Israel*, come down from the cross
Lk 1	16	[John] will bring back many of the sons of *Israel* to the Lord their God.
	54	[The Lord] has come to the help of *Israel* his servant,
	68	Blessed be the Lord, the God of *Israel*, for he has visited his people,
	80	[John] lived out in the wilderness until the day he appeared openly to *Israel*.
2	25	[Simeon] looked forward to *Israel*'s comforting
	32	[my eyes have seen the salvation which you have prepared,] the glory of your people *Israel*.
	34	this child . . . is destined for the fall and for the rising of many in *Israel*,
4	25	There were many widows in *Israel* . . . in Elijah's day,
	27	And in the prophet Elisha's time there were many lepers in *Israel*,
7	9	I tell you, not even in *Israel* have I found faith like this.
22	30	you will sit on thrones to judge the twelve tribes of *Israel*.
24	21	Our own hope had been that [Jesus] would be the one to set *Israel* free
Jn 1	31	it was to reveal [Christ] to *Israel* that I came baptising with water.
	47	When Jesus saw Nathanael coming he said of him, 'There is an *Israelite* who deserves the name, incapable of deceit.'
	49	Rabbi, you are the Son of God, you are the King of *Israel*.
3	10	[Jesus to Nicodemus:] You, a teacher in *Israel*, and you do not know these things!
12	13	Blessings on the King of *Israel*, who comes in the name of the Lord.
Ac 1	6	Are you going to restore the kingdom to *Israel*?
2	22	Men of *Israel*, listen to what I am going to say:
	36	the whole House of *Israel* can be certain that God has made this Jesus . . . Christ.
3	12	Peter . . . addressed them, 'Men *of Israel*, why are you so surprised at this?'
4	10	I am glad to tell you all, and would indeed be glad to tell the whole people of *Israel*,
	27	Herod and Pontius Pilate made an alliance with the pagan nations and the people of *Israel*, against your holy servant Jesus
5	21	the high priest . . . convened the Sanhedrin – this was the full Senate of *Israel* –
	31	God has now raised [Jesus] up . . . , to give repentance . . . through him to *Israel*.
	35	Men *of Israel*, be careful how you deal with these people.
7	23	(Ex 2 11) [Moses] decided to visit his countrymen, the sons of *Israel*.
	37	Moses . . . told the sons of *Israel* (Dt 18 15): God will raise up a prophet like myself for you
	42	(Am 5 25) Did you bring me victims and sacrifices . . . , you House of *Israel*?
9	15	to bring my name before pagans and . . . the people of *Israel*;

Ac 10	36	God sent his word to the people of *Israel*,
13	16	Men *of Israel*, and fearers of God, listen! [17] The God of our nation *Israel* chose our ancestors,
	17	
	23	God has raised up for *Israel* one of David's descendants, Jesus, as saviour,
	24	John . . . proclaimed a baptism of repentance for the whole people of *Israel*.
21	28	Men *of Israel*, help! This is the man who preaches . . . against the Law
28	20	it is on account of the hope of *Israel* that I wear this chain.
Rm 9	4	my brothers *of Israel* . . . were given . . . the covenants
	5	. . . [5] and from their flesh and blood came Christ
	6 ○	Not all those who descend from *Israel* [= Jacob] are *Israel* [= the people];
	27	Referring to *Israel* Isaiah had this to say (Is 10 22): Though *Israel* should have as many descendants as there are grains of sand on the seashore, only a remnant will be saved,
	31	while *Israel*, looking for a righteousness derived from law failed to do what the law required.
10	19	is it possible that *Israel* did not understand?
	21	referring to *Israel* [Isaiah] goes on (Is 65 2): Each day I stretched out my hand to a . . . rebellious people.
11	1	I, an *Israelite*, descended from Abraham
	2	(cf. 1 K 19 10) how [Elijah] complained to God about *Israel*'s behaviour?
	7	It was not *Israel* as a whole that found what it was seeking,
	25	One section of *Israel* has become blind, but this will last only until the whole pagan world has entered, [26] and then . . . the rest of *Israel* will be saved as well. As scripture says (cf. Is 59 20): The liberator will come from Zion,
	26	
1 Co 10	18	Look at the other *Israel*, the race,
2 Co 3	7	(cf. Ex 34 30) the *Israelites* could not bear looking at the face of Moses,
	13	(cf. Ex 34 33–35) Moses . . . put a veil over his face so that the *Israelites* would not notice the ending of what had to fade.
11	22	Hebrews, are they? So am I. *Israelites*? So am I.
Ga 6	16	Peace and mercy to all who follow this rule, who form the *Israel* of God.
Ep 2	12	you had no Christ and were excluded from membership of *Israel*,
Ph 3	5	I was born of the race of *Israel*
Heb 8	8	(Jr 31 31) I will establish a new covenant with the House of *Israel*
	10	(Jr 31 33) this is the covenant I will make with the House of *Israel*
11	22	(cf. Gn 50 24–25) Joseph recalled the Exodus of the *Israelites*
Rv 2	14	(cf. Nb 31 16; 25 1–2) Balaam, who taught Balak to set a trap for the *Israelites*
7	4	a hundred and forty-four thousand [were sealed as servants of God], out of all the tribes of *Israel*.
21	12	[Jerusalem] had twelve gates; . . . and over the gates were written the names of the twelve tribes of *Israel*;

JERUSALEM

1. the City and People of Jerusalem	2. the City and Citizens of the heavenly Jerusalem		
Jerusalem 140	1	*polis*	44/164
people of Jerusalem	2	*politeuma*	1
(=*Hierosolymitai*) 2 (Mk 1; Jn 7)	3	*sym-politēs*	1
Bethzatha 1			
Bethesda 1			
Siloam 3			
Z *Zion* 7			

1. THE CITY AND PEOPLE OF JERUSALEM

Mt 2 1   some wise men came to *Jerusalem* from the east.
   3   King Herod . . . was perturbed, and so was the whole of *Jerusalem*.
3 5   Then *Jerusalem* and all Judaea . . . made their way to [John],
4 5 1 The devil then took [Jesus] to the holy *city* and made him stand on the parapet of the Temple.
   25   Large crowds . . . from Galilee, the Decapolis, *Jerusalem*,
5 35 1 [do not swear] by *Jerusalem*, since that is the *city* of the great king.
15 1   Pharisees and scribes from *Jerusalem* then came to Jesus
16 21   Jesus . . . was destined to go to *Jerusalem* and suffer grievously
20 17   Jesus was going up to *Jerusalem*, and on the way he took the twelve to one side
   18   Now we are going up to *Jerusalem*, and the Son of Man is about to be handed over
21 1   When they were near *Jerusalem* and had come in sight of Bethphage
   5 Z (cf. Zc 9 9) Say to the daughter of *Zion*: Look, your king comes to you;
   10 1 when he entered *Jerusalem*, the whole *city* was in turmoil.
   17 1 he . . . went out of the *city* to Bethany
   18 1 returning to the *city* in the early morning, he felt hungry.
23 37   *Jerusalem, Jerusalem*, you that kill the prophets
26 18 1 Go to so-and-so in the *city* . . . and say to him, . . . It is at your house that I am keeping Passover
27 53   [the bodies of holy men came out of the tombs,] entered
     1 the Holy *City* and appeared to a number of people.
28 11 1 some of the guard went off into the *city* to tell the chief priests all that had happened.
Mk 1 5   All Judaea and all the *people of Jerusalem* made their way to [John],
3 8   [From Judaea,] *Jerusalem*, . . . great numbers . . . came to [Jesus].
   22   The scribes who had come down from *Jerusalem*
7 1   The Pharisees and some of the scribes who had come from *Jerusalem* gathered round [Jesus].
10 32   They were on the road, going up to *Jerusalem*; Jesus was walking on ahead of them;
   33   Now we are going up to *Jerusalem*, and the Son of Man is about to be handed over
11 1   When they were approaching *Jerusalem*, in sight of Bethphage
   11   He entered *Jerusalem* and went into the Temple.
   15   they reached *Jerusalem* and he went into the Temple
   19 1 when evening came he went out of the *city*.
   27   They came to *Jerusalem* again, and as Jesus was walking in the Temple,
14 13 1 Go into the *city* and you will meet a man carrying a pitcher
   16 1 The disciples . . . went to the *city* and . . . prepared the Passover.
15 41   many other women . . . who had come up to *Jerusalem* with him.
Lk 2 22   [Mary and Joseph] took [Jesus] up to *Jerusalem* to present him to the Lord
   25   in *Jerusalem* there was a man named Simeon.
   38   all who looked forward to the deliverance of *Jerusalem*.
   41   Every year [Jesus's] parents used to go to *Jerusalem*
   43   the boy Jesus stayed behind in *Jerusalem* without his parents knowing it.
   45   they went back to *Jerusalem* looking for him everywhere.
4 9   [the devil] led [Jesus] to *Jerusalem* and made him stand on the parapet of the Temple.

Lk 5 17   Pharisees and doctors of the Law who had come from every village in Galilee, from Judaea and from *Jerusalem*
6 17   a great crowd of people from all parts of Judaea and from *Jerusalem*
9 31   [Moses and Elijah] were speaking of his passing which he was to accomplish in *Jerusalem*.
   51   [Jesus] resolutely took the road for *Jerusalem*
   53   the people would not receive him because he was making for *Jerusalem*.
10 30   A man was once on his way down from *Jerusalem* to Jericho and fell into the hands of brigands;
13 4   those eighteen on whom the tower at *Siloam* fell and killed them. Do you suppose that they were more guilty than all the other people living in *Jerusalem*?
   22   Through towns and villages [Jesus] went teaching, making his way to *Jerusalem*.
   33   it would not be right for a prophet to die outside *Jerusalem*.
   34   [34] *Jerusalem, Jerusalem*, you that kill the prophets
17 11   on the way to *Jerusalem* he travelled along the border between Samaria and Galilee.
18 31   Now we are going up to *Jerusalem*, and everything that is written by the prophets . . . is to come true.
19 11   he went on to tell a parable, because he was near *Jerusalem*
   28   [Jesus] went on ahead, going up to *Jerusalem*.
   41 1 As he . . . came in sight of the *city* he shed tears over it
21 20   When you see *Jerusalem* surrounded by armies,
   24   *Jerusalem* will be trampled down by the pagans
22 10 1 as you go into the *city* you will meet a man carrying a pitcher
23 7   Herod . . . was also in *Jerusalem* at that time.
   19   [Barabbas] had been thrown into prison for causing a riot
     1 in the *city*
   28   Daughters of *Jerusalem*, do not weep for me;
24 13   a village called Emmaus, seven miles from *Jerusalem*,
   18   Cleopas answered him, You must be the only person staying in *Jerusalem* who does not know the things that have been happening there these last few days.
   33   They . . . returned to *Jerusalem*. There they found the Eleven assembled
   47   repentance . . . would be preached to all the nations, beginning from *Jerusalem*.
   49 1 Stay in the *city* . . . until you are clothed with the power from on high.
   52   [the apostles] went back to *Jerusalem* full of joy;
Jn 1 19   the Jews sent priests and Levites from *Jerusalem* to ask [John], 'Who are you?'
2 13   Just before the Jewish Passover Jesus went up to *Jerusalem*,
   23   During his stay in *Jerusalem* for the Passover many believed in his name
4 20   you say that *Jerusalem* is the place where one ought to worship.' [21] Jesus said: '. . . the hour is coming when you
   21   will worship the Father neither on this mountain [Gerizim] nor in *Jerusalem*.'
   45   the Galileans . . . [had] seen all that he had done at *Jerusalem*
5 1   there was a Jewish festival, and Jesus went up to *Jerusalem*.
   2   [2] Now at the Sheep Pool in *Jerusalem* there is a building, called *Bethzatha* (ᵛ*Bethesda*)
7 25   some of the *people of Jerusalem* were saying, 'Isn't this the man they want to kill?'
9 7   Go and wash in the Pool of *Siloam* (a name that means 'sent').
   11   Jesus . . . said to me, 'Go and wash at *Siloam*;'
10 22   the feast of the Dedication was being celebrated in *Jerusalem*
11 18   Bethany is only about two miles from *Jerusalem*,
   55   many of the country people who had gone up to *Jerusalem* to purify themselves
12 12   the crowds . . . heard that Jesus was on his way to *Jerusalem*.
   15 Z (cf. Zc 9 9) Do not be afraid, daughter of *Zion*; see, your king is coming,
19 20   the place where Jesus was crucified was not far from the
     1 *city*,
Ac 1 4   [Jesus] had told [the apostles] not to leave *Jerusalem*,
   8   you will be my witnesses not only in *Jerusalem* but throughout Judaea and Samaria, and indeed to the ends of the earth.
   12   from the Mount of Olives . . . [the apostles] went back to *Jerusalem*.
   19   Everybody in *Jerusalem* heard about [Judas's death]
2 5   there were devout men living in *Jerusalem* from every nation
   14   Men of Judaea, and all you who live in *Jerusalem*,
4 5   the rulers, elders and scribes had a meeting in *Jerusalem*
   16   It is obvious to everybody in *Jerusalem* that a miracle has been worked through them in public,

Ac	4 27	1	in this very *city* Herod and Pontius Pilate made an alliance . . . against your holy servant Jesus
	5 16		People even came crowding in from the towns round about *Jerusalem*,
	28		You have filled *Jerusalem* with your teaching,
	6 7		the number of disciples in *Jerusalem* was greatly increased,
	7 58	1	[they all rushed at Stephen,] sent him out of the *city* and stoned him.
	8 1		a bitter persecution started against the church in *Jerusalem*,
	14		the apostles in *Jerusalem* . . . sent Peter and John to [the Samaritans],
	25		they went back to *Jerusalem*, preaching the Good News to a number of Samaritan villages.
	26		set out at noon along the road that goes from *Jerusalem* down to Gaza,
	27		an Ethiopian had been on pilgrimage to *Jerusalem*;
	9 2		letters . . . that would authorise [Saul] to arrest and take to *Jerusalem* any followers of the Way,
	13		all the harm that [this man] has been doing to your saints in *Jerusalem*.
	21		Surely . . . this is the man who organised the attack in *Jerusalem* against the people who invoke this name,
	26		When [Saul] got to *Jerusalem* he tried to join the disciples.
	28		Saul now started to go round with them in *Jerusalem*,
	10 39		everything [Jesus] did throughout . . . Judaea and in *Jerusalem* itself:
	11 2		when Peter came up to *Jerusalem* the Jews criticised him
	22		The church in *Jerusalem* heard about this
	27		some prophets came down to Antioch from *Jerusalem*,
	12 10	1	[Peter and the angel] reached the iron gate leading to the *city*.
	25		Barnabas and Saul . . . came back from *Jerusalem*,
	13 13		John left [Paul and his friends] to go back to *Jerusalem*.
	27		the people of *Jerusalem* and their rulers . . . [fulfilled] the prophecies
	31		[Jesus] appeared to those who had accompanied him from Galilee to *Jerusalem*:
	15 2		It was arranged that Paul and Barnabas . . . should go up to *Jerusalem* and discuss the problem with the apostles
	4		When [Paul and Barnabas] arrived in *Jerusalem* they were welcomed by the church
	16 4		[Paul and Silas] passed on the decisions reached by the apostles and elders in *Jerusalem*,
	18 21		when [Paul] left he said, '. . . (ᵛ it is absolutely imperative that I keep the next feast at *Jerusalem*).'
	19 21		Paul made up his mind to go back to *Jerusalem* through Macedonia and Achaia.
	20 16		Paul . . . was anxious to be in *Jerusalem*, if possible, for the day of Pentecost.
	22		I am on my way to *Jerusalem*, but have no idea what will happen to me there,
	21 4		[the disciples] kept telling Paul not to go on to *Jerusalem*,
	11		[Paul] will be bound like this by the Jews in *Jerusalem* . . .
	12		¹². . . we . . . implored Paul not to go on to *Jerusalem*.
	13		¹³. . . Paul replied '. . . I am ready . . . to die in *Jerusalem*'
	15		we . . . went on up to *Jerusalem*.
	17		On our arrival in *Jerusalem* the brothers gave us a very warm welcome.
	29	1	They had . . . seen Trophimus the Ephesian in the *city* with [Paul],
	30	1	This roused the whole *city*;
	31		there was rioting all over *Jerusalem*.
	22 3	1	I . . . was born at Tarsus in Cilicia. I was brought up here in this *city*,
	5		bringing prisoners back from [Damascus] to *Jerusalem* for punishment.
	17		after I had got back to *Jerusalem* . . . I fell into a trance
	18		¹⁸. . . 'Hurry,' [the Lord] said, 'leave *Jerusalem* at once;
	23 11		You have borne witness for me in *Jerusalem*,
	24 11		I went up to *Jerusalem* on pilgrimage,
	12	1	it is not true that they ever found me arguing . . . in the Temple, in the synagogues, or about the *town*;
	25 1		Festus went up to *Jerusalem* from Caesarea.
	3		[The chief priests asked Festus] to have [Paul] transferred to *Jerusalem*.
	7		the Jews who had come down from *Jerusalem* surrounded [Paul],
	9		Are you willing to go up to *Jerusalem* and be tried . . . there?
	15		while [Festus] was in *Jerusalem* the chief priests and elders of the Jews laid information against [Paul],
	20		I asked him if he would be willing to go to *Jerusalem* to be tried
	24		the man about whom the whole Jewish community has petitioned me, both in *Jerusalem* and here,
	26 4		a life spent from the beginning among my own people and in *Jerusalem*,
	10		I [opposed the name of Jesus] in *Jerusalem*;
	20		I started preaching . . . to the people of . . . *Jerusalem*
	28 17		I was arrested in *Jerusalem* and handed over to the Romans.
Rm	9 33 Z		(Is 28 16) See how I lay in *Zion* a stone to stumble over,

	11 26 Z		(cf. Is 59 20) The liberator will come from *Zion*,
	15 19		all the way along, from *Jerusalem* to Illyricum, I have preached Christ's Good News
	25		I must take a present of money to the saints in *Jerusalem*,
	26		a generous contribution to the poor among the saints at *Jerusalem*.
	31		Pray that . . . the aid I carry to *Jerusalem* may be accepted by the saints.
1 Co	16 3		I will send your offering to *Jerusalem*
Ga	1 17		nor did I go up to *Jerusalem* to see those who were already apostles before me, . . . ¹⁸ . . . after three years I went up
	18		to *Jerusalem*
	2 1		It was not till fourteen years had passed that I went up to *Jerusalem* again.
	4 25		[Hagar] corresponds to the present *Jerusalem* that is a slave like her children.
1 P	2 6 Z		(Is 28 16) See how I lay in *Zion* a precious cornerstone
Rv	11 8 △	1	Their corpses will lie in the main street of the Great *City* . . . in which their Lord was crucified.
	13 △	1	a tenth of the *city* collapsed;

2. THE CITY AND CITIZENS OF THE HEAVENLY JERUSALEM

Ga	4 26		The *Jerusalem* above, however, is free and is our mother,
Ep	2 19 △	3	you are ᶠ*citizens like* (or: *fellow-citizens* with) all the saints,
Ph	3 20 ?	2	For us, our ᶠ*homeland* is in (lit. *citizenship* is that of) heaven,
Heb	11 10	1	[Abraham] looked forward to a *city* founded, designed and built by God.
	16		in fact they were longing for a better homeland
		1	. . . God . . . has founded the *city* for them.
	12 22 Z	1	what you have come to is Mount *Zion* and the *city* of the living God, the heavenly *Jerusalem*
	13 14	1	there is no eternal *city* for us in this life but we look for one in the life to come.
Rv	3 12	1	I will inscribe on [the victors] the name of . . . the *city* of my God, the new *Jerusalem*
	11 2	1	pagans . . . will trample on the holy *city* for forty-two months.
	14 1 Z	1	I saw Mount *Zion*, and standing on it a Lamb
	20	1	[in the winepress of God's anger] outside the *city* . . . [the whole vintage of the earth] was trodden
	20 9	1	[Satan's armies will besiege] the *city* that God loves.
	21 2	1	I saw the holy *city*, and the new *Jerusalem*, coming down from God
	10	1	*Jerusalem*, the holy *city*, coming down from God out of heaven,
	14	1	the *city* walls stood on twelve foundation stones,
	15	1	The angel . . . was carrying a golden measuring rod to measure the *city*
	16	1	the *city* is perfectly square, the length the same as its breadth.
		1	He measured the *city* with his rod
	18	1	the *city* [was] of pure gold, like polished glass. ¹⁹ The
	19	1	foundations of the *city* wall were faced with all kinds of precious stone
	21	1	the main street of the *city* was pure gold, transparent as glass.
	23	1	the *city* . . . was lit by the radiant glory of God
	22 14	1	[those who have washed their robes clean can come] into the *city*
	19	1	God will cut off his share of the tree of life and of the holy *city*,

JESUS CHRIST

1. Jesus – Christ, Christian – Antichrist	3: Christian
1: Who is Christ? and Who Christ is	4: (False) Christs, (False) Messiahs – Antichrist
2: Jesus Christ	2. He = Christ

1. JESUS – CHRIST, CHRISTIAN – ANTICHRIST

3	*christianos*	3	*Iēsous (Jesus)*	655/923
1	*christos*	540	*Messias (Messiah)*	2
2	*anti-christos*	5		
4	(*pseudo-*)*christos*	6		

For Jesus said *see* SAY – TELL – SPEAK 1.3:, 2.3:, 3.3:

1: WHO IS CHRIST? and WHO CHRIST IS

J = Jesus   M = Messiah

Mt 1 16 J of [Mary] was born *Jesus* who is called *Christ*.
2 1 J After *Jesus* had been born at Bethlehem . . .⁴ [Herod] . . .
4 enquired . . . where the *Christ* was to be born.
11 2 John in his prison had heard what *Christ* was doing and he sent his disciples to ask him,³ 'Are you the one who is to come . . ?'
16 13 J *Jesus* . . . put this question to his disciples, 'Who do people say the Son of Man is?'¹⁴ 'Some say . . . Elijah, and others Jeremiah or one of the prophets.'¹⁶ . . . Simon Peter spoke up, 'You are the *Christ*, . . . the Son of the living God.'
20 [Jesus] gave the disciples strict orders not to tell anyone that he was the *Christ*.
22 41 J *Jesus* put . . . this question [to the Pharisees],⁴² 'What is
42 your opinion about the *Christ*?'
26 63 J *Jesus* was silent. And the high priest said to him, '. . . tell us if you are the *Christ*, the Son of God.'
68 Play the prophet, *Christ*! Who hit you then?
27 17 Which do you want me to release for you: Barabbas, or *Jesus* who is called *Christ*?
J
22 J what am I to do with *Jesus* who is called *Christ*?
Mk 8 27 J *Jesus* . . . put this question to his disciples, 'Who do people say I am?'²⁸ '. . . John the Baptist,' they said, '. . . Elijah . . . one of the prophets.'²⁹ . . . Peter . . . said
29 '. . . You are the *Christ*.'
12 35 J while teaching in the Temple, *Jesus* said. 'How can the scribes maintain that the *Christ* is the son of David?'
14 61 J 'Are you the *Christ*, . . . the Son of the Blessed One?'
62 ⁶²'I am,' said *Jesus*
15 32 Let the *Christ*, the king of Israel, come down from the cross
Lk 2 11 Today . . . a saviour has been born to you; he is *Christ* the Lord.
26 [Simeon] would not see death until he had set eyes on the *Christ* of the Lord.
3 15 the people . . . were beginning to think that John might be the *Christ*,¹⁶ so John declared '. . . someone is coming . . . more powerful than I am,'
4 41 [devils] knew that [Jesus] was the *Christ*.
9 20 'who do you say I am?' '. . . The *Christ* of God,' [Peter] said.
20 41 [Jesus] then said to [the scribes], 'How can people maintain that the *Christ* is son of David?'
22 67 [the Sanhedrin] said to [Jesus], 'If you are the *Christ*, tell us.' 'If I tell you,' he replied, 'you will not believe me,'
23 2 We found this man . . . claiming to be *Christ*, a king,
35 let him save himself if he is the *Christ* of God, the Chosen One
39 One of the criminals hanging there abused him. 'Are you not the *Christ*?'
24 19 J *Jesus* of Nazareth . . . who proved he was a great prophet . . .²¹ Our own hope had been that he would be the one to set Israel free.
26 [Jesus to the disciples of Emmaus:] 'Was it not ordained that the *Christ* should suffer . . .?'
46 [Jesus to the apostles:] 'So you see how it is written that the *Christ* would suffer . . .'
Jn 1 20 [John] declared '. . , I am not the *Christ*.'
25 'Why are you baptising if you are not the *Christ*, and not Elijah, and not the prophet?'²⁶ John replied, '. . . there stands one among you . . .'
41 M [Andrew to Simon:] 'We have found the *Messiah*' – which
42 J means the *Christ* –⁴² and he took Simon to *Jesus*. . . .
45 ⁴⁵ Philip found Nathanael and said to him, 'We have found the one Moses wrote about in the Law, the one about whom the prophets wrote: he is *Jesus* son of Joseph, from Nazareth.'
J
3 28 [John] said: 'I myself am not the *Christ*; I am the one who has been sent in front of him.'
4 25 M [The Samaritan woman said to Jesus:] 'I know that *Messiah*
26 J – that is, *Christ* – 'is coming;' . . .²⁶ 'I . . .' said *Jesus*, '. . . am he'.
29 a man . . . has told me everything I ever did; I wonder if he is the *Christ*?
6 15 J *Jesus* . . . could see they were about to come and take him by force and make him king,
42 'Surely this is *Jesus*, son of Joseph, . . . How can he now say, "I have come down from heaven"?'
7 26 [Have the authorities] made up their minds that he is the *Christ*?
27 when the *Christ* appears no one will know where he comes from.
31 When the *Christ* comes, will he give more signs than this man?
41 some said, 'He is the *Christ*,' but others said, 'Would the
42 *Christ* be from Galilee?⁴² Does not scripture say that the *Christ* must be . . . from the town of Bethlehem?'
9 22 the Jews . . . had already agreed to expel from the synagogue anyone who should acknowledge [Jesus as the] *Christ*.
10 24 If you are the *Christ*, tell us plainly.
11 27 'Lord,' [Martha] said 'I believe you are the *Christ*, the Son of God,
12 34 The Law has taught us that the *Christ* will remain for ever.

Jn 20 31 J These [signs] are recorded so that you may believe that *Jesus* is the *Christ*, the Son of God,
Ac 2 31 what [David] foresaw . . . was the resurrection of the *Christ*:
32 J God raised this man *Jesus* to life, and all of us are witnesses to that.
36 the whole House of Israel can be certain that God has made
J this *Jesus* whom you crucified both Lord and *Christ*.
3 18 God carried out what he had foretold, . . . that his *Christ* would suffer.
20 [The Lord] will send you the *Christ* he has pre-destined, that
J is *Jesus*.
4 26 (Ps 2 2) princes making an alliance, against the Lord and against his *Anointed* [= *Christ*].
8 5 Philip . . . went to a Samaritan town and proclaimed the *Christ* to them.
9 22 Saul . . . was able to throw the Jewish colony at Damascus into complete confusion by the way he demonstrated that *Jesus* was the *Christ*.
17 3 [Paul expounded scripture to the Jews,] proving how it was ordained that the *Christ* should suffer and rise from the dead. And the *Christ*, he said, is this *Jesus* whom I am
J proclaiming to you.
18 5 [at Corinth] Paul devoted all his time to preaching, declaring
J to the Jews that *Jesus* was the *Christ*.
28 [Apollos] refuted the Jews in public and demonstrated from
J the scriptures that *Jesus* was the *Christ*.
26 23 [what the prophets and Moses said would happen:] that the
J *Christ* was to suffer
Rm 9 5 from [the] flesh and blood [of the Israelites] came *Christ*
1 Jn 2 22 J The man who denies that *Jesus* is the *Christ* – he is the liar, he is Antichrist;
5 1 J Whoever believes that *Jesus* is the *Christ* has been begotten by God;

2: JESUS CHRIST

C = Christ   CJ = Christ Jesus   JC = Jesus Christ

e = in Jesus, in Christ, in Jesus Christ, in Christ Jesus
(*en Iēsou, en Christō* etc.) 95

Mt 1 1 JC A genealogy of *Jesus Christ*, son of David, son of Abraham:
17 fourteen [generations] from the Babylonian deportation to
C *Christ*.
18 JC This is how *Jesus Christ* came to be born.
21 [Mary] will give birth to a son and you must name him *Jesus*, because he is the one who is to save his people from their sins.
25 [Mary] gave birth to a son; and [Joseph] named him *Jesus*.
3 13 Then *Jesus* appeared: he came from Galilee to the Jordan to be baptised by John.
16 As soon as *Jesus* was baptised he came up from the water,
4 1 *Jesus* was led by the Spirit out into the wilderness to be tempted
23 ʳHe (ᵛ *Jesus*) went round the whole of Galilee
8 10 When *Jesus* heard [the centurion] he was astonished
14 going into Peter's house *Jesus* found Peter's mother-in-law in bed
18 *Jesus* . . . gave orders to leave for the other side.
34 the whole town set out to meet *Jesus*;
9 9 *Jesus* . . . saw a man named Matthew sitting by the customs house,
10 a number of tax collectors and sinners came to sit at the table with *Jesus* and his disciples.
19 *Jesus* rose and, with his disciples, followed [the official].
27 As *Jesus* went on his way two blind men followed him
30 *Jesus* sternly warned them, 'Take care that no one learns about this'.
35 *Jesus* made a tour through all the towns and villages,
10 5 These twelve *Jesus* sent out,
11 1 *Jesus* . . . moved on from there to teach and preach in their towns.
12 1 *Jesus* took a walk one sabbath day through the cornfields.
15 *Jesus* . . . withdrew from the district.
13 1 *Jesus* left the house and sat by the lakeside,
53 When *Jesus* had finished these parables he left the district;
14 1 Herod . . . heard about the reputation of *Jesus*,
12 John's disciples . . . went off to tell *Jesus*.
13 *Jesus* . . . withdrew by boat to a lonely place
29 Peter . . . started walking towards *Jesus* across the water,
31 *Jesus* put out his hand at once and held him.
15 1 ʳPharisees and scribes from Jerusalem then came to *Jesus*
21 *Jesus* left that place and retired to the region of Tyre and Sidon.
29 *Jesus* went on from there and reached the shores of the Sea of Galilee.
16 21 JC *Jesus* (§ *Christ*) began to make it clear to his disciples that he was destined to go to Jerusalem and suffer grievously

Mt 17	1	*Jesus* took with him Peter and James and his brother John
	4	Peter spoke to *Jesus*. 'Lord, . . . it is wonderful for us to be here;'
	7	*Jesus* came up and touched them. 'Stand up,' he said
	8	when they raised their eyes they saw no one but only *Jesus*.
	9	*Jesus* gave them this order, 'Tell no one about the vision . . . '
	18	when *Jesus* rebuked it the devil came out of the boy
	19	the disciples came privately to *Jesus*. 'Why were we unable to cast it out?'
	25	before he could speak, *Jesus* said, 'Simon, what is your opinion? . . . '
18	1	the disciples came to *Jesus* and said, 'Who is the greatest in the kingdom of heaven?'
20	17	*Jesus* . . . took the Twelve to one side
	30	When [the two blind men] heard that it was *Jesus* who was passing by,
	32	*Jesus* . . . called [the two blind men] over and said, 'What do you want me to do for you?'
	34	*Jesus* felt pity for them and touched their eyes,
21	1	*Jesus* sent two disciples, ² saying to them, 'Go to the village facing you, . . . '
	6	the disciples . . . did as *Jesus* had told them.
	11	This is the prophet *Jesus* from Nazareth in Galilee.
	12	*Jesus* then went into the Temple and drove out all those who were selling and buying there;
	27	their reply to *Jesus* was, 'We do not know.'
23 10 C		you have only one Teacher, the *Christ*.
24	1	*Jesus* left the Temple,
26	4	[the chief priests and elders] made plans to arrest *Jesus*
	6	*Jesus* was at Bethany . . . when a woman came to him
	17	the disciples came to *Jesus* to say, 'Where do you want . . . to eat the passover?'
	19	The disciples did what *Jesus* told them
	26	*Jesus* took some bread, and when he had said the blessing he broke it
	36	*Jesus* came with [the disciples] to a small estate called Gethsemane;
	49	[Judas] went straight up to *Jesus* and said, 'Greetings, Rabbi,'
	50	they . . . seized *Jesus* and took him in charge.
	51	one of the followers of *Jesus* grasped his sword and drew it;
	57	The men who had arrested *Jesus* led him off to Caiaphas
	59	The chief priests . . . were looking for evidence against *Jesus*,
	69	You too [Peter] were with *Jesus* the Galilean.
	71	This man was with *Jesus* the Nazarene.
27	1	the chief priests . . . met in council to bring about the death of *Jesus*.
	11	*Jesus* . . . was brought before the governor, . . . 'Are you the king of the Jews?'
	20	The chief priests . . . had persuaded the crowd to demand . . . the execution of *Jesus*.
	26	[Pilate] ordered *Jesus* to be . . . handed over to be crucified.
	27	The governor's soldiers took *Jesus* with them
	37	the charge against him . . . read: This is *Jesus*, the King of the Jews.
	50	*Jesus*, again crying out in a loud voice, yielded up his spirit.
	54	the centurion, together with the others guarding *Jesus*,
	55	the same women who had followed *Jesus* from Galilee
	57	Joseph, who had himself become a disciple of *Jesus*.
	58	⁵⁸ This man went to Pilate and asked for the body of *Jesus*.
28	5	I know you are looking for *Jesus*,
	9	there, coming to meet them, was *Jesus*.
	16	the eleven disciples set out for Galilee, to the mountain where *Jesus* had arranged to meet them.
Mk 1	1 JC	The beginning of the Good News about *Jesus Christ*, the Son of God.
	9	*Jesus* came from Nazareth in Galilee and was baptised
	14	*Jesus* went into Galilee.
	24	[the unclean spirit shouted,] 'What do you want with us, *Jesus* of Nazareth? . . . I know who you are: the Holy One of God.' ²⁵ But *Jesus* said sharply, 'Be quiet!'
	25	
2	15	a number of tax collectors and sinners were also sitting at the table with *Jesus* and his disciples;
3	7	*Jesus* withdrew with his disciples to the lakeside,
5	6	Catching sight of *Jesus* from a distance, [the demoniac] ran up
	7	What do you want with me, *Jesus*, son of the Most High God?
	15	[The Gerasenes] came to *Jesus* and saw the demoniac sitting there,
	20	[the demoniac] proceeded to spread throughout the Decapolis all that *Jesus* had done for him.
	21	When *Jesus* had crossed . . . to the other side, [Jairus came up to him,]
	27	[A woman who had suffered from a haemorrhage for twelve years] had heard about *Jesus*,
	30	Immediately aware that power had gone out from him, *Jesus* turned round
6	30	The apostles rejoined *Jesus*

Mk 9	2	*Jesus* took with him Peter and James and John and . . . in their presence he was transfigured;
	4	[Elijah and Moses] were talking with *Jesus*.
	5	Peter spoke to *Jesus*: 'Rabbi, . . . it is wonderful for us to be here;'
	8	they saw no one with them any more but only *Jesus*.
	25	when *Jesus* saw how many people were pressing round him, he rebuked the unclean spirit.
	27	*Jesus* took [the boy] by the hand and helped him up,
	41 C	If anyone gives you a cup of water to drink because you belong to *Christ*,
10	14	when *Jesus* saw this he was indignant . . . 'Let little children come to me;'
	21	*Jesus* looked steadily at him and loved him, . . . 'Go and sell everything you own . . . '
	32	*Jesus* was walking on ahead of the [disciples]; they were in a daze,
	47	When [Bartimaeus] heard that it was *Jesus* of Nazareth, he began to shout . . . 'Son of David, *Jesus*, have pity on me.'
	50	he jumped up and went to *Jesus*.
11	7	they took the colt to *Jesus*
	33	their reply to *Jesus* was, 'We do not know.'
14	53	They led *Jesus* off to the high priest;
	55	The chief priests . . . were looking for evidence against *Jesus*
	60	The high priest . . . put this question to *Jesus*: 'Have you no answer to that?'
	67	[The servant girl to Peter:] 'You too were with *Jesus*, the man from Nazareth.'
15	1	the chief priests . . . had *Jesus* bound and . . . handed him over to Pilate.
	15	having ordered *Jesus* to be scourged, [Pilate] handed him over to be crucified.
	34	*Jesus* cried out in a loud voice, 'Eloi, Eloi,
	37	*Jesus* gave a loud cry and breathed his last.
	43	Joseph of Arimathaea . . . asked for the body of *Jesus*.
16	6	You are looking for *Jesus* of Nazareth,
Lk 1	31	You are to . . . bear a son, and you must name him *Jesus*.
2	21	they gave him the name *Jesus*,
	27	when the parents brought in the child *Jesus*
	43	the boy *Jesus* stayed behind in Jerusalem
	52	*Jesus* increased in wisdom, in stature, and in favour with God and men.
3	21	while *Jesus* after his own baptism was at prayer,
	23	When he started to teach, *Jesus* was about thirty
4	1	Filled with the Holy Spirit, *Jesus* . . . was led by the Spirit through the wilderness,
	14	*Jesus* . . . returned to Galilee; and his reputation spread
	34	What do you want with us, *Jesus* of Nazareth? I know who you are: the Holy One of God.
	35	*Jesus* said sharply, 'Be quiet! Come out of him!'
5	8	Simon Peter . . . fell at the knees of *Jesus* saying, 'Leave me, Lord;
	12	Seeing *Jesus* [the leper] fell on his face and implored him,
	19	they . . . lowered [the paralytic] and his stretcher . . . in front of *Jesus*.
6	11	they . . . began to discuss the best way of dealing with *Jesus*.
7	3	Having heard about *Jesus* [the centurion] sent some Jewish elders to him
	4	When they came to *Jesus* they pleaded earnestly with him.
	6	So *Jesus* went with them, and . . . the centurion sent word to him
	9	When *Jesus* heard these words he was astonished at [the centurion]
	19	[John] sent [two of his disciples] to ʳthe Lord (ᵛ *Jesus*)
8	28	Catching sight of *Jesus* [the demoniac] . . . cried out . . . 'What do you want with me, *Jesus*, son of the Most High God?
	30	'What is your name?' *Jesus* asked. 'Legion,' he said.
	35	when [the Gerasenes] came to *Jesus* they found [the demoniac] . . . sitting at the feet of *Jesus*,
	39	the man . . . spread throughout the town all that *Jesus* had done for him.
	40	On his return *Jesus* was welcomed by the crowd,
	41	Jairus . . . fell at *Jesus*' feet and pleaded with him to come to his house,
9	33	Peter said to *Jesus*, 'Master, it is wonderful for us to be here;
	36	after the voice had spoken, *Jesus* was found alone.
	42	*Jesus* rebuked the unclean spirit and cured the boy
	47	*Jesus* . . . took a little child
10	29	the [lawyer] . . . said to *Jesus*, 'And who is my neighbour?'
13	14	the synagogue official was indignant because *Jesus* had healed on the sabbath,
17	13	[The ten lepers] called to him, '*Jesus*! Master! Take pity on us.'
18	16	*Jesus* called the children to him
	37	they told [the blind man] that *Jesus* the Nazarene was passing by.
	38	[the blind man] called out, '*Jesus*, Son of David, have pity on me.'

Lk 18	40		*Jesus* stopped and ordered them to bring the man to him,
19	3		[Zacchaeus] was anxious to see what kind of man *Jesus* was,
	35		they took the colt to *Jesus*, and . . . helped *Jesus* on to it.
22	47		Judas . . . went up to *Jesus* to kiss him.
23	8		Herod was delighted to see *Jesus*;
	20		Pilate was anxious to set *Jesus* free
	25		[Pilate] handed *Jesus* over to them to deal with as they pleased.
	26		they seized on a man, Simon from Cyrene, . . . and made him shoulder the cross and carry it behind *Jesus*.
	42		'*Jesus*,' [the other criminal] said, 'remember me when you come into your kingdom.'
	52		[Joseph] went to Pilate and asked for the body of *Jesus*,
24	3		on entering [the tomb the women] discovered that the body of the Lord *Jesus* was not there.
	15		*Jesus* himself came up and walked by their side;
Jn 1	17	JC	grace and truth have come through *Jesus Christ*.
	29		seeing *Jesus* coming towards him, John said, 'Look, there is the lamb of God.'
	36		*Jesus* passed, and John stared hard at him and said, 'Look, there is the lamb of God.' [37] . . . the two disciples followed *Jesus*.
2	1		there was a wedding at Cana . . . The mother of *Jesus* was there,
	2		*Jesus* and his disciples had also been invited.
	3		the mother of *Jesus* said to him, 'They have no wine.'
	11		This was the first of the signs given by *Jesus*:
	13		Just before the Jewish Passover, *Jesus* went up to Jerusalem,
	24		*Jesus* knew them all and did not trust himself to them;
3	22		*Jesus* went . . . into the Judaean countryside . . . and baptised.
4	1		When ʳ*Jesus* (G the Lord) heard that the Pharisees had found out that ʳhe (lit. *Jesus*) was making and baptising more
	2		disciples than John – [2] though in fact it was his disciples who baptised, not *Jesus* himself –
	6		*Jesus*, tired by the journey, sat straight down by the well.
	44		ʳHe (lit. *Jesus*) himself had declared that there is no respect for a prophet in his own country,
	47		hearing that *Jesus* had arrived in Galilee from Judaea,
	54		the second sign given by *Jesus*, on his return from Judaea to Galilee.
5	1		there was a Jewish festival, and *Jesus* went up to Jerusalem.
	13		*Jesus* had disappeared into the crowd
	14		After a while *Jesus* met [the sick man] in the Temple and said, 'Now you are well again,
	15		The man . . . told the Jews that it was *Jesus* who had cured him. [16] It was because he did things like this on the sabbath that the Jews began to persecute *Jesus*.
6	1		*Jesus* went off to the other side of the Sea of Galilee
	3		*Jesus* climbed the hillside,
	11		*Jesus* took the loaves, gave thanks, and gave them out
	17		*Jesus* had still not rejoined [the disciples].
	19		they saw *Jesus* walking on the lake
	22		the crowd . . . saw that . . . *Jesus* had not got into the boat
	24		When the people saw that neither *Jesus* nor his disciples were there, they got into those boats . . . to look for *Jesus*.
	64		*Jesus* knew from the outset those who did not believe,
7	1		After this *Jesus* stayed in Galilee; he ᵛcould (G would) not stay in Judaea,
	14		When the festival was half over, *Jesus* went to the Temple
	28		as *Jesus* taught in the Temple, he cried out:
	37		*Jesus* stood there and cried out: 'If any man is thirsty,
	39		there was no Spirit as yet because *Jesus* had not yet been glorified.
8	1		*Jesus* went to the Mount of Olives.
	6		*Jesus* bent down and started writing on the ground with his finger.
	9		ʳ*Jesus* (ᵛ he) was left alone with the woman,
	59		*Jesus* hid himself and left the Temple.
9	11		The man called *Jesus* . . . made a paste,
	14		It had been a sabbath day when *Jesus* had made the paste,
	35		*Jesus* heard [the Jews] had driven [the man born blind] away,
10	23		*Jesus* was in the Temple walking up and down
11	5		*Jesus* loved Martha and her sister and Lazarus,
	13		[Lazarus is resting.] *Jesus* . . . referred to the death of Lazarus,
	17		*Jesus* found that Lazarus had been in the tomb for four days
	20		When Martha heard that *Jesus* had come she went to meet him.
	21		Martha said to *Jesus*, 'If you had been here, my brother would not have died,'
	30		*Jesus* had not yet come into the village;
	32		Mary went to *Jesus* . . . saying, 'Lord, if you had been here,
	33		At the sight of her tears . . . *Jesus* said in great distress,
	35		*Jesus* wept;
	38		*Jesus* reached the tomb:
	46		some of them went to tell the Pharisees what *Jesus* had done.
	51		[Caiaphas] made this prophecy that *Jesus* was to die for the nation
	54		*Jesus* no longer went about openly among the Jews,
	56		many [of the country people in Jerusalem] looked out for *Jesus*,

Jn 12	1		Six days before the Passover, *Jesus* went to Bethany, where Lazarus was, whom ʳhe (lit. *Jesus*) had raised from the dead.
	3		Mary . . . anointed the feet of *Jesus*,
	9		a large number of Jews . . . came not only on account of *Jesus* but also to see Lazarus
	11		it was on [Lazarus'] account that many of the Jews were . . . believing in *Jesus*.
	12		the crowds . . . heard that *Jesus* was on his way to Jerusalem
	14		*Jesus* found a young donkey and mounted it
	16		after *Jesus* had been glorified, [his disciples] remembered that this had been written about him
	21		[some Greeks] put this request to [Philip]: 'Sir, we should like to see *Jesus*.'
	22		Andrew and Philip together went to tell *Jesus*.
13	1		ʳHe (lit. *Jesus*) had always loved those who were his in the world,
	23		The disciple *Jesus* loved was reclining next to Jesus;
	25		leaning back on Jesus' breast he said, 'Who is it, Lord?'
16	19		*Jesus* knew that they wanted to question him,
17	3	JC	eternal life is this: to know you, the only true God, and *Jesus Christ* whom you have sent.
18	2		*Jesus* had often met his disciples there,
	4		Knowing everything that was going to happen to him, *Jesus* then came forward
	5		['Who are you looking for?'] They answered, '*Jesus* the Nazarene.'
	7		He asked them a second time, . . . They said, '*Jesus* the Nazarene.'
	12		The cohort and its captain and the Jewish guards seized *Jesus* and bound him.
	15		Simon Peter, with another disciple, followed *Jesus*. This disciple . . . went with *Jesus* into the high priest's palace,
	19		The high priest questioned *Jesus*
	22		one of the guards . . . gave *Jesus* a slap in the face,
	28		They then led *Jesus* from the house of Caiaphas to the Praetorium.
	33		Pilate . . . called *Jesus* to him, 'Are you the king of the Jews?'
19	1		Pilate then had *Jesus* taken away and scourged;
	5		*Jesus* then came out wearing the crown of thorns
	9		[Pilate] said to *Jesus*, 'Where do you come from?'
	13		Pilate had *Jesus* brought out,
	16		[The Jews] then took charge of *Jesus*.
	18		they crucified him with two others . . . with *Jesus* in the middle.
	19		a notice . . . *Jesus* the Nazarene, King of the Jews.
	20		the place where *Jesus* was crucified was not far from the city,
	23		When the soldiers had finished crucifying *Jesus* they took his clothing
	25		Near the cross of *Jesus* stood his mother and his mother's sister,
	33		When they came to *Jesus*, they found he was already dead,
	38		Joseph of Arimathaea, who was a disciple of *Jesus* . . . asked Pilate to let him remove the body of *Jesus*.
	40		They took the body of *Jesus*
	42		Since . . . the tomb was near at hand, they laid *Jesus* there.
20	2		Simon Peter, and the other disciple, the one *Jesus* loved.
	12		[Mary] saw two angels . . . sitting where the body of *Jesus* had been,
	14		[Mary] turned round and saw *Jesus* standing there, ʳthough she did not recognise him (lit. without knowing it was *Jesus*).
	19		*Jesus* came and stood among them. He said to them 'Peace be with you,'
	24		Thomas . . . was not with them when *Jesus* came.
	26		The doors were closed, but *Jesus* came in and stood among them.
	30		There were many other signs that *Jesus* worked
21	1		*Jesus* showed himself again to the disciples. It was by the Sea of Tiberias.
	4		there stood *Jesus* on the shore, though the disciples did not realise that it was Jesus.
	7		The disciple *Jesus* loved said to Peter, 'It is the Lord.'
	13		*Jesus* then stepped forward, took the bread and gave it to them,
	14		This was the third time that *Jesus* showed himself to the disciples
	20		Peter turned and saw the disciple *Jesus* loved following them
	21		Peter said to *Jesus*, 'What about him, Lord?'
	25		There were many other things that *Jesus* did;
Ac 1	1		I dealt with everything *Jesus* had done and taught
	11		this same *Jesus* will come back in the same way as you have seen him go
	14		several women, including Mary the mother of *Jesus*,
	16		Judas, who offered himself as a guide to the men who arrested Jesus
	21		the whole time that the Lord *Jesus* was travelling round with us,
2	22		*Jesus* the Nazarene was a man commended to you by God
	38	JC	every one of you must be baptised in the name of *Jesus Christ*
3	6	JC	in the name of *Jesus Christ* the Nazarene, walk!

Ac 3	13		it is the God of . . . our ancestors, who has glorified his servant *Jesus,*
	4 2		[The priests] were extremely annoyed at their teaching the people the doctrine of the resurrection from the dead by proclaiming the resurrection of *Jesus.*
		e	
	10	JC	by the name of *Jesus Christ* the Nazarene . . . this man is able to stand up
	13		[the Sanhedrin] recognised [Peter and John] as associates of Jesus;
	18		they . . . gave them a warning on no account to . . . teach in the name of *Jesus.*
	27		Herod and Pontius Pilate made an alliance . . . against your holy servant *Jesus*
	30		by stretching out your hand to heal . . . through the name of your holy servant *Jesus.*
	33		The apostles continued to testify to the resurrection of the Lord *Jesus*
5	30		it was the God of our ancestors who raised up *Jesus,* but it was you who had him executed
	40		[the Sanhedrin] warned [the apostles] not to speak in the name of *Jesus*
	42	CJ	their proclamation of the Good News of *Christ Jesus* was never interrupted.
6	14		We have heard [Stephen] say that *Jesus* the Nazarene is going to destroy this Place
7	55		Stephen . . . saw . . . *Jesus* standing at God's right hand.
	59		Stephen said in invocation, 'Lord *Jesus,* receive my spirit.'
8	12	JC	the Good News about the kingdom of God and the name of *Jesus Christ*
	16		[the Samaritans] had only been baptised in the name of the Lord *Jesus.*
	35		Philip proceeded to explain the Good News of *Jesus* to [the Ethiopian].
	37	JC	(ᵛ the eunuch said: 'I believe that *Jesus Christ* is the Son of God)
9	5		'Who are you, Lord?' . . . 'I am *Jesus,* and you are persecuting me.'
	17		I have been sent by the Lord *Jesus* who appeared to you
	20		[Saul] began preaching in the synagogues, *Jesus* the Son of God.
	27		how [Saul] had preached boldly at Damascus in the name of *Jesus.*
	34	JC	Peter said to him, 'Aeneas, *Jesus Christ* cures you:'
10	36	JC	the good news of peace was brought by *Jesus Christ*
	37		You must have heard about . . . *Jesus* of Nazareth . . . ³⁸ God had anointed him with the Holy Spirit
	48	JC	[Peter] then gave orders for [the pagans] to be baptised in the name of *Jesus Christ.*
11	17	JC	God was giving [the pagans] the identical thing he gave to us when we believed in the Lord *Jesus Christ*
	20		proclaiming the Good News of the Lord *Jesus* to [the Greeks] as well.
13	23		God has raised up for Israel one of David's descendants, *Jesus,* as Saviour,
	33		[God] has fulfilled [his promise] by raising *Jesus* from the dead.
15	11		we believe that we are saved . . . through the grace of the Lord *Jesus.*
	26	JC	[Barnabas and Paul] have dedicated their lives to the name of our Lord *Jesus Christ.*
16	7		the Spirit of *Jesus* would not allow [Paul and Silas to cross the frontier]
	18	JC	I order you in the name of *Jesus Christ* to leave that woman.
	31		Become a believer in the Lord *Jesus,* and you will be saved, and your household too.
17	7		claiming that there is another emperor, *Jesus.*
	18		[in Athens Paul] was preaching about *Jesus* and the resurrection,
18	25		[Apollos] was accurate in all the details he taught about *Jesus,*
19	4		[John] insisted that the people [he baptised] should believe in . . . *Jesus.*
	5		[the disciples of John at Ephesus] were baptised in the name of the Lord *Jesus,*
	13		some . . . Jewish exorcists tried pronouncing the name of the Lord *Jesus* over people . . . they used to say, 'I command you by the *Jesus* whose spokesman is Paul.'
	15		The evil spirit replied, '*Jesus* I recognise,
	17		the name of the Lord *Jesus* came to be held in great honour.
20	21	JC	[I have urged] both Jews and Greeks to turn to God and to believe in our Lord *Jesus* (ᵛ *Christ*).
	24		provided that . . . I have carried out the mission the Lord *Jesus* gave me
21	13		I am ready . . . to die . . . for the name of the Lord *Jesus.*
22	8		he said to me, 'I am *Jesus* the Nazarene, and you are persecuting me.'
24	24	CJ	[Felix] gave [Paul] a hearing on the subject of faith in *Christ Jesus.*
25	19		a dead man called *Jesus* whom Paul alleged to be alive.

Ac 26	9		I once thought it was my duty to use every means to oppose the name of *Jesus* the Nazarene.
	15		the Lord answered, 'I am *Jesus,* and you are persecuting me.'
28	23		[Paul tried] to persuade [the Roman Jews] about *Jesus,*
	31	JC	[Paul] teaching the truth about the Lord *Jesus Christ*
Rm 1	1	CJ	Paul, a servant of *Christ Jesus*
	4	JC	[This news is about the Son of God;] it is about *Jesus Christ* our Lord
	6		You are one of these [pagan] nations, and by his call belong to *Jesus Christ.*
		JC	
	7	JC	may God our Father and the Lord *Jesus Christ* send [you] grace and peace.
	8	JC	I thank my God through *Jesus Christ* for all of you
2	16	CJ	God, through *Christ Jesus,* judges the secrets of mankind.
3	22		the same justice of God that comes through faith to everyone . . . who believes in *Jesus Christ.*
		JC	
	24		justified through the free gift of his grace by being redeemed in *Christ Jesus.*
		e CJ	
	26		[God] justifies everyone who believes in *Jesus.*
4	24		if we believe in him who raised *Jesus* our Lord from the dead,
5	1	JC	through our Lord *Jesus Christ* . . . we are . . . at peace with God,
	6	C	at his appointed moment *Christ* died for sinful men.
	8	C	what proves that God loves us is that *Christ* died for us
	11		we are filled with joyful trust in God, through our Lord *Jesus Christ,*
		JC	
	15	JC	divine grace, coming through the one man, *Jesus Christ,* came to so many
	17	JC	one man, *Jesus Christ,* will cause everyone to reign in life who receives the free gift
	21	JC	thanks to the righteousness that comes through *Jesus Christ* our Lord.
6	3	CJ	when we were baptised in *Christ Jesus* we were baptised in his death;
	4	C	as *Christ* was raised from the dead by the Father's glory,
	8	C	having died with *Christ,* we shall return to life with him:
	9	C	*Christ,* . . . having been raised from the dead, will never die again.
	11		you too must consider yourselves to be dead to sin but alive for God in *Christ Jesus.*
		e CJ	
	23	e CJ	the present given by God is eternal life in *Christ Jesus* our Lord.
7	4	C	you, my brothers, who through the body of *Christ* are now dead to the Law,
	25	JC	Thanks be to God through *Jesus Christ* our Lord!
8	1	e CJ	those who are in *Christ Jesus* are not condemned,
	2	e CJ	the law of the spirit of life in *Christ Jesus* has set you free
	9	C	unless you possessed the Spirit of *Christ* you would not belong to him.
	10	C	if *Christ* is in you then your spirit is life itself because you have been justified;
	11		if the Spirit of him who raised *Jesus* . . . is living in you, then he who raised *Christ Jesus* . . . will give life to your own mortal bodies
		CJ	
	17	C	heirs with God and co-heirs with Christ,
	34	CJ	Could *Christ Jesus* [condemn us]? He . . . died for us
	35		Nothing . . . can come between us and the love of *Christ*
	35	C	. . . ³⁸ . . . not any power, ³⁹ or height or depth . . . can ever come between us and the love of God made visible in *Christ Jesus* our Lord.
		e CJ	
9	1	e C	I say it in union with *Christ* – it is the truth –
	3	C	I would willingly be . . . cut off from *Christ* if it could help my brothers of Israel,
10	4	C	the Law has come to an end with *Christ,*
	6	C	Do not tell yourself you have to bring *Christ* down . . .
	7	C	⁷or that you have to bring *Christ* back from the dead
	9		If your lips confess that *Jesus* is Lord . . . you will be saved.
	17	C	what is preached comes from the word of *Christ.*
12	5	e C	all of us, in union with *Christ,* form one body,
13	14	JC	Let your armour be the Lord *Jesus Christ;*
14	9	C	*Christ* both died and came to life, . . . so that he might be Lord both of the dead and of the living.
	10		We shall have to stand before the judgement seat of ʳGod
		C	(ᵛ *Christ*);
	14	e	I am perfectly aware, . . . and I speak for the Lord *Jesus,* that no food is unclean in itself;
	15		You are certainly not free to eat what you like if that means
		C	the downfall of someone for whom *Christ* died.
	18	C	If you serve *Christ* in this way you will please God
15	3	C	*Christ* did not think of himself:
	5	CJ	following the example of *Christ Jesus,* ⁶ so that . . . you may give glory to the God and Father of our Lord *Jesus Christ.*
	6		
		JC	
	7	C	treat each other in the same friendly way as *Christ* treated you.
	8	C	*Christ* became the servant of circumcised Jews
	16	CJ	He has appointed me as a priest of *Jesus Christ*
	17	e CJ	proud of what I, in union with *Christ Jesus,* have been able to do for God.

Rm 15 18 C what *Christ* himself has done to win the allegiance of the pagans,

19 C I have preached *Christ's* Good News . . . ²⁰ I have always,

20 however, made it an unbroken rule never to preach where

C *Christ's* name has already been heard.

29 C I shall arrive with rich blessings from *Christ*.

30 JC I beg you . . . by our Lord *Jesus Christ* . . . to help me

16 3 My greeting to Prisca and Aquila, my fellow workers in

e CJ *Christ Jesus*,

5 C Greetings to Epaenetus, the first of Asia's gifts to *Christ*;

7 Andronicus and Junias . . . who ˹became Christians before

e C me (lit. were before me in *Christ*)

9 e C Urban, my fellow worker in *Christ*;

10 e C Apelles who has gone through so much ˹for (lit. in) *Christ*;

16 C All the churches of *Christ* send greetings.

18 People like that are not slaves of ˹Jesus (lit. our saviour)

C *Christ*,

20 JC The grace of our Lord *Jesus* ˅*Christ*˺ be with you.

24 JC (˅ the grace of our Lord *Jesus Christ* be with you all. Amen.)

25 JC the Good News I preach, in which I proclaim *Jesus Christ*,

27 JC give glory therefore to [God] through *Jesus Christ*

1 Co 1 1 CJ Paul, appointed by God to be an apostle of *Christ Jesus*

2 e CJ to the holy people of *Jesus Christ*, who are called to take their place among all the saints . . . who pray to our

JC Lord *Jesus Christ*;

3 JC May God our Father and the Lord *Jesus Christ* send you grace and peace.

4 e CJ The graces you have received through *Jesus Christ*

6 C the witness to *Christ* has indeed been strong among you

7 JC while you are waiting for our Lord *Jesus Christ* to be revealed;

8 JC the last day, the day of our Lord *Jesus Christ*,

9 JC God by calling you has joined you to his Son, *Jesus Christ*;

10 JC I appeal to you, brothers, for the sake of our Lord *Jesus Christ*,

12 C 'I am for Paul,' . . . 'I am for *Christ*,' Has *Christ* been parcelled out?

17 C *Christ* did not send me to baptise, but to preach the Good News, and not to preach that in the terms of philosophy

C in which the crucifixion of *Christ* cannot be expressed.

23 C here are we preaching a crucified *Christ*; to the Jews an

24 obstacle . . . ²⁴ but to those who have been called,

C . . . a *Christ* who is the power and the wisdom of God.

30 e CJ you, God has made members of *Christ Jesus*

2 2 JC the only knowledge I claimed to have was about *Jesus*, and only about him as the crucified [*Christ*].

16 C we are those who have the mind of *Christ*.

3 1 e C I treated you as sensual men, still infants in *Christ*.

11 JC nobody can lay any other [foundation] than . . . *Jesus Christ*.

23 C you belong to *Christ*, and *Christ* belongs to God.

4 1 C People must think of us as *Christ's* servants,

10 C Here we are, fools for the sake of *Christ*, while you are the

e C learned men in *Christ*;

15 e C You might have thousands of guardians in *Christ*, but . . .

e C it was I who begot you in *Christ Jesus*

17 e CJ [Timothy] will remind you of the way that I live in *Christ*,

5 4 When you are assembled together in the name of the Lord *Jesus* . . . then with the power of our Lord *Jesus* he is to be handed over

7 C *Christ*, our passover, has been sacrificed;

6 11 you have been . . . justified through the name of the Lord

JC *Jesus Christ*

15 C You know, surely, that your bodies are members making

C up the body of *Christ*; do you think I can take parts of

C *Christ's* body and join them to the body of a prostitute?

7 22 C a freeman called in the Lord becomes *Christ's* slave.

8 6 for us there is one God . . . and there is one Lord,

JC *Jesus Christ*,

11 C the ruin of someone weak, of a brother for whom *Christ*

12 died. ¹² By . . . injuring their weak consciences, it would

C be *Christ* against whom you sinned.

9 1 I have seen *Jesus* our Lord.

12 we have put up with anything rather than obstruct the Good

C News of *Christ* in any way.

21 C I was free of the Law myself . . ., being under the law of

C *Christ*

10 4 they all drank from the spiritual rock . . . and that rock

C was *Christ*

9 C We are not to put the ˹Lord (˅ *Christ*) to the test:

16 C The blessing-cup . . . is a communion with the blood of

C *Christ*, and the bread . . . a communion with the body

C of *Christ*.

11 1 C Take me for your model, as I take *Christ*.

3 C *Christ* is the head of every man, . . . and God is the head

C of *Christ*.

23 the same night that he was betrayed, the Lord *Jesus* took some bread,

12 3 no one can be speaking under the influence of the Holy Spirit and say, 'Curse *Jesus*', and . . . no one can say,

1 Co 12 3 '*Jesus* is Lord' unless he is under the influence of the Holy Spirit.

12 Just as a human body, though it is made up of many parts,

C is a single unit . . ., so it is with *Christ*.

27 C you together are *Christ's* body; but each of you is a different part of it.

15 3 C *Christ* died for our sins,

12 C if *Christ* raised from the dead is what has been preached,

13 C If there is no resurrection of the dead, *Christ* himself cannot

14 C have been raised, ¹⁴ and if *Christ* has not been raised then our preaching is useless

15 C we swore in evidence before God that he had raised *Christ* to life.

16 C if the dead are not raised, *Christ* has not been raised,

17 C ¹⁷and if *Christ* has not been raised, you are still in your

18 e C sins. ¹⁸And . . . all who have died in *Christ* have perished.

19 e C ¹⁹If our hope in *Christ* has been for this life only, we are

20 C the most unfortunate of all people. ²⁰ But *Christ* has in fact been raised from the dead.

22 e C all men will be brought to life in *Christ*; ²³ but all of them

23 C in their proper order: *Christ* as the first-fruits and then,

C after the coming of *Christ*, those who belong to him.

31 e CJ the pride that I take in you in *Christ Jesus* our Lord.

57 C victory through our Lord *Jesus Christ*.

16 23 JC The grace of the Lord *Jesus* (˅ *Christ*) be with you.

24 e CJ My love is with you all in *Christ Jesus*.

2 Co 1 1 CJ Paul, . . . an apostle of *Christ Jesus*,

2 Grace and peace to you from God our Father and the

JC Lord *Jesus Christ*.

3 JC Blessed be the God and Father of our Lord *Jesus Christ*,

5 C as the sufferings of *Christ* overflow to us, so, through

C *Christ*, does our consolation

14 I hope that, . . . when the day of our Lord *Jesus* comes, . . . you can be as proud of us as we are of you.

19 CJ The Son of God, the *Christ Jesus* that we proclaimed among you . . . was never Yes and No:

21 It is God himself who assures us . . . of our standing in

C *Christ*,

2 10 if there has been anything to be forgiven, I have forgiven

C it for your sake in the presence of *Christ*.

12 C I went up to Troas to preach the Good News of *Christ*,

14 e C God . . . makes us, in *Christ*, partners of his triumph,

15 C We are *Christ's* incense to God

17 e C In *Christ*, we speak as . . . envoys of God and in God's presence.

3 3 C it is plain that you are a letter from *Christ*, drawn up by us,

4 C Before God, we are confident of this through *Christ*:

14 that same veil is still there . ., since ˹Christ alone can

e C remove it (lit. it is removed only in *Christ*).

4 4 to stop [unbelievers] seeing the light shed by the Good

C News of the glory of *Christ*,

5 CJ it is not ourselves that we are preaching, but *Christ Jesus* as the Lord, and ourselves as your servants for *Jesus* sake.

6 JC God's glory, the glory on the face of (˅ *Jesus*) *Christ*.

10 we carry with us in our body the death of *Jesus*, so that the life of *Jesus*, too, may always be seen in our body.

11 ¹¹Indeed, . . . we are consigned to our death every day, for the sake of *Jesus*, so that in our mortal flesh the life of *Jesus*, too, may be openly shown.

14 he who raised the Lord *Jesus* to life will raise us with *Jesus*

5 10 the truth about us will be brought out in the law court

C of *Christ*.

14 C the love of *Christ* overwhelms us

16 C Even if we did once know *Christ* in the flesh, that is not how we know him now.

17 e C for anyone who is in *Christ*, there is a new creation;

18 C It was God who reconciled us to himself through *Christ*

19 e C God in *Christ* was reconciling himself to the world,

20 C we are ambassadors for *Christ*; . . . the appeal that we make

C in *Christ's* name is: be reconciled to God.

6 15 C *Christ* is not the ally of Beliar,

8 9 JC Remember how generous the Lord *Jesus* was:

23 C the other two brothers . . . are a real glory to *Christ*.

9 13 C the way you accept and profess the gospel of *Christ*,

10 1 C by the gentleness and patience of *Christ*

5 every thought is our prisoner, captured to be brought into obedience to *Christ*.

7 C Anybody who is convinced that he belongs to *Christ* must go

C on to reflect that we all belong to *Christ*

14 C we did come all the way to you with the gospel of *Christ*.

11 2 C I arranged for you to marry *Christ* so that I might give you away as a chaste virgin to this one husband.

3 I am afraid . . . your ideas may get . . . turned away from

C simple devotion to *Christ*.

4 a new *Jesus*, different from the one that we preached,

10 C by *Christ's* truth in me,

13 These people are counterfeit apostles, . . . disguised as

C apostles of *Christ*.

23 C The servants of *Christ*? . . . so am I, and more than they:

2 Co 11 31		The God and Father of the Lord *Jesus* . . . knows that I am not lying.
12 2	e C	I know a man in *Christ* who, fourteen years ago, was caught up . . . into the third heaven.
9	C	so that the power of *Christ* may stay over me,
10	C	I am quite content with . . . the agonies I go through for *Christ's* sake.
19	e C	it is before God that we, in *Christ*, are speaking;
13 3	C	You want proof . . . that it is *Christ* speaking in me:
5	JC	Do you acknowledge that *Jesus Christ* is really in you?
13	JC	The grace of the Lord *Jesus Christ* . . . be with you all.
Ga 1 1	JC	Paul . . . an apostle . . . appointed by *Jesus Christ* and by God the Father
3	JC	We wish you the grace and peace of God our Father and of the Lord *Jesus Christ*,
6	C	you have turned away from the one who called you [by the grace of *Christ*]
7	C	some troublemakers among you want to change the Good News of *Christ*;
10	C	If I still wanted [men's approval], I should not be what I am – a servant of *Christ*.
12	JC	[the Good News] is something I learnt only through a revelation of *Jesus Christ*.
22	e C	[I] was still not known by sight to the churches ᶠof (lit. in) *Christ* in Judaea,
2 4	e JC	to spy on the liberty we enjoy in *Christ Jesus*,
16	CJ	we acknowledge that what makes a man righteous is . . . faith in *Jesus Christ*. We had to become believers in
	CJ	*Christ Jesus* no less than you had, and now we hold that
	C	faith in *Christ* rather than fidelity to the Law is what justifies us,
17	e C	if we were to admit that the result of ᶠlooking to Christ to justify us (lit. seeking to be justified in *Christ*) is to make us
	C	sinners . ., it would follow that *Christ* had induced us to sin,
19	C	I have been crucified with *Christ*,
20	C	I live now not with my own life but with the life of *Christ*
21	C	if the Law can justify us, there is no point in the death of *Christ*.
3 1		the plain explanation you have had of the crucifixion of
	JC	*Jesus Christ*?
13	C	*Christ* redeemed us from the curse of the Law
14	e JC	so that in *Jesus Christ* the blessing of Abraham might include the pagans,
16		the promises were addressed to Abraham and to his . . .
	C	posterity, which is *Christ*.
22	JC	the promise can only be given through faith in *Jesus Christ*
24	C	The Law was to be our guardian until the *Christ* came
26	e CJ	you are . . . sons of God through faith in *Christ Jesus*.
27	C	All baptised in *Christ*, you have all clothed yourselves in
	C	*Christ*,
28	e CJ	all of you are one in *Christ Jesus*.
29	C	by belonging to *Christ* you are . . . the heirs [Abraham] was promised.
4 14	CJ	you welcomed me . . . as if I were *Christ Jesus* himself.
19	C	until *Christ* is formed in you.
5 1	C	When *Christ* freed us, he meant us to remain free.
2	C	if you allow yourselves to be circumcised, *Christ* will be of no benefit to you
4		if you do look to the Law to make you *justified*, then you
	C	have separated yourselves from *Christ*,
6	e CJ	in *Christ Jesus* whether you are circumcised or not makes no difference
24	CJ	You cannot belong to *Christ Jesus* unless you crucify all self-indulgent passions
6 2		You should carry each other's troubles and fulfil the law of
	C	*Christ*.
12	CJ	they want to escape persecution for the cross of *Christ* (§ *Jesus*)
14		the only thing I can boast about is the cross of our Lord
	JC	*Jesus Christ*,
17		the marks on my body are those of *Jesus*.
18	JC	The grace of our Lord *Jesus Christ* be with your spirit,
Ep 1 1	CJ	Paul, . . . an apostle of *Christ Jesus*, to the saints who are
2	e CJ	faithful ᶠto (lit. in) *Christ Jesus*: ² Grace and peace to you
	JC	from God our Father and from the Lord *Jesus Christ*.
3	JC	Blessed be God the Father of our Lord *Jesus Christ*, who has blessed us with all the spiritual blessings of heaven in
	e C	*Christ*.
5	JC	that we should become his adopted sons, through *Jesus Christ*
10	e C	he would bring everything together ᶠunder (lit. in) *Christ*, as head,
12	e C	the people who would put their hopes in *Christ* before he came.
15	e	once having heard about your faith in the Lord *Jesus*,
17	JC	May the God of our Lord *Jesus Christ*, the Father of glory, give you a spirit of wisdom
20	e C	[the strength of his power] at work in *Christ*, when he used it to raise him from the dead
Ep 2 5	C	he brought us to life with *Christ* . . . ⁶ and raised us up with him and gave us a place with him in heaven, in *Christ Jesus*.
6	e CJ	
7	e CJ	his goodness towards us in *Christ Jesus*,
10	e CJ	We are God's work of art, created in *Christ Jesus*
12	C	you had no *Christ* and were excluded from membership of Israel,
13	e CJ	now in *Christ Jesus*, you that used to be so far apart from us
	C	have been brought very close, by the blood of *Christ*.
20	CJ	You are part of a building that has . . . *Christ Jesus* himself for its main cornerstone.
3 1	CJ	I, Paul, a prisoner of *Christ Jesus* for the sake of you pagans.
4	C	the depths that I see in the mystery of *Christ*.
6	e CJ	the same promise has been made to [the pagans], in *Christ Jesus*,
8	C	proclaiming to the pagans the infinite treasure of *Christ*
11	e CJ	the plan which he had had from all eternity in *Christ Jesus* our Lord.
17	C	so that *Christ* may live in your hearts through faith,
19	C	until, knowing the love of *Christ*, . . . you are filled with the utter fullness of God.
21	e CJ	glory be to him . . . in the Church and in *Christ Jesus*
4 7		Each one of us . . . has been given his own share of grace,
	C	given as *Christ* allotted it.
12		[To some, his gift was that they should be apostles; to some, prophets;] . . . so that the saints together . . . [build]
13	C	up the body of *Christ*. ¹³ In this way we . . become the perfect Man, fully mature with the fullness of *Christ* himself.
15	C	we shall grow in all ways into *Christ*, who is the head
20	C	that is hardly the way you have learnt from *Christ*, ²¹ unless
21	e	you failed to hear him properly when you were taught what the truth is in *Jesus*.
32	e C	forgiving each other as readily as God forgave you in *Christ*.
5 2	C	follow *Christ* by loving as he loved you,
5		nobody who actually indulges in fornication or . . . promiscuity . . . can inherit anything of the kingdom ᶠof (lit. of *Christ* and of) God.
	C	
14	C	Wake up from your sleep, rise from the dead, and *Christ* will shine on you.
20		you are giving thanks to God who is our Father in the name
	JC	of our Lord *Jesus Christ*.
21	C	Give way to one another in obedience to *Christ*.
23	C	as *Christ* is head of the Church and saves the whole body,
24		so is a husband the head of his wife; ²⁴ and as the Church submits to *Christ*, so should wives to their husbands,
25	C	Husbands should love their wives just as *Christ* loved the Church
29		A man . . . looks after [his own body]; and that is the way
	C	*Christ* treats the Church,
32		This mystery [marriage] has many implications; but I am
	C	saying that it applies to *Christ* and the Church.
6 5		Slaves, be obedient to . . . your masters . ., as you are
6	C	obedient to *Christ*: ⁶ . . . because you are slaves of
	C	*Christ*
23	JC	May God the Father and the Lord *Jesus Christ* grant peace . . . to all the brothers.
24	JC	May grace . . . be with all who love our Lord *Jesus Christ*.
Ph 1 1	CJ	Paul and Timothy, servants of *Christ Jesus*, to all the saints
	e CJ	in *Christ Jesus*,
2		the grace and peace of God our Father and of the Lord
	JC	*Jesus Christ*.
6		the One who began this good work in you will see that it is
	CJ	finished when the Day of *Christ Jesus* comes.
8	CJ	I miss you all, loving you as *Christ Jesus* loves you.
10	C	This will . . . prepare you for the Day of *Christ*, ¹¹ when you
11	JC	will reach the perfect goodness which *Jesus Christ* produces in us
13	e C	My chains, in *Christ*, have become famous
15	C	the rest preach *Christ* with the right intention,
17	C	The others, who proclaim *Christ* for jealous or selfish motives,
18	C	Whether from dishonest motives or in sincerity, *Christ* is proclaimed;
19		thanks to your prayers and to the help which will be given to
	JC	me by the Spirit of *Jesus Christ*,
20		My one hope . . . is that . . . I shall have the courage for
	C	*Christ* to be glorified in my body,
21	C	Life to me . . . is *Christ*, but then death would bring me something more;
23	C	I want to be gone and be with *Christ*,
26		another reason ᶠto give praise to Christ Jesus (lit. for pride in
	e CJ	*Christ Jesus*)
27		Avoid anything in your everyday lives that would be unworthy of the gospel of *Christ*,
29		[God] has given you the privilege not only of believing in
	C	*Christ*, but of suffering for him as well.
2 1	e C	If our life in *Christ* means anything to you,
5	e CJ	In your minds you must be the same as *Christ Jesus*.
10		so that all beings . . . should bend the knee at the name of *Jesus*

Ph	2 11	JC	that every tongue should acclaim *Jesus Christ* as Lord
	16	C	This would give me something to be proud of for the Day of *Christ*,
	19	e	I hope, in the Lord *Jesus*, to send Timothy to you
	21	JC	[I have nobody here as whole-heartedly concerned for your welfare as Timothy;] all the rest seem more interested in
		CJ	themselves than in ᵛ*Jesus Christ* (G *Christ Jesus*).
	30	C	It was for *Christ's* work that [Epaphroditus] came so near to dying,
	3 4	e CJ	we have our own glory ʳfrom (lit. in) *Christ Jesus*
	7	C	because of *Christ*, I have come to consider all these advantages
	8		that I had as disadvantages. ⁸ . . . nothing that can happen will outweigh the supreme advantage of knowing
		CJ	*Christ Jesus* my Lord. . . . I look on everything as so much
	9	C	rubbish if only I can have *Christ* ⁹ . . . I want only the
		C	perfection that comes through faith in *Christ*,
	12		I am still running, trying to capture the prize for which
		CJ	*Christ Jesus* captured me.
	14	e CJ	the prize for which God calls us upwards to receive in *Christ Jesus*.
	18		there are many who are behaving as the enemies of the cross
		C	of *Christ*.
	20		from heaven comes the saviour we are waiting for, the Lord
		JC	*Jesus Christ*,
	4 7		that peace of God . . . will guard your hearts and your
		e CJ	thoughts, in *Christ Jesus*.
	19	e CJ	God will fulfil all your needs, in *Christ Jesus*,
	21	e CJ	My greetings to every one of the saints in *Christ Jesus*.
	23	JC	May the grace of the Lord *Jesus Christ* be with your spirit.
Col	1 1	CJ	Paul, . . . an apostle of *Christ Jesus*, . . . ² to the saints in
	2	e C	Colossae, our faithful brothers in *Christ*:
	3	JC	God, the Father of our Lord *Jesus Christ*,
	4	e CJ	ever since we heard about your faith in *Christ Jesus*
	7		Epaphras . . . is one of ʳour (ᵛ your) closest fellow workers
		C	and a faithful deputy for us as *Christ's* servant.
	24	C	It makes me happy . . . in my own body to do what I can to make up all that has still to be undergone by *Christ* for the sake of his body, the Church.
	27	C	The mystery is *Christ* among you, your hope of glory:
	28		this is the wisdom in which we . . . instruct everyone, to
		e C	make them all perfect in *Christ*.
	2 2	C	until you really know God's secret, *Christ*, ³ in which all the jewels of wisdom and knowledge are hidden.
	5	C	I am . . . delighted . . . to see how firm your faith in *Christ* is.
	6	CJ	You must live your whole life according to the *Christ Jesus*, the Lord you have received
	8		some . . . empty, rational philosophy based on the principles
		C	of this world instead of on *Christ*.
	11	C	the complete stripping of your body of flesh. This is circumcision according to *Christ*.
	17	C	These were only pale reflections of what was coming: the
		C	ʳreality (lit. body) is *Christ*.
	20	C	If you have really died with *Christ* to the principles of this world,
	3 1	C	Since you have been brought back to true life with *Christ*, you must look for the things that are in heaven, where
		C	*Christ* is, sitting at God's right hand.
	3	C	now the life you have is hidden with *Christ* in God. ⁴ But
	4	C	when *Christ* is revealed . . . you too will be revealed in all your glory with him.
	11		there is no room for distinction between Greek and Jew, . . .
		C	slave and free man. There is only *Christ*, he is everything and he is in everything.
	13	C	The Lord (ᵛ*Christ*) has forgiven you: now you must do the same.
	15	C	may the peace of *Christ* reign in your hearts,
	16	C	Let the message of *Christ*, in all its richness, find a home with you.
	17		never say or do anything except in the name of the Lord *Jesus*,
	24	C	It is *Christ* the Lord that you are serving;
	4 3		asking God to show us opportunities for . . . proclaiming the
		C	mystery of *Christ*,
	12	CJ	Epaphras . . . this servant of *Christ Jesus*
1 Th	1 1		to the church in Thessalonika which is in God the Father and
		e JC	the Lord *Jesus Christ*;
	3		you have shown your faith in action, . . . in our Lord
		JC	*Jesus Christ*.
	10		now you are waiting for *Jesus*, his Son, whom he raised from the dead,
	2 7		we could have imposed ourselves on you with full weight, as
		C	apostles of *Christ*.
	14	e CJ	the churches of God in *Christ Jesus*
	15		the people who put the Lord *Jesus* to death, and the prophets too.
	19		the crown of which we shall be proudest in the presence of our Lord *Jesus*
	3 2		Timothy, who is God's helper in spreading the Good News of
		C	*Christ*,

1 Th	3 11		May God our Father himself, and our Lord *Jesus* Christ, make it easy for us to come to you.
	13		that you may be blameless in the sight of God our Father when our Lord *Jesus* Christ comes
	4 1	e	we urge you and appeal to you in the Lord *Jesus*
	2		the instructions we gave you on the authority of the Lord *Jesus*.
	14		We believe that *Jesus* died and rose again, and that it will be the same for those who have died in *Jesus*: God will bring them with him.
	16	e C	those who have died in *Christ* will be the first to rise,
	5 9	JC	to win salvation through our Lord *Jesus Christ*,
	18	e CJ	this is what God expects you to do in *Christ Jesus*.
	23		may you be kept . . . blameless, spirit, soul and body, for
		JC	the coming of our Lord *Jesus Christ*.
	28	JC	The grace of our Lord *Jesus Christ* be with you.
2 Th	1 1		to the Church in Thessalonika which is in God our Father and
		e JC	in the Lord *Jesus Christ*;
	2	JC	grace and peace from God the Father and the Lord *Jesus Christ*.
	7		when the Lord *Jesus* appears from heaven
	8		all who . . . refuse to accept the Good News of our Lord *Jesus*.
	12		the name of our Lord *Jesus* [Christ] will be glorified in you . . .
		JC	by the grace of our God and the Lord *Jesus Christ*.
	2 1	JC	To turn now, brothers, to the coming of our Lord *Jesus Christ*
	8		The Lord (§ *Jesus*) will kill [the Rebel] openly
	14		[God] called you to this so that you should share the glory of
		JC	our Lord *Jesus Christ*.
	16	JC	May our Lord *Jesus Christ* himself, and God our Father, . . . ¹⁷ comfort you
	3 5		May the Lord turn your hearts towards the love of God and
		C	the fortitude of *Christ*.
	6	JC	In the name of the Lord *Jesus Christ*, . . . we urge you to keep away from any of the brothers who refuses to work
	12	e JC	In the name of the Lord *Jesus Christ*, we . . . call on people of this kind to go on quietly working
	18	JC	May the grace of our Lord *Jesus Christ* be with you all.
1 Tm	1 1	CJ	Paul, apostle of *Christ Jesus* appointed by the command of
		CJ	God our saviour and of *Christ Jesus* our hope,
	2	CJ	mercy and peace from God the Father and from *Christ Jesus* our Lord.
	12	CJ	I thank *Christ Jesus* our Lord, who has given me strength,
	14		the grace of our Lord filled me with faith and with the love
		e CJ	that is in *Christ Jesus*.
	15	CJ	*Christ Jesus* came into the world to save sinners.
	16	JC	*Jesus Christ* meant to make me the greatest evidence of his inexhaustible patience
	2 5		there is only one mediator between God and mankind,
		CJ	himself a man, *Christ Jesus*,
	3 13		rewarded with great assurance in their work for the faith in
		e CJ	*Christ Jesus*.
	4 6		If you put all this to the brothers, you will be a good servant
		CJ	of *Christ Jesus*
	5 11		if their natural desires get stronger than their devotion to
		C	*Christ*,
	21	CJ	Before God, and before *Jesus Christ* and the angels he has chosen,
	6 3	JC	the sound teaching which is that of our Lord *Jesus Christ*,
	13	CJ	before *Jesus Christ*, who spoke up as a witness for the truth
	14		[the duty] of doing all that you have been told . . . until the
		JC	Appearing of our Lord *Jesus Christ*,
2 Tm	1 1	CJ	Paul, appointed by God to be an apostle of *Christ Jesus* in his
		e CJ	design to promise life in *Christ Jesus*;
	2		to Timothy . . . grace . . . from God the Father and from
		CJ	*Christ Jesus* our Lord.
	9	e CJ	This grace had already been granted to us, in *Christ Jesus*,
	10		before the beginning of time, ¹⁰ but it has only been
		CJ	revealed by the Appearing of our saviour *Christ Jesus*.
	13	e CJ	in the faith and love that are in *Christ Jesus*.
	2 1		Accept the strength . . . that comes from the grace ʳof (lit.
		e CJ	which is in) *Christ Jesus*.
	3		Put up with your share of difficulties, like a good soldier of
		CJ	*Christ Jesus*.
	8	JC	Remember . . . *Jesus Christ* risen from the dead,
	10	e CJ	so that . . . they may have the salvation that is in *Christ Jesus*
	3 12	e CJ	anybody who tries to live in [devotion to] *Christ* is certain to be attacked;
	15	e CJ	the wisdom that leads to salvation through faith in *Christ Jesus*.
	4 1	CJ	Before God and before *Christ Jesus* . . . ² proclaim the message
Tt	1 1	JC	Paul, . . . an apostle of *Jesus Christ*
	4	CJ	To Titus . . . peace from God the Father and from *Christ Jesus* our saviour.
	2 13		the Appearing of the glory of our great God and saviour
		CJ	*Christ Jesus*.
	3 6		the Holy Spirit which he has so generously poured over us
		JC	through *Jesus Christ* our saviour.

Phm 1 CJ — Paul, a prisoner of *Christ Jesus*
3 — wishing you . . . the peace of God our Father and the Lord
JC — *Jesus Christ.*
5 — I hear of the love . . . which you have for the Lord *Jesus*
6 C — all the good things that we are able to do for *Christ.*
8 e C — although in *Christ* I can have no diffidence about telling you to do . . . your duty,
9 — this is Paul writing, an old man now and still a prisoner of
CJ — *Christ Jesus.*
20 e C — put new heart into me, in *Christ.*
23 e CJ — Epaphras, a prisoner with me in *Christ Jesus,*
25 JC — May the grace of our Lord *Jesus Christ* be with your spirit.

Heb 2 9 — we do see in *Jesus* one who was for a short while made lower than the angels and is now crowned with glory
3 1 — *Jesus*, the apostle and the high priest of our religion.
6 C — *Christ* was faithful as a son, and as the master in the house.
14 C — we shall remain co-heirs with *Christ*
4 14 — Since in *Jesus*, the Son of God, we have the supreme high priest
5 5 C — Nor did *Christ* give himself the glory of becoming a high priest,
6 1 — Let us leave behind us then all the elementary teaching about
C — *Christ* and concentrate on its completion,
20 — [beyond the veil of the sanctuary] where *Jesus* has entered before us . . . to become a high priest of the order of Melchizedek,
7 22 — it is a greater covenant for which *Jesus* has become our guarantee.
9 11 C — But now *Christ* has come, as the high priest of all the blessings which were to come.
14 C — how much more effectively the blood of *Christ*, who offered himself . . . can purify our inner self
24 C — It is not as though *Christ* had entered a man-made sanctuary . . . it was heaven itself
28 C — *Christ* . . . offers himself only once . . . and when he appears a second time, it will not be to deal with sin
10 10 — for us to be made holy by the offering of his body made
JC — once and for all by *Jesus Christ.*
19 — through the blood of *Jesus* we have the right to enter the sanctuary,
11 26 C — [Moses] considered that the insults offered to the *Anointed* were something more precious than all the treasures of Egypt,
12 2 — Let us not lose sight of *Jesus*, who leads us in our faith
24 — [You have come] to *Jesus*, who leads us in our faith
13 8 JC — *Jesus Christ* is the same today as he was yesterday and as he will be for ever.
12 — *Jesus* too suffered outside the gate to sanctify the people
20 — the God of peace, who brought our Lord *Jesus* back from the dead to become the great Shepherd of the sheep
21 — [God] may turn us all into whatever is acceptable to himself
JC — through *Jesus Christ,*

Jm 1 1 JC — James, servant of God and of the Lord *Jesus Christ.*
2 1 JC — do not try to combine faith in *Jesus Christ* . . . with the making of distinctions between classes of people.

1 P 1 1 JC — Peter, apostle of *Jesus Christ* . . . to all . . . who have been
2 — chosen, [2] by the provident purpose of God . . . to be made
JC — . . . obedient to *Jesus Christ*
3 JC — Blessed be God the Father of our Lord *Jesus Christ* who
JC — [has raised] *Jesus Christ* from the dead,
7 JC — so that, when *Jesus Christ* is revealed, your faith will have been tested
11 C — The Spirit of *Christ* which was in [the prophets] foretold the
C — sufferings of *Christ* and the glories that would come after them,
13 JC — the grace that will be given you when *Jesus Christ* is revealed.
19 — [the ransom that was paid to free you was paid] in the precious
C — blood of a lamb without spot or stain, namely *Christ*;
2 5 JC — the spiritual sacrifices which *Jesus Christ* has made acceptable to God,
21 C — *Christ* suffered for you and left an example for you to follow the way he took.
3 15 C — reverence the Lord *Christ* in your hearts,
16 — those who slander you when you are living a good life in
e C — *Christ*
18 C — *Christ* himself . . . had died once for sins,
21 — the baptism . . . which is . . . a pledge made to God . . .
JC — through the resurrection of *Jesus Christ,*
4 1 — Think of what *Christ* suffered in this life, and then arm yourselves with the same resolution that he had:
11 — so that in everything God may receive the glory, through
JC — *Jesus Christ,*
13 C — If you can have some share in the sufferings of *Christ*, be glad,
14 — It is a blessing for you when they insult you for bearing the
C — name of *Christ*,
5 1 C — I am . . . a witness to the sufferings of *Christ*,
10 — the God of all grace who called you to eternal glory in
e C — *Christ*
14 e C — Peace to you all who are in *Christ*.

2 P 1 1 JC — Simeon Peter, servant and apostle of *Jesus Christ*; . . . through
JC — the righteousness of our God and saviour *Jesus Christ.*
2 — May you have more and more grace and peace as you come to know (§ God and *Jesus*) our Lord more and more.
8 — [these spiritual gifts] will bring you to a real knowledge of
JC — our Lord *Jesus Christ.*
11 — admittance into the eternal kingdom of our Lord and saviour
JC — *Jesus Christ.*
14 — I know the time for taking off this tent is coming soon, as our
JC — Lord *Jesus Christ* foretold to me.
16 JC — the power and the coming of our Lord *Jesus Christ*;
2 20 — anyone who has escaped the pollution of the world once by
JC — coming to know our Lord and saviour *Jesus Christ,*
3 18 — go on growing in . . . the knowledge of our Lord and saviour
JC — *Jesus Christ.*

1 Jn 1 3 JC — as we are in union with the Father and with his Son *Jesus Christ.*
7 — the blood of *Jesus*, his Son, purifies us from all sin.
2 1 JC — we have our advocate with the Father, *Jesus Christ*, who is just;
22 JC — The man who denies that *Jesus* is the *Christ* – he is the liar,
3 23 — His commandments are these: that we believe in the name of
JC — his Son *Jesus Christ*
4 2 JC — every spirit which acknowledges that *Jesus* the *Christ* has
3 — come in the flesh is from God; [3] but any spirit which will not say this of *Jesus* is not from God, but is the spirit of Antichrist,
15 — if anyone acknowledges that *Jesus* is the Son of God, God lives in him, and he in God.
5 5 — Who can overcome the world? Only the man who believes
6 JC — that *Jesus* is the Son of God: [6] *Jesus Christ* who came by water and blood,
20 e JC — We are in the true God, as we are in his Son, *Jesus Christ,*
2 Jn 3 — we shall have grace, mercy and peace from God the Father
JC — and from *Jesus Christ*, the Son of the Father.
7 JC — There are many deceivers . . . refusing to admit that *Jesus Christ* has come in the flesh.
9 C — If anybody does not keep within the teaching of *Christ* . . . he cannot have God with him:
Jude 1 JC — From Jude, servant of *Jesus Christ* . . . to those who are
JC — called . . . and kept safe for *Jesus Christ.*
4 — Certain people . . . were condemned for . . . rejecting our
JC — only Master and Lord, *Jesus Christ.*
5 — [r]the Lord ([v]*Jesus*) . . . destroyed the men who did not trust him.
17 JC — remember . . . what the apostles of our Lord *Jesus Christ* told you to expect.
21 JC — wait for the mercy of our Lord *Jesus Christ*
25 JC — To God, the only God, who saves us through *Jesus Christ* our Lord, be the glory,
Rv 1 1 JC — This is the revelation given by God to *Jesus Christ*
2 JC — it is the word of God guaranteed by *Jesus Christ.*
5 JC — [grace and peace to you] from *Jesus Christ*, the faithful witness,
9 e — through our union in *Jesus* I am your brother . . . I was on the island of Patmos for having . . . witnessed for *Jesus*;
11 15 — The kingdom of the world has become the kingdom of our
C — Lord and his *Christ*,
12 10 — Victory and . . . empire for ever have been won by our God,
C — and all authority for his *Christ*,
17 — all who obey God's commandments and bear witness for *Jesus.*
14 12 — there must be constancy in the saints who keep the commandments of God and faith in *Jesus.*
17 6 — [the woman] was . . . drunk with . . . the blood of the martyrs of *Jesus*;
19 10 — like you and all your brothers who are witnesses to *Jesus*. . . . The witness *Jesus* gave is the same as the spirit of prophecy.
20 4 — all who had been beheaded for having witnessed for *Jesus* and for having preached God's word, . . . they came to life, and reigned with *Christ*
6 C — they will be priests of God and of *Christ* and reign with him for a thousand years.
22 16 — I, *Jesus*, have sent my angel to make these revelations to you
20 — Amen; come, Lord *Jesus.*
21 — May the grace of the Lord *Jesus* be with you all. Amen.

3: CHRISTIAN

Ac 11 26 3 — It was at Antioch that the disciples were first called *Christians.*
26 28 — [Agrippa to Paul:] 'A little more, and your arguments would
3 — make a *Christian* of me.'
1 P 4 16 3 — if any one of you should suffer for being a *Christian*, then he is not to be ashamed of it; he should thank God that he has been called one.

4: (FALSE) CHRISTS, (FALSE) MESSIAHS – ANTICHRIST

Mt 24 5 — many will come using my name and saying, I am the *Christ*,

Mt 24	23		If anyone says to you then, Look, here is the *Christ*, or, He
	24	4	is there, do not believe it; ²⁴ for false *Christs* and false prophets will arise
Mk 13	21		if anyone says to you then, Look, here is the *Christ*, or He
	22	4	is there, do not believe it; ²² for false *Christs* and false prophets will arise
1 Jn 2	18	2	you were told that an *Antichrist* must come, and now several
		2	*antichrists* have already appeared;
	22		The man who denies that Jesus is the Christ – he is the liar,
		2	he is *Antichrist*,
4	3		any spirit which will not [acknowledge that Jesus the Christ
		2	has come in the flesh] . . . is the spirit of *Antichrist*,
2 Jn	7	2	They are the Deceiver; they are the *Antichrist*.

2. HE = CHRIST

ekeinos (6)

1 Jn 2	6	when one who claims to be living in [God] is living the same kind of life as ⌐*Christ* (lit. *he*) lived.
3	3	Surely everyone who entertains this hope must purify himself, must try to be as pure as ⌐*Christ* (lit. *he*).
	5	you know that *he* appeared in order to abolish sin, and that in him there is no sin;
	7	to live a holy life is to be holy just as *he* is holy;
	16	This has taught us love – that *he* gave up his life for us;
4	17	even in this world we have become as *he* is.

JEW – JEWISH

1	*ioudaios*	194	4 *ioudaikos*	1
2	*ioudaismos*	2	5 *ioudaikōs*	1
3	*ioudaizō*	1		

G = Jews//Greeks   P = Jews//Pagans

Mt 2	2		Where is the infant king of the *Jews*?
27	11		the governor put . . . this question, 'Are you the king of the *Jews*?'
	29		To make fun of him [the soldiers] knelt to him saying, 'Hail, king of the *Jews*!'
	37		the charge against him . . . read: This is Jesus, the King of the *Jews*.
28	15		to this day that is the story among the *Jews*.
Mk 7	3		the Pharisees, and the *Jews* in general, . . . never eat without washing their arms as far as the elbow;
15	2		Pilate questioned him, 'Are you the king of the *Jews*?'
	9		Do you want me to release for you the king of the *Jews*?
	12		what am I to do with the man you call king of the *Jews*?
	18		[the soldiers] began saluting him, 'Hail, king of the *Jews*!'
	26		The inscription . . . read: The King of the *Jews*.
Lk 7	3		[a centurion] sent some *Jewish* elders to [Jesus]
23	3		Pilate put . . . this question, 'Are you the king of the *Jews*?'
	37		If you are the king of the *Jews*, save yourself.
	38		an inscription: This is the King of the *Jews*.
	51		[Joseph] came from Arimathaea, a *Jewish* town,
Jn 1	19		the *Jews* sent priests and Levites [to John]
2	6		six stone water jars . . . , meant for the ablutions that are customary among the *Jews*:
	13		Just before the *Jewish* Passover
	18		The *Jews* intervened and said, 'What sign can you show us . . . ?'
	20		The *Jews* replied, 'It has taken forty-six years to build this sanctuary:
3	1		one of the Pharisees called Nicodemus, a leading *Jew*,
	22	○	Jesus went with his disciples into the *Judaean* countryside
	25		John's disciples had opened a discussion with a *Jew* about purification,
4	9		'You are a *Jew* and you ask me, a Samaritan, for a drink?' – *Jews*, in fact, do not associate with Samaritans.
	22		we worship what we do know: for salvation comes from the *Jews*.
5	1		Some time after this there was a *Jewish* festival,
	10		the *Jews* said to the man who had been cured, 'It is the sabbath;
	15		The man . . . told the *Jews* that it was Jesus who had cured him. ¹⁶ It was because he did things like this on the sabbath that the *Jews* began to persecute Jesus.
	18		that only made the *Jews* even more intent on killing [Jesus],
6	4		It was shortly before the *Jewish* feast of Passover.
	41		Meanwhile the *Jews* were complaining to each other about [Jesus],

Jn 6	52		the *Jews* started arguing with one another:
7	1		Jesus . . . could not stay in Judaea, because the *Jews* were out to kill him.
	2		As the *Jewish* feast of Tabernacles drew near,
	11		At the festival the *Jews* were on the look-out for him:
	13		no one spoke about [Jesus] openly, for fear of the *Jews*.
	15		The *Jews* were astonished and said, 'How did he learn to read?'
	35	G	The *Jews* then said to one another, ' . . . will he teach the Greeks?'
8	22		The *Jews* said to one another, 'Will he kill himself?'
	31		To the *Jews* who believed in him Jesus said:
	48		The *Jews* replied, 'Are we not right in saying that you are a Samaritan . . . ?'
	52		The *Jews* said, 'Now we know for certain that you are possessed.'
	57		The *Jews* then said, 'You are not fifty yet, and you have seen Abraham!'
9	18		the *Jews* would not believe that the man had been blind
	22		His parents spoke like this out of fear of the *Jews*, ⌐who (lit. for the *Jews*) had already agreed to expel from the synagogue anyone who should acknowledge Jesus as the Christ.
10	19		These words caused disagreement among the *Jews*.
	24		The *Jews* gathered round [Jesus]
	31		The *Jews* fetched stones to stone him,
	33		The *Jews* answered him, 'We are not stoning you for doing a good work
11	8		Rabbi, it is not long since the *Jews* wanted to stone you;
	19		many *Jews* had come to Martha and Mary
	31		the *Jews* who were in the house sympathising with Mary . . . followed her,
	33		At the sight of [Mary's] tears, and those of the *Jews* who followed her, Jesus said
	36		[Jesus wept;] and the *Jews* said, 'See how much he loved [Lazarus].'
	45		Many of the *Jews* who had come to visit Mary . . . believed in him,
	54		Jesus no longer went about openly among the *Jews*,
	55		The *Jewish* Passover drew near,
12	9		a large number of *Jews* heard that [Jesus] was there
	11		many of the *Jews* were leaving [the chief priests] and believing in Jesus.
13	33		as I told the *Jews*, where I am going, you cannot come.
18	12		The cohort and . . . the *Jewish* guards seized Jesus
	14		It was Caiaphas who had suggested to the *Jews*, 'It is better for one man to die for the people.'
	20		in the Temple where all the *Jews* meet together:
	31		The *Jews* answered, 'We are not allowed to put a man to death.
	33		Pilate . . . called Jesus to him, 'Are you the king of the *Jews*?'
	35		Pilate answered, 'Am I a *Jew*?'
	36		if my kingdom were of this world, my men would have fought to prevent my being surrendered to the *Jews*.
	38		Pilate . . . went out again to the *Jews*
	39		would you like me . . . to release the king of the *Jews*?
19	3		[The soldiers] kept . . . saying, 'Hail, king of the *Jews*!'
	7		'We have a Law,' the *Jews* replied
	12		the *Jews* shouted, 'If you set him free you are no friend of Caesar's;'
	14		'Here is your king,' said Pilate to the *Jews*.
	19		Pilate wrote out a notice . . . Jesus the Nazarene, King of the *Jews* . . . ²⁰ The notice was read by many of the *Jews*
	20		
	21		. . . ²¹ So the *Jewish* chief priests said to Pilate: 'You should not write King of the *Jews*, but This man said: I am King of the *Jews*.'
	31		the *Jews* asked Pilate to have . . . the bodies taken away.
	38		Joseph of Arimathaea, who was a disciple of Jesus – though a secret one because he was afraid of the *Jews* –
	40		following the *Jewish* burial custom.
	42		Since it was the *Jewish* Day of Preparation . . . they laid Jesus there.
20	19		the doors were closed . . . for fear of the *Jews*.
Ac 2	5		there were devout men, (§ *Jews*,) living in Jerusalem
	11		*Jews* and proselytes alike – Cretans and Arabs; we hear them preaching in our own language
	14	○	Peter . . . addressed them . . . : ⌐*Men of Judaea* (or: 'You *Jewish* men) . . . make no mistake about this,
9	22		[Saul] was able to throw the *Jewish* colony at Damascus into complete confusion
	23		the *Jews* worked out a plot to kill [Saul],
10	22		The centurion Cornelius, who is . . . highly regarded by the entire *Jewish* people,
	28		it is forbidden for *Jews* to mix with people of another race
	39		everything [Jesus] did throughout the countryside of ⌐*Judaea* (or: the *Jews*)
11	19	G	they usually proclaimed the message only to *Jews*.
12	3		[Herod beheaded James] and when he saw that this pleased the *Jews* he decided to arrest Peter

Ac 12 11 the Lord . . . has saved me from . . . all that the *Jewish* people were so certain would happen to me.

13 5 [Barnabas and Saul] proclaimed the word of God in the synagogues of the *Jews*,

6 at Paphos they came in contact with a *Jewish* magician called Bar-jesus.

43 many *Jews* and devout converts joined Paul and Barnabas,

45 P the *Jews*, prompted by jealousy, . . . contradicted everything Paul said.

50 the *Jews* worked upon some of the devout women

14 1 G At Iconium [Paul and Barnabas] went to the *Jewish* synagogue, and . . . a great many *Jews* and Greeks became believers. [2] Some of the *Jews*, however, . . . poisoned the minds of the pagans against the brothers.

2 P

4 some supported the *Jews*, others the apostles.

5 P a move was made by pagans as well as *Jews* to make attacks on them

19 some *Jews* arrived . . . and turned the people against the apostles.

16 1 G Timothy, whose mother was a *Jewess* who had become a believer; but his father was a Greek. . . . [3] . . . Paul . . . had him circumcised. This was on account of the *Jews*

3 G

20 [Paul and Silas] are *Jews* [21] and are advocating practices which it is unlawful for us as Romans to accept

17 1 Thessalonika, where there was a *Jewish* synagogue.

5 G The *Jews* . . . enlisted the help of a gang

10 G Paul and Silas . . visited the *Jewish* synagogue as soon as they arrived [in Beroea].

17 In the synagogue [Paul] held debates with the *Jews*

18 2 [Paul went to Corinth] where he met a *Jew* called Aquila [who] . . . had recently arrived from Italy because an edict of Claudius had expelled all the *Jews* from Rome.

4 G Every sabbath [Paul] used to hold debates in the synagogues, trying to convert *Jews* as well as Greeks.

5 Paul devoted all his time to preaching, declaring to the *Jews* that Jesus was the Christ.

12 the *Jews* made a concerted attack on Paul

14 Gallio said to the *Jews*, 'Listen, you *Jews*. If this were . . . a crime, I would not hesitate to attend to you;

19 [Paul] went alone to the synagogue to debate with the *Jews*.

24 An Alexandrian *Jew* named Apollos . . . with a sound knowledge of the scriptures,

28 by the energetic way [Apollos] refuted the *Jews* in public

19 10 G people from all over Asia, both *Jews* and Greeks, were able to hear the word of the Lord.

13 some itinerant *Jewish* exorcists tried pronouncing the name of the Lord Jesus . . . [14] Among those who did this were seven sons of Sceva, a *Jewish* chief priest.

14

17 G Everybody in Ephesus, both *Jews* and Greeks, heard about this episode.

33 The *Jews* pushed Alexander to the front . . . [34] When the people realised he was a *Jew*,

34

20 3 a plot organised against [Paul] by the *Jews*

19 the sorrows and trials that came to me through the plots of the *Jews*.

21 G urging both *Jews* and Greeks to turn to God

21 11 The man this girdle belongs to will be bound like this by the *Jews*

P

20 you see . . . how thousands of *Jews* have now become believers,

21 P you instruct all *Jews* living among the pagans to break away from Moses,

27 some *Jews* from Asia . . . stirred up the crowd and seized [Paul],

39 'I?' said Paul, 'I am a *Jew* and a citizen of . . . Tarsus in Cilicia.'

22 3 'I am a *Jew* . . . and was born at Tarsus in Cilicia.'

12 Ananias, . . . highly thought of by all the *Jews* living [in Damascus].

30 [the tribune] wanted to know what precise charge the *Jews* were bringing [against Paul],

23 12 the *Jews* held a secret meeting at which they made a vow not to eat or drink until they had killed Paul.

20 the *Jews* have made a plan to ask you to take Paul

27 This man had been seized by the *Jews*

24 5 [Paul] stirs up trouble among *Jews* the world over,

9 The *Jews* supported [Tertullus], asserting that these were the facts.

19 some *Jews* from Asia . . . – these are the ones who should have appeared before you

24 Felix came with his wife Drusilla who was a *Jewess*.

27 being anxious to gain favour with the *Jews*, Felix left Paul in custody.

25 2 The . . . leaders of the *Jews* informed [Festus] of the case against Paul,

7 As soon as Paul appeared, the *Jews* who had come down from Jerusalem surrounded him,

8 I have committed no offence whatever against either *Jewish* law, or the Temple,

Ac 25 9 Festus was anxious to gain favour with the *Jews*, so he said to Paul,

10 Paul replied, '. . . I have done the *Jews* no wrong,

15 the . . . elders of the *Jews* laid information against [Paul],

24 the man [Paul] against whom the whole *Jewish* community has petitioned me,

26 2 I consider myself fortunate . . . in that it is before you I am to answer today all the charges made against me by the *Jews*, [3] the more so because you are an expert in matters of custom . . . among the *Jews*.

3

4 My manner of life . . . is common knowledge among the *Jews*.

7 For that hope, Sire, I am actually put on trial by the *Jews*!

21 P This was why the *Jews* . . . tried to do away with me.

28 17 [Paul] called together the leading *Jews* [in Rome].

19 the *Jews* lodged an objection, and I was forced to appeal to Caesar,

29 (v. . . . the *Jews* went away, arguing vehemently among themselves)

Rm 1 16 the Good News . . . is the power of God saving all who have faith – *Jews* first, but Greeks as well –

G

2 9 G Pain and suffering will come . . . [to] *Jews* first, but [to] Greeks as well; [10] renown, honour and peace will come . . . [to] *Jews* first, but [to] Greeks as well.

10 G

17 If you call yourself a *Jew*,

28 To be a *Jew* is not just to look like [a *Jew*], . . . [29] The real *Jew* is the one who is inwardly [a *Jew*],

29

3 1 is a *Jew* any better off?

9 G *Jews* and Greeks are all under sin's dominion.

29 P Is God the God of *Jews* alone and not of the pagans too?

9 24 P whether we were *Jews* or pagans we are the ones he has called.

10 12 G scripture . . . makes no distinction between *Jew* and Greek: all belong to the same Lord

1 Co 1 22 G while the *Jews* demand miracles and the Greeks look for wisdom, [23] here are we preaching a crucified Christ; to the *Jews* an obstacle . . , to the pagans madness, [24] but to those who have been called, whether they are *Jews* or Greeks, a Christ who is the power and the wisdom of God.

23

24 P

G

9 20 I made myself a *Jew* to the *Jews*, to win the *Jews*;

10 32 G Never do anything offensive to anyone – to *Jews* or Greeks

12 13 G In the one Spirit we were all baptised, *Jews* as well as Greeks,

2 Co 11 24 five times I had the thirty-nine lashes from the *Jews*,

Ga 1 13 2 You must have heard of my career ⌐as a *practising Jew* (or: in *Judaism*)' . . [14] how I stood out ⌐among other Jews⌐ (lit. above the *Judaism*) of my generation.

14 2

2

2 13 The other *Jews* joined [Cephas] in this pretence . . . [14] . . . I said to Cephas . . , 'In spite of being a *Jew*, you live like pagans and not *like the Jews*, so you have no right to make the pagans *copy Jewish ways*.

14

P 5

P 3

15 P Though we were born *Jews* and not pagan sinners,

3 28 G there are not more distinctions between *Jew* and Greek, . . . but all of you are one in *Christ Jesus*.

Col 3 11 there is no room for distinction between Greek and *Jew* . . . There is only Christ:

G

1 Th 2 14 you . . . have been like the churches . . . in Judaea, in suffering the same treatment from your own countrymen as they have suffered from the *Jews*,

Tt 1 14 4 so that they stop taking notice of *Jewish* myths

Rv 2 9 people who profess to be *Jews* but are really members of the synagogue of Satan

3 9 the synagogue of Satan . . . those who profess to be *Jews*, but are liars,

---

JOHN THE BAPTIST

1. Zechariah, Elizabeth and John | 2. John

John	91	Elizabeth	9
1 *ho baptistēs*	12	Zechariah	9
2 *ho baptizōn*	3		

1. ZECHARIAH, ELIZABETH AND JOHN

Lk 1 5 a priest called *Zechariah* who belonged to the Abijah section of the priesthood, and he had a wife, *Elizabeth* by name, who was a descendant of Aaron. . . . [7] But they were childless: *Elizabeth* was barren and they were both getting on in years.

7

12 *Zechariah* . . . was overcome with fear. [13] But the angel said to him, '*Zechariah*, do not be afraid . . . Your wife *Elizabeth* is to bear you a son and you must name him John.'

13

18 *Zechariah* said to the angel, 'How can I be sure of this?'

Lk 1 21 — the people were waiting for *Zechariah* and were surprised that he stayed in the sanctuary so long.
24 — Some time later his wife *Elizabeth* conceived,
36 — [The angel said to Mary:] 'your kinswoman *Elizabeth* has, in her old age, herself conceived a son
40 — [Mary] went into *Zechariah's* house and greeted *Elizabeth*.
41 — [41] Now as soon as *Elizabeth* heard Mary's greeting, the child leapt in her womb and *Elizabeth* was filled with the Holy Spirit.
57 — the time came for *Elizabeth* to have her child, and she gave birth to a son;
59 — they were going to call him *Zechariah* after his father,
60 — [60] but his mother spoke up. 'No, . . . he is to be called *John*.'
63 — The father asked for a writing-tablet and wrote, His name is *John*.
67 — His father *Zechariah* was filled with the Holy Spirit and spoke this prophecy:
3 2 — [In the fifteenth year of Tiberius Caesar's reign] the word of God came to *John* son of *Zechariah*, in the wilderness.

2. JOHN

E = John//Elijah

Mt 3 1 1 — In due course *John the Baptist* appeared; he preached in the wilderness of Judaea and this was his message: [2] Repent,
4 — This man *John* wore a garment made of camel-hair
13 — Jesus . . . came from Galilee to the Jordan to be baptised by *John*. [14] *John* tried to dissuade him.
14 —
4 12 — Hearing that *John* had been arrested [Jesus] went back to Galilee,
9 14 — *John's* disciples came to [Jesus] and said, 'Why is it that . . . your disciples do not [fast]?'
11 2 — *John* in his prison had heard what Christ was doing
4 — Go back and tell *John* what you hear and see;
7 — Jesus began to talk to the people about *John*: 'What did you go out into the wilderness to see?
11 1 — of all the children born of women a greater than *John the Baptist* has never been seen; . . . [12] Since *John the Baptist* came, up to the present time, the kingdom of heaven has been subjected to violence . . . [13] Because it was towards *John* that all the prophecies . . . were leading; [14] (cf. Ml 3 23–24) and he . . . is the Elijah who was to return.
12 1 —
13 —
14 —
E
18 — *John* came, neither eating nor drinking, and they say, He is possessed.
14 2 1 — [Herod said of Jesus:] 'This is *John the Baptist* himself; he has risen from the dead, . . .' [3] . . . it was Herod who had arrested *John*, . . . because of Herodias . . . [4] For *John* had told him, 'It is against the Law for you to have her.'
3 —
4 —
8 1 — Give me *John the Baptist's* head, here, on a dish.
10 — [Herod] sent and had *John* beheaded in the prison.
16 14 E 1 — Some say he is *John the Baptist*, some Elijah,
17 13 E — [Jesus said, 'Elijah has come already.'] The disciples understood then that he had been speaking of *John the Baptist*.
1 —
21 25 — *John's* baptism: where did it come from: heaven or man?
26 — the people . . . all hold that *John* was a prophet.
32 — *John* came to you, a pattern of true righteousness, but you did not believe him,
Mk 1 4 2 — *John the Baptist* appeared in the wilderness, proclaiming a baptism of repentance
6 — *John* wore a garment of camel-skin,
9 — Jesus . . . was baptised in the Jordan by *John*.
14 — After *John* had been arrested, Jesus went into Galilee.
2 18 — One day when *John's* disciples and the Pharisees were fasting, some people came and said to [Jesus], 'Why is it that *John's* disciples . . . fast, but your disciples do not?'
6 14 2 — Some were saying, '*John the Baptist* has risen from the dead . . .' [15] Others said, 'He is Elijah;' . . . [16] But when Herod heard this he said, 'It is *John* whose head I cut off; he has risen from the dead.' [17] . . . Herod . . . had sent to have *John* arrested . . . because of Herodias . . . [18] For *John* had told Herod, 'It is against the law for you to have your brother's wife.'
16 E —
17 —
18 —
20 — Herod was afraid of *John*, knowing him to be a good and holy man,
24 2 — [Herodias said to her daughter, 'Ask for] the head of *John the Baptist*.' [25] '. . . I want you to give me *John the Baptist's* head, here and now, on a dish.'
25 1 —
8 28 E 1 — [Who do people say I am?'] '*John the Baptist* . . . others [say] Elijah;'
11 30 — *John's* baptism: did it come from heaven, or from man?
32 — everyone held that *John* was a real prophet.
Lk 3 15 — the people . . . were beginning to think that *John* might be the Christ, [16] so *John* declared . . . , 'I baptise you with water, but someone is coming . . . who . . . will baptise you with the Holy Spirit
16 —

Lk 3 20 — [Herod shut] *John* up in prison.
5 33 — *John's* disciples are always fasting and saying prayers,
7 18 — The disciples of *John* gave him all this news, and *John* . . .
20 1 — [19] sent them to the Lord . . . [20] . . . '*John the Baptist* has sent us . . . to ask, Are you the one who is to come . . . ?' [22] 'Go back and tell *John* what you have seen and heard;
22 —
24 — When *John's* messengers had gone [Jesus] began to talk to the people about *John* . . . [28] '. . . there is no one greater than *John*; yet the least in the kingdom of God is greater than he is.' [29] All the people who heard him, and the tax collectors too, acknowledged God's plan by accepting baptism from *John*;
28 —
29 —
33 1 — *John the Baptist* comes, not eating bread, not drinking wine, and you say, He is possessed.
9 7 E — some people were saying that *John* had risen from the dead, [8] others that Elijah had reappeared, . . . [9] But Herod said, '*John*? I beheaded him.
9 —
19 E 1 — ['Who do the crowds say I am?'] '*John the Baptist*; others [say] Elijah;'
11 1 — Lord, teach us to pray, just as *John* taught his disciples.
16 16 — Up to the time of *John* it was the Law and the Prophets;
20 4 — *John's* baptism: did it come from heaven, or from man?
6 — the people . . . are convinced that *John* was a prophet.
Jn 1 6 — A man came, sent by God, His name was *John*.
15 — [The Word was made flesh.] *John* appears as his witness.
19 — This is how *John* appeared as a witness.
26 E — ['Why are you baptising if you are not the Christ and not Elijah?'] *John* replied, 'I baptise with water; but there stands one among you
28 — This happened at Bethany, on the far side of the Jordan, where *John* was baptising.
32 — *John* also declared, 'I saw the Spirit coming down on him
35 — On the following day as *John* stood there again . . . [36] . . . [he] said, 'Look, there is the lamb of God.'
40 — One of these two who became followers of Jesus after hearing what *John* had said was Andrew,
3 23 — At the same time *John* was baptising at Aenon, near Salim, where there was plenty of water, . . . [24] This was before *John* had been put in prison. [25] Now some of *John's* disciples had opened a discussion with a Jew about purification, [26] so they went to *John* and said, '. . . the man to whom you bore witness is baptising now;' . . . [27] *John* replied: 'A man can lay claim only to what is given him from heaven.'
24 —
25 —
26 —
27 —
4 1 — [Jesus] was making and baptising more disciples than *John*
5 33 — You sent messengers to *John*, . . . [35] *John* was a lamp . . . [36] But my testimony is greater than *John's*:
36 —
10 40 — [Jesus] went back again to the far side of the Jordan . . . where *John* had once been baptising. [41] Many people . . . said, '*John* gave no signs; but all *John* said about this man was true;
41 —
Ac 1 5 — *John* baptised with water, but you . . . will be baptised with the Holy Spirit.
22 — from the time when *John* was baptising until the day when [Jesus] was taken up from us
10 37 — the recent happenings in Judaea . . . after *John* had been preaching baptism.
11 16 — *John* baptised with water, but you will be baptised with the Holy Spirit.
13 24 — [Jesus] whose coming was heralded by *John* when he proclaimed a baptism of repentance . . . [25] Before *John* ended his career he said, 'I am not the one you imagine me to be;
25 —
18 25 — [Apollos] had only experienced the baptism of *John*.
19 3 — 'How were you baptised?' . . . 'With *John's* baptism . . .'
4 — [4] '*John's* baptism,' said Paul, 'was a baptism of repentance; but he insisted that the people should believe in . . . Jesus.'

JOIN – ATTACH

1. Knit together – Join – Bind together: *sym-bibazō*

2. Yoke – Join – Unite: *zygos*
  a) Yoke
  b) Unite, Join together – Harness(ed) together

3. Join, Fit together – Joint, Bond: *harmos*

4. Attach, Fasten on – Joint: *kathaptō*

  a) Attach (oneself), Fasten on
  b) Joint

5. Cling to – Join – Attach: *kollaō*
  a) Cling to (a thing), Hold fast to – Join – (Be) Piled high (so as to touch)
  b) Cling to (a person) – Join, Go with, (Be) Joined to – Attach oneself to

B = Bond between a man and a woman

1. KNIT TOGETHER – JOIN – BIND TOGETHER: *SYM-BIBAZŌ*

sym-bibazo 3/7

Ep	4 16	the whole body is fitted and ┌joined together (or: *knit together*)
Col	2 2	It is all to *bind* you *together* in love and to stir your minds, so that your understanding may come to full development,
	19	it is the head that . . . *holds* the whole body *together*, with all its joints and sinews

2. YOKE – JOIN – UNITE: *ZYGOS*

3 (hetero-)zygeō 1	2 sy-zeugnymi	2
4 sy-zygos 1	1 zygos	5/6

a) Yoke

Mt	11 29 X	Shoulder my *yoke* and learn from me,
	30 X	my *yoke* is easy and my burden light.
Ac	15 10	It would only provoke God's anger . . . if you imposed on the disciples the very ┌burden (lit. *yoke*) that neither we nor our ancestors were strong enough to support
Ga	5 1	do not submit again to the *yoke* of slavery.
1Tm	6 1	All slaves 'under the *yoke*' must have unqualified respect for their masters,

b) Unite, Join together – Harness(ed) together

Mt	19 6 B	2 what God has *united*, man must not divide.
Mk	10 9 B	2 what God has *united*, man must not divide.
2 Co	6 14	3 Do not *harness* yourselves *in* an uneven *team* with unbelievers.
Ph	4 3	4 I ask you, Syzygus, to be truly a ┌'companion' (or: 'yoke-fellow') and to help [Evodia and Syntyche] in this.

3. JOIN, FIT TOGETHER – JOINT, BOND: *HARMOS*

2 harmos 1   1 syn-harmo-logeō 2

Ep	2 21	As every structure ┌is aligned on (lit. *is joined together* in) [Christ], all grow into one holy temple in the Lord;
	4 16	the whole body *is fitted* and joined together,
Heb	4 12	The word of God . . . can slip through the place where the soul is divided from the spirit, or *joints* from the marrow;

4. ATTACH, FASTEN ON – JOINT: *KATH-APTŌ*

1 haphē 2   2 kath-aptō 1

a) Attach (oneself), Fasten on

Ac	28 3	2 a viper . . . *attached itself* to [Paul's] hand.

b) Joint

Ep	4 16	[Christ is the head] by whom the whole body is fitted and ┌joined together (or: knit together), every *joint* adding its own strength,
Col	2 19	it is the head that adds strength and holds the whole body together, with all its *joints* and sinews

5. CLING TO – JOIN – ATTACH: *KOLLAŌ*

1 kollaō 12   2 pros-kollaō 2

a) Cling to (a thing), Hold fast to – Join – (Be) Piled high (so as to touch)

Lk	10 11	We wipe off the very dust of your town that *clings to* our feet.
Ac	8 29	The Spirit said to Philip, 'Go up and ┌meet (lit. *join*) that chariot'.
Rm	12 9	sincerely ┌prefer good to (lit. *hold fast to* good and hate) evil.
Rv	18 5	[Babylon's] sins have ┌reached up to (lit. been *piled high* as) heaven,

b) Cling to (a person) – Join, Go with, (Be) Joined to – Attach oneself to

Mt	19 5 B	(Gn 2 24) a man must leave father and mother, and *cling to* his wife,
Mk	10 7 B	2 (Gn 2 24) a man must leave father and mother, (ᵛ and *cling to* his wife)
Lk	15 15	[the prodigal son] ┌hired himself out to (lit. *attached himself to*) one of the local inhabitants
Ac	5 13	No one else ever dared to *join* [the disciples],
	9 26	[Saul] tried to *join* the disciples,
	10 28	it is forbidden for Jews to *mix with* people of another race

Ac	17 34	there were some who *attached themselves to* [Paul]
1 Co	6 16 B	a man who *goes with* a prostitute is one body with her . . .
	17 B	¹⁷ But anyone who *is joined to* the Lord is one spirit with him.
Ep	5 31 B	2 (Gn 2 24) a man must leave his father and mother and *be joined to* his wife,

JUDAEA

1. Judaea	4. Bethlehem
2. Arimathaea	5. Emmaus
3. Bethany and Bethphage	6. Jericho

1. JUDAEA

Judaea 44   Ephraim 1 (Jn 11)   1 polis 1/164

For Judaean *see* JEW – JEWISH

Mt	2 1	After Jesus had been born at Bethlehem in *Judaea*
	5	[the Christ was to be born] At Bethlehem in *Judaea*
	22	[Joseph] learnt that Archelaus had succeeded his father Herod as ruler of *Judaea*
	3 1	John the Baptist . . . preached in the wilderness of *Judaea*
	5	Jerusalem and all *Judaea* and the whole Jordan district made their way to [John],
	4 25	Large crowds followed [Jesus], coming from Galilee, the Decapolis, Jerusalem, *Judaea* and Transjordan.
	19 1	Jesus . . . came into the part of *Judaea* which is on the far side of the Jordan.
	24 16	those in *Judaea* must escape to the mountains;
Mk	1 5	All *Judaea* and all the people of Jerusalem made their way to [John],
	3 7	From *Judaea*, ⁸ Jerusalem, Idumaea, Transjordania . . . great numbers . . . came to [Jesus].
	10 1	[Jesus] came to the district of *Judaea* and the far side of the Jordan.
	13 14	those in *Judaea* must escape to the mountains;
Lk	1 5	In the days of King Herod of *Judaea*
	65	the whole affair was talked about throughout the hill country of *Judaea*.
	2 4	Joseph set out from the town of Nazareth in Galilee and travelled up to *Judaea*,
	3 1	when Pontius Pilate was governor of *Judaea*,
	4 44	[Jesus] continued his preaching in the synagogues of ┌*Judaea* (ᵛ Galilee).
	5 17	Pharisees and doctors of the Law who had come from every village in Galilee, from *Judaea* and from Jerusalem.
	6 17	a great crowd of people from all parts of *Judaea* and from Jerusalem
	7 17	this opinion of [Jesus] spread throughout *Judaea*
	21 21	those in *Judaea* must escape to the mountains,
	23 5	[Jesus] is inflaming the people with his teaching all over *Judaea*;
Jn	4 3	[Jesus] left *Judaea* and went back to Galilee.
	47	hearing that Jesus had arrived in Galilee from *Judaea*
	54	This was the second sign given by Jesus, on his return from *Judaea* to Galilee.
	7 1	After this Jesus stayed in Galilee; he could not stay in *Judaea*,
	3	his brothers said to him, 'Why not leave this place and go to *Judaea* . . . ?'
	11 7	[Jesus said] to the disciples, 'Let us go to *Judaea*.'
	54	1 Jesus . . . left the district for a *town* called *Ephraim*, in the country bordering the desert, and stayed there with his disciples.
Ac	1 8	you will be my witnesses not only in Jerusalem but throughout *Judaea* and Samaria.
	2 9	[devout men living in Jerusalem from] Mesopotamia, *Judaea* and Cappadocia,
	8 1	everyone except the apostles fled to the country districts of *Judaea* and Samaria.
	9 31	The churches throughout *Judaea*, Galilee and Samaria were now left in peace,
	10 37	You must have heard about the recent happenings in *Judaea*;
	11 1	The apostles and the brothers in *Judaea* heard that the pagans too had accepted the word of God,
	29	The disciples decided to send relief . . . to the brothers living in *Judaea*,
	12 19	before leaving *Judaea* to take up residence in Caesarea [Herod] gave orders for [the guards'] execution.
	15 1	some men came down from *Judaea* and taught the brothers,
	21 10	a prophet called Agabus arrived [in Caesarea] from *Judaea*

Ac 26 20	I started preaching . . . to the people of . . . Jerusalem and all the countryside of *Judaea,*
28 21	We have received no letters from *Judaea* about you,
Rm 15 31	Pray that I may escape the unbelievers in *Judaea,*
2 Co 1 16	for you to see me on my way to *Judaea.*
Ga 1 22	[I] was still not known by sight to the churches of Christ in *Judaea,*
1 Th 2 14	you . . . have been like the churches of God in Christ Jesus which are in *Judaea,*

2. ARIMATHAEA

Arimathaea 4   1 polis 1/164

Mt 27 57	When it was evening, there came a rich man of *Arimathaea,*
Mk 15 43	Joseph of *Arimathaea,* a prominent member of the Council, . . . boldly went to Pilate and asked for the body of Jesus.
Lk 23 51	1 [Joseph] came from *Arimathaea,* a Jewish *town,*
Jn 19 38	Joseph of *Arimathaea,* who was a disciple of Jesus – though a secret one

3. BETHANY and BETHPHAGE

Bethany   11   S Simon 2
B Bethphage   3

Mt 21 1	When they were near Jerusalem and had come in sight of *Bethphage* on the Mount of Olives, Jesus sent two disciples,
B	
17	[Jesus] . . . went out of the city [Jerusalem] to *Bethany* where he spent the night.
26 6 S	Jesus was at *Bethany* in the house of *Simon* the leper,
Mk 11 1	When they were approaching Jerusalem, in sight of *Bethphage* and *Bethany,* close by the Mount of Olives, he sent two of his disciples
B	
11	[Jesus] went out to *Bethany* with the Twelve. ¹² Next day as they were leaving *Bethany,* he felt hungry.
12	
14 3 S	Jesus was at *Bethany* in the house of *Simon* the leper;
Lk 19 29 B	when he was near *Bethphage* and *Bethany,* close by the Mount of Olives as it is called, he sent two of the disciples,
24 50	he took [the apostles] out as far as the outskirts of *Bethany,* and . . . ⁵¹ . . . was carried up to heaven.
Jn 11 1	a man named Lazarus who lived in the village of *Bethany* with the two sisters, Mary and Martha,
18	*Bethany* is only about two miles from Jerusalem,
12 1	Jesus went to *Bethany,* where Lazarus was,

4. BETHLEHEM

Bethlehem 8   1 polis 2/164

Mt 2 1	After Jesus had been born at *Bethlehem* in Judaea during the reign of King Herod,
5	[Herod asked the scribes where the Christ was to be born.] 'At *Bethlehem* in Judaea, . . . for this is what the prophet wrote (Mi 5 1): ⁶ And you *Bethlehem,* in the land of Judah, . . . out of you will come a leader . . .'
6	
8	[Herod] sent [the wise men] on to *Bethlehem.*
16	in *Bethlehem* and its surrounding district [Herod] had all the male children killed who were two years old or under,
Lk 2 4	1 Joseph . . . travelled up to Judaea, to the *town* of David called *Bethlehem,*
11	1 Today in the *town* of David a saviour has been born to you;
15	the shepherds said to one another, 'Let us go to *Bethlehem* . . .'
Jn 7 42	Does not scripture say that the Christ must be descended from David and come from the town of *Bethlehem?*

5. EMMAUS

Emmaus 1   Cleopas 1

| Lk 24 13 | two of [the disciples] were on their way to a village called *Emmaus,* seven miles from Jerusalem, |
| 18 | one of them, called *Cleopas,* answered him, 'You must be the only person staying in Jerusalem who does not know the things that have been happening there . . .' |

6. JERICHO

Jericho 7   Bar-timaeus   1
                Timaeus   1
                Rahab [Rachab]   3

Mt 1 5	Salmon was the father of Boaz, *Rahab* being his mother,
20 29	As they left *Jericho* a large crowd followed [Jesus].
Mk 10 46	They reached *Jericho;* and as [Jesus] left *Jericho* . . . *Bartimaeus* (that is, the son of *Timaeus*), a blind beggar, was sitting at the side of the road.
Lk 10 30	A man was once on his way down from Jerusalem to *Jericho* and fell into the hands of brigands;
18 35	as [Jesus] drew near to *Jericho* there was a blind man sitting at the side of the road begging;
19 1	[Jesus] entered *Jericho* and was going through the town ² when a man whose name was Zacchaeus made his appearance;
Heb 11 30	It was through faith that the walls of *Jericho* fell down (cf. Jos 6 20) . . . ³¹ It was by faith that *Rahab* the prostitute welcomed the spies (cf. Jos 2 1; 6 17)
31	
Jm 2 25	(cf. Jos 2 1) *Rahab* the prostitute, justified by her deeds

---

JUDGE – CONDEMN – PUNISH

---

1. Judge – Condemn: *dikazō*
1: Judge
2: Condemn, Condemnation
2. Condemn(ed): *kata-ginōskō*
3. Judge – Condemn – Punish
1: Judge, Judgement – Condemn, Punish: *krinō*
  a) the Judges
  b) Judge, Pass Judgement, Justice – (Be) Tried, On Trial – Decide, Make up one's mind
  c) Condemn, Pass Sentence – Condemnation – Punish(ment)
2: Condemn, Condemnation – Uncondemned, Without trial: *kata-krinō*

3: Judge, Distinguish (between), Discern – Criticise – Recognise, Interpret: *dia-krinō*
4. Justice, Judgement – Vengeance, Avenge – Retribution, Punish(ment): *dikē*
5. Punish(ment)
1: Punish(ment): *kolazō*
2: Punishment, Penalty: *timōreō*
6. Court, Tribunal
1: Court(s): *kritērion*
2: Court, Tribunal: *hēmera*
3: Court, Tribunal – Judgement seat, Bench, Chair of Judgement: *bēma*
4: Assizes, Courts: *agoraios*

1. JUDGE – CONDEMN: *DIKAZŌ*

2 dikastēs 2   1 kata-dikazō 5
              3 kata-dikē   1

1: JUDGE

| Ac 7 27 | (Ex 2 14) who appointed you . . . to be our leader and 2 *judge?* |
| 35 | 2 (Ex 2 14) Who appointed you to be our leader and *judge?* |

2: CONDEMN, CONDEMNATION

Mt 12 7	you would not have *condemned* the blameless.
37	it is by your words you will be . . . *condemned.*
Lk 6 37	do not *condemn,* and you will not be *condemned* yourselves;
Ac 25 15	the chief priests . . . laid information against [Paul], demanding his *condemnation.*
3	
Jm 5 6	It was you who *condemned* the innocent and killed them;

2. CONDEMN(ED): *KATA-GINŌSKŌ*

1 kata-ginōskō 3   2 a-kata-gnōstos 1

Ga 2 11	I opposed [Cephas] to his face, since he ᵣwas manifestly in the wrong (lit. stood *condemned*).
Tt 2 8	[be an example to them] in keeping all that you say so 2 ᵣwholesome (lit. *impossible to condemn*) that nobody can make objections to it;
1 Jn 3 20	[we will be able to quieten our conscience] whatever ᵣaccusations it may raise against us (lit. it may *condemn* us for), because God is greater than our conscience,
21	if we cannot *be condemned* by our own conscience, we need not be afraid in God's presence,

3. JUDGE – CONDEMN – PUNISH

1: JUDGE, JUDGEMENT – CONDEMN, PUNISH: *KRINŌ*

	3 *krima*	27	5 *ana-krinō*	7/16
•	1 *krinō*	115	7 *apo-krima*	1
	2 *krisis*	47	8 (*dikaio-*)*krisia*	1
	6 *kritērion*	2/3	9 *epi-krinō*	1
	4 *kritēs*	19	10 *pro-krima*	1
	11 *kritikos*	1		

a) the Judges

Barak 1   Jephthah 1
Gideon 1   Samson 1

Ac 13 20 — 4 [God] gave them *judges*, down to the prophet Samuel.
Heb 11 32 — There is not time for me to give an account of *Gideon, Barak, Samson, Jephthah*,

b) Judge, Pass Judgement, Justice – (Be) Tried, On Trial – Decide, Make up one's mind

ⓓ = the Devil is judged, condemned

Mt 5 21 — if anyone does kill he must ⌐answer for it before the court (lit. be brought to *judgement*). ²² . . . anyone who is angry with his brother will ⌐answer for it before the court (lit. be brought to *judgement*);
22 2
2
25 4 [your opponent] may hand you over to the *judge* and the 4 *judge* to the officer,
40 — if a man *takes* you *to law* and would have your tunic, let him have your cloak as well.
7 1 ⊖ Do not *judge*, and you will not be *judged*;
2 3/ because the *judgements* you ⌐give (lit. [use to] *judge*) are the ⊖ *judgements* you will get,
10 15 ⊖ 2 on the day of *Judgement* it will not go as hard with the land of Sodom . . . as with that town.
11 22 ⊖ 2 it will not go as hard on *Judgement* day with Tyre and Sidon 24 as with you . . . ²⁴ . . . it will not go as hard with the ⊖ 2 land of Sodom on *Judgement* day as with you.
12 18 — (Is 42 1–3) [my servant] will proclaim ⌐the true faith (lit. 2 *judgement*) to the nations . . . ²⁰ He will not break the 2 crushed reed . . . till he has led ⌐the truth (lit. *justice*) to victory:
20
27 4 Let [your sons = your experts] be your *judges*, then.
36 — for every unfounded word men utter they will answer on ⊖ 2 *Judgement* day,
41 ⊖ 2 On *Judgement* day the men of Nineveh will stand up with this 42 ⊖ 2 generation and condemn it . . . ⁴² On *Judgement* day the Queen of the South will rise up with this generation and condemn it,
19 28 — you will yourselves sit on twelve thrones to *judge* the twelve tribes of Israel.
23 23 — you hypocrites . . . have neglected the weightier matters of the Law – *justice*, mercy, good faith!
Lk 6 37 ⊖ Do not *judge*, and you will not be *judged* yourselves;
7 43 — Jesus said [to Simon], 'You ⌐are (lit. have *judged*) right'.
10 14 ⊖ 2 it will not go as hard with Tyre and Sidon at the *Judgement* as with you.
11 19 4 Let [your sons = your experts] be your *judges*, then.
31 ⊖ 2 On *Judgement* day the Queen of the South will rise up with 32 ⊖ the men of this generation and condemn them . . . ³² On 2 *Judgement* day the men of Nineveh will stand up with this generation and condemn it,
42 2 But alas for you Pharisees . . . who . . . overlook *justice*
12 14 4 My friend . . . who appointed me your *judge* . . .?
57 — Why not *judge* for yourselves what is right?
58 4 [your opponent] may drag you before the *judge* and the 4 *judge* hand you over to the bailiff
18 2 4 There was a *judge* in a certain town . . . who had neither fear of God nor respect for man.
6 4 You notice what the unjust *judge* has to say? ⁷ Now will not God see justice done . . .?
19 22 < 'You wicked servant!' [the master] said 'Out of your own mouth I ⌐condemn (or: *judge*) you.'
22 30 — you will sit on thrones to *judge* the twelve tribes of Israel.
23 24 9 Pilate then *gave* his *verdict*: their demand was to be granted.
Jn 3 17 X For God sent his Son into the world not to ⌐condemn (or: *judge*) the world, but so that through him the world might be saved.
5 22 ⊖ /2 the Father *judges* no one; he has entrusted all *judgement* X to the Son,
24 X whoever listens to my words . . . has eternal life; without 2 being brought to *judgement*
27 X because he is the Son of Man, [God] has appointed him 2 supreme *judge*.
30 X /2 I can only *judge* as I am told to [judge], and my *judging* is just,
7 24 — Do not keep *judging* according to appearances; let your /2 *judgement* be according to ⌐what is right (lit. right *judgement*).

Jn 7 51 — surely the Law does not allow us to *pass judgement* on a man without giving him a hearing . . .?
8 15 X You *judge* by human standards; I *judge* no one, ¹⁶ but if I 16 X /2 *judge*, my *judgement* will be sound.
26 X About you I have much to say and much to ⌐condemn (or: *judge*);
50 ⊖ Not that I care for my own glory, there is someone who takes care of that and is the *judge* of it.
9 39 3 It is for *judgement* that I have come into this world, so that those without sight may see
12 31 ● 2 Now ⌐sentence (or: *judgement*) is being *passed* on this world;
47 X If anyone hears my words and does not keep them faithfully, it is not I who shall ⌐condemn (or: *judge*) him, since I 48 X have come not to ⌐condemn (or: *judge*) the world . . . ⁴⁸ he who . . . refuses my words has his *judge* already; the word itself that I have spoken will *be his judge* on the last day.
16 8 — [the Advocate] will show the world how wrong it was, about 2 sin, and about who was in the right, and about *judgement*
11 ⓓ 2 . . . ¹¹ about *judgement*: proved by the prince of this world being already ⌐condemned (or: *judged*).
18 31 — Take [Jesus] yourselves, and *try* him by your own Law.
Ac 3 13 — you . . . disowned [Jesus] . . . after Pilate had *decided* to release him.
4 19 — You must *judge* whether . . . it is right to listen to you and not to God.
7 7 ⊖ (Gn 15 14) I will *pass judgement* on the nation that enslaves them
8 33 — (Is 53 8 G) He has been humiliated and ⌐has no one to 2 defend him (lit. *justice* has been denied).
10 42 X 4 God has appointed [Jesus] to *judge* everyone, alive or dead.
13 46 — since you do not ⌐think (lit. *judge*) yourselves worthy of eternal life,
15 19 — I ⌐rule (lit. *judge*), then, that instead of making things more difficult for pagans who turn to God . . .
16 4 — [Paul and Timothy] passed on the ⌐decisions reached (lit. decrees *decided* on) by the apostles
15 — If you really ⌐think (lit. *judge*) me a true believer in the Lord . . . stay with us;
17 31 ⊖ [God] has fixed a day when the whole world will be *judged*, and judged in righteousness, and he has appointed a man to be the judge. And God . . . proved this by raising this man from the dead.
18 15 4 I [Gallio] have no intention of *making* legal *decisions* about things like that.
20 16 — Paul had *decided* to pass wide of Ephesus
21 25 — we told [the pagans who have become believers] our *decisions*,
23 3 — How can you [Ananias] sit there to *judge* me according to the Law . . .?
6 — It is for our hope in the resurrection of the dead that I am *on trial*.
24 6 — We placed [Paul] under arrest, ⌄ intending to *judge* him according to our Law,⌐
10 4 [Felix,] I know that you have *administered justice* over this nation for many years,
21 — It is about the resurrection of the dead that I am *on trial* before you today.
25 9 ⊖ 3 when [Paul] began to treat of . . . the coming *Judgement*,
25 9 — [Festus] said to Paul, 'Are you willing to go up to Jerusalem 10 and *be tried* on these charges before me there?' ¹⁰ But Paul replied, 'I am standing before the tribunal of Caesar and this is where I should *be tried*.'
20 — I asked [Paul] if he would be willing to go to Jerusalem to *be tried* there
25 — when [Paul] himself appealed to the august emperor I *decided* to send him.
26 6 — it is for my hope in the promise made by God to our ancestor that I am *on trial*,
8 — Why ⌐does it seem incredible to you (lit. should you *judge* it unbelievable) that God should raise the dead?
27 1 — When it had been *decided* that we should sail for Italy,
Rm 2 1 — if you *pass judgement* you have no excuse. In *judging* others you *condemn* yourself, since you behave no differently from those you *judge*.
3 — when you *judge* those who behave like this while you are doing exactly the same, do you think you will escape ⊖ 3 God's *judgement*?
5 ⊖ 8 on that day of anger when his just *judgement* will be made known.
12 ⊖ — sinners who were under the Law will have that Law to *judge* them.
16 ⊖ — on the day when . . . God . . . *judges* the secrets of mankind.
27 — the man who keeps the Law, even though he has not been physically circumcised, is a living ⌐condemnation of (or: *judgement* on) the way you disobey the Law in spite of being circumcised
3 4 — (Ps 51 4 G) when you *are judged* you win your case.
6 ⊖ — it would mean God could never *judge* the world.
7 — I should not be ⌐judged to be (or: *condemned* as) a sinner at all.

Rm	5	16	3 after one single fall came *judgement* with a verdict of con-demnation,
	11	33 Θ	3 how impossible to penetrate [God's] ᶜmotives (lit. *judge-ments*) . . .!
	14	3	the scrupulous must not ᶜcondemn (or: *judge*) those who feel free to eat anything . . . ⁴ It is not for you to ᶜcondemn
		4	(or: *judge*) someone else's servant:
		5	If one man ᶜkeeps certain days as (lit. *judges* certain days) holier than others, and another ᶜconsiders (lit. *judges*) all days to be equally holy, each must be left free to hold his own opinion.
		10	you should never *pass judgement* on a brother or treat him with contempt . . . We shall all have to stand before the judgement seat of God . . . ¹³ Far from *passing judgement*
		13	on each other, therefore, you should *make up* your *mind* never to be the cause of your brother tripping or falling.
1 Co	2	2	the only knowledge I ᶜclaimed (lit. *decided*) to have was about Jesus,
		14	5 [the Spirit of God] can only be ᶜunderstood (lit. *judged*) by means of the Spirit.
		15	5 A spiritual man . . . is able to *judge the value* of everything,
		5	and his own *value* is not *to be judged* by other men.
	4	3	Not that it makes the slightest difference to me whether you,
		5	or indeed any human *tribunal*, *find* me *worthy* or not. I
		5	will not even *pass judgement* on myself.
	4	X 5/	the Lord alone is my *judge*. ⁵ There must be no *passing* of
		5	premature *judgement*.
	5	3	I . . . have already ᶜcondemned (or: *judged*) the man who did this thing
		12	It is not my business to *pass judgement* on those outside. Of
		13	those who are inside, you can surely *be the judges*. ¹³ But
		Θ	of those who are outside, God *is the judge*.
	6	1	How dare one of your members *take up* a complaint against another *in the lawcourts* of the unjust instead of before
		2	the saints? ² . . . it is the saints who are to 'judge the world'; and if the world is to *be judged* by you, how can
		3	6 you be unfit to *judge* trifling cases? ³ Since we are also
		4	to *judge* angels, it follows that we can judge matters of
		6	everyday life; ⁴ but when you have had *cases* of that kind, the people you appointed to try them were not even
		6	respected in the Church . . . ⁶ and so one brother *brings a*
		7	*court case* against another in front of unbelievers? ⁷ It is
		3	bad enough for you to have *lawsuits* at all against one another; oughtn't you to let yourselves be wronged . . .?
	7	37	if someone has firmly *made* his *mind up* . . . to keep his daughter as she is, he will be doing a good thing.
	10	15	*judge* for yourselves what I am saying.
		29	Why should my freedom ᶜdepend on (lit. *be judged* by) somebody else's conscience?
	11	13	ᶜAsk (lit. *Judge*) for yourselves if it is fitting for a woman to pray to God without a veil;
	14	24	[an uninitiated person] would find himself analysed and
		5	*judged* by everyone speaking;
2 Co	2	1	I *made up* my *mind* not to pay you a second distressing visit.
	5	14	the love of Christ overwhelms us when we *reflect* that if one man has died for all, then all men should be dead;
Col	2	16	never let anyone else *decide* what you should eat or drink,
2 Th	1	5 Θ	2 It all shows that God's *judgment* is just,
	2	12	[The reason why God is sending a power to delude people] is to ᶜcondemn (or: *pass judgement* on) all who refused to believe in the truth
1 Tm	5	21	10 keep these rules ᶜimpartially (lit. without *prejudging*)
		24	The faults of some people are obvious long before anyone
		2	ᶜmakes any complaint about (or: *passes judgement* on) them,
2 Tm	4	1 X	Christ Jesus who is to *be judge* of the living and the dead.
		8 X	the crown of righteousness . . . which the Lord, the righteous
		4	*judge*, will give to me
Tt	3	12	I have *decided* to spend the winter [at Nicopolis].
Heb	4	12	11 The word of God is something alive . . . it *can judge* the secret emotions and thoughts.
	6	2 Θ	[the fundamental *doctrines*:] the teaching about the resur-
		3	rection of the dead and eternal *judgement*.
	9	27 Θ	2 men only die once, and after that comes *judgement*,
	10	27 Θ	2 There will be left only the dreadful prospect of *judgement*
		30 Θ	(Dt 32 36) The Lord will *judge* his people.
	12	23	4 You have come to God himself, the supreme *Judge*,
	13	4 Θ	fornicators and adulterers will come under God's *judgement*.
Jm	2	4	4 you have . . . turned yourselves into *judges*, and corrupt [judges] at that
		12 Θ	Talk and behave like people who are going to *be judged* by the
		13 Θ	2 law of freedom, ¹³ because there will be *judgement* without
		2	mercy for those who have not been merciful; but the
		2	*merciful* need have no fear of *judgement*.
	3	1 Θ	3 those of us who teach can expect a stricter *judgement*.
	4	11	if you condemn the Law, you have stopped keeping it and
		12	4 become a *judge* over it. ¹² There is only one lawgiver and
		Θ 4/	he is the only *judge* . . . Who are you to *give a verdict on* your neighbour?

Jm	5	9	Do not make complaints against one another, brothers, so
		X /4	as not to be *brought to judgement* yourselves; the *Judge* is already to be seen waiting at the gates.
		12	do not swear . . . If you mean 'yes', you must say 'yes'; if you mean 'no', say 'no'. Otherwise you make yourselves
		Θ	2 liable to *judgement*.
1 P	1	17 Θ	If you are acknowledging as your Father one who . . . *judges* everyone according to what he has done,
	2	23 Θ	[Jesus] put his trust in the righteous *judge*.
	4	5 X	[the Lord] who is ready to *judge* the living and the dead.
		6	so that though . . . [the dead] had *been through the judge-ment* that comes to all humanity, they might come to God's life in the spirit.
		17 Θ	3 The time has come for the *judgement* to begin at the house-hold of God;
2 P	2	4	When angels sinned, God . . . sent them down to the
		Θ 2	underworld . . . to be held there till the day of *Judgement*.
		9 Θ	the Lord can . . . hold the wicked for their punishment
		2	until the day of *Judgement*,
		11	2 the angels . . . *make* no . . . ᶜaccusation (or: *judgement*) against [these self-willed people] in front of the Lord.
	3	7	by the same word, the present sky and earth are . . . being
		Θ	2 reserved until *Judgement* day
1 Jn	4	17 Θ	2 we can face the day of *Judgement* without fear;
Jude		6 Θ	2 [the Lord] has kept [the angels] down in the dark . . . *to be judged* on the great day.
		15 Θ	2 [the Lord will come] to pronounce *judgement* on all mankind
Rv	6	10 Θ	Master, how much longer will you wait before you ᶜpass sentence (or: *judge*) and take vengeance for our death . . .?
	11	18 Θ	now the time has come . . . for the dead to be *judged*,
	14	7 Θ	Fear God and praise him, because the time has come for
		2	him to sit in *judgement*;
	16	5 Θ	You are the holy He-Is-and-He-Was, the Just One, and ᶜthis is a (lit. you have *pronounced a*) just ᶜpunishment (or: *judgement*):
		7 Θ	2 Truly, Lord . . . the ᶜpunishments (or: *judgements*) you give are true and just.
	17	1 Θ	Come here and I will show you the ᶜpunishment given to
		3	(or: *judgement* given on) the famous prostitute
	18	20 Θ	God has *given judgement* for your accusation against [Babylon].
	19	2 Θ	2 [Our God] *judges* fairly, he punishes justly,
		11 X	[the rider on the white horse] is a *judge* with integrity, a warrior for justice.
	20	4 Θ	3 I saw those who are given the power to *be judges* take their seats on [the thrones].
		12 Θ	I saw . . . books opened which were the record of what they had done in their lives, by which the dead were
		14 Θ	*judged*. ¹³ The sea gave up all the dead . . . ¹⁴ . . . and every one was *judged* according to the way in which he had lived.

c) Condemn, Pass Sentence – Condemnation – Punish(ment)

Mt	23	33	2 how can you escape *being condemned* to hell?
Mk	12	40 Θ	3 The more severe will be the *sentence* [the scribes] receive.
Lk	19	22 <	'You wicked servant!' [the master] said 'Out of your own mouth I ᶜcondemn (or: *judge*) you.'
	20	47 Θ	3 The more severe will be the *sentence* [the scribes] receive.
	23	40	3 Have you no fear of God at all? . . . You got the same sentence
	24	20	our chief priests and our leaders handed [Jesus] over to be
		3	*sentenced* to death,
Jn	3	17 X	God sent his Son into the world not to ᶜcondemn (or: *judge*) the world, but so that through him the world might be
		18	saved. ¹⁸ No one who believes in him will be *condemned*; but whoever refuses to believe is *condemned* already . . .
		19	2 ¹⁹ On these grounds is *sentence* pronounced: . . . men have shown they prefer darkness
	5	29	those who did good will rise again to life; and those who did
		2	evil, to *condemnation*.
	8	26 X	About you I have much to say and much to ᶜcondemn (or: *judge*)
	12	31 ⦿	2 Now ᶜsentence (or: *judgement*) is being *passed* on this world;
		47	If anyone hears my words and does not keep them faithfully,
		X	it is not I who shall ᶜcondemn (or: *judge*) him, since I have come not to ᶜcondemn (or: *judge*) the world . . .
	6	11	[the Advocate will show the world how wrong it was] about
		Ⓓ	judgement: proved by the prince of this world being already ᶜcondemned (or: *judged*).
Ac	13	27	What the people of Jerusalem . . . did . . . was in fact to fulfil the prophecies . . . they *condemned* [Jesus]
Rm	2	2 Θ	3 We know that God *condemns* that sort of behaviour im-partially:
		27	the man who keeps the Law, even though he has not been physically circumcised, is a living ᶜcondemnation of (or: *judgement* on) the way you disobey the Law in spite of being circumcised
	3	7	I should not be ᶜjudged to be (or: *condemned* as) a sinner at all.

Rm	3 8 ⊖	3	[slanderers] are justly *condemned*.
	13 2	3	rebelling against God's decision . . . is bound to *be punished*.
	14 3		the scrupulous must not ⌐*condemn* (or: *judge*) those who feel free to eat anything . . . ⁴ It is not for you to ⌐*condemn*
	4		(or: *judge*) someone else's servant:
	22		consider the man fortunate who can make his decision without ⌐going against (lit. *condemning* himself through) his conscience.
1 Co	5 3		I . . . have already ⌐*condemned* (or: *judged*) the man who did this thing
	11 29		a person who eats and drinks without recognising the Body is eating and drinking his own *condemnation* . . . ³¹ If
	31	3	only we recollected ourselves, we should not be *punished*
	32 X?		like that. ³² But when the Lord does *punish* us like that, it is to correct us and stop us from being condemned with the world.
	34		eat at home, and then your meeting will not bring your *condemnation*.
		3	
2 Co	1 9	7	we were carrying our own death ⌐warrant (lit. *sentence*) with us,
Ga	5 10 ⊖	3	anybody who troubles you in future will *be condemned*,
2 Th	2 12		[God is sending a power to delude people] . . . to ⌐*condemn* (or: *pass judgement on*) all who refused to believe in the truth
1 Tm	3 6		[the elder-in-charge] should not be a new convert, in case
	ⓓ	3	pride might turn his head and then he might be *condemned* as the devil was [condemned].
	5 12	3	then people *condemn* [young widows] for being unfaithful to their original promise.
	24		The faults of some people are obvious long before anyone
		2	⌐*makes* any *complaint about* (or: *passes judgement on*) them,
Jm	4 11		Anyone who slanders a brother, or *condemns* him, is speaking against the Law and *condemning* the Law. But if you *condemn* the Law, you have . . . become a judge over it.
2 P	2 3 ⊖	3	for [false teachers] the *Condemnation*, pronounced so long ago, is at its work already,
	11	2	the angels . . . make no . . . . ⌐*accusation* (or: *judgement*) against [these self-willed people] in front of the Lord.
Jude	4	3	Certain people . . . were *condemned* for denying all religion,
	9	2	Not even the archangel Michael . . . dared to *denounce* [the devil] in the language of abuse;
Rv	6 10 ⊖		Master, how much longer will you wait before you ⌐*pass sentence* (or: *judge*) and take vengeance for our death . . .?
	16 5 ⊖		You are the holy He-Is-and-He-Was, the Just One, and ⌐this is (lit. *you have pronounced*) a just ⌐*punishment* (or: *judgement*):
	7 ⊖	2	Truly, Lord . . . the ⌐*punishments* (or: *judgements*) you give are true and just.
	17 1 ⊖	3	Come here and I will show you the ⌐*punishment* given to (or: *judgement* given on) the famous prostitute
	18 8 ⊖		The Lord God has *condemned* [Babylon], and he has great power.
	10 ⊖	2	Babylon . . . ⌐*doomed* (lit. *condemned*) as you are within a single hour.
	20 ⊖	3	God has given judgement for your *accusation* against [Babylon].
	19 2 ⊖	2/	[Our God] *punishes* justly and he has *condemned* the famous prostitute

2: CONDEMN, CONDEMNATION – UNCONDEMNED, WITHOUT TRIAL: *KATA-KRINŌ*

2 *kata-krima* 3		4 *a-kata-kritos* 2
1 *kata-krinō* 18		5 *auto-kata-kritos* 1
3 *kata-krisis* 2		

Mt	12 41		On Judgement day the men of Nineveh will stand up with this generation and *condemn* it . . . ⁴² On Judgement day
	42		the Queen of the South will rise up with this generation and *condemn* it,
	20 18		the Son of Man is about to be handed over . . . They will *condemn* him to death
	27 3		When he found that Jesus had been *condemned*, Judas . . was filled with remorse
Mk	10 33		They will *condemn* [the Son of Man] to death and will hand him over to the pagans,
	14 64		they all ⌐gave their verdict (lit. *condemned* him): [Jesus] deserved to die.
	16 16		he who does not believe will be *condemned*.
Lk	11 31		On Judgement day the Queen of the South will rise up with the men of this generation and *condemn* them . . . ³² On
	32		Judgement day the men of Nineveh will stand up with this generation and *condemn* it,
Jn	8 10		'Woman . . . Has no one *condemned* you?' ¹¹ 'No one, sir'
	11 X		she replied. 'Neither do I *condemn* you,' said Jesus
Ac	16 37	4	They flog Roman citizens in public and *without trial*
	22 25		Is it legal for you to flog a man who is a Roman citizen and
		4	⌐has not been brought to trial (lit. *uncondemned*)?

Rm	2 1		In judging others you *condemn* yourself,
	5 16		after one single fall came judgement with a verdict of
		2	*condemnation*.
	18	2	one man's fall brought *condemnation* on everyone,
	8 1	2	those who are in Christ Jesus are not *condemned*,
	3 ⊖		in that body God *condemned* sin.
	34		[When God acquits,] could anyone *condemn*?
	14 23		anybody who eats in a state of doubt is *condemned*, because he is not in good faith;
1 Co	11 32		when the Lord does punish us like that, it is to correct us
	⊖		and stop us from being *condemned* with the world.
2 Co	3 9	3	if there was any splendour in administering *condemnation*,
	7 3	3	I am not saying this to ⌐put any blame on (lit. *condemn*) you;
Tt	3 11	5	any man of that sort has already lapsed and *condemned* himself as a sinner.
Heb	11 7		By [Noah's] faith the world was *convicted*,
2 P	2 6 ⊖		The cities of Sodom and Gomorrah, these too [God] con-*demned* and reduced to ashes;

3: JUDGE, DISTINGUISH (BETWEEN), DISCERN – CRITICISE – RECOGNISE, INTERPRET: *DIA-KRINŌ*

1 *dia-krinō* 10/19		3 *a-dia-kritos* 1
2 *dia-krisis* 3		

Mt	16 3		You know how to ⌐read (lit. *interpret*) the face of the sky, but you cannot read the signs of the times.
Ac	11 2		when Peter came up to Jerusalem the Jews *criticised* him
	15 9 ⊖		God made no *distinction* between [the pagans] and us,
Rm	14 1		welcome [a person whose faith is not strong] all the same
		2	without ⌐starting an argument (lit. *criticising* his opinions).
1 Co	4 7		has anybody ⌐given you *some special right*?
	6 5		is there really not one reliable man among you to *settle differences* between brothers . . .?
	11 29		a person who eats and drinks without *recognising* the Body is eating and drinking his own condemnation.
	31		If only we ⌐*recollected* (or: *judged*) ourselves, we should not be punished like that.
	12 10	2	another [may have] the gift of *recognising* spirits;
	14 29		let two or three of [the prophets] speak, and the others ⌐attend to (lit. *judge*) them.
Heb	5 14	2	mature men with minds trained by practice to *distinguish between* good and bad.
Jm	2 4		you have ⌐used two *different standards* (or: *made distinctions*) ⌐in your mind (or: among yourselves), and turned yourselves into judges, and corrupt judges at that
	3 17 ⊖		the wisdom that comes down from above [has *no*] trace of
		3	*partiality* or hypocrisy in it.
Jude	9		the archangel Michael, when he ⌐was engaged in argument with the devil about (lit. *criticised* the devil concerning) the corpse of Moses,

4. JUSTICE, JUDGEMENT – VENGEANCE, AVENGE – RETRIBUTION, PUNISH(MENT): *DIKĒ*

3 *dikē* 3		4 *ek-dikos* 2
2 *ek-dikeō* 6		5 *hypo-dikos* 1
1 *ek-dikēsis* 9		

Lk	18 3		there was a widow who kept on coming to [the unjust judge]
		2	and saying, 'I want *justice* from you against my enemy!'
	5	2	since she keeps pestering me I must *give* this widow ⌐her just rights (lit. *justice*), or she will . . . worry me to death.
	7		will not God see *justice* done to his chosen who cry to him
	8		day and night . . .? ⁸ I promise you, he will see *justice* done to them, and done speedily.
	21 22		[when Jerusalem is besieged] this is the time of ⌐*vengeance* (or: *retribution*)
Ac	7 24		When [Moses] saw one of [his countrymen] being ill-treated he went to his defence and ⌐*rescued* (lit. *avenged*) the man by killing the Egyptian.
	28 4 ○	3	[Paul] must be a murderer . . . divine *vengeance* would not let him live.
Rm	3 19	5	[these words are] meant to . . . lay the whole world *open to* God's *judgement*;
	12 19	2	Never try to *get revenge*; leave that . . . to God's anger. As scripture says (Dt 32 35): *Vengeance* is mine – I will pay them back, the Lord promises.
	13 4		The authorities are there to serve God: they carry out God's
		4	*revenge* by punishing wrongdoers.
2 Co	7 11		what aching to see me, what concern for me, and what *justice done*!
	10 6	2	we are prepared to *punish* any disobedience.
1 Th	4 6	4	the Lord always *punishes* sins of that sort,
2 Th	1 8		[Jesus] will come . . . to impose ⌐the *penalty* (or: *justice*) on all who do not acknowledge God
	9	3	It will be their *punishment* to be lost eternally,

Heb 10 30		We are all aware who it was that said (Dt 32 35): *Vengeance* is mine; I will repay.
1 P 2 14		the governors as commissioned by [the Lord] to *punish* criminals
Jude 7	3	Sodom and Gomorrah . . . are ⌐paying (lit. undergoing the *punishment*) for their crimes in eternal fire.
Rv 6 10	2	Holy, faithful Master, how much longer will you wait before you . . . *take vengeance* for our death
19 2	2	[Our God] has condemned the famous prostitute . . . he has *avenged* his servants that she killed.

5. PUNISH(MENT)

1: PUNISH(MENT): *KOLAZŌ*

1 kolasis 2   2 kolazō 2

Mt 25 46 ●		they will go away to eternal *punishment*, and the virtuous to eternal life.
Ac 4 21	2	The court . . . released [Peter and John]; they could not think of any way to *punish* them,
2 P 2 9 ●	2	the Lord can . . . hold the wicked for their *punishment* until the day of Judgement,
1 Jn 4 18		to fear is to expect *punishment*, and anyone who is afraid is still imperfect in love.

2: PUNISHMENT, PENALTY: *TIMŌREŌ*

1 timōreō 2   3 epi-timia 1
2 timōria 1

Ac 22 5		bringing prisoners back from [Damascus] to Jerusalem for *punishment*.
26 11		I often went round the synagogues inflicting *penalties* . . . to force [the saints] to renounce their faith;
2 Co 2 6	3	The *punishment* already imposed by the majority on the man in question is enough;
Heb 10 29	2	anyone who tramples on the Son of God . . . will be condemned to a far severer *punishment*.

6. COURT, TRIBUNAL

1: COURT(S): *KRITĒRION*

kritērion 1/3

Jm 2 6		Isn't it always the rich who are against you? Isn't it always their doing when you are dragged before the *court*?

2: COURT, TRIBUNAL (lit. DAY [of judgement]): *HĒMERA*

hēmera 1/389

1 Co 4 3		Not that it makes the slightest difference to me whether you, or indeed any human *tribunal*, find me worthy or not.

3: COURT, TRIBUNAL – JUDGEMENT SEAT, BENCH, CHAIR OF JUDGEMENT: *BĒMA*

bēma 10/12

Mt 27 19		[Pilate] was seated in the *chair of judgement*,
Jn 19 13		Pilate . . . seated himself on the *chair of judgement*
Ac 18 12		the Jews . . . brought [Paul] before the *tribunal*.
16		[Gallio] sent them out of the *court*,
17		[the Jews] beat [Sosthenes] in front of the ⌐*court house* (or: *bench*).
25 6		[Festus] took his seat on the *tribunal* and had Paul brought in.
10		I am standing before the *tribunal* of Caesar
17		I . . . took my seat on the *tribunal*
Rm 14 10 Θ		We shall all have to stand before the *judgement seat* of God;
2 Co 5 10 X		all the truth about us will be brought out in the *law court* of Christ,

4: ASSIZES, COURTS: *AGORAIOS*

agoraios 1/2

Ac 19 38		If Demetrius [wants] to complain about anyone, there are the *assizes* and the proconsuls;

K

KEEP – GUARD

1. Keep: *tēreō*
- a) Keep watch, Guard – Under arrest, Held, Remanded – Put in prison, Jail, Custody
- b) Keep (safe), Preserve, Protect – Treasure, Store (up) – Hold on to, Keep on
- c) Keep oneself (in *or* from) – Avoid, Refrain, Be careful not to
- d) Keep = Reserve
- e) Keep = Observe, Obey, Heed

2. Guard – Keep: *phylassō*
- a) Prison, Jail, Imprison – Sentry, Warder, Gaoler – Guard, Restrain
- b) the Watches of the night (3-hour intervals)
- c) Guard, Keep (safe), Watch over – Take care of, Protect, Preserve
- d) Be on one's guard, Beware, Be careful not to – Abstain from, Avoid, Keep from
- e) Keep = Observe, Obey, Respect
- f) Phylacteries

3. Guard, Soldier – Executioner – Guardian
- 1: Guard: *koustōdia*
- 2: Bodyguard, Soldier – Executioner: *spekoulatōr*

- 3: Guardian – Keeper, Warden, Custodian: *(neō-)koros*

4. Guard, Keep (under observation), Look after – Custody: *phr-oureō*

5. Shut up, Imprison – Catch: *kleiō*

6. Captive, Prisoner – Fellow-prisoner – Make a prisoner, Lead captive: *aichm-(h)alōsia*

7. Keep, Hold fast (to), Cling to – Beware of, Be on one's guard – Guard, Imprison: *kat-echō*
- 1: Keep – Take to oneself, Hold fast (to), Cling to – Guard, Imprison
- 2: Beware of, Be on one's guard, Be careful – Take heed, Take care (imperatives)

8. Hold firmly (to), Cling to (figuratively), Keep (to): *krateō*

9. Store (up), Lay up, Reserve: *apo-keimai*

10. Treasure – Store up, Lay up – Treasury
- 1: Treasure – Store up treasures, Save up – Store, Lay up: *thēsauros*
- 2: Treasury – Treasure: *gaza*
  - a) the Treasury (of the Temple)
  - b) the (royal) Treasury

11. Keep from, Restrain from, Banish: *pauō*

---

1. KEEP: *TĒREŌ*

1	*tēreō*	71	4 *dia-tēreō*	2
2	*tērēsis*	3	5 *para-tēreō*	2/6
3	*syn-tēreō*	3		

a) Keep watch, Guard – Under arrest, Held, Remanded – Put in prison, Jail, Custody

Mt	27	36	[the soldiers] stayed there *keeping guard* over [Jesus].
		54	the centurion, together with the others *guarding* Jesus, had seen the earthquake
	28	4	The *guards* were so shaken . . . that they were like dead men.
Ac	4	3	2 they *held* [Peter and John] till the next day.
	5	18	2 they arrested the apostles and had them *put in the common gaol*.
	9	24	5 To make sure of killing [Saul, the Jews] *kept watch* on the gates
	12	5	All the time Peter was *under guard* the Church prayed to God
		6	guards *kept watch* at the main entrance to the prison.
	16	23	the gaoler was told to *keep* a close *watch* on [Paul and Silas].
	24	23	[Felix] gave orders . . . that Paul should be *kept under arrest*
	25	4	Festus replied that Paul would *remain in custody* in Caesarea,
		21	Paul put in an appeal ⌐for his case to be reserved (or: to be kept in custody) for the judgement of the august emperor, so I ordered him to be *remanded* until I could send him to Caesar.
2 P	2	4	When angels sinned, God . . . consigned them to the dark underground caves to be ⌐held there till (or: reserved for) the day of Judgement.
		9 Θ	the Lord can . . . ⌐hold (or: reserve) the wicked for their punishment until the day of Judgement,

b) Keep (safe), Preserve, Protect – Treasure, Store (up) – Hold on to, Keep on

Mt	9	17 <	3 they put new wine into fresh skins and both are *preserved*.
Mk	6	20	3 Herod was afraid of John . . . and ⌐*gave him his protection* (or: kept him in custody).

Mk	7	9	you get round the commandment of God in order to *preserve* your own tradition!
Lk	2	19	3 Mary . . . *treasured* all these things
		51	4 His mother *stored* up all these things in her heart.
Jn	17	11 Θ	*keep* those you have given me true to your name,
		12 X	I *kept* those you had given me true to your name.
		15	I am not asking you to remove them from the world, but to *protect* them from the evil one.
		Θ	
1 Co	7	37	if someone has firmly made his mind up . . . to *keep* his daughter as she is, he will be doing a good thing.
Ep	4	3	Do all you can to *preserve* the unity of the Spirit
1 Th	5	23	may you all be *kept safe* and blameless, spirit, soul and body, for the coming of our Lord Jesus Christ.
2 Tm	4	7	I have *kept* the faith;
1 Jn	5	18	anyone who has been begotten by God does not sin, because the begotten Son of God ⌐*protects* him (ᵛ *protects* himself);
		X	
Jude		1	From Jude . . . to those who are called, to those who are dear to God the Father and *kept safe* for Jesus Christ,
		Θ	
Rv	1	3	happy those who . . . ⌐*treasure* (or: observe) all that [this prophecy] says,
	3	3	do you remember how eager you were when you first heard the message? ⌐*Hold on* to (or: Keep) that.
		10	Because you have kept my commandment . . . I will *keep* you *safe* in the time of trial
	16	15	Happy is the man who has stayed awake and ⌐not taken off (lit. *keeps on*) his clothes
	22	7	Happy are those who ⌐*treasure* (or: observe) the prophetic message of this book.
		9	those who ⌐*treasure* (or: observe) what you have written in this book.

c) Keep oneself (in or from) – Avoid, Refrain, Be careful not to

Ac	15	29	you are to abstain from food sacrificed to idols . . . and from fornication. *Avoid* these, and you will do what is right.
		4	
2 Co	11	9	I was no burden to anyone . . . I *was* very *careful*, and I always shall *be careful*,
1 Tm	5	22	*keep* yourself pure.
Jm	1	27	unspoilt religion . . . is this: . . . *keeping* oneself uncontaminated by the world.
Jude		21	*keep* yourselves within the love of God

d) Keep = Reserve

Jn	2	10	you have *kept* the best wine till now.
	12	7	she had to *keep* this scent for the day of my burial.
Ac	25	21	Paul put in an appeal ⌐for his case to be *reserved* (or: to be kept in custody) for the judgement of the august emperor,
1 P	1	4 Θ	an inheritance . . . being *kept* for you in the heavens;
2 P	2	4	When angels sinned, God . . . consigned them to the dark underground caves to be ⌐*held* there till (or: *reserved* for) the day of Judgement.
		9 Θ	the Lord can . . . ⌐*hold* (or: *reserve*) the wicked for their punishment
		17	the dark underworld is the place *reserved* for [people who are like dried-up rivers].
	3	7 Θ	by the same word, the present sky and earth are destined for fire, and are only being *reserved* until Judgement day
Jude		6 ⑩	let me remind you of the angels who had supreme authority but did not keep it . . . [God] has *kept* them down in the dark . . . to be judged on the great day.
		Θ	
		13	shooting stars ⌐bound for (lit. for whom has been *reserved*) an eternity of black darkness.

e) Keep = Observe, Obey, Heed

Mt	19	17	if you wish to enter into life, *keep* the commandments.
	23	3	You must therefore do what they tell you and ⌐listen to (lit. *observe*) what they say;
	28	20	teach them to *observe* all the commands I gave you.
Jn	8	51	whoever *keeps* my word will never see death.
		52	you say, "Whoever *keeps* my word will never know the taste of death".
		55 X	But I do know [my Father], and I faithfully *keep* his word.
	9	16 X	This man cannot be from God: he does not *keep* the sabbath.
	14	15	If you love me you will *keep* my commandments.
		21	Anybody who receives my commandments and *keeps* them will be one who loves me;
		23	If anyone loves me he will *keep* my word,
		24	Those who do not love me do not *keep* my words.
	15	10	If you *keep* my commandments you will remain in my love,
		X	just as I have *kept* my Father's commandments

Jn	15 20	if they *kept* my word, they will *keep* yours as well.
	17 6	they have *kept* your word.
Ac	15 5	the pagans should be circumcised and instructed to *keep* the Law of Moses.
1 Co	7 19	2 what does matter is to *keep* the commandments of God.
Ga	4 10	5 You and your *keeping* of special days and months and seasons and years!
1 Tm	6 14	[I put to you the duty] of ᵣdoing (lit. *observing*) all that you have been told, with no faults or failures,
Jm	2 10	if a man *keeps* the whole of the Law, except for one small point . . . he is still guilty of breaking it all.
1 Jn	2 3	We can be sure that we know God only by *keeping* his commandments. ⁴ Anyone who says, 'I know him', and does not *keep* his commandments, is a liar . . . ⁵ But when anyone does *obey* what he has said, God's love comes to perfection in him.
	4	
	5	
	3 22	whatever we ask [God], we shall receive, because we *keep* his commandments
	24	Whoever *keeps* his commandments lives in God and God lives in him.
	5 3	this is what loving God is – *keeping* his commandments;
Rv	1 3	happy those who . . . ᵣtreasure (or: *observe*) all that [this prophecy] says,
	2 26	ᵣkeep working for me (lit. *keep* my works) until the end,
	3 3	do you remember how eager you were when you first heard the message? ᵣHold on to (or: *Keep*) that.
	8	you have *kept* my commandments and not disowned my name.
	10	Because you have *kept* my commandment . . . I will keep you safe in the time of trial
	12 17	the dragon . . . went away to make war on . . . all who *obey* God's commandments
	14 12	there must be constancy in the saints who *keep* the commandments of God and faith in Jesus.
	22 7	Happy are those who ᵣtreasure (or: *observe*) the prophetic message of this book.
	9	those who ᵣtreasure (or: *observe*) what you have written in this book.

2. GUARD – KEEP: *PHYLASSŌ*

1	*phylakē*	46	3	*phylax*	3
5	*phylakizō*	1	4	(*desmo-*)*phylax*	3
6	*phylaktērion*	1	7	*dia-phylassō*	1
2	*phylassō*	31			

a) Prison, Jail, Imprison – Sentry, Warder, Gaoler – Guard, Restrain

Mt	5 25	your opponent . . . may hand you over to the judge . . . and you will be thrown into *prison*.
	14 3	Herod . . . had arrested John . . . and put him in *prison*
	10	[the king] sent and had John beheaded in the *prison*.
	18 30 <	he had [his fellow servant] thrown into *prison*
	25 36 X	I was . . . in *prison* and you came to see me.
	39 X	[When did we see you] sick or in *prison* . . .?
	43 X	I was . . . sick and in *prison* and you never visited me.
	44 X	when did we see you . . . sick or in *prison* . . .?
Mk	6 17	Herod . . . had sent to have John arrested, and had him chained up in *prison*
	27	[One of the bodyguard] beheaded [John] in *prison*;
Lk	3 20	[Herod] added a further crime to all the rest by shutting John up in *prison*.
	8 29	they used to secure [the demoniac] with chains . . . to ₂ *restrain* him,
	12 58 <	the bailiff [may] have you thrown into *prison*.
	21 12	they will hand you over to the synagogues and to *imprisonment*,
	22 33	'Lord,' [Peter] answered 'I would be ready to go to *prison* with you, and to death.'
	23 19	[Barabbas] had been thrown into *prison* . . . for murder.
	25	[Pilate] released the man . . . who had been *imprisoned* for . . . murder,
Jn	3 24	This was before John had been put in *prison*.
Ac	5 19	the angel of the Lord opened the *prison* gates
	22	when the officials arrived at the *prison* they found [the apostles] were not inside,
	23	3 We found . . . the *warders* on duty at the gates,
	25	At this very moment . . . the men you *imprisoned* are in the Temple.
	8 3	Saul . . . went from house to house arresting both men and women and sending them to *prison*.
	12 4	[Herod] put Peter in *prison*, assigning four squads of four soldiers each to *guard* him . . . ⁵ All the time Peter was under guard in *prison* the Church prayed to God for him
	5	2
	6	3/ *guards* kept watch at the main entrance to the *prison*.
	10	[The angel and Peter] passed through two *guard posts* one after the other,
	17	[Peter] described to them how the Lord had led him out of *prison*.

Ac	12 19	3 Herod . . . had the *guards* questioned, and . . . gave orders for their execution.
	16 23	/4 [Paul and Silas were] thrown into *prison*, and the *gaoler* was told to keep a close watch on them. ²⁴ So . . . he threw them into the inner *prison*
	24	
	27	4/ When the *gaoler* woke and saw the *prison* doors wide open he drew his sword
	36	4 The *gaoler* reported the message to Paul . . . ³⁷ . . . Paul replied, '[The magistrates] flog Roman citizens . . . and throw us into *prison*, and then think they can push us out on the quiet!'
	37	
	40	From the *prison* [Paul and Silas] went to Lydia's house
	22 4	I even persecuted this Way to the death, and sent women as well as men to *prison*
	19	5 I used to go from synagogue to synagogue, *imprisoning* . . . those who believed in you;
	23 35	2 [the governor] ordered [Paul] to be *held* in Herod's praetorium.
	26 10	I myself threw many of the saints into *prison*,
	28 16	in Rome Paul was allowed to stay in lodgings of his own with the soldier who *guarded* him
	2	
2 Co	6 5	[we prove we are servants of God by great fortitude] when we are flogged, or sent to *prison*,
	11 23	The servants of Christ? . . . more than they . . . because I . . . have been sent to *prison* more often,
Heb	11 36	Some had to bear being . . . chained up in *prison*.
1 P	3 19 O	[Christ] went to preach to the spirits in *prison*.
Rv	2 10	the devil is going to send some of you to *prison*
	18 2	Babylon . . . has become . . . a *cage* for every foul spirit and a *cage* for every dirty, loathsome bird.
	20 7 ⓓ	Satan will be released from his *prison* and will come out to deceive all the nations

b) the Watches of the night (3-hour intervals)

Mt	14 25	In the fourth *watch* of the night [Jesus] went towards [the disciples],
	24 43	if the householder had known at what ᵣtime (lit. *watch*) of the night the burglar would come, he would have stayed awake
Mk	6 48	about the fourth *watch* of the night [Jesus] came towards them,
Lk	2 8	close by there were shepherds who . . . took it in turns to watch their flocks during the *watches* of the night.
	12 38	It may be in the second *watch* [the master] comes, or in the third,

c) Guard, Keep (safe), Watch over – Take care of, Protect, Preserve

Lk	2 8	close by there were shepherds who . . . took it in turns to ₂ *watch* their flocks
	4 10	7 (Ps 91 11) He will put his angels in charge of you to *guard* you,
	11 21	2 So long as a strong man fully armed *guards* his own palace, his goods are undisturbed;
Jn	12 25	2 anyone who hates his life in this world will *keep* it for the eternal life.
	17 12 X	2 I have *watched over* [those you had given me] and not one is lost
Ac	22 20	I was standing by in full agreement with [Stephen's] murderers, and *minding* their clothes.
2 Th	3 3 X	2 the Lord is faithful, and he will give you strength and *guard* you from the evil one,
1 Tm	6 20	2 My dear Timothy, take great *care of* all that has been entrusted to you.
2 Tm	1 12 X	2 he is able to *take care of* all that I have entrusted to him until that Day.
	14	You have been trusted to look after something precious; ₂ *guard* it with the help of the Holy Spirit who lives in us.
2 P	2 5 ⊖	2 it was only Noah he *saved* . . . along with seven others,
Jude	24 ⊖	2 Glory be to him who can *keep* you from falling

d) Be on one's guard, Beware, Be careful not to – Abstain from, Avoid, Keep from

Lk	12 15	2 *be on your guard* against avarice of any kind,
Ac	21 25	2 The pagans . . . must *abstain* from things sacrificed to idols,
2 Tm	4 15	2 *Be on your guard* against [Alexander] yourself, because he has been bitterly contesting everything that we say.
2 P	3 17	2 my friends; *be careful not to* get carried away by the errors of unprincipled people,
1 Jn	5 21	2 Children, *be on your guard* against false gods.

e) Keep = Observe, Obey, Respect

Mt	19 20	2 I have *kept* all these. What more do I need to do?
Mk	10 20	2 Master, I have *kept* all these from my earliest days,
Lk	11 28	2 Still happier those who hear the word of God and *keep* it!
	18 21	2 I have *kept* all these from my earliest days till now.
Jn	12 47	2 If anyone hears my words and does not *keep* them faithfully,
Ac	7 53	You who had the Law . . . are the very ones who have not ₂ *kept* it.

Ac 16 4	[Paul and Timothy] passed on the decisions reached by the 2 apostles . . . with instructions to *respect* them.
21 24	This will let everyone know . . . that you still regularly 2 *observe* the Law.
Rm 2 26	2 If a man who is not circumcised *obeys* the commandments of the Law, surely that makes up for not being circumcised?
Ga 6 13	2 they accept circumcision but do not *keep* the Law themselves;
1 Tm 5 21	2 I put it to you as a duty to *keep* these rules impartially

f) Phylacteries

Mt 23 5	Everything [the Pharisees and the scribes] do is done to 6 attract attention, like wearing broader *phylacteries*

3. GUARD, SOLDIER – EXECUTIONER – GUARDIAN

1: GUARD: *KOUSTŌDIA*

koustōdia 3

Mt 27 65	'You may have your *guard*' said Pilate to [the chief priests].
66	[the chief priests and the Pharisees] made the sepulchre secure, putting seals on the stone and mounting a *guard*.
28 11	some of the *guard* went off into the city to tell the chief priests all that had happened.

2: BODYGUARD, SOLDIER – EXECUTIONER: *SPEKOULATŌR*

spekoulatōr 1

Mk 6 27	the king at once sent one of the *bodyguard* with orders to bring John's head.

3: GUARDIAN – KEEPER, WARDEN, CUSTODIAN: *(NEŌ-)KOROS*

(neō-)koros 1

Ac 19 35	the city of the Ephesians is the *guardian* of the temple of great Diana

4. GUARD, KEEP (UNDER OBSERVATION), LOOK AFTER – CUSTODY: *PHR-OUREŌ*

phr-oureō 4

2 Co 11 32	in Damascus, the ethnarch of King Aretas *put guards* round the city
Ga 3 23	we were *being looked after* [by the Law] till faith was revealed.
Ph 4 7	[the] peace of God . . . will *guard* your hearts and your thoughts,
1 P 1 5	Through your faith, God's power will *guard* you until the salvation

5. SHUT UP, IMPRISON – CATCH: *KLEIŌ*

2 *kata-kleiō 2*   1 *syn-kleiō 4*

Lk 3 20	2 [Herod] added a further crime to all the rest by *shutting* John *up* in prison.
5 6	[the fishermen] *ʳnetted* (or: *caught*) such a huge number of fish that their nets began to tear,
Ac 26 10	2 I myself *ʳthrew* many of the saints *into* (or: *shut up* many of the saints in) prison,
Rm 11 32	God has *imprisoned* all men in their own disobedience only to show mercy
Ga 3 22	scripture *ʳmakes no exceptions* (lit. *includes* everyone; or: *confines* everyone) when it says that sin is master everywhere.
23	we were *ʳallowed no freedom* (lit. *imprisoned*) by the Law;

6. CAPTIVE, PRISONER – FELLOW-PRISONER – MAKE A PRISONER, LEAD CAPTIVE: *AICHM-(H)ALŌSIA*

2 *aichm-(h)alōsia 3*   5 *aichm-(h)alōtos 1*
4 *aichm-(h)alōteuō 1*   3 *syn-aichm-(h)alōtos 3*
1 *aichm-(h)alōtizō 4*

Lk 4 18	(Is 61 1) The spirit of the Lord . . . has sent me to . . . 5 proclaim liberty to *captives*
21 24	They will . . . be *led captive* to every pagan country;
Rm 7 23	This is what *makes* me *a prisoner* of that law of sin
16 7	[Greetings] to . . . Andronicus and Junias, my compatriots 3 and *fellow prisoners*

2 Co 10 5	every thought is our *prisoner*, [captured] to be brought into obedience to Christ.
Ep 4 8	4 (Ps 68 19) When [Christ] ascended to the height, he *ʳcap-* 2 *tured prisoners* (or: *captured captivity*),
Col 4 10	3 Aristarchus, who is here in prison with me, sends his greetings,
2 Tm 3 6	those men . . . *ʳget influence over* (lit. *captivate*) silly women who are obsessed with their sins
Phm 23	3 Epaphras, a *prisoner with* me in Christ Jesus, sends his greetings,
Rv 13 10	2 (cf. Jr 15 2) *Captivity* for those who *ʳare destined for* 2 (ᵛ *have led* others *into*) *captivity*;

7. KEEP, HOLD FAST (TO), CLING TO – BEWARE OF, BE ON ONE'S GUARD – GUARD, IMPRISON: *KAT-ECHŌ*

1 *kat-echō 15/18*   2 *pros-echō 12/24*
3 *ep-echō 1/5*   4 *syn-echō 1/12*

1: KEEP – TAKE TO ONESELF, HOLD FAST (TO), CLING TO – GUARD, IMPRISON

Lk 4 42	The crowds . . . wanted to *prevent* [Jesus] *leaving* them,
8 15	this is people . . . who have heard the word and *take it to themselves* and yield a harvest
14 9	you would have to go and *take* the lowest place.
22 63	4 the men who *guarded* Jesus were mocking and beating him.
Ac 27 40	hoisting the foresail to the wind, they *ʳheaded for* (lit. *kept* towards) the beach.
Rm 1 18	The anger of God is being revealed . . . against all the impiety . . . of men who *keep* truth *imprisoned*
7 6	now we are . . . *freed* by death from our *imprisonment*,
1 Co 11 2	You have done well in . . . *maintaining* the traditions
15 2	the gospel will save you only if you *keep* [believing] exactly what I preached to you
Ph 2 16	[you will shine in the world] because you are *ʳoffering it* 3 (or: *holding fast to*) the word of life.
1 Th 5 21	*hold on to* what is good
2 Th 2 6	you know, too, what is still *holding* him *back*
7	Rebellion is at its worst already, but . . . the one who is *holding* it *back* has first to be removed
Phm 13	I should have liked to *keep* [Onesimus] with me;
Heb 3 6	we are [Christ's] house, as long as we *cling to* our hope with the confidence that we glory in.
14	we shall remain co-heirs with Christ only if we *keep a grasp on* our first confidence
10 23	Let us *keep* firm in the hope we profess,

2: BEWARE OF, BE ON ONE'S GUARD, BE CAREFUL – TAKE HEED, TAKE CARE (IMPERATIVES)

Mt 6 1	2 *Be careful* not to parade your good deeds before men
7 15	2 *Beware of* false prophets
10 17	2 *Beware of* men: they will hand you over to sanhedrins
16 6	2 *be on your guard* against the yeast of the Pharisees and Sadducees
11	2 *Beware of* the yeast of the Pharisees and Sadducees.
12	2 he was telling them to *be on their guard* . . . against the teaching of the Pharisees and Sadducees.
Lk 12 1	2 *Be on your guard* against the yeast of the Pharisees
17 3	2 *Watch* yourselves!
20 46	2 *Beware of* the scribes who like to walk about in long robes
21 34	2 *Watch* yourselves, or your hearts will be coarsened with debauchery
Ac 5 35	2 Men of Israel, *be careful* how you deal with [the apostles].
20 28	2 *Be on your guard* for yourselves and for all the flock

8. HOLD FIRMLY (TO), CLING TO (FIGURATIVELY), KEEP (TO): *KRATEŌ*

krateō 20/47

Mk 7 3	the Pharisees . . . *ʳfollow* (lit. *cling to*) the tradition of the elders
4	There are also many other observances to *keep to* which have been handed down to them
8	You put aside the commandment of God to *cling to* human traditions.
9 10	[The disciples] *ʳobserved* the warning faithfully (lit. *kept* these words *to themselves*),
Lk 24 16	something *ʳprevented* them (lit. *kept* their eyes) from recognising [Jesus].
Jn 20 23	for those whose sins you *retain*, they are *retained*.
Ac 2 24	it was impossible for [Christ] to be *held in* [the] *power* [of Hades]
27 13	thinking their objective as good as *ʳreached* (lit. *grasped*), they weighed anchor

Col	2	19	A man of this sort is not *united to* the head,
2 Th	2	15	Stand firm . . . and *keep* the traditions
Heb	4	14	we must *never let go* of the faith that we have professed.
	6	18	*take a firm grip* on the hope that is held out to us.
Rv	2	1	Here is the message of the one who *holds* the seven stars in his right hand
		13	I know . . . that you still *hold firmly to* my name,
		14	some of you are ⌐followers of Balaam (lit. *clinging to* what Balaam taught),
		15	among you . . . there are some . . . who ⌐accept (lit. *cling to*) what the Nicolaitans teach.
		25	*hold firmly on to* what you already have until I come.
	3	11	*hold firmly to* what you already have,
	7	1	I saw four angels . . . *holding* the four winds of the world back

9. STORE (UP), LAY UP, RESERVE: *APO-KEIMAI*

apo-keimai 4

Lk	19	20	here is your pound. I put it away ⌐safely (lit. *stored*) in a piece of linen
Col	1	5	you show [love] towards all the saints because of the hope which is *stored* up for you in heaven.
2 Tm	4	8	all there is to come now is the crown of righteousness *reserved* for me,
Heb	9	27	men only ⌐die (lit. have death *reserved* for them) once,

10. TREASURE – STORE UP, LAY UP – TREASURY

1: TREASURE – STORE UP TREASURES, SAVE UP – STORE, LAY UP: *THĒSAUROS*

2 *thēsaurizō* 8	3 *apo-thēsaurizō 1*
1 *thēsauros 17*	

Mt	2	11	opening their *treasures*, [the wise men] offered him gifts of gold and frankincense and myrrh.
	6	19	2/ Do not *store up treasures* for yourselves on earth . . . ²⁰ But
		20	2/ *store up treasures* for yourselves in heaven . . . ²¹ For
		21	where your *treasure* is, there will your heart be also.
	12	35	A good man draws good things from his *store* of goodness; a bad man draws bad things from his *store* of badness.
	13	44 <	The kingdom of heaven is like *treasure* hidden in a field
		52 <	every scribe who becomes a disciple of the kingdom of heaven is like a householder who brings out from his *store*[room] things both new and old.
	19	21	sell what you own and give the money to the poor, and you will have *treasure* in heaven;
Mk	10	21	sell everything you own . . and you will have *treasure* in heaven;
Lk	6	45	A good man draws what is good from the *store* of goodness in his heart;
	12	21	2 So it is when a man *stores up treasure* for himself in place of making himself rich in the sight of God.
		33	Get yourselves . . . *treasure* that will not fail you, in heaven
		34	. . . ³⁴ For where your *treasure* is, there will your heart be also.
	18	22	Sell all that you own . . . and you will have *treasure* in heaven;
Rm	2	5	Your stubborn refusal to repent is only ⌐adding to (lit. 2 *laying up* for yourself) the anger God will have towards you
1 Co	16	2	each one of you must put aside what he can ⌐afford (lit. 2 *lay up* in proportion to his earnings),
2 Co	4	7	We are only the earthenware jars that hold this *treasure*,
	12	14	2 Children are not expected to *save up* for their parents,
Col	2	3	in [God's secret] all the ⌐jewels (lit. *treasures*) of wisdom and knowledge are hidden.
1 Tm	6	19	3 [by doing good the rich] can *save up* a good capital sum for the future
Heb	11	26	[Moses] considered that the insults offered to the Anointed were something more precious than all the *treasures* of Egypt,
Jm	5	3	2 It was a burning fire that you *stored up as your treasure* for the last days.
2 P	3	7	2 the present sky and earth are ⌐destined (lit. *laid up*) for fire

2: TREASURY – TREASURE: *GAZA*

2 *gaza* 1	3 *korbanas 1*
1 *gazo-phylakeion 5*	

a) the Treasury (of the Temple)

Mt	27	6	3 It is against the Law to put [blood-money] into the *treasury*;
Mk	12	41	[Jesus] sat down opposite the *treasury* and watched the people putting money into the *treasury*,

Mk	12	43	this poor widow has put more in than all who have contributed to the *treasury*;
Lk	21	1	[Jesus] saw rich people putting their offerings into the *treasury*;
Jn	8	20	[Jesus] spoke these words in the *Treasury*, . . . in the Temple.

b) the (royal) Treasury

Ac	8	27	he was a eunuch and . . . [the queen's] ⌐chief treasurer (lit. 2 superintendent of [the royal] *treasure*).

11. KEEP FROM, RESTRAIN FROM, BANISH: *PAUŌ*

pauō 1/15

1 P	3	10	(Ps 34 14) Anyone who wants to have a happy life . . . must *banish* malice from his tongue,

---

KING

1: (God, Jesus) the King – the Kingdom of God, of Heaven	*f*) Herod (Agrippa II)
	g) Melchizedek
2: (the People of God) Reign – Be king – Royal	*h*) Solomon and the Queen of the South
3: King, Kingdom (generally) – Emperor	5: Reign, Kingdom (figuratively)
	a) (Death, Sin) Reign
4: Particular kings	*b*) (Satan's) Kingdom – (the Angel of the Abyss as) Emperor
a) Aretas	
b) the Kandake or Queen of Ethiopia	*c*) (Grace) Reigns – (the) Royal (law)
c) Herod (the Great)	6: Palace, Royal Court
d) Herod (Antipas)	7: Court official
e) Herod (Agrippa I)	

2	*basileia*	60	6	*basileuō*	21
4	*basileia ep-ouranios*	1	5	*basileus*	109/115
3	*basileia tōn ouranōn*	33	7	*basilikos*	5
1	*basileia tou theou*	69	8	*basilissa*	4
9	*(ta) basileia*	1	11	*sym-basileuō*	2
10	*basileios*	1			

(163 and 2 bracketed totals)

X = Jesus as king   J = King of Israel, King of the Jews

1: (GOD, JESUS) THE KING – THE KINGDOM OF GOD, OF HEAVEN

Mt	2	2	X J	5	Where is the infant *king* of the Jews?
	3	2		3	the *kingdom of heaven* is close at hand.
	4	17		3	the *kingdom of heaven* is close at hand.
		23		2	[Jesus] . . . proclaiming the Good News of the *kingdom*
	5	3		3	How happy are the poor in spirit; theirs is the *kingdom of heaven*.
		10		3	Happy those who are persecuted in the cause of right: theirs is the *kingdom of heaven*.
		19		3	the man who infringes even one of the least of these commandments . . . will be considered the least in the *kingdom of heaven*; but the man who keeps them . . . will be considered great in the *kingdom of heaven*.
		20		3	if your virtue goes no deeper than that of the scribes and Pharisees, you will never get into the *kingdom of heaven*.
		35	Θ	5	[do not swear] by Jerusalem, since that is the city of the great *king*.
	6	10	Θ	2	[Our Father in heaven,] your *kingdom* come,
		13	Θ	2	(ᵛ For yours is the *kingdom*, the power and the glory . . .)
		33		2	Set your hearts on his *kingdom* first,
	7	21		3	It is not those who say to me, 'Lord, Lord', who will enter the *kingdom of heaven*,
	8	11			many will come from east and west to take their places with Abraham . . . at the feast in the *kingdom of heaven*;
		12		2	but the subjects of the *kingdom* will be turned out
	9	35		2	Jesus . . . proclaiming the Good News of the *kingdom*
	10	7		3	proclaim that the *kingdom of heaven* is close at hand.
	11	11		3	the least in the *kingdom of heaven* is greater than [John the Baptist] is.
		12		3	the *kingdom of heaven* has been subjected to violence
	12	28			the *kingdom of God* has overtaken you.
	13	11		3	the mysteries of the *kingdom of heaven* are revealed to you,
		19		2	When anyone hears the word of the *kingdom* without understanding,
		24		3	The *kingdom of heaven* may be compared to a man who sowed good seed
		31		3	The *kingdom of heaven* is like a mustard seed

Mt 13 33   3 The *kingdom of heaven* is like the yeast a woman took
    38   2 the good seed is the subjects of the *kingdom*;
    41 X 2 his angels . . . will gather out of his *kingdom* all things that provoke offences
    43 Θ 2 the virtuous will shine like the sun in the *kingdom* of their Father.
    44   3 The *kingdom of heaven* is like treasure hidden in a field
    45   3 the *kingdom of heaven* is like a merchant looking for fine pearls;
    47   3 the *kingdom of heaven* is like a dragnet cast into the sea
    52   3 every scribe who becomes a disciple of the *kingdom of heaven* is like a householder
16 19   3 [Peter,] I will give you the keys of the *kingdom of heaven*;
    28   some of these standing here . . . will not taste death before
       X 2 they see the Son of Man coming with his *kingdom*.
18 1   3 'Who is the greatest in the *kingdom of heaven*?' . . .
    3   3 '. . . unless you . . . become like little children you
    4   3 will never enter the *kingdom of heaven*. ⁴ . . . the one who makes himself as little as this little child is the greatest
          3 in the *kingdom of heaven*.'
    23   3 the *kingdom of heaven* may be compared to a king who decided to settle his accounts
19 12   there are eunuchs who have made themselves that way for
          3 the sake of the *kingdom of heaven*.
    14   3 it is to such as these [little children] that the *kingdom of heaven* belongs.
    23   3 it will be hard for a rich man to enter the *kingdom of heaven*.
    24   ²⁴ . . . it is easier for a camel to pass through the eye of
          3 a needle than for a rich man to enter the ᵛ*kingdom of heaven* (G *kingdom of God*).
20 1   3 the *kingdom of heaven* is like a landowner
    21   Promise that these two sons of mine may sit one at your
       X 2 right hand and the other at your left in your *kingdom*.
21 5 X J 5 Look, your *king* comes to you; he is humble, he rides on a donkey
    31   tax collectors and prostitutes are making their way into the *kingdom of God* before you.
    43   the *kingdom of God* will be taken from you and given to a people who will produce its fruit.
22 2   3 The *kingdom of heaven* may be compared to a king who gave a feast
23 13   Alas for you, scribes and Pharisees, . . . who shut up the
          3 *kingdom of heaven* in men's faces.
24 14   2 This Good News of the *kingdom* will be proclaimed to the whole world.
25 1   3 The *kingdom of heaven* will be like this: Ten bridesmaids took their lamps
    34 X 5 the *King* will say to those on his right hand, 'Come, . . .
          2 take for your heritage the *kingdom* prepared for you'
    40 X 5 the *King* will answer, '. . . in so far as you did this to one of the least of these brothers of mine,'
26 29   until the day I drink the new wine with you in the
       Θ 2 *kingdom* of my Father.
27 11 X J 5 'Are you the *King* of the Jews?' Jesus replied, 'It is you who say it'.
    29 X J 5 [the soldiers] knelt to him saying, 'Hail, *king* of the Jews!'
    37   the charge against him . . . read: 'This is Jesus, the
       X J 5 *King* of the Jews'.
    42 X J 5 He is the *king* of Israel; let him come down from the cross
Mk 1 15   the *kingdom of God* is close at hand.
  4 11   The secret of the *kingdom of God* is given to you,
    26   This is what the *kingdom of God* is like. A man throws seed on the land.
    30   What can we say the *kingdom of God* is like?
  9 1   there are some standing here who will not taste death before they see the *kingdom of God* come with power.
    47   it is better for you to enter into the *kingdom of God* with one eye,
10 14   it is to such as these [little children] that the *kingdom of God* belongs
    15   anyone who does not welcome the *kingdom of God* like a little child will never enter it.
    23   How hard it is for those who have riches to enter the
    24   *kingdom of God*!²⁴ . . . how hard it is to enter the
    25   *kingdom of God*! ²⁵ It is easier for a camel to pass through the eye of a needle than for a rich man to enter the *kingdom of God*.
11 10 X J 2 Blessings on the coming *kingdom* of our father David!
12 34   You are not far from the *kingdom of God*.
14 25   until the day I drink the new wine in the *kingdom of God*.
15 2 X J 5 Pilate questioned him, 'Are you the *king* of the Jews?'
    9 X J 5 Do you want me to release for you the *king* of the Jews?
    12 X J 5 what am I to do with the man you call *king* of the Jews?
    18 X J 5 [the soldiers] began saluting him, 'Hail, *king* of the Jews!'
    26 X J 5 the charge against him read: 'The *King* of the Jews'.
    32 X J 5 Let the Christ, the *king* of Israel, come down from the cross
    43   Joseph of Arimathaea, . . . who himself lived in hope of seeing the *kingdom of God*.
Lk 1 33 X J 6 [Jesus] will rule over the House of Jacob for ever and his
          2 *reign* will have no end.

Lk 4 43   I must proclaim the Good News of the *kingdom of God*
  6 20   How happy are you who are poor: yours is the *kingdom of God*.
  7 28   the least in the *kingdom of God* is greater than [John the Baptist] is.
  8 1   [Jesus] proclaiming the Good News of the *kingdom of God*.
   10   The mysteries of the *kingdom of God* are revealed to you;
  9 2   [Jesus] sent [the Twelve] out to proclaim the *kingdom of God* and to heal.
   11   [Jesus] talked to [the crowds] about the *kingdom of God*.
   27   there are some standing here who will not taste death before they see the *kingdom of God*.
   60   your duty is to go and spread the news of the *kingdom of God*.
   62   no one who looks back is fit for the *kingdom of God*.
10 9   The *kingdom of God* is very near to you.
   11   the *kingdom of God* is very near.
11 2 Θ 2 Father, may . . . your *kingdom* come;
   20   then know that the *kingdom of God* has overtaken you.
12 31   2/ set your hearts on ⌐his *kingdom* (ᵛ the *kingdom of God*), and these other things will be given you as well.
   32   2 it has pleased our Father to give you the *kingdom*.
13 18   What is the *kingdom of God* like? [A mustard seed.]
   20   What shall I compare the *kingdom of God* with? [Yeast.]
   28   there will be weeping . . . when you see Abraham and . . . all the prophets in the *kingdom of God*, and yourselves turned outside. ²⁹And men from east and west
   29   . . . will come to take their places at the feast in the *kingdom of God*.
14 15   Happy the man who will be at the feast in the *kingdom of God*!
16 16   since [the time of John], the *kingdom of God* has been preached,
17 20   Asked by the Pharisees when the *kingdom of God* was to come, he gave them this answer, 'The coming of the
   21   *kingdom of God* does not admit of observation ²¹ . . . the *kingdom of God* is among you.
18 16   it is to such as these [little children] that the *kingdom of God* belongs. ¹⁷ . . . anyone who does not welcome the
   17   *kingdom of God* like a little child will never enter it.
   24   How hard it is for those who have riches to make their way
   25   into the *kingdom of God*! ²⁵ Yes, it is easier for a camel to pass through the eye of a needle than for a rich man to enter the *kingdom of God*.
   29   there is no one who has left house, wife, . . . or children for the sake of the *kingdom of God* ³⁰ who will not be given repayment
19 11   the people . . . imagined that the *kingdom of God* was going to show itself then and there.
   38 X 5 Blessings on the *King* who comes, in the name of the Lord!
21 31   So with you when you see these things happening: know that the *kingdom of God* is near.
22 16   I shall not eat [the passover] again until it is fulfilled in the *kingdom of God*.
   18   I shall not drink wine until the *kingdom of God* comes.
   29   2 now I confer a *kingdom* on you, just as my Father conferred one on me:
   30 X 2 you will eat and drink at my table in my *kingdom*,
23 2 X 5 We found this man . . . claiming to be Christ, a *king*.
   3 X J 5 'Are you the *king* of the Jews?' 'It is you who say it' [Jesus] replied.
   37 X J 5 If you are the *king* of the Jews, save yourself.
   38 X J 5 Above him there was an inscription: 'This is the *King* of the Jews'.
   42 X 2 remember me when you come into your *kingdom*.
   51   [Joseph] came from Arimathaea, . . . and he lived in the hope of seeing the *kingdom of God*.
Jn 1 49   [Nathanael to Jesus:] Rabbi, you are the Son of God, you
       X J 5 are the *King* of Israel.
  3 3   unless a man is born ⌐from above (or: again), he cannot see the *kingdom of God*
   5   unless a man is born through water and the Spirit, he cannot enter the *kingdom of God*:
  6 15   Jesus . . . could see [the people] were about to come and
       X J 5 take him by force and make him *king*,
12 13 X J 5 Blessings on the *King* of Israel, who comes in the name of the Lord.
   15 X J 5 Do not be afraid, daughter of Zion; see, your *king* is coming, mounted on the colt of a donkey.
18 33 X J 5 Are you the *king* of the Jews?
   36 X 2/2 Mine is not a *kingdom* of this world; if my *kingdom* were of this world, my men would have fought . . . But my
       X 2 *kingdom* is not of this kind.
   37 X 5 'So you are a *king* then?' . . . 'It is you who say it' answered
       X 5 Jesus. 'Yes, I am a *king*.'
   39 X J 5 would you like me . . . to release the *king* of the Jews?
19 3   [The soldiers] kept coming up to him and saying, 'Hail,
       X J 5 *king* of the Jews!'
   12 X 5 anyone who makes himself *king* is defying Caesar.
   14 X J 5 'Here is your *king*' said Pilate to the Jews.

Jn 19 15 X J 5 'Do you want me to crucify your *king*?' . . . 'We have no king except Caesar'.

    19 X J 5 a notice . . . [which] ran: 'Jesus the Nazarene, *King* of the Jews'.

    21 X J 5 You should not write '*King* of the Jews', but 'This man said:
        X J 5 'I am *King* of the Jews'.

Ac 1 3 for forty days [Jesus] had continued to appear to [the apostles] and tell them about the *kingdom of God*.

    6 J 2 Lord, has the time come? Are you going to restore the *kingdom* of Israel?

    8 12 [the Samaritans] believed Philip's preaching of the Good News about the *kingdom of God* and the name of Jesus Christ,

   14 22 We all have to experience many hardships . . . before we enter the *kingdom of God*.

   17 7 They have broken every one of Caesar's edicts by claiming
      X 5 that there is another *emperor*, Jesus.

   19 8 [Paul] argued persuasively about the *kingdom of God*.

   20 25 none of you among whom I have gone about proclaiming
      2 the *kingdom* will ever see my face again.

   28 23 [Paul] put his case to [the Roman Jews], testifying to the *kingdom of God* and trying to persuade them about Jesus,

    31 [Paul in Rome] proclaiming the *kingdom of God* and teaching the truth about the Lord Jesus Christ

Rm 14 17 the *kingdom of God* does not mean eating and drinking this or that, it means righteousness and peace and joy

1 Co 4 20 the *kingdom of God* is not just words, it is power.

   6 9 people who do wrong will not inherit the *kingdom of God*:

    10 thieves, usurers, . . . and swindlers will never inherit the *kingdom of God*.

  15 24 After that will come the end, when [Christ] hands over the
      X ϴ 2 *kingdom* to God the Father,

    25 X 6 [Christ] must *be king* until he has put all his enemies under his feet

    50 flesh and blood cannot inherit the *kingdom of God*:

Ga 5 21 those who behave like this will not inherit the *kingdom of God*.

Ep 5 5 nobody who actually indulges in fornication . . . can
    X inherit anything of the *kingdom of God* and Christ.

Col 1 13 X 2 [God] has . . . created a place for us in the *kingdom* of the Son that he loves,

   4 11 these are the only ones working with me for the *kingdom of God*.

1 Th 2 12 ϴ 2 God, who is calling you to share the glory of his *kingdom*.

2 Th 1 5 the purpose of [God's judgement] is that you may be found worthy of the *kingdom of God*;

1 Tm 1 17 ϴ 5 To the eternal *King*, the undying, invisible and only God, be honour and glory

   6 15 ϴ 5 God, the . . . *King* of kings and the Lord of lords,

2 Tm 4 1 I put this duty to you, in the name of his Appearing and of
      X 2 his *kingdom*:

    18 X 4 The Lord will . . . bring me safely to his *heavenly kingdom*.

Heb 1 8 (Ps 45 6) to his Son he says: God, your throne shall last for
      X 2 ever and ever; and: his *royal* sceptre is the sceptre of virtue;

  12 28 2 We have been given possession of an unshakeable *kingdom*.

Jm 2 5 it is those who are poor according to the world that God
      2 chose, to be . . . heirs to the *kingdom* which he promised to those who love him.

2 P 1 11 X 2 you will be granted admittance into the eternal *kingdom* of . . . Jesus Christ.

Rv 1 9 2 I [John] am your brother and share . . . your *kingdom* and all you endure.

  11 15 X ϴ 2 The *kingdom* of the world has become [the kingdom] of
      6 our Lord and his Christ, and he will *reign* for ever and ever.

    17 We give thanks to you, Almighty Lord God, . . . for using
      ϴ 6 your great power and *beginning your reign*.

  12 10 ϴ Victory and power and *empire* for ever have been won *by our God*, and all authority for his Christ,

  15 3 ϴ 5 just and true are all your ways, *King* of nations.

  17 14 X 5 the Lamb is the Lord of lords and the *King* of kings,

  19 6 ϴ 6 The *reign* of the Lord our God Almighty *has begun*;

   16 X 5 On his cloak . . . there was a name written: The *King* of kings and the Lord of lords.

2: (THE PEOPLE OF GOD) REIGN – BE KING – ROYAL

Rm 5 17 it is even more certain that one man, Jesus Christ, will
      6 cause everyone to *reign* in life who receives the free gift

1 Co 4 8 6 Is it that . . . you are rich already, *in possession of your*
      6 *kingdom*, with us left outside? Indeed I wish you *were*
     11 really *kings*, and we could *be kings with* you!

2 Tm 2 12 X 11 If we hold firm, then we shall *reign with* him.

1 P 2 9 10 (Ex 19 6) you are a chosen race, a *royal* priesthood, a consecrated nation,

Rv 1 6 2 [Jesus Christ has] made us [a line of] *kings*, priests to serve his God

  5 10 2 [you bought men for God] and made them [a line of] *kings*
      6 and priests, to serve our God and to *rule* the world.

Rv 20 4 those who refused to worship the beast . . . came to life
    X 6 and *reigned* with Christ for a thousand years.

   6 X 6 they will be priests of God and of Christ and *reign* with him for a thousand years.

  22 5 6 They will *reign* for ever and ever.

3: KING, KINGDOM (GENERALLY) – EMPEROR

R = Roman emperor

Mt 4 8 2 the devil showed [Jesus] all the *kingdoms* of the world and their splendour.

  10 18 5 You will be dragged before governors and *kings* for my sake,

  11 8 5 those who wear fine clothes are to be found in *kings*' palaces.

  12 25 5 Every *kingdom* divided against itself is heading for ruin,

  17 25 5 From whom do the *kings* of the earth take toll or tribute?

  18 23 < 5 the kingdom of heaven may be compared to a *king* who decided to settle his accounts

  22 2 < 5 The kingdom of heaven may be compared to a *king* who gave a feast

   7 < 5 The *king* was furious. He despatched his troops,

   11 < 5 the *king* came in to look at the guests

   13 < 5 the *king* said to the attendants, 'Bind him hand and foot'

  24 7 2 nation will fight against nation, and *kingdom* against *kingdom*.

Mk 3 24 2/2 If a *kingdom* is divided against itself, that *kingdom* cannot last.

  13 8 2 nation will fight against nation, and *kingdom* against *kingdom*.

   9 5 you will stand before governors and *kings* for my sake,

Lk 4 5 2 the devil showed [Jesus] in a moment of time all the *kingdoms* of the world [6] and said to him, 'I will give you all this power and the glory of these [kingdoms],

  10 24 5 many prophets and *kings* wanted to see what you see,

  11 17 2 Every *kingdom* divided against itself is heading for ruin,

  14 31 5/5 what *king* marching to war against another *king* would not first sit down and consider . . . ?

  19 12 A man of noble birth went to a distant country to be
     < 2 appointed *king*

   14 his compatriots . . . sent a delegation to follow him with
     < 6 this message, 'We do not want this man to *be our king*'.

   15 < 2 on his return, having received his appointment as *king*,

   27 < 6 as for my enemies who did not want me *for* their *king*,

  21 10 2 Nation will fight against nation, and *kingdom* against *kingdom*.

   12 5 men will . . . bring you before *kings* and governors because of my name

  22 25 5 Among pagans it is the *kings* who lord it over them,

Jn 19 15 R 5 We have no *king* except Caesar.

Ac 4 26 5 (Ps 2 2) *Kings* on earth setting out to war . . . against the Lord and against his Anointed.

  9 15 my chosen instrument to bring my name before pagans
     5 and pagan *kings* and before the people of Israel;

  13 21 J 5 they demanded a *king*, and God gave them Saul

1 Tm 2 2 [there should be prayers offered for everyone] and especially
     5 for *kings* and others in authority,

  6 15 6 [our Lord Jesus Christ will be revealed] the King of *kings* and the Lord of lords,

Heb 11 33 [Gideon, . . . Samuel and the prophets] were men who
     2 through faith conquered *kingdoms*,

1 P 2 13 For the sake of the Lord, accept the authority of . . . the
     5 *emperor*,

   17 5 fear God and honour the *emperor*.

Rv 1 5 5 Jesus Christ, . . . the Ruler of the *kings* of the earth.

  6 15 5 all the earthly *rulers*, the governors and the commanders,

  10 11 You are to prophesy again, this time about many different
     5 nations and . . . *emperors*.

  16 12 all the water [of the Euphrates] dried up so that a way was
     5 made for the *kings* of the East to come in.

   14 [the three foul spirits] were . . . able to work miracles,
     5 going out to all the *kings* of the world to call them together for the war of the Great Day of God the Almighty.

  17 2 5 [Babylon] the one with whom all the *kings* of the earth have comitted fornication,

   9 R 5 The seven heads [of the beast] are also seven *emperors*.

   12 R 5 The ten horns [of the beast] are ten *kings* who have not yet
     2/5 been given their *royal power* but will have *royal authority* only for a single hour

   14 5 the Lamb is the Lord of lords and the King of *kings*,

   17 2 to agree together to put their *royal powers* at the beast's disposal

  18 2/5 the great city which has *authority* over all the *rulers* on earth.

  18 3 5 every *king* in the earth has committed fornication with [Babylon]

   7 8 I *am the queen* on my throne, [Babylon] says to herself,

   9 There will be mourning and weeping for [Babylon] by the
     5 *kings* of the earth

  19 16 On his cloak . . . there was a name written: The King of
     5 *kings* and the Lord of lords.

Rv 19 18 5 There will be the flesh of *kings* for you,
     19 5 Then I saw the beast, with all the *kings* of the earth and
            their armies,
  21 24 5 the *kings* of the earth will bring [the holy city] their treasures.

4: PARTICULAR KINGS

a) Aretas
Aretas 1

2 Co 11 32 5 When I was in Damascus, the ethnarch of *King Aretas* put
              guards round the city to catch me,

b) the Kandake or Queen of Ethiopia
kandake [Candace] 1   (of) Ethiopia* 2

Ac 8 27   an Ethiopian* . . . a eunuch and an officer at the court of
        8   the *kandake*, or *queen*, of Ethiopia*,

c) Herod (the Great)

Herod 11   Archelaus 1 (Mt 2 22)

Mt 2 1   5 After Jesus had been born . . . during the reign of *King
            Herod*,
     3   5 When *King Herod* heard this he was perturbed,
     7   Then *Herod* summoned the wise men to see him privately.
     9   5 Having listened to what the *king* had to say, [the wise men]
            set out.
    12   [the wise men] were warned in a dream not to go back to
            Herod,
    13   *Herod* intends to search for the child [Jesus] and do away
            with him.
    15   [Joseph] stayed [in Egypt] until *Herod* was dead.
    16   *Herod* was furious when he realised that he had been outwitted
            by the wise men,
    19   After *Herod*'s death, the angel of the Lord appeared in a dream
            to Joseph
    22   when [Joseph] learnt that *Archelaus* had succeeded his father
         6 *Herod* as *ruler* of Judaea he was afraid to go there,
Lk 1 5   5 In the days of *King Herod* of Judaea there lived a priest called
            Zechariah
Ac 23 35   [the governor of Caesarea] ordered [Paul] to be held in
            Herod's praetorium.

d) Herod (Antipas)

Herod   27   Philip* (son of Herod the Great and
Mariamne II) 2 (Mt; Mk 6)
H Herodias* 6   Philip* (son of Herod the Great and
Cleopatra) 1/3 (Lk 3)

Mt 14 1   At that time *Herod* the tetrarch heard about the reputation of
              Jesus,
      3   it was *Herod* who had arrested John, . . . and put him in
         H   prison because of Herodias*, his brother Philip's* wife.
      6   during the celebrations for *Herod*'s birthday, the daughter
         H   of Herodias* danced before the company, and so delighted
             Herod 7 that he promised . . . to give her anything she
             asked.
      9   5 The *king* was distressed
Mk 6 14 5 *King Herod* had heard about [Jesus], . . . 16 . . . *Herod*
     16   . . . said, 'It is John whose head I cut off;' . . . 17 Now it
     17   was this same *Herod* who had . . . had [John] chained
         H   up in prison because of Herodias*, his brother Philip's*
     18   wife whom he had married. 18 For John had told *Herod*,
             'It is against the law for you to have your brother's wife'.
     19 H   19 As for Herodias*, she . . . wanted to kill him; but she
     20   was not able to, 20 because *Herod* was afraid of John,
     21   on *Herod*'s birthday . . . he gave a banquet . . . 22 When
     22 H   the daughter of this same Herodias* came in and danced,
          5 she delighted *Herod* and his guests; so the *king* said to the
             girl, 'Ask me anything you like and I will give it to you'.
     23   2 23 '. . . '. . . even half my *kingdom*'.
     25 5 The girl hurried straight back to the *king* and made her
             request,
     26 5 The *king* was deeply distressed but, thinking of the oaths he
     27 5   had sworn . . . 27 . . . the *king* at once sent one of the
             bodyguard
  8 15   be on your guard against the yeast of the Pharisees and the
            yeast of *Herod*.
Lk 3 1   In the fifteenth year of Tiberius Caesar's reign, when Pontius
             Pilate was governor of Judaea, *Herod* tetrarch of Galilee,
             his brother Philip* tetrarch of the lands of Ituraea and
             Trachonitis,
     19   *Herod* the tetrarch, whom [John] criticised for his relations
         H   with his brother's wife Herodias* and for all the other
             crimes *Herod* had committed,
  8 3   Joanna the wife of *Herod*'s steward Chuza,

Lk 9 7   *Herod* the tetrarch had heard about all that was going on;
      9   *Herod* said, 'John? I beheaded him.'
  13 31   [Some Pharisees to Jesus:] '*Herod* means to kill you,' 32 He
             replied, 'You may go and give that fox this message':
  23 7   finding that [Jesus] came under *Herod*'s jurisdiction [Pilate]
      8   passed him over to *Herod* . . . 8 *Herod* was delighted to see
             Jesus;
     11   *Herod* . . . put a rich cloak on him and sent him back to
     12   Pilate. 12 And though *Herod* and Pilate had been enemies
             before, they were reconciled
     15   *Herod* . . . has sent him back to us.
Ac 4 27   in this very city *Herod* and Pontius Pilate made an alliance
             with the pagan nations and the peoples of Israel, against
             . . . Jesus
  13 1   In the church at Antioch the following were prophets and
             teachers: . . . Manaen, who had been brought up with
             Herod the tetrarch,

e) Herod (Agrippa I)

Herod 5

Ac 12 1   5 It was about this time that *King Herod* started persecuting
             certain members of the Church.
      6   On the night before *Herod* was to try him, Peter was sleeping
             between two soldiers,
     11   The Lord . . . has saved me from *Herod*
     19   *Herod* . . . gave orders for [the guards]' execution.
     20   the Tyrians and Sidonians . . . managed to enlist the support
          5 of Blastus, the *king*'s chamberlain, and through him nego-
          7 tiated a treaty, since their country depended . . . on *King
     21   [Herod's]* territory. 21 A day was fixed, and *Herod*,
          7 wearing his robes *of state* . ., made a speech

f) Herod (Agrippa II)

Agrippa 11   B Bernice* 3   Porcius* 1 (Ac 24)
Festus* 13

Ac 24 27   Felix was succeeded [as governor of Caesarea] by Porcius*
             Festus*
  25 1   Festus* went up to Jerusalem from Caesarea.
      4   Festus* replied that Paul would remain in custody in Caesarea,
      9   Festus* . . . said to Paul, 'Are you willing to go up to
             Jerusalem . . .?'
     12   Festus* . . . replied. 'You have appealed to Caesar; to
             Caesar you shall go'.
     13 B 5 *King Agrippa* and Bernice* arrived in Caesarea and paid their
     14   5 respects to Festus*. 14 . . . Festus* put Paul's case before
             the *king*.
     22   *Agrippa* said to Festus*, 'I should like to hear the man
             myself'.
     23 B   *Agrippa* and Bernice* arrived in great state . . . and Festus*
     24   ordered Paul to be brought in. 24 Then Festus* said,
          5 'King Agrippa*, and all here present with us, you see before
             you the man about whom the whole Jewish community has
     26   petitioned me, 26 . . . I have produced him before
          5 you all, and before you in particular, *King Agrippa*,
  26 1   *Agrippa* said to Paul, 'You have leave to speak on your own
      2   5 behalf'. And Paul . . . began his defence: 2 'I consider
          5 myself fortunate, *King Agrippa*, that it is before you'
      7   5 For that hope, *Sire*, I am actually put on trial by Jews!
     13   5 at midday as I was on my way, your *Majesty*, I saw a light
             brighter than the sun
     19   5 After that, *King Agrippa*, I could not disobey the heavenly
             vision.
     24   Festus* shouted out, 'Paul, you are out of your mind':
     25   Festus*, your Excellency, . . . I am not mad:
     26   5 The *king* understands these matters, and to him I now speak
     27   5 'King Agrippa*, do you believe in the prophets? I know you
     28   do.' 28 At this *Agrippa* said to Paul, 'A little more, and your
             arguments would make a Christian of me'.
     30   5 the *king* rose to his feet, with the governor (= Festus) and
         B   Bernice*
     32   *Agrippa* remarked to Festus*, 'The man could have been set
             free if he had not appealed to Caesar'.

g) Melchizedek

Melchizedek 1/9   Salem* 2

Heb 7 1   5 You remember that *Melchizedek*, king of Salem*, a priest of
             God Most High, went to meet Abraham who was on his
          5 way back after defeating the *kings*, and blessed him;
      2 5 2 . . . By the interpretation of his name, he is, first, '*king*
         5/5 of righteousness' and also *king* of Salem*, that is, '*king*
             of peace'; 3 he has no father, mother or ancestry, and his
             life has no beginning or ending; he is like the Son of God.
             He remains a priest for ever.

h) Solomon and the Queen of the South
Solomon 12

Mt	1	6	David was the father of *Solomon*, whose mother had been Uriah's wife,
		7	*Solomon* was the father of Rehoboam,
	6	29	not even *Solomon* in all his regalia was robed like one of these [flowers].
	12	42	8 On Judgement day the *Queen* of the South will rise up with this generation and condemn it, because she came from the ends of the earth to hear the wisdom of *Solomon* (cf. 1 K 10 1–10); and there is something greater than *Solomon* here.
Lk	11	31	8 On Judgement day the *Queen* of the South will rise up with the men of this generation and condemn them, because she came from the ends of the earth to hear the wisdom of *Solomon* (1 K 10 1–10); and there is something greater than *Solomon* here.
	12	27	not even *Solomon* in all his regalia was robed like one of these [flowers].
Jn	10	23	Jesus was in the Temple walking up and down in the Portico of *Solomon*,
Ac	3	11	Everyone came running towards [Peter, John and the lame man] . ., to the Portico of *Solomon*,
	5	12	[The believers] all used to meet . . . in the Portico of *Solomon*.
	7	47	(1 K 6 1) it was *Solomon* who actually built God's house

5: REIGN, KINGDOM (FIGURATIVELY)

a) (Death, Sin) Reign

Rm	5	14	6 death *reigned* over all from Adam to Moses, even though their sin . . . was not a matter of breaking a law.
		17	6 it is certain that death *reigned* over everyone as the consequence of one man's fall,
		21	6 sin *reigned* wherever there was death,
	6	12	6 you must not let sin *reign* in your mortal bodies

b) (Satan's) Kingdom – (the Angel of the Abyss as) Emperor

Mt	12	26	Ⓓ 2 if Satan casts out Satan, . . . how can his *kingdom* stand?
Lk	11	18	if [Satan] is divided against himself, how can his *kingdom* Ⓓ 2 stand?
Rv	9	11	Ⓓ 5 As their leader [the locusts] had their *emperor*, the angel of the Abyss.
	16	10	The fifth angel emptied his bowl over the throne of the beast 2 and its whole *empire* was plunged into darkness.

c) (Grace) Reigns – (the) Royal (law)

Rm	5	21	just as sin reigned wherever there was death, so grace will 6 *reign* to bring eternal life
Jm	2	8	7 the right thing to do is to keep the ⌜supreme (lit. *royal*) law of scripture (Lv 19 18): you must love your neighbour as yourself;

6: PALACE, ROYAL COURT

Lk	7	25	9 those who go in for fine clothes . . . are to be found at *court*!

7: COURT OFFICIAL

Jn	4	46	7 there was a *court official* [at Cana] whose son was ill at Capernaum
		49	7 'Sir', answered the *official* 'come down before my child dies.'

KISS – EMBRACE

1. Kiss: *phileō*	**2. Embrace – Put one's arms round – Take in one's arms:** *en-ankalizomai*

1. KISS: *PHILEŌ*

1 *philēma* 7   2 *kata-phileō* 6
3 *phileō* 3/25

Mt	26	48	3 The one I *kiss* . . . is [Jesus]. Take him in charge.
		49	2 [Judas said], 'Greetings, Rabbi', and *kissed* [Jesus].
Mk	14	44	3 The one I *kiss* . . . is [Jesus]. Take him in charge,
		45	the traitor . . . went straight up to Jesus and said, 'Rabbi!' 2 and *kissed* him.
Lk	7	38	2 [the woman who was a sinner] *covered* his feet *with kisses*

Lk	7	45	/2 You gave me no *kiss*, but she has been *covering* my feet *with kisses* ever since I came in.
	15	20	2 [His father] ran to the boy, clasped him in his arms and *kissed* him tenderly.
	22	47	3 Judas . . . went up to Jesus to *kiss* him.
		48	Judas, are you betraying the Son of Man with a *kiss*?
Ac	20	37	[the elders in Ephesus] put their arms round Paul's neck and 2 *kissed* him;
Rm	16	16	Greet each other with a holy *kiss*.
1 Co	16	20	Greet one another with a holy *kiss*.
2 Co	13	12	Greet one another with the holy *kiss*.
1 Th	5	26	Greet all the brothers with the holy *kiss*.
1 P	5	14	Greet one another with a *kiss* of love.

2. EMBRACE – PUT ONE'S ARMS ROUND – TAKE IN ONE'S ARMS: *EN-ANKALIZOMAI*
en-ankalizomai 2

Mk	9	36	[Jesus] took a little child . . . *put his arms round* him, and said
	10	16	[Jesus] *put his arms round* [the little children] . . . and gave them his blessing.

KNOW – UNDERSTAND

1. **Know – Recognise – Understand:** *ginōskō*
   1: (God) Knows, Acknowledges – the Foreknowledge of God
   2: (Jesus) Knew – (Jesus) Perceived
   3: Know – Recognise, Perceive – Understand (referring to things religious or moral)
   4: Ignorance, Without knowing – Fail to recognise
   5: Examine, Investigate – Go into – Decide
   6: Know personally, Recognise – Acquaintance, Friend
   7: Know sexually, Have sexual intercourse with
   8: Know – Realise, Understand, Recognise – Hear about, Find out (generally)
   9: Make known, Reveal – Want (a person) to know
2. **Know – Realise, Remember – Understand:** *oida*
   1: (God) Knows, Knows how to
   2: (Jesus) Knows
   3: Recognition of Jesus by devils, unclean spirits

4: (A person) Knows, Understands, Remembers
   a) Know, Realise – Understand, Be aware (of) – Remember (God, Jesus, things religious)
   b) Know, Have an idea (of), Remember (generally)
   5: Conscience – Awareness
3. **Know (well) – Understand:** *epistamai*
4. **Understand – Perception, Intelligence – Clever:** *syn-(h)iēmi*
5. **Realise, Perceive – Grasp, Comprehend – Consider:** *kata-lambanō*
6. **Perception, Grasp the meaning of – Mind:** *aisthanomai*
7. **Reason, Understanding – Mind:** *noeō*
   1: Understand – Perceive, See
   2: Mind – Reason, Understanding, Intelligence – Ideas
8. **Reason – Unreasoning – Unreasonable, Pointless:** *a-logos*
9. **Unskilled – Not to know:** *a-peiros*
10. **Layman – Uninitiated – Unskilled:** *idiōtēs*
11. **Come to oneself – Recover one's senses:** *ginomai en*

1. KNOW – RECOGNISE – UNDERSTAND: *GINŌSKŌ*

1	*ginōskō*	221	11	*(kardio-)gnōstēs*	2
4	*gnōrizō*	26	12	*dia-ginōskō*	2
3	*gnōsis*	29	17	*dia-gnōsis*	1
14	*gnōstēs*	1	2	*epi-ginōskō*	44
7	*gnōstos*	15	6	*epi-gnōsis*	20
15	*a-gnoēma*	1	8	*pro-ginōskō*	5
5	*a-gnoeō*	22	13	*pro-gnōsis*	2
9	*a-gnoia*	4			
10	*a-gnōsia*	2			
16	*a-gnōstos*	1			

1: (GOD) KNOWS, ACKNOWLEDGES – THE FOREKNOWLEDGE OF GOD

Mt	11	27	2 no one *knows* the Son except the Father, just as no one knows the Father except the Son
Lk	10	22	no one *knows* who the Son is except the Father
	16	15	God *knows* your hearts.
Jn	10	15	the Father *knows* me and I know the Father;
Ac	1	24	11 Lord, you ⌜can read (lit. *know*) everyone's heart;

Ac 2 23   13 [Jesus] was put into your power by the . . . *foreknowledge* of God,
   15 8   11 God . . . ⌐can read (lit. *knows*) everyone's heart,
      18   says the Lord who ⌐made this known (or: did these things, *known* [by him]) so long ago.
          7
Rm 8 29   8 They are the ones he ⌐chose (or: *knew*) specially long ago
   11 2   8 the people [God] ⌐chose (or: *knew*) specially long ago.
      33   How rich are the depths of God – how deep his wisdom and *knowledge* –
          3
1 Co 2 11 Ⓢ   the depths of God can only be *known* by the Spirit of God.
   3 20   (Ps 94 11) The Lord *knows* men's thoughts:
   8 3   any man who loves God is *known* by him.
   13 12   2 then I shall know as fully as I am *known*.
Ga 4 9   now that you have come to acknowledge God – or rather, now that God has *acknowledged* you –
Ph 4 6   if there is anything you need, pray for it, ⌐asking God for it (lit. letting God *know* of) with prayer and thanksgiving,
          4
2 Tm 19   (Nb 16 5 G) The Lord *knows* those who are his own
1 P 1 2   [Peter sends greetings to all those who have been chosen]
      13   by the ⌐provident purpose (lit. *foreknowledge*) of God
   20   8 [Christ] *known* since before the world was made,
1 Jn 3 20   God is greater than our conscience and he *knows* everything.

2: (JESUS) KNEW – (JESUS) PERCEIVED

Mt 7 23   I have never *known* you;
   11 27   no one knows the Son except the Father, just as no one
          2 *knows* the Father except the Son
   12 15   Jesus *knew* [that the Pharisees were plotting against him] and withdrew from the district.
   16 8   Jesus *knew* [what the disciples were saying among themselves], and he said, 'Men of little faith . . .'
   22 18   Jesus *was aware of* [the Pharisees'] malice and replied, 'You hypocrites!'
   26 10   Jesus ⌐noticed (or: *knew*) [that the disciples were indignant]. 'Why are you upsetting the woman?' he said to them.
Mk 2 8   2 Jesus, inwardly *aware* that this was what [the scribes] were thinking, said to them, 'Why do you have these thoughts . . .?'
   5 30   2 Immediately *aware* that power had gone out from him, Jesus turned round in the crowd
   8 17   Jesus *knew* [what the disciples were saying among themselves] and he said to them,
Lk 5 22   2 Jesus, *aware of* [the scribes and Pharisees'] thoughts, made them this reply,
   7 39   If this man were a prophet, he would *know* who this woman is
   8 46   Jesus said, '. . . I *felt* that power had gone out from me.'
   10 22   no one *knows* who the Son is except the Father, and who the Father is except the Son
Jn 1 48   'How do you *know* me?' said Nathanael [to Jesus].
   2 24   [many believed in his name] but Jesus *knew* them all and did not trust himself to them; ²⁵ he never needed evidence about any man; he *could tell* what a man had in him.
      25
   4 1   Jesus ⌐heard (lit. *knew*) that the Pharisees had found out that he was making . . . more disciples than John –
   5 6   Jesus saw [the sick man lying by the pool] and *knew* he had been in this condition for a long time,
      42   I *know* you too well: you have no love of God in you.
   6 15   Jesus . . . *could see* they were about to come . . . and make him king,
   10 14   I *know* my own [sheep] and my own know me, ¹⁵ just as the Father knows me and I *know* the Father;
      15
      27   I *know* [the sheep that belong to me] and they follow me.
   16 19   Jesus *knew* that [his disciples] wanted to question him,
   17 25   Father, . . . the world has not known you, but I have *known* you,
   21 17   Lord, you know everything; you *know* I love you.
2 Co 5 21   For our sake God made the ⌐sinless one (lit. one who had not *known* sin) into sin,

3: KNOW – RECOGNISE, PERCEIVE – UNDERSTAND (REFERRING TO THINGS RELIGIOUS OR MORAL)

Mt 7 16   2 You will be able to *tell* [false prophets] by their fruits.
   20   2 you will be able to *tell* [false prophets] by their fruits.
   9 30   Take care that no one *learns* about [the cure of the two blind men].
   11 27   2 no one *knows* the Son except the Father, just as no one
          2 *knows* the Father except the Son and those to whom the Son chooses to reveal him.
   12 7   if you had *understood* the meaning of the words (Ho 6 6): What I want is mercy, not sacrifice,
      33   the tree can be *told* by its fruit.
   13 11   the mysteries of the kingdom of heaven are ⌐revealed (lit. made *known*) to you,
   17 12   2 Elijah has come already and [the scribes] did not *recognise* him

Mt 24 33   when you see all these things: *know* that [the Son of Man] is near,
   39   [people] *suspected* nothing till the Flood came
   43   You may *be quite sure* of this that if the householder had *known* . . . he would have stayed awake
   50   [the servant's] master will come . . . at an hour he does not *know*.
Mk 4 13   Do you not understand this parable? Then how will you *understand* any of the parables?
   5 29   [the woman who had suffered from a haemorrhage] *felt* in herself that she was cured
   43   [Jesus] ordered them strictly not to let anyone *know* [about the raising of Jairus's daughter],
   9 32   5 [the disciples] did *not understand* what he said
   12 12   [the elders] *realised* that the parable was aimed at them,
   13 29   when you see these things happening: *know* that [the Son of Man] is near.
Lk 1 18   Zechariah said to the angel, 'How can I *be sure* [that I shall have a son]?'
   77   3 [you who will go before the Lord] to give his people *knowledge* of salvation
   6 44   every tree can be *told* by its own fruit:
   8 10   The mysteries of the kingdom of God are ⌐revealed (lit. made *known*) to you;
   9 45   5 [the disciples] did *not understand* [Jesus] when he said this;
   10 11   *be sure* of this; the kingdom of God is very near.
   22   no one *knows* who the Son is except the Father, and who the Father is except the Son and those to whom the Son chooses to reveal him.
   11 52   Alas for you lawyers who have taken away the key of
          3 *knowledge*!
   12 39   You may *be quite sure* of this, that if the householder had *known* . . . he would not have let anyone break through the wall
   46   [the servant's] master will come . . . at an hour he does not *know*.
   47   The servant who *knows* what his master wants, but has not even started to carry out those wishes, will receive . . . strokes
   48   The [servant] who did *not know* [his master's wishes] . . . will receive fewer strokes
   18 34   [the Twelve] could make nothing of [Jesus's prophecy of the Passion]; . . . they *had no idea* what it meant.
   19 42   If you in your turn had only *understood* on this day the message of peace!
   44   [Jerusalem,] you did not *recognise* your opportunity when God offered it!
   21 31   *know* that the kingdom of God is near.
   24 35   [the two disciples] told . . . how they had *recognised* [Jesus] at the breaking of bread.
Jn 1 10   He was in the world . . . and the world did not *know* him.
   3 10   You, a teacher in Israel, and you do not *know* these things!
   6 69   [Simon Peter answered, . . .] we *know* that you are the Holy One of God.
   7 17   if anyone is prepared to do [the] will [of the one who sent me], he will *know* whether my teaching is from God
   26   Can it be true the authorities have ⌐made up their minds (lit. *perceived*) that he is the Christ?
   27   we all know where he comes from, but when the Christ appears no one will *know* where he comes from.
   49   This rabble *knows* nothing about the Law –
   8 27   [The Jews] failed to *understand* that he was talking to them about the Father.
   28   When you have lifted up the Son of Man, then you will *know* that I am He
   32   [If you make my word your home] you will *learn* the truth
   43   you are unable to *understand* my language.
   52   Now we *know* for certain that you are possessed.
   55   [you say, 'He is our God'] although you do not *know* him.
   10 6   [the Pharisees] failed to *understand* what [Jesus] meant
   14   I know my own [sheep] and my own *know* me,
   38   then you will *know* ⌐for sure (lit. and *recognise*) that the Father is in me
   12 16   At the time his disciples did not *understand* this,
   13 7   At the moment you do not know what I am doing, but later you will *understand*.
   12   'Do you *understand*' [Jesus] said 'what I have done to you?'
   28   None of the others at table *understood* the reason [Jesus] said this [to Judas].
   35   By this love you have for one another, everyone will *know* that you are my disciples.
   14 7   If you ᵛ*know* (G had *known*) me, you ᵛ*know* (G would have known) my Father too. From this moment you *know* him and have seen him.
   9   Have I been with you all this time, Philip, . . . and you still do not *know* me?
   17   the world can never receive [that Spirit of truth] since it neither sees nor *knows* him; but you *know* him,
   20   On that day you will *understand* that I am in my Father
   31   the world must [be brought to] *know* that I love the Father

Jn 15	18		If the world hates you, ⌐remember (lit. *know*) that it hated me before you.
16	3		they have never *known* either the Father or myself.
17	3		eternal life is this: to *know* you, the only true God, and Jesus Christ whom you have sent.
	7		they *know* that all you have given me comes indeed from you;
	8		they have truly *accepted* this, that I came from you,
	23		the world will *realise* that it was you who sent me
	25		the world has not *known* you, but I have known you, and these have *known* that you have sent me.
Ac 1	7		It is not for you to *know* times or dates that the Father has decided
2	14	7	⌐make no mistake about (lit. *understand*) this, . . . ¹⁶ this is what the prophet spoke of:
	36		the whole House of Israel ⌐can be certain (lit. ought to *understand*) that God has made this Jesus whom you crucified both Lord and Christ.
4	10	7	⌐I am glad to tell you all (lit. *understand*) . . . that it was by the name of Jesus Christ . . . that this man is able to stand up perfectly healthy,
	16	7	It is *obvious* to everybody in Jerusalem that a miracle has been worked
8	30		Do you *understand* what you are reading?
9	42	7	The whole of Jaffa ⌐heard (lit. *knew*) about [the resurrection of Tabitha]
13	27	5	What the people of Jerusalem . . . did, though they did *not realise* it, was in fact to fulfil the prophecies
	38	7	I want you to *realise* that it is through [Jesus] that forgiveness of your sins is proclaimed.
17	19		How much of this new teaching . . . are we allowed to *know*? ²⁰ Some of the things you said seemed startling to us and we would like to ⌐find out (lit. *know*) what they mean.
	20		
	23	16	I noticed . . . that you had an altar inscribed: To An *Unknown* God.
19	15		Jesus I *recognise*, and I know who Paul is, but who are you?
22	14		The God of our ancestors has chosen you to *know* his will,
26	3	14	you *are an expert in* matters of custom and controversy among the Jews.
28	28	7	*Understand*, then, that this salvation of God has been sent to the pagans
Rm 1	19	7	what can be *known* about God is perfectly plain to [the pagans]
	21		[the pagans] *knew* God and yet refused to honour him as God
	28	6	[the pagans] refused to see it was rational to *acknowledge* God,
	32	2	[Enemies of God] *know* what God's verdict is:
2	18		if you *know* God's will [then why not teach yourself as well as the others?]
	20	3	your Law embodies all *knowledge* and truth,
3	17		(Is 59 8) They *know* nothing of the way of peace,
	20	6	all that law does is to ⌐tell us (lit. give us *knowledge* of) what is sinful.
6	6		We must *realise* that our former selves have been crucified with [Christ]
7	7		I should not have *known* what sin was except for the Law.
	15		I cannot *understand* my own behaviour.
10	2	6	I can swear to their fervour for God, but their zeal is ⌐misguided (lit. less *understandable*).
	19		is it possible that Israel did not *understand*?
11	34		(Is 40 13) Who could ever *know* the mind of the Lord?
15	14	3	I am quite certain that you are . . . perfectly well *instructed*
1 Co 1	5		you have been enriched in so many ways, especially in your ⌐teachers and preachers (lit. teaching and *knowledge*);
	21		it was God's wisdom that human wisdom should not *know* God,
2	8		It is a wisdom that none of the masters of this age have ever *known*, ⌐or (§ if they had *known* it) they would not have crucified the Lord
	11	Ⓢ	the depths of a man can only be *known* by his own spirit,
	14		An unspiritual person . . . does not accept anything of the Spirit of God: . . . it is beyond his *understanding*
	16		(Is 40 13) Who can *know* the mind of the Lord . . . ?
8	1	3/3	'We all have *knowledge*'; yes, this is so, but *knowledge* gives self-importance – it is love that makes the building grow.
	2		A man may imagine he *understands* something, but still not *understand* anything in the way that he ought to (§ *understand*).
	7	3	Some people . . . do not have this *knowledge*.
	10	3	Suppose someone sees you, a man who *understands*, eating in some temple of an idol; . . . ¹¹ . . . your *knowledge* could become the ruin of someone weak,
	11	3	
10	1		⌐I want to remind you . . . how (lit. I do not want you to *misunderstand* that) our fathers were all guided by a cloud
	5		
12	1		I want to ⌐clear up a wrong impression (lit. see that you do not *misunderstand*) about spiritual gifts.
	5		
	8	3	another may have the gift of preaching *instruction*
13	2	3	If I have the gift of prophecy, . . . *knowing* everything . . . but without love, then I am nothing at all.
	8	3	*knowledge* – . . . the time will come when it must fail. ⁹ For our *knowledge* is imperfect
	9		

1 Co 13	12		The *knowledge* that I have now is imperfect; but then I shall *know* as fully as I am known.
		2	
14	6		what use shall I be if all my talking . . . neither ⌐inspires you (lit. imparts *understanding*) nor instructs you?
		3	
	9		if your tongue does not produce intelligible speech, how can anyone *know* what you are saying?
	37	2	Anyone who claims to be a prophet . . . ought to *recognise* that what I am writing to you is a command from the Lord.
2 Co 2	14	3	through us [God] is spreading the *knowledge* of himself, like a sweet smell, everywhere.
4	6		God . . . has shone in our minds to radiate the light of the *knowledge* of God's glory,
		3	
5	16		Even if we did once know Christ in the flesh, that is not how we *know* him now.
6	6	3	We prove we are God's servants by our purity, *knowledge*,
8	7		You always have the most of everything – of faith, of eloquence, of *understanding*,
		3	
	9		⌐Remember (lit. You *know*) how generous the Lord Jesus was:
10	5	3	[we demolish] the arrogance that tries to resist the *knowledge* of God,
11	6	3	I may not be a polished speechmaker, but as for *knowledge*, that is a different matter;
13	5	2	Do you *acknowledge* that Jesus Christ is really in you?
Ga 2	9		[James, Cephas and John] shook hands with me, *recognising* the grace thus given me
3	7		Don't you ⌐see (lit. *understand* that) it is those who rely on faith who are the sons of Abraham?
4	9		now that you have come to *acknowledge* God – or rather, now that God has acknowledged you –
Ep 1	17	6	May . . . God . . . give you a spirit of . . . perception of what is revealed, to bring you to full *knowledge* of him.
3	19	/3	*knowing* the love of Christ, which is beyond all *knowledge*, you are filled with the utter fullness of God.
4	13	6	we are all to come to unity in our faith and in our *knowledge* of the Son of God,
5	5		For you ⌐can be quite certain (lit. should understand and *know*) that nobody who actually indulges in fornication or impurity . . . can inherit anything of the kingdom of God.
Ph 1	9	6	My prayer is that your love for each other may . . . never stop improving your *knowledge*
3	8	3	nothing can happen that will outweigh the supreme advantage of *knowing* Christ Jesus
	10		All I want is to *know* Christ and the power of his resurrection
Col 1	6	2	you heard about God's grace and *understood* what this really is.
	9	6	we ask God . . . that . . . you should reach the fullest *knowledge* of his will. ¹⁰ . . . showing the results in . . .
	10	6	good actions . . . and increasing your *knowledge* of God.
2	2	6	[my struggle for you] is all to . . . stir your minds . . . until you really *know* God's secret ³ in which all the jewels of wisdom and *knowledge* are hidden.
	3	3	
3	10	6	you have put on a new self which will progress towards *true knowledge*
1 Th 4	13	5	We want you ⌐to be quite certain (lit. not to *misunderstand*), brothers, about those who have died,
1 Tm 2	4	6	[God] wants everyone to . . . reach full *knowledge* of the truth.
4	3	2	abstaining from foods which God created to be accepted with thanksgiving by all who . . . *know* the truth.
6	20	3	Have nothing to do with . . . antagonistic beliefs of the '*knowledge*' which is not [knowledge] at all;
2 Tm 2	25	6	God may give them a change of mind so that they *recognise* the truth
3	1		You may ⌐be quite sure (lit. *perceive*) that in the last days there are going to be some difficult times.
	7	6	[Men who keep up only the appearance of religion] can never come to *knowledge* of the truth.
Tt 1	1	6	From Paul, . . . an apostle of Jesus Christ to bring those whom God has chosen to faith and to the *knowledge* of the truth
Phm	6	6	a sense of fellowship that will ⌐show you (lit. enable you to *perceive*) all the good things that we are able to do for Christ.
Heb 3	10		(Ps 95 10) How unreliable these people who refuse to *grasp* my ways!
8	11		(Jr 31 34) There will be no further need for neighbour to try to teach neighbour, . . . '[Learn to] *know* the Lord'.
10	26	6	If, after we have been given *knowledge* of the truth, we should deliberately commit any sins, then there is no . . . sacrifice for them.
	34		you happily accepted being stripped of your belongings, *knowing* that you owned something that was better and lasting.
Jm 1	3		you *understand* that your faith is only put to the test to make you patient.
2	20		Do *realise* . . . that faith without good deeds is useless.
5	20		he may ⌐be sure (lit. *know*) that anyone who can bring back a sinner from the wrong way . . . will be saving a soul
2 P 1	2	6	May you have more and more grace and peace as you come to *know* our Lord more and more.

2 P 1 3 6 By his divine power, [Christ] has . . . [brought] us to *know* God himself,

5 3 adding . . . *understanding* to your goodness, 6 self-control to
6 3 your *understanding*,

8 6 [these virtues] will bring you to a real *knowledge* of our Lord Jesus Christ.

20 ┌we must be most careful to remember (lit. *understand*) that the interpretation of scriptural prophecy is never a matter for the individual

2 20 anyone who has escaped the pollution of the world once by
6 coming to *know* our Lord

21 2 better . . . never to have ┌learnt (lit. *known*) the way of
2 holiness, than to *know* it and afterwards desert the holy rule

3 3 ┌We must be careful to remember (lit. *Understand*) that during the last days there are bound to be people who will be scornful,

17 8 You have ┌been warned about this (lit. *known* this *in advance*),

18 3 go on growing in the grace and in the *knowledge* of our Lord and saviour Jesus Christ.

1 Jn 2 3 We can *be sure* that we *know* God only by keeping his
4 commandments. ⁴ Anyone who says, 'I *know* him', and does not keep his commandments, is a liar,

5 We ┌can be sure (lit. *know*) that we are in God

13 I am writing to you, fathers, who [have come to] *know* the one who has existed since the beginning;

14 children, . . . you already *know* the Father . . . fathers, . . . you [have come to] *know* the one who has existed since the beginning;

18 several antichrists have already appeared; we *know* from this that these are the last days.

29 you must *recognise* that everyone whose life is righteous has been begotten by [God].

3 1 Because the world refused to *acknowledge* him, therefore it does not *acknowledge* us.

6 anyone who sins has never seen [God] or *known* him.

16 ┌This has taught us (lit. By this we have *known*) love – that he gave up his life for us;

19 [our love is something active;] only by this can we ┌be certain (lit. *know*) that we are children of the truth

24 We *know* that [God] lives in us by the Spirit that he has given us.

4 2 You can *tell* the spirits that come from God by this: every spirit which acknowledges . . . Jesus the Christ . . . is from God;

6 those who *know* God listen to us; . . . This is how we can *tell* the spirit of truth from the spirit of falsehood.

7 everyone who loves is begotten by God and *knows* God.

8 Anyone who fails to love can never have *known* God,

13 We can *know* that we are living in [God]

16 We ourselves have *known* and put our faith in God's love towards ourselves.

5 2 We ┌can be sure (lit. *know*) that we love God's children

20 the Son of God . . . has given us the power to *know* the true God.

2 Jn 1 my greetings to the Lady . . . whom I love in the truth – and . . . so do all who [have come to] *know* the truth –

Rv 2 23 all the churches *realise* that it is I who search heart and loins

24 all of you who have not . . . ┌learnt (lit. *known*) the secrets of Satan,

3 3 I shall come to you like a thief, without ┌telling you (lit. your *knowing*) at what hour to expect me.

9 I am going to make the synagogue of Satan . . . ┌admit (lit. *recognise*) that you are the people that I love.

4: IGNORANCE, WITHOUT KNOWING – FAIL TO RECOGNISE

Ac 3 17 9 neither you nor your leaders *had any idea* what you were really doing;

17 23 the God whom I proclaim is in fact the one whom you
5 already worship *without knowing* it.

30 9 God overlooked that sort of thing when men were *ignorant*, but now . . . everyone . . . must repent,

Rm 2 4 5 are you abusing his abundant goodness . . . *not realising* that this goodness of God is meant to lead you to repentance?

6 3 5 ┌You have been taught (lit. Do you *not know*) that when we were baptised in Christ Jesus we were baptised in his death;

10 3 5 *Failing to recognise* the righteousness that comes from God,

11 25 5 There is a hidden reason . . . of which I do not want you to be *ignorant*,

1 Co 14 38 5 ┌Unless he recognises (lit. If he *fails to recognise*) [that what I am writing to you is a command from the Lord], you should not recognise him.

15 34 10 there are some of you who seem *not to know* God at all;

2 Co 2 11 5 we ┌know well enough (lit. are not *ignorant* of) what [Satan's] intentions are.

Ep 4 18 9 [pagans] are estranged from the life of God, *without knowledge* because they have shut their hearts to it.

1 Tm 1 13 5 until I became a believer I had been acting in *ignorance*;
Heb 5 2 [every high priest] can sympathise with those who are
5 *ignorant* or uncertain

9 7 the high priest . . . must . . . take the blood to offer for
15 his own *faults* (§ *of ignorance*) and the people's.

1 P 1 14 Do not behave in the way that you liked to ┌before you learnt
9 the truth (lit. in the time of your *ignorance*),

2 15 God wants . . . to silence what fools are saying in their
10 *ignorance*.

2 P 2 12 5 these people who only insult anything that they *do not understand* are not reasoning beings,

5: EXAMINE, INVESTIGATE – GO INTO – DECIDE

Ac 23 15 12 bring [Paul] down to you, as though you meant to *examine* his case more closely;

24 22 12 I will *go into* your case.

25 21 Paul put in an appeal for his case to be reserved for the
17 ┌*judgement* (or: *decision*) of the august emperor,

6: KNOW PERSONALLY, RECOGNISE – ACQUAINTANCE, FRIEND

Mt 14 35 2 the local people *recognised* [Jesus]

Mk 6 54 2 people *recognised* [Jesus], ⁵⁵ and . . . brought the sick on stretchers

Lk 2 44 [Jesus's parents] went to look for him among their relations
7 and *acquaintances*.

23 49 7 All [Jesus's] *friends* stood at a distance;

24 16 something prevented [the disciples on the road to Emmaus]
2 from *recognising* [Jesus].

31 2 their eyes were opened and they *recognised* [Jesus];

Jn 18 15 5 This disciple . . . was *known* to the high priest,

16 7 the other disciple, the one *known* to the high priest, went out,

Ac 3 10 2 they *recognised* him as the man who used to sit begging

4 13 2 [the Sanhedrin] *recognised* [Peter and John] as associates of Jesus;

7 13 4 Joseph made himself *known* to his brothers,

26 5 8 [The Jews] have *known* me *for a long time*

1 Co 14 38 5 Unless he recognises this, you should *not recognise* him.

2 Co 6 9 5/2 [we are] ┌obscure (lit. *not known*) yet ┌famous (lit. *known*);

Ga 1 22 5 [I] was still *not known* by sight to the churches . . . in Judaea,

7: KNOW SEXUALLY, HAVE SEXUAL INTERCOURSE WITH

Mt 1 25 though [Joseph] had not *had intercourse with* [his wife], she gave birth to a son;

Lk 1 34 how can this come about, since I ┌am a virgin (lit. have not *known* man)?

8: KNOW – REALISE, UNDERSTAND, RECOGNISE – HEAR ABOUT, FIND OUT (GENERALLY)

Mt 6 3 your left hand must not *know* what your right is doing;

10 26 everything now hidden will be made ┌clear (lit. *known*).

16 3 You *know* how to read the face of the sky,

21 45 the chief priests and the scribes *realised* [Jesus] was speaking about them,

24 32 you *know* that summer is near.

25 24 Sir, . . . I had *heard* you were a hard man,

Mk 6 33 people saw [Jesus and the disciples] going, and many could
2 *guess* where;

38 'How many loaves have you?' . . . when they had *found out* they said, 'Five, and two fish'.

7 24 [Jesus] did not want anyone to *know* he was there, but he could not pass unrecognised.

9 30 [Jesus and the disciples] made their way through Galilee; and he did not want anyone to *know*,

13 28 you *know* that summer is near.

15 10 [Pilate] *realised* it was out of jealousy that the chief priests had handed Jesus over.

45 ┌Having been assured (lit. *Hearing*) [that Jesus was dead from] the centurion, [Pilate] granted the corpse to Joseph

Lk 1 4 2 so that your Excellency may *learn* how well founded the teaching is that you have received.

22 2 they *realised* that [Zechariah] had received a vision in the sanctuary.

2 43 the boy Jesus stayed behind in Jerusalem without his parents *knowing* it.

7 37 a woman came in, who had a bad name in the town. She had
2 *heard* [Jesus] was dining with the Pharisee

8 17 nothing [is] secret but it will be *known*

9 11 the crowds got to *know* [that Jesus had withdrawn to Bethsaida] and they went after him.

12 2 everything now hidden will be made ┌clear (lit. *known*).

Lk 16	4	I *know* what I will do to make sure that . . . there will be some to welcome me into their homes.
19	15	[the king] sent for those servants . . . to *find out* what profit each had made.
20	19	the scribes and the chief priests . . . *realised* that this parable was aimed at them.
21	20	When you see Jerusalem surrounded . . . you must *realise* that she will soon be laid desolate.
	30	you *know* that summer is now near.
23	7	2 *finding* that [Jesus] came under Herod's jurisdiction [Pilate] passed him over to Herod
24	18	You must be the only person staying in Jerusalem who does not *know* the things that have been happening there
Jn 4	53	The father *realised* that this was exactly the time when Jesus had said, 'Your son will live';
7	51	surely the Law does not allow us to pass judgement on a man without . . . *discovering* what he is about?
11	57	anyone who *knew* where [Jesus] was must inform [the Pharisees]
12	9	a large number of Jews *heard* that [Jesus] was [at Bethany]
19	4	I am going to bring [Jesus] out to you to let you *see* that I find no case.
Ac 1	19	7 Everybody in Jerusalem *heard about* [Judas's suicide]
9	24	*news* of [the Jews' plot] *reached* Saul.
	30	2 When the brothers *knew* [there was a plot to kill Saul], they took him to Caesarea.
12	14	2 [Rhoda] *recognised* Peter's voice
17	13	the Jews of Thessalonika *heard* that the word of God was being preached by Paul in Beroea
19	17	7 Everybody in Ephesus . . . *heard about* [the Jewish exorcists]
	34	2 [the Ephesians] *realised* [Paul] was a Jew,
	35	Is there anybody alive who does not *know* that the city of the Ephesians is the guardian of the temple of great Diana . . ?
20	34	you *know* for yourselves that the work I did earned enough to meet my needs
21	24	This will let everyone *know* there is no truth in the reports . . . about you
	34	the noise made it impossible for [the tribune] to *get* any positive *information*,
	37	The tribune said, 'You ⌐speak (lit. *know*) Greek, then?'
22	24	2 the tribune . . . ordered [Paul] to be examined . . . to *find out* the reason for the outcry against him.
	29	2 the tribune himself was alarmed when he *realised* that he had put a Roman citizen in chains,
	30	[the tribune] wanted to *know* what precise charge the Jews were bringing [against Paul].
23	6	Paul *was well aware* that one section was made up of Sadducees
	28	2 Wanting to *find out* what charge [the Jews] were making against [Paul], I brought him before their Sanhedrin.
24	8	2 you can *find out* for yourself the truth of all our accusations against this man.
	11	2 As you can *verify* for yourself, it is no more than twelve days since I went up to Jerusalem
25	10	2 I have done the Jews no wrong, as you very well *know*.
27	39	2 When day came [the crew] did not *recognise* the land,
28	1	2 we *discovered* that the island was called Malta.
	22	7 all we *know* about this sect is that opinion everywhere condemns it.
Rm 1	13	5 I want you to *know*, brothers, that I have often planned to visit you –
7	1	/5 those of you who ⌐have studied (lit. *know*) law will *know*
1 Co 4	19	I shall [want to] *know* not what these self-important people have to say, but what they can do,
14	7	if one note on [a flute or a harp] cannot be distinguished from another, how can you *tell* what [tune] is being played?
16	18	2 I hope you ⌐appreciate (lit. *recognise*) men like this.
2 Co 1	8	5 we should like you to *realise* . . . that the things we had to undergo in Asia were . . . a burden
	13	There are no hidden meanings in our letters besides what you
	14	2 can read for yourselves and *understand*. [14] And I hope
		2 that, although you do not *know* us very well yet, you will
		2 have come to *recognise* . . . that you can be . . . proud of us
2	4	I wrote to you . . . to let you *know* how much love I have for you.
	9	What I really wrote for . . . was to . . . *see* whether you are completely obedient.
3	2	you are yourselves our letter . . . that anybody can ⌐see (lit. *recognise*) and read,
13	6	we, as I hope you will [come to] *see*, have not failed [the test].
Ep 6	21	4 Tychicus . . . will ⌐tell you (lit. make you *understand*) [what I am doing]
	22	I am sending [Tychicus] to you . . . ⌐to give you (lit. that you will *know* all the) news about us
Ph 1	12	I ⌐am glad to tell you (lit. should like you to *know*) that the things that happened to me have actually been a help to the Good News.
	22	4 [death or] living in this body . . . I do not *know* what I should choose.

Ph 2	19	I shall be reassured by ⌐having (lit. *finding out* the) news of you.
	22	you *know* how [Timothy] has proved himself
4	5	Let your tolerance be ⌐evident to (lit. *known* by) everyone:
Col 4	7	4 Tychicus will ⌐tell you (lit. let you *know*) all the news about us
	8	I am sending [Tychicus] to you . . . ⌐to give you (lit. so that you will *know* all the) news about us
	9	4 [Tychicus and Onesimus] will ⌐tell you (lit. let you *know*) everything that is happening here.
1 Th 3	5	I sent to ⌐assure myself of (lit. *hear about*) your faith:
2 Tm 1	18	You *know* better than anyone else how much [Onesiphorus] helped me at Ephesus.
Heb 13	23	I want you to *know* that our brother Timothy has been set free.
1 P 3	7	husbands must always treat their wives with ⌐consideration
	3	(lit. *understanding*)

9: MAKE KNOWN, REVEAL – WANT (A PERSON) TO KNOW

Lk 2	15	let us go to Bethlehem and see this thing that has happened 4 which the Lord has *made known* to us.
	17	4 [the shepherds] ⌐repeated (lit *made known*) what they had been told about [the baby],
Jn 15	15	4 I have *made known* to you everything I have learnt from my Father.
17	26	4 I have *made* your name *known* to them and will continue to 4 *make* it *known*,
Ac 2	28	4 (Ps 16 11) You have *made known* the way of life to me,
15	17	7 says the Lord who ⌐made this [18] *known* (or: did these things,
	18	known [by him]) so long ago
Rm 9	22	4 God is ready to . . . *display* his power,
	23	4 those other people . . . to whom [God] wants to *reveal* the richness of his glory,
16	26	4 [a mystery] now so clear that it must be *broadcast* to pagans everywhere
1 Co 12	3	4 I *want* you *to understand* that . . . no one can be speaking under the influence of the Holy Spirit and say, 'Curse Jesus',
15	1	4 I want to ⌐remind you of (lit. *make known* to you) the gospel I preached to you.
2 Co 8	1	4 ⌐here is (lit. we want to *make known* to you) the news of the grace of God
Ga 1	11	4 I *want* you *to realise* this, the Good News I preached is not a human message
Ep 1	9	4 [God] has *let* us *know* the mystery of his purpose,
3	3	4 it was by a revelation that I was *given the knowledge* of the mystery,
	5	This mystery that has now been revealed through the Spirit 4 . . . was un*known* to any men in past generations;
	10	⌐the Sovereignties and Powers should learn (lit it should be 4 *made known* to the Sovereignties and Powers) . . . how comprehensive God's wisdom really is,
6	19	4 pray for me to be given an opportunity to . . . *give out* the mystery of the gospel
Col 1	27	4 It was God's purpose to *reveal* it to them and to show all the rich glory of this mystery to pagans.
2 P 1	16	4 we *brought* you *the knowledge of* the power and the coming of our Lord Jesus Christ;

2. KNOW – REALISE, REMEMBER – UNDERSTAND: *OIDA*

5	*historeō* 1	3	*syn-eidēsis* 31
1	*oida* 326	3	*syn-eidon* 2
		4	*syn-oida* 2

1: (GOD) KNOWS, KNOWS HOW TO

Mt 6	8	your Father *knows* what you need
	32	Your heavenly Father *knows* you need [food, drink and clothes].
24	36	as for that day and hour, nobody *knows* it . . . but the Father only.
Mk 13	32	as for that day or hour, nobody *knows* it . . . but the Father.
Lk 12	30	Your Father well *knows* you need [things to eat and drink].
Rm 8	27	God who knows everything in our hearts *knows* perfectly well what [the Spirit] means,
2 Co 11	11	Would I do that if I did not love you? God *knows* I do.
	31	God . . . *knows* that I am not lying.
12	2	I know a man in Christ who . . . was caught up – whether still in the body or out of the body, I do not know; God *knows* – right into the third heaven. [3] . . . this same person
	3	– whether in the body or out of the body, I do not know; God *knows* –
2 P 2	9	the Lord ⌐can (lit. *knows how* to) rescue the good from the ordeal,

2: (JESUS) KNOWS

Mt 9 4 ⌐*Knowing* (ᵛ Seeing) what was in [the scribes'] minds Jesus said,

12 25 *Knowing* what was in [the Pharisees'] minds [Jesus] said to them,

15 12 Do you *know* that the Pharisees were shocked when they heard what you said?

24 36 as for that day and hour, nobody *knows* it, neither the angels . . . nor the Son, no one but the Father only

25 12 < I tell you solemnly, I do not *know* you.

Mk 12 15 *Seeing through* their hypocrisy [Jesus] said to [the Pharisees],

13 32 as for that day or hour, nobody *knows* it, neither the angels . . . nor the Son; no one but the Father.

Lk 6 8 [Jesus] *knew* [the Pharisees'] thoughts;

9 47 Jesus *⌐knew* (ᵛ saw) what thoughts were going through [the disciples'] minds,

11 17 *knowing* what [the people] were thinking [Jesus] said to them,

13 25 < the master of the house . . . will answer, 'I do not *know* where you come from'.

27 < I do not *know* where you come from.

Jn 3 11 we speak only about what we *know*

5 32 there is another witness . . . and I *know* that his testimony is valid.

6 6 [Jesus] himself *knew* exactly what he was going to do.

61 Jesus *was aware* that his followers were complaining

64 Jesus *knew* from the outset those who did not believe,

7 15 How *⌐did he learn* (lit. does he *know* how) to read?

29 I *know* him because I have come from him

8 14 I *know* where I came from and where I am going; but you do not know

37 I *know* that you are descended from Abraham;

55 you do not *know* him [the Father]. But I *know* him, and if I were to say: I do not *know* him, I should be a liar . . . But I do *know* him, and I faithfully keep his word.

11 42 Father, . . . I *knew* indeed that you always hear me,

12 50 I *know* that [the Father's] commands mean eternal life.

13 1 Jesus *knew* that the hour had come for him to pass from this world

3 Jesus *knew* that the Father had put everything into his hands,

11 [Jesus] *knew* who was going to betray him,

18 I *know* the ones I have chosen.

16 30 Now we see that you *know* everything,

18 4 *Knowing* everything that was going to happen to him, Jesus then came forward

19 10 Surely you *know* I have power to release you . . . ?

28 Jesus *knew* that everything had now been completed,

21 15 Yes Lord, you *know* I love you,

16 Yes, Lord, you *know* I love you.

17 Lord, you *know* everything; you know I love you.

Rv 2 2 I *know* all about you: how hard you work and how much you put up with

9 I *know* the trials you have had, and how poor you are

13 I *know* where you live, in the place where Satan is enthroned,

19 I *know* all about you and how charitable you are;

3 1 I *know* all about you: how you are reputed to be alive and yet are dead.

8 I *know* all about you . . . you have kept my commandments

15 I *know* all about you: how you are neither cold nor hot.

19 12 the name written on [the rider] was *known* only to himself,

3: RECOGNITION OF JESUS BY DEVILS, UNCLEAN SPIRITS

Mk 1 24 I *know* who you are: the Holy One of God.

34 [Jesus] would not allow [the devils he cast out] to speak, because they *knew* who he was.

Lk 4 34 I *know* who you are: the Holy One of God.

41 [the devils] *knew* that [Jesus] was the Christ.

4: (A PERSON) KNOWS, UNDERSTANDS, REMEMBERS

a) Know, Realise – Understand, Be aware (of) – Remember (God, Jesus, things religious)

Mt 9 6 ⌐*to prove to you* (lit. so that you may *know*) that the Son of Man has authority on earth to forgive sins,

21 27 [John's baptism: where did it come from?] We do not *know*.

22 16 Master, we *know* that you are an honest man

29 You are wrong, because you *understand* neither the scriptures nor the power of God.

24 36 as for that day and hour, nobody *knows* it . . . but the Father only.

42 you do not *know* the day when your master is coming.

43 if the householder had *known* at what time of the night the burglar would come, he would have stayed awake

25 13 stay awake, because you do not *know* either the day or the hour.

Mt 25 26 So you *knew* that I reap where I have not sown . . . ?

26 70 [Peter] denied it . . . 'I do not *know* what you are talking about'

72 again, with an oath, [Peter] denied it, 'I do not *know* the man'.

74 Then [Peter] started . . . swearing, 'I do not *know* the man'.

Mk 2 10 ⌐*to prove to you* (lit. so that you may *know*) that the Son of Man has authority on earth to forgive sins,

4 13 Do you not *understand* this parable? Then how will you understand any of the parables?

10 19 You *know* the commandments:

11 33 [John's baptism: did it come from heaven?] We do not *know*.

12 14 Master, we *know* you are an honest man,

24 Is not the reason why you go wrong, that you *understand* neither the scriptures nor the power of God?

28 One of the scribes . . . had ᵛ *observed* (G *understood*) how well Jesus had answered them,

13 32 as for that day or hour, nobody *knows* it . . . but the Father.

33 you never *know* when the time will come.

35 you do not *know* when the master of the house is coming.

14 68 [Peter] denied it. 'I do not *know*, I do not understand, what you are talking about'

71 I do not *know* the man you speak of.

Lk 2 49 Did you not *know* that I must be busy with my Father's affairs?

5 24 ⌐*to prove to you* (lit. so that you may *know*) that the Son of Man has authority on earth to forgive sins,

9 55 (ᵛ You do not *know* to what spirit you belong.)

12 39 if the householder had *known* at what hour the burglar would come, he would not have let anyone break through the wall

18 20 You *know* the commandments:

19 22 So you *knew* I was an exacting man . . . ?

20 7 [the elders'] reply was that they did not *know* where [John's baptism] came from.

21 Master, we *know* that you say and teach what is right;

22 34 Peter, by the time the cock crows today you will have denied three times that you *know* me.

57 [Peter] denied it. 'Woman, . . . I do not *know* him'.

60 'My friend', said Peter 'I do not *know* what you are talking about'.

23 34 Father, forgive them; they do not *know* what they are doing.

Jn 1 26 there stands among you – un*known* to you – ²⁷ the one who is coming after me;

31 I did not *know* him myself,

33 I did not *know* him myself,

3 2 Rabbi, we *know* that you are a teacher who comes from God;

4 10 If you only *knew* what God is offering

22 You worship what you do not *know*; we worship what we do *know*;

25 I *know* that Messiah . . . is coming;

32 I have food to eat that you do not *know* about.

42 we *know* that he really is the saviour of the world.

5 13 The [sick] man *had* no *idea* who it was [who had cured him],

6 42 Surely this is Jesus . . . We *know* his father and mother.

7 27 we all *know* where he comes from, but when the Christ appears no one will know where he comes from.

28 you *know* me and you *know* where I came from . . . you do not *know* [the one who sent me],

8 14 I know where I came from and where I am going: but you do not *know* where I came from or where I am going.

19 You do not *know* me, nor do you know my Father; if you did *know* me, you would *know* my Father as well.

9 12 'Where is [Jesus]?' 'I don't *know*' [the blind man whom he had cured] answered.

21 we don't *know* how it is that he can see now, . . . who opened his eyes (§ we don't *know* either).

24 we *know* that this man is a sinner.

25 I don't *know* if he is a sinner; I only *know* that I was blind and now I can see.

29 we *know* that God spoke to Moses, but as for this man, we don't *know* where he comes from.

30 He has opened my eyes, and you don't *know* where he comes from!

31 We *know* that God doesn't listen to sinners,

10 4 the sheep follow [the shepherd] because they *know* his voice.

11 22 I *know* that . . . whatever you ask of God, he will grant you.

24 Martha said, 'I *know* he will rise again at the resurrection'

13 7 At the moment you do not *know* what I am doing, but later you will understand.

14 4 You *know* the way to the place where I am going.

5 Lord, we do not *know* where you are going, so how can we *know* the way?

7 If you ᵛ *know* (G had known) me, you ᵛ *know* (G would have known) my Father too.

15 21 they do not *know* the one who sent me.

16 18 We don't *know* what [Jesus] means.

30 Now we *see* that you know everything,

18 21 Ask my hearers what I taught: they *know* what I said.

19 35 ∆ This is the evidence of one who saw it . . . and **he** *knows* **he** speaks the truth

Jn 20	2	They have taken the Lord out of the tomb . . . and we don't *know* where they have put him.
	9	Till this moment [Peter and John] had failed to *understand* the teaching of scripture, that [Jesus] must rise from the dead.
	13	They have taken my Lord away . . . and I don't *know* where they have put him.
	14	[Mary] saw Jesus standing there, though she did not *recognise* him.
21	4	there stood Jesus on the shore, though the disciples did not *realise* that it was Jesus.
	12	[the disciples] *knew* quite well it was the Lord.
Ac 2	22	[Jesus] was a man commended to you by God . . . as you all *know*.
	30	[David] *knew* that God had sworn . . . to make one of his descendants succeed him on the throne,
3	17	I *know*, brothers, that neither you nor your leaders had any idea what you were really doing;
10	37	You ⌐must have heard (lit. *know*) about the recent happenings in Judaea;
12	11	'Now I *know* it is all true,' [Peter] said. 'The Lord really did send his angel'
Rm 2	2	We *know* that God condemns that sort of behaviour impartially:
3	19	all this that the Law says is said, as we *know*, for the benefit of those who are subject to the Law,
5	3	These sufferings bring patience, as we *know*,
6	9	Christ, as we *know*, having been raised from the dead will never die again.
7	14	The Law, of course, as we all *know*, is spiritual;
	18	I *know* of nothing good living in me –
8	22	the entire creation, as we *know*, has been groaning in one great act of giving birth;
	26	we ⌐cannot (lit. do not *know* how to) choose words in order to pray properly,
	28	We *know* that . . . God co-operates with all those who love him,
11	2	Do you ⌐remember (or: *know*) what scripture says of Elijah . . .?
15	29	I *know* that . . . I shall arrive with rich blessings from Christ.
1 Co 2	2	the only *knowledge* I claimed to have was about Jesus, and only about him as the crucified Christ.
	12	we have received the Spirit that comes from God, to teach us to *understand* the gifts that he has given us.
3	16	Didn't you *realise* that you were God's temple . . .?
6	2	As you *know*, it is the saints who are to judge the world;
	3	⌐Since (lit. *Remembering* that) we are also to judge angels . . . we can judge matters of everyday life;
	9	You *know* perfectly well that people who do wrong will not inherit the kingdom of God;
	15	You *know*, surely, that your bodies are members making up the body of Christ;
	19	Your body, you *know*, is the temple of the Holy Spirit,
7	16	If you are a wife, it may be your part to save your husband, for all you *know*; if a husband, for all you *know*, it may be your part to save your wife.
8	4	we *know* that idols do not really exist in the world
9	13	*Remember* that the ministers serving in the Temple get their food from the Temple
11	3	I want you to *understand* . . . that Christ is the head of every man,
13	2	If I have the gift of prophecy, *understanding* all the mysteries there are . . . but without love, then I am nothing at all.
14	16	Any uninitiated person . . . will *have no idea* what you are saying.
15	58	keep on working . . . *knowing* that, in the Lord, you cannot be labouring in vain.
2 Co 4	14	[we believe and speak,] *knowing* that he who raised the Lord Jesus to life will raise us
5	1	we *know* that . . . there is a house built by God for us,
	6	We are always full of confidence . . . when we *remember* that to live in the body means to be exiled from the Lord,
	11	*with* the fear of the Lord *in mind*
Ga 2	16	we *acknowledge* that what makes a man righteous is not obedience to the Law, but faith in Jesus Christ.
4	8	Once you ⌐were ignorant of (lit. did not *know*) God, and were enslaved to 'gods'
Ep 1	18	May [God] enlighten [you] so that you ⌐can see (lit. *understand*) what hope his call holds for you,
5	5	For you ⌐can be quite certain (lit. should *understand* and know) that nobody who actually indulges in fornication or impurity . . . can inherit anything of the kingdom of God.
6	8	You ⌐can be sure (lit. should *know*) that everyone . . . will be properly rewarded by the Lord for whatever work he has done well.
	9	employers, . . . do without threats, ⌐*remembering* (or: knowing) that [your slaves] and you have the same Master in heaven
Col 3	24	*knowing* that the Lord will repay you

Col 4	1	Masters, make sure that your slaves are given what is just and fair, *knowing* that you too have a Master in heaven.
1 Th 1	4	We *know*, brothers, . . . that you have been chosen,
4	5	not giving way to selfish lust like the pagans who do not *know* God.
5	2	you *know* very well that the Day of the Lord is going to come like a thief in the night.
2 Th 1	8	[Jesus] will come . . . to impose the penalty on all who do not *acknowledge* God
1 Tm 1	8	We *know*, of course, that the Law is good, but only provided it is treated like any law, ⁹ in the *understanding* that laws are not framed for people who are good.
	9	
2 Tm 1	12	I *know* who it is that I have put my trust in,
3	15	ever since you were a child, you have *known* the holy scriptures –
Tt 1	16	[Those who lack faith] claim to have *knowledge* of God but the things they do are nothing but a denial of him;
Heb 8	11	(Jr 31 34) There will be no further need for neighbour to try to teach neighbour . . . 'Learn to know the Lord'. No, they will all *know* me, the least no less than the greatest,
10	30	We *are* all *aware* who it was that said: Vengeance is mine;
Jm 4	4	don't you *realise* that making the world your friend is making God your enemy?
1 P 1	18	*Remember*, the ransom that was paid to free you . . . was not paid in anything corruptible.
2 P 1	12	I am continually recalling the same truths to you, even though you already *know* them
1 Jn 2	20	you have been anointed by the Holy One, and have all [received] the *knowledge*.
	21	It is not because you do not *know* the truth that I am writing to you but rather because you *know* it already
	29	You *know* that God is righteous –
3	2	all we *know* is, that when [the future] is revealed we shall be like [God]
	5	you *know* that [Christ] appeared in order to abolish sin,
	14	we have passed out of death and into life, and ⌐of this we can be sure (lit. we should *understand* this)
	15	murderers, as you *know*, do not have eternal life in them.
5	13	you who believe . . . may ⌐be sure (lit. *know*) that you have eternal life.
	15	*knowing* that whatever we may ask, he hears us, we *know* that we have already been granted what we asked of him.
	18	We *know* that anyone who has been begotten by God does not sin,
	19	We *know* that we belong to God,
	20	We *know*, too, that the Son of God has come,
Jude	5	I should like to remind you – though you ⌐have already learnt (lit. should *know*) it once and for all –
	10	[false teachers] abuse anything they do not *understand*; and the only things they do understand . . . will turn out to be fatal to them.
Rv 19	12	the name written on [the rider] was *known* only to himself,

b) Know, Have an idea (of), Remember (generally)

Mt 7	11	If you . . . *know* how to give your children what is good,
20	22	You do not *know* what you are asking
	25	You *know* that among the pagans the rulers lord it over them,
26	2	It will be Passover, as you *know*, in two days' time,
27	18	Pilate *knew* it was out of jealousy that [the elders] had handed [Jesus] over.
	65	Go and make all as secure as you *know* how.
28	5	I *know* you are looking for Jesus, who was crucified.
Mk 4	27 <	the seed is sprouting and growing; how, [the sower] does not *know*
5	33	the woman [with a haemorrhage] came forward, frightened . . . because she *knew* what had happened to her,
6	20	Herod was afraid of John, *knowing* him to be a good and holy man,
9	6	[Peter] did not *know* what to say; they were so frightened.
10	38	You do not *know* what you are asking
	42	You *know* that among the pagans their so-called rulers lord it over them,
14	40	[Jesus] found [the Twelve] sleeping . . . and they ⌐could find no answer for (lit. did not *know* how to answer) him.
Lk 8	53	they laughed at [Jesus], *knowing* she was dead.
9	33	[Peter] did not *know* what he was saying.
11	13	If you . . . *know* how to give your children what is good,
	44	you are like the unmarked tombs that men walk on without *knowing* it!
12	56	Hypocrites! You *know* how to interpret the face of the earth and the sky.
Jn 2	9 <	*Having* no idea where [the wine] came from – only the servants who had drawn the water *knew* – the steward called the bridegroom
3	8 <	you hear [the wind's] sound, but you cannot *tell* where it comes from or where it is going.
9	20	We *know* he is our son and we know he was born blind,
10	5 <	[the sheep] do not *recognise* the voice of strangers.

Jn 11 49 | Caiaphas . . . said, 'You don't seem to have *grasped* the situation at all'
12 35 | he who walks in the dark does not *know* where he is going.
13 17 | [No servant is greater than his master.] Now that you *know* this, happiness will be yours if you behave accordingly.
15 15 | a servant does not *know* his master's business;
18 2 | Judas the traitor *knew* the place well,
21 24 | we *know* that [this disciple's] testimony is true.
Ac 3 16 | the name of Jesus . . . brought back the strength of this man . . . who is well *known* to you.
5 2 | 4 ⌐with his wife's connivance (lit. having an *understanding with* his wife), [Ananias] kept back part of the proceeds,
7 | About three hours later [Ananias's] wife came in, not *knowing* what had taken place.
7 18 | a new king came to power in Egypt who *knew* nothing of Joseph.
40 | (Ex 32 1) we do not *understand* what has come over this Moses
12 9 | Peter followed him, but *had* no *idea* that what the angel did was all happening in reality;
12 | 3 As soon as he *realised* [that the angel had delivered him from prison Peter] went straight to the house of Mary the mother of John Mark,
14 6 | 3 [Paul and Barnabas] *came to hear of* [the intention at Iconium of stoning them],
16 3 | everyone *knew* [Timothy's] father was a Greek.
19 32 | most of [the assembly at Ephesus] did not even *know* why they had been summoned.
20 22 | I am on my way to Jerusalem, but *have* no *idea* what will happen to me there,
25 | I now ⌐feel sure (lit. *know*) that none of you . . . will ever see my face again.
29 | I *know* quite well that when I have gone fierce wolves will invade you
23 5 | I did not *realise* it was the high priest,
24 22 | Felix . . . *knew* more about the Way than most people,
26 4 | My manner of life from my youth . . . is common *knowledge* among the Jews.
27 | King Agrippa, do you believe in the prophets? I *know* you do.
Rm 6 16 | You *know* that if you agree to serve . . . a master you become his slaves.
7 7 | I should not . . . have *known* what it means to covet if the Law had not said
13 11 | you *know* 'the time' has come:
14 14 | I *am* perfectly well *aware*, of course, . . . that no food is unclean in itself;
1 Co 1 16 | there was the family of Stephanas . . . that I baptised too, but no one else as far as I can *remember*.
2 11 | the depths of a man can only be *known* by his own spirit,
5 6 | You must *know* how even a small amount of yeast is enough to leaven all the dough,
6 16 | As you *know*, a man who goes with a prostitute is one body with her.
8 1 | Now about food sacrificed to idols. 'We all have knowledge'; yes, ⌐that is so (lit. *we understand* that),
9 24 | All the runners at the stadium are trying to win, *remember*,
12 2 | You *remember* that, when you were pagans, whenever you felt irresistibly drawn, it was towards dumb idols?
14 11 | if I ⌐am ignorant of (lit. *do not know*) what the sounds mean, I am a savage to the man who is speaking,
16 15 | You *know* how the Stephanas family . . . have really worked hard
2 Co 1 7 | we *know* that . . . you will also share our consolations.
5 16 | we do not judge (lit. *know*) anyone by the standards of the flesh.
9 2 | I *know* how anxious you are to help;
12 2 | I *know* a man in Christ who . . . was caught up – whether still in the body (§ I do not *know*) or out of the body, I do not *know*; God knows – right into the third heaven. ³ I
3 | do *know*, however, that this same person – whether in the body or out of the body, I do not *know*; God knows – ⁴ was caught up into paradise
Ga 1 18 | 5 I went up to Jerusalem to ⌐visit (lit. *get to know*) Cephas
4 13 | that illness, as you *know*, gave me the opportunity to preach the Good News to you,
Ep 6 21 | I should like you to *know*, as well, what is happening to me
Ph 1 16 | they *know* that this is my invariable way of defending the gospel.
19 | I shall continue being happy, because I *know* this will help to save me,
25 | I ⌐feel sure (lit. *know*) I shall survive and stay with you all,
4 12 | I *know* how to be poor and I *know* how to be rich too.
15 | as you people of Philippi well *know*, . . . no other church helped me with gifts of money.
Col 2 1 | I want you to *know* that I do have to struggle hard for you,
4 6 | Talk to [those who are not Christians] agreeably . . . ⌐and try to (lit. *so that you may understand* how to) fit your answers to the needs of each one.
1 Th 1 5 | you ⌐observed (lit. *know*) the sort of life we lived when we were with you,

1 Th 2 1 | You *know* yourselves, my brothers, that our visit to you has not proved ineffectual.
2 | We had, as you *know*, been given rough treatment . . . at Philippi,
5 | You *know* very well . . . that never at any time have our speeches been simply flattery,
11 | You [can] *remember* how we treated every one of you as a father treats his children,
3 3 | As you *know*, [troubles] are bound to come our way:
4 | we warned you that we must expect to have persecutions to bear, and that is what has happened now, as you ⌐have found out (lit. *know*).
4 2 | You ⌐have not forgotten (lit. *remember*) the instructions we gave you
4 | [God wants] each one of you to *know* how to use the body that belongs to him in a way that is holy
5 12 | We appeal to you . . . to ⌐be considerate to (lit. *remember*) those who are working amongst you and are above you
2 Th 2 6 | you *know* . . . what is still holding [the Lord] back from appearing before his appointed time.
3 7 | You *know* how you are supposed to imitate us:
1 Tm 3 5 | how can any man who does not *understand* how to manage his own family have responsibility for the church of God?
15 | I wanted you to *know* how people ought to behave in God's family
2 Tm 1 15 | As you *know*, . . . all [those] from Asia refuse to have anything more to do with me.
2 23 | Avoid these . . . silly speculations, *understanding* that they only give rise to quarrels;
3 14 | You must keep to what you have been taught . . . *remember* who your teachers were,
Tt 3 11 | you will *know* that any man of that sort has already lapsed
Phm 21 | I am writing with complete confidence in your compliance, ⌐sure (lit. *knowing*) that you will do even more than I ask.
Heb 12 17 | As you *know*, . . . [Esau] was rejected
Jm 1 19 | *Remember* this, . . . be quick to listen but slow to speak
3 1 | Only a few of you . . . should be teachers, *bearing in mind* that those of us who teach can expect a stricter judgement.
4 17 | Everyone who *knows* what is the right thing to do and doesn't do it commits a sin.
1 P 5 9 | Stand up to [the devil], strong in . . . the *knowledge* that your brothers all over the world are suffering the same things.
2 P 1 14 | I *know* the time for taking off this tent is coming soon,
1 Jn 2 11 | the man who hates his brother . . . is in the darkness, not *knowing* where he is going,
3 Jn 12 | We too will vouch for [Demetrius] and you *know* that our testimony is true.
Rv 2 17 | to those who prove victorious I will give . . . a stone with a new name written on it, *known* only to the man who receives it.
3 17 | You say to yourself, 'I am rich . . .' never *realising* that you are wretchedly and pitiably poor,
7 14 | [Do you know who these people are?] I answered him, 'You ⌐can tell me (lit. *know*), my Lord'.
12 12 ⓓ | the devil has gone down to you in a rage, *knowing* that his days are numbered.

5: CONSCIENCE – AWARENESS

Ac 23 1 | 2 I have conducted myself before God with a perfectly clear *conscience*.
24 16 | 2 I . . . do my best to keep a clear *conscience* at all times before God and man.
Rm 2 15 | [pagans] can point to the substance of the Law engraved on their hearts – they can call a witness, that is, their own ² *conscience* –
9 1 | 2 it is the truth – my *conscience* in union with the Holy Spirit assures me of it too.
13 5 | 2 You must obey . . . also for *conscience*' sake.
1 Co 4 4 | 4 ⌐My conscience does not reproach me (lit. *I have nothing on my conscience*) at all,
8 7 | There are some [people] who have been so long ᵛ in the *awareness* of (G used to) idols that they eat this food as ² though it really had been sacrificed to the idol, and their ² *conscience* . . . is defiled by it.
10 | Suppose someone sees you . . . eating in some temple of an ² idol; his own *conscience* . . . may encourage him to eat food which has been offered to idols . . . ¹² By sinning ² in this way against your brothers, and injuring your ² weak *consciences*, it would be Christ against whom you sinned.
10 25 | Do not hesitate to eat anything that is sold in butchers' shops: ² there is no need to raise questions of *conscience*;
27 | 2 eat whatever is put in front of you, without asking questions
28 | 2 just to satisfy *conscience*. ²⁸ . . . out of consideration for the man that told you [the food was offered in sacrifice],
29 | 2 you should not eat, it for the sake of his *scruples*; ²⁹ his ² *scruples*, you see, not your own. Why should my freedom ² depend on somebody else's *conscience*?

2 Co	1	12	2	There is one thing we are proud of, and our *conscience* tells us it is true:
	4	2	2	the way we commend ourselves to every human [being with a] *conscience* is by stating the truth openly in the sight of God.
	5	11	2	I hope that in your *consciences* you know us too.
1 Tm	1	5	2	there should be love, coming out of a pure heart, a clear *conscience* and a sincere faith.
		19	2	[fight like a good soldier] with faith and a good *conscience* for your weapons.
	3	9	2	[Deacons] must be *conscientious* believers in the mystery of the faith.
	4	2	2	hypocrites whose *consciences* are branded as though with a red-hot iron:
2 Tm	1	3	2	I thank God, keeping my *conscience* clear and remembering my duty to him as my ancestors did,
Tt	1	15	2	those who have been corrupted . . . both in their minds and in their *consciences*.
Heb	9	9	2	None of the . . . sacrifices offered under these regulations can possibly bring any worshipper to perfection in his ⌐inner self (lit. *conscience*);
		14	2	the blood of Christ . . . can purify our ⌐inner self (lit. *conscience*) from dead actions
	10	2	2	the worshippers, when they had been purified once, would have no *awareness* of sins.
		22	2	let . . . our minds [be] . . . free from any trace of bad *conscience*
	13	18	2	We are sure that our own *conscience* is clear
1 P	2	19	2	there is some merit in putting up with the pains of unearned punishment if it is done ⌐for the sake (lit. in an *awareness*) of God
	3	16	2	[have your answer ready and] give it with courtesy and respect and with a clear *conscience*.
		21	2	the baptism which [is] a pledge made to God from a good *conscience*,

3. KNOW (WELL) – UNDERSTAND: *EPISTAMAI*

1 epistamai 14   2 epistēmōn 1

Mk	14	68		[Peter] denied it. 'I do not know, I do not *understand*, what you are talking about'
Ac	10	28		You *know* it is forbidden for Jews to mix with people of another race
	15	7		'My brothers,' [Peter] said 'you *know* perfectly *well* that . . . God made his choice among you'
	18	25		[Apollos] had only ⌐experienced (lit. *known*) the baptism of John.
	19	15		The evil spirit replied, 'Jesus I recognise, and I *know* who Paul is, but who are you?'
		25		'As you men *know*,' [Demetrius] said 'it is on this industry that we [silversmiths] depend for our prosperity.'
	20	18		You *know* my way of life has been
	22	19		[the Israelites] *know* that I used to [persecute] those who believed in you;
	24	10		I *know* that you have administered justice over this nation for many years,
	26	26		The king *understands* these matters,
1 Tm	6	4		[a false teacher] ⌐is simply ignorant (lit. does not *know* anything) and must be full of self-conceit
Heb	11	8		It was by faith that Abraham . . . set out without *knowing* where he was going.
Jm	3	13	2	If there are any wise or ⌐learned (lit. *understanding*) men among you, let them show it by their good lives,
	4	14		You never *know* what will happen tomorrow:
Jude		10		the only things [these false teachers] do *understand* – just by nature like unreasoning animals – will turn out to be fatal to them.

4. UNDERSTAND – PERCEPTION, INTELLIGENCE – CLEVER: *SYN-(H)IĒMI*

2 syn-(h)esis 7   1 syn-(h)iēmi 26
3 syn-(h)etos 4

Mt	11	25	3	I bless you, Father, . . . for hiding these things from the learned and the *clever*
	13	13		they . . . listen without hearing or *understanding*.
		14		(Is 6 9) You will listen and listen again, but not *understand*,
		15		(Is 6 10) this nation has grown coarse . . for fear they should . . . *understand* with their heart,
		19		When anyone hears the word of the kingdom without *understanding*, the evil one . . . carries off what was sown in his heart:
		23		the man who hears the word and *understands* it . . . yields a harvest

Mt	13	51		Have you *understood* all this?
	15	10		[Jesus] called the people to him and said, 'Listen and *understand*.'
	16	12		[the disciples] *understood* that he was telling them to be on their guard . . . against the teaching of the Pharisees
	17	13		The disciples *understood* then that he had been speaking of John the Baptist.
Mk	4	12		(Is 6 10) so that they may see . . . but not *perceive*;
	6	52		[the disciples] had not *seen what* the miracle of the loaves *meant*;
	7	14		Listen to me, . . . and *understand*.
	8	17		Do you not yet *understand*? Have you no *perception*?
		21		Are you still without *perception*?
	12	33	2	love [God] with all your heart, with all your *understanding*
Lk	2	47 X	2	all those who heard [Jesus] were astounded at his *intelligence*
		50		[Joseph and Mary] did not *understand* what [Jesus] meant.
	8	10		(Is 6 9) they may . . . listen but not *understand*.
	10	21	3	I bless you, Father, . . . for hiding these things from the learned and the *clever*
	18	34		[the Twelve] ⌐could make (lit. *understood*) nothing of [the prophecy of the Passion];
	24	45		[Jesus] opened their minds to *understand* the scriptures,
Ac	7	25		[Moses] thought his brothers *realised* that through him God would liberate them, but they did not *understand*.
	13	7	3	Sergius Paulus . . . was an extremely *intelligent* man.
	28	26		(Is 6 9) You will hear and hear again but not *understand*,
		27		(Is 6 10) they have shut their eyes for fear they should . . . *understand* with their heart,
Rm	3	11		(Ps 14 2) there is not one who *understands*, not one who looks for God.
	15	21		(Is 52 15) those who have never heard about [Christ] will *understand*.
1 Co	1	19	2	(Is 29 14) I shall . . . bring to nothing all the ⌐learning (or: *cleverness*) of the ⌐learned (or: *clever*).
2 Co	10	12		Measuring themselves against themselves . . . they are simply ⌐foolish (lit. without *intelligence*).
Ep	3	4	2	you will have some idea of the ⌐depths that I see in (lit. *perception* I have of) the mystery of Christ.
	5	17		do not be thoughtless but *recognise* what is the will of the Lord.
Col	1	9	2	what we ask God is that through perfect wisdom and spiritual *understanding* you should reach the fullest knowledge of his will.
	2	2	2	It is all . . . to stir your minds, so that your *understanding* may come to full development,
2 Tm	2	7	2	the Lord will show you how to *understand* it all.

5. REALISE, PERCEIVE – GRASP, COMPREHEND – CONSIDER: *KATA-LAMBANŌ*

kata-lambanō 5/15

Jn	1	5		a light that darkness could not *grasp*.
Ac	4	13		They were astonished at the assurance shown by Peter and John, *considering* they were uneducated laymen;
	10	34		The truth I have now come to *realise* . . . is that God does not have favourites.
	25	25		I *am satisfied* that [Paul] has committed no capital crime,
Ep	3	18		you will with all the saints have strength to *grasp* . . . the height and the depth;

6. PERCEPTION, GRASP THE MEANING OF – MIND: *AISTHANOMAI*

1 aisthanomai 1   3 aisthētērion 1
2 aisthēsis   1

Lk	9	45		[the prophecy] was hidden from [the disciples] so that they should not *see the meaning of* it,
Ph	1	9	2	My prayer is that your love for each other may increase . . . improving your knowledge and deepening your *perception*
Heb	5	14	3	mature men with *minds* trained by practice to distinguish between good and bad.

7. REASON, UNDERSTANDING – MIND: *NOEŌ*

4 noēma	4/6	1	nous	24
2 noeō	14	3	dia-noia	12
5 noun-echōs	1	6	dys-noētos	1

1: UNDERSTAND – PERCEIVE, SEE

| Mt | 15 | 17 | 2 | Can you not *see* that whatever goes into the mouth passes through the stomach . . .? |
| | 16 | 9 | 2 | Do you not yet *understand*? Do you not remember the five loaves . . .? |

| Mt | 16 | 11 | 2 | How could you fail to *understand* that I was not talking about bread? |

Mt 16 11   2   How could you fail to *understand* that I was not talking about bread?

24 15   2   when you see the disastrous abomination . . . (let the reader *understand*),

Mk 7 18   2   Can you not *see* that whatever goes into a man from outside cannot make him unclean,

8 17   2   Do you not yet *understand*? Have you no perception?

13 14   2   When you see the disastrous abomination . . . (let the reader *understand*),

Jn 12 40   2   (Is 6 10) he has hardened their heart, for fear they should . . . *understand* with their heart,

Rm 1 20   2   Ever since God created the world his everlasting power and deity – however invisible – have been ʳthere for the mind to see (lit. able to be *perceived*)

Ep 3 4   2   you will *have some idea of* the depths that I see in the mystery of Christ.

20   2   Glory be to him whose power . . . can do infinitely more than we can ask or *imagine*;

1 Tm 1 7   2   [false teachers] *understand* neither the arguments they are using nor the opinions they are upholding.

2 Tm 2 7   2   *Think over* what I have said, and the Lord will show you how to understand it all.

Heb 11 3   2   we *understand* that the world was created by one word from God,

2 P 3 16   6   some points in [Paul's] letter [are] *hard to understand*;

2: MIND – REASON, UNDERSTANDING, INTELLIGENCE – IDEAS

Mt 22 37   3   (Dt 6 5 G) You must love the Lord . . . with all your heart, with all your soul, and with all your *mind*.

Mk 12 30   3   (Dt 6 5 G) you must love the Lord . . . with all your *mind*

34   5   Jesus, seeing how *wisely* [the scribe] had spoken, said,

Lk 1 51   3   [God] has routed the proud in ʳthe *imagination* of their (or: *mind* and) heart.

10 27   3   (Dt 6 5 G) You must love the Lord . . . with all your *mind*,

24 45   [Jesus] opened their *minds* to understand the scriptures,

Rm 1 28   God has left [pagans] to their own irrational *ideas*

7 23   my body follows a different law that battles against the law which my *reason* dictates.

25   it is I who with my *reason* serve the Law of God,

11 23 Θ   (Is 40 13) Who could ever know the *mind* of the Lord?

12 2   let your behaviour change, modelled by your new *mind*.

14 5   each [man] must be left free to hold his own *opinion*.

1 Co 1 10   be united again in your ʳbelief and practice (lit. *mind* and judgement).

2 16 Θ? X   (Is 40 13) Who can know the *mind* of the Lord . . .? But we are those who have the *mind* of Christ.

14 14   if I use this gift [of tongues] in my prayers, my spirit may be praying but my *mind* is left barren. 15 . . . Surely I should pray not only with the spirit but with the *mind* as well? And sing praises not only with the spirit but with the *mind* as well?

19   when I am in the presence of the community I would rather say five words ʳthat mean something (lit. with my *mind*) than ten thousand words in a tongue.

2 Co 3 14   4   [the Israelites'] *minds* had been dulled;

4 4   4   the unbelievers whose *minds* the god of this world has blinded,

11 3   4   I am afraid that . . . your ʳ*ideas* (or: thoughts) may get corrupted

Ep 2 3   3   We all were . . . ruled entirely by our own physical desires and our own *ideas*;

4 17   [don't] go on living the ʳaimless (lit. vacant-*minded*) kind of life that pagans live. 18 *Intellectually* they are in the dark,

18   3

23   Your *mind* must be renewed by a spiritual revolution

Ph 4 7   that peace of God, which is so much greater than we can *understand*, will guard your hearts and your ʳthoughts (or: *minds*),

4

Col 1 21   3   you were . . . enemies, in *the way that you used to think* and the evil things that you did;

Col 2 18   people like that . . . inflating themselves to a false importance with their wordly *outlook*.

2 Th 2 2   do not let your *minds* get excited too soon . . . by any prediction

1 Tm 6 5   unending disputes by people who are neither *rational* nor informed

2 Tm 3 8   Men like this defy the truth . . . their *minds* are corrupt

Tt 1 15   the corruption is both in their *minds* and in their consciences.

Heb 8 10   3   (Jr 31 33) I will put my laws into their *minds* and write them on their hearts.

10 16   3   (Jr 31 33) I will put my laws into their hearts and write them on their *minds*.

1 P 1 13   3   Free your *minds* then, of encumbrances;

2 P 3 1   3   I have tried to awaken a true *understanding* in you by giving you a reminder:

1 Jn 5 20   3   the Son of God has come, and has given us the ʳpower (lit. *understanding*) to know the true God.

Rv 13 18   if anyone ʳis clever enough (lit. has enough *intelligence*) he may interpret the number of the beast:

17 9   Here there is need for cleverness, for a shrewd *mind*;

8. REASON – UNREASONING – UNREASONABLE, POINTLESS: A-LOGOS

     2 *logikos*   2   1 *a-logos* 3
     3 *logos*   1/334

Ac 18 14   If this were . . . a crime, I would ʳnot hesitate (lit. have *reason*) to attend to you;

25 27   It seems to me *pointless* to send a prisoner without indicating the charges against him.

Rm 12 1 ●   2   worship [God], I beg you, ʳ*in a way that is worthy of thinking beings* (or: spiritually).

1 P 2 2 ●   2   be hungry for nothing but milk – the [spiritual] *honesty* which will help you to grow up to salvation –

2 P 2 12   [false teachers] are *not reasoning* beings, but simply animals

Jude 10   the only things [false teachers] do understand – just by nature like *unreasoning* animals – will turn out to be fatal to them.

9. UNSKILLED – NOT TO KNOW: A-PEIROS

     a-peiros 1

Heb 5 13   anyone who is still living on milk ʳcannot digest (lit. does *not know*) the doctrine of righteousness

10. LAYMAN – UNINITIATED – UNSKILLED: IDIŌTĒS

     idiōtēs 5

Ac 4 13   [The Sanhedrin] were astonished at the assurance shown by Peter and John, considering they were uneducated *laymen*;

1 Co 14 16   Any *uninitiated person* will never be able to say Amen to your thanksgiving, if you only bless God with the spirit,

23   any *uninitiated people* or unbelievers . . . would say you were all mad;

24   if you were all prophesying and an unbeliever or *uninitiated person* came in, he would find himself . . . judged by everyone speaking,

2 Co 11 6   I may ʳnot be a *polished* (or: be *unskilled* as a) speechmaker,

11. COME TO ONESELF – RECOVER ONE'S SENSES: GINOMAI EN

     ginomai en (1)

Ac 12 11   It was only then that Peter *came to himself*.

L

LABOUR – TROUBLE

1. Drudge, Labour – Impediment: *mochthos*
  1: Drudge, Labour, Strain – Toil, Work
  2: an Impediment (in speech)
2. Work (hard), Labour – Trouble – Upset: *kopos*
  1: Work (hard), Labour, Toil – Trouble, Exertion – Tire(d), Weary

  2: to Trouble, Bother, Pester – Be a nuisance
3. (to) Trouble – (Be) Harassed: *skyllō*
  1: Trouble, Put (a person) to trouble – Bother
  2: (Be) Harassed – Exhausted
4. (Be) Tormented, Troubled – Make trouble, Make difficult for: *ochleō*

1. DRUDGE, LABOUR – IMPEDIMENT: *MOCHTHOS*

1 *mochthos* 3   2 *mogi(-lalos)* 1

1: DRUDGE, LABOUR, STRAIN – TOIL, WORK

2 Co 11 27		I have worked and *laboured*, often without sleep;
1 Th 2 9		Let me remind you . . . how hard we used to *work*, slaving night and day
2 Th 3 8		we worked night and day, slaving and *straining*,

2: AN IMPEDIMENT (IN SPEECH)

Mk 7 32	2	they brought [Jesus] a deaf man who had an *impediment* in his speech;

2. WORK (HARD), LABOUR – TROUBLE – UPSET: *KOPOS*

1 *kopiaō* 23   2 *kopos* 18

1: WORK (HARD), LABOUR, TOIL – TROUBLE, EXERTION – TIRE(D), WEARY

Mt 6 28		Think of the flowers growing in the fields; they never *have to work* or spin;
11 28		Come to me, all you who *labour* and are overburdened,
Lk 5 5		Master, . . . we *worked hard* all night long and caught nothing,
12 27		Think of the flowers; they never have to ⌐spin or weave (ᵛ *work* or spin)
Jn 4 6 X		Jesus, *tired* by the journey, sat straight down by the well.
38	2	I sent you to reap a harvest you had not *worked* for. Others *worked* for it; and you have come into the rewards of their *trouble*.
Ac 20 35		this is how we must *exert ourselves* to support the weak,
Rm 16 6		greetings to Mary who *worked* so hard for you;
12		[greetings] to Tryphaena and Tryphosa, who *worked hard* for the Lord; to my friend Persis who has ⌐done so much (lit. *toiled* so *hard*) for the Lord;
1 Co 3 8	2	each will duly be paid according to his share in the *work*.
4 12 ●		we *toil* and work for our living with our own hands.
15 10		I, or rather the grace of God that is with me, have *worked harder* than any of the others;
58	2	knowing that, in the Lord, you cannot be *labouring* in vain.
16 16		put yourselves at the service of people like this, and anyone who helps and *works* with them.
2 Co 6 5	2	[we show we are servants of God by great fortitude] when we are . . . *labouring*, sleepless,
10 15	2	we are not boasting without any measure, about *work* that was *done* by other people;
11 23	2	The servants of Christ? . . . so am I, and more than they: more, because I have *worked harder*,
27	2	I have *worked* and laboured, often without sleep; I have been hungry and thirsty
Ga 4 11		You make me feel I have wasted my ⌐time (lit. *efforts*) with you.
Ep 4 28		he should *work hard* at some useful manual work instead,
Ph 2 16		I had not run in the race and *exhausted myself* for nothing.
Col 1 29		It is for this I struggle *wearily* on,
1 Th 1 3	2	[we] constantly remember . . . how you have shown your faith in action, *worked* for love
1 Th 2 9	2	Let me remind you . . . ⌐how hard (lit. with what *exertion*) we used to work, slaving night and day
3 5	2	I was afraid . . . all our *work* might have been wasted.
5 12		We appeal to you . . . to be considerate to those who are *working* amongst you
2 Th 3 8	2	we worked night and day, *slaving* and straining,
1 Tm 4 10		the point of all our *toiling* and battling is that we have put our trust in the living God
5 17		The elders . . . are to be given double consideration, especially those who *are assiduous* in preaching and teaching.
2 Tm 2 6		it is the *working* farmer who has the first claim on any crop
Rv 2 2	2	I know all about you: how hard you *work* and how much you put up with.
3		you . . . have suffered for my name without *growing tired*.
14 13	2	Happy are those who die . . . they can rest for ever after their *work*,

2: TO TROUBLE, BOTHER, PESTER – UPSET – BE A NUISANCE

Mt 26 10	2	Why are you *upsetting* the woman?
Mk 14 6	2	Leave [this woman] alone. Why are you *upsetting* her?
Lk 11 7 <	2	Do not *bother* me. The door is bolted now,
18 5 <	2	since she keeps *pestering* me I must give this widow her just rights,
Ga 6 17	2	I want no more *trouble* from anybody after this;

3. (TO) TROUBLE – (BE) HARASSED: *SKYLLŌ*

skyllō 4

1: TROUBLE, PUT (A PERSON) TO TROUBLE – BOTHER

Mk 5 35		why *put* the Master *to* any further *trouble*?
Lk 7 6		Sir . . . do not *put* yourself *to trouble*;
8 49		Do not *trouble* the Master any further.

2: (BE) HARASSED – EXHAUSTED

Mt 9 36		the crowds . . . were *harassed* and dejected,

4. (BE) TORMENTED, TROUBLED – MAKE TROUBLE, MAKE DIFFICULT FOR: *OCHLEŌ*

2 *ochleō* 1   1   *en-ochleō* 2
3 *par-en-ochleō* 1

Lk 6 18 Ⓓ		People *tormented* by unclean spirits were also cured,
Ac 5 16 Ⓓ	2	People . . . came crowding in . . . bringing with them their sick and those *tormented* by unclean spirits,
15 19	3	I rule . . . that instead of *making* things more *difficult for* pagans who turn to God [we tell them to abstain from anything polluted by idols]
Heb 12 15		Be careful that . . . no root of bitterness should begin to grow and *make trouble*;

LAME – CRIPPLED – PARALYSED

1. Lame – Crippled: *chōlos*
2. Crippled – Maimed – Deformed: *kyllos*
3. Crippled – Maimed: *ana-pēros*
4. Paralysed – the Palsy: *para-lytikos*

1. LAME – CRIPPLED: *CHŌLOS*

chōlos 14

Mt 11 5		the blind see again, and the *lame* walk
15 30		large crowds came to [Jesus] bringing the *lame*, the crippled
31		The crowds were astonished to see . . . the cripples whole again, the *lame* walking

Mt	18	8	it is better for you to enter into life crippled or *lame*
	21	14	There were also blind and *lame* people who came to [Jesus] in the Temple
Mk	9	45	it is better for you to enter into life *lame*
Lk	7	22	the blind see again, the *lame* walk
	14	13	invite the poor, the crippled, the *lame*
		21	bring in here the poor, the crippled, the blind and the *lame*
Jn	5	3	and under these [porticoes of Bethzatha] were . . . sick people . . . *lame*, paralysed
Ac	3	2	there was a man being carried past. He was a *cripple* from birth; and they used to put him . . . near the Temple entrance
	8	7	several paralytics and *cripples* were cured
	14	8	a man . . . who had never walked . . . because his feet were *crippled* from birth
Heb	12	13	then the *injured* limb will not be wrenched, it will grow strong again

2. CRIPPLED – MAIMED – DEFORMED: *KYLLOS*

kyllos 4

Mt	15	30	the lame, the *crippled* . . . [Jesus] cured them
		31	The crowds were astonished to see . . . the *cripples* whole again, the lame walking
	18	8	it is better for you to enter life *crippled* or lame
Mk	9	43	it is better for you to enter life *crippled*

3. CRIPPLED – MAIMED: *ANA-PĒROS*

ana-pēros 2

Lk	14	13	invite the poor, the *crippled*, the lame
		21	bring in here the poor, the *crippled*, the blind and the lame

4. PARALYSED – THE PALSY: *PARA-LYTIKOS*

2 *para-lyō* 4/5   1 *para-lytikos* 10

Mt	4	24	the possessed, epileptics, the *paralysed*, were all brought to him
	8	6	My servant is lying at home *paralysed*
	9	2	bringing [to Jesus] a *paralytic* stretched out on a bed . . . Jesus said to the *paralytic* '. . . your sins are forgiven
		6	he said to the *paralytic*: 'Get up, and pick up your bed
Mk	2	3	some people came bringing him a *paralytic*
		4	they lowered the stretcher on which the *paralytic* lay
		5	Jesus said to the *paralytic* '. . . your sins are forgiven
		9	Which of these is easier, to say to the *paralytic*: Your sins are forgiven
		11	. . . he said to the *paralytic*: 'I order you: get up
Lk	5	18	2 some men appeared, carrying on a bed a *paralysed* man
		24	2 [Jesus] said to the *paralysed* man: 'I order you: get up
Ac	8	7	2 several *paralytics* and cripples were cured
	9	33	2 Aeneas, a *paralytic* who had been bedridden for eight years

---

LAW

1: Lawyer, (Doctor, Teacher, of the) Law | 2: The (Mosaic) Law
| 3: (Mosaic and other) laws

2	*nomikos*	9	10	*nomo-thetēs*	1
5	*nomimōs*	2	3	*a-nomos*	5/10
1	*nomos*	197	7	*a-nomōs*	2
4	*nomo(-didaskalos)*	3	8	*en-nomos*	2
9	*nomo-thesia*	1	11	*para-nomeō*	1
6	*nomo-theteō*	2			

P = Law // Prophets

1: LAWER, (DOCTOR, TEACHER, OF THE) LAW

Mt	22	35	[The Pharisees got together] and . . . one of them (§ a lawyer) put a question,
Lk	5	17	among the audience there were Pharisees and doctors of the Law
	7	30	by refusing baptism from [John] the Pharisees and the lawyers had thwarted what God had in mind for them.

Lk	10	25	2 a *lawyer* . . . said to [Jesus], 'Master, what must I do . . .?'
	11	45	2 A *lawyer* then spoke up. 'Master,' he said 'when you speak like this you insult us too.'
		46	2 Alas for you *lawyers* also . . . because you load on men burdens that are unendurable;
		52	2 Alas for you *lawyers* who have taken away the key of knowledge!
	14	3	2 Jesus addressed the *lawyers* and Pharisees. 'Is it against the law . . . to cure a man on the sabbath . . .?'
Ac	5	34	4 Gamaliel . . . was a doctor of the *Law* and respected by the whole people.
1 Tm	1	7	4 [some people] claim to be doctors of the *Law*
Tt	3	13	2 See to all the travelling arrangements for Zenas the *lawyer*

2: THE (MOSAIC) LAW

Mt	5	17 P	Do not imagine that I have come to abolish the *Law* or the Prophets.
		18	not one dot . . . shall disappear from the *Law*
	7	12 P	treat others as you would like them to treat you; that is the meaning of the *Law* and the Prophets.
	11	13 P	it was towards John that all the prophecies of the prophets and of the *Law* were leading;
	12	5	have you not read in the *Law* (Nb 28 9) that . . . the Temple priests break the sabbath without being blamed for it?
	15	6	you have made God's ʳword (ᵛ *law*) null and void by means of your tradition.
	22	36	which is the greatest commandment of the *Law*?
		40 P	On these two commandments hang the whole *Law*, and the Prophets also.
	23	23	you hypocrites . . . pay your tithe of mint . . . and have neglected the weightier matters of the *Law* –
Lk	2	22	when the day came for them to be purified as laid down by the *Law* of Moses (Lv 12 2), they took [Jesus] up to Jerusalem to present him to the Lord – ²³ observing what stands written in the *Law* of the Lord (Ex 13 2): Every first-born male must be consecrated to the Lord – ²⁴ and also to offer in sacrifice, in accordance with what is said in the *Law* of the Lord (Lv 5 7; 12 8), a pair of turtledoves
		23	
		24	
		27	the parents brought in the child Jesus to do for him what the *Law* required,
		39	[Joseph and Mary] had done everything the *Law* of the Lord required,
	10	26	[Jesus] said to [the lawyer], 'What is written in the *Law*?'
	16	16 P	Up to the time of John it was the *Law* and the Prophets;
		17	It is easier for heaven and earth to disappear than for one little stroke to drop out of the *Law*.
	24	44 P	everything written about me in the *Law* of Moses, in the Prophets and in the Psalms, has to be fulfilled.
Jn	1	17	the *Law* was given through Moses,
		45 P	We have found the one Moses wrote about in the *Law*, the one whom the prophets wrote: he is Jesus
	7	19	Did not Moses give you the *Law*? And yet not one of you keeps the *Law*!
		23	a man can be circumcised on the sabbath so that the *Law* of Moses is not broken,
		49	This rabble knows nothing about the *Law* – they are damned.
		51	surely the *Law* (Dt 1 16) does not allow us to pass judgement on a man without giving him a hearing . . .?
	8	5	Moses has ordered us in the *Law* (Lv 20 10; Dt 22 24) to condemn women like this to death by stoning.
		17	in your *Law* it is written (Dt 19 15) that the testimony of two witnesses is valid.
	10	34	Is it not written in your *Law* (Ps 82 6): I said, you are gods?
	12	34	The *Law* has taught us that the Christ will remain for ever.
	15	25	this was only to fulfil the words written in their *Law* (Ps 35 19): They hated me for no reason.
	18	31	Pilate said, '. . . try him by your own *Law*'.
	19	7	We have a *Law* . . . and according to that *Law* (Lv 24 16) he ought to die, because he has claimed to be the Son of God.
Ac	2	23	3 This man . . . you took and had crucified by [men] *outside* the Law.
	6	13	[Stephen] is always making speeches against . . . the Law.
	7	53	You . . . had the *Law* brought to you by angels
	13	15 P	After the lessons from the *Law* and the Prophets had been read, the presidents of the Synagogue sent [the apostles] a message:
		38	Through [Christ] justification from all sins which the *Law* of Moses was unable to justify [is offered]
	15	5	the pagans should be . . . instructed to keep the *Law* of Moses.
	18	13	We accuse [Paul] . . . of persuading people to worship God in a way that breaks the *Law*.
		15	if it is only quibbles about words . . . and about your own *Law*, then you must deal with it yourselves –
	21	20	thousands of Jews have now become believers, all of them staunch upholders of the *Law*,
		24	let everyone know . . . that you still regularly observe the *Law*.

Ac 21	28	This is the man who preaches . . . against the *Law*
22	3	I studied under Gamaliel and was taught the exact observance of the *Law* of our ancestors.
	12	Ananias, a devout follower of the *Law*
23	3	How can you . . . judge me according to the *Law*, and then
	11	ᵣbreak the Law by ordering (lit. *contrary to the Law* order) a man to strike me?
	29	the accusation concerned disputed points of their *Law*,
24	6	(ᵛ intending to judge [Paul] according to our *Law*)
	14 P	I worship the God of my ancestors, retaining my belief in all points of the *Law* and in what is written in the prophets;
25	8	I have committed no offence whatever against . . . Jewish *law*,
28	23 P	[Paul tried] to persuade [the Roman Jews] about Jesus, arguing from the *Law* of Moses and the prophets.
Ep 2	15	[Christ destroyed in his own person the hostility] caused by the rules and decrees of the *Law*.
Ph 3	5	As for the *Law*, I was a Pharisee; ⁶ . . . as far as the *Law* can make you perfect, I was faultless.
	6	
	9	I am no longer trying for perfection by my own efforts, the perfection that comes from the *Law*,

3: (MOSAIC AND OTHER) LAWS

Ac 19	39	if you want to ask any more questions you must raise them in the ᵣregular (or: *lawful*) assembly
	8	
Rm 2	12 7/	Sinners who were *not subject to the Law* will perish all the same, *without that Law*; sinners who were under the *Law*
	7/|	will have that *Law* to judge them ¹³ It is not listening to
	13	the *Law* but keeping ᵣit (lit. *the Law*) that will make people holy in the sight of God. ¹⁴ . . . pagans who never heard
	14	of the *Law* but are led by reason to do what the *Law* commands, may not actually 'possess' the *Law*, but they
	15	can be said to 'be' the *Law*. ¹⁵ They can point to the substance of the *Law* engraved on their hearts –
	17	if you really trust in the *Law* . . . ¹⁸ if you know God's will
	18	through the *Law* and can tell what is right . . . ²⁰ if you
	20	can teach the ignorant . . . because your *Law* embodies all knowledge and truth, ²¹ then why not teach yourself as
	23	well as the others? . . . ²³ By boasting about the *Law* and then disobeying ᵣit (lit. *the Law*), you bring God into contempt.
	25	It is a good thing to be circumcised if you keep the *Law*; but if you break the *Law*, you might as well have stayed uncircumcised.
	26	If a man who is not circumcised obeys . . . the *Law*, surely
	27	that makes up for not being circumcised? ²⁷ . . . the man who keeps the *Law*, even though he has not been physically circumcised, is a living condemnation of the way you disobey the *Law* in spite of being circumcised
	19	Now all this that the *Law* says is said . . . for the benefit of those who are subject to the *Law*,
	20	no one can be justified in the sight of God by keeping the *Law*: all that *Law* does is to tell us what is sinful.
	21 P	God's justice that was made known through the *Law* and the Prophets has now been revealed outside the *Law*,
	27	There is no room for [boasts]. What sort of *law* excludes them? The sort [of law] that tells us what to do? On the contrary,
	28	it is the *law* of faith, ²⁸ since . . . a man is justified by faith and not by doing something the *Law* tells him to do.
	31	Do we mean that faith makes the *Law* pointless? Not at all: we are giving the *Law* its true value.
4	13	The promise . . . was not made to Abraham . . . on account of any *law*
	14	If the world is only to be inherited by those who submit to
	15	the *Law*, then faith is pointless . . . ¹⁵ *Law* involves the possibility of punishment [for breaking the law] – only where there is no *law* can that be avoided.
	16	the promise depends on faith, so that it may . . . be available to all of Abraham's descendants, not only those who belong to the *Law* but also those who belong to the faith of Abraham
5	13	Sin existed in the world long before the *Law* was given. There was no *law* and so no one could be accused of the sin of 'law-breaking',
	20	When *law* came, it was to multiply the opportunities of falling,
6	14	you are living by grace and not by *law*.
	15	Does the fact that we are living by grace and not by *law* mean that we are free to sin?
7	1	those of you who have studied *law* will know that *laws* affect a person only during his lifetime.
	2	A married woman . . . has *legal* obligations to her husband while he is alive, but ᵣall these obligations come to an end (lit. she is discharged from [having to obey] that *law*) if the husband dies. ³ So . . . after her husband is
	3	dead ᵣher legal obligations come to an end (lit. she is exempt from that *law*), and she can marry someone else without becoming an adulteress.

Rm 7	4	you, my brothers, . . . through the body of Christ are now dead to the *Law*,
	5	our sinful passions, quite unsubdued by the *Law*, fertilised our bodies to make them give birth to death. ⁶ But now
	6	we are rid of the *Law*,
	7	Does it follow that the *Law* itself is sin? Of course not. What I mean is that I should not have known what sin was except for the *Law*. I should not for instance have known what it means to covet if the *Law* had not said (Ex 20 17) You shall not covet,
	8	when there is no *Law*, sin is dead.
	9	Once, when there was no *Law*, I was alive;
	12	The *Law* is sacred, and what it commands is sacred,
	14	The *Law* . . . is spiritual; but I am unspiritual;
	16	I have a self that acknowledges that the *Law* is good,
	21	In fact, this seems to be the *rule*, that every single time I want to do good it is something evil that comes to hand. ²² In my inmost self I dearly love God's *Law*, but ²³ I can
	22	see that my body follows a different *law* that battles against
	23	the *law* which my reason dictates. This is what makes me a prisoner of that *law* of sin which lives inside my body . . .
	25	²⁵ . . . it is I who with my reason serve the *Law* of God, and no less I who serve in my unspiritual self the *law* of sin.
8	2	the *law* of the spirit of life in Christ Jesus has set you free from the *law* of sin and death.
	3	God has done what the *Law* . . . was unable to do. God dealt with sin by sending his own Son in a body . . . and in that body God condemned sin. ⁴ He did this in order that the
	4	*Law*'s just demands might be satisfied in us,
	7	such a limitation never could and never does submit to God's *law*.
9	4	⁹ the *Law* and the ritual were drawn up for [the Israelites],
	31	Israel, looking for a righteousness derived from *law* failed to do what that *law* required.
10	4	the *Law* has come to an end with Christ, and everyone who has faith may be justified.
	5	When Moses refers to being justified [by the Law], he writes: those who keep the *Law* will draw life from it.
13	8	If you love your fellow men you have ᵣcarried out your obligations (lit. fulfilled the *Law*).
	10	Love . . . is the answer to every ᵣone of the commandments (lit. point of the *Law*).
1 Co 9	8	does not the *Law* itself say the same thing? ⁹ It is written
	9	in the *Law* of Moses (Dt 25 4): You must not put a muzzle on the ox
	20	I who am not a subject of the *Law* made myself a subject of the *Law* to those who are subjects of the *Law*, to win
	21 /3	those who are subject to the *Law*. ²¹ To *those who have*
	3/3	*no Law*, I was *free of the Law* myself (though not *free from*
	8/3	God's *law*, being *under the law* of Christ) to win *those who have no Law*.
14	21	In the written *Law* it says (Is 28 11): Through . . . the lips of foreigners I shall talk to the nation,
	34	women . . . must keep in the background as the *Law* itself lays it down (Gn 3 16).
15	56	sin gets its power from the *Law*.
Ga 2	16	we acknowledge that what makes a man righteous is not obedience to the *Law*, but faith in Jesus Christ . . . we hold that faith in Christ rather than fidelity to the *Law* is what justifies us, and that no one can be justified by keeping the *Law*.
	19	through the *Law* I am dead to the *Law*, so that now I can live for God.
	21	if the *Law* can justify us, there is no point in the death of Christ.
3	2	was it because you practised the *Law* that you received the Spirit? . . . ⁵ Does God give you the Spirit . . . because
	5	you practise the *Law* . . .?
	10	those who rely on the keeping of the *Law* are under a curse, since scripture says (Dt 27 26): Cursed be everyone who does not persevere in observing everything prescribed in the book of the *Law*. ¹¹ The *Law* will not justify anyone
	11	in the sight of God, because we are told: the righteous
	12	man finds life through faith. ¹² The *Law* is not even based
	13	on faith . . . ¹³ Christ redeemed us from the curse of the *Law* by being cursed for our sake,
	17	once God had expressed his will in due form no *law* . . .
	18	could cancel that . . . ¹⁸ If you inherit something ᵣas a legal right (lit. as the result of *law*), it does not come to
	19	you as the result of a promise . . . ¹⁹ What then was the purpose of adding the *Law*?
	21	Does this mean that there is opposition between the *Law* and the promises of God? Of course not. We could have been justified by the *Law* if the *Law* we were given had been capable of giving life,
	23	Before faith came, we were allowed no freedom by the *Law*;
	24	we were being looked after till faith was revealed. ²⁴ The *Law* was to be our guardian until the Christ came
4	4	God sent his Son . . . born a subject of the *Law*, ⁵ to redeem
	5	the subjects of the *Law*

Ga	4 21	You want to be subject to the *Law*? Then listen to what the *Law* says.
	5 3	Everyone who accepts circumcision is obliged to keep the whole *Law*. [4] But if you do look to the *Law* to make you
	4	justified, then you have separated yourselves from Christ,
	14	the whole of the *Law* is summarised in a single command (Lv 19 18): Love your neighbour
	18	If you are led by the Spirit, no *law* can touch you.
	23	There can be no *law* against things like [love, joy . . .]
	6 2	You should carry each other's troubles and fulfil the *law* of Christ.
	13	they accept circumcision but do not keep the *Law* themselves;
1 Tm	1 8	We know . . . that the *Law* is good, but only provided it is
	9	5/ treated *like any law*, [9] in the understanding that *laws* are not framed for people who are good.
2 Tm	2 5	an athlete . . . cannot win any crown unless he has ʳkept all
	5	the rules (lit. competed *according to the rules*) of the contest;
Tt	3 9	2 avoid pointless speculations . . . and disputes *about the Law* –
Heb	7 5	[the priests] are obliged by the *Law* (Dt 14 22) to take tithes
	11	6 the *Law* given to the nation rests on the [levitical priesthood]
	12	. . . [12] But any change in the priesthood must mean a change in the *Law* as well.
	16	[there appears a second priest] not by virtue of a *law* about physical descent, but by the power of an indestructible life.
	19	the *Law* could not make anyone perfect;
	28	The *Law* appoints high priests who are men subject to weakness; but the promise on oath, which came after the *Law*, appointed the Son who is made perfect for ever.
	8 4	there are other [priests] who make the offerings laid down by the *Law*
	6	6 it is a better covenant . . . ʳfounded (G *legally established*) on better promises.
	10	(Jr 31 33) I will put my *laws* into their minds
	9 19	Moses . . . announced all the commandments of the *Law*
	22	according to the *Law* almost everything has to be purified with blood;
	10 1	the *Law* . . . is quite incapable of bringing the worshippers to perfection,
	8	You did not want what the *Law* lays down as the things to be offered, that is: the sacrifices, the oblations
	16	(Jr 31 33) I will put my *laws* into their hearts
	28	Anyone who disregards the *Law* of Moses is . . . put to death
Jm	1 25	the man who looks steadily at the perfect *law* of freedom . . . will be happy in all that he does.
	2 8	keep the supreme *law* of scripture (Lv 19 18): you must love your neighbour . . . [9] but as soon as you make distinctions
	9	between classes of people, you are . . . under condemnation
	10	for breaking the *Law*. [10] . . . if a man keeps the whole of the *Law*, except for one small point . . . he is still guilty
	11	of breaking it all. [11] . . . if you commit murder, you do not have to commit adultery as well to become a breaker
	12	of the *Law*. [12] Talk and behave like people who are going to be judged by the *law* of freedom,
	4 11	Anyone who . . . condemns [a brother], is speaking against the *Law* and condemning the *Law*. But if you condemn the *Law*, you have stopped keeping ʳit (lit. the *Law*) and become
	12	10 a judge over it. [12] There is only one *law-giver* and he is the only judge and has the power to acquit or to sentence.

LEAN – BEND – BOW

---

1. **Lean (back) – Stoop, Bend over:** *ana-piptō*
2. **Bend, Bow down:** *syn-kamptō*
3. **Bend down, Stoop – Look into, Peer in:** *kyptō*
   1: Bend down, Stoop
   2: Look into, at – Peer in

4. **Bow – Lean – Unswervingly:** *klinō*
   1: Bow, Lower (one's head)
   2: (Daylight) Declines
   3: Unswervingly
   4: Lean on (figuratively)
   5: Lean towards (figuratively)

1. LEAN (BACK) – STOOP, BEND OVER: *ANA-PIPTŌ*

1 *ana-piptō* 2/12   2 *epi-piptō* 1/11

Jn	13 25	*leaning back* on Jesus' breast [John] said,
	21 20	the [disciple] who had *leaned* on Jesus' breast at the supper
Ac	20 10	2 Paul . . . ʳstooped to clasp (or: threw himself on [Eutychus], clasping) the boy to him.

2. BEND, BOW DOWN: *SYN-KAMPTŌ*

syn-kamptō 1

Rm	11 10	(Ps 69 23) may . . . their backs *bend* for ever.

3. BEND DOWN, STOOP – LOOK INTO, PEER IN: *KYPTŌ*

2   *kyptō* 2   1   *para-kyptō* 5
3   *kata-kyptō* 1   4   *syn-kyptō* 1

1: BEND DOWN, STOOP

Mk	1 7	2 I am not fit to ʳkneel down (lit. *stoop down*) and undo the strap of his sandals.
Lk	13 11	4 a woman . . . was *bent double* and ʳquite unable to stand (or: unable to stand quite) upright.
	24 12	ᵛPeter . . . *bent down* and saw the binding cloths but nothing else;
Jn	8 6 X	2 Jesus *bent down* and started writing on the ground with his finger.
	8 X	3 he *bent down* and wrote on the ground again.
	20 5	[John] ʳbent down (or: *peered in*) and saw the linen cloths lying on the ground,
	11	still weeping, [Mary of Magdala] *stooped to look inside*,

2: LOOK INTO, AT – PEER IN

Jn	20 5	[John] ʳbent down (or: *peered in*) and saw the linen cloths lying on the ground,
Jm	1 25	the man who *looks steadily at* the perfect law of freedom
1 P	1 12	Even the angels long to ʳcatch a glimpse of (lit. *peer into*) these things.

4. BOW – LEAN – UNSWERVINGLY: *KLINŌ*

1   *klinō* 4/7   3   *pros-klinō* 1
2   *a-klinēs* 1   4   *pros-klisis* 1

1: BOW, LOWER (ONE'S HEAD)

Lk	24 5	Terrified, the women *lowered* their ʳeyes (lit. faces towards the ground).
Jn	19 30 X	*bowing* his head [Jesus] gave up his spirit.

2: (DAYLIGHT) DECLINES

Lk	9 12	ʳIt was late afternoon (lit. The daylight had begun to *decline*)
	24 29	the day is ʳalmost over (lit. *declining*).

3: UNSWERVINGLY

Heb	10 23	2 Let us keep ʳfirm in (lit. *unswervingly*) the hope we profess,

4: LEAN ON (FIGURATIVELY)

Ac	5 36	3 Theudas . . . ʳcollected (lit. *leaned* [for support] *on*) about four hundred followers;

5: LEAN TOWARDS (FIGURATIVELY)

1 Tm	5 21	I put it to you as a duty to keep these rules impartially and
	4	never to be influenced ʳby favouritism (lit. into *leaning towards* [anyone]).

LEAVE

---

1. **Leave – Go (out), Come (out):** *ex-erchomai*
   1: (Satan, devils) Come out, Go out, Leave
   2: (Jesus) Leaves, Left, Goes out, Went out, Comes forth, Steps ashore
   3: (A person) Goes out, Went out, Comes out, Leaves, Sets off
      a) physically
      b) figuratively
   4: (Things, animals) Spread, Come (from, out of), Go out, Issue, Originate

2. **Leave – Come (out), Go (out):** *ek-poreuomai*
   1: (A person) Leaves, Sets out, Goes out, Went out, Comes (out)
   2: (Things, spirits) Come out (of, from), Issue, Go (out)

3. **Leave – Withdraw – Part, Separate:** *chōrizō*
   1: Leave, Go away, Part – Withdraw, Draw aside – Disappear
   2: Separate (from being married), Divide, Put asunder – Leave (one's spouse)

3: Come between (spiritually) – Separated (morally)
4. **Take leave of – Part with:** *apo-tassomai*
 1: Say good-bye to – Take leave of
 2: Part with – Renounce, Give up
5. **Leave – Forsake, Withdraw – Revolt:** *aph-istēmi*
 1: Leave, Withdraw, Depart – Leave alone
 2: Turn away, Forsake, Desert – Fall away, Revolt – Draw away, Convert
 3: Remove – Depose – Dismiss
6. **Withdraw – Slip away – Disappear:** *ek-neuō*
7. **Leave – Depart from:** *ap-allassō*
8. **Leave – Desert, (Be) Left – the Rest:** *leipō*
 1: Leave – Desert, Abandon, Forsake – Neglect
 2: Leave (figuratively)
 3: Remain, Remnant – Be left – Reserve

4: the Rest, the Other(s) – (Someone, No one) Else
5: Now – At last, Finally – Still
9. **Leave (out), Exclude:** *ek-ballō*
10. **Leave – Let – Give up:** *aph-iēmi*
 1: Leave – Leave alone – Desert, Neglect
 2: Leave = Let, Allow, Permit – Give in
 3: Leave (figuratively)–Bequeath, (Be) Left – Give up, Do without
 4: Give (a cry) – Yield up (one's spirit)
11. **Departure – Exodus:** *ex-(h)odos*
 1: the Exodus
 2: Departure – Passing (=Death)
12. **Leave, Go away, Move on:** *met-airo*
13. **Move – Leave – Pass:** *bainō*
 1: Move, Move on – Leave – Pass, Pass on
 2: Abandon, Desert

1. LEAVE – GO (OUT), COME (OUT): *EX-ERCHOMAI*

2 *ex-eimi* 4   1 *ex-erchomai* 222

1: (SATAN, DEVILS) COME OUT- GO OUT, LEAVE

Mt	8 32	[the devils] *came out* and made for the pigs;
	12 43	When an unclean spirit *goes out* of a man . . . ⁴⁴ Then it
	44	says, 'I will return to the home I *came from*'.
	17 18	the devil *came out* of the boy
Mk	1 25	Be quiet! *Come out* of him!
	26	And the unclean spirit . . . *went out* of him.
	5 8	*Come out* of the man, unclean spirit.
	13	the unclean spirits *came out* and went into the pigs,
	7 29	the devil *gone out* of your daughter.
	30	she . . . found the child lying on the bed and the devil *gone*.
	9 25	Deaf and dumb spirit, . . . *come out* of him and never enter him again.
	26	throwing the boy into violent convulsions it *came out* shouting,
	29	This is the kind . . . that can only *be driven out* by prayer.
Lk	4 35	Be quiet! *Come out* of him! And the devil . . . *went out* of him
	36	He gives orders to unclean spirits . . . and they *come out*.
	41	Devils too *came out* of many people,
	8 2	Mary surnamed the Magdalene, from whom seven demons had *gone out*,
	29	Jesus had been telling the unclean spirit to *come out* of the man.
	33	The devils *came out* of the man and went into the pigs,
	35	the people . . . found the man from whom the devils had *gone out*
	38	The man from whom the devils had *gone out* asked to be allowed to stay with him,
	11 14	when the devil had *gone out* the dumb man spoke,
	24	When an unclean spirit *goes out* of a man . . . it says, 'I will go back to the home I *came from*'.
Ac	8 7	unclean spirits . . . *came* shrieking *out* of many who were possessed,
	16 18	'I order you in the name of Jesus Christ to *leave* that woman.' The spirit *went out* of her then and there.
Rv	20 8	[Satan will be released from his prison] and will *come out* to deceive all the nations . . . and mobilise them for war.

2: (JESUS) LEAVES, LEFT, GOES OUT, WENT OUT, COMES FORTH, STEPS ASHORE

P = Jesus leaves with other people

Mt	13 1	That same day, Jesus *left* the house
	14 14	as he *stepped ashore* he saw a large crowd;
	21 17	he left them and *went out* of the city to Bethany
	24 1	Jesus *left* the Temple,
	26 30 P	they *left* for the Mount of Olives.
Mk	1 29 (P)	On *leaving* the synagogue, ʳhe (G they) went . . . straight to the house of Simon and Andrew.
	35	he got up and *left* the house, and went off to a lonely place
	38 Δ	Let us go elsewhere . . . so that I can preach there too, because that is why I *came*.
	2 13	He *went out* again to the shore of the lake;
	5 2	no sooner had he *left* the boat
	6 1	*Going* from that district, he went to his home town

Mk	6 34	as he *stepped ashore* he saw a large crowd;
	54 P	No sooner had they *stepped out* of the boat
	7 31	*Returning* from the district of Tyre, he went by way of Sidon
	8 27 P	Jesus and his disciples *left* for the villages round Caesarea Philippi.
	9 30 P	After *leaving* that place they made their way through Galilee;
	11 11 P	he *went out* to Bethany with the Twelve.
	12 P	Next day as they were *leaving* Bethany, he felt hungry.
	14 26 P	they *left* for the Mount of Olives.
Lk	4 42	When daylight came he *left* [the house] and made his way to a lonely place.
	5 8	*Leave* me, Lord, I am a sinful man.
	27	When he *went out* after this, he noticed a tax collector, Levi by name,
	6 12	he *went out* into the hills to pray;
	8 27	He was *stepping ashore* when a man . . . came towards him;
	11 53	When he *left* the house, the scribes and the Pharisees began a furious attack.
	13 31	some Pharisees came up. 'Go away' they said.
	21 37	In the daytime he would be in the Temple teaching, but would *go* and spend the night on the . . . Mount of Olives.
	22 39	He then *left* to make his way as usual to the Mount of Olives.
Jn	1 43	after Jesus had decided to *leave* for Galilee,
	4 43	Jesus *left* for Galilee.
	8 59	Jesus hid himself and *left* the Temple.
	10 39	[The Jews] wanted to arrest him then, but he ʳeluded (lit. *left*) them.
	18 1 P	Jesus *left* with his disciples and crossed the Kedron valley.
	4	Jesus then *came* [forward] and said, 'Who are you looking for?'
	19 5	Jesus then *came out* wearing the crown of thorns
	17	carrying his own cross he *went out* of the city to the place of the skull
Ac	1 21	the whole time that the Lord Jesus was ʳtravelling round
	O	(lit. *coming* and *going*) with us,

3: (A PERSON) GOES OUT, WENT OUT, COMES OUT, LEAVES, SETS OFF

a) physically

A = Angel   E = the Exodus

Mt	5 26	you will not *get out* [of prison] till you have paid the last penny.
	8 28	two demoniacs *came* towards him *out* of the tombs
	34	the whole town *set out* to meet Jesus;
	9 31	But when [the two blind men he had cured] had *gone*, they talked about him all over the countryside.
	32	They had only just *left* when a man was brought to him,
	10 11	stay with him until you *leave*.
	14	if anyone does not welcome you . . . , as you *walk out* of the house or town shake the dust from your feet.
	11 7	What did you *go out* into the wilderness to see? . . ⁸ Then what did you *go out* to see? . . . ⁹ Then what did you *go out* for? To see a prophet?
	8	
	9	
	12 14	the Pharisees *went out* and began to plot against him,
	13 3 <	Imagine a sower *going out* to sow.
	49 A	angels will ʳappear (lit. *come*) and separate the wicked from the just
	15 22	Then *out came* a Canaanite woman from that district
	18 28 <	as this servant *went out*, he happened to meet a fellow servant
	20 1 <	a landowner *going out* at daybreak to hire workers
	3 <	*Going out* at about the third hour
	5 <	At about the sixth hour and again at about the ninth hour, he *went out*
	6 <	at about the eleventh hour he *went out*
	22 10 <	So these servants *went out* on to the roads
	24 26	If . . . they say to you, 'Look, he is in the desert', do not *go* there;
	25 1 <	Ten bridesmaids . . . *went* to meet the bridegroom.
	6 <	The bridegroom is here! *Go out* and meet him.
	26 55	Am I a brigand, that you had to *set out* to capture me with swords and clubs?
	71	When [Peter] *went out* to the gateway
	75	Peter . . . *went* outside and wept bitterly.
	27 32	On their *way out*, they came across a man from Cyrene,
	53	[many holy men] *came out* of the tombs,
Mk	1 45	The [cured leper] *went away*, but then started talking about it freely
	2 12	the [cured paralytic] got up . . . and *walked out* in front of everyone,
	3 6	The Pharisees *went out* and . . . began to plot with the Herodians
	21	his relatives . . . *set out* to take charge of [Jesus],
	4 3 <	Imagine a sower *going out* to sow.
	6 10	If you enter a house anywhere, stay there until you *leave* the district.
	12	[the Twelve] *set off* to preach repentance;

Mk	6 24		[Herodias' daughter] *went out* and said to her mother,
	8 11		The Pharisees *came up* and started a discussion
	14 16		The disciples *set out* and went to the city
	48		Am I a brigand . . . that you had to *set out* to capture me with swords and clubs?
	68		[Peter] *went out* into the forecourt.
	16 8		the women *came* and ran away from the tomb
	20		while the Eleven, *going out*, preached everywhere,
Lk	1 22		When [Zechariah] *came out* he could not speak to them,
	7 24		What did you *go out* into the wilderness to see? . . .
	25		²⁵ . . . Then what did you *go out* to see? . . . ²⁶ Then
	26		what did you *go out* to see?
	8 5	<	A sower *went out* to sow his seed.
	35		the people *went out* to see what had happened.
	9 4		Whatever house you enter, stay there; and when you *leave* let it be from there.
	5		As for those who do not welcome you, when you *leave* their town shake the dust from your feet
	6		[the Twelve] *set out* and went from village to village
	10 10		whenever you enter a town and they do not make you welcome, *go* into its streets and say,
	12 59		you will not *get out* [of prison] till you have paid the very last penny.
	14 18	<	I have bought a piece of land and must *go* and see it.
	21	<	*Go out* quickly into the streets and alleys
	23	<	*Go* to the open roads and the hedgerows
	15 28		[The elder son] was angry then and refused to go in, and
		<	his father *came out* to plead with him;
	17 29		the day Lot *left* Sodom,
	22 52		Am I a brigand . . . that you had to *set out* with swords and clubs?
	62		[Peter] *went* outside and wept bitterly.
Jn	4 30		This ⌈brought people out (lit. made people *come out*) of the town
	8 9		they *went away* one by one, beginning with the eldest,
	10 9		Anyone who enters [the sheepfold] through me will . . .
		<	*go* freely in and *out* and be sure of finding pasture.
	11 31		When the Jews who were in the house sympathising with Mary saw her get up . . . and *go out*,
	44		The dead man *came out*, his feet and hands bound
	12 13		They took branches of palm and *went out* to meet him,
	13 30		As soon as Judas had taken the piece of bread he *went out*.
	31		. . . ³¹ When he had *gone* Jesus said: 'Now has the Son of Man been glorified.'
	18 16		the other disciple . . . *went out*,
	29		So Pilate *came* outside to them
	38		Pilate . . . *went out* again to the Jews
	19 4		Pilate *came* outside again and said to them, 'Look, I am going to bring him out to you'
	20 3		Peter *set out* with the other disciple to go to the tomb.
	21 3		They *went out* and got into the boat
Ac	7 3		(Gn 12 1) *Leave* your country and your family
	4		So [Abraham] *left* Chaldaea
	7	E	(Gn 15 14) after this they will *leave*,
	10 23		[Peter] was ready to *go off* with them,
	11 25		Barnabas then *left* for Tarsus to look for Saul,
	12 9		Peter *set off* and followed [the angel],
	10		[Peter and the angel] reached the iron gate leading to the city
		A	. . . they *went out* through it
	17		Then [Peter] *left* and went to another place.
	13 42	2	As [Barnabas and Paul] *left* they were asked to preach . . . on the following sabbath.
	14 20		The next day [Paul] and Barnabas *went off* to Derbe.
	15 40		Before Paul *left*, he chose Silas to accompany him
	16 3		Paul, who wanted to have [Timothy] ⌈as a travelling companion (lit. *going* with him),
	10		we lost no time in arranging ⌈a passage (lit. to *go*) to Macedonia.
	13		we *went* along the river outside the gates
	36		you can *go* now and be on your way (§ in peace).
	40		From the prison [Paul and Silas] *went* to Lydia's house . . .; then they *left*.
	17 15	2	Paul's escort . . . *went back* with instructions for Silas and Timothy
	33		After that Paul *left* [the Athenians],
	18 23		[Paul] spent a short time [at Antioch] before ⌈continuing his journey (lit. *leaving* and going) through the Galatian country
	20 1		Paul . . . *set out* for Macedonia.
	7	2	Paul was due to *leave* the next day,
	11		[Paul] *left* at daybreak.
	21 5		when our time was up we *set off*.
	8		The next day we *left* and came to Caesarea.
	22 18		*leave* Jerusalem at once;
	27 43	2	the centurion . . . gave orders that those who could swim should jump overboard . . . and so *get ashore*,
1 Co	5 10		To do that, you would have to *withdraw* from the world altogether.
2 Co	2 13		I . . . *went on* to Macedonia.
	6 17		(Is 52 11) *come away* from them and keep aloof,

2 Co	8 17		[Titus] is *visiting* you on his own initiative.
Ph	4 15		when I *left* Macedonia,
Heb	3 16	E	the people who were *brought out* of Egypt by Moses.
	11 8		(cf. Gn 12 1) that Abraham obeyed the call to *set out* for a country . . . and that he *set out* without knowing where he was going.
3 Jn	7		It was entirely for the sake of the name that they *set out*,
Rv	3 12		Those who prove victorious I will make into pillars in the sanctuary of my God, and they will ⌈*stay there* for ever (lit. never *leave*);
	6 2		[the rider of the white horse] *went away*, to go from victory to victory.
	14 15	A	Then another angel *came out* of the sanctuary,
	17	A	Another angel . . . *came out* of the temple
	18	A	the angel in charge of the fire *left* the altar
	15 6	A	*out came* the seven angels with the seven plagues,
	18 4		*Come out*, my people, away from [Babylon],

b) figuratively

Mt	2 6	X	(Mi 5 1) for *out* of you [Bethlehem] will *come* a leader
Jn	8 42	X	I have *come* here from God; yes, I have come from him;
	13 3	X	Jesus knew that . . . he had *come* from God and was returning to God,
	16 27	X	the Father himself loves you for . . . believing that I *came* from God.
	28	X	I *came* from the Father and have come into the world
	30	X	we believe that you *came* from God.
	17 8	X	they have truly accepted this, that I *came* from you,
Ac	15 24		We hear that some ⌈of our members (ᵛ who *come* from our people) have disturbed you with their demands
Heb	7 5		[priests] take tithes from the people, . . . although they too are *descended* from Abraham.
	13 13		Let us *go* to [Jesus], then, outside the camp,
1 Jn	2 19		Those rivals of Christ *came out* of our own number,
	4 1		there are many false prophets *come up*, now, in the world.
2 Jn	7		There are many deceivers *come* into the world,

4: (THINGS, ANIMALS) SPREAD, COME (FROM, OUT OF), GO OUT, ISSUE, ORIGINATE

Mt	9 26		the news *spread* all round the countryside.
	15 18		the things that come out of the mouth *come* from the heart,
	19		From the heart *come* evil intentions:
	24 27		like lightning ⌈striking in (lit. *coming* from) the east
Mk	1 28		his reputation rapidly *spread* everywhere,
	5 30		Immediately aware that power had *gone out* from him, Jesus turned
Lk	2 1		at this time Caesar Augustus *issued* a decree
	4 14		his reputation *spread* throughout the countryside.
	6 19		power *came out* of him that cured them all.
	7 17		this opinion of him *spread* throughout Judaea
	8 46		I felt that power had *gone out* from me.
Jn	19 34		immediately there *came out* blood and water.
	21 23		The rumour then *went out* among the brothers that this disciple would not die.
Ac	16 19		her masters saw ⌈that there was no hope of making any (lit. *go* their hope of making) more money out of her,
	28 3		a viper *brought out* by the heat attached itself to his hand.
Rm	10 18		(Ps 19 4) their voice has *gone out* through all the earth,
1 Co	14 36		Do you think the word of God *came out* of yourselves?
1 Th	1 8		it was from you that the word of the Lord [started to] *spread*
Jm	3 10		the blessing and the curse *come out* of the same mouth.
Rv	6 4		And *out came* another horse, bright red,
	9 3		*out* of the smoke *dropped* locusts
	14 20		[the whole vintage of the earth] was trodden until the blood that *came out* of the winepress [of God's anger] was up to the horses' bridles
	16 17		a voice shouted *coming* from the sanctuary, 'The end has come'.
	19 5		a voice *came* from the throne;
	21		the sword of the rider, which *came out* of his mouth,

2. LEAVE – COME (OUT), GO (OUT): *EK-POREUOMAI*

ek-poreuomai 34

1: (A PERSON) LEAVES, SETS OUT, GOES OUT, WENT OUT, COMES OUT

Mt	3 5		Jerusalem and all Judaea . . . *made their way* to [John the Baptist],
	20 29	X	As they *left* Jericho, a large crowd followed him.
Mk	1 5		all the people of Jerusalem *made their way* to [John the Baptist],

Mk	6 11		if any place does not welcome you . . , as you *walk away* shake off the dust
	10 17 X		He was *setting out* for a journey when a man ran up,
	46 X		and as he *left* Jericho with his disciples and a large crowd,
	11 19 X		when evening came ⌐he (G they) *went out* of the city.
	13 1 X		As he was *leaving* the Temple
Lk	3 7		[John] said . . . to the crowds who *came* to be baptised by him,
Ac	25 4		Festus replied that . . . he would be *going back* there shortly

2: (THINGS, SPIRITS) COME OUT (OF, FROM), ISSUE, GO (OUT)

Mt	4 4		(Dt 8 3) Man . . . [lives] on every word that *comes* from the mouth of God.
	15 11		it is what *comes out* of the mouth that makes [a man] unclean.
	18		the things that *come out* of the mouth come from the heart,
	17 21	Ⓓ	(ᵛ This is the kind [of spirit] that will *come out* only after prayer and fasting.)
Mk	7 15		it is the things that *come out* of a man that make him unclean.
	19		because it . . . *passes* into the sewer?
	20		It is what *comes out* of a man that makes him unclean.
	21		For it is from within . . . that evil intentions *emerge*:
	23		All these evil things *come* from within and make a man unclean.
Lk	4 22		the gracious words that *came* from his lips.
	37		reports of him *went* all through the surrounding countryside.
Jn	5 29		the hour is coming when the dead will *leave* their graves at the sound of his voice
	15 26	Ⓢ	When the Advocate comes, . . . the Spirit of truth who *issues* from the Father,
Ac	9 28	Ⓞ	Saul now started to ⌐go round (lit. come and *go*) with them in Jerusalem.
	19 12	Ⓓ	the evil spirits *came out* of them.
Ep	4 29		⌐Guard against foul talk (lit. Let no foul talk *come out* of your mouth);
Rv	1 16		*out* of his mouth came a sharp sword,
	4 5		Flashes of lightning were *coming* from the throne,
	9 17		fire, smoke and sulphur were *coming out* of [the horses'] mouths.
	18		the fire, the smoke and the sulphur *coming out* of their mouths,
	11 5		Fire can *come* from [the two witnesses'] mouths and consume their enemies
	16 14	Ⓓ	[they] were demon spirits . . . *going out* to all the kings of the world to call them together for the war of the Great Day
	19 15		From his mouth *came* a sharp sword,
	22 1		the river of life, *rising* from the throne of God and of the Lamb

3. LEAVE – WITHDRAW – PART, SEPARATE: *CHŌRIZŌ*

	2	*chōrizō* 13	6	*dia-chōrizō* 1
1	*ana-chōreō* 14	7	*ek-chōreō* 1
3	*apo-chōreō* 3	5	*hypo-chōreō* 2
4	*apo-chōrizō* 2		

1: LEAVE, GO AWAY, PART – WITHDRAW, DRAW ASIDE – DISAPPEAR

Mt	2 12		[the wise men] *returned* to their own country by a different way. ¹³ After they had *left*, the angel of the Lord appeared to Joseph in a dream
	13		
	14		Joseph . . . *left* that night for Egypt,
	22		[Joseph] *left* for the region of Galilee.
	4 12 X		Hearing that John had been arrested he *went back* to Galilee,
	7 23	3	(Ps 6 8) *away* from me, you evil men!
	9 24		*Get out* [of here]; the little girl is not dead,
	12 15 X		Jesus knew this and *withdrew* from the district.
	14 13 X		Jesus . . . *withdrew* by boat to a lonely place
	15 21 X		Jesus . . . *withdrew* to the region of Tyre and Sidon.
	27 5		[Judas] *made off*, and went and hanged himself.
Mk	3 7 X		Jesus *withdrew* with his disciples to the lakeside,
Lk	5 16 X	5	but he would always *go off* to some place where he could be alone and pray.
	9 10 X	5	he took [the apostles] with him and *withdrew* to . . . Bethsaida where they could be by themselves.
	33	6	As [Moses and Elijah] were *leaving* [Jesus], Peter said
	39	3	[the spirit] is slow to *leave* [my son]
	21 21	7	those inside the city must *leave* it,
Jn	6 15 X		Jesus . . . ⌐escaped back to (G *withdrew* into) the hills by himself.
Ac	1 4	2	[Jesus] had told [the apostles] not to *leave* Jerusalem,
	13 13	3	John *left* [Paul and his friends] to go back to Jerusalem.
	15 39	4	After a violent quarrel [Paul and Barnabas] *parted* [company],
	18 1	2	Paul *left* Athens

Ac	18 2		an edict of Claudius had ⌐expelled all the Jews from (lit. decreed that all Jews must *leave*) Rome.
	23 19		the tribune . . . *drew* [Paul's nephew] *aside* privately and asked, 'What is it you have to tell me?'
	26 31		When [the king and the governor] had *retired* they talked together
Phm	15	2	you have been ⌐deprived of (lit. *parted* from) Onesimus for a time, but . . . only so that you could have him back for ever,
Rv	6 14	4	the sky *disappeared* like a scroll rolling up

2: SEPARATE (FROM BEING MARRIED), DIVIDE, PUT ASUNDER – LEAVE (ONE'S SPOUSE)

Mt	19 6	2	what God has united, man must not *divide*.
Mk	10 9	2	what God has united, man must not *divide*.
1 Co	7 10	2	a wife must not *leave* her husband – ¹¹ or if she ⌐does
	11	2	*leave* him she must either remain unmarried or else make it up with her husband –
	15	2	if the unbelieving partner ⌐does not consent (lit. wants [the
		2/2	two partners] to *separate*), they may *separate*;

3: COME BETWEEN (SPIRITUALLY) – SEPARATED (MORALLY)

Rm	8 35	2	Nothing therefore can *come between* us and the love of Christ, . . . ³⁸ neither death nor life, . . . ³⁹ or height or
	39	2	depth . . . can ever *come between* us and the love of God
Heb	7 26 X	2	the ideal high priest would have to be . . . ⌐beyond the
		2	*influence* of (or: *separated* from) sinners,

4. TAKE LEAVE OF – PART WITH: *APO-TASSOMAI*

apo-tassomai 6

1: SAY GOOD-BYE TO – TAKE LEAVE OF

Mk	6 46 X		After *saying good-bye to* [the crowd] he went off into the hills to pray.
Lk	9 61		first let me go and *say good-bye to* my people at home.
Ac	18 18		Paul *took leave* of the brothers and sailed for Syria,
	21		⌐when he left (lit. as he *took his leave*) he said, 'I will come back'
2 Co	2 13		I *said good-bye to* them and went on to Macedonia.

2: PART WITH – RENOUNCE, GIVE UP

Lk	14 33		none of you can be my disciple unless he ⌐gives up (or: *parts with*) all his possessions.

5. LEAVE – FORSAKE, WITHDRAW – REVOLT: *APH-ISTĒMI*

1	*aph-istēmi* 14	4	*di-(h)istēmi* 1/3
3	*apo-stasia* 2	2	*meth-istēmi* 3/5

1: LEAVE, WITHDRAW, DEPART – LEAVE ALONE

Lk	2 37		[Anna] never *left* the Temple,
	4 13		Having exhausted all these ways of tempting [Jesus], the devil *left* him
	13 27	⬤	(Ps 6 8) *Away* from me, all you wicked men!
	24 51 X	4	he *withdrew* from them and was carried up to heaven.
Ac	5 38		*leave* these men *alone* and let them go.
	12 10		suddenly the angel *left* [Peter].
	15 38		[John Mark] who had ⌐deserted (or: *left*) [Paul and Barnabas] in Pamphylia
	19 9		[Paul] ⌐broke with (lit. *withdrew* from) them
	22 29		Those who were about to examine him [hurriedly] *withdrew*,
2 Co	12 8	Ⓓ	I have pleaded with the Lord . . . for [this angel of Satan] to *leave* me,
2 Tm	2 19		All who call on the name of the Lord must ⌐avoid sin (lit. *leave* sin *alone*).

2: TURN AWAY, FORSAKE, DESERT – FALL AWAY, REVOLT – DRAW AWAY, CONVERT

Lk	8 13		in time of trial they ⌐give up (or: *fall away*).
Ac	5 37		Judas the Galilean . . . who ⌐attracted (lit. *drew away*) crowds of supporters;
	19 26	2	this man Paul has persuaded and *converted* a great number of people
	21 21	3	you instruct all Jews living among the pagans to ⌐break
		3	*away* from (or: *forsake*) Moses,
2 Th	2 3	3	It cannot happen until the [Great] *Revolt* has taken place

1 Tm	4	1	during the last times there will be come who will *desert* the the faith
Heb	3	12	a wicked mind, so unbelieving as to *turn away* from the living God.

3: REMOVE – DEPOSE – DISMISS

Lk	16	4	2 to make sure that when I am ⌐*dismissed* from (or: *made to leave* my) office there will be some to welcome me
Ac	13	22	2 [God] ⌐*deposed* (or: *removed*) [Saul] and made David their king,

6. WITHDRAW – SLIP AWAY – DISAPPEAR: *EK-NEUŎ*
ek-neuō 1

Jn	5	13 X	Jesus had *disappeared* into the crowd

7. LEAVE – DEPART FROM: *AP-ALLASSŎ*
ap-allassō 1/3

Ac	19	12	⌐they were cured of their illnesses (lit. their illnesses *left* them) and the evil spirits came out of them.

8. LEAVE – DESERT, (BE) LEFT – THE REST: *LEIPŎ*

6	*leimma*	1	8	*epi-loipos*	1
1	*loipos*	55	9	*hypo-leimma*	1
4	*apo-leipō*	7	10	*hypo-leipō*	1
2	*kata-leipō*	24	11	*hypo-limpanō*	1
7	*kata-loipos*	1	5	*peri-leipomai*	2
3	*en-kata-leipo*	10			
			12	*sabachthani*	2

1: LEAVE – DESERT, ABANDON, FORSAKE – NEGLECT

Mt	4	13 X	2 *leaving* Nazareth he went and settled in Capernaum,
	16	4 X	2 *leaving* them standing there, he went away.
	19	5	2 (Gn 2 24) a man must *leave* father and mother, and cling to his wife,
	21	17 X	2 he *left* them
	27	46 Θ	12 (Ps 22 1) 'Eli, . . . lama *sabachthani*?' that is, 'My God,
		Θ	3 my God, why have you *deserted* me?'
Mk	10	7	2 (Gn 2 24) a man must *leave* father and mother,
	14	52	2 [the young man] *left* the cloth in their hands and ran away naked.
	15	34 Θ	12 (Ps 22 1) 'Eli, . . . lama *sabachthani*?' which means, 'My
		Θ	3 God, my God, why have you *deserted* me?'
Lk	5	28	2 *leaving* everything [Levi] got up and followed [Jesus].
	15	4	What man among you with a hundred sheep, losing one,
		<	2 would not *leave* the ninety-nine in the wilderness
Ac	2	27 Θ	2 (Ps 16 10) you will not *abandon* my soul to Hades
		31 Θ	3 Christ . . . is the one who was not *abandoned* to Hades,
	6	2	2 It would not be right for us to *neglect* the word of God so as to give out food;
	18	19	2 When they reached Ephesus, [Paul] *left* them,
2 Co	4	9	3 we have been persecuted, but never *deserted*;
Ep	5	31	2 (Gn 2 24) a man must *leave* his father and mother
2 Tm	4	10	3 Demas has *deserted* me for love of this life
		13	4 bring the cloak I *left* with Carpus in Troas,
		16	there was not a single witness to support me. Every one of
			3 them *deserted* me
		20	4 I left Trophimus ill at Miletus.
Tt	1	5	4 I *left* you *behind* in Crete . . . to get everything organised
Heb	10	25	3 Do not *stay away from* the meetings of the community, as some do,
	11	27	2 It was by faith that [Moses] *left* Egypt
	13	5	God himself has said (Jos 1 5): I will not fail you or
		Θ	3 *desert* you.
2 P	2	15	2 They have *left* the right path and wandered off
Jude		6	4 the angels who . . . *left* their appointed sphere;

2: LEAVE (FIGURATIVELY)

Mt	12	19	2 if a man's brother dies *leaving* a wife but no child,
		21	2 The second . . . too died *leaving* no children;
Lk	10	40	2 Lord, do you not care that my sister is *leaving* me to do the serving all by myself?
	20	31	2 all seven . . . died *leaving* no children.
Ac	21	3	2 After sighting Cyprus and *leaving* it to port,

Ac	24	27	2 being anxious to gain favour with the Jews, Felix *left* Paul in custody.
	25	14	2 There is a man here . . . whom Felix *left behind* in custody,
Rm	9	29 Θ	3 (Is 1 9) Had the Lord of hosts not *left* us some descendants
1 P	2	21 X	11 Christ suffered for you and *left* an example for you to follow

3: REMAIN, REMNANT – BE LEFT – RESERVE

Jn	8	9 X	2 Jesus *was left* alone with the woman
Rm	9	27 ●	9 (Is 10 22) only a *remnant* [of Israel] will be saved,
	11	3 ●	10 (1 K 19 10) I, and I only, *remain*, and they want to kill me.
		4 ●	2 (1 K 19 18) I have *kept* for myself seven thousand men
		5	who have not bent the knee to Baal. [5] Today the same
		●	6 thing has happened: there is a *remnant*, chosen by grace.
1 Th	3	1	2 we decided it would be best to *be left* without a companion at Athens,
	4	15	5 any of us who *are left* [alive] until the Lord's coming
		17	5 those of us who ⌐*are still* (lit. *are left*) [alive] will be taken up in the clouds,
Heb	4	1	the promise of reaching the place of rest he had for them
		2	still ⌐*holds good* (or: *remains*)
		6	4 It ⌐*is established* (lit. *remains*), then, that there would be some people who would reach [the place of rest],
		9	4 There must still be, therefore, a place of rest *reserved* for God's people,
	10	26	If . . . we should deliberately commit any sins, then there
		4	*is no longer* any sacrifice *left* for them.
1 P	4	2	8 for the ⌐*rest* (lit. *time which remains*) of his life on earth
Rv	3	2	revive what little you have *left*: it is dying fast.
	11	13	the ⌐*survivors* (or: *rest*) . . . could only praise the God of heaven.

4: THE REST, THE OTHER(S) – (SOMEONE, NO ONE) ELSE

Mt	22	6	and the *rest* seized his servants, . . . and killed them.
	25	11	The *other* bridesmaids arrived later.
	27	49	'Wait!' said the *rest* of them 'and see if Elijah will come to save him.'
Mk	4	19	the lure of riches and all the *other* passions
	16	13	These went back and told the *others*,
Lk	8	10	for the *rest* there are only parables,
	12	26	why worry about the *rest*?
	18	9	some people who . . . despised *everyone else*.
		11	I am not . . . like the *rest* of mankind,
	24	9	the women . . . told all this to the Eleven and to all the *others*.
		10	The *other* women . . . also told the apostles,
Ac	2	37	they . . . said to Peter and the *other* apostles,
	5	13	No one *else* ever dared to join them,
	15	17	7 (cf. Am 9 12 G) Then the *rest* of mankind . . . will look for the Lord,
	17	9	they made Jason and the *rest* give security
	27	44	the *rest* follow . . . on pieces of wreckage.
	28	9	the *other* sick people . . . came [to Paul] as well
Rm	1	13	in the hope that I might work as fruitfully among you as I have done among the *other* pagans.
	11	7	The *rest* were not allowed to see the truth;
1 Co	1	16	there was the family of Stephanas . . . but no one *else*
	7	12	The *rest* is from me and not from the Lord.
	9	5	[Have we not] the right . . . , like all the *other* apostles . . . ?
	11	34	The *other* [matters] I shall adjust when I come.
	15	37	you sow a bare grain, say of wheat or something ⌐like that (lit. *else*),
2 Co	12	13	Is there anything of which you have had less than the *other* churches . . . ?
	13	2	I give warning . . . to those who sinned before and to any *others*,
Ga	2	13	The *other* Jews joined [Cephas] in this pretence,
Ep	2	3	we were as much under God's anger as the *rest* of the world.
Ph	1	13	not only all over the Praetorium but ⌐everywhere (lit. in every *other* place),
	4	3	Clement and the *others* who worked with me.
1 Th	4	13	do not grieve about [those who have died], like the *other* [people] who have no hope.
	5	6	we should not go on sleeping as *everyone else* does,
1 Tm	5	20	reprimand them publicly, as a warning to the *rest*.
2 P	3	16	in the same way as they distort the *rest* of scripture
Rv	2	24	on the *rest* of you in Thyatira . . . I am not laying any special duty;
	8	13	at the sound of the *other* three trumpets
	9	20	the *rest* of the human race, who escaped these plagues,
	11	13	the ⌐*survivors* (or: *rest*) . . . could only praise the God of heaven.
	12	17	the dragon . . . went away to make war on the *rest* of her children,
	19	21	All the *rest* were killed by the sword of the rider,
	20	5	the *rest* of the dead did not come to life

5: NOW – AT LAST, FINALLY – STILL

Mt 26	45	You can sleep on *now* and take your rest.
Mk 14	41	You can sleep on *now* and take your rest.
Ac 27	20	the storm raged unabated until *at last* we gave up all hope of surviving.
1 Co 4	2	*Moreover*, what is expected of stewards
7	29	Those who *now* have wives should live as though they had none,
2 Co 13	11	*In the meantime*, brothers, we wish you happiness;
Ga 6	17	I want no more trouble from anybody *after this*;
Ep 6	10	*Finally*, grow strong in the Lord.
Ph 3	1	*Finally*, my brothers, rejoice in the Lord.
4	8	*Finally*, brothers, fill your minds with everything that is true,
1 Th 4	1	*Finally*, brothers, we urge you
2 Th 3	1	*Finally*, brothers, pray for us;
2 Tm 4	8	all there is to come *now* is the crown of righteousness reserved for me,
Heb 10	13	where he is *now* waiting until his enemies are made into a footstool for him.

9. LEAVE (OUT), EXCLUDE: *EK-BALLŌ*

ek-ballō 1/81

Rv 11	2	but *leave* out the outer court and do not measure it,

10. LEAVE – LET – GIVE UP: *APH-IĒMI*

2 an-(h)iēmi   2/4   3 par-(h)iēmi 1/2
1 aph-iēmi 94/146

1: LEAVE – LEAVE ALONE – DESERT, NEGLECT

Mt 3	15		Jesus replied [to John], '*Leave* it [like this] for the time being; . . . ' At this, John *gave in* to him. [16] As soon as Jesus was baptised he came up from the water,
4	11	⑩	Then the devil *left* [Jesus],
	20		[Simon and Andrew] *left* their nets at once and followed him.
	22		At once, *leaving* their boat and their father, [James and John] followed him.
5	24		*leave* your offering there before the altar, go and be reconciled with your brother first,
	40		if a man . . . would have your tunic, ⌐let him have (or: *give up* to him) your cloak as well.
8	22		Follow me, and *leave* the dead to bury their dead.
13	36	X	*leaving* the crowds, he went to the house;
15	14		*Leave* [the Pharisees] *alone*. They are blind men leading blind men;
18	12	<	Suppose a man has a hundred sheep . . . ; will he not *leave* the ninety-nine . . . ?
19	14		*Let* the little children *alone*, and do not stop them coming to me;
	27		[Peter to Jesus:] 'We have *left* everything and followed you.'
	29		everyone who has *left* houses, brothers, . . . for the sake of my name
22	22		they *left* [Jesus] *alone* and went away.
23	23		[you Pharisees] have *neglected* . . . justice, mercy, good faith! These you should have practised, without *neglecting* the others.
26	44	X	*Leaving* the disciples there, he went away again and prayed
	56		all the disciples *deserted* him and ran away.
27	49		'*Wait*!' said the rest of them 'and see if Elijah will come to save him.'
Mk 1	18		[Simon and Andrew] *left* their nets and followed him.
	20		*leaving* their father Zebedee . . . , [James and John] went after him.
	31		the fever *left* [Simon's mother-in-law]
4	36		*leaving* the crowd *behind* [the disciples] took [Jesus] . . . in the boat;
7	8		You [Pharisees and scribes] *put aside* the commandment of God to cling to human traditions.
8	13	X	*leaving* [the Pharisees] again and re-embarking he went away to the opposite shore.
10	28		[Peter to Jesus:] 'We have *left* everything and followed you.'
	29		there is no one who has *left* house, brothers, . . . or land for my sake . . . [30] who will not be repaid
12	12		[the chief priests] *left* him *alone* and went away.
13	34	<	like a man travelling abroad: he has *gone from* home,
14	6		[A woman poured ointment on his head.] Jesus said, '*Leave* her *alone*. Why are you upsetting her?'
	50		[the disciples] all *deserted* him and ran away.
15	36		⌐*Wait* and (or: Let us) see if Elijah will come and take him down.

Lk 5	11		[Simon, Andrew, James and John] *left* everything and followed him.
9	60		*Leave* the dead to bury their dead;
10	30		[the brigands] made off, *leaving* him half dead.
11	42	3	These you should have practised, without *leaving* the others [undone].
13	8	<	*leave* [the fig tree] one more year
18	28		[Peter to Jesus:] 'We *left* all we had to follow you.'
	29		no one who has *left* house, wife, . . . or children for the sake of the kingdom of God
Jn 4	3	X	he *left* Judaea and went back to Galilee.
	28		The woman *put down* her water jar and hurried back to the town
8	29	Θ	he who sent me is with me, and has not *left* me to myself,
10	12	<	The hired man . . . *abandons* the sheep
12	7		*Leave* her *alone*; she had to keep this scent for the day of my burial.
14	18	X	I will not *leave* you orphans; I will come back to you.
16	28	X	now I *leave* the world to go to the Father.
	32		the time will come . . . when you will be scattered, . . . *leaving* me alone,
Ac 5	38		*leave* these men *alone* and let them go.
Heb 13	5	Θ	2 God himself has said (Jos 1 5): I will not ⌐*fail* (lit. *leave*) you or desert you,

2: LEAVE = LET, ALLOW, PERMIT – GIVE IN

Mt 3	15		Jesus replied [to John], '*Leave* it [like this] for the time being; . . . ' At this, John *gave in* to him. [16] As soon as Jesus was baptised he came up from the water,
5	40		if a man . . . would have your tunic, ⌐*let him have* (or: give up to him) your cloak as well.
7	4		*Let* me take the splinter out of your eye,
8	22		Follow me, and *leave* the dead to bury their dead.
13	30		*Let* [the wheat and the darnel] both grow till the harvest;
19	14		*Let* the little children *alone*, and do not stop them coming to me;
23	13		You [scribes and Pharisees] who shut up the kingdom of heaven . . . , neither going in yourselves nor *allowing* others to go in
27	49		'*Wait*!' said the rest of them 'and see if Elijah will come to save him.'
Mk 1	34	X	he would not *allow* [the devils] to speak,
5	19		[the man who had been possessed begged to be allowed to stay with him.] Jesus would not *let* him
	37	X	he *allowed* no one to go with him except Peter and James and John
7	12		he is ⌐*forbidden* (lit. not *allowed*) from that moment to do anything for his father or mother.
	27		[Jesus to the Syrophoenician woman:] ⌐The children should (lit. *Let* the children) be fed first,
10	14		*Let* the little children come to me,
11	6		[the disciples untied the colt] and the men *let* them [go].
	16	X	Nor would he *allow* anyone to carry anything through the Temple.
15	36		⌐*Wait* and (or: *Let* us) see if Elijah will come and take him down.
Lk 6	42		*let* me take out the splinter that is in your eye,
8	51	X	he *allowed* no one to go in with him except Peter and John and James,
9	60		*Leave* the dead to bury their dead;
12	39		the householder . . . would not have *let* anyone break through the wall of his house.
13	8	<	*leave* [the fig tree] one more year
18	16		*Let* the little children come to me,
Jn 11	44		Jesus said to them, 'Unbind [Lazarus], *let* him go free'.
	48		If we *let* him go on in this way everybody will believe in him,
18	8		If I am the one you are looking for, *let* these others go.
Rv 2	20		[To the church in Thyatira:] you are ⌐*encouraging* (lit. *permitting*) the woman Jezebel
11	9		Men . . . will stare at [the] corpses [of the two witnesses] . . . , not *letting* them be buried,

3: LEAVE (FIGURATIVELY) – BEQUEATH, (BE) LEFT – GIVE UP, DO WITHOUT

Mt 8	15		the fever *left* [Peter's mother-in-law],
22	25		the first [brother] . . . died without children, *leaving* his wife to his brother;
23	38		Your house will *be left* to you desolate,
24	2		not a single stone here will *be left* on another,
	40		of two men in the fields one is taken, one *left*; [41] of two women
	41		at the millstone grinding, one is taken, one *left*.
Mk 1	31		the fever *left* [Peter's mother-in-law]
12	19		(Dt 25 5) if a man's brother dies leaving a wife but *leaving* no child,
	20		The first [brother] . . . died *leaving* no children . . . [22]and
	22		none of the seven *left* any children.

Mk 13	2	Not a single stone will *be left* on another:
Lk 4	39	the fever . . . *left* [Simon's mother-in-law].
13	35	Your house will *be left* to you.
17	34	two will be in one bed: one will be taken, the other *left*;
	35	two women will be grinding corn together: one will be taken, the other *left*.
	36	(ᵛ Two men will be out in the field: one will be taken, the other *left*.)
19	44	[Jerusalem, your enemies] will *leave* not one stone standing on another within you
21	6	the time will come when not a single stone will *be left* on another:
Jn 4	52	The fever *left* him . . . at the seventh hour.
14	27 X	Peace I *bequeath* to you,
Ac 14	17 Θ	[the living God] did not *leave* you without evidence of himself
Rm 1	27	their menfolk have *given up* natural intercourse
Ep 6	9	2 employers, . . . *do without* threats,
Heb 2	8 Θ	[God] has *left* nothing which is not under [the son of man's] command.
6	1	Let us *leave behind* [us] then all the elementary teaching about Christ
Rv 2	4	you ⌐have less love now than you used to (lit. are *leaving behind* your love of former days).

4: GIVE (A CRY) – YIELD UP (ONE'S SPIRIT)

Mt 27	50 X	Jesus, again crying out in a loud voice, *yielded up* his spirit.
Mk 15	37 X	Jesus *gave* a loud cry and breathed his last.

11. DEPARTURE – EXODUS: *EX-(H)ODOS*
ex-(h)odos 3

1: THE EXODUS

Heb 11	22	Joseph recalled the *Exodus* of the Israelites

2: DEPARTURE – PASSING (= DEATH)

Lk 9	31	[Moses and Elijah] were speaking of [Jesus's] ⌐passing (or: *departure*) which he was to accomplish in Jerusalem.
2 P 1	15	after my own *departure* you will still have a means to recall things

12. LEAVE, GO AWAY, MOVE ON: *MET-AIRŌ*
met-airō 2

Mt 13	53 X	When Jesus had finished these parables he *left* the district;
19	1 X	Jesus had now finished what he wanted to say, and he *left* Galilee

13. MOVE – LEAVE – PASS: *BAINŌ*
1 *meta-bainō 12*   2 *para-bainō 3*

1: MOVE, MOVE ON – LEAVE – PASS, PASS ON

Mt 8	34 X	they implored him to *leave* the neighbourhood.
11	1 X	Jesus . . . *moved on* from there to teach and preach
12	9 X	He *moved on* from there and went to their synagogue,
15	29 X	Jesus *went on* from there and reached the shores of the Sea of Galilee,
17	20	you could say to this mountain, 'Move from here to there', and it would *move*;
Lk 10	7	do not *move* from house to house.
Jn 5	24	whoever listens to my words, and believes in the one who sent me, . . . has *passed* from death to life.
O		
7	3 X	Why not *leave* this place and go to Judaea, and let your disciples see the works you are doing;
13	1 X O	Jesus knew that the hour had come for him to *pass* from this world to the Father.
Ac 18	7	Then he *left* the synagogue and moved to the house next door
1 Jn 3	14 O	we have *passed* out of death and into life,

2: ABANDON, DESERT

Mt 15	2	2 Why do your disciples ⌐break away from (or: *desert*) the tradition of the elders?
3		2 And why do you . . . ⌐break away from (or: *desert*) the commandment of God for the sake of your tradition?

Ac 1	25	2 this ministry and apostolate, which Judas *abandoned*

LITTLE

1. Little, Least – Small, Short, Tiny: *mikros*
  a) Little, Small, Least (applied to people) – Short, Young, Low(ly)
  b) a Little (time), a Little while, (a) Short (time)
  c) Small, Smallest, Little (generally) – Tiny
2. a Little – Short(ly), Briefly
  1: a Little – Small, Short – Briefly, For a short while: *brachys*
  2: Momentary, Soon over, Short-lived: *par-autika*
3. a Few, a Little – Short: *oligos*
  a) a Few (people)
  b) Short (time), a Little – For a short while

  c) (a) Few (things) – (a) Little – Small
4. Least – Very small – Inferior: *elachistos*
  a) Least (applied to people), Young, Inferior – Decrease, Grow smaller – Make lower
  b) Least, Very little, Slightest – a Small thing, Trifling, Tiny – Inferior
5. Shortened, Cut short: *koloboō*
6. Grow short, Be short: *sy-stellō*
7. (Have) Less: *hēsson*
8. (Be) Less, (Be) Inferior: *hystereō*
9. Narrow – Constraint – Be restricted: *stenos*
10. Light (in weight): *elaphros*
11. to Lighten (a weight): *kouphizō*

1. LITTLE, LEAST – SMALL, SHORT, TINY: *MIKROS*
2 *mikron 16*   1 *mikros 30*

G = Little, Less, Least // Great, Big

a) Little, Small, Least (applied to people) – Short, Young, Low(ly)

Mt 10	42	If anyone gives . . . water to one of these *little ones* . . . he will . . . not lose his reward.
11	11 G	the *least* in the kingdom of heaven is greater than [John the Baptist] is.
18	6	anyone who is an obstacle to bring down one of these *little ones* who have faith in me would be better drowned
	10	See that you never despise any of these *little ones*,
	14	Similarly, it is never the will of your Father . . . that one of these *little ones* should be lost.
Mk 9	42	anyone who is an obstacle to bring down one of these *little ones* who have faith, would be better thrown into the sea
15	40	Mary . . . the mother of James the *younger* and Joset,
Lk 7	28 G	the *least* in the kingdom of God is greater than [John the Baptist] is.
9	48 G	the *least* among you all, that is the one who is great.
12	32	There is no need to be afraid, *little* flock,
17	2	It would be better for him to be thrown into the sea . . . than that he should lead astray a single one of these *little ones*.
19	3	[Zacchaeus] was too *short* and could not see [Jesus] for the crowd
Ac 8	10 G	everyone believed what [Simon the magician] said; eminent citizens and ⌐ordinary (lit. *lesser*) people alike
26	22 G	I have stood firm to this day, testifying to great and *small* alike,
Heb 8	11 G	(Jr 31 34) they will all know me, the *least* no less than the greatest,
Rv 11	18 G	all who worship you, *small* or great,
13	16 G	[the second beast] compelled everyone – *small* and great . . . – to be branded
19	5 G	all who, great or *small*, revere him.
	18 G	There will be the flesh . . . of all kinds of men [for you] . . . , *small* and great.
20	12 G	I saw the dead, both great and *small*, standing in front of his throne,

b) a Little (time), a Little while, (a) Short (time)

Mt 26	73	2 A *little* later the bystanders came up and said to Peter,
Mk 14	70	2 a *little* later the bystanders . . . said to Peter,
Jn 7	33	I shall remain with you for only a *short* time now;
12	35	The light will be with you only a *little* longer now.
13	33	2 I shall ⌐not be with you much (lit. be with you only a *little*) longer.
14	19	2 In a *short* time the world will no longer see me;
16	16	2/2 In a *short* time you will no longer see me, and then a *short* time later you will see me again. ¹⁷ . . . What does he mean,
	17	
	18	2 'In a *short* time you will no longer see me, and then a *short* time later you will see me again' . . .? ¹⁸ What is
	19	2 this '*short* time'? . . . ¹⁹ Jesus . . . said, 'You are asking
		2 . . . what I meant by saying: In a *short* time you will no
		2 longer see me, and then a *short* time later you will see me again.'

Heb 10 37   2 (Is 26 20) Only a *little* while now, ⌐a very little while (lit.
                 just as long as that, only as long as that), and the one
                 that is coming will have come;
Rv 6 11   [the souls of all the people who had been killed on account
                 of the word of God] were told to be patient a *little* longer,
    20 3   [the dragon] must be released, but only for a *short* while;

c) Small, Smallest, Little (generally) – Tiny

Mt 13 32 G <   [A mustard seed] is the *smallest* of all the seeds,
   26 39   2   going on a *little* further [Jesus] fell on his face and prayed.
Mk 4 31 G <   a mustard seed . . . is the *smallest* of all the seeds on earth;
   14 35   2   going on a *little* further [Jesus] threw himself on the ground
                 and prayed
1 Co 5 6   even a *small amount* of yeast is enough to leaven all the dough,
2 Co 11 1   2 I only wish you were able to tolerate a *little* foolishness from
                 me.
       16   2 let me do a *little* boasting of my own.
Ga 5 9   A *little* yeast seems to be spreading through the whole batch
                 of you.
Jm 3 5 G   So is the tongue only a *tiny* part of the body, but it can proudly
                 claim that it does great things.
Rv 3 8   though ⌐you are not very strong (lit. the strength you can
                 muster is *small*) you have kept my commandments

2. A LITTLE – SHORT(LY), BRIEFLY

1: A LITTLE – SMALL, SHORT – BRIEFLY, FOR A SHORT WHILE: *BRACHYS*

brachys 7

Lk 22 58   *Shortly* afterwards someone else saw [Peter] and said,
Jn 6 7   Two hundred denarii would only buy enough to give them a
                 small [piece] each.
Ac 5 34   [Gamaliel] asked to have the men taken outside for ⌐a time
                 (lit. a *little*).
   27 28   after a *short* interval [the crew] sounded again
Heb 2 7   (Ps 8 6) *For a short while* you made him lower than the angels;
        9   we do see in Jesus one who was *for a short while* made lower
                 than the angels
   13 22   that is why I have written to you so *briefly*.

2: MOMENTARY, SOON OVER, SHORT-LIVED: *PAR-AUTIKA*

par-autika 1

2 Co 4 17   troubles *which are soon over* . . . train us for . . . eternal
                 glory

3. A FEW, A LITTLE – SHORT: *OLIGOS*

1 oligos 35/43   2 oligōs 1

M = Few, Little // Many, Much

a) (a) Few (people)

Mt 7 14 M   it is . . . a hard road that leads to life, and only a *few* find it
    9 37 M   The harvest is rich but the labourers [are] *few*,
   20 16 M   (ᵛ For many are called, but *few* are chosen.)
   22 14 M   For many are called, but *few* are chosen.
Mk 6 5   [Jesus] could work no miracle [in Nazareth], though he cured
                 a *few* sick people
Lk 10 2 M   The harvest is rich but the laboureres [are] *few*,
   13 23   Sir, will there be only a *few* saved?
1 P 3 20   that ark . . . saved only a *small group* [of] eight people
Rv 3 4   There are a *few* in Sardis . . . who have kept their robes from
                 being dirtied,

b) Short (time), a Little – For a short while

Mk 6 31   [Jesus] said to them 'You must . . . rest *for a while*';
Heb 12 10   Our human fathers were thinking of this *short* life
Jm 4 14   you are no more than a mist that is here *for a little* [while]
1 P 1 6   you may *for a short time* have to bear being plagued
    5 10   You will have to suffer only *for a little* [while]: . . . God
                 . . . will . . . support you.
2 P 2 18   2 they tempt back the ones who have only ⌐just (lit. *for a short
                 time*) escaped from paganism,
Rv 12 12   the devil has gone down to [earth and sea] . . . knowing that
                 his ⌐days are numbered (lit. time is *short*).
   17 10   once here he must stay *for a short while*.

c) (a) Few (things) – (a) Little – Small

Mt 15 34   How many loaves have you? Seven . . . and a *few* small fish.
   25 21 M   you have shown you can be faithful in ⌐small (lit. *few*)
                 [things,] I will trust you with ⌐greater (lit. many);

Mt 25 23 M   you have shown you can be faithful in ⌐small (lit. *few*)
                 [things], I will trust you with ⌐greater (lit. many).
Mk 1 19   Going on a *little* further [Jesus] saw James . . . and . . .
                 John;
    8 7   [The disciples] had a *few* small fish as well,
Lk 5 3   [Jesus] asked [Simon] to put out a *little* from the shore.
    7 47 M   the man who is forgiven *little* . . . shows *little* love.
   10 42 M   you worry . . . about so many things and yet *few* are needed,
                 indeed only one.
   12 48 M   The one who did not know . . . will receive *fewer* strokes.
Ac 26 28   A *little* more, and your arguments would make a Christian
                 of me.
      29   'Little' or more,' Paul replied
2 Co 8 15 M   (Ex 16 18) the man who gathered *little* did not go short.
Ep 3 3   I have just described it very *shortly*.
1 Tm 4 8   Physical exercises are ⌐useful enough (lit. of only *little* use)
    5 23   have a *little* wine for the sake of your digestion
Jm 3 5   Think how *small* a flame can set fire to a huge forest;
1 P 5 12   I write these *few* words to you through Silvanus.
Rv 2 14   I have *one or two* complaints to make:

4. LEAST – VERY SMALL – INFERIOR: *ELACHISTOS*

1 elachistos   14   4 elattoneō   1
2 elassōn, elatton 4   3 elattoō   3

G = Little, Less, Least // Great, Big

*a) Least (applied to people), Young, Inferior – Decrease, Grow smaller – Make
                 lower*

Mt 5 19 G   the man who infringes even one of the *least* of these command-
                 ments . . . will be considered the *least* in the kingdom of
                 heaven;
   25 40   in so far as you did this to one of the *least* of these brothers
                 of mine you did it to me.
      45   in so far as you neglected to do this to one of the *least* of
                 these you neglected to do it to me.
Jn 3 30   3   He must grow greater, I must grow *smaller*.
Rm 9 12 G 2   (Gn 25 23) the elder shall serve the *younger*,
1 Co 15 9   I am the *least* of the apostles;
Ep 3 8   I, who am less than the *least* of all the saints,
Heb 2 7 X 3   (Ps 8 6) For a short while you *made* him *lower* than the angels;
      9 X 3   we do see in Jesus one who was for a short while *made lower*
                 than the angels
      7 7 2   a blessing is given by a superior to an *inferior*.

b) Least, Very little, Slightest – a Small thing, Trifling, Tiny – Inferior

Mt 2 6   (Mi 5 1) Bethlehem . . . you are by no means *least* among the
                 leaders of Judah,
    5 19 G   the man who infringes even one of the *least* of these command-
                 ments . . . will be considered the least
Lk 12 26   if the *smallest things* . . . are outside your control, why worry
                 about the rest?
   16 10   The man who can be trusted in *little things* can be trusted in
                 great; the man who is dishonest in *little things* will be
                 dishonest in great.
   19 17   you have proved yourself faithful in a *very small thing*,
Jn 2 10   People generally serve the best wine first, and keep the
        2   ⌐cheaper (lit. *inferior*) sort till the guests have had plenty
                 to drink;
1 Co 4 3   Not that it makes the *slightest* difference to me whether you
                 . . . find me worthy or not.
      6 2   how can you be unfit to judge *trifling* cases?
2 Co 8 15   (Ex 16 18) the man who gathered little did not ⌐go short
        4   (lit. *have too little*).
1 Tm 5 9   Enrolment as a widow is permissible only for a woman at
        2   *least* sixty years old
Jm 3 4 G   the man at the helm can steer [ships] anywhere . . by con-
                 trolling a *tiny* rudder.

5. SHORTENED, CUT SHORT: *KOLOBOŌ*

koloboō 4

Mt 24 22   if that time had not been *shortened*, no one would have
                 survived; but *shortened* that time shall be, for the sake of
                 those who are chosen.
Mk 13 20   if the Lord had not *shortened* that time, no one would have
                 survived; but he did *shorten* the time,

6. GROW SHORT, BE SHORT: *SY-STELLŌ*

sy-stellō 1/2

1 Co 7 29   Brothers, this is what I mean: our time *is growing short*.

7. (HAVE) LESS: *HĒSSON*

1 *hēttaomai, hēssaomai* 1/3   2 *hēsson* 1/2

2 Co 12	13	Is there anything of which you have *had less* than the other churches . . .?
	15	2 Because I love you more, must I be loved the *less*?

8. (BE) LESS, (BE) INFERIOR: *HYSTEREŌ*

hystereō 2/16

2 Co 11	5	As far as I can tell, these arch-apostles have nothing ⌐more than I have (or: that makes me *inferior* to them).
12	11	there is not a thing these arch-apostles have that ⌐I do not have as well (or: *is any less* mine as well).

9. NARROW – CONSTRAINT – BE RESTRICTED: *STENOS*

1 *stenos* 3   2 *steno-chōreō* 3

Mt 7	13	Enter by the *narrow* gate,
	14	it is a *narrow* gate . . . that leads to life,
Lk 13	24	Try your best to enter by the *narrow* door,
2 Co 4	8	2 We are in difficulties on all sides, but never ⌐cornered (or: distressed);
6	12	2/2 Any *constraint* that you feel is not on our side; the *constraint* is in your own selves.

10. LIGHT (IN WEIGHT): *ELAPHROS*

2 *elaphria* 1   1 *elaphros* 2

Mt 11	30	my yoke is easy and my burden *light*.
2 Co 1	17	Do you think I was ⌐not sure of my own intentions (lit. 2 considering things only *lightly*) . . .?
4	17	the troubles . . . though they ⌐weigh little (lit. are *light*), train us for the carrying of a weight of eternal glory

11. TO LIGHTEN (A WEIGHT): *KOUPHIZŌ*

kouphizō 1

Ac 27	38	[the crew] *lightened* the ship by throwing the corn overboard

LONG – BROAD – DEEP

1. **Length, Lengthy, Long:** *makros*
2. **Breadth – Wide, Broad – Broaden,**   **Open wide:** *platos*
   3. **Depth – Deep:** *bathys*

1. LENGTH, LENGTHY, LONG: *MAKROS*

2 *makros*   2/4   1 *mēkos* 3
3 *makro(-chronios)*   1

Mk 12	40	the men who swallow the property of widows, while making 2 a show of *lengthy* prayers.
Lk 20	47	[the scribes] who swallow the property of widows, while 2 making a show of *lengthy* prayers.
Ep 3	18	you will . . . have strength to grasp the breadth and the *length*, the height and the depth;
6	3	3 (Ex 20 12) you will prosper and have a *long* life in the land.
Rv 21	16	The plan of the city is perfectly square, its *length* the same as its breadth.

2. BREADTH – WIDE, BROAD – BROADEN, OPEN WIDE: *PLATOS*

1 *platos* 4   3 *platys* 1
2 *platynō* 3

Mt 7	13	3 the road that leads to perdition is *wide* and spacious,
23	5	2 [the scribes and Pharisees] ⌐wearing (lit. *making*) broader phylacteries
2 Co 6	11	2 Corinthians, . . . our mind has been *opened wide* in front of you.

2 Co 6	13	2 *open* your minds *wide* in the same way.
Ep 3	18 ●	you will . . . have strength to grasp the *breadth* and the length, the height and the depth;
Rv 20	9	they will come swarming over the ⌐entire (lit. *breadth* of the) country
21	16	[the city's] length [is] the same as its *breadth*. . . . it was twelve thousand furlongs in length and in *breadth*, and equal in height.

3. DEPTH – DEEP: *BATHYS*

1 *bathos* 8   2 *bathys* 4
3 *bathynō* 1

Mt 13	5	[some seeds] sprang up straightaway, because there was no *depth* of earth;
Mk 4	5	Some seed . . . sprang up straightaway, because there was no *depth* of earth;
Lk 5	4	Put out into *deep* water
6	48	3 the man who . . . dug, and *dug deep*, and laid the foundations on a rock.
24	1	2 On the first day of the week, at the ⌐first sign (lit. *depth*) of dawn, they went to the tomb
Jn 4	11	2 You have no bucket . . . and the well is *deep*:
Ac 20	9	a young man called Eutychus who was sitting on the window-sill ⌐grew drowsy and was overcome by sleep and (or: fell 2 into a *deep* sleep, and finally, overcome by sleep,) fell to the ground
Rm 8	39 ○	[nothing, not any power] or height or *depth* . . . can ever come between us and the love of God
11	33 ⊖	How rich are the *depths* of God – [how deep] his wisdom and knowledge . . .!
1 Co 2	10 ⊖	the spirit reaches [the depths of] everything, even the *depths* of God.
2 Co 8	2	their constant cheerfulness and their ⌐intense (lit. *depths* of) poverty have overflowed in a wealth of generosity.
Ep 3	18 ●	you will . . . have strength to grasp the breadth and the length, the height and the *depth*;
Rv 2	24 ⓓ	2 all of you who have not . . . learnt the ⌐secrets (lit. *depths*) of Satan,

LOVE

1. Love *agapaō*	**5: Friend – Beloved – Dear**
1: the Love of God	**2. Love – Friend:** *phileō*
a) for his Son – the Beloved	1: the Love of God
b) for others	2: the Love of Jesus – (a) Friend
2: the Love of Jesus	3: the Love of man
3: the Love of man	*a)* for God
a) for God	*b)* for Jesus
b) for Jesus	*c)* for other men – Friend
c) for God and his neighbour	*d)* for various
d) for his neighbour	**3. Love, Affection – Without Love:**
e) for his wife	*stergō*
f) for others	**4. Friend:** *hetairos*
4: Love (generally)	

H = Love // Hate

For Faith, Hope and Love *see* HOPE – EXPECT – WAIT FOR 1.

1. LOVE: *AGAPAŌ*

1 *agapaō*   143   3 *agapētos* 62
2 *agapē* 115/117

1: THE LOVE OF GOD

a) for his Son – the Beloved

Mt 3	17	3 a voice spoke from heaven, 'This is my Son, the *Beloved*; my favour rests on him'.
12	18	(cf. Is 42 1) Here is my servant whom I have chosen, my 3 *beloved*, the favourite of my soul.
17	5	from the cloud there came a voice which said, 'This is my 3 Son, the *Beloved*; he enjoys by favour.'
Mk 1	11	3 a voice came from heaven, 'You are my Son, the *Beloved*; my favour rests on you'.
9	7	there came a voice from the cloud, 'This is my Son, the 3 *Beloved*'.

Mk 12 6 [The owner of the vineyard] had still someone left: his
< 3 *beloved* son. He sent him to them last of all.
Lk 3 22 3 a voice came from heaven, 'You are my Son, the *Beloved*;
my favour rests on you'.
9 35 a voice came from the cloud saying, 'This is my Son, the
3 ⌐Chosen One (ᵛ*Beloved*). Listen to him.'
20 13 the owner of the vineyard said, '. . . I will send them my
< 3 *dear* son.'
Jn 3 35 The Father *loves* the Son and has entrusted everything to
him.
10 17 The Father *loves* me, because I lay down my life in order to
take it up again.
15 9 As the Father has *loved* me, so I have loved you. Remain
in my love.
10 just as I have kept my Father's commandments and remain
in his *love*.
17 23 2/ the world will realise . . . that ᵛI (G you) have loved them
as much as you *loved* me.
24 they may always see the glory you have given me because you
loved me before the foundation of the world.
26 I have made your name known to them . . . so that the
2/ *love* with which you *loved* me may be in them,
Ep 1 6 [Blessed be God who chose us] to make us praise the glory o
his grace, his free gift to us in the *Beloved*.
Col 1 13 [God] has . . . created a place for us in the kingdom of the
2 Son that he *loves*,
2 P 1 17 3 This is my Son, the *Beloved*; he enjoys my favour.

b) for others

Jn 3 16 God *loved* the world so much that he gave his only Son,
14 21 anybody who loves me will be *loved* by my Father, and I shall
love him
23 If anyone loves me . . . my Father will *love* him,
17 23 the world will realise . . . that ᵛI (G you) have *loved* them
as much as you loved me.
Rm 1 7 3 To you all . . . who are God's *beloved* in Rome . . . may
God . . . send grace and peace.
5 8 2 what proves that God *loves* us is that Christ died for us while
we were still sinners.
8 39 [neither death nor life,] nor any created thing, can ever
2 come between us and the *love* of God made visible in Christ
Jesus our Lord.
9 13 H (Ml 1 2) I *showed* my *love* for Jacob and my hatred for Esau.
25 (Ho 2 25) I shall say . . . to a nation I never *loved*, 'I love
you'.
11 28 3 as the chosen people, [the Jews] are still *loved* by God,
[loved] for the sake of their ancestors.
2 Co 9 7 (cf. Pr 22 8 G) God *loves* a cheerful giver.
13 11 2 live in peace, and the God of *love* and peace will be with you.
13 2 The grace of the Lord Jesus Christ, the *love* of God and the
fellowship of the Holy Spirit be with you all.
Ep 2 4 /2 God *loved* us with so much *love* that . . . ⁵ when we were
dead . . . he brought us to life with Christ
5 1 3 Try, then, to imitate God, as children of his that he *loves*,
Col 3 12 You are God's chosen race, his saints; he *loves* you,
1 Th 1 4 We know, brothers, that God *loves* you and that you have
been chosen,
2 Th 2 16 May our Lord Jesus Christ himself, and God our Father
who has *given* us his love . . . ¹⁷ comfort you
Heb 12 6 (Pr 3 12) the Lord trains the ones that he *loves*
1 Jn 3 1 2 Think of the *love* that the Father has lavished on us, by
letting us be called God's children; and that is what we
are.
4 8 Anyone who fails to love can never have known God, because
9 2/2 God is *love*. ⁹ God's *love* for us was revealed when God sent
into the world his only Son so that we could have life
10 through him; ¹⁰ this is the *love* I mean: not our love for
11 God, but God's *love* for us when he sent his Son . . . ¹¹
. . . since God has *loved* us so much, we too should love
one another.
16 2 We ourselves have known and put our faith in God's *love*
2 towards ourselves. God is *love* and anyone who lives in
love lives in God, and God lives in him.
19 We are to love, then, because he *loved* us first.
Jude 1 From Jude . . . to those who are called, to those who are
dear to God the Father and kept safe for Jesus Christ,

2: THE LOVE OF JESUS

Θ = Jesus loves the Father

Mk 10 21 Jesus looked steadily at [the rich young man] and *loved* him,
Jn 11 5 Jesus *loved* Martha and her sister and Lazarus,
13 1 Jesus . . . had always *loved* those who were his . . . but now
he showed how perfect his *love* was.
23 The disciple Jesus *loved* was reclining next to Jesus;
34 love one another; just as I have *loved* you, you also must
love one another.

Jn 14 21 anybody who loves me will be loved by my Father, and I
shall *love* him
31 Θ the world must be brought to know that I *love* the Father
15 9 As the Father has loved me, so I have *loved* you. Remain in
10 2 my *love*. ¹⁰ If you keep my commandments you will remain
2 in my *love*, just as I have kept my Father's commandments
and remain in his love.
12 love one another, as I have *loved* you. ¹³ A man can have no
13 2 greater *love* than to lay down his life for his friends.
17 23 the world will realise . . . that ᵛI (G you) have *loved* them as
much as you loved me.
19 26 Seeing his mother and the disciple he *loved* standing near
her, Jesus said
21 7 The disciple Jesus *loved* said to Peter, 'It is the Lord'.
20 Peter turned and saw the disciple Jesus *loved* following them
Rm 8 35 2 Nothing . . . can come between us and the *love* of Christ,
37 we triumph by the power of him who *loved* us.
2 Co 5 14 2 the *love* of Christ overwhelms us when we reflect that if one
man has died for all, then all men should be dead;
Ga 2 20 I live in faith . . . in the Son of God who *loved* me and who
sacrificed himself for my sake.
Ep 3 19 2 the *love* of Christ . . . is beyond all knowledge,
5 2 follow Christ by loving as he *loved* you, giving himself up
in our place
25 Husbands should love their wives just as Christ *loved* the
Church and sacrificed himself for her
2 Th 2 13 brothers whom the Lord *loves*, . . . God chose you from the
beginning
Heb 1 9 H [God says to his Son,] (Ps 45 8) virtue you *love* as much as
you hate wickedness.
1 Jn 3 16 2 This has taught us *love* – that he gave up his life for us;
Rv 1 5 [Jesus Christ] *loves* us and has washed away our sins with
his blood,
3 9 I am going to make the synagogue of Satan . . . admit that
you are the people that I *love*.

3: THE LOVE OF MAN

a) for God

Lk 11 42 alas for you Pharisees! You . . . overlook justice and the
2 *love* of God!
Jn 5 42 2 I know you too well: you have no *love* of God in you.
Rm 8 28 God co-operates with all those who *love* him,
1 Co 2 9 we teach . . . all that God has prepared for those who *love*
him.
8 3 2 any man who *loves* God is known by him.
2 Th 3 5 2 May the Lord turn your hearts towards the *love* of God and
the fortitude of Christ.
Jm 1 12 He has proved himself, and will win . . . the crown that the
Lord has promised to those who *love* him.
2 5 it was those who are poor . . . that God chose . . . to be the
heirs to the kingdom which he promised to those who *love*
him.
1 Jn 4 10 this is the love I mean: not our *love* for God, but God's love
for us when he sent his Son

b) for Jesus

Jn 8 42 If God were your father, you would *love* me, since I have come
here from God;
14 15 If you *love* me you will keep my commandments.
21 Anybody who receives my commandments and keeps them
will be one who loves me; and anybody who *loves* me will
be loved by my Father, and I shall love him
23 If anyone *loves* me he will keep my word, and my Father will
love him,
24 Those who do not *love* me do not keep my words.
28 If you *loved* me you would have been glad to know that I am
going to the Father,
21 15 Simon son of John, do you *love* me more than these others do?
16 A second time he said to him, 'Simon son of John, do you
love me?
2 Co 5 14 2 the *love* of Christ overwhelms us
Ep 6 24 May grace and eternal life be with all who *love* our Lord Jesus
Christ.
Phm 5 2 I hear of the *love* and the faith which you have for the Lord
Jesus and for all the saints.
1 P 1 8 You did not see him, yet you *love* him;

c) for God and his neighbour

Mt 22 37 (Dt 6 5) You must *love* the Lord your God with all your
heart, with all your soul, and with all your mind. ³⁸ This is
the greatest and the first commandment. ³⁹ The second
39 resembles it (Lv 19 18): You must *love* your neighbour as
yourself. ⁴⁰ On these two commandments hang the whole
Law, and the Prophets also.

Mk 12	30	[this is the first commandment:] (Dt 6 5) you must *love* the Lord your God . . .³¹ The second is this (Lv 19 18): You
	31	must *love* your neighbour as yourself . . . ³² The scribe
	33	said to him, 'Well spoken . . .³³ To *love* him with all your heart, with all your understanding and strength, and to *love* your neighbour as yourself, this is far more important than any holocaust or sacrifice.'
Lk 10	27	(Dt 6 5) You must *love* the Lord your God . . . (Lv 19 18) and your neighbour as yourself.
1 Co 16	14	2 Let everything you do be done in *love*.
Heb 6	10	2 God would not . . . forget . . . the *love* that you have for his name or the services you have done . . . for the saints.
1 Jn 4	20 H	Anyone who says, 'I *love* God', and hates his brother, is a liar, since a man who does not *love* the brother that he can see cannot *love* God, whom he has never seen. ²¹ So
	21	this is the commandment that he has given us, that anyone who *loves* God must also *love* his brother.
5	1	whoever *loves* the Father that begot him *loves* the child
	2	whom he begets. ² We can be sure that we *love* God's
	3	children if we *love* God himself and do what he has com- 2 manded us; ³ this is what *loving* God is – keeping his commandments;

d) for his neighbour

Mt 5	43 H	it was said (Lv 19 18): You must *love* your neighbour and
	44 H	hate your enemy. ⁴⁴ But I say this to you: *love* your enemies
	46	. . .⁴⁶ For if you *love* those who *love* you, what right have you to claim any credit?
19	19	(Lv 19 18) you must *love* your neighbour as yourself.
Lk 6	27 H	*Love* your enemies, do good to those who hate you . . .³² If
	32	you *love* those who *love* you, what thanks can you expect?
	35 H	Even sinners *love* those who *love* them . . . ³⁵ Instead, *love* your enemies
Jn 13	34	*love* one another; just as I have loved you, you also must
	35	/2 *love* one another. ³⁵ By this *love* you have for one another, everyone will know that you are my disciples.
15	12	*love* one another, as I have loved you. ¹³ A man can have no
	13	2 greater *love* than to lay down his life for his friends . . .
	17	¹⁷ What I command you is to *love* one another.
Rm 12	9	2 Do not let your *love* be a pretence, . . .¹⁰ Love each other as much as brothers should,
13	8	Avoid getting into debt, except the debt of mutual *love*. If you *love* your fellow men you have carried out your
	9	obligations. ⁹ All the commandments . . are summed up in this single command (Lv 19 18): You must *love* your
	10	2 neighbour as yourself. ¹⁰ *Love* is the one thing that cannot 2 hurt your neighbour; that is why ⌐it (lit. *love*) is the answer to every one of the commandments.
14	15	if your attitude to food is upsetting your brother, then you 2 are hardly being guided by *charity*.
1 Co 4	21	2 do I come with a stick in my hand or in a spirit of *love* . . .?
16	24	2 My *love* is with you all in Christ Jesus.
2 Co 2	4	2 I wrote . . . to let you know how much *love* I have for you.
	8	2 I am asking you to give some definite proof of your *love* for [the man in question].
11	11	Would I do that if I did not *love* you? God knows I do.
12	15	Because I *love* you more, must I be *loved* the less?
Ga 5	13	2 Serve one another . . . in works of *love*, ¹⁴ since the whole of
	14	the Law is summarised in a single command (Lv 19 18): *Love* your neighbour as yourself.
Ep 1	15	2 I, having once heard about . . . the *love* that you show towards all the saints, [have never failed to remember you in my prayers]
4	2	2 Bear with one another *charitably*, in complete selflessness,
5	2	2 follow Christ by *loving* as he loved you,
Col 1	4	2 we heard about . . . the *love* that you show towards all the saints
1 Th 3	12	2 May the Lord be generous in increasing your *love*
4	9	you have learnt from God yourselves to *love* one another,
5	13	2 Have the greatest respect and *affection* for [those who are above you in the Lord]
2 Th 1	3	2 the *love* that you have for one another never stops increasing;
Phm	5	2 I hear of the *love* and the faith which you have for the Lord Jesus and for all the saints.
	7	2 I am so delighted, and comforted, to know of your *love*;
	9	2 I am appealing to your *love* instead,
Jm 2	8	the supreme law of scripture (Lv 19 18): you must *love* your neighbour as yourself;
1 P 1	22	let your *love* for each other be real and from the heart –
2	17	*Have* . . . *love* for our community; fear God and honour the emperor.
4	8	2 never let your *love* for each other grow insincere, since *love* 2 covers over many a sin.
5	14	2 Greet one another with a kiss of *love*.
2 P 1	7	[you will have to do your utmost, adding] kindness towards your fellow men to your devotion, and, to this kindness, 2 *love*.
1 Jn 2	10 H	anyone who *loves* his brother is living in the light
3	10	anybody . . . not *loving* his brother is no child of God's.

1 Jn 3	11	we are to *love* one another;
	14 H	we have passed out of death and into life . . . because we *love* our brothers. If you refuse to *love*, you must remain dead;
	18	our *love* is not to be just words or mere talk, but something real and active;
	23	His commandments are these: that we believe in the name of his Son . . . and that we *love* one another
4	7	let us *love* one another since love comes from God and everyone who *loves* is begotten by God and knows God.
	8	⁸Anyone who fails to *love* can never have known God, because God is love.
	11	since God has loved us so much, we too should *love* one
	12	another. ¹² . . . as long as we *love* one another God will live in us
	19	We are to *love*, then, because he loved us first.
2 Jn	1	From the Elder: my greetings to the Lady, the chosen one, and to her children, she whom I *love* in the truth –
	5	I am writing now . . . to plead: let us *love* one another.
3 Jn	1	to my dear friend Gaius, whom I *love* in the truth.

e) for his wife

Ep 5	25	Husbands should *love* their wives just as Christ loved the Church
	28 H	husbands must *love* their wives as [they love] their own bodies; for a man to *love* his wife is for him to love himself.
	33	each one of you must *love* his wife as he loves himself;
Col 3	19	Husbands, *love* your wives and treat them with gentleness.

f) for others

Mt 6	24 H <	No one can be the slave of two masters: he will either hate the first and *love* the second,
Lk 7	5	[this centurion] *is friendly towards* our people;
	42 <	[A creditor had two men in his debt,] he pardoned them both. Which of them will *love* him more?
11	43	Pharisees . . . *like* taking the seats of honour in the synagogues
16	13 H <	No servant can be the slave of two masters: he will either hate the first and *love* the second,
Jn 3	19 H	men have shown they *prefer* darkness to the light
12	43	[there were many who did believe in Jesus, but they did not admit it,] they ⌐put (lit. *loved*) honour from men before the honour that comes from God.
Ep 5	28 H	for a man to love his wife is for him to *love* himself.
2 Th 2	10	[Satan will] deceive those who are bound for destruction 2 because they would not grasp the *love* of the truth
2 Tm 4	8	the Lord . . . will give [the crown of righteousness] . . . to all those who have ⌐ longed for (lit. *loved*) his Appearing.
	10	Demas has deserted me for *love* of this life
1 P 3	10	(Ps 34 13) Anyone who wants to ⌐have a happy (lit. *love*) life . . . must banish malice from his tongue.
2 P 2	15	Balaam . . . ⌐thought he could profit best (lit. *loved* to profit) by sinning,
1 Jn 2	15	You must not *love* this passing world or anything that is in the world. The love of the Father cannot be in any man who *loves* the world,
Rv 12	11	even in the face of death [our brothers] ⌐would not cling to life (lit. did not *love* their life).

4: LOVE (GENERALLY)

Mt 24	12	2 with the increase of lawlessness, *love* in most men will grow cold;
Lk 7	47	her many sins must have been forgiven her, or she would not have shown such great *love*. It is the man who is forgiven little who shows little *love*.
Rm 5	5	2 the *love* of God has been poured into our hearts by the Holy Spirit which has been given us.
15	30	2 by our Lord Jesus Christ and the *love* of the Spirit . . . help me . . . by praying to God for me.
1 Co 8	1	2 knowledge gives self-importance – it is *love* that makes the building grow.
13	1	If I have all the eloquence of men or of angels, but speak
	2	2 without *love*, I am simply a gong booming . . . ² If I have 2 the gift of prophecy . . . but without *love*, then I am nothing at all. ³ If I give away all that I possess . . . but
	3	
	4	2/2 am without *love*, it will do me no good whatever. ⁴ *Love* is 2 always patient and (§ *love* is always) kind; it is never
	8	2/2 jealous; *love* is never boastful or conceited . . . ⁸ *Love* does not come to an end.
	13	In short, there are three things that last: faith, hope and 2/2 *love*; and the greatest of these is *love*.
14	1	2 You must want *love* more than anything else;
2 Co 6	6	We prove we are God's servants by our purity . . . by a 2 *love* free from affection;
8	7	You always have the most of everything – of faith, . . . and 2 the biggest share of our *affection* –
	8	2 I am just testing the genuineness of your *love*
	24	2 in front of all the churches, give them a proof of your *love*.

Ga 5 6   in Christ Jesus whether you are circumcised or not makes no difference – what matters is faith that makes its power 2 felt through *love*.

22 H 2 What the Spirit brings is very different: *love*, joy, peace,

Ep 1 4   [God] chose us . . . to be holy and spotless, and to live 2 through *love* in his presence,

3 17 2 planted in love and built on *love*, you will have strength

4 15 2 If we live by the truth and in *love*, we shall grow . . . into 16   Christ, who is the head ¹⁶ by whom the whole body is 2 . . . joined together . . . until it has built itself up, in *love*.

6 23 2 May God . . . and the Lord Jesus Christ grant peace, *love* and faith to all the brothers.

Ph 1 9 2 My prayer is that your *love* for each other may increase . . . improving your knowledge

16 2 [the rest of the brothers preach] out of nothing but *love*, as they know that this is my invariable way of defending the gospel.

2 1 2 If our life in Christ means anything to you, if *love* can 2 2 persuade at all, . . . ² . . . be united . . . in your *love*, with a common purpose and a common mind.

Col 1 8 2 [Epaphras] told us all about your *love* in the Spirit.

2 2 2 It is all to bind you together in *love* . . . so that your understanding may come to full development,

3 14   Over all these clothes, to keep them together and complete 2 them, put on *love*,

1 Th 1 3   [We] constantly remember . . . how you have shown your 2 faith in action, worked for *love* and persevered through hope,

3 6   Timothy . . . has given us good news of your faith and your 2 *love*,

5 8 2 let us put on faith and *love* for a breastplate, and the hope of salvation for a helmet.

1 Tm 1 5 2 there should be *love*, coming out of a pure heart, a clear conscience and a sincere faith.

14   the grace of our Lord filled me with faith and with the 2 *love* that is in Christ Jesus.

2 15   [a woman] will be saved by childbearing, provided she lives 2 a modest life and is constant in faith and *love*

4 12 2 be an example to all the believers . . . in your *love*, your faith and your purity.

6 11   You must aim to be saintly and religious, filled with faith 2 and *love*, patient and gentle.

2 Tm 1 7 2 God's gift was . . . the Spirit of power, and *love*, and self-control.

13   Keep as your pattern the sound teaching you have heard 2 from me, in the faith and *love* that are in Christ Jesus.

2 22 2 fasten your attention on holiness, faith, *love* and peace,

3 10   You know . . . what I have aimed at; . . . my faith, my 2 patience and my *love*;

Tt 2 2 2 The older men should be . . . sound in faith and *love* and constancy.

Heb 10 24 2 Let us . . . stir a response in *love* and good works.

1 Jn 2 5 2 when anyone does obey what he has said, God's *love* comes to perfection in him.

15 2 The *love* of the Father cannot be in any man who loves the world,

3 17   If a man . . . saw that one of his brothers was in need, but 2 closed his heart to him, how could the *love* of God be living in him?

4 7 2 let us love one another since *love* comes from God and everyone who loves is begotten by God and knows God.

12   as long as we love one another God will live in us and his 2 *love* will be complete in us.

16 2 God is love and anyone who lives in *love* lives in God, and God lives in him.

17 2 *Love* will come to its perfection in us when we can face the 18 2 day of Judgement without fear; . . . ¹⁸ In *love* there can 2 be no fear, but fear is driven out by perfect *love*: because 2 . . . anyone who is afraid is still imperfect in *love*.

2 Jn 3 2 In our life of truth and *love*, we shall have grace, mercy and peace

6 2 To *love* is to live according to [God's] commandments: this is the commandment . . . to live a life ^rof love (lit. in him).

3 Jn 6   [These brothers] are a proof to the whole Church of your 2 charity

Jude 2 2 wishing you all mercy and peace and *love*.

21 2 keep yourselves within the *love* of God

Rv 2 4 H 2 I have this complaint to make: you have less *love* now than you used to.

19 2 I know all about you and how *charitable* you are; I know your faith and devotion

20 9   they will . . . besiege the camp of the saints, which is the ^rcity that God *loves* (or: *beloved* city).

5: FRIEND – BELOVED – DEAR

Ac 15 25   [we are sending delegates] to you with Barnabas and Paul, 3 men we *highly respect*

Rm 12 19 3 Never try to get revenge; leave that, [my] *friends*, to God's anger.

16 5 3 Greetings to my *friend* Epaenetus,

8 3 [Greetings] to Ampliatus, my *friend* in the Lord;

9 3 [Greetings] to Urban . . . to my *friend* Stachys;

12 3 [Greetings] to my *friend* Persis

1 Co 4 14 3 I am saying all this . . . to bring you, as my *dearest* children, to your senses.

17 3 Timothy, my *dear* and faithful son in the Lord:

10 14 3 This is the reason, my *dear* [brothers], why you must keep clear of idolatry.

15 58 3 Never give in then, my *dear* brothers, never admit defeat;

2 Co 7 1 3 With promises like these made to us, *dear* brothers, let us wash off all that can soil either body or spirit,

12 19 3 it is all, my *dear* brothers, for your benefit.

Ep 6 21 3 my *dear* brother Tychicus . . . will tell you everything.

Ph 2 12 3 my *dear friends*, . . . work for your salvation

4 1 3 my brothers and *dear friends*, . . . remain faithful in the Lord. 3 I miss you very much, *dear friends*;

Col 1 7 3 Epaphras, who taught you, is one of our ^rclosest (lit. *beloved*) fellow workers

4 7   Tychicus will tell you all the news . . . He is a brother I 3 love very much,

9 3 With [Tychicus] I am sending Onesimus, that *dear* and faithful brother

14 3 Greetings from my *dear friend* Luke, the doctor,

1 Th 2 8 3 we . . . had come to *love* you so much,

1 Tm 6 2   those who have the benefit of [slaves'] services are believers 3 and *dear* to God.

2 Tm 1 2 3 [From Paul, appointed by God,] to Timothy, *dear* child of mine,

Phm 1 3 [From Paul,] to our *dear* fellow worker Philemon,

16 3 [You could have Onesimus back] as . . . a *dear* brother; especially [dear] to me,

Heb 6 9 3 you, [my] *dear* [people] . . . are in a better state

Jm 1 16 3 Make no mistake about this, my *dear* brothers:

19 3 Remember this, my *dear* brothers:

2 5 3 Listen, my *dear* brothers:

1 P 2 11 3 I urge you, [my] *dear* [people] . . . to keep yourselves free from the selfish passions

4 12 3 [My] *dear* [people], you must not think it unaccountable that you should be tested by fire.

2 P 3 1 3 [My] *friends*, this is my second letter to you,

8 3 there is one thing, [my] *friends*, that you must never forget:

14 3 So then, [my] *friends*, . . . do your best to live lives without spot or stain

15 3 our brother Paul, who is so *dear* to us, told you this when he wrote to you

17 3 You have been warned about this, [my] *friends*; be careful

1 Jn 2 7 3 [My] *dear* [people], this is not a new commandment

3 2 3 [My] *dear* [people], we are already the children of God

21 3 [My] *dear* [people], if we cannot be condemned by our own conscience, we need not be afraid in God's presence,

4 1 3 It is not every spirit, [my] *dear* [people], that you can trust;

7 3 [My] *dear* [people], let us love one another

11 3 [My] *dear* [people], . . . God has loved us so much,

3 Jn 1 3 From the Elder: greetings to [my] *dear friend* Gaius,

2 3 [My] *dear friend*, I hope everything is going happily with you

5 3 [My] *friend*, you have done faithful work

11 3 [My] *dear friends*, never follow such a bad example,

Jude 3 3 [My] *dear friends*, . . . I was eagerly looking forward to writing to you

17 3 remember, [my] *dear friends*, what the apostles of our Lord Jesus Christ told you to expect.

20 3 you, [my] *dear friends*, must use your . . . faith as your foundation and build on that,

2. LOVE – FRIEND: *PHILEŌ*

2	*phileō*	22/25	10	*phil(-anthrōpos)*	1
5	*philia*	1	11	*phil-autos*	1
1	*philos*	29	12	*phil(-(h)ēdonos)*	1
3	*phil(-adelphia)*	6	13	*philo-phronōs*	1
6	*phil(-adelphos)*	1	14	*philo(-prōteuō)*	1
7	*phil(-agathos)*	1	15	*philo(-teknos)*	1
8	*a-phil(-agathos)*	1	16	*philo(-theos)*	1
9	*phil(-andros)*	1	17	*pros-philēs*	1
4	*phil(-anthrōpia)*	2			

1: THE LOVE OF GOD

Jn 5 20 2 the Father *loves* the Son and shows him everything he does himself,

16 27 2 the Father himself *loves* you for loving me

Tt 3 4 4 the kindness and *love* of God our saviour for mankind were revealed,

Jm 2 23   Abraham put his faith in God, and . . . he was called 'the *friend* of God'.

2: THE LOVE OF JESUS – (A) FRIEND

Mt 11 19   The Son of Man came, eating . . . and they say, 'Look, . . . a *friend* of tax collectors and sinners'.
Lk 7 34   Look, . . . a *friend* of tax collectors and sinners.
   12 4   To you my *friends* I say: Do not be afraid of those who kill the body
Jn 3 29   the bridegroom's *friend* . . . is glad when he hears the bridegroom's voice.
   11 3   2 Lord, the man you *love* is ill.
      11   Our *friend* Lazarus is resting, I am going to wake him.
      36   2 the Jews said, 'See how much he *loved* him!'
   15 13   no greater love than to lay down his life for his *friends*.
      14   You are my *friends*, if you do what I command you.
      15   I call you *friends*, because I have made known to you everything I have learnt from my Father.
   20 2   [Mary of Magdala] came running to Simon Peter and the
      2   other disciple, the one Jesus *loved*.
Rv 3 19   2 I am the one who reproves and disciplines all those he *loves*:

3: THE LOVE OF MAN

a) for God

2 Tm 3 4   16 [People] preferring their own pleasure to being *lovers* of God.

b) for Jesus

Jn 16 27   2 the Father himself loves you for *loving* me
   21 15   2 Yes Lord, you know I *love* you.
      16   2 Yes, Lord, you know I *love* you.
      17   2 'Simon son of John, do you *love* me?' Peter was upset that he
      2   asked him the third time, 'Do you *love* me?' and said,
      2   'Lord, . . . you know I *love* you'.
1 Co 16 22 2 If anyone does not *love* the Lord, a curse on him.

c) for other men – Friend

Mt 10 37   2 Anyone who *prefers* father or mother to me is not worthy
      2   of me. Anyone who *prefers* son or daughter to me is not worthy of me.
Lk 7 6   the centurion sent word to [Jesus] by some *friends*:
   11 5   Suppose one of you has a *friend* and goes to him . . . to say,
      6   'My *friend*, lend me three loaves, 6 because a *friend* of
      8   mine on his travels has just arrived . . .' 8 I tell you, if the man does not get up and give it him for *friendship's* sake, persistence will be enough to make him get up
   14 10   [My] *friend*, move up higher.
      12   When you give a lunch . . . do not ask your *friends*, brothers,
   15 6   [What man among you] when he got home, [would not] call together his *friends* and neighbours?
      9   [What woman] when she had found [the drachma, would not] call together her *friends* and neighbours?
      29   you never offered me so much as a kid for me to celebrate with my *friends*.
   16 9   use money, tainted as it is, to win you *friends*,
   21 16   You will be betrayed even by parents . . . and *friends*;
   23 12 H   though Herod and Pilate had been enemies before, they ┌were reconciled (lit. became *friends*) that same day.
Jn 15 13   no greater love than to lay down his life for his *friends*.
   19 12   If you set [Jesus] free you are no *friend* of Caesar's;
Ac 10 24   Cornelius . . . had asked his relations and close *friends* to be there,
   19 31   some of the Asiarchs . . . were *friends* of [Paul],
   27 3   10 Julius ┌was considerate (lit. had *love* for his fellow-man) enough to allow Paul to go to his *friends*
   28 2   The inhabitants [of Malta] treated us with unusual ┌kindness
      4   (lit. *friendliness*).
      7   Publius . . . received us and entertained us ┌hospitably (lit.
      13   in the greatest *friendship*) for three days.
Rm 12 10   3 Love each other as much as brothers should *love*, and have a profound respect for each other.
1 Th 4 9   3 As for *loving* our brothers, there is no need for anyone to write to you about that,
Tt 2 4   [the older women should] show the younger women how they
      9/15   should *love* their husbands and *love* their children,
   3 15   2 Greetings to those who *love* us in the faith.
Heb 13 1   3 Continue to *love* each other like brothers,
1 P 1 22   3 You have . . . purified your souls until you can *love* like brothers, in sincerity;
   3 8   6 be sympathetic; *love* the brothers, have compassion
2 P 1 7   3 [add] *kindness* towards your fellow men to your devotion, and,
      3   to this *kindness*, love.
3 Jn 15   greetings from your *friends*; greet each of our *friends* by name.

d) for various

Mt 6 5   2 the hypocrites . . . *love* to say their prayers standing up in the synagogues
   23 6   2 [scribes and Pharisees,] ┌wanting (lit. *loving*) to take the place of honour at banquets
Lk 20 46   2 the scribes . . . *love* to be greeted obsequiously
Jn 12 25 H 2 Anyone who *loves* his life loses it; anyone who hates his life in this world will keep it for the eternal life.
   15 19 H   2 If you belonged to the world, the world would *love* you as its own; but because you do not belong to the world . . . the world hates you.
Ph 4 8   fill your minds with everything that is true, . . . everything
      17   that we *love* and honour,
2 Tm 3 2   11 People will ┌be self-centred (lit. *love themselves*) and [be]
      3   8 grasping . . . ³ heartless . . . and *enemies* of everything
      4   12 that is good; ⁴ they will be treacherous . . . *preferring* their own pleasure to being lovers of God.
Tt 1 8   7 [an elder must be] hospitable and a *friend* of all that is good;
Jm 4 4 H   5 making the world your *friend* is making God your enemy. Anyone who chooses the world for his *friend* turns himself into God's enemy.
3 Jn 9   14 Diotrephes . . . *seems to enjoy* being in charge of [the church].
Rv 22 15   These others must stay outside: . . . everyone of false speech
      2   and ┌false life (lit. who *loves* wrongdoing).

3. LOVE, AFFECTION – WITHOUT LOVE: STERGŌ

1 *a-storgos* 2   2 *philo-storgos* 1

Rm 1 31   [the pagans are] *without* brains, honour, *love* or pity.
   12 10   2 *Love* each other as much as brothers should love, and have a profound respect for each other.
2 Tm 3 3   [People will be] *heartless* and unappeasable;

4. FRIEND: HETAIROS

hetairos 4

Mt 11 16   like children shouting to ┌each other (their ▽ *friends*)
   20 13   My *friend*, I am not being unjust to you;
   22 12   How did you get in here, my *friend*, without a wedding garment?
   26 50   Jesus said to [Judas], 'My *friend*, do what you are here for'.

LUXURY – WANTONNESS

1. Luxury – Dissipation – Amuse oneself	2. Pleasure, Self-indulgence – Luxury: *spatalaō*
1: Luxury – Dissipation – Amuse oneself: *tryphē*	3. Wanton, Wantonness – Debauchery, Orgy – Luxury: *strēniaō*
2: Amuse oneself, Play: *paizō*	

1. LUXURY – DISSIPATION – AMUSE ONESELF

1: LUXURY – DISSIPATION – AMUSE ONESELF: TRYPHĒ

2 *tryphaō* 1   3 *en-tryphaō* 1
1 *tryphē* 2

Lk 7 25   those who . . . live *luxuriously* are to be found at court!
Jm 5 5   2 [an answer for the rich:] On earth you have *had a life of comfort* and luxury;
2 P 2 13   They are . . . men whose ┌only object (lit. idea of pleasure)
      /3   is *dissipation* all day long, and they *amuse themselves* deceiving you

2: AMUSE ONESELF, PLAY: PAIZŌ

paizō 1

1 Co 10 7   (Ex 32 6) After sitting down to eat and drink, the people got up to *amuse themselves*.

2. PLEASURE, SELF-INDULGENCE – LUXURY: SPATALAŌ

spatalaō 2

1 Tm 5 6   The [widow] who ┌*thinks only of pleasure* (or: is *self-indulgent*) is already dead

Jm 5 5   [an answer for the rich:] On earth you have *had a life of* comfort and ⸢*luxury* (or: *pleasure*);

3. WANTON, WANTONNESS – DEBAUCHERY, ORGY – LUXURY: *STRĒNIAŌ*

1 *strēniaō* 2   3 *kata-strēniaō* 1
2 *strēnos* 1

1 Tm 5 11

Rv 18 3
7
9

3 Do not accept young widows because if ⸢their *natural desires*
3   *get stronger* than (or: they *grow wanton* above) their dedication to Christ, they want to marry again,
every merchant [has] grown rich through [Babylon's]
2   *debauchery* (or: *wantonness*) . . . ⁷ Every one of her shows and *orgies* is to be matched by a torture . . . ⁹ There will be mourning and weeping for her by the kings of the earth who have fornicated with her and ⸢*lived* with her *in luxury* (or: have *been wanton* with her).

M

MAGIC	MAN – PEOPLE – WOMAN

1. Put a spell on, Bewitch: *baskainō*
2. Magic (arts): *peri-ergos*
3. Magi, Astrologers, Wise men – Magician, Sorcerer – Magic: *mageia*
4. Sorcery, Witchcraft – Sorcerers, Fortune-tellers: *pharmakeia*
5. Soothsaying – Telling fortunes: *pythōn* and *manteuomai*

1. Adam and Eve
2. Man, Men – People: *anthrōpos*
  1: Man = Adam
  2: Man, in relation to woman
  3: Individual Men
    a) Man = Jesus
    b) Individual Men known by name
    c) Individual Men unnamed
    d) Men = Citizens, People of a place – Man of a race
  4: Man = Self, Nature
  5: Man of God, Man dedicated to God
  6: Man, Human(ity) – People, Everybody, Everyone – Someone, Anybody
3. Man, Men: *anēr*
  1: Man, Men, distinct from woman
  2: Man as a Husband
  3: Individual Men
    a) Man = Jesus
    b) Individual Men known by name
    c) Men = Citizens, People of a place – Men of a race
    d) 'Brother-Men' = Brothers! Friends!
  4: Man, Men (generally)
4. Woman – Wife: *gynē*
  1: Woman
  2: Woman as a Wife or Widow
5. Male, Men(folk) and Female, Women: *arsēn* and *thēlys*
6. People, Crowds: *ochlos*
7. People: *laos*
  1: People(s), Nations, Tribes
  2: (the) People (of Israel, of God)
  3: People (generally)
8. (the) People, People's Assembly – Publicly, In public: *dēmos*
9. Nation: *ethnos*
  1: Nation(s)
  2: (the) Nation, People (of Israel, of God)
  3: Nation(s) = Pagans, Gentiles, Heathen

1. PUT A SPELL ON, BEWITCH: *BASKAINŌ*
baskainō 1

Ga	3 1	Are you people in Galatia mad? Has someone *put a spell on* you,

2. MAGIC (ARTS): *PERI-ERGOS*
peri-ergos 1/2

Ac	19 19	a number of [the believers] who had practised *magic* collected their books and made a bonfire of them in public.

3. MAGI, ASTROLOGERS, WISE MEN – MAGICIAN, SORCERER – MAGIC: *MAGEIA*

2 *mageia 1*	*Bar-jesus 1*
3 *mageuō 1*	= *Elymas 1*
1 *magos 6*	

Mt	2 1	some *wise men* came to Jerusalem from the east.
	7	Herod summoned the *wise men* to see him privately.
	16	Herod was furious when he realised that he had been out-witted by the *wise men*, and . . . had all the male children killed who were two years old or under, reckoning by the date he had been careful to ask the *wise men*.
Ac	8 9	3 Simon had already *practised magic arts* in the town and
	11	astounded the Samaritan people . . . [11] They had only been won over to him because of the long time he had
	2	spent working on them with his *magic*.
	13 6	at Paphos [Paul and Barnabas] came in contact with a Jewish *magician* called *Bar-jesus* . . . [8] . . . *Elymas*
	8	⌜*Magos* (or: the *sorcerer*) – as he was called in Greek – tried to . . . prevent the proconsul's conversion to the faith.

4. SORCERY, WITCHCRAFT – SORCERERS, FORTUNE-TELLERS: *PHARMAKEIA*

1 *pharmakeia 3*	2 *pharmakos 2*

Ga	5 20	[The results of self-indulgence are obvious:] idolatry, *sorcery*;
Rv	9 21	Nor did [the people] give up their murdering, or *witchcraft*,
	18 23	[Babylon,] all the nations were ⌜under your spell (lit. deceived by your *sorcery*).
	21 8	2 the legacy for cowards . . . for *fortune-tellers*, idolaters . . . is the second death in the burning lake
	22 15	2 These others must stay outside: dogs, *fortune-tellers*,

5. SOOTHSAYING – TELLING FORTUNES: *PYTHŌN* and *MANTEUOMAI*

1 *pythōn 1*	2 *manteuomai 1*

Ac	16 16	we met a slave-girl who was ⌜a soothsayer (lit. possessed by a spirit of *soothsaying*) and made a lot of money for her
	2	masters by *telling fortunes*.

1. ADAM AND EVE
Adam 9   E *Eve 2*

Lk	3 38	[Jesus, son of Joseph, . . .] son of *Adam*, son of God.
Rm	5 14	death reigned over all from *Adam* to Moses, even though their sin, unlike that of *Adam*, was not a matter of breaking a law. [Adam] prefigured the One to come,
1 Co	15 22	Just as all men die in *Adam*, so all men will be brought to life in Christ;
	45 X	The first man, *Adam* . . . became a living soul; but the last *Adam* has become a life-giving spirit.
2 Co	11 3 E	the serpent, with his cunning, seduced *Eve*,
1 Tm	2 13 E	*Adam* was formed first and *Eve* afterwards, [14] and it was not
	14	*Adam* who was led astray but the woman
Jude	14	Enoch, the seventh patriarch from *Adam*,

2. MAN, MEN – PEOPLE: *ANTHRŌPOS*

2 *anthrōpinos*	7	3 *anthrōpo(-ktonos)*	3
1 *anthrōpos*	464/552	5 (*phil-*)*anthrōpia*	2
4 *anthrōp(-areskos)*	2	6 (*phil-*)*anthrōpōs*	1

Θ = Man // God (the Father, the Lord, the Spirit, Heaven

For Son of Man *see* SON – DAUGHTER 1.1:d)

1: MAN = ADAM

Rm	5 12	sin entered the world through one *man*,
	19	by one *man*'s disobedience many were made sinners,
1 Co	15 21	Death came through one *man*
	45	(Gn 2 7) The first *man*, Adam . . . became a living soul;
	47	The first *man*, being from the earth, is earthly by nature; the second man is from heaven.

2: MAN, IN RELATION TO WOMAN

Mt	19 5	(Gn 2 24) a *man* must leave father and mother, and cling to his wife,
	10	If that is how things are between ⌜husband (or: *man*) and wife, it is not advisable to marry.
Mk	10 7	(Gn 2 24) a *man* must leave father and mother,
1 Co	7 1	it is a good thing for a *man* not to touch a woman;

Ep 5 31	(Gn 2 24) a *man* must leave his father and mother and be joined to his wife,

3: INDIVIDUAL MEN

a) Man = Jesus

Mt 11 19	The Son of Man came, eating and drinking, and they say, 'Look, a *man* who is a glutton and a drunkard,'
26 72	I do not know the *man*.
74	I do not know the *man*.
Mk 14 71	I do not know the *man* you speak of.
15 39	In truth this *man* was a son of God.
Lk 7 34	The Son of Man comes . . . and you say, 'Look, a *man* who is a glutton and a drunkard,'
23 4	I find no case against this *man*.
6	When Pilate heard this, he asked if the *man* were a Galilean;
14	You brought this *man* before me . . . . as a political agitator . . . I have . . . found no case against the *man* in respect of all the charges you bring against him.
47	This was a great and good *man*.
Jn 4 29	Come and see a *man* who has told me everything I ever did;
5 12	Who is the *man* who said to you, 'Pick up your mat and walk'?
7 46	There has never been anybody who has spoken like ˹him (lit. this *man*).
8 40	you want to kill me ˹when I tell (lit. a *man* who has told) you the truth
9 11	The *man* called Jesus . . . made a paste, daubed my eyes with it
16	This *man* cannot be from God: he does not keep the sabbath.
24	we know that this *man* is a sinner.
10 33 Θ	you are only a *man* and you claim to be God.
11 47	Here is this *man* working all these signs
50	it is better for one *man* to die for the people
18 14	It is better for one *man* to die for the people.
17	Aren't you another of that *man*'s disciples?
29	What charge do you bring against this *man*?
19 5	Pilate said, 'Here is the *man*'.
Ac 5 28	You . . . seem determined to fix the guilt of this *man*'s death on us.
Rm 5 15 Θ	divine grace, coming through the one *man*, Jesus Christ, came to so many as an abundant free gift.
1 Co 15 21	the resurrection of dead the has come through one *man*.
47	The first man, being from the earth, is earthly by nature; the second *man* is from heaven.
1 Tm 2 5 Θ	there is only one God, and there is only one mediator between God and mankind, himself a *man*, Christ Jesus,

b) Individual Men known by name

P = Paul

Mt 8 27	The *men* [the disciples] were astounded and said, 'Whatever kind of man is this?'
9 9	Jesus . . . saw a *man* named Matthew sitting by the customs house,
11 8	what did you go out to see? A *man* [John the Baptist] . . .?
26 24	alas for that *man* [Judas] by whom the Son of Man is betrayed! Better for that *man* if he had never been born!
27 32	they came across a *man* from Cyrene, Simon by name,
57	When it was evening, there came a rich *man* of Arimathaea, called Joseph,
Mk 14 21	alas for that *man* [Judas] by whom the Son of Man is betrayed! Better for that *man* if he had never been born!
Lk 2 25	Now in Jerusalem there was a *man* named Simeon. He was an upright and devout *man*;
7 25	what did you go out to see? A *man* [John the Baptist] . . .?
22 22	alas for that *man* [Judas] by whom [the Son of Man] is betrayed!
Jn 1 6	A *man* came, sent by God. His name was John.
3 1	There was one of the Pharisees, a *man* called Nicodemus,
Ac 4 13	[Peter and John] were uneducated ˹lay*men* (or: uneducated *men*) . . . ¹⁶ What are we going to do with these *men*?
16	
5 34	Gamaliel . . . asked to have the *men* [the apostles] taken outside for a time. ³⁵ Then he addressed the Sanhedrin, 'Men of Israel, be careful how you deal with these ˹people (or: *men*) . . .³⁸ . . . leave these *men* alone and let them go.'
35	
38	
6 13	This *man* [Stephen] is always making speeches against this Holy Place and the Law.
9 33	[At Lydda Peter] found a *man* called Aeneas,
10 26	Peter helped [Cornelius] up. 'Stand up,' he said 'I am only a *man* after all!'
14 15 P	We [Barnabas and Paul] are only human ˹beings (lit. *men*) like you.
15 26 P	[Barnabas and Paul,] *men* . . . who have dedicated their lives to the name of our Lord Jesus Christ.
16 17 P	These *men* [Paul and his companions] are the servants of the Most High God;
20 P	These ˹people (or: *men*) are causing a disturbance in our city.
Ac 16 35 P	the magistrates sent the officers with the order: 'Release those *men*'.
21 28 P	This is the *man* who preaches to everyone everywhere against our people,
22 26 P	The *man* is a Roman citizen.
23 9 P	We find nothing wrong with this *man*.
25 22 P	I should like to hear the *man* myself.
26 31 P	This *man* is doing nothing that deserves death
32 P	The *man* could have been set free if he had not appealed to Caesar.
28 4 P	That *man* must be a murderer.
Rm 7 24 P	What a wretched *man* I am!
2 Co 12 2 P	I know a *man* in Christ . . .³ . . . this same ˹person (or: *man*) . . .⁴ was caught up into paradise
3 P	
Jm 5 17	Elijah was a human ˹being (lit. *man*) like ourselves

c) Individual Men unnamed

Mt 8 9	I am a *man* under authority myself, and have soldiers under me;
12 10	a *man* was there [in the synagogue] . . . who had a withered hand
13	[Jesus] said to the *man*, 'Stretch out your hand'.
17 14	a *man* came up to [Jesus] . . . ¹⁵ 'Lord,' he said 'take pity on my son: he is a lunatic'
Mk 1 23	In their synagogue just then there was a *man* possessed by an unclean spirit,
3 1	there was a *man* there who had a withered hand
3	[Jesus] said to the *man* with the withered hand, 'Stand up out in the middle!'
5	[Jesus] said to the *man*, 'Stretch out your hand'.
5 2	a *man* with an unclean spirit came out from the tombs towards [Jesus].
8	Come out of the *man*, unclean spirit.
14 13	you will meet a *man* carrying a pitcher of water.
Lk 4 33	In the synagogue there was a *man* who was possessed by the spirit of an unclean devil,
5 18	some men appeared, carrying on a bed a paralysed *man*
20	Seeing their faith [Jesus] said, ˹'My friend (lit. *Man*), your sins are forgiven'.
6 6	a *man* was there whose right hand was withered.
7 8	I am a *man* under authority myself,
8 29	Jesus had been telling the unclean spirit to come out of the *man*.
33	The devils came out of the *man*
35	they found the *man* from whom the devils had gone out sitting at the feet of Jesus,
12 14	˹My friend (lit. *Man*) . . . who appointed me your judge . . .?
14 2	There in front of [Jesus] was a *man* with dropsy,
22 10	you will meet a *man* carrying a pitcher of water.
58	Peter replied, 'I am not, ˹my friend (lit. *man*)'.
60	˹'My friend (lit. *Man*),' said Peter 'I do not know what you are talking about.'
Jn 4 50	The *man* believed what Jesus had said
5 5	One *man* there had an illness which had lasted thirty-eight years,
9	The *man* was cured at once,
15	The *man* went back and told the Jews that it was Jesus who had cured him.
6 10	Jesus said to them, 'Make the ˹people (or: *men*) sit down'.
14	The ˹people (or: *men*), seeing this sign . . . said, 'This really is the prophet'
7 23	why are you angry with me for making a *man* whole and complete on a sabbath?
9 1	[Jesus] saw a *man* who had been blind from birth.
24	the Jews again sent for the *man* [who had been blind]
30	The *man* replied, 'Now here is an astonishing thing!'
Ac 4 9	you are questioning us today about an act of kindness to a ˹cripple (lit. crippled *man*),
14	they saw the *man* who had been cured standing by their side,
22	The *man* who had been miraculously cured was over forty years old.
19 16	the *man* with the evil spirit hurled himself at [the seven sons of Sceva]
2 Th 2 3 ●	It cannot happen until . . . the ˹Rebel (lit. *man* of sin), the Lost One, has appeared.
2 Tm 3 8	*Men* like this defy the truth . . . their minds are corrupt and their faith spurious.
Jude 4	Certain ˹people (or: *men*) have infiltrated among you, and they are the ones you had a warning about,
Rv 9 4	[the locusts were] told only to attack any *men* who were without God's seal
16 2	The first angel . . . emptied his bowl . . . on all the ˹people (or: *men*) who had been branded with the mark of the beast

d) Men = Citizens, People of a place – Man of a race

Lk 13 4	Do you suppose that [those eighteen on whom the tower at Siloam fell] were more guilty than all the other *people* living in Jerusalem?

Jn 4 28 — The woman . . . hurried back to the town [Sychar] to tell the *people*,
Ac 16 37 — They flog Roman *citizens* in public
21 39 — 'I?' said Paul 'I am a Jewish *man* and a citizen of the well-known city of Tarsus'
22 25 — Is it legal for you to flog a *man* who is a Roman citizen . . .?

4: MAN = SELF, NATURE

Rm 6 6 — our former *selves* have been crucified with [Christ]
7 22 — In my inmost *self* I dearly love God's Law,
1 Co 2 14 — [r]An unspiritual *person* (or: The unspiritual *man*) is one who does not accept anything of the Spirit of God . . . [15] A spiritual [man], on the other hand, is able to judge the value of everything,
2 Co 4 16 — though this outer *man* of ours may be falling into decay, the inner [man] is renewed day by day.
Ep 2 15 — This was to create one single New *Man* in himself out of the two of them
3 16 — may [the Father] give you the power through his Spirit for your hidden *self* to grow strong,
4 22 — You must give up your old way of life; you must put aside your old [r]*self* (or: *nature*) . . . [24] so that you can put on
24 — the new *self* that has been created in God's way,
Col 3 9 — You have stripped off your old behaviour with your old *self*,
1 P 3 4 — [Women, do not dress up for show;] all this should be [r]inside (lit. *part of the self*), in a person's heart,

5: MAN OF GOD, MAN DEDICATED TO GOD

1 Tm 6 11 — as a *man* dedicated to God, you must avoid all that.
2 Tm 3 17 — This is how the *man* who is dedicated to God becomes fully equipped and ready for any good work.

6: MAN, HUMAN(ITY) – PEOPLE, EVERYBODY, EVERYONE – SOMEONE, ANYBODY

Mt 4 4 — (Dt 8 3) *Man* does not live on bread alone
19 — [Jesus] said to them 'Follow me and I will make your fishers of *men*'.
5 13 — if salt becomes tasteless . . . it is good for nothing and can only be thrown out to be trampled underfoot by *men*.
16 — In the same way your light must shine in the sight of *men*,
19 — [the man] who infringes even one of the least of these commandments and teaches other *men* to do the same will be considered the least
6 1 — Be careful not to parade your good deeds before *men*
2 — this is what the hypocrites do . . . to win *men*'s admiration.
5 — they love to say their prayers standing up in the synagogues . . . for *people* to see them.
14 — if you forgive [r]others (lit. *people*) their failings, your heavenly
15 — Father will forgive you yours; [15] but if you do not forgive [r]others (lit. *people*), your Father will not forgive your failings either.
16 — the hypocrites . . . pull long faces to let *men* know they are fasting.
18 ⊖ — [put oil on your head,] so that [r]no one (lit. *no man*) will know you are fasting except your Father
7 9 — Is there a *man* among you who would hand his son a stone when he asked for bread?
12 — treat [r]others (lit. *people*) as you would like them to treat you;
9 8 — the crowd . . . praised God for giving such power to *men*.
10 17 — Beware of *men*: they will hand you over to sanhedrins
32 ⊖ — if anyone declares himself for me in the presence of *men*, I will declare myself for him
33 ⊖ — the one who disowns me in the presence of *men*, I will disown in the presence of my Father
35 — I have come to set a *man* against his father, a daughter against her mother,
36 — A *man*'s enemies will be those of his own household.
12 11 < — If any [r]one (lit. *man*) of you here had only one sheep and it fell down a hole . . . would he not . . . lift it out?
12 — Now a *man* is far more important than a sheep,
31 — every one of *men*'s sins and blasphemies will be forgiven,
35 — A good *man* draws good things from his store of goodness; a bad *man* draws bad things from his store of badness.
36 — for every unfounded word *men* utter they will answer
43 — When an unclean spirit goes out of a *man* it wanders through waterless country
45 — the *man* ends up by being worse than he was before.
13 24 < — The kingdom of heaven may be compared to a *man* who sowed good seed . . . [25] While *everybody* was asleep his enemy came,
25 < —
28 < — Some [r]enemy (lit. *man who is an enemy*) has done this
31 < — The kingdom of heaven is like a mustard seed which a *man* took and sowed in his field.

Mt 13 44 < — The kingdom of heaven is like treasure . . . which *someone* has found;
52 < — a [r]householder (lit. *man who is the head of his house*) . . . brings out from his storeroom things both new and old.
15 9 — (Is 29 13) the doctrines they teach are only *human* regulations.
11 — What goes into the mouth does not make a *man* unclean; it is what comes out of the mouth that makes the *man* unclean
18 — . . . [18] . . . the things that come out of the mouth come from the heart, and it is these that make a *man* unclean . . .
20 — [20] These are the things that make a *man* unclean. But to eat with unwashed hands does not make a *man* unclean.
16 13 ⊖ — Who do *people* say the Son of Man is?
23 ⊖ — the way you think is not God's way but *man*'s.
26 — What, then, will a *man* gain if he wins the whole world and ruins his life? Or what has a *man* to offer in exchange for his life?
17 22 — The Son of Man is going to be handed over into the power of *men*,
18 7 — alas for the *man* who provides [obstacles]!
12 — Suppose a *man* has a hundred sheep
23 < — the kingdom of heaven may be compared to a *man*, a king who decided to settle his accounts with his servants.
19 6 ⊖ — what God has united, *man* must not divide.
12 — there are eunuchs made so by *men*
26 ⊖ — For *men* . . . this is impossible; for God everything is possible.
20 1 < — the kingdom of heaven is like a [r]landowner (lit. *man who is the head of his house*)
21 25 ⊖ — John's baptism: where did it come from: heaven or *man*?
26 ⊖ — if we say from *man*, we have the people to fear,
28 < — A *man* had two sons.
33 < — There was a *man*, a landowner, who planted a vineyard;
22 2 < — The kingdom of heaven may be compared to a *man*, a king who gave a feast for his son's wedding.
11 < — the king . . . noticed one *man* who was not wearing a wedding garment,
16 — Master, . . . a *man*'s rank means nothing to you.
23 4 — [The scribes and the Pharisees] tie up heavy burdens and lay them on *men*'s shoulders,
5 — Everything they do is done to attract *people*'s attention,
7 — [the Pharisees love] having *people* call them Rabbi.
13 — Alas for you . . . who shut up the kingdom of heaven in *men*'s faces.
28 — you appear to *people* from the outside like good honest men,
25 14 < — It is like a *man* . . . who summoned his servants
24 < — I had heard you were a hard *man*,
Mk 1 17 — I will make you into fishers of *men*.
2 27 — The sabbath was made for *man*, not *man* for the sabbath;
3 28 — all *men*'s sins will be forgiven,
4 26 < — A *man* throws seed on the land.
7 7 — (Is 29 13) the doctrines they teach are only *human* regulations.
8 ⊖ — You put aside the commandment of God to cling to *human* traditions.
11 — If a *man* says to his father or mother: Anything I have . . . is Corban
15 — Nothing that goes into a *man* from outside can make him unclean; it is the things that come out of a *man* that make the *man* unclean . . . [18] . . . whatever goes into a *man*
18 —
20 — from outside cannot make him unclean . . . [20] . . . It is what comes out of a *man* that makes the *man* unclean.
21 — [21] For it is from within, from *men*'s hearts, that evil intentions emerge . . . [23] All these evil things come from within and make a *man* unclean.
23 —
8 24 — I can see *people*; they look like trees to me, but they are walking about.
27 — Who do *people* say I am?
33 ⊖ — the way you think is not God's way but *man*'s.
36 — What gain, then, is it for a *man* to win the whole world and ruin his life? [37] And indeed what can a *man* offer in exchange for his life?
37 —
9 31 — The Son of Man will be delivered into the hands of *men*;
10 9 ⊖ — what God has united, *man* must not divide.
27 ⊖ — For *men* . . . it is impossible, but not for God:
11 2 — you will find a tethered colt that [r]no one (lit. *no man*) has yet ridden.
30 ⊖ — John's baptism: did it come from heaven, or from *man*?
32 ⊖ — But dare we say from *man*?
12 1 < — A *man* planted a vineyard;
14 — a *man*'s rank means nothing to you,
13 34 < — It is like a *man* travelling abroad:
Lk 1 25 — it has pleased [the Lord] to take away the humiliation I suffered among *men*.
2 14 ⊖ — Glory to God in the highest heaven, and peace to *men* who enjoy his favour.
52 ⊖ — Jesus increased in wisdom . . . and in favour with God and *men*.
4 4 — (Dt 8 3) Scripture says: *Man* does not live on bread alone.
5 10 — from now on it is *men* you will catch.
6 22 — Happy are you when *people* hate you,
26 — Alas for you when [r]the world speaks (lit. *people speak*) well of you!

Lk	6	31	Treat ʳothers (lit. *people*) as you would like them to treat you.
		45	A good *man* draws what is good from the store of goodness in his heart;
		48	He is like the *man* who when he built his house . . . laid the foundations on rock;
		49	the *man* . . . built his house on soil,
	7	31	What description, then, can I find for the *men* of this generation?
	9	25	What gain, then, is it for a *man* to have won the whole world and to have lost . . . his very self?
		44	The Son of Man is going to be handed over into the power of *men.*
		56	(ᵛthe Son of Man did not come to destroy *men*'s lives but to save them.)
	10	30	A *man* was once on his way down from Jerusalem to Jericho
	11	24	When an unclean spirit goes out of a *man* it wanders through waterless country
		26	the *man* ends up by being worse than he was before.
		44	you are like the unmarked tombs that *men* walk on without knowing it!
		46	you load on *men* burdens that are unendurable,
	12	8	if anyone openly declares himself for me in the presence of *men*, the Son of Man will declare himself for him . . .
		9	⁹ But [the man] who disowns me in the presence of *men* will be disowned
		16 <	There was a rich *man* who . . . had a good harvest
		36	Be like *men* waiting for their master to return
	13	19 <	[The kingdom of God] is like a mustard seed which a *man* took and threw into his garden.
	14	16	There was a *man* who gave a great banquet,
		30	Here is a *man* who started to build and was unable to finish.
	15	4	What *man* among you with a hundred sheep, losing one, would not . . . go after the missing one . . . ?
		11 <	A *man* had two sons.
	16	1 <	There was a rich *man* and he had a steward
		15 Θ	You are the very ones who pass yourselves off as virtuous in *people*'s sight, but God knows your hearts. For what is thought highly of by *men* is loathsome in the sight of God.
		19	There was a rich *man* who used to dress in purple and fine linen
	18	2 Θ	There was a judge . . . who had neither fear of God nor respect for *man* . . . ⁴ . . . he said to himself, 'Maybe I have
		4 Θ	neither fear of God nor respect for *man*,'
		10 <	Two *men* went up to the Temple to pray,
		11 <	I thank you, God, that I am not . . . like the rest of *mankind*,
		27 Θ	Things that are impossible for *men* . . . are possible for God.
	19	12 <	A *man* of noble birth went to a distant country
		21 <	I was afraid of you; for you are an exacting *man*:
		22 <	So you knew I was an exacting *man*,
		30	you will find a tethered colt that ʳno one (lit. no *man*) has yet ridden.
	20	4 Θ	John's baptism: did it come from heaven, or from *man*?
		6 Θ	if we say from men, the people will all stone us,
		9 <	A *man* planted a vineyard
	21	26	[there will be] *men* dying of fear
	24	7	the Son of Man had to be handed over into the power of sinful *men*
Jn	1	4	All that came to be had life in [the Word] and that life was the light of *men*,
		9	The Word was the true light that enlightens all *men*; ʳand he (or: which [light]) was coming into the world.
	2	10	*People* generally serve the best wine first,
		25	[Jesus] never needed evidence about any *man*; he could tell what a *man* had in him.
	3	4	How can a grown *man* be born?
		19	*men* have shown they prefer darkness to the light
		27	A *man* can lay claim only to what is given him from heaven.
	5	7	ʳI have no one (lit. There is no *man*) to put me into the pool
		34	not that I depend on *human* testimony;
		41 Θ	As for *human* approval, this means nothing to me.
	7	22	you circumcise a *man* on the sabbath. ²³ . . . a *man* can be
		23	circumcised on the sabbath
		46	There has never been *anybody* who has spoken like him.
		51	surely the Law does not allow us to pass judgement on a *man* without giving him a hearing . . . ?
	8	17	(Dt 19 15) the testimony of two ʳwitnesses (lit. *men*) is valid.
		44 3	[The devil] was a murderer of *men* from the start;
	9	16	How could a *man* who is a sinner produce signs like this?
	12	43 Θ	they put honour from *men* before the honour that comes from God.
	16	21	A woman . . . forgets the suffering in her joy that a *man* has been born into the world.
	17	6	I have made your name known to the *men*
Ac	4	12	of all the names in the world given to *men*, this is the only one by which we can be saved.
		17	let us caution [Peter and John] never to speak to *anyone* in this name again.
	5	4 Θ	It is not to *men* that you have lied, but to God.
		29 Θ	Peter, . . . said, 'Obedience to God comes before obedience to *men*;'

Ac	5	38 Θ	If this enterprise . . . is of *human* origin it will break up of its own accord;
	10	28	I must not call *anyone* profane or unclean.
	12	22 Θ	It is a god speaking, not a *man*!
	14	11 Θ	These people are gods who have come down to us disguised as *men*.
	15	17	(Am 9 12) Then the rest of *mankind* . . . will look for the Lord,
	17	25 2	Nor is [God] dependent on anything that *human* hands can do for him,
		26	From one single stock [God] . . . created the whole *human* race so that they could occupy the entire earth,
		29	we have no excuse for thinking that the deity looks like anything in gold, silver or stone that has been carved . . . by a *man*.
		30	[God] is telling *everyone* everywhere that they must repent,
	18	13	We accuse this man . . . of persuading *people* to worship God in a way that breaks the Law.
	19	35	Is there *anybody* alive who does not know that the city of the Ephesians is the guardian of the temple of great Diana . . . !
	22	15	[Saul,] you are to be [Christ's] witness before all *mankind*,
	24	16 Θ	I . . . do my best to keep a clear conscience . . . before God and *man*.
	25	16	Romans are not in the habit of surrendering any *man*, until the accused confronts his accusers
	27	3 6	Julius was ʳconsiderate (lit. ʳhumane) enough to allow Paul to go to his friends
	28	2	The inhabitants treated us with unusual ʳkindness (lit. ʳhumanity).
Rm	1	18 5	The anger of God is being revealed . . . against all the impiety and depravity of *men*
		23 Θ	they exchanged the glory of the immortal God for . . . the image of mortal *man*,
	2	1	ʳIn judging others you (lit. You, the *man* who judges,) condemn yourself,
		3	you, the *man* who judges, judge those who behave like this while you are doing exactly the same,
		9	Pain and suffering will come to every *human* being who employs himself in evil
		16	on the day when . . . God . . . judges the secrets of *mankind*.
		29 Θ	A Jew like that may not be praised by *man*, but he will be praised by God.
	3	4 Θ	God will always be true even though *everyone* proves to be false;
		5	to use a *human* analogy
		28	a *man* is justified by faith
	4	6	David says the same: a *man* is happy if God considers him righteous,
	5	12	thus death has spread through the whole *human* race
		18	as one man's fall brought condemnation on *everyone*, so the good act of one man brings *everyone* life and makes them justified.
	6	19 2	If I may use *human* terms to help your natural weakness:
	7	1	laws affect a *person* only during his lifetime.
	9	20 Θ	what right have you, a *human* being, to cross-examine God?
	10	5	(Lv 18 5) ʳthose who keep (lit. the *man* who keeps) the Law will draw life from it.
	12	17	let *everyone* see that you are interested only in the highest ideals.
		18	Do all you can to live at peace with *everyone*.
	14	18 Θ	If you serve Christ in this way you will please God and be respected by *men*.
		20	all food is clean, but it becomes evil if by eating it you make *somebody* else fall away.
1 Co	1	25 Θ / Θ	God's foolishness is wiser than *human* wisdom, and God's weakness is stronger than *human* strength.
	2	5 Θ	I did this so that your faith should not depend on *human* philosophy
		9 Θ	we teach . . . things beyond the mind of *man*,
		11 Θ	the depths of a *man* can only be known by the *man*'s own spirit, not by any other *man*,
		13 Θ 2	we teach, not in the way in which ʳphilosophy (lit. *human* wisdom) is taught, but in the way that the Spirit teaches us:
	3	3	you are still unspiritual. Isn't that obvious . . . from the way
		4	that you go on behaving like ordinary *people*? ⁴ What could be more ʳunspiritual (lit. like mere *men*) than your slogans, 'I am for Paul' and 'I am for Apollos'?
		21	there is nothing to boast about in anything *human*:
	4	1	*People* must think of us as Christ's servants,
		3 Θ 2	Not that it makes the slightest difference to me whether you, or indeed any *human* tribunal, find me worthy or not.
		9	we have been put on show in front of the whole universe, angels as well as *men*.
	6	18	All the other sins ʳare committed (lit. a *man* may commit) outside the body;
	7	7	I should like *everyone* to be like me,
		23	do not be slaves of other *men*.
		26	it is good for a *man* to stay as he is.
	9	8	These may be only *human* comparisons,

1 Co 10 13		The trials that you have had to bear are no more than
	2	*people* normally have.
11 28		*Everyone* is to recollect himself before eating this bread
13 1		If I have all the eloquence of *men* or of angels, but speak without love, I am simply a gong booming
14 2 Θ		Anybody with the gift of tongues speaks to God, but not to other *people* . . . ³ On the other hand, [the man] who
3		prophesies does talk to other *people*,
15 19		If our hope in Christ has been for this life only, we are the most unfortunate of all *people*.
32		If my motives were only *human* ones, what good would it do me to fight the wild animals at Ephesus?
39		Everything that is flesh is not the same flesh: there is *human* flesh, animals' flesh,
2 Co 3 2		you are yourselves our letter . . . that *anybody* can see and read,
4 2		we commend ourselves to every *human being* with a conscience
5 11		we try to win *people* over.
8 21 Θ		we are trying to do right not only in the sight of God but also in the sight of *men*.
12 4		things which . . . cannot be put into *human* language.
Ga 1 1		Paul . . . an apostle who does not owe his authority to *men* or his appointment to any *human being* but who has been
Θ		appointed by Jesus Christ and by God the Father
10 Θ		So now whom am I trying to please – *man*, or God? Would you say it is *men*'s approval I am looking for? If I still wanted *men* to approve, I should not be what I am – a servant
11		of Christ. ¹¹ . . . the Good News I preached is not a
12		*human* message ¹² that I was given by *men*, it is something I learnt only through a revelation of Jesus Christ.
2 6		God ʳhas no favourites (lit. makes an exception for no *man*)
16		what makes a *man* righteous is not obedience to the Law,
3 15		Compare this, brothers, with what happens in ʳordinary life (lit. a *human* example). If a will has been drawn up in due form, ʳno one (lit. no *man*) is allowed to disregard it
5 3		*Everyone* who accepts circumcision is obliged to keep the whole Law.
6 1		if ʳone of (lit. a *man* among) you misbehaves, the more spiritual of you who set him right should do so in a spirit of gentleness,
7		where a *man* sows, there he reaps:
Ep 3 5		This mystery . . . was unknown to any *men* in past generations;
4 8		(Ps 68 19) When [Christ] ascended to the height . . . he gave gifts to *men*.
14		Then we shall not be . . . at the mercy of all the tricks *men* play
6 6 Θ		[Slaves, be obedient to your masters,] not only when you are
	4	under their eye, as if you had only to please *men*, but because you are slaves of Christ
7 Θ		Work hard . . . for the sake of the Lord and not for the sake of *men*.
Ph 2 7 Θ		[Christ] emptied himself . . . and became as *men* are; and being as all *men* are, ⁸ he was humbler yet,
4 5		Let your tolerance be evident to *everyone*:
Col 1 28		this is the Christ we proclaim, this is the wisdom in which we thoroughly train *everyone* and instruct *everyone*, to make *everyone* perfect in Christ.
2 8		Make sure that no one traps you . . . by some . . . ʳrational (lit. *human*) philosophy based on the principles of this world instead of on Christ.
22		an example of *human* doctrines and regulations!
3 22		[Slaves, be obedient to your masters,] not only when you are
	4	under their eye, as if you had only to please *men*, but wholeheartedly,
23 Θ		put your heart into [the work] as if it were for the Lord and not for *men*,
1 Th 2 4 Θ		we are not trying to please *men* but God,
6		nor have we ever looked for any special honour from *men*,
13 Θ		you accepted [the message] for what is really is, God's message and not some *human* thinking;
15 Θ		[the Jews are] the enemies of the whole *human* race,
4 8 Θ		anyone who objects is not objecting to a *human* [authority], but to God,
2 Th 3 2		pray that we may be preserved from the interference of bigoted and evil *people*,
1 Tm 2 1		there should be prayers offered for *everyone*
4		[God] wants *everyone* to be saved
5		there is only one mediator between God and *mankind*, himself a man, Christ Jesus,
4 10		we have put our trust in . . . the saviour of the whole *human race*
5 24		The faults of some *people* are obvious long before anyone makes any complaint about them,
6 5		unending disputes by *people* who are neither rational nor informed
9		dangerous ambitions . . eventually plunge ʳthem (lit. *men*) into ruin and destruction.
16		God] whom no *man* has seen and [no man] is able to see:
2 Tm 2 2		hand [everything that I teach] on to reliable *people*
3 2		[in the last days] *people* will be self-centred
13		these wicked *people*, these impostors will go from bad to worse,
Tt 1 14		so that they stop . . . doing what they are told to do by *people* who are no longer interested in the truth.
2 11		God's grace . . . has made salvation possible for the whole *human race*
3 2		be courteous and always polite to all kinds of *people*
4	5	the kindness and love of God . . . for *mankind* were revealed,
8		All this . . . will do nothing but good to *everybody*.
10		If a *man* disputes what you teach . . . have no more to do with him:
Heb 2 6		(Ps 8 5) What is *man* that you should spare a thought for him,
5 1		Every high priest has been taken out of *mankind* and is appointed to act for *men* in their relations with God,
6 16 Θ		*Men* . . . swear an oath by something greater than themselves,
7 8		in the one case it is ordinary mortal *men* who receive the tithes,
28		The Law appoints high priests who are *men* subject to weakness;
8 2 Θ		the true Tent of Meeting which the Lord, and not any *man*, set up.
9 27		*men* only die once,
13 6 Θ		(Ps 118 6) With the Lord to help me . . . what can *man* do to me?
Jm 1 7		That sort of *person* . . . must not expect that the Lord will give him anything.
19		brothers: every *man* should be quick to listen but slow to speak
2 20		you senseless *man*, . . . faith without good deeds is useless.
24		it is by doing something good . . . that a *man* is justified.
3 7	2	Wild animals and birds . . . can all be tamed by *man* . . .
8		⁸ but ʳnobody (lit. no *person*) can tame the tongue
9 Θ		we also use [the tongue] to curse *men* who are made in God's image:
1 P 2 4 Θ		He is the living stone, rejected by *men*
13		For the sake of the Lord, accept the authority of every
	2	*social* institution:
15		be good citizens, so as to silence what ʳfools (lit. foolish *people*) are saying in their ignorance.
4 2 Θ		he is not ruled by *human* passions but only by the will of God.
6 Θ		so that though . . . [the dead] had been through the judgement that comes to all *humanity*, they might come to God's life in the spirit.
2 P 1 21 Θ		no prophecy ever came from *man*'s initiative. When *men* spoke for God it was the Holy Spirit that moved them.
2 16		The dumb donkey put a stop to that prophet's madness when it talked like a *man*.
3 7		the present sky and earth . . . are only being reserved until Judgement day so that all ʳsinners (lit. sinful *people*) may be destroyed.
1 Jn 3 15	3	to hate your brother is to be a ʳmurderer (lit. *man*-killer),
	3	and ʳmurderers (lit. *man*-killers) . . . do not have eternal life in them.
5 9 Θ		We accept the testimony of *human* witnesses, but God's testimony is much greater,
Rv 4 7		the third animal had a *human* face,
8 11		many *people* died from drinking [the water turned to bitter wormwood].
9 5		the pain was to be the pain of a scorpion's sting for a *man*.
6		When this happens, *men* will long for death and not find it anywhere;
7		these locusts . . . had . . . faces that seemed *human*,
10		[the locusts] were able to injure *people* for five months.
15		These four angels . . . were released to destroy a third of the *human race*.
18		one third of the *human race* was killed.
20		the rest of the *human race* . . . refused . . . to stop worshipping devils.
11 13		seven thousand *persons* were killed in the earthquake,
13 13		it worked great miracles, even to calling down fire from heaven on to the earth while *people* watched.
18		the number of the beast . . . is the number of a *man*, the number 666.
14 4		they have been redeemed from amongst *men* to be the first-fruits for God
16 8		the sun . . . was made to scorch *people* with its flames;
9		⁹ but though *people* were scorched by the fierce heat of it, they cursed the name of God
18		[there was] the most violent earthquake that anyone has ever seen since there have been *men* on the earth.
21		great hailstones . . . fell from the sky on to the *people*. And the *people* cursed God
18 13		[there is nobody left to buy the traders' cargoes of goods;] their slaves, their *human cargo*
21 3		You see this city? Here God lives among *men*.
17		[the wall of the city] was a hundred and forty-four cubits high – the angel was using the ʳordinary (lit. *human* measure) cubit.

3. MAN, MEN: *ANĒR*

2	*andrizomai*	*1*	3	*andro(-phonos) 1*
1	*anēr*	*216*	4	*hyp- andros 1*
			5	*(phil-)andros 1*

1: MAN, MEN, DISTINCT FROM WOMAN

A = Adam

Mt 14	21	Those who ate numbered about five thousand *men*, to say nothing of women and children.
15	38	four thousand *men* had eaten, to say nothing of women and children.
Jn 1	13	[the Word] ≠ who was (G those who are) born not out of human stock or urge of the flesh or will of *man* but of God himself.
Ac 5	14	the numbers of *men* and women who came to believe in the Lord increased steadily.
8	3	Saul . . . went from house to house arresting both *men* and women and sending them to prison.
	12	they were baptised, both *men* and women,
9	2	[Saul] asked for letters . . . that would authorise him to arrest . . . any followers of the Way, *men* and women,
17	12	Many Jews became believers, and so did many Greek women . . . and a number of the *men*.
	34	there were some *men* who attached themselves to [Paul] . . . among them Dionysius the Areopagite and a woman called Damaris.
22	4	I . . . persecuted this Way . . . and sent women as well as *men* to prison.
1 Co 11	3	Christ is the head of every *man*, *man* is the head of woman, and God is the head of Christ.
	4	For a *man* to pray or prophesy with his head covered is a sign of disrespect to his head
	7	A *man* . . . is the image of God and reflects God's glory;
	8 A	but woman is the reflection of *man*'s glory. ⁸ For *man* did
	A	not come from woman; no, woman came from *man*;
	9	*man* was not created for the sake of woman, but woman was
	11 A	created for the sake of *man* . . . ¹¹ However, though woman
	A	cannot do without *man*, neither can *man* do without
	12 A	woman, in the Lord; ¹² woman may come from *man*,
	A	but *man* is born of woman – both come from God.
	14	long hair on a *man* is nothing to be admired,
16	13	Be awake to all the dangers; stay firm in the faith; ᵣbe
	2	brave (lit. *act like men*) and be strong.
1 Tm 2	8	I want the *men* to lift their hands up reverently in prayer . . . ⁹ Similarly . . . women are to wear suitable clothes
	12	I am not giving permission for a woman to teach or to tell a *man* what to do.

2: MAN AS A HUSBAND

Mt 1	16	Jacob was the father of Joseph the *husband* of Mary;
	19	Her *husband* Joseph . . . decided to divorce her informally.
Mk 10	2	Is it against the law for a *man* to divorce his wife?
	12	if a woman divorces her *husband* and marries another she is guilty of adultery;
Lk 1	34	Mary said to the angel, 'But how can this come about, since I ᵣam a virgin (lit. do not know *man*)?'
2	36	Anna . . . had ᵣbeen married (lit. lived with her *husband*) for seven years ³⁷ before becoming a widow.
16	18	the man who marries a woman divorced by her *husband* commits adultery.
Jn 4	16	'Go and call your *husband*' said Jesus to [the Samaritan woman] . . . ¹⁷ The woman answered, 'I have no *husband*'.
	17	He said to her, 'You are right to say, "I have no *husband*";
	18	¹⁸ for although you have had five *husbands*, the one you have now is not your *husband*.'
Ac 5	9	You hear those footsteps? They have just been to bury your *husband*;
	10	they . . . buried [Sapphira] by the side of her *husband*.
Rm 7	2	4/ A *married* woman . . . has legal obligations to her *husband* while he is still alive, but all these obligations to her
	3	*husband* come to an end if the *husband* dies. ³ So if she gives herself to another *man* while her *husband* is still alive she is legally an adulteress; but after her *husband* is dead . . . she can marry ᵣsomeone else (lit. another *man*) without becoming an adulteress.
1 Co 7	2	let [each man] have his own wife and each woman her own
	3	*husband*. ³ The *husband* must give his wife what she has the right to expect, and so too the wife to the *husband*. ⁴ The
	4	wife has no rights over her own body; it is the *husband* who has them. In the same way, the *husband* has no rights over his body; the wife has them.
	10	a wife must not leave her *husband* ¹¹ . . . she must . . . make
	11	it up with her *husband* – nor must a *husband* send his wife away,

1 Co 7	13	if a woman has an unbeliever for her *husband* . . . she must
	14	not leave her *husband*. ¹⁴ This is because the unbelieving *husband* is made one with the saints through his wife, and the unbelieving wife . . . through her ᵣhusband (lit. brother)
	16	If you are a wife, it may be your part to save your *husband*, for all you know; if a *husband*, for all you know, it may be your part to save your wife.
	34	The married woman . . . has to . . . devote herself to pleasing her *husband*.
	39	A wife is tied as long as her *husband* is alive. But if the *husband* dies, she is free to marry anybody she likes,
14	35	If [women] have any questions to ask, they should ask their *husbands* at home:
2 Co 11	2 X	I arranged for you to marry Christ so that I might give you away . . . to this one *husband*.
Ga 4	27	(Is 54 1) there are more sons of the forsaken one than sons of the ᵣwedded wife (lit. one with a *husband*).
Ep 5	22	Wives should regard their *husbands* as they regard the Lord,
	23	as Christ is head of the Church . . . so is a *husband* the head of his wife;
	24	as the Church submits to Christ, so should wives to their *husbands*, in everything.
	25	Husbands should love their wives just as Christ loved the Church
	28	*husbands* must love their wives as they love their own bodies;
	33	let every wife respect her *husband*.
Col 3	18	Wives, give way to your *husbands*,
	19	Husbands, love your wives
1 Tm 3	2	the president . . . must not have been ᵣmarried more than once (lit. *husband* to more than one woman),
	12	Deacons must not have been ᵣmarried more than once (lit. *husband* to more than one woman),
5	9	Enrolment as a widow is permissible only for a woman . . . who has had only one *husband*.
Tt 1	6	[an elder] must not have been ᵣmarried more than once (lit. *husband* to more than one woman),
2	4	[the older women should] show the younger women how
	5	they should love their *husbands* and love their children, ⁵ how they are to . . . do as their *husbands* tell them,
1 P 3	1	wives should be obedient to their *husbands*.
	5	the holy women . . . were tender and obedient to their *husbands*;
	7	*husbands* must always treat their wives with consideration
Rv 21	2	the new Jerusalem . . . as beautiful as a bride all dressed for her *husband*.

3: INDIVIDUAL MEN

a) Man = Jesus

Lk 24	19	Jesus of Nazareth . . . (G a *man*) who proved he was a great prophet
Jn 1	30	A *man* is coming after me who ranks before me
Ac 2	22	Jesus the Nazarene was a *man* commended to you by God
17	31	[God] has appointed a *man* to be the judge [when the whole world will be judged].
Ep 4	13 O	we are all to come to unity in our faith . . . until we become the perfect *Man*, fully mature with the fullness of Christ himself.

b) Individual Men known by name

P = Paul

Mk 6	20	Herod was afraid of John, knowing him to be a good and holy *man*,
Lk 1	27	a virgin betrothed to a *man* named Joseph,
5	8	[Peter said:] I am a sinful *man*.
8	41	there came a *man* named Jairus
9	30	there were two *men* there talking to [Jesus] . . . Moses and Elijah
	32	Peter and his companions . . . saw his glory and the two *men* standing with him.
19	2	a *man* whose name was Zacchaeus made his appearance;
	7	[Jesus] has gone to stay at a ᵣsinner's (lit. sinful *man*'s) house
23	50	Then a *man*, a member of the council arrived, an upright and virtuous *man* named Joseph.
Ac 3	14	you . . . demanded the reprieve of a *man* who was a murderer [Barabbas]
5	1	There was another *man*, however, called Ananias. He . . . agreed to sell a property;
	25	the *men* [the apostles] you imprisoned are in the Temple.
6	3	you, brothers, must select from among yourselves seven *men*
	5	of good reputation . . . ⁵ The whole assembly . . . elected Stephen, a *man* full of faith and of the Holy Spirit,
8	9	a *man* called Simon had already practised magic arts in the town
9	12	[Saul] had a vision of a *man* called Ananias
	13 P	several people have told me about this *man*

Ac 10 1   One of the ⌐centurions (lit. *men*, a centurion,) of the Italica cohort stationed in Caesarea was called Cornelius.

22   The centurion Cornelius . . . is an upright and God-fearing *man*,

11 12   we entered the *man*'s [Cornelius's] house.

24   [Barnabas] was a good *man*,

13 6   [Barnabas and Saul] came in contact with a Jewish *man* who was a magician called Bar-jesus. 7 This false prophet was one of the attendants of the proconsul Sergius Paulus who was an extremely intelligent *man*.

21   [our ancestors] demanded a king, and God gave them Saul . . . a *man* of the tribe of Benjamin.

22   (Ps 89 21) I have selected David . . . a *man* after my own heart,

15 22   the apostles . . . decided to choose ⌐delegates (lit. *men* from among them) . . . They chose Judas . . . and Silas, both leading *men* in the brotherhood,

25   we have decided . . . to elect ⌐delegates (lit. *men* from among us) and to send them to you

18 24   Apollos . . . was an eloquent *man*, with a sound knowledge of the scriptures,

19 37   These *men* [Gaius and Aristarchus] you have brought here are not guilty

21 11 P   The *man* this girdle belongs to will be bound like this by the Jews in Jerusalem,

22 12   Someone called Ananias, a devout ⌐follower of (lit. *man* who followed) the Law

23 27 P   This *man* had been seized by the Jews

30 P   there is a conspiracy against the *man*,

24 5 P   we find this *man* a perfect pest;

25 5 P   if there is anything wrong about the *man*, they can bring a charge against him.

14 P   There is a *man* here . . . whom Felix left behind in custody,

17 P   I . . . took my seat on the tribunal . . . and had the *man* brought in.

1 Co 13 11 P   I am a *man*, all childish ways are put behind me.

c) *Men = Citizens, People of a place – Men of a race*

Mt 12 41   On Judgement day the *men* of Nineveh will . . . condemn [this generation],

14 35   the local *people* [at Gennesaret] . . . spread the news through the whole neighbourhood

Lk 8 27   a *man* from the town [of the Gerasenes] who was possessed by devils came towards [Jesus];

11 32   On Judgement day the *men* of Nineveh will . . . condemn [this generation],

Ac 1 11   Why are you *men* from Galilee standing here looking into the sky?

2 14   Peter . . . addressed them in a loud voice: '*Men* of Judaea . . . listen carefully to what I say.'

22   *Men* of Israel, listen to what I am going to say:

3 12   Peter . . . addressed them, '*Men* of Israel, why are you so surprised at this?'

5 35   *Men* of Israel, be careful how you deal with these people.

8 27   ⌐an Ethiopian (lit. a *man* from Ethiopia) had been on pilgrimage to Jerusalem;

10 28   it is forbidden for Jewish *men* to mix with people of another race

11 20   Some of the *men* . . . who came from Cyprus and Cyrene, went to Antioch

13 16   *Men* of Israel, and fearers of God, listen!

16 9   a Macedonian *man* appeared and appealed to [Paul]

17 22   *Men* of Athens, I have seen for myself how extremely scrupulous you are in all religious matters,

19 35   *Citizens* of Ephesus! Is there anybody alive who does not know that the city of the Ephesians is the guardian of the temple of great Diana . . . ?

21 28 P   [some Jews seized Paul] shouting, '*Men* of Israel, help!'

22 3 P   I am a ⌐Jew (lit. Jewish *man*),

d) '*Brother-Men*' = *Brothers! Friends!*

Ac 1 16   Brother[-*men*], the passage of scripture had to be fulfilled

2 29   Brother[-*men*], no one can deny that . . . David himself is dead

37   What must we do, brother[-*men*]?

7 2   My brother[-*men*], my fathers, listen to what I have to say.

26   '*Friends*,' [Moses] said 'you are brothers:'

13 15   Brother[-*Men*], if you would like to address some words of encouragement . . . please do so.

26   My brother[-*men*], sons of Abraham's race,

38   My brother[-*men*], I want you to realise that it is through him that forgiveness of your sins is proclaimed.

14 15   *Friends*, what do you think you are doing?

15 7   My brother[-*men*], . . . God made his choice among you: the pagans were to learn the Good News from me

13   'My brother[-*men*],' [James] said 'listen to me.'

19 25   As *you men* know . . . it is on this industry that we depend for our prosperity.

22 1   My brother[-*men*], my fathers, listen to what I have to say

Ac 23 1   My brother[-*men*], . . . I have conducted myself . . . with a perfectly clear conscience.

6   Brother[-*Men*], I am a Pharisee and the son of Pharisees.

27 10   *Friends*, I can see this voyage will be dangerous

21   *Friends*, . . . if you had . . . not put out from **Crete**, you would have spared yourselves all this damage

25   So take courage, *friends*,

28 17   Brother[-*Men*], . . . I was arrested in Jerusalem

4: MAN, MEN (GENERALLY)

A = Angel

Mt 7 24   a sensible *man* . . . built his house on rock.

26   a stupid *man* . . . built his house on sand.

Mk 6 44   Those who had eaten the loaves numbered five thousand *men*.

Lk 5 12   a *man* appeared, covered with leprosy.

18   some *men* appeared, carrying . . . a paralysed man

6 8   [Jesus] said to the *man* with the withered hand,

7 20   the *men* [sent by John the Baptist] reached Jesus and said,

8 38   The *man* from whom the devils had gone out asked to be allowed to stay with [Jesus],

9 14   there were about five thousand *men*.

38   Suddenly a *man* in the crowd cried out.

11 31   the Queen of the South will rise up with the *men* of this generation and condemn them.

14 24 <   not one of those *men* who were invited shall have a taste of my banquet.

17 12   As [Jesus] entered one of the villages, ten ⌐lepers (lit. *men* with leprosy) came to meet him.

22 63   the *men* who guarded Jesus were mocking . . . him.

24 4 A   As they stood there not knowing what to think, two *men* in brilliant clothes suddenly appeared

Jn 6 10   as many as five thousand *men* sat down.

Ac 1 10 A   suddenly two *men* in white were standing near them

21   We must therefore choose ⌐someone who has (lit. one of the *men* who have) been with us

2 5   there were devout *men* living in Jerusalem

3 2   there was a *man* being carried past. He was a cripple from birth;

4 4   many . . . became believers, the total number of ⌐whom (lit. which *men*) had now risen to something like five thousand.

5 36   Theudas . . . collected about four hundred ⌐followers (lit. *men*);

6 11   [members of the Synagogue of Freedmen] procured some *men* to say,

8 2   some devout *people* . . . buried Stephen

9 7   The *men* travelling with Saul stood there speechless,

38   the disciples . . . sent two *men* with an urgent message for [Peter],

10 5   you must send ⌐someone (lit. *men*) to Jaffa and fetch a man called Simon,

17   the *men* sent by Cornelius arrived.

19   Some *men* have come to see you.

21   Peter went down . . . to the *men*,

30 A   I suddenly saw a *man* in front of me

11 3   you have been visiting ⌐the uncircumcised (lit. uncircumcised *men*)

11   three *men* stopped outside the house

14 8   A *man* sat there who had never walked in his life,

17 5   The Jews . . . enlisted the help of ⌐a gang (lit. some violent *men*) from the market place,

19 7   There were about twelve of these *men* [disciples of John at Ephesus].

20 30   there will be *men* coming forward with a travesty of the truth on their lips

21 23   We have four *men* here who are under a vow;

26   the next day Paul took the *men* along and was purified with them,

38   So you are not the Egyptian who . . . led those four thousand ⌐cut-throats (lit. *men* who were cut-throats)

23 21   There are more than forty of those *men* lying in wait for [Paul],

25 23   Agrippa and Bernice arrived . . . attended by . . . the ⌐city notables (lit. notable *men* of the city);

24   King Agrippa, and all the *men* here present with us, you see before you the man

Rm 4 8   (Ps 32 2) happy the *man* whom the Lord considers sinless.

11 4   (1 K 19 18) I have kept for myself seven thousand *men* who have **not** bent the knee to Baal.

1 Tm 1 9   laws are not framed for people who are good . . . they are . . . for ⌐murderers (lit. *man*-killers),

Jm 1 8   That sort of *person*, in two minds . . . must not expect that the Lord will give him anything.

12   Happy the *man* who stands firm when trials come.

20   God's righteousness is never served by *man*'s anger;

23   To listen to the word and not obey is like ⌐looking at your (lit. a *man* looking at his) own features in a mirror and then [immediately forgetting what you looked like].

Jm	2	2	suppose a *man* comes into your synagogue, beautifully dressed and with a gold ring on,
	3	2	the only *man* who could reach perfection would be someone who never said anything wrong

4. WOMAN, WIFE: *GYNĒ*

2 gynaikarion 1   1 gynē 216
3 gynaikeios 1

G = Woman, in general; M = Mary, mother of Jesus

1: WOMAN

B = Woman, the symbol of Babylon (= Rome)
E = Eve; C = Woman, the symbol of the Church

Mt	5	28		if a man looks at a *woman* lustfully, he has already committed adultery with her
	9	20		a *woman* . . . had suffered from a haemorrhage for twelve years,
		22		from that moment the *woman* was well again.
	11	11	G	of all the children born of *women*, a greater than John the Baptist has never been seen;
	13	33		The kingdom of heaven is like the yeast a *woman* took
	14	21		Those who ate numbered about five thousand men, to say nothing of *women* and children.
	15	22		Then out came a Canaanite *woman* . . . and started shouting,
		28		*Woman*, you have great faith.
		38		four thousand men had eaten, to say nothing of *women* and children.
	26	7		a *woman* came to [Jesus] with an alabaster jar
		10		Why are you upsetting the *woman*?
	27	55		many *women* were there, watching from a distance,
	28	5		the angel spoke; and he said to the *women*,
Mk	5	25		there was a *woman* who had suffered from a haemorrhage for twelve years,
		33		the *woman* came forward, frightened and trembling
	7	25		A *woman* whose little daughter had an unclean spirit heard about [Jesus] . . . [26] . . . the *woman* was a pagan,
		26		
	14	3		a *woman* came in with an alabaster jar
	15	40		There were some *women* watching from a distance.
Lk	1	42	G	Of all *women* you are the most blessed,
	4	26		Elijah . . . was sent to a *woman* who was a widow at Zarephath,
	7	28	G	of all the children born of *women*, there is no one greater than John;
		37		a *woman* came in, who had a bad name in the town.
		39		If this man were a prophet, he would know who this *woman* is
		44		[Jesus] turned to the *woman*, 'Simon,' he said 'you see this *woman*?'
		50		[Jesus] said to the *woman*, 'Your faith has saved you'
	8	2		certain *women* who had been cured of evil spirits
		43		there was a *woman* suffering from a haemorrhage
		47		Seeing herself discovered, the *woman* came forward trembling,
	10	38		a *woman* named Martha welcomed [Jesus] into her house.
	11	27		a *woman* in the crowd raised her voice
	13	11		a *woman* was there who . . . had been possessed by a spirit that left her enfeebled;
		12		*Woman*, you are rid of your infirmity
		21		[The kingdom of God] is like the yeast a *woman* took
	15	8		what *woman* with ten drachmas would not, if she lost one . . . search . . . till she found it?
	22	57		'*Woman*,' [Peter] said 'I do not know him.'
	23	27		Large numbers of people followed [Jesus], and of *women* too,
		49		All his friends stood . . . at a distance; so also did the *women*
		55		the *women* who had come from Galilee with Jesus . . . took note of the tomb
	24	22		some *women* from our group have astounded us:
		24		Some of our friends . . . found everything exactly as the *women* had reported,
Jn	2	4	M	Jesus said [to his mother], '*Woman*, why turn to me?'
	4	7		a Samaritan *woman* came to draw water,
		9		The Samaritan *woman* said to [Jesus], 'What? . . . you ask me, a Samaritan *woman*, for a drink?'
		11		'You have no bucket, sir,' ⌐she (ˇ the *woman*) answered
		15		'Sir,' said the *woman* 'give me some of that water'
		17		The *woman* answered, 'I have no husband'.
		19		'I see you are a prophet, sir' said the *woman*.
		21		[Jesus to the Samaritan woman:] Believe me, *woman*, the hour is coming
		25		The *woman* said to him, 'I know that Messiah . . . is coming'
		27	G	his disciples . . . were surprised to find him speaking to a *woman*,
		28		The *woman* put down her water jar and hurried back to the town

Jn	4	39		Many Samaritans . . . had believed in him on the strength of the *woman*'s testimony . . . [42] . . . they said to the *woman*, 'Now we no longer believe because of what you told us;'
		42		
	8	3		The scribes . . . brought a *woman* along who had been caught committing adultery;
		4		Master, this *woman* was caught in the very act of committing adultery,
		9		Jesus was left alone with the *woman*,
		10		[Jesus] said, '*Woman*, where are they?'
	16	21	G	A *woman* in childbirth suffers,
	19	26	M	Jesus said to his mother, '*Woman*, this is your son'.
	20	13		[The two angels said to Mary of Magdala:] '*Woman*, why are you weeping?'
		15		Jesus said, '*Woman*, why are you weeping?'
Ac	1	14		All these joined in continuous prayer, together with several *women*,
	5	14		the numbers of men and *women* who came to believe . . . increased
	8	3		Saul then worked for the total destruction of the Church . . . arresting both men and *women*
		12		[the Samaritan people] were baptised, both men and *women*,
	9	2		[Saul] asked for letters . . . that would authorise him to arrest . . . any followers of the Way, men or *women*,
	13	50		the Jews worked upon some of the devout *women* of the upper classes
	16	1		Timothy, ⌐whose mother (lit. the son of a *woman* who) was a Jewess
		13		We . . . preached to the *women* who had come to the meeting.
		14		One of these *women* was called Lydia,
	17	4		a number of rich *women* [were convinced and joined Paul and Silas].
		12		many Greek *women* from the upper classes and a number of the men [became believers].
		34		some . . . became believers, among them . . . a *woman* called Damaris,
	21	5		Together with the *women* and children they all escorted us on our way
	22	4		I . . . sent *women* as well as men to prison in chains
1 Co	7	1	G	it is a good thing for a man not to touch a *woman*;
		34		an unmarried *woman* . . . can devote herself to the Lord's affairs;
	9	5		[Have we not] the right to take a Christian *woman* round with us . . . ?
	11	3	G	man is the head of *woman*,
		5	G	For a *woman* . . . it is a sign of disrespect to her head if she prays or prophesies unveiled . . . [6] . . . a *woman* who will not wear a veil ought to have her hair cut off. If a *woman* is ashamed to have her hair cut off . . . she ought to wear a veil.
		6	G	
			G	
		7	G	*woman* is the reflection of man's glory. [8] For man did not come from *woman*; no, *woman* came from man; [9] and man was not created for the sake of *woman*, but *woman* was created for the sake of man. [10] That is the argument for *women*'s covering their heads with a symbol of the authority over them, out of respect for the angels. [11] However, though *woman* cannot do without man, neither can man do without *woman*, in the Lord; [12] *woman* may come from man, but man is born of *woman* – both come from God.
		8	G E	
		9	G	
		10	G	
		11		
			G	
		12	G E	
			G	
		13	G	Ask yourselves if it is fitting for a *woman* to pray to God without a veil.
		15	G	a *woman* . . . thinks long hair her glory
	14	34	G	*women* are to remain quiet at meetings
		35	G	it does not seem right for a *woman* to raise her voice at meetings.
Ga	4	4	M	God sent his Son, born of a *woman*,
1 Tm	2	9	G	*women* are to wear suitable clothes . . . their adornment is [10] to do the sort of good works that are proper for *women* who profess to be religious.
		10		
		11	G	During instruction, a *woman* should be quiet and respectful.
		12	G	I am not giving permission for a *woman* to . . . tell a man what to do.
		14	E	it was not Adam who was led astray but the *woman*
	3	11	G?	the *women* [= ? deaconesses ? deacons' wives] must be respectable, not gossips but sober and quite reliable.
2 Tm	3	6		men who insinuate themselves into families in order to get influence over silly *women* who are obsessed with their sins
			2	
Rv	2	20		the *woman* Jezebel . . . claims to be a prophetess,
	9	8	G	[the locusts had] hair like *women*'s hair,
	12	1	C	a great sign appeared in heaven: a *woman*,
		4	C	the dragon stopped in front of the *woman* as she was having the child,
		6	C	the *woman* escaped into the desert,
		13	C	the devil . . . sprang in pursuit of the *woman* . . . [14] but ⌐she (lit. the *woman*) was given a huge pair of eagle's wings
		14	C	
		15		the serpent vomited water from his mouth, like a river,
		16	C	after the *woman* . . . [16] but the earth came to the *woman*'s rescue . . . [17] . . . the dragon was enraged with the *woman*
		17	C	

Rv 14	4	G		These are the ones who have . . . not been defiled with *women*;
17	3	B		I saw a *woman* riding a scarlet beast . . . ⁴ The *woman* was
	4			dressed in purple . . . and glittered with gold . . . ⁶ I saw
	6	B		that ⌐she (lit. the *woman*) was drunk . . . with the blood
	7			of the saints . . . ⁷ . . . I will tell you the meaning of
	9	B		this *woman* . . . ⁹ . . . the seven heads are the seven hills,
		B		and the *woman* is sitting on them.
	18	B		The *woman* you saw is the great city [of Babylon]

2: WOMAN AS A WIFE OR WIDOW

Mt 1	20	M	Joseph, . . . do not be afraid to take Mary home as your *wife*,
	24	M	Joseph . . . took his *wife* to his home
5	31		It has also been said: (Dt 24 1) Anyone who divorces his *wife* must give her a writ of dismissal. ³² But I say this to
	32		you: everyone who divorces his *wife* . . . makes her an adulteress;
14	3		Herod . . . had arrested John . . . because of Herodias, his brother Philip's *wife*.
18	25		his master gave orders that he should be sold, together with his *wife* and children
19	3		Is it against the Law for a man to divorce his *wife* . . .?
	5		(Gn 2 24) a man must leave father and mother, and cling to his *wife*,
	8		Moses allowed you to divorce your *wives*,
	9		the man who divorces his *wife* . . . and marries another, is guilty of adultery;
	10		If that is how things are between husband and *wife*, it is not advisable to marry.
	29		everyone who has left houses . . . father, mother, (▽ *wife*,) children . . . for the sake of my name will be repaid
22	24		if a man dies childless, his brother is to marry the *widow*, his sister-in-law, to raise children for his brother.
	25		we had a case involving seven brothers; the first married and then died . . . leaving his *wife* to his brother . . .
	27		²⁷ . . . then last of all the *woman* herself died. ²⁸ Now
	28		at the resurrection to which of those seven will she be *wife* . . .?
27	19		as [Pilate] was seated in the chair of judgement, his *wife* sent him a message,
Mk 6	17		Herod . . . had sent to have John arrested . . . because of Herodias, his brother Philip's *wife*
	18		It is against the law for you to have your brother's *wife*.
10	2		Is it against the law for a man to divorce his *wife*?
	7		(Gn 2 24) a man must leave father and mother (▽ and be joined to his *wife*)
	11		The man who divorces his *wife* and marries another is guilty of adultery
12	19		(Dt 25 5) if a man's brother dies leaving a *wife* . . . the man must marry the *widow*
	20		there were seven brothers. The first married a *wife* and
	22		died leaving no children . . . ²² . . . Last of all the *woman*
	23		herself died. ²³ Now at the resurrection . . . whose *wife* will she be, since she had been ⌐married (lit. a *wife*) to all seven?
Lk 1	5		Zechariah . . . had a *wife* . . . who was a descendant of Aaron.
	13		Your *wife* Elizabeth is to bear you a son
	18		my *wife* is getting on in years.
	24		his *wife* Elizabeth conceived,
3	19		Herod . . . [was] criticised for his relations with his brother's *wife* Herodias
8	3		Joanna the *wife* of Herod's steward Chuza,
14	20		another said, 'I have just ⌐got married (lit. married a *wife*)'
	26		If any man comes to me without hating his . . . *wife*, children . . . he cannot be my disciple.
16	18		Everyone who divorces his *wife* and marries another is guilty of adultery.
17	32		Remember Lot's *wife*.
18	29		there is no one who has left house, *wife* . . . or children [who will not be given repayment]
20	28		if a man's ⌐married brother (lit. brother, having a *wife*) dies childless, the man must marry the *widow*
	29		there were seven brothers. The first, having married a *wife*,
	32		died childless . . . ³² Finally the *woman* herself died.
	33		³³ Now, as to the *woman* at the resurrection, to which of them will she be *wife* since she had been ⌐married (lit. *wife*) to all seven?
Ac 5	1		Ananias . . . and his *wife*, Sapphira, agreed to sell a property;
	2		² but with his *wife*'s connivance he kept back part of the proceeds
	7		[Ananias's] *wife* came in, not knowing what had taken place.
18	2		Aquila . . . and his *wife* Priscilla had recently left Italy
24	24		Felix came with his *wife* Drusilla
Rm 7	2		A married *woman* . . . has legal obligations to her husband while he is alive,
1 Co 5	1		one of you is living with his father's *wife*.

1 Co 7	2		let each man have his own *wife* and each woman her own
	3		husband. ³ The husband must give his *wife* what she has the right to expect, and so too the *wife* to the husband.
	4		⁴ The *wife* has no rights over her own body; it is the husband who has them. In the same way, the husband has no rights over his body; the *wife* has them.
	10		a *wife* must not leave her husband ¹¹ . . . nor must a husband
	11		send his *wife* away.
	12		If a brother has a *wife* who is an unbeliever . . . he must
	13		not send her away; ¹³ and if a *woman* has an unbeliever
	14		for her husband . . . she must not leave him. ¹⁴ This is because the unbelieving husband is made one with the saints through his *wife*, and the unbelieving *wife* is made one with the saints through her husband.
	16		If you are a *wife*, it may be your part to save your husband . . . if a husband . . . it may be your part to save your *wife*,
	27		If you are tied to a *wife*, do not look for freedom; if you are free of a *wife*, then do not look for a *wife*.
	29		Those who have *wives* should live as though they had none,
	33		a married man has to . . . devote himself to pleasing his *wife*;
	39		A *wife* is tied as long as her husband is alive.
Ep 5	22		*Wives* should regard their husbands as they regard the Lord,
	23		as Christ is head of the Church . . . so is a husband the head of his *wife*;
	24		as the Church submits to Christ, so should *wives* to their husbands, in everything.
	25		Husbands should love their *wives* just as Christ loved the Church
	28		husbands must love their *wives* . . . for a man to love his *wife* is for him to love himself.
	31		(Gn 2 24) a man must leave his father and mother and be joined to his *wife*,
	33		each one of you must love his *wife* as he loves himself; and let every *wife* respect her husband,
Col 3	18		*Wives*, give way to your husbands,
	19		Husbands, love your *wives*
1 Tm 3	2		the president . . . must not have been ⌐married more than once (lit. husband to more than one *woman*),
	12		Deacons must not have been ⌐married more than once (lit. husbands to more than one *woman*),
5	9		Enrolment as a widow is permissible only for a *woman* . . . who has ⌐had (lit. been *wife* to) only one husband.
Tt 1	6		[an elder] must not have been ⌐married more than once (lit. husband to more than one *woman*),
Heb 11	35		Some came back to their *wives* from the dead, by resurrection;
1 P 3	1		*wives* should be obedient to their husbands. Then . . . they may find themselves won over . . . by the way their *wives* behave,
	5		That is how the holy *women* of the past dressed themselves . . . and were . . . obedient to their husbands;
	7		husbands must always treat [their wives] with consideration in their life together, respecting a *woman*
Rv 19	7	X	[the Lamb's] *bride* is ready,
21	9	X	I will show you the *bride* that the Lamb has married.

5. MALE, MEN(FOLK) and FEMALE, WOMEN: *ARSĒN* and *THĒLYS*

1 *arsēn*	9	3 *thēlys* 5
2 *arseno*(-*koitēs*) 2		

Mt 19	4		(Gn 1 27) the creator from the beginning made them *male*
		3	and *female*
Mk 10	6		(Gn 1 27) from the beginning of creation God made them
		/3	*male* and *female*.
Lk 2	23		(Ex 13 2) Every first-born *male* must be consecrated to the Lord
Rm 1	26	3	their *women* have turned from natural intercourse to unnatural
	27		practices ²⁷ and . . . their *menfolk* have given up natural
		3	⌐intercourse (lit. relations with *women*) to be consumed with passion for each other, *men* doing shameless things with *men*
1 Co 6	9	2	people of immoral lives . . . *sodomites*, ¹⁰ . . . will never inherit the kingdom of God.
Ga 3	28	/3	there are no more distinctions between . . . *male* and *female*, but all of you are one in Christ Jesus.
1 Tm 1	10	2	[laws are framed] for *those who are immoral* with women or with boys
Rv 12	5		The woman brought a *male* child into the world,
	13		the devil . . . sprang in pursuit of the woman, the mother of the *male* child,

6. PEOPLE, CROWDS: *OCHLOS*

1 *ochlos* 174		2 *ochlo-poieō* 1

Mt 4	25		Large *crowds* followed [Jesus],

Mt	5	1	Seeing the *crowds*, [Jesus] went up the hill.
	7	28	his teaching made a deep impression on the *people*
	8	1	large *crowds* followed [Jesus].
		18	When Jesus saw the great *crowds* all about him he gave orders to leave for the other side.
	9	8	A feeling of awe came over the *crowd* when they saw this,
		23	Jesus . . . saw the flute-players, with the *crowd* making a commotion
		25	when the *people* had been turned out [Jesus] went inside
		33	the dumb man spoke and the *people* were amazed.
		36	when [Jesus] saw the *crowds* he felt sorry for them
	11	7	Jesus began to talk to the *people* about John:
	12	23	All the *people* were astounded and said, 'Can this be the Son of David?'
		46	[Jesus] was still speaking to the *crowds* when his mother and his brothers appeared;
	13	2	such *crowds* gathered round [Jesus] that he got into a boat and sat there. The *people* all stood on the beach,
		34	In all this Jesus spoke to the *crowds* in parables;
		36	leaving the *crowds*, [Jesus] went to the house;
	14	5	[Herod] had wanted to kill [John] but was afraid of the *people*,
		13	the *people* heard of this and, leaving the towns, went after [Jesus] on foot.
		14	as [Jesus] stepped ashore he saw a large *crowd*; and he took pity on them
		15	send the *people* away, and they can go . . . to buy themselves some food.
		19	[Jesus] gave orders that the *people* were to sit down on the grass; then he took the five loaves and . . . handed them to his disciples who gave them to the *crowds*.
		22	[Jesus] made the disciples . . . go on ahead . . . while he would send the *crowds* away. ²³ After sending the *crowds* away he went up into the hills by himself to pray.
	15	10	[Jesus] called the *people* to him and said, 'Listen . . .'
		30	large *crowds* came to [Jesus] bringing the lame . . . and many others . . . ³¹ The *crowds* were astonished to see the dumb speaking,
		32	I feel sorry for all these *people*; they have been with me for three days now and have nothing to eat.
		33	Where could we get enough bread . . . to feed such a *crowd*?
		35	[Jesus] instructed the *crowd* to sit down on the ground,
		36	the disciples . . . gave [the loaves] to the *crowds*.
		39	when [Jesus] had sent the *crowds* away he got into the boat
	17	14	As they were rejoining the *crowd* a man came up to [Jesus]
	19	2	Large *crowds* followed [Jesus], and he healed them there.
	20	29	As they left Jericho a large *crowd* followed [Jesus].
		31	the *crowd* scolded [the two blind men] and told them to keep quiet,
	21	8	⌐Great crowds of (lit. Very many) *people* spread their cloaks on the road . . . ⁹ The *crowds* who went in front of him . . . were all shouting: Hosanna
		11	the *crowds* answered, 'This is the prophet Jesus'
		26	we have the *people* to fear, for they all hold that John was a prophet.
		46	they were afraid of the *crowds*, who looked on [Jesus] as a prophet.
	22	33	his teaching made a deep impression on the *people*
	23	1	addressing the *people* and his disciples Jesus said,
	26	47	Judas . . . appeared, and with him a large ⌐number of men (or: *crowd*) armed with swords and clubs, sent by the chief priests and elders of the people.
		55	Jesus said to the *crowds*, 'Am I a brigand . . .?'
	27	15	At festival time it was the governor's practice to release a prisoner for the *people*,
		20	The chief priests and the elders . . . had persuaded the *crowd* to demand the release of Barabbas
		24	Pilate . . . washed his hands in front of the *crowd*
Mk	2	4	the *crowd* made it impossible to get [the paralytic to Jesus]
		13	all the *people* came to Jesus,
	3	9	[Jesus] asked his disciples to have a boat ready for him because of the *crowd*,
		20	[Jesus] went home again, and once more . . . a *crowd* collected
		32	A *crowd* was sitting round [Jesus]
	4	1	such a huge *crowd* gathered round [Jesus] that he got into a boat . . . The *people* were all along the shore,
		36	leaving the *crowd* behind [the disciples] took [Jesus] . . . in the boat;
	5	21	When Jesus had crossed again . . . to the other side, a large *crowd* gathered round him
		24	Jesus went with [Jairus] and a large *crowd* followed him;
		27	[the woman suffering from a haemorrhage] came up behind [Jesus] through the *crowd* and touched his cloak.
		30	Jesus turned round in the *crowd* and said, 'Who touched my clothes?'
		31	You see how the *crowd* is pressing round you and yet you say, 'Who touched me?'
	6	34	[Jesus] saw a large *crowd*; and he took pity on them

Mk	6	45	[Jesus] made his disciples . . . go on ahead . . . while he himself sent the *crowd* away.
	7	14	[Jesus] called the *people* to him again and said, 'Listen . . .'
		17	away from the *crowd*, his disciples questioned him about the parable.
		33	[Jesus] took [the deaf man] aside in private, away from the *crowd*,
	8	1	once again a great *crowd* had gathered,
		2	I feel sorry for [all] these *people*;
		6	[Jesus] instructed the *crowd* to sit down on the ground, and he took the seven loaves, and . . . his disciples . . . distributed them among the *crowd*.
		34	[Jesus] called the *people* and his disciples to him and said,
	9	14	they saw a large *crowd* round [the disciples]
		15	The moment they saw [Jesus] the whole *crowd* were struck with amazement
		17	A man answered [Jesus] from the *crowd*, 'Master, I have brought my son to you'
		25	when Jesus saw [how] *many people* were pressing round him, he rebuked the unclean spirit.
	10	1	again *crowds* gathered round him,
		46	[Jesus] left Jericho with his disciples and a large *crowd*,
	11	18	the *people* were carried away by his teaching.
		32	they had the *people* to fear, for everyone held that John was a real prophet.
	12	12	they would have liked to arrest [Jesus] . . . but they were afraid of the *crowds*.
		37	the great majority of the *people* heard this with delight.
		41	[Jesus] watched the *people* putting money into the treasury,
	14	43	Judas . . . came up with a ⌐number of men (or: *crowd*) armed with swords
	15	8	the *crowd* . . . began to ask Pilate the customary favour,
		11	The chief priests . . . had incited the *crowd* to demand that [Pilate] should release Barabbas for them
		15	Pilate, anxious to placate the *crowd*, released Barabbas
Lk	3	7	[John the Baptist] said . . . to the *crowds* who came to be baptised by him 'Brood of vipers, . . .'
		10	all the *people* asked John, 'What must we do, then?'
	4	42	The *crowds* went to look for [Jesus],
	5	1	[Jesus] was standing . . . by the Lake of Gennesaret, with the *crowd* pressing round him
		3	[Jesus] taught the *crowds* from the boat.
		15	large *crowds* would gather to hear [Jesus]
		19	the *crowd* made it impossible to find a way of getting [the paralytic] in,
		29	with them at table was a large *gathering* of tax collectors and others.
	6	17	there was a large *gathering* of his disciples with a great crowd of people
		19	everyone in the *crowd* was trying to touch [Jesus]
	7	9	Jesus . . . said to the *crowd* following him, '. . . not even in Israel have I found faith like this'.
		11	[Jesus] went to . . . Nain, accompanied by his disciples and a great *number of people*.
		12	a considerable *number of* the townspeople were with [the widow of Nain].
	8	4	With a large *crowd* gathering . . . [Jesus] used this parable:
		19	His mother and his brothers . . . could not get to [Jesus] because of the *crowd*.
		40	Jesus was welcomed by the *crowd*, for they were all there waiting for him.
		42	the *crowds* were almost stifling Jesus as he went.
		45	Master, it is the *crowds* round you, pushing.
	9	11	the *crowds* got to know [where Jesus was] and they went after him.
		12	Send the *people* away, and they can go . . . to find . . . food;
		16	[Jesus] took the five loaves and the two fish . . . and handed them to his disciples to distribute among the *crowd*.
		18	Who do the *crowds* say I am?
		37	a large *crowd* came to meet [Jesus].
		38	Suddenly a man in the *crowd* cried out . . . 'I implore you to look at my son'
	11	14	the dumb man spoke, and the *people* were amazed.
		27	a woman in the *crowd* raised her voice
		29	The *crowds* got even bigger
	12	1	the *people* had gathered in their thousands
		13	A man in the *crowd* said to him, 'Master, tell my brother to give me a share of our inheritance'.
		54	[Jesus] said again to the *crowds*, 'When you see a cloud . . . you say at once that rain is coming,'
	13	14	the synagogue official . . . addressed the *people* [present]. 'There are six days' he said 'when work is to be done.'
		17	all the *people* were overjoyed at all the wonders [Jesus] worked.
	14	25	Great *crowds* accompanied [Jesus] on his way
	18	36	[the blind man] heard the *crowd* going past
	19	3	[Zacchaeus] was anxious to see what kind of man Jesus was, but he . . . could not see him for the *crowd*;
		3	Some Pharisees in the *crowd* said to him, 'Master, check your disciples',

Lk 22	6	[Judas] looked for an opportunity to betray him to them without the *people* knowing.
	47	[Jesus] was still speaking when a ⌐*number of men* (or: *crowd*) appeared, and at the head of them . . . Judas,
23	4	Pilate then said to the chief priests and the *crowd*, 'I find no case against this man.'
	48	all the *people* . . . went home beating their breasts.
Jn 5	13	Jesus had disappeared into the *crowd* that filled the place.
6	2	a large *crowd* followed [Jesus],
	5	Jesus saw the *crowds* approaching
	22	the *crowd* . . . had stayed on the other side
	24	the *people* saw that neither Jesus nor his disciples were there,
7	12	*People* stood *in groups* whispering about [Jesus]. Some said . . . 'he is leading the *people* astray'.
	20	The *crowd* replied, 'You are mad!'
	31	There were many people in the *crowds*, however, who believed in [Jesus];
	32	rumours like this about [Jesus] were spreading among the *people*,
	40	Several people who had been listening in the *crowd* said, 'Surely he must be the prophet',
	43	So the *people* could not agree about [Jesus].
	49	This *rabble* knows nothing about the Law – they are damned.
11	42	I speak for the sake of ⌐all these (lit. the *people*) who stand round me,
12	9	a large *number* of Jews heard that [Jesus] was [at Bethany]
	12	The next day the *crowds* . . . heard that Jesus was on his way to Jerusalem.
	17	⌐All (lit. The *people*) who had been with [Jesus] when he called Lazarus out of the tomb
	18	it was because of this, too, that the *crowd* came out to meet [Jesus]:
	29	*People* . . . said it was a clap of thunder;
	34	The *crowd* answered, 'The Law has taught us that the Christ will remain for ever.'
Ac 1	15	there were about a hundred and twenty persons in the *congregation*
6	7	a large *group* of priests [in Jerusalem] made their submission to the faith.
8	6	The *people* united in welcoming the message Philip preached,
11	24	a large number of *people* were won over to the Lord.
	26	[Barnabas and Saul] were to live together . . . a whole year, instructing a large number of *people* [at Antioch].
13	45	When they saw the *crowds*, the Jews, prompted by jealousy . . . contradicted everything Paul said.
14	11	the *crowd* . . . shouted in the language of Lycaonia, 'These people are gods'
	13	The priests . . . proposing that [all] the *people* should offer sacrifice with them, brought garlanded oxen
	14	Barnabas and Paul . . . rushed into the *crowd*, shouting, ['What do you think you are doing?']
	18	Even this speech . . . was scarcely enough to stop the *crowd* offering [Barnabas and Paul] sacrifice.
	19	some Jews . . . turned the *people* against the apostles. They stoned Paul
16	22	The *crowd* . . . showed its hostility to [Paul and Silas],
17	5	2 The Jews . . . *stirred up a crowd*,
	8	This accusation alarmed the *citizens* and the city councillors
	13	the Jews of Thessalonika . . . went [to Beroea] to make trouble and stir up the *people*.
19	26	this man Paul has . . . converted a great number of *people*
	33	The Jews pushed Alexander to the front (⌐ of the *people*), and . . . some of the *crowd* shouted encouragement
	35	the town clerk eventually succeeded in calming the *crowd*,
21	27	some Jews . . . stirred up the *crowd* and seized [Paul],
	34	People in the *crowd* called out different things,
	35	the *crowd* became so violent that [Paul] had to be carried by the soldiers;
24	12	it is not true that they ever found me . . . stirring up the *mob*, either in the Temple . . . or about the town;
	18	I had been purified, and there was no *crowd* involved, and no disturbance.
Rv 7	9	I saw a huge *number*, impossible to count, *of people* from every nation, race, tribe and language;
17	15	The waters you saw . . . are all the peoples, the *populations*, the nations and the languages.
19	1	I seemed to hear the great sound of a huge *crowd* in heaven, singing, 'Alleluia!'
	6	I seemed to hear the voices of a huge *crowd*, like the sound of the ocean

7. PEOPLE: *LAOS*

laos 142

1: PEOPLE(S), NATIONS, TRIBES

Lk 2	31	you have prepared [the salvation] for all the *nations* to see,

Ac 4	25	(Ps 2 1) Why this arrogance among the nations, these futile plots among the *peoples*?
Rm 15	11	(Ps 117 1) Let all the pagans praise the Lord, let all the *peoples* sing his praises.
Rv 5	9	you bought men for God of every race, language, *people* and nation
7	9	I saw a huge number . . . of people from every nation, race, *tribe* and language;
10	11	You are to prophesy . . . about many different *nations* and countries and languages
11	9	Men out of every *people*, race, language and nation will stare at [the two witnesses'] corpses,
13	7	[the beast was] given power over every race, *people*, language and nation;
14	6	I saw another angel . . . sent to announce the Good News of eternity to . . . every nation, race, language and *tribe*.
17	15	The waters you saw . . . are all the *peoples*, the populations, the nations and the languages.

2: (THE) PEOPLE (OF ISRAEL, OF GOD)

Mt 1	21	Jesus . . . is the one who is to save his *people* from their sins.
2	4	[Herod] called together all the chief priests and the scribes of the *people*,
	6	(Mi 5 1) Bethlehem, . . . out of you will come a leader who will shepherd my *people* Israel.
4	16	(Is 9 1) The *people* that lived in darkness has seen a great light;
13	15	(Is 6 10) the heart of this *nation* has grown coarse,
15	8	(Is 29 13) This *people* honours me only with lip-service,
21	23	the chief priests and the elders of the *people* came to [Jesus]
26	3	the chief priests and the elders of the *people* assembled
	5	there must be no disturbance among the *people*.
	47	Judas . . . appeared, and with him a large number of men . . . sent by the chief priests and elders of the *people*.
27	1	all the chief priests and the elders of the *people* met in council to bring about the death of Jesus.
	25	the *people* . . . shouted back, 'His blood be on us and on our children!'
Mk 7	6	(Is 29 13) This *people* honours me only with lip-service,
14	2	there will be a disturbance among the *people*.
Lk 1	10	the whole congregation of the *people* was outside, praying.
	17	[John] will go before him . . . preparing for the Lord a *people* fit for him
	21	the *people* were waiting for Zechariah
	68	the God of Israel . . . has visited his *people*, he has come to their rescue
	77	[you will go before the Lord] to give his *people* knowledge of salvation
2	10	a joy to be shared by the whole *people*.
	32	[I have seen] a light to enlighten the pagans and the glory of your *people* Israel.
7	16	God has visited his *people*.
20	1	[Jesus] was teaching the *people* in the Temple
	6	the *people* will all stone us,
	9	[Jesus] went on to tell the *people* this parable:
	19	But for their fear of the *people*, the scribes and the chief priests would have liked to lay hands on [Jesus] that very moment,
21	23	great misery will descend on the land and wrath on this *people*.
	38	from early morning the *people* would gather round [Jesus] in the Temple
22	2	the chief priests and the scribes . . . mistrusted the *people*.
	66	there was a meeting of the elders of the *people*.
Jn 8	2	all the *people* came to [Jesus],
11	50	it is better for one man to die for the *people*, than for the whole nation to be destroyed.
18	14	It is better for one man to die for the *people*.
Ac 2	47	[the faithful] praised God and were looked up to by ⌐everyone (lit. all the *people*)
3	9	⌐Everyone (lit. All the *people*) could see [the lame man] walking and praising God,
	11	⌐Everyone (lit. All the *people*) came running towards [Peter and John] in great excitement . . . ¹² When Peter saw the *people* he addressed them,
	12	
	23	(Dt 18 19) The man who does not listen to that prophet is to be cut off from the *people*.
4	1	While [Peter and John] were still talking to the *people* the priests came up to them . . . ² They were extremely annoyed at their teaching the *people*
	2	
	8	Peter . . . addressed them, 'Rulers of the *people*, and elders!'
	10	I am glad to tell you all, and would indeed be glad to tell the whole *people* of Israel,
	17	to stop the whole thing spreading any further among the *people*, let us caution them

Ac 4 21 [the court] released [Peter and John] since all the *people* were giving glory to God for what had happened.
27 Herod and Pontius Pilate made an alliance with the pagan nations and the *peoples* of Israel against . . . Jesus
5 13 the *people* were loud in their praise . . . ¹²ª So many signs
12a and wonders were worked among the *people* at the hands of the apostles
20 tell the *people* all about this new Life.
25 the men you imprisoned are in the Temple . . . preaching to the *people.*
26 The captain went with his men and fetched [the apostles]. They were afraid to use force in case the *people* stoned them.
34 Gamaliel . . . was a doctor of the Law and respected by the whole *people,*
6 8 Stephen . . . began to work miracles and great signs among the *people.*
12 [some members of the Synagogue of Freedmen] turned the *people* against [Stephen] as well as the elders and scribes,
7 17 our *nation* in Egypt grew larger and larger,
34 (Ex 3 7) I have seen the way my *people* are ill-treated in Egypt,
10 2 [Cornelius] gave generously to ⌐Jewish causes (lit. the *people*)
42 [God] has ordered us to proclaim this to his *people*
12 11 The Lord . . . has saved me . . . from all that the Jewish *people* were so certain would happen to me.
13 15 if you would like to address some words of encouragement to the *congregation,* please do so.
17 The God of our *nation* Israel chose our ancestors, and made our *people* great when they were living as foreigners in Egypt;
24 [John] proclaimed a baptism of repentance for the whole *people* of Israel.
31 it is these same companions of [Jesus] who are now his witnesses before our *people.*
15 14 Simeon has described how God first arranged to enlist a *people* for his name out of the pagans.
18 10 I have so many *people* on my side in this city [Corinth]
19 4 [John] insisted that the *people* should believe in the one who was to come after him
21 28 This is the man who preaches to everyone everywhere against our *people,*
23 5 (Ex 22 27) You must not curse a ruler of your *people.*
26 17 I shall deliver you from the *people* and from the pagans,
23 the Christ . . . was to proclaim that light now shone for our *people* and for the pagans too.
28 17 I have done nothing against our *people*
26 (Is 6 9) Go to this *nation* and say:
27 (Is 6 10) the heart of this *nation* has grown coarse,
Rm 9 25 (Ho 2 25) I shall say to a *people* that was not mine, 'You are my *people*' . . . ²⁶ Instead of being told (Ho 1 10), 'You are no *people* of mine', they will now be called the sons of the living God.
10 21 (Is 65 2) I stretched out my hand to a disobedient and rebellious *people.*
11 1 (Ps 94 14) is it possible that God has rejected his *people*? Of course not. I . . . ² could never agree that God had rejected his *people,* [the people] he chose specially long ago.
15 10 (Dt 32 43) Rejoice, pagans, with his *people,*
1 Co 10 7 (Ex 32 6) After sitting down to eat and drink, the *people* got up to amuse themselves.
14 21 (Is 28 11) Through men speaking strange languages . . . I shall talk to the *nation,*
2 Co 6 16 (Lv 26 12) I will be their God and they shall be my *people.*
Tt 2 14 [Christ] sacrificed himself . . . to purify a *people* so that it could be his very own
Heb 2 17 a compassionate and trustworthy high priest . . . able to atone for ⌐human (lit. the *people's*) sins.
4 9 There must still be . . . a place of rest reserved for God's *people,*
5 3 [every high priest] has to make sin offerings for himself as well as for the *people.*
7 5 the descendants of Levi . . . are obliged . . . to take tithes from the *people,*
11 the Law given to the *nation* rests on [the levitical priesthood],
27 the other high priests [offer sacrifices] for their own sins and then for those of the *people,*
8 10 (Jr 31 33) I will be their God and they shall be my *people.*
9 7 the high priest . . . must . . . offer for his own faults and the *people's.*
19 after Moses had announced all the commandments of the Law to the *people,* he . . . sprinkled . . . all the *people,*
10 30 (Dt 32 36) The Lord will judge his *people.*
11 25 [Moses] chose to be ill-treated in company with God's *people*
13 12 Jesus too suffered outside the gate to sanctify the *people*
1 P 2 9 (cf. Is 43 21) you are . . . a consecrated nation, a *people* set apart to sing the praises of God . . . ¹⁰ Once you were not a *people* at all and now you are the *People* of God;
10
2 P 2 1 there were false prophets in the past history of our *people.*
Jude 5 the Lord rescued the *nation* from Egypt,
Rv 18 4 Come out, my *people,* away from [Babylon],

Rv 21 3 they shall be his ᵛ *people* (G *peoples*), and he will be their God;

3: PEOPLE (GENERALLY)

Mt 4 23 [Jesus] went round the whole of Galilee . . . curing all kinds of diseases and sickness among the *people.*
27 64 have the sepulchre kept secure . . . for fear his disciples . . . steal him away and tell the *people,* 'He has risen from the dead'.
Lk 3 15 A feeling of expectancy had grown among the *people,*
18 there were many other things [John] said to exhort the *people*
21 when all the . . . *people* had been baptised . . . heaven opened
6 17 there was . . . a great crowd of *people* from all parts of Judaea
7 1 When [Jesus] had come to the end of all he wanted the *people* to hear, he went into Capernaum.
29 All the *people* who heard [John] acknowledged God's plan
8 47 the woman . . . explained in front of all the *people* why she had touched [Jesus]
9 13 unless we are to . . . buy food for all these *people.*
18 43 all the *people* . . . gave praise to God for what had happened.
19 47 the scribes, with the support of the leading *citizens,* tried to do away with [Jesus],
48 the *people* as a whole hung on [Jesus's] words.
20 26 they were unable to find fault with anything [Jesus] had to say in *public;*
45 While all the *people* were listening [Jesus] said to the disciples,
23 5 [the Jews] persisted, 'He is inflaming the *people*'
13 Pilate then summoned the chief priests . . . and the *people.*
14 ¹⁴ 'You brought this man before me' he said 'as ⌐a political agitator (lit. a man leading the *people* into revolt).'
27 Large numbers of *people* followed [Jesus],
35 The *people* stayed there watching [Jesus].
24 19 Jesus . . . was a great prophet . . . in the sight of God and of the whole *people;*
Ac 5 37 Judas the Galilean . . . attracted ⌐crowds of (lit. many *people* as) supporters;
10 41 [God allowed Jesus to be seen,] not by the whole *people* but only by certain witnesses
12 4 Herod meant to try Peter in *public*
21 30 *people* came running from all sides;
36 the whole ⌐mob (lit. crowd of *people*) was after them, shouting, 'Kill [Paul]!'
39 Please give me permission to speak to the *people.*
40 Paul . . . gestured to the *people* with his hand.

8. (THE) PEOPLE, PEOPLE'S ASSEMBLY – PUBLICLY, IN PUBLIC: *DĒMOS*

1 *dēmos*	4	3 *dēm(-ēgoreō)* 1
2 *dēmosios*	4	

Ac 5 18 2 they arrested the apostles and had them put in the ⌐common
2 (or: *public*) gaol.
12 21 3 Herod . . . made a *public* speech to them.
22 The *people* acclaimed him with, 'It is a god speaking, not a man!'
16 37 2 They flog Roman citizens *in public*
17 5 [The Jews] made for Jason's house, hoping to find [Paul and
○ Silas] there and drag them off to the *People's Assembly;*
18 28 2 [Apollos] refuted the Jews *in public*
19 30 ○ Paul wanted to make an appeal to the *people,*
33 ○ [Alexander wanted] to explain things to the *people.*
20 20 2 I have preached to you . . . both *in public* and in your homes,

9. NATION: *ETHNOS*

2 *ethnikos*	4	1 *ethnos* 163
3 *ethnikōs*	1	

1: NATION(S)

Mt 4 15 (Is 8 23) Land of Zebulun! . . . Galilee of the ⌐*nations* (or: heathen)!
24 7 *nation* will fight against *nation,*
9 you will be hated by all the *nations* on account of my name.
14 This Good News . . . will be proclaimed to the whole world as a witness to all the *nations.*
25 32 All the *nations* will be assembled before [the Son of Man]
28 19 Go, therefore, make disciples of all the *nations;*
Mk 11 17 (Is 56 7) My house will be called a house of prayer for all the *peoples*
13 8 *nation* will fight against *nation,*
10 the Good News must . . . be proclaimed to all the *nations,*
Lk 21 10 *Nation* will fight against *nation,*
25 on earth *nations* [will be] in agony,

Lk 24 47   [it is written] that, in [Christ's] name, repentance . . . would be preached to all the *nations*, beginning from Jerusalem.
Ac 2 5   there were devout men living in Jerusalem from every *nation*
7 7   (Gn 15 14) I will pass judgement on the *nation* that enslaves them
45   the country we had conquered from the *nations* which were driven out by God as we advanced.
8 9   Simon had already practised magic arts . . . and astounded the Samaritan *people*.
10 35   anybody of any *nationality* who fears God . . . is acceptable to him.
13 19   [God] destroyed seven *nations* in Canaan,
14 16   In the past [God] allowed each *nation* to go its own way;
17 26   From one single stock [God] created ʳthe whole human race (lit. every *nation* of men)
Rm 4 17   (Gn 17 5) I have made you the ancestors of many *nations*
18   [Abraham] did become the father of many *nations*
10 19   (Dt 32 21) I will make you jealous of people who are not even a *nation*; I will make you angry with an irreligious *people*.
Ga 3 8   (Gn 12 3) In you all the ʳpagans (or: *nations*) will be blessed.
Rv 5 9   you bought men for God of every *race* . . . *people* and *nation*
7 9   I saw a huge number . . . of people from every *nation*, *race*, *tribe*
10 11   You are to prophesy . . . about many different nations and *countries*
11 9   Men out of every people, race, language and *nation* will stare at [the two witnesses'] corpses,
18   The *nations* were seething with rage
12 5   a male child . . . who was to rule all the *nations*
13 7   [the beast was] given power over every race, people, language and *nation*;
14 6   I saw another angel . . . sent to announce the Good News of eternity to . . . every *nation*, race, language and tribe.
8   Babylon . . . gave ʳthe whole world (lit. every *nation*) the wine of God's anger to drink.
15 3   just and true are all your ways, King of ʳnations (ᵛ *ages*).
16 19   the cities of the ʳworld (lit. *nations*) collapsed;
17 15   The waters you saw . . . are all the peoples . . . the *nations* and the languages
18 3   All the *nations* have been intoxicated by the wine of her prostitution;
23   all the *nations* were under your spell.

2: (THE) NATION, PEOPLE (OF ISRAEL, OF GOD)

Mt 21 43   the kingdom of God will be . . . given to a *people* who will produce its fruit.
Lk 7 5   [the centurion] is friendly towards our *people*;
23 2   We found this man inciting our *people* to revolt,
Jn 11 48   the Romans will come and destroy . . . our *nation*.
50   it is better for one man to die for the people, than for the whole *nation* to be destroyed. 51 . . . [Caiaphas] made this
51   prophecy that Jesus was to die for the *nation* – 52 and not for the *nation* only,
52
18 35   It is your own *people* and the chief priests who have handed you over to me;
Ac 10 22   Cornelius . . . is . . . highly regarded by the entire Jewish *people*,
24 2   the reforms this *nation* owes to your foresight [are matters we accept with all gratitude]
10   you have administered justice over this *nation* for many years,
17   I came to bring alms to my *nation*
26 4   My manner of life . . . a life spent from the beginning among my own *people* . . . is common knowledge among the Jews.
28 19   not that I had any accusation to make against my own *nation*.
1 P 2 9   (Ex 19 6) you are . . . a consecrated *nation*, a people set apart

3: NATION(S) = PAGANS, GENTILES, HEATHEN

Gog 1 (Rv 20)   *Magog 1* (Rv 20)

Mt 4 15   (Is 8 23) Land of Zebulun! . . . Galilee of the ʳnations (or: *heathen*)!
5 47   2 Even the *pagans* do as much, do they not?
6 7   2 In your prayers do not babble as the *pagans* do,
32   It is the *pagans* who set their hearts on all these things.
10 5   Do not turn your steps to *pagan* territory,
18   You will be dragged before governors . . . to bear witness before them and the *pagans*.
12 18   (Is 42 1-4) [my servant] will proclaim the true faith to the
21   *nations* . . . 21 in his name the *nations* will put their hope.
18 17   if he refuses to listen to the community, treat him like a *pagan* or a tax collector.
20 19   [the chief priests and scribes] will hand him over to the *pagans* to be mocked
25   among the *pagans* the rulers lord it over them,
Mk 10 33   the chief priests and the scribes . . . will condemn him to death and will hand him over to the *pagans*,

Mk 10 42   among the *pagans* their so-called rulers lord it over them,
Lk 2 32   [my eyes have seen] a light to enlighten the *pagans* and the glory of your people Israel.
12 30   It is the *pagans* of this world who set their hearts on all these things.
18 32   he will be handed over to the *pagans* and will be mocked,
21 24   They will . . . be led captive to every *pagan country*; and Jerusalem will be trampled down by the *pagans* until the age of the *pagans* is completely over.
22 25   Among *pagans* it is the kings who lord it over them,
Ac 4 25   (Ps 2 1) Why this arrogance among the ʳnations (or: *Gentiles*)
27   . . . ? 27 This is what has come true: . . . Herod and Pontius Pilate made an alliance with the *pagan nations* and the peoples of Israel,
9 15   this man is my chosen instrument to bring my name before *pagans*
10 45   Jewish believers . . . . were all astonished that the gift of the Holy Spirit should be poured out on the *pagans* too,
11 1   the *pagans* too had accepted the word of God,
18   God . . . can evidently grant even the *pagans* the repentance
13 46   since you have rejected [the word of God] we must turn to the *pagans*.
47   (Is 49 6) I have made you a light for the *nations*,
48   the *pagans* . . . thanked the Lord for his message;
14 2   Some of the Jews . . . poisoned the minds of the *pagans* against the brothers.
5   a move was made by *pagans* as well as Jews to make attacks on [the apostles]
27   [God] had opened the door of faith to the *pagans*.
15 3   [Paul and Barnabas] told how the *pagans* had been converted,
7   in the early days God made his choice among you: the *pagans* were to learn the Good News from me
12   the entire assembly . . . listened to Barnabas and Paul describing all the signs and wonders God had worked through them among the *pagans*.
14   Simeon has described how God first arranged to enlist a people for his name out of the *pagans*.
17   (Am 19 12) all the *pagans* who are consecrated to my name will look for the Lord,
19   instead of making things more difficult for *pagans* who turn to God, [let us tell them merely to abstain from anything polluted by idols]
23   The apostles . . . send greetings to the brothers of *pagan* [birth]
18 6   from now on I can go to the *pagans* with a clear conscience.
21 11   The man this girdle belongs to will be . . . handed over to the *pagans*.
19   [Paul] gave a detailed account of all that God had done among the *pagans*
21   you instruct all Jews living among the *pagans* to break away from Moses,
25   The *pagans* who have become believers . . . must abstain from things sacrificed to idols,
22 21   I am sending you out to the *pagans* far away.
26 17   (Jr 1 5, 7) I shall deliver you from the people and from the *pagans*,
20   I started preaching . . . also to the *pagans*, urging them to repent
23   the Christ . . . was to proclaim that light now shone for our people and for the *pagans* too.
28 28   this salvation of God has been sent to the *pagans*;
Rm 1 5   Through [Jesus Christ] we received . . . our apostolic mission to preach the obedience of faith to all *pagan nations*
13   I have often planned to visit you . . . in the hope that I might work as fruitfully among you as I have done among the other *pagans*.
2 14   *pagans* who never heard of the Law . . . are led by reason to do what the Law commands,
24   (Is 52 5 G) It is your fault that the name of God is blasphemed among the *pagans*.
3 29   Is God the God of Jews alone and not of the *pagans* too? Of the *pagans* too, most certainly,
9 24   whether we were Jews or *pagans* we are the one [God] has called.
30   the *pagans* who were not looking for righteousness found it all the same, a righteousness that comes of faith,
11 11   [the Jews'] fall . . . has saved the *pagans*
12   Think of the extent to which . . . the *pagan world* has benefited from [the Jews'] fall
13   Let me tell you *pagans* this: I have been sent to the *pagans* as their apostle,
25   One section of Israel has become blind, but this will last only until the whole *pagan world* has entered,
15 9   get the *pagans* to give glory to God for his mercy, as scripture says in one place (Ps 18 50): . . . I shall praise you among the *pagans*
10   (Dt 32 43 G) Rejoice, *pagans*, with his people,
11   (Ps 117 1) Let all the *pagans* praise the Lord,
12   (Is 11 10 G) The root of Jesse will appear, rising up to rule the *pagans*, and in him the *pagans* will put their hope.

Rm 15 16	I am to carry out my priestly duty by bringing the Good News . . . to the *pagans*, and so make ⌐them (lit. the *pagans*) acceptable as an offering,	
18	[I speak of] what Christ himself has done to win the allegiance of the *pagans*,	
27	the *pagans* . . . share the spiritual possessions of these poor people	
16 4	all the churches among the *pagans* [owe Prisca and Aquila a debt of gratitude]	
26	[the revelation of the mystery] must be broadcast to *pagans*	
1 Co 1 23	here are we preaching a crucified Christ; . . . to the *pagans* madness,	
5 1	This is a case of sexual immorality . . . that must be unparalleled even among *pagans*.	
10 20	the sacrifices that ⌐they (ᵛ the *pagans*) offer they sacrifice to demons.	
12 2	when you were *pagans* . . . you felt irresistably drawn . . . towards dumb idols	
2 Co 11 26	I have been . . . in danger from my own people and in danger from *pagans*;	
Ga 1 16	[God chose] to reveal his Son in me, so that I might preach the Good News about him to the *pagans*.	
2 2	I proclaim [the Good News] among the *pagans*;	
8	The same person whose action had made Peter the apostle of the circumcised had given me a similar mission to the *pagans*. ⁹ . . . we were to go to the *pagans* and they to the circumcised.	
9		
12	[Cephas's] custom had been to eat with the *pagans* . . .	
14	¹⁴ . . . I said to Cephas in front of everyone, 'In spite of being a Jew, you live *like the pagans* . . . so you have no right to make the *pagans* copy Jewish ways.' ¹⁵ . . . we were born Jews and not *pagan* sinners,	
3/ 15		
3 8	Scripture foresaw that God was going to use faith to justify the *pagans* and proclaimed . . . (Gn 12 3): In you all the *pagans* will be blessed.	
14	This was done so that in Christ Jesus the blessing of Abraham might include the *pagans*,	
Ep 2 11	Do not forget . . . that there was a time when you . . . were *pagans*	
3 1	I, Paul, a prisoner of Christ Jesus for the sake of you *pagans*	
6	*pagans* now share the same inheritance,	
8	I . . . have been entrusted with this special grace . . . of proclaiming to the *pagans* the infinite treasure of Christ	
4 17	I want to urge you . . . not to go on living the aimless kind of life that *pagans* live,	
Col 1 27	It was God's purpose . . . to show all the rich glory of this mystery to *pagans*.	
1 Th 2 16	they are hindering us from preaching to the *pagans* and trying to save them.	
4 5	[use the body that belongs to God honourably,] not giving way to selfish lust like the *pagans* who do not know God.	
1 Tm 2 7	I have been named . . . a teacher of the faith and the truth to the *pagans*.	
3 16	He was . . . proclaimed to the *pagans*,	
2 Tm 4 17	the Lord . . . gave me power, so that through me the whole message might be proclaimed for all the *pagans* to hear;	
1 P 2 12	Always behave honourably among *pagans*	
4 3	You spent quite long enough in the past living the sort of life that *pagans* live,	
3 Jn 7	It was entirely for the sake of the name that [the brothers] set out, without depending on the *pagans* for anything;	
2		
Rv 2 26	To those who prove victorious . . . I will give the authority over the *pagans*	
11 2	the outer court [of God's sanctuary] has been handed over to *pagans*	
15 4	(Ps 86 9) all the *pagans* will come and adore you	
19 15	From [the rider's] mouth came a sharp sword to strike the *pagans* with;	
20 3	[The angel] threw [Satan] into the Abyss . . . to make sure he would not deceive the *nations* again	
8	[Satan] will come out to deceive all the *nations* in the four quarters of the earth, Gog and *Magog*,	
21 24	[the Lamb was a lighted torch for the city.] The *pagan nations* will live by its light	
26	the *nations* will come, bringing their treasure	
22 2	the leaves of [the trees of life] are the cure for the *pagans*.	

MARRY – UNMARRIED

1. Betroth – Betrothed
1: Betroth, Arrange the marriage of: *harmozomai*

2: (Be) Betrothed: *mnēsteuō*
2. Marry – Wedding – Unmarried
1: Marry, (Be) Given in marriage

	– Wedding, Marriage – Get married, (Be) Unmarried: *gameō*	5: Live together: *syn-erchomai*
	2: Bridegroom, Bride – Daughter-in-law: *nymphios*	**3. Divorce** 1: Divorce – (Writ of) Dismissal: *apo-luō* and *apo-stasion*
	a) Bridegroom – Bride	2: Divorce, Send away: *aph-iēmi*
	b) Bridegroom, Bride (= Christ, the Church) – Wedding hall	**4. Mother-in-law – Father-in-law:** *pentheros*
	c) Daughter-in-law, Son's wife	**5. Widow:** *chēra*
	3: Take (a wife), Marry: *lambanō*	**6. Virgin, (Young) Girl, Unmarried – Bridesmaid – Girlhood, Virginity, Celibate:** *parthenos*
	4: Have (a wife, a husband): *echō*	

1. BETROTH – BETROTHED

1: BETROTH, ARRANGE THE MARRIAGE OF: *HARMOZOMAI*

harmozomai 1

2 Co 11 2 ●	I *arranged* for you *to marry* Christ so that I might give you away as a chaste virgin to this one husband.	

2: (BE) BETROTHED: *MNĒSTEUŌ*

mnēsteuō 3

Mt 1 18	His mother Mary was *betrothed* to Joseph;	
Lk 1 27	a virgin *betrothed* to a man named Joseph,	
2 5	[Joseph travelled up to Judaea] in order to be registered together with Mary, his *betrothed*,	

2. MARRY – WEDDING – UNMARRIED

1: MARRY, (BE) GIVEN IN MARRIAGE – WEDDING, MARRIAGE – GET MARRIED, (BE) UNMARRIED: *GAMEŌ*

1 *gameō*	28	2 *gamos*	16
5 *gamiskomai*	1	4 *a-gamos*	4
3 *gamizō*	7	6 *epi-gambreuō*	1

Mt 5 32	anyone who *marries* a divorced woman commits adultery.	
19 9	the man who divorces his wife – I am not speaking of fornication – and *marries* another, is guilty of adultery.' ¹⁰ The disciples said '. . . it is not advisable to *marry*.'	
10		
22 2 < 2	a king who gave a feast for his son's *wedding*. ³ He sent his	
3 < 2	servants to call those who had been invited to the *wedding*,	
4 < 2	but they would not come. ⁴ . . . 'Come to the *wedding*.'	
8 < 2	The *wedding* is ready; but . . . those who were invited proved to be unworthy.	
9 < 2	invite everyone you can find to the *wedding*.	
11 < 2	the king . . . noticed one man who was not wearing a	
12 < 2	*wedding* garment, ¹² '. . . How did you get in here without a *wedding* garment?'	
2		
24 6	(Dt 25 5) if a man dies childless, his brother is to *marry* the widow, . . . to raise children for his brother.	
25	the first [of seven brothers] *married* and then died without children, leaving his wife to his brother;	
30	at the resurrection men and women do not *marry*, nor are they *given in marriage*; no, they are like the angels	
3		
24 38	in those days before the Flood people were eating, drinking,	
/3	⌐taking wives, taking husbands (lit. *marrying, being married*),	
25 10 < 2	Those who were ready went in with him to the *wedding*	
Mk 6 17	Herodias, [Herod's] brother Philip's wife whom he had *married*.	
10 11	The man who divorces his wife and *marries* another is guilty of adultery . . . ¹² And if a woman divorces her husband and *marries* another she is guilty of adultery too.	
12		
12 25	when they rise from the dead, men and women do not *marry*, nor are they *given in marriage*; no, they are like the angels	
/3		
Lk 12 36 < 2	Be like men waiting for their master to return from the *wedding* [feast],	
14 8 < 2	When someone invites you to a *wedding* [feast], do not take . . . the place of honour.	
20 <	I have just *got married* and so am unable to come.	
16 18	Everyone who divorces his wife and *marries* another is guilty of adultery, and the man who *marries* a woman divorced by her husband commits adultery.	
17 27	People were . . . ⌐marrying wives and husbands (lit. *marrying, being married*) right up to the day Noah went into the ark,	
3		
20 34	The children of this world ⌐take wives and husbands (lit. *marry* and are *given in marriage*) (ᵛ are born and have their own children); ³⁵ but those who are judged worthy of a place in the other world . . . do not *marry* nor are *given in marriage*	
/5		
35		
3		

Jn 2	1	2 there was a *wedding* at Cana . . . ². . . Jesus and his
	2	2 disciples had also been invited to the *wedding*. ³ When
	3	they ran out of wine, ᵛsince the wine provided for the
		2 *wedding* was all finished,

1 Co 7   8   There is something I want to add for the sake of widows
   4 and *those who are not married*: it is a good thing for them
   9 to stay as they are, like me, ⁹ but if they cannot control
   the sexual urges, they should *get married*, since it is better
   10 to *be married* than to be tortured. ¹⁰ For the *married* I
   have sómething to say, and this is not from me but from
   11 the Lord: a wife must not leave her husband – ¹¹ or if
   4 she does leave him, she must either remain *unmarried*
   or else make it up with her husband
   28 if you *marry*, it is no sin, and it is not a sin for a young girl
   to *get married*.
   32   4 An *unmarried* man can devote himself to the Lord's affairs,
   33   . . . ³³ a *married* man has to bother about . . . pleasing
   34 his wife: ³⁴ he is torn two ways. In the same way an
   4 *unmarried* woman, like a young girl, can devote herself
   to the Lord's affairs; . . . The *married* woman . . . has
   to worry about . . . pleasing her husband.
   36 [the father] is not sinning if *there is a marriage*.
   38   3 the man who *sees* that his daughter is *married* has done a
   3 good thing but the man who *keeps* his daughter un*married*
   has done something even better.
   39 if the husband dies, [a woman] is free to *marry* anybody
   she likes, only it must be in the Lord.

1 Tm 4   3   [false teachers] will say *marriage* is forbidden,
   5 11 if [young widows'] natural desires get stronger than their
   dedication to Christ, they want to *marry* [again],
   14 it is best for young widows to *marry* [again] and have
   children

Heb 13   4   2 *Marriage* is to be honoured by all, and [marriages are] to
   be kept undefiled,

Rv 19   7 X   2 this is the time for the *marriage* of the Lamb.
   9 X   2 Happy are those who are invited to the *wedding* [feast] of
   the Lamb,

2: BRIDEGROOM, BRIDE – DAUGHTER-IN-LAW: *NYMPHIOS*

2 *nymphē*   8   3 *nymphōn* 4
1 *nymphios* 16

a) Bridegroom – Bride

Jn 2   9   the steward called the *bridegroom*
Rv 18 23   (Jr 25 10) never again will be heard the voices of *bridegroom*
   2 and *bride*.

b) Bridegroom, Bride (= Christ, the Church) – Wedding hall

Mt 9 15   3 Surely the ⌐*bridegroom*'s attendants (lit. sons of the *wedding*
   hall) would never think of mourning as long as the
   bridegroom is still with them? But the time will come for
   the *bridegroom* to be taken away
   22 10   3 the *wedding hall* was filled with guests.
   25   1 Ten bridesmaids . . . went to meet the *bridegroom*.
   5 The *bridegroom* was late, and they all grew drowsy
   6 The *bridegroom* is here! Go out and meet him!
   10 [The foolish bridesmaids] had gone off to buy [oil] when
   the *bridegroom* arrived.
Mk 2 19   3 Surely the ⌐*bridegroom*'s attendants (lit. sons of the *wedding*
   hall) would never think of fasting while the *bridegroom*
   20 is still with them? ²⁰ But the time will come for the
   bridegroom to be taken away
Lk 5 34 Surely you cannot make the ⌐*bridegroom*'s attendants
   3/ (lit. sons of the *wedding hall*) fast while the *bridegroom*
   35 is still with them? ³⁵ But the time will come . . . for the
   bridegroom to be taken away
Jn 3 29   2/ The *bride* is only for the *bridegroom*; and yet the *bridegroom*'s
   friend . . . is glad when he hears the *bridegroom*'s voice.
Rv 21   2   2 the new Jerusalem . . . as beautiful as a *bride* all dressed
   for her husband.
   9   2 Come here and I will show you the *bride* that the Lamb
   has married.
   22 17   2 The Spirit and the *Bride* say, 'Come.'

c) Daughter-in-law, Son's wife

Mt 10 35   2 I have come to set . . . a *daughter-in-law* against her mother-
   in-law.
Lk 12 53   2 [a household will be divided:] mother-in-law against *daughter-
   2 in-law, daughter-in-law* against mother-in-law.

3: TAKE (A WIFE), MARRY: *LAMBANŌ*

lambanō 6/257

Mk 12 19   (Dt 25 5) if a man's brother dies leaving a wife but no child,
   the man must ⌐*marry* the widow (lit. *take* the wife) to
   raise up children for his brother.

Mk 12 20   there were seven brothers. The first *married* a wife and
   21 then died leaving no children. ²¹ the second *married*
   the widow, and he too died . . . ; with the third it was
   the same,
Lk 20 28   (Dt 25 5) if a man's married brother dies childless, the man
   must ⌐*marry* the widow (lit. *take* the wife) to raise up
   children for his brother.
   29 there were seven brothers. The first, having *married* a wife,
   31 died childless. ³⁰ The second ³¹ and then the third ⌐*married*
   the widow (lit. *took* the wife).

4: HAVE (A WIFE, A HUSBAND): *ECHŌ*

echō (19)

Mt 14   4   It is against the Law for you to *have* [Herodias].
   22 28 at the resurrection to which of those seven will she be wife,
   since ⌐she had been married to them all (lit. all of them had
   had her)?
Mk 6 18   It is against the law for you to *have* your brother's wife.
   12 23 at the resurrection . . . whose wife will she be, since ⌐she had
   been married to all seven (lit. all seven of them had *had*
   her as wife)?
Lk 20 28   if a man's ⌐*married* brother (lit. brother, *having* a wife) dies
   childless,
   33 since ⌐she had been married to all seven (lit. all seven of
   them had *had* her as wife)?
Jn 3 29   ⌐The bride *is* only *for* the bridegroom (or: Only the bridegroom *has* the bride);
   4 17 'I *have* no husband.' [Jesus] said to her, 'You are right to
   18 say, I *have* no husband; ¹⁸ for although you have *had* five,
   the one you *have* now is not your husband.'
1 Co 5   1   one of you ⌐is living with (lit. *has*) his father's wife.
   7   2 let each man *have* his own wife and each woman *have* her
   own husband.
   12 if a brother *has* a wife who is an unbeliever, and she is content
   to live with him, he must not send her away; ¹³ and if a
   13 woman *has* an unbeliever for her husband, and he is content to live with her, she must not leave him.
   29 Those who *have* wives should live as though they *had* none,
Ga 4 27   (Is 54 1) there are more sons of the forsaken one than sons
   of the ⌐*wedded* wife (lit. wife who *has* a husband).

5: LIVE TOGETHER: *SYN-ERCHOMAI*

syn-erchomai 1/32

Mt 1 18   before they *came to live together* [Mary] was found to be with
   child

3. DIVORCE

1: DIVORCE – (WRIT OF) DISMISSAL: *APO-LUŌ* and *APO-STASION*

1 *apo-luō* 14/67   2 *apo-stasion* 3

Mt 1 19   Joseph . . . decided to *divorce* [Mary] informally.
   5 31 It has also been said (Dt 24 1): Anyone who *divorces* his wife
   2 must give her a ⌐*writ of dismissal* (or: *certificate of divorce*).
   32 ³² But I say this to you: everyone who *divorces* his wife,
   except for the case of fornication, makes her an adulteress;
   and anyone who marries a *divorced* woman commits
   adultery.
   19   3 Is it against the Law for a man to *divorce* his wife on any
   pretext whatever?
   7   2 why did Moses command that a writ of *dismissal* should be
   8 given in [cases of] *divorce*? ⁸ . . . Moses allowed you to
   9 *divorce* your wives, but . . . ⁹ . . . I say this to you: the
   man who *divorces* his wife – i am not speaking of fornication – and marries another, is guilty of adultery.
Mk 10   2   Is it against the law for a man to *divorce* his wife?
   4   2 Moses allowed us . . . to draw up a writ of *dismissal* and so to
   divorce.
   11 The man who *divorces* his wife and marries another is guilty
   12 of adultery . . . ¹² And if a woman *divorces* her husband
   and marries another
Lk 16 18   Everyone who *divorces* his wife and marries another . . . and
   the man who marries a woman *divorced* . . . commits
   adultery.

2: DIVORCE, SEND AWAY: *APH-IĒMI*

aph-iēmi 3/146

1 Co 7 11   nor must a husband ⌐*send* his wife *away* (or: *divorce* his wife).

1 Co 7 12		If a brother has a wife who is an unbeliever, and she is content to live with him, he must not ˹send her *away* (or: *divorce* her); ¹³ and if a woman has an unbeliever for her husband, . . . she must not ˹leave (lit. *divorce*) him.
13		

4. MOTHER-IN-LAW – FATHER-IN-LAW: *PENTHEROS*

1 penthera 6   2 pentheros 1

Mt 8 14	Jesus found Peter's *mother-in-law* in bed with fever.
10 35	I have come to set . . . a daughter-in-law against her *mother-in-law*.
Mk 1 30	Simon's *mother-in-law* had gone to bed with fever,
Lk 4 38	Simon's *mother-in-law* was suffering from . . . fever
12 53	[a household will be divided:] *mother-in-law* against daughter-in-law, and daughter-in-law against *mother-in-law*.
Jn 18 13	2 Annas was the *father-in-law* of Caiaphas,

5. WIDOW: *CHĒRA*

chēra 26

Mt 12 40	[Beware of the scribes] who swallow the property of *widows*,
42	A poor *widow* came and put in two small coins,
43	this poor *widow* has put more in than all
Lk 2 37	[Anna had been married for seven years] before becoming a *widow*.
4 25	There were many *widows* in Israel . . . ²⁶ but Elijah was not sent to any of these: he was sent to a *widow* at Zarephath,
26	
7 12	the only son of his mother, and she was a *widow*.
18 3 <	In the same town there was a *widow* who kept on coming to [the judge]
5 <	since she keeps pestering me I must give this *widow* her just rights,'
20 47	[Beware of the scribes] who swallow the property of *widows*,
21 2	he happened to notice a poverty-stricken *widow* putting in two small coins,
3	this poor *widow* has put in more than any of them;
Ac 6 1	the Hellenists made a complaint . . .: in the daily distribution their own *widows* were being overlooked.
9 39	all the *widows* stood round [Peter] in tears,
41	Peter . . . called in the saints and *widows* and showed them [Dorcas] was alive.
1 Co 7 8	There is something I want to add for the sake of *widows* and those who are not married: it is a good thing for them to stay as they are, like me,
1 Tm 5 3	Be considerate to *widows*; I mean those who are truly *widows*, ⁴ If a *widow* has children or grandchildren, they are to learn . . . to do their duty
4	
5	a *woman who is* really *widowed* and left without anybody can give herself up to God
9	Enrolment as a *widow* is permissible only for a woman at least sixty years old who has had only one husband.
11	Do not accept young *widows*
16	If a Christian woman has *widowed* relatives, she should support them and . . . enable [the Church] to support those who are genuinely *widows*.
Jm 1 27	Pure, unspoilt religion . . . is this: coming to the help of orphans and *widows* when they need it.
Rv 18 7	[Babylon] says to herself, '. . . I am no *widow* and shall never be in mourning.'

6. VIRGIN, (YOUNG) GIRL, UNMARRIED – BRIDESMAID – GIRLHOOD, VIRGINITY, CELIBATE: *PARTHENOS*

2 parthenia 1   1 parthenos 15

M = Mary

Mt 1 23 M	(Is 7 14) The *virgin* will conceive and give birth to a son
25 1 <	Ten ˹bridesmaids (or: *girls*) . . . went out to meet the bridegroom
7 <	all those ˹bridesmaids (or: *girls*) woke up and trimmed their lamps,
11 <	The other [foolish] ˹bridesmaids (or: *girls*) arrived later.
Lk 1 27 M	a *virgin* betrothed to a man named Joseph, . . . the *virgin's* name was Mary
2 36	2 Her days of *girlhood* over, [Anna] had been married for seven years
Ac 21 9	[Philip the evangelist] had four ˹*virgin* (or: *unmarried*) daughters who were prophets.
1 Co 7 25	About ˹remaining *celibate* (or: the *unmarried*), I have no directions from the Lord
28	it is not a sin for a *young girl* to get married.
34	In the same way an unmarried woman, like a *young girl*, can devote herself to the Lord's affairs;

1 Co 7 36	if there is anyone who feels that it would not be fair to his ˹*daughter* (or: *young girl*) to let her grow too old for marriage, . . . he is free to do as he likes: . . . ³⁷ On the other hand, if someone has firmly made his mind up . . . to keep his ˹*daughter* (or: *young girl*) as she is, he will be doing a good thing. ³⁸ . . . the man who sees that his ˹*daughter* (or: *young girl*) is married has done a good thing but the man who keeps [his daughter] unmarried has done something even better.
37	
38	
2 Co 11 2	I arranged for you to marry Christ . . as a chaste *virgin*
Rv 14 4 ○	The [one hundred and forty-four thousand] are the ones *who have kept their virginity* and not been defiled with women;

MARY AND JOSEPH

J *Joseph 14*   *Simeon* 2 (Lk 2)*
Mary 19

Mt 1 16 J	Jacob was the father of *Joseph* the husband of *Mary*; of her was born Jesus
18	This is how Jesus Christ came to be born. His mother *Mary* was betrothed to *Joseph* . . . she was . . . with child through the Holy Spirit.
J	
19 J	Her husband *Joseph*, being a man of honour . . . decided to divorce her informally. ²⁰ . . . the angel of the Lord . . . said, '*Joseph* son of David, do not be afraid to take *Mary* home as your wife . . .'
20 J	
24 J	²⁴ . . . *Joseph* . . . did what the angel of the Lord had told him to do:
2 11	[the Magi] saw the child with his mother *Mary*,
13 J	the angel . . . appeared to *Joseph* in a dream and said, 'Get up, take the child and his mother with you, and escape into Egypt,'
19 J	the angel of the Lord appeared in a dream to *Joseph* . . . ²⁰ and said, 'Get up, take the child and his mother . . . and go back to the land of Israel,'
13 55	Is not his mother the woman called *Mary* . . .?
Mk 6 3	This is the carpenter, surely, the son of *Mary* . . .?
Lk 1 27 J	a virgin betrothed to a man named *Joseph*, of the House of David; and the virgin's name was *Mary*.
30	the angel said to her, '*Mary*, do not be afraid;'
34	*Mary* said to the angel, 'But how can this come about . . .?'
38	'I am the handmaid of the Lord,' said *Mary*
39	*Mary* set out . . . ⁴⁰ She went into Zechariah's house . . .
41	⁴¹ Now as soon as Elizabeth heard *Mary's* greeting, the child leapt in her womb
46	*Mary* said: My soul proclaims the greatness of the Lord
56	*Mary* stayed with Elizabeth about three months
2 4 J	*Joseph* set out . . . to Judaea, to . . . Bethlehem . . . ⁵ in order to be registered together with *Mary*, his betrothed, who was with child.
5	
16 J	[the shepherds] found *Mary* and *Joseph*, and the baby
19	*Mary* . . . treasured all these things . . . in her heart.
25	in Jerusalem there was a man named Simeon* . . . an upright and devout man;
34	Simeon* blessed them and said to *Mary* his mother, 'You see this child . . .'
3 23 J	Jesus was . . . the son, as it was thought, of *Joseph* son of Heli,
4 22 J	They said, 'This is *Joseph's* son, surely?'
Jn 1 45	We have found the one Moses wrote about . . . the one about whom the prophets wrote: he is Jesus son of *Joseph*, from Nazareth.
J	
6 42 J	Surely this is Jesus son of *Joseph* . . . We know his father and mother.
Ac 1 14	[the apostles] joined in continuous prayer, together with several women, including *Mary* the mother of Jesus, and with his brothers.

MARY OF MAGDALA

M	*Mary*	*14*	*Salome 2 (Mk)*
	of Magdala, Magdalene	*12*	*Susanna 1 (Lk)*
C	*Mary (the wife of Clopas)*	*8*	*Chuza* 1 (Lk)*
	Joanna	*2 (Lk)*	*Clopas* 1 (Jn 19)*

Mt 27 56 M	Among [the women who had followed Jesus] were *Mary* of *Magdala*, *Mary* the mother of James and ˹*Joseph* (ᵛ *Joset*) and the mother of Zebedee's sons.
C	

Mt 27	61	M C	*Mary* of *Magdala* and the other *Mary* were there, sitting opposite the sepulchre.
28	1	M C	*Mary* of *Magdala* and the other *Mary* went to visit the sepulchre.
Mk 15	40	M C	There were some women . . . Among them were *Mary* of *Magdala*, *Mary* who was the mother of James the younger and Joset, and *Salome*.
	47	M C	*Mary* of *Magdala* and *Mary* the mother of Joset were watching and took note of where [Jesus] was laid.
16	1	M C	When the sabbath was over, *Mary* of *Magdala*, *Mary* the mother of James, and *Salome*, bought spices with which to go and anoint [Jesus].
	9	M	Having risen . . . [Jesus] appeared first to *Mary* of *Magdala* from whom he had cast out seven devils.
Lk 8	2	M	[With Jesus went the Twelve,] as well as certain women who had been cured of evil spirits and ailments: *Mary* surnamed the *Magdalene*, from whom seven demons had gone out,
	3		³ *Joanna* the wife of Herod's steward Chuza*, *Susanna*, and several others who provided for them out of their own resources.
24	10	M C	[The women told all this to the Eleven and to all the others.] The women were *Mary* of *Magdala*, *Joanna*, and *Mary* the mother of James. The other women with them also told the apostles.
Jn 19	25	C M	Near the cross of Jesus stood his mother and his mother's sister, *Mary* the wife of Clopas*, and *Mary* of *Magdala*.
20	1	M	It was very early on the first day of the week and still dark, when *Mary* of *Magdala* came to the tomb.
	11	M	Meanwhile *Mary* stayed outside near the tomb, weeping.
	16	M	Jesus said, 'Mary!' She knew him then and said to Him in Hebrew, 'Rabbuni!'
	18	M	*Mary* of *Magdala* went and told the disciples that she had seen the Lord

---

MASTER – LORD

1. Master
1: Master, Lord: *des-potēs*
  a) Master, Sovereign Lord (God or Christ)
  b) Master (of slaves, of servants, of a house)
2: Master of the house, Householder, (Land-)Owner: *oiko-des-potēs*
2. Lord, Master, Owner – Sir: *kyrios*
  a) the Lord (God), the Lord of hosts
  b) the Lord (Jesus), the Master – (Jesus addressed as) Sir
  c) Lord (God *or* Jesus)

  d) Master, Owner, Lord (God, Jesus *or* another) – Sir – Authority
  e) (an angel, a voice from heaven, addressed as) Lord
  f) (the angelic order of) Domination, Dominion
  g) (a christian church addressed as) Lady
  h) Master, Owner, (generally) – Sir, Lord – Lord it over, Have power over
3. (Jesus addressed as) Master: *epi-statēs*
4. (Your, His) Excellency: *kratistos*

1. MASTER

1: MASTER, LORD: *DES-POTĒS*
des-potēs 10

a) Master, Sovereign Lord (God or Christ)

Lk 2	29	Now, *Master*, you can let your servant go in peace,
Ac 4	24	*Master*, . . . it is you who made heaven and earth
2 Tm 2	21 X?	to avoid these faults . . . is the way for anyone to become a vessel . . . fit for ⌐the *Master* (or: a master) himself to use,
2 P 2	1 X	you too will have your false teachers, who will . . . disown the *Master* who purchased their freedom.
Jude	4 X	they were condemned for . . . rejecting our only *Master* and Lord, Jesus Christ.
Rv 6	10	Holy, faithful *Master*, how much longer will you wait before you pass sentence . . .?

b) Master (of slaves, of servants, of a house)

1 Tm 6	1 2	All slaves 'under the yoke' must have unqualified respect for their *masters*, . . . ² Slaves whose *masters* are believers
2 Tm 2	21 X?	to avoid these faults . . . is the way for anyone to become a vessel . . . fit for ⌐the Master (or: a *master*) himself to use,
Tt 2	9	Tell the slaves that they are to be obedient to their *masters*
1 P 2	18	Slaves must be respectful and obedient to their *masters*,

2: MASTER OF THE HOUSE, HOUSEHOLDER, (LAND-)OWNER: *OIKO-DES-POTĒS*

2 oiko-des-poteō 1   *1 oiko-des-potēs 12*

Mt 10	25	X	If they have called the *master of the house* Beelzebul,
13	27		The *owner's* servants went to him
	52		every scribe who becomes a disciple of the kingdom of heaven is like a *householder*
20	1	<	the kingdom of heaven is like a *landowner* going out at daybreak
	11	<	They took [the denarius], but grumbled at the *landowner*.
21	33	<	There was a man, a *landowner*, who planted a vineyard;
24	43		if the *householder* had known at what time of the night the burglar would come,
Mk 14	14		say to the *owner of the house* which he enters, "The Master says:"
Lk 12	39		if the *householder* had known at what hour the burglar would come,
13	25		Once the *master of the house* has . . . locked the door,
14	21	<	the *householder*, in a rage, said to his servant,
22	11		tell the *owner of the house*, "The Master has this to say to you:"
1 Tm 5	14 2		I think it is best for young widows to marry again and have children and ⌐a home to look after (lit. *look after a home*),

2. LORD, MASTER, OWNER – SIR: *KYRIOS*

5	kyria	2	1	kyrios	724
6	kyriakos	2	3	kyriotēs	4
2	kyrieuō	7	4	kata-kyrieuō	4

a) the Lord (God), the Lord of hosts

7 sabaōth (= of hosts) 2

Θ = Lord + God

Mt 1	20		the angel of the *Lord* appeared to [Joseph] in a dream
	22		to fulfil the words spoken by the *Lord* through the prophet (Is 7 14):
	24		Joseph . . . did what the angel of the *Lord* had told him to do:
2	13		the angel of the *Lord* appeared to Joseph in a dream
	15		This was to fulfil what the *Lord* had spoken through the prophet (Ho 11 1):
	19		the angel of the *Lord* appeared in a dream to Joseph
4	7	Θ	(Dt 6 16) You must not put the *Lord* your God to the test.
	10	Θ	(Dt 6 13) You must worship the *Lord* your God,
5	33		(cf. Ps 50 14) You must . . . fulfil your oaths to the *Lord*.
9	38		ask the *Lord* of the harvest to send labourers to his harvest.
11	25		I bless you, Father, *Lord* of heaven and of earth,
21	9		(Ps 118 26) Blessings on him who comes in the name of the *Lord*!
	42		(Ps 118 23) This was the *Lord's* doing
22	37	Θ	(Dt 6 5) You must love the *Lord* your God
	44		(Ps 110 1) The *Lord* said to my Lord:
23	39		(Ps 118 26) Blessings on him who comes in the name of the *Lord*!
27	10		(cf. Zc 11 13) just as the *Lord* directed me.
28	2		the angel of the *Lord*, descending from heaven,
Mk 5	19		tell them all that the *Lord* in his mercy has done for you.
11	9		(Ps 118 26) Blessings on him who comes in the name of the *Lord*!
12	11		(Ps 118 23) This was the *Lord's* doing
	29	Θ	(Dt 6 4) the *Lord* our God is the one Lord,
	30	Θ	(Dt 6 5) you must love the *Lord* your God with all your heart,
	36		(Ps 110 1) The *Lord* said to my Lord:
13	20		if the *Lord* had not shortened that time,
Lk 1	6		all the commandments and observances of the *Lord*.
	9		to enter the *Lord's* sanctuary
	11		there appeared to [Zechariah] the angel of the *Lord*,
	15		[John] will be great in the sight of the *Lord*; . . . ¹⁶ and he will bring back many of the sons of Israel to the *Lord* their
	16		God. ¹⁷ . . . he will go before him . . , preparing for the *Lord* a people fit for him.
	17	Θ	
	25		'The *Lord* has done this for me' [Elizabeth] said
	28		[Gabriel to Mary:] 'Rejoice, so highly favoured! The *Lord* is with you!
	32	Θ	The *Lord* God will give him the throne of his ancestor David;
	38		I am the handmaid of the *Lord*,
	45		that the promise made her by the *Lord* would be fulfilled.
	46		My soul proclaims the greatness of the *Lord*
	58		that the *Lord* had shown her so great a kindness,
	66		And indeed the hand of the *Lord* was with him.
	68	Θ	Blessed be the *Lord*, the God of Israel,
	76		you shall be called the Prophet of the Most High, for you will go before the *Lord*
2	9		The angel of the *Lord* appeared to them and the glory of the *Lord* shone round them.
	15		Let us go . . . and see this thing . . . which the *Lord* has made known to us.
	22		they took [Jesus] up to Jerusalem to present him to the *Lord*
	23		observing what stands written in the Law of the *Lord*: Every first-born male must be consecrated to the *Lord*
	24		in accordance with what is said in the Law of the *Lord*,

Lk 2 26   he would not see death until he had set eyes on the Christ of the *Lord*.

39   When they had done everything the Law of the *Lord* required,

4 8 ⊖   (Dt 6 13) You must worship the *Lord* your God,

12 ⊖   (Dt 6 16) You must not put the *Lord* your God to the test.

18   (Is 61 1) The spirit of the *Lord* has been given to me,

19   (Is 61 2) to proclaim the *Lord's* year of favour.

5 17   the Power of the *Lord* was behind his works of healing.

10 21   I bless you, Father, *Lord* of heaven and of earth,

27 ⊖   (Dt 6 5) You must love the *Lord* your God with all your heart,

13 35   (Ps 118 26) Blessings on him who comes in the name of the *Lord*!

19 38   (Ps 118 26) Blessings on the King who comes, in the name of the *Lord*!

20 37 ⊖   [Moses] calls the *Lord* the God of Abraham, the God of Isaac and the God of Jacob.

42   (Ps 110 1) The *Lord* said to my Lord:

Jn 5 4   ᵛ for at intervals the angel of the *Lord* came down into the pool,⸀

12 13   (Ps 118 26) Blessings on the King of Israel, who comes in the name of the *Lord*!

38   (Is 53 1) *Lord*, who could believe what we have heard said, and to whom has the power of the *Lord* been revealed?

Ac 1 24   *Lord*, you can read everyone's heart;

2 25   (Ps 16 8) I saw the *Lord* before me always,

34   (Ps 110 1) The *Lord* said to my Lord:

39 ⊖   for all those whom the *Lord* our God will call to himself.

3 20   so that the *Lord* may send the time of comfort.

22 ⊖   (Dt 18 15) The *Lord* God will raise up a prophet like myself for you,

4 26   (Ps 2 2) princes making an alliance, against the *Lord* and against his Anointed.

29   *Lord*, take note of their threats

5 9   So you and your husband have agreed to put the Spirit of the *Lord* to the test!

19   the angel of the *Lord* opened the prison gates

7 31   the voice of the *Lord* was heard, ³² I am the God of your ancestors,

33   The *Lord* said to him, 'Take off your shoes;'

49   (Is 66 1) 'what house could you build me,' says the *Lord*,

8 26   The angel of the *Lord* spoke to Philip

39   Philip was taken away by the Spirit of the *Lord*,

10 33   to hear what message ᵛ God (G the *Lord*) has given you for us.

12 7   suddenly the angel of the *Lord* stood there, and the cell was filled with light.

11   The *Lord* really did send his angel

17   [Peter] described . . . how the *Lord* had led him out of prison.

23   the angel of the *Lord* struck [Herod] down,

15 17   (Am 9 12 G) all the pagans who are consecrated to my name, will look for the *Lord*, says the *Lord* who made this ¹⁸ known so long ago.

17 24   Since the God who made the world . . . is himself *Lord* of heaven and earth, he does not make his home in shrines made by human hands.

Rm 4 8   (Ps 32 2) happy the man whom the *Lord* considers sinless.

9 28   (cf. Is 10 23) the *Lord* will execute his sentence on the earth.

29 /7   (Is 1 9) Had the *Lord of hosts* not left us some descendants we should now be like Sodom,

10 16   (Is 53 1) *Lord*, how many believed what we proclaimed?

11 3   (1 K 19 10) *Lord*, they have killed your prophets

34   (Is 40 13) Who could ever know the mind of the *Lord*?

12 19   (cf. Dt 32 35) 'vengeance is mine – I will pay them back,' the *Lord* promises.

14 11   (cf. Is 45 23) By my life – it is the *Lord* who speaks – every knee shall bend before me,

15 11   (Ps 117 1) Let all the pagans praise the *Lord*,

Co 3 20   (Ps 94 11) The *Lord* is not convinced by the arguments of the wise.

10 26   (Ps 24 1) for the earth and everything in it belong to the *Lord*.

14 21   (cf. Is 28 12) and still they will not listen to me, says the *Lord*.

2 Co 6 17   (cf. Is 52 11) keep aloof, says the *Lord*.

18   [I will] be your father, and you shall be my sons and daughters, says the Almighty *Lord*.

1 Tm 6 15   the King of kings and the *Lord* of lords,

2 Tm 2 19   (Nb 16 5) The *Lord* knows those who are his own

Heb 7 21   (Ps 110 4) The *Lord* has sworn an oath which he will never retract:

8 2   the true Tent of Meeting which the *Lord*, and not any man, set up.

8   (Jr 31 31) the days are coming – it is the *Lord* who speaks – when I will establish a new covenant

9   (Jr 31 32) and so I on my side deserted them. It is the *Lord* who speaks.

10   (Jr 31 33) this is the covenant I will make . . . when those days arrive – it is the *Lord* who speaks.

11   (Jr 31 34) Learn to know the *Lord*.

10 16   (Jr 31 33) the *Lord* then goes on to say: 'I will put my laws into their hearts'

Heb 10 30   (Ps 135 14) The *Lord* will judge his people.

12 5   (Pr 3 11) My son, when the *Lord* corrects you, do not treat it lightly;

6   (Pr 3 12) For the *Lord* trains the ones that he loves

13 6   (Ps 118 6) With the *Lord* to help me, I fear nothing:

Jm 1 7   That sort of person . . . must not expect that the *Lord* will give him anything.

3 9   We use [the tongue] to bless the *Lord* and Father,

4 10   Humble yourselves before the *Lord*

15   If it is the *Lord's* will, we shall still be alive

5 4   the cries of the reapers have reached the ears of the *Lord of* ⁷ *hosts*.

10   the prophets who spoke in the name of the *Lord*;

11   You have . . . understood the *Lord's* purpose, realising that the *Lord* is kind and compassionate.

1 P 1 25   (Is 40 8) the word of the *Lord* remains for ever.

3 12   (Ps 34 16, 15) the face of the *Lord* frowns on evil men, but the eyes of the *Lord* are turned towards the virtuous.

2 P 2 9   the *Lord* can rescue the good from the ordeal,

11   the angels . . . make no . . . accusation against them in front of the *Lord*.

3 8   with the *Lord*, 'a day' can mean a thousand years . . .

9   ⁹ The *Lord* is not being slow to carry out his promises

10   The Day of the *Lord* will come like a thief,

Jude 5   ʳthe *Lord* (ᵛ Jesus) rescued the nation from Egypt,

9   Let the *Lord* correct you.

Rv 1 8 ⊖   'I am the Alpha and the Omega' says the *Lord* God,

4 8 ⊖   (Is 6 3) Holy, Holy, Holy is the *Lord* God, the Almighty; he was, he is and he is to come.

11 ⊖   You are our *Lord* and our God, you are worthy of glory and honour

11 4   (Zc 4 14) the two olive trees . . . that stand before the *Lord* of the world.

15   The kingdom of the world has become the kingdom of our *Lord* and his Christ,

17 ⊖   We give thanks to you, Almighty *Lord* God, He-Is-and-He-Was,

15 3 ⊖   How great and wonderful are all your works, *Lord* God Almighty;

4   Who would not revere and praise your name, O *Lord*?

16 7 ⊖   Truly, *Lord* God Almighty, the punishments you give are true and just.

18 8 ⊖   The *Lord* God has condemned her, and he has great power.

19 6 ⊖   The reign of the *Lord* our God Almighty has begun;

21 22 ⊖   the *Lord* God Almighty and the Lamb were themselves the temple,

22 5 ⊖   the *Lord* God will be shining on them.

6 ⊖   the *Lord* God who gives the spirit to the prophets has sent his angel

b) the Lord (Jesus), the Master – (Jesus addressed as) Sir

Marana tha⎫
ᵛ *Maran (atha)*⎭ *1* (1 Co 16 22)

e = *en Kyriō* = in the Lord 55

Mt 3 3   (Is 40 3) Prepare a way for the *Lord*,

7 21   It is not those who say to me, '*Lord*, *Lord*',

22   When the day comes many will say to me, '*Lord*, *Lord*,'

8 2   *Sir*, . . . if you want to, you can cure me.

6   *Sir*, . . . my servant is lying at home

8   *Sir*, I am not worthy to have you under my roof;

21   *Sir*, let me go and bury my father first.

25   Save us, *Lord*, we are going down!

9 28   'Do you believe I can do this?' . . . '*Sir*, we do.'

12 8 ○   the Son of Man is *master* of the sabbath.

14 28   *Lord*, . . . tell me to come to you across the water.

30   *Lord*! Save me!

15 22   *Sir*, Son of David, take pity on me.

25   *Lord*, . . . help me.

27   Ah yes, *sir*; but even house-dogs can eat the scraps

16 22   Heaven preserve you, *Lord*;

17 4   *Lord*, . . . it is wonderful for us to be here;

15   *Lord*, . . . take pity on my son: he is a lunatic

18 21   *Lord*, how often must I forgive . . .?

20 30   *Lord*! Have pity on us, Son of David.

31   *Lord*! Have pity on us, Son of David.

33   *Lord*, let us have our sight back.

21 3   you are to say, 'The *Master* needs them'

22 43   Then how is it . . . that David . . . calls [Christ] *Lord* . . .?

44   (Ps 110 1) The Lord said to my *Lord*:

45   If David can call him *Lord*,

24 42   you do not know the day when your *master* is coming.

25 37   *Lord*, when did we see you hungry . . .?

44   *Lord*, when did we see you hungry . . .?

26 22   Not I, *Lord*, surely?

Mk 1 3   (Is 40 3) Prepare a way for the *Lord*,

2 28 ○   the Son of Man is *master* even of the sabbath.

7 28   Ah yes, *sir*, . . . but the house-dogs . . . can eat the children's scraps.

Mk 11	3	The *Master* needs it
12	36	(Ps 110 1) The Lord said to my *Lord*:
	37	David himself calls him *Lord*,
16	19	the *Lord* Jesus . . . was taken up into heaven:
	20	the *Lord* working with them and confirming the word
Lk 1	43	Why should I be honoured with a visit from the mother of my *Lord*?
2	11	a saviour has been born to you; he is Christ the *Lord*.
3	4	(Is 40 3) Prepare a way for the *Lord*,
5	8	Leave me, *Lord*; I am a sinful man.
	12	*Sir*, . . . if you want to, you can cure me.
6	5 ○	The Son of Man is *master* of the sabbath.
	46	Why do you call me, '*Lord, Lord*' . . .?
7	6	*Sir*, . . . do not put yourself to trouble;
	13	When the *Lord* saw her he felt sorry for her.
	19	[John] sent [two of his disciples] to ⌐the *Lord* (ᵛ Jesus)
9	54	*Lord*, do you want us to call down fire from heaven . . .?
	59	Another . . . replied, '(ᵛ *Lord*,) let me go and bury my father first'.
	61	Another said, 'I will follow you, *sir* but first let me go and say good-bye to my people'
10	1	After this the *Lord* appointed seventy-two others
	17	*Lord*, . . . even the devils submit to us
	39	Mary . . . sat down at the *Lord*'s feet and listened to him speaking.
	40	*Lord*, do you not care that my sister is leaving me to do the serving . . .?
	41	But the *Lord* answered: 'Martha,'
11	1	*Lord*, teach us to pray,
	39	the *Lord* said to him, 'Oh, you Pharisees!'
12	41	*Lord*, do you mean this parable for us . . .?
	42	The *Lord* replied, 'What sort of a steward . . .?
13	15	But the *Lord* answered him. 'Hypocrites!'
	23	*Sir*, will there be only a few saved?
17	5	The apostles said to the *Lord*, 'Increase our faith'.
	6	The *Lord* replied, 'Were your faith the size of a mustard seed . . .'
	37	'Where, *Lord*?' [the disciples] asked. He replied, 'Where the body is,'
18	6	the *Lord* said, 'You notice what the unjust judge has to say?'
	41	*Sir*, . . . let me see again.
19	8	Zacchaeus . . . said to the *Lord*, 'Look, *sir*, I am going to give half my property to the poor,'
	31	you are to say this, The *Master* needs it.
	34	they answered, 'The *Master* needs it'.
20	42	(Ps 110 1) The Lord said to my *Lord*:
	44	David here calls him *Lord*;
22	33	*Lord*, . . . I would be ready to go to prison with you,
	38	*Lord*, . . . there are two swords here now.
	49	*Lord*, shall we use our swords?
	61	and the *Lord* turned and looked straight at Peter, and Peter remembered what the *Lord* had said to him,
24	3	[the women] discovered that the body of the *Lord* Jesus was not there.
	34	Yes, it is true. The *Lord* has risen
Jn 1	23	(Is 40 3) Make a straight way for the *Lord*.
4	1	When ᵛ Jesus (G the *Lord*) heard that the Pharisees
	11	You have no bucket, *sir*,
	15	*Sir*, . . . give me some of that water,
	19	I see you are a prophet, *sir*
	49	*Sir*, . . . come down before my child dies.
5	7	*Sir*, . . . I have no one to put me into the pool
6	23	the place where the bread had been eaten (§ after the *Lord* had given thanks).
	34	*Sir*, . . . give us that bread always.
	68	*Lord*, who shall we go to? You have the message of eternal life,
8	11	'Has no one condemned you?' 'No one, *sir*,'
9	36	*Sir*, . . . tell me who he is so that I may believe in him.
	38	The man said, '*Lord*, I believe', and worshipped him.
11	2	It was the same Mary . . . who anointed the *Lord* with ointment
	3	*Lord*, the man you love is ill.
	12	*Lord*, if he is able to rest he is sure to get better.
	21	Martha said to Jesus, '(§ *Lord*,) if you had been here, my brother would not have died,
	27	Yes, *Lord*, I believe that you are the Christ,
	32	*Lord*, if you had been here, my brother would not have died.
	34	*Lord*, come and see.
	39	*Lord*, by now he will smell; this is the fourth day.
13	6	*Lord*, are you going to wash my feet?
	9	Then, *Lord*, . . . not only my feet,
	13 ●	You call me Master and *Lord*, and rightly; so I am. ¹⁴ If I,
	14	then, the *Lord* and Master, have washed your feet, you should wash each other's feet.
	25	Who is it, *Lord*?
	36	Simon Peter said, '*Lord*, where are you going?'
	37	(§ *Lord*,) why can't I follow you now?
14	5	*Lord*, we do not know where you are going,
	8	*Lord*, let us see the Father

Jn 14	22	*Lord*, what is all this about?
20	2	They have taken the *Lord* out of the tomb
	13	'They have taken my *Lord* away' she replied
	15 ○	[Mary to Jesus:] '*Sir*, if you have taken him away,
	18	Mary of Magdala went and told the disciples that she had seen the *Lord*
	20	The disciples were filled with joy when they saw the *Lord*,
	25	the disciples said, 'We have seen the *Lord*',
	28	Thomas replied, 'My *Lord* and my God!'
21	7	The disciple Jesus loved said to Peter, 'It is the *Lord*'. At these words 'It is the *Lord*', Simon Peter, who had practically nothing on, wrapped his cloak round him
	12	they knew quite well it was the *Lord*.
	15	Yes, *Lord*, you know I love you.
	16	Yes, *Lord*, you know I love you.
	17	*Lord*, you know everything; you know I love you.
	20	*Lord*, who is it that will betray you?
	21	Peter said to Jesus, 'What about him, *Lord*?'
Ac 1	6	*Lord*, has the time come?
	21	the whole time that the *Lord* Jesus was travelling round with us,
2	20	(Jl 3 4) before the great Day of the *Lord* dawns.
	21	(Jl 3 5) All who call on the name of the *Lord* will be saved.
	34	(Ps 110 1) The Lord said to my *Lord*:
	36 ●	God has made this Jesus whom you crucified both *Lord* and Christ.
	47	the *Lord* added to their community those destined to be saved.
4	33	The apostles continued to testify to the resurrection of the *Lord* Jesus
5	14	the numbers of men and women who came to believe in the *Lord* increased steadily.
7	59	*Lord* Jesus, receive my spirit.
	60	*Lord*, do not hold this sin against them;
8	16	they had only been baptised in the name of the *Lord* Jesus.
9	1	Saul was still breathing threats to slaughter the *Lord*'s disciples.
	5	'Who are you, *Lord*?' . . . 'I am Jesus, and you are persecuting me.'
	10	he heard the *Lord* say to him, 'Ananias!' . . . 'Here I am, *Lord*',
	11	the *Lord* said, 'You must go to Straight Street'
	13	*Lord*, several people have told me about this man
	15	The *Lord* replied, ' . . . this man is my chosen instrument'
	17	I have been sent by the *Lord* Jesus
	27	how the *Lord* had appeared to Saul
	28	Saul . . . preaching fearlessly in the name of the *Lord*.
	35	they were all converted to the *Lord*.
	42	many believed in the *Lord*.
10	36 ●	Jesus Christ is *Lord* of all men.
11	16	I remembered that the *Lord* had said,
	17	God was giving them the identical thing he gave to us when we believed in the *Lord* Jesus Christ;
	20	proclaiming the Good News of the *Lord* Jesus to them
	21	The *Lord* helped them, and a great number . . . were converted to the *Lord*.
	23 ᵛe	[Barnabas] urged them all to remain faithful ⌐to (ᵛ in) the *Lord*
	24	a large number of people were won over to the *Lord*.
13	2	while they were offering worship to the *Lord*
15	11	we believe that we are saved . . . through the grace of the *Lord* Jesus.
	26	men . . . who have dedicated their lives to the name of our *Lord* Jesus Christ.
16	15	If you really think me a true believer in the *Lord*,
	31	Become a believer in the *Lord* Jesus, and you will be saved,
18	8	Crispus . . . and his whole household . . . became believers in the *Lord*.
	25	[Apollos] had been given instruction in the Way of the *Lord*
19	5	they were baptised in the name of the *Lord* Jesus,
	13	some . . . Jewish exorcists tried pronouncing the name of the *Lord* Jesus
	17	the name of the *Lord* Jesus came to be held in great honour.
20	21	urging both Jews and Greeks to . . . believe in our *Lord* Jesus.
	24	the mission the *Lord* Jesus gave me
	35	remembering the words of the *Lord* Jesus,
21	13	I am ready . . . to die . . . for the name of the *Lord* Jesus.
22	8	'Who are you, *Lord*?' . . . 'I am Jesus the Nazarene,'
	10	'What am I to do, *Lord*?' The *Lord* answered, 'Stand up'
	19	'*Lord*,' I answered, 'it is because they know that I used to [imprison them];'
23	11	the *Lord* appeared to him and said, 'Courage!'
26	15	'Who are you, *Lord*?' And the *Lord* answered, 'I am Jesus,'
28	31	[Paul] teaching the truth about the *Lord* Jesus Christ
Rm 1	4	[This news] is about Jesus Christ our *Lord*
	7	may God the Father and the *Lord* Jesus Christ send grace and peace.
4	24	who raised Jesus our *Lord* from the dead,

Rm 5	1		through our *Lord* Jesus Christ, by faith we are judged righteous
	11		we are filled with joyful trust in God, through our *Lord* Jesus Christ,
	21		thanks to the righteousness that comes through Jesus Christ our *Lord*.
6	23 e		eternal life in Christ Jesus our *Lord*.
7	25		Thanks be to God through Jesus Christ our *Lord*!
8	39 e		the love of God made visible in Christ Jesus our *Lord*.
10	9 ●		If your lips confess that Jesus is *Lord*
	12		all belong to the same *Lord* who is rich enough, however many ask his help,
	13		(Jl 3 5) everyone who calls on the name of the *Lord* will be saved.
12	11		Work for the *Lord* with untiring effort
13	14		Let your armour be the *Lord* Jesus Christ;
14	4		It is not for you to condemn someone else's servant: whether he stands or falls it is his own *master's* business; he will stand, you may be sure, because the *Lord* has power to make him stand.
	6		The one who observes special days does so in honour of the *Lord*. The one who eats meat also does so in honour of the *Lord* . . . ; but then the man who abstains does that too in honour of the *Lord*,
	8		if we live, we live for the *Lord*; and if we die, we die for the *Lord*, so that alive or dead we belong to the *Lord*. ⁹ . . .
	9		Christ both died and came to life . . . so that he might
●	2		be *Lord* both of the dead and of the living.
	14 e		I speak ʳfor (lit. in) the *Lord* Jesus,
15	6		the God and Father of our *Lord* Jesus Christ.
	30		I beg you . . . , by our *Lord* Jesus Christ . . . , to help me
16	2 e		Give her, in [union with] the *Lord*, a welcome worthy of the saints,
	8 e		[Greetings] to Amphiatus, my friend in the *Lord*;
	11 e		to the household of Narcissus who ʳbelong to (lit. are in) the *Lord*;
	12 e		to Tryphaena and Tryphosa, who work hard ʳfor (lit. in) the *Lord*; to . . . Persis who has done so much ʳfor (lit. in) the *Lord*;
	13 e		Rufus, a chosen servant ʳof (lit. in) the *Lord*,
	18		People like that are not slaves of ʳJesus Christ (lit. Christ our *Lord*),
	20		The grace of our *Lord* Jesus Christ be with you.
	22 e		I, Tertius, . . . greet you in the *Lord*.
	24		(ᵛ The grace of our *Lord* Jesus Christ be with you all. Amen.)
1 Co 1	2		all the saints everywhere who pray to our *Lord* Jesus Christ;
	3		May God our Father and the *Lord* Jesus Christ send you grace and peace.
	7		while you are waiting for our *Lord* Jesus Christ to be revealed;
	8		the last day, the day of our *Lord* Jesus Christ,
	9		God by calling you has joined you to his Son, Jesus Christ our *Lord*;
	10		I appeal to you, brothers, for the sake of our *Lord* Jesus Christ,
2	8		they would not have crucified the *Lord* of glory;
4	4		the *Lord* alone is my judge.
	5		Leave that until the *Lord* comes:
	17 e		Timothy, my dear and faithful son in the *Lord*:
5	4		When we are assembled together in the name of the *Lord* Jesus, . . . then with the power of the *Lord* Jesus he is to be handed over to Satan
	5		so that . . . his spirit [may be] saved on the day of the *Lord*.
6	11		you have been . . . justified through the name of the *Lord* Jesus Christ
	13		But the body . . . is for the *Lord*, and the *Lord* for the body.
	14		God, who raised the *Lord* from the dead, will . . . raise us up too.
	17		anyone who is joined to the *Lord* is one spirit with him.
7	10		This is not from me but from the *Lord*:
	12		The rest is from me and not from the *Lord*.
	22 e		A slave, when he is called in the *Lord*, becomes the *Lord's* freedman,
	25		About remaining celibate, I have no directions from the *Lord* but give my own opinion as one who, by the *Lord's* mercy, has stayed faithful.
	39 e		she is free to marry anybody she likes, only it must be in the *Lord*.
8	6 ●		for us there is one God, . . . and there is one *Lord*, Jesus Christ, through whom . . . we exist.
9	1		I have seen Jesus our *Lord*. You are all my work in the *Lord*.
	2 e		you who are the seal of my apostolate in the *Lord*.
	5		like all the other apostles and the brothers of the *Lord* and Cephas?
	14		the *Lord* directed that those who preach the gospel should get their living from the gospel.
10	21		You cannot drink the cup of the *Lord* and the cup of demons. You cannot take your share at the table of the *Lord*
	22		and at the table of demons. ²² Do you want to make the *Lord* angry . . . ?

1 Co 11	11 e		neither can man do without woman, in the *Lord*;
	20	6	when you hold these meetings, it is not the *Lord's* Supper that you are eating,
	23		this is what I received from the *Lord* . . . that on the same night that he was betrayed, the *Lord* Jesus took some bread,
	26		Until the *Lord* comes, . . . you are proclaiming his death,
	27		anyone who eats the bread or drinks the cup of the *Lord* unworthily will be behaving unworthily towards the body and blood of the *Lord*.
12	3 ●		no one can say, 'Jesus is *Lord*' unless he is under the influence of the Holy Spirit.
	5		there are all sorts of service to be done, but always to the same *Lord*;
14	37		what I am writing to you is a command from the *Lord*.
15	21 e		the pride that I take in you in Christ Jesus our *Lord*.
	57		let us thank God for giving us the victory through our *Lord* Jesus Christ.
	58		keep on working at the *Lord's* work always, knowing that
	e		in the *Lord*, you cannot be labouring in vain.
16	10		[Timothy] is doing the *Lord's* work,
	19		Aquila and Prisca . . . send you their warmest wishes, in
	e		the *Lord*.
	22		If anyone does not love the *Lord*, a curse on him. ᵛMaran atha [the *Lord* is coming] (G *Marana* tha [Our *Lord*, come!]).
	23		The grace of the *Lord* Jesus be with you.
2 Co 1	2		Grace and peace to you from God our Father and the *Lord* Jesus Christ.
	3		Blessed be the God and Father of our *Lord* Jesus Christ,
	14		when the day of our *Lord* Jesus Christ comes,
2	12 e		the door was wide open for my work there in the *Lord*,
3	16		[The veil] will not be removed until they turn to the *Lord*.
	17		this *Lord* is the Spirit, and where the Spirit of the *Lord* is, there is freedom.
	18		we, . . . reflecting like mirrors the brightness of the *Lord*, all grow brighter . . . ; this is the work of the *Lord* who is Spirit.
4	5		it is not ourselves that we are preaching, but Christ Jesus as the *Lord*,
	14		he who raised the *Lord* Jesus to life
5	6		to live in the body means to be exiled from the *Lord*,
	8		we . . . want to be exiled from the body and make our home with the *Lord*.
8	9		Remember how generous the *Lord* Jesus was:
10	8		Maybe I do boast . . . about our authority, but the *Lord* gave it [to me]
11	17		What I am going to say now is not prompted by the *Lord*,
	31		The God and Father of the *Lord* Jesus
12	1		I will not move on to the visions and revelations I have had from the *Lord*.
	8		I have pleaded with the *Lord* three times for [the angel of Satan] to leave me,
13	10		the authority which the *Lord* gave me
	13		The grace of the *Lord* Jesus Christ . . . be with you all.
Ga 1	3		We wish you the grace and peace of God our Father and of the *Lord* Jesus Christ,
	19		James, the brother of the *Lord*,
5	10 e		united in the *Lord*, you will agree with me,
6	14		the only thing I can boast about is the cross of our *Lord* Jesus Christ,
	18		The grace of our *Lord* Jesus Christ be with your spirit,
Ep 1	2		Grace and peace to you from God our Father and from the *Lord* Jesus Christ.
	3		Blessed be God the Father of our *Lord* Jesus Christ,
	15 e		having once heard about your faith in the *Lord* Jesus,
	17		May the God of our *Lord* Jesus Christ, . . . give you a spirit of wisdom
2	21 e		all grow into one holy temple in the *Lord*;
3	11		according to the plan which [God] had had from all eternity
	e		in Christ Jesus our *Lord*,
4	1 e		I, the prisoner in the *Lord*,
	5 ●		There is one *Lord*, one faith, one baptism,
	17 e		I want to urge you in [the name of] the *Lord*,
5	8 e		but now you are light in the *Lord*;
	10		Try to discover what the *Lord* wants of you,
	17		recognise what is the will of the *Lord*.
	19		go on singing and chanting to the *Lord* in your hearts,
	20		giving thanks to God who is our Father in heaven in the name of our *Lord* Jesus Christ.
	22		Wives should ʳregard (ᵛ be subject to) their husbands as [ʳthey regard, ᵛ to] the *Lord*,
6	1 e		Children, be obedient to your parents in the *Lord*
	4		parents, . . . guide [your children] as the *Lord* does.
	7		Work hard and willingly, . . . for the sake of the *Lord* and not for the sake of men.
	8		everyone . . . will be properly rewarded by the *Lord*
	9		they and you [slaves and masters] have the same *Master* in heaven
	10 e		grow strong in the *Lord*,

Ep	6 21 e	Tychicus, my loyal helper in the *Lord,*	

Ep 6 21 e Tychicus, my loyal helper in the *Lord,*
   23 May God the Father and the *Lord* Jesus Christ grant peace
   24 . . . to all the brothers. ²⁴ May grace and eternal life be
        with all who love our *Lord* Jesus Christ.
Ph 1 2 We wish you the grace . . . of God our Father and of the
        Lord Jesus Christ.
   14 e most of the brothers have taken courage in the *Lord* from
        these chains of mine
   2 11 that every tongue should acclaim Jesus Christ as *Lord,*
   19 e I hope, in the *Lord* Jesus, to send Timothy to you soon,
   24 e I continue to trust, in the *Lord,* that I shall be coming
        soon myself.
   29 e Give [Epaphroditus] a most hearty welcome in the *Lord;*
   3 1 e rejoice in the *Lord.*
   8 the supreme advantage of knowing Christ Jesus my *Lord.*
   20 from heaven comes the saviour we are waiting for, the *Lord*
        Jesus Christ,
   4 1 e remain faithful in the *Lord*
   2 e come to an agreement with each other, in the *Lord;*
   4 e I want you to be . . . always happy in the *Lord;*
   5 the *Lord* is very near.
   10 e It is a great joy to me, in the *Lord,*
   23 May the grace of the *Lord* Jesus Christ be with your spirit.
Col 1 3 We have never failed to . . . give thanks for you to God,
        the Father of our *Lord* Jesus Christ,
   10 So you will be able to lead the kind of life which the *Lord*
        expects of you,
   2 6 You must live your whole life according to the Christ you
        have received – Jesus the *Lord;*
   3 13 The *Lord* (ᵛChrist) has forgiven you; forgive each other
   17 Remember the service that the *Lord* wants you to do,
   18 Wives, give way to your husbands, as you should in the
    e *Lord.*
   20 Children, be obedient to your parents always, because that
    e is what ʳwill please (lit. is pleasing in) the *Lord.*
   22 Slaves, be obedient . . . out of respect for the *Master.*
   23 put your heart into [your work] as if it were for the *Lord*
   24 . . , ²⁴ knowing that the *Lord* will repay you . . . It is
        Christ the *Lord* that you are serving;
   4 1 Masters, . . . you too have a *Master* in heaven.
   7 Tychicus . . . is . . . a loyal helper and companion in [the
    e service of] the *Lord.*
   17 Remember the service that ʳthe Lord wants you to do (lit.
    e you received in the *Lord*),
1 Th 1 1 to the Church in Thessalonika which is in God the Father
    e and the *Lord* Jesus Christ;
   3 how you have . . . persevered through hope, in our *Lord*
        Jesus Christ.
   6 you were led to become imitators of us, and of the *Lord;*
   8 it was from you that the word of the *Lord* started to spread
   2 15 the people who put the *Lord* Jesus to death,
   19 in the presence of our *Lord* Jesus when he comes;
   3 8 e you are still holding firm in the *Lord.*
   11 God our Father himself, and our *Lord* Jesus Christ,
   12 May the *Lord* be generous in increasing your love
   13 when our *Lord* Jesus Christ comes
   4 1 e we . . . appeal to you in the *Lord* Jesus
   2 the instructions we gave you on the authority of the *Lord*
        Jesus.
   6 the *Lord* always punishes sins of that sort,
   15 We can tell you this from the *Lord's* own teaching, that
        any of us who are left alive until the *Lord's* coming will
        not have any advantage over those who have died.
   16 ¹⁶. . . the *Lord* himself will come down from heaven;
   17 those who have died in Christ will . . . rise, ¹⁷ and then
        those of us who are still alive will be taken up . . . with
        them, to meet the *Lord* in the air.
   5 2 the Day of the *Lord* is going to come like a thief
   9 to win salvation through our *Lord* Jesus Christ,
   12 e those who are . . . above you in the *Lord*
   23 the coming of our *Lord* Jesus Christ.
   27 My orders, in the *Lord's* name, are . . .
   28 The grace of our *Lord* Jesus Christ be with you.
2 Th 1 1 to the Church in Thessalonika which is in God our Father
    e and the *Lord* Jesus Christ;
   7 when the *Lord* Jesus appears from heaven
   8 all who . . . refuse to accept the Good News of our *Lord*
        Jesus.
   9 excluded from the presence of the *Lord*
   12 the name of our *Lord* Jesus Christ will be glorified in you and
        you in him, by the grace of our God and the *Lord* Jesus
        Christ.
   2 1 To turn now . . . to the coming of our *Lord* Jesus Christ
   2 the Day of the *Lord* has already arrived.
   8 The *Lord* (§ Jesus) will kill him with the breath of his mouth
   13 brothers whom the *Lord* loves,
   14 that you should share the glory of our *Lord* Jesus Christ.
   16 May our *Lord* Jesus Christ himself, and God our Father,
        . . .¹⁷ comfort you
   3 1 Pray that the *Lord's* message may spread quickly,

2 Th 3 3 the *Lord* is faithful,
   4 e we, in the *Lord,* have every confidence that you are doing . . .
        all that we tell you.
   5 May the *Lord* turn your hearts towards the love of God and
        the fortitude of Christ.
   6 In the name of the *Lord* Jesus Christ, we urge you, brothers,
   12 e In the *Lord* Jesus Christ, we . . . call on people of this kind
   16 May the *Lord* of peace himself give you peace all the time . . .
        The *Lord* be with you all.
   18 May the grace of our *Lord* Jesus Christ be with you all.
1 Tm 1 2 peace from God the Father and from Christ Jesus our *Lord.*
   12 I thank Christ Jesus our *Lord,* who has given me strength,
   14 the grace of our *Lord* filled me with faith
   6 3 the sound teaching which is that of our *Lord* Jesus Christ,
   14 until the Appearing of our *Lord* Jesus Christ,
2 Tm 1 2 peace from God the Father and from Christ Jesus our *Lord.*
   8 you are never to be ashamed of witnessing to the *Lord,*
   2 19 All who call on the name of the *Lord* must avoid sin.
   22 in union with all those who call on the *Lord*
   24 a servant of the *Lord* is not to engage in quarrels,
   3 11 all the persecutions I have endured; and the *Lord* has rescued
        me from every one of them.
   4 8 the crown of righteousness . . . which the *Lord* . . . will give
        to me
   14 (Pr 24 12) the *Lord* will repay him for what he has done.
   17 the *Lord* stood by me
   18 The *Lord* will rescue me from all evil attempts on me,
   22 The *Lord* be with your spirit.
Phm 3 the peace of God our Father and the *Lord* Jesus Christ.
   5 the love . . . which you have for the *Lord* Jesus and for all
        the saints.
   16 e as a blood-brother as well as a brother in the *Lord.*
   20 e I am counting on you, in the *Lord;* put new heart into me, in
        Christ.
   25 May the grace of our *Lord* Jesus Christ be with your spirit.
Heb 1 10 It is you, *Lord,* who laid earth's foundations
   2 3 The promise was first announced by the *Lord* himself,
   7 14 So our *Lord* . . . came from Judah,
   13 20 the God of peace, who brought our *Lord* Jesus back from the
        dead
Jm 1 1 James, servant of God and of the *Lord* Jesus Christ.
   2 1 faith in Jesus Christ, our glorified *Lord,*
   5 7 be patient, brothers, until the *Lord's* coming.
   8 do not lose heart, because the *Lord's* coming will be soon.
   14 the elders . . . must anoint him with oil in the name of the
        Lord . . .¹⁵ . . . the *Lord* will raise him up again;
   15
1 P 1 3 Blessed be God the Father of our *Lord* Jesus Christ,
   2 3 (Ps 34 8) you have tasted the goodness of the *Lord.*
   3 15 (Is 8 13) Simply reverence the *Lord* Christ in your hearts,
2 P 1 2 as you come to know (§ God and Jesus) our *Lord* more and
        more.
   8 a real knowledge of our *Lord* Jesus Christ.
   11 the eternal kingdom of our *Lord* and saviour Jesus Christ.
   14 the time . . . is coming soon, as our *Lord* Jesus Christ fore-
        told to me.
   16 the coming of our *Lord* Jesus Christ;
   2 20 by coming to know our *Lord* and saviour Jesus Christ,
   3 2 the commandments of the *Lord* and saviour
   15 Think of our *Lord's* patience as your opportunity to be saved:
   18 the knowledge of our *Lord* and saviour Jesus Christ.
Jude 4 condemned for . . . rejecting our only Master and *Lord,*
        Jesus Christ.
   14 the *Lord* will come with his saints in their tens of thousands,
   17 the apostles of our *Lord* Jesus Christ
   21 the mercy of our *Lord* Jesus Christ
   25 the only God, who saves us through Jesus Christ our *Lord,*
Rv 1 10 6 it was the *Lord's* day and the Spirit possessed me,
   11 8 the Great City . . . in which their *Lord* was crucified.
   14 13 e Happy are those who die in the *Lord!*
   17 14 the Lamb is the *Lord* of lords and the King of kings,
   19 16 The King of Kings and the *Lord* of lords.
   22 20 Amen; come, *Lord* Jesus.
   21 May the grace of the *Lord* Jesus be with you all. Amen.

c) Lord (God or Jesus)

e = *en Kyriō* = in the Lord 2

Ac 8 22 Repent . . . and pray to the *Lord;*
   24 Pray to the *Lord* for me yourselves
   25 Having . . . proclaimed the word of the *Lord,*
   9 31 The churches . . . living in the fear of the *Lord,*
   12 24 The word of ᵛ God (G the *Lord*) continued to spread
   13 10 [Elymas,] why don't you stop twisting the straightforward
        ways of the *Lord?* ¹¹ Now watch how the right hand of the
   11 *Lord* will strike you:
   12 The proconsul . . . became a believer, being astonished by
        what he had learnt about the *Lord.*
   47 this is what the *Lord* commanded us to do
   48 the pagans . . . thanked the *Lord* for his message;
   49 the word of the *Lord* spread

Ac	14	3	the *Lord* supported all [Paul and Barnabas] said about his gift of grace,
		23	[Paul and Barnabas] commended [the disciples] to the *Lord* in whom they had come to believe.
	15	35	Paul and Barnabas . . . proclaimed the Good News, the word of the *Lord.*
		36	all the towns where we preached the word of the *Lord,*
		40	Paul . . . was commended by the brothers to the grace of ˅ God (G the *Lord*).
	16	14	the *Lord* opened [Lydia's] heart
		32	they preached the word of ˥the *Lord* (G God) to him
	18	9	the *Lord* spoke to Paul in a vision,
	19	10	people from all over Asia . . . were able to hear the word of the *Lord.*
		20	In this impressive way the word of the *Lord* spread
	20	19	I have served the *Lord* in all humility,
		28	Be on your guard . . . to feed the Church of ˥God (G the *Lord*)
		32	I commend you to ˥God (G the *Lord*)
	21	14	The *Lord's* will be done.
1 Co	1	31	(cf. Jr 9 23) if anyone wants to boast, let him boast ˥about (lit. in) the *Lord.*
	2	16	(Is 40 13) Who can know the mind of the *Lord* . . .?
	3	5	the different ways in which [Apollos and Paul] brought [you the faith] were assigned to them by the *Lord.*
	4	19	I will be visiting you soon, the *Lord* willing.
	7	17	what each one has is what the *Lord* has given him
		32	An unmarried man can devote himself to the *Lord's* affairs, all he need worry about is pleasing the *Lord;*
		34	an unmarried woman . . . can devote herself to the *Lord's* affairs;
		35	give your undivided attention to the *Lord.*
	10	9	We are not to put ˥the *Lord* (˅ Christ) to the test:
	11	32	when the *Lord* does punish us like that,
	16	7	I hope to spend some time with you, the *Lord* permitting.
2 Co	5	11	with the fear of the *Lord* in mind
	8	5	they offered their own selves first to ˥God (lit. the *Lord*) and, under God, to us.
		19	for the glory of ˥God (lit. the *Lord*),
		21	(Pr 3 4 G) we are trying to do right not only in the sight of ˥God (lit. the *Lord*) but also in the sight of men.
	10	17	(cf. Jr 9 23) If anyone wants to boast, let him boast ˥of (lit. in) the *Lord.*
		18	It is not the man who commends himself that can be accepted, but the man who is commended by the *Lord.*
2 Tm	1	16	I hope the *Lord* will be kind to all the family of Onesiphorus,
		18	May it be the *Lord's* will that he shall find the *Lord's* mercy on that Day.
	2	7	the *Lord* will show you how to understand it all.
Heb	12	14	the holiness without which no one can ever see the *Lord.*
1 P	2	13	For the sake of the *Lord,* accept the authority of every social institution:

d) Master, Owner, Lord (God, Jesus or another) – Sir – Authority

Mt	6	24	No one can be the slave of two *masters*:
	10	24	The disciple is not superior to his teacher, nor the slave to his *master.* 25 It is enough for the disciple that he should grow to be like his teacher, and the slave like his *master.*
	13	27	*Sir,* was it not good seed that you sowed . . .?
	18	25	his *master* gave orders that he should be sold,
		27	the servant's *master* felt so sorry for him that he let him go
		31	his fellow servants . . . went to their *master* and reported the whole affair
		32	the *master* sent for him.
		34	the *master* handed him over to the torturers
	20	8	the *owner* of the vineyard said to his bailiff,
	21	30	the second [son] . . . answered, 'Certainly, *sir,*' but did not go [to the vineyard].
		40	when the *owner* of the vineyard comes,
	24	45	What sort of servant . . . is . . . wise enough for the *master* to place him over his household . . .?
		46	Happy that servant if his *master's* arrival finds him at this employment.
		48	the dishonest servant who says to himself, 'My *master* is taking his time',
		50	his *master* will come on a day he does not expect
	25	11	'Lord, Lord,' [the other bridesmaids] said 'open the door for us.'
		18	the man who had received one [talent] . . . hid his *master's* money.
		19	the *master* of those servants came back
		20	'*Sir,*' he said 'you entrusted me with five talents; . . .'
		21	21 His master said to him, 'Well done, good and faithful servant; . . . come and join in your *master's* happiness'.
		22	'*Sir,*' he said 'you entrusted me with two talents; . . .'
		23	23 His master said to him, 'Well done, good and faithful servant; . . . come and join in your *master's* happiness'.
		24	'*Sir,*' said he 'I had heard you were a hard man,'
		26	his *master* answered him, 'You wicked and lazy servant!'

Mk	12	9	what will the *owner* of the vineyard do?
			you do not know when the *master* of the house is coming,
Lk	10	2	ask the *Lord* of the harvest to send labourers to his harvest.
	12	36	like men waiting for their *master* to return
		37	Happy those servants whom the *master* finds awake
		42	What sort of steward . . . is . . . wise enough for the *master* to place him over his household . . . ?
		43	Happy that servant if his *master's* arrival finds him at this employment.
		45	the servant who says to himself, 'My *master* is taking his time coming',
		46	his *master* will come on a day he does not expect
		47	The servant who knows what his *master* wants,
	13	8	*Sir,* . . . leave it one more year
		25	*Lord,* open to us
	14	21	The servant returned and reported this to his *master.*
		22	'*Sir,*' said the servant 'your orders have been carried out'
		23	Then the *master* said to his servant,
	16	3	Now that my *master* is taking the stewardship from me,
		5	he called his *master's* debtors one by one. . . . 'how much do you owe my *master*?'
		8	The *master* praised the dishonest steward for his astuteness.
			No servant can be the slave of two *masters*:
	19	16	*Sir,* your one pound has brought in ten.
		18	*Sir,* your one pound has made five.
		20	*Sir,* here is your pound. I put it away safely in a piece of linen
		25	But, *sir,* he has ten pounds
	20	13	Then the *owner* of the vineyard said, 'What am I to do?'
		15	what will the *owner* of the vineyard do to them?
Jn	13	16	no servant is greater than his *master,*
	15	15	a servant does not know his *master's* business;
		20	A servant is not greater than his *master.*
2 P	2	10 Δ 3	those who . . . have no respect for *authority.*
Jude		8 Δ 3	these people . . . disregard *authority,*

e) (an angel, a voice from heaven, addressed as) Lord

Ac	10	4	[Cornelius said to the angel:] 'What is it, *Lord*?'
		14	Peter answered, 'Certainly not, *Lord*;'
	11	8	I answered: 'Certainly not, *Lord*; nothing profane . . . has ever crossed my lips.'

f) (the angelic order of) Domination, Dominion

Ep	1	21	[God made Christ sit] far above every Sovereignty, Authority, Power, or *Domination,* or any other name that can be named,
Col	1	16 3	in [Christ] were created . . . Thrones, *Dominations,* Sovereignties, Powers

g) (a christian church addressed as) Lady

2 Jn		1 5	From the Elder: my greetings to the *Lady,* the chosen one, and to her children,
		5 5	I am writing now, dear *lady,* . . . to plead: let us love one another.

h) Master, Owner (generally) – Sir, Lord – Lord it over, Have power over

Mt	15	27	even house-dogs can eat the scraps that fall from their *master's* table.
	20	25 4	among the pagans the rulers *lord it over* them,
	27	63	˥Your Excellency (or: *Sir*) [=Pilate], we recall that this impostor said,
Mk	10	42 4	among the pagans their so-called rulers *lord it over* them,
Lk	19	33	As they were untying the colt, its *owners* said,
	22	25 2	Among pagans it is the kings who *lord it over* them,
Jn	12	21	[Some Greeks to Philip:] '*Sir,* we should like to see Jesus.'
Ac	16	16	a slave girl who was a soothsayer and made a lot of money for her *masters*
		19	her *masters* . . . seized Paul and Silas
		30	[The gaoler to Paul and Silas:] '*Sirs,* what must I do to be saved?'
	19	16 4	the man with the evil spirit hurled himself at them and *overpowered* [them]
	25	26	I have nothing definite that I can write to ˥his Imperial Majesty (lit. my *lord*) about [Paul];
Rm	6	9 2	Death *has no power over* [Christ] any more.
		14 2	sin will no longer *dominate* your life,
	7	1 2	laws ˥affect (lit. *have power over*) a person only during his lifetime.
1 Co	8	5	either in the sky or on earth – where there certainly seem to be 'gods' and 'lords' in plenty –
2 Co	1	24 2	We are not *dictators over* your faith,
Ga	4	1	an heir, even if he has actually ˥inherited (lit. become the *owner* of) everything, is no different from a slave
Ep	6	5	Slaves, be obedient to the men who are called your *masters* in this world;
		9	those of you who are *employers,* . . . you have the same Master in heaven
Col	3	22	Slaves, be obedient to the men who are called your *masters* in this world; . . . out of respect for the Master.

Col	4	1	*Masters*, make sure that your slaves are given what is just . . . , knowing that you too have a Master in heaven.
1 Tm	6	15	2 the King of kings and the Lord of *lords*,
1 P	3	6	like Sarah, who was obedient to Abraham, and called him her *lord*.
	5	3	4 Never *be a dictator over* any group that is put in your charge,
Rv	7	14 ○	I answered [the elder], 'You can tell me, my *lord*'.
	17	14	the Lamb is the Lord of *lords*
	19	16	The King of kings and the Lord of *lords*.

3. (JESUS ADDRESSED AS) MASTER: *EPI-STATĒS*

epi-statēs 7

Lk	5	5	'*Master*,' Simon replied 'we worked hard all night'
	8	24	*Master! Master!* We are going down!
		45	Peter and his companions said, '*Master*, it is the crowds round you, pushing'.
	9	33	Peter said to Jesus, '*Master*, it is wonderful for us to be here;'
		49	'*Master*,' [John] said 'we saw a man casting out devils'
	17	13	Jesus! *Master*! Take pity on us.

4. (YOUR, HIS) EXCELLENCY: *KRATISTOS*

kratistos 4

Lk	1	3	I . . . have decided to write an ordered account for you, Theophilus, 4 so that your *Excellency* may learn how well founded the teaching is
Ac	23	26	to his *Excellency* the governor Felix, greetings.
	24	2	Your *Excellency*, Felix . . . the reforms this nation owes to your foresight 3 are matters we accept,
	26	25	Festus, your *Excellency*, I am not mad;

MATTER – THING – AFFAIR

1. Matter – Question – Thing: *logos*
 a) (Judicial) Matter, Fact – Charge
 b) Cause of Argument, Case
 c) Thing – Happening – Affair
 d) a Question

2. Matter, Affair – Thing – Reality: *pragma*
3. Have to do with, Be about, Concern – Affair, Case: *ta kata, ta peri,* etc.

1. MATTER – QUESTION – THING: *LOGOS*

1 *logos* 11/334   2 *rhēma* 10/67

a) (Judicial) Matter, Fact – Charge

Mt	18	16	(Dt 19 15) the evidence of two or three witnesses is required to sustain any *charge*.
Ac	8	21	You have no share, no rights, in this *matter*:
	15	6	The apostles and elders met to look into the *matter*,
2 Co	13	1	(Dt 19 15) The evidence of three, or at least two, witnesses is necessary to sustain the *charge*.

b) Cause of Argument, Case

Mt	5	32	everyone who divorces his wife, except for the *case* of fornication, makes her an adulteress;
Ac	10	29	I should like to know *exactly why* you sent for me.
	19	38	If Demetrius and the craftsmen . . . ⌐want to complain (lit. have any *case to argue*) about anyone,
Ep	5	6	Do not let anyone deceive you with empty *arguments*:
Col	2	23	It may *be argued* that true wisdom is to be found in these [human doctrines and regulations],

c) Thing – Happening – Affair

Lk	1	37	2 for no*thing* is impossible to God.
		65	2 the whole *affair* was talked about
	2	15	2 Let us go . . . and see this *thing* that has happened
		19	2 Mary . . . treasured all these *things* . . . in her heart.
		51	2 His mother stored up all these *things* in her heart.
Ac	5	32	2 We are witnesses to all ⌐this (lit. these *things*), we and the Holy Spirit
	10	37	2 You must have heard about the recent *happenings* in Judaea;
	20	24	But life to me is not a *thing* to waste words on,
2 Co	12	4	2 [a man in Christ] was caught up into paradise and heard ⌐*things* (or: *words*) which . . . cannot be put into human language.

d) a Question

Mt	21	24	And I . . . will ask you a *question*, only one;
Mk	11	29	I will ask you a *question*, only one;
Lk	20	3	And I . . . will ask you a *question*.

2. MATTER, AFFAIR – THING – REALITY: *PRAGMA*

1 *pragma*   11   3 *prassō* 1/39
2 *pragmateia* 1

Mt	18	19	if two of you . . . agree to ask *anything* at all, it will be granted
Lk	1	1	accounts of the *events* that have taken place among us,
Ac	5	4	What put this ⌐*scheme* (lit. *thing*) into your mind?
	26	26	3 after all, these *things* were not done in a corner.
Rm	16	2	help [Phoebe] with *anything* she needs:
1 Co	6	1	How dare one of your members take up a *complaint* against another in the lawcourts of the unjust . . .?
2 Co	7	11	you have shown yourselves blameless in this *affair*.
1 Th	4	6	[God] wants nobody . . . to sin by taking advantage of a brother in these *matters*;
2 Tm	2	4	2 no soldier gets himself mixed up in the *affairs* of civilian life,
Heb	6	18	there would be two unalterable *things* . . . [by which] we . . . should have a strong encouragement
	10	1	since the Law has no more than a reflection of these *realities*, and no finished picture of them, it is quite incapable
	11	1	Only faith can . . . prove the existence of the *realities* that . . . remain unseen.
Jm	3	16	Wherever you find jealousy . . . you find disharmony, and wicked *things* of every kind

3. HAVE TO DO WITH, BE ABOUT, CONCERN – AFFAIR, CASE: *TA KATA, TA PERI,* etc.

6 *ta (tou patros)*	1	5 *ti pros (tina)?*	3
3 *ta kata*	5	2 *ti emoi (hēmin) kai soi?*	6
1 *ta peri (tinos)*	17	7 *(mēden) soi kai (tini)*	1
4 *ta pros (ton theon)*	3		

Mt	8	29	2 [The two demoniacs cried out:] What do you *want with* us, Son of God?
	27	4	5 What *is that to* us? . . . That is your concern.
		19	7 *Have* nothing *to do with* that man;
Mk	1	24	2 [the demoniac:] What do you *want with* us, Jesus of Nazareth?
	5	7	2 [the demoniac:] What do you *want with* me, Jesus, son of the Most High God?
		27 X	[the woman who suffered from a haemorrhage] had heard *about* Jesus, and . . . came up
Lk	2	49	6 I must be busy ⌐with my Father's *affairs* (or: in my father's house)
	4	34	2 [the demoniac:] Ha! What do you *want with* us, Jesus of Nazareth?
	8	28	2 [the demoniac:] What do you *want with* me, Jesus, son of the Most High God?
	22	37 X	Yes, what scripture *says about* me is even now reaching its fulfilment.
	24	19 X	All *about* Jesus of Nazareth
		27 X	[Jesus] explained to them the passages throughout the scriptures that *were about* himself.
Jn	2	4	2 Jesus said [to his mother], 'Woman, why *turn to* me?'
	21	22	5 What *does it matter to* you [Peter]?
		23	5 If I want him to stay . . . what *does it matter to* you?
Ac	1	3	[Jesus] had continued to . . . tell them *about* the kingdom of God.
	18	25 X	[Apollos] was accurate in all the details he taught *about* Jesus,
	23	11 X	You have borne witness ⌐for (or: *about*) me
		15	as though you meant to examine his *case* more closely;
	24	10	I can . . . speak with confidence in the defence of my *case*.
		22	Felix, who knew more *about* the Way than most people, adjourned the case, saying, 'When Lysias the tribune has come down I will go into your *case*'.
	25	14	3 Festus put Paul's *case* before the king.
	28	15	3 the brothers [in Rome] heard ⌐*of* (or: *something about*) our arrival
		31 X	[Paul spent two years] teaching the truth *about* the Lord Jesus Christ.
Rm	15	17	4 I have some reason to be proud ⌐*of* (or: *concerning*) what I, in union with Christ Jesus, have been able to do for God.
Ep	6	21	3 I should like you to know, as well, *what is happening to* me I am sending [Tychicus] . . . to give you news *about* us
Ph	1	12	3 the *things that happened to* me have actually been a help
		27	whether I come to you . . . or stay at a distance and only hear *about* you,
	2	19	I shall be reassured by ⌐having news of (lit. hearing *something about*) you.

Ph 2 20 I have nobody else like [Timothy] here, as whole-heartedly concerned ʳfor your welfare (lit. in your *affairs*):
Col 4 7 3 Tychicus will tell you all the news *about* me . . . [8] I am
8 sending him . . . to give you news *about* us
Heb 2 17 so that [Christ] could be a compassionate and trustworthy
4 high priest *of* God's *religion*,
5 1 Every high priest . . . is appointed to act for men in their
4 *relations with* God,

MEASURE

1. Measure (out), Deal (out) – Allowance, Ration, Amount (measured) – Without measure: *metreō*
2. Linear measure
- 1: a Mile (1619 yd, 1480 m): *milion*
- 2: a Furlong (201 yd, 184 m): *stadion*
- 3: a Fathom ($72\frac{1}{2}$ in, 184 cm): *orguia*
- 4: a Cubit (17 in, 44 cm): *pēchys*

3. Cubic measure
- 1: a Measure (of wheat: 99 gal., 450 litres): *koros*
- 2: a Measure (of oil: 10 gal., 45·5 litres): *batos*
- 3: a *metrētēs* (capacity of 9 gal., 40 litres)
- 4: a Measure (of flour: 3 gal., 14 litres): *saton*
- 5: a Tub (used for measuring, capacity 15 pints, 7·1 litres): *modios*
- 6: a Ration (of corn, of barley: $1\frac{3}{8}$ pints, 0·8 litre): *choinix*

4. Measures of weight
- 1: a Talent (75 lb, 34 kg): *talantiaios*
- 2: a Pound (a tenth of a *talantiaos:* 12 oz, 330 g): *litra*

5. a Pair of Scales, Balance: *zygos*
6. (In) Proportion: *ana-logia*

1. MEASURE (OUT), DEAL (OUT) – ALLOWANCE, RATION, AMOUNT (MEASURED) – WITHOUT MEASURE: *METREŌ*

2 *metreō*	*11*	3 *a-metros*	*2*
4 *metriōs*	*1*	6 *anti-metreō*	*1*
1 *metron*	*14*	7 *(sito-)metrion*	*1*
5 *metrio(-patheō)*	*1*		

Mt 7 2 /2 the *amount* you *measure out* is
2 ʳthe amount you will be given (lit. what you will be *measured out*).
23 32 ʳfinish off the work that your fathers began (lit. complete what your fathers began *measuring out*).
Mk 4 24 2 the *amount* you *measure out* is
2 ʳthe amount you will be given (lit. what you will be *measured out*).
Lk 6 38 a full *measure* . . . will be poured into your lap; because
/2 the *amount* you *measure out* is
6 the *amount* you will be *given back*.
12 42 7 to give them their ʳ*allowance* (or: *ration*) of food at the proper time?
Jn 3 34 he whom God has sent speaks God's own words: God gives him the Spirit without ʳreserve (lit. *measuring*).
Ac 20 12 they . . . were ʳgreatly encouraged (lit. encouraged without
4 *measure*).
Rm 12 3 Each of you must judge himself soberly by the ʳstandard of the (lit. *measure* of) faith God has given him.
2 Co 10 12 2 *Measuring* themselves against themselves, . . . they are
13 simply foolish. [13] We, on the other hand, are not . . .
3 *without a standard to measure against*: taking for our *measure* the yardstick which God gave us to *measure* with,
15 3 . . . [15] So we are not boasting *without any measure*,
Ep 4 7 Each one of us . . . has been given his own share of grace, given as Christ *allotted* it.
13 ʳfully mature with (lit. of *measurable* maturity against) the fullness of Christ himself.
16 every joint adding its own *measure* of strength, for each part to work according to its function.
Heb 5 2 5 [Every high priest] can ʳsympathise (lit. *measure* his feelings) with those who are ignorant or uncertain
Rv 11 1 Then I was given a long cane . . . and I was told, 'Go and
2 2 *measure* God's sanctuary, . . . [2] but leave out the outer
2 court and do not *measure* it,'
°21 15 /2 The angel . . . was carrying a gold *measuring* rod to *measure*
16 2 the city and its gates and wall. [16] . . . He *measured* the city with his rod and it was twelve thousand furlongs . . .
17 2 [17] He *measured* its wall, and this was using the ʳordinary cubit (lit. human *measure*).

2. LINEAR MEASURE

1: A MILE (1619 yd, 1480 m): *MILION*

milion 1

Mt 5 41 if anyone orders you to go one *mile*, go two [miles] with him.

2: A FURLONG (201 yd, 184 m): *STADION*

stadion 6/7

Mt 14 24 the boat, by now ᵛ far out (G several *furlongs* from the shore) on the lake,
Lk 24 13 a village called Emmaus, sixty *furlongs* [$6\frac{3}{4}$ miles, 11 km] from Jerusalem,
Jn 6 19 They had rowed twenty-five or thirty *furlongs* [3 or $3\frac{3}{8}$ miles, 4·6 or 5·5 km].
11 18 Bethany is only about fifteen *furlongs* [$1\frac{3}{4}$ miles, 2·8 km] from Jerusalem,
Rv 14 20 the blood that came out of the winepress was up to the horses' bridles as far away as sixteen hundred *furlongs*.
21 16 He measured the city with his rod and it was twelve thousand *furlongs* in length

3: A FATHOM ($72\frac{1}{2}$ in, 184 cm): *ORGUIA*

orguia 2

Ac 27 28 [The crew] took soundings and found twenty *fathoms*; after a short interval they . . . found fifteen *fathoms*.

4: A CUBIT (17 in, 44 cm): *PĒCHYS*

pēchys 4

Mt 6 27 Can any of you . . . add one single *cubit* to his span of life?
Lk 12 25 Can any of you . . . add one single *cubit* to his span of life?
Jn 21 8 they were only about two hundred *cubits* [$94\frac{1}{2}$ yards, 86·3 m] from land.
Rv 21 17 He measured its wall, and this was a hundred and forty-four *cubits* high

3. CUBIC MEASURE

1: A MEASURE (OF WHEAT: 99 gal., 450 litres): *KOROS*

koros 1

Lk 16 7 'how much do you owe?' 'One hundred *measures* of wheat' . . . '. . . write eighty.'

2: A MEASURE (OF OIL: 10 gal., 45·5 litres): *BATOS*

batos 1

Lk 16 6 ['How much do you owe . . . ?'] 'One hundred *measures* of oil' . . . '. . . write fifty.'

3: A *METRĒTĒS* (Capacity of 9 gal., 40 litres)

metrētēs 1

Jn 2 6 There were six stone water jars standing there . . . : each could hold two or three *metrētēs* [18 or 27 gallons, 80 or 120 litres].

4: A MEASURE (OF FLOUR: 3 gal., 14 litres): *SATON*

saton 2

Mt 13 33 like the yeast a woman took and mixed in with three *measures* of flour
Lk 13 21 like the yeast a woman took and mixed in with three *measures* of flour

5: A TUB (USED FOR MEASURING, Capacity 15 pints, 7·1 litres): *MODIOS*

modios 3

Mt 5 15 No one lights a lamp to put it under a *tub*;
Mk 4 21 Would you bring in a lamp to put it under a *tub* . . . ?
Lk 11 33 No one lights a lamp and puts it . . . under a *tub*,

6: A RATION (OF CORN, OF BARLEY: $1\frac{3}{8}$ pints, 0·8 litre): *CHOINIX*

choinix 2

Rv 6 6 A *ration* of corn for a day's wages, and three *rations* of barley for a day's wages,

4. MEASURES OF WEIGHT

1: A TALENT (75 lb, 34 kg): TALANTIAIOS

talantiaios 1

Rv 16 21   great hailstones weighing a *talent* each,

2: A POUND (A tenth of a *talantiaios*: 12 oz, 330 g): LITRA

litra 2

Jn 12 3   a *pound* of very costly ointment,
  19 39   a mixture of myrrh and aloes, weighing about a hundred
                pounds.

5. A PAIR OF SCALES, BALANCE: ZYGOS

zygos 1/6

Rv 6 5   [the] rider [of the black horse] was holding *a pair of scales*;

6. (IN) PROPORTION: ANA-LOGIA

ana-logia 1

Rm 12 6   If your gift is prophecy, then use it ⌐in *proportion* to your
                faith (or: as your faith suggests);

MERCY – PITY

1. Mercy, Have mercy, Pity – Alms:
eleos
  1: Mercy (of God, of Jesus) –
    Show mercy, Have mercy –
    Receive mercy (from God),
    Enjoy mercy
  2: 'Take pity', 'Have pity' – 'Have
    mercy' (Jesus is besought)
  3: (the spirit of) Mercy, Pity,
    Compassion
  4: Alms, Charity
  5: Pitiable, Unfortunate
2. Compassion, Pity, Mercy – Com-

passionate, Merciful: *oiktirmos*
3. Feel sorry (for), (Take) Pity, Have
  Compassion – (Be) Moved with
  pity: *splanchnizomai*
4. Be merciful to – Expiation:
  hilaskomai
  1: Be merciful to – Forgive – Be
    gracious to
  2: Expiate, Atone for – Sacrificial
    expiation
  3: Throne of mercy, Place of
    expiation
5. Forgive, Forgiveness: *aph-iēmi*

1. MERCY, HAVE MERCY, PITY – ALMS: ELEOS

4 *eleaō*	3	1 *eleeō*	29
5 *eleeinos*	2	2 *eleos*	27
6 *eleēmōn*	2	7 *an-eleēmōn*	1
3 *eleēmosynē*	13	8 *an-eleos*	1

1: MERCY (OF GOD, OF JESUS) – SHOW MERCY, HAVE MERCY – RECEIVE MERCY (FROM GOD), ENJOY MERCY

Mt 5 7   Happy the merciful: they shall have *mercy shown* them.
Mk 5 19   Go home to your people and tell them all that the Lord in
              his *mercy* has done for you.
Lk 1 50   2 his *mercy* reaches from age to age for those who fear him
    54   He has come to the help of Israel, . . . mindful of his
            2 *mercy*
    58   the Lord had shown [Elizabeth] ⌐so great a kindness (lit.
            2 such great *mercy*),
    72   2 Thus [the Lord] shows *mercy* to our ancestors, thus he
            remembers his holy covenant,
    78   2 [the forgiveness of his people's sins] by the tender *mercy*
            of our God
Rm 9 15   (Ex 33 19) I *have mercy* on whom I ⌐will (lit. *have mercy*),
    16   and I show pity to whom I please. [16] . . . the only thing
    18   4 that counts is . . . the *mercy* of God. . . . [18] . . . when
            God wants to *show mercy* he does,
    23   [God] puts up with [the people who make him angry] for
            the sake of those . . . ⌐to whom he wants to be merciful
            2 (lit. the recipients of his *mercy*),
  11 30   Just as you changed from being disobedient to God, and

Rm 11 31   now *enjoy mercy* because of their disobedience, [31] so those
            who are disobedient now – and only because of the
      2/ *mercy* shown to you – will also *enjoy mercy* eventually.
    32   [32] God has imprisoned all men in their own disobedience
            only to *show mercy* to all mankind.
  15 9   2 to get the pagans to give glory to God for his *mercy*,
1 Co 7 25   my own opinion as one who, by the Lord's *mercy*, has
            stayed faithful.
2 Co 4 1   Since we have *by an act of mercy* been entrusted with this
            work
Ga 6 16   2 Peace and *mercy* to all who follow this rule, who form the
            Israel of God.
Ep 2 4   2 God . . . was generous with his *mercy*:
Ph 2 27   [Epaphroditus] has been ill, . . . but God *took pity* on
            him, and on me
1 Tm 1 2   2 to Timothy, . . . wishing you grace, *mercy* and peace from
            God the Father and from Christ Jesus our Lord.
    13   *Mercy* . . . *was shown* me, because . . . I had been acting
            in ignorance;
    16   if *mercy has been shown* to me, it is [as evidence of Christ
            Jesus's] inexhaustible patience
2 Tm 1 2   2 to Timothy, . . . wishing you grace, *mercy* and peace from
            God the Father and from Christ Jesus our Lord.
    16   2 I hope the Lord will ⌐be kind (lit. grant *mercy*) to all the
            family of Onesiphorus,
    18   May it be the Lord's will that he shall find the Lord's
            2 *mercy* on that Day.
Tt 3 5   2 it was for no reason except his own ⌐compassion (or: *mercy*)
            that he saved us,
Heb 4 16   Let us be confident, . . . in approaching the throne of grace,
      2 that we shall have *mercy* from him
1 P 1 3   2 Blessed be God . . . who in his great *mercy* has given us a
            new birth
  2 10   once you ⌐were outside the (lit. did not *receive*) *mercy* and
            now you have been *given mercy*.
2 Jn 3   2 we shall have grace, *mercy* and peace from God the Father
            and from Jesus Christ.
Jude 2   2 wishing you all *mercy* and peace and love.
    21   keep yourselves within the love of God, and wait for the
      2 *mercy* of our Lord Jesus Christ

2: 'TAKE PITY', 'HAVE PITY' – 'HAVE MERCY' (JESUS IS BESOUGHT)

Mt 9 27   two blind men . . . shouting, '*Take pity* on us, Son of
            David.'
  15 22   a Canaanite woman . . . shouting, 'Sir, Son of David,
            take pity on me.'
  17 15   *take pity* on my son: he is a lunatic
  20 30   two blind men . . . shouted, 'Lord! *Have pity* on us, Son
    31   of David. . . . [31] Lord! *Have pity* on us, Son of David.'
Mk 10 47   [Bartimeus] began to shout . . . 'Son of David, Jesus,
    48   *have pity* on me. [48] Son of David, Jesus, *have pity* on me.
Lk 17 13   [Ten lepers] called to him, 'Jesus! Master! *Take pity* on us!'
  18 38   [the blind man] called out, 'Jesus, Son of David, *have pity*
    39   on me. [39] . . . Son of David, *have pity* on me.'

3: (THE SPIRIT OF) MERCY, PITY, COMPASSION

Mt 5 7   6 Happy the *merciful*: they shall have mercy shown them.
  9 13   2 (Ho 6 6) What I want is *mercy*, not sacrifice,
  12 7   2 (Ho 6 6) What I want is *mercy*, not sacrifice,
  18 33 <   [The master to the servant:] 'Were you not bound, then,
            to *have pity* on your fellow servant just as I *had pity*
            on you?'
  23 23   Alas for you, scribes and Pharisees, . . . who pay your
      2 tithe . . . and have neglected . . . justice, *mercy*, good
            faith!
Lk 10 37 <   [Which of these three proved himself a neighbour?] 'The
      2 one who took *pity* on him . . . ' Jesus said to him, 'Go,
            and do the same yourself.'
  16 24   Father Abraham, *pity* me and send Lazarus to . . . cool
            my tongue.
Rm 1 31   7 [pagans are] *without* brains, honour, love or *pity*.
  12 8   Let . . . those who *do works of mercy* do them cheerfully.
Heb 2 17   It was essential that [Christ] should in this way become
      6 completely like his brothers so that he could be a *com-
           passionate* . . . high priest
Jm 2 13   8 there will be judgement *without mercy* for those who have
      2/2 not been *merciful* themselves; but the *merciful* need have
            no fear of judgement.
  3 17   the wisdom that comes down from above . . . is full of
      2 *compassion*
Jude 22   4 When there are some who have doubts, ⌐reassure (G be
            compassionate towards) them;
    23   4 there are others to whom you must be ⌐kind (lit. *com-
            passionate*) with great caution,

4: ALMS, CHARITY

Mt	6 2	3	when you give *alms*, do not have it trumpeted before you;
	3	3	. . . ³ But when you give *alms*, your left hand must not
	4	3	know what your right is doing; ⁴ your *alms*giving must be secret,
Lk	11 41	3	give *alms* from what you have
	12 33	3	Sell your possessions and give *alms*.
Ac	3 2	3	they used to put [the cripple] down every day near the Temple entrance . . . so that he could beg *alms*
	3	3	When this man saw Peter and John . . . he begged *alms* from them.
	10	3	they recognised him as the man who used to sit begging *alms* at the Beautiful Gate
	9 36	3	Tabitha, . . . who never tired of . . . giving in *charity*.
	10 2	3	[Cornelius] gave *alms* generously to Jewish causes
	4	3	Your offering of prayers and *alms* . . . has been accepted by God.
	31	3	Cornelius, . . . your *alms* have been accepted . . . in the sight of God;
	24 17	3	I came to bring *alms* to my nation

5: PITIABLE, UNFORTUNATE

1Co	15 19	5	we are the most *unfortunate* of all people.
Rv	3 17	5	never realising that you are wretchedly and *pitiably* poor,

2. COMPASSION, PITY, MERCY – COMPASSIONATE, MERCIFUL: *OIKTIRMOS*

3 *oikteirō* 2   1 *oiktirmos* 5
2 *oiktirmōn* 3

Lk	6 36	Θ 2/2	Be *compassionate* as your Father is *compassionate*.
Rm	9 15	Θ 3	(Ex 33 19) I have mercy on whom I will, and I *show pity*
		Θ 3	to whom I ⌐please (lit. *show pity*).
	12 1	Θ	Think of God's *mercy*, my brothers,
2Co	1 3		Blessed be the God and Father of our Lord Jesus Christ,
		Θ	⌐a gentle Father (lit. the Father of all *mercies*)
Ph	2 1		if love can persuade at all, . . . or any tenderness and *sympathy*,
Col	3 12		You are God's chosen race . . . you should be clothed in sincere *compassion*,
Heb	10 28		Anyone who disregards the Law of Moses is ⌐ruthlessly put to death (lit. put to death without *compassion*)
Jm	5 11	Θ	2 the Lord is kind and *compassionate*.

3. FEEL SORRY (FOR), (TAKE) PITY, HAVE COMPASSION – (BE) MOVED WITH PITY: *SPLANCHNIZOMAI*

splanchnizomai 12

Mt	9 36	X	when [Jesus] saw the crowds he *felt sorry* for them
	14 14	X	he saw a large crowd; and he *took pity* on them
	15 32	X	Jesus . . . said, 'I *feel sorry* for all these people'
	18 27	<	the servant's master *felt* so *sorry* for him that he let him go
	20 34	X	Jesus *felt pity* for [the two blind men] and touched their eyes,
Mk	1 41	X	*Feeling sorry* for [the leper], Jesus stretched out his hand and touched him.
	6 34	X	he saw a large crowd; and he *took pity* on them
	8 2	X	I *feel sorry* for all these people; they . . . have nothing to eat.
	9 22	X	*have pity* on us and help us.
Lk	7 13	X	When the Lord saw [the widow] he *felt sorry* for her.
	10 33	<	a Samaritan traveller . . . was *moved with compassion* when he saw [the man who had fallen into the hands of brigands].
	15 20	<	his father saw him and was *moved with pity*.

4. BE MERCIFUL TO – EXPIATION: *HILASKOMAI*

1 *hilaskomai* 2   3 *hilastērion* 2
2 *hilasmos* 2   4 *hileōs* 2

1: BE MERCIFUL TO – FORGIVE – BE GRACIOUS TO

Mt	16 22		Peter started to remonstrate with him: ⌐Heaven preserve
		4	(lit. God *be gracious to*) you, Lord; . . . this must not happen to you'.
Lk	18 13		God, *be merciful to* me, a sinner.
Heb	8 12	4	(Jr 31 34) I will *forgive* their iniquities and never call their sins to mind.

2: EXPIATE, ATONE FOR – SACRIFICIAL EXPIATION

Rm	3 25		[Christ Jesus] was appointed by God to sacrifice his life ⌐so
		3	as to win reconciliation (lit. in order to be the *means of expiation*)
Heb	2 17		a compassionate and trustworthy high priest . . . able to *atone for* human sins.
1Jn	2 2		2 he is the *sacrifice that* ⌐*takes* our sins *away* (or: *expiates* our sins*), and not only ours, but the whole world's.
	4 10		[I mean] God's love for us when he sent his Son to be the
		2	*sacrifice that* ⌐*takes* our sins *away* (or: *expiates* our sins).

3: THRONE OF MERCY, PLACE OF EXPIATION

*cheroubein** 1

Heb	9 5	3	On top of [the ark] was the *throne of mercy*, and outspread over it were the glorious cherubs*.

5. FORGIVE, FORGIVENESS: *APH-IĒMI*

2 *aph-esis* 15/17   3 *par-(h)esis* 1
1 *aph-iemi* 49/146

Mt	6 12		[Our Father,] *forgive* us our debts, as we have *forgiven* those who are in debt to us . . . ¹⁴ Yes, if you *forgive* others
	14		their failings, your heavenly Father will *forgive* you yours;
	15		¹⁵ but if you do not *forgive* others, your Father will not *forgive* your failings either.
	9 2		Jesus said to the paralytic, ' . . . your sins are *forgiven*.'
	5		. . . ⁵ 'Now, which of these is easier: to say, "Your sins are *forgiven*", or to say, "Get up and walk"? ⁶But to
	6		prove to you that the Son of Man has authority on earth to *forgive* sins,' – he said to the paralytic – 'get up, . . .'
	12 31		every one of men's sins and blasphemies will be *forgiven*, but blasphemy against the Spirit will not be *forgiven*.
	32		³²And anyone who says a word against the Son of Man will be *forgiven*; but let anyone speak against the Holy Spirit and he will not be *forgiven* either in this world or in the next.
	18 21		Lord, how often must I *forgive* my brother if he wrongs me? As often as seven times? ²² Jesus answered, 'Not seven . . . but seventy-seven times'.
	27		the servant's master . . . ⌐cancelled (lit. *forgave* him) the debt . . .³² . . . "I ⌐cancelled (lit. *forgave* you) all that debt
	32		of yours" . . . ³⁴ And in his anger the master handed
	35		him over to the torturers . . . ³⁵And that is how my heavenly Father will deal with you unless you each *forgive* your brother from your heart.
	26 28		2 my blood . . . is to be poured out for many for the *forgiveness* of sins.
Mk	1 4	2	John the Baptist appeared . . . proclaiming a baptism of repentance for the *forgiveness* of sins.
	2 5		Jesus said to the paralytic, ' . . . your sins are *forgiven*' . . .
	7		⁷. . . He is blaspheming. Who can *forgive* sins but God?
	9		Which of these is easier: to say to the paralytic, 'Your sins are *forgiven*' or to say, 'Get up . . .'? ¹⁰ . . . the Son of
	10		Man has authority on earth to *forgive* sins,
	3 28		all men's sins will be *forgiven* . . . ²⁹ but let anyone blaspheme
	29	2	against the Holy Spirit and he will never have *forgiveness*:
	4 12		[to those who are outside everything comes in parables,] otherwise they might be converted and be *forgiven*.
	11 25		When you stand in prayer, *forgive* whatever you have against anybody, so that your Father in heaven may *forgive* your
	26		failings too. ²⁶ (ᵛ But if you do not *forgive*, neither will your Father in heaven *forgive* you your failings.)
Lk	1 77	2	[you will go before the Lord] to give his people knowledge of salvation through the *forgiveness* of their sins;
	3 3	2	[John proclaimed] a baptism of repentance for the *forgiveness* of sins,
	5 20		My friend, your sins are *forgiven* you, ²¹. . . Who can *forgive*
	21		sins but God alone? . . . . ²³ Which of these is easier to
	23		say, 'Your sins are *forgiven* you' or to say, 'Get up . . .'?
	24		²⁴. . . the Son of Man has authority on earth to *forgive* sins
	7 47		her many sins must have been *forgiven* her, or she would not have shown such great love. It is the man who is
	48		*forgiven* little who shows little love. ⁴⁸ Then [Jesus] said
	49		to her, 'Your sins are *forgiven*'. ⁴⁹. . . Who is this man, that he even *forgives* sins?
	11 4		[Father,] *forgive* us our sins, for we ourselves *forgive* each one who is in debt to us.
	12 10		Everyone who says a word against the Son of Man will be *forgiven*, but he who blasphemes against the Holy Spirit will not be *forgiven*.
	17 3		If your brother . . . is sorry, *forgive* him. ⁴And if he wrongs
	4		you seven times a day . . . and says, 'I am sorry', you must *forgive* him.

Lk 23	34		Jesus said, 'Father, *forgive* them; they do not know what they are doing'.
	24 47	2	that, in his name, repentance for the *forgiveness* of sins would be preached to all the nations,
Jn 20	23		For those whose sins you *forgive*, they are *forgiven*;
Ac 2	38	2	every one of you must be baptised in the name of Jesus Christ for the *forgiveness* of your sins,
5	31	2	to give repentance and *forgiveness* of sins through [Jesus] to Israel.
8	22		[Peter to Simon the magician:] 'Repent of this wickedness . . .; you may still be *forgiven* for thinking as you did;'
10	43	2	all who believe in Jesus will have their sins *forgiven* through his name.
13	38	2	it is through [Jesus] that *forgiveness* of your sins is proclaimed.
26	18	2	so that they may . . . receive, through faith in me, *forgiveness* of their sins
Rm 3	25 ○	3	first for the past, when sins *went unpunished* because [God] held his hand,
4	7		(Ps 32 1) Happy those whose crimes are *forgiven*,
Ep 1	7	2	in [Jesus] through his blood, we gain our freedom, the *forgiveness* of our sins.
Col 1	14	2	in [his Son] we gain our freedom, the *forgiveness* of our sins.
Heb 9	22	2	according to the Law, . . . if there is no shedding of blood, there is no *remission*.
10	18	2	When all sins have been *forgiven*, there can be no more sin offerings.
Jm 5	15		if [the sick man] has committed any sins, he will be *forgiven*.
1 Jn 1	9		if we acknowledge our sins, then God who is faithful and just will *forgive* our sins and purify us from everything that is wrong.
2	12		[your] sins have already been *forgiven* through his name;

MESOPOTAMIA

1. Mesopotamia	**2: "Babylon" = Rome**
2. Babylon	**3. Nineveh – Jonah**
1: Babylon	

1. MESOPOTAMIA

(of) *Chaldaea*	*1*	*Elamites**	*1*	1 *gē* 2/252	
Mesopotamia	*2*	*Medes**	*1*		
Haran [*Harran*]	*2*	*Parthians**	*1*		

Ac 2	9		Parthians*, Medes* and Elamites*; people from *Mesopotamia*,
7	2		The God of glory appeared to . . . Abraham, while he was
	3		in *Mesopotamia* before settling in *Haran* ³ and said to him:
	4	1	(Gn 12 1) Leave your *country* . . . ⁴ So he left ⌐Chaldaea
		1	(lit. the *country* of the *Chaldaeans*) and settled in *Haran*;

2. BABYLON

Babylon 12   1 *polis* 10/164

1: BABYLON

Mt 1	11		Josiah was the father of Jechoniah . . . Then the deportation to *Babylon* took place.
	12		After the deportation to *Babylon*: Jechoniah was the father of Shealtiel,
	17		The sum of generations is . . . fourteen from David to the *Babylonian* deportation; and fourteen from the *Babylonian* deportation to Christ
Ac 7	43		(Am 5 27) you carried the tent of Moloch . . . now I will exile you even further than *Babylon*.

2: "BABYLON" = ROME

1 P 5	13		Your sister in *Babylon*, who is with you among the chosen, sends you greetings;
Rv 11	8	1	Their corpses will lie in the main street of the Great *City* known by the symbolic names Sodom and Egypt,
	13	1	there was a violent earthquake, and a tenth of the *city* collapsed;
14	8		[Babylon] has fallen, *Babylon* the Great has fallen,

Rv 16	19	1	The Great *City* was split into three parts . . . *Babylon* the Great was not forgotten: God made her drink the full winecup of his anger.
17	5		on her forehead was written a name, a cryptic name: '*Babylon* the Great, the mother of all the prostitutes and all the filthy practices on the earth'.
	18	1	The woman you saw is the great *city*
18	2		*Babylon* the Great has fallen, and has become the haunt of devils
	10	1/1	Mourn, mourn for this great *city*, *Babylon*, so powerful a *city*,
	16	1	Mourn, mourn for this great *city*; for all the linen . . . that you wore,
	18	1	Has there ever been a *city* as great as this!
	19	1	Mourn, mourn for this great *city*
	21	1	That is how the great *city* of *Babylon* is going to be hurled down,

3. NINEVEH – JONAH

N *Ninevites, of Nineveh 3*   *Jonah 9*

Mt 12	39		The only sign [this generation] will be given is the sign of the
	40		prophet *Jonah*. ⁴⁰ For as (Jon 2 1) *Jonah* was in the belly of the sea-monster . . . so will the Son of Man be in the
	41 N		heart of the earth . . . ⁴¹ On Judgement Day the men *of Nineveh* will stand up . . . and condemn [this generation] because when *Jonah* preached (cf. Jon 3 3–9) they repented; and there is something greater than *Jonah* here.
16	4		The only sign [this generation] will be given is the sign of *Jonah*.
Lk 11	29		The only sign [this generation] will be given is the sign of
	30 N		*Jonah*. ³⁰ For just as *Jonah* became a sign to the *Ninevites*, so will the Son of Man . . . ³² On Judgement Day the men
	32 N		*of Nineveh* will stand up . . . and condemn [this generation], because when *Jonah* preached (cf. Jon 3 3–9) they repented; and there is something greater than *Jonah* here.

MID – AMONG

1: Among, (in the) Midst, (in the) Middle	2: Mid(-day, -night), the Middle (of the day, night)
a) Jesus Among, (in the) Midst, (in the) Middle – Surrounded (by)	3: Convey (between two parties)
b) Among, (in the) Midst, (in the) Middle – Between	4: Mediator, Intermediary

2 *mesitēs*	6	5 *mes-(h)ēmbria*	2
6 *mesiteuō*	1	3 *meso(-nyktion)*	4
7 *mesoō*	1	4 *mes(-ouranēma)*	3
1 *mesos*	59		

1: AMONG, (IN THE) MIDST, (IN THE) MIDDLE

a) Jesus Among, (in the) Midst, (in the) Middle – Surrounded (by)

Mt 18	20	where two or three meet in my name, I shall be there ⌐with (lit. in the *midst* of) them.
Mk 7	31	he went . . . ⌐right through (lit. through the *middle* of) the Decapolis region.
Lk 2	46	[his parents] found him in the Temple, sitting *among* the doctors,
4	30	he ⌐slipped through (lit. passed through the *middle* of) the crowd and walked away.
22	27	Yet here am I *among* you as one who serves!
24	36	[The apostles] were still talking about all this when he himself stood *among* them.
Jn 1	26	there stands one *among* you – unknown to you –
19	18	they crucified him with two others, one on either side with Jesus in the *middle*.
20	19	Jesus came and stood *among* them.
	26	The doors were closed, but Jesus came in and stood *among* them,
Ac 2	22	Jesus was a man commended to you by God by the miracles . . . that God worked through him when he was *among* you,
Rv 1	13	[I saw seven golden lamp-stands] and, *surrounded* by them, a figure like a Son of man,
2	1	the one who . . . lives *surrounded* by the seven golden lamp-stands:
7	17	the Lamb who is ⌐at (lit. in the *midst* of) the throne

b) Among, (in the) Midst, (in the) Middle – Between

Mt	10 16	I am sending you out like sheep *among* wolves;
	13 25 <	his enemy . . . sowed darnel *among* the wheat,
	49	the angels will appear and separate the wicked from the *midst* of the just
	14 6	the daughter of Herodias danced *before* the company,
	24	the boat, by now ˅ in the *middle* of (G several furlongs away from the shore on) the lake,
	18 2	[Jesus] set the child ⌐in front (lit. in the *middle*) of them.
Mk	3 3	[Jesus] said to the man with the withered hand, 'Stand up out in the *middle*!'
	6 47	When evening came, the boat was ⌐far out on (lit. in the *middle* of) the lake,
	9 36	[Jesus] then took a little child, set him ⌐in front (lit. in the *middle*) of them,
	14 60	The chief priest then stood up *before* the whole assembly
Lk	4 35	the demon, throwing the man down ⌐in front (lit. in the *middle*) of everyone, went out of him
	5 19	they . . . lowered [the paralytic] . . . down through the tiles into the *middle* of the gathering,
	6 8	Stand up! Come out into the *middle*.
	8 7 <	Some seed fell *amongst* thorns
	10 3	I am sending you out like lambs *among* wolves.
	17 11	[Jesus] travelled along the border *between* Samaria and Galilee.
	21 21	those ⌐inside (lit. in the *midst* of) the city must leave it,
	22 55	They had lit a fire in the *middle* of the courtyard and Peter sat down *among* them,
	23 45	The veil of the Temple was torn right down the *middle*:
Jn	7 14	7 ⌐When the festival was half over (lit. In the *middle* of the festival),
	8 3	making [the adulteress] stand there in ⌐full view (lit. the *middle*) of everybody,
		Jesus was left alone with the woman, who remained standing ⌐there (lit. in the *middle*).
Ac	1 15	One day Peter stood up ⌐to speak to the brothers (lit. *among* the brothers to speak)
	18	He fell headlong and burst at the *middle*,
	4 7	They made the prisoners [Peter and John] stand in the *middle*
	17 22	So Paul stood *before* the whole Council of the Areopagus
	33	Paul left their *midst*,
	23 10	the tribune . . . ordered his troops to . . . haul [Paul] out of their *midst* and bring him into the fortress.
	27 21	Paul stood up *among* the men. 'Friends,' he said 'if you had . . . not put out from Crete,'
1 Co	5 2	A man who does a thing like that ought to have been expelled from ⌐the community (lit. *among* you).
	6 5	is there really not one reliable man [among you] to settle differences *between* brothers . . .?
2 Co	6 17	(Is 52 11) come away from their *midst*
Ph	2 15	perfect children of God *among* a deceitful and underhand brood,
Col	2 14	He has . . . cancelled every record of the debt that we had to pay; he has done away with it (G from *between*) by nailing it to the cross;
1 Th	2 7	we ⌐were unassuming (lit. made ourselves humble in your *midst*).
2 Th	2 7	the one who is holding [rebellion] back has first to be ⌐removed (lit. away from *between*) ⁸ before the Rebel appears openly.
Heb	2 12	(Ps 22 22) I shall . . . praise you in ⌐full (lit. the *middle* of the) assembly;
Rv	4 6	In the *centre*, grouped round the throne itself, were four animals
	5 6	I saw, standing in the *midst* of the throne with its four animals and *among* the circle of the elders, a Lamb
	6 6	I seemed to hear a voice shout from *among* the four animals
	8 13	I heard an eagle, calling aloud as it flew ⌐high overhead (lit. in the *middle* of the sky; or: in *mid*-heaven),
	14 6	4 I saw another angel, flying ⌐high overhead (lit. in the *middle* of the sky; or: in *mid*-heaven),
	19 17	all the birds that were flying ⌐high overhead in the sky (lit. in the *middle* of the sky; or: in *mid*-heaven),
	22 2	[the river of life, . . . flowing] down the *middle* of the city street.

2: MID(-DAY, -NIGHT), THE MIDDLE (OF THE DAY, NIGHT)

Mt	25 6	at *mid*night there was a cry, 'The bridegroom is here!'
Mk	13 35	you do not know when the master of the house is coming, 3 evening, midnight, cockcrow, dawn;
Lk	11 5	3 Suppose one of you has a friend and goes to him in the *middle* of the night
Ac	8 26	5 Be ready to set out at ⌐noon (lit. *mid*day)
	16 25	3 ⌐Late (lit. Towards the *middle* of) that night Paul and Silas were praying
	20 7	3 Paul . . . preached a sermon that went on till the *middle* of the night.

Ac	22 6	5 I was . . . nearly at Damascus when about *mid*day a bright light from heaven suddenly shone round me.
	26 13	at *mid*day as I was on my way . . . I saw a light brighter than the sun
	27 27	about *mid*night the crew sensed that land . . . was near.

3: CONVEY (BETWEEN TWO PARTIES)

Heb	6 17 Θ	when God wanted to make the heirs to the promise thoroughly
	6	realise that his purpose was unalterable, he ⌐conveyed this by (or: guaranteed this with) an oath;

4: MEDIATOR, INTERMEDIARY

Ga	3 19	2 The Law was promulgated by angels assisted by an *intermediary*. ²⁰ Now there can only be an *intermediary* between two parties,
	20	2
1 Tm	2 5 X	2 there is only one *mediator* between God and mankind,
Heb	8 6 X	2 it is a better covenant of which [Christ] is the *mediator*,
	9 15 X	2 He brings a new covenant, as the *mediator*,
	12 24 X	2 Jesus, the *mediator* who brings a new covenant

MISERY – DANGER

1. Woe – Misery	2. Danger – Threat – Risk
1: Alas for (a person) – Woe to (a person) – Trouble: *ouai*	1: Danger–Peril–Threat: *kindynos*
2: Wretchedness – Misery: *talaipōria*	2: Hazardous – Risky: *epi-sphalēs*
	3: Risk: *para-boleuomai*

1. WOE – MISERY

1: ALAS FOR (A PERSON) – WOE TO (A PERSON) – TROUBLE: *OUAI*
ouai 46

Mt	11 21	*Alas for* you, Chorazin! *Alas for* you, Bethsaida! For if the miracles done in you had been done in Tyre and Sidon, they would have repented
	18 7	*Alas for* the world that there should be such obstacles! . . *alas for* the man who provides them!
	23 13	*Alas for* you, scribes and Pharisees, you hypocrites! You who shut up the kingdom of heaven in men's faces,
	15	*Alas for* you, scribes . . . who travel over sea and land to make a single proselyte,
	16	*Alas for* you, blind guides! You who say, 'If a man swears by the Temple . . .'
	23	*Alas for* you, scribes . . . who pay your tithe of mint
	25	*Alas for* you, scribes . . . who clean the outside of cup
	27	*Alas for* you, scribes . . . who are like whitewashed tombs
	29	*Alas for* you, scribes . . . who build the sepulchres of the prophets
	24 19	*Alas for* those with child, or with babies at the breast, when those days come!
	26 24	*alas for* that man by whom the Son of Man is betrayed!
Mk	13 17	*Alas for* those with child, or with babies at the breast, when those days come!
	14 21	*alas for* that man by whom the Son of Man is betrayed!
Lk	6 24	*alas for* you who are rich: you are having your consolation now.
	25	*Alas for* you who have your fill now: you shall go hungry. *Alas for* you who laugh now: you shall mourn and weep.
	26	*Alas for* you when the world speaks well of you!
	10 13	*Alas for* you, Chorazin! *Alas for* you, Bethsaida!
	11 42	*alas for* you Pharisees! You who pay your tithe of mint
	43	*Alas for* you Pharisees who like taking the seats of honour
	44	*Alas for* you, because you are like the unmarked tombs
	46	*Alas for* you lawyers also . . . because you load on men burdens
	47	*Alas for* you who build the tombs of the prophets,
	52	*Alas for* you lawyers who have taken away the key of knowledge!
	17 1	*alas for* the one who provides [obstacles]!
	21 23	*Alas for* those with child, or with babies at the breast,
	22 22	*alas for* that man by whom [the Son of Man] is betrayed!
1 Co	9 16	⌐I should be punished (lit. *Woe betide me*) if I did not preach [the gospel]!
Jude	11	⌐May [the false teachers] get what they deserve (lit. *Woe to* [the false teachers]), because they have followed Cain;

Rv	8 13	*Trouble, trouble, trouble*, for all the people on earth
	9 12	That was the first of the *troubles*; there are still two more *troubles* to come.
	11 14	That was the second of the *troubles*; the third *trouble* is to come quickly after it.
	12 12	for you, earth and sea, *trouble* is coming – because the devil has gone down to you
	18 10	⌜*Mourn, mourn* (or: *Alas, alas*) for this great city, Babylon, so powerful a city,
	16	⌜*Mourn, mourn* (or: *Alas, alas*) for this great city; for all the linen . . . that you wore, for all your finery of gold
	19	⌜*Mourn, mourn* (or: *Alas, alas*) for this great city . . . ruined within a single hour.

2: WRETCHEDNESS – MISERY: *TALAI-PŌRIA*

3 *talai-pōreō 1*   2 *talai-pōros 2*
1 *talai-pōria 2*

Rm	3 16	(Is 59 7) wherever they go there is ⌜havoc (lit. *misery*) and ruin.
	7 24	2 What a *wretched* man I am!
Jm	4 9	3 *Look at your wretched condition*, and weep for it in misery;
	5 1	Start crying, weep for the *miseries* that are coming to you.
Rv	3 17	2 you are *wretchedly* and pitiably poor,

2. DANGER – THREAT – RISK

1: DANGER – PERIL – THREAT: *KINDYNOS*

2 *kindyneuō 4*   1 *kindynos 9*

Lk	8 23	2 the boat started taking in water and they *found themselves in danger*.
Ac	19 27	2 This *threatens* . . . to reduce the sanctuary of . . . Diana to unimportance.
	40	2 We ⌜could easily be (lit. *are in peril* of being) charged with rioting
Rm	8 35	Nothing therefore can come between us and the love of Christ, even if we are . . . *being threatened* or even attacked.
1 Co	15 30	2 Why are we *living under* a constant *threat*?
2 Co	11 26	I have been in *danger* from rivers and in *danger* from brigands, in *danger* from my own people and in *danger* from pagans; in *danger* in the towns, in *danger* in the open country, *danger* at sea and *danger* from so-called brothers.

2: HAZARDOUS – RISKY: *EPI-SPHALĒS*

epi-sphalēs 1

Ac	27 9	navigation was already *hazardous*

3: RISK: *PARA-BOLEUOMAI*

para-boleuomai 1

Ph	2 30	[Epaphroditus] *risked* his life to give me the help that you were not able to give me yourselves.

MIX – ASSOCIATE

1. **Mix:** *kerannymi*
   a) Mix (a drink), Mixture – Undiluted
   b) Mix with, Unite in
   c) Arrange, Construct
2. **Mix, Mingle – Associate with:** *mignymi*

   a) Mix (with), Mingle – Mixture – Suffused
   b) Associate with, Have to do with
3. **Associate**
   1: Company, Associate(s): *homilia*
   2: Associate with, Have to do with: *syn-chraomai*

1. MIX: *KERANNYMI*

1 *kerannymi 3*   2 *syn-kerannymi 2*
3 *a-kratos*   *1*

a) Mix (a drink), Mixture – Undiluted

Rv	14 10	the wine of God's fury which ⌜is ready (lit. has been *mixed*), *undiluted*, in his cup of anger;
	18 6	[Babylon] is to ⌜have (lit. be *mixed*) a doubly strong cup of her own *mixture*.

b) Mix with, Unite in

Heb	4 2	hearing the message did them no good because ⌜they did not share the faith of (lit. they *were* not *united in* faith with) (G the message did not *mix with* faith in) those who listened.

c) Arrange, Construct

1 Co	12 24 Θ	2 God has *arranged* the body so that more dignity is given to the parts which are without it,

2. MIX, MINGLE – ASSOCIATE WITH: *MIGNYMI*

3 *migma   1*   2 *syn-ana-mignymi 3*
1 *mignymi 4*

a) Mix (with), Mingle – Mixture – Suffused

Mt	27 34	they gave him wine to drink *mixed* with gall,
Lk	13 1	the Galileans whose blood Pilate had *mingled* with that of their sacrifices.
Jn	19 39	3 Nicodemus . . . brought a *mixture* of myrrh and aloes,
Rv	8 7	hail and fire, *mixed* with blood, were dropped on the earth;
	15 2	I seemed to see a glass lake *suffused* with fire,

b) Associate with, Have to do with

1 Co	5 9	2 When I wrote . . . to you not to *associate with* people living immoral lives,
	11	2 you should not *associate with* a brother Christian who is leading an immoral life, or is a usurer, or idolatrous, or a slanderer, or a drunkard, or is dishonest;
2 Th	3 14	If anyone refuses to obey what I have written in this letter,
		2 . . . *have* nothing *to do with* him,

3. ASSOCIATE

1: COMPANY, ASSOCIATE(S): *HOM-ILIA*

hom-ilia 1

1 Co	15 33	Bad ⌜*associates* ruin (or: *company* ruins) the noblest people.

2: ASSOCIATE WITH, HAVE TO DO WITH: *SYN-CHRAOMAI*

syn-chraomai 1

Jn	4 9	Jews, in fact, do not *associate with* Samaritans.

MOCK – LAUGH

1. **Mock, Make fun of – Make a fool of:** *em-paizō*
2. **Scoff (at), Jeer (at), Mock – Make a fool of:** *myktērizō*
3. **Mock – Hold up to contempt:** *para-deigmatizō*
4. **Laugh (at), Mock:** *chleuazō*
5. **Laugh:** *gelaō*
   a) Laugh (at Jesus)
   b) Laugh
6. **Jokes:** *eu-trapelia*

1. MOCK, MAKE FUN OF – MAKE A FOOL OF: *EM-PAIZŌ*

2 *em-paiktēs   2*   4 *em-paigmos   1*
3 *em-paigmonē 1*   1 *em-paizō   13*

Mt	2 16	Herod was furious when he realised that he had been ⌜out-witted (lit. *made a fool of*) by the wise men,
	20 19 X	[The chief priests] will hand [the Son of Man] over to the pagans to be *mocked* and scourged
	27 29 X	To *make fun of* him [the soldiers] knelt to him . . . ³¹ And
	31 X	when they had finished *making fun of* him, they took off the cloak
	41 X	The chief priests with the scribes and elders *mocked* him
Mk	10 34 X	[The chief priests will hand the Son of Man over to the pagans,] who will *mock* him
	15 20 X	when [the soldiers] had finished *making fun of* him, they took off the purple
	31 X	The chief priests and the scribes *mocked* him
Lk	14 29	if he . . . found himself unable to finish the work, the onlookers would all start *making fun of* him
	18 32 X	[The Son of Man] will be handed over to the pagans and will be *mocked*,
	22 63 X	the men who guarded Jesus were *mocking* and beating him.

Lk	23	11 X	Herod, together with his guards, . . . *made fun of* him;
		36 X	The soldiers *mocked* him too,
Heb	11	36	4 Some [prophets] had to bear being ⸢*pilloried* (or: *publicly*
		4	*made a fool of*) and flogged,
2 P	3	3	during the last days there are bound to be ⸢*people who will*
		2/3	*be scornful* (lit. *mockers*), . . . and they will *make fun of* the promise
Jude		18	2 At the end of time . . . there are going to be *people who sneer* [at religion]

2. SCOFF (AT), JEER (AT), MOCK – MAKE A FOOL OF: *MYKTĒRIZŌ*

2 *myktērizō* 1   1 *ek-myktērizō* 2

Lk	16	14 X	The Pharisees, who loved money, . . . ⸢*laughed* at (or: *scoffed* at) him.
	23	35 X	As for the leaders, they *jeered* at him,
Ga	6	7 Θ	Don't delude yourself into thinking that God can be 2 ⸢*cheated* (lit. *made a fool of*):

3. MOCK – HOLD UP TO CONTEMPT: *PARA-DEIGMATIZŌ*

para-deigmatizō 1

Heb	6	6	They cannot be repentant if they have wilfully crucified the Son of God and *openly mocked* him.

4. LAUGH (AT), MOCK: *CHLEUAZŌ*

1 *chleuazō* 1   2 *dia-chleuazō* 1

Ac	2	13	2 Some, however, ⸢*laughed* [it off] (or: *mocked*). 'They have been drinking . . .' they said.
	17	32	At this mention of rising from the dead, some of them *burst out laughing*;

5. LAUGH: *GELAŌ*

2 *gelaō* 2   1 *kata-gelaō* 3
3 *gelōs* 1

a) Laugh (at Jesus)

Mt	9	24	[he said,] ' . . . the little girl is not dead, she is asleep'. And they *laughed* at him.
Mk	5	40	['The child is not dead, but asleep.'] But they *laughed* at him.
Lk	8	53	['she is not dead, but asleep'.] But they *laughed* at him,

b) Laugh

Lk	6	21	2 Happy you who weep now: you shall *laugh*.
		25	2 Alas for you who *laugh* now: you will mourn
Jm	4	9	3 be miserable instead of *laughing*, gloomy instead of happy.

6. JOKES: *EU-TRAPELIA*

eu-trapelia 1

Ep	5	4	There must be no coarseness, or salacious talk and *jokes*

MONEY

1. **Riches, Rich (man) – Grow rich, Make rich – Wealth, Money:** *ploutos*
2. **Riches – Money:** *chrēma*
3. **Money:** *mamōnas*
4. **Money:** *nomisma*
5. **Coins:** *kerma*
6. **Silver – Money:** *argyros*
   1: Silver pieces, Money – Silver
   2: Love of money – Lover of money
   3: Silver, Made of silver – Silversmith
7. **Gold:** *chrysos*
   1: Gold (= gold pieces)
   2: Gold, Golden – Made of gold – Gilded
8. **Bronze, Brass, Copper:** *chalkos*
   1: Copper (coins), Brass (coins) – Money
   2: Bronze, Made of bronze – Brass
   3: Coppersmith
9. **Specified coins and sums**
   1: a Talent: *talanton*
   2: a Pound: *mna*
   3: a Shekel, Silver coin: *statēr*
   4: a Half-shekel (two drachmas) – Drachma, Silver piece: *drachmē*
   5: Denarius, Penny: *dēnarion*
   6: Penny: *assarion*
   7: Farthing, Penny (quarter of an *assarion*): *kodrantēs*
   8: Small copper coins – Penny, Farthing: *lepton*
10. **Sum:** *kephalaion*
11. **Large fund, Liberal generosity:** *hadrotēs*
12. **Money changers:** *kermatistēs* and *kollybistēs*
13. **Bankers – Bank:** *tra-peza*

1. RICHES, RICH (MAN) – GROW RICH, MAKE RICH – WEALTH, MONEY: *PLOUTOS*

1 *plousios* 28	5 *ploutizō* 3	
4 *plousiōs* 4	2 *ploutos* 22	
3 *plouteō* 12		

P = Rich // Poor

Mt	13	22	2 the worries of this world and the lure of *riches* choke the word
	19	23	it will be hard for a *rich* man to enter the kingdom of heaven.
		24	²⁴ . . . it is easier for a camel to pass through the eye of a needle than for a *rich* man to enter the kingdom of heaven.
	27	57	there came a *rich* man of Arimathaea, called Joseph,
Mk	4	19	2 the worries of this world, the lure of *riches* . . . come in to choke the word,
	10	25	It is easier for a camel to pass through the eye of a needle than for a *rich* man to enter the kingdom of God.
	12	41 P	[Jesus] watched the people putting money into the treasury, and many of the *rich* put in a great deal.
Lk	1	53	3 The hungry [God] has filled with good things, the *rich* sent empty away.
	6	24 P	alas for you who are *rich*: you are having your consolation now.
	8	14	2 they are choked by the worries and *riches* and pleasures of life
	12	16 <	There was once a *rich* man who . . . had a good harvest from his land . . . ²¹ So it is when a man stores up treasure
		21	3 for himself in place of *making himself rich* in the sight of God.
	14	12 P	When you give a lunch . . . do not ask . . . *rich* neighbours . . . ¹³ No; when you have a party, invite the poor,
	16	1 <	There was a *rich* man and he had a steward
		19 < P	There was a *rich* man . . . ²⁰ And at his gate there lay a poor
		21 < P	man called Lazarus . . . ²¹ who longed to fill himself with
		22 < P	the scraps that fell from the *rich* man's table . . . ²² Now the poor man died . . . the *rich* man also died
	18	23	he was filled with sadness, for he was very *rich*.
		25	it is easier for a camel to pass through the eye of a needle than for a *rich* man to enter the kingdom of God.
	19	2	Zacchaeus made his appearance; he was . . . a *wealthy man*.
	21	1 P	[Jesus] saw *rich* [people] putting their offerings into the treasury;
Rm	2	4 Θ	2 are you abusing ⸢his abundant (lit. the *riches* of his) goodness,
	9	23 Θ	2 he wants to reveal the *richness* of his glory,
	10	12 Θ	3 all belong to the same Lord who is *rich* enough, however many ask his help,
	11	12	Think of the extent to which the world ⸢has benefited from 2/2 (lit. is *rich* through) their fall, the pagan world is *rich* through their defection –
		33 Θ	2 How *rich* are the depths of God . . .!
1 Co	1	5	5 you have been *enriched* in so many ways,
	4	8	3 you have everything you want . . . you are *rich* already,
2 Co	6	10 P	5 [we are] taken for paupers though we *make* others *rich*,
	8	2 P	their constant cheerfulness and their intense poverty have 2 overflowed in a *wealth* of generosity.
	9	X P	the Lord Jesus . . . was *rich*, but he became poor for your sake, to *make you rich* out of his poverty.
	9	11 P	5 *made richer* in every way, you will be able to do . . . generous things
Ep	1	7 Θ	2 Such is the *richness* of the grace ⁸ which he has showered on us
		18	2 you can see . . . what *rich* glories he has promised the saints will inherit
	2	4 Θ	God loved us with so much love that ⸢he was generous with his (lit. being *rich* in) mercy . . . he brought us to life
		7 Θ	2 This was to show . . . how infinitely *rich* he is in grace,
	3	8 X	2 [I proclaim] to the pagans the infinite *treasure* of Christ
		16 Θ	2 Out of ⸢his infinite (lit. the *richness* of his) glory, may he give you the power . . . for your hidden self to grow strong,
Ph	4	19 Θ	2 God will fulfil all your needs . . . as magnificently *lavishly* as only God can.
Col	1	27	2 It was God's purpose . . . to show all the *rich* glory of this mystery to pagans.
	2	2	It is all . . . to stir your minds, so that your understanding may come to ⸢full development (lit. the *richness* of fulfilment),
	3	16	4 Let the message of Christ, *in all its richness*, find a home with you.
1 Tm	6	9	3 People who long to *be rich* are a prey to temptation;

1 Tm 6	17		Warn [those who are] *rich* . . . not to set their hopes on *money*, which is untrustworthy, but on God who, out of his
		2	
	18	4	*riches*, gives us all that we need . . . ¹⁸ Tell them that
		3	they are to . . . *be rich* in good works,
Tt 3	6		[God] saved us . . . by renewing us with the Holy Spirit
		4	which he has so ⌐generously (lit. *richly*) poured over us
Heb 11	26		[Moses] considered that the insults offered to the Anointed
		2	were ⌐something more precious (lit. better *riches*) than all the treasures of Egypt,
Jm 1	10		[It is right for] the *rich* [brother] to be thankful that he has
	11		been humbled . . . ¹¹ . . . It is the same with the *rich man*: his business goes on; he himself perishes.
2	5 P		it was those who are poor according to the world that God
	6		chose, to be *rich* in faith . . . ⁶ . . . Isn't it always the *rich* who are against you?
5	1		Now an answer for the *rich*, . . . weep for the miseries that
	2		are coming to you. ² Your *wealth* is all rotting,
2 P 1	11	4	In this way you will be ⌐granted (lit. *richly* provided for) admittance into the eternal kingdom
Rv 2	9 P		I know . . . how poor you are – though you are *rich* –
3	17 P	/3	I am *rich*, I have *made a fortune*, and have everything I want,
	18		I warn you, buy from me the gold that has been tested in the
		3	fire to *make you really rich*,
5	12 X		The Lamb that was sacrificed is worthy to be given power,
		2	*riches*,
6	15		the *rich* [people] . . . took to the mountains to hide in caves
13	16 P		[The beast] compelled . . . *rich* and poor . . . to be branded on the right hand or on the forehead,
18	3	3	every merchant [has] *grown rich* through [Babylon's] debauchery,
	15	3	The traders . . . had *made a fortune* out of [Babylon]
	17	2	your *riches* are all destroyed within a single hour.
	19	3	[Babylon's] lavish living has *made a fortune* for every owner of a sea-going ship;

2. RICHES – MONEY: *CHRĒMA*

chrēma 7

Mk 10	23		How hard it is for those who have *riches* to enter the kingdom
	24		of God! ²⁴ . . . how hard it is (^v for those who trust in *riches*) to enter the kingdom of God!
Lk 18	24		How hard it is for those who have *riches* to make their way into the kingdom of God!
Ac 4	37		[Barnabas] brought the *money*, and presented to the apostles.
8	18		Simon . . . offered [Peter and John] some *money* . . . ²⁰ Peter
	20		answered, 'May your silver be lost for ever . . . for thinking that *money* could buy what God has given for nothing!'
24	26		[Felix] had hopes of receiving *money* from Paul,

3. MONEY: *MAMŌNAS*

mamōnas 4

Mt 6	24		You cannot be the slave both of God and of *money*.
Lk 16	9		use *money*, tainted as it is, to win you friends,
	11		If then you cannot be trusted with *money*, that tainted thing, who will trust you with genuine riches?
	13		You cannot be the slave both of God and of *money*.

4. MONEY: *NOMISMA*

nomisma 1

| Mt 22 | 19 | | Let me see the *money* you pay the tax with. |

5. COINS: *KERMA*

kerma 1

| Jn 2 | 15 | | [Jesus] scattered the money changers' *coins*, |

6. SILVER – MONEY: *ARGYROS*

3 *argyreos*	3	7 *phil-argyria* 1
1 *argyrion*	21	4 *phil-argyros* 2
2 *argyros*	4	5 *a-phil-argyros* 2
6 *argyro-kopos*	1	

1: SILVER PIECES, MONEY – SILVER

| Mt 10 | 9 | 2 | Provide yourselves with no gold or *silver*, not even with a few coppers |

Mt 25	18	<	the man who had received one [talent] . . . hid his master's *money*.
	27	<	you should have deposited my *money* with the bankers,
26	15		[The chief priests] paid [Judas] thirty *silver pieces*,
27	3		Judas . . . took the thirty *silver pieces* back . . . ⁵ And
	5		flinging down the *silver pieces* in the sanctuary he . . .
	6		went and hanged himself. ⁶ The chief priests picked up the *silver pieces*
	9		(Zc 11 13) They took the thirty *silver pieces*, the sum at which the precious One was priced
28	12		[The chief priests] handed a considerable sum of *money* to the soldiers
	15		The soldiers took the *money* and carried out their instructions,
Mk 14	11		[The chief priests] promised to give [Judas] *money*;
Lk 9	3		Take nothing for the journey: neither staff . . . nor *money*;
19	15		[the king] sent for those servants to whom he had given the *money*,
22	23	<	why did you not put my *money* in the bank?
	5		[The chief priests] agreed to give [Judas] *money*.
Ac 3	6		I have neither *silver* nor gold, but I will give you what I have:
7	16		the tomb that Abraham had bought ⌐and paid for (lit. with a sum of *silver*)
8	20		May your *silver* be lost for ever, and you with it,
19	19		The value of [the books of magic they burned] was calculated to be fifty thousand *silver pieces*.
20	33		I have never asked anyone for ⌐money (lit. gold or *silver*) or clothes;
1 P 1	18		the ransom that was paid to free you . . . was not paid in . . . *silver* [or] gold,

2: LOVE OF MONEY – LOVER OF MONEY

Lk 16	14	4	The Pharisees, who *loved money*, . . . laughed at [Jesus].
1 Tm 3	3	5	[A presiding elder] must *not be a lover of money*.
6	10	7	The *love of money* is the root of all evils,
2 Tm 3	2	4	People will be self-centred and ⌐grasping (lit. *lovers of money*);
Heb 13	5	5	⌐Put greed out of (lit. Be sure to have *no love of money* in) your lives

3: SILVER, MADE OF SILVER – SILVERSMITH

Ac 17	29		we have no excuse for thinking that the deity looks like
		2	anything in gold, *silver* or stone
19	24	6/3	A *silversmith* called Demetrius, who . . . [made] *silver* shrines of Diana,
1 Co 3	12		On this foundation you can build in gold, *silver* and jewels,
2 Tm 2	20	3	Not all the dishes in a large house are *made of* gold and *silver*,
Jm 5	3	2	All your gold and your *silver* are corroding away,
Rv 9	20	3	idols *made of* gold, *silver*, bronze, stone and wood
18	12	2	stocks of gold and *silver*, jewels and pearls,

7. GOLD: *CHRYSOS*

1 *chryseos* 18	3 *chrysos*	9
2 *chrysion* 13	5 *chryso(-daktylios)* 1
4 *chrysoō* 2	

S = Gold//Silver

1: GOLD (= GOLD PIECES)

Mt 10	9 S	3	Provide yourselves with no *gold* or silver, not even with a few coppers
Ac 3	6 S	2	I have neither silver nor *gold*, but I will give you what I have: in the name of Jesus Christ . . . walk!
20	33 S	2	I have never asked anyone for ⌐money (lit. *gold* or silver) or clothes;
Jm 5	3 S	3	All your *gold* and your silver are corroding away,
1 P 1	18		the ransom that was paid to free you . . . was not paid
		S 2	in . . . silver [or] *gold*, ¹⁹ but in the precious blood of . . . Christ;

2: GOLD, GOLDEN – MADE OF GOLD – GILDED

Mt 2	1	3	[the wise men] offered [the child] gifts of *gold* and frankincense and myrrh.
23	16	3	You who say, '. . . if a man swears by the *gold* of the Temple,
	17	3/3	he is bound'. ¹⁷ Fools and blind! For which is of greater worth, the *gold* or the Temple that makes the *gold* sacred?

Ac 17	29		we have no excuse for thinking that the deity looks like
		S 3	anything in *gold*, silver or stone
1 Co 3	12	S 2	On this foundation you can build in *gold*, silver and jewels,
1 Tm 2	9		women are . . . to be dressed . . . modestly, without
		2	braided hair or *gold* and jewellery
2 Tm 2	20	S	Not all the dishes in a large house are *made of gold* and silver;
Heb 9	4		[the Holy of Holies] to which belonged the *gold* altar of incense, and the ark of the covenant, plated all over with
		2/	*gold*. In this [was] kept the *gold* jar containing the manna,
Jm 2	2		suppose a man comes into your synagogue . . . with a
		5	*gold* ring on,
1 P 1	7	2	your faith will have been tested and proved like *gold* – only it is more precious [than gold],
	3	3 2	[Wives,] Do not dress up for show: . . . wearing *gold* bracelets and fine clothes;
Rv 1	12		I saw seven *golden* lamp-stands [13] and, surrounded by them,
	13		a figure like a Son of man, dressed in a long robe . . . with a *golden* girdle.
	20		The secret of . . . the seven *golden* lamp-stands is this
2	1		Here is the message of the one who . . . lives surrounded by the seven *golden* lamp-stands:
3	18	2	[Laodicea,] buy from me the *gold* that has been tested in the fire
4	4		Round the throne in a circle were twenty-four . . . elders with *golden* crowns on their heads
5	8		each one of [the elders] . . . had a *golden* bowl full of incense
8	3		Another angel . . . had a *golden* censer, . . . A large quantity of incense was given to him to offer, . . . on the *golden* altar that stood in front of the throne;
9	7	3	these locusts . . . had things that looked like *gold* crowns on their heads.
	13		I heard a voice come out of the four horns of the *golden* altar
	20	S	idols *made of gold*, silver, bronze, stone and wood
14	14		one like a son of man with a *gold* crown on his head
15	6		seven angels . . . wearing pure white linen . . . with *golden* girdles.
	7		One of the four animals gave the seven angels seven *golden* bowls filled with the anger of God
17	4	4/2	The woman . . . ⌐glittered (lit. was *gilded*) with *gold* and jewels and pearls, and she was holding a *gold* winecup
18	12	S 3	their stocks of *gold* and silver, jewels and pearls,
	16		mourn for this great city; for all . . . your ⌐finery (lit.
		4/2	*gilding*) of *gold* and jewels and pearls;
21	15		The angel . . . was carrying a *gold* measuring rod
	18	2	the city [was built] of pure *gold*, like polished glass.
	21	2	the main street of the city was pure *gold*, transparent as glass.

8. BRONZE, BRASS, COPPER: *CHALKOS*

3 *chalkeos* 1		1 *chalkos*		5
4 *chalkeus* 1		2 *chalko-libanon* 2		

1: COPPER (COINS), BRASS (COINS) – MONEY

Mt 10	9	Provide yourselves with no gold or silver, not even [a few] *coppers*
Mk 6	8	to take nothing for the journey except a staff – no bread, no haversack, no *coppers*
12	41	[Jesus] watched the people putting *money* into the treasury,

2: BRONZE, MADE OF BRONZE – BRASS

1 Co 13	1	If I . . . speak with love, I am simply ⌐a gong (lit. *bronze* booming)
Rv 1	15 2	[a Son of man,] his feet like *burnished bronze*
2	18 2	the Son of God who has . . . feet like *burnished bronze*:
9	20 3	idols *made of* gold, silver, *bronze*, stone and wood
18	12	every piece in ivory or fine wood, in *bronze* or iron or marble;

3: COPPERSMITH

2 Tm 4	14 4	Alexander the *coppersmith* has done me a lot of harm;

9. SPECIFIED COINS AND SUMS

1: A TALENT: *TALANTON*

talanton 15

Mt 18	24	they brought him a man who owed ten thousand *talents*;
25	15	To one [servant] he gave five *talents*, to another two, to a third one;

Mt 25	16	The man who had received the five *talents* promptly went and . . . made five more (ᵛ *talents*).
	20	The man who had received the five *talents* came forward bringing five more *talents*, 'Sir,' he said, 'you entrusted me with five *talents*; here are five more *talents*'
	22	the man with the two *talents* . . . said, '. . . you entrusted me with two *talents*; here are two more *talents*'
	24	Last came forward the man who had the one *talent*.
	25	I . . . hid your *talent* in the ground.
	28	take the *talent* from him and give it to the man who has the ten *talents*.

2: A POUND: *MNA*

mna 9

Lk 19	13	He summoned ten of his servants and gave them ten *pounds*.
	16	The first . . . said, 'Sir, your one *pound* has brought in ten'.
	18	the second . . . said, 'Sir, your one *pound* has made five'.
	20	the other . . . said, 'Sir, here is your *pound*. I put it away safely'
	24	Take the *pound* from him and give it to the man who has ten *pounds*.
	25	But, sir, he has ten *pounds*.

3: A SHEKEL, SILVER COIN: *STATĒR*

statēr 1

Mt 17	27	open [the fish's] mouth and there you will find a *shekel*;

4: A HALF-SHEKEL (TWO DRACHMAS) – DRACHMA, SILVER PIECE: *DRACHMĒ*

1 *drachmē* 3		2 *di-drachmon* 2	

Mt 17	24 2	the collectors of the *half-shekel* came to Peter and said,
	2	'Does your master not pay the *half-shekel*?'
Lk 15	8 <	what woman with ten *drachmas* would not, if she lost one *drachma*, . . . search . . . till she found it?
	9 <	I have found the *drachma* I lost.

5: DENARIUS, PENNY: *DĒNARION*

dēnarion 16

Mt 18	28 <	he happened to meet a fellow servant who owed him one hundred *denarii*;
20	2 <	He made an agreement with the workers for one *denarius* a day,
	9	those who were hired at about the eleventh hour . . . received one *denarius* each. [10] When the first came . . .
	10 <	they too received one *denarius* each.
	13 <	did we not agree on one *denarius*?
22	19	They handed him a *denarius*.
Mk 6	37	Are we to go and spend two hundred *denarii* on bread
12	15	Hand me a *denarius* and let me see it.
14	5	Ointment like this could have been sold for over three hundred *denarii*
Lk 7	41 <	one [creditor] owed him five hundred *denarii*, the other fifty.
10	35 <	[the Samaritan] took out the two *denarii* and handed them to the innkeeper.
20	24	Show me a *denarius*.
Jn 6	7	Philip answered, 'Two hundred *denarii* to give them a small piece [of bread] each'.
12	5	Why wasn't this ointment sold for three hundred *denarii* . . .?
Rv 6	6	A ration of corn for a ⌐day's wages (lit. *denarius*), and three rations of barley for a ⌐day's wages (lit. *denarius*),

6: PENNY: *ASSARION*

assarion 2

Mt 10	29	Can you not buy two sparrows for a *penny*?
Lk 12	6	Can you not buy five sparrows for two *pennies*?

7: FARTHING, PENNY (QUARTER OF AN *ASSARION*): *KODRANTĒS*

kodrantēs

Mt 5	26	you will not get out till you have paid the last *penny*.
Mk 12	42	A poor widow came and put in two *small coins*, the equivalent of a penny.

8: SMALL COPPER COINS – PENNY, FARTHING: *LEPTON*

lepton 3

Mk 12 42		A poor widow came and put in two small coins, the equivalent of a *penny*.
Lk 12 59		you will not get out till you have paid the very last *penny*.
21 2		[Jesus] happened to notice a poverty-stricken widow putting in two *small coins*,

10. SUM: *KEPHALAION*

kephalaion 2

Ac 22 28		It cost me a large *sum* to acquire this citizenship.
Heb 8 1		The ⌐great point (or: *sum*) of all that we have said is that we have a high priest of exactly this kind.

11. LARGE FUND, LIBERAL GENEROSITY: *HADROTĒS*

hadrotēs 1

2 Co 8 20		We hope that . . . there will be no accusations made about our administering such a *large fund*;

12. MONEY CHANGERS: *KERMATISTĒS* and *KOLLYBISTĒS*

2 *kermatistēs 1*   1 *kollybistēs 3*

Mt 21 12		Jesus then went into the Temple and . . . upset the tables of the *money changers*
Mk 11 15		[Jesus] went into the Temple and . . . upset the tables of the *money changers*
Jn 2 14	2	in the Temple [Jesus] found . . . the *money changers* sitting
15		at their counters . . . ¹⁵ . . . he . . . scattered the *money changers'* coins,

13. BANKERS – BANK: *TRA-PEZA*

1 *tra-peza 1/15*   2 *tra-pezitēs 1*

Mt 25 27	2	you should have deposited my money with the *bankers*,
Lk 19 23		why did you not put my money in the *bank*?

MORNING – EVENING

---

1. (Early) In the Morning – Dawn, Daybreak	2. Evening – Late
1: Dawn, Daybreak – Early in the morning: *orthros*	1: *hespera*
2: (Early) In the Morning – At Daybreak, Dawn: *prōi*	2: *opsia*

1. (EARLY) IN THE MORNING – DAWN, DAYBREAK

1: DAWN, DAYBREAK – EARLY IN THE MORNING: *ORTHROS*

2 *orthrinos 1*   1 *orthros 3*
3 *orthrizō 1*

Lk 21 38	3	from *early in the morning* the people would gather round [Jesus] in the Temple to listen to him.
24 1		On the first day of the week, at the first sign of *dawn*, [the women] went to the tomb
22	2	some women . . . went to the tomb *in the early morning*,
Jn 8 2		At *daybreak* [Jesus] appeared in the Temple again;
Ac 5 21		[the apostles] went into the Temple at *dawn* and began to preach.

2: (EARLY) IN THE MORNING – AT DAYBREAK, DAWN: *PRŌI*

1 *prōi 12*   3 *prōinos 2*
2 *prōia 2*

Mt 16 3		and *in the morning* [you say], 'Stormy weather today:'
20 1 <		a landowner going out *at daybreak* to hire workers

Mt 21 18		As [Jesus] was returning to the city *in the early morning*, he felt hungry.
27 1	2	When *morning* came, all the chief priests . . . met in council
Mk 1 35		*In the morning*, long before dawn, [Jesus] got up and left the house,
11 20		⌐Next (lit. *In the*) *morning*, as they passed by, they saw the fig tree withered to the roots.
13 35		you do not know when the master of the house is coming, evening, midnight, cockcrow, *dawn*;
15 1		First thing *in the morning*, the chief priests . . . had their plan ready.
16 2		very early *in the morning* on the first day of the week [the women] went to the tomb,
9		Having risen *in the morning* on the first day of the week, [Jesus] appeared first to Mary of Magdala
Jn 1 41		*Early* ⌐next (lit. *in the*) *morning* (G First), Andrew met his brother
18 28		They then led Jesus from the house of Caiaphas to the Praetorium. It was now *morning*.
20 1		It was *very early* on the first day of the week and still dark, when Mary of Magdala came to the tomb.
21 4	2	It was ⌐light (lit. *morning*) by now and there stood Jesus on the shore,
Ac 28 23		[Paul was] trying to persuade [the Roman Jews] about Jesus . . . This went on from *in the early morning* until evening,
Rv 2 28	3	I will give him the *Morning* Star.
22 16	3	I am of David's line, the root of David and the bright star *of the morning*.

2. EVENING – LATE

1: EVENING – LATE: *HESPERA*

hespera 3

Lk 24 29		[the two disciples from Emmaus] pressed him to stay with them. 'It is nearly *evening*,' they said
Ac 4 3		They arrested [John and Peter], but as it was already ⌐late (or: *evening*), they held them till the next day.
28 23		This went on from early morning until *evening*,

2: EVENING – LATE: *OPSIA*

2 *opse (3)*   1 *opsia 14*

Mt 8 16		That *evening* they brought [Jesus] many who were possessed by devils.
14 15		When *evening* came, the disciples . . . said, '. . . send the people away,'
23		When *evening* came, [Jesus] was there alone,
16 2		In the *evening* you say, 'It will be fine;'
20 8		In the *evening*, the owner of the vineyard said to the bailiff,
26 20		When *evening* came he was at table with the twelve disciples.
27 57		When it was *evening*, there came a rich man of Arimathaea, called Joseph,
Mk 1 32		That *evening*, after sunset, they brought to him all who were sick
4 35		With the coming of *evening* . . . he said to [the disciples], 'Let us cross over [the lake]'
6 47		When *evening* came, the boat was far out on the lake,
11 11	2	as it was now *late*, he went out to Bethany
19	2	when *evening* came ᵛ he (G they) went out of the city.
13 35	2	you do not know when the master of the house is coming, *evening*, midnight, cockcrow, dawn;
14 17		When *evening* came he arrived with the Twelve.
15 42		It was now *evening*, and since it was Preparation Day
Jn 6 16		That *evening* the disciples went down to the shore of the lake
20 19		In the *evening* . . . Jesus came and stood among them.

MOSES

Moses 80
A Aaron 5   Jannes 1
J Joshua 2   Jambres 1 (2 Tm 2 3)

E = Moses and Elijah   P = Moses and the Prophets

Mt 8 4		(cf. Lv 14 1–31) make the offering prescribed by *Moses*
17 3 E		Suddenly *Moses* and Elijah appeared to them; they were talking with [Jesus].
4 E		I will make three tents here, one for you, one for *Moses* and one for Elijah.

Mt 19	7	why did *Moses* command (Dt 24 1) that a writ of dismissal should be given in cases of divorce? ⁸ 'It was because you were so unteachable' [Jesus] said 'that *Moses* allowed you to divorce your wives,'
	8	
22	24	*Moses* said (cf. Dt 25 5–6) that if a man dies childless,
23	2	The scribes and the Pharisees occupy the chair of *Moses*.
Mk 1	44	(cf. Lv 14 1–31) make the offering for your healing prescribed by *Moses*
7	10	*Moses* said (Ex 20 12): 'Do your duty to your father and your mother,
9	4 E	Elijah appeared to them with *Moses*;
	5 E	let us make three tents, one for you, one for *Moses* and one for Elijah.
10	3	'What did *Moses* command you?' ⁴ '*Moses* allowed us' they said 'to draw up a writ of dismissal (Dt 24 1)
	4	
12	19	we have it from *Moses* in writing (cf. Dt 25 5–6), if a man's brother dies leaving a wife but no child,
	26	have you never read in the Book of *Moses*, in the passage about the Bush . . . (Ex 3 6): I am the God of Abraham,
Lk 1	5 A	Zechariah . . . had a wife, Elizabeth . . . who was a descendant of *Aaron*.
2	22	the day . . . for them to be purified as laid down by the Law of *Moses* (cf. Lv 12 2–5),
5	14	make the offering for your healing as *Moses* prescribed it (cf. Lv 14 1–31),
9	30 E	Suddenly there were two men there talking to [Jesus]; they were *Moses* and Elijah
	33 E	let us make three tents, one for you, one for *Moses* and one for Elijah.
16	29 P	They have *Moses* and the prophets, . . . let them listen to them.
	31 P	if they will not listen either to *Moses* or to the prophets,
20	28	we have it from *Moses* in writing (cf. Dt 25 5–6), that if a man's married brother dies childless,
	37	*Moses* himself implies that the dead rise again, in the passage about the bush (Ex 3 6)
24	27 P	starting with *Moses* and going through all the prophets, [Jesus] explained . . . the passages . . . that were about himself.
	44 P	everything written about me in the Law of *Moses*, in the Prophets, and in the Psalms,
Jn 1	17	the Law was given through *Moses*,
	45 P	We have found the one *Moses* wrote about in the Law, the one about whom the prophets wrote:
3	14	(cf. Nb 21 9) as *Moses* lifted up the serpent in the desert,
5	45	you place your hopes on *Moses*, and [Moses] will be your accuser. ⁴⁶ If you really believed ʳhim (lit. *Moses*) you would believe me too.
	46	
6	32	it was not *Moses* who gave you bread from heaven,
7	19	Did not *Moses* give you the Law?
	22	*Moses* ordered you to practise circumcision – not that it began with ʳhim (lit. *Moses*), it goes back to the patriarchs – . . . ²³ Now if a man can be circumcised on the sabbath so that the Law of *Moses* is not broken,
	23	
8	5	*Moses* has ordered us in the Law (cf, Lv 20 10; Dt 22 22) to condemn women like this to death by stoning,
9	28	we are disciples of *Moses*: ²⁹ we know that God spoke to *Moses*,
	29	
Ac 3	22	*Moses* . . . said (Dt 18 15, 18): 'The Lord God will raise up a prophet like myself for you,
6	11	We heard [Stephen] using blasphemous language against *Moses* and against God.
	14	We have heard [Stephen] say that Jesus . . . is going to . . . alter the traditions that *Moses* handed down to us.
7	20	(cf. Ex 2 2) It was at this period that *Moses* was born, a fine child and favoured by God.
	22	*Moses* was taught all the wisdom of the Egyptians
	29	(Ex 2 15) *Moses* fled . . . and went to stay in the land of Midian,
	31	(cf. Ex 3 3) *Moses* was amazed by what he saw.
	32	(cf. Ex 3 5f) *Moses* trembled and did not dare to look any more.
	35	It was the same *Moses* that they had disowned . . . who was now sent to be both leader and redeemer
	37	It was *Moses* who told the sons of Israel (Dt 18 15), 'God will raise up a prophet'
	40 A	(cf. Ex 32 1) [our ancestors] said to *Aaron*, Make some gods to be our leaders; we do not understand what has come over this *Moses* who led us out of Egypt.
	44	our ancestors possessed the Tent of Testimony that had been constructed according to the instructions God gave *Moses*,
	45 J	. . . ⁴⁵ It was handed down . . . until *Joshua* brought it into the country we had conquered
13	38	justification from all sins which the Law of *Moses* was unable to justify
15	1	Unless you have yourselves circumcised in the tradition of *Moses*
	5	insisting that the pagans should be circumcised and instructed to keep the Law of *Moses*.

Ac 15	21	*Moses* has always had his preachers in every town, and is read aloud in the synagogues
21	21	you instruct all Jews living among the pagans to break away from *Moses*,
26	22 P	nothing more than what the prophets and *Moses* himself said would happen:
28	23 P	trying to persuade them about Jesus, arguing from the Law of *Moses* and the prophets.
Rm 5	14	death reigned over all from Adam to *Moses*.
9	15	God said to *Moses* (Ex 33 19): I have mercy on whom I will,
10	5	When *Moses* refers to being justified by the Law, he writes (Lv 18 5): those who keep the Law will draw life from it.
	19	*Moses* answered this long ago (Dt 32 21): I will make you jealous
1 Co 9	9	It is written in the law of *Moses* (Dt 25 4): You must not put a muzzle on the ox
10	2	(cf. Ex 13 21; 14 22) [our fathers] were all baptised into *Moses* in this cloud and in this sea;
2 Co 3	7	(cf. Ex 34 30) the Israelites could not bear looking at the face of *Moses*,
	13	not like *Moses* (Ex 34 33), who put a veil over his face
	15	whenever *Moses* is read, the veil is over their minds.
2 Tm 3	8	(cf. Ex 7 11–22) just as *Jannes* and *Jambres* defied *Moses*:
Heb 3	2	[Christ] was faithful to the one who appointed him, just like *Moses*, . . . ³ but he has been found to deserve a greater glory than *Moses*.
	3	
	5	*Moses* was faithful in the house of God,
	16	all the people who were brought out of Egypt by *Moses*.
4	8 J	If *Joshua* had led them into this place of rest,
5	4 A	No one takes [the] honour [of priesthood] on himself, but each one is called by God, as *Aaron* was.
7	11 A	why was it still necessary for a new priesthood to arise, one of the same order as Melchizedek not counted as being 'of the same order as' *Aaron*?
	14	Judah, a tribe which *Moses* did not even mention when dealing with priests.
8	5	*Moses* . . . was warned by God (Ex 25 40) who said: '. . . make everything according to the pattern shown you'
9	4 A	In [the ark of the covenant] were kept the gold jar containing the manna, *Aaron's* branch that grew the buds,
	19	after *Moses* had announced all the commandments of the Law
10	28	(cf. Dt 17 6) Anyone who disregards the Law of *Moses* is ruthlessly put to death
11	23	It was by faith (Ex 2 2) that *Moses* . . . was hidden by his parents
	24	It was by faith that . . . *Moses* refused to be known as the son of Pharaoh's daughter
12	21	*Moses* said (cf. Dt 9 19): I am afraid,
Jude	9	the archangel Michael, when he was engaged in argument with the devil about the corpse of *Moses*,
Rv 15	3	[the conquerors of the beast] were singing the hymn of *Moses* (Ex 15), the servant of God,

MOUNTAIN – HILL

1. Mountain, Mount – Hill: *oros* a) Mountain, Hill(s) b) Mountain (=Gerizim) c) the Mount of Olives d) Mount Sinai – the Mountain of Moses e) Mount Zion f) the Mountain of the Transfiguration	**2. Amageddon** [Heb. *Har M^egiddōn*: the Hill of Megiddo]: *Ar Magedōn* **3. Hill:** *bounos* **4. Cliff, Steep bank:** *krēmnos* **5. Brow (of a hill):** *ophrys* **6. Valley, Ravine:** *pharanx* **7. Level:** *pedinos*

1. MOUNTAIN, MOUNT – HILL: *OROS*

2 *oreinē* 2   1 *oros* 63

a) *Mountain, Hill(s)*

Mt 4	8	taking [Jesus] to a very high *mountain*, the devil showed him all the kingdoms of the world
5	1	Seeing the crowds, [Jesus] went up the *hill*.
	14	A city built on a *hill*[-top] cannot be hidden.
8	1	After [Jesus] had come down from the *mountain*
14	23	After sending the crowds away [Jesus] went up into the *hills* by himself to pray.
15	29	Jesus . . . went up into the *hills*.
17	20	you could say to this *mountain*, 'Move from here to there',
18	12	will he not leave the ninety-nine [sheep] on the *hillside* and go in search of the stray?
21	21	even if you say to this *mountain*, 'Get up and throw yourself into the sea', it will be done.

Mt 24	16	then those in Judaea must escape to the *mountains*;
28	16	the eleven disciples set out for Galilee, to the *mountain* where Jesus had arranged to meet them.
Mk 3	13	[Jesus] now went up into the *hills* and summoned those he wanted.
5	5	All night and all day, among the tombs and in the *mountains*, [the demoniac] would howl
	11	there was there on the *mountainside* a great herd of pigs feeding,
6	46	[Jesus] went off into the *hills* to pray.
11	23	if anyone says to this *mountain*, 'Get up and throw yourself into the sea',
13	14	then those in Judaea must escape to the *mountains*;
Lk 1	39	Mary . . . went as quickly as she could to a town in the *hill country* of Judah.
	2	
	65	2 the whole affair was talked about throughout the *hill country* of Judaea.
3	5	(Is 40 4) Every valley will be filled in, every *mountain* and hill be laid low,
4	29	the brow of the *hill* their town [Nazareth] was built on,
6	12	[Jesus] went out into the *hills* to pray;
8	32	there was a large herd of pigs feeding there on the *mountain*, . . . ³³ . . . and the herd charged down the cliff into the lake
21	21	Then those in Judaea must escape to the *mountains*,
23	30	they will begin to say to the *mountains*, 'Fall on us!'; to the hills, 'Cover us!'
Jn 6	3	Jesus climbed the *hillside*, and sat down there with his disciples.
	15	Jesus . . . escaped back to the *hills* by himself.
1 Co 13	2	if I have faith in all its fulness, to move *mountains*,
Heb 11	38	[the prophets] went out to live in deserts and *mountains* and in caves and ravines.
Rv 6	14	and all the *mountains* and islands were shaken from their places.
	15	the whole population . . . took to the *mountains* to hide
	16	. . . ¹⁶ They said to the *mountains* and the rocks, 'Fall on us'
8	8	it was as though a great *mountain*, all on fire, had been dropped into the sea:
16	20	Every island vanished and the *mountains* disappeared;
17	9	the seven heads are the seven *hills*, and the woman is sitting on them.

b) Mountain (= Gerizim)

Jn 4	20	'Our fathers worshipped on this *mountain*, while you say that Jerusalem is the place where one ought to worship.'
	21	²¹ Jesus said: '. . . the hour is coming when you will worship the Father neither on this *mountain* nor in Jerusalem.'

c) the Mount of Olives
3 elaia 9/13   4 elaiōn 3

Mt 21	1	When they . . . had come in sight of Bethphage on the /3 *Mount* of *Olives*,
24	3	/3 when [Jesus] was sitting on the *Mount* of *Olives*
26	30	After psalms had been sung they left for the *Mount* of 3 *Olives*.
Mk 11	1	When they were . . . in sight of Bethphage and Bethany, /3 close by the *Mount* of *Olives*,
13	3	while [Jesus] was sitting facing the Temple, on the *Mount* 3 of *Olives*,
14	26	After psalms had been sung they left for the *Mount* of 3 *Olives*.
Lk 19	29	when [Jesus] was near Bethphage and Bethany, close by /4 the *Mount* of *Olives* as it is called,
	37	[Jesus] was approaching the downward slope of the *Mount* 3 of *Olives*,
21	37	[Jesus] would spend the night on the *hill* called [the Mount] 4 of *Olives*
22	39	[Jesus] then left to make his way as usual to the *Mount* 3 of *Olives*,
Jn 8	1	/3 Jesus went to the *Mount* of *Olives*.
Ac 1	12	/4 from the *Mount* of *Olives*, as it is called, they went back to Jerusalem,

d) Mount Sinai – the Mountain of Moses
Sinai 4

Ac 7	30	in the wilderness near *Mount Sinai*, an angel appeared to [Moses]
	38	the angel who had spoken to [Moses] on *Mount Sinai*;
Ga 4	24	The first [woman] who comes from *Mount Sinai*, and whose children are slaves, is Hagar – ²⁵ since ⌈*Mount Sinai*
	25	is (§ Hagar is *Mount Sinai*) in Arabia
Heb 8	5	(Ex 25 40) See that you make everything according to the pattern shown you on the *mountain*.
12	20	(Ex 19 13) If even an animal touches the *mountain*, it must be stoned.

e) Mount Zion

Heb 12	22	what you have come to is *Mount* Zion and the city of the living God, the heavenly Jerusalem
Rv 14	1	I saw *Mount* Zion, and standing on it a Lamb
21	10 Δ	(Ezk 40 2) [an angel] took me to the top of an enormous high *mountain*

f) the Mountain of the Transfiguration

Mt 17	1	Jesus took with him Peter and James and his brother John and led them up a high *mountain*
	9	As they came down from the *mountain* Jesus gave them this order,
Mk 9	2	Jesus took with him Peter and James and John and led them up a high *mountain*
	9	As they came down from the *mountain* he warned them to tell no one what they had seen,
Lk 9	28	[Jesus] took with him Peter and John and James and went up the *mountain* to pray.
	37	on the following day when they were coming down from the *mountain* a large crowd came to meet him.
2 P 1	18	when we were with [our Lord Jesus Christ] on the holy *mountain*.

2. ARMAGEDDON [Heb. *Har Mᵉgiddōn*: The Hill of Megiddo]: *AR MAGEDŌN*
Ar Magedōn 1

Rv 16	16	[The demon spirits] called the kings together at the place called, in Hebrew, *Armageddon*.

3. HILL: *BOUNOS*
bounos 2

Lk 3	5	every mountain and *hill* [will be] laid low,
23	30	to the mountains, "Fall on us!"; to the *hills*, "Cover us!"

4. CLIFF, STEEP BANK: *KRĒMNOS*
krēmnos 3

Mt 8	32	the whole herd [of pigs] charged down the *cliff* into the lake
Mk 5	13	the herd of about two thousand pigs charged down the *cliff* into the lake,
Lk 8	33	the herd charged down the *cliff* into the lake

5. BROW (OF A HILL): *OPHRYS*
ophrys 1

Lk 4	29	[the people of Nazareth] took [Jesus] up to the *brow* of the hill their town was built on,

6. VALLEY, RAVINE: *PHARANX*
pharanx 1

Lk 3	5	(Is 40 4) Every *valley* will be filled in,

7. LEVEL: *PEDINOS*
pedinos 1

Lk 6	17	[Jesus] then came down [from the hills with the Twelve] and stopped at a piece of *level* ground.

MOURN – LAMENT

1. Mourn, Grieve – Grief, Sorrow: *pentheō*	**4. (In) Tears – Weep** 1: Tear(s) – Weep: *dakruō*
2. (Be) Distress(ed), Grieve(d) – (Be) Sad, Sorrowful – Sorrow: *lypē*	2: Weep, Weeping – Cry – In tears: *klaiō*
3. Beat one's breast – Mourn: *koptō*	**5. Groan – Sigh – Grumble:** *stenazō*

6. **Lament, Lamentation:** *odyrmos*
7. **Sing dirges – Lament, Wail (over):** *thrēneō*
8. **Howl, Wail:** *ololuzō*
9. **Wailing – Clashing, Clanging:** *alalazō*
   a) Wailing
   b) Clashing, Clanging
10. **Gloomy**

1: (a) Gloomy look – Look sad: *skythr-ōpos*
2: (Be) Gloomy: *stygnazō*
   a) Gloomy – Lowering – Overcast
   b) (a person's) Face falls
3: Gloom(y), Dejection: *kat-ēpheia*
11. **Sigh:** *em-brimaomai*

R = Mourn, Weep, Grieve // Rejoice, Laugh

1. MOURN, GRIEVE – GRIEF, SORROW: *PENTHEŌ*

1 *pentheō* 10   2 *penthos* 5

Mt	5	5		Happy [those who] *mourn*: they shall be comforted.
	9	15		Surely the bridegroom's attendants would never think of *mourning* as long as the bridegroom is still with them?
Mk	16	10		[Mary of Magdala] then went to those who had been his companions, and who *were mourning* and in tears.
Lk	6	25	R	Alas for you who laugh now: you shall *mourn* and weep.
1 Co	5	2		How can you be so proud of yourselves? You should *be in mourning*.
2 Co	12	21		I shall *be grieving* over all those who sinned
Jm	4	9	R	Look at your wretched condition, and weep for it *in misery*;
		2		*be miserable* instead of laughing,
Rv	18	7		Every one of [Babylon's] shows and orgies is to be matched
		2		by a torture or a *grief* . . . she says to herself, . . . I am no
		2		widow and shall never be in *mourning*. ⁸ For that . . . the
	8	2		plagues will fall on her: disease and *mourning* and famine.
	11			There will be weeping and *distress* over her among all the traders of the earth
	15			The traders . . . will be . . . *mourning* and weeping. ¹⁶ They will be saying: 'Mourn,
	19			They will throw dust on their heads and say, ᵗwith tears and
		R		groans (lit. weeping and *sorrowing*): 'Mourn,
	21	4		2 there will be no more . . . *mourning* or sadness.

2. (BE) DISTRESS(ED), GRIEVE(D) – (BE) SAD, SORROWFUL – SORROW: *LYPĒ*

2 *lypē* 16   6 *peri-lypos* 5
1 *lypeō* 26   5 *syl-lypeō* 1
4 *a-lypos* 1

Mt	14	9		The king was *distressed* but . . . ordered [John the Baptist's head] to be given her,
	17	23		[The Son of Man is going to be handed over into the power of men;] And a great *sadness* came over them.
	18	31		His fellow servants were deeply *distressed* when they saw what had happened,
	19	22		the young man . . . went away *sad*, for he was a man of great wealth.
	26	22		[One of you is about to betray me.] They were greatly *distressed* and started asking him in turn, 'Not I, Lord, surely?'
	37	X		And *sadness* came over him, and great distress.
	38	X	3	My soul is *sorrowful* to the point of death. Wait here and keep awake with me.
Mk	3	5	X	5 *grieved* to find them so obstinate, he looked angrily round
	6	26		3 The king was deeply *distressed* but . . . he was reluctant to break his word
	10	22		[the young man] went away *sad*, for he was a man of great wealth.
	14	19		[One of you is about to betray me.] They were *distressed*
	34	X	3	My soul is *sorrowful* to the point of death.
Lk	18	23		3 [the rich aristocrat] was *filled with sadness*, for he was very
		24		3 rich. ²⁴ Jesus ᵗlooked at him (ᵛ saw he was *filled with sadness*) and said, 'How hard it is for those who have riches to make their way into the kingdom of God!'
	22	45		[Jesus] went to the disciples and found them sleeping for
		2		[sheer] *grief*.
Jn	16	6		2 Yet you are *sad* at heart because I have told you [that I am going to the one who sent me].
		20	R	/2 you will be *sorrowful*, but your *sorrow* will turn to joy.
		21	R	2 A woman in childbirth ᵗsuffers (lit. *is distressed*) . . . ²² So it
		22	R	2 is with you: you are *sad* now, but I shall see you again, and your hearts will be full of joy,
	21	17		Peter was *upset* that [Jesus] asked him the third time, 'Do you *love* me?'
Rm	9	2		2 my *sorrow* is so great, my mental anguish so endless,
	14	15		If your attitude to food is *upsetting* your brother, then you are hardly being guided by charity.

---

2 Co	2	1	2	I made up my mind not to pay you a second *distressing* visit. ² I may have ᵗhurt (lit. *grieved*) you, but if so I have
		2	R	ᵗhurt (lit. *grieved*) the only people who could give me any
			R	pleasure. ³ I wrote as I did to make sure that, when I came,
		3		I should not be *distressed* . . . ⁴ When I wrote to you . . .
		4	2	it was not to make you feel ᵗhurt (lit. *grieved*)
		5		Someone has been the *cause of pain*; and the *cause of pain* not to me, but to some degree . . . to all of you.
		7		the best thing now is to give him your forgiveness . . . or
			2	he might break down from so much *misery*.
	6	10	R	[we are] thought [most] *miserable* and yet we are always rejoicing;
	7	8		even if I *distressed* you by my letter, I do not regret it . . .
		9		I see that that letter did *distress* you . . . ⁹ but I am happy
			R	now – not because I ᵗmade you suffer (lit. *distressed* you), but because your ᵗsuffering (lit. *distress*) led to your repentance. Yours has been a kind of ᵗsuffering (lit. *distress*) that
		10	2	God approves . . . ¹⁰ ᵗTo suffer (lit. *Distress*) in God's
			2	way means changing for the better . . . but ᵗto suffer (lit. *distress*) as the world knows [suffering] brings death.
		11		¹¹ Just look at what ᵗsuffering (lit. being *distressed*) in God's way has brought you:
	9	7	R	2 Each one should give what he has decided . . , not grudgingly or because he is made to, for God loves a cheerful giver.
Ep	4	30	Ⓢ	you will only be *grieving* the Holy Spirit of God
Ph	2	27		God took pity on [Epaphroditus], and on me as well as him, and spared me what would have been ᵗone grief on top of
		28	2/2	another (lit. *grief* on top of *grief*). ²⁸ So I shall send him back as promptly as I can; then you will be happy to see him
			R	4 again, and that will *make* me *less sorry*.
1 Th	4	13		We want you to be quite certain, brothers, about those who have died, to make sure that you do not *grieve* about them, like the other people who have no hope.
Heb	12	11	R	2 any punishment is most ᵗpainful (lit. *distressing*) at the time and far from pleasant;
1 P	1	6	R	This is a cause of great joy for you, even though you may . . . have to bear being *plagued* by all sorts of trials;
	2	19	2	there is some merit in putting up with the ᵗpains (or: *griefs*) of unearned punishment if it is done for the sake of God

3. BEAT ONE'S BREAST – MOURN: *KOPTŌ*

2 *kopetos* 1   1 *koptō* 6/8

Mt	11	17		we sang dirges, and you wouldn't *be mourners*.
	24	30		all the peoples of the earth will *beat their breasts*;
Lk	8	52		They were all weeping and *mourning* for [Jairus's daughter],
	23	27		Large numbers of people followed [Jesus], and of women too, who *mourned* and lamented for him.
Ac	8	2		some devout people . . . buried Stephen and made great
			2	*mourning* for him.
Rv	1	7		(cf. Zc 12 10) all the races of the earth will *mourn* over [Jesus Christ].
	18	9		There will be *mourning* and weeping for [Babylon] by the kings of the earth

4. (IN) TEARS – WEEP

1: TEAR(S) – WEEP: *DAKRUŌ*

1 *dakru* 10   2 *dakruō* 1

Lk	7	38		her *tears* fell on [Jesus's] feet, and she wiped them away with her hair;
		44		she has poured out her *tears* over my feet
Jn	11	35	X	2 [At the sight of Mary's tears] Jesus *wept*;
Ac	20	19		[You know] how I have served the Lord . . . with all the ᵗsorrows (lit. *tears*) and trials that came to me through the plots of the Jews.
		31		for three years I never failed to keep you right, [shedding *tears* over each one of you.
2 Co	2	4	R	When I wrote to you, . . . in *tears*,
2 Tm	1	3	R	I remember your *tears* ⁴ and long to see you again to complete my happiness.
Heb	5	7		he offered up prayer and entreaty, aloud and in [silent]
		X		*tears*, to the one who had the power to save him out of death,
	12	17		when [Esau] wanted to obtain the blessing afterwards, he was rejected, . . . though he pleaded for it with *tears*,
Rv	7	17		(Is 25 8) God will wipe away all *tears* from their eyes.
	21	4		(Is 25 8) He will wipe away all *tears* from their eyes,

2: WEEP, WEEPING – CRY – IN TEARS: *KLAIŌ*

1 *klaiō* 40   2 *klauthmos* 9

Mt	2	18		2 (Jr 31 15) A voice was heard in Ramah, *sobbing* and loudly lamenting: it was Rachel *weeping* for her children,

Mt 8	12	2 into the dark, where there will be *weeping* and grinding of teeth.

Repeated in 13 42, 50; 22 13; 24 51; 25 30; Lk 13 28.

	26 75	[Peter] went outside and *wept* bitterly.
Mk 5	38	people *weeping* and wailing unrestrainedly.
	39	Why all this commotion and *crying*?
	14 72	[Peter] *burst into tears.*
	16 10	[Mary of Magdala] then went to those who had been his companions, and who *were mourning* and *in tears*
Lk 6	21 R	Happy you who *weep* now: you shall laugh.
	26	Alas for you who laugh now: you shall mourn and *weep.*
7	13	'Do not *cry*' [Jesus] said [to the widow of Nain]
	32	we sang dirges, and you wouldn't *cry.*
	38	She waited behind [Jesus] at his feet, *weeping,* and her tears fell on his feet,
8	52	They were all *weeping* and mourning for [Jairus's daughter], but Jesus said, 'Stop *crying*;'
	19 41 X	As he . . . came in sight of the city he *shed tears* over it
	22 62	[Peter] went outside and *wept* bitterly.
	23 28	Daughters of Jerusalem, do not *weep* for me; *weep* rather for yourselves and for your children.
Jn 11	31	[the Jews] followed [Mary], thinking that she was going to the tomb to *weep* there . . . [33] At the sight of her ⌐tears, and those (lit. *weeping,* and the *weeping*) of the Jews who followed her, Jesus said
	33	
	16 20 R	you will be *weeping* and wailing while the world will rejoice;
	20 11	Mary stayed outside near the tomb, *weeping.* Then, still *weeping,* she stooped to look inside,
	13	[The two angels] said, 'Woman, why are you *weeping*?'
	15	Jesus said, 'Woman, why are you *weeping*?'
Ac 9	39	all the widows stood round [Peter] *in tears,*
	20 37	2 now they *were* all *in tears;*
	21 13	What are you trying to do – weaken my resolution by your ⌐tears (lit. *weeping*)?
Rm 12	15 R	Rejoice with those who rejoice and ⌐be sad (lit. *weep*) with those ⌐in sorrow (lit. *weeping*).
1 Co 7	30 R	those who ⌐mourn (lit. *weep*) should live as though they had nothing to ⌐mourn (lit. *weep*) for;
Ph 3	18	I repeat it today *with tears,* there are many who are behaving as the enemies of the cross of Christ.
Jm 4	9 R	Look at your wretched condition, and *weep* for it in misery;
5	1	Start *crying,* ⌐weep (lit. howl) for the miseries that are coming to you.
Rv 5	4	I *wept* bitterly because there was nobody fit to open the scroll and read it, [5] but one of the elders said to me, 'There is no need to *cry*'
	5	
18	9	There will be mourning and *weeping* for [Babylon] by the kings of the earth
	11	There will be *weeping* and distress over her among all the traders of the earth
	15	The traders . . . will be . . . mourning and *weeping.* [16] They will be saying: 'Mourn,'
	19 R	They will throw dust on their heads and say, ⌐with tears and groans (lit. *weeping* and sorrowing): 'Mourn,'

5. GROAN – SIGH – GRUMBLE: *STENAZŌ*

2 *stenagmos* 2	3 *ana-stenazō* 1
1 *stenazō* 6	4 *sy-stenazō* 1

Mk 7	34 X	looking up to heaven he *sighed*; and he said to [the deaf man], 'Ephphatha',
8	12 X	3 *with a sigh* that came straight from the heart he said, 'Why does this generation demand a sign?'
Ac 7	34	(Ex 3 7) I have seen the way my people are ill-treated in Egypt, I have heard their *groans,*
Rm 8	22	4 till now the entire creation . . . has *been groaning* in one great act of giving birth; [23] . . . we too *groan* inwardly as we wait for our bodies to be set free.
	23	
	26 Ⓢ	2 the Spirit himself expresses our plea in ⌐a way (lit. *groans*) that could never be put into words,
2 Co 5	2	we *groan* as we wait with longing to put on our heavenly home
	4	Yes, we *groan* and find it a burden being still in this tent,
Heb 13	17 R	make this a joy for [your leaders] to do, and not ⌐a grief (lit. [something] to *groan* about)
Jm 5	9	Do not ⌐*make complaints* (or: *grumble*) against one another,

6. LAMENT, LAMENTATION: *ODYRMOS*

odyrmos 2

Mt 2	18	(Jr 31 15) A voice was heard in Ramah, sobbing and loudly *lamenting*:
2 Co 7	7 R	[Titus] has told us . . . ⌐how sorry you were and how concerned (lit. your *lamentation* and concern) for me,

7. SING DIRGES – LAMENT, WAIL (OVER): *THRĒNEŌ*

thrēneō 4

Mt 11	17	we *sang dirges,* and you wouldn't be mourners.
Lk 7	32	we *sang dirges,* and you wouldn't cry.
	23 27	Large numbers of . . . women [followed Jesus to Calvary] . . ., who mourned and *lamented* for him,
Jn 16	20 R	you will be weeping and *wailing* while the world will rejoice;

8. HOWL, WAIL: *OLOLUZŌ*

ololuzō 1

Jm 5	1	Now an answer for the rich. Start crying, ⌐weep (lit. *howl*) for the miseries that are coming

9. WAILING – CLASHING, CLANGING: *ALALAZŌ*

alalazō 2

a) Wailing

Mk 5	38	Jesus noticed . . . people weeping and *wailing* unrestrainedly.

b) Clashing, Clanging

1 Co 13	1	If I . . . speak without love, I am simply . . . a cymbal *clashing.*

10. GLOOMY

1: (A) GLOOMY LOOK – LOOK SAD: *SKYTHR-ŌPOS*

skythr-ōpos 2

Mt 6	16	When you fast do not put on a *gloomy look* as the hypocrites do:
Lk 24	17	[The disciples] stopped short, their *faces downcast.*

2: (BE) GLOOMY: *STYGNAZŌ*

stygnazō 2

a) Gloomy – Lowering – Overcast

Mt 16	3	Stormy weather today; the sky is red and *overcast.*

b) (a person's) Face falls

Mk 10	22	[the rich man's] *face fell* at these words and he went away sad,

3: GLOOM(Y), DEJECTION: *KAT-ĒPHEIA*

kat-ēpheia 1

Jm 4	9	be miserable instead of laughing, *gloomy* instead of happy.

11. SIGH: *EM-BRIMAOMAI*

em-brimaomai 2/5

Jn 11	33 X	At the sight of [Mary's] tears . . . Jesus said . . . with a *sigh* that came straight from the heart,
	38 X	Still *sighing,* Jesus reached the tomb:

MOUTH – TONGUE

1. Mouth: *stoma*
  1: Mouth – Lips (as an organ of speech)
    a) of God, of Jesus
    b) of various
  2: Force to speak, *or negatively,* Silence
  3: Mouth (generally)
  4: Mouths of creatures – the Mouth of the earth
2. Lips: *cheilos*
3. Tongue – Language – Lick
  1: Tongue – Language: *glōssa*
    a) Tongue, especially as an organ of speech
    b) Language – (Gift of) Tongues, (Speak with) Tongues
  2: Lick: *epi-leichō*
4. Tooth – Grinding (one's) teeth – Bite
  1: Tooth – Grinding (one's) teeth: *odous, brychō* and *trizō*
  2: Bite – Snap at – Gnaw
    a) Bite – Snap at: *daknō*
    b) Bite – Gnaw: *masaomai*
  3: Ivory: *elephantinos*
5. Throat: *larynx*

1. MOUTH: *STOMA*

1   *stoma*   76/78   3 *epi-stomizō* 1
2   *apo-stomatizō*   1

1: MOUTH – LIPS (AS AN ORGAN OF SPEECH)

a) of God, of Jesus

Mt 4 4		(Dt 8 3) Man does not live on bread alone but on every word that comes from the *mouth* of God.
	Θ	
5 2		[Jesus] ⌐began to speak (lit. opened his *mouth* [to speak]). This is what he taught them;
13 35		(Ps 78 2) I will ⌐speak (lit. open my *mouth* [and speak]) to you in parables
Lk 4 22		they were astonished by the gracious words that came from his *lips*.
11 54		[the scribes tried] to catch him out in something ⌐he might say (lit. [that might fall] from his *lips*).
22 71		We have heard it for ourselves from his own *lips*.
Ac 8 32		(Is 53 7) like a lamb that is dumb . . . he never opens his *mouth*.
22 14		God . . . has chosen you . . . to see the Just One and hear his own voice ⌐speaking (lit. from his *lips*),
2 Th 2 8		(Is 11 4) The Lord will kill [the Rebel] with the breath of his *mouth*
1 P 2 22		(Is 53 9) there had been no perjury in his *mouth*.

b) of various

Mt 12 34	⌐a man's words (lit. [the words] that leave a man's *lips*) flow out of what fills his heart.
15 11	it is what comes out of the *mouth* that makes [a man] unclean.
18	the things that come out of the *mouth* come from the heart,
18 16	(Dt 19 15) the ⌐evidence (lit. *mouth*) of two or three witnesses is required to sustain any charge.
21 16	(Ps 8 3) By the *mouths* of children . . . you have made sure of praise
Lk 1 64	At that instant [Zechariah's] ⌐power of speech returned (lit. *mouth* [and his tongue were] opened)
70	even as [God] proclaimed, by the *mouth* of his holy prophets
6 45	⌐a man's words (lit. [the words] that leave a man's *lips*) flow out of what fills his heart.
19 22	Out of your own *mouth* I condemn you.
21 15	I myself shall give you ⌐an eloquence (lit. a *mouth*) and a wisdom
Ac 1 16	the Holy Spirit, ⌐speaking through (lit. through the *mouth* of) David, foretells the fate of Judas,
3 18	God carried out what he had foretold, when he ⌐said through (lit. spoke through the *mouth* of) all his prophets
21	the universal restoration . . . which God proclaimed, speaking through (§ the *mouth* of) his holy prophets.
4 25	you it is who said . . . speaking through (§ the *mouth* of) our ancestor David,
8 35	Philip ⌐proceeded (lit. set his *lips*) to explain the Good News of Jesus to [the eunuch].
10 34	Peter ⌐addressed them (lit. opened his *mouth*) . . . he said, '. . . God does not have favourites'
15 7	the pagans were to learn the Good News from ⌐me (lit. my *lips*)
18 14	Before Paul could open his *mouth*, Gallio said to the Jews,
23 2	Ananias ordered his attendants to strike [Paul] on the *mouth*.
Rm 3 14	(Ps 10 7) bitter curses fill their *mouths*.
19	all this that the Law says . . . is meant to ⌐silence everyone (lit. shut everyone's *mouth*)
10 8	(Dt 30 14) The word . . . is very near to you, it is on your *lips* and in your heart.
9	If your *lips* confess that Jesus is Lord . . . you will be saved.
10	by confessing with your *lips* you are saved.
15 6	so that united in mind and ⌐voice (lit. *lips*) you may give glory to the God and Father of our Lord Jesus Christ.
2 Co 6 11	⌐we have spoken to you very frankly (lit. our *mouth* has been opened to you); our mind has been opened in front of you.
13 1	(Dt 19 15) The ⌐evidence (lit. *mouth*) of three, or at least two, witnesses is necessary to sustain the charge.
Ep 4 29	Guard against foul talk (§ coming from your *mouth*);
6 19	pray for me to be given an opportunity to open my *mouth* and . . . give out the mystery of the gospel
Col 3 8	you . . . must give all these things up: . . . abusive language and dirty talk (§ should not leave your *lips*);
Jm 3 10	the blessing and the curse come out of the same *mouth*.
2 Jn 12	I hope . . . to visit you and talk to you ⌐personally (lit. *mouth* to *mouth*),
3 Jn 14	I hope to see you soon and talk to you ⌐personally (lit. *mouth* to *mouth*).
Jude 16	[the false teachers,] with *mouths* full of boastful talk,
Rv 13 5	(Dn 7 8) the beast was allowed to *mouth* its boasts
6	it ⌐mouthed its (lit. opened its *mouth* in) blasphemies against God,

Rv 14 5	[The companions of the Lamb] never allowed a lie to pass their *lips* and no fault can be found in them.

2: FORCE TO SPEAK, or negatively, SILENCE

Lk 11 53	2 the Pharisees began . . . to *force answers* from [Jesus]
Tt 1 11	3 [the false teachers] have got to be *silenced*:

3: MOUTH (GENERALLY)

Mt 15 11	What goes into the *mouth* does not make a man unclean; it is what comes out of the mouth that makes him unclean . . .
17	whatever goes into the *mouth* passes through the stomach . . . [18] But the things that come out of the mouth come from the heart,
Jn 19 29	they held [a sponge soaked in vinegar] up to [Jesus's] *mouth*.
Ac 11 8	nothing profane or unclean has ever crossed my *lips*.
Rv 1 16	[I saw a figure like a Son of man.] Out of his *mouth* came a sharp sword, double-edged,
2 16	I shall soon come to you and attack these people with the sword out of my *mouth*.
3 16	since you are neither [cold nor hot] . . . I will spit you out of my *mouth*.
10 9	(Ezk 3 3) in your *mouth* [the scroll] will taste as sweet as honey. [10] . . . I . . . swallowed it; it was as sweet as honey in my *mouth*,
10	
11 5	Fire can come from [my two witnesses'] *mouths* and consume their enemies
16 13	from the ⌐jaws of dragon and beast and false prophet (lit. mouth of dragon, the mouth of beast, and the *mouth* of false prophet) I saw three foul spirits come;
19 15	From [the] *mouth* [of The Word of God] came a sharp sword
21	All the rest were killed by the sword of the rider, which came out of his *mouth*,

4: MOUTHS OF CREATURES – THE MOUTH OF THE EARTH

Mt 17 27	take the first fish . . . open its *mouth* and there you will find a shekel.
2 Tm 4 17	I was rescued from the lion's *mouth*.
Heb 11 33	These were men who through faith . . . could keep a lion's *mouth* shut,
Jm 3 3	Once we put a bit into the horse's *mouth*,
Rv 9 17	the horses had lions' heads, and fire, smoke and sulphur were coming out of their *mouths*. [18] . . . by these three plagues . . . coming out of their *mouths* . . . one third of the human race was killed. [19] All the horses' power was in their *mouths*
18	
19	
12 15	the serpent vomited water from his *mouth*, like a river . . .
16	[16] but the earth . . . opened its *mouth* and swallowed the river thrown up by the dragon's *jaws*.
13 2	the beast was like a leopard, with . . . a *mouth* like a ⌐lion (lit. lion's *mouth*);
16 13 Ⓓ	from the ⌐jaws of dragon and beast and false prophet (lit. *mouth* of dragon, the *mouth* of beast, and the mouth of false prophet) I saw three foul spirits come;

2. LIPS: *CHEILOS*

cheilos 6/7

Mt 15 8	(Is 29 13) This people honours me only with *lip*-service, while their hearts are far from me.
Mk 7 6	(Is 29 13) This people honours me only with *lip*-service, while their hearts are far from me.
Rm 3 13	(Ps 140 4) Vipers' venom is on their *lips*,
1 Co 14 21	(Is 28 11) through the *lips* of foreigners I shall talk to the nation,
Heb 13 15	(Is 57 19) let us offer God . . . a ⌐verbal sacrifice (or: tribute of *lips*) that is offered every time we acknowledge his name.
1 P 3 10	(Ps 34 14) Anyone who wants to have a happy life . . . must banish . . . deceitful conversation from his *lips*;

3. TONGUE – LANGUAGE – LICK

1: TONGUE – LANGUAGE: *GLŌSSA*

1 *glōssa* 50   2 (*hetero-*)*glōssos* 1

a) Tongue, especially as an organ of speech

Mk 7 33	[Jesus] took [the deaf man who had an impediment in his speech] aside . . . and touched his *tongue* with spittle
35	

Mk	7 35	. . . ³⁵ . . . the ligament of his *tongue* was loosened and he spoke clearly.

Mk 7 35 . . . ³⁵ . . . the ligament of his *tongue* was loosened and he spoke clearly.

Lk 1 64 [Zechariah's] ┌power of speech returned (lit. mouth and his *tongue* were opened) and he spoke

16 24 send Lazarus to . . . cool my *tongue*,

Ac 2 3 something appeared to [the apostles] that seemed like *tongues* of fire;

26 my *tongue* cried out with joy;

Rm 3 13 (Ps 5 10) Their throats are yawning graves; their *tongues* are full of deceit.

14 11 (Is 45 23) every *tongue* shall praise God.

1 Co 14 9 if your *tongue* does not produce intelligible speech, how can anyone know what you are saying?

Ph 2 11 every *tongue* should acclaim Jesus Christ as Lord,

Jm 1 26 Nobody must imagine that he is religious while . . . not keeping control over his *tongue*;

3 5 So is the *tongue* only a tiny part of the body,

6 the *tongue* is a flame . . . Among all the parts of the body, the *tongue* is a whole wicked world in itself:

8 nobody can tame the *tongue*

1 P 3 10 Anyone who wants to have a happy life . . . must banish malice from his *tongue*, deceitful conversation from his lips;

1 Jn 3 18 our love is not to be just words or mere *talk*, but something real and active.

Rv 16 10 Men were biting their *tongues* for pain,

b) Language – (Gift of) Tongues, (Speak with) Tongues

P = Speak with tongues // Prophesy

Mk 16 17 P [believers] will ┌have the gift of (or: speak in new) *tongues*;

Ac 2 4 They . . . all . . . began to speak foreign *languages*

11 we hear them preaching in our own *language* about the marvels of God.

10 46 they could hear them speaking strange *languages* and proclaiming the greatness of God.

19 6 P they began to speak with *tongues* and to prophesy.

1 Co 12 10 P [the Spirit gives] one, the power of miracles; another, prophecy . . . another [the gift of] *tongues* and another the ability to interpret ┌them (lit. the *tongues*).

28 God has given . . . the second [place] to prophets, . . . after them . . . those with many *languages*. ²⁹ . . . Are

30 . . . all of them prophets . . .?³⁰ . . . Do all speak strange *languages*, and all interpret them?

13 1 If I ┌have all the eloquence (lit. speak with the *tongues*) of men or of angels, but speak without love, I am simply a gong booming

8 gifts of prophecy . . . must fail; . . . the gift of *languages* . . . will not continue for ever;

14 2 P Anybody ┌with the gift of (or: who speaks with) *tongues* speaks to God . . . ³ . . . the man who prophesies does

4 P talk to other people . . . ⁴ The one ┌with the gift of (or: who speaks with) *tongues* talks for his own benefit, but the man who prophesies does so for the benefit of the

5 community. ⁵ While I should like you all to ┌have the gift

P of (or: speak with) *tongues*, I would much rather you could prophesy, since the man who prophesies is of greater

P importance than the man ┌with the gift of (or: who speaks with) *tongues*, unless of course the latter offers an interpretation

6 Now suppose . . . I am someone ┌with the gift of (or: who

P speaks with) *tongues*,

13 P anybody who ┌has the gift of (or: speaks with) *tongues*

14 must pray for the power of interpreting them. ¹⁴ For if

P I ┌use this gift (lit. speak with *tongues*) in my prayers, my spirit may be praying but my mind is left barren.

18 P I have a greater gift of *tongues* than all of you, ¹⁹ but . . . I

19 would rather say five words that mean something than ten

P thousand words in a *tongue*.

21 2 (Is 28 11) Through men speaking strange *languages* and through the lips of foreigners, I shall talk to the nation,

22 the strange *languages* are meant to be a sign . . . for unbelievers,

23 any uninitiated people . . . coming into a meeting . . .

P where everybody was speaking in *tongues*, would say you were all mad;

26 let everyone be ready with . . . a revelation, or ready to use

P his gift of *tongues*

27 P If there are people present with the gift of *tongues*, let only two or three, at the most, be allowed to use it,

39 be ambitious to prophesy, do not suppress the gift of *tongues*;

Rv 5 9 you bought men . . . of every race, *language*, people and nation

7 9 people from every nation, race, tribe and *language*;

10 11 You are to prophesy again . . . about many different nations and countries and *languages*

11 9 Men out of every people, race, *language* and nation will stare at [the two witnesses'] corpses,

13 7 [the beast was] given power over every race, people, *language* and nation;

Rv 14 6 announce the Good News of eternity to . . . every nation, race, *language* and tribe.

17 15 The waters . . . are all the peoples, the populations, the nations and the *languages*.

2: LICK: *EPI-LEICHŌ*

epi-leichō 1

Lk 16 21 Dogs even came and *licked* [Lazarus's] sores.

4. TOOTH – GRINDING (ONE'S) TEETH – BITE

1: TOOTH – GRINDING (ONE'S) TEETH: *ODOUS, BRYCHŌ* and *TRIZŌ*

3 brychō 1   1 odous 12   4 trizō 1
2 brygmos 7

Mt 5 38 (Ex 21 24) it was said: Eye for eye and *tooth* for *tooth*.

8 12 the subjects of the kingdom will be turned out into the dark,

2/ where there will be weeping and *grinding* of *teeth*.

13 42 throw them into the blazing furnace, where there will be

2/ weeping and *grinding* of *teeth*.

50 throw them into the blazing furnace where there will be

2/ weeping and *grinding* of *teeth*.

22 13 throw him out into the dark, where there will be weeping and

2/ *grinding* of *teeth*.

24 51 send him to the same fate as the hypocrites, where there

2/ will be weeping and *grinding* of *teeth*.

25 30 throw him out into the dark, where there will be weeping and

2/ *grinding* of *teeth*.

Mk 9 18 4/ [my son] foams at the mouth and *grinds* his *teeth* and goes rigid.

Lk 13 28 2/ there will be weeping and *grinding* of teeth, when you see . . . yourselves turned outside.

Ac 7 54 3/ They were infuriated . . . and *ground* their *teeth* at [Stephen].

Rv 9 8 [the locusts had] *teeth* like lions' [teeth].

2: BITE – SNAP AT – GNAW

a) Bite – Snap at: daknō

daknō 1

Ga 5 15 If you go *snapping at* each other and tearing each other to pieces, you had better watch

b) Bite – Gnaw: masaomai

masaomai 1

Rv 16 10 Men were *biting* their tongues for pain,

3: IVORY: *ELEPHANTINOS*

elephantinos 1

Rv 18 12 there is nobody left to buy their cargoes of . . . sandalwood, every piece of *ivory* or fine wood,

5. THROAT: *LARYNX*

larynx 1

Rm 3 13 (Ps 5 10) Their *throats* are yawning graves; their *tongues* are full of deceit.

MUST – OUGHT TO

1. **Must, Have to – Should, Ought to – Necessary:** *dēi*
2. **Must – Should, Ought to – Duty:** *chrē*
3. **Must, Have to:** *echō*
4. **Must, Have to – Ought to, Owe – Duty, Debt:** *opheilō*
   1: **Must, Have to – Ought to, Should – Duty, Obliged (to)**
2. **Debt, Debtor – Owe, Due – Have a right to**
5. **Must, Have to, Obliged (to) – Necessary, Essential, Indispensable – Force (to), Compel (to), Make (to):** *anankaios*
6. **Force (to), Compel (to) – Press into service:** *angareuō*
7. **Necessities, (Things) Needed:** *epi-tēdeios*

1. MUST, HAVE TO – SHOULD, OUGHT TO – NECESSARY:
DĒI
dei 104

Mt 16 21 X	Jesus began to make it clear . . . that he ʳwas destined to (lit. *had to*) . . . be put to death
17 10	Elijah *has to* come first
18 33	*Were you not bound*, then, *to* have pity on your fellow servant . . .?
23 23	These you *should* have practised, without neglecting the others.
24 6	You will hear of wars . . . this is something that *must* happen,
25 27	you *should* have deposited my money with the bankers,
26 35	Even if I *have to* die with you, I will never disown you.
54	how would the scriptures be fulfilled that say this is the way it *must* be?
Mk 8 31 X	the Son of Man ʳwas destined to (lit. *had to*) suffer grievously.
9 11	Elijah *has to* come first
13 7	you hear of wars . . . this is something that *must* happen,
10	the Good News *must* first be proclaimed to all the nations.
14	you see the disastrous abomination set up where it *ought* not to be
14 31	If I *have to* die with you, I will never disown you.
Lk 2 49 X	Did you not know that I *must* be busy with my Father's affairs?
4 43 X	I *must* proclaim the Good News . . . to the other towns too,
9 22 X	The Son of Man . . . ʳis destined to (lit. *must*) suffer grievously,
11 42	These you *should* have practised, without leaving the others undone.
12 12	when the time comes, the Holy Spirit will teach you what you *must* say.
13 14	There are six days . . . when work ʳis to (lit. *ought to*) be done.
16	ʳis it not right to untie her bonds (lit. *should* her bonds not have been untied) on the sabbath day?
33 X	the next day I *must* go on,
15 32	[it was only right] we *should* . . . rejoice, because your brother . . . has come to life;
17 25 X	first [the Son of Man] *must* suffer grievously
18 1	[Jesus] told them a parable about ʳthe need to (lit. how they *ought to*) pray continually
19 5 X	Zacchaeus . . . I *must* stay at your house today.
21 9	you hear of wars and revolutions . . . this is something that *must* happen
22 7	The day of Unleavened Bread came round, the day on which the passover *had to* be sacrificed,
37 X	these words of scripture *have to* be fulfilled in me:
24 7 X	the Son of Man *had to* be handed over into the power of sinful men
26 X	ʳWas it not ordained that the Christ should (lit. *Ought* not the Christ *to*) suffer . . .?
44 X	everything written about me . . . *has to* be fulfilled.
Jn 3 7 X	You *must* be born from above.
14 X	the Son of Man *must* be lifted up
30 X	He *must* grow greater, I [must] grow smaller.
4 4 X	he *had to* cross Samaria.
20	you say that Jerusalem is the place where one *ought to* worship.
24	those who worship *must* worship in spirit and truth.
9 4 X	I *must* carry out the work of the one who sent me;
10 16 X	there are other sheep I have . . . and these I *have to* lead as well.
12 34 X	The Son of Man *must* be lifted up
20 9 X	they had failed to understand the teaching of scripture, that he *must* rise from the dead.
Ac 1 16	scripture *had to* be fulfilled
21	We *must* therefore choose someone who . . . ²² can act with us as a witness to his resurrection.
3 21	[the Christ] whom heaven *must* keep till the universal restoration
4 12	of all the names in the world . . . this is the only one by which we ʳcan (lit. *must*) be saved.
5 29	Obedience to God ʳcomes (lit. *must* come) before obedience to men;
9 6	[Saul], you will be told what you *have to* do.
16	I myself will show [Saul] how much he himself *must* suffer for my name.
14 22	We all *have to* experience many hardships . . . before we enter the kingdom of God.
15 5	certain members . . . who had become believers objected, insisting that the pagans *should* be circumcised
16 30	[The gaoler:] what *must* I do to be saved?
7 3 X	ʳit was ordained that the Christ should (lit. the Christ *ought to*) suffer and rise from the dead.
18 21	(ᵛ It *is* absolutely *necessary* for me to celebrate the next festival in Jerusalem.)
19 21	Paul . . . said, 'I *must* go on to see Rome as well.'
36	[Citizens of Ephesus,] there *is* no *need* for you to get excited
20 35	we *must* exert ourselves to support the weak,
Ac 21 22	ᵛ Inevitably there ʳwill (lit. *must*) be a meeting of the whole body,
23 11	You have borne witness for me in Jerusalem, now you *must* do the same in Rome.
24 19	some Jews from Asia . . . *should* have appeared before you
25 10	I am standing before the tribunal of Caesar and this is where I *should* be tried.
24	[Paul] *ought* not to be allowed to remain alive.
26 9	I once thought ʳit was my duty to (lit. I *had to*) use every means to oppose the name of Jesus the Nazarene.
27 21	ʳif you had (lit. you *should* have) listened to me and not put out from Crete,
24	You ʳare destined to (lit. *must*) appear before Caesar,
26	we ʳare to (lit. *must*) be stranded on some island.
Rm 1 27	men doing shameless things with men and getting ʳan appropriate (lit. the *necessary*) reward for their perversion.
8 26	we cannot choose words in order to pray ʳproperly (lit. as we *should*),
12 3	I want to urge each one . . . not to ʳexaggerate his real importance (lit. think of himself more highly than he *should*)
1 Co 8 2	A man may imagine he understands something, but still not understand anything in the way that he *ought to*,
11 19	there *must* no doubt be separate groups among you,
15 25 X	[Christ] *must* be king until he has put all his enemies under his feet
53	our present perishable nature *must* put on imperishability
2 Co 2 3	I wrote . . . to make sure that . . . I *should* not be distressed by the very people who *should* have made me happy.
5 10	all the truth about us ʳwill (lit. *must*) be brought out in the law court of Christ,
11 30	If I ʳam to (lit. *must*) boast, then let me boast of my own feebleness.
12 1	*Must* I go on boasting . . .? But I will move on to the visions
Ep 6 20	pray that in proclaiming [the mystery of the gospel] I may speak as boldly as I *ought to*.
Col 4 4	pray that I may proclaim [the mystery of Christ] as clearly as I *ought to*.
6	try to fit your answers to the *needs* of each one.
1 Th 4 1	make more and more progress in the kind of life that you ʳare meant to (lit. *ought to*) live:
2 Th 3 7	You know how you *are supposed to* imitate us:
1 Tm 3 2	the president *must* have an impeccable character.
7	It is also *necessary* that people outside the Church should speak well of [the elder-in-charge]
15	ʳI wanted you to know how people ought to (lit. you *ought to* know how people) behave in God's family
5 13	[young widows] go round from house to house . . . to chatter when they *would be better* keeping quiet.
2 Tm 2 6	the working farmer . . . ʳhas (lit. *should* have) the first claim on any crop that is harvested.
24	a servant of the Lord ʳis not to (lit. *must* not) engage in quarrels,
Tt 1 7	[an elder] *must* be irreproachable
11	[False teachers] *have got to* be silenced: men of this kind ruin whole families, by teaching things that they *ought* not to,
Heb 2 1	We *ought*, then, *to* turn our minds . . . to what we have been taught,
9 26 X	[Christ] would *have to* suffer over and over again
11 6	anyone who comes to [God] *must* believe that he exists
1 P 1 6	you may for a short time *have to* bear being plagued by all sorts of trials,
2 P 3 11	you *should* be living holy and saintly lives
Rv 1 1	This is the revelation . . . about the things which ʳare now to (lit. *must* now) take place very soon;
4 1	Come up here: I will show you what ʳis to (lit. *must*) come
10 11	You ʳare to (lit. *must*) prophesy again,
11 5	if anybody does try to harm [my two witnesses] he ʳwill (lit. *must*) certainly be killed
13 10	the sword for those who ʳare to (lit. *must*) die by the sword.
17 10	once here, [the seventh emperor] *must* stay for a short while.
20 3 ⑩	[Satan] *must* be released, but only for a short while.
22 6	the Lord God . . . has sent his angel to reveal to his servants what ʳis soon to (lit. *must* soon) take place.

2. MUST – SHOULD, OUGHT TO – DUTY: *CHRĒ*
1 *chrē* 1   2 *chreia* 1/49

Ac 6 3	select from among yourselves seven men . . .; we will hand over this *duty* to them,
2	
Jm 3 10	the blessing and the curse come out of the same mouth. My brothers, this *must* be wrong

3. MUST, HAVE TO: *ECHŌ*
echō (1)

Lk 12 50 X	There is a baptism I *must* still receive,

4. MUST, HAVE TO – OUGHT TO, OWE – DUTY, DEBT:
OPHEILŌ

3	*opheilē*	3	1	*opheilō*	35
4	*opheilēma*	2	5	*chre-opheiletēs*	2
2	*opheiletēs*	7	6	*pros-opheilō*	1

1: MUST, HAVE TO – OUGHT TO, SHOULD – DUTY, OBLIGED (TO)

Mt 23	16		You . . . say . . . if a man swears by the gold of the Temple,
	18		he *is bound* . . . [18] if a man swears by the offering that is on the altar, he *is bound*.
Lk 17	10		when you have done all you have been told to do, say, '. . . we have done no more than our *duty*'.
Jn 13	14		you *should* wash each other's feet.
	19	7 X	according to that Law he *ought to* die, because he has claimed to be the Son of God.
Ac 17	29		we ⌐have no excuse for thinking (lit. *must* not think) that the deity looks like anything in gold,
Rm 8	12	2	there *is* no *necessity* for us to obey our unspiritual selves
15	1		We who are strong *have a duty to* put up with the qualms of the weak
	27		the pagans who share the spiritual possessions of these poor [saints] *have a duty to* help them with temporal possessions.
1 Co 5	10		you would *have to* withdraw from the world altogether [in order not to associate with people living immoral lives].
7	36		anyone who feels . . . that he *should* do something about [his daughter's marriage] . . . is free to do as he likes:
9	10		the ploughman *ought to* plough in expectation,
11	7		A man *should* certainly not cover his head,
	10		That is the argument for women's ⌐covering (lit. *having to* cover) their heads with a symbol of the authority over them,
2 Co 12	11		you are the ones who *should* have been commending me.
	14		Children ⌐are not expected to (lit. do not *have to*) save up for their parents,
Ga 5	3	2	Everyone who accepts circumcision *is obliged to* keep the whole Law.
Ep 5	28		husband *must* love their wives
2 Th 1	3		we *must* be continually thanking God for you, brothers,
2	13		we *must* be continually thanking God for you, brothers
Heb 2	17	X	[the Son of God] *should* in this way become completely like his brothers.
5	3		[the high priest] *has to* make sin offerings for himself as well as for the people.
	12		you *should* by this time have become masters,
1 Jn 2	6		the one who claims to be living in [God] ⌐is living (lit. *must* live) the same kind of life as Christ lived.
3	16		we, too, *ought to* give up our lives for our brothers.
4	11		since God has loved us so much, we too *should* love one another.
3 Jn	8		It *is* our *duty to* welcome men of this sort

2: DEBT, DEBTOR – OWE, DUE – HAVE A RIGHT TO

Mt 6	12	2/4	forgive us our *debts*, as we have forgive *those who are in debt* to us.
18	24	< 2	they brought [the king] a man who *owed* ten thousand talents;
	28	<	this servant . . . happened to meet a fellow servant who *owed* him one hundred denarii . . . 'Pay what you *owe* me' he said.
	30	<	he had him thrown into prison till he should pay the *debt*.
	32	< 3	You wicked servant . . . I cancelled all that *debt* of yours
	34	<	the master handed him over to the torturers till he should pay all his *debt*.
Lk 7	41	< 5/	a *creditor* . . . had two *men in his debt*; one *owed* him five hundred denarii
11	4		[Father,] forgive us our sins, for we ourselves forgive each one who is in *debt* to us.
13	4	2	those eighteen . . . Do you suppose that ⌐they were more guilty (lit. their *debt* was greater) . . . ?
16	5	< 5	[the steward] called his master's *debtors* one by one. To the first he said, 'How much do you *owe* my master?' . . .
	7	<	[7] To another . . . 'how much do you *owe*?'
Rm 1	14	4	I *owe a duty* to Greeks just as much as to barbarians,
4	4	4	If a man has work to show, his wages are not considered as a favour but as his *due*.
13	7	3	Pay every government official what he *has a right to* ask
	8		Avoid *getting into debt*, except the debt of mutual love.
15	27	2	[Macedonia and Achaia have decided to send a generous contribution] as it should be, since it is really repaying a *debt*:

---

1 Co 7	3	○ 3	The husband must give his wife what she *has the right to* expect,
Phm	18		if [Onesimus] . . . *owes* you anything, then let me pay for it.
	19	6	I will not add any mention of your own *debt* to me,

5. MUST, HAVE TO, OBLIGED (TO) – NECESSARY, ESSENTIAL, INDISPENSABLE – FORCE (TO), COMPEL (TO), MAKE (TO):
ANANKAIOS

3	*anankaios*	8	1	*anankē*	13/18
4	*anankastōs*	1	5	*ep-anankes*	1
2	*anankazō*	9			

Mt 14	22	2	[Jesus] *made* the disciples get into the boat
18	7		Obstacles indeed there *must* be,
Mk 6	45	2	[Jesus] *made* his disciples get into the boat
Lk 14	18		I have bought a piece of land and *must* go and see it.
	23	2	*force* people to come in to make sure my house is full;
23	17		(ᵛ [Pilate] was *under obligation* to release one man for them every feast day.)
Ac 10	24	3	Cornelius . . . had asked his relations and ⌐close (lit. *indispensable*) friends to be there,
13	46	3	We had to proclaim the word of God to you first,
15	28	5	It has been decided . . . not to saddle you with any burden beyond these *essentials*:
26	11	2	I often went round the synagogues inflicting penalties, trying . . . to *force* [the saints] to renounce their faith;
28	19	2	I was *forced* to appeal to Caesar,
Rm 13	5		You *must* obey . . . for conscience' sake.
1 Co 7	37		without any *compulsion* and in complete freedom of choice,
9	16		preaching the gospel . . . is a ⌐duty (lit. *necessity*) which has been laid on me;
12	22	3	the parts of the body that seem to be the weakest . . . are the *indispensable* ones;
2 Co 9	5	3	I have thought it *necessary* to ask these brothers to go on to you ahead of us,
	7		Each one should give what he has decided in his own mind, not grudgingly or because he is *made to*,
12	11	2	I have been talking like a fool, but you *forced* me to do it:
Ga 2	3	2	Titus . . . was not *obliged* to be circumcised.
	14	2	you have no right to *make* the pagans copy Jewish ways.
6	12	2	It is only self-interest that makes them want to *force* circumcision on you
Ph 1	24	3	for me to stay alive in this body is a more urgent *need* for your sake.
2	25	3	It is *essential* . . . to send brother Epaphroditus back to you.
Tt 3	14	3	All our people are to learn to occupy themselves in doing good works for their practical *needs* as well,
Phm	14		it would have been *forcing* your act of kindness,
Heb 7	12		any change in the priesthood *must* mean a change in the Law as well.
	27	X	[the high priest] who would not *need* to offer sacrifices every day,
8	3	3	this [high priest] too *must* have something to offer.
9	16	3	wherever a will is in question, the death of the testator *must* be established;
	23		the heavenly things themselves *have to* be purified by a higher sort of sacrifice
1 P 5	2	4	Be the shepherds of the flock of God . . . not simply ⌐as a duty (lit. [as though] *under obligation*) but gladly,
Jude	3		I have been *forced* to write to you

6. FORCE (TO), COMPEL (TO) – PRESS INTO SERVICE TO: *ANGAREUŌ*
angareuō 3

Mt 5	41		if anyone ⌐orders (lit. *forces*) you to go one mile, go two miles with him.
27	32		[the soldiers] ⌐enlisted [Simon] (lit. *pressed him into service*) to carry [Jesus's] cross.
Mk 15	21		[The soldiers] ⌐enlisted (lit. *pressed into service*) a passer-by, Simon of Cyrene . . . *to* carry [Jesus's] cross.

7. NECESSITIES, (THINGS) NEEDED: *EPI-TĒDEIOS*
epi-tēdeios 1

| Jm 2 | 16 | | without giving them these [bare] *necessities* of life, then what good is [wishing them well]? |

N

NAME – CALL

1. Name: *onoma*
  1: (God's) Name
  2: (Jesus's) Name
  3: Name – Named, (Be) Called
2. Acclaim with a Title – Designate: *pros-agoreuō*
3. Be called: *chrēmatizō*
4. (Be) Called, Named – Call: *legō*
5. Call, (Be) Called: *kaleō*
  1: Call (a name, a title), (Be) Called – (Be) Known as

  2: Consecrated, Dedicated, to (the name of God, of Jesus)
  3: Invoke, Call (up)on (God, Jesus)
  4: Appeal to (Caesar)
  5: (Jesus, God) Calls, Summons – Vocation
  6: (A person) Invites, Summons – Call (together), Convene
6. Call, Call out : *phōneō*
  1: Call (a name, a title)
  2: Call (over, on, out) – Summon, Invite

1. NAME: ONOMA

1	*onoma*	228/231	a:	*en (tō) onomati*	40
2	*onomazō*	10	b:	*epi tō onomati*	13
3	*ep-onomazō*	1	c:	*eis (to) onoma*	14

1: (GOD'S) NAME

Mt 6 9 — pray like this: Our Father . . . may your *name* be held holy,
21 9 a — (Ps 118 26) Blessings on him who comes in the *name* of the Lord!
23 39 — (Ps 118 26) you shall not see me any more until you say:
a — Blessings on him who comes in the *name* of the Lord!
28 19 c — baptise them in the *name* of the Father and of the Son and of the Holy Spirit,
Mk 11 9 a — (Ps 118 26) Blessings on him who comes in the *name* of the Lord!
Lk 1 49 — (Ps 11 9) the Almighty has done great things for me. Holy is his *name*,
11 2 — Say this when you pray: Father, may your *name* be held holy,
13 35 a — (Ps 118 26) Blessings on him who comes in the *name* of the Lord!
19 38 a — (Ps 118 26) Blessings on the King who comes, in the *name* of the Lord!
Jn 5 43 a — I have come in the *name* of my Father and you refuse to accept me; if someone else comes in his own name you will accept him.
10 25 a — The works I do in my Father's *name* are my witness;
12 13 — (Ps 118 26) Blessings on the King of Israel, who comes in
a — the *name* of the Lord.
28 — Father, glorify your *name*! . . . I have glorified it, and I will glorify it again.
17 6 — [Father,] I have made your *name* known to the men
11 a — Holy Father, keep ᵛ those you have given me true to your *name* (G those true to the name you have given me), so
12 — that they may be one like us. ¹² While I was with them, I
a — kept ᵛ those you had given me true to your *name* (G those true to the name you had given me).
26 — I have made your *name* known to them
Ac 15 14 — God . . . arranged to enlist a people for his *name* out of the pagans.
17 — (Am 9 12) all the pagans who are consecrated to my *name*,
Rm 2 24 — (Is 52 5) It is your fault that the *name* of God is blasphemed
9 17 — (Ex 9 16) I raised you up . . . to make my *name* known throughout the world.
15 9 — (Ps 18 50) I shall . . . sing to your *name*.
1 Tm 6 1 — the *name* of God and our teaching are not brought into disrepute.
2 Tm 2 19 — 2/ (Is 26 13 G) All who ⌜call on (or: name) the *name* of the Lord must avoid sin.
Heb 2 12 — (Ps 22 23) I shall announce your *name* to my brothers,
6 10 c — God would not . . . forget . . . the love that you have for his *name*
13 15 — Through him, let us offer God . . . a verbal sacrifice that is offered every time we acknowledge his *name*.
Jm 5 10 a — the prophets . . . spoke in the *name* of the Lord;
Rv 3 12 — I will inscribe on [those who proved victorious] the *name* of my God and the name of the city of my God . . . and my own new name as well.

Rv 11 18 — the time has come . . . for your servants the prophets, for the saints and for all who worship ⌜you (lit. your *name*) . . . to be rewarded.
13 6 — [the beast] mouthed its blasphemies . . . against his *name*, his heavenly Tent
14 1 — all with [the Lamb's] name and his Father's *name* written on their foreheads.
15 4 — Who would not revere and praise your *name*, O Lord?
16 9 — they cursed the *name* of God who had the power to cause such plagues,
22 4 — [his servants] will see him face to face, and his *name* will be written on their foreheads.

2: (JESUS'S) NAME

Mt 1 21 — [Mary] will give birth to a son and you must ⌜name him (lit. call him by the *name* of) Jesus, because he is the one who is to save his people from their sins.
23 — (Is 7 14) The virgin will . . . give birth to a son and they will call him by the *name* of Immanuel, [a name] which means 'God-is-with-us'.
25 — [Mary] gave birth to a son; and [Joseph] ⌜named him (lit. called him by the *name* of) Jesus.
7 22 — many will say to me, 'Lord, Lord, did we not prophesy in your *name*, cast out demons in your *name*, work many miracles in your *name*?'
10 22 — You will be hated by all men on account of my *name*;
12 21 — (Is 42 4 G) in [my servant's] *name* the nations will put their hope.
18 5 b — Anyone who welcomes a little child . . . in my *name* welcomes me.
20 c — where two or three meet in my *name*, I shall be there with them.
19 29 — everyone who has left houses . . . for the sake of my *name* will be repaid a hundred times over,
24 5 b — many will come using my *name* and saying, 'I am the Christ',
9 — you will be hated by all the nations on account of my *name*.
28 19 c — baptise them in the *name* of the Father and of the Son and of the Holy Spirit,
Mk 6 14 — King Herod had heard about [Jesus], since by now his *name* was well-known.
9 37 b — Anyone who welcomes one of these little children in my *name*, welcomes me;
38 — we saw a man who is not one of us casting out devils in
a — your *name*;
39 b — no one who works a miracle in my *name* is likely to speak evil of me.
13 6 b — Many will come using my *name* . . . and they will deceive many.
13 — You will be hated by all men on account of my *name*;
16 17 a — in my *name* [believers] will cast out devils;
Lk 1 31 — You are to . . . bear a son, and you must ⌜name him (lit. call him by the *name* of) Jesus.
2 21 — they ⌜gave him (lit. called him by) the *name* Jesus, [the name] the angel had given him before his conception.
9 48 b — Anyone who welcomes this little child in my *name* welcomes me;
49 a — Master . . . we saw a man casting out devils in your *name*,
10 17 — Lord . . . even the devils submit to us when we use your
a — *name*.
21 8 — Take care not to be deceived . . . because many will come
b — using my *name*
12 — men will . . . bring you before kings and governors because of my *name*
17 — You will be hated by all men on account of my *name*,
24 47 b — in his *name*, repentance . . . would be preached to all the nations,
Jn 1 12 — he gave power to become children of God, to all who believe
c — in the *name* of him
2 23 c — many believed in his *name* when they saw the signs that [Jesus] gave;
3 18 — whoever refuses to believe is condemned already, because
c — he has refused to believe in the *name* of God's only Son.
14 13 a — Whatever you ask for in my *name* I will do,
14 a — If you ask for anything in my *name*, I will do it.
26 a — the Holy Spirit, whom the Father will send in my *name*, will teach you everything
15 16 a — the Father will give you anything you ask him in my *name*.
21 — on ⌜my account (lit. account of my *name*) . . . they will do all this,
16 23 — anything you ask for from the Father he will grant in my
a — *name*.

Jn 16 24 a	Until now you have not asked for anything in my *name*.
26 a	When that day comes you will ask in my *name*;
17 11	Holy Father, keep ᵛ those you have given me true to your name (G those true to the *name* you have given me), so
a	that they may be one like us. ¹² While I was with them, I kept ᵛ those you had given me true to your name (G those
12	
a	true to the *name* you had given me).
20 31	believing [that Jesus is the Christ] you may have life through
a	his *name*.
Ac 2 21	(Jl 3 5) All who call on the *name* of the Lord will be saved.
38 b	every one of you must be baptised in the *name* of Jesus Christ
3 6 a	Peter said, '. . . in the *name* of Jesus Christ the Nazarene, walk!'
16	it is the *name* of Jesus which . . . has brought back the strength of this man . . . It is faith in that *name* that has restored this man to health,
4 7 a	By what power, and by whose *name* have you men done this?
10 a	it was by the *name* of Jesus Christ the Nazarene . . . that this man is able to stand up perfectly healthy . . . ¹² For
12	all [the names] given in the world given to men, this is the only ʳone (lit. *name*) by which we can be saved.
17 b	let us caution them never to speak to anyone in this *name* again. ¹⁸ So [the Sanhedrin] . . . gave them a warning on
18	
b	no account . . . to teach in the *name* of Jesus.
30	[Lord, help your servants] by stretching out your hand to heal . . . through the *name* of your holy servant Jesus.
5 28 b	We gave you a formal warning . . . not to preach in this *name*,
40	[the Sanhedrin] warned [the apostles] not to speak in the
b	*name* of Jesus
41	[the apostles] left . . . glad to have had the honour of suffering humiliation for the sake of the *name*.
8 12	the Good News about the kingdom of God and the *name* of Jesus Christ,
16 c	[the Samaritans] had . . . been baptised in the *name* of the Lord Jesus.
9 14	[Saul] has only come here . . . to arrest everybody who invokes your *name*.
15	this man is my chosen instrument to bring my *name* before pagans and pagan kings and before the people of Israel;
16	I myself will show [Saul] how much he himself must suffer for my *name*.
21	Surely . . . this is the man who organised the attack in Jerusalem against the people who invoke this *name* . . .?
27 a	[Saul] had preached boldly at Damascus in the *name* of Jesus. ²⁸ Saul now started to go round . . . preaching
28	
a	fearlessly in the *name* of the Lord.
10 43	all who believe in Jesus will have their sins forgiven through his *name*.
48 a	[Peter] gave orders for them to be baptised in the *name* of Jesus Christ.
15 26	[Barnabas and Paul] have dedicated their lives to the *name* of our Lord Jesus Christ.
16 18 a	Paul . . . said to the spirit, 'I order you in the *name* of Jesus Christ to leave that woman'.
19 5 c	[the disciples of John at Ephesus] were baptised in the *name* of the Lord Jesus,
13	2/ some itinerant Jewish exorcists tried *pronouncing* the *name* of the Lord Jesus
17	they were all greatly impressed, and the *name* of the Lord Jesus came to be held in great honour.
21 13	[Paul:] I am ready . . . to die . . . for the *name* of the Lord Jesus.
22 16	[Ananias said to Saul:] It is time you were baptised and had your sins washed away while invoking his *name*.
26 9	I once thought it was my duty to use every means to oppose the *name* of Jesus the Nazarene.
Rm 1 5	we received . . . our apostolic mission to preach the obedience of faith . . . in honour of his *name*.
10 13	(Jl 3 5) everyone who calls on the *name* of the Lord will be saved.
15 20	I have . . . made it an unbroken rule never to preach where ʳChrist's name has already been heard (lit. Christ has already been *named*).
2	
1 Co 1 2	all the saints everywhere who ʳpray to (lit. call upon the *name* of) our Lord Jesus Christ;
10	I do appeal to you, brothers, ʳfor the sake (lit. by the *name*) of our Lord Jesus Christ,
5 4 a	you are assembled together in the *name* of the Lord Jesus,
6 11 a	now you have been . . . justified through the *name* of the Lord Jesus Christ and through the Spirit of our God.
Ep 5 20 a	you are giving thanks to God who is our Father in the *name* of our Lord Jesus Christ.
Ph 2 9	God . . . gave him the *name* which is above all other names ¹⁰ so that all beings . . . should bend the knee at the *name*
10 a	
of Jesus	
Col 3 17 a	never say or do anything except in the *name* of the Lord Jesus,
2 Th 1 12	the *name* of our Lord Jesus Christ will be glorified in you and you in him,

2 Th 3 6 a	In the *name* of the Lord Jesus Christ, we urge you, brothers, to keep away from any of the brothers who refuses to work
2 Tm 2 19	2/ (Is 26 13 G) All who ʳcall on (or: *name*) the *name* of the Lord must avoid sin.
Heb 1 4	[the Son] is now as far above the angels as the *title* which he has inherited is higher than their own [name].
Jm 2 7	Aren't [the rich] the ones who insult the honourable *name* to which you have been dedicated?
5 14 a	[the elders] must anoint [the sick] with oil in the *name* of the Lord and pray over him.
1 P 4 14	It is a blessing for you when they insult you for bearing the
a	*name* of Christ,
1 Jn 2 12	my own children, whose sins have already been forgiven through his *name*;
3 23	His commandments are these: that we believe in the *name* of his Son Jesus Christ . . .
5 13 c	you who believe in the *name* of the Son of God may be sure that you have eternal life.
3 Jn 7	It was entirely for the sake of the *name* that [these brothers] set out,
Rv 2 3	[the angel of the church in Ephesus, you] have suffered for my *name* without growing tired.
13	[the angel of the church in Pergamum,] you still hold firmly to my *name*,
3 8	[the angel of the church in Philadelphia,] you have kept my commandments and not disowned my *name*.
12	I will inscribe on [those who prove victorious] . . . my own new *name*
14 1	people, all with [the Lamb's] *name* and his Father's name written on their foreheads.
19 12	the *name* written on him was known only to himself ¹³ . . .
13	He is known by the *name*, The Word of God.
16	On his cloak and on his thigh there was a *name* written: The King of kings and the Lord of lords.

3: NAME – NAMED, (BE) CALLED

Mt 10 2	These are the *names* of the twelve apostles: first, Simon who is called Peter,
41	Anyone who welcomes a prophet ʳbecause he is (lit. who is *called*) a prophet will have a prophet's reward; and anyone
c	who welcomes a holy man ʳbecause he is (lit. who is *called*) a holy man will have a holy man's reward.
c	
42	If anyone gives . . . water to one of these little ones ʳbecause he is (lit. who is *called*) a disciple . . . he will . . . not lose his reward.
c	
27 32	they came across a man from Cyrene, Simon by *name*,
57	there came a rich man of Arimathaea, *called* Joseph,
Mk 3 14	2 [Jesus] appointed twelve (ᵛ whom he *named* apostles);
16	[Jesus] appointed the Twelve: Simon to whom he gave the
17	*name* Peter, ¹⁷ James . . . and John . . . to whom he gave the *name* Boanerges or 'Sons of Thunder';
5 9 ⓓ	'What is your *name*?' Jesus asked. 'My *name* is legion,' answered 'for there are many of us.'
22	one of the synagogue officials came up, Jairus by *name*,
9 41	If anyone gives you a cup of water to drink ʳjust because you belong (lit. in the *name* of your belonging) to Christ . . .
a	he will . . . not lose his reward.
14 32	They came to a small estate *called* Gethsemane,
Lk 1 5	In the days of King Herod . . . there lived a priest *called* Zechariah . . . and he had a wife, Elizabeth by *name*, who was a descendant of Aaron.
13	Elizabeth is to bear you a son and you must ʳname him (lit. call him by the *name*) of John.
26	the angel Gabriel was sent by God to a town in Galilee *called* Nazareth, ²⁷ to a virgin betrothed to a man *named*
27	Joseph . . . and the virgin's *name* was Mary.
59	they were going to call him by the *name* of Zechariah after his father, ⁶⁰ but his mother spoke up, 'No . . . he is to
61	be called John.' ⁶¹ They said to her, 'But no one in your
63	family ʳhas (lit. is called by) that *name*', . . . ⁶³ [Zechariah] wrote, 'His *name* is John'.
2 25	in Jerusalem there was a man *named* Simeon.
5 27	[Jesus] noticed a tax collector, Levi by *name*,
6 13	[Jesus] summoned his disciples and picked out twelve of
14	2/2 them; he *called* them 'apostles': ¹⁴ Simon . . . he *called* Peter
22	Happy are you when people . . . denounce your *name* as criminal, on account of the Son of Man.
8 30 ⓓ	'What is your *name*?' Jesus asked [the demoniac]. 'Legion'
41	now there came a man *named* Jairus . . . an official of the synagogue.
10 20	your *names* are written in heaven.
38	a woman *named* Martha welcomed [Jesus] into her house.
16 20	at [the rich man's] gate there lay a poor man *called* Lazarus,
19 2	a man ʳwhose name was (lit. called by the *name* of) Zacchaeus made his appearance;
23 50	a member of the council arrived, an upright . . . man *named* Joseph.

Lk 24	13	two of [the disciples] were on their way to a village *called* Emmaus,
	18	one of them *called* Cleopas, answered [Jesus],
Jn 1	6	A man came, sent by God. His *name* was John.
3	1	There was one of the Pharisees *called* Nicodemus, a leading Jew,
5	43	I have come in the name of my Father . . . if someone else comes in his own *name* you will accept him.
	a	
10	3	one by one by the *name* of each [the good shepherd] calls his own sheep
18	10	The servant's *name* was Malchus.
Ac 5	1	another man . . . *called* Ananias . . . agreed to sell a property:
	34	One member of the Sanhedrin . . . a Pharisee *called* Gamaliel . . . stood up
8	9	a man *called* Simon had . . . practised magic arts
9	10	A disciple *called* Ananias . . . lived in Damascus
	11	ask . . . for someone *called* Saul, who comes from Tarsus.
	12	At this moment he is praying, 12 having had a vision of a man *called* Ananias . . . laying hands on him
	33	[At Lydda Peter] found a man *called* Aeneas, a paralytic who had been bedridden for eight years.
	36	At Jaffa there was a woman disciple *called* Tabitha, or Dorcas in Greek.
10	1	One of the centurions of the Italica cohort stationed in Caesarea was *called* Cornelius.
11	28	[some prophets came down to Antioch,] one of them whose *name* was Agabus . . . stood up and predicted
12	13	[Peter] knocked at the outside door and a servant *called* Rhoda came to answer it.
13	6	at Paphos they came in contact with a Jewish magician *called* Bar-jesus.
	8	Elymas Magos – as ⌐he was called (lit. the *name* means) in Greek – tried to stop them
16	1	[In Lystra] there was a disciple *called* Timothy,
	14	One of these women was *called* Lydia . . . She listened to us,
17	34	some . . . became believers, among them Dionysius the Areopagite and a woman *called* Damaris and others besides.
18	2	[Paul went to Corinth,] where he met a Jew *called* Aquila
	7	[Paul] moved to the house next door that belonged to a worshipper of God *called* Justus.
	15	if it is only quibbles about words and *names*, and about your own Law, then you must deal with it yourselves
	24	An Alexandrian Jew *named* Apollos . . . arrived in Ephesus.
19	24	A silversmith *called* Demetrius . . . employed a large number of craftsmen
20	9	a young man *called* Eutychus . . . fell to the ground three floors below.
21	10	a prophet *called* Agabus arrived from Judaea
27	1	Paul . . . [was] handed over to a centurion *called* Julius, of the Augustan cohort.
28	7	there were estates belonging to the prefect of the island [of Malta], whose *name* was Publius.
Rm 2	17	3 If you ⌐call yourself a (or: *bear the name* of] Jew [then why not teach yourself as well as the others?]
1 Co 1	13 c	Were you baptised in the *name* of Paul? 14 I am thankful that I never baptised any of you after Crispus and Gaius
	15 c	15 so none of you can say he was baptised in my *name*.
5	11	2 you should not associate with someone who is *called* a brother Christian who is leading an immoral life,
Ep 1	21	far above every Sovereignty, Authority . . . or any other *name* that can be *named*,
	O /2	
3	15	from [the Father] every family, whether spiritual or natural, 2 ⌐takes its name (lit. is *named*):
5	3	Among you ⌐there must be not even a mention of (lit. must 2 not even be *named*) fornication or impurity
Ph 2	9	God . . . gave him the name which is above all other *names*
4	3	Clement and the others who worked with me. Their *names* are written in the book of life.
1 P 4	16	if anyone of you should suffer for being a Christian, then . . . he should thank God that he has been *called* one.
3 Jn	15	greetings from your friends; greet each of our friends by *name*.
Rv 2	17	a stone with a new *name* written on it, known only to the man who receives it.
3	1	you are ⌐reputed to be alive (lit. alive in *name*) and yet are dead.
	5	I shall not blot [the] *names* [of those who prove victorious] out of the book of life, but acknowledge their *names* in the presence of my Father and his angels.
	12	I will inscribe on [those who prove victorious] . . . the *name* of the city of my God,
6	8	[the] rider [on the deathly pale horse] was *called* Plague,
8	11	this was the star called by the *name* Wormwood,
9	11 ⅅ	the angel of the Abyss, whose *name* in Hebrew is Abaddon, ⅅ or Apollyon as the *name* is in Greek.
13	1	I saw a beast . . . and its heads were marked with blasphemous *titles*.
	8	all people of the world will worship [the beast], that is, everybody whose *name* has not been written down . . . in the book of life of the sacrificial Lamb.

Rv 13	17	[the beast] made it illegal for anyone to buy or sell anything unless he had been branded with the *name* of the beast or with the number of its *name*.
14	11	There will be no respite . . . for those who worshipped the beast or . . . accepted branding with its *name*.
15	2	those who had fought against the beast and won, and against his statue and the number which is his *name*.
17	3	I saw . . . a scarlet beast which . . . had blasphemous *titles* written all over it.
	5	on [the woman's] forehead was written a [name,] cryptic *name*: Babylon the Great,
	8	the people of the world, whose *names* have not been written . . . in the book of life, will think [the beast] miraculous
21	12	over the [twelve] gates were written the *names* of the twelve tribes of Israel;
	14	each one of [the twelve foundation stones] bore the *name* of one of the twelve apostles of the Lamb.

2. ACCLAIM WITH A TITLE – DESIGNATE: *PROS-AGOREUŌ*

pros-agoreuō 1

Heb 5	10	[Jesus] was ⌐acclaimed by God *with the title* of (or: *designated by God*) high priest

3. BE CALLED: *CHRĒMATIZŌ*

chrēmatizō 2/9

Ac 11	26	It was at Antioch that the disciples *were* first *called* 'Christians'.
Rm 7	3	if [the wife] gives herself to another man while her husband is still alive, she *is* legally *called* an adulteress;

4. (BE) CALLED, NAMED – CALL: *LEGŌ*

1 *legō 55/2365*   2 *epi-legō 1*

Mt 1	16	of [Mary] was born Jesus who is *called* Christ.
2	23	[Joseph] settled in a town *called* Nazareth.
4	18	[Jesus] saw two brothers, Simon, who was *called* Peter, and . . . Andrew;
9	9	a man *named* Matthew
10	2	Simon who is *called* Peter,
13	55	Is not his mother the woman *called* Mary . . . ?
26	3	the high priest, ⌐whose name was (lit. who was *called*) Caiaphas,
	14	one of the Twelve, the man *called* Judas Iscariot,
	36	Jesus came . . . to a small estate *called* Gethsemane;
27	16	a notorious prisoner ⌐whose name was (lit. who was *called*) Barabbas.
	17	Jesus who is *called* Christ
	22	what am I to do with Jesus who is *called* Christ?
	33	they had reached a place *called* Golgotha, that is, *called* the place of the skull,
Mk 10	18	Jesus said to [the rich man], 'Why do you *call* me good?'
12	37	David himself *calls* him Lord (Ps 110 1)
15	7	a man *called* Barabbas was then in prison
	12	the man you *call* king of the Jews
Lk 18	19	Jesus said to [the rich aristocrat], 'Why do you *call* me good?'
20	37	Moses . . . *calls* the Lord the God of Abraham, (Ex 3 6)
22	1	The feast of Unleavened Bread, *called* the Passover, was now drawing near,
	47	a number of men appeared, and at the head of them the man *called* Judas,
Jn 4	5	[Jesus] came to the Samaritan town *called* Sychar,
	25	Messiah – ⌐that is, (or: who is *called*) Christ – is coming;
5	2	at the Sheep ᵛ Pool in Jerusalem there is a building *called* 2 (G [Gate) in Jerusalem there is a pool *called*) Bethzatha in Hebrew,
	18 X	[Jesus] *spoke of* God *as* his own Father,
9	11	The man *called* Jesus . . . made a paste,
10	35	the Law *uses the word* gods *of* those to whom the word of God was addressed,
11	16	Thomas – *known as* the Twin – said to the other disciples, 'Let us go too, and die with him'.
	54	Jesus . . . left the district for a town *called* Ephraim,
15	15	I shall not *call* you servants any more . . . I *call* you friends,
19	13	Pilate . . . seated himself on the chair of judgement at a place *called* the Pavement,
	17	[Jesus] went . . . to the place *called* [that] of the skull or, as it was in Hebrew, Golgotha,
20	24	Thomas, *called* the Twin, who was one of the Twelve, was not with them when Jesus came.
21	2	Simon Peter, Thomas *called* the Twin . . . were together.
Ac 3	2	the Temple entrance *called* the Beautiful Gate
6	9	the synagogue *called* the Synagogue of Freedmen,

Ac	9	36	a woman disciple whose name was Tabitha, or Dorcas as she was *called* in Greek,
	10	28	I must not *call* anyone profane or unclean.
	24	14	the Way which they ˹*describe as* (or: *call*) a sect
1 Co	8	5	even if there were things *called* gods, either in the sky or on earth [still for us there is one God]
Ep	2	11	you . . . were pagans physically, *termed* the Uncircumcised by those who *speak of* themselves as the Circumcision
Col	4	11	Jesus *called* Justus adds his greetings.
2 Th	2	4	This is the Enemy, the one who claims to be so much greater than all that men *call* 'god',
Heb	7	11	a new priesthood . . . not ˹*counted* as being (lit. to be *called*) 'of the same order as' Aaron
	9	2	a tent which . . . was *called* the Holy Place;
		3	beyond the second veil, an innermost part which was *called* the Holy of Holies
	11	24	Moses refused to be *known as* the son of Pharaoh's daughter
Rv	2	2	the impostors who *called* themselves apostles and proved they were liars,
		9	the people who ˹*profess to be* (lit. *call* themselves) Jews but are really members of the synagogue of Satan,
	3	9	those who ˹*profess to be* (lit. *call* themselves) Jews, but are liars,
	8	11	this was the star *called* by the name Wormwood,

5. CALL, (BE) CALLED: *KALEŌ*

1	kaleō	146	2	epi-kaleō	30
4	klēsis	11	7	meta-kaleomai	4
5	klētos	11	3	pros-kaleomai	29
8	anti-kaleō	1	6	syn-kaleō	8
9	eis-kaleomai	1			

1: CALL (A NAME, A TITLE), (BE) CALLED – (BE) KNOWN AS

Mt	1	21	[Mary] will give birth to a son and you must ˹*name* him (lit. *call* him by the name of) Jesus,
		23	(Is 7 14) The virgin will . . . give birth to a son and they will *call* him [by the name of] Immanuel,
		25	she gave birth to a son; and [Joseph] ˹*named* him (lit. *called* him by the name of) Jesus.
	2	23	He will be *called* a Nazarene.
	5	9	Happy the peacemakers: they shall be *called* sons of God.
		19	the man who infringes even one of the least of these commandments . . . will be ˹*considered* (or: *called*) the least . . . the man who keeps them and teaches them will be ˹*considered* (or: *called*) great in the kingdom of heaven.
	10	25	2 If they have *called* the master of the house Beelzebul, what will they not say of his household?
	21	13	(Is 56 7) my house will be *called* a house of prayer;
	22	43	how is it . . . that David . . . *calls* him Lord,
		45	If David can *call* him Lord, then how can he be his son?
	23	7	[The Pharisees like] having people *call* them Rabbi.
		8	You, however, must not allow yourselves to be *called* Rabbi,
		9	*call* no one on earth your father,
		10	Nor must you allow yourselves to be *called* teachers,
	27	8	the field is *called* the Field of Blood today.
Mk	11	17	(Is 56 7) My house will be *called* a house of prayer;
Lk	1	13	a son and you must ˹*name* him (lit. *call* him by the name of) John.
		31	You are to . . . bear a son, and you must ˹*name* him (lit. *call* him by the name of) Jesus.
		32	He . . . will be *called* Son of the Most High.
		35	the child . . . will be *called* Son of God.
		36	Elizabeth . . . herself conceived . . . she whom people *called* barren
		59	they were going to *call* him by the name of Zechariah after his father, ⁶⁰ but his mother spoke up. 'No . . . . he is to be *called* John.' ⁶¹ They said to her, 'But no one in your family ˹*has* (lit. is *called* by) that name', ⁶² and made signs to his father to find out what he wanted him *called*.
		60	
		61	
		62	
		76	And you, little child, you shall be *called* Prophet of the Most High,
	2	4	Joseph . . . travelled up to Judaea, to the town of David *called* Bethlehem,
		21	they ˹*gave* him (lit. *called* him by) the name Jesus, [the name] the angel had ˹*given* him (lit. *called* him by) before his conception.
		23	(cf. Ex 13 2) Every first-born male must be *called* consecrated to the Lord
	6	15	Simon *called* the Zealot,
		46	Why do you *call* me, 'Lord, Lord' and not do what I say?
	7	11	[Jesus] went to a town *called* Nain,
	8	2	Mary sur*named* the Magdalene
	9	10	[Jesus] withdrew to a town *called* Bethsaida
	10	39	[Martha] had a sister *called* Mary,
	15	19	I no longer deserve to be *called* your son;

Lk	15	21	I no longer deserve to be *called* your son.
	19	2	a man ˹whose name was (lit. *called* by the name of) Zacchaeus
		29	close by the Mount of Olives as it is *called*,
	20	44	David here *calls* him Lord;
	21	37	[Jesus] would spend the night on the hill *called* the Mount of Olives.
	22	3	Satan entered into Judas, sur*named* Iscariot,
		25	those who have authority over them are *given the title* Benefactor.
	23	33	they reached the place *called* The Skull,
Jn	1	42	You are Simon son of John; you are to be *called* Cephas
Ac	1	12	from the Mount of Olives, as it is *called*, [the apostles] went back to Jerusalem,
		19	the field came to be *called* the Bloody Acre, in their language Hakeldama.
		23	/2 Joseph *known as* Barsabbas, whose *surname* was Justus,
	3	11	Everyone came running . . . to the Portico of Solomon, as it is *called*,
	4	36	2 Joseph whom the apostles sur*named* Barnabas
	7	58	a young man *called* Saul.
	8	10	[Simon the magician] is the divine power that is *called* Great.
	9	11	You must go to ˹Straight Street (lit. the street that is *called* Straight)
	10	1	One of the centurions of ˹the Italica cohort (lit. the cohort *called* the Italica) . . . was called Cornelius.
		5	2 fetch [a man named] Simon, ˹*known as* (or: *called*) Peter,
		18	2 calling out to know if the Simon *known as* Peter was lodging there,
		32	2 send to Jaffa and fetch Simon *known as* Peter
	11	13	2 Send to Jaffa and fetch Simon *known as* Peter;
	12	12	2 Mary the mother of John sur*named* Mark,
		25	Barnabas and Saul . . . came back from Jerusalem, bringing 2 John sur*named* Mark with them.
	13	1	Simeon *called* Niger,
	14	12	They *addressed* Barnabas *as* Zeus, and . . . Paul [they called] Hermes.
	15	22	Judas *known as* Barsabbas
		37	John *called* Mark,
	27	8	we came to a place *called* Fair Havens,
		14	it was not long before a hurricane, the 'north-easter' as they *call* it, burst on them
		16	a small island *called* Cauda
	28	1	we discovered that the island was *called* Malta.
Rm	9	7	(Gn 21 12) through Isaac . . . will be carried on the line to be *called* yours,
		25	(Ho 2 25) I shall ˹say to (lit. *call*) a people that was not mine, '[You are] my people',
		26	(Ho 2 1) Instead of being told, 'You are no people of mine', they . . . will now be *called* the sons of the living God.
1 Co	15	9	I hardly deserve ˹the name (lit. to be *called* an) apostle;
Heb	2	11	[Christ] openly *calls* them brothers
	3	13	Every day, as long as this 'today' ˹lasts (lit. is still *called* 'today'), keep encouraging one another
	11	16	2 God is not ashamed to be *called* their God,
		18	(Gn 21 12) It is through Isaac that ˹your name (lit. the line to be *called* yours) will be carried on.
Jm	2	23	Abraham . . . was *called* 'the friend of God'.
1 P	1	17	2 If you are ˹*acknowledging as* (or: *calling*) your Father one who has no favourites . . . you must be scrupulously careful
	3	6	Sarah . . . was obedient to Abraham, and *called* him her lord.
1 Jn	3	1	Think of the love that the Father has lavished on us, by letting us be *called* God's children;
Rv	1	9	I was on the island *called* Patmos.
	11	8	the Great City *known by the* symbolic *names* Sodom and Egypt,
	12	9	The great dragon, the primeval serpent, *known as* the devil or Satan,
	16	16	They called the kings together at the place *called*, in Hebrew, Armageddon.
	19	11	a white horse . . . its rider was *called* Faithful and True;
		13	He is *known by the name*, The Word of God.

2: CONSECRATED, DEDICATED, TO (THE NAME OF GOD, OF JESUS)

| Ac | 15 | 17 | 2 (Am 9 12) all the pagans who are *consecrated to* my name, |
| Jm | 2 | 7 | Aren't [the rich] the ones who insult the honourable name *to* 2 which you have been *dedicated*? |

3: INVOKE, CALL (UP)ON (GOD, JESUS)

Ac	2	21	2 (Jl 3 5) All who *call on* the name of the Lord will be saved.
	7	59	2 Stephen *said in invocation*, 'Lord Jesus, receive my spirit'.
	9	14	[Saul] has only come here . . . to arrest everybody who 2 *invokes* your name.
		21	Surely . . . this is the man who organised the attack in 2 Jerusalem against the people who *invoke* this name,

Ac 22 16	2	It is time you . . . had your sins washed away while *invoking* his name.
Rm 10 12		all belong to the same Lord who is rich enough, however
	2	many ʳask his help (lit. *call on* him),
13	2	(Jl 3 5) everyone who *calls on* the name of the Lord will be saved.
14	2	But they will not ʳask his help (lit. *call on* him) unless they believe in him,
1 Co 1 2	2	all the saints everywhere who ʳpray to (lit. *call upon* the name of) our Lord Jesus Christ;
2 Co 1 23	2	By my life I *call* God to witness . . . the reason . . . I did not come to Corinth.
2 Tm 2 22	2	all those who *call on* the Lord with pure minds.

4: APPEAL TO (CAESAR)

Ac 25 11	2	I *appeal* to Caesar.
12	2	You have *appealed* to Caesar; to Caesar you shall go.
21	2	Paul *put in an appeal* for his case to be reserved for the judgement of the august emperor,
25	2	[Paul] himself *appealed* to the august emperor
26 32	2	The man could have been set free if he had not *appealed* to Caesar.
28 19	2	I was forced to *appeal* to Caesar,

5: (JESUS, GOD) CALLS, SUMMONS – VOCATION

Mt 2 15		(Ho 11 1) I *called* my son out of Egypt.
4 21		James son of Zebedee and his brother John . . . [Jesus] *called* them.
9 13		I did not come to *call* the virtuous, but sinners.
10 1	3	[Jesus] *summoned* his twelve disciples,
15 10	3	He *called* the people to him and said, 'Listen, and understand.'
32	3	Jesus *called* his disciples . . . and said, 'I feel sorry for all these people;'
18 2	3	he *called* a little child to him
20 16 <	5	(ᵛ for many are *called*, but few [are] chosen)
25	3	Jesus *called* [the other ten disciples] to him and said,
22 14 <	5	For many are *called*, but few [are] chosen.
Mk 1 20		[Jesus saw James and John.] He *called* them at once
2 17		I did not come to *call* the virtuous, but sinners.
3 13	3	He . . . *summoned* those he wanted.
23	3	he *called* [the scribes] to him and spoke to them in parables,
6 7	3	he *summoned* the Twelve and began to send them out in pairs
7 14	3	He *called* the people to him again and said, 'Listen to me, all of you,'
8 1	3	he *called* his disciples to him and said to them, ² 'I feel sorry for all these people;'
34	3	He *called* the people and his disciples to him and said,
10 42	3	Jesus *called* [the other ten disciples] to him and said
12 43	3	Then he *called* his disciples and said to them,
Lk 5 32		I have not come to *call* the virtuous, but sinners
9 1	6	He *called* the Twelve *together* and gave them . . . authority over all devils
14 7		He then told ʳthe guests (lit. those *invited*) a parable,
18 16		Jesus *called* the children to him and said, 'Let the little children come to me,'
Jn 2 2		Jesus and his disciples had also been *invited* [to the wedding at Cana].
Ac 2 39	3	The promise . . . was made . . . for all those who are far away, for all those whom the Lord . . . will *call* to himself.
13 2	3	I want Barnabas and Saul set apart for the work to which I have *called* them.
16 10	3	we lost no time . . . convinced that God had *called* us to bring [the Macedonians] the Good News.
Rm 1 1	5	Paul . . . has been *called* to be an apostle, and specially chosen to preach the Good News
6	5	by his *call* [you] belong to Jesus Christ
7	5	you . . . who are God's beloved in Rome, *called* to be saints,
4 17		God . . . *calls* into being what does not exist.
8 28	5	all those that [God] has *called* according to his purpose.
30		He *called* those he intended for this; those he *called* he justified,
9 12		[God's choice is free,] since it depends on the one who *calls*, not on human merit,
24		whether we are Jews or pagans we are the ones he has *called*.
11 29	4	God never takes back his gifts or revokes his ʳchoice (lit. *calling*).
1 Co 1 1	5	Paul, ʳappointed (or: *called*) by God to be an apostle,
2	5	to [those] . . . who are *called* to take their place among all the saints
9		God by *calling* you has joined you to his Son,
24	5	to those who have been *called*, whether they are Jews or Greeks, a Christ who is the power . . . of God.
26	4	Take yourselves for instance, brothers, at the time when you were *called*:
7 15		God has *called* you to a life of peace.
17		each one . . . should continue as he was when God's *call* reached him.

1 Co 7 18		If anyone had already been circumcised at the time of his *call*, he need not disguise it, and anyone who was uncircumcised at the time of his *call* need not be circumcised;
20	4	Let everyone stay ʳas he was (lit. in the *vocation* that was his) at the time of his call. ²¹ If, when you were *called*,
21		you were a slave, do not let this bother you . . . ²² A slave,
22		when he is *called* in the Lord, becomes the Lord's freedman, and a freeman *called* in the Lord becomes Christ's slave
24		. . . ²⁴ Each one of you . . . should stay as he was . . . at the time of his *call*.
Ga 1 6		I am astonished at the promptness with which you have turned away from the one who *called* you
15		God, who had specially chosen me while I was still in my mother's womb, *called* me through his grace
5 8		You were not prompted by him who *called* you!
13		My brothers, you were *called* . . . to liberty;
Ep 1 18	4	May he enlighten the eyes of your mind so that you can see what hope his *call* holds for you,
4 1	4/	lead a life worthy of the *vocation* to which you were *called*.
4	4	you were all *called* into one and the same hope ʳwhen you were *called* (or: by your *vocation*).
Ph 3 14	4	I am racing for the finish, for the prize to which God *calls* us upwards to receive in Christ Jesus.
Col 3 15		may the peace of Christ reign in your hearts . . . it is for this that you were *called*
1 Th 2 12		God . . . is *calling* you to share the glory of his kingdom.
4 7		We have been *called* by God to be holy, not to be immoral;
5 24		God has *called* you and he will not fail you.
2 Th 1 11	4	we pray . . . that our God will make you worthy of his *call*,
2 14		Through the Good News that we brought [God] *called* you
1 Tm 6 12		win for yourself the eternal life to which you were *called*
2 Tm 1 9	/4	[God] *called* us to ʳbe holy (lit. a holy *vocation*)
Heb 3 1	4	all you who are holy brothers and have had the same heavenly *call* should turn your minds to Jesus,
5 4		No one takes this honour on himself, but each one is *called* by God,
9 15		the people who were *called* to an eternal inheritance may . . . receive what was promised:
11 8		It was by faith that Abraham obeyed the *call* to set out
1 P 1 15		be holy in all you do, since it is the Holy One who has *called* you,
2 9		God . . . *called* you out of the darkness into his wonderful light.
21		[when you are punished after doing your duty,] this . . . is what you were *called* to do,
3 9		pay back with a blessing. That is what you are *called* to do,
5 10		the God of all grace . . . *called* you to eternal glory
2 P 1 3		By his divine power, he has . . . [brought] us to know God himself, who has *called* us
10	4	you have been *called* and chosen: work all the harder to justify it.
Jude 1	5	From Jude, servant of Jesus Christ . . . to those who are *called*, to those who are dear to God
Rv 17 14	5	[the ten kings] will be defeated by [the Lamb's] followers, the *called*, the chosen, the faithful.
19 9		Happy are those who are *invited* to the wedding feast of the Lamb,

6: (A PERSON) INVITES, SUMMONS – CALL (TOGETHER), CONVENE

Mt 2 7		Herod *summoned* the wise men to see him privately
18 32 <	3	the master ʳsent for (lit. *called*) [the wicked servant].
20 8 <		the owner of the vineyard said to his bailiff, '*Call* the workers'
22 3 <		[The king] sent his servants to *call* those who had been *invited* [to the wedding],
4 <		he sent some more servants. 'Tell those who have been *invited* . . . come to the wedding.'
8 <		The wedding is ready; but . . . those who were *invited* proved to be unworthy,
9 <		*invite* everyone you can find to the wedding.
25 14 <		a man . . . *summoned* his servants and entrusted his property to them.
Mk 3 31		His mother and brothers . . . sent in a message ʳasking for (lit. to *call*) him.
15 16	6	The soldiers . . . *called* the whole cohort *together*
44	3	Pilate . . . *summoned* the centurion
Lk 7 18	3	John, *summoning* two of his disciples, ¹⁹ sent them to the Lord
39		the Pharisee who had *invited* [Jesus] . . . said to himself,
14 8 <		When someone *invites* you to a wedding feast, do not take your seat in the place of honour. A more distinguished person than you may have been *invited*, ⁹ and the person
9 <		who *invited* you both may come and say, 'Give up your
10 <		place to this man' . . . ¹⁰ No; when you are ʳa guest (lit. *invited*), make your way to the lowest place . . .
<		so that, when ʳyour host (lit. the man who *invited* you) comes, he may say, 'My friend, move up higher'.

Lk 14 12   [Jesus] said to ⌐his host (lit. the man who had *invited* him),
            'When you give a lunch . . . do not ask your friends
            . . . or rich neighbours, for fear they repay your courtesy
   13   8   by *inviting* you *in return.* ¹³ No; when you have a party,
            invite the poor,'
   16   <   There was a man who gave a great banquet, and he *invited* a
            large number of people.
   17   <   he sent his servant to say to those who had been *invited,*
            'Come along; everything is ready now',
   24   <   not one of those who were *invited* shall have a taste of my
            banquet.
15 6   <   [when the man found the missing sheep, would he not]
        6   *call together* his friends and neighbours?
    9   <   when [the woman] had found [the lost drachma, would
        6   she not] *call together* her friends and neighbours?
   26   3   *Calling* one of the servants [the elder son] asked what it
            was all about.
16 5   <   3 he *called* his master's debtors one by one.
19 13   <   3 He *summoned* ten of his servants and gave them ten pounds.
23 13   6 Pilate then *summoned* the chief priests and the leading men
            and the people.
Ac 4 18   [the Sanhedrin] *called* [Peter and John in] and gave them a
            warning on no account to . . . teach
    5 21   6 the high priest . . . and his supporters *convened* the
            Sanhedrin – this was the full Senate of Israel –
       40   3 they had the apostles *called* [in],
    6 2   3 the Twelve *called* a full meeting of the disciples
    7 14   7 Joseph then sent ⌐for (lit. to *call*) his father Jacob
   10 23   9 Peter ⌐asked (lit. *invited*) [the men sent by Cornelius] in
            and gave them lodging.
       24   6 Cornelius . . . had ⌐asked (lit. *invited*) his relations and close
            friends to be there,
       32   7 [Cornelius,] you must send to Jaffa and ⌐fetch (lit. *invite*)
            Simon known as Peter
   13 7   3 The proconsul [Sergius Paulus] *summoned* Barnabas and Saul
   20 17   7 [Paul] sent ⌐for (lit. to *call*) the elders of the church of
            Ephesus.
   23 17   3 [Paul] *called* one of the centurions and said,
       18   3 The prisoner Paul *summoned* me
       23   3 [the tribune] *summoned* two of the centurions and said,
   24 2   Paul was *called,* and Tertullus opened for the prosecution,
       25   7 [Felix to Paul:] I will ⌐send for (lit. *call*) you when I find it
            convenient.
   28 17   6 After three days [Paul] *called together* the leading Jews.
1 Co 10 27   If an unbeliever *invites* you to his house . . . eat whatever
            is put in front of you,
Jm 5 14   3 If one of you is ill, he should ⌐send for (lit. *call*) the elders
            of the church,

6. CALL, CALL OUT: *PHŌNEŌ*

1 *phōneō* 25/43   2 *pros-phōneō* 2/7

1: CALL (A NAME, A TITLE)

Jn 13 13   You *call* me Master and Lord, and rightly; so I am.

2: CALL (OVER, ON, OUT) – SUMMON, INVITE

I = Invite   V = Vocation

Mt 20 32   Jesus . . . *called* [the two blind men over] and said,
   27 47   some of those who stood there . . . said, 'The man is *calling*
            [on] Elijah',
Mk 9 35   [Jesus] *called* the Twelve to him and said, 'If anyone wants
            to be first, he must make himself last of all'
   10 49   Jesus . . . said, '*Call* him [here].' So they *called* the blind
            man. 'Courage,' they said 'get up; he is *calling* you.'
   15 35   When some of those who stood by heard this, they said,
            'Listen, he is *calling* [on] Elijah'.
Lk 6 13 V 2 When day came [Jesus] *summoned* his disciples and picked
            out twelve of them;
    8 54   taking her by the hand [Jesus] *called to* her, 'Child, get up'.
   13 12   2 When Jesus saw [the crippled woman] he *called* her [over]
   14 12 I When you give a lunch . . . do not ⌐ask (lit. *invite*) your
            friends . . . or rich neighbours,
   16 2   [The rich man] *called* [for] the man and said, 'What is this
            I hear about you?'
   19 15   on his return, having received his appointment as king, he
            ⌐sent for (lit. *called*) those servants
Jn 1 48   Before Philip came to *call* you . . . I saw you
    2 9   the steward *called* the bridegroom
    4 16   'Go and *call* your husband' said Jesus to her 'and come back
            here.'
    9 18   the Jews would not believe that the man . . . had gained his
            sight, without first ⌐sending for (lit. *calling*) his parents
       24   the Jews again ⌐sent for (lit. *called*) the man
   10 3   < one by one [the shepherd] *calls* his own sheep and leads
            them out.

Jn 11 28   [Martha] went and *called* her sister Mary, saying in a low
            voice, 'The Master is here and ⌐wants to see (lit. is *calling*
            [for]) you.'
   12 17 ● [Jesus] *called* Lazarus out of the tomb
   18 33   Pilate . . . *called* Jesus to him, 'Are you the king of the Jews?'
Ac 9 41   Peter . . . *called* [in] the saints and widows and showed them
            [Tabitha] was alive.
   10 7   Cornelius *called* two of the slaves and a devout soldier of
            his staff,
       18   [the men sent by Cornelius were] *calling out* to know if the
            Simon known as Peter was lodging there.

NEAR – APPROACH – COME TO

---

1. Neighbour(s)
  1: *geitōn*
  2: *peri-oikeō*
2. Neighbouring – Next (to):
echomenos
3. (Be) Next door (to):
syn-(h)om-(h)oreō
4. Neighbour – Near: *plēsion*
  1: Neighbour
  2: Near – Nearly, Almost
5. Close inshore – Touch at
  1: Close inshore: *asson*
  2: Touch (at): *pros(-eaō)*
  3: Touch at: *para-ballō*
**6. Near, Close – Draw near, Approach
– Come up (to):** *engus*
  1: (the coming of the kingdom)
  Is close at hand, Near – Draw
  near, Be soon

  2: Near, Close to (Christ, God) –
  Draw near, Come near to **(God)**
  3: Near, Close at hand (generally)
  – Draw near, Approach, Come
  up – Be near
  4: Near, Close (figuratively)
**7. Approach, Come to – Closely –
Proselyte:** *pros-erchomai*
  1: Approach, Draw near, Come
  to **(God)**
  2: Come (to, up, forward),
  Approach, Go to (generally)
  3: Closely
  4: Proselyte, a Convert
8. Approach – Come over to: *pros-
poreuomai*
**9. Approach – Access, Way to come
to:** *pros-agōgē*

X = Approach, Come to, Jesus

1. NEIGHBOUR(S)

1: NEIGHBOUR(S): *GEITŌN*

geitōn 4

Lk 14 12   When you give a lunch . ., do not ask your . . . relations
        <   or rich *neighbours,*
   15 6   < [would he not] call together his friends and *neighbours?*
            'Rejoice with me . . . I have found my sheep'
        9   [what woman would not] call together her friends and
        <   *neighbours?* 'Rejoice with me . . . I have found the
            drachma'
Jn 9 8   His *neighbours* and people who earlier had seen him begging

2: NEIGHBOUR(S): *PERI-OIKEŌ*

1 *peri-oikeō* 1   2 *peri-oikos* 1

Lk 1 58   2 when [Elizabeth's] *neighbours* and relations heard that the
            Lord had shown her so great a kindness, they shared her
            joy.
       65   [Zechariah's power of speech returned.] All the *neighbours*
            were filled with awe

2. NEIGHBOURING – NEXT (TO): *ECHOMENOS*

echomenos 2/5

Mk 1 38   Let us go elsewhere, to the *neighbouring* country towns,
Heb 6 9   you are in a better state and *on the way to* salvation.

3. (BE) NEXT DOOR (TO): *SYN-(H)OM-(H)OREŌ*

syn-(h)om-(h)oreō 1

Ac 18 7   [Paul] left the synagogue and moved to the house *next
            door*

4. NEIGHBOUR – NEAR: *PLĒSION*

1 *plēsion* 17   2 *para-plēsion* 1

1: NEIGHBOUR

Mt 5 43   (Lv 19 18) You must love your *neighbour* and hate your
            enemy.

Mt 19	19	(Lv 19 18) you must love your *neighbour* as yourself.
22	39	The second [commandment] resembles [the first] (Lv 19 18): You must love your *neighbour* as yourself.
Mk 12	31	The second [commandment] is this (Lv 19 18): You must love your *neighbour* as yourself.
	33	To love [God] . . . and (Lv 19 18) to love your *neighbour* as yourself,
Lk 10	27	You must love the Lord your God . . . and (Lv 19 18) your *neighbour* as yourself.
	29	But [the lawyer] . . . said to Jesus, 'And who is my *neighbour*?'
	36	Which of these three . . . proved himself a *neighbour* to the man who fell into the brigands' hands?
Ac 7	27	But the man who was attacking his ⌐fellow countryman (lit. *neighbour*) pushed [Moses] aside.
Rm 13	9	(Lv 19 18) You must love your *neighbour* as yourself.
	10	Love is the one thing that cannot hurt your *neighbour*;
15	2	Each of us should think of his *neighbours* and help them to become stronger Christians.
Ga 5	14	(Lv 19 18) Love your *neighbour* as yourself.
Ep 4	25	You must speak the truth to ⌐one another (lit. your *neighbour*),
Jm 2	8	(Lv 19 18) you must love your *neighbour* as yourself;
4	12	Who are you to give a verdict on your *neighbour*?

2: NEAR – NEARLY, ALMOST

Jn 4	5	Sychar, *near* the land that Jacob gave to his son Joseph.
Ph 2	27	2 [Epaphroditus] has been ill, and *almost* died,

5. CLOSE INSHORE – TOUCH AT

1: CLOSE INSHORE: *ASSON*

asson 1

Ac 27	13	they . . . began to sail past Crete, *close inshore*.

2: TOUCH (AT): *PROS(-EAŌ)*

pros(-eaō) 1

Ac 27	7	The wind would not allow us to ⌐*touch* there (or: go on on further).

3: TOUCH AT: *PARA-BALLŌ*

para-ballō 1

Ac 20	15	The second day we ⌐*touched at* (or: crossed to) Samos

6. NEAR, CLOSE – DRAW NEAR, APPROACH – COME UP (TO): *ENGUS*

2 *engizō*   28⌐
3 *engizō* (perfect) 14⌐42   1 *engus* 31

1: (THE COMING OF THE KINGDOM) IS CLOSE AT HAND, NEAR – DRAW NEAR, BE SOON

Mt 3	2	3 Repent, for the kingdom of heaven *is close at hand*.
4	17	3 Repent, for the kingdom of heaven *is close at hand*.
10	7	3 proclaim that the kingdom of heaven *is close at hand*.
21 34	<	2 When vintage time *drew near* he sent his servants
24	32	as soon as . . . [the fig tree's] leaves come out, you know that summer is *near*. ³³ So with you when you see all
33	<	these things; know that he *is near*, at the very gates.
26	18	The Master says: 'My time *is near*.'
	45	3 the hour *has come* when the Son of Man is to be betrayed
Mk 1	15	3 the kingdom of God *is close at hand*.
13	28	as soon as . . . [the fig tree's] leaves come out, you know
29	<	that summer is *near*. ²⁹ So with you when you see these things happening: know that he *is near*, at the very gates.
Lk 10	9	3 The kingdom of God *is very near* to you.
	11	3 the kingdom of God *is very near*.
21	8	3 many will come . . . saying, '. . . The time *is near at hand*'.
	20	3 Jerusalem ⌐*will soon be* (or: *is close to* being) laid desolate.
	28	When these things begin to take place, . . . hold your heads high, because your liberation *is near at hand*.
	30	As soon as you see [trees] bud, you know that summer is
31	<	now *near*. ³¹ So with you . . .: know that the kingdom of God *is near*.
Ac 7	17	2 As the time *drew near* for God to fulfil the promise
Rm 13	11	our salvation is even *nearer* than it was when we were
	12	3 converted. ¹² The night is almost over, it *will be* daylight *soon*

Ph 4	5	the Lord is [very] *near*.
Heb 10	25	encourage each other to go [to the meetings]; the more so as you see the Day *drawing near*.
Jm 5	8	You too have to be patient; . . . the Lord's coming *will be soon*.
1 P 4	7	3 Everything *will soon* come to an end,
Rv 1	3	Happy the man who reads this prophecy, . . . because the Time *is close*.
22	10	Do not keep the prophecies in this book a secret, because the Time is *close*.

2: NEAR, CLOSE TO (CHRIST, GOD) – DRAW NEAR, COME NEAR TO (GOD)

Ep 2	13	you that used to be so far apart from us have been brought *very close*, by the blood of Christ.
	17	(Is 57 19) peace to you who were far away and peace to those who were *near at hand*.
Heb 7	19	2 the hope ⌐that *brings us nearer* (or: in which we *draw near*) to God.
Jm 4	8	2/2 The *nearer* you go to God, the *nearer* he will *come* to you.

3: NEAR, CLOSE AT HAND (GENERALLY) – DRAW NEAR, APPROACH, COME UP – BE NEAR

Mt 21	1	2 When they *were near* Jerusalem . . ., Jesus sent two disciples,
26 46	X	3 My betrayer *is* already *close at hand*.
Mk 11	1	2 When they were *approaching* Jerusalem, . . . he sent two of his disciples
14 42	X	3 My betrayer *is close at hand* already.
Lk 7	12	2 When he *was near* the gate of the town [of Nain]
12	33	2 treasure . . . in heaven where no thief can *reach* it
15	1	The tax collectors and the sinners . . . were all ⌐seeking
	X	his company (lit. *drawing near* him)
	25	2 as [the elder son] *drew near* the house, he could hear music and dancing.
18	35	2 as [Jesus] *drew near* to Jericho there was a blind man . . . begging.
40	X	2 when [the blind man] *came up*, [Jesus] asked him,
19	11	he went on to tell a parable, because he was *near* Jerusalem
	29	2 when he *was near* Bethphage . . . he sent two of the disciples,
	37	2 as he was *approaching* the downward slope of the Mount of Olives,
	41	2 As he *drew near* . . . the city he shed tears over it
22 47	X	2 Judas . . . *went up* to Jesus to kiss him.
24	15	as [the travellers to Emmaus] talked this over, Jesus himself 2 *came up* and walked by their side;
	28	2 When they *drew near* to [Emmaus]
Jn 3	23	John was baptising at Aenon *near* Salim,
6	19	they saw Jesus walking on the lake and coming ⌐towards (lit. *near*) the boat.
	23	other boats . . . had put in . . . *near* the place where the bread had been eaten.
11	18	Bethany is only about two miles ⌐from (lit. *near* to) Jerusalem,
	54	Jesus . . . left the district for a town called Ephraim, in the country *bordering on* the desert,
19	20	the place where Jesus was crucified was *not far from* the city,
	42	Since . . . the tomb was *near at hand*, they laid Jesus there.
Ac 1	12	from the Mount of Olives . . . they went back to Jerusalem, *a short distance away*, no more than a sabbath walk;
9	3	while [Saul] was travelling to Damascus and ⌐just before he 2 reached (lit. *approaching*) the city,
	38	Lydda is *not far from* Jaffa,
10	9	2 while they . . . *had only a short distance to go* before reaching Jaffa,
21	33	2 When the tribune *came up* he arrested Paul
22	6	2 I *was* on that journey and *nearly at* Damascus
23	15	we . . . are prepared to dispose of [Paul] before he *reaches* 2 you.
27	8	a place called Fair Havens, *near* the town of Lasea.

4: NEAR, CLOSE (FIGURATIVELY)

Lk 22	1	The feast of Unleavened Bread, called the Passover, was 2 now *drawing near*,
Jn 2	13	⌐Just before (lit. *Near* [the time of]) the Jewish feast of Passover.
6	4	It was ⌐shortly before (lit. *near*) the Jewish feast of Passover
7	2	As the Jewish feast of Tabernacles drew *near*,
11	55	The Jewish Passover drew *near*,
Rm 10	8 ●	(Dt 30 14) The word . . . is *very near* to you,
Ph 2	30	2 It was for Christ's work that [Epaphroditus] *came so near* to dying,
Heb 6	8	[a field] that grows brambles . . . is abandoned, and *practically* cursed.
8	13	anything old only gets more antiquated until in the end it ⌐*disappears* (lit. comes *near* to disappearing).

7. APPROACH, COME TO – CLOSELY – PROSELYTE: *PROS-ERCHOMAI*

2 *pros-ēlytos*   4   3 *a-pros-itos 1*
1 *pros-erchomai 87*

1: APPROACH, DRAW NEAR, COME TO (GOD)

1 Tm 6 16   3 [God] whose home is ⌜inaccessible (or: *unapproachable*) light,

Heb 4 16   Let us be confident . . . in *approaching* the throne of grace,
7 25   [Jesus] is living for ever to intercede for all who *come to* God through him.
10 1   the Law . . . is quite incapable of bringing ⌜the worshippers (lit. those who *draw near*) to perfection,
22   as we ⌜go in (lit. *draw near*) [to the sanctuary], let us be sincere in heart and filled with faith,
11 6   anyone who *comes to* [God] must believe that he exists
12 18   What you have *come to* is nothing known to the senses:
22   . . . [22] But what you have *come to* is Mount Zion and the city of the living God, the heavenly Jerusalem . . . , [23] . . . God himself, the supreme Judge, . . . [24] and to Jesus the mediator who brings a new covenant

1 P 2 4 X   He is the living stone . . . ; *set yourselves close to* him

2: COME (TO, UP, FORWARD), APPROACH, GO TO (GENERALLY)

Mt 4 3 X   the tempter *came* and said to [Jesus], 'If you are the Son of God'
11 X   Then the devil left him, and angels *appeared* and looked after him.
5 1 X   There he sat down and was ⌜joined (lit. *approached*) by his disciples.
8 2 X   A leper now *came up* and bowed low in front of him.
5 X   a centurion *came up* and pleaded with him. 'Sir, . . . my servant is . . . paralysed,'
19 X   One of the scribes then *came up* and said to him, 'Master, I will follow you'
25 X   [the disciples] *went to* him and woke him
9 14 X   John's disciples *came to* [Jesus] and said,
18 X   While he was speaking to them, *up came* one of the officials, . . . and said, 'My daughter has just died,'
20 X   Then from behind him *came* a woman, who had suffered . . . for twelve years,
28 X   when Jesus reached the house the blind man *came up* with him
13 10 X   the disciples *went up* to him and asked, 'Why do you talk to them in parables?'
27 <   The owner's servants *went to* him and said,
36 X   his disciples *came to* him and said, 'Explain the parable . . . to us'.
14 12   John's disciples *came* and took the body
15   the disciples *went to* him and said, '. . . send the people away,'
15 1 X   The Pharisees and scribes . . . *came to* Jesus and said,
12 X   the disciples *came to* him and said, '. . . the Pharisees were shocked'
23 X   his disciples *went* and pleaded with him. 'Give her what she wants,'
30 X   large crowds *came to* him bringing the lame, the crippled,
16 1 X   The Pharisees and Sadducees *came*, and to test him asked
17 7   Jesus *came up* [to Peter, James and John] and touched them. 'Stand up'
14 X   a man *came up to* him . . . '. . . my son . . . is a lunatic'
19 X   the disciples *came* privately *to* Jesus. 'Why were we unable to cast it out?'
24   the collectors of the half-shekel *came to* Peter
18 1 X   the disciples *came to* Jesus and said, 'Who is the greatest in the kingdom . . . ?'
21 X   Peter *went up to* him and said, 'Lord, how often must I forgive . . . ?'
19 3 X   Some Pharisees *approached* him, and to test him they said,
16 X   there was a man who *came to* him and asked, 'Master, what good deed must I do to possess eternal life?'
20 20 X   the mother of Zebedee's sons *came* with her sons to make a request of him,
21 14 X   There were also blind and lame people who *came to* him . . . and he cured them.
23 X   the chief priests and the elders of the people *came to* him and said,
28 <   A man had two sons. He *went* and said to the first, '. . . go and work in the vineyard today'. . . . [30] The man then
30 <   *went* and said the same thing to the second
22 23 X   some Sadducees . . . *approached* him and they put this question to him,
24 1 X   as [Jesus] was going away [from the Temple] his disciples *came up* to draw his attention to the Temple buildings.

Mt 24 3 X   the disciples *came* and asked him privately,
25 20 <   The man who had received the five talents *came forward* bringing five more.
22 <   Next the man with the two talents *came forward*.
24 <   Last *came forward* the man who had the one talent.
26 7 X   a woman *came to* him with an alabaster jar
17 X   the disciples *came to* Jesus to say, 'Where do you want us to make the preparations for . . . the passover?'
49 X   [Judas] *went* [straight] *up to* Jesus and said, 'Greetings, Rabbi',
50 X   they *came forward*, seized Jesus and took him in charge.
60   they could not find any [evidence against Jesus], though several lying witnesses *came forward*. Eventually two *stepped forward* [61] and made a statement.
69   a servant-girl *came up* [to Peter] and said, 'You too were with Jesus' . . . [73] A little later the bystanders *came up* and said to Peter, 'You are one of them for sure!'
73
27 58   [Joseph] *went* to Pilate and asked for the body of Jesus.
28 2   the angel of the Lord . . . *came* and rolled away the stone
9 X   the women *came up to* [Jesus] and . . . clasped his feet.
18   Jesus *came up* and spoke to [the disciples]. 'All authority . . . has been given to me.'

Mk 1 31   [Jesus] *went to* [Simon's mother-in-law] . . . and helped her up.
6 35 X   his disciples *came up to* him and said, '. . . it is getting very late,'
10 2 X   Some Pharisees *approached* him and asked, 'Is it against the law for a man to divorce his wife?'
12 28 X   One of the scribes . . . now *came up* . . . 'Which is the first of all the commandments?'
14 45 X   [Judas] *went* [straight] *up to* Jesus and said, 'Rabbi!'

Lk 7 14   [Jesus] *went up* and put his hand on the bier
8 24 X   [the disciples] *went to* rouse [Jesus]
44 X   [The woman] *came up* behind [Jesus] and touched the fringe of his cloak]
9 12 X   the Twelve *came to* him and said, 'Send the people away,'
42   The boy was still *moving towards* Jesus when the devil threw him to the ground
10 34 <   [The Samaritan] *went up* and bandaged his wounds
13 31 X   some Pharisees *came up*. 'Go away' they said.
20 27 X   Some Sadducees . . . *approached* him and they put this question to him,
23 36 X   [the soldiers] *approached* to offer him vinegar
52   [Joseph] *went to* Pilate and asked for the body of Jesus.
Jn 12 21   [Some Greeks] *approached* Philip . . . 'Sir, we should like to see Jesus'.
Ac 7 31   Moses . . . *went nearer* to look at [the burning bush]
8 29   The Spirit said to Philip, '*Go up* and meet that chariot'.
9 1   Saul . . . had *gone to* the high priest
10 28   it is forbidden to Jews to mix with people of another race and *visit* them,
12 13   [Peter] knocked at the outside door and a servant called Rhoda *came to* answer it.
18 2   [in Corinth Paul] met a Jew called Aquila . . . and his wife Priscilla . . . Paul *went to* [visit] them,
22 26   the centurion *went* and told the tribune;
27   So the tribune *came* and asked [Paul], '. . . are you a Roman citizen?'
23 14   [the Jews] *went to* the chief priests and elders,
28 9   the other sick people on the island *came* [to Paul] as well and were cured;

3: CLOSELY

1 Tm 6 3   Anyone who . . . does not keep ⌜closely (or: *attached*) to the sound teaching which is that of our Lord Jesus Christ . . . [4] is simply ignorant

4: PROSELYTE, A CONVERT

Mt 23 15   Pharisees, you . . . who travel over sea and land to make a
2   single *proselyte*,
Ac 2 11   2 Jews and *proselytes* alike – Cretans and Arabs; we hear them preaching in our own language
6 5   The whole assembly . . . elected . . . Nicolaus of Antioch,
2   a *convert* to Judaism.
13 43   2 many Jews and devout *converts* joined Paul and Barnabas

8. APPROACH – COME OVER TO: *PROS-POREUOMAI*

pros-poreuomai 1

Mk 10 35 X   James and John, the sons of Zebedee, *approached* him.

9. APPROACH – ACCESS, WAY TO COME TO: *PROS-AGŌGĒ*

pros-agōgē 3

Rm	5 2	it is . . . through Jesus that we have ᴿentered (lit. been given *access* to) this state of grace
Ep	2 18	Through him, both of us have . . . our *way to come to* the Father.
	3 12	This is why we are bold enough to *approach* God in complete confidence,

NEED

1. Need
  1: Need – Lack: *en-deēs*
  2: Need: *chreia*
2. Need – Lack – Be deprived of
  1: Need, Lack, Want – Be deprived of, Short of – Poverty: *hystereō*

2: Need, Lack – Short of – Fail: *leipō*
3: Deprived of (a person's company) – Separated from, Lost to: *ap-orphanizō*

1. NEED

1: NEED – LACK: *EN-DEĒS*

1 en-deēs 1   2 pros-deomai 1

Ac	4 34	None of their members was ever *in want*,
	17 25 Θ	2 [God] can never *be in need of* anything;

2: NEED: *CHREIA*

2   chreia 10/49   3 chrēzō 5
1 echō chreian   38

Mt	3 14	It is I who *need* baptism from you . . . and yet you come to me!
	6 8	your Father knows what you *need*
	32	3 Your heavenly Father knows you *need* them all.
	9 12	It is not the healthy who *need* the doctor,
	14 16	There is no *need* for them to go: give them something to eat yourselves.
	21 3 X	you are to say, 'The Master *needs* [the donkey and the colt] . . .'
	26 65	He has blasphemed. What *need of* witnesses *have* we now?
Mk	2 17	It is not the healthy who *need* the doctor,
	25	Did you never read what David did in his [time of] *need* when he and his followers were hungry . . . ?
	11 3 X	The Master *needs* [the colt]
	14 63	'What *need of* witnesses *have* we now?' [the high priest] said.
Lk	5 31	It is not those who are well who *need* the doctor,
	9 11	[Jesus] cured those who *were in need of* healing.
	10 42	[Martha, you worry and fret over so many things] and yet 2 few are *needed*, indeed only one.
	11 8	persistence will be enough to make him get up and give his 3 friend all he *wants*.
	12 30	3 Your Father well knows you *need* them.
	15 7	there will be more rejoicing . . . over one repentant sinner than over ninety-nine virtuous men who *have* no *need of* repentance.
	19 31 X	you are to say this, 'The Master *needs* [the colt].' . . . ³⁴ . . .
	34 X	they answered, 'The Master *needs* it'.
	22 71	What *need of* witnesses *have* we now?
Jn	2 25 X	he never *needed* evidence about any man;
	13 10	None who has taken a bath *needs* washing,
	29	Buy what we *need* for the festival,
	16 30 X	you know everything, and do not ᴿhave to wait for (lit. *need*) questions to be put into words
Ac	2 45	they sold their goods . . . and shared out the proceeds among themselves according to what each one *needed*.
	4 35	[the money] was then distributed to any members who might *be in need*.
	20 34	2 the work I did earned enough to meet my *needs* and those of my companions.
	28 10	2 [the Maltese] put on board the provisions we *needed*.
Rm	12 13	2 If any of the saints are in *need* you must share with them;
	16 2	3 help [Phoebe] with anything she *needs*;
1 Co	12 21	The eye cannot say to the hand, 'I do not *need* you,' nor can the head say to the *feet*, 'I do not *need* you.'
	24	[the improper parts get decorated] in a way that our more proper parts do not *need*.
2 Co	3 1	3 we *need* no letters of recommendation either to you or from you,
Ep	4 28	work instead, and be able to do some good by helping others that *are in need*.
	29	let your words be for the improvement of others, as ᴿoccasion 2 offers (lit. the *need* arises),

Ph	2 25	Epaphroditus . . . was sent as your representative to help 2 me when I *needed* someone to be my companion
	4 16	2 twice . . . you have sent me what I *needed*.
	19	2 In return my God will fulfil all your *needs*,
1 Th	1 8	We do not *need* to tell other people about [your faith]:
	4 9	As for loving our brothers, there *is* no *need* for anyone to write to you about that,
	12	[make a point of earning your living] so that you are seen to be respectable by those outside the Church, though you do not *have to depend on* them.
	5 1	You will not ᴿbe expecting (lit. *need*) us to write anything
Tt	3 14	All our people are to learn to occupy themselves in doing good 2 works for their practical *needs* as well,
Heb	5 12	you *need* someone to teach you all over again the elementary principles . . .; you have gone back to *needing* milk,
	7 11	2 why was it still *necessary* for a new priesthood to arise,
	10 36	You will *need* endurance to . . . gain what [God] has promised.
1 Jn	2 27	you do not *need* anyone to teach you;
	3 17	If a man . . saw that one of his brothers *was in need*, but closed his heart to him, how could the love of God be living in him?
Rv	3 17	You say to yourself, 'I am rich, . . . I have everything I *want*,'
	21 23	[the heavenly Jerusalem] did not *need* the sun or the moon for light,
	22 5	they will not *need* lamplight or sunlight,

2. NEED – LACK – BE DEPRIVED OF

1: NEED, LACK, WANT – BE DEPRIVED OF, SHORT OF – POVERTY: *HYSTEREŌ*

2 hysterēma 9   3   hysterēsis 2
1 hystereō 16   4 aph-ystereō   1

Mt	19 20	I have kept all these. What more do I *need* to do?
Mk	10 21	There is one thing you *lack*. Go and sell everything that you own
	12 44	3 she from the *little she had* has put in everything she possessed,
Lk	15 14	[the prodigal son] began to *feel the pinch*,
	21 4	2 she from the *little she had* has put in all she had to live on.
	22 35	When I sent you out without purse . . . *were* you *short of* anything?
Jn	2 3	they ᵛ ran out of wine, since the wine provided for the wedding was all finished (G began to *be short of* the wine provided for the wedding),
Rm	3 23	Both Jew and pagan sinned and *forfeited* God's glory,
1 Co	1 7	you will not *be without* any of the gifts of the Spirit
	8 8	we *lose* nothing if we refuse to eat,
	12 24	God has arranged the body so that more dignity is given to the parts which *are without* it,
	16 17	Stephanas, Fortunatus and Achaicus . . . make up for ᴿyour 2 absence (lit. the *lack* of your presence).
2 Co	8 14	[it is a question of balancing] what happens to be your surplus 2 now against their present *need* . . . they may have some- 2 thing to spare that will supply your own *need*.
	9 12	2 doing this holy service is not only supplying all the *needs* of the saints, but it is also increasing . . . thanksgiving
	11 5	these arch-apostles ᴿ*have nothing* more than I have (or: are not in the least inferior to me).
	9	When I . . . *ran out of* [money] . . . the brothers who came 2 from Macedonia provided me with everything I *wanted*.
	12 11	there is not a thing these arch-apostles have that I do *not have* as well.
Ph	2 30	[Epaphroditus] risked his life to give me ᴿthe help that you 2 *were not able* (lit. what I *needed* you) to give me yourselves.
	4 11	3 I am not talking about the *shortage* [of money]:
	12	I am ready for anything anywhere: . . . *poverty* or plenty.
Col	1 24	It makes me happy . . . to do what I can to make up all that 2 *has still* to be undergone by Christ
1 Th	3 10	We are earnestly praying . . . to be able to . . . make up any 2 *shortcomings* in your faith.
Heb	4 1	none of you must think that he has ᴿcome too late for (or: *been deprived of*) [the promise].
	11 37	[the prophets] were homeless, . . . they *were penniless* and were given nothing but ill-treatment.
	12 15	Be careful that no one *is deprived of* the grace of God
Jm	5 4	4 listen to the wages that you *kept back*, calling out;

2: NEED, LACK – SHORT OF – FAIL: *LEIPŌ*

1   leipō 6   3 an-ek-leiptos 1
2 ek-leipō 3/4   4   epi-leipō 1

Lk	12 33	3 Get yourselves . . . treasure *that will not fail* you, in heaven
	16 9	use money, tainted as it is, to win you friends, and thus make 2 sure that when it *fails* you, they will welcome you
	18 22	There is still one thing you *lack*.
	22 32	2 I have prayed for you, Simon, that your faith may not *fail*,

Lk 23 45	2	with the sun ʳeclipsed (lit. having *failed*), a darkness came over the whole land
Tt 1 5		The reason I left you behind in Crete was for you to get everything organised there that *needed* it, and appoint elders
3 13		make sure [Zenas and Apollos] have everything they *need*.
Heb 11 32	4	*There is not* time for me to give an account of Gideon,
Jm 1 4		you will become . . . complete, with no*thing missing*.
5		If there is any one of you who *needs* wisdom, he must ask God,
2 15		If one of the brothers or one of the sisters . . . *has not enough* food to live on, and one of you says to them, '. . . eat plenty,' . . . then what good is that?

3: DEPRIVED OF (A PERSON'S COMPANY) – SEPARATED FROM, LOST TO: *AP-ORPHANIZŌ*

ap-orphanizō 1

1 Th 2 17		A short time after we had been *separated from* you . . . we [longed] to see you face to face again,

NEW – OLD

1. New – Young
  1: New – Recently, Lately: *pros-phatos*
  2: New, Renew – Dedication: *kainos*
    a) New, Fresh, Latest – Renew, Be renewed
    b) Dedication – Inaugurate – Open (up)
  3: New – Young: *neos*
    a) New
    b) Young, Young man – Youth – Young women
2. Old – Elder
  1: Old – Grow old: *palaios*
  2: Old – Senate: *gerōn*
    a) Old, Old age – Grow old, Antiquated

  b) Senate (Council of elders)
  3: Old man, Older – Elder: *presbyteros*
    a) Old man, Older men, Eldest – Older women
    b) Elder (son)
    c) Ancestors, Men of old
    d) (the) Elders, the Jewish council
    e) (the) Elders of the Christian communities
    f) (the) Elders of the Revelation
  4: Old, Early, Ancient – Ancestor: *archaios*
    a) Ancient, Old, Early – Primeval
    b) Ancestor(s), Forefather(s)

Y = Old//Young   N = Old//New   O = New, Young(er)//Old

1. NEW – YOUNG

1: NEW – RECENTLY, LATELY: *PROS-PHATOS*

1 *pros-phatos 1*   2 *pros-phatōs 1*

Ac 18 2	2	[Paul] met a Jew called Aquila . . . He had *recently* left Italy
Heb 10 20		a *new* way which Jesus has opened for us,

2: NEW, RENEW – DEDICATION: *KAINOS*

1	*kainos 42*	4 *ana-kainōsis 2*
2	*kainotēs 2*	7 (*ta*) *en-kainia 1*
6	*ana-kainizō 1*	5 *en-kainizō 2*
3	*ana-kainoō 2*	

a) New, Fresh, Latest – Renew, Be renewed

Mt 9 17 O		people . . . put new wine into *fresh* skins
13 52	O	a householder who brings out from his storeroom things both *new* and old.
26 29		until the day I drink the *new* wine with you in the kingdom of my Father.
27 60		[Joseph of Arimathaea] put [Jesus's body] in his own *new* tomb . . . hewn out of the rock.
Mk 1 27		Here is a teaching that is *new*
2 21	O	No one sews a piece of unshrunken cloth on an old cloak; if he does, the patch pulls away from it, the *new* from the old, and the tear gets worse. ²² And nobody puts new wine into old wineskins; . . . New wine, *fresh* skins!
22	O	
14 25		until the day I drink the *new* wine in the kingdom of God.
16 17		believers . . . will have the gift of (§ *new*) tongues;
Lk 5 36 O		No one tears a piece from a *new* cloak to put it on an old cloak; if he does, not only will he have torn the *new* one, but the piece taken from the *new* will not match the old.
38		new wine must be put into *fresh* skins.
22 20		(Jr 31 31) This cup is the *new* covenant in my blood which will be poured out for you.
Jn 13 34		I give you a *new* commandment: love one another;

Jn 19 41		there was a garden, and in this garden a *new* tomb in which no one had yet been buried.
Ac 17 19		How much of this *new* teaching . . . are we allowed to know?
21		The one amusement the Athenians . . . seem to have, apart from discussing the *latest* ideas, is listening to lectures about them.
Rm 6 4		so that as Christ was raised from the dead . . . we too
O	2	might live a *new* life.
7 6 O	2	free to serve in the *new* spiritual way and not in the old way of a written law.
12 2		let your behaviour change, ʳmodelled by your new (lit.
4		through the *renewal* of your) mind.
1 Co 11 25		(Jr 31 31) This cup is the *new* covenant in my blood.
2 Co 3 6		the administrators of this *new* covenant, which is not a covenant of written letters but of the Spirit:
4 16	3	the inner man *is renewed* day by day.
5 17 O		for anyone who is in Christ, there is a *new* creation; the old creation has gone, and now the *new* [one] is here.
Ga 6 15		it does not matter if a person is circumcised or not; what matters is for him to become an altogether *new* creature.
Ep 2 15		[Jesus has made Jews and pagans into one people.] This was to create one single *New* Man in himself out of the two of them
4 24		[Your mind must be renewed,] so that you can put on the *new* self that has been created in God's way,
Col 3 10	O	you have put on a new self which will progress towards true
O	3	knowledge the more it *is renewed* in the image of its creator;
Tt 3 5	4	[God] saved us, by means of . . . rebirth and by *renewing* us with the Holy Spirit
Heb 6 6		it is impossible for [those who have received a share of the
6		Holy Spirit and yet have fallen away] to *be renewed* a second time.
8 8		(Jr 31 31) I will establish a *new* covenant with the House of Israel
13	O	By speaking of a *new* covenant, [God] implies that the first one is already old.
9 15		[Christ] brings a *new* covenant,
2 P 3 13		What we are waiting for is what he promised: the *new* heavens and *new* earth,
1 Jn 2 7 O		this is not a *new* commandment that I am writing to tell
8		you, . . . ⁸ Yet in another way, [it] . . . is a *new* commandment,
2 Jn 5		I am writing . . . not to give you any *new* commandment,
Rv 2 17		I will give . . . a stone with a *new* name written on it, known only to the man who receives it.
3 12		I will inscribe on [those who prove victorious] the name of the city of my God, the *new* Jerusalem which comes down from my God in heaven, and my own *new* name as well.
5 9		[The four animals and the twenty-four elders] sang a *new* hymn
14 3		[a hundred and forty-four thousand people] were singing a *new* hymn
21 1		I saw a *new* heaven and a *new* earth;
2		I saw the holy city, and the *new* Jerusalem, coming down from God
5		the One sitting on the throne spoke: 'Now I am making the whole of creation *new*'

b) Dedication – Inaugurate – Open (up)

Jn 10 22	7	the feast of *Dedication* was being celebrated in Jerusalem.
Heb 9 18	5	even the earlier covenant needed something to be killed in order to ʳtake effect (lit. be *inaugurated*),
10 20	5	a new way [into the sanctuary] which Jesus has *opened* for us, a living opening through the curtain, that is to say, his body.

3: NEW – YOUNG: *NEOS*

4	*neanias 3*	3 *neotēs 4*
2	*neaniskos 11*	6 *neo(-menia) 1*
1	*neos 23*	7 *neo(-phytos) 1*
5	*neōterikos 1*	8 *ana-neoō 1*

a) New

Mt 9 17 O		Nor do people put *new* wine into old wineskins; . . . they put *new* wine into fresh skins
Mk 2 22 O		nobody puts *new* wine into old wineskins; . . . *New* wine, fresh skins!
Lk 5 37 O		nobody puts *new* wine into old skins; if he does, the *new* wine will burst the skins . . . ³⁸ No; *new* wine must be
38		put into fresh skins. ³⁹ And nobody who has been drinking
39	O	old wine wants *new*.
1 Co 5 7		get rid of all the old yeast, and make yourselves into a
O		completely *new* batch of bread.
Ep 4 23 O	8	Your mind must *be renewed* by a spiritual revolution
Col 2 16		never let anyone else decide . . . whether you are to observe
6		. . . *New* Moons or Sabbaths.
3 10 O		you have put on a new self
1 Tm 3 6	7	[The president] should not be a *new* convert,
Heb 12 24		Jesus, the mediator who brings a *new* covenant

b) *Young, Young man – Youth – Young women*

A = Angel

Mt 19 20	2	The *young man* said to him, 'I have kept all these.'
22	2	the *young man* . . . went away sad,
Mk 10 20	3	he said to him, 'Master, I have kept all these from my ᶜearliest days (lit. *youth*)'.
14 51	2	A *young man* who followed [Jesus] had nothing on but a linen cloth.
16 5 A	2	On entering the tomb [the women] saw a *young man* in a white robe
Lk 7 14	2	*Young man*, I tell you to get up.
15 12		The *younger* [son] said . . . , 'Father, let me have the share of the estate that would come to me'. . . . ¹³ . . . the *younger* son . . . left for a distant country
13		
18 21	3	I have kept all these from my ᶜearliest days (lit. *youth*) till now.
22 26		the greatest among you must behave as if he were the *youngest*,
Jn 21 18 O		[Peter,] when you were *young* you put on your own belt
Ac 2 17 O	2	(Jl 3 1) your *young men* shall see visions,
5 6		The *younger men* . . . wrapped the body [of Ananias] in a sheet,
10	2	the *young men* . . . found [Sapphira] was dead,
7 58	4	at the feet of a *young man* called Saul.
20 9	4	A *young man* called Eutychus . . . fell to the ground three floors below.
23 17	4	Take this *young man* [= Paul's nephew] to the tribune;
18	2	Paul . . . requested me to bring this *young man* to you;
22	2	The tribune let the *young man* go
26 4	3	My manner of life from my *youth* . . . is common knowledge among the Jews.
1Tm 4 12	3	Do not let people disregard you because you are *young*,
5 1 O		treat the *younger men* as brothers ² and older women as you would your mother. Always treat *young women* . . . as if they were sisters.
2		
11 O		Do not accept *young* widows
14		I think it is best for *young* widows to marry again
2Tm 2 22	5	Instead of giving in to your impulses *like a young man*,
Tt 2 4 O		[the older women should] show the *younger women* how they should love their husbands and love their children,
6 O		you have got to persuade the *younger men* to be moderate
1P 5 5 O		To ᶜthe rest of you (lit. those of you who are *younger*) I say: do what the elders tell you,
1Jn 2 13	2	I am writing to you, *young men*, who have already overcome the Evil One;
14	2	I have written to you, *young men*, because you are strong

2. OLD – ELDER

1: OLD – GROW OLD: *PALAIOS*

2 *palaioō* 4		3 *palaiotēs* 1
1 *palaios* 19		

Mt 9 16		No one puts a piece of unshrunken cloth on to an *old* cloak . . . ¹⁷ Nor do people put new wine into *old* wineskins;
17 N		
13 52		a householder who brings out from his storeroom things both new and *old*.
N		
Mk 2 21 N		No one sews a piece of unshrunken cloth on an *old* cloak; if he does, the patch pulls away from it, the new from the *old*, . . . ²² And nobody puts new wine into *old* wineskins;
22 N		
Lk 5 36 N		No one tears a piece from a new cloak to put it on an *old* cloak; . . . the piece taken from the new will not match the *old*. ³⁷ And nobody puts new wine into *old* skins; . . . ³⁹ And nobody who has been drinking *old* wine wants new.
37 N		
39 N		
12 33	2	Get yourselves purses that do not ᶜwear out (lit. *grow old*),
Rm 6 6 N		our *former* selves have been crucified with him
7 6 N	3	free to serve in the new spiritual way and not [in] *the old way* of a written law.
1Co 5 7 N		get rid of all the *old* yeast, and make yourselves into a completely new batch of bread, . . . ⁸ let us celebrate the feast . . . by getting rid of all the *old* yeast of evil . . , having only the unleavened bread of . . . truth.
8		
2Co 3 14		that same veil is still there when the *old* covenant is being read
Ep 4 22		You must give up your [old] way of life; you must put aside your *old* self,
N		
Col 3 9		You have stripped off ᶜyour old (lit. that) behaviour with your *old* self,
N		
Heb 1 11		(Ps 102 26) all will vanish, though you remain, all ᶜwear out (lit. *grow old*) like a garment;
2		
8 13		By speaking of a new covenant, [God] implies that the first one is already *old*. Now anything *old* only gets more antiquated until in the end it disappears.
N 2/2		
1Jn 2 7 N		this is . . . an *old* commandment that you were given from the beginning, the ᶜoriginal (lit. *old*) commandment which was the message brought to you.

2: OLD – SENATE: *GERŌN*

2 *gēras* 1		4 *gerousia* 1
1 *gēraskō* 2		5 *graōdēs* 1
3 *gerōn* 1		

a) *Old, Old age – Grow old, Antiquated*

Lk 1 36	2	Elizabeth has, in her *old age*, . . . conceived a son,
Jn 3 4	3	How can a ᶜgrown man (lit. man who is *old*) be born?
21 18 Y		when you *grow old* . . . somebody else will put a belt round you
1Tm 4 7	5	Have nothing to do with godless myths and *old wives*' tales.
Heb 8 13		anything old only *gets* more *antiquated* until in the end it disappears.

b) *Senate (Council of elders)*

Ac 5 21	4	the high priest . . . convened the Sanhedrin – this was the full *Senate* of Israel –

3: OLD MAN, OLDER – ELDER: *PRESBYTEROS*

2 *presbyterion* 3		4 *presbytis* 1
1 *presbyteros* 66		5 *sym-presbyteros* 1
3 *presbytēs* 3		

a) *Old man, Older men, Eldest – Older women*

Lk 1 18	3	I am an *old man* and my wife is getting on in years.
Jn 8 9		they went away one by one, beginning with the *eldest*,
Ac 2 17 Y		(Jl 3 1) your *old men* shall dream dreams.
1Tm 5 1 Y		Do not speak harshly to a *man older than yourself*, but advise him as you would your own father; treat . . . ² *older women* as you would your mother.
2		
Tt 2 2 Y	3	The *older men* should be reserved, dignified, moderate, . . . ³ Similarly the *older women* should behave as though they were religious.
3	4	
Phm 9	3	this is Paul writing, an *old man* now

b) *Elder (son)*

Lk 15 25 Y		the *elder* son was out in the fields,

c) *Ancestors, Men of old*

Heb 11 2 O		It was for faith that our *ancestors* were commended.

d) *(the) Elders, the Jewish council*

P = High Priests and Elders   S = Scribes and Elders

Mt 15 2		Why do your disciples break away from the tradition of the *elders*?
O		
16 21		Jesus . . . was destined to go to Jerusalem and suffer grievously at the hands of the *elders* and chief priests and scribes,
P S		
21 23 P		the chief priests and the *elders* of the people came to [Jesus] and said, 'What authority have you . . .?'
26 3 P		the chief priests and the *elders* of the people assembled . . . ⁴ and made plans to arrest Jesus
47		Judas . . . appeared, and with him a large number of men armed with swords and clubs, sent by the chief priests and *elders* of the people.
P		
57		The men . . . led [Jesus] to Caiaphas the high priest, where the scribes and the *elders* were assembled.
S		
27 1 P		all the chief priests and the *elders* of the people met in council to bring about the death of Jesus.
3		Judas . . . took the thirty silver pieces back to the chief priests and *elders*.
P		
12 P		when [Jesus] was accused by the chief priests and the *elders* he refused to answer at all.
20 P		The chief priests and the *elders* . . . had persuaded the crowd to demand the release of Barabbas
41 P S		The chief priests with the scribes and *elders* mocked [Jesus]
28 12 P		[The chief priests] held a meeting with the *elders*
Mk 7 3 O		the Jews . . . follow the tradition of the *elders* and never eat without washing
5 O		Why do your disciples not respect the tradition of the *elders* . . .?
8 31 P S		the Son of Man was destined to . . . be rejected by the *elders* and the chief priests and the scribes,
11 27 P S		the chief priests and the scribes and the *elders* came to [Jesus]
14 43		Judas . . . came up with a number of men armed with swords and clubs, sent by the chief priests and the scribes and the *elders*.
P S		
53 P S		all the chief priests and the *elders* and the scribes assembled
Lk 7 3		[a centurion] sent some Jewish *elders* to [Jesus]
9 22		The Son of Man . . . is destined to . . . be rejected by the *elders* and chief priests and scribes
P S		
20 1		in the Temple . . . the chief priests and the scribes came up, together with the *elders*,
22 52		Jesus spoke to the chief priests and captains of the Temple guard and *elders* who had come for him.
P		

Lk 22 66 P S 2	there was a *meeting of the elders* of the people, attended by the chief priests and scribes.
Ac 4 5 S	the rulers, *elders* and scribes had a meeting in Jerusalem
8	Peter . . . addressed them, 'Rulers of the people, and *elders*!'
23 P	[Peter and John] went to the community and told them everything the chief priests and *elders* had said
6 12	Having . . . turned the people against [Stephen] as well as the *elders* and scribes,
S	
22 5 2	[I persecuted this Way to the death] as the high priest and the whole *council of elders* can testify,
23 14 P	[the Jews] went to the chief priests and *elders*,
24 1	the high priest Ananias came down with some of the *elders* and an advocate
25 15 P	the chief priests and *elders* of the Jews laid information against [Paul]

e) (the) Elders of the Christian communities

A = Apostles and Elders

Ac 11 30	They . . . delivered their contributions to the *elders* in the care of Barnabas and Saul.
14 23	In each of these churches [Paul and Barnabas] appointed *elders*,
15 2	it was arranged that Paul and Barnabas . . . should go up to Jerusalem and discuss the problem with the apostles and *elders*.
4 A	they were welcomed by the church and by the apostles and *elders*,
6 A	The apostles and *elders* met to look into the matter,
22 A	the apostles and *elders* decided to choose delegates to send to Antioch
23 A	The apostles and *elders*, your brothers, send greetings to the brothers of pagan birth in Antioch,
16 4 A	[Paul and Timothy] passed on the decisions reached by the apostles and *elders* in Jerusalem,
20 17	[Paul] sent for the *elders* of the church of Ephesus.
21 18	Paul went with us to visit James, and all the *elders* were present.
1.Tm 4 14 2	a spiritual gift . . . was given to you when the prophets spoke and the *body of elders* laid their hands on you;
5 17	The *elders* who do their work well . . . are to be given double consideration,
19	Never accept any accusation brought against an *elder* unless it is supported by two or three witnesses.
Tt 1 5	I left you behind in Crete . . . to . . . appoint *elders* in every town,
Jm 5 14	If one of you is ill, he should send for the *elders* of the church, and they must . . . pray over him.
1 P 5 1	/5 Now I have something to tell your *elders*: I am an *elder* ┌myself (lit. *with* them),
5	To ┌the rest of you (lit. those of you who are younger) I say; do what the *elders* tell you,
2 Jn 1	From the *Elder*: my greetings to the Lady, the chosen one,
3 Jn 1	From the *Elder*: greetings to my dear friend Gaius,

f) (the) Elders of the Revelation

Rv 4 4	Round the throne in a circle were twenty-four thrones and on them I saw twenty-four *elders* sitting, dressed in white robes
10	the twenty-four *elders* prostrated themselves before [the One sitting on the throne]
5 5	one of the *elders* said to me, '. . . the Lion of the tribe of Judah . . . has triumphed,
6	I saw, standing between the throne with its four animals and the circle of the *elders*, a Lamb
8	the four animals prostrated themselves before [the One sitting on the throne] and with them the twenty-four *elders*;
11	I heard the sound of an immense number of angels gathered round the throne and the animals and the *elders*;
14	the *elders* prostrated themselves to worship.
7 11	all the angels . . . were standing in a circle round the throne, surrounding the *elders* and the four animals,
13	One of the *elders* then spoke,
11 16	The twenty-four *elders* . . . in the presence of God, prostrated themselves
14 3	they were singing . . . in the presence of the four animals and the *elders*,
19 4	the twenty-four *elders* and the four animals prostrated themselves

4: OLD, EARLY, ANCIENT – ANCESTOR: *ARCHAIOS*

archaios 11

a) Ancient, Old, Early – Primeval

Lk 9 8	others [said] that one of the *ancient* prophets had come back to life.

Lk 9 19	others say [that you are] one of the ancient prophets come back to life.
Ac 15 7	[Peter] said, '. . . in the ┌early (or: *old*) days God made his choice among you:
21	Moses has ┌always (lit. since *ancient* times) had his preachers in every town,
21 16	Mnason . . . had been one of the *earliest* disciples.
2 Co 5 17 N	the *old* creation has gone, and now the new one is here.
2 P 2 5	Nor did [God] spare the world in *ancient* times:
Rv 12 9 ⑪	The great dragon, the *primeval* serpent, known as the devil or Satan,
20 2 ⑪	[The angel] overpowered the dragon, that *primeval* serpent

b) Ancestor(s), Forefather(s)

Mt 5 21	it was said to our *ancestors* (Ex 20 13): You must not kill;
33	it was said to our *ancestors* (Ex 20 7): You must not break your oath,

NIGHT – DARKNESS

1. Night: *nyx*	2: Gloom, Darkness, Dark: *zophos, gnophos*
a) Night and Day	*a)* Gloom, Darkness (of God in Old Testament times)
b) Night	
c) (Mid)night – (the middle of the) Night	*b)* Gloom, Dark (reserved for angels who have sinned)
2. Darkness, Dark	
1: Darkness, Dark, Darkened: *skotia*	3: Dark: *auchmēros*

1. NIGHT: *NYX*

1	*nyx*	61	5	*en-nycha*	1
3	*nychth-ēmeron*	1	2	*(meso)nyktion*	4
4	*dia-nyktereuō*	1			

a) Night and Day

6 hēmera 32/389

Mt 4 2	6/ [Jesus] fasted for forty *days* and forty *nights*,
12 40	(Jon 2 1) as Jonah was in the belly of the sea-monster for 6/ three *days* and three *nights*, so will the Son of Man be in the 6/ heart of the earth for three *days* and three *nights*.
Mk 4 27	/6 *Night* and *day*, . . . the seed is sprouting and growing;
5 5	/6 All *night* and all *day*, among the tombs . . , [the demoniac] would howl
Lk 2 37	/6 [Anna] never left the Temple, serving God *night* and *day*
6 12	4 [Jesus] *spent the* [whole] *night* in prayer to God. ¹³ When 6 *day* came he summoned his disciples and picked out twelve of them;
13	
17 31	6 When that *day* comes, anyone on the housetop . . . ³⁴ . . . 6 on that *night* two will be in one bed:
34	
18 7	6/ [God's] chosen who cry to him *day* and *night*
21 37	6 In the *daytime* [Jesus] would be in the Temple teaching, but would spend the *night* on . . . the Mount of Olives
Jn 9 4	6 As long as the *day* lasts I must carry out the work of the one who sent me; the *night* will soon be here when no one can work.
11 9	6 Are there not twelve hours in the *day*? A man can walk in 6 the *daytime* without stumbling . . .; ¹⁰ but if he walks at *night* he stumbles,
10	
Ac 9 24	To make sure of killing [Saul the Jews] kept watch on the 6/ gates [of Damascus] *day* and *night*, ²⁵ but when it was ┌dark (lit. *night*) the disciples took him
25	
20 31	/6 remembering how *night* and *day* for three years I never failed to keep you right,
26 7	the promise that our twelve tribes, constant in worship /6 *night* and *day*, hope to attain.
Rm 13 12	/6 The *night* is almost over, it will be *daylight* soon . . . ¹³ Let 6 us live decently as people do in the *daytime*:
13	
2 Co 11 25	3 I have been . . . once adrift in the open sea for *a night and a day*,
1 Th 2 9	/6 how hard we used to work, slaving *night* and *day*
3 10	/6 We are earnestly praying *night* and *day* to be able to see you face to face again
5 5	6 you are all sons of light and sons of the *day*: we do not belong to the *night* or to darkness,
7	*Night* is the time for sleepers to sleep and *night* is the time for 6 drunkards to be drunk, ⁸ but we belong to the *day* and we should be sober;
8	
2 Th 3 8	/6 we worked *night* and *day*, slaving and straining,
1 Tm 5 5	a woman who is really widowed . . . can . . . consecrate 6 all her *days* and *nights* to . . . prayer.

2 Tm	1	3	/6 *Night* and *day* I thank God,
Rv	4	8	6/ *day* and *night* [the four animals] never stop singing: Holy,
	7	15	6 they now stand in front of God's throne and serve him *day* and *night*
	8	12	6 for a third of the *day* there was no illumination, and the same with the *night*.
	12	10	6 the persecutor, who accused our brothers *day* and *night* before our God,
	14	11	/6 There will be no respite, *night* or *day*, for those who worshipped the beast
	20	10	6/ their torture will not stop, *day* or *night*, for ever and ever.
	21	25	(cf. Is 60 11) The gates of [the city] will never be shut by 6/ *day* – and there will be no *night* there –

b) Night

Mt	2	14	Joseph . . , taking the child and his mother with him, left that *night* for Egypt,
	14	25	In the fourth watch of the *night* [Jesus] went towards [the disciples], walking on the lake,
	26	31	You will all lose faith in me this *night*,
		34	[Peter] this very *night*, before the cock crows, you will have disowned me three times.
	28	13	His disciples came during the *night* and stole him away
Mk	1	35	5 In the morning, *long before dawn*, [Jesus] got up and left the house,
	6	48	about the fourth watch of the *night* he came towards [the disciples],
	14	30	this very *night*, before the cock crows twice, you will have disowned me
Lk	2	8	shepherds who lived in the fields and took it in turns to watch their flocks during the *night*.
	5	5	Master, . . . we worked hard all *night* long and caught nothing,
	12	20	This very *night* the demand will be made for your soul;
Jn	3	2	[Nicodemus] came to Jesus by *night*
	13	30	As soon as Judas had taken the piece of bread he went out. *Night* had fallen.
	19	39	Nicodemus . . . had first come to Jesus at *night-time*
	21	3	[the disciples] caught nothing that *night*.
Ac	5	19	at *night* the angel of the Lord opened the prison gates
	12	6	On the *night* before Herod was to try [Peter],
	16	9	One *night* Paul had a vision: a Macedonian appeared
		33	Late at *night* as it was, [the gaoler] took [Paul and Silas] to wash their wounds,
	17	10	When it was ⌐dark (lit. *night*) the brothers . . . sent Paul and Silas away
	18	9	One *night* the Lord spoke to Paul in a vision, 'Do not be afraid to speak out,'
	23	11	Next *night*, the Lord appeared to [Paul] and said, 'Courage!'
		23	Get two hundred soldiers ready to leave . . . by the third hour of the *night*
		31	The soldiers . . . took Paul and escorted him by *night* to Antipatris,
	27	23	Last *night* there was standing beside me an angel of the God to whom I belong
		27	On the fourteenth *night* we were being driven one way and another in the Adriatic,
1 Co	11	23	on the same *night* that he was betrayed, the Lord Jesus took some bread,
1 Th	5	2	the Day of the Lord is going to come like a thief in the *night*.
Rv	22	5	It will never be *night* again . . . the Lord God will be shining on them.

c) (Mid)night – (the middle of the) Night

Mt	25	6	at mid*night* there was a cry, 'The bridegroom is here!'
Mk	13	35	you do not know when the master of the house is coming, 2 evening, mid*night*, cockcrow, dawn;
Lk	11	5	Suppose one of you has a friend and goes to him in the 2 middle of the *night*
Ac	16	25	⌐Late that night (lit. Towards mid*night*) Paul and Silas were 2 praying
	20	7	Paul . . . preached a sermon that went on till the middle 2 of the *night*.
	27	27	On the fourteenth night we were being driven one way and another . . . , when about mid*night* the crew sensed that land . . . was near.

2. DARKNESS, DARK

L = Dark, Darkness//Light, Lighten

1: DARKNESS, DARK, DARKENED: *SKOTIA*

4 *skoteinos*	3	5 *skotoō*	3
2 *skotia*	17	1 *skotos*	30
3 *skotizō*	6		

Mt	4	16 L	2 (Is 9 1) The people that lived in *darkness* has seen a great light;

Mt	6	23	if your eye is diseased, your whole body will be all *darkness*.
		L 4	If then, the light inside you is *darkness*, what *darkness* that will be!
	8	12	the subjects of the kingdom will be turned out into the *dark*,
	10	27 L	2 What I say to you in the *dark*, tell in the daylight;
	22	13	Bind him hand and foot and throw him out into the *dark*,
	24	29	3 the sun will *be darkened*, the moon will lose its brightness,
	25	30	As for this good-for-nothing servant, throw him out into the *dark*,
	27	45	From the sixth hour there was *darkness* over all the land,
Mk	13	24	3 the sun will *be darkened*, the moon will lose its brightness,
	15	33	When the sixth hour came there was *darkness* over the whole land
Lk	1	79 L	to give light to those who live in *darkness* and the shadow of death,
	11	34 L	4 when [your eye] is diseased your body too will be in *darkness*.
		35 L	See to it . . . that the light inside you is not *darkness*.
		36	If . . . your whole body is filled with light, and no trace of L 4 *darkness*,
	12	3 L	2 whatever you have said in the *dark* will be heard in the daylight,
	22	53	this is the reign of *darkness*.
	23	44	It was now about the sixth hour and, with the sun ⌐eclipsed 3/ (ᵛ having *been darkened*), a *darkness* came over the whole land
Jn	1	5 L 2/2	a light that shines in the *dark*, a light that *darkness* could not overpower.
	3	19 L	2 men have shown they prefer *darkness* to light
	6	17 L	2 It was getting *dark* by now
	8	12 L	2 anyone who follows me will not be walking in the *dark*;
	12	35 L	2 Walk while you have the light, or the *dark* will overtake 2 you; he who walks in the *dark* does not know where he is going.
		46 L	2 so that whoever believes in me need not stay in the *dark* any more.
	20	1	2 It was very early . . . and still *dark*,
Ac	2	20	(Jl 3 4) The sun will be turned into *darkness* and the moon into blood
	13	11	everything went misty and *dark* for [Paul],
	26	18 L	2 so that [the pagans] may turn from *darkness* to light,
Rm	1	21	3 their empty minds *were darkened*.
	2	19	if you are convinced you can . . . be a beacon to those in L the *dark*,
	11	10	(Ps 69 23) may their eyes ⌐be struck incurably blind (lit. 3 *be darkened* so they cannot see)
	13	12	let us give up all the things we prefer to do under cover of the *dark*;
1 Co	4	5 L	[the Lord] will light up all that is hidden in the *dark*
2 Co	4	6 L	Let there be light shining out of *darkness*,
	6	14 L	Light and *darkness* have nothing in common,
Ep	4	18	5 Intellectually [the pagans] are *in the dark*,
	5	8 L	You were *darkness* once, but now you are light
		11 L	having nothing to do with the futile works of *darkness*
	6	12	we have to struggle . . . against . . . the Powers who originate the *darkness* in this world,
Col	1	13 L	[the Father] has taken us out of the power of *darkness*
1 Th	5	4 L	it is not as if you live in the *dark*, . . . ⁵ . . . we do not 5 belong to the night or to *darkness*,
1 P	2	9 L	God who called you out of the *darkness* into his wonderful light.
2 P	2	17	the *dark* underworld is the place reserved for them.
1 Jn	1	5 L	2 God is light; there is no *darkness* in him at all. ⁶ If we say 6 that we are in union with God while we are living in L *darkness*, we are lying
	2	8 L	2 the ⌐night is over (lit. *darkness* is passing away) and the 9 real light is already shining. ⁹ Anyone who claims to be 2 in the light but hates his brother is still in the *dark*. . . .
		11 L	2 ¹¹ the man who hates his brother . . . is in the *darkness*, L 2 not knowing where he is going in the *darkness*, because L 2 ⌐it is too dark to see (lit. the *darkness* has blinded his eyes)
Jude		13	like shooting stars bound for an eternity of ⌐black (lit. *gloom and*) *darkness*.
Rv	8	12	a third of the sun . . . moon and . . . stars were blasted, so that ⌐the light went out of a third of them (lit. a third of them *was darkened*)
	9	2 L	5 the sun and the sky were *darkened* by [the smoke],
	16	10	5 [the beast's] whole empire was *plunged into darkness*.

2: GLOOM, DARKNESS, DARK: *ZOPHOS, GNOPHOS*

1 *zophos* 5   2 *gnophos* 1

a) Gloom, Darkness (of God in Old Testament times)

Heb	12	18	What you have come to is nothing known to the senses: 2/ not a blazing fire, or a *gloom* turning to *total darkness*, or a storm;

b) Gloom, Dark (reserved for angels who have sinned)

2 P	2	4	When angels sinned, God . . . sent them down to the underworld and consigned them to the *dark* underground caves
		17	the dark ⌐underworld (lit. *gloom*) is the place reserved for [such self-willed people].
Jude		6	[God] has kept [the angels who sinned] down in the *dark*,
		13	like shooting stars bound for an eternity of ⌐black (lit. *gloom* and) darkness.

3: DARK: *AUCHMĒROS*

auchmēros 1

2 P	1	19 L	you will be right to depend on prophecy and take it as a lamp for lighting a way through the *dark*

NOAH – ENOCH

E *Enoch 3*   1 *kibōtos 4/6*
    Noah 8

Mt	24	37	As it was in *Noah*'s day, so it will be when the Son of Man comes. [38] For in those days before the Flood people were eating . . . right up to the day (Gn 7 7) *Noah* went
		38 1	into the *ark*,
Lk	3	36	[Jesus, son of Joseph . . . son] of *Noah*, son of Lamech,
		37 E	[37] son of Methuselah, son of *Enoch* . . . [38] . . . son of Adam, son of God.
	17	26	As it was in *Noah*'s day, so will it also be in the days of the Son of Man. [27] People were eating . . . right up to the
		27 1	day (Gn 7 7) *Noah* went into the *ark*, and the Flood came
Heb	11	5 E	It was because of his faith that *Enoch* was taken up and did not have to experience death:
		7 1	It was through his faith that *Noah*, (Gn 6 13) when he had been warned by God . . . built an *ark* to save his family.
1 P	3	20 1	when *Noah* was still building that *ark* which saved only . . . eight people
2 P	2	5	it was only *Noah* he saved, the preacher of righteousness, along with seven others,
Jude		14 E	It was with them in mind that *Enoch*, the seventh patriarch from Adam, made his prophecy

NOT ANY – NO

1. Not any – None: *ou-d-(h)eis*
  1: No one, Nobody – Not anyone – No (person)
  2: No (thing), Not any(thing), Nothing – Not at all – Without

2. Not any – No (person or thing): *pas* + negative

(doing) something

3. No: *ou*

1. NOT ANY – NONE: *OU-D-(H)EIS*

4 *mē-damōs*	2	6 *ou-damōs*	1
2 *mē-d-(h)eis*	89	1 *ou-d-(h)eis*	228
5 *mē-th-eis*	1	3 *ou-th-eis*	7

1: NO ONE, NOBODY – NOT ANYONE – NO (PERSON)

Mt	6	24	*No one* can be the slave of two masters:
	8	4	2 Mind you do *not* tell *anyone*,
		10	⌐nowhere (lit. in *no one*) in Israel have I found faith like this.
	9	16	*No one* puts a piece of . . . cloth on to an old cloak,
		30	2 Take care that *no one* learns about this.
	11	27	*no one* knows the Son except the Father,
	16	20	2 he gave . . . strict orders *not* to tell *anyone* that he was the Christ.
	17	8	they saw *no one* but only Jesus.
		9	2 Tell *no one* about the vision
	20	7	*no one* has hired us
	22	16	Master, . . . you are *not* afraid of *anyone*,
		46	*Not one* could think of anything to say in reply,
	24	36	as for that day and hour, *nobody* knows it,

Mk	1	44	2 Mind you ⌐say nothing (lit. do *not* say anything) to *anyone*,
	2	21	*No one* sews a piece of unshrunken cloth on an old clock;
	3	27	*no one* can make his way into a strong man's house
	5	3	*no one* could secure [the man with the unclean spirit] any more,
		4	*no one* had the strength to control him.
		37	[Jesus] allowed *no one* to go with him except Peter
		43	2 [Jesus] ordered them strictly *not* to let *anyone* know about it,
	7	24	[Jesus] did *not* want *anyone* to know he was [in Tyre],
		36	2 Jesus ordered them to tell *no one* about it,
	8	30	2 he gave them strict orders *not* to tell *anyone* about him.
	9	8	they saw *no one* with them any more but only Jesus.
		9	2 he warned them to tell *no one* what they had seen,
		39	*no one* who works a miracle in my name is likely to speak evil of me.
	10	18	*No one* is good but God alone.
		29	there is *no one* who has left house, brothers [who will not be repaid]
	11	2	you will find a tethered colt that *no one* has yet ridden.
		14	2 May *no one* ever eat fruit from you again
	12	14	you are *not* afraid of *anyone*,
		34	*no one* dared to question [Jesus] any more.
	13	32	as for that day or hour, *nobody* knows it,
	16	8	the women . . . ⌐said nothing to a soul (lit. did *not* say anything to *anyone*),
Lk	1	61	*no one* in your family has that name,
	3	14	2 ⌐No intimidation (lit. Do *not* harass *anyone*)!
	4	24	*no prophet* is ever accepted in his own country.
		26	Elijah was *not* sent to *any one* of these [widows in Israel]:
		27	there were many lepers in Israel, but *none* of these was cured.
	5	14	2 [Jesus] ordered him to tell *no one*,
		36	*No one* tears a piece from a new cloak
		37	*nobody* puts new wine into old skins;
		39	*nobody* who has been drinking old wine wants new.
	7	28	of all the children born of women, there is *no one* greater than John;
	8	16	*No one* lights a lamp to cover it
		43	there was a woman . . . whom *no one* had been able to cure.
		56	2 [Jesus] ordered them *not* to tell *anyone* what had happened.
	9	21	2 he gave them strict orders *not* to tell *anyone*
		36	The disciples . . . told *no one* anything of what they had seen.
		62	*no one* who looks back is fit for the kingdom of God.
	10	4	2 Salute *no one* on the road.
		22	*no one* knows who the Son is except the Father,
	11	13	*No one* lights a lamp and puts it . . . under a tub,
	14	24	*not one* of those . . . shall have a taste of my banquet.
	15	16	*no one* offered [the lost son] anything.
	16	13	*No servant* can be the slave of two masters:
	18	19	*No one* is good but God alone.
		29	there is *no one* who has left house, wife
	19	30	you will find a tethered colt that *no one* has yet ridden.
	23	53	[Joseph] put [Jesus] in a tomb . . . in which *no one* had yet been laid.
Jn	1	18	*No one* has ever seen God;
	3	2	*no one* could perform the signs that you do
		13	*No one* has gone up to heaven except . . . the Son of Man
		32	⌐his testimony is not accepted (lit. *no one* accepts his testimony);
	4	27	*none* of [the disciples] asked, 'What do you want from [this Samaritan]?'
	5	22	the Father judges *no one*;
	6	44	*No one* can come to me unless he is drawn by the Father
		65	*no one* could come to me unless the Father allows him.
	7	4	⌐if a man wants to be known he does not do (lit. *no one* who wants to be known does) things in secret;
		13	*no one* spoke about [Jesus] openly,
		19	*not one* of you keeps the Law!
		27	*no one* will know where [the Christ] comes from.
		30	*no one* laid a hand on [Jesus]
		44	*no one* actually laid hands on [Jesus]
	8	10	Has *no one* condemned you? [11] *No one*, sir
		15	I judge *no one*,
		20	*No one* arrested [Jesus],
		33	we have *never* been the slaves of *anyone*;
	9	4	the night will soon be here when *no one* can work.
	10	18	[I lay down my life;] *no one* takes it from me;
		29	*no one* can steal from the Father,
	13	28	*None* of the others at table understood the reason
	14	6	*No one* can come to the Father except through me.
	15	13	⌐A man can have no (lit. *No one* can have) greater love than to lay down his life for his friends.
		24	I had . . . performed such works . . . as *no one* else has ever done,
	16	5	*Not one* of you has asked, 'Where are you going?'
		22	that joy *no one* shall take from you.
	17	12	*not one* is lost except the one who chose to be lost,
	18	9	*Not one* of those you gave me have I lost.
		31	We are *not* allowed to put *a man* to death.
	19	41	there was . . . a new tomb in which *no one* had yet been buried.

Jn 21 12   *None* of the disciples was bold enough to ask, 'Who are you? (§ there is salvation in *no one* else)
Ac 4 12
    17   2 let us caution them *never* to speak to *anyone* in this name again.
  5 13   *No one* else ever dared to join [the apostles],
    23   we found *no one* inside [the prison].
  8 16   [the Holy Spirit] had *not* come down on *any* of [the Samaritans]
  9 7   2 The men travelling with Saul ... could see *no one*.
 10 28   2 I must *not* call *anyone* profane or unclean.
 11 19   2 they usually proclaimed the message ┌only (lit. to *no one* but) the Jews.
 18 10   *no one* will even attempt to hurt you.
 20 33   I have *never* asked *anyone* for money or clothes;
 23 22   2 Tell *no one* that you have given me this information.
 24 23   2 [Felix] then gave orders ... that *none* of [Paul's] own people should be prevented from seeing to his needs.
 25 11   *no one* has a right to surrender me to [the Jews].
Rm 12 17   2 ┌*Never* (lit. To *no one*) repay evil with evil
 13 8   2 ┌Avoid getting into (lit. Do *not* get into *anyone's*) debt,
 14 7   ┌The life and death of each of us has its influence on others (lit. *None* of us lives only to himself, and *none* of us dies only to himself)
1 Co 1 14   I am thankful that I *never* baptised *any* of you
  2 8   It is a wisdom that *none* of the masters of this age have ever known,
    11   ┌the depths of God can only be known by (lit. *no one* can know the depths of God except) the Spirit of God.
    15   [a spiritual man's] value is *not* to be judged by *other men*.
  3 11   For the foundation, *nobody* can lay any other ... that is [not] Jesus Christ.
    18   2 ┌Make no (lit. Let *no one* make any) mistake about it:
    21   2 ┌there is nothing to (lit. let *no one*) boast about ... anything human:
  6 5   is there really *not one* reliable man among you ...?
  8 4   idols do *not* really exist in the world and ... there is *no* god but the One.
  9 15   I would rather die ┌than let anybody (lit. that *no one* may) take away something that I can boast of.
 10 24   2 *Nobody* should be looking for his own advantage,
 12 3   *no one* can be speaking under the influence of the Holy Spirit and say, 'Curse Jesus', and ... *no one* can say, 'Jesus is Lord' unless he is under the influence of the Holy Spirit.
 14 2   Anybody with the gift of tongues speaks ... but ... *nobody* understands him
2 Co 5 16   we do *not* judge *anyone* by the standards of the flesh.
  7 2   We have *not* injured *anyone*, or ruined *anyone*, or exploited *anyone*.
 11 9   3 I was *no* burden to *anyone*;
Ga 3 11   The Law will *not* justify *anyone* in the sight of God,
    15   *no one* is allowed to disregard [a will]
  6 17   2 I want *no* more trouble from *anybody* after this;
Ep 5 6   2 Do *not* let *anyone* deceive you with empty arguments:
    29   ┌A man never (lit. *No one* ever) hates his own body,
Ph 2 20   I have *nobody* else like [Timothy] here,
  4 15   *no other* church helped me
Col 2 4   2 I say this to make sure that *no one* deceives you
    18   2 Do *not* ┌be taken in by people (lit. let *anyone* take you in)
1 Th 3 3   2 and ┌prevent any of you from being (lit. so that *none* of you would be) unsettled
  4 12   2 you ┌do not have to depend on them (lit. depend on *nobody*)
1 Tm 4 12   2 Do *not* let people disregard you because you are young,
  5 22   2 Do *not* be too quick to lay hands on *any man*,
  6 16   [God] whom *no man* has seen and [no man] is able to see;
2 Tm 2 4   *no* soldier gets himself mixed up in civilian life,
  4 16   there was *not* a single *witness* to support me.
Tt 2 15   2 *no one* is to question it.
  3 2   2 [Remind them that it is their duty] *not* to go slandering *other people*
Heb 6 13   ┌it was impossible for [God] to swear by anyone (lit. [God] could swear by *no one*) greater:
  7 13   [Judah,] a different tribe, ┌the members of which have never (lit. *no* members of which have ever) done service at the altar;
 12 14   the holiness without which *no one* can ever see the Lord.
Jm 1 13   2 ┌*Never*, when you have (lit. Let *no one*, having) been tempted, say, 'God sent the temptation'; God ... does *not* tempt *anybody*.
  3 8   *nobody* can tame the tongue
1 Jn 3 7   2 My children, do *not* let *anyone* lead you astray:
  4 12   *No one* has ever seen God;
Rv 2 17   to those who prove victorious I will give ... a new name ... ┌known only to (lit. that *no one* knows but) the man who receives it.
  3 7   when he opens, *nobody* can close, and when he closes, *nobody* can open:
    8   I have opened ... a door that *nobody* will be able to close
    11   2 let *nobody* take your prize away from you.
  5 3   there was *no one* ... who was able to open the scroll
    4   there was *nobody* fit to open the scroll

Rv 7 9   a huge number of people ┌impossible to (lit. that *no one* could) count,
 14 3   a hymn that ┌could only be learnt by (lit. *none* could learn but) the ... redeemed
 15 8   *no one* could go into [the temple]
 18 11   there is *nobody* left to buy [Babylon's] cargoes of goods;
 19 12   the name written on him ┌was known only to (lit. *none* knew but) himself

2: NO (THING), NOT ANY(THING), NOTHING – NOT AT ALL – WITHOUT (DOING) SOMETHING

Mt 2 6   6 (cf. Mi 5 1) Bethlehem, ... you are *by no means* least among the leaders of Judah,
  5 13   if salt becomes tasteless ... it is good for *nothing*,
 10 26   ┌everything that is now covered will (lit. *nothing* that is now covered will not) be uncovered,
 13 34   Jesus ... would ┌never speak to them except in (lit. speak to them in *nothing* but) parables.
 17 20   if your faith were the size of a mustard seed ... *nothing* would be impossible for you.
 21 19   Seeing a fig tree ... [Jesus] found *nothing* on it but leaves.
 23 16   If a man swears by the Temple, it ┌has no force (lit. is *nothing*);
    18   If a man swears by the altar it ┌has no force (lit. is *nothing*);
 26 62   Have you *no* answer to that?
 27 12   [Jesus] refused to answer *at all*.
    19   2 Have *nothing* to do with that man;
    24   Pilate saw that he was making *no* impression,
Mk 1 44   2 Mind you say *nothing* to anyone,
  5 26   2 [a woman] had spent all she had *without* being *any* the better for it,
  6 5   [Jesus] could work *no* miracle [in Nazareth],
    8   2 [Jesus] instructed [the Twelve] to take *nothing* for the journey
  7 12   he is ┌forbidden (lit. *not* allowed) ... to do *anything* for his father
    15   *Nothing* that goes into a man from outside can make him unclean;
  9 29   This is the kind ... that ┌can only be driven out by (lit. *nothing* can drive out except) prayer.
 11 13   Seeing a fig tree ... [Jesus] found *nothing* but leaves;
 14 60   Have you *no* answer to that?
    61   [Jesus] made *no* answer *at all*.
 15 4   Have you *no* reply *at all*?
    5   Jesus made *no* further reply.
 16 8   the women ... said *nothing* to a soul,
Lk 3 13   2 Exact *no* more than your rate.
  4 2   for forty days ... [Jesus] ate *nothing*
    35   2 the devil ... went out of [Jesus] *without* hurting him *at all*.
  5 5   we worked hard all night long and caught *nothing*,
  6 35   2 lend *without any* hope of return.
  9 3   2 Take *nothing* for the journey:
    36   The disciples ... told *no one anything* of what they had seen.
 10 19   *nothing* shall ever hurt you.
 12 2   ┌Everything that is now covered will (lit. *Nothing* that is now covered will not) be uncovered,
 18 34   [the Twelve] could make *nothing* of this;
 20 40   [the scribes] would *not* dare to ask [Jesus] *any* more questions.
 22 35   3 were you short of anything?' 'No (lit. Of *nothing*)' they said.
 23 4   I find ┌no case (lit. *nothing*) against this man.
    9   [Herod] questioned [Jesus] ... but *without* getting *any* reply.
    14   3 I have ... found *no* case against this man in respect of all the charges
    15   the man has done *nothing* that deserves death,
    22   I have found *no* case against him that deserves death,
    41   this man has done *nothing* wrong.
Jn 3 27   ┌A man can lay claim only (lit. *No* one can lay claim to *anything* except) to what is given him from heaven
  5 19   the Son can do *nothing* by himself; he can only do what he sees the Father doing:
    30   I can do *nothing* by myself;
  6 63   the flesh has *nothing* to offer.
  7 26   here [Jesus] is, speaking freely, and they have *nothing* to say to him!
  8 28   I do *nothing* of myself:
    54   If I were to seek my own glory that would be *no* glory *at all*;
  9 33   if this man were not from God, he ┌couldn't do a thing (lit. could do *nothing*).
 10 41   John gave *no* signs,
 11 49   Caiaphas ... said, 'You do *not* seem to have grasped the situation *at all*'
 12 19   You see, there is *nothing* you can do;
 14 30   the prince of this world is on his way. He has *no* power over me,
 15 5   cut off from me you can do *nothing*.
 16 23   you will *not* ask me *any* questions.
    24   Until now you have *not* asked for *anything* in my name.
    29   Now you are speaking plainly and *not* using metaphors!
 18 20   I have said *nothing* in secret.

Lk 18 38   I find *no* case against [Jesus].
   19 4   I find *no* case.
       11   You would have *no* power over me
   21 3   [the disciples] caught *nothing* that night.
Ac 4 14   they could find *no* answer.
       21 2 The court . . . released [Peter and John]; they could *not* think of *any* way to punish them,
    5 36   all [Theudas's] followers scattered and ⌐that was the end of them (lit. *nothing* more came of it).
    8 24 2 Pray . . . for me . . . so that *none* of the things you have spoken about may happen to me.
    9 8   Saul got up from the ground, but . . . he could see *nothing at all*,
   10 14 4 [Peter, kill and eat!] *Certainly not*, Lord;
       20 2 ⌐do not hesitate (lit. have *no* hesitation) about going back with them;
   11 8 4 [Peter, kill and eat!] But I answered: *Certainly not*, Lord;
       12 2 the Spirit told me to have *no* hesitation about going back with them.
   13 38 2 Though they found *nothing* to justify his death, they condemned him
   15 9 3 God made *no* distinction between [the pagans] and us,
       28 2 It has been decided . . . *not* to saddle you with *any* burden beyond these essentials.
   16 28 2 Do *not* do yourself *any* harm;
   17 21   ⌐The one amusement (lit. *No* other amusement did) the Athenians . . . seem to have
   18 17   Gallio refused to take *any* notice *at all*.
   19 27   This threatens . . . to reduce the sanctuary of the great goddess Diana to *unimportance*.
       36 2 there is *no* need for you . . . to do *anything* rash.
       40 2 there was *no* ground for it all, and we can give no reason for this gathering.
   20 20   I have *not* hesitated to do *anything* that would be helpful to you;
       24   life to me is *not a thing* to waste words on,
   21 24   there is *no* truth in the reports they have heard about you
   23 9   We find *nothing* wrong with this man.
       14 2 let *nothing* pass our lips until we have killed Paul.
       29 2 there was *no* charge deserving death
   25 10   I have done the Jews *no* wrong,
       11   there is *no* substance in the accusations
       17 2 I wasted *no* time but took my seat on the tribunal
       18   his accusers did *not* charge him with *any* of the crimes I had expected:
       25 2 I am satisfied that [Paul] has committed *no* capital crime,
   26 22   I have stood firm . . . saying *nothing* more than what the prophets and Moses himself said
       26 3 I now speak . . . confident that *nothing* of all this is lost on [King Agrippa];
       31   This man is doing *nothing* that deserves death
   27 22   There will be *no* loss of life *at all*,
       33 5 For fourteen days . . . you have been in suspense . . . eating *nothing*.
       34   *Not* a hair of your heads will be lost.
   28 5   [Paul] shook the creature off into the fire and came to *no* harm,
        6 2 they had waited a long time *without* seeing *anything* out of the ordinary happen to [Paul],
       17   I have done *nothing* against our people
       18 2 they found me guilty of *nothing* involving the death penalty;
Rm 8 1   those who are in Christ Jesus are *not* condemned,
   13 8 2 ⌐Avoid getting into (lit. Do *not* get into anyone's) debt for *anything*
   14 14   *no* food is unclean in itself;
1 Co 1 7 2 you will *not* be without *any* of the gifts of the Spirit
    4 4   my conscience does *not* reproach me *at all*,
    7 19   to be circumcised means *nothing* and to be uncircumcised means *nothing*:
    8 4   idols do *not really* exist in the world
    9 15   I have *not* exercised *any* of these rights,
   10 25 2 eat . . . there is *no* need to raise questions of conscience;
       27 2 eat whatever is put in front of you, *without* asking questions
   13 2 3 without love . . . I am *nothing at all*.
        3   without love it will do me *no* good whatever.
   14 10   *not one* of [the different languages in the world] is meaningless,
2 Co 6 3 2/2 We do *not* do *anything at all* that people might object to,
       10 2 [we are] taken . . . for people having *nothing* though we have everything.
    7 5   there was *no* rest for this body of ours.
        9 2 I am happy now – *not* because I made you suffer [*at all*], but because your suffering led to your repentance.
   11 5 2 As far as I can tell, these arch-apostles have *nothing* more than I have.
   12 11   Though I am ⌐a nobody (lit. *nothing*), there is *not a thing* these arch-apostles have that I do not have as well.
   13 7 2 We pray to God that you will do *nothing* wrong:
Ga 2 6   *not* that their importance ⌐matters (lit. is of *any* importance) to me . . . these leaders . . . had *nothing* to add to the Good News as I preach it.

Ga 4 1   an heir . . . is *no* different from a slave for as long as he remains a child.
       12   You have *never* treated me in an unfriendly way before;
    5 2   Christ will be of *no* benefit to you *at all*;
       10   united in the Lord, you will ⌐agree with me (lit. feel *no* differently),
    6 3 2 It is the people who are *not important* who often make the mistake of thinking that they are.
Ph 1 20   ⌐I shall never have to (lit. *Nothing* will make me) admit defeat,
       28 2 [you are] ⌐quite unshaken (lit. *not at all* shaken) by your enemies.
    2 3 2 There must be *no* competition among you,
    4 6 2 There is *no* need to worry;
2 Th 2 3 2 ⌐Never let anyone deceive you (lit. Do *not* be *at all* deceived by anyone) in this way.
    3 11   there are some of you who are living ⌐in idleness (lit. *without* doing *anything*),
1 Tm 4 4 2 *no* food is to be rejected,
    5 14 2 [young widows should] *not* give . . . *any* chance to raise a scandal about them;
       21 2 keep these rules . . . and *never* . . . be influenced by favouritism.
    6 4   [Anyone who teaches anything different] ⌐is simply ignorant (lit. knows *nothing*)
        7   We brought *nothing* into the world,
2 Tm 2 14 2 wrangling about words: ⌐all that this ever achieves is (lit. that achieves *nothing* but) the destruction of those who are listening.
Tt 1 15   to those who have been corrupted . . . *nothing* can be pure
    2 8 2 then any opponent will be at a loss, with *no* accusation to make against us.
    3 13 2 See to all the travelling arrangements and make sure that ⌐they have everything (lit. there is *nothing* else) they need.
Phm 14   I did *not* want to do *anything* without your consent;
Heb 2 8 2 [God] has left *nothing* which is not under [Christ's] command.
    7 14   Judah, a tribe which Moses ⌐did not even mention (lit. said *nothing* about) when dealing with priests.
       19   the Law could *not* make ⌐anyone (lit. *anything*) perfect;
   10 2 2 the worshippers . . . would have *no* awareness of sins.
Jm 1 4 2 you will become . . . complete, with *nothing* missing.
        6 2 he must ask with faith, and *no* trace of doubt,
1 P 3 6   live good lives ⌐and do not give way to fear or worry (lit. with no fear, *without any* worry *at all*).
1 Jn 1 5 2 there is *no* darkness in [God] *at all*.
3 Jn 7 2 [these brothers] set out, *without* depending on the pagans for *anything*;
Rv 2 10 2 Do *not* be afraid of (ᵛ *any* of) the sufferings that are coming to you;
    3 17   You say to yourself, 'I am rich . . . and ⌐have everything (lit. want *nothing*)'

2. NOT ANY – NO (PERSON OR THING): *PAS* + negative

    1   *pas*   18/1249 ⎫ + negative
    2   *ha-pas* 1/32 ⎭

Mk 7 18   ⌐whatever goes into a man from outside cannot (lit. *nothing* that goes into a man from outside can) make him unclean,
Lk 1 37   *nothing* is impossible to God.
   21 15 2 I myself shall give you . . . a wisdom that *none* of your opponents will be able to . . . contradict.
Jn 6 39   the will of [the Father] who sent me is that I should lose *nothing*
Ac 10 14   I have *never* yet eaten *anything* profane or unclean.
Ep 4 29   ⌐Guard against foul talk (lit. Let *no* foul talk come from your lips);
    5 5   *nobody* who . . . indulges in fornication or impurity or promiscuity . . . can inherit anything of the kingdom of God.
Heb 7 7   it is ⌐indisputable (lit. *without any* doubt) that a blessing is given by a superior to an inferior.
2 P 1 20   ⌐the interpretation of scriptural prophecy is never (lit. *no* interpretation of scriptural prophecy is) a matter for the individual.
1 Jn 2 21   *no* lie can come from the truth.
    3 15   ⌐murderers . . . do not (lit. *no* murderers may) have eternal life in them.
Rv 7 1   four angels . . . holding the four winds . . . back to keep them ⌐from blowing (lit. so they might *not* blow) over the land . . . or in *any* trees.
       16   neither the sun *nor any* scorching wind will ever plague them,
    9 4   [the locusts] were ⌐forbidden (lit. *not* allowed) to harm *any* fields or crops or *any* trees
   18 22   *never* again will [§ *any*] craftsmen of ⌐every (lit. *any*) skill be found [in Babylon]
   21 27   *Nothing* unclean may come into [the city]:

Rv 22 3 ᴿThe ban will be lifted (lit. There will *no* longer be *any* ban).

3. NO: *OU*

ou (12)

Mt 5 37   All you need say is 'Yes' if you mean yes, '*No*' if you mean *no*;

13 29 <   'Do you want us to go and weed [the darnel] out?'. . . he said, '*No*'

Jn 1 21   'Are you the Prophet?' [John] answered, '*No*'.

7 12   Some said, 'He is a good man'; others, '*No*'

21 5   'Have you caught anything, friends?'. . . they answered, '*No*',

2 Co 1 17   Do you really think. . . that I say Yes, yes, and *No, no*, at
18   the same time? ¹⁸. . . there is no Yes and *No* about
19   what we say to you. ¹⁹ The Son of God, the Christ Jesus
X   . . . was never Yes and *No*:

Jm 5 12   If you mean 'yes', you must say 'yes'; if you mean '*no*', say '*no*'.

NOT YET – NEVER

1. Not yet, Still not – No (one) yet: *ou-pō* | **2. Never – No(t) . . . ever: *ou-de-pote***

1. NOT YET, STILL NOT – NO (ONE) YET: *OU-PŌ*

4 *mē-de-pō* 1	2 *ou-de-pō* 4		
3 *mē-pō* 2	1 *ou-pō* 27		

Mt 16 9   Do you *not yet* understand?
24 6   the end will *not* be *yet*.
Mk 8 17   Do you *not yet* understand?
21   ᴿAre you still without perception (lit. Do you *still not* understand)?
11 2   you will find a tethered colt that *no* one has *yet* ridden.
13 7   the end will *not* be *yet*.
Lk 23 53   [Jesus was put] in a tomb . . . in which *no* one had *yet* been laid.
Jn 2 4   My hour has *not* come *yet*.
3 24   ᴿThis was before John had (lit. John had *not yet*) been put in prison.
6 17   Jesus had *still not* rejoined them.
7 6   The right time for me has *not* come *yet*,
8   I am *not* ᵛ*yet* going to this festival, because for me the time is *not* ripe *yet*.
30   his time had *not yet* come
39   /2 there was *no* Spirit *as yet* because Jesus had *not yet* been glorified.
8 20   his time had *not yet* come.
57   You are *not* fifty *yet*, and you have seen Abraham!
11 30   Jesus had *not yet* come into the village;
19 41   2 in this garden [there was] a new tomb in which *no* one had *yet* been buried.
20 9   2 *Till that moment* [the disciples] had *failed to* understand
17   I have *not yet* ascended to the Father.
Ac 8 16   2 *as yet* [the Spirit] had *not* come down on any of [the Samaritans]:
Rm 9 11   [Even more to the point is what was said to Rebecca] ᴿbefore her twin children were (lit. while her twin children were 3 *not yet*) born
1 Co 3 2   you were *not yet* ready for [the solid food];
8 2   A man may imagine he understands . . . but *still not* understand anything in the way that he ought to.
Ph 3 13   I am ᴿfar from (lit. *not yet*) thinking that I have already won.
Heb 2 8   we are *not yet* able to see that everything has been put under his command,
9 8   3 *no* one has the right to go into the sanctuary
11 7   Noah . . . had been warned by God of something that had 4 *never* been seen *before*,
12 4   you have *not yet* had to keep fighting to the point of death.
1 Jn 3 2   what we are to be in the future has *not yet* been revealed;
Rv 17 10   one [emperor] ᴿis yet to (lit. has *not yet*) come;
12   The ten horns are ten kings who have *not yet* been given their royal power

2. NEVER – NO(T) . . . EVER: *OU-DE-POTE*

2	*pote* 7	1 *ou-de-pote* 16	
4 *mē-de-pote* 1	3 *pō-pote* 7		

Mt 7 23   I have *never* known you;
9 33   *Nothing* like this has *ever* been seen in Israel
21 16   have you *never* read this: By the mouths of children . . . you have made sure of praise?
42   Have you *never* read in the scriptures: It was the stone, rejected by the builders that became the keystone . . .?
26 33   Though all lose faith in you, I will *never* lose faith.
Mk 2 12   We have *never* seen anything like this.
25   Did you *never* read what David did in his time of need . . .?
Lk 15 29   I have . . . *never* once disobeyed your orders, yet you *never* offered me so much as a kid
19 30   3 you will find a tethered colt that *no* one has *yet* ridden.
Jn 1 18   3 *No* one has *ever* seen God;
5 37   3 You have *never* heard his voice, you have [*never*] seen his shape,
6 35   3 He who comes to me will ᵛ*never* be hungry; he who believes 3 in me will *never* thirst.
7 46   There has *never* been anybody who has spoken like him.
8 33   3 we have *never* been the slaves of anyone;
Ac 10 14   I have *never* [yet] eaten anything profane or unclean;
11 8   nothing profane or unclean has *ever* crossed my lips.
14 8   A man sat there who had *never* walked in his life,
1 Co 9 7   2 *Nobody ever* paid money to stay in the army,
13 8   Love ᴿdoes not come to an end (lit. *never* ends).
Ep 5 29   2 A man *never* hates his own body,
1 Th 2 5   2 *never* at any time have our speeches been simply flattery,
2 Tm 3 7   4 [these silly women] can *never* come to knowledge of the truth.
Heb 1 5   2 God has *never* said to any angel: You are my Son,
13   2 God has *never* said to any angel: Sit at my right hand
10 1   the Law . . . ᴿis quite incapable of bringing (lit. can *never* bring) the worshippers to perfection,
11   sacrifices . . . ᴿare quite incapable of taking (lit. can *never* take) sins away.
2 P 1 10   2 If you do all these things there is *no* danger that you will *ever* fall away.
21   2 *no* prophecy *ever* came from man's initiative.
1 Jn 4 12   3 *No* one has *ever* seen God;

NOW – AT ONCE

1. Now – From now on: *arti*
a) Now, (the) Present, For the time being
b) From now on, Henceforth
2. Now, (the) Present – From now on: *nun*
a) Now, (the) Present
b)ⁱ From now on, Henceforth
3. Now: *deuro*
4. Already, Yet – Now: *ēdē*
5. (the) Present: *en-(h)istēmi*
6. Future – to Come, Coming: *mellō*
7. At once, Immediately, Straight(away): *euthus*
a) At once, Immediately – Directly, Straight(away) – No sooner than, As soon as

b) (Very) Soon
8. At once, Immediately – As soon as: *ex-autēs*
9. Immediately, Instantly – At once, At that instant: *para-chrēma*
10. Suddenly
1: *aiphnidios*
2: *aphnō*
3: *exapina*
11. Brief(ly) – Moment – Twinkling (of an eye)
1: Brief(ly), (For a) Moment, (an) Instant: *a-tomos*
2: Moment: *stigmē*
3: Twinkling (of an eye): *rhipē*

1. NOW – FROM NOW ON: *ARTI*

1 *arti* 30/36   2 *ap' arti* 6

a) *Now, (the) Present, For the time being*

Mt 3 15   Leave it like this *for the time being*;
9 18   My daughter has *just* died,
11 12   Since John the Baptist came, up to *this present time*, the kingdom of heaven has been subjected to violence
26 53   my Father . . . would *promptly* send more than twelve legions of angels to my defence
Jn 2 10   you have kept the best wine till *now*.
5 17   My Father ᴿgoes on working (lit. is working *now*), and so do I.
9 19   how is it that [the man born blind] is *now* able to see?
25   I only know that I was blind and *now* I can see.
13 7   *At the moment* you do not know what I am doing, but later you will understand.
19   2 I tell you this *now*, before it happens,

Jn 13 33	as I told the Jews, I am also telling you *now*, where I am going, you cannot come.
37	Why can't I follow you *now*?
16 12	I still have many things to say to you but they would be too much for you *now*.
24	Until *now* you have not asked for anything in my name.
31	Do you believe ᵗat last (lit. *now*)?
1 Co 4 11	To this day, *now*, we go without food and drink and clothes;
13	We are treated as the offal of the world, still to *this day*, the scum of the earth.
8 7	There are some who have *now* been so long used to idols that they eat this food as though it really had been sacrificed to the idol,
13 12	*Now* we are seeing a dim reflection in a mirror; but then we shall be seeing face to face. The knowledge that I have *now* is imperfect; but then I shall know as fully as I am known.
15 6	most of [the five hundred brothers] are *still* alive,
16 7	I do not want to make it ᵗonly (lit. *for the time being*) a passing visit to you
Ga 1 9	I am ᵗonly (lit. *now*) repeating what we told you before;
10	So *now* whom am I trying to please – man, or God?
4 20	I wish I were with you *now* so that I could know exactly what to say.
1 Th 3 6	Timothy is *now* back from you and he has given us good news
2 Th 2 7	Rebellion is at its work already . . . and the one who is *now* holding it back has first to be removed
1 P 1 6	you may *now* for a short time have to bear being plagued by all sorts of trials;
8	*still* without seeing him, you are already filled with a joy . . . because you believe;
1 Jn 2 9	Anyone who . . . hates his brother is *still* in the dark.
Rv 12 10	all authority for his Christ, *now* that the persecutor . . . has been brought down.

b) From now on, Henceforth

Mt 23 39	2 you shall not see me *any more*
26 29	2 *From now on*, I tell you, I shall not drink wine
64	2 *from this time onward* you will see the Son of Man seated at the right hand of the Power
Jn 14 7	2 *From this moment* you know [my Father] and have seen him.
Rv 14 13	2 Happy are those who die in the Lord! . . . *now* they can rest for ever

2. NOW, (THE) PRESENT – FROM NOW ON: *NUN*

1 *nun, nuni* (87)   2 *apo tou nun* 8

a) Now, (the) Present

Mt 24 21	there will be great distress such as, until *now*, since the world began, there never has been,
Mk 10 30	[there is no one who has left house, brothers . . .] who will not be repaid a hundred times over . . . *now* in this present time
13 19	in those days there will be such distress as, until *now*, has not been equalled since the beginning when God created the world,
Lk 2 29	*Now*, Master, you can let your servant go in peace,
6 21	Happy you who are hungry *now*: you shall be satisfied. Happy you who weep *now*: you shall laugh.
25	Alas for you who have your fill *now*: you shall go hungry. Alas for you who laugh *now*: you shall mourn
16 25	*Now* [Lazarus] is being comforted here
22 36	*now* if you have a purse, take it;
Jn 4 23	the hour will come – in fact it is ᵗhere already (lit. *now*) – when true worshippers will worship the Father in spirit
5 25	the hour will come – in fact it is ᵗhere already (lit. *now*) – when the dead will hear the voice of the Son of God,
6 42	How can he *now* say, 'I have come down from heaven'?
12 31	*Now* sentence is being passed on this world;
13 31	*Now* has the Son of Man been glorified
36	Where I am going you cannot follow me *now*;
15 22	but *as it is* they have no excuse for their sin.
24	but *as it is*, they have seen all this, and still they hate both me and my Father.
16 5	*now* I am going to the one who sent me.
22	So it is with you: you are sad *now*,
29	*Now* you are speaking plainly
17 5	*Now*, Father, it is time for you to glorify me
7	*Now*, at last they know that all you have given me comes indeed from you;
13	*now* I am coming to you
Ac 7 52	*now* you have become [the Just One's] betrayers, his murderers.
17 30	*now* [God] is telling everyone everywhere that they must repent,
Rm 3 21	God's justice . . . has *now* been revealed outside the Law,
26	[God makes his justice known; first, for the past . . .] then, for the *present* age, by showing positively that he is just,

Rm 5 9	is it likely that [Christ] would *now* fail to save us from God's anger?
11	through [Jesus Christ] we have *already* gained our reconciliation.
6 19	*now* you must put [your bodies] at the service of righteousness
21	[When you were slaves of sin] what did you get from this? Nothing but experiences that *now* make you blush,
22	*Now*, however, you have been set free from sin,
7 6	*now* we are rid of the Law,
8 1	those who are in Christ Jesus are not *now* condemned,
18	what we suffer in this ᵗlife (lit. *present* time) can never be compared to the glory . . . which is waiting for us.
22	From the beginning till *now* the entire creation . . . has been groaning in one great act of giving birth;
11 5	ᵗToday (lit. [*Now*,] at the *present* time) the same thing has happened: there is a remnant, chosen by grace.
30	Just as you . . . *now* enjoy mercy because of [the Jews'] disobedience, ³¹ so those who are disobedient *now* . . . will also enjoy mercy ᵗeventually (lit. *now*).
31	
13 11	salvation is *now* even nearer that it was when we were converted.
16 26	[I proclaim the revelation of a mystery kept secret,] but *now* so clear that it must be broadcast to pagans
1 Co 13 13	ᵗIn short (lit. *Now*), there are three things that last: faith, hope and love;
15 20	Christ has ᵗin fact (lit. *now*) been raised from the dead,
2 Co 5 16	if we did once know Christ in the flesh, that is not how we know him *now*.
6 2	Well, *now* is the favourable time; ᵗthis (lit. *now*) is the day of salvation.
Ga 1 23	their one-time persecutor was *now* preaching the faith
2 20	The life I *now* live in this body I live in faith:
3 3	Are you foolish enough *now* to end in outward observances what you began in the Spirit?
4 9	*now* that you have come to acknowledge God . . . how can you want to go back to elemental things like these . . . ?
25	[Hagar] corresponds to the *present* Jerusalem
29	as at that time the child born in the ordinary way persecuted the child born in the Spirit's way, so also *now*.
Ep 2 2	the ruler who governs the air . . . is *now* at work in the rebellious
13	*now* in Christ Jesus, you that used to be so far apart from us have been brought very close, by the blood of Christ.
3 5	This mystery . . . has *now* been revealed through the Spirit
10	[The mystery has been kept secret. Why?] So that the Sovereignties and Powers should learn [only] *now* . . . how comprehensive God's wisdom really is,
5 8	You were darkness once, but *now* [you are] light in the Lord;
Ph 1 20	My one hope . . . is that . . . *now* as always I shall have the courage for Christ to be glorified in my body,
Col 1 22	*now* he has reconciled you, by his death and in that mortal body.
26	a mystery hidden for generations . . . has *now* been revealed
3 8	*now* you, of all people, must give all these things up:
2 Th 2 6	you know, too, what is *still* holding [the Rebel] back
1 Tm 4 8	the usefulness of spirituality is unlimited, since it holds out the reward of life [here and] *now* and of the future life as well.
6 17	Warn those who are rich in ᵗthis (lit. the *present*) world's goods that they are not to . . . set their hopes on money, which is untrustworthy,
2 Tm 1 10	[this grace] has ᵗonly (lit. *now*) been revealed by the Appearing of our saviour Christ Jesus.
4 10	Demas has deserted me for love of ᵗthis life (lit. the *present* world)
Tt 2 12	we must . . . live good and religious lives here in this *present* world,
Phm 11	[Onesimus] will be useful to you *now*,
Heb 2 8	*At present* . . . we are not able to see that everything has been put under his command,
8 6	ᵗWe have seen that (lit. But *now*) [Christ] has been given a ministry of a far higher order,
9 24	Christ had entered . . . heaven itself, so that he could appear *now* in the actual presence of God
26	[Christ] has made his appearance once and for all, *now* at the end of the last age, to do away with sin
12 26	That time [God's] voice made the earth shake, but *now* he has given us this promise:
Jm 4 13	ᵗHere is the (lit. *Now* an) [answer] for those of you who talk like this: 'Today or tomorrow, we are off to this or that town;
5 1	*Now* [an answer] for the rich. Start crying,
1 P 1 12	the news [the prophets] brought of all the things which have *now* been announced to you . . . was for you
2 10	*now* you are the People of God;
25	You had gone astray . . . but *now* you have come back to the shepherd
3 21	That water is a type of the baptism which saves you *now*,
2 P 3 7	by the same word, the *present* sky and earth are destined for fire,

2 P	3	18

To him be glory, ⌜in time and in (lit. *now* and till the day of) eternity.

1 Jn	2	18
		28
	3	2
	4	3
Jude		25

now several antichrists have already appeared;
Live in Christ, ⌜then (lit. *now*), my children,
we are *already* the children of God
now [Antichrist] is here, already in the world.
To God . . . be the glory . . . which he had before time began, *now* and for ever.

b) From now on, Henceforth

Lk	1	48
	5	10
	12	52
	22	18
		69
Jn	8	11
Ac	18	6
2 Co	5	16

2 *from this day forward* all generations will call me blessed,
2 *from now on* it is men you will catch.
2 *from now on* a household . . . will be divided:
2 *from now on* . . . I shall not drink wine
2 *from now on*, the Son of Man will be seated at the right hand of the Power of God.
2 go away, and don't sin *any more*.
2 *from now on* I can go to the pagans with a clear conscience.
2 *From now onwards* . . . we do not judge anyone by the standards of the flesh.

3. NOW: *DEURO*

deuro 1|9

| Rm | 1 | 13 |

I have often planned to visit you – though until *now* I have always been prevented

4. ALREADY, YET – NOW: *ĒDĒ*

ēdē (19)

Mt	3	10
	5	28
	17	12
Lk	3	9
	12	49
	14	17
Jn	3	18
	4	36
	15	3
	19	28
Rm	13	11
1 Co	4	8
Ph	3	12
2 Th	2	7
2 Tm	2	18
1 Jn	2	8
	4	3

Even *now* the axe is laid to the roots of the trees,
if a man looks at a woman lustfully, he has *already* committed adultery with her in his heart.
Elijah has come *already*
even *now* the axe is laid to the roots of the trees,
how I wish [the earth] were blazing *already*!
Come along: everything is ready *now*.
whoever refuses to believe is condemned *already*,
Already the reaper is being paid his wages,
You are pruned *already*,
Jesus knew that everything had *now* been completed,
you know 'the time' has come: you must wake up *now*:
Is it that you *already* have everything you want – that you are rich *already* . . .?
Not that I have become perfect *yet*: I have not *yet* won,
Rebellion is at its work *already*, but in secret,
[Hymenaeus and Philetus] claim that the resurrection has *already* taken place.
the real light is *already* shining.
now [Antichrist] is here, *already* in the world.

5. (THE) PRESENT: *EN-(H)ISTĒMI*

en-(h)istēmi 7

Rm	8	38
1 Co	3	22
	7	26
Ga	1	4
2 Th	2	2
2 Tm	3	1
Heb	9	9

nothing ⌜that exists⌝ (lit. of the *present*), nothing still to come . . . ³⁹ . . . can ever come between us and the love of God
life and death, the *present* and the future, are all your servants;
I believe that in these *present* times of stress this is right:
[Jesus Christ,] in order to rescue us from this *present* wicked world sacrificed himself for our sins,
do not get . . . alarmed by . . . any letter claiming to come from us implying that the Day of the Lord [has] *already* [arrived].
in the last days there are *going to be* some difficult times.
it is a symbol for this *present* time.

6. FUTURE – TO COME, COMING: *MELLŌ*

mellō (19)

Mt	3	7
	12	32
Lk	3	7
	13	9
Ac	24	25
Rm	5	14 X

who warned you to fly from the retribution that is *coming*?
let anyone speak against the Holy Spirit and he will not be forgiven either in this world or in ⌜the next (lit. that *to come*).
who warned you to fly from the retribution that is *coming*?
[this fig tree] may bear fruit ⌜next year (lit. [sometime] in the *future*);
when [Paul] began to treat of . . . the *coming* Judgement, Felix took fright
Adam prefigured the One *to come*,

Rm	8	38
1 Co	3	22
Ep	1	21
Col	2	17
1 Tm	4	8
	6	19
Heb	2	5
	6	5
	9	11
	10	1
	11	20
	13	14
2 P	2	6

nothing that exists, nothing [still] *to come* . . . ³⁹ . . . can ever come between us and the love of God
life and death, the present and the *future*, are all your servants;
[Christ] is far above every Sovereignty . . . not only in this age but also in the age *to come*.
These were only pale reflections of [what was] *coming*:
the usefulness of spirituality is unlimited, since it holds out the reward of life here and now and of the *future* life as well.
[if the rich are generous] they can save up a good capital sum for the *future*
[God] did not appoint angels to be rulers of the world *to come*,
[As for those people who] appreciate . . . the powers of the world *to come* ⁶ and . . . have fallen away – it is impossible for them to be renewed a second time.
now Christ has come, as the high priest of all the ᵛ blessings which were *to come* (G realities).
the Law has no more than a reflection of these ⌜realities (lit. blessings *to come*).
Isaac gave his blessing to Jacob and Esau for the [still distant] *future*.
we look for [an eternal city] in the life *to come*.
[God] destroyed [Sodom and Gomorrah] completely, as a warning to anybody lacking reverence in the *future*.

7. AT ONCE, IMMEDIATELY, STRAIGHT(AWAY): *EUTHUS*

2 *eutheōs* 33   1 *euthus* (adv.) 54

a) At once, Immediately – Directly, Straight(away) – No sooner than, As soon as

Mt	3	16
	4	20
		22
	8	3
	13	5
		20
		21
	14	22
		27
		31
	20	34
	21	2
		3
	24	29
	25	15
	26	49
		74
	27	48
Mk	1	10
		12
		18
		20
		21
		23
		28
		29
		30
		42
		43
	2	8
		12
	3	6
	4	5
		15
		16
		17
		29
	5	2

As soon as Jesus was baptised he came up from the water,
2 [Simon and Andrew] left their nets *at once* and followed [Jesus].
2 *At once*, leaving the boat and their father, [James and John] followed [Jesus].
2 his leprosy was cured *at once*.
2 [the seeds] sprang up *straight away*,
The one who received [the seed] on patches of rock is the man who hears ᵗhe word and welcomes it *at once* with joy.
let some trial com... . . . and he falls away *at once*.
2 *Directly after this* [Jesus] made the disciples get into the boat
at once Jesus called out to [the disciples]
2 Jesus put out his hand *at once* and held [Peter].
2 [Jesus] touched their eyes, and *immediately* their sight returned
you will *immediately* find a tethered donkey and a colt with her.
The Master needs them and will send them back *directly*.
2 *Immediately* after the distress of those days the sun will be darkened,
2 The man who had received the five talents *promptly* went and traded with them and made five more.
2 [Judas] went *straight* up to Jesus
[Peter] started . . . swearing . . . *At that moment* the cock crew,
2 one of [those who stood there] *quickly* ran to get a sponge
No sooner had [Jesus] come up out of the water *than* he saw the heavens torn apart
Immediately afterwards the Spirit drove [Jesus] out into the wilderness
at once [Simon and Andrew] left their nets and followed [Jesus].
[Jesus] called [James and John] *at once*
as soon as the sabbath came [Jesus] . . . began to teach.
In their synagogue *just then* there was a man possessed by an unclean spirit,
his reputation *rapidly* spread everywhere,
[Jesus] went . . . *straight* to the house of Simon and Andrew.
Simon's mother-in-law had gone to bed with fever, and they told [Jesus] about her *straightaway*.
the leprosy left him *at once*
Jesus *immediately* sent [the cured leper] away
Jesus [was] *at once* inwardly aware that this was what they were thinking,
the man got up, picked up his stretcher *at once* and walked out
The Pharisees . . . *at once* began to plot with the Herodians
Some seed . . . sprang up *straightaway*,
Those on the edge of the path . . . are people who have *no sooner* heard [the word] *than* Satan comes and carries [it] away
those who receive the seed on patches of rock are people who . . . welcome [the word] *at once* with joy.
should some trial come . . . they fall away *at once*.
when the crop is ready, ⌜he loses no time: (lit. *immediately*) he starts to reap
no sooner had [Jesus] left the boat *than* a man with an unclean spirit came . . . towards him.

Mk	5 29	the source of the bleeding dried up *instantly*,
	30	*Immediately* aware that power had gone out from him, Jesus turned round
	42	The little girl got up *at once* . . . *At this* they were overcome with astonishment,
	6 25	The girl hurried *straight* back to the king and made her request,
	27	the king *at once* sent one of the bodyguard with orders to bring John's head.
	45	*Directly after this* [Jesus] made his disciples get into the boat
	50	[Jesus] *at once* spoke to [the disciples], and said, 'Courage! It is I! Do not be afraid.'
	54	*No sooner* had they stepped out of the boat *than* people recognised [Jesus],
	7 25	A woman whose little daughter had an unclean spirit heard about [Jesus] *straightaway*,
	35	the ligament of his tongue was *immediately* loosened
	8 10	*immediately*, getting into the boat with his disciples, [Jesus] went to the region of Dalmanutha.
	9 15	*The moment* they saw [Jesus] the whole crowd . . . ran to meet him.
	20	*as soon as* the spirit saw Jesus it threw the boy into convulsions,
	24	*Immediately* the father of the boy cried out, 'I do have faith.'
	10 52	*immediately* his sight returned and he followed [Jesus] along the road.
	11 2	Go off to the village . . . and *as soon as* you enter it you will find a tethered colt
	3	The Master needs [the colt] and will send it back here *directly*.
	14 43	Even *while* [Jesus] was still speaking, Judas . . . came up
	45	[Judas] went *straight* up to Jesus
	72	*At that moment* the cock crew for the second time,
	15 1	*First thing* in the morning, the chief priests . . . had their plan ready.
Lk	5 13	2 the leprosy left him *at once*
	6 49	*as soon as* the river bore down on [the house], it collapsed;
	12 36	2 Be . . . ready to open the door *as soon as* [the master] . . . knocks.
	54	2 When you see a cloud looming up in the west you say *at once* that rain is coming,
	14 5	Which of you here, if his son falls into a well, or his ox, will 2 not pull him out on a sabbath day *without hesitation*?
	17 7	2 Come and have your meal *immediately*
	21 9	2 this is something that must happen but the end is not *so soon*.
Jn	5 9	2 The man was cured *at once*,
	6 21	2 *in no time* [the boat] reached the shore
	13 30	*As soon as* Judas had taken the piece of bread he went out.
	32	God . . . will glorify [the Son of Man] ⸢*very soon* (or: *at once*)
	18 27	2 *at once* a cock crew.
	19 34	*immediately* there came out blood and water.
Ac	9 18	2 *Immediately* it was as though scales fell away from Saul's eyes
	20	2 [Saul] *immediately* began preaching in the synagogues,
	34	2 Aeneas got up *immediately*;
	10 16	then *suddenly* the container was drawn up to heaven again.
	12 10	2 *suddenly* the angel left [Peter].
	16 10	2 *Once* [Paul] had seen this vision we lost no time
	17 10	2 When it was dark the brothers *immediately* sent Paul . . . away
	14	2 the brothers arranged for Paul to go *immediately*
	21 30	2 the gates [of the Temple] were *at once* closed
	22 29	2 those who were about to examine [Paul] *hurriedly* withdrew,
Ga	1 17	2 I went off to Arabia *at once*
Jm	1 24	[To listen to the word and not obey is like looking at your 2 own features in a mirror] and *immediately* forgetting what you looked like.
Rv	4 2	2 *With that*, the Spirit possessed me

b) (Very) Soon

Jn	13 32	God . . . will glorify [the Son of Man] ⸢*very soon* (or: *at once*).
3 Jn	14	2 I hope to see you *soon* and talk to you personally.

8. AT ONCE, IMMEDIATELY – AS SOON AS: *EX-AUTĒS*
ex-autēs 6

Mk	6 25	I want you to give me John the Baptist's head, *here and now*, on a dish.
Ac	10 33	I sent for you *at once*, and you have been kind enough to come.
	11 11	Just *at that moment*, three men stopped outside the house where we were staying;
	21 32	[The tribune] *immediately* called out soldiers . . . and charged down on the crowd,
	23 30	I ⸢*hasten to send* (lit. am *immediately* sending) [Paul] to you,

Ph	2 23	I am hoping to send [Timothy to] you, *as soon as* I know something definite about my fate.

9. IMMEDIATELY, INSTANTLY – AT ONCE, AT THAT INSTANT: *PARA-CHRĒMA*
para-chrēma 18

Mt	21 19	*at that instant* the fig tree withered.
	20	What happened to the tree . . . that it withered *there and then*?
Lk	1 64	*At that instant* [Zechariah's] power of speech returned
	4 39	the fever . . . left [Simon's mother-in-law]. And she *immediately* got up and began to wait on them.
	5 25	*immediately* before their very eyes [the paralysed man] got up,
	8 44	[a woman] touched the fringe of his cloak; and the haemorrhage stopped *at that instant*.
	47	the woman . . . explained . . . how she had been cured *at that very moment*.
	55	[Jairus' daughter's] spirit returned and she got up *at once*.
	13 13	*at once* [the crippled woman] straightened up, and she glorified God.
	18 43	*instantly* [the blind man's] sight returned
	19 11	they imagined that the kingdom of God was going to show itself *then and there*.
	22 60	*At that instant*, while [Peter] was still speaking, the cock crew
Ac	3 7	*Instantly* his feet and ankles became firm,
	5 10	*Instantly* [Sapphira] dropped dead at [Peter's] feet.
	12 23	*at that moment* the angel of the Lord struck [Herod] down, because he had not given the glory to God.
	13 11	*That instant*, everything went misty and dark for [Elymas],
	16 26	All the doors *at once* flew open and the chains fell from all the prisoners.
	33	[the gaoler] was baptised *then and there* with all his household.

10. SUDDENLY

1: SUDDENLY: *AIPHNIDIOS*
2 *aiphnidios* 2   1 *ex-aiphnēs* 5

Mk	13 36	if he comes ⸢unexpectedly (lit. *suddenly*), he must not find you asleep.
Lk	2 13	*suddenly* with the angel there was a great throng of the heavenly host, praising God
	9 39	All at once a spirit will take hold of him, and give a *sudden* cry
	21 34	2 that day will be sprung on you *suddenly*, [35] like a trap.
Ac	9 3	*Suddenly* . . . there came a light from heaven all round [Saul].
	22 6	about midday a bright light from heaven *suddenly* shone round me.
1 Th	5 3	It is when people are saying, 'How quiet and peaceful it is' 2 that the worst *suddenly* happens,

2: SUDDENLY: *APHNŌ*
aphnō 3

Ac	2 2	*suddenly* they heard what sounded like a powerful wind from heaven,
	16 26	*Suddenly* there was an earthquake that shook the prison
	28 6	they were expecting [Paul] *at any moment* to swell up or drop dead on the spot.

3: SUDDENLY: *EXAPINA*
exapina 1

Mk	9 8	Then *suddenly*, when [the apostles] looked round, they saw no one with them any more

11. BRIEF(LY) – MOMENT – TWINKLING (OF AN EYE)

1: BRIEF(LY), (FOR A) MOMENT, (AN) INSTANT: *A-TOMOS*
1 *a-tomos* 1   2 *syn-temnō* 1
3 *syn-tomōs* 1

Ac	24 4	3 I beg you to give us a *brief* hearing.
Rm	9 28	2 (Is 10 22) *without* hesitation or *delay* the Lord will execute his sentence on the earth.
1 Co	15 52	This will be *instantaneous*, in the twinkling of an eye, when the last trumpet sounds.

MOMENT: *STIGMĒ*

stigmē 1

Lk 4 5   the devil showed [Jesus] in a *moment* (G of time) all the kingdoms of the world

3: TWINKLING (OF AN EYE): *RHIPĒ*

rhipē 1

Co 15 52   This will be instantaneous, in the *twinkling* of an eye, when the last trumpet sounds.

NUMBERS

1. Number – (Be) Counted, Numbered – Innumerable: *arithmeō*
2. Work out, Calculate, Count: *psēphizō*
3. One – First
  1: One – First: *heis*
    a) One (God, Christ, Adam) – (God) Alone
    b) One (person), One (of some people)
    c) One (day, hour) – First (day of the week) – Single (hour, day)
    d) One, One (of), Single, (generally)
    e) Unity – (to make, to be) One
    f) One (. . . other), First (. . . second) – One . . ., One
    g) Once, Once and for all – At the same time, At once
    h) Individually – Singular
  2: First: *prōtos*
    a) (God, Christ, is the) First
    b) (A person is) First – Leading (people)
    c) First (day)
    d) First (as an adjective, generally) – Front
    e) First (as an adverb) – At first, In the first place
4. Two, Both – Second – Half
  1: Two – Second – Both: *duō, amphoteroi*
    a) Two (people) – Second (person, angel) – Both
    b) Two (years, days, hours) – Second (day, watch)
    c) Two, Second, Both (generally)
    d) (in) Two
    e) Twice, (for) A second time – Doubly
  2: a Pair (of turtledoves) – a Yoke (of oxen): *zeugos*
  3: Half: *hēmisys*
5. Three – Third: *treis*
    a) Three (people) – (the) Third (person, angel)
    b) Three (lengths of time) – (the) Third (day, hour)
    c) Three, (the) Third, (generally)
    d) Three times – (for) the Third time
    e) a Third (of)
6. Four – Fourth – Quarter: *tessares*
    a) Four (people, angels) – (the) Fourth
    b) Four (lengths of time) – (the) Fourth (watch, day)
    c) Four, (the) Fourth, (generally)
    d) Four times
    e) Quarter
7. Five – Fifth: *pente*
    a) Five (people) – (the) Fifth (angel)
    b) Five (days, months)
    c) Five, (the) Fifth, (generally)
    d) Five times
8. Six – Sixth: *hektos*
    a) Six (days, hours, months) – (the) Sixth (month, hour)
    b) Six, (the) Sixth, (generally)
9. Seven – Seventh: *hepta*
    a) Seven (years, days) – (the) Seventh (day, hour)
    b) Seven, (the) Seventh, (generally)
    c) Seven times
10. Eight – Eighth: *oktō*
    a) Eight (days, years) – (the) Eighth (day)
    b) Eight, (the) Eighth, (generally)
11. (the) Ninth – Nine: *enatos*
12. Ten – Tenth – Tithe: *deka*
    a) Ten (days) – (the) Tenth (hour)
    b) Ten, (the) Tenth, (generally)
    c) (a) Tenth (of)
    d) Tithe – Pay (a) tithe, (a) Tenth – Take (a) tithe
13. Eleven – Eleventh: *hen-deka*
    a) the Eleven (remaining apostles)
    b) (the) Eleventh
14. Twelve – Twelfth: *dō-deka*
    a) the Twelve (apostles)
    b) (the) Twelve (tribes of Israel, patriarchs)
    c) Twelve (concerning the apostles, the tribes of Israel)
    d) Twelve (years, days, hours)
    e) Twelve, (the) Twelfth, (generally)
15. Other numbers

14	50	100	1 000
15	60	120	1 260
18	70	144	1 600
20	72	153	2 000
24	75	200	3 000
25	77	276	4 000
30	80	300	5 000
38	84	400	7 000
39	99	430	10 000
40		450	12 000
42		500	20 000
46		(616)	23 000
		666	50 000
			144 000

1. NUMBER – (BE) COUNTED, NUMBERED – INNUMERABLE: *ARITHMEŌ*

2	*arithmeō 3*	3	*an-arithmētos 1*
1	*arithmos 18*	4	*kat-arithmeō 1*

Mt 10 30   2 Why, every hair on your head has been *counted*.

Lk 12 7   2 Why, every hair on your head has been *counted*
  22 3   Judas . . . was *numbered* among the Twelve.
Jn 6 10   as many as five thousand men in *number* sat down.
Ac 1 17   4 [Judas betrayed Jesus] after having been one of our *number*
  4 4   the [total] *number* of [believers] had now risen to something like five thousand.
  5 36   Theudas . . . even collected a *number* of men, about four hundred [followers];
  6 7   the *number* of disciples in Jerusalem was greatly increased,
  11 21   a great *number* believed and were converted to the Lord.
  16 5   [the churches were] growing daily in *numbers*.
Rm 9 27   (Is 10 22) Israel should have as many descendants in *number* as there are grains of sand on the seashore,
Heb 11 12   3 there came from one man . . . more descendants *than could be counted*.
Rv 5 11   an immense number of angels gathered round . . . the elders; in *number* there were ten thousand times ten thousand of them
  7 4   I heard ⌐how many were (lit. the *number* of those) sealed: a hundred and forty-four thousand,
  9   2 I saw a huge number, impossible to *count*, of people
  9 16   I learnt ⌐how many there were (lit. the *number* of those) in their army: twice ten thousand times ten thousand mounted men was the *number*.
  13 17   [the beast] made it illegal for anyone to buy . . . anything unless he had been branded with the name of the beast or with the *number* of its name.
  18   if anyone is clever enough he may interpret the *number* of the beast: it is the *number* of a man, the *number* ⌐666 (ᵛ 616).
  15 2   [I saw] those who had fought against the beast and won, and against . . . the *number* which is his name.
  20 8   [Satan's] armies will be as many in *number* as the sands of the sea;

2. WORK OUT, CALCULATE, COUNT: *PSĒPHIZŌ*

1	*psēphizō 2*	3	*syn-kata-psēphizō 1*
2	*sym-psēphizō 1*		

Lk 14 28   which of you here, intending to build a tower, would not first . . . *work out* the cost . . .?
Ac 1 26   3 as the lot fell to Matthias, he was ⌐listed (lit. *counted*) as one of the ᵛ twelve (G eleven) apostles.
  19 19   2 The value of [the burnt books] was *calculated* to be fifty thousand silver pieces.
Rv 13 18   if anyone is clever enough he may ⌐interpret (lit. *work out*) the number of the beast:

3. ONE – FIRST

1: ONE – FIRST: *HEIS*

2	*ha-pax 14*	1	*heis*		317/339
4	*eph-a-pax 5*	5	*henotēs*		2
		3	*kath'heis, kath'hena 7*		

For Each One *see* WHOLE – ALL – EACH 4.

a) One (God, Christ, Adam) – (God) Alone

A = Adam

Mt 19 17   There is *one* [alone] who is good.
  23 8   You . . . must not allow yourselves to be called Rabbi, since you have only *one* Master . . . ⁹ You must call no one on
  9   earth your father, since you have only *one* Father, and
  10   he is in heaven. ¹⁰ Nor must you allow yourselves to be called teachers, for you have only *one* Teacher, the Christ.
Mk 2 7   Who can forgive sins but God *alone*?
  10 18   No one is good but God *alone*.
  12 29   (Dt 6 4) the Lord our God is the *one* Lord,
  32   Well spoken, . . . he is *one* and there is no other.
Lk 18 19   No one is good but God *alone*.
Jn 8 41   [The Jews said to Jesus], we have *one* father: God.
  10 16   there will be only one flock, and *one* shepherd.
  11 50   it is better for *one* man to die for the people,
  18 14   It is better for *one* man to die for the people.
Rm 3 30   there is only *one* God,
  5 12 A   sin entered the world through *one* man,
  15 A   If it is certain that through *one* [man's] fall so many died, it is even more certain that divine grace, coming through the *one* man, Jesus Christ, came to so many . . . ¹⁶ The results
  16 A   of the gift also outweigh the results of *one* [man's] sin:

Rm 16 17 A If it is certain that (§ through *one* man) death reigned over
         A everyone as the consequence of *one* [*man's*] fall, it is even
            more certain that *one* [man], Jesus Christ, will cause every-
            one to reign in life who receives the free gift . . . [18]
      18 A as *one* [*man's*] fall brought condemnation on everyone, so
            the good act of *one* [man] . . . makes them justified. [19] As
      19 A by *one* man's disobedience many were made sinners, so by
            one [*man's*] obedience many will be made righteous.

1 Co 8 4   there is no god but the *One*.
       6   there is *one* God . . . and there is *one* Lord, Jesus Christ,
2 Co 5 14   if *one* [man] had died for all, then all men should be dead;
      11 2 I arranged for you to marry . . . this *one* husband.
Ga 3 20   there can only be an intermediary between two parties, yet
            God is *one*.
Ep 4 5   There is *one* Lord, one faith, one baptism, [6] and *one* God who
       6   is Father of all,
1 Tm 2 5   there is only *one* God, and there is only *one* mediator between
            God and mankind, himself a man, Christ Jesus,
Heb 2 11   [the one] who sanctifies, and [the ones] who are sanctified,
            are of ʳthe same (lit. *one*) [stock];
Jm 2 19   You believe in the *one* God . . . but the demons have the
            same belief,
     4 12   There is only *one* lawgiver and he is the only judge

            b) One (person), One (of some people)

Mt 8 19   One of the scribes . . . said to him, 'Master, I will follow you'
     9 18   *one* of the officials . . . bowed low in front of [Jesus]
    10 42   If anyone gives . . . water to *one* of these little ones . . . he
            will . . . not lose his reward.
    16 14   Some say [the Son of Man] is . . . Jeremiah or *one* of the
            prophets.
    18 5   Anyone who welcomes ʳa (lit. *one*) little child . . . welcomes
            me.
       6   anyone who is an obstacle to bring down *one* of these little
            ones . . . would be better drowned
      10   See that you never despise *any* of these little ones,
      14   it is never the will of your Father . . . that *one* of these
            little ones should be lost.
      16   take *one* or two . . . witnesses
      24   they brought him ʳa man (lit. *one* [servant]) who owed ten
            thousand talents;
      28   this servant . . . happened to meet ʳa fellow servant (lit. *one*
            of his fellow servants)
    19 16   there was ʳa man (lit. *one*) who came to [Jesus]
    20 13   [The landowner] answered *one* of them and said, 'My
            friend,'
    22 35   to disconcert [Jesus], *one* of [the Pharisees] put a question,
    23 15   You . . . travel over sea and land to make a *single* proselyte,
    25 40   in so far as you did this to *one* of the least of these . . . you
            did it to me.
      45   in so far as you neglected to do this to *one* of the least of
            these, you neglected to do it to me.
    26 14   *one* of the Twelve, . . . Judas Iscariot, went to the chief
            priests
      21   *one* of you is about to betray me.
      47   Judas, *one* of the Twelve, appeared,
      51   *one* of the followers of Jesus grasped his sword
      69   ʳa (lit. *one*) servant-girl came up to [Peter]
    27 15   it was the governor's practice to release ʳa (lit. *one*) prisoner
      48   *one* of [those who stood there] quickly ran to get a sponge
Mk 5 22   *one* of the synagogue officials came up, Jairus by name,
     6 15   He is a prophet, like *one* of the prophets we used to have.
     8 28   [Who do people say I am?] John the Baptist, . . . others
            Elijah; others again, *one* of the prophets.
     9 17   ʳA (lit. *One*) [man] answered him from the crowd,
      37   Anyone who welcomes *one* of these little children . . .
            welcomes me;
      42   anyone who is an obstacle to bring down *one* of these little
            ones . . . would be better thrown into the sea
    10 17   ʳa (lit. *one*) man ran up, knelt before [Jesus]
    12 6 < He had still [some]*one* left: his beloved son.
      28   One of the scribes . . . had listened to them debating
      42   ʳA (lit. *One*) poor widow came and put in two small coins
    13 1   *one* of his disciples said to him, 'Look . . . Master!'
    14 10   Judas Iscariot, *one* of the Twelve, approached the chief
            priests
      18   *one* of you is about to betray me,
      20   It is *one* of the Twelve,
      43   Judas, *one* of the Twelve, came up with a number of men
      47   *one* of the bystanders drew his sword
      66   *one* of the high priest's servant-girls came up.
    15 6 ● Pilate used to release a ʳ(lit. *one*) prisoner for them,
Lk 15 7 ● there will be more rejoicing . . . over *one* repentant sinner
            than over ninety-nine virtuous men
      10 ● there is rejoicing among the angels . . . over *one* repentant
            sinner.
      15   [the prodigal son] hired himself out to *one* of the local
            inhabitants
      19   treat me as *one* of your paid servants.

Lk 15 26   Calling *one* of the servants [the elder son] asked what it was
            all about.
    17 2   It would be better for him to be thrown into the sea . . .
            than that he should lead astray [a single] *one* of these little
            ones.
      15   *one* of [the ten lepers] turned back praising God
    22 47   Judas, *one* of the Twelve, . . . went up to Jesus to kiss him.
      50   *one* of [Jesus's followers] struck out at the high priest's
            servant,
    23 17   (ᵛ At festival time [Pilate] was obliged to release *one* [person]
            to them.)
    24 18   *one* of [the two disciples on their way to Emmaus was] called
            Cleopas
Jn 1 40   *One* of these two who became followers of Jesus . . . was
            Andrew,
     6 8   *One* of his disciples, Andrew, . . . said,
      70   *one* of you is a devil. [71] [Jesus] meant Judas . . . *one* of the
      71   Twelve who was going to betray him.
     7 50   *One* of [the Pharisees], Nicodemus . . . who had come to
            Jesus earlier, said,
     8 9   [the scribes and Pharisees] went away ʳone by one (lit.
            [each] *one* individually),
    11 49   *One* of them, Caiaphas, the high priest that year,
    12 2   Lazarus was ʳamong (lit. *one* of) those at table.
       4   Judas, . . . *one* of his disciples,
    13 21   *one* of you will betray me.
      23   ʳThe disciple (lit. *One* of his disciples, whom) Jesus loved was
            reclining next to Jesus;
    18 22   *one* of the guards . . . gave Jesus a slap in the face,
      26   *One* of the high priest's servants . . . said [to Peter],
      39   according to a custom of yours I should release *one* [prisoner]
            at the Passover;
    19 34   *one* of the soldiers pierced his side
    20 24   Thomas . . . was *one* of the Twelve,
Ac 1 22   [We must choose] [some]*one* who . . . can act with us as a
            witness
      24   show us . . . which *one* of these two you have chosen
    11 28   *one* of them whose name was Agabus . . . stood up and
            predicted
    17 26 A From *one* [single stock God] . . . created the whole human
            race
    23 17   [Paul] called *one* of the centurions
Rm 3 10 ● (Ps 14 3) There is not a good man left, no, not *one*;
      12 ● (Ps 14 4) there is not one good man left, not [a single] *one*.
     9 10   Rebecca . . . was pregnant by *one* [man, by our] ancestor
            Isaac,
1 Co 4 6   it is not for any *one* of you, so full of your own importance,
            to go taking sides for *one* [man] against another.
     9 24   All the runners . . . are trying to win, but only *one* of them
            gets the prize.
    14 27   If there are people present with the gift of tongues . . .
            there must be [some]*one* to interpret.
Ga 3 20   there can only be an intermediary between two parties, not
            just *one*, yet God is *one*.
1 Tm 3 2   the president . . . must not have been ʳmarried more than
            once (lit. husband to more than *one* woman),
      12   Deacons must not have been ʳmarried more than once
            (lit. husbands to more than *one* woman),
     5 9   Enrolment as a widow is permissible only for a woman
            . . . who has had only *one* husband.
Tt 1 6   [an elder] must not have been ʳmarried more than once
            (lit. husband to more than *one* woman),
Heb 11 12   there came from *one* man [Abraham], who was already as
            good as dead himself, more descendants than could be
            counted,
Rv 4 8   ʳEach (lit. [Each] *one* individually) of the four animals had
            six wings
     5 5   *one* of the elders said to me,
     7 13   *One* of the elders then spoke,
    17 1   *One* of the seven angels that had the seven bowls came . . .
            to me,
    18 21   ʳa (lit. *one*) powerful angel picked up a boulder
    19 17   I saw ʳan (lit. *one*) angel standing in the sun,
    21 9   *One* of the seven angels . . . came to speak to me,

            c) One (day, hour) – First (day of the week) – Single (hour, day)

            D = First day of the week, Sunday

Mt 20 12   The men who came last . . . have done only *one* hour,
    26 40   So you had not the strength to keep awake with me *one* hour?
    28 1 D   towards dawn on the *first* day of the week, [the women] . . .
            went to visit the sepulchre.
Mk 14 37   Simon, . . . had you not the strength to keep awake *one* hour?
    16 2 D   very early in the morning on the *first* day of the week [the
            women] went to the tomb,
Lk 5 17   [Jesus] was teaching *one* day,
     8 22   *One* day, [Jesus] got into a boat
    17 22   you will long to see *one* of the days of the Son of Man
    20 1   *one* day . . . [Jesus] was teaching

Lk 22 59 about ᶠan (lit. *one*) hour later another man insisted, saying,
24 1 D On the *first* day of the week . . . [the women] went to the tomb
Jn 20 1 D It was very early on the *first* day of the week and still dark,
19 D In the evening of that same day, the *first* day of the week,
Ac 20 7 D On the *first* day of the week we met to break bread,
21 7 we . . . stayed *one* day with [the brothers at Ptolemais].
28 13 After *one* day [at Rhegium] a south wind sprang up
1 Co 10 8 twenty-three thousand met their downfall in *one* day.
16 2 D Every ᶠSunday (lit. *first* day of the week), each one of you must put aside what he can afford,
2 P 3 8 (Ps 90 4) with the Lord ᶠa (lit. *one*) day can mean a thousand years, and a thousand years is like ᶠa (lit. *one*) day.
Rv 17 12 ten kings . . . will have royal authority only for ᶠa (lit. *one*) single hour
18 8 within a *single* day the plagues will fall on [Babylon]:
10 Mourn . . . Babylon, . . . doomed as you are within a *single* hour.
17 your riches are all destroyed within a *single* hour.
19 mourn for this great city . . . ruined within a *single* hour.

d) One, One (of), Single, (generally)

Mt 5 18 not *one* dot, not *one* little stroke, shall disappear from the Law
19 the man who infringes even *one* of the least of these commandments . . . will be considered the least in the kingdom of heaven;
29 it will do you less harm to lose *one* part of you
30 it will do you less harm to lose *one* part of you
36 you cannot turn a *single* hair white or black.
41 if anyone orders you to go *one* mile, go two miles with him.
6 27 Can any of you . . . add *one* [single] cubit to his span of life?
29 not even Solomon . . . was robed like *one* of these [flowers].
10 29 yet not *one* [sparrow] falls to the ground without your Father knowing.
12 11 < If any [one] of you here had only *one* sheep and it fell down a hole on the sabbath day, would he not . . . lift it out?
13 46 < when [a merchant] finds *one* [pearl] of great value he . . . sells everything he owns and buys it.
17 4 I will make three tents here, *one* for you, *one* for Moses and *one* for Elijah.
18 12 Suppose a man has a hundred sheep and *one* of them strays; will he not leave the ninety-nine . . . ?
21 19 Seeing ᶠa (lit. *one*) fig tree by the road, [Jesus] went up to it
24 I . . . will ask you a question, only *one*;
25 15 < To *one* he gave five talents, . . . to a third *one*;
18 < the man who had received *one* went off and . . . hid his master's money.
24 < Last came forward the man who had the *one* talent.
27 14 [Jesus] offered no reply to *any* of the charges.
Mk 8 14 The disciples . . . had only *one* loaf with them in the boat.
9 5 let us make three tents, *one* for you, *one* for Moses and *one* for Elijah.
10 21 There is *one* thing you lack. Go and sell everything you own
11 29 I will ask you a question, only *one*;
14 20 It is one of the Twelve, one who is dipping into the ᶠsame (lit. *one*) dish with me.
Lk 5 3 [Jesus] got into *one* of the boats
12 Jesus was in *one* of the towns
9 33 let us make three tents, *one* for you, *one* for Moses and *one* for Elijah.
10 42 [you worry about so many things] and yet few are needed, indeed only *one*.
11 46 you load on men burdens that . . . you yourselves do not move ᶠa (lit. *one*) finger to lift.
12 6 yet not *one* [sparrow] is forgotten in God's sight.
27 not even Solomon . . . was robed like *one* of these [flowers].
13 10 [Jesus] was teaching in *one* of the synagogues,
15 4 < What man among you with a hundred sheep, losing *one*, would not leave the ninety-nine . . . ?
8 < what woman with ten drachmas would not, if she lost *one*, . . . search thoroughly till she found it?
16 17 It is easier for heaven and earth to disappear than for *one* little stroke to drop out of the Law.
17 34 on that night two will be in *one* bed:
18 22 There is still *one* thing you lack.
Jn 1 3 not *one* thing had its being but through [the Word].
6 22 the crowd . . saw that only *one* boat had been there,
7 21 *One* work I did, and you are all surprised by it.
9 25 I only know *one* thing: that I was blind and now I can see.
20 7 the cloth that had been over his head . . . was . . . rolled up in ᶠa (lit. *one*) place by itself.
Ac 12 10 [the angel and Peter] had walked the whole length of *one* street
24 21 unless it were to do with this *single* outburst, when I stood up among them and called out:
28 25 Paul had *one* last thing to say to [the Jews in Rome], 'How aptly the Holy Spirit spoke when he told your ancestors . . . :

Rm 5 16 after one *single* fall came judgement with a verdict of condemnation,
1 Co 11 5 if [a woman] prays . . . unveiled, ᶠshe might as well have (lit. it is *one* and the same thing as her having) her hair shaved off.
12 26 If *one* part is hurt, all parts are hurt with it.
2 Co 11 24 Five times I had the ᶠthirty-nine (lit. forty-less-*one*) lashes from the Jews.
Ga 5 14 the whole of the Law is summarised in a *single* command: Love your neighbour
Ph 3 13 ᶠAll (lit. *One* thing) I can say is that . . . ¹⁴ I am racing for the finish,
Heb 10 12 [Christ] has offered *one* [single] sacrifice for sins . . . ¹⁴ By virtue of that *one* [single] offering, he has achieved the eternal perfection of all whom he is sanctifying.
12 16 Esau . . . sold his birthright for *one* [single] meal.
Jm 2 10 if a man keeps the whole of the Law, except for *one* [small] point . . . he is still guilty of breaking it all.
Rv 6 1 I saw the Lamb break ᶠone (or: the *first*) of the seven seals, and I heard *one* of the four animals shout
8 13 I heard an ᶠ(lit. *one*) eagle, calling aloud
9 12 That was the *first* of the troubles;
13 I heard ᶠa (lit. *one*) voice come out of the four horns
13 3 *one* of [the beast's] heads seemed to have had a fatal wound
15 7 *One* of the four animals gave the seven angels seven golden bowls
21 21 The twelve gates were twelve pearls, each gate being made of a *single* pearl,

e) Unity – (to make, to be) One

Mt 19 5 (Gn 2 24) the two become *one* body
6 They are no longer two, therefore, but *one* body.
Mk 10 8 the two become *one* body. They are no longer two, therefore, but *one* body.
Lk 12 52 from now on ᶠa (lit. *one*) household of five will be divided:
14 18 all ᶠalike (lit. as *one*) started to make excuses.
Jn 10 16 there will be only *one* flock, and one shepherd.
30 The Father and I are *one*.
11 52 [Jesus was to die] to gather together in *unity* the scattered children of God.
17 11 Father, keep those you have given me true to your name, so that they may be *one* like us.
21 May they all be *one*. Father, may they be ᵛ*one* ᶠin us,
22 I have given them the glory you gave to me, that they may be
23 *one* as we are *one*. ²³ . . . may they be . . . completely *one*
Ac 4 32 The whole group of believers was united in heart and with *one* soul;
19 34 [the Ephesians] started shouting ᶠin unison (lit. with *one* voice),
Rm 12 4 Just as each *one* of our bodies has several parts . . . ⁵ so all of us, in union with Christ, form *one* body,
15 6 so that united in mind and with *one* voice you may give glory to . . . God
1 Co 3 8 It is all *one* who does the planting and who does the watering,
6 16 a man who goes with a prostitute is *one* body with her, since (Gn 2 24) the two . . . become *one* flesh.
17 anyone who is joined to the Lord is *one* spirit with him.
10 17 The fact that there is only *one* loaf means that . . . we form a *single* body because we all have a share in this *one* loaf.
12 9 Ⓢ another [man may have] the gift of healing, through this *one* Spirit . . . ¹¹ these are the work of *one* and the same Spirit . . . ¹² Just as a human body . . . is [a] *single* [unit] because all these parts, though many, make *one* body, so it is with Christ.
11 Ⓢ
12
13 Ⓢ In the *one* Spirit we were all baptised into *one* body, Jews
Ⓢ as well as Greeks . . . and *one* Spirit was given to us all to drink.
14 Nor is the body to be identified with any *one* of its many
19 parts . . . ¹⁹ If all the parts were ᶠthe same (lit. *one*),
20 how could it be a body? ²⁰ As it is, the parts are many but the body is *one*.
Ga 3 28 all of you are *one* in Christ Jesus.
Ep 2 14 [Christ] has made the two into *one* [people] . . . ¹⁵ . . . This
15 was to create *one* [single] New Man in himself out of the
16 two of them and . . . ¹⁶ . . . to unite them both in a
18 Ⓢ *single* Body and reconcile them with God . . . ¹⁸ Through him, both of us have in the *one* Spirit our way to come to the Father.
4 3 Ⓢ 5 Do all you can to preserve the *unity* of the Spirit
4 There is *one* Body, *one* Spirit, just as you were all called into *one* and the same hope when you were called.
5 There is one Lord, *one* faith, *one* baptism.
13 5 In this way we are all to come to *unity* in our faith and in our knowledge of the Son of God,
5 31 (Gn 2 24) the two will become *one* body.
Ph 1 27 you are *unanimous* in meeting the attack with firm resistance, *united* by your love
2 2 be united . . . with a common purpose and ᶠa common (ᵛ *one*) mind

Col 3 15	you were called together as parts of *one* body.
1 Jn 5 8	the Spirit, the water and the blood, . . . all three of them agree [on] the *one* [testimony].
Rv 17 13	[The ten kings] are all of *one* mind
17	God influenced their minds . . . to ˹agree together (lit. *unite*) to put their royal powers at the beast's disposal

f) One (. . . other), First (. . . second) – One . . , One

Mt 6 24	No one can be the slave of two masters: he will either hate the *first* and love the second, or treat the *first* with respect and the second with scorn.
20 21	Promise that these two sons of mine may sit *one* at your right hand and ˹the other (lit. *one*) at your left
24 40 41	Then of two men in the fields *one* is taken, *one* left; ⁴¹ of two women at the millstone grinding, *one* is taken, *one* left.
27 38	two robbers were crucified with him, *one* on the right and *one* on the left.
Mk 10 37	Allow us to sit *one* at your right hand and ˹the other (lit. *one*) at your left
14 19	[the Twelve] asked him, *one* ˹after another (lit. by *one*), 'Not I, surely?'
15 27	they crucified two robbers with him, *one* on his right and *one* on his left.
Lk 7 41	There was once a creditor who had two men in his debt; *one* owed him five hundred denarii, the other fifty.
16 13	No servant can be the slave of two masters: he will either hate the *first* and love the second, or treat the *first* with respect and the second with scorn.
17 34 35 36	two will be in one bed: *one* will be taken, the other left; ³⁵ two women will be grinding corn together: *one* will be taken, the other left. ³⁶ (ᵛ Two men will be in the field: *one* will be taken, the other left.)
18 10	Two men went up to the Temple . . . *one* a Pharisee, the other a tax collector.
23 39	*One* of the criminals . . . abused [Jesus] . . . ⁴⁰ But the other . . . rebuked him.
Jn 20 12	[Mary] saw two angels in white sitting where the body of Jesus had been, *one* at the head, ˹the other (lit. *one*) at the feet.
Ac 23 6	*one* section [of the Sanhedrin] was made up of Sadducees and the other of Pharisees,
Ga 4 22 24	Abraham had two sons, *one* by the slave-girl, and *one* by his freeborn wife . . . ²⁴ . . . the women stand for the two covenants. The *first* who comes from Mount Sinai . . . is Hagar
1 Th 5 11	So give encouragement *one* to ˹another (lit. *one*),
Tt 3 10	after a *first* and a second warning have no more to do with him:
Rv 17 10	Five of [the seven emperors] have already gone, *one* is here now,

g) Once, Once and for all – At the same time, At once

Rm 6 10	X	4	When [Christ] died, he died, *once for all*, to sin,
1 Co 15 6	X	4	[Jesus] appeared to more than five hundred of the brothers *at the same time*,
2 Co 11 25		2	three times I have been beaten with sticks; *once* I was stoned;
Ph 4 16		2	*once* or twice since my stay in Thessalonika you have sent me what I needed.
1 Th 2 18		2	I, Paul, tried ˹more than once (lit. *once* or twice) [to visit you]
Heb 6 4		2	As for those people who were *once* brought into the light . . .⁶ . . . it is impossible for them to be renewed a second time.
7 27	X	4	[the ideal high priest] would not need to offer sacrifices every day . . . because he has done this *once and for all* by offering himself.
9 7		2	the second tent is entered only *once* a year, and then by the high priest
12	X	4	[Christ] has entered the sanctuary *once and for all*,
26	X	2	he has made his appearance *once and for all*, now at the end of the last age,
27		2	Since men only die *once* . . . ²⁸ so Christ, too, offers himself
28	X	2	only *once* . . . and when he appears a second time, it will not be to deal with sin
10 2		2	the worshippers, when they had been purified *once*, would have no awareness of sins.
10		4	this will was for us to be made holy by the offering of his body made *once and for all* by Jesus Christ.
12 26		2	I shall make the earth shake *once* more . . . ²⁷ The words
27		2	'*once* more' show that . . . created things . . . are going to be changed,
1 P 3 18	X	2	Christ himself, innocent though he was, had died *once* for sins,
Jude 3		2	fight hard for the faith which has been *once and for all* entrusted to the saints.
5		2	you have already learnt it *once and for all*

h) Individually – Singular

Jn 8 9		3	[The scribes and the Pharisees] went away ˹one by one (lit. [each] one *individually*),
21 25		3	if ˹all [the things Jesus did] were written down (lit. they were written down *individually*), the world itself . . . would not hold all the books
Ac 21 19		3	[Paul] gave ˹a detailed account of all (lit. an account [of things] each *individually*) that God had done among the pagans
Rm 12 5		3	all of us, in union with Christ, form one body, and *individually* as parts of it we belong to each other.
1 Co 14 31		3	you can all prophesy ˹in turn (lit. *individually*),
Ga 3 16		3	scripture . . . uses the *singular*: to [Abraham's] posterity, which is Christ.
Ep 5 33		3	each ˹one of you (lit. *individually*) must love his wife as he loves himself;
Rv 4 8		3	˹Each (lit. [Each] one *individually*) of the four animals had six wings

2: FIRST: *PRŌTOS*

5	*prōteuō*	1	4	*prōto*(-*kath-edria*) 4
2	*prōton*	61	3	*prōto*(-*klisia*) 5
1	*prōtos*	97	6	(*deutero*-)*prōtos* 1
8	*prōtōs*	1	7	(*philo*-)*prōteuō* 1

a) (God, Christ, is the) First

For First-born *see* BEAR – BIRTH – CHILD 4. 3:

Ac 26 23	the Christ was . . . the *first* to rise from the dead,
Col 1 18	As [the Christ] is the Beginning, he was first to be born from the dead, so that he should *be* first in every way;
Rv 1 17	it is I, the *First* and the Last; I am the Living One,
2 8	Here is the message of the *First* and the Last,
22 13	I am the Alpha and the Omega, the *First* and the Last, the Beginning and the End.

b) (A person is) First – Leading (people)

A = Adam

Mt 10 2			These are the names of the twelve apostles: *first*, Simon who is called Peter,
19 30			Many who are *first* will be last, and the last, *first*.
20 8			pay [the workers] their wages, starting with the last arrivals and ending with the *first*.
10			When the *first* came, they expected to get more,
16			Thus the last will be *first*, and the *first*, last.
27			anyone who wants to be *first* among you must be your slave,
21 28			A man had two sons. He . . . said to the *first*, 'My boy, you go and work in the vineyard today'.
31			Which of the two did the father's will? 'The ᵛ *first* (G second)' they said.
36			[the landowner] sent some more servants, this time a larger number than the *first*,
22 25			we had a case involving seven brothers; the *first* married
Mk 6 21	○		[Herod] gave a banquet . . . for the ˹leading [figures] (or: *first* [men]) in Galilee.
9 35			If anyone wants to be *first*, he must make himself last of all
10 31			Many who are *first* will be last, and the last *first*.
44			anyone who wants to be *first* among you must be slave to all.
12 20			there were seven brothers. The *first* married a wife
Lk 13 30			there are those now last who will be *first*, and those now *first* who will be last.
14 18			The *first* [of those who had been invited] said, 'I have bought a piece of land and must go and see it.'
16 5			[the steward] called his master's debtors one by one. To the *first* he said,
19 16			The *first* [servant] came in
47	○		The chief priests . . . with the support of the ˹leading (or: *first*) [citizens], tried to do away with him,
20 29			there were seven brothers. The *first* . . . died childless.
Jn 5 4			ᵛ the *first* [person] to enter the water . . . was cured . . .¹
8 7			If there is one of you who has not sinned, let him be the *first* to throw a stone at her.
19 32			the soldiers . . . broke the legs of the *first* [man] . . . and then of the other.
Ac 13 50	○		the Jews worked upon some of . . . the ˹leading (or: *first*) [men] of the city
17 4			a great many God-fearing people and Greeks [joined Paul and Silas,] as well as a number of ˹rich (lit. *leading*) women.
25 2	○		The chief priests and *leaders* of the Jews informed [Festus] of the case against Paul,
28 7	○		there were estates belonging to the ˹prefect (lit. *first* [man]) of the island,
17	○		[Paul] called together the ˹leading (or: *first*) Jews.
1 Co 14 30			If one of the listeners receives a revelation, then the ˹man who is already speaking (lit. *first* speaker) should stop.

1 Co 15	45 A	The *first* man, Adam, . . . became a living soul; but the last Adam has become a life-giving spirit . . . ⁴⁷ The *first* man, being from the earth, is earthly by nature; the second is from heaven.
	47 A	
1 Tm 1	15	I myself am the ⌐greatest (lit. *first*) of [sinners];
	16	Jesus Christ meant to make me the ⌐greatest (lit. *first*) evidence of his inexhaustible patience
3 Jn	9	⁷ Diotrephes . . . seems to enjoy *being* ⌐in charge (lit. *first*) of [the church],
Rv 8	7	The *first* blew his trumpet and . . . hail and fire, mixed with blood were dropped on the earth;
	16 2	The *first* angel went and emptied his bowl over the earth;

c) First (day)

D = First day of the week, Sunday

Mt 26	17	on the *first* day of Unleavened Bread the disciples came to Jesus
Mk 14	12	On the *first* day of Unleavened Bread . . . his disciples said
	16 9 D	Having risen in the morning on the *first* day of the week,
Lk 6	1	⌐one sabbath (ᵛ on the second sabbath after the *first*) . . . his disciples were picking ears of corn,
	6	
Ac 20	18	You know what my way of life has been ever since the *first* day I set foot among you in Asia,
Ph 1	5	you have helped to spread the Good News from the *first* day you heard it

d) First (as an adjective, generally) – Front

Mt 12	45	⌐the man ends up by being worse than he was before (lit. the final state of the man is worse than the *first*).
	17 27	take the *first* fish that bites,
	22 38	This is the greatest and the *first* commandment.
	23 6	[Everything the Pharisees do is done to attract attention,] like wanting to take the ⌐place of honour (lit. the *first*) place) at banquets and the ⌐front (or: *first*) seats in the synagogues,
	3	
	4	
	27 64	This last piece of fraud would be worse than ⌐what went before (lit. the *first*).
Mk 12	28	Which is the *first* of all the commandments? ²⁹ Jesus replied, 'This is the *first* (Dt 6 4–5): Listen, Israel, the Lord our God is the one Lord',
	29	
	39	⁴ [the scribes like] to take the ⌐front (or: *first*) seats in the synagogues and the ⌐places of honour (lit. *first* places) at banquets;
	3	
Lk 2	2	This census – the *first* – took place while Quirinius was governor of Syria,
	10 5	² ⌐let your *first* words be (or: say first), 'Peace to this house!'
	11 26	⌐the man ends up by being worse than he was before (lit. the final state of the man is worse than the *first*).
	43	you Pharisees . . . like taking the ⌐seats of honour (lit. *first* seats) in the synagogues
	4	
	14 7	³ the guests . . . picked the ⌐places of honour (lit. *first* places).
	8 <	³ do not take your seat in the ⌐place of honour (lit. *first* place).
	15 22 <	Bring out the ⌐best (lit. *first*) robe and put it on him;
	20 46	⁴ the scribes . . . love . . . to take the ⌐front (or: *first*) seats in the synagogues and the ⌐places of honour (lit. *first* places) at banquets,
	3	
Ac 1	1	In my ⌐earlier (lit. *first*) work . . . I dealt with everything Jesus had done
	12 10	[The angel and Peter] passed through two guard posts ⌐one after the other (lit. the *first* then a second),
	13 33	As scripture says in the ⌐first (ᵛ second) psalm: You are my son:
	16 12	Philippi, . . . the ⌐principal (lit. *first*) city of that particular district of Macedonia,
Ep 6	2	The *first* commandment . . . is: Honour your father and mother,
1 Tm 5	12	[young widows want to marry again,] and then people condemn them for being unfaithful to their *original* promise.
2 Tm 2	6	² it is the working farmer who has the *first* claim on any crop that is harvested.
	4 16	The *first* time I had to present my defence, there was not a single witness to support me.
Heb 8	7	If that *first* covenant had been without a fault, there would have been no need for a second one to replace it.
	13	By speaking of a new covenant, he implies that the *first* [one] is already old.
9	1	The *first* covenant also had its laws governing worship,
	2	There was a tent which comprised two compartments: the *first* . . . was called the Holy Place;
	6	priests are constantly going into the ⌐outer (or: *first*) tent
	8	no one has the right to go into the sanctuary as long as the ⌐outer (or: *first*) tent remains standing;
	15	[Christ's] death took place to cancel the sins that infringed the ⌐earlier (lit. *first*) covenant.

Heb 9	18	even the ⌐earlier (lit. *first*) covenant needed something to be killed in order to take effect,
10	9	[Christ] is abolishing the *first* sort to replace it with the second.
2 P 2	20	anyone who . . . allows himself to be entangled by [the pollution of the world] a second time . . . will end up in a worse state than ⌐he began in (lit. the *first* he was in).
Rv 4	1	I . . . heard the ⌐same (lit. *first*) voice speaking to me,
	7	The *first* animal was like a lion,
13	12	This second beast was servant to the *first* beast . . . making the world . . . worship the *first* beast,
20	5	This is the *first* resurrection;
	6	Happy . . . are those who share in the *first* resurrection;
21	1	the *first* heaven and the *first* earth had disappeared
	4	The ⌐world of the past (lit. *first* world) has gone.
	19	the *first* [foundation was faced] with diamond, the second lapis lazuli,

e) First (as an adverb) – At first, In the first place

Mt 5	24	² go and be reconciled with your brother *first*,
6	33	² Set your hearts on his kingdom *first*, and on his righteousness,
7	5	² Take the plank out of your own eye *first*,
8	21	² let me go and bury my father *first*.
10	2	These are the names of the twelve apostles: *first*, Simon who is called Peter,
12	29	how can anyone make his way into a strong man's house . . . unless he has tied up the strong man *first*?
13	30	² *First* collect the darnel
17	10	² Why do the scribes say then that Elijah has to come *first*?
Mk 3	27	² Clean the inside of cup and dish *first*
		no one can make his way into a strong man's house . . . unless he has tied up the strong man *first*.
4	28	² the land produces *first* the shoot, then the ear,
7	27	² The children should be fed *first*,
9	11	² Why do the scribes say that Elijah has to come *first*?
	12	² True, . . . Elijah is to come *first*
13	10	² the Good News must *first* be proclaimed to all the nations.
16	9	² [Jesus] appeared *first* to Mary of Magdala
Lk 6	42	² Take the plank out of your own eye *first*,
9	59	² Let me go and bury my father *first*.
	61	² *first* let me go and say good-bye to my people at home.
10	5	² ⌐let your first words be (or: say *first*), 'Peace to this house!'
11	38	² The Pharisee . . . was surprised that [Jesus] had not *first* washed before the meal.
12	1	² [Jesus] began to speak, *first of all* to his disciples. 'Be on your guard against the yeast of the Pharisees'
14	28	which of you here, intending to build a tower, would not *first* . . . work out the cost . . . ?
	31	what king marching to war against another king would not ² *first* . . . consider whether . . . he could stand up to the other . . . ?
17	25	² *first* [the Son of Man] must suffer grievously
21	9	² this is something that must happen *first* but the end is not so soon.
Jn 1	15 X	He who comes after me ranks before me because he existed *before* me.
	30 X	A man is coming after me who ranks before me because he existed *before* me.
	41	≠ Early (G *First*) next morning, Andrew met his brother
2	10	² People generally serve the best wine *first*,
7	51	² surely the Law does not allow us *first* to pass judgement on a man without giving him a hearing . . . ?
10	40	[Jesus] went back again to the far side of the Jordan to stay ² in the district where John had ⌐once (or: *first*) been baptising.
12	16	² *At the time* his disciples did not understand this,
15	18	² remember that [the world] hated me *before* you.
18	13	² They took [Jesus] *first* to Annas,
19	39	² Nicodemus came as well – the same one who had *first* come to Jesus at night-time –
20	4	the other disciple . . . reached the tomb *first*;
	8	the other disciple who had reached the tomb *first* also went in;
Ac 3	26	² It was for you *in the first place* that God raised up his servant Jacob . . . sent our ancestors there [on a] *first* [visit],
7	12	
11	26	⁸ It was at Antioch that the disciples were *first* called 'Christians'.
13	46	² We had to proclaim the word of God to you *first*,
15	14	² Simeon has described how God *first* arranged to enlist a people for his name out of the pagans.
26	20	² I started preaching, *first* to the people of Damascus, then to those of Jerusalem
27	43	the centurion . . . gave orders that those who could swim should jump overboard *first*
Rm 1	8	² *First* I thank my God
	16	the Good News . . . is the power of God saving all who have ² faith – Jews *first*,
2	9	Pain . . . will come to every human being who employs himself in evil – Jews *first*, . . . ¹⁰ renown . . . will come to ² everyone who does good – Jews *first*,
	10	

Rm	3 2	2 *First*, the Jews are the people to whom God's message was entrusted.
	10 19	Moses answered this ⌐long ago (lit. *first*) (Dt 32 21):
	15 24	2 after *first* enjoying a little of your company, [I hope] to complete the rest of the journey
1 Co	11 18	2 *In the first place*, I hear that . . . there are separate factions among you,
	12 28	2 In the Church, God has given ⌐the first place to (lit. *in the first place*) apostles,
	15 3	Well then, *in the first place*, I taught you what I had been taught myself,
	46	2 *first* the one with the soul, not the spirit,
2 Co	8 5	2 they offered their own selves *first* to God
Ep	4 9	2 When [scripture] says, 'he ascended', what can it mean if not that he (ᵛ *first*) descended
1 Th	4 16	2 those who have died in Christ will ⌐be the first to rise (lit. rise *first*),
2 Th	2 3	2 It cannot happen until the Great Revolt has *first* taken place
1 Tm	2 1	2 My advice is that, *first of all*, there should be prayers offered
	13	Adam was formed *first* and Eve afterwards,
	3 10	2 [Deacons] are to be examined *first*,
	5 4	2 If a widow has children . . . they are to learn *first* [of all] to do their duty to their own families
2 Tm	1 5	2 the sincere faith . . . came *first* to live in your grandmother
Heb	7 2	2 By the interpretation of [Melchizedek's] name, he is, *first* 'king of righteousness'
Jm	3 17	the wisdom that comes down from above is ⌐essentially
		2 (lit. *first*) something pure;
1 P	4 17	2 if ⌐what we know now is only the beginning (lit. *first* is only what we know now), what will it be . . . ?
2 P	1 20	2 *At the same time*, . . . remember that the interpretation . . . is never a matter for the individual.
	3 3	2 We must be careful *first* to remember that . . . there are bound to be people who will be scornful,
1 Jn	4 19 Θ	We are to love, then, because he loved us *first*.
Rv	2 4	you have less love now than your *first* used to.
	5	repent, and do as you used to *at first*,
	19	I know how you are ⌐still making⌐progress (lit. doing more now than *at first*).

4. TWO, BOTH – SECOND – HALF

1: TWO – SECOND – BOTH: DUŌ, AMPHOTEROI

7	*deuteraios*	*1*	9	*di(-etēs)*	*1*
2	*deuteros*	*44*	5	*di(-etia)*	*2*
3	*dis*	*6*	10	*di-ploō*	*1*
1	*duō*	*133*	4	*di-ploos*	*4*
8	*deutero-(prōtos)*	*1*	6	*di(-psychos)*	*2*
			11	*amphoteroi*	*14*

a) Two (people) – Second (person, angel) – Both

Mt	4 18		[Jesus] saw *two* brothers, Simon . . . and . . . Andrew;
	21		[Jesus] saw another ⌐pair of (lit. *two*) brothers, James . . . and . . . John;
	6 24		No one can be the slave of *two* masters:
	8 28		*two* demoniacs came towards [Jesus] out of the tombs
	9 27		*two* blind men followed [Jesus]
	15 14	11	if one blind man leads another, *both* will fall into a pit.
	18 16		take one or *two* others along with you: the evidence of *two* or three witnesses is required to sustain any charge.
	19		if *two* of you . . . agree to ask anything at all, it will be
	20		granted to you by my Father . . . 20 For where *two* or three meet in my name, I shall be there with them.
	19 5 ●		(Gn 2 24) a man must . . . cling to his wife, and the *two*
	6		become one body. 6 They are no longer *two*, therefore,
	20 21		Promise that these *two* sons of mine may sit one at your right hand and the other at your left
	24		the other ten . . . were indignant with the *two* brothers.
	30		there were *two* blind men sitting at the side of the road.
	21 1		Jesus sent *two* disciples,
	28		A man had *two* sons . . . 30 The man . . . said the same thing
	30	2/	to the *second* [son] . . . 31 Which of the *two* did the father's
	31		will?
	22 26		[The first brother died without children;] the same thing
		2	happened with the *second* and third and so on to the seventh,
	24 40		Then of *two* men in the fields one is taken . . . 41 of *two*
	41		women at the millstone grinding, one is taken,
	26 37		[Jesus] took Peter and the *two* sons of Zebedee with him.
	60		Eventually *two* [lying witnesses] stepped forward
	27 21		Which of the *two* do you want me to release for you?
	38		At the same time *two* robbers were crucified with [Jesus],
Mk	6 7		[Jesus] summoned the Twelve and began to send them out ⌐in pairs (lit. *two* by *two*)

Mk	10 8 ●		(Gn 2 24) the *two* become one body. They are no longer *two*,
	35		James and John, the *two* sons of Zebedee, approached [Jesus].
	11 1		[Jesus] sent *two* of his disciples
	12 21	2	The *second* [brother] married the widow, and he too died . . . with the third it was the same,
	14 13		[Jesus] sent *two* of his disciples,
	15 27		they crucified *two* robbers with [Jesus],
	16 12		[Jesus] showed himself under another form to *two* of them
Lk	1 6	11	*Both* [Zechariah and Elizabeth] were worthy in the sight of God,
	7	11	[Zechariah and Elizabeth] were *both* getting on in years.
	6 39	11	Can one blind man guide another? Surely *both* will fall into a pit?
	7 18		John, summoning *two* of his disciples, 19 sent them to the Lord
	41		a creditor . . . had *two* men in his debt . . . 42 They were
	42	11	unable to pay, so he pardoned them *both*.
	9 30		there were *two* men there talking to [Jesus]; they were Moses and Elijah . . . 32 Peter and his companions . . . saw
	32		the *two* men
	10 1		the Lord appointed seventy-two others and sent them out . . . ⌐in pairs (lit. in *twos*)
	12 52		a household of five will be divided: three against *two* and *two* against three;
	15 11		A man had *two* sons.
	16 13		No servant can be the slave of *two* masters:
	17 34		on that night *two* men will be in one bed: one will be taken . . . 35 *two* women will be grinding corn together: one
	35		will be taken . . . 36 (ᵛ *Two* men will be in a field: one will
	36		be taken, one left).
	18 10		*Two* men went up to the Temple to pray,
	19 18	2	Then came the *second* [servant] and said, 'Sir, your one pound has made five'.
	29		[Jesus] sent *two* of the disciples,
	20 30	2	The *second* [brother] 31 and then the third married the widow.
	23 32		Now with [Jesus] they were also leading out *two* other criminals to be executed.
	24 4		*two* men in brilliant clothes suddenly appeared
	13		*two* of [the disciples] were on their way to . . . Emmaus.
Jn	1 35		as John stood there . . . with *two* of his disciples, Jesus
	37		passed . . . 37 . . . the *two* disciples followed Jesus . . .
	40		40 One of these *two* . . . was Andrew.
	8 17		(Dt 29 15) the testimony of *two* witnesses is valid.
	19 18		they crucified [Jesus] with *two* others,
	20 4		[Peter and the other disciple] *both* ran together,
	12		[Mary] saw *two* angels . . . where the body of Jesus had been.
	21 2		Simon Peter . . . and *two* more of his disciples were together.
Ac	1 10		suddenly *two* men in white were standing near [the apostles]
	23		[The apostles] nominated *two* candidates, Joseph . . . and Matthias
	24		Lord, . . . show us . . . which of these *two* you have chosen
	7 29		in the land of Midian . . . [Moses] became the father of *two* sons.
	8 38	11	Philip and the eunuch *both* went down into the water
	9 38		the disciples . . . sent *two* men [to Peter]
	10 7		Cornelius called *two* of the slaves
	19		the Spirit had to tell [Peter], '⌐Two (ᵛ Three) men have come to see you.'
	12 6		Peter was sleeping between *two* soldiers,
	19 16	11	the man with the evil spirit . . . overpowered [first] one and [then] *another*,
	22		[Paul] sent *two* of his helpers . . . ahead of him to Macedonia,
	23 23		[the tribune] summoned *two* of the centurions
1 Co	6 16 ●		the *two* . . . become one flesh.
	14 27		If there are people present with the gift of tongues, let only *two* or three . . . be allowed to use it . . . 29 As for prophets,
	29		let *two* or three of them speak,
	15 47 X	2	The *first* man . . . is earthly by nature; the *second* man is from heaven.
2 Co	13 1		The evidence of three, or at least *two*, witnesses is necessary to sustain the charge.
Ga	4 22		Abraham had *two* sons, one by the slave-girl, and one by his free-born wife.
Ep	2 14 ● 11		[Christ] is the peace between us, and has made ⌐the *two*
	15 ● 11		(or: *both*) into one [people] . . . 15 . . . to create one
	●		single New Man in himself out of the *two* of them and . . .
	16 ● 11		16 . . . to unite them *both* in a single Body and reconcile
	18 ● 11		them with God . . . 18 Through him, *both* of us have in the one Spirit our way to come to the Father.
	5 31 ●		(Gn 2 24) the *two* will become one body.
1 Tm	5 19		Never accept any accusation . . . unless it is supported by *two* or three witnesses.
Heb	10 28		Anyone who disregards the Law of Moses is ruthlessly put to death on the word of *two* witnesses or three;
Rv	8 8	2	The *second* angel blew his trumpet,
	11 3		I shall send my *two* witnesses to prophesy
	10		these *two* prophets have been a plague to the people of the world.
	14 8	2	A *second* angel followed [the first one],
	16 3	2	The *second* angel emptied his bowl over the sea,

b) Two (years, days, hours) – Second (day, watch)

Mt 2 16	9	Herod . . . had all the male children killed who were *two* years old or under,
26 2		It will be Passover, as you know, in *two* days' time,
Mk 14 1		It was *two* days before the Passover and the feast of Unleavened Bread,
Lk 6 1	8	Now ˹one sabbath (ᵛ on the *second* sabbath after the first) [Jesus] happened to be taking a walk through the corn-fields,
12 38	2	It may be in the *second* watch he comes, or in the third,
Jn 4 40		the Samaritans . . . begged [Jesus] to stay with them. He stayed for *two* days,
43		When the *two* days were over Jesus left for Galilee.
11 6		[Jesus] stayed where he was for *two* more days,
Ac 19 10		[Paul took his disciples apart to the lecture room of Tyrannus.] This went on for *two* years,
34		they all started shouting . . . and they kept this up for *two* hours,
24 27	5	When the *two* years came to an end, Felix was succeeded by Porcius Festus
28 13	7	on the *second* day we made Puteoli,
30	5	Paul spent the whole of the *two* years in his own rented lodging.

c) Two, Second, Both (generally)

Mt 5 41		if anyone orders you to go one mile, go *two* miles with him.
9 17	11	they put new wine into fresh skins, and *both* are preserved.
10 10		[Provide yourselves] with no haversack . . . ˹or spare tunic or (lit. no *two* tunics, no) footwear
29		Can you not buy *two* sparrows for a penny?
13 30	11	Let . . . *both* [wheat and darnel] grow till the harvest;
14 17		All we have with us is five loaves and *two* fish . . . ¹⁹ [Jesus] took the five loaves and the *two* fish,
19		
18 8		it is better for you . . . than to have *two* hands or *two* feet and be thrown into eternal fire.
9		it is better for you . . . than to have *two* eyes and be thrown into the hell of fire.
22 39	2	The *second* [commandment] resembles it: You must love your neighbour.
40		On these *two* commandments hang the whole Law,
25 15	<	To one he gave five talents, to another *two*,
17	<	The man who had received *two* made *two* more
22	<	Next the man with the *two* talents came forward. 'Sir,' he said 'you entrusted me with *two* talents; here are *two* more'
Mk 6 9		Do not take ˹a spare tunic (lit. *two* tunics).
38		How many loaves have you? . . . they said, 'Five, and *two* fish'. . . . ⁴¹ Then [Jesus] took the five loaves and the *two* fish . . . He also shared out the *two* fish among them all.
41		
9 43		it is better for you . . . than to have *two* hands and go to hell,
45		it is better for you . . . than to have *two* feet and be thrown into hell.
47		it is better for you . . . than to have *two* eyes and be thrown into hell
12 31	2	The *second* [commandment] is this: You must love your neighbour
42		A poor widow . . . put [into the treasury] *two* small coins,
Lk 2 24		(Lv 12 8) [Joseph and Mary went up to Jerusalem] to offer in sacrifice . . . a pair of turtledoves or *two* young pigeons.
3 11		If anyone has *two* tunics he must share with the man who has none,
5 2		[Jesus] caught sight of *two* boats close to the bank.
7	11	they filled ˹the *two* (lit. *both*) boats [with fish]
9 3		let none of you take ˹a spare tunic (lit. *two* tunics).
13		We have no more than five loaves and *two* fish . . . ¹⁶ Then [Jesus] took the five loaves and the *two* fish, raised his eyes to heaven,
16		
10 35		Next day, [the Samaritan] took out *two* denarii
12 6		Can you not buy five sparrows for *two* pennies?
21 2		[Jesus] happened to notice a poverty-stricken widow putting [into the treasury] *two* small coins,
22 38		there are *two* swords here now.
Jn 2 6		each [stone water jar] could hold ˹twenty or thirty gallons (lit. *two* or three metrētēs [18 or 27 gallons]).
4 54	2	This was the *second* sign given by Jesus,
6 9		There is a small boy here with five barley loaves and *two* fish;
Ac 7 13	2	it was on the *second* [visit] that Joseph made himself known to his brothers,
12 6		Peter was sleeping between two soldiers, fastened with ˹double (or: two) chains,
10	2	[Peter and the angel] passed through [two] guard posts ˹one after the other (lit. a first then a *second*),
13 33	2	As scripture says in the ˹first (ᵛ *second*) psalm:
21 33		the tribune . . . had [Paul] bound with *two* chains
23 8		the Sadducees say there is neither resurrection, nor angel, nor spirit, while the Pharisees accept ˹all three (lit. *both*).
Ga 4 24	11	the women stand for the *two* covenants.

Ph 1 23		I am ˹caught in this dilemma (lit. hard pressed between *two* [choices]): I want to be gone and be with Christ . . . ²⁴ . . . to stay alive . . . is a more urgent need
Tt 3 10	2	after a first and a *second* warning have no more to do with him:
Heb 6 18		so that there would be *two* unalterable things in which it was impossible for God to be lying,
8 7		If that first covenant had been without a fault, there would have been no need for a *second* [one] to replace it.
9 3	2	beyond the *second* veil, an innermost part . . . called the Holy of Holies
7	2	the *second* tent is entered . . . only by the high priest
10 9		[Christ] is abolishing the first sort to replace it with the *second*.
2 P 3 1	2	My friends, this is my *second* letter to you,
Rv 2 11	2	for those who prove victorious there is nothing to be afraid of in the *second* death.
4 7	2	the *second* [animal was] like a bull,
6 3	2/2	When [the Lamb] broke the *second* seal, I heard the *second* animal shout,
9 12		That was the first of the troubles; there are still *two* more to come.
11 4		[The two witnesses] are the *two* olive trees and the *two* lamps that stand before the Lord of the world.
14	2	That was the *second* of the troubles;
12 14		[the woman] was given ˹a huge pair of (lit. *two* huge) eagle's wings
13 11		I saw a [second] beast . . . it had *two* horns
19 20		the beast was taken prisoner, together with the false prophet . . . These *two* were thrown alive into the fiery lake
20 6	2	the *second* death cannot affect [those who share in the first resurrection]
14	2	This burning lake is the *second* death;
21 8	2	the legacy for cowards . . . is the *second* death in the burning lake of sulphur.
19	2	the *second* [foundation of the city was faced with] lapis lazuli,

d) (in) Two

Mt 27 51		the veil of the Temple was torn in *two*
Mk 15 38		the veil of the Temple was torn in *two*
Jm 1 8	6	That sort of person, in *two* minds, wavering between going different ways, must not expect . . . anything.
4 8	6	clear your ˹minds, you waverers (lit. hearts, you in *two* minds).

e) Twice, (for) A second time – Doubly

Mt 23 15	4	you make [the proselyte] *twice* as fit for hell as you are.
26 42	2	Again, a *second time*, [Jesus] went away and prayed:
Mk 14 30	3	before the cock crows *twice*, you will have disowned me three times.
72	2	the cock crew *for the second time*, and Peter recalled how Jesus had said to him, 'Before the cock crows *twice*, you will have disowned me three times'.
	3	
Lk 18 12	3	I fast *twice* a week;
Jn 3 4	2	Can he go back a *second time* into his mother's womb and be born again?
9 24	2	So the Jews ˹again sent (lit. sent a *second time*) for the man
21 16	2	A *second time* [Jesus] said to him, 'Simon . . , do you love me?'
Ac 10 15	2	Again, a *second time*, the voice spoke to [Peter],
11 9	2	And a *second time* the voice spoke from heaven,
1 Co 12 28		In the Church, God has given ˹the first place to apostles, the second to (lit. in the first place apostles, *in the second*) prophets,
	2	
2 Co 1 15	2	I had meant to come to you first, so that you would benefit *doubly*;
13 2	2	I gave warning when I was with you *the second time*
Ph 4 16	3	once or *twice* since my stay in Thessalonika you have sent me what I needed.
1 Th 2 18	3	I, Paul, tried ˹more than once (lit. once or *twice*) [to visit you],
1 Tm 5 17	4	The elders . . . are to be given *double* consideration,
Heb 9 28		Christ, too, offers himself only once . . . and when he appears a *second time*, it will not be to deal with sin
	2	
Jude 5	2	˹afterwards (lit. *secondly*) [the Lord] still destroyed the men who did not trust him.
12		barren trees . . . are . . . uprooted in the winter and so are *twice* dead;
	3	
Rv 18 6	10/4	[Babylon] must be *paid double* with *double* the amount she exacted. She is to have a *doubly* strong cup of her own mixture.
	4	
19 3	2	They sang ˹again (lit. *for a second time*), 'Alleluia!'

2: A PAIR (OF TURTLEDOVES) – A YOKE (OF OXEN): *ZEUGOS*

zeugos 2

Lk 2 24		(Lv 12 8) [Joseph and Mary went up to Jerusalem] to offer in sacrifice . . . a *pair* of turtledoves or two young pigeons.

Lk	14 19	I have bought five *yoke* of oxen and am on my way to try them out.

3: HALF: *HĒMISYS*

1 *hēmisys* 5   2 *hēmi(-ōron)* 1

Mk	6 23	I will give you anything you ask, even *half* my kingdom.
Lk	19 8	I am going to give *half* my property to the poor,
Rv	8 1	2 there was silence in heaven for about *half* an hour.
	11 9	Men out of every people . . . will stare at their corpses for three-and-a-*half* days,
	11	After the three-and-a-*half* days, God breathed life into them
	12 14	[the woman] was to be looked after for a year and twice a year and *half* a year.

5. THREE – THIRD: *TREIS*

1 *treis* 67/68   5 *tri(-etia)* 1
3 *tris* 12   6 *tri(-mēnos)* 1
4 *triton* 9   7 *tri(-stegos)* 1
2 *tritos* 47

a) Three (people) – (the) Third (person, angel)

Mt	18 16	the evidence of two or *three* witnesses is required to sustain any charge.
	20	where two or *three* meet in my name, I shall be there with them.
	22 26	[The first brother died leaving his wife to his brother;] the
	2	same thing happened with the second and *third*
Mk	12 21	The second [brother] married the widow, and he too died
	2	leaving no children; with the *third* it was the same,
Lk	10 36	Which of these *three* . . . proved himself a neighbour to the man . . .?
	12 52	a household of five will be divided: *three* against two and two against three;
	20 12 <	2 He still persevered and sent a *third* [servant];
	31	2 [The second] and then the *third* married the widow.
Ac	10 19	the Spirit had to tell [Peter], 'Two (ᵛ*Three*) men have come to see you.'
	11 11	*three* men . . . had been sent from Caesarea to fetch me,
1 Co	14 27	If there are people present with the gift of tongues, let only two or *three* . . . be allowed to use it. . . . ²⁹ As for prophets,
	29	let two or *three* of them speak,
2 Co	13 1	The evidence of *three*, or at least two, witnesses is necessary to sustain the charge.
1 Tm	5 19	Never accept any accusation brought against an elder unless it is supported by two or *three* witnesses.
Heb	10 28	Anyone who disregards the Law of Moses is . . . put to death on the word of two witnesses or *three*;
Rv	8 10	The *third* angel blew his trumpet,
	13	Trouble . . . for all the people on earth at the sound of the other [three] trumpets which the *three* angels are going to blow.
	14 9	2 A *third* angel followed, shouting aloud,
	16 4	2 The *third* angel emptied his bowl into the rivers

b) Three (lengths of time) – (the) Third (day, hour)

R = concerning the Resurrection of Jesus

Mt	12 40	as Jonah was in the belly of the sea-monster for *three* days and *three* nights, so will the Son of Man be in the heart of
	R	the earth for *three* days and *three* nights.
	15 32	these people . . . have been with me for *three* days now
	16 21	[Jesus] was destined . . . to be put to death and to be raised
	R 2	up on the *third* day.
	17 23 R	2 on the *third* day he will be raised to life again.
	20 3 <	2 [The landowner was] going out at about the *third* hour
	19 R	2 on the *third* day he will rise again.
	26 61 R	I have power to destroy the Temple of God and in *three* days build it up.
	27 40 R	So you would destroy the Temple and rebuild it in *three* days!
	63 R	this impostor said, . . . 'After *three* days I shall rise again'.
	64	⁶⁴ Therefore give the order to have the sepulchre kept
	R 2	secure until the *third* day,
Mk	8 2	these people . . . have been with me for *three* days now
	31	the Son of Man was destined . . . to be put to death, and
	R	after *three* days to rise again;
	9 31 R	*three* days after [the Son of Man] has been put to death he will rise again.
	10 34 R	[the pagans will] put him to death; and after *three* days he will rise again.
	14 58 R	I am going to destroy this Temple . . . and in *three* days build another,
	15 25	2 It was the *third* hour when they crucified him.
	29 R	So you would destroy the Temple and rebuild it in *three* days!

Lk	1 56	Mary stayed with Elizabeth about *three* months
	2 46	*Three* days later, they found [Jesus] in the Temple,
	4 25	in Elijah's day . . . heaven remained shut for *three* years and six months
	9 22	The Son of Man . . . is destined to suffer . . . and to be
	R 2	raised up on the *third* day.
	12 38	2 It may be in the second watch he comes, or in the *third*,
	13 7	for *three* years now I have been coming to look for fruit on this fig tree
	32	Learn that today and tomorrow I cast out devils and on the
	2	*third* day attain my end.
	18 33 R	2 on the *third* day he will rise again.
	24 7	the Son of Man had to be handed over . . . and rise again on
	R 2	the *third* day.
	21 R	2 ⸢two whole days have gone by (lit. this is the *third* day) since it all happened;
	46 R	2 it is written that the Christ would suffer and on the *third* day rise from the dead,
Jn	2 1	2 ⸢Three days later (lit. On the *third* day [afterwards]) there was a wedding at Cana
	19 R	Destroy this sanctuary, and in *three* days I will raise it up.
	20	It has taken forty-six years to build this sanctuary: are you
	R	going to raise it up in *three* days?
Ac	2 15	2 why, it is only the *third* hour of the day.
	5 7	About *three* hours later [Sapphira] came in,
	7 20	Moses . . . was looked after for *three* months in his father's house,
	9 9	For *three* days [Saul] was without his sight,
	10 40 R	2 ⸢three days (lit. on the *third* day) afterwards God raised him to life
	17 2	for *three* consecutive sabbaths [Paul] developed the arguments . . . for the [Jews in Thessalonika],
	19 8	[Paul] spoke out boldly . . . He did this for *three* months,
	20 3	[Paul made his way into Greece,] where he spent *three* months.
	31	5 night and day for *three* years I never failed to keep you right,
	23 23	2 Get two hundred soldiers ready to leave . . . by the *third* hour of the night
	25 1	*Three* days after his arrival . . . Festus went up to Jerusalem
	27 19	2 the *third* day [the crew] threw the ship's gear overboard
	28 7	Publius . . . received us and entertained us hospitably for *three* days.
	11	At the end of *three* months we set sail
	12	We put in at Syracuse and spent *three* days there;
	15	After *three* days [Paul] called together the leading Jews.
1 Co	15 4 R	2 [I taught you] that he was raised to life on the *third* day,
Ga	1 18	after *three* years I went up to Jerusalem to visit Cephas
Heb	11 23	Moses, when he was born, was hidden by his parents for
	6	*three* months;
Jm	5 17	[Elijah] prayed hard for it not to rain, and no rain fell for *three*-and-a-*half* years;
Rv	11 9	Men out of every people . . . will stare at [the two witnesses']
	11	corpses, for *three*-and-a-*half* days . . . ¹¹ After the *three*-and-a-*half* days, God breathed life into them

c) Three, (the) Third, (generally)

Mt	13 33	a woman . . . mixed [the yeast] in with *three* measures of flour
	17 4	if you wish, I will make *three* tents here,
Mk	9 5	Peter spoke to Jesus: '. . . let us make *three* tents,
Lk	9 33	Master, . . . let us make *three* tents,
	11 5	My friend, lend me *three* loaves,
	13 21	a woman . . . mixed [the yeast] in with *three* measures of flour
Jn	2 6	each [stone water jar] could hold ⸢twenty or thirty gallons (lit. two or *three* metrētēs [18 or 27 gallons]).
Ac	20 9	7 [Eutychus] fell to the ground *three* floors below.
	28 15	the brothers . . . came to meet us, as far as the Forum of Appius and the *Three* Taverns
1 Co	13 13	there are *three* things that last: faith, hope and love;
2 Co	12 2	2 a man in Christ . . . was caught up . . . right into the *third* heaven.
1 Jn	5 7	there are *three* witnesses, ⁸ the Spirit, the water and the
	8	blood, and all *three* of them agree.
Rv	4 7	2 the *third* animal had a human face,
	6 5	2/2 When [the Lamb] broke the *third* seal, I heard the *third* animal shout, 'Come'.
	6	*three* rations of barley for a day's wages,
	9 18	by these *three* plagues, the fire, the smoke and the sulphur . . . one third of the human race was killed.
	11 14	2 That was the second of the troubles; the *third* is to come from the jaws of dragon . . . I saw *three* foul spirits come;
	16 13	The Great City was split into *three* parts
	19	on the east there were *three* gates, on the north *three* gates, on the south *three* gates, and on the west *three* gates.
	21 13	2 the *third* [foundation of the city was faced with] turquoise,

d) Three times – (for) the Third time

Mt	26 34	3 before the cock crows, you will have disowned me *three times*.
	44	4 [Jesus] went away again and prayed *for the third time*,

Mt 26 75   3 Before the cock crows you will have disowned me *three times.*

Mk 14 30   before the cock crows twice, you will have disowned me
    3 *three times.*

    41   4 [Jesus] came back *a third time* and said to them 'You can sleep on now'

    72   Before the cock crows twice, you will have disowned me
    3 *three times.*

Lk 22 34   3 by the time the cock crows today you will have denied *three times* that you know me.

    61   Before the cock crows today you will have disowned me
    3 *three times.*

 23 22   4 *for the third time* [Pilate] spoke to them, 'Why? What harm has this man done?

Jn 13 38   3 before the cock crows you will have disowned me *three times.*

 21 14   4 This was *the third time* that Jesus showed himself to the disciples

    17   4 [Jesus] said to him *a third time,* 'Simon . . , do you love me?'
       4 Peter was upset that he asked him *the third time,*

Ac 10 16   [Peter saw something like a big sheet being let down to
    3 earth.] This was repeated *three times.*

 11 10   3 This was repeated *three times,* before the whole of [the sheet] was drawn up to heaven again.

1 Co 12 28   4 God has given in the first place apostles . . . *thirdly* teachers

2 Co 11 25 3/3 *three times* I have been beaten with sticks . . . *three times* I have been shipwrecked

  12 8   3 I have pleaded with the Lord *three times* for [the angel of Satan] to leave me,

    14   4 I am all prepared now to come to you *for the third time,*

  13 1   4 This will be *the third time* I have come to you.

e) A Third (of)

Rv 8 7 2/2 a *third* of the earth was burnt up, and a *third* of all trees,

   8   2 a *third* of the sea turned into blood,

   9   2 a *third* of all the living things in the sea were killed, and a
    2 *third* of all ships were destroyed.

  10   2 a huge star fell from the sky . . . and it fell on a *third* of all

  11   2 rivers . . . ¹¹ . . . a *third* of all water turned to bitter wormwood,

  12 2/2/2 a *third* of the sun and a *third* of the moon and a *third* of the
    2 stars were blasted, so that the light went out of a *third* of
    2 them and for a *third* of the day there was no illumination, and the same with the night.

 9 15   2 These four angels . . . were released to destroy a *third* of the human race.

  18   2 It was by these three plagues . . . that the *one third* of the human race was killed.

 12 4   2 [The dragon's] tail dragged a *third* of the stars from the sky and dropped them to the earth,

6. FOUR – FOURTH – QUARTER: *TESSARES*

1 tessares	30	4 tetradion	1
3 tetartaios	1	5 tetra(-mēnos)	1
2 tetartos	10	6 tetra-ploos	1

a) Four (people, angels) – (the) Fourth

Mk 2 3   some people came bringing [Jesus] a paralytic carried by *four* men,

Ac 12 4 /4 [Herod] put Peter in prison, assigning *four squads of four* soldiers each to guard him in turns.

 21 9   [Philip] had *four* virgin daughters who were prophets.

  23   We have *four* men here who are under a vow;

Rv 7 1   I saw *four* angels, standing at the four corners of the earth, holding the four winds of the world back

   2   another angel . . . called in a powerful voice to the *four* angels

 8 12   2 The *fourth* angel blew his trumpet,

 9 14   Release the *four* angels that are chained up at the great river Euphrates.

  15   These *four* angels . . . were released to destroy a third of the human race.

 16 8   2 The *fourth* angel emptied his bowl over the sun

b) Four (lengths of time) – (the) Fourth (watch, day)

Mt 14 25   2 In the *fourth* watch of the night [Jesus] went towards [the disciples],

Mk 6 48   2 about the *fourth* watch of the night [Jesus] came towards them,

Jn 4 35   5 *Four* months and then the harvest?

 11 17   Jesus found that Lazarus had been in the tomb for *four* days

  39   3 Lord, by now he will smell; this is the *fourth* day.

Ac 10 30   2 ⌐Three days ago (lit. At the end of the *fourth* day back from this precise hour) I was praying

c) Four, (the) Fourth, (generally)

Mt 24 31   [the Son of Man] will send his angels . . . to gather his chosen from the *four* winds,

Mk 13 27   [the Son of Man] will send the angels to gather his chosen from the *four* winds,

Jn 19 23   the soldiers , . . divided [Jesus's clothing] into *four* shares,

Ac 10 11   [Peter] saw . . . something like a big sheet being let down to earth by its *four* corners;

 11 5   I . . . had a vision of something like a big sheet being let down from heaven by its *four* corners.

 27 29   [the crew] dropped *four* anchors from the stern

Rv 4 6   In the centre, grouped round the throne . . . were *four* animals

   7   2 the *fourth* animal was like a flying eagle.

   8   Each of the *four* animals had six wings

 5 6   I saw, standing between the throne with its *four* animals and the circle of the elders, a Lamb

   8   the *four* animals prostrated themselves before [the Lamb]

  14   the *four* animals said, 'Amen';

 6 1   I heard one of the *four* animals shout . . , 'Come'.

   6   I seemed to hear a voice shout from among the *four* animals

   7   2 When [the Lamb] broke the *fourth* seal, I heard the voice of
    2 the *fourth* animal shout, 'Come'.

 7 1   I saw four angels, standing at the *four* corners of the earth, holding the *four* winds of the world back

  11   all the angels . . . surrounding the elders and the *four* animals, prostrated themselves

 9 13   I heard a voice come out of the *four* horns of the golden altar

 14 3   they were singing a new hymn in the presence of the *four* animals and the elders,

 15 7   One of the *four* animals gave the seven angels seven golden bowls

 19 4   the twenty-four elders and the *four* animals prostrated themselves

 20 8   [Satan] will come out to deceive all . . . in the *four* quarters of the earth,

 21 19   2 the *fourth* [foundation of the city wall was faced with] crystal,

d) Four times

Lk 19 8   6 if I have cheated anybody I will pay him back *four times* [the amount].

e) Quarter

Rv 6 8   2 [The four riders] were given authority over a *quarter* of the earth,

7. FIVE – FIFTH: *PENTE*

2 pemptos	4	1 pente	34
3 pentakis	1		

a) Five (people) – (the) Fifth (angel)

Mt 25 2 <   *Five* of [the bridesmaids] were foolish and *five* were sensible:

Lk 12 52   a household of *five* will be divided: three against two and two against three;

 16 28   [The rich man replied,] I have *five* brothers,

Jn 4 18   [Jesus said to the Samaritan woman,] you have had *five* [husbands]

Rv 9 1   2 the *fifth* angel blew his trumpet,

 16 10   2 The *fifth* angel emptied his bowl over the throne of the beast

 17 10   The seven heads are also seven emperors. *Five* of them have already gone,

b) Five (days, months)

Lk 1 24   Elizabeth conceived, and for *five* months she kept to herself.

Ac 20 6   We . . . met [the disciples] *five* days later at Troas,

 24 1   *Five* days later the high priest Ananias came down with some of the elders

Rv 9 5   [The locusts were to] give [people] pain for *five* months,

  10   [the locusts] were able to injure people for *five* months.

c) Five, (the) Fifth, (generally)

Mt 14 17   All we have with us is *five* loaves and two fish . . . ¹⁹ . . . [Jesus] took the *five* loaves and the two fish . . . and said the blessing.

 16 9   Do you not remember the *five* loaves for the five thousand . . .?

 25 15 <   To one he gave *five* talents, to another two,

  16 <   The man who had received the *five* talents promptly went
    <   . . . and made *five* more.

  20 <   The man who had received the *five* talents came forward
    <   bringing *five* more. 'Sir,' he said 'you entrusted me with
    <   *five* talents; here are *five* more that I have made.'

Mk 6 38   How many loaves have you? . . . *Five,* and two fish . . .
  41   ⁴¹ Then [Jesus] took the *five* loaves and the two fish,

 8 19   I broke the *five* loaves among the five thousand,

Lk 9 13   We have no more than *five* loaves and two fish . . . ¹⁶ Then
  16   [Jesus] took the *five* loaves and the two fish . . . and said the blessing over them;

Lk 12	6		Can you not buy *five* sparrows for two pennies?
14	19		I have bought *five* yoke of oxen and am on my way to try them out.
19	18	<	Sir, your one pound has made *five*. ¹⁹ . . . And you shall be
	19	<	in charge of *five* cities.
Jn 5	2		at the Sheep Pool in Jerusalem there is a building, called Bethzatha in Hebrew, consisting of *five* porticos;
6	9		There is a small boy here with *five* barley loaves and two fish;
	13		they . . . filled twelve hampers with scraps left over from the meal of *five* barley loaves.
1 Co 14	19		I would rather say *five* words that mean something than ten thousand words in a tongue.
Rv 6	9	2	[the Lamb] broke the *fifth* seal,
21	20	2	the *fifth* [foundation of the city wall was faced with] agate,

d) Five times

2 Co 11	24	3	*Five times* I had the thirty-nine lashes from the Jews;

8. SIX – SIXTH: *HEKTOS*

1 *hektos* 14   2 *hex* 10

a) Six (days, hours, months) – (the) Sixth (month, hour)

Mt 17	1	2	*Six* days later, Jesus took with him Peter and James and . . . John
20	5	<	At about the *sixth* hour . . . [the landowner] went out
27	45		From the *sixth* hour there was darkness over all the land
Mk 9	2	2	*Six* days later, Jesus took with him Peter and James and John
15	33		When the *sixth* hour came there was darkness over the whole land
Lk 1	26		In the *sixth* month the angel Gabriel was sent by God to [Mary]
	36		Elizabeth . . . whom people called barren is now in her *sixth* month
4	25	2	in Elijah's day . . . heaven remained shut for three years and *six* months
13	14	2	There are *six* days . . . when work is to be done.
23	44		It was now about the *sixth* hour and . . . a darkness came over the whole land
Jn 4	6		It was about the *sixth* hour.
12	1	2	*Six* days before the Passover, Jesus went to Bethany,
19	14		It was Passover Preparation Day, about the *sixth* hour.
Ac 10	9		Peter went to the housetop at about the *sixth* hour to pray.
18	11	2	Paul stayed [in Corinth] . . . for ⌐eighteen months (lit. a year and *six* months).
Jm 5	17	2	no rain fell for ⌐three-and-a-half years (lit. three years and *six* months);

b) Six, (the) Sixth, (generally)

Jn 2	6	2	There were *six* stone water jars standing there,
Ac 11	12	2	The *six* brothers here came with me as well,
Rv 4	8	2	Each of the four animals had *six* wings
6	12		when [the Lamb] broke the *sixth* seal, there was a violent earthquake
9	13		The *sixth* angel blew his trumpet,
	14		[a voice] spoke to the *sixth* angel with the trumpet,
16	12		The *sixth* angel emptied his bowl over the great river Euphrates;
21	20		the *sixth* [foundation of the city wall was faced with] ruby,

9. SEVEN – SEVENTH: *HEPTA*

2 *hebdomos* 9   1 *hepta* 86
3 *heptakis* 5

a) Seven (years, days) – (the) Seventh (day, hour)

Lk 2	36		Anna . . . had been married for *seven* years ³⁷ before becoming a widow.
Jn 4	52	2	The fever left [the boy] yesterday . . . at the *seventh* hour.
Ac 20	6		we stopped [at Troas] for ⌐a week (lit. *seven* days).
21	4		We . . . stayed [at Tyre] ⌐a week (lit. *seven* days).
	27		The *seven* days [of Paul's purification] were nearly over
28	14		we found some brothers [in Puteoli] and were much rewarded by staying ⌐a week (lit. *seven* days) with them.
Heb 4	4	2	one text says, referring to the *seventh* day: After all his work
		2	God rested on the *seventh* day.
11	30		the walls of Jericho fell down when the people had been round them for *seven* days.

b) Seven, (the) Seventh, (generally)

D = Deacons

Mt 12	45	Ⓓ	[the unclean spirit] goes off and collects *seven* other spirits

Mt 15	34		Jesus said to them, 'How many loaves have you?' 'Seven . . . and a few small fish.' . . . ³⁶ . . . he took the *seven*
	36		loaves and the fish,
	37		they collected what was left of the scraps, *seven* baskets full.
16	10		[Don't you remember] the *seven* loaves for the four thousand . . .?
22	25		we had a case involving *seven* brothers; the first . . . died
	26		without children, leaving his wife to his brother; ²⁶ the same thing happened with the second and third and so on
	28		to the *seventh* . . . ²⁸ Now at the resurrection to which of those *seven* will she be wife . . .?
Mk 8	5		'How many loaves have you?' 'Seven' they said.
	6		[Jesus] took the *seven* loaves, and . . . broke them
	8		they collected *seven* basketfuls of scraps left over.
	20		'When I broke the *seven* loaves for the four thousand, how many baskets full of scraps did you collect?' . . . they answered, 'Seven'.
12	20		there were *seven* brothers . . . ²² . . . none of the *seven* left
	22		any children . . . ²³ Now at the resurrection . . . whose
	23		wife will she be, since she had been married to all *seven*?
16	9	Ⓓ	[Jesus] appeared first to Mary of Magdala from whom he had cast out *seven* devils.
Lk 8	2	Ⓓ	Mary surnamed the Magdalene, from whom *seven* demons had gone out,
11	26	Ⓓ	[the unclean spirit] goes off and brings *seven* other spirits
20	29		there were *seven* brothers . . . ³¹ . . . the same with all
	31		*seven*, they died leaving no children . . . ³³ . . . at the
	33		resurrection, to which of them will she be wife since she had been married to all *seven*?
Ac 6	3	D	select from among yourselves *seven* men of good reputation,
13	19		[God] destroyed *seven* nations in Canaan,
19	14		*seven* sons of Sceva, a Jewish chief priest.
21	8	D	we called on Philip the evangelist, one of the *Seven*
Jude	14	2'	Enoch, the *seventh* patriarch from Adam,
Rv 1	4		From John, to the *seven* churches of Asia: grace and peace to you from him who is . . . and . . . from the *seven* spirits in his presence before his throne,
	11		Write down all that you see in a book, and send it to the *seven* churches
	12		I saw *seven* golden lamp-stands ¹³ and, surrounded by them, a figure like a Son of man . . . ¹⁶ In his right hand he was
	16		holding *seven* stars,
	20		The secret of the *seven* stars you have seen in my right hand, and of the *seven* golden lamp-stands is this: the *seven* stars are the angels of the *seven* churches, and the seven lamp-stands are the *seven* churches themselves.
2	1		Here is the message of the one who holds the *seven* stars in his right hand and who lives surrounded by the *seven* golden lamp-stands:
3	1		Here is the message of the one who holds the *seven* spirits of God and the *seven* stars:
4	5		there were *seven* flaming lamps burning, the *seven* Spirits of God.
5	1		there was a scroll that . . . was sealed with *seven* seals.
	5		the Lion of . . . Judah . . . will open the scroll and the *seven* seals of it.
	6		I saw . . . a Lamb that . . . had *seven* horns, and it had *seven* eyes, which are the *seven* Spirits God has sent out all over the world.
6	1		I saw the Lamb break one of the *seven* seals,
8	1	2	The Lamb then broke the *seventh* seal,
	2		I saw *seven* trumpets being given to the *seven* angels who stand in the presence of God . . . ⁶ The *seven* angels that
	6		had the *seven* trumpets now made ready to sound them.
10	3		*seven* claps of thunder made themselves heard ⁴ and when the
	4		*seven* thunderclaps had spoken . . . I heard a voice . . . say to me, 'Keep the words of the *seven* thunderclaps secret'
	7	2	when the *seventh* angel is heard sounding his trumpet, God's . . . intention will be fulfilled,
11	15	2	the *seventh* angel blew his trumpet,
12	3		a huge red dragon [appeared] which has *seven* heads and ten horns, and each of the *seven* heads crowned with a coronet.
13	1		I saw a beast . . .: it had *seven* heads and ten horns,
15	1		I saw . . . *seven* angels . . . bringing the *seven* plagues
	6		out came the *seven* angels with the *seven* plagues . . . ⁷ One
	7		of the four animals gave the *seven* angels *seven* golden
	8		bowls filled with the anger of God . . . ⁸ . . . no one could go into [the temple] until the *seven* plagues of the *seven* angels were completed.
16	1		a voice from the sanctuary [shouted] to the *seven* angels, 'Go, and empty the *seven* bowls of God's anger over the earth'.
	17	2	The *seventh* angel emptied his bowl into the air,
17	1		One of the *seven* angels that had the *seven* bowls came . . . to me,
	3		I saw a woman riding a scarlet beast which had *seven* heads

Rv 17	7		I will tell you the meaning of this woman, and of the beast . . . with the *seven* heads and the ten horns . . . ⁹ . . . the *seven* heads are the *seven* hills, and the woman is sitting on them. The seven heads are also *seven* emperors. ¹⁰ Five of them have already gone, one is here now, and one is yet to come . . . ¹¹ The beast . . . is at the same time the eighth and one of the *seven*
	9		
	11		
21	9		One of the *seven* angels that had the *seven* bowls full of the *seven* last plagues came to speak to me,
	20	2	the *seventh* [foundation of the city wall was faced with] gold quartz,

c) Seven times

Mt 18	21	3	how often must I forgive my brother . . .? As often as *seven times*? ²² Jesus answered, 'Not *seven*, I tell you, but ⌐seventy-seven times (or: seventy *seven times*).'
	22	3	
		3	
Lk 17	4	3/3	if [your brother] wrongs you *seven times* a day and *seven times* comes . . . and says, 'I am sorry', you must forgive him.

10. EIGHT – EIGHTH: *OKTŌ*

1 oktō	6	3 okta(-(h)ēmeros) 1
2 ogdoos	5	

a) Eight (days, years) – (the) Eight (day)

Lk 1	59	2	on the *eighth* day they came to circumcise [John the Baptist];
2	21		When the *eighth* day came and the child was to be circumcised, they gave him the name Jesus,
9	28		about *eight* days after this . . . [Jesus] went up the mountain
Jn 20	26		*Eight* days later the disciples were in the house again
Ac 7	8	2	[Abraham] circumcised [Isaac] on the *eighth* day.
9	33		Aeneas . . . had been bedridden for *eight* years.
25	6		After staying with them for *eight* or ten days at the most, [Festus] went down to Caesarea
Ph 3	5	3	[I, Paul] was circumcised when I was *eight* days old.

b) Eight, (the) Eighth, (generally)

1 P 3	20		Noah was . . . building that ark which saved . . . *eight* people
2 P 2	5	2	Nor did [God] spare the world in ancient times: it was only Noah he saved, . . . ⌐along with seven others (lit. as the *eighth*),
Rv 17	11	2	The beast . . . is at the same time the *eighth* and one of the seven [emperors],
21	20	2	the *eighth* [foundation of the city wall was faced with] malachite,

11. (THE) NINTH – NINE: *ENATOS*

1 enatos	10	2 ennea 1

Mt 20	5	<	At about the sixth hour and again at about the *ninth* hour, [the landowner] went out
27	45		there was darkness over all the land until the *ninth* hour.
	46		⁴⁶ And about the *ninth* hour, Jesus cried out
Mk 15	33		there was darkness over the whole land until the *ninth* hour. ³⁴ And at the *ninth* hour Jesus cried out
	34		
Lk 17	17	2	The other *nine* [lepers], where are they?
23	44		a darkness came over the whole land until the *ninth* hour.
Ac 3	1		Peter and John were going up to the Temple for the prayers at the *ninth* hour,
10	3		One day at about the *ninth* hour [Cornelius] had a vision
	30		I was praying in my house at the *ninth* hour,
Rv 21	20		the *ninth* [foundation of the city wall was faced with] topaz,

12. TEN – TENTH – TITHE: *DEKA*

1 deka	23	3 dekatos	3
2 dekatē	4	6 apo-dekateuō	1
5 dekatoō	2	4 apo-dekatoō	3

a) Ten (days) – (the) Tenth (hour)

Jn 1	39	3	they went and saw where [Jesus] lived . . . it was about the *tenth* hour.
Ac 25	6		After staying with them for eight or *ten* days at the most, [Festus] went down to Caesarea
Rv 2	10		you must face an ordeal for *ten* days.

b) Ten, (the) Tenth, (generally)

Mt 20	24		When the other *ten* [disciples] heard this they were indignant
25	1		the kingdom of heaven will be like this: *Ten* bridesmaids took their lamps and went to meet the bridegroom.

Mt 25	28	<	give [the talent] to the man who has the *ten* talents.
Mk 10	41		the other *ten* [disciples] . . . began to feel indignant with James and John,
Lk 15	8	<	what woman with *ten* drachmas would not, if she lost one, . . . search thoroughly till she found it?
17	12		*ten* lepers came to meet [Jesus].
	17		Were not all *ten* [lepers] made clean?
19	13	<	He summoned *ten* of his servants and gave them *ten* pounds.
	16	<	Sir, your one pound has brought in *ten*.
	17	<	you shall have the government of *ten* cities.
	24	<	give [the pound] to the man who has *ten* pounds.
	25	<	But, sir, he has *ten* pounds
Rv 12	3		a huge red dragon which had seven heads and *ten* horns [appeared]
13	1		[the beast] had seven heads and *ten* horns, with a coronet on each of its *ten* horns,
17	3		I saw . . . a scarlet beast which had seven heads and *ten* horns
	7		I will tell you the meaning . . . of the beast . . . with the seven heads and the *ten* horns.
	12		The *ten* horns are *ten* kings
	16		the *ten* horns . . . will turn against the prostitute,
21	20	3	the *tenth* [foundation of the city wall was faced with] emerald,

c) (a) Tenth (of)

Rv 11	13	3	a *tenth* of the city collapsed;

d) Tithe – Pay (a) tithe, (a) Tenth – Take (a) tithe

Mt 23	23	4	Alas for you . . . who *pay* your *tithe* of mint and dill . . . and have neglected the weightier matters of the Law
Lk 11	42	4	alas for you . . . who *pay* your *tithe* of mint . . . and overlook justice
18	12	6	[The Pharisee said this prayer:] I *pay tithes* on all I get.
Heb 7	2	2	it was to [Melchizedek] that Abraham gave a *tenth* of all that he had.
	4	2	(Gn 14 20) Abraham paid [Melchizedek] a *tenth* of the treasure he had captured.
	5	4	any of the descendants of Levi who are admitted to the priesthood are obliged . . . to *take tithes* from the people
	6	5	. . . ⁶ But [Melchizedek], who was not of the same descent, *took* his *tenth* from Abraham,
	8	2	it is ordinary mortal men who receive the *tithes*,
	9	2	It could be said that Levi himself, who receives *tithes*, actually *paid* ⌐them (lit. tithes), in the person of Abraham,
		5	

13. ELEVEN – ELEVENTH: *HEN-DEKA*

1 hen-deka	6	2 hen-dekatos 3

a) the Eleven (remaining apostles)

Mt 28	16		Meanwhile the *eleven* disciples set out for Galilee,
Mk 16	14		[Jesus] showed himself to the *Eleven* themselves while they were at table.
Lk 24	9		When the women returned from the tomb they told all this to the *Eleven*
	33		[The two disciples on their way to Emmaus] returned to Jerusalem. There they found the *Eleven* assembled together with their companions,
Ac 1	26		as the lot fell to Matthias, he was ⌐listed as one (lit. added to the number) of the ᵛ twelve (G *eleven*) apostles.
2	14		Then Peter stood up with the *Eleven* and addressed [the Jews] in a loud voice:

b) (the) Eleventh

Mt 20	6	<	2 at about the *eleventh* hour [the landowner] went out
	9	<	2 So those who were hired at about the *eleventh* hour . . . received one denarius each.
Rv 21	20		2 the *eleventh* [foundation of the city wall was faced with] sapphire

14. TWELVE – TWELFTH: *DŌ-DEKA*

1 dō-deka	63	3 dō-deka(-phylon) 1
2 dō-dekatos	1	

a) the Twelve (apostles)

Mt 10	1		[Jesus] summoned his *twelve* disciples, and gave them authority
	2		These are the names of the *twelve* apostles: first, Simon . . .
	5		⁵ These *twelve* Jesus sent out,
11	1		When Jesus had finished instructing his *twelve* disciples he moved on
20	17		[Jesus] took the *Twelve* (ᵛ disciples) to one side and said
26	14		one of the *Twelve*, the man called Judas Iscariot, went to the chief priests
	20		When evening came [Jesus] was at table with the *twelve* disciples.

Mt 26	47	Judas, one of the *Twelve*, appeared,
Mk 3	14	[Jesus] appointed *twelve*; they were to be his companions and to be sent out to preach . . . ¹⁶ And so he appointed the *Twelve*:
	16	
4	10	the *Twelve*, together with the others who formed his company, asked what the parables meant.
6	7	[Jesus] summoned the *Twelve* and began to send them out in pairs
9	35	[Jesus] called the *Twelve* to him and said, 'If anyone wants to be first, he must make himself . . . servant of all'.
10	32	taking the *Twelve* aside [Jesus] began to tell them what was going to happen to him:
11	11	[Jesus] went out to Bethany with the *Twelve*.
14	10	Judas Iscariot, one of the *Twelve*, approached the chief priests
	17	When evening came [Jesus] arrived with the *Twelve*.
	20	[One of you is about to betray me.] It is one of the *Twelve*,
	43	while he was still speaking, Judas, one of the *Twelve*, came up
Lk 6	13	[Jesus] summoned his disciples and picked out *twelve* of them;
8	1	With [Jesus] went the *Twelve*, ² as well as certain women
9	1	[Jesus] called the *Twelve* together and gave them power and authority over all devils
	12	the *Twelve* came to [Jesus] and said, 'Send the people away,'
18	31	taking the *Twelve* aside [Jesus] said to them, 'Now we are going up to Jerusalem,'
22	3	Satan entered into Judas . . . who was numbered among the *Twelve*.
	47	a number of men appeared, and at the head of them the man called Judas, one of the *Twelve*,
Jn 6	67	Jesus said to the *Twelve*, 'What about you, do you want to go away too?'
	70	Have I not chosen you, you *Twelve*? Yet one of you is a devil. ⁷¹ [Jesus] meant Judas . . , one of the *Twelve*, who was going to betray him.
	71	
20	24	Thomas, . . . one of the *Twelve*, was not with them when Jesus came.
Ac 1	26	as the lot fell to Matthias, he was listed ʳas one (lit. added to the number) of the ᵛ *twelve* (G eleven) apostles.
6	2	the *Twelve* called a full meeting of the disciples
1 Co 15	5	[Christ] appeared first to Cephas and secondly to the *Twelve*.
Rv 21	14	each one of [the twelve foundation stones] bore the name of one of the *twelve* apostles of the Lamb.

b) (the) Twelve (tribes of Israel, partriarchs)

Mt 19	28	you will . . . sit on twelve thrones to judge the *twelve* tribes of Israel.
Lk 22	30	you will sit on thrones to judge the *twelve* tribes of Israel.
Ac 7	8	Isaac [circumcised] Jacob, and Jacob . . . the *twelve* patriarchs.
26	7	3 [I am on trial for my hope in] the promise that our *twelve* tribes . . . hope to attain.
Jm 1	1	Greetings to the *twelve* tribes of the Dispersion.
Rv 21	12	over the gates were written the names of the *twelve* tribes of Israel;

c) Twelve (concerning the apostles, the tribes of Israel)

Mt 19	28	you will . . . sit on *twelve* thrones to judge the twelve tribes of Israel.
Rv 12	1	a woman [appeared] . . . with the *twelve* stars on her head for a crown.
21	12	The walls of [the city] . . . had *twelve* gates; at each of the *twelve* gates there was an angel,
	14	The city walls stood on *twelve* foundation stones, ʳeach one of which bore the name of (lit. on which were *twelve* names, each of) one of the *twelve* apostles of the Lamb.
	21	The *twelve* gates were *twelve* pearls,
22	2	the trees of life . . . bear *twelve* crops of fruit in a year

d) Twelve (years, days, hours)

Mt 9	20	a woman,ʹwho had suffered from a haemorrhage for *twelve* years . . . touched the fringe of his cloak,
Mk 5	25	there was a woman who had suffered from a haemorrhage for *twelve* years;
	42	The little girl [of Jairus] . . . began to walk about, for she was *twelve* years old.
Lk 2	42	When [Jesus] was *twelve* years old, they went up for the feast
8	42	[Jairus] had an only daughter about *twelve* years old,
	43	there was a woman suffering from a haemorrhage for *twelve* years,
Jn 11	9	Are there not *twelve* hours in the day?
Ac 24	11	it is no more than *twelve* days since I went up to Jerusalem

e) Twelve, (the) Twelfth, (generally)

Mt 14	20	they collected the scraps remaining, *twelve* baskets full.
26	53	my Father . . . would promptly send more than *twelve* legions of angels to my defence
Mk 6	43	They collected *twelve* basketfuls of scraps

Mk 8	19	how many baskets full of scraps did you collect? They answered, '*Twelve*'.
Lk 9	17	when the scraps remaining were collected they filled *twelve* baskets.
Jn 6	13	they . . . filled *twelve* hampers with scraps left over
Ac 19	7	There were about *twelve* of [the disciples of John at Ephesus].
Rv 21	20	2 the *twelfth* [foundation of the city wall was faced with] amethyst.

15. OTHER NUMBERS

FOURTEEN – 14

Mt 1	17	The sum of generations is therefore: *fourteen* from Abraham to David; *fourteen* from David to the Babylonian deportation; and *fourteen* from the Babylonian deportation to Christ
Ac 27	27	On the *fourteenth* night we were being driven one way and another in the Adriatic,
	33	For *fourteen* days . . . you have been in suspense,
2 Co 12	2	I know a man in Christ who, *fourteen* years ago, was caught up . . . right into the third heaven.
Ga 2	1	It was not till *fourteen* years had passed that I went up to Jerusalem again.

FIFTEEN – 15

Lk 3	1	In the *fifteenth* year of Tiberius Caesar's reign [the word of God came to John]
Jn 11	18	Bethany is only about ʳtwo miles (lit. *fifteen* furlongs [1⅘ miles]) from Jerusalem,
Ac 27	5	[we sailed] across the open sea off . . . Pamphylia, (ᵛ taking *fifteen* days) to reach Myra
	28	they sounded again and found *fifteen* fathoms.
Ga 1	18	I went up to Jerusalem to visit Cephas and stayed with him for *fifteen* days,

EIGHTEEN – 18

Lk 13	4	[Do you suppose] those *eighteen* on whom the tower at Siloam fell [were greater sinners]?
	11	a woman was there who for *eighteen* years had been possessed by a spirit
	16	Satan has held [this daughter of Abraham] bound these *eighteen* years

TWENTY – 20

Ac 27	28	They took soundings and found *twenty* fathoms;

TWENTY-FOUR – 24

Rv 4	4	Round the throne . . . were *twenty-four* thrones, and on them I saw *twenty-four* elders sitting,
	10	the *twenty-four* elders prostrated themselves before [the One sitting on the throne]
5	8	the four animals prostrated themselves before [the Lamb] and with them the *twenty-four* elders;
11	16	The *twenty-four* elders . . . prostrated themselves . . . worshipping God
19	4	the *twenty-four* elders . . . prostrated themselves

TWENTY-FIVE – 25

Jn 6	19	[The disciples] had rowed ʳthree or four miles (lit. *twenty-five* or thirty furlongs [3 or 3⅘ miles])

THIRTY – 30

Mt 13	8 <	Other [seeds] . . . produced their crop, some a hundredfold, some sixty, some *thirty*.
	23 <	the one who . . . understands [the word] . . . is the one who . . . produces now a hundredfold, now sixty, now *thirty*.
	26 15	[The chief priests] paid [Judas] *thirty* silver pieces,
	27 3	Judas . . . took the *thirty* silver pieces back to the chief priests
	9	(Zc 11 12) And they took the *thirty* silver pieces,
Mk 4	8 <	some seeds . . . yielded *thirty*, sixty, even a hundredfold.
	20 <	they hear the word and . . . yield a harvest, *thirty* and sixty and a hundredfold.

Lk 3 23   When he started to teach, Jesus was about *thirty* years old,
Jn 6 19   [The disciples] had rowed ⌐three or four miles (lit. twenty-five or *thirty* furlongs [3 or 3⅔ miles])

THIRTY-EIGHT – 38

Jn 5 5   One man there had an illness which had lasted *thirty-eight* years,

THIRTY-NINE – 39

2 Co 11 24   Five times I had the ⌐*thirty-nine* (lit. forty-less-one) lashes from the Jews; (cf. Dt 25 3)

FORTY – 40

     1 *tesserakonta* 16   2 *tesserakonta(-etēs)* 2

Mt 4 2   [Jesus] fasted for *forty* days and *forty* nights,
Mk 1 13   [Jesus] remained [in the wilderness] for *forty* days,
Lk 4 2   [Jesus was] being tempted there by the devil for *forty* days.
Ac 1 3   for *forty* days [Jesus] had continued to appear to [the apostles]
   4 22   The man who had been miraculously cured was over *forty* years old
   7 23   2 At the age of *forty* [Moses] decided to visit his countrymen,
     30   *Forty* years later, in the wilderness near Mount Sinai, an angel appeared to [Moses]
     36   It was Moses who . . . led them . . . through the wilderness for *forty* years.
     42   (Am 5 25) Did you bring me victims and sacrifices . . . for all those *forty* years . . .?
   13 18   2 for about *forty* years [God] took care of them in the wilderness.
     21   After *forty* years, [God deposed Saul]
   23 13   There were more than *forty* who took part in this conspiracy,
     21   There are more than *forty* [Jews] lying in wait for [Paul],
2 Co 11 24   Five times I had the ⌐*thirty-nine* (lit. *forty*-less-one) lashes from the Jews (cf. Dt 25 3);
Heb 3 10   (Ps 95 9, 10) [your ancestors challenged me . . . though they had seen what I could do] for *forty* years.
     17   those who made God angry for *forty* years were the ones who sinned

FORTY-TWO – 42

Rv 11 2   pagans . . . will trample on the holy city for *forty-two* months.
   13 5   For *forty-two* months the beast was allowed to mouth its boasts

FORTY-SIX – 46

Jn 2 20   It has taken *forty-six* years to build this sanctuary:

FIFTY – 50

pentēkonta 5

Mk 6 40   they sat down on the ground in squares of hundreds and *fifties*.
Lk 7 41   There was once a creditor who had two men in his debt; one owed him five hundred denarii, the other *fifty*.
   9 14   Get them to sit down in parties of about *fifty*.
   16 6   < [How much do you owe?] 'One hundred measures of oil' . . . 'Sit down straight away and write *fifty*'.
Jn 8 57   You are not *fifty* yet, and you have seen Abraham!

SIXTY – 60

Mt 13 8   < Other [seeds] . . . produced their crop, some a hundredfold, some *sixty*, some thirty.
     23   < the one who . . . hears the word . . . is the one who . . . produces now a hundredfold, now *sixty*, now thirty.
Mk 4 8   < some seeds . . . yielded thirty, *sixty*, even a hundredfold.
     20   < those who . . . hear the word . . . yield a harvest, thirty and *sixty* and a hundredfold.
Lk 24 13   two [disciples] were on their way to a village called Emmaus, *sixty* furlongs [7¼ miles] from Jerusalem,
1 Tm 5 9   Enrolment as a widow is permissible only for a woman at least *sixty* years old

SEVENTY – 70

Mt 18 22   [You must forgive your brother] not seven, . . . but ⌐*seventy*-seven times (or: *seventy* seven times).

Ac 23 23   Get two hundred soldiers ready to leave for Caesarea . . with *seventy* cavalry

SEVENTY-TWO – 72

Lk 10 1   the Lord appointed *seventy-two* others and sent them out
     17   The *seventy-two* came back rejoicing.

SEVENTY-FIVE – 75

Ac 7 14   Joseph then sent for . . . his whole family, a total of *seventy-five* people.

SEVENTY-SEVEN – 77

Mt 18 22   [You must forgive your brother] not seven, . . . but ⌐*seventy-seven* times (or: seventy seven times).

EIGHTY – 80

Lk 16 7   Here, take your bond and write *eighty*.

EIGHTY-FOUR – 84

Lk 2 37   [Anna] was now *eighty-four* years old and never left the Temple,

NINETY-NINE – 99

Mt 18 12   < Suppose a man has a hundred sheep and one of them strays; will he not leave the *ninety-nine* . . . and go in search of the stray? ¹³ . . . if he finds it, it gives him more joy than
     13   < do the *ninety-nine* that did not stray at all.
Lk 15 4   < What man among you with a hundred sheep, losing one, would not leave the *ninety-nine* . . . and go after the missing one . . .?
     7   < there will be more rejoicing in heaven over one repentant sinner than over *ninety-nine* virtuous men

A HUNDRED – 100

     1 *hekaton* 11   2 *hekatonta-plasiōn* 3
                    3 *hekatonta(-etēs)* 1

Mt 13 8   < Other [seeds] . . . produced their crop, some a *hundred*fold, some sixty, some thirty.
     23   < the one who . . . hears the word . . . is the one who . . . produces now a *hundred*fold, now sixty, now thirty.
   18 12   < Suppose a man has a *hundred* sheep and one of them strays;
     28   < this servant . . . happened to meet a fellow servant who owed him *one hundred* denarii;
   19 29   everyone who has left houses, brothers, sisters . . . will be repaid ⌐*a hundred* (G many) times over,
Mk 4 8   < some seeds . . . yielded thirty, sixty, even a *hundred*fold.
     20   < those who . . . hear the word . . . yield a harvest, thirty and sixty and a *hundred*fold.
   6 40   they sat down on the ground in squares of *hundreds* and fifties.
   10 30   [there is no one who has left house, brothers . . .] who will not be repaid *a hundred* times over,
Lk 8 8   < 2 some seed . . . produced its crop a *hundred*fold.
   15 4   < What man among you with a *hundred* sheep, losing one, would not . . . go after the missing one . . .?
   16 6   [How much do you owe my master?] *One hundred* measures of oil
     7   how much do you owe? *One hundred* measures of wheat
Jn 19 39   Nicodemus . . . brought a mixture of myrrh and aloes, weighing about *a hundred* pounds.
Rm 4 19   3 [When Abraham became the father of Isaac] he was about *a hundred* years old

A HUNDRED AND TWENTY – 120

Ac 1 15   One day . . . there were about *a hundred and twenty* persons in the congregation:

A HUNDRED AND FORTY-FOUR – 144

Rv 21 17   [The angel] measured [the] wall [of the city], and this was *a hundred and forty-four* cubits high

A HUNDRED AND FIFTY-THREE – 153

Jn 21 11   Simon Peter . . . dragged the net to the shore, full of big fish, *one hundred and fifty-three* of them;

TWO HUNDRED – 200

Mk	6 37	Are we to go and spend *two hundred* denarii on bread for them to eat?
Jn	6 7	*Two hundred* denarii would only buy enough to give them a small piece each.
	21 8	[the disciples] were only about *two hundred* cubits [111 yards] from land.
Ac	23 23	Get *two hundred* soldiers ready to leave for Caesarea . . . with seventy cavalry and *two hundred* auxiliaries;

TWO HUNDRED AND SEVENTY-SIX – 276

Ac 27 37   We were in all *two hundred and seventy-six* souls on board that ship.

THREE HUNDRED – 300

Mk	14 5	Ointment like this could have been sold for over *three hundred* denarii
Jn	12 5	Why wasn't this ointment sold for *three hundred* denarii . . .?

FOUR HUNDRED – 400

Ac	5 36	Theudas . . . collected about *four hundred* followers;
	7 6	(Gn 15 13) [Abraham's] descendants would be . . . oppressed for *four hundred* years.

FOUR HUNDRED AND THIRTY – 430

Ga 3 17   no law that came *four hundred and thirty* years later could cancel [God's will]

FOUR HUNDRED AND FIFTY – 450

Ac 13 20   [God put our ancestors in possession of Canaan] for about *four hundred and fifty* years.

FIVE HUNDRED – 500

Lk	7 41 <	There was once a creditor who had two men in his debt; one owed him *five hundred* denarii, the other fifty.
1 Co	15 6	[Christ] appeared to more than *five hundred* of the brothers at the same time,

666 or 616

Rv 13 18   the number of the beast . . . is the number of a man, the number ⌐666 (ˇ *616*).

A THOUSAND – 1 000

2 chilias 2   1 chilioi 8

2 P	3 8	(Ps 90 4) with the Lord 'a day' can mean *a thousand* years, and *a thousand* years is like a day.
Rv	5 11	an immense number of angels . . . there were ten thousand times ten thousand of them and *thousands* upon *thousands*,
	2/2	
	20 2	[The angel] overpowered the dragon . . . and chained him up for *a thousand* years.
	3	[The angel] threw [the dragon] into the Abyss . . . to make sure he would not deceive the nations again until the *thousand* years had passed.
	4	those who refused to worship the beast . . . reigned with Christ for *a thousand* years.
	5	the rest of the dead did not come to life until the *thousand* years were over.
	6	those who share in the first resurrection . . . will be priests . . . of Christ and reign with him for *a thousand* years.
	7	When the *thousand* years are over, Satan will be released

TWELVE HUNDRED AND SIXTY – 1 260

Rv	11 3	But I shall send my two witnesses to prophesy for those *twelve hundred and sixty* days,
	12 6	God had made a place of safety ready for [the woman] to be looked after in the *twelve hundred and sixty* days.

SIXTEEN HUNDRED – 1 600

Rv 14 20   the blood that came out of the winepress was up to the horses' bridles as far away as *sixteen hundred* furlongs.

TWO THOUSAND – 2 000

Mk 5 13   the herd of about *two thousand* pigs charged down the cliff into the lake,

THREE THOUSAND – 3 000

Ac 2 41   That very day about *three thousand* were added to their number.

FOUR THOUSAND – 4 000

Mt	15 38	Now *four thousand* men had eaten, to say nothing of women and children.
	16 10	[Don't you remember] the seven loaves for the *four thousand* . . .?
Mk	8 9	Now there had been about *four thousand* people.
	20	I broke the seven loaves for the *four thousand*,
Ac	21 38	So you are not the Egyptian who . . . led those *four thousand* cut-throats out into the desert?

FIVE THOUSAND – 5 000

1 pentakis-chilioi 6   2 chiliades pente 1

Mt	14 21	Those who ate numbered about *five thousand* men, to say nothing of women and children.
	16 9	Do you not remember the five loaves for the *five thousand* . . .?
Mk	6 44	Those who had eaten . . . numbered *five thousand* men.
	8 19	I broke the five loaves among the *five thousand*,
Lk	9 14	there were about *five thousand* men,
Jn	6 10	as many as *five thousand* men sat down.
Ac	4 4	many . . . became believers, the total number of whom had now risen to something like *five thousand*.
	2	

SEVEN THOUSAND – 7 000

1 heptakis-chilioi 1   2 chiliades hepta 1

Rm	11 4	(1 K 19 18) I have kept for myself *seven thousand* men who have not bent the knee to Baal.
Rv	11 13	*seven thousand* persons were killed in the earthquake,

TEN THOUSAND – 10 000

a) myrias, myrioi 11/12

Mt	18 24 <	they brought him a man who owed *ten thousand* talents;
Lk	12 1	people had gathered in their ⌐thousands (lit. *ten thousands*) so that they were treading on one another.
Ac	21 20	you see . . . how ⌐thousands (lit. *ten thousands*) of Jews have now become believers,
1 Co	4 15	You might have ⌐thousands (lit. *ten thousands*) of guardians in Christ, but not more than one father
	14 19	in the presence of the community I would rather say five words that mean something than *ten thousand* words in a tongue.
Heb	12 22	you have come to . . . the heavenly Jerusalem where the ⌐millions (lit. *ten thousands*) of angels have gathered
Jude	14	the Lord will come with his saints in their *tens of thousands*,
Rv	5 11	an immense number of angels gathered . . . there were *ten thousand* times *ten thousand* of them
	9 16	I learnt how many there were in their army: twice *ten thousand* times *ten thousand* mounted men.

b) deka chiliades 1

Lk 14 31   what king . . . would not . . . consider whether with *ten thousand* men he could stand up to the other who advanced against him with twenty thousand?

TWELVE THOUSAND – 12 000

Rv 7 5 From the tribe of Judah, *twelve thousand* had been sealed; from the tribe of Reuben, *twelve thousand*; from the tribe
6 of Gad, *twelve thousand*; [6] from the tribe of Asher, *twelve thousand*; from the tribe of Naphtali, *twelve thousand*; from
7 the tribe of Manasseh, *twelve thousand*; [7] from the tribe of Simeon, *twelve thousand*; from the tribe of Levi, *twelve
8 thousand*; from the tribe of Issachar, *twelve thousand*; [8] from the tribe of Zebulun, *twelve thousand*; from the tribe of Joseph, *twelve thousand*; and from the tribe of Benjamin, *twelve thousand* were sealed.

21 16 the city . . . was *twelve thousand* furlongs in length

TWENTY THOUSAND – 20 000

Lk 14 31 what king . . . would not . . . consider whether with ten thousand men he could stand up to the other who advanced against him with *twenty thousand*?

TWENTY-THREE THOUSAND – 23 000

1 Co 10 8 We must never fall into sexual immorality: some of them did and *twenty-three thousand* met their downfall in one day.

FIFTY THOUSAND – 50 000

Ac 19 19 The value of these [burnt books] was calculated to be ᵣ*fifty thousand* (lit. five times ten thousand) silver pieces.

A HUNDRED AND FORTY-FOUR THOUSAND – 144 000

Rv 7 4 I heard how many were sealed: *a hundred and forty-four thousand*, out of all the tribes of Israel.

14 1 I saw . . . a Lamb . . . with . . . *a hundred and forty-four thousand* people,

3 they were singing a new hymn . . . that could only be learnt by the *hundred and forty-four thousand* who had been redeemed from the world.

OBEY – SUBMIT – SUBJECT

1. Obey, Be obedient, to Submit to – Disobedience: *hyp-akouō*
  1: Obey, Be obedient to, Submit to – Listen to, Accept
  2: Disobedience
2. Obey, Be obedient – Disobedient: *peithō*
  1: Obey, Be obedient to, Listen to – Follow(er)
  2: (Be) Disobedient, Rebellious – Refuse to
3. Submit – Obey – (Be) Subject (to): *hypo-tassō*

4: (God, Christ) Subjects, Puts under – Be subjected (to), Submit (to God, Christ)
2: Submit (to a person), Obey, Be obedient (to) – Be subject (to), Under authority – Give way (to)
4. Submit (to slavery) – (Be) Held (in), Subject (to slavery): *en-echō*
5. Submit (to) – Defer (to): *hyp-eikō*
6. Undergo: *hyp-echō*
7. Under – Subject (to): *hypo*
8. to Tame, Control, Subdue: *damazō*

1. OBEY, BE OBEDIENT TO, SUBMIT TO – DISOBEDIENCE: *HYP-AKOUŌ*

2 *hyp-akoē* 15   3 *hyp-ēkoos* 3
1 *hyp-akouō* 21   4 *par-akoē* 3

1: OBEY, BE OBEDIENT TO, SUBMIT TO – LISTEN TO, ACCEPT

Mt	8 27	Whatever kind of man is this? Even the winds and the sea *obey* him.
Mk	1 27	he gives orders even to unclean spirits and they *obey* him.
	4 41	Who can this be? Even the wind and the sea *obey* him.
Lk	8 25	Who can this be, that gives orders even to the winds and waves and they *obey* him?
	17 6	you could say to this mulberry tree, 'Be uprooted and planted in the sea', and it would *obey* you.
Ac	6 7	a large group of priests *made their submission* to the faith,
	7 39	3 [Moses] is the man that our ancestors refused to *listen to*:
	12 13	[Peter] knocked at the outside door and a servant called Rhoda came to *answer* it.
Rm	1 5	Through [the Son of God] we received . . . our apostolic mission to preach the *obedience* of faith to all pagan nations
	5 19	As by one man's disobedience many were made sinners, so
X	2	by one man's *obedience* many will be made righteous.
	6 12	you must not let sin reign in your mortal bodies or command your *obedience* to bodily passions,
	16	2 if you agree to serve and *obey* a master you become his *obedient* slaves. You cannot be the slaves of sin . . . and
	2	at the same time slaves of *obedience* that leads to righteousness. [17] . . . you *submitted* without reservation *to* the creed you were taught.
	17	
	10 16	Not everyone, of course, *listens to* the Good News.
	15 18	What I am presuming to speak of . . . is only what Christ
	2	himself has done to win the *allegiance* of the pagans,
	16 19	2 Your ⌜fidelity (lit. *obedience*) to Christ . . . is famous everywhere,
	26	[the mystery is] so clear that it must be broadcast to pagans
	2	everywhere to bring them to the *obedience* of faith.
2 Co	2 9	What I really wrote for . . . was to . . . see whether you are
	3	completely *obedient*.
	7 15	2 [Titus] remembers how *willing* you have all been,
	10 5	every thought is our prisoner, captured to be brought into
	2	*obedience* to Christ.
	6	Once you have given your complete *obedience*, we are prepared to punish any disobedience.
Ep	6 1	Children, *be obedient to* your parents in the Lord – that is your duty.
	5	Slaves, *be obedient to* the men who are called your masters in this world . . . as you are obedient to Christ:
Ph	2 8 X	3 [Christ] was humbler yet, even to *accepting* death,
	12	So then, my dear friends, continue to *do as I tell you*, as you always have;
Col	3 20	Children, *be obedient to* your parents always, because that is what will please the Lord.
	22	Slaves, *be obedient to* the men who are called your masters in this world . . . out of respect for the Master.
2 Th	1 8	The Lord Jesus] will come in flaming fire to impose the penalty on all who . . . refuse to *accept* the Good News of our Lord Jesus.

2 Th	3 14	If anyone refuses to *obey* what I have written in this letter . . . have nothing to do with him,
Phm	21	2 I am writing with complete confidence in your *compliance*,
Heb	5 8 X	2 Although he was Son, he learnt to *obey* through suffering;
	9	he became for all who *obey* him the source of eternal salvation
	11 8	It was by faith that Abraham *obeyed* the call to set out
1 P	1 2	2 [greetings to all those who have been chosen] to *be* . . . *obedient to* Jesus Christ and sprinkled with his blood.
	14	2 make a habit of *obedience*:
	22	2 You have *been obedient to* the truth and purified your souls
	3 6	Sarah . . . *was obedient to* Abraham, and called him her lord.

2: DISOBEDIENCE

Rm	5 19	4 As by one man's *disobedience* many were made sinners, so by one man's obedience many will be made righteous.
2 Co	10 6	Once you have given your complete obedience, we are prepared to punish any *disobedience*.
	4	
Heb	2 2	4 If . . . every . . . *disobedience* brought its own punishment, [then we shall certainly not go unpunished]

2. OBEY, BE OBEDIENT – DISOBEDIENT: *PEITHŌ*

1 *peithomai* (+ dat.) 9/53   2 *a-peitheia* 7
5 *peith-archeō* 4   4 *a-peitheō* 5/14
3 *a-peithēs* 6

1: OBEY, BE OBEDIENT TO, LISTEN TO – FOLLOW(ER)

Ac	5 29	5 *Obedience* to God comes before obedience to men;
	32	5 God has given [the Holy Spirit] to those who *obey* him.
	36	when [Theudas] was killed, all his *followers* scattered
	37	[Judas] got killed too, and all his *followers* dispersed.
	39	[Gamaliel's] advice was ⌜accepted (lit. *obeyed*);
	23 21	[Paul's nephew said to the tribune,] Do not ⌜let them persuade you (or: *listen to* them).
	27 11	the centurion *took* more *notice of* the captain . . . than of what Paul was saying;
	21	5 Friends, [Paul said,] if you had *listened to* me and not put out from Crete, you would have spared yourselves . . . this damage
Rm	2 8	the unsubmissive . . . refused to take truth for their guide and ⌜took (lit. *followed*) depravity instead,
Ga	5 7	who made you less anxious to *obey* the truth?
Tt	3 1	5 it is their duty to *be obedient to* the officials and representatives of the government;
Heb	13 17	*Obey* your leaders and do as they tell you,
Jm	3 3	we put a bit into the horse's mouth, to make it *do what we want*,

2: (BE) DISOBEDIENT, REBELLIOUS – REFUSE TO

Lk	1 17	3 [John] will go before him to turn . . . the *disobedient* back to the wisdom that the virtuous have,
Ac	26 19	3 King Agrippa, I could not *disobey* the heavenly vision.
Rm	1 30	3 enemies of God, rude, . . . enterprising in sin, *rebellious* to parents [deserve to die]
	2 8	4 the unsubmissive . . . *refused* [to take] truth for their guide
	10 21	4 (Is 65 2) I stretched out my hand to a *disobedient* and rebellious people.
	11 30	4 Just as you [pagans] changed from *being disobedient to God*,
	2	and now enjoy mercy because of [the Jews'] *disobedience*,
	31	4 [31] so those who *are disobedient* now . . . will also enjoy
	32	mercy eventually. [32] God has imprisoned all men in their own *disobedience* only to show mercy
	2	
Ep	2 2	2 the ruler who governs the air . . . is at work in the *rebellious*.
	5 6	2 God's anger comes down on those who *rebel* against him.
Col	3 6	all this is the sort of behaviour that makes God angry ᵛ with the *disobedient*.
	2	
2 Tm	3 2	3 People will be . . . *disobedient* to their parents, ungrateful,
Tt	1 16	3 they are outrageously *rebellious* and quite incapable of doing good.
	3 3	3 there was a time when we too were ignorant, *disobedient* and misled
Heb	3 18	Those that [God] swore would never reach the place of rest
	4	. . . were those who had *been disobedient*.

Heb	4	6	those who first heard the Good News failed to reach [the place of rest] through their *disobedience.*
		11	some of you might copy this example of *disobedience* and be lost.

3. SUBMIT – OBEY – (BE) SUBJECT (TO): *HYPO-TASSŌ*

2 *hypo-tagē* 4   3 *an-hypo-taktos* 4
1 *hypo-tassō* 39

1: (GOD, CHRIST) SUBJECTS, PUTS UNDER – BE SUBJECTED (TO), SUBMIT (TO GOD, CHRIST)

Rm	8	7	to limit oneself to what is unspiritual is to be at enmity with God: such a limitation . . . never does *submit* to God's law.
	10	3	[the Jews] try to promote their own idea of [righteousness], instead of *submitting* to the righteousness of God.
1 Co	15	27	(Ps 8 7) everything is to *be put under* [Christ's] feet. – Though when it is said that everything *is subjected,* this clearly cannot include the One who *subjected* everything to him.
		28	[28] And when everything *is subjected* to him, then the Son himself *be subject* in his turn to the One who *subjected* all things to him,
2 Co	9	13	[the saints] give glory to God for the way you *accep* . . . the gospel of Christ,
Ep	1	22	(Ps 8 7) [God] has *put* all things *under* [Christ's] feet,
	5	24	as the Church *submits* to Christ, so should wives to their husbands,
Ph	3	21	[Jesus Christ] will transfigure these wretched bodies of ours into copies of his glorious body . . . by the same power with which he can *subdue* the whole universe.
Heb	2	5	[God] did not appoint ⌐angels to be the rulers of the world to come (lit. the world to come to *be subject* to angels),
		8	(Ps 8 7) You have ⌐put him in command of everything (lit *put* everything *under* his feet. Well then, if he has ⌐put him in command of everything (lit. *put* everything *under* his feet), he has left nothing which *is not under* [his command].
		3	At present . . . we are not able to see that everything has been *put under* [his command],
	12	9	we ought to be . . . willing to *submit* [ourselves] to our spiritual Father, to be given life.
Jm	4	7	*Give in* to God, then; resist the devil,
1 P	3	22	[Jesus Christ] has *made* the angels and Dominations and Powers *his subjects.*

2: SUBMIT (TO A PERSON), OBEY, BE OBEDIENT (TO) – BE SUBJECT (TO), UNDER AUTHORITY – GIVE WAY (TO)

Lk	2	51 X	[Jesus] came to Nazareth and lived *under* [his parents'] authority.
	10	17 ⓓ	Lord, . . . even the devils *submit* to us when we use your name.
		20 ⓓ	do not rejoice that the spirits *submit* to you:
Rm	8	20	creation . . . ⌐was made unable to attain its purpose (lit. *was subjected* to futility), it ⌐was made so (lit. *was subjected*) by God;
	13	1	You must all *obey* the governing authorities . . . [5] You must
		5	*obey,* therefore, not only because you are afraid of being punished but also for conscience' sake.
1 Co	14	32	Prophets can always ⌐control (lit. keep *in submission*) their prophetic spirits,
		34	women are to remain quiet at meetings . . .; they must *keep in the background* as the Law itself lays it down (cf. Gn 3 16).
	16	16	*put* yourselves ⌐at the service of (lit. *under*) people like this, and anyone who helps and works with them.
Ga	2	5	I refused . . . to *yield* in *submission* to such people
Ep	5	21	*Give way* to one another in obedience to Christ. [22] Wives should ⌐regard (lit. *submit* to) their husbands as they regard the Lord . . . [24] . . . as the Church submits to Christ,
		22	
Col	3	18	Wives, *give way* to your husbands, as you should in the Lord.
1 Tm	1	9	[laws are framed] for criminals and *revolutionaries,*
	2	11	a woman should be quiet ⌐and respectful (lit. in *submission*).
	3	4	[The elder-in-charge] must be a man who . . . brings his children up to *obey* him
Tt	1	6	[the elder's] children must be believers and not *uncontrollable*
		10	you have there a great many people who *need to be disciplined,*
	2	5	[the older women should show the younger women] how they are to . . . be gentle, and ⌐do as their husbands tell them (lit. *submissive* to their husbands),
		9	the slaves . . . are to *be obedient* to their masters
	3	1	it is their duty to *submit* and be obedient to the officials . . . of the government;
1 P	2	13	For the sake of the Lord, *accept the authority* of every social institution:

---

1 P	2	18	Slaves must *be* respectful and *obedient* to their masters,
	3	1	wives should *be obedient* to their husbands.
		5	the holy women of the past . . . *were* tender and *obedient* to their husbands;
	5	5	⌐do what the elders tell you (lit. *obey* the elders),

4. SUBMIT (TO SLAVERY) – (BE) HELD (IN), SUBJECT (TO SLAVERY): *EN-ECHŌ*

1 *en-echō* 1/3   2 *en-ochos* 1/10

Ga	5	1	do not *submit* again to the yoke of slavery.
Heb	2	15	[Christ] set free all those who had been ⌐*held* in (or: *subject* to) slavery

5. SUBMIT (TO) – DEFER (TO): *HYP-EIKŌ*

hyp-eikō 1

Heb	13	17	*Obey* your leaders and ⌐do as they tell you (lit. *submit* to them),

6. UNDERGO: *HYP-ECHŌ*

hyp-echō 1

Jude	7	Sodom and Gomorrah and the other nearby towns . . . are ⌐paying for their crimes (lit. *undergoing* their punishment) in eternal fire.

7. UNDER – SUBJECT (TO): *HYPO*

hypo (+ acc.) (25)

Mt	8	9	I am *under* authority myself, and have soldiers *under* me;
Lk	7	8	I am *under* authority myself, and have soldiers *under* me;
Rm	3	9	Jews and Greeks are all *under* sin's [dominion].
	6	14	sin will no longer dominate your life, since you are living ⌐by (lit. *under*) grace and not ⌐by (lit. *under*) law. [15] Does the fact that we are living ⌐by (lit. *under*) grace and not ⌐by (lit. *under*) law mean that we are free to sin?
		15	
	7	14	I am unspiritual; I have been sold ⌐as a slave to (lit. *under*) sin.
1 Co	9	20	I, who am not *a subject of* the Law made myself *a subject of* the Law to those who are *the subjects of* the Law, to win those who are *subject to* the Law.
Ga	3	10	those who rely on the keeping of the Law are *under* a curse,
		22	scripture . . . says that ⌐sin is master everywhere (lit. everything is *under* sin).
		25	Now that that time has come we are no longer *under* that guardian,
	4	2	[The heir] is *under* [the control of] guardians and administrators until he reaches the age fixed by his father.
		4 X	God sent his Son, . . . born *a subject of* the Law, [5]to redeem the *subjects of* the Law
		5	
		21	You want to be *subject to* the Law? Then listen to what the Law says.
	5	18	If you are led by the Spirit, ⌐no law can touch you (lit. you are not *under* the law).
1 Tm	6	1	All slaves *under* the yoke must have unqualified respect for their masters,
Jm	5	12	[Do not swear by heaven or by the earth.] Otherwise you make yourselves *liable* to judgement.
1 P	5	6	Bow down, then, ⌐before (lit. *under*) the power of God now, and he will raise you up on the appointed day;

8. TO TAME, CONTROL, SUBDUE: *DAMAZŌ*

damazō 4

Mk	5	4	no one had the strength to ⌐*control* (or: *subdue*) [the demoniac].
Jm	3	7	Wild animals and birds . . . can all be *tamed* by man, and often are *tamed;* [8] but nobody can *tame* the tongue –
		8	

OFFEN

1. Often – Various (times) – Frequent, Constant, Over again: *pollakis*	**2. Frequently, Often:** *pyknos* **3. How often:** *posakis*

1. OFTEN – VARIOUS (TIMES) – FREQUENT, CONSTANT, OVER AGAIN: POLLAKIS

1 *pollakis* 18   3 *poly*(-*tropos*) 1   2 *polys* 2/358

Mt 17 15   he is ˹always (lit. *often*) falling into the fire and *often* into the water.
Mk 5 4   he had *often* been secured with fetters
   9 22   [the spirit] has *often* thrown him into the fire and into the water,
Jn 18 2   Jesus had *often* met his disciples there,
Ac 26 11   I *often* . . . [tried] to force them to renounce their faith;
Rm 1 13   I have *often* planned to visit you
   15 22   2 I have *often* been kept from visiting you,
2 Co 8 22   we are sending a third brother, of whose keenness we have *often* had proof
   11 23   I have been sent to prison more [*often*], and whipped so many times [more], *often* almost to death.
   26   *Constantly* travelling, I have been in danger
   27   I have . . . laboured, *often* without sleep; I have been hungry and thirsty and *often* starving;
Ph 3 18   I have told you *often*,
2 Tm 1 16   Onesiphorus . . . has *often* been a comfort to me
Heb 1 1   3 At *various* times in the past . . . God spoke to our ancestors
   6 7   A field that has been well watered by *frequent* rain,
   9 25   he does not have to offer himself *again and again*,
   26   or else he would have had to suffer *over and over again* since the world began.
   10 11   priests . . . offering *over and over again* the same sacrifices
Jm 3 2   2 every one of us does something wrong, *over and over again*;

2. FREQUENTLY, OFTEN: PYKNOS

pyknos 4

Mk 7 3   the Pharisees . . . never eat without washing their arms ˹as far as the elbow (ᵛ *frequently*);
Lk 5 33   John's disciples are ˹always (lit. *often*) fasting
Ac 24 26   [Felix] sent for [Paul] *frequently*
1 Tm 5 23   have a little wine for the sake of . . . the *frequent* bouts of illness that you have.

3. HOW OFTEN: POSAKIS

posakis 3

Mt 18 21   *how often* must I forgive my brother . . .?
   23 37   Jerusalem . . .! *How often* have I longed to gather your children
Lk 13 34   Jersualem . . .! *How often* have I longed to gather your children,

---

ONE ANOTHER – EACH OTHER

1. (With, To, From) One another, Each other – Mutual: *allēlōn* | 2. One another, Each other: *he-autou*

1. (WITH, TO, FROM) ONE ANOTHER, EACH OTHER – MUTUAL: ALLĒLŌN

allēlōn 100

Mt 24 10   men will betray *one another* and hate *one another*.
   25 32   he will separate men *one from another*
Mk 4 41   [the disciples] said *to one another*, 'Who can this be?'
   8 16   they said *to one another*, 'It is because we have no bread'.
   9 34   because they had been arguing *between each other* which of them was the greatest.
   50   be at peace *with one another*.
   15 31   The chief priests and the scribes mocked him *among themselves*
Lk 2 15   the shepherds said *to one another*, 'Let us go to Bethlehem'
   4 36   they were all saying *to one another*, 'What teaching!'
   6 11   [the Pharisees] began to discuss *with one another* the best way of dealing with Jesus.
   7 32   like children shouting *to one another*
   8 25   [the disciples] said *to one another*, 'Who can this be . . .?'
   12 1   the people had gathered in their thousands so that they were treading on *one another*.
   20 14   When the tenants [of the vineyard] saw him they ˹put their heads together (lit. reasoned *with one another*). 'This is the heir,'

Lk 23 12   Herod and Pilate . . . were reconciled *with each other* that same day.
   24 14   [the disciples of Emmaus] were talking ˹together (lit. *with one another*)
   17   What matters are you discussing *with each other* as you walk along?
   32   they said *to each other*, 'Did not our hearts burn . . .?'
Jn 4 33   the disciples asked *one another*,
   5 44   you look *to one another* for approval
   6 43   Stop complaining *to each other*.
   52   the Jews started arguing *with one another*:
   11 56   [people] looked out for Jesus, saying *to one another*, . . . 'Will he come . . .?'
   13 14   you should wash *each other's* feet.
   22   The disciples looked at *one another*,
   34   love *one another*; just as I have loved you, you also must love *one another*. ³⁵ By this love you have for *one another*, everyone will know that you are my disciples.
   35
   15 12   love *one another*, as I have loved you.
   17   What I command you is to love *one another*.
   16 17   some of his disciples said *to one another*,
   19   You are asking *one another* what I mean by saying:
   19 24   [the soldiers] said *to one another*, '. . . let's throw dice to decide'
Ac 4 15   the Sanhedrin had a ˹private discussion (lit. discussion *with each other*)
   7 26   why are you hurting *each other*?
   15 39   After a violent quarrel [Paul and Barnabas] ˹parted company (lit. separated *from each other*),
   19 38   let them take ˹the case (lit. *each other*) to court.
   21 6   after saying good-bye *to each other*, we went aboard
   26 31   [the king and the governor] talked ˹together (lit. *with each other*)
   28 4   the natives . . . said *to one another*, 'That man must be a murderer:'
   25   [the Roman Jews] disagreed *among themselves*
Rm 1 12   to find encouragement among ˹you for our common (lit. *each other* of us through) faith.
   27   their menfolk [are] consumed with passion *for each other*,
   2 15   they have accusation and defence *of one another*,
   12 5   as parts of [Christ's body] we belong *to each other*.
   10   Love *each other* as much as brothers should, and ˹have a profound respect for each other (lit. try to outdo *each other* in respect).
   16   Treat ˹everyone (lit. *one another*) with equal kindness;
   13 8   Avoid getting into debt, except the debt of *mutual* love.
   14 13   Far from passing judgement on *each other*, therefore,
   19   let us adopt any custom that leads to . . . our *mutual* improvement;
   15 5   may [God] . . . help you all to be tolerant with *each other*,
   7   treat *each other* in the same friendly way as Christ treated you.
   14   you are . . . perfectly well . . . able to advise *each other*.
   16 16   Greet *each other* with a holy kiss.
1 Co 7 5   Do not refuse *each other* except by [mutual] consent,
   11 33   when you meet for the Meal, wait for *one another*.
   12 25   so that . . . ˹each part may be equally concerned for all the others (lit. all parts may be concerned *for each other*).
   16 20   Greet *one another* with a holy kiss.
2 Co 13 12   Greet *one another* with the holy kiss.
Ga 5 13   Serve *one another* . . . in works of love,
   15   If you go snapping at [each other] and tearing *each other* to pieces, you had better watch or you will destroy ˹the whole community (lit. *each other*).
   17   [self-indulgence and the Spirit] are . . . opposed *to each other*
   26   We must stop being conceited, provocative *to each other* and envious *of each other*.
   6 2   You should carry *each other's* troubles
Ep 4 2   Bear with *one another* charitably,
   25   we are all parts *of one another*.
   32   Be friends *with one another*, and kind, forgiving *each other*
   5 21   Give way *to one another* in obedience to Christ.
Ph 2 3   Always consider ˹the other person (lit. *each other*) to be better than yourself,
Col 3 9   never tell *each other* lies.
   13   Bear with *one another*;
1 Th 3 12   May the Lord . . . make you love *one another*
   4 9   you have learnt from God . . . to love *one another*,
   18   With such thoughts as these you should comfort *one another*.
   5 11   give encouragement *to each other*, and keep strengthening *one another*,
   15   you must all think of what is best *for each other* and for the community.
2 Th 1 3   the love that you have *for one another*
Tt 3 3   we lived then in wickedness and ill-will, hating *each other*
Heb 10 24   Let us be concerned *for each other*,
Jm 4 11   do not slander *one another*.
   5 9   Do not make complaints *against one another*,
   16   confess your sins *to one another*, and pray *for one another*,
1 P 1 22   let your love *for each other* be real

1 P	4	9	Welcome *each other* into your houses without grumbling.
	5	5	wrap yourselves in humility to be servants *of each other*,
		14	Greet *one another* with a kiss of love.
1 Jn	1	7	if we live our lives in the light, . . . we are in union *with one another*,
	3	11	we are to love *one another*;
		23	His commandments are these: that we believe . . . and that we love *one another*
	4	7	let us love *one another*
		11	since God has loved us so much, we too should love *one another*.
		12	as long as we love *one another* God will live in us
2 Jn		5	let us love *one another*.
Rv	6	4	[the second horse's] rider was given this duty: to . . . set people killing *each other*,
	11	10	the people of the world will . . . celebrate the event by giving presents *to each other*,

2. ONE ANOTHER, EACH OTHER: *HE-AUTOU*

he-autou (8)

1 Co	6	7	It is bad enough for you to have lawsuits at all against *one another*:
Ep	4	32	Be friends with one another, and kind, forgiving *each other* as readily as God forgave you in Christ.
	5	19	Sing . . . psalms and hymns when you are ⌐together (lit. *with each other*),
Col	3	13	Bear with one another; forgive *each other* as soon as a quarrel begins.
1 Th	5	13	Be at peace ⌐among yourselves (lit. *with one another*).
Heb	3	13	Every day . . . keep encouraging *one another*
1 P	4	8	never let your love for *each other* grow insincere,
		10	put yourselves at the service of ⌐others (lit. *each other*).

ORDER – REGULATION – INSTRUCT

1. Order, Give orders, Command – Tell (to): *keleuō*

2. Order, Give orders, Command – Tell (to), Instruct, Direct – Prescribed, Appointed, Arranged: *tassō*

3. Order, Tell (to), Instruct – Give instructions, Command, Give orders: *par-angellō*

4. Order, Give orders, Give instructions – Enjoin, Charge, Insist: *dia-stellomai*

5. Command, Tell (to) – Regulations, Orders: *en-tolē*
  a) Command(ments) of God, of Christ, of law
  b) Regulations, Instructions,

Orders, (generally)–Give orders, Tell (to) – Precepts

6. Regulations, Ordinances, Precepts – Commandments, Just demands, Decree: *dikaiōma*

7. Decree, Edict – Rules, Regulations, Legal demands – Decision: *dogma*

8. Rule, Yardstick, Standard: *kanōn*
  a) Rule
  b) Yardstick, Standard (length) – Sphere, Field of action

9. (In) Order, (Of the) Order (of): *taxis*
  a) Order, Put in order – (a) Turn
  b) (The) Order (of Melchizedek, of Aaron)

1. ORDER, GIVE ORDERS, COMMAND – TELL (TO): *KELEUŌ*

1 *keleuō* 26   2 *keleusma* 1

Mt	8	18	X	Jesus . . . *gave orders* to leave for the other side [of the lake]
	14	9		The king . . . *ordered* [the head of John the Baptist] to be given [to the daughter of Herodias],
		19	X	He *gave orders* that the people were to sit down on the grass;
		28	X	Lord, . . . *tell* me to come to you across the water.
	18	25	<	he had no means of paying, so his master *gave orders* that he should be sold,
	27	58		Pilate thereupon *ordered* [the body of Jesus] to be handed over [to Joseph of Arimathaea].
		64		*give the order* to have the sepulchre kept secure
Lk	18	40	X	Jesus stopped and *ordered* them to bring the [blind] man to him,
Ac	4	15		they *ordered* [Peter and John] to stand outside while the Sanhedrin had a private discussion.
	5	34		Gamaliel . . . ⌐asked (lit. *gave orders*) to have the men taken outside for a time.
	8	38		[The eunuch] *ordered* the chariot to stop,
	12	19		Herod . . . had the guards questioned, and . . . *gave orders* for their execution.
	16	22		the magistrates . . . *ordered* [Paul and Silas] to be flogged.
	21	33		the tribune . . . arrested Paul, ⌐had him (lit. *ordered* him to be) bound with two chains
		34		the tribune *ordered* Paul to be taken into the fortress.

Ac	22	24		the tribune ⌐had [Paul] (lit. *commanded* [Paul] to be) brought into the fortress
		30		[the tribune] *gave orders* for a meeting of the chief priests and the entire Sanhedrin;
	23	3		How can you . . . break the Law by *ordering* a man to strike me?
		10		the tribune . . . *ordered* his troops to . . . haul [Paul] out
		35		[the governor] *ordered* [Paul] to be held in Herod's praetorium.
	24	8		(ᵛ [the tribune Lysias intervened,] *ordering* [Paul's] accusers to appear before you)
	25	6		[Festus] ⌐had Paul (lit. *ordered* Paul to be) brought in.
		17		I . . . ⌐had the man (lit. *commanded* the man to be) brought in.
		21		I *ordered* [Paul] to be remanded
		23		Festus *ordered* Paul to be brought in.
	27	43		the centurion . . . *gave orders* that those who could swim should jump overboard
1 Th	4	16	2	the archangel will call out the *command* and the Lord himself will come down from heaven;

2. ORDER, GIVE ORDERS, COMMAND – TELL (TO), INSTRUCT, DIRECT – PRESCRIBED, APPOINTED, ARRANGED: *TASSŌ*

8	*taktos*	1	10	*epi-dia-tassomai* 1
3	*tassō*	8	4	*epi-tagē* 7
7	*dia-tagē*	2	2	*epi-tassō* 10
9	*dia-tagma*	1	5	*pros-tassō* 7
1	*dia-tassō*	16	6	*syn-tassō* 3

Mt	1	24	5	Joseph . . . did what the angel of the Lord had *told* him to do:
	8	4	5	make the offering *prescribed* by Moses,
	11	1	X	When Jesus had finished *instructing* his twelve disciples he moved on
	21	6	X	6 the disciples . . . did as Jesus had *told* them. ⁷ They brought the donkey and the colt,
	26	19	X	6 The disciples did what Jesus *told* them
	27	10	Θ	(Zc 11 13) they gave [the thirty silver pieces] for the potter's 6 field, just as the Lord *directed* me.
	28	16	X	the eleven disciples set out for Galilee, to the mountain 3 where Jesus had *arranged* to meet them.
Mk	1	27	X	2 [Jesus] *gives orders* even to unclean spirits and they obey him.
		44		5 make the offering for your healing *prescribed* by Moses
	6	27		the king . . . sent one of the bodyguard ⌐with orders (lit. 2 *giving him orders*) to bring John's head.
		39	X	2 [Jesus] *ordered* them to get all the people together in groups
	9	25	X	2 Deaf and dumb spirit, . . . I *command* you: come out of [the boy]
Lk	3	13		Exact no more than ⌐your rate (lit. the rate *prescribed* for you).
	4	36	X	2 He *gives orders* to unclean spirits with authority and power
	5	14		5 make the offering for your healing as Moses *prescribed* it,
	7	8		3 I am (§ *appointed* to be) under authority myself,
	8	25	X	2 Who can this be, that *gives orders* even to winds and waves and they obey him?
		31	X	2 [the devils] pleaded with [Jesus] not to *order* them to depart into the Abyss.
		55	X	he *told* them to give [Jairus's daughter] something to eat.
	14	22	<	2 Sir, . . . ⌐your orders have (lit. what you *ordered* has) been carried out
	17	9		Must he be grateful to the servant for doing what he was 10 *told*? ¹⁰ So with you: when you have done all you have been *told* to do, say, 'We are merely servants: we have done no more than our duty'.
Ac	7	44	Θ	the Tent of Testimony . . . had been constructed according to the *instructions* ⌐God gave (lit. *given* by God) to Moses,
		53		7 You . . . had the Law brought to you ⌐by (lit. at the *command* of) angels
	10	33	Θ	[Cornelius said to Peter,] Here we all are, assembled . . . to hear what ⌐message (lit. *instructions*) God has *given* you 5 for us.
		48		5 [Peter] *gave orders* for [the pagans] to be baptised in the name of Jesus Christ.
	12	21		8 A day was ⌐fixed (or: *appointed*), and Herod . . . made a speech
	13	48		3 all who were ⌐destined for (lit. *appointed* to) eternal life became believers.
	15	2		3 it was *arranged* that Paul and Barnabas . . . should go up to Jerusalem
	17	26		5 [God] *decreed* how long each nation should flourish
	18	2		an ⌐edict of (lit. *edict issued* by) Claudius had expelled all the Jews from Rome.
	20	13		[at Assos] we were to take Paul on board; this was what he had *arranged*,
	22	10	3	go into Damascus, and there you will be told what you have been *appointed* to do.
	23	2	2	Ananias *ordered* his attendants to strike [Paul] on the mouth.
		31		The soldiers carried out ⌐their orders (lit. what they had been *ordered* [to do]);

Ac 24 23   [Felix] *gave orders* to the centurion that Paul should be kept under arrest

28 23   3 [the Roman Jews] *arranged* a day with [Paul] and . . . visited him at his lodgings.

Rm 13 1 Θ 3 the civil authorities were *appointed* by God, [2] and so anyone
    2 who resists authority is rebelling against God's ⌐decision
16 26 Θ 7 (lit. *command*),
       it is all ⌐part of the way the eternal God wants things to be
    Θ 4 (lit. *according to the command of the eternal God*).

1 Co 7 6   4 This is a suggestion, not a *rule*:
17   each one . . . should continue as he was when God's call reached him. This is the *ruling* that I give in all the churches.
25 X 4 About remaining celibate, I have no *directions* from the Lord
9 14 X   the Lord *directed* that those who preach the gospel should get get their living from the gospel.
11 34   The other matters I shall ⌐adjust (lit. *arrange*; or: *give instructions* about) when I come.
16 1   Now about the collection made for the saints: you are to do as I *told* the churches in Galatia too.
15   3 [the Stephanas family] have really ⌐worked hard (lit. *directed* themselves) to help the saints.

2 Co 8 8   4 It is not an *order* that I am giving you;
Ga 3 15   If a will has been drawn up . . . no one is allowed to disregard
     10 it or *add further arrangements* to it.
19   The Law was *promulgated* by angels, assisted by an intermediary.

1 Tm 1 1 Θ 4 From Paul, apostle . . . by the *command* of God our saviour
Tt 1 3 Θ 4 by the *command* of God our saviour, I have been commissioned to proclaim [his decision].
5   appoint elders . . . in the way that I *told* you:
2 15   4 this is what you are to say . . . with full *authority*,
Phm 8   2 in Christ I can have no diffidence about *telling* you to do whatever is your duty,
Heb 11 23   Moses . . . was hidden by his parents . . . they defied the
      9 royal *edict*

3. ORDER, TELL (TO), INSTRUCT – GIVE INSTRUCTIONS, COMMAND, GIVE ORDERS: *PAR-ANGELLŌ*

2 par-angelia 5   1 par-angellō 31

Mt 10 5 X   These twelve Jesus sent out, *instructing* them as follows: Do not turn your steps to pagan territory,
15 35 X   he *instructed* the crowd to sit down on the ground,
Mk 6 8 X   he *instructed* [the Twelve] to take nothing for the journey
8 6 X   he *instructed* the crowd to sit down on the ground,
Lk 5 14 X   He *ordered* [the leper] to tell no one,
8 29 X   Jesus had been *telling* the unclean spirit to come out of the man.
56 X   he *ordered* [Jairus and his wife] not to tell anyone what had happened.
9 21 X   he *gave* [the disciples] strict *orders* not to tell anyone [that he was the Christ]
Ac 1 4 X   he had *told* [the disciples] not to leave Jerusalem,
4 18   [the Sanhedrin] *gave* [Peter and John] ⌐a warning (lit. *an order*) on no account . . . to teach in the name of Jesus.
5 28   We ⌐gave you a formal warning (lit. *gave you an instruction, an order*) . . . not to preach in this name,
     2
40   [the Sanhedrin] ⌐warned (lit. *ordered*) [the apostles] not to speak in the name of Jesus
10 42 X   he has *ordered* us to proclaim this to his people
15 5   [certain Pharisees insisted] that the pagans should *be circumcised* and *instructed* to keep the Law of Moses.
16 18   Paul . . . said to the spirit, 'I *order* you in the name of Jesus Christ to leave that woman'.
23   the gaoler was *told* to keep a close watch on [Paul and Silas].
24   2 [24] So, following his *instructions*, he threw them into the inner prison
17 30 Θ   God . . . is *telling* everyone everywhere that they must repent,
23 22   The tribune let the young man go ⌐with this caution (lit. *giving* him this *instruction*), 'Tell no one that you have given me this information'.
30   I . . . have ⌐notified (lit. *given orders* to) his accusers that they must state their case against him in your presence.
1 Co 7 10   For the married I have ⌐something to say (lit. *an instruction to give*), and this is not from me but from the Lord:
     X
11 17   Now that I am on the subject of *giving instructions*, I cannot say that you have done well
1 Th 4 2   2 You have not forgotten the *instructions* we gave you
11   make a point of . . . earning your living, just as we *told* you to,
2 Th 3 4   you are doing and will go on doing all that we *tell* you . . .
6   [6] . . . we *urge* you . . . to keep away from any of the brothers who refuses to work
10   We *gave* you a *rule* when we were with you;
12   we *order* . . . people of this kind to go on quietly working
1 Tm 1 3   *insist* that certain people stop teaching strange doctrines

1 Tm 1 5   2 The only purpose of this *instruction* is that there should be love,
18   2 these are the *instructions* that I am giving you:
4 11   This is what you are to ⌐enforce (lit. *instruct*) in your teaching.
5 7   ⌐remind (lit. *instruct*) [the widows] of all this, too, so that their lives may be blameless.
6 13   I *put* to you *the duty* [14] of doing all that you have been told,
17   ⌐Warn (lit. *instruct*) those who are rich in this world's goods that they are not to look down on other people;

4. ORDER, GIVE ORDERS, GIVE INSTRUCTIONS – ENJOIN, CHARGE, INSIST: *DIA-STELLOMAI*

dia-stellomai 8

Mt 16 20 X   he *gave* the disciples *strict orders* not to tell anyone that he was the Christ.
Mk 5 43 X   he *ordered* them strictly not to let anyone know [that the daughter of Jairus was raised to life],
7 36 X   Jesus *ordered* them to tell no one about [the healing of the deaf man], but the more he *insisted*, the more widely they published it.
    X
8 15 X   he *gave* [the disciples] this ⌐warning (lit. *order*), '. . . be on your guard against the yeast of the Pharisees'
9 9 X   he ⌐warned (lit. *enjoined*) [the three apostles] to tell no one what they had seen,
Ac 15 24   some of our members have disturbed you with their demands . . . They acted without any ⌐authority from (lit. *instructions given* by) us,
Heb 12 20   [The Hebrews] were appalled at the *order that was given*:

5. COMMAND, TELL (TO) – REGULATIONS, ORDERS: *EN-TOLĒ*

3 en-talma   3   1 en-tolē 67
2 en-tellomai 16

a) Command(ments) of God, of Christ, of law

Mt 4 6   2 (Ps 91 11) He will ⌐put you in his angels' charge (lit. *command* the angels on your behalf),
5 19   the man who infringes even one of the least of these *commandments* . . . will be considered the least
15 3   why do you . . . break away from the *commandment* of God . . . ?
4   2 God ⌐said (lit. *commanded*, saying): Do you duty to your father and mother
17 9   2 Jesus *gave* them this *order*, 'Tell no one about the vision'
19 7   2 why did Moses *command* that a writ of dismissal should be given in cases of divorce?
17   if you wish to enter into life, keep the *commandments*.
22 36   which is the greatest *commandment* of the Law?
38   This is the greatest and the first *commandment*.
40   On these two *commandments* hang the whole Law,
28 20   teach them to observe all ⌐the commands I gave (lit. I
     2 *commanded*) you.
Mk 7 8   You put aside the *commandment* of God to cling to human traditions. [9] . . . How ingeniously you get round the
9   *commandment* of God
10 3   2 What did Moses *command* you?
5   [Moses] wrote this *commandment* for you.
19   You know the *commandments* (Ex 20 12–16): You must not kill;
12 28   Which is the first of all the *commandments*?
31   There is no *commandment* greater than these.
Lk 1 6   [Zechariah and Elizabeth] observed all the *commandments* and observances of the Lord
4 10   (Ps 91 11) He will ⌐put his angels in charge of you (lit.
     2 *command* the angels on your behalf)
18 20   You know the *commandments*: You must not commit adultery;
23 56   on the sabbath day [the women] rested, as the ⌐Law (lit. *commandment*) required.
Jn 8 5   2 Moses has *ordered* us in the Law to condemn women like this to death by stoning.
10 18   this is the *command* I have been given by my Father.
12 49   what I had to speak was *commanded* by the Father . . . [50] and
50   I know that his *commands* mean eternal life.
13 34   I give you a new *commandment*:
14 15   If you love me you will keep my *commandments*.
21   Anybody who receives my *commandments* and keeps them will be one who loves me;
31   2 I am doing exactly what the Father *told* me.
15 10   If you keep my *commandments* you will remain in my love, just as I have kept my Father's *commandments* and remain in his love.
12   This is my *commandment*: love one another,
14   2 You are my friends, if you do what I *command* you.
17   2 What I *command* you is to love one another.
Ac 1 2   2 [Jesus] *gave* his *instructions* . . . and was taken up to heaven.

Ac 13 47	2	this is what the Lord *commanded* us to do when he said (Is 49 6): I have made you a light for the nations,
Rm 7 8		it was this *commandment* that sin took advantage of to produce all kinds of covetousness in me,
	9	when the *commandment* came, sin came to life
	10	the *commandment* was meant to lead me to life but it turned out to mean death for me,
	11	sin took advantage of the *commandment* to mislead me,
	12	The Law is sacred, and *what it commands* is sacred,
	13	sin, thanks to the *commandment*, was able to exercise all its sinful power.
13 9		All the *commandments* . . . are summed up in this single [command]: You must love your neighbour
1 Co 7 19		what does matter is to keep the *commandments* of God.
14 37		what I am writing to you is a *command* from the Lord.
Ep 2 15		[Christ destroyed in his own person the hostility] caused by the *rules* and *decrees* of the Law.
6 2		The first *commandment* . . . is: Honour your father and mother,
1 Tm 6 14		[I put to you the duty] of doing *all that you have been told*,
Heb 7 5		any of the descendants of Levi who are admitted to the priesthood are ˞ obliged (lit. *commanded*) by the Law to take tithes from the people,
16		[a second Melchizedek, who is a priest] not by virtue of a law ˞about physical descent (lit. of a physical *commandment*),
18		The earlier *commandment* is thus abolished.
9 19		Moses . . . announced all the *commandments* of the Law to the people,
20	2	(Ex 24 8) This is the blood of the covenant that God has *laid down* for you.
2 P 2 21		It would even have been better for him never to have learnt the way of holiness, than to know it and afterwards desert the holy *rule*.
3 2		[remember] the *commandments* . . . which you were given by the apostles.
1 Jn 2 3		We can be sure that we know God only by keeping his *commandments*. ⁴ Anyone who says, 'I know him', and does not keep his *commandments*, is a liar,
7		this is not a new *commandment* that I am writing to tell you, but an old *commandment* . . . the original *commandment* which was the message brought to you. ⁸ Yet in another way, what I am writing to you . . . is a new *commandment*;
3 22		whatever we ask him, we shall receive, because we keep his *commandments*
23		His *commandments* are these: that we believe in the name of his Son . . . and that we love one another as he *told* us to.
24		Whoever keeps his *commandments* lives in God
4 21		this is the *commandment* that he has given us,
5 2		we love God's children if we love God himself and do *what he has commanded* us; ³ this is what loving God is – keeping his *commandments*; and his *commandments* are not difficult,
2 Jn 4		your children have been living the life of truth as we were *commanded* by the Father.
5		I am writing now, . . . not to give you any new *commandment*,
6		To love is to live according to his *commandments*: this is the *commandment* . . . to live a life of love.
Rv 12 17		the dragon . . . went away to make war on . . . all who obey God's *commandments* and bear witness for Jesus.
14 12		there must be constancy in the saints who keep the *commandments* of God and faith in Jesus.

b) Regulations, Instructions, Orders, (generally) – Give orders, Tell (to) – Precepts

Mt 15 9	3	(Is 29 13) the doctrines they teach are only human *regulations*.
Mk 7 7	3	(Is 29 13) the doctrines they teach are only human *regulations*.
13 34 <	2	a man travelling abroad . . . has *told* the doorkeeper to stay awake.
Lk 15 29 <		I have slaved for you and never once disobeyed your *orders*,
Jn 11 57		The chief priests and Pharisees had by now given their *orders*:
Ac 17 15		Paul's escort . . . went back with *instructions* for Silas and Timothy to rejoin Paul as soon as they could.
Col 2 22	3	an example of human doctrines and *regulations*!
4 10		you were sent some *instructions* about [Mark];
Tt 1 14		[make them sound in the faith] so that they stop . . . doing what they are *told* to do by people who are no longer interested in the truth.
Heb 11 22	2	Joseph . . . *made the arrangements for* his own burial.

6. REGULATIONS, ORDINANCES, PRECEPTS – COMMANDMENTS, JUST DEMANDS, DECREE: *DIKAIŌMA*

dikaiōma 6/10

Lk 1 6		[Zechariah and Elizabeth] observed all the commandments and ˞observances (lit. *ordinances*) of the Lord.
Θ		
Rm 1 32		They know what God's ˞verdict (lit. just *decree*) is:

Rm 2 26		If a man who is not circumcised obeys the *commandments* of the Law, surely that makes up for his not being circumcised?
8 4		[God] did this in order that the Law's *just demands* might be satisfied in us,
Heb 9 1		The first covenant also had its *regulations* governing worship,
10		they are *rules* about the outward life, connected with foods and drinks

7. DECREE, EDICT – RULES, REGULATIONS, LEGAL DEMANDS – DECISION: *DOGMA*

1 *dogma* 5 2 *dogmatizō* 1

Lk 2 1		Caesar Augustus issued a *decree* for a census of the whole world to be taken.
Ac 16 4		[Paul and Timothy] passed on the *decisions* reached by the apostles
17 7		[Paul and Silas] have broken every one of Caesar's *edicts*
Ep 2 15		[Christ destroyed in his own person the hostility] caused by the rules and *decrees* of the Law.
Col 2 14		[God] has . . . cancelled every record of the ˞debt that we had to pay (lit. *legal demands* [standing] against us);
20	2	why do you still ˞let *rules dictate to you* (or: *submit to regulations*), as though you were still living in the world?

8. RULE, YARDSTICK, STANDARD: *KANŌN*

kanōn 4

a) Rule

Ga 6 16		Peace and mercy to all who follow this *rule*,

b) Yardstick, Standard (length) – Sphere, Field of action

2 Co 10 13		[We are] taking for our measure the ˞yardstick (or: *standard*) which God gave us to measure with,
15		we trust that . . . we shall get taller and taller, when judged ˞by our own *standard* (or: in our own *sphere*). ¹⁶ I mean,
16		we shall be carrying the gospel to places far beyond you, without encroaching on anyone else's ˞*field* (or: *sphere*),

9. (IN) ORDER, (OF THE) ORDER (OF): *TAXIS*

2 *tagma* 1   3 *ana-tassomai* 1
1 *taxis* 10

a) Order, Put in order – (a) Turn

Lk 1 1	3	many others have undertaken to ˞ draw up (lit. *put in order*) accounts of the events that have taken place among us,
8		Now it was the *turn* of Zechariah's section to serve and he was exercising his priestly office before God
1 Co 14 40		let everything be done with propriety and in *order*.
15 23		[all men will be brought to life in Christ;] but all of them 2 in their proper *order*:
Col 2 5		I am . . . delighted to find you all in ˞harmony (lit. *order*)

b) (The) Order (of Melchizedek, of Aaron)

Heb 5 6		(Ps 110 4) You are a priest of the *order* of Melchizedek, and for ever.
10		[Jesus] was acclaimed by God with the title of high priest of the *order* of Melchizedek.
6 20		Jesus has . . . become a high priest of the *order* of Melchizedek, and for ever.
7 11		why was it still necessary for a new priesthood to arise, one of the same *order* as Melchizedek not counted as being 'of the same *order* as' Aaron?
17		You are a priest of the *order* of Melchizedek, and for ever.
21		you are a priest (ᵛ of the *order* of Melchizedek), and for ever.

OTHER – DIFFERENT

1. Other, Another – Different – More: *allos*
a) Another's, Someone else's, Anybody else's – Of others, Other men's, Not one's own (*allotrios*)
b) Other (people), Another (person), Someone else – More (people) – Some . . . Others

c) Other (things), Another (animal), Different – More, Second
2. Other, Another: *heteros*
a) Other (people), Another, Second (person) – Someone else
b) Other (things), Another (place), Next – Different, Strange, Unnatural

3. **Different, Other, At variance (with):** *para*
4. **Differ – Various:** *dia-pherō*
5. **a Kind, Sort**
  1: Of one kind or another,

Various, Different – All sorts of, Manifold, Comprehensive: *poikilos*
2: a Kind, Sort: *genos*
3: Form, Kind: *eidos*

Θ, X, Ⓢ = 'Other', 'Different' with some reference to God, Jesus, the Spirit

1. OTHER, ANOTHER – DIFFERENT – MORE: *ALLOS*

3 allachothen	1	5 allōs	1
4 allachou	1	2 allotrios	7/14
1 allos	157	6 allotri(-epi-skopos)	1

a) Another's, Someone else's, Anybody else's – Of others, Other men's, Not one's own (allotrios)

Lk 16 12		if you cannot be trusted with what is ˹not yours (lit.
	2	*another's*)
Rm 14 4 X	2	It is not for you to condemn *someone else's* servant:
15 20	2	I had no wish to build on *other* men's foundations;
2Co 10 15		we are not boasting without any measure, about work done
	2	by *other* people;
16	2	without encroaching on *anyone else's* field,
1Tm 5 22	2	never make yourself an accomplice to *anyone else's* sin;
Heb 9 25		like the high priest going into the sanctuary year after
	2	year with the blood that is *not his own*,
1 P 4 15		None of you should ever deserve to suffer for being a
	6	murderer, . . . or an informer *on others*;

b) Other (people), Another (person), Someone else – More (people) – Some . . . others . . .

Mt 4 21		[Jesus] saw *another* pair of brothers, James . . . and . . . John;
8 9		I . . . have soldiers under me; and I say to one man: Go, . . . to *another*: Come
16 14		Some say he is John the Baptist, *others* Elijah, and yet others Jeremiah
19 9		the man who divorces his wife . . . and marries *another*,
20 3 <		Going out at about the third hour he saw *others* standing idle
6 <		at about the eleventh hour he went out and found ˹more men (lit. *others*) standing round,
21 8		*others* were cutting branches from the trees
36 <		he sent some *more* servants,
41 <		He will . . . lease the vineyard to *other* tenants
22 4 <		he sent some *more* servants.
26 71		*another* servant girl saw [Peter] and said
27 42		He saved *others*; . . . he cannot save himself.
61		Mary of Magdala and the *other* Mary were there,
28 1		Mary of Magdala and the *other* Mary went to visit the sepulchre.
Mk 6 15		*Others* said, 'He is Elijah'; *others* again, 'He is a prophet',
8 28		*others* [say you are] Elijah; *others* again, one of the prophets.
10 11		The man who divorces his wife and marries *another*
12		And if a woman divorces her husband and marries *another*
11 8		*others* [spread] greenery which they had cut in the fields.
12 4 <		he sent *another* servant to them;
5 <		he sent *another* . . . then a number of *others*,
9 <		the owner . . . will . . . give the vineyard to *others*.
32 Θ		(cf. Dt 4 35) he is one and there is no *other*.
15 31		He saved *others*, . . . he cannot save himself.
41		there were many *other* women there who had come up to Jerusalem with him.
Lk 5 29		with them at table was a large gathering of tax collectors and *others*.
7 8		I say to one man: Go, and he goes; to *another*: Come here,
19 X		Are you the one who is to come, or must we wait for *someone else*?
20 X		Are you the one who is to come, or have we to wait for *someone else*?
9 8		[Some said] that Elijah had reappeared, still *others* . . . one of the ancient prophets
19		John the Baptist; *others* Elijah; and *others* say one of the ancient prophets
20 16 <		[the owner] will . . . give the vineyard to *others*.
22 59		*another* [man] insisted, . . . 'This fellow was certainly with him.
35		He saved *others*, . . . let him save himself
Jn 4 37		one sows, *another* reaps;
38		*Others* worked for [the harvest]; and you have come into the rewards of their trouble.
5 7		while I am still on the way, *someone else* gets there before me.
32 Θ		there is *another* witness who can speak on my behalf,
43 X		if *someone else* comes in his own name you will accept him.
7 12		Some said, 'He is a good man'; *others*, 'No, he is leading the people astray'.
41		*others* said, 'He is the Christ,' but then some said, 'Would the Christ be from Galilee?'

Jn 9 9		*Some* said, 'Yes, it is the same one.' *Others* said, 'No, he only looks like him.'
16		some of the Pharisees said . . . *Others* said,
10 21		*Others* said, 'These are not the words of a man possessed by a devil.'
12 29		*others* said, 'It is an angel speaking to him.'
14 16 ●		I will ask the Father, and he will give you *another* Advocate
15 24 X		If I had not performed such works among them as no one *else* has ever done,
18 15		Simon Peter, with *another* disciple, followed Jesus.
16		the *other* disciple . . . went out,
34		Do you ask this of your own accord, or have *others* spoken to you about me?
19 18		they crucified him with two *others*,
32		the soldiers . . . broke the legs of the first man . . . and then of the *other*.
20 2		[Mary of Magdala] came running to Simon Peter and the *other* disciple.
3		So Peter set out with the *other* disciple
4		the *other* disciple . . . reached the tomb first;
8		Then the *other* disciple . . . also went in;
25		When the *other* disciples said, 'We have seen the Lord,' [Thomas] answered,
21 2		Simon Peter, Thomas . . . and two *more* of his disciples were together.
8		The *other* disciples came on in the boat,
18		*somebody else* will put a belt round you
Ac 2 12		they asked *one another* what it all meant.
4 12 X		(Ⓢ salvation comes through no *other* [person])
15 2		it was arranged that Paul and Barnabas and *others* of the church should go up to Jerusalem
19 32		˹everybody was shouting (lit. some were shouting, and *others* were shouting)
21 34		˹People in the crowd called out (lit. Some in the crowd called out, *others* shouted)
1Co 1 16		the family of Stephanas . . . I baptised too, but no one *else* as far as I can remember.
3 10		I laid the foundations, on which *someone else* is doing the building.
9 2		Even if I were not an apostle to *others*, I should still be an apostle to you
12		*Others* are allowed these rights over you
27		having been an announcer to *others* myself,
10 29		Why should my freedom depend on *somebody else's* conscience?
12 8		*another* may have the gift of preaching instruction given him
9		by the same Spirit; ⁹ . . . *another* the gift of faith . . .
10		*another* again the gift of healing, . . . ¹⁰ one the power of miracles; *another* prophecy; *another* the gift of recognising spirits; *another* the gift of tongues and *another* the ability to interpret them.
14 19		I would rather say five words that mean something to *others* than ten thousand words in a tongue.
29		As for prophets, let two or three of them speak, and the *others* attend to them.
30		If one or *other* of the listeners receives a revelation,
2Co 8 13		This does not mean that to give relief to *others* you ought to make things difficult for yourselves:
11 4 X		any newcomer has only to proclaim a new Jesus, ˹different from (lit. *other* than) the one that we preached,
Ph 3 4		Take any ˹man (lit. *other*) who thinks he can rely on what is physical:
1Th 2 6		we have never looked for any special honour from men, either from you or *anybody else*,
Heb 11 35		Some came back to their wives from the dead, . . . *others* submitted to torture . . . ³⁶ Some had to bear being pilloried
Rv 7 2		Then I saw *another* angel
8 3		*Another* angel . . . came and stood at the altar.
10 1		Then I saw *another* powerful angel
14 6		Then I saw *another* angel,
8		*Another*, second, angel followed him,
9		*Another*, third, angel followed,
15		Then *another* angel came out of the sanctuary,
17		*Another* angel . . . came out of the temple in heaven,
18		the *other* angel in charge of the fire left the altar
17 10		Five of [the seven emperors] have already gone, one is here now, and the *other* is yet to come;
18 1		I saw *another* angel come down from heaven

c) Other (things), Another (animal), Different – More, Second

Mt 2 12		[the wise men] returned to their own country by a *different* way.
5 39		offer him the *other* [cheek] as well;
10 23		If they persecute you in one town, take refuge in the next; ˹and if they persecute you in ˹that (lit. the *other*), take refuge in *another*.
12 13		his hand was better, as sound as the *other* [one].
13 5 <		[some seeds fell on the edge of the path . . .] *Others* fell on patches of rock
7 <		*Others* fell among thorns,

Mt 13 8 < *Others* fell on rich soil
24 He put *another* parable before them [The good seed and the darnel],
31 He put *another* parable before them [The grain of mustard seed],
33 He told them *another* parable [The yeast].
21 33 Listen to *another* parable [The wicked husbandmen].
25 16 < The man who had received the five talents . . . made five *more*.
17 < The man who had received two made two *more*
20 < The man who had received the five talents came forward bringing five *more*.
22 < here is *more* than that I have made.
Mk 1 38 4 Let us go *elsewhere*, to the neighbouring country towns,
4 5 < ⌐Some (lit. *Other*) seed fell on rocky ground
7 < ⌐Some (lit. *Other*) seed fell into thorns,
8 < And ⌐some (lit. *other*) seed fell into rich soil
18 < there are *others* who receive the seed in thorns.
36 there were *other* boats with him.
7 4 There are also many *other* observances which have been handed down
12 31 ● There is no *other* commandment greater than these.
14 58 ● and in three days [I am going to] build *another* [Temple],
Lk 6 29 To the man who slaps you on one cheek, present the *other* cheek too;
Jn 6 22 the crowd . . . saw that only one boat and no *other* had been there,
23 *Other* boats, however, had put in from Tiberias,
10 1 3 anyone who . . . gets [into the sheepfold] in *some other way* is a thief
16 ● there are *other* sheep I have
20 30 There were many *other* signs that Jesus worked
21 25 There were many *other* things that Jesus did;
Ac 19 32 everybody was shouting *different* things
21 34 People in the crowd called out *different* things,
1 Co 3 11 X For the foundation, nobody can lay any *other* than the one which has already been laid, that is Jesus Christ.
15 39 human flesh is *different*, animals' flesh is *different*, the flesh of birds is *different*, and the flesh of fish is *different*.
41 The sun has a *different* brightness, the moon has a *different* brightness, and the stars a *different* brightness,
2 Co 1 13 There are no hidden meanings in our letters *besides* what you can read for yourselves
11 8 I was robbing *other* churches
Ga 1 7 ● Not that there can be ⌐more than one (lit. any *other*) Good News;
5 10 I feel sure that . . . you will ⌐agree with (lit. feel no *different* from) me,
1 Tm 5 25 the good that people do can be obvious; but even when it is ⌐not (lit. *otherwise*), it cannot be hidden for ever.
Heb 4 8 5 God would not . . . have spoken so much of *another* day.
Jm 5 12 do not swear by heaven or by the earth, or use any *other* oaths at all.
Rv 2 24 I am not laying any ⌐special (lit. *other*; or: *different*) duty;
6 4 out came *another* horse, bright red,
12 3 Then a *second* sign appeared in the sky,
13 11 Then I saw a *second* beast;
15 1 ⌐What I saw next (lit. *Another* sign I saw), in heaven, was a great and wonderful sign;
18 4 ⌐A new (lit. *Another*) voice spoke from heaven;
20 12 the book of life was opened, and *other* books opened

2. OTHER, ANOTHER: *HETEROS*

1 *heteros* 96/98   2 *hetero(-didaskaleō)* 2
3 *heterōs* 1   4 *hetero(-glōssos)* 1
5 *hetero(-zygeō)* 1

a) Other (people), Another, Second (person) – Someone else

Mt 6 24 No one can be the slave of two masters: he will either hate the
< first and love the *second*, or treat the first with respect and
< the *second* with scorn.
8 21 *Another* [man], one of his disciples, said to him,
11 3 Are you the one who is to come, or have we got to wait for
X *someone else*?
16 It is like children shouting to ⌐*each other* (ᵛ their companions)
15 30 bringing . . . the blind, the dumb, and many *others*;
16 14 Some say he is John the Baptist, . . . and *others* Jeremiah
Lk 7 41 < one owed him five hundred denarii, the *other* fifty.
8 3 Susanna, and several *others* who provided for them out of their own resources
9 59 *Another* to whom he said, 'Follow me,'
61 *Another* said, 'I will follow you, sir,
10 1 After this the Lord appointed seventy-two *others*
11 16 *Others* asked him, as a test, for a sign
14 19 < *Another* said, 'I have bought five yoke of oxen
20 < Yet *another* said, 'I have just got married

Lk 14 31 what king marching to war against *another* king . . .?
16 7 To *another* he said, 'And you, sir, how much do you owe?'
13 No servant can be the slave of two masters: he will either hate
< the first and love the *second*, or treat the first with respect and
< the *second* with scorn.
18 Everyone who divorces his wife and marries *another* is guilty of adultery,
17 34 two will be in one bed: one will be taken, the *other* left;
35 two women will be grinding corn together: one will be taken, the *other* left;
36 (ᵛ two men will be in the field: one will be taken, the *other* left;)
18 10 Two men went up to the Temple to pray, one a Pharisee, the
< *other* a tax collector.
19 20 < Next came the *other* [servant] and said, 'Sir, here is your pound.
20 11 < he persevered and sent a *second* servant;
22 58 someone else saw [Peter] and said, 'You are another of them.'
23 32 with him they were also leading out two *other* criminals to be executed.
40 the *other* [robber] spoke up and rebuked him. 'Have you no fear of God at all?
Ac 1 20 (Ps 109 8) Let *someone else* take his office.
2 13 ⌐Some (lit. *Others*), however, laughed it off. 'They have been drinking too much new wine'
7 18 (Ex 1 8) until ⌐a new (lit. *another*) king came to power
8 34 X is the prophet referring to himself or *someone else*?
15 35 Paul and Barnabas . . . with many *others* . . . proclaimed the Good News,
17 7 X there is *another* emperor, Jesus.
34 and *others* besides [became believers].
27 1 Paul and some *other* prisoners were handed over to a centurion
Rm 2 1 In judging *others* you condemn yourself,
21 [If you call yourself a Jew,] why not teach yourself as well as the *others*?
7 3 if she gives herself to *another* man while her husband is still alive, she is legally an adulteress; but after her husband is dead . . . she can marry *someone else* without becoming an adulteress.
4 X you, . . . who . . . are now dead to the Law, can now give yourselves to *another* [husband],
13 8 If you love ⌐your fellow men [lit. *others*] you have carried out your obligations.
1 Co 3 4 What could be more unspiritual than your slogans, one: 'I am for Paul', and the *other*: 'I am for Apollos'?
4 6 it is not for you . . . to go taking sides for one man against *another*.
6 1 How dare one of your members take up a complaint against *another* in the lawcourts . . .?
10 24 Nobody should be looking for his own advantage, but everybody for the *other* man's.
29 ⌐his (lit. *another's*) scruples, you see, not your own.
12 9 and *another* [may have] the gift of faith
10 *another* [may have] the gift of tongues
14 17 However well you make your thanksgiving, the *other* [person] gets no benefit from it.
21 (Is 28 11) Through men speaking strange languages and
○ through the lips of *foreigners*,
2 Co 8 8 I am just testing the genuineness of your love against the keenness of *others*.
Ga 1 19 [I stayed with Cephas.] I did not see any of the *other* apostles;
6 4 if you find anything to boast about [in your conduct], it will at least be something of your own, not just something better than ⌐your neighbour has (lit. *others* have).
Ep 3 5 This mystery . . . was unknown to any men in ⌐past (lit. *other*) generations;
Ph 2 4 so that nobody thinks of his own interests first but everybody thinks of *other people's* interests instead.
2 Tm 2 2 hand it on to reliable people so that they in turn will be able to teach *others*.
Heb 7 11 X why was it still necessary for ⌐a new (lit. *another*) priesthood to arise . . .?
15 X a *second* Melchizedek, who is a priest [. . . by the power of an indestructible life.]
11 36 ⌐Some (lit. *Others*) had to bear being pilloried and flogged,

b) Other (things), Another (place), Next –
Different, Strange, Unnatural

Mt 10 23 If they persecute you in one town, take refuge in the *next*;
12 45 [the unclean spirit] goes off and collects seven *other* spirits
Mk 16 12 X [Jesus] showed himself under *another* form to two of [the disciples]
Lk 3 18 there were many *other* things [John the Baptist] said to announce the Good News
4 43 I must proclaim the Good News . . . to the *other* towns too,
5 7 their companions in the *other* boat
6 6 on *another* sabbath he went into the synagogue
8 6 < ⌐Some (lit. *Other*) seed fell on rock,
7 < ⌐Some (lit. *Other*) seed fell amongst thorns
8 < And ⌐some (lit. *other*) seed fell into rich soil

Lk	9	29	As [Jesus] prayed, the aspect of his face ʳwas changed (lit. became *different*)
		X 56	they went off to *another* village.
	11	26	[the unclean spirit] goes off and brings seven *other* spirits
	22	65	[the guards] continued ʳheaping (lit. to heap *other*) insults on [Jesus].
Jn	19	37	and again, [in] *another* [place] scripture says:
Ac	2	4	they . . . began to speak ʳ*foreign* (or: *other*) languages
		40	[Peter] spoke to them for a long time using many *different* arguments,
	4	12	of all the names in the world given to men, ʳthis is the only X (lit. there is no *other*) one by which we can be saved.
	12	17	[Peter] left and went to *another* place.
	13	35	This is explained by *another* text:
	17	21	The one amusement the Athenians . . . seem to have, ʳapart from (lit. *other* than) discussing the latest ideas,
	23	6	one section was made up of Sadducees and the *other* of Pharisees,
Rm	7	23	I can see that my body follows a *different* law
	8	39	[neither death nor life] . . . nor any *other* created thing, can ever come between us and the love of God
	13	9	All the *other* commandments . . . are summed up in this single command:
1 Co	14	21	4 (Is 28 11) Through men speaking *strange* languages and through the lips of foreigners, I shall talk to the nation,
	15	40	the heavenly bodies have a ʳbeauty of their own (lit. *different* beauty) and the earthly bodies a *different* one.
2 Co	6	14	5 Do not harness yourselves in an *uneven* team with unbelievers.
	11	4 ⑤	you have only to receive a [new] spirit, *different* from the one you have already received, or a [new] gospel, *different* from the one you have already accepted
Ga	1	6	I am astonished at the promptness with which you . . . have decided to follow a *different* [version of the] Good News.
Ph	3	15	3 If there is some point on which you see things *differently*, God will make it clear to you;
1 Tm	1	3	2 insist that certain people stop teaching *strange* doctrines
		10	[laws are] for liars and for perjurers—and for everything *else* that is contrary to the sound teaching
	6	3	2 Anyone who teaches *anything different* [is simply ignorant]
Heb	5	6	and in *another* text:
	7	13	our Lord, of whom these things were said, belonged to a *different* tribe,
Jm	2	25	Rahab . . . welcomed the messengers and showed them a *different* way to leave.
Jude		7	The fornication of Sodom and Gomorrah and the other nearby towns was equally *unnatural*,

3. DIFFERENT, OTHER, AT VARIANCE (WITH): *PARA*

para + accusative (2)

Ga	1	8	if anyone preaches a version of the Good News ʳ*different* from (or: *other* than) the one we have already preached to you
	9		. . . he is to be condemned. ⁹ . . . if anyone preaches a version of the Good News ʳ*different* from (or: *other* than) the one you have already heard, he is to be condemned.

4. DIFFER – VARIOUS: *DIA-PHERŌ*

1 *dia-pherō* 2/13   2 *dia-phoros* 2

Rm	12	6	2 Our gifts *differ* according to the grace given us.
1 Co	15	41	the stars *differ* from each other in brightness.
Ga	4	1	an heir . . . *is no different* from a slave for as long as he remains a child.
Heb	9	10	2 they are rules about . . . washing at *various* times,

5. A KIND, SORT

1: OF ONE KIND OR ANOTHER, VARIOUS, DIFFERENT – ALL SORTS OF, MANIFOLD, COMPREHENSIVE: *POIKILOS*

1 *poikilos* 10   2 *poly-poikilos* 1

Mt	4	24	those who were suffering from diseases and painful complaints *of one kind or another* . . . were all brought to [Jesus],
Mk	1	34	[Jesus] cured many who were suffering from diseases *of one kind or another*;

Lk	4	40	all those who had friends suffering from diseases *of one kind or another* brought them to [Jesus],
Ep	3	10 Θ	2 the Sovereignties . . . should learn . . . how ʳ*comprehensive* (or: *manifold*) God's wisdom really is,
2 Tm	3	6	silly women . . . are obsessed with their sins and follow one craze *after another*
Tt	3	3	we too were . . . enslaved by *different* passions and luxuries;
Heb	2	4	God . . . confirmed their witness with . . . miracles *of all kinds*,
	13	9	Do not let yourselves be led astray by *all sorts of* strange doctrines:
Jm	1	2	you will always ʳhave your trials (lit. be facing *various* trials)
1 P	1	6	you may for a short time have to bear being plagued by *all sorts of* trials;
	4	10 Θ	like good stewards responsible for all these *different* graces of God, put yourselves at the service of others.

2: A KIND, SORT: *GENOS*

genos 6/21

Mt	13	47	the kingdom of heaven is like a dragnet . . . that brings in a haul of all *kinds*.
	17	21	(ᵛ This is the *kind* [of spirit] that can only be driven out by prayer and fasting.)
Mk	9	29	This is the *kind* . . . that can only be driven out by prayer.
1 Co	12	10	[One may have the power of miracles,] another ʳthe gift of tongues (lit. many *kinds* of ecstatic utterance)
		28	[God has given the first place to apostles . . .;] after them . . . those with ʳmany languages (lit. many *kinds* of language)
	14	10	There are any number of ʳ*different* (lit. *kinds* of) languages in the world,

3: FORM, KIND: *EIDOS*

eidos 1/5

1 Th	5	22	avoid every *form* of evil.

OWN ACCORD

1. (Of) One's own accord – By, Of, From, oneself: *aph-he-autou*   2. (Of) Its own accord – Of itself: *auto-matos*

1. (OF) ONE'S OWN ACCORD – BY, OF, FROM, ONESELF: *APH-HE-AUTOU*

aph-he-autou 14

Jn	5	19 X	the Son can do nothing *by himself*;
		30 X	I can do nothing *by myself*;
	7	17 X	he will know . . . whether my doctrine is *my own*.
		18	When a man's doctrine is *his own* he is hoping to get honour for himself;
		28 X	I have not come *of myself*:
	8	28 X	you will know . . . that I do nothing *of myself*:
		42 X	not that I came ʳbecause I chose (lit. *of my own accord*),
	10	18 X	I lay [my life] down *of my own free will*,
	11	51	[Caiaphas] did not speak *in his own person*,
	14	10 X	The words I say to you I do not speak *as from myself*:
	15	4	a branch cannot bear fruit all *by itself*, . . . neither can you
	16	13	the Spirit of truth . . . will not be speaking *as from himself*
	18	34	Do not ask this *of your own accord*,
2 Co	3	5	not that we are qualified in ourselves to claim anything as *our own* [work]:

2. (OF) ITS OWN ACCORD – OF ITSELF: *AUTO-MATOS*

auto-matos 2

Mk	4	28	*Of its own accord* the land produces first the shoot, then the ear,
Ac	12	10	the iron gate . . . opened *of its own accord*;

P

PARABLE – MYTH

1. **Parable:** *para-bolē*
2. **Metaphor, Figure of speech – Proverb – Parable:** *par-oimia*
3. **Allegory:** *all-ēgoreō*
4. **Myth:** *mythos*

1. PARABLE: *PARA-BOLĒ*
para-bolē 50

Mt 13	3	[Jesus] told [the people] many things in *parables*.
	10	Why do you talk to them in *parables*?
	13	The reason I talk to them in *parables* is that they look without seeing
	18	You . . . are to hear the *parable* of the sower.
	24	He put another *parable* before them [The darnel],
	31	He put another *parable* before them [The mustard seed],
	33	He told them another *parable* [The yeast],
	34	In all this Jesus spoke to the crowds in *parables*; indeed, he
	35	would never speak to them except in *parables*. ³⁵ This was to fulfil the prophecy (Ps 78 2); I will speak to you in *parables*
	36	Explain the *parable* about the darnel . . . to us.
	53	When Jesus finished these *parables* he left the district;
15	15	Explain the *parable* for us [On clean and unclean].
21	33	Listen to another *parable* [The wicked husbandmen],
	45	When they heard his *parables*, the chief priests and the scribes realised he was speaking about them,
22	1	Jesus began to speak to them in *parables* once again [The wedding feast],
24	32	Take the fig tree as a *parable*:
Mk 3	23	he . . . spoke to [the scribes] in *parables*, 'How can Satan cast out Satan?'
4	2	He taught them many things in *parables*,
	10	the Twelve . . . asked what the *parables* meant.
	11	to those who are outside everything comes in *parables*,
	13	Do you not understand this *parable* [The sower]? Then how will you understand any of the *parables*?
	30	What *parable* can we find for [the kingdom of God]?
	33	Using many *parables* like these, he spoke the word to them,
	34	He would not speak to [the people] except in *parables*, but he explained everything to his disciples when they were alone.
7	17	his disciples questioned him about the *parable* [On clean and unclean].
12	1	He went on to speak to them in *parables*,
	12	[the chief priests and scribes] realised that the *parable* was aimed at them [The wicked husbandmen],
13	28	Take the fig tree as a *parable*:
Lk 4	23	No doubt you will quote me the *saying*, 'Physician, heal yourself'
5	36	He also told them this *parable* [The old and the new],
6	39	He also told a *parable* to them [The splinter and the plank],
8	4	he used this *parable*: [The sower]
	9	his disciples asked him what this *parable* might mean,
	10	for the rest there are only *parables*, so that they may see but not perceive,
	11	This, then, is what the *parable* means: the seed is the word of God.
12	16	Then he told them a *parable* [On hoarding possessions]:
	41	Lord, do you mean this *parable* [The watchful servant] for us, or for everyone?
13	6	He told this *parable*: 'A man had a fig tree
14	7	He then told the guests a *parable* [On choosing places at table],
15	3	he spoke this *parable* to them: [The lost sheep]
18	1	he told them a *parable* [The unscrupulous judge and the importunate widow]
	9	He spoke the following *parable* [The Pharisee and the publican]
19	11	he went on to tell a *parable* [The pounds],
20	9	he went on to tell the people this *parable*:
	19	[the scribes and the chief priests] realised that this *parable* was aimed at them.
21	29	he told them a *parable*, 'Think of the fig tree and indeed every tree.'
Heb 9	9	it is a *symbol* for this present time.
11	19	*figuratively* [speaking, Abraham] was given back Isaac from the dead.

2. METAPHOR, FIGURE OF SPEECH – PROVERB – PARABLE: *PAR-OIMIA*
par-oimia 5

Jn 10	6	Jesus told them this *parable* [The gate of the sheepfold]
16	25	I have been telling you all this in *metaphors*, the hour is coming when I shall no longer speak to you in *metaphors*;
	29	His disciples said, 'Now you are speaking plainly and not using *metaphors*!'
2 P 2	22	What he has done is exactly as the *proverb* rightly says: The dog goes back to his own vomit, and: When the sow has been washed, it wallows in the mud.

3. ALLEGORY: *ALL-ĒGOREŌ*
all-ēgoreō 1

Ga 4	24	This can be regarded as an *allegory*: the women stand for the two covenants.

4. MYTH: *MYTHOS*
mythos 5

1 Tm 1	4	[insist that certain people stop] taking notice of *myths* and endless genealogies;
4	7	Have nothing to do with godless *myths* and old wives' tales.
2 Tm 4	4	instead of listening to the truth, [people] will turn to *myths*.
Tt 1	14	so that [the Cretans] stop taking notice of Jewish *myths*
2 P 1	16	we were not any cleverly invented *myths* that we were repeating when we brought you the knowledge of . . . our Lord Jesus Christ;

PASSOVER – PENTECOST

1. **Passover:** *pascha*
2. **Pentecost:** *pentēkostē*

1. PASSOVER: *PASCHA*
pascha 29

L: Passover = Passover lamb

Mt 26	2		It will be *Passover*, as you know, in two days' time,
	17	L	Where do you want us to make the preparations for you to eat the *passover*?
	18		My time is near. It is at your house that I am keeping *Passover* with my disciples. ¹⁹ The disciples . . . prepared
	19	L	the *Passover*.
		L	
Mk 14	1		It was two days before the *Passover* and the feast of Unleavened Bread,
	12	L	On the first day of Unleavened Bread, when the *Passover* lamb was sacrificed, his disciples said to him, 'Where do you want us to go and make the preparations for you to eat the *passover*?'
		L	
	14	L	Where is my dining room in which I can eat the *passover* with my disciples?
	16	L	The disciples . . . prepared the *Passover*.
Lk 2	41		[Jesus's] parents used to go to Jerusalem for the feast of the *Passover*
22	1•		The feast of Unleavened Bread, called the *Passover*, was now drawing near,
	7		The day of Unleavened Bread came round, the day on which
	8	L	the *passover* had to be sacrificed, ⁸ and [Jesus] sent Peter and John, saying, 'Go and make the preparations for us to eat the *passover*'.
	11	L	Where is the dining room in which I can eat the *passover* with my disciples?
	13	L	They set off . . . and prepared the *Passover*.

Lk 22 15 L	I have longed to eat this *passover* with you before I suffer;
Jn 2 13	Just before the Jewish *Passover* Jesus went up to Jerusalem,
23	During [Jesus's] stay in Jerusalem for the *Passover*
6 4	It was shortly before the Jewish feast of *Passover*.
11 55	The Jewish *Passover* drew near, and many of the country people . . . had gone up to Jerusalem (§ before the *Passover*) to purify themselves
12 1	Six days before the *Passover*, Jesus went to Bethany,
13 1	before the festival of the *Passover* . . . Jesus knew that the hour had come for him to pass from this world to the Father.
18 28 L	they would be defiled and unable to eat the *passover*.
39	according to a custom of yours I should release one prisoner at the *Passover*;
19 14	It was *Passover* Preparation Day, about the sixth hour.
Ac 12 4	Herod meant to try Peter in public after the end of *Passover* week.
1Co 5 7 L	get rid of all the old yeast . . . Christ, our *passover*, has been sacrificed;
Heb 11 28	It was by faith that [Moses] kept the *Passover* and sprinkled the blood

2. PENTECOST: *PENTĒKOSTĒ*

pentēkostē 3

Ac 2 1	When *Pentecost* day came round, [the Twelve] had all met in one room,
20 16	Paul . . . was anxious to be in Jerusalem . . . for the day of *Pentecost*.
1Co 16 8	I shall be staying at Ephesus until *Pentecost*

PAUL

1. Paul, his friends and fellow workers
1: Paul and Barnabas
2: John Mark, Luke and Demas
3: Timothy, Silas and Judas Barsabbas
4: Titus
5: Apollos
6: Aristarchus, Gaius, Tychicus and Trophimus

2. Paul writes to or of
1: the Colossians, the Laodiceans
2: the Corinthians
   a) Aquila and Priscilla
   b) Stephanas, Crispus and others
3: the Philippians
4: the Romans

1. PAUL, HIS FRIENDS AND FELLOW WORKERS

1: PAUL AND BARNABAS

Paul	157	*Eutychus**	1 (Ac 20)
S {*Saul*	15	J *Jason*	4 (Ac 17)
S {*Saoul*	8	*Mnason**	1 (Ac 21)
B *Barnabas*	28	*Sosthenes**	1 (1 Co 1)
Joseph	1 (Ac 4)		

Ac 4 36 B	There was a Levite of Cypriot origin called *Joseph* whom the apostles surnamed *Barnabas* (which means 'son of encouragement').
7 58 S	The witnesses [of the stoning of Stephen] put down their clothes at the feet of a young man called *Saul*.
8 1 S	*Saul* entirely approved of the killing.
3 S	*Saul* then worked for the total destruction of the church,
9 1 S	*Saul* was still breathing threats to slaughter the Lord's disciples.
4 S	He fell to the ground, and then he heard a voice saying, '*Saul*, Saul (G *Saoul, Saoul*), why are you persecuting me?'
8 S	*Saul* got up from the ground, but . . . he could see nothing
11 S	the Lord said, 'You must . . . ask at the house of Judas for someone called *Saul*, who comes from Tarsus. At this moment he is praying,'
17 S	Ananias . . . entered the house, and at once laid his hands on [Saul] and said, 'Brother ⌐Saul (G *Saoul*), I have been sent by the Lord Jesus'
22 S	*Saul's* power increased steadily . . . ²³ . . . the Jews [in Damascus] worked out a plot to kill him, ²⁴ but news
24 S	of it reached *Saul*.

Ac 9 27 B	*Barnabas* . . . took charge of [Saul], introduced him to the apostles.
11 22 B	The church in Jerusalem . . . sent *Barnabas* to Antioch. . . . ²⁴ . . . he was a good man, filled with the Holy Spirit and with faith.
25 B S	[Barnabas] then left for Tarsus to look for *Saul*, ²⁶ and . . . brought him to Antioch.
30 B S	[The disciples decided to send relief to the brothers in Judaea.] They . . . delivered their contributions to the elders in the care of *Barnabas* and *Saul*.
12 25 B S	*Barnabas* and *Saul* . . . came back from Jerusalem, bringing John Mark with them.
13 1 B	In the church Antioch at the following were prophets and teachers: *Baanabas*, Simeon called Niger, and Lucius of Cyrene, Manaen, who had been brought up with Herod the tetrarch, and *Saul*. ² One day . . . the Holy Spirit said,
2 S	
B S	'I want *Barnabas* and *Saul* set apart for the work to which I have called them'.
7 B S	The proconsul summoned *Barnabas* and *Saul* and asked to hear the word of God,
9 S	Then *Saul*, whose other name is *Paul*, looked [Elymas] full in the face
13	*Paul* and his friends went by sea from Paphos to Perga
16	*Paul* stood up, held up a hand for silence and began to speak:
43 B	many Jews and devout converts joined *Paul* and *Barnabas*
45	the Jews . . . used blasphemies and contradicted everything *Paul* said.
46 B	Then *Paul* and *Barnabas* spoke out boldly. 'We . . . must turn to the pagans.'
50 B	the Jews worked on some of the devout women . . . and persuaded them to turn against *Paul* and *Barnabas*
14 9	as [the cripple] listened to *Paul's* preaching, he managed to catch his eye.
11	When the crowd saw what *Paul* had done they shouted . . .
12 B	'These people are gods . . .' ¹² They addressed *Barnabas* as Zeus, and since *Paul* was the principal speaker they called him Hermes.
14 B	When the apostles *Barnabas* and *Paul* heard what was happening they tore their clothes,
19	They stoned *Paul* . . . ²⁰ . . . he stood up . . . The next day he and *Barnabas* went off to Derbe.
20 B	
15 2 B	after *Paul* and *Barnabas* had had a long argument with these men it was arranged that *Paul* and *Barnabas* and others of the church should go up to Jerusalem and discuss the problem
B	
12 B	they listened to *Barnabas* and *Paul* describing all the signs and wonders God had worked through them
22 B	the apostles and elders decided to choose delegates to send to Antioch with *Paul* and *Barnabas* . . . They chose Judas known as Barsabbas and Silas . . . ²⁵ . . . we have decided unanimously to elect delegates and to send them to you with *Barnabas* and *Paul*
25 B	
35 B	*Paul* and *Barnabas* . . . stayed on in Antioch,
36 B	On a later occasion *Paul* said to *Barnabas*, 'Let us go back . . .' ³⁷ *Barnabas* suggested taking John Mark, ³⁸ but *Paul* was not in favour of taking along the very man who had deserted them . . . ³⁹ After a violent quarrel they parted company, and *Barnabas* sailed off with Mark to Cyprus. ⁴⁰ Before *Paul* left, he chose Silas to accompany him
37 B	
38	
39 B	
40	
16 3	*Paul* wanted to have [Timothy] as a travelling companion,
9	One night *Paul* had a vision: a Macedonian appeared . . . 'Come across to Macedonia and help us'.
14	[At Philippi] Lydia . . . listened to us, and the Lord opened her heart to accept what *Paul* was saying.
17	This girl [who was a soothsayer] started following *Paul* and the rest of us . . . ¹⁸ . . . until *Paul* lost his temper one day and said to the spirit, 'I order you . . . to leave that woman'. . . . ¹⁹ . . . her masters . . . seized *Paul* and Silas and dragged them to the law courts
18	
19	
25	Late that night *Paul* and Silas were praying and singing
28	*Paul* shouted [to the gaoler] at the top of his voice, '. . . we are all here'. ²⁹ The gaoler . . . threw himself at the feet of *Paul* and Silas,
29	
36	The gaoler reported the message to *Paul*, 'The magistrates have sent an order for your release;' . . . ³⁷ 'What!' *Paul* replied
37	
17 2	[In Thessalonika] *Paul* as usual introduced himself [at the synagogue]
4	Some [of the Jews in Thessalonika] were convinced and joined *Paul* and Silas . . . ⁵ The Jews . . . made for Jason's house, hoping to find them there . . . ; ⁶ however, they found only Jason and some of the brothers, and these they dragged before the city council shouting, . . . ⁷ . . . 'they have been staying at Jason's.'
5 J	
6 J	
7 J	
9 J	they made Jason and the rest give security before setting them free.
10	When it was dark the brothers immediately sent *Paul* and Silas away to Beroea,

Ac 17	13	When the Jews of Thessalonika heard that the word of God was being preached by *Paul* in Beroea as well, they went there to make trouble . . . ¹⁴ So the brothers arranged for
	14	
	15	*Paul* to go immediately as far as the coast, . . . ¹⁵ *Paul's* escort took him as far as Athens, and went back with instructions for Silas and Timothy to rejoin Paul as soon
	16	as they could. ¹⁶ *Paul* waited for them in Athens
	22	*Paul* stood before the whole Council of the Areopagus
	33	After that *Paul* left them,
18	5	[in Corinth] *Paul* devoted all his time to preaching,
	9	the Lord spoke to *Paul* in a vision, 'Do not be afraid to speak out,'
	12	the Jews [of Corinth] made a concerted attack on *Paul* and
	14	brought him before the tribunal. . . . ¹⁴ Before *Paul* could open his mouth, Gallio said
	18	After staying on for some time, *Paul* took leave of the brothers
19	1	While Apollos was in Corinth, *Paul* made his way overland as far as Ephesus,
	4	'John's baptism' said *Paul* 'was a baptism of repentance'
	6	the moment *Paul* had laid hands on them the Holy Spirit came down on them,
	11	So remarkable were the miracles worked by God at *Paul's* hands
	13	some itinerant Jewish exorcists . . . used to say, 'I command you by the Jesus whose spokesman is *Paul*'. ¹⁵ The
	15	evil spirit replied, 'Jesus I recognise, and I know who *Paul* is, but who are you?'
	21	*Paul* made up his mind to go back to Jerusalem
	26	[Demetrius said:] '. . . this man *Paul* has . . . converted a great number of people
	29	the mob rushed to the theatre dragging along two of *Paul's* Macedonian travelling companions, Gaius and Aristarchus.
	30	³⁰ Paul wanted to make an appeal to the people,
20	1	*Paul* sent for the disciples and . . . set out for Macedonia.
	7	*Paul* was due to leave [Troas] the next day, and he preached a sermon that went on till the middle of the night. . . .
	9	⁹ and as *Paul* went on and on, a young man called Eutychus* . . . grew drowsy and . . . fell to the ground three floors
	10	below. . . . ¹⁰ *Paul* went down and . . . said 'there is still life in him.'
	13	we set sail for Assos, where we were to take *Paul* on board;
	16	*Paul* has decided to pass wide of Ephesus
	37	[the elders at Ephesus] put their arms round *Paul's* neck and kissed him;
21	4	[the disciples at Tyre] kept telling *Paul* not to go on to Jerusalem,
	11	[Agabus] took *Paul's* girdle . . . and said, '. . . The man this girdle belongs to will be bound like this by the Jews in Jerusalem,'
	13	ʳhe (lit. *Paul*) replied, 'What are you trying to do . . .?'
	16	Some of the disciples from Caesarea accompanied us and took us to the house of a Cypriot with whom we were to lodge; he was called Mnason* and had been one of the earliest disciples.
	18	The next day *Paul* went with us to visit James,
	26	the next day *Paul* took the men along and . . . visited the Temple
	29	[Some Jews from Asia] thought that *Paul* had brought [Trophimus the Ephesian] into the Temple. ³⁰ . . .
	30	people . . . seized *Paul* and dragged him out of the Temple . . . ³² . . . the crowd . . . stopped beating *Paul* when
	32	they saw the tribune and the soldiers.
	37	Just as *Paul* was being taken to the fortress, he asked the tribune if he could have a word with him.
	39	'I?' said *Paul* 'I am a Jew . . . Please give me permission to speak to the people.' ⁴⁰ The man gave his consent and
	40	*Paul* . . . gestured to the people
22	7 S	I fell to the ground and heard a voice saying, ʳSaul, Saul (G *Saoul, Saoul*), why are you persecuting me?'
	13 S	[Ananias] said, 'Brother ʳSaul (G *Saoul*), receive your sight'.
	25	*Paul* said to the centurion on duty, 'Is it legal for you to flog a . . . Roman citizen?'
	28	'I was born to [Roman citizenship]' said *Paul*.
	30	[the tribune] brought *Paul* down and stood him in front of [the Sanhedrin]
23	1	*Paul* looked steadily at the Sanhedrin
	3	*Paul* said to [the high priest Ananias], 'God will surely strike you,'
	5	*Paul* answered, 'Brothers, I did not realise it was the high priest,'
	6	*Paul* was well aware that one section [of the Sanhedrin] was made up of Sadducees and the other of Pharisees,
	10	the tribune, afraid that they would tear *Paul* to pieces, ordered his troops to . . . haul him out
	12	the Jews . . . made a vow not to eat or drink until they had killed *Paul*.
	14	We have made a solemn vow to let nothing pass our lips until we have killed *Paul*.

Ac 23	16	the son of *Paul's* sister heard of the ambush . . . and . . .
	17	told *Paul*, ¹⁷ ʳwho (lit. *Paul* then) called one of the centurions and said, 'Take this young man to the tribune;' . . .
	18	¹⁸ So the man . . . reported, 'The prisoner *Paul* . . . requested me to bring this young man to you;'
	20	The Jews have made a plan to ask you to take *Paul* down to the Sanhedrin
	24	provide horses for *Paul*, and deliver him unharmed to Felix the governor.
	31	The soldiers . . . took *Paul* and escorted him by night to Antipatris.
	33	On arriving at Caesarea the escort . . . handed *Paul* over to [the governor].
24	1	the high priest Ananias came down with some of the elders and an advocate named Tertullus, and they laid information against *Paul* before the governor.
	10	When the governor motioned him to speak, *Paul* answered:
	24	Felix . . . sent for *Paul* and gave him a hearing on the subject of faith in Christ Jesus. . . . ²⁶ . . . he had hopes of
	26	receiving money from *Paul*, . . . ²⁷ . . . being anxious to gain favour with the Jews, Felix left *Paul* in custody.
	27	
25	2	The chief priests . . . informed [Festus] of the case against *Paul* . . . ⁴ But Festus replied that *Paul* would remain in
	4	custody in Caesarea . . . ⁶ . . . he went down to Caesarea and . . . took his seat on the tribunal and had *Paul* brought
	6	in.
	8	*Paul's* defence was this, 'I have committed no offence . . .'
	9	⁹ Festus was anxious to gain favour with the Jews, so he said to *Paul*, 'Are you willing to go up to Jerusalem and be
	10	tried . . . before me there?' ¹⁰ But *Paul* replied, 'I am standing before the tribunal of Caesar'
	14	Festus put *Paul's* case before the king [Agrippa].
	19	some argument . . . about a dead man called Jesus whom *Paul* alleged to be alive.
	21	*Paul* put in an appeal
	23	Festus ordered *Paul* to be brought in.
26	1	Agrippa said to *Paul*, 'You have leave to speak on your own behalf'. And *Paul* held up his hand and began his defence:
	14 S	I heard a voice saying to me in Hebrew, ʳSaul, Saul (G *Saoul, Saoul*), why are you persecuting me?'
	24	Festus shouted out, '*Paul*, you are out of your mind;' . . .
	25	²⁵'Festus, your Excellency,' answered *Paul* 'I am not mad:'
	28	Agrippa said to *Paul*, 'A little more, and your arguments would make a Christian of me'. ²⁹ 'Little or more,' *Paul*
	29	replied 'I wish . . . all who have heard me today would come to be as I am'
27	1	*Paul* and some other prisoners were handed over to a centurion called Julius,
	3	Julius was considerate enough to allow *Paul* to go to his friends [in Sidon]
	9	navigation was already hazardous . . . so *Paul* gave them this warning, ¹⁰ '. . . this voyage will be dangerous'
	11	But the centurion took more notice of the captain . . . than of what *Paul* was saying;
	21	*Paul* stood up among the [shipwrecked] men. 'Friends, . . . if you had listened to me and not put out from Crete,
	24	[the angel] said, 'Do not be afraid, *Paul*.'
	31	*Paul* said to the centurion and his men, 'Unless [the crew] stay on board you cannot hope to be saved'.
	33	*Paul* urged them all to have something to eat.
	43	the centurion was determined to bring *Paul* safely through,
28	3	[Landed in Malta,] *Paul* had collected a bundle of sticks
	8	Publius' father was in bed, suffering from . . . dysentery. *Paul* went in to see him,
	15	When *Paul* saw [the brothers in Rome] he . . . took courage.
	16	in Rome *Paul* was allowed to stay in lodgings of his own
	25	*Paul* had one last thing to say to [the Roman Jews]
Rm 1	1	From *Paul*, . . . ⁷ To you all, . . . who are God's beloved in Rome,
1Co 1	1	I, *Paul*, . . . together with brother Sosthenes*, send greetings ² to the church of God in Corinth,
	12	these slogans that you have, like: 'I am for *Paul*', 'I am for Apollos', . . . ¹³ Was it *Paul* that was crucified for you?
	13	Were you baptised in the name of *Paul*?
3	4	What could be more unspiritual than your slogans, 'I am for *Paul*' and 'I am for Apollos'? ⁵ After all, what is Apollos
	5	and what is *Paul*? They are servants
	22	*Paul*, Apollos, . . . the world, . . . are all your servants;
9	6 B	Are *Barnabas* and I the only ones who are not allowed to stop working?
16	21	This greeting is in my own hand – *Paul*.
2Co 1	1	From *Paul*, appointed by God to be an apostle of Christ Jesus, . . . to the church of God at Corinth,
10	1	this is *Paul* himself appealing to you
Ga 1	1	From *Paul* to the churches of Galatia,
2	1 B	I went up to Jerusalem again. I went with *Barnabas* and took Titus with me.
	9 B	James, Cephas and John, these leaders, these pillars, shook hands with *Barnabas* and me as a sign of partnership:

Ga	2	13	The other Jews joined [Cephas] in this pretence, and even
		B	*Barnabas* felt himself obliged to copy their behaviour.
	5	2	It is I, *Paul*, who tell you this: if you allow yourselves to be circumcised,
Ep	1	1	From *Paul*, appointed by God to be an apostle of Christ Jesus, to the saints who are faithful in Christ Jesus:
	3	1	So I, *Paul*, a prisoner of Christ Jesus for the sake of the pagans
Ph	1	1	From *Paul* and *Timothy*, servants of Christ Jesus,
Col	1	1	From *Paul*, appointed by God to be an apostle of Christ Jesus, . . . [2] to the saints in Colossae,
		23	the Good News . . . of which I, *Paul*, have become the servant.
	4	10 B	*Mark*, the cousin of *Barnabas*
		18	Here is a greeting in my own handwriting – *Paul*.
1 Th	1	1	From *Paul*, *Silvanus* and *Timothy*, to the Church in Thessalonika
	2	18	we tried hard to come and visit you; I, *Paul*, tried more than once,
2 Th	1	1	From *Paul*, *Sivanus* and *Timothy*, to the church in Thessalonika
	3	17	From me, *Paul*, these greetings in my own handwriting,
1 Tm	1	1	From *Paul*, apostle of Christ Jesus . . , [2] to *Timothy*,
2 Tm	1	1	From *Paul*, appointed by God to be an apostle of Christ Jesus . . .; [2] to *Timothy*, dear child of mine,
Tt	1	1	From *Paul*, servant of God, . . . [4] To *Titus*, true child of mine
Phm		1	From *Paul*, a prisoner of Christ Jesus and from our brother *Timothy*; to our dear fellow worker Philemon,
		9	this is *Paul* writing, an old man now
		19	[if Onesimus owes you anything,] I, *Paul*, shall pay it back
2 P	3	15	our brother *Paul*, who is so dear to us, told you this when he wrote to you with the wisdom that is his special gift.

2: JOHN MARK, LUKE AND DEMAS

	John [Mark]	5		Theophilus*	2	(Lk 1; Ac 1)
	Mark	8		Mary*	1	
L	Luke	3		Rhoda*	1	(Ac 12)
	Crescens	1	(2 Tm)			
D	Demas	3				

Lk	1	3	I . . . have decided to write an ordered account for you, *Theophilus*,
Ac	1	1	In my earlier work, *Theophilus*, I dealt with everything Jesus had done and taught
	12	12	[Peter] went straight to the house of *Mary* the mother of *John Mark* . . . [13] He knocked at the outside door and a servant called *Rhoda* came to answer it.
		13	
		25	Barnabas and Saul . . . came back from Jerusalem, bringing *John Mark* with them.
	13	5	[Barnabas and Saul] landed at Salamis and proclaimed the word of God in the synagogues of the Jews; *John* acted as their assistant.
		13	Paul and his friends went from Paphos to Perga in Pamphylia where *John* left them to go back to Jerusalem.
	15	37	Barnabas suggested taking *John Mark* . . . [39] . . . Barnabas sailed off with *Mark* to Cyprus.
		39	
Col	4	10	Aristarchus . . . sends his greetings, and so does *Mark*, the cousin of Barnabas
		14 L D	Greetings from my dear friend *Luke*, the doctor, and also from *Demas*.
2 Tm	4	10 D	*Demas* has deserted me for love of this life and gone to Thessalonika, *Crescens* has gone to Galatia and Titus to Dalmatia; [11] only *Luke* is with me. Get *Mark* to come and bring him with you; I find him a useful helper in my work.
		11 L	
Phm		24 D L	[Epaphras sends his greetings;] so do my colleagues *Mark*, *Aristarchus*, *Demas* and *Luke*.
1 P	5	13	Your sister in Babylon . . . sends you greetings; so does my son, *Mark*.

3: TIMOTHY, SILAS AND JUDAS BARSABBAS

	Timothy	24		Alexander*	2	(1 & 2 Tm)
S	Silas	13		Carpus*	1	
S	Silvanus	4		Eunice*	1	(2 Tm)
J	Judas [Barsabbas]	3		Hermogenes*	1	
	Barsabbas	1	(Ac 15)	Hymenaeus*	2	(1 & 2 Tm)
	Erastus	1	(Ac 19)	Lois*	1	
	Onesiphorus	2	(2 Tm)	Philetus*	1	(2 Tm)
				Phygelus*	1	

Ac	15	22	the apostles and elders decided to . . . send to Antioch with Paul and Barnabas . . . *Judas* known as *Barsabbas* and *Silas*, both leading men in the brotherhood,
		J	
		S	
		27 J S	we are sending you *Judas* and *Silas*,
		32 J S	*Judas* and *Silas*, being themselves prophets, spoke for a long time, encouraging . . . the brothers.

Ac	15	38 S	[They went back to those who had sent them.] ([v] But *Silas* thought he would stay there.)
		40 S	Before Paul left [Antioch], he chose *Silas* to accompany him
	16	1	[At Lystra] there was a disciple called *Timothy*, whose mother was a Jewess who had become a believer; but his father was a Greek.
		19 S	[the soothsayer's] masters . . . seized Paul and *Silas* and dragged them to the law courts
		25 S	Late that night Paul and *Silas* were praying and singing God's praises,
		29 S	The gaoler . . . threw himself trembling at the feet of Paul and *Silas*,
	17	4 S	Some of [the Jews in Thessalonika] were convinced and joined Paul and *Silas*
		10 S	When it was dark the brothers immediately sent Paul and *Silas* away to Beroea,
		14 S	the brothers arranged for Paul to go . . , leaving *Silas* and *Timothy* behind. [15] Paul's escort . . . went back with instructions for *Silas* and *Timothy* to rejoin Paul as soon as they could.
		15 S	
	18	5 S	After *Silas* and *Timothy* had arrived from Macedonia, Paul devoted all his time to preaching,
	19	22	[Paul] sent two of his helpers, *Timothy* and *Erastus*, ahead of him to Macedonia,
	20	4	[Paul] was accompanied by Sopater . . . and *Timothy*,
Rm	16	21	*Timothy*, who is working with me, sends his greetings;
1 Co	4	17	I have sent you *Timothy*, my dear and faithful son in the Lord:
	16	10	If *Timothy* comes, . . . [11] . . . nobody is to be scornful of him.
2 Co	1	1	From Paul, . . . and from *Timothy*, one of the brothers, to the church of God at Corinth
		19 S	the Christ Jesus that we proclaimed among you – I mean *Silvanus* and *Timothy* and I –
Ph	1	1	From Paul and *Timothy*, servants of Christ Jesus, to all the saints in Christ Jesus,
	2	19	I hope . . . to send *Timothy* to you soon,
Col	1	1	From Paul . . . and from our brother *Timothy* [2] to the saints in Colossae,
1 Th	1	1 S	From Paul, *Silvanus* and *Timothy*, to the Church in Thessalonika
	3	2	[we] sent our brother *Timothy*, who is God's helper in spreading the Good News of Christ,
		6	*Timothy* is now back from you
2 Th	1	1 S	From Paul, *Silvanus* and *Timothy*, to the Church in Thessalonika
1 Tm	1	2	[from Paul] to *Timothy*, true child of mine in the faith;
		18	*Timothy*, my son, these are the instructions that I am giving you: . . . [19] . . . Some people have put conscience aside . . . [20] I mean men like Hymenaeus* and Alexander*, whom I have handed over to Satan
		20	
	6	20	My dear *Timothy*, take great care of all that has been entrusted to you.
2 Tm	1	2	[From Paul] to *Timothy*, dear child of mine, . . . [5] . . . I am reminded of the sincere faith which you have; it came first to live in your grandmother Lois*, and your mother Eunice*,
		5	
		15	Phygelus* and Hermogenes* and all the others from Asia refuse to have anything more to do with me. [16] I hope the Lord will be kind to all the family of Onesiphorus,
		16	
	2	17	Talk of this kind corrodes like gangrene, as in the case of Hymenaeus* and Philetus*,
	4	13	When you come, bring the cloak I left with Carpus* in Troas, and the scrolls, . . . [14] Alexander* the coppersmith has done me a lot of harm;
		14	
		19	Greetings to Prisca and Aquila, and the family of *Onesiphorus*.
Phm		1	From Paul . . . and from our brother *Timothy*; to our dear fellow worker Philemon,
Heb	13	23	our brother *Timothy* has been set free. If he arrives in time, he will be with me when I see you.
1 P	5	12 S	I write these few words to you through *Silvanus*, who is a brother I know I can trust,

4: TITUS

Titus 13

2 Co	2	13	I was so continually uneasy in mind at not meeting brother *Titus* [at Troas], I . . . went on to Macedonia.
	7	6	God . . . comforted us, by the arrival of *Titus*,
		13	we had the even greater happiness of finding *Titus* so happy; . . . [14] . . . our boasting to *Titus* has proved to be . . . true
		14	
	8	6	we have asked *Titus*, since he has already made a beginning, to bring this work of mercy to the same point of success among you,
		16	I thank God for putting into *Titus's* heart the same concern for you that I have myself.

2 Co	8	23	*Titus* . . . is my own colleague and fellow worker in your interests;
	12	18	*Titus* went at my urging, and I sent the brother that came with him. Can *Titus* have exploited you?
Ga	2	1	I went up to Jerusalem again. I went with Barnabas and took *Titus* with me.
		3	Even though *Titus* who had come with me is a Greek, he was not obliged to be circumcised.
2 Tm	4	10	*Titus* [has gone] to Dalmatia;
Tt	1	4	[From Paul] to *Titus*, true child of mine in the faith that we share,

5: APOLLOS

Apollos 10 Zenas 1 (Tt)

Ac	18	24	An Alexandrian Jew named *Apollos* now arrived in Ephesus. He was an eloquent man, with a sound knowledge of the scriptures.
	19	1	While *Apollos* was in Corinth, Paul made his way overland as far as Ephesus,
1 Co	1	12	all these slogans that you have, like: 'I am for Paul', 'I am for *Apollos*', 'I am for Cephas',
	3	4	What could be more unspiritual than your slogans, 'I am for Paul' and 'I am for *Apollos*'? [5] After all, what is
		5	*Apollos* and what is Paul? They are servants who brought the faith to you. . . . [6] I did the planting, *Apollos* did
		6	the watering,
		22	Paul, *Apollos*, Cephas, the world, . . . are all your servants;
	4	6	in everything I have said here, brothers, I have taken *Apollos* and myself as an example
	16	12	As for our brother *Apollos*, I begged him to come to you with the brothers
Tt	3	13	See to all the travelling arrangements for *Zenas* the lawyer and *Apollos*, and make sure they have everything they need.

6: ARISTARCHUS, GAIUS, TYCHICUS AND TROPHIMUS

Aristarchus	*5*	*Secundus*	*1* ⎫
Artemas	*1 (Tt)*	*Sopater* (the son	⎬ (Ac 20)
Gaius	*2 (Ac)*	of) *Pyrrhus 1*	⎭
Jesus Justus 1 (Col)		F *Trophimus*	*3*
		T *Tychicus*	*5*

Ac	19	29	the [Ephesian] mob rushed to the theatre dragging along two of Paul's Macedonian travelling companions, *Gaius* and *Aristarchus*.
	20	4	[Paul] was accompanied by *Sopater*, son of *Pyrrhus*, who came from Beroea; *Aristarchus* and *Secundus* who came from Thessalonika; *Gaius* from Doberus, and Timothy,
		T F	as well as *Tychicus* and *Trophimus* who were from Asia.
	21	19 F	[The Jews] had . . . previously seen *Trophimus* the Ephesian in [Jerusalem] with [Paul],
	27	2	we had *Aristarchus* with us, a Macedonian of Thessalonika.
Ep	6	21 T	my dear brother *Tychicus*, my loyal helper in the Lord,
Col	4	7 T	*Tychicus* will tell you all the news about me.
		10	*Aristarchus*, who is here in prison with me, sends his greetings,
		11	and so does Mark . . . [11] and *Jesus Justus* adds his greetings.
2 Tm	4	12 T	I have sent *Tychicus* to Ephesus.
		20 F	I left *Trophimus* ill at Miletus.
Tt	3	12 T	As soon as I have sent *Artemas* or *Tychicus* to you, lose no time in joining me at Nicopolis,
Phm		24	my colleagues Mark, *Aristarchus*, Demas and Luke [send greetings].

2. PAUL WRITES TO OR OF

1: THE COLOSSIANS, THE LAODICEANS

| *Apphia* | *1* | *Epaphras* | *3* | *Onesimus 2* |
| *Archippus* | *2* | *Nympha* | *1* | *Philemon 1* |

Col	1	7	*Epaphras*, who taught you, is one of our closest fellow workers and a faithful deputy for ⌜us⌝ (ᵛ you) as Christ's servant,
	4	9	*Onesimus*, that dear and faithful brother who is a fellow citizen of yours.
		12	*Epaphras*, your fellow citizen, . . . never stops battling for you, praying that you will never lapse
		15	Please give my greetings to the brothers at Laodicea and to *Nympha* and the church which meets in her house.
		17	Give *Archippus* this message: Remember the service that the Lord wants you to do,

Phm		1	From Paul . . . and from our brother Timothy; to our dear fellow worker *Philemon*, [2] our sister *Apphia*, our
		2	fellow soldier *Archippus* and the church that meets in your house;
		10	I am appealing to you for a child of mine, whose father I became while wearing these chains: I mean *Onesimus*. [11] He . . . will be useful to you now,
		23	*Epaphras*, a prisoner with me . . . , sends his greetings;

2: THE CORINTHIANS

a) *Aquila* and *Priscilla*

| *Aquila 6* | *Prisca* | *3* |
| | =*Priscilla 3* | |

Ac	18	2	[In Corinth Paul] met a Jew called *Aquila* whose family came from Pontus. He and his wife *Priscilla* had recently left Italy . . . [3] . . . they were tentmakers,
		18	Paul . . . sailed for Syria, accompanied by *Priscilla* and *Aquila*.
		26	*Priscilla* and *Aquila* . . . took an interest in [Apollos] and gave him further instruction about the Way.
Rm	16	3	My greetings to *Prisca* and *Aquila*, my fellow workers in Christ Jesus, [4] who risked death to save my life:
1 Co	16	19	*Aquila* and *Prisca*, with the church that meets at their house, send you their warmest wishes, in the Lord.
2 Tm	4	19	Greetings to *Prisca* and *Aquila*, and the family of Onesiphorus.

b) *Stephanas*, *Crispus* and others

Achaicus	*1*	*Lucius*	*1*
Chloe	*1*	*Phoebe*	*1*
Crispus	*2*	*Quartus*	*1*
Erastus	*2*	*Sosipater*	*1*
Fortunatus	*1*	*Stephanas*	*3*
Gaius	*2*	*Tertius*	*1*
Jason	*1*	*Tit(i)us Justus 1*

Ac	18	7	[In Corinth Paul] moved to the house next door [to the synagogue] that belonged to a worshipper of God called (§ *Titius*, ᵛ *Titus*) *Justus*. [8] *Crispus*, president of the synagogue, and his whole household, all became believers in the Lord.
		8	
Rm	16	1	I commend to you our sister *Phoebe*, a deaconess of the church at Cenchreae. [2] . . . she has looked after a great many people, myself included.
		21	Timothy . . . sends his greetings; so do my compatriots, *Lucius*, *Jason* and *Sosipater*. [22] I, *Tertius*, who wrote out
		22	this letter, greet you in the Lord.
		23	Greetings from *Gaius*, who is entertaining me and from the whole church that meets in his house. *Erastus*, the city treasurer, sends his greetings; so does our brother *Quartus*.
1 Co	1	11	From what *Chloe's* people have been telling me . . . it is clear that there are serious differences among you.
		14	I am thankful that I never baptised any of you after *Crispus*
		16	and *Gaius* . . . [16] Then there was the family of *Stephanas*,
	16	15	the *Stephanas* family, who were the first-fruits of Achaia, have really worked hard to help the saints.
		17	I am delighted that *Stephanas*, *Fortunatus* and *Achaicus* have arrived; they make up for your absence.
2 Tm	4	20	*Erastus* remained at Corinth,

3: THE PHILIPPIANS

Clement	*1*	*Lydia*	*2*
Epaphroditus	*2*	*Syntyche*	*1*
Evodia	*1*	*Syzygus*	*1*

Ac	16	14	One of these women [at Philippi] was called *Lydia*, a devout woman . . . who was in the purple-dye trade. . . . the Lord opened her heart to accept what Paul was saying.
		40	From the prison [Paul and Silas] went to *Lydia's* house
Ph	2	25	*Epaphroditus* . . . was sent as your representative to help me when I needed someone to be my companion in working
	4	2	I appeal to *Evodia* and I appeal to *Syntyche* to come to agreement with each other, in the Lord; [3] and I ask you,
		3	⌜*Syzygus*⌝ (or: [my] loyal comrade), to be truly a 'companion' and to help them in this. These women were a help to me when I was fighting to defend the Good News – and so, at the same time, were *Clement* and the others who worked with me.
		18	I am fully provided now that I have received from *Epaphroditus* the offering that you sent,

4: THE ROMANS

Ampliatus	*Eubulus*	*Mary*	*Phlegon*
Andronicus	*Hermas*	*Narcissus*	*Pudens*
Apelles	*Hermes*	*Nereus*	*Rufus*
Aristobulus	*Herodion*	*Olympas*	*Stachys*
Asyncritus	*Julia*	*Patrobas*	*Tryphaena*
Claudia	*Junias*	*Persis*	*Tryphosa*
Epaenetus	*Linus*	*Philologus*	*Urban*

Rm 16 5 Greetings to my friend *Epaenetus*, the first of Asia's gifts to
     6 Christ; ⁶ greetings to *Mary* who worked so hard for you;
     7 ⁷ to those outstanding apostles *Andronicus* and *Junias*, my
       compatriots and fellow prisoners who became Christians
     8 before me; ⁸ to *Ampliatus*, my friend in the Lord;
     9 ⁹ to *Urban*, my fellow worker in Christ; to my friend
    10 *Stachys*; ¹⁰ to *Apelles* who has gone through so much
       for Christ; to everyone who belongs to the household of
    11 *Aristobulus*; ¹¹ to my compatriot *Herodion*; to those in
    12 the household of *Narcissus* who belong to the Lord; ¹² to
       Tryphaena and *Tryphosa*, who work hard for the Lord;
       to my friend *Persis* who has done so much for the Lord;
    13 ¹³ to *Rufus*, a chosen servant of the Lord, and to his mother
       who has been a mother to me too. ¹⁴ Greetings to *Asyn-
    14 critus, Phlegon, Hermes, Patrobas, Hermas*, and all the
    15 brothers who are with them; ¹⁵ to *Philologus* and *Julia,
       Nereus* and his sister, and *Olympas* and all the saints who
       are with them.

2 Tm 4 21 Greetings to you from *Eubulus, Pudens, Linus, Claudia* and
       all the brothers.

PAY – REWARD – PRIZE

1. Pay: *histēmi*
2. Pay – Repay: *tinō*
3. Pay – Repay – Reward: *didōmi*
   1: Pay, Payment – Give (money)
   2: Repay, Pay back – Reward –
     Retribution
4. Wages, Pay – Hire – Reward:
   misthos
   1: Hire – Wages, Pay – Paid
     Servant, Hired man

2: Wages (figuratively) – Reward
5. Wages, Pay – Live on, (financial)
   Support: *ops-ōnion*
6. (financial) Accounts: *logos*
7. Prize: *brabeion*
   1: Prize
   2: (Be) Disqualified from winning
     a prize

1. PAY: *HISTĒMI*

histēmi 1/152

Mt 26 15 (Zc 11 12) They *paid* [Judas] thirty pieces of silver.

2. PAY – REPAY: *TINŌ*

1 *tinō* 1   2 *apo-tinō* 1

2 Th 1 9 ʳIt will be their punishment to be (lit. They will *pay* [the
       price] with the punishment of being) lost eternally,
Phm 19 2 I, Paul, shall *pay* it *back*

3. PAY – REPAY – REWARD: *DIDŌMI*

2 *didōmi* 12/415   3 *ant-apo-didōmi* 5/7
1 *apo-didōmi* 25/48 4 *ant-apo-doma* 2
              5 *ant-apo-dosis* 1

1: PAY, PAYMENT – GIVE (MONEY)

Mt 5 26 you will not get out till you have *paid* the last penny.
  18 25 < he had no means of *paying*, so his master gave orders that
         he should be sold, . . . to ʳmeet (lit. the) debt.
    26 < Give me time . . . and I will *pay* the whole sum.
    28 < *Pay* what you owe me
    29 < Give me time and I will *pay* you.
    30 < he had him thrown into prison till he should *pay* the debt.
    34 < the master handed him over to the torturers till he should
         pay all his debt.
  20 4 < 2 You go to my vineyard too and I will *give* you a fair wage.
    8 < 2 Call the workers and *pay* them their wages,
    14 < 2 I choose to *pay* the last-comer as much as [I *pay*] you.
  22 17 2 Is it permissible to *pay* taxes to Caesar or not?

Mt 27 10 2 they *gave* [the thirty pieces of silver] for the potter's field.
Mk 12 14 2 Is it permissible to *pay* taxes to Caesar or not? Should we
       2/2 *pay*, ʳyes or no (lit. or not *pay*)?
  14 11 2 They promised to *give* [Judas] money;
Lk 7 42 < They were unable to *pay*,
  10 35 < Look after him . . . and . . . I will *make good* any extra
         expense you have.
  12 59 you will not get out till you have *paid* the very last penny.
  20 22 2 Is it permissible for us to *pay* taxes to Caesar or not?
  22 5 2 They . . . agreed to *give* [Judas] money.
  23 2 2 We found this man . . . opposing *payment* of the tribute to
         Caesar,
Rm 13 7 *Pay* every government official what he has a right to ask
Heb 7 4 2 Abraham *paid* [Melchizedek] a tenth of the treasure he had
       captured.
Rv 18 6 [Babylon] is to be *paid* ʳin her own coin (lit. as she herself
       paid).

2: REPAY, PAY BACK – REWARD – RETRIBUTION

Mt 6 4 Θ your Father who sees all that is done in secret will *reward*
       you.
    6 Θ your Father who sees all that is done in secret will *reward*
       you.
   18 Θ your Father who sees all that is done in secret will *reward*
       you.
  16 27 X (cf. Ps 62 12) he will *reward* each one according to his be-
       haviour.
Lk 14 12 do not ask your . . . relations or rich neighbours, for fear
     4 they *repay* your courtesy by inviting you in return.
  14 Θ 3/3 that [the poor] cannot *pay* you *back* means that . . . *repay-
       ment* will be made to you when the virtuous rise again.
  19 8 [Zacchaeus:]' . . . if I have cheated anybody I will ʳ*pay* (or:
       give) him *back* four times the amount.'
Rm 2 6 Θ (Ps 62 12) [God] will *repay* each one as his works deserve.
  11 9 (Ps 69 22 G) May their own table prove a trap for them
     4 . . . let that be their ʳ*punishment* (lit. *retribution*).
  12 17 Never *repay* evil with evil
  19 Θ 3 (Dt 32 25) vengeance is mine – I will *pay* them *back*,
Col 3 24 X 5 anyone who does wrong will be *repaid* in kind
1 Th 5 15 Make sure that people do not try to ʳtake revenge (lit. *repay*
       evil with evil);
2 Th 1 6 Θ 3 God will very rightly *repay* with injury those who are injuring
       you,
1 Tm 5 4 children . . . are to learn first of all to . . . *repay* their
       debt to their parents,
2 Tm 4 14 X (Ps 62 12) the Lord will *repay* him for what he has done.
Heb 10 30 3 (Dt 32 35) Vengeance is mine; I will *repay*.
1 P 3 9 Never *pay back* one wrong with another,

4. WAGES, PAY – HIRE – REWARD: *MISTHOS*

4 *misthios*	2	2 *misthōtos*	3
7 *misthōma*	1	3 *misth-apo-dosia*	3
5 *misthoomai*	2	8 *misth-apo-dotēs*	1
1 *misthos*	29	6 *anti-misthia*	2

1: HIRE – WAGES, PAY – PAID SERVANT, HIRED MAN

Mt 20 1 < 5 like a landowner going out . . . to *hire* workers for his
       vineyard.
    7 < 5 no one has *hired* us
    8 < Call the workers and pay them their *wages*,
Mk 1 20 2 leaving their father Zebedee with the ʳmen he *employed* (or:
       hired men)
Lk 10 7 the labourer deserves his ʳ*wages* (or: *pay*);
  15 17 < 4 How many of my father's *paid servants* have more food than
       they want,
    19 < 4 treat me as one of your *paid servants*.
Jn 4 36 < the reaper is being paid his *wages*,
  10 12 < 2 The *hired man*, since he is not the shepherd . ., abandons
       the sheep
    13 < 2 this is because he is only a *hired man*
Ac 1 18 [Judas] bought a field with the *money he was paid* for his
       crime.
  28 30 7 Paul spent the whole of the two years in his own *rented*
       [lodging].
Rm 4 4 If a man has work to show, his *wages* are not considered as a
       favour
1 Tm 5 18 The worker deserves his *pay*.
Jm 5 4 listen to the *wages* you kept back, calling out;

2: WAGES (FIGURATIVELY) – REWARD

Mt 5 12 your *reward* will be great in heaven;

Mt	5 46	if you love those who love you, what right have you to claim any ⌐credit (or: reward)?
	6 1	by [parading your good deeds] you will lose all *reward* from your Father in heaven.
	2	when you give alms, do not have it trumpeted before you; this is what the hypocrites do . . . they have had their *reward*.
	5	when you pray, do not imitate the hypocrites; they love to [pray] . . . at the street corners . . . they have had their *reward*.
	16	When you fast do not put on a gloomy look as the hypocrites do: . . . they have had their *reward*.
	10 41	Anyone who welcomes a prophet . . . will have a prophet's *reward*;
	42	If anyone gives so much as a cup of cold water to one of these little ones . . . he will . . . not lose his *reward*.
Mk	9 41	If anyone gives you a cup of water . . . he will . . . not lose his *reward*.
Lk	6 23	your *reward* will be great in heaven.
	35	You will have a great *reward*, and you will be sons of the Most High,
Rm	1 27	6 men . . . getting an appropriate *reward* for their perversion.
1 Co	3 8	each will duly ⌐be paid (lit. receive his *wages*) according to his share in the work.
	14	If his structure stands up to it, he will get his *wages*;
	9 17	If I had chosen this work myself, I might have ⌐been paid (lit. got a *reward*) for it, . . . ¹⁸ Do you know what my
	18	*reward* is? It is . . . to be able to offer the Good News free,
2 Co	6 13	6 as ⌐a fair exchange (lit. *repayment*), open your minds in the same way.
Heb	2 2	every . . . disobedience brought its own proper ⌐punishment
	3	(lit. *reward*),
	10 35	3 Be as confident now, . . . since the *reward* is so great.
	11 6 Θ	8 God . . . *rewards* those who try to find him.
	26	3 [Moses] had his eyes fixed on the *reward*.
2 P	2 13	[they will] ⌐get (ᵛ *suffer*) their *reward* of evil for the evil that they do.
	15	Balaam . . . who thought he could ⌐profit best (lit. gain a *reward*) by sinning,
2 Jn	8	Watch yourselves, or all our work will be lost and not get the *reward* it deserves.
Jude	11	Many . . . have rushed to make the same mistake as Balaam and for the same *reward*;
Rv	11 18	the time has come for . . . all who worship you . . . to be
	Θ	
	22 12 X	I shall . . . [bring] the *reward* to be given to every man according to what he deserves.

5. WAGES, PAY – LIVE ON, (FINANCIAL) SUPPORT: *OPS-ŌNION*

ops-ōnion 4

Lk	3 14	[John to the soldiers:] 'Be content with your *pay*!'
Rm	6 23 ●	the *wage* [paid] by sin is death;
1 Co	9 7	Nobody ever ⌐paid *money* to stay (or: at his own expense stayed) in the army,
2 Co	11 8	I was robbing other churches, *living on* them so that I could serve you.

6. (FINANCIAL) ACCOUNTS: *LOGOS*

1 logos 4/334   2 el-logaō 1

Mt	18 23 <	a king who decided to settle his *accounts* with his servants.
	25 19	the master of those servants came back and went through his
	<	*accounts* with them.
Lk	16 2 <	Draw me up an *account* of your stewardship
Ph	4 17	what is valuable to me is the interest that is mounting up in your *account*.
Phm	18	if he . . . owes you anything, then ⌐let me pay for it (lit.
	2	*charge it to my account*).

7. PRIZE: *BRABEION*

1 brabeion 2   2 kata-brabeuō 1

1: PRIZE

1 Co	9 24	All the runners . . . are trying to win, but only one of them gets the *prize*.
Ph	3 14	I am racing for the finish, for the *prize* to which God calls us upwards

2: (BE) DISQUALIFIED FROM WINNING A PRIZE

Col	2 18	2 Do not be ⌐taken in (lit. *disqualified from winning the prize*) by people who like grovelling to angels

PEACE – RECONCILE

1. Peace – Live in peace, Be at peace – Make peace: *eirēnē*	2. Reconcile (Be) Reconciled: *katallassō*

1. PEACE – LIVE IN PEACE, BE AT PEACE – MAKE PEACE: *EIRĒNĒ*

1 eirēnē	90/92	4 eirēnēn poieō 2
2 eirēneuō	4	5 eirēno-poieō 1
3 eirēnikos	2	6 eirēno-poios 1

Mt	5 9	6 Happy the *peacemakers*: they shall be called sons of God.
	10 13	if the house deserves it, let your *peace* descend on it;
	34	Do not suppose that I have come to bring *peace* to the earth: it is not *peace* I have come to bring but, a sword.
Mk	5 34	My daughter, . . . go in *peace* and be free from your complaint.
	9 50	2 Have salt in yourselves and *be at peace* with one another.
Lk	1 79	to guide our feet into the way of *peace*.
	2 14	Glory to God . . . and *peace* to men who enjoy his favour.
	29	Now, Master, you can let your servant go in *peace*,
	7 50	Your faith has saved you; go in *peace*.
	8 48	your faith has restored you to health; go in *peace*.
	10 5	let your first words be, 'Peace to this house!' ⁶ And if a man
	6	of *peace* lives there, your *peace* will go and rest on him;
	11 21	So long as a strong man fully armed guards his own palace, his goods are ⌐undisturbed (lit. [left] in *peace*);
	12 51	Do you suppose that I am here to bring *peace* on earth?
	14 32	he would send envoys to sue for *peace*.
	19 38	*Peace* in heaven and glory in the highest heavens!
	42	If you . . . had only understood . . . the message of *peace*!
	24 36	ᵛ [Jesus] said to [the apostles], 'Peace be with you!'
Jn	16 33	*Peace* I bequeath to you, my own *peace* I give you,
		I have told you all this so that you may find *peace* in me.
	20 19	Jesus . . . said to them, 'Peace be with you',
	21	he said to them again, 'Peace be with you'.
	26	'Peace be with you', he said.
Ac	7 26	when [Moses] came across some of [his countrymen] fighting, he tried to reconcile them [together] in *peace*.
	9 31	The churches . . . were now left in *peace*,
	10 36	it was to [the people of Israel] that the good news of *peace* was brought by Jesus Christ
	12 20	the Tyrians and Sidonians . . . ⌐negotiated a treaty (lit. sued for *peace*) [with Herod],
	15 33	the brothers wished [Judas and Silas] *peace* and they went back
	16 36	you can go now and go on your way in *peace*.
	24 2	Your Excellency, Felix, the unbroken *peace* we enjoy and the reforms this nation owes to your foresight [we accept]
Rm	1 7	may God our Father and the Lord Jesus Christ send grace and *peace*.
	2 10	renown, honour and *peace* will come to everyone who does good
	3 17	(Is 59 8) They know nothing of the way of *peace*,
	5 1	by faith we ⌐are [judged] (ᵛ should be) righteous and at *peace* with God.
	8 6	life and *peace* can only come with concern for the spiritual.
	12 18	2 Do all you can to *live at peace* with everyone
	14 17	the kingdom of God . . . means righteousness and *peace*
		let us adopt any custom that leads to *peace*
	15 13	May the God of hope bring you such joy and *peace* in your faith
	33	May the God of *peace* be with you all! Amen.
	16 20	The God of *peace* will soon crush Satan beneath your feet.
1 Co	1 3	May God our Father and the Lord Jesus Christ send you grace and *peace*.
	7 15	God has called you to a life of *peace*.
	14 33	God is not a God of disorder but of *peace*.
	16 11	Send [Timothy] ⌐happily (lit. in *peace*) on his way to come back to me;
2 Co	1 2	Grace and *peace* to you from God our Father and the Lord Jesus Christ.
	13 11	2/ *live in peace*, and the God of love and *peace* will be with you.
Ga	1 3	We wish you the grace and *peace* of God our Father and of the Lord Jesus Christ,
	5 22	What the Spirit brings is . . . love, joy, *peace*,
	6 16	*Peace* and mercy to all who follow this rule, who form the Israel of God.
Ep	1 2	Grace and *peace* to you from God our Father and from the Lord Jesus Christ.
	2 14	[Christ] is the *peace* between [Jew and pagans], and has made the two into one . . ., destroying in his own person the hostility
	15	¹⁵ caused by the rules . . . of the Law. This was . . . by
		4 ⌐restoring (or: *making*) *peace* ¹⁶ through the cross, to unite them . . . and reconcile them with God. . . . . ¹⁷ Later he
	17	came to bring the good news of [peace], *peace* to you who were far away and *peace* to those who were near at hand.

Ep	4 3	Do all you can to preserve the unity of the Spirit by the *peace* that binds you together.
	6 15	eagerness to spread the gospel of *peace*
	23	May God the Father and the Lord Jesus Christ grant *peace*, love and faith to all the brothers.
Ph	1 2	We wish you the grace and *peace* of God our Father and of the Lord Jesus Christ.
	4 7	that *peace* of God, which is so much greater than we can understand, will guard your hearts
	9	the God of *peace* will be with you
Col	1 2	Grace and *peace* to you from God our Father.
	20	God wanted . . . all things to be reconciled through him . . . 5 when he *made peace* by his death on the cross.
	3 15	may the *peace* of Christ reign in your hearts
1 Th	1 1	wishing you grace and *peace*.
	5 3	It is when people are saying, 'How quiet and peaceful it is (lit. What *peace* and security)' that the worst suddenly happens,
	13	2 *Be at peace* among yourselves.
	23	May the God of *peace* make you perfect
2 Th	1 2	wishing you grace and *peace* from God the Father and the Lord Jesus Christ
	3 16	May the Lord of *peace* himself give you *peace*
1 Tm	1 2	to Timothy, . . . wishing you grace, mercy and *peace* from God the Father and from Christ Jesus our Lord.
2 Tm	1 2	to Timothy, . . . wishing you grace, mercy and *peace* from God the Father and from Christ Jesus our Lord.
	2 22	fasten your attention on holiness, faith, love and *peace*,
Tt	1 4	To Titus, . . . wishing you grace and *peace* from the Father and from Christ Jesus our saviour.
Phm	3	wishing you the grace and *peace* of God our Father and the Lord Jesus Christ.
Heb	7 2	[Melchizedek] is . . . also king of Salem, that is, 'king of *peace*';
	11 31	Rahab . . . welcomed the spies in *peace* and so was not killed with the unbelievers.
	12 11	3 but later . . . [punishment] bears fruit ⌐in (lit. that *makes for peace* and goodness.
	14	Always be wanting *peace* with all people,
	13 20	I pray that the God of *peace* . . . . 21 may make you ready to do his will
Jm	2 16	⌐I wish you well (lit. Go in *peace*); keep yourself warm and eat plenty,
	3 17	3 the wisdom that comes down from above . . . *makes for peace*,
	18	4/ *Peacemakers*, when they work for *peace*, sow the seeds which will bear fruit in holiness.
1 P	1 2	Grace and *peace* be with you more and more.
	3 11	(Ps 34 14) he must seek *peace* and pursue it.
	5 14	*Peace* to you all who are in Christ.
2 P	1 2	May you have more and more grace and *peace* as you come to know our Lord more and more.
	3 14	do your best to live lives without spot or stain so that [the Lord] will find you at *peace*.
2 Jn	3	we shall have grace, mercy and *peace* from God the Father and from Jesus Christ.
3 Jn	15	*Peace* be with you; greetings from your friends; greet each of our friends by name.
Jude	2	wishing you all mercy and *peace* and love.
Rv	1 4	grace and *peace* to you from him who is, who was, and who is to come, from the seven spirits . . . 5 and from Jesus Christ,
	6 4	out came another horse, bright red, and its rider was given this duty: to take away *peace* from the earth

2. RECONCILE, (BE) RECONCILED: *KAT-ALLASSŌ*

2	kat-allagē 4	4	di-allassō 1
1	kat-allassō 6	5	syn-allassō 1
3	apo-kat-allassō 3		

Mt	5 24	4 leave your offering there before the altar, go and be *reconciled* with your brother first,
Ac	7 26	when [Moses] came across some of [his countrymen] fighting, 5 he tried to *reconcile* them [together] in peace.
Rm	5 10	When we were *reconciled* to God by the death of his Son, we were still enemies; now that we have been *reconciled*, surely we may count on being saved by the life of his Son?
	11	Lord Jesus Christ, through whom we have already gained 2 our *reconciliation*.
	11 15	2 [my own people's] rejection meant the *reconciliation* of the world,
1 Co	7 11	if [a wife] does leave [her husband], she must either remain unmarried or else ⌐make it up (or: be *reconciled*) with her husband
2 Co	5 18	It was God who *reconciled* us to himself through Christ and gave us the work of handing on this *reconciliation*. 19 In 2 other words, God in Christ was *reconciling* the world to himself, . . . and he has entrusted to us the news that they

2 Co	5 20	2 are *reconciled*. 20 . . . the appeal that we make in Christ's name is: be *reconciled* to God.
Ep	2 16	3 to unite [Jew and pagan] in a single Body and *reconcile* them with God.
Col	1 20	3 [God wanted] all things to be *reconciled* through [Christ] and for him, . . . when he made peace by his death on the cross. 21 Not long ago, you were foreigners and enemies . . . 22 but now he has *reconciled* you, . . . in that mortal body.
	22	3

PETER AND THE TWELVE

1. Lists of the Apostles	5. Thomas the Twin
2. Simon Peter and Andrew	6. James the younger, Simon, Jude,
3. James and John, the sons of	apostles and brothers of the Lord
Zebedee	7. Judas Iscariot and Matthias
4. Philip and Bartholomew/Nathanael	

For Matthew/Levi *see* TAX 3.

1. LISTS OF THE APOSTLES

Mt 10 2-4	Mk 3 16-19	Lk 6 13-16	Ac 1 13, 25-26
2 These are the names of the twelve apostles: first, Simon who is called *Peter*, and his brother *Andrew*;	16 And so he appointed the Twelve: Simon to whom he gave the name *Peter*,	13 he . . . picked out twelve . . . [calling] them 'apostles': 14 Simon whom he called *Peter*, and his brother *Andrew*;	13 *Peter* and *John*,
James the [son] of Zebedee and his brother *John*;	17 *James* the [son] of Zebedee, and *John* the brother of James, . . . 18 then *Andrew*,	*James*, *John*,	*James* and *Andrew*,
3 *Philip* and *Bartholomew* [= Nathanael]; *Thomas*, and *Matthew* the tax collector;	*Philip*, *Bartholomew*, *Matthew*, *Thomas*,	*Philip*, *Bartholomew*, 15 *Matthew*, *Thomas*,	*Philip* and *Thomas*, *Bartholomew* and *Matthew*,
James the [son] of Alphaeus, and *Thaddeus* [= Jude];	*James* the [son] of Alphaeus, *Thaddeus*,	*James* [son] of Alphaeus,	*James* [son] of Alphaeus
4 *Simon* the Zealot	*Simon* the Zealot	*Simon* called the Zealot, 16 *Judas* [= Thaddeus] [son? brother?] of James,	and *Simon* the Zealot, and *Jude* [son? brother?] of James. . . . .
and *Judas* Iscariot,	19 and *Judas* Iscariot,	and *Judas* Iscariot	25 to take over this . . . apostolate, which *Judas* abandoned . . . 26 the lot fell to *Matthias*,

2. SIMON PETER AND ANDREW

	Peter (= *Petros*)	154		Aeneas*	2	(Ac 9)
S	*Simon*	50		Ananias*	3	(Ac 5)
	Simeon	2	(Ac 15; 2 P)	Cornelius*	8	(Ac 10)
K	*Cephas*	9		Dorcas*	2	(Ac 9)
	[son] of *John*	4	(Jn 1; 21)	Sapphira*	1	(Ac 5)
	son of *Jonah* = *Bar-iōna*	} 1	(Mt 16)	Simon* (the tanner)	4	(Ac 9; 10)
				Tabitha*	2	(Ac 9)
A	*Andrew*	13		Caesarea* Philippi*	2	(Mt 16; Mk 8)

Mt 4 18 S [Jesus] saw two brothers, *Simon*, who was called *Peter*, and
         A   his brother *Andrew*; . . . they were fishermen.
   10 2 S These are the names of the twelve apostles: first, *Simon* who
         A   is called *Peter*, and his brother *Andrew*; James . . . and
              . . . John;
   14 28   It was *Peter* who answered. '. . . tell me to come to you
      29   across the water.' 29 'Come' said Jesus. Then *Peter* . . .
              started walking . . . across the water.
   15 15   *Peter* said to him, 'Explain the parable for us'.
   16 13   When Jesus came to the region of Caesarea* Philippi* he
              put this question to his disciples, 'Who do people say the
      16 S   Son of Man is?' . . . 16 Then *Simon Peter* spoke up, 'You are
      17   the Christ, . . . the Son of the living God'. 17 Jesus replied,
         S   '*Simon son of Jonah*, you are a happy man! . . . my Father
      18   in heaven [revealed this to you]. 18 So I now say to you:
              You are *Peter* and on this rock I will build my Church.'
      22   *Peter* started to remonstrate with [Jesus]. 'Heaven preserve
      23   you, Lord;' . . . 23 But he turned and said to *Peter*, 'Get
              behind me, Satan!'
   17 1   Jesus took with him *Peter* and James and . . . John and led
              them up a high mountain . . . 2 There . . . he was trans-
       4   figured . . . 4 Then *Peter* spoke to Jesus. 'Lord, . . . it is
              wonderful for us to be here';
      24   the collectors of the half-shekel came to *Peter* and said, 'Does
      25   your master not pay the half-shekel?' 25 . . . Jesus said,
         S   '*Simon*, what is your opinion? From whom do the kings
              of the earth take . . . tribute?'
   18 21   *Peter* . . . said, 'Lord, how often must I forgive my brother
              . . .?'
   19 27   Then *Peter* spoke. '. . . We have left everything and followed
              you. What are we to have, then?'
   26 33   *Peter* said, 'Though all lose faith in you, I will never lose
      35   faith'. . . . 35 *Peter* said to him, 'Even if I have to die with
              you, I will never disown you'.
      37   [At Gethsemane Jesus] took *Peter* and the two sons of
              Zebedee with him. And sadness came over him,
      40   he said to *Peter*, 'So you had not the strength to keep awake
              with me one hour?'
      58   *Peter* followed him at a distance, and when he reached the
              high priest's palace, he went in
      69   *Peter* was sitting outside in the courtyard, . . . 73 . . . the
      73   bystanders . . . said to *Peter*, 'You are one of them for sure!'
      75   *Peter* remembered what Jesus had said, 'Before the cock
              crows you will have disowned me three times'.
Mk 1 16   As [Jesus] was walking along by the Sea of Galilee he saw
      S A   *Simon* and his (lit. *Simon's*) brother *Andrew* casting a
              net
      29   [Jesus] went with James and John straight to the house of
      30 S A *Simon* and *Andrew*. 30 Now *Simon's* mother-in-law had
              gone to bed with fever,
      36 S   [Jesus went off to a lonely place and prayed.] *Simon* and his
              companions set out in search of him,
    3 16 S   so he appointed the Twelve: *Simon* to whom he gave the name
      18 A   *Peter*, 17 James . . . and John . . .; 18 then *Andrew*,
    5 37   [Jesus] allowed no one to go with him [to Jairus's house]
              except *Peter* and James and John
    8 27   Jesus and his disciples left for the villages round Caesarea*
      29   Philippi*, . . . 'Who do people say I am?' . . . 29 . . .
              Peter spoke up . . . 'You are the Christ',
      32   *Peter* started to remonstrate with him. 33 But . . . he re-
      33   buked *Peter* and said to him, 'Get behind me, Satan!'
    9 2   Jesus took with him *Peter* and James and John and led them
              up a high mountain where . . . he was transfigured: . . .
       5   5 Then *Peter* spoke to Jesus: 'Rabbi, . . . let us make three
              tents,'
   10 28   *Peter* took this up. '. . . We have left everything and followed
              you.'
   11 21   *Peter* remembered. 'Look, Rabbi, . . . the fig tree you cursed
              has withered away.'
   13 3 A *Peter*, James, John and *Andrew* questioned him privately,
       4   'Tell us, when is this going to happen . . .?'
   14 29   *Peter* said, 'Even if all lose faith, I will not'.
      33   [At Gethsemane] he took *Peter* and James and John with him
      37 S he said to *Peter*, '*Simon*, are you asleep?'
      54   *Peter* had followed [Jesus] at a distance, right into the high
              priest's palace,
      66   While *Peter* was down below in the courtyard, one of the
      67   high priest's servant-girls came up. 67 She saw *Peter* . . .
      70   and said, 'You too were with Jesus,' . . . 70 . . . A little
              later the bystanders . . . said to *Peter*, 'You are one of
      72   them for sure!' . . . 72 . . . the cock crew for the second time,
              and *Peter* recalled how Jesus had said
   16 7   you must go and tell his disciples and *Peter*, 'He is going
              before you to Galilee;'
Lk 4 38 S [Jesus] went to *Simon's* house. Now *Simon's* mother-in-law
              was suffering from a high fever
    5 3 S [Jesus] got into one of the boats – it was *Simon's* – and . . .
       4 S   4 . . . he said to *Simon*, 'Put out into deep water and pay
       5 S   out your nets for a catch'. 5 'Master,' *Simon* replied 'we
              worked hard . . . and caught nothing,'

Lk 5 8 S When *Simon Peter* saw [the catch] he fell at the knees of
      10   Jesus . . . 9 For he [was] completely overcome . . .; 10 so
         S   also were James and John . . . who were *Simon's* partners.
         S   But Jesus said to *Simon*, '. . . from now on it is men you
              will catch'.
    6 14 S [Jesus picked out twelve:] *Simon* whom he called *Peter*, and
         A   his brother *Andrew*;
    8 45   *Peter* and his companions said, 'Master, it is the crowds
              round you, pushing'.
      51   when he came to [Jairus's] house he allowed no one to go in
              with him except *Peter* and John and James
    9 20   'But . . . who do you say I am?' It was *Peter* who spoke up.
              'The Christ of God'
      28   he took with him *Peter* and James and John and went up the
              mountain to pray.
      32   *Peter* and his companions were heavy with sleep, but they
              kept awake
      33   *Peter* said to Jesus, 'Master, . . . let us make three tents,'
   12 41   *Peter* said, 'Lord, do you mean this parable for us, or for
              everyone?'
   18 28   *Peter* said, '. . . We left all we had to follow you.'
   22 8   he sent *Peter* and John, saying, 'Go and make the prepara-
              tions for us to eat the passover'.
      31 S *Simon, Simon*! Satan . . . has got his wish to sift you all like
              wheat;
      34   I tell you, *Peter*, by the time the cock crows today
      54   *Peter* followed at a distance. 55 They had lit a fire in the . . .
      55   courtyard and *Peter* sat down among them,
      58   *Peter* replied, 'I am not, my friend!'
      60   'My friend,' said *Peter* 'I do not know what you are talking
      61   about.' . . . the cock crew 61 and the Lord turned and look-
              ed straight at *Peter*, and *Peter* remembered what the Lord
              had said . . . 62 And he . . . wept bitterly.
   24 12 v *Peter* . . . went running to the tomb.]
      34 S The Lord has risen and has appeared to *Simon*.
Jn 1 40   One of these two who became followers of Jesus after hearing
         A   what John [the Baptist] had said was *Andrew*, the brother
      41 S   of *Simon Peter*. 41 Early next morning [Andrew] met his
              brother *Simon* and said to him, 'We have found the
      42   Messiah'. . . . 42 and he took [Simon] to Jesus. Jesus looked
         S   hard at him and said, 'You are *Simon* son of *John*; you are
         K   to be called *Cephas*' – meaning *Rock*.
      44 A Philip came from the same town, Bethsaida, as *Andrew* and
              Peter.
    6 8 A S *Andrew*, *Simon Peter's* brother, said, 9 'There is a small boy
              here with five barley loaves and two fish;'
      68 S *Simon Peter* answered, 'Lord, who shall we go to?'
   12 22 A Philip went to tell *Andrew*, and *Andrew* and Philip together
              went to tell Jesus.
   13 6 S He came to *Simon Peter* . . . 8 'Never!' said *Peter* 'You
       8   shall never wash my feet. Jesus replied, 'If I do not wash
       9   you, you can have nothing in common with me'. 9 'Then,
         S   Lord,' said *Simon Peter* 'not only my feet,'
      24 S *Simon Peter* signed to [the disciple Jesus loved]
      36 S *Simon Peter* said, 'Lord, where are you going?' . . . 37 *Peter*
      37   said to him, 'Why can't I follow you now?'
   18 10 S *Simon Peter*, who carried a sword, drew it . . . 11 Jesus
      11   said to *Peter*, 'Put your sword back in its scabbard;'
      15 S *Simon Peter*, with another disciple, followed Jesus. . . .
      16   16 . . . *Peter* stayed outside the door [of the high priest's
      17   palace]. So the other disciple . . . brought *Peter* in. 17 The
              maid on duty at the door said to *Peter*, 'Aren't you another
      18   of that man's disciples?' . . . 18 . . . the servants and guards
              had lit a charcoal fire . . .; so *Peter* stood there too, warm-
              ing himself
      25 S *Simon Peter* stood there warming himself, . . . 26 One of the
      26   high priest's servants, a relation of the man whose ear *Peter*
      27   had cut off, said, 'Didn't I see you in the garden with
              him?' 27 Again *Peter* denied it;
   20 2 S [Mary of Magdala] came running to *Simon Peter* and the
       3   other disciple . . . 3 So *Peter* set out with the other disciple
       4   to go to the tomb. 4 They ran together, but the other
              disciple, running faster than *Peter*, reached the tomb first;
       6 S   . . . 6 *Simon Peter* . . . now came up,
   21 2 S *Simon Peter*, . . . the [sons] of Zebedee . . . were together.
       3 S   3 *Simon Peter* said, 'I'm going fishing'.
       7   The disciple Jesus loved said to *Peter*, 'It is the Lord'. . . .
         S   *Simon Peter*, who had practically nothing on, wrapped his
              cloak round him and jumped into the water.
      11 S *Simon Peter* went aboard and dragged the net to the shore,
      15 S After the meal Jesus said to *Simon Peter*, '*Simon* [son] of
              John, do you love me more than these others do?'
   21 16 S *Simon* [son] of *John*, do you love me?
      17 S '*Simon* [son] of *John*, do you love me?' *Peter* was upset that
              he asked him the third time,
      20   *Peter* turned and saw the disciple Jesus loved following them
      21   . . . 21 Seeing him, *Peter* said to Jesus, 'What about him,
              Lord?'
Ac 1 13   [the apostles] went to the upper room where they were staying;
         A   there were *Peter* and John, James and *Andrew*,

Ac 1 15   *Peter* stood up to speak to the brothers
  2 14   Then *Peter* stood up with the Eleven and addressed them
    37   they . . . said to *Peter* and the apostles, 'What must we do,
    38   brothers?' [38] 'You must repent,' *Peter* answered
  3 1   when *Peter* and John were going up to the Temple . . . there
    3   was a [cripple] being carried past. [3] When this man
    4   saw *Peter* and John . . . he begged from them. [4] Both
    6   *Peter* and John looked straight at him . . . [6] but *Peter*
      said, 'I have neither silver nor gold,'
    11   Everyone came running . . . to . . . where the man was still
    12   clinging to *Peter* and John. [12] When *Peter* saw the people
      he addressed them,
  4 8   *Peter*, filled with the Holy Spirit, addressed them, 'Rulers of
      the people,'
    13   [The Sanhedrin] were astonished at the assurance shown by
      Peter and John,
    19   But *Peter* and John retorted, 'You must judge whether . . .
      it is right to listen to you and not to God.'
  5 1   There was another man, . . . called Ananias*. He and his
      wife, Sapphira*, agreed to sell a property; [2] but . . . he
    3   kept back part of the proceeds, . . . [3] 'Ananias*,' *Peter*
    4   said . . . [4] . . . It is not to men that you have lied, but to
    5   God.' [5] When he heard this Ananias* fell down dead. . . .
    8   [7] About three hours later his wife came in, . . . [8] *Peter*
      challenged her, 'Tell me, was this the price . . .?' . . .
    9   [9] *Peter* then said, 'So you and your husband have agreed'
    15   in the hope that at least the shadow of *Peter* might fall across
      some of [the sick]
    29   *Peter* and the apostles said, 'Obedience to God comes before
      obedience to men;'
  8 14   the apostles in Jerusalem . . . sent *Peter* and John to
      [Samaria],
    20   *Peter* answered [Simon the magician], 'May your silver be
      lost for ever,'
  9 32   *Peter* . . . came to the saints living down in Lydda. [33] There
    33   he found a man called Aeneas*, a paralytic . . . [34] *Peter*
    34   said to him, 'Aeneas*, Jesus Christ cures you:'
    36   At Jaffa there was a woman disciple called Tabitha*, or
      Dorcas* [= Gazelle] in Greek, . . . [37] . . . she got ill and
    38   died, . . . [38] . . . so when the disciples heard that *Peter* was
    39   [at Lydda], they sent two men . . . [39] *Peter* went back with
      them . . . and . . . they took him to the upstairs room,
      . . . showing him . . . clothes Dorcas* had made . . .
    40   [40] *Peter* . . . said, 'Tabitha*, stand up'. She opened her
      eyes, looked at *Peter*, and sat up.
    43   [Peter] stayed some time in Jaffa, lodging with a leather-tanner
      called Simon*.
  10 1   One of the centurions of the Italica cohort stationed in
      Caesarea was called Cornelius*.
    3   he had a vision in which . . . the angel of God . . . called out
    5   to him, 'Cornelius*! . . . [5] . . . you must send someone to
    6 S   Jaffa and fetch a man called *Simon*, known as *Peter*, [6] who
      is lodging with Simon* the tanner'
    9   Next day, . . . *Peter* went to the housetop . . . to pray. [10] He
    13   . . . fell into a trance. . . . [13] A voice then said to him, 'Now
    14   *Peter*; kill and eat!' [14] But *Peter* answered, 'Certainly not,
    17   Lord;' . . . [17] *Peter* was still worrying about the meaning
      of the vision . . . when the men sent by Cornelius* arrived.
      They had asked where Simon*'s house was and they were
    18   now standing at the door, [18] calling out to know if the
    19 S   *Simon* known as *Peter* was lodging there. [19] *Peter's* mind
      was still on the vision and the Spirit had to tell him, 'Some
    21   men have come to see you.' . . . [21] *Peter* went down and
    22   said to them, ' . . . why have you come?' [22] They said,
      'The centurion Cornelius* . . . was directed . . . to send
      for you'
    24   Cornelius* was waiting for them. . . . [25] . . . as *Peter*
    25   reached the house Cornelius* went out . . . and prostrated
    26   himself. [26] But *Peter* helped him up. . . . [30] Cornelius*
      replied, ' . . . I suddenly saw a man . . . in shining robes.
    32 S   [31] He said, "Cornelius*, your prayer has been heard . . .
      [32] So now you must send to Jaffa and fetch *Simon* known
    34   as *Peter* who is lodging in the house of Simon* the tanner,"
      . . . [34] Then *Peter* addressed them: ' . . . anybody of any
      nationality who fears God . . . is acceptable to him.'
    44   While *Peter* was still speaking the Holy Spirit came down on
    45   all the listeners. [45] Jewish believers who had accompanied
    46   *Peter* were all astonished . . . [46] . . . *Peter* . . . then said,
      [47] 'Could anyone refuse . . . baptism . . .?'
  11 2   when *Peter* came up to Jerusalem the Jews criticised him
    4   . . . [4] *Peter* in reply gave them the details . . . : [7] 'Then I
    7   heard a voice that said to me, "Now, *Peter*; kill and eat!" '
    13   [Cornelius] had seen an angel . . . who said, 'Send to Jaffa
     S   and fetch *Simon* known as *Peter*;'
  12 3   [Herod] decided to arrest *Peter* . . . [5] All the time *Peter* was
    5   under guard the Church prayed to God for him . . . [6] . . .
    6   *Peter* was sleeping between two soldiers . . . [7] Then
    7   suddenly the angel of the Lord . . . tapped *Peter* on the
      side and woke him. . . . [9] [Peter] followed him . . .
    11   [11] [In the street] *Peter* came to himself.

Ac 12 14   [The servant Rhoda] recognised *Peter's* voice and . . . ran
      inside with the news that *Peter* was standing at the main
      entrance.
    16   *Peter*, meanwhile, was still knocking,
    18   the soldiers . . . could not imagine what had become of
      Peter.
  15 7   *Peter* stood up and addressed them: 'My brothers, . . . God
      made his choice among you: the pagans were to learn the
      Good News from me'
    14   [James:] *Simeon* has described how God first arranged to
      enlist a people for his name out of the pagans.
1 Co 1 12   these slogans that you have, like: 'I am for Paul,' . . . 'I am
     K   for *Cephas*',
  3 22 K   Paul, . . . *Cephas*, . . . are all your servants;
  9 5   [Have we not] the right to take a Christian woman round with
     K   us, like all the other apostles and . . . *Cephas*?
  15 5 K   [Christ] appeared first to *Cephas* and secondly to the Twelve.
Ga 1 18 K   I went up to Jerusalem to visit *Cephas*
  2 7   I had been commissioned to preach the Good News to the
      uncircumcised just as *Peter* had been commissioned to
    8   preach it to the circumcised. [8] The same person whose
      action had made *Peter* the apostle of the circumcised had
    9   given me a similar mission to the pagans. [9] So, James,
     K   *Cephas* and John, these leaders, these pillars, shook hands
      with Barnabas and me
    11 K   When *Cephas* came to Antioch, however, I opposed him to
      his face,
    14 K   I said to *Cephas* . . . , ' . . . you have no right to make the
      pagans copy Jewish ways'.
1 P 1 1   *Peter*, apostle of Jesus Christ, sends greetings to all those
      living among foreigners in the Dispersion
2 P 1 1 S   From ⌜*Simeon* (ᵛ*Simon*) *Peter*, servant and apostle of Jesus
      Christ;

3. JAMES AND JOHN, THE SONS OF ZEBEDEE

James	21	*Demetrius**	1 ⎫	
John	34	*Diotrephes**	1 ⎬ (3 Jn)	
Z [son(s)] of *Zebedee*	10	*Gaius**	1 ⎭	
Boanerges	1 (Mk 3)	*Zebedee**	2	(Mt 4; Mk 1 20)

Mt 4 21 Z   [Jesus] saw another pair of brothers, *James* [son] of *Zebedee*
      and his brother *John*; they were in their boat with their
      father Zebedee*, mending their nets, and he called them.
  10 2   These are the names of the twelve apostles: . . . Simon . . .
     Z   Andrew; *James* the [son] of *Zebedee*, and his brother *John*;
  17 1   Jesus took with him Peter and *James* and his brother *John*
      and . . . [2] . . . in their presence he was transfigured:
  20 20 Z   the mother of *Zebedee's* sons came with her sons to make a
      request of [Jesus],
  26 37 Z   He took Peter and the two sons of *Zebedee* with him [at
      Gethsemane]. And sadness came over him,
  27 56   Among [the women at Golgotha] were Mary of Magdala . . .
     Z   . . . and the mother of *Zebedee's* sons.
Mk 1 19 Z   [Jesus] saw *James* [son] of *Zebedee* and his brother *John*;
    20   they too were in their boat, . . . [20] and, leaving their father
      Zebedee* in the boat, . . . they went after him.
    29   [Jesus] went with *James* and *John* straight to the house of
      Simon and Andrew.
  3 17 Z   [he appointed the Twelve:] *James* the [son] of *Zebedee* and
      John the brother of *James*, to whom he gave the name
      Boanerges or 'Sons of Thunder';
  5 37   [Jesus] allowed no one to go with him [to Jairus's house]
      except Peter and *James* and *John* the brother of *James*.
  9 2   Jesus took with him Peter and *James* and *John* and . . . in
      their presence he was transfigured:
    38   *John* said to him, 'Master, we saw a man . . . casting out
      devils in your name';
  10 35 Z   *James* and *John*, the sons of *Zebedee*, approached him.
      'Master, . . . we want you to do us a favour.' . . .
    41   [41] . . . the other ten . . . began to feel indignant with
      James and *John*,
  13 3   Peter, *James*, *John* and Andrew questioned him privately,
      [4] 'Tell us, when is this going to happen . . .?'
  14 33   [at Gethsemane] he took Peter and *James* and *John* with him.
      And a sudden fear came over him,
Lk 5 10   [Peter and his companions were overcome by the catch;]
     Z   so also were *James* and *John*, sons of *Zebedee*, who were
      Simon's partners.
  6 14   [he picked out twelve:] Peter, and his brother Andrew;
      James, *John*,
  8 51   When he came to [Jairus's] house he allowed no one to go in
      with him except Peter and *John* and *James*,
  9 28   he took with him Peter and *John* and *James* and went up the
      mountain to pray.
    49   *John* spoke up. 'Master, . . . we saw a man casting out
      devils in your name,'

Lk 9 54   the disciples *James* and *John* said, 'Lord, do you want us to call down fire from heaven to burn them up?'

22 8   he sent Peter and *John*, saying, 'Go and make the preparations for us to eat the passover'.

Jn 21 2 Z   Simon Peter, . . . the [sons] of *Zebedee* . . . were together.

Ac 1 13   [the apostles] went to the upper room where they were staying; there were Peter and *John*, James and Andrew,

3 1   when Peter and *John* were going up to the Temple . . .

3   ² . . . there was a [cripple] being carried past. . . . ³ when this man saw Peter and *John* . . . he begged from them.

4   Both Peter and *John* looked straight at him and said, 'Look at us'.

11   the man was still clinging to Peter and *John*.

4 13   [The Sanhedrin] were astonished at the assurance shown by Peter and *John*,

19   But Peter and *John* retorted, 'You must judge whether . . . it is right to listen to you and not to God.'

8 14   the apostles in Jerusalem . . . sent Peter and *John* to [Samaria],

12 2   [Herod] beheaded *James* the brother of *John*,

Ga 2 9   James, Cephas and *John*, these leaders, these pillars, shook hands with Barnabas and me as a sign of partnership:

3 Jn 1   From the Elder: greetings to my dear friend Gaius*,

9   but Diotrephes*, who seems to enjoy being in charge of [the church], refuses to accept us.

12   Demetrius* has been approved by everyone,

Rv 1 1   This is the revelation given . . . to Jesus Christ . . .; he sent his angel to make it known to his servant *John*,

4 ?   From *John*, to the seven churches of Asia:

9 ?   My name is *John*, and through our union in Jesus I am your brother . . . I was on the island of Patmos for having preached God's word,

22 8 ?   I, *John*, am the one who heard and saw these things.

4. PHILIP AND BARTHOLOMEW/NATHANAEL

Philip 16   B *Bartholomew 4*
               N *Nathanael* *6*

Mt 10 3 B   [These are the names of the twelve apostles: . . .] *Philip* and *Bartholomew*; Thomas, and Matthew

Mk 3 18 B   [he appointed the Twelve: . . .] *Philip, Bartholomew,* Matthew, Thomas,

Lk 6 14 B   [he picked out twelve; . . .] *Philip, Bartholomew,* Matthew, Thomas,

Jn 1 43   Jesus . . . met *Philip* and said, 'Follow me'. ⁴⁴ *Philip* came

44   from the same town, Bethsaida, as Andrew and Peter.

45 N   *Philip* found *Nathanael* and said to him, 'We have found the one Moses wrote about . . , the one about whom the prophets wrote: he is Jesus . . . from Nazareth'. ⁴⁶ 'From

46 N   Nazareth?' said *Nathanael* 'Can anything good come from that place?' 'Come and see' replied *Philip*. ⁴⁷ When Jesus

47 N   saw *Nathanael* coming he said of him, 'There is an Israelite who deserves the name, incapable of deceit'. ⁴⁸ 'How do you

48 N   know me?' said *Nathanael*. 'Before *Philip* came to call you,' said Jesus 'I saw you under the fig tree.' ⁴⁹ *Nathanael*

49 N   answered, 'Rabbi, you are the Son of God',

6 5   Jesus . . . said to *Philip*, 'Where can we buy some bread for these people to eat?'. . . . ⁷ *Philip* answered, 'Two hundred

7   denarii would only buy enough to give them a small piece each'.

12 21   [some Greeks] approached *Philip*, who came from Bethsaida in Galilee, and put this request to him, 'Sir, we should like to see Jesus'. ²² *Philip* went to tell Andrew, and Andrew

22   and *Philip* together went to tell Jesus.

14 8   *Philip* said, 'Lord, let us see the Father and then we shall be satisfied'. ⁹ 'Have I been with you all this time, *Philip*,'

9   said Jesus 'and you still do not know me? To have seen me is to have seen the Father,'

21 2 N   Simon Peter, Thomas . . . *Nathanael* from Cana in Galilee, . . . were together

Ac 1 13 B   [the apostles] went to the upper room where they were staying; there were . . . *Philip* and Thomas, *Bartholomew* and Matthew,

5. THOMAS THE TWIN

Thomas 11   D *Didymus* [= the Twin] *3*

Mt 10 3   [These are the names of the twelve apostles: . . .] Philip and Bartholomew; *Thomas*, and Matthew

Mk 3 18   [he appointed the Twelve: . . .] Philip, Bartholomew, Matthew, *Thomas*,

Lk 6 15   [he picked out twelve: . . . Philip, Bartholomew,] Matthew, *Thomas*,

Jn 11 16 D   Then *Thomas* – known as the *Twin* – said to the other disciples, 'Let us go too, and die with him'.

Jn 14 5   *Thomas* said, 'Lord, we do not know where you are going, so how can we know the way?'

20 24 D   *Thomas*, called the *Twin*, who was one of the Twelve, was not with them when Jesus came. . . . ²⁶ Eight days later

26   the disciples were in the house again and *Thomas* was with them. . . . Jesus came in . . . ²⁷ Then he spoke to

27   *Thomas*. 'Put your finger here; . . . Doubt no longer but believe.' ²⁸ *Thomas* replied, 'My Lord and my God!'

28

21 2 D   Simon Peter, *Thomas* called the *Twin*, Nathanael . . . were together

Ac 1 13   [the apostles] went to the upper room where they were staying; there were . . . Philip and *Thomas*,

6. JAMES THE YOUNGER, SIMON, JUDE, APOSTLES AND BROTHERS OF THE LORD

   James   *21*   S *Simon* (the Zealot) *6*
     [son] of *Alphaeus* *4*   *Joseph*   *4*
    = ? *Levi*   *1* (Mk 2)   = *Joses*   *1* (Mt 13)
 J *Jude/Judas*   *6*   *Joset*   *3* (Mk)
    = ? *Thaddaeus* *2*|(Mt 10)
    or *Lebbaeus*   *2*|(Mk 3)

Mt 10 3   [These are the names of the twelve apostles: . . .] *James* the [son] of *Alphaeus*, and ᵀ*Thaddaeus* (ᵛ *Lebbaeus*); ⁴ *Simon*

4 S   the Zealot

13 55   Is not [Jesus's] mother the woman called Mary, and his

S   brothers *James* and ᵀ*Joseph* (ᵛ *Joses*) and *Simon* and

J   *Jude*?

27 56   Among [the women at Golgotha] were Mary of Magdala, Mary the mother of *James* and *Joseph*,

Mk 2 14   [Jesus] saw *Levi* the [son] of Alphaeus,

3 18   [he appointed the Twelve: . . .] *James* the [son] of *Alphaeus*,

S   ᵀ*Thaddaeus* (ᵛ *Lebbaeus*), *Simon* the Zealot

6 3   This is the carpenter, surely, the son of Mary, the brother of

J S   *James* and ᵀ*Joset* (ᵛ *Joseph*) and *Jude* and *Simon*?

15 40   Among [the women at Golgotha] were Mary of Magdala, Mary who was the mother of *James* the younger and *Joset*,

47   Mary of Magdala and Mary the [mother] of *Joset*,

16 1   Mary of Magdala, Mary the [mother] of *James*, and Salome, bought spices

Lk 6 15 S   [he picked out twelve: . . .] *James* [son] of *Alphaeus*, Simon

16 J   called the Zealot, ¹⁶ *Judas* son [? or brother?] of *James*

24 10   The women [who told the Eleven] were Mary of Magdala, Joanna, and Mary the [mother] of *James*.

Jn 14 22 J   *Judas* – this was not Judas Iscariot – said to him, '. . . Do you intend to show yourself to us and not to the world?'

Ac 1 13   [the apostles] went to the upper room where they were staying;

S   there were . . . *James* [son] of *Alphaeus* and *Simon* the

J   Zealot, and *Jude* son [? or brother?] of *James*.

12 17   [Peter] described . . . how the Lord had led him out of prison. He added, 'Tell *James* and the brothers'.

15 13   When [Barnabas and Paul] had finished it was *James* who spoke.

21 18   Paul went with us to visit *James*, and all the elders were present.

1 Co 15 7   then [Jesus] appeared to *James*, and then to all the apostles;

Ga 1 19   I did not see any of the other apostles; I only saw *James*, the brother of the Lord,

2 9   So, *James*, Cephas and John, these leaders, these pillars, shook hands with Barnabas and me as a sign of partnership:

12   after certain friends of *James* arrived [Cephas] stopped [eating with pagans]

Jm 1 1   From *James*, servant of God and of the Lord Jesus Christ. Greetings to the twelve tribes of the Dispersion.

Jude 1 J   From *Jude*, servant of Jesus Christ and brother of *James*;

7. JUDAS ISCARIOT AND MATTHIAS

  Judas   *22*   *Matthias*   *2*⎫
  [son] of *Simon*   *3*   *Joseph**   *1*⎪ (Ac 1)
  Iscariot   *11*   *Barsabbas** *1*⎬
                   Justus*   *1*⎭

Mt 10 4   [These are the names of the twelve apostles: . . .] and *Judas Iscariot*, the one who was to betray him.

26 14   one of the Twelve, the man called *Judas Iscariot*, went to the chief priests

25   *Judas*, who was to betray him, asked in his turn, 'Not I, Rabbi, surely?'

47   *Judas*, one of the Twelve, appeared, and with him a large number of men

27 3   *Judas* his betrayer was filled with remorse

Mk 3 19   [he appointed the Twelve: . . .] and *Judas Iscariot*, the man who was to betray him.

Mk 14 10   *Judas Iscariot*, one of the Twelve, approached the chief priests with an offer to hand Jesus over to them.

43   *Judas*, one of the Twelve, came up with a number of men

Lk 6 16   [he picked out twelve: . . .] and *Judas Iscariot* who became a traitor.

22 3   Then Satan entered into *Judas*, surnamed *Iscariot*, who was numbered among the Twelve.

47   a number of men appeared, and at the head of them the man called *Judas*, one of the Twelve, who went up to Jesus to kiss him. [48] Jesus said, '*Judas*, are you betraying the Son of Man with a kiss?'

Jn 6 71   [One of you is a devil.] He meant *Judas* [son] of *Simon Iscariot*, since this was the man, one of the Twelve, who was going to betray him.

12 4   *Judas Iscariot* – one of his disciples, the man who was to betray him – said, 'Why wasn't this ointment sold . . .?'

13 2   the devil had already put it into the mind of *Judas Iscariot* [son] of *Simon*, to betray him.

26   [Jesus] dipped the piece of bread and gave it to *Judas* [son] of *Simon Iscariot*. [27] At that moment . . . Satan entered him. Jesus then said, 'What you are going to do, do quickly'.

29   . . . [29] Since *Judas* had charge of the common fund, some of them thought Jesus was telling him, 'Buy what we need for the festival'.

14 22   *Judas* – this was not [Judas] *Iscariot* – said to him, '. . . Do you intend to show yourself to us and not to the world?'

18 2   *Judas* the traitor knew [Gethsemane] well, . . . [3] and ʳhe
3   (lit. *Judas*) brought the cohort to this place . . . [5] . . .
5   *Judas* the traitor was standing among them.

Ac 1 16   the passage of scripture had to be fulfilled in which the Holy Spirit . . . foretells the fate of *Judas*, . . . [20] . . . it says: . . . Let someone else take his office.

23   Having nominated two candidates, Joseph* known as Barsabbas*, whose surname was Justus*, and *Matthias*, [24] they prayed, 'Lord, . . . show us . . . which of these two you have chosen [25] to take over this ministry and

25   apostolate, which *Judas* abandoned to go to his proper place'. [26] . . . as the lot fell to *Matthias*, he was listed as

26   one of the twelve apostles.

PHARISEE

| 1: the Pharisees | 3: the Pharisees and the Herodians |
| 2: the Pharisees and the Sadducees | |

Pharisaios	98		*Gamaliel*	2 (Ac 5, 22)
Saddoukaios	14	N	*Nicodemus*	5
Hērōdianos	3		*Simon*	3 (Lk 7)

1: THE PHARISEES

L = Lawyers and Pharisees   P = Priests and Pharisees
S = Scribes and Pharisees

Mt 5 20 S   if your virtue goes no deeper than that of the scribes and *Pharisees*,

9 11   When the *Pharisees* saw this, they said to his disciples, 'Why does your master eat with tax collectors and sinners?'

14   [John's disciples:] 'Why is it that we and the *Pharisees* fast, but your disciples do not?'

34   the *Pharisees* said, 'It is through the prince of devils that he casts out devils'.

12 2   The *Pharisees* . . . said to [Jesus], 'Look, your disciples are doing something that is forbidden on the sabbath'.

14   the *Pharisees* . . . began to plot against him,

24   when the *Pharisees* heard this they said, 'The man casts out devils only through Beelzebul,'

38 S   Then some of the scribes and *Pharisees* spoke up. 'Master, . . . we should like to see a sign from you.'

15 1 S   *Pharisees* and scribes from Jerusalem then came to Jesus and said, 'Why do your disciples break away from the tradition of the elders?'

12   Do you know that the *Pharisees* were shocked . . .?

19 3   Some *Pharisees* approached him, . . . to test him

21 45   When they heard his parables, the chief priests and the
P   *Pharisees* realised he was speaking about them,

22 41   While the *Pharisees* were gathered round, Jesus put to them this question, 'What is your opinion about the Christ?'

23 2 S   The scribes and the *Pharisees* occupy the chair of Moses.

13 S   Alas for you, scribes and *Pharisees*, you hypocrites!
             Repeated in 23 15, 23, 25, 27, 29.

26   Blind *Pharisee*! Cleanse the inside of cup and dish first

Mt 27 62 P   the chief priests and the *Pharisees* went in a body to Pilate

Mk 2 16 S   When the scribes of the *Pharisee* party saw him eating with sinners and tax collectors,

18   One day when John's disciples and the *Pharisees* were fasting, some people came and said to [Jesus], 'Why is it that John's disciples and the disciples of the *Pharisees* fast, but your disciples do not?'

24   the *Pharisees* said to him, 'Look, why are [your disciples] doing something on the sabbath day that is forbidden?'

7 1 S   The *Pharisees* and some of the scribes . . . gathered round him,

3   the *Pharisees* . . . never eat without washing their arms

5 S   these *Pharisees* and scribes asked him, 'Why do your disciples not respect the tradition of the elders . . .?'

8 11   The *Pharisees* . . . demanded of him a sign from heaven,

10 2   Some *Pharisees* . . . asked, 'Is it against the law for a man to divorce his wife?'

Lk 5 17 L   among the audience there were *Pharisees* and doctors of the Law

21 S   The scribes and the *Pharisees* began to think this over. 'Who is this man . . .?'

30 S   The *Pharisees* and their scribes complained to his disciples

33   John's disciples are always fasting . . , and the disciples of the *Pharisees* too, but yours go on eating and drinking.

6 2   Some of the *Pharisees* said, 'Why are you doing something that is forbidden on the sabbath day?'

7 S   The scribes and the *Pharisees* were watching him to see if he would cure a man on the sabbath,

7 30 L   by refusing baptism from [John] the *Pharisees* and the lawyers had thwarted what God had in mind for them.

36   One of the *Pharisees* invited him to a meal. When he arrived
37   at the *Pharisee*'s house . . . [37] a woman came in, who had a bad name in the town. She had heard he was dining with the *Pharisee* and had brought with her an alabaster jar of ointment.

39   When the *Pharisee* who had invited him saw this, he said to himself, 'If this man were a prophet, he would know who
40   this woman is . . .' [40] Then Jesus . . . said, '*Simon*, I have something to say to you'.

43   'The one who was pardoned more, I suppose' said *Simon*.

44   '*Simon*,' [Jesus] said 'you see this woman?'

11 37   a *Pharisee* invited him to dine at his house. . . . [38] The
38   *Pharisee* . . . was surprised that he had not . . . washed
39   before the meal. [39] But the Lord said to him, 'Oh you *Pharisees*! You clean the outside of cup and plate,'

42   alas for you *Pharisees*! You who pay your tithe of mint and rue

43   Alas for you *Pharisees* who like taking the seats of honour in the synagogues

53 S   the scribes and the *Pharisees* began a furious attack on him

12 1   Be on your guard against the yeast of the *Pharisees* – that is, their hypocrisy.

13 31   some *Pharisees* came up. 'Go away' they said. '. . . Herod means to kill you.'

14 1   on a sabbath day he had gone for a meal to the house of one
3   of the leading *Pharisees*; . . . [3] and Jesus addressed the
L   lawyers and *Pharisees*. 'Is it against the law . . . to cure a man on the sabbath day, or not?'

15 2 S   the *Pharisees* and the scribes complained. 'This man . . . welcomes sinners'

16 14   The *Pharisees*, who loved money, . . . laughed at him.

17 20   Asked by the *Pharisees* when the kingdom of God was to come, [Jesus] gave them this answer,

18 10   Two men went up to the Temple to pray, one a *Pharisee*, the
11   other a tax collector. [11] The *Pharisee* . . . said this prayer to himself,

19 39   Some *Pharisees* in the crowd said to him 'Master, check your disciples',

Jn 1 24 P   these [priests and Levites] had been sent by the *Pharisees*,

3 1 N   There was one of the *Pharisees* called *Nicodemus*, a leading Jew, [2] who came to Jesus by night and said,

4 N   *Nicodemus* said, 'How can a grown man be born?'

9 N   'How can that be possible?' asked *Nicodemus*.

4 1   the *Pharisees* had found out that he was making . . . more disciples than John

7 32   The *Pharisees* heard that rumours like this about him were
P   spreading among the people, so the *Pharisees* and chief priests sent the Temple police to arrest him.

45 P   The police went back to the chief priests and *Pharisees*

47   'So' the *Pharisees* answered 'you have been led astray as
48   well? [48] Have any of the authorities believed in him? Any of the *Pharisees*?'

50 N   *Nicodemus* . . . said to them, [51] 'But surely the Law does not allow us to pass judgement on a man without giving him a hearing . . .?'

8 3 S   the scribes and *Pharisees* brought a woman along who had been caught committing adultery;

13   the *Pharisees* said to him, 'You are testifying on your own behalf;'

Jn	9	13	They brought the man who had been blind to the *Pharisees*.
		15	the *Pharisees* asked him how he had come to see,
		16	some of the *Pharisees* said, 'This man cannot be from God:'
		40	some *Pharisees* who were present said to him, 'We are not blind, surely?'
	11	46	some of [those who had seen the raising of Lazarus] went to tell the *Pharisees* what Jesus had done.
		47 P	the chief priests and *Pharisees* called a meeting.
		57 P	The chief priests and *Pharisees* had by now given their orders . . . so that they could arrest him.
	12	19	the *Pharisees* said to one another, '. . . look, the whole world is running after him!'
		42	there were many who did believe in him, even among the leading men, but they did not admit it, through fear of the *Pharisees*
	18	3 P	a detachment of guards sent by the chief priests and the *Pharisees*,
	19	39 N	*Nicodemus* came as well – the same one who had first come to Jesus at night-time –
Ac	5	34 L	a *Pharisee* called *Gamaliel*, who was a doctor of the Law and respected by the whole people,
	15	5	certain members of the *Pharisees*' party who had become believers objected,
	22	3	Paul said '. . . I was brought up here . . . I studied under *Gamaliel*'
	26	5	[Paul:] I followed the strictest party in our religion and lived as a *Pharisee*.
Ph	3	5	a Hebrew born of Hebrew parents . . . As for the Law, I was a *Pharisee*;

2: THE PHARISEES AND THE SADDUCEES

Mt	3	7	when he saw a number of *Pharisees* and *Sadducees* coming for baptism [John] said to them, 'Brood of vipers,'
	16	1	The *Pharisees* and *Sadducees* came, and to test [Jesus] they asked him if he would show them a sign from heaven.
		6	be on your guard against the yeast of the *Pharisees* and *Sadducees*.
		11	Beware of the yeast of the *Pharisees* and *Sadducees*. [12] . . .
		12	he was telling them to be on their guard . . . against the teaching of the *Pharisees* and *Sadducees*.
	22	23	some *Sadducees* – who deny that there is a resurrection – approached him
		34	when the *Pharisees* heard that he had silenced the *Sadducees* they got together
Mk	12	18	some *Sadducees* – who deny that there is a resurrection – came to him
Lk	20	27	Some *Sadducees* – those who say that there is no resurrection – approached him
Ac	4	1	the priests came up to [Peter and John], accompanied by the captain of the Temple and the *Sadducees*.
	5	17	Then the high priest intervened with . . . the party of the *Sadducees*.
	23	6	Now Paul was well aware that one section [of the Sanhedrin] was made up of *Sadducees* and the other of *Pharisees*, so he called out . . , 'Brothers, I am a *Pharisee* and the son of *Pharisees*. It is for our hope in the resurrection of the dead that I am on trial.'[7] . . . a dispute broke out between the *Pharisees* and *Sadducees*, . . . [8] For the *Sadducees* say there is neither resurrection, nor angel, nor spirit, while the *Pharisees* accept all three. [9] . . . some of the scribes from the *Pharisees*' party . . . protested strongly, 'We find nothing wrong with this man.'
		7	
		8	
		9 S	

3: THE PHARISEES AND THE HERODIANS

Mt	22	15	the *Pharisees* went away to work out . . . how to trap [Jesus] in what he said. [16]And they sent their disciples to him, together with the *Herodians*,
		16	
Mk	3	6	The *Pharisees* went out [of the synagogue] and at once began to plot with the *Herodians* against him,
	8	15	be on your guard against the yeast of the *Pharisees* and the yeast of Herod.
	12	13	they sent to him some *Pharisees* and some *Herodians* to catch him out in what he said.

PILATE – BARABBAS

	Pontius Pilate	4	1	*hēgemōn*	9/20
	Pilate	51	2	*hēgemoneuō*	1/2
B	*Barabbas*	11			
J	*Joseph*	6			

Mt	27	2	1	[The chief priests] had [Jesus] bound, and led him away to hand him over to (*v Pontius*) *Pilate*, the *governor*.
		11	1/1	Jesus . . . was brought before the *governor*, and the *governor* put to him this question,
		13		*Pilate* then said to him, 'Do you hear how many charges they have brought against you?' [14] But to the *governor's* complete amazement, he offered no reply to any of the charges. [15]At festival time it was the *governor's* practice to release a prisoner for the people, . . . [16] Now there was at that time a notorious prisoner whose name was *Barabbas*. [17]. . . *Pilate* said to [the crowd], 'Which do you want me to release for you: *Barabbas*, or Jesus . . .?'
		14	1	
		15	1	
		16		
		17	B	
			B	
		20		The chief priests and the elders . . . had persuaded the crowd to demand the release of *Barabbas* . . . [21] So when the *governor* . . . asked them, 'Which of the two do you want me to release for you?' they said, '*Barabbas*'. [22] 'But in that case,' *Pilate* said to them, 'what am I to do with Jesus . . .?'
		21	B	
			1	
		22	B	
		24		*Pilate* saw that he was making no impression [on the crowd]
		26	B	he released *Barabbas*
		27	1	The *governor's* soldiers took Jesus with them into the Praetorium
		57	J	there came a rich man of Arimathaea, called *Joseph*, who had himself become a disciple of Jesus. [58] This man went to *Pilate* and asked for the body of Jesus. *Pilate* thereupon ordered it to be handed over. [59] So *Joseph* took the body, wrapped it in a clean shroud
		58		
		59	J	
		62		the chief priests and the Pharisees went in a body to *Pilate* . . . [65] 'You may have your guard' said *Pilate*
		65		
	28	14	1	should the *governor* come to hear of this, we undertake to put things right with him
Mk	15	1		the whole Sanhedrin . . . handed [Jesus] over to *Pilate*. [2] *Pilate* questioned him, 'Are you the king of the Jews?' . . . [4] *Pilate* questioned him again, 'Have you no reply at all? . . .' [5] But, to *Pilate's* amazement, Jesus made no further reply.
		2		
		4		
		5		
		7	B	Now a man called *Barabbas* was then in prison with the rioters who had committed murder
		9		*Pilate* answered them, 'Do you want me to release for you the king of the Jews?' . . . [11] The chief priests, however, had incited the crowd to demand that he should release *Barabbas* . . . instead. [12] Then *Pilate* spoke again. '. . . what am I to do with the man you call king of the Jews?'
		11		
		12	B	
		14		'Why?' *Pilate* asked them
		15	B	*Pilate* . . . released *Barabbas* for them
		43	J	*Joseph* of Arimathaea, a prominent member of the Council . . . boldly went to *Pilate* and asked for the body of Jesus. [44] *Pilate*, astonished that he should have died so soon, . . . enquired if he was already dead. [45] Having been assured of this by the centurion, he granted the corpse to *Joseph* [46] who . . . took Jesus down from the cross,
		44		
		45		
			J	
Lk	3	1		In the fifteenth year of Tiberius Caesar's reign, when *Pontius Pilate was governor* of Judaea . . . [2] . . . the word of God came to John
			2	
	13	1		the Galileans whose blood *Pilate* had mingled with that of their sacrifices.
	20	20	1	to enable [the scribes and chief priests] to hand [Jesus] over to the jurisdiction and authority of the *governor*.
	23	1		The whole assembly . . . brought [Jesus] before *Pilate*. [2] They began their accusation . . . [3]*Pilate* put to him this question,
		3		
		4		*Pilate* then said to the chief priests and the crowd, 'I find no case against this man'.
		6		*Pilate* . . . asked if the man were a Galilean;
		11		Herod . . . sent him back to *Pilate*. [12] And though Herod and *Pilate* had been enemies before, they were reconciled that same day.
		12		
		13		*Pilate* then summoned the chief priests . . . [14] '. . . I . . . have found no case against the man . . .'
		18	B	Give us *Barabbas*!
		20		*Pilate* was anxious to set Jesus free
		24		*Pilate* then gave his verdict: their demand was to be granted.
		50	J	an upright and virtuous man named *Joseph*. [51]. . . He came from Arimathaea . . . [52] This man went to *Pilate* and asked for the body of Jesus.
		52		
Jn	18	29		*Pilate* . . . said, 'What charge do you bring against this man?'
		31		*Pilate* said, 'Take him yourselves, and try him by your own Law'.
		33		*Pilate* . . . called Jesus to him, 'Are you the king of the Jews?'
		35		*Pilate* answered, 'Am I a Jew?'
		37		'So you are a king then?' said *Pilate*.
		38		'Truth?' said *Pilate* 'What is that?'
		40	B	'Not this man,' they said 'but *Barabbas*'. Barabbas was a brigand.
	19	1		*Pilate* then had Jesus taken away and scourged;
		4		*Pilate* said, 'Here is the man'.

Jn 19	6	*Pilate* said, 'Take him yourselves and crucify him: I can find no case against him'.
	8	[He has claimed to be the Son of God.] When *Pilate* heard them say this his fears increased. ⁹. . . he said to Jesus, 'Where do you come from?'
	10	*Pilate* then said to him, 'Are you refusing to speak to me?'
	12	From that moment *Pilate* was anxious to set him free,
	13	*Pilate* had Jesus brought out, and seated himself on the chair of judgement
	15	'Do you want me to crucify your king?' said *Pilate*.
	19	*Pilate* wrote out a notice and had it fixed to the cross;
	21	the Jewish chief priests said to *Pilate*, 'You should not write "King of the Jews", . . .' ²²*Pilate* answered, 'What I have written, I have written'.
	22	
	31	the Jews asked *Pilate* to have the legs broken
	38 J	*Joseph* of Arimathaea, who was a disciple of Jesus – though a secret one . . . – asked *Pilate* to let him remove the body of Jesus. *Pilate* gave permission.
Ac 3	13	the same Jesus you handed over and then disowned in the presence of *Pilate* after [Pilate] had decided to release him. ¹⁴ It was you who . . . demanded the reprieve of a murderer.
	14 (B)	
4	27	Herod and *Pontius Pilate* made an alliance with the pagan nations and the people of Israel, against . . . Jesus.
13	28	[the Jews] condemned [Jesus] and asked *Pilate* to have him executed.
1 Tm 6	13	Jesus Christ, who spoke up as a witness for the truth in front of *Pontius Pilate*,

---

PLACE – ROOM

1. Place – Room: *topos*	**2. Be room (for) – Hold, Contain:** *chōreō*
a) Place, Spot, Locality	a) Be room (for), Make room (for), Keep a place for – Hold, Contain
b) (Holy) Place	
c) Place, Room (for)	b) Accept, Receive
d) Place = Opportunity, Chance	**3. Spacious:** *eury-chōros*

1. PLACE – ROOM: *TOPOS*

1 *topos* 95   2 *en-topios* 1

a) Place, Spot, Locality

Mt 12	43	When an unclean spirit goes out of a man it wanders through waterless ʳ country (lit. *places*)
14	13	Jesus . . . withdrew by boat to a lonely *place*
	15	the disciples . . . said, 'This is a lonely *place* . . .'
	35	the ʳlocal people (lit. people of the *place* [Gennesaret]) recognised [Jesus]
24	7	There will be famines and earthquakes ʳhere and there (lit. in many *places*).
27	33	they had reached a *place* called Golgotha, that is, the *place* of the skull,
28	6	[Jesus] has risen . . . Come and see the *place* where he lay,
Mk 1	35	[Jesus] went off to a lonely *place* and prayed there.
	45	Jesus . . . had to stay outside in *places* where nobody lived.
6	11	if any *place* does not welcome you . . . walk away
	31	You must come away to some lonely *place* all by yourselves and rest for a while;
	32	So they went off in a boat to a lonely *place* where they could be by themselves.
	35	This is a lonely *place* and it is getting very late,
13	8	There will be earthquakes ʳhere and there (lit. in many *places*);
15	22	They brought Jesus to the *place* called Golgotha, which means the *place* of the skull.
16	6	he has risen . . . here is the *place* where they laid him.
Lk 4	17 ○	Unrolling the scroll [Jesus] found the *place* where it is written:
	37	reports of [Jesus] went ʳall through (lit. through every *place* in) the surrounding countryside.
	42	When daylight came [Jesus] left the house and made his way to a lonely *place*.
6	17	[Jesus] then came down with [the Twelve] and stopped at a ʳpiece (lit. *place*) of level ground
9	12	Send the people away . . . for we are in a lonely *place* here.
10	1	the Lord appointed seventy-two others and sent them out . . . to all the towns and *places* he himself was to visit.
	32	a Levite who came to the *place* saw him, and passed by
11	1	[Jesus] was in a certain *place* praying,
	24	When an unclean spirit goes out of a man it wanders through waterless ʳcountry (lit. *places*)

Lk 16	28	[send Lazarus] give them warning so that they do not come to this *place* of torment too.
19	5	When Jesus reached the *spot* he . . . spoke to him: 'Zacchaeus, come down.'
21	11	There will be . . . famines ʳhere and there (lit. in many *places*);
22	40	When they reached the *place* [Jesus] said to [the disciples], 'Pray not to be put to the test'.
23	33	When they reached the *place* called The Skull, they crucified him
Jn 5	13	Jesus had disappeared into the crowd that filled the *place*.
6	10	There was plenty of grass ʳthere (lit. in that *place*),
	23	Other boats . . . had put in from Tiberias, near the *place* where the bread had been eaten.
10	40	[Jesus] went . . . to the far side of the Jordan to stay in the *district* where John had once been baptising.
11	6	[Jesus] stayed in the *place* where he was for two more days
	30	Jesus . . . was still at the *place* where Martha had met him.
18	2	Judas the traitor knew the *place* well,
19	13	Pilate . . . seated himself on the chair of judgement at a *place* called the Pavement,
	17	[Jesus] went out of the city to the *place* of the skull,
	20	the *place* where Jesus was crucified was not far from the city,
	41	At the *place* where he had been crucified there was a garden,
20	7	the cloth that had been over his head . . . was . . . rolled up in a *place* by itself.
Ac 4	31	As [the apostles] prayed, the ʳhouse (lit. *place*) where they were assembled rocked;
7	7	they will leave, and worship me in this *place*.
	33	(Ex 3 5) the *place* where you are standing is holy ground.
12	17	[Peter] left and went to another *place*.
16	3	Paul . . . had [Timothy] circumcised. This was on account of the Jews in the *locality*
21	12 ²	we and *everybody there* implored Paul not to go
27	2	a vessel . . . bound for ʳports (lit. *places*) on the Asiatic coast,
	8	we came to a *place* called Fair Havens,
	29	afraid that we might run aground somewhere on a ʳreef (lit. rocky *place*), they dropped four anchors
	41	the cross-currents carried them into a ʳshoal and (lit. *place* where) the vessel ran aground.
28	7	ʳIn that neighbourhood (lit. In the neighbourhood of that *place*) there were estates belonging to the prefect of the island,
Rm 9	26	(Ho 2 1) ʳInstead of being (or: In the very *place* where they were) told, 'You are no people of mine',
1 Co 1	2	all the saints ʳeverywhere (lit. in every *place*) who pray to our Lord Jesus Christ;
2 Co 2	14	God who . . . through us is spreading the knowledge of himself, like a sweet smell, ʳeverywhere (lit. in every *place*).
1 Th 1	8	the news of your faith in God has spread ʳeverywhere (lit. to every *place*).
1 Tm 2	8	In every *place*, then, I want the men to lift their hands up reverently in prayer,
Heb 11	8	Abraham obeyed the call to set out for a ʳcountry (lit. *place*) that was the inheritance given to him
2 P 1	19	depend on prophecy and take it as a lamp for lighting a way through ʳthe dark (lit. a dark *place*)
Rv 12	6	the woman escaped into the desert, where God had made a *place* of safety ready.
	14	she was given a huge pair of eagle's wings to fly away . . . into the desert, to the *place* where she was to be looked after
16	16	They called the kings together at the *place* called, in Hebrew, Armageddon.
18	17	All the captains and ʳseafaring men (lit. everyone sailing to a *place*),

b) (Holy) Place

Mt 24	15	the disastrous abomination . . . set up in the Holy *Place*
Jn 4	20	you say that Jerusalem is the *place* where one ought to worship.
11	48	the Romans will come and destroy the Holy *Place* and our nation.
Ac 6	13	This man is always making speeches against this Holy *Place*
	14	Jesus the Nazarene is going to destroy this *Place*
7	49	(Is 66 1) what house could you build me, what *place* could you make for my rest?
21	28	This is the man who preaches to everyone . . . against this *place*. Now he has profaned this Holy *Place* by bringing Greeks into the Temple.

c) Place, Room (for)

Mt 26	52	Jesus then said, 'Put your sword back in its *place*, for all who draw the sword will die by the sword.'
Lk 2	7	there was no *room* for them at the inn.
14	9 <	'Give up your *place* to this man' . . . And then . . . you would have to go and take the lowest *place*.
	10 <	when you are a guest, make your way to the lowest *place*
	22 <	Sir . . . your orders have been carried out and there is still *room*.

Jn 14 2   There are many rooms in my Father's house . . . I am going
      3 ●   now to prepare a *place* for you, ³ and after I have gone and
       ●   prepared you a *place*, I shall return
  20 25   Unless I . . . can put my finger into the ᵛ holes (G *place*)
        [the nails] made . . . I refuse to believe.
Ac 1 25   to take over this ministry and apostolate, the *place* which
      ○   Judas abandoned to go to his proper *place*.
Rm 9 26   (Ho 2 1) ᴵInstead of being (or: In the very place where they
        were) told, 'You are no people of mine',
1 Co 14 16   ᴵAny (lit. Anyone in the *position* of an) uninitiated person
        will never be able to say Amen to your thanksgiving,
Heb 8 7   If that first covenant had been without a fault, there would
        have been no need for a second one to re*place* it.
Rv 2 5   if you will not repent, I shall come . . . and take your lamp-
        stand from its *place*.
  6 14   all the mountains and islands were shaken from their *places*.
  12 8   [the dragon and his angels] were defeated and ᴵdriven out of
        (lit. there was no longer any *room* for them in) heaven.
  20 11   (cf. Dn 2 35) In his presence, earth and sky vanished, ᴵleaving
        no trace (lit. and there was no longer any *room* for them).

d) Place = Opportunity, Chance

Ac 25 16   Romans are not in the habit of surrendering any man, until
        the accused . . . is given an *opportunity* to defend himself
        against the charge.
Rm 12 19   ᴵleave that (lit. give *place*) . . . to God's anger.
  15 23   having no more ᴵ work to do (lit. *opportunity* to work) here,
        ²⁴ I hope to see you on my way to Spain
Ep 4 27   you will give the devil a *foothold*.
Heb 12 17   [Esau] ᴵwas unable to elicit (lit. could obtain no *opportunity*
        for) a change of heart [in his father].

2. BE ROOM (FOR) – HOLD, CONTAIN: *CHŌREŌ*

chōreō 7/10

a) Be room (for), Make room (for), Keep a place for – Hold, Contain

Mk 2 2   so many people collected that there *was no room* left, even
        in front of the door.
Jn 2 6   each [of the six stone water jars] *could hold* twenty or thirty
        gallons.
  21 25   the world itself . . . would not *hold* all the books that would
        have to be written [about the things that Jesus did].
2 Co 7 2   *Keep a place for* us in your hearts.

b) Accept, Receive

Mt 19 11   It is not everyone who can *accept* what I have said,
  12   Let anyone *accept* it who can *accept* it.

3. SPACIOUS: *EURY-CHŌROS*

eury-chōros 1

Mt 7 13   the road that leads to perdition is wide and *spacious*,

PLAN – COUNCIL

1. Purpose, Objective – Plan, Design,
Predetermine: *pro-thesis*

2. Plan, Plot – Counsel, Council:
sym-boulion
3. Sanhedrin – Council: *syn-(h)edrion*

1. PURPOSE, OBJECTIVE – PLAN, DESIGN, PREDETERMINE: *PRO-THESIS*

1 *pro-thesis* 8/12   2 *pro-tithemai* 3

Ac 11 23   [Barnabas] urged them all to remain faithful to the Lord
        with heartfelt ᴵdevotion (lit. *purpose*);
  27 13   thinking their *objective* as good as reached, they . . . began
        to sail past Crete,
Rm 1 13   2 I have often *planned* to visit you –
  3 25   2 [Christ Jesus] was ᴵappointed (or: *designed*) by God to
        sacrifice his life
  8 28   God co-operates . . . with all those that he has called
      Θ   according to his *purpose*.
  9 11   In order ᴵto stress that God's choice is free (lit. that God's
      Θ   selective *purpose* might stand), [Rebecca was told:]

Ep 1 9   He has let us know . . . the [hidden] plan he so kindly ᴵmade
    Θ 2   (lit. *designed beforehand*) in Christ [from the beginning]
  11 Θ   we were . . . chosen from the beginning, under the *predetermined plan* of the one who guides all things as he
decides by his own will;
  3 11 Θ   the *plan* which [God] had from all eternity in Christ
Jesus our Lord.
2 Tm 1 9 Θ   [God] has saved us . . . for his own *purpose*
  3 10   You know . . . how I have lived, ᴵwhat I have aimed at
(lit. and my *objectives*);

2. PLAN, PLOT – COUNSEL, COUNCIL: *SYM-BOULION*

5	*bouleuomai* 4/6	2 *sym-boulion*	3	
6	*bouleutēs* 2	1 *sym-boulion lambanō* 5		8
3	*epi-boulē* 4	7 *sym-boulos*	1	
4	*sym-bouleuō* 4			

Mt 12 14   the Pharisees . . . ᴵbegan to *plot* (or: *took counsel*) against
[Jesus],
  22 15   the Pharisees went away to *work out* [between them] how to
trap [Jesus] in what he said.
  26 4   4 [the chief priests and the elders] *made plans* to arrest Jesus
by some trick
  27 1   the chief priests and the elders of the people *met in council*
to bring about the death of Jesus.
  7   [the chief priests] ᴵ*discussed the matter* (or: *took counsel*)
and bought the potter's field
  28 12   [The chief priests] held a meeting with the elders and, after
some *discussion*, handed a considerable sum of money to
the soldiers
Mk 3 6   2 The Pharisees . . . began to *plot* with the Herodians against
[Jesus],
  15 1   the chief priests together with the elders and scribes . . . had
      2   their *plan* ready.
  43   6 Joseph of Arimathaea, a prominent member of the *Council*,
Lk 14 31   what king marching to war against another king would not
      5   first . . . *consider* whether with ten thousand men he could
stand up to the other . . . ?
  23 50   6 Then a member of the *council* arrived, an upright and virtuous
man named Joseph.
Jn 18 14   4 It was Caiaphas who had ᴵsuggested to (lit. *counselled*) the
Jews, 'It is better for one man to die for the people'.
Ac 9 23   4 the Jews *worked out a plot* to kill [Saul], ²⁴ but news of
  24   3 ᴵit (lit. the *plot*) reached Saul.
  20 3   3 [Paul] was leaving [Greece] by ship for Syria when a *plot*
organised against him by the Jews made him decide to go
back by way of Macedonia.
  19   3 all the sorrows and trials that came to me through the *plots*
of the Jews.
  23 30   3 My information is that there is a *conspiracy* against [Paul],
  25 12   2 Festus conferred with his *advisers*
  27 39   5 they *planned* to run the ship aground
Rm 11 34   7 (Is 40 13) Who could ever be [the Lord's] *counsellor*?
2 Co 1 17   Do you think I was not sure of my own intentions when I
    5/5   *planned* this? Do you really think that when I am *making
my plans*, my motives are ordinary human ones . . . ?
Rv 3 18   4 I ᴵwarn (lit. *counsel*) you, buy from me the gold that has been
tested in the fire

3. SANHEDRIN – COUNCIL: *SYN-(H)EDRION*

syn-(h)edrion 22

Mt 5 22   if a man calls his brother 'Fool' he will answer for it before
the *Sanhedrin*;
  10 17   Beware of men: they will hand you over to *sanhedrins*
  26 59   The chief priests and the whole *Sanhedrin* were looking for
evidence against Jesus,
Mk 13 9   Be on your guard: they will hand you over to *sanhedrins*,
  14 55   The chief priests and the whole *Sanhedrin* were looking for
evidence against Jesus
  15 1   the chief priests together with the elders and scribes, in short
the whole *Sanhedrin*, had their plan ready.
Lk 22 66   there was a meeting of the elders of the people, attended by
the chief priests and scribes. [Jesus] was brought before
their *council*.
Jn 11 47   the chief priests and Pharisees called a *meeting*.
Ac 4 15   they ordered [Peter and John] to stand outside while the
Sanhedrin had a private discussion.
  5 21   the high priest . . . and his supporters convened the *Sanhedrin*
– this was the full Senate of Israel –
  27   [the captain of the Temple and his men] brought [the apostles]
in to face the *Sanhedrin*,

Ac	5	34	One member of the *Sanhedrin*, however, a Pharisee called Gamaliel . . . asked to have the men taken outside
		41	[the apostles] left the presence of the *Sanhedrin* glad to have the honour of suffering
	6	12	[the Jews] brought [Stephen] before the *Sanhedrin*.
		15	The members of the *Sanhedrin* all looked intently at Stephen,
	22	30	[the tribune] gave orders for a meeting of the chief priests and the entire *Sanhedrin*;
	23	1	Paul looked steadily at the *Sanhedrin* and began to speak,
		6	Paul . . . called out in the *Sanhedrin*,
		15	it is up to you and the *Sanhedrin* together to apply to the tribune to bring [Paul] down to you,
		20	The Jews have made a plan to ask you to take Paul down to the *Sanhedrin* tomorrow,
		28	I brought [Paul] before their *Sanhedrin*.
	24	20	I stood before the *Sanhedrin*,

POOR – HUMBLE – LOWLY

1. **Poor, Poverty-stricken:** *penēs*	3. **Humble, Lowly, Poor – Humility –**
2. **Poor – Poverty – Poor man,**	**Humiliate, to Humble, Abuse:**
Pauper: *ptōchos*	*tapeinōsis*

R = Poor//Rich

1. POOR, POVERTY-STRICKEN: *PENĒS*
1 *penēs* 1   2 *penichros* 1

| Lk | 21 | 2 R | 2 a *poverty-stricken* widow putting . . . two small coins [into the treasury], |
| 2 Co | 9 | 9 | (Ps 112 9) He was free in almsgiving, and gave to the *poor*. |

2. POOR – POVERTY – POOR MAN, PAUPER: *PTŌCHOS*
2 *ptōcheia* 3   1 *ptōchos* 34
3 *ptōcheuō* 1

Mt	5	3	How happy are the *poor* in spirit; theirs is the kingdom of heaven.
	11	5	the Good News is proclaimed to the *poor*;
	19	21	sell what you own and give the money to the *poor*,
	26	9	This [ointment] could have been sold at a high price and the money given to the *poor*. ¹⁰ Jesus . . . said . . . ¹¹ '. . . You have the *poor* with you always.
		11	
Mk	10	21	sell everything you own and give the money to the *poor*,
	12	42 R	A *poor* widow came and put . . . two small coins [into the treasury], . . . ⁴³ . . . [Jesus] . . . said . . . '. . . this *poor* widow has put more in than all who have contributed to the treasury;
		43	
	14	5	Ointment like this could have been sold for over three hundred denarii and the money given to the *poor*;
		7	You have the *poor* with you always,
Lk	4	18	(Is 61 1) He has sent me to bring the good news to the *poor*,
	6	20 R	How happy are you who are *poor*: yours is the kingdom of God.
	7	22	the Good News is proclaimed to the *poor*
	14	13 R	when you have a party, invite the *poor*,
		21	Go out quickly into the streets . . . and bring in here the *poor*,
	16	20 R	at [the rich man's] gate there lay a *poor* man called Lazarus . . . ²² Now the *poor* man died and was carried away . . . to the bosom of Abraham. The rich man also died
		22 R	
	18	22	Sell all that you own and distribute the money to the *poor*,
	19	8	Zacchaeus . . . said to the Lord, '. . . I am going to give half my property to the *poor*,
	21	3 R	this *poor* widow has put . . . more [into the treasury] than any of them;
Jn	12	5	Why wasn't this ointment sold for three hundred denarii, and the money given to the *poor*?
		6	[Judas] said this, not because he cared about the *poor*,
		8	You have the *poor* with you always,
	13	29	some of [the disciples] thought Jesus was telling [Judas] . . . to give something to the *poor*.
Rm	15	26	a generous contribution to the *poor* among the saints at Jerusalem.
2 Co	6	10 R	[we are] taken for *paupers* though we make others rich,

2 Co	8	2	[the] constant cheerfulness [of the churches in Macedonia]
		2	and their intense *poverty* have overflowed in a wealth of generosity.
	9	X R 3	the Lord Jesus . . . was rich, but he *became poor* for your
		X R 2	sake, to make you rich out of his *poverty*.
Ga	2	10	The only thing [James, Cephas and John] insisted on was that we should remember to help the *poor*, as indeed I was anxious to do.
	4	9	how can you want to go back to elemental things like these, that ʳcan do nothing and give nothing (lit. are weak and *poor*), and be their slaves?
Jm	2	2	suppose a man comes into your synagogue, beautifully dressed . . ., and at the same time a *poor man* comes in,
		R	
		3	you tell the *poor man*, 'Stand over there'
		R	
		5 R	it was [those who are] *poor* according to the world that God chose, to be rich in faith . . . ⁶ In spite of this, you have no respect for [anybody who is] *poor*.
		6 R	
Rv	2	9	[Write to the angel of the church in Smyrna and say,] I know . . . how *poor* you are – though you are rich
		R 2	
	3	17	[Laodicea,] you say to yourself, 'I am rich,' . . . never realising that you are wretchedly . . . *poor*,
		R	
	13	16	[The second beast] compelled everyone – small and great, rich and *poor*, slave and citizen – to be branded . . . ¹⁷ . . . with the name of the beast
		R	

3. HUMBLE, LOWLY, POOR – HUMILITY – HUMILIATE, TO HUMBLE, ABUSE: *TAPEINŌSIS*

1 *tapeinoō*	14	5 *tapeino-phrōn*	1
2 *tapeinos*	8	3 *tapeino-phrosynē*	7
4 *tapeinōsis*	4		

E = Humble//Exalt

Mt	11	29 X	2 learn from me, for I am gentle and *humble* in heart,
	18	4	the one who *makes* himself as *little* as this little child is the greatest in the kingdom of heaven.
	23	12 E	Anyone who exalts himself will be *humbled*, and anyone who *humbles* himself will be exalted.
		E	
Lk	1	48	4 [the Lord] has looked upon his *lowly* handmaid.
		52	He has pulled down princes from their thrones and exalted the *lowly*.
		E 2	
	3	5	(Is 40 4) every mountain and hill [will be] *laid low*,
	14	11 E	everyone who exalts himself will be *humbled*, and the man who *humbles* himself will be exalted.
	18	14 E	everyone who exalts himself will be *humbled*, but the man who *humbles* himself will be exalted.
Ac	8	33 X	4 (Is 53 8 G) He has been *humiliated* and has no one to defend him.
	20	19	3 I have served the Lord ʳin (G *feeling*) all *humility*
Rm	12	16	never be condescending but make real friends with the *poor*.
		E 2	
2 Co	7	6	2 God comforts the *miserable*, and he comforted us, by the arrival of Titus,
	10	1	2 this is Paul himself . . . – I, the man who is so *humble* when he is facing you, but bullies you when he is at a distance.
	11	7 E	Or was I wrong, ʳlowering (or: *abusing*) myself so as to lift you high . . .?
	12	21	I am afraid . . . my God may ʳmake me ashamed (lit. *humble* me) on your account
Ep	4	2	Bear with one another charitably, ʳin complete selflessness (lit. with *feelings of humility*), gentleness and patience.
		3	
Ph	2	3	3 everybody is to be *self-effacing*
		8 X E	[Jesus] was *humbler* yet, even to accepting death,
	3	21	4 [the Lord Jesus Christ] will transfigure these *wretched* bodies of ours
	4	12	I know how to be *poor* and I know how to be rich too.
Col	2	18	3 people who like *grovelling* to angels and worshipping them;
		23	It may be argued that true wisdom is to be found in these, 3 with their . . . *self-abasement*, and their severe treatment of the body;
	3	12	you should be clothed in sincere compassion, in kindness and 3 (G *feelings of*) *humility*, gentleness and patience.
Jm	1	9 E	2 It is right for the *poor* brother to be proud of his high rank,
		10	4 ¹⁰ and the rich one to be thankful that he has been *humbled*,
	4	6	(Pr 3 34) God opposes the proud but he gives generously to 2 the *humble*.
		10 E	*Humble* yourselves before the Lord and he will lift you up.
1 P	3	8	5 love the brothers, have compassion and be *self-effacing*
	5	5	do what the elders tell you, and all wrap yourselves in (G 3 *feelings of*) *humility* to be servants of each other, because (Pr 3 34) God refuses the proud and will always favour the *humble*. ⁶ ʳBow down (lit. *Humble* yourselves), then, before the power of God now, and he will raise you up on the appointed day;
		6 E 2/	

POTTERY – CLAY

1. Potter – Earthenware – Tiles: *kerameus*
  1: Potter – Earthenware
  2: Tiles
2. Earthen, Earthenware: *ostrakinos*

3. Lump of clay: *phyrama*
4. Clay – Mud: *pēlos*
  1: (the potter's) Clay
  2: Mud, Clay – Paste
5. (to) Mould, Form: *plassō*

[1. POTTER – EARTHENWARE – TILES: *KERAMEUS*

    1 *kerameus 3*   3 *keramos 1*
    2 *keramikos 1*

1: POTTER – EARTHENWARE

Mt 27	7	they . . . bought the *potter's* field with [the thirty silver pieces]
	10	they gave [the thirty silver pieces] for the *potter's* field,
Rm 9	21	Surely a *potter* can do what he likes with the clay?
Rv 2	27	2 [authority] to . . . shatter [the pagans] like *earthenware* jars.

2: TILES

Lk 5	19	they . . . lowered [the paralytic] and his stretcher down through the *tiles*

2. EARTHEN, EARTHENWARE: *OSTRAKINOS*

    ostrakinos 2

2 Co 4	7 ○	We are only the *earthenware* jars that hold this treasure,
2 Tm 2	20	Not all the dishes in a large house are made of gold and silver; some are made of wood or *earthenware*:

3. LUMP OF CLAY: *PHYRAMA*

    phyrama 1/5

Rm 9	21	It is surely for [the potter] to decide whether he will use a particular *lump of clay* to make a special pot or an ordinary one?

4. CLAY – MUD: *PĒLOS*

    pēlos 6

1: (THE POTTER'S) CLAY

Rm 9	21	Surely a potter can do what he likes with the *clay*?

2: MUD, CLAY – PASTE

Jn 9	6	[Jesus] spat on the ground, made a *paste* with the spittle, put ⌐this (lit. the *paste*) over the eyes of the blind man,
	11	The man called Jesus . . . made a *paste*,
	14	It had been a sabbath day when Jesus made the *paste*
	15	He put a *paste* on my eyes,

5. (TO) MOULD, FORM: *PLASSŌ*

    2 *plasma 1*   1 *plassō 2*

Rm 9	20	2 ⌐The pot has no right to say to the potter (lit. Can *something moulded* say to the person who *moulded* it): Why did you make me this shape?
1 Tm 2	13 ⊖	Adam was *formed* first and Eve afterwards,

POWER – ABLE TO

1. Power – Be able to, Can – Could, Possible: *dynamai*
  1: Power, Strength – Be able to, Can – Could
    a) (God) Can, Has the power to, Is able to – Power (of God, of the Spirit)
    b) (Jesus) Can, Is able to – Power (of Jesus)
    c) Power (of angels)
    d) Power, Strength (of the Evil One) – (Satan) Can, Could
    e) (A person) Can, Is able to, Is made strong – (A person's) Ability, Power, Strength
    f) Power (generally) – (A thing, an animal) Can – (It is) Possible
  2: Can (not) – Could (not) – Impossible
    a) Impossible (to God) – (God) Could not
    b) (Jesus) Can (not), Is (not) able to, Could (not)
    c) (Satan) Can (not)
    d) (A person) Can (not), Is (not) able to, Could (not) – (No one) Can, Impossible (for a person)
    e) (A thing) Can (not), Could (not) – (Nothing) Can
  3: (the angelic order of) Power
  4: the Powers (of heaven, in the heavens)
  5: Miracle, Miraculous powers
2. Strength, Power – Strong, Mighty – Could: *ischuō*
  1: Strength, Power, Force – Powerful, Mighty, Strong

    a) (God's) Strength, Power – (God is) Strong, Mighty
    b) (Jesus is) Powerful, Mighty
    c) (Angels') Strength – (Angels are) Powerful, Mighty
    d) (A person is) Strong, Healthy, Powerful – (A man's) Strength
    e) Force, Power, Strength (generally)
  2: Can (not) – (Not to) Have the strength to
    a) (The underworld) Can (not) – (The dragon) Is (not) Strong
    b) (A person) Is (not) able to, Could (not), Has (not) the strength to
    c) (A thing) Could (not), Has (no) force, Is good for (nothing)

3. Might, Power, Strength – Strong, Mighty: *kratos*
  1: the Almighty
  2: Might, Power, Strength – Strong
    a) (God's) Power, Might, Strength
    b) (Jesus's) Power
    c) (the devil's) Power
    d) Become strong, Grow strong, Be strong
4. Strengthen: *sthenoō*
5. Can, Could – Be in one's power to, Have the means of: *echō*
6. Oppress – Be in the power of: *kata-dynasteuō*
7. Violence, Violent – (to) Subject to violence, Force, Press: *bia*
8. Possible, Impossible – Not right, Can (not): *en-dechomai*

W = Power, Strength // Weakness   G = Power // Glory

1. POWER – BE ABLE TO, CAN – COULD, POSSIBLE: *DYNAMAI*

    1 *dynamai 209*   3 *dynatos 32*
    2 *dynamis 120*   8 *a-dynateō 2*
    7 *dynamoō 2*   4 *a-dynatos 10*
    6 *dynateō 3*   5 *en-dynamoō 7*

1: POWER, STRENGTH – BE ABLE TO, CAN – COULD

a) (God) Can, Has the power to, Is able to – Power (of God, of the Spirit)

Mt 3	9	God *can* raise children for Abraham from these stones.
6	13 G	2 (ᵛ For the kingdom, the *power* and the glory are yours for ever, Amen.)
10	28	fear him rather who *can* destroy both body and soul in hell.
19	26	For men . . . this is impossible; for God everything is possible.
22	29	2 you understand neither the scriptures nor the *power* of God.
26	64	2 you will see the Son of Man seated at the right hand of the *Power*
Mk 2	7	Who *can* forgive sins but God?
10	27	For men . . . it is impossible, but not for God: because everything is *possible* for God.
12	24	2 you understand neither the scriptures nor the *power* of God?
14	36	3 Abba (Father)! . . . Everything is *possible* for you.
	62	2 you will see the Son of Man seated at the right hand of the *Power*
Lk 1	35	2 the *power* of the Most High will cover you with its shadow.
	49	3 for the *Almighty* has done great things for me.
3	8	God *can* raise children for Abraham from these stones.
4	14 Ⓢ	2 Jesus, with the *power* of the Spirit in him, returned to Galilee;
5	17	2 the *Power* of the Lord was behind his works of healing.
	21	Who *can* forgive sins but God alone?
18	27	3 Things that are impossible for men . . . are *possible* for God.
22	69	2 the Son of Man will be seated at the right hand of the *Power* of God.
24	49 Ⓢ	2 until you are clothed with the *power* from on high.
Ac 1	8 Ⓢ	2 you will receive *power* when the Holy Spirit comes on you

Ac 8 10   2 [Simon the magician] is the divine *power* that is called great.
    20 32   I commend you to God, and to the word of his grace that *has power to* build you up

Rm 1 16   2 the Good News . . . is the *power* of God saving all who have faith
     20   2 Ever since God created the world his everlasting *power* and deity . . . have been there for the mind to see in the things he has made.
   4 21   3 convinced that God had *power* to do what he had promised.
   9 17   (Ex 9 16 G) I raised you up, to use you as a means of showing
      2   my *power*
     22   3 God is ready to show his anger and display his *power*,
  11 23   3 God *is* perfectly *able to* graft them back again;
  14 4   6 he will stand . . . because the Lord *has power to* make him stand.
  15 13 Ⓢ 2 the *power* of the Holy Spirit will remove all bounds to hope.
    19 Ⓢ 2 by the power of signs and wonders, by the *power* of the Holy Spirit.
  16 25   Glory to him who *is able to* give you the strength to live according to the Good News

1 Co 1 18   2 those of us who are on the way [to salvation] see [the language
      2   of the cross] as God's *power* to save.
    24   2 a Christ who is the *power* and the wisdom of God.
   2 4   2 in . . . the sermons that I gave, there . . . [was] only a
     5 W 2 demonstration of the *power* of the Spirit. [5] And I did this
      2   so that your faith should . . . depend . . . on the *power* of God.
   6 14   2 God . . . will by his *power* raise us up too.
Co 4 7   2 such an overwhelming *power* comes from God
   6 7   [We prove we are God's servants] by the word of truth and
      G 2   by the *power* of God;
   9 8   6 there is no limit to the blessings which God *can* send you
  12 9 W 2 my *power* is at its best in weakness.
  13 4 W 2 [Christ] lives now through the *power* of God. So . . . we
      2   shall live with him, through the *power* of God,
Ep 1 19 G 2 how infinitely great is the *power* that he has exercised for us
   3 7   a gift of grace from God who gave it to me by his own
      2   *power*.
    20   2/ Glory be to him whose *power*, working in us, *can* do infinitely more than we can ask or imagine;

1 Th 1 5   the Good News . . . came to you not only as words, but as
      2   *power* and as the Holy Spirit
2 Th 1 11   2 we pray continually that our God will . . . by his *power* fulfil all your desires for goodness
2 Tm 1 8   2 but with me, bear the hardships . . , relying on the *power* of God
    12   3 I have no doubt at all that he *is able to* take care of all that I have entrusted to him
Heb 5 7   [Christ] offered up prayer and entreaty . . . to the one who *had the power to* save him out of death,
  11 19   3 God *had the power* even to raise the dead;
Jm 4 12   he is the only judge and *has the power to* acquit or to sentence.
1 P 1 5   2 Through your faith, God's *power* will guard you
2 P 1 3   2 By his divine *power*, he has given us all the things that we need for life
Jude 24   Glory be to him who *can* keep you from falling and bring you safe to his glorious presence,
Rv 4 11 G 2 you are worthy of glory and honour and *power*,
   7 12   2 honour and *power* and strength to our God
  11 17   2 We give thanks to you . . . for using your great *power*
  12 10   2 Victory and *power* and empire for ever have been won by our God,
  15 8 G 2 The smoke from the glory and the *power* of God filled the temple
  19 1 G 2 Victory and glory and *power* to our God!

b) (Jesus) Can, Is able to – Power (of Jesus)

Mt 8 2   Sir, . . . if you want to, you *can* cure me.
   9 28   Do you believe I *can* do this?
  24 30 G 2 they will see the Son of Man coming . . . with *power* and great glory.
  26 61   This man said, 'I *have power to* destroy the Temple of God'
Mk 1 40   If you want to . . . you *can* cure me.
   5 30   aware that *power* had gone out from him, Jesus turned round
   9 22   if you *can* [do] anything, have pity on us
    23   If you *can*? . . . Everything is possible for anyone who has faith.
  13 26   they will see the Son of Man coming in the clouds with great
      G 2   *power* and glory;
Lk 4 36   2 He gives orders to unclean spirits with authority and *power*
   5 12   Sir, . . . if you want to, you *can* cure me.
   6 19   2 *power* came out of him that cured them all.
   8 46   I felt that *power* had gone out from me.
  21 27 G 2 they will see the Son of Man coming in a cloud with *power* and great glory.
  24 19   Jesus . . . proved he was a great prophet by ⌐the things he said and did (lit. his *powerful* words and deeds)
Jn 6 52   How *can* this man give us his flesh to eat?
  11 37   *could* he not have prevented this man's death?
Ac 10 38   2 God had anointed him with the Holy Spirit and with *power*,

Rm 1 4   Jesus Christ . . . was proclaimed Son of God in all his
      2   *power*,
1 Co 5 4   When you are assembled together in the name of the Lord
      2   Jesus, . . . then with the *power* of our Lord Jesus he is to be handed over to Satan
2 Co 12 9   I shall be very happy to make my weaknesses my special
      W 2   boast so that the *power* of Christ may stay over me,
  13 3   6 you have known him not as a weakling, but *as a power* among you?
Ph 3 10   2 All I want to know is Christ and the *power* of his resurrection
    21   He will [transfigure these wretched bodies of ours] with the same *power*
Col 1 29   2 helped only by his *power* driving me irresistibly.
2 Th 1 7   when the Lord Jesus appears from heaven with the angels
      2   of his *power*.
Heb 1 3   2 sustaining the universe by his *powerful* command;
   2 18   he *is able to* help others who are tempted.
   5 2   he *can* sympathise with those who are ignorant
   7 25   his *power* to save is utterly certain,
2 P 1 16   2 we brought you the knowledge of the *power* and the coming of our Lord Jesus Christ;
Rv 5 12 G 2 The Lamb . . . is worthy to be given *power*, riches, . . . glory and blessing.

c) Power (of angels)

2 P 2 11   2 the angels in their great strength and *power*

d) Power, Strength (of the Evil One) – (Satan) Can, Could

Mk 3 23   How *can* Satan cast out Satan?
Lk 10 19   I have given you power to tread underfoot . . . the whole
      2   *strength* of the enemy;
Jn 10 21   *could* a devil open the eyes of the blind?
Rv 13 2   2 the dragon had handed over to [the beast] his own *power*

e) (A person) Can, Is able to, Is made strong – (A person's) Ability, Power, Strength

Mt 6 27   *Can* any of you . . . add one single cubit to his span of life?
  12 29   *can* anyone make his way into a strong man's house . . . ?
  19 12   Let anyone accept this who *can*.
    25   Who *can* be saved, then?
  20 22   'Can you drink the cup that I am going to drink?' . . 'We can.'
  25 15   To one he gave five talents, . . . each in proportion to his
     < 2   *ability*.
Mk 2 7   Who *can* forgive sins but God?
   4 33   he spoke the word to them, so far as they *were capable of* understanding it.
   8 4   Where *could* anyone get bread . . . in a deserted place like this?
   9 3   whiter than any earthly bleacher *could* make them.
    23   3 Everything is *possible* for anyone who has faith.
    29   This is the kind [of demon] . . . that *can* only be driven out by prayer.
    39   no one who works a miracle in my name ⌐is likely to (lit. *can*) speak evil of me.
  10 26   In that case . . . who *can* be saved?
    38   'Can you drink the cup that I must drink . . . ?' [39] . . .
    39   'We can.'
  14 7   you *can* be kind to [the poor] whenever you wish,
Lk 1 17   2 With the spirit and *power* of Elijah, he will go before him
   5 21   Who *can* forgive sins but God alone?
   6 39   *Can* one blind man guide another?
    42   How *can* you say to your brother, 'Brother, let me take out the splinter . . .'?
   9 1   2 He called the Twelve together and gave them *power* and authority
  12 25   *Can* any of you . . . add a single cubit to his span of life?
  14 31   what king . . . would not first . . . consider whether . . .
      3   he *could* stand up to the other . . . ?
  18 26   In that case . . . who *can* be saved?
Jn 3 4   How *can* a grown man be born? *Can* he go back into his mother's womb . . . ?
   5 44   How *can* you believe, since you look to one another for approval . . . ?
   6 60   This is intolerable language. How *could* anyone accept it?
Ac 3 12   2 as though we had made this man walk by our own *power* or holiness?
   4 7   2 By what *power*, and by whose name have you men done this?
    33   2 The apostles continued to testify . . . with great *power*,
   6 8   2 Stephen was filled with grace and *power*
   7 22   3 Moses . . . became a man *with power* both in his speech and his actions.
   8 31   How *can* I . . . unless I have someone to guide me?
   9 22   5 Saul's *power increased* steadily,
  10 47   *Could* anyone refuse the water of baptism to these people . . . ?
  11 17   3 ⌐who was I to (lit. how *could* I) stand in God's way?
  17 19   How much of this new teaching . . . *are we allowed to* know?
  18 24   Apollos . . . was an eloquent man, with a sound ⌐knowledge
      3   of (lit. *ability* in) the scriptures,

Ac 24 8   if you ask him you *can* find out for yourself the truth of all our accusations

     11   As you *can* verify for yourself, it is no more than twelve days since I went

     25 5   3 Let ʳyour authorities (lit. those who are *in power*) come down with me

     26 32   This man *could* have been set free

     27 39   they planned to run the ship aground . . . if they *could*.

     43   He gave orders that those who *could* swim should jump overboard

Rm 4 20   5 Abraham . . . drew *strength* from faith

     15 1 W 3 We who are *strong* have a duty to put up with the qualms of the weak

     14   I am quite certain that you *are* . . . *able to* advise each other.

1 Co 1 26 W 3 how many of you were . . . ʳinfluential (lit. *powerful*) people . . . ?

     4 19   I shall want to know not what these self-important people

     2   have to say, but *what they can* [do],

     6 5   not one reliable man among you ʳto (lit. who *can*) settle differences

     7 21   if you should *have the chance of* being free, accept it.

     10 13   You can trust God not to let you be tried beyond your *strength*, and with any trial he will give you . . . the *strength* to bear it.

     14 31   you *can* all prophesy in turn,

2 Co 1 4   so that we *can* offer others . . . consolation

     8   the things we had to undergo in Asia were more of a burden

     2   than we *could* [carry],

     8 3 O 2 they gave not only as much as they *could* [afford], but far more than they *could*,

     12 10 W 3 it is when I am weak that I am *strong*.

     13 9 W 3 We are only too glad to be weak provided you are *strong*.

Ep 3 4   you ʳwill (lit. *can*) have some idea of the depths that I see in the mystery of Christ.

     16   2 may he give you the *power* through his Spirit for your hidden self to grow strong,

     6 10   5 *grow strong* in the Lord, with the strength of his power.

     11   ¹¹ Put God's armour on so as to *be able to* resist the devil's tactics.

     13   you must rely on God's armour, or you will not *be able to*

     16   put up any resistance . . . ¹⁶ always carrying the shield of faith so that you *can* [use it to] put out the burning arrows of the evil one.

Ph 4 13   There is nothing I cannot master with the help of the One

     5   who *gives me strength*.

Col 1 11   7 You will ʳhave in you the strength (lit. be *made strong* in

     2   all the *strength*), based on his own glorious power, never to give in,

1 Th 2 7   we *could* have imposed ourselves on you with full weight,

     9   How *can* we thank God enough for you . . . ?

1 Tm 1 12   5 I thank Jesus Christ our Lord, who has *given me strength*,

2 Tm 1 7   God's gift was not a spirit of timidity, but the Spirit of

     2   *power*,

     2 1   5 *Accept the strength* . . . that comes from the grace of Christ Jesus.

     4 17   5 the Lord stood by me and *gave me power*,

Tt 1 9   3 so that he *can* [be counted on for] both expounding the sound doctrine and refuting those who argue against it.

Heb 11 11   2 Sarah . . . was made *able to* conceive, because she believed that he who had made the promise would be faithful to it.

     34 W 7 They were weak people who were *given strength*,

Jm 3 2   3 he would *be able to* control every part of himself.

Rv 3 8   2 though you are not very *strong*, you have kept my commandments

     6 17   the Great Day of his anger has come, and who *can* survive it?

     13 4   Who *can* compare with the beast?

     17 13   2 They are all of one mind in putting their *strength* at the beast's disposal,

f) Power (generally) – (A thing, an animal) Can – (It is) Possible

Mt 12 34   Brood of vipers, how *can* your speech be good . . . ?

     24 24   great signs and portents, enough to deceive even the chosen,

     3   if that were *possible*.

     26 9   This [ointment] *could* have been sold at a high price

     39   3 My Father, . . . if it is *possible*, let this cup pass me by.

Mk 4 32   so that the birds of the air *can* shelter in its shade.

     9 1   2 before they see the kingdom of God come with *power*.

     13 22   3 signs and portents to deceive the elect, if that were *possible*.

     14 5   Ointment like this *could* have been sold for over three hundred denarii

     35   3 [Jesus] prayed that, if it were *possible*, this hour might pass him by.

Jn 1 46   *Can* anything good come from that place?

     3 9   How *can* that be [possible]?

Ac 20 16   3 Paul . . . was anxious to be in Jerusalem, if *possible*, for the day of Pentecost.

     27 12   the majority were in favour of putting out from there ʳin the hope (lit. with the *possibility*) of wintering at Phoenix

---

Rm 12 18   3 Do all you can if *possible* to live at peace with everyone.

1 Co 4 20   2 the kingdom of God is not just words, it is *power*.

     14 11   but if I am ignorant of ʳwhat the sounds mean (lit. the

     O 2   *force* of the sounds), I am a savage to the man who is speaking,

     15 43 W 2 the thing that is sown is weak but what is raised is *powerful*;

     56   2 sin gets its *power* from the Law.

2 Co 10 4   Our war is not fought with weapons of flesh, yet they are

     3   *strong* enough . . . to demolish fortresses.

Ga 3 21   if the Law we were given had *been capable of* giving life.

     4 15   you would even have gone so far as to pluck out your eyes

     3   if that was *possible* and give them to me.

2 Tm 3 5   2 They will keep up the outward appearance of religion but will have rejected the inner *power* of it.

     15   ʳfrom these you can learn (lit. these *can* teach you) the wisdom that leads to salvation

Heb 6 5   2 the good message of God and the *powers* of the world to come

     7 16   2 [who is a priest] not by virtue of a law . . . but by the *power* of an indestructible life.

     11 34   [Gideon, . . . Samuel and the prophets could] put out

     2   ʳblazing (lit. *powerful*) fires

Jm 1 21   accept . . . the word which has been planted in you and *can* save your souls.

     2 14   ʳWill (lit. *Can*) that faith save him?

     3 12   *Can* a fig tree give you olives . . . ?

Rv 1 16   2 his face was like the sun shining with all its *force*.

     14 3   a hymn that *could* only be learnt by the hundred and forty-four thousand

     18 3   2 every merchant [has] grown rich through (§ the *power* of) her debauchery.

2: CAN (NOT) – COULD (NOT) – IMPOSSIBLE

a) Impossible (to God) – (God) Could not

Lk 1 37   8 [Elizabeth has conceived,] for nothing is *impossible* to God.

Heb 6 18   4 two unalterable things in which it was *impossible* for God to be lying,

b) (Jesus) Can (not), Is (not) able to, Could (not)

Mt 26 53   do you think that I *cannot* appeal to my Father . . . ?

     27 42   he *cannot* save himself.

Mk 1 45   Jesus *could* no longer go openly into any town,

     6 5   he *could* work no miracle there,

     7 24   he . . . did not want anyone to know he was there, but he *could* not pass unrecognised.

     15 31   he *cannot* save himself.

Jn 5 19   the Son *can* do nothing by himself; [he can do] only what he sees the Father doing:

     30   I *can* do nothing by myself;

     9 33   if this man were not from God, he *could*n't do a thing.

     11 37   *could* he not have prevented this man's death?

2 Tm 2 13   he *cannot* disown his own self.

Heb 4 15   it is not as if we had a high priest who was in*capable of* feeling our weaknesses with us;

c) (Satan) Can (not)

Mk 3 26   if Satan . . . is divided, he *cannot* stand either

d) (A person) Can (not), Is (not) able to, Could (not) – (No one) Can, Impossible (for a person)

Mt 5 36   you *cannot* turn a single hair white or black.

     6 24   No one *can* be the slave of two masters: . . . You *cannot* be the slave both of God and of money.

     9 15   Surely the bridegroom's attendants ʳwould never (lit. *could* not) think of mourning . . . ?

     10 28   Do not be afraid of those who kill the body but *cannot* kill the soul.

     16 3   you *cannot* read the signs of the times.

     17 16   your disciples *were unable to* cure him.

     19   Why were we *unable to* cast it out?

     20   if your faith were the size of a mustard seed . . . nothing

     8   would be *impossible* for you.

     19 26   4 For man . . . this is *impossible*; for God everything is possible.

     22 46   from that day no one ʳdared to (lit. *could*) ask him any further questions.

Mk 2 4   the crowd made it im*possible* to get the man to him,

     19   Surely the bridegroom's attendants ʳwould never (lit. *could* not) think of fasting . . . ? As long as they have the bridegroom with them, they *could* not think of fasting.

     3 20   they *could* not even have a meal.

     27   no one *can* make his way into a strong man's house

     5 3   no one *could* secure [the demoniac] any more,

     6 19   Herodias . . . *was not able to* [kill John],

     9 28   Why were we *unable to* cast it out?

     10 27   4 For man . . . it is *impossible*, but not for God:

Lk 1 20   you will . . . *have no power of* speech until this has happened.

     22   [Zechariah] *could* not speak to them,

     5 34   Surely you *cannot* make the bridegroom's attendants fast . . . ?

     8 19   His mother and his brothers . . . *could* not get to him

Lk 9 40 your disciples . . . *could* not [cast it out].
11 7 < I *cannot* get up to give it you.
12 26 If the smallest things . . . are outside your *control*,
13 11 she *was* . . . quite un*able to* stand upright.
14 20 < I have just got married and so *am* un*able to* come.
26 If any man comes to me without hating his father, . . . he *cannot* be my disciple.
27 Anyone who does not carry his cross . . . *cannot* be my disciple.
33 none of you *can* be my disciple unless he gives up all his possessions.
16 2 < you ʳare not to (lit. *cannot*) be my steward any longer.
13 No servant *can* be the slave of two masters: . . . You *cannot* be the slave both of God and of money.
26 between us and you a great gulf has been fixed, to stop anyone . . . ʳcrossing (lit. *being able to* cross) from our side to yours,
18 27 4 Things that are *impossible* for men . . . are possible for God.
19 3 [Zacchaeus] *could* not see [Jesus] for the crowd;
20 36 they *can* no longer die,
21 15 an eloquence . . . that none of your opponents will *be able to* resist
Jn 3 2 no one *could* perform the signs that you do
3 unless a man is born from above, he *cannot* see the kingdom of God.
5 unless a man is born through water and the Spirit, he *cannot* enter the kingdom of God:
27 ʳA man can lay claim only to (lit. No man *can* lay claim to more than) what is given him from heaven.
6 44 No one *can* come to me unless he is drawn by the Father
65 no one *could* come to me unless the Father allows him.
7 7 The world *cannot* hate you, but it does hate me,
34 where I am you *cannot* come.
36 where I am you *cannot* come.
8 21 Where I am going, you *cannot* come.
22 Where I am going, you *cannot* come.
43 you *are* un*able to* understand my language.
9 4 the night will soon be here when no one *can* work.
16 How *could* a sinner produce signs like this?
10 29 no one *can* steal from the Father.
12 39 they *were* un*able to* believe because, as Isaiah says (Is 6 9f)
13 33 where I am you *cannot* come.
36 Where I am going you *cannot* follow me now;
37 Why *can*'t I follow you now?
14 17 that Spirit of truth whom the world *can* never receive
15 5 cut off from me you *can* do nothing.
16 12 I still have many things to say to you but ʳthey would be too much for you (lit. you *could* not bear them) now.
Ac 4 16 a miracle has been worked through them in public, and we *cannot* deny it.
20 We *cannot* promise to stop proclaiming what we have seen and heard.
5 39 [if this movement] does in fact come from God you will . . . *be* un*able to* destroy them,
13 38 justification from all sins which the Law of Moses *was* un*able to* justify
14 8 4 his feet (§ *had no strength* and) were crippled from birth;
15 1 Unless you have yourselves circumcised . . . you *cannot* be saved
19 40 we *can* give no reason for this gathering.
21 34 the noise made it im*possible* for him to get any positive information,
24 13 neither *can* they prove any of the accusations
25 11 no one *has a right to* surrender me to them.
27 31 Unless those men stay on board you *cannot* [hope to] be saved.
Rm 8 8 People who are interested only in unspiritual things *can* never be pleasing to God.
15 1 We who are strong have a duty to put up with the qualms
W 4 of ʳthe weak (lit. those who *have no strength*)
1 Co 2 14 [to] one who does not accept anything of the Spirit of God . . . ʳit is beyond his understanding (lit. he *cannot* understand it)
3 1 I myself *was* un*able to* speak to you as people of the Spirit:
2 . . .² . . . you ʳwere not ready for (lit. *could* not take) it; and indeed, you ʳare still not ready for (lit. still *cannot* take) it
11 nobody *can* lay any other [foundation] than . . . Jesus Christ.
10 21 You *cannot* drink the cup of the Lord and the cup of demons. You *cannot* take your share at the table of the Lord and at the table of demons.
12 3 no one *can* say, 'Jesus is Lord' unless he is under the influence of the Holy Spirit.
2 Co 3 7 the Israelites *could* not [bear] looking at the face of Moses,
13 8 We *have no power to* resist the truth;
1 Tm 6 7 we *can* take nothing out of [the world];
16 [God] whom no man *is able to* see
2 Tm 3 7 [silly women who] *can* never come to knowledge of the truth.
Heb 3 19 it was because they were unfaithful that they *were* not *able to* reach [the place of rest].

Heb 6 6 4 it is *impossible* for [those who were once brought into the light and fell away] to be renewed a second time.
11 6 4 it is *impossible* to please God without faith,
Jm 3 8 nobody *can* tame the tongue
4 2 You have an ambition that you *cannot* satisfy;
1 Jn 3 9 he *cannot* sin when he has been begotten by God.
4 20 a man who does not love the brother that he can see *cannot* love God, whom he has never seen.
Rv 2 2 I know you *cannot* stand wicked men,
3 8 I have opened in front of you a door that nobody will *be able to* close
5 3 there was no one . . . who *was able to* open the scroll
7 9 I saw a huge number, im*possible* to count, of people from every nation,
13 17 [the second beast] made it ʳillegal (lit. im*possible*) for anyone to buy or sell anything unless he had been branded
15 8 no one *could* go into [the temple]

e) (A thing) Can (not), Could (not) – (Nothing) Can

Mt 5 14 A city built on a hill-top *cannot* be hidden.
7 18 A sound tree *cannot* bear bad fruit,
26 42 if this cup *cannot* pass by without my drinking it,
Mk 3 24 If a kingdom is divided against itself, that kingdom *cannot* last. ²⁵ . . . that household *can* never stand.
25
7 15 Nothing that goes into a man from outside *can* make him unclean
18 whatever goes into a man from outside *cannot* make him unclean,
Jn 10 35 scripture *cannot* be rejected.
15 4 a branch *cannot* bear fruit all by itself,
Ac 2 24 God raised him to life, freeing him from the pangs of Hades;
3 for it was im*possible* for him to be held in its power
27 15 The ship . . . *could* not be turned head-on to the wind,
Rm 8 3 4 God had done what the Law . . . *was* un*able to* [do].
7 such a limitation never *could* and never does submit to God's law.
39 neither death . . . nor any created thing, *can* ever come between us and the love of God
1 Co 12 21 The eye *cannot* say to the hand, 'I do not need you',
15 50 flesh and blood *cannot* inherit the kingdom of God:
1 Tm 5 25 the good that people do *can* be obvious;
Heb 9 9 None of the . . . sacrifices . . . *can possibly* bring any worshipper to perfection
10 1 the Law . . . *is* quite in*capable of* bringing the worshippers to perfection,
4 4 Bulls' blood and goats' blood are ʳuseless (or: *powerless*) for taking away sins,
11 sacrifices which *are* quite in*capable of* taking sins away.
Rv 9 20 idols . . . that *can* neither see nor hear nor move

3: (THE ANGELIC ORDER OF) POWER

Rm 8 38 2 no angel, no prince, . . . not any *power* . . .³⁹ . . . can ever come between us and the love of God
1 Co 15 24 when he hands over the kingdom to God the Father, having
2 done away with every sovereignty, authority, and *power*.
Ep 1 21 [God made Christ sit at his right hand,] far above every
2 Sovereignty, Authority, *Power*, or Domination,
1 P 3 22 [Jesus Christ] is at God's right hand, now that he has made
2 the angels and Dominations and *Powers* his subjects.

4: THE POWERS (OF HEAVEN, IN THE HEAVENS)

Mt 24 29 2 the *powers* of heaven will be shaken.
Mk 13 25 2 the *powers* in the heavens will be shaken.
Lk 21 26 2 the *powers* of heaven will be shaken.

5: MIRACLE, MIRACULOUS POWERS

Mt 7 22 2 Lord, did we not . . . work many *miracles* in your name?
11 20 X 2 the towns in which most of his *miracles* had been worked,
21 X 2 if the *miracles* done in you had been done in Tyre and Sidon
23 X 2 if the *miracles* done in you had been done in Sodom,
13 54 X 2 Where did the man get this wisdom and these *miraculous powers*?
58 X 2 he did not work many *miracles* there
14 2 John the Baptist . . . has risen from the dead, and that is
X 2 why *miraculous powers* are at work in him.
Mk 6 2 X 2 What is this wisdom . . , and these *miracles* that are worked through him?
5 X 2 he could work no *miracle* there,
14 John the Baptist has risen from the dead, and that is why
X 2 *miraculous powers* are at work in him.
9 39 2 no one who works a *miracle* in my name is likely to speak evil of me.

Lk 10 13 X 2 if the *miracles* done in you had been done in Tyre and Sidon,
19 37 the whole group of disciples joyfully began to praise God
X 2 . . . for all the *miracles* they had seen.
Ac 2 22 X 2 a man commended to you by God by the *miracles* and portents and signs that God worked through him when he was among you,
8 13 Simon . . . was astonished when he saw the wonders and
2 great *miracles* that took place.
19 11 2 So remarkable were the *miracles* worked by God at Paul's hands
Rm 15 19 2 by the *power* of signs and wonders, by the power of the Holy Spirit.
1 Co 12 10 2 one [may have] the power of *miracles*;
28 2 after them, *miracles*, and after them the gift of healing;
29 2 . . . [29] . . . Do they all have [the gift of] *miracles* . . .?
2 Co 12 12 You have seen done among you all the things that mark the
2 true apostle . . .: the signs, the marvels, the *miracles*.
Ga 3 5 Θ? 2 Does God give you the Spirit so freely and work *miracles* among you because you practise the Law . . .?
2 Th 2 9 when the Rebel comes, Satan will set to work: there will
○ 2 be all kinds of *miracles* and a deceptive show of signs and portents,
Heb 2 4 God himself confirmed their witness with signs and marvels
2 and *miracles*

2. STRENGTH, POWER – STRONG, MIGHTY – COULD: *ISCHUŌ*

2 ischuō	28	4 kat-ischuō	3
1 ischyros	29	5 en-ischuō	2
3 ischys	10	6 ex-ischuō	1

1: STRENGTH, POWER, FORCE – POWERFUL, MIGHTY, STRONG

a) (God's) Strength, Power – (God is) Strong, Mighty

1 Co 1 25 W God's weakness is *stronger* than human strength.
Ep 1 19 3 This you can tell from the strength of his *power* [20] at work in Christ
6 10 3 grow strong in the Lord, with the strength of his *power*.
2 Th 1 9 excluded from the presence of the Lord and from the glory
G 3 of his *strength*
1 P 4 11 if you are a helper, help as though every action was done
3 ⌜at God's orders (lit. with *strength* supplied by God);
Rv 7 12 G 3 Praise and glory and . . . power and *strength* to our God for ever
18 8 The Lord God has condemned [Babylon], and he ⌜has great *power* (or: is *mighty*).

b) (Jesus is) Powerful, Mighty

Mt 3 11 the one who follows me is more *powerful* than I am,
Mk 1 7 Someone is following me, someone who is more *powerful* than I am,
Lk 3 16 someone is coming, someone who is more *powerful* than I am,
Rv 5 12 G 3 The Lamb . . . is worthy to be given power, . . . *strength*, . . . glory and blessing.

c) (Angels') Strength – (Angels are) Powerful, Mighty

2 P 2 11 3 the angels in their greater *strength* and power make no complaint
Rv 5 2 I saw a *powerful* angel who called with a loud voice,
10 1 I saw another *powerful* angel coming down from heaven,
18 2 ⌜At the top of his (lit. In a *powerful*) voice he shouted, 'Babylon has fallen,'
21 a *powerful* angel picked up a boulder

d) (A person is) Strong, Healthy, Powerful – (A man's) Strength

Mt 9 12 2 It is not the *healthy* who need the doctor,
12 29 how can anyone make his way into a *strong* man's house . . . unless he has tied up the *strong* man first?
Mk 2 17 2 It is not the *healthy* who need the doctor,
3 27 no one can make his way into a *strong* man's house . . . unless he has tied up the *strong* man first
12 30 (Dt 6 5) you must love the Lord your God with . . . all
3 your *strength*.
33 3 To love him with all your . . . *strength* . . . is far more important than any holocaust
Lk 10 27 (Dt 6 5) You must love the Lord your God with . . . all
3 your *strength*.
11 21 So long as a *strong* man fully armed guards his own palace,
22 his goods are undisturbed; [22] but when someone *stronger* than he is attacks and defeats him, the [*stronger*] man takes away all the weapons he relied on
21 36 4 Stay awake, praying at all times for the *strength* to survive all that is going to happen,
22 43 5 an angel appeared to [Jesus], coming from heaven to *give* him *strength*.
Ac 9 19 5 after taking some food [Saul] *regained* his *strength*.

Ac 19 16 2 the man with the evil spirit . . . *handled* them so *violently* that they fled
27 16 2 We . . . *managed* with some difficulty to bring the ship's boat under control.
1 Co 1 27 W it was to . . . shame what is *strong* that [God] chose what is weak by human reckoning;
4 10 W we have no power, but you are ⌜influential (lit. *powerful*);
10 22 are we *stronger* than [the Lord] is?
Ep 3 18 6 you will with all the saints *have strength to* grasp the breadth
Ph 4 13 2 There is nothing I *cannot* [master] with the help of the One who gives me strength.
Heb 11 34 weak people who were given strength, to be *brave* in war
1 Jn 2 14 I have written to you, young men, because you are *strong*
Rv 6 15 all the earthly rulers, the . . . rich people and the ⌜men of influence (lit. *powerful* men) . . . took to the mountains
19 18 There will be the flesh of kings for you, and the flesh of great generals and ⌜heroes (lit. *mighty* men),

e) Force, Power, Strength (generally)

Mt 14 30 as soon as [Peter] felt the *force* of the wind, he took fright and began to sink.
Lk 15 14 that country experienced a *severe* famine,
23 23 their shouts were ⌜growing louder (lit. becoming more
4 *powerful*).
Ac 19 20 In this impressive way the word of the Lord spread more and
2 more widely and ⌜successfully (lit. *strongly*).
2 Co 10 10 W He writes powerful and *strongly*[-worded] letters
Heb 5 7 he offered up prayer and entreaty, ⌜aloud (lit. *forcefully*) and in silent tears,
6 18 so that we . . . should have a *strong* encouragement
Jm 5 16 2 the heartfelt prayer of a good man works very *powerfully*.
Rv 18 10 Babylon, so *powerful* a city,
19 6 the voices of a huge crowd, like . . . the *great* roar of thunder,

2: CAN(NOT) – (NOT TO) HAVE THE STRENGTH TO

a) (The underworld) Can(not) – (The dragon) Is (not) strong

Mt 16 18 4 the gates of the underworld *can* never hold out against [the Church].
Rv 12 8 [The dragon fought back with his angels,] but they ⌜were
2 defeated (lit. proved not to *be the stronger*)

b) (A person) Is (not) able to, Could (not), Has (not) the strength to

Mt 8 28 2 two demoniacs . . . – creatures so fierce that no one *could* pass that way.
26 40 2 So you ⌜had not *the strength to* (or: *could* not) keep awake with me one hour?
Mk 5 4 2 no one *had the strength to* control [the demoniac].
9 18 2 I asked your disciples to cast it out and they *were unable to*.
14 37 2 *Had* you not *the strength to* keep awake one hour?
Lk 8 43 a woman suffering from a haemorrhage . . ., whom no one
2 had *been able to* cure.
13 24 2 many will try to enter and will not *succeed*.
14 6 2 to this they *could* find no answer.
29 2 he laid the foundations and then found himself un*able to* finish the work,
30 2 Here is a man who . . . *was* un*able to* finish.
16 3 2 Dig? I am not *strong* [enough].
20 26 2 they *were unable to* find fault with anything he had to say
Jn 21 6 2 they *could* not haul [the net] in.
Ac 6 10 2 they *could* not get the better of [Stephen] because of his wisdom,
15 10 2 the very burden that neither we nor our ancestors *were strong* [enough] *to* support?
25 7 2 many serious accusations which they *were unable to* substantiate.

c) (A thing) Could (not), Has (no) force, Is good for (nothing)

Mt 5 13 2 [the salt] *is good for* nothing,
Lk 6 48 2 when the river was in flood it . . . *could* not shake [that house],
Ga 5 6 whether you are circumcised or not ⌜makes no difference
2 (lit. *has no force*)
Heb 9 17 2 it is not meant to *have any effect* while the testator is still alive.

3. MIGHT, POWER, STRENGTH – STRONG, MIGHTY: *KRATOS*

3 krataioō	4	1 kratos	12
4 krataios	1	2 panto-kratōr	10

1: THE ALMIGHTY

2 Co 6 18 2 [I will] be your father, . . . says the *Almighty* Lord.

Rv	1	8	'I am the Alpha and the Omega' says the Lord God, who is, 2 who was, and who is to come, the *Almighty*.
	4	8	2 Holy, holy, holy is the Lord God, the *Almighty*;
	11	17	2 We give thanks to you, *Almighty* Lord God, He-Is-and-He-Was,
	15	3	How great and wonderful are all your works, Lord God 2 *Almighty*,
	16	7	2 Truly, Lord God *Almighty*, the punishments you give are true and just.
		14	to call [all the kings of the world] together for the war of 2 the Great Day of God the *Almighty*
	19	6	2 The reign of the Lord our God *Almighty* has begun;
		15	2 the wine of *Almighty* God's fierce anger.
	21	22	2 the Lord God *Almighty* and the Lamb were themselves the temple,

2: MIGHT, POWER, STRENGTH – STRONG

a) (God's) Power, Might, Strength

Lk	1	51	[the Almighty] has shown the *power* of his arm,
Ac	19	20	⌐In this impressive way (lit. *Powerfully*; G *By* his *power*) the word of the Lord spread more and more widely and successfully.
Ep	1	19	This you can tell from the *strength* of his power ²⁰ at work in Christ,
	6	10	grow strong in the Lord, with the *strength* of his power.
Col	1	11	You will have in you the strength, based on his own glorious G *power*, never to give in,
1Tm	6	16	to him be honour and everlasting *power*. Amen.
1 P	5	6	4 Bow down, then, before the *power* of God
		11	His *power* lasts for ever and ever.
Jude		25 G	To God . . . be the glory, majesty, ⌐authority (or: *might*) and power, which he had before time began,
Rv	5	13	To the One who is sitting on the throne and to the Lamb, G be all praise, honour, glory and *power*, for ever and ever.

b) (Jesus's) Power

1 P	4	11 G	to [Jesus Christ] alone belong all glory and *power* for ever and ever.
Rv	1	6 G	[to Jesus Christ] be glory and *power* for ever and ever.
	5	13 G	to the Lamb, be all praise, honour, glory and *power*, for ever and ever.

c) (the devil's) Power

Heb	2	14	by his death [Christ] could take away all the power of the devil, who had *power* over death,

d) Become strong, Grow strong, Be strong

Lk	1	80	3 the child [John] grew up and his spirit ⌐matured (lit. *became strong*).
	2	40	3 the child [Jesus] grew ⌐to maturity (lit. and *became strong*),
1Co	16	13	3 stay firm in the faith; be brave and *be strong*.
Ep	3	16	may [the Father] give you the power through his Spirit for 3 your hidden self to *grow strong*,

4. STRENGTHEN: *STHENOŌ*

sthenoō 1

1 P	5	10 G	God . . . will confirm, *strengthen* and support you.

5. CAN, COULD – BE IN ONE'S POWER TO, HAVE THE MEANS OF: *ECHŌ*

echō (9)

Mt	18	25	he ⌐had no *means of* paying (or: *could* not pay) [the ten thousand talents],
Mk	14	8	She has done ⌐what *was in* her *power* [to do] (or: what she *could*):
Lk	12	4	Do not be afraid of those who kill the body and after that *can* do no more.
	14	14	that they *cannot* pay you back means that you are fortunate,
Jn	14	30 ⒟	the prince of this world . . . *has no power* over me,
Ac	4	14	[the members of the Sanhedrin] *could* find no answer.
Ep	4	28	he should . . . *be able to* do some good by helping others that are in need.
Heb	6	13 ⊖	[God] swore by his own self, since it was im*possible* for him to swear by anyone greater:
2 P	1	15	after my own departure you will still *have a means to* recall these things

6. OPPRESS – BE IN THE POWER OF: *KATA-DYNASTEUŌ*

kata-dynasteuō 2

Ac	10	38 ⒟	Jesus went about . . . curing all who had *fallen into the power* of the devil.
Jm	2	6	Isn't it always the rich who ⌐*are against* (or: *oppress*) you?

7. VIOLENCE, VIOLENT – (TO) SUBJECT TO VIOLENCE, FORCE, PRESS: *BIA*

1	bia	4	2	biazō 2
4	biaios	1	3	para-biazomai 2
5	biastēs	1		

Mt	11	12 ●	2 the kingdom of heaven has been *subjected to violence* and the 5 *violent* are taking it by storm.
Lk	16	16 ●	2 the kingdom of God has been preached, and by *violence* everyone is getting in.
	24	29	3 [the two disciples] *pressed* [Jesus to stay]
Ac	2	2	4 they heard what sounded like a *powerful* wind from heaven,
	5	26	The captain with his men . . . were afraid to use *force* in case the people stoned them.
	16	15	[Lydia] sent us an invitation: '. . . come and stay with us' 3 and she *would take no refusal*.
	21	35	the crowd *became so violent* that [Paul] had to be carried by the soldiers;
	24	7	(ᵛ the tribune Lysias . . . took [Paul] out of our hands by *force*)
	27	41	the stern began to break up with the *pounding* of the waves.

8. POSSIBLE, IMPOSSIBLE – NOT RIGHT, CAN(NOT): *EN-DECHOMAI*

1	en-dechomai 1	2	an-en-dektos 1

Lk	13	33	it ⌐would not *be right for* a prophet to (or: *cannot* [be] that a prophet might) die outside Jerusalem.
	17	1	2 ⌐*Obstacles are sure to* (lit. It is *impossible* that obstacles should not) come,

PRECIOUS – EXPENSIVE

1. Precious, Costly, Expensive – Special – Price, Value, Money: *timē*	**1:** Spend – Expense, Cost
	2: Without expense = Free (of charge)
2. (Very) Costly, Expensive – Precious: *poly-telēs*	**4. Expense:** *ops-ōnion*
3. Expense: *dapanaō*	**5. Send:** *pros-an-(h)aliskō*

1. PRECIOUS, COSTLY, EXPENSIVE – SPECIAL – PRICE, VALUE, MONEY: *TIMĒ*

5	timaō	2/21	7	bary-timos 1
1	timē	16/41	4	en-timos 3/5
2	timios	11/13	8	(iso-)timos 1
6	timiotēs	1	3	poly-timos 3

Mt	13	46 <	3 when [a merchant] finds [a pearl] *of great value*
	26	7	7 an alabaster jar of *the most expensive* ointment,
	27	6	It is against the Law to put this into the treasury; it is blood-X *money*.
		9	(cf. Zc 11 13) they took the thirty pieces, the ⌐*sum* (or: *price*) X 5/5 at which the *precious* [One] was *priced* by children of Israel,
Lk	7	2	A centurion . . . had a servant, ⌐a favourite of his (or: 4 *valued highly* by him), who was sick
Jn	12	3	3 Mary brought in a pound of *very costly* ointment,
Ac	4	34	all those who owned . . . houses would sell them, and bring the *money* from them, ³⁵ to . . . the apostles;
	5	2	[Ananias] kept back part of the *proceeds* [of the sale of his 3 property] . . . ³ 'Ananias,' Peter said 'how can Satan have so possessed you that you should . . . keep back part of the *money* from the land?'
	7	16	the tomb that Abraham had bought ⌐and paid for (lit. at a *price* in money) from the sons of Hamor,
	19	19	Some believers . . . collected their books [of magic] and made a bonfire of them in public. The *value* of these was calculated to be fifty thousand silver pieces.

Ac 20	24	2 life to me is not *precious* enough a thing to waste words on,
Rm 9	21	It is surely for [the potter] to decide whether he will use a particular lump of clay to make a ⌐*special* (or: *valuable* pot or an ordinary one?
1 Co 3	12	On this foundation you can build in gold, silver and ⌐*jewels* 2 (lit. *precious* stones),
6	20	[You are not your own property;] you have been bought ⌐and paid for (lit. at a *price*).
7	23	You have all been bought ⌐and paid for (lit. at a *price*);
Col 2	23	once the flesh starts to protest [against these regulations], they are ⌐no use (lit. of no *value*) at all.
1 Tm 5	17	The elders who do their work well . . . are to be given double ⌐*consideration* (or: *remuneration*),
2 Tm 2	20	some [dishes in a large house] are kept for *special* occasions
	21	. . .²¹ Now, to avoid these faults . . . is the way for anyone to become a vessel for *special* occasions
Jm 5	7	2 how patiently [a farmer] waits for the *precious* fruit of the ground
1 P 1	7	your faith will have been tested and próved like gold – only 3 it is more *precious* than gold,
19 X	2	[the ransom for you was paid] in the *precious* blood of a lamb without . . . stain, namely Christ;
2	4	the living stone, rejected by men but chosen by God and X 4 *precious* to him;
6 X	4	(Is 28 16) See how I lay in Zion a *precious* cornerstone that I have chosen
	7	for you who are believers, it is *precious*;
2 P 1	1	8 to all who ⌐*treasure* (lit. have accepted as *precious*) the same faith as ourselves,
	4	[God] has given us the guarantee of something very great 2 and ⌐*wonderful* (lit. *precious*) to come:
Rv 17	4	2 The woman . . . glittered with gold and ⌐*jewels* (lit. *precious* stones) and pearls, . . . every piece in . . . ⌐*fine* (lit. 2 *precious*) wood,
18	12	2 [the traders'] stocks of gold and silver, ⌐*jewels* (lit. *precious* stones) and pearls,
	16	mourn for this great city [Babylon]; for all . . . your finery 2 of gold and ⌐*jewels* (lit. *precious* stones) and pearls;
	19	6 mourn for this great city whose *lavish living* has made a fortune for every owner of a sea-going ship;
21 11	2	[The new Jerusalem] glittered like some *precious* jewel
	19	The foundations of the city wall were faced with all kinds of 2 *precious* stone:
	26	the nations will come, bringing their treasure and their ⌐*wealth* (or: *honour*).

2. (VERY) COSTLY, EXPENSIVE – PRECIOUS: *POLY-TELĒS*

poly-telēs 3

Mk 14	3	an alabaster jar of *very costly* ointment,
1 Tm 2	9	women are to . . . be dressed . . . modestly, without . . . *expensive* clothes;
1 P 3	4	the ornament of a sweet and gentle disposition – this is what is *precious* in the sight of God.

3. EXPENSIVE: *DAPANAŌ*

1	*dapanaō 5*	4 *ek-dapanaō 1*
2	*dapanē 1*	5 *pros-dapanaō 1*
3	*a-dapanos 1*	

1: SPEND – EXPENSE, COST

Mk 5	26	after long . . . treatment under various doctors, [the woman] had *spent* all she had
Lk 10	35	5 I will make good any *extra expense* you have.
14	28	which of you here, intending to build a tower, would not 2 first . . . work out the *cost* . . .?
15	14	When [the prodigal] had *spent* it all,
Ac 21	24	take these men along and . . . *pay* [all] *the expenses* connected with the shaving of their heads.
2 Co 12 15 ○	/4	I am perfectly willing to *spend* what I have, and to *be expended*, in the interests of your souls.
Jm 4	3	you have prayed for something to ⌐*indulge* (or: *spend* in) your own desires.

2: WITHOUT EXPENSE = FREE (OF CHARGE)

1 Co 9	18	my reward . . . is this: to be able to offer the Good News 3 *free*,

4. EXPENSE: *OPS-ŌNION*

ops-ōnion 1/4

1 Co 9	7	No one ever ⌐*paid money* to stay (or: at his own *expense* stayed) in the army,

5. SPEND: *PROS-AN-(H)ALISKŌ*

pros-an-(h)aliskō 1

Lk 8	43	a woman . . . whom no one had been able to cure (ᵛ though she had *spent* all she had on doctors).

PREPARE – READY

1. Prepare – Ready – Make ready: *hetoimazō*
1: (A person, an angel, is) Ready, Prepared (to) – Make ready (to)
2: Prepare, Make ready (a banquet, the Passover) – Make preparations (for)
3: Prepare (a way)

4: Prepare (generally) – Ready
2. Prepare – Ready – Preparation Day: *skeuazō*
1: Prepare – (Get, Be) Ready
2: Preparation Day – Day of Preparation
3. (Be) Ready, (Be) Ripe: ⌐*para-didōmi*

1. PREPARE – READY – MAKE READY: *HETOIMAZŌ*

5	*hetoimasia 1*	3	*hetoimōs 3*
1	*hetoimazō 41*	4	*pro-hetoimazō 2*
2	*hetoimos 17*		

1: (A PERSON, AN ANGEL, IS) READY, PREPARED (TO) – MAKE READY (TO)

Mt 24	44	2 you too must stand *ready* because the Son of Man is coming at an hour you do not expect.
25 10 <	2	Those who were *ready* went in with [the bridegroom] to the wedding hall
Lk 12	40	2 You too must stand *ready*, because the Son of Man is coming at an hour you do not expect.
22	33	2 Lord, . . . I would be *ready* to go to prison with you, and to death.
Ac 21	13	3 I am *ready* not only to be tied up but even to die
23	15	2 we, on our side, are *prepared* to dispose of [Paul]
	21	2 They are *ready* now and only waiting for your order to be given.
	23	*Get* two hundred soldiers *ready* to leave for Caesarea
2 Co 10	6	2 we are *prepared* to punish any disobedience.
12	14	3 I am [all] *prepared* now to come to you for the third time,
Ep 6	15	[stand your ground,] wearing for shoes on your feet the 5 ⌐*eagerness* (lit. *readiness*) to spread the gospel of peace
2 Tm 2	21	an athlete . . . cannot win any crown unless he has [kept] *ready* all the rules of the contest;
Tt 3	1	2 Remind them that it is their duty to . . . be *ready* to do good at every opportunity;
1 P 3	15	2 always have your answer *ready* for people who ask you the reason for the hope that you all have.
4 5 X	3	the judge who is *ready* to judge the living and the dead.
Rv 8	6	The seven angels that had the seven trumpets now *made ready* to sound them.
9	15	These four angels had been *put* [there] *ready* for this hour
19	7	[The Lamb's] bride is *ready*,
21	2	I saw . . . the new Jerusalem . . , as beautiful as a bride all dressed and *ready* for her husband.

2: PREPARE, MAKE READY (A BANQUET, THE PASSOVER) – MAKE PREPARATIONS (FOR)

Mt 22 4 <		I have my banquet all *prepared*, my oxen and fattened cattle 2 have been slaughtered, everything is *ready*. Come to the wedding.
8 <	2	The wedding is *ready*;
26	17	Where do you want us to *make the preparations* for you to eat the passover?
	19	The disciples . . . *prepared* the Passover.
Mk 14	12	Where do you want us to go and *make the preparations* for you to eat the passover?

Mk 14 15   2/ He will show you a large upper room . . , all *prepared. Make*
                the preparations for us there.
      16   The disciples . . . *prepared* the Passover.
Lk 14 17 < 2 Come along: everything is *ready* now.
   17 8   ᵣGet my supper laid (lit. *Get my supper ready*);
   22 8   Go and *make the preparations* for us to eat the passover.
       9   Where do you want us to *prepare* it?
      12   The man will show you a large upper room . . . *Make the*
                preparations there. ¹³ They set off and . . . *prepared* the
                Passover.

3: PREPARE (A WAY)

Mt 3 3   (Is 40 3) *Prepare* a way for the Lord,
Mk 1 3   (Is 40 3) *Prepare* a way for the Lord,
Lk 1 76   you, little child, . . . will go before the Lord to *prepare* the
                way for him.
    3 4   (Is 40 3) *Prepare* a way for the Lord,
Rv 16 12   so that a way was *made* for the kings of the East

4: PREPARE (GENERALLY) – READY

Mt 20 23   seats at my right hand . . . belong to those ᵣto whom they
        Θ   have been allotted (lit. for whom they have been *prepared*)
                by my Father.
   25 34 Θ   the kingdom *prepared* for you since the foundation of the
                world.
      41 Θ   the eternal fire *prepared* for the devil and his angels.
Mk 10 40   seats at my right hand . . . belong to those ᵣto whom they
        Θ   have been allotted (lit. for whom they have been *prepared*).
   15 1   the chief priests . . . had their plan *ready*.
Lk 1 17   [John] will go before him . . , *preparing* for the Lord a
                people fit for him.
    2 31 Θ   the salvation which you have *prepared* for all the nations to
                see,
    9 52   [Jesus] sent messengers ahead . . . to *make preparations* for
                him,
   12 20   this hoard ᵣof yours (lit. you have *prepared*), whose will it be
                then?
      47 <   The servant who . . . has not even ᵣstarted (lit. *prepared*)
                to carry out [his master's] wishes,
   23 56   [the women] *prepared* spices and ointments.
   24 1   they went to the tomb with the spices they had *prepared*.
Jn 7 6   2 any time is ᵣthe right time (lit. a time *prepared*) for you.
   14 2 X   I am going now to *prepare* a place for you,
       3 X   after I have gone and *prepared* you a place,
Rm 9 23 Θ   4 people he had *prepared* for this glory long ago.
1 Co 2 9 Θ   all that God has *prepared* for those who love him.
2 Co 9 5   to . . . make sure in advance that the gift you promised is
             2 all *ready*,
   10 16   2 not boasting of the work *already* done.
Ep 2 10   We are . . . created . . . to live the good life ᵣas from the
        Θ   4 beginning (lit. *prepared from the beginning* as) he had meant
                us to live it.
Phm   22   will you *get* a place *ready* for me to stay in?
Heb 11 16 Θ   God . . . has ᵣfounded (lit. *prepared*) the city for them.
1 P 1 5   2 the salvation [which has been] *prepared* is revealed at the end
                of time.
Rv 9 7   these locusts were like horses ᵣarmoured (lit. *prepared*) for
                battle;
   12 6 Θ   the woman escaped into the desert, where God had *made* a
                place of safety *ready*,

2. PREPARE – READY – PREPARATION DAY: *SKEUAZŌ*

           1 *kata-skeuazō*   6/11   3 *para-skeuazō*   4
           4 *epi-skeuazomai*   1   2 *para-skeuē*   6
                                       5 *a-para-skeuastos 1*

1: PREPARE – (GET, BE) READY

Mt 11 10   (Ml 3 1) my messenger . . . will *prepare* your way before you.
Mk 1 2   (Ml 3 1) my messenger . . . will *prepare* your way.
Lk 1 17   [John] will go before him . . , preparing for the Lord a
                people ᵣfit (or: *ready*) for him.
    7 27   (Ml 3 1) my messenger . . . will *prepare* the way before you.
Ac 10 10   3 [Peter] was looking forward to his meal, but before it *was*
                ready he fell into a trance
   21 15   4 we ᵣpacked (lit. *got ready*) and went on up to Jerusalem.
1 Co 14 8   if no one can be sure which call the trumpet has sounded, who
             3 will *be ready* for the attack?
2 Co 9 2   3 Achaia has *been ready* since last year.
       3   3 to make sure . . . that you really *are ready*

2 Co 9 4   5 If some of the Macedonians . . . found you *unprepared*,
Heb 9 2   ᵣThere was a tent (lit. A tent was *prepared*) which comprised
                two compartments:
       6   ᵣUnder these provisions (lit. With everything *prepared* like
                this), priests [enter] the outer tent

2: PREPARATION DAY – DAY OF PREPARATION

Mt 27 62   2 Next day, . . . when *Preparation* [Day] was over,
Mk 15 42   2 it was *Preparation* [Day] (that is, the vigil of the sabbath),
Lk 23 54   2 It was *Preparation* Day
Jn 19 14   2 It was Passover *Preparation* [Day],
      31   2 It was *Preparation* [Day],
      42   2 Since it was the Jewish [Day of] *Preparation* . . , they laid
                Jesus [in the tomb].

3. (BE) READY, (BE) RIPE: *PARA-DIDŌMI*

para-didōmi 1/119

Mk 4 29   when the crop *is ready* [a man] starts to reap because the
                harvest has come.

PRESS – INSIST

1. **Press down:** *piezō*
2. **Press (upon), Hem in:** *syn-echō*
3. **(Be) Wedged in, Stuck fast:** *ereidō*
4. **Press (round, on):** *syn-thlibō*
5. **Press (round, in, on) – Insist:** *epi-keimai*
6. **Press upon – Insist:** *eph-istēmi*
7. **Insist:** *di-ischyrizomai*

1. PRESS DOWN: *PIEZŌ*

piezō 1

Lk 6 38   a full measure, *pressed down*, shaken together, and running
                over, will be poured into your lap;

2. PRESS (UPON), HEM IN: *SYN-ECHŌ*

syn-echō 2/12

Lk 8 45   Master, it is the crowds ᵣround you, pushing (lit. *hemming*
                you *in* and pressing on you).
   19 43   [Jerusalem,] your enemies . . . will encircle you and *hem*
                you *in* on every side;

3. (BE) WEDGED IN, STUCK FAST: *EREIDŌ*

ereidō 1

Ac 27 41   The bows were *wedged in* and stuck fast,

4. PRESS (ROUND, ON): *SYN-THLIBŌ*

           2 *thlibō 2/10*   3 *apo-thlibō 1*
           1 *syn-thlibō 2*

Mt 7 14   2 it is a narrow gate and a hard (or: *narrow*) road that leads
                to life,
Mk 3 9   2 to keep [Jesus] from being *crushed* [by the crowd].
    5 24   a large crowd followed [Jesus]; they were *pressing all round*
                him.
      31   You see how the crowd is *pressing round* you and yet you
                say, 'Who touched me?'
Lk 8 45   Master, it is the crowds ᵣround you, pushing (lit. *hemming*
             3 you *in* and *pressing on* you).

5. PRESS (ROUND, IN, ON) – INSIST: *EPI-KEIMAI*

epi-keimai 3/7

Lk 5 1   with the crowd *pressing round* [Jesus] listening to the word
                of God,

Lk 23 23	But they kept on ⌐shouting (lit. *insisting*) at the top of their voices, demanding that he should be crucified.
Ac 27 20	the storm ⌐raged (lit. *pressed upon* us) unabated

6. PRESS UPON – INSIST: *EPH-ISTĒMI*

1 *eph-istēmi* 1/21   2 *epi-stasis* 1/2

2 Co 11 28 Δ	2 ⌐my daily preoccupation (lit. the daily *pressure upon* me): my anxiety for all the churches.
2 Tm 4 2	proclaim the message and, welcome or unwelcome, *insist* on it.

7. INSIST: *DI-ISCHYRIZOMAI*

1 *di-ischyrizomai* 2   2 *ep-ischyō* 1

Lk 22 59	another man *insisted*, saying, 'This fellow was certainly with him.'
23 5	2 But they ⌐persisted (lit. *insisted*), 'He is inflaming the people'
Ac 12 15	but [Rhoda] *insisted* that it was true [that it was Peter knocking].

PREVENT – HINDER – STRAIN

1. Prevent, Stop – Oppose, Hinder – Forbid, Refuse: *kōluō*	**2. Prevent – Obstruct, Keep from – Hinder, Obstacle:** *en-koptō*
1: Prevent, Stop – Oppose, Hinder – Forbid	**3. Thing that hinders, Encumbrance:** *onkos*
2: Refuse, Withold – Forbid	**4. Strain out, Strain off:** *di-(h)ylizō*

1. PREVENT, STOP – OPPOSE, HINDER – FORBID, REFUSE: *KŌLUŌ*

1 *kōluō*   23   3 *dia-kōluō* 1
2 *a-kōlytōs* 1

1: PREVENT, STOP – OPPOSE, HINDER – FORBID

Mt 3 14	3 [Jesus came to John for baptism.] John tried to *dissuade* him.
19 14	Let the little children alone, and do not *stop* them coming to me;
Mk 9 38	we saw a man who is not one of us casting out devils in your name; and . . . we tried to *stop* him. 39 But Jesus said, 'You must not *stop* him'
39	
10 14	Let the little children come to me; do not *stop* them;
Lk 9 49	we saw a man casting out devils in your name, and . . . we tried to *stop* him. 50 But Jesus said . . , 'You must not *stop* him'
50	
11 52	you lawyers . . . have *prevented* others going in who wanted to.
18 16	Let the little children come to me, and do not *stop* them;
23 2	We found [Jesus] . . . *opposing* payment of the tribute to Caesar.
Ac 8 36	the eunuch said, '. . . is there anything to *stop* me being baptised?'
11 17	who was I to *stand in God's way*?
16 6 ⓢ	[Paul and Timothy] travelled through Phrygia . . . having been ⌐told by the Holy Spirit *not to* preach (or: *prevented* by the Holy Spirit from preaching) the word in Asia.
24 23	[Felix] gave orders . . . that none of [Paul's] own people should be *prevented* from seeing to his needs.
27 43	[The soldiers planned to kill the prisoners.] But the centurion . . . *would not let* them do what they intended.
28 31	[Paul spent the two years] teaching the truth . . . without 2 *hindrance* from anyone.
Rm 1 13	I have often planned to visit you – though until now I have always been *prevented* –
1 Co 14 39	by all means be ambitious to prophesy, do not *suppress* the gift of tongues;
1 Th 2 16	[the Jews] are *hindering* us from preaching to the pagans
1 Tm 4 3	[false teachers] will say marriage is *forbidden*,
Heb 7 23	there used to be a great number of those other priests, because death *put an end* to each one of them;
2 P 2 16	The dumb donkey *put a stop* to that prophet's madness
3 Jn 10	[Diotrephes] *prevents* the other people who would have liked to [welcome our brothers] from doing it,

2: REFUSE, WITHOLD – FORBID

Lk 6 29	to the man who takes your cloak from you, do not *refuse* your tunic.
Ac 10 47	Could anyone *refuse* the water of baptism to these people, now they have received the Holy Spirit . . .?

2. PREVENT – OBSTRUCT, KEEP FROM – HINDER, OBSTACLE: *EN-KOPTŌ*

2 *en-kopē* 1
1 *en-koptō* 5

Ac 24 4	I do not want to ⌐*take up too much* of your *time* (or: *be a hindrance* to you),
Rm 15 22	That is the reason why I have been *kept from* visiting you so long,
1 Co 9 12	2 we have put up with anything rather than *obstruct* the Good News of Christ in any way.
Ga 5 7	who ⌐*made you less anxious to* obey (or: *hindered* you from obeying) the truth?
1 Th 2 18 ⓓ	we tried hard to . . . visit you . . . but Satan *prevented* us.
1 P 3 7	This will stop anything from *coming in the way of* your prayers.

3. THING THAT HINDERS, ENCUMBRANCE: *ONKOS*

onkos 1

Heb 12 1	we too, then, should throw off every*thing that hinders* us, especially . . . sin

4. STRAIN OUT, STRAIN OFF: *DI-(H)YLIZŌ*

di-(h)ylizō 1

Mt 23 24	You blind guides! *Straining out* gnats and swallowing camels!

PRIEST

1: the Chief Priests, High Priest	
2: a Priest, the Priest	orders – (Jesus as) High Priest
3: the Priesthood of the old and new	4: the Priesthood of the new order
	5: the Priest(s) of Zeus

4 *hierateia*	2	8 *hier-ourgeō* 1	
5 *hierateuma*	2	3 *hierōsynē* 3	
6 *hierateuō*	1	9 *arch-(h)ieratikos* 1	
2 *hiereus*	32	1 *arch-(h)iereus* 122	
7 *hieros*	1/2		

1: THE CHIEF PRIESTS, HIGH PRIEST

Abiathar 1 (Mk 2)		*Alexander** 1 ⎫	
Ananias 2 (Ac 23; 24)		*John** 1 ⎬(Ac 4)	
Annas 4 (Lk 3; Jn 18; Ac 4)		*Jonathan** 1 ⎭	
C *Caiaphas* 9			
Sceva 1 (Ac 19)			

E = Chief priests and elders   S = Chief priests and scribes

Mt 2 4 S	[Herod] called together all the *chief priests* and the scribes
16 21 E S	Jesus . . . was destined to . . . suffer grievously at the hands of the elders and *chief priests* and scribes,
20 18 S	the Son of Man is about to be handed over to the *chief priests* and scribes.
21 15 S	the *chief priests* and the scribes were indignant.
23 E	the *chief priests* and the elders . . . came to [Jesus]
45	the *chief priests* and the Pharisees realised [Jesus] was speaking about them,
26 3 E C	the *chief priests* and the elders . . . assembled in the palace of the *high priest*, whose name was *Caiaphas*,
14	Judas Iscariot went to the *chief priests*
47 E	a large number of men armed with swords and clubs, sent by the *chief priests* and elders
51 C	one of the followers of Jesus . . . struck out at the *high priest's* servant,

Mt 26	57 C S E	The men who had arrested Jesus led him off to *Caiaphas* the *high priest*, where the scribes and the elders were assembled.
	58 C	Peter followed him at a distance, and when he reached the *high priest's* palace, he went in
	59	The *chief priests* and the whole Sanhedrin were looking for evidence against Jesus,
	62 C	The *high priest* then . . . said to [Jesus], 'Have you no answer to that?'
	63 C	the *high priest* said to him, 'I put you on your oath . . . to tell us if you are the Christ,'
	65 C	the *high priest* tore his clothes
27	1 E	all the *chief priests* and the elders . . . met in council to bring about the death of Jesus.
	3 E	Judas . . . took the thirty silver pieces back to the *chief priests* and elders.
	6	The *chief priests* picked up the silver pieces
	12 E	when [Jesus] was accused by the *chief priests* and elders he refused to answer
	20 E	the *chief priests* and the elders . . . had persuaded the crowd to demand the release of Barabbas
	41 S E	The *chief priests* with the scribes and elders mocked him
	62	the *chief priests* and the Pharisees went in a body to Pilate
28	11 E	some of the guard went off . . . to tell the *chief priests* all that had happened.
Mk 2	26	[David] went into the house of God when *Abiathar* was *high priest*, and ate the loaves of offering
8	31 E S	the Son of Man was destined to . . . be rejected by the elders and the *chief priests* and the scribes,
10	33 S	the Son of Man is about to be handed over to the *chief priests* and the scribes.
11	18 S	This came to the ears of the *chief priests* and the scribes,
	27 S E	the *chief priests* and the scribes and the elders came to him,
14	1 S	the *chief priests* and the scribes were looking for a way to arrest Jesus
	10	Judas . . . approached the *chief priests* with an offer to hand Jesus over to them.
	43 S E	Judas . . . came up with a number of men . . . sent by the *chief priests* and the scribes and the elders.
	47 C	one of the bystanders . . . struck out at the *high priest's* servant,
	53 E S C	They led Jesus off to the *high priest*; and all the *chief priests* and the elders and the scribes assembled there.
	54 C	Peter had followed him . . . right into the *high priest's* palace,
	55	The *chief priests* and the whole Sanhedrin were looking for evidence against Jesus
	60 C	The *high priest* then stood up before the whole assembly and put this question to Jesus,
	61 C	The *high priest* put a second question to him, 'Are you the Christ . . .?' ⁶² 'I am,' said Jesus . . . ⁶³ The *high priest* tore his robes,
	63 C	
	66 C	one of the *high priest's* servant-girls came up.
15	1 E S	First thing in the morning, the *chief priests* together with the elders and scribes . . . had their plan ready
	3	the *chief priests* brought many accusations against him.
	10	[Pilate] realised it was out of jealousy that the *chief priests* had handed Jesus over.
	11	The *chief priests* . . . had incited the crowd to demand . . . Barabbas
	31 S	The *chief priests* and the scribes mocked him
Lk 3	2 C	during the pontificate of *Annas* and *Caiaphas*, the word of God came to John
9	22 E S	The Son of Man . . . is destined to . . . be rejected by the elders and *chief priests* and scribes
19	47 S	The *chief priests* and the scribes . . . tried to do away with him,
20	1 S E	in the Temple . . . the (ᵛchief) *priests* and the scribes came up, together with the elders,
	19 S	the scribes and the *chief priests* would have liked to lay hands on him
22	2 S	the *chief priests* and the scribes were looking for some way of doing away with him,
	4	[Judas] went to the *chief priests* and the officers of the guard to discuss a scheme for handing Jesus over to them.
	50 C	one of [Jesus's] followers struck out at the *high priest's* servant,
	52 E	Jesus spoke to the *chief priests* and captains of the Temple guard and elders who had come for him.
	54 C	they took him to the *high priest's* house.
	66 E S	there was a meeting of the elders . . , attended by the *chief priests* and scribes.
23	4	Pilate then said to the *chief priests* and the crowd,
	10 S	the *chief priests* and scribes were [at Herod's palace], violently pressing their accusations.
	13	Pilate then summoned the *chief priests* and the leading men and the people.
24	20	our *chief priests* and our leader handed him over

Jn 7	32	the *chief priests* and the Pharisees sent the Temple police to arrest him.
	45	The police went back to the *chief priests* and Pharisees
11	47	the *chief priests* and Pharisees called a meeting.
	49 C	*Caiaphas*, the *high priest* that year, said, '. . . ⁵⁰ . . . it is better for one man to die for the people,' . . . ⁵¹ . . . it was as *high priest* that he made this prophecy.
	51 C	
	57	The *chief priests* and Pharisees had by now given their orders:
12	10	the *chief priests* decided to kill Lazarus as well,
18	3	a detachment of guards sent by the *chief priests* and the Pharisees,
	10 C	Simon Peter . . . wounded the *high priest's* servant,
	13 C	They took [Jesus] first to *Annas*, because [Annas] was the father-in-law of *Caiaphas*, who was *high priest* that year.
	14 C	¹⁴ It was *Caiaphas* who had suggested to the Jews, 'It is better for one man to die'
	15 C	This disciple, who was known to the *high priest*, went with Jesus into the *high priest's* palace,
	16 C	the other disciple, the one known to the *high priest*, went out,
	19 C	the *high priest* questioned Jesus about his disciples and his teaching.
	22 C	Is that the way to answer the *high priest*?
	24 C	Then *Annas* sent him . . . to *Caiaphas* the *high priest*.
	26 C	One of the *high priest's* servants . . . said,
	28 C	They then led Jesus from the house of *Caiaphas* to the Praetorium.
	35	It is your own people and the *chief priests* who have handed you over to me:
19	6	the *chief priests* and the guards shouted, 'Crucify him!'
	15	The *chief priests* answered, 'We have no king except Caesar'.
	21	the Jewish *chief priests* said to Pilate, 'You should not write "King of the Jews"',
Ac 4	6 C E S 9	[the rulers, elders and scribes had a meeting] with *Annas* the *high priest*, *Caiaphas*, ᵛ Jonathan* (G John*), Alexander* and all the members of the *high-priestly* families.
	23 E	[the apostles] went to the community and told them everything the *chief priests* and elders had said
5	17	Then the *high priest* intervened with all his supporters
	21	When the *high priest* arrived, he and his supporters convened the Sanhedrin
	24	the *high priest* demanded an explanation [from the apostles].
7	1	The *high priest* asked [Stephen], 'Is this true?'
9	1	Saul . . . had gone to the *high priest*
	14	[Saul] holds a warrant from the *chief priests*
	21	for the sole purpose of arresting [the people who invoke this name] to have them tried by the *chief priests*?
19	14	seven sons of *Sceva*, a Jewish *chief priest*.
22	5 E	[I even persecuted this Way to the death,] as the *high priest* and the whole council of elders can testify,
	30	[the tribune] gave orders for a meeting of the *chief priests* and the entire Sanhedrin;
23	2	At this the *high priest Ananias* ordered his attendants to strike [Paul] on the mouth.
	4	The attendants said, 'It is God's *high priest* you are insulting!'
	5	⁵ Paul answered, 'Brothers, I did not realise it was the *high priest*,'
24	14 E	[the Jews] went to the *chief priests* and elders,
	1 E	the *high priest Ananias* came down with some of the elders and an advocate.
25	2	The *chief priests* and leaders of the Jews informed [Festus] of the case against Paul,
	15 E	the *chief priests* and elders of the Jews laid information against [Paul],
26	10	I myself threw many of the saints into prison, acting on authority from the *chief priests*,
	12	I was going to Damascus, armed with full powers . . . from the *chief priests*,

2: A PRIEST, THE PRIEST
Abijah 1 (Lk 1 5)

Mt 8	4 2	Jesus said to [the leper], '. . . go and show yourself to the *priest*
12	4 2	[Have you not read] how [David] . . . ate the loaves of offering . . . which were for the *priests* alone?
	5 2	have you not read . . . that on the sabbath day the Temple *priests* break the sabbath without being blamed for it?
Mk 1	44 2	[Jesus ordered the leper,] '. . . go and show yourself to the *priest*,'
2	26 2	[David] ate the loaves of offering which only the *priests* are allowed to eat,
Lk 1	5 2	In the days of King Herod of Judaea there lived a *priest* called Zechariah who belonged to the *Abijah* section of the priesthood, and he had a wife . . . who was a descendant of Aaron.

Lk 1 8 6 Zechariah . . . was *exercising his priestly office* before God
   9 4 [9] when it fell to him by lot, as the *ritual* custom was, to enter the Lord's sanctuary
5 14 2 [Jesus] ordered [the leper] . . , '. . . show yourself to the *priest*'
6 4 2 [So you have not read] how [David] . . . took the loaves of offering . . . which only the *priests* are allowed to eat?
10 31 2 a *priest* happened to be travelling down the same road, but when he saw the man, he passed by
17 14 2 [Jesus] said [to the ten lepers], 'Go and show yourselves to the *priest*'.
20 1 2 the ([v] chief) *priests* and the scribes came up, together with the elders,
Jn 1 19 2 the Jews sent *priests* and Levites from Jerusalem
Ac 4 1 2 the *priests* came up to [Peter and John], accompanied by the captain of the Temple and the Sadducees.
6 7 2 a large group of *priests* made their submission to the faith.
1 Co 9 13 7 Remember that the ministers *serving* [in the Temple] get their food from the Temple

3: THE PRIESTHOOD OF THE OLD AND NEW ORDERS – (JESUS AS) HIGH PRIEST

M *Melchizedek* 9

L = the Levitical priesthood

Heb 2 17 It was essential that [Jesus] should . . . become completely like his brothers so that he could be a compassionate and
   X trustworthy *high priest* of God's religion, able to atone for human sins.
3 1·X Jesus, the apostle and the *high priest* of our religion.
4 14 X in Jesus, the Son of God, we have the supreme *high priest*
  15 who has gone through to the highest heaven, . . . [15] . . .
  X it is not as if we had a *high priest* who was incapable of feeling our weaknesses with us;
5 1 L Every *high priest* . . . is appointed to act for men in their relations with God,
5 X Nor did Christ give himself the glory of becoming *high priest*, but he had it from [his Father],
6 X M 2 (Ps 110 4) You are a *priest* of the order of *Melchizedek*,
10 X [the Son] was acclaimed by God with the title of *high priest*
  M of the order of *Melchizedek*.
6 20 X where Jesus has entered before us . . , to become a *high*
  M *priest* of the order of *Melchizedek*,
7 1 M 2 *Melchizedek*, king of Salem, a *priest* of God Most High,
3 went to meet Abraham . . . [3] . . . he is like the Son of
  M 2 God. He remains a *priest* for ever.
5 L 4 any of the descendants of Levi who are admitted to the *priesthood* are obliged by the Law to take tithes from the people,
10 M when *Melchizedek* came to meet [Abraham].
11 L 3 if perfection had been reached through the levitical *priesthood* . . , why was it still necessary for a new *priesthood*
  X 2 to arise, one of the same order as *Melchizedek* not counted
  M as being of the same order as Aaron? [12] But any change in
12 the *priesthood* must mean a change in the Law as well.
  L 3
14 [our Lord] came from Judah, a tribe which Moses did not
  L 2 even mention when dealing with *priests*.
15 X M 2 a second *Melchizedek* who is *priest* [16] not by virtue of a law about physical descent,
17 X M 2 You are a *priest* of the order of *Melchizedek*,
20 L 2 The others . . . were made *priests* without any oath; [21] but
21 he with an oath sworn by the one who declared to him:
  X 2 . . . you are a *priest*, and for ever, [v] of the order of
  M *Melchizedek*.
23 L 2 there used to be a great number of those other *priests*,
24 because death put an end to each one of them; [24] but this
  X 3 one, because he remains for ever, can never lose his *priesthood*.
26 X To suit us, the ideal *high priest* would have to be holy, . . .
27 and raised up above the heavens; [27] one who would not
  L need to offer sacrifices every day, as the other *high priests* do for their own sins
28 L The Law appoints *high priests* who are men subject to weakness;
8 1 X we have a *high priest* [who is made perfect for ever].
3 L X It is the duty of every *high priest* to offer gifts and sacrifices,
4 X 2 if he were on earth, he would not be a *priest* at all,
9 6 L 2 *priests* are constantly going into the outer tent . . . [7] but the
7 second tent is entered only once a year, and then only by the
  L *high priest*
11 X now Christ has come, as the *high priest* of all the blessings which were to come. . . . [12] and he has entered the sanctuary once and for all,
25 he does not have to offer himself again and again, like the
  L *high priest* going into the sanctuary year after year
10 11 L 2 All the *priests* stand at their duties every day, offering over and over again the same sacrifices . . . [12] He, on the other hand, has offered one single sacrifice

Heb 10 21 X 2 we have the supreme *high priest* over all the house of God.
13 11 The bodies of the animals whose blood is brought into the
  L sanctuary by the *high priest*

4: THE PRIESTHOOD OF THE NEW ORDER

Rm 15 16 He has appointed me as a priest of Jesus Christ, and I am to
8 *carry out* my *priestly duty* by bringing the Good News from God to the pagans,
1 P 2 5 5 so that you too, the holy *priesthood* that offers the spiritual sacrifices which Jesus Christ has made acceptable to God, may be living stones making a spiritual house.
9 5 you are . . . a royal *priesthood*, . . . a people set apart to sing the praises of God
Rv 1 6 2 [Jesus Christ] made us a line of kings, *priests* to serve his God and Father;
5 10 [you bought men for God of every race] and made them a
2 line of kings and *priests*, to . . . rule the world.
20 6 2 [those who refused to worship the beast] will be *priests* of God and of Christ and reign with them

5: THE PRIEST(S) OF ZEUS

Ac 14 13 2 The [v] *priests* (G *priest*) of Zeus-outside-the-Gate . . . brought garlanded oxen to the gates.

PROMISE – VOW – OATH

---

1. **Promise:** *ep-angelia*
  1: Promise (in religious senses)
  2: Promise (generally)
2. **Promise, Pledge:** *pistis*
3. **Vow:** *euchē*
4. **Vow, Bind by oath – Votive offerings:** *ana-thematizō*
5. **Oath – Adjure:** *horkos*
	1: (God's) Oath
	2: Oath (generally)
	3: Break an oath – Perjurer
	4: Adjure, Put on oath – Exorcist(s)
	6. **Swear:** *omnuō*
	  1: (God) Swears
	  2: Swear (generally)

1. PROMISE: *EP-ANGELIA*

1	*ep-angelia*	52	3 *ep-angelma*	2
2	*ep-angellomai*	13/15	4 *pro-ep-angellō*	2

1: PROMISE (IN RELIGIOUS SENSES) – (GOD) MAKES A PROMISE

Lk 24 49 I am sending down to you what the Father has *promised*.
Ac 1 4 [Jesus] had told [the apostles] not to leave Jerusalem, but to wait there for what the Father had *promised*.
2 33 [Jesus] has received from the Father the Holy Spirit, who was *promised*,
39 The *promise* [that was made] is for you and your children, and for all those who are far away,
7 5 2 God . . . *promised* to give [this land] to [Abraham]
17 the time drew near for God to fulfil the *promise* he had solemnly made to Abraham,
13 23 To keep his *promise*, God has raised up for Israel . . . Jesus, as Saviour,
32 It was to our ancestors that God made the *promise* but [33] it is to us . . . that he has fulfilled it,
26 6 it is for my hope in the *promise* made by God to our ancestors that I am on trial,
Rm 1 2 4 the Good News that God *promised long ago* through his prophets
4 13 The *promise* of inheriting the world was not made to Abraham and his descendants on account of any law but on account of the righteousness which consists in faith. [14] If the world
14 is only to be inherited by those who submit to the Law, then faith is pointless and the *promise* worth nothing.
16 what fulfils the *promise* depends on faith,
20 Since God had *promised* it, Abraham refused to . . . doubt it,
21 . . . [21] convinced that God had power to do what he had
2 *promised*.
9 4 the *promises* were made to [my brothers of Israel].

Rm	9	8	it is only the children of the *promise* who will count as the true descendants [of Abraham]. [9] The actual words in which the *promise* was made were:
		9	
	15	8	so that God could faithfully carry out the *promises* made to the patriarchs,
2Co	1	20	however many the *promises* God made, the Yes to them all is in [Jesus].
	7	1	With *promises* like these made to us, . . . let us wash off all that can soil either body or spirit,
Ga	3	14	so that through faith we might receive the *promised* Spirit.
		16	the *promises* were addressed to Abraham and to . . . his posterity, which is Christ.
		17	no law . . . could . . . make the *promise* meaningless.
		18	it was precisely in the form of a *promise* that God made his gift to Abraham.
		19	2 until the posterity came to whom the *promise* was addressed.
		21	Does this mean that there is opposition between the Law and the *promises* of God?
		22	the *promise* can only be given through faith in Jesus Christ.
		29	you are the posterity of Abraham, the heirs he was *promised*.
	4	23	the child of the free woman was born as the result of a *promise*,
		28	you, . . . like Isaac, are children of the *promise*,
Ep	1	13	you too have been stamped with the seal of the Holy Spirit of the *Promise*.
	2	12	you . . . were . . . aliens with no part in the covenants with their *Promise*;
	3	6	the same *promise* has been made to [pagans], in Christ Jesus, through the gospel.
	6	2	The first commandment that has a *promise* attached to it is: Honour your father and mother
1Tm	4	8	the usefulness of spirituality is unlimited, since it [r]holds out the reward of (lit. *promises*) life here and now
2Tm	1	1	Paul . . . an apostle of Christ Jesus in his design to *promise* life in Christ Jesus;
Tt	1	2	2 to give them the hope of the eternal life that was *promised* so long ago by God.
Heb	4	1	the *promise* of reaching the place of rest · . . still holds good,
	6	12	those who have the faith and the perseverance to inherit the *promises*.
		13	2 When God *made the promise* to Abraham, he swore by his own self,
		15	Abraham persevered and saw the *promise* fulfilled.
		17	God wanted to make the heirs to the *promise* thoroughly realise that his purpose was unalterable,
	7	6	[Melchizedek] gave his blessing to [Abraham] the holder of the *promises*.
	8	6	it is a better covenant of which [Christ] is the mediator, founded on better *promises*.
	9	15	so that the people who were called to an eternal inheritance may actually receive what was *promised*;
	10	23	2 the one who *made the promise* is faithful.
		36	You will need endurance to . . . gain what he has *promised*.
	11	9	By faith [Abraham] arrived . . . in the *Promised* Land, and lived there . . . with Isaac and Jacob, who were heirs with him of the same *promise*.
		11	2 Sarah . . . believed that he who had *made the promise* would be faithful to it.
		13	All these died in faith, before receiving any of the [things that had been] *promised*,
		17	[Abraham] offered to sacrifice his only son even though the *promises* had been made to him
		33	[Gideon, . . . Samuel and the prophets] were men who . . . did what was right and earned the *promises*.
		39	These are all heroes of faith, but they did not receive what was *promised*.
	12	26	2 [God] has *given* us this *promise*: I shall make the earth shake once more
Jm	1	12	2 the crown that the Lord has *promised* to those who love him.
	2	5	2 the kingdom which [God] *promised* to those who love him.
2P	1	4	3 [God] has [r]given us the guarantee of (lit. *promised* us) something very great and wonderful to come:
	3	4	they will make fun of the *promise* and ask, 'Well, where is this coming?'
		9	The Lord is not being slow to carry out his *promises*,
		13	3 What we are waiting for is what he *promised*:
1Jn	2	25	2/ what is *promised* to you by his own *promise* is eternal life.

2: PROMISE (GENERALLY)

Mk	14	11	2 [the chief priests] *promised* to give [Judas] money;
Ac	23	21	They are ready now and only waiting for your [r]order (lit. *promise*) to be given.
2Co	9	5	4 to . . . make sure in advance that the gift you *promised* is all ready,
Ga	3	18	If you inherit something as a legal right, it does not come to you as the result of a *promise*,
2P	2	19	2 They may *promise* freedom but they themselves are slaves,

2. PROMISE, PLEDGE: *PISTIS*

pistis 1/242

| 1Tm | 5 | 12 | people condemn [young widows] for being unfaithful to their original *promise*. |

3. VOW: *EUCHĒ*

euchē 2/3

| Ac | 18 | 18 | [Paul] had his hair cut off because of a *vow* he had made. |
| | 21 | 23 | We have four men here who are under a *vow*; |

4. VOW, BIND BY OATH – VOTIVE OFFERINGS: *ANA-THEMATIZŌ*

| 2 *ana-thema* 1/6 | 1 *ana-thematizō* 3/4 |
| 3 *ana-thēma* 1 | |

Lk	21	5	the Temple . . . was adorned with fine stonework and 3 *votive offerings*,
Ac	23	12	the Jews . . . *made a vow* not to eat or drink until they had killed Paul.
		14	they went to the chief priests . . . and told them, 'We have /2 [r]made (lit. *bound* ourselves *by oath* with) a solemn *vow*
		21	they have *vowed* not to eat or drink until they have got rid of him.

5. OATH – ADJURE: *HORKOS*

3	*horkizō*	2	5 *epi-*(h)*orkeō*	1
1	*horkos*	10	6 *epi-*(h)*orkos*	1
2	*hork-ōmosia*	4	7 *ex-*(h)*orkistēs*	1
4	*en-*(h)*orkizō*	1	8 *ex-*(h)*orkizō*	1

1: (GOD'S) OATH

Lk	1	73	[God remembers] the *oath* he swore to our father Abraham
Ac	2	30	[David] knew that God had sworn him an *oath* to make one of his descendants succeed him on the throne,
Heb	6	17	[God] conveyed this by an *oath*;
	7	20	2 this was not done without the taking of an *oath*. The others 2 . . . were made priests without any *oath*; [21] but he with
		21	2 an *oath* [sworn] by the one who declared to him (Ps 110 4): The Lord has sworn an oath
		28	2 the promise on *oath* . . . appointed the Son who is made perfect for ever.

2: OATH (GENERALLY)

Mt	5	33	(cf. Ps 50 14) You must . . . fulfil your *oaths* to the Lord.
	14	7	[Herod] promised on *oath* to give her anything she asked.
		9	. . . [9] The king was distressed but, thinking of the *oaths* he had sworn . . , he ordered [John the Baptist's head] to be given her,
	26	72	again, with an *oath*, [Peter] denied it, 'I do not know the man'.
Mk	6	26	thinking of the *oaths* he had sworn . . , [Herod] was reluctant to break his word to her.
Heb	6	16	between men, confirmation by an *oath* puts an end to all dispute.
Jm	5	12	do not swear by heaven or by the earth, or use any *oaths* at all.

3: BREAK AN OATH – PERJURER

| Mt | 5 | 33 | 5 (Lv 19 12) You must not *break* your *oath*, |
| 1Tm | 1 | 10 | [Laws are not framed for people who are good. On the contrary they are] 6 for liars and for *perjurers* |

4: ADJURE, PUT ON OATH – EXORCIST(S)

Mt	26	63	8 the high priest said to [Jesus], 'I *put* you *on oath* by the living God to tell us if you are the Christ, the Son of God'.
Mk	5	7	Ⓓ 3 Swear by God you will not (lit. I *adjure* you by God not to) torture me!'
Ac	19	13	7 some itinerant Jewish *exorcists* tried pronouncing the name of the Lord Jesus over people who were possessed by evil spirits; they used to say, 'I [r]command (or: *adjure*) you by the Jesus whose spokesman is Paul'.

1 Th 5 27 | 4 My orders (lit. I *adjure* you), in the Lord's name, . . . that this letter . . . be read to all the brothers.

6. SWEAR: *OMNUŌ*

1 $\begin{Bmatrix} omnumi \\ omnuō \end{Bmatrix}$ 26   2 *syn-ōmosia 1*

1: (GOD) SWEARS

Lk 1 73 | [God remembers] the oath he *swore* to our father Abraham
Ac 2 30 | [David] knew that God had *sworn* him an oath to make one of his descendants succeed him on the throne,
Heb 3 11 | (Ps 95 11) in anger, I *swore* that not one would reach the place of rest I had for them.
18 | Those he *swore* would never reach the place of rest
4 3 | (Ps 95 11) in anger, I *swore* that not one would reach the place of rest I had for them.
6 13 | God . . . *swore* by his own self, since it was impossible for him to *swear* by anyone greater:
7 21 | (Ps 110 4) The Lord has *sworn* [an oath] which he will never retract: you are a priest,

2: SWEAR (GENERALLY)

Mt 5 34 | do not *swear* at all, either by heaven, . . . [35] or by the earth, . . . or by Jerusalem, . . . [36] Do not *swear* by your own head either,
23 16 | Alas for you . . . who say, 'If a man *swears* by the Temple it has no force; but if a man *swears* by the gold of the Temple, he is bound'. . . . [18] Or else, 'If a man *swears* by
18 | the altar it has no force; but if a man *swears* by the offering that is on the altar, he is bound'. . . . [20] Therefore,
20 | when a man *swears* by the altar he is *swearing* by that and everything on it. [21] And when a man *swears* by the Temple
21 | he is *swearing* by that and by the One who dwells in it. [22] And when a man *swears* by heaven he is *swearing* by the
22 | throne of God and by the One who is seated there.
26 74 | Then [Peter] started calling down curses on himself and *swearing*. 'I do not know the man'.
Mk 6 23 | [Herod] *swore* [her an oath], 'I will give you anything you ask, even half my kingdom'.
14 71 | [Peter] started calling down curses on himself and *swearing* 'I do not know the man you speak of'.
Ac 23 13 | 2 There were more than forty who took part in this *conspiracy*,
Heb 6 16 | Men . . . *swear* [an oath] by something greater than themselves,
Jm 5 12 | do not *swear* by heaven or by the earth, or use any oaths at all.
Rv 10 6 | [the angel] *swore* by the One who lives for ever and ever,

---

PROPHET

1: (the Law and) the Prophets
2: the Prophets (of the Old Testament) – Prophecies
3: the Prophet Isaiah
4: (specific) Prophets (of the Old Testament)
5: (John the Baptist as) Prophet
6: The Prophet (expected as Messiah – Dt 18 15)
7: (Jesus as) Prophet
8: the (Christian) Prophets – Prophecy
9: (false) Prophet(s)
10: (the Cretan) Prophet [? Epimenedes of Knossos]

3 *pro-phēteia* 19   5   *pro-phētikos* 2
1 *pro-phētēs* 144   6   *pro-phētis* 2
2 *pro-phēteuo* 28   4 (*pseudo-*)*pro-phētēs* 11

A = Prophet//Apostle

1: (THE LAW AND) THE PROPHETS

Mt 5 17 | Do not imagine that I have come to abolish the Law or the *Prophets*.

Mt 7 12 | always treat others as you would like them to treat you; that is the meaning of the Law and the *Prophets*.
11 13 | 2/ it was towards John that all the *prophecies* of the *prophets* and of the Law were leading;
22 40 | On these two commandments hang the whole Law and the *Prophets* also.
Lk 16 16 | Up to the time of John it was the Law and the *Prophets*;
29 | They have Moses and the *prophets*, . . . let them listen to them.
31 | If they will not listen either to Moses or to the *prophets*,
24 25 | You foolish men! So slow to believe the full message of the *prophets*!
27 | starting with Moses and going through all the *prophets*, [Jesus] explained . . . the passages . . . that were about himself.
44 | everything written about me in the Law of Moses, and in the *Prophets* and in the Psalms, has to be fulfilled.
Jn 1 45 | We have found the one Moses wrote about in the Law, the one about whom the *prophets* wrote: he is Jesus son of Joseph, from Nazareth.
Ac 13 15 | After the lessons from the Law and the *Prophets* had been read,
27 | to fulfil the ʳprophecies (lit. words of the *prophets*) read on every sabbath.
24 14 | retaining my belief in all points of the Law and in what is written in the *prophets*;
26 22 | saying nothing more than what the *prophets* and Moses himself said would happen;
28 23 | [Paul] put his case to [the Roman Jews], . . . trying to persuade them about Jesus, arguing from the Law of Moses and the *prophets*.
Rm 3 21 | God's justice that was made known through the Law and the *Prophets*

2: THE PROPHETS (OF THE OLD TESTAMENT) – PROPHECIES

Zechariah 2 (Mt 23; Lk 11)   *Barachiah* 1* (Mt 23)

Mt 2 23 | In this way the words spoken through the *prophets* were to be fulfilled: He will be called a Nazarene.
5 12 | this is how they persecuted the *prophets* before you.
13 17 | many *prophets* and holy men longed to see what you see,
16 14 | ['Who do people say the Son of Man is?'] 'Some say . . . John the Baptist, . . . and others . . . one of the *prophets*'.
23 29 | You who build the sepulchres of the *prophets* . . . [30] saying,
30 | 'We would never have joined in shedding the blood of the *prophets*, had we lived in our fathers' day'. [31] So! . . . You
31 | are the sons of those who murdered the *prophets*!
35 | the blood of every holy man that has been shed . . , from . . . Abel the Holy to . . . *Zechariah* son of Barachiah*
37 | Jerusalem, you that kill the *prophets*
26 56 | all this happened to fulfil the *prophecies* in scripture
Mk 6 15 | [Jesus] is a prophet, like the *prophets* we used to have.
8 28 | ['Who do people say I am?'] 'John the Baptist, . . . others . . . one of the *prophets*.'
Lk 1 70 | as [God] proclaimed, by the mouth of his holy *prophets*
6 23 | This was the way their ancestors treated the *prophets*.
9 8 | [some people were saying that John had risen from the dead,] others that . . . one of the ancient *prophets* had come back to life.
19 | ['Who do the crowds say I am?'] 'John the Baptist; others . . . one of the ancient *prophets* come back to life'.
10 24 | many *prophets* and kings wanted to see what you see,
11 47 | you who build the tombs of the *prophets*, the men your ancestors killed!
49 A | I will send them *prophets* and apostles; some they will slaughter
50 | . . , [50] so that this generation will have to answer for
51 | every *prophet*'s blood that has been shed . . , [51] from . . . Abel to . . . *Zechariah*,
13 28 | when you see Abraham . . . and all the *prophets* in the kingdom of God,
34 | Jerusalem, you that kill the *prophets*
18 31 | everything that is written by the *prophets* about the Son of Man is to come true.
Jn 8 52 | Abraham is dead, and the *prophets* are dead, . . . [53] Are you
53 | greater than our father Abraham . . .? The *prophets* are dead too.
Ac 3 18 | God . . . said through all his *prophets* that his Christ would suffer.
21 | the universal restoration which God proclaimed, speaking through his holy *prophets*.
24 | all the *prophets* that have ever spoken, from Samuel onwards, have predicted these days.
25 | You are the heirs of the *prophets*, the heirs of the covenant God made with our ancestors
7 52 | Can you name a single *prophet* your ancestors never persecuted?

Ac 10 43   It is to [Jesus] that all the *prophets* bear this witness:

26 27   King Agrippa, do you believe in the *prophets*?

Rm 1 2   [the Good News that God] promised long ago through his *prophets* in the scriptures.

11 3   (1K 19 10) Lord, they have killed your *prophets* . . . and I [Elijah] only, remain,

16 26   [a mystery] now so clear that it must be broadcast to pagans everywhere . . . This is only what ⌜scripture has predicted 5 (lit. the *prophetic* writings say),

1Th 2 15   [the Jews,] the people who put the Lord to death, and the *prophets* too.

Heb 1 1   At various times . . . God spoke to our ancestors through the *prophets*;

11 32   There is not time for me to give an account of Gideon, . . . Samuel and the *prophets*.

Jm 5 10   For your example . . . in submitting with patience, take the *prophets* who spoke in the name of the Lord;

1 P 1 10   It was this salvation that the *prophets* were looking . . . for; 2 their *prophecies* were about the grace which was to come to you.

2 P 1 19   5 we have confirmation of what was said in *prophecies*;

20   3 the interpretation of scriptural *prophecy* is never a matter for

21   3 the individual. 21 Why? Because no *prophecy* ever came from man's initiative. When men spoke for God it was the Holy Spirit that moved them.

3 2   recalling to you what was said in the past by the holy
A   *prophets*

3: THE PROPHET ISAIAH
Isaiah 22

Mt 1 22   all this took place to fulfil the words spoken by the Lord through the *prophet* (Is 7 14): The virgin will conceive

3 3   [John the Baptist] was the man the *prophet Isaiah* spoke of when he said (Is 40 3): A voice cries

4 14   In this way the *prophecy* of *Isaiah* was to be fulfilled (Is 8 23f): 15 Land of Zebulon!

8 17   This was to fulfil the *prophecy* of *Isaiah* (Is 53 4): He took our sickness away

12 17   This was to fulfil the *prophecy* of *Isaiah* (Is 42 1f): 18 Here is my servant

13 14   3 this *prophecy* of *Isaiah* (Is 6 8f) is being fulfilled: You will listen and listen again, but not understand,

15 7   Hypocrites! It was you *Isaiah* meant when he so rightly 2 *prophesied* (Is 29 13): 8 This people honours me only with lip-service,

21 4   This took place to fulfil the *prophecy* (Zc 9 9; Is 62 11): 6 . . . Look, your king comes to you;

Mk 1 2   It is written in the book of the *prophet Isaiah* (Ml 3 1): Look, I am going to send my messenger . . . (Is 40 3): 3 A voice cries

7 6   2 It was of you hypocrites that *Isaiah* so rightly *prophesied* (Is 29 13): This people honours me only with lip-service,

Lk 3 4   as it is written in the book of the sayings of the *prophet Isaiah* (Is 40 3f): A voice cries

4 17   they handed [Jesus] the scroll of the *prophet Isaiah*. . . . he found the place where it is written (Is 61 1f): The Spirit of the Lord has been given to me,

Jn 1 23   I am, as *Isaiah prophesied* (Is 40 3): a voice that cries

6 45   It is written in the *prophets* (Is 54 13): They will all be taught by God,

12 38   this was to fulfil the words of the *prophet Isaiah* (Is 53 1): Lord, who could believe what we have heard said . . .?

39   as *Isaiah* says again (cf. Is 6 9–10): He has blinded their eyes,

41   *Isaiah* said this when he saw [Christ's] glory (cf. Is 6 1–6), and his words referred to Jesus.

Ac 7 48   as the *prophet* says (Is 66 1–2): 49 With heaven my throne

8 28   [the eunuch] was reading the *prophet Isaiah* (Is 53 7f) . . .

30   30 . . . Philip . . . heard him reading the *prophet Isaiah*

34   the eunuch . . . said, 'Tell me, is the *prophet* referring to himself . . .?'

28 25   How aptly the Holy Spirit spoke when he told your ancestors through the *prophet Isaiah* (Is 6 9f): 26 . . . You will hear and hear again but not understand,

Rm 9 27   Referring to Israel *Isaiah* had this to say (Is 10 22–23G): . . . only a remnant will be saved,

29   As *Isaiah* foretold (Is 1 9): Had the Lord of hosts not left us some descendants

10 16   As *Isaiah* says (Is 53 1): Lord, how many believed what we proclaimed?

20   *Isaiah* said more clearly (Is 65 1): I have been found by those who did not seek me, . . . 21 and referring to Israel he goes on (Is 65 2): Each day I stretched out my hand to a disobedient . . . people.

15 12   *Isaiah* too has this to say (Is 11 10G): The root of Jesse will appear,

4: (SPECIFIC) PROPHETS (OF THE OLD TESTAMENT)

(*Amos*)	(Ac 7; 15)		J	*Jeremiah*	3
Anna	*1* (Lk 2)			*Joel*	*1* (Ac 2)
Daniel	*1* (Mt 24)			(*Micah*)	(Mt 2)
(*Habakkuk*)	(Ac 13)		S	*Samuel*	3
H *Hosea*	*1*		Z	(*Zechariah*, a Minor Prophet)
				Phanuel*	*1* (Lk 2)

Mt 2 5   [Herod enquired where the Christ was to be born.] At Bethlehem . . , for this is what the *prophet* wrote (Mi 5 1): And you, Bethlehem,

15   This was to fulfil what the Lord had spoken through the
H   *prophet* (Ho 11 1): I called my son out of Egypt.

17   It was then that the words spoken through the *prophet*
J   *Jeremiah* were fulfilled (Jr 31 15): A voice was heard in Ramah,

12 39   The only sign [this generation] will be given is the sign of the *prophet* Jonah.

13 35   This was to fulfil the *prophecy* (Ps 78 2): I will speak to you in parables

16 14 J   Some say [the Son of Man] is . . . Elijah, and others *Jeremiah* or one of the prophets.

21 4 Z   This took place to fulfil the *prophecy* (Zc 9 9; Is 62 11): . . . Look, your king comes to you,

24 15   when you see the disastrous abomination, of which the *prophet Daniel* spoke (Dn 9 27),

27 9 J Z   The words of the *prophet Jeremiah* were then fulfilled (Zc 11 12f; Jr 32 6f): And they took the thirty silver pieces,

Lk 1 67   Zechariah was filled with the Holy Spirit and spoke this 2 *prophecy*:

2 36   6 There was a *prophetess* also, *Anna* the daughter of Phanuel* . . . She . . . spoke of the child [Jesus]

4 27   in the *prophet* Elisha's time there were many lepers in Israel,

Jn 11 51   2 it was as high priest that [Caiaphas] made this *prophecy* that Jesus was to die for the nation

Ac 2 16   this is what the *prophet* (§*Joel*) spoke of (Jl 3 1): 17 . . . I will pour out my spirit

30   since David was a *prophet*, . . . 31 . . . he . . . spoke about . . . the resurrection of the Christ (Ps 16 9):

3 24 S   all the prophets that have ever spoken, from *Samuel* onwards,

7 42   God turned away from them . . , as scripture says in the book of the *prophets* (Am 5 25f): Did you bring me sacrifice . . .?

13 20 S   [God] gave [Israel] judges, down to the *prophet Samuel*.

40   be careful – or what the *prophets* say will happen to you (Hab 1 5): . . . be amazed, and perish!

15 15   This is entirely in harmony with the words of the *prophets*, since the scriptures say (Am 9 11): 16 . . . I shall . . . rebuild the fallen House of David;

Rm 9 25 H   That is exactly what God says in *Hosea* (Ho 2 25): I shall say . . . 'You are my people',

Heb 11 32   There is not time for me to give an account of Gideon,
S   . . . *Samuel* and the prophets.

2 P 2 16   The dumb donkey put a stop to that *prophet*'s [Balaam's] madness

Jude 14   2 It was with them in mind that Enoch . . . *made his prophecy*

5: (JOHN THE BAPTIST AS) PROPHET

Mt 11 9   what did you go out for? To see a *prophet*? Yes, I tell you, and much more than a *prophet*:

14 5   the people . . . regarded John as a *prophet*.

21 26   the people . . . all hold that John was a *prophet*.

Mk 11 32   everyone held that John was a real *prophet*.

Lk 1 76   you shall be called *Prophet* of the Most High,

7 26   what did you go out to see? A *prophet*? Yes, I tell you, and much more than a *prophet*:

20 6   the people . . . are convinced that John was a *prophet*.

6: THE PROPHET (EXPECTED AS MESSIAH – Dt 18 15)

Jn 1 21   'Are you the *Prophet*?' [John] answered, 'No'.

25   Why are you baptising if you are not the Christ, and not Elijah, and not the *prophet*?

6 14 X   The people . . . said, 'This really is the *prophet* who is to come into the world'.

7 40 X   Several people . . . said, 'Surely he must be the *prophet*',

Ac 3 22   Moses . . . said (Dt 18 15): The Lord God will raise up a *prophet* like myself . . . 23 The man who does not listen to
23 X   that *prophet* is to be cut off from the people
X

7 37 X   (Dt 18 15) God will raise up a *prophet* like myself

7: (JESUS AS) PROPHET

Mt	13 57	Jesus said to [the people of Nazareth], 'A *prophet* is only despised in his own country'
	21 11	This is the *prophet* Jesus from Nazareth in Galilee.
	46	the crowds . . . looked on [Jesus] as a *prophet*.
	26 68	2 'Play the prophet (or: *Prophesy*), Christ! Who hit you then?
Mk	6 4	A *prophet* is only despised in his own country,
	15	Others said . . , 'He is a *prophet*, like the prophets we used to have'.
	14 65	2 'Play the prophet (or: *Prophesy*)!
Lk	4 24	no *prophet* is ever accepted in his own country.
	7 16	A great *prophet* has appeared among us; God has visited his people.
	39	If this man were a *prophet*, he would know who this woman is
	13 33	it would not be right for a *prophet* to die outside Jerusalem.
	22 64	2 'Play the prophet (or: *Prophesy*) . . . Who hit you then?
	24 19	Jesus of Nazareth . . . who proved he was a great *prophet*
Jn	4 19	'I see you are a *prophet*, sir' said the [Samaritan] woman.
	44	[Jesus] had declared that there is no respect for a *prophet* in his own country.
	7 52	see for yourself: *prophets* do not come out of Galilee.
	9 17	'He is a *prophet*' replied the man [who had been born blind].

8: THE (CHRISTIAN) PROPHETS – PROPHESY

Agabus 2 (Ac 11; 21)	*Manaen* 1 } (Ac 13)
Lucius 1 (Ac 13)	*Simeon Niger* 1 } (Ac 13)

T = Prophesy//Speak with tongues

Mt	7 22	2 did we not *prophesy* in your name . . .?
	10 41	Anyone who welcomes a *prophet* because he is a *prophet* will have a *prophet*'s reward;
	23 34	I am sending you *prophets* and wise men and scribes;
Ac	2 17	2 (Jl 3 1) Their sons and daughters shall *prophesy*,
	18	Even on my slaves, men and women, in those days, I will 2 pour out my spirit (§ and they will *prophesy*).
	11 27	some *prophets* came down from Antioch to Jerusalem,
	28	[28] and one of them whose name was *Agabus* . . . predicted that a famine would spread over the whole empire.
	13 1	In the church at Antioch the following were *prophets* and teachers: Barnabas, *Simeon* called *Niger*, and *Lucius* of Cyrene, *Manaen* . . . and Saul.
	15 32	[At Antioch] Judas and Silas, being themselves *prophets*, spoke for a long time,
	19 6 T	2 [the disciples at Ephesus] began to speak with tongues and to *prophesy*.
	21 9	2 [Philip] had four virgin daughters who were *prophets*.
	10	[at Caesarea] a *prophet* called *Agabus* arrived from Judaea
Rm	12 6	3 If your gift is *prophecy*, then use it as your faith suggests;
1Co	11 4	2 For a man to pray or *prophesy* with his head covered is a sign of disrespect to his head. [5] For a woman, however, it is
	5	2 a sign of disrespect to her head if she prays or *prophesies* unveiled;
	12 10 T	3 [One may have the gift of preaching . . ,] another, *prophecy*;
	28	God has given the first place to apostles, the second to
	29 T A	*prophets*, . . . [29] Are all of them apostles, or all of them
	10 T A	. . . *prophets*?
	13 2 T	3 If I have the gift of *prophecy*, . . . but without love,
	8	Love does not come to an end. But if there are gifts of
	9 T 3/2	*prophecy*, . . . they must fail; . . . [9] For our . . . *prophesying* is imperfect.
	14 1	hope for the spiritual gifts as well [as love], especially
	T	2 *prophecy*.
	3 T	2 the man who *prophesies* does talk to other people, . . .
	4 T	2 [4] . . . the man who *prophesies* does so for the benefit
	5	of the community. [5] While I should like you all to have the
	T	2 gift of tongues, I would much rather you could *prophesy*,
	T	2 since the man who *prophesies* is of greater importance . . .
	6	[6] . . . what use shall I be it all my talking . . . 'tells you
	T	3 nothing (lit. makes no *prophecy*) . . .?
	22	the strange languages are meant to be a sign . . . for un-
	T	3 believers, while . . . *prophecy* is a sign . . . for believers.
	24 T	2 if you were all *prophesying* and an unbeliever . . . came in,
	29 T	As for *prophets*, let two or three of them speak, and the others attend to them.
	31 T	2 you can all *prophesy* in turn,
	32	*Prophets* cannot always control their *prophetic* spirits,
	37	Anyone who claims to be a *prophet* or inspired
	39 T	2 by all means be ambitious to *prophesy*,
Ep	2 20 A	You are part of a building that has the apostles and *prophets* for its foundations,
	3 5	This mystery that has now been revealed through the Spirit
	A	to his holy apostles and *prophets*

Ep	4 11 A	to some, [Christ's] gift was that they should be apostles; to some, *prophets*;
1 Th	5 20	3 [Never try to suppress the Spirit] or treat [the gift of] *prophecy* with contempt.
1 Tm	1 18	3 remember the *words* once *spoken* over you *by the prophets*.
	4 14	a spiritual gift which was given to you 'when the prophets 3 spoke (lit. in a *prophecy*)
Rv	1 3	3 Happy the man who reads this *prophecy*,
	10 7	as he announced in the Good News told to his servants the *prophets*.
	11	2 you are to *prophesy* again, this time about many different nations
	11 3	2 I shall send my two witnesses to *prophesy* . . , wearing sackcloth.
	6	3 so that it does not rain as long as they are *prophesying*;
	10	these two *prophets* have been a plague to the people of the world.
	18	the time has come . . . for your servants the *prophets* . . . to be rewarded.
	16 6	they spilt the blood of the saints and the *prophets*,
	18 20 A	Now heaven, celebrate [Babylon's] downfall, and all you saints, apostles and *prophets*;
	24	In [Babylon] you will find the blood of *prophets* and saints,
	19 10	3 The witness Jesus gave is the same as the spirit of *prophecy*.
	22 6	the Lord God who gives the spirit to the *prophets* has sent his angel
	7	3 Happy are those who treasure the *prophetic* message of this book.
	9	I am a servant just like you and like your brothers the *prophets*
	10	3 Do not keep the *prophecies* in this book a secret.
	18	3 This is my solemn warning to all who hear the *prophecies* in this book:
	19	3 if anyone cuts anything out of the *prophecies* in this book,

9: (FALSE) PROPHET(S)

J = Jezebel 1

Mt	7 15	4 Beware of false *prophets*
	24 11	4 Many false *prophets* will arise;
	24	4 false Christs and false *prophets* will arise
Mk	13 22	4 false Christs and false *prophets* will arise
Lk	6 26	4 This was the way their ancestors treated the false *prophets*.
Ac	13 7	4 [A Jewish magician called Bar-jesus.] This false *prophet* was one of the attendants of the proconsul
2 P	2 1	4 there were false *prophets* in the past history of our people,
1 Jn	4 1	4 there are many false *prophets*, now, in the world.
Rv	2 20 J	6 *Jezebel* who claims to be a *prophetess*,
	16 13	4 from the jaws of dragon and beast and false *prophet* I saw three foul spirits come;
	19 20	4 the beast was taken prisoner, together with the false *prophet*
	20 10	the lake of fire and sulphur, where the beast and the false 4 *prophet* are,

10: (THE CRETAN) PROPHET [= ? EPIMENEDES OF KNOSSOS]

Tt	1 12	one of their own *prophets* . . . said, 'Cretans were never anything but liars,'

PURE – INNOCENT – SIMPLE

1. Sweep, Swept (clean): *saroō*	2: Unstained, Without spot, Un-contaminated: *a-spilos*
2. Clean, Pure – Cleanse, Make clean, Clear – Purification: *katharos*	3: Spotless, Without blemish, Perfect – Faultless, Blameless, Innocent – Pure: *a-mōmos*
3. Pure: *pistikos*	**9. Blameless, Irreproachable**
4. Pure, Purify, Purification – Chaste – Sincere: *hagnos*	1: *an-en-klētos*
	2: *an-epi-lēmptos*
5. Sincerity – Sincere, Pure: *eili-krinēs*	**10. Blameless, Faultless – Innocent:** *a-memptos*
6. Without hypocrisy – Sincere, Genuine: *an-hypo-kritos*	**11. Innocent:** *a-thōos*
7. Guileless, Innocent – Genuine: *a-keraios*	**12. Innocent, Simple:** *a-kakos*
8. Unstained, Without spot – Innocent	**13. Simple, Single – Simplicity:** *ha-plotēs*
1: Undefiled, Unstained, Unspoilt: *a-miantos*	

1. SWEEP, SWEPT (CLEAN): *SAROŌ*

saroō 3

Mt 12 44		finding [the house] unoccupied, *swept* and tidied, [the unclean spirit goes off and collects seven other spirits]
Lk 11 25		finding [the house] *swept* and tidied, [the unclean spirit then goes off]
15 8		what woman . . . would not, if she lost one [drachma], . . . *sweep out* the house

2. CLEAN, PURE – CLEANSE, MAKE CLEAN, CLEAR – PURIFICATION: *KATHAROS*

5 *kathairō*	1	6	*katharotēs*	1
3 *katharismos*	7	7	*dia-kathairō*	1
1 *katharizō*	31	8	*dia-katharizō*	1
2 *katharos*	27	4	*ek-kathairō*	2

X = Jesus makes clean   L = Cure leprosy (Cleanse)

Mt 3 12 X	8	he will *clear* his threshing floor and gather his wheat into the barn;
5 8	2	Happy the *pure* in heart: they shall see God.
8 2		A leper now came up . . . 'Sir, . . . if you want to you can ⌐cure
3 X L		(lit. *cleanse*) me.' ³ 'Of course I want to! Be ⌐cured
X L		(lit. *clean*)!' And his leprosy was ⌐cured (lit. *cleansed*) at once.
10 8 L		Cure the sick, . . . *cleanse* the lepers,
11 5 X L		the blind see again, . . . lepers are *cleansed*,
23 25		you hypocrites! You who *clean* the outside of cup and dish
26		. . . ²⁶ . . . *Clean* the inside of cup and dish first so that
2		the outside may become *clean* as well.
27 59	2	Joseph took the body [of Jesus], wrapped it in a *clean* shroud
Mk 1 40		A leper . . . pleaded . . .: 'If you want to . . . you can ⌐cure
41 X L		(lit. *clean*) me'. . . . ⁴¹ . . . 'Of course I want to! . . .
42 X L		Be ⌐cured (lit. *clean*)!' ⁴² And . . . he was ⌐cured (lit.
X L		*cleansed*).
44 X L 3		make the offering for your ⌐healing (lit. *cleansing*) prescribed by Moses
7 19		Thus he pronounced all foods *clean*.
Lk 2 22	3	when the day came for them to be *purified* as laid down by the Law of Moses, they took [Jesus] up to Jerusalem
3 17 X	7	His winnowing-fan is in his hand to *clear* his threshing-floor
4 27		there were many lepers in Israel, but none of these was ⌐cured
L		(lit. *cleansed*), except the Syrian, Naaman.
5 12 X L		'Sir, . . . if you want to, you can ⌐cure (lit. *cleanse*) me.'
13 X L		¹³ 'Of course I want to! Be ⌐cured (lit. *cleansed*)!' And
14		the leprosy left him at once. ¹⁴ [Jesus] ordered him to tell no one. 'But . . . make the offering for your ⌐healing (lit.
X L 3		*cleansing*) as Moses prescribed it,'
7 22 X L		the blind see again, . . . lepers are *cleansed*,
11 39		You *clean* the outside of cup and plate,
41		Instead, give alms from what you have and then indeed
2		everything will be *clean* for you.
17 14		'Go and show yourselves to the priests'. Now as they were
X L		going away they were *cleansed*.
17 X L		Were not all ten [lepers] *made clean*?
Jn 2 6		six stone water jars . . , meant for the ⌐ablutions that are
3		(lit. *purification* that is) customary among the Jews
3 25		some of John's disciples had opened a discussion with a Jew
3		about *purification*,
13 10	2	No one who has taken a bath needs washing, he is *clean* all
11	2	over. You are *clean*, though not all of you are. ¹¹ He knew who was going to betray him, that was why he said,
2		'though not all of you are *clean*'.
15 2		every branch that does bear fruit [my Father] ⌐prunes (lit.
3 ⊖ 5		*cleans*) to make it bear even more. ³ You are ⌐pruned (lit.
2		*cleaned*) already, by means of the word that I have spoken to you.
Ac 10 15 ⊖		What God has *made clean*, you have no right to call profane.
11 9 ⊖		What God has *made clean*, you have no right to call profane.
15 9 ⊖		God . . . *purified* [the pagans'] hearts by faith.
18 6		Your blood be on your own heads; from now on I can go to
2		the pagans [with a] *clear* [conscience].
20 26	2	I swear that my conscience is *clear* as far as all of you are concerned.
Rm 14 20	2	Of course all food is *clean*, but it becomes evil if by eating it you make somebody else fall away.
1Co 5 7	4	⌐get rid (lit. *cleanse* yourselves) of all the old yeast,
2Co 7 1		let us *wash off* all that can soil either body or spirit,
Ep 5 26 X		[Christ] *made* [the Church] *clean* by washing her in water with a form of words,
1Tm 1 5	2	love, coming out of a *pure* heart,
3 9	2	[Deacons] must be ⌐conscientious believers in (lit. of *clear* conscience guarding) the mystery of the faith.

2Tm 1 3	2	keeping my conscience *clear* and remembering my duty to [God] as my ancestors did,
2 21	4	to ⌐avoid (lit. keep *clear* of) these faults . . . is the way for anyone to become a vessel for special occasions, fit for the Master himself to use,
22	2	in union with all those who call on the Lord with *pure* minds.
Tt 1 15	2/2	To all who are *pure* themselves, everything is *pure*; but to those who have been corrupted . . . nothing can be *pure*
2 14 X		He sacrificed himself for us in order to . . . *purify* a people so that it could be his very own
Heb 1 3		[the Son] has ⌐destroyed the defilement of (lit. attained
X 3		*purification* from) sin,
9 13 X		The blood of goats and bulls and the ashes of a heifer are sprinkled on those who have incurred defilement and they
6		restore the *holiness* (or: *purity*) of their outward lives;
14		¹⁴ how much more effectively the blood of Christ . . . can
X		*purify* our inner self
22		according to the Law almost everything has to be *purified* with blood;
23		only the copies of heavenly things can be *purified* in this way,
10 2		the worshippers, when they had been *purified* once, would have no awareness of sins.
22	2	our minds sprinkled . . . and our bodies washed with *pure* water,
Jm 1 27	2	*Pure*, unspoilt religion, in the eyes of God our Father is this:
4 8		*Clean* your hands, you sinners, and clear your minds, you waverers.
1P 1 22	2	let your love for each other be ⌐real (lit. *pure*) and from the heart
2P 1 9		without [these virtues] a man is blind . . ; he has forgotten
3		how his past sins were *washed away*.
1Jn 1 7	2	if we live our lives in the light, . . . the blood of Jesus . . .
9 X		*purifies* us from all sin. . . . ⁹ . . . if we acknowledge our
X		sins, then God . . . will . . . *purify* us from everything that is wrong.
Rv 15 6	2	the seven angels with the seven plagues, wearing *pure* white linen,
19 8	2	His bride . . . has been able to dress herself in dazzlingly *pure* white linen,
14	2	Behind him, dressed in linen of dazzlingly *pure* white, rode the armies of heaven
21 18	2/2	the city [was built] of *pure* gold, like ⌐polished (lit. *clear*) glass.
21	2	. . . ²¹ . . . the main street of the city was *pure* gold, transparent as glass.

3. PURE: *PISTIKOS*

pistikos 2

Mk 14 3		an alabaster jar of very costly ointment, *pure* nard.
Jn 12 3		a pound of very costly ointment, *pure* nard,

4. PURE, PURIFY, PURIFICATION – CHASTE – SINCERE: *HAGNOS*

3 *hagneia*	2	1	*hagnos*	8
5 *hagnismos*	1	6	*hagnōs*	1
2 *hagnizō*	7	4	*hagnotēs*	2

Jn 11 55		many of the country people who had gone up to Jerusalem
2		*purify* themselves
Ac 21 24		[We have four men here who are under a vow;] take these
26	2	men along and be *purified* with them . . . ²⁶ So the next
2		day Paul took the men along and was *purified* with them, and he visited the Temple to give notice of the time when
5		the period of *purification* would be over
24 18	2	I had been *purified*, and there was no crowd involved, and no disturbance.
2Co 6 6	4	We prove we are God's servants by our *purity*, knowledge,
7 11		In every way you have shown yourselves *blameless* in this affair.
11 2		I arranged for you to marry Christ so that I might give you away as a *chaste* virgin to this one husband.
3		I am afraid that . . . your ideas may get corrupted and turned
4		away from simple (§ and *pure*) devotion to Christ.
Ph 1 17		The others, who proclaim Christ for ⌐jealous or selfish motives
6		(lit. [the sake of] intrigue and not *sincerely*)
4 8		fill your minds with everything that is . . . good and *pure*,
1Tm 4 12	3	be an example . . . in . . . your faith and your *purity*.
5 2	3	Always treat young women ⌐with propriety (lit. in all *purity*),
22		never make yourself an accomplice in anybody else's sin; keep yourself *pure*.
Tt 2 5		[the older women should show the younger women] how they are to be sensible and *chaste*,
Jm 3 17		the wisdom that comes down from above is essentially something *pure*;

Jm 4 8	2	Clean your hands, you sinners, and ʳclear (lit. *purify*) your minds, you waverers.
1 P 1 22	2	You have . . . *purified* your souls until you can love like brothers, in sincerity;
3 2		[some husbands may find themselves won over] when they see how ʳfaithful (lit. *chaste*) and conscientious [their wives] are.
1 Jn 3 3 X	2	Surely everyone who entertains this hope must *purify* himself, must try to be as *pure* as Christ.

5. SINCERITY – SINCERE, PURE: *EILI-KRINĒS*

1 *eili-krineia* 3   2 *eili-krinēs* 2

1 Co 5 8		let us celebrate the feast, then, by . . . having only the unleavened bread of *sincerity* and truth.
2 Co 1 12		we have always treated everybody . . . with the reverence and *sincerity* which come from God,
2 17		In Christ, we speak [as men of] *sincerity*,
Ph 1 10	2	This will help you to become *pure* and blameless,
2 P 3 1	2	I have tried to awaken a ʳtrue (lit. *sincere*) understanding in you

6. WITHOUT HYPOCRISY – SINCERE, GENUINE: *AN-HYPO-KRITOS*

an-hypo-kritos 6

Rm 12 9		ʳDo not let your love be a pretence (lit. *Let your love be genuine*),
2 Co 6 6		We prove we are God's servants by . . . a love *free from affection*;
1 Tm 1 5		love, coming out of . . . a *sincere* faith.
2 Tm 1 5		I am reminded of the *sincere* faith which you have;
Jm 3 17		nor is there any trace of partiality or *hypocrisy* in [the wisdom that comes down from above].
1 P 1 22		You have . . . purified your souls until you can love like brothers, *in sincerity*;

7. GUILELESS, INNOCENT – GENUINE: *A-KERAIOS*

a-keraios 3

Mt 10 16		be cunning as serpents and yet as ʳharmless (or: *innocent*) as doves.
Rm 16 19		I only hope that you are also wise in what is good, and *innocent* of what is bad.
Ph 2 15		[Do all that has to be done without complaining or arguing] and then you will be innocent and ʳgenuine (or: *guileless*),

8. UNSTAINED, WITHOUT SPOT – INNOCENT

1: UNDEFILED, UNSTAINED, UNSPOILT: *A-MIANTOS*

a-miantos 4

Heb 7 26 X		To suit us, the ideal high priest would have to be holy, innocent and *uncontaminated*,
13 4		marriages are to be kept *undefiled*, because fornicators and adulterers will come under God's judgement.
Jm 1 27		Pure, *unspoilt* religion, in the eyes of God our Father is this:
1 P 1 4		[we have] the promise of an inheritance that can *never* be spoilt or *soiled*

2: UNSTAINED, WITHOUT SPOT, UNCONTAMINATED: *A-SPILOS*

a-spilos 4

1 Tm 6 14		[the duty] of doing all that you have been told, *with no faults or failures*,
Jm 1 27		Pure, unspoilt religion, in the eyes of God our Father is this: . . . keeping oneself *uncontaminated* by the world.
1 P 1 19 X		[the ransom that was paid to free you] in the precious blood of a lamb *without* spot or *stain*,
2 P 3 14		do your best to live lives *without spot* or stain

3: SPOTLESS, WITHOUT BLEMISH, PERFECT – FAULTLESS, BLAMELESS, INNOCENT – PURE: *A-MŌMOS*

1 *a-mōmos* 8   2 *a-mōmētos* 1

Ep 1 4		[God] chose us in Christ, to be holy and *spotless*, and to live through love in his presence,

Ep 5 27		so that . . . [the Church] would be glorious, with no speck or wrinkle . . . but holy and *faultless*.
Ph 2 15		then you will be innocent and genuine, *perfect* children of God among a deceitful and underhand brood,
Col 1 22		Now you are able to appear before [God] holy, *pure* and blameless
Heb 9 14 X		how much more effectively the blood of Christ, who offered himself as the *perfect* sacrifice . ., can purify our inner self
1 P 1 19 X		[the ransom that was paid to free you] in the precious blood of a lamb *without spot* or stain,
2 P 3 14	2	do your best to live lives *without* spot or *stain*
Jude 24		Glory be to him who can . . . bring you safe to his glorious presence, *innocent* and happy.
Rv 14 5		They never allowed a lie to pass their lips and *no fault* can be found in them.

9. BLAMELESS, IRREPROACHABLE

1: *AN-EN-KLĒTOS*

an-en-klētos 5

1 Co 1 8		[God] will keep you steady and *without blame*
Col 1 22		Now you are able to appear before [God] holy, pure and *blameless*
1 Tm 3 10		They are . . . only [to be] admitted to serve as deacons if there is *nothing against them*.
Tt 1 6		each of [the elders] must be a man *of irreproachable character*.
7		[an elder] must be *irreproachable*:

2: *AN-EPI-LĒMPTOS*

an-epi-lēmptos 3

1 Tm 3 2		the president must ʳhave *an impeccable character* (or: be *irreproachable*).
5 7		remind them of all this, . . . so that their lives may be *blameless*.
6 14		[the duty] of doing all that you have been told, *with no faults or failures*,

10. BLAMELESS, FAULTLESS – INNOCENT: *A-MEMPTOS*

1 *a-memptos* 5   2 *a-memptōs* 2

Lk 1 6		[Zechariah and Elizabeth] ʳscrupulously (or: *faultlessly*) observed all the commandments
Ph 2 15		[Do all that has to be done without complaining or arguing] and then you will be *innocent* and genuine,
3 6		as far as the Law can make you perfect, I was *faultless*.
1 Th 2 10	2	our treatment of you . . . has been *impeccably* right and fair.
3 13 Θ		may [the Lord] so confirm your hearts in holiness that you may be *blameless* in the sight of our God
5 23	2	may you all be kept safe and *blameless*, spirit, soul and body,
Heb 8 7		If that first covenant had been *without a fault*, there would have been no need for a second one to replace it.

11. INNOCENT: *A-THŌOS*

a-thōos 2

Mt 27 4		'I have sinned;' [Judas] said 'I have betrayed *innocent* blood.'
24		Pilate . . . said, 'I am *innocent* of this (ᵛ just) man's blood.'

12. INNOCENT, SIMPLE: *A-KAKOS*

a-kakos 2

Rm 16 18		People like that . . . are slaves of their own appetites, confusing the *simple*-minded with their . . . persuasive arguments.
Heb 7 26 X		To suit us, the ideal high priest would have to be holy, *innocent* and uncontaminated,

13. SIMPLE, SINGLE – SIMPLICITY: *HA-PLOTĒS*

ha-plotēs 4/8

2 Co 1 12		we have always treated everybody . . . with the ʳreverence (ᵛ *simplicity*) and sincerity which come from God,

2 Co 11	3		I am afraid that . . . your ideas may get corrupted and turned away from ⌐simple devotion to (lit. *simplicity* towards) Christ.
Ep 6	5		Slaves, be obedient to . . . your masters . . , with deep respect and ⌐sincere loyalty (lit. *single*-mindedness),
Col 3	22		Slaves, be obedient to . . . your masters . . . ⌐wholeheartedly (lit. *single*-mindedly),

PUT – SET – APPOINT

1. Put, Lay, Set – Appoint, Destine – Trust: *tithēmi*
1: Put – Lay (upon, up, in)
  a) Put – Lay (on, in)
  b) Put (in non-physical senses) – Lay (upon, up)
2: Set before – Put before
  a) Set before (a person) – Distribute (among) – Serve
  b) Put (a parable, an explanation) before
3: Put down, Deposit – Commit (to), Entrust (to) – Trust
4: Appoint, Commission – Destine (for)
5: Lay down (one's life for)
2. Set, Place, Put – Appoint: *histēmi*
1: Set, Place, Put – Make stand (in a place)
2: Establish, Make, Fix – Confirm, Sustain
3: Place, Set (a person over), Put (in charge of) – Appoint

4: Move (to a place) – Create a place for – Transfer
3. Put (on), Lay (on) – Foundation, Founding: *ballō*
1: Put, Lay – Put on, Lay (hands) on – Piece, Patch
2: Foundation – Founding
  a) the Foundation, Making (of the world)
  b) the Founding (of a dynasty)
4. Put: *didōmi*
5. Appoint(ed), Predstine(d): *procheirizomai*
6. Laid, Set, Placed – Destined: *keimai*
1: (Be) Laid, Set, Placed
2: (Be) Destined, Put – Set up, Laid down
3: Be (within reach, in the power of, present)
7. Appoint: *cheiro-toneō*
8. Set up (a tent): *pēgnymi*

1. PUT, LAY, SET – APPOINT, DESTINE – TRUST: *TITHĒMI*

1	*tithēmi*	92/99	2	*epi-tithēmi* 20/40
6	*ana-tithemai*	2	8	*hypo-tithēmi* 2
7	*apo-tithemai*	2/9	5	*para-thēkē* 3
9	*kata-tithēmi*	1/3	3	*para-tithēmi* 19
10	*ek-thetos*	1	11	*pro-thesmia* 1
4	*ek-tithēmi*	4	12	*pro-tithemai* 1/3

1: PUT – LAY (UPON, UP, IN)

a) *Put – Lay* (*on, in*)

Mt 5	15			No one lights a lamp to *put* it under a tub;
14	3		7	Herod . . . had arrested John, chained him up and *put* him in prison
21	7		2	They brought the donkey and the colt, then they *laid* their cloaks on their backs
23	4		2	[The scribes and Pharisees] tie up heavy burdens and *lay* them on men's shoulders,
27	29		2	having twisted some thorns into a crown they *put* this on his head
	37		2	Above his head was *placed* the charge against him;
	60			[Joseph] *put* [the body of Jesus] in his own new tomb
Mk 4	21			Would you bring in a lamp to *put* it under a tub or under the bed? Surely you will *put* it on the lamp-stand?
6	29			John's disciples . . . came and took his body and *laid* it in a tomb.
	56			they *laid* [down] the sick in the open spaces,
15	46		9	[Joseph] *laid* [Jesus] in a tomb which had been hewn out of the rock.
	47			Mary of Magdala and Mary . . . took note of where he was *laid*.
16	6			he has risen, . . . here is the place where they *laid* him.
Lk 5	18			a paralysed man whom they were trying to bring in and *lay* [down] in front of [Jesus].
6	48			the man who . . . *laid* the foundations [of his house] on rock;
8	16			No one lights a lamp to . . . *put* it under a bed. No, he *puts* it on a lamp-stand
11	33			No one lights a lamp and *puts* it in some hidden place
14	29			if he *laid* the foundation and then found himself unable to finish the work,
15	5	< 2		when he found [the missing sheep], would he not joyfully *take* it on his shoulders . . .?
23	26		2	they seized on a man, Simon from Cyrene, . . . and ⌐made him shoulder the cross and carry it (lit. *laid* the cross on him to carry)

Lk 23	53			[Joseph] took [the body of Jesus] down, . . . and *put* him in a tomb
	55			the women . . . took note of the tomb and ⌐of the position of the body (lit. how the body had been *laid* there).
Jn 9	6 X	2		[Jesus] made a paste with the spittle, *put* this over the eyes of the blind man
	15 X	2		He *put* a paste on my eyes,
11	34			[Jesus said,] 'Where have you *put* [Lazarus]?'
13	4 X			he got up from table, ⌐removed (or: *laid* [aside]) his outer garment and . . ⌐wrapped [a towel] round his waist;
19	2	2		the soldiers twisted some thorns into a crown and *put* it on his head,
	19			Pilate wrote out a notice and ⌐had it fixed to (lit *put* it on) the cross;
	41			a new tomb in which no one had yet been ⌐buried (lit. *laid*). 42. . . they *laid* Jesus there.
20	2	2		They have taken the Lord out of the tomb . . . and we don't know where they have *put* him.
	13			They have taken my Lord away . . . and I don't know where they have *put* him.
	15			Sir, if you have taken him away, tell me where you have *put* him,
Ac 3	2			He was a cripple from birth; and they used to *put* him [down] every day near the Temple entrance
4	3			[The priests] arrested [Peter and John], but as it was already late, they ⌐held them (lit. *put* them in custody) till the next day
	35			[those who owned . . . houses would sell them, and bring the money . . ,] to ⌐present it to (lit. *put* it at the feet of) the apostles;
	37			[Barnabas] sold [a piece of land] and brought the money, and ⌐presented it to (lit. *put* it at the feet of) the apostles
5	2			[Ananias] kept back part of the proceeds [of a sale], and brought the rest and ⌐presented it to (lit. *put* it at the feet of) the apostles.
	15			the sick were even taken out into the street and *laid* on beds
	18			[the Sadducees] arrested the apostles and had them *put* in the common gaol.
	25			the men you ⌐imprisoned (lit. *put* in prison) are in the Temple.
7	16			their bodies were . . . ⌐buried (lit. *laid*) in the tomb that Abraham had bought
	19	10		[This new king] ill-treated our ancestors, forcing them to *expose* their babies
	21	4		after [Moses] had been *exposed*, Pharaoh's daughter adopted him
	58	7		The witnesses *put down* their clothes at the feet of a young man called Saul.
9	37			they washed [Tabitha] and *laid* her [out] in a room upstairs.
12	4			[Herod] *put* Peter in prison,
13	29			they took him down from the tree and ⌐buried (lit. *laid*) him in a tomb.
28	3	2		Paul had collected a bundle of sticks and was *putting* them on the fire
	10	2		they *put* [on board] the provisions we needed.
1 Co 12	18 ⊖			God *put* all the separate parts into the body on purpose.
16	2			each one of you must *put* aside what he can afford,
2 Co 3	13			Moses, who *put* a veil over his face
Rv 1	17 X			I fell . . . at his feet, but he ⌐touched me with (lit. *laid* on me) his right hand
	10	2		he *put* his right foot in the sea and his left foot on the land
	11	9		Men of every . . . nation will stare at [the] corpses [of the two witnesses] . . ., not letting them be ⌐buried (lit. *laid* in the tomb),

b) *Put* (*in non-physical senses*) *– Lay* (*upon, up*)

Mt 12	18 ⊖			(Is 42 1) I will ⌐endow him with (lit. *put* upon him) my spirit,
22	44 ⊖			(Ps 110 1) I will *put* your enemies under your feet?
24	51			The master will cut him off and *send* him to the same fate as the hypocrites.
Mk 3	16 X	2		Simon ⌐to whom he gave (lit. *on* whom he *set*) the name Peter,
	17 X	2		James . . . and John . . . ⌐to whom he gave (lit. *on* whom he *set*) the name Boanerges
4	30 X			What can we say the kingdom of God is like? What parable can we ⌐find for it (lit. *put* it in)?
12	36 ⊖			(Ps 110 1) I will *put* your enemies under your feet.
Lk 1	66			All those who heard of it ⌐treasured it (lit. *laid* it [up]) in their hearts.
9	44			you must ⌐have (lit. *put*) these words constantly in your mind: The Son of Man is going to be handed over into the power of men.
10	30	2		they took all [the man] had, ⌐beat (lit. *laid* blows *upon*) him
12	46			The master will cut him off and *send* him to the same fate as the unfaithful.
20	43 ⊖			(Ps 110 1) I will ⌐make your enemies (lit. *set* your enemies as) a footstool for you.

Lk 21 14		⌐Keep (lit. *Put*) this carefully in [your] mind: you are not to prepare your defence,
Ac 2 35 ⊖		(Ps 110 1) until he has ⌐make your enemies (lit. *set* your enemies as) a footstool for you.
5 4		What *put* this scheme into your mind?
15 10	2	It would only provoke God's anger . . . if you *imposed* on the disciples the very burden
28		It has been decided by the Holy Spirit and by ourselves
⑧	2	not to *saddle* you with any burden beyond these essentials:
16 23		⌐[Paul and Silas] were given many lashes (lit. Many lashes
	2	were *laid upon* them)
18 10	2	no one will even attempt to ⌐hurt (lit. *lay hands on*) you.
19 21		Paul ⌐made up (lit. *set*) his mind to go back to Jerusalem
27 12		the majority were ⌐for (lit. *set* on) putting out from there
Rm 9 33 ⊖		(Is 28 16) See how I *lay* in Zion a stone to stumble over,
14 13		you should make up your mind never to ⌐be the cause of your brother (lit. *put* in the way of your brother any cause of) tripping
16 4	8	[Christ Jesus] who *risked* death to save my life:
1Co 3 10		I succeeded as an architect and *laid* the foundations, . . .
11		[11] For the foundation, nobody can *lay* any other than . . . Jesus Christ.
15 25 ⊖		(Ps 110 1) until he has *put* all his enemies under his feet
Heb 1 13 ⊖		(Ps 110 1) I will ⌐make your enemies (lit. *set* your enemies as) a footstool for you.
10 13		(Ps 110 1) until his enemies are ⌐made into (lit. *set* as) a footstool for him.
1P 2 6 ⊖		(Is 28 16) See how I *lay* in Zion a precious cornerstone that I have chosen
2P 2 6		Sodom and Gomorrah . . . he destroyed . . . completely, ⌐as (lit. *setting*) a warning to anybody lacking reverence in the future;
Rv 22 18	2	if anyone ⌐adds anything to (lit. *puts* anything *on*) [the prophe-
⊖	2	cies in this book], God will ⌐add to (lit. (*put on*) him every plague

2: SET BEFORE — PUT BEFORE

a) Set before (a person) — Distribute (among) — Serve

Mk 6 41		he handed [the loaves and fish] to the disciples to
	3	⌐*distribute* among (or: *set before*) the people.
8 6	3	he handed [the seven loaves] to his disciples to *distribute*;
7	3	and they *distributed* them among the crowd. [7] They had a few small fish as well, and . . . he . . . ordered them to
	3	be *distributed* also.
Lk 9 16		he . . . handed [the loaves and fish] to his disciples to
	3	⌐*distribute* among (or: *set before*) the crowd.
10 8	3	eat what is *set before* you.
11 6		a friend of mine . . . has just arrived . . . and I have
	3	nothing to ⌐offer (lit. *set before*) him;
Jn 2 10		People generally *serve* the best wine first,
Ac 16 34		Afterwards he took them home and ⌐gave them a meal
	3	(lit. *set* food *before* them),
1Co 10 27	3	eat whatever is *put in front of* you,

b) Put (a parable, an explanation) before

Mt 13 24 X	3	He *put* another parable before them [the darnel],
31 X	3	He *put* another parable before them [the mustard seed],
Ac 11 4	4	Peter in reply ⌐gave them (lit. *set out*) the details
17 3		[Paul developed the arguments from scripture for them,]
	3	explaining and ⌐proving (lit. *laying down*) how it was ordained that the Christ should suffer and rise from the dead.
18 26		Priscilla and Aquila . . . took an interest in [Apollos] and
	4	⌐gave him further (lit. *laid out* in more detail his) instruction about the Way.
25 14	6	Festus *put* Paul's case *before* the king.
28 23	4	[Paul] *put* his case to [the Roman Jews],
Ga 2 2	6	I *laid before* the leading men the Good News as I proclaim it among the pagans;
1Tm 4 6	8	If you *put* all this to the brothers, you will be a good servant of Christ Jesus

3: PUT DOWN, DEPOSIT — COMMIT (TO), ENTRUST (TO) — TRUST

Lk 12 48		when a man has had a great deal ⌐given him on trust (lit.
	3	*committed* to him), even more will be expected of him.
19 21		you are an exacting man: you pick up what you have not
<		*put down*
22 <		an exacting man, picking up what I have not *put down*
23 46 X	3	Father, into your hands I *commit* my spirit.
Ac 14 23	3	[Paul and Barnabas] *commended* [the elders] to the Lord
20 32	3	I *commend* you to God (ⱽ G the Lord), and to the word of his grace
1Co 9 18		my reward . . . is this: . . . to be able to *offer* the Good News free,

2Co 5 19 ⊖		God . . . has *entrusted* to us the news that [men] are reconciled.
1Tm 1 18	3	these are the instructions that I am ⌐giving (lit. *committing* to) you:
6 20	5	take great care of *all that has been entrusted* to you.
2Tm 1 12	5	[God] is able to take care of *all that* I have *entrusted* to him
14	5	You have *been trusted to look after* something precious;
2 2		You have *heard* everything that I teach in public; ⌐hand it
	3	on (lit. *commit* it) to reliable people
1P 4 19	3	even those whom God allows to suffer must *trust* themselves to the constancy of the creator

4: APPOINT, COMMISSION — DESTINE (FOR)

Jn 15 16 X		I *commissioned* you to go out and bear fruit,
Ac 1 7		It is not for you to know times or dates that the Father
⊖		has *decided* by his own authority,
13 47 ⊖ ?		(Is 49 6) I have ⌐made you (lit. *appointed* you to be) a light for the nations,
20 28		all the flock of which the Holy Spirit has ⌐made you (lit.
⑧		*appointed* you to be) the overseers,
Rm 3 25 ⊖	12	[Christ Jesus] who was *appointed* by God to sacrifice his life
4 17 ⊖		(Gn 17 5) I have ⌐made you (lit. *appointed* you to be) the ancestor of many nations
1Co 12 28 ⊖		In the Church, God has ⌐given (lit. *appointed* in) the first place . . . apostles, the second . . . prophets, the third . . . teachers;
Ga 4 2		[An heir] is under the control of guardians . . . until he
11		reaches the age *fixed* by his father.
1Th 5 9 ⊖		God never ⌐meant us to experience (lit. *destined* us for) the Retribution, but to win salvation
1Tm 1 12		Christ Jesus our Lord . . . judged me faithful enough to
X		*call* me into his service
2 7 X		I have been *named* a herald and apostle
2Tm 1 11 X		I have been *named* [the] herald [of the Good News],
Heb 1 2 ⊖		the Son that he has *appointed* to inherit everything
1P 2 8		[Unbelievers] stumble . . .; it was the fate ⌐in store (lit. *destined*) for them.

5: LAY DOWN (ONE'S LIFE FOR)

Jn 10 11 <		the good shepherd is one who *lays down* his life for his sheep.
15 X		I *lay down* my life for my sheep.
17 X		The Father loves me, because I *lay down* my life . . . [18] . . .
18 X		I *lay* it *down* of my own free will, and as it is in my power to *lay* it *down*, so it is in my power to take it up again;
13 37		'I will *lay down* my life for you.' [38] '*Lay down* your life for
38		me? . . . before the cock crows you will have disowned me three times'.
15 13		A man can have no greater love than to *lay down* his life for his friends.
1Jn 3 16 X		This has taught us love — that he ⌐gave up (lit. *laid down*) his life for us: and we, too, ought to ⌐give up (lit. *lay down*) our lives for our brothers.

2. SET, PLACE, PUT — APPOINT: *HISTĒMI*

2	*histēmi* 14/152	3 *meth-istēmi* 2/5
1	*kath-istēmi* 20/21	

1: SET, PLACE, PUT — MAKE STAND (IN A PLACE)

Mt 4 5 ①	2	The devil then took [Jesus] to the holy city and ⌐made him
	2	*stand* (or: *set* him) on the parapet of the Temple.
18 2 X	2	he called a little child to him and *set* the child in front of them.
25 33 X	2	[The Son of Man] will *place* the sheep on his right hand and the goats on his left.
Mk 9 36 X	2	He then took a little child, *set* him in front of them,
Lk 4 9 ①	2	[the devil] led [Jesus] to Jerusalem and ⌐made him *stand* (or: *set* him) on the parapet of the Temple.
9 47 X	2	he took a little child and *set* him by his side
Jn 8 3		The scribes and Pharisees brought a woman along who had been caught committing adultery; and ⌐making her *stand* (or: *placing* her) there in full view
Ac 7 60 X	2	Lord, do not ⌐hold (lit. *set*) this sin against them;
Jm 3 6		*Put* among all the parts of the body, the tongue is a whole wicked world in itself:

2: ESTABLISH, MAKE, FIX — CONFIRM, SUSTAIN

Mt 18 16		(Dt 19 15) the evidence of two or three witnesses is required
	2	to ⌐*sustain* (or: *establish*) any charge.

Ac 17 31	Θ	2	[God] has *fixed* a day when the whole world will be judged,
Rm 3 31			Do we mean that faith makes the Law pointless? Not at all:
		2	we are *giving the Law its true value* (lit. *confirming the* Law).
5 19			As by one man's disobedience many were *made* sinners, so by one man's obedience many will be *made* righteous.
10 3			Failing to recognise the righteousness that comes from God,
		2	they try to *promote* their own idea of it,
2 Co 13 1			(Dt 19 15) The evidence of three or, at least two, witnesses is
		2	necessary to ʳ*sustain* (or: *establish*) the charge.
Heb 10 9	X	2	[Christ] is abolishing the first sort [of sacrifice] to ʳ*replace it* with (lit. *establish*) the second.
Jm 4 4			don't you realise that [making] the world your friend is *making* God your enemy?
2 P 1 8			If you have a generous supply of [kindness, love, devotion, . . .], they will not ʳ*leave* (lit. *make*) you ineffectual or unproductive:

3: PLACE, SET (A PERSON OVER), PUT (IN CHARGE OF) – APPOINT

Mt 24 45	<		What sort of servant . . . is . . . wise enough for the master to *place* him over his household . . . ?
47	<		he will *place* him over everything he owns.
25 21	<		you have shown you can be faithful in small things, I will ʳ*trust you with* (lit. *put you in charge of*) greater;
23	<		you have shown you can be faithful in small things, I will ʳ*trust you with* (lit. *put you in charge of*) greater;
Lk 12 14			My friend, . . . who *appointed* me your judge . . . ?
42			What sort of steward . . . is . . . wise enough for the master to *place* him over his household . . . ?
44	<		he will *place* him over everything he owns.
Ac 6 3			select from among yourselves seven men of good reputation . . . ; we will ʳ*hand over this duty to them* (lit. *appoint them to this duty*)
7 10			Pharaoh . . . *made* [Joseph] governor of Egypt
27			(Ex 2 14) who *appointed* you . . . to be our leader and judge?
35			(Ex 2 14) Who *appointed* you to be our leader and judge?
Tt 1 5			I left you behind in Crete . . . to . . . *appoint* elders
Heb 5 1			Every high priest . . . is *appointed* to act for men in their relations with God,
7 28			The Law *appoints* high priests who are men subject to weakness;
8 3			ʳIt is the duty of every high priest (lit. *Every high priest is appointed*) to offer gifts and sacrifices,

4: MOVE (TO A PLACE) – CREATE A PLACE FOR – TRANSFER

1 Co 13 2		3	if I have faith . . . to *move* mountains,
Col 1 13	Θ	3	[the Father] has . . . *created a place for* us in the kingdom of the Son

3. PUT (ON), LAY (ON) – FOUNDATION, FOUNDING: *BALLŌ*

1	*ballō*	44/122	3	*kata-bolē*	11
5	*blēteon*	1	2	*epi-ballō*	15/18
6	*kata-ballō*	1/2	4	*epi-blēma*	4

1: PUT, LAY – PUT ON, LAY (HANDS) ON – PIECE, PATCH

Mt 5 25			you will be ʳ*thrown into* (or: *put in*) prison.
9 16		2/4	No one *puts* a ʳ*piece* (or: *patch*) of unshrunken cloth *on* to an old cloak;
17			Nor do people *put* new wine into old wineskins;
10 34	X X		Do not suppose that I have come to *bring* peace to the earth: it is not peace I have come to *bring*, but a sword.
25 27			you should have *deposited* my money with the bankers,
26 12			When she ʳ*poured* (lit. *put*) this ointment on my body,
50		2	they . . . ʳ*seized* (lit. *laid hands on*) Jesus and took him in charge.
27 6			It is against the Law to *put* this [money] into the treasury;
Mk 2 21		4	No one sews a ʳ*piece* (or: *patch*) of unshrunken cloth on an old cloak; . . . ²² And nobody *puts* new wine into old wineskins;
22			
7 33	X		[Jesus] *put* his fingers into the man's ears
11 7		2	they took the colt to Jesus and ʳ*threw* (or: *laid*) their cloaks on its back,
12 41			[Jesus] watched the people *putting* money into the treasury,
42			and many of the rich *put* in a great deal. ⁴² A poor widow came and *put* in two small coins, . . . ⁴³ . . . 'this poor widow has *put* in more than all who have contributed to the treasury; ⁴⁴ for they have all *put* in money they had over, but she . . . has *put* in everything she possessed,'
43			
44			
14 46		2	The others ʳ*seized* (lit. *laid hands on*) [Jesus] and took him in charge.

Lk 5 36		4/2	No one tears a *piece* from a new cloak to *put it on* an old cloak; if he does, . . . the *piece* taken from the new will not match the old.
37			nobody *puts* new wine into old skins; . . . ³⁸ No; new wine
38		5	*must be put* into fresh skins.
9 62		2	Once the hand is *laid on* the plough, no one who looks back is fit for the kingdom of God.
12 49			I have come to *bring* fire to the earth,
58			the bailiff [may] have you ʳ*thrown into* (or: *put in*) prison.
13 8			leave [the fig tree] one more year and give me time to . . . ʳ*manure* (lit. *put manure on*) it;
20 19		2	the scribes . . . would have liked to *lay hands on* [Jesus]
21 1			[Jesus] saw rich people *putting* their offerings into the treasury; ² then he happened to notice a poverty-stricken widow *putting* in two small coins, ³ and he said, '. . . this poor widow has *put* in more than any of them; ⁴ for these have ʳ*contributed* (lit. *put in*) money they had over, but she has . . . *put* in all she had to live on.'
2			
3			
4			
12		2	men will ʳ*seize* (lit. *lay hands on*) you
23 19			This man had been ʳ*thrown into* (or: *put in*) prison for causing a riot
Jn 3 24			This was before John had been ʳ*put in* (or: *thrown into*) prison.
5 7			I have no one to *put* me into the pool
7 30		2	They would have arrested him then, but . . . no one *laid* a hand *on* him.
44		2	Some would have liked to arrest him, but no one actually *laid* hands *on* him.
12 6			[Judas] was in charge of the common fund and used to help himself to ʳthe contributions (lit. *what people put in*).
13 2			the devil had already *put* it into the mind of Judas . . . to betray him.
5	X		he then ʳ*poured* (lit. *put*) water into a basin
18 11			*Put* your sword [back] in its scabbard;
20 25			Unless I . . . can *put* my finger into the holes [the nails] made, and unless I can *put* my hand into his side, I refuse to believe. Give me your hand; *put* it into my side.
27			
Ac 4 3		2	[The priests] ʳ*arrested* (lit. *laid hands on*) [Peter and John],
5 18		2	[the Sadducees] ʳ*arrested* (lit. *laid hands on*) the apostles
12 1		2	Herod started ʳ*persecuting* (lit. *laying* hands violently *on*) certain members of the Church.
21 27		2	some Jews from Asia . . . stirred up the crowd and ʳ*seized* (lit. *laid hands on*) [Paul], ²⁸ shouting,
1 Co 7 35		2	I say this only to help you, not to *put* a halter round your necks,
Heb 6 1		6	without ʳgoing over the fundamental doctrines (lit. *laying* the foundations) again:
Jm 3 3			Once we *put* a bit into the horse's mouth, . . . we have the whole animal under our control.
Rv 2 10			the devil is going to ʳ*send* some of you to (or: *put* some of you in) prison
14			Balaam, who taught Balak to *set* a trap for the Israelites
22			I ʳ*am consigning* (lit. *will put*) [Jezebel] to bed,
24	X		But on the rest of you . . . I am not *laying* any special duty:
14 16			[the angel] ʳ*set his sickle to work on* (lit. *put* his sickle *in*) the earth,
19			the angel ʳ*set his sickle to work on* (lit. *put* his sickle *in*) the earth and harvested the whole vintage . . . and *put* it into a huge winepress,

2: FOUNDATION – FOUNDING

a) the Foundation, Making (of the world)

Mt 13 35		3	(cf. Ps 78 2) I will . . . expound things hidden since the *foundation* ᵛ of the world.
25 34		3	the kingdom prepared for you since the *foundation* of the world.
Lk 11 50		3	every prophet's blood that has been shed since the *foundation* of the world,
Jn 17 24		3	Father, . . . you loved me before the *foundation* of the world.
Ep 1 4		3	Before the world was *made*, he chose us,
Heb 4 3		3	God's work was undoubtedly all finished at the ʳbeginning (lit. *foundation*) of the world;
9 26		3	or else [Christ] would have had to suffer over and over again since the world ʳbegan (lit. *was made*).
1 P 1 20		3	though [Christ was] known since before the world was *made*,
Rv 13 8		3	everybody whose name has not been written down since the *foundation* of the world in the book of life
17 8		3	the people . . . whose names have not been written since the ʳbeginning (lit. *foundation*) of the world in the book of life,

b) the Founding (of a dynasty)

Heb 11 11		3	It was equally by faith that Sarah . . . was made able to ʳ*conceive* (lit. *found* a posterity),

4. PUT: *DIDŌMI*

didōmi 11/415

Lk	6 38		a full measure . . . will be ⌐poured (lit. *put*) into your lap;
	7 44		you ⌐poured (lit. *put*) no water over my feet,
	12 51	X	Do you suppose that I am here to *bring* peace on earth?
	15 22	<	the father said to his servants, '. . . *put* a ring on his finger'
	19 23	<	why did you not *put* my money in the bank?
2 Co	8 16	Θ	I thank God for *putting* into Titus' heart the same concern for you
Heb	8 10	Θ	(Jr 31 33) I will *put* my laws into their minds
	10 16	Θ	(Jr 31 33) I will *put* my laws into their hearts
Rv	3 8	X	I have ⌐opened in front of you a (lit. *put* in front of you an open) door
	13 16		He compelled everyone . . . to ⌐be branded (lit. have a brand-mark *put*) on the right hand or on the forehead,
	17 17	Θ	God ⌐influenced (lit. *put* into) their minds to do what he intended,

5. APPOINT(ED), PREDESTINE(D): *PRO-CHEIRIZOMAI*

pro-cheirizomai 3

Ac	3 20	Θ	the Lord . . . will send you the Christ he has *predestined*,
	22 14	Θ	The God of our ancestors has ⌐chosen (lit. *appointed*) you to know his will
	26 16	X	I have appeared to you . . . to *appoint* you as my servant

6. LAID, SET, PLACED DESTINED: *KEIMAI*

1	*keimai 14/24*		4	*para-keimai 2*
3	*epi-keimai 4/7*		2	*pro-keimai 5*

1: (BE) LAID SET, PLACED

Mt	3 10		Even now the axe *is laid* to the roots of the trees,
	5 14		A city ⌐built (lit. *set*) on a hill-top cannot be hidden,
Lk	3 9		even now the axe *is laid* to the roots of the trees,
	12 19		you have plenty of good things *laid by* for many years to come;
Jn	2 6		six stone water jars ⌐standing (lit. *set*) [there], meant for the ablutions
	11 38	3	it was a cave with a stone *placed* to close the opening.
	19 29		A jar full of vinegar ⌐stood (lit. *was placed*) there,
	21 9	/3	they saw that there was . . . a charcoal fire *set* with fish *laid* cooking on it.
1 Co	3 11		For the foundation, nobody can lay any other than the one which has already been *laid*, that is Jesus Christ.

Rv	4 2		I saw a throne ⌐standing (lit. *set*) in heaven,

2: (BE) DESTINED, PUT – SET UP, LAID DOWN

Lk	2 34	X	this child . . . is *destined* for the fall and for the rising of many
Ph	1 16		⌐this is my invariable way of defending (lit. I have been *put* [here] to defend) the gospel.
1 Co	9 16	3	preaching the gospel . . . is a duty which has been *laid on* me;
1 Th	3 3		⌐these [troubles] are bound to come our way (lit. we have been *destined* for these):
1 Tm	1 9		laws are not *framed* for people who are good.
Heb	9 10	3	they are rules about the outward life, . . . intended to be *in force* only until it should be time to reform them.
Rv	21 16		The plan of the city *is* perfectly square,

3: BE (WITHIN REACH, IN THE POWER OF, PRESENT)

Rm	7 18	4	though the will to do what is good ⌐is in me (lit. *is within reach*), the performance is not,
	21	4	every single time I want to do good it is something evil that *comes to hand.*
2 Co	8 12	2	As long as the readiness *is* [there], a man is acceptable with whatever he can afford;
Heb	6 18	2	take a firm grip on the hope that is *held out* to us.
	12 1	2	we . . . should . . . keep running steadily the race ⌐we have started (lit. that *is before* us).
	2	2	for the sake of the joy which *was* still in the future, [Jesus] endured the cross,
Jude	7	2	The fornication of Sodom and Gomorrah . . . *is* a warning to us

7. APPOINT: *CHEIRO-TONEŌ*

cheiro-toneō 2

Ac	14 23		In each of these churches [Paul and Barnabas] *appointed* elders,
2 Co	8 19		the same brother . . . has been ⌐elected (or: *appointed*) by the churches to be our companion

8. SET UP (A TENT): *PĒGNYMI*

pēgnymi 1

Heb	8 2 Θ		the true Tent of Meeting which the Lord, and not any man, *set up.*

Q

QUARREL – DISPUTE

1. Quarrel, Argue, Dispute – Protest – Fight: *machē*
2. Wrangle, Quarrel – Contention – Strife, Fighting: *eris*
3. Unending dispute, Endless Wrangle: *dia-para-tribē*
4. Dispute, Argue: *philo-neikia*
5. Speak against, Say that . . . not – Contradict, (Make an) Objection – Argue, Dispute: *anti-legō*

6. Contradiction – Dispute – Refractory: *anti-thesis*
7. Dissension, Disagreement: *dicho-stasia*
8. Selfish ambition, Selfishness – Rivalry – Quarrel: *eritheia*
9. Rebellion, Revolt – Rebel: *para-pikrasmos*

---

1. QUARREL, ARGUE, DISPUTE – PROTEST – FIGHT: *MACHĒ*

1	*machē* 4	6	*(logo-)machia* 1
2	*machomai* 4	7	*(theo-)machos* 1
3	*a-machos* 2	8	*(thērio-)macheō* 1
4	*dia-machomai* 1	9	*(thymo-)macheō* 1
5	*(logo-)macheō* 1		

Jn 6 52 — 2 the Jews started *arguing* with one another:
Ac 5 39 — 7 you might find yourselves *fighting* against God.
7 26 — 2 [Moses] came across some of [his countrymen] ⌐*fighting* (or: *quarrelling*),
12 20 — 9 Herod was *on bad terms* with the Tyrians and Sidonians.
23 9 — some of the scribes from the Pharisees' party stood up and 4 *protested strongly*.
1 Co 15 32 — If my motives were only human ones, what good would it do 8 me to *fight* the wild animals at Ephesus?
2 Co 7 5 — [in] Macedonia . . . we found trouble on all sides: *quarrels* outside, misgivings inside.
1 Tm 3 3 — 3 [The president must be] kind and ⌐*peaceable* (lit. *not quarrelsome*).
6 4 — [A false teacher] must be full of self-conceit – with a craze 6 for . . . *arguing* about words.
2 Tm 2 14 — 5 there is to be no *wrangling* about words:
23 — these . . . silly speculations . . . only give rise to *quarrels*:
24 — 2 a servant of the Lord is not to *engage in quarrels*,
Tt 3 2 — 3 [Remind them that it is their duty] *not to go* slandering other people or *picking quarrels*,
9 — avoid . . . the quibbles and *disputes* about the Law
Jm 4 1 — Where do these wars and *battles* between yourselves first start? . . . ² . . . you *fight* to get your own way by force.

---

2. WRANGLE, QUARREL – CONTENTION – STRIFE, FIGHTING: *ERIS*

1 *eris* 9   2 *erizō* 1

Mt 12 19 X — 2 (cf. Is 42 2) [My servant] will not *brawl* or shout,
Rm 1 29 — [men] are . . . addicted to envy, murder, *wrangling*.
13 13 — Let us live decently . . : no . . . *wrangling* or jealousy.
1 Co 1 11 — it is clear that there are ⌐*serious differences* (or: *quarrels*) among you.
3 3 — all the jealousy and *wrangling* that there is among you,
2 Co 12 20 — I am afraid . . . that when I come . . . there will be *wrangling*, jealousy,
Ga 5 20 — [the results of self-indulgence are obvious:] feuds and *wrangling*, jealousy,
Ph 1 15 — some of [the brothers] are [announcing the Message] just out of rivalry and *competition*,
1 Tm 6 4 — All that can come of this is jealousy, ⌐*contention* (or: *strife*),
Tt 3 9 — avoid . . . the *quibbles* and disputes about the Law

---

3. UNENDING DISPUTE, ENDLESS WRANGLE: *DIA-PARA-TRIBĒ*

dia-para-tribē 1

1 Tm 6 5 — [All that can come of this is jealousy, . . .] and *unending disputes* by people who are neither rational nor informed

---

4. DISPUTE, ARGUE: *PHILO-NEIKIA*

1 *philo-neikia* 1   2 *philo-neikos* 1

Lk 22 24 — A *dispute* arose also between [the apostles] about which should be reckoned the greatest,
1 Co 11 16 — 2 To anyone who might still want to *argue*: it is not the custom . . . in the churches of God.

---

5. SPEAK AGAINST, SAY THAT . . . NOT – CONTRADICT, (MAKE AN) OBJECTION – ARGUE, DISPUTE: *ANTI-LEGŌ*

1	*anti-legō* 11	3	*an-anti-rrhētos*
2	*anti-logia* 4	4	*an-anti-rrhētōs* 1

Lk 2 34 — this child . . . is destined . . . to be a sign that is ⌐*rejected* X (lit. *spoken against*)
20 27 — Some Sadducees – those who *say that* there is *no* resurrection – approached him
21 15 — an eloquence and a wisdom that none of your opponents will be able to resist or *contradict*.
Jn 19 12 — anyone who makes himself king is *defying* Caesar.
Ac 4 14 — but when they saw the man who had been cured . ., they could find no *contradictory answer*.
10 29 — 4 That is why I *made no objection* to coming when I was sent for;
13 45 — the Jews . . . *contradicted* everything Paul said.
19 36 — 3 *Nobody can contradict* this and there is no need for you to get excited
28 19 — but the Jews *lodged an objection*, and I was forced to appeal to Caesar,
22 — all we know about this sect is that opinion everywhere ⌐*condemns* (lit. *speaks against*) it.
Rm 10 21 — (Is 65 2 G) Each day I stretched out my hand to a disobedient and *rebellious* people.
Tt 1 9 — so that he can be counted on for . . . refuting [those] *who argue against* [sound doctrine].
2 9 — Tell the slaves that they are to . . . do what [their masters] want without any *argument*.
Heb 6 16 — confirmation [of a promise] by an oath puts an end to all 2 *dispute*.
7 7 — 2 it is in*disputable* that a blessing is given by a superior to an inferior.
12 3 X — 2 Think of the way he stood such *opposition* from sinners
Jude 11 — 2 they have *rebelled* just as Korah did – and share the same fate.

---

6. CONTRADICTION – DISPUTE – REFRACTORY: *ANTI-THESIS*

1 *anti-thesis* 1   2 *anti-dia-tithemai* 1

1 Tm 6 20 — Have nothing to do with the . . . ⌐*antagonistic beliefs* (or: *contradictions*) of the 'knowledge' which is not knowledge at all;
2 Tm 2 25 — [A servant of the Lord] has to be gentle when he corrects 2 *people who dispute* what he says,

---

7. DISSENSION, DISAGREEMENT: *DICHO-STASIA*

dicho-stasia 2

Rm 16 17 — be on your guard against anybody who encourages ⌐*trouble* (lit. *dissensions*)
Ga 5 20 — [the results of self-indulgence are obvious:] *disagreements*, factions,

---

8. SELFISH AMBITION, SELFISHNESS – RIVALRY – QUARREL: *ERITHEIA*

eritheia 7

Rm 2 8 — for the *unsubmissive* . . . there will be anger and fury.
2 Co 12 20 — I am afraid . . . that when I come . . . there will be wrangling, . . . ⌐*intrigues* (or: *selfish ambitions*) and backbiting
Ga 5 20 — jealousy, bad temper and *quarrels*;

Ph	1 17	The others, who proclaim Christ *for* [jealous or] *selfish motives*, do not mind
	2 3	There must be no ⌐competition (or: *rivalry*) among you,
Jm	3 14	if at heart you have . . . a *self-seeking ambition*, never make any claims for yourself
	16	Wherever you find jealousy and *ambition*, you find disharmony,

9. REBELLION, REVOLT – REBEL: *PARA-PIKRASMOS*

2 *para-pikrainō* 1   1 *para-pikrasmos* 2

Heb	3 8	(Ps 95 8) do not harden your hearts, as happened in the *Rebellion*, on the Day of Temptation in the wilderness,
	15	(Ps 95 8) do not harden your hearts, as happened in the *Rebellion*,
	16	/2 *Rebellion*, ¹⁶ those who *rebelled* . . . were all the people who were brought out of Egypt

---

QUIET – SILENCE

---

1. **Calm:** *galēnē*	**5.** **Silence, Quiet – Be silent, Keep quiet:** *sigaō*
2. **Quiet(en) – Keep calm:** *kata-stellō*	**6.** **Silence, Quiet – Be silent, Keep quiet:** *siōpaō*
3. **Quiet – Tranquil – Undisturbed:** *ēremos*	**7.** **Silence – Be quiet, Be silent:** *phimoō*
4. **Remain quiet – Rest – Silence:** *hēsychios*	

1. CALM: *GALĒNĒ*

galēnē 3

Mt	8 26	[Jesus] stood up and rebuked the winds and the sea; and all was *calm* again.
Mk	4 39	the wind dropped, and all was *calm* again.
Lk	8 24	[the wind and the rough water] subsided and it was *calm* again.

2. QUIET(EN) – KEEP CALM: *KATA-STELLŌ*

kata-stellō 2

Ac	19 35	the town clerk eventually succeeded in *calming* the crowd
	36	⌐there is no need for you to get excited or (lit. you should *keep quiet* and not) do anything rash.

3. QUIET – TRANQUIL – UNDISTURBED: *ĒREMOS*

ēremos 1

1 Tm	2 2	[there should be prayers offered for everyone] so that we may be able to live religious . . . lives in peace and *quiet*.

4. REMAIN QUIET – REST – SILENCE: *HĒSYCHIOS*

1 *hēsychazō* 5   3 *hēsychios* 2
2 *hēsychia* 4

Lk	14 4	[Is it against the law to cure a man on the sabbath or not?] They *remained silent*,
	23 56 ○	on the sabbath day they *rested*, as the Law required.
Ac	11 18	This account ⌐satisfied (lit. *silenced*) [the Jews of Jerusalem],
	21 14	we ⌐gave up the attempt (lit. *remained quiet*),
	22 2	When they realised [Paul] was speaking in Hebrew, the *silence* was even greater than before.

1 Th	4 11	make a point of *living quietly*,
2 Th	3 12	2 we order [those who are living in idleness] to go on *quietly* working
1 Tm	2 2	[there should be prayers offered for everyone] so that we may be able to live religious . . . lives in *peace* and quiet.
	11	2 During instruction, a woman should be *quiet* . . . ¹² I am not giving permission for a woman to teach . . . A woman
	12	2 ought *not to speak*
1 P	3 4	[Women, your ornament] should be . . . the ornament of a sweet and ⌐gentle (or: *quiet*) disposition

5. SILENCE, QUIET – BE SILENT, KEEP QUIET: *SIGAŌ*

1 *sigaō* 10   2 *sigē* 2

Lk	9 36	The disciples *kept silence* and . . . told no one what they had seen.
	18 39	The people in front scolded [the blind man] and told him to *keep quiet*, but he shouted all the louder,
	20 26	[Give back to Caesar what belongs to Caesar;] his answer took them by surprise and they were *silenced*.
Ac	12 17	With a gesture of his hand [Peter] *stopped* them *talking*,
	15 12	This *silenced* the entire assembly, and they listened to Barnabas and Paul . . . ¹³ When they ⌐had finished (lit. *were quiet*) it was James who spoke.
	13	
	21 40	2 When all was quiet again [Paul] spoke to them in Hebrew.
Rm	16 25	I proclaim . . . the revelation of a mystery *kept secret* for endless ages,
1 Co	14 28	If there is no interpreter present, [people with the gift of tongues] must *keep quiet* in church
	30	If one of the listeners receives a revelation, then the man who is already speaking should ⌐stop (lit. *be silent*).
	34	women are to *remain quiet* at meetings
Rv	8 1	2 The Lamb then broke the seventh seal, and there was *silence* in heaven for about half an hour.

6. SILENCE, QUIET – BE SILENT, KEEP QUIET: *SIŌPAŌ*

siōpaō 10

Mt	20 31	the crowd scolded [the two blind men] and told them to *keep quiet*,
	26 63 X	[The high priest said, 'Have you no answer to that?'] But Jesus *was silent*.
Mk	3 4	[Jesus] said to them, 'Is it against the law on the sabbath day to do good, or to do evil . . . ?' But they *said nothing*.
	4 39	[Jesus] said to the sea, '*Quiet* [now]! Be calm!'
	9 34	[The disciples] *said nothing* because they had been arguing which of them was the greatest.
	10 48	many of them scolded [the blind man] and told him to *keep quiet*,
	14 61 X	[The high priest put this question to Jesus, 'Have you no answer to that?'] But he *was silent* and made no answer at all.
Lk	1 20	[The angel said to Zechariah,] you will be *silenced* and have no power of speech
	19 40	I tell you, if [the disciples] *keep silence* the stones will cry out.
Ac	18 9	the Lord spoke to Paul in a vision, 'Do not be afraid to speak out, nor allow yourself to be *silenced*:

7. SILENCE – BE QUIET, BE SILENT: *PHIMOŌ*

phimoō 6/7

Mt	22 12 <	'How did you get in here . . . without a wedding garment?' And the man *was silent*.
	34	the Pharisees heard that [Jesus] had *silenced* the Sadducees
Mk	1 25	Jesus said [to the unclean spirit], '*Be quiet*! Come out of him!'
	4 39	[Jesus] said to the sea, '*Quiet now*! ⌐*Be calm* (or: *Be silent*)!'
Lk	4 35	Jesus said [to the unclean spirit], '*Be quiet*! Come out of him!'
1 P	2 15	God wants you to be good citizens, so as to *silence* what fools are saying in their ignorance.

R

RECEIVE – ACCEPT

1. Receive, Accept – Get (back): *lambanō*
  a) Receive (the Holy Spirit)
  b) Receive (the gospel message)
  c) Receive, Accept (a person) – Get (a person) back–Welcome
  d) Receive, Accept, Be given (a thing) – Welcome–Get (back)

2. Receive, Accept, Welcome: *dechomai*
  a) (God, Jesus) Receives, Welcomes – Acceptable, Of favour (to God)

  b) Accept, Welcome, Receive (the word of God, the kingdom)
  c) Welcome, Receive, Accept (a person)
  d) a Reception – Party
  e) Accept (a thing)
  f) Receive (a thing)
  g) Receive = Take

3. Welcome, Make (a person) welcome: *syn-agō*

4. Receive, Be given, Get – Gain, Recover – (Be) Repaid: *komizō*

1. RECEIVE, ACCEPT – GET (BACK): *LAMBANŌ*

1	*lambanō*	123/257	5	*meta-lambanō*	3/7
6	*lēmpsis*	1	9	*meta-lēmpsis*	1
7	*anti-lambanomai*	1/3	2	*para-lambanō*	13/50
3	*apo-lambanō*	8/9	4	*pros-lambanomai*	6/12
8	*hypo-lambanō*	1/5	10	*pros-lēmpsis*	1

a) *Receive (the Holy Spirit)*

Jn 7 39   [Jesus] was speaking of the Spirit which those who believed in him were to *receive*;

14 17   [The Father will give you] that Spirit of truth whom the world can never *receive*

20 22   *Receive* the Holy Spirit.

Ac 2 33   [Jesus] has *received* from the Father the Holy Spirit,
    38   you will *receive* the gift of the Holy Spirit.

8 15   [the apostles] prayed for the Samaritans to *receive* the Holy Spirit . . . [17] . . . and they *received* the Holy Spirit.
  17
  19   Give me the same power . . . so that anyone I lay my hands on will *receive* the Holy Spirit.

10 47   now [the pagans] have *received* the Holy Spirit just as much as we have

19 2   Did you *receive* the Holy Spirit when you became believers?

1 Co 2 12   instead of the spirit of the world, we have *received* the Spirit that comes from God,

2 Co 11 4   you have only to receive a new spirit, different from the one you have already *received* . . . and you welcome it

Ga 3 2   was it because you practised the Law that you *received* the Spirit . . .?

14   This was done . . . so that through faith we might *receive* the promised Spirit.

b) *Receive (the gospel message)*

1 Co 11 23   2 this is what I *received* from the Lord, and . . . passed on to you:

15 1   2 I want to remind you of . . . the gospel that you *received*
  3   2 I taught you what I had ⸢been taught (lit. *received*) myself,

Ga 1 9   if anyone preaches a version of the Good News different from the one you have already ⸢heard (lit. *received*), he is to be condemned . . . [11] . . . the Good News I preached
  2
  12   2 is not a human message [12] that I ⸢was given by (lit. *received* from) men,

Ph 4 9   Keep doing all the things that you learnt from me and have
  2   ⸢been taught (lit. *received*)

Col 2 6   2 live your whole life according to the Christ you have *received*

1 Th 2 13   2 as soon as you ⸢heard (lit. *received*) the message that we brought . . . you accepted it

4 1   we urge you . . . to make more and more progress in the
  2   kind of life that . . . God wants, as you ⸢learnt (lit. *received*) from us,

2 Th 3 6   live according to the tradition ⸢we passed on to you (lit. you
  2   *received* from us).

c) *Receive, Accept (a person) – Get (a person) back – Welcome*

Θ = Receive God   X = Receive Jesus

Mk 14 65 Δ X   the attendants ⸢rained blows on him (lit. *received* him with blows).

Lk 15 27   3 your father has killed the calf . . . because he has *got* [your brother] *back* safe and sound.

Jn 1 11   He came to his own domain and his own people did not
  12 X 2/   *accept* him. [12] But to all who did *accept* him he gave power
5 43   X   I have come in the name of my Father and you refuse to *accept* me; if someone else comes in his own name you will *accept* him.

13 20 X Θ   whoever *welcomes* the one I send *welcomes* me, and whoever *welcomes* me *welcomes* the one who sent me.

Ac 24 27   Felix ⸢was succeeded by (lit. *received* as his successor) Porcius Festus

28 2   4 The inhabitants [of Malta] . . . *made* us all *welcome*,

Rm 11 15   Since [the] rejection [of the Jews] meant the reconciliation of
  10   the world, do you know what their ⸢admission (or: *acceptance*) will mean?

14 1   4 If a person's faith is not strong enough, *welcome* him all the
  3   4 same . . . [3] . . . since God has *welcomed* them.

15 7   It can only be to God's glory, then, for you to ⸢treat (lit.
  4   *accept*) each other in the same [friendly] way as Christ
  4   ⸢treated (lit. *accepted*) you.

Phm 17   4 *welcome* [Onesimus] as you would me;

Heb 11 35   Some ⸢came back to (lit. were *received* by) their wives from the dead, by resurrection;

2 Jn 10   If anyone comes to you bringing a different doctrine, you must not *receive* him in your house

3 Jn 8   8 it is our duty to *welcome* men of this sort

d) *Receive, Accept, Be given (a thing) – Welcome – Get (back)*

G = Receive the gospel message

Mt 7 8   the one who asks always *receives*; the one who searches always finds;

10 8   You *received* without charge, give without charge.
  41   Anyone who welcomes a prophet . . . will *have* a prophet's reward; and anyone who welcomes a holy man . . . will *have* a holy man's reward.

13 20   The one who received [the seed] on patches of rock is the
  G   man who hears the word and *welcomes* it at once with joy.

19 29   everyone who has left houses, brothers . . . will *be repaid* a hundred times over,

20 9   those who were hired at about the eleventh hour . . .
  10 <   *received* one denarius each. [10] When the first came, they
  <   expected to *get* more, but they too *received* one denarius each.

21 22   if you have faith, everything you ask for in prayer you will *receive*.

25 16 <   The man who had *received* the five talents . . . made five more.

18 <   the man who had *received* one [talent] . . . hid his master's money.

20 <   The man who had *received* the five talents came forward bringing five more.

24 <   Last came forward the man who had *received* the one talent.

Mk 4 16   those who receive the seed on patches of rock are people who,
  G   when first they hear the word, *welcome* it . . . with joy.

10 30   [there is no one who has left house, brothers . . .] who will not *be repaid* a hundred times over.

11 24   everything you ask and pray for, believe that you have *received* it already,

12 40   The more severe will be the sentence [the scribes] *receive*.

Lk 6 34   if you lend to those from whom you hope to *receive*, what thanks can you expect? Even sinners lend to sinners to
  3   *get back* the same amount.

11 10   the one who asks always *receives*; the one who searches always finds;

16 25   remember that during your life ⸢good things came your way
  < 3   (lit. you *received* good things), just as bad things came the way of Lazarus.

18 30   [there is no one who has left house, wife . . . who will not *be given repayment* many times over

19 12   A man of noble birth went to a distant country to ⸢be appoint-
  <   ed king (lit. *receive* a kingdom).

15 <   on his return, having *received* his appointment as king, he sent for those servants

20 47   The more severe will be the sentence [the scribes] *receive*.

23 41   3 we are ⸢paying (lit. *receiving* due payment) for what we did.

Jn 1 16   from his fulness we have, all of us, *received*
3 11 G   you people ⸢reject (lit. will not *accept*) our evidence.
32   He . . . bears witness . . . even if his testimony is not
33 G   *accepted*; [33] though all who do *accept* his testimony are attesting the truthfulness of God;

4 36 <   the reaper *is being paid* his wages,

Jn	5 34	not that I ʳdepend on (lit. *accept*) human testimony;
	41	As for human approval, ʳthis means nothing to me (lit. I do not *accept* it).
	6 7	Two hundred denarii would only buy enough [bread] ʳto give them a small piece each (lit. for each of them to *receive* a small piece).
	7 23	a man can ʳbe circumcised (lit. *receive* circumcision) on the sabbath
	10 18	this is the command I have *been given* by my Father.
	12 48 G	he who . . . ʳrefuses (lit. will not *accept*) my words has his judge already: the word itself
	13 30	As soon as Judas had ʳtaken (lit. *received*) the piece of bread he went out.
	16 24	Ask and you will *receive*, and so your joy will be complete.
	17 8 G	they have truly *accepted* this, that I came from you,
	19 30	After Jesus had ʳtaken (or: *received*) the vinegar he said,
Ac	1 8	you will *receive* power when the Holy Spirit comes on you,
	3 3	[the lame man] begged (G to *receive* [something]) from [Peter and John] . . . ⁵ He turned to them expectantly, hoping to *get* something from them,
	5	
	10 43	all who believe in Jesus will ʳhave their sins forgiven (lit. *receive* forgiveness of their sins)
	16 24	following his instructions as he'd *received* them, [the gaoler] threw [Paul and Silas] into the inner prison
	17 15	Paul's escort . . . went back ʳwith (lit. having *received*) instructions for Silas and Timothy to rejoin Paul
	20 24	I have carried out the mission ʳthe Lord Jesus gave me (lit. I *received* from the Lord Jesus)
	35	There is more happiness in giving than in *receiving*.
	25 16	the accused . . . *is given* an opportunity to defend himself against the charge.
	26 10	I . . . threw many . . . saints into prison, acting on authority *received* from the chief priests,
	18	so that [the pagans] may . . . *receive* . . . forgiveness of their sins
Rm	1 5	Through [Jesus Christ] we *received* grace and our apostolic mission to preach
	27	3 their menfolk . . . *getting* an appropriate reward for their perversion,
	4 11	when [Abraham] was circumcised later it was *received* only as a sign
	5 11	through our Lord Jesus Christ . . . we have already *gained* our reconciliation.
	17	Jesus Christ will cause everyone to reign in life who *receives* the free gift . . . of being made righteous.
	8 15	The spirit you *received* is not the spirit of slaves . . . it is the spirit of sons that you *received*,
	13 2	anyone who resists authority is rebelling against God's decision, and such ʳan act is bound to be punished (lit. people are bound to *receive* their punishment).
1 Co	2 12	instead of the spirit of the world, we have *received* the Spirit that comes from God,
	3 8	each will duly *be paid* according to his share in the work.
	14	If his structure stands up to [the fire], he will *get* his wages;
	4 7	What do you have that *was* not *given* to you? And if it *was given*, how can you boast as though it *were* not *given*?
	14 5	the man who prophesies is of greater importance . . . unless of course [the man with the gift of tongues] offers an interpretation so that the church may *get* some benefit.
2 Co	11 4	you have only to *receive* a new spirit, different from the one you have already received . . . and you welcome it
	24	Five times I had the thirty-nine lashes from the Jews;
Ga	4 5	3 [God sent his Son] to enable us to ʳbe adopted (lit. *receive* adoption) as sons.
Ph	4 15	no other church helped me with gifts ʳof money (lit. and *receipts*).
	6	
Col	3 24	3 ʳthe Lord will repay you by making (lit. you will *receive* payment from the Lord when he makes) you his heirs.
	4 10	you ʳwere sent (lit. have *received*) some instructions about [Mark];
	17	Remember the service that ʳthe Lord wants you to do (lit. you have *received* in the Lord),
1 Tm	4 3	9 God created [foods] to be *accepted* with thanksgiving
	6 2	7 those who have [the benefit of] their services are . . . dear to God.
2 Tm	2 6	5 it is the working farmer who *has* the first claim on any crop
Heb	4 16	Let us be confident . . . that we shall *have* mercy from him and find grace
	6 7	5 A field that . . . gives the crops that are wanted . . . *is given* God's blessing;
	7 5	any of the descendants of Levi who are *admitted* to the priesthood are obliged . . . to take tithes
	8	in the one case it is ordinary mortal men who *receive* the tithes,
	9	Levi himself, who *receives* tithes, actually paid them,
	9 15	[Christ] brings a new covenant . . . so that the people who were called . . . may . . . *receive* what was promised:
	10 26	we have *been given* knowledge of the truth,
	11 8	Abraham . . . set out for a country that was the inheritance *given* to him

Heb	11 11	by faith . . . Sarah . . . ʳwas made able (lit. *was given* the ability) to conceive,
	36	Some *had* to bear being pilloried and flogged,
	12 10	5 [God punishes us] for our own good, so that we may *share* his own holiness.
	28	2 We have *been given* [possession of] a unshakeable kingdom.
Jm	1 7	That sort of person, in two minds, . . . must not expect ʳthat the Lord will give him anything (lit. to *receive* anything from the Lord).
	3 1	those of us who teach ʳcan expect (lit. will *receive*) a stricter judgement.
	4 3	when you do pray and don't *get* it, it is because you have not prayed properly,
	5 7	a farmer . . . patiently . . . waits for the precious fruit of the ground until it has *had* the autumn rains
1 P	4 10	Each one of you has *received* a special grace, so, . . . put yourselves at the service of others.
2 P	1 17	[Christ] ʳwas honoured and glorified by (lit. *received* honour and glory from) God the Father,
1 Jn	2 27	you have not lost the anointing that ʳhe gave you (lit. you *received*),
	3 22	whatever we ask him, we shall *receive*,
	5 9 G	We *accept* the testimony of human witnesses, but God's testimony is much greater,
2 Jn	4	your children have been living . . . ʳas we were commanded by (lit. following the commandment *received* from) the Father.
	8	3 Watch yourselves, or all our work will be lost and not *get* the reward it deserves.
3 Jn	7	It was . . . for the sake of the name that they set out, without ʳdepending on the pagans for anything (lit. *accepting* anything from the pagans);
Rv	2 17	to those who prove victorious I will give . . . a stone with a new name written on it, known only to the man who *receives* it.
	28	[To those who prove victorious I will give the authority] which I myself have *been given* by my Father,
	3 3 G	do you remember how eager you were when you first *received* and heard the message?
	4 11	you are worthy ʳof (lit. to *be given*) glory and honour and power,
	5 12	The Lamb . . . is worthy to *be given* power, riches,
	14 9	those who . . . have ʳhad themselves branded (lit. *accepted* the brand-mark) [will be made to drink the wine of God's fury]
	11	There will be no respite . . . for those who . . . *accepted* branding with its name.
	17 12	The ten horns are ten kings who have not yet *been given* their royal power but will *have* royal authority
	18 4	Come out . . . away from her, so that you do not share in her crimes and *have* the same plagues to bear.
	19 20	[the false prophet] had deceived all who had ʳbeen branded (lit. *accepted* the brand-mark)
	20 4	I saw . . . those who . . . would not *have* the brand-mark on their foreheads
	22 17	all who want it may *have* the water of life,

2. RECEIVE, ACCEPT, WELCOME: *DECHOMAI*

1	*dechomai*	56	13	*dia-dechomai*	1
4	*dektos*	5	14	*eis-dechomai*	1
8	*dochē*	2	12	*epi-dechomai*	2
9	*ana-dechomai*	2	7	*hypo-dechomai*	4
2	*apo-dechomai*	7	3	*para-dechomai*	6
10	*apo-dektos*	2	5	*pros-dechomai*	6/14
11	*apo-dochē*	2	6	*eu-pros-dektos*	5

a) (God, Jesus) Receives, Welcomes – Acceptable, Of favour (to God)

Lk	4 19	4 (Is 61 2) [God sent me] to proclaim the Lord's year *of favour*
Ac	7 59 X	Stephen said in invocation, 'Lord Jesus, *receive* my spirit'.
	10 35	anybody . . . who fears God and does what is right is *acceptable* to him.
Rm	15 16	4 I am to carry out my priestly duty . . . and so make [the pagans] *acceptable* as an offering,
2 Co	6 2	4 [God] says (Is 49 8): At the *favourable* time, I have listened to you; . . . Well, now is the *favourable* time;
	17	14 (Zp 3 20) I will *welcome* you
Ph	4 18	I have received . . . the offering that you sent . . . the sacrifice that God *accepts* and finds pleasing.
1 Tm	2 3	[To offer prayers for everyone] is right, and will ʳplease (lit. be *something acceptable* to) God
	5 4	[children are to] repay their debt to their parents because this is ʳwhat pleases (lit. *what is acceptable* to) God.
Heb	12 6	3 the Lord . . . punishes all those that he *acknowledges* as his sons.
1 P	2 5	[you are] the holy priesthood that offers the spiritual sacrifices which Jesus Christ has *made acceptable* to God,
	6	

b) Accept, Welcome, Receive (the word of God, the kingdom)

Mt 11	14	he, if you will ⌐believe me (lit. *accept* it), is the Elijah who was to return.
Mk 4	20	3 they hear the word and ⌐accept (or: *welcome*) it and yield a harvest,
10	15	anyone who does not *welcome* the kingdom of God like a little child will never enter it.
Lk 8	13	Those on the rock are people who . . . *welcome* the word with joy.
18	17	anyone who does not *welcome* the kingdom of God like a little child will never enter it.
Ac 2	41	2 they *accepted* what [Peter] said and were baptised.
7	38	[Moses] ⌐was entrusted with (or: *received*) words of life to hand on to ᵛus (G you).
8	14	Samaria had *accepted* the word of God,
11	1	the pagans too had *accepted* the word of God,
17	11	[the Jews at Beroea] *welcomed* the word very readily;
22	18	3 leave Jerusalem at once; they will not *accept* the testimony you are giving about me.
24	15	5 I hold the same hope in God as they ⌐do (lit. *accept*) that there will be a resurrection
1 Co 2	14	An unspiritual person . . . does not *accept* anything of the Spirit of God:
2 Co 6	1	we beg you . . . not to neglect the grace of God that you have *received*.
11	4	you have only to receive . . . a new gospel, different from the one you have already *accepted* – and you welcome in
Ep 6	17	*accept* salvation . . . and [receive] the word of God from the Spirit to use as a sword.
1 Th 1	6	with the joy of the Holy Spirit . . . you *took to* the gospel,
2	13	as soon as you heard the message . . . you *accepted* it
2 Th 2	10	they would not *grasp* the love of the truth
1 Tm 1	15	Here is a saying that you can rely on and ⌐nobody should doubt (lit. which is worth full *acceptance*):
4	9	that is a saying that you can rely on and ⌐nobody should doubt (lit. which is worth full *acceptance*).
Heb 11	17	[Abraham] offered to sacrifice his only son even though ⌐the promises had been made to him (lit. he had *received* the promises)
Jm 1	21	*accept* and submit to the word which has been planted in you

c) Welcome, Receive, Accept (a person)

Θ = Receive God   X = Welcome Jesus

Mt 10	14	if anyone does not *welcome* you or listen to what you have to say . . . walk out of the house
40 X		Anyone who *welcomes* you *welcomes* me; and those who
41 X Θ		*welcome* me *welcome* the one who sent me. ⁴¹ Anyone who *welcomes* a prophet . . . will have a prophet's reward; and anyone who *welcomes* a holy man . . . will have a holy man's reward.
18	5 X	Anyone who *welcomes* a little child like this in my name *welcomes* me.
Mk 6	11	if any place does not *welcome* you . . . walk away
9	37	Anyone who *welcomes* . . . little children in my name,
X Θ		*welcomes* me; and anyone who *welcomes* me *welcomes* not me but the one who sent me.
Lk 4	24	4 no prophet is ever *accepted* in his own country.
8	40 X	2 Jesus was *welcomed* by the crowd,
9	5	As for those who do not *welcome* you, . . . leave their town
11	2	[Jesus] *made* [the crowds] *welcome*
48 X		Anyone who *welcomes* this little child in my name *welcomes*
X Θ		me; and anyone who *welcomes* me *welcomes* the one who sent me.
53 X		the people [in a Samaritan village] would not *receive* [Jesus]
10	8	Whenever you go into a town where they *make* you *welcome*,
10		eat what is set before you . . . ¹⁰ But whenever you enter a town and they do not *make* you *welcome*, go out
38 X	7	a woman named Martha *welcomed* him into her house.
15	2	5 This man . . . *welcomes* sinners and eats with them.
16	4	I know what I will do to make sure that . . . there will be some to *welcome* me into their homes.
9		win . . . friends, and thus make sure that . . . they will *welcome* you into the tents of eternity.
19	6 X	7 [Zacchaeus] hurried down and ⌐welcomed him joyfully.
Jn 4	45 X	the Galileans *received* him well,
Ac 3	21 X	heaven must ⌐keep (lit. *receive*) [Jesus] till the universal restoration comes
15	4	When [Paul and Barnabas] arrived in Jerusalem they were
3		*welcomed* by the church
17	7	[The people who have been turning the whole world upside
7		down] have been ⌐staying (lit. *welcomed*) at Jason's.
18	27	2 the brothers . . . wrote asking the disciples to *welcome* [Apollos]
21	17	2 On our arrival in Jerusalem the brothers *gave* us *a* very warm *welcome*.
28	7	9 Publius . . . *received* us and entertained us . . . for three days.
30		2 Paul . . . . *welcomed* all who came to visit him,

Rm 16	2	5 *Give* [Phoebe], in union with the Lord, *a welcome* worthy of saints,
2 Co 7	15	[Titus] remembers . . . with what deep respect you *welcomed* him.
8	12	6 As long as the readiness is there, a man is *acceptable* with whatever he can afford;
11	16	let no one take me for a fool; but if you must, then ⌐treat (lit. *accept*) me as a fool
Ga 4	14 X	you *welcomed* me as an angel of God, as if I were Christ Jesus
Ph 2	29	5 *Give* [Epaphroditus] a most hearty *welcome*, in the Lord;
Col 4	10	if [Mark] comes to you, *give* him *a* [warm] *welcome*
Heb 11	31	Rahab the prostitute *welcomed* the spies and so was not killed with the unbelievers.
Jm 2	25	Rahab the prostitute, justified by her deeds because she
7		*welcomed* the messengers
3 Jn	9	I have written a note for the members of the church but
10		Diotrephes . . . refuses to *accept* us. ¹⁰ . . . As if that were
12		not enough, he not only refuses to *welcome* our brothers,
12		but prevents . . . other people . . . from doing it,

d) a Reception – Party

Lk 5	29	8 In [Jesus's] honour Levi held a great *reception* in his house,
14	13	8 when you have a *party*, invite the poor,

e) Accept (a thing)

Ac 16	21	[Paul and Silas] are advocating practices which it is unlawful
3		. . . to *accept* or follow.
24	3	2 [your reforms] are matters we *accept* . . . with all gratitude.
Rm 15	31	6 pray . . . that the aid I carry to Jerusalem may be *accepted* by the saints.
2 Co 8	17	[Titus] ⌐did what we asked him (lit. *accepted* our commission);
1 Tm 5	19	3 Never *accept* any accusation brought against an elder unless it is supported by two or three witnesses.
Heb 10	34	5 you happily *accepted* being stripped of your belongings,
11	35	5 others submitted to torture, refusing to *accept* release

f) Receive (a thing)

Ac 7	45	13 [The Tent of Testimony] was *handed down* from one ancestor of ours to another
22	5	⌐they even sent me with (lit. I even *received*) letter to their brothers in Damascus.
28	21	We have *received* no letters from Judaea about you,
Ph 4	18	I have *received* from Epaphroditus the offering that you sent,

g) Receive = Take

Lk 2	28	[Simeon] *took* [the child Jesus] into his arms and blessed God;
16	6	Here, *take* your bond; sit down straight away and write fifty.
7		Here, *take* your bond and write eighty.
22	17	*taking* a cup [Jesus] gave thanks

3. WELCOME, MAKE (A PERSON) WELCOME: *SYN-AGŌ*

syn-agō 3/59

Mt 25	35 X	I was a stranger and you *made* me *welcome*;
38 X		When did we see you a stranger and *make* you *welcome* . . .?
43 X		I was a stranger and you never *made* me *welcome*,

4. RECEIVE, BE GIVEN, GET – GAIN, RECOVER – (BE) REPAID: *KOMIZŌ*

komizō 11/12

Mt 25	27 <	on my return I would have *recovered* my capital with interest.
2 Co 5	10	each of us will ⌐get (or: *receive*) what he deserves for the things he did in the body, good or bad.
Ep 6	8	everyone . . . will be properly *rewarded* by the Lord
Col 3	25	anyone who does wrong will be *repaid* in kind
Heb 10	36	You will need endurance to . . . *gain* what [God] has promised.
11	13	All these died in faith, before *receiving* any of the things that had been promised
19		[Abraham] *was given back* Isaac from the dead.
39		These are all heroes of faith, but they did not *receive* what was promised.
1 P 1	9	you are sure of *receiving* the end to which your faith looks forward, that is, the salvation of your souls.
5	4	you will *be given* the crown of unfading glory.
2 P 2	13	[These people will] ⌐get their *reward* of (ᵛ suffer) evil for the evil that they do.

REJECT – AVOID – ESCAPE

1. **Reject, Rejection – Throw off, Cast away:** *apo-* and *ek-ballō*
2. **Reject:** *apo-dokimazō*
3. **Reject – Push aside, Thrust away:** *ap-ōtheomai*
4. **Reject, Refuse – Throw off – Give up:** *apo-tithemai*
   1: Reject, Refuse (a person) – Object (to) – Disregard, Flout
   2: Throw off, Lay aside – Give up, Put away – Put off
5. **Disown – Deny – Renounce, Reject:** *arneomai*
6. **Renounce – Have none of:** *apo-legō*
7. **Have nothing to do with, Avoid – Refuse – Excuse:** *par-aiteomai*
   1: Have nothing to do with, Avoid – Refuse (to)
   2: Excuse, Make excuses – Ask to escape

8. **Avoid, Have nothing to do with, Steer clear of:** *peri-(h)istēmi*
9. **Avoid, Have nothing to do with:** *apo-trepō*
10. **Avoid:** *ek-klinō*
11. **Avoid – Draw back, Shrink from – Intend not to:** *stellomai*
    1: Avoid, Keep from – Intend not to
    2: Draw back, Shrink from – Hesitate, Falter – Stop doing
12. **Avoid – Keep from, Abstain:** *ap-echō*
13. **Flee – Escape (from, to) – Shun:** *pheugō*
    1: Flee, Run away, Escape – Take refuge
    2: (figuratively) Flee, Fly from, Shun – Escape from, Survive – Avoid, Evade, Vanish

1. REJECT, REJECTION – THROW OFF, CAST AWAY: APO- and EK-BALLŌ

1 *apo-ballō* 2	3 *apo-bolē* 1/2
2 *apo-blētos* 1	4 *ek-ballō* 1/81

Mk 10 50   *throwing off* his cloak, [the blind man] jumped up and went to Jesus.

Lk 6 22   4 Happy are you when people . . . ⌜denounce (lit. *cast out*) your name as criminal, on account of the Son of Man.

Rm 11 15   3 [the] *rejection* [of the Jews] meant the reconciliation of the world,

1Tm 4 4   2 no food is *to be rejected*,

Heb 10 35   ⌜Be as confident now (lit. Do not *throw away* your confidence), then, since the reward is so great.

2. REJECT: APO-DOKIMAZŌ

apo-dokimazō 9

Mt 21 42 X   (Ps 118 22) It was the stone *rejected* by the builders that became the keystone.

Mk 8 31 X   the Son of Man was destined . . . to be *rejected* by the elders
   12 10 X   (Ps 118 22) It was the stone *rejected* by the builders that became the keystone.

Lk 9 22 X   The Son of Man . . . is . . . to be *rejected* by the elders
   17 25 X   he must suffer grievously and be *rejected* by this generation.
   20 17 X   (Ps 118 22) It was the stone *rejected* by the builders that became the keystone

Heb 12 17   when [Esau] wanted to obtain the blessing afterwards, he was *rejected*

1P 2 4 X   He is the living stone, *rejected* by men but chosen by God
     7 X   (Ps 118 22) the stone *rejected* by the builders has proved to be the keystone,

3. REJECT – PUSH ASIDE, THRUST AWAY: AP-ŌTHEOMAI

ap-ōtheomai 6

Ac 7 27   the man who was attacking his fellow countryman *pushed* [Moses] *aside*.
     39   our ancestors . . . *pushed* [Moses] *aside*, turned back to Egypt in their thoughts,
   13 46   since you have *rejected* [the word of God] . . . we must turn to the pagans.

Rm 11 1   (Ps 94 14) is it possible that God has *rejected* his people?
    2   Of course not. I . . . ² could never agree that God had *rejected* his people,

1Tm 1 19   Some people have *put* conscience *aside* and wrecked their faith in consequence.

4. REJECT, REFUSE – THROW OFF – GIVE UP: APO-TITHEMAI

1	*a-theteō* 10/16	3 *apo-thesis*	2
4	*meta-tithēmi* 1/6	2 *apo-tithemai*	8/9

1: REJECT, REFUSE (A PERSON) – OBJECT (TO) – DISREGARD, FLOUT

Mk 6 26   [Herod] was deeply distressed but . . . he was reluctant to ⌜break his word to (lit. *refuse*) [Herodias' daughter].

Lk 10 16 X   anyone who *rejects* you *rejects* me, and those who *reject* me
     Θ   *reject* the one who sent me.

Jn 12 48 X   he who *rejects* me and refuses my words has his judge already:

Ga 1 6   I am astonished at the promptness with which you have
    4   *turned away* from the one who called you

1Th 4 8 Θ   anyone who *objects* is not *objecting to* a human authority, but to God,

Jude 8 X   these people . . . not only . . . *disregard* authority, but abuse the glorious angels as well.

2: THROW OFF, LAY ASIDE – GIVE UP, PUT AWAY – PUT OFF

Ac 7 58   2 The witnesses *put down* their clothes at the feet of a young man called Saul.

Rm 13 12   2 let us *give up* all the things we prefer to do under cover of the dark;

Ga 2 21   I cannot bring myself to ⌜*give up* (or: *reject*) God's gift:

Ep 4 22   2 you must *put aside* your old self . . ²⁴ so that you can put on the new self
    25   2 ⌜there must be no more (lit. *put away*) lies: You must speak the truth

Col 3 8   2 you . . . must *give* all these things *up*: getting angry, being bad-tempered,

Heb 12 1   2 we . . . should *throw off* everything that hinders us, especially the sin that clings so easily,

Jm 1 21   2 *do away with* all the impurities . . . that are still left in you

1P 2 1   2 Be sure, then, you ⌜are never (lit. *lay aside* [being]) spiteful, or deceitful,
    3 21   3 the baptism . . . is not the *washing off* of physical dirt

2P 1 14   3 I know the time for *taking off* this tent is coming soon,

5. DISOWN – DENY – RENOUNCE, REJECT: ARNEOMAI

1 *arneomai* 33	2 *ap-arneomai* 11

Mt 10 33   the one who *disowns* me in the presence of men, I will *disown* in the presence of my Father
   16 24   2 If anyone wants to be a follower of mine, let him *renounce* himself
   26 34   2 before the cock crows you will have *disowned* me three times.
     35   2 Even if I have to die with you, I will never *disown* you.
     70   [Peter] *denied* it . . . 'I do not know what you are talking about'
     72   again, with an oath, [Peter] *denied* it, 'I do not know the man'.
     75   2 Before the cock crows you will have *disowned* me three times.

Mk 8 34   2 If anyone wants to be a follower of mine, let him *renounce* himself
   14 30   2 before the cock crows twice, you will have *disowned* me three times.
     31   2 If I have to die with you, I will never *disown* you.
     68   [Peter] *denied* it. 'I do not know . . . what you are talking about'
     70   But again [Peter] *denied* it.
     72   2 Before the cock crows twice, you will have *disowned* me three times.

Lk 8 45   'Who touched me?' . . . they all *denied* that they had,
    9 23   If anyone wants to be a follower of mine, let him *renounce* himself
   12 9   the man who *disowns* me in the presence of men will be
         2 *disowned* in the presence of God's angels.
   22 34   2 by the time the cock crows today you will have *denied* three times that you know me.
     57   [Peter] *denied* it. 'Woman, . . . I do not know him.'
     61   2 Before the cock crows today, you will have *disowned* me three times.

Jn 1 20   [John] not only ⌜declared (lit. *denied* [the assertion]) but he declared quite openly, 'I am not the Christ'.
   13 38   before the cock crows you will have *disowned* me three times.
   18 25   'Aren't you another of his disciples?' [Peter] *denied* it
     27   Again Peter *denied* it; and at once a cock crew.

Ac 3 13   the same Jesus you . . . *disowned* in the presence of Pilate
    14   It was you who ᵛaccused (G *disowned*) the Holy One,
   4 16   a miracle has been worked through [Peter and John] in public, and we cannot *deny* it.
   7 35   It was the same Moses that they had *disowned* . . . who was now sent to be both leader and redeemer

1Tm 5 8   Anyone who does not look after his own relations . . . has ⌜*rejected* (or: *renounced*) the faith

2Tm 2 12   If we *disown* [Christ Jesus], then he will *disown* us. ¹³ We
    13   may be unfaithful, but he is always faithful, for he cannot *disown* his own self.

2 Tm	3 5	They will keep up the outward appearance of religion but will have *rejected* the inner power of it.
Tt	1 16	They claim to have knowledge of God but the things they do *are* nothing but *a denial* of him;
	2 12	what we have to do is to *give up* everything that does not lead to God,
Heb	11 24	Moses *refused* to be known as the son of Pharaoh's daughter
2 P	2 1	false teachers . . . will . . . *disown* the Master who purchased their freedom.
1 Jn	2 22	The man who *denies* that Jesus is the Christ – he is the liar, he is Antichrist; and he is *denying* the Father as well as the Son, [23] because no one who has the Father can *deny* the Son,
	23	
Jude	4	Certain people . . . were condemned for . . . *rejecting* our only Master and Lord, Jesus Christ.
Rv	2 13	you . . . did not *disown* your faith in me
	3 8	you have . . . not *disowned* my name.

6. RENOUNCE – HAVE NONE OF: *APO-LEGŌ*

apo-legō 1

2 Co	4 2	we ˹will have none of˺ (or: have *renounced*) the reticence of those who are ashamed,

7. HAVE NOTHING TO DO WITH, AVOID – REFUSE – EXCUSE: *PAR-AITEOMAI*

par-aiteomai 10/12

1: HAVE NOTHING TO DO WITH, AVOID – REFUSE (TO)

1 Tm	4 7	*Have nothing to do with* godless myths and old wives' tales.
	5 11	*Do not accept* young widows
2 Tm	2 23	*Avoid* these futile and silly speculations,
Tt	3 10	If a man disputes what you teach . . . *have no more to do with* him:
Heb	12 25	Make sure that you never *refuse* to listen when [Jesus] speaks. The people who *refused* to listen to the warning . . . could not escape their punishment,

2: EXCUSE, MAKE EXCUSES – ASK TO ESCAPE

Lk	14 18	all alike started to *make excuses*. The first said, 'I have bought a piece of land and must go and see it. Please ˹accept my apologies (lit. have me *excused*)˺.' [19] Another said, 'I have bought five yoke of oxen . . . Please ˹accept my apologies (lit. have me *excused*)˺.'
	19	
Ac	25 11	I do not *ask to be spared* the death penalty.

8. AVOID, HAVE NOTHING TO DO WITH, STEER CLEAR OF: *PERI-(H)ISTĒMI*

peri-(h)istēmi 2/4

2 Tm	2 16	*Have nothing to do with* pointless philosophical discussions
Tt	3 9	*avoid* pointless speculations, and . . . genealogies,

9. AVOID, HAVE NOTHING TO DO WITH: *APO-TREPŌ*

2 *apo-trepō 1*   1 *ek-trepō 1/5*

1 Tm	6 20	Timothy, . . . *have nothing to do with* the pointless philosophical discussions . . . of the 'knowledge' which is not knowledge at all;
2 Tm	3 5	2 *Have nothing to do with* people like that.

10. AVOID: *EK-KLINŌ*

ek-klinō 1/3

Rm	16 17	be on your guard against anybody who encourages trouble . . . *Avoid* them.

11. AVOID – DRAW BACK, SHRINK FROM – INTEND NOT TO: *STELLOMAI*

2 *stellomai 2*   1 *hypo-stellō 4*
                   3 *hypo-stolē 1*

1: AVOID, KEEP FROM – INTEND NOT TO

2 Co	8 20	2 in this way ˹there will be no (lit. we can *avoid*) accusations
2 Th	3 6	2 *keep away from* any of the brothers who refuses to work

2: DRAW BACK, SHRINK FROM – HESITATE, FALTER – STOP DOING

Ac	20 20	I have not ˹*hesitated* to do (or: *shrunk from* doing) anything that would be helpful to you;
	27	I have without *faltering* put before you the whole of God's purpose
Ga	2 12	after certain friends of James arrived [Cephas] *stopped doing* this
Heb	10 38	(Hab 2 4 G) if he *draws back*, my soul will take no pleasure in him
	39	3 You and I are not the sort of people who *draw back*,

12. AVOID – KEEP FROM, ABSTAIN: *AP-ECHŌ*

ap-echō 6/15

Ac	15 20	*abstain* from anything polluted by idols,
	29	you are to *abstain* from food sacrificed to idols,
1 Th	4 3	God . . . wants you to *keep away from* fornication,
	5 22	*avoid* every form of evil.
1 Tm	4 3	[false teachers will] lay down rules about *abstaining* from foods which God created
1 P	2 11	*keep* yourselves *free from* the selfish passions that attack the soul.

13. FLEE – ESCAPE (FROM, TO) – SHUN: *PHEUGŌ*

1	*pheugō 31*	4	*kata-pheugō 2*
5	*phygē 1*	6	*dia-pheugō 1*
3	*apo-pheugō 3*	2	*ek-pheugō 8*

1: FLEE, RUN AWAY, ESCAPE – TAKE REFUGE

Mt	2 13	take the child and his mother with you and *escape* into Egypt,
	8 33	The swineherds *ran off* and made for the town,
	10 23	If they persecute you in one town, *take refuge* in the next; [v] and if they persecute you in that, *take refuge* in another.
	24 16	those in Judaea must *escape* to the mountains;
	20	5 Pray that you will not have to *escape* in winter
	26 56	all the disciples deserted [Jesus] and *ran away*
Mk	5 14	The swineherds *ran off* and told their story in the town
	13 14	those in Judaea must *escape* to the mountains;
	14 50	[the disciples] deserted [Jesus] and *ran away*.
	52	[They caught hold of a young man,] but he left the cloth in their hands and *ran away* naked.
	16 8	the women . . . *ran away* from the tomb
Lk	8 34	The swineherds . . . *ran off*
	21 21	those in Judaea must *escape* to the mountains,
Jn	6 15 X	Jesus . . . [v] *escaped* back (G withdrew) to the hills by himself.
	10 5 <	[The sheep] never follow a stranger but *run away* from him:
	12 <	The hired man . . . *runs away* as soon as he sees a wolf
Ac	7 29	Moses *fled* . . . and . . . went to stay in the land of Midian,
	14 6	4 [Paul and Barnabas] *went off for safety* to Lycaonia
	16 27	2 the gaoler . . . was about to commit suicide, presuming that the prisoners had *escaped*.
	19 16	2 [the sons of Sceva] *fled* from that house . . . badly mauled.
	27 30	some of the crew tried to *escape* from the ship
	42	The soldiers planned to kill the prisoners for fear that any 6 should swim off and *escape*.
2 Co	11 33	I had to be let down . . . through a window in order to 2 *escape*.
Jm	4 7 ①	resist the devil, and he will *run away* from you.
Rv	12 6	the woman *escaped* into the desert,

2: (FIGURATIVELY) FLEE, FLY FROM, SHUN – ESCAPE FROM, SURVIVE – AVOID, EVADE, VANISH

Mt	3 7	who warned you to *fly from* the retribution . . .?
	23 33	how can you *escape* being condemned to hell?
Lk	3 7	who warned you to *fly from* the retribution . . .?
	21 36	2 [Pray] for the strength to *survive* all that is going to happen,
Rm	2 3	2 do you think you will *escape* God's judgement?
1 Co	6 18	˹*Keep away from* (or: *Shun*) fornication.
	10 14	you must *keep clear of* idolatry.

1Th 5 3		the worst suddenly happens . . . and there will be no way 2 for anybody to *evade* it.
1Tm 6 11		as a man dedicated to God you must *avoid* [the love of money, dangerous ambitions]
2Tm 2 22		⌐Instead of (lit. *Avoid*) giving in to your impulses like a young man,
Heb 2 3		2 we shall certainly not ⌐go unpunished (lit. *escape* punishment) if we neglect this salvation
6 18		4 so that we, now we have *found safety*, should have a strong encouragement to take a firm grip on the hope
11 34		[The prophets could] ⌐emerge unscathed from (lit. *escape* the edge of the sword in) battle.
12 25		The people who refused to listen to the warning . . . could 2 not *escape* their punishment,
2P 1 4		3 you will be able . . . to *escape* corruption in a world that is sunk in vice.
2 18		[false teachers] tempt back the ones who have only just 3 *escaped* from paganism,
20		3 anyone who has *escaped* the pollution of the world once . . . and then allows himself to be entangled by it a second time . . . will end up in a worse state than he began in.
Rv 9 6		men . . . will want to die and death will *evade* them.
12 6		the woman *escaped* into the desert,
16 20		Every island *vanished* and the mountains disappeared;
20 11		In his presence, earth and sky *vanished*,

REJOICE – GLAD – HAPPY

---

1. **Joy, Delight, Rejoice – (Be) Happy,**
   Be glad, Be delighted – Joyful,
   Overjoyed: *chairō*
2. **Joy, Gladness – Rejoice, Exult, Be**
   glad: *agalliaō*
3. **Have Joy from a person:** *oninamai*
4. **Rejoice, Celebrate, Make merry –**
   Be glad, Happy: *eu-phrainō*
5. **Glad(ly):** *asmenōs*
6. **Pleasure – Gladly – Delight:**
   hēdonē
   1: Pleasure(s)
   2: Gladly, With delight – Delight (in), Like (to)
7. **(Be) Pleased (with), Delight (in):**
   eu-dokeō
   1: (God) Is pleased (with), De-

lights (in) – Enjoy (God's)
favour – to Please (God)
2: (A person) Is pleased (with),
Delights (in) – Desire,
Choose – Goodwill
8. **to Please, Delight, (Be) Acceptable**
   (to): *areskō*
   1: to Please (God) – (Be)
   Pleasing, Acceptable (to
   God, to the Lord)
   2: to Please, Delight (a person)
   – (Be) Acceptable (to a
   person)
9. **Pleasure – Happiness, Enjoyment:**
   apo-lausis
10. **Cheerful, Cheerfulness:** *hilaros*
11. **Happy – Fortunate – Blessed:**
    makarios

S = Joy // Sadness, Sorrow

---

1. JOY, DELIGHT, REJOICE – (BE) HAPPY, BE GLAD, BE
DELIGHTED – JOYFUL, OVERJOYED: *CHAIRŌ*

1 *chairō* 64/74	3 *syn-chairō* 7
2 *chara*	59

Mt 2 10		The sight of the star ⌐filled [the Magi] (lit. made them *re-* 2 *joice*) with *delight*,
5 12		*Rejoice and be glad*,
13 20		the man who hears the word and welcomes it at once with 2 *joy*.
44 <		2 he hides [the treasure] again, goes off *happy*,
18 13 <		if he finds [the sheep that strayed], ⌐it gives him more joy than do (lit. he *rejoices* more in it than in) the ninety-nine
25 21 <		good and faithful servant, . . . come and join in your 2 master's *happiness*.
23 <		good and faithful servant, . . . come and join in your 2 master's *happiness*.
28 8		2 Filled with awe and great *joy* [Mary of Magdala and the other Mary] . . . ran to tell the disciples.
Mk 4 16		people who, when first they hear the word, welcome it at 2 once with *joy*.
14 11		[the chief priests] *were delighted* to hear [Judas Iscariot's offer to hand Jesus over to them],
Lk 1 14		[Zechariah, Elizabeth is to bear you a son.] He will be your 2/ *joy* and delight and many will *rejoice* at his birth,
28		[Gabriel] went in and said to [Mary], ⌐*Rejoice* (or: Hail), so highly favoured!'
58		[Elizabeth gave birth to a son;] her neighbours and relations 3 . . . *shared* her *joy*.

Lk 2 10		2 I bring you news of great *joy*, [a joy] to be shared by the whole people. [11] . . . a saviour has been born to you;
6 23		[when people hate you . . .] *Rejoice* . . . and dance for joy,
8 13		Those [seeds] on the rock are people who, when they first 2 hear it, welcome the word with *joy*.
10 17		2 The seventy-two came back *rejoicing*. 'Lord,' they said 'even the devils submit to us when we use your name.' [18] He
20		said to them . . . [20] 'Yet do not *rejoice* that the spirits submit to you; *rejoice* rather that your names are written in heaven.'
13 17		all the people *were overjoyed* at all the wonders [Jesus] worked.
15 5 <		when he found [the sheep], would he not *joyfully* take it on
6 <	3	his shoulders [6] . . . *Rejoice with* me . . . I have found my
7	2	sheep that was lost. [7] . . . there will be more *rejoicing* in heaven over one repentant sinner . . .
9 <	3	*Rejoice with* me . . . I have found the drachma I lost. [10] . . .
10 <	2	there is *rejoicing* among the angels of God over one repentant sinner.
32 <		it was only right we should celebrate and *rejoice*, because your brother . . . is found.
19 6		[Zacchaeus] hurried down and welcomed [Jesus] *joyfully*.
37		the whole group of disciples *joyfully* began to praise God
22 5		[the chief priests] *were delighted* and agreed to give [Judas] money.
23 8		Herod *was delighted* to see Jesus;
24 41		2 [Jesus appeared to the apostles.] Their *joy* was so great that they still could not believe it,
52		2 [the apostles] went back to Jerusalem full of *joy*;
Jn 3 29	/2	the bridegroom's friend, who . . . listens, *is glad* with *joy* 2 when he hears the bridegroom's voice. This same *joy* I feel, and now it is complete.
4 36		thus sower and reaper *rejoice* together.
8 56		Abraham rejoiced to think that he would see my Day; he saw it and *was glad*.
11 15 X		[Lazarus is dead;] and for your sake I *am glad* I was not there
14 28		If you loved me you *would have been glad* to know that I am going to the Father,
15 11 X		2 I have told you this so that my own *joy* may be in you and 2 your *joy* be complete.
16 20 S		you will be weeping and wailing while the world will *rejoice*
21 S	2	. . . but your sorrow will turn to *joy*. [21] A woman . . . when she has given birth . . . forgets the suffering in the
22	2	*joy* that a man has been born into the world. [22] . . . I S shall see you again, and your hearts *will be full of joy*, and 2 that *joy* no one shall take from you.
24	2	Ask and you will receive, and so your *joy* will be complete.
17 13 X	2	I say these things to share my *joy* with [those you had given me] to the full.
20 20		The disciples *were filled with joy* when they saw the Lord,
Ac 5 41		[the apostles] left . . . the Sanhedrin *glad* to have had the honour of suffering humiliation for the sake of the name.
8 8		[Philip proclaimed the Christ . . .] As a result there was 2 great *rejoicing* in that town [in Samaria]
39		the [baptised] eunuch . . . went on his way *rejoicing*.
11 22		[Barnabas] could see for himself that God had given grace, and this *pleased* him,
12 14		[Rhoda] recognised Peter's voice and was so overcome with 2 *joy* that, instead of opening the door, she ran inside
13 48		It made the pagans *very happy* to hear this and they thanked the Lord for his message.
52		2 the disciples were filled with *joy* and the Holy Spirit.
15 3		[Paul and Barnabas] told how the pagans had been con- verted, and this news was received with the greatest 2 *satisfaction* by the brothers.
31		The community read [the letter from the apostles and elders] and *were delighted* with the encouragement it gave them.
Rm 12 12		If you have hope, this will *make you cheerful*. Do not give up if trials come;
15		*Rejoice* with those who *rejoice* and be sad with those in sorrow.
14 17		the kingdom of God . . . means righteousness and peace 2 and *joy* brought by the Holy Spirit.
15 13		2 May the God of hope bring you such *joy* and peace in your faith
32		2 if God wills, I shall be feeling *very happy* when I come to enjoy a period of rest among you.
16 19		Your fidelity to Christ . . . is famous everywhere, and that *makes* me *very happy* about you.
1Co 7 30		those who are *enjoying* life should live as though there were nothing to *laugh about*;
12 26		3 If one part is given special honour, all parts *enjoy* it *together*.
13 6	/3	Love *takes no pleasure* in other people's sins but *delights* in the truth;
16 17		I *am delighted* that Stephanas, Fortunatus and Achaicus have arrived;
2Co 1 24		2 We . . . are fellow workers with you for your *happiness*; in the faith you are steady enough.

2Co	2 3 S		I wrote . . . to make sure that, when I came, I should not be distressed by the very people who should have *made* me *happy*.
		2	I am sure . . . I could never be *happy* unless you were.
	6 10 S		[we are] thought most miserable and yet we are always *rejoicing*;
	7 4	2	I am so proud of you that in all our trouble . . . my *joy* is overflowing.
	7		[Titus] has told us . . . how concerned [you were] for me, and so I *am happier* now than I was before.
	9 S		I *am happy* now . . . because your suffering led to your repentance.
	13	/2	we *had the* even greater *happiness* of finding Titus so *happy*; thanks to you all, he has no more worries;
	16		I *am very happy* knowing that I can rely on you so completely.
	8 2	2	[the] constant *cheerfulness* [of the brothers in Macedonia] and their intense poverty have overflowed in a wealth of generosity.
	13 9		We *are only too glad* to be weak provided you are strong.
	11		In the meantime, brothers, ⌐[we wish you]┐ *happiness* (or: farewell).
Ga	5 22	2	the Spirit brings . . . love, *joy*, peace,
Ph	1 4	2	every time I pray for all of you, I pray with *joy*,
	18		Whether from dishonest motives or in sincerity, Christ is proclaimed; and that *makes* me *happy*; 19 and I shall
	19		*continue being happy*,
	25		I shall . . . stay with you all, and help you to progress in
		2	the faith and even increase your *joy* in it;
	2 2		be united in your convictions . . . That is the one thing
		2	which would make me completely *happy*.
	17		if my blood has to be shed . . . I shall still *be happy* and
	18	3/	*rejoice* with all of you, 18 and you must *be* just as *happy*
		3	and *rejoice* with me.
	28 S		you will *be happy* to see [Epaphroditus] again . . . 29 Give
	29	2	him a most ⌐hearty (lit. *joyful*)┐ welcome, in the Lord;
	3 1		Finally, my brothers, *rejoice* in the Lord.
	4 1	2	my brothers and dear friends . . . you are my *joy* and my crown.
	4		I want you to *be happy*, [always happy] in the Lord; I repeat, what I want is your *happiness*.
	10		It *is* a great *joy* to me, in the Lord,
Col	1 11	2	You will have . . . the strength . . . to bear anything *joyfully*, 12 thanking the Father who has made it possible for you to join the saints
	24		It *makes* me *happy* to suffer for you,
	2 5		I am . . . *delighted* to find you all in harmony and to see how firm your faith in Christ is.
1 Th	1 6 Ⓢ	2	it was with the *joy* of the Holy Spirit that you took to the gospel, in spite of the great opposition
	2 19	2	What do you think is our pride and our *joy*? You are . . .
	20	2	20 you are our pride and our *joy*.
	3 9	2	How can we thank God enough for you, for all the *joy* ⌐we feel (lit. with which we *rejoice*)┐ before our God on your account?
	5 16		*Be happy* at all times;
2 Tm	1 4	2	[I] long to see you again to complete my *happiness*.
Phm	7	2	I am so *delighted*, and comforted, to know of your love;
Heb	10 34	2	you *happily* accepted being stripped of your belongings,
	12 2 X	2	for the sake of the *joy* which was still in the future, [Jesus] endured the cross,
	11 S	2	any punishment is most painful at the time, and far from *pleasant*;
	13 17	2	Obey your leaders . . . because they . . . look after your souls; make this a *joy* for them to do, and not a grief
Jm	1 2	2	try to treat [your trials] as a *happy* privilege;
	4 9 S	2	be miserable instead of laughing, gloomy instead of *happy*.
1 P	1 8	2	you are already filled with a *joy* so glorious that it cannot be described,
	4 13		If you can have some share in the sufferings of Christ, *be glad*, because you will *enjoy* a much greater gladness when his glory is revealed.
1 Jn	1 4	2	We are writing this to you to make ⌐our (ⱽ your)┐ own *joy* complete.
2 Jn	4		It has *given* me *great joy* to find that your children have been living the life of truth
	12	2	I hope instead to . . . talk to you personally, so that ⌐our (ⱽ your)┐ *joy* may be complete.
3 Jn	3		It *was a* great *joy* to me when some brothers came . . . 4 It
	4	2	is always my greatest *joy* to hear that my children are living according to the truth.
Rv	11 10		the people of the world will *be glad* about [the death of the two witnesses] and celebrate the event
	19 7		*let us be glad* and joyful . . . because this is the time for the marriage of the Lamb.

2. JOY, GLADNESS – REJOICE, EXULT, BE GLAD: *AGALLIAŌ*

1 *agalliaō* 11   2 *agalliasis* 5

Mt	5 12		[when people abuse you . . .] Rejoice and *be glad*.

Lk	1 14		[Zechariah, Elizabeth is to bear you a son.] He will be your
		2	*joy* and *delight*
	44	2	the child in my womb leapt for *joy*.
	47		my spirit *exults* in God my saviour;
	10 21 X		*filled with joy* by the Holy Spirit, [Jesus] said,
Jn	5 35		for a time you were content to *enjoy* the light that [John] gave.
	8 56		Abraham *rejoiced* to think that he would see my Day; he saw it and was glad.
Ac	2 26 X		(Ps 16 9) my heart was glad and my tongue *cried out with joy*;
	46	2	[the faithful] shared their food *gladly*
	16 34		[The gaoler] and the whole family *celebrated* their conversion to belief in God.
Heb	1 9 X		(Ps 14 8) God, your God, has anointed you with the oil of *gladness*,
1 P	1 6 S		This is a cause of great *joy* for you, even though you may for a short time have to bear being plagued . . . 8 . . . you
	8		are already ⌐filled (lit. *rejoicing*)┐ with a joy so glorious that it cannot be described,
	4 13		be glad, because you will *enjoy* a much greater *gladness* when [Christ's] glory is revealed.
Jude	24	2	Glory be to him who can keep you . . . innocent and *happy*.
Rv	19 7		*let us be* . . . *joyful* . . . because this is the time for the marriage of the Lamb.

3. HAVE JOY FROM A PERSON: *ONINAMAI*

oninamai 1

Phm	20		⌐I am counting on you (lit. let me *have joy* from you; or: let me derive some benefit from you), in the Lord;

4. REJOICE, CELEBRATE, MAKE MERRY – BE GLAD, HAPPY: *EU-PHRAINŌ*

1 *eu-phrainō* 14   2 *eu-phrosynē* 2

Lk	12 19 <		My soul, . . . take things easy, eat, drink, *have a good time*.
	15 23		Bring the calf we have been fattening, and kill it; we are going to *have* a feast, *a celebration*,
	24 <		they began to *celebrate*.
	29 <		you never offered me so much as a kid for me to *celebrate* with my friends.
	32 <		it was only right we should *celebrate* and rejoice, because your brother . . . is found.
	16 19 <		There was a rich man who used to . . . ⌐feast (lit. *celebrate*)┐ magnificently every day.
Ac	2 26 X		(Ps 16 9) my heart *was glad* and my tongue cried out with joy;
	28 X	2	(Ps 16 11) you will fill me with *gladness* through your presence.
	7 41		(cf. Ex 32 6) [the sons of Israel] made a bull calf and offered sacrifice to the idol. They *were perfectly happy* with something they had made for themselves.
	14 17	2	[God] gives you food and makes you *happy*.
Rm	15 10		(Dt 32 43) *Rejoice*, pagans, with his people,
2Co	2 2 S		I have hurt the only people who could *give* me any *pleasure*.
Ga	4 27		(Is 54 1) *Shout for joy*, you barren women . . . Break into shouts of joy and gladness,
Rv	11 10		the people of the world will be glad about [the death of the two witnesses] and *celebrate* the event
	12 12		Let the heavens *rejoice* and all who live there; but for you, earth and sea, trouble is coming
	18 20		Now heaven, *celebrate* [Babylon's] downfall,

5. GLAD(LY): *ASMENŌS*

asmenōs 1

Ac	21 17		On our arrival in Jerusalem the brothers gave us a very ⌐warm (lit. *glad*)┐ welcome.

6. PLEASURE – GLADLY – DELIGHT: *HĒDONĒ*

1 *hēdeōs* 5	3 (*phil-*) (*h*)*ēdonos* 1
2 *hēdonē* 5	4 *syn-*(*h*)*edomai* 1

1: PLEASURE(S)

Lk	8 14	2	they are choked by the worries and riches and *pleasures* of life

2Tm	3	4	[people] will be treacherous and reckless . . . preferring their
		3	own *pleasure* to God.
Tt	3	3	there was a time when we too were . . . enslaved by different
		2	passions and ˹luxuries (lit. *pleasures*);
Jm	4	1	Where do these wars . . . first start? Isn't it precisely in the
		2	*desires* fighting inside your own selves?
		3	when you do pray and don't get it, it is because . . . you
		2	have prayed for something to indulge your own ˹*desires*
		2	(or: *pleasures*).
2 P	2	13	2 [such self-willed people's] only object is *dissipation* all day
			long,

2: GLADLY, WITH DELIGHT – DELIGHT (IN), LIKE (TO)

Mk	6	20	Herod was afraid of John . . . and yet he *liked to* listen to
			him.
	12	37	the great majority of the people heard this *with delight*.
Rm	7	22	4 I ˹*dearly love* (or: *delight* in) God's Law,
2Co	11	19	You are all wise men and can ˹*cheerfully* (or: *gladly*) tolerate
			fools,
	12	9	I shall ˹*be very happy* to (lit. *gladly*) make my weaknesses
			my special boast
		15	I ˹*am perfectly willing* (lit. *gladly* [allow myself]) to spend
			what I have, and to be expended, in the interests of your
			souls.

7. (BE) PLEASED (WITH), DELIGHT (IN): *EU-DOKEŌ*

1 *eu-dokeō* 21   2 *eu-dokia* 9

1: (GOD) IS PLEASED (WITH), DELIGHTS (IN) – ENJOY (GOD'S) FAVOUR – TO PLEASE (GOD)

Mt	3	17	This is my Son, the Beloved; ˹my favour rests on (lit. I *am*
			well *pleased* with) him.
	11	26	2 Yes, Father, for that is what it *pleased* you to do.
	12	18	(Is 42 1) Here is . . . my beloved, ˹the favourite of my soul
			(lit. in whom my soul *is* well *pleased*).
	17	5	This is my Son, the Beloved; ˹he *enjoys* my *favour* (or: I *am*
			very *pleased* with him).
Mk	1	11	You are my Son, the Beloved; ˹my favour rests on (lit. I *am*
			well *pleased* with) you.
Lk	2	14	2 Glory to God . . . and peace to men ˹who *enjoy* his *favour*
		2	(or: with whom he *is pleased*).
	3	22	You are my Son, the Beloved; ˹my favour rests on (lit. I *am*
			well *pleased* with) you.
	10	21	2 Yes, Father, for that is what it *pleased* you to do.
	12	32	it has *pleased* your Father to give you the kingdom.
1Co	1	21	˹God wanted (lit. it *pleased* God) to save those who have
			faith through the foolishness of the message
	10	5	most of [our fathers] failed to *please* God
Ga	1	15	God . . . ˹chose (lit. *was pleased*) ¹⁶ to reveal his Son in me,
Ep	1	5	[God determined] that we should become his adopted sons
		2	. . . for his own ˹kind (lit. *pleasure* and) purposes.
		9	He has let us know the mystery of his purpose, ˹the hidden
		2	plan he so kindly made: lit. which it *was* his *pleasure* to
			fulfil) in Christ from the beginning
Ph	2	13	2 It is God, for his own loving ˹purpose (lit. *pleasure*), who
			puts both the will and the action into you.
Col	1	19	˹God wanted (lit. it *pleased* God for) all perfection to be
			found in [Christ]
Heb	10	6	(Ps 40 7) You *took* no *pleasure* in holocausts or sacrifices
			for sin;
		8	(Ps 40 7) you *took* no *pleasure* in [the sacrifices for sin];
		38	if [the righteous man] draws back, my soul will *take* no
			pleasure in him.
2 P	1	17	This is my Son, the Beloved; ˹he *enjoys* my *favour* (or: I
			am very *pleased* with him).

2: (A PERSON) IS PLEASED (WITH), DELIGHTS (IN) – DESIRE, CHOOSE – GOODWILL

Rm	10	1	2 my heart's *delight* – and what I pray to God for – would be
			that [the Jews] were saved.
	15	26	Macedonia and Achaia have ˹decided (lit. *been pleased*) to
			send a generous contribution to the poor among the saints
			at Jerusalem. ²⁷ ˹A generous contribution as it should be
	27		(lit. they *were pleased* to quite rightly), since it is really
			repaying a debt:
2Co	5	8	we . . . ˹want (lit. would *be pleased*) to be exiled from the
			body
	12	10	I *am* quite *content* with my weaknesses, and with insults,
			hardships, persecutions, and the agonies I go through for
			Christ's sake.

Ph	1	15	2 the rest preach Christ with ˹the right intention (lit. *goodwill*),
1Th	2	8	we ˹were eager (lit. would have *been pleased*) to hand over
			to you . . . our whole lives
	3	1	we ˹decided it would be best (lit. *were pleased*) to be left
			without a companion at Athens,
2Th	1	11	we pray continually that our God will . . . fulfil all your
		2	*desires* for goodness
	2	12	[God is sending a power to delude people] to condemn all
			who . . . *chose* wickedness

8. TO PLEASE, DELIGHT, (BE) ACCEPTABLE (TO): *ARESKŌ*

6	*areskeia* 1	4	*eu-aresteō* 3
1	*areskō* 17	2	*eu-arestos* 9
3	*arestos* 4	7	*eu-arestōs* 1
5	(*anthrōp-*)*areskos* 2		

1: TO PLEASE (GOD) – (BE) PLEASING, ACCEPTABLE (TO GOD, TO THE LORD)

Jn	8	29	3 I always do what *pleases* [the Father].
Rm	8	8	People who are interested only in unspiritual things can
			never *be pleasing* to God.
	12	1	[worship God] by offering your living bodies as a holy
		2	sacrifice, truly *pleasing* to God.
		2	discover the will of God and know what is good, what it is
		2	that ˹God wants (lit. *is acceptable* [to God]),
	14	18	2 If you serve Christ in this way you will *please* God and be
			respected by men.
1Co	7	32	all [an unmarried man] need worry about is *pleasing* the
			Lord; ³³ but a married man has to . . . devote himself
			to *pleasing* his wife.
2Co	5	9	Whether we are living in the body or exiled from it, we are
		2	intent on *pleasing* [the Lord].
Ep	5	10	2 Try to discover ˹what the Lord wants of (lit. what *is accept-*
			able to the Lord from) you,
Ph	4	18	I have received from Epaphroditus the offering that you
			sent . . . the sacrifice that God accepts and *finds pleasing*.
Col	1	10	lead the kind of life which the Lord expects of you, a life
		6	*acceptable* to him in all its aspects;
	3	20	be obedient to your parents always, because that is what will
		2	*please* the Lord.
1Th	2	4	when we are speaking, we are not trying to *please* men but
			God,
		15	the people who put the Lord Jesus to death . . . have been
			. . . acting in a way that cannot *please* God and makes
			them the enemies of the whole human race,
	4	1	the life that ˹God wants (lit. *is acceptable* [to God]),
Heb	11	5	4 before his assumption it is attested that [Enoch] had *pleased*
		4	God. ⁶ Now it is impossible to *please* God without faith,
	12	28	7 Let us . . . worship God in the way that he finds *acceptable*,
	13	16	Keep doing good works and sharing your resources, for
		4	these are sacrifices that *please* God.
		21	2 [may God] turn us all into whatever *is acceptable* to himself
1 Jn	3	22	we keep his commandments and live the kind of life that ˹he
		3	wants (lit. *pleases* him).

2: TO PLEASE, DELIGHT (A PERSON) – (BE) ACCEPTABLE (TO A PERSON)

Mt	14	6	the daughter of Herodias danced . . . and so *delighted* Herod
Mk	6	22	When the daughter of this same Herodias . . . danced, she
			delighted Herod and his guests;
Ac	6	2	3 It would not ˹be right (lit. *be acceptable*) for us to neglect
			the word of God so as to give out food;
		5	The whole assembly ˹approved of (lit. *accepted*) this proposal
			[to select deacons]
	12	3	3 when [Herod] saw that this *pleased* the Jews he decided to
			arrest Peter as well.
Rm	15	1	We . . . have a duty to put up with the qualms of the weak
		2	without ˹thinking of (lit. *pleasing*) ourselves. ² Each of us
			should ˹think of (lit. *please*) his neighbours and help them
		3	to become stronger Christians. ³ Christ did not ˹think of
		X	(lit. *please*) himself:
1Co	7	33	a married man has to . . . devote himself to *pleasing* his
			wife.
		34	The married woman . . . has to . . . devote herself to
			pleasing her husband.
	10	33	I try to ˹be helpful to (lit. *please*) everyone at all times,
Ga	1	10	Would you say it is ˹men's approval I am looking for (lit.
			men I am trying to *please*)? If I still wanted ˹that (lit. to
			please men), I should not be . . . a servant of Christ.
Ep	6	6	[Slaves, be obedient to your masters] not only when you are
		5	under their eye, as if you had only to *please* men, but
			because you are slaves of Christ
Col	3	22	Slaves, be obedient to . . . your masters . . . not only when
		5	you are under their eye, as if you had only to *please* men,
			but wholeheartedly,

2 Tm	2 4	[a soldier] must ꜛbe at the disposal of (lit. *be acceptable* to) the man who enlisted him;
Tt	2 9	the slaves . . . are to be obedient to their masters and always
	2	do what ꜛthey want (lit. *pleases* them)

9. PLEASURE – HAPPINESS, ENJOYMENT: *APO-LAUSIS*

apo-lausis 2

1 Tm	6 17	God . . . gives us all that we need for our ꜛ*happiness* (or: *enjoyment*).
Heb	11 25	[Moses] chose to be ill-treated . . . rather than to enjoy for a time the *pleasures* of sin.

10. CHEERFUL, CHEERFULNESS: *HILAROS*

1 hilaros 1   2 hilarotēs 1

Rm	12 8	2 Let . . . those who do works of mercy do them *cheerfully*.
2 Co	9 7 S	(Pr 22 8) God loves a *cheerful* giver.

11. HAPPY – FORTUNATE – BLESSED: *MAKARIOS*

1 makarios   50   3 makarizō 2
2 makarismos   3

Mt	5 3	How *happy* are the poor in spirit; theirs is the kingdom of heaven.
	4	*Happy* the gentle: they shall have the earth for their heritage.
	5	*Happy* those who mourn: they shall be comforted.
	6	*Happy* those who hunger and thirst for what is right: they shall be satisfied.
	7	*Happy* the merciful: they shall have mercy shown them.
	8	*Happy* the pure in heart: they shall see God.
	9	*Happy* the peacemakers: they shall be called sons of God.
	10	*Happy* those who are persecuted in the cause of right: theirs is the kingdom of heaven. 11 *Happy* are you when people abuse you . . . on my account.
	11	
	11 6	*happy* is the man who does not lose faith in me.
	13 16	*happy* are your eyes because they see, your ears . . .
	16 17	Simon son of Jonah, you are a *happy* man! Because it was not flesh and blood that revealed this to you but my Father
	24 46	*Happy* that servant if his master's arrival finds him at this employment.
Lk	1 45	*blessed* is she who believed that the promise made her by the Lord would be fulfilled.
	48	3 all generations will *call* me *blessed*,
	6 20	How *happy* are you who are poor: yours is the kingdom of God.
	21	*Happy* you who are hungry now: you shall be satisfied. *Happy* you who weep now: you shall laugh.
	22	*Happy* are you when people hate you . . . on account of the Son of Man.
	7 23	*happy* is the man who does not lose faith in me.
	10 23	*Happy* the eyes that see what you see,
	11 27	*Happy* the womb that bore you
	28	Still *happier* those who hear the word of God and keep it!
	12 37	*Happy* those servants whom the master finds awake . . .
	38	38 . . . *happy* those servants if he finds them ready.
	43	*Happy* that servant if his master's arrival finds him at this employment. 44 . . . he will place him over everything he owns.
	14 14	[invite the poor;] that they cannot pay you back means that you are *fortunate*,
	15	*Happy* the man who will be at the feast in the kingdom of God!
	23 29	*Happy* are those who are barren, the wombs that have never borne, the breasts that have never suckled!
Jn	13 17	[you should wash each other's feet . . .] *happiness* will be yours if you behave accordingly.
	20 29	*Happy* are those who have not seen and yet believe.
Ac	20 35	Jesus, who himself said, 'There is more *happiness* in giving than in receiving'.
	26 2	I consider myself *fortunate*, King Agrippa, in that it is before you I am to answer today all the charges
Rm	4 6	2 David says the same: a man is *happy* if God considers him righteous, irrespective of good deeds: 7 (Ps 32 1,2) *Happy* those whose crimes are forgiven . . . 8 *happy* the man whom the Lord considers sinless.
	7	
	8	
	9	2 Is this *happiness* meant only for the circumcised . . .?
	14 22	consider the man *fortunate* who can make his decision without going against his conscience.
1 Co	7 40	[a widow] would be *happier* . . . if she stayed as she is
Ga	4 15	What has become of ꜛthis enthusiasm you had (lit. the 2 *happiness* you spoke about)?

1 Tm	1 11 Θ	the Good News of the glory of the *blessed* God,
	6 15 Θ	[our Lord Jesus Christ] will be revealed by God, the *blessed* and only Ruler of all,
Tt	2 13	we are waiting in hope for the ꜛ*blessing* (or: *happiness*) which will come with the Appearing of the glory of . . . Jesus.
Jm	1 12	*Happy* the man who stands firm when trials come.
	25	[the man who looks steadily at the perfect law of freedom] will *be happy* in all that he does.
	5 11	3 it is those who had endurance that we *say* are the *blessed* ones.
1 P	3 14	if you do have to suffer for being good, you will count it a *blessing*.
	4 14	It is a *blessing* for you when they insult you for bearing the name of Christ,
Rv	1 3	*Happy* the man who reads this prophecy, and happy those who listen to him, if they treasure all that it says,
	14 13	*Happy* are those who die in the Lord!
	16 15	*Happy* is the man who has stayed awake and not taken off his clothes so that he does not go out naked
	19 9	*Happy* are those who are invited to the wedding feast of the Lamb,
	20 6	*Happy* and blessed are those who share in the first resurrection;
	22 7	*Happy* are those who treasure the prophetic message of this book.
	14	*Happy* are those who will have washed their robes clean, so that they will have the right to feed on the tree of life

---

REMEMBER – FORGET

1. Remember – Memorial – Remind: *mimnēskomai*	**2:** (Not to) Remember
1: Remember, Recall – Memorial – Remind	**2. Forget:** *lanthanomai*
	1: Forget, Forgotten
	2: (Never to) Forget

1. REMEMBER – MEMORIAL – REMIND: *MIMNĒSKOMAI*

1	*mimnēskomai*	23	4 *ana-mimnēskō*	6
7	*mneia*	3/7	6 *ana-mnēsis*	4
5	*mneian poieomai*	4	11 *ep-ana-mimnēskō*	1
10	*mnēmēn poieomai*	1	3 *hypo-mimnēskō*	7
2	*mnēmoneuō*	21	9 *hypo-mnēsis*	3
8	*mnēmosynon*	3		

1: REMEMBER, RECALL – MEMORIAL – REMIND

Mt	5 23	if you . . . *remember* [at the altar] that your brother has something against you [go and be reconciled with him first]
	26 13	wherever . . . this Good News is proclaimed, what [this 8 woman] has done will be told also, in *remembrance* of her.
	75	Peter *remembered* what Jesus had said, 'Before the cock crows
	27 63	we *recall* that this impostor said, . . . 'After three days I shall rise again'.
Mk	11 21	4 Peter *remembered*. 'Look, Rabbi, . . . the fig tree you cursed has withered away.'
	14 9	wherever . . . the Good News is proclaimed, what [this 8 woman] has done will be told also, in *remembrance* of her.
	72	4 Peter *recalled* how Jesus had said to him, 'Before the cock crows
Lk	1 54 Θ	[God] has come to the help of Israel . . *mindful of* his mercy
	72 Θ	[God] *remembers* his holy covenant,
	16 25	*remember* that during your life good things came your way,
	17 32	2 *Remember* Lot's wife.
	22 19 ●	6 This is my body which will be given for you; do this as a *memorial* of me.
	61	3 Peter *remembered* what the Lord had said to him,
	23 42 X	'Jesus,' [the other criminal] said 'remember me when you come into your kingdom.'
	24 6	he has risen. *Remember* what he told you
	8	[the women] *remembered* [Jesus's] words.
Jn	2 17	his disciples *remembered* the words of scripture (Ps 69 10): Zeal for your house will devour me.
	22	his disciples *remembered* that he had said this, and they believed the scripture
	12 16	after Jesus had been glorified, [his disciples] *remembered* that this had been written about him (Is 40 9; Zc 9 9)
	14 26 ●	3 the Holy Spirit . . . will . . . *remind* you of all I have said to you.

Jn 15 20   2 *Remember* the words I said to you: A servant is not greater than his master,

16 4   I have told you all this, so that when the time for it comes
  2 you may *remember* that I told you.

Ac 10 4   Your offering of prayers and alms . . . has ʳbeen accepted
Θ 8   by (lit. gone up as your *memorial* before) God.

31   Cornelius, . . . your alms have been ʳaccepted as a sacrifice
Θ   (lit. *remembered*) in the sight of God;

11 16   I *remembered* that the Lord had said, 'John baptised with water,

20 31   2 be on your guard, *remembering* how night and day for three years I never failed to keep you right,

35   2 we must exert ourselves to support the weak, *remembering* the words of the Lord Jesus.

Rm 1 9   5 I never fail to *mention* you in my prayers,

15 15   The reason why I have written to you, and put some things
11   rather strongly, is to *refresh your memories,*

1 Co 4 17   4 Timothy . . . will *remind* you of the way that I live in Christ,

11 2   You have done well in *remembering* me so constantly

24 ● 6 This is my body, which is for you; do this as a *memorial* of
25 ●   me. ²⁵ . . . This cup is the new covenant in my blood.

6 Whenever you drink it, do this as a *memorial* of me.

2 Co 7 15   4 [Titus] *remembers* how willing you all have been,

Ga 2 10   2 we should *remember* [to help] the poor, as indeed I was anxious to do.

Ep 1 16   5 [I] have never failed to *remember* you in my prayers

2 11   2 Do *not forget,* then, that there was a time when you . . . were pagans

Ph 1 3   7 I thank my God ʳwhenever I think (lit. for every *memory* I have) of you;

Col 4 18   2 *Remember* the chains I wear.

1 Th 1 2   5 We always *mention* you in our prayers . . . ³ and constantly
3   2 *remember* before God . . . how you have shown your faith in action,

2 9   2 Let me *remind* you, brothers, how hard we used to work,

3 6   7 Timothy is . . . telling us that you always *remember* us with pleasure

2 Th 2 5   2 Surely you *remember* me telling you about this when I was with you?

2 Tm 1 3   7 I always *remember* you in my prayers;
4   I *remember* your tears and long to see you again . . . ⁵ . . .
5   9 I am *reminded* of the sincere faith which you have;
6   4 I am *reminding* you now to fan into a flame the gift that God gave you

2 8 ● 2 *Remember* the Good News . . , 'Jesus Christ risen from the
14   3 dead, . . .' ¹⁴ *Remind* them of this;

Tt 3 1   3 *Remind* them that it is their duty to be obedient to the officials

Phm 4   5 I always *mention* you in my prayers and thank God for you,

Heb 2 6 Θ   (Ps 8 5) What is man that you should *spare a thought for* him . . . ?

10 3   6 the sins are *recalled* year after year in the sacrifices.

32   4 *Remember* all the sufferings that you had to meet . . . in earlier days;

11 15   2 They can hardly have ʳmeant (lit. been *recalling*) the country they came from,

22   2 Joseph *recalled* the Exodus of the Israelites

13 3   *Keep in mind* those who are in prison, as though you were in prison with them;

7   2 *Remember* your leaders . . . and . . . imitate their faith.

2 P 1 12   3 I am continually *recalling* the same truths to you . . . ¹³ I
13   am sure it is my duty . . . to keep stirring you up with
15   9 *reminders* . . . ¹⁵ And I shall take care that after my own
10   departure you will still have a means to *recall* these things *to memory.*

3 1   I have tried to awaken a true understanding in you by giving
2   9/ you a *reminder:* ² *recalling* to you what was said in the past by the holy prophets.

3 Jn 10   3 I shall ʳtell (lit. *remind*) everyone how [Diotrephes] has behaved,

Jude 5   3 I should like to *remind* you . . . how the Lord rescued the nation from Egypt,

17   *remember,* my dear friends, what the apostles . . . told you to expect

Rv 2 5   [Write to the angel of the church in Ephesus and say,]
2   ʳThink (lit. *Remember*) where you were before you fell;

3 3   2 [Sardis,] do you *remember* how eager you were when you first heard the message?

16 19 Θ   Babylon the Great was *not forgotten;* God made her drink the full winecup of his anger.

18 5 Θ   2 [Come out, my people, away from Babylon;] God *has her crimes in mind;*

2: (NOT TO) REMEMBER

Mt 16 9   2 Do you not *remember* the five loaves for the five thousand . . . ?

Mk 8 18   2 do you not *remember* [how I broke the five loaves among the five thousand]?

Jn 16 21   when [a woman] has given birth to the child she ʳforgets
2   (lit. does not *remember*) the suffering

Heb 8 12 Θ   (Jr 31 34) I . . . never *call* their sins *to mind.*

10 17 Θ   (Jr 31 34) I will never *call* their sins *to mind,*

2. FORGET: *LANTHANOMAI*

2   *lēthē*   1   1 *epi-lanthanomai* 8
3   *ek-lanthanomai* 1   4 *epi-lēsmonē*   1

1: FORGET, FORGOTTEN

Mt 16 5   The disciples . . . had *forgotten* to take any food.

Mk 8 14   The disciples had *forgotten* to take any food

Lk 12 6 Θ   not one [sparrow] is *forgotten* in God's sight.

Ph 3 13   I *forget* the past and I strain ahead for what is still to come;

Heb 6 10 Θ   God would not be so unjust as to *forget* all you have done,

12 5   3 Have you *forgotten* that encouraging text . . . ?

Jm 1 24   [To listen to the word and not obey is like looking at your own features in a mirror] and immediately *forgetting* what you looked like.

25   the man who looks steadily at the perfect law of freedom –
4   not listening and then *forgetting* . . . will be happy

2 P 1 9   2 [without these virtues a man] has *forgotten* how his past sins were washed away.

2: (NEVER TO) FORGET

Heb 13 2   ʳremember always (lit. never *forget*) to welcome strangers

16   ʳKeep doing (lit. Never *be forgetful in*) good works

REPENT

1. **Regret, Repent, Think better of – Change one's mind, Retract – Irrevocable:** *meta-melomai*
2. **Repent, Repentance, Change of heart – Be sorry:** *meta-noeō*
3. **Change one's mind:** *meta-ballō*

1. REGRET, REPENT, THINK BETTER OF – CHANGE ONE'S MIND, RETRACT – IRREVOCABLE: *META-MELOMAI*

1 *meta-melomai* 6   2 *a-meta-melētos* 2

Mt 21 29   [The first son] answered, 'I will not go', but afterwards
<   *thought better of it* and went.

32   you refused to *think better of it* and believe in [John].

27 3   Judas . . . was *filled with remorse* and took the thirty silver pieces back to the chief priests

Rm 11 29 Θ   2 God *never* takes back his gifts or ʳ*revokes* (or: *repents* of) his choice.

2 Co 7 8   even if I distressed you by my letter, I do not *regret* it. I did *regret* it before, . . . but I am happy how

10   To suffer in God's way means changing for the better and
2   *leaves no regrets,*

Heb 7 21 Θ   (Ps 110 4) The Lord has sworn an oath which he will never *retract:*

2. REPENT, REPENTANCE, CHANGE OF HEART – BE SORRY: *META-NOEŌ*

1 *meta-noeō* 34   3 *a-meta-noētos* 1
2 *meta-noia* 22

Mt 3 2   *Repent,* for the kingdom of heaven is close at hand.

8   2 if you *are repentant,* produce the appropriate fruit,

11   2 I baptise you in water for *repentance.*

4 17   *Repent,* for the kingdom of heaven is close at hand.

11 20   [Jesus] began to reproach the towns in which most of his miracles had been worked, because they ʳrefused to *repent.*

21   Tyre and Sidon . . . would have *repented* long ago

12 41   when Johan preached [the men of Nineveh] *repented;*

Mk 1 4   John the Baptist appeared in the wilderness, proclaiming a
2   baptism of *repentance*

15   *Repent,* and believe the Good News.

6 12   [the Twelve] set off to preach *repentance;*

Lk 3 3   [John] went through the whole Jordan district proclaiming
2   a baptism of *repentance*

Lk 3 8 2 if you *are repentant*, produce the appropriate fruits,
5 32 2 I have not come to call the virtuous, but sinners to *repentance*.
10 13 Tyre and Sidon . . . would have *repented* long ago
11 32 when Jonah preached [the men of Nineveh] *repented*;
13 3 unless you *repent* you will all perish
5 unless you *repent* you will all perish
15 7 there will be more rejoicing in heaven over one *repentant* sinner than over ninety-nine virtuous men who have no
2 need of *repentance*.
10 there is rejoicing among the angels of God over one *repentant* sinner.
16 30 if someone comes to them from the dead, they will *repent*.
17 3 If your brother . . . *is sorry*, forgive him. [4] And if he wrongs
4 you seven times a day and seven times comes back to you and says, 'I *am sorry*', you must forgive him.
24 47 2 that, in [Christ's] name, *repentance* for the forgiveness of sins would be preached to all the nations,
Ac 2 38 You must *repent* . . . and every one of you must be baptised
3 19 you must *repent* and turn to God, so that your sins may be wiped out,
5 31 God has now raised him up to be leader and saviour, to
2 give *repentance* and forgiveness of sins
8 22 *Repent* of this wickedness of yours, [Simon]
11 18 2 God . . . can evidently grant even the pagans the *repentance* that leads to life.
13 24 2 John . . . proclaimed a baptism of *repentance*
17 30 God . . . is telling everyone everywhere that they must *repent*,
19 4 2 John's baptism . . . was a baptism of *repentance*;
20 21 [I have preached to you,] urging both Jews and Greeks to
2 ⸢turn to (lit. *repentance* before) God
26 20 I started preaching . . . also to the pagans, urging them to
/2 *repent* and turn to God, proving their *change of heart* by their deeds.
Rm 2 4 Or are you abusing [God's] . . . toleration, not realising that this goodness of God is meant to lead you to
5 2/3 *repentance*? [5] Your stubborn *refusal to repent* is only adding to [his] anger
2 Co 7 9 2 your suffering led you to *repentance*. . . . [10] To suffer
10 in God's way means ⸢changing for the better (lit.
2 *repentance* leading towards salvation)
12 21 all those who sinned before and have still not *repented* of the impurities . . . they committed.
2 Tm 2 25 2 God may give them a *change of mind* so that they recognise the truth and [26] come to their senses,
Heb 6 1 without going over the fundamental doctrines again: the
2 *turning away* from dead actions
6 2 They cannot *be repentant* if they have wilfully crucified the Son of God
12 17 though [Esau] pleaded for it with tears, he was unable to
2 elicit a *change of heart*.
2 P 3 9 The Lord . . . is being patient with you all, wanting . . .
2 everybody to be brought to *change his ways*.
Rv 2 5 *repent*, and do as you used to at first, or else, if you will not *repent*, I shall come to you
16 You must *repent*, or I shall soon come to you
21 I have given [Jezebel] time to reform but she is not willing
22 to *change her* adulterous *life*. [22] Now I am consigning . . . all her partners in adultery to troubles that will test them severely, unless they *repent* of their practices;
3 3 Hold on to [the message]. *Repent*.
19 *repent* in real earnest.
9 20 The rest of the human race . . . refused . . . to ⸢abandon (lit. *repent* of) the things they had made with their
21 own hands . . . [21] Nor did they ⸢give up (lit. *repent* of) their murdering, or witchcraft,
16 9 they would not *repent* and praise [God].
11 instead of *repenting* for what they had done, they cursed . . . God

3. CHANGE ONE'S MIND: *META-BALLŌ*

meta-ballō 1

Ac 28 6 [the Maltese] *changed their minds* and began to say [Paul] was a god.

REST – RELIEVE – REFRESH

1. **Seventh-day rest, Sabbath rest:** *sabbatismos*
2. **Relief – Rest – Peace (of mind):** *an-(h)esis*
3. **Rest, Give rest (to a person), Relieve – Refresh:** *ana-pauō*
4. **Refresh – Reassure, Relieve – Comfort:** *ana-psychō*

1. SEVENTH-DAY REST, SABBATH REST: *SABBATISMOS*

sabbatismos 1

Heb 4 9 There must still be . . . [a place of rest] reserved for God's people, the *seventh-day rest*,

2. RELIEF – REST – PEACE (OF MIND): *AN-(H)ESIS*

an-(h)esis 4/5

2 Co 2 13 ⸢I was so continually uneasy in mind (lit. My mind had no *rest*) at not meeting brother Titus there,
7 5 Even after we had come to Macedonia . . . there was no *rest* for this body of ours.
8 13 This does not mean that to give *relief* to others you ought to make things difficult for yourselves:
2 Th 1 7 [God will] reward you . . . with the same *peace* as he will give us,

3. REST, GIVE REST (TO A PERSON), RELIEVE – REFRESH: *ANA-PAUŌ*

1	*ana-pauō*	*12*	6	*syn-ana-pauomai*	*1*
3	*ana-pausis*	*5*	4	*kata-pauō*	*3/4*
5	*ep-ana-pauō*	*2*	2	*kata-pausis*	*9*

R = Rest in the Promised Land

Mt 11 28 Come to me . . . and I will *give* you *rest*.
29 3 (Jr 6 16) learn from me . . . and you will find *rest* for your souls.
12 43 an unclean spirit . . . wanders through waterless country
Ⓓ 3 looking for a place to *rest*,
26 45 You can sleep on now and *take* your *rest*.
Mk 6 31 You must come away to some lonely place . . . and *rest* for a while;
14 41 You can sleep on now and *take* your *rest*.
Lk 10 6 5 your peace will go and *rest on* him;
11 24 an unclean spirit . . . wanders through waterless country
Ⓓ 3 looking for a place to *rest*,
12 19 My soul, . . . *take things easy*, eat, drink, have a good time.
Ac 7 49 Θ 2 (Is 66 1) what place could you make for my *rest*?
Rm 2 17 5 if you really ⸢trust in (lit. *rest on*) the Law [then why not teach yourself as well as the others?]
15 32 I shall be feeling very happy when I come to [enjoy a period
6 of] *rest among* you.
1 Co 16 18 [Stephanas, Fortunatus and Achaicus] have ⸢settled (lit. *relieved*) my mind
2 Co 7 13 thanks to you all, [Titus] has ⸢no more worries (lit. had his mind *relieved*);
Phm 7 brother, . . . you have ⸢put new heart into (lit. *refreshed* the feelings of) the saints.
20 brother, . . . ⸢put new heart into me (lit. *relieve* my mind), in Christ.
Heb 3 11 Θ R 2 (Ps 95 11) not one would reach the [place of] *rest* I had for them.
18 [the disobedient] he swore would never reach the [place of]
Θ R 2 *rest*
4 1 Θ R 2 the promise of reaching the [place of] *rest* . . . still holds good,
3 R 2 We . . . who have faith, shall reach a [place of] *rest*, as in the text (Ps 95 11): . . . not one would reach the [place
Θ R 2 of] *rest* I had for them.
4 Θ 4 (Gn 2 2) After all his work God *rested* on the seventh day.
5 Θ R 2 (Ps 95 11) They shall not reach the [place of] *rest*
8 Θ R 4 If Joshua had *led* [the Israelites] *into* this [place of] *rest*, God would not later on have spoken so much of another day.
10 Θ R 2/4 to reach the [place of] *rest* is to *rest* after your work, as
11 God did after his. [11] We must therefore do everything
Θ R 2 we can to reach this [place of] *rest*,
1 P 4 14 Ⓢ you have . . . the Spirit of God *resting* on you.
Rv 4 8 3 the four animals . . . never ⸢stopped (lit. *rested* from) singing: 'Holy, Holy, Holy is the Lord God'
6 11 they were told to ⸢be patient (lit. *rest*) a little longer,
14 11 3 no ⸢*respite* (or: *rest*), night or day, for those who worshipped the beast
13 Happy indeed, the Spirit says; now they can *rest* for ever after their work,

4. REFRESH – REASSURE, RELIEVE – COMFORT: *ANA-PSYCHŌ*

1 *ana-psychō 1* 3 *eu-psycheō 1*
2 *ana-psyxis 1*

Ac 3 20 you must repent . . . so that the Lord may send the time of
2 ⸢*comfort* (or: *refreshing*).

Ph 2 19	3	I shall be ⸢reassured (or: relieved) by having news of you.
2 Tm 1 16		[Onesiphorus] has often *been a comfort to me*

RIGHT – LEFT

1: Right *and* Left Hands	2: Right(-hand), Starboard – Left (-hand), Port

3 *aristeros* 4   1 *dexios* 54   2 *eu-ōnymos* 9

1: RIGHT and LEFT HANDS

Mt 5 30		if your *right* hand should cause you to sin, cut it off
6 3	3	when you give alms, your *left* hand must not know what your *right* [hand] is doing;
27 29 X		[Jesus,] a reed in his *right* hand
Lk 6 6		a man was there whose *right* hand was withered.
Ac 2 33 ⊖		raised to the heights by God's *right* hand, [Jesus] has received from the Father the Holy Spirit,
3 7		Peter then took [the lame man] by the *right* hand and helped him to stand up.
5 31 ⊖		By his own *right* hand God has now raised [Jesus] up to be leader and saviour,
Ga 2 9		James, Cephas and John . . . ⸢shook hands with (lit. grasped the *right* hand of) Barnabas and me as a sign of partnership:
Rv 1 16 X		In his *right* hand [the Son of Man] was holding seven stars,
17 X		he touched me with his *right* hand and said, 'Do not be afraid;'
20 X		The secret of the seven stars you have seen in my *right* hand . . . is this:
2 1 X		Here is the message of the one who holds the seven stars in his *right* hand
5 1 ⊖		I saw that in the *right* hand of the One sitting on the throne there was a scroll
7 X		The Lamb came . . . to take the scroll from the *right* hand of the One sitting on the throne,
10 5		the angel . . . raised his *right* hand to heaven, ⁶ and swore
13 16		[the beast] compelled everyone . . . to be branded on the *right* hand or on the forehead,

2: RIGHT(-HAND), STARBOARD – LEFT(-HAND), PORT

Mt 5 29		If your *right* eye should cause you to sin, tear it out
39		if anyone hits you on the *right* cheek, offer him the other as well;
20 21 X /2		Promise that these two sons of mine may sit one at your *right* hand and the other at your *left*
23 X /2		as for seats at my *right* hand and my *left*, these are not mine to grant;
22 44 ⊖		(Ps 110 1) The Lord said to my Lord: Sit at my *right* hand
25 33 X	2	[the Son of Man] will place the sheep on his *right* hand and the goats on his *left*.
34 X		the King will say to those on his *right* hand, 'Come, you whom my Father has blessed . . .'
41 X	2	Next [the King] will say to those on his *left* hand, 'Go away from me, with your curse upon you . . .'
26 64 ⊖		you will see the Son of Man seated at the *right* hand of the Power
27 38 X	2	two robbers were crucified with [Jesus], one on the *right* and one on the *left*.
Mk 10 37 X /3		[James and John] said to him, 'Allow us to sit one at your *right* hand and the other at your *left* in your glory'.
40 X /2		as for seats at my *right* hand or my *left*, these are not mine to grant;
12 36 ⊖		(Ps 110 1) The Lord said to my Lord: Sit at my *right* hand
14 62 ⊖		you will see the Son of Man seated at the *right* hand of the Power
15 27 X	2	they crucified two robbers with [Jesus], one on his *right* and one on his *left*.
16 5		On entering the tomb they saw a young man . . . seated on the *right-hand* side,
19 ⊖		the Lord Jesus . . . was taken up into heaven: there at the *right* hand of God he took his place,
Lk 1 11		there appeared to [Zechariah] the angel of the Lord, standing on the *right* of the altar of incense.
20 42 ⊖		(Ps 110 1) The Lord said to my Lord: Sit at my *right* hand
22 50		one of them . . . cut off the *right* ear [of the high priest's servant]
69 ⊖		the Son of Man will be seated at the *right* hand of the Power of God.
23 33 X /3		they crucified [Jesus] there and the two criminals also, one on the *right*, the other on the *left*.

Jn 18 10		Simon Peter . . . wounded the high priest's servant, cutting off his *right* ear.
21 6		Throw the net out to *starboard* and you'll find something.
Ac 2 25		with [the Lord] at my *right* hand nothing can shake me.
34 ⊖		(Ps 110 1) The Lord said to my Lord: Sit at my *right* hand
7 55 ⊖		[Stephen] saw . . . Jesus standing at God's *right* hand.
56 ⊖		I can see . . . the Son of Man standing at the *right* hand of God.
21 3	2	After sighting Cyprus and leaving it to *port*, we sailed to Syria
Rm 8 34 ⊖		at God's *right* hand [Christ Jesus] stands
2 Co 6 7 ○	3	armed with the weapons of righteousness in the *right* hand and in the *left*,
Ep 1 20 ⊖		[God] used [his power] . . . to make [Jesus] sit at his *right* hand,
Col 3 1 ⊖		in heaven, where Christ is, sitting at God's *right* hand.
Heb 1 3 ⊖		[the Son] has gone to take his place in heaven at the *right* hand of divine Majesty.
13 ⊖		God has never said to any angel (Ps 110 1): Sit at my *right* hand
8 1 ⊖		a high priest . . . [who] has his place at the *right* of the throne of divine Majesty in the heavens,
10 12 ⊖		[Jesus Christ has] taken his place for ever, at the *right* hand of God,
12 2 ⊖		Jesus, who . . . from now on has taken his place at the *right* of God's throne.
1 P 3 22 ⊖		Jesus Christ, who has entered heaven and is at God's *right* hand,
Rv 10 2 /2		[the angel] put his *right* foot in the sea and his *left* foot on the land

RIGHTEOUS – JUSTIFY – VIRTUE

1. Righteous(ness), Virtuous, Holy (man) – Just, Honest, Good, Upright – Justify, Acquit, (Prove) Right: *dikaios*	2. Goodness, Virtue, Excellence – Praises: *aretē* 1: Goodness, Virtue, Excellence 2: Praises, Triumphs

1. RIGHTEOUS(NESS), VIRTUOUS, HOLY (MAN) – JUST, HONEST, GOOD, UPRIGHT – JUSTIFY, ACQUIT, (PROVE) RIGHT: *DIKAIOS*

5 *dikaiōma* 4/10	6 *dikaiōsis*	2
3 *dikaioō* 39	1 *dikaiosynē*	91
2 *dikaios* 80	8 *dikaio(-krisia)*	1
4 *dikaiōs* 5	7 *en-dikos*	2

Mt 1 19	2	Joseph, being a man *of honour*
3 15		it is fitting that we should . . . do all that *righteousness* demands.
5 6		Happy those who hunger and thirst for *what is right*:
10		Happy those who are persecuted in the *cause of right*:
20		if your *virtue* goes no deeper than that of the scribes and Pharisees,
45	2	your Father in heaven . . . causes . . . his rain to fall on *honest* and dishonest men alike.
6 1		Be careful not to parade your ⸢good deeds (lit. *righteousness*) before men
33		Set your hearts on his kingdom first, and on his *righteousness*,
9 13	2	I did not come to call the *virtuous*, but sinners.
10 41	2/2	anyone who welcomes a *holy man* because he is a *holy man* will have a *holy man*'s reward.
11 19	3	Yet wisdom has been *proved right* by her ⸢actions (ᵛ children).
12 37	3	it is by your words you will be *acquitted*, and by your words condemned.
13 17	2	many prophets and *holy men* longed to see what you see,
43	2	the *virtuous* will shine like the sun (cf. Dn 12 3)
49	2	the angels will . . . separate the wicked from the *just*
20 4	2	You go to my vineyard too and I will give you a *fair* wage.
21 32		John came to you, a pattern of true *righteousness*,
23 28	2	you appear to people from the outside like *good honest men*, but inside you are full of hypocrisy and lawlessness.
29	2	Pharisees, . . . who . . . decorate the tombs of *holy men*,
35	2	you will draw down on yourselves the blood of every *holy man* that has been shed on earth, from the blood of Abel the *Holy*
25 37	2	the *virtuous* will say to him in reply, 'Lord, when did we see you hungry . . .?'
46	2	they will go . ., and the *virtuous* to eternal life.
27 19 X	2	[Pilate,] have nothing to do with that *holy man*;
24 X	2	I am innocent of this *good man*'s blood
Mk 2 17	2	I did not come to call the *virtuous*, but sinners.

Mk	6 20	2	Herod was afraid of John, knowing him to be a *good* and holy man,
Lk	1 6	2	[Zechariah and Elizabeth] were ⌐*worthy* (or: *righteous*) in the sight of God,
	17	2	to turn . . . the disobedient back to the wisdom that the *virtuous* have,
	75		to serve [God] in holiness and *virtue*
	2 25	2	Simeon . . . was an *upright* and devout man;
	5 32	2	I have not come to call the *virtuous*, but sinners
	7 29 Θ	3	All the people who heard him, and the tax collectors too, ⌐*acknowledged* God's plan (lit. *justified* God) by accepting baptism from John;
	35	3	Wisdom has been *proved right* by all her children.
	10 29	3	But the [lawyer] was anxious to *justify* himself and said to Jesus, 'And who is my neighbour?'
	12 57	2	Why not judge for yourselves what is *right*?
	14 14	2	repayment will be made to you when the *virtuous* rise again.
	15 7	2	more rejoicing . . . over one repentant sinner than over ninety-nine *virtuous* men
	16 15	3	You are the very ones who ⌐*pass yourselves off as virtuous* (or: *justify yourselves*) in people's sight,
	18 9	2	some people who prided themselves on being *virtuous*
	14	3	[The tax collector] . . . went home again ⌐*at rights* [with God] (or: *justified*); the other did not.
	20 20	2	[the scribes and the chief priests] sent agents [to Jesus] to pose as ⌐*men devoted to the Law* (lit. *honest men*), and to fasten on something he might say
	23 41	4	in our case ⌐we deserved it (lit. it is *fair*): we are paying for what we did.
	47 X	2	the centurion . . . said, 'This was a [great and] *good man*.'
	50	2	an upright and *virtuous* man named Joseph.
Jn	5 30		I can only judge as I am told to judge, and my judging is ⌐*just*,
	X	2	
	7 24	2	Do not keep judging according to appearances; let your judgement be according to *what is right*,
	16 8		[the Advocate] will show the world how wrong it was about
	10 X		. . . who was *in the right*, . . . [10] about who was *in the right*: proved by my going to the Father
	X		
	17 25 Θ	2	Father, *Righteous One*, the world has not known you,
Ac	3 14		It was you who ⌄accused (G denied) the Holy One, the *Just One*,
	X	2	
	4 19	2	You must judge whether in God's eyes it is *right* to listen to you and not to God.
	7 52		[your ancestors] killed those who foretold the coming of the *Just One*,
	X	2	
	10 22	2	The centurion Cornelius, who is an *upright* and God-fearing man,
	35		anybody of any nationality who fears God and does *what is right* is acceptable to him.
	13 10	2	[Elymas,] you enemy of all ⌐*true religion* (lit. *righteousness*)
	38	3	Through [Christ] *justification* from all sins which the Law
	39	3	of Moses was unable to *justify* [39] is offered to every believer.
	17 31 Θ		[God] has fixed a day when the whole world will be judged, and judged in *righteousness*,
	22 14		The God of our ancestors has chosen you [Saul] to . . . see the *Just One*,
	X	2	
	24 15	2	there will be a resurrection of *good men*
	25		when [Paul] began to treat of *righteousness*
Rm	1 17 Θ		this is what reveals the ⌐*justice* (or: *righteousness*) of God to us: it shows how faith leads to faith, or as scripture says (Hab 2 4): The *upright* man finds life through faith.
	2 5 Θ	8	that day of anger when God's *just* judgements will be made known.
	13	2	It is not *holy* to listen to the Law, but keeping it . . . will *make* people *holy* (or: *justify* people) in the sight of God.
	3 4		(Ps 51 4 G) in all you say ⌐your *justice* shows (lit. you may be *justified*), and when you are judged you win your case.
	Θ	3	
	5 Θ	3	our lack of holiness makes God demonstrate his *integrity*,
	8	7	they are *justly* condemned.
	10	2	(Ps 14 1) There is not a *good man* left,
	20	3	(Ps 143 2) no one can be *justified* in the sight of God by keeping the Law: . . . [21] God's ⌐*justice* (or: *righteousness*)
	21 Θ		
	22		. . . has now been revealed outside the Law, [22] since it is the same ⌐*justice* (or: *righteousness*) of God that comes through faith to everyone,
	Θ	2	
	24	3	both [Jew and pagan] are *justified* through the free gift of his grace by being redeemed in Christ Jesus . . . [25] . . .
	25		
	Θ		In this way God makes his ⌐*justice* (or: *righteousness*) known; first, for the past, . . . [26] then, for the present age, by showing positively that he is *just*, and that he *justifies* everyone who believes in Jesus.
	26 Θ	2	
		3	
	28	3	a man is *justified* by faith and not by doing something the Law tells him to do.
	30 Θ	3	God . . . will *justify* the circumcised because of their faith and [justify] the uncircumcised through their faith.
	4 2	3	If Abraham was *justified* as a reward for doing something, he would really have had something to boast about,
	3		(Gn 15 6) Abraham put his faith in God, and this faith was considered as *justifying* him.

Rm	4 5		when a man has nothing to show except faith in the one who *justifies* sinners, then his faith is considered as *justifying* him. [6] And David says the same (Ps 32 1f): a man is happy is God considers him *righteous*, irrespective of good deeds:
	Θ	3/	
	6		
	9		[Abraham's] faith, we say, was considered as *justifying* him,
	11		when [Abraham] was circumcised . . . it was only as a sign and guarantee that the faith he had before his circumcision *justified* him. In this way Abraham became the ancestor of all uncircumcised believers, so that they too might be considered *righteous*;
	13		the promise of inheriting the world was . . . made . . . on account of the *righteousness* which consists in faith.
	22		This is the faith that was considered as *justifying* [Abraham].
	25	6	Jesus who was put to death for our sins and raised to life to *justify* us.
	5 1	3	by faith we are ⌐*judged righteous* (or: *justified*) and at peace with God,
	7	2	It is not easy to die even for a *good* man
	9	2	Having died to *make* us *righteous*,
	16	5	after many falls comes grace with its verdict of *acquittal*.
	17		everyone . . . who receives the free gift . . . of being *made righteous*.
	18 X	5	the *good act* of one man brings everyone to life and makes them *justified*.
		6	
	19	2	by one man's obedience many will be made *righteous*.
	21 X		grace will reign to bring eternal life thanks to the *righteousness* that comes through Jesus Christ our Lord.
	6 7	3	When a man dies . . . he ⌐has finished with (lit. is *acquitted* from) sin.
	13		you should make every part of your body into a *holy* weapon fighting on the side of God;
	16		You cannot be slaves of sin that leads to death and . . . slaves of obedience that leads to *righteousness*.
	18		You have been freed from the slavery of sin, but only to become slaves of *righteousness*.
	19		you must put [your bodies] at the service of *righteousness*
	20		When you were slaves of sin, you felt no obligation to *righteousness*.
	7 12	2	The Law is sacred, and what it commands is sacred, *just* and good.
	8 10		your body may be dead . . . because of sin, but . . . your spirit is life itself because you have been *justified*;
	30 Θ	3/3	those he called he *justified*, and with those he *justified* he shared his glory.
	33 Θ	3	(Is 50 9) When God *acquits*, [34] could anyone condemn?
	9 30		the pagans who were not looking for *righteousness* found a *righteousness* all the same, a *righteousness* that comes of faith, [31] while Israel, looking for a *righteousness* derived from law failed to do what that law required. [32] Why . . . ? Because they relied on good deeds instead of . . . faith.
	31		
	10 3 Θ		Failing to recognise the *righteousness* that comes from God, [the Jews] try to promote their own idea of ⌐it (⌄*righteousness*), instead of submitting to the *righteousness* of God. [4] But now the Law has come to an end with Christ, and everyone who has faith may be *justified*. [5] When Moses refers to *being justified* by the Law, he writes: Those who keep the Law will draw life from it. [6] But the *righteousness* that comes from faith says this:
	Θ		
	4		
	5		
	6		
	10		By believing from the heart you are made *righteous*;
	14 17		the kingdom of God . . . means *righteousness* and peace and joy brought by the Holy Spirit.
1 Co	1 30 X		Christ Jesus . . . has become our wisdom, and our *virtue*, and our holiness, and our freedom.
	4 4	3	my conscience does not reproach me at all, but that does not prove that I am *acquitted*; the Lord alone is my judge.
	6 11	3	you have been washed clean, and sanctified, and *justified* through the name of the Lord Jesus Christ and the Spirit of our God.
	15 34	4	Come to your senses, behave *properly*,
2 Co	3 9		if there was any splendour in administering condemnation, there must be very much greater splendour in administering *justification*.
	5 21		God made the sinless one into sin, so that in him we might become the *goodness* of God
	Θ		
	6 7		[We prove we are God's servants] by being armed with the weapons of *righteousness*
	14		*Virtue* is no companion for crime.
	9 9 Θ		(Ps 112 9) his ⌐*good deeds* (lit. *righteousness*) will never be forgotten.
	10		[God will] make the harvest of your ⌐*good deeds* (lit. *righteousness*) a larger one,
	11 15		[Satan's] servants . . . disguise themselves as the servants of *righteousness*.
Ga	2 16	3	what *makes* a man *righteous* is not obedience to the Law, but faith in Jesus Christ. We . . . hold that faith in Christ rather than fidelity to the Law is what *justifies* us (Ps 143 2), and that no one can be *justified* by keeping the Law. [17] Now if we were to admit that the result of looking to Christ to *justify* us is to make us sinners
		3	
		3	
	17	3	

Ga	2 21	if the Law can *justify* us, there is no point in the death of Christ.
	3 6	Abraham . . . put his faith in God, and this faith was considered as *justifying* him.
	8 ⊖ 3	Scripture foresaw that God was going to use faith to *justify* the pagans, and proclaimed the Good News long ago when Abraham was told (Gn 12 3): In you all the pagans will be blessed.
	11 3	The Law will not *justify* anyone in the sight of God, because
	2	we are told (Hab 2 4): the *righteous man* finds life through faith.
	21	We could have been *justified* by the Law if the Law . . . had been capable of giving life,
	24	The Law was to be our guardian until Christ came and we
	3	could be *justified* by faith.
	5 4 3	if you do look to the Law to *make you justified*, then you have separated yourselves from Christ,
	5ˢ	look to faith for those rewards that *righteousness* hopes for,
Ep	4 24	the new self . . . created in God's way, in the *goodness* and holiness of the truth.
	5 9	the effects of the light are seen in complete goodness and *right living* and truth.
	6 1	Children, be obedient to your parents in the Lord – that is
	2	⌐your duty (lit. *right*).
	14	stand your ground, with . . . *integrity* for a breastplate
Ph	1 7 2	It is only ⌐natural (lit. *right*) that I should feel like this towards you all,
	11	the *perfect goodness* which Jesus Christ produces in us
	3 6	as far as the Law can make you ⌐perfect (lit. *righteous*), I was faultless.
	9	I am no longer trying for ⌐perfection (lit. *righteousness*) by my own efforts, . . . but I want only the ⌐perfection (lit.
	⊖	*righteousness*) that comes through faith in Christ, and is from God
	4 8	fill your minds with everything that is true, . . . everything
	2	that is *good* and pure,
Col	4 1 2	Masters, make sure that your slaves are given what is *just* and fair.
1 Th	2 10 4	our treatment of you . . . has been impeccably *right* and fair.
2 Th	1 5 ⊖ 2	It all shows that God's judgement is *just*,
	6 ⊖ 2	God will very *rightly* repay with injury those who are injuring you,
1 Tm	1 9 2	laws are not framed for *people who are good*.
	3 16 X 3	He was . . . ⌐attested (lit. *justified*) by the Spirit,
	6 11	You must aim to be *saintly* and religious,
2 Tm	2 22	fasten your attention on *holiness*, faith, love
	3 16	All scripture . . . can be used for . . . guiding people's lives and teaching them to be *holy*.
	4 8 X /2	the crown of *righteousness* . . . which the Lord, the *righteous* judge, will give to me
Tt	1 8 2	[an elder should be] sensible, *moral*, devout
	2 12 4	we must . . . live *good* and religious lives
	3 5	it was not because [God] was concerned with any *righteous* actions we might have done ourselves; . . . ⁷ [but] so
	7	
	X 3	that we should be *justified* by his grace [through Jesus Christ],
Heb	1 9	(Ps 45 8) *virtue* you love as much as you hate wickedness.
	2 2	If . . . every . . . disobedience brought its own ⌐proper (lit.
	7	*just*) punishment,
	5 13	anyone who is still living on milk cannot digest the doctrine of *righteousness*
	7 2	By the interpretation of his name, [Melchizedek] is, first, 'king of *righteousness*'
	10 38 2	(Hab 2 4) The *righteous man* will live by faith,
	11 4	It was because of his faith that Abel offered God a better sacrifice than Cain, and for that he was declared to be
	2	*righteous*
	7	By his faith . . . [Noah] was able to claim the *righteousness* which is the reward of faith.
	33	[Gideon . . . and the prophets] were men who through faith . . . did *what is right*
	12 11	any punishment . . . bears fruit in peace and *goodness*.
	23 2	You have . . . been placed with the spirits of the ⌐saints (or: *righteous*)
Jm	1 20 ⊖	God's *righteousness* is never served by man's anger;
	2 21 3	Abraham . . . was *justified* by his deed, because he offered his son Isaac
	23	Abraham put his faith in God, and this was counted as
	24	*making* him *justified*; . . . ²⁴ You see now that it is by doing something good, and not only by believing, that a
	25 3	man is *justified*. ²⁵ . . . Rahab the prostitute [was]
	3	*justified* by her deeds
	3 18	Peacemakers . . . sow the seeds which will bear fruit in *holiness*.
	5 6 (X) 2	It was you who condemned the ⌐innocent (lit. *righteous*) and killed them;
	16 2	the heartfelt prayer of a *good man* works very powerfully.
1 P	2 23 ⊖ 4	[Christ] put his trust in the *righteous* judge. ²⁴ He was
	24	bearing our faults . . . so that we might die to our faults and live for *holiness*;

1 P	3 12	(Ps 34 16) the eyes of the Lord are turned towards the
	2	*virtuous*.
	14	if you do have to suffer for *being good*, you will count it a blessing.
	18 X 2	Christ himself, ⌐innocent (lit. *righteous*) though he was, had died once for sins,
	4 18 2	If it is hard for a *good man* to be saved, what will happen to . . . sinners?
2 P	1 1	to all who treasure the same faith as ourselves, given through
	X	the *righteousness* of our God and saviour Jesus Christ.
	13	2 I am sure it is ⌐my duty (lit. *right* for me) . . . to keep stirring you up with reminders,
	2 5	it was only Noah he saved, the preacher of *righteousness*,
	7 2	he rescued Lot, . . . a *holy man* who had been sickened by
	8 2	. . . these vile people . . . ⁸ for that *holy man* . . . was
	2	outraged in his *good* soul by [their] crimes
	21	It would . . . have been better for him never to have learnt the way of *holiness*, than to . . . desert the holy rule
	3 13	we are waiting for . . . the new heavens and new earth, the place where *righteousness* will be at home.
1 Jn	1 9 ⊖ 2	God who is faithful and *just* will forgive our sins
	2 1	we have our advocate with the Father, Jesus Christ, who is
	X 2	*just*;
	29 ⊖ 2	You know that God is *righteous* – then you must recognise that everyone whose life is *righteous* has been begotten by him.
	3 7 X /2/2	to live a *holy* life is to be *holy* just as he is *holy*; ⁸ to lead a sinful life is to belong to the devil, . . . ¹⁰ . . . anybody
	10	not living a *holy* life . . . is no child of God's.
	12 2	[Cain's] life was evil and his brother lived a *good* life.
Rv	15 3 ⊖ 2	How . . . *just* and true are all your ways, King of nations.
	4	You alone are holy, and all the pagans will come and adore
	⊖ Δ 5	you for the many *acts of justice* you have shown.
	16 5 ⊖ 2	You are the *holy* He-Is-and-He-Was,
	7	Lord God Almighty, the punishments you give are true and
	⊖ 2	*just*.
	19 2 ⊖ 2	He judges fairly, he punishes *justly*,
	8 5	her linen is made of the *good deeds* of the saints.
	11 X	[the rider of the white horse] is a judge [and warrior] with *integrity* for justice.
	22 11	2/ let *those who do good* go on doing good.

2. GOODNESS, VIRTUE, EXCELLENCE – PRAISES: *ARETĒ*

aretē 5

1: GOODNESS, VIRTUE, EXCELLENCE

Ph	4 8	fill your minds with . . . everything that can be thought *virtuous* or worthy of praise.
2 P	1 3	God himself . . . has called us by his own glory and ⌐good-ness (or: *excellence*).
	5	you will have to [add] *goodness* to the faith that you have, understanding to your *goodness*,

2: PRAISES, TRIUMPHS

1 P	2 9	a people set apart to sing the ⌐praises (or: *triumphs*) of God

---

RISE – RAISE – HIGH

1. Rise, Arise, Get up – Raise – Resurrection: egeirō
1: Rise (up), Raise (up) = Stand up, Get up – Lift (up), Help to stand
2: Rise (up), Rouse = Wake up, Get up (from sleeping)
3: Rise(n), (Be) Raise(d), from the dead – Resurrection
4: Arise, Raise (up) = Appear – Make (to be), Arouse, Stir up
5: Rise (against)

2. Rise, Arise – Raise – Resurrection: an-(h)istēmi
1: Rise = Stand up, Get up
2: Rise(n) again, Raise (up), from the dead – Resurrection
3: Arise, Rise, Raise up = Appear, Come forward, Intervene

4: Rise (against)
5: Arise = Leave, Set out

3. Rise: ana-tellō
1: (a star) Rises, (the sun) Comes up, (light) Dawns
2: (Christ) Springs (from)

4. Go up, Come up – Rise – Climb: ana-bainō
1: Ascend, Go up, Come up, to heaven
2: Go up, Come up, to Jerusalem
3: Go up, Travel up, to a person, to a place
4: Get (up), Climb, into a boat – Go aboard
5: Lift on, Help on, Set on, (to) an animal – Ride
6: Go up(wards), Come up, Climb up – Rise (up), Emerge

7: Rise, Arise (figuratively) – Come up, Move up
8: Dais – Step(s)
5. Go up – Climb: an-erchomai
6. Lift up, Hoist up – Keep up – Rise up: airō
  1: Hoist (up, aboard) – Weigh (anchor)
  2: Lift up, Raise, one's hand(s)
  3: Hold high, Lift up – Keep in suspense
  4: Rise up – Haughty, Put on airs – Become proud, Claim to be great
7. Take (a person) up, Bring (a person) up: an-agō

8. High, Height – Lift(ed) – Exalted: hypsoō
  1: the Most High
  2: On high, In the highest heavens, To the height – Heaven(s)
  3: Jesus Lifted up, Raised (up, high, above), Exalted
  4: Exalt(ed), Lift(ed) up – Haughty, Proud – Thought highly of, High rank, Made great
  5: High, Height
9. Lift up (oneself, one's head) – Stand: ana-kyptō

1. RISE, ARISE, GET UP – RAISE – RESURRECTION: *EGEIRŌ*

1	egeirō	144	4 ep-egeirō 2
6	egersis	1	5 ex-egeirō 2
2	di-egeirō	6	3 syn-egeirō 3

1: RISE (UP), RAISE (UP) = STAND UP, GET UP – LIFT (UP), HELP TO STAND

Mt 8 15   [Jesus] touched [Peter's mother-in-law's] hand and the fever left her, and she *got up* and began to wait on him.
    26 X   [Jesus] *stood up* and rebuked the winds and the sea;
9 5   which of these is easier: to say, 'Your sins are forgiven', or
6   to say, '*Get up* and walk'? [6] . . . he said to the paralytic,
7   '*Get up*, and pick up your bed . . .' [7] And the man *got up* and went home.
    19 X   Jesus *rose* and, with his disciples, followed [the official].
12 11   If any one of you here had only one sheep and it fell down a hole on the sabbath day, would he not . . . *lift* it out?
17 7   Jesus came up and touched [the disciples]. '*Stand up*,' he said 'do not be afraid.'
Mk 1 31   [Simon's mother-in-law had gone to bed with fever. Jesus]
    X   took her by the hand and *helped* her *up*.
2 9   Which of these is easier: to say . . ., 'Your sins are forgiven'
11   or to say, '*Get up* . . . and walk'? . . . [11] he said to the
12   paralytic, 'I order you: *get up* . . .' [12] And the man *got up* . . . and walked out in front of everyone,
3 3   [Jesus] said to the man with the withered hand, '*Stand up* out in the middle!'
9 27 X   Jesus . . . *helped* [the boy] *up*, and he was able to stand.
10 49   they called the blind man. 'Courage,' they said '*get up*; he is calling you.'
Lk 5 23   Which of these is easier: to say, 'Your sins are forgiven you'
24   or to say, '*Get up* and walk'? [24] . . . he said to the paralysed man, 'I order you: *get up* . . .'
6 8   [Jesus] said to the man with the withered hand, '*Stand up*! Come out into the middle.'
13 25   the master of the house has *got up* and locked the door,
Jn 5 8   *Get up*, pick up your sleeping-mat and walk.
11 29   Mary *got up* quickly and went to [Jesus].
13 4   [Jesus] *got up* from table . . . and, taking a towel, wrapped it round his waist;
14 31   ⌐Come (lit. *Get up*) now, let us go.
Ac 3 7   Peter . . . took [the lame man] by the hand and *helped* him *to stand* up.
9 8   Saul *got up* from the ground,
10 26   Peter *helped* [Cornelius] *up*. '*Stand up*, . . . I am only a man . . .!'
Jm 5 15 ⊖   The prayer of faith will save the sick man and the Lord will *raise* him up again;
Rv 11 1 ○   ⌐'Go (lit. *Get up*) and measure God's sanctuary,

2: RISE (UP), ROUSE = WAKE UP, GET UP (FROM SLEEPING)

Mt 1 24   When Joseph *woke up* he did what the angel . . . had told him to do:
2 13   the angel of the Lord appeared to Joseph . . . and said, '*Get up*, take the child and his mother with you, and escape
14   . . .' [14] So Joseph *got up* and . . . left that night for Egypt,
20   [The angel of the Lord appeared in a dream to Joseph in
21   Egypt and said:] *Get up*, . . . [21] So Joseph *got up* and . . . went back to the land of Israel.
8 25   [his disciples] *woke* him saying, 'Save us, Lord, we are going down!'
25 7   all those bridesmaids *woke up* and trimmed their lamps,
26 46   [Jesus found the disciples sleeping and said,] *Get up*!
Mk 4 27   while [the sower] sleeps, when he *is awake*, the seed is sprouting

Mk 4 38   [Jesus] was in the stern . . . asleep. They *woke* him and said
    39 X 2   . . . 'We are going down!' [39] And he *woke up* and rebuked the wind
14 42   [Jesus found the disciples sleeping and said,] *Get up*!
Lk 8 24   2   [the disciples] went to *rouse* him saying, '. . . We are going
    X 2   down!' Then he *woke up* and rebuked the wind
11 8   if the man does not get up . . . for friendship's sake, persistence will be enough to make him *get up*
Ac 12 7   [The angel] tapped Peter on the side and *woke* him. 'Get up!'
Rm 13 11   the time has come: you must *wake up* from your sleep now:

3: RISE(N), (BE) RAISE(D), FROM THE DEAD – RESURRECTION

7 *kum* 1 (Mk 5 41)   8 *nekros* 48/130

X = the Resurrection of Jesus

Mt 9 25   [Jesus] went inside and took the little girl by the hand; and she *stood up*.
10 8   /8   Cure the sick, *raise* the dead,
11 5   8/   the deaf hear, and the *dead are raised*
14 2   [Jesus] is John the Baptist himself; he has *risen* from the dead,
16 21 X   Jesus began to make it clear . . . that he was destined . . . to be *raised up* on the third day.
17 9 X   Tell no one about the vision until the Son of Man has *risen* 8 from the *dead*.
23 X   they will put him to death, and on the third day he will be *raised* [to life again].
20 19   [the chief priests] will hand him over to the pagans to be
    X   . . . crucified; and on the third day he will *rise* again.
26 32 X   after my *resurrection* I shall go before you to Galilee.
27 52   [Jesus yielded up his spirit;] the bodies of many holy men
53 X /6   *rose* [from the dead], [53] and these, after his *resurrection*, came out of the tombs,
63 X   this impostor said, . . . 'After three days I shall *rise again*'.
64   [64] Therefore . . . have the sepulchre kept secure . . . for fear his disciples . . . steal him away and tell the people,
    X /8   'He has *risen* from the *dead*'.
28 6 X   [Jesus] has *risen*, as he said he would . . . [7] . . . go quickly
7 X /8   and tell his disciples, 'He has *risen* from the *dead*'
Mk 5 41   7   [Jesus] said to her, 'Talitha, *kum*!' which means, 'Little girl, I tell you to *get up*!'
6 14   /8   Some were saying, 'John the Baptist has *risen* from the *dead*.'
16   Herod . . . said, 'It is John . . . he has *risen* [from the dead]'.
12 26   8/   Now about the *dead rising again*, have you never read . . .?
14 28 X   after my *resurrection* I shall go before you to Galilee.
16 6   You are looking for Jesus . . . who was crucified: he has
    X   *risen*, he is not here.
14   He reproached [the Eleven] for their incredulity . . . because they had refused to believe those who had seen him after
    X /8   he had *risen* (ᵛ from the *dead*).
Lk 7 14   [Jesus] said, 'Young man, I tell you to *get up*'. [15] And the
15   8   *dead man* sat up
22   8/   the deaf hear, the *dead are raised*
8 54   [Jesus] called to her, 'Child, *get up*'. [55] And her spirit returned and she got up at once.
9 7   /8   some people were saying that John had *risen* from the *dead*,
22   X   The Son of Man . . . is destined . . . to be put to death, and to be *raised up* on the third day.
20 37   8/   Moses himself implies that the *dead rise again*,
24 6 X   He is not here; he has *risen*.
34 X   The Lord has *risen* and has appeared to Simon.
Jn 2 19 X   Destroy this sanctuary, and in three days I will *raise* it up.
20   [20] . . . It has taken forty-six years to build this sanctuary:
    X   are you going to *raise* it up in three days? [21] But he was speaking of the sanctuary that was his body, [22] and when
22
    X /8   Jesus *rose* from the *dead*, his disciples . . . believed the scripture
5 21   /8   as the Father *raises* the dead and gives them life, so the Son gives life to anyone he chooses;
12 1   Jesus went to Bethany, where Lazarus was, whom he had
    /8   *raised* from the *dead*.
9   8   [many Jews came] to see Lazarus whom [Jesus] had *raised* from the *dead*.
17   8   [Jesus] called Lazarus out of the tomb and *raised* him from the *dead*
21 14   This was the third time that Jesus showed himself to the
    X /8   disciples after *rising* from the *dead*.
Ac 3 15 X   you killed the prince of life. God, however, *raised* him from the *dead*,
4 10   Jesus Christ the Nazarene, the one you crucified, whom God
    X /8   *raised* from the *dead*,
5 30 X   it was the God of our ancestors who *raised* up Jesus, but it was you who had him executed
10 40 X   three days afterwards God *raised* him [to life]
13 30 X   [They asked Pilate to have him executed.] But God *raised*
8   him from the *dead*,

Ac 13 37 X The one whom God has *raised* up, however, has not experienced corruption.

26 8 Why does it seem incredible to you that God should *raise*
8 the *dead*?

Rm 4 24 X /8 we believe in him who *raised* Jesus our Lord from the *dead*,
25 X 25 Jesus who was put to death for our sins and *raised* [to
life] to justify us.

6 4 X we . . . joined him in death, so that as Christ was *raised*
8 from the *dead* . . . we too might live a new life.

9 X /8 Christ . . . having been *raised* from the *dead* will never die
again.

7 4 X you . . . can now give yourselves . . . to him who *rose* from
8 the *dead*

8 11 X /8 if the Spirit of him who *raised* Jesus from the *dead* is living in
X /8 you, then he who *raised* Jesus from the *dead* will give life
to your own mortal bodies

34 X Christ Jesus . . . not only died for us – he *rose* (v from the
8 *dead*),

10 9 X if you believe in your heart that God *raised* [Jesus] from the
8 *dead*, then you will be saved.

1 Co 6 14 X God, who *raised* the Lord [from the dead], will by his power
5 *raise* us up too.

15 4 X · [I taught you] that he was *raised* [to life] on the third day, in
accordance with the scriptures;

12 X /8 If Christ [was] *raised* from the *dead* . . . how can some of you
13 be saying that there is no resurrection of the dead? 13 If there
is no resurrection . . . Christ himself cannot have been

14 X *raised*, 14 and if Christ has not been *raised* then our
15 preaching is useless and your believing it is useless; 15 . . .
X we . . . have committed perjury before God, because we
swore in evidence before God that he had *raised* Christ
X /8 [to life] whom he did not *raise* if it is true that the *dead
are* not *raised*.

16 X 8// For if the *dead are* not *raised*, Christ has not been *raised*,
17 X 17 and if Christ has not been *raised*, you are still in your
sins . . . 20 But Christ has in fact been *raised* from the
20 X *dead*, the first-fruits of all who have fallen asleep.
8

29 8 what do people hope to gain by being baptised for the *dead*?
8/ If the *dead* are not ever going to be *raised*, why be baptised
on their behalf?

32 8/ If the *dead are* not *raised*, you say (Is 22 13), 'Let us eat
and drink today; tomorrow we shall be dead.'

35 8/ Someone may ask, 'How *are* dead people *raised* . . .?'

42 It is the same with the resurrection of the dead: the thing
that is sown is perishable but what *is raised* is imperishable; 43 the thing that is sown is contemptible but what
43 *is raised* is glorious; the thing that is sown is weak but what
44 *is raised* is powerful; 44 when it is sown it embodies the
soul, when it *is raised* it embodies the spirit.

52 8/ the *dead* will *be raised*, imperishable, and we shall be changed
as well,

2 Co 1 9 /8 rely . . . only on God, who *raises* the *dead* [to life].

4 14 X he who *raised* the Lord Jesus [to life] will *raise* us with Jesus

5 15 he died for all . . . so that living men should live no longer
X for themselves, but for him who died and *was raised* to
life for them.

Ga 1 1 [Paul] has been appointed by Jesus Christ and by God the
X /8 Father who *raised* Jesus from the *dead*.

Ep 1 20 X /8 [God] used [his power] to *raise* [Jesus] from the *dead*

2 6 3 [God] *raised* us *up with* [Christ]

5 14 *Wake up* from your sleep, rise from the dead,

Col 2 12 3 by baptism . . . you have been *raised up with* [Christ] through
X your belief in the power of God who *raised* him from the
8 *dead*.

3 1 3 Since you have been ⌐brought back to true life (lit. *raised*)⌐
with Christ, you must look for the things that are in heaven,

1 Th 1 10 X you are now waiting for Jesus, his Son, whom he *raised* from
8 the *dead*, to come from heaven to save us

2 Tm 2 8 X Remember the Good News that I carry, Jesus Christ *risen*
8 from the *dead*,

Heb 11 19 [Abraham] was confident that God had the power even to
/8 *raise* the *dead*; and so . . . he was given back Isaac from
the dead.

1 P 1 21 X Through him you now have faith in God, who *raised* him
8 from the *dead*

4: ARISE, RAISE (UP) = APPEAR – MAKE (TO BE), AROUSE, STIR UP

Mt 3 9 Θ God can *raise* children for Abraham from these stones.

11 11 of all the children born of women, a greater than John the
Baptist has never ⌐been seen (lit. *appeared*)⌐;

12 42 On Judgement day the Queen of the South will *rise up* with
this generation and condemn it,

24 11 Many false prophets will *arise*;
24 false Christs and false prophets will *arise*

Mk 13 22 false Christs and false prophets will *arise*

Lk 1 69 Θ [the God of Israel] has *raised* up for us a power for salvation

3 8 Θ God can *raise* children for Abraham from these stones.

Lk 7 16 Everyone . . . praised God saying, 'A great prophet has
appeared among us';

11 31 On Judgement day the Queen of the South will *rise* up with
the men of this generation and condemn them,

Jn 6 18 The wind was strong, and the sea was ⌐getting rough (lit.
2 *arising*)⌐

7 52 prophets do not ⌐come out of (lit. *appear* in) Galilee.

Ac 13 22 Θ [God] *made* David their king,
23 Θ God has v *raised* up (G brought) for Israel one of David's
descendants, Jesus, as Saviour,

50 4 [the Jews] ⌐persuaded them to turn (lit. *aroused* ill-feeling)⌐
against Paul and Barnabas

14 2 4 the Jews . . . refused to believe, and they *stirred up* ill-
feeling and poisoned the minds of the pagans against the
brothers.

Rm 9 17 Θ 5 (Ex 9 16) he says to Pharaoh: It was for this I *raised* you
up, to use you as a means of showing my power

Ph 1 17 The others . . . do not mind if they *make* my chains heavier
to bear.

2 P 1 13 2 I am sure it is my duty . . . to keep *stirring* you *up* with
reminders,

3 1 2 I have tried to ⌐awaken (or: *arouse*) a true understanding
in you by giving you a reminder:

5: RISE (AGAINST)

Mt 24 7 For nation will ⌐fight (lit. *rise*) against nation, and kingdom
against kingdom.
Repeated in Mk 13 8; Lk 21 10.

2. RISE, ARISE – RAISE – RESURRECTION: *AN-(H)ISTĒMI*

2	*ana-stasis* 42		3	*ex-an-(h)istēmi* 3
1	*an-(h)istēmi* 108		6	*kat-eph-istēmi* 1
4	*ep-an-(h)istēmi* 2		7	*par-(h)istēmi* 1/41
5	*ex-ana-stasis* 1			

1: RISE = STAND UP, GET UP

Mt 9 9 [Jesus] said to [Matthew], 'Follow me'. And he *got up* and
followed him.

26 62 The high priest then *stood up* and said to [Jesus], 'Have you
no answer to that?'

Mk 1 35 X In the morning, long before dawn, [Jesus] *got up* and left the
house

2 14 [Jesus] said to [Levi], 'Follow me'. And he *got up* and
followed him.

9 27 Jesus took [the boy] by the hand and helped him up, and
he was able to *stand* [up].

14 57 Some *stood up* and submitted this false evidence against
[Jesus],

60 The high priest then *stood up* . . . and put this question to
Jesus,

Lk 4 16 X [Jesus] went into the synagogue . . . he *stood up* to read,

29 They *sprang to their feet* and hustled [Jesus] out of the
town;

39 [The fever left Simon's mother-in-law.] And she immediately
got up and began to wait on them.

5 25 immediately before their very eyes [the paralysed man]
got up,

28 leaving everything [Levi] *got up* and followed [Jesus].

6 8 [the man with a withered hand] ⌐came out (lit. *got up*) and
stood there.

10 25 There was a lawyer who, to disconcert [Jesus], *stood up* and
said

11 7 < I cannot *get up* to give [three loaves to] you.
8 < if the man does not *get up* . . . for friendship's sake, persistence will be enough to make him get up

17 19 *Stand up* and go on your way. Your faith has saved you.

22 45 X When he *rose* from prayer he went to the disciples
46 *Get up* and pray not to be put to the test.

23 1 The whole assembly then *rose*, and they brought [Jesus]
before Pilate.

Jn 11 31 the Jews . . . saw [Mary] *get up* . . . quickly and go out,

Ac 1 15 One day Peter *stood up* to speak to the brothers

5 6 The younger men *got up*, wrapped the body [of Ananias]
in a sheet,

34 One member of the Sanhedrin . . . a Pharisee called
Gamaliel . . . *stood up*

8 26 The angel . . . spoke to Philip saying, ⌐'Be ready to (lit.
Get up and) set out at noon'

9 6 [Saul,] *get up* now and go into the city,

11 You must *get up* and go to Straight Street and ask . . . for
. . . Saul,

18 [Saul] was baptised ⌐there and then (lit. on the spot, having
got up),

Ac 9	34		Aeneas, Jesus Christ cures you: *get up* . . . Aeneas *got up* immediately;
	39		Peter *got up* and went back with [the two men] straightaway,
10	13		˹Now (lit. *Get up*), Peter; kill and eat!
	20		˹Hurry (lit. *Get up* and go) down, and do not hesitate about going back with them;
	23		Next day, [Peter] ˹was ready to go (lit. *got up* and went) off with them,
	26		Peter helped [Cornelius] up. 'Stand up,' he said
11	7		˹Now (lit. *Get up*), Peter; kill and eat!
	28		Agabus, seized by the Spirit, *stood up* and predicted
12	7		[The angel] tapped Peter on the side and woke him. '*Get up!*' he said
13	16		Paul *stood up*, held up a hand for silence and began to speak:
14	10		'Get to your feet – *stand up*', and the cripple jumped up
	20		[Paul] *stood up* and went back to the town.
15	7		after the discussion had gone on a long time, Peter *stood up* and addressed them.
22	10		*Stand up* and go into Damascus,
	16		˹It is time you were (lit. *Get up* and be) baptised
23	9		some of the scribes from the Pharisees' party *stood up* and protested
26	16		*get up* and stand on your feet,
	30		At this the king *rose to his feet*, with the governor and Bernice and those who sat there with them.
1 Co 10	7		(Ex 32 6) After sitting down to eat and drink, the people *got up* to amuse themselves.

2: RISE(N) AGAIN, RAISE (UP), FROM THE DEAD – RESURRECTION

8 *nekros* 29/130

X = the Resurrection of Jesus

Mt 22	23	2	Sadducees . . . deny that there is a *resurrection*
	28	2	at the *resurrection* to which of those seven will she be wife . . .?
	30	2	at the *resurrection* men and women do not marry;
	31	2/8	as for the *resurrection* of the *dead*, have you never read . . .?
Mk 5	42		The little girl *got up* at once and began to walk about,
8	31	X	the Son of Man was destined . . . to be put to death, and after three days to *rise again*;
9	9	X	[Jesus] warned them to tell no one what they had seen, until after the Son of Man had *risen* from the *dead*. [10] They
10	X	/8	observed the warning . . . though among themselves they
		/8	discussed what '*rising* from the *dead*' could mean.
	31	X	three days after [the Son of Man] has been put to death he will *rise again*.
10	34	X	[the pagans will] put him to death; and after three days he will *rise again*.
12	18	2	Sadducees . . . deny that there is a *resurrection*
	23	2/	Now at the *resurrection*, when they *rise again*, whose wife will she be . . .?
	25	/8	when they *rise* from the *dead*, men and women do not marry;
16	9	X	Having *risen* in the morning on the first day of the week, [Jesus] appeared first to Mary of Magdala
Lk 8	55		[Child, get up.] And her spirit returned and she *got up* at once.
9	8		[people were saying about Jesus] that one of the ancient prophets had *come back to life*
	19		others say [you are] one of the ancient prophets *come back to life*.
14	14	2	repayment will be made to you when the virtuous *rise again*.
16	31		Abraham said [to the rich man], '. . . they will not be con-
		/8	vinced even if someone should *rise* from the *dead*'.
18	33	X	they will put him to death; and on the third day he will *rise again*.
20	27	2	Sadducees . . . say that there is no *resurrection*
	33	2	Now, at the *resurrection*, to which of them will she be wife
	35		since she had been married to all seven? . . . [35] . . .
		2	those who are judged worthy of a place . . . in the *resur-*
	36	8	*rection* from the *dead* do not marry [36] because they can
		2	no longer die, for . . . being children of the *resurrection* they are sons of God.
24	7	X	the Son of Man had to . . . be crucified and *rise again* on the third day.
	46	X	it is written that the Christ would suffer and on the third
		/8	day *rise* from the *dead*,
Jn 5	29		[The dead will leave their graves:] those who did good will
		2/2	*rise again* to life; and those who did evil will *rise again* to condemnation.
6	39		the will of him who sent me is that I should lose nothing
	40		. . . and that I should *raise* it *up* on the last day. [40] . . . whoever sees the Son and believes in him . . . I shall *raise* him *up* on the last day.
	44		I will *raise* him *up* at the last day.
	54		Anyone who does eat my flesh . . . has eternal life, and I shall *raise* him *up* on the last day.
Jn 11	23		'Your brother' said Jesus to her 'will *rise again*.' [24] Martha
	24	/2	said, 'I know he will *rise again* at the *resurrection* on the
	25	○ 2	last day'. [25] Jesus said: I am the *resurrection* (§ and the life).
20	9	X	the teaching of scripture [is] that [Jesus] must *rise* from the
		8	*dead*.
Ac 1	22		[We must choose] someone who . . . can act with us as a
		X 2	witness to his *resurrection*.
2	24	X	God *raised* him [to life], freeing him from the pangs of
		ᵛ	Hades (G death);
	31	2	[David] foresaw and spoke about . . . the *resurrection* of the *Christ*,
	32	X	God *raised* this man Jesus [to life], and all of us are witnesses to that.
3	26	X	It was for you in the first place that God *raised up* his servant
4	2		[The priests] were extremely annoyed at [the apostles']
		2	teaching the people the doctrine of the *resurrection* from
		8	the *dead*
	33	X 2	The apostles continued to testify to the *resurrection* of the Lord Jesus with great power,
9	40		Tabitha, *stand up* . . . [41] Peter *helped* her *to her feet*, then
	41		he called in the saints . . . and showed them she was alive.
10	41	X	we have eaten and drunk with him after his *resurrection*
		8	from the *dead*
13	33	X	[God] has fulfilled [his promise], by *raising* Jesus [from the
	34	X /8	*dead*] . . . [34] The fact that God *raised* him from the *dead*, never to return to corruption, is no more than what he had declared:
17	3	X	it was ordained that the Christ should suffer and *rise* from
		8	the *dead*.
	18	2	because [Paul] was preaching about Jesus and the *resur-rection*, [people] said, 'He sounds like a propagandist for some outlandish gods'.
	31	X /8	God has . . . proved this by *raising* this man from the *dead*.
	32	2/8	[32] At this mention of *rising* from the *dead*, some of them burst out laughing;
23	6	2	It is for our hope in the *resurrection* of the *dead* that I am on trial.
	8	2	the Sadducees say there is neither *resurrection*, nor angel, nor spirit, while the Pharisees accept all three.
24	15	2	there will be a *resurrection* of good men and bad men alike.
	21	2/8	It is about the *resurrection* of the *dead* that I am on trial before you today.
26	23	X 2	the Christ was to suffer and . . . as the first to *rise* from the
		8	*dead*, he was to proclaim that light now shone for our people
Rm 1	4	X 2	[Jesus] was proclaimed Son of God . . . through his *resur-*
		8	*rection* from the *dead*.
6	5	X 2	in union with Christ we . . . imitate him in his *resurrection*.
1 Co 15	12	2	how can some . . . be saying that there is no *resurrection* of
	13	8/2/8	the *dead*? [13] If there is no *resurrection* of the *dead*, Christ himself cannot have been raised,
	21	2/8	the *resurrection* of the *dead* has come through one man.
	42	2/8	It is the same with the *resurrection* of the *dead*:
Ep 5	14	/8	Wake up from your sleep, *rise* from the *dead*,
Ph 3	10	X 2	All I want is to know . . . the power of his *resurrection* and to share his sufferings by reproducing the pattern of his
	11		death. [11] That is the way I can hope to take my place in
		5/8	the *resurrection* of the *dead*.
1 Th 4	14	X	Jesus died and *rose again*, and . . . it will be the same for those who have died in Jesus: God will bring them with him.
	16	8/	those who *have died* in Christ will be the first to *rise*,
2 Tm 2	18		[Hymenaeus and Philetus] have gone right away from the
		2	truth and claim that the *resurrection* has already taken place.
Heb 6	2	2	[let us concentrate on] the teaching about the *resurrection*
		8	of the *dead* and eternal judgement.
11	35	8/2	Some came back to their wives from the *dead*, by *resurrec-tion*; and others submitted to torture . . . so that they would *rise again* to a better life.
1 P 1	3	X 2	[God] has given us a new birth as his sons, by *raising* Jesus
		8	Christ from the *dead*, so that we have a sure hope
3	21	X	[the baptism is] a pledge made to God from a good con-science, through the *resurrection* of Jesus Christ,
Rv 20	5		[The souls of all who had been beheaded came to life.] This
		2/8	is the first *resurrection*; the rest of the *dead* did not come to life until the thousand years were over. [6] Happy and
	6	2	blessed are those who share in the first *resurrection*;

3: ARISE, RISE, RAISE UP = APPEAR, COME FORWARD, INTERVENE

Mt 12	41		On Judgement day the men of Nineveh will ˹*stand up* (lit. *arise*) with this generation and condemn it,
22	24		(cf. Dt 25 5) his brother is to marry the widow . . . to *raise* children for his brother.
Mk 12	19	3	(cf. Dt 25 5) the man must marry the widow to *raise up* children for his brother.

Lk	2 34	2	this child [Jesus] is destined for the fall and for the *rising* of many in Israel,
	11 32		On Judgement day the men of Nineveh will ⌐stand up (lit. *arise*) with this generation and condemn it,
	20 28	3	(cf. Dt 25 5) the man must marry the widow to *raise up* children for his brother.
Ac	3 22 Θ		(Dt 18 15) The Lord God will *raise up* a prophet . . . from among your own brothers;
	5 17		Then the high priest *intervened* with all his supporters
	36		Theudas . . . ⌐became notorious (lit. *appeared*) not so long ago.
	37		then there ⌐was (lit. *appeared*) Judas the Galilean,
	6 9		certain people *came forward* to debate with Stephen,
	7 18		[our nation grew larger and larger] until a new king ⌐came to power (lit. *arose*) in Egypt who knew nothing of Joseph.
	37 Θ		(Dt 18 15) God will *raise up* a prophet like myself for you from among your own brothers.
	15 5 3		certain members of the Pharisees' party . . . ⌐objected (lit. *rose*, or: *came forward*), insisting that the pagans should be circumcised
	20 30		Even from your own ranks there will be men *coming forward* with a travesty of the truth on their lips
Rm	15 12 X		(Is 11 10) The root of Jesse will appear, *rising up* to rule the pagans,
Heb	7 11 X		why was it still necessary for a new priesthood to *arise* . . .?
	15 X		This becomes even more clearly evident when there *appears* a second Melchizedek,

4: RISE (AGAINST)

Mt	10 21	4	children will *rise* against their parents
Mk	3 26		if Satan has ⌐rebelled (lit. *risen*) against himself . . . he cannot stand either
	13 12	4	children will *rise* against their parents
Ac	15 5 3		certain members of the Pharisees' party . . . ⌐objected (lit. *rose*, or: *came forward*), insisting that the pagans should be circumcised
	18 12	6	the Jews ⌐made a concerted attack on (lit. *rose* in concert against) Paul and brought him before the tribunal.

5: ARISE = LEAVE, SET OUT

Mk	7 24 X		He *left* that place and set out for the territory of Tyre.
	10 1 X		*Leaving* there, he came to the district of Judaea
Lk	1 39		Mary *set out* . . . and went as quickly as she could to a town in the hill country of Judah.
	4 38 X		*Leaving* the synagogue he went to Simon's house.
	15 18 <		I will *leave* this place and go to my father
	20 <		So he *left* the place and went back to his father.
	24 12		⌐Peter, however, *went* running to the tomb . . .⌐
	33		[The disciples] *set out* that instant and returned to Jerusalem.
Ac	4 26	7	(Ps 2 2) Kings on earth *setting out* [to war], princes making an alliance, against the Lord
	8 27		[Philip] *set off* on his journey.

3. RISE: *ANA-TELLŌ*

1 ana-tellō 9   2 ana-tolē 5/10

1: (A STAR) RISES, (THE SUN) COMES UP, (LIGHT) DAWNS

Mt	2 2	2	We saw his star ⌐as it *rose* (or: in the east)
	9	2	there in front of them was the star they had seen ⌐*rising* (or: in the east);
	4 16 ●		(Is 9 1) on those who dwell in the land and shadow of death a light has *dawned*.
	5 45 Θ		your Father . . . *causes* his sun *to rise* on bad men as well as good,
	13 6		as soon as the sun *came up* [the shoots] were scorched
Mk	4 6		when the sun *came up* it was scorched
	16 2		[the women] went to the tomb, just as the sun was *rising*.
Lk	1 78 ●	2	God . . . from on high will bring the *rising* [Sun] to visit us,
	12 54		When you see a cloud *looming up* in the west you say . . . that rain is coming,
Jm	1 11		the scorching sun *comes up*,
2 P	1 19 ●		take [prophecy] as a lamp for lighting a way through the dark until . . . the morning star *rises* in your minds.
Rv	7 2	2	I saw another angel rising ⌐where the sun *rises* (or: in the East),
	16 12 2		the great river Euphrates . . . dried up so that a way was made for the kings of ⌐the East (or: where the sun *rises*) to come in.

2: (CHRIST) SPRINGS (FROM)

Heb	7 14		everyone knows [our Lord] ⌐came (lit. *sprang*) from Judah,

4. GO UP, COME UP – RISE – CLIMB: *ANA-BAINŌ*

6	*bēma*	1/12	8	pros-ana-bainō	1
1	*ana-bainō*	77/81	5	syn-ana-bainō	2
4	*ana-bathmos*	2	2	epi-bainō	4/6
7	*ana-bibazō*	1	3	epi-bibazō	3

1: ASCEND, GO UP, COME UP, TO HEAVEN

Jn	1 51		you will see . . . above the Son of Man, the angels of God *ascending* and descending.
	3 13 X		No one has *gone up* to heaven except the one who came down from heaven,
	6 62 X		What if you should see the Son of Man *ascend* to where he was before?
	20 17 X		I have not yet *ascended* to the Father. But . . . find the brothers, and tell them: I am *ascending* to my Father
Ac	2 34 X		David himself never *went up* to heaven;
	10 4		Your offering of prayers and alms . . . has ⌐been accepted by (lit. *ascended* to speak for you to) God.
Rm	10 6		(Dt 30 12) Do not tell yourself . . .: Who will *go up* to heaven?
Ep	4 8 X		(Ps 68 19) When he *ascended* to the height, he captured prisoners . . . ⁹ When it says, 'he *ascended*', what can it mean if not that he descended right down to the lower regions of the earth? ¹⁰ The one who *rose* higher than all the heavens . . . is none other than the one who descended.
	9 X		
	10 X		
Rv	4 1		*Come up* here: I will show you what is to come in the future.
	8 4		the smoke of the incense *went up* in the presence of God
	11 12		they heard a loud voice from heaven say to [the two witnesses], '*Come up* here', and . . . they *went up* to heaven in a cloud.

2: GO UP, COME UP, TO JERUSALEM

Mt	20 17 X		Jesus was *going up* to Jerusalem, and on the way he took the Twelve to one side
	18 X		Now we are *going up* to Jerusalem,
Mk	10 32 X		They were on the road, *going up* to Jerusalem;
	33 X		Now we are *going up* to Jerusalem,
	15 41 X	5	there were many other women there who had *come up* to Jerusalem *with* [Jesus].
Lk	2 42 X		When he was twelve years old, they *went up* for the feast as usual.
	18 31 X		Now we are *going up* to Jerusalem,
	19 28 X		he went on ahead, *going up* to Jerusalem.
Jn	2 13 X		Just before the Jewish Passover Jesus *went up* to Jerusalem.
	5 1 X		there was a Jewish festival, and Jesus *went up* to Jerusalem.
	7 8 X		*Go up* to the festival yourselves: I am not (ᵛ yet) *going up* to this festival . . . ¹⁰ However, after his brothers had ⌐left (lit. *gone up*) for the festival, he *went up* as well.
	10 X		
	11 55		many of the country people . . . had *gone up* to Jerusalem
	12 20		Among those who *went up* to worship at the festival were some Greeks.
Ac	11 2		Peter *came up* to Jerusalem
	13 31 X	5	he appeared to those who had *accompanied* him *up* from Galilee to Jerusalem:
	15 2		it was arranged that Paul and Barnabas . . . should *go up* to Jerusalem
	18 22 △		[Paul] *went up* to greet the church. Then he came down to Antioch
	21 4	2	[the disciples] kept telling Paul not to *go on* to Jerusalem,
	12		we . . . implored Paul not to *go up* to Jerusalem.
	15		we packed and *went on up* to Jerusalem.
	24 11		I *went up* to Jerusalem on pilgrimage,
	25 1		Festus *went up* to Jerusalem from Caesarea.
	9		Are you willing to *go up* to Jerusalem and be tried . . . there?
Ga	2 1		It was not till fourteen years had passed that I *went up* to Jerusalem . . . ² I *went up* there as the result of a revelation,
	2		

3: GO UP, TRAVEL UP, TO A PERSON, TO A PLACE

Mk	15 8		the crowd *went up* and began to ask Pilate the customary favour,
Lk	2 4		Joseph set out from . . . Nazareth in Galilee and *travelled up* to Judaea, to . . . Bethlehem,
	18 10		Two men *went up* to the Temple to pray,
Jn	7 14 X		When the festival was half over, Jesus *went up* to the Temple
Ac	3 1		Peter and John were *going up* to the Temple for the prayers

4: GET (UP), CLIMB, INTO A BOAT – GO ABOARD

Mt	14 32		as they *got* into the boat the wind dropped.
Mk	6 51 X		he *got* into the boat with them, and the wind dropped.
Jn	21 11		Simon Peter *went aboard* and dragged the net to the shore,
Ac	21 2	2	we found a ship bound for Phoenicia, so we *went on board*

Ac 27 2   2 We *boarded* a vessel from Adramyttium

5: LIFT ON, HELP ON, SET ON, (TO) AN ANIMAL – RIDE

Mt 21 5 X   2 (Zc 9 9) your king comes to you; he is humble, he *rides* on a donkey
Lk 10 34   3 [The Samaritan] *lifted* [the wounded man] *on* to his own ˹mount (lit. animal),
   19 35 X   3 throwing their garments over [the colt's] back they *helped* Jesus *on* to it.
Ac 23 24   3 provide ˹horses (lit. animals) ˹for Paul (lit. to *set* Paul *on*),

6: GO UP(WARDS), COME UP, CLIMB UP – RISE (UP), EMERGE

Mt 3 16 X   As soon as Jesus was baptised he *came up* from the water,
    5 1 X   Seeing the crowds, he *went up* the hill.
   13 48   7 the fishermen *haul* [the dragnet] *up* ashore;
   14 23 X   After sending the crowds away he *went up* into the hills.
   15 29 X   he *went up* into the hills.
   17 27   take the first fish that ˹bites (lit. *comes up*),
Mk 1 10 X   No sooner had he *come up* out of the water than he saw the heavens torn apart
    3 13 X   He now *went up* into the hills
Lk 5 19   they *went up* on to the flat roof and lowered [the paralytic] down
    9 28 X   he took with him Peter and John and James and *went up* the mountain to pray.
   19 4   [Zacchaeus] *climbed* a sycamore tree to catch a glimpse of Jesus
Jn 10 1   anyone who does not enter the sheepfold through the gate, but ˹*gets* (lit. *climbs*) in some other way is a thief
Ac 1 13   [the apostles] *went up* to the upper room where they were staying;
    8 31   [the eunuch] invited Philip to ˹*get* (lit. *climb*) in and sit by his side.
      39   after they had *come up* out of the water again Philip was taken away by the Spirit of the Lord,
   10 9   Peter *went up* to the housetop
   20 11   [Paul] *went back upstairs* where he broke bread
Rv 7 2   I saw another angel *rising* where the sun rises,
    9 2   When [the angel] unlocked the shaft of the Abyss, smoke *poured up*
   11 7   the beast that *comes up* out of the Abyss is going to make war on them and overcome them
   13 1   Then I saw a beast *emerge* from the sea:
      11   I saw a second beast; it *emerged* from the ground;
   14 11   the smoke of their torture will *go up* for ever and ever.
   17 8   The beast you have seen . . . is yet to *come up* from the Abyss,
   19 3   The smoke of [Babylon] will *go up* for ever and ever.
   20 9   [Satan's armies] will *come* ˹*swarming* (lit. *up*) over the entire country

7: RISE, ARISE (FIGURATIVELY) – COME UP, MOVE UP

Lk 14 10 <   8 My friend, *move up* higher.
   24 38   why are these doubts *rising* in your hearts?
Ac 7 23   [Moses] ˹decided (lit. it *arose* in [Moses's] mind) to visit his countrymen,
   21 31   They would have killed [Paul] if a report had not ˹*reached* (lit. *come up* to) the tribune . . . that there was rioting
1 Co 2 9   we teach . . . things ˹beyond (lit. that have not *arisen in*) the mind of man,

8: DAIS – STEP(S)

Ac 12 21   6 Herod, . . . enthroned on a *dais* made a speech to them.
   21 35   4 When Paul reached the *steps*, the crowd became . . . violent
      40   4 Paul, standing at the top of the *steps*, gestured to the people

5. GO UP – CLIMB: *AN-ERCHOMAI*

an-erchomai 3

Jn 6 3 X   Jesus *climbed* the hillside,
Ga 1 17   nor did I *go up* to Jerusalem to see those who were already apostles before me,
      18   I *went up* to Jerusalem to visit Cephas

6. LIFT UP, HOIST UP – KEEP UP – RISE UP: *AIRŌ*

2 *airō* 8/101   1   *ep-airō* 8/19
                      3   *hyper-airō*   3

1: HOIST (UP, ABOARD) – WEIGH (ANCHOR)

Ac 27 13   2 they *weighed* anchor and began to sail past Crete,
      17   2 They *hoisted* [the ship's boat] aboard and with the help of tackle bound cables round the ship;
      40   *hoisting* the foresail to the wind, they headed for the beach

2: LIFT UP, RAISE, ONE'S HAND(S)

Lk 24 50 X   *lifting up* his hands [Jesus] blessed the [apostles].
1 Tm 2 8   In every place . . . I want the men to *lift* their hands *up* reverently in prayer,
Rv 10 5   2 Then the angel . . . *raised* his right hand to heaven, ⁶ and swore

3: HOLD HIGH, LIFT UP – KEEP IN SUSPENSE

Mt 4 6   2 (Ps 91 12) his angels . . . will *support* you on their hands
   21 21   2 if you say to this mountain, '˹Get up (lit. *Be lifted up*)!' . . . it will be done.
Mk 11 23   2 if anyone says to this mountain, '˹Get up (lit. *Be lifted up*)! . . . it will be done for him,
Lk 4 11   2 (Ps 91 12) [his angels] will *hold* you *up* on their hands
   21 28   stand erect, *hold* your heads *high*, because your liberation is near at hand.
Jn 10 24   2 How much longer are you going to *keep us in suspense*?
   13 18   (Ps 41 10) Someone who shares my table ˹rebels (lit. *lifts up* his heel) against me.
Ac 1 9   [Jesus] was *lifted up* while they looked on, and a cloud took him from their sight.

4: RISE UP – HAUGHTY, PUT ON AIRS – BECOME PROUD, CLAIM TO BE GREAT

2 Co 10 5   [We demolish] the arrogance that ˹tries to resist (lit. *rises up* against) the knowledge of God;
   11 20   [You can cheerfully tolerate] somebody who . . . ˹orders you about (lit. acts *haughtily*)
   12 7   3 In view of the extraordinary nature of these revelations, to stop me from *getting* too *proud* I was given a thorn in the flesh, an angel of Satan to beat me and stop me from
            3 *getting* too *proud*!
2 Th 2 4   3 This is the Enemy, the one who *claims to be* so much *greater* than all that men call 'god',

7. TAKE (A PERSON) UP, BRING (A PERSON) UP: *AN-AGŌ*

an-agō 4/23

Lk 2 22   [Jesus's parents] *took* him *up* to Jerusalem to present him to the Lord
    4 5 ⓓ   ˹leading him to a height (or: *taking* him *up*), the devil showed [Jesus] . . . all the kingdoms of the world
Rm 10 7   [Do not tell yourself] you have to *bring* Christ ˹back (lit. *up*) from the dead
Heb 13 20 Θ   God . . . *brought* our Lord Jesus ˹back (lit *up*) from the dead

8. HIGH, HEIGHT – LIFT(ED) – EXALTED: *HYPSOŌ*

3 *hypsēlos*	11	4	*hypsos*	6
2 *hypsistos*	13	6	*hypsēlo(-phroneō)*	1
5 *hypsōma*	2	7	*hyper-(h)ypsoō*	1
1 *hypsoō*	20			

E = Height, Heaven // Earth, Below   H = Exalted // Humble

1: THE MOST HIGH

Mk 5 7   2 What do you want with me, Jesus, son of the *Most High* God?
Lk 1 32   2 [Jesus] will be called Son of the *Most High*.
      35   2 the power of the *Most High* will cover you with its shadow.
      76   2 [John the Baptist,] you shall be called Prophet of the *Most High*,
    6 35   2 you will be sons of the *Most High*,
    8 28   2 What do you want with me, Jesus, son of the *Most High* God?
Ac 7 48   2 the *Most High* does not live in a house that human hands have built:

Ac	16 17	2	Here are the servants of the *Most High* God;
Heb	7 1	2	Melchizedek, . . . a priest of God *Most High*,

2: ON HIGH, IN THE HIGHEST HEAVENS, TO THE HEIGHT – HEAVEN(S)

Mt	21 9	2	Hosanna in the *highest* [heavens]!
Mk	11 10	2	Hosanna in the *highest* [heavens]!
Lk	1 78	4	from *on high* [God] will bring the rising Sun to visit us,
	2 14 E	2	Glory to God in the *highest* [heaven], and peace to men
	19 38	2	Peace in heaven and glory in the *highest* [heavens]!
	24 49	4	Stay in the city . . . until you are clothed with the power from *on high*.
Ep	4 8	4	(Ps 68 19) When [Christ] ascended to the *height*, he captured prisoners,
Heb	1 3	3	[the Son] has gone to take his place in *heaven* at the right hand of divine Majesty.

3: JESUS LIFTED UP, RAISED (UP, HIGH, ABOVE), EXALTED

Jn	3 14		the Son of Man must be *lifted up* as Moses *lifted up* the serpent in the desert,
	8 28		When you have *lifted up* the Son of Man then you will know that I am He
	12 32		when I am *lifted up* from the earth I shall draw all men to myself.
	34		How can you say, 'The Son of Man must be *lifted up*'?
Ac	2 33		[Jesus is] *raised to the heights* by God's right hand,
	5 31		By his own right hand God has now *raised* him *up*
Ph	2 9 H	7	God *raised* him *high* and gave him the name which is above all other names
Heb	7 26	3	the ideal high priest would have to be . . . *raised up above* the heavens;

4: EXALT(ED), LIFT(ED) UP – HAUGHTY, PROUD – THOUGHT HIGHLY OF, HIGH RANK, MADE GREAT

Mt	11 23		as for you, Capernaum, did you want to be *exalted* as high as heaven? You shall be thrown down to hell.
	23 12 H H		Anyone who *exalts* himself will be humbled, and anyone who humbles himself will be *exalted*.
Lk	1 52 H		(cf. 1 S 2 7) [God] has pulled down princes from their thrones and *exalted* the lowly.
	10 15		as for you, Capernaum, did you want to be *exalted* high as heaven?
	14 11 H H		everyone who *exalts* himself will be humbled, and the man who humbles himself will be *exalted*.
	16 15	3	what is *thought highly of* by men is loathsome in the sight of God.
	18 14 H		everyone who *exalts* himself will be humbled, but the man who humbles himself will be *exalted*.
Ac	13 17		The God of our nation Israel . . . *made* our people *great*
Rm	11 20	3	Rather than making you *proud*, that should make you afraid.
	12 16 H	3	never be ⌜condescending (lit. *haughty*) but make real friends with the poor.
2 Co	10 5	5	[We demolish] the *arrogance* that tries to resist the knowledge of God;
	11 7 H		was I wrong, lowering myself so as to *lift* you *high* . . .?
1 Tm	6 17 H	6	Warn those who are rich in this world's goods that they are not to ⌜look down on (lit. be *haughty* towards) other people;
Jm	1 9 H	4	It is right for the poor brother to be proud of his *high rank*,
	4 10 H		Humble yourselves before the Lord and he will *lift* you *up*.
1 P	5 6 H		Bow down . . . before the power of God now, and he will *raise* you *up* on the appointed day;

5: HIGH, HEIGHT

Mt	4 8	3	taking [Jesus] to a very *high* mountain, the devil showed him all the kingdoms of the world
	17 1	3	Jesus took with him Peter and James and . . . John and led them up a *high* mountain
Mk	9 2	3	[Jesus] led [Peter, James and John] up a *high* mountain
Ac	13 17	3	(Ex 6 1) ⌜by divine power (lit. with arm [raised] *high*) he led [our people] out [of Egypt],
Rm	8 39 O	5	[neither death nor life,] or *height* or depth . . . can ever come between us and the love of God
Ep	3 18 ●	4	you will . . . grasp the breadth and the length, the *height* and the depth;
Rv	21 10	3	[the angel] took me to the top of an enormous *high* mountain,
	12	3	The walls of [the city] were of a great *height*,
	16	4	the city . . . was twelve thousand furlongs in length and in breadth, and equal in *height*.

9. LIFT UP (ONESELF, ONE'S HEAD) – STAND: *ANA-KYPTŌ*

ana-kyptō 4

Lk	13 11		[a woman] was bent double and quite unable to ⌜stand upright (or: *lift up her head*).
	21 28		When these things begin to take place, *stand erect*, hold your heads high,
Jn	8 7 X		[Jesus] ⌜looked up (lit. *lifted up his head*, or: *stood up*) and said, 'If there is one of you who has not sinned, let him be the first to throw a stone at her'.
	10 X		[Jesus] ⌜looked up (lit. *lifted up his head*, or: *stood up*) and said, 'Woman, where are they?'

RIVER – FLOW – FOUNTAIN

1. River – Flood: *potamos*
   1: River, Stream – Flood, Torrent – Current, Spate
   2: the River Euphrates
   3: the Jordan, with Transjordania
   4: Fountains, Streams (of living water) – the River (of the water of life)
2. Flow, Flood – Melt – Pour
   1: Flow – Flood: *rheō*
      a) Flow
      b) Flow of blood – Haemorrhage
      c) Seasonal watercourse – Valley
   2: Melt: *tēkō*
   3: Flood: *plē-m-myra*
   4: Flood: *kata-klysmos*
   5: Gush, Pour forth – Flow: *bruō*

6: Pour out: *ek-cheō*
   a) Pour (wine, perfume, oil) – Be spilled, Run out
   b) Pour out, Empty out (the bowls of God's anger)
   c) Pour out (God's spirit, love)
   d) Pour out, Shed, Spill (blood)
   e) Pour out (generally) – Running over, Rush down – Scatter
3. Fountain, Spring, Well – Source: *pēgē*
   a) Water-spring, Fountain, Well
   b) Source (of a haemorrhage)
4. Well – Shaft – Draw out
   1: Well – Shaft – Pit: *phrear*
      a) a Well
      b) (the) Shaft (of the Abyss)
   2: Draw (out, off) – Bucket: *antleō*

1. RIVER – FLOOD: *POTAMOS*

1 *potamos 17*   2 *potamo(-phorētos) 1*

1: RIVER, STREAM – FLOOD, TORRENT – CURRENT, SPATE

Mt	7 25		Rain came down, *floods* rose . . . against that house, and it did not fall . . . ²⁷ . . . *floods* rose . . . and struck that house, and it fell;
	27		
Lk	6 48		when the *river* was in flood it bore down on that house but could not shake it . . . ⁴⁹ . . . as soon as the *river* bore down on it, it collapsed;
	49		
Ac	16 13		we went along the *river* outside the gates
2 Co	11 26		Constantly travelling, I have been in danger from *rivers* and in danger from brigands,
Rv	8 10		a huge star . . . fell on a third of all *rivers* and springs;
	12 15		the serpent vomited water . . . like a *river*, after the woman,
	16	2	to sweep her away in the *current*, ¹⁶ but the earth . . . swallowed the *river*
	16 4		The third angel emptied his bowl into the *rivers* and water-springs and they turned into blood.

2: THE RIVER EUPHRATES

Euphrates 2

Rv	9 14		Release the four angels that are chained up at the great *river Euphrates*.
	16 12		The sixth angel emptied his bowl over the great *river Euphrates*;

3: THE JORDAN, WITH TRANSJORDANIA

Jordan 15			
	Aenon*	*1* (Jn 3)	Idumaea* *1* (Mk 3)
	Bethany* (*Bethabara**)	*1* (Jn 1)	
	Salim*	*1* (Jn 3)	

Mt	3 5		Then . . . the whole *Jordan* district made their way to [John],
	6		⁶ . . . they were baptised by him in the *river Jordan*
	13		[Jesus] came . . . to the *Jordan* to be baptised by John.
	4 15		(Is 8 23) Way of the sea on the far side of *Jordan*, Galilee of the nations!

Mt	4	25	Large crowds . . . coming from Galilee . . . and *Trans-jordania*.
	19	1	Jesus . . . came into the part of Judaea which is on the far side of the *Jordan*.
Mk	1	5	they were baptised by [John] in the *river Jordan*
		9	Jesus . . . was baptised in the *Jordan* by John.
	3	8	[From Judaea] . . . Idumaea*, *Transjordania* . . great numbers . . . came to [Jesus].
	10	1	[Jesus] came to the district of Judaea and the far side of the *Jordan*.
Lk	3	3	[John] went through the whole *Jordan* district
	4	1	Jesus left the *Jordan*
Jn	1	28	This happened at Bethany* (ᵛ Bethabara*), on the far side of the *Jordan*,
	3	23	At the same time John was baptising at Aenon* near Salim*,
		26	the man who was with you on the far side of the *Jordan* . . . is baptising now;
	10	40	[Jesus] went back again to the far side of the *Jordan* to stay in the district where John had once been baptising.

4: FOUNTAINS, STREAMS (OF LIVING WATER) – THE RIVER (OF THE WATER OF LIFE)

| Jn | 7 | 38 | From his breast shall flow *fountains* of living water. |
| Rv | 22 | 1 | the *river* of life, rising from the throne of God and of the Lamb and flowing crystal-clear ² down the middle of the city street. On either side of the *river* were the trees of life, |

2. FLOW, FLOOD – MELT – POUR

1: FLOW – FLOOD: *RHEŌ*

| 2 | *rheō* | 1 | | 3 | (haimo-)rrhoeō 1 | | Kedron [Kidron] 1 |
| 1 | *rhysis* | 3 | | 4 | cheima-rrhous 1 | | |

a) Flow

| Jn | 7 | 38 | 2 From his breast shall *flow* fountains of living water. |

b) Flow of blood – Haemorrhage

Mt	9	20	3 a woman, who had suffered from a *haemorrhage* for twelve years,
Mk	5	25	a woman who had suffered from a *haemorrhage* for twelve years;
Lk	8	43	a woman suffering from a *haemorrhage* for twelve years . . .
		44	⁴⁴ . . . the *haemorrhage* stopped at that instant.

c) Seasonal watercourse – Valley

| Jn | 18 | 1 | 4 Jesus left . . . and crossed the *Kedron* valley. |

2: MELT: *TĒKŌ*

tēkō 1

| 2 P | 3 | 12 | the sky will dissolve in flames and the elements *melt* in the heat. |

3: FLOOD: *PLĒ-M-MYRA*

plē-m-myra 1

| Lk | 6 | 48 | when the river was in *flood* it bore down on that house |

4: FLOOD: *KATA-KLYSMOS*

| 1 *kata-klysmos* 4 | | 2 *kata-klyzō* 1 |

Mt	24	38	in those days before the *Flood* people were eating, drinking,
		39	they suspected nothing till the *Flood* came and swept all away.
Lk	17	27	People were eating and drinking . . . and the *Flood* came and destroyed them all.
2 P	2	5	[God] sent the *Flood* over a disobedient world.
	3	6	2 the world of that time was destroyed by being *flooded* by water.

5: GUSH, POUR FORTH – FLOW: *BRUŌ*

bruō 1

| Jm | 3 | 11 | does any water supply *give a flow* of fresh water and salt water out of the same pipe? |

6: POUR OUT: *EK-CHEŌ*

4	ana-chysis	1		5	(haimat-)ek-chysia	1
3	kata-cheō	2		6	hyper-ek-chynnō	1
1	ek-cheō	16		7	epi-cheō	1
2	ek-chynnō	11		8	pros-chysis	1

a) Pour (wine, perfume, oil) – Be spilled, Run out

Mt	9	17	the [old] skins burst, the wine *runs out*,
	26	7	3 a woman came to [Jesus] . . . and *poured* [ointment] on his head as he was at table.
Mk	14	3	3 a woman came in . . . and *poured* the ointment on [Jesus's] head.
Lk	5	37	2 the new wine will burst the skins and then *run out*,
	10	34	7 [the Samaritan] bandaged his wounds, *pouring* oil and wine on them.

b) Pour out, Empty out (the bowls of God's anger)

Rv	16	1	I heard a voice . . . shouting to the seven angels, 'Go, and *empty* the seven bowls of God's anger over the earth'.
		2	² The first angel went and *emptied* his bowl over the earth;
		3	The second angel *emptied* his bowl over the sea,
		4	The third angel *emptied* his bowl into the rivers
		8	The fourth angel *emptied* his bowl over the sun
		10	The fifth angel *emptied* his bowl over the throne of the beast
		12	The sixth angel *emptied* his bowl over the great river Euphrates;
		17	The seventh angel *emptied* his bowl into the air,

c) Pour out (God's spirit, love)

Ac	2	17	(Jl 3 1 f) In the days to come . . . I will *pour out* my spirit on all mankind . . . ¹⁸ Even on my slaves, men and women, in those days, I will *pour out* my spirit.
		18	
		33	[Jesus] has received from the Father the Holy Spirit . . . and what you see and hear is the *outpouring* of that Spirit.
	10	45	2 the gift of the Holy Spirit should be *poured out* on the pagans too,
Rm	5	5	2 the love of God has been *poured* into our hearts by the Holy Spirit which has been given us.
Tt	3	6	[God] has so generously *poured* [the Holy Spirit] over us through Jesus Christ our saviour.

d) Pour out, Shed, Spill (blood)

Mt	23	35	you will draw down on yourselves the blood of every holy man that has been *shed* on earth,
	26	28	2 this is my blood . . . which is to be *poured out* for many
Mk	14	24	2 This is my blood . . . which is to be *poured out* for many.
Lk	11	50	this generation will have to answer for every prophet's blood that has been *shed*
	22	20	This cup is the new covenant in my blood which will be *poured out* for you.
Ac	22	20	2 when the blood of your witness Stephen was being *shed*, I was standing by in full agreement with his murderers,
Rm	3	15	(Is 59 7) Their feet are swift when blood is to be *shed*,
Heb	9	22	5 if there is no *shedding* of blood, there is no remission.
	11	28	8 It was by faith that [Moses] kept the Passover and *sprinkled* the blood
Rv	16	6	they *spilt* the blood of the saints and the prophets,

e) Pour out (generally) – Running over, Rush down – Scatter

Lk	6	38	6 a full measure, pressed down, shaken together, and *running over*, will be ʳpoured (lit. put) into your lap;
Jn	2	15 X	[Jesus] drove them all out of the Temple, . . . *scattered* the money changers' coins,
Ac	1	18	2 [Judas] burst open, and all his entrails *poured out*.
1 P	4	4	people cannot understand why you no longer hurry off with them to join this [flood which is] *rushing down* to ruin,
Jude		11	2 they have *rushed* to make the same mistake as Balaam and for the same reward;

3. FOUNTAIN, SPRING, WELL – SOURCE: *PĒGĒ*

pēgē 11

a) Water-spring, Fountain, Well

Jn	4	6	Jacob's *well* is [at Sychar] and Jesus . . . sat straight down by the *well*.
		14 ●	the water that I shall give will turn into a *spring* inside him, welling up to eternal life.
Jm	3	11	does any *water supply* give a flow of fresh water and salt water out of the same pipe?
2 P	2	17	People like this are dried-up ʳrivers (lit. *fountains*),
Rv	7	17 ●	the Lamb . . . will lead [the chosen] to *springs* of living water;
	8	10	a huge star . . . fell on a third of all rivers and *springs*;
	14	7	the maker of heaven . . . and sea and every *water-spring*
	16	4	The third angel emptied his bowl into the rivers and *water-springs* and they turned into blood.

Rv 21 6 ● I will give water from the *well* of life free to anybody who is thirsty;

b) Source of a haemorrhage

Mk 5 29 the *source* of the bleeding dried up instantly,

4. WELL – SHAFT – DRAW OUT

1: WELL – SHAFT – PIT: *PHREAR*

phrear 7

a) a Well

Lk 14 5 Which of you here, if his son falls into a *well*, or his ox, will not pull him out . . .?
Jn 4 11 the *well* is deep: how could you get this living water? [12] . . .
12 Jacob . . . gave us this *well* and drank from it himself

b) (the) Shaft (of the Abyss)

Rv 9 1 I saw a star . . . and he was given the key to the *shaft* leading down to the Abyss. [2] When he unlocked the *shaft* of the Abyss, smoke poured up out of the Abyss from the *shaft* . . . the sun and the sky were darkened by ʳit (lit. the smoke from the *shaft*),

2: DRAW (OUT, OFF) – BUCKET: *ANTLEŌ*

2 antlēma 1   1 antleō 4

Jn 2 8 'Draw some out now' [Jesus] told them 'and take it to the steward.'
9 the servants who had *drawn* the water knew [where the wine came from]
4 7 a Samaritan woman came to *draw* water,
11 2 You have no *bucket*, sir . . . and the well is deep:
15 Sir, . . . give me some of that water, so that I may . . . never have to come here again to *draw* water.

ROD – STAFF – CLUB

1. Staff, Rod: *rhabdos*
1: Staff, Stick (for walking)
2: Sceptre – Rod
3: Rod – Staff – Branch
4: Flog with sticks – Beat with rods
5: Officers (who carried a staff)
2. Club – Cudgel: *xylon*

1. STAFF, ROD: *RHABDOS*

2 rhabdizō 2   3 rhabd-ouchos 2
1 rhabdos 12

1: STAFF, STICK (FOR WALKING)

Mt 10 10 [Provide yourselves] with no haversack . . . or footwear or a *staff*,
Mk 6 8 take nothing for the journey except a *staff*
Lk 9 3 Take nothing for the journey: neither *staff*, nor haversack,
Heb 11 21 Jacob . . . blessed each of Joseph's sons, leaning on the end of his *stick* as though bowing to pray.

2: SCEPTRE – ROD

Heb 1 8 (Ps 45 7) his royal *sceptre* is the *sceptre* of virtue;
Rv 2 27 I myself have been given [authority] by my Father, to rule them with an iron *sceptre*
12 5 The woman brought a male child into the world . . . to rule all the nations with an iron *sceptre*,
19 15 [The Word of God] will rule [the pagans] with an iron *sceptre*,

3: ROD – STAFF – BRANCH

Heb 9 4 In this were kept the gold jar containing . . . Aaron's *branch* that grew the buds, and the stone tablets
Rv 11 1 I was given a long *cane* as a measuring rod,

4: FLOG WITH STICKS – BEAT WITH RODS

Ac 16 22 the magistrates had [Paul and Silas] stripped and ordered 2 them to be *flogged*.
1 Co 4 21 do I come with a *stick* in my hand or in a spirit of love . . .?
2 Co 11 25 2 three times I have been *beaten with sticks*; once I was stoned;

5: OFFICERS (WHO CARRIED A STAFF)

Ac 16 35 3 the magistrates sent the *officers* with the order: 'Release those men.'
38 3 The *officers* reported [Paul's words] to the magistrates,

2. CLUB – CUDGEL: *XYLON*

xylon 5/20

Mt 26 47 Judas . . . appeared, and with him a large number of men armed with swords and *clubs*,
55 Am I a brigand, that you had to set out to capture me with swords and *clubs*?
Mk 14 43 Judas . . . came up with a number of men armed with swords and *clubs*,
48 Am I a brigand . . . that you had to set out to capture me with swords and *clubs*?
Lk 22 52 Am I a brigand . . . that you had to set out with swords and *clubs*?

ROME – ROMAN – LATIN

R	*Rome* [=*Rhōmē*]	8	*Italy*	4
2	*rhōmaikos*	1	*Italica*	1 (Ac 10)
1	*rhōmaios*	12	*Forum of Appius*	1
3	*rhōmaisti*	1	*Puteoli*	1
			Rhegium	1 (Ac 28)
			Syracuse	1
			Three Taverns	1

Lk 23 38 Above [Jesus] there was an inscription (ᵛ in the Greek, 2 *Latin* and Hebrew scripts):
Jn 11 48 1 the *Romans* will come and destroy the Holy Place and our nation.
19 20 3 the writing was *in Hebrew, Latin and Greek.*
Ac 2 10 1 visitors *from Rome* – [11] Jews and proselytes alike – Cretans and Arabs; we hear them preaching in our own language
10 1 One of the centurions of the *Italica* cohort stationed at Caesarea was called Cornelius.
16 21 [These people . . . are Jews] and they are advocating 1 practices which it is unlawful for us as *Romans* to accept or follow.
37 1 [The magistrates] flog *Roman* citizens in public
38 the magistrates . . . were horrified to hear the men were 1 *Roman* [citizens].
18 2 a Jew called Aquila . . . and his wife Priscilla had recently left *Italy* because an edict of Claudius had expelled all R the Jews from *Rome.*
19 21 R [Paul] said 'I must go on to see *Rome* as well.'
22 25 1 Paul said . ., 'Is it legal for you to flog a . . . *Roman* [citizen] . . .?' [26] . . . the centurion went and told the 26 tribune; . . . 'This man is a *Roman* [citizen]'. [27] So the 27 1 tribune came and asked him, 'Tell me, are you a *Roman* [citizen]?'
29 the tribune himself was alarmed when he realised that he 1 had put a *Roman* [citizen] in chains.
23 11 the Lord appeared to [Paul] and said, '. . . You . . . must [bear witness for me] in *Rome.*'
R
27 1 I . . . discovered that [Paul] was a *Roman* [citizen].
R
25 16 1 *Romans* are not in the habit of surrendering any man, until the accused confronts his accusers
27 1 When it had been decided that we should sail for *Italy*,
6 [At Myra] the centurion found an Alexandrian ship leaving for *Italy* and put us aboard.
28 12 We put in at *Syracuse* and spent three days there;
13 [13] from there we followed the coast up to *Rhegium*. . . .
14 on the second day we made *Puteoli*, [14] where we found some brothers and were much rewarded by staying a week with them. And so we came to *Rome*. [15] . . . the
15 R brothers there . . . came to meet us, as far as the *Forum*
16 *of Appius* and the *Three Taverns*. . . . [16] On our arrival
R in *Rome* Paul was allowed to stay in lodgings of his own
17 1 I was arrested in Jerusalem and handed over to the *Romans*.
Rm 1 7 R To you all . . . who are God's beloved in *Rome*,

Rm 1 15 R	it is this that makes me want to bring the Good News to you too in *Rome*.	
2Tm 1 17 R	as soon as he reached *Rome*, [Onesiphorus] really searched hard for me	
Heb 13 24	The saints of *Italy* send you greetings.	

ROPE – TIE – CHAIN

1. Cords – Ropes: *schoinion*
2. Lashings – Guy-ropes: *zeuktēria*
3. Undergird with cables: *hypo-zōnnymi*
4. Strap – Thong: *himas*
5. Control – Bridle, Bit – Muzzle
  1: Control – Bridle – Bit: *chalinos*
  2: Muzzle: *kēmoō*
  3: Muzzle: *phimoō*
6. Plait – Twist – Entangle: *plekō*
  a) Plait, Twist (the crown of thorns)
  b) Plait, Braid (the hair)
  c) (Be) Entangled (figuratively) – (Be) Involved

7. Noose: *brochos*
8. Tie, Bind – Chain – Prison(er): *deō*
  a) Tie up, Tether, Secure – Bind, (up), Bandage – Ligament, Sinew
  b) (Be) Tied, Bound (figuratively) – Chain (up) – Bonds
  c) Prisoner, Gaol, Prison – Chain (up), Bind, Tie up – Custody
9. Chains: *seira*
10. Chain: *halysis*
11. Fetter(s): *pedē*
12. the Stocks: *xylon*

1. CORDS – ROPES: *SCHOINION*
schoinion 2

Jn 2 15	Making a whip out of some *cord*, [Jesus] drove them all out
Ac 27 32	the soldiers cut the boat's *ropes*

2. LASHINGS – GUY-ROPES: *ZEUKTĒRIA*
zeuktēria 1

Ac 27 40	[the crew] loosened the *lashings* of the rudders;

3. UNDERGIRD WITH CABLES: *HYPO-ZŌNNYMI*
hypo-zōnnymi 1

Ac 27 17	with the help of tackle [the crew] *bound cables round* the ship;

4. STRAP – THONG: *HIMAS*
himas 4

Mk 1 7	I am not fit to kneel down and undo the *strap* of his sandals.
Lk 3 16	I am not fit to undo the *strap* of his sandals;
Jn 1 27	I am not fit to undo his sandal-*strap*.
Ac 22 25	when they had *strapped* him down Paul said to the centurion . . , 'Is it legal for you to flog . . . a Roman citizen . . .?'

5. CONTROL – BRIDLE, BIT – MUZZLE

1: CONTROL – BRIDLE – BIT: *CHALINOS*
1 *chalinos* 2   2 *chalin-agōgeō* 2

Jm 1 26	2	Nobody must imagine that he is religious while . . . not *keeping control over* his tongue;
3 2		someone who never said anything wrong . . . would be able
3	2/	to *control* every part of himself. [3] Once we put a *bit* into the horse's mouth . . . we have the whole animal under our control.
Rv 14 20		the blood . . . was up to the horses' *bridles*

2: MUZZLE: *KĒMOŌ*
kēmoō 1

1 Co 9 9	(Dt 25 4) You must not *put a muzzle on* the ox when it is treading out the corn.

3: MUZZLE: *PHIMOŌ*
phimoō 1/7

1 Tm 5 18	(Dt 25 4) You must not *muzzle* an ox when it is treading out the corn;

6. PLAIT – TWIST – ENTANGLE: *PLEKŌ*

1 *plekō*	3	2 *em-plekō*	2
3 *plegma*	1	4 *em-plokē*	1

a) Plait, Twist (the crown of thorns)

Mt 27 29	having *twisted* some thorns into a crown they put this on [Jesus's] head
Mk 15 17	[the soldiers] *twisted* some thorns into a crown and put it on [Jesus].
Jn 19 2	the soldiers *twisted* some thorns into a crown and put it on his head,

b) Plait, Braid (the hair)

1 Tm 2 9	3 women are to wear suitable clothes . . . without *braided* [hair] or gold and jewellery
1 P 3 3	4 Do not dress up for show: *doing up* your hair, wearing . . . fine clothes.

c) (Be) Entangled (figuratively) – (Be) Involved

2 Tm 2 4	2 In the army, no soldier ˹gets himself *mixed up in* (or: *involves* himself *in*) civilian life,
2 P 2 20	2 anyone who has escaped the pollution of the world once . . . and who then allows himself to *be entangled* by it a second time . . . will end up in a worse state than he began in.

7. NOOSE: *BROCHOS*
brochos 1

1 Co 7 35	I say this only to help you, not to ˹put a halter round your necks (lit. throw a *noose* over you),

8. TIE, BIND – CHAIN – PRISON(ER): *DEŌ*

1 *deō*	43	8	*desmōtēs*	2
9 *desmē*	1	7	*desmo(-phylax)*	3
6 *desmeuō*	3	10	*kata-deō*	1
3 *desmios*	16	11	*peri-deō*	1
2 *desmos*	18	12	*syn-deō*	1
4 *desmōtērion*	4	5	*syn-desmos*	4

a) Tie up, Tether, Secure – Bind (up), Bandage – Ligament, Sinew

Mt 12 29	<	how can anyone make his way into a strong man's house . . . unless he has *tied up* the strong man first?
13 30		/9 collect the darnel and *tie* it in *bundles* to be burnt,
21 2		you will immediately find a *tethered* donkey
22 13		*Bind* him hand and foot and throw him out into the dark,
Mk 3 27	<	no one can make his way into a strong man's house . . . unless he has *tied up* the strong man first.
5 3		no one could *secure* [the demoniac] any more, even with a chain; [4] because he had often been *secured* with . . . chains
4		but had snapped the chains
7 35		2 the *ligament* of [the deaf-mute's] tongue was loosened
11 2		you will find a *tethered* colt
4		They went off and found a colt *tethered*
Lk 8 29		6 they used to *secure* [the demoniac] with chains and fetters
2		. . . but he would always break the *fastenings*,
10 34		10 [The Samaritan] went up and *bandaged* his wounds,
19 30		you will find a *tethered* colt
Jn 11 44		The dead man came out, his feet and hands *bound* with bands
11		of stuff and a cloth (§ *tied*) round his face.
19 40		They took the body of Jesus and *wrapped* it . . . in linen cloths,
Col 2 19		the head . . . holds the whole body together, with all its
○ 5		joints and *sinews*

b) (Be) Tied, Bound (figuratively) – Chain (up) – Bonds

B = Bond between a man and a woman   Ⓓ = Satan in chains

Mt 16 19	●	whatever you *bind* on earth shall be considered *bound* in heaven;
18 18	●	whatever you *bind* on earth shall be considered *bound* in heaven;
23 4		6 [the scribes and the Pharisees] *tie up* heavy burdens

Lk 13 16 ⑩		And this . . . daughter of Abraham whom Satan has *held bound* these eighteen years – was it not right to untie her *bonds* on the sabbath day?
	2	
Ac 8 23		[Simon,] you are trapped in the bitterness of gall and the *chains* of sin.
	5	
Rm 7 2 B		A married woman . . . ┌has (lit. is *bound* by) legal obligations to her husband while he is alive,
1 Co 7 27 B		If you are *tied* to a wife, do not look for freedom; if you are free of a wife, then do not look for one.
39 B		A wife is *tied* as long as her husband is alive.
Ep 4 3		Do all you can to preserve the unity of the Spirit by the peace that *binds* you *together*.
	5	
Col 3 14	5	Over all these clothes, to *keep* them *together* and complete them, put on love.
2 Tm 2 9		it is on account of [Christ] that I have my own hardships to bear, even to being chained like a criminal – but they cannot *chain up* God's news.
Jude 6 ⑩	2	[God] has kept them . . . in spiritual *chains*, to be judged on the great day.
Rv 9 14		Release the four angels that are *chained up* at the great river Euphrates.
20 2 ⑩		[An angel] overpowered the dragon . . . and *chained him up* for a thousand years.

c) Prisoner, Gaol, Prison – Chain (up), Bind, Tie up – Custody

Mt 11 2	4	Now John in his *prison* had heard what Christ was doing
14 3		it was Herod who had arrested John, *chained* him *up* and put him in prison
27 2		They had [Jesus] *bound*, and led him away
15		At festival time it was the governor's practice to release a *prisoner* . . . ¹⁶ Now there was at that time a notorious
16	3	
	3	*prisoner* whose name was Barabbas.
Mk 6 17		Herod . . . had sent to have John arrested, and had him *chained up* in prison
15 1		They had Jesus *bound* and took him away
6	3	At festival time Pilate used to release a *prisoner* . . . ⁷ Now a man called Barabbas was then *in prison* with the rioters
7		
Jn 18 12		the Jewish guards seized Jesus and *bound* him.
		Annas [Jesus], still *bound*, to Caiaphas the high priest.
Ac 5 21	4	[the Sanhedrin] sent to the *gaol* for [the apostles]
23	4	We found the *gaol* securely locked
9 2		[Saul was authorised] to ┌arrest (lit. *bind*) and take to Jerusalem any followers of the Way . . . that he could find.
14		[Saul] holds a warrant . . . to ┌arrest (lit. *take prisoner*) anybody who invokes your name.
21		this . . . man . . . came here for the sole purpose of ┌arresting them (lit. *taking* them *prisoner*) to have them tried
12 6		Peter was sleeping between two soldiers, *fastened* with double chains
16 23	7	[Paul and Silas were] thrown into prison, and the *gaoler* was told to keep a close watch on them.
25	3	Paul and Silas were praying and singing God's praises, while the other *prisoners* listened.
26	4 2	an earthquake . . . shook the *prison* to its foundations . . . and the *chains* fell from all the prisoners.
27	7 3	the *gaoler* . . . was about to commit suicide, presuming that the *prisoners* had escaped.
36	7	The *gaoler* reported the message to Paul,
20 22 ○		a *prisoner* already in spirit, I am on my way to Jerusalem,
23	2	the Holy Spirit . . . has made it clear enough that *imprisonment* and persecution await me.
21 11		[Agabus] took Paul's girdle, and *tied up* his own feet and hands, and said, '. . . the man this girdle belongs to will be *bound* like this by the Jews'
13		I am ready . . . to be *tied up*
33		the tribune . . . had [Paul] *bound* with two chains
22 4	6	I . . . sent women as well as men to prison *in chains*
5		When I set off [for Damascus] it was with the intention of bringing *prisoners* back from there to Jerusalem
29		the tribune . . . had *put* a Roman citizen *in chains*
23 18	3	The *prisoner* Paul . . . requested me to bring this young man to you;
29	2	there was no charge deserving death or *imprisonment*.
24 27		Felix left Paul *in custody*.
25 14	3	There is a man here . . . whom Felix left behind *in custody*,
27	3	It seems to me pointless to send a *prisoner* without indicating the charges against him.
26 29	2	I wish that . . . all . . . would come to be as I am – except for these *chains*.
31	2	This man is doing nothing that deserves death or *imprisonment*.
27 1	8	Paul and some other *prisoners* were handed over to a centurion
42	8	The soldiers planned to kill the *prisoners*
28 17	3	I was ┌arrested (lit. made a *prisoner*) in Jerusalem and handed over to the Romans.
Ep 3 1	3	I, Paul, a *prisoner* of Christ Jesus for the sake of you pagans
4 1	3	I, the *prisoner* in the Lord, implore you

Ph 1 7	2	you have shared . . . both my *chains* and my work defending . . . the gospel.
13	2	My *chains*, in Christ, have become famous
14		the brothers have taken courage in the Lord from these *chains* of mine
	2	
17	2	The others . . . do not mind if they make my *chains* heavier to bear.
Col 4 3		for the sake of [the mystery of Christ] I *am in chains*;
18	2	Remember the *chains* I wear.
2 Tm 1 8		you are never to be ashamed of . . . the Lord, or . . . of me for being his *prisoner*;
	3	
2 9	2	I have my own hardships to bear, even to being *chained* like a criminal
Phm 1	3	From Paul, a *prisoner* of Christ Jesus . . . to . . . Philemon,
9	3	this is Paul writing, an old man now and . . . still a *prisoner* of Christ Jesus.
10		a child of mine, whose father I became while wearing these *chains*: I mean Onesimus.
	2	
13	2	I am in the *chains* that the Good News has brought me.
Heb 10 34	3	you . . . shared in the sufferings of *those* [who were] *in prison*,
11 36	2	Some had to bear being . . . *chained up* in prison.
13 3	3	Keep in mind *those* [who are] *in prison*, as though you were *in prison with* them;
12		

9. CHAINS: *SEIRA*

seira 1

2 P 2 4		When angels sinned, God . . . sent them down to the underworld and consigned them to the ┌dark underground caves (ᵛ *chains* of darkness)

10. CHAIN: *HALYSIS*

halysis 11

Mk 5 3		no one could secure [the demoniac] any more, even with a *chain*; ⁴ because he had often been secured with fetters and *chains* but had snapped the *chains*
4		
Lk 8 29		they used to secure [the demoniac] with *chains* and fetters
Ac 12 6		Peter was sleeping between two soldiers, fastened with double *chains*,
7		the *chains* fell from [Peter's] hands.
21 33		the tribune . . . had [Paul] bound with two *chains*
28 20		it is on account of the hope of Israel that I wear this *chain*.
Ep 6 20		[give out the mystery of the gospel] of which I am an ambassador *in chains*;
2 Tm 1 16		Onesiphorus . . . has never been ashamed of my *chains*.
Rv 20 1		I saw an angel come down from heaven with . . . an enormous *chain*.

11. FETTER(S): *PEDĒ*

pedē 3

Mk 5 4		[the demoniac] had often been secured with *fetters* and chains but had snapped the chains and broken the *fetters*,
Lk 8 29		they used to secure [the demoniac] with chains and *fetters*

12. THE STOCKS: *XYLON*

xylon 1/20

Ac 16 24		[the gaoler] fastened [the] feet [of Paul and Silas] in the *stocks*.

ROUND – ROLL

1. **Go round – to Round a Point:** *perierchomai*
2. **Encircling:** *kyklō*
   a) Circle–Gather round–Round
   b) Encircle, Surround, Besiege
   c) Round about – (Go) Round, Make a tour
3. **Round, About – Those round, Followers:** *peri*
4. **Stand round, Surround – Cling to:** *peri-(h)istēmi*
5. **Put round, Wear – Beset on every side:** *peri-keimai*
6. **Put round – Put on, Clothe:** *peri-tithēmi*
7. **Wheel – Cycle:** *trochos*
8. **Roll, Roll up**
   1: Roll – Writhe – Wallow: *kyliō*
   2: Roll up – Fold up: *helissō*
   3: Roll up (a scroll): *ptyssō*
   4: Roll up: *en-tylissō*

1. GO ROUND – TO ROUND A POINT: *PERI-ERCHOMAI*
peri-erchomai 2/4

Ac 28 13	from [Syracuse] we ʳfollowed the coast up (lit. *went round*) to Rhegium.
1 Tm 5 13	[young widows] learn to . . . *go round* from house to house;

2. ENCIRCLING: *KYKLŌ*

4	*kykleuō 1*	3	*kyklothen 3*
1	*kyklō 8*	5	*peri-kykloō 1*
2	*kykloō 4*		

a) Circle – Gather round – Round

Mk 3 34	looking round at those sitting *in a circle* about him, [Jesus] said,
Jn 10 24	2 The Jews *gathered round* [Jesus]
Ac 14 20	2 The disciples *came crowding round* [Paul] but . . . he stood up
Heb 11 30 ○	2 the walls of Jericho fell down when the people had *been round* them for seven days.
Rv 4 3	3 There was a rainbow *encircling* the throne, and this looked like an emerald.
4	3 *Round* the throne *in a circle* were twenty-four thrones,
6	In the centre, *grouped round* the throne itself, were four animals
8	3 Each of the four animals . . . had eyes *all the way round* as well as inside;
5 11	an immense number of angels gathered *round* the throne and the animals and the elders;
7 11	all the angels . . . were standing *in a circle round* the throne,

b) Encircle, Surround, Besiege

Lk 19 43	Yes, [Jerusalem,] a time is coming when your enemies will raise fortifications all round you, . . . *encircle* you
5	
21 20	2 you see Jerusalem *surrounded* by armies,
Rv 20 9	4 they will . . . *besiege* the camp of the saints, which is the city that God loves.

c) Round about – (Go) Round, Make a tour

Mk 6 6	[Jesus] *made a tour* round the villages, teaching.
36	they can go to the farms and villages *round about*,
Lk 9 12	they can go to the farms and villages *round about*
Rm 15 19	all the way *round*, from Jerusalem to Illyricum,

3. ROUND, ABOUT – THOSE ROUND, FOLLOWERS: *PERI*

1	*peri*	(+ acc.)	(2)	3 *perix 1*
2	*hoi peri*		(2)	

Mt 8 18	Jesus saw the great crowds *all about* him
Mk 3 32	A crowd was sitting *round* [Jesus]
4 10	the Twelve, together with the others ʳwho formed his company (lit. *round* him), asked what the parables meant.ʳ
2	
Lk 22 49	2 His *followers*, seeing what was happening, said,
Ac 5 16	3 People even came crowding in from the towns *round about* Jerusalem,

4. STAND ROUND, SURROUND – CLING TO: *PERI-(H)ISTĒMI*

1 *peri-(h)istēmi 2/4*   2 *eu-peri-statos 1*

Jn 11 42	I speak for the sake of all these who *stand round* me,
Ac 25 7	the Jews who had come down from Jerusalem *surrounded* [Paul],
Heb 12 1	we . . . should throw off everything that hinders us, especially the sin that *clings* so easily,
2	

5. PUT ROUND, WEAR – BESET ON EVERY SIDE: *PERI-KEIMAI*
peri-keimai 5

Mk 9 42	[he] would be better thrown into the sea with a great millstone *put round* his neck.
Lk 17 2	It would be better for him to be thrown into the sea with a millstone *put round* his neck
Ac 28 20	it is on account of the hope of Israel that I *wear* this chain.
Heb 5 2	[every high priest] lives ʳin the limitations of (lit. *beset on every side* by) weakness.
12 1	With so many witnesses in a great cloud *on every side* of us,

6. PUT ROUND – PUT ON, CLOTHE: *PERI-TITHĒMI*

2 *peri-thesis 1*   1 *peri-tithēmi 8*

Mt 21 33	a man . . . planted a vineyard; he ʳfenced it round (lit. *put a fence round* it),
27 28	[the soldiers] stripped [Jesus] and *made* him *wear* a scarlet cloak,
48	one . . . ran to get a sponge which he dipped in vinegar, and *putting* it *on* a reed, gave it him
Mk 12 1	A man planted a vineyard; he ʳfenced it round (lit. *put a fence round* it),
15 17	[The soldiers] twisted some thorns into a crown and *put* it *on* him.
36	Someone . . . soaked a sponge in vinegar and, *putting* it *on* a reed, gave it him to drink
Jn 19 29	*putting* a sponge soaked in vinegar *on* a hyssop stick they held it up to his mouth.
1 Co 12 23	the least honourable parts of the body . . . we *clothe* with the greatest care.
1 P 3 3	2 Do not dress up for show: . . . *wearing* gold [bracelets]

7. WHEEL – CYCLE: *TROCHOS*
trochos 1

Jm 3 6	[the tongue] sets fire to the whole *wheel* of ʳcreation (or: existence).

8. ROLL, ROLL UP

1: ROLL – WRITHE – WALLOW: *KYLIŌ*

3	*kyliō 1*	5	*ana-kyliō 1*
4	*kylismos 1*	1	*apo-kyliō 3*
		2	*pros-kyliō 2*

Mt 27 60	2 [Joseph] *rolled* a large stone across the entrance of the tomb
28 2	the angel of the Lord . . . came and *rolled* away the stone
Mk 9 20	3 the boy . . . fell to the ground and lay *writhing* there,
15 46	2 [Joseph] *rolled* a stone against the entrance to the tomb.
16 3	Who will *roll* away the stone for us from the entrance to the tomb? ⁴ But . . . the stone . . . had already been *rolled back*.
4	5
Lk 24 2	They found that the stone had been *rolled* away from the tomb.
2 P 2 22	4 When the sow has been washed, it *wallows* in the mud.

2: ROLL UP – FOLD UP: *HELISSŌ*
helissō 2

Heb 1 12	X	(Ps 102 26) [the heavens wear out like a garment;] you will ʳroll (or: *fold*) them *up* like a cloak,
Rv 6 14		the sky disappeared like a scroll *rolling up*

3: ROLL UP (A SCROLL): *PTYSSŌ*
ptyssō 1

Lk 4 20	X	[Jesus] then *rolled up* the scroll, gave it back to the assistant and sat down.

4: ROLL UP: *EN-TYLISSŌ*
en-tylissō 1/3

Jn 20 7	the cloth that had been over [Jesus's] head . . . was . . . *rolled up* in a place by itself.

RULE – AUTHORITY – LEADER

1. Rule, Manage – Leader, Official, Ringleader: *pro-(h)istēmi*	2: the Prince (of devils, of this world), the Ruler (of the air)
2. Reign, Rule – Be arbiter (in): *brabeuō*	3: (the angelic order of) Sovereignty, Principality
3. Rule, Lead – Ruler, Prince – Leader, Officer: *archōn*	4: Ruler, Leader, Magistrate – Leading (men), the Authorities – Jurisdiction, Rule
1: (Jesus the) Ruler, Leader, Chief – (Jesus) Rules, Leads – (Jesus the) Prince	5: Tetrarch
	6: Tribune, Commander, Captain

a) Lysias the Tribune
b) Tribune, Commander, General – Captain, Army officer
7: various specific functionaries
8: Centurion
a) *hekatont-archēs*
b) *kentyriōn*
4. **Authority – Power:** *ex-ousia*
a) Authority, Power – Exercise authority (over), Dominate, Make one's authority felt
b) (the angelic order of) Authority, Power
5. **Have authority (over):** *auth-enteō*
6. **Guide – Leader – Governor:** *hēgeomai*
1: Guide – Lead
2: Leader – Governor – Teacher
a) various

b) Governors Felix, Festus and Quirinius
7. **Proconsul, Governer:** *anth-ypatos*
8. **Officer at court, High official – Ruler, Sovereign, Prince:** *dynastēs*
9. **Magistrates – Officers – Captain:** *strat-ēgos*
a) Magistrates
b) Officers of the (Temple) police, Captain(s) of the (Temple) guard
10. **Captain – Leader:** *kybernēsis*
a) Captain of a ship – Pilot
b) Leader within the church
11. **Direct – Guide – Helmsman:** *euthynō*
12. **Rule – Control:** *kratōr*
13. **Faction leaders:** Theudas, Judas the Galilean

1. RULE, MANAGE – LEADER, OFFICIAL, RINGLEADER: *PRO-(H)ISTĒMI*

1 *pro-(h)istēmi* 6/8   2 *prōto-statēs* 1

Ac 24	5	2 [Paul] is a *ringleader* of the Nazarene sect.
Rm 12	8	Let . . . the *officials* be diligent,
1Th 5	12	be considerate to those who . . . *are above* you (or: *are leaders* of you)
1Tm 3	4	[The elder-in-charge] must be a man who *manages* his own family well . . . ⁵ how can any man who does not understand how to *manage* his own family have responsibility for the church . . . ?
	12	Deacons must . . . *manage* their children and families well.
5	17	The elders who *do their work* well *while they are in charge* (or: *rule* well) are to be given double consideration

2. REIGN, RULE – BE ARBITER (IN): *BRABEUŎ*

brabeuō 1

Col 3	15	may the peace of Christ *reign* (or: *rule*) in your hearts,

3. RULE, LEAD – RULER, PRINCE – LEADER, OFFICER: *ARCHŎN*

4	*archē*	12/56	14	*ep-archeia*	1
9	*archō*	2/86	15	*ep-archeios*	1
1	*archōn*	34/37	16	*ethn-archēs*	1
6	*arch-ēgos*	4	3	*hekatont-archēs*	15
11	*archi(-poimēn)*	1	5	*hekatont-archos*	5
12	*archi-tel-ōnēs*	1	10	*polit-archēs*	2
13	*(asi-)archēs*	1	8	*tetra-archeō*	3
2	*chili-archos*	22	7	*tetra-archēs*	4

1: (JESUS THE) RULER, LEADER, CHIEF – (JESUS) RULES, LEADS – (JESUS THE) PRINCE

Ac 3	15	6 you killed the *prince* of life.
5	31	6 God has now raised him up to be *leader* and saviour,
Rm 15	12	9 (Is 11 10 G) The root of Jesse will appear, rising up to *rule* the pagans,
Heb 2	10	6 the *leader who would take them* to their salvation.
12	2	6 Let us not lose sight of Jesus, who *leads* us in our faith
1P 5	4	11 When the *chief shepherd* appears, you will be given the crown of unfading glory.
Rv 1	5	Jesus Christ . . . the *Ruler* of the kings of the earth.

2: THE PRINCE (OF DEVILS, OF THIS WORLD), THE RULER (OF THE AIR)

Mt 9	34	It is through the *prince* of devils that [Jesus] casts out devils.
12	24	through Beelzebul, the *prince* of devils.
Mk 3	22	It is through the *prince* of devils that he casts devils out.
Lk 11	15	It is through Beelzebul, the *prince* of devils, that he casts out devils.
Jn 12	31	now the *prince* of this world is to be overthrown.
14	30	the *prince* of this world is on his way. He has no power over me,
16	11	the *prince* of this world being already condemned.
Ep 2	2	you were . . . obeying the *ruler* who governs the air,

3: (THE ANGELIC ORDER OF) SOVEREIGNTY, PRINCIPALITY

Rm 8	38	4 no angel, no ʳprince (or: *principality*), nothing that exists, nothing still to come, not any power,
1Co 15	24	4 having done away with every *sovereignty*, authority and power.
Ep 1	21	[God made Christ sit at his right hand,] far above every 4 *Sovereignty*, Authority, Power, or Domination,
3	10	4 the *Sovereignties* and Powers should learn . . . how comprehensive God's wisdom really is,
6	12	4 we have to struggle . . . against the *Sovereignties* and the Powers who originate the darkness in this world, the spiritual army of evil in the heavens.
Col 1	16	in [Christ] were created all things . . . Thrones, Dominations, 4 *Sovereignties*, Powers
2	10	4 [Christ] is the head of every *Sovereignty* and Power
15	4 [God] got rid of the *Sovereignties* and the Powers,

4: RULER, LEADER, MAGISTRATE – LEADING (MEN), THE AUTHORITIES – JURISDICTION, RULE

Mt 20	25	among the pagans the *rulers* lord it over them,
Mk 10	42	among the pagans ʳtheir so-called rulers (lit. those who are 9 supposed to *rule*) lord it over them,
Lk 12	11	4 When they take you before . . . *magistrates* and authorities,
58	when you go ʳto court (lit. before a *magistrate*) with your opponent, try to settle with him on the way,
14	1	on a sabbath day [Jesus] had gone for a meal to the house of one of the *leading* Pharisees
18	18	A *member* of one of the *leading families* put this question to [Jesus], '. . . what have I to do to inherit eternal life?'
20	20	4 to hand [Jesus] over to the *jurisdiction* and authority of the governor.
23	13	Pilate then summoned the chief priests and the *leading men* and the people.
35	the *leaders* . . . jeered at him. 'He saved others,' they said
24	20	our chief priests and our *leaders* handed [Jesus] over
Jn 3	1	Nicodemus, a *leading* Jew,
7	26	Can it be true the *authorities* have made up their minds that he is the Christ?
48	Have any of the *authorities* believed in him?
12	42	there were many who did believe in him, even among the *leading men*,
Ac 3	17	neither you nor your *leaders* had any idea what you were really doing;
4	5	the *rulers* [of the Jews], elders and scribes had a meeting
8	Then Peter . . . addressed them, '*Rulers* of the people, and elders!'
26	(Ps 2 2) *princes* making an alliance, against the Lord and against his Anointed.
7	27	who appointed you . . . to be our *leader* and judge?
35	Who appointed you to be our *leader* and judge? . . . [Moses] was now sent to be both *leader* and redeemer through the angel
13	27	What the people of Jerusalem and their *rulers* did . . . was in fact to fulfil the prophecies
14	5	with the connivance of the *authorities* a move was made by pagans as well as Jews to make attacks on [Paul and Barnabas]
16	19	[the masters of the slave-girl] dragged [Paul and Silas] ʳto the law courts (lit before the *magistrates*)
23	5	(Ex 22 27) You must not curse a *ruler* of your people.
Rm 8	38	4 no angel, no ʳprince (or: *principality*), nothing that exists, nothing still to come, not any power,
13	3	Good behaviour is not afraid of *magistrates*;
1Co 2	6	we have a wisdom to offer . . . not a philosophy . . . of the *masters* of our age . . . ⁷ The hidden wisdom of God . . .
8 Δ	⁸ . . . is a wisdom that none of the *masters* of this age have ever known,
Tt 3	1	4 it is their duty to be obedient to the *officials* and representatives of the government;
Jude	6	4 the angels who had *supreme authority* but did not keep it

5: TETRARCH

(Tetrarchies:)

Lysanias 1	Abilene*	1
	Ituraea*	1
	Trachonitis*	1

Mt 14	1	7 Herod the *tetrarch* heard about the reputation of Jesus,
Lk 3	1	8 Pontius Pilate was governor of Judaea, Herod *tetrarch* of 8 Galilee, his brother Philip *tetrarch* of the lands of Ituraea* 8 and Trachonitis*, Lysanias *tetrarch* of Abilene*,
19	7 Herod the *tetrarch* . . . ²⁰ added a further crime to all the rest by shutting John up in prison.
9	7	7 Herod the *tetrarch* had heard about all that was going on;

| Ac | 13 | 1 | | In the church at Antioch . . . [there was] Manaen, who had |
| | | 7 | | been brought up with Herod the *tetrarch*, |

6: TRIBUNE, COMMANDER, CAPTAIN

a) Lysias the Tribune

Claudius 1 (Ac 23 26)   Lysias 3

Ac	21	31	2	a report . . . reached the *tribune* of the cohort
		32	2	the crowd . . . stopped beating Paul when they saw the *tribune* and the soldiers.
		33	2	the *tribune* . . . had [Paul] bound with two chains
		37	2	Paul . . . asked the *tribune* if he could have a word with him.
	22	24	2	the *tribune* had [Paul] brought into the fortress
		26	2	the centurion went and told the *tribune*;
		27	2	the *tribune* came and asked [Paul], 'Tell me, are you a Roman citizen?'
		28	2	The *tribune* replied, 'It cost me a large sum to acquire this citizenship'.
		29	2	the *tribune* himself was alarmed
	23	10	2	the *tribune* . . . ordered his troops to go down
		15	2	it is up to . . . the Sanhedrin . . . to apply to the *tribune* to bring [Paul] down to you,
		17	2	Take this young man to the *tribune*;
		18	2	So the man took him to the *tribune*,
		19	2	the *tribune* took him by the hand
		22	2	The *tribune* let the young man go
		26		*Claudius Lysias* to his Excellency the governor Felix, greetings.
	24	7	2	(ᵛ the *tribune Lysias* intervened . . .)
		22	2	When *Lysias* the *tribune* has come down I will go into your case.

b) Tribune, Commander, General – Captain, Army officer

Mk	6	21	2	Herod . . . gave a banquet . . . for his *army officers*
Jn	18	12	2	The cohort and its *captain* and the Jewish guards seized Jesus
Ac	25	23	2	Agrippa and Bernice . . . entered the audience chamber attended by the *tribunes*
Rv	6	15	2	all the earthly rulers, the governors and the *commanders* . . . took to the mountains to hide in caves
	19	18	2	There will be the flesh of kings for you, and the flesh of *great generals*

7: VARIOUS SPECIFIC FUNCTIONARIES

Lk	19	2	12	Zacchaeus . . . one of the *senior tax collectors* and a wealthy man.
Ac	17	6	10	[the Jews] found Jason and some of the brothers, and these they dragged before the *city council*,
		8	10	This accusation alarmed the citizens and the *city councillors*
	19	31	13	some of the *Asiarchs*, who were friends of [Paul's],
	23	34	14	The governor [Felix] . . . asked [Paul] what *province* he came from.
	25	1	15	Three days after his arrival in ⌜the *province* (or: the *office of provincial ruler*), Festus went up to Jerusalem
2 Co	11	32	16	in Damascus, the *ethnarch* of King Aretas put guards round the city

8: CENTURION

a) hekatont-archēs

Cornelius

| Ac | 10 | 1 | 3 | One of the *centurions* of the Italica cohort . . . called Cornelius |
| | | 22 | 3 | The *centurion* Cornelius . . . was directed by a holy angel |

Julius 2

Ac	27	1	3	Paul and some other prisoners were handed over to a *centurion* called *Julius*, of the Augustan cohort
		3		*Julius* was considerate enough to allow Paul to go to his friends
		6	3	the *centurion* found an Alexandrian ship leaving for Italy
		11	3	But the *centurion* took more notice of the captain . . . than of what Paul was saying;
		31	3	Paul said to the *centurion* and his men,
		43	3	the *centurion* was determined to bring Paul safely through, and would not let them do what they intended

Others

| Mt | 8 | 5 | 5 | When [Jesus] went into Capernaum a *centurion* came up and pleaded with him |
| | | 8 | 5 | The *centurion* replied, 'Sir, I am not worthy to have you under my roof;' |

Mt	8	13	3	to the *centurion* Jesus said, 'Go back, then; you have believed, so let this be done for you'.
	27	54	5	the *centurion*, together with the others guarding Jesus, had seen the earthquake
Lk	7	2	5	A *centurion* [in Capernaum] had a servant . . . who was sick and near death.
		6	3	the *centurion* sent word to [Jesus] by some friends:
	23	47	3	the *centurion* . . . gave praise to God
Ac	21	32	3	[The tribune] immediately called out soldiers and *centurions*,
	22	25	5	Paul said to the *centurion* on duty,
		26	3	When he heard this the *centurion* went and told the tribune;
	23	17	3	[Paul] called one of the *centurions* and said,
		23	3	[the tribune] summoned two of the *centurions*
	24	23	3	[Felix] then gave orders to the *centurion* that Paul should be kept under arrest

b) kentyriōn

17 kentyriōn 3

Mk	15	39	17	The *centurion* . . . said, 'In truth this man was a son of God'.
		44	17	Pilate . . . summoned the *centurion* and enquired if [Jesus] was already dead. ⁴⁵ Having been assured of this by the
		45	17	*centurion*, he granted the corpse to Joseph

4. AUTHORITY – POWER: *EX-OUSIA*

| | 1 ex-ousia   93/103 | 3 kat-ex-ousiazō 2 |
| | 2 ex-ousiazō   4 | |

a) Authority, Power – Exercise authority (over), Dominate, Make one's authority felt

Mt	7	29	X	[Jesus] taught them with *authority*,
	8	9		For I am under *authority* myself,
	9	6	X	the Son of Man has *authority* on earth to forgive sins,
		8	X	the crowd . . . praised God for giving such *power* to men.
	10	1		[Jesus] gave [the Twelve] *authority* over unclean spirits
	20	25	3	among the pagans . . . their great men *make their authority felt*.
	21	23	X	What *authority* have you for acting like this? And who gave you this *authority*?
			X	
		24	X	I will then tell you my *authority* for acting like this.
		27	X	Nor will I tell you my *authority* for acting like this.
	28	18	X	All *authority* in heaven and on earth has been given to me.
Mk	1	22	X	[Jesus] taught them with *authority*.
		27	X	Here is a teaching that is new . . . and with *authority* behind it:
	2	10	X	the Son of Man has *authority* on earth to forgive sins,
	3	15		[Jesus appointed twelve] with *power* to cast out devils
	6	7		[Jesus] summoned the Twelve . . . giving them *authority* over the unclean spirits.
	10	42	3	among the pagans . . . their great men *make their authority felt*.
	11	28	X	What *authority* have you for acting like this? Or who gave you *authority* to do these things?
			X	
		29	X	answer me and I will tell you my *authority* for acting like this.
		33	X	Nor will I tell you my *authority* for acting like this.
	13	34		a man travelling abroad . . . left his servants in *charge*, each with his own task;
Lk	4	6	Ⓓ	[the devil] said to him, 'I will give you all this *power* . . .'
		32		his teaching made a deep impression on them because [Jesus] spoke with *authority*.
			X	
		36	X	He gives orders to unclean spirits with *authority* and power
	5	24	X	the Son of Man has *authority* on earth to forgive sins,
	7	8		For I am under *authority* myself,
	9	1		[Jesus] called the Twelve together and gave them power and *authority*
	10	19		I have given you *power* to tread underfoot serpents and scorpions and the whole strength of the enemy;
	12	5	Θ	fear him who . . . has the *power* to cast into hell.
		11		When they take you before . . . magistrates and *authorities*, do not worry
	19	17		my good servant . . . you shall have ⌜the government of (lit. *authority* over) ten cities.
	20	2	X	Tell us . . . what *authority* have you for acting like this? Or who is it that gave you this *authority*?
			⟨	
			X	
		8	X	Nor will I tell you my *authority* for acting like this.
		20		to hand [Jesus] over to the jurisdiction and *authority* of the governor.
	22	25	2	those who *have authority* over [pagans] are given the title Benefactor.
		53	Ⓓ	this is your hour; this is the ⌜reign (lit. *power*) of darkness.
	23	7		[Jesus] came under Herod's *jurisdiction*
Jn	1	12		to all who did accept him he gave *power* to become children of God,
	5	27	X	[the Father] has ⌜appointed him (lit. given him *authority* to be) supreme judge.

Jn	7	1	X ○	Jesus . . . ⌐could not (lit. had not the *power* to; G would not) stay in Judaea, because the Jews were out to kill him.
10	18	X X	as it is in my *power* to lay [my life] down, so it is in my *power* to take it up again;
17	2	X	through the *power* over all mankind that you have given him,
19	10		I have *power* to release you and I have *power* to crucify you
	11		You would have no *power* over me . . . if it had not been given you from above;
Ac	1	7	Θ	times . . . that the Father has decided by his own *authority*,
5	4		after you had sold [the land] wasn't the money ⌐yours to do with as you liked (lit. entirely in your *power*)?
8	19		Give me the same *power*
9	14		[Saul] holds ⌐a warrant (lit. *authority*) from the chief priests to arrest everybody who invokes your name.
26	10		[Paul,] acting on *authority* from the chief priests,
	12		I was going to Damascus, armed with full *powers* and a commission from the chief priests,
	18	⒟	so that [the pagans] may turn . . . from the *dominion* of Satan to God,
Rm	9	21		Surely a potter ⌐can do what he likes with (lit. has complete *power* over) the clay?
13	1		You must all obey the governing *authorities*. Since . . . the
		Θ	civil *authorities* were appointed by God.
	2		anyone who resists *authority* is rebelling against God's decision,
	3		If you want to live without being afraid of *authority*, you must live honestly
1 Co	6	12	2	I am not going to let anything *dominate* me.
7	4	2	The wife *has* no ⌐rights (lit. *authority*) over her body; it is
		2	the husband who has them . . . the husband *has* no ⌐rights (lit. *authority*) over his body; the wife has them
	37		if someone has firmly made his mind up . . . ⌐in complete freedom of choice (lit. by the *authority* solely of his own choosing),
11	10		That is the argument for women's covering their heads with a symbol of the *authority* over them,
2 Co	10	8		Maybe I do boast rather too much about our *authority*,
10	10		with the *authority* which the Lord gave me
Ep	2	2	⒟	the ruler who ⌐governs (lit. has *authority* over) the air,
Col	1	13	⒟	[the Father] has taken us out of the *power* of darkness
Tt	3	1		it is their duty to be obedient to the officials and ⌐representatives of the government (lit. the *authorities*);
Jude		25		To God, the only God . . . be the glory, majesty, authority
		Θ	and *power*,
Rv	2	26		To those who prove victorious . . . I will give the *authority* over the pagans ²⁷ which I myself have been given by my Father,
6	8		[The four riders] were given *authority* over a quarter of the earth,
9	3		locusts . . . were given a *power* like the *powers* that scorpions have on the earth:
	10		[the locusts] ⌐were able (or: had the *power*) to injure people for five months.
	19		All the horses' *power* was in their mouths
11	6		[The two witnesses] ⌐are able (or: have the *power*) to lock up the sky . . . they ⌐are able (or: have the *power*) to turn water into blood
12	10		Victory and power . . . have been won by our God, and all
		X	*authority* for his Christ.
13	2		the dragon had handed over to [the beast] his own power and
		⒟	his throne and his worldwide *authority*.
	4		They prostrated themselves in front of the dragon because he had given the beast his *authority*;
	5		For forty-two months the beast was allowed . . . to ⌐do whatever it wanted (lit. exercise its *authority*);
	7		[the beast was] given *power* over every race, people, language and nation;
	12		This second beast was servant to the first beast, and extended its *authority* everywhere,
14	18		the angel in *charge* of the fire left the altar
16	9	Θ	God who had the *power* to cause such plagues,
17	12		ten kings who . . . will have royal *authority* only for a single hour
	13		[The ten kings] are all of one mind in putting their strength and their *powers* at the beast's disposal,
18	1		another angel . . . with great *authority* given to him;
20	6		the second death ⌐cannot affect (lit. has no *power* over) them

b) (the angelic order of) Authority, Power

1 Co	15	24		[Christ] hands over the kingdom to God . . . having done away with every sovereignty, *authority* and power.
Ep	1	21		[God made Christ sit at his right hand,] far above every Sovereignty, *Authority*, Power, or Domination,
3	10		the Sovereignties and *Powers* should learn . . . how comprehensive God's wisdom really is,
6	12		we have to struggle . . . against the Sovereignties and the *Powers* who originate the darkness in this world, the spiritual army of evil in the heavens.

Col	1	16		in [Christ] were created all things . . . Thrones, Dominations, Sovereignties, Powers
2	10		[Christ] is the head of every Sovereignty and *Power*.
	15		[God] got rid of the Sovereignties and the *Powers*,
1 P | 3 | 22 | | now . . . [Christ] has made the angels and *Authorities* and Powers his subjects.

5. HAVE AUTHORITY (OVER): *AUTH-ENTEŌ*

auth-enteō 1

1 Tm | 2 | 12 | I am not giving permission for a woman . . . to ⌐tell a man what to do (lit. *have authority* over men).

6. GUIDE – LEADER – GOVERNOR: *HĒGEOMAI*

1	*hēgemōn*	11/20	5	*kath-ēgētēs*	2
8	*hēgemoneuō*	1/2	3	*hod-hēgeō*	5
7	*hēgemonia*	1	4	*hod-hēgos*	5
6	*hēgeomai*	2/22	9	*pro-(h)ēgeomai*	1
2	*hēgoumenos*	6			

1: GUIDE – LEAD

Mt	15	14	4	[The Pharisees] are blind men *leading* blind men; and if on
		3	blind man *leads* another, both will fall into a pit.
23	16	4	Alas for you, blind *guides*!
	24	4	You blind *guides*! Straining out gnats and swallowing camels!
Lk	6	39	3	Can one blind man *guide* another?
Jn	16	13	Ⓢ 3	the Spirit of truth . . . will *lead* you to the complete truth,
Ac	1	16	4	Judas . . . offered himself as a *guide* to the men who arrested Jesus
8	31		How can I [understand what I am reading] unless I have
		3	someone to *guide* me?
Rm	2	19	4	if you [who call yourself a Jew] are convinced you can *guide*
		3	the blind
12	10	9	⌐have a profound respect for each other (lit. try to *outdo* each other in respect)
Rv | 7 | 17 | X 3 | the Lamb . . . will *lead* them to springs of living water;

2: LEADER – GOVERNOR – TEACHER

a) various

Mt	2	6		(Mi 5 1) you, Bethlehem . . . are by no means least among
		X /2	the *leaders* of Judah, for out of you will come a *leader* who will shepherd my people Israel.
10	18	2	You will be dragged before *governors* and kings for my sake,
23	10	5	Nor must you allow yourselves to be called *teachers*, for you
		X 5	have only one *Teacher*, the Christ.
Mk	13	9	2	you will stand before *governors* and kings for my sake,
Lk	3	1	7	In the fifteenth year of Tiberius Caesar's *reign*,
21	12		men will . . . bring you before kings and *governors* because of my name
22	26	2	the *leader* [among you must behave] as if he were the one who serves.
Ac	7	10	2	Pharaoh . . . made [Joseph] *governor* of Egypt
14	12	6	Paul was the *principal* speaker
15	22	6	Judas [Barsabbas] and Silas, both *leading* men in the brotherhood,
Heb	13	7	2	Remember your *leaders*, who preached the word of God to you,
	17	2	Obey your *leaders* . . . because they . . . look after your souls;
	24	2	Greetings to all your *leaders* and to all the saints.
1 P | 2 | 14 | | [accept the authority of] the *governors* as commissioned by [the Lord] to punish criminals

b) Governors Felix, Festus and Quirinius

Governor Felix

Felix 9   Drusilla* 1

Ac	23	24	provide horses for Paul, and deliver him unharmed to *Felix* the *governor*.
	26	Claudius Lysias to his Excellency the *governor* Felix, greetings.
	33	the escort delivered the letter to the *governor*
24	1	[the high priest and some of the elders] laid information against Paul before the *governor*.
	2	Your Excellency, *Felix*, . . . the reforms this nation owes to your foresight [we accept]
	10	When the *governor* motioned him to speak, Paul answered:
	22	*Felix*, who knew more about the Way than most people, adjourned the case,
	24	*Felix* came with his wife Drusilla* who was a Jewess.

Ac 24 25   *Felix* took fright and said, 'You may go for the present'
      27   *Felix* was succeeded by Porcius Festus and, being anxious
            to gain favour with the Jews, *Felix* left Paul in custody.
   25 14   There is a man here . . . whom *Felix* left behind in custody,

Governor Festus

Ac 26 30   the king rose to his feet, with the *governor*

Governor Quirinius

Quirinius 1

Lk 2 2   8 This census . . . took place while *Quirinius was governor* of
            Syria,

7. PROCONSUL, GOVERNOR: *ANTH-YPATOS*

anth-ypatos 5   Gallio   3
                   Sergius Paulus 1

Ac 13 7   [In Cyprus the magician Elymas] was one of the attendants of
            the *proconsul Sergius Paulus*
       8   Elymas . . . tried . . . to prevent the *proconsul*'s conversion
            to the faith.
      12   The *proconsul* . . . became a believer, being astonished by
            what he had learnt about the Lord.
   18 12   while *Gallio* was *proconsul* of Achaia, the Jews made a con-
            certed attack on Paul
      14   *Gallio* said to the Jews, 'Listen, you Jews. If this were a
            misdemeanour . . . I would not hesitate to attend to you;
      17   *Gallio* refused to take any notice at all.
   19 38   there are the assizes and the *proconsuls*;

8. OFFICER AT COURT, HIGH OFFICIAL – RULER, SOVEREIGN, PRINCE: *DYNASTES*

dynastes 3

Lk 1 52   [The Almighty] has pulled down *princes* from their thrones
Ac 8 27 ○ he was a eunuch and an *officer at* the *court* of the kandake,
            or queen, of Ethiopia,
1 Tm 6 15 Θ] God, the blessed and only *Ruler* of all,

9. MAGISTRATES – OFFICERS – CAPTAIN: *STRAT-ĒGOS*

strat-ēgos 10

a) Magistrates

Ac 16 20   they charged [Paul and Silas] before the *magistrates* and said,
            'These people are causing a disturbance in our city.'
      22   the *magistrates* . . . ordered them to be flogged
      35   the *magistrates* sent the officers with the order: 'Release
            those men'.
      36   The *magistrates* have sent an order for your release;
      38   The officers reported this to the *magistrates*,

b) Officers of the (Temple) police, Captain(s) of the (Temple) guard

Lk 22 4   [Judas] went to the chief priests and the *officers of the* Temple
            guard
      52   Jesus spoke to the chief priests and *captains of the* Temple
            guard and elders
Ac 4 1   the priests came up to [Paul and John], accompanied by the
            captain of the Temple and the Sadducees.
    5 24   the *captain* of the Temple and the chief priests heard this
            news
      26   The *captain* went with his men and fetched [Peter and the
            apostles].

10. CAPTAIN – LEADER: *KYBERNĒSIS*

2 kybernēsis 1   1 kybernētēs 2

a) Captain of a ship – Pilot

Ac 27 11   the centurion took more notice of the *captain* . . . than of
            what Paul was saying;
Rv 18 17   All the *captains* and seafaring men,

b) Leader within the church

1 Co 12 28   2 helpers, good *leaders*, those with many languages.

11. DIRECT – GUIDE – HELMSMAN: *EUTHYNŌ*

2 euthynō 1/2   1 kat-euthynō 3

Lk 1 79 X   *guide* our feet into the way of peace.
1 Th 3 11   May God . . . and our Lord Jesus Christ ⌐make it easy for us
         Θ X   to come (lit. *direct* us) to you.
2 Th 3 5 X   May the Lord *turn* your hearts towards the love of God
Jm 3 4   2 no matter how big [ships] are . . . the *man at the helm* can
            steer them

12. RULE – CONTROL: *KRATŌR*

1 (kosmo-)kratōr 1   2 peri-kratēs 1

Ac 27 16   2 We . . . managed with some difficulty to *bring* the ship's
            boat *under control*.
Ep 6 12   we have to struggle . . . against the Sovereignties and the
            Powers who ⌐originate (lit. *rule* over) the darkness in this
            world,

13. FACTION LEADERS: THEUDAS, JUDAS THE GALILEAN

Judas 1   Thuedas 1

Ac 5 36   *Theudas* . . . collected about four hundred followers . . .
      37   [37] And then there was *Judas* the Galilean . . . who attracted
            crowds of supporters;

RUN – QUICKLY

1. **Run – a Course:** *trechō*
   1: Run (up, under the lee of), Hurry – Make a run, Charge, Set a course
   2: Run a Race (figuratively), upon one's Course, Career
2. **Stadium:** *stadion*

3. Hurry, Make haste, Lose no time – Promptly, Quickly: *speudō*
4. Quick(ly), Speedily, Fast – Soon, Shortly, In (good) time – At once, Straight away: *tachy*
5. Swift(ly): *oxys*

1. RUN – A COURSE: *TRECHŌ*

1	trechō	20	10	dromos	3
5	kata-trechō	1	11	(euthy-)dromeō	2
6	eis-trechō	1	12	pro-dromos	1
7	hypo-trechō	1	13	syn-dromē	1
8	peri-trechō	1			
4	pro-trechō	2			
2	pros-trechō	3			
3	syn-trechō	3			
9	epi-syn-trechō	1			

1: RUN (UP, UNDER THE LEE OF), HURRY – MAKE A RUN, CHARGE, SET A COURSE

Mt 27 48   one of [those who stood there] quickly *ran* to get a sponge
   28 8   the women . . . *ran* to tell the disciples.
Mk 5 6   Catching sight of Jesus from a distance, [the demoniac]
            ran up and fell at his feet
    6 33   3 from every town they all *hurried* to the place on foot
      55   8 [people] started *hurrying* all through the countryside
    9 15   2 the whole crowd . . . *ran* to greet [Jesus].
      25   9 when Jesus saw how many people were ⌐pressing round (lit.
            running up towards) him, he rebuked the unclean spirit.
   10 17   2 [Jesus] was setting out on a journey when a man *ran up*,
   15 36   Someone *ran* and soaked a sponge in vinegar
Lk 15 20 < [the lost son's] father saw him . . . He *ran* to the boy,
   19 4   4 [Zacchaeus] *ran* ahead and climbed a sycamore tree
   24 12   ᵛ Peter . . . went *running* to the tomb . . .⌐
Jn 20 2   [Mary of Magdala] came *running* to Simon Peter
       4   /4 They *ran* together, but the other disciple, *running ahead*
            faster than Peter, reached the tomb first;
Ac 3 11   3 Everyone came *running* towards [Peter and John] . . . to the
            Portico of Solomon,
    8 30   2 ['Go up and meet that chariot'.] Philip *ran up*,
   12 14   6 [Rhoda] *ran inside* with the news that Peter was standing at
            the main entrance.
   16 11   11 we *made* a straight *run* for Samothrace;
   21 1   11 we *set* a straight *course* and arrived at Cos;
      30   13 people came *running* from all sides;

Ac 21 32	5	[the tribune] *charged down* on the crowd,
27 16	7	We *ran under the lee* of a small island called Cauda
1 Co 9 24		All the *runners* in the *races* at the stadium are trying to win, but only one of them gets the prize. You must run in the same way, meaning to win.
Rv 9 9		the noise of [the] wings [of the locusts] sounded like a great *charge* of horses and chariots into battle.

2: RUN A RACE (FIGURATIVELY), UPON ONE'S COURSE, CAREER

Ac 13 25	10	Before John ended his *career* he said,
20 24	10	provided that when I finish my *race* I have carried out the mission the Lord Jesus gave me
Rm 9 16		the only thing that counts is not what human beings want or ʳtry to do (lit. how they *run*), but the mercy of God.
1 Co 9 24		All the *runners* at the stadium are trying to win, but only one of them gets the prize. You must run in the same way, meaning to win . . . ²⁶ That is how I *run*, intent on winning;
Ga 2 2		privately I laid before the leading men the Good News . . . for fear [the course] I was ʳadopting (lit. *running*) or had already ʳadopted (lit. *run*) would not be allowed.
5 7		You ʳbegan your race (lit. *were running*) well: who made you less anxious to obey the truth?
Ph 2 16		I had not *run in the race* and exhausted myself for nothing.
2 Th 3 1		pray that the Lord's message may ʳspread quickly (lit. *run* everywhere), and be received with honour
2 Tm 4 7	10	I have run the *race* to the finish; I have kept the faith;
Heb 6 20		[beyond the veil] where Jesus has entered ʳbefore us (lit. as a *forerunner*)
X 12		
12 1		[we should] *keep running* steadily in the race we have started.
1 P 4 4	3	people cannot understand why you no longer *hurry off with* them to join this flood which is rushing down to ruin.

2. STADIUM: *STADION*

stadion 1/7

1 Co 9 24		All the runners in the races at the *stadium* are trying to win, but only one of them gets the prize.

3. HURRY, MAKE HASTE, LOSE NO TIME – PROMPTLY, QUICKLY: *SPEUDŌ*

3 *speudō* 4/6	2 *spoudazō* 1/10
4 *spoudaios* 1/4	1 *spoudē* 2/12

Mk 6 25		The girl hurried ʳstraight (lit. *quickly*) back to the king and made her request,
Lk 1 39		Mary . . . went *as quickly as* she could to a town in the hill country of Judah.
2 16	3	[the shepherds] *hurried* away and found Mary and Joseph,
19 5	3	'Zacchaeus, come down. *Hurry*, because I must stay at your house today.' ⁶ And he *hurried* down
6	3	
Ac 22 18	3	'Hurry,' [the Lord] said 'leave Jerusalem at once;'
Ph 2 28	4	I shall send [Epaphroditus] back ʳ*as promptly as* (or: as eagerly as) I can;
Tt 3 12	2	ʳ*lose no time* in joining (or: do your best to join) me at Nicopolis,

4. QUICK(LY), SPEEDILY, FAST – SOON, SHORTLY, IN (GOOD) TIME – AT ONCE, STRAIGHT AWAY: *TACHY*

2 *tacheōs* 10	1 *tachy* 18
4 *tachinos* 2	5 *tachys* 1
3 *tachos* 7	

Mt 5 25		Come to terms with your opponent *in good time*
28 7		go *quickly* and tell his disciples,
8		the women came *quickly* away from the tomb and ran to tell the disciples.
Mk 9 39		no one who works a miracle in my name is likely *straight away* to speak evil of me.
Lk 14 21 <	2	Go *quickly* into the streets and alleys of the town and bring in here the poor,
15 22 <		*Quick!* Bring out the best robe
16 6 <	2	Here, take your bond; sit down *straight away* and write fifty.
18 8 Θ	3	[God] will see justice done to them, and done *speedily*.
Jn 11 29		Hearing this, Mary got up *quickly* and went to [Jesus].
31	2	When the Jews . . . saw [Mary] get up so *quickly* and go out, they followed her,

Jn 13 27		What you are going to do, do *quickly*.
20 4		the other disciple, running *faster* than Peter, reached the tomb first;
Ac 12 7	3	the angel of the Lord stood there . . . 'Get up!' he said ʳ'Hurry! (or: Quickly!)'
17 15		Paul's escort . . . went back with instructions for Silas and Timothy to rejoin Paul *as soon as* they could.
22 18	3	'Hurry,' [the Lord] said 'leave Jerusalem *at once*;'
25 4	3	Festus replied . . . that he would be going back [to Caesarea] *shortly* himself.
Rm 16 20 Θ	3	God . . . will *soon* crush Satan beneath your feet.
1 Co 4 19	2	I will be visiting you *soon*,
Ga 1 6	2	I am astonished at the *promptness* with which you have turned away from the one who called you
Ph 2 19	2	I hope . . . to send Timothy to you *soon*,
24	2	I continue to trust . . . that I shall be coming *soon* myself.
2 Th 2 2	2	please do not get excited *too soon* . . . by any prediction
1 Tm 3 14		At the moment of writing to you, I am hoping that I may be with you *soon*;
5 22	2	Do not be *too quick* to lay hands on any man,
2 Tm 4 9	2	Do your best to come and see me *as soon as* you can.
Heb 13 19		pray that I may come back to you all the *sooner*.
23		If [Timothy] arrives *in time*, he will be with me when I see you.
Jm 1 19	5	be *quick* to listen but slow to speak
2 P 1 14	4	the time for taking off this tent is coming *soon*,
2 1	4	your false teachers . . . will destroy themselves very *quickly*.
Rv 1 1		This is the revelation given by God . . . so that he could tell his servants about the things which are now to take place very *soon*;
3		
2 16 X		You must repent, or I shall *soon* come to you
3 11 X		*Soon* I shall be with you: hold firmly to what you already have,
11 14		the third [trouble] is to come *quickly* after [the second].
22 6		God . . . has sent his angel to reveal to his servants what is *soon* to take place.
3		
7 X		Very *soon* now, I shall be with you again.
12 X		Very *soon* now, I shall be with you again,
20		The one who guarantees these revelations repeats his promise: I shall indeed be with you *soon*.
X		

5. SWIFT(LY): *OXYS*

oxys 1/8

Rm 3 15	(Is 59 7) Their feet are *swift* when blood is to be shed,

---

RUSH – SPRING – LEAP

---

1. Rush, Charge (at) – Make a move to: *hormaō*	**1: Spring up, Jump up – Fly at, Hurl oneself at**
2. Rush – Jump, Spring up: *pēdaō*	**2: Spring up (of water) – Well up**
3. Spring: *hallomai*	**4. Leap (for joy) – Dance:** *skirtaō*

1. RUSH, CHARGE (AT) – MAKE A MOVE TO: *HORMAŌ*

1 *hormaō* 5	3 *hormēma* 1
2 *hormē* 2	

Mt 8 32		the whole herd *charged* down the cliff and into the lake
Mk 5 13		the herd . . . *charged* down the cliff and into the lake
Lk 8 33		the herd *charged* down the cliff into the lake
Ac 7 57		the members of the council . . . *rushed* at [Stephen]
14 5	2	a *move* was made by pagans as well as Jews to make attacks on [Paul and Barnabas]
19 29		the [Ephesian] mob *rushed* to the theatre
Jm 3 4	2	the man at the helm can steer [ships] ʳanywhere he likes (lit. to wherever he wishes to *make a move*) by controlling a tiny rudder.
Rv 18 21	3	That is how *forcefully* the great city of Babylon is going to be hurled down,

2. RUSH – JUMP, SPRING UP: *PĒDAŌ*

1 *ana-pēdaō* 1	3 *eis-pēdaō* 1
2 *ek-pēdaō* 1	

Mk 10 50	throwing off his cloak, [the blind man] *jumped up* and went to Jesus

Ac 14 14   2 Barnabas and Paul . . . *rushed* into the crowd,
   16 29   3 The gaoler . . . *rushed* in, threw himself trembling at the feet of Paul and Silas,

3. SPRING: *HALLOMAI*

1   *hallomai 3*   3 *ex-(h)allomai 1*
2 *eph-allomai 1*

1: SPRING UP, JUMP UP – FLY AT, HURL ONESELF AT

Ac 3 8   3 [the lame man] *jumped up*, stood, and . . . went with them into the Temple, walking and *jumping* and praising God.
   14 10   the cripple [of Lystra] *jumped up* and began to walk.

   19 16   2 the man with the evil spirit *hurled himself at* [the exorcists] and overpowered [them]

2: SPRING UP (OF WATER) – WELL UP

Jn 4 14   the water that I shall give will turn into a spring inside him, *welling up* to eternal life.

4. LEAP (FOR JOY) – DANCE: *SKIRTAŌ*

skirtaō 3

Lk 1 41   as soon as Elizabeth heard Mary's greeting, the child *leapt* in her womb
      44   the child in my womb *leapt* for joy.
    6 23   [when people hate you] Rejoice . . . and *dance* for joy,

S

SACRIFICE – ALTER

1. Sacrifice: *thysia*
   a) Sacrifice (according to the old testament)
   b) Sacrifice (of Christ, of Christians)
   c) (Pagan) Sacrifice – Offer (in) sacrifice

2. Sacrifices for sin – Holocausts – Libation
   1: Holocausts – Sacrifices for sin: *holo-kautōma* and *peri hamartias*
   2: Pour as a libation: *spendō*
3. Alter
   1: *bōmos*
   2: *thysiastērion*

1. SACRIFICE: *THYSIA*

2 *thuō* 7/14	3 *hiero-thytos* 1
1 *thysia* 28	

a) Sacrifice (according to the old testament)

Mt 9 13	(Ho 6 6) What I want is mercy, not *sacrifice*.
12 7	(Ho 6 6) What I want is mercy, not *sacrifice*,
Mk 12 33	To love [God] with all your heart . . . and to love your neighbour as yourself, this is far more important than any holocaust or *sacrifice*.
14 12	On the first day of Unleavened Bread, when the Passover lamb was *sacrificed*
2	
Lk 2 24	[they took the child Jesus up to Jerusalem] to offer in *sacrifice*, in accordance with . . . the Law of the Lord, a pair of turtledoves
13 1	the Galileans whose blood Pilate had mingled with that of their *sacrifices*.
22 7	The day of Unleavened Bread came round, . . . on which the passover had to be *sacrificed*,
2	
Ac 7 42	(Am 5 25) Did you bring me victims and *sacrifices* in the wilderness . . , you House of Israel?
1 Co 10 18	Look at the other Israel, the race, where those who eat the *sacrifices* are in communion with the altar.
Heb 5 1	Every high priest . . . is appointed to . . . offer gifts and *sacrifices* for sins;
7 27	[To suit us, the ideal high priest would have to be] one who would not need to offer *sacrifices* every day, as the other high priests do for their own sins and then for those of the people,
8 3	It is the duty of every high priest to offer gifts and *sacrifices*,
9 9	None of the gifts and *sacrifices* offered under these regulations can possibly bring any worshipper to perfection in his inner self;
10 1	the Law . . . is quite incapable of bringing the worshippers to perfection, with the same *sacrifices* repeatedly offered
5	(Ps 40 6) You who wanted no *sacrifice* or oblation,
8	(Ps 40 6) You did not want . . . the *sacrifices*, the oblations, the holocausts and the sacrifices for sin,
11	All the priests stand at their duties every day, offering over and over again the same *sacrifices* which are quite incapable of taking sins away.
26	If . . . we should deliberately commit any sins, then there is no longer any *sacrifice* for them.
11 4	It was because of his faith that Abel offered God a better *sacrifice* than Cain,

b) Sacrifice (of Christ, of Christians)

Rm 12 1	worship [God] . . . in a way that is worthy of thinking beings, by offering your living bodies as a *sacrifice*,
1 Co 5 7 X	2 Christ, our passover, has been *sacrificed*;
Ep 5 2	Christ . . . [gave] himself up in our place as a fragrant offering and a *sacrifice* to God.
X	
Ph 2 17	if my blood has to be shed as part of your own *sacrifice* . . . I shall still be happy
4 18	the offering that you sent, a sweet fragrance – the *sacrifice* that God accepts
Heb 9 23	the heavenly things themselves have to be purified by a higher sort of *sacrifice* than this.
Δ	
26	[Christ] has made his appearance once and for all, . . . to do away with sin by *sacrificing* himself.
X	
10 12 X	[Christ] has offered one single *sacrifice* for sins,

Heb 13 15	Through [Christ], let us offer God an unending *sacrifice* of praise, . . . every time we acknowledge his name. [16] Keep doing good works and sharing your resources, for these are *sacrifices* that please God.
16	
1 P 2 5	you too, the holy priesthood that offers the spiritual *sacrifices* which Jesus Christ has made acceptable to God,

c) (Pagan) Sacrifices – Offer (in) sacrifice

Ac 7 41	(Ex 32 6) [the Israelites] made a bull calf and offered *sacrifice* to the idol.
14 13	The priests of Zeus-outside-the-Gate, proposing that all the people should *offer sacrifices* with them, brought garlanded oxen to the gates.
2	
18	Even this speech, however, was scarcely enough to stop the crowd *offering* [Paul and Barnabas] *sacrifice*.
2	
1 Co 10 20	2/2 the *sacrifices* that they *offer* they *sacrifice* to demons who are not God.
28	3 if someone says to you, 'This food was *offered in sacrifice*', then . . . you should not eat it,

2. SACRIFICES FOR SIN – HOLOCAUSTS – LIBATION

1: HOLOCAUSTS – SACRIFICES FOR SIN: *HOLO-KAUTŌMA* and *PERI HAMARTIAS*

1 *holo-kautōma* 3	2 *peri hamartias* 2
	3 *peri hamartiōn* 1

Mk 12 33	To love [God] . . . and to love your neighbour . . . is far more important than any *holocaust* or sacrifice.
Heb 5 3	3 [every high priest] has to ʳmake sin offerings (lit. *offer sacrifices for sin*) for himself as well as for the people.
10 6	/2 (Ps 40 6) You took no pleasure in *holocausts* or *sacrifices for sin*;
8	(Ps 40 6) You did not want . . . the *holocausts* and the *sacrifices for sin*,
2	

2: POUR AS A LIBATION: *SPENDŌ*

spendō 2

Ph 2 17	if my blood has to be ʳshed as part of (lit. *poured as a libation* upon) your own sacrifice . . . I shall still be happy
2 Tm 4 6	my life is already being *poured* [away] *as a libation*,

3. ALTER

1: ALTAR: *BŌMOS*

bōmos 1

Ac 17 23	[Men of Athens,] I noticed . . . that you had an *altar* inscribed: To An Unknown God.

2: ALTAR: *THYSIASTĒRION*

thysiastērion 23

Mt 5 23	if you are bringing your offering to the *altar* . . , [24] leave your offering there before the *altar*, go and be reconciled with your brother first,
24	
23 18	[You say,] 'If a man swears by the *altar* it has no force; but if a man swears by the offering [that is on the altar], he is bound'. [19] You blind men! For which is of greater worth, the offering or the *altar* that makes the offering sacred? [20] Therefore when a man swears by the *altar* he is swearing by that and everything on it.
19	
20	
35	Zechariah . . . whom you murdered between the sanctuary and the *altar*.
Lk 1 11	there appeared to [Zechariah] the angel of the Lord, standing on the right of the *altar* of incense.
11 51	Zechariah, who was murdered between the *altar* and the sanctuary.
Rm 11 3	(1 K 19 10) Lord, they have killed your prophets and broken down your *altars*.

1 Co	9 13	those serving at the *altar* can claim their share from the *altar* itself.
	10 18	those who eat the sacrifices are in communion with the *altar*.
Heb	7 13	our Lord . . . belonged to a different tribe, the members of which have never done service at the *altar*;
	13 10	We have our own *altar* from which those who serve the tabernacle have no right to eat.
Jm	2 21	Abraham . . . offered his son Isaac on the *altar*?
Rv	6 9	I saw underneath the *altar* the souls of all the people who had been killed on account of the word of God,
	8 3	Another angel, who had a golden censer, came and stood at the *altar*. A large quantity of incense was given to him to offer with the prayers of all the saints on the golden *altar*.
	5	the angel took the censer and filled it with the fire from the *altar*,
	9 13	I heard a voice come out of the four horns of the golden *altar*
	11 1	Go and measure God's sanctuary, and the *altar*,
	14 18	the angel in charge of the fire left the *altar*
	16 7	I heard the *altar* itself say, 'Truly, Lord God Almighty, the punishments you give are . . . just'.

SAMARIA

Samaria 11   Sychar 1 (Jn 4)   1 polis 9/164
Samaritan 11

Mt	10 5	1	Do not turn your steps to pagan territory, and do not enter any *Samaritan* town;
Lk	9 25		These [messengers] . . . went into a *Samaritan* village to make preparations for [Jesus], [53] but the people would not receive him because he was making for Jerusalem.
	10 33		a *Samaritan* traveller who came upon him was moved with compassion
	17 11		[Jesus] travelled along the border between *Samaria* and Galilee.
	16		[one of the lepers] threw himself at the feet of Jesus and thanked him. The man was a *Samaritan*.
Jn	4 4		This meant that [Jesus] had to cross *Samaria*. [5] On the way
	5	1	he came to the *Saamritan* town called *Sychar*, . . . [6] Jacob's well is there
	7		a *Samaritan* woman came to draw water, . . . [8] [Jesus's]
	8	1	disciples had gone into the *town* to buy food. [9] The *Samaritan* [woman] said to him, 'What? You are a Jew and you ask me, a *Samaritan*, for a drink?' – Jews, in fact, do not associate with *Samaritans*.
	9		
	28	1	The woman . . . hurried back to the *town* to tell the people, [29] 'Come and see'
	30	1	This brought people out of the *town* and they started walking towards [Jesus].
	39	1	Many *Samaritans* of that *town* had believed in him on the strength of the woman's testimony
	40		the *Samaritans* . . . begged him to stay with them. He stayed for two days,
	8 48		Are we not right in saying that you are a *Samaritan* and possessed by a devil?
Ac	1 8		you will be my witnesses not only in Jerusalem but throughout Judaea and *Samaria*,
	8 1		a bitter persecution started against the church in Jerusalem, and everyone except the apostles fled to the country districts of Judaea and *Samaria*. . . . [5] One of them was Philip who
	5		
	8	1	went to a *Samaritan* town and proclaimed the Christ to them. . . . [8] As a result there was great rejoicing in that *town*. [9] Now a man called Simon had already practised magic arts in the *town* and astounded the *Samaritan* people.
	9	1	
	14		When the apostles in Jerusalem heard that *Samaria* had accepted the word of God, they sent Peter and John to them,
	25		they went back to Jerusalem, preaching the Good News to a number of *Samaritan* villages.
	9 31		The churches throughout Judaea, Galilee and *Samaria* were now left in peace,
	15 3		as [Barnabas and Saul] passed through Phoenicia and *Samaria* they told how the pagans had been converted,

SAME – LIKE – SUCH

1. the Same – Equal: *autos*
  1: the Same (God, Lord, Christ, Spirit)

2: the Same, Equally
2. the Same, Equal, Like – Balance, Equality: *isos*

3. Equally, Likewise: *para-plēsiōs*
4. In the same way, Likewise, This is how – As, So, Too – Like, the Same (as): *hōs, kata, houtōs*
5. (Be) Like, Similar(ly), the Same – Compare – In the same way, Likewise: *homoioō*

1: (Be) like, Similar – Compare, (Be) Compared (to) – Imitation, Disguise
2: the Same – Similarly, In the same way, Likewise – Too, Also
6. Compare, Comparison – Class, Rank (with): *syn-krinō*
7. Such, Such as – Like this, So – This, These: *hoios*

1. THE SAME – EQUAL: *AUTOS*

(ho) autos (55)

1: THE SAME (GOD, LORD, CHRIST, SPIRIT)

Rm	10 12	X	[scripture] makes no distinction between Jew and Greek: all belong to *the same* Lord
1 Co	12 4	X	There is a variety of gifts but always *the same* Spirit; [5] there are all sorts of service to be done, but always to *the same* Lord; [6] working in all sorts of different ways in different people, it is *the same* God who is working in all of them.
	5	X	
	6	Θ	
	8		One . . . may have the gift of preaching instruction given him by *the same* Spirit; [9] and another the gift of faith given by *the same* Spirit;
	9		
	11		All these are the work of one and *the same* Spirit,
Heb	1 12	X	(Ps 102 27) [the heavens] will be changed. But yourself, you ⌐never change (lit. are *the same*)
	13 8	X	Jesus Christ is *the same* today as he was yesterday and as he will be for ever.

2: THE SAME, EQUALLY

Mt	26 44	[Jesus] prayed for the third time, repeating *the same* words.
	27 44	Even the robbers . . . taunted him [in] *the same* [way].
Mk	14 39	Again [Jesus] went away and prayed, saying *the same* words.
Lk	2 8	In ⌐the countryside close by (lit. *the same* region) there were shepherds who lived in the fields
	23 40	You got *the same* sentence as he did, but . . . we deserved it:
Ac	14 1	At Iconium ⌐similarly [Barnabas and Paul] went (or: they went together) to the Jewish synagogue,
	15 27	Judas and Silas . . . will confirm by word of mouth ⌐what (lit. *the same*) we have written
Rm	2 1	you ⌐behave no differently from (lit. are behaving [in] *the same* [way] as) those you judge.
	9 21	It is surely for [the potter] to decide whether he will use ⌐a particular (lit. *the same*) lump of clay to make a special pot or an ordinary one?
	12 4	each [body] has several parts and ⌐each part has a separate (lit. not *the same*) function,
1 Co	1 10	⌐make up the differences between you (lit. say *the same* things), and instead of disagreeing among yourselves . . . be united again in *the same* belief and *the same* practice.
	10 3	all ate *the same* spiritual food [4] and all drank *the same* spiritual drink,
	4	
	11 5	it is a sign of disrespect to her head if [a woman] *prays* . . . unveiled; ⌐she might as well have (lit. it is *the same* as her having) her hair shaved off.
	12 25	[God arranged the body so that] each part may be *equally* concerned for all the others.
	15 39	Everything that is flesh is not *the same* flesh;
2 Co	1 6	this should be a consolation to you, supporting you in patiently bearing *the same* sufferings as we bear.
	3 14	indeed, to this very day, *that same* veil is still there when the old covenant is being read,
	18	we . . . all grow brighter as we are turned into *the same* image that we reflect;
	4 13	we have *the same* spirit of faith
	6 13	I speak as if to children of mine: as ⌐a fair (lit. an *equal*) exchange, open your minds as well.
	8 16	I thank God for putting into Titus' heart *the same* concern for you
	12 18	[Titus] and I have always been guided by *the same* spirit and trodden *the same* tracks.
Ph	1 30	You and I are together in *the same* fight as you saw me fighting before
	2 2	⌐be united in your (lit. have *the same*) convictions and ⌐united in your (lit. *the same*) love, with a common purpose and ⌐a common (lit. *the same*) mind.
	18	you must be *just as* happy and rejoice with me.
	3 1	It is no trouble to me ⌐to repeat (lit. write *the same* as) what I have already written to you,
	16	let us go forward on *the same* road that has brought us where we are

<table>
<tr><td>1 Th 2 14</td><td>[you have suffered] *the same* treatment from your own country-men as [the churches in Judaea] have suffered from the Jews.</td></tr>
</table>

1 Th 2 14 [you have suffered] *the same* treatment from your own country-men as [the churches in Judaea] have suffered from the Jews.

Heb 2 14 Since all the children share [the same] blood and flesh, [Christ] too shared equally in *the same* things,

4 11 some of you might ⌐copy this (lit. fall following *the same*) example of disobedience

6 11 every one of you should go on showing *the same* earnestness

10 1 [the Law] is quite incapable of bringing the worshippers to perfection, with *the same* sacrifices repeatedly offered year after year.

11 priests stand at their duties . . . offering over and over again *the same* sacrifices

11 9 Isaac and Jacob . . . were heirs with [Abraham] of *the same* promise.

Jm 3 10 the blessing and the curse come out of *the same* mouth . . .

11 ¹¹ Does any water supply give a flow of fresh water and salt water out of *the same* pipe?

1 P 4 1 arm yourselves with *the same* resolution that [Christ] had:

4 people cannot understand why you no longer hurry off with them to join *this same* flood which is rushing down to ruin,

5 9 your brothers all over the world are suffering *the same* [things].

2 P 3 7 by *the same* word, the present sky and earth are destined for fire

2. THE SAME, EQUAL, LIKE – BALANCE, EQUALITY; *ISOS*

1 isos 8	3 is(-angelos) 1	
2 isotēs 3	4 iso(-psychos) 1	
	5 iso(-timos) 1	

Mt 20 12 you have treated [the men who came last] *the same* as us,

Mk 14 56 their evidence was ⌐conflicting (lit. not *the same*).

59 their evidence was ⌐conflicting (lit. not *the same*).

Lk 6 34 Even sinners lend to sinners to get back *the same* [amount].

20 36 3 [the dead] are ⌐*the same* as (or: *equal* to) the angels, and . . . sons of God.

Jn 5 18 X [Jesus] spoke of God as his own Father, and so made himself God's *equal*.

Ac 11 17 God was giving [the pagans] the *identical* thing he gave to us

2 Co 8 13 This does not mean that to give relief to others you ought to make things difficult for yourselves: it is a question of

14 2 balancing ¹⁴ what happens to be your surplus now against

2 their present need . . . That is how we strike a *balance*:

Ph 2 6 X [Christ] did not cling to his *equality* with God

20 4 I have nobody else *like* [Timothy] here,

Col 4 1 Masters, make sure that your slaves are given what is just

2 and *fair*,

2 P 1 1 5 From Simeon Peter . . . to all who treasure ⌐*the same* faith as ourselves (or: the faith *the same* as we [do]),

Rv 21 16 [the new Jerusalem] was twelve thousand furlongs in length and in breadth, and *equal* in height.

3. EQUALLY, LIKEWISE: *PARA-PLĒSIŌS*

para-plēsiōs 1

Heb 2 14 Since all the children share [the same] blood and flesh, [Christ] too shared *equally* in it,

4. IN THE SAME WAY, LIKEWISE, THIS IS HOW – AS, SO, TOO – LIKE, THE SAME (AS): *HŌS, KATA, HOUTŌS*

1 hōs (69)	8 kata ta auta 3	10 houtōs (56)
3 hōs-autōs 17	7 kath-aper (3)	
4 hōsei (2)	6 kath-ōs (22)	
2 hōsper (17)	9 kath-ōsper 1	
5 hōsperei 1		

Mt 5 12 10 [Rejoice when people persecute you;] *this is how* they persecuted the prophets before you.

16 10 [A lamp on the lamp-stand shines for everyone.] *In the same way* your light must shine in the sight of men,

6 10 your will be done, on earth *as* in heaven.

12 forgive us our debts, *as* we have forgiven those who are in debt to us.

7 17 10 *In the same way*, a sound tree produces good fruit

29 [Jesus] taught them with authority, and not *like* their own scribes.

10 25 It is enough for the disciple that he should grow to be *like* his teacher, and the slave *like* his master.

12 40 2 *as* Jonah was in the belly of the sea-monster for three days

10 and three nights, *so* will the Son of Man be in the heart of the earth

Mt 12 45 10 the man ends up by being worse . . . *That is what* will happen to this evil generation.

13 40 2/10 *just as* the darnel is gathered up . ., *so* it will be at the end of time.

17 12 they . . . treated [Elijah] as they pleased; and the Son of Man

10 will suffer *similarly* at their hands.

18 3 unless you . . . become *like* little children you will never enter the kingdom of heaven.

35 10 [The master handed him over to the torturers] and *that is how* my heavenly Father will deal with you

19 19 (Lv 19 18) You must love your neighbour *as* yourself.

20 5 again at about the ninth hour, [the landowner] went out and

3 did *the same*.

26 10 [Among the pagans the rulers lord it over them.] *This* is not to happen among you.

28 2 *just as* the Son of Man came not to be served but to serve,

21 30 3 The man then . . . said *the same* [thing] to the second [son]

36 he sent some more servants . . . and they dealt with them

3 *in the same way*.

22 30 at the resurrection men and women . . . are *like* the angels in heaven.

39 (Lv 19 18) You must love your neighbour *as* yourself.

23 28 [You are like whitewashed tombs.] *In the same way* you appear to people from the outside like good honest men,

24 33 10 [When leaves have come out, you know that summer is near.] *So* with you . . .: know that [the Son of Man] is near,

37 2/10 *As* it was in Noah's day, *so* will it be when the Son of Man comes.

39 10 they suspected nothing till the Flood came . . . It will be *like* this when the Son of Man comes.

25 14 2 [The kingdom of heaven] is *like* a man on his way abroad

17 The man who had received two [talents] made two more

3 *in the same way*.

32 2 [the Son of Man] will separate men . . . *as* the shepherd separates sheep from goats.

Mk 1 22 un*like* the scribes, [Jesus] taught them with authority.

4 26 10/ *This is what* the kingdom of God is *like*. A man throws seed on the land.

31 [The kingdom of God] is *like* a mustard seed

10 15 anyone who does not welcome the kingdom of God *like* a little child will never enter it.

43 10 [Among the pagans their rulers lord it over them.] *This* is not to happen among you,

12 21 The second [brother] married the widow . . .; with the third

3 it was *the same*,

25 when they rise from the dead, men and women . . . are *like* the angels in heaven.

31 (Lv 19 18) You must love your neighbour *as* yourself.

33 (Lv 19 18) to love your neighbour *as* yourself . . . is far more important

13 29 [When leaves come out, you know that summer is near.]

10 *So* with you . . .: know that [the Son of Man] is near,

34 [You never know when the time will come.] It is *like* a man travelling abroad:

14 31 [Peter said, 'I will never disown you'.] And they all said

3 *the same*.

Lk 6 23 8 *This was the way* their ancestors treated the prophets.

26 8 *This was the way* their ancestors treated the false prophets.

36 6 Be compassionate *as* your Father is compassionate.

40 the fully trained disciple will always be *like* his teacher.

10 27 (Lv 19 18) You must love . . . your neighbour *as* yourself.

11 30 6/10 *just as* Jonah became a sign . . . *so* will the Son of Man

13 5 [The tower at Siloam fell and killed eighteen people;] you will

3 all perish ⌐*as* they did (lit. *in the same way*).

15 7 10 [Rejoice with me, I have found my sheep.] *In the same way*, I tell you, there will be . . . rejoicing in heaven over one repentant sinner

10 10 [I have found the drachma I lost.] *In the same way* . . . there is rejoicing among the angels . . . over one repentant sinner.

17 24 2 *as* the lightning flashing from one part of heaven lights up the

10 other, *so* will the Son of Man be when his day comes.

26 6/10 *As* it was in Noah's day, *so* will it also be in the days of the Son of Man.

30 8 It will be *the same* when the day comes for the Son of Man to be revealed.

20 31 3 And *the same* with all seven [brothers], they died

21 31 [As soon as fig trees bud, you know that summer is near.]

10 *So* with you . . .: know that the kingdom of God is near.

22 20 3 [Jesus took some bread and gave thanks.] He did *the same* with the cup after supper,

26 10 [Among pagans the kings lord it over them.] *This* must not happen with you . . . the greatest among you must behave *as* [if he were] the youngest, the leader *as* [if he were] the one who serves.

44 4 his sweat fell to the ground *like* greats drops of blood.

Jn 3 8 10 The wind blows wherever it pleases . . . *That is how* it is with all who are born of the Spirit.

5 21 2/10 *as* the Father raises the dead and gives them life, *so* the Son gives life to anyone he chooses;

Jn 7 46 10 There has never been anybody who has spoken *like* him.
10 15 6 [I know my own and my own know me,] *just as* the Father knows me and I know the Father;
13 34 6 *just as* I have loved you, you also must love one another.
15 4 6/10 *As* a branch cannot bear fruit all by itself . . . *neither* can you unless you remain in me.
9 6 *As* the Father has loved me, so I have loved you.
12 6 love one another, *as* I have loved you.
17 18 6 *As* you sent me into the world, I have sent them into the world,
20 21 6 *As* the Father sent me, so am I sending you.
Ac 3 22 (Dt 18 15) God will raise up a prophet *like* myself for you,
7 37 (Dt 18 15) God will raise up a prophet *like* myself for you
8 32 (Is 53 7) *Like* a sheep that is led to the slaughter-house, *like*
10 a lamb that is dumb in front of its shearers, *like* these he never opens his mouth.
Rm 5 12 10 *thus* death has spread through the whole human race because everyone has sinned.
18 /10 *as* one man's fall brought condemnation on everyone, *so* the good act of one man . . . makes them justified.
19 2/10 *As* by one man's disobedience many were made sinners, *so* by one man's obedience many will be made righteous.
21 2/10 *just as* sin reigned wherever there was death, *so* grace will reign
6 4 2 we . . . joined him in death, so that *as* Christ was raised
10 from the dead . . . we *too* might live a new life.
11 10 [Christ died to sin,] you *too* must consider yourselves to be dead to sin
19 2/10 *as* once you put your bodies at the service of vice . . . *so* now you must put them at the service of righteousness.
8 26 3 The Spirit, too, *likewise* comes to help us in our weakness.
36 we are . . . reckoned *as* sheep for the slaughter.
11 30 2 *Just as* you changed from being disobedient to God . . .
31 10 ³¹ *so* those who are disobedient now
12 4 7/10 *Just as* each of our bodies has several parts . . . ⁵ *so* all of
5 us, in union with Christ, form one body,
13 9 (Lv 19 18) You must love your neighbour *as* yourself.
1 Co 2 11 the depth of a man can only be known by his own spirit . . .
10 and *in the same way* the depths of God can only be known by the Spirit of God.
7 7 I should like everyone to be *like* me,
10 33 6 *just as* I try to be helpful to everyone at all times,
11 1 6 Take me for your model, *as* I take Christ.
25 3 *In the same way* [Jesus] took the cup after supper,
12 12 7 *Just as* a human body, though it is made up of many parts, is
10 a single unit . . . *so* it is with Christ.
13 11 When I was a child, I used to talk *like* a child, and think *like* a child, and argue *like* a child,
14 9 [if no one can be sure which call the trumpet has sounded,
10 who will be ready for the attack?] It is *the same* with you: if your tongue does not produce intelligible speech,
15 8 5 [Christ] appeared to me too; it was *as though* I was born when no one expected it.
22 2/10 *Just as* all men die in Adam, *so* all men will be brought to life in Christ.
42 10 It is *the same* with the resurrection of the dead:
2 Co 1 5 6/10 Indeed, *as* the sufferings of Christ overflow to us, *so*, through Christ, does our consolation overflow
2 17 we do not go round offering the word of God for sale, *as* many other people do.
3 13 7 not *like* Moses, who put a veil over his face
11 3 the serpent . . . seduced Eve, and I am afraid that *in the same way* your ideas may get corrupted
Ga 2 7 6 I had been commissioned to preach the Good News to the uncircumcised *just as* Peter . . . to the circumcised.
4 14 you welcomed me *as* an angel of God, *as* [if I were] Christ Jesus himself.
29 2 *as* at that time the child born in the ordinary way persecuted
10 the child born in the Spirit's way, *so also* now
Ep 4 32 6 Be . . . kind, forgiving each other *as* [readily as] God forgave you in Christ.
5 2 6 follow Christ by loving *as* he loved you,
8 be *like* children of light,
22 Wives should regard their husbands *as* they regard the Lord,
23 ²³ since *as* Christ is head of the Church . . . so is a husband the head of his wife; ²⁴ and *as* the Church submits to
24 Christ, *so* should wives to their husbands . . . ²⁵ Husbands
25 10 should love their wives *just as* Christ loved the Church
6
28 10/ *In the same way*, husbands must love their wives *as* they love their own bodies;
29 A man . . . looks after [his own body]; and *that is the way* Christ treats the Church,
6 5 Slaves, be obedient to . . . your masters . . . *as* you are obedient to Christ:
Ph 2 8 being *as* all men [are, Christ] was humbler yet,
3 17 6 study them *as* you used to study us.
Col 3 13 10 The Lord has forgiven you; now you must do *the same*.
23 put your heart into [your work] *as* [if it were] for the Lord and not for men,
1 Th 2 7 *Like* a mother feeding and looking after her own children,
8 10 ⁸ we felt *so* . . . towards you,

1 Th 2 11 we treated every one of you *as* a father treats his children,
4 14 10 Jesus died and rose again, and . . . it will be *the same* for those who have died in Jesus: God will bring them with him.
5 2 the Day of the Lord is going to come *like* a thief in the night.
3 2 the worst suddenly happens, *as* [suddenly as] labour pains come on a pregnant woman . . . ⁴ But it is not as if you
4 live in the dark . . . for that Day to overtake you *like* a thief.
1 Tm 2 9 3 *Similarly* . . . women are to wear suitable clothes
3 8 3 *In the same way*, deacons must be respectable men
11 3 *In the same way*, the women must be respectable,
5 1 Do not speak harshly to a man older than yourself, but advise him *as* [you would] your own father; treat the younger
2 men *as* brothers ² and older women *as* [you would] your mother. Always treat young women . . . *as* [if they were] sisters.
25 3 *In the same way*, the good that people do can be obvious;
2 Tm 2 3 Put up with your share of difficulties, *like* a good soldier of Christ Jesus.
Tt 2 3 3 *Similarly*, the older women should behave as though they were religious,
6 3 *In the same way*, . . . persuade the younger men to be moderate
Heb 1 11 /4 all wear out *like* a garment; ¹² you will roll them up *like* a cloak, and *like* a garment they will be changed.
12
3 2 [Christ] was faithful to the one who appointed him, just *like* Moses, who stayed faithful in all his house;
4 10 2 to reach the place of rest is to rest after your work, *as* God did after his.
5 4 9 each one is called [to be a high priest] by God, *as* Aaron [was].
9 28 10 *so* Christ, too, offers himself only once to take the faults of many on himself,
12 5 Have you forgotten that . . . text in which you are addressed *as* sons?
7 God is treating you *as* his sons.
Jm 2 8 (Lv 19 18) you must love your neighbour *as* yourself;
17 10 Faith is *like that*: if good works do not go with it, it is quite dead.
26 10 *in the same way* faith is dead if it is separated from good deeds
3 5 10 [Men can steer ships by controlling a tiny rudder.] *So* is the tongue only a tiny part of the body,
1 P 2 2 *like* babies you should be hungry for nothing but milk
3 5 10 *That was how* the holy women of the past dressed themselves
5 8 your enemy the devil is prowling round *like* a roaring lion,
2 P 3 10 The Day of the Lord will come *like* a thief.
1 Jn 1 7 if we live our lives in the light, *as* he is in the light, we are in union with one another,
2 6 we are in God only when the one who claims to be living in
10/6 him is living (G *the same*) [kind of life] *as* Christ lived.
3 3 6 everyone who entertains this hope must . . . try to be *as* [pure as] Christ.
7 6 to live a holy life is to be holy *just as* [God] is holy;
4 17 6 even in this world we have become *as* [God] is.
Rv 2 18 the Son of God . . . has eyes *like* a burning flame
3 3 I shall come to you *like* a thief,
5 10 Those who prove victorious will be dressed, *like* [these], in white robes;
21 Those who prove victorious I will allow to share my throne, *just as* I was victorious myself
16 15 This is how it will be: I shall come *like* a thief.
18 21 10 *That is how* the great city of Babylon is going to be hurled down,
21 2 I saw the holy city . . . *as* [beautiful as] a bride all dressed for her husband.

5. (BE) LIKE, SIMILAR(LY), THE SAME – COMPARE – IN THE SAME WAY, LIKEWISE: *HOMOIOŌ*

4 *homoiōma*	6	6 *homoio(-pathēs)*	2
3 *homoioō*	15	8 *aph-omoioō*	1
1 *homoios*	45	9 *par-(h)omoiazō*	1
2 *homoiōs*	31	10 *par-(h)omoios*	1
7 *homoiōsis*	1		
5 *homoiotēs*	2		

1: (BE) LIKE, SIMILAR – COMPARE, (BE) COMPARED (TO) – IMITATION, DISGUISE

Mt 6 8 [In your prayers do not babble as the pagans do.] Do not
3 *be like* them;
7 24 everyone who listens to these words of mine and acts on them will *be like* a sensible man . . . ²⁶ But everyone who
26 3 listens to these words . . . and does not act on them will
3 *be like* a stupid man
11 16 3 What ʳdescription (lit. *comparison*) can I find for this generation? It is *like* children shouting to each other

Mt 13 24	3	The kingdom of heaven may *be compared* to a man who sowed good seed
31		The kingdom of heaven is *like* a mustard seed
33		The kingdom of heaven is *like* the yeast a woman took
44		The kingdom of heaven is *like* treasure hidden in a field
45		the kingdom of heaven is *like* a merchant looking for fine pearls;
47		the kingdom of heaven is *like* a dragnet cast into the sea
52		every scribe who becomes a disciple . . . is *like* a householder who brings out from his storeroom things both new and old.
18 23	3	the kingdom of heaven may *be compared* to a king who decided to settle his accounts
20 1		the kingdom of heaven is *like* a landowner going out at day-break to hire workers
22 2	3	The kingdom of heaven may *be compared* to a king who gave a feast for his son's wedding.
39		The second [commandment] *resembles* [the first one]:
23 27	9	scribes and Pharisees . . . *are like* whitewashed tombs
25 1	3	the kingdom of heaven will *be like* this: Ten bridesmaids took their lamps and went to meet the bridegroom.
Mk 4 30	3	What can we say the kingdom of God *is like*? What parable can we find for it? [31] It is *like* a mustard seed
7 13	10	you make God's word null and void for the sake of your tradition . . . And you do many other things *like* [this].
Lk 6 47		Everyone who . . . listens to my words and acts on them –
48		I will show you what he is *like*. [48] He is *like* the man who . . . laid the foundations on rock . . . . [49] But the one who
49		listens and does nothing is *like* the man who built his house . . . with no foundations.
7 31	3	What ꞈdescription (lit. *comparison*), then, can I find for the men of this generation? What are they *like*? [32] They are
32		*like* children shouting to one another
12 36		Be *like* men waiting for their master to return
13 18	/3	What is the kingdom of God *like*? What shall I *compare* it
19		with? [19] It is *like* a mustard seed
20	3/	What shall I *compare* the kingdom of God with? [21] It is
21		*like* the yeast a woman took
Jn 8 55		if I were to say: I do not know [the Father], I should be a liar, *as* you are liars yourselves.
9 9		Some said [about the blind man who had been cured], 'Yes, it is the same one'. Others said, 'No, he only *looks like* him'.
Ac 14 11	3	These people are gods who have come down to us *disguised* as men.
15	6	We are only human beings *like* you.
17 29		we have no excuse for thinking that the deity *looks like* anything in gold,
Rm 1 23	4	they exchanged the glory of the immortal God for a worthless *imitation*, for the image of mortal man,
5 14	4	their sin, *unlike* that of Adam, was not a matter of breaking a law.
6 5	4	If in union with Christ we have *imitated* his death, we shall also [imitate] him in his resurrection.
8 3	4	God dealt with sin by sending his own Son in a body ꞈas physical as (lit. *like*) any sinful body,
9 29	3	(Is 1 9) Had the Lord of hosts not left us some descendants we should now [be like] Sodom, we should *be like* Gomorrah.
Ga 5 21		[The results of self-indulgence are obvious:] envy; drunkenness, orgies and *similar* things.
Ph 2 7	4	[Christ Jesus assumed] the condition of a slave, and became *as* men are;
Heb 2 17	3	It was essential that [Jesus] should . . . *become completely like* his brothers
4 15	5	[Jesus] has been tempted in every way ꞈthat we are (lit. as *one similar* [to us]), though he is without sin.
7 3	8	[Melchizedek] *is like* the Son of God. He remains a priest for ever.
15	5	This becomes . . . evident when there appears ꞈa second (lit. *one similar to*) Melchizedek,
Jm 3 9	7	we also use [the tongue] to curse men who are made in God's ꞈ*image* (or: *likeness*):
5 17	6	Elijah was a human being *like* ourselves
1 Jn 3 2		we shall be *like* [God] because we shall see him as he really is.
Jude 7		The fornication of Sodom and Gomorrah . . . was *equally* unnatural,
Rv 1 13		surrounded by [golden lamp-stands], a figure *like* a Son of man,
15		his feet [were] *like* burnished bronze when it has been refined in a furnace,
2 18		the Son of God . . . has . . . feet *like* burnished bronze:
4 3		the Person sitting there looked *like* a diamond and a ruby. There was a rainbow . . . and this looked *like* an emerald.
6		Between the throne and myself was a sea that seemed to be made of glass, *like* crystal.
7		The first animal was *like* a lion, the second *like* a bull, the third animal had a human face, and the fourth was *like* a flying eagle.

Rv 9 7	4/	ꞈTo look at (lit. For *comparison*), these locusts were *like* horses armoured for battle; they had things that looked *like* gold crowns on their heads, and faces that seemed human,
10		[The locusts'] tails were *like* scorpions',
19		[the locusts'] tails were *like* snakes,
11 1		I was given a long cane *as* a measuring rod
13 2		the beast was *like* a leopard, with paws like a bear and a mouth like a lion;
4		Who can *compare* with the beast?
11		the second beast] had two horns *like* a lamb, but made a noise like a dragon.
14 14		I saw . . . sitting on [a cloud], one *like* a son of man
18 18		Has there ever been a city *as* great as this!
21 11		[the new Jerusalem] glittered *like* some precious jewel of crystal clear diamond.
18		the city [was built] of pure gold, *like* polished glass.

2: THE SAME – SIMILARLY, IN THE SAME WAY, LIKEWISE – TOO, ALSO

Mt 22 26		[The first brother married and died without children;]
	2	*the same* [thing happened with] the second
26 35	2	all the disciples said *the same*.
27 41		[The passers-by jeered at Jesus.] The chief priests . . .
	2	mocked him *in the same way*.
Mk 4 16	2	*Similarly*, those who receive the seed on patches of rock are people who [have no root in them]
15 31		[The passers-by jeered at Jesus.] The chief priests . . . mocked
	2	him among themselves *in the same way*.
Lk 3 11		If anyone has two tunics he must share with the man who has
	2	none, and the one with something to eat must do *the same*.
5 10	2	[Peter was overcome by the catch;] *so also* were James and John,
33		John's disciples are always fasting . . . and the disciples of
	2	the Pharisees *too*, but yours go on eating and drinking.
6 31	2	Treat others *the same* as you would like them to treat you.
10 32	2	[A priest passed by on the other side.] *In the same way* a Levite
37	2	Go, and do *the same* yourself.
13 3		unless you repent you will all perish ꞈas [those Galileans]
	2	did (lit. *likewise*).
16 25	2	during your life good things came your way, *just as* bad things came the way of Lazarus.
17 28	2	It will be *the same* as it was in Lot's day:
31		anyone on the housetop . . . must not come down to collect [his possessions], nor must anyone in the fields turn back
	2	ꞈeither (lit. *in the same way*).
22 36		if you have a purse, take it; if you have a haversack, do
	2	*the same*;
Jn 5 19	2	whatever the Father does the Son does *too*.
6 11		Jesus took the loaves . . . and gave them out . . . he then
	2	did *the same* with the fish,
21 13	2	Jesus . . . gave [the bread] to them, and *the same* with the fish.
Rm 1 27		[their women have turned to unnatural practices] and . . .
	2	their menfolk have *similarly* given up natural intercourse
1 Co 7 3		The husband must give his wife what she has the right to
	2	expect, and *so too* the wife to the husband. [4] The wife has
4		no rights over her own body; it is the husband who has
	2	them. *In the same way*, the husband has no rights over his body;
22	2	A slave . . . becomes the Lord's freedman, ꞈand (lit. *similarly*) a freeman . . . becomes Christ's slave.
Heb 9 21	2	[Moses] sprinkled the tent . . . with blood *in the same way*.
Jm 2 25		[Abraham was justified by his deed.] There is another example
	2	of *the same kind*: Rahab
1 P 3 1	2	*In the same way*, wives should be obedient to their husbands.
7	2	*In the same way*, husbands must always treat their wives with consideration in their life together,
5 5	2	*Likewise* to those who are young among you I say: do what the elders tell you,
Jude 8	2	Nevertheless, these [heretics] are doing *the same*:
Rv 2 15	2	and among you, *too*, there are some as bad who accept what the Nicolaitans teach.
8 12	2	for a third of the day there was no illumination, and *the same* with the night.

6. COMPARE, COMPARISON – CLASS, RANK (WITH): *SYN-KRINŌ*

2 en-krino 1   1 syn-krino 2/3

2 Co 10 12	2	We are not being so bold as to ꞈrank (or: *class*) ourselves, or [invite] *comparison*, with certain people who write their own references . . . and *comparing* themselves to themselves, they are simply foolish.

7. SUCH, SUCH AS – LIKE THIS, SO – THIS, THESE: *HOIOS*

2 *hoios* 14/15	3 *toiosde*	*1*
1 *toioutos* (56)		

Mt	9	8	they praised God for giving *such* power to men.
	18	5	Anyone who welcomes a little child *like this* . . .welcomes me.
	19	14	Let the little children alone . . . for it is to *such* [as these] that the kingdom of heaven belongs.
	24	21	2 (Dn 12 1) there will be great distress *such as*, until now, . . . there never has been,
Mk	4	33	Using many parables *like these*, [Jesus] spoke the word to them,
	6	2	What is this wisdom that has been granted [Jesus], and ʳ*these* (or: *such*) miracles that are worked through him?
	9	3	2 his clothes became . . . ʳwhiter than any (lit. *such as* no) earthly bleacher could make them.
		37	Anyone who welcomes one of ʳ*these* (or: *such*) little children in my name, welcomes me,
	10	14	Let the little children come to me; . . . for it is to *such* [as these] that the kingdom of God belongs.
	13	19	2 (Dn 12 1) there will be *such* distress *as*, until now, has not been *equalled*
Lk	9	9	who is this I hear *such* [reports] about?
	18	16	Let the little children come to me . . . for it is to *such* [as these] that the kingdom of God belongs.
Jn	4	23	*that is the kind of* worshipper the Father wants.
	8	5	Moses has ordered us in the Law to condemn women *like this* to death by stoning.
	9	16	How could a sinner produce signs *like this*?
Ac	16	24	ʳfollowing his (lit. having received *such*) instructions, [the gaoler] threw them into the inner prison
	19	25	[Demetrius] called a general meeting of his own men with others in the *same* trade.
	22	22	Rid the earth of ʳthe (lit. *such* a) man!
	26	29	I wish before God that . . . you . . . would come to be *as* I am
Rm	1	32	those who behave *like this* deserve to die
	2	2	God condemns *that sort of* behaviour impartially:
		3	you judge those who behave *like this* while you are doing exactly the same,
	9	6	2 ʳDoes this mean that (lit. Is it *so that*) God has failed to keep his promise?
	16	18	People *like that* are not slaves of Jesus Christ,
1 Co	5	1	ʳThis is a case of (lit. *Such*) sexual immorality among you that must be unparalleled even among pagans.
		5	ʳhe (lit. *this* [man]) is to be handed over to Satan
		11	you should not even eat a meal with people *like that*.
	7	15	in ʳ*these* (or: *such*) circumstances, the brother or sister is not tied;
		28	ʳThey (lit. *Such* [people]) will have their troubles, though, in their married life,
	11	16	To anyone who might still want to argue: ʳit (lit. *such*) is not the custom with us,
	15	48	2/ *As* this earthly man was, *so* are we on earth; and
			2/ *as* the heavenly man is, *so* are we in heaven.
	16	16	put yourselves at the service of people *like this*,
		18	I hope you appreciate men *like this*.
2 Co	2	6	The punishment already imposed . . . on [the man] *in question* is enough; ⁷ and the best thing now is to give him your
		7	forgiveness . . . or ʳhe (lit. [the man] *in question*) might break down from so much misery.
	3	4	we are confident of *this* through Christ:
		12	Having ʳ*this* (or: *such* a) hope, we can be quite confident;
	10	11	ʳThe (lit. *Such* a) man who said that can remember this:
		2	whatever we are like (lit. *such as* we are) in the words of our letters . . . ʳthat is what we shall be like (lit. *such* we shall be) in our actions when we are present.
	11	13	ʳ*These* (or: *Such*) people are counterfeit apostles,
	12	2	I know a man in Christ ʳwho (lit. *and this* [man]) . . . was
		3	caught up . . . right into the third heaven. ³ . . . *this same* [person] . . . ⁴ was caught up into paradise . . .
		5	⁵ I will boast about a man *like that*,
		20	I am afraid . . . that when I come I may find you ʳdifferent
		2	from what (lit. not *as*) I want you to be, and you may find
		2	that I am not *as* you would like me to be;
Ga	5	21	those who behave *like this* will not inherit the kingdom of God.
		23	[the Spirit brings] gentleness and self-control. There can be no law against things *like that*,
	6	1	set ʳhim (lit. *such* [a man]) right . . . in a spirit of gentleness,
Ep	5	27	[the Church] would be glorious, with no speck . . . or anything *like that*,
Ph	1	30	2 [We] are together in the same fight *as* you saw me fighting before
	2	29	people *like him* are to be honoured.
1 Th	1	5	2 you observed *the sort of* [life we lived] when we were with you,
2 Th	3	12	we order . . . people *of this kind* to go on quietly working
2 Tm	3	11	[you know] the persecutions . . . that came to me in places

2 Tm	3	11	2/2 *like* Antioch, Iconium and Lystra – ʳall the (lit. *such*) persecutions I have endured;
Tt	3	11	any man *of that sort* has already lapsed
Phm		9	*this* is Paul writing, an old man now
Heb	7	26	ʳthe ideal (lit. *such* a) high priest would have to be holy,
	8	1	we have a high priest *of exactly this kind*.
	11	14	People who use *such* [terms] about themselves make it quite plain that they are in search of their real homeland.
	12	3	Think of the way he stood *such* opposition from sinners
	13	16	*these* are sacrifices that please God
Jm	4	16	Pride *of this kind* is always wicked.
2 P	1	17	3 the Sublime Glory itself spoke in *such* a voice to him and said, 'This is my Son'
3 Jn		8	it is our duty to welcome men *of this sort*
Rv	16	18	there were flashes of lightning and . . . the most violent earthquake ʳthat anyone (lit. *such* and so great *as* no one)
		2	has ever seen

SATISFY – ENOUGH

1. Satisfy – Enough: *hikanos*	**Feed:** *chortazō*
2. Suffice, Be enough – Be content with – Satisfied: *arkeō*	**4. Have enough (food):** *korennymi*
3. (Be) Satisfied (with enough food) –	**5. It is enough – It is all over – It will do:** *ap-echō*

1. SATISFY – ENOUGH: *HIKANOS*

hikanos 4/40

Mk	15	15	Pilate, anxious to *placate* the crowd, released Barabbas
Lk	22	38	'Lord, . . . there are two swords here now.' [Jesus] said to them, 'That is *enough*!'
Ac	17	9	[the city councillors] made Jason and the rest give ʳsecurity (lit. *satisfaction*) before setting them free.
2 Co	2	6	The punishment already imposed . . . on the man in question is *enough*;

2. SUFFICE, BE ENOUGH – BE CONTENT WITH – SATISFIED: *ARKEŌ*

1 *arkeō* 8	3 *aut-arkeia* 2	
2 *arketos* 3	4 *aut-arkēs* 1	

Mt	6	34	2 Each day has *enough* trouble of its own.
	10	25	2 It is *enough* for the disciple that he should grow to be like his teacher.
	25	9	There may not be *enough* [oil] for us and for you;
Lk	3	14	No extortion! *Be content* with your pay!
Jn	6	7	Two hundred denarii would only buy *enough* [bread] to give them a small piece each.
	14	8	let us see the Father and then we shall *be satisfied*.
2 Co	9	8	3 [God] will make sure that you will always have *all you need* for yourselves . . . and still have something to spare for . . . good works.
	12	9	My grace is *enough* for you: my power is at its best in weakness.
Ph	4	11	4 I have learnt to *manage* on whatever I have,
1 Tm	6	6	3 Religion . . . does bring large profits, but only to those who *are content with what they have*.
		8	as long as we have food and clothing, let us *be content* with that.
Heb	13	5	Put greed out of your lives and *be content* with whatever you have.
1 P	4	3	2 You spent quite long *enough* in the past living the sort of life that pagans live,
3 Jn		10	As if that were not *enough*, [Diotrephes] . . . prevents the other people . . . from [accepting us],

3. (BE) SATISFIED (WITH ENOUGH FOOD) – FEED: *CHORTAZŌ*

chortazō 15

Mt	5	6	Happy those who hunger and thirst for what is right: they shall be *satisfied*.
	14	20	They all ate ʳas much as they wanted (lit. and were *satisfied*)
	15	33	Where could we get enough bread . . . to *feed* such a crowd?
		37	They all ate ʳas much as they wanted (lit. and were *satisfied*),
Mk	6	42	They all ate ʳas much as they wanted (lit. and were *satisfied*).
	7	27	The children should be *fed* first,
	8	4	Where could anyone get bread to *feed* these people in a deserted place like this?

Mk	8 8	They ate ʳas much as they wanted (lit. and were *satisfied*),
Lk	6 21	Happy you who are hungry now: you shall be *satisfied*.
	9 17	They all ate ʳas much as they wanted (lit. and were *satisfied*),
	16 21	[Lazarus] longed to *fill himself* with the scraps that fell from the rich man's table.
Jn	6 26	you are . . . looking for me . . . because you had all the bread ʳyou wanted to eat (lit. and were *satisfied*).
Ph	4 12	I am ready for anything . . .: ʳfull stomach or empty stomach (lit. being *fed* or being *hungry*),
Jm	2 16	I wish you well; keep yourself warm and *eat plenty*.
Rv	19 21	all the birds were *gorged* with their flesh.

4. HAVE ENOUGH (FOOD): *KORENNYMI*

korennymi 2

Ac	27 38	When they had ʳeaten what they wanted (lit. *had enough* to eat) they lightened the ship by throwing the corn overboard
1 Co	4 8	Is it that you *have everything you want* . . .?

5. IT IS ENOUGH – IT IS ALL OVER – IT WILL DO: *AP-ECHŌ*

ap-echō 1/15

Mk	14 41 Δ	*It is all over.* The hour has come.

SAVE – CURE

1. **Hosanna** [= Heb., Aram. 'Save, now!']
2. **Rescue, Save, Deliver (from)**
   1: *ex-(h)aireō*
   2: *rhuomai*
3. **Save, Saviour – Salvation – Cure, Heal:** *sōzō*
   a) Save, (Be) Saved (from sin, spiritual death) – Salvation – Saviour
   b) Save (from physical death), Rescue – Safe
   c) Save = Cure, Heal – Restore to health – (Make) Well again
4. **(Be) Cured, Healed – Healthy, Sound, Whole:** *hygiainō*

a) (Be) Cured, Healed, Well again–Healthy, Sound, Whole
b) Sound (teaching), Healthy (faith), Wholesome (words)
5. **Cure, Heal:** *therapeuō*
6. **Cure, Heal – Doctor, Physician:** *iaomai*
7. **Restore:** *apo-kath-istēmi*
   a) Restore (to health) – Cure
   b) Restore = Set right, See that (a thing) is as it should be (once more)
8. **Recover (from illness, disability)**
   1: *kalōs echō*
   2: *kompsoteron echō*
9. **Eye ointment, Salve:** *kollyrion*

X = Jesus works a cure, rescues, delivers (from)

1. HOSANNA [= Heb., Aram. 'Save, now!']

ōsanna 6

Mt	21 9	*Hosanna* to the Son of David! . . . *Hosanna* in the highest heavens!
	15	*Hosanna* to the Son of David
Mk	11 9	*Hosanna!* Blessings on him who comes in the name of the Lord!
	10	*Hosanna* in the highest heavens!
Jn	12 13	*Hosanna!* Blessings on the King of Israel, who comes in the name of the Lord.

2. RESCUE, SAVE, DELIVER (FROM)

1: RESCUE, SAVE, DELIVER (FROM): *EX-(H)AIREŌ*

ex-(h)aireō 6/8

Ac	7 10 Θ	[God] *rescued* [Joseph] from all his miseries
	34 Θ	(Ex 3 8) I have seen the way my people are ill-treated in Egypt, . . . and I have come down to *liberate* them.
	12 11 Θ	The Lord really did send his angel and has *saved* me from Herod
	23 27	This man had been seized by the Jews . . . but I . . . ʳgot him away (or: *rescued* him),
	26 17 X	(Jr 1 8) I shall *deliver* you from the people and from the pagans, to whom I am sending you
Ga	1 4 X	[Jesus Christ,] in order to *rescue* us from this present wicked world sacrificed himself for our sins,

2: RESCUE, SAVE, DELIVER (FROM): *RHUOMAI*

rhuomai 17

Mt	6 13 Θ	do not put us to the test, but *save* us from ʳthe evil one (or: evil).
	27 43 Θ	(Ps 22 9) now let God *rescue* [Jesus] if he wants him.
Lk	1 74 Θ	[God swore] that he would grant us, free from fear, to be *delivered* from the hands of our enemies, to serve him
Rm	7 24	Who will *rescue* me from this body doomed to death?
	11 26 X	the rest of Israel will be saved as well. As scripture says (cf. Is 59 20): The *liberator* will come from Zion,
	15 31	Pray that I may ʳescape (lit. be *saved* from) the unbelievers in Judaea,
2 Co	1 10 Θ	[God] *saved* us from dying, as he will *save* us again; yes, that is our firm hope in him, that in the future he will *save* us again.
Col	1 13 Θ	[The Father] has *taken* us *out* of the power of darkness and created a place for us in the kingdom of the Son
1 Th	1 10 X	you are now waiting for Jesus . . . to come from heaven to *save* us from the retribution which is coming.
2 Th	3 2	pray that we may be *preserved* from the interference of bigoted and evil people,
2 Tm	3 11 X	the Lord has *rescued* me from every [persecution].
	4 17 X	I was *rescued* from the lion's mouth. [18] The Lord will
	18 X	*rescue* me from all evil attempts on me,
2 P	2 7 Θ	[God] *rescued* Lot . . . [9] These are all examples of how the
	9 Θ	Lord can *rescue* the good from the ordeal,

3. SAVE, SAVIOUR – SALVATION – CURE, HEAL: *SŌZŌ*

3	*sōtēr*	24	6	*sōtērios*	1
2	*sōtēria*	45	1	*sōzō*	108
5	*sōtērion*	4	4	*dia-sōzō*	8

L = Save // Lose, Destroy

a) Save, (Be) Saved (from sin, spiritual death) – Salvation – Saviour

Mt	1 21	you must name him Jesus, because he is the one who is to *save* his people from their sins.
	10 22	the man who stands firm to the end will be *saved*.
	18 11 L	(ᵛ For the Son of Man came to *save* what was lost.)
	19 25	Who can be *saved*, then?
	24 13	the man who stands firm to the end will be *saved*.
Mk	8 35 L	anyone who loses his life for my sake, and for the sake of the gospel, will *save* it.
	10 26	In that case . . . who can be *saved*?
	13 13	the man who stands firm to the end will be *saved*.
	16 16	He who believes and is baptised will be *saved*;
Lk	1 47	my spirit exults in God my *saviour*.
	69 2	[God] has raised up for us a power for *salvation* in the House of . . . David, even as he proclaimed . . . [71] that he would
	71 2	*save* us from our enemies
	77	[You will go before the Lord,] to give his people knowledge
	2	of *salvation* through the forgiveness of their sins;
	2 11 3	Today in the town of David a *saviour* has been born to you;
	30 5	my eyes have seen the *salvation* [31] which you have prepared for all the nations to see,
	3 6 5	(Is 40 5 G) all mankind shall see the *salvation* of God.
	7 50	[Jesus] said to the woman, 'Your faith has *saved* you;
	8 12	the devil . . . carries away the word from their hearts in case they should believe and be *saved*.
	9 24 L	anyone who loses his life for my sake, that man will *save* it.
	56 L	(ᵛ For the Son of Man did not come to destroy men's lives but to *save* them.)
	13 23	Sir, will there be only a few *saved*?
	18 26	In that case . . . who can be *saved*?
	19 9 2	Today *salvation* has come to this house, because [Zacchaeus] too is a son of Abraham; [10] for the Son of Man has come
	10 L	to seek out and *save* what was lost.
Jn	3 17 L	God sent his Son into the world not to condemn the world, but so that through him the world might be *saved*.
	4 22 2	*salvation* comes from the Jews,
	42 3	we know that he really is the *saviour* of the world.
	5 34	it is for your *salvation* that I speak of this.
	10 9 L	I am the gate. Anyone who enters through me will be *safe*:
	12 47	I have come not to condemn the world, but to *save* the world
Ac	2 21	(Jl 3 5) All who call on the name of the Lord will be *saved*.
	40	[Peter] urged [the Jews], '*Save* yourselves from this perverse generation'.
	47	the Lord added to their community those destined to be *saved*.
	4 12 2	For (§ there is *salvation* in no one else;) of all the names in the world given to men, this is the only one by which we can be *saved*.
	5 31 3	God has now raised [Jesus] up to be leader and *saviour*,
	11 14	Peter . . . has a message for you that will *save* you and your entire household.

Ac 13 23 3 God has raised up for Israel . . . Jesus, as *Saviour*,
   26 2 My brothers, . . . this message of *salvation* is meant for you.
   47 (Is 49 6) I have made you a light for the nations, so that my
      2 *salvation* may reach the ends of the earth.
15 1 Unless you have yourselves circumcised . . . you cannot be
      saved.
   11 we believe that we are *saved* . . . through the grace of the
      Lord Jesus.
16 17 Here are the servants of the Most High God; they have come
      2 to tell you how to *be saved*!
   30 [The gaoler said to Paul and Silas,] Sirs, what must I do to be
      saved?
   31 Become a believer in the Lord Jesus, and you will be *saved*,
      and your household too.
28 28 5 this *salvation* of God has been sent to the pagans;
Rm 1 16 2 the Good News . . . is the power of God *saving* all who have
      faith
 5 9 Having died to make us righteous, is it likely that he would
   10 now fail to *save* us from God's anger? [10] . . . now that we
      have been reconciled, surely we may count on being *saved*
      by the life of his Son?
 8 24 we must be content to hope that we shall be *saved*
 9 27 (Is 10 22 G) Though Israel should have as many descendants
      as there are grains of sand . . . only a remnant will be
      saved,
10 1 2 I pray to God for [the Jews] to be *saved*.
    9 If your lips confess that Jesus is Lord . . . you will be *saved*.
   10 2 by confessing with your lips you are *saved*.
   13 (Jl 3 5) everyone who calls on the name of the Lord will be
      saved.
11 11 2 [the Jews'] fall . . . has ʳ*saved* (lit. obtained the *salvation*
      of) the pagans
   14 the purpose of it is to make my own people envious of you,
      and in this way *save* some of them.
   26 after this the rest of Israel will be *saved* as well.
13 11 2 our *salvation* is even nearer than it was when we were con-
      verted.
1 Co 1 18 The language of the cross may be illogical to those who are
      not on the way to salvation, but those of us who are on the
    L way ʳsee it as God's power to *save* (or: to be *saved* see it as
      God's power).
   21 God wanted to *save* those who have faith through the foolish-
      ness of the message that we preach.
 3 15 if [the structure] is burnt down, [the builder] will be the loser,
      and though he is *saved* himself, it will be as one who has
      gone through fire.
 5 5 he is to be handed over to Satan so that . . . his spirit [may
    L be] *saved* on the day of the Lord.
 7 16 If you are a wife, it may be your part to *save* your husband,
      for all you know; if a husband, for all you know, it may be
      your part to *save* your wife.
 9 22 I made myself all things to all men in order to *save* some at
      any cost;
10 33 [I am anxious] for the advantage of everybody else, so that
      they may be *saved*.
15 2 the gospel will *save* you only if you keep believing
2 Co 1 6 2 When we are made to suffer, it is for your . . . *salvation*.
 2 15 L We are Christ's incense to God for those who are being *saved*
      and for those who are not;
 6 2 2 (Is 49 8) on the day of *salvation* I came to your help. Well . . .
      2 this is the day of *salvation*.
 7 10 To suffer in God's way means ʳchanging for the better (lit.
      2 repentance leading towards *salvation*) and leaves no
      regrets,
Ep 1 13 Now you too . . . have heard . . . the good news of your
      2 *salvation*,
 2 5 it is through grace that you have been *saved*
    8 it is by grace that you have been *saved*, through faith;
 5 23 3 Christ is head of the Church and *saves* the whole body,
 6 17 5 you must accept *salvation* from God to be your helmet
Ph 1 19 [Christ is proclaimed;] and . . . I know this will help to
      2 *save* me,
   28 This would be the sure sign that they will lose and you will
    L 2 be *saved*.
 2 12 2 work for your *salvation* 'in fear and trembling'.
 3 20 L 3 from heaven comes the *saviour* we are waiting for, the Lord
      Jesus
1 Th 2 16 they are hindering us from preaching to the pagans and
      trying to *save* them.
 5 8 2 let us put on . . . the hope of *salvation* for a helmet. [9] God
    9 2 . . . meant us . . . to win *salvation* through our Lord
      Jesus Christ,
2 Th 2 10 they would not grasp the love of the truth which could have
    L *saved* them.
   13 2 God chose you from the beginning to *be saved*
1 Tm 1 1 Paul, apostle of Christ Jesus appointed by the command of
      3 God our *saviour* and of Christ Jesus
   15 Christ Jesus came into the world to *save* sinners.
 2 3 3/ God our *saviour* [4] . . . wants everyone to be *saved* and reach
    4 full knowledge of the truth.

1 Tm 2 15 [a woman] will be *saved* by childbearing, provided she lives
      a modest life
 4 10 3 the living God . . . is the *saviour* of the whole human race
   16 in this way you will *save* both yourself and those who listen
      to you.
2 Tm 1 9 [God] has *saved* us and called us to be holy
   10 [This grace] has . . . been revealed by the Appearing of our
      3 *saviour* Christ Jesus.
 2 10 I bear it all for the sake of those who are chosen, so that
      2 . . . they may have the *salvation* that is in Christ Jesus
 3 15 from [the holy scriptures] you can learn the wisdom that
      2 leads to *salvation* through faith in Christ Jesus.
Tt 1 3 3 by the command of God our *saviour*, I have been commissioned
      to proclaim [the Good News].
    4 To Titus, . . . wishing you grace and peace from God . . .
      3 and from Christ Jesus our *saviour*.
 2 10 [the slaves] must show complete honesty . . . so that they
      are in every way a credit to the teaching of God our
      3 *saviour*.
   11 6 God's grace has been revealed and it has *made salvation
      possible* for the whole human race
   13 we are waiting in hope for the blessing which will come with
      3 the Appearing of the glory of our . . . God and *saviour*
      Christ Jesus
 3 4 3 when the kindness and love of God our *saviour* for mankind
    5 were revealed, [5] . . . he *saved* us, by . . . renewing us with
    6 the Holy Spirit [6] which he has so generously poured over
      3 us through Jesus Christ our *saviour*.
Heb 1 14 [angels] are all spirits . . . sent to help those who will be the
      2 heirs of *salvation*.
 2 3 2 we shall . . . not go unpunished if we neglect this *salvation*
   10 it was appropriate that God . . . should make perfect . . .
      2 the leader who would take them to their *salvation*.
 5 9 having been made perfect, [Christ] became for all who obey
      2 him the source of eternal *salvation*
 6 9 we are sure you are in a better state and on the way to
      2 *salvation*.
 7 25 [Christ's] power to *save* is utterly certain, since he is living
      for ever to intercede for all who come to God through him.
 9 28 when [Christ] appears a second time, it will . . . be to . . .
      2 reward with *salvation* those who are waiting for him.
Jm 1 21 submit to the word which . . . can *save* your souls.
 2 14 Will that faith *save* [someone who has never done a good act]?
 4 12 There is only one lawgiver and he . . . has the power to ʳacquit
    L or to sentence (lit. *save* or to destroy).
 5 20 anyone who can bring back a sinner from the wrong way
      . . . will be *saving* a soul from death
1 P 1 5 2 God's power will guard you until the *salvation* . . . is revealed
      at the end of time.
    9 you are sure of the end to which your faith looks forward,
   10 2/2 that is, the *salvation* of your souls. [10] It was this *salvation*
      that the prophets were . . . searching so hard for.
 2 2 you should be hungry for nothing but milk – the spiritual
      2 honesty which will help you to grow up to *salvation*
 3 21 That water is a type of the baptism which *saves* you now,
 4 18 (Pr 11 31 G) If it is hard for a good man to be *saved*, what will
      happen to . . . the sinners?
2 P 1 1 From . . . Peter . . . to all who treasure the same faith . . .
      3 given through the righteousness of our God and *saviour*
      Jesus Christ.
   11 you will be granted admittance into the . . . kingdom of our
      3 Lord and *saviour* Jesus Christ.
 2 20 anyone who has escaped the pollution of the world once by
      3 coming to know our Lord and *saviour* Jesus Christ,
 3 2 [I am] recalling to you what was said in the past by . . . the
      3 Lord and *saviour*
   15 2 Think of our Lord's patience as your opportunity to *be saved*:
   18 3 go on growing . . . in the knowledge of our Lord and *saviour*
      Jesus Christ.
1 Jn 4 14 3 the Father sent his Son as *saviour* of the world.
Jude 3 I was . . . looking forward to writing to you about the
      2 *salvation* that we all share,
   23 when there are some to be *saved* from the fire, pull them out;
   25 3 To God, the only God, who *saves* us through Jesus Christ
      our Lord, be the glory . . . which he had before time began,
Rv 7 10 2 ʳVictory (lit. *Salvation*) ʳto (or: is of) our God, who sits on
      the throne, and to the Lamb!
12 10 2 ʳVictory (lit. *Salvation*) and power and empire for ever have
      been won by our God,
19 1 2 ʳVictory (lit. *Salvation*) ʳto (or: is of) our God!

b) Save (from physical death), Rescue – Safe

Mt 8 25 L [the disciples] woke [Jesus] saying, 'Save us, Lord, we are
      going down!'
14 30 [Peter] began to sink. 'Lord! *Save* me!' he cried.
16 25 L anyone who wants to *save* his life will lose it; but anyone who
      loses his life for my sake will find it.
24 22 if that time had not been shortened, no one would have ʳsurvived
      (lit. been *saved*); but shortened that time shall be, for the
      sake of those who are chosen.

Mt 27 40		Then *save* yourself! If you are God's son, come down from the cross!
	42	He *saved* others . . . he cannot *save* himself.
	49	Wait . . . and see if Elijah will come to *save* him.
Mk 3 4		Is it against the law on the sabbath day . . . to *save* life, or to kill?
	8 35 L	anyone who wants to *save* his life will lose it;
	13 20	if the Lord had not shortened that time, no one would have ⌜survived (lit. been *saved*);
	15 30	Then *save* yourself: come down from the cross!
	31	He *saved* others, . . . he cannot *save* himself.
Lk 6 9 L		is it against the law on the sabbath . . . to *save* life, or to destroy it?
	8 50	[Jesus] spoke to [Jairus], 'Do not be afraid, only have faith and [your daughter] will be *safe*'.
	9 24 L	anyone who wants to *save* his life will lose it;
	23 35	He *saved* others, . . . let him *save* himself if he is the Christ of God.
	37	If you are the king of the Jews, *save* yourself.
	39	Are you not the Christ? . . . *Save* yourself and us as well.
Jn 12 27		What shall I say: Father, *save* me from this hour?
Ac 7 25	2	through [Moses] God would ⌜liberate them (lit. afford them *safety*),
23 24	4	provide horses for Paul, and *deliver* him *unharmed* to Felix the governor.
27 20		at last we gave up all hope of ⌜surviving (lit. being *saved*).
31		Unless those men stay on board you cannot hope to be *saved*.
34	2	your *safety* is [not] in doubt.
43	4	the centurion was determined to *bring* Paul *safely through*, and would not let [the soldiers] do what they intended . . .
44	4	⁴⁴ . . . In this way all came *safe* [and sound] to land.
28 1	4	Once we had *come safely through*, we discovered that the island was called Malta.
4	4	That man must be a murderer; he may have ⌜escaped (lit. been *saved* from) the sea, but divine vengeance would not let him live.
2Tm 4 18		The Lord will rescue me . . . and bring me *safely* to his heavenly kingdom.
Heb 5 7		[Jesus] offered up prayer and entreaty . . . to the one who had the power to *save* him out of death,
11 7	2	Noah . . . built an ark to *save* his family.
Jm 5 15		The prayer of faith will *save* the sick man and the Lord will raise him up again;
1 P 3 20	4	Noah was still building that ark which *saved* only a small group of eight people
Jude 5		the Lord *rescued* the nation from Egypt,

c) Save = Cure, Heal – Restore to health – (Make) Well again

Mt 9 21		[the woman with a haemorrhage] said to herself, 'If I can only touch his cloak I shall be *well again*'.
	22	'Courage, my daughter, your faith has *restored* you *to health*'. And from that moment the woman was *well again*.
14 36	4	all those who touched [the fringe of his cloak,] were *completely cured*.
Mk 5 23		lay your hands on [my daughter] to *make* her *better* ⌜and save her life (lit. so that she can go on living).
28		If I can touch even his clothes . . . I shall be *well again*.
34		your faith has *restored* you *to health*; go in peace and be free from your complaint.
6 56		all those who touched him were *cured*.
10 52		Jesus said to [the blind man], 'Go; your faith has ⌜*saved* (or: *cured*) you.
Lk 7 3		Having heard about Jesus [the centurion] sent some Jewish elders to him to ask him to come and *heal* his servant.
8 36		Those who had witnessed it told . . . how the man who had been possessed came to be *healed*.
48		'My daughter,' [Jesus] said [to the woman who had a haemorrhage] 'your faith has *restored* you *to health*; go in peace.'
17 19		[Jesus] said to [the leper], 'Stand up . . . your faith has ⌜*saved* (or: *cured*) you.'
18 42		Jesus said to [the blind man], 'Receive your sight. Your faith has ⌜*saved* (or: *cured*) you.'
Jn 11 12		Lord, if [Lazarus] is able to rest he is sure to *get better*.
Ac 4 9		you are questioning us today about an act of kindness to a cripple and asking us how he was *healed*,
14 9		Seeing that the man had the faith to be *cured*, ¹⁰ Paul said in a loud voice, 'Get to your feet
Jm 5 15		The prayer of faith will *save* the sick man and the Lord will raise him up again;

4. (BE) CURED, HEALED – HEALTHY, SOUND, WHOLE: *HYGIAINŌ*

1 hygiainō 12   2 hygiēs 12

a) (Be) Cured, Healed, Well again – Healthy, Sound, Whole

Mt 12 13 X	2	his hand was better, as *sound* as the other one.

Mt 15 31 X	2	The crowds were astonished to see . . . the cripples *whole* again,
Mk 5 34		[Jesus] said [to the woman with a haemorrhage] 'your faith has restored you to health; go in peace and be ⌜free from (lit. *healed* of) your complaint.'
	X 2	
Lk 5 31		It is not those [who are] *well* who need the doctor, but the sick.
	X 2	
7 10 X		the messengers . . . found the servant *in perfect health*.
15 27		your father has killed the calf we had fattened because he has got [your brother] back [safe and] *sound*.
Jn 5 4		ᵛ. . . the first person to enter the water after this disturbance was *cured* . . .⌝
	2	
6 X	2	Jesus . . . said, 'Do you want to be *well again*?'
9 X	2	The man was *cured* at once.
11 X	2	the man who *cured* me told me, 'Pick up your mat and walk'.
14 X	2	Jesus met him . . . and said, 'Now you are *well again*, be sure not to sin any more,
15		The man . . . told the Jews that it was Jesus who had *cured* him.
7 23 X	2	why are you angry with me for *making* a man *whole* . . . on a sabbath?
Ac 4 10 X		it was by the name of Jesus Christ . . . that this man is able to stand up *perfectly healthy* . . . today.
	2	
3 Jn 2		I hope . . . that you are as *well* physically as you are spiritually.

b) Sound (teaching), Healthy (faith), Wholesome (words)

1Tm 1 10		[laws are framed] for everything . . . that is contrary to the *sound* teaching
6 3		Anyone who . . . does not keep to the *sound* teaching which is that of our Lord Jesus Christ [is simply ignorant]
2Tm 1 13		Keep as your pattern the *sound* teaching you have heard from me,
4 3		The time is sure to come when, far from being content with *sound* teaching, people will be avid for the latest novelty
Tt 1 9		[the elder] must have a firm grasp of . . . the *sound* doctrine
13		you will have to be severe in correcting [men of this kind], and *make* them *sound* in the faith
2 1		It is for you, then, to preach the behaviour which goes with *healthy* doctrine.
2		The older men should be reserved, dignified, moderate, *sound* in faith
8	2	[Be an example to younger men] in keeping all that you say so *wholesome* that nobody can make objections to it;

5. CURE, HEAL: *THERAPEUŌ*

2 therapeia 2/3   1 therapeuō 42/43

Mt 4 23 X		[Jesus] went round . . . *curing* all kinds of diseases and sickness . . . ²⁴ . . . those who were suffering from diseases . . . were all brought to him, and he *cured* them.
24	X	
8 7 X		'I will come . . . and *cure* him' said Jesus [to the centurion].
16 X		with a word [Jesus] *cured* all who were sick.
9 35 X		Jesus made a tour . . . *curing* all kinds of diseases
10 1		[Jesus] gave [the Twelve] authority over unclean spirits with power . . . to *cure* all kinds of diseases
8		*Cure* the sick, raise the dead, cleanse the lepers,
12 10		Is it against the law to *cure* a man on the sabbath day?
15 X		Many followed [Jesus] and he *cured* them all,
22	X	they brought to [Jesus] a blind and dumb demoniac; and he *cured* him,
14 14 X		[Jesus] took pity on [the crowd] and *healed* their sick.
15 30	X	the lame, the crippled, the blind, the dumb . . . [were] put down at his feet, and he *cured* them.
17 16		your disciples . . . were unable to *cure* [my lunatic son]
18 X		the devil came out of the boy who was *cured* from that moment.
19 2 X		Large crowds followed [Jesus] and he *healed* them there.
21 14	X	blind and lame people . . . came to [Jesus] . . . and he *cured* them,
Mk 1 34 X		[Jesus] *cured* many who were suffering from diseases of one kind or another;
3 2 X		they were watching [Jesus] to see if he would *cure* him on the sabbath day,
10 X		[Jesus] had *cured* so many that all who were afflicted . . . were crowding forward to touch him.
6 5 X		[Jesus] could work no miracle [in Nazareth], though he *cured* a few sick people
13		[the Twelve] anointed many sick people with oil and *cured* them.
Lk 4 23		No doubt you will quote me the saying, 'Physician, *heal* yourself'
40 X		laying his hands on each [sick person Jesus] *cured* them.
5 15 X		large crowds would gather . . . to have their sickness *cured*,
6 7		The scribes and the Pharisees were watching [Jesus] to see if he would *cure* a man on the sabbath,
	X	
18 X		People tormented by unclean spirits were also *cured*,

Lk	7 21	X	[Jesus] *cured* many people of diseases and afflictions
	8 2	X	certain women who had been *cured* of evil spirits [accompanied Jesus].
	43		there was a woman suffering from a haemorrhage . . . whom no one had been able to *cure*.
	9 1		[Jesus] gave [the Twelve] power . . . to *cure* diseases,
	6		[the Twelve] went from village to village . . . *healing* everywhere.
	11	2	[Jesus] cured those who were in need of *healing*.
	10 9		*Cure* those . . . who are sick [in the town where they make you welcome].
	13 14 X		the synagogue official was indignant because Jesus had *healed* on the sabbath, and . . . he said, '. . . Come and be *healed* on one of those days and not on the sabbath.'
	14 3		'Is it against the law' [Jesus] asked 'to *cure* a man on the sabbath, or not?'
Jn	5 10	X	the Jews said to the man who had been *cured*, 'It is the sabbath;
Ac	4 14		[the Sanhedrin] saw the man who had been *cured*
	5 16		People . . . came crowding in . . . bringing with them their sick and those tormented by unclean spirits, and all of them were *cured*
	8 7		several paralytics and cripples were *cured* [in Samaria].
	28 9		the other sick people [in Malta] came as well and were *cured*;
Rv	13 3		this deadly injury [to one of the beast's heads] had *healed*
	12		the first beast . . . had had the fatal wound and had been *healed*.
	22 2	2	the leaves [of the trees of life] are the *cure* for the pagans.

6. CURE, HEAL – DOCTOR, PHYSICIAN: *IAOMAI*

3 iama	3	4 iasis	3
1 iaomai	26	3 iatros	7

Mt	8 8	X	just give the word and my servant will be *cured*.
	13	X	the servant was *cured* at that moment.
	9 12	2	It is not the healthy who need the *doctor*, but the sick.
	13 15		(Is 6 10) they have shut their eyes, for fear they should . . . be converted and be *healed* by me.
	15 28	X	from that moment her daughter was *well again*.
Mk	2 17	2	It is not the healthy who need the *doctor*, but the sick.
	5 26	2	after long and painful treatment under various *doctors*, . . . [the woman] was getting worse . . . ²⁹ . . . she felt in herself that she was *cured* of her complaint.
	29	X	
Lk	4 23	2	No doubt you will quote me the saying, '*Physician*, heal yourself'
	5 17	X	the Power of the Lord was behind his [works of] *healing*.
	31	2	It is not those who are well who need the *doctor*, but the sick.
	6 18		[a great crowd of people] had come to hear him and to be *cured* of their diseases.
	19	X	power came out of [Jesus] that *cured* them all.
	7 7	X	give the word and let my servant be *cured*.
	8 43	2	a woman suffering from a haemorrhage . . . (ᵛ . . . had spent all she possessed on *doctors*)
	47	X	[the woman with a haemorrhage] explained . . . how she had been *cured* at that very moment.
	9 2		[Jesus] sent [the Twelve] out to proclaim the kingdom of God and to *heal*.
	11	X	[Jesus] *cured* those who were in need of healing.
	42	X	Jesus rebuked the unclean spirit and *cured* the boy
	13 32	X 4	today and tomorrow I cast out devils and work *cures* and on the third day attain my end.
	14 4	X	so [Jesus] took the man and *cured* him
	17 15	X	Finding himself *cured*, one of [the lepers] turned back praising God
	22 51	X	touching [the high priest's servant's] ear [Jesus] *healed* him.
Jn	4 47	X	[a court official] asked [Jesus] to come and *cure* his son as he was at the point of death.
	5 13		The man who had been *cured* had no idea who it was,
	12 40		(Is 6 9) [God] has blinded their eyes . . . for fear they should see with their eyes . . . and turn to me for *healing*.
	X		
Ac	4 22	4	The man who had been miraculously *cured* was over forty years old.
	30		[Lord, help your servants] by stretching out your hand to *heal* and to work miracles . . . through the name of . . . Jesus.
	X 4		
	9 34	X	Aeneas, Jesus Christ *cures* you: get up and fold up your sleeping mat.
	10 38	X	Jesus went about . . . *curing* all who had fallen into the power of the devil.
	28 8		after a prayer [Paul] laid his hands on [Publius' father] and *healed* him.
	27		they have shut their eyes, for fear they should . . . be converted and be *healed* by me.
1 Co	12 9	3	another again [may have] the gift of *healing*, through this one Spirit;

1 Co	12 28	3	after [miracles] the gift of *healing*; helpers, good leaders,
	30		[Do they all have the gift of miracles,] or all have the gift of *healing*?
	3		
Col	4 14	2	Greetings from my dear friend Luke, the *doctor*,
Heb	12 13		the injured limb will not be wrenched, it will *grow strong* again,
Jm	5 16		confess your sins . . . and pray . . . and this will *cure* you;
1 P	2 24	X	(Is 53 5) through [Christ's] wounds you have been *healed*.

7. RESTORE: *APO-KATH-ISTĒMI*

1 apo-kath-istēmi, -anō 8   2 apo-kata-stasis 1

a) Restore (to health) – Cure

Mt	12 13	'Stretch out your hand'. He stretched it out and his hand was ⌐*better* (or: *restored*), as sound as the other one.
Mk	3 5	his hand was ⌐*better* (or: *restored*).
	8 25	he saw clearly; he was *cured*,
Lk	6 10	his hand was ⌐*better* (or: *restored*).

b) Restore = Set right, See that (a thing) is as it should be (once more)

Mt	17 11	Elijah is to come to *see that* everything *is once more as it should be*;
Mk	9 12	Elijah is to come first and to *see that* everything *is as it should be*;
Ac	1 6	Are you going to *rest re* the kingdom to Israel?
	3 21	2 heaven must keep [Jesus] till the universal *restoration* comes
Heb	13 19	I ask you . . . to pray that I may ⌐*come back* (lit. be *restored*) to you.

8. RECOVER (FROM ILLNESS, DISABILITY)

1: RECOVER: *KALŌS ECHŌ*

kalōs echō 1

Mk	16 18	[believers] will lay their hands on the sick, who will *recover*.

2: RECOVER: *KOMPSOTERON ECHŌ*

kompsoteron echō 1

Jn	4 52	[The father] asked them when the boy had begun to *recover*.

9. EYE OINTMENT, SALVE: *KOLLYRION*

kollyrion 1

Rv	3 18	buy from me . . . *eye ointment* to put on your eyes so that you are able to see.

SAY – TELL – SPEAK

1. Speak – Say – Tell: *laleō*
  1: (God, Scripture) Speaks, Says – Inexpressible
    a) (God) Speaks, Says, Talks
    b) (the Spirit) Speaks, Says
    c) (Voices from/in heaven) Speak
    d) (Scripture, the Prophets) Speak, Say
    e) Inexpressible, Unutterable – Indescribable
  2: (an Angel, a Devil) Speaks, Says
    a) (Angels) Speak, Say, Tell
    b) (a Devil, the Devil) Speaks
  3: (Jesus) Speaks, Tells, Talks (to), Says, Preaches
  4: (A person) Speaks, Says, Talks
    a) (A person) Speaks (in a language, in tongues)
    b) (A person) Speaks, Says, Talks (concerning Jesus, the word of God) – Preaches, Proclaims
    c) Speak, Say, Talk (generally) – Discuss – (Be) Told

  5: (the Dumb, the Dead) Speak – (the Power of) Speech
  6: (Things, Creatures) Speak, Make a noise
2. Say – Speak, Tell – Word: *legō*
  1: (God) Says, Speaks, Tells – (the) Words (of God)
    a) (God) Says, Speaks – (the Words (of God)
    b) (the Spirit) Says, Tells
    c) Voices from/in heaven) Say, Speak, Tell – Shout – Words
    d) (Scriptures, the Prophets) Say, Speak, Tell – Word(s) spoken
    e) the Word (of the Kingdom = the Gospel) Message
    f) Not to be said, Unutterable
  2: (an Angel, a Devil) Says, Tells – Words
    a) (an Angel) Says, Tells, Calls – Words
    b) (Devils, the Devil, Unclean spirits) Say

3: (Jesus) Says, Tells, Speaks –
Word(s), Message
    a) the Word
    b) (Jesus) Says, Speaks (to
      God his Father)
    c) (Jesus in heaven) Says,
      Replies (to a person) –
      Message
    d) (Jesus while teaching) Says,
      Tells, Speaks, Talks –
      Word(s), Message
    e) (I) Tell (you), (I) Say (to
      you)
    f) (Jesus) Said
4: (A person, an animal) Says
    a) (A person, an animal) Says
      (in prayer, in praise)
    b) (A person) Says, Tells (of
      Christ) – Words, the Mes-
      sage (of Jesus, Gospel
      teaching)
    c) (A person) Says (to), Tells
      (another)
    d) (Specific people) Say, Tell
5: (Things and Personifications)
    Say
6: Advocate
7: Forewarn – Foretell – Already
    told
8: Speak (against)
9: Argue, Argument – Discuss,
    Debate, Talk (among)
10: Account, Reason – Answer
11: Claim (to be), Speak of (a
    person, oneself) as, Give out
    (that)

12: to Mean – Language
    a) to Mean
    b) Language
3. Say, Tell: *phēmi*
    1: (God) Says
    2: (an Angel or God) Says
    3: (Jesus) Says
    4: (A person) Says – Assert, Allege
    5: Reputation, Report, News –
      Spread (a story)
4. Answer, Reply – Speak, Say (in
    response): *apo-krinomai*
    1: (A heavenly voice) Speaks (in
      response)
    2: (Jesus) Answers, Replies (to a
      person)
    3: (A person) Answers, Replies,
      Says (in response)
5. Speak, Talk
    1: Report, Give an Account of,
      Describe – Tell of – Inexpress-
      ible: *di-(h)ēgeomai*
    2: Speak, Talk: *phthengomai*
    3: Make a speech: *(dem-)ēgoreō*
    4: Reply: *hypo-lambanō*
    5: Talk: *hom-ileō*
    6: Discuss, Confer – Argue: *ballō*
    7: Chatter – Gossip: *phlyareō*
    8: Nonsense: *lēros*
    9: Ask one another, Question –
      Discussion, Debate, Contro-
      versy – Argue, Dispute:
      sy-zēteō
    10: Discuss, consult, Confer: *pros-*
      ana-tithemai
    11: Speak (to), Address: *pros-phōneō*

1. SPEAK – SAY – TELL: *LALEŌ*

1	*laleō*	298/299	7	*ek-laleō*	1
3	*lalia*	3	8	*an-ek-lalētos*	1
6	*a-lalētos*	1	9	*(mogi-)lalos*	1
4	*dia-laleō*	2	5	*pros-laleō*	2
			2	*syl-laleō*	6

1: (GOD, SCRIPTURE) SPEAKS, SAYS – INEXPRESSIBLE

a) (God) Speaks, Says, Talks

Lk 1 55 according to ⌐the promise he made (lit. what he *said*) to our
    ancestors
Jn 9 29 we know that God *spoke* to Moses,
Ac 7 6 The actual words used when God *spoke* to him are that his
    descendants would be exiles
   44 the Tent of Testimony [was] constructed according to the
    instructions ⌐God gave (lit. given by him who *spoke* to)
    Moses,
1 Co 14 21 (Is 28 11) through the lips of foreigners, I shall *talk* to the
    nation,
Heb 5 5 [Christ] had it from the one who *said* to him (Ps 2 7): You
    are my son,
  11 18 ⌐[Abraham] had been told (lit. it had been *said* to him)
    (Gn 21 12): It is through Isaac
  12 25 Make sure that you never refuse to listen when he *speaks*.

b) (the Spirit) Speaks, Says

Mt 10 20 it is not you . . . ; the Spirit of your Father will be *speaking*
    in you.
Mk 13 11 it is not you who will be *speaking*: it will be the Holy Spirit.
Jn 16 13 [the Spirit of Truth] will not be *speaking* as from himself but
    will *say* only what he has learnt;

c) (Voices from/in heaven) Speak

Rv 1 12 I turned round to see whose voice had *spoken* to me,
  4 1 I saw a door open in heaven and heard the same voice *speak-*
    ing to me,
 10 3 At this, seven claps of thunder ⌐made themselves heard (lit.
   4 *spoke* with their voices) [4] and when the seven thunderclaps
    had *spoken*, . . . a voice [said] 'Keep the words ⌐of the
    seven thunderclaps (lit. the seven thunderclaps have
    spoken) secret . . .'
   8 I heard the voice I had heard from heaven *speaking* to me
    again.

d) (Scripture, the Prophets) Speak, Say

Lk 1 70 Θ even as [the Lord] *proclaimed*, by the mouth of his holy
    prophets
 24 25 You foolish men! So slow to believe the full message ⌐of
    (lit. *spoken* by) the prophets!

Jn 12 41 Isaiah said this . . . and ⌐his words referred to (lit. he was
    speaking about) Jesus (cf. Is 6 1–6).
Ac 2 31 what [David] foresaw and *spoke* about was the resurrection
    of the Christ (Ps 16 10)
  3 21 Θ the universal restoration . . . which God *proclaimed*, [speak-
    ing] through his holy prophets.
   24 all the prophets that have ever *spoken* . . . have predicted
    these days.
 26 22 [I have said] nothing more than what the prophets and Moses
    himself *said*
 28 25 Ⓢ How aptly the Holy Spirit *spoke* when he told your ancestors
    (Is 6 9–10)
Rm 3 19 all this that the Law says is *said* . . . for the benefit of those
    who are subject to the law,
Heb 1 1 Θ At various times . . . God *spoke* to our ancestors through
   2 Θ the prophets; but [2] in our own time, . . . he has *spoken*
    to us through his Son,
  3 5 [Moses acted] as witness to the things which were to be
    divulged later;
  4 8 Θ God would not later on have *spoken* so much of another day.
  7 14 Judah, a tribe which Moses did not even *mention*
  9 19 after Moses had *announced* all the commandments of the
    Law to the people,
Jm 5 10 the prophets who *spoke* in the name of the Lord;
2 P 1 21 When men *spoke* for God it was the Holy Spirit that moved
    them.
  3 16 [Paul] always writes like this when he ⌐deals with (lit. *speaks*
    on) this sort of subject,

e) Inexpressible, Unutterable – Indescribable

Rm 8 26 the Spirit himself expresses our plea in a ⌐way (lit. groaning)
  6 *that could never be put into words*,
1 P 1 8 you are already filled with a joy *so glorious that it cannot be*
  8 *described*,

2: (AN ANGEL, A DEVIL) SPEAKS, SAYS

(a) (Angels) Speak, Say, Tell

Lk 1 19 I am Gabriel . . . and I have been sent to *speak* to you
   45 blessed is she who believed ⌐that the promise made her (lit.
    that what was *said* to her) by the Lord would be fulfilled.
  2 17 When [the shepherds] saw the child they repeated ⌐what
    (G the message) they had been *told* about him,
   20 it was exactly as [the shepherds] had been *told*.
Jn 12 29 others said, 'It was an angel *speaking* to him.'
Ac 7 38 it was only through Moses that our ancestors could communi-
    cate with the angel who had *spoken* to him
  8 26 The angel of the Lord *spoke* to Philip
 10 7 When the angel who *said* this had gone, Cornelius called
    two [slaves]
 23 9 Suppose a spirit has *spoken* to him, or an angel?
 27 25 I trust in God that things will turn out just as I was *told*;
Heb 2 2 If a promise that was ⌐made (lit. *spoken*) through angels
    proved to be so true
Rv 17 1 One of the seven angels that had the seven bowls came to
    speak to me,
 21 9 One of the seven angels . . . came to *speak* to me,
   15 The angel that was *speaking* to me was carrying a gold
    measuring rod

b) (a Devil, the Devil) Speaks

Mk 1 34 [Jesus] also cast out many devils, but he would not allow
    them to *speak*,
Lk 4 41 [Jesus] would not allow them to *speak* because they knew
    that he was the Christ.
Jn 8 44 when [the devil] *speaks* lies he is ⌐drawing on (lit. *speaking*
    from) his own store,

3: (JESUS) SPEAKS, TELLS, TALKS (TO), SAYS, PREACHES

J = Jesus (*Iēsous*) 8/923

Mt 9 18 While he was *speaking* to them, up came one of the officials,
 12 46 He was still *speaking* to the crowds when his mother and
    his brothers appeared;
 13 3 he *told* [the people] many things in parables.
   10 Why do you *talk* to them in parables?
   13 The reason I *talk* to them in parables is that they look with-
    out seeing
   33 He *told* them another parable,
   34 J In all this *Jesus spoke* to the crowds in parables; indeed, he
    would never *speak* to them except in parables.
 14 27 J at once *Jesus* called out to [the disciples], saying, 'Courage!'
 23 1 J Then *addressing* the people and his disciples *Jesus* said,
 26 47 He was still *speaking* when Judas, one of the Twelve, appeared,
 28 18 J *Jesus* came up and *spoke* to [the eleven disciples]. He said,
    'All authority in heaven and on earth has been given to
    me.'

Mk	2 2	He was *preaching* the word to them
	7	How can this man *talk* like that? He is blaspheming.
	4 33	Using many parables . . . he *spoke* the word to them . . .
	34	³⁴ He would not *speak* to them except in parables,
	5 35	While he was still *speaking* some people arrived
	6 50	he at once *spoke* to them, and said, 'Courage! It is I!'
	8 32	he *said* ᵣall this (lit. these words) quite openly.
	12 1	He went on to *speak* to them in parables,
	14 43	while he was still *speaking*, Judas, one of the Twelve, came up
	16 19 J	And so the Lord *Jesus*, after he had *spoken* to them, was taken up into heaven:
Lk	2 50	But [his parents] did not understand ᵣwhat he meant (lit. the meaning of what he was *telling* them).
	5 4	When he had finished *speaking* he said to Simon, 'Put out into deep water
	21	Who is this man *talking* blasphemy?
	8 49	While he was still *speaking*, someone arrived from the house
	9 11	He made [the crowds] welcome and *talked* to them about the kingdom of God;
	11 37	He had just finished *speaking* when a Pharisee invited him to dine
	22 47	He was still *speaking* when a number of men appeared,
	24 6	Remember what he *told* you when he was still in Galilee:
	32	Did not our hearts burn within us as he *talked* to us on the road . . . ?
	44	This is what I meant when I *said*, while I was still with you,
Jn	3 11	I tell you most solemnly, we *speak* only about what we know
	34	he whom God has sent *speaks* God's own words:
	4 26	I who am *speaking* to you . . . I am he.
	27	his disciples returned and were surprised to find him *speaking* to a woman, though none of them asked, . . . 'Why are you *talking* to her?'
	6 63	The words I have *spoken* to you are spirit and they are life.
	7 17	if anyone is prepared to do [the will of the one who sent me], he will know. . . whether ᵣmy doctrine (lit. what I *say*) is my own.
	26	here he is, *speaking* freely, and [the authorities] have nothing to say to him!
	46	There has never been anybody who has *spoken* like him.
	8 12 J	When *Jesus spoke* to the people again, he said: 'I am the light of the world;'
	20	He *spoke* these words in the Treasury, while teaching
	25	'Who are you?' Jesus answered: 'ᵣWhat I have *told* you from the outset (or: Why should I *speak* to you in the first place?).
	26	²⁶ About you I have much to *say* . . . and what I have learnt from [the one who sent me] I *declare* to the world.'
	28	what the Father has taught me is what I *preach*;
	30	As he was *saying* this, many came to believe in him.
	38	What I, for my part, *speak* of is what I have seen with my Father;
	40	As it is, you want to kill me when I *tell* you the truth
	43 3	Do you know why you cannot take in *what* I *say*?
	9 37	You are looking at [the Son of Man]; he is *speaking* to you.
	10 6	they failed to understand what he meant by *telling* [the parable] to them.
	12 36 J	Having *said* this, *Jesus* left them and kept himself hidden.
	48	the word itself that I have *spoken* will be . . . judge on the last day.
	49	what I have *spoken* does not come from myself; no, what I was to say, what I had to *speak*, was commanded by the Father . . . ⁵⁰ . . . what the Father has told me to *speak* is what I *speak*.
	50	
	14 10	The words I say to you I do not *speak* as from myself: it is the Father,
	25	I have *said* these things to you while still with you;
	30	I shall not *talk* with you any longer,
	15 3	You are pruned already, by means of the word that I have *spoken* to you.
	11	I have *told* you this so that my own joy may be in you.
	22	if I had not *spoken* to them, they would have been blameless;
	16 1	I have *told* you all this so that [your faith] may not be shaken.
	4	I have *told* you all this, so that . . . you may remember that I told you.
	6	you are sad at heart because I have *told* you this.
	18	What is this 'short time'? We don't know what he ᵣmeans (lit. is *talking* about).
	25	I have been *telling* you all this in metaphors, the hour is coming when I shall no longer *speak* to you in metaphors;
	29	Now you are *speaking* plainly and not using metaphors!
	33	I have *told* you all this so that you may find peace in me.
	17 1 J	After *saying* this, *Jesus* raised his eyes to heaven
	13	while still in the world I *say* these things to share my joy
	18 20	I have *spoken* openly for all the world to hear; . . . I have *said* nothing in secret. ²¹ But why ask me? Ask my hearers what I ᵣtaught (lit. *told*) them: they know
	21	
	23	If there is something wrong in what I *said*, point it out;
	19 10	Pilate then said to him, 'Are you refusing to *speak* to me?
Ac	3 22	The Lord God will raise up a prophet . . . you must listen to whatever he *tells* you.

Ac	9 27	the Lord had appeared to Saul and *spoken* to him on his journey,
	22 9	The people with me saw the light but did not hear his voice as he *spoke*
2 Co	13 3	You want proof, you say, that it is Christ *speaking* in me:
Heb	2 3	The promise was first *announced* by the Lord himself,

4: (A PERSON) SPEAKS, SAYS, TALKS

a) (a Person) Speaks (in a language, in tongues)

Mk	16 17	believers: . . . they will ᵣhave the gift of (lit. *speak* in) tongues;
Ac	2 4	They were all filled with the Holy Spirit, and began to *speak* foreign languages
	6	each one bewildered to hear these men *speaking* his own language.
	7	'Surely' they said, 'all these men *speaking* are Galileans?
	11	we hear them *preaching* in our own language about the marvels of God.
	10 46	they could hear them *speaking* strange languages and proclaiming the greatness of God.
	19 6	the Holy Spirit came down on them, and they began to *speak* with tongues
1 Co	12 30	Do all *speak* strange languages, and all interpret them?
	13 1	If I have all the eloquence of men or of angels, but *speak* without love, I am simply a gong booming
	14 2	Anybody ᵣwith the gift of (lit. who *speaks* in) tongues *speaks* to God, . . . nobody understands him when he talks in the spirit
	4	The one ᵣwith the gift of (lit. who *speaks* in) tongues talks for his own benefit . . . ⁵ While I should like you all to ᵣhave the gift of (lit. *speak* in) tongues, I would much rather you could prophesy, since the man who prophesies is of greater importance than the man ᵣwith the gift of (lit. who *speaks* in) tongues, unless [there is] an interpretation
	5	
	6	suppose, my dear brothers, I am someone ᵣwith the gift of (lit. who *speaks* in) tongues, and I come to visit you, what use shall I be if all my *talking* reveals nothing new . . . ?
	13	anybody who ᵣhas the gift of (lit. *speaks* in) tongues must pray for the power of interpreting them.
	18	I thank God that I ᵣhave a greater gift of (lit. *speak* more in) tongues than all of you,
	23	unbelievers, coming into a meeting . . . where everybody was *speaking* in tongues, would say you were all mad;
	27	If there are people present ᵣwith the gift of (lit. who *speak* in) tongues, let only two or three . . . be allowed to use it . . . one at a time . . . ²⁸ If there is no interpreter present, they must . . . *speak* only to themselves and to God.
	28	
	39	by all means be ambitious to prophesy, do not suppress ᵣthe gift of (lit. *speaking* in) tongues,

b) (a Person) Speaks, Says, Talks (concerning Jesus, the word of God) – Preaches, Proclaims

Jn	1 37	Hearing [John] *say* this, the two disciples followed Jesus.
	4 42 3	Now we no longer believe because of *what* you *told* us; we have heard him ourselves and we know
Ac	4 1	While [Peter and John] were still *talking* to the people the priests came up to them,
	17	let us caution them never to *speak* to anyone in this name again.
	20	We cannot promise to stop *proclaiming* what we have seen and heard.
	29	Lord, . . . help your servants to *proclaim* your message with all boldness,
	31	they were all filled with the Holy Spirit and began to *proclaim* the word of God boldly.
	5 20	Go and stand in the Temple, and *tell* the people all about this new Life.
	40	[the Sanhedrin] warned [the apostles] not to *speak* in the name of Jesus
	6 10	it was the Spirit that prompted what [Stephen] *said*.
	8 25	Having . . . *proclaimed* the word of the Lord, [Peter and John] went back
	9 29	After [Saul] had *spoken* to the Hellenists,
	10 44	While Peter was still *speaking* the Holy Spirit came down on all
	11 14	Peter; he ᵣhas a message for (lit. will *say* words to) you that will save you
	15	I had scarcely begun to *speak* when the Holy Spirit came down on them
	19	they usually *proclaimed* the message only to Jews.
	20	Some . . . went to Antioch where they started *preaching* to the Greeks,
	13 42	[Barnabas and Paul] were asked to *preach* on the same theme
	43 5	in their *talks* with them Paul and Barnabas urged them to remain faithful
	45	the Jews, prompted by jealousy, . . . contradicted everything Paul *said*.
	46	We had to *proclaim* the word of God to you first,

Ac 14	1	At Iconium . . . they *spoke* so effectively that a great many [believed].
	9	as [the cripple] listened to Paul *preaching*, he managed to catch his eye.
	25	after *proclaiming* the word at Perga [Paul and Barnabas] went down to Attalia
16	6	having been told by the Holy Spirit not to *preach* the word in Asia.
	13	We sat down and *preached* to the women [of Philippi]
	14	the Lord opened [Lydia's] heart to accept what Paul was saying.
	32	[Paul and Silas] *preached* the word of the Lord to [the gaoler]
17	19	How much of this new teaching you were *speaking* about are we allowed to know?
18	9	the Lord spoke to Paul in a vision, 'Do not be afraid to *speak* [out],
	25	An Alexandrian Jew named Apollos . . . *preached* with great spiritual earnestness
21	39	Paul . . . 'Please give me permission to *speak* to the people.'
23	7	As soon as [Paul] *said* this a dispute broke out between the Pharisees and Sadducees,
26	26	The king understands these matters, and to him I now *speak*
28	20	5 That is why I have asked to see you and *talk* to you,
1 Co 2	6	still we have ⌜a wisdom to offer (lit. [words of] wisdom to *speak* to) those who have reached maturity: . . . ⁷ The
	7	hidden wisdom of God ⌜which we teach (lit. of which we *speak*) in our mysteries
	13	we ⌜teach (lit. *speak*), not in the way philosophy is taught, but in the way that the Spirit teaches us:
3	1	I myself was unable to *speak* to you as people of the Spirit:
14	3	On the other hand, the man who prophesies does *talk* to other people,
	19	I would rather *say* five words that mean something than ten thousand words in a tongue.
	29	As for prophets, let two or three of them *speak*,
2 Co 2	17	In Christ, we *speak* as men of sincerity, as envoys of God
4	13	(Ps 116 10) I believed, and therefore I *spoke* – we too believe and therefore we too *speak*,
Ep 5	19	⌜Sing the words and (lit. *Say* and sing the) tunes of the psalms and hymns
6	20	pray that in proclaiming [the gospel] I may *speak* as boldly as I ought
Ph 1	14	most of the brothers . . . are getting more and more daring in *announcing* the Message (§ of God)
Col 4	3	*proclaiming* the mystery of Christ . . . ⁴ pray that I may
	4	*proclaim* it as clearly as I ought.
1 Th 2	2	it was our God who gave us the courage to *proclaim* his Good News
	4	when we are *speaking*, we are not trying to please men but God,
	16	[the Jews] are hindering us from *preaching* to the pagans
Tt 2	1	It is for you, then, to *preach* the behaviour which goes with healthy doctrine.
	15	this is what you are to *say*,
Heb 2	5	the world to come, and that world is what we are talking about.
6	9	in spite of what we have just *said*, we are sure you are in a better state
13	7	Remember your leaders, who *preached* the word of God to you,
1 P 4	11	If you ⌜are a speaker, speak (lit. *speak*, do so) in words which seem to come from God;

c) Speak, Say, Talk (generally) – Discuss – (Be) Told

X = Speak, Say, Talk to Jesus

Mt 10	19	do not worry about how to *speak* or what [to say]; what you are to *say* will be given to you
	20	it is not you who will be *speaking*; the Spirit of your Father will be
12	34	how can ⌜your speech (lit. what you *say*) be good when you are evil? For ⌜a man's words flow (lit. what a man's mouth *says* flows) out of what fills his heart.
	36	for every unfounded word men *utter* they will answer on Judgement day,
	46 X	his mother and his brothers . . . were anxious to *have a word* with him.
	47 X	(ᵛ Someone said to him, 'Your mother and brothers are here and would like to *speak* to you.')
17	3 X	2 Moses and Elijah appeared to them; they were *talking with* him.
	5	[Peter] was still *speaking* when suddenly a bright cloud covered them
26	13	wherever [the] Good News is proclaimed, what she has done will be *told* also,
	73	3 You are one of them for sure! Why, your ⌜accent (or: *speech*) gives you away.
Mk 5	36	Jesus had overheard ⌜this remark of theirs (lit. the words they had *said*)
9	4 X	2 Elijah appeared to them with Moses; and they were *talking with* Jesus.

Mk 11	23	if anyone says . . . believing that what he *says* will happen, it will
13	11	do not worry beforehand about what to *say*; no, *say* whatever is given to you . . . because it is not you who will be speaking: it will be the Holy Spirit.
14	9	wherever . . . the Good News is proclaimed, what she has done will be *told* also,
	31 X	[Peter] *repeated* still more earnestly, 'If I have to die with you, I will
Lk 1	65	4 the whole affair was *talked about* throughout the hill country
2	15	the shepherds *said* to one another, 'Let us go to Bethlehem and see
	18	everyone . . . was astonished at what the shepherds *had to say*.
	33	the child's father and mother stood there wondering at the things that were being *said* about him,
	38	[Anna] *spoke* of the child to all
4	36	2 they were all *saying* to one another, 'What teaching!
6	11	4 [the Pharisees and the scribes] began to *discuss* the best way of dealing with Jesus.
	45	⌜a man's words flow (lit. what a man's mouth *says* flows) out of what fills his heart.
9	30 X	2 Suddenly there were two men there *talking with* him; they were Moses and Elijah
12	3	what you have ⌜whispered (lit. *spoken* into someone's ear) in hidden places will be proclaimed on the housetops.
22	4	[Judas] went to the chief priests and the officers . . . to *discuss* a scheme for handing Jesus over
	60	while [Peter] was still *speaking*, the cock crew,
24	36	They were still *talking* about all this when [Jesus] himself stood among them
Jn 3	31	he who is born of the earth . . . *speaks* in an earthly way.
7	13	no one *spoke* about [Jesus] openly, for fear of the Jews.
	18	When a ⌜man's doctrine is his own (lit. man *speaks* on his own [authority]) he is hoping to get honour for himself;
	46	There has never been anybody who has *spoken* like him.
9	21	[Our son who was born blind] is old enough: let him *speak* for himself.
Ac 6	11	We heard [Stephen] ⌜using (lit. *speaking* in) blasphemous language
9	6	go into the city, and you will be *told* what you have to do.
20	30	from your own ranks there will be ⌜men with a travesty of the truth on their lips (lit. men *speaking* seductively in order) to induce
22	10	Damascus, . . . there you will be *told* what . . . to do.
23	18	Paul . . . requested me to bring this young man to you; he has something to *tell* you.
	22	7 *Tell* no one that you have given me this information.
25	12	2 Festus *conferred* with his advisers
26	31	they *talked* together and agreed, ⌜This man is doing nothing
28	21	We have received no . . . ⌜story of anything (lit. person's *saying* anything) to your discredit.
Rm 7	1	those of you who have studied law will ⌜know (lit. follow me when I *say*)
15	18	What I am presuming to *speak* of . . . is only what Christ himself has done
1 Co 9	8	This may be to *talk* only [of] human [comparisons],
12	3	no one can be *speaking* under the influence of the Holy Spirit and say, 'Curse Jesus',
13	11	When I was a child, I used to *talk* like a child,
14	9	if your tongue does not produce intelligible speech, how can anyone know what you are *saying*? You will be *talking* to the air.
	11	I am a savage to the man who is *speaking*, and ⌜he (lit. the man who is *speaking*) is a savage to me.
	34	women are to remain quiet . . . they have no permission to *speak*;
	35	it does not seem right for a woman to *raise her voice* at meetings.
15	34	⌜you should be ashamed (lit. I *say* this to your shame).
2 Co 7	14	our boasting . . . has proved to be as true as anything we ever *said*
11	17	What I am going to *say* now is . . . *said* as if in a fit of folly,
	23	The servants of Christ? I must be mad to *say* this, but so am I,
12	4	things which must not and cannot be *put into* human *language*.
	19	it is before God that we, in Christ, are *speaking*;
Ep 4	25	(Zc 8 16) You must *speak* the truth to one another,
1 Th 1	8	We do not need to *tell* other people about [your] faith,
1 Tm 5	13	[young widows] learn to be gossips and meddlers . . . and to *chatter*
Heb 11	4	Though [Abel] is dead, he still *speaks* by faith.
Jm 1	19	be quick to listen but slow to *speak* and slow to rouse your temper;
	2 12	*Talk* and behave like people who are going to be judged by the law of freedom,
1 P 3	10	(Ps 34 14) Anyone who wants to have a happy life . . . must banish . . . deceitful *conversation* from his lips
1 Jn 4	5	they are of the world, and so they *speak* [the language] of the world

2 Jn	12		I hope instead to visit you and *talk* to you personally,
3 Jn	14		I hope to see you soon and *talk* to you personally.
Jude	15		all the defiant things *said* against [the Lord] by irreligious sinners. They are mischief-makers . . . with mouths full of boastful *talk*,
	16		

5: (THE DUMB, THE DEAD) SPEAK – (THE POWER OF) SPEECH

Mt	9	33	when the devil was cast out, the dumb man *spoke*
	12	22	[Jesus] cured him so that the dumb man could *speak*
	15	31	The crowds were astonished to see the dumb *speaking*,
Mk	7	32	9 a deaf man who had an impediment in his *speech*;
		35	the ligament of his tongue was loosened and he *spoke* clearly.
		37	he makes the deaf hear and the dumb *speak*.
Lk	1	20	you will be silenced and have no power of *speech* until this has happened.
		22	When [Zechariah] came out he could not *speak* to them,
		64	At that instant his power of speech returned and he *spoke*
	7	15	the dead man sat up and began to *talk*,
	11	14	when the devil had gone out the dumb man *spoke*,

6: (THINGS, CREATURES) SPEAK, MAKE A NOISE

Heb	12	24	blood for purification which ┌pleads more insistently (lit. *speaks* better) than Abel's.
Rv	13	5	(Dn 7 8) the beast was allowed to *mouth* its boasts
		11	a second beast . . . it had two horns . . . but *made a noise* like a dragon.
		15	the statue of the beast was able to *speak*,

2. SAY – SPEAK, TELL – WORD: *LEGŌ*

1	*legō*	2082/2365
2	*legō + apokrinomai*	147
8	*logion*	4
10	*logios*	1
3	*logos*	318/334
11	(aischro-)*logia*	1
12	batta-*logeō*	1
13	(chrēsto-)*logia*	1
7	*dia-lektos*	6
5	*dia-legomai*	13
9	*dia-logismos*	4/14
6	*dia-logizomai*	9/16
14	*logo(-macheō)*	1
15	*logo(-machia)*	1
16	(mataio-)*logia*	1
17	(mataio-)*logos*	1
18	(mōro-)*logia*	1
19	(pithanō-)*logia*	1
20	(poly-)*logia*	1
4	(pro-)*legō*	15
21	*syl-logizomai*	1
22	*rhēma*	58/67
23	*rhētōr*	1
24	*a-rrhētos*	1
25	*epos*	1

1: (GOD) SAYS, SPEAKS, TELLS – (THE) WORDS (OF GOD)

[a] (God) Says, Speaks – (the) Words (of God)

Mt	3	17	a voice *spoke* from heaven, 'This is my Son, the Beloved;
	4	4	22 Man [lives] on every *word* that comes from the mouth of God (cf. Dt 8 3).
	17	5	from the cloud there came a voice which *said*, 'This is my Son,
	22	44	(Ps 110 1) The Lord *said* to my Lord: Sit at my right hand
Mk	12	26	God *spoke* to [Moses] and *said*: I am the God of Abraham,
		36	(Ps 110 1) The Lord *said* to my Lord: Sit at my right hand
Lk	2	29	Master, you can let your servant go in peace, just as you ┌promised (lit. gave your *word*);
		22	
	3	2	22 the *word* of God came to John son of Zechariah,
	9	35	a voice came from the cloud *saying*, 'This is my Son, the Chosen One.
	11	49	the Wisdom of God *said*, 'I will send them prophets
	12	20	God *said* to him, 'Fool! This very night the demand will be made for your soul;
	20	42	(Ps 110 1) The Lord *said* to my Lord: Sit at my right hand
Jn	1	33	he who sent me to baptise with water had *said* to me,
	3	34	22 he whom God has sent speaks God's own *words*:
	8	47	22 A child of God listens to the *words* of God:

Jn	10	34	Is it not written in your Law (Ps 82 6): I *said*, You are gods?
	12	50	what the Father has *told* me to speak is what I speak.
	17	8	22 I have given them the ┌teaching (lit. *words*) you gave to me,
Ac	2	17	In the days to come – it is the Lord who *speaks* (Jl 3 1) – I will pour out my spirit
		34	(Ps 110 1) The Lord *said* to my Lord: Sit at my right hand
	7	3	[God] *said* to [Abraham] (Gn 12 1), 'Leave your country
		7	'I will pass judgement on the nation that enslaves them' God *said* (Gn 15 14)
		33	The Lord *said* to [Moses] (Ex 3 5), 'Take off your shoes;
		38	8 it was [Moses] who was entrusted with *words* of life to hand on to ᵛ us (G you).
		49	With heaven my throne and earth my footstool, what house could you build me – it is the Lord who *speaks* (Is 66 2) – . . . ?
	13	22	of [David, God] approved *in* these *words*, 'I have selected David (cf. 1 S 13 14; Ps 89 21; Is 44 28)
		34	that God raised him from the dead . . . is no more than what he had *declared* (Is 55 3):
	15	17	Then the rest of mankind . . . will look for the Lord, *says* the Lord (Am 9 12)
Rm	3	2	8 the Jews are the people to whom God's ┌*message* was (or: 8 *oracles* were) entrusted.
		4	3 (Ps 51 6) In all you *say* your justice shows,
	9	6	Does this mean that God has failed to keep his ┌promise 3 (lit. *word*)?
		12	Rebecca was *told*: the elder shall serve the younger, (Gn 25 23)
		15	God *said* to Moses (Ex 33 19): I have mercy on whom I will,
		26	(Ho 2 1) Instead of being *told*, 'You are no people of mine',
		28	3 the Lord will execute his *sentence* on the earth (cf. Is 10 23 G).
	11	4	What did God *say* to that? (1 K 19 18)
	12	19	vengeance is mine – I will pay them back, the Lord ┌promises (lit. *says*) (Dt 32 35).
	14	11	By my life – it is the Lord who *speaks* (Is 45 23) – every knee shall bend before me,
2 Co	4	6	It is the same God that *said* (cf Gn 1 3), 'Let there be light
	6	16	We have God's *word* for it (Lv 26 11–12; Ex 37 27): I will make my home among them
		17	come away from them and keep aloof, *says* the Lord (Is 52 11).
		18	I will welcome you and be your father . . . *says* the Almighty Lord (2 S 7 14; Is 43 6; Jr 31 9).
Ga	3	16	the promises were *addressed* to Abraham and to his descendants
1 Tm	4	5	3 the *word* of God and the prayer make [food] holy.
Heb	1	5	God has never *said* to any angel: You are my Son (Ps 2 7),
		6	he *says* (Dt 32 43 G; Ps 97 7): Let all the angels of God worship him.
		7	About the angels, he *says*: (Ps 104 4)
		13	God has never *said* to any angel: (Ps 110 1)
	3	10	(Ps 95 10) I was angry with that generation and *said*: How unreliable
	4	2	3 hearing the ┌message (or: *word*) did them no good because they did not share the faith
		12	3 The *word* of God is something alive and active:
	5	6	[Christ was given glory by the one who] *said* also: (Ps 110 4)
	6	14	[God] swore by his own self . . . *saying*: (Gn 22 17)
	7	21	the one who *declared* to him (Ps 110 4): The Lord has sworn an oath
	8	8	God does find fault . . . he *says* (Jr 31 31): See, the days are coming – it is the Lord who *speaks* –
		9	(Jr 31 32) and so I on my side deserted them. It is the Lord who *speaks*.
		10	(Jr 31 33) this is the covenant I will make . . . when those days arrive – it is the Lord who *speaks*.
		13	By *speaking* of a new covenant, he implies that the first one is [old].
	10	16	the Lord then goes on to *say*: (Jr 31 33)
		30	We are all aware who it was that *said* (Dt 32 35): Vengeance is mine;
	11	3	22 the world was created by one *word* from God,
	12	19	[What you have come to is not] the great voice ┌speaking 22 which (lit. whose *words*) made everyone that heard it beg 3 that no more *words* should be said to them.
		26	now he has given us this promise, *saying*: (Hg 2 6)
	13	5	God himself has *said* (Dt 31 6): I will not fail you
1 P	4	11	8 If you are a speaker, speak in ┌*words* (or: *oracles*) which seem to come from God;
2 P	3	5	3 the earth was formed by the *word* of God
		7	3 by the same *word*, the present sky and earth are destined for fire,
Rv	1	8	'I am the Alpha and the Omega' *says* the Lord God,
	17	17	3 until the time when God's *words* should be fulfilled.
	19	9	3 All the things you have written are true ┌*messages* (or: 3 *words*) from God.
	21	5	Then the One sitting on the throne *spoke*: 'Now I am making the whole of creation new' he *said*. . . . ⁶ And then he *said*, 'It is already done.
		6	

b) (The Spirit) Says, Tells

Ac	8	29	The Spirit *said* to Philip, 'Go up and meet that chariot.'

Ac 10	19	the Spirit had to *tell* [Peter], 'Some men have come to see you.
11	12	the Spirit *told* me to have no hesitation about going back with them.
13	2	the Holy Spirit *said*, 'I want Barnabas and Saul set apart
20	23	the Holy Spirit . . . has made it clear enough by *saying* that imprisonment and persecution await me.
21	11	[Agabus] tied up his own feet and hands, and said, 'This is what the Holy Spirit *says*,
1 Tm 4	1	The Spirit has explicitly *said* that . . . there will be some who desert the faith
Rv 2	7	If anyone has ears to hear, let him listen to what the Spirit is *saying* to the churches:
		Repeated at 2 11, 17, 29; 3 6, 13, 22.
14	13	Happy indeed, the Spirit *says*; now they can rest for ever
22	17	The Spirit and the Bride *say*, 'Come'.

c) (Voices from/in heaven) Say, Speak, Tell – Shout – Words

Ac 11	7	I heard a voice that *said* to me, 'Now, Peter; kill and eat!'
2 Co 12	4	[I know a man who] was caught up into paradise and heard
	22	ʳthings (or: *words*) which must not . . . be put into human language.
Rv 1	3	3 Happy the man who reads these *words* of prophecy, and happy those who listen to him,
4	1	[I] heard the same voice speaking to me, the voice like a trumpet, *saying*, 'Come up here;
5	5	one of the elders *said* to me, 'There is no need to cry:
6	1	I heard one of the four animals *shout* in a voice like thunder, 'Come'.
	3	I heard the second animal *shout*, 'Come'.
	5	I heard the third animal *shout*, 'Come'.
	6	I seemed to hear a voice [shout] from among the four animals [and] *say*, 'A ration of corn
	7	I heard the voice of the fourth animal *shout*, 'Come'.
	11	[the souls of the martyrs] were *told* to be patient a little longer,
7	13	One of the elders then *spoke*, ʳand asked (lit. *replying* to) me,
	14	he *said*, 'these are the people who have been through the great persecution
9	4	[the locusts] were ʳforbidden (lit. *told* not) to harm any fields
	14	[the voice from the four horns of the altar] *spoke* to the sixth angel
10	4	I heard a voice from heaven *say* to me, 'Keep the words of the seven thunderclaps secret
	8	I heard the voice I had heard from heaven . . . 'Go', it *said*
	11	Then I was *told*, 'You are to prophesy again,
11	1	I was given a long cane . . . and I was *told*, 'Go and measure
	12	they heard a loud voice from heaven *say* to them, 'Come up here,'
	15	voices could be heard shouting in heaven, *calling*,
12	10	Then I heard a *shout* from heaven, 'Victory and power
14	13	Then I heard a voice from heaven *say* to me, 'Write down:
16	1	I heard a voice from the sanctuary *shouting* to the seven angels,
	17	a voice *shouted* from the sanctuary, 'The end has come'.
18	4	I heard [a new voice] *say*, 'Come out, my people, away
19	5	a voice came from the throne; it *said*, 'Praise our God,
21	3	I heard a loud voice *call* from the throne, 'You see this city?
	5	3 Write this: that *what* I am *saying* is sure and will come true.
22	6	3 ʳAll that you have written is (lit. These *words* are) sure and will come true.
	7	3 Happy are those who treasure the prophetic ʳmessage (or: 3 *words*) of this book.
	9	I am a servant just . . . like those who treasure ʳwhat you 3 have written (lit. the *words*) in this book.
	10	3 Do not keep the ʳprophecies (lit. prophetic *words*) . . . secret,
	18	3 to all who hear the ʳprophecies (lit. prophetic *words*) in this book:
	19	if anyone cuts anything out of the ʳprophecies (lit. prophetic 3 *words*) in this book,

d) (Scriptures, the Prophets) Say, Speak, Tell – Word(s) spoken

Mt 1	22	to fulfil the *words spoken* by the Lord through the prophet (Is 7 14), *saying*: The virgin will conceive
2	15	to fulfil what the Lord *had spoken* through the prophet (Ho 11 1), *saying*: I called my son out of Egypt.
	17	It was then that the *words spoken* through the prophet Jeremiah were fulfilled, when he *said*: A voice was heard in Ramah,
	23	In this way the *words spoken* through the prophets were to be fulfilled: He will be called a Nazarene.
3	3	This was the man the prophet Isaiah *spoke* of (Is 40 3) when he *said*: A voice cries in the wilderness:
4	14	In this way the ʳprophecy of Isaiah was (lit. *words spoken* by Isaiah were) to be fulfilled, when he *said* (Is 8 23 – 9 1): Land of Zebulun!
5	21	it was *said* to our ancestors (Ex 20 13): You must not kill;

Mt 5	27	it was *said* (Ex 20 14): You must not commit adultery.
	31	It has also been *said* (cf. Dt 24 1): Anyone who divorces his wife
	33	it was *said* to our ancestors (Ex 20 7): You must not break your oath.
	38	it was *said* (Ex 21 24): Eye for eye and tooth for tooth.
	43	it was *said* (Lv 19 18): You must love your neighbour
8	17	to fulfil the ʳprophecy of (lit. *words spoken* by) Isaiah, when he *said* (Is 53 4): He took our sickness away
12	17	to fulfil the ʳprophecy of (lit. *words spoken* by) Isaiah, when he *said* (Is 42 1–4): Here is my servant
13	14	in their case this prophecy of Isaiah (Is 6 9f) is being fulfilled where it *says*: You will listen and listen again,
	35	to fulfil the ʳprophecy (lit. *words spoken* by the prophet, when he *said*) (Ps 78 2): I will speak to you in parables
15	4	God *said* (Ex 20 12): Do your duty to your father and mother
	6	3 you have made God's ʳword (ᵛ law) null and void by means of your tradition.
	7	It was you Isaiah ʳmeant (lit. was *speaking* of) when he so rightly prophesied (Is 29 13): This people honours me only with lip-service,
19	5	[the creator] *said* (Gn 2 24): . . . a man must leave father and mother,
21	4	to fulfil the ʳprophecy (lit. *words spoken* by the prophet, when he *said*) (Zc 9 9): Say to the daughter of Zion:
22	24	Moses *said* (Dt 25 5–6) that if a man dies childless,
	31	read ʳwhat (lit. the *words*) God himself *said* (Ex 3 6) to you: I am the God of Abraham,
	43	David, moved by the Spirit, calls him Lord, where he *says*: (Ps 110 1)
24	15	the disastrous abomination, of which the prophet Daniel *spoke* (Dn 9 27; 11 31; 12 11),
27	9	The *words* of the prophet Jeremiah were then fulfilled, when he *said* (Jr 19 12–13; cf. Jr 19 1; 32 7–9): And they took the thirty silver pieces,
Mk 7	10	Moses *said* (Ex 20 12): Do your duty to your father and your mother,
	13	3 you make God's *word* null and void for the sake of your tradition
12	36	David himself, moved by the Holy Spirit, *said*: (Ps 110 1)
15	28	(ᵛ And the scripture was fulfilled where it *says* (Is 53 12): And he was reckoned among criminals.)
Lk 2	24	sacrifice, in accordance with what is *said* in the Law of the Lord, (Lv 12 8)
3	4	3 it is written in the book of the *sayings* of the prophet Isaiah: (Is 40 3–5)
4	12	It has been *said* (Dt 6 16): You must not put the Lord . . . to the test.
20	42	David himself *says* in the Book of Psalms: (Ps 110 1)
Jn 1	23	I am, as Isaiah ʳprophesied (lit. the prophet *said*) (Is 40 3): a voice that cries in the wilderness:
7	38	As scripture *says* (? Is 48 21), From his breast shall flow fountains
	42	Does not scripture *say* (cf. 2 S 7 12; Ps 89 4–5; Mi 5 1) that the Christ must be descended from David . . .?
10	35	the Law *uses the word* gods of those to whom the word of God was addressed,
12	38	3/ to fulfil the *words* of the prophet Isaiah when he *said* (Is 53 1): Lord, who could believe
	39	as Isaiah *says* again (cf. Is 6 9–10): He has blinded their eyes,
	41	Isaiah *said* this when he saw his glory (Is 6 4),
15	25	3 to fulfil the *words* written in their Law (Ps 35 19): They hated me
19	24	In this way [the words of] scripture were fulfilled (ᵛ where it *says*) (Ps 22 19): They shared out my clothing
	37	in another place (Zc 12 10) scripture *says*: They will look on the one
Ac 2	16	this is what the prophet (§ Joel) *spoke* of (Jl 3 1): . . . I will pour out my spirit
	25	David *says* of him (Ps 16 8–11): I saw the Lord before me always,
	34	these *words* are [David's] (Ps 110 1). The Lord said to my Lord:
3	22	Moses, for example, *said* (Dt 18 15): The Lord God will raise up a prophet
4	25	you it is who *said* through the Holy Spirit and . . . David, your servant (Ps 2 1–2): Why this arrogance among the nations . . .?
7	37	Moses . . . *told* the sons of Israel (Dt 18 15), 'God will raise up a prophet
	48	as the prophet *says*: (Is 66 1–2)
8	34	is the prophet (Is 53 7–8) *referring* to himself or someone else?
13	35	ʳThis is explained by another text (lit. Which is why [scripture] (Ps 16 10) also *says*): You will not allow your holy one to experience corruption.
	40	be careful – or what the prophets *say* (Hab 1 5) will happen to you.
15	15	3 the *words* of the prophets, since the scriptures [*say*] (Am 9 11–12): After that I shall return

Ac 28 25   [the Holy Spirit] *told* your ancestors through the prophet Isaiah: (Is 6 9–10)

Rm 3 19   all this that the Law *says* is said . . . for the benefit of those who are subject to the Law,

     4 3   scripture *says* (Gn 15 6): Abraham put his faith in God,

       6   David *says* the same: (Ps 32 1–2)

      18   as [Abraham] had been ⌐promised (lit. *told*) (Gn 15 5): Your descendants will be as many

     7 7   if the Law had not *said* (Ex 20 17) You shall not covet.

     9 9   3   The actual *words* in which the promise was made (Gn 18 10) were: I shall visit you

      17   in scripture (Ex 9 16) [God] *says* to Pharaoh: It was for this

      25   That is exactly what God *says* in Hosea (Ho 2 1): I shall say to a people

   10 11   scripture (Is 28 16 G) *says*: those who believe in him

     16   Isaiah *says* (Is 53 1): Lord, how many believed what we proclaimed?

     19   Moses *answered* this long ago (Dt 32 21): I will make you jealous

     20   Isaiah *said* more clearly (Is 65 1): I have been found by those who did not seek me,

     21   he ⌐goes on (lit. *says*) (Is 65 2): Each day I stretched out my hand

   11 2   Do you remember what scripture *says* of Elijah – how he complained

     9   David *says* (Ps 69 23–24): May their own table prove a trap

   13 9   All the commandments . . . are summed up in this single
        3   ⌐command (lit. *saying*) (Lv 19 18): You must love your neighbour as yourself.

   15 10   And [scripture] *says* in another place (Dt 32 43): Rejoice, pagans,

     12   Isaiah too has this to *say* (Is 11 10 G): The root of Jesse will appear,

1 Co 9 8   does not the Law itself *say* the same thing? (Dt 25 4)

     10   is there not an obvious *reference* to ourselves?

   14 21   I shall talk to the nation, and still they will not listen to me, *says* the Lord (Is 28 11).

     34   [women] must keep in the background as the Law itself *lays down* (cf. Gn 3 16).

   15 27   when it is *said* (Ps 110 1) that everything is subjected,

     54   3   the *words* of scripture (cf. Is 25 8; Ho 13 14) will come true: Death is swallowed up in victory.

2 Co 6 2   [God] *says* (Is 49 8): At the favourable time, I have listened to you;

Ga 3 16   scripture does not *use a* plural *word* as if there were several descendants,

     4 30   Does not scripture (Gn 21 10) *say*: Drive away that slave-girl

     5 14   the whole of the Law is summarised in a single ⌐command
        3   (lit. *saying*) (Lv 19 18): Love your neighbour as yourself.

Ep 4 8   It was *said* (Ps 68 19 G) that [Christ] would [give] gifts to men.

1Tm 5 18   scripture (Dt 25 4) *says*: You must not muzzle an ox

Heb 2 6   there is a passage that shows us this. It (Ps 8 5–7 G) ⌐runs (lit. *says*): What is man

     3 7   The Holy Spirit *says* (Ps 95 7, 11): If only you would listen to him

     15   In this *saying* (Ps 95 7): If only you would listen to him

     4 3   as ⌐in the text (lit. has been *said*) (Ps 95 11): And so, in anger, I swore

      4   as one text (Gn 2 2) *says*, referring to the seventh day:

      7   much later, [God] *said* 'today' through David in the text (Ps 95 7)

     7 13   our Lord, of whom these things were *said*, belonged to a different tribe,

     28   3   the ⌐promise (lit. *word* [given]) on oath . . . appointed the Son

   10 15   The Holy Spirit . . . *says* (Jr 31 33–34), first: This is the covenant

Jm 2 11   It was the same person who *said* (Ex 20 14), 'You must not commit adultery' that also *said* (Ex 20 13) 'You must not kill'.

     23   scripture (Gn 15 6) . . . *says*: Abraham put his faith in God,

     4 5   you don't think scripture is wrong when it *says*: the spirit which he sent . . . wants us for himself alone?

      6   as scripture (Pr 3 34) *says*: God opposes the proud

2 P 1 19   3   we have confirmation of *what was said* in prophecies;

     3 2   [a reminder] recalling to you ⌐what was said in the past (lit.
      22   the *words* of prediction *spoken*) by the holy prophets

Jude 14 Δ   It was with them in mind that Enoch . . . *said*, 'I tell you, the Lord will come

e) the Word (of the Kingdom = the Gospel) Message

Mt 13 19   3   When anyone hears the *word* of the kingdom without understanding,

     20   3   the man who hears the *word* and welcomes it at once

     21   3   let some trial come . . . on account of the *word*, and he falls away

     22   3   the man who hears the *word*, but the worries of this world
        3   . . . choke the *word* and so he produces nothing.

Mt 13 23   3   the man who hears the *word* and understands it;

Mk 2 2   3   [Jesus] was preaching the *word* to them

     4 14   3   What the sower is sowing is the *word*. ¹⁵ Those on the edge of
     15   3   the path where the *word* is sown . . . Satan comes and
        3   carries away the *word* that was sown in them.

     16   3   people who, when they first hear the *word*, welcome it at once

     17   3   should some trial come . . . on account of the *word*, they fall away

     18   3   These have heard the *word*, ¹⁹ but the worries of this world
     19   3   . . . choke the *word*, and so it produces nothing.

     20   3   they hear the *word* and accept it and yield a harvest,

     33   3   Using many parables like these, [Jesus] spoke the *word* to them,

   16 20   3   the Lord . . . confirming the *word* by the signs that accompanied it.

Lk 1 2   3   those who from the outset were eyewitnesses and ministers of the *word*,

     5 1   3   the crowd pressing round him listening to the *word* of God,

     8 11   3   the seed is the *word* of God.

     12   3   the devil comes and carries away the *word* from their hearts

     13   3   people who, when they first hear it, welcome the *word* with joy.

     15   3   people . . . who have heard the *word* and take it to themselves

     21   3   My mother and my brothers are those who hear the *word* of God

   11 28   3   Still happier those who hear the *word* of God and keep it!

Jn 5 38   3   you have never seen his shape, and his *word* finds no home in you

     8 55   3   But I do know him, and I faithfully keep his *word*.

   10 35   3   those to whom the *word* of God was addressed,

   14 24   3   ᵛ my (G the) *word* (§ that you are listening to) is not my own: it is [the word] of the one who sent me.

   17 6   3   you gave them to me, and they have kept your *word*.

     14   3   I passed your *word* on to them,

     17   3   your *word* is truth.

Ac 4 4   3   many of those who had listened to their *message* became believers,

     29   3   help your servants to proclaim your *message* with all boldness.

     31   3   all [the apostles] began to proclaim the *word* of God boldly.

     6 2   3   It would not be right for us to neglect the *word* of God

      4   3   [we will] devote ourselves . . . to the service of the *word*.

      7   3   The *word* of the Lord continued to spread:

     8 4   3   Those who had escaped went . . . preaching the *message* of the Good News.

     14   3   Samaria had accepted the *word* of God,

     25   3   Having . . . proclaimed the *word* of the Lord, they went back

   10 36   3   It is true, God sent his *word* to the people of Israel,

     44   3   the Holy Spirit came down on all ⌐the listeners (lit. those listening to the *word*).

   11 1   3   the pagans too had accepted the *word* of God,

     19   3   they usually proclaimed the *message* only to Jews.

   12 24   3   The *word* of God (G the Lord) continued to spread

   13 5   3   [Barnabas and Paul] landed at Salamis and proclaimed the *word* of God

      7   3   The proconsul . . . asked to hear the *word* of God,

     26   3   this *message* of salvation is meant for you.

     44   3   almost the whole town assembled to hear the *word* of God.

     46   3   We had to proclaim the *word* of God to you first,

     48   3   the pagans . . . thanked the Lord for his *message*;

     49   3   Thus the *word* of the Lord spread through the whole countryside.

   14 3   3   the Lord supported ⌐all they said about (lit. their *message* of) his gift of grace,

     25   3   after proclaiming the *word* at Perga they went down to Attalia

   15 7   3   the pagans were to learn the *message* of the Good News from me

     35   3   Paul and Barnabas . . . proclaimed . . . the *word* of the Lord.

     36   Let us go back and visit all the towns where we preached
        3   the *word*

   16 6   3   having been told by the Holy Spirit not to preach the *word* in Asia.

     32   3   they preached the *word* of the Lord to [the gaoler]

   17 11   3   Here [at Beroea] the Jews . . . welcomed the *word* very readily;

     13   3   the *word* of God was being preached by Paul in Beroea as well,

   18 5   3   Paul devoted all his time to ⌐preaching (lit. the *word*),

     11   3   Paul stayed there preaching the *word* of God . . . for eighteen months.

   19 10   3   both Jews and Greeks were able to hear the *word* of the Lord.

     20   3   In this impressive way the *word* of the Lord spread more and more

   20 32   3   I commend you to God, and to the *word* of his grace,

1 Co 14 36   3   Do you think the *word* of God came out of yourselves?

2 Co 2 17   3   At least we do not go round offering the *word* of God for sale,

     4 2   3   no deceitfulness or watering down the *word* of God;

2 Co	5 19	3	God . . . has entrusted to us the ᶜnews (lit. *message*) that they are reconciled.
	6 7	3	[we are God's servants] by the *word* of truth and by the power of God;
Ga	6 6	3	People under instruction in the *word* should always contribute
Ep	1 13	3	Now you too, in him, have heard the *message* of the truth
	6 17	22	receive the *word* of God from the Spirit to use as a sword.
Ph	1 14	3	the brothers . . . are getting more and more daring in announcing the *Message* (§ of God)
	2 16	3	you are offering [the world] the *word* of life.
Col	1 5	3	you heard of this . . . announced in the *message* of the truth.
	25	3	God made me responsible for delivering God's *message* to you,
1 Th	1 6	3	it was with the joy of the Holy Spirit that you took to the ᶜgospel (lit. *word*),
	8	3	it was from you that the *word* of the Lord started to spread
	2 13	3	as soon as you heard the *message* that we brought as God's [message], you accepted it for what it really is, God's *message*
	4 15	3	We can tell you this from the Lord's own ᶜteaching (lit. *word*),
2 Th	3 1	3	pray that the Lord's *message* may spread quickly.
2 Tm	2 9	3	they cannot chain up God's ᶜnews (lit. *message*).
	15	3	[a man who] has kept a straight course with the *message* of the truth.
	4 2	3	proclaim the *message* and, welcome or unwelcome, insist on it.
Tt	1 3	3	at the appointed time, [God] revealed his ᶜdecision (lit. *word*),
	2 5	3	so that the *message* of God is never disgraced.
Heb	5 13	3	anyone who is still living on milk cannot digest the ᶜdoctrine (lit. *word*) of righteousness
	6 1	3	Let us leave behind . . . all the elementary ᶜteaching (lit. *message*) about Christ and concentrate on its completion,
	5	22	[those people who have] appreciated the good *message* of God
	13 7	3	Remember your leaders, who preached the *word* of God to you,
Jm	1 18	3	[God] made us his children by the *message* of the truth
	21	3	accept and submit to the *word* which has been planted in you
	22	3	you must do what the *word* tells you, and not just listen
	23	3	To listen to the *word* and not obey is like looking at your own features in a mirror
1 P	1 23	3	your new birth was . . . from the everlasting *word*
	25	22	(Is 40 8) the *word* of the Lord remains for ever. What is this
		22	*word*? It is the Good News
	2 8	3	[unbelievers] stumble . . . because they do not believe in the *word*;
	3 1	3	if there are some husbands who have not yet obeyed the *word*,
1 Jn	1 10	3	To say that we have never sinned is . . . to show that his *word* is not in us.
	2 5	3	when anyone does ᶜobey what he has said (lit. keep his *word*), God's love comes to perfection in him.
	14	3	young men, . . . God's *word* has made its home in you,
Rv	1 2	3	John . . . swears it is the *word* of God guaranteed by Jesus Christ;
	9	3	I was on the island of Patmos for having preached God's *word*
	6 9	3	all the people who had been killed on account of the *word* of God,
	20 4	3	the souls of all who had been beheaded . . . for having preached God's *word*,

f) Not to be said, Unutterable

2 Co	12 4	24	[I know a man in Christ who] heard things *which must not be said* and cannot be put into human language.

2: (AN ANGEL, A DEVIL) SAYS, TELLS – WORDS

a) (an Angel) Says, Tells, Calls – Words

Mt	1 20		the angel of the Lord appeared to [Joseph] in a dream and *said*,
	2 13		the angel of the Lord appeared to Joseph in a dream and *said*, 'Get up, . . . escape into Egypt and stay there until I *tell* you,
	20		[the angel] *said*, 'Get up, . . . go back to the land of Israel,
	28 5	2	the angel *spoke*; and he *said* to the women, 'There is no need for [fear].
	7		He has risen from the dead . . . Now I have *told* you.
Mk	16 6		he *said* to them, 'There is no need for alarm.
Lk	1 13		the angel *said* to him, 'Zechariah, do not be afraid,
	19	2	The angel ᶜreplied (lit. *said* in *reply*), 'I am Gabriel . . .
	20	3	²⁰ Listen! Since you have not believed my *words* . . . you will be silenced
	28		[Gabriel] went in and *said* to [Mary], 'Rejoice, so highly favoured!
	29	3	She was deeply disturbed by these *words*
	30		the angel *said* to her, 'Mary, do not be afraid;

Lk	1 35		'The Holy Spirit will come upon you' the angel ᶜanswered (lit. *said* in *answer*)
	38	22	[Mary said], 'Let *what you have said* be done to me.'
	2 10		the angel *said* [to the shepherds], 'Do not be afraid.
	13		suddenly . . . there was a great throng of the heavenly host, praising God and ᶜsinging (or: *saying*):
	17	22	When they saw the child they repeated ᶜwhat (G the *message*) they had been told about him,
	24 5		the two men *said* to [the women], 'Why look among the dead
	23		they had seen a vision of angels who *declared* [Jesus] was alive.
Jn	20 13		[The two angels] *said*, 'Woman, why are you weeping?
Ac	1 11		[The two men in white] *said*, 'Why are you . . . looking into the sky?
	5 19		the angel of the Lord opened the prison gates and *said* as he led [the apostles] out,
	8 26		The angel of the Lord spoke to Philip *saying*, ' . . . set out at noon
	10 3		he distinctly saw the angel of God come into his house and *call out* to him 'Cornelius!' ⁴ . . . 'Your offering of prayers and alms' the angel *answered* 'has been accepted
	11 13		he had seen an angel . . . who *said*, 'Send to Jaffa and fetch Simon
	12 7		'Get up!' [the angel] *said* 'Hurry!'
	8		The angel then *said* 'Put on your belt and sandals.' After he had done this, the angel next *said*, 'Wrap your cloak round you
	27 24		[the angel] *said*, 'Do not be afraid, Paul.
Heb	2 2	3	If ᶜa promise that was made through (lit. the *word* given by) angels proved to be so true
Jude	9		all [the archangel Michael] *said* was, 'Let the Lord correct you.'
Rv	5 12		[an immense number of angels] ᶜshouting (lit. *saying* in a loud voice), 'The Lamb that was sacrificed is worthy
	7 2		[the angel carrying God's seal] *called* in a powerful voice to the four angels
	12		All the angels . . . prostrated themselves . . . worshipping God with these *words*, 'Amen.
	10 9		I asked [the angel] to give me the small scroll, and he *said*, 'Take it and eat it;
	14 7		[The angel sent to announce the Good News of eternity] was *calling* in a loud voice, 'Fear God and praise him,
	8		A second angel followed him, *calling* in a loud voice, 'Babylon has fallen,
	9		A third angel followed, *shouting* aloud, 'All those who worship the beast
	18		the angel in charge . . . shouted aloud to the one with the sharp sickle, *saying*: 'Put your sickle in
	16 5		I heard the angel of water *say*, 'You are the holy He-Is-and-He-Was,
	17 1		One of the seven angels . . . came to speak to me, and *said*, 'Come
	7		The angel *said* to me, 'Don't you understand? Now I will *tell* you the meaning of this woman,
	15		The angel ᶜcontinued (lit. then *said*), 'The waters you saw,
	18 2		At the top of his voice he shouted these *words*, 'Babylon has fallen,
	21		as [the powerful angel] hurled [the boulder] into the sea, he *said*,
	19 9		The angel *said*, 'Write this: . . .', and he ᶜadded (lit. also *said*), 'All the things you have written are true
	10		he *said* to me, 'Don't do that: I am a servant just like you
	17		I saw an angel . . . and he shouted aloud, *saying* to all the birds
	21 9		One of the seven angels . . . came to speak to me, and *said*, 'Come
	22 6		The angel *said* to me, 'All that you have written is sure
	9		he *said*, 'Don't do that: I am a servant just like you
	10		This, too, he *said* to me, 'Do not keep the prophecies . . . secret,

b) (Devils, the Devil, Unclean spirits) Say

X = Say to Jesus

Mt	4 3	X	the tempter came and *said* to him, 'If you are the Son of God,
	6	X	'If you are the Son of God' he *said*, 'throw yourself down;
	9	X	'I will give you all these' he *said* 'if you fall at my feet
	8 31	X	the devils pleaded with Jesus, *saying*: 'If you cast us out,
	12 44		Then [the unclean spirit] *says*, 'I will return to the home I came from'.
Mk	3 11	X	the unclean spirits . . . would fall down before him and shout (§ *saying*), 'You are the Son of God!'
	5 9	X	'My name is legion,' [the unclean spirit] *answered*,
	12	X	the unclean spirits begged him, *saying*: 'Send us to the pigs,
Lk	4 3	X	the devil *said* to him, 'If you are the Son of God
	6	X	[the devil] *said* to him, 'I will give you all this power
	9	X	'If you are the Son of God,' he *said* to him, 'throw yourself down
	41	X	Devils too came out of many people, howling and *saying* 'You are the Son of God.'

Lk 11 24   not finding [a place to rest, the unclean spirit] *says*, 'I will go back to the home I came from.'
Ac 19 15   2 The evil spirit ⌐replied (lit. *said* in reply), 'Jesus I recognise,

3: (JESUS) SAYS, TELLS, SPEAKS – WORD(S), MESSAGE

J = Jesus (= *Iēsous*) 223/923

a) the Word

Jn 1 1   3/3 In the beginning was the *Word*: the *Word* was with God and
    3   the *Word* was God.
    14   3 The *Word* was made flesh
1 Jn 1 1   3 the *Word* who is life – this is our subject.
Rv 19 13   3 He is known by the name, The *Word* of God.

b) (Jesus) Says, Speaks (to God his Father)

Mt 11 25 J   2 At that time, *Jesus exclaimed, saying*: 'I bless you, Father,
   26 39   he fell on his face and prayed. 'My Father,' he *said*,
     42   a second time he went away and prayed: 'My Father,' he *said*,
     44   /3 he went away again and prayed . . . *repeating* the same *words*.
   27 46 J   *Jesus* cried out in a loud voice (§ *saying*), 'Eli, Eli,
Mk 14 36   'Abba (Father)!' he *said*. 'Everything is possible for you.'
     39   /3 he went away and prayed, *saying the same words*.
Lk 10 21   filled with joy by the Holy Spirit, he *said*, 'I bless you, Father,
   22 42   'Father,' he *said*, 'if you are willing, take this cup away from me.
   23 34 J   *Jesus said*, 'Father, forgive them;
     46 J   when *Jesus* had cried out . . . he *said*, 'Father, into your hands I commit my spirit'. With these *words* he breathed his last.
Jn 11 41 J   *Jesus* lifted up his eyes and *said*: 'Father, I thank you . . .
     42   [42] . . . you always hear me, but I *speak* for the sake of all these
     43   When he had *said* this, he cried in a loud voice, 'Lazarus, here!'
   12 27   What shall I *say*? Father, save me from this hour?
   17 1   [he] raised his eyes to heaven and *said*: 'Father, the hour has come:
Heb 2 12   [he calls them brothers] ⌐in the text (lit. when he *says*): I shall announce your name to my brothers,
   10 5   this (Ps 40 7–9 G) is what he *said*, on coming into the world: 'You . . . wanted no sacrifice . . . [7] then I *said*, . . .
     7
     8   I am coming to obey your will.' [8] Notice that he *says* first:
     9   You did not want . . . sacrifices . . . ; [9] and then he *says*: Here I am! I am coming to obey your will.

c) (Jesus in heaven) Says, Replies (to a person) – Message

Mt 25 12 <   2 [the bridegroom] ⌐replied (lit. *said* in reply), 'I tell you solemnly, I do not know you.'
     34   the King will *say* to those on his right hand, 'Come, you whom my Father has blessed,
     40   2 the King will *say* in *answer*, 'I tell you . . . in so far as you did this
     41   Next he will *say* to those on his left hand, 'Go away from me,
     45   2 Then he will *say* in *answer*, 'I tell you . . . in so far as you neglected to do this
Lk 13 25   2 [the master of the house] will *say* in answer, 'I do not know [you].'
     27   he will *reply* (§ *saying*), 'I do not know where you come from.
Ac 9 4   he heard a voice *saying*, 'Saul, Saul, why are you persecuting me?'
     10   he heard the Lord *say* to him, 'Ananias!'
     15   The Lord *replied*, 'You must go all the same,
   18 9   the Lord *spoke* to Paul in a vision, 'Do not be afraid to speak out,
   22 7   I fell to the ground and heard a voice *saying*, 'Saul, Saul,
     8   he *said* to me, 'I am Jesus the Nazarene,
     10   The Lord *answered*, 'Stand up and go into Damascus,
     18   'Hurry,' he *said*, 'leave Jerusalem at once;
     21   Then he *said* to me, 'Go! I am sending you out to the pagans
   23 11   the Lord appeared to him and *said*, 'Courage!
   26 14   I heard a voice *saying* to me in Hebrew, 'Saul, Saul,
     15   the Lord *answered*, 'I am Jesus, and you are persecuting me.'
2 Co 12 9   the Lord has *said*, 'My grace is enough for you:
Heb 1 3   sustaining the universe by his powerful ⌐command (lit.
     22   *word*);
Rv 1 11   [a voice like a trumpet] which *said*, 'Write down all that you see in a book
     17   he touched me with his right hand and *said*, 'Do not be afraid; it is I,
   2 1   Here is the *message* of the one who holds the seven stars
     8   Here is the *message* of the First and Last, who was dead and has come to life again:
     12   Here is what *said* of the one who has the sharp sword, double-edged:
     18   Here is the *message* of the Son of God

Rv 2 24   [on all who have not] learnt the secrets of Satan, as they are called, to you I *say* I am not laying any special duty;
   3 1   Here is the *message* of the one who holds the seven spirits of God
     7   Here is the *message* of the holy and faithful one
     14   Here is the *message* of the Amen, the faithful, the true witness,
   18 4   I heard [a new voice] *say*, 'Come out, my people, away
   22 20   The one who guarantees these revelations ⌐repeats his promise (lit. *says*): I shall indeed be with you soon.

d) (Jesus while teaching) Says, Tells, Speaks, Talks – Word(s), Message

Mt 4 17 J   *Jesus* began his preaching with the *message*, 'Repent,
   7 24   3 everyone who listens to these *words* of mine and acts
     26   3 everyone who listens to these *words* of mine and does not act
     28 J   *Jesus* had now finished ⌐what he wanted to say (lit. his
     3   *message*).
   8 8   /3 just ⌐give (lit. *say*) the *word* and my servant will be cured.
     16   3 He cast out the spirits with a *word* and cured all
   9 5   which of these is easier: to *say*, 'Your sins are forgiven', or to *say*, 'Get up and walk'?
   10 27   What I *say* to you in the dark, tell in the daylight;
   11 7 J   *Jesus* began to *talk* to the people about John:
   15 12   3 the Pharisees were shocked when they heard *what* you *said*
     23   3 he answered [the Canaanite woman] not a *word*.
   16 11   I was not *talking* about bread [when I said]: Beware of the yeast
     12   they understood that he was *telling* them to be on their guard,
   17 13   The disciples understood then that he had been *speaking* of John
   19 1 J   *Jesus* had now finished ⌐what he wanted to say (lit. his
     3   *message*),
     11   3 It is not everyone who can accept *what* I have *said*
     22   3 when the young man heard these *words* he went away sad,
   20 21   ⌐Promise (lit. *Say*) that these two sons of mine may sit . . . in your kingdom.
   21 24   I will then *tell* you my authority for acting like this.
     25   If we say [John's baptism is] from heaven, he will *retort*,
     27   Nor will I *tell* you my authority for acting like this.
     45   the chief priests and the scribes realised he was *speaking* about them,
   22 1 J   2/ *Speaking* in reply, *Jesus* began to talk to them in parables once again.
     15   the Pharisees went away to work out . . . how to trap him in
     3   *what* he *said*.
     17   *Tell* us your opinion, then. Is it permissible to pay taxes . . ?
   24 3   *Tell* us, when is this going to happen . . ?
     35   3 Heaven and earth will pass away, but my *words* will never pass away.
   26 1 J   3 *Jesus* had now finished ⌐all he wanted to say (lit. his *message*), and he *told* his disciples, 'It will be Passover,
     18   The Master *says*: My time is near.
     63   *tell* us if you are the Christ, the Son of God.
     75 J   22/ Peter remembered ⌐what (lit. the *words*) *Jesus* had *said*, 'Before the cock crows
   27 43   he did *say*, 'I am the son of God.'
     63   this impostor *said*, while he was still alive, 'After three days I shall rise again.'
   28 6   he has risen, as he *said* he would.
Mk 2 9   Which of these is easier: to *say* to the paralytic, 'Your sins are forgiven' or to *say*, 'Get up, . . . and walk'?
   3 9   he ⌐asked (lit. *told*) his disciples to have a boat ready for him
     23   he called [the scribes] to him and *spoke* to them in parables
   4 2   in the course of his teaching he *said* to [the people], 'Listen!
   5 31   the crowd is pressing round you and yet you *say*, 'Who touched me?'
     43   [he] *told* them to give [the little girl] something to eat.
   8 7   he said a blessing and *ordered* [the fish] to be distributed also.
     32   3 he said ⌐all this (lit. these *words*) quite openly.
     38   3 if anyone . . . is ashamed of me and of my *words*,
   9 10   3 [Peter, James and John] observed the *warning* [not to tell anyone] faithfully,
     32   22 [the disciples] did not understand *what* he *said* and were afraid to ask him.
   10 22   3 [the rich young man's] face fell at these *words* and he went away sad,
     24   3 the disciples were astounded at these *words*.
     32   taking the Twelve aside he began to *tell* them what was going to happen
   11 6 J   [The two disciples] gave the answer *Jesus* had *told* them,
     39   answer me and I will *tell* you my authority for acting like this.
     31   If we say from heaven, he will *say*, 'Then why did you refuse to believe him?'
     33   Nor will I *tell* you my authority for acting like this.
   12 12   they realised that the parable was ⌐aimed (lit. *told*) at them,
     13   3 they sent to him some [men] to catch him out in *what* he *said*.
     32   what you have *said* is true: that [God] is one
     35 J   2 *Jesus* in reply *said*, 'How can the scribes maintain . . ?
     38   In his teaching he *said*, 'Beware of the scribes

Mk 13	4		*Tell* us, when is this going to happen,
	5	J	*Jesus* began to *tell* them, 'Take care that no one deceives you.
	31	3	Heaven and earth will pass away, but my *words* will not pass away.
	37		what I *say* to you I *say* to all: Stay awake!
14	14		The Master *says*: Where is my dining room . . ?
	16		the disciples . . . found everything as he had *told* them,
	58		We heard him *say*, 'I am going to destroy this Temple
	72	J 22/	Peter recalled ⌐how (lit. the *words*) *Jesus* had *said* to him, 'Before the cock crows
16	7		there you will see him, just as he *told* you.
Lk 2	50	22	[his parents] did not understand what he meant by his *words*.
4	22	3	[all] were astonished by the gracious *words* that came from his lips.
	32	3	he *spoke* with authority.
	36	3	What ⌐teaching (lit. a *message*)! He gives orders to unclean spirits
5	5	22	If you *say* so, I will pay out the nets.
	23		Which of these is easier: to *say*, 'Your sins are forgiven you' or to *say*, 'Get up and walk'?
	36		He also *told* them this parable, 'No one tears a piece from a new cloak
6	39		He also *told* a parable to them, 'Can one blind man guide another?
	46		Why do you call me, 'Lord, Lord' and not do what I *say*?
	47	3	Everyone who comes to me and listens to my *words* and acts on them
7	1	22	When he had come to the end of ⌐all (lit. the *words*) he wanted the people to hear,
	7	/3	⌐give (lit. *say*) the *word* and let my servant be cured.
	24		he began to *talk* to the people about John,
	40	J	*Jesus* ⌐took him up and (lit. in reply) *said*, 'Simon, I have something to *say* to you.' '*Speak*, Master,' was the reply.
8	4		With a large crowd gathering . . . he ⌐used (lit. *told*) this parable:
	8		*Saying* this he cried, 'Listen, anyone who has ears to hear!'
9	26	3	if anyone is ashamed of me and of my *words*,
	28	3	about eight days after *this* had been *said*,
	44	3	you must have these *words* constantly in your ⌐mind (lit. ears):
	45	22/22	they did not understand ⌐him when he said this (lit these *words*); . . . they were afraid to ask him about *what* he had just *said*.
10	39	3	Mary . . . sat down at the Lord's feet and listened to him *speaking*.
	40		Please *tell* her to help me.
11	27		as he was *speaking*, a woman in the crowd raised her voice
	45		Master, . . . when you *speak* like this you insult us too.
12	13		Master, *tell* my brother to give me a share of our inheritance.
	16		he *told* them a parable, *saying*: There was once a rich man
	41		Lord, ⌐do you mean (lit. are you *telling*) this parable for us
13	6		He *told* this parable: 'A man had a fig tree
	17		When he *said* this, all his adversaries were covered with confusion.
14	7		He then *told* the guests a parable . . . He *said* this, [8] 'When someone invites you to a wedding feast,
15	3		he *spoke* this parable to them (§ *saying*): [4] 'What man among you with a hundred sheep
18	1		he *told* them a parable about the need to pray . . . [2] 'There was a judge in a certain town' he *said*
	9		He *spoke* the following parable . . . [10] 'Two men went up to the Temple
	34	22	*what* he *said* was quite obscure to [the Twelve], they had no idea what ⌐it meant (lit. he meant when he *said* it).
19	11		he went on to *tell* a parable, because he was near Jerusalem
	12		Accordingly he *said*, 'A man of noble birth went to a distant country
	28		When he had *said* this he went on ahead, going up to Jerusalem.
	32		The messengers . . . found everything just as he had *told* them.
20	2		*Tell* us, . . . what authority have you for acting like this?
	5		If we say from heaven, he will *say*, 'Why did you refuse to believe him?'
	8		Nor will I *tell* you my authority for acting like this.
	9		he went on to *tell* the people this parable: 'A man planted a vineyard
	19		they realised that this parable was ⌐aimed (lit. *told*) at them.
	20	3	[they sent agents] to fasten on *something* he might *say*
	21		Master, we know that you *say* and teach what is right:
	26	22	they were unable to find fault with *anything* he had *to say* in public.
	39		Some scribes then spoke up. 'Well ⌐put (lit. *spoken*), Master'
21	29		he *told* them a parable, 'Think of the fig tree
	33	3	Heaven and earth will pass away, but my *words* will never pass away.
22	11		The Master has this to *say* to you: Where is the dining room
	13		They set off and found everything as he had *told* them,
	61	3/	Peter remembered ⌐what (lit. the *words*) the Lord had *said* to him, 'Before the cock crows

Lk 22	67		'If you are the Christ, *tell* us.' 'If I *tell* you,' he *replied*, 'you will not believe me,
24	8	22	And [the women from Galilee] remembered his *words*.
	19	3	Jesus of Nazareth . . . who proved he was a great prophet by the *things* he *said* and did in the sight of God
	40		(ᵛ And as he *said* this he showed them his hands and feet.)
	44	3	This is *what* I [meant when I] *said*, while I was still with you,
Jn 1	47	J	When *Jesus* saw Nathanael coming he *said* of him, 'There is an Israelite
	50	J 2	*Jesus* ⌐replied (lit. *said* in reply), 'You believe that just because I *said*: I saw you under the fig tree.
2	5		His mother said to the servants, 'Do whatever he *tells* you.'
	21		he was *speaking* of the sanctuary that was his body,
	22	J 3/	his disciples remembered that he had *said* this, and they believed the scripture and the *words Jesus* had *said*.
3	7		Do not be surprised when I *say*: You must be born from above.
	12		If you do not believe me when I *speak* about things in this world, how are you going to believe me when I *speak* to you about heavenly things?
4	10		If only you knew . . . who it is that is *saying* to you: Give me a drink,
	29		Come and see a man who has *told* me everything I ever did;
	39		she said, 'He *told* me all I have ever done,'
	41	3	when he *spoke* to them many more came to believe;
	50	J	'Go home,' *said Jesus*, 'your son will live.' The man believed
		J 3/	⌐what (lit. the *words*) *Jesus* had *said* and started on his way;
	53	J	this was exactly the time when *Jesus* had *said*, 'Your son will live';
5	11		the man who cured me *told* me, 'Pick up your mat and walk'.
	12		Who is the man who *said* to you, 'Pick up your mat and walk'?
	24	3	whoever listens to my *words*, and believes . . . has eternal life;
	34		it is for your salvation that I *speak* of this.
	47	22	if you refuse to believe what [Moses] wrote, how can you believe *what* I *say*?
6	6		He only *said* this to test Philip;
	36		as I have *told* you, you can see me and still you do not believe.
	41		he had *said*, 'I am the bread that came down from heaven'.
	42		How can he now *say*, 'I have come down from heaven'?
	59		He ⌐taught this doctrine (lit. *said* the same thing) at Capernaum, in the synagogue.
	60	3	This is intolerable *language*. How could anyone accept it?
	63	22	The *words* I have spoken to you are spirit and they are life.
	65		This is why I *told* you that no one could come to me
	68	22	Lord, who shall we go to? You have the *message* of eternal life,
	71		He ⌐meant (lit. was *speaking* of) Judas son of Simon Iscariot,
7	9		Having *said* that, he stayed behind in Galilee.
	36	3	What ⌐does he mean (lit. is the meaning of his *words*) when he *says*: 'You will look for me and will not find me:
	39		He was *speaking* of the Spirit which those who believed in him were to receive;
	40	3	Several people who had ⌐been listening (lit. heard these *words*) said, 'Surely he must be the prophet',
8	5		Moses has ordered us in the Law to condemn women like this to death by stoning. What have you to *say*?
	20	22	He spoke these *words* in the Treasury,
	22		Will he kill himself? Is that what he means by *saying*, 'Where I am going, you cannot come'?
	24		I have *told* you already: You will die in your sins.
	27		[The Jews] failed to understand that he was *talking* to them about the Father.
	31	3	If you make my *word* your home you will indeed be my disciples,
	33		⌐what do you mean (lit. how can you *say*), 'You will be made free?'
	37	3	you want to kill me because ⌐nothing I say has (lit. my *word* has not) penetrated into you.
	43	3	Do you know why you cannot take in *what* I *say*?
	45		I *speak* the truth and for that very reason, you do not believe me.
	46		If I *speak* the truth, why do you not believe me?
	51	3	whoever keeps my *word* will never see death.
	52	3	Abraham is dead, . . . and yet you *say*, 'Whoever keeps my *word* will never know the taste of death'.
	55		if I were to *say*: I do not know him, I should be a liar,
9	6		Having *said* this, he spat on the ground, made a paste with the spittle,
	11		The man called Jesus . . . daubed my eyes with [the paste] and *said* to me, 'Go and wash at Siloam';
10	6	J	*Jesus told* them this parable but they failed to understand
	19	3	These *words* caused disagreement among the Jews.
	21	22	These are not the *words* of a man possessed by a devil:
	24		If you are the Christ, *tell* us plainly.
	25		I have *told* you, but you do not believe
	36		you say . . ., 'You are blaspheming', because he *says*, 'I am the Son of God'.
11	11		He *said* that and then ⌐added (lit. *said* afterwards), 'Our friend Lazarus is resting,

Jn 11 13 J   The *phrase Jesus used* referred to the death of Lazarus, but they thought that by 'rest' he ˹meant (lit. was *speaking* of)˺ 'sleep', so ¹⁴ *Jesus* ˹put (lit. *said*)˺ it plainly, 'Lazarus is dead;

14 J

40 J   *Jesus replied* [to Martha], 'Have I not *told* you that if you believe you will see the glory of God?'

12 33   By these *words* he indicated the kind of death he would die.

34   How can you *say*, 'The Son of Man must be lifted up'?

44 J   *Jesus declared* publicly: 'Whoever believes in me believes . . . in the one who sent me,

47   22 If anyone hears my *words* and does not keep them faithfully, it is not I who shall condemn him,

48   22 he who rejects me and refuses my *words* has his judge already: 3   the *word* itself that I have spoken

49   what I was to *say*, what I had to speak, was commanded by the Father

13 11   He knew who was going to betray him, that was why he *said*, 'though not all of you are [clean]'.

18   I am not *speaking* about all of you:

19   I *tell* you this now, before it happens, so that . . . you may believe that I am He.

21 J   Having *said* this, *Jesus* was troubled in spirit and *declared*,

22   '. . . one of you will betray me'. ²² The disciples looked at one another, wondering which he ˹meant (lit. was *speaking* of)˺.

24   Simon Peter signed to [the disciple Jesus loved] and said, 'Ask who it is he ˹means (lit. is *speaking* of)˺'

33   I *tell* you, as I told the Jews, where I am going you cannot come.

14 2   There are many rooms in my Father's house; if there were not, I should have *told* you.

10   22/ The *words* I *say* to you I do not speak as from myself:

23 J   2 *Jesus* ˹replied (lit. *said* in reply)˺: 'If anyone loves me he will 3   keep my *word*,

24   3 Those who do not love me do not keep my *words*. And 3   ˅my (G the) *word* (§ that you are listening to) is not my own: it is [the word] of the one who sent me.

26   the Advocate . . . will . . . remind you of all I have *said* to you.

28   You heard me *say*: I am going away, and shall return.

29   I have *told* you this now before it happens, so that when it does happen you may believe.

15 3   3 You are pruned already, by means of the *word* that I have spoken to you.

7   22 If . . . my *words* remain in you, you may ask what you will and you shall get it.

20   3/ Remember the *words* I *said* to you: A servant is not greater 3   than his master. If they . . . kept my *word*, they will keep yours as well.

16 4   I have told you all this, so that when the time for it comes you may remember that I *told* you. I did not *tell* you this from the outset, because I was with you;

7   Still, I must *tell* you the truth: it is for your own good that I am going

12   I still have many things to *say* to you

15   Everything the Father has is mine; that is why I *said*: All he tells you will be taken from what is mine.

17   What ˹does he mean (lit. is he *saying* to us)˺, 'In a short time you will no longer see me . . .'?

18   What is this 'short time'? We don't know what he ˹means (lit. is *talking* about)˺.

19   You are asking one another what I meant by *saying*: In a short time you will no longer see me,

26   I do not *say* that I shall pray to the Father for you,

29   Now you are speaking plainly and not ˹using (lit. *talking* in)˺ metaphors!

17 8   22 I have given them the ˹teaching (lit. *words*)˺ you gave to me,

14   3 I passed your *word* on to them, and the world hated them,

18 1 J   After he had *said* all this *Jesus* left with his disciples

6   When [Jesus] *said*, 'I am he', they moved back

8   I have *told* you that I am he

9   3/ This was to fulfil the *words* he had *spoken*, 'Not one of those you gave me have I lost'.

21   Ask my hearers what I taught: they know what I *said*.

32 J   3/ This was to fulfil the *words Jesus* had *spoken* indicating the way he was going to die.

19 21   You should not write 'King of the Jews', but 'This man *said*: I am King of the Jews'.

28 J   *Jesus* knew that everything had now been completed, and

30 J   . . . he *said*: 'I am thirsty' . . . ³⁰ After *Jesus* had taken the vinegar he *said*, 'It is accomplished';

20 15   Sir, . . . *tell* me where you have put him,

18   Mary of Magdala . . . *told* the disciples that she had seen the Lord and that he had *said* these things to her.

20   [Jesus said to the disciples, 'Peace be with you',] and having *said* this showed them his hands and his side.

22   After *saying* this he breathed on them and *said*: 'Receive the Holy Spirit.

Jn 21 17   Peter was upset that he ˹asked (lit. *said* this to)˺ him the third time, 'Do you love me?'

19   In these *words* he indicated the kind of death by which Peter would give glory to God. After *saying* this he *said*, 'Follow me'.

23 J   *Jesus* had not *said* to Peter, 'He will not die',

Ac 1 3   he had continued to appear to them and *tell* them about the kingdom of God.

9   As he *said* this he was lifted up while they looked on,

11 16   22 I remembered ˹that the Lord had (lit. the *words* of the Lord when he)˺ *said*, 'John baptised with water,

20 35 J   3 I did this . . . remembering the *words* of the Lord *Jesus*, who himself *said*, 'There is more happiness in giving than in receiving'.

Rm 10 17   22 what is preached comes from the *word* of Christ.

Col 3 16   3 Let the *message* of Christ, in all its richness, find a home with you.

1 Tm 6 3   Anyone who . . . does not keep to the sound ˹teaching (lit. 3   *message*)˺ which is that of our Lord Jesus Christ [is simply ignorant]

1 Jn 2 7   3 the original commandment . . . was the *message* brought to you.

Rv 3 8   3 you have kept my ˹commandments (lit. *word*)˺

10   3 Because you have kept my ˹commandment (lit. *word*)˺ to endure trials, I will keep you safe

e) (I) tell (you), (I) say (to you)

Mt 5 20   I *tell* you, if your virtue goes no deeper than that of the scribes . . . you will never get into the kingdom of heaven.

22   I *say* this to you: anyone who is angry with his brother will answer for it before the court;

28   I *say* this to you: if a man looks at a woman lustfully, he has . . . committed adultery with her in his heart.

32   I *say* this to you: everyone who divorces his wife . . . makes her an adulteress;

34   I *say* this to you: do not swear at all,

39   I *say* this to you: offer the wicked man no resistance.

44   I *say* this to you: love your enemies

6 25   That is why I am *telling* you not to worry about your life and what you are to eat,

29   I *assure* you that not even Solomon . . . was robed like one of these.

8 11   And I *tell* you that many will come from east and west to take their places with Abraham

11 22   I *tell* you that it will not go as hard . . . with Tyre and Sidon as with you.

24   I *tell* you that it will not go as hard with the land of Sodom . . . as with you.

12 6   Now here, I *tell* you, is something greater than the Temple.

31   And so I *tell* you, every one of men's sins and blasphemies will be forgiven,

36   So I *tell* you this, that for every unfounded word men utter they will answer on Judgement day,

16 18   So I now *say* to you: You are Peter

17 12   I *tell* you that Elijah has come already

18 10   I *tell* you that their angels . . . are continually in the presence of my Father in heaven.

22   Not seven, I *tell* you, but seventy-seven times.

19 9   Now I *say* this to you: the man who divorces his wife . . . is guilty of adultery.

24   I *tell* you again, it is easier for a camel to pass through the eye of a needle than for a rich man to enter the kingdom of heaven.

21 43   I *tell* you . . . that the kingdom of God will be taken from you

23 39   I ˹promise (lit. *tell* you)˺, you shall not see me any more

26 29   From now on, I *tell* you, I shall not drink wine

64   I *tell* you that from this time onward you will see the Son of Man seated at the right hand of the Power

Mk 2 11   I *order* you: get up, pick up your stretcher, and go off home.

5 41   Little girl, I *tell* you to get up.

9 13   I *tell* you that Elijah has come

11 24   I *tell* you therefore: everything you ask and pray for, believe that you have it already, and it will be yours.

Lk 5 24   I *order* you: get up, and pick up your stretcher and go home.

6 27   I *say* this to you who are listening: Love your enemies,

7 9   I *tell* you, not even in Israel have I found faith like this.

14   Young man, I *tell* you to get up.

28   I *tell* you, . . . there is no one greater than John;

47   I *tell* you that her sins, her many sins, must have been forgiven her

10 12   I *tell* you, . . . it will not go as hard with Sodom as with that town.

24   I *tell* you that many prophets and kings wanted to see what you see,

11 8   I *tell* you, . . . persistence will be enough to make him get up and give his friend all he wants.

9   So I *say* to you: Ask, and it will be given to you;

12 4   To you my friends I *say*: Do not be afraid of those who kill the body

Lk	12	8	I *tell* you, if anyone openly declares himself for me . . . the Son of Man will declare himself for him
		22	That is why I am *telling* you not to worry about your life
		27	I *assure* you, not even Solomon . . . was robed like one of these.
		51	Do you suppose that I am here to bring peace . . .? No, I *tell* you, but rather division.
		59	I *tell* you, you will not get out till you have paid the very last penny.
	13	3	They were not [greater sinners than any other Galileans], I *tell* you.
		5	They were not, I *tell* you. No; but unless you repent you will all perish as they did.
		24	I *tell* you, many will try to enter and will not succeed.
		35	I ʳpromise (lit. *tell*) you, you shall not see me
	14	24	I *tell* you, not one of those who were invited shall have a taste of my banquet.
	15	7	I *tell* you, there will be more rejoicing . . . over one repentant sinner than over ninety-nine virtuous men
		10	I *tell* you, there is rejoicing among the angels of God over one repentant sinner.
	16	9	I *tell* you this: use money, tainted as it is, to win you friends,
	17	34	I *tell* you, on that night two will be in one bed:
	18	8	I ʳpromise (lit. *tell*) you, he will see justice done to them,
		14	This man, I *tell* you, went home again at rights with God;
	19	26	I *tell* you, to everyone who has will be given more;
		40	I *tell* you, if [my disciples] keep silence the stones will cry out.
	22	16	I *tell* you, I shall not eat [the passover] again
		18	from now on, I *tell* you, I shall not drink wine
		34	I *tell* you, Peter, by the time the cock crows today you will have denied three times that you know me.
		37	I *tell* you these words of scripture have to be fulfilled in me:
Jn	4	35	I *tell* you: Look around you, look at the fields; already they are white, ready for harvest!

f) Jesus said (to the apostles, disciples)

Mt	4	19		Simon, Andrew
	8	22	J	disciple
		26		disciples
	9	9		Matthew
		37		disciples
	10	5		Twelve
	13	11		2 disciples
		37		2 disciples
		52		disciples
	14	16	J	disciples
		18		disciples
		27		disciples
		29		Peter
		31		Peter
	15	13		2 disciples
		16		Peter
		24		2 disciples
		32	J	disciples
		34	J	disciples
	16	6	J	disciples
		8	J	disciples
		13		disciples
		15		disciples
		17	J	2 Peter
		23		Peter
		24	J	disciples
	17	7		Peter, James, John
		9		Peter, James, John
		11		2 Peter, James, John
		17	J	2 disciples
		20		disciples
		22		disciples
		25		Simon
	18	3		disciples
		22	J	Peter
	19	11		disciples
		14	J	disciples
		23	J	disciples
		26	J	disciples
		28	J	Peter
	20	17		Twelve
		22	J	2 sons of Zebedee
		23		sons of Zebedee
		25	J	apostles
	21	2		two disciples
		21	J	2 disciples
	24	2		2 disciples
		4	J	2 disciples
	26	10	J	disciples
		18		disciples
		21		Twelve
		23		Twelve
	26	25		Judas

Mt	26	26		disciples
		27		disciples
		31	J	disciples
		36		disciples
		38		disciples
		40		Peter
		45		disciples
		50	J	Judas
		52	J	apostle
	28	18		Eleven
Mk	1	17	J	Simon, Andrew
		38		disciples
	2	14		Levi
	4	11		disciples
		13		disciples
		35		disciples
		40		disciples
	6	10		Twelve
		31		apostles
		37		2 disciples
		38		disciples
		50		disciples
	7	18		disciples
		20		disciples
	8	1		disciples
		15		disciples
		17	Jᵛ	disciples
		21		disciples
		27		disciples
		33		Peter
	9	29		disciples
		31		disciples
		35		Twelve
		36		Twelve
		39	J	John
	10	11		disciples
		14		disciples
		23	J	disciples
		24	J	2 disciples
		27	J	disciples
		36		sons of Zebedee
		38	J	sons of Zebedee
		39	J	sons of Zebedee
		42	J	disciples
		49	J	disciples
	11	2		two disciples
		22	J	2 Peter
	12	43		disciples
	13	2	J	disciple
	14	6	J	disciples
		13		two disciples
		18	J	Twelve
		20		Twelve

Mk	14	22		Twelve
		24		Twelve
		27	J	disciples
		30	J	Peter
		32		disciples
		34		disciples
		37		Peter
		41		disciples
	16	15		Eleven
Lk	5	4		Simon
		10	J	Simon
		27		Levi
	6	20		disciples
	8	10		disciples
		22		disciples
		25		disciples
	9	3		Twelve
		13		Twelve
		14		disciples
		18		disciples
		20		disciples
		22		disciples
		43		disciples
		48		disciples
		50	J	John
		55		James and John
	10	2		72 disciples
		18		72 disciples
		23		disciples
	11	2		disciples
		5		disciples
	12	1		disciples
		22		disciples
		42		Peter
	16	1		disciples
	17	1		disciples
		6		apostles
		22		disciples
		37		disciples
	18	16		disciples
		29		disciples
		31		Twelve
	19	30		two disciples
	20	45		disciples
	21	3		disciples
		5		disciples
		8		disciples
	22	8		Peter and John
		10		Peter and John
		15		apostles
		17		apostles
		19		apostles
		20		apostles
		25		apostles
		34		Peter
		35		apostles
		36		apostles
		38		apostles
		40		disciples
		46		disciples
		48	J	Judas
		51	J	2 his followers

Lk	24	7		disciples
		17		disciples from Emmaus
		19		disciples from Emmaus
		25		disciples from Emmaus
		36		disciples
		38		disciples
		41		disciples
		44		disciples
		46		disciples
Jn	1	38	J	John's disciples
		39		John's disciples
		42	J	Simon
		43	J	Philip
		48	J	2 Nathanael
		51		Nathanael
	4	32		disciples
		34	J	disciples
	6	5	J	Philip
		10	J	disciples
		12		disciples
		20		disciples
		61	J	his followers
		65		his followers
		67	J	Twelve
	11	4	J	disciples
		7		disciples
	12	7	J	Judas Iscariot
		23	J	2 Andrew and Philip
	13	7	J	2 Peter
		10	J	2 Peter
		12		disciples
		27	J	Judas
		28		Judas
		29	J	Judas
		31	J	disciples (Eleven)
	14	6	J	Thomas
		9	J	Philip
	16	19		disciples (Eleven)
	18	11	J	Peter
	19	27		(John)
	20	19		disciples
		21	J	disciples
		26		disciples
		27		Thomas
		29	J	Thomas
	21	5	J	disciples
		6		disciples
		10	J	disciples
		12	J	disciples
		15	J	Peter
		—		Peter
		16		Peter
		—		Peter
		17		Peter
		—	J	Peter
		22	J	Peter
Ac	1	7		apostles
1 Co	11	24		apostles
		25		apostles

(to the scribes, Pharisees, chief priests, lawyers, Sadducees or Jews)

Mt	8	20	J	scribe
	9	4	J	scribes
		12		Pharisees
	12	3		Pharisees
		11		Pharisees
		25		Pharisees
		39		2 scribes . . .
	15	3		2 Pharisees . . .
	16	2		2 Pharisees . . .
	19	4		2 Pharisees . . .
		8		Pharisees . . .
	21	16	J	chief priests . . .
		24	J	2 chief priests . . .
		31	J	chief priests . . .
		42	J	chief priests . . .
	22	18	J	Pharisees
		20	J	Pharisees
		21		Pharisees
		29	J	2 Sadducees
		42		Pharisees
		43		Pharisees
	26	64	J	high priest
Mk	2	8	J	scribes
		17	J	scribes
		25		Pharisees

Mk	2	27		Pharisees
	3	4		Pharisees
	5	36	J	synagogue official
	7	6		Pharisees . . .
		9		Pharisees . . .
	8	12		Pharisees . . .
	10	3		2 Pharisees . . .
		5	J	Pharisees . . .
	11	29	J	chief priests . . .
		33	J	chief priests
	12	15		Pharisees . . .
		16		Pharisees . . .
		17	J	Pharisees . . .
		34	J	scribe
	14	62	J	high priest
Lk	4	21		Jews
	5	22	J	2 scribes . . .
		31	J	2 Pharisees . . .
		34	J	Pharisees . . .
	6	3	J	2 Pharisees
		5		Pharisees
		9	J	scribes . . .
	7	43		Simon the Pharisee
	10	26		lawyer

Lk 10 28		lawyer
30	J	lawyer
37	J	lawyer
11 39		Pharisees
46		lawyers
13 15	2	synagogue official
32		Pharisees
14 3	J 2	lawyers . . .
5ᵛ		2 lawyers . . .
15 11		Pharisees . . .
16 15		Pharisees
17 20		2 Pharisees
19 40		2 Pharisees
20 3		2 chief priests . . .
8	J	chief priests . . .
23		scribes . . .
25		scribes . . .
34	J	Sadducees
Lk 20 41		scribes
22 52	J	chief priests . . .
Jn 2 19	J	2 Jews
5 19	J	Jews
6 43	J	2 Jews
53	J	Jews
7 16		Jews
8 7		scribes . .
14	J	2 Pharisees
23		Jews
25	J	Jews
28	J	Jews
31	J	Jews
39	J	Jews
42	J	Jews
58	J	Jews
9 41	J	Pharisees
13 33	J	Jews
Mk 10 51	J	2 blind man
52	J	blind man
11 14		2 fig tree
17		dealers in the Temple
14 2		2 Pilate
Lk 2 49		Mary and Joseph
4 3		stones
23		people of Nazareth
24		people of Nazareth
5 13		leper
20		paralytic
24		paralytic
6 8		man with a withered hand
10		man with a withered hand
7 13		widow of Nain
14		widow of Nain's son
22		2 John's disciples
48		woman with ointment
50		woman with ointment
8 48		woman
54		Jairus's daughter
9 58	J	a man
59		a second man
60		the second man
62	J	a third man
10 41		2 Martha
11 17		some people
28		woman in crowd
12 14		man in crowd
13 12	J	crippled woman
14 12		host
16		fellow guest
17 14		ten lepers
17	J	2 Samaritan leper
Lk 17 19		Samaritan leper
18 19	J	aristocrat
22	J	aristocrat
42	J	blind man
19 5	J	Zacchaeus
9	J	Zacchaeus
42		Jerusalem
46		dealers in the Temple
23 28	J	women
43		good thief
Jn 2 4	J	his mother
7	J	servants
8		servants
16		dealers in the Temple
3 3	J	2 Nicodemus
10	J	2 Nicodemus
4 7	J	Samaritan woman
10	J	2 Samaritan woman
13	J	2 Samaritan woman
16	Jᵛ	Samaritan woman
17	J	Samaritan woman
21	J	Samaritan woman
26	J	Samaritan woman
48	J	court official
5 6	J	sick man
8	J	sick man
14		sick man
7 6	J	his brothers
8 10	J	adulterous woman
11	J	adulterous woman
9 7		man born blind
35		man born blind
37	J	man born blind
11 23	J	Martha
25	J	Martha
18 4		guards . . .
5	Jᵛ	guards . . .
19 26	J	his mother
20 15	J	Mary of Magdala
16	J	Mary of Magdala
17	J	Mary of Magdala

(to devils, to those possessed by demons)

Mt 4 4		2 the devil
10	J	Satan
8 32		devils
Mk 1 25		a man possessed
5 8		unclean spirit
19		demoniac
Mk 9 25		unclean spirit
Lk 4 8	J	2 the devil
12	J	2 the devil
35		a devil
8 38		demoniac

(to the crowds, to the people)

Mt 5 2		crowds
8 10		people
9 24	J	crowd
12 49		crowd
13 3		crowd
24		crowd
31		crowd
57	J	people of Nazareth
15 10		people
23		2 people & disciples
16 55	J	crowds
Mk 1 15		people
2 19	J	people
3 3		2 people
34		people
4 9		people
21		crowd
24		crowd
26		crowd
30		crowd
5 30		crowd
39		people
7 14		people
8 34		people & disciples
9 1		people & disciples
19		2 crowd ?
14 48	J	2 people
Lk 4 43		crowds
7 9		crowd
8 21		2 crowd
45	J	crowd
46	J	crowd
Lk 8 52		people
9 23		crowd
41	J	2 crowd
11 29		crowds
12 15		crowd
54		crowds
13 2		2 people
18		crowd?
20		crowd?
23		crowd?
14 25		crowds
18 6		crowd
24	J	people
27		people
20 17		people
21 10		crowd
Jn 6 26	J	2 crowd
29	J	2 crowd
32	J	crowd
35	J	crowd
7 21	J	2 crowd
28		crowd
33	J	crowd
37		crowd
8 12		crowd
21		crowd
9 39	J	crowd
10 7	J	crowd
11 34		people
39		people
44	J	people
12 30	J	2 people
35	J	crowd

(to various)

Mt 3 15	J	2 John the Baptist
4 3		stones
8 3		leper
4	J	leper
7		centurion
13	J	centurion
9 2	J	paralytic
6		paralytic
15	J	John's disciples
22	J	woman
28	J	two blind men
29		two blind men
30		two blind men
11 4	J	2 John's disciples
12 13		man with a withered hand
48		2 man in crowd
15 26		2 Canaanite woman
28	J	2 Canaanite woman
19 17		rich young man
20 21		mother of Zebedee's sons
32		two blind men
21 13		dealers in the Temple
19		fig tree
Mt 28 9		women at tomb
10	J	women at tomb
Mk 1 41		leper
44		leper
2 5	J	paralytic
10		paralytic
3 3		man with a withered hand
5		man with a withered hand
4 39		sea
5 34		woman
41		Jairus's daughter
6 4	J	people of Nazareth
7 27		Syrophoenician woman
29		Syrophoenician woman
34		deaf mute
8 26		blind man
9 23	J	father of epileptic
10 18	J	rich young man
21		rich young man

4: (A PERSON, AN ANIMAL) SAYS

a) (A person, an animal) Says (in prayer, in praise)

Mt 6 7   12 In your prayers do not *babble* as the pagans do, for they 20 think that by *using* many *words* they will make themselves heard.

7 21   It is not those who *say* to me, 'Lord, Lord' who will enter the kingdom of heaven,

22   When the day comes many will *say* to me, 'Lord, Lord,'

23 39   until you *say* (Ps 118 26): Blessings on him who comes in the name of the Lord!

25 11 <   The other bridesmaids arrived later. 'Lord, Lord,' they *said* 'open the door for us.'

Mk 2 12   they . . . all . . . praised God *saying*, 'We have never seen anything like this.'

Lk 1 46   Mary *said*: 'My soul proclaims the greatness of the Lord

2 28   [Simeon] *said*: 'Now, Master, you can let your servant go in peace,

7 16   Everyone . . . praised God *saying*, 'A great prophet has appeared among us;'

11 2   *Say* this when you pray: 'Father, may your name be held holy,

13 25   you may find yourself knocking on the door, *saying*, 'Lord, open to us' . . . ²⁶ Then you will find yourself *saying*, 'We once ate and drank in your company;

35   till the time comes when you *say*: 'Blessings on him who comes in the name of the Lord!'

18 13   The tax collector . . . beat his breast and *said*: 'God, be merciful to me, a sinner'.

19 38   They *cried out* (Ps 118 26): Blessings on the King who comes, in the name of the Lord!'

23 47   the centurion . . . gave praise to God and *said*, 'This was a great and good man'.

Ac 1 24   they prayed, (§ *saying*,) 'Lord, . . . show us which of these two you have chosen'

4 24   they lifted up their voice to God all together, 'Master,' they ⌐prayed (lit. *said*)

7 59   As they were stoning him, Stephen *said* in invocation, 'Lord Jesus, receive my spirit'. ⁶⁰ Then he . . . *said* aloud, 'Lord, do not hold this sin against them'; and ⌐with these words (lit. having *said* this) he fell asleep.

11 18   they gave glory to God. 'God' they *said* 'can evidently grant even the pagans . . . repentance'

1 Co 14 16   Any uninitiated person will never be able to *say* Amen to your thanksgiving, . . . for he will have no idea what you are *saying*.

Ep 5 14		That is why it is *said*: Wake up from your sleep,
26		[Christ] made [the Church] clean by washing her in water
○ 22		with a *form of words*,
Heb 13 6		and so we can *say* with confidence (Ps 118 6): With the Lord to help me, I fear nothing:
Rv 4 8		day and night [the four animals] never stopped *singing* (Is 6 3): 'Holy, holy, holy'
10		the twenty-four elders . . . threw down their crowns in front of the throne, *saying*, 'You are our Lord'
5 9		[The four animals and the twenty-four elders] sang a new hymn, *saying*, 'You are worthy to take the scroll'
13		I heard all the living things in creation . . . *crying*, 'To the
14		. . . Lamb, be all praise, . . .' [14] And the four animals *said*, 'Amen';
6 10		They shouted aloud, *saying*, 'Holy, faithful Master,'
7 10		They shouted aloud, *saying*, 'Victory to our God,'
11 17		[The twenty-four elders . . . prostrated themselves . . . worshipping God] ⌐with these words (lit. *saying*), 'We give thanks to you, Almighty Lord God,'
15 3		they were singing the hymn of Moses, the servant of God, and of the Lamb, *saying*: 'How great and wonderful
16 7		I heard the altar itself *say*, 'Truly, Lord God Almighty,
19 1		the great sound of a huge crowd in heaven, *singing*, 'Alleluia!
3		. . .' [3] They *sang* again, 'Alleluia! . . .'
4		the twenty-four elders and the four animals . . . worshipped God . . . and they *cried*, 'Amen, Alleluia'.
6		I seemed to hear the voices of a huge crowd, like the sound of the ocean . . , *answering*, 'Alleluia!'
22 17		The Spirit and the Bride *say*, 'Come'. Let everyone who listens *answer*, 'Come'.

b) (A person) Says, Tells (of Christ)—Words, the Message (of Jesus, Gospel teaching)

Mt 8 4		Mind you do not *tell* anyone,
10 7		as you go, *proclaim* that the kingdom of heaven is at hand.
14	3	if anyone does not . . . listen to *what* you have *to say*, . . shake the dust from your feet.
27		What I say to you in the dark, *tell* in the daylight;
16 20		he gave the disciples strict orders not to *tell* anyone that he was the Christ.
17 9		*Tell* no one about the vision
21 5		(Zc 9 9) *Say* to the daughter of Zion: Look, your king comes to you;
28 7		go quickly and *tell* his disciples, 'He has risen from the dead
Mk 1 44		Mind you *say* nothing to anyone,
7 36		Jesus ordered them to *tell* no one about it,
8 30		he gave them strict orders not to *tell* anyone about him.
16 7		you must go and *tell* his disciples . . , 'He is going before to Galilee;'
8		[the women] *said* nothing to a soul, for they were afraid.
Lk 1 4	3	so that your Excellency may learn how well founded the *teaching* is that you have received.
5 14		He ordered him to *tell* no one.
8 56		he ordered them not to *tell* anyone what had happened.
9 21		he gave them strict orders not to *tell* anyone anything about this.
31		[Moses and Elijah] were *speaking* of his passing
10 9		*say*, 'The kingdom of God is very near to you.'
24 10		The other women with them also *told* the apostles, [11] but this
11	22	*story* of theirs seemed pure nonsense,
23		they came back to *tell* us they had seen a vision of angels . . .
24		[24] Some of our friends went to the tomb and found everything as the women had *reported*,
Jn 1 15		This is the one of whom I *said*: He who comes after me ranks before me
30		This is the one I spoke of when I *said*: A man is coming after me
3 28		You yourselves can bear me out: I *said*: I myself am not the Christ;
4 39		Many Samaritans . . . believed in him on the strength of the
3		woman's *testimony* [when she said], 'He told me all I have ever done,'
9 17		'What have you to *say* about him yourself, now that he has opened your eyes?' 'He is a prophet,' *replied* the man.
27		I have *told* you once and you wouldn't listen.
10 41		all [John] *said* about this man was true;
11 51		[Caiaphas] did not *speak* in his own person, it was as high priest
15 20	3	if they kept my *word*, they will keep yours as well.
17 20	3	I pray . . . for those also who through their *words* will believe in me.
19 35		he knows he *speaks* the truth
20 17		Go and find ˅ the (G my) brothers, and *tell* them: I am ascending to my Father
Ac 2 14	22	listen carefully to *what* I *say*.
22	3	listen to *what* I am going *to say*.
29		⌐no one can deny (lit. we can *say* with certainty) that . . . David himself is dead
40	3	He spoke to them for a long time using many *arguments*

Ac 2 41	3	They were convinced by his *arguments*,
5 5		When he heard ⌐this (lit. these *words*) Ananias fell down dead.
20	22	tell the people ⌐all about (lit. the *words* concerning) this new Life.
6 5	3	The whole assembly approved of this *proposal*.
14		We have heard him *say* that Jesus . . . is going to destroy this Place
8 6		The people united in welcoming the message Philip *preached*,
10 22		Cornelius . . . was directed by a holy angel to . . . listen to *what* you have *to say*.
44	22	While Peter was still speaking these *words* the Holy Spirit came down on all the listeners.
11 14	22	[Peter] has a *message* for you that will save you
13 15	3	if you would like to address some *words* of encouragement to the congregation, please ⌐do so (lit. *speak*).
42		As they left they were asked to ⌐preach on the same theme (lit. say the same *words*) the following sabbath.
14 12	22	since Paul was the ⌐principal speaker (lit. messenger of the *word*) they called him Hermes.
15 32	3	Judas and Silas, being themselves prophets, ⌐spoke for a long time (lit. made a long *speech*),
17 7		They have broken every one of Caesar's edicts by ⌐claiming (lit. *saying*) that there is another emperor, Jesus.
19 4		[John] ⌐insisted that the people should (lit. *told* people to) believe in . . . Jesus.
26		this man Paul has . . . converted a great number of people ⌐with his argument (lit. by *saying*) that gods made by hand are not gods
20 2	3	he said many *words* of encouragement
7	3	he preached a *sermon* that went on till the middle of the night.
36		When he had finished *speaking* he knelt down with them
21 21	3	⌐authorising (lit. *telling*) them not to circumcise their children
22 22	3	So far they had listened to him, but at these *words* they began to shout,
26 22		I have . . . [testified] to great and small alike, *saying* nothing more than what the prophets . . . said would happen:
25	22	I am speaking ⌐nothing but the (lit. *words* of) sober truth.
28 24		some were convinced by what he *said*,
25	22/	Paul had one last ⌐thing (lit. *word*) to *say* to them, '. . . the Holy Spirit . . . told your ancestors through the prophet Isaiah (Is 6 9-10): [26] Go to this nation and *say*: You will
26		hear and hear again but not understand,
29		(˅ When [Paul] had *said* this, the Jews went away . . .)
Rm 4 9	3	[Abraham's] faith, we *say*, was considered as justifying him,
10 8	22/22	(Dt 30 14) The *word*, that is the *word* of the faith we proclaim, is very near to you, it is on your lips
18	22	(Ps 19 4) their *message* [has gone out] to the ends of the world.
12 3		I want to ⌐urge (lit. *tell*) each one among you not to exaggerate his real importance.
15 8		⌐The reason (lit. I am *telling* you,) Christ became the servant of circumcised Jews . . . not only so that God could faithfully carry out the promises
18		what Christ himself has done to win the allegiance of the pagans, using *what* I have *said* and done
1 Co 1 5	3	I thank him that you have been enriched in so many ways, especially in ⌐your teachers and preachers (lit. *word* and enlightenment);
17	3	Christ [sent] me . . . to preach the Good News, and not to preach that in the *terms* of philosophy in which the crucifixion of Christ cannot be expressed.
18	3	The *language* of the cross may be illogical to those who are not on the way to salvation,
2 1	3	when I came to you, it was not with any show of *oratory* or
4	3	philosophy, . . . [4] and in my *speeches* and the sermons that I gave, there were none of the arguments that belong to philosophy;
13	3	we teach, not in the ⌐way (lit. learned *words*) in which philosophy is taught, but in the way that the Spirit teaches us;
6 5		⌐You should be ashamed (lit. I *say* it to your shame):
7 6		⌐This (lit. What I *say*) is a suggestion, not a rule:
8		There is something I want to ⌐add (lit. *say*) for the sake of widows and those who are not married:
12		The rest ⌐is from me (lit. I am *saying*) . . . not . . . the Lord.
35		I *say* this only to help you,
10 15		I *say* to you as sensible people: judge for yourselves what I am saying.
12 8	3	One may have the gift of *preaching* with wisdom given him
3		by the Spirit; another may have the gift of *preaching* instruction given him by the same Spirit;
15 2	3	if you keep believing exactly ⌐what (lit. the *word*) I preached
51		to you I will *tell* you something that has been secret:
2 Co 10 10	3	[Paul] is . . . only half a man and ⌐no preacher at all (lit. his *speaking* is useless).
11	3	whatever we are like in the *words* of our letters when we are absent, that is what we shall be like in our actions when we are present.
Ga 1 9		I am only ⌐repeating (lit. *saying*) what we told you before:
3 17		⌐my point is (lit. I *tell* you) this: once God has expressed his will
5 2		It is I, Paul, who *tell* you this:

Ga 5 16 — Let me *put it* like this: if you are guided by the Spirit
Ep 4 17 — ⌐In particular (lit. I *tell* you), I want to urge you . . . not to [live] the aimless kind of life
5 32 — This mystery has many implications; but I am *saying* it applies to Christ and the Church.
6 19 — pray for me to be given [an opportunity] to open my mouth
3 ⌐and speak (lit. for *speech*) without fear
Col 2 4 — I *say* this to make sure that no one deceives you
4 3 — asking God to show us opportunities for [announcing] the
3 *message*
1 Th 1 5 — when we brought the Good News to you, it came to you not
3 only as *words*,
4 15 — We can *tell* you this from the Lord's own teaching,
18 — 3 With such ⌐thoughts (lit. *words*) as these you should comfort one another.
2 Th 2 5 — Surely you remember me *telling* you about this when I was with you?
15 — 3 keep the traditions that we taught you, whether by *word* [of mouth] or by letter.
3 14 — 3 If anyone refuses to obey what ⌐I have written (lit. we have
3 *said*) in this letter,
1 Tm 1 15 — 3 Here is a *saying* that you can rely on and nobody should doubt;
3 1 — 3 Here is a *saying* that you can rely on:
4 6 — 3 show that you have really digested the ⌐teaching (lit. *words*) of the faith and the good doctrine
9 — 3 that is a *saying* that you can rely on and nobody should doubt it.
5 17 — especially those elders who are assiduous in ⌐preaching and
3 teaching (lit. *word* and doctrine)
2 Tm 1 13 — 3 Keep as your pattern the sound ⌐teaching (lit. *words*) you have heard from me,
2 7 — Think over what I have *said*,
11 — 3 Here is a *saying* that you can rely on:
4 15 — [Alexander] has been bitterly contesting ⌐everything that we
3 *say* (lit. our *words*)
Tt 1 9 — 3 [an elder] must have a firm grasp of the unchanging *message* of the tradition,
2 8 — 3 keeping ⌐all that you say (lit. your *speech*) so wholesome that nobody can make objections to it;
3 8 — 3 This is *doctrine* that you can rely on.
Heb 5 11 — 3 On this subject we have many *things to say*, and ⌐they are difficult to explain (lit. it is difficult to *tell* you an explanation of them).
12 — you need someone to teach you all over again the elementary
8 principles of interpreting God's *oracles*;
8 1 — The great point of all that we have *said* is that we have a high priest
11 — (Jr 31 34) There will be no further need for . . . brother to *say* to brother, 'Learn to know the Lord'.
13 22 — 3 take these *words* of advice kindly;
Jude 17 — 22 remember . . . *what* the apostles . . . *told* you to expect.
18 — [18] 'At the end of time', they *told* you, 'there are going to be people who sneer at religion . . .'

c) (A person) Says (to), Tells (another)

X = Say to, Tell, Jesus

Mt 3 9 — do not presume to *tell* yourselves, 'We have Abraham for our father,' because, I *tell* you, God can raise children for Abraham
5 22 — if a man ⌐calls (lit. *says* to) his brother 'Fool' he will answer for it before the Sanhedrin; and if a man ⌐calls (lit. *says* to) him 'Renegade' he will answer for it in hell fire.
37 — 3 ⌐All you need say is (lit. Let *what* you *say* be) 'Yes' if you mean yes, 'No' if you mean no;
7 4 — How dare you *say* to your brother, 'Let me take the splinter out
11 2 X — John . . . sent his disciples to ⌐ask (lit. *say* to) [Jesus], [3] 'Are you the one who is to come . . . ?'
18 — John came . . . and they *say*, 'He is possessed'.
19 — The Son of Man came . . . and they *say*, 'Look, a glutton
12 36 — 22 for every unfounded *word* men utter they will answer on Judgement day, [37] 3 since it is by your *words* you will be
3 acquitted, and by your *words* condemned
48 X — to the man who *told* him this Jesus replied, 'Who is my mother?'
13 30 < — at harvest time I shall *say* to the reapers: First collect the darnel
15 5 — you *say*, 'If anyone *says* to his [parents]; 'Anything I have . . . is dedicated to God
16 2 — In the evening you *say*, 'It will be fine;'
13 — Who do people *say* the Son of Man is?
15 — But you, . . . who do you *say* I am?
17 10 — Why do the scribes *say* then that Elijah has to come first?
20 — you could *say* to this mountain, 'Move'
18 17 — if he refuses to listen to these, *report* it to the community;
21 3 — If anyone *says* anything to you, you are to *say*, 'The Master needs them.'
16 — Do you hear what they are *saying*?
21 — if you *say* to this mountain, 'Get up

Mt 21 24 X — '. . . if you *tell* me the answer to [my question], I will then tell you my authority for acting like this. [25] John's baptism:
25 — where did it come from: heaven or man?' . . . 'If we *say* from heaven, he will retort, "Then why did you refuse to believe him?"; [26] but if we *say* from man, we have the
26 — people to fear, . . .'
22 4 — 'Tell those who have been invited' he said, 'that I have my banquet all prepared,
23 < — some Sadducees—who ⌐deny that there is a resurrection (lit. *say* that there is no resurrection)—approached him
46 X — 3 Not one could think of ⌐anything (lit. a *word*) to say in reply.
23 3 — do what [the scribes and Pharisees] *tell* you . . .; but do not be guided by what they do: since they do not practise what they *preach*.
16 — Alas for you, blind guides! You who *say*, 'If a man swears by the Temple,
30 — [Alas for you, scribes and Pharisees . . .!] You who build the sepulchres of the prophets . . ,] *saying*, 'We would never have joined in shedding the blood of the prophets,
24 5 — many will come using my name and *saying*, 'I am the Christ',
23 — If anyone *says* to you then, 'Look, here is the Christ' . . . do not believe it;
26 — If . . . they *say* to you, 'Look, he is in the desert', do not go there;
26 18 — Go to so-and-so in the city . . . and *say* to him, 'The Master says:'
25 — Judas . . . asked in his turn, 'Not I, Rabbi, surely?' ⌐They are your own words (lit. You have *said* it)' answered Jesus.
35 X — all the disciples *said* the same.
64 — [Jesus to the high priest:] ⌐'The words are your own (lit. 'You have *said* it').
70 — 'I do not know what you are *talking* about' [Peter] said.
27 11 — [Pilate:] 'Are you the king of the Jews?' Jesus replied, 'It is you who *say* it'.
14 X 22 — [Jesus] offered no reply to any of the *charges*.
19 — [Pilate's] wife sent ⌐him a message (lit. to *say* to him), 'Have nothing to do with that man;'
28 13 — This is what you must *say*: 'His disciples came during the night
15 — 3 to this day this is the *story* among the Jews.
Mk 1 30 X — 3 they *told* [Jesus] about [Simon's mother-in-law] at once
45 — [the leper] started talking about [his cure] freely and telling
3 the *story* everywhere,
2 18 X — some people came and *said* to [Jesus], 'Why is it that John's disciples . . . fast . . .?'
5 33 X — the woman . . . fell at his feet and *told* him the whole truth.
36 — 3 Jesus had overheard this *remark* of theirs
7 11 — But you *say*, 'If a man *says* to his father or mother:'
29 X — 3 [Jesus] said to her, 'For ⌐saying this (lit. this *saying*) you may go home happy:'
8 27 — Who do people *say* I am?
29 — But you, . . . who do you *say* I am?
9 11 — Why do the scribes *say* that Elijah has to come first?
18 — I ⌐asked (lit. *told*) your disciples to cast [the demon] out
10 28 X — Peter ⌐took this up (lit. began to *say* [to Jesus]). 'What about us?
11 3 — If anyone *says* to you, 'What are you doing?' *say*, 'The Master needs it'
6 — They ⌐gave the answer (lit. *said* what) Jesus had told them,
23 — if anyone *says* to this mountain, 'Get up'
31 X — If we *say* [John's baptism came] from heaven, he will say,
32 X — 'Then why did you refuse to believe him?' [32] But dare we *say* from man?
12 18 — Sadducees . . . ⌐deny that there is a resurrection (lit. *say* that there is no resurrection)
35 — How can the scribes ⌐maintain (lit. *say*) that the Christ is the son of David?
13 6 — Many will come using my name and *saying*, 'I am he',
21 — if anyone *says* to you then, 'Look, here is the Christ' . . , do not believe it;
14 14 — *say* to the owner of the house which he enters, 'The Master says:
31 X — And they all *said* the same [as Peter].
68 — [Peter:] 'I do not know . . . what you are *talking* about
15 2 — Pilate questioned him, 'Are you the king of the Jews?' 'It is you who *say* it' he answered.
Lk 3 8 — do not think of *telling* yourselves, 'We have Abraham for our father'
4 23 X — No doubt you will *quote* the saying
5 15 — 3 ⌐His reputation (lit. *Word* of him) continued to grow,
39 — 'The old [wine] is good' he *says*.
6 42 — How can you *say* to your brother, 'Brother, let me take out the splinter that is in your eye' . . . ?
7 6 X — the centurion sent *word* to him by some friends:
17 — 3 this ⌐opinion (lit. *word*) of him spread thoughout Judaea
19 X — [John] sent [two of his disciples] to the Lord to ⌐ask (lit. *say*), 'Are you the one who is to come . . . ?'
20 X — John the Baptist has sent us to you, to ⌐ask (lit. *say*), 'Are you the one who is to come . . . ?'
33 — you *say* [of John], 'He is possessed'.

Lk 7 34 you *say* [of the Son of Man], 'Look', a glutton'

9 20 But you, . . . who do you *say* I am?

33 X [Peter] did not know what he was *saying*, 34 As he *spoke*, a cloud came and covered them
34 X

54 Lord, do you want us to *call* down fire from heaven . . .?

10 5 Whatever house you go into, ʳlet your first words be (lit. *say* first), 'Peace to this house!'

10 whenever you go into a town and they do not make you welcome, go out into its streets and *say*, 'We wipe off the very dust of your town that clings to our feet,'

11 18 Since you *assert* that it is through Beelzebul that I cast out devils.

12 3 whatever you have *said* in the dark will be heard in the daylight,

11 do not worry about how to defend yourselves or what to *say*,

12 the Holy Spirit will teach you what you must *say*.

19 < I will *say* to my soul: My soul, you have plenty of good things laid by

55 when the wind is from the south you *say* it will be hot,

13 32 You may go and ʳgive that fox this message (lit. *say* to that fox):

14 9 the person who invited you both may come and *say*, 'Give up your place to this man'.

10 so that, when your host comes, he may *say*, 'My friend, move up higher'.

15 18 < I will . . . go to my father and *say*: Father, I have sinned

17 6 you could *say* to this mulberry tree, 'Be uprooted'

7 Which of you . . . would *say* to [your servant] . . , 'Come and have your meal immediately'? 8 Would he not be more
8
10 likely to *say*, 'Get my supper laid;' . . .? . . . 10 So with you: when you have done all you have been told to do, *say*, 'We are merely servants'.

21 there will be no one to *say*, 'Look here!'

23 They will *say* to you, 'Look there!'

18 6 You notice what the unjust judge has to *say*?

19 15 < [the king] ʳsent for (lit. *said* to call) those servants to whom he had given the money,

31 you are to *say* this, 'The Master needs it'.

20 3 X 'Tell me: 4 John's baptism: did it come from heaven, or from
5 X man?' 5 . . . 'If we *say* from heaven, he will say, "Why did
6 X you refuse to believe him?"; 6 and if we *say* from man, the people will all stone us,'

41 How can people ʳmaintain (lit. *say*) that the Christ is son of David?

21 5 some were *talking* about the Temple, remarking how it was adorned with fine stonework

8 many will come using my name and *saying*, 'I am he'

22 11 *tell* the owner of the house, 'The Master has this to say to you:'

60 'My friend,' said Peter 'I do not know what you are *talking* about.'

70 'So you are the Son of God then?' He answered, 'It is you who *say* I am.'
X

23 3 X 'Are you the king of the Jews?' 'It is you who *say* it' he replied.

9 X 3 [Herod] questioned [Jesus] ʳat some length (lit. in many *words*).

29 the days will surely come when people will *say*, 'Happy are those who are barren,'

30 (Ho 10 8) Then they will begin to *say* to the mountains, 'Fall on us!'

Jn 1 22 they said to [John], 'Who are you? . . . What have you to *say* about yourself?'

4 17 X You are right to *say*, 'I have no husband'; 18 for although
18 X you have had five, the one you have now is not your husband. You spoke the truth there.

20 you *say* that Jerusalem is the place where one ought to worship.

35 ʳHave you not got a saying (lit. Do you not *say*): Four months and then the harvest?

37 3 here the *proverb* holds good: one sows, another reaps;

5 15 The man went back and *told* the Jews that it was Jesus who had cured him.

7 26 X here he is, speaking freely, and they have nothing to *say* to him!

8 6 X They ʳasked him this (lit. *said* this to him) as a test,

48 X Are we not right in *saying* that you are a Samaritan . . .?

54 my glory is conferred by . . . the one of whom you *glory*, 'He is our God'

9 19 Is this man really your son who you *say* was born blind?

22 His parents *spoke* like this out of fear of the Jews,

41 since you *say*, 'We see', your guilt remains.

10 36 X you *say* to someone the Father has consecrated . ., 'You are blaspheming',

11 3 X The sisters sent ʳthis message (lit. to *say*) to Jesus,

28 X When [Martha] had *said* this, she went and called her sister Mary, *saying* in a low voice, 'The Master is here'

46 some of them went to *tell* the Pharisees what Jesus had done.

12 6 [Judas] *said* this, not because he cared about the poor,

22 Philip went to *tell* Andrew, and Andrew and Philip together
X went to *tell* Jesus.

Jn 12 29 People standing by, who heard this, *said* it was a clap of thunder; others *said* 'It was an angel speaking to him'.

13 13 X You call me Master and Lord, and *say* rightly;

24 X Simon Peter . . . said, ʳAsk (lit. *Say*) who it is he means',

14 9 X how can you *say*, 'Let us see the Father'?

18 16 the other disciple . . . *spoke* to the woman who was keeping the door

34 ['Are you the king of the Jews?'] Jesus replied, 'Do you ʳask (lit. *say*) this of your own accord, or have others *spoken* to you about me?'

37 X 'So you are a king then?' said Pilate. 'It is you who *say* it' answered Jesus.

38 X 'Truth?' said Pilate . . . and ʳwith (lit. having *said*) that he went out again to the Jews

19 8 3 ʳWhen Pilate heard [the Jews] say this (lit. Hearing these *words*)

13 3 Hearing these *words*, Pilate had Jesus brought out,

20 14 As she *said* this [Mary of Magdala] turned round and saw Jesus

21 20 X the [disciple] who had . . . *said* to him, 'Lord, who is it that will betray you?'

23 The *rumour* then went out among the brothers that this disciple would not die.

Ac 4 23 everything the chief priests and elders had *said* to them.

5 8 'Tell me, was this the price you sold the land for?' 'Yes,' [Sapphira] *said*

24 3 When the captain of the Temple and the chief priests heard ʳthis news (lit. these *words*) they wondered what this could mean.

38 What I ʳsuggest (lit. *say*), therefore, is that you leave these men alone

7 22 3 Moses . . . became a man with power both in his *speech* and his actions.

26 'Friends,' [Moses] *said* '. . . why are you hurting each other?' 27 . . . (Ex 2 14) 'And who appointed you' [the
27 man who was attacking his fellow countryman] *said* 'to
29 3 be our . . . judge? . . .' 29 Moses fled when he heard ʳthis (lit. these *words*)

35 It was the same Moses that they had disowned when they *said* (Ex 2 14), 'Who appointed you to be our . . . judge?'

40 [our ancestors] *said* to Aaron (Ex 32 1), 'Make some gods to be our leaders;'

8 24 Pray to the Lord for me . . . so that none of the things you have *spoken* about may happen to me.

11 8 I ʳanswered (lit. *said*): 'Certainly not, Lord;'

22 3 The Church in Jerusalem heard ʳabout this (lit. this *spoken* about)

13 15 the presidents of the synagogue sent ʳthem a message (lit. to *say* to them): 'Brothers,'

15 5 certain members of the Pharisees' party . . . ʳobjected, insisting (lit. got up to *say*) that the pagans should be circumcised

24 3 We hear that some of our members have disturbed you with their ʳdemands (lit. *words*)

27 3 we are sending you Judas and Silas, who will confirm by *word* [of mouth] what we have written

16 35 the magistrates sent the officers ʳwith the order (lit. to *say*): 'Release those men'.

36 3 The gaoler reported ʳthe message (lit. these *words*) to Paul.

38 22 The officers reported ʳthis (lit. these *words*) to the magistrates,

17 18 Does this parrot know what he's *talking* about?

28 as indeed some of ʳyour own writers (ᵛ your own people) have *said*:

18 15 3 if it is only quibbles about *words* and names,

24 10 [Apollos] was an *eloquent* man,

19 40 When he had ʳfinished this speech (lit. *said* this) [the town clerk] dismissed the assembly.

20 38 3 what saddened them most ʳwas his saying (lit. in the *words* he had *said* was that) they would never see his face again.

21 4 they kept *telling* Paul not to go on to Jerusalem,

23 do as we ʳsuggest (lit. *say*).

37 [Paul] asked the tribune if he could ʳhave a word with him (lit. *say* something).

22 10 X I *said*: 'What am I to do, Lord?'

19 X Lord, I ʳanswered (lit. *said*), it is because they know that I used to . . . [imprison and flog] those who believed in you;

24 the tribune ʳordered [Paul] (lit. *said* [Paul] was) to be examined under the lash,

27 *Tell* me, are you a Roman citizen?

23 8 the Sadducees *say* there is neither resurrection, nor angel, nor spirit, while the Pharisees accept all three.

12 the Jews . . . made a vow ʳnot to eat (lit. *saying* they would not eat) or drink until they had killed Paul.

30 I . . . have notified his accusers that they must *state* [their case] against him in your presence.

24 10 When the governor motioned him to *speak*, Paul answered:

20 At least let those who are present *say* what crime they found me guilty of

25 20 I ʳasked (lit. *said* to) [Paul] if he would be willing to go to Jerusalem

Ac 26	1		You have leave to *speak* on your own behalf.
	15	X	Then I *said*: Who are you, Lord?
27	11		the centurion took more notice of the captain . . . than of what Paul was *saying*;
	35		⌐With these words (lit. Having *said* this) [Paul] took some bread,
28	6		they changed their minds and began to *say* [Paul] was a god.
Rm 2	22		⌐you forbid (lit. you who *say* do not commit) adultery,
3	5		if our lack of holiness makes God demonstrate his integrity, how can we *say* God is unjust when – ⌐to use a human analogy (lit. I *speak* as a man) – he gets angry with us in return?
	8		Some slanderers have accused us of ⌐teaching (lit. *saying*) this,
4	1		⌐Apply this to Abraham (lit. What then shall we *say* of Abraham?)
6	1		⌐Does it follow that we should (lit. What then shall we *say*? Should we) remain in sin . . .?
	19		⌐If I may use human terms (lit. I *speak* in an entirely human way)
7	7		⌐Does it follow that the Law itself is (lit. What then shall we *say*? Is the Law itself) sin?
8	31		After *saying* this, what can we add?
9	1		I *say* it in union with Christ – it is the truth –
	14		⌐Does it follow that God is (lit. What then shall we *say*? Is God) unjust?
	19		You will ⌐ask (lit. *say* to me), 'In that case,
	30		⌐From this it follows that (lit. What then shall we *say*? That) the pagans . . . found [righteousness]
10	6		(cf. Dt 30 11–14) Do not *tell* yourself you have to bring Christ down
	18		⌐Let me put the question (lit. But I *say*): is it possible that they did not hear?
	19		⌐A second question (lit. But I *say*): is it possible that Israel did not understand?
11	1		⌐Let me put a further question (lit. I *say*) then (Ps 94 14): is it possible that God has rejected his people?
	11		⌐Let me put another question (lit. I *say*) then: have the Jews fallen for ever . . .?
	13		⌐Let me (lit. I) *tell* you pagans this:
	19		You will *say*, 'Those branches were cut off'
16	18		People like that . . . [confuse] the simple-minded with their
		13	pious and persuasive ⌐arguments (lit. *language*).
1 Co 1	10		I do appeal to you . . . to ⌐be united (lit. *say* the same thing) again in your belief and practice.
	12		What I ⌐mean are (lit. am *talking* about) all those slogans that you have,
	15		none of you can *say* he was baptised in my name.
2	4		in my speeches and . . . sermons . . . there were none of
		3	the ⌐arguments (lit. *words*) that belong to philosophy;
3	4		What could be more unspiritual than your ⌐slogans (lit. *saying*), 'I am for Paul'?
4	19		I shall want to know not ⌐what these self-important people
		3	have to say (lit. the *words* of these self-important people), but what they can do,
	20	3	the kingdom of God is not just *words*, it is power.
10	28		if someone *says* to you, 'The food was offered in sacrifice',
	29		his scruples, ⌐you see (lit. I *say*), not your own.
11	22		What am I to *say* to you? Congratulate you?
12	3		no one can be speaking under the influence of the Holy Spirit and *say*, 'Curse Jesus', and on the other hand no one can *say*, 'Jesus is Lord' unless he is under the influence of the Holy Spirit.
14	9	3	if your tongue does not produce intelligible *speech*, how can anyone know what you are saying?
	19	3	I would rather say five ⌐words that mean something than ten
		3	thousand *words* in a tongue.
	23		any uninitiated people . . . would *say* you were all mad;
15	12		how can some of you be *saying* that there is no resurrection of the dead?
	35		Someone may ⌐ask (lit. *say*), 'How are dead people raised . . .?'
2 Co 1	18		there is no Yes and No about *what* we *say* to you.
6	13		I *speak* as if to children of mine:
7	3		I am not *saying* this to put any blame on you;
8	7		You always have the most of everything – of faith, of
		3	*eloquence*, of understanding,
	8		It is not an order that I am ⌐giving (lit. *telling*) you;
9	3		to make sure . . . that you really are ready as I *said* you would be.
	4		we should be humiliated – to *say* nothing of yourselves –
11	6	3	I may not be a polished *speech*maker,
	16		As I *said* before, let no one take me for a fool;
	21		I ⌐hope you are ashamed (lit. *speak* to your shame) . . . I am still *talking* as a fool
12	6		I should only be *speaking* the truth;
Ga 2	14		I *said* to Cephas in front of everyone, 'In spite of being a Jew,'
3	15		⌐Compare this . . . with what happens in ordinary life (lit. I *speak* as a man).
4	1		⌐Let me put this another way (lit. Now I *say*):
	21		⌐You (lit. Are you *telling* me you) want to be subject to the Law?

Ep 4	29	3	Guard against foul *talk*;
5	4	18	There must be no coarseness, or salacious *talk*
	6		Do not let anyone deceive you with empty ⌐arguments (lit. *words*).
	12		The things which are done in secret are things that people are ashamed even to *speak* of;
Ph 3	18		I have ⌐told you often, and I ⌐repeat (lit. *say*) it today with tears,
4	4		I ⌐repeat (lit. *say* it again), what I want is your happiness.
	11		I am not *talking* about shortage of money:
Col 2	4		to make sure that no one deceives you with specious ⌐arguments (lit. *words*).
3	8	19	you . . . must give these things up: getting angry, . . abusive language, dirty *talk*;
	11		never *say* or do anything except in the name of the Lord Jesus,
4	6	3	⌐Talk to them agreeably (lit. Let your *words* to them be agreeable)
	17		⌐Give Archippus this message (lit. *Say* to Archippus):
1 Th 2	5	3	never . . . have our *speeches* been simply flattery,
	13		you accepted [God's message] for what it really is, God's
		3	message, and not some human *thinking* (lit. *statement*).
5	3		It is when people are *saying*, 'How . . . peaceful it is' that the worst suddenly happens,
2 Th 2	2	3	do not get . . . alarmed by any . . . ⌐rumour (lit. *word*) or any letter claiming to come from us,
	17		[May our Lord Jesus Christ] strengthen you in everything good that you do or *say*.
1 Tm 1	6		some people . . . have . . . taken a road that leads to empty
	7	16	⌐speculation (lit. *chattering*); 7 they claim to be doctors of the Law but they understand neither ⌐the arguments they are using (lit. what they are *saying*) nor the opinions they are upholding.
2	7		I am *telling* the truth and no lie
4	12		be an example to all the believers in ⌐the way you speak and
		3	behave (lit. your *speech* and behaviour),
6	4		[Anyone who teaches anything different] must . . . [have] a
	15		craze for . . . arguing about *words*.
2 Tm 2	14	14	there is to be no wrangling about *words*:
	17	3	*Talk* of this kind corrodes like gangrene;
	18		the men who have gone right away from the truth ⌐and claim (lit. *saying*) that the resurrection has already taken place.
Tt 1	10	17	you have there a great many *people who* . . . *talk* nonsense
	12		It was one of themselves . . . who *said*, 'Cretans were never anything but liars,'
Phm	19		⌐I will not add any mention (lit. to *say* nothing) of your own debt to me,
	21		I am . . . sure that you will do even more than I ⌐ask (lit. *say*).
Heb 7	9	/25	It could be *said* in a *word* that Levi . . . actually paid [tithes],
9	5		This is not the time to ⌐go into greater (lit. *speak* in) detail about this.
	20		[Moses sprinkled . . . the people,] *saying* as he did so (Ex 24 8): This is the blood of the covenant
11	14		People who ⌐use such terms (lit *speak* in this way) . . . make it quite plain that they are in search of their real homeland (cf. Gn 23 4; 47 9).
	32		⌐Is there any need to (lit. What shall I) *say* more?
12	21		The whole scene was so terrible that Moses *said* (Dt 9 19): I am afraid,
Jm 1	13		Never, when you have been tempted, *say*, 'God sent the temptation';
2	3		you take notice of the well-dressed man, and *say*, 'Come this way . . .'; then you *tell* the poor man, 'Stand over there'
	14		someone who has never done a single good act but ⌐claims (lit. *says*) that he has faith.
	16		one of you *says* to them, 'I wish you well;'
	18		This is the way to *talk* to people of that kind:
3	2		the only man who could reach perfection would be someone
		3	who never ⌐said anything wrong (lit. erred in *speech*)
4	13		you who ⌐talk like this (lit. *say*): 'Today or tomorrow, we are
	15		off to this or that town;' . . . 15 The most you should ever *say* is: 'If it is the Lord's will, we shall still be alive to do this or that'.
1 P 3	1	3	they may find themselves won over, without a *word* [spoken], by the way their wives behave,
2 P 2	3		They will eagerly try to buy you for themselves with insidious
		3	*speeches*,
3	4		[they will] ⌐ask (lit. *say*), 'Well, where is this coming?'
1 Jn 1	6		If we *say* that we are in union with God
	8		If we *say* we have no sin in us
	10		To *say* that we have never sinned is to call God a liar
2	4		Anyone who *says*, 'I know [God]',
	6		the one who ⌐claims to be (lit. *says* he is) living in [God]
	9		Anyone who ⌐claims to be (lit. *says* he is) in the light
3	18	3	our love is not to be just *words* or mere talk,
4	20		Anyone who *says*, 'I love God', and hates his brother, is a liar,
5	16		there is a sin that is death, and I will not *say* that you must pray about that.

2 Jn	10	you must not . . . even ʳgive him a greeting (lit. *say* a greeting to him).
	11	To ʳgreet him (lit. *say* a greeting to him) would make you a partner in his wicked work.
3 Jn	10	I shall tell everyone . . . about the wicked ʳaccusations (lit. 3 *words*) [Diotrephes] has been circulating against us.
Jude	15	to pronounce judgement on all mankind and to sentence the 3 wicked . . . for all the defiant *things said* against him
Rv	2 24	all of you who have not . . . learnt the secrets of Satan, as they are *called*,
	7 14	I ʳanswered (lit. *said* to) him, 'You can tell me, my lord.'
	10 9	I went to the angel and ʳasked (lit. *told*) him to give me the small scroll,
	12 11	3 by the blood of the Lamb and by the ʳwitness (lit. *word*) of their martyrdom,
	13 4	they prostrated themselves in front of the beast, *saying*, 'Who can compare with the beast?'
	18 10	They will *say*: 'Mourn, mourn for this great city, Babylon,'
	16	They will be *saying*: 'Mourn, mourn for this great city;
	18	[all those who make a living from the sea will be] ʳcrying out (lit. *saying*), 'Has there ever been a city as great as this!'
	19	They will . . . *say*, with tears and groans: 'Mourn, mourn for this great city . . .'

d) (specific people) Say, Tell

(Apostles, disciples) Say (to)

Mt	6 31	disciples	Mk	8 19	disciples to Jesus
	8 21	disciples to Jesus		20	disciples to Jesus
	25	disciples to Jesus		28	disciples to Jesus
	27	disciples to each other		—	disciples to Jesus
	13 10	disciples to Jesus		29	2 Peter to Jesus
	36	disciples to Jesus	9 5		2 Peter to Jesus
	51	disciples to Jesus		11	Peter, James and John to Jesus
	14 15	disciples to Jesus	10 26		disciples to each other
	17	disciples to Jesus		35	sons of Zebedee to Jesus
	26	disciples		37	sons of Zebedee to Jesus
	28	2 Peter to Jesus			
	30	Peter to Jesus		39	sons of Zebedee to Jesus
	33	disciples to Jesus			
	15 12	disciples to Jesus	11 21		Peter to Jesus
	15	2 Peter to Jesus	13 1		disciples to Jesus
	23	disciples to Jesus	14 12		disciples to Jesus
	33	disciples to Jesus		19	disciples to Jesus
	34	disciples to Jesus		44	Judas to the crowd armed with swords
	16 7	disciples			
	14	disciples to Jesus		45	Judas to Jesus
	16	2 Peter to Jesus		68	Peter to the servant-girl
	22	Peter to Jesus			
	17 4	2 Peter to Jesus	Lk 5 5		2 Peter to Jesus
	10	disciples to Jesus		8	Peter to Jesus
	19	disciples to Jesus	8 24		disciples to Jesus
	25	Peter to collectors		25	disciples to each other
	26	Peter to Jesus			
	18 1	disciples to Jesus		45	Peter and others to Jesus
	21	Peter to Jesus			
	19 10	disciples to Jesus	9 12		Twelve to Jesus
	25	disciples to Jesus		13	Twelve to Jesus
	27	2 Peter to Jesus		19	2 disciples to Jesus
	20 22	sons of Zebedee to Jesus		20	2 Peter to Jesus
				33	Peter to Jesus
	21 20	disciples to Jesus		49	2 John to Jesus
	24 3	disciples to Jesus		54	James and John to Jesus
	26 8	disciples	10 17		The seventy-two to Jesus
	15	Judas to the chief priests			
	17	disciples to Jesus	11 1		a disciple to Jesus
	22	disciples	12 41		Peter to Jesus
	25	2 Judas to Jesus	17 5		apostles to Jesus
	33	2 Peter to Jesus		37	2 disciples to Jesus
	35	Peter to Jesus	18 28		Peter to Jesus
	48	Judas to the crowd armed with swords	19 34		two disciples to owner of the colt
	49	Judas to Jesus	22 9		Peter and John to Jesus
	70	Peter to the servant-girl		33	Peter to Jesus
	27 4	Judas to the chief priests and elders		35	apostles to Jesus
				38	apostles to Jesus
	64	disciples to people		49	followers of Jesus to Jesus
Mk	1 37	disciples to Jesus			
	4 38	disciples to Jesus		57	Peter to the servant-girl
	41	disciples			
	5 31	disciples to Jesus		60	Peter to a man
	6 35	disciples to Jesus	24 18		2 Cleopas to Jesus
	37	disciples to Jesus			
	38	disciples to Jesus			
	8 5	disciples to Jesus			

Lk	24 19	"disciples from Emmaus" to Jesus	Ac	8 30	Philip to the eunuch
	29	"disciples from Emmaus" to Jesus		37ᵛ	Philip to the eunuch
	32	"disciples from Emmaus" to each other	9 5		Saul to the Lord [on the road to Damascus]
	34	the Eleven and others to the "disciples from Emmaus"		34	Peter to Aeneas
				40	Peter to Tabitha
Jn	1 41	Andrew to Simon	10 14		Peter to the angel
	45	Philip to Nathanael		21	Peter to Cornelius's messengers
	46	Nathanael to Philip		26	Peter to Cornelius
	—	Philip to Nathanael		34	Peter to Cornelius and his relations
	48	Nathanael to Jesus	11 4		Peter to the brothers in Jerusalem
	4 27	disciples to Jesus			
	31	disciples to Jesus	12 11		Peter
	33	disciples to each other		17	Peter to the people in Mary's house
	6 8	Andrew to Jesus	13 10		Paul to Elymas
	60	followers of Jesus		16	Paul to the Jews at Antioch in Pisidia
	9 2	disciples to Jesus			
	11 8	disciples to Jesus		46	Paul and Barnabas to the same
	12	disciples to Jesus	14 10		Paul to cripple at Lystra
	16	Thomas to disciples		15	Barnabas and Paul to crowd at Lystra
	12 4	Judas			
	13 6	Peter to Jesus		18	Barnabas and Paul to crowd at Lystra
	8	Peter to Jesus			
	9	Peter to Jesus	15 7		Peter to apostles and elders
	24	Peter to [John]			
	25	[John] to Jesus		13	2 James to apostles and elders
	36	Peter to Jesus			
	37	Peter to Jesus		36	Paul to Barnabas
	14 5	Thomas to Jesus	16 18		Paul to soothsaying spirit
	8	Philip to Jesus			
	22	Judas to Jesus		28	Paul to gaoler
	16 17	disciples to each other		31	Paul and Silas to gaoler
	18	disciples to each other	18 6		Paul to the Jews of Corinth
	29	disciples to Jesus		21	Paul to the Jews of Ephesus
	18 17	Peter to the servant-girl	19 2		Paul to disciples in Ephesus
	25	Peter to a bystander		3	Paul to disciples in Ephesus
	20 25	disciples to Thomas			
	—	Thomas to disciples		4	Paul to disciples in Ephesus
	28	2 Thomas to Jesus		21	Paul to disciples in Ephesus
	21 3	Peter to Thomas and others	20 10		Paul
	—	disciples to Peter		18	Paul to elders of the Church in Ephesus
	7	[John] to Peter			
	15	Peter to Jesus	21 14		disciples
	16	Peter to Jesus		37	Paul to the tribune
	17	Peter to Jesus		39	Paul to the tribune
	21	Peter to Jesus		40	Paul to the Jews
Ac	1 6	apostles	22 25		Paul to the centurion
	15	Peter to 120 brothers	23 1		Paul to Sanhedrin
	2 40	Peter to crowd at Pentecost		3	Paul to Ananias
	3 4	Peter and John to cripple	25 10		Paul to Festus
	6	Peter to cripple	27 10		Paul to the others in the ship
	4 8	Peter to Sanhedrin			
	19	2 Peter and John to Sanhedrin		21	Paul to the others in the ship
	5 3	Peter to Ananias			
	29	2 Peter and apostles to Sanhedrin		31	Paul to the centurion and his men
	6 2	Twelve to disciples		33	Paul to the others in the ship
	7 56	Stephen before Sanhedrin	28 17		Paul to leading Jews in Rome
	8 20	Peter to Simon the magician			

(Jews, chief priests and Pharisees) Say (to)

Mt	2 5	chief priests and scribes to Herod	Mt	9 11	Pharisees to the disciples
	8 19	scribe to Jesus		34	Pharisees
	9 3	scribes to each other	12 2		Pharisees to Jesus
				10	Pharisees to Jesus

Mt 12 24	Pharisees
38	2 scribes and Pharisees to Jesus
15 1	scribes and Pharisees to Jesus
19 3	Pharisees to Jesus
7	Pharisees to Jesus
21 16	chief priests and scribes to Jesus
23	chief priests and elders to Jesus
25	chief priests and elders
27	2 chief priests and elders to Jesus
31	chief priests and elders to Jesus
41	chief priests and elders to Jesus
22 16	disciples of the Pharisees, and Herodians, to Jesus
21	disciples of the Pharisees, and Herodians, to Jesus
24	Sadducees to Jesus
42	Pharisees to Jesus
26 5	chief priests and elders to Jesus
62	two false witnesses to Sanhedrin
63ᵛ	2 chief priests and elders to Jesus
65	the Sanhedrin
66	2 the Sanhedrin
27 4	chief priests and elders to Judas
6	chief priests
41	chief priests, scribes and elders to Jesus
63	chief priests
28 13	chief priests to soldiers
Mk 2 16	scribes and Pharisees to disciples
24	Pharisees to Jesus
3 22	scribes
30	scribes
10 4	Pharisees to Jesus
11 28	chief priests, scribes and elders to Jesus
31	chief priests, scribes and elders
33	2 chief priests, scribes and elders to Jesus
12 14	Pharisees and Herodians to Jesus
16	Pharisees and Herodians to Jesus
18	Sadducees to Jesus
32	scribe to Jesus
14 2	chief priests and scribes
60	high priest to Jesus
61	high priest to Jesus
63	high priest to Sanhedrin
15 31	chief priests and scribes
Lk 5 21	scribes and Pharisees
30	scribes and Pharisees to disciples
33	scribes and Pharisees to Jesus
6 2	Pharisees to disciples
Lk 7 4	elders to Jesus
39	Simon the Pharisee to himself
—	Simon the Pharisee to himself
43	2 Simon the Pharisee to Jesus
10 25	lawyer to Jesus
27	2 lawyer to Jesus
29	lawyer to Jesus
37	lawyer to Jesus
11 45	2 lawyer to Jesus
13 14	2 synagogue official to the crowd
31	Pharisees to Jesus
15 2	Pharisees and scribes
19 39	Pharisees to Jesus
20 2	chief priests, scribes and elders to Jesus
5	chief priests, scribes and elders
16	chief priests, scribes and elders, and/or people
21	chief priests and scribes to Jesus
24	chief priests and scribes to Jesus
28	Sadducees to Jesus
39	2 scribes to Jesus
22 67	elders, chief priests and scribes to Jesus
70	elders, chief priests and scribes to Jesus
71	elders, chief priests and scribes
23 35	leaders of the people
Jn 1 22	priests and Levites to John the Baptist
25	priests and Levites to John the Baptist
2 18	2 Jews to Jesus
20	Jews to Jesus
5 10	Jews to the paralytic
6 42	Jews to each other
52	Jews to each other
7 11	Jews to each other
12	people
—	people
15	Jews
25	people
35	Jews to each other
45	chief priests and Pharisees to police
52	2 Pharisees to Nicodemus
8 4	scribes and Pharisees to Jesus
13	Pharisees to Jesus
19	Pharisees to Jesus
22	Jews to each other
25	Jews to Jesus
39	2 Jews to Jesus
41	2 Jews to Jesus
48	2 Jews to Jesus
52	Jews to Jesus
57	Jews to Jesus
9 16	Pharisees
—	Pharisees
17	Pharisees to man born blind
19	Jews to parents of man born blind
24	Jews to man born blind
26	Jews to man born blind
Jn 9 28	Jews to man born blind
34	2 Jews to man born blind
40	Pharisees to Jesus
10 20	Jews
21	Jews
24	Jews to Jesus
11 34	Martha and Mary
36	Jews
37	Jews
47	chief priests and Pharisees
12 19	Pharisees to each other
18 30	2 Jews to Pilate
31	Jews to Pilate
19 6	chief priests and guards to Pilate
12	Jews to Pilate
21	chief priests to Pilate
Ac 4 16	Sanhedrin
5 28	high priest to apostles
7 1	high priest to Stephen
18 13	Jews to proconsul
21 20	elders of Church to Paul
22 22	Jews
23 4	high priest's attendants to Paul
9	scribes and Pharisees to Sanhedrin and proconsul
14	Jews to chief priests and elders
28 21	Paul to leading Jews in Rome

(John the Baptist and his disciples) Say (to)

Mt 3 2	John the Baptist
7	John the Baptist to Pharisees and Sadducees
14	John the Baptist to Jesus
9 14	John the Baptist's disciples to Jesus
14 4	John the Baptist to Herod
Mk 1 7	John the Baptist
6 18	John the Baptist to Herod
Lk 3 7	John the Baptist to the crowds
11	2 John the Baptist to all the people
13	John the Baptist to tax collectors
14	John the Baptist to soldiers
Lk 3 16	John the Baptist to all the people
7 20	John the Baptist's disciples to Jesus
Jn 1 15	John the Baptist
21	John the Baptist to priests and Levites
26	2 John the Baptist to priests and Levites
29	John the Baptist
32	John the Baptist
36	John the Baptist
38	two disciples of John to Jesus
3 26	John's disciples to John
27	2 John the Baptist to his disciples
Ac 13 25	John the Baptist

(Pilate) Says (to)

Mt 27 11	to Jesus
13	to Jesus
17	to the crowd
21	2 to the crowd
22	to the crowd
24	to the crowd
Mk 15 4	to Jesus
9	2 to the crowd
12	2 to the crowd
14	to the crowd
Lk 23 3	to Jesus
4	to the chief priests and the crowd
14	to the chief priests, the leading men and the people
Lk 23 22	to the chief priests, the leading men and the people
Jn 18 31	to the Jews
33	to Jesus
37	to Jesus
38	to Jesus
—	to the Jews
19 4	to the Jews
5	to the Jews
6	to the chief priests and the guards
9	to Jesus
10	to Jesus
14	to the Jews

(Demonicas) Say (to)

Mt 8 29	two demoniacs to Jesus
Mk 1 24	a man possessed to Jesus
5 7	a demoniac to Jesus
Lk 8 28	a demoniac to Jesus
30	a demoniac to Jesus

(Crowd, people, men) Say (to)

Mt 9 33	people
12 23	people
13 54	people
21 9	crowds
10	people in Jerusalem
11	crowds
26 28	people to Jesus
27 21	crowd to Pilate
22	crowd to Pilate
23	crowd to Pilate
25	2 people to Pilate
Mk 1 27	people
3 32	crowd (?) to Jesus
5 35	people to Jairus
Mk 6 2	people in synagogue
7 37	people
9 26	people
11 5	some men to the disciples
14 65	crowd (?) to Jesus
Lk 1 66	people
3 10	people to John the Baptist
4 22	people of Nazareth
36	people to each other

Book	Ch	V	Description
Lk	5	26	people
	9	18	crowds
	12	54	crowds
	14	30	onlookers
	19	7	crowd
	20	16	the people? scribes?
		21	agents of scribes and chief priests to Jesus
		24	agents of scribes and chief priests to Jesus
	23	2	assembly
		5	assembly
		18	chief priests, leading men and the people
		21	chief priests, leading men and the people
Jn	6	14	people
		25	people to Jesus
		28	people to Jesus
		30	people to Jesus
		34	people to Jesus
	7	31	believers in crowd
Jn	7	40	believers in crowd
		41	believers in crowd
		—	unbelievers in crowd
	9	8	people
		9	people
		—	people
		10	people to the man born blind
		12	people to the man born blind
	10	41	people
	11	56	country people in Jerusalem
	18	40	Jews to Pilate
Ac	2	7	crowd
		12	crowd
		13	crowd
		37	crowd to Peter and the other apostles
	6	11	men
	8	10	everyone in Samaritan town
	9	21	people of Damascus
	14	11	crowd in Lystra

(Various people) Say (to)

Book	Ch	V	Description
Mt	2	2	wise men
		8	Herod to wise men
	8	2	leper to Jesus
		6	centurion to Jesus
		9	centurion to his servant
	9	18	official to Jesus
		21	sick woman to herself
		27	two blind men to Jesus
		28	two blind men to Jesus
	11	17	children
	12	47	a man to Jesus
	13	27	servants to owner of field
		28	servants to owner
	14	2	Herod to his court
	15	22	Canaanite woman to Jesus
		25	Canaanite woman to Jesus
		27	Canaanite woman to Jesus
	17	15	epileptic's father to Jesus
		24	collectors of the half-shekel to Peter
	18	26	servant to king
		28	servant to servant
		29	servant to servant
		32	king to servant
	19	16	rich young man to Jesus
		18	rich young man to Jesus
		20	rich young man to Jesus
	20	4	landowner to workers
		6	landowner to workers
		7	workers to landowner
		—	landowner to workers
		8	landowner to bailiff
		11	workers to landowner
		13	2 landowner to worker
		21	mother of Zebedee's sons to Jesus
		30	two blind men to Jesus
Mt	20	31	two blind men to Jesus
		33	two blind men to Jesus
	21	15	children
		28	man to his son
		29	son to father
		30	man to second son
		—	2 second son to father
		37	landowner
		38	tenants to each other
	22	4	king to servants
		8	king to servants
		12	king to guest
		13	king to attendants
	24	48	dishonest servant to himself
	25	8	foolish bridesmaids to sensible ones
		9	2 sensible bridesmaids to foolish ones
		20	servant to master
		22	servant to master
		24	servant to master
		26	2 master to servant
		37	2 the virtuous to King, Son of Man
		44	2 evildoers to King, son of Man
	26	61	two false witnesses to Sanhedrin
		69	servant-girl to Peter
		71	servant-girl to bystanders
		73	bystanders to Peter
	27	29	soldiers to Jesus
		40	passers-by to Jesus
		47	some bystanders
		49	other bystanders
		54	centurion and soldiers
Mk	1	40	leper to Jesus
	3	21	Jesus's relatives
	5	23	Jairus to Jesus
		28	sick woman to herself
	6	14	some people
		15	other people
		—	other people
		16	Herod
		22	Herod to daughter of Herodias
Mk	6	24	daughter to Herodias
		—	Herodias to daughter
		25	daughter of Herodias to Herod
	7	28	2 Syrophoenician woman to Jesus
	8	24	blind man to Jesus
	9	21	father of epileptic to Jesus
		24	father of epileptic to Jesus
	10	47	Bartimaeus to Jesus
		49	people to Bartimaeus
		51	Bartimaeus to Jesus
	12	6	owner of vineyard
		7	tenants to each other
	14	57	false witnesses
		67	servant-girl to Peter
		69	servant-girl to bystanders
		70	bystanders to Peter
		71	bystanders
	15	29	passers-by to Jesus
		35	bystanders
		36	bystander
		39	centurion
	16	3	women to each other
Lk	1	18	Zechariah to angel
		24	Elizabeth
		34	Virgin Mary to angel
		38	Virgin Mary to angel
		42	Elizabeth to Mary
		60	2 Elizabeth to her relations
		61	relations to Elizabeth
		63	Zechariah
		67	Zechariah
	2	34	Simeon to Virgin Mary
		48	Virgin Mary to Jesus
	3	12	tax collectors to John the Baptist
	5	12	leper to Jesus
	7	8	centurion to soldiers
		32	children
		49	Jesus's fellow guests to each other
	8	49	man to Jairus
	9	7	some people
		9	Herod
		38	father of epileptic to Jesus
		57	man to Jesus
		59	a second man to Jesus
		61	a third man to Jesus
	10	35	Samaritan to innkeeper
		40	Martha to Jesus
	11	5	man to his friend
		7	2 friend to the man
		15	some people
		27	woman to Jesus
	12	13	man to Jesus
		17	rich man to himself
		18	rich man to himself
		45	servant to himself
	13	7	owner of vineyard
		23	someone to Jesus
	14	15	a fellow guest to Jesus
Lk	14	17	servant to guests
		18	guest to servant
		19	second guest to servant
		20	third guest to servant
		21	master to servant
		22	servant to master
		23	master to servant
	15	6	man to neighbours
		9	woman to neighbours
		12	younger son to father
		21	younger son to father
		22	father to servants
		27	servant to elder son
		29	2 elder son to father
		31	father to elder son
	16	2	rich man to steward
		3	steward to himself
		5	steward to debtor
		6	debtor to steward
		—	steward to debtor
		7	steward to second debtor
		—	second debtor to steward
		—	steward to second debtor
		24	rich man to Abraham
		25	Abraham to rich man
		27	rich man to Abraham
		29	Abraham to rich man
		30	rich man to Abraham
		31	Abraham to rich man
	17	4	your brother to you
		13	ten lepers to Jesus
	18	3	widow to judge
		4	judge to himself
		18	rich aristocrat to Jesus
		21	rich aristocrat to Jesus
		26	listeners to Jesus
		38	blind man to Jesus
		41	blind man to Jesus
	19	8	Zacchaeus to Jesus
		13	king-elect to servants
		14	his compatriots
		16	servant to king
		17	king to servant
		18	second servant to king
		19	king to second servant
		20	third servant to king
		22	king to third servant
		24	king to bystanders
		25	bystanders to king
		33	owner of colt to two disciples
	20	13	owner of vineyard
		14	tenants to each other
	21	7	people in the Temple to Jesus
	22	56	servant-girl to bystanders
		59	second man to bystanders
		64	guards to Jesus
	23	37	soldiers to Jesus
		39 v	good thief to Jesus
		42	good thief to Jesus

Jn 2 3	Virgin Mary to Jesus	
5	Virgin Mary to servants	
10	steward to bridegroom	
3 2	Nicodemus to Jesus	
4	Nicodemus to Jesus	
9	2 Nicodemus to Jesus	
4 9	Samaritan woman to Jesus	
11	Samaritan woman to Jesus	
15	Samaritan woman to Jesus	
17	2 Samaritan woman to Jesus	
19	Samaritan woman to Jesus	
25	Samaritan woman to Jesus	
28	Samaritan woman to people of Sychar	
42	people of Sychar to Samaritan woman	
49	official to Jesus	
51	servants to official	
52	servants to official	
7 3	Jesus's "brothers" to Jesus	
50	Nicodemus to Pharisees	
8 11	adulteress to Jesus	
9 9	man born blind to people	
12	man born blind to people	
15	man born blind to Pharisees	
20	2 parents of man born blind to the Jews	
23	parents of man born blind to the Jews	
30	2 man born blind to the Jews	
36	2 man born blind to Jesus	
11 21	Martha to Jesus	
24	Martha to Jesus	
27	Martha to Jesus	
32	Mary to Jesus	
39	Martha to Jesus	
49	Caiaphas to chief priests and Pharisees	
12 21	Greeks to Philip	
18 7	men who arrested Jesus to Jesus	
17	servant-girl to Peter	
22	guard to Jesus	
25	bystander to Peter	
26	high priest's servant to Peter	
19 3	soldiers to Jesus	
24	soldiers to each other	
20 2	Mary of Magdala to Peter and [John]	

Jn 20 13	Mary of Magdala to angels
15	Mary of Magdala to gardener (= Jesus)
Ac 5 23	officials to Sanhedrin
35	Gamaliel to Sanhedrin
6 13	false witnesses
8 19	Simon the magician to the apostles
24	2 Simon the magician to Peter
31	eunuch to Philip
34	2 eunuch to Philip
37ᵛ	eunuch to Philip
9 10	Ananias to the Lord
17	Ananias to Saul
10 4	Cornelius to angel
22	Cornelius's servants to Peter
11 3	circumcised brothers to Peter
12 15	Mary's household to Rhoda
—	Mary's household to Rhoda
16 9	Macedonian to Paul
15	Lydia to apostles
17	slave-girl soothsayer
20	slave-girl's masters to magistrates
17 18	Athenians to Paul
19	Athenians to Paul
32	Athenians to Paul
18 14	Gallio to the Jews
19 3	John's disciples at Ephesus to Paul
13	Jewish exorcists to people possessed
25	Demetrius to silversmiths
28	silversmiths
21 11	Agabus to apostles
22 13	Ananias to Saul
14	Ananias to Saul
26	centurion to tribune
27	tribune to Paul
23 20	Paul's nephew to tribune
23	tribune to two centurions
24 2	Tertullus
22	Felix to Paul
25 9	2 Festus to Paul
14	Festus to Agrippa
26 31	Festus, Agrippa and others among themselves
28 4	Maltese to each other
21	leading Jews in Rome to Paul
Rv 6 16	(Ho 10 8) rulers . . , slaves and citizens to mountains

5: (THINGS AND PERSONIFICATIONS) SAY

Rm 9 20	The pot has no right to *say* to the potter: Why did you make me this shape?
10 6	the righteousness that comes from faith *says* this (Dt 30 11–14):
8	On the positive side it *says*: The word . . . is very near to you,
1 Co 12 15	If the foot were to *say*, 'I am not a hand'
16	If the ear were to *say*, 'I am not an eye,'
21	The eye cannot *say* to the hand, 'I do not need you',

Rv 3 17	[Write to the angel of the church in Laodicea:] You *say to* yourself, 'I am rich,'
8 13	I heard an eagle, *calling* aloud . ., 'Trouble . . . for all the people on earth'
13 14	[the second beast] was able to win over the people of the world ʳand persuade (lit. *telling*) them to put up a statue in honour of the beast
18 7	I am the queen on my throne, [Babylon] *says* to herself,

6: ADVOCATE

Tertullus 2

Ac 24 1		the high priest Ananias came down with some of the elders
	23	and an *advocate* named *Tertullus*, and they laid information
2		against Paul before the governor. ² Paul was called, and *Tertullus* opened for the prosecution,

7: FOREWARN – FORETELL – ALREADY TOLD

Mt 24 25	X	4	I have *forewarned* you.
Mk 13 23	X	4	I have *forewarned* you of everything.
Ac 1 16	Ⓢ	4	the passage of scripture had to be fulfilled in which the Holy Spirit . . . *foretells* the fate of Judas,
Rm 9 29		4	As Isaiah *foretold* (Is 1 9): Had the Lord of hosts not left us some descendants
2 Co 7 3		4	I have *already told* you, you are in our hearts
13 2		4/4	I *gave warning* when I was with you . . . and I *give warning* now, too, . . . that when I come again, I shall have no mercy.
Ga 1 9		4	I am only repeating what we *told* you *before*:
5 21		4/4	I *warn* you now, as I *warned* you before:
1 Th 3 4		4	we *warned* you that we must expect to have persecutions
4 6		4	the Lord always punishes sins of that sort, as we *told* you *before*
Heb 4 7		4	[God] said . . . in the text *already quoted* (Ps 95 7): If only you would listen to him today:
2 P 3 2		4	recalling to you what was *said in the past* by the holy prophets
Jude 17		4	remember . . . what the apostles . . . ʳtold you to expect (lit. *foretold*).

8: SPEAK (AGAINST)

Mt 5 11		Happy are you when people abuse you and . . . *speak* all kinds of calumny against you on my account.
12 32	/3	anyone who *says* a *word* against the Son of Man will be forgiven; but let anyone *speak* against the Holy Spirit and he will not be forgiven
Lk 12 10	/3	Everyone who *says* a *word* against the Son of Man will be forgiven, but he who blasphemes against the Holy Spirit will not be forgiven.
22 65		[the soldiers] ʳcontinued heaping insults on him (lit. *said* many other things against him, insulting him).
Ac 6 11	22	We heard [Stephen] using blasphemous *language* against Moses and against God.
13	22	[Stephen] is always making *speeches* against the Holy Place and the Law.
Tt 2 8	△	[keep] all you *say* so wholesome that . . . any opponent will be at a loss, with ʳno accusation to make (lit. nothing to *say*) against us.

9: ARGUE, ARGUMENT – DISCUSS, DEBATE, TALK (AMONG)

Mt 16 7	6	[the disciples] ʳ*said* to (or: thought among) themselves, 'It is because we have not brought any bread.'
8	6	Men of little faith, why are you ʳ*talking* (or: thinking) among yourselves about having no bread?
21 25	6	[the chief priests and elders] *argued* it out this way among themselves,
Mk 2 6	6	some scribes were sitting there, and they ʳ*thought* (or: *said*) to themselves, ⁷ 'How can this man talk like that?'
8 16	6	[the disciples] *said* to one another, 'It is because we have no bread.'
17	6	Why are you ʳ*talking* (or: thinking) about having no bread?
9 33	6	What were you *arguing* about on the road?
34	5	[the disciples] had been *arguing* which of them was the greatest.
11 31	6	[the chief priests, scribes and elders] *argued* it out this way among themselves:
Lk 9 46	9	An *argument* started between [the disciples] about which of them was the greatest.
20 5	21	[the chief priests and scribes] *argued it out* this way *among themselves*,
14	6	when the tenants saw [the owner's son] they ʳput their heads together (lit. *argued* it over).
24 17	3	What *matters* are you discussing as you walk along?
Ac 17 2	5	for three consecutive sabbaths [Paul] *developed the arguments* from scripture

Ac 17	17	5	In the synagogue [in Athens Paul] *held debates* with the Jews
	21		The one amusement the Athenians . . . seem to have, apart from *discussing* the latest ideas,
18	4	5	Every sabbath [in Corinth Paul] used to *hold debates* in the synagogues,
	19	5	When they reached Ephesus . . . [Paul] went alone to the synagogue to *debate* with the Jews.
19	8	5	[At Ephesus Paul] began by going to the synagogue, where he . . . *argued* persuasively about the kingdom of God.
	9	5	[Paul] took his disciples apart to *hold* daily *discussions* in the lecture room of Tyrannus.
20	7	5	Paul was due to leave [Ephesus] the next day, and he ⌐preached a sermon that (lit. *discussed* things with [the brothers] and what he said) went on till the middle of the night.
	9	5	as Paul ⌐went (lit. *argued*) on and on, a young man called Eutychus . . . grew drowsy
24	12	5	it is not true that they ever found me *arguing* with anyone or stirring up the mob,
	25	5	when [Paul] began to *treat of* righteousness . . . and the coming Judgement, Felix took fright
1 Co 3	20	9	God is not convinced by the *arguments* of the wise.
Ph 2	14	9	Do all that has to be done without complaining or *arguing*
1 Tm 2	8	9	I want the men to lift their hands up reverently in prayer, with no anger or *argument*.
Heb 12	5	5	Have you forgotten that encouraging text in which you are *addressed* as sons (Pr 3 11–12 G)?
Jude	9	5	Not even the archangel Michael, when he was *engaged in argument* with the devil . ., dared to denounce him

10: ACCOUNT, REASON – ANSWER

Mt 12	36	3	for every unfounded word men . . . will [give an] ⌐answer (or: *account*).
Ac 19	40	3	we can give no *reason* for this gathering
Rm 14	12	3	It is to God . . . that each of us must give an *account* of himself.
Ph 4	15	3	no other church helped me ⌐with (lit. in *terms* of) gifts of money,
Heb 4	13	3	everything is . . . open to the eyes of . . . whom we must give an *account* of ourselves.
13	17	3	your leaders . . . must give an *account* of the way they look after your souls.
1 P 3	15	3	people who ask the *reason* for the hope you all have
4	5	3	They will have to [give an] *answer* for it [to] the judge [of] the living and the dead.

11: CLAIM (TO BE), SPEAK OF (A PERSON, ONESELF) AS, GIVE OUT (THAT)

Lk 23	2		We found this man inciting . . . revolt, . . . and *claiming* to be Christ, a king.
Jn 5	18		[Jesus] *spoke of* God *as* his own Father,
Ac 4	32		no one *claimed* for his own [use] anything that he had,
5	36		[Theudas] *claimed* to be someone important,
8	9		[Simon] had *given it out* that he was someone momentous,
Ep 2	11		there was a time when you [were] termed the Uncircumcised by those who *speak of* themselves *as* the Circumcision
Rv 2	20		you are encouraging the woman Jezebel who *claims* to be a prophetess,

12: TO MEAN – LANGUAGE

a) to Mean

Jn 1	38		[the two disciples] answered, 'Rabbi' – which *means* Teacher
4	25		I know that Messiah – that ⌐is (lit. *means*) Christ – is coming;
20	16		[Mary] said to him in Hebrew, 'Rabbuni!' – which *means* Master.
Ac 9	36		At Jaffa there was a woman disciple called Tabitha, or Dorcas [Gazelle] as it *means* in Greek,

b) Language

Ac 1	19	7	the field came to be called the Bloody Acre, in their *language* Hakeldama.
2	6	7	each one bewildered to hear these men speaking his own *language*,
	8	7	How does it happen that each of us hears them in his own *language*?
21	40	7	[Paul] spoke to [the crowd in Jerusalem] in the Hebrew *language*.
22	2	7	When [the people] realised he was speaking in the Hebrew *language*
26	14	7	I heard a voice saying to me in the Hebrew *language*, 'Saul Saul, why are you persecuting me?'

3. SAY, TELL: *PHĒMI*

2	*phaskō* 3	1	*phēmi*	67
5	*phasis* 1	3	*dia-phēmizō*	3
4	*phēmē* 2			

1: (GOD) SAYS

1 Co 6	16	the two, as ⌐it is (lit. he [= God]) *said* (Gn 2 24), become one flesh.
Heb 8	5	Moses . . . was warned by God who *said* (Ex 25 40): See that you make everything according to the pattern shown you on the mountain.

2: (AN ANGEL or GOD) SAYS

Ac 10	31	He *said*, 'Cornelius, your prayer has been heard'

3: (JESUS) SAYS

Mt 26	61	[two witnesses] made a statement, 'This man *said*, "I have power to destroy the Temple"'

(to the apostles and disciples)

J = *Jesus* (= *Iēsous*) 8/923

Mt 17 26 J	Peter		Mk 9 12	Peter, James and John
26 34 J	Peter		10 29 J	Peter

(to other people)

Mt 4	7 J	the devil	Mt 27 11 J	Pilate
19	18 J	rich young man	Mk 12 24 J	Sadducees
21	21 J	rich young man	Lk 7 44	Simon the Pharisee
21	27	chief priests and elders	22 70	Sanhedrin
22	37	Pharisee	23 3	Pilate

4: (A PERSON) SAYS – ASSERT, ALLEGE

Ac 24	9	2	The Jews supported [Tertullus], *asserting* that these were the facts.
25	19	2	a dead man called Jesus whom Paul *alleged* to be alive.
Rm 1	22	2	⌐The more they *called* themselves philosophers, the more stupid they grew,
3	8	2	Some slanderers have ⌐accused us of teaching (lit. *said* that we teach) this,
1 Co 7	29		this is what I ⌐mean (lit. *say*): our time is growing short.
10	15		judge for yourselves what I am *saying*.
	19		⌐Does this mean that (lit. What. What then am I *saying*? That) the . . . idol itself is real?
15	50		⌐put it this way (lit. I *say*): flesh and blood cannot inherit the kingdom of God:

(Apostles and disciples) Say (to)

Mk 9	38	John to Jesus	Ac 16	37	Paul to officers
14	29	Peter to Jesus	17	22	Paul to Athenians
Lk 22	58	Peter to servant-girl	22	2	Paul to Jews
				27	Paul to tribune
Ac 2	38ᵛ	Peter to crowd at Pentecost		28	Paul to tribune
			23	5	Paul to Sanhedrin
7	2	Stephen to Sanhedrin		17	Paul to centurion
10	28	Peter to Cornelius's relations and friends	26	25	Paul to Festus

(Specific people) Say (to)

Mt 8	8	centurion to Jesus	Lk 15	17	prodigal son
13	28	master to servants	22	58	man to Peter
	29	master to servants	23	40	good thief to second thief
14	8	daughter of Herodias to Herod	Jn 1	23	John to priests and Levites
25	21	master to servant	9	38	man born blind to Jesus
	23	master to servant	18	29	Pilate to Jews
27	23	Pilate to crowd	Ac 8	36	eunuch to Philip
	65	Pilate to chief priests and Pharisees	10	30	Cornelius to Peter
			16	30	gaoler to Paul and Silas
Mk 10	20	rich young man to Jesus	19	35	town clerk to Ephesians
Lk 7	40	Simon the Pharisee to Jesus	21	37	tribune to Paul

Ac	23	18	centurion to tribune	Ac	25	22	Festus to Agrippa
		35	Felix to Paul		26	24	Festus to Agrippa
	25	5	Festus to chief priests and leaders		26	1	Agrippa to Paul
						24	Festus to Paul
						32	Agrippa to Festus
				2 Co	10	10	someone

5: REPUTATION, REPORT, NEWS – SPREAD (A STORY)

Mt	9	26	4 the *news* spread all round the countryside.
		31	[Jesus cured two blind men:] they ⌐talked about him (lit. 3 *spread his fame*) all over the countryside.
	28	15	3 to this day that ⌐is the story (lit. story is *widespread*) among the Jews.
Mk	1	45	3 the [leper] started talking about [his cure] freely and *telling* the story everywhere,
Lk	4	14	4 Jesus . . . returned to Galilee; and his *reputation* spread through the countryside.
Ac	21	31	5 [The mob] would have killed [Paul] if a *report* had not reached the tribune of the cohort

4. ANSWER, REPLY – SPEAK, SAY (IN RESPONSE): *APO-KRINOMAI*

> 1 *apo-krinomai* 87/234   3 *ant-apo-krinomai* 2
> 2 *apo-krisis*   4

1: (A HEAVENLY VOICE) SPEAKS (IN RESPONSE)

| Ac | 11 | 9 | And a second time the voice *spoke* from heaven, |

2: (JESUS) ANSWERS, REPLIES (TO A PERSON)

J = *Jesus* (= *Iēsous*) 29/923

Mt	15	23	he *answered* [the Canaanite woman] not a word.
	26	62	The high priest . . . said to him, '*Have* you no *answer* to that?'
	27	12	he ⌐refused to answer at all (lit. *answered* nothing).
		14	he *offered* no *reply* to any of the charges.
Mk	12	28	One of the scribes who had . . . observed how well Jesus had *answered* [the Sadducees],
	14	60	The high priest . . . put this question to Jesus, '*Have* you no *answer* to that?'
		61	he was silent and *made* no *answer* at all.
	15	4	Pilate questioned him again, '*Have* you no *reply* at all?'
		5 J	But . . . *Jesus* made no further *reply*.
Lk	2	47	all those who heard him were astounded at his intelligence 2 and his *replies*.
	20	26	2 his *answer* took them by surprise and they were silenced.
	23	9	[Herod] questioned him at some length; but ⌐without getting any reply (lit. he *answered* nothing).
Jn	18	22	Is that the way ⌐to (lit. you) *answer* the high priest?
	19	9	2 *Jesus* made [Pilate] no *answer*.

Jesus replies to, answers (the disciples)

Jn	6	70	J	Twelve	Jn	13	26	J	[John]
	9	3	J	disciples			36	J	Peter
	11	9	J	disciples			38	J	Peter
	13	8	J	Peter		16	31	J	disciples

(the Jews)

Mk	12	29	J	scribe	Jn	8	54	J	Jews
Jn	5	17	Jᵛ	Jews		10	25	J	Jews
	8	19	J	Pharisees			32	J	Jews
		34	J	Jews			34	J	Jews
		49	J	Jews		18	20	J	Jews

(Pilate)

Lk	23	3	J	Pilate	Jn	18	37	J	Pilate
Jn	18	34	J	Pilate		19	11	J	Pilate
		36	J	Pilate					

(others)

Lk	4	4	J	the devil	Jn	18	8	J	guards
	8	50	J	Jairus			23		guard
Jn	3	5	J	Nicodemus					

3: (A PERSON) ANSWERS, REPLIES, SAYS (IN RESPONSE)

Θ = Reply to God: X = Reply to Jesus

Mt	22	46 X	from that day no one ⌐dared to ask him any further questions (lit. was capable of *answering* a word to him),
Mk	9	6	[Peter] did not know what to *say*; they were so frightened.
	11	29 X	*answer* me and I will tell you my authority for acting like this.

Mk	11	30 X	John's baptism: did it come from heaven, or from man? *Answer* me that.
	12	34 X	Jesus, seeing how wisely [the scribe] had *spoken*, said,
	14	40 X	[Peter, James and John] could *find* no *answer* for him.
Lk	10	28 X	'You have *answered* right,' said Jesus [to the lawyer]
	14	6 X	3 to this [the lawyers and Pharisees] could *find* no *answer*.
	20	7 X	⌐their reply was (lit. they *replied*) that they did not know where [John's baptism] came from.
	22	68 X	[Jesus to Sanhedrin:] '. . . if I question you, you will not *answer*.
Jn	1	22	[priests and Levites to John:] Who are you? We must take 2 back an *answer* to those who sent us.
Ac	22	8 X	I [Paul] *answered*: 'Who are you, Lord?'
	25	4	Festus *replied* [to chief priests and leaders of the Jews] that Paul would remain in custody
		16	I [Festus] *told* [the Jews] that Romans are not in the habit of surrendering any man,
Rm	9	20 Θ	what right have you, a human being, to ⌐cross-examine 3 (lit. *answer back*) God?
Col	4	6	try to ⌐fit your answers to the needs of each one (lit. *answer* each one according to his needs).

(Apostles and disciples) Reply (to)

Mk	8	4	disciples to Jesus	Ac	5	8	Peter to Sapphira
Jn	1	49	Nathanael to Jesus		10	46	Peter to brothers
	6	7	Philip to Jesus		21	13	Paul to brothers
		68	Peter to Jesus				in Caesarea
	21	5	disciples to Jesus		24	10	Paul to Felix
Ac	3	12	Peter to the people				

(Chief priests and Jews) Answer

Jn	7	47	Pharisees to police	Jn	19	7	Jews to Pilate
	8	33	Jews to Jesus			15	Jews to Pilate
	10	33	Jews to Jesus				

(Specific people) Reply to

Mt	8	8	centurion to Jesus	Jn	9	25	man born blind
Mk	9	17	man in crowd to				to Jews
			Jesus			27	man born blind
Lk	23	40	good thief to				to Jews
			second thief		12	34	crowd to Jesus
Jn	1	21	John the Baptist		18	5	guards to Jesus
			to priests and			35	Pilate to Jesus
			Levites		19	22	Pilate to chief
	5	7	sick man to Jesus				priests
		11	sick man to Jews	Ac	9	13	Ananias to the
	7	20	crowd to Jesus				Lord
		46	police to Pharisees		22	28	tribune to Paul
	9	11	man born blind		24	25	Felix to Paul
			to people		25	12	Festus to Paul

5. SPEAK, TALK

1: REPORT, GIVE AN ACCOUNT OF, DESCRIBE – TELL OF – INEXPRESSIBLE: *DI-(H)ĒGEOMAI*

> 1 *di-(h)ēgeomai* 8   3 *ek-di-(h)ēgeomai* 2
> 4 *di-(h)ēgēsis* 1   5 *an-ek-di-(h)ēgētos* 1
> 2 *ex-(h)ēgeomai* 6

Mk	5	16	those who had witnessed it *reported* what had happened to the demoniac
	9	9	he warned them to *tell* no one what they had seen,
Lk	1	1	4 many others have undertaken to draw up *accounts* of the events that have taken place among us,
	8	39	Go back home . . . and *report* all that God has done for you.
	9	10	On their return the apostles *gave* [Jesus] *an account of* all they had done.
	24	35	2 [the disciples from Emmaus] *told their story of* what had happened on the road
Jn	1	18 X	No one has ever seen God; it is the only Son . . . who has 2 ⌐*made him known* (lit. *given an account of* him).
Ac	8	33	(Is 53 8) Who will ever *talk about* his descendants . . .?
	9	27	Barnabas . . . introduced [Saul] to the apostles, and *explained* how the Lord had appeared to Saul
	10	8	2 Cornelius called two of the slaves . . , *told* them what had happened, and sent them off to Jaffa.
	12	17	[Peter] *described* . . . how the Lord had led him out of prison.
	13	41	(Hab 1 5) I am doing something . . . that you would not 3 believe if you were to be *told* of it.
	15	3	3 [Paul and Barnabas] *told* how the pagans had been converted,
		12	2 they listened to Barnabas and Paul *describing* all the signs and wonders God had worked through them among the pagans.
		14	2 Simeon has *described* how God first arranged to enlist a people for his name out of the pagans.
	21	19	2 [Paul] *gave a* detailed *account of* all that God had done among the pagans

2 Co	9 15	5 Thanks be to God for his *inexpressible* gift!
Heb	11 32	There is not time for me to *give an account of* Gideon, . . and the prophets.

2: SPEAK, TALK: *PHTHENGOMAI*

1 *phthengomai* 3 2 *apo-phthengomai* 3

Ac	2 4	They . . . began to speak foreign languages as the Spirit
	2	gave them ⌐the gift of speech (lit. to *speak*).
	14	2 Peter . . . *addressed* [the crowd] in a loud voice:
	4 18	[the Sanhedrin] called [the apostles] in and gave them a warning on no account to ⌐*make statements* (lit. *speak*) or teach in the name of Jesus.
	26 15	2 I am *speaking* nothing but the sober truth,
2 P	2 16	The dumb donkey put a stop to that prophet's madness when it *talked* like a man.
	18	⌐With their high-flown talk (lit. *Talking* in a high-flown manner) . . . they tempt back the ones who have only just escaped from paganism,

3: MAKE A SPEECH: *(DĒM-)ĒGOREŌ*

(dēm-)ēgoreō 1

Ac	12 21	Herod, wearing his robes of state and enthroned on a dais, *made a speech* to them.

4: REPLY: *HYPO-LAMBANŌ*

hypo-lambanō 1/5

Lk	10 30 X	Jesus *replied*: 'A man was once on his way down from Jerusalem to Jericho'

5: TALK: *HOM-ILEŌ*

1 *hom-ileō* 4 2 *syn-(h)om-ileō* 1

Lk	24 14	[the disciples from Emmaus] were *talking* together about all that had happened.
	15	as they *talked* [this over and discussed it together] Jesus himself came up
Ac	10 27	2 *Talking together* [Peter and Cornelius] went in to meet all the people assembled there,
	20 11	[Paul] carried on *talking* till he left at daybreak.
	24 26	[Felix] sent for [Paul] frequently and *had talks* with him.

6: DISCUSS, CONFER – ARGUE: *BALLŌ*

2 *anti-ballō* 1 1 *sym-ballō* 2/7

Lk	24 17	[Jesus] said to the [disciples from Emmaus], 'What matters are you *discussing* as you walk along?'
Ac	4 15	they ordered [Peter and John] to stand outside while the Sanhedrin *had a private discussion.*
	17 18	Even a few Epicurean and Stoic philosophers ⌐*argued* (or: *conferred*) with [Paul in Athens].

7: CHATTER – GOSSIP: *PHLYAREŌ*

1 *phlyareō* 1 2 *phlyaros* 1

1 Tm	5 13	2 [young widows] learn to be *gossips* and meddlers in other people's affairs, and to chatter when they would be better keeping quiet.
3 Jn	10	I shall tell everyone . . . about the wicked accusations [Diotrephes] has been ⌐*circulating* (lit. *chattering*) against us.

8: NONSENSE: *LĒROS*

lēros 1

Lk	24 11	[The women told the apostles what they had seen at the tomb,] but this story of theirs seemed pure *nonsense*, and they did not believe them.

9: ASK ONE ANOTHER, QUESTION – DISCUSSION, DEBATE, CONTROVERSY – ARGUE, DISPUTE: *SY-ZĒTEŌ*

1 *sy-zeteō* 10	3 *zētēma* 5		
4 *sy-zētēsis* 1	2 *zētēsis* 7		
5 *sy-zētētēs* 1	6 *ek-zetesis* 1		

Mk	1 27	The people were so astonished that they started *asking each other* what it all meant.
	8 11	The Pharisees came up and started a *discussion with* [Jesus];

Mk	9 10	*among* themselves [Peter, James and John] *discussed* what 'rising from the dead' could mean.
	14	they saw a large crowd round [the other disciples] and some scribes *arguing* with them.
	16	What are you *arguing* about *with* them?
	12 28	One of the scribes who had listened to them *debating*
Lk	22 23	[The disciples] began to *ask one another* which of them it could be
	24 15	as [the two disciples] *talked* this over, Jesus himself came up
Jn	3 25	2 some of John's disciples had opened a *discussion* with a Jew about purification,
	16 19	You are *asking one another* what I meant
Ac	6 9	certain people came forward to *debate with* Stephen,
	9 29	after Saul had spoken to the Hellenists, and *argued with* them,
	15 2	2 after Paul and Barnabas had had a long *argument* with these men it was arranged that [they] should go up to Jerusalem
	3	and *discuss the problem*
	7	2 after the *discussion* had gone on for a long time, Peter stood up
	18 15	3 if it is only *quibbles* about words . . . deal with it yourselves:
	23 29	3 I found that the accusation concerned *disputed points* of their Law,
	25 19	3 they had some *argument* or other with him about their own religion
	20	2 Not feeling qualified to deal with *questions* of this sort, [Festus] asked [Paul]
	26 3	3 you are an expert in matters of custom and *controversy* among the Jews.
	28 29	4 (ᵛ The Jews went away, *arguing* earnestly *among themselves*.)
1 Co	1 20	5 Where are any of our ⌐*thinkers* (lit. *debaters*) today?
1 Tm	1 4	myths and endless genealogies . . . are only likely to raise
	6	⌐*irrelevant doubts* (lit. *controversies*)
	6 4	2 [such a person] must be full of self-conceit, with a craze for *questioning* everything and arguing about words.
2 Tm	2 23	2 Avoid these futile and silly *speculations*,
Tt	3 9	2 avoid pointless *speculations* . . . and the quibbles and disputes

10: DISCUSS, CONSULT, CONFER: *PROS-ANA-TITHEMAI*

pros-ana-tithemai 1

Ga	1 16	I did not stop to *discuss* [the call to preach to the pagans] with any human being,

11: SPEAK (TO), ADDRESS: *PROS-PHŌNEŌ*

pros-phōneō 3/7

Lk	23 20	Pilate . . . *addressed* them again,
Ac	21 40	[Paul] *spoke to* them in Hebrew.
	22 2	When they realised [Paul] was *speaking* in Hebrew, the silence was even greater than before.

SEA – SHORE

1. Sea – Lake
  1: Sea – Lake: *thalassa*
  a) (the) Sea
  b) (the Mediterranean) Sea
  c) (the) Red Sea
  d) Sea (of Galilee), Lake (Tiberias)
  e) Sea (of glass), (glass) Lake
  2: the Depths – the Open Sea: *pelagos*
  a) (the) Depths
  b) (the) Open Sea (off Cilicia and Pamphylia)
  3: Lake: *limnē*
  a) Lake (of Gennesaret or Galilee)
  b) Lake (of fire), (the burning) Lake

2. Waves, Rough (water) – (Be) Tossed
  1: Waves: *kyma*
  2: Waves: *salos*
  3: Waves, Rough (water) – Tossed to and fro: *klydōn*

3. Sink – Plunge – Be drowned
  1: to Sink – Be drowned: *kata-pontizō*
  2: to Sink – Plunge, Drag down: *bythizō*

4. Shore, Beach – Coastal region – Sand
  1: Beach, Shore: *aigialos*
  2: (Sea-)Shore: *cheilos*
  3: Coastal region, Seaboard: *par-(h)alios*
  4: Sand: *ammos*

5. Bay: *kolpos*

6. Harbour – to Moor, Tie up – Run aground
  1: Harbour, Haven: *limēn*
  2: Moor, Tie up, Make fast: *pros-ormizō*
  3: Run aground: *ek-piptō*
  4: Run aground: *epi-kellō*

7. Sponge: *spongos*

1. SEA – LAKE

1: SEA – LAKE: *THALASSA*

1 *thalassa* 92 3 *para-thalassios* 1
2 *di-thalassos* 1

a) (the) Sea

Mt	13 47	the kingdom of heaven is like a dragnet cast into the *sea*
	18 6	[he] would be better drowned in the depths of the *sea*

Mt	21 21	if you say to this mountain, 'Get up and throw yourself into the *sea*',
	23 15	Pharisees . . . who travel over *sea* and land to make a single proselyte,
Mk	9 42	[he] would be better thrown into the *sea*
	11 23	if anyone says to this mountain. 'Get up and throw yourself into the *sea*',
Lk	17 2	It would be better for him to be thrown into the *sea*
	6	you could say to this mulberry tree, 'Be uprooted and planted in the *sea*',
	21 25	on earth [there will be] nations in agony, bewildered by the clamour of the *ocean* and its waves;
Ac	4 24	it is you who make heaven and earth and *sea*,
	14 15	the living God who made heaven and earth and the *sea*
Rm	9 27	(Is 10 22) Though Israel should have as many descendants as there are [grains of] sand ⌐on the seashore (lit. by the *sea*),
2 Co	11 26	I have been in danger from rivers and in danger . . . at *sea*
Heb	11 12	(Gn 22 17) as many [descendants] as the stars of heaven or the [grains of] sand on the *seashore*.
Jm	1 6	a person who has doubts is like the waves thrown up in the *sea* when the wind drives.
Jude	13	[the wicked are] like wild *sea* waves capped with shame as if with foam:
Rv	5 13	everything that lives in the air, and on the ground, and under the ground, and in the *sea*,
	7 1	to keep [the winds] from blowing over the land or the *sea* or in the trees.
	2	another angel . . . called . . . to the four angels whose duty was to devastate land and *sea*, ³ 'Wait before you do any
	3	damage on land or at *sea* or to the trees,'
	8 8	it was as though a great mountain . . . had been dropped into the *sea*: a third of the *sea* turned into blood, ⁹ a third of
	9	all the living things in the *sea* were killed,
	10 2	[the angel] put his right foot in the *sea* and his left foot on the land
	5	the angel . . . standing on the *sea* and the land, . . . ⁶ . . .
	6	swore by the One who . . . made heaven . . . and earth . . . and the *sea* and all it holds,
	8	the angel standing on *sea* and land.
	12 12	for you, earth and *sea*, trouble is coming – because the devil has gone down to you in a rage,
	18	ᵛ I (G It) was standing on the *seashore*.
	13 1	I saw a beast emerge from the *sea*:
	14 7	worship the maker of heaven and earth and *sea*
	16 3	The second angel emptied his bowl over the *sea*, and it turned into blood . . . and every living creature in the *sea* died.
	18 17	All the captains and *seafaring* men . . . will be keeping a safe distance.
	19	mourn for [Babylon] whose lavish living has made a fortune for every owner of a *sea*-going ship;
	21	a powerful angel picked up a boulder . . . and . . . hurled it into the *sea*,
	20 8	[Satan's] armies will be as many as the sands of the *sea*;
	13	The *sea* gave up all the dead who were in it;
	21 1	the first heaven and the first earth had disappeared now, and there was no longer any *sea*.

b) (the Mediterranean) Sea

A *Adriatic* 1

Ac	10 6	[At Jaffa] Simon the tanner whose house is by the *sea*.
	32	the house of Simon the tanner, by the *sea*.
	17 14	the brothers arranged for Paul to go immediately as far as the ⌐coast (lit. *sea*),
	27 27 A	On the fourteenth night we were being driven one way and another in the *Adriatic*,
	30	the crew . . . lowered the ship's boat into the *sea*
	38	they lightened the ship by throwing the corn overboard into the *sea*.
	40	They slipped the anchors and left them to the *sea*, . . .
	41 2	⁴¹ But the *cross-currents* carried them into a shoal and the vessel ran aground.
	28 4	That man . . . [Paul] may have escaped the *sea*, . . .

c) (the) Red Sea

4 *erythros* 2

Ac	7 36	4/ Moses . . . led them out across the *Red Sea*
1 Co	10 1	our fathers . . . all passed through the *sea*. ² They were all baptised into Moses in this cloud and in this *sea*;
	2	
Heb	11 29	4/ It was by faith they crossed the *Red Sea* as easily as dry land,

d) Sea (of) Galilee, Lake (Tiberias)

Mt	4 13	3 Capernaum, a *lakeside* town on the borders of Zebulun and Naphtali.
	15	(Is 8 23) Way of the *sea* on the far side of Jordan.
	18	As [Jesus] was walking by the *Sea* of Galilee he saw . . . Simon . . . and his brother Andrew; they were making a cast in the *lake* with their net,

Mt	8 24	Without warning a storm broke over the *lake*,
	26	[Jesus] rebuked the winds and the *sea*;
	27 ●	Whatever kind of man is this? Even the winds and the *sea* obey him.
	32	the whole herd charged down the cliff into the *lake*
	13 1	Jesus left the house and sat by the *lake*side,
	14 24	the boat, by now far out on the *lake*, was battling with a heavy sea,
	25	[Jesus] went towards [the disciples], walking on the *lake*,
	26	²⁶ and when the disciples saw him walking on the *lake* they were terrified.
	15 29	Jesus . . . reached the shores of the *Sea* of Galilee,
	17 27	go to the *lake* and cast a hook; take the first fish that bites,
Mk	1 16	As [Jesus] was walking along by the *Sea* of Galilee he saw Simon and his brother Andrew casting a net in the *lake*
	2 13	He went out again to the shore of the *lake*;
	3 7	Jesus withdrew with his disciples to the *lake*[side],
	4 1	Again he began to teach by the *lake*side, . . . he got into a boat on the *lake* and sat there. The people were . . . at the ⌐water's (lit. *lake*'s) edge.
	39	he . . . rebuked the wind and said to the *sea*, 'Quiet now!'
	41 ●	Who can this be? Even the wind and the *sea* obey him.
	5 1	the country of the Gerasenes on the other side of the *lake*,
	13	the herd . . . charged down the cliff into the *lake*, and ⌐there (lit. in the *lake*) they were drowned.
	21	[Jesus] stayed by the *lake*side.
	6 47	the boat was far out on the *lake*, and [Jesus] was alone on the land. . . . ⁴⁸ he came towards them walking on the lake . . . ⁴⁹
	48	
	49	. . . when they saw him walking on the *lake* they . . . cried out;
	7 31	[Jesus] went by way of Sidon towards the *Sea* of Galilee.
Jn	6 1	Jesus went off to the other side of the *Sea* of Galilee – or of Tiberias –
	16	the disciples went down to the shore of the *lake* and ¹⁷ got
	17	into a boat to make for Capernaum on the other side of the the *lake*. ¹⁸ The wind was strong, and the *lake* was getting
	18	
	19	rough. ¹⁹ They . . . saw Jesus walking on the *lake*
	22	the crowd . . . stayed on the other side of the *lake*
	25	When they found [Jesus] on the other side of the *lake*, they said to him,
	21 1	Jesus showed himself again . . . by the *Sea* of Tiberias,
	7	Simon Peter . . . jumped into the ⌐water (lit. *sea*).

e) Sea (of glass), (glass) Lake

Rv	4 6	Between the throne and myself was a *sea* that seemed to be made of glass, like crystal.
	15 2	I seemed to see a glass *lake* suffused with fire, and standing by the *lake* of glass, those who had fought against the beast and won,

2: THE DEPTHS – THE OPEN SEA: *PELAGOS*

pelagos 2

a) (the) Depths

Mt	18 6	[he] would be better drowned in the *depths* of the sea

b) (the) Open Sea (off Cilicia and Pamphylia)

Ac	27 5	[we sailed under the lee of Cyprus,] then across the *open sea* off Cilicia and Pamphylia,

3: LAKE: *LIMNĒ*

limnē 11

a) Lake (of Gennesaret or Galilee)

Lk	5 1	[Jesus] was standing one day by the *Lake* of Gennesaret,
	2	he caught sight of two boats close to the bank of the *lake*.
	8 22	Let us cross over to the other side of the *lake*.
	23	a squall came down on the *lake*
	33	the herd charged down the cliff into the *lake* and were drowned.

b) Lake (of fire), (the burning) Lake

Rv	19 20	[The beast and the false prophet] were thrown into the fiery *lake* of burning sulphur.
	20 10	the devil . . . will be thrown into the *lake* of fire and sulphur,
	14	Death and Hades were thrown into the burning *lake*. This
	15	burning *lake* is the second death; ¹⁵ and anybody whose name could not be found written in the book of life was thrown into the burning *lake*.
	21 8	the legacy for . . . idolaters or any other sort of liars, is the second death in the burning *lake* of sulphur.

2. WAVES, ROUGH (WATER) – (BE) TOSSED

1: WAVES: *KYMA*

kyma 4

Mt	8 24	the *waves* were breaking right over the boat.
	14 24	the boat . . . was ⌐battling with a heavy sea (lit. being tossed by rough *waves*),

Mk 4 37   the *waves* were breaking into the boat
Jude   13 ○ [the wicked are] like wild sea *waves* capped with shame as if
                with foam;

2: WAVES: *SALOS*

salos 1

Lk 21 25   There will be . . . nations . . . bewildered by the clamour of
                the ocean and its *waves*;

3: WAVES, ROUGH (WATER) – TOSSED TO AND FRO: *KLYDŌN*

1 *klydōn* 2   2 *klydōnizō* 1

Lk 8 24   [Jesus] rebuked the wind and the *rough water*;
Ep 4 14 ○ 2 Then we shall not be . . . *tossed one way and another* by every
                wind of doctrine,
Jm 1 6   a person who has doubts is like the *waves* thrown up in the
                sea when the wind drives.

3. SINK – PLUNGE – BE DROWNED

1: TO SINK – BE DROWNED: *KATA-PONTIZŌ*

kata-pontizō 2

Mt 14 30   [Peter] took fright and began to *sink*.
   18 6   [he] would *be* better *drowned* in the depths of the sea

2: TO SINK – PLUNGE, DRAG DOWN: *BYTHIZŌ*

bythizō 2

Lk 5 7   they filled the two boats to *sinking* point.
1 Tm 6 9 ○ dangerous ambitions which eventually *plunge* them into ruin
                and destruction.

4. SHORE, BEACH – COASTAL REGION

1: BEACH, SHORE: *AIGIALOS*

aigialos 6

Mt 13 2   The people all stood on the *beach*,
      48   When [the dragnet] is full, the fishermen haul it a*shore*;
Jn 21 4   It was light by now and there stood Jesus on the *shore*,
Ac 21 5   When we reached the *beach*, we knelt down and prayed;
   27 39   [the crew] could make out a kind of bay with a *beach;*
      40   they headed for the *beach*.

2: (SEA-)SHORE: *CHEILOS*

cheilos 1/7

Heb 11 12   (Gn 22 17) as many [descendants] as the stars of heaven or the
                grains of sand on the sea*shore*.

3: COASTAL REGION, SEABOARD: *PAR-(H)ALIOS*

par-(h)alios 1

Lk 6 17   a great crowd of people from all parts of Judaea and from
                Jerusalem and from the *coastal region* of Tyre and Sidon

4: SAND: *AMMOS*

ammos 5

Mt 7 26   a stupid man . . . built his house on *sand*.
Rm 9 27   (Is 10 22) Though Israel should have as many descendants as
                there are [grains of] *sand* ⌐on the seashore (lit. by the sea),
                only a remnant will be saved,
Heb 11 12   there came from one man . . . more descendants than could
                be counted, as many as . . . the [grains of] *sand* on the
                seashore.
Rv 12 18   ⌄ I (G He) was standing on the ⌐seashore (lit. *sand* by the sea).
   20 8   [Satan's] armies will be as many as the *sands* of the sea;

5. BAY: *KOLPOS*

kolpos 1/6

Ac 27 39   [the crew] could make out a kind of *bay* with a beach;

6 HARBOUR – TO MOOR, TIE UP – RUN AGROUND

1: HARBOUR, HAVEN: *LIMĒN*

limēn 2/3

Ac 27 12   since the *harbour* [Fair Havens] was unsuitable for wintering,
                the majority were for putting out from there in the hope of
                wintering at Phoenix – a *harbour* in Crete,

2: MOOR, TIE UP, MAKE FAST: *PROS-ORMIZŌ*

pros-ormizō 1

Mk 6 53   [Jesus and his disciples] came to land at Gennesaret and
                tied up.

3: RUN AGROUND: *EK-PIPTŌ*

ek-piptō 3/10

Ac 27 17   afraid of *running aground* on the Syrtis banks, they floated out
                the sea-anchor
      26   we are to *be stranded* on some island.
      29   afraid that we might *run aground* somewhere on a reef, they
                dropped four anchors

4: RUN AGROUND: *EPI-KELLŌ*

epi-kellō 1

Ac 27 41   the cross-currents carried them into a shoal and the vessel
                ran aground.

7. SPONGE: *SPONGOS*

spongos 3

Mt 27 48   one of them quickly ran to get a *sponge* which he dipped in
                vinegar
Mk 15 36   Someone ran and soaked a *sponge* in vinegar
Jn 19 29   putting a *sponge* soaked in vinegar on a hyssop stick they held
                it up to his mouth.

SEAL

1: (God) Seals, Sets his seal on (a person) – Mark with the seal (of God)	2: Seal – Seal up – Put (one's) seal to
1 *sphragis* 16 3 *kata-sphragizō* 1 2 *sphragizō* 15	

1: (GOD) SEALS, SETS HIS SEAL ON (A PERSON) – MARK WITH THE SEAL (OF GOD)

Jn 6 27   2 on [the Son of Man] the Father, God himself, has *set his
                seal*.
2 Co 1 22   2 [God has anointed us,] *marking* us *with his seal* and giving
                us . . . the Spirit,
Ep 1 13   2 you too have been *stamped with the seal* of the Holy Spirit
    4 30   2 the Holy Spirit of God who has *marked* you *with his seal*
Rv 7 2   I saw another angel . . , carrying the *seal* of the living God;
       3   2 Wait . . . until we have *put the seal on* the foreheads of the
                servants of our God.
       4   2 Then I heard how many were *sealed*: a hundred and forty-
                four thousand were *sealed*, out of all the tribes of Israel.
       5   ⁵ From the tribe of Judah, twelve thousand had been
       8   2 *sealed;* . . . ⁸ . . . and from the tribe of Benjamin, twelve
                thousand were *sealed*.
Rv 9 4   [the locusts] were . . . told only to attack any men who were
                without God's *seal* on their foreheads.

2: SEAL – SEAL UP – PUT (ONE'S) SEAL TO

Mt 26 66   2 they went and made the sepulchre secure, *putting seals on*
                the stone and mounting a guard.
Jn 3 33   all who do accept his testimony ⌐are attesting (lit. would
              2 *put their seal to*) the truthfulness of God.
Rm 4 11   when [Abraham] was circumcised it was only as a sign and
                ⌐guarantee (lit. *seal*) that the faith he had before . . . justified
                him.
   15 28   2 when I have . . . ⌐officially handed over (lit. *put my seal to*)
                what has been raised, I shall set out for Spain
1 Co 9 2   I should still be an apostle to you who are the *seal* of my
                apostolate
2 Tm 2 19   God's solid foundation stone is still in position, and this is
                the ⌐inscription (lit. *seal*) on it (Nb 16 5): 'The Lord knows
                those who are his own' and 'All who call on the name of the
                Lord must avoid sin'.

Rv	5	1	3	a scroll that had writing on back and front and was *sealed* with seven *seals*.
		2		Is there anyone worthy to open the scroll and break the *seals* of it?
		5		the Root of David . . . will open the scroll and the seven *seals* of it.
		9		You are worthy to take the scroll and break the *seals* of it,
	6	1		I saw the Lamb break one of the seven *seals*,
		3		When he broke the second *seal*,
		5		When he broke the third *seal*,
		7		When he broke the fourth *seal*,
		9		When he broke the fifth *seal*,
		12		when he broke the sixth *seal*,
	8	1		The Lamb then broke the seventh *seal*, and there was silence in heaven
	10	4	2	ᵣKeep the words of the seven thunderclaps secret (lit. *Seal up* the words of the seven thunderclaps)
	20	3		[The angel] threw [the dragon] into the Abyss, and shut the
		2		entrance and *sealed* it over him,
	22	10	2	Do not ᵣkeep the prophecies in this book a secret (lit. *seal up* the prophecies in this book),

---

SECRET – MYSTERY

---

1. **Secret – Keep to oneself – Hide, Hidden:** *kryptō*
2. **Hidden – Quietly, Privately – Not knowing:** *lanthanō*
3. **Mystery – Secret – Hidden truth, Hidden purpose:** *mystērion*
4. **Riddle, Puzzle:** *ainigma*

1. SECRET – KEEP TO ONESELF – HIDE, HIDDEN: *KRYPTŌ*

5 *kryphaios* 2	4 *apo-kryphos* 3
6 *kryphē* 1	3 *apo-kryptō* 4
7 *kryptē* 1	8 *en-kryptō* 1
1 *kryptō* 19	9 *peri-krybō* 1
2 *kryptos* 17	

Mt	5	14		A city built on a hill-top cannot be *hidden*.
	6	4	2	your almsgiving must be *secret*, and your Father who sees
			2	all that is done in *secret* will reward you.
		6	2	pray to your Father who is in that *secret* place, and your
			2	Father who sees all that is done in *secret* will reward you.
		18	5	so that no one will know you are fasting except your Father who sees all that is done in *secret*; and your Father who
			5	sees all that is done in *secret* will reward you.
	10	26		everything that is now covered will be uncovered, and
			2	everything now *hidden* will be made clear.
	11	25	Θ	I bless you, Father . . . for *hiding* these things from the learned and the clever
	13	33	8	The kingdom . . . is like the yeast a woman . . . *mixed in* with three measures of flour
		35		(Ps 78 2) I will . . . expound things *hidden* since the foundation of the world.
		44	<	The kingdom . . . is like treasure *hidden* in a field which someone has found; he *hides* it again . . . and buys the field.
	25	18		the man who had received one [talent] went off . . . and *hid* his master's money.
		25		I was afraid, and . . . *hid* your talent in the ground.
Mk	4	22	2	there is nothing *hidden* but it must be disclosed, nothing
			4	kept *secret* except to be brought to light.
Lk	1	24	9	Elizabeth conceived, and for five months she *kept to herself*.
	8	17	2/4	nothing is *hidden* but it will be made clear, nothing *secret* but it will be known and brought to light.
	10	21	Θ 3	I bless you, Father . . . for *hiding* these things from the learned and the clever
	11	33	7	No one lights a lamp and puts it in some *hidden place* or under a tub,
	12	2	2	everything now *hidden* will be made clear.
	13	21		[The kingdom] is like the yeast a woman . . . *mixed in* with three measures of flour
	18	34		what [Jesus] said was quite *obscure* to them, they had no idea what it meant.
	19	42		[Jerusalem,] the message of peace . . . is *hidden* from your eyes!
Jn	7	4	2	if a man wants to be known he does not do things in *secret*;
		10	X 2	[Jesus] went up as well, but quite *privately*, without drawing attention to himself.
	8	59	X	Jesus *hid* himself and left the Temple.
	12	36	X	Having said this, Jesus left them and *kept himself hidden*.
	18	20	X	Jesus answered, '. . . I have said nothing in *secret*'.
	19	38		Joseph of Arimathaea . . . was a disciple of Jesus – though a *secret* one

Rm	2	16	2	the day when . . . God . . . . . . judges the *secrets* of mankind.
		29	2	The real Jew is the one who is ᵣinwardly (lit. *secretly*) a Jew, and the real circumcision is in the heart
1Co	2	7	3	The *hidden* wisdom of God which we teach in our mysteries
	4	5	2	the Lord . . . will light up *all that is hidden* in the dark
	14	25	2	[an unbeliever] would find his *secret* thoughts laid bare,
2Co	4	2	2	we will have none of the ᵣreticence (lit. *secrets*) of those who are ashamed,
Ep	3	9	3	Through all the ages, [the mystery] has been *kept hidden* in God,
	5	12	6	The things which are done *in secret* are things that people are ashamed even to speak of;
Col	1	26	3	the message . . . was a mystery *hidden* for generations
	2	3	4	[God's secret] in which all the jewels of wisdom and knowledge are *hidden*.
	3	3		the life you have is *hidden* with Christ in God.
1Tm	5	25		the good that people do can be obvious; but even when it is not, it cannot be *hidden* for ever.
Heb	11	23		Moses, when he was born, was *hidden* by his parents for three months;
1P	3	4	2	[Women, do not dress up for show;] all this should be ᵣinside (lit. *hidden*) in a person's heart,
Rv	2	17		to those who prove victorious I will give the *hidden* manna
	6	15		slaves and citizens took to the mountains to *hide* in caves . . .
		16		¹⁶ . . . Fall on us and *hide* us away from the One who sits on the throne and from the anger of the Lamb.

2. HIDDEN – QUIETLY, PRIVATELY – NOT KNOWING: *LANTHANŌ*

1 *lanthanō* 6   2 *lathra*

Mt	1	19	2	Joseph . . . decided to divorce [Mary] ᵣinformally (or: *quietly*).
	2	7	2	Herod summoned the wise men to see him *privately*.
Mk	7	24	X	[Jesus] could not pass ᵣunrecognised (lit. *hidden*).
Lk	8	47		Seeing herself ᵣdiscovered (lit. no longer *hidden*), the woman came forward trembling,
Jn	11	28		[Martha] called her sister Mary, saying ᵣin a low voice
			2	(lit. *privately*), 'The Master is here . . .'
Ac	16	37	2	[the magistrates] think they can push us out *on the quiet*!
	26	26		I now speak . . . confident that nothing is ᵣlost on (lit. *hidden* from) him;
Heb	13	2		some people have entertained angels *without knowing* it.
2P	3	5		[the unbelievers] are choosing ᵣto forget (lit. *not to know*) that there were heavens at the beginning,
		8		there is one thing . . . that ᵣyou must never forget (lit. ought not to be *hidden* from you):

3. MYSTERY – SECRET – HIDDEN TRUTH, HIDDEN PURPOSE: *MYSTĒRION*

mystērion 28

Mt	13	11		the *mysteries* of the kingdom of heaven are revealed to you [disciples], but they are not revealed to [other people].
Mk	4	11		The *secret* of the kingdom of God is given to you, but to those who are outside everything comes in parables,
Lk	8	10		The *mysteries* of the kingdom of God are revealed to you;
Rm	11	25		There is a *hidden reason* for all this . . . One section of Israel has become blind, but this will last only until the whole pagan world has entered,
	16	25		the Good News . . . the revelation of a *mystery* kept secret for endless ages, ²⁶ but now so clear that it must be broadcast
1Co	2	1		I came to you . . . simply to tell you ᵣwhat God had guaranteed (ᵛ God's *mystery*).
		7		The hidden wisdom of God which we teach in our *mysteries*
	4	1		People must think of us as . . . stewards entrusted with the *mysteries* of God.
	13	2		If I have the gift of prophecy, understanding all the *mysteries* there are . . .
	14	2		Anybody with the gift of tongues . . . talks in the spirit about *mysterious things*.
	15	51		I will tell you *something that has been secret*: that we are not all going to die,
Ep	1	9		[God] has let us know the *mystery* of his purpose, the hidden plan he so kindly made in Christ
	3	3		it was by a revelation that I was given the knowledge of the *mystery*
		4		you will have some idea of the depths that I see in the *mystery* of Christ.
		9		[I have been entrusted with this special grace] of explaining how the *mystery* is to be dispensed. Through all the ages, this has been kept hidden in God,
	5	32		[Husbands should love their wives just as Christ loved the Church.] This *mystery* has many implications;
	6	19		pray for me to . . . speak without fear and give out the *mystery* of the gospel
Col	1	26		[God's message] was a *mystery* hidden for generations . . . and has now been revealed

Col	1 27	It was God's purpose . . . to show all the rich glory of this *mystery* to pagans. [It] is Christ among you,
	2 2	so that your understanding may come to full development, until you really know God's (§ Christ's) *secret*
	4 3	Pray for us . . . asking God to show us opportunities for . . . proclaiming the *mystery* of Christ,
2 Th	2 7 ○	Rebellion is at its work already, but in *secret*,
1 Tm	3 9	[Deacons] must be conscientious believers in the *mystery* of the faith.
	16	the *mystery* of our religion is very deep indeed: He was made visible in the flesh . . . taken up in glory.
Rv	1 20 ○	The *secret* of the seven stars . . . is this:
	10 7	when the seventh angel is heard sounding his trumpet, God's ⌐*secret intention* (or: *hidden purpose*) will be fulfilled,
	17 5 ○	on [the woman's] forehead was written . . . a *cryptic* name: Babylon the Great
	7 ○	I will tell you the ⌐*meaning* (or: *secret*) of this woman, and of the beast

4. RIDDLE, PUZZLE: *AINIGMA*

ainigma 1

1 Co	13 12	Now we are ⌐*seeing a dim reflection in* (lit. *looking as though trying to solve a riddle into*) a mirror;

SEE

1. Eye: *ophthalmos*
  1: Eye, Eyes
  2: Lift up, Raise, the eyes
2. See, Saw – Vision – Appear: *horaō*
  1: (God) Sees, Looks down
  2: (Jesus) Sees, Saw
  3: (a person) Sees, Saw
    a) See (God) – (God is) Invisible
    b) See (Jesus, Jesus's signs) – Vision – (Jesus) Appears (to a person)
    c) See a Vision – a Vision Appears (to a person)
    d) See (generally)
  4: Overlook
3. See – Vision – Appearance: *opsis*
  1: See – Eyewitness
  2: Vision – Appear
  3: Appearance(s) – Mirror
  4: 'Look forward' – Turn head-on, Face into
  5: Short-sighted
4. See, Look (at) – Watch (out), Take care: *blepō*
  1: See, See again – Look at
    a) (God) Sees, Looks upon
    b) (Jesus) Looks at, Looks round, Looks up
    c) (a person) Sees, Looks at
    d) (the spiritually or physically blind) See, Look – See again, Sight

  e) (angels) Look at – (things can, cannot) See, Look
  2: Watch out, Be on your guard – Take care (that), Take notice (of), Be careful (that)
5. See, Watch – Spectacle – Theatre: *theaomai*
  1: See – Notice – Watch
    a) (Jesus) Sees, Saw, Noticed – (Jesus) Watched
    b) (a person, a spirit) Sees, Saw – (a person) Watches
  2: Spectacle, a Sight – Theatre – Publicly exposed
6. See: *augazō*
7. Notice, Perceive – Look at: *kata-noeō*
8. Give attention (to), Heed, Watch – Notice: *ep-echō*
9. Stare (at), Gaze (at), Peer (at) – (Have one's eyes) Fixed (on), Look intently (at): *a-tenizō*
10. Look for, Have eyes for – See (that), Look to, Be on your guard: *skopeō*
11. Appearance, Aspect, Sight – Shape, Form: *eidos*
12. Watch – Observation: *para-tēreō*
13. Spy, Spies
  1: Spy (on), Spies – Informer: *kata-skopeō*
  2: (Secret) Agent, Spy: *en-ka-thetos*

D = See death, See corruption

1. EYE: *OPHTHALMOS*

2 *omma*	2	3	*ophthalmo(-doulia)* 2
1 *ophthalmos* 100		4	*(mon-)ophthalmos* 2

1: EYE, EYES

Mt	5 29	If your right *eye* should cause you to sin, tear it out
	38	You have learnt how it was said (Ex 21 24): *Eye* for *eye*
	6 22	The lamp of the body is the *eye*. It follows that if your *eye* is sound, your whole body will be filled with light. 23 But if your *eye* is diseased, your whole body will be all darkness.
	73	Why do you observe the splinter in your brother's *eye* and never notice the plank in your own *eye*? 4 How dare you say to your brother, 'Let me take the splinter out of your *eye*', when all the time there is a plank in your own *eye*?
	5	5 Hypocrite! Take the plank out of your own *eye* first, and then you will *see* clearly enough to take the splinter out of your brother's *eye*.

Mt	9 29 30	[Jesus] touched their *eyes* saying, 'Your faith deserves it, so let this be done for you'. 30 And their ⌐*sight* returned (lit. *eyes* opened).
	13 15	(cf. Is 6 10) they have shut their *eyes*, for fear they should see with their *eyes*,
	16	happy are your *eyes* because they see, your ears because they hear!
	18 9	if your *eye* should cause you to sin, tear it out . . . it is better for you to enter into life with one *eye*, than to have two *eyes* and be thrown into the hell of fire.
	20 15	Why (§ should your *eyes*) be envious because I am generous?
	33	'Lord, let us have our ⌐*sight* back (lit. *eyes* opened)'. 34 Jesus
	34	felt pity for them and touched their *eyes*, and . . . their sight returned
	21 42	(Ps 118 23) This was the Lord's doing and it is wonderful to ⌐*see* (lit. *our eyes*)
	26 43	[Jesus] found them sleeping, their *eyes* were so heavy.
Mk	7 22	[It is from men's hearts that evil intentions emerge:] indecency, ⌐*envy* (lit. *the evil eye*),
	8 18	Have you *eyes* that do not see . . . ?
	23	putting spittle on his *eyes* and laying his hands on him, [Jesus] asked, 'Can you see anything?' 24 The man . . . was beginning to see . . . 25 Then he laid his hands on the man's *eyes* again and he saw clearly;
	25	
	9 47	if your *eye* should cause you to sin, tear it out; it is better for you to enter into the kingdom of God with one *eye*, than to have two *eyes* and be thrown into hell
	12 11	(Ps 118 23) This was the Lord's doing and it is wonderful to ⌐*see* (lit. *our eyes*)
	14 40	[Jesus] found them sleeping, their *eyes* were so heavy;
Lk	2 30	my *eyes* have seen the salvation which you have prepared
	4 20	all *eyes* in the synagogue were fixed on [Jesus].
	6 41 42	Why do you observe the splinter in your brother's *eye* and never notice the plank in your own *eye*? 42 How can you say to your brother, 'Brother, let me take out the splinter that is in your *eye*', when you cannot see the plank in your own *eye*? Hypocrite! Take the plank out of your own *eye* first, and then you will see clearly enough to take out the splinter . . . in your brother's *eye*.
	10 23	Happy the *eyes* that see what you see,
	11 34	The lamp of your body is your *eye*. When your *eye* is sound, your whole body too is filled with light;
	19 42	alas, [the message of peace] is hidden from your *eyes*!
	24 16	something prevented ⌐*them* (lit. *their eyes*) from recognising [Jesus].
	31	their *eyes* were opened and they recognised [Jesus];
Jn	9 6	[Jesus] made a paste with the spittle, put this over the *eyes* of the blind man,
	10	Then how do your *eyes* come to be open?
	11	Jesus . . . made a paste, daubed my *eyes* with it and . . .[could see.
	14	It had been a sabbath day when Jesus . . . opened the man's *eyes*,
	15	He put a paste on my *eyes*, and . . . I can see.
	17	What have you to say about him yourself, now that he has opened your *eyes*?
	21	we don't know . . . who opened his *eyes*.
	26	How did he open your *eyes*?
	30	Now here is an astonishing thing! He has opened my *eyes*, and you don't know where he comes from! . . . 32 Ever since the world began it is unheard of for anyone to open the *eyes* of a man who was born blind;
	32	
	10 21	could a devil open the *eyes* of the blind?
	11 37	He opened the *eyes* of the blind man, could he not have prevented this man's death?
	12 40	(cf. Is 6 10) He has blinded their *eyes* . . . for fear they should see with their *eyes*
Ac	1 9	a cloud took [Jesus] from their ⌐*sight* (lit. *eyes*)
	9 8	even with his *eyes* wide open [Saul] could see nothing at all,
	18	it was as though scales fell away from Saul's *eyes* and he could see again.
	40	Tabitha . . . opened her *eyes*,
	26 18	[I am sending you to the pagans] to open their *eyes*,
	28 27	(Is 6 10) They have shut their *eyes*, for fear they should see with their *eyes*,
Rm	3 18	(Ps 36 2) there is no fear of God before their *eyes*.
	11 8	(cf. Dt 29 3) God has given them . . . unseeing *eyes*
	10	(Ps 69 24) may their *eyes* be ⌐*struck incurably blind* (lit. *darkened so they cannot see*),
1 Co	2 9	(Is 64 3) we teach . . . the things that no *eye* has seen
	12 16	If the ear were to say, 'I am not an *eye*, and so I do not belong to the body', would that mean that it was not a part of the body? 17 If your whole body was just one *eye*, how would you hear anything?
	17	
	21	The *eye* cannot say to the hand, 'I do not need you',
	15 52	in the twinkling of an *eye* . . . we shall be changed
Ga	3 1	Has someone put a spell on you, in spite of the plain explanation you have had (§ put before your *eyes*) of the crucifixion of Jesus Christ?

Ga	4 15	you would even have gone so far as to pluck out your *eyes* and give them to me.
Ep	1 18	May [the Father] enlighten the *eyes* of your mind
	6 6	[Slaves, be obedient to your masters;] not only when you are under their *eye*,
	(3)	
Col	3 22	Slaves, be obedient to . . . your masters in this world; not only when you are under their *eye*,
	(3)	
Heb	4 13 Θ	everything . . . is open to the *eyes* of the one to whom we must give account of ourselves.
1 P	3 12 Θ	(Ps 34 16) the *eyes* of the Lord are turned towards the virtuous.
2 P	2 14	with their *eyes* always looking for adultery, men with an infinite capacity for sinning,
1 Jn	1 1	Something which . . . we have seen with our own *eyes* . . . – this is our subject.
	2 11	the man who hates his brother . . . is in the darkness, not knowing where he is going, because ⌈it is too dark to see (lit. the darkness has blinded his *eyes*).
	16	nothing the world has to offer – the sensual body, the lustful *eye*, . . . – could ever come from the Father
Rv	1 7	It is [Jesus Christ] who is coming on the clouds; ⌈everyone (lit. every *eye*) will see him,
	14 X	[I saw a figure like a Son of man,] his *eyes* like a burning flame,
	2 18 X	the Son of God . . . has *eyes* like a burning flame
	3 18	buy from me . . . *eye* ointment to put on your *eyes* so that you are able to see.
	4 6	In the centre . . . were four animals with many *eyes* . . .
	8	⁸ Each of the four animals had . . . *eyes* all the way round as well as inside.
	5 6 X	I saw . . . a Lamb . . .; it had seven horns and it had seven *eyes*,
	7 17	God will wipe away all tears from their *eyes*.
	19 12 X	His *eyes* were flames of fire . . .; the name written on him was . . . The Word of God.
	21 4	[God] will wipe away all tears from their *eyes*;

2: LIFT UP, RAISE, THE EYES

6 *airō* 1/101   5 *ep-airō* 7/19

Mt	17 8	5/ when [Peter, James and John] *raised their eyes* they saw no one but only Jesus.
Lk	6 20 X	5/ *fixing his eyes* on his disciples [Jesus] said:
	16 23	5/ [the rich man] ⌈*looked up* (lit. *lifted up his eyes*) and saw Abraham a long way off with Lazarus
	18 13	5/ The tax collector stood some distance away, not daring even to *raise his eyes* to heaven;
Jn	4 35	5/ ⌈*Look around you*, (lit. *Lift up your eyes* and) look at the fields; already they are white, ready for harvest!
	6 5 X	5/ ⌈*Looking up* (lit. *Raising his eyes*), Jesus saw the crowds
	11 41 X	6/ Jesus *lifted up his eyes* and said: 'Father, I thank you
	17 1 X	5/ Jesus *raised his eyes* to heaven and said: 'Father, the hour has come:

2. SEE, SAW – VISION – APPEAR: *HORAŌ*

2	*horama* 12	6	*aph-oraō* 2	
1	*horaō* 455	9	*kath-oraō* 1	
4	*horasis* 4	7	*eph-oraō* 2	
8	*horatos* 1	10	*hyper-(h)oraō* 1	
3	*a-(h)oratos* 5	5	*pro-(h)oraō* 4	

A = Appear (to) = Be seen (by)

1: (GOD) SEES, LOOKS DOWN

Lk	1 25	The Lord has done this for me . . . now that ⌈it has pleased him (lit. he has *looked down*) to take away the humiliation I suffered among men.
	7	
Ac	4 29	7 Lord, ⌈take note of (lit. *look down* on) their threats
	7 34	(Ex 3 7) I have *seen* (§ I have *seen*) the way my people are ill-treated in Egypt,

2: (JESUS) SEES, SAW

Mt	3 16	Jesus . . . *saw* the Spirit of God descending like a dove
	4 18	he *saw* two brothers, Simon . . . and . . . Andrew;
	21	Going on from there he *saw* another pair of brothers,
	5 1	*Seeing* the crowds, he went up the hill.
	8 14	Jesus ⌈*found* (lit. *saw*) Peter's mother-in-law in bed with fever.
	18	When Jesus *saw* the great crowds . . . he gave orders to leave for the other side [of Lake Tiberius].
	9 2	*Seeing* their faith, Jesus said to the paralytic, 'Courage,
	4	⌈*Knowing* (ᵛ*Seeing*) what was in their minds Jesus said, 'Why do you have such wicked thoughts in your hearts?'
	9	As Jesus was walking on from there he *saw* a man named Matthew

Mt	9 22	Jesus turned round and *saw* [the woman with a haemorrhage];
	23	Jesus reached the official's house and *saw* the flute-players,
	36	when he *saw* the crowds he felt sorry for them
	14 14	as he stepped ashore he *saw* a large crowd; and he took pity on them and healed their sick.
	21 19	*Seeing* a fig tree by the road, he went up to it
Mk	1 10	he *saw* the heavens torn apart and the Spirit . . . descending on him.
	16	As he was walking along by the Sea of Galilee he *saw* Simon
	19	Going on a little further, he *saw* James
	2 5	*Seeing* their faith, Jesus said to the paralytic, 'My child, your sins are forgiven'.
	14	As he was walking on he *saw* Levi
	5 32	he continued to look all round to *see* who had done it.
	6 34	as he stepped ashore he *saw* a large crowd; and he took pity on them
	48	He could *see* [the disciples] were worn out with rowing, turning and *seeing* his disciples, he rebuked Peter
	8 33	
	9 25	Jesus *saw* how many people were pressing round him,
	10 14	when Jesus *saw* this he was indignant and said to them, 'Let the little children come to me;
	11 13	*Seeing* a fig tree in leaf some distance away, he went to *see* if he could find any fruit on it,
	12 15	Hand me a denarius and let me *see* it.
	34	Jesus, *seeing* how wisely he had spoken, said, 'You are not far from the kingdom of God'.
Lk	5 2	he *caught sight of* two boats close to the bank.
	20	*Seeing* their faith he said, 'My friend, your sins are forgiven you'.
	7 13	When the Lord *saw* [the widow of Nain] he felt sorry for her.
	9 47	Jesus ⌈*knew* (ᵛ *saw*) what thoughts were going through their minds,
	13 12	When Jesus *saw* [the crippled woman] he called her over
	17 14	When he *saw* [the ten lepers] he said, 'Go and show yourselves to the priests'.
	18 24	Jesus *looked at* him and said, 'How hard it is for those who have riches to make their way into the kingdom of God!'
	19 41	As he . . . *came in sight of* the city he shed tears over it
	21 1	As he looked up he *saw* rich people putting their offerings into the treasury; ² then he happened to *notice* a poverty-stricken widow putting in two small coins,
	2	
	22 43 A	an angel *appeared* to him . . . to give him strength.
Jn	1 47	Jesus *saw* Nathanael coming . . . ⁴⁸. . . 'Before Philip came to call you,' said Jesus 'I *saw* you under the fig tree.'
	48	
	50	You believe that just because I said: I *saw* you under the fig tree.
	3 11 Δ	we . . . witness only to what we have *seen*
	32	[He who comes from heaven] bears witness to the things he has *seen* and heard,
	5 6	when Jesus *saw* [the lame man] lying there . . . he said, 'Do you want to be well again?'
	6 46	the one who comes from God . . . has *seen* the Father.
	8 38	What I, for my part, speak of is what I have *seen* with my Father;
	57	You are not fifty yet, and you have *seen* Abraham!
	9 1	he *saw* a man who had been blind from birth.
	11 33	*At the sight of* [Mary's] tears . . . Jesus said in great distress,
	34	Lord, come and *see*.
	16 22	I shall *see* you again, and your hearts will be full of joy,
	19 26	*Seeing* his mother and the disciple he loved standing near her, Jesus said . . . , 'Woman, this is your son'.
Ac	2 27 D	(Ps 16 10) you will not . . . allow your holy one to ⌈*experience* (lit. *see*) corruption.
	31 D	[David] is the one . . . whose body did not ⌈*experience* (lit. *see*) corruption.
	13 35 D	(Ps 16 10) You will not allow your holy one to ⌈*experience* (lit. *see*) corruption.
	37 D	The one whom God has raised up . . . has not ⌈*experienced* (lit. *seen*) corruption.

3: (A PERSON) SEES, SAW

a) See (God) – (God is) Invisible

Mt	5 8	Happy the pure in heart: they shall *see* God.
Jn	1 18	No one has ever *seen* God; it is the only Son . . . who has made him known.
	3 11 Δ	we . . . witness only to what we have *seen*
	5 37	you have never *seen* his shape,
	6 46	Not that anybody has *seen* the Father, except the one who comes from God:
	14 7	From this moment you know [the Father] and have *seen* him . . . ⁹. . . To have seen me is to have *seen* the Father,
	9	
Ac	2 25	5 (Ps 16 8) I *saw* the Lord before me always,
	7 2 A	The God of glory *appeared* to our ancestor Abraham,

Ac 7 30 A | an angel *appeared* to [Moses] in the flames of a bush that
31 /2 | was on fire. [31]Moses was amazed by *seeing what he saw.*
35 A | the angel . . . had *appeared* to [Moses] in the bush.
55 | Stephen . . . *saw* the glory of God, and Jesus standing at God's right hand.
Rm 1 20 | Ever since God created the world his everlasting power and
3 | deity – however *invisible* – have been there for the mind
9 | to *see* in the things he has made.
Ga 3 8 Δ | Scripture *foresaw* that God was going to use faith to justify the pagans,
Col 1 15 | [Christ] is the image of the *unseen* God
1Tm 1 17 | To . . . the undying, *invisible* and only God, be honour and glory
6 16 | no man has *seen* and no man is able to *see* [God]:
Heb 11 27 | [Moses] held to his purpose like a man who could *see* the
3 | *Invisible.*
12 14 | Always be wanting peace . . . and the holiness without
Δ | which no one can ever *see* the Lord.
1 Jn 3 2 | we shall be like [God] because we shall *see* him as he really is.
4 20 | a man who does not love the brother that he can see cannot love God, whom he has never *seen.*
3 Jn 11 | the person who does what is wrong has never *seen* God.
Rv 22 4 | [the servants of God] will *see* him face to face,

b) See (Jesus, Jesus's signs) – Vision – (Jesus) Appears (to a person)

Mt 2 11 | going into the house [the wise men] *saw* the child with his mother Mary,
8 34 | as soon as [the Gadarenes] *saw* [Jesus] they implored him to leave the neighbourhood.
9 8 | A feeling of awe came over the crowd when they *saw* this,
11 | When the Pharisees *saw* this, they said to his disciples, 'Why does your master eat with tax collectors . . .?'
12 38 | Master, . . . we should like to *see* a sign from you.
13 17 | many prophets and holy men longed to *see* what you see, and never *saw* it;
14 26 | the disciples *saw* [Jesus] walking on the lake
16 28 | there are some . . . here who will not taste death before they *see* the Son of Man coming with his kingdom.
17 8 | when they raised their eyes they *saw* no one but only Jesus.
9 2 | [9] . . . 'Tell no one about the *vision* until the Son of Man has risen from the dead'.
21 15 | *At the sight of* the wonderful things he did . . . the chief priests and the scribes were indignant.
20 | The disciples were amazed when they *saw* it.
38 < | the tenants *saw* the son [of the landowner]
23 39 | you shall not *see* me any more until you say: Blessings on him who comes in the name of the Lord!
24 30 | they will *see* the Son of Man coming on the clouds of heaven
25 37 | Lord, when did we *see* you hungry and feed you . . .? [38] When
38 | did we *see* you a stranger and make you welcome . . .?
39 | [39] When did we *see* you sick or in prison and go to see you?
44 | Lord, when did we *see* you hungry . . .?
26 64 | you will *see* the Son of Man seated at the right hand of the Power
28 7 | he is going before you to Galilee; it is there you will *see* him.
10 | go and tell my brothers that . . . they will *see* me [in Galilee].
17 | When [the disciples] *saw* him they fell down before him,
Mk 2 12 | We have never *seen* anything like this.
16 | the scribes . . . *saw* him eating with sinners
5 6 | *Catching sight of* Jesus from a distance, [the demoniac] ran up and fell at his feet
14 | the people came to *see* what had really happened.
16 | those who had *witnessed* it reported . . . what had become of the pigs.
22 | *seeing* [Jesus, Jairus] fell at his feet
6 33 | people *saw* [Jesus and his disciples] going, and many could guess where;
49 | [the disciples] *saw* him walking on the lake
50 | they had all *seen* him and were terrified.
9 8 | [Peter, James and John] *saw* no one with them any more but only Jesus [9] . . . he warned them to tell no one what they had *seen,*
15 | The moment they *saw* him the whole crowd . . . ran to greet him.
20 | as soon as the spirit *saw* Jesus it threw the boy into convulsions,
12 28 | One of the scribes . . . had *observed* (G understood) how well Jesus had answered them,
13 26 | they will *see* the Son of Man coming in the clouds
14 62 | you will *see* the Son of Man seated at the right hand of the Power
15 32 | Let the Christ . . . come down from the cross now, for us to *see* it and believe.
39 | The centurion . . . had *seen* how he had died, and he said, 'In truth this man was a son of God'.
16 7 | He is going before you to Galilee; it is there you will *see* him,
Lk 2 15 | Let us go to Bethlehem and *see* this thing that has happened which the Lord has made known to us.

Lk 2 17 | When [the shepherds] *saw* the child they repeated what they had been told about him,
20 | the shepherds went back . . . praising God for all they had heard and *seen;*
26 | It had been revealed to [Simeon] . . . that he would not see death until he had *set eyes on* the Christ of the Lord.
30 | my eyes have *seen* the salvation
48 | [Joseph and Mary] were overcome when they *saw* [Jesus],
5 8 | When Simon Peter *saw* this he fell at the knees of Jesus
12 | *Seeing* Jesus [the leper] fell on his face
26 | We have *seen* strange things today.
7 22 | Go back and tell John what you have *seen* and heard:
8 20 | Your mother and brothers . . . want to *see* you.
28 | *Catching sight of* Jesus [the demoniac] gave a shout,
34 | When the swineherds *saw* what had happened they ran off
35 | the people went out to *see* what had happened.
36 | Those who had *witnessed* it told them how the man who had been possessed came to be healed.
9 9 | [Herod] was anxious to *see* him.
32 | Peter and his companions . . . kept awake and *saw* his glory
36 | The disciples . . . told no one what they had *seen.*
10 24 | many prophets and kings wanted to *see* what you see, and never *saw* it;
11 38 | The Pharisee *saw* this and was surprised that he had not first washed before the meal.
13 35 | you shall not *see* me till the time comes
17 15 | *Finding* himself cured, one of [the ten lepers] turned back
22 | A time will come when you will long to *see* one of the days of the Son of Man and will not *see* it.
18 43 | all the people who *saw* it gave praise to God
19 3 | [Zacchaeus] was anxious to *see* what kind of man Jesus was
4 | . . . [4] so he . . . climbed a sycamore tree to *catch a glimpse of* Jesus
7 | They all complained when they *saw* what was happening. 'He has gone to stay at a sinner's house' they said.
37 | the whole group of disciples joyfully began to praise God . . . for all the miracles they had *seen.*
20 14 < | when the tenants *saw* the son they put their heads together.
21 27 | they will *see* the Son of Man coming in a cloud
23 8 | Herod was delighted to *see* Jesus; he had . . . been wanting for a long time to *set eyes on* him; moreover, he was hoping to *see* some miracle worked by him.
47 | When the centurion *saw* what had taken place, he gave praise to God
49 | the women who had accompanied him from Galilee . . . *saw* all this happen.
24 24 | Some of our friends went to the tomb . . . but of [Jesus] they *saw* nothing.
34 A | The Lord has risen and has *appeared* to Simon.
39 | *Look* at my hands and feet . . . Touch me and *see* for yourselves; a ghost has no flesh and bones
Jn 1 39 | 'Come and *see*' he replied; so they went and *saw* where he lived,
46 | 'Come and *see*' replied Philip.
4 29 | Come and *see* a man who has told me everything I ever did;
45 | the Galileans received him well, having *seen* all that he had done at Jerusalem
48 | So you will not believe unless you *see* signs and portents!
6 2 | a large crowd followed him, [impressed by (lit. having *seen*) the signs he gave by curing the sick.
14 | The people, *seeing* this sign that he had given, said,
26 | you are not looking for me because you have *seen* the signs
30 | What sign will you give [to show us (lit. for us to *see*) that we should believe in you?
36 | you [can] *see* me and still you do not believe.
8 56 | Your father Abraham rejoiced to think that he would *see* my Day; he *saw* it and was glad.
9 37 | Jesus said, 'You are *looking at* [the Son of Man]; he is speaking to you'.
11 32 | as soon as [Mary] *saw* him she threw herself at his feet,
40 | Have I not told you that if you believe you will *see* the glory of God?
12 21 | [some Greeks] put this request to [Philip], 'Sir, we should like to *see* Jesus'.
40 | (Is 6 10) He has blinded their eyes, . . . for fear they should *see*
41 | Isaiah said this when he *saw* his glory,
14 9 | To have *seen* me is to have seen the Father,
15 24 | they have *seen* all [my works],
16 16 | then a short time later you will *see* me again.
17 | What does he mean, '. . . then a short time later you will *see* me again' . . .?
19 | You are asking one another what I meant by saying: . . . then a short time later you will *see* me again.
19 6 | When they *saw* him the chief priests . . . shouted, 'Crucify him!
33 | When they came to Jesus, they *found* he was already dead,
35 | This is the evidence of one who *saw* it –
37 | (Zc 12 10 Th) They will *look on* the one whom they have pierced.

Jn 20	8		the other disciple . . . *saw* and he believed.
	18		Mary of Magdala . . . told the disciples that she had *seen* the Lord
	20		The disciples were filled with joy when they *saw* the Lord,
	25		When the disciples said, 'We have *seen* the Lord', [Thomas] answered, 'Unless I *see* the holes . . . in his hands . . . I refuse to believe'.
	27		*look*, here are my hands . . . Doubt no longer but believe.
	29		You believe because you can *see* me. Happy are those who have not *seen* and yet believe.
Ac 2	31	5	[David] *foresaw* and spoke about . . . the resurrection of the Christ.
4	20		We cannot promise to stop proclaiming what we have *seen* and heard.
7	55		Stephen . . . *saw* the glory of God, and Jesus . . . at God's right hand.
9	10	2	Ananias . . . had a *vision* in which he heard the Lord say to him, 'Ananias!'
	17 A		the Lord Jesus . . . *appeared* to you on your way here
	27 A		the Lord had *appeared* to Saul and spoken to him on his journey,
13	31 A		[Jesus] *appeared* to those who had accompanied him from Galilee to Jerusalem.
18	9	2	One night the Lord spoke to Paul in a *vision*, 'Do not be afraid to speak out,
22	14		The God of our ancestors has chosen you . . . to *see* the Just One
	15		you are to be his witness . . , testifying to what you have *seen*
	18		then I *saw* him. 'Hurry,' he said 'leave Jerusalem at once;
26	13		I *saw* a light brighter than the sun come down from heaven.
	16 A		I have *appeared* to you for this reason: to appoint you as my servant and as witness of this [vision] in which you have
	A		*seen* me, and of others in which I shall *appear* to you.
1 Co	2 9		(Is 64 3) We teach . . . the things that no eye has *seen*
9	1		I have *seen* Jesus our Lord.
15	5 A		he *appeared* first to Cephas and secondly to the Twelve.
	6 A		[6] Next he *appeared* to more than five hundred of the brothers at the same time . . . [7] then he *appeared* to James, and then
	7 A		
	8 A		to all the apostles; [8] and last of all he *appeared* to me too;
1 Tm	3 16 A		He was . . . *seen* by angels, proclaimed to the pagans,
Heb	2 8		At present . . . we are not able to *see* that everything has been put under his command,
9	28 A		when [Christ] *appears* a second time, it will not be to deal with sin
11	13		they *saw* [the promised things] in the far distance and welcomed them,
12	2	6	Let us ʳ*not lose sight of* (or: *fix our eyes on*) Jesus,
	14 Δ		Always be wanting peace with all people, and the holiness without which no one can ever *see* the Lord.
1 P	1 8		You did not *see* him, yet you love him; and still without *seeing* him, you are already filled with a joy
1 Jn	1 1		Something which . . . we have *seen* with our own eyes . . . – this is our subject. [2] That life was made visible: we *saw* it and we are giving our testimony . . . [3] What we have *seen* and heard we are telling you
	2		
	3		
3	6		anyone who sins has never *seen* him or known him.
Rv	1 7		It is he who is coming on the clouds; ʳeveryone (lit. every eye) will *see* him,
	17		When I *saw* him, I fell in a dead faint at his feet,
5	6		I *saw* . . . a Lamb that seemed to have been sacrificed;

c) See a Vision – a Vision Appears (to a person)

Mt 17	3 A		Suddenly Moses and Elijah *appeared* to [Peter, James and John];
Mk 9	4 A		Elijah *appeared* to [Peter, James and John] with Moses;
16	5		On entering the tomb [the women] *saw* a young man in a white robe
Lk 1	11 A		Then there *appeared* to him the angel of the Lord . . .
	12		[12] The *sight* disturbed Zechariah
	22		they realised that [Zechariah] had ʳreceived (lit. *seen*) a vision in the sanctuary.
9	31 A		[They were Moses and Elijah] *appearing* in glory,
24	23		[the women] came back to tell us they had *seen* a vision of angels
Jn 1	33		'The man on whom you *see* the Spirit come down . . . is the the one who is going to baptise with the Holy Spirit'.
	34		[34] Yes, I have *seen* and I am the witness that he is the Chosen One of God.
	50		'You believe that just because I said: I saw you under the fig tree. You will *see* greater things than that.' [51] And then he added, '. . . you will *see* heaven laid open
	51		
Ac 2	3 A		something *appeared* to [the apostles] that seemed like tongues of fire;
	17	/4	(Jl 3 1) your young men shall *see* visions,
7	44		[God told Moses] to make an exact copy of the pattern he had ʳbeen shown (lit. *seen*).
9	12	/2	[Saul is praying,] having ʳhad (lit. *seen*) a *vision* of a man called Ananias

Ac 10	3	/2	[Cornelius] ʳhad (lit. *saw*) a *vision* in which he distinctly saw the angel of God
	17	2	Peter was still worrying over the meaning of the *vision* he had *seen*, when the men sent by Cornelius arrived . . . [19] Peter's mind was still on the *vision*
	19	2	
11	5	/2	I . . . ʳhad (lit. *saw*) a *vision* of something like a big sheet being let down from heaven
	6		I watched [the sheet] intently and *saw* all sorts of animals
	13		[Cornelius] had *seen* an angel standing in his house
12	9	2	Peter followed [the angel], but . . . he thought he was seeing a vision.
16	9 A	/2	One night Paul ʳhad (lit. *saw*) a *vision*: a Macedonian appeared
	10	/2	Once [Paul] had *seen* this *vision* we lost no time in arranging a passage to Macedonia,
Col 2	18		people like that are always going on about some *vision* they have (ᵛ not) had,
Heb 8	5		(Ex 25 40) *See* that you make everything according to the pattern shown you on the mountain
Rv 1	2		John has written down everything he *saw* and . . . it is the word of God guaranteed by Jesus Christ.
	12		I *saw* seven golden lamp-stands
	19		Now write down all that you *see*
	20		The secret of the seven stars you have *seen* in my right hand . . . is this:
4	1		[in my vision,] I *saw* a door open in heaven
5	1		I *saw* that in the right hand of the One sitting on the throne there was a scroll . . . [2] Then I *saw* a powerful angel
	2		
	11		In my *vision*, I heard the sound of an immense number of angels
6	1		I *saw* the Lamb break one of the seven seals,
	2 A		Immediately a white horse *appeared*,
	5 A		Immediately a black horse *appeared*,
	8 A		Immediately another horse *appeared*, deathly pale,
	9		I *saw* underneath the altar the souls of all the people who had been killed
	12		In my *vision*, . . . [the Lamb] broke the sixth seal,
7	1		I *saw* four angels . . . holding the four winds of the world back
	2		I *saw* another angel rising where the sun rises,
	9		After that I *saw* a huge number . . . of people
8	2		I *saw* . . . the seven angels who stand in the presence of God.
	13		In my *vision*, I heard an eagle, calling aloud
9	1		I *saw* a star that had fallen from heaven on to the earth,
	17	4/	In my *vision* I *saw* the horses, and the riders
10	1		I *saw* another powerful angel coming down from heaven,
	5		Then the angel that I had *seen* . . . raised his right hand to heaven,
11	19 A		the ark of the covenant could be *seen* inside [the sanctuary].
12	1 A		Now a great sign *appeared* in heaven: a woman,
	3 A		a second sign *appeared* in the sky, a huge red dragon
13	1		I *saw* a beast emerge from the sea:
	2		I *saw* that the beast was like a leopard,
	11		Then I *saw* a second beast; it emerged from the ground;
14	1		Next [in my vision] I *saw* Mount Zion, and standing on it a Lamb
	6		I *saw* another angel, flying high overhead,
	14		Now [in my vision] I *saw* a white cloud
15	1		What I *saw* next, in heaven, was a great and wonderful sign:
	2		I [seemed to] *see* a glass lake suffused with fire,
	5		in my *vision*, the sanctuary . . . opened in heaven,
16	13		from the jaws of dragon and beast and false prophet I *saw* three foul spirits come;
17	3		I *saw* a woman riding a scarlet beast
	6		I *saw* that [the woman] was drunk, drunk with the blood of the saints, . . . and when I *saw* her, I was completely mystified.
	8		The beast you have *seen* once was and now is not;
	12		The ten horns you *saw* are ten kings
	15		The waters you *saw* . . . are all the people,
	16		the time will come when the ten horns you *saw* and the beast will turn against the prostitute,
	18		The woman you *saw* is the great city
18	1		After this, I *saw* another angel come down from heaven,
19	11		I *saw* heaven open, and a white horse appear;
	17		I *saw* an angel standing in the sun,
	19		I *saw* the beast, with all the kings of the earth
20	1		I *saw* an angel come down from heaven
	4		I *saw* some thrones, and [I saw] those who are given the power to be judges take their seats on them.
	11		Then I *saw* a great white throne
	12		I *saw* the dead, both great and small, standing in front of his throne,
21	1		Then I *saw* a new heaven and a new earth;
	2		I *saw* the holy city, and the new Jerusalem,
	22		I *saw* that there was no temple in the city

d) See (generally)

Mt 2	2		'Where is the infant king of the Jews?' [the wise men] asked. 'We *saw* his star as it rose
	9		the star [the wise men] had *seen* rising . . . went forward

Mt	2	10	The *sight* of the star filled [the wise men] with delight,
		16	Herod was furious when he *realised* that he had been out-witted by the wise men,
	3	7	[John] *saw* a number of Pharisees and Sadducees coming for baptism
	4	16 ●	(Is 9 1) The people that lived in darkness has *seen* a great light;
	5	16	your light must shine in the sight of men, so that, *seeing* your good works, they may give the praise to your Father
	8	4	*Mind* you do not tell anyone,
	9	30	*Take care* that no one learns about this.
	11	8	what did you go out to *see*? A man wearing fine clothes?
		9	what did you go out for? To *see* a prophet?
	12	2	The Pharisees *noticed* [that the disciples picked ears of corn and ate them]
	13	14	(Is 6 9 G) You will . . . ʳsee and see again, but not perceive (lit. look and look [again], but not *see*).
		15	(cf. Is 6 10) they have shut their eyes, for fear they should *see* with theirs eyes,
	16	6	*Keep your eyes open*, and be on your guard against the yeast of the Pharisees
	18	10	*See* that you never despise any of these little ones,
		31 <	His fellow servants were deeply distressed when they *saw* what had happened,
	20	3 <	Going out at about the third hour [the landowner] *saw* others . . . idle in the market place
	21	32	Even after *seeing* this, you refused to think better of it
	22	11 <	When the king came in . . . he *noticed* one man who was not wearing a wedding garment,
	24	6	ʳdo not be (lit. *see* that you are not) alarmed, for this is something that must happen,
		15	So when you *see* the disastrous abomination [those in Judaea must escape to the mountains]
		33	So with you when you *see* all these things:
	26	8	When they *saw* this, the disciples were indignant;
		58	Peter . . . sat down with the attendants to *see* what the end would be.
		71	another servant-girl *saw* [Peter]
	27	3	When he *found* that Jesus had been condemned, Judas . . . was filled with remorse
		4	That is ʳyour concern (lit. for you to *see* [to]).
		24	Pilate *saw* that he was making no impression . . . So he . . . said, 'I am innocent of this man's blood. It is ʳyour concern (lit. for you to *see* [to]).'
		49	Wait . . . and *see* if Elijah will come to save him.
		54	the centurion, together with the others guarding Jesus, had *seen* the earthquake
	28	6	Come and *see* the place where [Jesus] lay,
Mk	1	44	*Mind* you say nothing to anyone,
	4	12	(Is 6 9) they may ʳsee and see again, but not perceive (lit. look and look [again,] but not *see*).
	6	38	'How many loaves have you?' [Jesus] asked. 'Go and *see*.'
	7	2	[the Pharisees] *noticed* that some of his disciples were eating with unclean hands,
	8	15	*Keep your eyes open*; be on your guard against the yeast of the Pharisees
		24	I can see people; they look like trees to me, but ʳthey are (lit. I [can] *see* them) walking about.
	9	1 ●	there are some standing here who will not taste death before they *see* the kingdom of God come with power.
		14	[Jesus, Peter, James and John] *saw* a large crowd
		38	Master, we *saw* a man . . . casting out devils in your name;
	11	20	Next morning . . . they *saw* the fig tree withered to the roots.
	13	14	When you *see* the disastrous abomination . . . then those in Judaea must escape to the mountains;
		29	So with you when you *see* these things happening:
	14	67	[The servant-girl] *saw* Peter warming himself there,
		69	The servant-girl *saw* [Peter] . . . again
	15	36	Wait and *see* if Elijah will come to take him down.
Lk	2	26 D	It had been revealed to [Simeon] . . . that he would not *see* death until he had set eyes on the Christ of the Lord.
	3	6 ●	(Is 40 5) all mankind shall *see* the salvation of God.
	7	25	Then what did you go out to *see*? A man dressed in fine clothes?
		26	Then what did you go out to *see*? A prophet? Yes, . . . and much more than a prophet;
		39	When the Pharisee . . . *saw* this, he said to himself, 'If this man were a prophet, he would know
	8	47	*Seeing* herself discovered, the woman came forward trembling,
	9	27 ●	there are some standing here who will not taste death before they *see* the kingdom of God.
		49	Master, . . . we *saw* a man casting out devils in your name,
		54	*Seeing* this, the disciples James and John said, 'Lord, do you want us to call down fire from heaven . . .?'
	10	31 <	when [a priest] *saw* the [wounded] man, he passed by . . .
		32 <	³² In the same way a Levite . . . *saw* him, and passed by
		33 <	. . . ³³ But a Samaritan traveller . . . was moved with compassion when he *saw* him.
	12	15	*Watch*, and be on your guard against avarice of any kind,
		54	When you *see* a cloud . . . you say at once that rain is coming,
Lk	13	28	Then there will be weeping . . . when you *see* Abraham and Isaac and Jacob . . . in the kingdom of God, and yourselves turned outside.
	14	18 <	I have bought a piece of land and must go and *see* it.
	15	20 <	his father *saw* [the prodigal son] and was moved with pity.
	16	23 <	[the rich man] *saw* Abraham a long way off with Lazarus
	18	15	when the disciples *saw* this they turned them away.
	21	20	When you *see* Jerusalem surrounded by armies, you must realise that she will soon be laid desolate.
		29	ʳThink of (lit. Now *see*) the fig tree and indeed every tree.
		31	So with you when you *see* these things happening:
	22	49	His followers, *seeing* what was happening, said, 'Lord, shall we use our swords?'
		56	as [Peter] was sitting there by the blaze a servant-girl *saw* him,
		58	someone else *saw* [Peter] and said, 'You are another of them'.
Jn	3	3 ○	unless a man is born from above, he cannot *see* the kingdom of God.
		36 ○	anyone who refuses to believe in the Son will never *see* life:
	6	22	the crowd . . . *saw* that only one boat had been there,
		24	the people *saw* that neither Jesus nor his disciples were there,
	7	52	Go into the matter, and *see* for yourself: prophets do not come out of Galilee.
	11	31	the Jews . . . *saw* [Mary] get up . . . and go out,
	12	9	a large number of Jews . . . came . . . to *see* Lazarus
	18	26	Didn't I *see* you in the garden with [Jesus]?
	21	21	*Seeing* [the disciple Jesus loved], Peter said to Jesus, 'What about him, Lord?'
Ac	3	3	this [lame] man *saw* Peter and John on their way into the Temple
		9	Everyone could *see* [the lame man] walking and praising God,
		12	When Peter *saw* the people he addressed them,
	6	15 A	[Stephen's] face *appeared* to them like the face of an angel.
	7	24	[Moses] *saw* one of [his countrymen] being ill-treated
		26	[Moses] *came across* some of [his countrymen] fighting,
	8	18	Simon *saw* that the Spirit was given through the imposition of hands by the apostles,
		23	*it is plain to* me that you are trapped in . . . the chains of sin.
		39	the eunuch never *saw* [Philip] again
	9	35	[the paralytic got up immediately;] everybody . . . *saw* him,
		40	[Tabitha] *looked* at Peter and sat up.
	11	23	[Barnabas] could *see* for himself that God had given grace,
	12	3	when [Herod] *saw* that this pleased the Jews he decided to arrest Peter as well.
		16	they . . . were amazed to *see* [that it really was] Peter himself.
	13	12	The proconsul, who had *watched* everything, became a believer,
		36 D	David . . . has certainly ʳexperienced (lit. *seen*) corruption.
		41	(Hab 1 5 D) *Cast your eyes around you*, mockers; be amazed, and perish!
		45	When they *saw* the crowds, the Jews, prompted by jealousy, used blasphemies
	14	9	*Seeing* that the man had the faith to be cured, [Paul said in a loud voice, 'Get to your feet – stand up']
		11	the crowd *saw* what Paul had done
	15	6	The apostles and elders met to *look into* the matter,
	16	19	her masters *saw* that there was no hope of making any more money out of her,
		27	the gaoler woke and *saw* the doors wide open
		40	[Paul and Silas] *saw* all the brothers [in Lydia's house]
	18	15	ʳdeal with (lit. *see* to) it yourselves – I have no intention of making legal decisions about things like that.
	19	21	I must go on to *see* Rome as well.
	20	25	I now feel sure that none of you . . . will ever *see* my face again.
	21	29	5 They had . . . *previously seen* Trophimus the Ephesian in the city with [Paul],
		32	the crowd . . . stopped beating Paul when they *saw* the tribune and the soldiers.
	28	4	the natives *saw* the creature hanging from [Paul's] hand
		15	When Paul *saw* [the brothers] he thanked God
		20	That is why I have asked to *see* you and talk to you,
		26	(Is 6 9 G) You will . . . ʳsee and see again, but not perceive (lit. look and look [again] but not *see*).
		27	(cf. Is 6 10) they have shut their eyes, for fear they should *see* with their eyes,
Rm	1	11	I am longing to *see* you
	11	22 ●	ʳDo not forget that (lit. *See* how) God can be severe as well as kind,
	15	21 ●	(Is 52 15 G) Those who have never been told about him will *see* him,
1 Co	8	10	Suppose someone *sees* you, a man who understands, eating in some temple of an idol;
	16	7	I do not want to make it only a passing visit to *see* you
Ga	1	19	I did not *see* any of the other apostles;
	2	7	they *recognised* that I had been commissioned to preach the Good News to the uncircumcised
		14	I *saw* they were not respecting the true meaning of the Good News,

Ga	6	11	*Take good note of* what I am adding in my own handwriting
Ph	1	27	whether I come to you and *see* for myself, or stay at a distance . . . I shall know that you are unanimous
		30	You and I are together in the same fight as you *saw* me fighting before
	2	23	I am hoping to send [Timothy] you, as soon as I ʳknow something definite about my fate (lit. can *see* my fate *more clearly*).
		28	you will be happy to *see* [Epaphroditus] again,
	4	9	Keep doing all the things that you learnt from me and have . . . *seen* that I do.
Col	1	16 ●	in [Christ] were created all things . . .; everything *visible* and everything *invisible*,
	2	1	I do have to struggle hard for . . . so many others who have never *seen* me face to face.
1 Th	2	17	we had an especially strong desire . . . to *see* you face to face again,
	3	6	Timothy is . . . telling us that you . . . want to *see* us quite as much as we want to see you.
		10	We are earnestly praying . . . to be able to *see* you face to face again
2 Tm	5	15	*Make sure* that people do not try to take revenge;
	1	4	[I] long to *see* you again
Heb	3	9 ●	(Ps 95 9) your ancestors challenged me . . . though they had *seen* what I could do
	11	5 D	Enoch . . . did not have to ʳ experience (lit. *see*) death:
		23	(Ex 2 2) his parents . . . *saw* [Moses] was such a fine child.
	13	23	Timothy . . . will be with me when I *see* you.
Jm	2	24	You *see* now that it is by doing something good . . . that a man is justified.
	5	11	You have heard of the patience of Job, and ʳunderstood (lit. *seen*) the Lord's purpose,
1 P	3	10	(Ps 34 13) Anyone who wants to ʳhave (lit. *see*) a happy life . . . must banish malice from his tongue,
1 Jn	3	1 ●	ʳThink of (lit. Now *see*) the love that the Father has lavished on us,
	4	20	a man who does not love the brother that he can *see* cannot love God, whom he has never seen.
	5	16	If anybody *sees* his brother commit a sin . . . he has only to pray, and God will give life to the sinner
3 Jn		14	I hope to *see* you soon
Rv	4	3 A	the Person sitting there *looked* like a diamond and a ruby.
		4	There was a rainbow encircling the throne, and this *looked* like an emerald.
	12	13	the devil *found* himself thrown down to the earth,
	18	7 ○	[Babylon] says to herself. . . . I . . . shall never ʳbe in (lit. *see*) mourning.
	19	10	ʳDon't do that (lit. No; *see*): I am a servant just like you
	22	9	ʳDon't do that (lit. *See*): I am a servant just like you

4: OVERLOOK

Ac	17	30 Θ	10 God *overlooked* that sort of thing when men were ignorant, but now he is telling everyone . . . that they must repent,

3. SEE – VISION – APPEARANCE: *OPSIS*

5	*opsis*	1/3	10	*ep-optēs*	1
6	*optanō*	1	3	*ep-opteuō*	2
1	*optasia*	4	4	*es-optron*	2
7	*ant-ophthalmeō*	1	11	*my-ōpazō*	1
8	*aut-optēs*	1	2	*pros-ōpon*	3/76
9	*kat-optrizō*	1	12	*eu-pros-ōpeō*	1

1: SEE – EYEWITNESS

Lk	1	2	these [accounts] were handed down to us by those who
		8	were *eyewitnesses* and ministers of the word,
1 P	2	12	Always behave honourably among pagans so that they can
		3	*see* your good works for themselves
	3	2	[Husbands who have not yet obeyed the word may find
		3	themselves won over,] when they *see* how faithful . . . [their wives] are.
2 P	1	16	10 we had *seen* [Christ's] majesty *for ourselves*.

2: VISION – APPEAR

Lk	1	22	they realised that [Zechariah] had ʳreceived (lit. *seen*) a *vision*
	24	23	[the women] came back to tell us they had seen a *vision* of angels
Ac	1	3	6 for forty days [Christ] had *continued to appear* to them
	26	19	King Agrippa, I could not disobey the heavenly *vision*.
2 Co	12	1	I will move on to the *visions* . . . I have had from the Lord.

3: APPEARANCE(S) – MIRROR

Jn	7	24	5 Do not keep judging according to *appearances*;
1 Co	13	12	4 Now we are seeing a dim reflection in a *mirror*; but then we shall be seeing face to face.

2 Co	3	18	9 we, with our unveiled faces *reflecting like mirrors* the brightness of the Lord, all grow brighter and brighter
	5	12	have an answer ready for the people who can boast more about *what they seem* than what they are.
	10	7	2 ʳFace plain facts (lit. Look things in the face; or: You are looking at things *superficially*).
Ga	6	12	12 It is only ʳself-interest (lit. [the intention of] *making a good showing*) that makes them want to force circumcision on you —
Jm	1	11	2 the flower falls; what *looked* so beautiful now disappears.
		23	To listen to the word and not obey is like looking at your own features in a *mirror*

4: 'LOOK FORWARD' = TURN HEAD-ON, FACE INTO

Ac	27	15	7 The ship . . . could not be *turned head-on* to the wind,

5: SHORT-SIGHTED

2 P	1	9	11 without [these virtues] a man is blind or else *short-sighted*; he has forgotten how his past sins were washed away.

4. SEE, LOOK (AT) – WATCH (OUT), TAKE CARE: *BLEPŌ*

7	*blemma*	1	5	*dia-blepō*	3
1	*blepō*	131/133	3	*em-blepō*	11
2	*ana-blepō*	25	6	*epi-blepō*	3
8	*ana-blepsis*	1	4	*peri-blepō*	7
9	*apo-blepō*	1	10	*pro-blepō*	1

1: SEE, SEE AGAIN – LOOK AT

a) (God) Sees, Looks upon

Mt	6	4	your Father who *sees* all that is done in secret will reward you.
		6	your Father who *sees* all that is done in secret will reward you.
		18	your Father who *sees* all that is done in secret will reward you.
Lk	1	48	6 he has *looked upon* his lowly handmaid.
Heb	11	40	10 God has ʳmade provision for us to (lit. *previously seen* [to it] that we should) have something better,

b) (Jesus) Looks at, Looks round, Looks up

Mt	14	19	2 [Jesus] *raised his eyes* to heaven and said the blessing.
	19	26	3 Jesus *gazed at* them. 'For men' he told them 'this is impossible;
Mk	3	5	4 he *looked* angrily *round* at [the people in the synagogue],
		34	4 *looking round* at those sitting in a circle about him, he said, 'Here are my mother and my brothers.
	5	31	You *see* how the crowd is pressing round you
		32	4 he continued to *look all round* to see who had [touched him].
	6	41	2 [Jesus] *raised his eyes* to heaven and said the blessing;
	7	34	2 *looking up* to heaven he sighed;
	10	21	3 Jesus *looked steadily at* [the rich young man] and loved him,
		23	4 Jesus *looked round* and said to his disciples, 'How hard it is for those who have riches to enter the kingdom of God!'
		27	3 Jesus *gazed at* them. 'For men' he said 'it is impossible,
	11	11	4 He *looked all round* him, but . . . went out to Bethany
	13	2	Master! *Look at* the size of those buildings!
Lk	6	10	4 he *looked round* at them all and said to the man, 'Stretch out your hand'.
	9	16	2 [Jesus] *raised his eyes* to heaven, and said the blessing
		38	6 Master! . . . I implore you to *look at* my son:
	19	5	2 Jesus . . . *looked up* and spoke to him: 'Zacchaeus,
	20	17	3 he *looked hard at* them and said, 'Then what does this text . . . mean?
	21	1	2 As he *looked up* he saw rich people putting their offerings into the treasury;
	22	61	3 the Lord turned and *looked straight at* Peter,
Jn	1	42	3 Jesus *looked hard at* him and said, 'You are Simon son of John;
	5	19	the Son can do nothing by himself; he can only do what he *sees* the Father doing:

c) (a person) Sees, Looks at

X = See, Look at, Jesus, his signs

Mt	5	28	if a man *looks at* a woman lustfully, he has already committed adultery
	6	26	3 *Look at* the birds in the sky.
	7	3	Why do you *observe* the splinter in your brother's eye . . .?
		5	5 then you will *see clearly* [enough] to take the splinter out of your brother's eye.
	11	4 X	Go back and tell John what you hear and *see*;
	13	16 X	happy are your eyes because they *see*,

Mt 13 17 X		many prophets . . . longed to see what you *see*, and never saw it;
14 30		as soon as [Peter] ⌐felt (lit. *saw*) the force of the wind, he took fright and began to sink.
15 31 X		The crowds were astonished to *see* the dumb speaking,
24 2		You *see* all these [buildings]? . . . not a single stone here will be left on another:
Mk 9 8	4	Then suddenly, when [the disciples] *looked round*, they saw no one with them any more but only Jesus.
14 67	3	[The servant-girl] saw Peter warming himself there, *stared at* him and said, 'You too were with Jesus,
16 4	2	when [the women] *looked* they could see that the stone . . . had already been rolled away.
Lk 6 41		Why do you *observe* the splinter in your brother's eye . . .?
42		⁴² . . . you cannot *see* the plank in your own eye? Hypocrite! Take the plank out of your own eye first, and then you
5		will *see clearly* [enough] to take out the splinter
7 44		'Simon,' [Jesus] said 'you *see* this woman?'
8 16		he puts [the lamp] on a lamp-stand so that people may *see* the light when they come in.
9 62		Once the hand is laid on the plough, no one who *looks* back is fit for the kingdom of God.
10 23 X		Happy the eyes that *see* what you *see*, ²⁴ . . . many prophets
24 X		. . . wanted to see what you *see*, and never saw it;
11 33		No one . . . puts [the lamp] in ˢome hidden place . . , but on the lamp-stand so that people may *see* the light
21 30		As soon as you *see* [trees] bud, you know that summer is now near.
24 12		ᵛ Peter . . . *saw* the binding cloths but nothing else . . .⌐
Jn 1 29 X		*seeing* Jesus coming towards him, John said, 'Look, there is the lamb of God
36 X	3	Jesus passed, and John *stared hard at* him and said, 'Look, there is the lamb of God'.
11 9		A man can walk in the daytime without stumbling, because he has the light of this world to *see* by;
13 22		The disciples *looked at* one another,
20 1		Mary . . . *saw* that the stone had been moved away from the tomb
5		[the other disciple] *saw* the linen cloths lying on the ground,
21 9		[the disciples] *saw* that there was . . . a charcoal fire with fish cooking on it.
20		Peter . . . *saw* the disciple Jesus loved following them –
Ac 1 9 X		[Jesus] was lifted up while they *looked on*,
11		Why are you . . . standing here *looking into* the sky?
2 33		what you *see* and hear is the outpouring of that Spirit.
3 4		Peter and John looked straight at [the lame man] and said, 'Look at us'.
4 14		[the Sanhedrin] *saw* the man who had been cured standing by their side,
8 6		they had heard of the miracles [Philip] worked or . . . they *saw* them for themselves.
12 9		Peter . . . thought he was *seeing* a vision.
Rm 7 23		I can *see* that my body follows a different law
8 24		[salvation lies] in hope, not for what we can *see*, or we should not be hoping – nobody hopes for something which he can already *see*. ²⁵ But having this hope for what we cannot yet
25		*see*, we are able to go on waiting for it
1 Co 1 26		⌐Take (lit. *Look at*) yourselves for instance, brothers,
10 18		*Look at* the other Israel, the race,
13 12 ●		Now we are *seeing* a dim reflection in a mirror;
16 10		If Timothy comes, ⌐show him (lit. *see*) that he has nothing to be afraid of in you:
2 Co 4 18		so we have no eyes for things that are *visible*, but only for things that are *invisible*; for *visible* things last only for a time, and the *invisible* things are eternal.
7 8		I *see* that that letter did distress you,
10 7		⌐Face plain facts (lit. *Look* things in the face, or: You are *looking at* things superficially).
12 6		I am not going to [boast], in case anyone should begin to think I am better than he can actually *see* and hear me to be.
Col 2 5		I am . . . delighted to *find* you all in harmony
Heb 2 9 X		we do *see* in Jesus one who . . . is now crowned with glory
3 19		We *see* . . . that it was because they were unfaithful that they were not able to reach it.
10 25		you *see* the Day drawing near.
11 1		Only faith can . . . prove the existence of the realities that at present remain *unseen*.
3		no apparent cause can account for the things we can *see*.
7		Noah . . . had been warned by God of something that had never been *seen* before,
26	9	[Moses] *had his eyes fixed on* the reward.
Jm 2 22		There you *see* it: faith and deeds were working together;
2 P 2 8	7	[Lot] was outraged . . . by the crimes that he *saw* and heard of every day.
Rv 1 11		Write down all that you *see* in a book,
12 X		I turned round to *see* who had spoken to me,
5 3		there was no one . . . who was able to open the scroll and ⌐read (lit. *look at*) it.
4		there was nobody fit to open the scroll and ⌐read (lit. *look at*) it,

Rv 11 9		Men out of every people . . . will *stare at* [the] corpses [of the two witnesses]
16 15		Happy is the man who has . . . not taken off his clothes so that he does not . . . ⌐expose his shame (lit. allow his shame to be *seen*).
17 8		the people of the world . . . will think it miraculous when they *see* how the beast once was and now is not
18 9		the kings of the earth . . . *see* the smoke as [Babylon] burns,
18		[All the seafaring men will be keeping a safe distance,] *watching* the smoke as [Babylon] burns,
22 8		I, John, am the one who heard and *saw* these things. When I had heard and *seen* them all, I knelt at the feet of the angel

d) (the spiritually or physically blind) See, Look – See again, Sight

Mt 11 5	2	the blind *see again*, and the lame walk,
12 22		they brought to [Jesus] a blind and dumb demoniac; and he cured him, so that the dumb man could speak and *see*.
13 13		they *look* without *seeing* and listen without hearing
14		(Is 6 9) You will . . . ⌐*see and see again, but not perceive* (lit. *look and look* [again], but not see).
15 31		The crowds were astonished to see the dumb speaking, the cripples whole again . . . and the blind *with their sight*,
20 34	2	immediately their *sight returned*
Mk 4 12		(Is 6 9) they may ⌐*see and see again, but not perceive* (lit. *look and look* [again], but not see);
8 18		Have you eyes that do not *see*, ears that do not hear?
23	/2	'Can you *see* anything?' ²⁴ The man, who was *beginning* to
24		*see*, replied, 'I can *see* people; they look like˙trees to me, but they are walking about'.
25	5/3	[the blind man] *saw clearly*; he was cured, and he could see everything plainly
10 51	2	'Master, let me *see again*.' ⁵² Jesus said to him, 'Go: your faith
52	2	has saved you'. And immediately his *sight returned*
Lk 4 18	2	(Is 61 1 G) The Lord . . . has sent me . . . to proclaim liberty
8		to captives and to the blind *new sight*,
7 21	2	[Jesus] gave the gift of *sight* to many who were blind.
22	2	the blind *see again*, the lame walk,
8 10		they may *see* but not *perceive*,
18 41	2	'Sir, . . . let me *see again*.' ⁴² Jesus said to him, 'Receive your
42	2	*sight*. Your faith has saved you.' ⁴⁶ And instantly his
43	2	*sight returned*
Jn 9 7		the blind man went off and washed himself, and came away with his *sight restored*.
11	2	I went [to Siloam], and when I washed I could *see*.
15	2	when the Pharisees asked him how he had *come to see*, he said, 'He put a paste on my eyes, and I washed, and I can *see*'.
18	2	the Jews would not believe that the man . . . had *gained his sight*, without first sending for ⌐his parents (lit. the parents
2		of the man who had *been given his sight*)
19		how is it that he is now able to *see*?
21		we don't know how it is that he can *see* now,
25		I was blind and now I can *see*.
39		I have come into this world so that those ⌐without sight (lit. who cannot *see*) may *see* and those ⌐with sight (lit. who can *see*) turn blind.
41		since you say, 'We *see*', your guilt remains.
Ac 9 8		even with his eyes wide open [Saul] could *see* nothing at all,
9		For three days [Saul] was without his *sight*,
12		[Saul] is praying having had a vision of a man called Ananias
2		. . . laying hands on him to *give* him *back his sight*.
17	2	I have been sent . . . so that you may *recover your sight*
18	2	[Saul] could *see again*.
13 11		[Elymas,] for a time you will not *see* the sun.
22 11		The light had been so dazzling that I ⌐was blind (lit. could not *see*)
13	3	'Saul, *receive your sight*'. Instantly . . . I was able to *see* him.
28 26	2/2	(Is 6 9 G) You will . . . ⌐*see and see again, but not perceive* (lit. *look and look* [again], but not see).
Rm 11 8		(Dt 29 3) God has given them . . . *unseeing* eyes
10		(Ps 69 24) may their eyes be ⌐struck incurably blind (lit. darkened so they cannot *see*),
Rv 3 18		put [eye ointment] on your eyes so that you are able to *see*.

e) (angels) Look at – (things can, cannot) See, Look

Mt 18 10		angels . . . are continually ⌐in the presence of (lit. *looking at* the face of) my Father in heaven.
Ac 27 12 ○		Phoenix – a harbour in Crete, ⌐facing (lit. *looking*) south-west and north-west.
Rv 9 20		the idols . . . can neither *see* nor hear nor move –

2: WATCH OUT, BE ON YOUR GUARD – TAKE CARE (THAT), TAKE NOTICE (OF), BE CAREFUL (THAT)

Mt 24 4		*Take care* that no one deceives you;
Mk 4 24		*Take notice* of what you are hearing.
8 15		Keep your eyes open; *be on your guard* against the yeast of the Pharisees
12 38		*Beware* of the scribes who like to walk about in long robes,
13 9		*Take care* that no one deceives you.
9		*Be on your guard*: they will hand you over to sanhedrins;

Mk	13	23		You therefore must *be on your guard*. I have forewarned you of everything.
		33		*Be on your guard,* stay awake,
Lk	8	18		So *take care* how you hear;
	21	8		*Take care* not to be deceived.
Ac	13	40		So *be careful* – or what the prophets say will happen to you.
1 Co	3	10		Everyone doing the building must work *carefully*.
	8	9		Only *be careful* that you do not make use of this freedom in a way that proves a pitfall for the weak.
	10	12		The man who thinks he is safe must *be careful* that he does not fall.
Ga	5	15		you had better *watch* or you will destroy the whole community.
Ep	5	15		So *be very careful* about the sort of lives you lead,
Ph	3	2		*Beware* of dogs! *Watch out* for the people who are making mischief. *Watch out* for the cutters.
Col	2	8		*Make sure* that no one . . . deprives you of your freedom
	4	17		*Remember* the service that the Lord wants you to do,
Heb	3	12		*Take care*, brothers, that there is not in any one of your community a wicked mind,
	12	25		*Make sure* that you never refuse to listen when he speaks.
Jm	2	3	6	you *take notice* of the well-dressed man,
2 Jn		8		*Watch* yourselves, or all ⌜your (ᵛ our) work will be lost

5. SEE, WATCH – SPECTACLE – THEATRE: *THEAOMAI*

2	*theaomai*	22		1	*the-ōreō*	57
5	*theatrizō*	1		6	*the-ōria*	1
3	*theatron*	3		4	*ana-the-ōreō*	2

1: SEE – NOTICE – WATCH

a) (Jesus) Sees, Saw, Noticed – (Jesus) Watched

Mk	5	38		Jesus *noticed* all the commotion, with people weeping and wailing
	12	41		[Jesus] *watched* the people putting money into the treasury,
Lk	5	27	2	When he went out after this, he *noticed* a tax collector, Levi by name,
	10	18		I *watched* Satan fall like lightning from heaven.
Jn	1	38	2	Jesus turned round, *saw* [the two disciples of John] following
	6	5	2	Looking up, Jesus *saw* the crowds approaching

b) (a person, a spirit) Sees, Saw – (a person) Watches

Θ, X, Ⓢ = See God, See Jesus (and his signs), See the Spirit

Mt	6	1		Be careful not to parade your good deeds before men to attract their *notice*;
	11	7	2	What did you go out into the wilderness to *see*?
	22	11	< 2	the king came in to *look at* the guests
	23	5	2	Everything [the Pharisees] do is done to attract *attention,*
	27	55		many women were there, *watching* from a distance,
	28	1		Mary of Magdala and the other Mary went to ⌜visit (lit. *see*) the sepulchre.
Mk	3	11	X	the unclean spirits, whenever they *saw* [Jesus], would fall down before him
	5	15		[the people] *saw* the demoniac sitting there,
	15	40		There were some women *watching* from a distance,
		47		Mary of Magdala and Mary the mother of Joset were *watching and took note of* where [Jesus] was laid.
	16	4		when [the women] looked they could *see* that the stone . . . had already been rolled back.
		11	X	they did not believe [Mary of Magdala] when they heard her say . . . that she had *seen* [Jesus].
		14	X 2	[Jesus] reproached them . . . because they had refused to believe those who had *seen* him after he had risen.
Lk	7	24	2	What did you go out into the wilderness to *see*?
	14	29		if he . . . found himself unable to finish the work, the *onlookers* would all start making fun of him
	21	6		All these things you are *staring at* now – the time will come when not a single stone will be left on another: ⌝
	23	35	X	The people stayed there *watching* him.
		48	X	when all the people who had gathered . . . *saw* what had happened, they went home beating their breasts.
		55	2	[The women] *took note of* the tomb and of the position of the body.
	24	37	X	In a state of alarm and fright, [the disciples] thought they were *seeing* a ghost.
		39	X	a ghost has no flesh and bones as you can *see* I have.
Jn	1	14	X 2	we *saw* his glory,
		32	Ⓢ 2	I *saw* the Spirit coming down on [Jesus] from heaven like a dove
	2	23	X	many believed in his name when they *saw* the signs that he gave,
	4	19	X	I *see* you are a prophet, sir
		35	2	Look around you, *look at* the fields; already they are . . . ready for harvest!

Jn	6	19	X	They had rowed three or four miles when they *saw* Jesus walking on the lake
		40	X	whoever *sees* the Son and believes in him shall have eternal life,
		62	X	What if you should *see* the Son of Man ascend to where he was before?
	7	3	X	Why not . . . let your disciples [in Judaea] *see* the works you are doing;
	8	51	D	whoever keeps my word will never *see* death.
	9	8		people who earlier had *seen* him begging said, 'Isn't this the man who used to sit and beg?'
	10	12	<	The hired man . . . runs away as soon as he *sees* a wolf coming,
	11	45	X 2	Many of the Jews who . . . had *seen* what he did believed in him.
	12	19		You *see*, there is nothing you can do;
		45	X Θ	whoever *sees* me, *sees* the one who sent me.
	14	17	Ⓢ	the world can never receive [the Spirit] since it neither *sees* nor knows him;
		19	X	In a short time the world will no longer *see* me; but you will *see* me,
	16	10	X	[the Advocate will show the world] who was in the right: proved by my going to the Father and your *seeing* me no more;
		16	X	In a short time you will no longer *see* me,
		17	X	What does he mean, 'In a short time you will no longer *see* me,
		19	X	You are asking one another what I meant by saying: In a short time you will no longer *see* me,
	17	24	X	they may always *see* the glory you have given me
	20	6		Simon Peter . . , *saw* the linen cloths on the ground,
		12		[Mary stooped to look inside,] and *saw* two angels
		14	X	[Mary] turned round and *saw* Jesus standing there,
Ac	1	11	X 2	Jesus will come back in the same way as you have *seen* him go [into heaven].
	3	16		the name of Jesus . . . has brought back the strength of this man whom you *see* here
	4	13		[The members of the Sanhedrin] were astonished ⌜at (lit. to *see*) the assurance shown by Peter and John,
	7	56	X	'I can *see* heaven thrown open' [Stephen] said 'and the Son of Man standing at the right hand of God.'
	8	13		Simon . . . was astonished when he *saw* the wonders . . . that took place.
	9	7		though [the men travelling with Saul] heard the voice they could *see* no one.
	10	11		[Peter] *saw* heaven thrown open and something like a big sheet being let down to earth
	17	16		[Paul's] soul was revolted *at the sight of* a city given over to idolatry.
		22		Men of Athens, I have *seen* for myself how extremely scrupulous you are in all religious matters,
		23	4	I *noticed*. . . that you had an altar inscribed: To An Unknown God.
	19	26		Now you must have *seen* and heard how . . . this man Paul has . . . persuaded and converted a great number of people
	20	38		[Paul had said] they would never *see* his face again.
	21	20		you *see* . . . how thousands of Jews have now become believers,
		27	2	some Jews from Asia *caught sight of* [Paul] in the Temple and stirred up the crowd
	22	9	2	The people with me *saw* the light but did not hear his voice
	25	24		you *see* before you the man [Paul] about whom the whole Jewish community has petitioned me,
	27	10		I can *see* this voyage will be dangerous
	28	6		[the Maltese] waited a long time without *seeing* anything out of the ordinary happen to [Paul],
Rm	15	24	2	I hope to *see* you on my way to Spain
Heb	7	4		Now ⌜think (lit. *see*) how great [Melchizedek] must have been,
	13	7	4	as you *reflect on* the outcome of their lives, imitate their faith.
1 Jn	1	1	X 2	Something . . . that we have *watched* and touched with our hands: the Word, who is life – this is our subject.
	3	17		If a man who is rich . . . *saw* that one of his brothers was in need, but closed his heart to him, how could the love of God be living in him?
	4	12	Θ 2	No one has ever *seen* God;
		14	X 2	We ourselves *saw* and we testify that the Father sent his Son as saviour of the world.
Rv	11	11		[the two witnesses] stood up, and everybody who *saw* it happen was terrified; ¹² then . . . while their enemies were *watching*, they went up to heaven in a cloud.
		12		

2: SPECTACLE, A SIGHT – THEATRE – PUBLICLY EXPOSED

| Lk | 23 | 48 | 6 | when all the people who had gathered for the *spectacle* saw what had happened, they went home beating their breasts. |
| Ac | 19 | 29 | 3 | the mob rushed to the *theatre* |

Ac 19 31	some of the Asiarchs . . . sent messages imploring [Paul]
3	not to take the risk of going into the *theatre*.
1 Co 4 9	3 we have been put *on show in front of* the whole universe, angels as well as men.
Heb 10 33	5 sometimes [you were] yourselves *publicly exposed* to insults and violence,

6. SEE: *AUGAZŌ*

augazō 1

| 2 Co 4 4 X | the god of this world has blinded [the minds of the unbelievers], to stop ⌐them *seeing* (or: the dawning on them of) the light shed by the Good News of the glory of Christ, |

7. NOTICE, PERCEIVE – LOOK AT: *KATA-NOEŌ*

kata-noeō 9/14

Mt 7 3	Why do you . . . never ⌐*notice* (or: think of) the plank in your own [eye]?
Lk 6 41	Why do you . . . never ⌐*notice* (or: think of) the plank in your own [eye]?
20 23	[Jesus] ⌐*was aware of* (or: *perceived*) their cunning and said, 24 'Show me a denarius.
Ac 7 31	[Moses] went nearer to *look at* [the burning bush]
32	Moses trembled and did not dare to *look* any more.
11 6	I *watched* [this sheet] intently and saw all sorts of animals
27 39	they ⌐could *make out* (or: *noticed*) a kind of bay with a beach.
Jm 1 23	To listen to the word and not obey is like *looking at* your own
24	features in a mirror and then, 24 after a quick *look*, going off and immediately forgetting what you looked like.

8. GIVE ATTENTION (TO), HEED, WATCH – NOTICE: *EP-ECHŌ*

ep-echō 3/5

Lk 14 7	[Jesus] had *noticed* how [the guests] picked the places of honour.
Ac 3 5	[The lame man] ⌐turned to them expectantly (lit. *gave* them *all his attention*),
1 Tm 4 16	*Take* great *care* about what you do and what you teach;

9. STARE (AT), GAZE (AT), PEER (AT) – (HAVE ONE'S EYES) FIXED (ON), LOOK INTENTLY (AT): *A-TENIZŌ*

a-tenizō 14

Lk 4 20	all eyes in the synagogue were *fixed* on [Jesus].
22 56	a servant-girl saw [Peter], *peered* at him, and said, 'This person was with him too'.
Ac 1 10	They were still *staring* into the sky when suddenly two men . . . were standing near them
3 4	Peter and John *looked straight* at [the lame man]
12	Why are you *staring* at us . . .?
6 15	The members of the Sanhedrin all *looked intently* at Stephen,
7 55	Stephen, filled with the Holy Spirit, *gazed* into heaven
10 4	[Cornelius] *stared* at the vision in terror
11 6	I *watched* [this sheet] *intently* and saw all sorts of animals
13 9	Paul *looked* [Elymas] *full in the face*
14 9	⌐he managed to catch his eye (lit. [Paul] *looked intently* at him).
23 1	Paul *looked steadily* at the Sanhedrin and began to speak,
2 Co 3 7	the Israelites could not bear *looking* at the face of Moses,
13	Moses . . . put a veil over his face so that the Israelites would not ⌐*notice* (lit. *fix their eyes* on) the ending of what had to fade.

10. LOOK FOR, HAVE EYES FOR – SEE (THAT), LOOK TO, BE ON YOUR GUARD: *SKOPEŌ*

1 skopeō 6   2 epi-skeptomai 1/11

Lk 11 35	*See* [to it] then that the light inside you is not darkness.
Ac 6 3	2 ⌐select from among yourselves (lit. *look* among yourselves *for*) seven men of good reputation
Rm 16 17	*be on your guard* against anybody who encourages trouble
2 Co 4 18	we *have* no *eyes for* things that are visible, but only for things that are invisible;

Ga 6 1	set [your brother] right . . . ⌐not forgetting that (lit. *looking to* yourselves in case) you may be tempted yourselves.
Ph 2 4	everybody ⌐thinks of (lit. *looks for*) other people's interests
3 17	with us as the example you have, *look out for* people of this kind;

11. APPEARANCE, ASPECT, SIGHT – SHAPE, FORM: *EIDOS*

2 eidea 1   1 eidos 5

Mt 28 3	2 [The angel's] ⌐face (lit. *appearance*) was like lightning,
Lk 3 22 Ⓢ	the Holy Spirit descended on [Jesus] in bodily *shape*, like a dove.
9 29 X	As [Jesus] prayed, the *aspect* of his face was changed
Jn 5 37	you have never seen [my Father's] *shape*
2 Co 5 7 ○	[We are always full of confidence,] going as we do by faith and not by *sight*
1 Th 5 22	avoid every *form* of evil.

12. WATCH – OBSERVATION: *PARA-TĒREŌ*

1 para-tēreō 4/6   2 para-tērēsis 1

Mk 3 2 X	they were *watching* [Jesus] to see if he would cure [the man with a withered hand] on the sabbath day,
Lk 6 7 X	The scribes and the Pharisees were *watching* [Jesus] to see if he would cure a man on the sabbath.
14 1 X	on a sabbath day [Jesus] had gone for a meal to the house of one of the leading Pharisees; and they *watched* him closely.
17 20	The coming of the kingdom of God does not admit of
2	*observation*
20 20 X	they ⌐waited their opportunity (lit. *watched*) and sent agents to pose as men devoted to the Law,

13. SPY, SPIES

1: SPY (ON), SPIES – INFORMER: *KATA-SKOPEŌ*

1 (allotri-)epi-skopos 1   2 kata-skopeō 1   3 kata-skopos 1

Ga 2 4	some who do not really belong to the brotherhood have
2	. . . crept in to *spy on* the liberty we enjoy in Christ Jesus,
Heb 11 31	It was by faith that Rahab the prostitute welcomed the
3	*spies*
1 P 4 15	None of you should ever deserve to suffer for being a murderer, a thief, a criminal or an *informer*;

2: (SECRET) AGENT, SPY: *EN-KA-THETOS*

en-ka-thetos 1

| Lk 20 20 | they ⌐waited their opportunity (lit. watched) and sent *agents* to pose as men devoted to the Law, |

SEEK – PURSUE

1. Seek, Look for, Search for: *zēteō*
  1: Seek, Look for – Set one's heart on, Aim at (God or the things of God)
  2: Look for, Ask for, Search for (Jesus)
  3: Seek (the life of) – Want (to kill)
  4: Look for, Search for (generally) – Ask for
2. Search: *ereunaō*

  1: Search - Explore – Study deeply
  2: Search into (men's hearts)
3. Pursue – Follow – Persecute: *diōkō*
  1: Pursue, Set off in pursuit – Go out in search of – Follow
  2: Pursue, Follow (figuratively) Aim (at), Seek, Look for
  3: Persecute

1. SEEK, LOOK FOR, SEARCH FOR: *ZĒTEŌ*

| 1 | *zēteō* 117 | 3 | *ek-zēteō* 7 |
| 4 | *ana-zēteō* 3 | 2 | *epi-zēteō* 13 |

F = Search // Find

1: SEEK, LOOK FOR – SET ONE'S HEART ON, AIM AT (GOD OR THE THINGS OF GOD)

Mt	6	33	*Set your hearts on* his kingdom first, and on his righteousness,
Lk	12	31	*set your hearts on* his kingdom, and these other things will be given you as well.
Jn	5	30	my *aim* is to do not my own will, but the will of him who sent me.
		44	you . . . ⌐are not concerned with (lit. *do not seek*) the approval that comes from the one God
	7	18	When a man's doctrine is his own he is hoping to get honour for himself; but when he ⌐is working for (lit. *seeks*) the honour of one who sent him, then he is sincere
Ac	15	17	3 (Am 9 12 G) Then the rest of mankind . . . will *look for* the Lord,
	17	27 F	[God] did this so that all nations might *seek* ᵛ the deity (G God)
Rm	2	7	For those who *sought* renown and honour . . . by always doing good . . . eternal life;
	3	11	(Ps 14 2) there is not one who understands, not one who 3 *looks for* God.
	10	20 F	(Is 65 1) I have been found by those who did not *seek* me,
	11	7 F	2 It was not Israel as a whole that found what it was *seeking*,
Ga	2	17	if we were to admit that the result of *looking to* Christ to justify us is to make us sinners like the rest,
Col	3	1	you must *look for* the things that are in heaven, where Christ is,
Heb	11	6	3 God . . . rewards those who *try to find* him.
		14	2 People who use such terms about themselves . . . *are in search of* their real homeland.
	13	14	2 there is no eternal city for us in this life but we *look for* one in the life to come.
1 P	1	10	3 It was this salvation that the prophets were *looking* and searching *for*;

2: LOOK FOR, ASK FOR, SEARCH FOR (JESUS)

Mt	2	13	escape into Egypt . . . because Herod intends to *search for* the child
	12	47	(ᵛ your brothers are . . . *seeking* a word with you.)
	28	5	I know you are *looking for* Jesus,
Mk	1	37 F	Everybody is *looking for* you.
	3	32	Your mother and brothers and sisters are outside *asking for* you
	16	6	You are *looking for* Jesus of Nazareth, who was crucified:
Lk	2	44	4 [Jesus's parents] went to *look for* him among their relations
		45 F	4 [Jesus's parents] went back to Jerusalem *looking for* him
		48	See how worried your father and I have been, *looking for* you.
		49	Why were you *looking for* me?
	4	42	2 The crowds went to *look for* him.
	24	5 F	Why *look* among the dead *for* someone who is alive?
Jn	6	24 F	the people . . . crossed to Capernaum to *look for* Jesus.
		26	you are . . . *looking for* me . . . because you had all the bread you wanted to eat.
	7	11	At the festival [of Tabernacles] the Jews *were on the look-out for* [Jesus]:
		34 F	You will *look for* me and will not find me:
		36 F	What does he mean . . .: You will *look for* me and will not find me:
	8	21	I am going away; you will *look for* me
	11	56	[the country people who had gone up to Jerusalem for the Passover] *looked out for* Jesus,
	13	33	I shall not be with you much longer. You will *look for* me,
	18	4	[Jesus said to the soldiers with Judas,] Who are you *looking for*?
		7	He asked them a second time, 'Who are you *looking for*?'
		8	If I am the one you are *looking for*, let these others go.
	20	15	Jesus said [to Mary of Magdala], 'Who are you *looking for*?

3: SEEK (THE LIFE OF) – WANT (TO KILL)

Mt	2	20	those who *wanted* to kill the child are dead.
Mk	11	18	the chief priests . . . *tried to find* some way of doing away with [Jesus];
Lk	19	47 F	The chief priests and the scribes . . . *tried to do away with* [Jesus],
	22	2	the chief priests and the scribes were *looking for* some way of doing away with [Jesus],
Jn	5	18	that only made the Jews even more *intent on* killing [Jesus],
	7	1	the Jews ⌐were out (lit. *sought*) to kill [Jesus].
		19	Why do you *want* to kill me?
		20	Who *wants* to kill you?
		25	Isn't this the man they *want* to kill?
	8	37	in spite of that you *want* to kill me
		40	you *want* to kill me when I tell you the truth
	11	8	it is not long since the Jews *wanted* to stone you; are you going back again [to Judaea]?

Ac	21	31	[The Jews] ⌐would have killed (lit. *sought* to kill) [Paul]
Rm	11	3	(1 K 19 10) I, and I only, remain, and they *want* to kill me.

4: LOOK FOR, SEEK, SEARCH FOR (GENERALLY) – ASK FOR

Mt	6	32	2 [eat? . . . drink?] It is the pagans who *set their hearts on* all these things.
	7	7 F	*search*, and you will find . . . ⁸ For . . . the one who *searches*
		8	always finds;
	12	39	2 It is an evil and unfaithful generation that *asks for* a sign!
		43 ⓓ F	an unclean spirit . . . wanders . . . *looking for* a place to rest, and cannot find one.
		46	[Jesus's] brothers . . . were ⌐anxious (lit. *seeking*) to have a word with him.
	13	45 < F	the kingdom of heaven is like a merchant *looking for* fine pearls;
	16	4	2 It is an evil and unfaithful generation that *asks for* a sign!
	18	12 <	will he not leave the ninety-nine [sheep] . . . and *go in search of* the stray?
	21	46	though [the chief priests and scribes] ⌐would have liked (lit. *sought*) to arrest [Jesus] they were afraid of the crowds,
	26	16	[Judas] *looked for* an opportunity to betray [Jesus].
		59 F	The chief priests and the whole Sanhedrin were *looking for* evidence against Jesus,
Mk	8	11	The Pharisees . . . ⌐demanded (lit. *sought*) of [Jesus] a sign from heaven;
		12	Why does this generation ⌐demand (lit. *look for*) a sign?
	12	12	[the chief priests and scribes] ⌐would have liked (lit. *sought*) to arrest [Jesus],
	14	1	the scribes were *looking for* a way to arrest Jesus by some trick
		11	[Judas] *looked for* a way of betraying him when the opportunity should occur.
		55 F	The chief priests . . . were *looking for* evidence against Jesus
Lk	5	18 F	some men appeared, carrying on a bed a paralysed man whom they were *trying* to bring in
	6	19	everyone in the crowd was *trying* to touch [Jesus]
	9	9	Herod . . . ⌐was anxious (lit. *sought*) to see [Jesus]
	11	9 F	*search*, and you will find; . . . ¹⁰ For . . . the one who *searches*
		10	always finds;
		16	Others *asked* him, as a test, *for* a sign from heaven;
		24 ⓓ F	an unclean spirit . . . wanders . . . *looking for* a place to rest, and not finding one
		29	This is a wicked generation; it is *asking for* a sign.
		50	3 this generation will have to ⌐answer for (lit. *look* to itself *for*) every prophet's blood
		51	3 this generation will have to ⌐answer for (lit. *look* to itself *for*) it all.
	12	29	you must not *set your hearts on* things to eat . . . ³⁰ It is
		30	2 the pagans . . . who *set their hearts on* all these things.
		48	When a man has had a great deal given him, a great deal will be ⌐demanded of (lit. *looked for* from) him;
	13	6 < F	A man had a fig tree . . . He came *looking for* fruit on it but
		7 < F	found none.⁷ . . . for three years now I have been coming to *look for* fruit on this fig tree
		24	many will *try* to enter [by the narrow door] and will not succeed.
	15	8 < F	what woman . . . would not . . . *search* thoroughly till she found [the lost drachma]?
	17	33	Anyone who *tries* to preserve his life will lose it;
	19	3	[Zacchaeus] ⌐was anxious (lit. *sought*) to see what kind of man Jesus was,
		10 X	the Son of Man has come to *seek out* and save what was lost.
	20	19	the scribes and the chief priests ⌐would have liked (lit. *sought*) to lay hands on [Jesus]
	22	6	[Judas] *looked for* an opportunity to betray [Jesus]
Jn	1	38	Jesus . . . said, 'What ⌐do you want (lit. *are you looking for*)?' They answered, 'Rabbi, . . . where do you live?'
	4	23 ⊖	that is the kind of worshipper the Father ⌐wants (lit. *is looking for*).
		27 X	none of them asked, 'What ⌐do you want (lit. *are you seeking*)?' from her?'
	7	4	if a man ⌐wants (lit. *seeks*) to be known he does not do things in secret;
		18	When a man's doctrine is his own he is ⌐hoping (lit. *seeking*) to get honour for himself; but when he is working for the honour of one who sent him, then he is sincere
		30	They ⌐would have arrested (lit. *sought* to arrest) [Jesus]
	8	50 X ⊖	Not that I ⌐care for (lit. *seek*) my own glory, there is someone who ⌐takes care of (lit. *seeks*) that
	10	39	They ⌐wanted (lit. *sought*) to arrest [Jesus] then, but he eluded them.
	16	19	You are *asking* [one another] what I meant
	19	12	Pilate ⌐was anxious (lit. *sought*) to set [Jesus] free,
Ac	9	11	[Ananias,] you must go . . . and *ask* at the house of Judas *for* someone called Saul, who comes from Tarsus.
	10	19	the Spirit had to tell [Peter], 'Some men have come ⌐to see (lit. *looking for*) you.'
		21	Peter went down and said . . , 'I am the man you are *looking for*'

Ac 11 25 F	4	Barnabas then left for Tarsus to *look for* Saul,
12 19 F	2	Herod put out an unsuccessful *search* for [Peter];
13 7	2	the proconsul Sergius Paulus . . . *asked* to hear the word of God,
8		Elymas . . . tried to stop [Barnabas and Saul] ˹so as (lit. *seeking*) to prevent the proconsul's conversion to the faith.
11		[Elymas] groped about *to find* someone to lead him by the hand.
16 10		Once [Paul] had seen this vision we ˹lost no time in arranging (lit. *looked for*) a passage to Macedonia,
17 5 F		[The Jews] made for Jason's house, ˹hoping to find (lit. *looking for*) [Paul and Silas] there [to] drag them off to the People's Assembly,
19 39	2	if you ˹want to ask any more questions (lit. have anything else to *ask*) you must raise them in the regular assembly,
27 30		some of the crew *tried* to escape from the ship
Rm 10 3		Failing to recognise the righteousness that comes from God, [the Jews] *try* to promote their own idea of it,
1 Co 1 22		the Greeks *look for* wisdom,
4 2 F		What is ˹expected of (lit. *looked for* in) stewards is that each one should be found worthy of his trust.
7 27		If you are tied to a wife, do not *look for* freedom; if you are free of a wife, then do not *look for* one.
10 24		Nobody should be *looking for* his own advantage, but everybody for the other man's.
33		I try to be helpful . . . not ˹anxious for (lit. *seeking*) my own advantage but [for] the advantage of everybody else,
13 5		[Love] is never rude or ˹selfish (lit. *seeking* after its own ends);
14 12		˹concentrate on (lit. *search for*) those [gifts] which will grow to benefit the community.
2 Co 12 14		it is you I ˹want (lit. am *looking for*), not your possessions.
13 3		you ˹want (lit. *seek*) proof . . . that it is Christ speaking in me:
Ga 1 10		Would you say it is men's approval I am *looking for*?
Ph 2 21		all the rest seem ˹more interested in themselves than in (lit. to *seek* after their own interests rather than those of) Jesus Christ.
4 17	2	It is not your gift that I ˹value (lit. *seek*); what ˹is valuable
	2	to me (lit. I am *looking for*) is the interest that is mounting up in your account.
1 Th 2 6		nor have we ever *looked for* any special honour from men,
2 Tm 1 17 F		as soon as [Onesiphorus] reached Rome, he really *searched* hard *for* me and found out where I was.
Heb 8 7		If that first covenant had been without a fault, there would have been no need (§ to *look*) for a second one to replace it.
12 17 F	3	when [Esau] wanted to obtain the blessing afterwards, he was rejected . . . though he *pleaded for* it with tears,
1 P 3 11		(Ps 34 15) [Anyone who wants to have a happy life] must *seek* peace and pursue it.
5 8 ⓓ		the devil is prowling round like a roaring lion, *looking for* someone to eat.
Rv 9 6 F		When this happens, men will ˹long for (lit. *search for*) death and not find it anywhere;

2. SEARCH: *EREUNAŌ*

1 *ereunaō* 6	2 *ex-ereunaō* 1
3 *an-ex-ereunētos* 1	

1: SEARCH – EXPLORE – STUDY DEEPLY

Jn 5 39		You *study* the scriptures, . . . now these same scriptures testify to me.
7 52		*Go into* the matter, and see for yourself: prophets do not come out of Galilee.
Rm 11 33 Θ	3	how impossible to *penetrate* [God's] motives or understand his methods!
1 Co 2 10 Ⓢ		the Spirit *reaches the depths* of everything, even the depths of God.
1 P 1 10		It was this salvation that the prophets were looking and
11	2/	*searching* so hard for; . . . [11] . . . they *tried to find out* at what time and in what circumstances all this was to be expected.

2: SEARCH INTO (MEN'S HEARTS)

Rm 8 27 Θ	God who *knows everything* in our hearts knows perfectly well what he means,
Rv 2 23 X	it is I who *search heart and loins*

3. PURSUE – FOLLOW – PERSECUTE: *DIŌKŌ*

1 *diōkō* 46	4 *kata-diōkō* 1
3 *diōktēs* 1	5 *ek-diōkō* 1
2 *diōgmos* 10	

1: PURSUE, SET OFF IN PURSUIT – GO OUT IN SEARCH OF – FOLLOW

Mk 1 36	4	Simon and his companions *set out in search of* [Jesus],
Lk 17 23		They will say to you, 'Look, [the Son of Man is] there!' . . . do not *set off in pursuit*;
Ac 26 11		I even *pursued* [the saints] into foreign cities.
Rv 12 13 ⓓ		the devil . . . *sprang in pursuit of* the woman,

2: PURSUE, FOLLOW (FIGURATIVELY) – AIM (AT), SEEK, LOOK FOR

Rm 9 30		the pagans who were not *looking for* righteousness found it all the same . . . [31] while Israel, *looking for* a righteousness derived from law failed to do what that law required.
31		
12 13		you should ˹make hospitality your special care (lit. *pursue* [the practice of] hospitality).
14 19		let us ˹adopt (lit. *follow*) any custom that leads to peace
1 Co 14 1		You must ˹want love more than anything else (lit. *seek* above all love);
Ph 3 12		I am still *running in pursuit*, trying to capture the prize
14		I am *racing for* the finish, for the prize
1 Th 5 15		you must all ˹think, of (lit. *seek*) what is best for each other
1 Tm 6 11		You must *aim* to be saintly and religious, filled with faith and love, patient and gentle,
2 Tm 2 22		˹fasten your attention on (lit. *aim at*) holiness, faith, love and peace,
Heb 12 14		Always be ˹wanting (lit. *seeking*) peace
1 P 3 11		(Ps 34 15) [Anyone who wants to have a happy life] must seek peace and *pursue* it.

3: PERSECUTE

X = Persecute Jesus

Mt 5 10		Happy [those who are] *persecuted* in the cause of right:
11		Happy are you when people . . . *persecute* you . . . on my account.
12		this is how they *persecuted* the prophets before you.
44		pray for those who *persecute* you
10 23		If they *persecute* you in one town, take refuge in the next; ᵛ and if they *persecute* you in that, take refuge in another.˺
13 21	2	let some trial come, or some *persecution* on account of the word, and he falls away at once.
23 34		you will . . . *hunt* [the prophets] from town to town;
Mk 4 17	2	should some trial come, or some *persecution* on account of the word, they fall away at once.
10 30		[there is no one] who will not be repaid a hundred times
	2	over . . . not without *persecutions*
Lk 11 49		I will send them prophets and apostles; some they will slaughter and *persecute*,
21 12		men will seize you and *persecute* you;
Jn 5 16 X		It was because he did things like this on the sabbath that the Jews began to *persecute* Jesus.
15 20 X		If they *persecuted* me, they will *persecute* you too;
Ac 7 52		Can you name a single prophet your ancestors never *persecuted*?
8 1	2	a bitter *persecution* started against the church in Jerusalem,
9 4 X		Saul, Saul, why are you *persecuting* me?
5 X		I am Jesus, and you are *persecuting* me.
13 50		the Jews . . . persuaded [the leading men] ˹to turn against
	2	(lit. into a *persecution* of) Paul and Barnabas
22 4		I even *persecuted* this Way to the death,
7 X		Saul, why are you *persecuting* me?
8 X		I am Jesus the Nazarene, and you are *persecuting* me.
26 14 X		Saul, why are you *persecuting* me?
15 X		I am Jesus, and you are *persecuting* me.
Rm 8 35		Nothing . . . can come between us and the love of Christ,
	2	even if we are . . . *being persecuted*,
12 14		Bless those who *persecute* you:
1 Co 4 12		when we are *hounded*, we put up with it;
15 9		I *persecuted* the Church of God,
2 Co 4 9		we have been *persecuted*, but never deserted;
12 10	2	I am quite content with . . . *persecutions* . . . for Christ's sake.
Ga 1 13		You must have heard . . . how merciless I was in *persecuting* the Church of God,
23		their one-time *persecutor* was now preaching the faith
4 29		the child born in the ordinary way *persecuted* the child born in the Spirit's way,
5 11		if I still preach circumcision, why am I still *persecuted*?
6 12		they want to escape *persecution* for the cross of Christ
Ph 3 6		as for working for religion, I was a *persecutor* of the Church;
1 Th 2 15		the people who put the Lord Jesus to death . . . have been
	5	*persecuting* us,
2 Th 1 4		we can take special pride in you for your constancy and faith
	2	under all the *persecutions*
1 Tm 1 13		I used to be a blasphemer and ˹did all I could to injure and
	3	(lit. as a *persecutor* tried to) discredit the faith.

2 Tm	3	11			2 [you know] the *persecutions* and hardships that came to me in places like Antioch, Iconium and Lystra – all the

2 Tm 3 11 2 [you know] the *persecutions* and hardships that came to me in places like Antioch, Iconium and Lystra – all the
　2 *persecutions* I have endured; and the Lord has rescued me from every one of them. [12] . . . anybody who tries to live
12　in devotion to Christ is certain to be *attacked*;

SEND

1. Send: *apo-stellō*
1: (the Son, the Spirit, is) Sent
2: Send (out) on a mission – Apostle
3: Send (out) – Let go – Start
4: Letter, Send a letter – Write (to)

2. Send: *pempō*
1: (the Son, the Spirit, is) Sent
2: Send (out) on a mission
3: Send – Commission – Messenger
4: Send for – Fetch, Bring (*meta-pempō*)

3. (Be) Ambassadors, Envoys – Delegation: *presbeuō*

A = Angels are sent
T = the Twelve Apostles are sent
J = John the Baptist is sent
P = Apostles//Prophets
S = Saul–Paul, the Apostle

1. SEND: *APO-STELLŌ*

1	*apo-stellō*	131	7	(*pseud-*)*apo-stolos*	1
5	*apo-stolē*	4	8	*syn-apo-stellō*	1
2	*apo-stolos*	79	6	*epi-stellō*	3
4	*ex-apo-stellō*	13	3	*epi-stolē*	23

1: (THE SON, THE SPIRIT, IS) SENT

Mt 10 40　those who welcome me welcome the one who *sent* me.
　15 24　I was *sent* only to the lost sheep of the house of Israel.
Mk 9 37　anyone who welcomes me welcomes . . . the one who *sent* me.
Lk 4 18　(Is 58 6) The spirit of the Lord . . . has *sent* me to bring the Good News to the poor,
　43　I must proclaim the Good News . . . because that is what I was *sent* to do.
　9 48　anyone who welcomes me welcomes the one who *sent* me.
　10 16　those who reject me reject the one who *sent* me.
　24 49 Ⓢ 4 I am *sending* down to you what the Father has promised.
Jn 3 17　God *sent* his Son into the world not to condemn the world, but so that through him the world might be saved.
　34　he whom God has *sent* speaks God's own words:
　5 36　the works my Father has given me to carry out . . . testify that the Father has *sent* me.
　38　you do not believe in the one he has *sent*.
　6 29　This is working for God: you must believe in the one he has *sent*.
　57　As I who am *sent* by the living Father, myself draw life from the Father,
　7 29　but I know him because . . . it was he who *sent* me.
　8 42　not that I came because I chose, no, I was *sent*, and by him.
　10 36　you say to someone the Father has consecrated and *sent* into the world, You are blaspheming,
　11 42　I speak . . . so that they may believe it was you who *sent* me.
　17 3　eternal life is this: to know you, the only true God, and Jesus Christ whom you have *sent*.
　8　they have . . . believed that it was you who *sent* me.
　18　As you *sent* me into the world, I have sent them into the world,
　21　Father, may they be one in us, . . . so that the world may believe it was you who *sent* me.
　23　may they be so completely one that the world will realise that it was you who *sent* me
　25　these have known that you have *sent* me.
　20 21　As the Father *sent* me, so I am sending you.
Ac 3 20　he will *send* you the Christ he has predestined, that is Jesus,
　26　It was for you in the first place that God raised up his servant and *sent* him to bless you
Ga 4 4　4 God *sent* his Son, born of a woman, born a subject of the Law,
　6 Ⓢ 4 God has *sent* the Spirit of his Son into our hearts:
Heb 3 1　the same heavenly call should turn your minds to Jesus, the
　2　*apostle* and the high priest of our religion.
1 P 1 12　those who preached to you the Good News through the Holy
　Ⓢ　Spirit *sent* from heaven,
1 Jn 4 9　God *sent* into the world his only Son so that we could have life through him;
　10　God's love for us when he *sent* his Son to be the sacrifice that takes our sins away.

1 Jn 4 14　we testify that the Father *sent* his Son as saviour of the world.

2: SEND (OUT) ON A MISSION – APOSTLE

Mt 10 2 T　2 These are the names of the twelve *apostles*:
　5 T　These twelve Jesus *sent out*, instructing them as follows:
　16 T　I am *sending* you *out* like sheep among wolves;
　11 10 J　(Ml 3 1) Look, I am going to *send* my messenger before you; he will prepare your way before you.
　13 41 A　The Son of Man will *send* his angels
　23 34　I am *sending* you prophets and wise men and scribes:
　37　Jerusalem, you that kill the prophets and stone those who are *sent* to you!
　24 31 A　he will *send* his angels . . . to gather his chosen
Mk 1 2 J　(Ml 3 1) Look, I am going to *send* my messenger before you;
　6 7 T　he summoned the Twelve and began to *send* them *out* in pairs
　30 T　2 The *apostles* rejoined Jesus
　13 27 A　he will *send* the angels to gather his chosen
Lk 1 19 A　I am Gabriel . . . and I have been *sent* to speak to you
　26 A　the angel Gabriel was *sent* by God to a town . . . called Nazareth,
　6 13　When day came he summoned his disciples and picked out
　T　2 twelve of them; he called them *apostles*.
　7 27 J　(Ml 3 1) See, I am going to *send* my messenger before you; he will prepare the way before you.
　9 2 T　he *sent* them *out* to proclaim the kingdom of God and to heal.
　10 T　2 the *apostles* gave [Jesus] an account of all they had done.
　10 1　the Lord appointed seventy-two others and *sent* them *out* ahead of him, in pairs,
　3　I am *sending* you *out* like lambs among wolves.
　11 49 P　the Wisdom of God said, 'I will *send* them prophets and
　2　*apostles*;'
　13 34　Jerusalem, you that kill the prophets and stone those who are *sent* to you!
　17 5 T　2 The *apostles* said to the Lord, 'Increase our faith.'
　22 14 T　2 he took his place at table, and the *apostles* with him.
　35 T　When I *sent* you *out* without purse or haversack or sandals,
　24 10 T　2 The other women . . . also told the *apostles*.
Jn 1 6 J　A man came, *sent* by God. His name was John.
　3 28 J　I myself am not the Christ; I am the one who has been *sent* in front of him.
　4 38 T　I *sent* you to reap a harvest you had not worked for.
　13 16 <　2 no *messenger* is greater than the man who sent him.
　17 18 T　2 As you sent me into the world, I have *sent* them into the world,
Ac 1 2 T　2 he gave his instructions to the *apostles* he had chosen
　25　[show us which of these two you have chosen] to take over
　T　5 this ministry and *apostolate*, which Judas abandoned
　26　as the lot fell to Matthias, he was listed as one of the ᵛ twelve
　T　2 (G eleven) *apostles*.
　2 37 T　2 [the Jews] said to Peter and the *apostles*, 'What must we do, brothers?'
　42　[the first Christians] remained faithful to the teaching of the
　T　2 *apostles*,
　43 T　2 the many miracles . . . worked through the *apostles*
　4 33 T　2 The *apostles* continued to testify to the resurrection of the Lord Jesus
　35 T　2 to present [the money] to the *apostles*;
　36 T　2 Joseph whom the *apostles* surnamed Barnabas . . . [37] . . .
　37　owned a piece of land and he sold it and brought the money
　T　2 . . . to the *apostles*.
　5 2　[Ananias] kept back part of the proceeds, and brought the
　T　2 rest . . . to the *apostles*.
　18 T　2 [the Sadducees] arrested the *apostles*
　29 T　2 Peter and the *apostles* said, 'Obedience to God comes before obedience to men;'
　40 T　2 [the Sanhedrin] had the *apostles* called in . . . [and] warned them not to speak in the name of Jesus
　6 6 T　2 They presented [the seven] to the *apostles*, who prayed and laid their hands on them.
　7 34　(Ex 3 10) come here and let me *send* you into Egypt.
　35　It was the same Moses . . . who was now *sent* to be both leader and redeemer
　8 1 T　2 everyone except the *apostles* fled
　14 T　2/ the *apostles* in Jerusalem . . . *sent* Peter and John to [Samaria],
　18　When Simon saw that the Spirit was given through the
　T　2 imposition of hands by the *apostles*,
　9 17　Brother Saul, I have been *sent* by the Lord Jesus
　27 T　2 Barnabas . . . introduced [Saul] to the *apostles*,
　10 20　it was I who ᶠtold them to come (lit. *sent* them).
　36　God *sent* his word to the people of Israel,
　11 1 T　2 The *apostles* and the brothers in Judaea heard that the pagans too had accepted the word of God,
　22　4 The church in Jerusalem . . . *sent* Barnabas to Antioch.
　12 11 A　4 The Lord really did *send* his angel and has saved me from Herod
　13 26　4 this message of salvation is ᶠmeant (lit. *sent*) for you.
　14 4　The people in [Iconium] were divided, some supported the
　S　2 Jews, others the *apostles*,

Ac 14	14	S	2	the *apostles* Barnabas and Paul . . . tore their clothes,
15	2			it was arranged that Paul and Barnabas . . . should go up
		T	2	to Jerusalem and discuss the problem with the *apostles* and elders.
	4	T	2	they were welcomed by the church and by the *apostles* and elders,
	6	T	2	The *apostles* and elders met to look into the matter,
	22	T	2	the *apostles* and elders decided to choose delegates to send to Antioch
	23	T	2	The *apostles* and elders, your brothers, send greetings to the brothers of pagan birth
	27			Accordingly we are *sending* you Judas and Silas,
	33			[Judas and Silas] went back to those who had *sent* them.
16	4			[Paul and Timothy] passed on the decisions reached by
		T	2	the *apostles* and elders in Jerusalem,
19	22			[Paul] *sent* two of his helpers, Timothy and Erastus, ahead of him to Macedonia,
22	21	S	4	I am *sending* you *out* to the pagans far away.
26	17			(Jr 1 7) I shall deliver you from the people and from the
		S		pagans, to whom I am *sending* you
28	28			this salvation of God has been *sent* to the pagans;
Rm 1	1			Paul, a servant of Christ Jesus who has been called to be an
		S	2	*apostle*,
	5	S	5	Through [Jesus Christ] we received grace and our *apostolic mission*
10	15			they will never have a preacher unless one is *sent*,
11	13	S	2	I have been *sent* to the pagans *as their apostle*, and I am proud of being [sent].
16	7		2	[Greetings] to those outstanding *apostles* Andronicus and Junias,
1 Co 1	1	S	2	I, Paul, appointed by God to be an *apostle*,
	17	S		Christ did not *send* me to baptise, but to preach the Good News,
4	9	S	2	God has put us *apostles* at the end of his parade,
9	1	S	2	I am an *apostle* and I have seen Jesus our Lord. . . .
	2	S	2	[2] Even if I were not an *apostle* to others, I should still be
		S	5	. . . to you who are the seal of my *apostolate* in the Lord.
9	5			to take a Christian woman round with us, like all the other
		T	2	*apostles* and the brothers of the Lord and Cephas?
12	28	P	2	In the church, God has given the first place to *apostles*, the second to prophets, the third to teachers; . . .
	29	P	2	[29] Are all of them *apostles*, or all of them prophets, or all of them teachers?
15	7			then [Jesus] appeared to James, and then to all the
	9	T	2	*apostles*; [8] last of all . . . to me too; . . . [9] I am the
		S	2	least of the *apostles*; in fact . . . I hardly deserve the name
			2	*apostle*;
2 Co 1	1	S	2	From Paul, appointed by God to be an *apostle* of Christ Jesus,
8	23		2	the other two brothers, who are *delegates* of the churches, are a real glory to Christ.
11	5		2	As far as I can tell, these arch-*apostles* have nothing more than I have.
	13		7	These people are counterfeit *apostles*, they are dishonest
			2	workmen disguised as *apostles* of Christ.
12	11		2	there is not a thing these arch-*apostles* have that I do not have as well.
	12			You have seen done among you all the things that mark
			2	the true *apostle* . . .: the signs, the marvels, the miracles.
	17			through one of the men that I have *sent* you?
	18		8	I *sent* the brother that came with Titus.
Ga 1	1	S	2	From Paul . . . an *apostle* who does not owe his authority to men . . . but [to] Jesus Christ,
	17			nor did I go up to Jerusalem to see those who were already
		T	2	*apostles* before me,
	19	T	2	I did not see any of the other *apostles* [but Cephas]; I only saw James,
2	8	T	5	The same person whose action had made Peter an *apostle* of the circumcised had given me a similar mission to the pagans.
Ep 1	1	S	2	From Paul, appointed by God to be an *apostle* of Christ Jesus,
2	20	P	2	You are part of a building that has the *apostles* and prophets for its foundations,
3	5			This mystery that has now been revealed through the
		P	2	Spirit to his holy *apostles* and prophets
4	11	P	2	to some [Christ's] gift was that they should be *apostles*; to some, prophets;
Col 1	1	S	2	From Paul, appointed by God to be an *apostle* of Christ Jesus,
1 Th 2	7			we could have imposed ourselves on you with full weight,
		S	2	as *apostles* of Christ.
1 Tm 1	1	S	2	From Paul, *apostle* of Christ Jesus appointed by the command of God
2	7	S	2	I have been named a herald and *apostle* of [Christ's mediation]
2 Tm 1	1	S	2	From Paul, appointed by God to be an *apostle* of Christ Jesus, I have been named [the] herald [of the Good News],
	11	S	2	its *apostle* and its teacher.
4	12			I have *sent* Tychicus to Ephesus.

Tt 1	1	S	2	From Paul, servant of God, an *apostle* of Jesus Christ
Heb 1	14	A		spirits whose work is service, *sent* to help those who will be the heirs of salvation.
1 P 1	1	T	2	Peter, an *apostle* of Jesus Christ, sends greetings to all those living among foreigners in the Dispersion
2 P 1	1	T	2	From Simon Peter, servant and *apostle* of Jesus Christ;
3	2			recalling to you what was said in the past by the holy prophets and the commandments of the Lord and saviour
		P	2	which you were given by the *apostles*.
Jude	17	T	2	remember . . . what the *apostles* of our Lord Jesus Christ told you to expect.
Rv 1	1			This is the revelation given by God to Jesus Christ . . . he
		A		*sent* his angel to make it known to his servant John,
2	2			[Ephesus,] I know . . . how you tested the impostors who
			2	called themselves *apostles*
5	6			a Lamb that . . . had seven horns, and . . . seven eyes, which are the seven Spirits God has *sent* out all over the world.
18	20			Now heaven, celebrate [Babylon's] downfall, and all you
		P	2	saints, *apostles* and prophets:
21	14			The city walls stood on twelve foundation stones, each one
		T	2	of which bore the name of one of the twelve *apostles* of the Lamb.
22	6	A		the Lord God . . . has *sent* his angel to reveal to his servants what is soon to take place.

3: SEND (OUT) – LET GO – START

Mt 2	16			Herod . . . ⌐had all the male children killed (lit. *sent* and killed all the male children)
8	31	X		the devils pleaded with Jesus, 'If you cast us out, *send* us into the herd of pigs.'
14	35			When the local people recognised him they ⌐spread (lit. *sent*) the news through the whole neighbourhood
20	2	<		[The landowner] *sent* [the workers] to his vineyard.
21	1	X		Jesus *sent* two disciples, [2] saying '. . . you will . . . find a tethered donkey and a colt
	3	X		The Master needs them and will *send* them back directly.
	34	<		[the landowner] *sent* his servants to the tenants . . . [35] But
	36	<		the tenants . . . thrashed one, . . . [36] Next he *sent* some
	37	<		more servants . . . [37] Finally he *sent* his son
22	3	<		[The king] *sent* his servants to call those who had been
	4	<		invited . . . [4] Next he *sent* some more servants.
	16			[the Pharisees] *sent* their disciples to [Jesus],
27	19			[Pilate's] wife *sent* him a message,
Mk 3	31			[Jesus's] mother and brothers . . . *sent* in a message asking for him.
4	29			when the crop is ready, he . . . *starts* to reap
5	10	X		[the unclean spirit] begged [Jesus] earnestly not to *send* them out of the district.
6	17			it was this same Herod who had *sent* to have John arrested,
	27			the king . . . *sent* one of the bodyguard with orders to bring John's head.
8	26	X		Jesus *sent* [the blind man of Bethsaida] home,
11	1	X		he *sent* two of his disciples [2] and said to them '. . . you will find a tethered colt
	3	X		The Master needs it and will *send* it back here directly.
12	2	<		he *sent* a servant to the tenants . . . [3] But they . . . *sent* him
	3	<		away empty-handed. [4] Next he *sent* another servant . . .
	4	<		[5] And he *sent* another . . . [6] He had still . . . his beloved
	6	<		son. He *sent* him to them last of all.
	13			they *sent* to [Jesus] some Pharisees . . . to catch him out
14	13	X		he *sent* two of his disciples
Lk 1	53	Θ	4	the rich [he has] *sent* empty away.
4	18	X		(Is 58 6) to ⌐set the downtrodden free (or: let the downtrodden *go* free),
7	3			[the centurion] *sent* some Jewish elders to [Jesus]
	20			John the Baptist has *sent* us to you, to ask, 'Are you the one who is to come . . .?'
9	52	X		[Jesus took the road for Jerusalem] and *sent* messengers ahead of him.
14	17	<		he *sent* his servant to say to those who had been invited 'Come
	32			[the king] would *send* envoys to sue for peace.
19	14			his compatriots . . . *sent* a delegation to follow him
	29	X		he *sent* two of the disciples, telling them, [30] . . . you will find a tethered colt
	32	X		the *messengers* . . . found everything just as he had told them.
20	10	<		he *sent* a servant to the tenants . . . But the tenants
	11	<	4	*sent* him away empty-handed. [11] But he persevered and
		<	/4	*sent* a second servant; they . . . *sent* him away empty-handed.
	20			[the scribes and the chief priests] *sent* agents to . . . fasten on something he might say
22	8	X		he *sent* Peter and John, saying, 'Go and make the preparations for . . . the passover.'
Jn 1	19			the Jews *sent* priests and Levites . . . to ask [John], 'Who are you?'

Jn	1 24	these men had been *sent* by the Pharisees,
	5 33	You *sent* messengers to John, and he gave his testimony to the truth:
	7 32	the Pharisees *sent* the Temple police to arrest him.
	9 7	Go and wash in the Pool of Siloam (a name that means '*sent*').
	11 3	The sisters *sent* this message to Jesus,
	18 24	Annas *sent* [Jesus] . . . to Caiaphas the high priest.
Ac	5 21	the high priest . . . and his supporters . . . *sent* to the gaol for [the apostles] to be brought.
	7 12	4 Jacob . . . *sent* our ancestors off to Egypt]
	14	Joseph then *sent* for his father Jacob
	9 30	4 the brothers . . . *sent* [Saul] off . . . to Tarsus.
	38	when the disciples heard that Peter was [at Jaffa] they *sent* two men . . . for him.
	10 8	[Cornelius called two slaves] and *sent* them off to Jaffa.
	17	the men *sent* by Cornelius arrived.
	11 11	three men stopped outside the house . . .; they had been *sent* from Caesarea to fetch me.
	13	*Send* to Jaffa and fetch Simon known as Peter;
	30	[The disciples] *delivered* their contributions to the elders
	13 15	the presidents of the synagogue *sent* . . . a message [to Paul and his companions]:
	16 35	the magistrates *sent* the officers [to the gaol] with the order: Release those men.
	36	The magistrates have *sent* an order for your release;
	17 14	4 the brothers *arranged* for Paul *to go* . . . as far as the coast,
Ph	2 25	2 Epaphroditus . . . was *sent* as your representative to help me

4: LETTER, SEND A LETTER – WRITE (TO)

Ac	9 2	3 [Saul had] asked for *letters* addressed to the synagogues in Damascus,
	15 20	6 [I rule that] we *send a letter* [to the pagans] telling them merely to abstain from . . . idols . . . and from blood.
	30	[The delegates] went down to Antioch, where they . . . 3 delivered the *letter*.
	21 25	6 The pagans . ., as we *wrote when we told* them *of* our decisions, must abstain from . . . idols, from blood,
	22 5	3 they even sent me with *letters* to their brothers in Damascus.
	23 25	5 [The tribune] wrote a *letter* in these terms: Claudius Lysias to his Excellency the governor Felix, greetings.
	33	3 the escort delivered the *letter* to the governor
Rm	16 22	3 I, Tertius, who wrote out this *letter*, greet you
1 Co	5 9	3 When I wrote in my *letter* to you not to associate with people living immoral lives,
	16 3	I will send your offering to Jerusalem by the hand of whatever 3 men you give *letters* of reference to;
2 Co	3 1	3 we need no *letters* of recommendation either to you or from you,
	2 ○	3 you are yourselves our *letter*, written in our hearts,
	3 ○	3 it is plain that you are a *letter* from Christ, . . . written . . . with the Spirit of the living God,
	7 8	3 even if I distressed you by my *letter*, I do not regret it. . . . 3 I see that that *letter* did distress you,
	10 9	3 I do not want you to think of me as someone who only 3 frightens you by *letter*.
	10	Someone said, 'He writes powerful and strongly-worded 3 *letters* but . . .
	11	3 whatever we are like in . . . our *letters* . ., that is what we shall be like in our actions
Col	4 16	3 After this *letter* has been read among you, send it on to be read in the church of the Laodiceans;
1 Th	5 27	3 this *letter* is to be read to all the brothers.
2 Th	2 2	3 do not get excited . . . by . . . any *letter* claiming to come from us,
	15	keep the traditions that we taught you, whether by word of 3 mouth or by *letter*.
	3 14	3 If anyone refuses to obey what I have written in this *letter*, take note of him
	17	greetings in my own handwriting, which is the mark of 3 genuineness in every *letter*;
Heb	13 22	6 that is why I have *written* to you so briefly.
2 P	3 1	3 this is my second *letter* to you,
	16	3 [Paul] always *writes* like this when he deals with this sort of subject, and this makes some points [in his letter] hard to understand;

2. SEND: *PEMPŌ*

1 *pempō* 79	2 *meta-pempō* 9
3 *ana-pempō* 5	5 *sym-pempō* 2
4 *ek-pempō* 2	

1: (THE SON, THE SPIRIT, IS) SENT

Jn	4 34	My food is to do the will of the one who *sent* me,

Jn	5 23	Whoever refuses honour to the Son refuses honour to the Father who *sent* him.
	24	whoever . . . believes in the one who *sent* me, has eternal life;
	30	my aim is to do . . . the will of him who *sent* me.
	37	the Father who *sent* me bears witness to me himself.
	6 38	not to do my own will, but to do the will of the one who *sent* me.
	39	the will of him who *sent* me is that I should lose nothing
	44	No one can come to me unless he is drawn by the Father who *sent* me,
	7 16	My teaching is not from myself: it comes from the one who *sent* me;
	18	when [a man] is working for the honour of one who *sent* him, there is one who *sent* me and I really come from him.
	28	
	33	I shall go back to the one who *sent* me.
	8 16	I am not alone: the one who *sent* me is with me;
	18	the Father who *sent* me is my witness too.
	26	the one who *sent* me is truthful,
	29	he who *sent* me is with me,
	9 4	I must carry out the work of the one who *sent* me;
	12 44	Whoever believes in me believes not in me but in the one who *sent* me,
	45	whoever sees me, sees the one who *sent* me.
	49	what I had to say . . . was commanded by the Father who *sent* me.
	13 20	whoever welcomes the one I send welcomes me, and whoever welcomes me welcomes the one who *sent* me.
	14 24	my word is not my own: it is the word ᵛ of the one (G of the Father) who *sent* me;
	26 Ⓢ	the Holy Spirit, whom the Father will *send* in my name, because they do not know the one who *sent* me.
	15 21	
	26 Ⓢ	the Advocate . . . whom I shall *send* to you from the Father,
	16 5	now I am going to the one who *sent* me.
	7 Ⓢ	but if I do go, I will *send* [the Advocate] to you.
Rm	8 3	God dealt with sin by *sending* his own Son in a body as physical as any sinful body,

2: SEND (OUT) ON A MISSION

Lk	4 26	Elijah was not *sent* to any [of the widows in Israel]: he was sent to a widow at Zarephath,
Jn	1 33 J	he who *sent* me to baptise with water
	13 16 <	no messenger is greater than the man who *sent* him.
	20	whoever welcomes the one I send welcomes me, and whoever welcomes me welcomes the one who sent me.
	20 21 T	As the Father sent me, so am I *sending* you.
Ac	13 4 S	4 [Barnabas and Saul,] *sent on their mission* by the Holy Spirit,
	15 22	the apostles and elders decided to choose delegates to *send* to Antioch
	25	we have decided . . . to elect delegates and to *send* them to you with Barnabas and Paul,
1 Co	4 17	I have *sent* you Timothy . . .: he will remind you of the way that I live in Christ,
1 Th	3 2	[we] sent our brother Timothy, . . . to keep you firm
	5	That is why . . . I *sent* to assure myself of your faith
Rv	22 16 A	I, Jesus, have *sent* my angel to make these revelations to you

3: SEND – COMMISSION – MESSENGER

Mt	2 8	[Herod summoned the wise men] and *sent* them on to Bethlehem.
	11 2	John . . . *sent* his disciples to ask [Christ], 'Are you the one who is to come . . .?'
	14 10	[Herod] *sent* and had John beheaded in the prison.
	22 7	The king . . . *despatched* his troops, destroyed those murderers
Mk	5 12 X	the unclean spirits begged him, '*Send* us to the pigs,'
Lk	7 6	the centurion *sent* word to [Jesus] . . .: 'Sir, . . . I am not worthy to have you under my roof;'
	10	when the *messengers* got back to the house they found the servant in perfect health.
	19	[John, summoning two of his disciples,] *sent* them to the Lord to ask, 'Are you the one who is to come . . .?'
	15 15	[the prodigal son] hired himself out to one of the local inhabitants ʳput him on (lit. *sent* him) to his farm
	16 24	*send* Lazarus to dip the tip of his finger in water
	27	I beg you then to *send* Lazarus to my father's house,
	20 11 <	[the owner of the vineyard] *sent* a second servant; . . .
	12 <	¹² He still persevered and *sent* a third; . . . ¹³ . . . 'What
	13 <	am I to do? I will *send* them my dear son.'
	23 7	finding that [Jesus] came under Herod's jurisdiction [Pilate] 3 *passed* him *over* to Herod
	11	3 Herod . . . *sent* him back to Pilate.
	15	3 Herod . . . has *sent* him back to us.
Jn	1 22	Who are you? We must take back an answer to those who *sent* us.
Ac	10 5	you must *send* someone to Jaffa and fetch a man called Simon, known as Peter,

Ac	10	32	you must *send* to Jaffa and fetch Simon known as Peter
		33	So I *sent* for you at once, and you have been kind enough to come.
	11	29	The disciples decided to *send* relief . . . to the brothers living in Judaea.
	17	10	4 When it was dark the brothers . . . *sent* Paul and Silas *away* to Beroea,
	19	31	some of the Asiarchs . . . *sent* messages imploring [Paul] not to take the risk of going into the theatre [at Ephesus].
	20	17	[Paul] *sent* for the elders of the church of Ephesus.
	23	30	I hasten to *send* [Paul] to you,
	25	21	3 I ordered [Paul] to be remanded until I could *send* him to Caesar.
		25	I decided to *send* [Paul to the emperor].
		27	It seems to me pointless to *send* a prisoner without indicating the charges against him.
1 Co	16	3	I will *send* your offering to Jerusalem by the hand of whatever men you give letters of reference to;
2 Co	8	18	5 As [Titus's] companion we are *sending* the brother who is famous in all the churches
		22	5 To accompany these, we are *sending* a third brother,
	9	3	I am *sending* the brothers
Ep	6	22	I am *sending* [Tychicus] to you
Ph	2	19	I hope . . . to *send* Timothy to you soon,
		23	That is why [Timothy] is the one that I am hoping to *send* you
		25	It is essential . . . to *send* brother Epaphroditus back to you.
		28	I shall *send* him back as promptly as I can;
	4	16	twice since my stay in Thessalonika you have *sent* me what I needed.
Col	4	8	I am *sending* [Tychicus] to you
2 Th	2	11 Θ	God is *sending* a power to delude them
Tt	3	12	As soon as I have *sent* Artemas or Tychicus to you,
Phm		12	3 I am *sending* [Onesimus] back to you,
1 P	2	14	[accept the authority of] the governors as *commissioned* by [the Lord]
Rv	1	11	Write down all that you see in a book, and *send* it to the seven churches
	11	10	the people of the world will . . . celebrate the event by ⌐giving (lit. *sending*) presents to each other,
	14	15	⌐Put (lit. *send*) your sickle in and reap;
		18	⌐Put (lit. *send*) your sickle in and cut all the bunches off the vine

4: SEND FOR – FETCH, BRING (*META-PEMPŌ*)

Ac	10	5	2 *send* someone to Jaffa and *fetch* a man called Simon, known as Peter,
		22	2 Cornelius . . . was directed by a holy angel to *send* [for you] *and bring* you to his house
		29	2 I made no objection to coming when I was *sent for*; but I
			2 should like to know exactly why you *sent for* me.
	11	13	2 Send to Jaffa and *fetch* Simon known as Peter;
	20	1	2 Paul *sent for* the disciples
	24	24	2 Felix . . . *sent for* Paul and gave him a hearing . . . ²⁶ . . .
		26	2 he *sent for* him frequently and had talks with him.
	25	3	2 [the leaders of the Jews asked Festus] to *have* [Paul] *transferred* to Jerusalem.

3. (BE) AMBASSADORS, ENVOYS – DELEGATION: *PRESBEUŌ*

1 *presbeia* 2   2 *presbeuō* 2

Lk	14	32	[the king] would send *envoys* to sue for peace.
	19	14	his compatriots . . . sent a *delegation* to follow him
2 Co	5	20 ●	2 we *are ambassadors* for Christ; it is as though God were appealing through us,
Ep	6	20 ●	2 [the mystery of the gospel] of which I *am an ambassador* in chains;

SHADOW

1: Shadow, Shade – Cover with shadow, Overshadow – a Shadow falls	2: (the) Shadow (of death, of things to come, of a change)

1   *skia*   7   4   *kata-skiazō* 1
3   *apo-skiasma* 1   2   *epi-skiazō*   5

1: SHADOW, SHADE – COVER WITH SHADOW, OVERSHADOW – A SHADOW FALLS

| Mt | 17 | 5 | 2 suddenly a bright cloud *covered* them *with shadow*, |

Mk	4	32	so that the birds of the air can shelter in its *shade*.
	9	7	2 a cloud came, *covering* them *in shadow*;
Lk	1	35	The Holy Spirit will come upon you . . . and the power of the
			2 Most High will *cover* you *with its shadow*.
	9	34	2 a cloud came and *covered* them *with shadow*;
Ac	5	15	/2 in the hope that at least the *shadow* of Peter might *fall across* some of them
Heb	9	5	On top of [the ark] was the throne of mercy, and ⌐outspread
		4	over (lit. *overshadowing*) it were the glorious cherubs.

2: (THE) SHADOW (OF DEATH, OF THINGS TO COME, OF A CHANGE)

Mt	4	16	(Is 9 1) on those who dwell in the land and *shadow* of death a light has dawned.
Lk	1	79	(Is 9 1) to give light to those who live in darkness and the *shadow* of death,
Col	2	17	These were only ⌐pale reflections (lit. the *shadow*) of what was coming: the reality is Christ.
Heb	8	5	[priests] only maintain the service of a model or a ⌐reflection (lit. *shadow*) of the heavenly realities.
	10	1	the Law has no more than a ⌐reflection (lit. *shadow*) of these realities,
Jm	1	17	with [the Father] there is no such thing as alteration, no
		3	*shadow* of a change.

SHAKE – STIR UP – PROVOKE

1. **Shake (off, out):** *tinassō*
2. **Be shaken, Be unsettled, Be moved:** *sainō*
3. **Wavering, Erratic – Restless, Not keeping still:** *a-kata-statos*
4. **Throw into convulsions, Convulse:** *sparassō*
5. **Shake – Move – Stir up:** *kineō*
   a) Move, (Make a) movement – Shake, Wag – Remove
   b) Stir up, Rouse – Turn (a person) against
6. **Shake, Unshakeable – Stir up:** *saleuō*
   a) Shake, Sway, Rock – Unshakeable, Immovable
   b) Stir up – Get excited, Agitated
7. **Quake, Shake – Stir up, Incite:** *seiō*
   a) Quake, Shake (violently) – Storm
   b) Stir up, Incite – (Be) in Turmoil
8. **Stir up, Incite – Work upon (a person's) feelings:** *par-otrynō*
9. **Stir up – Provoke – Quarrel:** *par-oxynō*
   a) Stir, up Arouse – Provoke a response
   b) Quarrel – (Be) Revolted, Provoked – Take offence
10. **Stir up, Provoke, Be a spur to – Drive to resentment:** *erethizō*
11. **Instigate, Put up to – Procure, Suborn:** *hypo-ballō*
12. **Provoke, Provocative – Challenging:** *pro-kaleomai*

1. SHAKE (OFF, OUT): *TINASSŌ*

2 *apo-tinassō* 2   1 *ek-tinassō* 4

Mt	10	14	if anyone does not welcome you . . , as you walk out . . . *shake* the dust from your feet.
Mk	6	11	as you walk away *shake off* the dust from under your feet
Lk	9	5	2 when you leave their town *shake* the dust from your feet
Ac	13	51	[Paul and Barnabas] *shook* the dust from their feet
	18	6	When [the Jews] . . . started to insult him, [Paul] took his cloak and *shook* it *out* in front of them,
	28	5	2 [Paul] *shook* [the viper] *off* into the fire

2. BE SHAKEN, BE UNSETTLED, BE MOVED: *SAINŌ*

sainō 1

| 1 Th | 3 | 3 | and prevent any of you from *being unsettled* by the present troubles. |

3. WAVERING, ERRATIC – RESTLESS, NOT KEEPING STILL: *A-KATA-STATOS*

a-kata-statos 2

| Jm | 1 | 8 | That sort of person, . . . *wavering* between going different ways, |
| | 3 | 8 | the tongue . . . is a pest *that will not keep still*, |

4. THROW INTO CONVULSIONS, CONVULSE: *SPARASSŌ*

1 *sparassō* 3	2 *sy-sparassō* 2

Mk	1 26	Ⓓ	the unclean spirit *threw* the man *into convulsions* and . . . went out of him.
	9 20	Ⓓ	2 as soon as the spirit saw Jesus it *threw* the boy *into convulsions*,
	26	Ⓓ	*throwing* the boy *into* (G violent) *convulsions* [the spirit] came out shouting,
Lk	9 39	Ⓓ	All at once a spirit will take hold of [my son] . . . and *throw* [him] *into convulsions*
	42	Ⓓ	2 the devil *threw* him to the ground *in convulsions*.

5. SHAKE – MOVE – STIR UP: *KINEŌ*

1 *kineō* 8	3 *meta-kineō* 1
2 *kinēsis* 1	4 *a-meta-kinētos* 1
	5 *syn-kineō* 1

a) Move, (Make a) Movement – Shake, Wag – Remove

Mt	23 4		will [the scribes and Pharisees] lift a finger to *move* [the burdens they impose]? Not they!
	27 39		(Ps 22 7) The passers-by jeered at him; they *shook* their heads
Mk	15 29		(Ps 22 7) The passers-by jeered at him; they *shook* their heads
Jn	5 3		2 crowds of sick people . . . ᵛ waiting for the water to *move*; ⁴ for at intervals the angel . . . came down into the pool,
Ac	17 28	●	it is in [God] that we live, and *move*, and exist,
1 Co	15 58		4 ⌐never admit defeat (lit. be *immovable*)
Col	1 23		3 never letting yourselves ⌐drift away (lit. be *shaken*) from the hope promised by the Good News.
Rv	2 5		or else . . . I shall come to you and ⌐take (lit. *remove*) your lamp-stand from its place.
	6 14		all the mountains and islands were *shaken* from their places.

b) Stir up, Rouse – Turn (a person) against

Ac	6 12	5 Having in this way *turned* (or: *stirred up*) the people *against* [Stephen]
	21 30	This *roused* the whole city [of Jerusalem];
	24 5	[Paul] *stirs up* trouble among Jews the world over,

6. SHAKE, UNSHAKEABLE – STIR UP: *SALEUŌ*

1 *saleuō* 15	2 *a-saleutos* 2

a) Shake, Sway, Rock – Unshakeable, Immovable

Mt	11 7	What did you go out into the wilderness to see? A reed *swaying* in the breeze?
	24 29	the powers of heaven will be *shaken*.
Mk	13 25	the powers in the heavens will be *shaken*.
Lk	6 38	a full measure, pressed down, *shaken* [together], and running over,
	48	when the river was in flood it bore down on that house but could not *shake* it,
	7 24	What did you go out into the wilderness to see? A reed *swaying* in the breeze?
	21 26	the powers of heaven will be *shaken*.
Ac	2 25	(Ps 16 8) with [the Lord] at my right hand nothing can *shake* me.
	4 31	the house where they were assembled *rocked*;
	16 26	an earthquake that *shook* the prison to its foundations.
	27 41	The bows were wedged in and ⌐stuck fast (lit. remained 2 *immovable*),
Heb	12 26 ⊖	That time his voice *made* the earth *shake*, but now he has given us this promise: I shall make the earth shake once more and . . . heaven as well. ²⁷ The words 'once more' show that since the things *being shaken* are created things, they are going to be changed, so that the un*shakeable* things will be left. ²⁸ We have been given possession of an 2 *unshakeable* kingdom.
	27	
	28	

b) Stir up – Get excited, Agitated

Ac	17 13	The Jews of Thessalonika . . . went [to Beroea] to . . . *stir up* the people.
2 Th	2 2	please do not *get excited* . . . or alarmed by any prediction

7. QUAKE, SHAKE – STIR UP, INCITE: *SEIŌ*

2 *seiō* 5	3 *ana-seiō* 2
1 *seismos* 14	

a) Quake, Shake (violently) – Storm

Mt	8 24	Without warning a *storm* broke over the lake,
	24 7	There will be famines and [earth]*quakes*
	27 51	2 [Jesus yielded up his spirit.] At that, . . . the earth *quaked*; the rocks were split;
	54	the centurion . . . had seen the [earth]*quake*
	28 2	all at once there was a violent [earth]*quake*
	4	2 The guards were ⌐so *shaken*, (or: *shaking* and) so frightened of [the angel], that they were like dead men.
Mk	13 8	There will be [earth]*quakes* here and there;
Lk	21 11	There will be great [earth]*quakes* and plagues
Ac	16 26	Suddenly there was an [earth]*quake* that shook the prison to its foundations.
Heb	12 26 ⊖	2 (Hg 2 6) I shall *make* the earth *shake* once more and . . heaven as well.
Rv	6 12	there was a violent [earth]*quake*
	13	2 a fig tree when a high wind *shakes* it;
	8 5	immediately there came peals of thunder . . . and ⌐the earth shook (lit. an [earth]*quake*).
	11 13	Immediately, there was a violent [earth]*quake*, and a tenth of the city collapsed; seven thousand persons were killed in the [earth]*quake*
	19	flashes of lightning, peals of thunder and an [earth]*quake*,
	16 18	flashes of lightning and peals of thunder and a violent [earth-]*quake* such that no one had ever seen as [earth]*quake* so violent.

b) Stir up, Incite – (Be) in Turmoil

Mt	21 10	2 when [Jesus] entered Jerusalem, the whole city was *in turmoil*
Mk	15 11	3 The chief priests . . . had *incited* the crowd to demand . . . Barabbas
Lk	23 5 X	3 But [the chief priests] persisted, 'He is *inflaming* the people . . .'

8. STIR UP, INCITE – WORK UPON (A PERSON'S) FEELINGS: *PAR-OTRYNŌ*

par-otrynō 1

Ac	13 50	the Jews *worked upon* some of the devout women of the upper classes

9. STIR UP – PROVOKE – QUARREL: *PAR-OXYNŌ*

1 *par-oxynō* 2	2 *par-oxysmos* 2

a) Stir up, Arouse – Provoke a response

Heb	10 24	2 Let us be concerned for each other, to *stir a response* in love and good works.

b) Quarrel – (Be) Revolted, Provoked – Take offence

Ac	15 39	2 After a violent *quarrel* [Paul and Barnabas] parted company,
	17 16	[Paul's] whole soul *was revolted* at the sight of a city [Athens] given over to idolatry.
1 Co	13 5 ●	[love] does not *take offence*,

10. STIR UP, PROVOKE, BE A SPUR TO – DRIVE TO RESENTMENT: *ERETHIZŌ*

erethizō 2

2 Co	9 2	your zeal has ⌐been a spur to (or: *stirred up*) many more.
Col	3 21	Parents, never *drive* your children *to resentment* or you will make them feel frustrated.

11. INSTIGATE, PUT UP TO – PROCURE, SUBORN: *HYPO-BALLŌ*

hypo-ballō 1

Ac	6 11	So [members of the synagogue] ⌐*procured* some men to (or: *put up* some men *to*) say,

12. PROVOKE, PROVOCATIVE – CHALLENGING: *PRO-KALEOMAI*

pro-kaleomai 1

Ga	5 26	We must stop being conceited, *provocative* and envious.

SHARE – PARTNER

1. Share, (in) Common – Partnership, Communion: *koinōneō*
  1: Share (materially), (in) Common – Contribute (to) – Partnership

2: Share (spiritually) – Join in, Take part (in) – (spiritual) Fellowship, Union, Communion

2. Share, Take a share – Partner, Companion: *met-echō*

Θ, X, Ⓢ, Ⓓ = Sharing in or with God, Christ, the Spirit, demons

1. SHARE, (IN) COMMON – PARTNERSHIP, COMMUNION: *KOINŌNEŌ*

3 *koinōneō*	8	4 *koinos*	4/14
1 *koinōnia*	19	6 *syn-koinōneō*	3
7 *koinōnikos*	1	5 *syn-koinōnos*	4
2 *koinōnos*	10		

1: SHARE (MATERIALLY), (IN) COMMON – CONTRIBUTE (TO) – PARTNERSHIP

Lk	5 10	2	James and John . . . who were Simon's *partners*.
Ac	2 42		These remained faithful to . . . the ⌐brotherhood (lit. *fellowship*),
	44	4	The faithful all lived together and owned everything in *common*;
	4 32	4	everything [the believers] owned was held in *common*.
Rm	12 13	3	If any of the saints are in need you must *share* with them;
	15 26		Macedonia and Achaia have decided to send a [generous] *contribution* to the poor among the saints at Jerusalem.
2 Co	8 4		begging us for the favour of *sharing* in this service to the saints
	23	2	Titus . . . is my own *colleague* and fellow worker in your interests;
	9 13		[the saints] give glory to God for . . . your *sympathetic generosity* to them
Ga	2 9		these leaders . . . shook hands with Barnabas and me as a sign of *partnership*:
	6 6	3	People under instruction should always *contribute* something to the support of the man who is instructing them.
Ph	1 5		remembering how you have *helped* to spread the Good News
	4 15	3	no other church ⌐*helped* (or: *entered into partnership* with) me with gifts of money.
1 Tm	6 18	7	Tell [the rich] that they are . . . to be generous and *willing to share*
Heb	10 33	2	[all the sufferings that you had to meet,] sometimes as *associates* of others who were treated in the same way.
	13 16		Keep doing good works and *sharing* [your resources], for these are sacrifices that please God.
2 Jn	11	3	To greet him would make you a *partner* in his wicked work.

2: SHARE (SPIRITUALLY) – JOIN IN, TAKE PART (IN) – (SPIRITUAL) FELLOWSHIP, UNION, COMMUNION

Mt	23 30	2	We would never have *joined in* shedding the blood of the prophets,
Ac	2 42		These remained faithful to . . . the ⌐brotherhood (lit. *fellowship*),
Rm	11 17	5	like shoots of wild olive, you have been grafted among the rest to *share* with them the rich sap
	15 27	3	the pagans who *share* the spiritual possessions of these poor people have a duty to help them with temporal possessions.
1 Co	1 9 X		God by calling you has *joined* you to his Son,
	9 23	5	I still do this, for the sake of the gospel, to *have a share* in its blessings,
	10 16 X		The blessing-cup . . . is a *communion* with the blood of Christ,
	X		and the bread . . . is a *communion* with the body of Christ.
	18	2	those who eat the sacrifices are in *communion* with the altar.
	20 Ⓓ	2	I have no desire to see you in *communion* with demons.
2 Co	1 7	2	we know that, *sharing* our sufferings, you will also share our consolations.
	6 14		Light and darkness have nothing in *common*.
	13 13 Ⓢ		The grace of the Lord Jesus Christ, the love of God and the *fellowship* of the Holy Spirit be with you all.
Ep	5 11		Try to discover what the Lord wants of you, ⌐having nothing to do with (lit. *taking part in* none of) the futile works of darkness
Ph	1 7	5	you have *shared* the privileges which have been mine;
	2 1 Ⓢ		if love can persuade at all, or the Spirit that we have in *common*,
Ph	3 10		All I want is to know Christ . . . and to *share* his sufferings
	4 14	6	it was good of you to *share* with me in my hardships.
1 Tm	5 22	3	never ⌐make yourself an accomplice (lit. *share*) in anybody else's sin;
Tt	1 4	4	To Titus, true child of mine in the faith that we *share*
Phm	6		I pray that this faith will give rise to a [sense of] *fellowship*
	17	2	if all that we have in *common* means anything to you,
Heb	2 14	3	Since all the children *share* the same blood and flesh, he [who sanctifies] too shared equally in it,
1 P	4 13	3	If you can have some *share* in the sufferings of Christ,
	5 1	2	with you I *have a share* in the glory that is to be revealed,
2 P	1 4 Θ	2	you will be able to *share* the divine nature
1 Jn	1 3 Θ X		so that you too may be in *union* with us, as we are in *union* with the Father and with his Son Jesus Christ.
	6 Θ		If we say that we are in *union* with God while we are living in darkness, we are lying . . . [7] But if we live our lives in the light . . . we are in *union* with one another,
	7		
Jude	3	4	I was eagerly looking forward to writing to you about the salvation *that we* [all] *share*,
Rv	1 9	5	through our union in Jesus I am your brother and *share* your sufferings,
	18 4	6	Come out, my people, away from [Babylon], so that you do not *share* in her crimes

2. SHARE, TAKE A SHARE – PARTNER, COMPANION: *MET-ECHŌ*

1 *met-echō*	8	2 *met-ochos*	6
4 *met-ochē*	1	3 *sym-met-ochos*	2

Lk	5 7	2	they signalled to their ⌐*companions* (or: *partners*) in the other boat
1 Co	9 10		the thresher [ought] to thresh in the expectation of *getting his share*.
	12		Others are allowed to *share* these rights over you
	10 17		though there are many of us, we form a single body because we all *have a share* in this one loaf.
	X		
	21 X Ⓓ		You cannot *take your share* at the table of the Lord and at the table of demons.
	30		If I *take my share* with thankfulness, why should I be blamed for food for which I have thanked God?
2 Co	6 14	4	Virtue is no *companion* for crime.
Ep	3 6	3	pagans now *share* the same inheritance,
	5 7	3	Make sure that you are not *included with* [those who rebel against God].
Heb	1 9	2	(Ps 45 8) God . . . has anointed you . . . above all your ⌐*rivals* (lit. *companions*).
	2 14		Since all the children share the same blood and flesh, he [who sanctifies] too *shared* equally in it,
	3 1	2	all you who are holy brothers and have ⌐had (lit. *shared*) the same heavenly call
	14 X	2	we shall ⌐remain co-heirs (lit. *take our share*) with Christ
	5 13		anyone who is still ⌐living on (lit. *taking his share* of) milk cannot digest the doctrine of righteousness
	6 4 Ⓢ	2	those people who . . . received a *share* of the Holy Spirit, . . . [6] and yet in spite of this have fallen away – it is impossible for them to be renewed
	7 13		our Lord . . . *belonged* to a different tribe,
	12 8	2	If you were not getting this training, ⌐as all of you are (lit. in which all of you *share*), then you would not be sons but bastards.

SHEPHERD – FLOCK – HERD

1. Shepherd, Pastor – Tend, Look after – Flock: *poimainō*

2. Herd (of pigs): *agelē*

1. SHEPHERD, PASTOR – TEND, LOOK AFTER – FLOCK: *POIMAINŌ*

2 *poimainō*	11	4 *poimnion*	5
1 *poimēn*	18	5 (archi-)*poimēn*	1
3 *poimnē*	5		

Mt	2 6		(Mi 5 1) Bethlehem, . . . out of you will come a leader who
	X	2	will *shepherd* my people Israel.
	9 36		when [Jesus] saw the crowds he felt sorry for them because they were harassed and dejected, like sheep without a *shepherd*.
	25 32		[the Son of Man] will separate men one from another as the *shepherd* separates sheep from goats.

Mt 26 31 X		(Zc 13 7) I shall strike the *shepherd* and the sheep of the
	3	*flock* will be scattered,
Mk 6 34		[Jesus] took pity on [the crowd] because they were like sheep
		without a *shepherd*.
14 27 X		(Zc 13 7) I shall strike the *shepherd* and the sheep will be
		scattered,
Lk 2 8		there were *shepherds* who lived in the fields and took it in
	3	turns to watch their *flocks* during the night.
15		the *shepherds* said to one another, 'Let us go to Bethlehem'
18		everyone who heard it was astonished at what the *shepherds*
		had to say.
20		the *shepherds* went back glorifying and praising God
12 32	4	There is no need to be afraid, little *flock*,
17 7	2	Which of you, with a servant ploughing or *minding* [sheep],
		would say to him
Jn 10 2		The one who enters through the gate [of the sheepfold] is the
<		*shepherd* of the [flock]
11 X		I am the good *shepherd*: the good *shepherd* is one who lays
12		down his life for his sheep. [12] The hired man, since he is not
		the *shepherd* . . ., abandons the sheep
14 X		I am the good *shepherd*; I know my own and my own know me,
16	3	there are other sheep I have . . . there will be only one *flock*,
X		and one *shepherd*.
21 16 ●	2	Jesus said to [Simon], 'Look after my sheep'.
Ac 20 28	4	Be on your guard for . . . all the *flock* of which the Holy
	2	Spirit has made you the overseers, to ˹feed (lit. *tend*) the
29		Church of God . . . [29] . . . fierce wolves will invade you
	4	and will have no mercy on the *flock*.
1 Co 9 7	2/3	Who has there ever been that ˹kept (lit. *tended*) a *flock* and
	3	did not feed on the milk from his *flock*?
Ep 4 11		to some, [Christ's] gift was that they should be . . . *pastors*
		and teachers;
Heb 13 20		the God of peace, who brought our Lord Jesus back from
X		the dead to become the great *Shepherd* of the sheep
1 P 2 25 X		now you have come back to the *shepherd* and guardian of your
		souls.
5 2	2/4	*Be the shepherds* of the *flock* of God that is entrusted to you:
3	4	. . . [3] . . . be an example that the whole *flock* can follow.
4 X	5	[4] When the chief *shepherd* appears, you will be given the
		crown of unfading glory.
Jude 12		They are a dangerous obstacle to your community meals,
O	2	quite shamelessly only *looking after* themselves.
Rv 2 27		[the authority over the pagans] which I myself have been
X	2	given by my Father, to *rule* them with an iron sceptre
7 17 X	2	the Lamb who is at the throne will *be* their *shepherd*
12 5 X	2	the son who was to *rule* all the nations with an iron sceptre,
19 15 X	2	he is the one who will *rule* [the pagans] with an iron sceptre,

2. HERD (OF PIGS): *AGELĒ*

agelē 7

Mt 8 30		some distance away there was a large *herd* of pigs feeding,
31		send us into the *herd* of pigs.
32		the whole *herd* charged down the cliff into the lake
Mk 5 11		there was there on the mountainside a great *herd* of pigs
		feeding,
13		the *herd* . . . charged down the cliff into the lake,
Lk 8 32		there was a large *herd* of pigs feeding there on the mountain,
33		the *herd* charged down the cliff into the lake

SHINE – LIGHT

1. Light, Lantern – Shine – Bright:
phainō
  1: Light, Dawn – Shine (on), Give
    light to, Flash – Filled with
    light, Bright
  2: Lanterns
2. Shine – Bright, Magnificent –
Lamp: *lampō*
  1: Shine, Light up – Bright,
    Shining
  2: Magnificent, Gorgeous, Rich

  3: Lamp(s), Torch(es)
3. Lamp – Lamp-stand: *lychnos*
4. Radiant light, Dawn – Clear,
Transparent: *augazō*
5. Brightness, Light: *phengos*
6. Lightning, Flash, Ray(s) – Brilliant,
Dazzling: *astrapē*
7. Dazzling(ly): *stilbō*
8. Glamour– Luxury: *liparos*

H = Light from heaven

For Light//Darkness *see* NIGHT – DARKNESS 2. 1: *under the sign* L

1. LIGHT, LANTERN – SHINE – BRIGHT: *PHAINŌ*

2 *phainō*	10/31	6	*phōtismos* 2
9 *phanos*	1	3	*phōtizō* 11
1 *phōs*	69/71	7	*epi-phainō* 2/4
5 *phōstēr*	2	10	*epi-phauskō* 1
4 *phōteinos*	5	8	*epi-phōskō* 2

1: LIGHT, DAWN – SHINE (ON), GIVE LIGHT TO, FLASH – FILLED WITH LIGHT, BRIGHT

Mt 4 16		(Is 9 1) The people that lived in darkness has seen a great
X		*light*; . . . a *light* has dawned.
5 14		You are the *light* of the world.
16		your *light* must shine in the sight of men,
6 22		The lamp of the body is the eye. It follows that if your eye
23	4	is sound, your whole body will be *filled with light*. [23]
		If then, the *light* inside you is darkness, what darkness that
		will be!
10 27		What I say to you in the dark, tell in the [day]*light*;
17 2		[Jesus's] clothes became as white as the *light*.
5 H	4	a *bright* cloud covered them with shadow,
24 27		the coming of the Son of Man will be like lightning striking
	2	in the east and *flashing* far into the west.
28 1	8	towards *dawn* on the first day of the week, Mary of Magdala
		. . . went to visit the sepulchre.
Lk 1 79 X	7	[our God will bring the rising sun] to *give light to* those
		who live in darkness
2 32 X		a *light* to enlighten the pagans
8 16		he puts [the lamp] on a lamp-stand so that people may see the
		light when they come in.
11 34		The lamp of your body is your eye. When your eye is sound,
35	4	your whole body too is *filled with light*; . . . [35] See to
36		it then that the *light* inside you is not darkness. [36] If,
	4	therefore, your whole body is *filled with light*, and no
	4	trace of darkness, it will be *light* entirely, as when the
	3	lamp *shines on* you with its rays.
12 3		whatever you have said in the dark will be heard in the
		[day]*light*,
16 8		the children of this world are more astute . . . than are the
		children of *light*.
23 54		It was Preparation Day and the sabbath was ˹imminent
	8	(lit. *dawning*).
Jn 1 4 X	/2	that life was the *light* of men, [5] a *light* that *shines* in the dark,
5		[a light] that darkness could not overpower.
7 X		[John] came as a witness . . . to speak for the *light*, . . .
8 X		[8] He was not the *light*, only a witness to speak for the
X		*light*.
9 X	/3	The Word was the true *light* that *enlightens* all men; and
		˹he (or: the light) was coming into the world.
3 19 X		though the *light* has come into the world men have shown they
X		prefer darkness to the *light* because their deeds were evil.
20 X		[20] and indeed, everybody who does wrong hates the *light*
21 X		and avoids ˹it (lit. the *light*) . . . [21] but the man who lives
X		by the truth comes out into the *light*,
5 35	2	John was a lamp alight and *shining*, and for a time you were
		content to enjoy the *light* that he gave.
8 12 X		I am the *light* of the world; anyone who follows me . . .
X		will have the *light* of life.
9 5 X		I am the *light* of the world.
11 9		A man can walk in the daytime without stumbling because
10		he has the *light* of this world to see by; [10] but . . . at night
		he stumbles, because there is no *light*
12 35 X		The *light* will be with you only a little longer now. Walk
36 X		while you have the *light*. . . . [36] While you still have the
X		*light*, believe in the *light* and you will become sons of *light*.
46 X		I, the *light*, have come into the world,
Ac 9 3 H		there came a *light* from heaven all round [Saul].
12 7		the angel of the Lord stood there, and ˹the cell was filled with
H		light (lit. a *light* shone in the cell).
13 47		(Is 49 6) I have made you a *light* for the nations,
16 29		The gaoler called for *lights*,
22 6 H		a bright *light* from heaven suddenly shone round me. . . .
9 H		[9] The people with me saw the *light*
11 H		The *light* had been so dazzling that I was blind
26 13 H		I saw a *light* brighter than the sun come down from heaven.
18 Θ		so that [the pagans] may turn from darkness to *light*,
23		as the first to rise from the dead, [the Christ] was to proclaim
X		that *light* now shone for our people and for the pagans too.
27 20		For a number of days both the sun and the stars ˹were
	7	invisible (or: did not *shine*)
Rm 2 19		[If you call yourself a Jew, . . .] if you are convinced you can
		. . . be a *beacon* to those in the dark,
13 12		it will be daylight soon – let us . . . arm ourselves [and appear]
		in [the] *light*.
1 Co 4 5 X	3	the Lord . . . will *light up* all that is hidden in the dark
2 Co 4 4 X	6	to stop ˹them seeing (or: the dawning on them of) the *light*
		shed by the Good News of the glory of Christ,

2 Co	4	6	It is the same God that said, 'Let there be *light* shining out of
		Θ 6	darkness', who has shone in our minds to *radiate the light* of knowledge of God's glory,
	6	14	*Light* and darkness have nothing in common.
	11	14 ⓓ	Satan himself goes disguised as an angel of *light*,
Ep	1	18 ⓓ 3	May [God] *enlighten* the eyes of your mind
	3	9 3	this special grace . . . of ᴿexplaining (lit. *bringing to light*) how the mystery is to be dispensed.
	5	8	now you are *light* in the Lord; be like children of *light*,
		9	[9] for the effects of the *light* are seen in complete goodness and right living and truth.
		13	anything exposed by the *light* will ᴿbe illuminated (or: become visible) [14] and anything ᴿilluminated (or: thus visible) turns
		14 X /10	into *light*. That is why it is said: . . . Christ will *shine* on you.
Ph	2	15 2/5	you will *shine* in the world like *bright stars*
Col	1	12 Θ	to join the saints and with them to inherit the *light*.
1 Th	5	5	you are all sons of *light* and sons of the day:
1 Tm	6	16	[the blessed and only Ruler of all] whose home is in inaccessible *light*,
		Θ	
2 Tm	1	10 3	Christ Jesus . . . has ᴿproclaimed (lit. *brought to light*) life and immortality
Heb	6	4 3	those people who were once *brought into the light*,
	10	32 3	all the sufferings that you had to meet after you *received the light*,
Jm	1	17	all that is good . . . comes down from the Father of all *light*;
		Θ	
1 P	2	9	a people set apart to sing the praises of God out of the darkness into his wonderful *light*.
		Θ	
2 P	1	19	you will be right to depend on prophecy and take it as a *lamp* for *lighting* a way through the dark
		2	
1 Jn	1	5 Θ	God is *light*; there is no darkness in him at all.
		7 Θ	if we live our lives in the *light*, as [God] is in the *light*, we are in union with one another, and the blood of Jesus, his Son, purifies us
	2	8 /2	the night is over and the real *light* is already *shining*.
		9	Anyone who claims to be in the *light* but hates his brother is still in the dark. [10] But anyone who loves his brother is living in the *light*
		10	
Rv	1	16 H 2	[a Son of man,] his face was like the sun *shining* with all its force.
	8	12	a third of the sun and a third of the moon and a third of the stars were blasted, so that the *light* went out of a third of them
		2	
	18	1 H 3	(Ezk 43 2) the earth was *lit up* with [the angel's] glory.
		23 /2	(Jr 25 10) [Babylon,] never again will *shine* the *light* of the lamp,
	21	11 H 5	[Jerusalem] *glittered* like some precious jewel
		23 2	[Jerusalem] did not need the sun or the moon for *light*, since
		Θ 3	it was *lit* by the radiant glory of God and the Lamb was a lighted torch for it. [24] (Is 60 3) The pagan nations will live
		24	
		H	by its *light*
	22	5	they will not need lamp*light* nor sun*light*, because the Lord
		Θ 3	God will be *shining* on them.

2: LANTERNS

Jn	18	3 9	[Judas] brought the cohort to [Gethsemane] with *lanterns* and torches and weapons.

2. SHINE – BRIGHT, MAGNIFICENT – LAMP: *LAMPŌ*

1	*lampas* 9	6	*lamprotēs* 1
3	*lampō* 7	7	*ek-lampō* 1
2	*lampros* 9	4	*peri-lampō* 2
5	*lamprōs* 1		

1: SHINE, LIGHT UP – BRIGHT, SHINING

Mt	5	15	No one lights a lamp to put it under a tub; they put it on the
		3	lamp-stand where it *shines* for everyone in the house.
		16 3	[16] In the same way your light must *shine* in the sight of men,
	13	43 7	the virtuous will *shine* like the sun in the kingdom
	17	2 H 3	[Jesus] was transfigured: his face *shone* like the sun
Lk	2	9 H 4	the glory of the Lord *shone round* [the shepherds].
	17	24 3	as the lightning flashing from one part of heaven *lights up* the other,
Ac	10	30	Cornelius replied, . . . 'I suddenly saw a man in front of me
		H 2	in *shining* robes'.
	12	7 H 3	ᴿthe cell was filled with light (lit. a light *shone* in the cell).
	26	13 H 6	I saw a light *brighter* than the sun come down from heaven.
		H 4	It *shone* brilliantly round me
2 Co	4	6 3	It is the same God that said, 'Let there be light *shining* out of
		Θ 3	darkness', who has *shone* in our minds
Rv	15	6 2	seven angels . . . wearing pure ᴿwhite (lit. *bright*) linen,

Rv	19	8 2	[The Lamb's bride] has been able to dress herself in *dazzling* white linen,
	22	1	the angel showed me the river of life, . . . flowing ᴿcrystal-
		2	clear (lit. as *bright* as crystal)
		16 X 2	I, Jesus, . . . am . . . the *bright* star of the morning.

2: MAGNIFICENT, GORGEOUS, RICH

Lk	16	19 5	a rich man who used to . . . feast *magnificently* every day.
	23	11 2	Herod . . . put a *rich* cloak on [Jesus]
Jm	2	2 2	a man comes into your synagogue, ᴿbeautifully (lit. *magnificently*) dressed . . . and at the same time a poor man comes
		3	in, in shabby clothes, [3] and you take notice of the ᴿwell-
		2	dressed (lit. *magnificently*-dressed) man,
Rv	18	14 2	gone for ever . . . is your life of *magnificence* and ease.

3: LAMP(S), TORCH(ES)

Mt	25	1 <	Ten bridesmaids took their *lamps* and went to meet the
		3 <	bridegroom. . . . [3] the foolish ones did take their *lamps*,
		4 <	but they brought no oil, [4] whereas the sensible ones took
		7 <	flasks of oil as well as their *lamps*.
		8 <	all those bridesmaids . . . trimmed their *lamps*, [8] and the foolish ones said . . . 'Give us some of your oil: our *lamps* are going out.'
Jn	18	3	[Judas] brought the cohort to [the garden] . . . with *lanterns* and *torches*
Ac	20	8	A number of *lamps* were lit in the upstairs room where we were assembled.
Rv	4	5 ●	there were seven flaming *lamps* burning, the seven Spirits of God.
	8	10	a huge star fell from the sky, burning like a ᴿball of fire (lit. *torch*),

3. LAMP – LAMP-STAND: *LYCHNOS*

2 lychnia 12   1 lychnos 14

Mt	5	15	No one lights a *lamp* to put it under a tub; they put it on the
		2	*lamp-stand* where it shines
	6	22	The *lamp* of the body is the eye.
Mk	4	21	Would you bring in a *lamp* to put it under a tub . . . ?
		2	Surely you will put it on the *lamp-stand*?
Lk	8	16	No one lights a *lamp* to cover it with a bowl . . . No, he puts
		2	it on a *lamp-stand* so that people may see the light
	11	33	No one lights a *lamp* and puts it in some hidden place . . .
		34 2/	but on the *lamp-stand* . . . [34] The *lamp* of your body is your eye.
		36	as when the *lamp* shines on you with its rays.
	12	35	See that you are dressed for action and have your *lamps* lit.
	15	8	what woman . . . would not, if she lost one [drachma], light a *lamp* . . . and search thoroughly till she found it?
Jn	5	35	John was a *lamp* alight and shining
Heb	9	2 2	the first [compartment of the tent] in which the *lamp-stand* . . . [was] kept,
2 P	1	19	take [prophecy] as a *lamp* for lighting a way through the dark
Rv	1	12 2	I saw seven golden *lamp-stands* [13] and, surrounded by ᴿthem
		13 2	(lit. the *lamp-stands*), a figure like a Son of man,
		20 2	The secret of . . . the seven golden *lamp-stands* is this: . . .
		2	the seven *lamp-stands* are the seven churches
	2	1	Here is the message of the one who . . . lives surrounded
		2	by the seven golden *lamp-stands*:
		5 2	I shall . . . take your *lamp-stand* from its place.
	11	4	[My three witnesses] are the two olive trees and the two
		2	ᴿlamps (or: *lamp-stands*) that stand before the Lord of the world.
	18	23	(Jr 25 10) [Babylon,] never again will shine the light of the *lamp*,
	21	23 X	the Lamb was a ᴿlighted torch (or: *lamp*) for [Jerusalem].
	22	5	[the servants of God] will not need *lamp*light or sunlight, because the Lord God will be shining on them.

4. RADIANT LIGHT, DAWN – CLEAR, TRANSPARENT: *AUGAZŌ*

1	*augazō* 1	4	*di-augazō* 1
2	*augē* 1	5	*di-augēs* 1
3	*ap-augasma* 1	6	*tēl-augōs* 1

Mk	8	25 6	[the blind man] saw *clearly*;
Ac	20	11 2	[Paul] carried on talking till he left at *daybreak*.
2 Co	4	4	to stop ᴿthem seeing (or: the *dawning* on them of) the light shed by the Good News of the glory of Christ,

Heb	1	3 X	3 [The Son] is the *radiant light* of God's glory and the perfect copy of his nature,
2 P	1	19	4 until the ⌐dawn comes (lit. day *dawns*)
Rv	21	21	5 the main street of the city was pure gold, *transparent* as glass.

5. BRIGHTNESS, LIGHT: *PHENGOS*

phengos 3

Mt	24	29	(Is 13 10) the sun will be darkened, the moon will lose its *brightness*,
Mk	13	24	(Is 13 10) the sun will be darkened, the moon will lose its *brightness*,
Lk	11	33	one . . . puts [a lamp] . . . on the lamp-stand so that people may see the *light*

6. LIGHTNING, FLASH, RAY(S) – BRILLIANT, DAZZLING: *ASTRAPĒ*

1 *astrapē* 9	4 *ex-astraptō* 1
2 *astraptō* 2	3 *peri-astraptō* 2

Mt	24	27	the coming of the Son of Man will be like *lightning* striking in the east and flashing far into the west.
	28	3	[The angel's] face was like *lightning*, his robe white as snow.
Lk	9	29	As [Jesus] prayed, the aspect of his face was changed and his clothing became brilliant as *lightning*.
		H 4	
	10	18	[Jesus said to the seventy-two:] 'I watched Satan fall like *lightning* from heaven.'
	11	36	your whole body . . . will be light entirely, as when the lamp shines on you with its *rays*.
	17	24	/2 as the *lightning flashing* from one part of heaven lights up the other,
	24	4 H 2	two men in *brilliant* clothes suddenly appeared at [the women's] side.
Ac	9	3 H 3	there came a light from heaven *flashing all round* [Saul].
	22	6 H 3	about midday a bright light from heaven suddenly *shone round* me.
Rv	4	5	*Flashes of lightning* were coming from the throne,
	8	5	there came peals of thunder and *flashes of lightning*, and the earth shook.
	11	19	Then came *flashes of lightning*, peals of thunder and an earthquake, and violent hail.
	16	18	there were *flashes of lightning* and peals of thunder and the most violent earthquake

7. DAZZLING(LY): *STILBŌ*

stilbō 1

Mk	9	3 H	[Jesus's] clothes became *dazzlingly* white (ᵛ like snow),

8. GLAMOUR – LUXURY: *LIPAROS*

liparos 1

Rv	18	14	[Babylon,] gone for ever . . . is your life of magnificence and ⌐ease (lit. *glamour*).

SHIP – SAIL

1. Boat, Ship – Sail (to, from, etc.): *ploion*
2. Put out (to sea), Sail (from), Set sail: *an-agō*
3. Drift away (metaphorically): *para-rheō*
4. Ship – Shipwreck: *naus*
  a) Ship-owner – Vessel – Crew, Sailors
  b) Shipwreck

5. Ship's boat: *skaphē*
6. Bows – Stern: *prymna* and *prōra*
7. Rudder: *pēdalion*
8. Anchor: *ankyra*
9. Sail
  1: Foresail: *artemōn*
  2: Mainsail: *histion*

1. BOAT, SHIP – SAIL (TO, FROM, etc.): *PLOION*

2	*pleō*	6	9	*kata-pleō*	1
3	*ploiarion*	6	10	*dia-pleō*	1
1	*ploion*	66	6	*ek-pleō*	3
5	*ploos*	3	7	*hypo-pleō*	2
4	*apo-pleō*	4	11	*para-pleō*	1
8	(*brady-*)*ploeō*	1			

Mt	4	21	[Jesus] saw . . . James . . . and . . . John . . . in their *boat*
		22	leaving the *boat* and their father, they followed him
	8	23	[Jesus] got into the *boat* followed by his disciples
		24	the waves were breaking right over the *boat*.
	9	1	[Jesus] got back in the *boat*, crossed the water and came to his own town.
	13	2	[Jesus] got into a *boat* and sat there.
	14	13	Jesus . . . withdrew by *boat* to a lonely place
		22	he made the disciples get into the *boat*
		24	the *boat*, by now far out on the lake, was battling with a heavy sea,
		29	Peter got out of the *boat* and started walking . . . across the water,
		32	as [Jesus and Peter] got into the *boat* the wind dropped.
		33	The men in the *boat* bowed down before [Jesus]
	15	39	[Jesus] got into the *boat* and went to the district of Magadan.
Mk	1	19	[Jesus] saw James . . . and . . . John . . . in their *boat*,
		20	leaving their father Zebedee in the *boat* . . . they went after [Jesus].
	3	9	3 [Jesus] asked . . . to have a *boat* ready for him because of the crowd.
	4	1	he got into a *boat* on the lake and sat there.
		36	they took [Jesus], just as he was, in the *boat*; and there were other *boats* with him.
		37	the waves were breaking into the *boat* so that the *boat* was almost swamped.
	5	2	no sooner had [Jesus] left the *boat* than a man with an unclean spirit came . . . towards him.
		18	As [Jesus] was getting into the *boat*, the man who had been possessed begged to be allowed to stay with him.
		21	Jesus had crossed again in the *boat* to the other side,
	6	32	So [the apostles and Jesus] went off in a *boat* to a lonely place
		45	[Jesus] made his disciples get into the *boat*
		47	the *boat* was far out on the lake, and [Jesus] was alone on the land.
		51	[Jesus] got into the *boat* with them, and the wind dropped.
		54	No sooner had they stepped out of the *boat* than people . . .
		55	. . . brought the sick
	8	10	getting into the *boat* with his disciples, [Jesus] went to the region of Dalmanutha.
		14	The disciples . . . had only one loaf with them in the *boat*.
Lk	5	2	3 [Jesus] caught sight of two *boats* close to the bank.
		3	[Jesus] got into one of the *boats* – it was Simon's – and . . . taught the crowds from the *boat*.
		7	they signalled to their companions in the other *boat* . . . they filled the two *boats* to sinking point.
		11	bringing their *boats* back to land, they left everything and followed [Jesus].
	8	22	he got into a *boat* with his disciples
		23	as they *sailed* [Jesus] fell asleep.
		26	9 [Jesus and his disciples] *came to land* in the country of the Gerasenes,
		37	Jesus . . . got into the *boat* and went back.
Jn	6	17	[the disciples] got into a *boat* to make for Capernaum
		19	they saw Jesus walking on the lake and coming towards the *boat*.
		21	They were for taking [Jesus] into the *boat*, but in no time the *boat* reached the shore.
		22	3 the crowd . . . saw that only one *boat* had been there, and that Jesus had not got into the *boat* with his disciples,
		23	3 Other *boats*, however, had put in from Tiberias,
		24	3 the people . . . got into those *boats* and crossed to Capernaum
	21	3	[The disciples] went out and got into the *boat* but caught nothing that night.
		6	Throw the net out to starboard of the *boat*
		8	3 The other disciples came on in the *boat*, towing the net
Ac	13	4	[Barnabas and Saul] went down to Seleucia and from there *sailed* to Cyprus.
	14	26	4 [Paul and Barnabas] *sailed* for Antioch,
	15	39	6 Barnabas *sailed off* with Mark to Cyprus.
	18	18	6 Paul . . . *sailed* for Syria,
	20	6	6 We ourselves *left* Philippi *by ship*
		13	We were now to go on ahead by ⌐sea (lit. *ship*), so we set sail for Assos,
		15	4 The next day we *sailed* from [Mitylene] and arrived opposite Chios.
		16	11 Paul had decided to *pass wide* of Ephesus
		38	[The elders of Ephesus] escorted [Paul] to the *ship*.
	21	2	we found a *ship* bound for Phoenicia, so we went on board
		3	2 After sighting Cyprus and leaving it to port, we *sailed* to Syria and put in at Tyre, since the *ship* was to unload her cargo there.

Ac 21	6	after saying good-bye to each other, we went *aboard*
	7	5 The end of our *sea-voyage* from Tyre came when we landed at Ptolemais,
27	1	4 it had been decided that we should *sail* for Italy,
	2	/2 We boarded a *vessel* from Adramyttium ⌐*bound* (lit. *sailing*) for ports on the Asiatic coast,
	4	7 From there we put to sea again . . . we *sailed under the lee* of Cyprus,
	5	10 then *sailed across* the open sea off Cilicia and Pamphylia,
	6	/2 the centurion found an Alexandrian *ship* ⌐*leaving* (lit. *sailing*) for Italy
	7	8/7 For some days we *made* little *headway* . . . so we *sailed under the lee* of Crete
	9	5 *navigation* was already hazardous
	10	5/ this *voyage* will be dangerous . . . [for] the *ship*
	15	The *ship* was caught . . . so we had to . . . let ourselves be driven
	17	They . . . bound cables round the *ship*;
	19	[the sailors] threw the *ship's* gear overboard
	22	There will be no loss of life at all, only of the *ship*.
	24	2 God grants you the safety of all who are *sailing* with you.
	30	When some of the crew tried to escape from the *ship* and
	31	lowered the ship's boat into the sea . . . ³¹ Paul said . . , 'Unless those men stay on *board* you cannot hope to be saved'.
	37	We were in all two hundred and seventy-six souls on [board] that *ship*.
	38	they lightened the *ship* by throwing the corn overboard
	39	[the crew] planned to run the *ship* aground on [the beach]
	44	the rest [got ashore] . . . on pieces of wreckage from the *ship*.
28	11	we set sail in a *ship* that had wintered in the island;
Jm 3	4	think of *ships* . . . the man at the helm can steer them any-where . . . by controlling a tiny rudder.
Rv 8	9	a third of all *ships* were destroyed
18	17	2 All the captains and *seafaring* men . . . will be keeping a safe distance,
	19	[Babylon] has made a fortune for every owner of a sea-going *ship*;

2. PUT OUT (TO SEA), SAIL (FROM), SET SAIL: *AN-AGŌ*

1 *an-agō* 14/23   2 *ep-an-agō* 2/3

Lk 5	3	2 [Jesus] asked [Simon] to *put out* a little from the shore.
	4	2 When [Jesus] had finished speaking he said to Simon, '*Put out* into deep water and pay out your nets for a catch'.
8	22	[Jesus] got into a boat with his disciples . . . they *put out* to sea,
Ac 13	13	Paul and his friends ⌐went by (lit. *put out* to) sea from Paphos to Perga
16	11	*Sailing* from Troas we made a straight run for Samothrace;
18	21	Then [Paul] *sailed* from Ephesus.
20	3	[Paul] was *leaving by ship* for Syria.
	13	We were now to go on ahead by sea, so we *set sail* for Assos,
21	1	When we had . . . *put out* to sea, we set a straight course and arrived at Cos;
	2	we found a ship bound for Phoenicia, so we went on board and *sailed* in her.
27	2	We boarded a vessel from Adramyttium bound for ports on the Asiatic coast, and *put out* to sea;
	4	From [Sidon] we *put out* to sea again . . . we sailed under the lee of Cyprus,
	12	the majority were for *putting out* from there in the hope of wintering at Phoenix
	21	if you had listened to me and not *put out* from Crete,
28	10	when we *sailed* [the inhabitants of Malta] put on board the provisions we needed;
	11	we *set sail* in a ship that had wintered in the island;

3. DRIFT AWAY (METAPHORICALLY): *PARA-RHEŌ*

para-rheō 1

Heb 2	1	We ought . . . to turn our minds more attentively than before to what we have been taught, so that we do not *drift away*.

4. SHIP – SHIPWRECK: *NAUS*

3 *naus*   1   2 *nau-ageō*   2
1 *nautēs* 3   4 *nau-klēros* 1

a) Ship-owner – Vessel – Crew, Sailors

Ac 27	11	the centurion took more notice of the captain and the
	4	*ship's owner* than of what Paul was saying;

Ac 27	27	the *crew* sensed that land of some sort was near.
	30	some of the *crew* tried to escape from the ship
	41	3 the *vessel* ran aground.
Rv 18	17	All the captains and seafaring men, *sailors* . . . will be keeping a safe distance,

b) Shipwreck

2 Co 11	25	2 three times I have been *shipwrecked*
1 Tm 1	19 ○	2 Some people have . . . *wrecked* their faith

5. SHIP'S BOAT: *SKAPHĒ*

skaphē 3

Ac 27	16	We . . . managed with some difficulty to bring the *ship's boat* under control.
	30	the crew . . . lowered the *ship's boat* into the sea
	32	the soldiers cut the *boat's* ropes and let it drop away.

6. BOWS – STERN: *PRYMNA* and *PRŌRA*

2 *prōra* 2   1 *prymna* 3

Mk 4	38	[Jesus] was in the *stern*, his head on the cushion, asleep.
Ac 27	29	[the crew] dropped four anchors from the *stern*
	30	the crew . . . lowered the ship's boat into the sea as though
	2	to lay out anchors from the *bows*,
	41	2/ The *bows* were . . . stuck fast, while the *stern* began to break up

7. RUDDER: *PĒDALION*

pēdalion 2

Ac 27	40	[the crew] loosened the lashings of the *rudders*;
Jm 3	4	the man at the helm can steer [ships] . . . by controlling a tiny *rudder*.

8. ANCHOR: *ANKYRA*

ankyra 4

Ac 27	29	they dropped four *anchors* from the stern
	30	the crew . . . lowered the ship's boat into the sea as though to lay out *anchors* from the bows,
	40	They slipped the *anchors* and left them to the sea,
Heb 6	19 ○	[In hope] we have an *anchor* for our soul,

9. SAIL

1: FORESAIL: *ARTEMŌN*

artemōn 1

Ac 27	40	hoisting the *foresail* to the wind, they headed for the beach.

2: MAINSAIL: *HISTION*

histion 1

Ac 27	17	they floated out the ⌐sea-anchor (or: *mainsail*) and so let themselves drift.

SHOW – REVEAL – OPEN

---

1. **Show, Let (a person) see, Demonstrate – Point (to, out), Publicity – Warn, Tell, Make clear:** *deiknymi*
2. **Show oneself, Appear, Reveal – Open(ly), (Make) Known, Manifest – Clear, Plain, (Be) Seen:** *phainō*
   a) applied to God, Christ, the works of God
   b) applied to various
   c) Ghost
   d) (Be) Invisible

3. **Disclose, Show – Clear – Uncertain:** *dēloō*
   1: Disclose, Show, Indicate – Tell – Clear, Obvious, Evident
   2: Uncertain – Unmarked – Untrustworthy
4. **Open, Exposed:** *trachēlizō*
5. **Openly, Plainly, (in) Public – Explicitly, Expressly:** *par-rhēsia*
6. **Divine Revelation, (the Spirit) Reveals, (God) Warns – (an angel)**

Directs, Instructs: *chrēmatizō*
7. Uncover, Unveil – Reveal, Revela-tion – Appear: *apo-kalyptō*
1: Uncover, Lay bare – Unveil, Lift (a veil)
2: Reveal, Revelation, Make known – Appear – Show, Make clear
8. to Open
1: to Open: *an-oigō*

a) to Open (a thing) – (Be) Opened, Wide open
b) (The heavens, the sky) Opens – (Heaven) Opened
c) Open (eyes, ears, mouth, heart, mind) – (Be) Opened
d) Open (a book, a seal)
e) to Open = to Explain
f) Open (the womb)
2: Unroll, Open (a scroll, a book): *ana-ptyssō*

---

1. SHOW, LET (A PERSON) SEE, DEMONSTRATE – POINT (TO, OUT), PUBLICITY – WARN, TELL, MAKE CLEAR: *DEIKNYMI*

1	*deiknymi, deiknuō* 33	2	*en-deiknymi*	11
7	*deigmatizō*	2	11 *en-deigma*	1
8	*ana-deiknymi*	2	6 *en-deixis*	4
9	*ana-deixis*	1	3 *epi-deiknymi*	7
5	*apo-deiknymi*	4	4 *hypo-deiknymi*	6
10	*apo-deixis*	1		

Mt 1 19   7 Joseph . . . wanting to spare [Mary] *publicity*,
  3 7   4 who *warned* you to fly from the retribution that is coming?
  4 8 Ⓓ the devil *showed* [Jesus] all the kingdoms of the world
  8 4   [Jesus to the leper:] go and *show* yourself to the priest
 16 1 X 3 The Pharisees . . . asked if he would *show* them a sign
 21 X   Jesus began to *make it clear* to his disciples that he was des-tined to . . . suffer
 22 19   3 *Let me see* the money you pay the tax with.
 24 1   3 [Jesus's] disciples came up to *draw* his *attention to* the Temple buildings.
Mk 1 44   go and *show* yourself to the priest,
 14 15   [The owner of the house] will *show* you a large upper room
Lk 1 80   9 until the day [John the Baptist] *appeared openly* to Israel.
 3 7   4 who *warned* you to fly from the retribution that is coming?
 4 5 Ⓓ the devil *showed* [Jesus] . . . all the kingdoms of the world
 5 14   go and *show* yourself to the priest
 6 47 X 4 I will *show* you what he is like.
 10 1 X 8 the Lord *appointed* seventy-two others
 12 5 X 4 I will ⌜*tell* (or: *warn*) you whom to fear:
 17 14   3 Go and *show* yourselves to the priests.
 20 24   *Show* me a denarius.
 22 12   The man will *show* you a large upper room
 24 40 X ᵛ. . . he *showed* them his hands and feet⌝
Jn 2 18 X   What sign can you *show* us to justify what you have done?
 5 20 Θ the Father loves the Son and *shows* him everything he does
   Θ himself, and he will *show* him even greater things
 10 32 X I have *done* many good works for you *to see*,
 14 8 X Philip said, 'Lord, *let us see* the Father . . .' ⁹ . . . Jesus
 9 X said to him, '. . . how can you say, "*Let us see* the Father"?'
 20 20 X [Jesus] *showed* them his hands and his side.
Ac 1 24 Θ 8 *show* us . . . which of these two you have chosen
 2 22 Θ 5 Jesus . . . was a man ⌜ commended (lit. *pointed out*) to you by God by the miracles
 7 3 Θ [God to Abraham:] go to the land I will *show* you.
 9 16 X 4 I myself will *show* [Saul] how much he himself must suffer
 39   3 *showing* [Peter] tunics and other clothes Dorcas had made
 10 28 Θ God has *made it clear* to me that I must not call anyone profane
 18 28   3 [Apollos] *demonstrated* . . . that Jesus was the Christ.
 20 35   4 I did this to *show* you that this is how we must exert ourselves
 25 7   5 accusations which [the Jews] were unable to *substantiate*
Rm 2 15   2 [The pagans] can *point to* the substance of the Law engraved on their hearts
 3 25 Θ 6/6 God *makes* his justice *known*; . . . ²⁶ . . . by *showing* posi-
 26   tively that he is just,
 9 17 Θ 2 (Ex 9 16) I raised you up, to use you as a means of *showing* my power
 22 Θ 2 although God is ready to *show* his anger
1 Co 2 4 10 in my speeches . . . [there was] only a *demonstration* of the power of the Spirit.
 4 9 Θ 5 God has *put* us apostles [*on*] at the end of his *parade*,
 12 31   I am going to *show* you a way that is better than any of them.
2 Co 8 24   So then, in front of all the churches, ⌜give them a proof
 2/6 (lit. *show* them a *demonstration*) of your love,
Ep 2 7 Θ 2 This was to *show* . . . how infinitely rich he is in grace.
Ph 1 28   6 This would be the *sure sign* that they will lose
Col 2 15 Θ 7 he got rid of the Sovereignties . . . and *paraded* them in public,
2 Th 1 5 11 It all *shows* that God's judgement is just,
 2 4   5 the Enemy, the one who . . . ⌜claims that he is (lit. *publicises* himself as being) God.
1 Tm 1 16   if mercy has been shown to me, it is because Jesus Christ
 X 2 meant to *make* me the greatest *evidence* of his . . . patience
 6 15 Θ [Jesus Christ] will *be revealed* by God, the blessed and only Ruler of all,
2 Tm 4 14   Alexander the coppersmith has ⌜*done* me a lot of harm (or:
 2 *displayed* a lot of spitefulness towards me);

Tt 2 10 2 [the slaves] must *show* complete honesty at all times,
 3 2 2 [remind them] to ⌜be . . . polite (lit. *show* politeness) to all
Heb 6 10 2 the love that you have *demonstrated* for [God's] name
 11 2 you should go on *showing* the same earnestness to the end,
 17   God wanted to ⌜make the heirs to the promise thoroughly
 Θ 3 realise (lit. *show* the heirs to the promise) that his purpose was unalterable,
 8 5 Θ (Ex 25 40) make everything according to the pattern *shown* you on the mountain.
Jm 2 18   I will prove to you that I have faith by *showing* you my good deeds – now you prove to me that you have faith without any good deeds to *show*.
 3 13   If there are any wise . . . men among you, let them *show* it by their good lives,
Rv 1 1 Θ so that he could *tell* his servants *about* the things which are now to take place very soon;
 4 1   Come up here: I will *show* you what is to come in the future.
 17 1   Come here and I will *show* you the punishment given to the famous prostitute
 21 9   Come here and I will *show* you the bride that the Lamb has married.
 10   he . . . *showed* me Jerusalem, the holy city,
 22 1   the angel *showed* me the river of life,
 6   the Lord . . . has sent his angel to *reveal* to his servants what is soon to take place.
 8   I knelt at the feet of the angel who had *shown* [these things] to me,

---

2. SHOW ONESELF, APPEAR, REVEAL – OPEN(LY), (MAKE) KNOWN, MANIFEST – CLEAR, PLAIN, (BE) SEEN: *PHAINŌ*

2	*phainō*	22/31	14 *a-phanēs*	1
1	*phaneroō*	49	15 *a-phantos*	1
3	*phaneros*	18	9 *ana-phainō*	2
6	*phanerōs*	3	10 *em-phanēs*	2
7	*phanerōsis*	2	4 *em-phanizō*	10
12	*phantasia*	1	11 *epi-phainō*	3/4
8	*phantasma*	2	5 *epi-phaneia*	6
13	*phantazomai*	1	16 *epi-phanēs*	1

a) applied to God, Christ, the works of God

Θ = God is revealed, made known
X = Christ appears, is revealed: his Appearing

Mt 1 20 2 the angel of the Lord *appeared* to [Joseph] in a dream
 2 7   [Herod] asked [the wise men] the exact date on which the
 2 star had *appeared*,
 13 2 the angel of the Lord *appeared* to Joseph in a dream
 19 2 the angel of the Lord *appeared* in a dream to Joseph in Egypt
 12 16 X 3 [Jesus cured them,] but warned them not to make him *known*.
 24 30 X 2 then the sign of the Son of Man will *appear* in heaven;
Mk 1 45 X 6 Jesus could no longer go *openly* into any town,
 3 12 X 3 he warned [the unclean spirits] . . . not to make him *known*.
 6 14 X 3 by now [Jesus's] name was *well-known*.
 16 9 X 2 [Jesus] *appeared* first to Mary of Magdala
 12 X [Jesus] *showed himself* under another form to two of them
 14 X he *showed himself* to the Eleven themselves while they were at table.
Lk 19 11 9 the kingdom of God was going to *show itself* then and there.
Jn 1 31 X it was to *reveal* [Jesus] to Israel that I came
 2 11 X He *let* his glory *be seen*, and his disciples believed in him.
 7 4 X since you are doing all this, you should *let* the whole world *see*.
 10 X he went [to the festival] . . . but quite privately, ⌜without
 6 *drawing attention to* himself (or: *not openly*).
 9 3 Θ he was born blind so that the works of God might *be displayed* in him.
 14 21 X 4 I shall . . . *show myself* to [anybody who receives my com-mandments]
 22 X 4 Do you intend to *show yourself* to us and not to the world?
 17 6 Θ I have *made* your name *known* to the men
 21 1 X Jesus *showed himself* again to the disciples . . . and ⌜it happened like this (lit. this is how he *revealed himself*):
 14 X This was the third time that Jesus *showed himself* to the disciples
Ac 2 20 16 (Jl 3 4 G) the great (§ and all-*revealing*) Day of the Lord
 10 3 6 [Cornelius] had a vision in which he *distinctly* saw the angel of God come into his house
 40 X 10 God raised [Jesus] to life and allowed him to *be seen*,
Rm 1 19 3 what can be known about God is *perfectly plain* to [men] since God himself has *made it plain*.
 3 21 Θ God's justice . . . has now *been revealed* outside the Law,
 10 20 Θ 10 (Is 65 1) I . . . have *revealed myself* to those who did not consult me;
 16 26 [the revelation of a mystery] now so *clear* that it must be broadcast to pagans
1 Co 12 7 7 The particular way in which the Spirit is ⌜given (lit. *manifested*) to each person is for a good purpose.

2 Co 2 14		God who . . . through us is ⌐spreading (lit. *revealing*) the knowledge of himself, like a sweet smell, everywhere.
4 2	7	we commend ourselves . . . by *stating* the truth *openly*
10 X		so that the life of Jesus . . . may always be *seen* in our body.
11 X		so that in our mortal flesh the life of Jesus . . . may be *openly shown.*
Col 1 26 X		the message which was a mystery . . . has now been *revealed* to his saints.
3 4 X		when Christ is *revealed* – and he is your life – you too will be *revealed* in all your glory with him.
4 4 X		pray that I may *proclaim* [the mystery of Christ] as *clearly* as I ought.
2 Th 2 8		The Lord . . . will annihilate [the Rebel] with his [glorious] *appearance* at his coming.
X 5		
1 Tm 3 16 X		He was *made visible* in the flesh,
6 14		[I put to you the duty] of doing all that you have been told
X 5		. . . until the *Appearing* of our Lord Jesus Christ,
2 Tm 1 10 X /5		[this grace of God] has only been *revealed* by the *Appearing* of our saviour Christ Jesus.
4 1 X 5		I put this duty to you, in the name of his *Appearing* and of his kingdom:
8 X 5		all those who have longed for his *Appearing.*
Tt 1 3		at the appointed time [God] *revealed* his decision,
2 11	11	God's grace has *been revealed*, and it has made salvation possible for the whole human race
13 X 5		we are waiting in hope for . . . the *Appearing* of the glory of our great God and saviour Christ Jesus.
3 4	11	when the kindness and love of God . . . *were revealed,*
Heb 9 24 X	4	Christ had entered . . . heaven itself, so that he could *appear* in the actual presence of God on our behalf.
26 X		[Christ] has *made his appearance* . . . to do away with sin by sacrificing himself.
12 21 ⊖	13	The whole *scene* was so terrible that Moses said:
1 P˙ 1 20 X		[Christ] has been *revealed* only in our time, the end of the ages, for your sake.
5 4 X		When the chief shepherd *appears*, you will be given the crown of unfading glory.
1 Jn 1 2 X		That life was *made visible* . . . and we are . . . telling you of
X		the eternal life which . . . has been *made visible* to us.
2 28 X		Live in Christ . . . so that if he *appears*, we may have full confidence,
3 2		what we are to be in the future has not yet been *revealed*; all we know is, that when it is *revealed* we shall be like him
5 X		he *appeared* in order to abolish sin;
8		It was to undo all that the devil has done that the Son of
X		God *appeared.*
10	3	In this way we *distinguish* the children of God from the children of the devil:
4 9		God's love for us was *revealed* when God sent into the world his only Son
Rv 15 4		[Lord,] all the pagans will . . . adore you for the many acts of justice you have *shown.*

b) applied to various

Mt 6 5		the hypocrites . . . love to say their prayers standing up in
	2	the synagogues . . . ⌐for people to see them (lit. to *be seen* by people).
16	2	they pull long faces to ⌐let men know (lit. *make it known* to men that) they are fasting.
18	2	so that ⌐no one will know (lit. it is not *known* to anybody that) you are fasting except your Father
9 33	2	Nothing like this has ever *been seen* in Israel
13 26 <	2	the darnel *appeared* as well.
23 27	2	whitewashed tombs that ⌐look (lit. *appear* to be) handsome on the outside,
28	2	In the same way you *appear* to people from the outside like good honest men,
27 53		[the bodies of many holy men] came out of the tombs . . .
	4	and *appeared* to a number of people.
Mk 4 22		there is nothing hidden but it must be *disclosed*, nothing
	3	kept secret except to be *brought to light.*
14 64		You heard the blasphemy. ⌐What is your finding (lit. How
	2	does it *appear* to you)?
Lk 8 17	3	nothing is hidden but it will be made *clear*, nothing secret
	3	but it will be known and *brought to light.*
9 8	2	others [were saying] that Elijah had *reappeared*,
24 11	2	this story of theirs *seemed* pure nonsense,
Jn 3 21		the man who lives by the truth comes out into the light, so that it may be *plainly seen* that what he does is done in God.
Ac 4 16	3	It is *obvious* to everybody in Jerusalem that a miracle has been worked through [Peter and John] in public,
7 13	3	Joseph *made himself known* to his brothers, and told Pharaoh about his family.
21 3 ○	9	⌐After sighting Cyprus (lit. After Cyprus *appeared*)
23 15	4	⌐apply to the tribune (lit. *make it plain* to the tribune that he should) bring [Paul] down to you,
22	4	Tell no one that you have ⌐given (lit. *revealed* to) me this information.

Ac 24 1		[the high priest and some elders] ⌐laid information (lit.
	4	*appeared*) against Paul before the governor.
25 2		leaders of the Jews ⌐informed [Festus] of the case (lit.
	4	*appeared* before him) against Paul,
15		the chief priests and elders of the Jews ⌐laid information
	4	(lit. *appeared*) against [Paul],
23	12	Agrippa and Bernice arrived in great ⌐state (lit. *show*)
27 20	11	For a number of days both the sun and the stars ⌐were *invisible* (or: did not shine)
Rm 2 28	3	To be a Jew is not just to ⌐look like (lit. *appear*) a Jew, and circumcision is more than a physical ⌐operation (lit.
	3	*appearance*)
7 13	2	sin, to *show itself* in its true colours, used that good thing to kill me;
1 Co 3 13	3	the work of each builder is going to be *clearly revealed*
4 5		the Lord . . . will light up all that is hidden in the dark and *reveal* the secret intentions of men's hearts.
11 19	3	there must no doubt be separate groups among you, to *distinguish* those who are to be trusted.
14 25	3	[an unbeliever] would find his secret thoughts *laid bare*,
2 Co 3 3		it is *plain* that you are a letter from Christ, drawn up by us,
5 10		the truth about us will be *brought out* in the law court of Christ,
11		⌐God knows us for what we really are (lit. We are *clearly revealed* to God), and I hope that in your consciences you *know* us too.
7 12		it was to *make* ⌐you realise (lit. *plain*) . . . your own concern for us.
11 6		surely we have *made* this *plain*, speaking on every subject in front of all of you.
13 7	2	not that we want to *appear* as the ones who have been successful
Ga 5 19	3	When self-indulgence is at work the results are *obvious*:
Ep 3 9		[I, Paul have been entrusted with this special grace] of
	2	*explaining* how the mystery is to be dispensed.
5 13		anything exposed by the light will ⌐be illuminated (or: become *visible*) [14] and anything ⌐illuminated (or: thus
14		*visible*) turns into light.
Ph 1 13	3	My chains, in Christ, have become *famous*
1 Tm 4 15	3	⌐everyone will be able to see (lit. it will be *clear* to all) how you are advancing.
Heb 9 8		⌐no one has the right to go into the sanctuary (lit. the way into the sanctuary is not *open*) as long as the outer tent remains standing;
11 3	2	no *apparent* cause can account for the things we can see.
14	4	People who use such terms about themselves *make it quite plain* that they are in search of their real homeland.
Jm 4 14	2	you are no more than a mist that ⌐is here (lit. *appears*) for a little while and then disappears.
1 P 4 18		(Pr 11 31 G) If it is hard for a good man to be saved, ⌐what will happen to the wicked and to sinners (lit. where will
	2	the wicked and sinners *appear*)?
1 Jn 2 19		[the rivals of Christ] left us, ⌐to prove (lit. necessarily *showing*) that not one of them ever belonged to us.
3 10	3	In this way we *distinguish* the children of God from the children of the devil:
Rv 3 18		buy . . . white robes . . . ⌐and cover your shameful nakedness (lit. so that your shameful nakedness is not *revealed*),

c) Ghost

Mt 14 26	8	the disciples saw him walking on the lake . . . 'It is a *ghost*' they said,
Mk 6 49		when [the disciples] saw him walking on the lake they thought
	8	it was a *ghost*

d) (Be) Invisible

Lk 24 31		[the apostles] recognised him; but he had ⌐vanished from
X 15		(lit. become *invisible* to) their sight.
Heb 4 13	14	No created thing can ⌐hide from (lit. remain *invisible* to) [the word of God];

3. DISCLOSE, SHOW – CLEAR – UNCERTAIN: *DĒLOŌ*

1	*dēloō* 7	6	*a-dēlotēs* 1
2	*dēlos* 3	7	*kata-dēlos* 1
4	*a-dēlos* 2	8	*ek-dēlos* 1
5	*a-dēlōs* 1	3	*pro-dēlos* 3

1: DISCLOSE, SHOW, INDICATE – TELL – CLEAR, OBVIOUS, EVIDENT

Mt 26 73	2	[Peter,] your accent ⌐gives you away (lit. *makes it obvious*).
1 Co 1 11		what Chloe's people have been *telling* me . . . is . . . that there are serious differences among you.
3 13		the work of each builder is going to be clearly revealed when the day comes and *discloses* it.
15 27	2	this *clearly* cannot include the One who subjected everything to him.

Ga 3 11   2 The Law will *obviously* not justify anyone in the sight of God,
Col 1 8   it was [Epaphras] who *told* us *all about* your love
1 Tm 5 24   3 The faults of some people are *obvious* long before anyone makes any complaint about them,
       25   3 the good that people do can be *obvious*;
2 Tm 3 9   8 their foolishness . . . must become *obvious* to everybody.
Heb 7 14   3 ⌐everyone knows (lit. it is *evident* that) [our Lord] came from Judah,
      15   7 This becomes even more clearly *evident* when there appears a second Melchizedek, who is a priest
      9 8 ⓢ By this, the Holy Spirit *is showing* that no one has the right to go into the sanctuary
    12 27   The words once more *show* that since the things being shaken are created things, they are going to be changed,
1 P 1 11 ⓢ The Spirit of Christ . . . foretold the sufferings of Christ . . . and [the prophets] tried to find out at what time . . . all this was ⌐to be expected (lit. being *disclosed* for).
2 P 1 14 X I know the time for taking off this tent is coming soon, as our Lord Jesus Christ ⌐foretold (lit. *disclosed*) to me.

2: UNCERTAIN – UNMARKED – UNTRUSTWORTHY

Lk 11 44   4 you are like the *unmarked* tombs that men walk on without knowing it!
1 Co 9 26   5 That is how I run, ⌐intent on winning (lit. not *without making a good showing*)
    14 8   4 if ⌐no one can be sure (lit. all are *uncertain*) which call the trumpet has sounded, who will be ready for the attack?
1 Tm 6 17   Warn those who are rich . . . that they are not . . . to set
      6   their hopes on money, which is *untrustworthy*,

4. OPEN, EXPOSED: *TRACHĒLIZŌ*
trachēlizō 1

Heb 4 13   everything is uncovered and *open* to the eyes of the one to whom we must give account of ourselves.

5. OPENLY, PLAINLY, (IN) PUBLIC – EXPLICITLY, EXPRESSLY: *PAR-RHĒSIA*
2 rhētōs 1   *1 par-rhēsia 13/31*

Mk 8 32 X   he said all this *quite openly*.
Jn 7 4   if a man wants to be known *openly* he does not do things in secret;
    13   Yet no one spoke about [Jesus] *openly*, for fear of the Jews.
    26 X   And here he is, speaking *freely*,
    10 24 X   If you are the Christ, tell us *plainly*.
    11 14 X   Jesus put it *plainly*, 'Lazarus is dead;'
    54 X   Jesus no longer went about *openly* among the Jews,
    16 25   the hour is coming when I shall . . . tell you about the Father *in plain words*.
      29 X   His disciples said, 'Now you are speaking *plainly*'
    18 20 X   I have spoken *openly* for all the world to hear;
Ac 2 29   Brothers, ⌐no one can deny (lit. I can confidently state, or: I can state *plainly*) that . . . David . . . ³¹ . . . foresaw and spoke about . . . the resurrection of the Christ:
    28 31   [Paul spent two years] teaching . . . with complete ⌐freedom (or: confidence) and without hindrance from anyone.
Col 2 15 X   he got rid of the Sovereignties and the Powers, and paraded them *in public*,
1 Tm 4 1 ⓢ   2 The Spirit has *explicitly* said that . . . some . . . will desert the faith

6. DIVINE REVELATION, (THE SPIRIT) REVEALS, (GOD) WARNS – (AN ANGEL) DIRECTS, INSTRUCTS: *CHRĒMATIZŌ*
2 chrēmatismos 1   *1 chrēmatizō 7/9*

Mt 2 12   [the Magi] were *warned* in a dream not to go back to Herod,
    22   being *warned* in a dream [Joseph] left for the region of Galilee.
Lk 2 26   It had been *revealed* to [Simeon] by the Holy Spirit that he would not see death until he had set eyes on the Christ
Ac 10 22   Cornelius . . . was *directed* by a holy angel to send for you
Rm 11 4   [Elijah complained to God about Israel's behaviour.] What
      2   did ⌐God (lit. *divine revelation*) say to that?
Heb 8 5   Moses . . . was ⌐*warned* (or: *instructed*) by *God* who said: See that you make everything according to the pattern
    11 7   Noah . . . had been ⌐*warned* (or: *instructed*) by *God* of something that had never been seen before,
    12 25   The people who refused to listen to the *warning* from a voice on earth could not escape their punishment,

7. UNCOVER, UNVEIL – REVEAL, REVELATION – APPEAR: *APO-KALYPTŌ*

3 *ana-kalyptō*	2	1 *apo-kalyptō*	26
2 *apo-kalypsis*	18	4 *a-kata-kalyptos*	2

1: UNCOVER, LAY BARE – UNVEIL, LIFT (A VEIL)

H = Uncover the head, the face

Mt 10 26   Everything that is now covered will be *uncovered*, and everything now hidden will be made clear.
Lk 2 35   so that the secret thoughts of many will be *laid bare*.
    12 2   Everything that is now covered will be *uncovered*,
1 Co 11 5 H   For a woman . . . it is a sign of disrespect to her head if she
      4   prays or prophesies *unveiled*;
    13 H   Ask yourselves if it is fitting for a woman to pray to God
      4   *without a veil*;
2 Co 3 14   3 a veil never *lifted*, since Christ alone can remove it.
    18 H   3 we, with our *unveiled* faces reflecting like mirrors the brightness of the Lord,

2: REVEAL, REVELATION, MAKE KNOWN – APPEAR – SHOW, MAKE CLEAR

Mt 11 25   I bless you, Father . . . for hiding these things from the learned . . . and *revealing* them to mere children.
    27   no one knows the Father except the Son and those to whom the Son chooses to *reveal* him.
    16 17   it was not flesh and blood that *revealed* this to you but my Father in heaven.
Lk 2 32   2 a light ⌐to enlighten (lit. for the *revelation* to) the pagans
    10 21   I bless you, Father . . . for hiding these things from the learned . . . and *revealing* them to mere children.
    22   no one knows . . . who the Father is except the Son and those to whom the Son chooses to *reveal* him.
    17 30   It will be the same when the day comes for the Son of Man to be *revealed*.
Jn 12 38   (Is 53 1) to whom has the power of the Lord been *revealed*?
Rm 1 17   it *shows* how faith leads to faith,
    18   The anger of God is being *revealed* from heaven against all . . . impiety
    2 5   that day of anger when [God's] just judgement will be
      2   *made known*.
    8 18   the glory, as yet *unrevealed*, which is waiting for us.
    19   2 The whole creation is eagerly waiting for God to *reveal* his sons.
    16 25   2 I proclaim Jesus Christ, the *revelation* of a mystery kept secret for endless ages, ²⁶ but now . . . clear
1 Co 1 7   2 you are waiting for our Lord Jesus Christ to be *revealed*;
    2 10   the very things that God has *revealed* to us through the Spirit,
    3 13   That day will *reveal* [the work of each builder] with fire, and the fire will test the quality
    14 6   2 what use shall I be if all my talking *reveals* nothing new . . .?
    26   2 At all your meetings, let everyone be ready with a psalm or a sermon or a *revelation*,
    30   2 If one of the listeners receives a *revelation*, then the man who is already speaking should stop.
2 Co 12 1   2 I will move on to the visions and *revelations* I have had from the Lord.
    7   2 In view of the extraordinary nature of these *revelations*, to stop me from getting too proud I was given a thorn in the flesh,
Ga 1 12   [the Good News I preached] is something I learnt only
      2   through a *revelation* of Jesus Christ.
    16   [God chose] to *reveal* his Son in me,
    2 2   2 I went [to Jerusalem] as the result of a *revelation*,
    3 23   Before faith came, we . . . were being looked after till faith was *revealed*.
Ep 1 17   May the God of our Lord Jesus Christ . . . give you . . .
      2   perception of what is *revealed*,
    3 3   2 it was by a *revelation* that I was given the knowledge of the mystery,
    5   This mystery . . . has now been *revealed* through the Spirit to his holy apostles and prophets
Ph 3 15   If there is some point on which you see things differently, God will *make* it *clear* to you;
2 Th 1 7   2 when the Lord Jesus *appears* from heaven
    2 3   [The Day of the Lord] cannot happen until . . . the Rebel, the Lost One, has *appeared*.
    6   you know . . . what is still holding [the Rebel] back from *appearing* before his appointed time.
    8   [the one who is holding Rebellion back has first to be removed] before the Rebel *appears* openly.
1 P 1 5   the salvation which has been prepared is *revealed* at the end of time.
    7   2 when Jesus Christ is *revealed*, your faith will have been tested

1 P	1 12	It was *revealed* to [the prophets] that the news they brought . . . was for you and not for themselves.
	13	2 the grace that will be given you when Jesus Christ is *revealed*.
	4 13	you will enjoy a much greater gladness when [Christ's] glory 2 is *revealed*.
	5 1	I have a share in the glory that is to be *revealed*.
Rv	1 1	2 This is the *revelation* given by God to Jesus Christ

8. TO OPEN

1: TO OPEN: *AN-OIGŌ*

1 *an-oigō* 78   2 *di-an-oigō* 8
3 *an-oixis* 1

a) to Open (a thing) – (Be) Opened, Wide open

Mt	2 11	*opening* their treasures, [the Magi] offered [the child Jesus] gifts of gold
	7 7	knock, and the door will be *opened* to you.
	8	the one who knocks will always have the door *opened* to him.
	25 11 <	The other bridesmaids . . . said 'open the door for us.'
	27 52	the tombs *opened*
Lk	11 9	knock, and the door will be *opened* to you.
	10	the one who knocks will always have the door *opened* to him.
	12 36 <	Be like men waiting for their master . . . ready to *open* the door
	13 25 <	you may find yourself knocking on the door, saying, 'Lord, *open* to us'
Jn	10 3 <	the gatekeeper ⌐lets [the shepherd] in (lit. *opens* [the gate] to [the shepherd]),
Ac	5 19	at night the angel of the Lord *opened* the prison gates
	23	when we ⌐unlocked (lit. *opened*) the door we found no one inside.
	12 10	the iron gate . . . *opened* of its own accord;
	14	instead of *opening* the door, [the servant] ran inside
	16	they *opened* the door and were amazed to see that it really was Peter himself.
	14 27 Θ	[God] had *opened* the door of faith to the pagans.
	16 26	All the doors *flew open*
	27	When the gaoler . . . saw the doors *wide open* he drew his sword
Rm	3 13	(Ps 5 10) Their throats are *yawning* graves;
1 Co	16 9	[at Ephesus] a big and important door has *opened* for my work
2 Co	2 12	the door was *wide open* for my work [in Troas] in the Lord,
Col	4 3 Θ	asking God to ⌐show us opportunities for (lit. *open* a door for our) announcing the message
Rv	3 7 X	when he *opens*, nobody can close, and when he closes, nobody can *open*:
	8 X	I have *opened* in front of you a door that nobody will be able to close
	20	I am standing at the door, knocking. If one of you . . . *opens* the door, I will come in to share his meal,
	4 1	in my vision I saw a door *open* in heaven
	9 2	[A star had fallen from heaven and he was given the key to the shaft.] When he ⌐unlocked (lit. *opened*) the shaft of the Abyss, smoke poured up
	11 19	[The seventh angel blew his trumpet.] Then the sanctuary of God in heaven *opened*,
	15 5	the sanctuary . . . *opened* in heaven,

b) (The heavens, the sky) Opens – (Heaven) Opened

Mt	3 16	As soon as Jesus was baptised . . . the heavens *opened* and he saw the Spirit of God
Lk	3 21	while Jesus after his . . . baptism was at prayer, heaven *opened*
Jn	1 51	you will see heaven [laid] *open* and, above the Son of Man, the angels of God ascending and descending.
Ac	7 56	2 'I can see heaven *thrown open*' [Stephen] said
	10 11	[Peter] saw heaven [thrown] *open* and something like a big sheet being let down
Rv	19 11	I saw heaven *open*, and a white horse appear;

c) Open (eyes, ears, mouth, heart, mind) – (Be) Opened

4 *ephphatha* 1

Mt	5 2 X	Then he ⌐began (lit. *opened* his mouth) to speak.
	9 30 X	[Jesus touched the eyes of the two blind men.] And their ⌐sight returned (lit. eyes were *opened*).
	13 35 X	(Ps 78 2) I will *speak* (lit. *open* my mouth) to you in parables
	17 27	take the first fish . . . *open* its mouth
	20 33 X	Lord, let us have our ⌐sight back (lit. eyes *opened*).
Mk	7 34 X	4 [Jesus] said to [the deaf man], '*Ephphatha*', that is, 'Be *opened*'. 35 And his ears were *opened*,
	35 X 2/	

Lk	1 64	[Zechariah's] ⌐power of speech returned (lit. mouth [and his tongue were] *opened*)
	24 31	2 [At table Jesus took the bread.] And their eyes were *opened* and they recognised him;
	45 X	2 [Jesus] *opened* their minds to understand the scriptures,
Jn	9 10 X	they said to [the man born blind], 'Then how do your eyes come to be *open*?'
	14 X	It had been a sabbath day when Jesus . . . *opened* the man's eyes,
	17 X	What have you to say about him . . . now that he has *opened* your eyes?
	21	we don't know . . . who *opened* his eyes.
	26 X	How did he *open* your eyes?
	30 X	Now here is an astonishing thing! He has *opened* my eyes, and you don't know where he comes from! . . . 32 Ever since the world began it is unheard of for anyone to *open* the eyes of a man who was born blind;
	32	
	10 21 D	could a devil *open* the eyes of the blind?
	11 37 X	He *opened* the eyes of the blind man,
Ac	8 32 X	(Is 53 7) like a lamb that is dumb . . . he never *opens* his mouth.
	35	Philip ⌐proceeded to explain (lit. *opened* his mouth and explained) the Good News
	9 8	even with his eyes *wide open* [Saul] could see nothing
	40	Peter . . . said, 'Tabitha, stand up'. She *opened* her eyes,
	10 34	Peter ⌐addressed (lit. *opened* his mouth and spoke to) them:
	16 14 Θ? 2	the Lord *opened* [Lydia's] heart to accept what Paul was saying.
	18 14	Before Paul could *open* his mouth, Gallio said
	26 18	[I am sending you to the pagans] to *open* their eyes, so that they may turn from darkness to light,
2 Co	6 11	Corinthians, ⌐we have spoken (lit. our mouths have been *opened*) to you very frankly;
Ep	6 19	3 pray for me to be given an opportunity to *open* my mouth and speak without fear
Rv	12 16	the earth . . . *opened* its mouth and swallowed the river
	13 6	[the beast] ⌐mouthed its (lit. *opened* its mouth in) blasphemies against God,

d) Open (a book, a seal)

Lk	4 17 X	ᵛ *Unrolling* (G *Opening*) the scroll [of the prophet Isaiah] he found the place
Rv	5 2	Is there anyone worthy to *open* the scroll and break the seals
	3	there was no one . . . who was able to *open* the scroll and read it.
	4	there was nobody fit to *open* the scroll and read it,
	5 X	the Lion of the tribe of Judah . . . will *open* the scroll and the seven seals of.
	9 X	You are worthy to take the scroll and ⌐break (lit. *open*) the seals of it,
	6 1 X	I saw the Lamb ⌐break (lit. *open*) one of the seven seals . . .
	3 X	3 When he ⌐broke (lit. *opened*) the second seal, I heard the second animal shout . . . 5 When he ⌐broke (lit. *opened*) the third seal, I heard the third animal shout . . . 7 When he ⌐broke (lit. *opened*) the fourth seal, I heard the voice of the fourth animal . . . 9 When he ⌐broke (lit. *opened*) the fifth seal, I saw underneath the altar . . . 12 when he ⌐broke (lit. *opened*) the sixth seal, there was a violent earthquake
	5 X	
	7 X	
	9	
	12 X	
	X	
	8 1 X	The Lamb then ⌐broke (lit. *opened*) the seventh seal,
	10 2	In his hand [the angel] had a small scroll, ⌐unrolled (lit. *open*);
	8	take that *open* scroll out of the hand of the angel
	20 12	the book of life was *opened*, and other books *opened*

e) to Open = to Explain

Lk	24 32 X	2 Did not our hearts burn within us as he . . . *explained* the scriptures to us?
Ac	17 3	[Paul developed the arguments from scripture for the Jews,] 2 *explaining* . . . how it was ordained that the Christ should suffer

f) Open (the womb)

Lk	2 23	2 (Ex 13 2) Every ⌐first born male (lit. male [child] that *opens* the womb) must be consecrated to the Lord

2: UNROLL, OPEN (A SCROLL, A BOOK): *ANA-PTYSSŌ*

ana-ptyssō 1

Lk	4 17 X	ᵛ *Unrolling* (G *Opening*) the scroll [of the prophet Isaiah] he found the place

SHUT – CLOSED

1. Shut, Close, Lock – Key: *kleiō*
  a) Key
  b) Shut, Close (a door) – Shut, Locked
  c) (Heaven is) Shut – Lock up (the sky)
  d) Close, Shut up (a person's heart)

2. Shut, Close (a person's eyes): *kam-muō*
3. Keep Shut – Fence, Hedge: *phrassō*
  a) Keep shut, (Be) Closed to
  b) Fence, Hedgerow, Hedge
4. to Stop (a person's ears): *syn-echō*

1. SHUT, CLOSE, LOCK – KEY: *KLEIŌ*

1 *kleiō* 16	3 *apo-kleiō* 1
2 *kleis* 6	

a) Key

Mt 16 19	2	I will give you the *keys* of the kingdom of heaven: whatever you bind on earth shall be considered bound in heaven;
Lk 11 52	2	Alas for you lawyers who have taken away the *key* of knowledge.
Rv 1 18	2	I hold the *keys* of death and of the underworld.
3 7	2	Here is the message of the holy and faithful one who has the *key* of David,
9 1	2	the fifth angel . . . was given the *key* to the shaft leading down to the Abyss.
20 1	2	I saw an angel come down from heaven with the *key* of the Abyss

b) Shut, Close (a door) – Shut up, Locked

Mt 6 6		when you pray, go to your private room and . . . *shut* your door,
23 13		scribes and Pharisees, you . . . who *shut up* the kingdom of heaven in men's faces,
25 10 <		[The five bridesmaids] who were ready went in with [the bridegroom] to the wedding hall and the door was *closed*.
Lk 11 7 <		Do not bother me. The door is ⌐bolted (lit. *shut up*) now,
13 25 <	3	Once the master of the house has got up and *locked* the door,
Jn 20 19		the doors were *closed* . . . for fear of the Jews,
26		The doors were *closed*, but Jesus came in
Ac 5 23		We found the gaol securely ⌐locked (lit. *shut up*)
21 30		people . . . seized Paul and dragged him out of the Temple, and the gates were *closed*
Rv 3 7		Here is the message of the holy and faithful one who has the key of David, so that when he opens, nobody can *close*, and when he *closes*, nobody can open.
X 8		I have opened in front of you a door that nobody will be able to *close*.
20 3		[The angel] threw [the dragon] into the Abyss, and *shut* the entrance and sealed it over him,
21 25		The gates of [the city] will never be *shut* by day

c) (Heaven is) Shut – Lock up (the sky)

Lk 4 25		in Elijah's day . . . heaven remained *shut* for three years and six months
Rv 11 6		[My two witnesses] are able to *lock up* the sky so that it does not rain

d) Close, Shut up (a person's heart)

1 Jn 3 17		If a man . . . saw that one of his brothers was in need, but *closed* his heart to him,

2. SHUT, CLOSE (A PERSON'S EYES): *KAM-MUŌ*

kam-muō 2

Mt 13 15	(Is 6 10) the heart of this nation has grown coarse, . . . they have *shut* their eyes,
Ac 28 27	(Is 6 10) the heart of this nation has grown coarse, . . . they have *shut* their eyes,

3. KEEP SHUT – FENCE, HEDGE: *PHRASSŌ*

1 *phragmos* 4   2 *phrassō* 3

a) Keep shut, (Be) Closed to

Rm 3 19	2	all this that the Law says . . . is meant to ⌐silence everyone (lit. *keep* every mouth *shut*)
2 Co 11 10	2	this cause of boasting will never be ⌐taken from (lit. *closed to*) me in the regions of Achaia.

Ep 2 14 ●		Christ has made the two [Jew and pagan] into one and broken down the barrier ⌐which used to keep them apart (lit. *kept shut*),
Heb 11 33	2	[Gideon, . . . Samson, . . .] were men who . . . could *keep* a lion's mouth *shut*,

b) Fence, Hedgerow, Hedge

Mt 21 33 <		a man . . . planted a vineyard; he *fenced* it round,
Mk 12 1 <		A man planted a vineyard; he *fenced* it round,
Lk 14 23 <		Go to the open roads and the *hedgerows*

4. TO STOP (A PERSON'S EARS): *SYN-ECHŌ*

syn-echō 1/12

Ac 7 57	At this all the members of the council *stopped* their ears [with their hands]; then they all rushed at [Stephen],

SIGN

1. Sign – Indicate – Miracle: *sēmeion*
1: Sign (of miraculous power) – Miracle
  a) Signs (and) Portents, Miracles (and) Wonders
  b) Sign (of the power of Jesus, of God) – Miracle

2: Sign (generally), Indicate – Signal, Mark – Outstanding, Notorious
2. Make signs (to), Signal (to), Motion (to): *neuō*
3. Motion, Gesture: *kata-seiō*

1. SIGN – INDICATE – MIRACLE: *SĒMEION*

2	*sēmainō*	6	3	*epi-sēmos* 2
1	*sēmeion*	77	6	*eu-sēmos* 1
4	*sēmeioomai*	1	7	*para-sēmos* 1
5	*a-sēmos*	1	8	*sys-sēmon* 1

1: SIGN (OF MIRACULOUS POWER) – MIRACLE

a) Signs (and) Portents, Miracles (and) Wonders

9 *teras* 16

Mt 24 24	/9	false Christs and false prophets will arise and produce great *signs* and *portents*,
Mk 13 22	9	false Christs and false prophets will arise and produce *signs* and *portents*
Jn 4 48	/9	So you will not believe unless you see *signs* and *portents*!
Ac 2 19	9/	(Jl 3 3) I will display *portents* in heaven above and *signs* on earth below.
22	9/	Jesus the Nazarene was a man commended to you by God by the *miracles* and *portents* and *signs* that God worked through him
43	9/	The many *miracles* and *signs* worked through the apostles made a deep impression on everyone.
4 30	9	by stretching out your hand to heal and to work *miracles* and *marvels* through the name of your holy servant Jesus.
5 12	/9	So many *signs* and *wonders* were worked among the people at the hands of the apostles
6 8	9/	Stephen . . . began to work *miracles* and great *signs* among the people.
7 36	9/	Moses . . , after performing *miracles* and *signs* in Egypt, led them out
14 3	/9	the Lord supported all [Paul and Barnabas] said about his gift of grace, allowing *signs* and *wonders* to be performed by them.
15 12	9	they listened to Barnabas and Paul describing all the *signs* and *wonders* God had worked through them among the pagans.
Rm 15 19		[what I have said and done] by the power of *signs* and *wonders*, by the power of the Holy Spirit.
2 Co 12 12	9	all the things that mark the true apostle . . .: the *signs*, the *marvels*, the miracles.
2 Th 2 9	/9	Satan will set to work: there will be all kinds of miracles and a deceptive show of *signs* and *portents*,
Heb 2 4	/9	God himself confirmed their witness with *signs* and *marvels* and miracles of all kinds,

b) Signs (of the power of Jesus, of God) – Miracle

Mt 12 38	[some of the scribes and Pharisees:] 'Master, . . . we should like to see a *sign* from you.'

Mt 12	39	[Jesus] replied, 'It is an evil and unfaithful generation that asks for a *sign*!'
16	1	to test him [the Pharisees and Sadducees] asked if he would show them a *sign* from heaven.
	3	[Jesus] replied, '. . . You know how to read the face of the sky, but you cannot read the *signs* of the times. ⁴ It is an evil and unfaithful generation that asks for a *sign*!'
	4	
24	3	the disciples came and asked him privately, 'Tell us, . . . what will be the *sign* of your coming and of the end of the world?'
	30	then the *sign* of the Son of Man will appear in heaven;
Mk 8	11	The Pharisees . . . demanded of him a *sign* from heaven, to test him.
	12	Why does this generation demand a *sign*? I tell you solemnly, no *sign* shall be given to this generation.
13	4	[Peter, James, John and Andrew questioned him privately,] 'Tell us, . . . what *sign* will there be that all this is about to be fulfilled?'
16	17	These are the *signs* that will be associated with believers: in my name they will cast out devils; they will have the gift of tongues;
	20	[the apostles] preached everywhere, the Lord . . . confirming the word by the *signs* that accompanied it.
Lk 2	34	You see this child: he is destined . . . to be a *sign* that is rejected
11	16	Others asked him, as a test, for a *sign* from heaven;
	29	This is a wicked generation; it is asking for a *sign*. The only *sign* it will be given is the *sign* of Jonah. ³⁰ For just as Jonah became a *sign* to the Ninevites, so will the Son of Man be to this generation.
	30	
21	7	'Master,' [the disciples] said '. . . what *sign* will there be that [the destruction of the Temple] is about to take place?'
	11	[he said to them,] 'There will be . . . fearful sights and great *signs* from heaven.'
	25	There will be *signs* in the sun and moon and stars;
23	8	Herod . . . was hoping to see some *miracle* worked by [Jesus].
Jn 2	11	This was the first of the *signs* given by Jesus;
	18	The Jews . . . said, 'What *sign* can you show us to justify what you have done?'
	23	many believed in his name when they saw the *signs* that he gave,
3	2	no one could perform the *signs* that you do unless God were with him.
4	54	This was the second *sign* given by Jesus,
6	2	a large crowd followed him, impressed by the *signs* he gave by curing the sick.
	14	The people, seeing this *sign* that he had given, said, 'This really is the prophet who is to come into the world'.
	26	Jesus answered: '. . . you are not looking for me because you have seen the *signs*'
	30	[the people] said, 'What *sign* will you give to show us that we should believe in you?'
7	31	many people . . . were saying, 'When the Christ comes, will he give more *signs* than this man?'
9	16	Others [of the Pharisees] said, 'How could a sinner produce *signs* like these?'
10	41	Many people . . . said, 'John gave no *signs*,'
11	47	[The chief priests and the Pharisees:] 'Here is this man [Jesus] working all these *signs* . . .'
12	18	the crowd . . . had heard that he had given this *sign*.
	37	Though [the crowd] had been present when he gave so many *signs*, they did not believe in him;
20	30	There were many other *signs* that Jesus worked
Ac 4	16	It is obvious to everybody in Jerusalem that a *miracle* has been worked through [Peter] and John in public,
	22	The man who had 'been miraculously cured (lit. in this way been cured as a *sign*)
8	6	The people united in welcoming the message Philip preached, either because they had heard of the *miracles* he worked or because they saw them
	13	Simon . . . was astonished when he saw the *wonders* and great miracles that took place.
Rm 4	11	when [Abraham] was circumcised later it was only as a *sign* and guarantee that the faith he had before . . . justified him.
1 Co 1	22	while the Jews demand *miracles* and the Greeks look for wisdom,
14	22	the strange languages are meant to be a *sign* . . . for unbelievers,
2 Co 12	12	You have seen done among you all the 'things that mark (lit. *signs* of) the true apostle.
Rv 12	1	Now a great *sign* appeared in heaven: a woman, adorned with the sun,
	3	a second *sign* appeared in the sky, a huge red dragon
13	13	[the second beast] worked great *miracles*, . . . ¹⁴ Through the *miracles* which it was allowed to do . . . it was able to win over the people of the world
	14	
15	1	What I saw next, in heaven, was a great and wonderful *sign*: seven angels were bringing the seven plagues
16	14	[the three foul spirits were] able to work *miracles*,

Rv 19	20	the false prophet who had worked *miracles* on the beast's behalf

2: SIGN (GENERALLY), INDICATE – SIGNAL, MARK – OUTSTANDING, NOTORIOUS

Mt 26	48	the traitor had arranged a *sign* with them. 'The one I kiss . . . is the man.'
27	16 3	there was at that time a *notorious* prisoner whose name was Barabbas.
Mk 14	44 8	the traitor had arranged a *signal* with them. 'The one I kiss . . . is the man.'
Lk 2	12	here is a *sign* for you: you will find a baby . . . lying in a manger.
Jn 12	33 2	By these words [Jesus] *indicated* the kind of death he would die.
18	32 2	This was to fulfil the words Jesus had spoken *indicating* the way he was going to die.
21	19 2	In these words [Jesus] *indicated* the kind of death by which Peter would give glory to God.
Ac 11	28 2	Agabus . . . 'predicted (lit. *indicated*) that a famine would spread over the whole empire.
21	39 5	I am a Jew and a citizen of the 'well-known city of (lit. city that is not *unremarkable*) Tarsus
25	27 2	It seems to me pointless to send a prisoner without *indicating* the charges against him.
28	11 7	[the ship] came from Alexandria and her *figurehead* was the Twins.
Rm 16	7 3	[Greetings] to those *outstanding* apostles Andronicus and Junias,
1 Co 14	9 6	if your tongue does not produce *intelligible* speech, how can anyone know what you are saying?
2 Th 3	14 4	If anyone refuses to obey what I have written in this letter, 'take note of (or: *mark*) him
	17	my own handwriting, which is the *mark* of genuineness in every letter;
Rv 1	1 2	This is the revelation given by God to Jesus Christ . . .; he sent his angel to 'make it known (lit. *indicate* it) to his servant John,

2. MAKE SIGNS (TO), SIGNAL (TO), MOTION (TO): *NEUŌ*

1	neuō 2	4 epi-neuō 1
2	dia-neuō 1	5 kata-neuō 1
3	en-neuō 1	

Lk 1	22 2	[Zechariah] could only *make signs* to them, and remained dumb.
	62 3	[They] *made signs* to [John's] father to find out what he wanted him called.
5	7 5	they *signalled* to their companions in the other boat to come and help them;
Jn 13	24	Simon Peter *signed* to [the disciple Jesus loved]
Ac 18	20 4	[The Jews in Ephesus] asked [Paul] to stay longer but he 'declined (lit. did not *make a sign* [of assent]),
24	10	When the governor *motioned* him to speak, Paul answered:

3. MOTION, GESTURE: *KATA-SEIŌ*

kata-seiō 4

Ac 12	17	With a *gesture* of his hand [Peter] stopped them talking,
13	16	Paul . . . 'held up a (lit. *motioned* with his) hand for silence and began to speak:
19	33	[Paul] 'raised (lit. *motioned* with) his hand for silence
21	40	Paul, standing at the top of the steps, *gestured* to the people with his hand.

SING – PLAY MUSIC

1. Sing – Psalm(s) – Hymn(s)
1: Sing – Inspired songs, Spiritual songs, Hymn: *adō*
2: Psalms – Hymns: *psalmos*
a) Chant Psalms – Sing Hymns
b) (the Book of) Psalms
3: (Sing) Psalms, Hymns – Sing praise: *hymneō*

2. Play music

1: Minstrel: *mousikos*
2: Cymbal: *kymbalon*
3: Flute – Play the pipes: *aulos*
4: Harp – Harpist, Harper: *kithara*
5: Trumpet: *salpinx*

3. Dance
1: Dancing: *choros*
2: Dance: *orcheomai*

1. SING – PSALM(S) – HYMN(S)

1: SING – INSPIRED SONGS, SPIRITUAL SONGS, HYMN: *ADŌ*

2 adō 5   1 ōdē 7

Ep	5 19	*Sing* the words and tunes of the psalms and hymns when you 2 are together, and *go on singing* and chanting to the Lord in your hearts,
Col	3 16	2 With gratitude in your hearts *sing* psalms and hymns and *inspired songs* to God;
Rv	5 9	2 [the four animals and the twenty-four elders] *sang* a new *hymn*

	14 3	2/ There in front of the throne they were *singing* a new *hymn*..,
		   a *hymn* that could only be learnt by the hundred and forty-
		   four thousand who had been redeemed

	15 3	[those who had fought against the beast and won] were 2/ *singing* the *hymn* of Moses, the servant of God, and the *song* of the Lamb:

2: PSALMS – HYMNS: *PSALMOS*

2 psallō 5   1 psalmos 7

a) Chant Psalms – Sing Hymns

Rm	15 9	2 (Ps 18 49) For this I shall . . . *sing* to your name.
1 Co	14 15	2 Surely I should . . . *sing* [praises] not only with the spirit but 2 *sing* with the mind as well?
	26	At all your meetings, let everyone be ready with a *psalm* or a sermon or a revelation.
Ep	5 19	Sing the words and tunes of the *psalms* and hymns when you 2 are together, and *go on* singing and *chanting* to the Lord in your hearts,
Col	3 16	With gratitude in your hearts sing *psalms* and hymns and inspired songs to God;
Jm	5 13	2 if anyone is feeling happy, he should *sing* [a psalm].

b) (the Book of) Psalms

Lk	20 42	David himself says in the Book of *Psalms* (Ps 110 1): The Lord said to my Lord:
	24 44	everything written about me in the Law of Moses, in the Prophets and in the *Psalms*, has to be fulfilled.
Ac	1 20	Now in the Book of *Psalms* it says (Ps 69 25): Let his camp be reduced to ruin,
	13 33	As scripture says in the first (ᵛ second) *psalm*: You are my son:

3: (SING) PSALMS, HYMNS – SING PRAISE: *HYMNEŌ*

1 hymneō 4   2 hymnos 2

Mt	26 30 X	After *psalms had been sung* they left for the Mount of Olives.
Mk	14 26 X	After *psalms had been sung* they left for the Mount of Olives.
Ac	16 25	Paul and Silas were praying and *singing* God's praises
Ep	5 19	2 Sing the words and tunes of the psalms and *hymns*
Col	3 16	2 With gratitude in your hearts sing psalms and *hymns*
Heb	2 12	(Ps 22 22) I shall . . . *praise* you in full assembly

2. PLAY MUSIC

1: MINSTREL: *MOUSIKOS*

mousikos 1

Rv	18 22	Never again in you, Babylon, will be heard the song of harpists and *minstrels*, the music of flute and trumpet;

2: CYMBAL: *KYMBALON*

kymbalon 1

1 Co	13 1	If I . . . speak without love, I am simply a gong booming or a *cymbal* clashing.

3: FLUTE – PLAY THE PIPES: *AULOS*

1 auleō 3   3 aulos 1
2 aulētēs 2

Mt	9 23	2 Jesus . . . saw the *flute-players*,
	11 17	We *played the pipes* for you, and you wouldn't dance;
Lk	7 32	We *played the pipes* for you, and you wouldn't dance;

1 Co	14 7	Think of ᴿa musical instrument (lit. something inanimate
		3 that gives out sound), a *flute* or a harp: if one note on it
		   cannot be distinguished from another, how can you tell
		   what tune is being *played on the flute* . . .?

Rv	18 22	Never again in you, Babylon, will be heard the . . . ᴿmusic 2 (lit. *players*) *of flute* and trumpet;

4: HARP – HARPIST, HARPER: *KITHARA*

1 kithara 4   3 kithar-ōdos 2
2 kitharizō 2

1 Co	14 7	Think of ᴿa musical instrument (lit. something inanimate that
		   gives out sound), a flute or a *harp*: if one note on it cannot
		   be distinguished from another, how can you tell what tune
		2 is being *played* on the flute or *on the harp*?

Rv	5 8	each of [the twenty-four elders] was holding a *harp*
	14 2	3 I heard a sound . . . it seemed to be the sound of *harpists* 2/ *playing* their *harps*.

	15 2	those who had fought against the beast and won . . . all had
		   harps from God, ³ and they were singing the hymn of
		   Moses . . . and the song of the Lamb:

	18 22	3 Never again in you, Babylon, will be heard the song of *harpists* and minstrels,

5: TRUMPET: *SALPINX*

2 salpinx 11   1 salpizō 12
3 salpistēs 1

Mt	6 2	when you give alms, do not have it *trumpeted* before you;
	24 31	2 [the Son of Man] will send his angels with a loud *trumpet*.
1 Co	14 8	2 if no one can be sure which call the *trumpet* has sounded, who will be ready for the attack?
	15 52	2 This will be instantaneous . . . when the last *trumpet* [sounds]. It will *sound* and the dead will be raised, imperishable,
1 Th	4 16	2 At the *trumpet* of God . . . the Lord himself will come down from heaven;
Heb	12 19	[What you have come to is nothing known to the senses: 2 not] *trumpeting* thunder or the great voice speaking
Rv	1 10	2 I heard a voice behind me, shouting like a *trumpet*,
	4 1	I . . . heard the same voice speaking to me, the voice like a 2 *trumpet*,
	8 2	2 I saw seven *trumpets* being given to the seven angels
	6	2 The seven angels that had the seven *trumpets* now made ready to *sound* them.
	7	The first *blew his trumpet* and . . . hail and fire . . . were dropped on the earth;
	8	The second angel *blew his trumpet*, and it was as though a great mountain . . . had been dropped into the sea;
	10	The third angel *blew his trumpet*, and a huge star fell from the sky,
	12	The fourth angel *blew his trumpet*, and a third of the sun [was] blasted,
	13	Trouble . . . for all the people on earth at the sound of the 2/ other three *trumpets* which the three angels are going to *blow*.
	9 1	the fifth angel *blew his trumpet*, and I saw a star
	13	The sixth angel *blew his trumpet*, and I heard a voice
	14	2 [the voice] spoke to the sixth angel with the *trumpet*, and said, 'Release the four angels that are chained up
	10 7	at the time when the seventh angel is heard *sounding his* *trumpet*, God's secret intention will be fulfilled,
	11 15	the seventh angel *blew his trumpet*, and voices could be heard shouting, '. . . our Lord . . . will reign for ever and ever'.
	18 22	Never again in you, Babylon, will be heard . . . the ᴿmusic 3 (lit. *players*) *of flute* and *trumpet*;

3. DANCE

1: DANCING: *CHOROS*

choros 1

Lk	15 25	as [the elder son] drew near the house, he could hear music and *dancing*.

2: DANCE: *ORCHEOMAI*

orcheomai 4

Mt	11 17	We played the pipes for you, and you wouldn't *dance*;
	14 6	the daughter of Herodias *danced* before the company,
Mk	6 22	When the daughter of this same Herodias came in and *danced*, she delighted Herod
Lk	7 32	We played the pipes for you, and you wouldn't *dance*;

SIT – LIE

1. Sit: *kath-izō*
1: Sit
  a) Sit down – a Seat
  b) Sit (on an animal), Mount – Ride
2: Sit (in a seat of glory)
3: Sit up (having been brought back to life)

2. Sit – Be sitting: *kath-ēmai*
1: Sit
  a) Sit
  b) Sit (on an animal), Mount – Rider
2: Sit (in a seat of glory)

3. Sit – Lay – Bed: *klinō*
1: Sit down (to eat) – Place at table – Steward of a feast
2: Lay
3: Bed – Stretcher

4. Sit – Lie: *keimai*
1: Sit at table – Dine – Those at table, Guests
2: Lie, Be laid (generally) – Gone to bed – Bedridden
3: Lie with – the Marriage-bed

5. Sit down (to eat): *ana-piptō*

6. Lie in bed – Stretched out: *ballō*

7. Throne: *thronos*
1: Throne
  a) of God, of Christ, of the Twelve, etc.
  b) of others
2: the Order of angels

8. Stretcher – Mat, Sleeping-mat – Bedridden: *krabatos*

9. Cushion – Pillow: *pros-kephalaion*

1. SIT: *KATH-IZŌ*

4	*kath-edra*	3	7	*epi-kath-izō*	1	
2	*kath-ezomai*	7	8	*para-kath-ezomai*	1	
1	*kath-izō*	43/46	3	*(prōto-)kath-edria*	4	
5	*ana-kath-izō*	2	6	*syn-kath-izō*	2	

1: SIT

a) Sit down – a Seat

Mt	5	1	X	There he *sat down* and was joined by his disciples.
	13	48		the fishermen haul [the dragnet] ashore; then, *sitting down*, they collect the good ones in a basket
	21	12	4	Jesus . . . upset . . . the *chairs* of those who were selling pigeons.
	23	6	3	[the scribes and the Pharisees want] to take . . . the front *seats* in the synagogues
	26	36		⌐Stay (or: *Sit*) here while I go over there to pray.
	55	X	2	I *sat* teaching in the Temple day after day
Mk	9	35	X	he *sat down*, called the Twelve to him
	11	15	4	[Jesus] upset . . . the *chairs* of those who were selling pigeons.
	12	39	3	[the scribes like] to take the front *seats* in the synagogues
	41	X		He *sat down* opposite the treasury and watched the people
	14	32		⌐Stay (or: *Sit*) here while I pray.
Lk	2	46	X	2 they found him in the Temple, *sitting* among the doctors,
	4	20	X	He then rolled up the scroll, gave it back to the assistant and *sat down*.
	5	3	X	Then he *sat down* and taught the crowds from the boat.
	10	39	8	Mary . . . *sat down* at the Lord's feet and listened
	11	43	3	Alas for you Pharisees who like taking the *seats* of honour in the synagogues
	14	28		which of you here, intending to build a tower, would not first *sit down* and work out the cost . . .?
		31		Or again, what king marching to war . . . would not first *sit down* and consider . . .?
	16	6		Here, take your bond; *sit down* straight away and write fifty.
	20	46	3	the scribes . . . like to . . . take the front *seats* in the synagogues
	22	55	6	They had lit a fire and were *sitting* round it in the middle of the courtyard and Peter sat down among them,
Jn	4	6	X	2 Jesus, tired by the journey, *sat* straight *down* by the well.
	8	2	X	[Jesus] *sat down* and began to teach them.
	11	20	2	Mary *remained sitting* in the house.
	20	12	2	[Mary] saw two angels in white *sitting* where the body of Jesus had been,
Ac	8	31		[the eunuch] invited Philip to get in and *sit* by his side.
	13	14		[Paul and his friends] went to synagogue . . . and *took* their *seats*.
	16	13		We *sat down* and preached to the women
	20	9	2	a young man . . . was *sitting* on the window-sill
1 Co	10	7		(Ex 32 6) After *sitting down* to eat and drink, the people got up to amuse themselves.

b) Sit (on an animal), Mount – Ride

Mt	21	7	X	7 They brought the donkey and the colt . . . and he *sat* on them.
Mk	11	2		you will find a tethered colt that no one has yet *ridden*.
		7	X	they took the colt to Jesus . . . and he *sat* on it.
Lk	19	30		you will find a tethered colt that no one has yet *ridden*.
Jn	12	14	X	Jesus found a young donkey and *mounted* it

2: SIT (IN A SEAT OF GLORY)

Mt	19	28	X	when . . . the Son of Man *sits* on his throne of glory, you will yourselves sit on twelve thrones
	20	21		Promise that these two sons of mine may *sit* one at your right hand and the other at your left
		23		Jesus said, '. . . as for ⌐seats (lit. *sitting*) at my right hand and my left, [it is] not mine to grant;
	23	2	/4	The scribes and the Pharisees ⌐occupy (lit. *sit* on) the *chair* of Moses.
	25	31	X	the Son of Man . . . will *take his seat* on his throne of glory.
Mk	10	37		Allow us to *sit* one at your right hand and the other at your left
		40		as for ⌐seats (lit. *sitting*) at my right hand or my left, [it is] not mine to grant;
	16	19		the Lord Jesus . . . was taken up into heaven: there at the right hand of God he *took his place*;
Jn	19	13		Pilate . . . *seated himself* on the chair of judgement
Ac	2	30	X	God had sworn [David] an oath to make one of his descendants ⌐succeed him (lit. *sit*) on the throne.
	6	15	2	The ⌐members of (lit. people *seated* in) the Sanhedrin all looked intently at Stephen,
	12	21		Herod . . . *enthroned* on a dais, made a speech
	25	6		[Festus] *took his seat* on the tribunal and had Paul brought in.
		17		I wasted no time but *took my seat* on the tribunal . . . and had the man brought in.
1 Co	6	4		the people you appointed to ⌐try (lit. *sit* [in judgement] over) them were not even respected in the Church.
Ep	1	20	X	[God] used [his power] to raise him from the dead and to make him *sit* at his right hand,
	2	6	X	6 God . . . *gave* us *a place with* [Christ] in heaven,
2 Th	2	4		the Enemy . . . *enthrones* himself in God's sanctuary
Heb	1	3	X	the Son . . . has gone to *take his place* in heaven at the right hand of divine Majesty
	8	1	X	a high priest of exactly this kind . . . *has his place* at the right of the throne of divine Majesty
	10	12	X	He has . . . *taken his place* for ever, at the right hand of God,
	12	2	X	Jesus . . . has *taken his place* at the right of God's throne.
Rv	3	21		Those who prove victorious I will allow to ⌐share (lit. *sit* near me on) my throne, just as I was victorious myself and *took my place* with my Father on his throne.
	20	4	X	I saw some thrones, and I saw those who are given the power to be judges *take their seats* on them.

3: SIT UP (HAVING BEEN BROUGHT BACK TO LIFE)

Lk	7	15	5	the dead man [in Nain] *sat up* and began to talk,
Ac	9	40	5	[Dorcas] opened her eyes, looked at Peter and *sat up*.

2. SIT – BE SITTING: *KATH-ĒMAI*

1 *kath-ēmai* 89/91   2 *syn-kath-ēmai* 2

1: SIT

a) Sit

Mt	4	16		[On the] people that ⌐lived (or: *sat*) in darkness . . . who ⌐dwell (or: *sit*) in the land and shadow of death a light has dawned.
	9	9		Jesus . . . saw a man named Matthew *sitting* by the customs house,
	11	16		this generation . . . is like children shouting to each other as they *sit* in the market place:
	13	1	X	Jesus left the house and *sat* by the lakeside,
		2	X	he got into a boat and *sat* there.
	15	29	X	he went up into the hills. He *sat* there,
	20	30		there *were* two blind men *sitting* at the side of the road.
	24	3	X	he *was sitting* on the Mount of Olives
	26	58		Peter . . . *sat down* with the attendants
		69		Meanwhile Peter *was sitting* outside in the courtyard,
	27	36		[the soldiers] *sat down* and stayed there keeping guard over [Jesus]
		61		Mary of Magdala and the other Mary were there, *sitting* opposite the sepulchre.
	28	2		the angel of the Lord . . . rolled away the stone and *sat* on it.
Mk	2	6		Now some scribes *were sitting* there,
		14		[Jesus] saw Levi . . . *sitting* by the customs house,
	3	32		A crowd *was sitting* round [Jesus]
		34		looking round at those *sitting* in a circle about him, [Jesus] said,
	4	1	X	he got into a boat on the lake and *sat* there.
	5	15		They . . . saw the demoniac *sitting* there,
	10	46		a blind beggar *was sitting* at the side of the road.
	13	3	X	he *was sitting* facing the Temple, on the Mount of Olives
	14	54	2	Peter . . . *was sitting with* the attendants warming himself at the fire.

Mk	16	5	On entering the tomb they saw a young man in a white robe *seated* on the right hand side
Lk	1	79	[you will go before the Lord] to give light to those who ⌐live (or: *sit*)⌐ in darkness and the shadow of death
	5	17	among ⌐the audience (lit. those *sitting*)⌐ there were Pharisees and doctors of the Law
		27	a tax collector, Levi by name, [was] *sitting* by the customs house,
	7	32	[the people of this generation] are like children shouting to one another while they *sit* in the market place:
	8	35	they found [the demoniac] . . . *sitting* at the feet of Jesus,
	10	13	[Tyre and Sidon] would have repented long ago *sitting* in sackcloth and ashes.
	18	35	there was a blind man *sitting* at the side of the road begging
	22	55	They had lit a fire in the middle of the courtyard and Peter *sat down* among them ⁵⁶ and as he *was sitting* there by the blaze a servant-girl saw him,
		56	
Jn	2	14	in the Temple [Jesus] found . . . the money changers *sitting* at their counters
	6	3 X	Jesus climbed the hillside, and *sat down* there with his disciples.
	9	8	Isn't this the man who used to *sit* and beg?
Ac	2	2	the noise . . . filled the entire house in which [the brothers] *were sitting*
	3	10	the man . . . used to *sit* begging at the Beautiful Gate
	8	28	as [the Ethiopian] *sat* in his chariot he was reading
	14	8	A man *sat* there who had never walked in his life
	26	30	2 the king rose to his feet, with . . . those who *sat* there with them.
1 Co	14	30	If one of the ⌐listeners (lit. people *sitting down*)⌐ receives a revelation, then the man who is already speaking should stop.
Jm	2	3	you say [to the well-dressed man], 'Come this way to ⌐the best seats (lit. *sit* in the best place)⌐'; then you tell the poor man, . . . 'You can *sit* on the floor by my foot-rest'.
Rv	14	14 X	I saw a white cloud, and *sitting* on it, one like a son of man
		15 X	another angel . . . shouted aloud to the one *sitting* on the cloud,
		16 X	the one *sitting* on the cloud set his sickle to work on the earth,
	17	1	the famous prostitute . . . rules *enthroned* beside abundant waters,
		9	the seven heads are the seven hills, and the woman *is sitting* on them.
		15	The waters you saw, beside which the prostitute *was sitting*, are all the peoples,

b) Sit (on an animal), Mount – Rider

Jn	12	15 X	(Zc 9 9) your king is coming, *mounted* on the colt of a donkey.
Rv	6	2	a white horse appeared, and the *rider* on it was holding a bow;
		4	out came another horse, bright red, and its *rider* was given this duty: to take away peace from the earth
		5	a black horse appeared and its *rider* was holding a pair of scales;
		8	another horse appeared, deathly pale, and its *rider* was called Plague,
	9	17	I saw the horses, and the *riders*
	17	3	I saw a woman *riding* a scarlet beast
	19	11 X	I saw . . . a white horse appear; its *rider* was called Faithful and True;
		18	There will be the flesh of kings for you . . . the flesh of horses and their *riders*
		19	all the kings of the earth . . . gathered together to fight the *rider*
		X	
		21 X	All the rest were killed by the sword of the *rider*,

2: SIT (IN A SEAT OF GLORY)

Mt	19	28	you will yourselves *sit* on twelve thrones
	22	44 X	(Ps 110 1) The Lord said to my Lord: *Sit* at my right hand
	23	22	when a man swears by heaven he is swearing by the throne of God and by the One who *is seated* there.
		Θ	
	26	64 X	you will see the Son of Man *seated* at the right hand of the Power
	27	19	[Pilate] *was seated* in the chair of judgement
Mk	12	36 X	(Ps 110 1) The Lord said to my Lord: *Sit* at my right hand
	14	62 X	you will see the Son of Man *seated* at the right hand of the Power
Lk	20	42 X	(Ps 110 1) The Lord said to my Lord: *Sit* at my right hand
	22	30	you will *sit* on thrones to judge the twelve tribes of Israel.
		69 X	the Son of Man will *be seated* at the right hand of the Power of God
Ac	2	34 X	(Ps 110 1) The Lord said to my Lord: *Sit* at my right hand
	23	3	How can you *sit* there to judge me according to the Law . . .?
Col	3	1 X	Christ is [in heaven], *sitting* at God's right hand.
Heb	1	13 X	(Ps 110 1) *Sit* at my right hand and I will make your enemies a footstool for you.
Rv	4	2 Θ	I saw . . . the One who was *sitting* on the throne,
		3 Θ	the Person *sitting* there looked like a diamond and a ruby.
		4	on [twenty-four thrones] I saw twenty-four elders *sitting*

Rv	4	9 Θ	the animals . . . gave thanks to the One *sitting* on the throne,
		10 Θ	the twenty-four elders prostrated themselves before ⌐him (lit. the One *sitting* on the throne)⌐
	5	1 Θ	I saw that in the right hand of the One *sitting* on the throne there was a scroll
		7	[The Lamb took the scroll] from the right hand of the One *sitting* on the throne,
		Θ	
		13 Θ	To the One who is *sitting* on the throne and to the Lamb, be all . . . honour, glory and power,
	6	16 Θ	hide us away from the One who *sits* on the throne and from the anger of the Lamb.
	7	10 Θ	Victory to our God, who *sits* on the throne, and to the Lamb!
		15 Θ	the One who *sits* on the throne will spread his tent over them.
	11	16	The twenty-four elders, *enthroned* in the presence of God,
	18	7	I *am* the queen *on my throne*, [Babylon] says to herself,
	19	4 Θ	[the twenty-four elders] worshipped God *seated* there on his throne,
	20	11 Θ	I saw a great white throne and the One who was *sitting* on it.
	21	5 Θ	Then the One *sitting* on the throne spoke:

3. SIT – LAY – BED: *KLINŌ*

8	*klinarion*	1	9	*klisia* 1
1	*klinē*	8	2	*ana-klinō* 6
6	*klinidion*	2	5	*archi-tri-klinos* 3
7	*klinō*	2/7	3	*kata-klinō* 5
			4	(*prōto-)klisia* 5

1: SIT DOWN (TO EAT) – PLACE AT TABLE – STEWARD OF A FEAST

Mt	8	11	2 many will come from east and west to *take their places* with Abraham and Isaac and Jacob *at the feast* in the kingdom of heaven;
	14	19	2 [Jesus] gave orders that the people were to *sit down* on the grass;
	23	6	4 [the scribes and the Pharisees want] to take the *place* of honour at banquets
Mk	6	39	[Jesus] ordered [the disciples] to get all the people together in groups *sitting down* on the green grass,
			2
	12	39	4 [the scribes like] to take . . . the *places* of honour at banquets
Lk	7	36 X	3 [Jesus] arrived at the Pharisee's house and *took his place* at table
	9	14	3/9 *Get* them *to sit down* in ⌐parties (lit. *sittings*)⌐ of about fifty.
		15	3 [The disciples] did so and *made* them *sit down*.
	12	37 <	2 the master . . . will . . . *sit* them *down at table* and wait on them.
	13	29	2 men from east and west . . . will come to *take their places at the feast* in the kingdom of God.
	14	7	4 [Jesus] had noticed how [the guests] picked the *places* of honour.
		8 <	3/4 do not *take your seat* in the *place* of honour.
	20	46	4 the scribes . . . like . . . to take . . . the *places* of honour at banquets,
	24	30 X	3 while [Jesus] *was* with [the disciples] *at table*, he took the bread
Jn	2	8	5 Draw some out now . . . and take it to the *steward*.
		9	5 the *steward* tasted the water, and it had turned into wine . . .
			5 the *steward* called the bridegroom

2: LAY

Mt	8	20 X	7 the Son of Man has nowhere to *lay* his head.
Lk	2	7 X	2 [Mary] gave birth to a son . . . and *laid* him in a manger
	9	58 X	7 the Son of Man has nowhere to *lay* his head.

3: BED – STRETCHER

Mt	9	2	some people appeared, bringing him a paralytic stretched out on a *bed*.
		6	[Jesus] said to the paralytic, 'Get up, and pick up your *bed* and go off home'.
Mk	4	21	Would you bring in a lamp to put it . . . under the *bed*?
	7	30	[the Syrophoenician woman] went off to her home and found the child lying on the *bed*
Lk	5	18	some men appeared, carrying on a *bed* a paralysed man
		19	6 [the men] lowered him and his *stretcher* down through the tiles . . . in front of Jesus.
		24	[Jesus] said to the paralysed man, 'I order you: get up, and pick up your *stretcher* and go home.'
	8	16	No one lights a lamp . . . to put it under a *bed*.
	17	34	on that night two will be in one *bed*: one will be taken, the other left;
Ac	5	15	8 the sick were even taken out into the streets and laid on *beds*

Rv 2 22		I am consigning [Jezebel] to *bed*, and all her partners in adultery to troubles

4. SIT – LIE: *KEIMAI*

3 *keimai* 10/24	1	*ana-keimai* 14	6	(*arseno-*)*koitēs* 2
5 *koitē*	4	4 *syn-ana-keimai* 7	2	*kata-keimai* 12

1: SIT AT TABLE – DINE – THOSE AT TABLE, GUESTS

Mt 9 10 X		While he *was at dinner* . . . a number of tax collectors and sinners came to *sit at the table with* Jesus and his disciples.
14 9	4	thinking of . . . his *guests*, [Herod] [10] had John beheaded
22 10 <		the wedding hall was filled with *guests*.
11 <		the king came in to look at the *guests*
26 7 X		a woman . . . poured [ointment] on his head as he *was at table*.
20 X		When evening came he *was at table* with the twelve disciples.
Mk 2 15 X	2	When Jesus *was at dinner* . . . a number of tax collectors and
4		sinners were also *sitting at the table with* Jesus and his disciples;
6 22		When the daughter of this same Herodias . . . danced, she
4		delighted Herod and his *guests*;
26		thinking of . . . his *guests*, [Herod] was reluctant to break his word to her.
14 3		Jesus was at Bethany in the house of Simon the leper; he
X	2	*was at dinner* when a woman came in
18 X		while they *were at table* eating, Jesus said,
16 14		[Jesus] showed himself to the Eleven themselves while they *were at table*.
Lk 5 29 X	2	Levi held a great reception in his house, and with them *at table* was a large gathering of tax collectors and others.
7 37 X	2	[The woman] had heard he *was dining* with the Pharisee and had brought with her an alabaster jar of ointment.
49	4	Those who *were with him at table* began to say to themselves,
14 10	4	everyone with you *at the table* will see you honoured.
15	4	one of those gathered *round the table* said to him, 'Happy the man who will be at the feast in the kingdom of God!'
22 27		who is the greater: the one *at table* or the one who serves? The one *at table*, surely?
Jn 6 11		Jesus took the loaves, gave thanks, and gave them out to all who *were sitting* ready:
12 2		They gave a dinner for [Jesus in Bethany] . . . and Lazarus was among *those at table*.
13 23		The disciple Jesus loved was *reclining* next to Jesus;
28		None of the others *at table* understood the reason he said this [to Judas]
1 Co 8 10	2	Suppose someone sees you, a man who understands, *eating* in some temple of an idol;

2: LIE, BE LAID (GENERALLY) – GONE TO BED – BEDRIDDEN

Mt 28 6 X ○	3	Come and see the place where he *lay*,
Mk 1 30	2	Simon's mother-in-law had *gone to bed* with fever,
2 4	2	they lowered the stretcher on which the paralytic *lay*.
Lk 2 12 X	3	you will find a baby . . . *lying* in a manger.
16 X	3	[the shepherds] found . . . the baby *lying* in the manger.
5 25	2	[the paralysed man] got up, picked up what he *had been lying* on and went home
11 7	5	my children and I are *in bed*; I cannot get up
23 53 ○		[Joseph] put [the body of Jesus] in a tomb . . . in which no
3		one *had* yet *been laid*.
Jn 5 3	2	under these [five porticos] *were* (lit. *lay*) crowds of sick people
6	2	Jesus saw [the sick man] *lying* there
20 5		[the other disciple] bent down and saw the linen cloths
3		*lying* on the ground,
6	3	Simon Peter . . . saw the linen cloths *lying* on the ground,
7		the cloth that had been over [Jesus's] head . . . was not
3		*lying* with the linen cloths but rolled up in a place by itself.
12 X ○		[Mary] saw two angels . . . sitting where the body of Jesus
3		had *been* (lit. *lain*)
Ac 9 33	2	[Peter] found . . . a paralytic who had been *bedridden* for eight years.
28 8	2	Publius' father was *in bed*, suffering from feverish attacks
2 Co 3 15	3	today, when Moses is read, the veil *is* (lit. *lies*) over their minds.
1 Jn 5 19	3	the whole world *lies* in the power of the Evil One.

3: LIE WITH – THE MARRIAGE-BED

Rm 9 10	5	Rebecca . . . *was pregnant by* (lit. *had lain with*) our ancestor Isaac,

Rm 13 13	5	no drunken orgies, no *promiscuity* or licentiousness,
1 Co 6 9	6	people *of immoral lives*, idolaters . . . will never inherit the kingdom of God.
1 Tm 1 10	6	[laws are framed] for *those who are immoral* with women or with boys or *with men*,
Heb 13 4		Marriage is to be honoured by all, and *marriages are* (lit. the *marriage-bed* is) to be kept undefiled,
5		

5. SIT DOWN (TO EAT): *ANA-PIPTŌ*

ana-piptō 10/12

Mt 15 35		[Jesus] instructed the crowd to *sit down* on the ground,
Mk 6 40		they *sat down* on the ground in squares of hundreds and fifties.
8 6		[Jesus] instructed the crowd to *sit down* on the ground,
Lk 11 37		a Pharisee invited him to dine at his house. He went in and
X		*sat down* at the table.
14 10 <		when you are a guest, make your way to the lowest place and *sit* there,
17 7 <		Which of you, with a servant . . . would say to him when he returned from the fields, 'Come and *have your meal*
22 14 X		When the hour came he *took his place* at table, and the apostles with him.
Jn 6 10		Jesus said to them, 'Make the people *sit down*' . . . as many as five thousand men *sat down*.
13 12		When [Jesus] had washed their feet . . . he went back to
X		(lit. and *sat down* at) the table.

6. LIE IN BED – STRETCHED OUT: *BALLŌ*

ballō 5/122

Mt 8 6		my servant *is lying* at home paralysed,
14		Jesus found Peter's mother-in-law *in bed* with fever.
9 2		some people appeared, bringing him a paralytic *stretched out* on a bed.
Mk 7 30		[the Syrophoenician woman] found the child *lying* on the bed
Lk 16 20		at [the rich man's] gate there *lay* a poor man called Lazarus,

7. THRONE: *THRONOS*

thronos 62

1: THRONE

a) of God, of Christ, of the Twelve, etc.

Mt 5 34		(Is 66 1) heaven . . . is God's *throne*;
19 28 X		when . . . the Son of Man sits on his *throne* of glory, you will yourselves sit on twelve *thrones* to judge the twelve tribes of Israel.
23 22		when a man swears by heaven he is swearing by the *throne* of God
25 31 X		the Son of Man . . . will take his seat on his *throne* of glory,
Lk 1 32 X		The Lord God will give him the *throne* of his ancestor David;
22 30		you will sit on *thrones* to judge the twelve tribes of Israel.
Ac 2 30		God had sworn [David] . . . to make one of his descendants
X		succeed him on the *throne*,
7 49		(Is 66 1) With heaven my *throne* and earth my footstool,
Heb 1 8 X		(Ps 45 7) to his Son [God] says: God, your *throne* shall last for ever and ever;
4 16		Let us be confident, then, in approaching the *throne* of grace,
8 1		we have a high priest of exactly this kind. He has his place at the right of the *throne* of divine Majesty in the heavens,
12 2		from now on [Jesus] has taken his place at the right of God's *throne*.
Rv 1 4		grace and peace to you . . . from the seven spirits in his presence before his *throne*,
3 21 X		Those who prove victorious I will allow to share my *throne*, just as I . . . took my place with my Father on his *throne*.
4 2		I saw a *throne* standing in heaven, and the One who was
3		sitting on the *throne*, [3] . . . There was a rainbow encircling the *throne* and this looked like an emerald. [4] Round the
4		*throne* in a circle were twenty-four *thrones*, and on them (lit. the *thrones*) I saw twenty-four elders sitting,
5		Flashes of lightning were coming from the *throne* . . . and in front of the *throne* there were seven flaming lamps burning,
6		Between the *throne* and myself was a sea that seemed to be made of glass . . . In the centre of the *throne* grouped round the *throne* itself, were four animals
9		the animals glorified . . . the One sitting on the *throne*,

Rv	4 10	the twenty-four elders prostrated themselves before ⌐him (lit. the One sitting on the *throne*) . . . and threw down their crowns in front of the *throne*,
	5 1	in the right hand of the One sitting on the *throne* there was a scroll
	6	I saw, standing between the *throne* with its four animals and the circle of the elders, a Lamb
	7	The Lamb came forward to take the scroll from the right hand of the One sitting on the *throne*,
	11	an immense number of angels gathered round the *throne*
	13	To the One who is sitting on the *throne* and to the Lamb, be all praise,
	6 16	hide us away from the One who sits on the *throne*
	7 9	I saw a huge number . . . of people . . . standing in front of the *throne* and in front of the Lamb . . . ¹⁰ They shouted
	10	aloud, 'Victory to our God, who sits on the *throne*,
	11	all the angels who were standing in a circle round the *throne* . . . prostrated themselves before the *throne*,
	15	they now stand in front of God's *throne* . . . and the One who sits on the *throne* will spread his tent over them.
	17	the Lamb . . . is at the *throne*
	8 3	the golden altar . . . stood in front of the *throne*;
	11 16	The twenty-four elders, ⌐enthroned (lit. sitting on their *thrones*) in the presence of God, prostrated themselves
	12 5	the child was taken straight up to God and to his *throne*,
	14 3	There in front of the *throne* [the hundred and forty-four thousand] were singing a new hymn
	16 17	a voice shouted from the sanctuary (§ coming from the *throne*)
	19 4	God [was] seated there on his *throne* . . . ⁵ Then a voice
	5	came from the *throne*; it said, 'Praise our God,
	20 4	I saw some *thrones*, and I saw those who are given the power to be judges take their seats on them.
	11	I saw a great white *throne* and the One who was sitting on it.
	12	I saw the dead . . . standing in front of his *throne*,
	21 3	I heard a loud voice call from the *throne*,
	5	Then the One sitting on the *throne* spoke:
	22 1 X	the angel showed me the river of life, rising from the *throne* of God and of the Lamb
	3 X	The *throne* of God and of the Lamb will be in its place in the city;

b) of others

Lk	1 52	[God] has pulled down princes from their *thrones*
Rv	2 13 ⒟	[Pergamum,] the place where Satan ⌐is enthroned (lit. has his *throne*) . . . Antipas was killed in your own town, where Satan lives.
	13 2 ⒟	the dragon had handed over to [the beast] his own power and his *throne*
	16 10	The fifth angel emptied his bowl over the *throne* of the beast

2: THE ORDER OF ANGELS

Col	1 16	*Thrones*, Dominations, Sovereignties, Powers – all things were created through [Christ]

8. STRETCHER – MAT, SLEEPING-MAT – BEDRIDDEN: *KRABATOS*
krabatos 11

Mk	2 4	they lowered the *stretcher* on which the paralytic lay.
	9	Get up, pick up your *stretcher* and walk.
	11	get up, pick up your *stretcher*, and go off home. ¹² And the
	12	man got up, picked up his *stretcher* at once and walked out
	6 55	people . . . brought the sick on *stretchers* to wherever they heard [Jesus] was.
Jn	5 8	Get up, pick up your *sleeping-mat* and walk. ⁹ The man . . .
	9	picked up his *mat* and walked away. Now that day happened
	10	to be the sabbath, ¹⁰ so the Jews said to the man, '. . . you
	11	are not allowed to carry your *sleeping-mat*.' ¹¹ He replied, 'But the man who cured me told me, "Pick up your *mat* and walk"'.
Ac	5 15	the sick were even taken out into the streets and laid on beds and *sleeping-mats*
	9 33	There they found a man . . . who had been *bedridden* for eight years.

9. CUSHION – PILLOW: *PROS-KEPHALAION*
pros-kephalaion 1

Mk	4 38	[Jesus] was in the stern, his head on the *cushion*, asleep.

SLAVE – SERVE – MINISTER

1. **Slaves:** *sōma*
2. **Servant, Slave:** *oiketēs*
3. **Serve – Slave, Servant – Be the slave of:** *douleuō*
   1: Servant, Handmaid, Slave (of the Lord) – Be the slave of, Serve (God, Christ)
   2: Slave, Servant – Be the slave of, Serve
   3: Slave, Servant (figuratively) – Slavery
4. **Servant:** *pais*
   1: Servant (of God)
      a) Jesus
      b) Israel, David
   2: Servant (generally) – Servant-girl, Slave-girl, Maid
5. **Serve – Servant:** *therapeuō*
   1: Serve (God) – Servant (of God)
   2: Servants – Household
6. **Serve – Servant, Attendant – Assistant:** *hyp-ēreteō*
   1: Servant (of God) – Serve (God) – Minister (of the word)
   2: Attendant, Assistant (of the Temple, the synagogue) – Officer, Guard

7. Serve, Attend (generally) – Assistant
8. **Serve – Attend, Wait upon:** *par-(h)edreuō*
9. **Service, Serve, Servant – Ministry, Minister, Administration – Deacon:** *dia-koneō*
   1: (Gospel) Ministry, Mission – (Apostolic) Service, Administration – Servant (of God)
   2: Service = (financial) Relief, Aid
   3: Deacon, Deaconess – Serve as deacon
   4: Serve (generally), Wait on – Look after, Administer, Minister to – Servant, Attendant, Helper
10. **Service, Serve, Servant – Ministry, Minister:** *leit-ourgeō*
    1: Service, Ministry, Duty (to God) – Servant, Minister (of God)
    2: Service (to the saints) – Serve, Minister to (Paul)

F = Slave, Servant//Free(d) man

1. SLAVES: *SŌMA*
sōma 1/142

Rv	18 13	[the traders'] *slaves*, their human cargo.

2. SERVANT, SLAVE: *OIKETĒS*
oiketēs 4

X = Servant of Christ

Lk	16 13	No *servant* can be the slave of two masters:
Ac	10 7	Cornelius called two of the *slaves*
Rm	14 4 X	It is not for you to condemn someone else's *servant*:
1 P	2 18	*Slaves* must be respectful and obedient to their masters,

3. SERVE – SLAVE, SERVANT – BE THE SLAVE OF: *DOULEUŌ*

6	*doulē*	3	7	*doulos* (adj.)	2
5	*douleia*	5	10	*doul-agōgeō*	1
2	*douleuō*	25	8	*kata-douloō*	2
4	*douloō*	8	9	*(ophthalmo-)doulia*	2
1	*doulos* (noun)	124	3	*syn-doulos*	10

1: SERVANT, HANDMAID, SLAVE (OF THE LORD) – BE THE SLAVE OF, SERVE (GOD, CHRIST)

Mt	6 24	2	You cannot *be the slave* both *of* God and of money.
Lk	1 38	6	'I am the *handmaid* of the Lord,' said Mary
	48	6	he has looked upon his lowly *handmaid*.
	2 29		Now, Master, you can let your *servant* go in peace.
	16 13	2	No servant can be the slave of two masters: . . . You cannot *be the slave* both *of* God and of money.
	17 10		say, 'We are merely *servants*: we have done no more than our duty'.
Jn	15 15		I shall not call you *servants* any more, because a servant does not know his master's business; I call you friends.
Ac	2 18		(Jl 3 2) Even on my ⌐*slaves*, men and women (lit. *male slaves*
		6	and *female slaves*), . . . I will pour out my spirit.
	4 29		now, Lord, . . . help your *servants* to proclaim your message
	16 17		Here are the *servants* of the Most High God;
	20 19	2	I have *served* the Lord in all humility,
Rm	1 1		From Paul, a *servant* of Christ Jesus who has been called to be an apostle,
	6 22		Now . . . you have been set free from sin, you have been
		F 4	*made slaves* of God,

Rm 7 6   2 now we are . . . free to *serve* in the new spiritual way and not the old way of a written law.
    25   2 it is I who with my reason *serve* the Law of God,
12 11   2 'Work for (lit. *Serve*) the Lord with untiring effort
14 18   2 If you *serve* Christ in this way you will please God
16 18   2 People like that *are* not *slaves* of Jesus Christ, they are [slaves] of their own appetites,
1 Co 7 22 F   a freeman called in the Lord becomes Christ's *slave*.
Ga 1 10   If I still wanted [men's approval], I should not be what I am – a *servant* of Christ.
Ep 6 6   [Slaves, be obedient to your masters] because you are *slaves* of Christ and wholeheartedly do the will of God.
    7   2 'Work hard and (lit. *Serve*) willingly, but do it for the sake of the Lord
Ph 1 1   From Paul and Timothy, *servants* of Christ Jesus,
2 22   you know how [Timothy] has proved himself by 'working 2 (lit. *serving*) with me on behalf of the Good News
Col 1 7   Epaphras . . . is one of our closest 'fellow workers (lit. 3 *fellow servants*)
3 24   2 It is Christ the Lord that you are *serving*;
4 7   3 Tychicus . . . is . . . a loyal helper and *companion in the service* of the Lord.
    12   Epaphras, . . . this *servant* of Christ Jesus
1 Th 1 9   other people tell us how . . . you broke with idolatry when 2 you . . . *became servants* of the real living God;
2 Tm 2 24   a *servant* of the Lord is not to engage in quarrels,
Tt 1 1   From Paul, *servant* of God,
Jm 1 1   From James, *servant* of God,
1 P 2 16 F   You are *slaves* of no one except God, so behave like free men,
2 P 1 1   From Simeon Peter, *servant* and apostle of Jesus Christ;
Jude 1   From Jude, *servant* of Jesus Christ
Rv 1 1   This is the revelation given by God to Jesus Christ so that he could tell his *servants* about the things which are now to take place very soon; he sent his angel to make it known to his *servant* John,
2 20   by her teaching [Jezebel] is luring my *servants* away
6 11   they were told to be patient a little longer, until . . . their 3 *fellow servants* and brothers had been killed
7 3   Wait . . . until we have put the seal on the foreheads of the *servants* of our God.
10 7   just as he announced in the Good News told to his *servants* the prophets
11 18   the time has come for . . . your *servants* the prophets . . . to be rewarded.
15 3   they were singing the hymn of Moses, the *servant* of God, and of the Lamb;
19 2   [God] has avenged his *servants* that [Babylon] killed.
    5   Praise our God, you *servants* of his
    10   3 I am a *servant just like* you and all your brothers
22 3   The throne of God and of the Lamb will be in its place in the city; his *servants* will worship him,
    6   the Lord God . . . has sent his angel to reveal to his *servants* what is soon to take place.
    9   3 I am a *servant just like* you and like your brothers the prophets

2: SLAVE, SERVANT – BE THE SLAVE OF, SERVE
Malchus* 1 (Jn 18 10)

Mt 6 24   2 No one can *be the slave of* two masters: . . . You cannot 2 *be the slave* both of God and *of* money.
8 9   I say to . . . my *servant*: Do this, and he does it.
10 24   the *slave* [is not superior] to his master. 25 It is enough for 25 . . . the *slave* [that he should be] like his master.
13 27   The owner's *servants* went to him
    28   the *servants* said, 'Do you want us to . . . weed [the darnel] out?'
18 23   a king who decided to settle his accounts with his *servants*.
    26   the *servant* threw himself down at his master's feet.
    27   the *servant*'s master felt . . . sorry for him
    28   /3 as this *servant* went out, he happened to meet a *fellow servant*
    29   3 His *fellow servant* fell at his feet
    31   3 His *fellow servants* were deeply distressed
    32   You wicked *servant*, . . . I cancelled all that debt of yours
    33   3 Were you not bound, then, to have pity on your *fellow servant* . . .?
21 34   he sent his *servants* to the tenants to collect his produce.
    35   the tenant seized his *servants*,
    36   he sent some more *servants*
22 3   [The king] sent his *servants* to call those who had been invited [to the feast],
    4   he sent some more *servants*.
    6   the rest seized his *servants*,
    8   he said to his *servants*, 'The wedding is ready;'
    10   these *servants* went out to the roads
24 45   What sort of *servant* . . . is faithful and wise enough . . .?
    46   Happy that *servant* if his master's arrival finds him at this employment.

Mt 24 48   as for the dishonest *servant* who says to himself, 'My master
    49   3 is taking his time', 49 and sets about beating his *fellow*
    50   *servants* . ., 50 'his (lit. this *servant*'s) master . . . will cut him off
25 14   a man on his way abroad summoned his *servants*
    19   the master of those *servants* came back
    21   Well done, good and faithful *servant*; . . . come and join in your master's happiness.
    23   Well done, good and faithful *servant*;
    26   You wicked and lazy *servant*!
    30   As for this good-for-nothing *servant*, throw him out into the dark,
26 51   one of the followers of Jesus . . . struck out at the high priest's *servant*,
Mk 12 2   he sent a *servant* to the tenants to collect . . . his share
    4   he sent another *servant* to them;
13 34   a man travelling abroad . . . has . . . left his *servants* in charge,
14 47   one of the bystanders . . . struck out at the high priest's *servant*,
Lk 7 2   A centurion there had a *servant*, . . . 3 . . . he sent . . . to [Jesus] to ask him to come and heal his *servant*.
    3
    8   I say to . . . my *servant*: Do this, and he does it.
    10   the messengers . . . found the *servant* in perfect health.
12 37   Happy those *servants* whom the master finds awake
    43   Happy that *servant* if his master's arrival finds him at this employment.
    45   But as to the *servant* who says to himself, 'My master is taking his time coming', . . . 46 'his (lit. this *servant*'s)
    46   master will . . . cut him off
    47   The *servant* who knows what his master wants, but has not even started to carry out those wishes,
14 17   [the man] sent his *servants* to say to those who had been invited [to the banquet], 'Come'
    21   The *servant* returned and reported this to his master . . . [who] in a rage said to his *servant*, 'Go . . . and bring in here the poor,'
    22   'Sir,' said the *servant* 'your orders have been carried out'
    23   the master said to his *servant*, 'Go to the open roads'
15 22   the father [of the prodigal] said to his *servants*, 'Quick! Bring out the best robe'
    29   [the elder son] answered his father, 'Look, all these years I 2 have *slaved for* you'
16 13   2 No *servant* can *be the slave of* two masters . . . you cannot 2 *be the slave* both of God and *of* money.
Lk 17 7   Which of you, with a *servant* ploughing . ., would say to him . . .?
    9   Must he be grateful to the *servant* for doing what he was told?
19 13   He summoned ten of his *servants* and gave them ten pounds.
    15   on his return, . . . he sent for those *servants*
    17   Well done, my good *servant*
    22   You wicked *servant*!
20 10   he sent a *servant* to the tenants to get his share of the produce
    11   he . . . sent a second *servant*;
22 50   one of [Jesus's followers] struck out at the high priest's *servant*,
Jn 4 51   his *servants* met him with the news that his boy was alive.
8 33 F   2 We are descended from Abraham and we have never *been the slaves of* anyone
13 16   no *servant* is greater than his master,
15 15   because a *servant* does not know his master's business;
    20   A *servant* is not greater than his master,
18 10   Simon Peter . . . wounded the high priest's *servant*, . . . The *servant*'s name was Malchus*.
    18   the *servants* and guards . . . were standing there warming themselves;
    26   One of the high priest's *servants* . . . said, 'Didn't I see you in the garden with [Jesus]?'
Ac 7 6   (Gn 15 13f) God [said] that [Abraham's] descendants would 4 be exiles in a foreign land, where they would *be slaves* . . . for four hundred years. 7 But I will pass judgement on the 2 nation that *enslaves* them . . . and after this they will leave,
Rm 6 16   You know that if you agree to *serve* and obey a master you become his *slaves*.
9 12   2 (Gn 25 23) the elder [Esau] shall *serve* the younger [Jacob],
1 Co 7 21 F   If, when you were called, you were a *slave*, do not let this 22 F   bother you; . . . 22 A *slave*, when he is called in the Lord, becomes the Lord's freedman,
12 13   In the one Spirit we were all baptised, Jews as well as Greeks, F *slaves* as well as citizens,
Ga 3 28 F   there are no distinctions between Jew and Greek, *slave* and free,
4 1   an heir . . . is no different from a *slave*
Ep 6 5   *Slaves*, be obedient to . . . your masters . . . 6 not only when 6 9 you are *serving* under their eye, as if you had only to please men,
    8 F   You can be sure that everyone, whether a *slave* or a free man,
Ph 2 7   [Christ Jesus] emptied himself to assume the condition of a *slave*,

Col	3	11 F	in [the] image [of the creator] there is no room for distinction between Greek and Jew, . . . *slave* and free man.
		22 9	*Slaves*, be obedient to . . . your masters . . . not only when you are *serving* under their eye, as if you had only to please men,
	4	1	Masters, make sure that your *slaves* are given what is just and fair,
1 Tm	6	1	All *slaves* 'under the yoke' must have unqualified respect for their masters,
		2	2 [Slaves] whose masters are believers . . . should *serve* them all the better,
Tt	2	9	Tell the *slaves* that they are to be obedient to their masters
Phm		16	[you have been deprived of Onesimus only so that you could have him back for ever,] not as a *slave* any more, but something much better than a *slave*, a dear brother;
Rv	6	15 F	the whole population, *slaves* and citizens, took to the mountains
	13	16 F	[The beast] compelled everyone – small and great, . . . *slave* and citizen – to be branded
	19	18 F	There will be the flesh of kings for you, . . . and of all kinds of men, citizens and *slaves*, small and great.

3: SLAVE, SERVANT (FIGURATIVELY) – SLAVERY

Mt	20	27	anyone who wants to be first among you must be your *servant*,
Mk	10	44	anyone who wants to be first among you must be *slave* to all.
Jn	8	34 35	everyone who commits sin is a *slave*. [35] Now the *slave's* place in the house is not assured,
Rm	6	6	2 to free us from the *slavery* of sin.
		17 18	You were once *slaves* of sin, but . . . you submitted . . . to the creed you were taught. [18] You may have been freed from the *slavery* of sin, but only to become ['slaves'] of
		19	7 righteousness. [19] . . . as once you put your bodies *at the service* of vice . . , so now you must put them *at the service of* righteousness . . . [20] When you were *slaves* of sin, you felt no obligation to righteousness,
		20 F	
	8	15	5 The spirit you received is not the spirit of *slaves* bringing fear into your lives again; it is the spirit of sons
		21 F	5 [creation still retains the hope] of being freed, like us, from its *slavery* to decadence.
1 Co	7	15	if the unbelieving partner does not consent, they may separate; in these circumstances, the brother or sister is not 'tied (lit. *bound in service*):
		4	
		23 F	do not be the *slaves* of other men.
	9	19 F	4 though I am not a slave of any man I have *made* myself the *slave of* everyone
		27	10 I treat my body hard and *make* it *obey* me,
2 Co	4	5	it is not ourselves that we are preaching, but Christ Jesus . . , and ourselves as your *servants* for Jesus's sake.
	11	20 8	[you can cheerfully tolerate fools,] yes, even to tolerating somebody who *makes slaves of* you,
Ga	2	4 8	some who do not really belong to the brotherhood . . . want to *reduce* us all *to slavery*.
	4	3	4 before we came of age we were [as good as] *slaves* to the elemental principles of this world,
		7	it is this that makes you a son, you are not a *slave* any more;
		8 9	2 Once you were ignorant of God, and *enslaved* to 'gods' . . .; [9] . . . how can you want to go back to elemental things 2 . . . and *be their slaves*?
		24 F	5 The first [covenant] . . , whose children are *slaves*, is Hagar
		25 F	[25] . . . and she corresponds to the present Jerusalem that 2 *is a slave* like her children.
	5	1 F	5 do not submit again to the yoke of *slavery*.
		13 F	2 *Serve* one another . . . in works of love,
Tt	2	3	the older women should behave as though they were religious, with no scandalmongering 'and no habitual (lit. without 4 *being slaves to*) winedrinking
	3	3	2 there was a time when we too were . . . *enslaved* by different passions
Heb	2	15	5 [Christ] set free all those who had been held in *slavery* all their lives by the fear of death.
2 P	2	19 F	[Self-willed people] may promise freedom but they themselves are [slaves], *slaves* to corruption; because if anyone lets 4 himself be dominated by anything, then he is a *slave* to it;

4. SERVANT: *PAIS*

2 *paidiskē* 13   1 *pais* 15/24

1: SERVANT (OF GOD)

a) Jesus

Mt	12	18	(Is 42 1) Here is my *servant* whom I have chosen,
Ac	3	13	it is the God of . . . our ancestors, who has glorified his *servant* Jesus,

Ac	3	26	God raised up his *servant* and sent him to bless you
	4	27	an alliance . . . against your holy *servant* Jesus
		30	to work miracles . . . through the name of your holy *servant* Jesus.

b) Israel, David

Lk	1	54 69	He has come to the help of Israel his *servant*, he has raised up for us a power for salvation in the House of his *servant* David,
Ac	4	25	speaking through our ancestor David, your *servant*:

2: SERVANT (GENERALLY) – SERVANT-GIRL, SLAVE-GIRL, MAID

Mt	8	6	Sir, . . . my *servant* is lying at home paralysed
		8	just give the word and my *servant* will be cured.
		13	the *servant* was cured at that moment.
	14	2	[Herod] said to his 'court (lit. *servants*), 'This is John the Baptist'
	26	69	2 a *servant-girl* came up to Peter and said, 'You too were with Jesus'
Mk	14	66	2 one of the high priest's *servant-girls* came up [to Peter]
		69	2 The *servant-girl* saw [Peter]
Lk	7	7	give the word and let my *servant* be cured.
	12	45	the servant who . . . sets about beating the *menservants* and 2 the *maids*,
	15	26	Calling one of the *servants* [the elder son] asked what it was all about.
	22	56	2 a *servant-girl* saw [Peter],
Jn	18	17	2 The *maid* on duty at the door said to Peter,
Ac	12	13	2 [Peter] knocked at the outside door and a *servant* called Rhoda came to answer it.
	16	16	2 we met a *slave-girl* who was a soothsayer
Ga	4	22 F	2 Abraham had two sons, one by a *slave-girl*, and one by his 2 free-born wife. [23] The child of the *slave-girl* was born in the ordinary way;
		23 F	
		30 F	2 Does not scripture say (Gn 21 10): Drive away that *slave-girl* 2 and her son; this *slave-girl's* son is not to share the inheritance with the son of the free woman? [31] . . . we are the children, not of the *slave-girl*, but of the free-born wife.
		31 F	2

5. SERVE – SERVANT: *THERAPEUŌ*

1 *therapeia* 1/3   3 *therapōn* 1
2 *therapeuō* 1/43

1: SERVE (GOD) – SERVANT (OF GOD)

Ac	17	25	2 Nor is [God] dependent on 'anything that' human hands 2 *can do for* him (or: being *served* by human hands)
Heb	3	5	3 Moses was faithful in the House of God, as a *servant*, . . . [6] but Christ was faithful as a son,

2: SERVANTS – HOUSEHOLD

Lk	12	42 <	What sort of steward . . . is faithful and wise enough for the master to place him over his 'household (or: *servants*) . . .?

6. SERVE – SERVANT, ATTENDANT – ASSISTANT: *HYP-ĒRETEŌ*

2 *hyp-ēreteō* 3   1 *hyp-ēretēs* 20

1: SERVANT (OF GOD) – SERVE (GOD) – MINISTERS (OF THE WORD)

Lk	1	2	those who from the outset were eyewitnesses and *ministers* of the word,
Ac	13	36	2 when David . . . had *served* God's purposes he died;
	26	16	[I am Jesus.] I have appeared to you . . . to appoint you as my *servant* and as witness of this vision in which you have seen me,
1 Co	4	1	People must think of us as Christ's *servants*,

2: ATTENDANT, ASSISTANT (OF THE TEMPLE, THE SYNAGOGUE) – OFFICER, GUARD

Mt	5	25	or [your opponent] may hand you over to the judge and the judge to the 'officer (or: *attendant*),
	26	58	when [Peter] reached the high priest's palace, he went in and sat down with the *attendants*
Mk	14	54	Peter had followed him . . . into the high priest's palace, and was sitting with the *attendants*

Mk 14 65		the *attendants* rained blows on [Jesus].
Lk 4 20		[In the synagogue Jesus] rolled up the scroll, gave it back to the *assistant* and sat down.
Jn 7 32	○	the ʳPharisees sent the ʳTemple police (lit. *officers*) to arrest [Jesus].
45		The ʳpolice (lit. *officers*) went back to the chief priests and Pharisees
46		The ʳpolice (lit. *officers*) replied, 'There has never been anybody who has spoken like him'.
18 3		[Judas] brought the cohort to this place together with [a detachment of] *guards*
12		The cohort . . . and the Jewish *guards* seized Jesus
18		the servants and *guards* had lit a charcoal fire
22		one of the *guards* standing by gave Jesus a slap in the face,
36		if my kingdom were of this world, my *men* would have fought
19 6		the chief priests and the *guards* shouted, 'Crucify him!
Ac 5 22		when the *officials* arrived at the prison they found [the apostles] were not inside.
26		The captain went with his *men* and fetched them.

3: SERVE, ATTEND (GENERALLY) – ASSISTANT

Ac 13 5		[Barnabas and Saul] landed at Salamis and proclaimed the word of God in the synagogues . . .; John acted as their *assistant*.
20 34	2	the work I did ʳearned enough (lit. *served*) to meet my needs
24 23	2	[Felix] then gave orders . . . that none of [Paul's] own people should be prevented from ʳ*seeing to* his *needs* (or: *attending* him).

7. SERVE – ATTEND, WAIT UPON: *PAR-(H)EDREUŌ*

1 *par-(h)edreuō* 1   2 *eu-par-(h)edros* 1

1 Co 7 35	2	to make sure that . . . you *give your* undivided *attention to* the Lord.
9 13		those *serving* at the altar can claim their share from the altar itself.

8. SERVICE, SERVE, SERVANT – MINISTRY, MINISTER, ADMINISTRATION – DEACON: *DIA-KONEŌ*

1 *dia-koneō* 37   3 *dia-konos* 30
2 *dia-konia* 34

1: (GOSPEL) MINISTRY, MISSION – (APOSTOLIC) SERVICE, ADMINISTRATION – SERVANT (OF GOD)

Ac 1 17	2	[Judas] after having been one of our number and actually sharing this *ministry* of ours.
25	2	to take over this *ministry* and apostolate, which Judas abandoned
6 4	2	[we will] continue to devote ourselves to prayer and to the *service* of the word.
12 25	2	Barnabas and Saul completed their ʳtask (lit. *ministry*) and came back from Jerusalem.
20 24	2	provided that when I finish my race I have carried out the *mission* the Lord Jesus gave me
21 19	2	[Paul] gave a detailed account of all that God had done among the pagans through his *ministry*.
Rm 11 13	2	I have been sent to the pagans as their apostle, and I am proud of *being sent*,
12 7	2/2	if [your gift is] *administration*, then use it for *administration*;
13 4	3	The state is there to *serve* God for your benefit . . . The authorities are there to *serve* God:
1 Co 3 5	3	what is Apollos and what is Paul? They are *servants* who brought the faith to you.
12 5	2	there are all sorts of *service* to be done, but always to the same Lord;
16 15	2	the Stephanas family . . . have really worked hard ʳto help (lit. in the *service* of) the saints.
2 Co 3 3		you are a letter from Christ, ʳdrawn up (lit. *being sent*) by us,
6	3	[God] has given us the qualifications to be the *administrators* of this new covenant,
8		then how much greater will be the brightness that surrounds
9	2	the *administering* of the Spirit? ⁹ For if there was any splendour in administering condemnation, there must be
	2	very much greater splendour in *administering* justification.
4 1	2	we have . . . been entrusted with this [work of] *administration*,
5 18	2	God . . . gave us the [work of] *handing on* this reconciliation,
6 3	2	We do nothing that people might object to, so as not to bring discredit on our function as God's *servants*. ⁴ Instead, we
4	3	prove we are *servants* of God by great fortitude

2 Co 11 8	2	I was robbing other churches, living on them so that I could *serve* you.
15	3	[Satan's] servants, too, disguise themselves as the *servants* of righteousness.
23	3	The *servants* of Christ [are they]? . . . so am I, and more than they:
Ep 3 7	3	I have been made the *servant* of that gospel
4 12	2	the saints together make a unity in the work of *service*,
Col 1 7	3	Epaphras . . . is . . . a faithful deputy for us as Christ's *servant*.
23	3	the Good News, . . . of which I, Paul, have become the *servant*.
25	3	I became the *servant* of the Church
4 17	2	Remember the *service* that the Lord wants you to do,
1 Th 3 2	3	Timothy, who is God's ʳhelper (ᵛ *servant*) in spreading the Good News of Christ
1 Tm 1 12		Christ Jesus our Lord . . . judged me faithful enough to call me into his *service*
4 6	3	you will be a good *servant* of Christ Jesus
2 Tm 4 5	2	make the preaching of the Good News your life's work, in thoroughgoing *service*.
11	2	I find [Mark] a useful helper in my ʳwork (lit. *ministry*).
1 P 1 12	2	the news they brought . . . was ʳfor you and not for (lit. *being sent* to you and not to) themselves.

2: SERVICE = (FINANCIAL) RELIEF, AID

Ac 11 29	2	The disciples decided to send *relief* . . . to the brothers living in Judaea.
15 25		First . . . I must ʳtake a present of money (lit. go to *be of service*) to the saints in Jerusalem.
31	2	Pray that . . . the *aid* I carry to Jerusalem may be accepted by the saints.
2 Co 8 4		[the churches in Macedonia gave far more than they could afford,] begging and begging us for the favour of sharing
	2	in this *service* to the saints
19	2	this errand of mercy that . . . we ʳhave undertaken (lit. are *being of service* in)
9 1	2	on the subject of [offering your] *services* to the saints,
12	2	*doing* this holy service is not only supplying all the needs of
13	2	the saints, . . . ¹³ By offering this *service*, you show them what you are,

3: DEACON, DEACONESS – SERVE AS DEACON

Rm 16 1	3	our sister Phoebe, a *deaconess* of the church at Cenchreae.
Ph 1 1	3	From Paul and Timothy . . . to all the saints in Christ Jesus, together with their presiding elders and *deacons*.
1 Tm 3 8	3	*deacons* must be respectable men . . . ¹⁰ They are . . . only
10		[to be] admitted to *serve as deacons* if there is nothing against them. ¹¹In the same way, the women [? deaconesses; ? deacons' wives] must be respectable, not gossips but
12	3	sober and quite reliable. ¹² *Deacons* must not have been married more than once.
13		Those . . . who *carry out* their *duties* well *as deacons* will earn a high standing

4: SERVE (GENERALLY), WAIT ON – LOOK AFTER, ADMINISTER, MINISTER TO – SERVANT, ATTENDANT, HELPER

Ⓓ = Serve Satan

Mt 4 11		Then the devil left [Jesus], and angels appeared and *looked after* him.
8 15		the fever left [Peter's mother-in-law], and she got up and began to *wait on* [Jesus].
20 26	3	anyone who wants to be great among you must be your *servant*,
28 X		the Son of Man came not to be *served* but to *serve*,
22 13 <	3	the king said to the *attendants*, 'Bind him hand and foot'
23 11	3	The greatest among you must be your *servant*.
25 44		Lord, when did we see you hungry or thirsty . . . and did not *come to* your *help*?
27 55		many women . . . had followed Jesus from Galilee and *looked after* him.
Mk 1 13		[Jesus] was with the wild beasts, and the angels *looked after* him.
31		the fever left [Simon's mother-in-law] and she began to *wait on* them.
9 35	3	If anyone wants to be first, he must make himself . . . *servant* of all.
10 43	3	anyone who wants to become great among you must be your *servant*,
45 X		the Son of Man himself did not come to be *served* but to *serve*,
15 41		These [women] used to follow [Jesus] and *look after* him when he was in Galilee.

Lk	4 39	[Simon's mother-in-law] immediately got up and began to *wait on* them.
	8 3	[certain women] who *provided for* [Jesus and the Twelve] out of their own resources.
	10 40 2	Martha who was distracted with all the *serving* said, 'Lord, do you not care that my sister is leaving me to do the *serving* all by myself?'
	12 37	the master . . . will . . . sit [the servants] down at table and *wait on* them.
	17 8 <	make yourself tidy and *wait on* me while I eat and drink.
	22 26	the leader [among you must behave] as if he were the *one who serves*. 27 For who is the greater: the one at table or the *one who serves*? The one at table, surely? Yet here am I among you as *one who serves*!
	27 X	
Jn	2 5 3	[Jesus's] mother said to the *servants*, 'Do whatever he tells you'.
	9 3	only the *servants* who had drawn the water knew [where the wine came from]
	12 2	They gave a dinner for [Jesus at Bethany]; Martha *waited on* them
	26	If a man *serves* me, he must follow me, wherever I am, my *servant* will be there too. If anyone *serves* me, my Father will honour him.
	3/	
Ac	6 1 2	in the daily *distribution* [the Hellenists'] widows were being overlooked.
	2	It would not be right for us to neglect the word of God so as to *give out* food;
	19 22	[Paul] sent two of his ʳhelpers (or: *assistants*) ahead of him to Macedonia,
Rm	15 8 X 3	The reason Christ became the *servant* of circumcised Jews
2 Co	3 7 2	if the *administering* of death . . . was accompanied by such a brightness . . . 9 . . . if there was any splendour in *administering* condemnation,
	9 2	
	8 20	We hope that . . . there will be no accusations made about our *administering* such a large fund;
	11 15 ⑪ 3	there is no need to be surprised when [Satan's] *servants*, too, disguise themselves as the servants of righteousness.
Ga	2 17	it would follow that Christ ʳhad induced us (lit. was an *assistant*) to sin, which would be absurd.
	X 3	
Ep	6 21 3	Tychicus, my loyal *helper* in the Lord,
Col	4 7 3	Tychicus . . . is . . . a loyal *helper* and companion in the service of the Lord.
2 Tm	1 18	You know . . . how much [Onesiphorus] ʳhelped (ᵛ me) (or: *assisted*) at Ephesus.
Phm	13	I should have liked to keep [Onesimus] with me . . . to ʳhelp (or: *attend*) me while I am in . . . chains
Heb	1 14 2	[angels] are all spirits whose work is service, sent to ʳhelp (or: *attend*) those who will be the heirs of salvation.
	6 10	God would not be so unjust as to forget . . . the love that you have for his name or the *services* [you have] *done*, and the *services* you are still doing, for the saints.
1 P	4 10	like good stewards responsible for all these different graces of God, *put yourselves at the service of* others. 11 If you are a . . . *helper*, help as though every action was done at God's orders;
	11	
Rv	2 19 2	I know your faith and ʳdevotion (lit. *service*)

9. SERVICE, SERVE, SERVANT – MINISTRY, MINISTER: *LEIT-OURGEŌ*

3 *leit-ourgeō*	3	4 *leit-ourgikos*	1
1 *leit-ourgia*	6	2 *leit-ourgos*	5

1: SERVICE, MINISTRY, DUTY (TO GOD) – SERVANT, MINISTER (OF GOD)

Lk	1 23	When [Zechariah's] time of *service* came to an end
Ac	13 2 3	One day while they were *offering worship* to the Lord
Rm	13 6 2	all government officials are God's ʳofficers (or: *ministers*).
	15 16 2	[God] has appointed me a ʳpriest (or: *minister*) of Jesus Christ,
Ph	2 17	if my blood has to be shed as part of your own sacrifice and ʳoffering (or: *service*)
Heb	1 7 2	(cf. Ps 104 4) He makes his angels winds and his *servants* flames of fire.
	14 4	[angels] are all spirits *whose work is service*,
	8 2 X 2	[our high priest] is the *minister* of the sanctuary
	6 X	[Christ] has been given a *ministry* of a far higher order,
	9 21	[Moses] sprinkled the tent and all the *liturgical* vessels with blood
	10 11 3	All the priests stand *at their duties* every day,

2: SERVICES (TO THE SAINTS) – SERVE, MINISTER TO (PAUL)

Rm	15 27 3	the pagans who share the spiritual possessions of these poor people have a duty to ʳhelp (lit. *be of service to*) them with temporal possessions.

2 Co	9 12	doing this *holy service* is not only supplying all the needs of the saints,
Ph	2 25	Epaphroditus . . . was sent ʳas your representative to help me when I needed (lit. to *minister* to my needs for) someone to be my companion in working
	2	
	30	he risked his life to ʳgive me the help (lit. render me the *service*) that you were not able to give me yourselves.

SLEEP – WAKE

1. Sleep, Asleep, Fall asleep – Die – Dream
  1: Sleep, Fall asleep – Drowsy: *hypnos*
  2: Sleep, Fall asleep: *kath-eudō*
    a) Sleep, Asleep – Fall asleep
    b) Be asleep = Be (as, among the) dead
  3: Fall asleep: *koimaomai*
    a) Fall asleep, Be sleeping – Sleep, Rest
    b) Fall asleep = Die
  4: Drowsy, Doze – Asleep: *nystazō*
  5: Sluggish – Numbness, Stupor: *kata-nyxis*

  6: In a dream: *kat' onar*
  7: Dream – Delusion: *en-(h)ypnion*
2. Awake – Watchful
  1: Awake – Alert – Alive: *grēgoreō*
    a) Stay, Be, Keep awake – Alert, Vigilant, On guard
    b) Awake = Alive
  2: Stay awake – Wakeful, Sleepless – Watch over, Look after: *agr-(h)ypneō*
3. Wake, Woke – Awake: *ex-(h)ypnizō*

1. SLEEP, ASLEEP, FALL ASLEEP – DIE – DREAM

1: SLEEP, FALL ASLEEP – DROWSY: *HYPNOS*

1 *hypnos* 6   2 *aph-ypnoō* 1

Mt	1 24	When Joseph woke up from his *sleep* he did what the angel of the Lord had told him to do:
Lk	8 23 X 2	as they sailed [Jesus] *fell asleep*.
	9 32	Peter and his companions were heavy with *sleep*,
Jn	11 13	The phrase Jesus used referred to the death of Lazarus, but they thought that by 'rest' he meant '*sleep*',
Ac	20 9	as Paul went on and on . . . Eutychus . . . ʳgrew *drowsy* and was (or: was brought into a deep *sleep*, finally becoming) ʳovercome (lit. brought down) by *sleep* and fell to the ground three floors below.
Rm	13 11 ○	the time has come: you must wake up from your *sleep* now:

2: SLEEP, FALL ASLEEP: *KATH-EUDŌ*

kath-eudō 22

a) Sleep, Asleep – Fall asleep

Mt	8 24 X	the waves were breaking right over the boat. But he was *asleep*.
	13 25 <	While everybody was *asleep* his enemy . . . sowed darnel
	25 5 <	The bridegroom was late, and [the ten bridesmaids] grew drowsy and *fell asleep*.
	26 40	[Jesus] came back to the disciples and found them *sleeping*,
	43	[Jesus] came back again and found them *sleeping*, their eyes were so heavy.
	45	You can *sleep* on now and take your rest.
Mk	4 27 <	while [the sower] *sleeps*, when he is awake, the seed is sprouting
	38 X	he was in the stern, his head on the cushion, *asleep*.
	13 36 <	[stay awake,] . . . [the master] must not find you *asleep*.
	14 37	[Jesus] came back and found them *sleeping*, and he said to Peter, 'Simon, are you *asleep*?
	40	once more he . . . found them *sleeping*, their eyes were so heavy;
	41	You can *sleep* on now and take your rest.
Lk	22 46	'Why are you *asleep*?' [Jesus] said to them. 'Get up and pray . . .'
1 Th	5 6 ○	we should not go on *sleeping*, as everyone else does, but stay wide awake and sober. 7 Night is the time for *sleepers* to *sleep*
	7	

b) Be asleep = Be (as, among the) dead

Mt	9 24	[Jesus said,] '. . . the little girl is not dead, she is *asleep*'.
Mk	5 39	[Jesus] said to them '. . . The child is not dead, but *asleep*'.
Lk	8 52	Jesus said, 'Stop crying; she is not dead, but *asleep*'.
Ep	5 14 ○	Wake up from your *sleep*, rise from the dead,
1 Th	5 10	[Jesus] died for us so that, alive or *dead*, we should still live united to him.

3: FALL ASLEEP: *KOIMAOMAI*

1 *koimaomai* 18   2 *koimēsis* 1

a) Fall asleep, Be sleeping – Sleep, Rest

Mt 28	13	This is what you must say, 'His disciples . . . stole him away while we were *asleep*'.
Lk 22	45	[Jesus] went to the disciples and found them *sleeping* for sheer grief.
Jn 11	11	Our friend Lazarus is *resting*, I am going to wake him.
	12	[12] The disciples said to him, 'Lord, if he is able to *rest*, he is sure to get better'. [13] The phrase Jesus used referred to
	13	the death of Lazarus, but they thought that by '*rest*' he meant 'sleep',
	2	
Ac 12	6	Peter was *sleeping* between two soldiers,

b) Fall asleep = Die

Mt 27	52	the bodies of many holy men rose from *the dead*,
Jn 11	11	Our friend Lazarus is *resting*, I am going to wake him.
Ac 7	60	with these words [Stephen] *fell asleep*.
13	36	David . . . *died*; he was buried with his ancestors
1 Co 7	39	if the husband *dies*, [the wife] is free to marry anybody she likes,
11	30	In fact that is why many of you . . . have *died*.
15	6	though some [of the five hundred brothers] have *died*;
	18	[if Christ has not been raised] all who have *died* in Christ have perished.
	20	Christ has in fact been raised from the dead, the first fruits of all who have *fallen asleep*.
	51	we are not all going to *die*, but we shall all be changed.
1 Th 4	13	We want you to be quite certain, brothers, about those who have *died* . . . [14] We believe that Jesus died and rose
	14	again, and that it will be the same for those who have *died* in Jesus: God will bring them with him. [15] We . . . who
	15	are left alive . . . will not have any advantage over those who have *died*
2 P 3	4	Everything goes on as it has since the Fathers *died*, as it has since it began at the creation.

4: DROWSY, DOZE – ASLEEP: *NYSTAZŌ*

nystazō 2

Mt 25	5 <	[the ten bridesmaids] grew *drowsy* and fell asleep.
2 P 2	3 ○	Destruction is not *asleep* [for the false teachers].

5: SLUGGISH – NUMBNESS, STUPOR: *KATA-NYXIS*

kata-nyxis 1

Rm 11	8	(Is 29 10) God has given them a *sluggish* spirit, unseeing eyes

6: IN A DREAM: *KAT' ONAR*

kat' onar 6

Mt 1	20	the angel of the Lord appeared to [Joseph] *in a dream* and said, '. . . do not be afraid to take Mary home as your wife'
2	12	[the wise men] were warned *in a dream* not to go back to Herod,
	13	the angel of the Lord appeared to Joseph *in a dream* and said, '. . . escape into Egypt'
	19	the angel of the Lord appeared *in a dream* to Joseph in Egypt [20] and said, '. . . go back to the land of Israel'
	22	. . . [22] . . . being warned *in a dream* he left for the region of Galilee.
27	19	[Pilate's] wife sent him a message, '. . . I have been upset all day *by a dream* [I had] about [Jesus]'.

7: DREAM – DELUSION: *EN-(H)YPNION*

1 *en-(h)ypniazomai* 2   2 *en-(h)ypnion* 1

Ac 2	17	/2 (Jl 3 1) your old men shall *dream dreams*.
Jude	8	in their *delusions* [these people] . . . defile their bodies and disregard authority,

2. AWAKE – WATCHFUL

1: AWAKE – ALERT – ALIVE: *GRĒGOREŌ*

1 *grēgoreō* 23   2 *dia-grēgoreō* 1

a) Stay, Be, Keep awake – Alert, Vigilant, On guard

Mt 24	42	*stay awake*, because you do not know the day when your master is coming.

Mt 24	43 <	if the householder had known . . . he would have *stayed awake*
25	13	*stay awake*, because you do not know either the day or the hour.
26	38	[Jesus] said to them, '. . . Wait here and *keep awake* with me'.
	40	So you had not the strength to *keep awake* with me one hour?
	41	You should *be awake*, and praying not to be put to the test.
Mk 13	34 <	[the man] has told the doorkeeper to *stay awake*.
	35	So *stay awake*, because you do not know when the master . . . is coming,
	37	I say to all: *Stay awake*!
14	34	he said to them '. . . Wait here, and *keep awake*.'
	37	Simon, are you asleep? Had you not the strength to *keep awake* one hour?
	38	You should *be awake*, and praying not to be put to the test.
Lk 9	32	2 [Peter and his companions] *kept awake* and saw his glory
12	37	Happy those servants whom the master finds *awake*
	39	the householder . . . ([v] would have *kept awake* and) would not have let anyone break through the wall of his house.
Ac 20	31	So be *on your guard*,
1 Co 16	13	*Be awake* to all the dangers; stay firm in the faith;
Col 4	2	be thankful as you *stay awake* to pray.
1 Th 5	6	*stay wide awake* and sober.
1 P 5	8	Be calm but *vigilant*,
Rv 3	2	*Wake up*; revive what little you have left:
	3	If you do not *wake up*, I shall come to you like a thief,
16	15	I shall come like a thief. Happy is the man who has *stayed awake*

b) Awake = Alive

1 Th 5	10	so that, *alive* or dead, we should still live united to [Jesus Christ]

2: STAY AWAKE – WAKEFUL, SLEEPLESS – WATCH OVER, LOOK AFTER: *AGR-(H)YPNEŌ*

1 *agr-(h)ypneō* 4   2 *agr-(h)ypnia* 2

Mk 13	33	Be on your guard, *stay awake*, because you never know when the time will come.
Lk 21	36	*Stay awake*, praying at all times
2 Co 6	5	2 labouring, *sleepless*, starving.
11	27	2 often *without sleep*; I have been hungry and thirsty and often starving;
Ep 6	18	Pray all the time . . . Never get tired of *staying awake* to pray
Heb 13	17	Obey your leaders . . . because . . . they *look after* your souls;

3. WAKE, WOKE – AWAKE: *EX-(H)YPNIZŌ*

1 *ex-(h)ypnizō* 1   2 *ex-(h)ypnos* 1

Jn 11	11 ○	Our friend Lazarus is resting, I am going to *wake* him.
Ac 16	27	2 When the gaoler *woke* . . . he drew his sword

SMELL – INCENSE – SPICE

1. **Smell – Fragrance:** *osmē*
   a) Smell – Stench – Scent, Fragrance
   b) Smell, Fragrance, Sweet-smelling (metaphorically)
2. **Incense – Frankincense**
   1: Incense – Altar of incense – (to) Burn incense: *thymiama*
   2: Frankincense – Censer: *libanos*
   a) Frankincense
   b) Censer
3. **Spice, Spices**
   1: Spice, Spices
   a) *arōma*
   b) *amōmon*
   2: Myrrh – Aloes: *smyrna, aloē*
   3: Nard: *nardos*
   4: Cinnamon: *kinnamōmon*
4. **Ointment, Oil of Myrrh Perfume:** *myron*

1. SMELL – FRAGRANCE: *OSMĒ*

1 *osmē*	6	4 *ozō*	1
3 *os-phrēsis* 1		2 *eu-ōdia*	3

a) Smell – Stench – Scent, Fragrance

Jn 11	39	4 Lord, by now [Lazarus] will *smell*; this is the fourth day.
12	3	the house was full of the *scent* of the ointment.
1 Co 12	17	If your whole body was just one . . . ear, how would you *smell* anything?
	3	

b) Smell, Fragrance, Sweet-smelling (metaphorically)

2 Co 2 14	God . . . is spreading the knowledge of himself, [like] a *sweet smell*, everywhere. ¹⁵ We are ⌐Christ's incense (lit.
15	the *sweet smell* of Christ) to God for those who are being
	2 saved and for those who are not; ¹⁶ for the last, the *smell*
16	of death that leads to death, for the first the *sweet smell* of life that leads to life.
Ep 5 2	[Christ] loved you, giving himself up in our place as a
/2	*sweet-smelling* and *fragrant* offering and as a sacrifice to God.
Ph 4 18	I have received from Epaphroditus the offering that you
/2	sent, a *sweet-smelling fragrance* – the sacrifice that God accepts and finds pleasing.

2. INCENSE – FRANKINCENSE

1: INCENSE – ALTAR OF INCENSE – (TO) BURN INCENSE: *THYMIAMA*

1 *thymiama* 6   3 *thymiatērion* 1
2 *thymiaō* 1

Lk 1 9	it fell to [Zechariah] by lot . . . to enter the Lord's sanctuary
10	2/ and *burn incense* there. ¹⁰ And at the hour of *incense* the
11	whole congregation was outside, praying. ¹¹ Then there appeared to him the angel of the Lord, standing on the right of the altar of *incense*.
Heb 9 4	3 [the Holy of Holies] to which belonged the gold *altar of incense*,
Rv 5 8	a golden bowl full of *incense* made of the prayers of the saints.
8 3	A large quantity of *incense* was given to [the angel] to offer with the prayers of all the saints on the golden altar . . .
4	⁴ and . . . the smoke of the *incense* went up in the presence of God
18 13	the myrrh and ⌐ointment (lit. frankincense) and *incense*;

2: FRANKINCENSE – CENSER: *LIBANOS*

1 *libanos* 2   2 *libanōtos* 2

a) Frankincense

Mt 2 11	[the wise men] offered [the child] gifts of gold and *frankincense* and myrrh.
Rv 18 13	the myrrh and ⌐ointment (lit. *frankincense*) and incense;

b) Censer

Rv 8 3	2 Another angel, who had a golden *censer*, came and stood at the altar.
5	2 Then the angel took the *censer* and filled it with the fire

3. SPICE, SPICES

1: SPICE, SPICES

a) arōma

arōma 4

Mk 16 1	Mary of Magdala, Mary . . . and Salome, bought *spices* with which to go and anoint [Jesus].
Lk 23 56	[the women] prepared *spices* and ointments.
24 1	they went to the tomb with the *spices* they had prepared.
Jn 19 40	[Joseph of Arimathaea and Nicodemus] took the body of Jesus and wrapped it with the *spices* in linen

b) amōmon

amōmon 1

Rv 18 13	the cinnamon and *spices*, the myrrh and ⌐ointment (lit. frankincense) and incense;

2: MYRRH – ALOES: *SMYRNA, ALOĒ*

1 *aloē* 1   2 *smyrna* 2
3 *smyrnizō* 1

Mt 2 11	[the wise men] offered [the child] gifts of gold and frankincense
	2 and *myrrh*.
Mk 15 23	3 They offered [Jesus] wine *mixed with myrrh*, but he refused it.
Jn 19 39	2/ Nicodemus . . . brought a mixture of *myrrh* and *aloes*,

3: NARD: *NARDOS*

nardos 2

Mk 14 3	a woman came in with an alabaster jar of very costly ointment, pure *nard*.
Jn 12 3	Mary brought in a pound of very costly ointment, pure *nard*,

4: CINNAMON: *KINNAMŌMON*

kinnamōmon 1

Rv 18 13	the *cinnamon* and spices, the myrrh and ⌐ointment (lit. frankincense) and incense;

4. OINTMENT, OIL OF MYRRH – PERFUME: *MYRON*

1 *myron* 14   2 *myrizō* 1

Mt 26 7	a woman came to [Jesus] with an alabaster jar of the most expensive *ointment*,
12	When she poured this *ointment* on my body, she did it to prepare me for burial.
Mk 14 3	a woman came in with an alabaster jar of very costly *ointment*, pure nard. ⁴ Some . . . said . ., 'Why this waste of
4	*ointment*? ⁵ *Ointment* like this could have been sold for
5	over three hundred denarii'
8	2 she has *anointed* my body beforehand for its burial.
Lk 7 37	[the woman] had brought with her an alabaster jar of *ointment*,
38	she covered his feet with kisses and anointed them with the *ointment*.
46	she has anointed my feet with *ointment*.
23 56	[the women] prepared spices and ⌐ointments (or: *perfumes*).
Jn 11 2	It was the same Mary . . . who anointed the Lord with *ointment*
12 3	Mary brought in a pound of very costly *ointment*, pure nard, and with it anointed the feet of Jesus . . .; the house was full of the scent of the *ointment*.
5	Why wasn't this *ointment* sold for three hundred denarii . . .?
Rv 18 13	the cinnamon and spices, the *myrrh* and ⌐ointment (lit. frankincense) and incense;

SNAKE – DRAGON – SCORPION

1. Reptile, Crawling animal – Snake, Serpent	3: Frog: *batrachos*
1: Reptile – Crawling animal: *herpeton*	**3. Dragon:** *drakōn*
2: Serpent, Snake: *ophis*	**4. Scorpion – Sting**
2. Viper – Asp – Frog	1: Scorpion: *skorpios*
1: Viper: *echidna*	2: Sting – Goad: *kentron*
2: Asp – Viper, Adder: *aspis*	a) Sting
	b) Goad

1. REPTILE, CRAWLING ANIMAL – SNAKE, SERPENT

1: REPTILE – CRAWLING ANIMAL: *HERPETON*

herpeton 4

Ac 10 12	[the sheet] contained every possible sort of animal . . . walking, *crawling* or flying ones.
11 6	I . . . saw . . . everything possible that could walk, *crawl* or fly.
Rm 1 23	they exchanged the glory of . . . God for . . . the image of . . . birds, of quadrupeds and *reptiles*.
Jm 3 7	Wild animals and birds, *reptiles* and fish can all be tamed by man,

2: SERPENT, SNAKE: *OPHIS*

ophis 14

Mt 7 10	[Who] would hand [his son] a *snake* when he asked for a fish?
10 16	be cunning as *serpents* and yet as harmless as doves.
23 33	[Scribes and Pharisees, you hypocrites!] *Serpents*,
Mk 16 18	[believers] will pick up *snakes* in their hands,
Lk 10 19	I have given you power to tread underfoot *serpents* and scorpions

Lk 11	11	[What father would] hand [his son] a *snake* instead of a fish?
Jn 3	14	[the Son of Man must be lifted up] as Moses lifted up the
	O	*serpent* in the desert,
1 Co 10	9	We are not to put the Lord to the test: some of [our fathers] did and they were killed by *snakes*.
2 Co 11	3 ⓓ	the *serpent*, with his cunning, seduced Eve,
Rv 9	19	[the horses'] tails were like *snakes*,
12	9 ⓓ	The great dragon, the primeval *serpent*, known as the devil or Satan . . . had deceived all the world,
	14	[the woman] was given a huge pair of eagle's wings to
	ⓓ	fly away from the *serpent* into the desert,
	15 ⓓ	the *serpent* vomited water from his mouth, like a river, after the woman,
20	2 ⓓ	the dragon, that primeval *serpent* . . . is the devil and Satan,

2. VIPER – ASP – FROG

1: VIPER: *ECHIDNA*

echidna 5

Mt 3	7	[John said to the Pharisees,] Brood of *vipers*, who warned you
12	34	Brood of *vipers*, how can your speech be good when you are evil?
23	33	[Scribes and Pharisees, you hypocrites!] Serpents, brood of *vipers*,
Lk 3	7	[John] said, therefore, to the crowds . . , 'Brood of *vipers*,
Ac 28	3	a *viper* brought out by the heat attached itself to [Paul's] hand.

2: ASP – VIPER, ADDER: *ASPIS*

aspis 1

Rm 3	13	(Ps 140 4) *Vipers'* venom is on their lips,

3: FROG: *BATRACHOS*

batrachos 1

Rv 16	13	I saw three foul spirits . . . they looked like *frogs*

3. DRAGON: *DRAKŌN*

drakōn 13

Rv 12	3 ⓓ	a second sight appeared . . . a huge red *dragon* which had seven heads and ten horns,
	4 ⓓ	the *dragon* stopped in front of the woman
	7 ⓓ	Michael and his angels attacked the *dragon*. The *dragon* fought back with his angels,
	9 ⓓ	The great *dragon*, the primeval serpent, known as the devil or Satan . . . had deceived all the world,
	13 ⓓ	the *devil* found himself thrown down to the earth,
	16 ⓓ	the earth . . . swallowed the river thrown up by the *dragon*'s jaws.
	17 ⓓ	the *dragon* was enraged with the woman
13	2 ⓓ	the *dragon* had handed over to [the beast] his own power
	4 ⓓ	[People] prostrated themselves in front of the *dragon*
	11	a second beast . . . made a noise like a *dragon*.
16	13 ⓓ	from the jaws of the *dragon* . . . I saw three foul spirits come;
20	2 ⓓ	[an angel] overpowered the *dragon* . . . which is the devil and Satan

4. SCORPION – STING

1: SCORPION: *SKORPIOS*

skorpios 5

Lk 10	19	I have given you power to tread underfoot serpents and *scorpions*
11	12	[What father would] hand [his son] a *scorpion* if he asked for an egg?
Rv 9	3	locusts . . . were given the powers that *scorpions* have
	5	the pain was to be the pain of a *scorpion*'s sting
	10	[The locusts'] tails were like *scorpions*',

2: STING – GOAD: *KENTRON*

kentron 4

a) Sting

1 Co 15	55 O	(Ho 13 14 G) Death, where is your *sting*? [56] Now the *sting*
	56	of death is sin, and sin gets its power from the Law.

Rv 9	10	[The locusts'] tails were like scorpions', with *stings*,

b) Goad

Ac 26	14	It is hard for you, kicking like this against the *goad*.

SODOM

Gomorrah 4	L Lot 4	1 *polis* 2/164
Sodom 9		

Sodom = Babylon = Rome (Rv)

Mt 10	15	on the day of Judgement it will not go as hard with the land of *Sodom* and *Gomorrah* as with that town.
11	23	if the miracles done in [Capernaum] had been done in *Sodom*, it would have been standing yet. [24] . . . it will not go as
	24	hard with the land of *Sodom* on Judgement day as with you.
Lk 10	12	on that day it will not go as hard with *Sodom* as with that town.
17	28 L	It will be the same as it was in *Lot*'s day: people were eating and drinking . . . and building, [29] (cf. Gn 19) but the
	29 L	day *Lot* left *Sodom*, God rained fire and brimstone from heaven
	32 L	[Nor must anyone in the fields turn back either.] (cf. Gn 19 26) Remember *Lot*'s wife.
Rm 9	29	(Is 1 9) Had the Lord . . . not left us some descendants we should now be like *Sodom*, we should be like *Gomorrah*.
2 P 2	6	1 (cf. Gn 19) The *cities of Sodom* and *Gomorrah*, these too [God] condemned and reduced to ashes . . . [7] he rescued
	7 L	*Lot*, however, a holy man who had been sickened by the shameless way in which these vile people behaved
Jude	7	The fornication of *Sodom* and *Gomorrah* and the other nearby
	1	*towns* was equally unnatural,
Rv 11	8	[Babylon,] the Great City known by the symbolic names *Sodom* and Egypt,

---

SON – DAUGHTER

1. Son: *huios*	e) Sons (of Israel) – Israelites
1: (Jesus the) Son	3: Sons, Children = Men, People
a) the Son of God	(generally) – Subjects, Experts,
b) the son of Mary and Joseph	Heirs
c) the son of David	4: Foal
d) the Son of Man	**2. Daughter:** *thygatēr*
2: (Men as) Sons	1: Daughter (literally and gener-
a) Sons (of God) – Adopted as	ally)
(his) sons	2: Daughter (of Zion = Jerusalem)
b) Sons (of specified people)	3: Daughter (in a wider sense) –
c) Sons (literally and generally)	Descendant
d) Sons (in a wider sense) –	**3. Bastards:** *nothos*
Descendants	

1. SON: *HUIOS*

1 *huios*	243/380	3 *huio-thesia*	5
2 *huios (tou) theou*	49	5 *huios anthrōpou*	4 (Jn 5; Heb; Rv)
4 *huios tou anthrōpou*	84		

1: (JESUS THE) SON

a) the Son of God

Mt 2	15	(Ho 11 1) I called my *son* out of Egypt.
3	17	This is my *Son*, the Beloved; my favour rests on him.
4	3	2 If you are the *Son of God*, tell these stones to turn into loaves.
	6	2 If you are the *Son of God* . . . throw yourself down;
8	29	2 What do you want with us, *Son of God*?
11	27	no one knows the *Son* except the Father, just as no one knows the Father except the *Son* and those to whom the *Son* chooses to reveal him.
14	33	2 The men in the boat . . . said, 'Truly, you are the *Son of God*'.
16	16	Simon Peter spoke up, 'You are the Christ . . . the *Son* of the living God'.
17	5	This is my *Son*, the Beloved; he enjoys my favour.
24	36	as for that day . . . nobody knows it, neither the angels . . . nor the *Son*,

Mt 26 63   I put you on oath . . . to tell us if you are the Christ, the
     2   *Son of God*.

27 40   2 Then save yourself! If you are *God's son*, come down from
     the cross!

43   2 now let God rescue him . . . For he did say, 'I am the *son of
     God*'.

54   [the centurion and the guards] were terrified and said, 'In
     2 truth this was a *son of God*.'

28 19   baptise [disciples of all the nations] in the name of the Father
     and of the *Son* and of the Holy Spirit,

Mk 1 1   The beginning of the Good News about Jesus Christ, ᵛ the
     2 *Son of God*ᵀ.

11   You are my *Son*, the Beloved; my favour rests on you.

3 11   the unclean spirits . . . would . . . shout, 'You are the
     2 *Son of God*!

5 7   What do you want with me, Jesus, *son* of the Most High God?

9 7   This is my *Son*, the Beloved. Listen to him.

13 32   as for that day . . . nobody knows it, neither the angels
     . . . nor the *Son*;

14 61   Are you the Christ, . . . the *Son* of the Blessed One?

15 39   2 The centurion. . . said, 'In truth this man was a *son of God*'.

Lk 1 32   He will be great and will be called *Son* of the Most High.

35   2 so the child will be holy and will be called *Son of God*.

3 22   You are my *Son*, the Beloved; my favour rests on you.

4 3   2 If you are the *Son of God*, tell this stone to turn into a loaf.

9   2 If you are the *Son of God* . . . throw yourself down from here,

41   Devils too came out of many people, howling, 'You are the
     2 *Son of God*'.

8 28   What do you want with me, Jesus, *son* of the Most High God?

9 35   This is my *Son*, the ᵀChosen One (ᵛ Beloved). Listen to
     him.

10 22   no one knows who the *Son* is except the Father, and who the
     Father is except the *Son* and those to whom the *Son*
     chooses to reveal him.

22 70   2 Then they all said, 'So you are the *Son of God* then?' He
     answered, 'It is you who say I am'.

Jn 1 18   ᵛ the only *Son* (G God, only-begotten), who is nearest to the
     Father's heart,

34   Yes, I have seen and I am the witness that he is the ᵛ Chosen
     2 One (G *Son*) of God.

49   2 Nathanael answered, 'Rabbi, you are the *Son of God*,'

3 16   God loved the world so much that he gave his only *Son*,

17   God sent his *Son* into the world not to condemn the world . . .

18   whoever refuses to believe is condemned already, because he
     2 has refused to believe in the name of *God's* only *Son*.

35   The Father loves the *Son* and has entrusted everything to
     him. ³⁶ Anyone who believes in the *Son* has eternal life,

36   but anyone who refuses to believe in the *Son* will never see
     life:

5 19   the *Son* can do nothing by himself; he can do only what he
     sees the Father doing: and whatever the Father does the
     Son does too. ²⁰ For the Father loves the *Son* and shows

20   him everything he does himself,

21   as the Father raises the dead . . . so the *Son* gives life to

22   anyone he chooses; ²² for the Father . . . has entrusted all

23   judgement to the *Son*, ²³ so that all may honour the *Son* as
     they honour the Father. Whoever refuses honour to the
     Son refuses honour to the Father

25   the hour will come . . . when the dead will hear the voice of
     2 the *Son of God*.

26   the Father, who is the source of life, has made the *Son* the
     source of life;

6 40   whoever sees the *Son* and believes in him shall have eternal
     life,

8 36   if the *Son* makes you free, you will be free indeed.

9 35   [Jesus to the man who was born blind:] Do you believe in the
     2 *Son* of ᵀMan (ᵛ *God*)?

10 36   you say to someone the Father has . . . sent . . . 'You are
     2 blaspheming', because he says, 'I am the *Son of God*'.

11 4   This sickness will end . . . in God's glory and through it the
     2 *Son of God* will be glorified.

27   2 I believe that you are the Christ, the *Son of God*, the one who
     was to come into this world.

14 13   so that the Father may be glorified in the *Son*.

17 1   Father, . . . glorify your *Son* so that your *Son* may glorify you:

19 7   according to that Law he ought to die, because he has claimed
     2 to be the *Son of God*.

20 31   These [signs] are recorded so that you may believe that Jesus
     2 is the Christ, the *Son of God*,

Ac 8 37   (ᵛ [the eunuch] replied, 'I believe that Jesus Christ is the
     2 *Son of God*'.)

9 20   2 [Saul] began preaching in the synagogues, 'Jesus is the *Son
     of God*'.

13 33   (Ps 2 7) You are my *son*: today I have become your father.

Rm 1 3   This news is about the *Son* of God who . . . was a descendant
     of David:

4   2 [Jesus] was proclaimed *Son of God* in all his power through
     his resurrection

9   The God I worship . . . by preaching the Good News of his
     Son

Rm 5 10   When we were reconciled to God by the death of his *Son*,
     we were still enemies.

8 3   God dealt with sin by sending his own *Son* in a body as
     physical as any sinful body,

29   the ones [God] chose specially long ago . . . to become true
     images of his *Son*,

32   God did not spare his own *Son*, but gave him up to benefit us
     all,

1 Co 1 9   God by calling you has joined you to his *Son*, Jesus Christ;

15 28   the *Son* himself will be subject in his turn to the One who
     subjected all things to him,

2 Co 1 19   2 The *Son of God*, the Christ Jesus . . . was never Yes and No:

Ga 1 16   [God called me through his grace and chose] to reveal his
     Son in me,

2 20   The life I now live in this body I live in faith: faith in the
     2 *Son of God* who loved me

4 4   when the appointed time came, God sent his *Son*, born of a
     woman,

6   The proof that you are sons is that God has sent the Spirit
     of his *Son* into your hearts:

Ep 4 13   we are all to come to unity in our faith and in our knowledge
     2 of the *Son* of God,

Col 1 13   [the Father] has . . . created a place for us in the kingdom of
     the *Son* that he loves,

1 Th 1 10   you are now waiting for Jesus, his *Son* . . . to come from
     heaven

Heb 1 2   in our own time, the last days, [God] has spoken to us through
     his *Son*,

5   God has never said to any angel (Ps 2 7): You are my *Son* . . .
     or (2 S 7 14): I will be a father to him and he a *son* to me.

8   to his *Son* he says: God, your throne shall last for ever and
     ever;

3 6   Christ was faithful as a *son*,

4 14   2 in Jesus, the *Son of God*, we have the supreme high priest

5 5   [Christ] had [the glory of becoming high priest] from the one
     who said to him (Ps 2 7): You are my *son*, today I have
     become your father,

8   Although he was *Son*, he learnt to obey through suffering;

6 6   2 they have wilfully crucified the *Son of God* and openly mocked
     him.

7 3   2 [Melchizedek] is like the *Son of God*.

28   the promise on oath . . . appointed the *Son* who is made
     perfect for ever.

10 29   2 anyone who tramples on the *Son of God* . . . will be condemned

2 P 1 17   This is my *Son*, the Beloved: he enjoys my favour.

1 Jn 1 3   we are in union with the Father and with his *Son* Jesus Christ.

7   the blood of Jesus, his *Son*, purifies us from all sin.

2 22   The man who denies that Jesus is the Christ . . . is Antichrist;
     and he is denying the Father as well as the *Son*,

23   no one who has the Father can deny the *Son*, and to acknowl-
     edge the *Son* is to have the Father as well.

24   you will live in the *Son* and in the Father;

3 8   2 It was to undo all that the devil has done that the *Son of God*
     appeared.

23   [God's] commandments are these: that we believe in the
     name of his *Son* Jesus Christ and that we love one another

4 9   God sent into the world his only *Son* so that we could have
     life through him,

10   this is the love I mean: . . . God's love for us when he sent
     his *Son*

14   the Father sent his *Son* as saviour of the world.

15   2 If anyone acknowledges that Jesus is the *Son of God*, God
     lives in him,

5 5   Who can overcome the world? Only the man who believes
     2 that Jesus is the *Son of God*:

9   this is God's testimony, given as evidence for his *Son*.

10   2 Everybody who believes in the *Son of God* has this testimony
     inside him; and anyone who will not believe God is making
     God out to be a liar, because he has not trusted the testi-
     mony God has given about his *Son*.

11   God has given us eternal life and this life is in his *Son*;

12   anyone who has the *Son* has life, anyone who does not have
     2 the *Son of God* does not have life.

13   2 you who believe in the name of the *Son of God* . . . have
     eternal life.

20   2 We know, too, that the *Son of God* has come . . . We are in
     the true God, as we are in his *Son*, Jesus Christ.

2 Jn 3   we shall have grace . . . from God the Father and from Jesus
     Christ, the *Son* of the Father.

9   those who keep to what [Christ] taught can have the Father
     and the *Son* with them.

Rv 2 18   2 the *Son of God* who has eyes like a burning flame

b) the son of Mary and Joseph

Mt 1 21   [Mary] will give birth to a *son*

23   (Is 7 14) The virgin will conceive and give birth to a *son*

25   [Mary] gave birth to a *son*;

13 55   This is the carpenter's *son*, surely?

Mk 6 3   This is the carpenter, surely, the *son* of Mary,

Lk 1 31   You are to conceive and bear a *son*,

Lk	2 7	[Mary] gave birth to a *son*, her first-born.
	3 23	Jesus was . . . the *son*, as it was thought, of Joseph
	4 22	This is Joseph's *son*, surely?
Jn	1 45	he is Jesus *son* of Joseph, from Nazareth
	6 42	Surely this is Jesus *son* of Joseph . . . We know his father and mother.

c) the Son of David

Mt	1 1	Jesus Christ, *son* of David, *son* of Abraham:
	9 27	Take pity on us, *Son* of David.
	12 23	Can this be the *Son* of David?
	15 22	Sir, *Son* of David, take pity on me.
	20 30	Have pity on us, *Son* of David.
	31	Have pity on us, *Son* of David.
	21 9	Hosanna to the *Son* of David!
	15	Hosanna to the *Son* of David
	22 42	the Christ? Whose *son* is he? 'David's' they told him.
	45	If David can call him Lord, then how can he be his *son*?
Mk	10 47	*Son* of David, Jesus, have pity on me.
	48	*Son* of David, have pity on me.
	12 35	How can the scribes maintain that the Christ is the *son* of David?
	37	David himself calls him Lord, in what way then can he be his *son*?
Lk	18 38	Jesus, *Son* of David, have pity on me.
	39	*Son* of David, have pity on me.
	20 41	How can people maintain that the Christ is *son* of David?
	44	David here calls him Lord; how then can he be his *son*?

d) the Son of Man

Mt	8 20	4 the *Son of Man* has nowhere to lay his head.
	9 6	4 the *Son of Man* has authority on earth to forgive sins,
	10 23	you will not have gone the round of the towns of Israel before 4 the *Son of Man* comes.
	11 19	4 The *Son of Man* came, eating and drinking,
	12 8	4 the *Son of Man* is master of the sabbath.
	32	4 anyone who says a word against the *Son of Man* will be forgiven;
	40	4 so will the *Son of Man* be in the heart of the earth for three days and three nights.
	13 37	4 The sower of the good seed is the *Son of Man*.
	41	4 The *Son of Man* will send his angels
	16 13	4 Who do people say the *Son of Man* is?
	27	4 the *Son of Man* is going to come in the glory of his Father
	28	some of these . . . will not taste death before they see the 4 *Son of Man* coming with his kingdom.
	17 9	4 Tell no one about the vision until the *Son of Man* has risen from the dead.
	12	4 the *Son of Man* will suffer similarly at their hands.
	22	4 The *Son of Man* is going to be handed over into the power of men;
	18 11	4 (ᵛ For the *Son of Man* has come to save what was lost)
	19 28	4 when . . . the *Son of Man* sits on his throne of glory,
	20 18	4 the *Son of Man* is about to be handed over to the chief priests and scribes.
	28	4 the *Son of Man* came not to be served but to serve,
	24 27	4 the coming of the *Son of Man* will be like lightning
	30	4 then the sign of the *Son of Man* will appear in heaven; then 4 too all the peoples of the earth . . . will see the *Son of Man* coming on the clouds of heaven
	37	4 As it was in Noah's day, so will it be when the *Son of Man* comes.
	39	4 It will be like this when the *Son of Man* comes.
	44	4 the *Son of Man* is coming at an hour you do not expect.
	25 31	4 When the *Son of Man* comes in his glory,
	26 2	4 the *Son of Man* will be handed over to be crucified.
	24	4 The *Son of Man* is going to his fate, as the scriptures say he 4 will, but alas for that man by whom the *Son of Man* is betrayed!
	45	4 Now the hour has come when the *Son of Man* is to be betrayed
	64	4 you will see the *Son of Man* seated at the right hand of the Power and coming on the clouds of heaven.
Mk	2 10	4 the *Son of Man* has authority on earth to forgive sins,
	28	4 the *Son of Man* is master even of the sabbath.
	8 31	4 he began to teach them that the *Son of Man* was destined to suffer grievously,
	38	4 if anyone . . . is ashamed of me . . . the *Son of Man* will also be ashamed of him
	9 9	he warned them to tell no one what they had seen, until 4 after the *Son of Man* had risen from the dead.
	12	4 how is it that the scriptures say about the *Son of Man* that he is to suffer grievously . . . ?
	31	4 The *Son of Man* will be delivered into the hands of men;
	10 33	4 the *Son of Man* is about to be handed over to the chief priests and the scribes.
	45	4 the *Son of Man* himself did not come to be served
	13 36	4 they will see the *Son of Man* coming in the clouds with great power and glory;

Mk	14 21	4 the *Son of Man* is going to his fate, as the scriptures say he 4 will, but alas for that man by whom the *Son of Man* is betrayed!
	41	4 the *Son of Man* is to be betrayed into the hands of sinners.
	62	4 you will see the *Son of Man* seated at the right hand of the Power
Lk	5 24	4 the *Son of Man* has authority on earth to forgive sins,
	6 5	4 The *Son of Man* is master of the sabbath.
	22	Happy are you when people . . . denounce your name as 4 criminal, on account of the *Son of Man*.
	7 34	4 The *Son of Man* comes, eating and drinking,
	9 22	4 The *Son of Man* . . . is destined to suffer grievously, to be rejected
	26	4 if anyone is ashamed of me . . . of him the *Son of Man* will be ashamed
	44	4 The *Son of Man* is going to be handed over into the power of men.
	56	4 (ᵛ The *Son of Man* came not to destroy souls but to save them)
	58	4 the *Son of Man* has nowhere to lay his head.
	11 30	just as Jonah became a sign to the Ninevites, so will the 4 *Son of Man* be to this generation.
	12 8	4 the *Son of Man* will declare himself for him in the presence of God's angels.
	10	4 Everyone who says a word against the *Son of Man* will be forgiven,
	40	4 the *Son of Man* is coming at an hour you do not expect.
	17 22	4 you will long to see one of the days of the *Son of Man*
	24	4 as the lightning . . . so will be the *Son of Man* when his day comes.
	26	As it was in Noah's day, so will it also be in the days of the 4 *Son of Man*.
	30	4 It will be the same when the day comes for the *Son of Man* to be revealed.
	18 8	4 when the *Son of Man* comes, will he find any faith on earth?
	31	4 everything that is written by the prophets about the *Son of Man* is to come true.
	19 10	4 the *Son of Man* has come to seek out and save what was lost.
	21 27	4 they will see the *Son of Man* coming in a cloud with . . . glory.
	36	4 the strength . . . to stand with confidence before the *Son of Man*.
	22 22	4 The *Son of Man* does indeed go to his fate even as it has been decreed,
	48	4 Judas, are you betraying the *Son of Man* with a kiss?
	69	4 the *Son of Man* will be seated at the right hand of the Power of God.
	24 7	4 the *Son of Man* had to be handed over into the power of sinful men
Jn	1 51	4 you will see . . . above the *Son of Man*, the angels of God ascending and descending.
	3 13	No one has gone up to heaven except the one who came down 4 from heaven, the *Son of Man* who is in heaven;
	14	4 the *Son of Man* must be lifted up
	5 27	5 because he is the *Son of Man*, [the Father] has appointed him supreme judge.
	6 27	4 work for . . . the kind of food the *Son of Man* is offering you,
	53	4 if you do not eat the flesh of the *Son of Man* and drink his blood, you will not have life in you.
	62	4 What if you should see the *Son of Man* ascend to where he was before?
	8 28	4 When you have lifted up the *Son of Man*, then you will know that I am He
	9 35	Jesus . . . said to [the man who was born blind], 'Do you 4 believe in the *Son of* ʳ*Man* (ᵛ *God*)?'
	12 23	4 Now the hour has come for the *Son of Man* to be glorified.
	34	4 How can you say, 'The *Son of Man* must be lifted up'? Who 4 is this *Son of Man*?
	13 31	4 Now has the *Son of Man* been glorified, and in him God has been glorified.
Ac	7 56	4 I can see . . . the *Son of Man* standing at the right hand of God.
Heb	2 6	(Ps 8 4) What is man that you should spare a thought for him, 5 the *son of man* that you should care for him?
Rv	1 13	surrounded by [seven golden lamp-stands], a figure like a 5 *Son of man*, dressed in a long robe
	14 14	5 I saw a white cloud and, sitting on it, one like a *son of man*

2: (MEN AS) SONS

a) Sons (of God) – Adopted as (his) sons

Mt	5 9	2 Happy the peacemakers: they shall be called *sons of God*.
	45	[love your enemies;] in this way you will be *sons* of your Father
Lk	6 35	love your enemies . . . and you will be *sons* of the Most High,
	20 36	2 being children of the resurrection they are *sons of God*.
Rm	8 14	2 Everyone moved by the Spirit is a *son of God*.
	15	The spirit you received . . . is ʳthe *spirit of sons* (lit. the 3 spirit of *adoption as sons*), and it makes us cry out, 'Abba, Father!'

Rm 8 19	The whole creation is eagerly waiting for ⌐God to reveal his sons (lit. the revelation of the *sons of God*).
2	
23	we too groan inwardly as we wait to *be made sons* and for our bodies to be set free.
9 4	[brothers of Israel] were *adopted as sons*,
26	(Ho 2 1) they will now be called the *sons* of the living God.
2 Co 6 18	you shall be⌐my *sons* and daughters, says the Almighty Lord.
Ga 3 26	you are, all of you, *sons of God* through faith in Christ Jesus.
4 5	[God sent his Son] to enable us to *be adopted as sons*. ⁶ The proof that you are *sons* is that God has sent the Spirit of his Son into our hearts: the Spirit that cries, 'Abba, Father', ⁷ and it is this that makes you a *son*, you are not a slave any more; and if God has made you *son*, then he has made you heir.
6	
7	
Ep 1 5	[God chose us] determining that we should *become* his *adopted sons*, through Jesus Christ
Heb 2 10	it was [God's] purpose to bring a great many of his *sons* into glory,
12 5	Have you forgotten that encouraging text in which you are addressed as *sons* (Pr 3 11 f)? My *son*, when the Lord corrects you . . . do not get discouraged . . . ⁶ For the Lord . . . punishes all those that he acknowledges as *sons*. ⁷ . . . God is treating you as his *sons*. Has there ever been any *son* whose father did not train him? ⁸ If you were not getting this training . . . you would not be *sons* but bastards.
6	
7	
8	
Rv 21 7	the one who proves victorious (2 S 7 14); . . . I will be his God and he a *son* to me.

b) Sons (of specified people)

Mt 17 15	[A man came up to Jesus.] 'Lord,' he said 'take pity on my *son*'
20 20	the mother of Zebedee's *sons* came with her *sons* . . . ²¹ . . . She said to [Jesus], 'Promise that these two *sons* of mine may sit one at your right hand and the other at your left . . .'
21	
23 35	Zechariah *son* of Barachiah whom you murdered
26 37	[Jesus] took Peter and the two *sons* of Zebedee with him.
27 56	Among them were Mary of Magdala . . . and the mother of Zebedee's *sons*.
Mk 9 17	Master, I have brought my *son* to you; there is a spirit of dumbness in him,
10 35	James and John, the *sons* of Zebedee,
46	Bartimaeus (that is, the *son* of Timaeus), a blind beggar,
Lk 1 13	Your wife Elizabeth is to bear you a *son* [John the Baptist]
36	Elizabeth has, in her old age . . . conceived a *son*,
57	Elizabeth . . . gave birth to a *son*;
3 2	the word of God came to John *son* of Zechariah,
5 10	James and John, *sons* of Zebedee,
7 12	a dead man was being carried out for burial, the only *son* of his mother, and she was a widow.
9 38	I implore you to look at my *son*: he is my only child . . . ⁴¹ . . . Jesus said . . . 'Bring your *son* here.'
41	
Jn 1 42	You are Simon *son* of John; you are to be called Cephas
4 5	Sychar, near the land that Jacob gave to his *son* Joseph.
12	Jacob . . . drank from [this well] himself with his *sons* and his cattle
46	there was a court official there whose *son* was ill at Capernaum
47	⁴⁷ . . . he went and asked [Jesus] to come and cure his *son*
50	your *son* will live.
53	Your *son* will live;
9 19	Is this man really your *son* who you say was born blind? . . . ²⁰ . . . We know he is our *son*
20	
Ac 7 21	Pharaoh's daughter . . . brought [Moses] up as her own *son*.
29	Moses . . . went to stay in the land of Midian, where he became the father of two *sons*.
13 21	God gave them Saul *son* of Kish,
16 1	Timothy, ⌐whose mother was (lit. who was the *son* of) a Jewess who had become a believer;
19 14	Among those who did this were seven *sons* of Sceva, a Jewish chief priest.
23 6	I am a Pharisee and the *son* of Pharisees.
16	the *son* of Paul's sister heard of the ambush they were laying
Rm 9 9	(Gn 18 10) I shall visit you . . . and Sarah will have a *son* [= Isaac].
Ga 4 22	Abraham had two *sons*, one by the slave-girl [= Ishmael], and one by his free-born wife [= Isaac].
30	(Gn 21 10) Drive away that slave-girl and her *son*: this slave-girl's *son* is not to share the inheritance with the *son* of the free woman.
Heb 11 21	Jacob, when he was dying, blessed each of Joseph's *sons*,
24	Moses refused to be known as the *son* of Pharaoh's daughter
Jm 2 21	Abraham . . . was justified by his deed, because he offered his *son* Isaac
Rv 12 5	The woman brought a male child into the world, the *son* who was to rule all the nations

c) Sons (literally and generally)

Mt 7 9	Is there a man among you who would hand his *son* a stone . . .?

Mt 10 37	Anyone who prefers *son* or daughter to me is not worthy of me.
21 37 <	Finally he sent his *son* to them. 'They will respect my *son*' he said. ³⁸ But when the tenants saw the *son*, they said . . . 'This is the heir . . .'
38 <	
22 2 <	a king who gave a feast for his *son*'s wedding.
Mk 12 6 <	He had still someone left: his beloved *son*. He sent him to them last of all. 'They will respect my *son*' he said.
Lk 11 11	What father among you would hand his *son* a stone . . .?
12 53	the father divided against the *son*, *son* against father,
14 5	Which of you here, if his ⌐*son* (ᵛ *donkey*) falls into a well, or his ox, will not pull him out . . .?
15 11 <	A man had two *sons*.
13 <	the younger *son* . . . left for a distant country
19 <	I no longer deserve to be called your *son*;
21 <	his *son* said, 'Father, I have sinned against heaven and against you. I no longer deserve to be called your *son*.'
24 <	this *son* of mine was dead and has come back to life;
25 <	the elder *son* was out in the fields,
30 <	for this *son* of yours, when he comes back . . . you kill the calf we had been fattening.
20 13 <	the owner of the vineyard said, . . . 'I will send them my dear *son*.'
Jn 8 35	the slave's place in the house is not assured, but the *son*'s place is assured.
Ac 2 17	(Jl 3 1) ᵛ Their (G *your*) *sons* and daughters shall prophesy,

d) Sons (in a wider sense) – Descendants

Mt 1 20	Joseph *son* of David,
23 31	You are the *sons* of those who murdered the prophets!
Mk 3 28	⌐all men's sins (lit. all the sins of the *sons* of men) will be forgiven,
Lk 19 9	this man [Zacchaeus] too is a *son* of Abraham;
Jn 19 26	Woman, this is your *son*.
Ac 7 16	the tomb that Abraham had bought . . . from the *sons* of Hamor,
13 26	My brothers, *sons* of Abraham's race,
Ga 3 7	it is those who rely on faith who are the *sons* of Abraham
Ep 3 5	This mystery that has now been revealed . . . was unknown to any ⌐men (lit. *sons*)
Heb 7 5	any of the *descendants* of Levi who are admitted to the priesthood are obliged by the Law to take tithes
1 P 5 13	Your sister in Babylon . . . sends you greetings; so does my *son*, Mark.

e) Sons (of Israel) – Israelites

Mt 27 9	(cf. Zc 11 13) the sum at which the precious One was priced by *children* of Israel,
Lk 1 16	[John the Baptist] will bring back many of the *sons* of Israel to the Lord
Ac 5 21	the high priest . . . and his supporters convened the Sanhedrin – this was the full Senate of ⌐Israel (lit. the *sons* of Israel)
7 23	[Moses] decided to visit his countrymen, the *sons* of Israel.
37	It was Moses who told the *sons* of Israel,
9 15	this man is my chosen instrument to bring my name . . . before the *people* of Israel;
10 36	God sent his word to the *people* of Israel,
9 27	(cf. Is 10 22) Though Israel should have as many *descendants* as there are grains of sand
2 Co 3 7	the *Israelites* could not bear looking at the face of Moses,
13	Moses, who put a veil over his face so that the *Israelites* would not notice the ending of what had to fade.
Heb 11 22	Joseph recalled the Exodus of the *Israelites*
Rv 2 14	Balaam, who taught Balak to set a trap for the *Israelites*
7 4	a hundred and forty-four thousand, out of all the tribes of ⌐Israel (lit. the *sons* of Israel).
21 12	over the gates were written the names of the twelve tribes of ⌐Israel (lit. the *sons* of Israel);

3: SONS, CHILDREN = MEN, PEOPLE (GENERALLY) – SUBJECTS, EXPERTS, HEIRS

Mt 8 12	the *subjects* of the kingdom will be turned out into the dark,
9 15	the ⌐bridegroom's *attendants* (lit. *sons* of the wedding hall)
12 27	through whom do your own *experts* cast [devils] out?
13 38	the good seed is the *subjects* of the kingdom; the darnel, the *subjects* of the evil one;
17 25	From whom do the kings . . . take toll or tribute? From their *sons* or from foreigners? ²⁶ . . . Well then, the *sons* are exempt.
26	
23 15	you make [a proselyte] twice ⌐as fit for (lit. as much a *son* of) hell
Mk 2 19	the ⌐bridegroom's *attendants* (lit. *sons* of the wedding hall)
3 17	James . . . and John . . . Boanerges or 'Sons of Thunder';
Lk 5 34	the ⌐bridegroom's *attendants* (lit. *sons* of the wedding hall)
10 6	if a ⌐man (lit. *son*) of peace lives there, your peace will go and rest on him;
11 19	through whom do your own *experts* cast [devils] out?

Lk	16 8	the *children* of this world are more astute . . . than are the *children* of light.
	20 34	The *children* of this world take wives and husbands,
	36	being *children* of the resurrection they are sons of God.
Jn	12 36	believe in the light and you will become *sons* of light.
	17 12	not one is lost except the ⌐one who chose to be lost (lit. *son* of perdition),
Ac	3 25	You are the *heirs* of the prophets, [the heirs] of the covenant
	4 36	Barnabas (which means 'son of encouragement')
	13 10	[Elymas,] You utter fraud . . . you *son* of the devil,
Ep	2 2	the spirit who is at work in the ⌐rebellious (lit. rebel *subjects*)
	5 6	God's anger comes down on ⌐those who rebel against him (lit. rebel *subjects*).
Col	3 6	this is the sort of behaviour that makes God angry (∨ ⌐with those who resist him (lit. with *sons* of disobedience)).
1 Th	5 5	you are all *sons* of light and *sons* of the day:
2 Th	2 3	the Rebel, the ⌐Lost One (lit. *Son* of perdition),

4: FOAL

Mt	21 5	(Zc 9 9) a colt, the *foal* of a beast of burden.

3. DAUGHTER: *THYGATĒR*

1 *thygatēr* 28   2 *thygatrion* 2

1: DAUGHTER (LITERALLY AND GENERALLY)

Mt	9 18	My *daughter* has just died,
	10 35	(Mi 7 6) I have come to set a man against his father, a *daughter* against her mother,
	37	Anyone who prefers son or *daughter* to me is not worthy of me.
	14 6	the *daughter* of Herodias danced before the company,
	15 22	My *daughter* is tormented by a devil.
	28	from that moment her *daughter* was well again.
Mk	5 23	2 [Jairus pleaded with Jesus:] 'My *little daughter* is desperately sick.'
	35	Your *daughter* is dead: why put the Master to any further trouble?
	6 22	the *daughter* of this same Herodias came in and danced,
	7 25	2 A [Syrophoenician] woman whose *little daughter* had an unclean spirit . . . ²⁶ . . . begged [Jesus] to cast the devil out of her *daughter*.
	26	
	29	For saying this, you may go home happy: the devil has gone out of your *daughter*.
Lk	2 36	There was a prophetess also, Anna the *daughter* of Phanuel,
	8 42	[Jairus] had an only *daughter* . . . who was dying.
	49	Your *daughter* has died.
	12 53	[a household will be divided . . .] mother against *daughter*, *daughter* against mother,
Ac	2 17	(Jl 3 1) ∨ Their (G your) sons and *daughters* shall prophesy,
	7 21	Pharaoh's *daughter* adopted [Moses]
	21 9	Philip the evangelist . . . had four virgin *daughters* who were prophets.
Heb	11 24	Moses refused to be known as the son of Pharaoh's *daughter*

2: DAUGHTER (OF ZION = JERUSALEM)

Mt	21 5	(Zc 9 9) Say to the *daughter* of Zion:
Jn	12 15	Do not be afraid, *daughter* of Zion;

3: DAUGHTER (IN A WIDER SENSE) – DESCENDANT

Mt	9 22	[Jesus said to the woman who suffered from a haemorrhage:] '. . . my *daughter*, your faith has restored you to health.'
Mk	5 34	[Jesus said to the woman who suffered from a haemorrhage:] 'My *daughter* . . . your faith has restored you to health;'
Lk	1 5	Zechariah . . . had a wife, Elizabeth . . . who was a *descendant* of Aaron.
	8 48	[Jesus said to the woman who suffered from a haemorrhage:] 'My *daughter* . . . your faith has restored you to health;'
	13 16	this woman, a *daughter* of Abraham whom Satan has held bound these eighteen years
	23 28	*Daughters* of Jerusalem, do not weep for me;
2 Co	6 18 Θ	you shall be my sons and *daughters*,

3. BASTARDS: *NOTHOS*

nothos 1

Heb	12 8	If you were not getting this training . . . then you would not be sons but *bastards*.

SPARE

1: Spare, Have mercy – Sparing, Thin – Austerity	2: Refrain from – Not to be going to

1 *pheidomai* 10   3 *a-pheidia* 1
2 *pheidomenōs* 2

1: SPARE, HAVE MERCY – SPARING, THIN – AUSTERITY

Ac	20 29	when I have gone fierce wolves will invade you and will have no *mercy* on the flock.
Rm	8 32 Θ	God did not *spare* his own Son,
	11 21	God did not spare the natural branches, and he is not likely to *spare* you.
	Θ	
1 Co	7 28	[those who marry] will have their troubles . . . in their married life, and I should like to *spare* you that.
2 Co	1 23	the reason why I did not come to Corinth . . . was to *spare* your feelings.
	9 6	2/2 *thin* sowing means *thin* reaping; the more you sow, the more you reap.
	13 2	when I come again, I shall have no *mercy*.
Col	2 23	their self-imposed devotions, their self-abasement, and their ³ ⌐severe treatment of (lit. *austerity* toward) the body;
2 P	2 4 Θ	When angels sinned, God did not *spare* them: . . . ⁵ Nor did
	5 Θ	he *spare* the world in ancient times:

2: REFRAIN FROM – NOT TO BE GOING TO

2 Co	12 6	If I should decide to boast, . . . I should only be speaking the truth; but I am ⌐not going to (or: *refraining*),

SPIRIT – SOUL – PERSON

1. Spirit – Breath	3: Breathe on: *em-physaō*
1: Spirit: *pneuma*	4: Choke, Stifle – Throttle, Strangle – Drown: *pnigō*
a) Holy Spirit, the Spirit (of God, of Jesus, of Truth) – Holy Ghost	**2. Soul – Person – Life**
b) the Spirit, Heart, Mind (of a person) – Inwardly, Spiritual	1: Soul – Person – Life: *psychē*
	a) Soul – Heart, Mind (of a person)
c) Spirit, Spiritual (in various and indefinite senses) – Inspired	b) Unspiritual, Animal, Natural – Embodying the soul (not the spirit), Physical
d) Spirit, Ghost	c) Life – Person, People – Living beings
e) (Unclean, Foul) Spirits – (Evil) Spirits	2: Persons, People
f) Spirit = (Breath of) Life – Breathe	a) *onoma*
2: Spiritual: *logikos*	b) *pros-ōpon*

B = Spirit or Soul//Flesh or Body

1. SPIRIT – BREATH

1: SPIRIT: *PNEUMA*

1 *pneuma*	286/378	5 *pnoē*	1/2
2 *pneuma hagion*	90	6 *em-pneō*	1
3 *pneumatikos*	26	7 (*theo-*)*pneustos*	1
4 *pneumatikōs*	2		

e = *en tō pneumati* (*hagiō*), lit. in the (Holy) Spirit

a) *Holy Spirit, the Spirit (of God, of Jesus, of Truth) – Holy Ghost*

Mt	1 18	2 Mary . . . was found to be with child through the *Holy Spirit*.
	20	2 she has conceived what is in her by the *Holy Spirit*.
	3 11 e	2 he will baptise you with the *Holy Spirit* and fire.
	16	Jesus . . . saw the *Spirit* of God descending like a dove
	4 1	Jesus was led by the *Spirit* out into the wilderness
	10 20	the *Spirit* of your Father will be speaking in you.
	12 18	(Is 42 1) I will endow [my servant] with my *spirit*,
	28 e	if it is through the *Spirit* of God that I cast devils out,
	31	blasphemy against the *Spirit* will not be forgiven;
	32	2 let anyone speak against the *Holy Spirit* and he will not be forgiven either in this world or in the next.
	22 43 e	how is it . . . that David, moved by the *Spirit*, calls [Christ] Lord . . .?

Mt 28 19 / 2 make disciples of all the nations; baptise them in the name of the Father and of the Son and of the *Holy Spirit*,

Mk 1 8 ᵛe / 2 but he will baptise you with the *Holy Spirit*.
10 [Jesus] saw the heavens torn apart and the *Spirit*, like a dove, descending on him.
12 Immediately afterwards the *Spirit* drove him out into the wilderness
3 29 / 2 let anyone blaspheme against the *Holy Spirit* and he will never have forgiveness:
12 36 e / 2 David himself, moved by the *Holy Spirit*, said (Ps 110 1): The Lord
13 11 / 2 it is not you who will be speaking: it will be the *Holy Spirit*.

Lk 1 15 / 2 Even from his mother's womb [John] will be filled with the *Holy Spirit*,
35 / 2 The *Holy Spirit* will come upon you
41 / 2 Elizabeth was filled with the *Holy Spirit*.
67 / 2 Zechariah was filled with the *Holy Spirit* and spoke this prophecy:
2 25 / 2 the *Holy Spirit* rested on [Simeon]. ²⁶ It had been revealed
26 / 2 to him by the *Holy Spirit* that he would not see death until he had set eyes on the Christ
27 e ʳPrompted by (lit. In) the *Spirit* he came to the Temple:
3 16 e / 2 he will baptise you with the *Holy Spirit* and fire.
22 / 2 the *Holy Spirit* descended on [Jesus] in bodily shape, like a dove.
4 1 / 2 Filled with the *Holy Spirit*, Jesus left the Jordan and was led
e by the *Spirit* through the wilderness,
14 / 2 Jesus, with the power of the *Spirit* in him, returned to Galilee;
18 (Is 61 1) The *Spirit* of the Lord has been given to me,
10 21 ᵛe / 2 filled with joy by the *Holy Spirit*, [Jesus] said,
11 13 / 2 how much more will the heavenly Father give the *Holy Spirit* to those who ask him!
12 10 / 2 he who blasphemes against the *Holy Spirit* will not be forgiven.
12 / 2 when the time comes, the *Holy Spirit* will teach you what you must say.

Jn 1 32 I saw the *Spirit* coming down on [Jesus] from heaven like a dove and resting on him.
33 e / 2 The man on whom you see the *Spirit* come down and rest is the one who is going to baptise with the *Holy Spirit*.
3 5 unless a man is born through water and the *Spirit*, he cannot enter the kingdom of God: ⁶ . . . what is born of the *Spirit* is spirit.
8 The wind blows wherever it pleases; . . . That is how it is with all who are born of the *Spirit*.
34 he whom God has sent speaks God's own words: God gives him the *Spirit* without reserve.
7 39 [Jesus] was speaking of the *Spirit* which those who believed in him were to receive; for there was no *Spirit* (ᵛ given) as yet
14 17 [the Father will give you another Advocate,] that *Spirit* of truth whom the world can never receive
26 / 2 the Advocate, the *Holy Spirit*, whom the Father will send in my name, will teach you everything
15 26 When the Advocate comes, . . . the *Spirit* of truth who issues from the Father, he will be my witness.
16 13 when the *Spirit* of truth comes he will lead you to the complete truth,
20 22 / 2 [Jesus] breathed on them and said: 'Receive the *Holy Spirit*.'

Ac 1 2 / 2 to the apostles he had chosen through the *Holy Spirit*,
5 e but you, not many days from now, will be baptised with the / 2 *Holy Spirit*.
8 / 2 you will receive power when the *Holy Spirit* comes on you,
16 the passage of scripture had to be fulfilled in which the / 2 *Holy Spirit*, speaking through David, foretells the fate of Judas,
2 4 / 2 They were all filled with the *Holy Spirit*, and began to speak foreign languages as the *Spirit* gave them the gift of speech.
17 (Jl 3 1-2) I will pour out my *spirit* on all mankind. . . .
18 ¹⁸ Even on my slaves, men and women, . . . I will pour out my *spirit*.
33 / 2 [Jesus] has received from the Father the *Holy Spirit*, who was promised, and what you see and hear is the outpouring of that Spirit.
38 / 2 you will receive the gift of the *Holy Spirit*.
4 8 / 2 Then Peter, filled with the *Holy Spirit*, addressed them, 'Rulers of the people,'
25 / 2 you it is who said through the *Holy Spirit*, and speaking through . . . David (Ps 2 1),
31 / 2 they were all filled with the *Holy Spirit*
5 3 how can Satan have so possessed you that you should lie / 2 to the *Holy Spirit* . . .?
9 So you and your husband have agreed to put the *Spirit* of the Lord to the test!
32 / 2 We are witnesses to all this, we and the *Holy Spirit* whom God has given to those who obey him.
6 3 select from among yourselves seven men . . . filled with the *Spirit* and with wisdom; . . . ⁵ The whole assembly . . .
5 / 2 elected Stephen, a man full of faith and of the *Holy Spirit*,

Ac 6 10 They found they could not get the better of [Stephen] because of his wisdom, and because it was the *Spirit* that prompted what he said.
7 51 / 2 You stubborn people, . . . You are always resisting the *Holy Spirit*,
55 / 2 Stephen, filled with the *Holy Spirit*, gazed into heaven
8 15 / 2 [Peter and John] went down [to Samaria], and prayed for the Samaritans to receive the *Holy Spirit*, . . . ¹⁷ . . . Then
17 / 2 they laid hands on them, and they received the *Holy Spirit*.
18 / 2 When Simon saw that the ᵛ Holy¹ *Spirit* was given through the imposition of hands by the apostles, he offered them some money. ¹⁹ 'Give me the same power . . . so that anyone I
19 lay my hands on will receive the *Holy Spirit*.'
29 The *Spirit* said to Philip, '. . . meet that chariot,'
39 Philip was taken away by the *Spirit* of the Lord,
9 17 so that you may recover your sight and be filled with the / 2 *Holy Spirit*.
31 The churches (G church) . . . were now left in peace, building themselves up, . . . and filled with the consolation of the / 2 *Holy Spirit*.
10 19 the *Spirit* had to tell [Peter], 'Some men have come to see you'.
38 / 2 God had anointed [Jesus] with the *Holy Spirit* and with power,
44 / 2 While Peter was still speaking the *Holy Spirit* came down on all the listeners.
45 Jewish believers . . . were astonished that the gift of the / 2 *Holy Spirit* should be poured out on the pagans too.
47 Could anyone refuse the water of baptism to these people, / 2 now they have received the *Holy Spirit* just as much as we have?
11 12 the *Spirit* told me to [go] back with [the three men from Caesarea]. . . . ¹⁵ I had scarcely begun to speak when the
15 / 2 *Holy Spirit* came down on them . . . as it came on us in the beginning, ¹⁶ and I remembered that the Lord had
16 e / 2 said, '. . . you will be baptised with the *Holy Spirit*.'
24 / 2 [Barnabas] was a good man, filled with the *Holy Spirit* and with faith.
28 Agabus, seized by the *Spirit*, stood up and predicted . . . a famine
13 2 / 2 the *Holy Spirit* said, 'I want Barnabas and Saul set apart . . .'
4 / 2 ⁴ So these two, sent on their mission by the *Holy Spirit*, went down to Seleucia
9 / 2 Saul . . . filled with the *Holy Spirit*, looked [Elymas] full in the face
52 / 2 the disciples were filled with joy and the *Holy Spirit*.
15 8 God . . . showed his approval of [the pagans] by giving the / 2 *Holy Spirit* to them
28 / 2 It has been decided by the *Holy Spirit* and by ourselves
16 6 / 2 [Paul and Timothy were] told by the *Holy Spirit* not to preach the word in Asia. ⁷ . . . they thought to cross [the frontier]
7 into Bithynia, but . . . the *Spirit* of Jesus would not allow them,
19 2 / 2 'Did you receive the *Holy Spirit* . . .? ' . . . No, we were / 2 never even told there was such a thing as a *Holy Spirit*'
6 / 2 the moment Paul had laid hands on them the *Holy Spirit* came down on them,
20 23 / 2 the *Holy Spirit* . . . has made it clear enough that imprisonment and persecution await me.
28 / 2 for all the flock of which the *Holy Spirit* has made you the overseers,
21 4 Speaking in the *Spirit*, they kept telling Paul not to go on to Jerusalem
11 / 2 This is what the *Holy Spirit* says, 'The man this girdle belongs to will be bound'
28 25 / 2 How aptly the *Holy Spirit* spoke when he told your ancestors

Rm 1 4 B Jesus Christ our Lord who, in the order of the spirit, the *spirit* of holiness that was in him, was proclaimed Son of God
5 5 the love of God has been poured into our hearts by the / 2 *Holy Spirit* which has been given us.
8 9 Your interests . . . are in the spiritual, since the *Spirit* of God has made his home in you. In fact, unless you possessed the *Spirit* of Christ you would not belong to him. . . . ¹¹ and
11 if the *Spirit* of him who raised Jesus from the dead is living in you, then he who raised Jesus from the dead will give
B life to your own mortal bodies through his *Spirit* living in you.
13 if by the *Spirit* you put an end to the misdeeds of the body you will live.
14 Everyone moved by the *Spirit* is a son of God. . . . ¹⁶ The
16 *Spirit* himself and our spirit bear united witness that we are children of God.
8 23 all of us who possess the first-fruits of the *Spirit*,
26 The *Spirit* too comes to help us in our weakness. . . . the
27 *Spirit* himself expresses our plea . . . ²⁷ and God . . . knows perfectly well . . . that the pleas of the saints expressed by the *Spirit* are according to the mind of God.
9 1 e / 2 it is the truth – my conscience in union with the *Holy Spirit* assures me of it

Rm	14 17		the kingdom of God . . . means righteousness and peace
		e 2	and joy brought by the *Holy Spirit*.
	15 13	2	such joy and peace . . . that the power of the *Holy Spirit* will remove all bounds to hope.
	16		and so make [the pagans] acceptable as an offering, made
		e 2	holy by the *Holy Spirit*
	19		[to win the allegiance of the pagans] by the power of the [Holy] *Spirit*
	30		I beg you, brothers, by our Lord Jesus Christ and the love of the *Spirit*, to help me
1 Co	2 4		a demonstration of the power of the *Spirit*.
	10		the very things that God has revealed to us through the *Spirit*, for the *Spirit* reaches the depths of everything,
	11		the depths of God can only be known by the *Spirit* of God.
	12		instead of the spirit of the world, we have received the *Spirit* that comes from God,
	13		we teach . . . in the way that the *Spirit* teaches us: we teach spiritual things spiritually.
	14		An unspiritual person . . . does not accept anything of the *Spirit* of God . . . because it can only be understood *by*
		4	*means of the Spirit*.
	3 16		Didn't you realise that . . . the *Spirit* of God was living among you?
	6 11 e		now you have been . . . justified through . . . the *Spirit* of our God.
	19	2	Your body . . . is the temple of the *Holy Spirit*, who is in you
	7 40		I too have the *Spirit* of God, I think.
	12 3		no one can be speaking ʳunder the influence of (lit. in) the [Holy] *Spirit* and say, 'Curse Jesus', and on the other hand,
		e	no one can say, 'Jesus is Lord' unless he is ʳunder the
		e 2	influence of (lit. in) the *Holy Spirit*
	4		There is a variety of gifts but always the same *Spirit*; . . .
	7		⁷ The particular way in which the *Spirit* is given to each
	8		person is for a good purpose. ⁸ One may have the gift of preaching with wisdom given him by the *Spirit*; another may have the gift of preaching instruction given him by the
	9 e		same *Spirit*; ⁹ and another the gift of faith given by the same *Spirit*; another again the gift of healing, through this
	11 e		one *Spirit*; . . . ¹¹ All these are the work of one and the
	13 e		same *Spirit*, . . . ¹³ In the one *Spirit* we were all baptised, . . . and the one *Spirit* was given to us all to drink.
2 Co	1 22		giving us the pledge, the *Spirit*, that we carry in our hearts.
	3 3		you are a letter from Christ, . . . written . . . with the *Spirit* of the living God,
	17		this Lord is the *Spirit*, and where the *Spirit* of the Lord is, there is freedom.
	5 5		God . . . has given us the pledge of the *Spirit*.
	13 13		The grace of the Lord Jesus Christ, the love of God and the
		2	fellowship of the *Holy Spirit* be with you all.
Ga	3 2		was it because you practised the Law that you received the
	3		*Spirit* . . . ? ³ Are you foolish enough to end in outward
	5 B		observances what you began in the *Spirit*? . . . ⁵ Does God give you the *Spirit* because you practise the Law . . . ?
	14		so that through faith we might receive the promised *Spirit*.
	4 6		God has sent the *Spirit* of his Son into our hearts.
	29 B		the child born in the ordinary way persecuted the child born in the *Spirit*'s way.
	5 5		Christians are told by the *Spirit* to look to faith for those rewards that righteousness hopes for.
	16 B		if you are guided by the *Spirit* you will be in no danger of
	17 B		yielding to self-indulgence, ¹⁷ since self-indulgence is the
	18 B		opposite of the *Spirit*, the *Spirit* is totally against such a thing, . . . ¹⁸ If you are led by the *Spirit*, no law can touch you.
	22 B		What the *Spirit* brings is . . . love, joy, peace,
	25 B		Since the *Spirit* is our life, let us be directed by the *Spirit*.
	6 8 B		if [a man] sows in the field of the *Spirit* he will get from ʳit (lit. the *Spirit*) a harvest of eternal life.
Ep	1 13		you too have been stamped with the seal of the [Holy]
		2	*Spirit* of the Promise.
	2 22		you too . . . are being built into a house where God lives, in the *Spirit*.
	3 5 e		This mystery that has now been revealed through the *Spirit* to his holy apostles and prophets
	16		may he give you the power through his *Spirit* to grow strong,
	4 3		Do all you can to preserve the unity of the *Spirit* by the peace that binds you together.
	30	2	otherwise you will only be grieving the *Holy Spirit* of God who has marked you with his seal
	5 18		Do not drug yourselves with wine . . .; be filled with the
		e	*Spirit*.
	6 17		you must accept . . . the word of God from the *Spirit* to use as a sword.
	18 e		Pray all the time, . . . in the *Spirit*
Ph	1 19		I know this will help to save me, thanks to . . . the help which will be given to me by the *Spirit* of Jesus.
	2 1 Δ		if love can persuade at all, ʳor (or: in) the *Spirit* that we have in common,
	3 3 B		we who worship in accordance with the *Spirit* of God;

Col	1 8		it was [Epaphras] who told us all about your love in the
		e	*Spirit*.
1 Th	1 5		when we brought the Good News to you, it came to you not
		e 2	only as words, but as power and as the *Holy Spirit*
	6	2	it was with the joy of the *Holy Spirit* that you took to the gospel
	4 8	2	God, who gives you his *Holy Spirit*.
	5 19		Never try to suppress the *Spirit*.
2 Th	2 13		God chose you from the beginning to be saved by the sanctifying *Spirit*
1 Tm	3 16 B e		He was made visible in the flesh, attested by the *Spirit*,
	4 1		The *Spirit* has explicitly said that . . . there will be some who will desert the faith
2 Tm	1 14	2	guard [the sound teaching] with the help of the *Holy Spirit* who lives in us.
	3 16	7	All scripture is *inspired* by God and can be profitably used for teaching,
Tt	3 5		[God] saved us, by means of the cleansing water of rebirth
		2	and by renewing us with the *Holy Spirit* which he has so generously poured over us through Jesus Christ
Heb	2 4		God himself confirmed their witness . . . by freely giving
		2	the gifts of the *Holy Spirit*.
	3 7	2	The *Holy Spirit* says (Ps 95 7): If only you would listen to him today;
	6 4		those . . . who were once brought into the light, . . . and
		2	received a share of the *Holy Spirit* . . . ⁷ . . . and yet in spite of this have fallen away – it is impossible for them to be renewed a second time.
	9 8	2	the *Holy Spirit* is showing that no one has the right to go into the sanctuary as long as the outer tent remains standing:
	14		how much more effectively the blood of Christ, who offered
		B	himself as the perfect sacrifice to God through the eternal *Spirit*,
	10 15	2	The *Holy Spirit* assures us of this;
	29		you may be sure that anyone who . . . insults the *Spirit* of grace, will be condemned to a far severer punishment.
1 P	1 2		[chosen] by the provident purpose of God the Father, to be made holy by the *Spirit*, obedient to Jesus Christ
	11		The *Spirit* of Christ which was in [the prophets] foretold the sufferings of Christ
	12		those who preached to you the Good News through the
		e 2	*Holy Spirit* sent from heaven,
	4 14		you have the *Spirit* of glory, the Spirit of God resting on you.
2 P	1 21	2	When men spoke for God it was the *Holy Spirit* that moved them.
1 Jn	3 24		We know that he lives in us by the *Spirit* that he has given us.
	4 13		he lets us share his *Spirit*.
	5 6		with the *Spirit* as another witness – since the *Spirit* is the truth –
	8		[so that there are three witnesses,] the *Spirit*, the water and the blood,
Jude	20		use your most holy faith as your foundation and build on that,
		e 2	praying in the *Holy Spirit*; keep yourselves within the love of God
Rv	1 10		it was the Lord's day and the *Spirit* possessed me,
	2 7		If anyone has ears to hear, let him listen to what the *Spirit* is saying to the churches:
			Repeated in Rv 2 11, 17, 29; 3 6, 13, 22
	4 2		With that, the *Spirit* possessed me
	14 13		Happy are those who die in the Lord! Happy indeed, the *Spirit* says; now they can rest for ever after their work,
	22 17		The *Spirit* and the Bride say, 'Come'.

b) the Spirit, Heart, Mind (of a person) – Inwardly, Spiritual

Mt	5 3		How happy are the poor in *spirit*; theirs is the kingdom of heaven.
	26 41 B		The *spirit* is willing, but the flesh is weak.
Mk	2 8 X		Jesus, *inwardly* aware that this was what they were thinking,
	8 12 X		with a sigh that came straight from the *heart* [Jesus] said,
	14 38 B		The *spirit* is willing, but the flesh is weak.
Lk	1 47		my *spirit* exults in God my saviour;
	80		Meanwhile the child [Jesus] grew up and his *spirit* matured.
Jn	11 33		Jesus said in great distress, with a sigh that came straight
		X	from the *heart*,
	13 21 X		Jesus was troubled in *spirit*
	19 30 Δ		bowing his head [Jesus] gave up his *spirit*.
Ac	17 16		Paul waited for them in Athens and there his whole *spirit* was revolted
	18 25		[Apollos] preached with great *spiritual* earnestness
	19 21		Paul made up his *mind* to go back to Jerusalem through Macedonia
Rm	1 9		The God I worship *spiritually*
	2 29		the real circumcision is in the *heart* – something not of the letter
	7 6		in the new *spiritual* way and not the old way of a written law.
	8 4		us, who behave not as our unspiritual nature but as the
		B	*spirit* dictates.
	5 B		the *spiritual* are interested in *spiritual* things. ⁶ . . . life
	6		and peace can only come with concern for the *spiritual*.
	9 B		⁹ Your interests . . . are . . . in the *spiritual*,

Rm 8 10 B   if Christ is in you then your *spirit* is life itself
   15   The spirit you received is not the *spirit* of slaves . . .; it is the *spirit* of sons,
   16   The Spirit himself and our *spirit* bear united witness that we are children of God.
  11 8   (Is 29 10) God has given them a sluggish *spirit*,
  12 11   Work for the Lord . . . with great earnestness of *spirit*,
1 Co 2 11   the depths of a man can only be known by his own *spirit*,
  3 1 B 3   I myself was unable to speak to you as [people] *of the Spirit*:
  5 3 B   Though I am far away in body, I am with you in *spirit*,
   4   When you are assembled together in the name of the Lord Jesus, and I am *spiritually* present with you,
   5 B   so that his sensual body may be destroyed and his *spirit* saved on the day of the Lord.
  6 17 B   anyone who is joined to the Lord is one *spirit* with him.
  7 34   all [an unmarried woman] need worry about is being holy
   B   in body and *spirit*.
  14 2   nobody understands [a man with the gift of tongues] when he talks in the *spirit* about mysterious things.
   14   if I use [the gift of tongues] in my prayers, my *spirit* may be praying but my mind is left barren. [16] . . . Surely I should
   15   pray not only with the *spirit* but with the mind as well? And sing praises not only with the *spirit* but with the mind as well? [16] Any uninitiated person will never be able to
   16   say Amen to your thanksgiving, if you only bless God with the *spirit*,
   32   Prophets can always control their prophetic *spirits*,
  15 45   the last Adam has become a life-giving *spirit*.
  16 18   They have settled my *mind*, and yours too;
2 Co 2 13   I was so continually uneasy in *mind* at not meeting brother Titus
  4 13   as we have the same *spirit* of faith that is mentioned in scripture . . . we too believe
  6 6 e   We prove we are God's servants . . . by a *spirit* of holiness,
  7 1 B   let us wash off all that can soil either body or *spirit*,
   13   thanks to you all, [Titus] has ᵣno more worries (lit. been granted peace of *spirit*);
  12 18   You know that [Titus] and I have always been guided by the same *spirit*
Ga 6 18   The grace of our Lord Jesus Christ be with your *spirit*,
Ep 1 17   May the God of our Lord Jesus Christ . . . give you a *spirit* of wisdom
  4 23   Your mind must be renewed by a *spiritual* revolution
Ph 1 27   so that . . . I shall know that you are un*animous* in meeting the attack with firm resistance,
  4 23   May the grace of our Lord Jesus Christ be with your *spirit*.
Col 2 5 B   I may be absent in body, but in *spirit* I am there among you,
1 Th 5 23 B   may you all be kept safe and blameless, *spirit*, soul and body,
2 Tm 4 22   The Lord be with your *spirit*.
Phm 25   May the grace of our Lord Jesus Christ be with your *spirit*.
Heb 4 12   The word of God . . . can slip through the place where the soul is divided from the *spirit*,
  12 9   we ought to be even more willing to submit ourselves to our
   B   *spiritual* Father,
   23   You have . . . been placed with the *spirits* of the saints
Jm 2 26 B   A body dies when it is separated from the *spirit*, and . . . faith is dead if it is separated from good deeds.
1 P 3 4   the ornament of a sweet and gentle *disposition*
   18 X B   In the body he was put to death, in the *spirit* he was raised to life,
  4 6 B   so that . . . [the dead] might come to God's life in the *spirit*.
Jude 19   These un*spiritual* and selfish people are nothing but mischief-makers.
Rv 17 3   [The angel] took me in *spirit* to a desert,
  21 10   In the *spirit*, he took me to the top of an enormous high mountain

c) Spirit, Spiritual (in various and indefinite senses) — Inspired

Lk 1 17 e   With the *spirit* and power of Elijah, [John the Baptist] will go before [the Lord]
  9 55   (ᵛ You do not know to what *spirit* you belong.)
Jn 3 6 B   what is born of the Spirit is *spirit*.
  4 23 e   true worshippers will worship the Father in *spirit* and truth:
   24   . . . [24] God is *spirit*, and those who worship must worship
   e   in *spirit* and truth.
  6 63 B   It is the *spirit* that gives life, the flesh has nothing to offer. The words I have spoken to you are *spirit* and they are life.
Ac 20 22   you see me a prisoner already ᵣin (or: of the) *spirit*;
Rm 1 11 3   to strengthen you by sharing a *spiritual* gift with you,
  7 14 B 3   The Law . . . is *spiritual*; but I am unspiritual;
  8 2   the law of the *spirit* of life in Christ Jesus has set you free from the law of sin and death.
  15 27 B 3   the pagans who share the *spiritual possessions* of these poor people have a duty to help them with ᵣtemporal (lit. physical) possessions.
1 Co 2 12   instead of the *spirit* of the world, we have received the Spirit that comes from God,
   13   we teach . . . in the way that the Spirit teaches us: we teach
   3/3   *spiritual* things *spiritually*.

1 Co 2 15 3   A *spiritual* man . . . is able to judge the value of everything,
  4 21   It is for you to decide: do I come with a stick in my hand or in a *spirit* of love and goodwill?
  9 11 B 3   If we have sown *spiritual things* for you,
  10 3 3   all ate the same *spiritual* food [4] and all drank the same
   4 3/3   *spiritual* drink, since they all drank from the *spiritual* rock
  12 1 3   I want to clear up a wrong impression about *spiritual gifts*.
   10   [to] another, [the Spirit gives] the gift of recognising *spirits*;
  14 1 3   hope for the *spiritual gifts* . . ., especially prophecy.
   12   since you aspire to ᵣspiritual gifts (lit. *spirits*), concentrate on those which will grow to benefit the community.
   37 3   Anyone who claims to be a prophet or *inspired*
  15 44 3   when it is sown it embodies the soul, when it is raised it
   3   embodies the *spirit*. If the soul has its own embodiment,
   46 3   so does the *spirit* have its own embodiment, . . . [46]
   3   first the one with the soul, not the *spirit*, and after that the
   3   one with the *spirit*.
2 Co 3 6   this new covenant, which is not a covenant of written letters but of the *Spirit*: the written letters bring death, but the *Spirit* gives life.
   8   how much greater will be the brightness that surrounds the administering of the *Spirit*!
   18   this is the work of the Lord who is *Spirit*.
  11 4   you have only to receive a new *spirit*, different from the one you have already received, . . . and you welcome it with open arms.
Ga 6 1 3   if one of you misbehaves, the more *spiritual* of you who set him right should do so in a *spirit* of gentleness,
Ep 1 3 3   Blessed be God . . . who has blessed us with all the *spiritual* blessings of heaven
  2 18 e   Through [Christ], both of us have in the one *Spirit* our way to come to the Father.
  4 4   There is one Body, one *Spirit*,
  5 19   Sing the words and tunes of the psalms and hymns and
   3   *inspired* songs when you are together,
Col 1 9 3   what we ask God is that through perfect wisdom and *spiritual* understanding you should reach the fullest knowledge of his will.
  3 16 3   sing psalms and hymns and *inspired* songs to God;
2 Th 2 2   please do not get excited too soon or alarmed by any ᵣprediction (lit. *intuition*) or rumour or any letter
2 Tm 1 7   God's gift was not a *spirit* of timidity, but the Spirit of power, and love,
Jm 4 5 Δ   the *spirit* which he sent to live in us wants us for himself alone?
1 P 2 5 3   so that you too, the holy priesthood that offers the *spiritual*
   3   sacrifices . . . may be living stones making a *spiritual* house.
  3 19 Δ   and, in the spirit, [Christ] went to preach to the *spirits* in prison.
1 Jn 4 1   It is not every spirit . . . that you can trust; test all *spirits*, to see if they come from God, . . . [2] You can tell the *spirits*
   2   that come from God by this: every *spirit* which acknowledges that Jesus the Christ has come in the flesh is from God;
   3   [3] but any *spirit* which will not say this of Jesus is not from
   6   God, but is [the spirit] of Antichrist, . . . [6] . . . those who know God listen to us; . . . this is how we can tell the *spirit* of truth from the *spirit* of falsehood.
Rv 1 4   grace and peace to you from him who is, who was, and who is to come, from the seven *spirits* in his presence before his throne, [5] and from Jesus Christ,
  3 1   Here is the message of the one who holds the seven *spirits* of God
  4 5   in front of the throne there were seven flaming lamps burning, the seven *Spirits* of God.
  5 6   [the Lamb] had seven horns, and it had seven eyes, which are the seven *Spirits* God has sent out all over the world.
  11 8 4   the Great City known by the *symbolic* names Sodom and Egypt,
  19 10   The witness Jesus gave is the same as the *spirit* of prophecy.
  22 6   the Lord God who gives the *spirit* to the prophets

d) Spirit, Ghost

Lk 24 37   [the apostles] thought they were seeing a *ghost*.
  39 B   a *ghost* has no flesh and bones as you can see I have.
Ac 23 8   the Sadducees say there is neither . . . angel nor *spirit*.
  9   Suppose a *spirit* has spoken to [Paul], or an angel?
Heb 1 14   they are all *spirits* whose work is service,

e) (Unclean, Foul) Spirits — (Evil) Spirits

Mt 8 16   [Jesus] cast out the *spirits* [of the possessed] with a word
  10 1   [Jesus] gave [the Twelve] authority over unclean *spirits*
  12 43   When an unclean *spirit* goes out of a man it wanders . . .
  45   [45] it then goes off and collects seven other *spirits* more evil than itself,
Mk 1 23   In their synagogue . . . there was a man possessed by an unclean *spirit*,
  26   the unclean *spirit* threw the man into convulsions and . . . went out of him.
  27   he gives orders even to unclean *spirits* and they obey him.

Mk	3	11	the unclean *spirits*, whenever they saw him, would fall down before him
		30	This was because they were saying, 'An unclean *spirit* is in him.'
	5	2	a man with an unclean *spirit* came out from the tombs towards him.
		8	Jesus had been saying to him, 'Come out of the man, unclean *spirit*.'
		13	With that, the unclean *spirits* came out and went into the pigs,
	6	7	giving [the Twelve] authority over the unclean *spirits*.
	7	25	A woman whose little daughter had an unclean *spirit*
	9	17	Master, I have brought my son to you; there is a *spirit* of dumbness in him,
		20	as soon as the *spirit* saw Jesus it threw the boy into convulsions,
		25	he rebuked the unclean *spirit*, 'Deaf and dumb *spirit*, . . . come out of him'
Lk	4	33	In the synagogue there was a man who was possessed by the *spirit* of an unclean devil,
		36	He gives orders to unclean *spirits* with authority and power and they come out.
	6	18	People tormented by unclean *spirits* were also cured,
	7	21	he cured many people of diseases . . . and of evil *spirits*,
	8	2	certain women who had been cured of evil *spirits* and ailments:
		29	Jesus had been telling the unclean *spirit* to come out of the man.
	9	39	All at once a *spirit* will take hold of [my son], and give a sudden cry
		42	Jesus rebuked the unclean *spirit*
	10	20	Yet do not rejoice that the *spirits* submit to you;
	11	24	When an unclean *spirit* goes out of a man it wanders . . .
		26	[26] it then goes off and brings seven other *spirits* more wicked than itself,
	13	11	a woman . . . who for eighteen years had been possessed by a *spirit* that left her enfeebled;
Ac	5	16	People . . . came crowding in . . . bringing . . . those tormented by unclean *spirits*,
	8	7	There were . . . unclean *spirits* that came shrieking out of many who were possessed,
	16	16	we met a girl who was ⌐a soothsayer (lit. possessed by an oracular *spirit*)
		18	Paul . . . said to the *spirit*, I order you in the name of Jesus Christ to leave that woman.
	19	12	they were cured of their illnesses, and the evil *spirits* came out of them.
		13	some . . . exorcists tried pronouncing the name of the Lord Jesus over people who were possessed by evil *spirits*;
		15	The evil *spirit* replied, 'Jesus I recognise, . . .' [16] and the man
		16	with the evil *spirit* hurled himself at them
Ep	2	2	obeying the ruler who governs the air, the *spirit* who is at work in the rebellious.
	6	12	it is not against human enemies that we have to struggle, but
	B	3	against the Sovereignties . . , the *spiritual* army of evil in the heavens.
1 Tm	4	1	there will be some who will desert the faith and choose to listen to deceitful *spirits* and doctrines that come from the devils;
Rv	16	13	I saw three foul *spirits* come; they looked like frogs [14] and in
		14	fact were demon *spirits*, able to work miracles,
	18	2	Babylon has fallen, . . . and become . . . a lodging for every foul *spirit*.

f) Spirit = (Breath of) Life – Breathe

Mt	27	50 X	Jesus . . . yielded up his *spirit*.
Lk	8	55	[the] *spirit* [of Jairus' daughter] returned and she got up
	23	46 X	Father, into your hands I commit my *spirit*.
Jn	19	30 X Δ	bowing his head [Jesus] gave up his *spirit*.
Ac	7	59	Stephen said . . , 'Lord Jesus, receive my *spirit*.'
	9	1 6	Saul was still *breathing* threats to slaughter the Lord's disciples.
	17	25 5	it is he who gives everything – including life and *breath* – to everyone.
2 Th	2	8	(Is 11 4) The Lord will kill him with the *breath* of his mouth
Rv	11	11	(cf. Ez 37 5, 10) God *breathed* life into them and they stood up,
	13	15	[The second beast] was allowed to ⌐breathe (lit. give the *breath of*) life into this statue,

2: SPIRITUAL: *LOGIKOS*

logikos 2

Rm	12	1	worship [God], I beg you, ⌐in a way that is worthy of thinking beings (or: *spiritually*),
1 P	2	2	you should be hungry for nothing but milk – the *spiritual* [honesty] which will help you to grow up to salvation –

3: BREATHE ON: *EM-PHYSAŌ*

em-physaō 1

Jn	20	22	[Jesus] *breathed on* [the disciples] and said: Receive the Holy Spirit.

4: CHOKE, STIFLE – THROTTLE, STRANGLE – DROWN: *PNIGŌ*

2 *pniktos 3*		3 *apo-pnigō 3*	
4 *pnigō 2*		1 *sym-pnigō 5*	

Mt	13	7 < 3	the thorns grew up and *choked* [the grain].
		22	the worries of this world and the lure of riches *choke* the word
	18	28 4	he seized him by the throat and *began to throttle* him.
Mk	4	7 <	the thorns grew up and *choked* [the grain],
		19	the worries of this world, . . . and all other passions come in to *choke* the word.
	5	13	the herd of . . . pigs charged . . . into the lake, and there
		4	they were *drowned*.
Lk	8	7 < 3	the thorns grew with [the seed] and *choked* it.
		14	they are *choked* by the worries and riches and pleasures of life
		33 3	the herd charged . . . into the lake and were *drowned*.
		42	the crowds *were almost stifling* Jesus as he went [to Jairus' house].
Ac	15	20	[I rule that] we send [the pagans] a letter telling them merely
		2	to abstain from . . . [the meat of] *strangled animals* and from blood.
		29	you are to abstain from food sacrificed to idols, . . . from
		2	[the meat of] *strangled animals*,
	21	25	The pagans . . . must abstain from . . . [the meat of]
		2	*strangled animals*

2. SOUL – PERSON – LIFE

1: SOUL – PERSON – LIFE: *PSYCHĒ*

1 *psychē*	103	3 *(di-)psychos 2*	
2 *psychikos*	6	5 *(iso-)psychos 1*	
4 *a-psychos*	1	6 *sym-psychos 1*	

a) Soul – Heart, Mind (of a person)

Mt	10	28	Do not be afraid of those who kill the body but cannot kill
		B	the *soul*; fear him rather who can destroy both body and
		B	*soul* in hell.
	11	29	and you will find rest for your *souls*.
	12	18 Θ	(Is 42 1) my beloved, the favourite of my *soul*.
	22	37	(Dt 6 5) You must love the Lord your God with all your heart, with all your *soul*, and with all your mind.
	26	38 X	My *soul* is sorrowful to the point of death.
Mk	12	30	(Dt 6 5) you must love the Lord your God . . . with all your *soul*,
	14	34 X	My *soul* is sorrowful to the point of death.
Lk	1	46	My *soul* proclaims the greatness of the Lord and my spirit exults in God my saviour;
	2	35	and a sword will pierce your own *soul* too
	10	27	(Dt 6 5) You must love the Lord your God . . . with all your *soul*,
	12	19	I will say to my *soul*: My *soul*, you have plenty of good things
		20	. . . [20] . . . This very night the demand will be made for your *soul*;
Jn	10	24	⌐How much longer are you going to keep ⌐us (lit. our *minds*) in suspense?
	12	27 X	my *soul* is troubled.
Ac	2	27 X	(Ps 16 10) you will not abandon my *soul* to Hades
	4	32	The whole group of believers was united, heart and *soul*;
	14	2	Some of the Jews . . . poisoned the *minds* of the pagans against the brothers.
		22	[Paul and Barnabas] put fresh *heart* into the disciples,
	15	24	We hear that some of our members have . . . unsettled your *minds*.
1 Co	15	45	(Gn 2 7) The first man, Adam, . . . became a living *soul*;
2 Co	12	15	I am perfectly willing to spend what I have . . . in the interests of your *souls*.
Ep	6	6	because you are slaves of Christ and *wholeheartedly* do the will of God.
Ph	1	27	so that . . . I shall know that you are unanimous in meeting the attack . . . ⌐united by your love (lit. with a single *mind*) for the faith of the gospel
	2	2 6	be united in your . . . love, with a *common* ⌐purpose (lit. *heart*) and a common mind.
		20 5	I have nobody else like [Timothy] here, as whole*heartedly* concerned for your welfare:
Col	3	23	Whatever your work is, put your *heart* into it
1 Th	5	23 B	may you all be kept safe and blameless, spirit, *soul* and body, for the coming of our Lord Jesus Christ.
Heb	4	12	the word of God . . . can slip through the place where the *soul* is divided from the spirit,
	6	19	[In this hope] we have an anchor for our *soul*,
	10	38 Θ	(Ha 2 4) if [the righteous man] draws back, my *soul* will take no pleasure in him.
		39	we are the sort who keep faithful until our *souls* are saved.
	12	3	then you will not give up ⌐for want of courage (lit. or lose *heart*).

| Heb | 13 | 17 | | [your leaders] must give an account of the way they look after your *souls*; |

Jm 1 8 3 That sort of person, in two *minds*, wavering between going different ways,
21 accept and submit to the word which . . . can save your *souls*.
4 8 3 clear your minds, you ⌐waverers (lit. in two *minds*).
5 20 anyone who can bring back a sinner from the wrong way . . . will be saving a *soul* from death
1 P 1 9 you are sure of the end to which your faith looks forward, that is, the salvation of your *souls*.
22 You have been obedient to the truth and purified your *souls*
2 11 B keep yourselves free from the selfish passions that attack the *soul*.
25 you have come back to the shepherd and guardian of your *souls*.
4 19 even those whom God allows to suffer must trust their *souls* to the constancy of the creator
2 P 2 8 [Lot] was outraged in his good *soul* by the crimes that he saw and heard of
14 [wicked men] will seduce any *soul* which is at all unstable.
3 Jn 2 B I hope . . . that you are as well ⌐physically as you are spiritually (lit. in your body as you are in your *soul*).
Rv 6 9 I saw underneath the altar the *souls* of all the people who had been killed
18 14 All the fruits you had set your *hearts* on have failed you;
20 4 I saw the *souls* of all who had been beheaded . . .; they came to life,

b) Unspiritual, Animal, Natural – Embodying the soul (not the spirit), Physical

1 Co 2 14 2 An *unspiritual* person is one who does not accept anything of the Spirit of God:
15 44 B 2 when it is sown it embodies the ⌐*physical* (or: *soul*), when it is
B 2 raised it embodies the spirit. If the ⌐*physical* (or: *soul*) has
46 2 its own embodiment, so does the spirit . . . ⁴⁶ . . . first
2 the ⌐*physical one* (or: *one with the soul*), not the spirit, and after that, the one with the spirit.
Jm 3 15 2 principles of this kind are not the wisdom that comes down from above: they are only earthly, *animal* and devilish.
Jude 19 2 These unspiritual and *selfish* people are nothing but mischief-makers.

c) Life – Person, People – Living beings

P = Person, People

Mt 2 20 X those who wanted ⌐to kill the child (lit. the child's *life*) are dead.
6 25 That is why I am telling you not to worry about your *life* and what you are to eat, . . . Surely *life* means more than food
10 39 Anyone who finds his *life* will lose it; anyone who loses his *life* for my sake will find it.
16 25 anyone who wants to save his *life* will lose it; but anyone who
26 loses his *life* for my sake will find it. ²⁶ What, then, will a man gain if he wins the whole world and ruins his *life*? Or what has a man to offer in exchange for his *life*?
20 28 X the Son of Man came . . . to give his *life* as a ransom for many.
Mk 3 4 Is it against the law on the sabbath day . . . to save *life*, or to kill?
8 35 anyone who wants to save his *life* will lose it: but anyone who
36 loses his *life* for my sake . . . will save it. ³⁶ What gain, then, is it for a man to win the whole world and ruin his
37 *life*? ³⁷ And indeed what can a man offer in exchange for his *life*?
10 45 X the Son of Man . . . [came] to give his *life* as a ransom for many.
Lk 6 9 is it against the law on the sabbath to . . . save *life*, or to destroy it?
9 24 anyone who wants to save his *life* will lose it; but anyone who loses his *life* for my sake, that man will save it.
56 (ᵛ For the Son of Man has not come to destroy men's *lives* but to save them.)
12 22 That is why I am telling you not to worry about your *life*
23 and what you are to eat, . . . ²³ For *life* means more than food,
14 26 If a man comes to me without hating his father, . . . yes and his own *life* too,
17 33 Anyone who tries to preserve his *life* will lose it; and anyone who loses it will keep it safe.
21 19 Your endurance will win you your *lives*.
Jn 10 11 the good shepherd is one who lays down his *life* for his sheep.
15 I lay down my *life* for my sheep.
17 The Father loves me, because I lay down my *life* in order to take it up again.
12 25 Anyone who loves his *life* loses it; anyone who hates his *life* in this world will keep it for the eternal life.
13 37 Peter said to him, . . . 'I will lay down my *life* for you.'
38 ³⁸ 'Lay down your *life* for me?' answered Jesus.

Jn 15 13 A man can have no greater love than to lay down his *life* for his friends.
Ac 2 41 P That very day about three thousand *people* were added to their number.
43 The many miracles and signs worked through the apostles made a deep impression on *everyone*.
3 23 P (Dt 18 19) The *person* who does not listen to that prophet is to be cut off from the people.
7 14 Joseph then sent for his father Jacob and his whole family,
P a total of seventy-five *people*.
15 26 [Barnabas and Paul] who have dedicated their *lives* to the name of our Lord Jesus Christ.
20 10 we run the risk of losing not only . . . the ship but also our *lives*
24 But *life* to me is not a thing to waste words on,
27 10 we run the risk of losing . . . our *lives* as well.
22 There will be no loss of *life*, only of the ship.
37 P We were in all 276 *souls* on board that ship.
Rm 2 9 Pain and suffering will come to every human *being* who employs himself in evil
11 3 (1 K 19 10) Lord, . . . I, and I only, remain, and they want ⌐to kill me (lit. my *life*).
13 1 P ⌐You must all (lit. Every *person* must) obey the governing authorities.
16 4 [my fellow workers in Christ Jesus] who risked death to save my *life*:
1 Co 14 7 4 Think of a ⌐musical instrument (lit. *lifeless* thing that gives out sounds), a flute or a harp:
2 Co 1 23 By my *life*, I call God to witness
Ph 2 30 [Epaphroditus] risked his *life* to give me . . . help
1 Th 2 8 we were eager to hand over to you not only the Good News but our whole *lives* as well.
1 P 3 20 P that ark which saved only a small group of eight *people*
1 Jn 3 16 he gave up his *life* for us; and we, too, ought to give up our *lives* for our brothers.
Rv 8 9 a third of all the *living* things in the sea were killed,
12 11 even in the face of death they would not cling to *life*.
16 3 every living *creature* in the sea died.
18 13 P their slaves, their human ⌐cargo (lit. *lives*).

2: PERSONS, PEOPLE

a) onoma 3/231

Ac 1 15 there were about 120 *persons* in the congregation:
Rv 3 4 There are a few *people* in Sardis, it is true, who have kept their robes from being dirtied,
11 13 seven thousand *persons* were killed in the earthquake,

b) pros-ōpon 1/76

2 Co 1 11 the more *people* there are asking for help for us, the more will be giving thanks when it is granted to us.

SPIT – FOAM – VOMIT

1. Spit – Spittle: *ptuō*	**3. Vomit – Spit out**
2. Foam – Foam at the mouth: *aphrizō*	1: Vomit: *ex-erama*
	2: Spit out: *emeō*

1. SPIT – SPITTLE: *PTUŌ*

| 2 | *ptuō* | 3 | | 4 | *ek-ptuō* | 1 |
| 3 | *ptysma* | 1 | | 1 | *em-ptuō* | 6 |

Mt 26 67 they spat in Jesus' face and hit him with their fists;
27 30 [the soldiers] *spat* on [Jesus] and took the reed and struck him on the head with it.
Mk 7 33 X 2 He touched [the deaf man's] tongue with *spittle*.
8 23 X 2 putting *spittle* on [the blind man's] eyes and laying his hands on him, he asked, 'Can you see anything?'
10 34 [the pagans] will mock [the Son of Man] and *spit* at him
14 65 Some of them started *spitting* at [Jesus]
15 19 [The soldiers] struck [Jesus's] head with a reed and *spat* on him;
Lk 18 32 [the Son of Man] will be mocked, maltreated and *spat* on,
Jn 9 6 X 2/3 [Jesus] *spat* on the ground, made a paste with the *spittle*, put this over the eyes of the blind man,
Ga 4 14 you never showed the least sign of being revolted ⌐or disgusted
4 by (lit. nor did you *spit* at) my disease

2. FOAM – FOAM AT THE MOUTH: *APHRIZŌ*

1 *aphrizō* 2   3 *ep-aphrizō* 1
2 *aphros* 1

Mk	9 18	when [the spirit of dumbness] takes hold of [my son] it throws him to the ground, and he *foams* [*at the mouth*]
	20	as soon as the spirit saw Jesus it threw the boy into convulsions, and he fell to the ground . . . *foaming* [*at the mouth*],
Lk	9 39 2	All at once a spirit will take hold of [my son] and. . . throw the boy into convulsions with *foaming* [*at the mouth*]
Jude	13 3	[these wicked people are] like wild sea waves capped with shame as if with *foam*;

3. VOMIT – SPIT OUT

1: VOMIT: *EX-ERAMA*

ex-erama 1

2 P	2 22	(Pr 26 11) The dog goes back to his own *vomit*

2: SPIT OUT: *EMEŌ*

emeō 1

Rv	3 16 X	since you are neither [cold nor hot] but only lukewarm, I will *spit* you *out* of my mouth.

STAND

Stand, Stood – Stand firm, Stop – Stand before
1: Stand (up, by, beside), (Be) Standing, Stood
2: Stand (before an authority) – Be brought (before), Made to stand (before)

3: Stand before = Come (up, by) – Appear
4: Stand (still) – Stop – Stay
5: Stand (fast), Last – Stand firm
6: Stand (transitively) – Put (forward), Present, Offer – Show, Prove

STAND, STOOD – STAND FIRM, STOP – STAND BEFORE

1	*histēmi, histanō*	137/152	3 *eph-istēmi*	20/21
6	*stasis*	1/9	2 *par-(h)istēmi*	38/41
4	*stēkō*	11	5 *syn-(h)istēmi, -anō*	7/16

A = Angel

1: STAND (UP, BY, BESIDE), (BE) STANDING, STOOD

Mt	6 5	the hypocrites . . . love to say their prayers *standing up* in the synagogues
	12 46	his mother and his brothers . . . were *standing* outside and were anxious to have a word with [Jesus].
	47	(§ Your mother and your brothers are *standing* outside, asking to speak to you.)
	13 2	The people all *stood* on the beach.
	16 28	there are some of these *standing* here who will not taste death before they see the Son of Man coming with his kingdom.
	20 3	[the landowner] saw [other workers] *standing* idle in the market place . . . ⁶ . . . he went out and found more men
	6	*standing* round and he said to them, 'Why have you been *standing* here idle all day?'
	24 15	you see the disastrous abomination . . . ⌐*set up* (or: *standing*) in the Holy Place
	26 73	A little later the by*standers* came up and said to Peter,
	27 47	some of those who *stood* there . . . said, 'The man is calling on Elijah',
Mk	3 31 4	His mother and brothers now arrived and, *standing* outside, sent in a message asking for [Jesus].
	9 1	there are some *standing* here who will not taste death before they see the kingdom of God come with power.
	11 5	some men *standing* there said, 'What are you doing, untying that colt?'
	25 4	when you *stand* in prayer, forgive whatever you have against anybody,
	13 14	you see the disastrous abomination ⌐*set up* (or: *standing*) where it ought not to be

Mk	14 47	2 one of the by*standers* . . . struck out at the high priest's servant,
	69	2 The servant-girl . . . started telling the by*standers*, 'This
	70	2 fellow is one of them'. ⁷⁰ . . . A little later the by*standers* themselves said to Peter, 'You are one of them for sure!'
	15 35	2 some of those who *stood by* . . . said, 'Listen, he is calling on Elijah'.
	39	2 The centurion, who was *standing* in front of him . . . said, 'In truth this man was a son of God'.
Lk	1 11 A	Then there appeared . . . the angel of the Lord, *standing* on the right of the altar of incense.
	19 A ●2	I am Gabriel who *stand* in God's presence,
	4 39 X 3	⌐Leaning (lit. *Standing*) over [Simon's mother-in-law Jesus] rebuked the fever
	5 1 X	he was *standing* one day by the Lake of Gennesaret,
	6 8	'Stand up! Come out ⌐into (lit. and *stand* in) the middle.' And he came out and *stood* there.
	7 14	[Jesus] put his hand on the bier and the bearers *stood still*,
	38	[The woman] ⌐waited (lit. *stood*) behind him at his feet . . . and anointed them with the ointment.
	8 20	Your mother and brothers are *standing* outside
	9 27	there are some *standing* here who will not taste death before they see the kingdom of God,
	32 5	Peter and his companions . . . saw his glory and the two men *standing with* him.
	13 25	you may find yourself *standing* outside knocking on the door,
	17 12	ten lepers . . . *stood* some way off ¹³ and called to [Jesus],
	18 11	The Pharisee *stood* there and said this prayer to himself,
	13	The tax collector *stood* some distance away, not daring even to raise his eyes to heaven;
	19 8	Zacchaeus *stood* [his ground] and said to the Lord, '. . . I am going to give half my property to the poor,
	24 2	[the king] said to those *standing by*, 'Take the pound from him
	23 10	the chief priests and the scribes ⌐were (lit. *stood*) there, violently pressing their accusations.
	49	All his friends *stood* at a distance;
	24 36 X	[Jesus] himself *stood* among them and said . . ., 'Peace be with you!'
Jn	1 26 X 4	there *stands* among you – unknown to you – ²⁷ the one who is coming after me;
	35	On the following day . . . John *stood* there again
	3 29	the bridegroom's friend, who *stands* [there] and listens, is glad
	7 37 X	Jesus *stood* [there] and cried out: 'If any man is thirsty, let him come to me!'
	11 56	[the country people] *stood* [about] in the Temple,
	12 29	People *standing* by . . . said it was a clap of thunder;
	18 5	Judas the traitor was *standing* among them.
	18	the servants and guards . . . were *standing* [there] warming themselves; so Peter *stood* [there] too,
	22 2	one of the guards *standing by* gave Jesus a slap in the face,
	25	Simon Peter *stood* [there] warming himself,
	19 25	Near the cross of Jesus *stood* his mother . . . ²⁶ Seeing his
	26 2	mother and the disciple he loved *standing* [near her], Jesus said
	20 14 X	[Mary of Magdala] turned round and saw Jesus *standing* [there],
	19 X	Jesus came and *stood* among [the disciples].
	26 X	The doors were closed, but Jesus came in and *stood* among them.
	21 4 X	It was light now and there *stood* Jesus on the shore,
Ac	1 10 A 2	suddenly two men in white were *standing* near [the disciples],
	11	Why are you men from Galilee *standing* here looking into the sky?
	2 14	Peter *stood up* with the Eleven and addressed them
	3 8	[the lame man] jumped up, *stood*, and began to walk,
	4 10	it was by the name of Jesus Christ . . . that this man is able
	2	to *stand up* perfectly healthy,
	14	[the Sanhedrin] saw the man who had been cured *standing* by their side.
	5 20	Go and *stand* in the Temple, and tell the people all about this new Life.
	23	We found . . . the warders ⌐on duty (lit. *standing*) at the gates,
	25	the men you imprisoned are in the Temple . . . *standing* [there] preaching to the people.
	7 33	(Ex 3 5) the place where you are *standing* is holy ground.
	55 X	Stephen . . . saw . . . Jesus *standing* at God's right hand.
	56 X	I can see . . . the Son of Man *standing* at the right hand of God.
	9 7	The men travelling with Saul *stood* there speechless,
	39 2	all the widows *stood* round [Peter] in tears,
	10 17 3	the men sent by Cornelius . . . were now *standing* at the door,
	30 A	Cornelius replied, '. . . I suddenly saw a man *standing* in front of me
	11 13 A	[Cornelius] had seen an angel *standing* in his house
	12 14	Peter was *standing* at the main entrance.
	16 9	Paul had a vision: a Macedonian appeared ⌐and appealed (lit. to *stand* and appeal) to him
	17 22	Paul *stood* before the whole Council of the Areopagus and made this speech:

Ac	21 40		Paul, *standing* at the top of the steps, gestured to the people with his hand.
	22 13	3	[Ananias] *stood beside* me and said, 'Brother Saul, receive your sight'.
	20	3	when the blood of . . . Stephen was being shed, I was *standing by*
	25		Paul said to the centurion ⌐on duty (lit. *standing* there), 'Is it legal for you to flog . . . a Roman citizen . . .?'
	23 2	2	Ananias ordered ⌐his *attendants* (or: those *standing by* him) to strike [Paul]
	4	2	⌐The *attendants* (or: Those *standing by*) said, 'It is God's high priest you are insulting!'
	24 21		I *stood up* among them and called out:
	26 16		[the Lord said,] get up and *stand* on your feet,
	27 21		Paul *stood up* among the men.
	23 A	2	Last night there was *standing beside* me an angel of . . . God
Rm	5 2		we have entered this ⌐state of grace (lit. grace in which we *stand*) in which we can boast about looking forward to God's glory.
Heb	10 11		All the priests *stand* at their duties every day,
Jm	2 3		you tell the poor man, '*Stand* over there'
	5 9 X		the Judge is already to be seen ⌐waiting (lit. *standing*) at the gates.
Rv	3 20 X		Look, I am *standing* at the door, knocking.
	5 6 X		I saw, *standing* between the throne . . . and . . . the elders, a Lamb
	7 1 A		I saw four angels, *standing* at the four corners of the earth,
	9		I saw a huge number . . . of people . . . *standing* in front of the throne and in front of the Lamb,
	11 A		the angels . . . were *standing* in a circle round the throne,
	8 2 A ●		I saw . . . the seven angels who *stand* in the presence of God.
	3 A		Another angel . . . came and *stood* at the altar.
	10 5 A		the angel . . . *standing* on the sea and the land, raised his right hand to heaven,
	8 A		take that open scroll out of the hand of the angel *standing* on sea and land.
	11 4 ●		These are the two olive trees and the two lamps that *stand* before the Lord of the world.
	11		God breathed life into [the two witnesses] and they *stood up* on their feet,
	12 18 ᵛ		I (G He) was *standing* on the seashore.
	14 1 X		I saw Mount Zion, and *standing* on it a Lamb
	15 2		I seemed to see . . . *standing* by the lake of glass, those who had fought against the beast and won,
	18 10		[the kings of the earth] ⌐keep (lit. *stand*) at a safe distance from fear of her agony,
	15		The traders . . . will be *standing* at a safe distance from fear of her agony,
	17		All the captains and seafaring men . . . will be ⌐keeping (lit. *standing* at) a safe distance,
	19 17 A		I saw an angel *standing* in the sun,
	20 12		I saw the dead, both great and small, *standing* in front of his throne,

2: STAND (BEFORE AN AUTHORITY) – BE BROUGHT (BEFORE), MADE TO STAND (BEFORE)

Mt	27 11 X		Jesus, then, ⌐was brought (or: *stood*) before the governor,
Mk	13 9		you will *stand* before governors and kings for my sake,
Lk	21 36		Stay awake, praying at all times for the strength to . . . *stand* [with confidence] before the Son of Man.
Ac	4 7		[The Sanhedrin] *made* the prisoners *stand* in the middle
	5 27		they had *brought* [the apostles] in to face the Sanhedrin,
	22 30		[the tribune] brought Paul down and *stood* him in front of [the Sanhedrin].
	24 20		I *stood* before the Sanhedrin,
	25 10		I am *standing* before the tribunal of Caesar
	18		When *confronted* with [Paul], his accusers did not charge him with any of the crimes I had expected;
	26 6		it is for my hope in the promise made by God . . . that I ⌐am (lit. *stand*) on trial,
	27 24	2	Do not be afraid, Paul. You are destined to *appear* before Caesar,
Rm	14 10	2	We shall all have to *stand* before the judgement seat of God;
Col	1 22 X	2	he has reconciled you . . . you are able to *appear* before him holy,
Jude	24		Glory be to him who can . . . *bring* you safe to his . . . presence,

3: STAND BEFORE = COME (UP, BY) – APPEAR

Mk	4 29 ○	2	he starts to reap because the harvest has *come*.
Lk	2 9 A	3	The angel of the Lord *appeared* to [the shepherds]
	38	3	[Anna] *came by* just at that moment and began to praise God;
	10 40	3	Martha who was distracted with all the serving *came up* to him and said,
	20 1	3	while [Jesus] was teaching . . . the chief priests and the scribes *came up*,

Lk	21 34	3	Watch yourselves, or . . . that day will ⌐be sprung on (lit. *come upon*) you suddenly,
	24 4 A	3	two men in brilliant clothes suddenly *appeared* at their side.
Ac	4 1	3	While [Peter and John] were still talking . . . the priests *came up*
	6 12	3	[some members of the Synagogue of Freedmen] ⌐took Stephen by surprise (lit. *came up* on Stephen),
	11 11	3	Just at that moment three men ⌐stopped (or: *came up*) outside the house
	12 7 A	3	Then suddenly the angel of the Lord *stood* [there], and the cell was filled with light.
	17 5	3	The Jews . . . *made for* Jason's house, hoping to find [Paul and Silas] there
	23 11 X	3	Next night, the Lord *appeared* to [Paul]
	27	3	I *came on the scene* with my troops and got [Paul] away,
	28 2	3	they lit a huge fire because it had ⌐started (lit. *come on*) to rain
1 Th	5 3	3	It is when people are saying, 'How quiet and peaceful it is' that the worst suddenly *happens*,
2 Tm	4 6	3	the time has *come* for me to be gone.

4: STAND (STILL) – STOP – STAY

Mt	2 9		the star . . . *halted* over the place where the child was.
	20 32 X		Jesus *stopped*, called [the two blind men] over
Mk	10 49 X		Jesus *stopped* and said, 'Call [the blind man] here'.
Lk	5 2		[Jesus] caught sight of two boats ⌐close to (lit. *standing* by) the bank.
	6 17 X		[Jesus] *stopped* at a piece of level ground
	7 14		[Jesus] put his hand on the bier and the bearers *stood still*,
	8 44		the haemorrhage *stopped* at that instant.
	18 40 X		Jesus *stopped* and ordered them to bring the [blind] man to him,
	23 35		The people *stayed* there watching [Jesus].
	24 17		[the two disciples on their way to Emmaus] *stopped short*, their faces downcast.
Jn	6 22		the crowd that had *stayed* on the other side saw that . . . Jesus had not got into the boat with his disciples,
	18 16		Peter *stayed* outside the door.
	20 11		Meanwhile Mary *stayed* outside near the tomb, weeping.
Ac	8 38		[The eunuch] ordered the chariot to *stop*,
	11 11	3	Just at that moment three men ⌐stopped (or: came up) outside the house
Rv	12 4 ①		the dragon *stopped* in front of the woman as she was having the child,

5: STAND (FAST), LAST – STAND FIRM

Mt	12 25		no town, no household divided against itself can *stand*.
	26 ①		Now if Satan casts out Satan . . . how can his kingdom *stand*?
Mk	3 24		If a kingdom is divided against itself, that kingdom cannot *last*. And if a household is divided against itself, that household can never *stand*. Now if Satan . . . is divided,
	25		
	26 ①		he cannot *stand* either
Lk	11 18 ①		if [Satan] is divided against himself, how can his kingdom *stand*?
	19 8		Zacchaeus *stood* [his ground] and said to the Lord, '. . . I am going to give half my property to the poor,
Jn	8 44 ①	4	[the devil] ⌐was never grounded (lit. has never *stood*) in the truth;
Ac	26 22		I have *stood* [firm] to this day, testifying to great and small
Rm	11 20		if you still ⌐hold firm (lit. *stand* [firm]), it is only thanks to your faith.
	14 4	4	It is not for you to condemn someone else's servant: whether he *stands* or falls it is his own masters' business; he will *stand*, you may be sure, because the Lord has power to make him *stand*.
1 Co	7 37		if someone ⌐has firmly made his mind up (lit. firmly *stands* fast in his heart) . . . to keep his daughter as she is, he will be doing a good thing.
	10 12		The man who thinks he ⌐is safe (lit. will *stand*) must be careful that he does not fall.
	15 1		I want to remind you of the gospel . . . in which you are *firmly established*;
	16 13	4	*stay firm* in the faith;
2 Co	1 24		in the faith you *are steady* [enough].
Ga	5 1	4	*Stand firm* . . . and do not submit again to the yoke of slavery.
Ep	6 11		⌐resist (lit. *stand against*) the devil's tactics . . . . . . you must rely on God's armour, or you will not be able to . . . have enough resources to ⌐hold (lit. *stand*) [your ground].
	13		
	14		So *stand* [your ground], with truth buckled round your waist,
Ph	1 27	4	I shall know that you are unanimous in meeting the attack ⌐with firm resistance (lit. *standing firm*),
	4 1	4	⌐remain faithful (lit. *stand firm*) in the Lord.

Col 1 17   Before anything was created, [Christ] existed, and ⌐he holds
      5   all things in unity (lit. all things *stand* [fast] in him).
   4 12   [Epaphras prays] that you will . . . always ⌐hold perfectly
        and securely to (lit. *stand* perfectly and securely in) the
        will of God.
1 Th 3 8   Now we can breathe again, as you are still ⌐holding (lit.
      4   *standing) firm* in the Lord.
2 Th 2 15   4 *Stand firm*, then, brothers, and keep the traditions
2 Tm 2 19   God's solid foundation stone *is still in position*,
Heb 9 8   no one has the right to go into the sanctuary as long as the
      6   outer tent *remains standing*;
1 P 5 12   I write these few words . . . to encourage you ⌐never to let
        go (lit. to *stand* [firm] in) this true grace of God
2 P 3 5   there were heavens at the beginning, and . . . the earth
      5   *was formed* by the word of God
Rv 6 17   the Great Day of his anger has come, and who can ⌐survive
        it (lit. *stand* [fast] then) ?

6: STAND (TRANSITIVELY) = PUT (FORWARD), PRESENT, OFFER – SHOW, PROVE

Mt 26 53 Θ 2 my Father . . . would promptly ⌐send (lit. *put* forward) more
        than twelve legions of angels to my defence
Lk 2 22   2 they took [Jesus] up to Jerusalem to *present* him to the Lord
Ac 1 3 X 2 [Jesus] had *shown* himself alive to them after his Passion
   23   Having ⌐nominated (lit. *put* forward) two candidates [they
        prayed]
   6 6   They *presented* these [seven men of good reputation] to the
        apostles,
   13   they *put up* false witnesses [before the Sanhedrin]
   9 41   2 [Peter] *showed* them [Tabitha] was alive.
   23 24   2 *provide* horses for Paul, and deliver him unharmed to Felix
   33   On arriving at Caesarea the escort . . . ⌐handed Paul over
        (lit. *presented* Paul) to [the governor].
   24 13   2 neither can they *prove* any of the accusations . . . against me
Rm 3 5   5 our lack of holiness makes God *demonstrate* his integrity,
   5 8   5 what *proves* that God loves us is that Christ died for us
   6 13   you must not let any part of your body ⌐turn into (lit. be
      2   *offered* as) an unholy weapon fighting on the side of sin;
      2   you should . . . *offer* yourselves to God,
   16   2 if you ⌐agree (lit. *offer*) to serve and obey a master you become
        his slaves.
   19   2 as once you *put* your bodies *at the service* of vice . . . so now
      2   you must *put* them *at the service* of righteousness
   12 1   2 [worship God] by *offering* your living bodies as a holy
        sacrifice,
1 Co 8 8   2 Food, of course, cannot *bring us in touch* with God:
2 Co 4 14 Θ 2 he who raised the Lord Jesus to life will . . . *put* us [by his
        side]
   6 4   5 we ⌐*prove* we are (or: commend ourselves as) servants of God
        by great fortitude
   7 11   5 In every way you have *shown* yourselves blameless in this
        affair.
   11 2   I arranged for you to marry Christ so that I might ⌐give you
      2   away (lit. *present* you) as a chaste virgin to this one husband.
Ga 2 18   If I were to return to a position I had already abandoned, I
      5   should be ⌐admitting (or: *proving*) I had done something
        wrong.
Ep 5 27 X [Christ washed the Church clean] so that when he ⌐took (lit.
      2   *presented*) her to himself he would be glorious,
Col 1 28   this is the wisdom in which we . . . instruct everyone, to
      2   ⌐make (lit. *present*) them all perfect in Christ.
2 Tm 2 15 2 Do all you can to *present* yourself in front of God as a man
        who has come through his trials,

STAR – SUN – MOON

1. **Star:** *astēr*
2. **Morning Star:** *phōs-phoros*
3. **Sun – Moon:** *hēlios* and *selēnē*

  1: Sun – Moon
  2: Sun(rise), (the rising) Sun
  3: Sunset, the Setting Sun

1. STAR: *ASTĒR*
1 *astēr* 24   2 *astron* 4

Mt 2 2   We saw his *star* ⌐as it rose (or: in the east)
   7   Herod . . . asked them the exact date on which the *star* had
        appeared,
   9   the *star* they had seen ⌐rising (or: in the east) . . . went for-
        ward
   10   The sight of the *star* filled them with delight,

Mt 24 29   the sun will be darkened . . , the *stars* will fall from the sky
Mk 13 25   the *stars* will come falling from heaven
Lk 21 25   2 There will be signs in the sun and moon and *stars*;
Ac 7 43   2 (Am 5 26) you carried . . . the *star* of the god Rephan,
   27 20   2 For a number of days both the sun and the *stars* were invisible
1 Co 15 41   The sun has its brightness, the moon a different brightness,
        and the *stars* a different brightness, and the *stars* differ
        from ⌐each other (lit. other *stars*) in brightness.
Heb 11 12   there came from one man . . . more descendants than could
      2   be counted, as many as the *stars* of heaven
Jude 13   [the wicked are] like shooting *stars* bound for an eternity of
        black darkness.
Rv 1 16   In his right hand [the Son of Man] was holding seven *stars*,
   20   The secret of the seven *stars* you have seen . . . is this: the
        seven *stars* are the angels of the seven churches,
   2 1   Here is the message of the one who holds the seven *stars* in his
        right hand
   28 X [To the victorious] I will give . . . the Morning *Star*.
   3 1   Here is the message of the one who holds . . . the seven *stars*:
   6 13   (Is 34 4) the *stars* of the sky fell on to the earth
   8 10   a huge *star* fell from the sky, burning like a ball of fire, . . .
   11   [11] this was the *star* called Wormwood,
   12   a third of the *stars* were blasted,
   9 1   I saw a *star* that had fallen from heaven onto the earth,
   12 1   a great sign appeared in heaven: a woman, . . . with the
        twelve *stars* on her head for a crown;
   4   [The dragon's] tail dragged a third of the *stars* from the sky
   22 16 X I am . . . the root of David and the bright *star* of the morning.

2. MORNING STAR: *PHŌS-PHOROS*
phōs-phoros 1

2 P 1 19 X take [the prophecy] as a lamp . . . until the dawn comes and
        the *morning star* rises in your minds.

3. SUN – MOON: *HĒLIOS* and *SELĒNĒ*
1 *hēlios* 32   2 *selēnē* 9

1: SUN – MOON

Mt 5 45   your Father . . . causes his *sun* to rise on bad men as well as
        good,
   13 43   the virtuous will shine like the *sun* in the kingdom of their
        Father.
   17 2   [Jesus's] face shone like the *sun*
   24 29 /2 the *sun* will be darkened, the *moon* will lose its brightness, the
        stars will fall from the sky
Mk 13 24 /2 the *sun* will be darkened, the *moon* will lose its brightness,
      [25] the stars will come falling from heaven
Lk 21 25 /2 There will be signs in the *sun* and *moon* and stars;
   23 45   It was now about the sixth hour and, with the *sun* eclipsed, a
        darkness came over the whole land
Ac 2 20   The *sun* will be turned into darkness and the *moon* into blood
        before the great Day of the Lord dawns.
   13 11   [Elymas,] for a time you will not see the *sun*.
   26 13   I saw a light brighter than the *sun* come down from heaven.
   27 20   For a number of days both the *sun* and the stars were invisible
1 Co 15 41 /2 The *sun* has its brightness, the *moon* a different brightness,
        and the stars a different brightness, and the stars differ from
        ⌐each other (lit. other stars) in brightness.
Rv 1 16   [The Son of Man's] face was like the *sun* shining with all its
        force.
   6 12 /2 The *sun* went as black as coarse sackcloth; the *moon* turned
        red as blood all over, [13] and the stars . . . fell
   7 16   neither the *sun* nor scorching wind will ever plague [the chosen]
   8 12 /2 a third of the *sun* and a third of the *moon* . . . were blasted,
   9 2   smoke poured up out of the Abyss . . . so that the *sun* and the
        sky were darkened
   10 1   I saw another powerful angel . . .; his face was like the *sun*,
   12 1   a great sign appeared in heaven: a woman, adorned with the
      /2   *sun*, standing on the *moon*
   16 8   The fourth angel emptied his bowl over the *sun*
   19 17   I saw an angel standing in the *sun*,
   21 23 /2 the [heavenly] city did not need the *sun* or the *moon* for light,
   22 5   they will not need lamplight or *sun*light,

2: SUN(RISE), (THE RISING) SUN

Mt 13 6   as soon as the *sun* came up [the seeds] were scorched
Mk 4 6   when the *sun* came up [the seed] was scorched
   16 2   [The three women] went to the tomb, just as the *sun* was
        rising.
Jm 1 11   the scorching *sun* comes up, and the grass withers,

Rv	7 2	I saw another angel rising ⌐where the *sun* rises (or: in the east),
	16 12	a way was made for the kings of ⌐the East (lit. where the *sun* rises) to come in.

3: SUNSET, THE SETTING SUN

3 *duō, dynō 2*   4 *epi-duō 1*

Mk	1 32	/3 after *sunset*, they brought to [Jesus] all who were sick
Lk	4 40	/3 At *sunset* all those who had friends suffering from diseases . . . brought them to [Jesus],
Ep	4 26	/4 never let the *sun set* on your anger

STAY – LIVE

1. Stay – Remain: *ep-echō*
2. Stay – Remain – Come to rest: *kath-izō*
3. Stay – Remain – Live: *menō*
  1: Stay, Live – Wait – Remain, Spend (time)
  2: Live (in a person) – Remain (in), Dwell (in) – Make a home (within), Rest (on)
  3: Continue to, Persist in – Keep to, Persevere in – Stay, Remain (in a state)
  4: Stand (fast) – Last, Endure – Stay (behind), Remain (for ever)
  5: Remain (a possession)
4. Live, Living, Be alive – Life: *zōē*
  1: (the) Living (God) – (God) Lives
  2: Live, Be alive – Life
  3: (eternal, everlasting) Life – Live (after the resurrection, for salvation)
  4: (the four) Living creatures, Animals (in Revelation)
5. Life – Live on: *bios*
  1: Life, of Living
  2: Live on, Life's earnings – Property, Possessions, Goods
6. Live – Dwell – Settle: *kat-oikeō*

  1: Live (at, in), Settle (in), Dwell– Inhabitant
  2: (God) Lives (in), Dwells (in), Makes his home (in)
  3: Live (in), Dwell (within), figuratively – Settle, Set up house (in)
  4: Live with, Life together
7. Live (in, on), Dwell: *kath-ēmai*
8. Be at home (with), Live (in), Make one's home (in): *en-dēmeō*
9. Live in a continuous state of: *dia-teleō*
10. (Be, Go, Do) Continuously, Constantly – (Be) Devoted to, Faithful in (doing) – Persist: *kartereō*
11. Stay – Stop – Spend time: *dia-tribō*
12. Spend time: *poieō*
13. Spend a night in the open, Camp: *aulizomai*
  1: Spend the night(s) in the open
  2: Camp, Encampment
14. to Winter – Pass, Spend, the winter: *para-cheimazō*
15. Lodge, Stay, Be the guest of – Lodging, Guest room, Inn: *kata-luma*
16. Inn, Innkeeper: *pan-docheion*
17. Colony: *kolōnia*

1. STAY – REMAIN: *EP-ECHŌ*

ep-echō 1/5

Ac	19 22	[Paul] *remained* for a time in Asia.

2. STAY – REMAIN – COME TO REST: *KATH-IZŌ*

kath-izō 5/46

Mt	26 36	[Jesus] said to his disciples, '⌐*Stay* (or: Sit) here while I go over there to pray'.
Mk	14 32	Jesus said to his disciples, '⌐*Stay* (or: Sit) here while I pray'.
Lk	24 49	*Stay* in the city [of Jerusalem] then,
Ac	2 3	tongues of fire . . . *came to rest* on the head of each of them.
	18 11	Paul *stayed* [at Corinth] . . . for eighteen months.

3. STAY – REMAIN – LIVE: *MENŌ*

1	*menō 118/120*	2	*epi-menō 17*
8	*monē 2*	3	*hypo-menō 7/17*
9	*kata-menō 2*	7	*para-menō 3*
5	*dia-menō 5*	4	*pros-menō 7*
6	*em-menō 4*		

1: STAY, LIVE – WAIT – REMAIN, SPEND (TIME)

Mt	10 11	ask for someone trustworthy and *stay* with him until you leave.
	15 32	4 they have ⌐been (lit. *stayed*) with me for three days now
	26 38	*Wait* here and keep awake with me.
Mk	6 10	If you enter a house anywhere, *stay* there
	8 2	4 they have ⌐been (lit. *stayed*) with me for three days now

Mk	14 34		*Wait* here, and keep awake.
Lk	1 56		Mary *stayed* with Elizabeth about three months
	2 43	X 3	the boy Jesus *stayed* behind in Jerusalem without his parents knowing it.
	8 27		nor did [the man who was possessed by devils] *live* in a house, but in the tombs.
	9 4		Whatever house you enter, *stay* there;
	10 7		*Stay* in the same house,
	19 5	X	Zacchaeus . . . I must *stay* at your house today.
	22 28	5	You are the men who have ⌐stood by (lit. *remained* with) me faithfully in my trials;
	24 29	X	but they pressed him to *stay* with them. 'It is nearly evening,'
		X	they said . . . So he went in to *stay* with them.
Jn	1 38	X	Rabbi . . . where do you *live*?
	39	X	they went and saw where he *lived*, and *stayed* with him the rest of that day.
	2 12		but they *stayed* there only a few days.
	4 40	X	the Samaritans . . . begged him to *stay* with them. He *stayed* for two days,
	7 9	X	he *stayed* behind in Galilee.
	8 35	<	Now the ⌐slave's place in the house is not assured (lit. slave may not always *remain* in the house), but the ⌐son's place is assured (lit. son will always *remain* there).
	10 40	X	He went back again to the far side of the Jordan to *stay* in the district
	11 6	X	he *stayed* where he was for two more days
	54	X	Jesus . . . left the district for a town called Ephraim . . . and *stayed* there with his disciples.
	14 25	X	I have said these things to you while ⌐still (lit. *remaining*) with you;
	19 31		to prevent the bodies *remaining* on the cross during the sabbath
Ac	1 13	9	they went to the upper room where they were *staying*;
	9 43		Peter *stayed* on some time in Jaffa,
	10 48	2	[the converted pagans] begged [Peter] to *stay* on for some days.
	15 34	2	(ᵛ But Silas decided to *stay* [at Antioch].)
	16 15		come and *stay* with us:
	17 14	3	⌐leaving Silas and Timothy behind (lit. while Silas and Timothy *remained*) [at Beroea].
	18 3		when [Paul] found they were tentmakers, of the same trade as himself, he *lodged* with them,
	18	4	After *staying* on for some time [at Corinth], Paul . . .
	20		[the Jews at Ephesus] asked him to *stay* longer
	20 15		after *stopping* at Trogyllium,
	21 4	2	we . . . *stayed* [at Tyre] a week.
	7		we landed at Ptolemais, where we greeted the brothers and *stayed* one day with them.
	8		we came to Caesarea. Here we called on Philip . . . and *stayed* with him.
	10	2	When we had ⌐been (lit. *stayed*) there several days
	27 31		Unless those men *stay* on board you cannot hope to be saved.
	28 12	2	We put in at Syracuse and *spent* three days there.
	14	2	we were much rewarded by *staying* a week with [the brothers at Puteoli].
	16		Paul was allowed to *stay* in lodgings of his own
	30	6	Paul *spent* the whole of the two years in his own rented lodging.
1Co	16 6	9	I may be *staying* with you, perhaps even passing the winter,
	7	2	I hope to *spend* some time with you,
	8	2	In any case I shall be *staying* at Ephesus until Pentecost
Ga	1 18	2	I went up to Jerusalem to visit Cephas and *stayed* with him for fifteen days,
Ph	1 24	2	but for me to *stay* alive in this body is a more urgent need for your sake. ²⁵ . . . I feel sure I shall ⌐survive (lit.
	25	/7	*remain* [alive]) and *stay* with you all,
1Tm	1 3	4	please *stay* at Ephesus,
2Tm	4 20		Erastus *remained* at Corinth,
1Jn	2 19		if they had belonged, they would have *stayed* with us;

2: LIVE (IN A PERSON) – REMAIN (IN), DWELL (IN) – MAKE A HOME (WITHIN), REST (ON)

Jn	1 32	Ⓢ	I saw the Spirit coming down on him from heaven like a dove and *resting* on him.
	33	Ⓢ	The man on whom you see the Spirit come down and *rest*
	3 36		the anger of God *stays* on him.
	5 38		and his word *finds* no *home in* you
	6 56		He who eats my flesh and drinks my blood *lives* in me and I [live] in him.
	14 2	8	There are many ⌐rooms (lit. *places to dwell*) in my Father's house;
	10		it is the Father, *living* in me, who is doing this work.
	17	Ⓢ	but you know [the Spirit], because he ⌐is (lit. *remains*) with you.
	23	8	If anyone loves me . . . we shall come to him and make our *home* with him.
	15 4		*Make your home* in me, as I make mine in you. As a branch cannot bear fruit all by itself, but must *remain* part of the vine, neither can you unless you *remain* in me.
	5		Whoever *remains* in me, with me in him, bears fruit in plenty;

Jn 15	6	Anyone who does not *remain* in me is like a branch that has been thrown away
	7	If you *remain* in me and my words *remain* in you,
1 Jn 2	6	only when the one who claims to be *living* in him is living the same kind of life as Christ lived.
	14	because . . . God's word has *made its home* in you,
	24	*Keep alive* in yourselves what you were taught in the beginning: as long as what you were taught in the beginning *is alive* in you, you will *live* in the Son and in the Father;
	27	⌐But you have not lost the anointing (lit. The anointing *remains*) that he gave you . . . and as it has taught you, so you must *stay* in him.
	28	*Live* in Christ, then, my children,
3	6	anyone who *lives* in God does not sin,
	9	because God's seed *remains* inside him,
	15	murderers . . . do not have eternal life ⌐in (lit. *dwelling* within) them.
	17	how could the love of God be *living* in him?
	24	Whoever keeps his commandments *lives* in God and God [*lives*] in him. We know that he *lives* in us by the Spirit that he has given us.
4	12	as long as we love one another God will *live* in us
	13	We can know that we are *living* in him and he [is living] in us
	15	If anyone acknowledges that Jesus is the Son of God, God *lives* in him, and he in God.
	16	anyone who lives in love *lives* in God, and God *lives* in him.
2 Jn	2	because of the truth that *lives* in us

3: CONTINUE TO, PERSIST IN – KEEP TO, PERSEVERE IN – STAY, REMAIN (IN A STATE)

Lk 1	22	5 [Zechariah] could only make signs to them, and *remained* dumb.
Jn 8	7	2 As they *persisted* with their questions, [Jesus] looked up and said,
	31	If you *make* my word *your home* you will indeed be my disciples.
12	24	unless a wheat grain falls on the ground and dies, it *remains* only a single grain;
	46	so that whoever believes in me need not *stay* in the dark any more.
15	9	*Remain* in my love,
	10	you will *remain* in my love, just as I . . . *remain* in his love.
Ac 11	23	4 [Barnabas] urged them all to *remain* faithful to the Lord with heartfelt devotion;
12	16	2 Peter, meanwhile, ⌐was still knocking (lit. *continued* to knock),
13	43	4 Paul and Barnabas urged them to *remain* faithful to the grace God had given them.
14	22	6 encouraging [the disciples] to *persevere* in the faith.
27	41	The bows were wedged in and ⌐stuck fast (lit. *remained* stuck),
Rm 6	1	2 Does it follow that we should *remain* in sin so as to let grace have greater scope?
11	22	Do not forget that God . . . is kind to you, but only for as long as ⌐he chooses to be (lit. you *continue* in his kindness).
	23	2 the Jews, if they ⌐give up (lit. do not *persist* in) their unbelief, [will find themselves] grafted back
1 Co 7	8	I want to add for the sake of widows and those who are not married: it is a good thing for them to *stay* as they are,
	11	if [a wife] does leave [her husband], she must either *remain* unmarried or else make it up with her husband
	20	Let everyone *stay* as he was at the time of his call.
	24	Each one of you . . . should *stay* as he was before God at the time of his call.
	40	[a widow] would be happier . . . if she *stayed* as she is
Ga 3	10	6 (Dt 27 26) Cursed be everyone who does not *persevere* in observing everything prescribed
Col 1	23	2 as long as you *persevere* and stand firm on the solid base of the faith,
1 Tm 2	15	[a woman] will be saved by childbearing, provided she lives a modest life and *is constant* in faith and love and holiness.
4	16	2 ⌐always do (lit. *continue* to do; or: *persist* in doing) this,
5	5	a woman who is really widowed . . . can . . . ⌐consecrate all her days and nights to (lit. *remain* all her days and nights in) petitions and prayer.
2 Tm 2	13	[Christ] ⌐is always (lit. *remains*) faithful, for he cannot disown his own self.
3	14	You must *keep to* what you have been taught
Heb 7	3	[Melchizedek] *remains* a priest for ever.
8	9	6 (Jr 31 32 G) They ⌐abandoned (lit. did not *keep to*) that covenant of mine,
13	1	*Continue* to love each other like brothers,
Jm 1	25	the man who looks steadily at the perfect law of freedom and 7 ⌐makes that his habit (lit. *keeps to* it constantly) . . . will be happy
1 Jn 2	10	anyone who loves his brother is *living* in the light
3	15	If you refuse to love, you must *remain* dead;
4	16	anyone who *lives* in love lives in God, and God lives in him.
2 Jn	9	If anybody does not *keep* within the teaching of Christ . . . he cannot have God with him: only those who *keep to* what he taught can have the Father and the Son with them.

4: STAND (FAST) – LAST, ENDURE – STAY (BEHIND), REMAIN (FOR EVER)

Mt 10	22	3 the man who *stands firm* to the end will be saved.
11	23	Sodom, it would have been *standing* yet.
Mk 13	13	3 the man who *stands firm* to the end will be saved.
Jn 6	27	work for food that *endures* to eternal life,
9	41	your guilt *remains*.
12	34	X The Law has taught us that the Christ will *remain* for ever.
15	16	I commissioned you . . . to bear fruit, fruit that will *last*;
21	22	I want [John] to *stay* behind till I come,
	23	I want him to *stay* behind till I come.
Rm 9	11	In order ⌐to stress that God's choice is free (lit. that God's selective purpose might *stand*),
1 Co 3	14	If his structure *stands up to* [the fire], he will get his wages;
13	13	In short, there are three things that *last*: faith, hope and love;
15	6	most of [these brothers] ⌐are still alive (lit. *remain*).
2 Co 3	11	there must be much more [splendour] in what is going to *last* for ever.
	14	to this very day, that same veil ⌐is still (lit. *remains*) there
9	9	(Ps 112 9) his good deeds will ⌐never be forgotten (lit. *last* for ever).
Ga 2	5	I was so determined ⌐to safeguard for you the true meaning of the Good News (lit. that the true meaning of the Good 5 News should *last* for you),
2 Tm 2	12	If we *hold firm*, then we shall reign with [Christ Jesus].
Heb 1	11	X 5 (Ps 102 27) all will vanish, though you *remain*,
7	23	there used to be a great number of those other priests, because death ⌐put an end to each one of them (lit. *stopped them* 24 X 7/ from *remaining*); 24 but this one, because he *remains* for ever, can never lose his priesthood.
10	34	you owned something that was better and *lasting*.
12	27	so . . . the unshakeable things will ⌐be left (lit. *stand fast*).
13	14	there is no ⌐eternal (lit. *lasting*) city for us in this life
Jm 1	12	3 Happy the man who *stands firm* when trials come.
1 P 1	23	the . . . word of the living and ⌐eternal (lit. *lasting*) God.
	25	(Is 40 8) the word of the Lord *remains* for ever.
2 P 3	4	5 [Scornful people say,] Everything ⌐goes on (lit. *stays*) . . as it has since it began at the creation.
1 Jn 2	17	anyone who does the will of God *remains* for ever.
Rv 17	10	once here, [the seventh emperor] must *stay* for a short while.

5: REMAIN (A POSSESSION)

Ac 5	4 Δ	While you still owned the land, wasn't it yours to keep (lit. While the land *remained*, did it not *remain* yours)?

4. LIVE, LIVING, BE ALIVE – LIFE: *ZŌĒ*

1 zaō	140	4 zōo-poieō	11
2 zōē	135	7 ana-zaō	2
3 zōon	20/23	6 sy-zaō	3
5 zōo-goneō	3	8 sy-zōo-poieō	2

D = Life, Living // Death, Dead

1: (THE) LIVING (GOD) – (GOD) LIVES

Mt 16	16	You are the Christ, . . . the Son of the *living* God.
26	63	I put you on oath by the *living* God
Jn 6	57	I, who am sent by the *living* Father, myself draw life from the Father,
Ac 14	15	We have come . . . to make you turn from these empty idols to the *living* God
Rm 9	26	they will now be called the sons of the *living* God.
14	11	(Is 45 23) By my *life* – it is the Lord who speaks – every knee shall bend before me,
2 Co 3	3	you are a letter from Christ . . . written . . . with the Spirit of the *living* God,
6	16	that is what we are – the temple of the *living* God.
1 Th 1	9	you . . . became servants of the real, *living* God;
1 Tm 3	15	I wanted you to know how people ought to behave in God's family – that is, in the Church of the *living* God,
4	10	we have put our trust in the *living* God
Heb 3	12	there is not in any one of your community a wicked mind, so unbelieving as to turn away from the *living* God.
9	14	we do our service to the *living* God.
10	31	It is a dreadful thing to fall into the hands of the *living* God.
12	22	you have come to . . . the city of the *living* God, the heavenly Jerusalem
1 P 1	23	your new birth was . . . from the everlasting word of the *living* and eternal God.
Rv 4	9	the animals . . . gave thanks to the One sitting on the throne, who *lives* for ever and ever,

Rv 4 10   the twenty-four elders prostrated themselves . . . to worship the One who *lives* for ever and ever,

7 2   I saw another angel . . . carrying the seal of the *living* God;

10 6   [the angel] swore by the One who *lives* for ever and ever,

15 7   God . . . *lives* for ever and ever.

2: LIVE, BE ALIVE – LIFE

Mt 9 18 D   My daughter has just died, but come and lay your hand on her and ʳher life will be saved (lit. she will *live*).

27 63 X   this impostor said, *while he was still alive*, 'After three days I shall rise again'.

Mk 5 23   Do come and lay your hands on [my little daughter] to make her better ʳ and save her life (lit. so that she will *live*).

Lk 2 36   [Anna] had ʳbeen married (lit. *lived* with her husband) for seven years

12 15 2   a man's *life* is not made secure by what he owns,

16 25 D 2   remember that during your *life* good things came your way,

Jn 4 50   Go home . . . your son will *live*.

51   his servants met him with the news that his boy *was alive*.

53   this was exactly the time when Jesus had said, 'Your son will *live*';

Ac 7 19 5   [The new king of Egypt forced our ancestors] to expose their babies to prevent their *surviving*.

8 33 X 2   (Is 53 8) his *life* on earth has been cut short!

9 41 D   [Tabitha got ill and died.] Peter . . . showed them she *was alive*.

10 42 D   God has appointed [Jesus] to judge everyone, *alive* or dead.

17 25 2   it is [God] who gives everything – including *life* and breath – to everyone.

28   it is in [God] that we *live*, and move, and exist,

20 12 D   [Eutychus was picked up dead.] They took the boy away *alive*.

22 22   [Paul] is not fit to *live*!

25 24   [Paul] ought not to be allowed to *remain alive*.

26 5   I . . . *lived* as a Pharisee.

28 4   divine vengeance would not let [Paul] *live*.

Rm 7 1   laws affect a person only during his *lifetime* . . . ² A married
2   woman . . . has legal obligations to her husband while he
3 D   *is alive* . . . ³ So if she gives herself to another man while
D   her husband *is still alive*, she is legally an adulteress;

8 38 D 2   neither death not *life* . . . ³⁹ . . . can ever come between us and the love of God

14 7 D   The *life* and death of each of us has its influence on others;
8 D   ⁸ if we *live*, we live for the Lord . . . so . . . *alive* or dead
9   we belong to the Lord. ⁹ This explains why Christ both died and came to life, it was so that he might be Lord both
D   of the dead and of the *living*.

1Co 3 22 D 2   the world, *life* and death . . . all are your servants;

7 39 D   A wife is tied as long as her husband *is alive*.

9 14   the Lord directed that those who preach the gospel should *get their living* from the gospel.

15 19 2   If our hope in Christ has been for this *life* only, we are the most unfortunate of all people.

36 D 4   Whatever you sow . . . has to die before it is *given* [new] *life*
45   (Gn 2 7) The first man, Adam . . . became a *living* soul;

2Co 1 8   we despaired of *coming through alive*.

4 11 D   while [we *are*] *still alive*, we are consigned to our death every day

5 15 D   [Christ] died for all . . . so that *living* [men] should [live] no longer for themselves,

6 9 D   [we are] said to be dying and here *are* we *alive*;

7 3 D 6   you are in our hearts – *together* we *live* or together we die.

Ga 2 14   In spite of being a Jew, you *live* like the pagans

20   I *live* now not with my own [life] but with [the life] of Christ who lives in me. [The life] I now *live* in this body I live in faith:

Ph 1 20   My one hope . . . is that . . . I shall have the courage for
D 2   Christ to be glorified in my body, whether by my *life* or
22   by my death. ²¹ Life to me, of course, is Christ . . . ²² but . . . if *living* in this body means doing work which is having good results – I do not know what I should choose.

1Th 4 15 D   any of us who are left *alive* until the Lord's coming will not have any advantage over those who have died.

17   then those who *are still alive* will be taken up in the clouds,

1Tm 5 6   The [widow] who thinks only of pleasure is already dead
D   while she *is still alive*:

2Tm 4 1 D   Christ Jesus . . . is to be judge of the *living* and the dead,

Heb 2 15   [Christ can] set free all those who had been held in slavery all their *lives* by the fear of death.

7 3 2   [Melchizedek's] *life* has no beginning or ending;
8 D   [Melchizedek] is declared to *be still alive*.

9 17 D   a will . . . is not meant to have any effect while the testator *is still alive*.

Jm 4 14 2   You never know what will happen in your *life* tomorrow:
15   If it is the Lord's will, we shall *still be alive* to do this

1P 4 5 D   the judge . . . is ready to judge the *living* and the dead.

Rv 11 11 2   God breathed *life* into [the two witnesses] and they stood up,

13 14   the beast . . . had been wounded by the sword and still *lived*.

Rv 16 3 D 2   every *living* creature in the sea died.

19 20   [the beast and the false prophet] were thrown *alive* into the fiery lake of burning sulphur.

3: (ETERNAL, EVERLASTING) LIFE – LIVE (AFTER THE RESURRECTION, FOR SALVATION)

Mt 4 4 2   (Dt 8 3) Man does not *live* on bread alone

7 14 2   it is . . . a hard road that leads to *life*,

18 8 2   it is better for you to enter into *life* crippled . . . ⁹ . . . it is
9 2   better for you to enter into *life* with one eye,

19 16 2   what good deed must I do to possess eternal *life*? ¹⁷ . . . if
17 2   you wish to enter into *life*, keep the commandments.

29   everyone who has left houses . . . or land for the sake of my name will . . . inherit eternal *life*.

22 32 D   God is God, not of the dead, but of the *living*.

25 46 2   the virtuous [will go] to eternal *life*.

Mk 9 43 2   it is better for you to enter into *life* crippled . . . ⁴⁵ . . . it is
45 2   better for you to enter into *life* lame,

10 17 2   what must I do to inherit eternal *life*?

30 2   [there is no one] who will not be repaid . . . in the world to come, eternal *life*.

12 27 D   He is God, not of the dead, but of the *living*.

16 11 D X   they did not believe . . . when they heard . . . that he *was alive*.

Lk 4 4 2   (Dt 8 3) Man does not *live* on bread alone.

10 25 2   what must I do to inherit eternal *life*?

28   'You have answered right,' said Jesus 'do this and *life is yours*.'

15 13   the younger son . . . squandered his money on a *life* of debauchery.

24 D 7   this son of mine was dead and has *come back to life*;

32 D   your brother . . . was dead and has come to *life*.

17 33   Anyone who tries to preserve his life will lose it; and anyone
5   who loses it will keep it safe (lit. *be made alive*).

18 18 2   what have I to do to inherit eternal *life*?

30 2   [there is no one who has left house . . .] who will not be given . . . eternal *life*.

20 38 D   he is God, not of the dead, but of the *living*; for to him all men *are* in fact *alive*.

24 5 D X   Why look among the dead for someone who *is alive*?

23 D X   angels . . . declared he *was alive*.

Jn 1 4 X 2/2   All that came to be had *life* in him (ᵛ In him was *life*) and
2   that *life* was the light of men,

3 15 2   everyone who believes may have eternal *life* in [the Son of Man].

16 D   [God] gave his only Son, so that everyone who believes in
2   him . . . may have eternal *life*.

36 2   Anyone who believes in the Son has eternal *life*, but anyone
2   who refuses to believe in the Son will never see *life*.

4 10 2   he would have given you *living* water. ¹¹ . . . how could you
11   get this *living* water?

14   the water that I shall give will turn into a spring inside him,
2   welling up to eternal *life*.

36 2   the reaper . . . is bringing in the grain for eternal *life*,

5 21 D 4   as the Father raises the dead and *gives* them *life*, so the Son
4   *gives life* to anyone he chooses;

24 2   whoever listens to my words . . . has eternal *life* . . . he has
D 2   passed from death to *life*.

25   the dead will hear the voice of the Son of God, and all who
D   hear it will *live*.

26 Θ 2   the Father, who is the source of *life*, has made the Son the
X   source of *life*;

29 2   those who did good will rise again to *life*;

39   You study the scriptures, believing that in them you have
40 2   eternal *life* . . . ⁴⁰ and yet you refuse to come to me for
2   *life*!

6 27 D 2   work for food that endures to eternal *life*,

33 2   the bread of God is that which . . . gives *life* to the world.

35 2   I am the bread of *life*.

40   whoever sees the Son and believes in him shall have eternal
2   *life*,

47 2   everybody who believes has eternal *life*.

48 D 2   I am the bread of *life*. ⁴⁹ Your fathers ate the manna . . . and they are dead;

51   I am the *living* bread which has come down from heaven.
D   Anyone who eats this bread will *live* for ever; and the
2   bread that I shall give is my flesh, for the *life* of the world.

53   if you do not eat the flesh of the Son of Man . . . you will
54 2   not find *life* in you. ⁵⁴ Anyone who does eat my flesh and
2   drink my blood has eternal *life*,

57 X   As I, who am sent by the living Father, myself *draw life* from
58   the Father, so whoever eats me will *draw life* from me. ⁵⁸
D   . . . anyone who eats this bread will *live* for ever.

63 4   It is the spirit that *gives life* . . . The words I have spoken
2   to you are spirit and they are *life*,

68 2   You have the message of eternal *life*,

7 38   [Let the man drink who believes in me!] From his breast shall flow fountains of *living* water.

Jn	8	12	2 anyone who follows me . . . will have the light of *life*.
	10	10	2 I have come so that [my sheep] may have *life*
		28	2 I give [my sheep] eternal *life*; they will never be lost
	11	25 X	2 I am the resurrection (§ and the *life*). If anyone believes in me, even though he dies he will *live*, ²⁶ and whoever *lives*
		26 D	and believes in me will never die.
	12	25	anyone who hates his life in this world will keep it for the eternal *life*.
		50	2 I know that [the Father's] commands mean eternal *life*.
	14	6 X	2 I am the Way, the Truth and the *Life*.
		19 X	you will see me, because I *live* and you will *live*.
	17	2	2 let [your Son] give eternal *life* to all those you have entrusted to him. ³ And eternal *life* is this: to know you . . . and
		3	2 Jesus Christ whom you have sent.
	20	31	These [signs] are recorded so that . . . believing this you may have *life* through his name.
Ac	1	3 X D	He had shown himself *alive* to [the apostles] after his Passion
	2	28	2 (Ps 16 11) You have made known the way of *life* to me,
	3	15 X D 2	you killed the prince of *life*.
	5	20	2 Go . . . and tell the people all about this new *Life*.
	7	38	[Moses] was entrusted with words of *life* to hand on to us.
	11	18	God . . . can evidently grant even the pagans the repentance that leads to *life*.
	13	46	2 since you do not think yourselves worthy of eternal *life*, we must turn to the pagans.
		48	2 all who were destined for eternal *life* became believers.
	25	19 X D	they had some argument . . . about a dead man called Jesus whom Paul alleged to *be alive*.
Rm	1	17	(Hab 2 4) The upright man *finds life* through faith.
	2	7	For those who sought renown . . . by always doing good there will be eternal *life*;
	4	17 D	4 God . . . *brings* the dead *to life* and calls into being what does not exist.
	5	10 X D 2	surely we may count on being saved by the *life* of his Son?
		17 D	2 Jesus Christ will cause everyone to reign in *life* who receives the free gift . . . of being made righteous.
		18	2 the good act of one man brings everyone *life*
		21 D	2 grace will reign to bring eternal *life*
	6	2 D	We are dead to sin, so how can we continue to *live* in it?
		4 D	[we] joined [Christ] in death, so that . . . we too might live a new *life*.
		8 X	6 we believe that . . . we shall *return to life with* [Christ]:
		10 X D	When [Christ] died, he died, once for all, to sin, so his *life* now is *life* with God;
		11 D	consider yourselves to be dead to sin but *alive* for God
		13 D	consider yourselves dead men brought back to *life*;
		22 D	you get a reward leading to your sanctification and . . . eternal *life*. ²³ . . . the present given by God is eternal
		23 D	2 *life* in Christ
	7	9 D	Once, when there was no Law, I *was alive*; but when the commandment came, sin *came to life* ¹⁰ and I died: the
		10	7 commandment was meant to lead me to *life* but it turned
		D	out to mean death for me,
	8	2 D	2 the law of the spirit of *life* in Christ Jesus has set you free from the law of sin and death.
		6 D	2 *life* and peace can only come with concern for the spiritual.
		10 D	2 your spirit is *life* itself because you have been justified;
		11 D	4 he who raised Jesus from the dead will *give life* to your own mortal bodies
		12	there is no necessity for us . . . to *live* unspiritual [lives]. ¹³ If you do *live* in that way, you are doomed to die; but
		13 D	if by the Spirit you put an end to the misdeeds of the body you will *live*.
	10	5	(Lv 18 5) those who keep the Law will *draw life* from it.
	11	15	do you know what [the Jews'] admission will mean? Nothing less than ⌜a resurrection (lit. *life*) from the dead!
		D	2
	12	1	[worship God] by offering your *living* bodies as a holy sacrifice,
	14	8 D	if we live, we *live* for the Lord . . . ⁹ This explains why Christ both died and *came to life*, it was so that he might be
		9 X D	Lord both of the dead and of the *living*.
1 Co	15	22 D	4 all men will be *brought to life* in Christ;
		45	4 the last Adam has become a *life-giving* spirit.
2 Co	2	16	[for those who are being saved we are] the sweet smell of *life* that leads to *life*.
		D 2/2	
	3	6 D	4 the written letters bring death, but the Spirit *gives life*.
	4	10	we carry with us in our body the death of Jesus, so that the *life* of Jesus, too, may always be seen in our body.
		X	2
		11	we are consigned to our death every day . . . so that in our mortal flesh the *life* of Jesus, too, may be openly shown.
		X D 2	
		12 D 2	¹² So death is at work in us, but *life* in you.
	5	4 D	2 we want . . . to have what must die taken up into *life*.
		15	[Christ] died for all . . . so that living men should *live* no longer for themselves, but for him who died and was raised to life for them.
	13	4 X	he was crucified . . . and [still] he *lives* now through the power of God . . . we are weak . . . but we shall *live* with him,
Ga	2	19 D	I am dead to the Law, so that now I can *live* for God . . . ²⁰ and I live now not with my own life but with the life of
		20	
		X	Christ who *lives* in me. [The life] I now live in this body I *live* in faith:

Ga	3	11	(Hab 2 4) the righteous man *finds life* through faith.
		12	(Lv 18 15) The man who practises these precepts *finds life* through practising them.
		21	We could have been justified by the Law if the Law we were given had been capable of *giving life*,
		4	
	5	25	Since the Spirit *is our life*, let us be directed by the Spirit.
	6	8	if [a man] sows in the field of the Spirit he will get from it a harvest of eternal *life*.
		2	
Ep	2	5 X D 8	when we were dead through our sins, [God] *brought us to life with* Christ
	4	18 Θ	2 [the pagans] are estranged from the *life* of God,
Ph	1	21 D	*Life* to me, of course, is Christ, but then death would bring me something more;
	2	16	2 you are offering [the world] the word of *life*.
	4	3	[The] names [of those who worked with me] are written in the book of *life*.
		2	
Col	2	13 X D 8	You were dead, . . . [God] has *brought* you *to life with* [Christ],
		20	why do you still let rules dictate to you, as though you were still *living* in the world?
		D	
	3	3 D	2 now the *life* you have is hidden with Christ in God. ⁴ But when
		4	2 Christ is revealed – and he is your *life* – you too will be revealed in all your glory with him.
		7	it is the way in which you used to *live* when you were surrounded by people doing the same thing,
1 Th	3	8 ○	now we can ⌜breathe (lit. *live*) again, as you are still holding firm in the Lord.
	5	10 X D	[Jesus Christ] died for us so that . . . we should still *live* united to him.
1 Tm	1	16	other people . . . would later have to trust in [Christ] to come to eternal *life*.
		2	
	4	8	2 spirituality . . . holds out the reward of *life* here and now and of the future [life] as well;
	6	12	2 win for yourself the eternal *life* to which you are called
		13	5 before God the *source* of all *life* . . . I put to you the duty ¹⁴ of doing all that you have been told,
		19	2 this is the way [the rich] can save up a good capital sum for the future if they want to make sure of the only *life* that is real.
2 Tm	1	1	From Paul, appointed by God to be an apostle . . . in his design to promise *life* in Christ Jesus;
		X	2
		10 D	2 Christ Jesus . . . has proclaimed *life* and immortality through the Good News;
	2	11 X D 6	If we have died with him, then we shall *live with* him.
	3	12	anybody who tries to *live* in devotion to Christ is certain to be attacked;
Tt	1	2	[God has chosen Paul] to give them the hope of . . . eternal *life*
		2	
	2	12	we must . . . *live* good and religious [lives] here in this present world,
	3	7	we should . . . become heirs looking forward to inheriting eternal *life*.
		2	
Heb	4	12	The word of God is something *alive* and active:
	7	16 X	2 [Christ is a priest] by the power of an indestructible *life*.
		25 X	[Christ] *is living* for ever to intercede for all who come to God
	10	20	[Brothers, through the blood of Jesus we have the right to enter the sanctuary,] by . . . a *living* opening through the curtain, that is to say, his body.
		X Δ	
		38	(Hab 2 4) The righteous man will *live* by faith,
	12	9	we ought to be . . . willing to submit ourselves to our spiritual Father, to *be given life*.
Jm	1	12	2 the man who stands firm . . . will win the prize of *life*,
1 P	1	3	God . . . has given us a new birth . . . by raising Jesus Christ from the dead, so that we have ⌜sure (lit. *living*) hope
	2	4 X	He is the *living* stone . . . set yourselves close to him ⁵ so that you too . . . may be *living* stones making a spiritual house.
		5	
		24	[Christ] was bearing our faults . . . so that we might die to our faults and *live* for holiness.
		D	
	3	7	2 a woman . . . is equally an heir to the *life* of grace.
		10	2 (Ps 34 13) Anyone who wants to have a happy *life* . . . must banish malice from his tongue;
		18	In the body [Christ] was put to death, in the spirit he was *raised to life*,
		X D 4	
	4	6	the dead had to be told the Good News as well, so that . . . they might *come to* God's *life* in the spirit.
		D	
2 P	1	3	2 [Christ] has given us all the things that we need for *life* and for true devotion.
1 Jn	1	1 X 2/2	the Word, who is *life* . . . is our subject. ² That *life* was made visible: we . . . are . . . telling you of . . . eternal *life*
		2 X	2
	2	25	2 what is promised to you . . . is eternal *life*.
	3	14 D	2 we have passed out of death and into *life*, . . . because we love our brothers.
		15	2 murderers . . . do not have eternal *life* in them.
	4	9	God sent into the world his only Son so that we could *have life* through him;
	5	11	2/2 God has given us eternal *life* and this *life* is in his Son;
		12	2 ¹² anyone who has the Son has *life*, anyone who does not
		13	2 have the Son does not have *life*. ¹³ . . . you who believe in

1 Jn	5 13		the name of the Son of God may be sure that you have
		2	eternal *life*.
	16		If anybody sees his brother commit a sin that is not a deadly
		D 2	sin, he has only to pray, and God will give *life* to the sinner
	20 X	2	This is the true God, this is eternal *life*.
Jude	21		keep yourselves within the love of God and wait for . . .
		2	eternal *life*.
Rv	1 18 X D		I am the *Living* [One], I was dead and now I *am to live* for
			ever and ever,
	2 7	2	those who prove victorious I will feed from the tree of *life*
	8		Here is the message of the First and the Last, who was dead
		X D	and has *come to life* again:
	10	2	keep faithful, and I will give you the crown of *life*
	3 1 D		you are reputed to *be alive* and yet are dead.
	5		I shall not blot [the] names [of those who prove victorious]
		2	out of the book of *life*,
	7 17	2	the Lamb . . . will lead them to springs of *living* water;
	13 8		everybody whose name has not been written down . . . in
		2	the book of *life* of the sacrificial Lamb [will worship the
			beast].
	17 8		All the people of the world, whose names have not been
		2	written . . . in the book of *life*,
	20 4 D		all who had been beheaded . . . *came to life* and reigned with
	5 D		Christ . . . [5] . . . the rest of the dead did not *come to life*
			until the thousand years were over.
	12 D	2	the book of *life* was opened,
	15		anybody whose name could not be found written in the book
		2	of *life* was thrown into the burning lake.
	21 6 D	2	I will give water from the well of *life* free to anybody who is
			thirsty;
	27	2	only those who are listed in the Lamb's book of *life* [may come
			to the city].
	22 1	2	the angel showed me the river of *life*, rising from the throne of
			God and of the Lamb
	2	2	On either side of the river were the trees of *life*,
	14		those who will have washed their robes clean . . . will have
		2	the right to feed on the tree of *life*
	17	2	all who want it may have the water of *life*, and have it free.
	19		if anyone cuts anything out of the prophecies in this book, God
		2	will cut off his share of the tree of *life*

4: (THE FOUR) LIVING CREATURES, ANIMALS (IN REVELATION)

Rv	4 6	3	In the centre . . . were four *animals* with many eyes . . .
	7	3/3	[7] The first *animal* was like a lion, the second *animal* was like
		3	a bull, the third *animal* had a human face, and the fourth
	8	3/3	*animal* was like a flying eagle. [8] Each of the four *animals*
	9	3	had six wings . . . [9] . . . the *animals* glorified . . . the
			One sitting on the throne.
	5 6	3	I saw, standing between the throne with its four *animals* and
	8		the circle of the elders, a Lamb . . . [8] . . . when he took
		3	[the scroll] the four *animals* prostrated themselves before
			him
	11		I heard the sound of an immense number of angels gathered
		3	round the throne and the *animals* and the elders;
	14	3	the four *animals* said, 'Amen';
	6 1	3	I heard one of the four *animals* shout . . , 'Come'.
	3	3	I heard the second *animal* shout, 'Come'.
	5	3	I heard the third *animal* shout, 'Come'.
	6	3	I seemed to hear a voice shout from among the four *animals*
	7	3	I heard the voice of the fourth *animal* shout, 'Come'.
	7 11		the angels . . . were . . . surrounding the elders and the four
		3	*animals*,
	14 3		There in front of the throne they were singing . . . in the
		3	presence of the four *animals* and the elders,
	15 7	3	One of the four *animals* gave the seven angels seven golden
			bowls
	19 4	3	the twenty-four elders and the four *animals* prostrated them-
			selves and worshipped God

5. LIFE – LIVE ON: *BIOS*

3	*bioō*	1	4 *biōsis* 1
1	*bios*	10	2 *biōtikos* 3

1: LIFE, OF LIVING

Lk	8 14		people . . . are choked by the worries and riches and pleasures
			of *life*
	21 34		Watch yourselves, or your hearts will be coarsened with
		2	debauchery . . . and the cares *of life*,
Ac	26 4	4	My [manner of] *life* from my youth, [a life] spent . . . among
			my own people . . . is common knowledge among the
			Jews.

1 Co	6 3	2	we can judge [matters] *of* [everyday] *life*; [4] but when you have
	4	2	had cases 「of that kind (lit. *concerning* [everyday] *life*),
			the people you appointed to try them were not even respected
			in the Church.
1 Tm	2 2		[there should be prayers offered for everyone] so that we
			may be able to live religious and reverent *lives* in peace
2 Tm	2 4		In the army, no soldier gets himself mixed up in [civilian] *life*,
1 P	4 2	3	for the rest of his *life* on earth [a person with bodily suffering]
			is not ruled by human passions

2: LIVE ON, LIFE'S EARNINGS – PROPERTY, POSSESSIONS, GOODS

Mk	12 44		[the poor widow] from the little she had has put in everything
			she possessed, all she *had to live on*.
Lk	8 43		there was a woman . . . whom no one had been able to cure
			(ᵛ though she had spent all her *life's earnings* on doctors).
	15 12		the father divided the *property* between [his two sons].
	30		this son of yours . . . comes back after swallowing up your
			property
	21 4		[this poor widow] from the little she had has put in all she
			had to live on.
1 Jn	2 16		the sensual body, the lustful eye, pride in *possessions* . . .
			come from the world;
	3 17		If a man who was rich enough in this world's *goods* saw that
			one of his brothers was in need, but closed his heart to him,
			how could the love of God be living in him?

6. LIVE – DWELL – SETTLE: *KAT-OIKEŌ*

2	*oikeō*	6 ⎫	7 *kat-oikia* 1
4	*oikeō meta*	2 ⎬ 8	8 *kat-oikizō* 1
1	*kat-oikeō*	44	9 *en-kat-oikeō* 1
6	*kat-oikēsis*	1	3 *en-oikeō* 6
5	*kat-oikētērion*	2	10 *syn-oikeō* 1

1: LIVE (AT, IN), SETTLE (IN), DWELL – INHABITANT

Mt	2 23		[Joseph] *settled* in a town called Nazareth.
	4 13 X		leaving Nazareth [Jesus] went and *settled* in Capernaum,
Mk	5 3	6	[the demoniac] *lived* in the tombs
Lk	13 4		all the other people *living* in Jerusalem?
Ac	1 19		Everybody *living* in Jerusalem heard about [the fate of Judas]
	20		(Ps 69 26) Let his camp be reduced to ruin, Let there be no
			one to *live* in it.
	2 5		there were devout men *living* in Jerusalem
	9		people 「from (lit. who *live* in) Mesopotamia, Judaea and
			Cappadocia,
	14		Men of Judaea, and all you who *live* in Jerusalem,
	4 16		It is obvious to everybody *living* in Jerusalem
	7 2		God . . . appeared to . . . Abraham, while he was in
	4		Mesopotamia before *settling* in Haran . . . [4] So he left
			Chaldaea and *settled* in Haran . . . God made him . . .
			come to this land where you are *living* today.
	9 22		[Saul] was able to throw the 「Jewish colony (lit. Jews who
			lived) at Damascus into complete confusion
	32		Peter . . . came to the saints *living* down in Lydda.
	35		everybody who *lived* in Lydda and Sharon
	11 29		The disciples decided to send relief . . . to the brothers
			living in Judaea.
	13 27		What the people 「of (lit. *living* in) Jerusalem and their rulers
			did . . . was in fact to fulfil the prophecies
	17 26		[God] not only created the whole human race so that they
			could 「*occupy* (or: *inhabit*) the entire earth, but he decreed
	7		. . . what the boundaries of [each nation's] 「territory
			(lit. *habitation*) should be.
	19 10		people *living* all over Asia . . . were able to hear the word of
			the Lord.
	17		Everybody *living* in Ephesus . . . heard about this episode;
	22 12		Ananias . . . highly thought of by all the Jews *living* there,
Heb	11 10		[Abraham] *lived* . . . in tents while he looked forward to a
			city founded . . . by God.
2 P	2 8	9	[Lot,] that holy man, *living* among [the people of Sodom],
Rv	2 13		[Pergamum,] where you *live*, in the place where Satan is
			enthroned,
	3 10		to test the 「people (lit. *inhabitants*) of the world.
	6 10		before you . . . take vengeance for our death on the
			inhabitants of the earth?
	8 13		trouble for all the *inhabitants* of the earth
	11 10		the 「people (lit. *inhabitants*) of the world will be glad . . .
			because these two prophets have been a plague to the
			「people (lit. *inhabitants*) of the world.
	13 8		all 「people (lit. *inhabitants*) of the world will worship [the
			beast],
	12		making the world and all its 「people (lit. *inhabitants*) worship
			the first beast,

Rv 13 14		[the beast] was able to win over the ⌐people (lit. *inhabitants*)┐ of the world and persuade ⌐them (lit. the *inhabitants*)┐ to put up a statue in honour of the beast
17 2		[the prostitute] who has made all the *population* of the world drunk with the wine of her adultery
8		the ⌐people (lit. *inhabitants*)┐ of the world . . . will think [the beast] miraculous

2: (GOD) LIVES (IN), DWELLS (IN), MAKES HIS HOME (IN)

Mt 23 21		when a man swears by the Temple he is swearing . . . by the One who *dwells* in it.
Ac 7 48		the Most High does not *live* in a house that human hands have built.
17 24		God who made the world . . . does not *make his home* in shrines made by human hands.
Rm 8 9 Ⓢ	2	the Spirit of God has *made his home* in you.
11 Ⓢ	2	if the Spirit of him who raised Jesus from the dead is *living* in you, then he . . . will give life to your own mortal
Ⓢ	3	bodies through his Spirit *living* in you.
1 Co 3 16		Didn't you realise that you are God's temple and that the
Ⓢ	2	Spirit of God was *living* among you?
2 Co 6 16	3	(Lv 26 11) I will *make my home* among them and live with them; I will be their God and they shall be my people.
Ep 2 22	5	[a house] *where* God *lives*, in the Spirit.
3 17		so that Christ may *live* in your hearts through faith,
1 Tm 6 16	2	[God] ⌐whose home is (lit. who *lives*)┐ in inaccessible light,
2 Tm 1 14 Ⓢ	3	with the help of the Holy Spirit who *lives* in us.

3: LIVE (IN), DWELL (WITHIN), FIGURATIVELY – SETTLE, SET UP HOUSE (IN)

Mt 12 45 Ⓓ		seven other spirits more evil . . . go in and *set up house* [in the man],
Lk 11 26 Ⓓ		seven other spirits more wicked . . . go in and *set up house* [in the man],
Rm 7 17	3	the thing behaving in that way is not my self but sin *living* in me
18	2	I know of nothing good *living* in me
20	2	sin which *lives* in me.
Col 1 19		God wanted all perfection to ⌐be found (lit. *dwell*)┐ in [Christ]
2 9		In [Christ's] body *lives* the fullness of divinity.
3 16	3	Let the message of Christ, in all its richness, *find a home* with you.
2 Tm 1 5	3	the sincere faith which . . . came first to *live* in your grandmother
Jm 4 5 △	8	the spirit which [God] *sent to live* in us wants us for himself alone?
2 P 3 13		the new heavens and new earth . . . where righteousness will *be at home*.
Rv 2 13 Ⓓ		Antipas was killed in your own town, where Satan *lives*.
18 2 Ⓓ	5	Babylon . . . has become the ⌐haunt (or: *dwelling*)┐ of devils

4: LIVE WITH, LIFE TOGETHER

1 Co 7 12		If a brother has a wife who is an unbeliever, and she is
13	4	content to *live with* him, he must not send her away; [13] and if a woman has an unbeliever for her husband, and he is
4		content to *live with* her, she must not leave him.
1 P 3 7		husbands must always treat their wives with consideration
10		in their *life together*,

7. LIVE (IN, ON), DWELL: KATH-ĒMAI

kath-ēmai 5/91

Mt 4 16		(Is 9 1) The people that ⌐lived (or: sat)┐ in darkness . . . those who ⌐dwell (or: sit)┐ in the land and shadow of death
Lk 1 79		(Is 9 1) to give light to those who *live* in darkness and the shadow of death,
21 35		[that day] will come down on every man *living* on the face of the earth.
Rv 14 6		another angel, . . . sent to announce the Good News of eternity to all who *live* on the earth,

8. BE AT HOME (WITH), LIVE (IN), MAKE ONE'S HOME (IN): EN-DĒMEŌ

en-dēmeō 3

2 Co 5 6		to *live* in the body means to be exiled from the Lord,
8		we . . . want to be exiled from the body and ⌐make our (or: *be at*)┐ *home* with the Lord.

2 Co 5 9		Whether we are *living* in the body or exiled from it, we are intent on pleasing [the Lord].

9. LIVE IN A CONTINUOUS STATE OF: DIA-TELEŌ

dia-teleō 1

Ac 27 33		For fourteen days . . . you have *been* in suspense, going hungry

10. (BE, GO, DO) CONTINUOUSLY, CONSTANTLY – (BE) DEVOTED TO, FAITHFUL IN (DOING) – PERSIST: KARTEREŌ

2 *kartereō* 1		1 *pros-kartereō* 10	
		3 *pros-karterēsis* 1	

Mk 3 9		[Jesus] asked his disciples to have a boat *ready* for him because of the crowd,
Ac 1 14		All [the apostles] joined in *continuous* prayer,
2 42		These *remained faithful* to the teaching of the apostles,
46		They *went* as a body to the Temple every day
6 4		[we will] continue to *devote* ourselves to prayer
8 13		After his baptism Simon . . . *went round constantly* with Philip,
10 7		Cornelius called two of the slaves and a *devout* soldier of his staff . . . and sent them off to Jaffa.
Rm 12 12		Do not give up if trials come; and *keep on* praying.
13 6		all government officials . . . *serve* God by collecting taxes.
Ep 6 18	3	*Never get tired of* staying awake to pray for all the saints;
Col 4 2		*Be persevering* in your prayers
Heb 11 27	2	[Moses] *held to his purpose* like a man who could see the Invisible.

11. STAY – STOP – SPEND TIME: DIA-TRIBŌ

2 (*chrono-*)*tribeō* 1		1 *dia-tribō* 10

Jn 3 22		Jesus went . . . into the Judaean countryside and *stayed* with them there
11 54		Jesus . . . left the district for a town called Ephraim . . . and *stayed* there with his disciples.
Ac 12 19		before leaving Judaea to ⌐take up residence (or: *stay*)┐ in Caesarea [Herod] gave orders for the execution [of the guards].
14 3		[at Iconium] Paul and Barnabas *stayed* on for some time,
28		[Paul and Barnabas] *stayed* [at Antioch] with the disciples for some time.
15 35		Paul and Barnabas, however, *stayed* on in Antioch,
16 12		After *spending* a few days [at Philippi]
20 6		we . . . met them five days later at Troas, where we *stopped* for a week.
16	2	to avoid *spending* time in Asia,
25 6		After *staying* with them for eight or ten days at the most, [Festus] went down to Caesarea
14		[King Agrippa's and Bernice's] ⌐visit (lit. *stay*)┐ lasted several days

12. SPEND TIME: POIEŌ

poieō 5/567

Ac 15 33		[Judas and Silas] *spent* some time there, and then the brothers wished them peace and they went back
18 23		[at Antioch, Paul] *spent* a short time before continuing his journey
20 3		[Paul made his way into Greece] where he *spent* three months.
2 Co 11 25		I have ⌐been┐ . . . once adrift in the open sea for a night and a day (lit. once *spent* a night and a day adrift in the open sea)
Jm 4 13		Today or tomorrow, we are off to this or that town; we are going to *spend* a year there,

13. SPEND A NIGHT IN THE OPEN, CAMP: AULIZOMAI

1 *aulizomai* 2		3 *ep-aulis* 1	
2 (*agr-*)*auleō* 1			

1: SPEND THE NIGHT(S) IN THE OPEN

Mt 21 17 X		[Jesus] went out of the city to Bethany where he *spent the night*.

Lk	2	8	In the countryside close by there were shepherds who ⌐lived
		2	in (lit. *spent the nights in the open* among) the fields
	21	37 X	[Jesus] would *spend the night* on . . . the Mount of Olives.

2: CAMP, ENCAMPMENT

Ac	1	20	3 (Ps 69 26) Let his *camp* be reduced to ruin,

14. TO WINTER – PASS, SPEND THE WINTER: *PARA-CHEIMAZŌ*

2 *para-cheimasia* 1   1 *para-cheimazō* 4

Ac	27	12	since the harbour [of Fair Havens] was unsuitable for
		2	*wintering*, the majority were for putting out from there in the hope of *wintering* at Phoenix
	28	11	At the end of three months we set sail in a ship that had *wintered* in the island [of Malta];
1 Co	16	6	I may be staying with you, perhaps even *passing the winter*,
Tt	3	12	lose no time in joining me at Nicopolis, where I have decided to *spend the winter*.

15. LODGE, STAY, BE THE GUEST OF – LODGING, GUEST ROOM, INN: *KATA-LUMA*

1 *kata-luma* 3   2 *kata-luō* 2/17

Mk	14	14	Where is my ⌐dining (lit. *guest*) *room* in which I can eat the passover with my disciples?
Lk	2	7	there was no room for [Joseph and Mary] at the *inn*.
	9	12	2 the people . . . can go to the villages . . . to find *lodging* and food;
	19	7 X	2 He has gone to ⌐*stay* (or: *be a guest*) at a sinner's house
	22	11	Where is the ⌐dining (lit. *guest*) *room* in which I can eat the passover with my disciples?

16. INN, INNKEEPER: *PAN-DOCHEION*

1 *pan-docheion* 1   2 *pan-docheus* 1

Lk	10	34	[the Samaritan] carried him to the *inn* and looked after him.
		35	2 ³⁵ Next day, he . . . handed [two denarii] to the *innkeeper*.

17. COLONY: *KOLŌNIA*

kolōnia 1

Ac	16	12	Philippi [was] a Roman *colony* and the principal city of that particular district of Macedonia.

STEPHEN – PHILIP

1: The Seven 'Deacons' | 3: Philip
2: Stephen

Stephen	2	Philip	16	S Simon* 4
Nicanor	1	Prochorus	1	
Nicolaus	1	Timon	1	
Parmenas	1			

1: THE SEVEN 'DEACONS'

Ac	6	5	[Select seven men of good reputation.] The whole assembly . . . elected *Stephen*, a man full of faith and of the Holy Spirit, together with *Philip*, *Prochorus*, *Nicanor*, *Timon*, *Parmenas*, and *Nicolaus* of Antioch, a convert to Judaism.

2: STEPHEN

Ac	6	8	*Stephen* was filled with grace and power and began to work miracles
	7	9	certain people came forward to debate with *Stephen*,
		59	As they were stoning him, *Stephen* said in invocation,
	8	2	There were some devout people . . . who buried *Stephen*
	11	19	Those who had escaped during the persecution that happened because of *Stephen*

Ac	22	20	when the blood of your witness *Stephen* was being shed, I was standing by in full agreement

3: PHILIP

Ac	8	5	*Philip* . . . went to a Samaritan town and proclaimed the Christ to them. ⁶ The people united in welcoming the message *Philip* preached,
		6	
		9 S	Now a man called Simon* had already practised magic arts in the town
		12	when [the people of the town] believed *Philip*'s preaching of the Good News . . . they were baptized, . . . ¹³ and even Simon* himself became a believer. After his baptism [Simon*] . . . went round constantly with *Philip*,
		13	
		S	
		18 S	When Simon* saw that the Spirit was given through the imposition of hands by the apostles, he offered them some money.
		24 S	'Pray to the Lord for me yourselves,' Simon* replied
		26	The angel of the Lord spoke to *Philip* saying, 'Be ready to set out at noon
		29	The Spirit said to *Philip*, 'Go up and meet that chariot.'
		30	³⁰ When *Philip* ran up, he heard [the eunuch] reading Isaiah . . . ³¹ . . . So he invited *Philip* to get in
		31	
		34	The eunuch turned to *Philip* and said, '. . . is the prophet referring to himself or someone else?' ³⁵ . . . *Philip* proceeded to explain the Good News of Jesus to him.
		35	
		37	ᵛ *Philip* said: 'If you believe with all your heart, I can [baptise you] . . .' ³⁸ *Philip* and the eunuch both went down into the water and *Philip* baptised him.
		38	
		39	*Philip* was taken away by the Spirit of the Lord, . . . ⁴⁰ *Philip* found that he had reached Azotus and continued his journey proclaiming the Good News in every town
		40	
	21	8	[in] Caesarea . . . we called on *Philip* the evangelist, one of the Seven, and stayed with him. ⁹ He had four virgin daughters who were prophets.

STEWARD – GUARDIAN

1. **Steward, Administrator – the Office, Commission, of Stewardship – Entrusted with, Responsible for:** *oiko-nomeō*
2. **Steward, Bailiff, Guardian – Commission:** *epi-tropos*
3. **Oversee, Watch over, Be careful (that) – Office of a Bishop, Be a presiding elder, Guardian:** *epi-skopeō*
4. **Chamberlain:** *ho epi tou koitōnos*

1. STEWARD, ADMINISTRATOR – THE OFFICE, COMMISSION, OF STEWARDSHIP – ENTRUSTED WITH, RESPONSIBLE FOR: *OIKO-NOMEŌ*

3 *oiko-nomeō* 1   1 *oiko-nomos* 10
2 *oiko-nomia* 9

Lk	12	42	What sort of *steward*, then, is faithful and wise enough for the master to place him over his household . . . ?
	16	1	There was a rich man and he had a *steward* who was denounced to him for being wasteful with his property. ² He called for the man and said, '. . . Draw me up an account of your *stewardship* because you are not to *be my steward* any longer.' ³ Then the *steward* said to himself, 'Now that my master is taking the *stewardship* from me, what am I to do? . . . ⁴ Ah, I know what I will do to make sure that when I am dismissed from *office* there will be some to welcome me into their homes.' . . . ⁸ The master praised the dishonest *steward* for his astuteness.
		2	
			2/3
		3	2
		4	2
		8	
Rm	16	23	Erastus, the city *treasurer*, sends his greetings;
1 Co	4	1	People must think of us as Christ's servants, *stewards* entrusted with the mysteries of God. ² What is expected of *stewards* is that each one should be found worthy of his trust.
		2	
	9	17	2 this work . . . is a *responsibility* which has been put into my hands.
Ga	4	2	[An heir] is under the control of guardians and *administrators* until he reaches the age fixed by his father.
Ep	1	10	[God has let us know the mystery of his purpose,] to ⌐act upon (lit. *put into commission*) when the times had run their course to the end;
		Θ 2	
	3	2 Θ 2	I have been *entrusted* by God *with* the grace he meant for you,
		9 Θ 2	[I have been entrusted with this special grace] of explaining how the mystery is to be *dispensed*.
Col	1	25	I became the servant of the Church when God made me
		2	*responsible for* delivering God's message to you,

1 Tm	1	4	myths . . . are only likely to raise irrelevant doubts instead of
	Θ	2	furthering the ⌐designs (lit. *commissions*; or: *stewardship*) of God
Tt	1	7	as president, [the elder] will be God's *representative*,
1 P	4	10	like good *stewards responsible for* all these different graces of God, put yourselves at the service of others.

2. STEWARD, BAILIFF, GUARDIAN – COMMISSION: *EPI-TROPOS*

2 *epi-trope* 1   1 *epi-tropos* 3

Mt	20	8 <	the owner of the vineyard said to his *bailiff*, 'Call the workers
Lk	8	3	Joanna the wife of Herod's *steward* Chuza,
Ac	26	12	I was going to Damascus, armed with full powers and a
		2	*commission* from the chief priests,
Ga	4	2	[An heir] is under the control of *guardians* and administrators

3. OVERSEE, WATCH OVER, BE CAREFUL (THAT) – OFFICE OF A BISHOP, BE A PRESIDING ELDER, GUARDIAN: *EPI-SKOPEŌ*

2 *epi-skopē* 2/4   1 *epi-skopos* 5
3 *epi-skopeō* 2

Ac	1	20	2 (Ps 109 8) Let someone else take his *office*.
	20	28	Be on your guard . . . for all the flock of which the Holy Spirit has made you the *overseers*,
Ph	1	1	From Paul and Timothy . . . to all the saints . . , together with their ⌐*presiding elders* (or: *bishops*) and deacons.
1 Tm	3	1	2 To want to *be a presiding elder* is to want to do a noble work.
		2	² That is why the *president* must have an impeccable character.
Tt	1	7	Since, as *president*, [the elder] will be God's *representative*, he must be irreproachable:
Heb	12	15 O	3 *Be careful* that no one is deprived of the grace of God
1 P	2	25 X	now you have come back to the shepherd and *guardian* of your souls.
	5	2	3 Be the shepherds of the flock of God . . . ⌄*watch over it*⌐, not simply as a duty but gladly,

4. CHAMBERLAIN: *HO EPI TOU KOITŌNOS*

ho epi tou koitōnos 1   *Blastus* 1

Ac	12	20	the Tyrians and Sidonians . . . managed to enlist the support of *Blastus*, the king's *chamberlain*, and through him negotiated a treaty,

STONE – JEWEL

1. Rock – Rocky ground, Patches of rock: *petra*
2. (a) Stone: *psēphos*
3. Stone – Pavement: *lithos*
   a) Stone
   b) Pavement
   c) (Precious) Stones
4. to Stone: *lithazō* and *litho-boleō*

5. Marble: *marmaros*
6. Pearl(s): *margaritēs*
7. Specific jewels
8. Crystal – Glass
   1: Crystal: *krystallos*
   2: Glass: *hyalos*

1. ROCK – ROCKY GROUND, PATCHES OF ROCK: *PETRA*

1 *petra* 15   2 *petr-ōdēs* 4

Mt	7	24 <	a sensible man who built his house on *rock*.
		25 <	that house . . . did not fall; it was founded on *rock*.
	13	5 <	2 [Other seed] fell on *patches of rock* where they found little soil
		20 <	2 The one who received it on *patches of rock* is the man who . . .²¹ . . . has no root in him,
	16	18 ●	You are Peter and on this *rock* I will build my Church.
	27	51	the earth quaked; the *rocks* were split;
		60	[Joseph] put [the body of Jesus] in his own new tomb which he had hewn out of the *rock*.
Mk	4	5 <	2 Some seed fell on *rocky ground* where it found little soil
		16 <	2 those who receive the seed on *patches of rock* are people who . . .¹⁷ . . . have no root in them,
	15	46	[Joseph] laid him in a tomb which had been hewn out of the *rock*.

Lk	6	48 <	the man who when he built his house . . . laid the foundations on *rock*;
	8	6 <	Some seed fell on *rock*,
		13 <	Those on the *rock* are people who . . . have no root;
Rm	9	33 X	(Is 8 14) See how I lay in Zion a stone to stumble over, a *rock* to trip me up
1 Co	10	4 X	[our fathers] all drank from the spiritual *rock* that followed
		X	them as they went, and that *rock* was Christ.
1 P	2	8 X	(Is 8 14) a stone to stumble over, a *rock* to bring men down.
Rv	6	15	the whole population . . . took to the mountains to hide . . . among the *rocks*.
		16	They said to the mountains and the *rocks*, 'Fall on us'

2. (A) STONE: *PSĒPHOS*

psēphos 2/3

Rv	2	17	to those who prove victorious I will give . . . a white *stone* – a *stone* with a new name written on it,

3. STONE – PAVEMENT: *LITHOS*

2 *lithinos* 3   3 *litho-strōton* 1
1 *lithos* 60

a) Stone

Mt	3	9	God can raise children for Abraham from these *stones*.
	4	3	If you are the Son of God, tell these *stones* to turn into loaves.
		6	(Ps 91 12) in case you hurt your foot against a *stone*.
	7	9	Is there a man among you who would hand his son a *stone* when he asked for bread?
	21	42 X	(Ps 118 22) It was the *stone* rejected by the builders that became the keystone.
		44 X	(§ Anyone who falls on that *stone* will be dashed to pieces . . .)
	24	2	[the Temple] . . . not a single *stone* here will be left on another *stone*:
	27	60	[Joseph] then rolled a large *stone* across the entrance of the tomb
		66	they . . . made the sepulchre secure, putting seals on the *stone*
	28	2	the angel of the Lord . . . rolled away the *stone*
Mk	5	5	[the Gerasene demoniac] would howl and gash himself with *stones*
	12	10 X	(Ps 118 22) It was the *stone* rejected by the builders that became the keystone.
	13	1	'Look at the size of those *stones*, Master!' . . . ² And Jesus
		2	said to him, '. . . Not a single *stone* will be left on another *stone*:'
	15	46	[Joseph] then rolled a *stone* against the entrance to the tomb
	16	3	Who will roll away the *stone* for us from the entrance to the tomb?
		4	the *stone* – which was very big – had already been rolled back.
Lk	3	8	God can raise children for Abraham from these *stones*.
	4	3	tell this *stone* to turn into a loaf.
		11	(Ps 91 12) in case you hurt your foot against a *stone*.
	11	11	What father among you would ⌄ hand his son a *stone* when he asked for bread?⌐
	17	2	It would be better for him to be thrown into the sea with a mill*stone* put round his neck
	19	40	if [my disciples] keep silence the *stones* will cry out.
		44	[Jerusalem, your enemies] will leave not one *stone* standing on another *stone* within you
	20	17 X	(Ps 118 22) It was the *stone* rejected by the builders that became the keystone
		18 X	Anyone who falls on that *stone* will be dashed to pieces;
	21	5	When some were . . . remarking how [the Temple] was adorned with fine *stone*work . . , he said, ⁶ '. . . the
		6	time will come when not a single *stone* will be left on another *stone*:'
	22	41	[Jesus] withdrew from [the disciples], about a *stone*'s throw away,
	24	2	[The women] found that the *stone* had been rolled away from the tomb,
Jn	2	6	2 six *stone* water jars . . . for the ablutions
	8	7	let him be the first to throw a *stone* at her.
		59	[the Jews] picked up *stones* to throw at [Jesus];
	10	31	The Jews fetched *stones* to stone [Jesus].
	11	38	[Lazarus's tomb] was a cave with a *stone* to close the opening.
		39	³⁹ Jesus said, 'Take the *stone* away'. . . . ⁴¹ So they took
		41	away the *stone*.
	20	1	Mary of Magdala . . . saw that the *stone* had been moved away from the tomb
Ac	4	11 X	(Ps 118 22) [Jesus] is the *stone* rejected by you the builders,
	17	29	we have no excuse for thinking that the deity looks like anything in gold, silver or *stone*

Rm 9 32 X   [the Jews] stumbled over the stumbling *stone*
    33 X   (Is 8 14) See how I lay in Zion a *stone* to stumble over, a rock to trip men up
2 Co 3 3   2 written . . . not on *stone* tablets but on the tablets of your living hearts,
    7   the administering of death, in the written letters engraved on *stones*,
1 P 2 4 X   [Jesus] is the living *stone*, rejected by men but chosen by God and precious to him; set yourselves close to him [5] so that you too . . . may be living *stones* making a spiritual house. [6] As scripture says (Is 28 16): See how I lay in Zion a
    5
    6   precious corner*stone* that I have chosen . . . [7] . . . (Ps
    7 X   118 22) the *stone* rejected by the builders has proved to be
        X   the keystone, [8] (Is 8 14) a *stone* to stumble over, a rock to
    8 X   bring men down.
Rv 9 20   2 idols made of gold, silver, bronze, *stone* and wood
  18 21   a powerful angel picked up a *boulder* like a great millstone, and . . . hurled it into the sea,

b) Pavement
Gabbatha 1

Jn 19 13   Pilate . . . seated himself on the chair of judgement at a
    3   place called the *Pavement*, in Hebrew *Gabbatha*.

c) (Precious) Stones

1 Co 3 12   On this foundation you can build in gold, silver and ⌐jewels (lit. precious *stones*),
Rv 4 3   the Person sitting [on the throne] looked like a diamond
      Θ   *stone* and a ruby.
  17 4   The [prostitute] . . . glittered with gold and ⌐jewels (lit. precious *stones*) and pearls,
  18 12   [the traders'] stocks of gold and silver, ⌐jewels (lit. precious *stones*) and pearls,
  16   Mourn . . . for all your finery of gold and ⌐jewels (lit. precious *stones*) and pearls;
  21 11   [Jerusalem] had all the radiant glory of God and glittered like some ⌐precious jewel (lit. priceless *stone*) of crystal-clear ⌐diamond (or: jasper) *stone*.
  19   The foundations of the city wall were faced with all kinds of precious *stone*:

4. TO STONE: *LITHAZŌ* and *LITHO-BOLEŌ*

1   *lithazō* 9   2 *litho-boleō* 7
3   *kata-lithazō* 1

X = to stone Jesus

Mt 21 35   the tenants seized [the landowner's] servants, thrashed one,
    <   2   . . . and *stoned* a third.
  23 37   2 Jerusalem, you that . . . *stone* those who are sent to you!
Lk 13 34   2 Jerusalem, you that . . . *stone* those who are sent to you!
  20 6   3 the people will all *stone* us, for they are convinced that John was a prophet.
Jn 8 5   Moses has ordered us . . . to condemn women like this to [death by] *stoning*.
  10 31 X   The Jews fetched stones to *stone* him, [32] so Jesus said to them,
  32   'I have done many good works for you to see . . .; for
      X   which of these are you *stoning* me?' [33] The Jews answered
  33 X   him, 'We are not *stoning* you for doing a good work but for blasphemy:'
  11 8 X   it is not long since the Jews wanted to *stone* you; are you going back again?
Ac 5 26   [The guards] were afraid to use force in case the people *stoned* them.
  7 58   2 [the people] sent [Stephen] out of the city and *stoned* him.
  59   2 . . .[59] As they were *stoning* him, Stephen said in invocation,
  14 5   2 a move was made . . . to *stone* [Paul and Barnabas]
  19   They *stoned* Paul and dragged him outside the town.
2 Co 11 25   three times I have been beaten with sticks; once I was *stoned*;
Heb 11 37   They were *stoned*, or sawn in half,
  12 20   (Ex 19 13) If even an animal touches the mountain, it must
    2   be *stoned*.

5. MARBLE: *MARMAROS*
marmaros 1

Rv 18 12   every piece in ivory or fine wood, in bronze or iron or *marble*;

6. PEARL(S): *MARGARITĒS*
margaritēs 9

Mt 7 6 <   do not throw your *pearls* in front of pigs,
  13 45   the kingdom of heaven is like a merchant looking for fine
  46 <   *pearls*; [46] when he finds ⌐one (lit. a *pearl*) of great value he . . . sells everything . . . and buys it.
1 Tm 2 9   women are to . . . be dressed quietly . . , without braided hair or gold and ⌐jewellery (lit. *pearls*)
Rv 17 4   The [prostitute] . . . glittered with gold and jewels and *pearls*,
  18 12   [the traders'] stocks of gold and silver, jewels and *pearls*,
  16   Mourn . . . for all your finery of gold and jewels and *pearls*;
  21 21   The twelve gates were twelve *pearls*, each gate being made of a single *pearl*,

7. SPECIFIC JEWELS

10 *a-methystos*	1	1 *iaspis*	4
11 *bēryllos*	1	13 *sapphiros*	1
12 *chalkēdōn*	1	2 *sardion*	2⌐
4 *chryso-lithos*	1⌐	3 *sard-onyx*	1⌐
5 *chryso-prasos*	1⌐	8 *smaragdinos*	1⌐
6 *hyakinthinos*	1⌐	9 *smaragdos*	1⌐
7 *hyakinthos*	1⌐	14 *topazion*	1

Rv 4 3 Θ   the Person sitting [on the throne] looked like a *diamond* stone
    Θ 2   and a *ruby*. There was a rainbow encircling the throne, and
  8   this looked like an *emerald*.
  9 17   6 the riders with their breastplates of flame colour, ⌐hyacinth-(or: sapphire-)blue
  21 11   [Jerusalem] had all the radiant glory of God and glittered like some ⌐precious jewel (lit. priceless stone) of crystal[-clear] ⌐diamond (or: jasper) stone.
  18   The wall was built of ⌐diamond (or: jasper), and the city of pure gold,
  19   The foundations of the city wall were faced with all kinds of precious stone: the first with ⌐diamond (or: jasper),
  13   the second ⌐lapis lazuli (or: sapphire),
  12   the third ⌐turquoise (or: chalcedony),
  9   the fourth ⌐crystal (or: emerald),
  20 3   [20] the fifth ⌐agate (or: sardonyx),
  2   the sixth ⌐ruby (or: carnelian),
  4   the seventh ⌐gold quartz (or: chrysolite),
  11   the eighth ⌐malachite (or: beryl),
  14   the ninth *topaz*,
  5   the tenth ⌐emerald (or: chrysoprase),
  7   the eleventh ⌐sapphire (or: hyacinth)
  10   and the twelfth *amethyst*.

8. CRYSTAL – GLASS

1: CRYSTAL: *KRYSTALLOS*
2 *krystallizō* 1   1 *krystallos* 2

Rv 4 6   a sea that seemed to be made of glass, like *crystal*.
  21 11   [Jerusalem] glittered like some ⌐precious jewel (lit. priceless
    2   stone) of *crystal*[-clear] ⌐diamond (or: jasper) stone.
  22 1   the river of life, . . . flowing *crystal*[-clear]

2: GLASS: *HYALOS*
1 *hyalinos* 3   2 *hyalos* 2

Rv 4 6   a sea that seemed to be *made of glass*, like crystal.
  15 2   a *glass* lake suffused with fire, and standing by the lake *of glass*, those who had fought against the beast and won,
  21 18   2 the city [was built] of pure gold, like polished *glass*.
  21   the main street of the city was pure gold, transparent as
    2   *glass*.

STRAIGHT – CROOKED

1. Straight – Right – Smooth
  1: Straight(en), Right – Restore, Reform: *orthos*
  2: Straight(en), Make straight – Right: *euthys*
  3: Smooth: *leios*
2. Rough – Rugged, Rocky – Reef: *trachys*

3. Winding, Crooked – Perverse, Deceitful: *skolios*
  a) Physically: Winding, Crooked – Corner
  b) Figuratively: Crooked, Perverse Deceitful
4. Swerve – Miss, Shoot wide – Go off: *a-stocheō*

1. STRAIGHT – RIGHT – SMOOTH

1: STRAIGHT(EN), RIGHT – RESTORE, REFORM: *ORTHOS*

3	*orthos* 2	2	*an-orthoō* 3
1	*orthōs* 4	6	*ep-an-orthōsis* 1
4	*ortho(-podeō)* 1	7	*di-orthōma* 1
5	*ortho(-tomeō)* 1	8	*di-orthōsis* 1
		9	*epi-di-orthoō* 1

P = Physical sense

Mk	7 35	the ligament of his tongue was loosened and he spoke ⌜*clearly* (or: *plainly*)
Lk	7 43	Jesus said [to Simon], 'You are *right*'.
	10 28	'You have answered *right*,' said Jesus 'do this and life is yours.'
	13 13 P	2 at once [the crippled woman] *straightened* up,
	20 21	Master, we know that you say and teach what is *right*.
Ac	14 10	Paul said [to the cripple] . . ., 'Get to your feet – stand up *straight*',
	P 3	
	15 16	(Am 9 11) I shall . . . rebuild the fallen House of David
	2	. . . and *restore* it.
	24 2	7 the unbroken peace . . . and the *reforms* this nation owes to your foresight
Ga	2 14	4 they were not ⌜*respecting* (lit. *being straight* with) the true meaning of the Good News,
2 Tm	2 15	5 a man who . . . has kept a *straight* course with the message of the truth.
	3 16	All scripture . . . can profitably be used for teaching, for
	6	refuting error, for ⌜*guiding* (lit. *putting right*) people's lives
Tt	1 5	9 The reason I left you behind in Crete was for you to *get* everything *organised* that needed it
Heb	9 10	rules . . . intended to be in force only until it should be
	8	time to *reform* them.
	12 12	2 ⌜*hold up* (lit. *straighten*) your limp arms and steady your trembling knees
	13	3 (Pr 4 26 G) ⌜*smooth* out (or: make *straight*) the path you tread;

2: STRAIGHT(EN), MAKE STRAIGHT – RIGHT: *EUTHYS*

3	*euthynō* 1/2	5	*kat-euthynō* 1/3
1	*euthys* (adj.) 8	2	*euthy(-dromeō)* 2
4	*euthytēs* 1		

Mt	3 3	(Is 40 3 G) Prepare a way for the Lord, make his paths *straight*.
		Repeated in Mk 1 3 *and* Lk 3 4;
Lk	3 5	(cf. Is 40 4 G) winding ways will be *straightened* and rough roads made smooth.
Jn	1 23	3 (Is 40 3 G) Make a *straight* way for the Lord.
Ac	8 21	[Simon the magician,] God can see how your heart is ⌜*warped* (lit. *not straight*; or: *not right*)
	9 11	You must go to *Straight* Street and ask . . . for . . . Saul;
	13 10	why don't you stop twisting the *straight*forward ways of the Lord?
	16 11	2 we made a *straight* run for Samothrace;
	21 1	2 we set a *straight* course and arrived at Cos;
1 Th	3 11	May God . . . and our Lord Jesus Christ, ⌜*make it easy* (lit.
	5	*make* the *way straight*) for us to come to you.
Heb	1 8	4 (Ps 45 7) his royal sceptre is the sceptre of ⌜*virtue* (or:
	4	*righteousness*);
2 P	2 15	They have left the *right* path and wandered off

3: SMOOTH: *LEIOS*

leios 1

Lk	3 5	(cf. Is 40 4 G) rough roads [will be] made *smooth*.

2. ROUGH – RUGGED, ROCKY – REEF: *TRACHYS*

trachys 2

Lk	3 5	(cf. Is 40 4 G) and *rough* roads [will be] made smooth.
Ac	27 29	afraid that we might run aground somewhere on a *reef*,

3. WINDING, CROOKED – PERVERSE, DECEITFUL: *SKOLIOS*

skolios 4

a) physically: Winding, Crooked – Corner

Lk	3 5	(cf. Is 40 4 G) *winding* ways will be straightened

b) figuratively: Crooked, Perverse, Deceitful

Ac	2 40	Save yourselves from this *perverse* generation.
Ph	2 15	you will be innocent . . . among a *deceitful* and underhand brood,
1 P	2 18	Slaves must be . . . obedient to their masters, not only when they are kind . . . but also when they are *unfair*.

4. SWERVE – MISS, SHOOT WIDE – GO OFF: *A-STOCHEŌ*

a-stocheō 3

1 Tm	1 6	There are some people who have *gone off* the straight course and taken a road that leads to empty speculation;
	6 21	by adopting [antagonistic beliefs], some have ⌜*gone right away from* (or: *shot far wide of*) the faith.
2 Tm	2 18	[Hymenaeus and Philetus] have ⌜*gone right away from* (or: *missed*) the truth

---

STREET – PATH – WAY

---

1. Square – Street
1: Market place – Square: *agora*
2: Street: *plateia*
3: Street – Lane – Alley: *rhymē*
2. Path – Way
1: Path: *tribos* and *trochia*
2: Path (to be walked in) – Footsteps (to be followed): *ichnos*
  a) Path – Steps, Tracks – Way
  b) Untraceable – Impenetrable

3: Way: *hodos*
  a) Way, Road – Journey – Travelling Companion
  b) Crossroads – Thoroughfares – Byroads
  c) Way, Road (figuratively)
  d) The Way = Christianity
4: Follow the right path – Walk onward uprightly – Model oneself (on): *stoicheō*

1. SQUARE – STREET

1: MARKET PLACE – SQUARE: *AGORA*

1 *agora* 11　　2 *agoraios* 1/2

Mt	11 16	children shouting to each other as they sit in the *market place*:
	20 3	about the third hour he saw others standing idle in the *market place*
	23 7	[scribes and Pharisees like] being greeted obsequiously in the *market places*
Mk	6 56	wherever [Jesus] went . . . they laid down the sick in the *open spaces*,
	7 4	on returning from the *market place* [the Pharisees and the Jews in general] never eat without first sprinkling themselves.
	12 38	Beware of the scribes who like to . . . be greeted obsequiously in the *market squares*,
Lk	7 32	children shouting to one another while they sit in the *market place*:
	11 43	Alas for you Pharisees who like . . . being greeted obsequiously in the *market squares*!
	20 46	scribes who . . . love to be greeted obsequiously in the *market squares*,
Ac	16 19	they seized Paul and Silas and dragged them to the law courts in the *market place*
	17 5 ○	2 The Jews . . . enlisted the help of a gang *from the market place*,
	17	in the *market place* [in Athens, Paul] had debates every day with anyone who would face him.

2: STREET: *PLATEIA*

plateia 9

Mt	6 5	hypocrites . . . love to say their prayers . . . at the *street corners*
	12 19	(Is 42 2) nor will anyone hear [my servant's] voice in the *streets*.
Lk	10 10	whenever you enter a town and they do not make you welcome, go out into its *streets* and say,
	13 26	We once ate and drank in your company; you taught in our *streets*
	14 21	Go out quickly into the *streets* and alleys of the town
Ac	5 15	the sick were even taken out into the *streets*
Rv	11 8	[The] corpses [of the two witnesses] will lie in the main *street* of the Great City
	21 21	the main *street* of the city was pure gold,
	22 2	[the river of life flowed] down the middle of the city *street*.

3: STREET – LANE – ALLEY: *RHYMĒ*
rhymē 4

Mt	6 2	this is what the hypocrites do in . . . the *streets*
Lk	14 21	Go out quickly into the streets and *alleys* of the town
Ac	9 11	go to Straight *Street* and ask . . . for someone called Saul, who comes from Tarsus.
	12 10	[Peter and the angel] walked the whole length of one *street*

2. PATH – WAY

1: PATH: *TRIBOS* and *TROCHIA*
tribos 3

Mt	3 3	(Is 40 3 G) Prepare a way for the Lord, make his *paths* straight.

Repeated in Mk 1 3: Lk 3 4

trochia 1

Heb	12 13	(Pr 4 26) smooth out the *path* you tread;

2: PATH (TO BE WALKED IN) – FOOTSTEPS (TO BE FOLLOWED): *ICHNOS*

1 *ichnos* 3   2 *an-ex-ichniastos* 2

a) Path – Steps, Tracks – Way

Rm	4 12	those who . . . follow our ancestor Abraham along the *path* of faith he trod before he had been circumcised.
2 Co	12 18	[Titus] and I have always been guided by the same spirit and trodden in the same *tracks*.
1 P	2 21 X	Christ . . . left an example for you to follow the *way* he took.

b) Untraceable – Impenetrable

Rm	11 33	2 How rich are the depths of God . . . and how *impossible to penetrate* his motives or [understand] his ʳmethods (lit. ways)!
Ep	3 8	2 proclaiming to the pagans the *infinite* treasure of Christ

3: WAY: *HODOS*

3 *hodeuō*	*1*	5	*amph-odon*	*1*
1 *hodos*	*100*	6	*syn-(h)odeuō*	*1*
4 *hodoi-poreō*	*1*	7	*syn-(h)odia*	*1*
2 *hodoi-poria*	*2*	8	*di-ex-(h)odos*	*1*

a) Way, Road – Journey – Travelling Companion

Mt	2 12	[the wise men] returned to their own country by a different *way*.
	4 15	(Is 8 23) Land of Zebulun! . . . *Way* of the sea
	5 25	Come to terms with your opponent in good time while you are still on the *way* to the court with him.
	8 28	Two demoniacs . . . so fierce that no one could pass that *way*.
	10 5	Do not ʳturn your steps (lit. take the *way*) to pagan territory,
	10	[Provide yourselves] with no haversack for the *journey*
	13 4	some seeds fell on the edge of the *path*,
	19	this is the man who received the seed on the edge of the *path*.
	15 32	I do not want to send them off hungry, they might collapse on the *way*.
	20 17	on the *way* [to Jerusalem, Jesus] took the Twelve to one side
	30	there were two blind men sitting at the side of the *road*.
	21 8	people spread their cloaks on the *road*, while others were cutting branches . . . and spreading them in his *path*.
	19	Seeing a fig tree by the *road*, [Jesus] went up to it
	22 10	these servants went out on the *roads*
Mk	2 23	his disciples began to pick ears of corn as they ʳwent (lit. made their *way*) along.
	4 4	some of the seed fell on the edge of the *path*,
	15	Those on the edge of the *path* where the word is sown
	6 8	take nothing for the *journey* except a staff
	8 3	If I send them off home hungry they will collapse on the *way*;
	27	On the *way* he put this question to his disciples, 'Who do people say I am?'
	9 33	What were you arguing about on the *road*?
	34	they had been arguing on the *road* about which of them was the greatest.
	10 17	[Jesus] was setting out on a *journey* when a man ran up,
	32	[Jesus and his disciples] were on the *road*, going up to Jerusalem;
	46	a blind beggar was sitting at the side of the *road*.
	52	[the blind man's] sight returned and he followed him along the *road*.
	11 4	5 They . . . found a colt tethered near a door in the *open street*.
	8	Many people spread their cloaks on the *road*,

Lk	2 44	7 [Jesus's parents] assumed he was with the *caravan*, and it was only after a day's *journey* that they went to look for him
	8 5	some [seed] fell on the edge of the *path*
	12	Those on the edge of the *path* are people who have heard [the word]
	9 3	Take nothing for the *journey*;
	57	they met a man on the *road* who said to Jesus 'I will follow you
	10 4	Salute no one on the *road*.
	31	a priest happened to be travelling down the same *road*,
	33	3 a Samaritan ʳtraveller (lit. who *was on a journey* and) who came upon [the wounded man]
	11 6	a friend of mine on his *travels* has just arrived.
	12 58	when you go to court with your opponent, try to settle with him on the *way*,
	14 23	Go to the [open] *roads* . . . and force people to come in
	18 35	there was a blind man sitting at the side of the *road* begging
	19 36	people spread their cloaks in the *road*
	24 32	as he talked to us on the *road* and explained the scriptures to us
	35	they told their story of what had happened on the *road*
Jn	4 6	2 Jesus, tired by the *journey*, sat straight down by the well.
Ac	1 12 ○	from the Mount of Olives . . . to Jerusalem, a short distance away, no more than a sabbath ʳwalk (lit. *journey*);
	8 26	set out at noon along the *road* that goes from Jerusalem down to Gaza,
	36	Further along the *road* [Philip and the eunuch] came to some water,
	39	the eunuch . . . went on his *way* rejoicing.
	9 7	6 The *men travelling* with Saul stood there speechless,
	17	I have been sent by the Lord Jesus who appeared to you on your *way* here
	27	Barnabas . . . explained how the Lord had appeared to Saul . . . on his *journey*,
	10 9	4 while [Cornelius's slaves] *were still on their journey*
	25 3	[The Jews] were . . . preparing an ambush to murder [Paul] on the *way*.
	26 13	at midday as I was on my *way* . . . I saw a light brighter than the sun
2 Co	11 26	2 Constantly *travelling*, I have been in danger from rivers and . . . brigands,
1 Th	3 11	May God . . . and our Lord Jesus Christ ʳmake it easy for us to come (lit. smooth our *path*) to you.
Jm	2 25	Rahab . . . showed [the messengers] a different *way* to leave.
Rv	16 12	all the water [of the great river Euphrates] dried up so that a *way* was made for the kings of the East

b) Crossroads – Thoroughfares – Byroads

Mt	22 9	8 go to the *crossroads* . . . and invite everyone you can find to the wedding.

c) Way, Road (*figuratively*)

Mt	3 3	(Is 40 3) Prepare a *way* for the Lord, make his paths straight.
	7 13	the *road* that leads to perdition is wide and spacious . . .
	14	[14] it is a narrow gate and a hard *road* that leads to life,
	11 10	(Ml 3 1) I am going to send my messenger . . . he will prepare your *way* before you.
	21 32	John came to you, ʳa pattern (lit. in the *way*) of true righteousness,
	22 16	Master, we know that you . . . teach the *way* of God in an honest way,
Mk	1 2	(Ml 3 1) I am going to send my messenger . . . he will prepare your *way*.
	3	(Is 40 3) Prepare a *way* for the Lord, make his paths straight.
	12 14	Master, we know . . . that you teach the *way* of God in all honesty.
Lk	1 76	for you will go before the Lord to prepare the *way* for him.
	79	to guide our feet into the *way* of peace.
	3 4	(Is 40 3) Prepare a *way* for the Lord, make his paths straight.
	5	(cf. Is 40 4) winding ways will be straightened and rough *roads* made smooth.
	7 27	(Ml 3 1) I am going to send my messenger . . . he will prepare your *way* before you.
	20 21	Master, we know that you . . . teach the *way* of God in all honesty.
Jn	1 23	(Is 40 3) Make a straight *way* for the Lord.
	14 4	'You know the *way* to the place where I am going.' [5] Thomas said, 'Lord, we do not know where you are going, so how can we know the *way*?' [6] Jesus said: 'I am the *Way*, the Truth and the Life. No one can come to the Father except through me.'
	5	
	6 ○	
Ac	2 28	(Ps 16 11) You have made known the *way* of life to me,
	13 10	why don't you stop twisting the straightforward *ways* of the Lord?
	14 16	In the past [God] allowed each nation to go its own *way*;
	16 17	they have come to tell you ʳhow (lit. the *way*) to be saved!
Rm	3 16	(Is 59 7) ʳwherever (lit. whichever *way*) they go there is havoc
	17	(Is 59 8) They know nothing of the *way* of peace.

Rm 11	33	how impossible to penetrate [God's] motives or [understand] his ʳmethods (lit. *ways*)!
1 Co 4	17	[Timothy] will remind you of the *way* that I live in Christ,
12	31	I am going to show you a *way* that is better than any of them.
Heb 3	10	(Ps 95 10) How unreliable these people who refuse to grasp my *ways*!
9	8	no one has the right ʳto go (lit. of *way*) into the sanctuary as long as the outer tent remains standing;
10	20	[through the blood of Jesus we have the right to enter] by a new *way* which he has opened for us,
Jm 1	8	That sort of person, in two minds, wavering between going different *ways*,
5	20	anyone who can bring back a sinner from the wrong *way* that he has taken
2 P 2	2	the *Way* of Truth will be brought into disrepute
15	They have left the right *path* and wandered off to follow the *path* of Balaam
21	It would have been better for him never to have learnt the *way* of holiness,
Jude	11	they have ʳfollowed (lit. gone along the *path* of) Cain;
Rv 15	3	How . . . just and true are all your *ways*, King of nations.

d) The Way = Christianity

Ac 9	2	authorise [Saul] to arrest and take to Jerusalem any followers of the *Way* . . . that he could find.
18	25	[Apollos] had been given instruction in the *Way* of the Lord . . . ²⁶ Priscilla and Aquila . . . gave him further instruction about the *Way*.
26	
19	9	some of the congregation . . . began attacking the *Way* in front of the others,
23	a rather serious disturbance broke out [in Ephesus] in connection with the *Way*.
22	4	I even persecuted this *Way* to the death,
24	14	it is according to the *Way* which they describe as a sect that I worship the God of my ancestors,
22	Felix, who knew more about the *Way* than most people,

4: FOLLOW THE RIGHT PATH – WALK ONWARD UPRIGHTLY – MODEL ONESELF (ON): *STOICHEŌ*

1 *stoicheō* 5   2 *sy-stoicheō* 1

Ac 21	24	you still ʳregularly observe (lit. *walk uprightly* within) the Law.
Rm 4	12	[those uncircumcised who] *follow* our ancestor Abraham *along the path* of faith he trod before he had been circumcised.
Ga 4	25	2 [Hagar] *corresponds* to the present Jerusalem that is a slave
5	25	Since the Spirit is our life, let us ʳbe directed by (lit. *follow*) the Spirit.
6	16	Peace and mercy to all who *follow* this rule,
Ph 3	16	let us *go forward on the road* that has brought us to where we are.

STRETCH OUT

1. Stretch out (a hand): *ek-petannymi*
2. Stretch, Stretch out: *ek-teinō*
  1: Stretch out a hand
  2: Stretch out (a person)

3: Stretch (figuratively) – Prolong, Extend
4: Lay out (an anchor)

1. STRETCH OUT (A HAND): *EK-PETANNYMI*

ek-petannymi 1

Rm 10	21	Θ	(Is 65 2) I *stretched out* my hand to a disobedient . . . people.

2. STRETCH, STRETCH OUT: *EK-TEINŌ*

2	*ek-teinō*	3/16	5	*para-teinō* 1
3	*ep-ek-teinomai*	1	6	*pro-teinō* 1
4	*hyper-ek-teinō*	1	1	*tēn cheira ek-teinō* 13

1: STRETCH OUT A HAND

Mt 8	3	X	Jesus *stretched out his hand*, touched [the leper] and said, '. . . Be cured!'
12	13		[Jesus] said to the man [with a withered hand], '*Stretch out your hand*'. He *stretched* it *out* and his hand was better,
2	
49	X	*stretching out his hand* towards his disciples [Jesus] said, 'Here are my mother and my brothers.'
14	31	X	Jesus *put out his hand* at once and held [Peter].

Mt 26	51		one of the followers of Jesus ʳgrasped (lit. *stretched out his hand* for) his sword
Mk 1	41	X	Feeling sorry for [the leper], Jesus *stretched out his hand* and touched him.
3	5		[Jesus] said to the man [with a withered hand], '*Stretch out your hand*'. He *stretched* it *out* and his hand was better.
2	
Lk 5	13	X	Jesus *stretched out his hand*, touched [the leper] and said '. . . Be cured!'
6	10		[Jesus] said to the man, '*Stretch out your hand*'. He did so, and his hand was better.
22	53		When I was among you in the Temple day after day you never ʳmoved to lay hands on (lit. *stretched out a hand* against) me.
Jn 21	18		when you grow old you will *stretch out your hands*, and somebody else will . . . take you where you would rather not go.
Ac 4	30	Θ	[Lord, help your servants] by *stretching out your hand* to heal and to work miracles
26	1		Paul *held up his hand* and began his defence:

2: STRETCH OUT (A PERSON)

Ac 22	25	6	when they had ʳstrapped him down (lit. *stretched* him *out* ʳwith (or: for the) straps) Paul said, 'Is it legal for you to flog . . . a Roman citizen . . .?'

3: STRETCH OUT (FIGURATIVELY) – PROLONG, EXTEND

Ac 20	7	5	[Paul] preached a sermon that *went on* till the middle of the night.
2 Co 10	14	4	we are not *stretching further than we ought*;
Ph 3	13	3	I *strain ahead* for what is still to come; ¹⁴ I am racing for the finish,

4: LAY OUT (AN ANCHOR)

Ac 27	30		some of the crew . . . lowered the ship's boat into the sea
2		as though to *lay out* anchors from the bows,

STUMBLE – FALL

1. Obstacle: *spilas*
2. Stumble – Trip: *pros-koptō*
3. Trip up, Stumble, Fall – (Be an) Obstacle (to), Cause to sin – Offend: *skandalon*
4. Fall, Stumble – Make a mistake: *ptaiō*
5. Fall: *piptō*
  1: Fall, Fell – Collapse – Drop
  2: Fall, Fell (figuratively)

3: Fall = Sin(s), Trespass(es) – Failing, Fault
4: Fall, Fell (to the ground in awe, fear, before) – Throw oneself (down), Prostrate oneself
5: Fall on, Fell on – Hurl oneself against
6: Fall upon, Fell upon (figuratively) – Come down on
6. Headlong: *prēnēs*

1. OBSTACLE: *SPILAS*

spilas 1

Jude	12	They are ʳa [dangerous] *obstacle* to (or: *blemishes* on) your community meals,

2. STUMBLE – TRIP: *PROS-KOPTŌ*

1	*pros-komma*	6	2 *pros-koptō* 5/8
4	*pros-kopē*	1	3 *a-pros-kopos* 3

X = Jesus as a cause of stumbling

Jn 11	9	2	A man can walk in the daytime without *stumbling* . . . ¹⁰ but
10	2	if he walks at night he *stumbles*,
Ac 24	16		I . . . do my best to keep a ʳclear conscience (lit. conscience *that will not trip me up*)
3	
Rm 9	32	X	2/ they *stumbled* over the *stumbling*-stone
33	X	(cf. Is 8 14) See how I lay in Zion a stone to *stumble over*, a rock to trip men up
14	13		make up your mind never to be the cause of your brother *tripping* or falling.
20		all food . . . becomes evil if by eating it you *make* somebody else *fall away* . . . ²¹ . . . the best course is to abstain
21	2	from . . . anything . . . that would *make* your brother *trip* (ᵛ or fall or weaken)

1 Co 8 9   do not make use of this freedom in a way that proves a *pitfall* for the weak.

10 32   3 ˥Never do anything offensive to anyone (lit. Do *not* ever *cause* anyone else *to trip up*) –

2 Co 6 3   We do nothing that people might ˥object to (lit. see as 4 *something to stumble over*),

Ph 1 10   3 This will help you to become pure and ˥blameless (lit. *sure-footed*)

1 P 2 8   (cf. Is 8 14) [the stone rejected by the builders has proved to X be] a stone to *stumble over*, a rock to bring men down.

2 They *stumble* over it because they do not believe in the word;

3. TRIP UP, STUMBLE, FALL – (BE AN) OBSTACLE (TO), CAUSE TO SIN – OFFEND: *SKANDALON*

1 *skandalizō* 30   2 *skandalon* 15

X = Jesus as a cause of falling, of offence

Mt 5 29   If your right eye should *cause* you *to sin*, tear it out

30   if your right hand should *cause* you *to sin*, cut it off

11 6   happy is the man who ˥does not lose faith in me (lit. does not X *stumble* where I am concerned).

13 21   let some trial come or some persecution on account of the word, and he *falls away* at once.

41   The Son of Man will send his angels and they will gather 2 out of his kingdom all *things that provoke offences* and all who do evil,

57 X   [the people of Nazareth] ˥would not accept (lit. were *offended at*) [Jesus].

15 12 X   the Pharisees were *shocked* when they heard what you said

16 23   2 [Peter,] you are an *obstacle* in my *path*, because the way you think is not God's way but man's

17 27 X   so as not to *offend* these people . . . give [a shekel] to them

18 6   anyone who *is an obstacle to bring down* one of these little ones who have faith in me would be better drowned

7   2 Alas for the world that there should be such *obstacles*!

2   *Obstacles* indeed there must be, but alas for the man who

8   2 provides ˥them (lit. such *obstacles*)! ⁸ If your hand or your

9   foot should *cause* you *to sin*, cut it off . . . ⁹ and if your eye should *cause* you *to sin*, tear it out

24 10   [you will be hated by all] and then many will *fall away*;

26 31 X   You will all ˥lose faith in (lit. *fall away* from) me this night,

33 X   for the scripture says: I shall strike the shepherd . . .

X   ³³ . . . Peter said, 'Though all ˥lose faith in (lit. *fall away* from) you, I will never ˥lose faith (lit. *fall away*)'.

Mk 4 17   should some trial come . . . they *fall away* at once.

6 3 X   [the people of Nazareth] ˥would not accept (lit. were *offended at*) [Jesus].

9 42   anyone who *is an obstacle to bring down* one of these little ones who have faith, would be better thrown into the sea

43   if your hand should *cause* you *to sin*, cut if off;

45   if your foot should *cause* you *to sin*, cut it off;

47   if your eye should *cause* you *to sin*, tear it out;

14 27 X   You will all ˥lose faith (lit. *fall away*) . . . ²⁹ Peter said,

29 X   'Even if all ˥lose faith (lit. *fall away*), I will not'.

Lk 7 23   happy is the man who ˥does not lose faith in me (lit. does not X *stumble* where I am concerned).

17 1   2 *Obstacles* are sure to come, but alas for the one who provides

2   them! ² It would be better for him to be thrown into the sea . . . than that he should ˥lead astray (lit. *trip up*) a single one of these little ones.

Jn 6 61 X   Does this *upset* you? ⁶² What if you should see the Son of Man ascend to where he was before?

16 1   I have told you all this so that ˥your faith may not be shaken

X   (lit. you will not *stumble*).

Rm 9 33 X   (cf. Is 8 14) I lay in Zion a stone to stumble over, a rock to

2   *trip* [men] *up* –

11 9   (Ps 69 23 G) May their own table prove . . . a snare and a

2   *pitfall* –

14 13   make up your mind never to be the cause of your brother

2   *tripping* or *falling*.

21   the best course is to abstain from . . . anything . . . that would make your brother trip (ᵛ or *fall* or weaken)

16 17   2 be on your guard against anybody who . . . puts *difficulties in the way* of the doctrine

1 Co 1 23 X   2 we are preaching a crucified Christ; to the Jews an *obstacle that they cannot get over*,

8 13   since food can be the *occasion of* my brother's *downfall*, I shall never eat meat again in case I am the *cause of* a brother's *downfall*.

2 Co 11 29   when any man is *made to fall*, I am tortured.

Ga 5 11 X   2 If I did that now, would there be any *scandal* of the cross?

1 P 2 8   (cf. Is 8 14) [the stone rejected by the builders has proved to

X   2 be] a stone to stumble over, a rock to *bring* [men] *down*.

1 Jn 2 10   anyone who loves his brother . . . need not be afraid of

2   *stumbling*;

Rv 2 14   2 Balaam . . . taught Balak to set ˥a trap (lit. an *obstacle*) for the Israelites

4. FALL, STUMBLE – MAKE A MISTAKE: *PTAIŌ*

1 *ptaiō* 5   2 *a-ptaistos* 1

Rm 11 11   have the Jews fallen for ever, or have they just *stumbled*?

Jm 2 10   if a man keeps the whole of the Law, except for one small point at which he *fails*, he is still guilty of breaking it all.

3 2   every one of us ˥does something wrong (lit. *makes mistakes*) . . . the only man who could reach perfection would be someone who never ˥said anything wrong (lit. *made any mistake* in what he said)

2 P 1 10   If you do all these things there is no danger that you will ever *fall away*.

Jude 24   2 Glory be to him who can keep you *from falling* and bring you safe to his glorious presence,

5. FALL: *PIPTŌ*

1	*piptō*	90		3	*epi-piptō*	11
9	*ptōsis*	2		12	*para-piptō*	1
10	*apo-piptō*	1		2	*para-ptōma*	20
7	*kata-piptō*	3		8	*peri-piptō*	3
11	*(dio-)petēs*	1		4	*pros-piptō*	8
5	*ek-piptō*	7/10		13	*sym-pipto*	
6	*em-piptō*	7				

K = Fall = Be killed

1: FALL, FELL – COLLAPSE – DROP

Mt 7 25   gales . . . hurled themselves against that house, and it did < not *fall*:

27 < /9   gales . . . struck that house, and it *fell*; and what a *fall* it had!

10 29   not one [sparrow] *falls* to the ground without your Father knowing.

12 11   6 If any one of you here had only one sheep and it *fell* down a hole . . . would he not . . . lift it out?

13 4 <   some seeds *fell* on the edge of the path . . . ⁵ Others *fell* on

5   patches of rock where they found little soil . . ⁷ Others

7 <   *fell* among thorns, and the thorns . . . choked them.

8 <   ⁸ Others *fell* on rich soil

15 14   if one blind man leads another, both will *fall* into a pit.

27   house-dogs can eat the scraps that *fall* from their master's table.

17 15   my son . . . is always *falling* into the fire or into the water.

21 44   (§ Anyone who *falls* on that stone will be dashed to pieces; anyone it *falls* on will be crushed.)

24 29   the stars will *fall* from the sky

Mk 4 4 <   some of the seed *fell* on the edge of the path . . . ⁵ Some

5 <   seed *fell* on rocky ground where it found little soil . . .

7 <   ⁷ Some seed *fell* into thorns, and the thorns . . . choked

8 <   it . . . ⁸ And some seeds *fell* into rich soil

9 20   the spirit . . . threw the boy into convulsions, and he *fell* to the ground

13 25   the stars will come *falling* from heaven

Lk 6 39   6 Can one blind man guide another? Surely both will *fall* into a pit?

49 < 13   as soon as the river bore down on [the house], it *collapsed*;

8 5 < /7   some [seed] *fell* on the edge of the path . . . ⁸ Some seed *fell*

6 <   on rock . . . ⁷ Some seed *fell* amongst thorns and the

7 <   thorns . . . choked it. ⁸ And some seed *fell* into rich soil

8   and . . . produced its crop

14 <   As for the part that *fell* into thorns, this is people who . . . are choked by the worries . . . of life

13 4   the tower at Siloam *fell* [on eighteen people] and killed them

14 5   Which of you here, if his son *falls* into a well . . . will not pull him out . . . ?

16 21   [Lazarus] longed to fill himself with the scraps that *fell* from the rich man's table.

20 18   Anyone who *falls* on that stone will be dashed to pieces; anyone it *falls* on will be crushed.

21 24 K   [this people] will *fall* by the edge of the sword

23 30   (Ho 10 8) Then they will begin to say to the mountains, '*Fall* on us!'

Jn 12 24   unless a wheat grain *falls* on the ground and dies it remains only a single grain;

Ac 5 5   When he heard this Ananias *fell* down dead.

10   Instantly [Sapphira] *dropped* dead at [Peter's] feet.

9 18   10 it was as though scales *fell away* from Saul's eyes

12 7   5 the chains *fell* from [Peter's] hands.

15 16   (Am 9 11) I shall . . . rebuild the *fallen* House of David;

19 35   the city of the Ephesians is the guardian of . . . [Diana's]

11   statue that *fell* from heaven

Ac 20	9		Eutychus . . . *fell* to the ground three floors below.
27	32	5	the soldiers cut the boat's ropes and let it *drop* [away].
	41	8	the cross-currents ᴿcarried them into (lit. caused them to *fall into*) a shoal
28	6	7	they were expecting [Paul] . . . to swell up or *drop* dead on the spot.
1 Co 10	8 K		twenty-three thousand *met their downfall* in one day.
Heb 3	17		(Nb 14 29) [the] dead bodies [of those who sinned] were *left lying* in the wilderness.
	K		
11	30		It was through faith that the walls of Jericho *fell down*
Jm 1	11		(Is 40 8) the scorching sun comes up, and the grass withers, the flower *falls*;
	5		
1 P 1	24	5	(Is 40 8) The grass withers, the flower *falls*.
Rv 6	13		(Is 34 4 G) the stars of the sky *fell* on to the earth
	16		(Ho 10 8) They said to the mountains, . . . '*Fall* on us
8	10		(cf. Is 14 12) a huge star *fell* from the sky . . . and it *fell* on a third of all rivers
9	1		I saw a star that had *fallen* from heaven on to the earth,
11	13		a tenth of the city *collapsed*;
16	19		the cities of the world *collapsed*;
17	10 K		Five of [the seven emperors] have already ᴿgone (lit. *fallen*), one is here now, and one is yet to come;

2: FALL, FELL (FIGURATIVELY)

Lk 2	34	9	this child . . . is destined for the *fall* and for the rising of many in Israel,
10	18 Ⓓ		I watched Satan *fall* like lightning from heaven.
	30	8	A man was once on his way down from Jerusalem to Jericho and *fell into* [the hands of] brigands;
	36	6	Which of these three . . . proved himself a neighbour to the man who *fell into* [the hands of] brigands?
11	17		a household divided against itself *collapses*.
16	17		It is easier for heaven and earth to disappear than for one little stroke to *drop* out of the Law.
Ac 1	26		the lot *fell* to Matthias,
13	11		ᴿeverything went misty and dark for (lit. mistiness and darkness *fell* upon) [Elymas]
Rm 9	6	5	Does this mean that ᴿGod has failed to keep his promise (lit. God's promise has *fallen*)?
11	22		Do not forget that God . . . is severe to those who *fell*,
14	4		whether [someone else's] servant stands or *falls* it is his own master's business;
1 Co 10	12		The man who thinks he is safe must be careful that he does not *fall*.
13	8		Love does not ᴿcome to an end (lit. *fall*),
Ga 5	4	5	you have . . . *fallen* from grace.
1 Tm 3	6		[The elder-in-charge] should not be a new convert, in case . . . he might ᴿbe condemned (lit. *fall* in the same way) as the devil was condemned.
	7	6	people outside the Church should speak well of him, so that he never . . . *falls* into the devil's trap.
6	9	6	People who long to be rich ᴿare a prey to (lit. *fall* into) temptation,
Heb 4	11		some of you might copy this example of disobedience and *be lost*.
6	6	12	[For those who were once brought into the light] and yet in spite of this have *fallen away* – it is impossible . . . to be renewed a second time.
10	31	6	It is a dreadful thing to *fall* into the hands of the living God.
Jm 1	2	8	you will always ᴿhave your (lit. *fall into* differing) trials
5	12		you make yourselves liable to *fall* under the judgement.
2 P 3	17	5	be careful . . . people, not to *fall* from the firm ground that you are standing on.
Rv 2	5		Think where you were before you *fell*;
7	16		neither the sun nor scorching wind will ever ᴿplague (lit. *fall* on) them,
14	8		(Is 21 9) Babylon has *fallen*, Babylon the Great has *fallen*,
18	2		(Is 21 9) Babylon has *fallen*, Babylon the Great has *fallen*.

3: FALL = SIN(S), TRESPASS(ES) – FAILING, FAULT

Mt 6	14	2	if you forgive others their *failings*, your . . . Father will forgive you yours; 15 but if you do not forgive others, your
	15	2	Father will not forgive your *failings* either.
Mk 11	25		forgive whatever you have against anybody, so that your
	26	2	Father . . . may forgive your *failings* too. 26 (ᵛ But if you do not forgive others, your Father will not forgive your
		2	*failings* either.)
Rm 4	25	2	Jesus . . . was put to death for our *sins*
5	15	2	the gift itself considerably outweighed the *fall* . . . it is certain that through one man's *fall* so many died,
		2	
	16	2	now after many *falls* comes grace with its verdict of acquittal;
	17	2	death reigned over everyone as the consequence of one man's *fall*,
	18	2	one man's *fall* brought condemnation on everyone,
	20		When law came, it was to multiply the [opportunities of]
		2	*falling*,

Rm 11	11		have the Jews *fallen* for ever, or have they just stumbled?
		2	Obviously [they have] not [fallen] for ever: their *fall*, though, has saved the pagans . . . 12 Think of the extent to
	12		which the world . . . has benefited from their *fall* and defection –
2 Co 5	19		God in Christ was reconciling the world to himself, not
		2	holding men's *faults* against them,
Ga 6	1	2	if one of you ᴿmisbehaves (lit. has some *fault* detected), the more spiritual of you . . . should [set him right]
Ep 1	7	2	in [Christ] . . . we gain . . . the forgiveness of our *sins*.
2	1	2	you were dead, through the *crimes* and the sins [in which you used to live]
	5	2	we were dead through our *sins*,
Col 2	13	2	You were dead, because you were *sinners* . . . [God] has
		2	brought you to life . . . he has forgiven us all our *sins*.

4: FALL, FELL (TO THE GROUND IN AWE, FEAR, BEFORE) – THROW ONESELF (DOWN), PROSTRATE ONESELF

Mt 2	11		[the wise men] saw the child with his mother Mary, and *falling* [to their knees] they did him homage.
4	9	X	'I will give you all these' [the devil] said [to Jesus] 'if you *fall* [at my feet] and worship me.'
17	6		the disciples *fell* on their faces, overcome with fear.
18	26	<	the servant ᴿthrew himself down (lit. *fell down* and prostrated himself) [at his master's feet].
	29	<	His fellow servant *fell* [at his feet] and implored him,
26	39	X	[Jesus] *fell* on his face and prayed.
Mk 3	11	4	the unclean spirits . . . would *fall down before* him and shout, 'You are the Son of God!'
5	22		Jairus . . . seeing [Jesus], *fell* at his feet
	33		the woman [with a haemorrhage] came forward . . . and . . .
		4	*fell* [at Jesus's feet]
7	25		A woman whose little daughter had an unclean spirit . . .
		4	*fell* at [Jesus's] feet.
14	35	X	[Jesus] *threw himself* on the ground and prayed that . . . this hour might pass him by.
Lk 5	8	4	Simon Peter . . . *fell* at the knees of Jesus
	12		Seeing Jesus [the leper] *fell* on his face and implored him.
8	28	4	Catching sight of Jesus [the demoniac] gave a shout, *fell* [at his feet] and cried out
	41		Jairus . . . *fell* at Jesus's feet and pleaded with him to come to his house,
	47		the woman [with a haemorrhage] came forward trembling
		4	and *falling* [at Jesus's feet] explained . . . why she had touched him
17	16		[one of the ten lepers] *threw himself* at the feet of Jesus
Jn 11	32		Mary . . . *threw herself* at [Jesus's] feet,
18	6		[the cohort and the guards] moved back and *fell* to the ground.
Ac 9	4		[Saul] *fell* to the ground and then he heard a voice
10	25		Cornelius . . . ᴿknelt (lit. *fell*) at [Peter's] feet and prostrated himself.
16	29	4	The gaoler . . . *threw himself* . . . at the feet of Paul and Silas,
22	7		I *fell* to the ground and heard a voice saying, 'Saul,
26	14	7	We all *fell* to the ground,
1 Co 14	25		[If you were all prophesying and an unbeliever came in, he would] *fall* on his face and worship God,
Rv 1	17		When I saw [the Son of Man], I *fell* in a dead faint at his feet,
4	10		the twenty-four elders *prostrated themselves* before [the One sitting on the throne]
5	8		the four animals *prostrated themselves* before [the Lamb] and with them the twenty-four elders;
	14		the four animals said, 'Amen'; and the elders *prostrated themselves* to worship.
7	11		All the angels . . . *prostrated themselves* before the throne, and touched the ground with their foreheads worshipping God
11	16		The twenty-four elders . . . *prostrated themselves and touched the ground* with their foreheads worshipping God
19	4		the twenty-four elders and the four animals *prostrated themselves* and worshipped God
	10		I ᴿknelt (lit. *fell*) at [the angel's] feet to worship him,
22	8		I, John . . . ᴿknelt (lit. *fell*) at the feet of the angel . . . to worship him;

5: FALL ON, FELL ON – HURL ONESELF AGAINST

Mt 7	25	4	gales blew and *hurled themselves against* that house,
Mk 3	10	3	all who were afflicted . . . were *crowding forward to touch* [Jesus].
Lk 15	20	3	[his father] ᴿclasped him in his arms (lit. *fell on* his neck) and kissed him tenderly.
Ac 20	10	3	Paul . . . ᴿstooped to clasp (or: *threw himself on*) [Eutychus]
	37	3	[the elders of Ephesus] ᴿput their arms round (lit. *fell on*) Paul's neck and kissed him;

6: FALL UPON, FELL UPON (FIGURATIVELY) – COME DOWN ON

Lk	1	12	The sight disturbed Zechariah and ⌐he was overcome with
		3	fear (lit. fear *fell upon* him).
Ac	8	16 ⑤	3 [the Holy Spirit] had not *come down on* any of [the Samaritans]:
	10	44 ⑤	3 the Holy Spirit *came down on* all the listeners.
	11	15 ⑤	3 the Holy Spirit *came down on* [the pagans] in the same way as it came on us
	19	17	Everybody in Ephesus . . . heard about this episode; ⌐they
		3	were all greatly impressed (lit. fear *fell upon* them),
Rm	15	3	3 (Ps 69 10) the insults of those who insult you *fall on* me
Rv	11	11	⌐everybody who saw it happen was terrified (lit. great fear
		3	*fell upon* everybody who saw it happen);

6. HEADLONG: *PRĒNĒS*

prēnēs 1

Ac	1	18 Δ	[Judas fell] *headlong* [and] burst open, and all his entrails poured out.

SUFFER – ANGUISH

---

1. **Suffer, Suffering:** *paschō*
   1: (Jesus) Suffers – the Passion, Sufferings (of Christ)
   2: Suffer (generally) – Be hurt, Bear hardship
   3: Suffer = Experience
2. **Suffering, Distress, Anguish – Trial, Trouble, Tribulation – Persecution:** *thlipsis*
3. **Distress, Worry – Suffer:** *steno-chōria*
4. **Suffer, Be in a state – Distress, Anguish – Overwhelm:** *syn-echō*
5. **Great distress, Anguish – Be worried, Be troubled:** *adēmoneō*
6. **Distress, Hardship – Trouble:** *anankē*
7. **Sorrow, (Be) Distressed – Anguish, Be in agony:** *odunē*
8. **Anguish:** *agōnia*
9. **Pain, Anguish – Be sickened, Be annoyed – Oppressed:** *ponos*
10. **Torment, Torture – Pain – Distress:** *basanos*
    1: Pain, Agony – Torture, Torment – Distress, Outrage
    2: Torment, Torture (in Hades)
    3: Torture, Torment (devils, demons)
11. **Birthpangs, Labour pains:** *ōdin*

1. SUFFER, SUFFERING: *PASCHŌ*

1	*paschō*	41	5	*(homoio-)pathēs*	2
2	*pathēma*	14/16	10	*(metrio-)patheō*	1
8	*pathētos*	1	11	*pro-paschō*	1
9	*kako-patheia*	1	6	*sym-paschō*	2
3	*kako-patheō*	3	7	*sym-patheō*	2
4	*syn-kako-patheō*	2	12	*sym-pathēs*	1

1: (JESUS) SUFFERS – THE PASSION, SUFFERINGS (OF CHRIST)

Mt	16	21	he was destined to . . . *suffer* grievously at the hands of the elders
	17	12	the Son of Man will *suffer* similarly at their hands.
Mk	8	31	the Son of Man was destined to *suffer* grievously,
	9	12	the Son of Man . . . is to *suffer* grievously
Lk	9	22	The Son of Man . . . is destined to *suffer* grievously,
	17	25	he must *suffer* grievously
	22	15	I have longed to eat this passover with you before I *suffer*;
	24	26	Was it not ordained that the Christ should *suffer* and so enter into his glory?
		46	it is written that the Christ would *suffer* and on the third day rise from the dead,
Ac	1	3	He had shown himself alive to them after his *Passion*
	3	18	God . . . said . . . that his Christ would *suffer*.
	17	3	it was ordained that the Christ should *suffer* and rise from the dead.
	26	23	8 [the prophets and Moses said] that the Christ was to *suffer*
2 Co	1	5	2 the *sufferings* of Christ overflow to us,
Ph	3	10	2 All I want is to know Christ and . . . to share his *sufferings*
Heb	2	9	Jesus . . . is now crowned with glory . . . because he
		2	⌐submitted to (lit. *suffered*) death;
		10	it was appropriate that God . . . should make perfect,
		2	through *suffering*, the leader who would take them to their salvation.
		18	because he has himself ⌐been through (lit. *suffered*) temptation
	4	15	it is not as if we had a high priest who was incapable of
		7	⌐feeling our weaknesses with us (lit. *sympathising* with us in our weaknesses);
	5	8	he learnt to obey through *suffering*;
	9	26	or else he would have had to *suffer* over and over again
	13	12	Jesus too *suffered* outside the gate
1 P	1	11	2 The Spirit of Christ . . . foretold the *sufferings* of Christ

1 P	2	21	Christ *suffered* for you
		23	when he *was tortured* he made no threats
	3	18	Christ himself . . . had ⌐died (ᵛ*suffered*) once for sins,
	4	1	Think what Christ *suffered* in this life,
		13	2 If you can have some share in the *sufferings* of Christ, be glad,
	5	1	2 I am . . . a witness to the *sufferings* of Christ,

2: SUFFER (GENERALLY) – BE HURT, BEAR HARDSHIP

Mt	27	19	I have *been upset* all day by a dream I had about [Jesus].
Mk	5	26	after long ⌐and *painful treatment* (or: *suffering*) under various doctors,
Lk	13	2	Do you suppose these Galileans who *suffered* like that were greater sinners than any other Galileans?
Ac	9	16	I myself will show [Paul] he himself must *suffer* for my name.
	28	5	[Paul] shook the [viper] off . . . and ⌐came to (lit. *suffered*) no harm,
Rm	8	17	6 we are . . . coheirs with Christ, *sharing* his *sufferings* so as to share his glory.
		18	2 *what* we *suffer* in this life can never be compared to the glory . . . which is waiting for us.
1 Co	12	26	/6 If one part [of the body] *is hurt*, all parts *are hurt with* it.
2 Co	1	5	2 the *sufferings* of Christ overflow to us,
		6	a consolation to you, supporting you in patiently bearing
		/2	the same *sufferings* as we ⌐bear (lit. *suffer*).
		7	2 sharing our *sufferings*, you will also share our consolations.
Ga	3	4	Have all the ⌐experiences (or: *sufferings*) you underwent been wasted?
Ph	1	29	[God] has given you the privilege . . . of *suffering* for [Christ]
Col	1	24	2 It makes me happy to *suffer* for you, as I am [suffering] now,
1 Th	2	2	11 We had . . . *been given rough treatment* and been grossly insulted at Philippi
		14	you . . . have been like the churches . . . in Judaea, in *suffering* the same treatment
2 Th	1	5	it is for the sake of [the kingdom of God] that you *are suffering* now.
2 Tm	1	8	you are never to be ashamed of witnessing to the Lord, . .
		4	but *with* me, *bear the hardships*
		12	I am *experiencing* [fresh] *hardships* here
	2	3	4 *Put up with your share of difficulties*, like a good soldier of Christ Jesus.
		9	3 I *have* [my own] *hardships* to bear,
	3	11	2 [you know] the persecutions and *hardships* that came to me in places like Antioch, Iconium and Lystra
	4	5	3 *be brave under trials*; make the preaching of the Good News your life's work,
Heb	10	32	2 Remember all the *sufferings* that you had to meet
		34	7 you . . . *shared in the sufferings* of those who were in prison,
Jm	5	10	9 For your example . . . in ⌐*submitting* (or: *suffering*) in patience, take the prophets
		13	3 If any one of you *is in trouble*, he should pray;
1 P	2	19	there is some merit in putting up with the pains of unearned ⌐*punishment* (lit. *suffering*) if it is done for the sake of God
		20	²⁰ . . . The merit . . . is in bearing it patiently when you ⌐*are punished* after (lit. *suffer* for) doing your duty.
	3	8	12 you should all agree among yourselves and *be sympathetic*;
		14	if you do [have to] *suffer* for being good, you will count it a blessing.
		17	it is better to *suffer* for doing right than for doing wrong.
	4	1	anyone who in this life has bodily *suffering* has broken with sin,
		15	None of you should ever deserve to *suffer* for being a murderer,
		19	even those whom God allows to *suffer* must trust themselves to the constancy of the creator
	5	9	strong in . . . the knowledge that your brothers all over the
		2	world *are suffering* the same things.
		10	You will have to *suffer* only for a little while:
Rv	2	10	Do not be afraid of the *sufferings* that are coming to you:

3: SUFFER = EXPERIENCE

Ac	14	15	5 We are only ⌐human beings (lit. men of human *experience*) like you.
Ga	3	4	Have all the ⌐*experiences* (or: sufferings) you underwent been wasted?
Heb	5	2	10 [Every high priest] can *sympathise with* those who are ignorant or uncertain
Jm	5	17	5 Elijah was a ⌐human being (lit. man of human *experience*)

2. SUFFERING, DISTRESS, ANGUISH – TRIAL, TROUBLE, TRIBULATION – PERSECUTION: *THLIPSIS*

2 *thlibō* 9/10   1 *thlipsis* 45

Mt	7	14	2 it is a narrow gate and a ⌐*hard* (or: narrow) road that leads to life,
	13	21	but let some *trial* come, or some persecution on account of the word, and he falls away at once.

Mt 24	9	They will hand you over to *be tortured* and put to death;
	21	then there will be great *distress*
	29	Immediately after the *distress* of those days
Mk 4	17	should some *trial* come, or some persecution on account of the word, they fall away at once.
13	19	For in those days there shall be such *distress* as, until now, has not been equalled
	24	in those days, after that time of *distress*, the sun will be darkened,
Jn 16	21	but when [a woman] has given birth to the child she forgets the *suffering*
	33	In the world you will have *trouble*,
Ac 7	10	[God] rescued [Joseph] from his *miseries*
	11	a famine came that caused much *suffering* throughout Egypt and Canaan,
11	19	the *persecution* that happened because of Stephen
14	22	We all have to experience many *hardships*
20	23	the Holy Spirit . . . has made it clear enough that imprisonment and *persecution* await me.
Rm 2	9	*Pain* and suffering will come to every human being who employs himself in evil
5	3	we can boast about our *sufferings*. These *sufferings* bring patience,
8	35	Nothing . . . can come between us and the love of Christ, even if we are *troubled* or worried, or being persecuted,
12	12	Do not give up if *trials* come;
1 Co 7	28	[Those who marry] will have their *troubles*, though,
2 Co 1	4	[God] comforts us in all our *sorrows*, so that we can offer others, in their *sorrows*, the consolation that we have received
	6	2 When we are made to *suffer*, it is for your consolation
	8	the *things* we had to *undergo* in Asia were more of a burden than we could carry,
2	4	When I wrote to you, in deep *distress* and anguish of mind,
4	8	2 We are *in difficulties* on all sides, but never ⌐cornered (or: distressed);
	17	the *troubles* which are soon over, though they weigh little, train us for the carrying of a weight of eternal glory
6	4	great fortitude in [time of] *suffering*: in times of hardship and distress;
7	4	in all our *trouble* I am filled with consolation
	5	2 we found *trouble* on all sides: quarrels outside, misgivings inside.
8	2	throughout great trials by *suffering*, their constant cheerfulness and their intense poverty have overflowed in a wealth of generosity.
	13 O	This does not mean that to give relief to others you ought to *make things difficult* for yourselves:
Ep 3	13	never lose confidence just because of the *trials* that I go through on your account:
Ph 1	17	The others . . . do not mind if they *make* my chains *heavier to bear*.
4	14	it was good of you to share with me in my *hardships*.
Col 1	24 X	all that has still to be *undergone* by Christ for the sake of . . . the Church.
1 Th 1	6	you took to the gospel in spite of the great ⌐opposition (lit. *suffering*) all round you.
3	3	[to] prevent any of you from being unsettled by the present *troubles*.
	4	2 we warned you that we must expect to have *persecutions* [to bear],
	7	your faith has been a great comfort to us in the middle of our own troubles and *sorrows*;
2 Th 1	4	your constance and faith under all the persecutions and *troubles* you have to bear.
	6	/2 God will very rightly repay with *injury* those who are *injuring* you, ⁷ and reward you, who are *suffering* now, with . . . peace
	7	2
1 Tm 5	10	[The widow] must be a woman known for . . . the way in which she has . . . helped *people who are in trouble*
		2
Heb 10	33	by being yourselves publicly exposed to insults and *violence*,
11	37	2 they were penniless and were ⌐given nothing but (lit. *persecuted* and received) ill-treatment.
Jm 1	27	coming to the help of orphans and widows ⌐when they need it (lit. in their *distress*),
Rv 1	9	My name is John, and through our union in Jesus I . . . share your *sufferings*,
2	9	[Smyrna,] I know the *trials* you have had, . . . ¹⁰ Do not be afraid of the sufferings that are coming to you: . . . you must face an *ordeal* for ten days.
	10	
	22	I am consigning . . . all her partners in adultery to *troubles* that will test them severely,
7	14	These are the people who have been through the great *persecution*,

3. DISTRESS, WORRY – SUFFER: *STENO-CHŌRIA*

2 *steno-chōreō* 1/3   1 *steno-chōria* 4

Rm 2	9	Pain and *suffering* will come to every human being who employs himself in evil

Rm 8	35	Nothing . . . can come between us and the love of Christ even if we are troubled or *worried*, or being persecuted,
2 Co 4	8	We are in difficulties on all sides, but never ⌐cornered (or: distressed);
		2
6	4	great fortitude in times of suffering: in times of hardship and *distress*;
12	10	I am quite content with . . . the *agonies* I go through for Christ's sake.

4. SUFFER, BE IN A STATE – DISTRESS, ANGUISH – OVERWHELM: *SYN-ECHŌ*

1 *syn-echō* 7/12   2 *syn-ochē* 2

Mt 4	24	those who were *suffering* from diseases and painful complaints of one kind or another,
Lk 4	38	Simon's mother-in-law was *suffering* from a high fever
8	37	The entire population of the Gerasene territory *was in a state of panic*
12	50 X	There is a baptism I must still receive, and how great is my *distress* till it is over!
21	25	2 on earth [there will be] nations in *agony*, bewildered by the clamour of the ocean
Ac 28	8	Publius' father was in bed, *suffering* from feverish attacks'
2 Co 2	4	2 When I wrote to you, in deep distress and *anguish* of mind,
5	14 O	this is because the love of Christ *overwhelms* us
Ph 1	23 O	I *am caught* in this dilemma: I want to be gone and be with Christ, . . . ²⁴ but for me to stay alive . . . is a more urgent need for your sake.

5. GREAT DISTRESS, ANGUISH – BE WORRIED, BE TROUBLED: *ADĒMONEŌ*

adēmoneō 3

Mt 26	37 X	sadness came over him, and *great distress*.
Mk 14	33 X	a sudden fear came over him, and *great distress*.
Ph 2	26	[Epaphroditus] *is worried* because you heard about his illness.

6. DISTRESS, HARDSHIP – TROUBLE: *ANANKĒ*

anankē 5/18

Lk 21	23	great ⌐misery (or: *distress*) will descend on the land
1 Co 7	26	in these present [times of] *stress* [celibacy] is right:
2 Co 6	4	great fortitude in [times of] *hardship* and distress:
12	10	I am quite content with . . . the *agonies I go through* for Christ's sake.
1 Th 3	7	your faith has been a great comfort to us in the middle of our *troubles* and sorrows;

7. SORROW, (BE) DISTRESSED – ANGUISH, BE IN AGONY: *ODUNĒ*

1 *odunaō* 4   2 *odunē* 2

Lk 2	48	See how ⌐worried (or: *anguished*) your father and I have been, looking for you.
16	24	I *am in agony* in these flames.
	25	Lazarus . . . is being comforted here while you *are in agony*.
Ac 20	38	what ⌐saddened (or: *distressed*) them most was [Paul's] saying they would never see his face again.
Rm 9	2	2 my mental *anguish* [is] so endless,
1 Tm 6	10	some . . . have . . . ⌐given their souls any number of fatal wounds (lit. pierced their souls with any number of *sorrows*).
		2

8. ANGUISH: *AGŌNIA*

agōnia 1

Lk 22	44 X	In his *anguish* [Jesus] prayed even more earnestly,

9. PAIN, ANGUISH – BE SICKENED, BE ANNOYED – OPPRESSED: *PONOS*

1 *ponos* 4   2 *kata-poneō* 2
3 *dia-poneō* 2

Ac 4	2	3 [the priests] *were* extremely *annoyed* at [the apostles'] teaching the people

Ac	7 24	When [Moses] saw one of [his countrymen] being ill-treated
	2	he . . . rescued the *oppressed* man
	16 18	3 Paul *lost his temper* one day and . . . said to the spirit,
Col	4 13	[Epaphras] 「works hard for (lit. takes great *pains* over) you,
2 P	2 7	2 Lot . . . had *been sickened* by the shameless way in which these vile people behaved
Rv	16 10	Men were biting their tongues for *pain*,
	11	they cursed the God of heaven because of their *pains* and sores.
	21 4	there will be no more . . . mourning or 「*sadness* (or: *pain*).

10. TORMENT, TORTURE – PAIN – DISTRESS: *BASANOS*

2 *basanismos* 6   1 *basanizō* 12
4 *basanistēs* 1   3 *basanos* 3

1: PAIN, AGONY – TORTURE, TORMENT – DISTRESS, OUTRAGE

Mt	4 24	3 those who were suffering from diseases and *painful complaints* of one kind or another . . . were all brought to [Jesus],
	8 6	my servant is lying at home paralysed and in great *pain*.
	14 24	the boat, by now far out on the lake, was 「battling with a heavy sea (lit. being *tormented* by the waves),
	18 34	4 the master handed [the wicked servant] over to the *torturers*
Mk	6 48	[Jesus] could see they were 「worn out (lit. becoming *distressed*) with rowing,
2 P	2 8	[Lot] was *outraged* in his good soul by the crimes that he saw
Rv	9 5	[the locusts were] to *give* [the people] *pain* for five months,
	2/2	and the *pain* was to be the *pain* of a scorpion's sting.
	11 10	these two prophets have *been a plague to* the people of the world.
	12 2	[The woman] was pregnant, and in *labour*, crying aloud in the pangs of childbirth.
	18 7	Every one of [Babylon's] shows and orgies is to be matched
	2	by a *torture* or a grief.
	10	[the kings of the earth will] keep at a safe distance from fear
	2	of [Babylon's] *agony*.
	15	The traders . . . will be standing at a safe distance from fear
	2	of [Babylon's] *agony*,

2: TORMENT, TORTURE (IN HADES)

Lk	16 23	3 In his *torment* in Hades [the rich man] looked up and saw Abraham
	28	give [my brothers] warning so that they do not come to this
	3	place of *torment* too.
Rv	14 10	[those who worship the beast] will be *tortured* in the presence of the holy angels
	11	2 the smoke of their *torture* will go up for ever and ever.
	20 10	their *torture* will not stop, day or night, for ever and ever.

3: TORTURE, TORMENT (DEVILS, DEMONS)

Mt	8 29	What do you want with us, Son of God? Have you come here to *torture* us before the time?
Mk	5 7	Swear by God you will not *torture* me!
Lk	8 28	I implore you, do not *torture* me.

11. BIRTHPANGS, LABOUR PAINS: *ŌDIN*

1 *ōdin* 4   3 *syn-ōdinō* 1
2 *ōdinō* 3

Mt	24 8	this is only the beginning of the *birthpangs*.
Mk	13 8	This is the beginning of the *birthpangs*.
Ac	2 24 ○	God raised [Jesus] to life, freeing him from the *pangs* of ᵛ Hades (G death);
Rm	8 22	the entire creation . . . has been groaning in one great
	3	*painful act of giving birth*;
Ga	4 19	2 my children! I must go through the *pain of giving birth* to you all over again,
	27	(Is 54 1) Break into shouts of joy . . , you who were never
	2	*in labour*.
1 Th	5 3	the worst suddenly happens, as suddenly as *labour pains* come on a pregnant woman;
Rv	12 2	2 [The woman was] crying aloud in the *pangs* of childbirth.

SWEET – GENTLE – KINDLY

1. Sweet(ness) – Fresh (water): *glykys*	*b)* Gentle – Unassuming – Kind(ly): *ēpios*
2. Gentle – Kindly – Courteous	
1: Gentle – Meek – Humble	2: Courteous, Gentle, Kind(ly):
a) Gentle(ness) – Meek(ness),	*epi-eikēs*
Humility – Courtesy: *praus*	

1. SWEET(NESS) – FRESH (WATER): *GLYKYS*

glykys 4

Jm	3 11	does any water supply give a flow of *fresh* water and salt water out of the same pipe?
	12	No more can sea water give you *fresh* water.
Rv	10 9	(Ezk 3 3) in your mouth [the scroll] will taste as *sweet* as honey. ¹⁰ . . . it was as *sweet* as honey in my mouth,
	10	

2. GENTLE – KINDLY – COURTEOUS

1: GENTLE – MEEK – HUMBLE

a) Gentle(ness) – Meek(ness), Humility – Courtesy: praus

2 *praus* 4   3 *prau-pathia* 1
1 *prautēs* 11

Mt	5 4	2 (Ps 37 11) Happy the *gentle*: they shall have the earth for their heritage.
	11 29 X	2 learn from me, for I am *gentle* and humble in heart,
	21 5 X	2 (Zc 9 9) your king comes to you; he is *humble*, he rides on a donkey
1 Co	4 21	do I come with a stick . . . or in a spirit of love and *goodwill*?
2 Co	10 1 X	this is Paul himself appealing to you by the *gentleness* and patience of Christ
Ga	5 23	[the Spirit brings love, joy, peace . . .] *gentleness*
	6 1	if one of you misbehaves . . . you who set him right should do so in a spirit of *gentleness*,
Ep	4 2	Bear with one another . . . in complete selflessness, *gentleness* and patience.
Col	3 12	you should be clothed in sincere compassion, in kindness . . . *gentleness* and patience.
1 Tm	6 11	You must aim to be saintly . . . filled with faith and love,
	3	patient and *gentle*.
2 Tm	2 25	[the servant of the Lord] has to be *gentle* when he corrects people who dispute what he says,
Tt	3 2	[it is their duty] to be courteous and always *polite* to all
Jm	1 21	accept 「*and submit to* (lit. with *humility*) the word which . . . can save your souls.
	3 13	If there are any wise . . . men among you, let them show it . . . with *humility* and wisdom in their actions.
1 P	3 4	this should be inside . . . imperishable: the ornament of a
	2	sweet and *gentle* disposition
	16	[Always have your answer ready.] But give it with *courtesy* and respect

b) Gentle – Unassuming – Kind(ly): ēpios

ēpios 2

1 Th	2 7	we could have imposed ourselves on you . . . Instead, we were *unassuming*.
2 Tm	2 24	a servant of the Lord . . . has to be *kind* to everyone,

2: COURTEOUS, GENTLE, KIND(LY): *EPI-EIKĒS*

epi-eikēs 4/5

1 Tm	3 3	[The elder-in-charge must not be] hot-tempered, but 「*kind* (or: forbearing)
Tt	3 2	[Remind them] not to go . . . picking quarrels, but to be *courteous*
Jm	3 17	the wisdom that comes down from above . . . makes for peace, and is *kindly* and considerate;
1 P	2 18	Slaves must be respectful . . . to their masters, not only when they are kind and *gentle* but also when they are unfair.

SYRIA – ANTIOCH

S	*Syria* 8	*Antioch* 14	
	Syrian 1	of *Antioch* 1 (Ac 6)	
		Seleucia 1 (Ac 13)	

Mt	4 24 S ○	[Jesus's] fame spread throughout *Syria*,
Lk	2 2 S	Quirinius was governor of *Syria*,
	4 27	in the prophet Elisha's time . . . none of [the lepers] was
	S	cured, except the *Syrian*, Naaman.
Ac	6 5	[The assembly] elected Stephen, . . . and Nicolaus *of Antioch*, a convert to Judaism.
	11 19	Those who had escaped during the persecution . . . travelled as far as Phoenicia and Cyprus and *Antioch*,
	20	Some of them . . . who came from Cyprus and Cyrene, went to *Antioch*
	22	The church in Jerusalem . . . sent Barnabas to *Antioch*.
	26	when [Barnabas] found [Saul] he brought him to *Antioch* . . . It was at *Antioch* that the disciples were first called 'Christians'.
	27	some prophets came down to *Antioch* from Jerusalem,
	13 1	In the church at *Antioch* the following were prophets and teachers: Barnabas, Simeon . . , Lucius . . , Manaen . . . and Saul.

Ac	13 4	[Saul and Barnabas] went down to *Seleucia* and from there sailed to Cyprus.
	14 26	from [Attalia Paul and Barnabas] sailed for *Antioch*,
	15 22	the apostles . . . decided to choose delegates to send to *Antioch* with Paul and Barnabas . . . They chose Judas . . . and Silas,
	23 S	The apostles . . . send greetings to the brothers of pagan birth in *Antioch*, *Syria* and Cilicia.
	30	The party left and went down to *Antioch*,
	35	Paul and Barnabas . . . stayed on in *Antioch*,
	41 S	[Paul] travelled through *Syria* and Cilicia,
	18 18 S	Paul took leave of the brothers and sailed for *Syria*,
	22	[Paul] came down to *Antioch*
	20 3 S	[Paul] was leaving by ship for *Syria*
	21 3	After sighting Cyprus and leaving it to port, we sailed to *Syria*
Ga	1 21 S	After that I went to *Syria* and Cilicia,
	2 11	When Cephas came to *Antioch* . . . I opposed him to his face,

TABLE

1: (food-)Table
2: Tables (of the money changers)

3: Table (in the Holy Place)

tra-peza 14/15

1: (FOOD-)TABLE

Mt 15 27		even house-dogs can eat the scraps that fall from their master's *table*.
Mk 7 28		the house-dogs under the *table* can eat the children's scraps.
Lk 16 21		[Lazarus] longed to fill himself with the scraps that fell from the rich man's *table*.
22 21		here with me on the *table* is the hand of the man who betrays me.
30	X	you will eat and drink at my *table* in my kingdom,
Ac 6 2		It would not be right for us to neglect the word of God so as to ⌐give out food (lit. serve [at the] *tables*);
16 34		[the gaoler] took [Paul and Silas] home and ⌐gave them a meal (lit. set a *table* for them),
Rm 11 9		(Ps 69 23) May their own *table* prove a trap for them,
1 Co 10 21	X	You cannot take your share at the *table* of the Lord and at the *table* of demons.
Ⓓ		

2: TABLES (OF THE MONEY CHANGERS)

Mt 21 12	Jesus . . . upset the *tables* of the money changers
Mk 11 15	[Jesus] upset the *tables* of the money changers
Jn 2 15	[Jesus] scattered the money changers' coins, knocked their *tables* over

3: TABLE (IN THE HOLY PLACE)

Heb 9 2	(cf. Ex 25 23–30) the first [compartment], in which the lampstand, the *table* and the presentation loaves were kept, was called the Holy Place;

TAKE – BRING – LEAD

1. Take, Bring: *lambanō*
  1: Take, Bring (a person)
  2: Seize, Take hold of (a person) – Capture, Arrest
  3: (Jesus is) Taken up (to heaven)
  4: Take (a thing) – Bring, Collect
  5: Attain, Grasp, Lay hold on (a thing) – Get – Win
  6: Take (= Eat, Drink)
  7: Take by surprise, Catch (out) – Overtake
  8: Take (figuratively) – Bring – Hand down (to)
2. Carry, Bear – Take (off, away, up) – Support: *bastazō*
3. Take away: *airō*
  1: Take (up, away), Carry (off), Bear – Collect, Fetch, Pick up – Move, Remove
  2: Do away with, Sweep away – "Away(with)!", "Kill!" – Expel
  3: Take (a person's life) – Cut short (a life)
  4: Tear away (from) – Pull away (from)
4. Take away – Cut off: *haireō*
  1: Take (away, up) from – Cut off, Tear out
  2: Take away (sins)

5. (Be) Taken (up, away) – (Be) Brought, Carried (back): *meta-tithēmi*
6. Bring, Carry – Take – Produce: *pherō*
  1: Bring, (Be) Brought, Take (to) – Carry (in, away)
  2: Burden, Be burdened – Load, Unload
  3: Wear, Bear (on a person)
  4: Bring (an accusation, a case, against) – Cast (a vote against)
  5: Bring, Carry, Bear (figuratively) – Lead (into) – Produce
  6: Bear (fruit) – Yield, Produce
7. Bring, Brought: *komizō*
8. Lead (away, out) – Bring – Take: *agō*
  1: Lead away, Lead out (to) – Bring (out, to) – Take (to)
    a) Lead, Bring, Take (to a place)
    b) Lead out, Bring out (of Egypt)
    c) Lead away (to), Bring (before), Take (to a person in authority)
    d) Lead (figuratively) to, Be led (to) – Bring (upon)

    e) Bring down (from heaven)
  2: Direct, Control
  3: Bring in
    a) Bring in
    b) Bring in (figuratively) – Introduce
    c) Put in (at a port)

9. To, Dead to (death) – End in (death): *pros* + accusative
10. Escort – Conduct: *kath-istēmi*
11. Escort – Send a person on his way – Help a person on his journey: *pro-pempō*

1. TAKE, BRING: *LAMBANŌ*

1	*lambanō*	121/257		8	*meta-lambanō*	4/7
4	*ana-lambanō*	13		2	*para-lambanō*	37/50
11	*ana-lēmpsis*	1		9	*sym-para-lambanō*	4
12	*apo-lambanō*	1/9		14	*sym-peri-lambanō*	1
5	⌐*kata-lambanō*	12/15		10	*pro-lambanō*	2/3
3	*epi-lambanomai*	19		7	*pros-lambanomai*	6/12
13	*hypo-lambanō*	1/5		6	*syl-lambanō*	9/16

1: TAKE, BRING (A PERSON)

Mt	1 20		2	Joseph . . . do not be afraid to *take* Mary [home] as your wife,
	24		2	[Joseph] *took* his wife to [his home]
	2 13		2	*take* the child and his mother with you . . . ¹⁴ So Joseph got
	14		2	up and, *taking* the child and his mother with him, left that night for Egypt,
	20		2	Get up, *take* the child and his mother with you and go back
	21		2	. . . ²¹ So Joseph got up and, *taking* the child and his mother with him, went back to the land of Israel.
	4 5	Ⓓ	2	The devil then *took* [Jesus] to the holy city
	8	Ⓓ	2	*taking* [Jesus] to a very high mountain, the devil showed him all the kingdoms of the world
	12 45	Ⓓ	2	it then goes off and ⌐*collects* (or: *brings*) seven other spirits more evil than itself,
	16 22		7	*taking* [Jesus] *aside*, Peter started to remonstrate with him.
	17 1	X	2	Jesus *took* [with him] Peter and James and his brother John and led them up a high mountain
	18 16		2	*take* one or two others along with you:
	20 17	X	2	Jesus . . . *took* the Twelve to one side
	24 40		2	Then of two men in the fields one is *taken*, one left; ⁴¹ of two women at the millstone grinding, one is *taken*, one left.
	41		2	
	26 37	X	2	[Jesus] *took* Peter and the two sons of Zebedee with him.
	27 27		2	The governor's soldiers *took* Jesus [with them] into the Praetorium
Mk	4 36		2	they *took* [Jesus], just as he was, in the boat;
	5 40	X	2	*taking* [with him] the child's father and mother . . . he went into the place where the child lay.
	7 33	X	12	He *took* [the deaf man] aside in private, away from the crowd,
	8 23	X	3	He *took* the blind man by the hand and led him outside the village.
	32		7	*taking* [Jesus] *aside*, Peter started to remonstrate with him.
	9 2	X	2	Jesus *took* [with him] Peter and James and John
	36	X	2	He then *took* a little child, set him in front of them,
	10 32	X	2	*taking* the Twelve aside he began to tell them what was going to happen
	14 33	X	2	he *took* Peter and James and John with him.
Lk	9 10	X	2	[Jesus] *took* them [with him] and withdrew to a town called Bethsaida
	28	X	2	[Jesus] *took* [with him] Peter and John and James
	47	X	3	[Jesus] *took* a little child and set him by his side
	11 26	Ⓓ	2	it then goes off and *brings* seven other spirits more wicked than itself,
	14 4	X	3	[Jesus] *took* the man and cured him
	17 34		2	two will be in one bed: one will be *taken*, the other left; ³⁵ two women will be grinding corn together: one will be
	35			
	36		2	*taken*, the other left. ³⁶ (ᵛ Two men will be out in the fields: one will be *taken*, the other left.)
			2	
	18 31	X	2	*taking* the Twelve aside [Jesus] said to them,
Jn	6 21		2	They were for *taking* [Jesus] into the boat,
	14 3	X	2	I shall return to *take* you with me;
	18 3			[Judas] *brought* the cohort to this place together with a detachment of guards
	31			Pilate said, '*Take* him yourselves, and try him by your own Law'.
	19 1			Pilate then had Jesus *taken* [away] and scourged;
	6			*Take* him yourselves and crucify him;
	16		2	They then *took* [charge of] Jesus, ¹⁷ and carrying his own cross he went out of the city
	27			from that moment the disciple ⌐made a place for [Mary] in (lit. *took* [Mary] into) his home.

Ac 9 25 the disciples *took* [Saul] and let him down from the top of the wall, lowering him in a basket.
27 3 Barnabas . . . *took* [charge of Saul], introduced him to the apostles,
12 25 9 Barnabas and Saul . . . came back from Jerusalem, *bringing* John Mark *with* them.
15 14 Θ God . . . arranged to ⌐enlist (lit. *take*) a people for his name out of the pagans.
37 9 Barnabas suggested *taking* John Mark, [38] but Paul was not
38 9 in favour of *taking along* the very man who had deserted them in Pamphylia
39 2 Barnabas sailed off ⌐with (lit. *taking*) Mark to Cyprus.
16 3 9 Paul . . . *took* [Timothy] and had him circumcised.
33 2 [the gaoler] *took* [Paul and Silas] to wash their wounds,
17 5 7 The Jews . . . ⌐enlisted the help of (lit. *took*) a gang from the market place,
19 3 [The Athenians] ⌐invited [Paul] to accompany them (lit. *took* [Paul] and led him) to the Council of the Areopagus,
18 26 When Priscilla and Aquila heard [Apollos] speak . . . they
7 *took* [an interest in] him
20 13 4 we set sail for Assos, where we were to *take* Paul *on board*;
14 4 When [Paul] rejoined us at Assos we *took* him *aboard* and went on to Mitylene.
21 24 2 *take* these men along and be purified with them
26 2 So the next day Paul *took* the men along
32 2 [The tribune] ⌐called out (lit. *took* his) soldiers . . . and charged down on the crowd,
23 18 2 the man *took* [the son of Paul's sister] to the tribune,
19 3 the tribune *took* [the young man] by the hand
31 4 The soldiers . . . *took* Paul and escorted him by night to Antipatris.
Ga 2 1 9 I went up to Jerusalem . . . with Barnabas and *took* Titus *with* me.
2 Tm 4 11 4 *Get* Mark *to come* and bring him with you;
Heb 2 16 X 3 it was not the angels that he *took* [to himself];
5 1 Every high priest has been *taken* out of mankind
8 9 Θ 3 (Jr 31 32) I *took* them by the hand to bring them out of the land of Egypt.

2: SEIZE, TAKE HOLD OF (A PERSON) – CAPTURE, ARREST

Mt 14 31 X 3 Jesus put out his hand at once and *held* [Peter].
21 35 < the tenants *seized* his servants,
39 < they *seized* [the heir] and threw him out of the vineyard
26 55 6 Am I a brigand, that you had to set out to *capture* me with swords and clubs?
Mk 9 18 Ⓓ 5 when [the spirit of dumbness] *takes hold of* [my son] it throws him to the ground,
12 3 < [the tenants] *seized* the man, thrashed him and sent him away
8 < they *seized* him and killed him
14 48 6 Am I a brigand . . . that you had to set out to *capture* me with swords and clubs?
Lk 5 26 They were all ⌐astounded (lit. *seized* with astonishment)
7 16 Everyone was ⌐filled (lit. *seized*) with awe
9 39 Ⓓ All at once a spirit will *take hold of* [my son],
22 54 6 They *seized* [Jesus] then and led him away,
23 26 3 they *seized on* a man, Simon from Cyrene
Jn 18 12 6 The cohort and its captain and the Jewish guards *seized* Jesus
Ac 1 16 6 Judas . . . offered himself as a guide to the men who *arrested* Jesus
12 3 6 [Herod] decided to *arrest* Peter as well,
16 19 3 [the slave-girl's] masters . . . *seized* Paul and Silas
18 17 3 they all ⌐turned on (lit. *seized*) Sosthenes . . . and beat him
20 10 14 Paul . . . stooped to *clasp* [Eutychus] to him.
21 30 3 people . . . *seized* Paul and dragged him out of the Temple,
33 3 the tribune . . . *arrested* Paul . . . and enquired who he was
23 27 6 This man had been *seized* by the Jews
26 21 6 the Jews *laid hands on* me . . . and tried to do away with me.
1 Co 10 13 The trials that ⌐you have had to bear (lit. have *taken a hold on* you) are no more than people normally have.
Ph 3 12 I am still running, trying to capture the prize for which
X 5 Christ Jesus *captured* me.

3: (JESUS IS) TAKEN UP (TO HEAVEN)

Mk 16 19 4 the Lord Jesus . . . was *taken up* into heaven: there at the right hand of God he took his place,
Lk 9 51 11 the time drew near for [Jesus] to *be taken up* to heaven,
Ac 1 2 [Jesus] gave his instructions to the apostles . . . and was
4 *taken up* to heaven.
9 13 he was lifted up while they looked on, and a cloud *took* him from their sight.
11 4 Jesus . . . has been *taken up* from you into heaven,
22 [We must choose] someone who was with us right from the time when John was baptising until the day when [Jesus]
4 was *taken up*
1 Tm 3 16 4 He was made visible in the flesh, . . . *taken up* in glory.

4: TAKE (A THING) – BRING, COLLECT

F = Catch fish

Mt 5 40 if a man takes you to law and would ⌐have (lit. *take*) your tunic, let him have your cloak as well.
8 17 X (Is 53 4) He *took* our sicknesses *away* and carried our diseases for us.
10 38 Anyone who does not *take* his cross . . . is not worthy of me.
13 31 The kingdom of heaven is like a mustard seed which a man
< *took* and sowed in his field.
33 < The kingdom of heaven is like the yeast a woman *took* and mixed in with three measures of flour
14 19 X he *took* the five loaves and the two fish,
15 26 It is not fair to *take* the children's food and throw it to the house-dogs.
36 X he *took* the seven loaves and the fish,
16 5 The disciples . . . had forgotten to *take* any food . . . [7] And
7 they said to themselves, 'It is because we have not *brought* any bread'.
9 Do you not remember . . . the number of baskets you *collected*?
10 Or the seven loaves . . . and the number of baskets you *collected*?
17 24 the *collectors* of the half-shekel came to Peter
25 From whom do the kings of the earth *take* toll or tribute?
27 you will find a shekel; *take* it and give it to them
20 11 They *took* [one denarius each], but grumbled at the landowner.
21 34 < he sent his servants to the tenants to *collect* his produce.
25 1 < Ten bridesmaids *took* their lamps . . . [3] the foolish ones did
3 < *take* their lamps, but they *brought* no oil, [4] whereas the
4 < sensible ones *took* flasks of oil
26 26 X Jesus *took* some bread . . . and gave it to the disciples.
27 'Take it and eat;' he said 'this is my body.' [27] Then he
X *took* a cup, and . . . gave it to them.
52 all who *draw* the sword will die by the sword.
27 6 The chief priests *picked up* the silver pieces
9 (cf. Zc 11 13) they *took* the thirty silver pieces,
24 Pilate . . . *took* some water,
30 [the soldiers] *took* the reed and struck [Jesus] on the head
48 one of them quickly ran to *get* a sponge
59 So Joseph *took* the body,
28 15 The soldiers *took* the money and carried out their instructions,
Mk 6 41 X he *took* the five loaves and the two fish,
7 27 it is not fair to *take* the children's food and throw it to the house-dogs.
8 6 X he *took* the seven loaves, and after giving thanks he broke them
14 The disciples had forgotten to *take* any food
12 2 < he sent a servant to the tenants to *collect* . . . his share of the produce from the vineyard.
14 22 X [Jesus] *took* some bread . . . and gave it to them, 'Take it,'
23 X he said 'this is my body.' [23] Then he *took* a cup, and . . . gave it to them,
Lk 5 5 F we worked hard all night long and *caught* nothing,
9 [Simon Peter] and all his companions were completely
F 6 overcome by the catch they had ⌐made (lit. *taken*);
6 4 [David] *took* the loaves of offering and ate them
9 16 X he *took* the five loaves and the two fish,
13 19 [The kingdom of God] is like a mustard seed which a man
< *took* and threw into his garden:
21 < It is like the yeast a woman *took* and mixed in with three measures of flour
22 17 *Take* this [cup] and share it among you,
19 X he *took* some bread, and when he had given thanks, broke it,
24 30 X he *took* the bread and said the blessing;
43 X he *took* [a piece of grilled fish] and ate before their eyes.
Jn 6 11 X Jesus *took* the loaves, gave thanks,
10 17 X I lay down my life in order to *take* it *up* again. [18] . . . as it is
18 X in my power to lay it down, so it is in my power to *take* it *up* again;
12 3 Mary *brought in* a pound of very costly ointment, pure nard,
13 They *took* branches of palm and went out to meet [Jesus],
13 4 X [Jesus] got up . . . and, *taking* a towel, wrapped it round his waist;
12 X When he had . . . *put on* his clothes again he went back to the table.
26 X He dipped the piece of bread, *took* it *out* and gave it to Judas
16 14 Ⓢ all he tells you will be *taken* from what is mine.
15 Ⓢ All he tells you will be *taken* from what is mine.
19 23 the soldiers . . . *took* his clothing and divided it into four shares,
40 They *took* the body of Jesus
21 13 X Jesus . . . *took* the bread and gave it to [the disciples],
Ac 7 43 4 (Am 5 26 G) you *carried* the tent of Moloch on your shoulders and the star of the god Rephan.
10 16 4 suddenly the container was *drawn up* to heaven again.
17 9 [the city councillors] ⌐made Jason and the rest give security (lit. *took* security from Jason and the rest) before setting them free.

Ac 27 35   [Paul] *took* some bread, gave thanks . . . broke it and began to eat.
1 Co 11 23 X   the Lord Jesus *took* some bread, [24] and . . . broke it,
2 Co 11 20   yes, even tolerating somebody who . . . ⌐imposes on you (lit. *takes* your property),
         ○
Ep 6 13   4 you must ⌐rely on (lit. *take up*) God's armour,
   16   4 [stand your ground,] always *carrying* the shield of faith
Ph 2 7 X   [Jesus] emptied himself to *assume* the condition of a slave,
Heb 9 19   Moses . . . *took* the calves' blood, the goats' blood and some water,
Rv 3 11   hold firmly to what you already have, and let nobody *take* your prize away from you.
   5 7 X   The Lamb came forward to *take* the scroll . . . [8] and when
      8 X   he *took* it, the four animals . . . [9] . . . sang a new hymn:
      9 X   You are worthy to *take* the scroll and break the seals of it,
   6 4   its rider was given this duty: to *take away* peace from the earth
   8 5   the angel *took* the censer and filled it with the fire from the altar
   10 8   'Go,' [the voice] said 'and *take* that open scroll . . .'
      9   *Take* [the scroll] and eat it . . . [10] So I *took* it out of the angel's hand, and swallowed it;
      10
   11 17 ⊖   We give thanks to you, . . . God, . . . for ⌐using (lit. *taking up*) your great power

5: ATTAIN, GRASP, LAY HOLD ON (A THING) – GET – WIN

Lk 20 20   3 [the chief priests] sent agents . . . to *fasten* on something [Jesus] might say
Jn 1 5   that life was the light of men, . . . a light that darkness could not *grasp*.
    △   5
   3 27   A man can ⌐lay claim only to (lit. *lay hold* only *on*) what is given him from heaven.
Rm 9 30   5 the pagans who were not looking for righteousness ⌐found
      5   (or: *attained*) it all the same,
1 Co 9 24   All the runners at the stadium are trying to win, but only one of them *gets* the prize. You must run in the same way,
   25   5 meaning to ⌐*win* (or: *get* it). [25] All the fighters at the games go into strict training; they do this just to *win* a wreath that will wither away, but we do it for a wreath that will never wither.
2 Co 11 8   I was *robbing* other churches living on them so that I could serve you.
Ep 3 18   5 you will . . . have strength to *grasp* the breadth and the length, the height and the depth;
Ph 3 12   /5 I have not yet *won*, but I am still running, trying to *capture*
   13   the prize for which Christ Jesus captured me. [13] . . . I am
      5   far from thinking that I have already *won*.
1 Tm 6 12   3 *win* for yourself the eternal life to which you were called
   19   they can save up a good capital sum for the future if they
      3   want to ⌐*make sure of* (lit. *attain*) the only life that is real.
Jm 1 12   the man who stands firm when trials come . . . will *win* the prize of life,

6: TAKE (= EAT, DRINK)

Mk 15 23 X   They offered him wine . . . but he ⌐refused (lit. did not *take*) it.
Jn 13 30   As soon as Judas had ⌐*taken* (or: *received*) the piece of bread he went out.
   19 30 X   After Jesus had ⌐*taken* (or: *received*) the vinegar he said, 'It is accomplished';
Ac 2 46   8 [the faithful] ⌐*shared* (lit. *took*) their food gladly and generously,
   9 19   after *taking* some food [Saul] regained his strength.
   27 33   8 Paul urged them all to ⌐*have* (lit. *take*) something to eat . . .
      7   'you have been in suspense . . . and ⌐*eating* (lit. *taking*)
   34   8 nothing. [34] Let me persuade you to ⌐*have* (lit. *take*)
   36   7 something to eat . . .' [36] Then they all . . . *took* something to eat themselves.
1 Co 11 21   10 everyone *is in such a hurry to* ⌐start (lit. *take*) his own supper
1 Tm 4 4   no food is to be rejected, provided grace is ⌐said for it (lit. said before it is *taken*):

7: TAKE BY SURPRISE, CATCH (OUT) – OVERTAKE

Lk 20 26   3 his answer *took* them *by surprise* and they were silenced.
Jn 8 3   The scribes . . . brought a woman along who had been
      5   *caught* committing adultery;
   4   5 this woman was *caught* in the very act of committing adultery,
   12 35   5 Walk while you have the light, or the dark will *overtake* you;
2 Co 12 16   I *took* you *in* by a trick.
Ga 6 1   10 if one of you ⌐misbehaves (lit. is *caught* misbehaving) . . . set him right

---

1 Th 5 4   5 it is not as if you live in the dark . . . for that Day to *overtake* you like a thief.

8: TAKE (FIGURATIVELY) – BRING – HAND DOWN (TO)

Mk 7 4   There are also many other observances which have been
      2   *handed down* to them
Jn 5 44   How can you believe, since you ⌐look to (lit. *draw on*) one another for approval . . .?
Ac 1 20   (Ps 109 8) Let someone else *take* his office.
   25   [show us which of these two you have chosen] to *take* [over] this ministry . . . which Judas abandoned
   7 53   You . . . had the Law *brought* to you by angels
   24 25   I will send for you when ⌐I find it convenient (lit. there is an
      8   opportunity for me to *take*).
   28 15   Paul . . . thanked God and *took* courage.
Rm 7 8   it was this commandment that sin *took* advantage of
   11   sin *took* advantage of the commandment to mislead me,
2 Tm 1 5   Then I ⌐am reminded of (lit. *bring* to mind) the sincere faith which you have;
Heb 2 2   every infringement . . . *brought* its own proper punishment,
   3   ⌐The promise (lit. The salvation *brought*) was first announced by the Lord himself.
   16 X   3 he *took* [to himself] descent from Abraham.
   5 4   No one *takes* this honour on himself,
   11 29   the Egyptians, ⌐trying to do (lit. *taking* [a chance] on doing) the same, were drowned.
Jm 5 10   For your example, brothers, in submitting with patience, *take* the prophets
2 P 1 9   he ⌐has (lit. *takes* as) forgotten how his past sins were washed away.

2. CARRY, BEAR – TAKE (OFF, AWAY, UP) – SUPPORT: *BASTAZŌ*

    1 *bastazō 27*   2 *dys-bastaktos 2*

Mt 3 11   I am not fit to ⌐*carry* (or: *take off*) his sandals;
   8 17 X   (Is 53 4) He took our sicknesses away and *carried* our diseases for us.
   20 12   we have ⌐done a heavy day's work (lit. *borne* the burden of the day) in all the heat.
   23 4   2 [The Pharisees] tie up (ᵛ *unendurably*) heavy burdens and lay them on men's shoulders,
Mk 14 13   you will meet a man *carrying* a pitcher of water.
Lk 7 14   [Jesus] put his hand on the bier and the *bearers* stood still,
   10 4   *Carry* no purse, no haversack, no sandals.
   11 27   Happy the womb that *bore* you
   46   2 you load on men burdens that are *unendurable*,
   14 27   Anyone who does not *carry* his cross . . . cannot be my disciple.
   22 10   you will meet a man *carrying* a pitcher of water.
Jn 10 31   The Jews *fetched* stones to stone [Jesus],
   12 6   [Judas] was in charge of the common fund and used to ⌐help *himself to* (or: *take*) the contributions.
   16 12   I still have many things to say to you but they would be too much for you to *bear* now.
   19 17 X   *carrying* his own cross he went out of the city
   20 15   Sir, if you have *taken* him *away*, tell me where you have put him,
Ac 3 2   there was a man being *carried* past. He was a cripple from birth;
   9 15   [Saul] is my chosen instrument to *bring* my name before pagans
   15 10   It would only provoke God's anger now, surely, if you imposed on the disciples the very burden that neither we nor our ancestors were strong enough to *support*?
   21 35   [Paul] had to be *carried* by the soldiers;
Rm 11 18   you do not *support* the root; it is the root that [supports] you
   15 1   We who are strong have a duty to *put up with* the qualms of the weak
Ga 5 10   anybody who troubles you in future will ⌐be condemned (lit. *bear* [God's] judgement),
   6 2   You should *carry* each other's troubles and fulfil the law of Christ.
   5   Everyone has his own burden to *carry*.
   17   the marks I *carry* on my body are those of Jesus.
Rv 2 2   I know you cannot *stand* wicked men . . . [3] I know, too,
   3   that you have patience, and ⌐have suffered (lit. are *bearing* [up]) for my name
   17 7   I will tell you the meaning of this woman, and of the beast ⌐she is riding (lit. which is *carrying* her),

3. TAKE AWAY: *AIRŌ*

    1 *airō 90/101*   2 *ap-airō 3*

C = Carry the cross   S = Take away sin

1: TAKE (UP, AWAY), CARRY (OFF), BEAR – COLLECT, FETCH, PICK UP – MOVE, REMOVE

Mt	9 6	*pick up* your bed and go off home.
	15	2 the time will come for the bridegroom to be *taken away* from them,
	11 29 ●	┌Shoulder (lit. *Bear*) my yoke and learn from me,
	13 12	from anyone who has not, even what he has will be *taken away*.
	14 12	John's disciples came and *took* the body and buried it;
	20	they *collected* the scraps remaining, twelve baskets full.
	15 37	they *collected* what was left of the scraps, seven baskets full.
	16 24 C	If a man wants to be a follower of mine, let him . . . *take up* his cross and follow me.
	17 27	cast a hook; *take* the first fish that bites,
	20 14	*Take* your earnings and go.
	21 43	the kingdom of God will be *taken* from you and given to a people who will produce its fruit.
	24 17	if a man is on the housetop, he must not come down to *collect* his belongings;
	18	if a man is in the fields, he must not turn back to *fetch* his cloak.
	25 28	*take* the talent from him and give it to the man who has the five talents.
	29	from the man who has not, even what he has will be *taken away*.
	27 32 C	they came across a man from Cyrene, Simon by name, and enlisted him to *carry* his cross.
Mk	2 3	some people came bringing [Jesus] a paralytic *carried* by four men,
	9	Get up, *pick up* you stretcher and walk
	11	I order you: get up, *pick up* your stretcher, and go off home.
	12	the man got up, *picked up* his stretcher at once and walked out
	20	2 the time will come for the bridegroom to be *taken away* from them,
	4 15	Satan comes and *carries away* the word that was sown in them.
	6 8	[Jesus] instructed them to *take* nothing for the journey
	29	John's disciples . . . came and *took* his body
	43	They *collected* twelve basketfuls of scraps of bread
	8 8	they *collected* seven basketfuls of the scraps left over.
	19	how many baskets full of scraps did you *collect*?
	20	how many baskets full of scraps did you *collect*?
	34 C	If anyone wants to be a follower of mine, let him . . . *take up* his cross and follow me.
	13 15	if a man is on the housetop, he must not come down to . . .
	16	*collect* any of his belongings; ¹⁶ if a man is in the fields, he must not turn back to *fetch* his cloak.
	15 21 C	They enlisted a passer-by, Simon of Cyrene, . . . to *carry* his cross.
	24	[the soldiers] shared his clothing, casting lots to decide what each should *get*.
	16 18	they will *pick up* snakes in their hands, and be unharmed
Lk	5 24	I order you: get up, and *pick up* your stretcher and go home.
	25	²⁵ And immediately . . . he got up, *picked up* what he had been lying on
	35	2 the time will come . . . for the bridegroom to be *taken away* from them;
	6 29	to the man who *takes* your cloak from you, do not refuse your tunic.
	30	do not ask for your property back from the man who ┌robs (or: *takes* it from) you.
	8 12	the devil comes and *carries away* the word from their hearts in case they should believe and be saved.
	18	from anyone who has not, even what he thinks he has will be *taken away*.
	9 3	*Take* nothing for the journey:
	17	when the scraps remaining were *collected* they filled twelve baskets.
	23 C	If anyone wants to be a follower of mine, let him . . . *take up* his cross every day.
	11 22	the stronger man *takes away* all the weapons he relied on and shares out his spoil.
	52	Alas for you lawyers who have *taken away* the key of knowledge!
	17 31	When that day comes, anyone on the housetop . . . must not come down to *collect* [his possessions],
	19 21	you are an exacting man: you *pick up* what you have not put down
	22	So you knew I was an exacting man, *picking up* what I have not put down . . .?
	24	*Take* the pound from him and give it to the man who has ten pounds
	26	from the man who has not, even what he has will be *taken away*
	22 36	if you have a purse, *take* it;
Jn	1 29 S	Look, there is the lamb of God that *takes away* the sin of the world.
	2 16	*Take* all this *out* of here and stop turning my Father's house into a market.
	5 8	Get up, *pick up* your sleeping-mat and walk. ⁹ The man was cured at once, and he *picked up* his mat and walked away.
	9	

Jn	5 10	It is the sabbath; you are not allowed to *carry* your sleeping-mat.
	11	the man who cured me told me, '*Pick up* your mat and walk'.
	12	¹² They asked, 'Who is the man who said to you, "*Pick up* your mat . . ."'?
	8 59	At this they *picked up* stones to throw at [Jesus];
	11 39	Jesus said, '*Take* the stone *away*' . . . ⁴¹ So they *took away* the stone.
	41	
	16 22	that joy no one shall *take* from you.
	17 15	I am not asking you to *remove* them from the world, but to protect them from the evil one.
	19 31	the Jews asked Pilate to have . . . the bodies *taken away*.
	38	Joseph of Arimathaea . . . asked Pilate to let him *remove* the body of Jesus.
	20 1	Mary of Magdala . . . saw that the stone had been *moved away* from the tomb
	2	They had *taken* the Lord *out* of the tomb
	13	They have *taken* my Lord *away* . . . and I don't know where they have put him.
	15	Sir, if you have *taken* him *away*, tell me where you have put him,
Ac	8 33	(Is 53 8 G) He has been humiliated and ┌has no one to defend him (lit. all his defenders have been *removed*).
	20 9	Eutychus . . . was *picked up* dead.
	21 11	[Agabus] *took* Paul's girdle, and tied up his own feet and hands,
1 Co	6 15	do you think I can *take* parts of Christ's body and join them to the body of a prostitute?
Rv	18 21	a powerful angel *picked up* a boulder like a great millstone,

2: DO AWAY WITH, SWEEP AWAY – "AWAY (WITH)!", "KILL!" – EXPEL

Mt	24 39	they suspected nothing till the Flood came and *swept* all *away*.
Lk	23 18	*Away* with him! Give us Barabbas!
Jn	11 48 ○	the Romans will come and ┌destroy (or: *sweep away*) the Holy Place
	15 2	Every branch in me that bears no fruit [my Father] ┌cuts *away* (or: *does away with*),
	19 15	*Take* him *away*! *Take* him *away*!
Ac	21 36	the whole mob was after [Paul], shouting, '*Kill* him!'
	22 22	┌Rid the earth of (lit. *Away with*) the man!
1 Co	5 2	A man who does a thing like that ought to have been *expelled* from the community.
Ep	4 31	┌Never have (lit. *Do away with*) grudges against others,
Col	2 14	[Christ] has *done away with* [every record of the debt we had to pay]
1 Jn	3 5 S	[Christ] appeared in order to ┌abolish (or: *do away with*) sin,

3: TAKE (A PERSON'S LIFE) – CUT SHORT (A LIFE)

Jn	10 18	No one *takes* [my life] from me; I lay it down of my own free will,
Ac	8 33	(Is 53 8 G) his life on earth has been *cut short*.

4: TEAR AWAY (FROM) – PULL AWAY (FROM)

Mt	9 16	the patch [of unshrunken cloth] *pulls away* from the cloak
Mk	2 21	the patch *pulls away* from [the cloak], the new from the old,

4. TAKE AWAY – CUT OFF: *HAIREŌ*

4	an-(h)aireō 2/24	3	ex-(h)aireō 3/8
1	aph-aireō 10	5	kath-aireō 1/9
2	peri-(h)aireō 4		

1: TAKE (AWAY, UP) FROM – CUT OFF, TEAR OUT

Mt	5 29	3 If your right eye should cause you to sin, *tear it out*
	18 9	3 if your eye should cause you to sin, *tear it out*
	26 51	[one of the followers of Jesus] struck out at the high priest's servant, and *cut off* his ear.
Mk	14 47	one of the bystanders . . . struck out at the high priest's servant, and *cut off* his ear.
Lk	1 25	it has pleased [the Lord] to *take away* the humiliation I suffered among men.
	10 42	It is Mary who has chosen the better part; it is not to be *taken from* her.
	16 3	Now that my master is *taking* the stewardship *from* me, what am I to do?
	22 50	one of [the followers] struck out at the high priest's servant, and *cut off* his right ear.
Ac	7 21	(cf. Ex 2 5) after [Moses] had been exposed, Pharaoh's daughter ┌adopted him (or: *took* him *up*)
	4	
	19 27	5 It could end up by *taking away* all the prestige of [Diana]

Ac 23 27		3	[The tribune] came on the scene with [his] troops and *got* [Paul] *away*,
	27 20		at last ⌐we gave up all hope of surviving (lit. all hope of surviving was *taken away* from us).
	40	2	They ⌐slipped (lit. *cut off*) the anchors and left them to the sea,
2 Co 3 16		2	[The veil is over their minds.] It will not be *removed* until they turn to the Lord.
Heb 10 9 X		4	He is *abolishing* the first sort to replace it with the second
Rv 22 19			if anyone *cuts* anything out of the prophecies in this book, God will *cut off* his share of the tree of life

2: TAKE AWAY (SINS)

Rm 11 27		(Is 27 9 G) this is the covenant I will make with them when I *take* their sins *away*.
Heb 10 4		Bulls' blood and goats' blood are useless for *taking away* sins.
11	2	the same sacrifices . . . are quite incapable of *taking* sins *away*.

5. (BE) TAKEN (UP, AWAY) – (BE) BROUGHT, CARRIED (BACK): *META-TITHĒMI*

2 meta-thesis 1/3   1 meta-tithēmi 3/6

Ac 7 16			[the] bodies [of Jacob and our ancestors] were *brought back* to Shechem
Heb 11 5			Enoch was *taken up* and . . . was not to be found because
Θ	/2		God had *taken* him. This was because before his *assumption* . . . he had pleased God.

6. BRING, CARRY – TAKE – PRODUCE: *PHERŌ*

1		*pherō*	66/68	4		*ek-pherō*	8
6		*phoreō*	6	5		*eis-pherō*	8
7		*phortion*	6	19		*par-eis-pherō*	1
14		*phortizō*	2	15		*epi-pherō*	2
9		*ana-pherō*	5/10	20		*eu-phoreō*	1
8		*apo-pherō*	6	11		*para-pherō*	4
17		*apo-phortizomai*	1	13		*peri-pherō*	3
3		*(karpo-)phoreō*	8	21	*(potamo-)phorētos*		1
18		*(karpo-)phoros*	1	16		*pro-pherō*	2
10		*kata-pherō*	4	2		*pros-pherō*	17/46
12		*dia-pherō*	3/13	22		*sym-pherō*	1/15

1: BRING, (BE) BROUGHT, TAKE (TO) – CARRY (IN, AWAY)

Mt 4 24		2	those who were suffering from diseases . . . were all *brought* to [Jesus], and he cured them.
5 23		2	if you are *bringing* your offering to the altar and there remember that your brother has something against you, [go and be reconciled with him first]
8 16		2	they *brought* [Jesus] many who were possessed by devils.
9 2		2	some people appeared, *bringing* [Jesus] a paralytic
32		2	a man was *brought* to [Jesus], a dumb demoniac.
12 22		2	they *brought* to [Jesus] a blind and dumb demoniac;
14 11			The head [of John the Baptist] was *brought in* on a dish and given to the girl who *took* it to her mother.
18			[We have five loaves and two fish.] *Bring* them here to me
35		2	the local people . . . *took* all that were sick to [Jesus],
17 1 X		9	Jesus . . . *led* [Peter, James and John] up a high mountain
16		2	I *took* [my son] to your disciples and they were unable to cure him.
17			*Bring* [the lunatic boy] here to me.
19 13		2	People *brought* little children to [Jesus],
22 19		2	They *handed* [Jesus] a denarius
25 20			The man who had received the five talents came forward *bringing* five more.
		2	
Mk 1 32			they *brought* to [Jesus] all who were sick and those who were possessed by devils.
2 3			some people came *bringing* [Jesus] a paralytic carried by four men, 4 but . . . the crowd made it impossible to
4		2	⌐get (lit. *bring*) the man to him,
6 27			the king . . . sent one of the bodyguard with orders to *bring* John's head. 28 The man . . . *brought* the head on a dish
28			
55		13	[people] *brought* the sick on stretchers to wherever they heard [Jesus] was.
7 32			they *brought* [Jesus] a deaf man
8 22			some people *brought* to [Jesus] a blind man
23 X		4	[Jesus] took the blind man by the hand and *led* him outside the village.
9 2 X		9	Jesus . . . *led* [Peter, James and John] up a high mountain
17			Master, I have *brought* my son to you . . . 18 . . . I asked
19			your disciples to cast [the spirit] out and they were unable
20			to. 19 . . . [Jesus] said, '. . . *Bring* him to me.' 20 They *brought* the boy to him,

Mk 10 13		2	People were *bringing* little children to [Jesus],
11 2			Untie [the tethered colt] and *bring* it here.
7			they *took* the colt to Jesus
16		12	[Jesus would not] allow anyone to *carry* anything through the Temple.
12 15			Why do you set this trap for me? *Hand* me a denarius . . .
16			16 They *handed* him one
14 36 Θ		11	Abba (Father)! . . . *Take* this cup away from me. But let it be as you, not I, would have it.
15 1		8	the chief priests . . . had Jesus bound and *took* him *away* and handed him over to Pilate.
22		4	They *brought* Jesus to the place called Golgotha,
Lk 5 18			some men appeared, *carrying* on a bed a paralysed man whom
19		5	they were trying to *bring in* . . . 19 But . . . the crowd made
5			it impossible to find a way of ⌐getting him in (lit. *bringing* him in),
12 11		5	When they *take* you before synagogues . . . do not worry
15 22			Quick! *Bring* [out] the best robe and put it on him;
23			*Bring* the calf we have been fattening, and kill it; we are going to have a feast,
16 22 ●		8	the poor man died and was *carried away* . . . to the bosom of Abraham.
18 15		2	People even *brought* little children to [Jesus],
22 42 Θ		11	Father, . . . if you are willing, *take* this cup away from me.
23 14		2	'You *brought* this man before me' [Pilate] said 'as a political agitator.'
26			they seized on a man, Simon from Cyrene, . . . and made him shoulder the cross and *carry* it behind Jesus.
24 1			they went to the tomb ⌐with (lit. *carrying*) the spices
51 ●		9	Now as [Jesus] blessed them, he withdrew from them ˅ and was *carried* up to heaven.⌐
Jn 2 8			Draw some out now . . . and *take* it to the steward. They ⌐did (lit. *took* it to him);
4 33			Has someone been *bringing* [Jesus] food?
19 29		2	they *held* [the sponge soaked in the vinegar] up to his mouth.
39			Nicodemus . . . *brought* a mixture of myrrh and aloes,
20 27			[Jesus] spoke to Thomas, '*Put* your finger here; look, here are my hands. *Give* me your hand; put it into my side.'
21 10			*Bring* some of the fish you have just caught.
18			somebody else will put a belt round you and *take* you where you would rather not go.
Ac 4 34			those who owned land or houses would sell them, and *bring* the money
37			[Barnabas] sold [his land] and *brought* the money,
5 2			[Ananias] kept back part of the proceeds, and *brought* the rest
6		4	The younger men . . . *carried* [Ananias] out and buried [him].
9		4	They have just been to bury your husband; they will *carry*
10		4	you *out*, too. 10 . . . the young men . . . *carried* [Sapphira] *out* and buried her by the side of her husband.
15		4	the sick were even *taken out* into the streets
16			People . . . came crowding in . . . *bringing* with them their sick
7 42		2	(Am 5 25) Did you ⌐bring (or: offer) me . . . sacrifices in the wilderness . . .?
14 13			The ˅ priests (G priest) of Zeus-outside-the-Gate . . . *brought* garlanded oxen to the gates.
19 12		8	handkerchiefs . . . which had touched [Paul] were *taken* to the sick,
19		22	[some believers] who had practised magic *collected* their books and made a bonfire of them
27 15			we had to give way to [the wind] and let ourselves be ⌐driven (or: *carried*).
17			they floated out the sea-anchor and so let themselves ⌐drift (lit. be *carried*).
27		12	we were being ⌐driven (or: *carried*) *one way and another* in the Adriatic,
1 Co 16 3			I will send your offering to Jerusalem ⌐by the hand of (lit.
8			*carried* by) whatever men you give letters of reference to;
1 Tm 6 7		5/4	We *brought* nothing into the world, and we can *take* nothing out of it;
2 Tm 4 13			When you come, *bring* the cloak I left with Carpus in Troas,
Heb 13 11		5	The bodies of the animals whose blood is *brought* into the sanctuary . . . are burnt outside the camp,
Jude 12			[These people] are like clouds blown about by the winds and
11			*bringing* no rain,
Rv 12 15			the serpent vomited water . . . like a river, after the woman,
21			to *sweep* her *away* in the current,
17 3		8	[The angel] *took* me in spirit to a desert,
21 10		8	In the spirit, [the angel] *took* me to the top of an enormous high mountain,
24			the kings of the earth will *bring* [Jerusalem] their treasures . . .
26			26 and the nations will come, *bringing* their treasure and their wealth.

2: BURDEN, BE BURDENED – LOAD, UNLOAD

Mt 11 28		14	Come to me, all you who labour and *are overburdened*,

Mk 11 30 X 7 Yes, my yoke is easy and my *burden* light.
   23 4 7 [The Pharisees] tie up (ᵛ unendurably) heavy *burdens* and lay them on men's shoulders,
Lk 11 46 14 Alas for you lawyers also . . . because you *load* on men
   7/7 *burdens* that are unendurable, *burdens* that you yourselves do not move a finger to lift.
Ac 21 3 17 we . . . put in at Tyre, since the ship was to *unload* her cargo there.
   27 10 7 we run the risk of losing . . . the *cargo* and the ship
Ga 6 5 7 Everyone has his own *burden* to carry.

3: WEAR, BEAR (ON A PERSON)

Mt 11 8 6 those who *wear* fine clothes are to be found in palaces.
Jn 19 5 X 6 Jesus . . . came out *wearing* the crown of thorns
Rm 13 4 6 the *bearing* of the sword has its significance.
1 Co 15 49 ○ 6 we, who have ⸢been modelled on (lit. *worn* the likeness of)
   ○ 6 the earthly man, ⸢will be (ᵛare) ⸢modelled on (lit. *wearing* the likeness of) the heavenly man.
Jm 2 3 6 you take notice of the *well-dressed* man (lit. man *wearing* fine clothes),

4: BRING (AN ACCUSATION, A CASE, AGAINST) – CAST (A VOTE AGAINST)

Jn 18 29 What charge do you *bring* against this man?
Ac 25 7 10 the Jews . . . surrounded [Paul], ⸢making (lit. *bringing* [forward]) many serious accusations
   18 [Paul's accusers did not ⸢charge him with (lit. *bring* a charge against him involving) any of the crimes I had expected;
   26 10 10 when [the saints] were sentenced to death I *cast* my vote against them.
2 P 2 11 the angels . . . ⸢make (lit. *bring*) no complaint or accusation against [the glorious ones]
Jude 9 Not even the archangel Michael . . dared to ⸢denounce
   15 (lit. *bring* an accusation against) [the devil]

5: BRING, CARRY, BEAR (FIGURATIVELY) – LEAD (INTO) – PRODUCE

Mt 6 13 Θ 5 And do not ⸢put (lit. *bring*; or: *lead*) us to the test,
Lk 6 45 16 A good man ⸢draws (or: *produces*) what is good from the
   16 store of goodness in his heart; a bad man ⸢draws (or:
   16 *produces*) what is bad from the store of badness.
   11 4 Θ 5 And do not ⸢put (lit. *bring*; or: *lead*) us to the test.
Ac 2 2 suddenly they heard ⸢what sounded like a powerful wind from heaven (lit. the sound a powerful wind from heaven might *produce*),
   12 10 [The angel and Peter] reached the iron gate *leading* to the city.
   13 49 12 the word of the Lord ⸢spread (lit. was *carried*) through the whole countryside.
   17 20 5 Some of the things you ⸢said (lit. *brought* to our ears) seemed startling to us
   20 9 10 a young man called Eutychus . . . ⸢grew (lit. was *brought*
   10 to be) drowsy and was ⸢overcome (lit. *brought down*) by sleep and fell to the ground three floors below.
Rm 3 5 how can we say God is unjust when . . . he ⸢gets angry with
   Θ 15 (lit. *brings* his anger *upon*) us in return?
2 Co 4 10 13 always, wherever we may be, we *carry* with us in our body the death of Jesus,
Ep 4 14 13 Then we shall not be . . . *carried* along by every wind of doctrine,
Heb 1 3 X [The Son] is the radiant light of God's glory . . . *sustaining* the universe by his powerful command;
   6 1 Let us leave behind us then all the elementary teaching about Christ and ⸢concentrate on (lit. *bring* ourselves to) its completion,
   9 16 wherever a will is in question, the death of the testator must be *established*;
   28 X 9 (Is 53 12) Christ . . . offers himself only once to *take* the faults of many *on* himself,
   13 9 11 Do not *let* yourselves *be led* astray by all sorts of strange doctrines;
   13 Let us go to [Jesus], then, outside the camp, and ⸢share (lit. *bear*) his degradation.
1 P 1 13 put your trust in . . . the grace that will be ⸢ given (lit. *brought* to) you when Jesus Christ is revealed.
   2 24 X 9 [Christ] was *bearing* our faults in his own body on the cross,
2 P 1 5 19 ⸢do your utmost yourselves, adding (lit. *bring* yourselves with the utmost energy *to* add) goodness to the faith that you have,
   17 Θ [Christ] was honoured . . . by God . . . when the Sublime Glory itself ⸢spoke to him and said (lit. was *brought* to him [saying]) . . . ¹⁸ We heard this ourselves, ⸢spoken (lit.
   18 *brought*) from heaven,

2 P 1 21 no prophecy ever ⸢came from (lit. was *produced* by) man's initiative. When men spoke for God it was the Holy Spirit that ⸢moved them (lit. *brought* them to).
2 Jn 10 ⓢ If anyone comes to you *bringing* a different doctrine, you must not receive him

6: BEAR (FRUIT) – YIELD, PRODUCE

Mt 7 18 A sound tree cannot *bear* bad fruit, nor a rotten tree *bear* good fruit.
   13 23 the man who hears the word and understands it . . . is the
   3 one who *yields* a harvest
Mk 4 8 some seeds . . . produced crop; and *yielded* thirty, sixty, even a hundredfold.
   20 there are those who . . . hear the word and accept it and
   3 *yield* a harvest,
   28 3 Of its own accord the land *produces* . . . the shoot,
Lk 8 15 people . . . who have heard the word and take it to them-
   3 selves . . . *yield* a harvest
   12 16 20 There was once a rich man who . . . *had a good harvest* from his land,
Jn 12 24 if [a wheat grain] dies, it *yields* a rich harvest.
   15 2 Every branch in me that *bears* no fruit [my Father] cuts away, and every branch that does *bear* fruit he prunes to
   4 make it *bear* even more . . . ⁴ . . . As a branch cannot
   5 *bear* fruit all by itself . . . neither can you . . . ⁵ . . .
   8 Whoever remains in me, with me in him, *bears* fruit in plenty . . . ⁸ It is to the glory of my Father that you should *bear* much fruit,
   16 I commissioned you to go out and to *bear* fruit,
Ac 14 17 [God] sends you rain from heaven, ⸢he makes your crops
   18 grow when they should (lit. and *fruitful* times [of the year]),
Rm 7 4 you . . . can now give yourselves . . . to him who rose from
   5 3 the dead to *make* us *productive* for God. ⁵ Before our conversion our sinful passions . . . fertilised our bodies to
   3 make them ⸢give birth to (lit. *bear* fruit for) death.
Col 1 6 3 [the Good News] is spreading all over the world and *producing* the same results as it has among you
   10 you will be able to lead . . . a life acceptable to [God] . . .
   3 ⸢showing the results (lit. *bearing* fruit) in . . . good actions
Heb 6 8 4 [a field] that *grows* brambles and thistles is abandoned,

7. BRING, BROUGHT: *KOMIZŌ*

komizō 1/12

Lk 7 37 [a woman] had *brought* with her an alabaster jar of ointment.

8. LEAD (AWAY, OUT) – BRING – TAKE: *AGŌ*

1	agō	58/67	14	ep-eis-agōgē	1
6	an-agō	5/23	15	par-eis-aktos	1
2	ap-agō	17	16	par-eis-agō	1
9	syn-ap-agō	3	10	ep-agō	3
5	kat-agō	9	12	met-agō	2
11	(cheir-)agōgeō	2	17	peri-agō	1/6
13	(cheir-)agōgos	1	8	pro-agō	4/20
3	ex-agō	12	7	pros-agō	5
4	eis-agō	11			

X = Lead Jesus

1: LEAD AWAY, LEAD OUT (TO) – BRING (OUT, TO) – TAKE (TO)

a) Lead, Bring, Take (to a place)

Mt 4 1 X 6 Jesus was *led* by the Spirit *out* into the wilderness
   21 2 Untie [the tethered donkey and the colt] and *bring* them to me.
   7 [The disciples] *brought* the donkey and the colt,
   27 31 X 2 [the soldiers] *led* him *away* to crucify him.
Mk 14 44 X 2 Take [the one I kiss] in charge, and . . . *lead* him *away*,
   15 16 X 2 The soldiers *led* him *away* to the inner part of the palace,
   20 X 3 They *led* him *out* to crucify him.
Lk 4 1 X 6 Jesus . . . was *led* by the Spirit *out* through the wilderness,
   5 X 6 ⸢leading him *to a height* (or: taking him up), the devil showed him . . . all the kingdoms of the world
   9 X Then [the devil] *led* him to Jerusalem
   29 X [the Nazarenes] *took* him *up* to the brow of the hill
   40 all those who had friends suffering from diseases . . *brought* them to [Jesus],
   5 11 5 *bringing* their boats [back] to land, [Simon and his companions] left everything and followed [Jesus]
   9 41 7 *Bring* your son *here*.

Lk 10 34   [the Samaritan] *carried* [the wounded man] to the inn
13 15   Is there one of you who does not untie his ox . . . on the
   2   sabbath and *take* it *out* for watering?
18 40   Jesus stopped and ordered them to *bring* [the blind man] to him,
19 27   as for my enemies . . . *bring* them here and execute them
   30   Untie [the tethered colt] and *bring* it here.
   35   So they *took* the colt to Jesus,
23 26 X 2 As they were *leading* him *away* they seized on a man, Simon from Cyrene,
   32 X with him they were also *leading out* two other criminals
24 50 3 [Jesus] *took* [the apostles] *out* as far as the outskirts of Bethany,
Jn 1 42   [Andrew] *took* Simon to Jesus.
10 3   one by one [the shepherd] calls his own sheep and *leads* them *out.*
19 4 X Pilate said . . , 'I am going to *bring* him *out* to you'
   13 X Pilate had Jesus *brought out,*
Ac 5 19 3 the angel . . . opened the prison gates and . . . *led* [the apostles] *out,*
8 32 X (Is 53 7) Like a sheep that is *led away* to the slaughter-house,
9 2   [Saul] asked for letters . . . that would authorise him to arrest and *take* to Jerusalem any followers of the Way,
   8 11 they had to *lead* [Saul] into Damascus by the hand
   21   [Saul] came here for the sole purpose of ⌐arresting [Christians] to have them tried by (lit. *taking* them as prisoners before) the chief priests
   30 5 the brothers . . . *took* [Saul] to Caesarea,
   39 6 on his arrival they *took* [Peter] to the upstairs room
11 26   [Barnabas] *brought* [Saul] to Antioch.
12 17 3 [Peter] described . . . how the Lord had *led* him *out* of prison.
   19   Herod . . . gave orders ⌐for [the] execution [of Peter's guards]
○   2 (lit. for them to be *led away* to execution)
13 11 13 [Elymas] groped about to find *someone to lead him* by the hand.
16 30   [The gaoler threw himself at the feet of Paul and Silas,] and
   8   *escorted* them out,
   34 6 [the gaoler] *took* them home and gave them a meal
   37 3 [The magistrates] must come and *escort* us *out* themselves.
   39 3 They came, (§ *brought* them *out*) and begged them to leave the town.
17 15   Paul's escort *took* him as far as Athens,
   19   [The Athenians] ⌐invited [Paul] to accompany them (lit. *took* him) to the Council of the Areopagus,
20 12   They *took* [Eutychus] away alive,
21 16   Some of the disciples . . . *took* us to the house of . . . Mnason
   34   the tribune ordered Paul to be *taken* into the fortress.
   38 3 So you are not the Egyptian who . . . *led* those four thousand cut-throats *out* into the desert?
22 5   I set off . . . with the intention of *bringing* prisoners back from [Damascus] to Jerusalem for punishment.
   11 11 I was blind and my companions had to *take* me by the hand;
23 10   the tribune . . . ordered his troops to . . . *bring* [Paul] into the fortress.
   17 2/ *Take* this young man to the tribune . . . ¹⁸ So the man *took*
   18   [the son of Paul's sister] to the tribune, and reported, '. . . Paul . . . requested me to *bring* this young man to you
   31   The soldiers . . . took Paul and *escorted* him . . . to Antipatris.
24 7 2 ⱽ the tribune Lysias intervened and *took* [Paul] out of our hands by force,
27 27   the crew sensed that ⌐land of some sort was near (lit. we were
   7   being *brought* to land of some sort).
1 Co 9 5 17 [Have we not every right to] *take* a Christian woman round with us?
1 Th 4 14   it will be the same for those who have died in Jesus: God will *bring* them with him.
2 Tm 4 11   Get Mark to come and *bring* him with you;
Rv 13 10 2 (Jr 15 2) Captivity for those who ⌐are destined for (ⱽ *lead* [others] into) captivity;

b) Lead out, Bring out (of Egypt)

Ac 7 36 3 It was Moses who . . . *led* them *out* across the Red Sea
   40 3 (Ex 32 1 G) this Moses . . . *led* us *out* of Egypt.
13 17 3 By divine power . . . [God] *led* [our people] *out* [of Egypt].
Heb 8 9 3 (Jr 31 32) I took them by the hand to *bring* them *out* of the land of Egypt.

c) Lead away (to), Bring (before), Take (to a person in authority)

Mt 10 18   You will be *dragged* before governors . . . to bear witness
18 24 7 they *brought* [the king] a man who owed ten thousand talents;
26 57 X 2 The men who had arrested Jesus *led* him *off* to Caiaphas
27 2 X 2 They had him bound, and *led* him *away* . . . to Pilate,
Mk 13 11   when they *lead* you *away* to hand you over, do not worry
14 53 X 2 They *led* Jesus *off* to the high priest;
Lk 21 12 2 men will . . . *bring* you before kings . . . because of my name

---

Lk 22 54 X [The soldiers] seized him then and *led* him *away,*
   66 X 2 He was *brought* before [the Sanhedrin],
23 1 X [the Sanhedrin] *brought* him before Pilate.
Jn 7 45   [the Pharisees] said to [the police], 'Why haven't you
   X   *brought* him?'
8 3   The scribes and Pharisees *brought* a woman along who had been caught committing adultery;
9 13   They *brought* the man who had been blind to the Pharisees
18 13 X They *took* him first to Annas,
   28 X they *led* Jesus from the house of Caiaphas to the Praetorium.
Ac 5 21   [the Sanhedrin] sent to the gaol for [the apostles] to be *brought.*
   26   The captain went with his men and *fetched* them.
   27   When they had *brought* them in to face the Sanhedrin, the high priest demanded an explanation.
6 12   they . . . *brought* [Stephen] before the Sanhedrin.
9 27   Barnabas . . . ⌐introduced (or: *brought*) [Saul] to the apostles,
12 4 6 Herod meant to ⌐try Peter in public (lit. *bring* him before the people) after the end of Passover week . . . ⁶ On the night
   6 8 before Herod was to ⌐try him (lit. *bring* him before the people), Peter was sleeping
16 20   [The slave-girl soothsayer's masters] charged [Paul and Silas]
   7   having *brought* them *before* the magistrates
17 5   [The Jews hoped] to find [Paul and Silas at Jason's house]
   8   and *drag* them *off* to the People's Assembly;
18 12   the Jews . . . *brought* [Paul] before the tribunal.
19 37   These men you have *brought* here are not guilty of any sacrilege
22 30 5 [the tribune] *brought* Paul *down* and stood him in front of [the Sanhedrin].
23 15 5 apply to the tribune to *bring* [Paul] *down*
   20 5 The Jews have made a plan to ask you to *take* Paul *down* to the Sanhedrin tomorrow,
   28 5 I *brought* him before their Sanhedrin.
25 6   [Festus] had Paul *brought* in.
   17   I . . . had the man *brought* in.
   23   Festus ordered Paul to be *brought* in.
26 8 that is why I have *produced* [Paul] before you all,

d) Lead (figuratively) to, Be led (to) – Bring (upon)

Ⓢ = being led by the Spirit

Mt 7 13 2 the road that *leads* to perdition is wide and spacious,
   14 2 it is a narrow gate and a hard road that *leads* to life,
Jn 10 16   there are other sheep I have . . . and these I have to *lead* as well.
Ac 5 28 10 You . . . seem determined to ⌐fix (lit. *bring*) the guilt of this man's death on us.
13 23 X God has ⱽ raised up (G *brought*) for Israel . . . Jesus, as Saviour,
Rm 2 4   this goodness of God is meant to *lead* you to repentance
8 14 Ⓢ Everyone *moved* by the Spirit is a son of God.
12 16 9 ⌐Make real friends (lit. *Bring* yourself *into* real *contact*) with the poor.
1 Co 12 2 △ when you were pagans, whenever you felt irresistibly *drawn,*
   2   ⌐it was (lit. are *drawn*) towards dumb idols
Ga 2 13 9 even Barnabas ⌐felt himself obliged (or: *brought* himself) to copy [the] behaviour [of the group that insisted on circumcision].
   5 18 Ⓢ If you are *led* by the Spirit, no law can touch you.
2 Tm 3 6   silly women . . . ⌐follow (lit. are *led* into) one craze after another
1 P 3 18 7 Christ . . . died for the guilty, to *lead* us *to* God.
2 P 2 1   false teachers . . . will ⌐destroy themselves very quickly
   10   (lit. *bring upon* themselves a speedy perdition).
   5 10 [God] *sent* the Flood *over* a disobedient world.
3 17 9 be careful not to get *carried* away by the errors of unprincipled people,

e) Bring down (from heaven)

Rm 10 6 5 Do not tell yourself you have to *bring* Christ *down*

2: DIRECT, CONTROL

Jm 3 3   Once we put a bit into the horse's mouth . . . we have the
   12   whole animal under our *control.*
   4   no matter how big [ships] are . . . the man at the helm can
   12   steer them . . . by *controlling* a tiny rudder.

3: BRING IN

a) Bring in

Lk 2 27 X 4 the parents *brought* in the child Jesus
14 21 4 *bring* in here the poor, the crippled, the blind
22 54 X 4 they *took* him to the high priest's house.
Jn 18 16   the other disciple . . . spoke to the woman who was keeping
   4   the door and *brought* Peter *in.*

Ac 7 45   4 Joshua *brought* [the Tent of Testimony] *into* the country we had conquered

9 8   they had to lead [Saul] ᶠ*into* Damascus by the hand (lit. by
4   the hand to *bring* him *into* Damascus).

21 28   4 [Paul] has profaned this Holy Place by *bringing* Greeks *into* the Temple.

29   4 They . . . thought that Paul had *brought* [the Ephesian] *into* the Temple.

37   4 Paul was being *taken into* the fortress,

22 24   4 the tribune had [Paul] *brought into* the fortress

b) Bring in (figuratively) – Introduce

Ac 9 27   Barnabas . . . ᶠ*introduced* (or: brought) [Saul] to the apostles

Ga 2 4 15 some . . . have furtively *crept in* to spy on the liberty we enjoy in Christ Jesus,

Heb 1 6 X 4 when [God] *brings* the First-born *into* the world, he says:

2 10   it was [God's] purpose to *bring* a great many of his sons into the glory,

7 19 14 [The Law] is replaced by something better [now] *introduced* – the hope that brings us nearer to God.

2 P 2 1 16 you too will have your false teachers, who will *insinuate* their own disruptive views

c) Put in (at a port)

Ac 27 3   5 Next day we *put in* at Sidon, and Julius [allowed] Paul to go to his friends

28 12   5 We *put in* at Syracuse and spent three days there

9. TO, LEAD TO (DEATH) – END IN (DEATH): *PROS*

pros (+ accusative) (5)

Jn 11 4   This sickness will *end* not *in* death but in God's glory

Jn 5 16   If anybody sees his brother commit a sin that ᶠis not a deadly sin (lit. will not *lead to* his death), he has only to pray, and God will give life to the sinner – not those who commit ᶠa deadly sin (lit. a sin that *leads to* death); for there is a sin that ᶠis (lit. *leads to*) death . . .

17   ¹⁷ Every kind of wrongdoing is sin, but not all sin ᶠis deadly (lit. *leads to* death).

10. ESCORT – CONDUCT: *KATH-ISTĒMI*

kath-istēmi 1/21

Ac 17 15   ᶠPaul's escort (lit. those who were *escorting* Paul) took him as far as Athens,

11. ESCORT – SEND A PERSON ON HIS WAY – HELP A PERSON ON HIS JOURNEY: *PRO-PEMPŌ*

pro-pempō 9

Ac 15 3   the church [at Antioch] *saw* [Paul and Barnabas] *off*,

20 38   [the elders of the church at Ephesus] *escorted* [Paul] to the ship.

21 5   when . . . we set off . . . they all *escorted* us *on our way*

Rm 15 24   I hope to . . . ᶠcomplete the rest of the journey (lit. *be sent on my way*) with your good wishes.

1 Co 16 6   I may be staying with you . . . to make sure that it is you who *send* me *on my way* wherever my travels take me.

11   *Send* [Timothy] happily *on his way* to come back to me;

2 Co 1 16   coming back to you again . . . for you to *see* me *on my way* to Judaea.

Tt 3 13   See to all the *travelling arrangements* for Zenas the lawyer

3 Jn 6   it would be a very good thing if you could *help* [the brothers] *on their journey*

TAX

| 1. Tax, Taxes – Tribute: *kēnsos* | 3. Tax collector – Tax office, Customs house – Pay (tax), Toll: *telos* |
| 2. Tax, Taxes – Tribute: *phoros* | |

1. TAX, TAXES – TRIBUTE: *KĒNSOS*

kēnsos 4

Mt 17 25   From whom do the kings of the earth take toll or *tribute*?

Mt 22 17   Is it permissible to pay *taxes* to Caesar or not?
19   Let me see the money you pay the *tax* with.

Mk 12 14   Is it permissible to pay *taxes* to Caesar or not?

2. TAX, TAXES – TRIBUTE: *PHOROS*

phoros 5

Lk 20 22   Is it permissible for us to pay *taxes* to Caesar or not?

23 2   We found this man . . . opposing payment of the *tribute* to Caesar,

Rm 13 6   [You must obey the law for conscience' sake.] This is also the reason why you must pay *taxes*, . . . ⁷ Pay every government official what he has a right to ask – *tax* if *taxes*, toll if toll, respect if respect or honour if honour.

3. TAX COLLECTOR – TAX OFFICE, CUSTOMS HOUSE – PAY (TAX), TOLL: *TELOS*

4	*teleō*	2/28		*Matthew*	5
2	*telos*	3/41	M {	= ? *Levi*	3
1	*tel-ōnēs*	21		[son] of *Alphaeus**	1
3	*tel-ōnion*	3	Z	*Zacchaeus*	3
5	(*archi-*)*tel-ōnēs*	1			

Mt 5 46   Even the *tax collectors* do as much,

9 9 M 3 Jesus . . . saw a man named *Matthew* sitting by the *customs house*, and he said to him, 'Follow me'. . . .

10   ¹⁰ . . . a number of *tax collectors* and sinners came to sit at the table with Jesus . . .

11   ¹¹ . . . the Pharisees . . . said to his disciples, 'Why does your master eat with *tax collectors* and sinners?'

10 3 M   [the twelve apostles: . . .] Thomas, and *Matthew* the *tax collector*;

11 19   The Son of Man . . , a friend of *tax collectors* and sinners.

17 24 4 Does your master not *pay* the half-shekel?

25 2 From whom do the kings of the earth take *toll* or tribute?

18 17   if he refuses to listen to the community, treat him like a pagan or a *tax collector*.

21 31   *tax collectors* and prostitutes are making their way into the kingdom of God before you. ³² For John came to you, . . .

32   but you did not believe him, and yet the *tax collectors* and prostitutes did.

Mk 2 14 M   [Jesus] saw *Levi* (ᵛ James), [the son] of Alphaeus*, sitting by the
3   *customs house*, and he said to him, 'Follow me'. . .

15   ¹⁵ . . . a number of *tax collectors* and sinners were also

16   sitting at the table with Jesus . . . ¹⁶ . . . the scribes . . . said to his disciples, 'Why does he eat with *tax collectors* and sinners?'

3 18 M   [the Twelve . . .] *Matthew*, Thomas,

Lk 3 12   *tax collectors* too . . . came for baptism,

5 27 M   [Jesus] noticed a *tax collector*, *Levi* by name, sitting by the
29 M 3 *customs house*, and said to him, 'Follow me'. . . . ²⁹ In his honour *Levi* held a great reception in his house and with them at table was a large gathering of *tax collectors* and

30   others. ³⁰ The Pharisees and their scribes complained to his disciples and said, 'Why do you eat and drink with *tax collectors* and sinners?'

6 15 M   [he called them 'apostles'; . . .] *Matthew*, Thomas,

7 29   [Jesus said,] 'All the people who heard [John], and the *tax collectors* too, . . . [accepted] baptism

34   The Son of Man, . . . a friend of *tax collectors* and sinners.

15 1   The *tax collectors* and the sinners . . . were all seeking [Jesus's] company

18 10   Two men went up to the Temple to pray, one a Pharisee, the other a *tax collector*. ¹¹ The Pharisee . . . said this

11   prayer . . , 'I thank you, God, that . . . I am not like this *tax collector* here.' . . . ¹³ The *tax collector* stood some

13   distance away, . . . and said, 'God, be merciful to me, a sinner'.

19 2 Z   a man whose name was *Zacchaeus* made his appearance; he
5   was one of the senior *tax collectors* and a wealthy man.

5 Z   *Zacchaeus*, come down. Hurry, because I must stay at your house today.

8 Z   *Zacchaeus* . . . said to the Lord, '. . . I am going to give half my property to the poor,'

Ac 1 13   [the apostles] went up to the upper room . . .; there were . . .
M   Bartholomew and *Matthew*,

Rm 13 6   [You must obey the law for conscience' sake.] This is also
7 4 the reason why you must *pay* taxes, . . . ⁷ Pay every government official what he has a right to ask – tax if taxes,
2/2   *toll* if *toll*, respect if respect or honour if honour.

TEACHING

1. Master – Teaching – Instruction
1: Master – Teach – Instructed: *didaskō*
  a) "Master", "Teacher" = Jesus
  b) (Jesus) Teaches, Taught
  c) (God, the Spirit, the Apostles) Teach, Taught – Teacher – Doctrine, Instruction
  d) Teach, Taught – Teacher, Doctor – Doctrine
2: Master, Rabbi
  a) Rabbi = Jesus

  b) various
3: Instructed, Informed, Told – Hear, Receive Information: *kat-ēcheō*
4: (Be) Initiated – Ready: *myeō*
5: Lecture room, Hall: *scholē*
2. Teach – Discipline: *paideuō*
1: Teach, Train, Guardian – Correct, Discipline, Punish
2: Ignorant – Futile, Senseless
3. Teach, Advise – Warn – Admonish: *nou-theteō*

1. MASTER – TEACHING – INSTRUCTION

1: MASTER – TEACH – INSTRUCTED: *DIDASKŌ*

3	*didachē*	30	9	(kalo-)*didaskalos* 1
7	*didaktikos*	2	8	(hetero-)*didaskaleō* 2
5	*didaktos*	3	6	(nomo-)*didaskalos* 3
4	*didaskalia*	21	10	(pseudo-)*didaskalos* 1
2	*didaskalos*	59	11	(theo-)*didaktos* 1
1	*didaskō*	97		

a) "Master", "Teacher" = Jesus

Mt 8 19 2 One of the scribes . . . said to him, 'Master, I will follow you wherever you go.'
  9 11 2 Why does your *master* eat with tax collectors and sinners?
  10 24 2 The disciple is not superior to his *teacher*,
      25   It is enough for the disciple that he should grow to be like his *teacher*,
  12 38 2 *Master*, . . . we should like to see a sign from you.
  17 24 2 Does your *master* not pay the half-shekel?
  19 16 2 *Master*, what good deed must I do to possess eternal life?
  22 16 2 *Master*, we know that you . . . teach the way of God in an honest way,
      24 2 *Master*, Moses said that if a man dies childless,
      36 2 *Master*, which is the greatest commandment of the Law?
  23 8   You . . . must not allow yourselves to be called Rabbi,
        2 since you have only one *Master*,
  26 18 2 The *Master* says: my time is near.
Mk 4 39 2 *Master*, do you not care? We are going down!
  5 35 2 why put the *Master* to any further trouble?
  9 17 2 *Master*, I have brought my son to you;
     38 2 *Master*, we saw a man . . . casting out devils in your name;
  10 17 2 Good *master*, what must I do to inherit eternal life?
     20 2 *Master*, I have kept all these from my earliest days.
     35 2 *Master*, . . . we want you to do us a favour.
  12 14 2 *Master*, we know you are an honest man,
     19 2 *Master*, we have it from Moses in writing,
     32 2 Well spoken, *Master*; what you have said is true:
  13 1 2 Look at the size of those stones, *Master*!
  14 14 2 The *Master* says: where is my dining room . . .?
Lk 6 40 2 The disciple is not superior to his *teacher*; the fully trained
        2 disciple will always be like his *teacher*.
  7 40 2 'Simon, I have something to say to you'. 'Speak, *Master*'
  8 49 2 Do not trouble the *Master* any further.
  9 38 2 *Master*, . . . I implore you to look at my son:
  10 25 2 *Master*, what must I do to inherit eternal life?
  11 45 2 '*Master*,' [the lawyer] said, 'when you speak like this you insult us too.'
  12 13 2 *Master*, tell my brother to give me a share of our inheritance.
  18 18 2 Good *Master*, what have I to do to inherit eternal life?
  19 39 2 *Master*, check your disciples,
  20 21 2 *Master*, we know that you say . . . what is right:
     28 2 *Master*, we have it from Moses in writing,
     39 2 Some scribes then spoke up. 'Well put, *Master*' they said
  21 7 2 *Master*, when will this happen . . .?
  22 11 2 The *Master* has this to say to you: Where is the dining room in which I can eat the passover . . .?
Jn 1 38 2 They answered, 'Rabbi,' – which means *Teacher*
  3 2 2 Rabbi, we know that you are a *teacher* who comes from God;
  8 4 2 *Master*, this woman was caught in the very act of committing adultery,
  11 28   [Martha] called her sister Mary, saying . . . 'The *Master*
        2 is here and wants to see you.'
  13 13 2 You call me *Master* and Lord . . .; so I am. [14] If I, then,
     14 2 the Lord and *Master*, have washed your feet,
  20 16   [Mary of Magdala] knew him then and said . . . 'Rabbuni!'
        2 – which means *Master*.

b) (Jesus) Teaches, Taught

Mt 4 23   He went round the whole of Galilee *teaching* in their synagogues,
  5 2   Then he began to speak. This is what he *taught* them:
  7 28 3 his *teaching* made a deep impression on the people [29] because
     29   he *taught* them with authority.
  9 35   Jesus made a tour through all the towns and villages, *teaching* in their synagogues,
  11 1   Jesus . . . moved on from there to *teach* and preach in their towns.
  13 54   coming to his home town, he *taught* the people in their synagogue
  21 23   He had gone into the Temple and was *teaching*,
  22 16   Master, we know that you . . . *teach* the way of God in an honest way,
     33 3 his *teaching* made a deep impression on the people who heard it.
  26 55   I sat *teaching* in the Temple day after day
Mk 1 21   he went to the synagogue [at Capernaum] and began to
     22 /3 *teach*. [22] And his *teaching* made a deep impression on them because . . . he *taught* them with authority.
     27 3 Here is a *teaching* . . . with authority behind it:
  2 13   the people came to him, and he *taught* them.
  4 1   Again he began to *teach* by the lakeside.
    2   He *taught* them many things in parables, and in the course of
       3 his *teaching* he said to them,
  6 2   he began *teaching* in the synagogue [at Nazareth]
    6   He made a tour round the villages, *teaching*,
    34   he set himself to *teach* [the people] at some length.
  8 31   he began to *teach* [the disciples] that the Son of Man was destined to suffer grievously,
  9 31   he was *instructing* his disciples; '. . . The Son of Man will be delivered into the hands of men;
  10 1   and again he *taught* [the crowds],
  11 17   he *taught* [those who were buying and selling in the Temple] and said, '. . . My house will be called a house of prayer
    18 3 the people were carried away by his *teaching*.
  12 14   Master, we know . . . that you *teach* the way of God in all honesty.
    35   while *teaching* in the Temple, Jesus said, 'How can the scribes . . .?'
    38 3 In his *teaching* he said, 'Beware of the scribes
  14 49   I was among you *teaching* in the Temple day after day
Lk 4 15   He *taught* in their synagogues
    31 /3 He . . . *taught* them on the sabbath. [32] And his *teaching* made a deep impression on them
    32
  5 3   he . . . *taught* the crowds from the boat.
    17   he was *teaching* one day, and among the audience there were Pharisees
  6 6   on another sabbath he went into the synagogue and began to *teach*,
  11 1   Lord, *teach* us to pray, just as John taught his disciples.
  13 10   One sabbath day he was *teaching* in one of the synagogues,
    22   Through towns and villages he went *teaching*,
    26   you *taught* in our streets
  19 47   He *taught* in the Temple every day.
  20 1   while he was *teaching* the people in the Temple and proclaiming the Good News,
    21   Master, we know that you say and *teach* what is right; you . . . *teach* the way of God in all honesty.
  21 37   In the daytime he would be in the Temple *teaching*,
  23 5   He is inflaming the people with his *teaching* all over Judaea;
Jn 6 59   He *taught* the doctrine at Capernaum, in the synagogue.
  7 14   Jesus went to the Temple and began to *teach*.
    16 3 My *teaching* is not from myself: it comes from the one who sent me;
    17 3 he will know whether my *teaching* is from God or . . . my own.
    28   as Jesus *taught* in the Temple,
    35   will he *teach* the Greeks?
  8 2   he appeared in the Temple again; and as all the people came to him, he . . . began to *teach* them.
    20   He spoke these words in the Treasury, while *teaching* in the Temple.
  18 19   The high priest questioned Jesus about his disciples and his
    20 3/ *teaching*. [20] Jesus answered, '. . . I have always *taught* in the synagogue and in the Temple.
Ac 1 1   everything Jesus had done and *taught*

c) (God, the Spirit, the Apostles) Teach, Taught – Teacher – Doctrine, Instruction

Mt 5 19   but the man who keeps [the least of these commandments] and *teaches* them will be considered great in the kingdom of heaven.
  28 20   *teach* [all the nations] to observe all the commands I gave you.
Mk 6 30   The apostles rejoined Jesus and told him all they had done and *taught*.
Lk 12 12 Ⓢ the Holy Spirit will *teach* you what you must say.
Jn 6 45 5 (Is 54 13) They will all be *taught* by God.

Jn	7	16	3 My *teaching* is not from myself: it comes from the one who sent me:
		17	3 he will know whether my *teaching* is from God or . . . my own.
	8	28	what the Father has *taught* me is what I preach;
	9	34	Are you trying to *teach* us, . . . and you a sinner through and through
	14	26 ⑤	but the Advocate, the Holy Spirit, . . . will *teach* you everything
Ac	2	42	3 These remained faithful to the *teaching* of the apostles
	4	2	[The priests] were extremely annoyed at [Peter and John's] *teaching* the people
		18	[the Sanhedrin] gave [Peter and John] a warning on no account to . . . *teach* in the name of Jesus.
	5	21	[the apostles] went into the Temple at dawn and began to *preach*.
		25	the men you imprisoned are . . . *preaching* to the people.
		28	We gave you a formal warning . . not to *preach* in this name,
		3	. . . You have filled Jerusalem with your *teaching*,
		42	[The apostles] *preached* every day both in the Temple and in private houses,
	11	26	[Barnabas and Saul] were to live together [at Antioch] a whole year, *instructing* a large number of people.
	13	1	In the church at Antioch the following were prophets and
		2	*teachers*: Barnabas, Simeon called Niger, and Lucius of Cyrene, Manaen . . . and Saul.
		12	The proconsul . . . became a believer, being astonished
	Θ	3	by *what he had learnt* about the Lord.
	15	35	Paul and Barnabas . . . *taught* and proclaimed the Good News,
	17	19	3 How much of this new *teaching* . . . are we allowed to know?
	18	11	Paul stayed [in Corinth] *preaching* the word of God
		25	[Apollos] was accurate in all the details he *taught* about Jesus,
	20	20	I have preached to you, and *instructed* you
	21	21	you *instruct* all Jews living among the pagans to break away from Moses,
		28	This is the man who *preaches* to everyone everywhere against our people,
	28	31	proclaiming the kingdom of God and *teaching* the truth about the Lord Jesus Christ.
Rm	6	17	you submitted without reservation to the ⌜creed (lit. pattern
		3	of *teaching*) you were taught
	12	7	4/ if [your gift is] *teaching*, then use it for *teaching*.
	15	4	everything that was written long ago in the scriptures was
		4	meant to *teach* us something about hope
	16	17	be on your guard against anybody who . . . puts difficulties
		3	in the way of the *doctrine* you have been taught.
1 Co	2	13 ⑤	5 we teach . . . in the way that the Spirit *teaches* us:
	4	17	the way that I live in Christ, as I *teach* it everywhere
	12	28	God has given the first place to apostles, the second to pro-
		29	2 phets, the third to *teachers*; . . . ²⁹ Are all of them apostles,
		2	or all . . . prophets, or all . . . *teachers*?
	14	6	what use shall I be if my talking . . . neither inspires you
		3	nor *instructs* you?
		26	At all your meetings, let everyone be ready with a psalm
		3	or ⌜a *sermon* (or: *instruction*)
Ga	1	12	[the Good News I preached is not a human message] that I was given by men, in Christ, it is something I ⌜learnt (lit. was *taught*) through a revelation
Ep	4	11	to some, [Christ's] gift was that they should be . . . pastors
		2	and *teachers*,
		21	[that is hardly the way you have learnt from Christ] unless you failed to hear him properly when you were *taught* what the truth is in Jesus.
Col	1	28	this is the wisdom in which we thoroughly . . . *instruct* everyone,
	2	7	you must be . . . held firm by the faith you have been *taught*,
	3	16	Teach each other, and ⌜*advise* (or: *instruct*) each other, in all wisdom.
1 Th	4	9	11 you have ⌜learnt (lit. been *taught*) from God yourselves to love one another,
2 Th	2	15	keep the traditions that we *taught* you,
1 Tm	1	10	[laws are for] perjurors — and for everything else that is
		4	contrary to the sound *teaching* [that goes with the Good News]
	2	7	I have been named a herald and apostle of [Christ's sacrifices]
		2	and . . . a *teacher* of the faith and the truth to the pagans.
		12	I am not giving permission for a woman to *teach*
	3	2	7 The president must . . . be . . . a good *teacher*;
	4	6	you will . . . show that you have really digested the ⌜*teaching*
		4	(lit. words) of the faith and the good *doctrine* which you have always followed.
		11	This is what you are to enforce in your *teaching*.
		16	4 Take great care about what you do and what you *teach*;
	5	17	especially those [elders] who are assiduous in preaching and
		4	*teaching*.
	6	1	4 so that the name of God and our *teaching* are not brought into disrepute.
		2	This is what you are to *teach* them to believe

1 Tm	6	3	Anyone who teaches anything different, and does not keep
		4	to the . . . *doctrine* which is in accordance with true religion,
2 Tm	1	11	[Jesus has proclaimed life and immortality through the Good News;] and I have been named its herald, its apostle and
		2	its *teacher*.
	2	2	they in turn will be able to *teach* others.
		24	7 a servant of the Lord . . . has to be . . . a good *teacher*,
	3	10	4 You know . . . what I have *taught*,
		16	4 All scripture . . . can profitably be used for *teaching*
	4	2	Refute falsehood, correct error, call to obedience — but do
		3	all . . . with the intention of *teaching*.
		3	The time is sure to come when, far from being content with
		4	sound *teaching*, people will be avid for . . . novelty
Tt	1	9	[the president] must have a firm grasp of the unchanging
		3	message of the *tradition*, so that he can be counted on for
		4	. . . expounding the sound *doctrine*.
	2	1	4 preach the behaviour which goes with healthy *doctrine*.
		3	9 the older women . . . are to be the *teachers* of the right behaviour
		7	4 when you are *teaching*, be an example . . . in your sincerity
		10	4 [the slaves] must [be] in every way a credit to the *teaching* of God
Heb	5	12	2 when you should by this time have become *masters*, you need someone to *teach* you all over again.
	6	2	3 [fundamental doctrines:] the *teaching* about baptisms and the laying-on of hands;
	8	11	(Jr 31 34) There will be no further need for neighbour to try to *teach* neighbour,
Jm	3	1	2 Only a few of you, my brothers, should be *teachers*,
1 Jn	2	27	you do not need anyone to *teach* you; the anointing [Christ] gave *teaches* you everything; you are anointed with truth, . . . and as it has *taught* you, so you must stay in him.
2 Jn		9	3 If anybody does not keep within the *teaching* of Christ, . . . he cannot have God with him: only those who keep
		3	to *what he taught* can have the Father and the Son with them.
		10	If anyone comes to you ⌜bringing a different (or: not bringing
		3	this) *doctrine* you must not receive him

d) Teach, Taught – Teacher, Doctor – Doctrine

Mt	5	19	the man who infringes even one of the least of these commandments and *teaches* others to do the same
	15	9	4/ (Is 29 13) the *doctrines* they *teach* are only human regulations.
	16	12	[Jesus] was telling [the disciples] to be on their guard . . .
		3	against the *teaching* of the Pharisees
	28	15	The soldiers . . . carried out their *instructions*,
Mk	7	7	4/ (Is 29 13) the *doctrines* they *teach* are only human regulations.
Lk	2	46	2 they found him in the Temple, sitting among the *doctors*,
	3	12	[tax collectors] said to [John the Baptist], 'Master, what must we do?
	5	17	6 among the audience there were Pharisees and *doctors* of the Law
	11	1	Lord, teach us to pray, just as John *taught* his disciples.
Jn	3	10	2 'You, [Nicodemus] a *teacher* in Israel, and you do not know these things!' replied Jesus.
Ac	5	34	6 Gamaliel, who was a *doctor* of the Law and respected by the whole people,
	15	1	some men . . . *taught* the brothers, 'Unless you have yourselves circumcised
Rm	2	20	[If you call yourself a Jew,] if you can teach the ignorant and
		21	2/ *instruct* the unlearned . . , ²¹ then why not *teach* yourself as well as *teaching* the others?
1 Co	2	13	5 we teach, not in the way in which philosophy is *taught*,
	11	14	[Ask yourselves] whether nature itself does not *tell* you that long hair on a man is nothing to be admired,
Ep	4	14	Then we shall not be . . . carried along by every wind of
		4	*doctrine*
Col	2	22	4 an example of human *doctrines* and regulations!
1 Tm	1	3	8 to insist that certain people stop *teaching* strange doctrines
		7	6 they claim to be *doctors* of the Law
	4	1	there will be some who will desert the faith and choose to
		4	listen to . . . *doctrines* that come from the devils;
	6	3	8 Anyone who *teaches* anything different, and does not keep to . . . the doctrine which is in accordance with true religion,
2 Tm	4	3	2 people will . . . collect themselves a whole series of *teachers*
Tt	1	11	men of this kind ruin whole families, by *teaching* things that they ought not to,
Heb	13	9	Do not let ⌜yourselves be led astray by all sorts of strange
		3	*doctrines*;
2 P	2	1	10 you too will have your false *teachers*,
Rv	2	14	[Pergamum,] some of you ⌜are followers (lit. accept the
		3/	*teaching*) of Balaam, who *taught* Balak to set a trap for the Israelites . . . ¹⁵ and among you, too, there are some
	15		3 . . . who accept what the Nicolaitans *teach*.
	20		by her *teaching* [Jezebel] is luring my servants away . . .
	24		3 ²⁴ But . . . all of you who have not accepted this *teaching*

2: MASTER, RABBI

1 rabbi 15   2 rabbuni 2

a) Rabbi = Jesus

Mt 26 25		Judas, who was to betray him, asked in his turn, 'Not I, *Rabbi*, surely?'
	49	[Judas] went straight up to Jesus and said, 'Greetings, *Rabbi*!'
Mk 9 5		Peter spoke to Jesus: '*Rabbi*, . . . it is wonderful for us to be here;
	10 51	2 '*Rabbuni*,' the blind man said . . . 'Master, let me see again.'
	11 21	Look, *Rabbi*, . . . the fig tree you cursed has withered away.
	14 45	when the traitor came, he went straight up to Jesus and said, '*Rabbi*!' and kissed him.
Jn 1 38		*Rabbi*, – which means Teacher – where do you live?
	49	*Rabbi*, you are the Son of God, you are the King of Israel.
	3 2	*Rabbi*, we know that you are a teacher who comes from God;
	4 31	*Rabbi*, do have something to eat;
	6 25	*Rabbi*, when did you come here?
	9 2	*Rabbi*, who sinned, this man or his parents . . .?
	11 8	*Rabbi*, it is not long since the Jews wanted to stone you;
	20 16	2 [Mary of Magdala] said to him in Hebrew' '*Rabbuni*!' – which means Master.

b) various

Mt 23 7		[The scribes and Pharisees love] having people call them *Rabbi*. [8] You, however, must not allow yourselves to be called *Rabbi*, since you have only one Master,
Jn 3 26		so they went to John and said, '*Rabbi*,

3: INSTRUCTED, INFORMED, TOLD – HEAR, RECEIVE INFORMATION: *KAT-ĒCHEŌ*

kat-ēcheō 8

Lk 1 4		so that your Excellency may learn how well founded the *teaching* is that you have *received*.
Ac 18 25		[Apollos] had been *given instruction* in the Way of the Lord
	21 21	they have *heard* that you instruct all Jews living among the pagans to break away from Moses,
	24	there is no truth in the reports they have *heard* about you
Rm 2 18		[If you call yourself a Jew,] if you know God's will ⌐through (lit. having been *instructed* in) the Law
1 Co 14 19		I would rather say five ⌐words that mean something (lit. meaningful words to *instruct* others) than ten thousand words in a tongue.
Ga 6 6		People under *instruction* should always contribute something to the support of the man who is *instructing*.

4: (BE) INITIATED – READY: *MYEŌ*

myeō 1

Ph 4 12		I know how to be poor and I know how to be rich too. I have *been through my initiation*

5: LECTURE ROOM, HALL: *SCHOLĒ*

scholē 1

Ac 19 9		[Paul] took his disciples apart to hold daily discussions in the *lecture room* of Tyrannus.

2. TEACH – DISCIPLINE: *PAIDEUŌ*

2	*paideia*	6	3	*paid-agōgos 3*
1	*paideuō*	13	5	*a-paideutos 1*
4	*paideutēs*	2		

1: TEACH, TRAIN, GUARDIAN – CORRECT, DISCIPLINE, PUNISH

Lk 23 16		[Pilate said, 'The man has done nothing that deserves death,] so I shall have him *flogged* and then let him go.'
	22	so I shall have him *punished* and then let him go.
Ac 7 22		Moses was *taught* all the wisdom of the Egyptians
	22 3	I studied under Gamaliel and was *taught* the exact observance of the Law of our ancestors.
Rm 2 20		4 [If you call yourself a Jew,] if you can *teach* the ignorant and instruct the unlearned
1 Co 4 15		3 You might have thousands of *guardians* in Christ, but not more than one father
	11 32	when the Lord does punish us like that, it is to *correct* us
2 Co 3 24		3 The Law was to be our *guardian* until the Christ came . . . [25] Now that that time has come we are no longer
	25	3 under that *guardian*,

Ep 6 4		2 parents, . . . in bringing [your children] up *correct* them and guide them as the Lord does.
1 Tm 1 20		Hymenaeus and Alexander, whom I have handed over to Satan to *teach* them not to be blasphemous.
2 Tm 2 25		[a servant of the Lord] has to be gentle when he *corrects* people who dispute what he says,
	3 16	All scripture . . . can profitably be used for . . . guiding people's lives and *teaching* them to be holy.
Tt 2 12		[God's grace has] *taught* us that . . . we have to . . . give up everything that does not lead to God,
Heb 12 5		2 (Pr 3 11) My son, when the Lord *corrects* you, do not treat it lightly; but do not get discouraged when he reprimands you. [6] (Pr 3 12) For the Lord *trains* the ones that he loves and he punishes all those that he acknowledges as his sons.
	6	
	7	2 [7] Suffering is part of your *training*; . . . Has there ever been any son whose father did not *train* him? [8] If you
	8	2 were not getting this *training* . . . you would not be sons but bastards. [9] . . . we have all had our human
	9	2
	10	4 fathers who *punished* us . . . [10] Our human fathers were thinking of this short life when they *punished* us . . . but he does it all for our own good, so that we may share his
	11	2 own holiness. [11] . . . any *punishment* is most painful at the time,
Rv 3 19		(cf. Pr 3 12) I am the one who reproves and *disciplines* all those he loves:

2: IGNORANT – FUTILE, SENSELESS

2 Tm 2 23		5 Avoid these *futile* and silly speculations,

3. TEACH, ADVISE – WARN – ADMONISH: *NOU-THETEŌ*

2 nou-thesia 3   1 nou-theteō 8

Ac 20 31		I never failed to ⌐keep you *right* (or: *warn* you), shedding tears over each one of you.
Rm 15 14		you are . . . able to *advise* each other.
1 Co 4 14		I am saying all this . . . to *bring* you, as my dearest children, to *your senses*.
	10 11	2 All this . . . was written down to be a *lesson* for us
Ep 6 4		parents, . . . in bringing [your children] up, correct them and 2 *guide* them as the Lord does.
Col 1 28		this is the wisdom in which we ⌐thoroughly train (or: *admonish*) everyone and instruct everyone,
	3 16	Teach each other, and *advise* each other, in all wisdom,
1 Th 5 12		be considerate to those who . . . are above you in the Lord as your *teachers*.
	14	*warn* the idlers, give courage to those who are apprehensive,
2 Th 3 15		[If anyone refuses to obey what I have written,] regard him as . . . a brother in need of *correction*.
Tt 3 10		2 after a first and a second *warning*, have no more to do with him:

TELL – PREACH – PROCLAIM

1. Tell – Preach – Proclaim: angellō
  1: The Good News, Gospel – Tell, Proclaim, the Good News – (Gospel-)Messenger, Evangelist
  2: Tell – Report, Give an account of – Messenger
  3: Profess – Claim (to be)
2. Acknowledge, Declare – Praise – Confess: homo-logeō
  1: Acknowledge, Declare oneself (for), Profess – Praise – Bless, Thank – Confess, Confession
    of faith, Religion
  2: Confess, Acknowledge (sins)
  3: Declare, Tell, Admit
3. Preach – Proclaim, Announce – Herald: kēryssō
4. Utter – Expound: ereugomai
5. Inform, Tell – Show, Imply Information: mēnuō

1. TELL – PREACH – PROCLAIM: *ANGELLŌ*

9	*angelia*	2	10	*ep-angellomai*	2/15
12	*angellō*	1	1	*eu-angelion*	76
6	*angelos*	6/176	8	*eu-angelistēs*	3
5	*an-angellō*	13	2	*eu-angelizomai*	54
3	*ap-angellō*	46	14	*ex-angellō*	1
13	*kat-angeleus*	1	15	*par-angellō*	1/31
4	*kat-angellō*	18	11	*pro-kat-angellō*	2
7	*di-angellō*	3	16	*pro-eu-angelizomai*	1

: THE GOOD NEWS, GOSPEL – TELL, PROCLAIM, THE GOOD NEWS – (GOSPEL-)MESSENGER, EVANGELIST

Mt	4	23	[Jesus] went round the whole of Galilee . . . proclaiming the *Good News* of the kingdom
	9	35	Jesus made a tour through all the towns . . . proclaiming the *Good News* of the kingdom
	11	4	3 Go back and *tell* John what you hear and see; [5] the blind
		5	2 see . . . and (Is 61 1) the *Good News is proclaimed* to the poor;
		10	[John] of whom scripture says (Ml 3 1): Look, I am going to send my *messenger* before you;
	12	18	3 (Is 42 1) Here is my servant . . . he will *proclaim* the true faith to the nations.
	24	14	This *Good News* of the kingdom will be proclaimed to the whole world
	26	13	wherever in all the world this *Good News* is proclaimed,
	28	8	3 the women . . . ran to *tell* the disciples [that Jesus had risen]
Mk	1	1	The beginning of the *Good News* about Jesus Christ.
		2	6 (Ml 3 1) I am going to send my *messenger* before you; he will prepare your way.
		14	[Jesus] *proclaimed* the *Good News* from God. [15] . . . the
		15	kingdom of God is close at hand . . . believe the *Good News*.
	5	19	3 *tell* them all that the Lord . . . has done for you.
	8	35	anyone who loses his life for my sake, and for the sake of the *gospel*, will save it.
	10	29	there is no one who has left house, brothers . . . for my sake and for the sake of the *gospel* [30] who will not be repaid a hundred times over,
	13	10	the *Good News* must first be proclaimed to all the nations.
	14	9	wherever throughout all the world the *Good News* is proclaimed,
	16	10	[Mary of Magdala] went to those who had been his companions . . . and *told* them [that she had seen Jesus].
		13	3 These [two] went back and *told* the others,
		15	proclaim the *Good News* to all creation.
Lk	2	10	2 I *bring* you *news* of great joy . . . [11] . . . a saviour has been born to you;
	3	18	2 [John continued] to *announce the Good News* to them.
	4	18	2 (Is 61 1,2) The spirit of the Lord . . . has sent me to *bring the good news* to the poor, to proclaim liberty to captives
		43	2 I must *proclaim the Good News* of the kingdom of God to the other towns too,
	7	22	3 Go back and *tell* John what you have seen and heard: the
			2 blind see again . . . the *Good News is proclaimed* to the poor
		27	[John] of whom scripture says (Ml 3 1): See, I am going to send my *messenger* before you;
	8	1	2 [Jesus] made his way . . . preaching and *proclaiming the Good News* of the kingdom of God.
	9	6	2 [the Twelve] set out . . . *proclaiming the Good News*
		60	7 Leave the dead . . . go and *spread the news* of the kingdom of God.
	16	16	Up to the time of John it was the Law and the Prophets; since then, the kingdom of God *has been preached*,
	20	1	2 [Jesus] was teaching the people in the Temple and *proclaiming the Good News*,
	24	9	3 When the women returned from the tomb they *told* all this to the Eleven
Jn	4	25	5 when [the Messiah] comes he will *tell* us everything.
	16	13 Ⓢ	5 the Spirit of truth . . . will *tell* you of the things to come.
		14 Ⓢ	5 He will glorify me, since all [the Spirit] *tells* you will be taken from what is mine.
		15 Ⓢ	5 All he *tells* you will be taken from what is mine.
		25	3 the hour is coming when I shall . . . *tell* you about the Father in plain words.
	20	18	12 Mary of Magdala went and *told* the disciples that she had seen the Lord
Ac	3	18	11 God carried out what he had *foretold*, when he said through all his prophets that his Christ would suffer.
		24	4 all the prophets . . . have *predicted* these days.
	4	2	[the priests and the Sadducees] were extremely annoyed at
			4 their teaching . . . by *proclaiming* the resurrection of Jesus.
	5	42	2 [The apostles] preached every day . . . and their *proclamation of the Good News* of Christ Jesus was never interrupted.
	7	52	11 [your ancestors] killed those who *foretold* the coming of the Just One,
	8	4	2 Those . . . went from place to place *preaching the Good News*.
		12	2 [the Samaritans] believed Philip's *preaching of the Good News* about the kingdom of God
		25	2 [Peter and John] went back to Jerusalem, *preaching the Good News* to a number of Samaritan villages.
		35	Starting . . . with this text of scripture [of Isaiah's] Philip
			2 proceeded to *explain the Good News* of Jesus to [the eunuch].
		40	2 Philip . . . continued his journey *proclaiming the Good News* in every town
	10	36	God sent his word to the people of Israel, and it was to them that the *good news* of peace *was brought* by Jesus Christ
	11	20	Some . . . who came from Cyprus and Cyrene . . . started

Ac	11	20	2 preaching to the Greeks *proclaiming the Good News* of the Lord Jesus
	13	5	4 at Salamis [Barnabas and Saul] *proclaimed* the word of God in the synagogues of the Jews;
		32	2 We have come here to *tell* you the *Good News*. It was to our ancestors that God made the promise but [33] it is to us . . . that he has fulfilled it,
		38	4 it is through [Jesus] that forgiveness of your sins is *proclaimed*.
	14	7	2 [in Lycaonia Paul and Barnabas] *preached the Good News*.
		15	2 We have *come with good news* to make you turn from these empty idols to the living God
		21	2 Having *preached the Good News* in [Derbe] . . . they went back through Lystra
	15	7	the pagans were to learn the *Good News* from me
		35	2 Paul and Barnabas . . . taught and *proclaimed the Good News*, the word of the Lord.
		36	4 all the towns where we *preached* the word of the Lord,
	16	10	we lost no time in arranging a passage to Macedonia, convinced that God had called us to *bring* them the *Good News*.
		17	4 they have *come to tell* you how to be saved!
		21	4 [They are Jews] and are *advocating* practices which it is unlawful for us as Romans to accept or follow.
	17	3	4 the Christ . . . is this Jesus whom I am *proclaiming* to you.
		13	4 the word of God *was being preached* by Paul in Beroea as well,
		18	2 because he was *preaching about* Jesus and the resurrection,
		13	others said, '[Paul] sounds like a *propagandist* for some outlandish gods'.
		23	[Men of Athens,] the God whom I *proclaim* is . . . the one whom you already worship without knowing it.
		30	5 God . . . is *telling* everyone everywhere that they must repent,
	20	20	5 I have *preached* to you, and instructed you both in public and in your homes,
		24	provided that . . . I have carried out the mission . . . to bear witness to the *Good News* of God's grace.
		27	5 I have without faltering *put before* you the whole of God's purpose.
	21	8	8 Philip the *evangelist*, one of the Seven,
	26	20	3 [Paul said to Agrippa,] I started *preaching* . . . urging them to repent
		23	the Christ . . . as the first to rise from the dead . . . was to
			4 *proclaim* that light now shone for our people and for the pagans too.
Rm	1	1	Paul . . . specially chosen [to preach] the *Good News* [of] God
		9	The God I worship spiritually by preaching the *Good News* of his Son
		15	2 it is this that makes me want to *bring the Good News* to you too in Rome. [16] For I am not ashamed of the *Good News*:
		16	it is the power of God saving all who have faith
	2	16	on the day when, according to the *Good News I preach*, God, through Jesus Christ, judges the secrets of mankind.
	9	17	7 (Ex 9 16) I raised you up . . . to *make* my name *known* throughout the world.
	10	15	2 (Is 52 7) The footsteps of those who ⸢*bring* (or: *proclaim*) good [news] is a welcome sound.
		16	Not everyone . . . listens to the *Good News*.
	11	28	The Jews are enemies of God only with regard to the *Good News* . . . for your sake; but as the chosen people, they are . . . loved for the sake of their ancestors.
	15	16	I am to carry out my priestly duty by *bringing the Good News* from God to the pagans,
		19	I have preached Christ's *Good News* to the utmost of my capacity.
		20	2 an unbroken rule never to *preach* where Christ's name has already been heard.
		21	5 (cf. Is 52 15) Those who have never *been told about* him will see him,
	16	25	Glory to him who is able to give you the strength to live according to the *Good News I preach*, and in which I proclaim Jesus Christ,
1 Co	1	17	2 Christ did not send me to baptise, but to *preach the Good News*,
	2	1	when I came to you, it was not with any show of oratory or
			4 philosophy, but simply to *tell* you what God had guaranteed.
	4	15	it was I who begot you in Christ Jesus by *preaching the Good News*.
	9	12	we have put up with anything rather than obstruct the *Good News* of Christ in any way.
		14	4/ the Lord directed that those who *preach the gospel* should get their living from the *gospel*.
		16	2 *preaching the gospel* . . . is a duty which has been laid on me;
			2 I should be punished if I did not *preach the gospel*! . . . [18] Do you know what my reward is? It is this: in my
	18		2/ *preaching*, to be able to offer the *Good News* free, and not insist on the rights which the *gospel* gives me.
		23	I still do this, for the sake of the *gospel*, to have a share in its blessings.
	11	26	4 every time you eat this bread . . . you are *proclaiming* [the Lord's] death,

1Co 14	25	3	[an unbeliever] would . . . worship God, *declaring* that God is among you indeed.
15	1	/2	the *gospel* I *preached* to you . . . [2] . . . will save you only if
		2	you keep believing exactly what I *preached* to you
2 Co 2	12		I went up to Troas to preach the *Good News* of Christ,
4	3		If our *gospel* does not penetrate the veil, then the veil is
	4		on . . . [4] the unbelievers whose minds the god of this world has blinded, to stop them seeing the light shed by the *Good News* of the glory of Christ,
8	18		the brother who is famous in all the churches for *spreading the gospel*.
9	13		the way you accept and profess the *gospel* of Christ,
10	14		we did come all the way to you with the *gospel* of Christ.
	16	2	[we shall get taller,] I mean, we shall be *carrying the gospel* to places far beyond you,
11	4		you have only to receive . . . a new *gospel*, different from the one you have already accepted – and you welcome it with open arms.
	7		was I wrong, lowering myself so as to lift you high, by
		2	*preaching the gospel* of God to you and taking no fee for it?
Ga 1	6		I am astonished . . . you have turned away from the one who called you . . . to follow a different version of the *Good News*. [7] Not that there can be more than one [Good News]; it is merely that some trouble makers . . . want to change
	8	2	the *Good News* of Christ; [8] . . . if anyone preaches a
		/2	version of *the Good News* different from the one we have
		2	already *preached* to you . . . he is to be condemned!
	9	2	[9] . . . if anyone *preaches* a version of *the Good News* different from the one you have already heard, he is to be condemned!
	11	/2	the *Good News* I *preached* is not a human message
	16	2	[God chose] to reveal his Son in me, so that I might *preach* the Good News about him to the pagans.
	23	2	their one-time persecutor was now *preaching* the faith
2	2		[I went up to Jerusalem] and I laid before the leading men the *Good News* as I proclaim it among the pagans;
	5		to safeguard for you the true meaning of the *Good News*,
	7		I had been commissioned to *preach the Good News* to the uncircumcised just as Peter had been commissioned to [preach it] to the circumcised.
	14		they were not respecting the true meaning of the *Good News*,
3	8	16	Scripture . . . *proclaimed the Good News long ago* when Abraham was told (Gn 12 3): In you all the pagans will be blessed.
4	13	2	that illness gave me the opportunity to *preach the Good News* to you,
Ep 1	13		Now you . . . have heard the message of the truth and the *good news* of your salvation,
2	17	2	[Christ] came to *bring the good news* of peace,
3	6		the same promise has been made to [pagans] . . . through the *gospel*.
	8		I . . . have been entrusted with this special grace . . . of
		2	*proclaiming* to the pagans the infinite treasure of Christ
4	11		to some, [Christ's] gift was that they should be apostles; to
		8	some, prophets; to some, *evangelists*;
6	15		[So stand your ground,] wearing for shoes . . . the eagerness to *spread the gospel* of peace
	19		pray for me to be given an opportunity to . . . give out the mystery of the *gospel*
Ph 1	5		remembering how you have helped to *spread the Good News*
	7		you have shared the privileges which have been mine: . . . establishing the *gospel*.
	12		the things that happened to me have actually been a help to the *Good News*.
	16		[some preach Christ] out of nothing but love, as they know that this is my invariable way of defending the *gospel*.
	17	4	[17] The others . . . *proclaim* Christ for jealous or selfish motives,
	18	4	But does it matter? . . . Christ is *proclaimed*; and that makes me happy;
	27		Avoid anything . . . that would be unworthy of the *gospel* of Christ . . . united by your love for the faith of the *gospel*
2	22		[Timothy] has proved himself by working with me on behalf of the *Good News* like a son
4	3		[Evodia and Syntyche] were a help to me when I was fighting to defend the *Good News*
	15		In the early days of the *Good News* . . . no other church helped me
Col 1	5		The *Good News* [6] which has reached you is spreading all over the world
	23		the hope promised by the *Good News*, which you have heard, which has been preached to the whole human race,
	28	4	this is the Christ we *proclaim*,
1 Th 1	5		when we *brought the Good News* to you, it came to you not only as words,
2	2		it was our God who gave us the courage to proclaim his *Good News* to you
	4		it was God who decided that we were fit to be entrusted with the *Good News*,

1 Th 2	8		we were eager to hand over to you not only the *Good News* but our whole lives as well.
	9		we used to work . . . while we were proclaiming God's *Good News* to you.
3	2		Timothy, who is God's helper in *spreading the Good News* of Christ,
2 Th 1	8		[The Lord Jesus] will come . . . to impose the penalty on all who . . . refuse to accept the *Good News* of our Lord Jesus,
2	14		[God chose you to be saved.] Through the *Good News* that we *brought* he called you to this
1 Tm 1	11		[the sound teaching] that goes with the *Good News* of the glory of the blessed God,
2 Tm 1	8		with me, bear the hardships for the sake of the *Good News*,
	10		Christ Jesus . . . proclaimed life and immortality through the *Good News*;
2	8		the *Good News* that I carry, 'Jesus Christ risen from the dead . . .'
4	5	8	make the *preaching of the Good News* your life's work,
Phm	13		the chains that the *Good News* has brought me.
Heb 2	12	2	(Ps 22 23) I shall *announce* your name to my brothers,
4	2	2	We *received the Good News* exactly as [our ancestors] did;
	6	2	those who first *heard the Good News* failed to reach [the place of rest] through their disobedience,
1 P 1	12		the news [the prophets] brought of all the things which have
		5/2	now been *announced* to you, by those who *preached* to you the *Good News*
	25	2	the word of the Lord . . . is the *Good News that has been brought* to you.
2	9		(cf. Is 43 21) you are a chosen race . . . to ˹sing the praises
		14	(lit. *proclaim* the triumphs) of God who called you
4	6	2	the dead had to be *told the Good News* as well,
	17		what will [the judgement] be when it comes down to those who refuse to believe God's *Good News*?
1 Jn 1	2	3	we are . . . *telling* you of the eternal life which was with the Father
	3	3	What we have seen and heard we are *telling* you
	5	9	This is what we have heard from him, and the *message* that
		5	we are *announcing* to you: God is light;
3	11	9	This is the *message* as you heard it from the beginning: that we are to love one another;
Rv 10	7		God's secret intention will be fulfilled, just as [he announced]
		2	in the *Good News told* to his servants the prophets.
14	6	2	I saw another angel, flying high overhead, sent to *announce* the *Good News* of eternity to all who live on the earth,

2: TELL – REPORT, GIVE AN ACCOUNT OF – MESSENGER

Mt 2	8	3	when you have found [the child], ˹let me know (lit. *tell* me),
8	33		The swineherds ran off and made for the town, where they
		3	*told the* whole story,
14	12	3	John's disciples . . . went off to *tell* Jesus.
28	10	3	go and *tell* my brothers that they must leave for Galilee;
	11	3	some of the guard went off . . . to *tell* the chief priests all that had happened.
Mk 5	14	3	The swineherds . . . *told their story* in the town
6	30	3	The apostles . . . *told* [Jesus] all they had done and taught,
Lk 1	19	2	I am Gabriel . . . I have been sent to . . . *bring* you this *good news*.
7	18	3	The disciples of John *gave him all this news* [of Jesus's renown],
	24	6	When John's *messengers* had gone [Jesus] began to talk
8	20	3	[Jesus] was *told*, 'Your mother and your brothers . . . want to see you.'
	34	3	the swineherds . . . *told their story* in the town
	36	3	Those who had witnessed it *told* them how the man who had been possessed came to be healed.
	47	3	the woman . . . *explained* . . . why she had touched [Jesus]
9	36	3	The disciples . . . *told* no one what they had seen.
	52	6	[Jesus] sent *messengers* ahead of him.
13	1	3	some people . . . *told* [Jesus] about the Galileans
14	21	3	The servant returned and *reported* this to his master.
18	37	3	they *told* [the blind man] that Jesus the Nazarene was passing by.
Ac 4	23	3	[Peter and John] *told* them everything the chief priests and elders had said to them.
5	22	3	[the guards] went back and *reported*, [We found the gaol securely locked]
	25	3	a man arrived ˹with fresh news (lit. and *told* them): . . . the men . . . are standing there preaching to the people.
11	13	3	[Cornelius] *told* us he had seen an angel
12	14	3	[Rhoda] ran inside ˹with the news (lit. to *tell* them) that Peter was standing at the main entrance.
	17	3	*Tell* James and the brothers.
14	27	5	[Paul and Barnabas] *gave an account of* all that God had done with them.
15	4	5	they . . . *gave an account of* all that God had done with them.
	27	3	Judas and Silas . . . will *confirm by word of mouth* what we have written
16	36	3	The gaoler *reported* the message to Paul,
	38	3	The officers *reported* this to the magistrates,

Ac 19 18   5 Some . . . came forward to admit ʳin detail (lit. and *give an account of*) how they had used spells
   21 26   7 Paul . . . visited the Temple to *give notice* of the time when . . . the offering would have to be presented
   22 26   3 the centurion went and *told* the tribune;
   23 16   the son of Paul's sister . . . made his way into the fortress and *told* Paul, ¹⁷ who called one of the centurions and said, 'Take this young man to the tribune; he has something to *tell* him' . . . ¹⁹ . . . the tribune . . . asked, 'What is it you have to *tell* me?'
      17   3
      19   3
      30 15 I . . . have ʳnotified (or: given order to) his accusers that they must state their case against him in your presence.
   28 21   nor has any countryman of yours arrived here with any *report* or story of anything to your discredit.
         3
Rm 1 8   4 your faith *is spoken of* all over the world.
2 Co 7 7   5 [Titus] has *told* us all about how you want to see me . . . and how concerned for me [you are],
 Th 1 9   3 other people *tell* us how we started the work among you,
    3 6   2 Timothy . . . has *given* us *good news* of your faith
Jm 2 25   6 Rahab . . . welcomed the *messengers* and showed them a different way to leave.

3: PROFESS – CLAIM (TO BE)

1 Tm 2 10   to do the sort of good works that are proper for women who *profess* to be religious.
         10
    6 21 10 by ʳadopting (lit. *professing*) [the 'knowledge' which is not knowledge at all] some have gone right away from the faith.

2. ACKNOWLEDGE, DECLARE – PRAISE – CONFESS: *HOMO-LOGEŌ*

1	*homo-logeō*	26	5	*anth-omo-logeomai*	1
3	*homo-logia*	6	2	*ex-(h)omo-logeō*	9/10
4	*homo-logoumenōs*	1			

1: ACKNOWLEDGE, DECLARE ONESELF (FOR), PROFESS – PRAISE, BLESS, THANK – CONFESS, CONFESSION OF FAITH, RELIGION

X = Confess, Acknowledge, Declare oneself for, Jesus Christ

Mt 10 32 X   if anyone *declares himself* for me in the presence of men, I will *declare myself* for him in the presence of my Father
   11 25   2 Jesus exclaimed, 'I *bless* you, Father . . . for hiding these things from the learned
Lk 2 38   5 [Anna] came by just at that moment and began to *praise* God;
   10 21   2 [Jesus] said, 'I *bless* you, Father . . . for hiding these things from the learned
   12 8 X if anyone openly *declares himself* for me in the presence of men, the Son of Man will *declare himself* for him in the presence of God's angels.
Jn 9 22   the Jews . . . had already agreed to expel from the synagogue anyone who should *acknowledge* Jesus as the Christ
         X
   12 42   there were many who did believe in him . . . but they did not ʳadmit it (lit. *declare themselves*), through fear of the Pharisees
         X
Ac 23 8   the Sadducees say there is neither resurrection, nor angel, nor spirit, while the Pharisees ʳaccept (lit. *acknowledge*) all three.
Rm 10 9 X If your lips *confess* that Jesus is Lord and if you believe . . . you will be saved. ¹⁰ . . . by *confessing* with your lips you are saved.
      10
   14 11   2 (Is 45 23 G) every tongue shall *praise* God.
   15 9   2 (Ps 18 50) For this I shall *praise* you among the pagans
2 Co 9 13   [the saints] give glory to God for the way you accept and *profess* the gospel of Christ,
         3
Ph 2 11 X 2 every tongue should *acclaim* Jesus Christ as Lord.
1 Tm 3 16   4 ʳWithout any doubt, (lit. Let us *acknowledge* that) the mystery of our religion is very deep indeed:
    6 12   the eternal life to which you were called when you ʳmade (lit. *professed*) your profession
      /3
      13   Jesus Christ . . . ʳspoke up as a witness for the truth (lit. *professed* the truth as a witness)
         3
Tt 1 16   [those who lack faith] *claim* to have knowledge of God but the things they do are nothing but a denial of him;
Heb 3 1   3 Jesus, the apostle and the high priest of our *religion*.
   4 14   3 we must never let go of the *faith* that we have *professed*.
   10 23   3 Let us keep firm in the hope we *confess*,
   11 13   [our ancestors,] *recognising* that they were only strangers . . . on earth
   13 15   let us offer God an unending sacrifice of praise . . . that is offered every time we *acknowledge* his name.
1 Jn 2 23 X to *acknowledge* the Son is to have the Father as well.
    4 2 X every spirit which *acknowledges* that Jesus the Christ has come in the flesh is from God; ³ but any spirit which will not ʳsay (lit. *acknowledge*) this of Jesus is not from God,
         3
         X
      15 X If anyone *acknowledges* that Jesus is the Son of God, God lives in him,

2 Jn 7   There are many deceivers . . . refusing to ʳadmit (lit. *acknowledge*) that Jesus Christ has come in the flesh.
         X
Rv 3 5   I shall . . . *acknowledge* their names in the presence of my Father

2: CONFESS, ACKNOWLEDGE (SINS)

Mt 3 6   2 as they were baptised by [John] . . . they *confessed* their sins.
Mk 1 5   2 as they were baptised by [John] . . . they *confessed* their sins.
Ac 19 18   2 Some believers, too, came forward to ʳadmit (or: *confess*) in detail how they had used spells
Jm 5 16   2 So *confess* your sins to one another,
1 Jn 1 9   if we ʳacknowledge (or: *confess*) our sins, then God . . . will forgive our sins

3: DECLARE, TELL, ADMIT

Mt 7 23 X Then I shall *tell* them to their faces: I have never known you;
   14 7   [Herod] ʳpromised (lit. *declared*) on oath to give [the daughter of Herodias] anything she asked.
Jn 1 20   [John the Baptist] not only *declared*, but he *declared* quite openly, 'I am not the Christ'.
Ac 7 17 Θ   the time drew near for God to fulfil the promise he had *solemnly made* to Abraham.
   24 14   What I do *admit* to you is this: it is according to the Way which they describe as a sect that I worship the God of my ancestors,

3. PREACH – PROCLAIM, ANNOUNCE – HERALD: *KĒRYSSŌ*

2	*kērygma*	8	3	*kēryx*	3
1	*kēryssō*	61	4	*pro-kēryssō*	1

J = John the Baptist

Mt 3 1 J John the Baptist appeared; he *preached* in the wilderness of Judaea
    4 17 X Jesus began his *preaching* with the message, 'Repent . . .'
      23   [Jesus] went round the whole of Galilee teaching in their synagogues, *proclaiming* the Good News of the kingdom
         X
    9 35 X Jesus made a tour through all the towns . . . *proclaiming* the Good News of the kingdom
   10 7   *proclaim* that the kingdom of heaven is close at hand.
      27   what you hear in whispers, *proclaim* from the housetops.
   11 1 X Jesus . . . moved on . . . to teach and *preach* in their towns.
   12 41   2 when Jonah *preached* [the men of Nineveh] repented;
   24 14   This Good News of the kingdom will be *proclaimed* to the whole world
   26 13   wherever in all the world this Good News is *proclaimed*,
Mk 1 4 J John the Baptist appeared in the wilderness, *proclaiming* a baptism of repentance for the forgiveness of sins . . . ⁷ In the course of his *preaching* he said, 'Someone is following me, someone who is more powerful than I am,'
    7 J
   14 X Jesus went into Galilee. There he *proclaimed* the Good News from God.
      38   Let us go elsewhere, to the neighbouring country towns, so that I can *preach* there too . . . ³⁹ And he went all through Galilee, *preaching* in their synagogues
      39 X
         X
      45   [The leper] started *talking about* it freely and telling the story everywhere,
    3 14   [Jesus] appointed twelve . . . to be sent out to *preach*,
    5 20   the man [with the unclean spirit] went off and proceeded to ʳspread (or: *proclaim*) . . . all that Jesus had done for him.
    6 12   [The Twelve] set off to *preach* repentance;
    7 36   the more [Jesus] insisted, the more widely they *published* [the cure].
   13 10   the Good News must first be *proclaimed* to all the nations.
   14 9   wherever throughout all the world the Good News is *proclaimed*,
   16 15   *proclaim* the Good News to all creation.
      20   [the apostles] *preached* everywhere, the Lord . . . confirming the word
Lk 3 3 J [John,] *proclaiming* a baptism of repentance for the forgiveness of sins,
    4 18   (Is 61 1, 2) The spirit of the Lord . . . has sent me to bring the good news to the poor, to *proclaim* liberty to captives . . . ¹⁹ to *proclaim* the Lord's year of favour.
         X
      19 X
      44 X [Jesus] *continued his preaching* in the synagogues of Judaea.
    8 1 X [Jesus] made his way through towns and villages *preaching*, and proclaiming the Good News of the kingdom of God.
      39   the man went off and ʳspread (or: *proclaimed*) throughout the town all that Jesus had done for him.
    9 2   [Jesus] sent [the Twelve] out to *proclaim* the kingdom of God
   11 32   2 when Jonah *preached* [the men of Nineveh] repented;
   12 3   what you have whispered . . . will be *proclaimed* on the housetops.

Lk 24 47	in [Christ's] name, repentance for the forgiveness of sins would be *preached* to all the nations,	

Ac 8 5   Philip . . . went to a Samaritan town and *proclaimed* the Christ to them.

9 20   [in Damascus Saul] began *preaching* in the synagogues, 'Jesus is the Son of God'.

10 37 J   after John had been *preaching* baptism.

42   [Jesus] has ordered us to *proclaim* this to his people and to tell them that God has appointed him to judge everyone,

13 24 J 4 [Jesus's] coming was heralded by John when he *proclaimed* a baptism of repentance

15 21   Moses has always had his *preachers* in every town, and is read aloud in the synagogues

19 13   I command you by the Jesus whose *spokesman* is Paul.

20 25   you among whom I have gone about *proclaiming* the kingdom

28 31   [Paul,] *proclaiming* the kingdom of God and teaching the truth about the Lord Jesus Christ

Rm 2 21   You *preach* against stealing, yet you steal;

10 8   (Dt 30 14) The word, that is the faith we *proclaim*, is very near to you,

14   they will not hear of him unless they get ⌐a preacher (lit. someone to *preach*), [15] and they will never have ⌐a preacher (lit. anyone to *preach*) unless one is sent,

16 25   Glory to him who is able to give you the strength to live according to the Good News I preach, and in which I [2] *proclaim* Jesus Christ.

1 Co 1 21   God wanted to save those who have faith through the foolish- [2] ness of the *message* that we preach.

23   here we are *preaching* a crucified Christ;

2 4   [2] in my speeches and the *sermons* that I gave, there were none of the arguments that belong to philosophy;

9 27   I treat my body hard . . . for, having been an *announcer* myself, I should not want to be disqualified.

15 11   what matters is that I *preach* what they [preach],

12   if Christ raised from the dead is what has *been preached*,

14   [2] if Christ has not been raised then our *preaching* is useless

2 Co 1 19   The Son of God . . . that we *proclaimed* among you . . . was never Yes and No:

4 5   it is not ourselves that we are *preaching*, but Christ Jesus as the Lord,

11 4   any newcomer has only to *proclaim* a new Jesus, different from the one that we *preached*,

Ga 2 2   [in Jerusalem] I laid before the leading men the Good News as I *proclaim* it among the pagans;

5 11   if I still *preach* circumcision, why am I still persecuted?

Ph 1 15   It is true . . . the rest *preach* Christ with the right intention,

Col 1 23   the Good News, which you have heard, which has been *preached* to the whole human race,

1 Th 2 9   we used to work . . . while we were *proclaiming* God's Good News to you.

1 Tm 2 7   [Christ is the evidence of this] and I have been named a [3] *herald* and apostle of it

3 16   the mystery of our religion . . . [has been] . . . *proclaimed* to the pagans,

2 Tm 1 11   [3] [the Good News;] and I have been named its *herald*, its apostle and its teacher.

4 2   *proclaim* the message and, welcome or unwelcome, insist on it.

17   the Lord stood by me . . . so that through me the whole [2] *message* might be [proclaimed]

Tt 1 3   [God] revealed his decision and, by the command of God [2] . . . I have been commissioned to *proclaim* it.

1 P 3 19 X   in the spirit, [Christ] went to *preach* to the spirits in prison.

2 P 2 5   [3] Noah . . . the *preacher* of righteousness,

Rv 5 2   I saw a powerful angel who *called* with a loud voice, 'Is there anyone worthy to open the scroll . . . ?'

4. UTTER – EXPOUND: *EREUGOMAI*

ereugomai 1

Mt 13 35 X   (Ps 78 2 G) I will . . . *expound* things hidden since the foundation of the world.

5. INFORM, TELL – SHOW, IMPLY – INFORMATION: *MĒNUŌ*

mēnuō 4

Lk 20 37   Moses himself *implies* that the dead rise again, in the passage about the bush

Jn 11 57   anyone who knew where [Jesus] was must *inform* [the chief priests and the Pharisees]

Ac 23 30   My *information* is that there is a conspiracy against [Paul],

1 Co 10 28   out of consideration for the man that *told* you, you should not eat [sacrificed food], for the sake of his scruples;

TEMPLE – SANCTUARY

1. Temple: *hieron*
  1: the Temple (at Jerusalem)
  2: Sanctuary, Temple (to other gods)
2. Temple, Sanctuary – Shrine: *naos*
  1: Temple, Sanctuary (of God)

  2: Shrine, Temple (of Diana/Artemis)
3. House (of God = the Temple): *ta (tou patros)*
4. Parapet (of the Temple): *pterygion*

1. TEMPLE: *HIERON*

1 *hieron* 71   2 *hiero(-syleō)* 1

1: THE TEMPLE (AT JERUSALEM)

Mt 4 5   The devil . . . made [Jesus] stand on the parapet of the *Temple*.

12 5   have you not read . . . that . . . the *Temple* priests break the sabbath without being blamed for it? [6] Now here . . . is something greater than the *Temple*.

21 12   Jesus then went into the *Temple* and drove out all those who were selling and buying ⌐(lit. within the *Temple*);

14   There were also blind and lame people who came to [Jesus] in the *Temple*, and he cured them.

15   the children [were] shouting, 'Hosanna to the Son of David' in the *Temple*,

23   [Jesus] had gone into the *Temple* and was teaching,

24 1   Jesus left the *Temple*, and . . . his disciples came up to draw his attention to the *Temple* buildings.

26 55   I sat teaching in the *Temple* day after day

Mk 11 11   [Jesus] entered Jerusalem and went into the *Temple*.

15   [Jesus] went into the *Temple* and began driving out those who were selling and buying ⌐(lit. within the *Temple*) . . .

16   [16] Nor would he allow anyone to carry anything through the *Temple*.

27   Jesus was walking in the *Temple*,

12 35   Later, while teaching in the *Temple*, Jesus said, 'How can the scribes maintain that the Christ is the son of David?'

13 1   As [Jesus] was leaving the *Temple* one of his disciples said to him, 'Look . . . at the size of those buildings!'

3   [Jesus] was sitting facing the *Temple*, on the Mount of Olives,

14 49   I was among you teaching in the *Temple* day after day

Lk 2 27   Prompted by the Spirit [Simeon] came to the *Temple*;

37   [Anna] never left the *Temple*, serving God night and day

46   Three days later [Joseph and Mary] found [Jesus] in the *Temple*,

4 9   [the devil] made [Jesus] stand on the parapet of the *Temple*.

18 10   Two men went up to the *Temple* to pray,

19 45   [Jesus] went into the *Temple* and began driving out those who were selling.

47   [Jesus] taught in the *Temple* every day.

20 1   [Jesus] was teaching the people in the *Temple*

21 5   some were talking about the *Temple*, remarking how it was adorned with fine stonework and votive offerings,

37   In the daytime [Jesus] would be in the *Temple* teaching,

38   from early morning the people would gather round him in the *Temple*

22 52   Jesus spoke to the chief priests and captains of the *Temple* guard and elders

53   I was among you in the *Temple* day after day

24 53   [the apostles] were continually in the *Temple* praising God.

Jn 2 14   in the *Temple* [Jesus] found people selling cattle. . . [15] Making a whip out of some cord, he drove them all out of the *Temple*,

5 14   After a while Jesus met [the sick man] in the *Temple*

7 14   When the festival was half over, Jesus went to the *Temple*

28   Then . . . Jesus taught in the *Temple*,

8 2   At daybreak [Jesus] appeared in the *Temple* again;

20   [Jesus] spoke these words in the Treasury, while teaching in the *Temple*.

59   Jesus hid himself and left the *Temple*.

10 23   Jesus was in the *Temple* walking . . . in the Portico of Solomon.

11 56   [the country people] looked out for Jesus, saying to one another as they stood about in the *Temple*, '. . . Will he come . . . ?'

18 20   I have always taught in the synagogue and in the *Temple*

Ac 2 46   [The faithful] went as a body to the *Temple* every day

3 1   when Peter and John were going up to the *Temple* for the prayers at the ninth hour, [2] it happened that there was a man being carried past . . . they used to put him down . . . near the *Temple* entrance . . . so that he could beg from the people going in to the *Temple*. [3] . . . this man saw Peter and John on their way into the *Temple*

8   [the cripple] went with [Peter and John] into the *Temple*,

10   [people] recognised him as the man who used to sit begging at the Beautiful Gate of the *Temple*.

Ac	4	1	the priests came up . . . accompanied by the captain of the *Temple*

Ac 4 1   the priests came up . . . accompanied by the captain of the *Temple*
  5 20   stand in the *Temple*, and tell the people all about this new Life.
  21   [the apostles] went into the *Temple* and began to preach.
  24   the captain of the *Temple* and the chief priests heard this news
  25   the men you imprisoned are in the *Temple*
  42   They preached every day both in the *Temple* and in private houses,
  21 26   Paul took the men along and . . . visited the *Temple* . . .
  27   ²⁷ . . . some Jews from Asia caught sight of him in the *Temple* and stirred up the crowd and seized him, ²⁸ shouting, '. . . he has profaned this Holy Place by bringing
  28
  29   Greeks into the *Temple*.' ²⁹ They . . . thought that **Paul** had brought [Trophimus] into the *Temple*. ³⁰ . . . they seized Paul and dragged him out of the *Temple*,
  30
  22 17   Once . . . when I was praying in the *Temple*, I fell into a trance
  24 6   [Paul] has even attempted to profane the *Temple*.
  12   it is not true that they ever found me arguing with anyone . . ., either in the *Temple*, in the synagogues, or about the town.
  18   it was in connection with these [offerings] that they found me in the *Temple*;
  25 8   I have committed no offence whatever against . . . the *Temple*,
  26 21   the Jews laid hands on me in the *Temple* and tried to do away with me.
Co 9 13   the ministers serving [in the Temple] get their food from the *Temple*

2: SANCTUARY, TEMPLE (TO OTHER GODS)

Ac 19 27   This threatens . . . to reduce the *sanctuary* of the great goddess Diana to unimportance.
Rm 2 22   2 you despise idols, yet you rob their *temples*.

2. TEMPLE, SANCTUARY – SHRINE: *NAOS*

1 *naos* 45   2 *neō(-koros)* 1

1: TEMPLE, SANCTUARY (OF GOD)

X = the Body of Jesus as Temple, Sanctuary
C = Christian(s) as Temple, Sanctuary

Mt 23 16   You . . . say, 'If a man swears by the *Temple*, it has no force; but if a man swears by the gold of the *Temple*, he is bound'.
  17   ¹⁷ . . . which is of greater worth, the gold or the *Temple* that makes the gold sacred?
  21   when a man swears by the *Temple* he is swearing by . . . the One who dwells in it.
  35   you murdered [Zechariah] between the *sanctuary* and the altar.
  26 61 X   I have power to destroy the *Temple* of God and in three days build it up.
  27 5   flinging down the silver pieces in the *sanctuary* [Judas] . . . went and hanged himself.
  40   So you would destroy the *Temple* and rebuild it in three days!
  51   the veil of the *Temple* was torn in two
Mk 14 58 X   I am going to destroy this *Temple* made by human hands,
  15 29   So you would destroy the *Temple* and rebuild it in three days!
  38   the veil of the *Temple* was torn in two
Lk 1 9   it fell to [Zechariah] by lot . . . to enter the Lord's *sanctuary*
  21   people . . . were surprised that [Zechariah] stayed in the *sanctuary* so long. ²² When he came out . . . they realised that he had received a vision in the *sanctuary*.
  22
  23 45   The veil of the *Temple* was torn right down the middle;
Jn 2 19 X   Destroy this *sanctuary*, and in three days I will raise it up.
  20   It has taken forty-six years to build this *sanctuary*:
  21 X   [Jesus] was speaking of the *sanctuary* that was his body,
Ac 17 24   God who made the world . . . does not make his home in *shrines* made by human hands,
1 Co 3 16 C   Didn't you realise that you were God's *temple* . . .? ¹⁷ If anybody should destroy the *temple* of God, God will destroy him, because the *temple* of God is sacred; and you are that [temple].
  17 C
    C
  6 19 C   Your body . . . is the *temple* of the Holy Spirit,
2 Co 6 16 C   The *temple* of God has no common ground with idols, and that is what we are – the *temple* of the living God.
    C
Ep 2 21 C   As every structure is aligned on [Christ], all grow into one holy *temple* in the Lord.
2 Th 2 4   the Enemy . . . enthrones himself in God's *sanctuary*
Rv 3 12   Those who prove victorious I will make into pillars in the *sanctuary* of my God,

Rv 7 15   [the saints] now . . . serve [God] day and night in his *sanctuary*;
  11 1   Go and measure God's *sanctuary*,
  2   leave out the outer court of the *sanctuary* and do not measure it,
  19   the *sanctuary* of God in heaven opened, and the ark of the covenant could be seen inside ⌐it (lit. the *sanctuary*).
  14 15   Then another angel came out of the *sanctuary*,
  17   Another angel . . . came out of the *temple* in heaven,
  15 5   the *sanctuary*, the Tent of the Testimony, opened in heaven, ⁶ and out of the *sanctuary* came . . . seven angels,
  6
  8   the power of God filled the *temple* so that no one could go into ⌐it (lit. the *sanctuary*)
  16 1   I heard a voice from the *sanctuary* shouting to the seven angels,
  17   a voice shouted from the *sanctuary*, 'The end has come'.
  21 22   I saw that there was no *temple* in the city since the Lord God Almighty and the Lamb were themselves the *temple*,

2: SHRINE, TEMPLE (OF DIANA/ARTEMIS)

Ac 19 24   Demetrius . . . employed a large number of craftsmen making silver *shrines* of Diana,
  35   2 the city of the Ephesians is the guardian of the *temple* of great Diana

3. HOUSE (OF GOD = THE TEMPLE): *TA (TOU PATROS)*

ta (tou patros) 1

Lk 2 49   I must be busy ⌐with my Father's affairs (or: in my Father's Δ   house)

4. PARAPET (OF THE TEMPLE): *PTERYGION*

pterygion 2

Mt 4 5   The devil . . . made [Jesus] stand on the *parapet* of the Temple.
Lk 4 9   [the devil] made [Jesus] stand on the *parapet* of the Temple.

TEST

1. Test – Tempt – Try: *peirazō*
   1: Tempt (God) – Put (the Spirit) to the test
   2: Tempt (Jesus) – Tempter, Temptation
   3: Test (Jesus) – Set a trap for, Try to Disconcert – Trial
   4: Test, Examine, Trial – Tempt(er), Temptation
   5: Try, Attempt
2. Test – Decide – Fail: *dokimazō*
   1: Test, Examine, Approve – Try, Trial, Prove, Proof – Persevere
   2: Make a decision – See fit to, See as rational
   3: Fail a test, (Be) Disqualified – Irrational, Incapable – Rejected, Worthless
3. Proof, Demonstration – Prove
   1: *tekmērion*
   2: *elenchos*

1. TEST – TEMPT – TRY: *PEIRAZŌ*

4 *peira* 2   1 *peirazō* 39
5 *peiraomai* 1   6 *a-peirastos* 1
2 *peirasmos* 21   3 *ek-peirazō* 4

1: TEMPT (GOD) – PUT (THE SPIRIT) TO THE TEST

Mt 4 7   3 (Dt 6 16) You must not *put the Lord your God to the test*.
Lk 4 12   3 (Dt 6 16) You must not *put the Lord your God to the test*.
Ac 5 9 ⑤   So you and your husband have agreed to *put the Spirit of the Lord to the test*!
  15 10   It would only ⌐provoke God's anger (lit. be *putting* God *to the test*) now, surely, if you imposed on the disciples the very burden . . . we . . . were [not] strong enough to support?
1 Co 10 9   3 We are not to *put the Lord to the test*: some of [our fathers] ⌐did (lit. *put* him *to the test*), and they were killed
Heb 3 8   (Ps 95 9) do not harden your hearts, as happened . . . on the Day of *Temptation* in the wilderness, ⁹ when your ancestors *challenged* me and tested me,
  9   2
Jm 1 13   6 God *cannot be tempted* to do anything wrong, and he does not tempt anybody.

2: TEMPT (JESUS) – TEMPTER, TEMPTATION

Mt	4 1	Then Jesus was led by the Spirit out into the wilderness to be *tempted* by the devil . . .[3] . . . the *tempter* came and said to him, 'If you are the Son of God, tell these stones to turn into loaves'.
	3	
Mk	1 13	he remained [in the wilderness] for forty days, and was *tempted* by Satan.
Lk	4 2	[Jesus was] being *tempted* there by the devil for forty days.
	13	2 Having exhausted all these ways of *tempting* him, the devil left him.
Heb	2 18	because he has himself been through *temptation* he is able to help others who are tempted.
	4 15	we have [a high priest] who has been *tempted* in every way that we are, though he is without sin.

3: TEST (JESUS) – SET A TRAP FOR, TRY TO DISCONCERT – TRIAL

Mt	16 1	The Pharisees and Sadducees came, and to *test* him, they asked if he would show them a sign from heaven.
	19 3	Some Pharisees . . . to *test* him . . . said, 'Is it against the Law for a man to divorce his wife . . .?'
	22 18	Jesus . . . replied, 'You hypocrites! Why do you *set this trap for* me?'
	35	to *disconcert* him, one [Pharisee] put a question, [36] 'Master, which is the greatest commandment of the Law?'
Mk	8 11	The Pharisees . . . demanded of him a sign from heaven, to *test* him.
	10 2	Some Pharisees . . . asked, 'Is it against the law for a man to divorce his wife?' They were *testing* him.
	12 15	Seeing through their hypocrisy he said to them, 'Why do you *set this trap for* me?'
Lk	10 25	3 There was a lawyer who, to *disconcert* him, . . . said to him, 'Master, what must I do to inherit eternal life?'
	22 28	2 You are the men who have stood by me faithfully in my *trials*;
Jn	8 6	[The scribes and Pharisees] asked him this as a *test*, looking for something to use against him.

4: TEST, EXAMINE, TRIAL – TEMPT(ER), TEMPTATION

Mt	6 13	2 do not put us to the *test*, but save us from the evil one.
	26 41	You should be awake, and praying not to be put to the *test*.
		2
Mk	14 38	You should be awake, and praying not to be put to the *test*.
		2
Lk	8 13	these have no root; they believe for a while, and in time of *trial* they give up.
		2
	11 4	2 do not put us to the *test*.
	22 40	2 [Jesus said to the disciples,] Pray not to be put to the *test*.
	46	2 Get up and pray not to be put to the *test*.
Jn	6 6	[Jesus said, 'Where can we buy some bread for these people to eat?'] He only said this to *test* Philip.
Ac	20 19	[Paul said,] I have served the Lord . . . with all the sorrows and *trials* that came to me through the plots of the Jews.
		2
1 Co	7 5	in case Satan should take advantage of your weakness to *tempt* you.
	⒟ 2	
	10 13	2 The *trials* that you have had to bear are no more than people normally have. You can trust God not to let you be *tried*
		2 beyond your strength, and with any *trial* he will give you a way out of it
2 Co	13 5	*Examine* yourselves to make sure you are in the faith; test yourselves.
Ga	4 14	2 my disease that was such a *trial* to you;
	6 1	you may be *tempted* yourselves.
1 Th	3 5 ⒟	I was afraid the *Tempter* might have *tried* you too hard,
1 Tm	6 9	People who long to be rich are a prey to *temptation*;
Heb	2 18	because [Christ] has himself been through temptation he is able to help others who are *tempted*.
	11 17	It was by faith that Abraham, when *put to the test*, offered up Isaac.
	36	4 Some *had to bear* being pilloried or flogged,
	37	They were stoned, (ᵛ *tempted*) or sawn in half,
Jm	1 2	2 you will always have your *trials* but, when they come, try to treat them as a happy privilege;
	12	2 Happy the man who stands firm when *trials* come. He has proved himself, and will win the prize of life, . . . [13] Never, when you have been *tempted*, say, 'God sent the *temptation*'; God cannot be tempted to do anything wrong, and he does not *tempt* anybody. [14] Everyone who is *tempted* is attracted and seduced by his own desire.
	13	
	14	
1 P	1 6	you may for a short time have to bear being plagued by all sorts of *trials*;
		2
	4 12	you must not think it unaccountable that you should be *tested* by fire.
		2
2 P	2 9	2 the Lord can rescue the good from the *ordeal*,
Rv	2 2	I know . . . how you *tested* the impostors who called themselves apostles and proved they were liars.

Rv	2 10	the devil is going to send some of you to prison to *test* you,
	3 10	2 I will keep you safe in the time of *trial* which is going to come for the whole world, to *test* the people of the world.

5: TRY, ATTEMPT

Ac	9 26	When he got to Jerusalem [Saul] *tried* to join the disciples.
	16 7	[Paul and his companions] thought (lit. *tried*) to cross [the frontier] into Bithynia,
	24 6	[Paul] has even *attempted* to profane the Temple.
	26 21	5 the Jews laid hands on me in the Temple and *tried* to do away with me.
Heb	11 29	4 the Egyptians, *trying* to [cross the Red Sea], were drowned.

2. TEST – DECIDE – FAIL: *DOKIMAZŌ*

6	*dokimasia*	1	5 *dokimion*	2
1	*dokimazō*	22	4 *dokimos*	7
3	*dokimē*	7	2 *a-dokimos*	8

1: TEST, EXAMINE, APPROVE – TRY, TRIAL, PROVE, PROOF – PERSEVERE

Θ = to Tempt God

Lk	12 56	Hypocrites! You know how to *interpret* the face of the earth and the sky. How is it you do not know how to *interpret* these times?
	14 19	I have bought five yoke of oxen and am on my way to *try* them *out*.
Rm	2 18	if you know God's will through the Law and *can tell* what is right,
	5 4	3/3 patience brings *perseverance*, and *perseverance* brings hope,
	12 2	This is the only way to *discover* the will of God
	14 18	If you serve Christ in this way you will please God and be *ʳrespected* (lit. *approved*) by men.
		4
	16 10	4 [Greetings] to Apelles who has *gone through so much* for Christ;
1 Co	3 13	the fire will *test* the quality of each man's work.
	11 19	4 to distinguish those who are ʳto be trusted (or: *approved*).
	28	Everyone is to ʳrecollect (or: *examine*) himself before eating this bread
	16 3	I will send your offering to Jerusalem by the hand of whatever men you ʳgive [letters of] *reference to* (or: *approve*);
2 Co	2 9	3 What I really wrote for, after all, was to *test* you
	8 2	3 throughout great *trials* by suffering, their constant cheerfulness and . . . poverty have overflowed in . . . generosity.
	8	I am just *testing* the genuineness of your love
	22	a third brother, of whose keenness we have often *had proof*
	9 13	3 By offering this service, you ʳshow (lit. *prove* to) them what you are,
	10 18	It is not the man who commends himself that can be ʳaccepted (lit. *approved*).
		4
	13 3	4 You want *proof* . . . that it is Christ speaking in me:
	5	*Examine* yourselves . . .; test yourselves.
	7	not that we want to appear as the ones who have ʳbeen successful (lit. *passed the test*)
		4
Ga	6 4	Let each of you *examine* his own conduct;
Ep	5 10	*Try to discover* what the Lord wants of you,
Ph	1 10	so that you can always *recognise* what is best.
	2 22	3 you know how [Timothy] has *proved* himself
1 Th	2 4	God . . . can ʳread (lit. *examine*) our inmost thoughts.
	5 21	ʳthink before you do anything (lit. *test* everything) – hold on to what is good
1 Tm	3 10	They are to be *examined* first,
2 Tm	2 15	Do all you can to present yourself in front of God as a man who *has come through his trials*,
		4
Heb	3 9 Θ	6 (Ps 95 9) when your ancestors challenged me and *tested* me,
Jm	1 3	5 your faith is only *put to the test* to make you patient,
	12	4 He has *proved* himself, and will win the prize of life,
1 P	1 7	5 your faith will have been *tested* [and proved] like gold – only it is more precious than gold, which is corruptible even though it *bears testing* by fire –
1 Jn	4 1	It is not every spirit . . . that you can trust; *test* them,

2: MAKE A DECISION – SEE FIT TO, SEE AS RATIONAL

Rm	1 28	[the pagans] refused to *see it was rational* to acknowledge God,
	14 22	consider the man fortunate who can *make* his *decision* without going against his conscience.
1 Th	2 4	It was God who *decided* that we were *fit* to be entrusted with the Good News,

3: FAIL A TEST, (BE) DISQUALIFIED – IRRATIONAL, INCAPABLE – REJECTED, WORTHLESS

Rm	1 28	2	God has left [the pagans] to their own *irrational* ideas
1 Co	9 27	2	I should not want to be *disqualified*.
2 Co	13 5		Examine yourselves to make sure you are in the faith; test yourselves. Do you acknowledge that Jesus Christ is really in you? If not, you have *failed the test*, ⁶ but we . . . have
	6	2	
	7	2	not *failed* [it]. ⁷ . . . not that we want to appear as the ones who have been successful – we would rather that you did well even though we *failed*.
		2	
2 Tm	3 8	2	their minds are corrupt and their faith *spurious*.
Tt	1 16	2	they are . . . rebellious and quite *incapable* of doing good.
Heb	6 8		[a field] that grows brambles and thistles is ⌐abandoned (lit. *rejected*; or: *worthless*),
		2	

3. PROOF, DEMONSTRATION – PROVE

1: PROOF, DEMONSTRATION – PROVE: *TEKMĒRION*

tekmērion 1

Ac	1 3	[Jesus] had shown himself alive . . . after his Passion by many *demonstrations*:

2: PROOF, DEMONSTRATION – PROVE: *ELENCHOS*

elenchos 1

Heb	11 1	Only faith can . . . *prove* [the existence of] the realities that at present remain unseen.

THINK – CONSIDER

1. Suppose – Think – Expect: *oiomai*
2. Suppose – Imagine – Think: *hypo-lambanō*
3. Think – Suppose, Imagine, Assume: *nomizō*
4. Think, Feel – Be interested (in), View, Outlook – Set the mind (on): *phroneō*
5. Ponder (over): *sym-ballō*
6. Opinion, Judgement, Mind – Advice, Suggestion – Decide, Purpose: *gnōmē*
7. Thought(s) – Think over, Ponder, Mind – Design: *en-thymeomai*
8. Think, Thought – Reckon (as), Count (as): *logizomai*
  1: Think, Wonder – Thought, Intention, Design
  2: Think (of as), Thought(s) – Consider (as), Count (as), Reckon (as)

9. Think, Decide – Seem, Recognise (as): *dokeō*
  1: Think, Be (of the) opinion, Decide – Expect – Imagine, Suppose
  2: Seem (to be), Reckon (as), Recognise (as) – Regard (as), So-called – Think (of as)
10. Think, Consider – Count (as), Look on (as) – Esteem: *hēgeomai*
11. Regard (as), Look on (as), Hold (to be) – Consider (as), Count (as): *echō*
12. Think, Thought – Consider – Suspicion: *kata-noeō*
  1: Consider (as), Think (of as) – (the) Thought (that)
  2: Think, Thought – Imagine – Intention
  3: Suspicion
13. Consider, Think of: *kata-manthanō*

1. SUPPOSE – THINK – EXPECT: *OIOMAI*

oimai, oiomai 3

Jn	21 25	the world itself, I *suppose*, would not hold all the books that would have to be written.
Ph	1 17	The others . . . ⌐do not mind if (lit. *think*) they make my chains heavier to bear.
Jm	1 7	That sort of person . . . must not *expect* that the Lord will give him anything.

2. SUPPOSE – IMAGINE – THINK: *HYPO-LABMANŌ*

hypo-lambanō 2/5

Lk	7 43	The one who was pardoned more, I *suppose*
Ac	2 15	These men are not drunk, as you *imagine*;

3. THINK – SUPPOSE, IMAGINE, ASSUME: *NOMIZŌ*

nomizō 15

Mt	5 17	Do not *imagine* that I have come to abolish the Law
	10 34	Do not *suppose* that I have come to bring peace to the earth;
	20 10	When the first [labourers] came [to be paid], they *expected* to get more,
Lk	2 44	[Jesus's parents] *assumed* he was with the caravan,
	3 23	Jesus was . . , it was *thought*, the son of Joseph
Ac	7 25	[Moses] *thought* his brothers realised that through him God would liberate them,
	8 20	May your silver be lost for ever, and you with it, for *thinking* that money could buy what God has given for nothing!
	14 19	They stoned Paul and dragged him outside the town, *thinking* he was dead.
	16 13	we went along the river outside the gates [of Philippi] as it was the sabbath and ᵛ this was a customary (G there we *thought* might be a) place for prayer.
	27	the gaoler . . . was about to commit suicide, *presuming* that the prisoners had escaped.
	17 29	we have no excuse for *thinking* that the deity looks like anything in gold,
	21 29	[the Jews] *thought* that Paul had brought [Trophimus] into the Temple.
1 Co	7 26	I *believe* that . . . this is right:
	36	if there is anyone who *feels* that it would not be fair to his daughter
1 Tm	6 5	people who . . . *imagine* that religion is a way of making a profit.

4. THINK, FEEL – BE INTERESTED (IN), VIEW, OUTLOOK – SET THE MIND (ON): *PHRONEŌ*

3	*phrēn*	2	5	*phren(-apataō)* 1
2	*phronēma*	4	6	*phren(-apatēs)* 1
1	*phroneō*	20/26	7	(*hypsēlo-*)*phroneō* 1
4	*phrontizō*	1	8	(*philo-*)*phronōs* 1

Mt	16 23		the way you *think* is not God's way but man's.
Mk	8 33		the way you *think* is not God's way but man's.
Ac	28 7		Publius . . . entertained us ⌐hospitably (lit. with the greatest
		8	*feelings* of friendship) for three days.
	22		We think it would be as well to hear your own account of your ⌐position (lit. *views*);
Rm	8 5		The unspiritual *are interested* only in what is unspiritual, but the spiritual [are interested] in spiritual things. ⁶ It is death
	6	2	to ⌐limit oneself to (lit. *be interested* only in) what is unspiritual; life and peace can only come with ⌐concern for
	7	2	(lit. *setting one's mind* on) the spiritual. ⁷ That is because
		2	to ⌐limit oneself (lit. *be interested* only in) what is unspiritual is to be at enmity with God:
	27	Ⓢ 2	God who knows everything in our hearts knows perfectly well what he *means*,
	11 20		Rather than making you *feel* proud, that should make you afraid.
	12 3		I want to urge each one among you not to exaggerate his real importance above what he should *think* of himself. Each of you ⌐must (lit. should *think* to) judge himself soberly never ⌐be (lit. *feel*) condescending
	16		The one who ⌐observes (lit. *thinks* of) special days ⌐does (lit. *thinks*) so in honour of the Lord.
1 Co	13 11		When I was a child, I used to . . . *think* like a child, and argue like a child,
	14 20	3/3	you are not to be childish in your *outlook* . . . *mentally* you must be adult.
Ga	5 10		I feel sure that, united in the Lord, you will ⌐agree with (lit. *feel* no different from) me,
	6 3		It is the people who are not important who often ⌐make the mistake of (lit. delude their *minds* by) thinking that they are.
		5	
Ph	1 7		It is only natural that I should *feel* like this towards you all,
	2 5		*In your minds* you must *be* the same as Christ Jesus:
	3 15		We . . . must all *think* in this way. If there is some point on which you ⌐see things (lit. *think*) differently, God will make it clear to you;
	19		the things they *think* [important] are earthly things.
	4 10		It is a great joy to me . . . that at last you have shown some *concern* for me again; though of course you were *concerned* before, and only lacked an opportunity.
Col	3 2		*Let your thoughts be* on heavenly things, not on the things that are on the earth,
1 Tm	6 17		Warn those who are rich . . . that they are not to ⌐look down
		7	on (lit. *think* haughtily of) other people;
Tt	1 10		a great many people who . . . talk nonsense and try to make
		6	⌐others (G other men's *minds*) believe it,
	3 8	4	so that those who now believe in God may keep their *minds* constantly occupied in doing good works.

5. PONDER (OVER): SYM-BALLŌ
sym-ballō 1/7

Lk 2 19 — Mary . . . treasured all these things and *pondered* them in her heart.

6. OPINION, JUDGEMENT, MIND – ADVICE, SUGGESTION – DECIDE, PURPOSE: GNŌMĒ
gnōmē 9

Ac 20 3 — a plot . . . made [Paul] *decide* to go back by way of Macedonia.
1 Co 1 10 — be united again in your ⌐belief⌐ and practice (lit. *mind and judgement*).
7 25 — About remaining celibate, I have no directions from the Lord but give my own *opinion*
40 — [A widow] would be happier, in my *opinion*, if she stayed as she is
2 Co 8 10 — I am only ⌐making a *suggestion* (or: giving some *advice*)
Phm 14 — I did not want to do anything without your ⌐*consent* (lit. *opinion*);
Rv 17 13 — [The ten kings] are all of one *mind* in putting their . . . powers at the beast's disposal,
17 Θ — God influenced their minds to ⌐do what he intended (lit. carry out his *purpose*), ⌐to agree together (lit. and be of one *mind* to) put their royal powers at the beast's disposal

7. THOUGHT(S) – THINK OVER, PONDER, MIND – DESIGN: EN-THYMEOMAI

2 *en-thymeomai* 2   3 *di-en-thymeomai* 1
1 *en-thymēsis* 4

Mt 1 20 — 2 [Joseph] had *made up his mind* to do this when the angel of the Lord appeared to him
9 4 — Knowing ⌐what was in their *minds* (or: their *thoughts*) Jesus
2 said, 'Why do you have such wicked *thoughts* in your hearts?'
12 25 — Knowing ⌐what was in their *minds* (or: their *thoughts*) he said to them,
Ac 10 19 — 3 Peter's *mind* was still on the vision
17 29 — anything in gold, silver or stone that has been carved or *designed* by a man.
Heb 4 12 — The word of God . . . can judge the secret ⌐emotions (lit. *designs*) and thoughts.

8. THINK, THOUGHT – RECKON (AS), COUNT (AS): LOGIZOMAI

4 *logismos* 2   3 *dia-logismos* 11/14
1 *logizomai* 41   2 *dia-logizomai* 14/16
5 *ana-logizomai* 1 6 *el-logeō* 1

1: THINK, WONDER – THOUGHT, INTENTION, DESIGN

Mt 15 19 — 3 from the heart come evil *intentions*:
16 7 — 2 [the disciples] ⌐said to (or: *thought* among) themselves, 'It is because we have not brought any bread'. 8 Jesus knew it,
8 — and he said, 'Men of little faith, why are you ⌐talking (or:
2 *thinking*) among yourselves about having no bread?'
21 25 — 2 [the chief priests and elders] ⌐argued (or: *thought*) it out this way among themselves,
Mk 2 6 — 2 some scribes were sitting there, and they ⌐*thought* (or: said) to themselves, 7 '. . . He is blaspheming, . . .' 8 Jesus,
8 — 2 inwardly aware that this was what they were *thinking*, said
2 to them, 'Why do you have these *thoughts* in your hearts?'
7 21 — 3 it is from within, from men's hearts, that evil *intentions* emerge:
8 16 — 2 [the disciples] ⌐said to (or: *thought* among) one another, 'It is because we have no bread'. 17 . . . 'Why are you ⌐talking
2 (or *thinking*) about having no bread?'
17 —
11 31 — [the chief priests and the scribes and elders] ⌐argued (or:
2 *thought*) it out this way among themselves: 'If we say from heaven,'
Lk 1 29 — 2 [Mary] was deeply disturbed by these words and ⌐asked *herself* (or: *wondered*) what this greeting could mean,
2 35 — 3 so that the secret *thoughts* of many may be laid bare.
3 15 — 2 the people . . . were beginning to *think* that John might be the Christ,
5 21 — 2 The scribes and the Pharisees began to *think this over*, saying
22 'Who is this man . . . ?' 22 But Jesus, aware of their
3/2 *thoughts*, made them this reply, 'What are these *thoughts* you *have* in your hearts?'
6 8 — 3 But he knew their *thoughts*;
9 47 — 3 Jesus knew what *thoughts* were going through their minds,

Lk 12 17 — [a rich man who, having had a good harvest from his land, *thought* to himself, 'What am I to do?'
24 38 — < 2 why are these ⌐doubts (lit. *thoughts*) rising in your hearts?
Rm 1 21 — 3 they made nonsense ⌐out of logic (lit. of their *thinking*)
14 1 — 3 without starting an argument over *opinions*.
1 Co 3 20 — (cf. Ps 94 11) God is not convinced by the ⌐arguments (or *thoughts*) of the wise.
Jm 2 4 — Can't you see that you have . . . turned yourselves into judges, ⌐and corrupt judges at that (lit. open to evil
3 *thoughts*)?

2: THINK (OF AS), THOUGHT(S) – CONSIDER (AS), COUNT (AS) RECKON (AS)

Mk 15 28 — (ᵛ So the scripture came true where it says (Is 53 12), He was *considered* a criminal.)
Lk 22 37 — these words of scripture have to be fulfilled in me (Is 53 12) He ⌐let himself be (or: was) *taken for* a criminal.
Jn 11 50 — you fail to ⌐*see* that it is better for one man to die for the people
Ac 19 27 — This threatens . . . to reduce the sanctuary of the great goddess Diana to ⌐unimportance (lit. being *considered* unimportant).
Rm 2 3 — when you judge . ., do you *think* you will escape God's judgement?
15 — 4 [pagans] have . . . their own ⌐inner mental dialogue (or
4 *thoughts*).
26 — If a man . . . obeys the . . . Law, surely that ⌐makes up for, not (lit. *counts as*) being circumcised?
3 28 — as we *see* it, a man is justified by faith
4 3 — (Gn 15 6) Abraham put his faith in God, and this faith was
4 Θ *considered* as justifying him. 4 If a man has work to show his wages are not *considered* as a favour but as his due
5 — 5 but when a man has nothing to show except faith . .
6 — then his faith is *considered* as justifying him. 6 And David
Θ says the same: a man is happy if God *considers* him righteous irrespective of good deeds:
8 Θ — (Ps 32 2) happy the man whom the Lord *considers* sinless.
9 Θ — (Gn 15 6) [Abraham's] faith . . . was *considered* as justifying
10 Θ — him, 10 but when was ⌐this (lit. the *considering*) done?
11 Θ — so that [uncircumcised believers] too might be *considered* righteous.
22 Θ — (Gn 15 6) This is the faith that was *considered* as justifying
23 — him. 23 Scripture however does not refer only to him but
Θ to us as well when it says that his faith was thus '*considered*'
24 Θ — 24 our faith too will be '*considered*' if we believe in him who raised Jesus
5 13 — before the Law was given . . . no one could ⌐be accused of
6 (lit. have *imputed* [against them]) the sin of 'law-breaking'
6 11 — you must *consider* yourselves to be dead to sin
8 18 — I *think* that what we suffer in this life can never be compared to the glory . . . which is waiting for us.
36 — (Ps 44 22) we are . .. *reckoned* as sheep for the slaughter.
9 8 — it is only the children of the promise who will *count* as the true descendants [of Abraham].
14 14 — if someone *thinks* that a particular food is unclean, then it is unclean for him.
1 Co 4 1 — People must *think* of us as Christ's servants,
13 5 — [love] ⌐is not resentful (lit. does not *think* evil).
11 — When I was a child, I used to . . . think like a child, and ⌐argue (lit. *consider*) as a child,
2 Co 3 5 — not that we are qualified in ourselves to ⌐claim (lit. *think*) anything as our own work:
5 19 — God in Christ was reconciling the world to himself, not
Θ ⌐holding (lit. *counting*) men's faults against them,
10 2 — the confident assurance I *mean* to show when I come face to face with people I could name who *think* we go by ordinary human motives.
4 — 4 We demolish *sophistries*,
7 — Anybody who is convinced that he belongs to Christ must go on to ⌐*reflect* (lit. *consider*) that we all belong to Christ
11 5 — The man who said that can ⌐remember (lit. *consider*) this:
⌐As far as I can tell (lit. I *reckon*), these arch-apostles have nothing more than I have.
12 6 — in case anyone should [begin to] *think* I am better than he can actually see and hear me to be.
Ga 3 6 — (Gn 15 6) Abraham . . . put his faith in God, and this faith
Θ was *considered* as justifying him.
Ph 3 13 — I am far from *thinking* that I have already won.
4 8 — fill your *minds* with everything that is true, . . . noble, . . . good and pure,
2 Tm 4 16 — may they not ⌐be held accountable (lit. come into a *reckoning*) for it.
Heb 11 19 — [Abraham] ⌐was confident (lit. *considered*) that God had the power even to raise the dead;
12 3 — 5 *Think* of the way [Jesus] stood such opposition from sinners,
Jm 2 23 — (Gn 15 6) Abraham put his faith in God, and this was
Θ *counted* as making him justified;
1 P 5 12 — Silvanus, who is a brother I *know* I can trust,

9. THINK, DECIDE – SEEM, RECOGNISE (AS): *DOKEŌ*

dokeō 63

1: THINK, BE (OF THE) OPINION, DECIDE – EXPECT – IMAGINE, SUPPOSE

Mt 3	9	do not *presume* to tell yourselves, 'We have Abraham for our father'
6	7	the pagans . . . *think* that by using many words they will make themselves heard.
17	25	Simon, what *is* your *opinion*? From whom do the kings of the earth take . . . tribute?
18	12	⌐Tell me. (lit. What do you *think*?) Suppose a man has a hundred sheep
21	28	What *is* your *opinion*? A man had two sons.
22	17 X	Tell us your *opinion*, then. Is it permissible to pay taxes to Caesar or not?
	42	What *is* your *opinion* about the Christ? Whose son is he?
24	44	the Son of Man is coming at an hour you do not *expect*.
26	53	do you *think* that I cannot appeal to my Father . . .?
	66	'What *is* your *opinion*?' They answered, 'He deserves to die'.
Mk 6	49	when [the disciples] saw [Jesus] walking on the lake they *thought* it was a ghost
Lk 1	3	I . . . have *decided* to write an ordered account for you
8	18	from anyone who has not, even what he *thinks* he has will be taken away.
10	36	Which of these three, do you *think*, proved himself a neighbour . . .?
12	40	the Son of Man is coming at an hour you do not *expect*.
	51	Do you *suppose* that I am here to bring peace on earth?
13	2	Do you *suppose* these Galileans . . . were greater sinners than any other Galileans? . . .⁴ Or those eighteen . . .?
	4	Do you *suppose* that they were more guilty . . .?
19	11	[the people] *imagined* that the kingdom of God was going to show itself then and there.
24	37	[the disciples] *thought* they were seeing a ghost.
Jn 5	39	You study the scriptures, *believing* that in them you have eternal life;
	45	Do not *imagine* that I am going to accuse you before the Father;
11	13	[the disciples] *thought* that by 'rest' [Jesus] meant 'sleep',
	31	[the Jews] followed [Mary], *thinking* that she was going to the tomb [of Lazarus]
	56	What do you *think*? Will [Jesus] come to the festival or not?
13	29	some of [the Twelve] *thought* Jesus was telling [Judas], 'Buy what we need for the festival'
16	2	the hour is coming when anyone who kills you will *think* he is doing a holy duty
20	15	*Supposing* [Jesus] to be the gardener, [Mary] said, 'Sir . . , tell me where you have put him,'
Ac 12	9	Peter . . . *thought* he was seeing a vision.
15	22	the apostles and elders *decided* to choose delegates
	25	we have *decided* unanimously to elect delegates
	28 Ⓢ	It has been *decided* by the Holy Spirit and by ourselves
	34	(ᵛ But Silas *thought* he would stay there.)
26	9	I once *thought* it was my duty to use every means to oppose the name of Jesus
27	13	*thinking* their objective as good as reached, they . . . began to sail past Crete,
1 Co 3	18	if any one of you *thinks* of himself as wise, in the ordinary sense of the word,
7	40	I too have the Spirit of God, I *think*.
8	2	A man may *imagine* he understands something,
10	12	The man who *thinks* he is safe must be careful that he does not fall.
11	16	To anyone who might still ⌐want (lit. *decide*) to argue: it is not the custom with us,
12	23	it is those *thought* the least honourable parts of the body that we clothe with the greatest care.
14	37	Anyone who ⌐claims to be (lit. *imagines* he is) a prophet
2 Co 11	16	let no one take me *for* a fool;
12	19	you have been *thinking* that our defence has been addressed to you,
Ga 6	3	It is the people who are not important who often make the mistake of *thinking* that they are.
Ph 3	4	Take any man who *thinks* he can rely on what is physical:
Heb 4	1	none of you must *think* that he has come too late
10	29	⌐you may be sure (lit. do you not *suppose*) that anyone who tramples on the Son of God . . . will be condemned to a far severer punishment.
12	10	Our human fathers . . . could only do what they *thought* best;
Jm 1	26	Nobody must *imagine* that he is religious while he still goes on deceiving himself
4	5	Surely you don't *think* scripture is wrong when it says: the spirit . . . wants us for himself alone?

2: SEEM (TO BE), RECKON (AS), RECOGNISE (AS) – REGARD (AS), SO-CALLED – THINK (OF AS)

Mk 10	42	among the pagans their *so-called* rulers lord it over them,
Lk 22	24	A dispute arose . . . among [the apostles] about which should be *reckoned* the greatest.
Ac 17	18	He ⌐sounds like (lit. *seems* to be) a propagandist for some outlandish gods.
25	27	It *seems* to me pointless to send a prisoner without indicating the charges against him.
1 Co 4	9	instead, it *seems* to me, God has put us apostles at the end of the parade,
12	22	it is precisely the parts of the body that *seem* to be the weakest which are the indispensable ones;
2 Co 10	9	I do not want you to *think* of me as someone who only frightens you by letter.
Ga 2	2 ●	I laid before those *regarded* as the leading men the Good News as I proclaim it among the pagans;
	6 ●	these people who are ⌐acknowledged (lit. *recognised*) leaders – not that their importance matters to me . . . – these *recognised* leaders, as I say, had nothing to add to the Good News as I preach it.
	●	
	9 ●	James, Cephas and John, these *recognised* leaders, . . . shook hands with Barnabas and me
Heb 12	11	any punishment is most painful . . . and ⌐far from (lit. does not *seem* [to be]) pleasant;

10. THINK, CONSIDER – COUNT (AS), LOOK ON (AS) – ESTEEM: *HĒGEOMAI*

hēgeomai 20/22

Ac 26	2	I *consider* myself fortunate, King Agrippa, in that it is before you I am to answer . . . the charges made against me
2 Co 9	5	I have *thought* it necessary to ask these brothers to go on to you ahead of us,
Ph 2	3	Always *consider* the other person to be better than yourself,
	6 X	His state was divine, yet he did not ⌐cling (lit. *think* of clinging) to his equality with God
	25	It is essential, I *think*, to send brother Epaphroditus back to you.
3	7	I [have come to] *consider* all these advantages that I had as disadvantages. ⁸ . . . I *believe* nothing can happen that will outweigh the supreme advantage of knowing Christ Jesus my Lord . . . I *look* on everything as so much rubbish if only I can have Christ
	8	
1 Th 5	13	⌐Have the greatest respect and (lit. *Esteem* them with the greatest) affection
2 Th 3	15	you are not to *regard* him as an enemy
1 Tm 1	12 X	Christ Jesus our Lord, who . . . *judged* me faithful enough to call me into his service
6	1	All slaves . . . must ⌐have unqualified respect for (lit. *look* with unqualified respect *on*) their masters,
Heb 10	29	anyone who . . . ⌐treats (lit. *counts*) the blood of the covenant which sanctifies him as if it were not holy,
11	11	Sarah . . . *believed* that he who had made the promise would be faithful to it.
	26	[Moses] *considered* that the insults offered to the Anointed were something more precious than all the treasure of Egypt,
Jm 1	2	try to ⌐treat (lit. *think* of) [your trials] as a happy privilege;
2 P 1	13	I ⌐am sure (lit. *consider*) it is my duty . . . to keep stirring you up with reminders,
2	13	men ⌐whose only object is (lit. who *think* with enjoyment of) dissipation all day long,
3	9	The Lord is not being slow to carry out his promises, as anybody else might *think* he could be called slow;
	15	*Think* of our Lord's patience as your opportunity to be saved;

11. REGARD (AS), LOOK ON (AS), HOLD (TO BE) – CONSIDER (AS), COUNT (AS): *ECHŌ*

echō (5)

Mt 14	5	the people, who *regarded* John as a prophet,
21	26	the people . . . all *hold* that John was a prophet.
	46	the crowds . . . *looked* on [Jesus] as a prophet.
Mk 11	32	everyone *held* that John was a real prophet.
Phm	17	if ⌐all that we have in common means anything to you (lit. you *consider* me your partner), welcome [Onesimus] as you would me;

12. THINK, THOUGHT – CONSIDER – SUSPICION: *KATA-NOEŌ*

2	*noēma*	4/6	6	*epi-noia*	1
1	*kata-noeō*	7/14	3	*hypo-noeō*	3
5	*dia-noēma*	1	7	*hypo-noia*	1
4	*en-noia*	2			

1: CONSIDER (AS), THINK (OF AS) – (THE) THOUGHT (THAT)

Mt 7 3   Why do you . . . never ⌐notice (or: *think of*) the plank in your own [eye]?

Lk 6 41   Why do you . . . never ⌐notice (or: *think of*) the plank in your own [eye]?

12 24   *Think of* the ravens. They do not sow or reap;

27   *Think of* the flowers; they never have to spin or weave;

Rm 4 19   Even the *thought* that his body was past fatherhood . . . did not shake [Abraham's] belief.

Heb 3 1   you . . . should *turn your minds to* Jesus, the apostles and the high priest of our religion.

10 24   Let us ⌐be concerned for (lit. *consider*) each other,

2: THINK, THOUGHT – IMAGINE – INTENTION

Lk 11 17   5 knowing *what they were thinking* [Jesus] said to them, 'Every kingdom divided against itself

Ac 8 22   6 you may still be forgiven for *thinking* as you did;

13 25   3 I am not the one you *imagine* me to be;

25 18   his accusers did not charge him with any of the crimes I 3 had *expected*;

27 27   3 the crew *sensed* that land of some sort was near.

2 Co 2 11 ⑩   2 we know well enough what [Satan's] *intentions* are.

10 5   2 every *thought* is our prisoner, captured to be brought into obedience to Christ.

11 3   2 I am afraid that . . . your ⌐ideas (or: *thoughts*) may get corrupted

Ph 4 7   and that peace of God, which is so much greater than we can 2 understand, will guard your hearts and your ⌐thoughts (or: *minds*),

Heb 4 12   The word of God . . . can judge the secret emotions and 4 *thoughts*.

1 P 4 1   4 arm yourselves with the same *resolution* that [Christ] had:

3: SUSPICION

1 Tm 6 4   All that can come of this is jealousy, . . . and wicked ⌐mis-7 trust (lit. *suspicions*) of one another;

13. CONSIDER, THINK OF: *KATA-MANTHANŌ*

kata-manthanō 1

Mt 6 28   *Think of* the flowers growing in the fields;

THROUGH

1: Through (God, the Spirit, Jesus, the name of Jesus) | 2: (God is) Through (all)

dia + gen. (76)
dia + acc. (2)

1: THROUGH (GOD, THE SPIRIT, JESUS, THE NAME OF JESUS)

Mk 6 2   What . . . [are] these miracles that are worked *through* him?

Jn 1 3   *Through* [the Word] all things came to be,

7   [John] came . . . so that everyone might believe *through* him.

10   [The Word] was in the world that had its being *through* him.

17   though the Law was given *through* Moses, grace and truth have come *through* Jesus Christ.

3 17   God sent his Son into the world . . . so that *through* him the world might be saved.

10 9   I am the gate [of the sheepfold]. Anyone who enters *through* me will be safe:

14 6   I am the Way . . . No one can come to the Father except *through* me.

Ac 1 2   the apostles [Jesus] had chosen *through* the Holy Spirit,

2 22   the miracles . . . that God worked *through* [Jesus]

3 16   It is faith ⌐in that name (lit. *through* [Jesus]) that restored this man to health,

4 25   you it is who said *through* the Holy Spirit

30   stretching out your hand to heal . . . *through* the name of your holy servant Jesus.

10 36   the good news of peace was brought *by* Jesus Christ

43   all who believe in Jesus will have their sins forgiven *through* his name.

11 28   Agabus, ⌐seized by (lit. *through*) the Spirit, . . . predicted . . . a famine

Ac 15 11   we are saved . . . *through* the grace of the Lord Jesus.

18 27   [Apollos] was able *by* God's grace to help the believers

21 4   Speaking ⌐in (lit. *through*) the Spirit, they kept telling Paul not to go on to Jerusalem,

Rm 1 5   *through* [Jesus Christ] we received grace and our apostolic mission

8   I thank my God *through* Jesus Christ for all of you

2 16   on the day when . . . God, *through* Jesus Christ, judges the secrets of mankind.

5 1   *through* our Lord Jesus Christ . . . we are judged righteous 2 and at peace with God, ² since it is . . . *through* Jesus that we have entered this state of grace

5   the love of God has been poured into our hearts *by* the Holy Spirit

9   is it likely that ⌐he would now fail to save us (lit. we should not be saved *through* him) from God's anger?

11   we are filled with joyful trust in God, *through* our Lord Jesus Christ, *through* whom we have . . . gained our reconciliation.

17   If it is certain that death reigned over everyone as the consequence of one man's fall, it is even more certain that ⌐one man, Jesus Christ, will cause everyone to (lit. *through* one man, Jesus Christ, everyone will) reign in life

21   grace will reign to bring eternal life ⌐thanks to (lit. *through*) the righteousness that comes *through* Jesus Christ our Lord.

7 25   Thanks be to God *through* Jesus Christ our Lord.

8 37   These are the trials through which we triumph, ⌐by the power of (lit. *through*) him who loved us.

11 36   all is *by* [God] and for him.

15 30   I beg you, brothers, *by* our Lord Jesus Christ and *through* the love of the Spirit,

16 27   [God] alone is wisdom; give glory therefore to him *through* Jesus Christ

1 Co 1 10   I do appeal to you, brothers, ⌐for the sake (lit. *through* the name) of our Lord Jesus Christ,

2 10   These are the very things that God has revealed to us *through* the Son,

8 6   there is one God, the Father, from whom all things come and for whom we exist; and there is one Lord, Jesus Christ, *through* whom all things come and *through* whom we exist.

15 21   Death came through one man and in the same way the resurrection of the dead has come *through* one man.

57   let us thank God for giving us the victory *through* our Lord Jesus Christ.

2 Co 1 5   as the sufferings of Christ overflow to us, so, *through* Christ, does our consolation overflow.

20   it is 'through him' that we answer Amen to the praise of God.

3 4   we are confident of this *through* Christ:

4 5   we are preaching . . . Christ Jesus as the Lord, and ourselves as your servants ⌐for Jesus' sake (ᵛ *through* Jesus).

5 18   It was God who reconciled us to himself *through* Christ

Ga 1 1   Paul . . . an apostle who . . . has been appointed *by* Jesus Christ and [by] God the Father

Ep 1 5   [God chose us,] determining that we should become his adopted sons, *through* Jesus Christ

2 18   *Through* him, both of us [Jew and pagan] have in the one Spirit our way to come to the Father.

3 16   may [the Father] give you the power *through* his Spirit for your hidden self to grow strong,

Ph 1 11   the perfect goodness ⌐which Jesus Christ produces in us for (lit. *through* Jesus Christ to) the glory and praise of God.

Col 1 16   all things were created *through* [the Son] and for him.

20   [God wanted] all things to be reconciled *through* him and for him,

3 17   giving thanks to God the Father *through* [the Lord Jesus].

1 Th 4 2   the instructions we gave you ⌐on the authority of (lit. *through*) the Lord Jesus.

5 9   God . . . meant us . . . to win salvation *through* our Lord Jesus Christ,

2 Tm 1 14   guard [the sound teaching] ⌐with the help of (lit. *through*) the Holy Spirit

Tt 3 6   the Holy Spirit which he has . . . poured over us *through* Jesus Christ

Heb 1 2   the Son . . . *through* whom he made everything there is.

2 3   The promise was first announced *by* the Lord himself

10   God, for whom everything exists and *through* whom everything exists,

7 21   [Jesus was made a priest] with an oath sworn *by* the one who declared to him: . . . you are a priest,

25   he is living for ever to intercede for all who come to God *through* him.

9 14   Christ . . . offered himself as the perfect sacrifice to God *through* the eternal Spirit,

13 15   *Through* [Jesus], let us offer God an unending sacrifice of praise,

21   [I pray that God may] turn us all into whatever is acceptable to himself *through* Jesus Christ,

1 P 1 21   *Through* [Christ] you now have faith in God,

23   your new birth was . . . ⌐from (lit. *through*) the everlasting word of . . . God.

1 P	2	5	the spiritual sacrifices ⌜which Jesus Christ has (lit. *through* Jesus Christ) made acceptable to God,
		14	[accept the authority of] the governors as commissioned *by* [the Lord]
	4	11	so that in everything God may receive the glory, *through* Jesus Christ,
1 Jn	2	12	you . . . whose sins have already been forgiven *through* his name;
	4	9	God sent into the world his only Son so that we could have life *through* him;
Jude		25	To . . . the only God, who saves us *through* Jesus Christ our Lord,

2: (GOD IS) THROUGH (ALL)

Ep	4	6	one God who is Father of all, over all, *through* all and within all.

THROW – DROP

1. Throw, Cast – Strike down – Drop: *ballō*	**2. Throw (down), Fling, Wave – Drop, Cast down – Downcast:** *rhiptō*
1: Throw, Cast, Fling – Strike down – Drop, Hurl down	**3. Throw to the ground, Dash down:** *rhēgnymi*
2: (Make a) Cast (with) a net – Throw, Drop, a net	**4. Throw down, Hurl over:** *kata-krēmnizō*

1. THROW, CAST – STRIKE DOWN – DROP: *BALLŌ*

1	*ballō*	79/122		6	*kata-ballō*	1/2
3	*bolē*	1		7	*ek-ballō*	1/81
2	*bolizō*	2		8	*ek-bolē*	1
4	*amphi-ballō*	1		9	*em-ballō*	1
5	*amphi-blēstron*	1		10	*epi-ballō*	1/18

1: THROW, CAST, FLING – STRIKE DOWN – DROP, HURL DOWN

Ⓓ = the Devil is (over)thrown   P = Throw into prison
L = Cast lots

Mt	3	10		any tree which fails to produce good fruit will be cut down and *thrown* on the fire.
	4	6	X	If you are the Son of God . . . *throw* yourself down;
	5	13		if salt becomes tasteless, what can make it salty again? It . . . can only be *thrown* out
		25	P	Come to terms with your opponent . . . or . . . you may be ⌜*thrown* into (or: put in) prison.
		29		If your right eye should cause you to sin, . . . *throw* it away; for it will do you less harm . . . than to have your whole body *thrown* into hell . . . ³⁰ And if your right hand should cause you to sin, . . . *throw* it away;
		30		
	6	30		the grass in the field which is there today and *thrown* into the furnace tomorrow,
	7	6		do not *throw* your pearls in front of pigs,
		19		Any tree that does not produce good fruit is . . . *thrown* on the fire.
	13	42		[the angels] will *throw* [all who do evil] into the blazing furnace,
		48		[the fishermen] *throw* away those [fish] that are no use.
		50		[the angels will appear] to *throw* [the wicked] into the blazing furnace
	15	26		It is not fair to take the children's food and *throw* it to the house-dogs.
	18	8		If your hand or foot should cause you to sin, . . . *throw* it away: it is better . . . than to . . . be *thrown* into eternal fire. ⁹ And if your eye should cause you to sin, . . . *throw* it away: it is better . . . than to . . . be *thrown* into the hell of fire.
		9		
		30	P	the other [servant] . . . had him *thrown* into prison
	21	21		even if you say to this mountain, 'Get up and *throw* yourself into the sea', it will be done.
	27	35	L	they shared out [Jesus's] clothing by *casting* lots.
Mk	4	26		A man *throws* seed on the land.
		37	10	the waves were ⌜breaking (lit. *throwing* themselves) into the boat
	7	27		it is not fair to take the children's food and *throw* it to the house-dogs.
	9	22		[the spirit] has often *thrown* [my son] into the fire and into the water,
		42		anyone who . . . [brings] down one of these little ones . . . would be better *thrown* into the sea
		45		better . . . than to have two feet and be *thrown* into hell
		47		better . . . than to have two eyes and be *thrown* into hell

Mk	11	7		[the disciples] *threw* their cloaks on [the colt's] back, and [Jesus] sat on it.
		23		if anyone says to this mountain, 'Get up and *throw* yourself into the sea,
	15	24	L	they . . . shared out [Jesus's] clothing, *casting* lots
Lk	3	9		any tree which fails to produce good fruit will be . . . *thrown* on the fire.
	4	9	X	If you are the Son of God, . . . *throw* yourself down
	12	5	Θ 9	fear him who . . . has the power to *cast* into hell.
		28		the grass of the field which is there today and *thrown* into the furnace tomorrow,
		58		try to settle with [your opponent] . . . or he may . . . have you ⌜*thrown* into (or: put in) prison.
			P	
	13	19		a mustard seed which a man . . . *threw* into his garden
	14	35		[if salt loses its taste] people *throw* it out.
	22	41	3	[Jesus] withdrew from them, about a stone's *throw* away,
	23	19	P	[Barabbas] had been ⌜*thrown* into (or: put in) prison for causing a riot
		25		[Pilate] released the man they asked for, who had been ⌜*imprisoned* (or: *thrown* into prison) for rioting
			P	
		34	L	[the soldiers] *cast* lots to share out [Jesus's] clothing.
Jn	3	24	P	This was before John had been ⌜*put* in (or: *thrown* into) prison.
	8	7		[Jesus] . . . said, 'If there is one of you who has not sinned, let him be the first to *throw* a stone at her.'
		59		At this [the Jews] picked up stones to *throw* at [Jesus]
	12	31	Ⓓ	the prince of this world is to be ᵛ over*thrown* (G *cast* out).
	15	6		Anyone who does not remain in me is like a branch that has been *thrown* away – he withers; these branches are . . . *thrown* on the fire,
	19	24	L	They *cast* lots for my clothes.
	21	7		Simon Peter . . . jumped (lit. *flung* himself) into the water.
Ac	16	23	P	[Paul and Silas] were . . . *thrown* into prison,
		24	P	[the gaoler] *threw* them into the inner prison
		37	P	They . . . *threw* us into prison,
	22	23		They were yelling, waving their cloaks and *throwing* dust into the air,
	27	14	○	it was not long before a hurricane . . . ⌜burst (lit. *struck* down) on them
		18	8	they began to *jettison* the cargo,
	28	2	○	They ⌜took *soundings* and found twenty fathoms; . . . they *sounded* again and found fifteen fathoms.
			2	
		38	7	they lightened the ship by *throwing* the corn overboard
2 Co	4	9	6	we have been . . . *knocked* down, but never killed;
Rv	2	10	P	the devil is going to ⌜*send* some of you to (lit. *throw* some of you into) prison
		22		Now I ⌜am consigning (lit. will *throw*) her to bed,
	4	10		the twenty-four elders . . . *threw* down their crowns in front of the throne,
	6	13		like figs ⌜*dropping* (or: *cast*) from a fig tree when a high wind shakes it;
	8	5		fire from the altar, which [the angel] then *threw* down on the earth;
		7		hail and fire, mixed with blood, were *dropped* on the earth;
		8		it was as though a great mountain, all on fire, had been *dropped* into the sea.
	12	4		Its tail dragged a third of the stars from the sky and *dropped* them to the earth.
		9	Ⓓ	The great dragon . . . known as the devil . . . was *hurled* down, *hurled* down to the earth and his angels were *hurled* down with him
			Ⓓ	
		10	Ⓓ	now that the persecutor . . . has been ⌜brought (lit. *flung*) down.
		13	Ⓓ	As soon as the devil found himself *thrown* down to the earth, he sprang in pursuit of the woman,
		15		the serpent ⌜*vomited* (lit. *hurled*) water from his mouth, like a river,
		16		the earth . . . swallowed the river *thrown* up by the dragon's jaws.
	18	19		They will *throw* dust on their heads
		21		a powerful angel picked up a boulder . . . and as he *hurled* it into the sea, he said, 'That is how . . . Babylon is going to be *hurled* down,
	19	20		[The beast and the false prophet] were *thrown* alive into the Abyss,
	20	3	Ⓓ	[The angel] *threw* [the dragon] into the Abyss, and shut the entrance
		10	Ⓓ	the devil . . . will be *thrown* into the lake of fire and sulphur,
		14		Death and Hades were *thrown* into the burning lake
		15		¹⁵ and anybody whose name could not be found written in the book of life was *thrown* into the burning lake.

2: (MAKE A) CAST (WITH) A NET – THROW, DROP, A NET

Mt	4	18	5	Simon . . . and his brother Andrew . . . were *making a cast* in the lake with their *net*,
	13	47		the kingdom of heaven is like a dragnet *cast* into the sea
	17	27		go to the lake and *cast* a hook;
Mk	1	16	4	Simon and his brother Andrew *casting a net* in the lake

Jn 21 6   *Throw* the net out . . . So they *dropped* the net,

2. THROW (DOWN), FLING, WAVE – DROP, CAST DOWN – DOWNCAST: *RHIPTŌ*

1 *rhiptō* 8		3 *apo-rhiptō* 1	
		2 *epi-rhiptō* 2	

Mt 9 36 ○   the crowds . . . were harassed and *dejected*, like sheep without a shepherd,

15 30   large crowds came to him bringing the lame, . . . the dumb and many others; these they ⌐put down (lit. *dropped*) at his feet,

27 5   *flinging down* the silver pieces in the sanctuary [Judas] . . . went and hanged himself.

Lk 4 35   the devil, *throwing* the man down in front of everyone, went out of him

17 2   It would be better for him to be *thrown* into the sea

19 35   2 *throwing* their garments over [the colt's] back they helped Jesus on to it.

Ac 22 23   They were yelling, *waving* their cloaks

27 19   they *threw* the ship's gear overboard

29   they *dropped* four anchors from the stern

43   [The centurion] gave orders that those who could swim should ⌐jump (lit. *throw* themselves) overboard

1 P 5 7 ○   2 (Ps 55 22) ⌐unload (lit. *throw*) all your worries on to [God],

3. THROW TO THE GROUND, DASH DOWN: *RHĒGNYMI*

rhēgnymi, rhēssō 2/7

Mk 9 18   when [the spirit of dumbness] takes hold of [my son] it *throws him to the ground*,

Lk 9 42   the devil *threw* [the boy] *to the ground* in convulsions.

4. THROW DOWN, HURL OVER: *KATA-KRĒMNIZŌ*

kata-krēmnizō 1

Lk 4 29   [everyone in the synagogue] sprang to their feet and . . . took [Jesus] up to the brow of the hill . . . , intending to *throw* him *down* the cliff,

TIME – DAY – HOUR

1. **Time**: *chronos*
2. **Time – Opportunity**
   1: Time – Opportunity: *kairos*
     a) Time – Season
     b) For a time, For a while
     c) (Have) Time (to, for), Opportunity – Timely, Opportune, Convenient
   2: Opportunity, Chance: *aph-ormē*
3. **Lifetime, Span of life, Age – Contemporary:** *hēlikia*
4. **Day – Time – Daily**
   1: Day – Time: *hēmera*
     a) (special or feast) Day(s)
     b) the Days, the Time (of the Passion, Resurrection and Ascension)
     c) the Day(s), the Time (of God's action)
     d) Day(s), Time (generally)

     e) Today, This day
     f) (Time of the) Day, Daylight
     g) (each, every) Day, Daily
   2: Daily: *ep-iousios*
5. **Yesterday – Tomorrow – (the) Next day**
   1: Yesterday: *echthes*
   2: Tomorrow – (the) Next day: *aurion*
   3: (the) Next day: *tē hetera*
6. **Hour – Time:** *hōra*
     a) Hour (of the day) – the Time
     b) (Jesus's) Hour
     c) the Hour, the Time (of Judgement)
     d) the Hour = the Moment, the Time, the Instant
     e) an Hour
     f) an Hour = a Time, a Moment

1. TIME: *CHRONOS*

1 *chronos*	54	3 (*makro-*)*chronios* **1**
2 *chrono(-tribeō)*	**1**	

Mt 2 7   [Herod] asked [the wise men] the exact ⌐date on (lit. *time* at) which the star had appeared,

16   [Herod] had all the male children killed who were two years old or under, reckoning by the ⌐date (lit. *time*) he had been careful to ask the wise men.

Mt 25 19   Now a long *time* after, the master of those servants came back

Mk 2 19   ⌐As long as (lit. For the *time*) they have the bridegroom with them, they could not think of fasting.

9 21   ⌐How long (lit. For what *time*) has this been happening to him?

Lk 1 57   the *time* came for Elizabeth to have her child,

4 5   the devil showed [Jesus] in a moment (G of *time*) all the kingdoms of the world

8 27   for a long *time* [the demoniac] had worn no clothes,

29   It was a devil that had seized on him a great many *times*,

18 4   [I want justice from you against my enemy!] For a long *time* [the judge] refused,

20 9   A man planted a vineyard . . . and went abroad for a long *while*.

23 8   Herod . . . had been wanting for a long *time* to set eyes on [Jesus];

Jn 5 6   Jesus . . . knew [the sick man] had been in this condition for a long *time*,

7 33   I shall remain with you for only a short *time* now;

12 35   The light will be with you only a little ⌐longer (lit. *time*) now.

14 9   Have I been with you all this *time*, Philip . . . and you still do not know me?

Ac 1 6   Lord, has the *time* come? Are you going to restore the kingdom to Israel? [7] He replied, 'It is not for you to know *times* or dates that the Father has decided by his own authority,

21   We must . . . choose someone who has been with us the whole *time* that the Lord Jesus was travelling round with us,

3 21   heaven must keep [Jesus] till the *time* the universal restoration comes which God proclaimed,

7 17   the *time* drew near for God to fulfil the promise

23   At the *age* of forty [Moses] decided to visit his countrymen,

8 11   [The Samaritan people] had only been won over to [Simon] because of the long *time* he had spent working on them with his magic.

13 18   for a *time* of about forty years [God] took care of [our nation] in the wilderness.

14 3   Paul and Barnabas stayed on for some *time* [at Iconium],

28   [Paul and Barnabas] stayed there with the disciples for some *time*.

15 33   [Judas and Silas] spent some *time* [in Antioch], and then . . . they went back to those who had sent them.

17 30   God overlooked that sort of thing at the *time* when men were ignorant,

18 20   [The Jews] asked [Paul] to stay ⌐longer (lit. for more *time*) but he declined,

23   [Paul] spent a short *time* [in Antioch] before continuing his journey

19 22   [Paul] remained for a *time* in Asia.

20 16   2   Paul had decided to pass wide of Ephesus so as to avoid spending *time* in Asia.

18   You know what my way of life has been ⌐ever (lit. all the *time*) since the first day I set foot among you in Asia.

27 9   A great deal of *time* had been lost,

Rm 7 1   laws affect a person only during his life*time*.

16 25   I proclaim . . . the revelation of a mystery kept secret for endless *ages*,

1 Co 7 39   A wife is tied ⌐as long as (lit. for the *time*) her husband is alive.

16 7   I hope to spend some *time* with you,

Ga 4 1   an heir . . . is no different from a slave for ⌐as long as (lit. the *time*) he remains a child.

4   when the appointed *time* came, God sent his Son.

Ep 6 3   3   (Ex 20 12) you will . . . ⌐have a long life (lit. be a long *time*) in the land.

1 Th 5 1   You will not be expecting us to write anything . . . about 'times and seasons',

2 Tm 1 9   This grace had already been granted to us, in Christ Jesus, before the beginning of *time*,

Tt 1 2   the eternal life . . . was promised ⌐so long ago (lit. before eternal *times*) by God.

Heb 4 7   God fixed another day when, ⌐much later (lit. after a long *time*), he said 'today' through David

5 12   you should by this *time* have become masters,

11 32   There is not *time* for me to give an account of Gideon . . . and the prophets.

1 P 1 17   you must be scrupulously careful ⌐as long as (lit. during the *time*) you are living away from home.

20   [Christ] has been revealed only in our *time*, the end of the ages, for our sake.

4 2   for the ⌐rest (lit. remaining *time*) of his life on earth [Christ] is . . . ruled . . . only by the will of God. [3] You spent

3   quite ⌐long (lit. *time*) enough in the past living the sort of life that pagans live,

Jude 18   At the end of *time* . . . there are going to be people who sneer at religion

Rv 2 21   I have given her *time* to reform

6 11   Each of them was given a white robe, and they were told to be patient a little ⌐longer (lit. more *time*),

10 6   [the angel] swore . . . 'The *time* of waiting is over;

Rv 20 3 [Satan] must be released, but only for a short *while*.

2. TIME – OPPORTUNITY

1: TIME – OPPORTUNITY: *KAIROS*

1	kairos 86	4	eu-kairia	2
7	a-kaireō 1	5	eu-kairos	2
8	a-kairōs 1	6	eu-kairōs	2
3	eu-kaireō 3	2	pros-kairos	4

a) Time – Season

Mt 8 29 Have you come here to torture us before the *time*?
11 25 At that *time* Jesus exclaimed, 'I bless you, Father,
12 1 At that *time* Jesus took a walk one sabbath day
13 30 at harvest *time* I shall say to the reapers:
14 1 At that *time* Herod . . . heard about the reputation of Jesus,
16 3 You know how to read the face of the sky, but you cannot read the signs of the *times*.
21 34 When vintage *time* drew near he sent his servants to the tenants
41 other tenants . . . will deliver the produce to him when the *season* arrives,
24 45 What sort of servant . . . is faithful . . . enough for the master to place him over his household to give teem their food at the [proper] *time*?
26 18 The Master says: My *time* is near.
Mk 1 15 The *time* has come . . . and the kingdom of God is close at hand.
10 30 [there is no one who has left house, brothers . . .] who will not be repaid a hundred times over . . . now in this present *time* and, in the world to come, eternal life.
11 13 it was not the *season* for figs.
12 2 When the *time* came, he sent a servant to the tenants
13 33 you never know when the *time* will come.
Lk 1 20 my words . . . will come true at their [appointed] *time*,
4 13 the devil left [Jesus], to return at the [appointed] *time*.
8 13 in *time* of trial they give up.
42 What sort of steward . . . is faithful . . . enough for the master to place him over his household to give them their allowance of food at the [proper] *time*?
56 How is it you do not know how to interpret these *times*?
13 1 It was just about this *time* that some people arrived
18 30 [there is no one who has left house, wife . . .] who will not be given repayment many times over in this present *time* and, in the world to come, eternal life.
19 44 you did not recognise your ⌐opportunity (or: *time*) when God offered it!
20 10 When the *time* came, he sent a servant to the tenants
21 8 the *time* is near at hand.
24 Jerusalem will be trampled down by the pagans until the *age* of the pagans is completely over.
36 Stay awake, praying at all *times*
Jn 5 4 ᵛfor at ⌐intervals (lit. *times*) the angel of the Lord came down into the pool . . .⌐
7 6 The [right] *time* for me has not come yet, but any [time] is the [right] *time* for you . . . ⁸ Go up to the festival yourselves: . . . for me the *time* is not ripe yet.
Ac 1 7 It is not for you to know times or *dates* that the Father has decided
3 20 [You must repent] so that the Lord may send the *time* of comfort.
7 20 It was at this *period* that Moses was born,
12 1 It was about this *time* that King Herod started persecuting certain members of the Church.
13 11 [Elymas,] for a *time* you will not see the sun.
14 17 [God] sends you rain from heaven, ⌐he makes your crops grow when they should (lit. and fruitful *times* [of the year]),
17 26 [God] decreed ⌐how long (lit. for what *time*) each nation should flourish
19 23 It was during this *time* that a rather serious disturbance broke out
Rm 3 26 [God makes his justice known,] for the present *age*, by showing positively that he is just,
5 6 at his appointed *moment* Christ died for sinful men.
8 18 what we suffer in this ⌐life (lit. present *time*) can never be compared to the glory . . . which is waiting for us.
9 9 (Gn 18 10) I shall visit you at such and such a *time*, and Sarah will have a son.
11 5 ⌐Today (lit. [Now,] at the present *time*,) the same thing has happened: there is a remnant, chosen by grace.
13 11 Besides, you know the *time* has come: you must wake up now:
1 Co 4 5 There must be no passing of ⌐premature judgement (lit. judgement before the *time*).
7 29 Brothers, this is what I mean: our *time* is growing short.
2 Co 6 2 (Is 49 8) At the favourable *time*, I have listened to you . . . Well, now is the favourable *time*;

2 Co 8 14 [it is a question of balancing] what happens to be your surplus now against their ⌐present need (lit. need at the present *time*),
Ga 4 10 You and your special days and months and *seasons* and years!
6 9 we shall get our harvest at the [proper] *time*.
Ep 1 10 [God has let us know] the hidden plan he so kindly made in Christ from the beginning to act upon when the *times* had run their course to the end:
2 12 ⌐do not forget, I say, that (lit. remember that at that *time*) you had no Christ
5 16 This may be a wicked age, but ⌐your lives should redeem it⌐ (lit. you should make the most of the *time*).
6 18 Pray all the *time* . . . in the Spirit
Col 4 5 make the best use of your *time* with [those who are not Christians].
1 Th 2 17 A short *time* (G within an hour) after we had been separated from you . . . we had an especially strong desire . . . to see you
5 1 You will not be expecting us to write anything to you . . . about times and *seasons*,
2 Th 2 6 you know . . . what is still holding [the Rebel] back from appearing before his [appointed] *time*.
1 Tm 2 6 [Christ] is the evidence of this, sent at the appointed *time*,
4 1 during the last *times* there will be some who will desert the faith
6 15 [our Lord Jesus Christ,] at the due *time* will be revealed by God,
2 Tm 3 1 in the last days there are going to be some difficult *times*.
4 3 The *time* is sure to come when . . . people will be avid for the latest novelty
6 the *time* has come for me to be gone.
Tt 1 3 at the appointed *time*, [God] revealed his decision,
Heb 9 9 it is a symbol for this present *time*.
10 they are rules about the outward life . . . intended to be in force only until it should be *time* to reform them.
11 11 It was equally by faith that Sarah, in spite of being past ⌐the (lit. that *time* of her) age, was made able to conceive,
15 They can hardly have meant the country they came from, since they had the ⌐opportunity (or: *time*) to go back to it;
1 P 1 5 God's power will guard you until the salvation which . . . is revealed at the end of *time*.
11 they tried to find out at what *time* and in what circumstances all this was to be expected.
4 17 The *time* has come for the judgement to begin
5 6 Bow down . . . now, and [God] will raise you up ⌐on the appointed day (lit. at the *time*);
Rv 1 3 the *Time* is close.
11 18 now the *time* has come . . . for the dead to be judged,
12 12 the devil has gone down to [the earth and the sea] in a rage, knowing that his ⌐days are numbered (lit. *time* is short).
14 (Dn 7 25) [the woman] was to be looked after for a ⌐year (lit. *season*) and twice a ⌐year (lit. *season*) and half a ⌐year (lit. *season*).
22 10 Do not keep the prophecies in this book a secret, because the *Time* is close.

b) For a time, For a while

Mt 13 21 2 he has no root in him, he ⌐does not last (lit. continues *for a time*);
Mk 4 17 they have no root in them, they ⌐do not last (lit. continue 2 *for a time*);
Lk 8 13 they believe for a *while*, and in time of trial they give up.
1 Co 7 5 Do not refuse each other except . . . for an agreed *time*,
2 Co 4 18 2 visible things [last only] *for a time*, and the invisible things are eternal.
Heb 11 25 [Moses] chose to be ill-treated in company with God's people 2 rather than to enjoy *for a time* the pleasures of sin.

c) (Have) Time (to, for), Opportunity – Timely, Opportune, Convenient

Mt 26 16 4 from that moment [Judas] looked for an *opportunity* to betray him.
Mk 6 21 5 An *opportunity* [to kill John the Baptist] came on Herod's birthday
31 3 the apostles *had* no *time* even to eat.
14 11 6 [Judas] looked for a way of betraying him *when the opportunity should occur*.
Lk 19 44 you did not recognise your ⌐opportunity (or: *time*) when God offered it!
22 6 4 [Judas] looked for an *opportunity* to betray [Jesus] to them
Ac 17 21 3 The one thing the Athenians . . . seem to *have time* for . . . is listening to lectures of [the latest ideas].
24 25 I will send for you when I find it *convenient*.
1 Co 16 12 3 [Apollos] will come as soon as he ⌐can (lit. *has time* to).
Ga 6 10 While we have the *chance*, we must do good to all,
Ph 4 10 at last you have shown some concern for me again; though 7 of course you were concerned before, and only *lacked an opportunity*.
2 Tm 4 2 6 proclaim the message and, ⌐welcome (or: *convenient*) or 8 ⌐unwelcome (or: *inconvenient*), insist on it.

Heb 4 16	Let us be confident . . . that we shall . . . find grace ⌐when
5	we are in need of help (lit. in *timely* help).
11 15	They can hardly have meant the country they came from, since they had the ⌐*opportunity* (or: time) to go back to it;

2: OPPORTUNITY, CHANCE: *APH-ORMĒ*

aph-ormē 7

Rm 7 8	it was this commandment that sin took advantage of the *opportunity* of to produce all kinds of covetousness in me,
11	sin took advantage of the *opportunity* provided by the commandment
2 Co 5 12	we are simply giving you ⌐reasons (lit. an *opportunity*) to be proud of us,
11 12	I intend to go on . . . leaving no *opportunity* for those people who are looking for an *opportunity* to claim equality with us
Ga 5 13	this liberty will provide an *opening* for self-indulgence
1 Tm 5 14	it is best for young widows to marry again . . . and not give the enemy any *chance* to raise a scandal about them;

3. LIFETIME, SPAN OF LIFE, AGE – CONTEMPORARY: *HĒLIKIA*

1 *hēlikia 6/8*   2 *syn-(h)ēlikiōtēs 1*

Mt 6 27	Can any of you . . . add one single cubit to his ⌐*span of life* (or: stature)?
Lk 12 25	Can any of you . . . add a single cubit to his ⌐*span of life* (or: stature)?
Jn 9 21	He is ⌐old enough (lit. *of age*): let him speak for himself . . .
23	23 This was why his parents said, 'He is ⌐old enough (lit. *of age*); ask him'.
Ga 1 14	2 I stood out among other ⌐Jews *of my generation* (or: Jewish contemporaries of mine),
Ep 4 13	we become the perfect Man, ⌐fully mature (lit. of full *age*) with the fullness of Christ himself.
Heb 11 11	Sarah, in spite of being past ⌐the (lit. that time of her) *age*, was made able to conceive,

4. DAY – TIME – DAILY

1: DAY – TIME: *HĒMERA*

1	*hēmera*	*360/389*	5	*eph-ēmeros 1*
2	*sēmeron*	*41*	3	*(mes-)(h)ēmbria 2*
4	*kath-ēmerinos*	*1*	6	*(okta-)(h)ēmeros 1*

For Day and Night *see* NIGHT – DARKNESS 1. a)

a) (special or feast) Day(s)

Mk 14 12	On the first *day* of Unleavened Bread . . . the Passover lamb was sacrificed,
Lk 2 43	When [Jesus's parents] were on their way home after the ⌐feast (lit. *days*), the boy Jesus stayed behind
4 16	[Jesus] went into the synagogue on the sabbath *day* as he usually did.
13 14	There are six *days* . . . when work is to be done. Come and be healed on one of those [days] and not on the sabbath *day*.
16	was it not right to untie [this woman's] bonds on the sabbath *day*?
14 5	Which of you here, if his son falls into a well . . . will not pull him out on a sabbath *day* without hesitation?
22 7	The *day* of Unleavened Bread came round . . . on which the passover had to be sacrificed,
23 54	It was Preparation *Day*
Jn 5 9	The man was cured . . . Now that *day* happened to be the sabbath,
7 37	On the last *day* and greatest day of the festival [of Tabernacles], Jesus . . . cried out:
9 14	It had been a sabbath *day* when Jesus . . . opened the man's eyes,
19 31	It was Preparation [Day], and . . . that sabbath was a *day* of special solemnity
Ac 2 1	When Pentecost *day* came round, they had all met in one room,
12 3	[Herod] decided to arrest Peter as well. This was during the *days* of Unleavened Bread,
13 14	[Paul and his friends] went to synagogue on the sabbath *day*
16 13	we went . . . outside the gates as it was the sabbath *day* and this was a customary place for prayer.
20 6	We ourselves left Philippi . . . after the *days* of Unleavened Bread

Ac 20 16	[Paul] was anxious to be in Jerusalem . . . for the *day* of Pentecost.
Rm 14 5	one man keeps certain *days* as holier than ⌐others (lit. other *days*), and another considers all *days* to be equally holy,
6	The one who observes special *days* does so in honour of the Lord.
Ga 4 10	You and your special *days* and months and seasons and years!
Heb 4 4	(Gn 2 2) God rested on the seventh *day*.

b) the Days, the Time (of the Passion, Resurrection and Ascension)

S = Sunday (the Lord's Day)

Mt 9 15	the *time* will come for the bridegroom to be taken away
12 40	(Jon 2 1) as Jonah was in the belly of the sea-monster for three *days* and three nights, so will the Son of Man be in the heart of the earth for three *days* and three nights.
16 21	Jesus began to make it clear . . . that he was destined . . to be put to death and to be raised up on the third *day*.
17 23	on the third *day* he will be raised to life again.
20 19	on the third *day* [the Son of Man] will rise again.
26 61	I have power to destroy the Temple of God and in three *days* build it up.
27 40	So you would destroy the Temple and rebuild it in three *days*!
63	After three *days* I shall rise again.
64	have the sepulchre kept secure until the third *day*,
Mk 2 20	the *time* will come for the bridegroom to be taken away from them, and then, on that *day*, they will fast.
8 31	the Son of Man was destined . . . after three *days* to rise again;
9 31	three *days* after [the Son of Man] has been put to death he will rise again.
10 34	after three *days* [the Son of Man] will rise again.
14 58	I am going to destroy this Temple . . . and in three *days* build another,
15 29	So you would destroy the Temple and rebuild it in three *days*!
Lk 5 35	the *time* will come . . . for the bridegroom to be taken away from them; that will be the *time* when they will fast.
9 22	The Son of Man . . . is destined . . . to be raised up on the third *day*.
51	the *time* drew near for him to be taken up to heaven,
18 33	on the third *day* [the Son of Man] will rise again.
23 7	Herod . . . was also in Jerusalem at that *time*.
12	Herod and Pilate . . . were reconciled that same *day*.
24 7	the Son of Man had to . . . rise again on the third *day*.
13 S	That very same *day*, two of them were on their way to . . . Emmaus,
18	You must be the only person staying in Jerusalem who does not know the things that have been happening there these last few *days*.
21	⌐two whole days have gone by (lit. this is the third *day*) since it all happened;
46	the Christ would suffer and on the third *day* rise from the dead,
Jn 2 19	Destroy this sanctuary, and in three *days* I will raise it up.
20	are you going to raise [this sanctuary] up in three *days*?
12 7	she had to keep this scent for the *day* of my burial.
20 19 S	In the evening of that same *day*, the first [day] of the week, the doors were closed in the room where the disciples were,
26 S	Eight *days* later the disciples were in the house again
Ac 1 2	[I dealt with everything Jesus had done] until the *day* he . . . was taken up to heaven.
3	for forty *days* [Jesus] had continued to appear to them
5	you, not many *days* from now, will be baptised with the Holy Spirit.
15	One *day* Peter stood up to speak to the brothers
22	[We must choose] someone who was with us . . . until the *day* when [Jesus] was taken up from us
10 40	three *days* afterwards God raised him to life
13 31	for many *days* [Jesus] appeared to those who had accompanied him
1 Co 15 4	[Jesus] was raised to life on the third *day*,
Heb 5 7	During his ⌐life (lit. *days*) on earth, [Christ] offered up prayer and entreaty,
10 16	(Jr 31 33) This is the covenant I will make with them when those *days* arrive;
Rv 1 10 S	it was the Lord's *day* and the Spirit possessed me,

c) the Day(s), the Time (of God's action)

N = the Days of Noah or of Lot

Mt 7 22	When the *day* comes many will say to me, 'Lord, Lord, did we not prophesy in your name . . .?'
10 15	on the *day* of Judgement it will not go as hard with the land of Sodom and Gomorrah as with that town.
11 22	it will not go as hard on Judgement *day* with Tyre and Sidon as with you.
24	it will not go as hard with the land of Sodom on Judgement *day* as with you.
12 36	for every unfounded word men utter they will answer on Judgement *day*,

Mt 24	19		Alas for those with child . . . when those *days* come!
	22		if that *time* had not been shortened, no one would have survived; but shortened that *time* shall be, for the sake of those who are chosen.
	29		after the distress of those *days* the sun will be darkened,
	36		as for that *day* and hour, nobody knows it,
	37	N	As it was in Noah's *day*, so will it be when the Son of Man comes.
	38	N	in those *days* before the Flood people were eating, drinking . . . right up to the *day* Noah went into the ark,
		N	
	42		you do not know the *day* when your master is coming.
	50	<	his master will come on a *day* he does not expect
25	13		So stay awake, because you do not know either the *day* or the hour.
26	29		I shall not drink wine until the *day* I drink the new wine with you
Mk 13	17		Alas for those with child . . . when those *days* come!
	19		in those *days* there will be such distress as, until now, has not been equalled . . . ²⁰ And if the Lord had not shortened
	20		that *time*, no one would have survived; but he did shorten the *time* for the sake of the elect
	24		in those *days* . . . the sun will be darkened,
	32		as for that *day* or hour, nobody knows it,
14	25		I shall not drink any more wine until the *day* I drink the new wine
Lk 10	12		on that *day* it will not go as hard with Sodom as with that town.
12	46	<	his master will come on a *day* he does not expect
17	22		A *time* will come when you will long to see one of the *days* of the Son of Man and will not see it.
	24		as the lightning flashing from one part of heaven lights up the other, so will be the Son of Man in his *day*.
	26	N	As it was in Noah's *day*, so will it also be in the *days* of the Son of Man. ²⁷ People were eating and drinking . . . right up to the *day* Noah went into the ark,
	27		
		N	
	28	N	It will be the same as it was in Lot's *day*: people were eating and drinking . . . ²⁹ but the *day* Lot left Sodom, God destroyed them all. ³⁰ It will be the same when the *day* comes for the Son of Man to be revealed.
	29	N	
	30		
	31		When that *day* comes, anyone on the housetop . . . must not come down
19	42		If you . . . had only understood on this *day* the message of peace!
	43		a *time* is coming when your enemies . . . will encircle you
21	6		the *time* will come when not a single stone will be left on another:
	22		this is the *time* of vengeance
	23		Alas for those with child . . . when those *days* come!
	34		that *day* will be sprung on you suddenly,
23	29		the *days* will surely come when people will say, 'Happy are those who are barren,
Jn 6	39		the will of him who sent me is that I should lose nothing . . . and that I should raise it up on the last *day*. ⁴⁰ Yes, it is my
	40		Father's will that . . . I shall raise him up on the last *day*.
	44		I will raise him up at the last *day*.
	54		I shall raise [anyone who does eat my flesh] up on the last *day*.
8	56		Abraham rejoiced to think that he would see my *Day*;
11	24		I know [Lazarus] will rise again . . . on the last *day*.
12	48		the word itself . . . will be his judge on the last *day*.
14	20		On that *day* you will understand that I am in my Father
16	23		When that *day* comes, you will not ask me any questions.
	26		When that *day* comes, you will ask in my name;
Ac 2	17		(Jl 3 1f) In the *days* to come . . . I will pour out my spirit . . . ¹⁸ Even on my slaves, men and women, in those *days*, I will pour out my spirit. ¹⁹ I will display portents . . . ²⁰ . . . before the great *Day* of the Lord dawns.
	18		
	20		
3	24		all the prophets . . . have predicted these *days*.
13	41		(Hab 1 5) I am doing something in your own *days* that you would not believe if you were to be told of it.
17	31		[God] has fixed a *day* when the whole world will be judged,
Rm 2	5		Your stubborn refusal to repent is only adding to the anger God will have towards you on that *day* of anger
	16		on the *day* when . . . God . . . judges the secrets of mankind.
13	12		The night is almost over, it will be *daylight* soon
1 Co 1	8		he will keep you . . . without blame until the last *day*, the [day] of our Lord Jesus Christ.
3	13		the work of each builder is going to be clearly revealed when the *day* comes.
5	5		he is to be handed over to Satan so that . . . his spirit [may be] saved on the *day* of the Lord.
2 Co 1	14		when the *day* of our Lord Jesus comes . . . you can be as proud of us as we are of you.
6	2		(Is 49 8) on the *day* of salvation I came to your help. Well, . . . this is the *day* of salvation.
Ep 4	30		the Holy Spirit of God . . . has marked you with his seal for you to be set free when the *day* comes.
Ph 1	6		the One who began this good work in you will see that it is finished when the *Day* of Christ Jesus comes.
	10		This will . . . prepare you for the *Day* of Christ,

Ph 2	16		This would give me something to be proud of for the *Day* of Christ,
1 Th 5	2		the *Day* of the Lord is going to come like a thief in the night.
	4		it is not as if you live in the dark . . . for that *Day* to overtake you like a thief.
2 Th 1	10		It will be their punishment to be . . . excluded from the presence of the Lord . . . on that *day* when he comes to be glorified
2	2		do not get . . . alarmed by any prediction . . . implying that the *Day* of the Lord has already arrived.
2 Tm 1	12		he is able to take care of all that I have entrusted to him until that *Day*.
	18		May it be the Lord's will that [Onesiphorus] shall find the Lord's mercy on that *Day*.
3	1		in the last *days* there are going to be some difficult times.
4	8		all there is to come now is the crown of righteousness . . . which the Lord . . . will give to me on that *Day*;
Heb 1	2		in our own time, the last *days*, [God] has spoken to us through his Son,
4	7		God fixed another *day* when, much later, he said 'today' through David in the text already quoted (Ps 95 7):
	8		God would not later on have spoken so much of another *day*.
8	8		(Jr 31 31f) See, the *days* are coming . . . ¹⁰ . . . this is the covenant I will make with the House of Israel when those *days* arrive
	10		
10	16		(Jr 31 33) This is the covenant I will make with them when those *days* arrive;
	25		you see the *Day* drawing near.
Jm 5	3		It was a burning fire that you stored up as your treasure for the last *days*.
	5	Δ	in the *time* of slaughter you went on eating to your heart's content.
1 P 2	12		behave honourably among pagans so that they can . . . when the *day* of reckoning comes, give thanks to God
3	20	N	it was long ago, in the *days* when Noah was still building that ark
2 P 1	19		take [prophecy] as a lamp for lighting a way through the dark until the ʳdawn comes (lit. *day* dawns)
2	9		the Lord can . . . hold the wicked for their punishment until the *day* of Judgement,
3	3		during the last *days* there are bound to be people who will be scornful,
	7		by the same word, the present sky and earth are . . . only being reserved until Judgement *day*
	10		The *Day* of the Lord will come like a thief,
	12		you wait and long for the *Day* of God to come,
	18		To him be glory, ʳin time and in (lit. now and to the *day* of) eternity.
1 Jn 4	17		Love will come to its perfection in us when we can face the *day* of Judgement without fear;
Jude	6		[God] has kept [the angels] down in the dark, in spiritual chains, to be judged on the great *day*.
Rv 6	17		the Great *Day* of his anger has come,
9	6		ʳWhen this happens (lit. In those *days*), men will long for death and not find it anywhere;
	15		These four angels had been put there ready for this hour of this *day* of this month of this year,
10	7		at the *time* when the seventh angel is heard sounding his trumpet, God's secret intention will be fulfilled,
16	14		[they] were demon spirits . . . going out to all the kings of the world to call them together for the war of the Great *Day* of God the Almighty.

d) Day(s), Time (generally)

Mt 2	1		Jesus had been born at Bethlehem . . . during the ʳreign (lit. *days*) of King Herod,
3	1		In ʳdue course (lit. those *days*) John the Baptist appeared;
11	12		Since John ʳthe Baptist came (lit. the Baptist's *days*), up to this present time,
13	1		That same *day*, Jesus left the house
15	32		these people . . . have been with me for three *days* now and have nothing to eat.
17	1		Six *days* later, Jesus took with him Peter and James and . . . John
20	2		[The landowner] made an agreement with the workers for one denarius a *day*,
	6		Why have you been standing here idle all *day*?
	12		we have done a heavy *day*'s work in all the heat.
22	23		That *day* some Sadducees . . . approached [Jesus]
	46		from that *day* no one dared to ask [Jesus] any further questions.
23	30		We would never have joined in shedding the blood of the prophets, had we lived in our fathers' *day*.
26	2		It will be Passover . . . in two *days*' time,
28	20		I am with you ʳalways; (lit. all the *days*,) yes, to the end of time.
Mk 1	9		It was at this *time* that Jesus came from Nazareth in Galilee and was baptised
	13		[Jesus] remained [in the wilderness] for forty *days*,
2	1		[Jesus] returned to Capernaum some *time* later,

Mk	4 35	With the coming of evening that same *day*, [Jesus] said to them, 'Let us cross over to the other side'.
	6 21	┌An opportunity (lit. A convenient *time*) came on Herod's birthday
	8 1	And ┌now (lit. at about that *time*) once again a great crowd had gathered,
	2	these people . . . have been with me for three *days* now
	9 2	Six *days* later, Jesus took with him Peter and James and John
	14 1	It was two *days* before the Passover
Lk	1 5	In the *days* of King Herod . . . there lived a priest called Zechariah
	7	they were both getting on in ┌years (lit. *days*).
	18	my wife is getting on in ┌years (lit. *days*).
	20	you will be silenced . . . until the *day* this has happened.
	23	When his *time* of service came to an end [Zechariah] returned home.
	24	Some *time* later his wife Elizabeth conceived,
	25	The Lord has done this for me . . . ┌now that (lit. in these *days* when) it has pleased him to take away the humiliation I suffered
	39	Mary set out at that *time* and went . . . to a town in . . . Judah.
	59	on the eighth *day* they came to circumcise the child;
	75	[God swore that he would grant us] to serve him in holiness . . . all our *days*.
	80	[John] lived out in the wilderness until the *day* he appeared openly to Israel.
	2 1	Now at this *time* Caesar Augustus issued a decree for a census
	6	the *time* came for [Mary] to have her child,
	21	When the eighth *day* came . . . the child was to be circumcised,
	22	the *day* came for [Mary and Jesus] to be purified
	36	Anna . . . was well on in ┌years (lit. *days*).
	44	it was only after a *day*'s journey that [Jesus's parents] went to look for [Jesus].
	46	Three *days* later, they found him in the Temple,
	4 2	[Jesus was] being tempted there by the devil for forty *days*. During that *time* he ate nothing
	25	There were many widows in Israel . . . in Elijah's *day*,
	5 17	[Jesus] was teaching one *day*,
	6 12	it was about this *time* that [Jesus] went out into the hills to pray;
	23	Rejoice when that *day* comes and dance for joy,
	8 22	One *day*, [Jesus] got into a boat with his disciples
	9 28	about eight *days* after this . . . [Jesus] took with him Peter and John and James
	36	The disciples kept silence and, at that *time*, told no one what they had seen.
	37	on the following *day* . . . a large crowd came to meet [Jesus].
	15 13	A few *days* later, the younger son . . . left
	20 1	one *day* . . . [Jesus] was teaching the people in the Temple
Jn	1 39	[the two disciples] stayed with [Jesus] the rest of that *day*.
	2 1	Three *days* later there was a wedding at Cana
	12	[Jesus] went down to Capernaum with his mother and the brothers, but they stayed there only a few *days*.
	4 40	[Jesus] stayed [in Sychar] for two *days*,
	43	When the two *days* were over Jesus left for Galilee.
	11 6	when he heard that Lazarus was ill he stayed where he was for two more *days*
	17	Jesus found that Lazarus had been in the tomb for four *days*
	53	From that *day* [the chief priests] were determined to kill [Jesus].
	12 1	Six *days* before the Passover, Jesus went to Bethany,
Ac	2 41	That very *day* about three thousand were added to their number.
	5 36	Some *time* ago there was Theudas who became notorious
	37	then there was Judas the Galilean, at the *time* of the census,
	6 1	About this *time*, when the number of disciples was increasing, the Hellenists made a complaint
	7 8	[Abraham] circumcised [Isaac] on the eighth *day*.
	26	The next *day*, when [Moses] came across some of them fighting, he tried to reconcile them.
	41	It was ┌then (lit. at that *time*) that they made a bull calf
	45	Here [the Tent of Testimony] stayed until the *time* of David.
	8 1	That *day* a bitter persecution started against the church
	9 9	For three *days* [Saul] was without his sight,
	19	[Saul] spent only a few *days* . . . in Damascus,
	23	Some *time* passed, and the Jews worked out a plot to kill [Saul],
	37	the *time* came when [Tabitha] got ill and died,
	43	Peter stayed on some *time* in Jaffa,
	10 3	One *day* at about the ninth hour [Cornelius] had a vision
	30	┌Three days ago (lit. At the end of the fourth *day* backward from this precise hour) I was praying
	48	[the pagans] begged [Peter] to stay on for some *days*.
	11 27	┌While they were there (lit. In those *days*) some prophets came down to Antioch from Jerusalem,
	12 21	A *day* was fixed, and Herod . . . made a speech to them.
	15 7	in the early *days* God made his choice among you:
	36	┌On a later occasion (lit. Some *days* later) Paul said to Barnabas, 'Let us go back and . . . see how the brothers are doing'.

Ac	16 12	After a few *days* in [Philippi] [13] we went along the river
	18	[The slave-girl followed Paul and Silas] every *day*
	18 18	After staying on for some *time*, Paul took leave of the brothers
	20 6	We . . . met them five *days* later at Troas, where we stopped for ┌a week (lit. seven *days*).
	18	You know what my way of life has been ever since the first *day* I set foot among you in Asia,
	21 4	We . . . stayed [at Tyre] ┌a week (lit. seven *days*).
	5	when our *time* was up we set off.
	7	at Ptolemais . . . we greeted the brothers and stayed one *day* with them.
	10	we had been [at Caesarea] several *days*
	15	Some *days* after this we . . . went on up to Jerusalem.
	26	the next *day* Paul took the men along and was purified with them, and he visited the Temple to give notice of the time when the *period* of purification would be over . . . [27] The seven *days* were nearly over when some Jews . . . caught sight of him
	38	So you are not the Egyptian who started the ┌recent revolt (lit. revolt a short *time* ago) . . .?
	24 1	Five *days* later . . . Ananias came . . . before the governor.
	11	it is no more than twelve *days* since I went up to Jerusalem
	24	Some *days* later Felix came with his wife Drusilla
	25 1	Three *days* after his arrival . . . Festus went up to Jerusalem
	6	After staying with them for eight or ten *days* at the most, [Festus] went down to Caesarea
	13	Some *days* later King Agrippa and Bernice arrived in Caesarea . . . [14] Their visit lasted several *days*,
	27 5	[we sailed] across the open sea . . . ᵛ taking ┌a fortnight (lit. fifteen *days*) to reach Myra in Lycia.
	7	For some *days* we made little headway,
	20	For a number of *days* both the sun and the stars were invisible
	33	For fourteen *days*. . . you have been in suspense,
	28 7	Publius . . . entertained us hospitably for three *days*.
	12	We put in at Syracuse and spent three *days* there;
	13	After one *day* [in Rhegium] a south wind sprang up
	14	[in Puteoli] we found some brothers and were much rewarded by staying ┌a week (lit. seven *days*) with them.
	17	After three *days* [Paul] called together the leading Jews.
	23	[the Roman Jews] arranged a *day* with [Paul]
Rm	8 36	(Ps 44 22) For your sake we are being massacred ┌daily (lit. all the *day* long),
	10 21	(Is 65 2) ┌Each day (lit. All *day* long) I stretched out my hand to a disobedient . . . people.
1 Co	10 8	twenty-three thousand [Israelites] met their downfall in one *day*.
2 Co	4 16	the inner man is renewed *day* by *day*.
Ga	1 18	I . . . stayed with [Cephas] for fifteen *days*,
Ep	5 16	┌This may be a wicked age (lit. These may be wicked *days*),
	6 13	you must rely on God's armour, or you will not be able to put up any resistance when the ┌worst (lit. evil *day*) happens,
Ph	1 5	you have helped to spread the Good News from the *day* you . . . heard it right up to the present.
	3 5	6 I was circumcised when I was eight *days* old.
Col	1 6	[the Good News is] producing the same results as it has among you ever since the *day* when you heard about God's grace
	9	ever since the *day* [Epaphras] told us [about your love in the Spirit], we have never failed to pray for you,
Heb	3 8	(Ps 95 8) do not harden your hearts, as happened . . . on the Day of Temptation in the wilderness,
	7 3	[Melchizedek's] ┌life has (lit. *days* have) no beginning or ending;
	8 9	(Jr 31 32) I made [a covenant] with their ancestors on the *day* I took them by the hand to bring them out of . . . Egypt.
	10 32	Remember all the sufferings that you had to meet after you received the light, in earlier *days*;
	11 30	the walls of Jericho fell down when the people had been round them for seven *days*.
	12 10	Our human fathers were thinking of ┌this short life (lit. these few *days*) when they punished us,
1 P	3 10	(Ps 34 13) Anyone who wants ┌a happy life (lit. happy *days*) . . . must banish malice from his tongue;
2 P	2 8	[Lot] was outraged in his good soul by the crimes that he saw . . . *day* after *day*.
	13	They are . . . men whose only object is dissipation all *day* long,
	3 8	(Ps 90 4) with the Lord, 'a *day*' can mean a thousand years, and a thousand years is like a *day*.
Rv	2 10	you must face an ordeal for ten *days*.
	13	you still hold firmly to my name, and did not disown your faith in me even in the *days* when . . . Antipas was killed
	11 3	I shall send my two witnesses to prophesy for those twelve hundred and sixty *days*,
	6	it does not rain ┌as long as (lit. on the *days* when) they are prophesying;
	9	Men out of every people . . . will stare at their corpses, for three-and-a-half *days*,

Rv 11	11		After the three-and-a-half *days*, God breathed life into them
12	6		the woman escaped into the desert . . . to be looked after in the twelve hundred and sixty *days*.
18	8		within a single *day*, the plagues will fall on [Babylon]:

e) Today, This day

Mt 6	11	2	[Our Father . . .] Give us *today* our daily bread.
	30	2	the grass in the field . . . is there *today* and thrown into the furnace tomorrow,
11	23	2	Capernaum, . . . if the miracles done in you had been done in Sodom, it would have been standing ⌐yet (lit. *today*).
16	3	2	in the morning [you say], 'Stormy weather *today*; the sky is red and overcast'.
21	28	2	My boy, you go and work in the vineyard *today*.
27	8	2	this is why the field is called the Field of Blood *today*.
	19	2	I have been upset all *today* by a dream I had about [Jesus].
28	15	/2	⌐to this day (lit. to this *day today*) that is the story among the Jews.
Mk 14	30	2	*this day*, this very night . . . you will have disowned me three times.
Lk 2	11	2	*Today* in the town of David a saviour has been born
4	21	2	This text is being fulfilled *today* even as you listen.
5	26	2	We have seen strange things *today*.
12	28	2	the grass in the field . . . is there *today* and thrown into the furnace tomorrow.
13	32	2	Learn that *today* and tomorrow I cast out devils and on the third day attain my end. [33] But for *today* and tomorrow and the next day I must go on,
	33	2	
19	5	2	Zacchaeus, . . . I must stay at your house *today*.
	9	2	*Today* salvation has come to this house,
22	34	2	by the time the cock crows *today* you will have denied three times that you know me.
	61	2	Before the cock crows *today*, you will have disowned me three times.
23	43	2	*today* you will be with me in paradise.
Ac 2	29	2	[David's] tomb is ⌐still with us (lit. with us to this *day*).
4	9	2	you are questioning us *today* about an act of kindness to a cripple,
13	33	2	(Ps 2 7) You are my son: *today* I have become your father.
19	40	2	We could easily be charged with rioting for *today*'s happenings.
20	26	/2	so ⌐here and now (lit. on this *day today* and in front of you) I swear that my conscience is clear
22	3	2	I was as full of duty towards God as you are *today*.
23	1		to this *day* I have conducted myself before God with a perfectly clear conscience.
24	21	2	It is about the resurrection . . . that I am on trial . . . *today*.
26	2	2	I consider myself fortunate, King Agrippa, in that it is before you I am to answer *today* all the charges made against me
	22		I have stood firm to this *day*, testifying to great and small alike,
	29	2	I wish before God that . . . all who have heard me *today* would come to be as I am
27	33	2	Till today makes days . . . you have been in suspense,
Rm 11	8	/2	(Dt 29 3) God has given [the Jews] a sluggish spirit . . . and they are still like that ⌐to this day (lit. to this *day today*).
2 Co 3	14	/2	⌐to this very day (lit. to this *day today*), that same veil is still there when the old covenant is being read . . . [15] Yes,
	15	2	even *today* . . . the veil is over their minds.
Heb 1	5	2	(Ps 2 7) You are my Son, *today* I have become your father;
3	7	2	(Ps 95 7) If only you would listen to him *today*;
	13		Every day, as long as this '*today*' lasts, keep encouraging one another
	15	2	(Ps 95 7) If only you would listen to him *today*;
4	7	2	God fixed another day when . . . he said '*today*' through David in the text already quoted (Ps 95 7): If only you would listen to him *today*;
5	5	2	(Ps 2 7) You are my son, *today* I have become your father,
13	8	2	Jesus Christ is the same *today* as he was yesterday and as he will be for ever.
Jm 4	13		Here is the answer for those of you who talk like this:
		2	'*Today* or tomorrow, we are off'

f) (Time of the) Day, Daylight

Lk 4	42		When *daylight* came [Jesus] . . . made his way to a lonely place.
9	12		⌐It was late afternoon (lit. *Daylight* was beginning to fade)
22	66		When *day* broke there was a meeting of the elders of the people,
24	29		[the two disciples] pressed [Jesus] to stay with them . . . they said '. . . the *day* is almost over.'
Ac 2	15		These men are not drunk, as you imagine; why, it is only the third hour of the *day*.
8	26	3	Be ready to set out ⌐at mid*day* (or: south) along the road that goes from Jerusalem down to Gaza,
12	18		When *daylight* came there was a great commotion among the soldiers,
16	35		When it was *daylight* the magistrates sent the officers with the order: 'Release those men'.

Ac 22	6	3	about mid*day* a bright light from heaven suddenly shone round me.
23	12		When it was *day*, the Jews held a secret meeting
26	13		at mid*day* . . . I saw a light
27	29		[the crew] prayed for *daylight*.
	33		Just before *daybreak* Paul urged them all to have something to eat.
	39		When *day* came [the crew] did not recognise the land,
Rm 13	12		The night is almost over, it will be *daylight* soon

g) (each, every) Day, Daily

Mt 6	34		Each *day* has enough trouble of its own.
26	55		I sat teaching in the Temple ⌐*day* after (lit. every) *day*
Mk 14	49		I was . . . teaching in the Temple ⌐*day* after (lit. every) *day*
Lk 9	23		let him . . . take up his cross every *day* and follow me.
11	3		give us each *day* our daily bread,
16	19		There was a rich man who used to . . . feast magnificently every *day*.
17	4		if [your brother] wrongs you seven times a *day* . . . forgive him.
19	47		[Jesus] taught in the Temple every *day*.
22	53		I was among you in the Temple ⌐*day* after (lit. every) *day*
Ac 2	46		[The faithful] went as a body to the Temple every *day*
	47		⌐*Day* (lit. Each) *day* the Lord added to their community those destined to be saved
3	2		they used to put [the cripple] down every *day* near the Temple entrance
5	42		[The apostles] preached every *day*
6	1	4	in the *daily* distribution their own widows were being overlooked.
16	5		the churches grew . . . *daily* in numbers.
17	11		every *day* [the Jews at Beroea] studied the scriptures
	17		[Paul] held debates with the Jews . . . every *day*
19	9		[Paul held] *daily* discussions in the lecture room of Tyrannus.
1 Co 15	31		I face death every *day*,
2 Co 11	28		there is my *daily* preoccupation: my anxiety for all the churches.
Heb 3	13		Every *day* . . . keep encouraging one another
7	27		[the ideal high priest] would not need to offer sacrifices every *day*, as the other high priests do for their own sins
10	11		All the priests stand at their duties every *day*, offering over and over again the same sacrifices
Jm 2	15		If one of the brothers . . . has not enough food ⌐to live on
	5		(lit. for *each day*)

2: DAILY: *EP-IOUSIOS*

ep-iousios 2

Mt 6	11		Give us today our *daily* bread.
Lk 11	3		give us each day our *daily* bread,

5. YESTERDAY – TOMORROW – (THE) NEXT DAY

1: YESTERDAY: *ECHTHES*

echthes 3

Jn 4	52		The fever left [the boy] *yesterday* . . . at the seventh hour.
Ac 7	28		Do you intend to kill me as you killed the Egyptian *yesterday*?
Heb 13	8		Jesus Christ is the same today as he was *yesterday* and as he will be for ever.

2: TOMORROW – (THE) NEXT DAY: *AURION*

2 aurion 14   I tē ep-aurion 17

Mt 6	30	2	the grass in the field . . . is there today and thrown into the furnace *tomorrow*,
	34	2/2	do not worry about *tomorrow*: *tomorrow* will take care of itself.
27	62		*Next day*, that is, when Preparation Day was over,
Mk 11	12		*Next day* as they were leaving Bethany, [Jesus] felt hungry.
Lk 10	35	2	*Next day*, [the Samaritan] took out two denarii and handed them to the innkeeper.
12	28	2	the grass in the field . . . is there today and thrown into the furnace *tomorrow*,
13	32	2	Learn that today and *tomorrow* I cast out devils and on the third day attain my end. [33] But for today and *tomorrow* and the next day I must go on,
	33	2	
Jn 1	29		*The next day*, seeing Jesus coming towards him, John said,
	35		On *the following day* . . . John stood there again with two of his disciples.
	43		*The next day*, after Jesus had decided to leave for Galilee, he met Philip.
6	22		*Next day*, the crowd . . . saw that only one boat had been there,

Jn 12	12	*The next day* the crowds . . . heard that Jesus was on his way to Jerusalem.
Ac 4	3	[The priests] arrested [Peter and John], but as it was already
	5	2/2 late, they held them till *the next day* . . . ⁵ *The next day* the rulers . . . had a meeting in Jerusalem
10	9	*Next day* . . . they . . . had only a short distance to go before reaching Jaffa,
	23	*Next day*, [Peter] was ready to go off with [the men sent by Cornelius],
	24	They reached Caesarea *the following day*.
14	20	*The next day* [Paul] and Barnabas went off to Derbe.
20	7	Paul was due to leave *the next day*, and he preached a sermon
21	8	*The next day* we left and came to Caesarea.
22	30	*The next day* . . . [the tribune] freed Paul
23	20	The Jews have made a plan to ask you to take Paul down to
	2	the Sanhedrin *tomorrow*,
	32	*Next day* [the soldiers] left the mounted escort to go on with [Paul]
25	6	*the next day* [Festus] took his seat on the tribunal and had Paul brought in.
	22	2 'I should like to hear the man myself'. '*Tomorrow*' [Festus]
	23	answered 'you shall hear him.' ²³ So *the next day* Agrippa and Bernice arrived in great state
1 Co 15	32	2 (Is 22 13) Let us eat and drink today; *tomorrow* we shall be dead.
Jm 4	13	Here is the answer for those of you who talk like this: 'Today
	14	2 or *tomorrow* we are off . . .' ¹⁴ You never know what will 2 happen *tomorrow*:

3: (THE) NEXT DAY: *TĒ HETERA*

tē hetera 2

Ac 20	15	*The second day* we touched at Samos
27	3	*Next day* we put in at Sidon,

6. HOUR – TIME: *HŌRA*

1 hōra 106   2 (hēmi-)(h)ōron 1

a) Hour (of the day) – the Time

Mt 14	15	This is a lonely place, and the *time* has slipped by;
20	3	< Going out at about the third *hour* [the owner of the vineyard] saw [other workers]
	5	< At about the sixth [hour] and again at about the ninth *hour*, he went out
	9	< those who were hired at about the eleventh *hour* . . . received one denarius each.
27	45	From the sixth *hour* there was darkness over all the land until
	46	the ninth *hour*. ⁴⁶ And about the ninth *hour*, Jesus cried out . . , 'Eli, Eli, lama sabachthani?'
Mk 6	35	⌐it (lit. the *hour*) was getting very late, and his disciples . . . said, '. . . ⌐it (lit. the *hour*) is getting very late.
11	11	as ⌐it (lit. the *hour*) was now late, [Jesus] went out to Bethany
15	25	It was the third *hour* when they crucified him.
	33	When the sixth *hour* came there was darkness over the whole
	34	land until the ninth *hour*. ³⁴ And at the ninth *hour* Jesus cried out . . , 'Eloi, Eloi, lama sabachthani?'
Lk 1	10	at the *hour* of incense the whole congregation was . . . praying.
14	17	When the *time* for the banquet came, he sent his servant to say to those who had been invited,
22	14	When the *hour* came [Jesus] took his place at table,
23	44	It was now about the sixth *hour* and . . . a darkness came over the whole land until the ninth *hour*.
Jn 1	39	[The two disciples went with Jesus.] It was about the tenth *hour*.
4	6	Jesus . . . sat straight down by the well. It was about the sixth *hour*.
	52	He asked them ⌐when (lit. at what *hour*) the boy had begun to recover. 'The fever left him . . . at the seventh *hour*.'
	53	⁵³ The father realised that this was exactly the *time* when Jesus had said, 'Your son will live';
19	14	It was Passover Preparation Day, about the sixth *hour*.
Ac 2	15	These men are not drunk . . . why, it is only the third *hour* of the day.
3	1	Peter and John were going up to the Temple for the prayers at the ninth *hour*,
10	3	One day at about the ninth *hour* [Cornelius] had a vision
	9	Peter went to the housetop at about the sixth *hour* to pray.
	30	⌐Three days ago (lit. At the end of the fourth day backwards from this precise *hour*) I was praying in my house at the ninth [hour],
23	23	Get . . . ready to leave for Caesarea by the third *hour* of the night

b) (Jesus's) Hour

Mt 26	45	Now the *hour* has come when the Son of Man is to be betrayed
Mk 14	35	[Jesus] prayed that, if it were possible, this *hour* might pass him by.
	41	The *hour* has come. Now the Son of Man is to be betrayed
Jn 2	4	My *hour* has not come yet.
7	30	his *time* had not yet come
8	20	his *time* had not yet come.
12	23	Now the *hour* has come for the Son of Man to be glorified.
	27	Father, save me from this *hour*? But it was for this very reason that I have come to this *hour*.
13	1	Jesus knew that the *hour* had come for him to pass from this world
16	32	the ⌐*time* (lit. *hour*) will come – in fact it has come already – when you will be scattered,
17	1	Father, the *hour* has come: glorify your Son

c) the Hour, the Time (of Judgement)

Mt 24	36	as for that day and *hour*, nobody knows it,
	44	the Son of Man is coming at an *hour* you do not expect.
	50	< his master will come . . . at an *hour* he does not know.
25	13	you do not know either the day or the *hour*.
Mk 13	32	as for that day or *hour*, nobody knows it,
Lk 12	39	< if the householder had known at what *hour* the burglar would come, he would not have let anyone break through the wall . . . ⁴⁰ . . . the Son of Man is coming at an *hour* you
	40	do not expect.
	46	< his master will come . . . at an *hour* he does not know.
Jn 5	25	the *hour* will come . . . when the dead will hear the voice of the Son of God,
	28	the *hour* is coming when the dead will leave their graves
1 Jn 2	18	⌐these are the last days (lit. this is the last *hour*) . . . now several antichrists have already appeared; we know from this that ⌐these are the last days (lit. this is the last *hour*).
Rv 3	3	I shall come to you like a thief, without telling you at what *hour* to expect me.
	10	I will keep you safe in the *time* of trial
9	15	These four angels had been put there ready for this *hour* of this day of this month of this year,
14	7	Fear God . . . because the *time* has come for him to sit in judgement;
	15	Put your sickle in and reap: harvest *time* has come

d) the Hour = the Moment, the Time, the Instant

Mt 8	13	the servant [of the centurion] was cured at that *moment*.
9	22	from that *moment* the woman [with a haemorrhage] was well again.
10	19	what you are to say will be given to you when the *time* comes;
15	28	from that *moment* [the] daughter [of the Canaanite woman] was well again.
17	18	the devil came out of the boy who was cured from that *moment*.
18	1	At this *time* the disciples came to Jesus
26	55	It was at this *time* that Jesus said to the crowds,
Mk 13	11	say whatever is given to you when the *time* comes,
Lk 2	38	[Anna] came by just at that *moment* and began to praise God;
7	21	It was ⌐just then (lit. at that *moment*) that [Jesus] cured many people
10	21	It was ⌐then (lit. at this *time*) that, filled with joy by the Holy Spirit, [Jesus] said,
12	12	when the *time* comes, the Holy Spirit will teach you what you must say.
13	31	Just at this *time* some Pharisees came up.
20	19	the scribes and the chief priests would have liked to lay hands on [Jesus] that very *moment*,
Jn 16	4	when the *time* for it comes you may remember that I told you.
	21	● A woman in childbirth suffers, because her *time* has come;
19	27	from that *moment* the disciple made a place for [Jesus's mother] in his home.
Ac 16	18	The spirit went out of [the slave-girl] ⌐then and there (lit. at that same *moment*).
	33	[the gaoler] was baptised ⌐then and there (lit. at the same *time*)
22	13	*Instantly* my sight came back and I was able to see [Ananias].
Rm 13	11	⌐you must wake up now (lit. now is the *time* for you to wake up):
1 Co 4	11	To this ⌐day (lit. very *moment*), we go without food
15	30	Why are we living under a ⌐constant threat (lit. threat from one *moment* to the next)?
Rv 11	13	⌐Immediately (lit. At that *moment*), there was a violent earthquake,

e) an Hour

Mt 20	12	The men who came last . . . have done only one *hour*,
26	40	So you had not the strength to keep awake with me one *hour*?
Mk 14	37	Had you not the strength to keep awake one *hour*?

Lk 22	59	About an *hour* later another man insisted, saying, 'This fellow was certainly with him.'
Jn 11	9	Are there not twelve *hours* in the day?
Ac 5	7	About three *hours* later [Ananias's] wife came in,
19	34	[the Ephesians] kept [shouting] for two *hours*.
Rv 8	1	2 there was silence in heaven for about *half an hour*.
17	12	[the ten kings] will have royal authority only for a single *hour*,
18	10	Mourn . . . Babylon, . . . doomed as you are within a single *hour*.
	17	your riches are all destroyed within a single *hour*.
	19	mourn for this great city . . . ruined within a single *hour*.

f) an Hour = a Time, a Moment

Lk 22	53 ●	this is your *hour*; this is the reign of darkness.
24	33	[the two disciples on their way to Emmaus] set out that *instant* and returned to Jerusalem.
Jn 4	21 ●	the *hour* is coming when you will worship the Father neither on this mountain nor in Jerusalem . . . ²³ But the *hour*
	23 ●	will come . . . when true worshippers will worship the Father in spirit and truth;
5	35	for a *time* you were content to enjoy the light that [John] gave.
16	2	the *hour* is coming when anyone who kills you will think he is doing a holy duty for God.
	25 ●	the *hour* is coming when I shall no longer speak to you in metaphors;
2 Co 7	8	that letter did distress you, at least for a *time*;
Ga 2	5	I refused . . . to yield to such people for one *moment*.
1 Th 2	17	A short time (G Within an *hour*) after we had been separated from you . . . we had an especially strong desire . . . to see you
Phm	15	you have been deprived of Onesimus for a *time*, but it was only so that you could have him back for ever,

TOUCH

1. Touch: *haptomai*	**3. Touch:** *pros-psauō*
2. Touch: *thinganō*	

1. TOUCH: *HAPTOMAI*

1 *haptomai* 35   2 *psēl-(h)aphaō* 4

Mt 8	3	X	Jesus stretched out his hand, *touched* [the leper]
	15	X	[Jesus] *touched* [Peter's mother-in-law's] hand and the fever left her,
9	20		a woman, who had suffered from a haemorrhage for twelve years . . . *touched* the fringe of his cloak,
	21		If I can only *touch* his cloak I shall be well again.
	29	X	[Jesus] *touched* [the] eyes [of the two blind men]
14	36		[people were] begging [Jesus] just to let them *touch* the fringe of his cloak. And all those who *touched* it were . . . cured.
17	7	X	Jesus came up and *touched* [Peter, James and John].
20	34	X	Jesus felt pity for [the two blind men] and *touched* their eyes,
Mk 1	41	X	Jesus stretched out his hand and *touched* [the leper].
3	10		all who were afflicted in any way were crowding forward to *touch* [Jesus].
5	27		[a woman suffering from a haemorrhage] *touched* [Jesus's] cloak. ²⁸ 'If I can *touch* even his clothes,' she had told
	28		herself 'I shall be well again.' . . . ³⁰ . . . Jesus turned
	30		round in the crowd and said, 'Who *touched* my clothes?'
	31		³¹ His disciples said to him, 'You see how the crowd is pressing round you and yet you say, "Who *touched* me?"'
6	56		[people were] begging [Jesus] to let them *touch* even the fringe of his cloak. And all those who *touched* him were cured.
7	33	X	[Jesus] *touched* [the deaf man's] tongue with spittle.
8	22	X	some people brought to [Jesus] a blind man whom they begged him to *touch*.
10	13	X	People were bringing little children to [Jesus], for him to *touch* them.
Lk 5	13	X	Jesus stretched out his hand, *touched* [the leper]
6	19		everyone in the crowd was trying to *touch* [Jesus]
7	14	X	[the Lord] went up and *put his hand on* the bier
	39		If this man were a prophet, he would know who this woman is that is *touching* him and what a bad name she has.
8	44		[a woman suffering from a haemorrhage] *touched* the fringe of his cloak . . . ⁴⁵ Jesus said, 'Who *touched* me?' . . .
	45		
	46		⁴⁶ . . . Jesus said, 'Somebody *touched* me. I felt that power had gone out from me.' ⁴⁷ . . . the woman came forward
	47		trembling, and falling at his feet explained . . . why she had *touched* him
18	15	X	People even brought little children to [Jesus], for him to *touch* them;

Lk 22	51	X	*touching* [the high priest's servant's] ear he healed him.
24	39		2 *Touch* me and see for yourselves; a ghost has no flesh and bones
Jn 20	17		Do not ⌐cling to (lit. *touch*)¬ me, because I have not yet ascended to the Father.
Ac 17	27		[God] did this so that all nations might seek the deity and, 2 by *feeling* [their way] towards him, succeed in finding him.
1 Co 7	1 O		it is a good thing for a man not to *touch* a woman;
2 Co 6	17		(Is 52 11) *Touch* nothing that is unclean, and I will welcome you
Col 2	21		It is forbidden to *pick up* this, it is forbidden to taste that, it is forbidden to touch something else;
Heb 12	18		What you have come to is nothing ⌐known to the senses (lit. 2 *palpable*)¬:
1 Jn 1	1		2 Something . . . that we have . . . *touched* with our hands: the Word, who is life – this is our subject.
5	18 ⓓ		the Evil One does not *touch* [anyone who has been begotten by God].

2. TOUCH: *THINGANŌ*

thinganō 3

Col 2	21	It is forbidden to pick up this, it is forbidden to taste that, it is forbidden to *touch* something else;
Heb 11	28	by faith . . . [Moses] sprinkled the blood to prevent the Destroyer from *touching* any of the first-born sons o Israel.
12	20	(Ex 19 13) If even an animal *touches* the mountain, it must be stoned.

3. TOUCH: *PROS-PSAUŌ*

pros-psauō 1

Lk 11	46	you load on men burdens that . . . you yourselves do not move a finger to ⌐lift (lit. *touch*)¬.

TREE – WOOD

1. Tree	**7. Plank – Speck, Splinter – Log, Beam**
1: Tree: *dendron*	1: Plank: *sanis*
2: Tree (of life): *xylon*	2: Speck, Splinter and Plank, Log, Beam: *karphos* and *dokos*
2. Forest: *hulē*	**8. Reed – Cane, Rod:** *kalamos*
3. Branches – Leaves – Palm	**9. Fig – Sycamore – Mulberry**
1: Branch – Twig, Shoot: *klados*	1: Fig: *sukē*
2: Palm branches, Palms: *baion* and *phoinix*	2: Sycamore (Sycomore): *suko-morea*
3: Greenery – Leafy branches: *stibas*	3: Mulberry – Sycamine: *suka-minos*
4: Leaves: *phyllon*	**10. Thorn – Bush – Thistle**
4. Root – Uproot: *rhiza*	1: Thorns, Thornbushes: *akantha*
5. Sap – Richness: *piotēs*	2: Bush – Brambles: *batos*
6. Wood – Sticks	*a)* the Burning Bush
1: Wood – Scented wood, Sandal-wood: *xylon* and *thyinos*	*b)* Brambles
2: Sticks: *phryganon*	3: Thorn – Pain: *skolops*
	4: Thistles: *tri-bolos*

1. TREE

1: TREE: *DENDRON*

dendron 25

Mt 3	10	Even now the axe is laid to the roots of the *trees*, so that any *tree* which fails to produce good fruit will be cut down.
7	17	a sound *tree* produces good fruit but a rotten *tree* bad fruit.
	18	A sound *tree* cannot bear bad fruit, nor a rotten *tree* bear good fruit.
	19	Any *tree* that does not produce good fruit is cut down
12	33	Make a *tree* sound and its fruit will be sound; make a *tree* rotten and its fruit will be rotten. For the *tree* can be told by its fruit.
13	32	[the mustard seed] becomes a *tree*
21	8	others were cutting branches from the *trees*
Mk 8	24	people . . . look like *trees* to me, but they are walking about.

Lk	3	9

the axe is laid to the roots of the *trees*, so that any *tree* which fails to produce good fruit will be cut down

	6	43
		44

There is no sound *tree* that produces rotten fruit, nor again a rotten *tree* that produces sound fruit. [44] For every *tree* can be told by its own fruit:

	13	19
	21	29

[the mustard seed] grew and became a *tree*,
Think of the fig [tree] and indeed every *tree*.

Jude		12

[Certain people who have infiltrated among you are] like barren *trees* which are then uprooted in the winter

Rv	7	1

[I saw four angels holding the four winds back] to keep them from blowing . . . in the *trees*.

		3

Wait before you do any damage on land or at sea or to the *trees*,

	8	7

The first [angel] blew his trumpet and . . . a third of all *trees* . . . was burnt.

	9	4

[The locusts] were forbidden to harm any fields or crops or *trees*

2: TREE (OF LIFE): *XYLON*
xylon 5/20

Rv	2	7

Those who prove victorious I will feed from the *tree* of life set in God's paradise.

	22	2

On either side of the river were the *trees* of life, which bear twelve crops of fruit in a year . . . and the leaves ʳof which (lit. of each *tree*) are the cure for the pagans.

		14

[those who will have washed their robes clean] will have the right to feed on the *tree* of life

		19

if anyone cuts anything out of the prophecies in this book, God will cut off his share of the *tree* of life

2. FOREST: *HULĒ*
hulē 1

Jm	3	5

Think how small a flame can set fire to a huge *forest*.

3. BRANCHES – LEAVES – PALM

1: BRANCH – TWIG, SHOOT: *KLADOS*
1 klados 11   2 klēma 4

Mt	13	32

the birds of the air come and shelter in its *branches*.

	21	8

others were cutting *branches* from the trees and spreading them in [Jesus's] path.

	24	32

as soon as [the] *twigs* [of the fig tree] grow supple and its leaves come out, you know that summer is near.

Mk	4	32

[the mustard] puts out big *branches* so that the birds of the air can shelter in its shade.

	3	28

as soon as [the] *twigs* [of the fig tree] grow supple and its leaves come out, you know that summer is near.

Lk	13	19

a mustard seed . . . became a tree, and the birds of the air sheltered in its *branches*.

Jn	15	2
		4
		5
		6

2 Every *branch* in me that bears no fruit, [my Father] cuts away,
2 a *branch* cannot bear fruit all by itself,
2 I am the vine, you are the *branches*.
2 Anyone who does not remain in me is like a *branch* that has been thrown away – he withers;

Rm	11	16
		17
		18
		19
		21

all the *branches* are holy if the root is holy.
No doubt some of the *branches* have been cut off,
even if you think yourself superior to the other *branches*, remember . . . it is the root that supports you.
You will say, 'Those *branches* were cut off on purpose to let me be grafted in!'
God did not spare the natural *branches*, and he is not likely to spare you.

2: PALM BRANCHES, PALMS: *BAION* and *PHOINIX*
2 baion 1   1 phoinix 2

Jn	12	13
Rv	7	9

2/ They took *branches* of *palm* and went out to meet [Jesus]
a huge number of people . . . dressed in white robes and holding *palms* in their hands.

3: GREENERY – LEAFY BRANCHES: *STIBAS*
stibas 1

Mk	11	8

others [spread] *greenery* which they had cut in the fields.

4: LEAVES: *PHYLLON*
phyllon 6

Mt	21	19

Seeing a fig tree . . . [Jesus] went up to it and found nothing on it but *leaves*.

	24	32

as soon as . . . [the] *leaves* [of the fig tree] come out, you know that summer is near.

Mk	11	13

Seeing a fig tree in *leaf* some distance away, [Jesus] went to see if he could find any fruit on it, but . . . he found nothing but *leaves*.

	13	28

as soon as . . . [the] *leaves* [of the fig tree] come out, you know that summer is near.

Rv	22	2

the *leaves* [of the trees of life] are the cure for the pagans.

4. ROOT – UPROOT: *RHIZA*
1 rhiza 14/17   2 ek-rhizoō 4
3 rhizoō   2

Mt	3	10
	13	6
		21
		29
	15	13

Even now the axe is laid to the *roots* of the trees,
not having any *roots*, [the seeds] withered away.
[The one who received the seed on patches of rock] has no *root* in him, he does not last;
2 you might ʳpull up (lit. *uproot*) the wheat with [the darnel].
2 Any plant my heavenly Father has not planted will be *pulled up by the roots*.

Mk	4	6
		17
	11	20

not having any *roots*, [some seed] withered away.
[those who receive the seed on patches of rock] have no *root* in them, they do not last;
[the disciples] saw the fig tree withered to the *roots*.

Lk	3	9
	8	13
	17	6

the axe is laid to the *roots* of the trees.
these have no *root*; they believe for a while,
2 Be *uprooted* and planted in the sea.

Rm	11	16
		17
		18

all the branches are holy if the *root* is holy.
like shoots of wild olive, you have been grafted among the rest to share with them (§ the *root* and) the rich sap provided by the olive tree itself.
you do not support the *root*; it is the *root* that supports you.

Ep	3	17

3 ʳplanted (lit. *rooted*) in love and built on love, [18] you will . . . have strength

Col	2	7
1 Tm	6	10
Heb	12	15

3 you must be *rooted* in [Christ] and built on him.
The love of money is the *root* of all evils.
Be careful that . . . no *root* of bitterness should begin to grow and make trouble.

Jude		12

2 [Certain people who have infiltrated among you are] like barren trees which are then *uprooted* in the winter

5. SAP – RICHNESS: *PIOTĒS*
piotēs 1

Rm	11	17

you have been grafted among the rest to share with them (§the root and) the *rich sap* provided by the olive tree itself.

6. WOOD – STICKS

1: WOOD – SCENTED WOOD, SANDALWOOD: *XYLON* and *THYINOS*
3 thyinos 1   2 xylinos   2
1 xylon   4/20

Lk	23	31

if men use the green *wood* like this, what will happen when it is dry?

1 Co	3	12

On this foundation you can build . . . in *wood*, grass and straw.

2 Tm	2	20

2 in a large house . . . some [dishes] are made of *wood* and earthenware.

Rv	9	20
	18	12

[the rest of the human race refused to abandon] the idols made
2 of gold, silver, bronze, stone and *wood*,
3/ nobody left to buy . . . all the *sandalwood*, every piece in ivory or fine *wood*,

2: STICKS: *PHRYGANON*
phryganon 1

Ac	28	3

Paul had collected a bundle of *sticks*

7. PLANK – SPECK, SPLINTER – LOG, BEAM

1: PLANK: *SANIS*

sanis 1

Ac 27 44   the rest [should] follow either on *planks* or on pieces of wreckage.

2: SPECK, SPLINTER and PLANK, LOG, BEAM: *KARPHOS* and *DOKOS*

1 *karphos 6*   2 *dokos 6*

Mt 7 3		Why do you observe the *splinter* in your brother's eye and never notice the *plank* in your own?
4	2	How dare you say to your brother, 'Let me take the *splinter*
5	2	out of your eye', when all the time there is a *plank* in your own? [5] . . . Take the *plank* out of your own eye first, and then you will see clearly enough to take the *splinter* out of your brother's eye.
Lk 6 41		Why do you observe the *splinter* in your brother's eye and
42	2	never notice the *plank* in your own? [42] How can you say . . , 'Brother, let me take the *splinter* that is in your
	2	eye', when you cannot see the *plank* in your own? Hypo-
	2	crite! Take the *plank* out of your own eye first, and then you will see clearly enough to take out the *splinter* that is in your brother's eye.

8. REED – CANE, ROD: *KALAMOS*

kalamos 11|12

M = Measure

Mt 11 7		What did you go out into the wilderness to see? A *reed* swaying in the breeze?
12 20	<	(Is 42 3) He will not break the crushed *reed*.
27 29		[the soldiers] placed a *reed* in his right hand.
30		they took the *reed* and struck [Jesus] on the head with it.
48		one of them quickly ran to get a sponge . . . and putting it on a *reed*, gave it him to drink.
Mk 15 19		[the soldiers] struck his head with a *reed*
36		Someone . . . putting [a sponge] on a *reed*, gave it him to drink,
Lk 7 24		What did you go out into the wilderness to see? A *reed* swaying in the breeze?
Rv 11 1	M	I was given a long cane as a measuring *rod*, and I was told, 'Go and measure . . '
21 15	M	[the angel] was carrying a gold measuring *rod* to measure the city.
16	M	[the angel] measured the city with his *rod*.

9. FIG – SYCAMORE – MULBERRY

1: FIG: *SUKĒ*

1 *sukē 16*   2 *sukon 4*

Mt 7 16	2	Can people pick grapes from thorns, or *figs* from thistles?
21 19		Seeing a *fig tree* . . . [Jesus] found nothing on it but leaves. And he said to it, 'May you never bear fruit again'; and at that instant the *fig tree* withered.
20		What happened to the *fig tree* . . . that it withered there and then?
21		if you have faith . . . you [will] do what I have done to the *fig tree*,
24 32		Take the *fig tree* as a parable.
Mk 11 13		Seeing a *fig tree* in leaf some distance away . . . [Jesus] found nothing but leaves; for it was not the season for
	2	*figs*.
20		[the disciples] saw the *fig tree* withered to the roots.
21		the *fig tree* you cursed has withered away.
13 28		Take the *fig tree* as a parable.
Lk 6 44	2	people do not pick *figs* from thorns,
13 6		A man had a *fig tree* planted in his vineyard,
7		for three years now I have been coming to look for fruit on this *fig tree*,
21 29		Think of the *fig tree* and indeed every tree.
Jn 1 48		[Nathanael,] I saw you under the *fig tree*.
50		You believe that just because I said: I saw you under the *fig tree*.
Jm 3 12		/2 Can a *fig tree* give you olives . . . or the vine give *figs*?
Rv 6 13		the stars . . . fell . . . like [figs] dropping from a *fig tree*

2: SYCAMORE (SYCOMORE): *SUKO-MOREA*

suko-morea 1

Lk 19 4   [Zacchaeus] climbed a *sycamore tree* to catch a glimpse of Jesus

3: MULBERRY – SYCAMINE: *SUKAMINOS*

sukaminos 1

Lk 17 6   Were your faith the size of a mustard seed you could say to this *mulberry tree*, 'Be uprooted and planted in the sea',

10. THORN – BUSH – THISTLE

1: THORNS, THORNBUSHES: *AKANTHA*

1 *akantha 14*   2 *akanthinos 2*

Mt 7 16		Can people pick grapes from *thorns*, or figs from thistles?
13 7		[some seeds] fell among *thorns*, and the *thorns* . . . choked them.
22		The one who received the seed in *thorns* is the man who hears the word . . . but produces nothing.
27 29		[the soldiers] twisted some *thorns* into a crown
Mk 4 7		Some seed fell into *thorns*, and the *thorns* grew up and choked it.
18		there are others who receive the seed in *thrrns*.
15 17	2	[the soldiers] twisted some *thorns* into a crown
Lk 6 44		people do not pick figs from *thorns*,
8 7		Some seed fell amongst *thorns* and the *thorns* . . . choked it.
14		the part that fell into *thorns*, this is people who . . . do not reach maturity.
Jn 19 2		the soldiers twisted some *thorns* into a crown
5	2	Jesus then came out wearing the crown of *thorns*
Heb 6 8		[a field] that grows *brambles* and thistles is abandoned.

2: BUSH – BRAMBLES: *BATOS*

batos 5

a) the Burning Bush

Mk 12 26	in the Book of Moses, in the passage about the *Bush* (Ex 3 1f),
Lk 20 37	Moses himself implies . . . in the passage about the *bush*,
Ac 7 30	an angel appeared to [Moses] in the flames of a *bush*
35	the angel . . . had appeared to [Moses] in the *bush*

b) Brambles

Lk 6 44   people do not . . . gather grapes from *brambles*.

3: THORN – PAIN: *SKOLOPS*

skolops 1

2 Co 12 7 ○   I was given a *thorn* in the flesh.

4: THISTLES: *TRI-BOLOS*

tri-bolos 2

Mt 7 16	Can people pick . . . figs from *thistles*?
Heb 6 8	[a field] that grows brambles and *thistles* is abandoned.

TRIBE

1: (the twelve) Tribes (of Israel, collectively)	sons of Jacob, individually)
2: (the twelve) Tribes (of Israel,	3: Tribe(s), People(s), Race

Asher	2	Levi	3	1	*phylē*	31	
Benjamin	4	Manasseh	1	2	(*dōdeka-*)*phylon*	1	
Gad	1	Naphtali	3	3	*sym-phyletēs*	1	
Issachar	1	Reuben	1				
Joseph	9	Simeon	1				
Judah	10	Zebulun	3				

1: (THE TWELVE) TRIBES (OF ISRAEL, COLLECTIVELY)

In Rv 7 8 the tribe of *Joseph* replaces that of *Ephraim*. *Dan* is omitted; the full complement of twelve is made up by the addition of *Manasseh*, one of the two sons of Joseph.

Mt 19 28		you will . . . sit on twelve thrones to judge the twelve *tribes* of Israel.
Lk 22 30		you will sit on thrones to judge the twelve *tribes* of Israel.
Ac 26 7	2	[I am on trial for my hope in] the promise that our twelve *tribes* . . . hope to attain.
Jm 1 1		From James . . . greetings to the twelve *tribes* of the Dispersion.
Rv 7 4		I heard how many were sealed: a hundred and forty-four thousand, out of all the *tribes* of Israel. [5] From the *tribe*
5		of *Judah*, twelve thousand had been sealed; from the *tribe* of *Reuben*, twelve thousand; from the *tribe* of *Gad*, twelve
6		thousand; [6] from the *tribe* of *Asher*, twelve thousand; from the *tribe* of *Naphtali*, twelve thousand; from the *tribe* of
7		*Manasseh*, twelve thousand; [7] from the *tribe* of *Simeon*, twelve thousand; from the *tribe* of *Levi*, twelve thousand;
8		from the *tribe* of *Issachar*, twelve thousand; [8] from the *tribe* of *Zebulun*, twelve thousand; from the *tribe* of *Joseph*, twelve thousand; and from the *tribe* of *Benjamin*, twelve thousand were sealed.
21 12		over the gates [of the new Jerusalem] were written the names of the twelve *tribes* of Israel;

2: (THE TWELVE) TRIBES (OF ISRAEL, SONS OF JACOB, INDIVIDUALLY)

a) Asher

Lk 2 36		There was a prophetess also, Anna the daughter of Phanuel, of the *tribe* of *Asher*.

b) Benjamin

Ac 13 21		God gave them Saul son of Kish, a man of the *tribe* of *Benjamin*.
Rm 11 1		I, [Paul], an Israelite, descended from Abraham through the *tribe* of *Benjamin*,
Ph 3 5		I was born of the race of Israel and of the *tribe* of *Benjamin*,

c) Joseph

Jn 4 5		Sychar, near the land that Jacob gave to his son *Joseph*.
Ac 7 9		The patriarchs were jealous of *Joseph* and sold him into slavery
13		*Joseph* made himself known to his brothers, and told Pharaoh
14		about *Joseph*'s family. [14] *Joseph* then sent for his father Jacob
18		a new king came to power in Egypt who knew nothing of *Joseph*.
Heb 11 21		By faith, Jacob, when he was dying, blessed each of *Joseph*'s sons,
22		It was by faith that, when he was about to die, *Joseph* recalled the Exodus of the Israelites and made the arrangements for his own burial.

d) Judah

Mt 1 2		Jacob [was] the father of *Judah* and his brothers,
3		*Judah* was the father of Perez and Zerah, Tamar being their mother,
2 6		(Mi 5 1) And you, Bethlehem, in the land of *Judah*, you are by no means least among the leaders of *Judah*,
Lk 1 39		Mary set out . . . and went . . . to a town in the hill country of *Judah*.
3 33		Hezron, son of Perez, son of *Judah*,
Heb 7 13		our Lord . . . belonged to a different *tribe*, the members of which have never done service at the altar;
14		[14] everyone knows he came from *Judah*, a *tribe* which Moses did not even mention when dealing with priests.
8 8		(Jr 31 31) I will establish a new covenant with the House of Israel and the House of *Judah*,
Rv 5 5		the Lion of the *tribe* of *Judah*, the Root of David, has triumphed,

e) Levi, Levite, Levitical

4 *leuitēs* 3   5 *leuitikos* 1

Lk 10 32		4 In the same way a *Levite* . . . saw [the wounded man], and passed by
Jn 1 19		4 the Jews sent priests and *Levites* from Jerusalem to ask [John], 'Who are you?'
Ac 4 36		4 There was a *Levite* of Cypriot origin called Joseph
Heb 7 5		the descendants of *Levi* who are admitted to the priesthood are obliged by the Law to take tithes from the people,
9		It could be said that *Levi* himself, who receives tithes, actually paid them, in the person of Abraham,

---

Heb 7 11		5 if perfection had been reached through the *levitical* priesthood . . . why was it still necessary for a new priesthood to arise . . .?

f) Zebulun, Naphtali

Mt 4 13		Capernaum, a lakeside town on the borders of *Zebulun* and *Naphtali*.
15		(Is 8 23) Land of *Zebulun*! Land of *Naphtali*! Way of the sea on the far side of Jordan, Galilee of the nations!

3: TRIBE(S), PEOPLE(S), RACE

Mt 24 30		all the *peoples* of the earth will beat their breasts;
1 Th 2 14	3	you . . . have been . . . suffering the same treatment from your own ⌐countrymen (lit. *tribesmen*)
Rv 1 7		all the ⌐*races* (or: *tribes*) of the earth will mourn over him.
5 9		you bought men for God of every ⌐*race* (or: *tribe*), language, people and nation
7 9		I saw a huge number . . . of people from every nation, *race*, tribe and language;
11 9		Men out of every people, *race*, language and nation will stare at [the] corpses [of the two witnesses],
13 7		[the beast was] given power over every *race*, people, language and nation;
14 6		I saw another angel . . . sent to announce the Good News . . . to . . . every nation, *race*, language and tribe.

TRUE – AMEN

1. True, Truly – Genuine *gnēsios*
2. the Truth, True, Truly – Real, Really: *a-lētheia*
  1: the Truth, Truly, Really – True, Valid, Real – Truthful(ness)
  2: I tell you truly – I assure you
3. Amen
  1: *amēn legō hymin*

a) I tell you solemnly – Truly, I say to you
b) I tell you most solemnly – Truly, Truly I say to you – In truth, I tell you
  2: Amen (after a doxology)
  3: the Amen (= Jesus)
  4: Amen

1. TRUE, TRULY – GENUINE: *GNĒSIOS*

1 *gnēsios* 4   2 *gnēsiōs* 1

2 Co 8 8		I am just testing the *genuineness* of your love
Ph 2 20	2	[Timothy is] *wholeheartedly* concerned for your welfare:
4 3		I ask you, Syzygus, to be *truly* a companion and to help them in this.
1 Tm 1 2		to Timothy, *true* child of mine in the faith; wishing you grace, mercy and peace
Tt 1 4		To Titus, *true* child of mine in the faith that we share, wishing you grace and peace

2. THE TRUTH, TRUE, TRULY – REAL, REALLY: *A-LĒTHEIA*

1: THE TRUTH, TRULY, REALLY – TRUE, VALID, REAL – TRUTHFUL(NESS)

1 *a-lētheia* 108/109	2 *a-lēthinos* 28
3 *a-lēthēs* 26	4 *a-lēthōs* 15/18
5 *a-lētheuō* 2	

Θ, Χ, Ⓢ, Ⓓ = Truth/True applied to God, Jesus, the Spirit, the Devil

Mt 14 33		4 *Truly*, you are the Son of God.
22 16 X		3 Master, we know that you are ⌐an honest man (lit. *true*) and teach the way of God ⌐in an honest way (lit. with the
X		*truth*),
26 73		4 You are one of [Jesus's companions] *for sure*!
27 54		4 *In truth* this was a son of God.
Mk 5 33		the woman [who had touched Jesus] came forward . . . and told him the whole *truth*.
12 14 X		3 Master, we know you are ⌐an honest man (lit. *true*) . . . and that you teach the way of God ⌐in all honesty (lit. with the
X		*truth*).
32 X		The scribe said to him, 'Well spoken, Master; what you have said is *true*: that he is one and there is no other.
14 70		4 You are one of them *for sure*! Why, you are a Galilean.
15 39		4 *In truth* this man was a son of God.
Lk 16 11	2	If then you cannot be trusted with money . . . who will trust you with *genuine* [riches]?

Lk	20	21	X	Master, we know that you . . . teach the way of God ᵣin all honesty (lit. with the *truth*).
	22	59		This fellow was *certainly* with him. Why, he is a Galilean.
Jn	1	9	2	The Word was the *true* light
		14	X	the only Son of the Father, full of grace and *truth*.
		17	X	grace and *truth* have come through Jesus Christ.
		47	4	There is ᵣan Israelite who deserves the name (lit. *truly* an Israelite), incapable of deceit.
	3	21		the man who lives by the *truth* comes out into the light,
		33	Θ 3	all who do accept his testimony are attesting the *truthfulness* of God,
	4	18	3	You are right to say, 'I have no husband' . . . You spoke *the truth* there.
		23	2/	*true* worshippers will worship the Father in spirit and *truth* . . . ²⁴ . . . those who worship must worship in spirit and *truth*.
		37	2	here the proverb holds *good*: one sows, another reaps;
		42	4	we know that [Jesus] *really* is the saviour of the world.
	5	31		Were I to testify on my own behalf, my testimony would not
		32	3	be *valid*; ³² but there is another witness . . . and I know
			Θ 3	that his testimony is *valid*.
		33		[John] gave his testimony to the *truth*:
	6	14	4	This *really* is the prophet who is to come into the world.
		32	2	it is my Father who gives you the bread from heaven, the *true* bread;
		55	3/3	my flesh is *real* food and my blood is *real* drink.
	7	18	X 3	when [a man] is working for the honour of one who sent him, then he is *sincere*
		26	4	Can it be *true* the authorities have made up their minds that he is the Christ?
		28	2	there is one who sent me and I *really* come from him,
		40	4	*Surely* he must be the prophet,
	8	13	3	You are testifying on your own behalf; your testimony is not *valid*.
		14	3 X	I am testifying on my own behalf, but my testimony is still *valid*,
		16	X 2	my judgement will be *sound*, because I am not alone:
		17	3	it is written that the testimony of two witnesses is *valid*.
		26	Θ 3	the one who sent me is *truthful*,
		31	4	If you make my word your home you will *indeed* be my disciples,
		32		you will learn the *truth* and the *truth* will make you free.
		40	X	you want to kill me when I tell you the *truth*
		44	Ⓓ	The devil . . . was never grounded in the *truth*; there is no Ⓓ *truth* in him at all:
		45	X	I speak the *truth* and . . . you do not believe me.
		46	X	If I speak the *truth*, why do you not believe me?
	10	41	3	all [John] said about [Jesus] was *true*,
	14	6	X	I am the Way, the *Truth* and the Life.
		17	Ⓢ	[the Father will give you] that Spirit of *truth* whom the world can never receive
	15	1	2	I am the *true* vine,
		26	Ⓢ	the Spirit of *truth* . . . will be my witness.
	16	7	X	Still, I must tell you the *truth*: it is for your own good that I am going
		13	Ⓢ	when the Spirit of *truth* comes he will lead you to the complete *truth*,
	17	3	2	eternal life is this: to know you, the only *true* God,
		8	4	they have *truly* accepted this, that I came from you,
		17	Θ	Consecrate them in the *truth*; your word is *truth*.
		19		I consecrate myself so that they too may be consecrated in *truth*.
	18	37	X	I came into the world . . . to bear witness to the *truth*; and all who are on the side of *truth* listen to my voice.
		38		'Truth?' said Pilate 'What is that?'
	19	35	2	This is the evidence of one who saw it – *trustworthy* evidence, 3 and he knows he speaks the *truth* –
	21	24	3	we know that his testimony is *true*.
Ac	4	27		This is *what has come true*: . . . an alliance . . . against your holy servant Jesus
	10	34		The *truth* I have now come to realise . . . is that God does not have favourites,
	12	9	3	Peter . . . had no idea that what the angel did was all happening *in reality*;
		11	4	Now I know it is all *true* . . . the Lord really did send his angel
	26	25		I am speaking nothing but the sober *truth*.
Rm	1	18		The anger of God is being revealed . . . against all the impiety of men who keep *truth* imprisoned in their wickedness.
		25	Θ	they have given up divine *truth* for a lie.
	2	2		We know that God condemns that sort of behaviour ᵣimpartially (lit. *rightly and according to the truth*):
			Θ	
		8		for the unsubmissive who refused to take *truth* for their guide . . . there will be anger and fury.
		20		your Law embodies all knowledge and *truth*,
	3	4	Θ 3	God will always be *true* even though everyone proves to be false;
		7	Θ	my untruthfulness makes God demonstrate his *truthfulness*
	9	1		I say it in union with Christ – it is the *truth* –
Rm	15	8	Θ	Christ became the servant of circumcised Jews . . . so that God could ᵣfaithfully carry (lit. show his *truthfulness* by carrying) out the promises made to the patriarchs,
1 Co	5	8		let us celebrate the feast . . . having only the unleavened bread of sincerity and *truth*.
	13	6		Love . . . delights in the *truth*;
2 Co	4	2		we commend ourselves to every human being with a conscience . . . by stating the *truth* openly in the sight of God.
	6	7		[We prove we are God's servants] by the word of *truth* and by the power of God;
		8	3	[we are] taken for impostors while we are *genuine*;
	7	14		our boasting to Titus has proved to be as *true* as anything that we ever said to you was *true*.
	11	10	X	by Christ's *truth* in me, this cause of boasting will never be taken from me
	12	6		If I should decide to boast . . . I should only be speaking the *truth*;
	13	8		We have no power to resist the *truth*; only to further ᵣit (lit. the *truth*).
Ga	2	5		I was . . . determined to safeguard for you the *true meaning* of the Good News,
		14		they were not respecting the *true meaning* of the Good News [in Antioch],
	4	16	5	Is it *telling* you *the truth* that has made me your enemy?
	5	7		who made you less anxious to obey the *truth*?
Ep	1	13		Now you too . . . have heard the message of the *truth* and the good news of your salvation,
	4	15	5	If we *live by the truth* and in love, we shall grow in all ways into Christ,
		21	X	you were taught what the *truth* is in Jesus.
		24		you can put on the new self that has been created in God's way, in the goodness and holiness of the *truth*.
		25		You must speak the *truth* to one another,
	5	9		the effects of the light are seen in complete goodness . . . and *truth*.
	6	14		stand your ground, with *truth* buckled round your waist,
Ph	1	18		Whether from dishonest motives or in *sincerity*, Christ is proclaimed;
	4	8	3	fill your minds with everything that is *true*, everything that is noble,
Col	1	5		it was announced in the message of the *truth*.
		6		you heard about God's grace and understood what this *really* is.
1 Th	1	9	2	you were converted . . . and became servants of the *real*, living God;
	2	13		as soon as you heard the message . . . you accepted it for 4 what it *really* is, God's message
2 Th	2	10		they would not grasp the love of the *truth*
		12		[God is sending a power] to condemn all who refused to believe in the *truth*
		13		God chose you . . . to be saved . . . by faith in the *truth*.
1 Tm	2	4		[God] wants everyone to . . . reach full knowledge of the *truth*.
		7		I have been named a herald and apostle of it and – I am telling the *truth* and no lie – a teacher of the faith and the *truth* to the pagans,
	3	15		the Church of the living God . . . upholds the *truth* and keeps it safe.
	4	3		God created [foods] to be accepted with thanksgiving by all who believe and who know the *truth*.
	6	5		[All that can come of this is jealousy, contention] and unending disputes by people who are neither rational nor ᵣinformed (lit. aware of the *truth*)
2 Tm	2	15		[Do all you can to keep] a straight course with the message of the *truth*.
		18		[Hymenaeus and Philetus] have gone right away from the *truth*
		25		God may give [people who dispute what is said] a change of mind so that they recognise the *truth*
	3	7		[silly women who are obsessed with their sins] can never come to knowledge of the *truth*.
		8		Men like this defy the *truth*
	4	4		instead of listening to the *truth*, they will turn to myths.
Tt	1	1		From Paul . . . to bring those whom God has chosen to faith and to the knowledge of the *truth*
		13	3	[Cretans were never anything but liars;] that is a *true* statement.
		14		people . . . are no longer interested in the *truth*.
Heb	8	2	2	[Christ] is the minister . . . of the *true* Tent of Meeting which the Lord, and not any man, set up.
	9	24		It is not as though Christ had entered a man-made sanctuary 2 which was only modelled on the *real* one;
	10	22	2	So as we go in, let us be *sincere* in heart
		26		If, after we have been given knowledge of the *truth*, we should . . . commit any sins, then there is no longer any sacrifice for them.
Jm	1	18		[God] made us his children by the message of the *truth*
	3	14		never . . . cover up the *truth* with lies
	5	19		if one of you strays away from the *truth*, and another brings him back to it, [he will be saving a soul from death]

1 P	1	22	You have been obedient to the *truth* and purified your souls
	5	12	3 never . . . let go this *true* grace of God
2 P	1	12	I am continually recalling the same *truths* to you,
	2	2	the Way of *Truth* will be brought into disrepute
		22	3 What he has done is exactly as the proverb *rightly* says: The dog goes back to his own vomit
1 Jn	1	6	we are lying because we are not living the *truth*.
		8	If we say we have no sin in us, we are . . . refusing to admit the *truth*;
	2	4	Anyone who says, 'I know him', and does not keep his commandments, is a liar, refusing to admit the *truth*.
		5	4 when anyone does obey what he has said, *truly* God's love comes to perfection in him.
		8	what is ⌜being carried out in your lives as it was in his (lit. 3 as *true* for you as it was for him), is a new commandment; 2 . . . the *real* light is already shining.
		21	It is not because you do not know the *truth* that I am writing to you but rather because you . . . know that no lie can come from the *truth*.
		27	3 you are anointed with *truth*, not with a lie,
	3	18	our love is not to be just words or mere talk, but something *real* and active; ¹⁹ only by this can we be certain that we are [children] of the *truth*
	4	6	This is how we can tell the spirit of *truth* from the spirit of falsehood.
	5	6 Ⓢ	the Spirit is the *truth*
		20	2 the Son of God . . . has given us the power to know the *true* 2 [God]. We are in the *true* [God], as we are in his Son, Jesus 2 Christ. This is the *true* God,
2 Jn		1	my greetings to the Lady, the chosen one, and to her children, she whom I love in the *truth* – and I am not the only one,
		2	for so do all who have come to know the *truth* – ² because
		3	of the *truth* that lives in us . . . ³ In our life of *truth* and love, we shall have grace, mercy and peace
3 Jn		1	your children have been living the life of *truth*
		1	greetings to my dear friend Gaius, whom I love in the *truth*.
		3	some brothers . . . told of your faithfulness to the *truth*, and
		4	of your life in the *truth*. ⁴ It is always my greatest joy to hear that my children are living according to the *truth*.
		8	it is our duty to . . . contribute our share to their work for the *truth*.
		12	Demetrius has been approved . . . by the *truth* itself. We too will vouch for him and you know that our testimony is 3 *true*.
Rv	3	7 X	2 Here is the message of the holy and *faithful* [one]
		14 X	2 Here is the message of the Amen, the faithful, the *true* witness,
	6	10 Θ	2 Holy, *faithful* Master, how much longer will you wait . . .?
	15	3	2 just and *true* are all your ways,
	16	7	2 the punishments you give are *true* and just.
	19	2	2 He judges *fairly*, he punishes justly,
		9	2 All the things you have written are *true* messages from God.
		11 X	I saw . . . a white horse appear; its rider was called Faithful 2 and *True*;
	21	5	Write this: that what I am saying is sure and [will come] 2 *true*.
	22	6	2 All that you have written is sure and [will come] *true*:

2: I TELL YOU TRULY – I ASSURE YOU

6	*a-lēthōs legō hymin*	2
7	*ep' a-lētheias legō hymin*	1
8	*legō hymin a-lēthōs*	1

Lk	4	25	7 There were many widows in Israel, *I chn assure you*, in Elijah's day,
	9	27	8 *I tell you truly*, there are some standing here who will not taste death before they see the kingdom of God.
	12	44	6 *I tell you truly*, [the master] will place him over everything he owns.
	21	3	6 *I tell you truly*, this poor widow has put in more than any of [the rich people];

3. AMEN
amēn 135

1: *AMĒN LEGŌ HYMIN*

a) *I tell you solemnly – Truly, I say to you*

1	*amēn legō hymin*	46
2	*amēn legō soi*	4

Note: only the (Greek) clause preceded by 1 or 2 above is quoted below.

Mt	5	18	1 till heaven and earth disappear, not one dot . . . shall disappear from the Law

Mt	5	26	2 you will not get out till you have paid the last penny.
	6	2	1 [the hypocrites] have had their reward.
		5	1 [the hypocrites] have had their reward.
		16	1 [the hypocrites] have had their reward.
	8	10	1 nowhere in Israel have I found faith like this.
	10	15	1 on the day of Judgement it will not go as hard with the land of Sodom and Gomorrah as with that town.
		23	1 you will not have gone the round of the towns of Israel before the Son of Man comes.
		42	1 he will most certainly not lose his reward.
	11	11	1 of all the children born of women, a greater than John . . . has never been seen;
	13	17	1 many prophets and holy men longed to see what you see,
	16	28	1 there are some of these standing here who will not taste death before they see the Son of Man coming with his kingdom.
	17	20	1 if your faith were the size of a mustard seed you could say to this mountain, 'Move from here to there', and it would move;
	18	3	1 unless you . . . become like little children you will never enter the kingdom of heaven.
		13	1 if he finds [the lost sheep], it gives him more joy than do the ninety-nine that did not stray at all.
		18	1 whatever you bind on earth shall be considered bound in heaven;
		19	1 if two of you on earth agree to ask anything at all, it will be granted to you
	19	23	1 it will be hard for a rich man to enter the kingdom of heaven.
		28	1 when all is made new . . . you will yourselves sit on twelve thrones
	21	21	1 if you have faith and do not doubt at all, . . . even if you say to this mountain, 'Get up and throw yourself into the sea', it will be done.
		31	1 tax collectors and prostitutes are making their way into the kingdom of God before you.
	23	36	1 all of this will recoil on this generation.
	24	2	1 not a single stone here will be left on another:
		34	1 before this generation has passed away all these things will have taken place.
		47	1 [the master] will place him over everything he owns.
	25	12 <	1 I do not know you.
		40	1 in so far as you did this to one of the least of these brothers of mine, you did it to me.
		45	1 in so far as you neglected to do this to one of the least of these, you neglected to do it to me.
	26	13	1 wherever . . . this Good News is proclaimed, what she has done will be told also,
		21	1 one of you is about to betray me.
		34	2 this very night . . . you will have disowned me three times.
Mk	3	28	1 all men's sins will be forgiven,
	8	12	1 no sign shall be given to this generation.
	9	1	1 there are some standing here who will not taste death before they see the kingdom of God
		41	1 he will most certainly not lose his reward.
	10	15	1 anyone who does not welcome the kingdom of God like a little child will never enter it.
		29	1 there is no one who has left house, brothers . . . for my sake [who will not be repaid]
	11	23	1 if anyone says to this mountain, 'Get up and throw yourself into the sea', . . . it will be done for him.
	12	43	1 this poor widow has put more in than all who have contributed to the treasury;
	13	30	1 before this generation has passed away all these things will have taken place.
	14	9	1 wherever . . . the Good News is proclaimed, what she has done will be told also,
		18	1 one of you is about to betray me,
		25	1 I shall not drink any more wine
		30	2 this day . . . you will have disowned me three times.
Lk	4	24	1 no prophet is ever accepted in his own country.
	12	37	1 [the master] will put on an apron . . . and wait on [the servants].
	18	17	1 anyone who does not welcome the kingdom of God like a little child will never enter it.
		29	1 there is no one who has left house, wife . . . for the sake of the kingdom of God [who will not be given repayment]
	21	32	1 before this generation has passed away all will have taken place.
	23	43	2 today you will be with me in paradise.

b) *I tell you most solemnly – Truly, Truly I say to you – In truth, I tell you*

3	*amēn, amēn legō hymin*	20
4	*amēn, amēn legō soi*	5

Note: only the (Greek) clause preceded by 3 or 4 above is quoted below.

Jn	1	51	3 you will see heaven laid open and . . . the angels of God ascending and descending.
	3	3	4 unless a man is born from above, he cannot see the kingdom of God.

Jn	3	5	4 unless a man is born through water and the Spirit, he cannot enter the kingdom of God;
		11	4 we speak only about what we know and witness only to what we have seen
	5	19	3 the Son . . . can do only what he sees the Father doing:
		24	3 whoever listens to my words . . . has eternal life;
		25	3 the hour will come . . . when the dead will hear the voice of the Son of God,
	6	26	3 you are . . . looking for me . . . because you had all the bread you wanted to eat.
		32	3 it was not Moses who gave you bread from heaven,
		47	3 everybody who believes has eternal life.
		53	3 if you do not eat the flesh of the Son of Man and drink his blood, you will not have life in you.
	8	34	3 everyone who commits sin is a slave.
		51	3 whoever keeps my word will never see death.
		58	3 before Abraham ever was, I Am.
	10	1	3 anyone who does not enter the sheepfold through the gate . . . is a thief
		7	3 I am the gate of the sheepfold.
	12	24	3 unless a wheat grain falls on the ground and dies, it remains only a single grain;
	13	16	3 no servant is greater than his master,
		20	3 whoever welcomes the one I send welcomes me,
		21	3 one of you will betray me.
		38	4 before the cock crows you will have disowned me three times.
	14	12	3 whoever believes in me will perform the same works as I do myself.
	16	20	3 you will be weeping and wailing while the world will rejoice;
		23	3 anything you ask for from the Father he will grant in my name.
	21	18	4 when you were young you put on your own belt

2: AMEN (AFTER A DOXOLOGY)

Mt	6	13	(ᵛ For yours is the kingdom . . . for ever. *Amen*.)
Rm	1	25	the creator . . . is blessed for ever. *Amen*!
	9	5	Christ . . . is above all, God for ever blessed! *Amen*.
	11	36	To [God] be glory for ever! *Amen*.
	16	27	give glory therefore to [God] . . . for ever and ever. *Amen*.
2 Co	1	20	That is why it is 'through [Christ]' that we answer *Amen* to the praise of God.
Ga	1	5	to [God] be glory for ever and ever. *Amen*.
Ep	3	21	glory be to [God] . . . in the Church and in Christ Jesus for ever and ever. *Amen*.
Ph	4	20	Glory to God, our Father, for ever and ever. *Amen*.
1 Tm	1	17	To the eternal King . . . be honour and glory for ever and ever. *Amen*.
	6	16	to [God] be honour and everlasting power. *Amen*.
2 Tm	4	18	To [the Lord] be glory for ever and ever. *Amen*.
Heb	13	21	to [Jesus Christ] be glory for ever and ever. *Amen*.
1 P	4	11	to [God] alone belong all glory . . . for ever and ever. *Amen*.
	5	11	[God's] power lasts for ever and ever. *Amen*.
2 P	3	18	To [Jesus Christ] be glory, in time and in eternity. *Amen*.
Jude		25	To God . . . be the glory . . . which he had before time began, now and for ever. *Amen*.
Rv	1	6	to [Jesus Christ] be glory and power for ever and ever. *Amen*. ⁷ It is he who is coming on the clouds . . . This is the truth. *Amen*.
	5	14	the four animals said, '*Amen*';
	7	12	[All the angels worshipped God] with these words, '*Amen*. Praise and glory . . . to our God for ever and ever. *Amen*.'
	19	4	the twenty-four elders and the four animals prostrated themselves . . . and they cried, '*Amen*, Alleluia'.

3: THE AMEN (= JESUS)

Rv	3	14	Here is the message of the *Amen* (cf. Is 65 16), the faithful, the true witness,

4: AMEN

Mk	16	20	[the Eleven] preached everywhere, the Lord . . . confirming the word by the signs that accompanied it. (ᵛ*Amen*.)
Rm	15	33	May the God of peace be with you all! *Amen*.
	16	24	(ᵛ May the grace of our Lord Jesus Christ be with you all. *Amen*.)
1 Co	14	16	Any uninitiated person will never be able to say *Amen* to your thanksgiving, if you only bless God with the spirit,
	16	24	My love is with you all in Christ Jesus, (ᵛ*Amen*.)
Ga	6	18	The grace of our Lord Jesus Christ be with your spirit, my brothers. *Amen*.
1 Th	3	13	may [the Lord] so confirm your hearts in holiness that you may be blameless . . . when our Lord Jesus Christ comes with all his saints. (ᵛ*Amen*.)
Phm		25	May the grace of our Lord Jesus Christ be with your spirit. (ᵛ*Amen*.)

Heb	13	25	Grace be with you all. (ᵛ *Amen*).
Rv	22	20	*Amen*; come, Lord Jesus.
		21	May the grace of the Lord Jesus be with you all. *Amen*.

TURN – RETURN

1. Turn, Turn off – Upset: *trepō*
  1: Turn, Turn off – Wrench, Put out of joint
  2: Upset, Knock over
2. Turn aside, Turn away: *ek-klinō*
3. Turn, Turn away, Turn back – Return: *strephō*
  1: Turn, Turn round – Twist, Distort
  2: Overturn, Upset
  3: Turn away
    a) Turn away – Banish – Desert

    b) Pervert, Perverse – Subvert
  4: Turn (to), Turn back (figuratively) – Be converted – Come back (to one's senses)
  5: Return – Come back (to), Go back (to) – Turn back
4. Go back (to), Come back (to), Return: *ana-kamptō*
5. Return: *ep-an-agō*

1. TURN, TURN OFF – UPSET: *TREPŌ*

2	*ana-trepō*	2/3	3	*peri-trepō* 1
1	*ek-trepō*	4/5		

1: TURN, TURN OFF – WRENCH, PUT OUT OF JOINT

Ac	26	24	3 Festus shouted out, 'Paul, . . . all that learning of yours is ᵊdriving (lit. *turning*) you mad'.
1 Tm	1	6	some people . . . have gone off the straight course and ᵊtaken a road (lit. *taken a turning off*) that leads to empty speculation;
	5	15	some [young widows] . . . have *left* us to follow Satan.
2 Tm	4	4	instead of listening to us they will *turn* to myths.
Heb	12	13	then the injured limb will not be *wrenched*,

2: UPSET, KNOCK OVER

Jn	2	15 X	2 he . . . scattered the money-changers' coins, *knocked* their tables *over*
2 Tm	2	18	[Hymenaeus and Philetus] claim that the resurrection has already taken place. ᵊSome people's faith cannot stand 2 up to them (lit. *upsetting* the faith of some people).

2. TURN ASIDE, TURN AWAY: *EK-KLINŌ*

ek-klinō 2/3

Rm	3	12	All have *turned aside*, tainted all alike;
1 P	3	11	(Ps 34 14) he must ᵊnever yield to (lit. *turn away* from) evil but must practise good;

3. TURN, TURN AWAY, TURN BACK – RETURN: *STREPHŌ*

8	*strebloō*	1	5	*dia-strephō*	7
3	*strephō*	19/21	9	*ek-strephō*	1
6	*ana-strephō*	2/10	1	*epi-strephō*	36
4	*apo-strephō*	9	10	*epi-strophē*	1
7	*kata-strephō*	2/3	2	*hypo-strephō*	36

1: TURN, TURN ROUND – TWIST, DISTORT

Mt	5	39	3 if anyone hits you on the right cheek, ᵊoffer (lit. *turn*) him the other as well;
	7	6	3 [the pigs] may . . . *turn* on you and tear you to pieces.
	9	22 X	3 Jesus *turned round* and saw [the woman with a haemorrhage];
	16	23 X	3 he *turned* and said to Peter, 'Get behind me, Satan!'
Mk	5	30 X	Jesus *turned round* in the crowd
	8	33 X	*turning* and seeing his disciples, he rebuked Peter
Lk	7	9 X	3 Jesus . . . was astonished at [the centurion] and, *turning round*, said to the crowd
		44 X	3 Then he *turned* to the woman.
	9	55 X	3 he *turned* and rebuked [James and John],
	10	23 X	3 *turning* to his disciples he spoke to them in private,
	14	25	Great crowds accompanied him on his way and he *turned*
		X	3 and spoke to them.
	22	61 X	3 the Lord *turned* and looked straight at Peter,
	23	28 X	3 Jesus *turned* to them and said, 'Daughters of Jerusalem,'

Jn 1 38 X 3 Jesus *turned round*, saw [John's two disciples] following
20 14 3 [Mary of Magdala] *turned round* and saw Jesus standing there,
16 3 [Mary] knew him then and *turned round* and said to him in Hebrew, 'Rabbuni!'
21 20 Peter *turned* and saw the disciple Jesus loved following them
Ac 9 40 Peter . . . *turned* to the dead woman and said, 'Tabitha, stand up'.
13 10 5 why don't you stop *twisting* the straightforward ways of the Lord?
16 18 Paul lost his temper one day and *turned round* and said to the spirit, 'I order you . . . to leave that woman'.
20 30 5 there will be men coming forward with a ⌐travesty (lit. *distortion*) of the truth on their lips
2 P 3 16 8 these are the points that uneducated and unbalanced people *distort*,
Rv 1 12 I *turned round* to see who had spoken to me, and when I *turned* I saw seven golden lamp-stands

2: OVERTURN, UPSET

Mt 21 12 X 7 he *upset* the tables of the money changers
Mk 11 15 X 7 he *upset* the tables of the money changers

3: TURN AWAY

a) Turn away – Banish – Desert

Mt 5 42 4 if anyone wants to borrow, do not *turn away*.
Ac 3 26 4 God raised up his servant and sent him to bless you by *turning* every one of you from your wicked ways.
7 42 3 God *turned away* from them and abandoned them to the worship of the army of heaven,
Rm 11 26 X 4 (Is 59 20 G) The liberator . . . will *banish* godlessness from Jacob.
2 Tm 1 15 4 all the others from Asia ⌐refuse to have anything more to do with (or: have *turned away* from) me.
Tt 1 14 4 [make them sound in the faith] so that they stop . . . doing what they are told to do by people who ⌐are no longer interested in (lit. have *turned away* from) the truth.
Heb 12 25 4 how shall we escape if we *turn away* from a voice that warns us from heaven?
2 P 2 21 2 better . . . never to have learnt the way of holiness, than to know it and afterwards *desert* the holy rule

b) Pervert, Perverse – Subvert

Mt 17 17 5 'Faithless and *perverse* generation!' Jesus said
Lk 9 41 5 'Faithless and *perverse* generation!' Jesus said
23 2 5 We found this man ⌐inciting our people to revolt (lit. *subverting* our people),
14 4 You brought this man before me . . . as a ⌐political agitator (lit. [man who was] *subverting* our people).
Ph 2 15 5 then you will be . . . perfect children of God among a deceitful and ⌐underhand (lit. *perverse*) brood,

4: TURN (TO), TURN BACK (FIGURATIVELY) – BE CONVERTED – COME BACK (TO ONE'S SENSES)

Mt 13 15 (cf. Is 6 10) they have shut their eyes, for fear they should . . . ⌐be converted (or: *turn back* [to me])
Mk 4 12 (cf. Is 6 10) [everything comes in parables,] so that they may see . . . but not understand, otherwise they might ⌐be converted (or: *turn back* [to me])
Lk 1 16 [John] will ⌐bring back (lit. *turn back*) many of the sons of Israel to the Lord their God.
17 (Ml 3 24) [John] will go before [the Lord] to *turn* the hearts of fathers towards their children
22 32 Simon, . . . once you have ⌐recovered (lit. *come back* [to yourself]), you in your turn must strengthen your brothers.
Jn 12 40 3 (cf. Is 6 10) he has hardened their heart, for fear they should . . . *turn* to me for healing.
Ac 3 19 you must repent and *turn* [to God], so that your sins may be wiped out,
7 39 3 our ancestors . . . *turned back* to Egypt in their thoughts,
9 35 everybody who lived in Lydda . . . saw [the paralytic Peter had cured], and they *were* all *converted* to the Lord.
11 21 [at Antioch] a great number believed and *were converted* to the Lord.
13 8 5 Elymas . . . tried to stop [Paul and Barnabas speaking] so as to prevent the proconsul's *conversion* to the faith.
46 3 since you have rejected [the word of God], we must *turn* to the pagans.
14 15 We have come with good news to *make* you *turn* from these empty idols to the living God.
15 3 10 as [Paul and Barnabas] passed through Phoenicia and Samaria they told how the pagans had *been converted*,
19 instead of making things more difficult for pagans who *turn* to God,

Ac 26 18 so that [the pagans] may *turn* from darkness to light,
20 I started preaching . . . to the pagans, urging them to repent and *turn* to God,
28 27 (cf. Is 6 10) they have shut their eyes, for fear they should . . . ⌐be converted (or: *turn back* [to me])
2 Co 3 16 [The veil is over their minds.] It will not be removed until they *turn* to the Lord.
Ga 4 9 how can you want to *go back* to elemental things like these . . .?
1 Th 1 9 you broke with idolatry when you *were converted* to God
2 Tm 4 4 4 instead of ⌐listening (lit. *turning* their attention) to the truth they will turn to myths.
Tt 3 11 9 you will know that any man [who disputes what you teach] has already *lapsed*
Jm 5 19 if one of you strays from the truth, and another ⌐brings (lit. *turns*) him back, 20 he may be sure that anyone who can ⌐bring back (lit. *turn back*) a sinner from the wrong way . . . will be saving a soul from death
1 P 2 25 now you have *come back* to the shepherd

5: RETURN – COME BACK (TO), GO BACK (TO) – TURN BACK

Mt 10 13 O if [the house] does not [deserve your peace], let your peace *come back* to you.
12 44 Ⓓ [the unclean spirit] says, 'I will *return* to the home I came from'.
24 18 if a man is in the fields, he must not *turn back* to fetch his cloak.
26 52 4 ⌐Put your sword back (lit. *Return* your sword to its place),
27 3 O 3 Judas . . . ⌐took the thirty silver pieces back (lit. *returned* the thirty silver pieces) to the chief priests
Mk 13 16 if a man is in the fields, he must not *turn back* to fetch his cloak.
14 40 X 2 once more he *came back* and found [the apostles] sleeping,
Lk 1 56 2 Mary . . . *went back* home.
2 20 2 the shepherds *went back* . . . praising God
39 [Mary and Joseph] *went back* . . . to their own town of Nazareth.
43 2 When [Mary and Joseph] were ⌐on their **way** (lit. *going back*) [home] after the feast,
45 2 they *went back* to Jerusalem looking for [Jesus] everywhere.
4 1 X 2 Jesus ⌐left (lit. *returned* from) the Jordan
14 X 2 Jesus . . . *returned* to Galilee;
7 10 2 when the messengers *got back* to the house they found the servant in perfect health.
8 37 X 2 Jesus . . . got into the boat and *went back*.
39 2 [Jesus to the demoniac:] *Go back* home . . . and report all that God has done for you.
40 X 2 On his *return* Jesus was welcomed by the crowd,
55 O her spirit *returned* [to Jairus's daughter] and she got up at once.
9 10 2 On their *return* the apostles gave him an account of all they had done.
10 17 2 The seventy-two [disciples] *came back* rejoicing.
11 24 Ⓓ 2 [the unclean spirit] says, 'I will *go back* to the home I came from'.
17 4 2 if he wrongs you seven times a day and seven times *comes back* to you and says, 'I am sorry', you must forgive him.
15 2 one of [the lepers] *turned back* praising God
18 2 no one has *come back* to give praise to God, except this foreigner.
31 nor must anyone in the fields *turn back* either.
19 12 < 2 A man . . . went to a distant country to be appointed king and afterwards *returned*.
23 48 2 all the people . . . *went back* [home] beating their breasts.
56 2 Then [the women] *returned* [from the tomb] and prepared spices
24 9 2 the women *returned* from the tomb
33 2 [The two disciples] *returned* to Jerusalem [from Emmaus].
52 2 [The apostles] *went back* to Jerusalem full of joy;
Ac 1 12 2 from the Mount of Olives . . . [the apostles] *went back* to Jerusalem,
5 22 6 the officials . . . *went back* and reported.
8 25 2 [Peter and John] *went back* to Jerusalem,
28 2 [The eunuch] was now ⌐on his way (lit. *going back*) home;
12 25 2 [Barnabas and Saul] completed their task, and *came back* from Jerusalem,
13 13 2 John left [Paul and his friends] to *go back* to Jerusalem,
34 O 2 God raised him from the dead, never to *return* to corruption,
14 21 2 [Paul and Barnabas] *went back* . . . to Antioch.
15 16 Θ 6 (Am 9 11 G) I shall *return* and rebuild the fallen House of David;
36 Paul said to Barnabas, 'Let us *go back* and visit all the towns where we preached'
20 3 2 a plot . . . made [Paul] decide to *go back* by way of Macedonia.
21 6 2 we went aboard and they *returned* home.
22 17 2 after I had got back to Jerusalem, . . . I fell into a trance
23 32 2 [the soldiers] left the mounted escort to go on with [Paul] and *returned* to the fortress.

Ga	1	17		2 later [I] *went straight back* from [Arabia] to Damascus.
Heb	7	1		2 Abraham . . . was ⌐on his way back (lit. *going back*) after defeating the kings,
2 P	2	22		(Pr 26 11) The dog *goes back* to his own vomit

4. GO BACK (TO), COME BACK (TO), RETURN: *ANA-KAMPTŌ*

ana-kamptō 4

Mt	2	12		[the wise men] were warned in a dream not to *go back* to Herod,
Lk	10	6		if a man of peace lives there, your peace will go and rest on
			○	him; if not, it will *come back* to you.
Ac	18	21		[Paul to the Jews in Ephesus:] I will *come back* another time, God willing.
Heb	11	15		They can hardly have meant the country they came from, since they had the opportunity to *go back* to it;

5. RETURN: *EP-AN-AGŌ*

ep-an-agō 1/3

| Mt | 21 | 18 | X | As he was *returning* to the city in the early morning, he felt hungry. |

TYRE – SIDON

Canaanite	*1* (Mt 15)	Sidonian	*2*		1 *polis 1/164*	
Phoenicia	*3*	⌐Tyre	*11*			
Ptolemais	*1* (Ac 21)	T⌐Tyrian	*1*			
Syro-phoenician	*1* (Mk 7)	Zarephath [*Sarepta*]	*1* (Lk 4)			
Sidon	*10*					

Mt	11	21	T		if the miracles done in you had been done in *Tyre* and *Sidon*, they would have repented long ago . . . ²² . . . it will not
		22	T		go as hard on Judgement day with *Tyre* and *Sidon* as with you.
	15	21	T		Jesus . . . withdrew to the region of *Tyre* and *Sidon*. ²² Then
		22	T		out came a *Canaanite* [woman] . . . and started shouting, 'Sir, . . . take pity on me.
Mk	3	8	T		[From] the region of *Tyre* and *Sidon*, great numbers . . came to [Jesus].
	7	24	T		[Jesus] set out for the territory of *Tyre* (ᵛ and *Sidon*).
		26			[A woman fell at his feet.] Now the woman was a pagan, by birth a *Syrophoenician*,
		31	T		Returning from the district of *Tyre*, [Jesus] went by way of *Sidon* . . . right through the Decapolis region.
Lk	4	26			[There were many widows in Israel,] but Elijah was not sent to any one of these (1 K 17 9): he was sent to a widow at *Zarephath* [*Sarepta*], a *Sidonian* town.
	6	17	T		there was . . . a great crowd of people . . . from the coastal region of *Tyre* and *Sidon*
	10	13	T		if the miracles done in you had been done in *Tyre* and *Sidon*, they would have repented long ago . . . ¹⁴ . . . it will not
		14	T		go as hard with *Tyre* and *Sidon* at the Judgement as with you.
Ac	11	19			Those who had escaped during the persecution . . . travelled as far as *Phoenicia* and Cyprus and Antioch,
	12	20	T		Herod was on bad terms with the *Tyrians* and *Sidonians*. However, they . . . negotiated a treaty, since their country depended for its food supply on King Herod's territory.
	15	3			[Paul and Barnabas] passed through *Phoenicia* and Samaria
	21	2			we found a ship bound for *Phoenicia*, so we went on board
		3	T		. . . ³ . . . we sailed to Syria and put in at *Tyre*, since the
		5			ship was to unload her cargo there . . . ⁵ . . . when our time was up . . . they all escorted us on our way till we
	7	7	T	1	were out of the *town* . . . ⁷ The end of our voyage from
			T		*Tyre* came when we landed at *Ptolemais*,
	27	3			Next day we put in at *Sidon*,

V

VESSEL – BASKET – BAG

1. Vessel, Container
  1: Vessel, Container – Thing that belongs, Property: *skeuos*
     a) Vessel, Container – Pot, Jar, Bowl
     b) Vessel = Body
     c) Things that belong (to a ship) – (Ship's) Gear, Tackle
     d) Property, Possessions
     e) Instrument – Article, Piece, Thing
  2: Container, Vessel – Flask: *angos*
2. Jar, Pot, Jug
  1: Jar: *stamnos*
  2: Pitcher, Jar: *keramion*
  3: Water-jar: *hydria*
  4: Alabaster jar: *alabastros*
  5: Pot, Jug: *xestēs*

3. (Wine-)Skins: *askos*
4. Bowl – Basin
  1: Basin: *niptēr*
  2: Bowl: *phialē*
5. Dish, Plate
  1: Dish, Platter, Plate: *pinax*
  2: Dish: *tryblion*
  3: Dish: *par-opsis*
  4: Bronze dishes, Copper Bowls, Brass vessels: *chalkion*
6. Basket, Hamper
  1: *kophinos*
  2: *spyris*
  3: *sarganē*
7. Haversack, Bag: *pēra*
8. Purse, Fund
  1: Purse: *ballantion*
  2: Common fund, Communal purse: *glōsso-komon*

---

1. VESSEL, CONTAINER

1: VESSEL, CONTAINER – THING THAT BELONGS, PROPERTY: *SKEUOS*

2 *skeuē* 1   1 *skeuos* 23

a) Vessel, Container – Pot, Jar, Bowl

Lk	8 16	No one lights a lamp to cover it with a *bowl*
Jn	19 29	A *jar* full of vinegar stood there,
Ac	10 11	[Peter] saw . . . *something* like a big sheet being let down to earth
	16	then suddenly the *container* was drawn up to heaven again.
	11 5	I . . . had a vision of *something* like a big sheet being let down from heaven
Rm	9 21	It is surely for [the potter] to decide whether he will use a particular lump of clay to make a special *pot* or an ordinary one? ²² . . . God . . . patiently puts up with the ˹people (lit. *vessels*) who make him angry, . . . ²³ He puts up with them for the sake of those other ˹people (lit. *vessels*), to whom he wants to be merciful, . . . ²⁴ Well, we are those people;
	22	
	23 ○	
	○	
2 Co	4 7 ○	We are only the earthenware *jars* that hold this treasure,
2 Tm	2 20	Not all the ˹dishes (lit. *vessels*) in a large house are made of gold and silver; some are made of wood or earthenware
	21	to avoid these faults . . . is the way for anyone to become a *vessel* for special occasions,
	○	
Heb	9 21	[Moses] sprinkled the tent and all the liturgical *vessels* with blood
Rv	2 27	to . . . shatter [the pagans] like earthenware *pots*.

b) Vessel = Body

1 Th	4 4	[God wants] each one of you to know how to use the *body* that belongs to him in a way that is holy and honourable,
1 P	3 7	husbands must always treat their wives with consideration . . ., respecting a woman as one who, though she may be ˹the weaker partner (lit. considered the weaker *vessel*), is equally an heir to the life of grace.

c) Things that belong (to a ship) – (Ship's) Gear, Tackle

Ac	27 17	they floated out the ˹sea-anchor (or: mainsail)
	19	2 they threw the [ship's] *gear* overboard

d) Property, Possessions

Mt	12 29	how can anyone make his way into a strong man's house and burgle his *property* . . .?
Mk	3 27	no one can make his way into a strong man's house and burgle his *property*
Lk	17 31	anyone on the housetop, with his *possessions* in the house,

e) Instrument – Article, Piece, Thing

Mk	11 16	Nor would [Jesus] allow anyone to carry *anything* through the Temple.
Ac	9 15	this man is my chosen *instrument* to bring my name before pagans
Rv	18 12	all the sandalwood, every *piece* in ivory ˹or (lit. and every *piece* in) fine wood,

2: CONTAINER, VESSEL – FLASK: *ANGOS*

1 *angeion* 1   2 *angos* 1

Mt	13 48	the fishermen . . . collect the good [fish] in a ˹basket (lit. 2 *container*).
	25 4	the sensible [bridesmaids] took *flasks* of oil as well as their lamps.

---

2. JAR, POT, JUG

1: JAR: *STAMNOS*

stamnos 1

Heb	9 4	in [the ark of the covenant] were kept the gold *jar* containing the manna, . . . and the stone tablets

2: PITCHER, JAR: *KERAMION*

keramion 2

Mk	14 13	you will meet a man carrying a *pitcher* of water.
Lk	22 10	you will meet a man carrying a *pitcher* of water.

3: WATER-JAR: *HYDRIA*

hydria 3

Jn	2 6	There were six stone *water jars* standing there, meant for the ablutions . . . ⁷ Jesus said to the servants, 'Fill the *jars* with water',
	7	
	4 28	The [Samaritan] woman put down her *water jar* and hurried back to the town

4: ALABASTER JAR: *ALABASTROS*

alabastros 4

Mt	26 7	a woman came to him with an *alabaster jar* of the most expensive ointment,
Mk	14 3	a woman came in with an *alabaster jar* of very costly ointment, pure nard. She broke the *jar* and poured the ointment on his head.
Lk	7 37	a woman came in . . . She . . . brought with her an *alabaster jar* of ointment.

5: POT, JUG: *XESTĒS*

xestēs 1

Mk	7 4	many other observances . . . concerning the washing of cups and *pots* and bronze dishes.

---

3. (WINE–)SKINS: *ASKOS*

askos 12

Mt	9 17	Nor do people put new wine into old *wineskins*; if they do, the *skins* burst, the wine runs out, and the *skins* are lost. No; they put new wine into fresh *skins* and both are preserved.
Mk	2 22	nobody puts new wine into old *wineskins*; if he does, the wine will burst the *skins*, and the wine is lost and the *skins* too. No! New wine, fresh *skins*!
Lk	5 37	nobody puts new wine into old *skins*; if he does, the new wine will burst the *skins* and then run out, and the *skins* will be lost. ³⁸ No; new wine must be put into fresh *skins*.
	38	

4. BOWL – BASIN

1: BASIN: *NIPTĒR*

niptēr 1

Jn 13 5 [Jesus] then poured water into a *basin* and began to wash the disciples' feet

2: BOWL: *PHIALĒ*

phialē 12

Rv 5 8 the four animals . . . and with them the twenty-four elders; each one of them . . . . had a golden *bowl* full of incense
15 7 One of the four animals gave the seven angels seven golden *bowls* filled with the anger of God
16 1 empty the seven *bowls* of God's anger over the earth.
2 The first angel went and emptied his *bowl* over the earth;
3 The second angel emptied his *bowl* over the sea,
4 The third angel emptied his *bowl* into the rivers and water-springs
8 The fourth angel emptied his *bowl* over the sun
10 The fifth angel emptied his *bowl* over the throne of the beast
12 The sixth angel emptied his *bowl* over the great river Euphrates;
17 The seventh angel emptied his *bowl* into the air,
17 1 One of the seven angels that had the seven *bowls* came to speak to me,
21 9 One of the seven angels that had the seven *bowls* full of the seven last plagues

5. DISH, PLATE

1: DISH, PLATTER, PLATE: *PINAX*

pinax 5

Mt 14 8 Give me John the Baptist's head, here, on a *dish*.
11 The head was brought in on a *dish*
Mk 6 25 I want you to give me John the Baptist's head, here and now, on a *dish*.
28 The man . . . brought the head on a *dish*
Lk 11 39 You clean the outside of cup and *plate*,

2: DISH: *TRYBLION*

tryblion 2

Mt 26 23 Someone who has dipped his hand into the *dish* with me
Mk 14 20 It is one of the Twelve, one who is dipping into the same *dish* with me.

3: DISH: *PAR-OPSIS*

par-opsis 2

Mt 23 25 You who clean the outside of cup and *dish* . . . [26] . . .
26 Clean the inside of cup and *dish* first

4: BRONZE DISHES, COPPER BOWLS, BRASS VESSELS: *CHALKION*

chalkion 1

Mk 7 4 many other observances . . . concerning the washing of cups and pots and *bronze dishes*.

6. BASKET, HAMPER

1: BASKET, HAMPER: *KOPHINOS*

kophinos 6

Mt 14 20 they collected the scraps remaining, twelve *baskets* full.
16 9 Do you not remember the five loaves . . . and the number of *baskets* you collected?
Mk 6 43 They collected twelve *basket*fuls
8 19 how many *baskets* full of scraps did you collect?
Lk 9 17 when the scraps remaining were collected they filled twelve *baskets*.
Jn 6 13 they . . . filled twelve *hampers* with scraps

2: BASKET, HAMPER: *SPYRIS*

spyris 5

Mt 15 37 they collected what was left of the scraps, seven *baskets* full.
16 10 [Do you not remember] the number of *baskets* you collected?
Mk 8 8 they collected seven *basket*fuls of the scraps left over.
20 how many *baskets* full of scraps did you collect?
Ac 9 25 the disciples . . . let [Saul] down from the top of the wall, lowering him in a *basket*.

3: BASKET, HAMPER: *SARGANĒ*

sarganē 1

2 Co 11 33 I had to be let down over the wall in a *hamper*

7. HAVERSACK, BAG: *PĒRA*

pēra 6

Mt 10 10 [Provide yourselves] with no *haversack* for the journey or spare tunic
Mk 6 8 [Jesus] instructed them to take nothing for the journey except a staff – no bread, no *haversack*,
Lk 9 3 [Jesus to the Twelve:] Take nothing for the journey: neither staff, nor *haversack*,
10 4 [Jesus to the seventy-two:] Carry no purse, no *haversack*,
22 35 When I sent you out without purse or *haversack* . . ., were you short of anything?
36 But now if you have a purse, take it; if you have a *haversack*, do the same;

8. PURSE, FUND

1: PURSE: *BALLANTION*

ballantion 4

Lk 10 4 Carry no *purse*, no haversack,
12 33 Get yourselves *purses* that do not wear out,
22 35 When I sent you out without *purse* or haversack . . ., were you short of anything?
36 But now if you have a *purse*, take it; if you have a haversack, do the same;

2: COMMON FUND, COMMUNAL PURSE: *GLŌSSO-KOMON*

glōsso-komon 2

Jn 12 6 [Judas] was in charge of the *common fund* and used to help himself to the contributions.
13 29 Since Judas had charge of the *common fund*, some of them thought Jesus was . . . telling him to give something to the poor.

VICTORY – CONQUER

| 1. Victory – Conquer, Defeat, Overcome – Triumph (over): *nikaō* | 2. Lead in triumphal procession: *thriambeuō* |

1. VICTORY – CONQUER, DEFEAT, OVERCOME – TRIUMPH (OVER): *NIKAŌ*

| 1 *nikaō* 28 | 2 *nikos* 4 |
| 3 *nikē* 1 | 4 *hyper-nikaō* 1 |

Mt 12 20 (cf. Is 42 3) He will not break the crushed reed . . . till he has
2 led the truth to *victory*:
Lk 11 22 someone stronger than he is attacks and *defeats* him,
Jn 16 33 X I have *conquered* the world.
Rm 3 4 Θ (Ps 51 6 G) when you are judged you *win your case*.
8 37 4 These are the trials through which we *triumph*, by the power of him who loved us.
12 21 ʳResist (lit. Do not be *overcome* by) evil and *conquer* it with good.
1 Co 15 54 2 (cf. Is 25 8) Death is swallowed up in *victory*.
55 2 (cf. Ho 13 14) Death, where is your *victory*?
57 2 let us thank God for giving us the *victory* through our Lord Jesus Christ.

1 Jn	2 13	you . . . have already *overcome* the Evil One;
	14	you have *overcome* the Evil One.
	4 4	you have already *overcome* these false prophets, because you are from God
	5 4	anyone who has been begotten by God has already *overcome* the world; this is the *victory* ⌐over (lit. that has *overcome*) the world – our faith. ⁵ Who can *overcome* the world?
	3/	
	5	
Rv	2 7	those who *prove victorious* I will feed from the tree of life
	11	for those who *prove victorious* there is nothing to be afraid of in the second death.
	17	to those who *prove victorious* I will give the hidden manna
	26	To those who *prove victorious* . . . I will give the authority over the pagans
	3 5	Those who *prove victorious* will be dressed . . . in white robes;
‾	12	Those who *prove victorious* . . . will stay [in the sanctuary of my God] for ever;
	21	Those who *prove victorious* I will allow to share my throne, just as I *was victorious* myself and took my place with my Father on his throne.
	X	
	5 5	There is no need to cry: the Lion . . . of Judah . . . has *triumphed*,
	X	
	6 2	he was given the *victor's* crown and he went away, to go [from victory] to *victory*.
	11 7	the beast . . . is going to . . . *overcome* [my two witnesses] and kill them.
	12 11	They have *triumphed over* [the dragon] by the blood of the Lamb
	13 7	[The beast] was allowed to make war against the saints and *conquer* them,
	15 2	I seemed to see . . . those who had *fought* against the beast and won,
	17 14 X	the Lamb is the Lord of lords . . . and he will *defeat* them
	21 7	[Water from the well of life] is the rightful inheritance of the one who *proves victorious*;

2. LEAD IN TRIUMPHAL PROCESSION: *THRIAMBEUŌ*

thriambeuō 2

2 Co	2 14 Θ	God . . . *makes* us, in Christ, *partners of* his *triumph*,
Col	2 15	[God] got rid of the Sovereignties and the Powers, and paraded them in public, (§ *leading* them) behind him *in* his *triumphal procession*.
	X	

VOICE – SOUND

1. **Voice – Sound – Shout:** *phōnē*
   1: Voice
     a) Voice (*of* God)
     b) Voice (*of* Jesus)
     c) Voice (*of* angels, from heaven)
     d) Voice (generally) – Words spoken, Language
     e) Raise the Voice
     f) Voiceless = Dumb – Meaningless
   2: Cry out, Shout (with a loud, at the top of one's) Voice
   3: Voice = Sound, Noise
   4: Voice = Music, (musical) Sound, Song
   5: the Cock Crows, Cockcrow
2. **Voice – Sound, Note:** *phthongos*
     a) Voice
     b) (musical) Sound, Note
3. **Shout, Cry, Cry out**
   1: Shout, Cry out: *kraugē*
     a) (generally)
     b) (in supplication)
     c) (in acclamation)
   2: Cry, Cry out, Shout: *boē*
4. **Sound – Noisy:** *ēchos*
5. **Roar, Roaring**
   1: *mykaomai*
   2: *ōruomai*
   3: *rhoizēdon*
6. **Thunder:** *brontē*

1. VOICE – SOUND – SHOUT: *PHŌNĒ*

1	*phōnē*	140	4	*epi-phōneō*	4
2	*phōneō*	18/43	5	*pros-phōneō*	2/7
3	*a-phōnos*	4	7	*sym-phōnia*	1
6	*ana-phōneō*	1			

1: VOICE

a) Voice (of God)

Mt	3 17	a *voice* spoke from heaven, 'This is my Son,
	17 5	from the cloud there came a *voice* which said, 'This is my Son,
Mk	1 11	a *voice* came from heaven, 'You are my Son,
	9 7	there came a *voice* from the cloud, 'This is my Son,
Lk	3 22	a *voice* came from heaven, 'You are my Son,

Lk	9 35	a *voice* came from the cloud saying, 'This is my Son,
	36	after the *voice* had spoken, Jesus was found alone.
Jn	5 37	You have never heard [the Father's] *voice*,
	12 28	A *voice* came from heaven, 'I have glorified [my name],
	30	It was not for my sake that this *voice* came, but for yours.
Ac	7 31	the *voice* of the Lord was heard,
Heb	3 7	(Ps 95 7) If only you would listen to ⌐him (lit. his *voice*) today;
	15	(Ps 95 7) If only you would listen to ⌐him (lit. his *voice*) today;
	4 7	(Ps 95 7) If only you would listen to ⌐him (lit. his *voice*) today;
	12 19	the great *voice* speaking . . . made everyone that heard it beg that no more should be said to them.
	26	That time his *voice* made the earth shake,
2 P	1 17	the Sublime Glory itself ⌐spoke (lit. extended its *voice*) to him and said, 'This is my Son . . .' ¹⁸ We heard this *voice* ourselves, spoken from heaven,
	18	

b) Voice (of Jesus)

Jn	3 29	the bridegroom's friend . . . is glad when he hears the bridegroom's *voice*.
	<	
	5 25	the hour will come . . . when the dead will hear the *voice* of the Son of God,
	28	the hour is coming when the dead will leave their graves at the sound of his *voice*:
	10 3 <	the sheep hear [the shepherd's] *voice* . . . ⁴ . . . and the sheep follow because they know his *voice*.
	4 <	
	16	there are other sheep I have that . . . will listen to my *voice*,
	27	The sheep that belong to me listen to my *voice*;
	18 37	all who are on the side of truth listen to my *voice*.
Ac	9 4	[Saul] fell to the ground, and then he heard a *voice*
	7	though [the men travelling with Saul] heard the *voice* they could see no one.
	22 7	I fell to the ground and heard a *voice*
	9	The people who saw the light but did not hear his *voice*
	14	The God of our ancestors has chosen you . . . to see the Just One and hear his own *voice* speaking,
	26 14	I heard a *voice* saying to me in Hebrew, 'Saul, Saul, why are you persecuting me?'
Rv	1 15	his *voice* [was] like the sound of the ocean.
	3 20	If one of you hears ⌐me calling (lit. my *voice*) and opens the door, I will come in

c) Voice (of angels, from heaven)

Ac	10 13	A *voice* then said to him, 'Now, Peter; kill and eat!'
	15	Again, a second time, the *voice* spoke to [Peter], 'What God has made clean, you have no right to call profane'.
	11 7	I heard a *voice* that said to me, 'Now, Peter; kill and eat!'
	9	And a second time the *voice* spoke from heaven, 'What God has made clean, you have no right to call profane'.
1 Th	4 16	the *voice* of the archangel will call out the command and the Lord himself will come down from heaven;
Rv	1 10	I heard a *voice* behind me, shouting like a trumpet,
	12	I turned round to ⌐see who (lit. look for the *voice* that) had spoken to me,
	4 1	I . . . heard the same *voice* speaking to me, [the voice] like a trumpet,
	5	Flashes of lightning were coming from the throne, and ⌐the sound of (or: *voices* and) peals of thunder,
	5 2	a powerful angel . . . called with a loud *voice*,
	12	[the angels were] ⌐shouting (lit. saying in a loud *voice*), 'The Lamb . . . is worthy to be given power,
	6 1	I heard one of the four animals shout in a *voice* like thunder,
	6	I seemed to hear a *voice* shout from among the four animals
	7	I heard the *voice* of the fourth animal shout;
	8 5	immediately there came peals of thunder (§ and *voices*; or: and noises) and flashes of lightning,
	13	I heard an eagle, calling ⌐aloud (lit. in a loud *voice*)
	9 13	I heard a *voice* come out of the four horns of the golden altar
	10 4	when the seven thunderclaps had spoken . . . I heard a *voice* from heaven
	7	when the *voice* of the seventh angel is heard . . . God's secret intention will be fulfilled,
	8	I heard the *voice* I had heard from heaven speaking to me again.
	11 12	ⱽ they (G I) heard a loud *voice* from heaven say to them, 'Come up here',
	15	*voices* could be heard shouting in heaven,
	19	Then came flashes of lightning, ⌐peals of (lit. *voices* and; or: noises and) thunder and an earthquake,
	12 10	I heard a *voice* shout from heaven,
	14 7	[The angel] was calling in a loud *voice*, 'Fear God and praise him,
	9	A third angel followed, shouting ⌐aloud (lit. in a loud *voice*),
	13	Then I heard a *voice* from heaven say to me, 'Write down: Happy are those who die in the Lord!
	16 1	I heard a *voice* from the sanctuary
	17	a *voice* shouted from the sanctuary, 'The end has come'.
	18	there were flashes of lightning and ⌐peals of (lit. *voices* and; or: noises and) thunder
	18 4	A new *voice* spoke from heaven;

Rv 19	5	a *voice* came from the throne; it said, 'Praise our God,
21	3	I heard a loud *voice* call from the throne,

d) Voice (generally) – Words spoken, Language

Mt 2	18	(Jr 31 15) A *voice* was heard in Ramah, . . . it was Rachel weeping
Lk 17	15	one of [the ten lepers] turned back praising God at the top of his *voice*
19	37	the whole group of disciples . . . began to praise God at the top of their *voices*
Jn 10	5 <	[the sheep] do not recognise the *voice* of strangers.
Ac 12	14	[Rhoda] recognised Peter's *voice*
22	The people acclaimed [Herod] with, 'It is ⌐a god speaking (lit. the *voice* of a god), not a man!'
13	27	What the people of Jerusalem and their rulers did, . . . was in fact to fulfil the ⌐prophecies (lit. *words spoken* by the prophets)
14	10	Paul said in a loud *voice*, 'Get to your feet – stand up',
26	24	Festus ⌐shouted out (lit. cried in a loud *voice*), 'Paul, you are out of your mind;
1 Co 14	10	There are any number of different *languages* in the world, and not one of them is meaningless, [11] but if I am ignorant of what the ⌐sounds (or: *languages*) mean, I am a savage to the man who is speaking,
11	
Ga 4	20	I wish I were with you now so that I could know . . . *what to say*;
2 P 2	16	The dumb donkey put a stop to that prophet's madness ⌐when it talked like a man (lit. with a man's *voice*).
Rv 18	23	(Jr 25 10) never again will be heard the *voices* of bridegroom and bride.
19	6	I seemed to hear the ⌐*voices* (or: sound) of a huge crowd,

e) Raise the Voice
9 *airō* 2/101   8 *ep-airō* 4/19

Lk 11	27	8/ a woman in the crowd *raised her voice* and said, 'Happy the womb that bore you
17	13	9/ [ten lepers] ⌐called to him (lit. *raised their voices*), 'Jesus! Master! Take pity on us.'
Ac 2	14	Then Peter stood up with the Eleven and addressed them ⌐in 8/ a loud voice (lit. *raising his voice*):
4	24	9/ [the apostles] *lifted up their voice* to God all together.
14	11	8/ the crowd . . . ⌐shouted (lit. *raised their voices*, saying) . . , 'These people are gods
22	22	8/ [the Jews] began to ⌐shout (lit. *raise their voices*), 'Rid the earth of the man!'

f) Voiceless = Dumb – Meaningless

Ac 8	32	3 (Is 53 7) like a lamb that is *dumb* in front of its shearers . . . he never opens his mouth.
1 Co 12	2	3 you felt irresistibly drawn . . . towards *dumb* idols
14	10	There are any number of different languages in the world, and not one of them is *meaningless*,
3	
2 P 2	16	3 The *dumb* donkey put a stop to that prophet's madness

2: CRY OUT, SHOUT (WITH A LOUD, AT THE TOP OF ONE'S) VOICE

Mt 3	3	(Is 40 3) A *voice* cries in the wilderness:
11	16	5 this generation . . . is like children *shouting* to each other
12	19 X	[My servant] will not . . . shout, nor will anyone hear his *voice* in the streets.
27	46 X	about the ninth hour, Jesus cried out in a loud *voice*, 'Eli, Eli,
50 X	Jesus, again crying out in a loud *voice*, yielded up his spirit.
Mk 1	3	(Is 40 3) A *voice* cries in the wilderness:
26	⒟	2/ with a loud cry (lit. *crying out* with a loud *voice*) [the unclean spirit] went out of him.
5	7	⒟	[the demoniac] shouted at the top of his *voice*, 'What do you want with me, Jesus,
15	34 X	at the ninth hour Jesus cried out in a loud *voice*, 'Eloi, Eloi,
37 X	Jesus gave a loud *cry* and breathed his last.
Lk 1	42	6 [Elizabeth] ⌐gave (lit. *raised her voice* in) a loud cry and said, 'Of all women you are the most blessed,
3	4	(Is 40 3) A *voice* cries in the wilderness:
4	33	⒟	the spirit of an unclean devil . . . shouted at the top of its *voice*,
7	32	5 [The men of this generation] are like children *shouting* to one another
8	8 X	2 [Jesus] *cried*, 'Listen, anyone who has ears to hear!'
28	⒟	Catching sight of Jesus [the demoniac] gave a shout . . . and cried out at the top of his *voice*, 'What do you want with me,
16	24	2 [the rich man] *cried out*, 'Father Abraham, pity me
23	21	4 [the Jews] *shouted* back, 'Crucify him'
23	[the Jews] kept on shouting at the top of their *voices*, demanding that he should be crucified. And their ⌐shouts (lit. *voices*) were growing louder.
46 X	2/ when Jesus had *cried out* in a loud *voice*, he said, 'Father, into your hands I commit my spirit'.
Jn 1	23	(Is 40 3) I am . . . a *voice* that cries in the wilderness:

Jn 11	43 X	[Jesus] cried in a loud *voice*, 'Lazarus, here! Come out!'
Ac 7	57	At this all the members of the council shouted out in a loud *voice* and stopped their ears with their hands;
60	[Stephen] ⌐said aloud (lit. cried in a loud *voice*), 'Lord, do not hold this sin against them';
8	7	⒟	unclean spirits . . . came shrieking with loud *voices* out of many who were possessed,
12	22	4 The people *acclaimed* [Herod] with, 'It is a god speaking,
16	28	2/ Paul *shouted* at the top of his *voice*, 'Don't do yourself any harm';
19	34	they all started shouting ⌐in unison (lit. with one *voice*), 'Great is Diana of the Ephesians!'
21	34	4 People in the crowd *called out* different things,
22	24	the tribune had [Paul] brought into the fortress . . . to find out 4 the reason for the *outcry* against him.
24	21	[Let those who are present say what crime they found me guilty of,] unless it were to do with this single *outburst*,
Rv 6	10	[all the people who had been killed] shouted ⌐aloud (lit. in a loud *voice*),
7	2	another angel . . . called in a powerful *voice*
10	[I saw a huge number of people.] They shouted ⌐aloud (lit. in a loud *voice*), 'Victory to our God,
10	3	[another angel] shouted ⌐so loud (lit. in such a loud *voice*), it was like a lion roaring.
14	15	another angel . . . shouted ⌐aloud (lit. in a loud *voice*) . . , 'Put your sickle in and reap;
18	2/ the angel . . . shouted ⌐aloud (lit. in a loud *voice*) . . , 'Put your sickle in
18	2	At the top of his *voice* [the angel] shouted, 'Babylon has fallen,
19	17	an angel . . . shouted ⌐aloud (lit. in a loud *voice*) . . , 'Come here. Gather together at the great feast that God is giving.

3: VOICE = SOUND, NOISE

Lk 1	44	the moment the *sound* of your greetings reached my ears, the child in my womb leapt for joy.
Jn 3	8	The wind blows wherever it pleases; you hear its *sound*, but you cannot tell where it comes from or where it is going.
Ac 2	6	[They heard what sounded like a powerful wind from heaven,] and at this *sound* they all assembled,
1 Co 14	11	if I am ignorant of what the *sounds* (or: *languages*) mean, I am a savage to the man who is speaking,
Rv 1	15	his voice [was] like the *sound* of the ocean.
4	5	Flashes of lightning were coming from the throne, and ⌐the *sound* of (or: voices and) peals of thunder,
5	11	I heard the *sound* of an immense number of angels
8	5	immediately there came peals of thunder (§ and voices; or: and *noises*) and flashes of lightning,
9	9	the *noises* of [the locusts'] wings *sounded* like a great charge of horses and chariots into battle.
10	3	seven claps of thunder made ⌐themselves (lit. their *noise*) heard
11	19	Then came flashes of lightning, ⌐peals of (lit. voices and; or: *noises* and) thunder and an earthquake,
14	2	I heard a *sound* coming out of the sky like the *sound* of the ocean or the *roar* of thunder;
16	18	there were flashes of lightning and ⌐peals of (lit. voices and; or: *noises* and) thunder
18	22	(Jr 25 10) Never again in you, Babylon, will . . . the *sound* of the mill be heard;
19	1	I seemed to hear the great *sound* of a huge crowd in heaven,
6	I seemed to hear the ⌐*voices* (or: sound) of a huge crowd, like the *sound* of the ocean or the [great] *roar* of thunder,

4: VOICE = MUSIC, (MUSICAL) SOUND, SONG

Mt 24	31	he will send his angels with a ⌐loud trumpet (ᵛ trumpet that has a very loud *sound*)
Lk 15	25	7 as [the elder son] drew near the house, he could hear *music* and dancing.
1 Co 14	7	Think of a *musical* instrument . . . [8] . . . if no one can be sure which *call* the trumpet has *sounded*, who will be ready for the attack?
8	
Rv 8	13	Trouble . . . for all the people on earth at the *sound* of the other three trumpets
14	2	it seemed to be the *sound* of harpists playing their harps.
18	22	Never again in you, Babylon, will be heard the *song* of harpists and minstrels,

5: THE COCK CROWS, COCKCROW
10 *alektōr* 12   11 *alektoro-phōnia* 1

Mt 26	34	10/2 this very night, before the *cock crows*, you will have disowned me three times.
74	[Peter] started . . . swearing, 'I do not know the man'. At

Mt	26	75	10/2

Mt 26 75 10/2 — 10/2 that moment the *cock crew*, [75] and Peter remembered what
10/2 Jesus had said, 'Before the *cock crows* you will have disowned me three times'.
Mk 13 35 — you do not know when the master of the house is coming,
11 midnight, *cockcrow*, dawn;
14 30 10/2 this day . . . before the *cock crows* twice, you will have disowned me three times.
68 [Peter] denied it, 'I do not know . . . what you are talking about' . . . And he went out into the forecourt ([v] and a
10/2 *cock crew*).
72 10/2 the *cock crew* for the second time, and Peter recalled how
10/2 Jesus had said to him, 'Before the *cock crows* twice, you will have disowned me three times'.
Lk 22 34 10/2 by the time the *cock crows* today you will have denied three times that you know me.
60 while [Peter] was still speaking, the *cock crew*, [61] . . . and
61 Peter remembered what the Lord had said to him, 'Before
10/2 the *cock crows* today you will have disowned me three times'.
Jn 13 38 10/2 before the *cock crows* you will have disowned me three times.
18 27 10/2 Again Peter denied it; and at once a *cock crew*.

2. VOICE – SOUND, NOTE: *PHTHONGOS*

phthongos 2

a) *Voice*

Rm 10 18 (Ps 19 5) their *voice* has gone out through all the earth,

b) *(musical) Sound, Note*

1 Co 14 if one *note* on [a musical instrument] cannot be distinguished from another, how can you tell what tune is being played?

3. SHOUT, CRY, CRY OUT

1: SHOUT, CRY OUT: *KRAUGĒ*

2 *kraugazō* 9		1 *krazō* 55	
3 *kraugē* 6		4 *ana-krazō* 5	

a) *Shout, Cry out (generally)*

Mt 8 29 ⑩ [Two demoniacs] stood there *shouting*, 'What do you want with us,
12 19 X 2 (Is 42 2) [My servant] will not brawl or *shout*, nor will anyone hear his voice in the streets.
14 26 when the disciples saw [Jesus] walking on the lake they . . . *cried out* in fear.
25 6 < 3 at midnight there was a *cry*, 'The bridegroom is here!'
27 23 [the Jews] *shouted* all the louder, 'Let him be crucified!'
50 X *crying out* in a loud voice, yielded up his spirit.
Mk 1 23 ⑩ 4 there was a man possessed by an unclean spirit, and it *shouted*,
3 11 ⑩ the unclean spirits . . . would fall down before him and
⑩ *shout*, 'You are the Son of God!'
5 5 ⑩ All night and all day . . . [the demoniac] would *howl*
7 ⑩ [the demoniac] *shouted* at the top of his voice, 'What do you want with me, Jesus . . .?'
6 49 [the disciples] saw [Jesus] walking on the lake . . . and
4 *cried out*;
9 26 ⑩ [the deaf and dumb spirit] came out *shouting*,
15 13 [The Jews] *shouted* back, 'Crucify him!'
14 [the Jews] *shouted* all the louder, 'Crucify him!'
Lk 4 33 ⑩ 4 the spirit of an unclean devil . . *shouted* at the top of its voice,
41 ⑩ 2 Devils too came out of many people, *howling*,
8 28 ⑩ 4 Catching sight of Jesus [the demoniac] *gave a shout* . . . and *cried out* at the top of his voice, 'What do you want with me,
9 39 ⑩ a spirit will take hold of [my son], and *give a sudden cry*
23 18 4 as one man *howled*, 'Away with him! Give us Barabbas!'
Jn 1 15 John . . . *cries out* and proclaims: 'This is the one of whom I said: He who comes after me ranks before me
7 28 X as Jesus taught in the Temple, he *cried out*: 'Yes, you know me
37 X Jesus stood there and *cried out*: 'If any man is thirsty, let him come to me!'
11 43 X 2 [Jesus] *cried out* in a loud voice, 'Lazarus, here! Come out!'
12 44 X Jesus declared ⌐publicly (lit. *crying out*): 'Whoever believes in me believes . . . in the one who sent me,
18 40 2 [the Jews] *shouted*: 'Not this man, . . . but Barabbas'.
19 6 2 the chief priests and the guards *shouted*, 'Crucify him!'
12 2 Pilate was anxious to set him free, but the Jews *shouted*, 'If you set him free you are no friend of Caesar's;
15 2 'Take him away . . .!' [the Jews] ⌐said (lit. *cried*). 'Crucify him!'
Ac 7 57 At this all the members of the council *shouted out* in a loud voice and stopped their ears with their hands;
14 14 Barnabas and Paul . . . rushed into the crowd, *shouting*, [15] 'Friends, what do you think you are doing?'

Ac 16 17 This girl started following Paul and the rest of us and *shouting* 'Here are the servants of the Most High God;
21 28 [some Jews seized Paul,] *shouting*, 'Men of Israel, help!'
36 the whole mob was after them, *shouting*, 'Kill him!'
22 23 2 [The Jews] were *yelling* . . . and throwing dust into the air,
23 6 Paul . . . *called out* in the Sanhedrin, 'Brothers, I am [a] Pharisee
9 3 The *shouting* grew louder,
24 21 I stood up among them and *called out*: It is about the resurrection of the dead that I am on trial
Rm 9 27 Referring to Israel Isaiah ⌐had this to say (lit. *cried*) (Is 10 22–23):
Ep 4 31 3 Never . . . lose your temper, or *raise your voice* to anybody
Rv 7 2 another angel . . . *called* in a powerful voice to the four angels
10 3 [the angel] *shouted* ⌐so loud (lit. in such a loud voice), it was like a lion roaring. ⌐At this (lit. At his *shout*), seven claps of thunder made ⌐themselves (lit. their noise) heard
12 2 [The woman] was . . . in labour, *crying aloud* in the pangs of childbirth
14 15 another angel . . . *shouted* ⌐aloud (lit. in a loud voice) . . . 'Put your sickle in and reap;
18 2 At the top of his voice [the angel] *shouted*, 'Babylon has fallen,
18 [All the seafaring men will be keeping a safe distance, watching the smoke as she burns and *crying out*, 'Has there ever been a city as great as this!' [19] They will throw dust on
19 their heads and ⌐say (lit. *shout*), with tears and groans 'Mourn, mourn for this great city
19 17 an angel standing in the sun . . . *shouted* ⌐aloud (lit. in a loud voice) to all the birds
21 4 3 there will be . . . no more ⌐mourning (lit. *crying out*) or sadness.

b) *Shout, Cry out (in supplication)*

Mt 9 27 two blind men followed [Jesus] *shouting*, 'Take pity on us,
14 30 [Peter] began to sink. 'Lord! Save me!' he *cried*.
15 22 a Canaanite woman . . . started *shouting*, 'Sir . . , take pity on me.
23 Give her what she wants . . . because she is *shouting* after us
20 30 two blind men . . . *shouted*, 'Lord! Have pity on us . .
31 [31] And the crowd scolded them . . . but they only *shouted* more loudly,
Mk 9 24 the father of the boy *cried out*, 'I do have faith.
10 47 [Bartimaeus] began to *shout* . . , 'Son of David, Jesus, have pity on me'. [48] And many of them scolded him . . . but he
48 only *shouted* all the louder,
Lk 18 39 [the blind man] *shouted* all the louder, 'Son of David, have pity on me
Ac 7 60 [Stephen] ⌐said aloud (lit. *cried* in a loud voice), 'Lord, do not hold this sin against them';
Rm 8 15 you received . . . the spirit of sons, and it makes us *cry out* 'Abba, Father!'
Ga 4 6 God has sent the Spirit of his Son into our hearts: the Spirit that *cries*, 'Abba, Father',
Heb 5 7 X Ⓢ 3 [Christ] offered up prayer and entreaty, *crying aloud* and in silent tears, to the one who had the power to save him out of death,
Jm 5 4 listen to the wages that you kept back, *calling out*; realise that the cries of the reapers have reached the ears of the Lord
Rv 6 10 [All the people who had been killed] *shouted* ⌐aloud (lit. in a loud voice), 'Holy, faithful Master,

c) *Shout, Cry out (in acclamation)*

Mt 21 9 The crowds who went in front of him and those who followed were all *shouting*: 'Hosanna to the Son of David!'
15 At the sight . . . of the children *shouting*, 'Hosanna to the Son of David' . . . the chief priests . . . were indignant.
Mk 11 9 those who went in front and those who followed were all *shouting*, 'Hosanna!'
Lk 1 42 3 [Elizabeth] *gave* (lit. raised her voice in) a loud *cry* and said 'Of all women you are the most blessed,
19 40 I tell you, if these keep silence the stones will *cry out*.
Jn 12 13 2 They . . . went out to meet him, *shouting*, 'Hosanna!'
Ac 19 28 This speech roused [the silversmiths] to fury, and they started to *shout*, 'Great is Diana of the Ephesians!'
32 By now everybody was *shouting* different things
34 they all started *shouting* ⌐in unison (lit. with one voice), 'Great is Diana of the Ephesians!'
Rv 7 10 [I saw a huge number of people.] They *shouted* ⌐aloud (lit. in a loud voice), 'Victory to our God,

2: CRY, CRY OUT, SHOUT: *BOĒ*

1 *boaō* 12		3 *ana-boaō* 1	
2 *boē* 1			

Mt 3 3 (Is 40 3) A voice *cries* in the wilderness:

Mt 27 46 X 3 about the ninth hour, Jesus *cried out* in a loud voice, 'Eli, Eli,
Mk 1 3 (Is 40 3) A voice *cries* in the wilderness:
 15 34 X at the ninth hour Jesus *cried out* in a loud voice, 'Eloi, Eloi,
Lk 3 4 (Is 40 3) A voice *cries* in the wilderness:
 9 38 Suddenly a man in the crowd *cried out*. 'Master, . . . I implore you to look at my son:
 18 7 Now will not God see justice done to his chosen who *cry* to him day and night . . .?
 38 [the blind man] *called out*, 'Jesus, Son of David, have pity on me'.
Jn 1 23 (Is 40 3) I am . . . a voice that *cries* in the wilderness:
Ac 8 7 ⒟ unclean spirits . . . came *shrieking* with a loud voice out of many who were possessed,
 17 6 [the Jews] dragged [Jason] before the city council, *shouting*,
 25 24 the whole Jewish community . . . [is] *loudly protesting* that [Paul] ought not to be allowed to remain alive.
Ga 4 27 (Is 54 1) Break into *shouts* of joy and gladness, you who were never in labour.
Jm 5 4 2 the *cries* of the reapers have reached the ears of the Lord

4. SOUND – NOISY: *ĒCHOS*

2 *ĕcheō 1*   3 *ex-ĕcheō 1*
1 *ĕchos 4*

Lk 4 37 *reports* of [Jesus] went all through the surrounding country-side.
 21 25 nations in agony, bewildered by the *clamour* of the ocean and its waves;
Ac 2 2 suddenly they heard what *sounded* like a powerful wind from heaven,
1 Co 13 1 2 If I . . . speak without love, I am simply a ⌐gong *booming*
 2 (or: *noisy* gong) or a cymbal clashing.
1 Th 1 8 it was from you that the word of the Lord started to ⌐spread
 3 (lit. *sounded forth*)
Heb 12 19 [What you have come to is nothing known to the senses: not a fire] or ⌐*trumpeting* thunder (lit. the *sound* of a trumpet) or the great voice speaking

5. ROAR, ROARING

1: ROAR, ROARING: *MYKAOMAI*
mykaomai 1

Rv 10 3 [the angel] shouted so loud, it was like a lion *roaring*.

2: ROAR, ROARING: *ŌRUOMAI*
ōruomai 1

1 P 5 8 the devil is prowling round like a *roaring* lion,

3: ROAR, ROARING: *RHOIZĒDON*
rhoizēdon 1

2 P 3 10 The Day of the Lord will come like a thief, and then *with a roar* the sky will vanish,

6. THUNDER: *BRONTĒ*

brontē 12

Mk 3 17 [Jesus appointed the Twelve:] James . . . and John . . , to whom he gave the name Boanerges or 'Sons of *Thunder*';
Jn 12 29 People standing by . . . said it was [a clap of] *thunder*; others said, 'It was an angel speaking to him'.
Rv 4 5 Flashes of lightning were coming from the throne, and ⌐the sound of (or: voices and) [peals of] *thunder*,
 6 1 I heard one of the four animals shout in a voice like *thunder*,
 8 5 immediately there came peals of *thunder* (§ and voices; or: and noises) and flashes of lightning,
 10 3 seven [claps of] *thunder* made themselves heard [4] and when the
 4 seven *thunderclaps* had spoken . . . I heard a voice from heaven say to me, 'Keep the words of the seven *thunderclaps* secret
 11 19 Then came flashes of lightning, ⌐peals of (lit. voices and; or: noises and) *thunder* and an earthquake,
 14 2 I heard a sound coming out of the sky like . . . a roar of *thunder*;
 16 18 there were flashes of lightning and ⌐peals of (lit. voices and; or: noises and) *thunder*
 19 6 I seemed to hear the voices of a huge crowd, like . . . the great roar of *thunder*,

WAR – ARMY – WEAPONS

1. **(Make, Wage) War, Battle – Attack, Fight:** *polemos*
2. **Army – Serve as a Soldier – Fight:** *strateia*
   - a) Soldier(s), Troops – Army
   - b) Stay, Serve, in the army – Enlisted – Fellow-soldier, Companion in arms
   - c) Fight, Battle against – (Wage) War, Warfare
   - d) the Army of heaven – (Heavenly) Host
3. **Cohort, Company, Band of soldiers:** *speira*
4. **Legion:** *legiōn*

5. **Auxiliary Spearmen:** *dexio-labos*
6. **Weapons, Armour**
   - 1: Weapons, Armour – Arm oneself: *hoplon*
   - 2: Breastplate – Body-armour: *thōrax*
     - a) Breastplate
     - b) Body-armour, Scales
   - 3: Helmet: *peri-kephalaia*
   - 4: Shield: *thyreos*
   - 5: Sword: *machaira*
   - 6: Sword: *rhomphaia*
   - 7: Lance, Spear: *lonchē*
   - 8: Arrows, Darts: *belos*
   - 9: a Bow: *toxon*
   - 10: Scabbard, Sheath: *thēkē*

1. (MAKE, WAGE) WAR, BATTLE – ATTACK, FIGHT: *POLEMOS*

2 *polemeō*	7	3 *polemon poieō*	4
1 *polemos 14/18*			

Mt 24	6	You will hear of *wars* and rumours of *wars*;
Mk 13	7	When you hear of *wars* and rumours of *wars*, do not be alarmed,
Lk 14	31	what king marching to *war* against another king would not first . . . consider
21	9	when you hear of *wars* and revolutions, do not be frightened,
1 Co 14	8	if no one can be sure which call the trumpet has sounded, who will be ready for the *attack*?
Heb 11	34	[Gideon, Barak, Samson . . .] were given strength, to be brave in *war*
Jm 4	1	Where do these *wars* and battle between yourselves first start? . . . ² You want something . . . so you fight ʳto get your way by force (lit. and *wage war*).
	2	
Rv 2 16 X	2	I shall . . . *attack* these people with the sword out of my mouth.
9	7	(J1 2 4) these locusts were like horses armoured for *battle*;
	9	(J1 2 5) the noise of their wings sounded like a great charge of horses . . . into *battle*.
11	7	(Dn 7 21) the beast that comes out of the Abyss is going to *make war* on [the two witnesses]
	3	
12	7	*war* broke out in heaven, when Michael with his angels *attacked* the dragon. The dragon *fought* back with his angels,
Ⓓ	2/2	
17 Ⓓ	3	the dragon . . . went away to *make war* on the rest of her children.
13	4	How could anybody ʳdefeat (lit. *fight* against) [the beast]?
	7	3 (Dn 7 21) [The beast] was allowed to *make war* against the saints
16	14	demon spirits . . . going out to all the kings of the world to call them together for the *war*
17	14	2 [the ten kings] will *go to war* against the Lamb;
19	11	its rider was called Faithful and True; he is a judge with integrity, a *warrior* for justice.
X	2	
	19	I saw the beast, with all the kings of the earth and their armies, gathered together to *fight* the rider
	3	
20	8	[Satan] will come out to . . . mobilise [the nations] for *war*.

2. ARMY – SERVE AS A SOLDIER – FIGHT: *STRATEIA*

4 *strateia*	2	7	*strato-logeō*	1
2 *strateuma*	8	8	*strato-pedon*	1
3 *strateuomai*	7	9	*anti-strateuomai*	1
5 *stratia*	2	6	*sy-stratiōtēs*	2
1 *stratiōtēs*	26			

a) Soldier(s), Troops – Army

Mt 8	9	I . . . have *soldiers* under me; and I say to one man: Go, and he goes;
22	7	2 The king . . . despatched his *troops*, destroyed those murderers and burnt their town.

Mt 27	27	The governor's *soldiers* took Jesus with them into the Praetorium
	28 12	[the chief priests] handed a considerable sum of money to the *soldiers*
Mk 15	16	The *soldiers* led [Jesus] away to the inner part of the palace,
Lk 3	14	3 Some *soldiers* asked [John the Baptist] in their turn,
7	8	I . . . have *soldiers* under me; and I say to one man: Go, and he goes;
21	20	8 When you see Jerusalem surrounded by *armies* . . . she will soon be laid desolate.
23	11	2 Then Herod, together with his *guards*, treated [Jesus] with contempt
	36	The *soldiers* mocked [Jesus] too,
Jn 19	2	the *soldiers* twisted some thorns into a crown and put it on his head,
	23	When the *soldiers* had finished crucifying Jesus they took his clothing and divided it into four shares, one for each *soldier* . . . ²⁴ . . . This is exactly what the *soldiers* did.
	24	
	32	the *soldiers* came and broke the legs of the first man
	34	one of the *soldiers* pierced his side with a lance;
Ac 10	7	Cornelius called . . . a devout *soldier* of his staff
12	4	[Herod] put Peter in prison, assigning four squads of four *soldiers* each to guard him in turns.
	6	Peter was sleeping between two *soldiers*,
	18	there was a great commotion among the *soldiers*,
21	32	[the tribune] called out *soldiers* . . . and charged down on the crowd, who stopped beating Paul when they saw . . . the *soldiers*.
	35	[Paul] had to be carried by the *soldiers*;
23	10	the tribune, afraid that they would tear Paul to pieces, 2 told his *troops* to go down
	23	Get two hundred *soldiers* ready to leave for Caesarea . . . with seventy cavalry and two hundred auxiliaries;
	27	2 I came on the scene with my *troops* and got [Paul] away,
	31	The *soldiers* carried out their orders; they took Paul
27	31	Paul said to the centurion and his ʳmen (lit. *troops*),
	32	the *soldiers* cut the boat's ropes
	42	The *soldiers* planned to kill the prisoners
28	16	in Rome Paul was allowed to stay in lodgings of his own with the *soldier* who guarded him.
2 Tm 2	3	Put up with your share of difficulties, like a good *soldier* of Christ Jesus.
Rv 9 16 ○	2	I learnt how many there were in their *army*: twice ten thousand times ten thousand mounted men.
19 19 ○	2	I saw the beast, with all the kings of the earth and their *armies*, gathered together to fight the rider

b) Stay, Serve, in the army – Enlisted – Fellow-soldier, Companion in arms

1 Co 9	7	3 Nobody ever paid money to *stay in the army*,
Ph 2	25	6 Epaphroditus . . . my *companion* in working and *battling*,
2 Tm 2	4	3 *In the army*, no soldier gets himself mixed up in civilian life, because he must be at the disposal of the man who 7 *enlisted* him;
Phm	2	6 our *fellow-soldier* Archippus

c) Fight, Battle against – (Wage) War, Warfare

Rm 7	23	9 my body follows a different law that *battles against* the law which my reason dictates.
2 Co 10	3	3/4 the muscles that we *fight* with are not flesh. ⁴ Our *war* is not 4 fought with weapons of flesh.
1 Tm 1	18	3 I ask you . . . to *fight* ʳlike a good soldier (lit. the good 4 *fight*)
Jm 4	1	3 the desires *fighting* inside your own selves
1 P 2	11	3 keep yourselves free from the selfish passions that *attack* the soul.

d) the Army of heaven – (Heavenly) Host

Lk 2	13	suddenly with the angel there was a great throng of the 5 heavenly *host*,
Ac 7 42 ○	5	God . . . abandoned them to the worship of the *army* of heaven,
Rv 19	14	2 Behind [The Word of God] . . . rode the *armies* of heaven
	19	I saw the beast, with all the kings of the earth . . . gathered 2 together to fight the rider and his *army*.

3. COHORT, COMPANY, BAND OF SOLDIERS: *SPEIRA*

speira 7

Mt 27	27	The governor's soldiers . . . collected the whole *cohort* round [Jesus].

Mk 15	16	The soldiers . . . called the whole *cohort* together.
Jn 18	3	[Judas] brought the *cohort* to this place together with a detachment of guards
	12	The *cohort* and its captain and the Jewish guards seized Jesus
Ac 10	1	One of the centurions of the Italica *cohort* . . . was called Cornelius.
21	31	a report . . . reached the tribune of the *cohort* that there was rioting all over Jerusalem.
27	1	Paul and some other prisoners were handed over to a centurion called Julius, of the Augustan *cohort*.

4. LEGION: *LEGIŌN*

legiōn 4

Mt 26	53	my Father . . . would promptly send more than twelve *legions* of angels to my defence
Mk 5	9 ⑩	My name is *legion* . . . for there are many of us.
	15	They . . . saw the demoniac sitting there . . . who had had the *legion* in him before
Lk 8	30 ⑩	'What is your name?' Jesus asked. '*Legion*' he said

5. AUXILIARY SPEARMEN: *DEXIO-LABOS*

dexio-labos 1

Ac 23	23	Get two hundred soldiers ready . . . with seventy cavalry and two hundred *auxiliaries*;

6. WEAPONS, ARMOUR

1: WEAPONS, ARMOUR – ARM ONESELF: *HOPLON*

3 *hoplizō*	1	4 *kath-oplizō*	1
1 *hoplon*	6	2 *pan-hoplia*	3

b = employed in a purely literal sense

Lk 11	21	4 So long as a strong man *fully armed* guards his own palace, his goods are undisturbed; ²² but when someone stronger than he is attacks and defeats him, the stronger man takes away *all the weapons* he relied on
22	2	
Jn 18	3 b	[Judas] brought the cohort to this place . . . with lanterns and torches and *weapons*.
Rm 6	13	you must not let any part of your body turn into an unholy *weapon* fighting on the side of sin; you should, instead . . . make every part of your body into a *weapon* fighting on the side of God;
13	12	let us give up all the things we prefer to do under cover of the dark; let us *arm* ourselves and appear in the light.
2 Co 6	7	[We prove we are God's servants] by being armed with the *weapons* of righteousness in the right hand and in the left,
10	4	Our war is not fought with *weapons* of flesh, yet they are strong enough . . . to demolish fortresses.
Ep 6	11	2 Put God's *armour* on so as to be able to resist the devil's tactics.
13		2 you must rely on God's *armour*, or you will not be able to put up any resistance
1 P 4	1	3 *arm* yourselves with the same resolution that [Christ] had:

2: BREASTPLATE – BODY-ARMOUR: *THŌRAX*

thōrax 5

a) Breastplate

Ep 6	14	stand your ground, with truth buckled round your waist, and integrity for a *breastplate*,
1 Th 5	8	let us put on faith and love for a *breastplate*, and the hope of salvation for a helmet.
Rv 9	9	[The locusts] had body-armour like iron *breastplates*,
17		I saw . . . the riders [of the army of the four angels] with their *breastplates* of flame colour,

b) Body-armour, Scales

Rv 9	9	[The locusts] had ⌐body-armour (or: chests) like iron breastplates,

3: HELMET: *PERI-KEPHALAIA*

peri-kephalaia 2

Ep 6	17	you must accept salvation from God to be your *helmet* and receive . . . the Spirit to use as a sword.
1 Th 5	8	let us put on . . . the hope of salvation for a *helmet*.

4: SHIELD: *THYREOS*

thyreos 1

Ep 6	16	always carrying the *shield* of faith so that you can use it to put out the burning arrows of the evil one.

5: SWORD: *MACHAIRA*

machaira 29

Mt 10	34 ●	it is not peace I have come to bring, but a *sword*.
26	47	Judas . . . appeared, and with him a large number of men armed with *swords* and clubs,
51		one of the followers of Jesus grasped his *sword* and drew it;
52		Put your *sword* back, for all who draw the *sword* will die by the *sword*.
55		Am I a brigand, that you had to set out to capture me with *swords* and clubs?
Mk 14	43	Judas . . . came up with a number of men armed with *swords* and clubs,
47		one of the bystanders drew his *sword* and struck out at the high priest's servant,
48		Am I a brigand . . . that you had to set out to capture me with *swords* and clubs?
Lk 21	24	[This people] will fall by the edge of the *sword*
22	36	if you have no *sword*, sell your cloak and buy one,
38		there are two *swords* here now.
49		Lord, shall we use our *swords*?
52		Am I a brigand . . . that you had to set out with *swords* and clubs?
Jn 18	10	Simon Peter, who carried a *sword*, drew it
11		Put your *sword* back in its scabbard;
Ac 12	2	[Herod] ⌐beheaded (lit. put to the *sword*) James the brother of John,
16	27	When the gaoler . . . saw the doors wide open he drew his *sword*
Rm 8	35	Nothing . . . can come between us and the love of Christ, even if we are troubled . . . or even attacked with a *sword*.
13	4 ●	the bearing of the *sword* has its significance.
Ep 6	17 ●	receive the word of God from the Spirit to use as a *sword*.
Heb 4	12	The word of God . . . cuts like any double-edged *sword* but more finely:
11	34	[Gideon, Barak, Samson . . .could] ⌐emerge unscathed from battle (lit. escape death by the *sword*).
37		[Some] were . . . ⌐beheaded (lit. put to the *sword*);
Rv 6	4	[The second rider] was given a huge *sword*.
13	10	the *sword* for those who are to die by the *sword*.
14		the beast . . . had been wounded by the *sword* and still lived.

6: SWORD: *RHOMPHAIA*

rhomphaia 7

Lk 2	35	a *sword* will pierce your own soul too
Rv 1	16	out of [the] mouth [of the Son of man] came a sharp *sword*, double-edged,
2	12	Here is the message of the one who has the sharp *sword*, double-edged:
16		I shall soon . . . attack these people with the *sword* out of my mouth.
6	8	[Plague and Hades] were given authority . . . to kill by the *sword*, by famine, by plague and wild beasts.
19	15	From [the] mouth [of The Word of God] came a sharp *sword* to strike the pagans with;
21		the rest were killed by the *sword* of the rider, which came out of his mouth,

7: LANCE, SPEAR: *LONCHĒ*

lonchē 1

Jn 19	34	one of the soldiers pierced his side with a *lance*;

8: ARROWS, DARTS: *BELOS*

belos 1

Ep 6	16 ⑩	you can use [the shield of faith] to put out the burning *arrows* of the evil one.

9: A BOW: *TOXON*

toxon 1

Rv 6	2	the rider on [the white horse] was holding a *bow*;

10: SCABBARD, SHEATH: *THĒKĒ*

thēkē 1

Jn 18 11   Jesus said to Peter, 'Put your sword back in its *scabbard*;

WATER – BAPTISE – WASH

1. Water – Moisture – Sweat
1: Water: *hydōr*
  a) Water of baptism
  b) Water – Ocean – Waterless, Arid
2: Moisture
  a) Moisture: *ikmas*
  b) Green (wood): *hygros*
3: Sweat: *hidrōs*
2. Baptise – Wash – Dip: *baptizō*
  a) Baptise, Baptism
  b) Baptism = Passion
  c) Wash, Washing – Ritual Ablutions
  d) Dip, Dipped – Soak, Drench
3. Wash – Bath, Bathe – Cleanse
1: Wash – Bath, Bathe – Cleanse: *louō*

  a) Washed by Christ
  b) Wash – Bath, Bathe
2: Wash: *niptō*
  a) Ritual Washing – Without washing, Unwashed
  b) Wash feet
  c) Wash oneself
3: Wash: *plynō*
4. Pour out upon – Wet – Wash: *brechō*
5. Sprinkle – Purify by sprinkling: *rhantizō*
6. Fuller, Bleacher – Shrunk, Unshrunken: *gnapheus*
7. Swim – Pool: *kolymbaō*
  a) Swim
  b) Pool

1. WATER – MOISTURE – SWEAT

1: WATER: *HYDŌR*

1 *hydōr*   79   2 *an-(h)ydros 4*
3 *hydro(-poteō) 1*

a) Water of baptism

Mt 3 11   I baptise you in *water* . . . he will baptise you with the Holy Spirit
  16   As soon as Jesus was baptised he came up from the *water*,
Mk 1 8   I have baptised you with *water*, but he will baptise you with the Holy Spirit.
  10   No sooner had [Jesus] come up out of the *water* than he saw the heavens torn apart
Lk 3 16   I baptise you with *water* . . . he . . . with the Holy Spirit
Jn 1 26   I baptise with *water*;
  31   I came baptising with *water* . . . ³² . . . I saw the Spirit
  33   he who sent me to baptise with *water* had said to me, 'The man on whom you see the Spirit . . . is the one who is going to baptise with the Holy Spirit.'
  3 5   unless a man is born through *water* and the Spirit, he cannot enter the kingdom of God:
  23   At the same time John was baptising at Aenon . . . where there was plenty of *water*,
Ac 1 5   John baptised with *water*, but you . . . will be baptised with the Holy Spirit.
  8 36   [Philip and the eunuch] came to some *water*, and the eunuch said, 'Look, there is some *water* here; is there anything
  38   to stop us being baptised? . . . ³⁸ . . . both went down into the *water* and Philip baptised him. ³⁹ But after they
  39   had come up out of the *water* again Philip was taken away by the Spirit
  10 47   Could anyone refuse the *water* of baptism to these people, now they have received the Holy Spirit . . .?
  11 16   John baptised with *water* but you will be baptised with the Holy Spirit.
Ep 5 26   [Christ sacrificed himself for the Church] to make her holy. He made her clean by washing her in *water* with a form of words,
Heb 10 22   our minds sprinkled . . . and our bodies washed with pure *water*.
1 P 3 20   that ark which saved . . . eight people 'by *water*' . . . ²¹ That
  21   *water* is a type of the baptism

b) Water – Ocean – Waterless, Arid

L = Living water, Water of life

Mt 8 32   the whole herd . . . perished in the *water*.
  12 43   2 an unclean spirit . . . wanders through *waterless* country
  14 28   tell me to come to you across the *water*.
  29   Peter . . . started walking towards Jesus across the *water*,
  17 15   he is always falling into the fire or into the *water*.
  27 24   Pilate . . . took some *water*, washed his hands
Mk 9 22   it has often thrown him . . . into the *water*, in order to destroy him.

Mk 9 41   If anyone gives you a cup of *water* to drink,
  14 13   you will meet a man carrying a pitcher of *water*.
Lk 7 44   you poured no *water* over my feet.
  8 24   Then he . . . rebuked . . . the rough *water*;
  25   Who can this be, that gives orders even to winds and ʳwaves (lit. *water*) and they obey him?
  11 24   2 an unclean spirit . . . wanders through *waterless* country
  16 24   Father Abraham . . . send Lazarus to dip the top of his finger in *water*
  22 10   you will meet a man carrying a pitcher of *water*.
Jn 2 7   Fill the jars with *water*,
  9   the steward tasted the *water*, and it had turned into wine .
      the servants who had drawn the *water*
  4 7   a Samaritan woman came to draw *water*,
  10 L   he would have given you living *water*.
  11 L   how could you get this living *water*?
  13   Whoever drinks this *water* will get thirsty again; ¹⁴ but
  14 L   anyone who drinks the *water* that I shall give will never
  L   be thirsty again: the *water* that I shall give will turn into a
  15 L   ʳspring (lit. fountain of *water*) inside him, welling up to eternal life. ¹⁵ Sir . . . give me some of that *water*,
  46   Cana in Galilee, where he had changed the *water* into wine.
  5 3   crowds of sick people . . . ᵛ waiting for the *water* to move;
  4   ⁴ . . . the *water* was disturbed, and the first person to enter the *water* after this disturbance was cured . . .
  7   I have no one to put me into the pool when the *water* is disturbed;
  7 38 L   From his breast shall flow fountains of living *water*.
  13 5   [Jesus] then poured *water* into a basin and began to wash the disciples' feet
  19 34   one of the soldiers pierced his side . . . and immediately there came out blood and *water*.
1 Tm 5 23   3 You should give up drinking only *water* and have a little wine
Heb 9 19   [Moses] took the calves' blood, the goats' blood and some *water*,
Jm 3 12   No more can sea water give you fresh *water*.
2 P 2 17   2 People like this are ʳdried-up (lit. *waterless*) rivers,
  3 5   the earth was formed by the word of God out of *water* and between the *waters*,
  6   the world . . . was destroyed by being flooded by *water*.
1 Jn 5 6   Jesus Christ who came by *water* and blood, not with *water* only, but with *water* and blood;
  8   [there are three witnesses,] the Spirit, the *water* and the blood,
Jude 12   [these people] are like clouds blown about by the winds and
  2   ʳbringing no rain (lit. *without water*)
Rv 1 15   [a figure like a Son of man,] his voice like the sound of the *ocean*.
  7 17 L   the Lamb . . . will lead them to springs of living *water*;
  8 10   a huge star fell from the sky . . . on a third of all rivers and
  11   ʳsprings (lit. *water* sources); ¹¹ . . . a third of all *water* turned to bitter wormwood, so that many people died from drinking this *water*.
  11 6   they are able to turn *water* into blood
  12 15   the serpent vomited *water* from his mouth, like a river,
  14 2   I heard a sound . . . like the sound of the *ocean*
  7   the maker of heaven . . . and sea and every *water*-spring.
  16 4   The third angel emptied his bowl into the rivers and *water*-springs and they turned into blood. ⁵ Then I heard the
  5   angel of *water* say, 'You are . . . the Just One . . .'
  12   The sixth angel emptied his bowl over the . . . Euphrates; all the *water* dried up
  17 1   the famous prostitute who rules enthroned beside abundant *waters*,
  15   The *waters* . . . are all the peoples, the populations, the nations
  19 6   I seemed to hear . . . the sound of the *ocean*
  21 6 L   I will give *water* from the well of life free to anybody who is thirsty;
  22 1 L   the angel showed me the river (§ of the *water*) of life,
  17 L   all who want it may have the *water* of life, and have it free.

2: MOISTURE

a) Moisture: ikmas

ikmas 1

Lk 8 6   Some seed . . . withered away, having no *moisture*.

b) Green (wood): hygros

hygros 1

Lk 23 31   if men use the *green* wood like this,

3: SWEAT: *HIDRŌS*

hidrōs 1

Lk 22 44   [Jesus's] *sweat* fell to the ground like great drops of blood.

2. BAPTISE – WASH – DIP: *BAPTIZŌ*

2 *baptisma*	20	3	*baptō* 4
4 *baptismos*	3	5	*em-baptō* 2
1 *baptizō*	74/76		

a) Baptise, Baptism

Mt 3	6	they were *baptised* by [John] in the river Jordan
	7	[John] saw a number of Pharisees and Sadducees coming for
	2	*baptism*
	11	I *baptise* you in water for repentance . . . he will *baptise* you with the Holy Spirit and fire.
	13	[Jesus] came . . . to the Jordan to be *baptised* by John. [14] John
	14	tried to dissuade him. 'It is I who need *baptism* from you'
	16	As soon as Jesus was *baptised* he came up from the water,
21	25 2	John's *baptism*: where did it come from: heaven or man?
28	19	make disciples of all the nations; *baptise* them in the name of the Father and of the Son and of the Holy Spirit,
Mk 1	4	⌐John the Baptist appeared in the wilderness, (ᵛ John appeared,
	/2	*baptising* in the wilderness and) proclaiming a *baptism* of repentance for the forgiveness of sins. [5] . . . and as they were *baptised* by him in the river Jordan they confessed their sins.
	8	I have *baptised* you with water, but he will *baptise* you with the Holy Spirit.
	9	Jesus . . . was *baptised* in the Jordan by John.
11	30 2	John's *baptism*: did it come from heaven, or from man?
16	16	He who believes and is *baptised* will be saved;
Lk 3	3 2	[John] proclaiming a *baptism* of repentance for the forgiveness of sins,
	7	[John] said, therefore, to the crowds who came to be *baptised*
	12	There were tax collectors too who came for *baptism*,
	16	I *baptise* you with water . . . he will *baptise* you with the Holy Spirit and fire.
	21	when all the people had been *baptised* and while Jesus after his own *baptism* was at prayer, heaven opened
7	29	the people . . . and the tax collectors too, acknowledged
	/2	God's plan by ⌐accepting (lit. being *baptised* with) *baptism* from John; [30] but by refusing *baptism* from him the
	30	Pharisees and the lawyers had thwarted what God had in mind for them.
20	4 2	John's *baptism*: did it come from heaven, or from man?
Jn 1	25	Why are you *baptising* if you are not the Christ, and not
	26	Elijah, and not the prophet? [26] . . . I *baptise* with water
	28	. . . [28] This happened at Bethany . . . where John was
		baptising.
	31	it was to reveal [Christ] to Israel that I came *baptising* with water.
	33	he who sent me to *baptise* with water had said to me, 'The man on whom you see the Spirit . . . is the one who is going to *baptise* with the Holy Spirit'.
3	22	Jesus went . . . into the Judaean countryside . . . and *baptised*.
	23	At the same time John was *baptising* at Aenon . . . and people were going there to be *baptised*.
	26	the man to whom you bore witness, is *baptising* now;
4	1	[Jesus] was making and *baptising* more disciples than John –
	2	[2] though in fact it was his disciples who *baptised*, not Jesus himself –
10	40	[Jesus] went . . . where John had once been *baptising*.
Ac 1	5	John *baptised* with water but you . . . will be *baptised* with the Holy Spirit.
	22	[the whole time that the Lord Jesus was travelling round with
	2	us] . . . right from the time when John was *baptising*
2	38	every one of you must be *baptised* in the name of Jesus Christ
	41	[the Jews] accepted what [Peter] said and were *baptised*.
8	12	[the Samaritan people] were *baptised*, both men and women,
	13	After his *baptism* Simon [the magician] . . . went round constantly with Philip,
	16	[the Samaritans] had only been *baptised* in the name of the Lord Jesus.
	36	the eunuch said, 'Look, there is some water here; is there
	38	anything to stop me being *baptised*'? [38] . . . both went down into the water and Philip *baptised* him.
9	18	[Saul] was *baptised* there and then,
10	37	You must have heard about the recent happenings in Judaea; about Jesus of Nazareth and how he began in Galilee,
	2	after John had been preaching *baptism*. [38] God had anointed him with the Holy Spirit and with power,
	47	Could anyone refuse the water of *baptism* to these people, now they have received the Holy Spirit . . .? [48] [Peter] then
	48	gave orders for [Cornelius and his family] to be *baptised* in the name of Jesus Christ.
11	16	John *baptised* with water, but you will be *baptised* with the Holy Spirit.
13	24	[Jesus's] coming was heralded by John when he proclaimed a
	2	*baptism* of repentance for the whole people of Israel.
16	15	After [Lydia] and her household had been *baptised*
	33	[the gaoler] was *baptised* then and there with all his household
18	8	A great many Corinthians . . . became believers and were *baptised*.

Ac 18	25 2	[Apollos] had only experienced the *baptism* of John.
19	3	'Then how were you *baptised*?' [Paul] asked. 'With John's
	4 2	*baptism*' [the disciples at Ephesus] replied. [4] 'John's *baptism*' said Paul 'was a *baptism* of repentance; but he insisted that the people should believe in . . . Jesus.'
	5	[5] When they heard this, they were *baptised* in the name of the Lord Jesus,
22	16	It is time you were *baptised* and had your sins washed away while invoking his name
Rm 6	3	when we were *baptised* in Christ Jesus we were *baptised* in his
	4 2	death; [4] in other words, when we were *bpatised* we went into the tomb with him and joined him in death,
1 Co 1	13	Were you *baptised* in the name of Paul? [14] I am thankful that
	14	I never *baptised* any of you after Crispus and Gaius [15] so
	15	none of you can say he was *baptised* in my name. [16] Then
	16	there was the family of Stephanas . . . that I *baptised* too,
	17	but no one else . . . [17] For Christ did not send me to *baptise*, but to preach the Good News,
10	2	[our fathers] were all *baptised* into Moses in this cloud and in this sea,
12	13	In the one Spirit we were all *baptised* . . . and one Spirit was given to us all to drink.
15	29 ○	what do people hope to gain by being *baptised* for the dead?
	○	. . . why be *baptised* on their behalf?
Ga 3	27	*baptised* in Christ, you have all clothed yourselves in Christ,
Ep 4	5 2	There is one Lord, one faith, one *baptism*,
Col 2	12	You have been buried with [Jesus], when you were baptised;
	2	and by *baptism*, too, you have been raised up with him
Heb 6	2 4	[the fundamental doctrines:] the teaching about *baptisms* . . .
1 P 3	21 2	the *baptism* which saves you now, and which is not the washing off of physical dirt

b) Baptism = Passion

Mk 10	38	Jesus said to [James and John], 'Can you drink the cup that I
	/2	must drink, or be *baptised* with the *baptism* with which I must be *baptised*?' [39] . . . 'The cup . . . you shall drink,
	39	and with the *baptism* with which I must be *baptised* you
	2/	shall be *baptised*,'
Lk 12	50 2/	There is a *baptism* I must still ⌐receive (lit. be *baptised* with)

c) Wash, Washing – Ritual Ablutions

Mk 7	4	they never eat without first ⌐sprinkling themselves (ᵛ bathing). There are also many other observances . . . concerning the
	4	*washing* of cups
Lk 11	38	The Pharisee . . . was surprised that [Jesus] had not first *washed* before the meal.
Heb 9	10	they are rules about the outward life, connected with foods
	4	. . . and *washing* at various times,

d) Dip, Dipped – Soak, Drench

Mt 26	23 5	Someone who has *dipped* his hand into the dish with me,
Mk 14	20 5	It is one of the Twelve, one who is *dipping* into the same dish with me.
Lk 16	24 3	send Lazarus to *dip* the tip of his finger in water
Jn 13	26	It is the one . . . to whom I give the piece of bread that I
	3/3	shall *dip* in the dish. He *dipped* the piece of bread and gave it to Judas
Rv 19	13 3	his cloak was *soaked* in blood.

3. WASH – BATH, BATHE – CLEANSE

1: WASH – BATH, BATHE – CLEANSE: *LOUŌ*

| 1 *louō* | 6 | 3 *apo-louō* 2 |
| 2 *loutron* | 2 | |

a) Washed by Christ

Ac 22	16 3	[Saul,] it is time you were baptised and had your sins *washed* away while invoking his name.
1 Co 6	11 3	but now you have been *washed* clean, and sanctified,
Ep 5	26 2	to make [the Church] holy . . . by *washing* her in water with a form of words,
Tt 3	5 2	[God] saved us, by means of the *cleansing* water of rebirth and by renewing us with the Holy Spirit
Heb 10	22	our minds sprinkled and free from any trace of bad conscience and our bodies *washed* with pure water.
Rv 1	5	Jesus Christ . . . has ᵛ *washed* away (G released us from) our sins with his blood,

b) Wash – Bath, Bathe

Jn 13	10	No one who has *taken a bath* needs washing,
Ac 9	37	[Tabitha] died, and they *washed* her and laid her out in a room upstairs.
16	33	[the gaoler] took [Paul and Silas] to *wash* their wounds,
2 P 2	22	When the sow has been *washed*, it wallows in the mud.

2: WASH: *NIPTŌ*

1 *niptō* 17   2   *a-niptos* 2
3 *apo-niptō* 1

a) Ritual Washing – Without washing, Unwashed

Mt 15 2   your disciples . . . do not *wash* their hands when they eat food.

     20   2 to eat with *unwashed* hands does not make a man unclean.

Mk 7 2   [the Pharisees] noticed that some of [Jesus's] disciples were

     2   eating with unclean hands, that is, *without washing* them.

     3   the Pharisees . . . never eat without *washing* their arms as far as the elbow;

b) Wash feet

Jn 13 5   [Jesus] began to *wash* the disciples' feet

     6   Lord, are you going to *wash* my feet?

     8   'Never!' said Peter 'You shall never *wash* my feet.' . . . 'If I do not *wash* you, you can have nothing in common with me'.

     10   No one who has taken a bath needs *washing*,

     12   When he had *washed* their feet

     14   If I, then, the Lord and Master, have *washed* your feet, you should *wash* each other's feet.

1 Tm 5 10   [a widow] must . . . [have] shown hospitality to strangers and *washed* the saints' feet,

c) Wash oneself

Mt 6 17   when you fast, put oil on your head and *wash* your face,

     27 24   3 Pilate . . . *washed* his hands in front of the crowd

Jn 9 7   'Go and *wash* in the Pool of Siloam.' . . . So the blind man . . . *washed himself*, and came away with his sight restored.

     11   Jesus . . . said to me, 'Go and *wash* at Siloam'; so I went, and when I *washed* I could see.

     15   He put a paste on my eyes, and I *washed*, and I can see.

3: WASH: *PLYNŌ*

plynō 3

Lk 5 2   The fishermen . . . were *washing* their nets.

Rv 7 14   they have *washed* their robes white again in the blood of the Lamb,

     22 14   Happy are those who will have *washed* their robes clean, so that they will have the right to feed on the tree of life

4. POUR OUT UPON – WET – WASH: *BRECHŌ*

brechō 2/7

Lk 7 38   the tears [of the woman who was a sinner] ⌐fell on (lit. *poured out upon*) [Jesus's] feet,

     44   you poured no water over my feet, but she has *poured out* her tears over my feet

5. SPRINKLE – PURIFY BY SPRINKLING: *RHANTIZŌ*

2 *rhantismos* 2   1 *rhantizō* 5

Mk 7 4   [the Pharisees] never eat without first *sprinkling* themselves (ᵛ bathing).

Heb 9 13   The blood . . . and the ashes of a heifer are *sprinkled* on those who have incurred defilement

     19   Moses . . . *sprinkled* the book itself and all the people, . . .

     21   ²¹ After that, he *sprinkled* the tent and all the liturgical vessels with blood

     10 22   as we go in . . . our minds *sprinkled* and free from any trace of bad conscience

     12 24   2 a blood for ⌐purification (lit. *sprinkling*) which pleads more insistently than Abel's.

1 P 1 2   2 obedient to Jesus Christ and *sprinkled* with his blood.

6. FULLER, BLEACHER – SHRUNK, UNSHRUNKEN: *GNAPHEUS*

2 *gnapheus* 1   1 *a-gnaphos* 2

Mt 9 16   No one puts a piece of *unshrunken* cloth on to an old cloak,

Mk 2 21   No one sews a piece of *unshrunken* cloth on an old cloak;

     9 3   2 his clothes became . . . whiter than any earthly *bleacher* could make them.

---

7. SWIM – POOL: *KOLYMBAŌ*

2 *kolymbaō* 1   3 *ek-kolymbaō* 1
1 *kolymbēthra* 4

a) Swim

Ac 27 42   The soldiers planned to kill the prisoners for fear that any

     43   3 should *swim off* and escape. ⁴³ But the centurion . . . gave

       2 orders that those who could *swim* should jump overboard first

b) Pool

Jn 5 2   at the Sheep *Pool* in Jerusalem there is a building, called Bethzatha in Hebrew,

     4   ᵛ at intervals the angel of the Lord came down into the *pool*,

     7   Sir . . . I have no one to put me into the *pool*

     9 7   [Jesus] said to [the blind man], 'Go and wash in the *Pool* of Siloam'.

WEAKEN – SICKNESS

---

1. Weak – Fade – Collapse
  1: Weaken, Lose heart – Grow weary in, Tire of: *en-kakeō*
  2: Collapse, Give up, (Get) Discouraged – Faint, Trembling: *ek-luō*
  3: Drooping, Limp: *par-(h)iēmi*
  4: Fade away, Perish – Unfading, Never to wither: *marainomai*
  5: (the) Weak, Helpless, Unable – Weaken – Weakness, Qualms, Scruples: *a-stheneia*
  6: Weaken (a person's resolution): *syn-thryptō*

2. Sick – Sickness – Sick people
  1: (the) Sick – Sickness, Ailment, Infirmity – Suffering: *a-stheneia*
  2: Disease, Sickness – a Craze (for): *nosos* and *malakia*
  3: Affliction, Complaint – Plague: *mastix*
  4: Sick, Sick people – Ill: *a-rrhōstos*

  5: the Sick, (Those who) are sick – (Be) In a wretched condition: *kakōs echō*
  6: Faint, (Become) Wanting – Sick man: *kamnō*

3. Specific Diseases, Complaints and Invalids
  1: Leper - Leprosy: *lepra*
  2: Sores – Covered with sores: *helkos*
  3: Gangrene: *gangraina*
  4: Fever – Feverish bouts: *pyretos*
  5: Plague, Pestilence – Pest: *loimos*
  6: Dysentery: *dys-enterion*
  7: Dropsy: *hydrōpikos*
  8: Itching: *knēthō*
  9: Swell up: *pimprēmi*
  10: Epilectic – Lunatic: *selēniazomai*
  11: Scales (covering the eyes): *lepis*

1. WEAK – FADE – COLLAPSE

1: WEAKEN, LOSE HEART – GROW WEARY IN, TIRE OF: *EN-KAKEŌ*

en-kakeō 6

Lk 18 1   a parable about the need to pray continually and never *lose heart*.

2 Co 4 1   Since we have . . . been entrusted with this work of administration, there is no *weakening* on our part.

     16   [God will raise us.] That is why there is no *weakening* on our part,

Ga 6 9   We must never get *tired of* doing good

Ep 3 13   I beg you, never *lose confidence* just because of the trials that I go through

2 Th 3 13   never grow *tired of* doing what is right.

2: COLLAPSE, GIVE UP, (GET) DISCOURAGED – FAINT, TREMBLING: *EK-LUŌ*

1 *ek-luō* 5   2 *para-luō* 1/5

Mt 15 32   I do not want to send them off hungry, they might *collapse* on the way.

Mk 8 3   If I send them off home hungry they will *collapse* on the way;

Ga 6 9   if we don't *give up* the struggle we shall get our harvest at the proper time.

Heb 12 3   then you will not *give up* for want of courage.

     5   (Pr 3 11 G) do not *get discouraged* when [the Lord] reprimands you.

     12   2 (Is 35 3) hold up your limp arms and steady your *trembling* knees

3: DROOPING, LIMP: *PAR-(H)IĒMI*

par-(h)iēmi 1/2

Heb 12 12   (Is 35 3) hold up your *limp* arms

4: FADE AWAY, PERISH – UNFADING, NEVER TO WITHER: *MARAINOMAI*

1 *marainomai* 1	2 *a-marantinos* 1
	3 *a-marantos* 1

Jm	1 11	the scorching sun comes up, and the grass withers . . . It is the same with the rich man: . . . he . . . *perishes*.
1 P	1 4	[we have] the promise of an inheritance that can never be 3 spoilt or soiled and *never fade away*,
	5 4	2 you will be given the crown of *unfading* glory.

5: (THE) WEAK, HELPLESS, UNABLE – WEAKEN – WEAKNESS, QUALMS, SCRUPLES: *A-STHENEIA*

3 *a-stheneia* 15/24	2 *a-stheneō* 15/35
4 *a-sthenēma* 1	1 *a-sthenēs* 19/25

W = Weakness // Strength, Power

Mt	26 41		The spirit is willing, but the flesh is *weak*.
Mk	14 38		The spirit is willing, but the flesh is *weak*.
Lk	13 11		a woman was there who for eighteen years had been possessed 3 by a spirit that left her *enfeebled*;
Ac	20 35		2 this is how we must exert ourselves to support the *weak*.
Rm	4 19		Even the thought that his body was past fatherhood . . . did 2 not ⌐*shake* (lit. *weaken*) [Abraham's] belief.
	5 6		We were still *helpless* when . . . Christ died for sinful men.
	6 19		3 If I may use human terms to help your natural *weakness*:
	8 3		God has done what the Law, because of our unspiritual 2 nature, was *unable* to do.
	26		3 The Spirit too comes to help us in our *weakness*.
	14 1		2 If a person's faith is *not strong* enough, welcome him all the 2 same . . . ² People range from those who believe they may eat any sort of meat to those whose faith is so *weak* they dare not eat anything except vegetables . . . ²¹ . . . the
	21		best course is to abstain from . . . anything . . . that 2 would make your brother trip or fall or *weaken* in any way.
	15 1	W	4 We who are strong have a duty to put up with the *qualms* of the weak
1 Co	1 25	W	*God's weakness* is stronger than human strength.
	27	W	to shame what is strong . . . [God] chose what is *weak* by human reckoning;
	2 3	W	3 *Far from* relying on any *power* of my own, I came among you in great fear and trembling
	4 10	W	we have *no power*, but you are influential;
	8 7		Some people . . . eat this food as though it really had been sacrificed . . . and their conscience, being *weak*, is defiled by
	9		it . . . ⁹ Only be careful that you do not make use of this freedom in a way that proves a pitfall for the *weak*.
	10		¹⁰ Suppose someone sees you . . . eating in some temple of an idol; his own conscience, even if it is *weak*, may encourage him to eat food which has been offered to idols.
	11		¹¹ In this way your knowledge could become the ruin of
	12	2/2	someone *weak* . . . ¹² By . . . injuring their *weak* consciences, it would be Christ against whom you sinned.
	9 22		For the *weak* I made myself *weak* with the *weak*.
	11 30		In fact that is why many of you are *weak* and ill
	12 22		it is precisely the parts of the body that seem to be the *weakest* which are the indispensable ones;
	15 43	W	3 the thing that is sown is *weak* but what is raised is powerful;
2 Co	10 10	W	when [Paul] is with you you see only ⌐half a man (lit. a *weak* presence [of a man]) and no preacher at all.
	11 21		2 I hope you are ashamed of us for being *weak* with you
	29	2/2	When any man has had *scruples*, I have had *scruples* with him;
	30		3 If I am to boast, then let me boast of my own *feebleness*.
	12 5		I will boast about . . . my *weaknesses*.
	9	W	3 [the Lord] has said, '. . . my *power* is at its best in *weakness*'.
		W	3 So I shall be very happy to make my *weaknesses* my special
	10		boast . . . ¹⁰ and that is why I am quite content with my W3/2 *weaknesses* . . . For it is when I am *weak* that I am strong.
	13 3	W	2 you have known [Christ] not as a *weakling*, but as a power
	4	W	among you. ⁴ Yes, but he was crucified through *weakness* 2 . . . So then, we are *weak*, as he was,
	9	W	2 We are only too glad to be *weak* provided you are strong.
Ga	4 9		how can you want to go back to elemental things like these, that *can do nothing*
1 Th	5 14		give courage to those who are apprehensive, care for the *weak*
Heb	4 15		it is not as if we had a high priest [in Jesus] who was incapable 3 of feeling our *weaknesses* with us;
	5 2		[every high priest] can sympathise with those who are . . . 3 uncertain because he too lives in the limitations of *weakness*.
	7 18		The earlier commandment is thus abolished, because it was ⌐neither effective nor useful (lit. both *weak* and useless),
	28		The Law appoints high priests who are men subject to 3 *weakness*;
	11 34	W	3 [Gideon and the prophets] were *weak* people who were given strength [through faith],

1 P	3 7	respecting a woman . . . though she may be the *weaker* partner,

6: WEAKEN (A PERSON'S RESOLUTION): *SYN-THRYPTŌ*

syn-thryptō 1

Ac	21 13	What are you trying to do – ⌐*weaken* my resolution (or: break my heart) by your tears?

2. SICK – SICKNESS – SICK PEOPLE

1: (THE) SICK – SICKNESS, AILMENT, INFIRMITY – SUFFERING: *A-STHENEIA*

2 *a-stheneia* 9/24	3 *a-sthenēs* 6/25
1 *a-stheneō* 20/35

Mt	8 17		2 (Is 53 4) He took our *sicknesses* away and carried our diseases for us.
	10 8		Cure the *sick*, raise the dead.
	25 36	X	[I was] *sick* and you visited me,
	39	X	3 [When did we see you] *sick* or in prison . . .?
	43	X	3 I was . . . *sick* and in prison and you never visited me.
	44	X	3 Lord, when did we see you . . . *sick* or in prison . . .?
Mk	6 56		wherever [Jesus] went . . . they laid down the *sick* in the open spaces,
Lk	4 40		all those who had *sick* [friends] suffering from diseases of one kind or another brought them to [Jesus],
	5 15		large crowds would gather to hear him and to have their 2 *sickness* cured,
	8 2		certain women who had been cured of evil spirits and 2 *ailments*:
	9 2		[Jesus] sent [the Twelve] out to proclaim the kingdom of God and to heal (ᵛ the *sick*)
	10 9		3 Cure those in [the town] who are *sick*,
	13 12		Jesus . . . said [to the crippled woman], 'Woman, you are 2 rid of your *infirmity*'
Jn	4 46		there was a court official there whose son was *ill* at Capernaum
	5 3		under these [five porticos] were crowds of *sick people*
	5		2 One man there had an *illness* which had lasted thirty-eight years,
	7		'Sir,' replied the *sick* man 'I have no one to put me into the pool'
	6 2		a large crowd . . . impressed by the signs he gave by curing the *sick*.
	11 1		a man named Lazarus . . . lived in the village of Bethany with the two sisters, Mary and Martha, and he was *ill*. ² It was
	2		the same Mary, the sister of the *sick* [man] Lazarus, who anointed the Lord
	3		Lord, the man you love is *ill*.
	4		2 Jesus said, 'This *sickness* will end . . . in God's glory . . .'
	6		⁶ yet when he heard that Lazarus was *ill* he stayed where he was
Ac	4 9		you are questioning us today about an act of kindness to a 3 *cripple*,
	5 15		3 the *sick* were even taken out into the streets
	16		People . . . came crowding . . . bringing with them their 3 *sick*
	9 37		[Tabitha] got *ill* and died,
	19 12		handkerchiefs . . . which had touched [Paul] were taken to the *sick*, and they were cured of their illnesses,
	28 9		2 the other *sick people* on the island [of Malta] came as well and were cured;
Ga	4 13		2 that *illness* gave me the opportunity to preach the Good News to you,
Ph	2 26		you heard about [Epaphroditus's] *illness*. ²⁷ It is true that he 27 has been *ill*, and almost died,
1 Tm	5 23		have a little wine for the sake of your digestion and the frequent 2 bouts of *illness* that you have.
2 Tm	4 20		I left Trophimus *ill* at Miletus.
Jm	5 14		If one of you is *ill*, he should send for the elders of the church,

2: DISEASE, SICKNESS – A CRAZE (FOR): *NOSOS* and *MALAKIA*

2 *nosēma* 1	4 *malakia* 3
3 *noseō* 1
1 *nosos* 11

Mt	4 23	/4	[Jesus] went round the whole of Galilee . . . curing all kinds of *diseases* and *sickness* among the people.
	24		those who were suffering from *diseases* and painful complaints of one kind or another . . . were all brought to him,
	8 17		(Is 53 4) He took our sicknesses away and carried our *diseases* for us.

Mt	9 35	Jesus made a tour through all the towns . . . curing all kinds of *diseases* and *sickness*.
	/4	
	10 1	[Jesus gave the Twelve] power . . . to cure all kinds of *diseases* and *sickness*.
	/4	
Mk	1 34	[Jesus] cured many who were suffering from *diseases* of one kind or another;
Lk	4 40	all those who had friends suffering from *diseases* of one kind or another brought them to him,
	6 18	[a great crowd] had come . . . to be cured of their *diseases*.
	7 21	[Jesus] cured many people of *diseases* and afflictions
	9 1	[Jesus gave the Twelve] power and authority . . . to cure *diseases*,
Jn	5 4	2 ᵛ the first person . . . was cured of any *ailment* he suffered from¹
Ac	19 12	they were cured of their *illnesses*,
1 Tm	6 4	[Anyone who teaches anything different] is simply ignorant
	3	. . . with a *craze* for questioning everything

3: AFFLICTION, COMPLAINT – PLAGUE: *MASTIX*

mastix 4/6

Mk	3 10	all who were *afflicted* in any way were crowding forward to touch [Jesus].
	5 29	[the woman with a haemorrhage] was cured of her *complaint*.
	34	go in peace and be free from your *complaint*.
Lk	7 21	[Jesus] cured many people of diseases and *afflictions*

4: SICK, SICK PEOPLE – ILL: *A-RRHŌSTOS*

a-rrhōstos 5

Mt	14 14	[Jesus] saw a large crowd; and he . . . healed their *sick*.
Mk	6 5	[Jesus] could work no miracle there, though he cured a few *sick people*
	13	[the Twelve] anointed many *sick people* with oil
	16 18	they will lay their hands on the *sick*, who will recover.
1 Co	11 30	In fact that is why many of you are weak and *ill*

5: THE SICK, (THOSE WHO) ARE SICK – (BE) IN A WRETCHED CONDITION: *KAKŌS ECHŌ*

kakōs echō 11

Mt	4 24	those who were *sick*, suffering from diseases and painful complaints
	8 16	[Jesus] cured all who were *sick*.
	9 12	It is not the healthy who need the doctor, but the *sick*.
	14 35	the local people . . . took all that were *sick* to him,
	17 15	Lord, . . . take pity on my son: he is a lunatic and *in a wretched state*;
Mk	1 32	they brought to him all who were *sick* and those who were possessed by devils.
	34	he cured many who were *sick*, suffering from diseases of one kind or another;
	2 17	It is not the healthy who need the doctor, but the *sick*.
	6 55	[people] brought the *sick* on stretchers to wherever . . . he was.
Lk	5 31	It is not those who are well who need the doctor, but the *sick*.
	7 2	A centurion . . . had a servant . . . who was *sick* and near death.

6: FAINT, (BECOME) WANTING – SICK MAN: *KAMNŌ*

kamnō 2

Heb	12 3	then you will not give up for *want* of courage.
Jm	5 15	The prayer of faith will save the *sick man*

3. SPECIFIC DISEASES, COMPLAINTS AND INVALIDS

1: LEPER – LEPROSY: *LEPRA*

2 lepra 4   1 lepros 9

Mt	8 2	A *leper* now came up and bowed low in front of [Jesus].
	3	2 Jesus stretched out his hand . . . And his *leprosy* was cured at once.
	10 8	Cure the sick . . . cleanse the *lepers*,
	11 5	*lepers* are cleansed, and the deaf hear,
	26 6	Jesus was at Bethany in the house of Simon the *leper*,
Mk	1 40	A *leper* came to [Jesus] and pleaded on his knees:
	42	2 And the *leprosy* left him at once and he was cured.
	14 3	Jesus was at Bethany in the house of Simon the *leper*;
Lk	4 27	in the prophet Elisha's time there were many *lepers* in Israel,
	5 12	2 a man appeared, covered with *leprosy* . . . ¹³ Jesus stretched
	13	2 out his hand, touched him . . . And the *leprosy* left him at once.

Lk	7 22	*lepers* are cleansed, and the deaf hear,
	17 12	ten *lepers* came to meet [Jesus].

2: SORES – COVERED WITH SORES: *HELKOS*

2 helkoomai 1   1 helkos 3

Lk	16 20	at [the rich man's] gate there lay a poor man called Lazarus,
	21	2 *covered with sores*, ²¹ . . . Dogs even came and licked his *sores*.
Rv	16 2	on all the people who had been branded with the mark of the beast . . . there came disgusting and virulent *sores*.
	11	they cursed . . . God . . . because of their pains and *sores*.

3: GANGRENE: *GANGRAINA*

gangraina 1

2 Tm	2 17	Talk of this kind corrodes like *gangrene*,

4: FEVER – FEVERISH BOUTS: *PYRETOS*

2 pyressō 2   1 pyretos 6

Mt	8 14	2 Jesus found Peter's mother-in-law in bed *with fever*. ¹⁵ He
	15	touched her hand and the *fever* left her,
Mk	1 30	2 Simon's mother-in-law had gone to bed *with fever* . . .
	31	³¹ [Jesus] went to her . . . and helped her up. And the *fever* left her
Lk	4 38	Simon's mother-in-law was suffering from a high fever . . .
	39	³⁹ . . . [Jesus] rebuked the *fever* and it left her.
Jn	4 52	The *fever* left him yesterday . . . at the seventh hour.
Ac	28 8	Publius' father was in bed, suffering from *feverish attacks* and dysentery.

5: PLAGUE, PESTILENCE – PEST: *LOIMOS*

loimos 2

Lk	21 11	There will be great earthquakes and *plagues* and famines
Ac	24 5 ○	we find this man [Paul] a perfect *pest*;

6: DYSENTERY: *DYS-ENTERION*

dys-enterion 1

Ac	28 8	Publius' father was in bed, suffering from feverish attacks and *dysentery*.

7: DROPSY: *HYDRŌPIKOS*

hydrōpikos 1

Lk	14 2	There in front of [Jesus] was a man with *dropsy*,

8: ITCHING: *KNĒTHŌ*

knēthō 1

2 Tm	4 3	people will ʳbe avid for the latest novelty (lit. have *itching* ears) and collect themselves a whole series of teachers

9: SWELL UP: *PIMPRĒMI*

pimprēmi 1

Ac	28 6	they were expecting [Paul] at any moment to *swell up*

10: EPILEPTIC – LUNATIC: *SELĒNIAZOMAI*

selēniazomai 2

Mt	4 24	the possessed, *epileptics*, the paralysed, were all brought to him,
	17 15	Lord . . . take pity on my son: he is a *lunatic*

11: SCALES (COVERING THE EYES): *LEPIS*

lepis 1

Ac	9 18	it was as though *scales* fell away from Saul's eyes

WHERE FROM

pothen (22)

Mt 13	54	*Where* did the man get this wisdom and these miraculous powers?
	56	*where* did the man get it all?
21	25	John's baptism: *where* did it come *from*: heaven or man?
Mk 6	2	*Where* did the man get all this?
12	37	David himself calls him Lord, ⌐in what way (lit. *from where*) then can he be his son?
Lk 13	25	I do not know *where* you come *from*.
	27	I do not know *where* you come *from*.
20	7	their reply was that they did not know *where* [John's baptism] came *from*.
Jn 1	48	'*From where*) do you know me?' said Nathanael.
2	9	Having no idea *where* [the wine] came *from* . . . the steward called the bridegroom
3	8	you cannot tell *where* [the wind] comes *from* or where it is going.
4	11	⌐how (lit. *from where*) could you get this living water?
7	27	we all know *where* he comes *from*, but when the Christ appears no one will know *where* he comes *from*. ²⁸ . . .
	28	Jesus . . . cried out: 'Yes, you know . . . *where* I came *from*.'
8	14	I know *where* I came *from* and where I am going; but you do not know *where* I come *from* or where I am going.
9	29	[the Jews said,] 'We don't know *where* this man comes *from*'.
	30	³⁰ The [blind] man replied, '. . . He has opened my eyes, and you don't know *where* he comes *from*!'
19	9	[Pilate] said to Jesus, '*Where* do you come *from*?'
Jm 4	1	*Where* do these wars (§ come *from*) and (§ *where* do these) battles between yourselves first start?

WHOLE – ALL – EACH

1. All, the Whole (of), Entire – At all – Complete: *holos*
  1: All (the world), (the) Whole (world)
  2: All, (the) Whole (of) – Entire
  3: All (as adverb) – Absolutely – At all
  4: (Be) Complete, Perfect, Whole – Health

2. All: *pas*
  1: All (people)
    a) All (as pronoun or adjective) – Everyone, Everybody
    b) All (as pronoun or adjective) – Anyone (who), Everyone (who), Whoever – Every
    c) All = Entire, As a whole

  2: All (things)
    a) All, Everything, the Whole – Whatever
    b) All (as adjective)
    c) All = the Whole
    d) All = Perfect, Full, Complete
    e) All, Any (generally)
    f) Certainly, No doubt – In every way, In everything – At all, Completely

  3: All (places)
    a) All = the Whole
    b) All (places), Every (place), Everywhere – From, on, all sides – All round, All over

  4: All (time)

3. Any, Whatever: *hoios dēpotoun*

4. Each, Each one – Every, Every one: *hekastos*

1. ALL, THE WHOLE (OF), ENTIRE – AT ALL – COMPLETE: *HOLOS*

1	*holos*	109	4	*holo-klēria*	1
7	*di' holou*	1 } 110	3	*holo-klēros*	2
2	*holōs*	4	5	*holo-telēs*	1
			6	*kath-olou*	1

1: ALL (THE WORLD), (THE) WHOLE (WORLD)

Mt 16	26	What . . . will a man gain if he wins the *whole* world . . .?
24	14	The Good News of the kingdom will be proclaimed to the *whole* world
26	13	wherever in *all* the world this Good News is proclaimed,
Mk 8	36	What gain . . . is it for a man to win the *whole* world . . .?
14	9	wherever throughout *all* the world the Good News is proclaimed,
Lk 9	25	What gain . . . is it for a man to have won the *whole* world . . .?
Ac 11	28	Agabus . . . predicted that a famine would spread over the *whole* empire.
Rm 1	8	the way in which your faith is spoken of ⌐all over (lit. over *all*) the world.

1 Jn 2	2	he is the sacrifice that takes our sins away, and not only ours, but the *whole* world's.
5	19	the *whole* world lies in the power of the Evil One.
Rv 3	10	the time of trial which is going to come for the *whole* world,
12	9	The great dragon . . . who had deceived *all* the world,
13	3	the *whole* world had marvelled and followed the beast.
16	14	demon spirits . . . going out to the kings of *all* the world

2: ALL, (THE) WHOLE (OF) – ENTIRE

Mt 1	22	*all* this took place to fulfil the words spoken by the Lord
4	23	[Jesus] went round the *whole* of Galilee teaching
	24	His fame spread through *all* Syria,
5	29	it will do you less harm to lose one part of you than to have your *whole* body thrown into hell.
	30	it will do you less harm to lose one part of you than to have your *whole* body go to hell.
6	22	if your eye is sound, your *whole* body will be filled with light.
	23	if your eye is diseased, your *whole* body will be all darkness.
9	26	the news spread round the *whole* countryside
	31	[the two blind men] talked about [Jesus] through *all* the countryside.
13	33	like the yeast a woman took and mixed in with three measures of flour till it was *all* leavened.
14	35	When the local people recognised [Jesus] they spread the news through the *whole* neighbourhood
20	6	Why have you been standing here idle *all* day?
22	37	(Dt 6 5) You must love the Lord your God with *all* your heart, with *all* your soul, and with *all* your mind.
	40	On these two commandments hang the *whole* Law, and the Prophets also.
26	56	*all* this happened to fulfil the prophecies in scripture.
	59	The chief priests and the *whole* Sanhedrin were looking for evidence against Jesus,
27	27	The governor's soldiers . . . collected the *whole* cohort round [Jesus].
Mk 1	28	[Jesus's] reputation rapidly spread everywhere, through *all* the surrounding Galilean countryside.
	33	The *whole* town came crowding round the door,
	39	[Jesus] went through the *whole* of Galilee,
6	55	[the people] started hurrying through the *whole* countryside
12	30	(Dt 6 5) you must love the Lord your God with *all* your heart, with *all* your soul, with *all* your mind and with *all* your strength.
	33	(Dt 6 5) To love him with *all* your heart, with *all* your understanding and *all* your strength . . . is far more important than any holocaust
	44	but [the widow] from the little she had has put in [to the treasury] everything she possessed, *all* she had to live on.
14	55	The chief priests and the *whole* Sanhedrin were looking for evidence against Jesus
15	1	the chief priests together with the elders and scribes, in short the *whole* Sanhedrin
	16	The soldiers . . . called the *whole* cohort together.
	33	there was darkness over the *whole* land
Lk 1	65	the whole affair was talked about ⌐throughout (lit. through *all*) the hill country of Judaea.
4	14	[Jesus's] reputation spread through *all* the countryside.
5	5	Master, . . . we worked hard *all* night long
7	17	this opinion of [Jesus] spread ⌐throughout (lit. through *all*) Judaea
8	39	the man went off and spread ⌐throughout (lit. through *all*) the town all that Jesus had done for him.
	43	a woman . . . (ᵛ who had spent *all* she had on doctors)
10	27	(Dt 6 5) You must love the Lord your God with *all* your heart, with *all* your soul, with *all* your strength, and with *all* your mind,
11	34	When your eye is sound, your *whole* body too is filled with light; . . . ³⁶ If, therefore, your *whole* body is filled with light, . . . it will ⌐be light entirely (lit. *all* be light),
13	21	It is like the yeast a woman took and mixed in with three measures of flour till it was ⌐leavened all through (lit. *all* leavened).
23	5	He is inflaming the people with his teaching ⌐all over (lit. over *all*) Judaea;
	44	a darkness came over the *whole* land
Jn 4	53	[the official] and *all* his household believed.
9	34	and you a sinner *through and through*, since you were born!
11	50	it is better for one man to die for the people, than for the *whole* nation to be destroyed.
13	10	No one who has taken a bath needs washing, he is ⌐clean all over (lit. *all* clean).
Ac 2	2	the noise of [the wind] filled the *entire* house
	47	[the believers] were looked up to by ⌐everyone (lit. *all* the people).
5	11	This made a profound impression on the *whole* Church
7	10	Pharaoh . . . made [Joseph] governor of Egypt and put him in charge of *all* the royal household.

Ac	7 11	a famine came that caused much suffering ˹throughout (lit. through *all*) Egypt and Canaan
	8 37	(ᵛ Philip said, 'If you believe with *all* your heart, . . .)
	9 31	The churches ˹throughout (lit. through *all*) Judaea, Galilee and Samaria were now left in peace,
	42	The *whole* of Jaffa heard about it
	10 22	Cornelius, who is . . highly regarded by the *entire* Jewish people,
	37	You must have heard about the recent happenings in *all* [of] Judaea,
	11 26	[Barnabas and Saul] were to live together in that church a *whole* year,
	13 6	They travelled the *whole* length of the island,
	49	the word of the Lord spread through the *whole* countryside.
	15 22	the *whole* church concurred with this.
	18 8	Crispus, . . . and his *whole* household, all became believers
	19 27	Diana . . . a goddess venerated over *all* Asia,
	21 30	This roused the *whole* city;
	31	there was rioting ˹all over (lit. in *all*) Jerusalem
	28 30	Paul spent the *whole* [of the] two years in his own rented lodging.
Rm	8 36	(Ps 44 22) For your sake we are being massacred ˹daily (lit. *all* day long),
	10 21	(Is 65 2) ˹Each (lit. *All*) day I stretched out my hand to a disobedient . . . people.
	16 23	Greetings from Gaius . . . and from the *whole* church that meets in his house.
1 Co	5 6	even a small amount of yeast is enough to leaven *all* the dough.
	12 17	If your *whole* body was just one eye, how would you hear anything? If it was *all* just one ear, how would you smell anything?
	14 23	any . . . unbelievers, coming into a meeting of the *whole* church
2 Co	1 1	From Paul . . . to all the saints in the *whole* of Achaia.
Ga	5 3	Everyone who accepts circumcision is obliged to keep the *whole* Law.
	9	The yeast seems to be spreading through the *whole* batch of you.
Ph	1 13	My chains . . . have become famous not only ˹all over (lit. through *all*) the Praetorium but everywhere,
1 Th	4 10	this is what you are doing with all the brothers throughout the *whole* of Macedonia.
	5 23	may ˹you all (lit. your *whole* being) be kept safe and blameless,
Tt	1 11	men of this kind ruin *whole* families,
Heb	3 2	(Nb 12 7) [Jesus] was . . . just like Moses, who stayed faithful in *all* his house,
	5	(Nb 12 7) Moses was faithful in *all* the house of God,
Jm	2 10	if a man keeps the *whole* of the Law, except for one small point . . , he is still guilty of breaking it all.
	3 2	someone who never said anything wrong . . . would be able to control ˹every part (lit. *all*) of himself. ³ Once we put a bit into the horse's mouth . . . we have the *whole* animal under our control.
	6	the tongue . . . infects the *whole* body;
Rv	6 12	[the sixth seal broken,] ˹the moon turned red as blood all over (lit. *all* the moon turned red as blood),

3: ALL (AS AN ADVERB) – ABSOLUTELY – AT ALL

Mt	5 34	2 do not swear *at all*,
Jn	19 23	7 [Jesus's] undergarment was seamless, woven [*all*] *in one piece*
Ac	4 18	[Peter and John were given] a warning ˹on no account to (lit.
	6	*absolutely* not to) . . . teach in the name of Jesus.
1 Co	5 1	2 I have been told *as an undoubted fact* that one of you is living with his father's wife.
	6 7	2 It is bad enough for you to have lawsuits *at all* against one another:
	15 29	2 If the dead are not ˹ever (lit. *at all*) going to be raised,

4: (BE) COMPLETE, PERFECT, WHOLE – HEALTH

Jn	7 23	why are you angry with me for making a man whole and *complete* on a sabbath?
Ac	3 16	4 It is faith . . . that has restored this man to ˹health (or:
	4	*wholeness*),
1 Th	5 23	5 May the God of peace make you *perfect* and holy;
Jm	1 4	3 so that you will become fully-developed, *complete*,

2. ALL: *PAS*

1	*pas*	1212/1249	3	*pantōs*	9
7	*pantachē*	1	5	*pantothen*	3
4	*pantachou*	7	2	*ha-pas*	31/32
6	*pantē*	1			

1: ALL (PEOPLE)

a) All (as a pronoun) – Everyone, Everybody

Mt	5 15	[people] put [a lamp] on the lamp-stand where it shines for *everyone* in the house.
	8 16	[Jesus] cured *all* who were sick.
	10 22	You will be hated by *all* [men] on account of my name;
	11 28	Come to me, *all* [you] who labour
	12 15	[Jesus] cured [them] *all*,
	13 56	His sisters, too, are they not *all* here with us?
	14 20	[They] *all* ate as much as they wanted,
	15 37	[They] *all* ate as much as they wanted,
	19 11	It is not *everyone* who can accept what I have said,
	21 26	we have the people to fear, for [they] *all* hold that John was a prophet.
	22 10	these servants went out on to the roads and collected together *everyone* they could find,
	27	last of *all* the woman herself died.
	28	to which of those seven will she be wife, since she had been married to [them] *all*?
	23 8	you are *all* brothers.
	24 39	2 they suspected nothing till the Flood came and swept *a* away.
	25 5	[the bridesmaids] *all* grew drowsy and fell asleep.
	26 27	'Drink *all* [of you] from this,' [Jesus] said ²⁸ 'for this is my blood,'
	31	You will *all* lose faith in me this night,
	33	Though *all* lose faith in you, I will never lose faith.
	52	*all* who draw the sword will die by the sword.
	56	Then *all* the disciples deserted him and ran away.
	70	[Peter] denied it in front of [them] *all*.
	27 22	They *all* said, 'Let him be crucified!'
Mk	1 27	2 ˹The people (lit. *All*) were so astonished
	37	*Everybody* is looking for you.
	2 12	the [paralytic] got up . . . and walked out in front of *everyone*, so that [they] were *all* astounded
	5 20	*everyone* was amazed.
	40	[Jesus] turned [them] *all* out and . . . went into the place where the child lay.
	6 39	[Jesus] ordered [the disciples] to get *all* [the people] together in groups on the green grass,
	41	[Jesus] also shared out the two fish among [them] *all*.
	42	[They] *all* ate as much as they wanted.
	50	[they] had *all* seen him and were terrified.
	7 14	Listen to me, *all* [of you], and understand.
	9 35	If anyone wants to be first, he must make himself last of *all* and servant of *all*.
	49	*everyone* will be salted with fire.
	10 44	anyone who wants to be first among you must be slave to *all*.
	11 32	2 everyone held that John was a real prophet.
	12 22	Last of *all* the woman herself died.
	43	this poor widow has put more in than *all* who have contributed to the treasury; ⁴⁴ for they have *all* put in money they had over,
	13 13	You will be hated by *all* [men] on account of my name;
	37	what I say to you I say to all: Stay awake!
	14 23	[Jesus] gave [the cup] to [the Twelve], and *all* drank from it.
	27	You will *all* lose faith,
	29	Even if *all* lose faith, I will not.
	31	And [they] *all* said the same.
	50	they *all* deserted him and ran away.
	64	[they] *all* gave their verdict: he deserved to die.
Lk	1 63	[Zechariah] wrote, 'His name is John' And they were *all* astonished.
	66	*All* those who heard of it treasured it in their hearts.
	71	that he would save us . . . from the hands of *all* who hate us.
	2 3	*everyone* went to his own town to be registered.
	18	*everyone* who heard it was astonished
	38	[Anna] spoke of the child to *all* who looked forward to the deliverance of Jerusalem.
	47	*all* those who heard [the child Jesus] were astounded
	3 15	A feeling of expectancy had grown among the people, ˹who (lit. *all*) were beginning to think that John might be the Christ,
	16	John declared before [them] *all*, '. . . someone is coming . . . who is more powerful than I am,'
	4 15	*everyone* praised [Jesus].
	20	˹all eyes (lit. the eyes of *all*) in the synagogue were fixed on [Jesus].
	22	[Jesus] won the approval of *all*,
	28	*everyone* in the synagogue was enraged.
	40	2 *all* those who had friends suffering from diseases . . . brought them to [Jesus],
	5 9	[Peter] and *all* ˹his companions (lit. who were with him) were completely overcome by the catch they had made;
	26	2 They were *all* astounded and praised God,
	6 10	[Jesus] looked round at them *all*
	19	power came out of [Jesus] that cured them *all*.
	7 16	*Everyone* was filled with awe and praised God

Lk	8 40	Jesus was welcomed by the crowd, for [they] were *all* waiting for him.
	45	Jesus said, 'Who touched me?' When [they] *all* denied that they had,
	52	[They] were *all* weeping and mourning for [Jairus's daughter],
	9 15	2 [the disciples] made them *all* sit down.
	17	[They] *all* ate as much as they wanted,
	23	Then to *all* he said, 'If anyone wants to be a follower of mine,'
	43	*everyone* was awestruck by the greatness of God. At a time when *everyone* was full of admiration for all he did, he said
	48	For the least among you *all*, that is the one who is great.
	12 41	Lord, do you mean this parable for us, or for *everyone*?
	13 3	unless you repent you will *all* perish as they did.
	5	you will *all* perish as they did.
	17	*all* ⌐his adversaries (lit. those who opposed him) were covered with confusion,
	14 18	*all* alike started to make excuses.
	29	the onlookers would *all* start making fun of him
	17 27	the Flood came and destroyed them *all*.
	29	God rained fire and brimstone from heaven and it destroyed them *all*.
	19 7	[They] *all* complained when they saw what was happening.
	20 38	he is God, not of the dead, but of the living; for to him *all* [men] are in fact alive.
	21 3	this poor widow has put in [to the treasury] more than ⌐any (lit. *all*) of them; ⁴ for these have *all* contributed money they had over,
	4	
	17	You will be hated by *all* [men] on account of my name,
	35	[that day] will come down on ⌐every living man (lit. *all* those who live) on the face of the earth.
	22 70	Then [they] *all* said, 'So you are the Son of God then?'
Jn	1 7	He came as a witness, . . . so that *everyone* might believe through him,
	16	from his fullness we have, *all* [of us], received
	2 15	[In the Temple he found people selling cattle.] Making a whip out of some cord, he drove them *all* out
	24	Jesus knew them *all* and did not trust himself to them;
	3 26	the man to whom you bore witness, is baptising now; and *everyone* is going to him.
	31	He who comes from above is above ⌐*all* [others] (or: everything); . . . He who comes from heaven (§ is above ⌐*all* [others] (or: everything))
	5 23	so that *all* may honour the Son
	28	the hour is coming when ⌐the dead will leave their graves (lit. *all* who lie in their graves will leave them)
	6 45	(Is 54 13) They will *all* be taught by God,
	7 21	you are *all* surprised
	10 8	*All* ⌐others (lit. those) who have come are thieves and brigands;
	29	The Father who gave them to me is greater than *anyone*,
	11 48	If we let him go on in this way *everybody* will believe in him,
	12 32	I shall draw ⌐*all* [men] (ᵛ everything) to myself.
	13 10	You too are clean, though not *all* [of you] are.
	11	that was why he said, 'though not *all* [of you] are'.
	18	I am not speaking about *all* of you:
	35	By this love you have for one another, *everyone* will know that you are my disciples.
	17 21	May [they] *all* be one.
Ac	1 14	*All* [these] joined in continuous prayer,
	24	Lord, you can read *everyone's* heart;
	2 1	When Pentecost day came round, they had *all* met in one room,
	4	[They] were *all* filled with the Holy Spirit,
	7	They were (ᵛ *all*) amazed and astonished. 'Surely' they said 'all these [men] speaking are Galileans?'
	12	*Everyone* was amazed
	14	*all* you who live in Jerusalem,
	32	God raised this man Jesus to life, and *all* of us are witnesses to that.
	39	The promise that was made is for you . . , and for *all* those who are far away,
	44	The faithful *all* lived together
	45	they sold their goods . . . and shared out the proceeds among ⌐themselves (lit. *all*) according to what each one needed.
	3 16	it is the name of Jesus which . . . has brought back the strength of this man ⌐whom you see here (lit. in front of you *all*)
	4 10	I am glad to tell you *all*
	21	*all* [the people] were giving glory to God
	31	2 [they] were *all* filled with the Holy Spirit,
	33	The apostles . . . were *all* given great respect.
	5 5	Ananias fell down dead. This made a profound impression on *everyone* present.
	11	This made a profound impression on the whole Church and on *all* who heard it.
	12	[They] *all* used to meet by common consent in the Portico of Solomon.
	16	2 *all* of them were cured.
	17	the high priest intervened with *all* his supporters
	36	when [Theudas] was killed, *all* his followers scattered
	37	[Judas the Galilean] got killed too, and *all* his followers dispersed.

Ac	6 15	The members of the Sanhedrin *all* looked intently at Stephen,
	8 1	*everyone* except the apostles fled
	10	*everyone* believed what [Simon the magician] said;
	9 14	[Saul] holds a warrant from the chief priests to arrest *everybody* who invokes your name.
	21	*All* [Saul's] hearers were amazed.
	26	the disciples . . . were *all* afraid of [Saul]:
	32	Peter ⌐visited one place after another (lit. travelled across everything; or: travelled to *everyone*)
	40	Peter sent them *all* out of the room
	10 33	Here we are *all*, assembled in front of you to hear ⌐what (lit. the *whole*) message God has given you for us.
	36	Jesus Christ is Lord of *all* [men].
	38	Jesus went about . . . curing *all* who had fallen into the power of the devil.
	44	the Holy Spirit came down on *all* the listeners.
	11 23	[Barnabas] urged them *all* to remain faithful to the Lord
	16 3	2 *everyone* knew [Timothy's] father was a Greek.
	26	the chains fell from *all* [the prisoners].
	28	2 Don't do yourself any harm; we are *all* here.
	32	[Paul and Silas] preached the word of the Lord to [the gaoler] and to *all* his family.
	33	2 [the gaoler] was baptised then and there with *all* his household.
	17 7	⌐They (lit. *All* these [people]) have broken [every one of] Caesar's edicts
	25	it is [God] who gives everything . . . to *everyone*.
	30	now [God] is telling *everyone* everywhere that they must repent,
	31	God has ⌐publicly proved thiṣ (lit. proved this to *all* [men]) by raising this man from the dead.
	18 17	at once they *all* turned on Sosthenes,
	19 17	they were *all* greatly impressed,
	19	a number of them who had practised magic collected their books and made a bonfire of them ⌐in public (lit. in front of them *all*).
	34	they *all* started shouting in unison, 'Great is Diana of the Ephesians!'
	20 25	I now feel sure that ⌐none (lit. *all*) of you among whom I have gone about proclaiming the kingdom will ⌐ever (lit. never) see my face again.
	26	my conscience is clear as far as *all* of you are concerned.
	36	[Paul] knelt down with them *all* and prayed.
	37	By now they were *all* in tears;
	21 5	they *all* escorted us on our way
	20	thousands of Jews have now become believers, *all* of them staunch upholders of the Law,
	24	This will let *everyone* know there is no truth in the reports they have heard
	28	This is the man who preaches to *everyone* everywhere against our people,
	22 3	I was as full of duty towards God as you *all* are today.
	25 24	King Agrippa, and *all* here present with us,
	26 14	We *all* fell to the ground, and I heard a voice
	29	*all* who have heard me today
	27 24	God grants you the safety of *all* who are sailing with you.
	33	2 Paul urged them *all* to have something to eat.
	35	[Paul] gave thanks to God in front of them *all*,
	36	Then they *all* plucked up courage
	44	*all* came safe and sound to land.
	28 2	[The Maltese] made us *all* welcome,
	30	[Paul] welcomed *all* who came to visit him,
Rm	1 8	I thank my God . . . for *all* of you
	3 9	Jews and Greeks are *all* under sin's dominion.
	12	(Ps 14 3) *All* have turned aside, tainted 'all alike (lit. together);
	22	it is the same justice of God that comes through faith to *everyone* (ᵛ and over *everyone*) . . . who believes in Jesus Christ
	23	⌐Both Jew and pagan (lit. *All*) sinned and forfeited God's glory,
	4 11	Abraham became the ancestor of *all* uncircumcised believers,
	16	so that [the promise] may be . . . available to *all* of Abraham's descendants,
	5 12	death has spread through the whole human race because *everyone* has sinned.
	8 32	God did not spare his own Son, but gave him up to benefit us *all*,
	9 7	not *all* the descendants of Abraham are his true children.
	10 12	*all* belong to the same Lord who is rich enough, ⌐however many (lit. for *all* who) ask his help,
	16	Not *everyone*, of course, listens to the Good News.
	11 32	God has imprisoned *all* men in their own disobedience only to show mercy to *all* mankind.
	13 7	Pay ⌐every government official (lit. *all*) what ⌐he has (lit. they have) a right to ask
	14 10	We shall *all* have to stand before the judgement seat of God;
	15 33	May the God of peace be with you *all*!
	16 19	Your fidelity to Christ . . . is ⌐famous everywhere (lit. well known to *all*),
	24	(ᵛ May the grace of our Lord Jesus Christ be with you *all*. Amen.)

1 Co	1 2	*all* the saints everywhere who pray to our Lord Jesus Christ;
	10	I do appeal to you, brothers, . . . to ⸢be united again in your belief (lit. have *all* [of you] the same language)
	4 13	We are treated as the offal of ⸢the world (lit. *everyone*),
	8 1	We *all* have knowledge;
	7	⸢Some people, however, (lit. *All*) do not have this knowledge.
	9 19	though I am ⸢not a slave to any man (lit. free in relation to *everyone*) I have made myself the slave of *everyone*
	22	I made myself all things to *all* [men] in order to save some ⸢at any cost (lit. completely);
	24	*All* the runners at the stadium are trying to win,
	10 1	our fathers were *all* guided by a cloud . . . and . . . they
	2	*all* passed through the sea. ² They were *all* baptised into Moses . . .; ³ *all* ate the same spiritual food ⁴ and *all*
	3	
	4	drank the same spiritual drink,
	17	though there are many of us, we form a single body because we *all* have a share in this one loaf.
	33	I try to be helpful to *everyone* at all times,
	12 6	working in all sorts of different ways in different people, it is the same God who is working in *all* of them.
	13	In the one Spirit we were *all* baptised, . . . and one Spirit was given to us *all* to drink.
	29	Are *all* of them apostles, or *all* of them prophets, or *all* of them teachers? Do they *all* have the gift of miracles,
	30	³⁰ or *all* the gift of healing? Do *all* speak strange languages, and *all* interpret them?
	14 5	I would like you *all* to have the gift of tongues,
	18	I have a greater gift of tongues than *all* of you,
	23	a meeting of the whole church where *everybody* was speaking in tongues,
	24	if you were *all* prophesying and an unbeliever . . . came in, he would find himself analysed by *everyone* and judged by *everyone* speaking;
	31	you can *all* prophesy in turn, so that *everybody* will learn something and *everybody* will be encouraged.
	15 8	last of *all* [Christ] appeared to me too ;
	10	I . . . have worked harder than ⸢any of the others (lit. *all* of them);
	22	Just as *all* men die in Adam, so *all* [men] will be brought to life in Christ;
	28	the Son himself will be subject in his turn to the One who subjected all things to him, so that God may be all in all.
	51	we are not *all* going to die, but we shall *all* be changed.
	16 24	My love is with you *all* in Christ Jesus.
2 Co	2 3	I am sure you *all* know that I could never be happy unless you *all* were.
	5	Someone has been the cause of pain . . . not to me, but . . . to *all* of you.
	3 18	we . . . *all* grow brighter and brighter, as we turn into the image that we reflect;
	5 10	For the truth about us *all* will be brought out in the law court of Christ,
	14	if one man has died for *all*, then *all* [men] should be dead;
	15	¹⁵ and the reason he died for *all* was so that living men should live . . . for him
	7 13	thanks to you *all*, [Titus] has no more worries;
	15	[Titus] remembers how willing you have *all* been,
	9 13	your sympathetic generosity to them and to *all*.
	11 6	speaking on every subject ⸢in front of *all* of you (or: in every way).
	13 2	I give warning . . . to those who sinned before and to ⸢any (lit. *all*) others,
	13	the love of God . . . be with you *all*.
Ga	2 14	I said to Cephas in front of *everyone*,
	3 26	you are, all of you, sons of God
	28	*all* of you are one in Christ Jesus.
	6 10	we must do good to *all*,
Ep	2 3	We *all* were among them too in the past,
	3 9	explaining (ᵛ to *all*) how the mystery is to be dispensed.
	4 6	one God who is Father of *all*, through *all* and within *all*.
	13	In this way we are *all* to come to unity in our faith
	6 24	May grace . . . be with *all* who love our Lord Jesus Christ.
Ph	1 4	every time I pray for *all* of you, I pray with joy,
	7	It is only natural that I should feel like this towards you *all*, since you have *all* shared the privileges which have been mine:
	8	God knows how much I miss you *all*,
	25	I feel sure I shall survive and stay with you *all*,
	2 17	I shall . . . rejoice with *all* of you,
	21	*all* [the rest] seem more interested in themselves than in Jesus Christ.
	26	[Epaphroditus] misses you *all*
1 Th	1 2	We . . . thank God for you *all*,
	7	This has made you the great example to *all* believers in Macedonia and Achaia.
	3 12	May the Lord . . . make you love one another and ⸢the whole human race (lit. *everyone*)
	5 5	you are *all* sons of light
	14	be patient with *everyone*.
	15	you must [all] think what is best for each other and for ⸢the community (lit. *everyone*).

2 Th	1 3	the love that you have for one another never stops increasing [among you *all*];
	10	when he comes to be . . . seen in his glory by *all* who believe in him;
	2 12	to condemn *all* who refuse to believe in the truth
	3 2	faith is not given to *everyone*.
	16	The Lord be with you *all*.
	18	May the grace of our Lord Jesus Christ be with you *all*.
1 Tm	2 2	[there should be prayers offered] especially for kings and ⸢others (lit. *all*) in authority,
	6	[Christ Jesus] sacrificed himself as a ransom for them *all*.
	4 15	*everyone* will be able to see how you are advancing.
	5 20	reprimand them ⸢publicly (lit. in front of *everyone*),
2 Tm	2 24	a servant of the Lord . . . has to be kind to *everyone*,
	3 9	their foolishness . . . must become obvious to *everyone*.
	12	⸢anybody (lit. *everybody*) who tries to live in devotion to Christ is certain to be attacked;
	4 8	not only to me but to *all* those who have longed for his Appearing.
	16	there was not a single witness to support me. ⸢Every one (lit. *All*) of them deserted me
Tt	3 15	*All* those who are with me send their greetings. . . . Grace be with you *all*.
Heb	1 14	they are *all* spirits whose work is service,
	2 11	the one who sanctifies, and the ones who are sanctified, are [*all*] of the same stock.
	3 16	those who rebelled . . . were *all* the people who were brought out of Egypt
	5 9	he became for *all* who obey him the source of eternal salvation
	8 11	(Jr 31 34) they will *all* know me, the least no less than the greatest,
	11 13	*All* these died in faith,
	39	These are *all* heroes of faith,
	12 8	If you were not getting this training, as *all* of you are,
	14	Always be wanting peace with *all* [people],
	23	God himself, the ⸢supreme Judge (lit. Judge of *all*),
	13 4	Marriage is to be honoured by *all*,
		Grace be with you *all*.
Jm	1 5	God, who gives to *all* freely
	3 2	⸢every one (lit. *all*) of us ⸢does (lit. do) something wrong, over and over again;
1 P	2 17	Have respect for *everyone*
	3 8	you should *all* agree among yourselves
	5 5	To the rest of you I say: . . . *all* wrap yourselves in humility
	14	Peace to you *all* who are in Christ.
2 P	3 9	The Lord is . . . being patient with you *all*,
1 Jn	2 19	Those rivals of Christ came out of our own number, but ⸢they had never really belonged (lit. *all* were not ours);
	20	you . . . have *all* received the knowledge.
2 Jn	1	so do *all* who have come to know the truth
3 Jn	12	Demetrius has been approved by *everyone*,
Jude	15	to pronounce judgement on *all* [mankind]
Rv	13 16	He compelled *everyone* – small and great, rich and poor,
	18 17	*All* the captains and seafaring men,
	19	⸢every owner of a sea-going ship (lit. *all* who have ships on the sea);
	24	⸢all the blood that was ever shed on earth (lit. the blood of *all* who were slaughtered on earth).

(*as an adjective*)

(*applied to men*)

Lk 6 26	⸢the world (lit. *all* men)	Ph 4 5	⸢everyone (lit. *all* men)
Jn 17 2	all mankind	1 Th 2 15	⸢the whole human race (lit. *all* men)
Ac 22 15	all mankind		
Rm 5 12	⸢the whole human race (lit. *all* men)	1 Tm 2 1	⸢everyone (lit. *all* men)
18	⸢everyone (lit. *all* men)	4	⸢everyone (lit. *all* men)
—	⸢everyone (lit. *all* men)	4 10	⸢the whole human race (lit. *all* men)
12 17	⸢everyone (lit. *all* men)	Tt 2 11	⸢the whole human race (lit. *all* men)
18	⸢everyone (lit. *all* men)	3 2	*all* [kinds of] people
1 Co 7 7	⸢everyone (lit. *all* men)		
15 19	*all* people		
2 Co 3 2	⸢anybody (lit. *all* men)		

(*applied to nations, peoples, races, tribes, pagans*)

Mt 24 9	*all* the nations	Mk 11 17	*all* the people
14	*all* the nations	13 10	*all* the nations
30	*all* the peoples of the earth	Lk 2 31	*all* the nations
25 32	*all* the nations	21 24	⸢every pagan country (lit. *all* the nations)
28 19	*all* the nations		

Lk 24 47	all the nations
Ac 2 5	[r]every nation (lit. all the nations)
14 16	[r]each nation (lit. all the nations)
15 17	all the pagans
Rm 15 11	all the pagans
—	all the peoples
16 26	[r]pagans every-where (lit. all pagans)

Ga 3 8	all the pagans
2 Tm 4 17	all the pagans
Rv 1 7	all the races
7 4	all the tribes
12 5	all the nations
14 8	[r]the whole world (lit. all the nations)
15 4	all the pagans
18 3	all the nations
23	all the nations

Rv 7 11	all the angels
13 8	all the people of the world
18 17	all the captains
19 5	all the servants [of God]

Rv 19 18	all citizens and slaves
21 8	[r]any other sort of (lit. all) liars

In all

Ac 19 7 — [r]There were about twelve of these men (lit. These men were *in all* about twelve).

27 37 — We were *in all* two hundred and seventy-six souls on board that ship.

(applied to churches)

Rm 16 4	all the churches
16	all the churches
1 Co 4 17	all the churches
7 17	all the churches
1 Co 14 33	all the churches
2 Co 8 18	all the churches
11 28	all the churches
Rv 2 23	all the churches

(applied to disciples, apostles, brothers, saints, the beloved of God)

Mt 26 35	all the disciples
Ac 15 3	all the [r]members of the church (lit. brothers)
18 23	all the followers
20 32	all the sanctified
Rm 1 7	all God's beloved
16 15	all the saints
1 Co 15 7	all the apostles
16 20	all the brothers
2 Co 1 1	all the saints
13 12	all the saints
Ga 1 2	all the brothers
Ep 1 15	all the saints
3 8	all the saints
Ep 3 18	all the saints
6 18	all the saints
Ph 1 1	all the saints
4 22	all the saints
Col 1 4	all the saints
1 Th 3 13	all the saints
4 10	all the brothers
5 26	all the brothers
27	all the brothers
2 Tm 4 21	all the brothers
Phm 5	all the saints
Heb 13 24	all the saints
Rv 8 3	all the saints
22 21[v]	all the saints

(various)

Mt 1 17	[r]the sum of (lit. all) generations
2 4	all the chief priests
16	all the male children
4 24	all who were suffering
11 13	all the prophets
12 23	all the people
14 35	all the sick
21 12	all the sellers
25 7	all the bridesmaids
31	all the angels
27 1	all the chief priests and elders
Mk 1 5	all the people of Jerusalem
32	all the sick
7 3	[r]the Jews in general (lit. all the Jews)
14 53	all the chief priests and elders and scribes
Lk 1 48	all generations
65	all the neighbours
7 35	all the children [of Wisdom]
9 1	all devils
11 50	[r]every prophet (lit. all prophets)
13 2	[r]any other Galilean (lit. all Galileans)
4	all the people of Jerusalem
27	all [r]you wicked men (lit. evil-doers)
28	all the prophets
14 10	[r]everyone with you at table (lit. all the guests)
15 1	all the tax collectors and the sinners
23 48	all the people
49	all [Jesus's] friends
24 9	all the others

Lk 24 27	all the prophets
Jn 18 20	all the Jews
Ac 1 19	[r]everybody in (lit. all the people of) Jerusalem
3 18	all [God's] prophets
24	all the prophets
25	all the families
4 16	[r]everybody in (lit. all the people of) Jerusalem
9 35	everybody who lived in Lydda and Sharon
39	all the widows
10 43	all the prophets
17 21	[all] the Athenians
18 2	all the Jews
19 10	[r]people from all over Asia (lit. all the people of Asia)
17	[r]everybody in Ephesus, both Jews and Greeks (lit. all the Jews and Greeks in Ephesus)
21 18	all the elders
21	all Jews
22 12	all the Jews
24 5	[r]Jews the world over (lit. all the Jews)
26 4	[all] the Jews
Rm 1 5	all pagan nations
9 6	all those who descend from Israel
1 Co 15 25	[all] the enemies
2 Tm 1 15	all [r]the others (lit. those) from Asia
Heb 1 6	all the angels
12 6	all [God's] sons
13 24	all your leaders
Jude 15	[all] the wicked

b) All

(as a pronoun =) Anyone (who), Everyone (who), Whoever

Mt 5 22	*anyone* who is angry with his brother
28	[r]if a man (lit. *anyone* who) looks at a woman lustfully,
32	*everyone* who divorces his wife
7 8	[r]the one (lit. *anyone*) who asks always receives;
21	It is not [r]those who say (lit. *everyone* who says), 'Lord, Lord',
24	*everyone* who listens to these words of mine
26	*everyone* who listens to these words of mine
10 32	[r]if anyone (lit. *anyone* who) declares himself for me
13 19	[r]When anyone (lit. *Anyone* who) hears the word of the kingdom without understanding,
19 29	*everyone* who has left houses, brothers, . . . or land for the sake of my name
25 29	to *everyone* who has will be given more,
Lk 6 30	Give to *everyone* who asks you,
47	*Everyone* who comes to me and listens to my words
11 4	for we ourselves forgive *each one* who is in debt to us.
10	[r]the one (lit. *anyone*) who asks always receives;
12 8	[r]if anyone (lit. *anyone* who) openly declares himself for me
10	*Everyone* who says a word against the Son of Man
48	[r]When a man (lit. *Anyone* who) has had a great deal given him,
14 11	*everyone* who exalts himself will be humbled,
33	[r]none of you can be my disciple unless he gives up all possessions (lit. *anyone* among you who does not give up all his possessions cannot be my disciple).
16 16	the kingdom of God has been preached, and by violence *everyone* is getting in.
18	*Everyone* who divorces his wife
18 14	*everyone* who exalts himself will be humbled,
19 26	to *everyone* who has will be given more;
20 18	*Anyone* who falls on that stone will be dashed to pieces;
Jn 3 8	That is how it is with *all* who are born of the Spirit.
15	so that *everyone* who believes may have eternal life in him.
16	so that *everyone* who believes in him may not be lost
20	*everybody* who does wrong hates the light
4 13	*Whoever* drinks this water will get thirsty again;
6 40	*whoever* sees the Son and believes in him
45	[r]to hear the teaching of the Father . . . is to come (lit. *whoever* hears the teaching of the Father . . . comes) to me.
8 34	*everyone* who commits sin is a slave.
11 26	*whoever* lives and believes in me will never die.
12 46	*whoever* believes in me need not stay in the dark any more.
16 2	*anyone* who kills you will think he is doing a holy duty for God.
18 37	*all* who are on the side of truth listen to my voice.
19 12	*anyone* who makes himself king is defying Caesar.
Ac 2 21	*All* who call on the name of the Lord will be saved.
43	*all* who believe in Jesus will have their sins forgiven
13 39	[Through him justification from all sins . . .] is offered to [r]every believer (lit. *whoever* believes).
Rm 1 16	it is the power of God saving *all* who have faith
2 1	[r]no matter who you are (lit. *whoever* you are), if you pass judgement you have no excuse.
10	renown, honour and peace will come to *everyone* who does good
10 4	*everyone* who has faith may be justified.
11	(Is 28 16) [r]those who believe (lit. *whoever* believes) in him will have no cause for shame,
13	(Jl 3 5) *everyone* who calls on the name of the Lord will be saved.
12 3	I want to urge [r]each one (lit. *whoever* is) among you
1 Co 9 25	[r]All the fighters at the games go (lit. *Whoever* fights at the games goes) into strict training;
16 16	put yourselves at the service of people like this, and *anyone* who helps . . . them
Ga 3 10	(Dt 27 26 G) Cursed be *everyone* who does not persevere in observing . . . the Law.
13	(cf. Dt 21 23) Cursed be *everyone* who is hanged on a tree.
2 Tm 2 19	*All* who call on the name of the Lord must avoid sin.
Heb 2 9	he had to experience death for *all* mankind.
5 13	*anyone* who is still living on milk cannot digest the doctrine of righteousness
1 P 3 15	always have your answer ready for [r]people who ask (lit. *whoever* asks) you the reason for the hope that you all have.
1 Jn 2 23	[r]no one who has the Father can deny the Son (lit. *anyone* who denies the Son does not have the Father),

1 Jn 2 29 you must recognise that *everyone* whose life is righteous has been begotten by [God].
3 3 *everyone* who entertains this hope must purify himself,
4 *Anyone* who sins at all breaks the law,
6 *anyone* who lives in God does not sin, and *anyone* who sins has never seen him
9 ⌜No one who has been begotten by God sins (lit. *Whoever* has been begotten by God does not sin);
10 *anybody* not living a holy life . . . is no child of God's.
15 ⌜to hate your brother is to be (lit. *anyone* who hates his brother is) a murderer,
4 7 *everyone* who loves is begotten by God
5 1 *Whoever* believes that Jesus is the Christ has been begotten by God; and *whoever* loves the Father that begot him loves the child whom he begets.
18 *anyone* who has been begotten by God does not sin,
2 Jn 9 ⌜If anybody (lit. *Anybody* who) does not keep within the teaching of Christ
Rv 22 15 These others must stay outside: dogs, . . . and *everyone* of false speech and false life.
19 if *anyone* cuts anything out of the prophecies in this book,

(*as an adjective*=) *Every, Any, Each*

(*applied to Man*)

Jn 1 9 ⌜all men (lit. *every* man)
2 10 ⌜people (lit. *every* man)
Rm 3 4 ⌜everyone (lit. *every* man)
1 Co 11 3 *every* man
4 ⌜a (lit. *any*) man
Ga 5 3 ⌜everyone (lit. *every* man)
Col 1 28 ⌜everyone (lit. *every* man)
— ⌜everyone (lit. *every* man)
— ⌜them all (lit. *every* man)
Jm 1 19 *every* man

(*various*)

Mt 13 52 *every* scribe
Lk 2 23 *every* first-born male
6 40 ⌜the (lit. *every*) fully trained disciple
Ac 2 43 ⌜everyone (lit. *every* spirit)
3 23 ⌜the man (lit. *every* soul)
10 35 *any* nationality
Rm 2 9 *every* human being
3 19 ⌜everyone (lit. *every* mouth)
13 1 ⌜you all (lit. *each* person)
14 11 *every* knee
— *every* tongue
1 Co 11 5 ⌜a (lit. *every*) woman
15 24 *every* sovereignty
— *every* authority and power
Ep 1 21 *every* Sovereignty
— *any* [other] name
Ph 2 9 ⌜all other names (lit. *any* name)
10 [*every*] knee
11 *every* tongue
4 21 *every one* of the saints
Col 1 15 ⌜all creation (lit. *every* creature)
Col 1 23 ⌜the whole human race (lit. *every* creature)
2 10 *every* Sovereignty and Power
2 Th 3 6 *any* brother
1 Tm 4 4 ⌜everything God has created (lit. *every* creature)
Heb 5 1 *every* high priest
8 3 *every* high priest
10 11 ⌜all the priests (lit. *every* priest)
1 Jn 4 2 *every* spirit
3 *any* spirit
Rv 5 9 *every* race
6 15 ⌜slaves and citizens (lit. *every* slave and citizen)
7 9 *every* nation, race, tribe, and language
13 7 *every* race, people, language and nation
14 6 *every* nation, race, language and tribe
16 3 *every* living creature

c) *All* = *Entire, As a whole*

(*applied to the Jewish people*)

Mt 27 25 the people *to a man*
Lk 2 10 the *whole* people
3 21 2 *all* the people
7 29 *all* the people
8 47 *all* the people
9 13 *all* these people
18 43 *all* the people
19 48 2 the people *as a whole*
20 6 2 the people . . . *all*
45 *all* the people
21 38 *all* the people
24 19 the *whole* people
Jn 8 2 *all* the people
Ac 3 9 ⌜everyone (lit. *all* the people)
11 ⌜everyone (lit *all* the people)
4 10 the *whole* people of Israel
5 34 the *whole* people
10 41 the *whole* people
13 24 the *whole* people of Israel
25 24 2 the *whole* Jewish community
Heb 9 19 *all* the people
— *all* the people

(*applied to the crowd*)

Mt 13 2 The people *all*
Mk 2 13 *all* the people
4 1 The people . . . *all*
9 15 the *whole* crowd
11 18 *all* the people
Lk 1 10 the *whole* congregation
6 19 ⌜everyone in the (lit. the *whole*) crowd
Lk 8 37 2 the *entire* population
13 17 *all* the people
19 37 2 the *whole* group of disciples
23 1 2 the *whole* assembly
Ac 21 27 the *whole* crowd

(*various*)

Mt 2 3 the *whole* of Jerusalem
8 34 the *whole* town
21 10 the *whole* city
Mk 1 5 *all* Judaea
16 15 2 the *whole* world
— *all* creation
Lk 2 1 the *whole* world
Ac 2 36 the *whole* House of Israel
5 21 the *full* Senate of Israel
6 5 the *whole* assembly
7 14 his *whole* family
10 2 the *whole* of his household
11 14 your *entire* household
Ac 13 44 the *whole* town
15 12 the *entire* assembly
17 26 the *whole* human race
20 28 *all* the flock [of believers]
22 5 the *whole* council of elders
30 the *entire* Sanhedrin
Rm 3 19 the *whole* world
4 16 *all* of Abraham's descendants
11 26 ⌜the rest (lit. *all*) of Israel
Col 1 6 ⌜all over the (lit. over the *whole*) world

2: ALL (THINGS)

a) *All, Everything, the Whole – Whatever* (*as a pronoun or used with a pronoun*)

Mt 4 9 I will give you *all* these
5 18 not one dot . . . shall disappear from the Law until ⌜its purpose (lit. *all*) is achieved.
6 32 It is the pagans who set their hearts on *all* these [things].
2 Your heavenly Father knows you need them *all*.
33 *all* these [other things] will be given you as well.
7 12 ⌜always treat others as you would like them to treat you (lit. do *all* that you would like others to do);
8 33 The swineherds . . . told the *whole* [story],
11 27 *Everything* has been entrusted to me by my Father;
13 34 In *all* this Jesus spoke to the crowds in parables;
44 he . . . sells ᵛ *everything*⌝ (or: what) he owns
46 he . . . sells *everything* he owns
51 Have you understood *all* this?
56 where did the man get it *all*?
15 17 *whatever* goes into the mouth passes through the stomach
17 11 Elijah is to come to see that *everything* is once more as it should be;
18 25 his master gave orders that he should be sold together with . . . *all* ⌜his possessions (lit. that he possessed),
26 I will pay the *whole* [sum].
31 they went to their master and reported the *whole* [affair] to him.
19 20 I have kept *all* these.
26 for God *everything* is possible.
21 22 if you have faith, *everything* you ask for in prayer you will receive.
22 4 *everything* is ready. Come to the wedding.
23 3 You must therefore do ⌜what (lit. *everything*) they tell you
20 he is swearing by [the altar] and by *everything* on it.
36 *all* of this will recoil on this generation.
24 2 You see *all* these? . . . not a single stone here will be left on another:
8 *All* this is only the beginning of the birthpangs.
33 So with you when you see *all* these [things];
34 before this generation has passed away *all* these [things] will have taken place.
28 11 2 to tell the chief priests *all* that had happened.
20 teach them to observe *all* [the commands] I gave you.
Mk 3 28 ⌜all men's sins will be forgiven (lit. *all* will be forgiven to men)
4 11 to those who are outside *everything* comes in parables,
34 he explained *everything* to his disciples when they were alone.
5 26 [the sick woman] had spent *all* she had
6 30 The apostles . . . told him *all* they had done
7 37 He has done *all* [things] well,
8 25 2 [the blind man] could see *everything* plainly
9 12 Elijah is to come first and to see that *everything* is as it should be;
23 *Everything* is possible for anyone who has faith

Mk 10 20   I have kept *all* these from my earliest days.
      27   *everything* is possible for God.
      28   We have left *everything*
  11 11   [Jesus] looked ʳall (lit. at *everything*) round him,
      24   *everything* you ask and pray for,
  12 44   [the widow] has put in [to the treasury] *everything* she possessed,
  13 4   what sign will there be that *all* this is about to be fulfilled?
      23   I have forewarned you of *everything*.
      30   before this generation has passed away *all* these [things] will have taken place.
  14 36   Father! . . . *Everything* is possible for you.
Lk 1 3   after carefully going over *the whole* [story] from the beginning,
  2 20   praising God for *all* they had heard and seen;
      39   When they had done *everything* the Law of the Lord required,
  5 11   they left *everything* and followed him.
      28   leaving *everything* [Levi] got up and followed him.
  7 18   The disciples of John ʳgave him all this news (lit. informed him of *all* this),
  9 7   Herod . . . had heard about *all* that was going on;
      43   everyone was full of admiration for *all* he did,
  10 22   *Everything* has been entrusted to me by my Father;
  11 41   and then indeed *everything* will be clean for you.
  12 30   It is the pagans . . . who set their hearts on *all* these [things].
  15 13   the younger son got together *everything* he had
      14   When he had spent it *all*,
      31   My son, . . . *all* I have is yours.
  16 14   The Pharisees . . . heard *all* this
      26   But that is not *all*;
  17 10   when you have done *all* you have been told to do,
  18 12   I pay tithes on *all* I get.
      21   I have kept *all* these from my earliest days
      22   Sell *all* that you own
      31   *everything* that is written by the prophets about the Son of Man
  21 12   before *all* this happens,
      22   when *all* that scripture says must be fulfilled.
      32   before this generation has passed away *all* will have taken place.
      36   praying at all times for the strength to survive *all* that is going to happen,
  24 9   When the women returned from the tomb they told *all* this to the Eleven
      14   they were talking together about *all* that had happened.
      21   And this is not *all*:
      25   You foolish men! So slow to believe ʳthe full message of the prophets (lit. *all* that the prophets foretold)!
      44   *everything* written about me in the Law of Moses,
Jn 1 3   Through him *all* [things] came to be,
  3 31   He who comes from above is above ʳall [others] (or: *all* [things]); . . . He who comes from heaven (§ is above ʳall [others]; or: *all* [things]))
      35   The Father loves the Son and has entrusted *everything* to him.
  4 25   2 when [the Messiah] comes he will tell us *everything*.
      29   Come and see a man who has told me *everything* I ever did;
      39   He told me *all* I have ever done,
      45   the Galileans received him well, having seen *all* that he had done at Jerusalem
  5 20   the Father loves the Son and shows him *everything* he does himself,
  6 37   *All* that the Father gives me will come to me,
  10 29   The Father who gave them to me is greater than *all*,
      41   *all* [John] said about [Jesus] was true;
  12 32   I shall draw ʳall [men] (ᵛ *everything*) to myself.
  13 3   Jesus knew that the Father had put *everything* into his hands,
  14 26   the Holy Spirit . . . will teach you *everything* and remind you of *all* I have said to you.
  15 15   I have made known to you *everything* I have learnt from my Father.
      21   it will be on my account that they will do *all* this,
  16 15   *Everything* the Father has is mine;
      30   Now we see that you know *everything*,
  17 7   they know that *all* you have given me comes indeed from you;
      10   *all* I have is yours
  18 4   Knowing *everything* that was going to happen to him, Jesus then came forward
  19 28   Jesus knew that *everything* had now been completed,
  21 17   Lord, you know *everything*; you know I love you,
Ac 1 1   In my earlier work . . . I dealt with *everything* Jesus had done and taught
  2 44   2 The faithful . . . owned *everything* in common;
  3 21   heaven must keep [Jesus] till the ʳuniversal restoration (lit. restoration of *everything*) comes
      22   (cf. Dt 18 18–19) you must listen to *whatever* he tells you.
  4 24   it is you who have made heaven and earth and sea, and *everything* in them;
      32   *everything* [the believers] owned was held in common.
  7 50   (Is 66 2) Was not *all* this made by my hand?
  10 8   2 Cornelius . . . told them ʳwhat (lit. *all* that) had happened.
      33   Here we all are, assembled in front of you to hear ʳwhat message (lit. *all* that) God has given you for us.

Ac 10 39   I, and those with me, can witness to *everything* [Jesus] did
  11 10   2 *the whole* [of it] was drawn up to heaven again.
  13 29   When they had carried out *everything*
      38   justification from *all* [sins] which the Law of Moses was unable to justify
  14 15   God who made heaven and earth and the sea and *all* that these hold.
  17 24   the God who made the world and *everything* in it
      25   it is he who gives *everything* . . . to everyone.
  22 10   go into Damascus, and there you will be told ʳwhat (lit. *all*) you have been appointed to do.
  24 8   you can find out for yourself the truth ʳof all our accusations against this man (lit. about *all* that we accuse this man of).
      14   retaining my belief in *all* ʳpoints of (lit. that there is in) the Law
  26 2   *all* ʳthe charges made against me by the Jews (lit. the Jews charge me with),
Rm 8 28   ʳby turning *everything* to their good God co-operates with (ᵛ *everything* turns to the good of) [all] those who love him,
      32   [God] will not refuse us *anything*
      37   *All* [these] are the trials through which we triumph,
  9 5   Christ who is above *all*,
  11 36   *All* that exists comes from him;
  14 2   those who believe they may eat ʳany sort of meat (lit. *everything*)
      20   Of course *all* [food] is clean,
      23   ʳevery act done in bad faith (lit. *everything* that does not proceed from [good] faith) is a sin.
1 Co 1 5   I thank [God] that you have been enriched in ʳso many ways (lit. *everything*)
  2 10   the Spirit reaches the depths of *everything*,
      15   A spiritual man . . . is able to judge the value of *everything*,
  3 21   *everything* is yours: 22 Paul, Apollos, Cephas, the world, life and death, the present and the future, are *all* yours;
      22
  6 12   ʳFor me there are no forbidden things (lit. To me *everything* is permitted)'; maybe, but not *everything* does good. I agree ʳthere are no forbidden things for (lit. *everything* is permitted to) me, but I am not going to let anything dominate me.
  8 6   one God, the Father, from whom ʳall things come (lit. *everything* comes) . . . and there is one Lord, Jesus Christ, through whom ʳall things come (lit. *everything* comes)
  9 12   we have put up with ʳanything (lit. *everything*) rather than obstruct the Good News of Christ in any way.
      22   I made myself *all* [things] to all [men]
      23   and I still do [*all*] this, for the sake of the gospel,
      25   All the fighters . . . ʳgo into strict training (lit. keep away from *everything*);
  10 23   ʳFor me there are no forbidden things (lit. To me *everything* is permitted)'; but not *everything* does good. True, ʳthere are no forbidden things (lit. *everything* is permitted), but it is not *everything* that helps the building to grow.
      25   ʳDo not hesitate to eat anything (lit. Eat *everything*) that is sold in butchers' shops:
      27   eat *whatever* is put in front of you,
      31   whatever you do . . . do [it] *all* for the glory of God.
  11 12   woman . . . man . . . —*everything* comes from God.
  12 6   it is the same God who is ʳworking (lit. doing *everything*) in all of them.
      11   ʳAll these are (lit. *All* this is) the work of one and the same Spirit,
      19   If *all the parts* were the same, how could it be a body?
  13 7   [love] ʳis always ready to excuse, to trust, to hope, and to endure whatever comes (lit. excuses *everything*, trusts *everything*, hopes *everything*, and endures *everything*).
  14 26   but it must ʳalways (lit. *all*) be for the common good.
      40   let *everything* be done with propriety
  15 26   (Ps 8 6) *everything* is to be put under [Christ's] feet.
      27   ²⁷ – Though when it is said that *everything* is subjected, this clearly cannot include the One who subjected *everything* to him. ²⁸ And when *everything* is subjected to him, the Son himself will be subject . . . to the One who subjected *all* [things] to him, so that God may be *all* in all.
      28
  16 14   Let *everything* you do be done in love.
2 Co 4 15   *all* this is for your benefit,
  5 18   [The old creation is gone, and now the new one is here.] It is *all* God's work.
  6 10   [we are taken] for people having nothing though we have *everything*.
Ga 3 10   (Dt 27 26) Cursed be everyone who does not persevere in observing *everything* prescribed in . . . the Law.
      22   scripture ʳmakes no exceptions (lit. covers *everything*)
  4 1   an heir, even if he has actually inherited *everything*, is no different from slave
Ep 1 10   that [God] would bring *everything* together under Christ, as head, [everything] in the heavens and [everything] on earth.
      11   the one who guides *all* [things]

Ep	1 22	(Ps 8 6) [God] has put *all* [things] under [Christ's] feet, and made him, as the ruler of *everything*, the head of the Church; ²³ which is his body, the fullness of him who fills ⌐the *whole* creation (lit. *all* in all).
	23	
	3 9	God, the creator of *everything*.
	20	Glory be to him whose power . . . can do infinitely more than [*all*] we can ask or imagine;
	4 10	The one who rose higher than all the heavens to fill *all* [things]
	5 13	*anything* exposed by the light will be illuminated ¹⁴ and *anything* illuminated turns into light.
	14	
	20	so that ⌐always (lit. for *everything*) and everywhere you are giving thanks to God who is our Father
	6 13	2 [you will not] ⌐have enough resources to (lit. having done *all*) hold your ground.
	21	Tychicus . . . will tell you *everything*.
Ph	2 14	Do *all* [that has to be done] without complaining
	3 8	⌐nothing can happen higher that will (lit. the loss of *everything* could not) outweigh . . . knowing Christ Jesus my Lord. For him I have accepted the loss of *everything*.
	21	the same power with which we can subdue ⌐the *whole* universe (lit. *everything*).
	4 13	⌐There is nothing I cannot master (lit. I can master *everything*) with the help of the One who gives me strength.
	18	I have *everything* that I need
Col	1 16	in him ⌐were created all things (lit. was created *everything*) in heaven and on earth: [*everything*] visible and [*everything*] invisible, . . . ⌐all things were (lit. *everything* was) created through him and for him. ¹⁷Before *anything* was created, he existed, and he holds *all things* in unity.
	17	
	20	[God wanted] *all* [things] to be reconciled through him and for him,
	2 22	things that [*all*] perish by their very use
	3 8	you, of all people, must give *all* these [things] up: getting angry, . . . dirty talk;
	11	There is only Christ: he is *everything* and he is in everything.
	14	Over *all* these [clothes] . . . put on love.
	17	⌐never say or do anything except (lit. *Whatever* you can say or do, [say and do] *everything*) in the name of the Lord Jesus,
	4 7	Tychicus will tell you *all* [the news] about me.
	9	They will tell you *everything* that is happening here.
1 Th	4 6	the Lord always punishes ⌐sins (lit. *everything*) of that sort.
	5 21	think before you do *anything*—hold on to what is good.
2 Th	2 4	the Enemy, the one who claims to be so much greater than *all* that men call 'god',
1 Tm	2 2	first of *all*, there should be prayers
	4 8	⌐the usefulness of spirituality is unlimited (lit. spirituality is useful in *everything*),
	6 13	God ⌐the source of life (lit. who gives life to *everything*)
	17	God who . . . gives us *all* that we need for our happiness.
2 Tm	2 10	I bear it *all* for the sake of those who are chosen,
Tt	1 15	To all who are pure themselves, *everything* is pure;
Heb	1 2	the Son that [God] has appointed to inherit *everything*
	3	[The Son] is . . . the perfect copy of [God's] nature, sustaining the *universe* by his powerful command.
	11	(Ps 102 26–27) *all* will vanish, though you remain,
	2 8	(Ps 8 6) You have put him in command of *everything*. Well then, if he has put him in command of *everything*, . . . At present . . . we are not able to see that *everything* has been put under his command.
	10	God, for whom *everything* exists and through whom *everything* exists,
	3 4	God built *everything* that exists.
	4 13	*everything* is uncovered
	7 2	it was to [Melchizedek] that Abraham gave a tenth of *all* that he had.
	8 5	(cf. Ex 25 40) See that you make *everything* according to the pattern shown you on the mountain.
	9 22	almost *everything* has to be purified with blood;
Jm	2 10	if a man keeps the whole of the Law, except for one small point . ., he is still guilty of breaking it *all*.
1 P	4 7	*Everything* will soon come to an end,
2 P	1 3	he has given us *all* [the things] that we need for life
	3 4	*Everything* goes on as it has since the Fathers died,
	11	*everything* is coming to an end
1 Jn	2 16	⌐nothing (lit. *everything*) the world has to offer . . . could ⌐ever (lit. *never*) come from the Father
	27	the anointing he gave teaches you *everything*;
	3 20	God . . . knows *everything*.
	5 4	⌐everyone who has been (lit. *everything* which is) begotten by God has already overcome the world;
Jude	5	you have already learnt ⌐it (lit. *all* this) once and for all
Rv	4 11	you made all the *universe*
	5 13	then I heard *all* [the living things] in creation – ⌐everything (lit. every creature) that lives in the air, and on the ground, and under the ground, and in the sea, crying,
	21 5	Now I am making ⌐the *whole* of creation (lit. *everything*) new

b) All (as an adjective)

Mt	10 30	⌐every hair (lit. *all* the hairs)
	13 32	*all* the seeds

Mt	13 41	*all* things that provoke offences
	23 5	⌐Everything they do (lit. *All* their actions)
	24 47	⌐everything he owns (lit. *all* his goods)
	26 1	⌐all he wanted to say (lit. *all* his sermons)
Mk	4 13	⌐any of (lit. *all*) the parables
	31	*all* the seeds
	32	⌐the biggest shrub of them all (lit. the biggest of *all* the shrubs)
	7 19	*all* foods
	23	*all* these evil things
	12 28	*all* the commandments
	33	⌐any holocaust (lit. *all* the holocausts)
Lk	1 6	*all* the commandments
	65	⌐the *whole* affair (lit. *all* the events)
	2 19	*all* these ⌐things (lit. events)
	51	*all* these ⌐things (lit. events)
	3 19	*all* the [other] crimes
	20	*all* the ⌐rest (lit. crimes)
	7 1	*all* ⌐he wanted these people to hear (lit. these words)
	12 7	⌐every hair (lit. *all* the hairs)
	44	⌐everything he owns (lit. *all* his possessions)
	13 17	*all* the wonders
	14 33	*all* his possessions
	19 37	*all* the miracles
	21 29	⌐every tree (lit. *all* trees)
	24 27	*all* the prophets
Jn	10 4	*all* his own flock
Ac	1 18	*all* his entrails
	5 20	*all* ⌐about (lit. the words of) this new Life.
	7 10	*all* his miseries
	10 12	⌐every possible sort (lit. *all* sorts) of animal
	13 22	⌐my *whole* purpose (lit. *all* my wishes)
	16 26	*all* the doors
	26 3	⌐matters of custom (lit. *all* the customs) and controversy
Rm	12 4	⌐each part [of the body] (lit. *all* parts)
1 Co	12 12	*all* these parts [of the body]
	26	*all* parts [of the body]
	13 2	*all* the mysteries
	— 3	⌐all that I possess (lit. *all* my possessions)
Ep	6 16	*all* the burning arrows of the evil one
Ph	1 4	⌐every time I pray (lit. *all* my prayers)
Col	2 3	*all* the jewels
	13	*all* our sins
2 Th	1 4	*all* the persecutions
1 Tm	6 10	*all* evils
2 Tm	3 11	[*all*] the persecutions
Heb	4 4	*all* his ⌐work (lit. works)
	9 21	*all* the liturgical vessels
1 Jm	8	wavering between going ⌐different (lit. *all*) ways
2 P	3 16	⌐his letter (lit. *all* his letters)
Jude	15	*all* the wicked things they have done
	—	*all* the defiant things said
Rv	18 14	⌐your life (lit. *all* the things) of magnificence and ease.
	19 17	*all* the birds
	21	*all* the birds

c) All = the Whole

Mt	6 29	*all* his regalia
	8 32	the *whole* herd
	18 32	*all* that debt
	34	*all* his debt
Mk	5 33	the *whole* truth
Lk	4 6	2 *all* this power
	7	⌐it shall all (lit. *all* this will) be yours
	10 19	the *whole* strength
	12 18	*all* my grain
	27	*all* his regalia
	21 4	*all* she had to live on
Jn	5 22	*all* judgement
	16 13	the *complete* truth
Ac	7 22	*all* the wisdom
	8 27	⌐treasurer (lit. guard over *all* her treasures)
	12 11	*all* [the Jewish people's expectations]
	20 27	the *whole* of God's purpose
Rm	8 22	the *entire* creation
	15 14	⌐perfectly well instructed (lit. filled with *all* knowledge)
1 Co	13 2	⌐knowing everything (lit. *all* knowledge)
	—	faith *in all its fullness*
2 Co	1 4	*all* our ⌐sorrows (lit. sorrow)
	7 4	*all* our trouble
	9 8	⌐all you need (lit. *all* sufficiency)
Ga	5 14	the *whole* of the Law
Ep	3 19	the *utter* fullness of God
	4 16	the *whole* body
Col	1 19	*all* perfection
	2 9	⌐your own fulfilment (lit. *all* perfection)
	19	the *whole* body
1 Th	3 9	*all* the joy
1 Tm	1 16	2 *all* his inexhaustible patience
1 P	1 24	*all* its glory

1 P	5	7	*all* your worries
Rv	13	12	⌐*extended its authority* (lit. exercised *all* its power)

d) All = Perfect, Full, Complete

Mt	3	15	*all* [that] righteousness [demands]
Ac	4	29	*all* boldness
	5	23	⌐*securely locked* (lit. locked with *complete* security)
	17	11	⌐*very readily* (lit. with *complete* readiness)
	20	19	*all* humility
	23	1	a *perfectly* clear conscience
	28	31	*complete* freedom
2 Co	12	12	⌐*unfailingly produced* (lit. produced in *all* patience)
Ep	1	8	*all* wisdom
	4	2	*complete* selflessness
	6	18	⌐on every possible occasion (lit. with *all* prayer)
Ph	1	9	⌐*deepening your perception* (lit. in *all* judgement)
		20	⌐*have the courage* (lit. act with *perfect* boldness)
	2	29	⌐*a most hearty welcome* (lit. a welcome with *all* gladness)
Col	1	9	*perfect* wisdom
		10	a life acceptable . . . in *all* its aspects
		11	⌐*never to give in, but* (lit. with *complete* patience)
		28	*perfect* wisdom
	2	2	*full* development
		3	*all* wisdom
1 Tm	1	15	⌐*nobody should doubt* (lit. worthy of *complete* acceptance)
	3	4	⌐*and be well-behaved* (lit. in *all* propriety)
	4	9	⌐*nobody should doubt it* (lit. worthy of *complete* acceptance)
	5	2	with *all* propriety
	6	1	*unqualified* respect
2 Tm	4	2	with *all* patience
Tt	2	10	*complete* honesty
		15	*full* authority
	3	2	⌐*and always polite* (lit. with *complete* politeness)
Jm	1	2	⌐*a happy privilege* (lit. *perfect* happiness)
1 P	2	18	⌐*and obedient* (lit. in *complete* obedience)
2 P	1	5	⌐*do your utmost* (lit. act with *perfect* zeal)
Jude		3	⌐*eagerly* (lit. in *all* eagerness)

e) All, Any (generally)

Mt	3	10	*any* tree
	4	4	*every* word
		23	*all kinds of* disease
		—	[*all kinds of*] sickness
	5	11	*all kinds of* calumny
	7	17	*every* sound tree
		19	*any* tree
	9	35	*all kinds of* diseases
		—	[*all kinds of*] sickness
	10	1	*all kinds of* diseases
		—	[*all kinds of*] sickness
	12	31	*everyone* of man's sins
		36	*every* unfounded word
	13	47	*all* kinds
	15	13	*any* plant
	18	16	*any* charge
		19	ask *anything* at all
	19	3	*any* pretext *whatever*
	23	27	*every kind of* corruption
		35	⌐the blood of every holy man (lit. *all* the holy blood)
	28	18	*all* authority
Lk	3	9	*any* tree
	4	13	*all* these ways of tempting
	11	42	*all sorts of* garden herbs
	12	15	avarice *of any kind*
Jn	15	2	*every* branch
Ac	13	10	⌐*utter fraud* (lit. full of *all* treachery)
		—	⌐*impostor* (lit. full of *all* facile ways)
		—	*all* true religion
	24	3	*all* gratitude
	27	20	*all* hope
Rm	1	18	*all* impiety
		29	*all sorts of* depravity
	7	8	*all kinds of* covetousness
	15	13	⌐such (lit. *all*) joy and peace
1 Co	1	5	enriched in . . . ⌐your teachers (lit. *all* teaching)
		—	⌐preachers (lit. *all* knowledge)
	6	18	*all* ⌐the other sins (lit. sin)
2 Co	1	3	*all* consolation
		4	*all* our ⌐sorrows (lit. sorrow)
	4	2	*every* human being with a conscience
	7	1	*all* that can soil
	8	7	⌐the most (lit. *all*) keenness
	9	8	*no limit to* the blessings
		—	*all sorts of* good works
		11	*all* the generous things
	10	5	⌐the arrogance (lit. *every* arrogant thing)
		—	*every* thought
		6	*any* disobedience

2 Co	13	1	⌐the (lit. *every*) charge
Ga	6	6	contribute ⌐something (lit. in *all* good things)
Ep	1	3	*all* ⌐the spiritual blessings (lit. spiritual blessing)
	2	21	*every* structure
	3	15	*every* family
	4	14	*every* wind
		19	indecency *of every kind*
		31	⌐Never have (lit. Do not have *any*) grudges
			any sort of spitefulness
	5	3	impurity *in any of its forms*
		9	*complete* goodness
	6	18	praying . . . on *every* possible occasion
Ph	1	3	⌐whenever I think of you (lit. at *every* recollection)
	4	7	greater than ⌐we can understand (lit. *all* understanding)
		19	*all* ⌐your needs (lit. need)
Col	1	10	*all* the good actions
		11	*all* the strength
	4	12	*all* the will of God
1 Th	3	7	*all* our own troubles
	5	22	*every* form
2 Th	1	11	⌐all your desires (lit. *every* desire)
	2	9	*all kinds of* miracles
		10	*everything* evil that can deceive
		17	*everything* good
	3	17	*every* letter
1 Tm	5	10	*all kinds of* good work
2 Tm	2	21	*any* good work
	3	16	*all* scripture
		17	*any* good work
	4	18	*all* evil attempts
Tt	1	16	incapable of ⌐doing good (lit. *any* good work)
	2	14	*all* wickedness
	3	1	do ⌐good at every opportunity (lit. *every* good work)
Phm		6	*all* the good things
Heb	2	2	*every* disobedience
	3	4	*every* house
	4	12	*any* sword
	6	16	*all* dispute
	9	19	*all* the commandments
	12	1	*everything* that hinders us
		11	*any* punishment
	13	21	*any kind of* good action
Jm	1	17	*all* that is good
			everything that is perfect
		21	*all* ⌐the impurities (lit. impurity)
	3	7	*All* wild animals and birds
		16	wicked things *of every kind*
	4	16	*All* pride of this kind
1 P	1	15	*all* you do
	2	1	you ⌐are never (lit. do not do *anything*) spiteful
		—	or *anything* deceitful
		—	or say *anything* critical of each other
		13	*every* social institution
	5	10	*all* grace
1 Jn	1	7	*all* sin
		9	*everything* that is wrong
	4	1	*every* spirit
	5	17	*every kind of* wrong-doing
Rv			⌐everyone (lit. *every* eye)
	5	13	*all* the living things in creation
	7	17	*all* tears
	8	7	*every* blade of grass
	11	6	*any* plague
	18	2	*every* foul spirit
		—	[*every*] loathsome bird
		12	*all* the sandalwood
		—	*every* piece in ivory
		—	[*every* piece in] fine wood
	21	4	*all* tears
		19	*all kinds of* precious stone

f) Certainly, No doubt – In every way, In everything – At all, Completely

Lk	4	23	3 *No doubt* you will quote me the saying,
Ac	17	22	how extremely scrupulous you are in *all* [religious] *matters*
	18	21	3 (ᵛ It is *absolutely* necessary for me to keep the coming feast in Jerusalem)
	20	35	I did ⌐this (lit. *everything*) to show you that this is how
	21	22	3 *Inevitably* there will be a meeting of the whole body,
	24	3	[the unbroken peace and reforms] are matters we accept
		6	⌐always (lit. in *everything*) and everywhere,
	28	4	3 That man ⌐must be (lit. is *certainly*) a murderer;
Rm	3	2	[Is there any advantage in being circumcised?] A great advantage in *every* way.
		9	3 are we any better off? Not *at all*?
1 Co	5	10	3 I was not meaning to *include all* . . . who are sexually immoral
	9	10	3 *Clearly* this was written for our sake
		22	3 in order to save some [people] ⌐at any cost (lit. *completely*);
	10	33	I try to be helpful to everyone ⌐at all times (lit. in *everything*),

1 Co	11 2	You have done well in remembering me ʳso constantly (lit. in everything)
	16 12	ʳhe was quite firm that he did not want to go yet (lit. he did
	3	not at all want to go yet)
2 Co	2 9	to . . . see whether you are completely obedient.
	4 8	We are in difficulties ʳon all sides (lit. in everything),
	6 4	we prove [in everything that] we are servants of God
	7 11	In every way you have shown yourselves blameless in this affair.
	14	as true as anything we ever said to you.
	16	I am very happy knowing that I can rely on you [so] completely.
	8 7	You always have the most of everything
	9 8	[God] will make sure that you will always have all you need for yourselves in every possible circumstance.
	11	made richer in every way,
	11 6	surely we have made this plain, speaking on every subject and ʳin front of all of you (or: in every way).
	9	I was very careful . . . not to be a burden to you in any way,
Ep	1 23	[the Church] is his body, the fullness of him who fills ʳthe whole creation (or: everything completely).
	4 15	we shall grow in all ways into Christ,
	5 24	so should wives [submit] to their husbands, in everything.
	6 16	ʳalways (lit. in all things) carrying the shield of faith
Ph	1 18	ʳwhether from dishonest motives or in sincerity (lit. In every way)
	4 6	ʳif there is anything you need (lit. in everything), pray
	12	I am ready for anything anywhere.
Col	1 18	[Christ] should be first in every way;
	3 11	There is only Christ: he is everything and he is in everything.
	20	Children, be obedient to your parents ʳalways (lit. in everything),
	22	Slaves, be obedient [in everything] to . . . your masters
1 Th	5 18	for all things give thanks to God,
2 Th	3 16	May the Lord of peace himself give you peace all the time and in every way.
1 Tm	2 1	first of all, there should be prayers offered for everyone
	3 11	the women must be respectable [in every way],
2 Tm	2 7	the Lord will show you how to understand all that (lit. completely).
	4 5	Be careful ʳalways (lit. in everything) [to choose the right course;]
Tt	2 7	in everything you do, make yourself an example
	9	the slaves . . . are to be obedient [in everything] to their
	10	masters . . . ¹⁰ . . . so that they are in every way a credit to the teaching of God
Heb	2 17	It was essential that [Christ] should [in this way] become completely like his brothers
	4 15	we have [a high priest] who has been tempted in every way that we are,
	13 18	we are certainly determined to behave honourably in everything [we do];
Jm	5 12	Above all, . . . do not swear
1 P	4 8	Above all, never let your love for each other grow insincere,
	11	so that in everything God may receive the glory,
3 Jn	2	I hope ʳeverything is going happily with you (lit. you are well in everything)

3: ALL (PLACES)

a) All = the Whole

Mt	2 16	all its surrounding district	Ac	1 8	ʳthroughout (lit. through all) Judaea
	3 5	all Judaea		17 26	the entire earth
	—	the whole Jordan district		19 26	ʳeverywhere in (lit. in all) Asia
	27 45	all the land		26 20	all the countryside of Judaea
Lk	3 3	the whole Jordan district	Rm	9 17	ʳthroughout (lit. through all) the world
	4 25	ʳthroughout the (lit. through the whole) land		10 18	through all the earth
	6 17	all [parts of] Judaea	Rv	5 6	ʳall over (lit. over all) the world
	7 17	ʳall over (lit. over all) the countryside			
	21 35	on ʳthe face of (lit. all) the			

b) All (places), Every (place), Everywhere – From, on, all sides – All round, All over

Mt	4 8	the devil showed [Jesus] all the kingdoms of the world
	35	Jesus made a tour through all the towns and villages,
	19 25	Every kingdom divided against itself is heading for ruin,
Mk	21 28	4 [Jesus's] reputation rapidly spread everywhere, through all the surrounding Galilean countryside.
	45	5 people from all around would come to him.
	6 33	from every town they all hurried to the place on foot
	16 20	4 while they, going out, preached everywhere,
Lk	3 5	Every valley will be filled in, every mountain and hill be laid low,

Lk	4 5	the devil showed [Jesus] . . . all the kingdoms of the world
	37	reports of [Jesus] went ʳall through (lit. through all) the surrounding countryside.
	5 17	among the audience there were Pharisees and doctors of the Law who came from every village in Galilee,
	9 6	they set out and went from village to village proclaiming
	4	the Good News and healing everywhere.
	10 1	the Lord appointed seventy-two others and sent them out . . . to all the towns and places he himself was to visit.
	11 17	Every kingdom divided against itself is heading for ruin,
	19 43	5 [Jerusalem,] your enemies will raise fortifications all round you,
Ac	8 40	proclaiming the Good News in every town as far as Caesarea
	9 32	Peter ʳvisited one place after another (lit. went through every place; or: went to everyone)
	15 36	Let us go back and visit all the towns where we preached the word of the Lord,
	17 30	4 [God] is telling everyone everywhere that they must repent,
	21 28	7 This is the man who preaches to everyone everywhere against our people,
	24 3	[the unbroken peace and reforms] are matters we accept,
	4	always and everywhere,
	26 11	I often went ʳround (lit. into all) the synagogues inflicting penalties,
	28 22	4 all we know about this sect is that opinion everywhere condemns it.
1 Co	1 2	to the holy people of Jesus Christ, who are called to take their place among the saints ʳeverywhere (lit. in every place)
	4 17	Timothy . . . will remind you of the way that I live in Christ,
	4	as I teach it everywhere
2 Co	2 14	God who . . . is spreading the knowledge of himself, like a sweet smell, ʳeverywhere (lit. in all places).
	7 5	we found trouble on all sides;
Ep	4 10	The one who rose higher than all the heavens
Ph	1 13	My chains . . . have become famous not only all over the Praetorium but ʳeverywhere (lit. in all other [places]),
1 Th	1 8	news of your faith in God has spread ʳeverywhere (lit. in all places).
1 Tm	2 8	In every place . . . I want the men to lift their hands up reverently in prayer,
Heb	9 4	5 the ark of the covenant, plated all over with gold.
Rv	6 14	all the mountains and (§ all [the]) islands were shaken from their places.
	16 20	ʳEvery island (lit. All the islands) vanished

4: ALL (TIME)

Mt	28 20	always (lit. for all time)	Rm	14 5	ʳall days (lit. every day)
Lk	1 75	all our days	1 Co	15 30	ʳconstant threat (lit. threat all the time)
	21 36	at all times			
Ac	1 21	the whole time	Ep	3 21	ʳgeneration to (lit. every) generation
	5 42	every day			
	13 27	on every sabbath		6 18	all the time
	15 21	every sabbath	Heb	2 15	all their lives
	17 17	every day	Jude	25	before all time
	18 4	every sabbath		—	for ever
	20 18	ʳever (lit. all the time) since			

3. ANY, WHATEVER: HOIOS DĒPOTOUN

hoios dēpotoun 1

Jn	5 4	ᵛ . . . the first person to enter the water . . . was cured of any ailment he suffered from.

4. EACH, EACH ONE – EVERY, EVERY ONE: HEKASTOS

1 hekastos 65/80   3 heis hekastos 15
2 hekastote 1

Mt	16 27	when [the Son of Man] comes, he will reward each [one] according to his behaviour.
	18 35	unless you each forgive your brother from your heart.
	25 15	To [his servants] he gave . . . each in proportion to his ability.
	26 22	3 [The disciples] were greatly distressed and each one started asking him in turn,
Mk	13 34	[he] left his servants in charge, each with his own task;
Lk	2 3	everyone went each to his own town to be registered.
	4 40	3 laying his hands on each one [Jesus] cured them.
	6 44	every tree can be told by its own fruit:
	13 15	ʳIs there one of you who does not (lit. Each of you would) untie his ox
	16 5	3 Then he called his master's debtors ʳone by (lit. each) one.
Jn	6 7	Two hundred denarii would only buy enough to give them a small piece each.

Jn	7 53	They ˹all (lit. *each*) went home.
	16 32	you will be scattered, *each* going his own way and leaving me alone.
	19 23	they took [Jesus's] clothing and divided it into four shares, one for *each* soldier.
Ac	2 3	3 [the tongues of fire] came to rest on the head of *each one* of them.
	6	3 *each one* bewildered to hear these men speaking his own language.
	8	How does it happen that *each* of us hears them in his own native language?
	38	˹every one (lit. *each*) of you must be baptised in the name of Jesus Christ
	3 26	to bless you by turning every one (lit. *each*) of you from your wicked ways.
	4 35	[the money] was then distributed to ˹any members (lit. *each* [member]) who might be in need.
	11 29	The disciples decided to send relief, *each* to contribute what he could afford,
	17 27	3 [God] is not far from ˹any (lit. *each one*) of us,
	20 31	3 I never failed to keep you right, shedding tears over *each one* of you.
	21 19	[Paul] gave ˹a detailed account of all (lit. an account [of things] *each* individually) that God had done among the pagans
	26	3 the offering would have to be presented on behalf of *each one* of them.
Rm	2 6	He will repay *each* [one] as his works deserve.
	12 3	*Each* of you must judge himself soberly
	14 5	*each* must be left free to hold his own opinion.
	12	It is to God, therefore, that *each* of us must give an account of himself.
	15 2	*Each* of us should think of his neighbours and help them
1 Co	1 12	What I mean are ˹all these slogans that you have (lit. these things that *each* of you keeps saying) like: 'I am for Paul',
	3 5	the different ways in which they brought [the faith] were assigned to *each* of them by the Lord.
	8	*each* will duly be paid according to his share in the work.
	10	˹Everyone (lit. *Each* [one]) doing the building must work carefully.
	13	the work of *each* builder is going to be clearly revealed . . . the fire will test the quality of *each* man's work.
	4 5	Then will be the time for *each* [one] to have whatever praise he deserves.
	7 2	let *each* man have his own wife and *each* woman her own husband.
	7	˹everybody (lit. *each*) has his own particular gifts from God,
	17	what *each* [one] has is what the Lord has given him and ˹he (G *each*) should continue as he was
	20	Let ˹everyone (lit. *each*) stay as he was at the time of his call.
	24	*Each* [one] of you, my brothers, should stay as he was
	11 21	when the time comes to eat, ˹everyone (lit. *each*) is in such a hurry to start his own supper
	12 7	The particular way in which the Spirit is given to *each* [person] is for a good purpose.
	11	[the same Spirit] distributes different gifts to ˹different people (lit. *each*) just as he chooses.
	18	3 God put ˹all the separate (lit. *each one* of the) parts into the body
	14 26	At all your meetings, let ˹everyone (lit. *each*) be ready with a psalm
	15 23	˹all of them in their (lit. *each* in his) proper order: Christ as the first-fruits
	38	*each* sort of seed gets its own sort of body.
	16 2	Every Sunday, *each* [one] of you must put aside what he can afford,
2 Co	5 10	*each* of us will get what he deserves for the things he did in the body,
	9 7	*Each* [one] should give what he has decided in his own mind,
Ga	6 4	Let *each* of you examine his own conduct;
	5	˹Everyone (lit. *Each*) has his own burden to carry.
Ep	4 7	3 *Each one* of us, however, has been given his own share of grace.
	16	3 every joint adding its own strength, for *each* ˹separate part (lit. *one*) to work according to its function.
	25	(Zc 8 16) You too, *each* must speak the truth to one another,
	5 33	you too, *each* ˹one of you (lit. individually), must love his wife
	6 8	˹everyone (lit. *each*), whether a slave or a free man, will be properly rewarded by the Lord
Ph	2 4	so that ˹nobody thinks (lit. *each* does not think) of his own interests first but ˹everybody (lit. *each* [one]) thinks of other people's
Col	4 6	3 try to fit your answers to the needs of *each one*.
1 Th	2 11	3 we treated ˹every (lit. *each*) one of you as a father treats his children,
	4 4	[God wants] *each* [one] of you to know how to use the body that belongs to him
2 Th	1 3	3 the love *each one* of you has for one another never stops increasing;

Heb	3 13	˹Every (lit. *Each*) day . . . keep encouraging one another
	6 11	˹every one (lit. *each*) of you should go on showing the same earnestness to the end,
	8 11	There will be no further need for ˹neighbour (lit. *each* [one]) to try to teach [his] neighbour, or ˹brother (lit. *each* [one]) to say to [his] brother, . . . (Jr 31 34)
	11 21	Jacob, when he was dying, blessed *each* of Joseph's sons,
Jm	1 14	˹Everyone (lit. *Each*) who is tempted is attracted and seduced by his own wrong desire.
1 P	1 17	your Father . . . judges ˹everyone (lit. *each* [one]) according to what he has done,
	4 10	*Each* [one] of you has received a special grace,
2 P	1 15	after my own departure you will still have a means to recall these things to memory ˹at any (or: *each*) time.
Rv	2 23	I . . . give *each* [one] of you what your behaviour deserves.
	5 8	*each* of the twenty-four elders was holding a harp
	6 11	*Each* [of the martyrs] was given a white robe,
	20 13	˹every (lit. *each*) [one] was judged according to the way in which he had lived.
	21 21	3 The twelve gates were twelve pearls, *each one* of the gates being made of a single pearl,
	22 2	the trees of life, which bear twelve crops . . . in a year, one in *each* month,
	12	I shall be with you again, bringing the reward [for] ˹every (lit. *each*) man according to what he deserves.

WILL – WANT

1. Will – Want – Decide (to), Choose (to): *boulomai* 1: Purpose, Intention, Will (of God, Christ, the Spirit) – (God, the Spirit) Chooses (to), Wants 2: (a person) Wants (to), Would like (to) – (a person) Decides (to), Determines (to), Means (to) **2. Want – Will:** *thelō* 1: the Will (of God) – (God, the Lord) Wills, Wants – (God's) Purpose	2: (God and Jesus) Will, Would have – the Will (of God and Jesus) 3: (Jesus) Wants (to) 4: Want, Would like (to), Wish (to) **3. Of one's own free will, Willingly, By choice – Spontaneous, Deliberately:** *hekōn* **4. On one's own initiative, Spontaneously:** *auth-airetos*

1. WILL – WANT – DECIDE (TO), CHOOSE (TO): *BOULOMAI*

2 *boulē*	12	3 *bouleuomai*	2/6
4 *boulēma*	3	1 *boulomai*	37

1: PURPOSE, INTENTION, WILL (OF GOD, CHRIST, THE SPIRIT) – (GOD, THE SPIRIT) CHOOSES (TO), WANTS

Mt	11 27	X	no one knows the Father except the Son and those to whom the Son *chooses* to reveal him.
Lk	7 30	2	by refusing baptism from [John] the Pharisees and the lawyers had thwarted *what* God *had in mind* for them.
	10 22	X	no one knows . . . who the Father is except the Son and those to whom the Son *chooses* to reveal him.
	22 42		Father, . . . if you are *willing*, take this cup away from me.
Ac	2 23	2	[Jesus] was put into your power by the deliberate *intention* and foreknowledge of God,
	4 28	2	[This alliance against Jesus was] only to bring about the very thing that you in . . . your ˹wisdom (lit. *purpose*) had pre-determined should happen.
	13 36	2	when David in his own time had served God's *purpose* he died;
	20 27	2	I have . . . put before you the whole of God's *purpose*.
Rm	9 19	4	how can God ever blame anyone, since no one can oppose his *will*?
1 Co	12 11	Ⓢ	the same Spirit . . . distributes different gifts to different people just as he *chooses*.
Ep	1 11	2	we were . . . chosen . . . under the predetermined plan of the one who guides all things as he decides by ˹his own (lit. the *purpose* within his) will;
Heb	6 17	2	God *wanted* to make the heirs to the promise thoroughly realise that his *purpose* was unalterable,
Jm	1 18		By his own *choice* [the Father of all light] made us his children
2 P	3 9		[the Lord] is being patient with you all, *wanting* nobody to be lost

2: (A PERSON) WANTS (TO), WOULD LIKE (TO) – (A PERSON) DECIDES (TO), DETERMINES (TO), MEANS (TO)

Mt	1 19	Joseph . . . *decided* to divorce [Mary] informally.
Mk	15 15	Pilate, ⸢anxious (lit. *wishing*) to placate the crowd, released Barabbas for them
Lk	23 51	2 [Joseph] had not consented to *what the others had planned*
Jn	11 53	3 From that day they were *determined* to kill [Jesus].
	12 10	3 the chief priests *decided* to kill Lazarus as well,
	18 39	*would* you *like* me, then, to release the king of the Jews?
Ac	5 28	You . . . seem *determined* to fix the guilt of this man's death on us.
	33	they *wanted* to put [Peter and the apostles] to death.
	38	2 If this *enterprise* . . . is of human origin it will break up of its own accord;
	12 4	Herod *meant* to try Peter in public after the end of Passover week.
	15 37	Barnabas ⸢suggested taking (lit. *wanted* to take) John Mark,
	17 20	we *would like* to find out what [the things you said] mean.
	18 15	[Gallio said,] I *have* no *intention* of making legal decisions about things like that.
	27	When Apollos ⸢thought of crossing (lit. *decided* to cross) over to Achaia, the brothers encouraged him
	19 30	Paul *wanted* to make an appeal to the people,
	22 30	since [the tribune] *wanted* to know what precise charge the Jews were bringing [against Paul], he . . . gave orders for a meeting
	23 28	*Wanting* to find out what charge they were making against [Paul], I brought him before their Sanhedrin.
	25 20	I asked [Paul] if he *would be willing* to go to Jerusalem.
	22	I *should like* to hear the man myself.
	27 12	2 the majority *planned* (lit. *decided*) to put out from there
	42	2 The soldiers ⸢planned (lit. *decided*) to kill the prisoners
	43	But the centurion was *determined* to bring Paul safely through,
	4	and would not let them do *what they intended.*
	28 18	[the Romans] ⸢would have (lit. *wanted* to) set me free,
1 Co	4 5	2 [the Lord will] reveal the secret *intentions* of men's hearts.
2 Co	1 15	I had *meant* to come to you first . . . ¹⁷ Do you think I was
	17	not sure of my own *intentions* when I planned this?
Ph	1 12	⸢I am glad to tell you (lit. I *want* you to know) . . . that the things that happened to me have actually been a help to the Good News.
1 Tm	2 8	I *want* the men to lift their hands reverently in prayer,
	5 14	I *think it is best* for young widows to marry again
	6 9	People who *long* to be rich are a prey to temptation;
Tt	3 8	I *want* you to be quite uncompromising in teaching all this,
Phm	13	I *should have liked* to keep [Onesimus] with me;
Jm	3 4	the man at the helm can steer [the ships] anywhere he *likes* by controlling a tiny rudder.
	4 4	Anyone who *chooses* the world for his friend turns himself into God's enemy.
1 P	4 3	You spent quite long enough in the past living the sort of life
	4	that pagans *would like* to live,
2 Jn	12	There are several things I have to tell you, but I have *thought it best* not to trust them to paper and ink.
3 Jn	10	[Diotrephes] not only refuses to welcome our brothers, but prevents the other people who *would have liked* to from doing it,
Jude	5	I *should like* to remind you . . . how the Lord . . . destroyed the men who did not trust him.

2. WANT – WILL: *THELŌ*

2 *thelēma* 62   1 *thelō* 209
3 *thelēsis* 1

1: THE WILL (OF GOD) – (GOD, THE LORD) WILLS, WANTS – (GOD'S) PURPOSE

Mt	6 10	2 [Our Father in heaven, may] your *will* be done,
	7 21	2 It is . . . the person who does the *will* of my Father [who will enter the kingdom of heaven]
	9 13	(Ho 6 6) What I *want* is mercy, not sacrifice.
	12 7	(Ho 6 6) What I *want* is mercy, not sacrifice,
	50	2 Anyone who does the *will* of my Father in heaven . . . is my brother
	18 14	2 It is never the *will* of your Father . . . that one of these little ones should be lost.
	26 42	My Father, . . . if this cup cannot pass by without my drinking it, your *will* be done!
	27 43	(Ps 22 9) He puts his trust in God; now let God rescue him if he *wants* him.
Mk	3 35	2 Anyone who does the *will* of God . . . is my brother
Jn	4 34	2 My food is to do the *will* of the one who sent me,
	6 39	2 Now the *will* of him who sent me is that I should lose nothing
	40	2 . . . ⁴⁰ Yes, it is my Father's *will* that whoever sees the Son and believes in him shall have eternal life,

Jn	7 17	2 and if anyone is prepared to do his *will*, he will know whether my teaching is from God or whether my doctrine is my own.
	9 31	2 God does listen to men who . . . do his *will*.
Ac	13 22	I have selected David . . , a man after my own heart, who will
		2 carry out my whole *purpose*.
	18 21	2 I will come back another time, God *willing*.
	21 14	2 we gave up the attempt, saying, 'The Lord's *will* be done'.
	22 14	The God of our ancestors has chosen you [Saul], to know his
		2 *will*,
Rm	1 10	[we] ask to be allowed at long last the opportunity to visit you,
		2 if [God] so *wills*.
	2 18	2 [If you call yourself a Jew,] you know God's *will* through the Law
	9 18	when God *wants* to show mercy he does, and when he *wants* to harden someone's heart he does so.
	22	although God *is ready* to show his anger . . . he patiently puts up with the people who make him angry,
	12 2	2 This is the only way to discover the *will* of God
	15 32	2 Then, if God *wills*, I shall . . . come to enjoy a period of rest among you.
1 Co	1 1	2 I, Paul, appointed ⸢by (lit. through the *will* of) God to be an apostle . . . send greetings
	4 19	I will be visiting you soon, the Lord *willing*,
	12 18	God put all the separate parts into the body *on purpose*.
	15 38	[You sow a bare grain,] then God gives it the sort of body that he has *chosen*.
2 Co	1 1	2 From Paul, appointed ⸢by (lit. through the *will* of) God to be an apostle of Christ Jesus,
	8 5	[the Macedonians] offered their own selves . . . ⸢under (lit.
		2 through the *will* of) God, to us.
Ga	1 4	[Jesus Christ] sacrificed himself for our sins, in accordance
		2 with the *will* of God our Father,
Ep	1 1	2 From Paul, appointed ⸢by (lit. through the *will* of) God to be an apostle of Christ Jesus,
	5	[God determined] that we should become his adopted sons,
		2 through Jesus Christ for his own kind *purposes*,
	9	2 [God] has let us know the mystery of his *purpose* . . . ¹¹ . . .
	11	we were . . . chosen . . . under the predetermined plan of the one who guides all things as he decides by ⸢his own (lit. the *purpose* within his) *will*;
	5 17	2 do not be thoughtless but recognise what is the *will* of the Lord.
	6 6	2 you are slaves of Christ and wholeheartedly do the *will* of God.
Col	1 1	2 From Paul, appointed ⸢by (lit. through the *will* of) God to be an apostle of Christ Jesus,
	9	2 you should reach the fullest knowledge of [God's] *will*.
	27	It was God's *purpose* to reveal . . . this mystery to pagans.
	4 12	2 always hold perfectly and securely to the *will* of God.
1 Th	4 3	2 What God *wants* is for you all to be holy.
	5 18	2 give thanks to God, because this is what God *expects* you to do
1 Tm	2 4	[God our saviour] *wants* everyone to be saved
2 Tm	1 1	2 From Paul, appointed ⸢by (lit. through the *will* of) God to be an apostle of Christ Jesus
Heb	2 4	God himself confirmed their witness with signs and marvels
		3 . . , and by ⸢freely (lit. *willingly*) giving the gifts of the Holy Spirit.
	10 5	(Ps 40 7) You . . . *wanted* no sacrifice or oblation,
	7	(Ps 40 9) God, here I am! I am coming to obey your *will*.
	8	[Christ] says first: You did not *want* . . . the sacrifices,
	9	[Christ] says (Ps 40 9): Here I am! I am coming to obey your
		2 *will*.
	10	2 this *will* was for us to be made holy by the offering of his body made once and for all by Jesus Christ.
	36	2 You will need endurance to do God's *will*
	13 21	[I pray that the God of peace] may make you ready to do his
		2 *will* in any kind of good (ᵛ *action*);
Jm	4 15	The most you should ever say is: 'If it is the Lord's *will*, we shall still be alive to do this or that'.
1 P	2 15	2 God *wants* you to be good citizens,
	3 17	2/ And if it is the ⸢*will* of (lit. *will purposed* by) God that you should suffer, it is better to suffer for doing right
	4 2	[anyone who has bodily suffering has broken with sin] because for the rest of his life . . . he is not ruled by human
		2 passions but only by the *will* of God.
	19	even those ⸢whom God allows to suffer (lit. who suffer by the
		2 *will* of God) must trust themselves to the constancy of the creator
1 Jn	2 17	2 anyone who does the *will* of God remains for ever.
	5 14	We are quite confident that if we ask [God] for anything, and
		2 it is in accordance with his *will*, he will hear us;
Rv	4 11	2 it was only by your *will* that everything was made and exists.

2: (GOD AND JESUS) WILL, WOULD HAVE – THE WILL (OF GOD AND JESUS)

Mt	26 39	My Father, . . . let it be as you, not I, *would have* it.
Mk	14 36	Abba! . . . let it be as you, not I, *would have* it.

Lk 22	42		Father, . . . if you are willing, take this cup away from me.
		2	Nevertheless, let your *will* be done, not mine.
Jn 5	30	2/2	my aim is to do not my own *will*, but the *will* of him who sent me.
6	38	2	I have come from heaven, not to do my own *will*, but to do
		2	the *will* of the one who sent me.

3: (JESUS) WANTS (TO)

Mt 8	2	'Sir, . . . if you *want* to, you can cure me.' ³ Jesus stretched
	3	out his hand . . . and said, 'Of course I *want* to! Be cured!'
15	32	I do not *want* to send [these people] off hungry,
17	4	Lord, . . . if you *wish*, I will make three tents here,
23	37	Jerusalem, . . . how often have I *longed* to gather your children,
26	17	Where do you *want* us to make the preparations for you to eat the passover?
27	34	[Jesus] tasted [the wine] but ʳrefused (lit. did not *want*) to drink.
Mk 1	40	'If you *want* to' [the leper] said 'you can cure me'. ⁴¹ . . . 'Of
	41	course I *want* to!' [Jesus] said. 'Be cured!'
3	13	[Jesus] summoned those he *wanted*.
6	48	[Jesus] ʳwas going (lit. *wanted*) to pass them by, but . . . they saw him
7	24	[Jesus] went into a house and did not *want* anyone to know he was there,
9	30	they made their way through Galilee; and [Jesus] did not *want* anyone to know,
14	12	Where do you *want* us to . . . make the preparations for you to eat the passover?
Lk 5	12	'Sir, . . . if you *want* to, you can cure me,' ¹³ Jesus stretched
	13	out his hand . . . and said, 'Of course I *want* to! Be cured!'
9	54	Lord, do you *want* us to call down fire from heaven to burn them up?
12	49	I have come to bring fire to the earth, and how I *wish* it were blazing already!
13	34	Jerusalem, . . . how often have I *longed* to gather your children,
22	9	Where do you *want* us to prepare [the passover]?
Jn 1	43	The next day, ʳafter Jesus had decided (lit. when Jesus *wanted*) to leave for Galilee, he met Philip
5	21	as the Father raises the dead . . . so the Son gives life to anyone he *chooses*;
7	1	he ᵛcould not (G did not *want* to) stay in Judaea, because the Jews were out to kill him.
17	24	Father, I *want* those you have given me to be with me where I am,
21	22	If I *want* him to stay behind till I come, what does it matter to you?
	23	Jesus had . . . said . ., 'If I *want* him to stay behind till I come'.

4: WANT, WOULD LIKE (TO), WISH (TO)

Mt 1	9	Joseph, . . . *wanting* to spare [Mary] publicity, decided to divorce her informally.
2	18	(Jr 31 15) it was Rachel weeping . ., ʳrefusing (lit. not *wanting*) to be comforted
5	40	if a man ʳtakes (lit. *wants* to take) you to law and would have your tunic, let him have your cloak as well.
	42	if anyone *wants* to borrow, do not turn away.
7	12	always treat others as you *would like* them to treat you;
11	14	if you ʳwill (lit. *would like*) to believe me, [John the Baptist] is the Elijah who was to return.
12	38	Master, . . . we *should like* to see a sign from you.
13	28 <	Do you *want* us to go and weed [the darnel] out?
14	5	[Herod] had *wanted* to kill [John] but was afraid of the people,
15	28	Woman, you have great faith. Let your *wish* be granted.
16	24	If anyone *wants* to be a follower of mine, let him renounce himself
	25	anyone who *wants* to save his life will lose it;
17	12	Elijah has come already and they did not recognise him but treated him as they ʳpleased (lit. *wished*);
18	23 <	a king . . . *decided* to settle his accounts with his servants.
	30 <	the other [servant] *would* not agree; . . . he had him thrown into prison till he should pay the debt.
19	17	if you *wish* to enter into life, keep the commandments.
	21	If you *wish* to be perfect, go and sell what you own
20	14 <	I *choose* to pay the last-comer as much as I pay you. ¹⁵ Have
	15 <	I no right to do what I *like* with my own?
	21	[Jesus] said [to the mother of Zebedee's sons], 'What is it you *want*?'
	26	anyone who *wants* to be great among you must be your servant,
	27	anyone who *wants* to be first among you must be your slave,
	32	Jesus . . . said [to the two blind men], 'What do you *want* me to do for you?'

Mt 21	29 <		[My boy, you go and work in the vineyard today.] I *will* not go,
	31 <	2	Which of the two did the father's *will*?
22	3 <		those who had been invited . . . *would* not come.
23	4		[the scribes] lay [heavy burdens] on men's shoulders, but ʳwill they (lit. *would* they *like* to) lift a finger to move them?
	37		Jerusalem, . . . how often have I longed to gather your children . . . and you ʳrefused (lit. *would* not *have* it)!
26	15		What are you *prepared* to give me if I hand [Jesus] over to you?
27	15		it was the governor's practice to release a prisoner . . ., anyone they *chose*.
	17		Which do you *want* me to release for you: Barabbas, or Jesus . . .?
	21		Which of the two do you *want* me to release for you?
Mk 6	19		Herodias . . . *wanted* to kill [John];
	22		Ask me anything you *like* and I will give it you.
	25		I *want* you to give me John the Baptist's head,
	26		[Herod] ʳwas reluctant (lit. did not *want*) to break his word
8	34		If anyone *wants* to be a follower of mine, let him renounce himself
	35		anyone who *wants* to save his life will lose it;
9	13		Elijah has come and they have treated him as they ʳpleased (lit. *wished*).
	35		If anyone *wants* to be first, he must make himself last of all
10	35		'Master,' [James and John] said to him 'we *want* you to do us a favour.'
	36		What is it you *want* me to do for you?
	43		anyone who *wants* to become great among you must be your servant,
	44		anyone who *wants* to be first among you must be slave to all.
	51		What do you *want* me to do for you?
12	38		Beware of the scribes who *like* to walk about in long robes,
14	7		you can be kind to [the poor] whenever you *wish*,
15	9		Do you *want* me to release for you the king of the Jews?
	12		what ʳam I (ᵛ do you *want* me) to do with the man you call king of the Jews?
Lk 1	62		[they] made signs to [Zechariah] to find out what he *wanted* [the child] called.
4	6 ⑩		I give [all this power] to anyone I *choose*.
5	39		nobody who has been drinking old wine *wants* new.
6	31		Treat others as you *would like* them to treat you.
8	20		Your mother and brothers . . . *want* to see you.
9	23		If anyone *wants* to be a follower of mine, let him renounce himself
	24		anyone who *wants* to save his life will lose it;
10	24		many prophets and kings *wanted* to see what you see,
	29		the man was *anxious* to justify himself and said to Jesus, 'And who is my neighbour?'
12	47 <	2	The servant who knows what his master *wants*, but has not
	<	2	even started to carry out those *wishes*, will receive . . . many strokes of the lash
13	31		Herod *means* to kill you.
	34		Jerusalem, . . . how often have I longed to gather yous children . . . and you ʳrefused (lit. *would* not *have* it)!
14	28		which of you here, *intending* to build a tower, would not first sit down and work out the cost . . .?
15	28		[The elder son] was angry then and ʳrefused (lit. did not *want*) to go in,
16	26		between us and you a great gulf has been fixed, to stop anyone, if he *wanted* to, crossing from our side to yours,
18	4 <		[I want justice from you against my enemy.] For a long time [the judge] ʳrefused (lit. did not *want* to),
	13		The tax collector stood some distance away, not *daring* even to raise his eyes to heaven;
	41		'What do you *want* me to do for you?' 'Sir' he replied 'let me see again.'
19	14 <		We do not *want* this man to be our king.
	27 <		as for my enemies who did not *want* me for their king, . execute them
20	46		Beware of the scribes who *like* to walk about in long robes
23	8		[Herod] had been *wanting* for a long time to set eyes on [Jesus];
	20		Pilate was *anxious* to set Jesus free
	25	2	[Pilate] handed Jesus over to them to deal with as they ʳpleased (lit. *wished*).
Jn 1	13		[the Word] ≠ was (G were) born not out of human stock or
		2/2	urge (lit. *will*) of the flesh or *will* of man but of God himself.
3	8		The wind blows wherever it ʳpleases (lit. *wishes*) . . . That is how it is with all who are born of the Spirit.
5	6		[Jesus said [to the sick man], 'Do you *want* to be well again?'
	35		for a time you ʳwere content (lit. *wanted*) to enjoy the light that [John] gave.
	40		you ʳrefuse (lit. do not *want*) to come to me for life!
6	11		Jesus took the loaves, gave thanks . . .; he then did the same with the fish, giving out as much as was *wanted*.
	21		[The disciples] *were for* taking [Jesus] into the boat,
	67		Jesus said to the Twelve, 'What about you, do you *want* to go away too?'

Jn	7 17	if anyone is *prepared* to do [God's] will, he will know whether my teaching is from God or whether my doctrine is my own.
	44	Some *would have liked* to arrest [Jesus], but no one actually laid hands on him.
	8 44	you *prefer* to do what your father wants.
	9 27	Why do you *want* to hear it all again? Do you *want* to become his disciples too?
	12 21	[Some Greeks put this request to Philip,] Sir, we *should like* to see Jesus.
	15 7	you may ask what you *will* and you shall get it.
	16 19	Jesus knew that [the disciples] *wanted* to question him,
	21 18	when you were young you . . . walked where you *liked*; but when you grow old . . . somebody else will . . . take you where you *would rather* not go.
Ac	2 12	they asked one another what it all *meant*.
	7 28	(Ex 2 14) Do you *intend* to kill me as you killed the Egyptian . . .?
	39	This is the man that our ancestors ʳrefused (lit. did not *want*) to listen to:'
	10 10	[Peter] felt hungry and was *looking forward* to his meal,
	14 13	The priests of Zeus . . , *proposing* that all the people should offer sacrifice with them, brought garlanded oxen
	16 3	Paul . . . *wanted* to have [Timothy] as a travelling companion,
	17 18	Does this parrot know what ʳhe's talking about (lit. he *wants* to get across)?
	20	we would like to find out what [the things you said] *mean*.
	19 33	Alexander . . . raised his hand for silence *in the hope of being able* to explain things to the people.
	24 6	(ᵛ *intending* to judge [Paul] according to our Law,)
	27	being *anxious* to gain favour with the Jews, Felix left Paul in custody.
	25 9	Festus was *anxious* to gain favour with the Jews, so he said to Paul, 'Are you *willing* to go up to Jerusalem and be tried . . . there?'
	26 5	[the Jews] could testify, if they *would*, that I . . . lived as a Pharisee.
Rm	1 13	I *want* you to know, brothers, that I have often planned to visit you
	7 15	I fail to carry out the things I *want* to do, and I find myself doing the very things I hate. ¹⁶ . . . I act against my own *will*,
	18	though the *will* to do what is good is in me, the performance is not, ¹⁹ with the result that instead of doing the good things I *want* to do, I carry out the sinful things I do not *want*.
	20	²⁰ When I act against my *will*, then, it is not my true self doing it, but sin which lives in me. ²¹ . . . every single time I *want* to do good it is something evil that comes to hand.
	9 16	the only thing that counts is not what human beings *want* or try to do, but the mercy of God.
	11 25	I do not *want* you to be ignorant [of the reason for all this]
	13 3	If you *want* to live without being afraid of authority, you must live honestly
	16 19	I only ʳhope (lit. *wish*) that you are also wise in what is good,
1 Co	4 21	ʳIt is for you to decide (lit. What *would* you *like*: do I come with a stick in my hand or in a spirit of love . . .?
	7 7	I *should like* everyone to be like me,
	32	I *would like* to see you free from all worry.
	36	[the father] is free to do as he *likes*:
	37	if someone has firmly made his mind up, without any compulsion and in complete freedom of *choice*, to keep his daughter as she is, he will be doing a good thing.
	39	[the widow] is free to marry anybody she *likes*,
	10 1	I *want* to remind you, brothers, how our fathers were all guided by a cloud above them
	20	I have no *desire* to see you in communion with demons.
	27	If an unbeliever invites you to his house, go if you *want* to,
	11 3	what I *want* you to understand is that Christ is the head of every man,
	12 1	I *want* to clear up a wrong impression about spiritual gifts.
	14 5	I *should like* you all to have the gift of tongues,
	19	I *would rather* say five words that mean something than ten thousand words in a tongue.
	35	If [the women] ʳhave any questions to ask (lit. *would like* to ask any questions), they should ask their husbands at home:
	16 7	I do not *want* to make it only a passing visit
	12	2 Apollos . . . was quite firm that he did not *want* to go yet
2 Co	1 8	we *should like* you to realise . . . that the things we had to undergo in Asia were more of a burden than we could carry,
	5 4	we groan . . . in this tent, not that we *want* to strip it off, but to put the second garment over it
	8 10	you were the first, a year ago, not only in taking action but even in *deciding* to. ¹¹ So now . . . let the results be worthy . . . of the *decision* you made so promptly.
	11 12	[I am] leaving no opportunity for those people who are *looking for* an opportunity to claim equality with us in what they boast of.
	12 6	If I should ʳdecide (lit. *wish*) to boast, I should not be made to look foolish,

2 Co	12 20	I am afraid . . . that when I come I may find you different from what I *want* you to be, and you may find that I am not as you *would like* me to be;
Ga	1 7	some troublemakers among you *want* to change the Good News
	3 2	ʳLet me (lit. I *should like* to) ask you one question:
	4 9	how can you *want* to go back to elemental things like these . . .?
	17	by separating you from me, they *want* to win you over to themselves
	20	I *wish* I were with you now
	21	You *want* to be subject to the Law?
	5 17	you do not always carry out you [good] *intentions*.
	6 12	It is only ʳself-interest (lit. *wanting* to put on a good show) that make them want to force circumcision on you
	13	they only *want* you to be circumcised so that they can boast of the fact.
Ep	2 3	We all were among them too in the past, . . . ruled entirely by our own physical *desires* and our own ideas;
Ph	2 13	It is God . . . who puts both the *will* and the action into you.
Col	2 1	I *want* you to know that I do have to struggle hard for you,
	18	Do not be taken in by people who *like* grovelling to angels
1 Th	2 18	we ʳtried hard (lit. *should have liked*) to come and visit you
	4 13	We *want* you to be quite certain . . . about those who have died,
2 Th	3 10	We gave you a rule when we were with you: not to let anyone have any food if he ʳrefused (lit. did not *want*) to do any work.
1 Tm	1 7	they *claim* to be doctors of the Law
	5 11	young widows . . . *want* to marry again,
2 Tm	2 26	[they may] come to their senses, once out of the trap where the devil caught them and kept them enslaved to his *will*.
	3 12	anybody who ʳtries (lit. *wants*) to live in devotion to Christ is certain to be attacked;
Phm	14	I did not *want* to do anything without your consent;
Heb	12 17	when [Esau] *wanted* to obtain the blessing . . . he was rejected
	13 18	we are certainly *determined* to behave honourably in everything we do;
Jm	2 20	ʳDo (lit. Surely you *want* to) realise . . . that faith without good deeds is useless.
1 P	3 10	(Ps 34 13) Anyone who *wants* to have a happy life . . . must banish malice from his tongue,
2 P	1 21	2 no prophecy ever came from man's *initiative*.
	3 5	They are *choosing* to forget that . . . the earth was formed by the word of God
3 Jn	13	There were several things I had to tell you but I *would rather* not trust them to pen and ink.
Rv	2 21	[Jezebel] is not *willing* to change her adulterous life.
	11 5	Fire can come from [the] mouths [of my two witnesses] and consume their enemies if anyone ʳtries (lit. *wants*) to harm them; and if anybody does ʳtry (lit. *want*) to harm them he will certainly be killed in this way.
	6	[My two witnesses] are able to . . strike the whole world with any plague as often as they *like*.
	22 17	all who *want* it may have the water of life, and have it free.

3. OF ONE'S OWN FREE WILL, WILLINGLY, BY CHOICE – SPONTANEOUS, DELIBERATELY: *HEKŌN*

3 *akōn* 1		4 *hekousios* 1	
1 *hekōn* 2		2 *hekousiōs* 2	

Rm	8 20	It was not ʳfor any fault on the part of (lit. *through the will of*) creation that it was made unable to attain its purpose,
1 Co	9 17	If I had ʳchosen this work myself (lit. *done this work by my own choice*), I might have been paid for it, but as I have not [done it] *by my own choice*, it is a responsibility which has been put into my hands.
Phm	14	it would have been forcing your act of kindness, which should be *spontaneous*.
Heb	10 26	If, after we have been given knowledge of the truth, we should *deliberately* commit any sins, then there is no . . . sacrifice for them.
1 P	5 2	Be the shepherds of the flock of God . . , not simply as a duty but ʳgladly (or: *willingly*), because God wants it;

4. ON ONE'S OWN INITIATIVE, SPONTANEOUSLY: *AUTH-AIRETOS*

auth-airetos 2

2 Co	8 3	[the Macedonians] gave not only as much as they could afford, but far more, and quite *spontaneously*,
	17	[Titus] is visiting you *on his own initiative*.

WIND – CLOUD – RAIN

1. the Air: *aēr*
2. the Wind
  1: Wind – Gale – Breeze: *anemos*
    a) Wind – Gale – Breeze
    b) (the four) Winds (of the world)
  2: the South(erly) Wind: *notos*
  3: the North-easter: *eur-akylōn*
  4: (the wind) Blows, Blew: *pneō*
  5: (the wind) Drives: *rhipizō*
  6: Hurricane: *typhōnikos*
3. Storm, Stormy
  1: Storm, Tempest, Whirlwind: *thyella*
  2: Storm, Stormy weather: *cheimōn*
  3: Storm(y): *lailaps*
4. Cloud – Fog, Mist – Vapour
  1: Cloud(s): *nephelē*
    a) (the) Clouds (of heaven)
    b) Cloud(s)
    c) Cloud (figuratively)

  2: Cloud, Mist, Vapour: *atmis*
  3: Fog, Mist: *homichlē*
  4: Misty: *achlys*
5. the Rain
  1: Rain: *brochē*
  2: Rain: *huetos*
  3: Rain: Shower: *ombros*
  4: the Autumn rains, the Spring rains: *proimos* and *opsimos*
  5: Rainbow: *iris*
  6: Hail, Hailstones: *chalaza*
6. Summer – Fine, Fair (weather)
  1: Summer: *theros*
  2: Fine, Fair (weather): *eu-dia*
7. Winter – Snow
  1: Late autumn, Winter: *phthin-opōrinos*
  2: Winter: *cheimōn*
  3: Snow: *chiōn*

1. UHE AIR: *AĒR*

aēr 7

Ac 22 23	They were yelling . . . and throwing dust into the *air*,
1 Co 9 26	that is how I fight, not beating the *air*.
14 9	if your tongue does not produce intelligible speech . . . you will be talking to the *air*.
Ep 2 2	you were following the way of this world, obeying the ruler who governs the *air*,
1 Th 4 17	those of us who are still alive will be taken up in the clouds . . . to meet the Lord in the *air*.
Rv 9 2	smoke poured up out of the Abyss . . . so that the sun and the ⌐sky (lit. *air*) were darkened by it,
16 17	The seventh angel emptied his bowl into the *air*,

2. THE WIND

1: WIND – GALE – BREEZE: *ANEMOS*

2 anemizō 1   1 anemos 31

a) Wind – Gale – Breeze

Mt 7 25 <	*gales* blew and hurled themselves against that house, and it did not fall:
27 <	*gales* blew and struck that house, and it fell;
8 26	[Jesus] rebuked the *winds* and the sea; and all was calm again.
27	Whatever kind of man is this? Even the *winds* and the sea obey him.
11 7	What did you go out into the wilderness to see? A reed swaying in the *breeze*?
14 24	the boat . . . was battling with a heavy sea, for there was a head*wind*.
30	as soon as [Peter] felt the force of the *wind*, he took fright
32	as [Jesus and Peter] got into the boat the *wind* dropped.
Mk 4 37	Then ⌐it began to blow a gale (lit. a stormy *gale* arose)
39	[Jesus] rebuked the *wind* and said to the sea, 'Quiet now! Be calm!' And the *wind* dropped, and all was calm again.
41	Who can this be? Even the *wind* and the sea obey him.
6 48	[Jesus] could see [the disciples] were worn out with rowing, for the *wind* was against them;
51	[Jesus] got into the boat with them, and the *wind* dropped.
Lk 7 24	What did you go out into the wilderness to see? A reed swaying in the *breeze*?
8 23	When a ⌐squall (lit. stormy *wind*) came down on the lake the boat started taking in water
24	[Jesus] rebuked the *wind* and the rough water;
25	Who can this be, that gives orders even to *winds* . . . and they obey him?
Jn 6 18	⌐The wind was strong (lit. A high *wind* was blowing), and the sea was getting rough.
Ac 27 4	as the *winds* were against us we sailed under the lee of Cyprus,
7	The *wind* would not allow us to touch there,
14	it was not long before a (§ *wind*, a) hurricane, the 'north-easter' as they call it, burst on them from across the island.
15	[15] The ship was caught and could not be turned head-on to the *wind*,
Ep 4 14 ○	Then we shall not be . . . carried along by every *wind* of doctrine,

Jm 1 6	a person who has doubts is like the waves thrown up in the sea when the *wind* drives.
3 4	no matter how big [the ships] are, even if a *gale* is driving them, the man at the helm can steer them . . . by controlling a tiny rudder.
Jude 12	[Certain people who have infiltrated among you] are like clouds blown about by the *winds* and bringing no rain,
Rv 6 13	the stars . . . fell on to the earth like figs dropping from a fig tree when a high *wind* shakes it;
7 1	I saw four angels . . . holding the four winds of the world back to keep ⌐them (lit. any *wind*) from blowing over the land

b) (the four) Winds (of the world)

Mt 24 31	[the Son of Man] will send his angels . . . to gather his chosen from the four *winds*,
Mk 13 27	[the Son of Man] will send the angels to gather his chosen from the four *winds*,
Rv 7 1	I saw four angels . . . holding the four *winds* of the world back to keep ⌐them (lit. any *wind*) from blowing over the land

2: THE SOUTH(ERLY) WIND: *NOTOS*

notos 3/7

Lk 12 55	when the *wind* is blowing *from the south* you say it will be hot,
Ac 27 13	A ⌐*southerly* breeze sprang up (lit. *southerly wind* blew lightly) and . . . they weighed anchor
28 13	After one day [at Rhegium] a *south wind* sprang up

3: THE NORTH-EASTER: *EUR-AKYLŌN*

eur-akylōn 1

Ac 27 14	it was not long before a hurricane, the '*north-easter*' as they call it, burst on them from across the island.

4: (THE WIND) BLOWS, BLEW: *PNEŌ*

1 *pneō*	7	3 *pnoē* 1/2
2 *pneuma* 2/378		4 *hypo-pneō* 1

Mt 7 25 <	gales *blew* and hurled themselves against that house, and it did not fall:
27 <	gales *blew* and struck that house, and it fell;
Lk 12 55	when the wind is *blowing* from the south you say it will be hot,
Jn 3 8	2/ The *wind blows* wherever it pleases; you hear its sound, but you cannot tell where it comes from or where it is going.
6 18	⌐The wind was strong (lit. A high wind was *blowing*), and the sea was getting rough.
Ac 2 2	3 suddenly they heard what sounded like a powerful *wind* from heaven,
27 13	4 A ⌐*southerly* breeze sprang up (lit. southerly wind *blew lightly*),
40	hoisting the foresail to the *wind*, they headed for the beach.
Heb 1 7	2 (Ps 104 4) He makes his angels *winds*
Rv 7 1	I saw four angels . . . holding the four winds of the world back to keep ⌐them (lit. any wind) from *blowing* over the land

5: (THE WIND) DRIVES: *RHIPIZŌ*

rhipizō 1

Jm 1 6	a person who has doubts is like the waves thrown up in the sea when the wind *drives*.

6: HURRICANE: *TYPHŌNIKOS*

typhōnikos 1

Ac 27 14	it was not long before a *hurricane*, the 'north-easter' as they call it, burst on them from across the island.

3. STORM, STORMY

1: STORM, TEMPEST, WHIRLWIND: *THYELLA*

thyella 1

Heb 12 18	What you have come to is nothing known to the senses: not a blazing fire, . . . or a *storm*;

2: STORM, STORMY WEATHER: *CHEIMŌN*

2 *cheimazō* 1   1 *cheimōn* 2/6

Mt 16 3 *Stormy weather* today; the sky is red and overcast.
Ac 27 18 2 As we were *making* very *heavy weather* of it, the next day
           they began to jettison the cargo,
      20 For a number of days . . . the *storm* raged unabated until at
           last we gave up all hope of surviving.

3: STORM(Y): *LAILAPS*

lailaps 3

Mk 4 37 Then ⌐it began to blow a gale (lit. a *stormy* gale arose)
Lk 8 23 When a ⌐squall (lit. *stormy* wind) came down on the lake the
           boat started taking in water
2 P 2 17 People like this are dried-up rivers, fogs swirling in the *wind*,

4. CLOUD – FOG, MIST – VAPOUR

1: CLOUD(S): *NEPHELĒ*

1 *nephelē* 25   2 *nephos* 1

a) (the) Clouds (of heaven)

Mt 17 5 suddenly a bright *cloud* covered [Jesus, Peter, James and
           John] with shadow, and from the *cloud* there came a voice
           which said, 'This is my Son,
   24 30 they will see the Son of Man coming on the *clouds* of heaven
   26 64 you will see the Son of Man . . . coming on the *clouds* of
           heaven.
Mk 9 7 a *cloud* came, covering [Jesus, Peter, James and John] in
           shadow; and there came a voice from the *cloud*, 'This is my
           Son,
   13 26 they will see the Son of Man coming in the *clouds*
   14 62 you will see the Son of Man . . . coming with the *clouds* of
           heaven.
Lk 9 34 a *cloud* came and covered them with shadow; and when
           [Moses and Elijah] went into the *cloud* the disciples were
           afraid. 35 And a voice came from the *cloud* saying, 'This is
           my Son,
   21 27 they will see the Son of Man coming in a *cloud*
Ac 1 9 a *cloud* took [Jesus] from their sight.
1 Co 10 1 our fathers were all guided by a *cloud* above them and . . .
           they all passed through the sea. 2 They were all baptised
       2 into Moses in this *cloud* and in this sea;
1 Th 4 17 those of us who are still alive will be taken up in the *clouds*
           . . . to meet the Lord in the air.
Rv 1 7 [Jesus Christ] is coming on the *clouds*;
   10 1 I saw another powerful angel coming down from heaven,
           wrapped in a *cloud*,
   11 12 [the two witnesses] went up to heaven in a *cloud*.
   14 14 I saw a white *cloud* and, sitting on ⌐it (lit. the *cloud*), one like
       15 a son of man . . . 15 Then another angel . . . shouted
       16 aloud to the one sitting on the *cloud*, 'Put your sickle in
           and reap . . .' 16 Then the one sitting on the *cloud* set his
           sickle to work on the earth,

b) Cloud(s)

Lk 12 54 When you see a *cloud* looming up in the west you say . . .
           that rain is coming,
Jude 12 They are like *clouds* blown about by the winds and bringing
           no rain,

c) Cloud (figuratively)

Heb 12 1 2 With so many witnesses in a great *cloud* on every side of us,
           we too . . . should throw off everything that hinders us,

2: CLOUD, MIST, VAPOUR: *ATMIS*

atmis 2

Ac 2 19 (Jl 3 3 G) (§ blood and fire and a *cloud* of smoke)
Jm 4 14 you are no more than a *mist* that is here for a little while

3: FOG, MIST: *HOMICHLĒ*

homichlē 1

2 P 2 17 People like this are dried-up rivers, *fogs* swirling in the wind,

4: MISTY: *ACHLYS*

achlys 1

Ac 13 11 That instant, everything went *misty* and dark for [Elymas],

5. THE RAIN

1: RAIN: *BROCHĒ*

1 *brechō* 5/7   2 *brochē* 2

Mt 5 45 your Father . . . *causes* . . . his *rain to fall* on honest and
           dishonest men alike.
    7 25 2 *Rain* came down, floods rose,
      27 2 *Rain* came down, floods rose,
Lk 17 29 the day Lot left Sodom, God *rained* fire and brimstone from
           heaven
Jm 5 17 Elijah . . . prayed hard for it not to *rain*, and no *rain* fell
Rv 11 6 [The two witnesses] are able to lock up the sky so that ⌐it does
           not rain (lit. no *rain* can *rain*)

2: RAIN: *HUETOS*

huetos 5

Ac 14 17 [God] sends you *rain* from heaven, he makes your crops grow
   28 2 [the inhabitants of Malta] lit a huge fire because [it had started
           to] *rain*
Heb 6 7 A field that has been well watered by frequent *rain* . . . gives
           the crops that are wanted
Jm 5 18 [Elijah] prayed again and the sky gave *rain*
Rv 11 6 [The two witnesses] are able to lock up the sky so that ⌐it does
           not rain (lit. no *rain* can rain)

3: RAIN, SHOWER: *OMBROS*

ombros 1

Lk 12 54 When you see a cloud looming up in the west you say . . .
           that *rain* is coming, and so it does.

4: THE AUTUMN RAINS, THE SPRING RAINS: *PROIMOS* AND *OPSIMOS*

1 *opsimos* 1   2 *proimos* 1

Jm 5 7 Think of a farmer: how patiently he waits for the precious
       2 fruit of the ground until it has had the *autumn rains* and the
           spring rains!

5: RAINBOW: *IRIS*

iris 2

Rv 4 3 There was a *rainbow* encircling the throne, and this looked like
           an emerald.
   10 1 I saw another powerful angel coming down from heaven,
           wrapped in a cloud, with a *rainbow* over his head;

3: HAIL, HAILSTONES: *CHALAZA*

chalaza 4

Rv 8 7 *hail* and fire, mixed with blood, were dropped on the earth;
   11 19 Then came flashes of lightning, peals of thunder and an
           earthquake, and violent *hail*.
   16 21 great *hailstones* weighing a talent each, fell from the sky on the
           people. They cursed God for sending a plague of *hail*.

6. SUMMER – FINE, FAIR (WEATHER)

1: SUMMER: *THEROS*

theros 3

Mt 24 32 as soon as . . . leaves come out, you know that *summer* is
           near.
Mk 13 28 as soon as . . . leaves come out, you know that *summer* is
           near.
Lk 21 30 As soon as you see [the fig tree and indeed every tree] bud,
           you know that *summer* is now near.

2: FINE, FAIR (WEATHER): *EU-DIA*

eu-dia 1

Mt 16 2 It will be *fine*; there is a red sky,

7. WINTER – SNOW

1: LATE AUTUMN, WINTER: *PHTHIN-OPŌRINOS*

phthin-opōrinos 1

| Jude | 12 | They are like . . . barren trees which are . . . uprooted in the *winter* and so are twice dead; |

2: WINTER: *CHEIMŌN*

cheimōn 4/6

Mt	24 20	Pray that you will not have to escape in *winter* or on a sabbath.
Mk	13 18	Pray that this may not be in *winter*.
Jn	10 22	It was the time when the feast of Dedication was being celebrated in Jerusalem. It was *winter*,
2 Tm	4 21	[Timothy], do your best to come before the *winter*.

3: SNOW: *CHIŌN*

chiōn 3

Mt	28 3	[the] robe [of the angel of the Lord was] white as *snow*.
Mk	9 3	[Jesus's] clothes became dazzlingly white, ʳwhiter (ᵛ *snow* white, more) than any earthly bleacher could make them.
Rv	1 14	[The] head [of the Son of Man] and his hair were white as white wool or as *snow*,

---

WIPE – WIPE OUT

1. **Wipe – Wipe off:** *ek-massō*
2. **Wipe – Wipe out, Cancel:** *ex-a-leiphō*

 a) Wipe away
 b) Wipe out, Cancel – Blot out

1. WIPE – WIPE OFF: *EK-MASSŌ*

1 ek-massō 5   2 apo-massomai 1

Lk	7 38	her tears fell on his feet, and she *wiped* them *away* with her hair;
	44	she has poured out her tears over my feet and *wiped* them *away* with her hair.
	10 11	2 We *wipe off* the very dust of your town that clings to our feet,
Jn	11 2	Mary . . . anointed the Lord with ointment and *wiped* his feet with her hair.
	12 3	Mary . . . anointed the feet of Jesus, *wiping* them with her hair;
	13 5 X	[Jesus] began to wash the disciples' feet and to *wipe* them with the towel he was wearing.

2. WIPE – WIPE OUT, CANCEL: *EX-A-LEIPHŌ*

ex-a-leiphō 5

a) Wipe away

| Rv | 7 17 Θ | (Is 25 8) and God will *wipe away* all tears from their eyes. |
| | 21 4 Θ | (Is 25 8) He will *wipe away* all tears from their eyes; |

b) Wipe out, Cancel – Blot out

Ac	3 19	so that your sins may be *wiped out*,
Col	2 14 Θ	He has . . . *cancelled* every record of the debt that we had to pay . . . by nailing it to the cross;
Rv	3 5 X	I shall not *blot* [the] names [of the victorious] *out* of the book of life,

---

WISE – SOBER

1. **Wisdom, Wise – Philosophy:** *sophia*
   a) Wisdom, Wise
   b) Philosophy, Philosopher
2. **Wise, Sensible – In one's full senses – Sober:** *phronimos*
   a) Wise, Sensible, Astute
   b) In one's full senses, In one's

 right mind – Sober, Modest – Reasonable, Sane
3. **Be sober, Temperate – Be calm, Steady – Come to one's senses:** *nēphō*
4. **Self-control, Temperance – Intemperance:** *en-krateia*

F = Sensible, Wise // Foolish, Mad

---

1. WISDOM, WISE – PHILOSOPHY: *SOPHIA*

1 sophia	51	4 kata-sophizomai	1
3 sophizō	2	5 philo-sophia	1
2 sophos	20	6 philo-sophos	1

a) Wisdom, Wise

Mt	11 19	*wisdom* has been proved right by her ʳactions (ᵛ children).
	25	I bless you, Father . . . for hiding these things from the
	2	*learned* and the clever and revealing them to mere children.
	12 42	the Queen of the South . . . came . . . to hear the *wisdom* of Solomon; and there is something greater than Solomon here.
	13 54 X	Where did the man get this *wisdom* and these miraculous powers? 55 This is the carpenter's son, surely?
	23 34	2 I am sending you prophets and *wise men* and scribes:
Mk	6 2 X	What is this *wisdom* that has been granted him . . .?
Lk	2 40 X	[Jesus] grew to maturity, and he was filled with *wisdom*;
	52 X	Jesus increased in *wisdom*, in stature, and in favour with God and men.
	7 35	*Wisdom* has been proved right by all her children.
	10 21	I bless you, Father . . . for hiding these things from the
	2	*learned* and the clever
	11 31	the Queen of the South . . . came . . . to hear the *wisdom* of Solomon;
	49	the *Wisdom* of God said, 'I will send them prophets and apostles;
	21 15	I myself shall give you . . . a *wisdom* that none of your opponents will be able to resist or contradict.
Ac	6 3	select from among yourselves seven men . . . filled with the Spirit and with *wisdom*,
	10	They found they could not get the better of [Stephen] because of his *wisdom*,
	7 10	[God] rescued [Joseph] from all his miseries by making him *wise* enough to attract the attention of Pharaoh king of Egypt,
	19	4 [The] new king ʳexploited (lit. *was too clever for*) our race and ill-treated our ancestors,
	22	Moses was taught all the *wisdom* of the Egyptians
Rm	1 14	I owe a duty to Greeks just as much as to barbarians, to the
	F 2	*educated* just as much as to the uneducated,
	22 F	2 The more they called themselves ʳphilosophers (or: *wise*), the more stupid they grew,
	11 33	How rich are the depths of God – how deep his *wisdom* and knowledge
	16 19	2 I only hope that you are also *wise* in what is good, and innocent of what is bad.
	27	2 [God] alone is *wise*; give glory therefore to him through Jesus Christ
1 Co	1 17	Christ did not send me . . . to preach [the Good News] in the terms of ʳphilosophy (or: *wisdom*)
	19	/2 (Is 29 14) I shall destroy the *wisdom* of the *wise*
	20	2 Where are the ʳphilosophers (or: *wise*) now? . . . Do you see now how God has shown up the foolishness of human
	21 F	*wisdom*? 21 If it was God's *wisdom* that human *wisdom* should not know God, it was because God wanted to save those who have faith through the foolishness of the message
	22	that we preach. 22 . . . while . . . the Greeks look for
	F	*wisdom*, 23 here are we preaching a crucified Christ . . ,
	24	to the pagans madness, 24 but to those who have been
	X	called, . . . a Christ who is the power and the *wisdom* of
	25 F	2 God. 25 For God's foolishness is *wiser* than human
	26	[wisdom],
	27	Take yourselves for instance, . . . how many of you were
	F 2	*wise* in the ordinary sense of the word . . .? 27 No, it was to shame the *wise* that God chose what is foolish by human reckoning.
	30 X	Christ Jesus . . . has become our *wisdom*, and our virtue, and our holiness,
	2 1	brothers, when I came to you, it was not with any show of
	4	oratory or ʳphilosophy (or: *wisdom*) . . . 4 and in my speeches . . . there were none of the arguments that belong to
	5	ʳphilosophy (or: *wisdom*) . . . 5 And I did this so that your faith should not depend on human ʳphilosophy (or: *wisdom*) . . . 6 But still we have a *wisdom* to offer those
	6	who have reached maturity: not a ʳphilosophy (or: *wisdom*)
	7	of our age . . . 7 The hidden *wisdom* of God which we teach . . . God predestined to be for our glory
	13 F	we teach, not in the way in which ʳphilosophy (or: *wisdom*) is taught, but in the way that the Spirit teaches us:
	3 10	2 I ʳsucceeded as an (lit. *was a wise*) architect and laid the foundations.
	18	2 if any one of you thinks of himself as *wise* . . . then he must
	19 F	2 learn to be a fool before he really can be *wise*. 19 Why?
	F	Because the *wisdom* of this world is foolishness to God. As scripture says (Jb 5 13): . . . God is not convinced by the
	20	arguments of the *wise*; 20 or . . . (Ps 94 11): The Lord
	2	knows *wise men*'s thoughts: he knows how useless they are;

1 Co	6	5	2 is there really not one ⌐reliable (lit. *wise*) man among you to settle differences between brothers . . .?
	12	8	One may have the gift of preaching with *wisdom* given . . . by the Spirit;
2 Co	1	12	by the grace of God we have [treated you with sincerity] ⌐without ulterior motives (lit. and not through worldly *wisdom*).
Ep	1	8	[Such is the richness of the grace] which [God] has showered on us in all *wisdom* and insight,
		17	May the God of our Lord Jesus Christ, the Father of glory, give you a spirit of *wisdom* and perception of what is revealed,
	3	10	the Sovereignties . . . should learn . . . how comprehensive God's *wisdom* really is,
	5	15 F	2 be very careful about the sort of lives you lead, like *intelligent* and not like senseless people.
Col	1	9	what we ask God is that through perfect *wisdom* and spiritual understanding you should reach the fullest knowledge of his will.
		28	this is the Christ we proclaim, this is the *wisdom* in which we . . . instruct everyone,
	2	3 X	in [God's secret] all the jewels of *wisdom* . . . are hidden.
		23	It may be argued that true *wisdom* is to be found in these [human doctrines and regulations],
	3	16	Teach each other, and advise each other, in all *wisdom*.
	4	5	Be ⌐tactful (lit. *wise*) with those who are not Christians
2 Tm	3	15	3 from [the holy scriptures] you can *learn the wisdom* that leads to salvation through faith in Christ Jesus.
Jm	1	5	If there is any one of you who needs *wisdom*, he must ask God,
	3	13	2 If there are any *wise* or learned men among you, let them show it by their good lives, with humility and *wisdom* in their actions.
		15	principles of this kind are not the *wisdom* that comes down from above: they are only earthly,
		17	the *wisdom* that comes down from above is . . . something pure:
2 P	1	16	3 It was not any *cleverly invented* myths that we were repeating when we brought you the knowledge . . . of our Lord Jesus Christ;
	3	15	Paul . . . told you this when he wrote to you with the *wisdom* that is his special gift.
Rv	5	12 X	The Lamb that was sacrificed is worthy to be given power, riches, *wisdom*,
	7	12	Praise and glory and *wisdom* . . . to our God for ever and ever.
	13	18	There is need for *shrewdness* here: if anyone is clever enough he may interpret the number of the beast:
	17	9	Here there is need for cleverness, for a *shrewd mind*; the seven heads are the seven hills,

b) Philosophy, Philosopher

7 *epikoureios* 1   8 *stōikos* 1

Ac	17	18	7/8/6 Even a few *Epicurean* and *Stoic* philosophers argued with [Paul in Athens].
Rm	1	22 F	2 The more they called themselves ⌐philosophers (or: wise), the more stupid they grew,
1 Co	1	17	Christ did not send me . . . to preach [the Good News] in the terms of ⌐philosophy (or: wisdom)
		20	2 Where are the ⌐philosophers (or: wise) now?
	2	1	brothers, when I came to you, it was not with any show of oratory or ⌐philosophy (or: wisdom) . . . ⁴ and in my speeches . . . there were none of the arguments that belong
		4	
		5	to ⌐philosophy (or: wisdom) . . . ⁵ And I did this so that your faith should not depend on human ⌐philosophy (or: wisdom) . . . ⁶ But still we have a wisdom to offer those who have reached maturity: not a ⌐philosophy (or: wisdom) of our age [but the hidden wisdom of God]
		6	
		13 F	we teach, not in the way in which ⌐philosophy (or: wisdom) is taught, but in the way that the Spirit teaches us;
Col	2	8	Make sure that no one traps you . . . by some secondhand, empty, rational *philosophy* based on the principles of this world
		5	

2. WISE, SENSIBLE – IN ONE'S FULL SENSES – SOBER: *PHRONIMOS*

5	*phronēsis*	2	7 *sō-phronismos* 1
1	*phronimos*	14	8 *sō-phronizō* 1
6	*phronimōs*	1	9 *sō-phronōs* 1
3	*sō-phrōn*	4	4 *sō-phrosynē* 3
2	*sō-phroneō*	6	

a) Wise, Sensible, Astute

Mt	7	24 F	everyone who listens to these words of mine and acts on them will be like a *sensible* man who built his house on rock.
	10	16	be *cunning* as serpents and yet as harmless as doves.
	24	45	What sort of servant . . . is faithful and *wise* enough for the master to place him over his household . . .?

Mt	25	2 F	Five of [the bridesmaids] were foolish and five were *sensible*:
		4 F	the *sensible* [ones] took flasks of oil as well as their lamps.
		8 F	the foolish ones said to the *sensible* [ones], 'Give us some of your oil:
		9	⌐they (lit. the *sensible* [ones]) replied, 'There may not be enough for us and for you;
Lk	1	17	[John] will go before him to turn . . . the disobedient back to the *wisdom* that the virtuous have,
		5	
	12	42	What sort of steward . . . is faithful and *wise* enough for the master to place him over his household . . .?
	16	8	6 The master praised the dishonest steward for his *astuteness*. For the children of this world are more *astute* in dealing with their own kind than are the children of light.
Rm	11	25	I do not want you to be ignorant [of the hidden reason for all this] in case (Pr 3 7) you ⌐think you know more than you do (lit. become *wise* in your own conceit).
	12	16	(Pr 3 7) Do not allow yourself to become ⌐self-satisfied (lit. *wise* in your own conceit).
1 Co	4	10 F	we are fools for the sake of Christ, while you are the *learned* [men] in Christ,
	10	15	I say to you as *sensible* [people]: judge for yourselves what I am saying.
2 Co	11	19 F	You are all *wise* [men] and can cheerfully tolerate fools,
Ep	1	8	[Such is the richness of the grace] which [God] has showered on us in all wisdom and *insight*.
		5	
1 Tm	3	2	3 the president . . . must be temperate, ⌐discreet (or: sensible) and courteous;
Tt	1	8	3 [the president must be] a man who is . . . *sensible*, moral, devout
	2	4	8 [the older women should] *show* the younger women ⌐how they should love (lit. *the sense of* loving) their husbands and
		5	3 . . . their children, ⁵ how they are to be *sensible* and chaste,

b) In one's full senses, In one's right mind – Sober, Modest – Reasonable, Sane

Mk	5	15	They came to Jesus and saw the demoniac sitting there, clothed and *in his full senses*,
		2	
Lk	8	35	2 they found the man . . . clothed and *in his full senses*;
Ac	26	25 F	4 I am speaking nothing but the *sober* truth.
Rm	12	3	2 Each of you must judge himself *soberly* by the standard of the faith God has given him.
2 Co	5	13 F	2 if we are being *reasonable* now, it is for your sake.
1 Tm	2	9	4 women are . . . to be dressed quietly and *modestly*,
		15	4 [a woman] will be saved . . . provided she lives a *modest* life and is constant in faith
2 Tm	1	7	7 God's gift was . . . the Spirit of power, and love, and *self-control*.
Tt	2	2	3 The older men should be reserved, dignified, *moderate*,
		6	2 you have got to persuade the younger men to *be moderate*
		12	9 we must be *self-restrained* and live good and religious lives
1 P	4	7	2 to pray better, keep a ⌐calm (or: sane) and sober mind.

3. BE SOBER, TEMPERATE – BE CALM, STEADY – COME TO ONE'S SENSES: *NĒPHŌ*

2	*nēphalios*	3	3 *ana-nēphō* 1
1	*nēphō*	6	4 *ek-nēphō* 1

1 Co	15	34	4 *Come to your senses*, behave properly, and leave sin alone;
1 Th	5	6	*stay* wide awake and *sober*.
		8	we belong to the day and we should *be sober*;
1Tm	3	2	2 the president . . . must be *temperate*, discreet and courteous;
		11	2 the women must be respectable, . . . *sober* and quite reliable.
2Tm	2	26	[God may give your opponents a change of mind so that they] 3 *come to their senses*,
	4	5	⌐*Be careful* always to choose (or: *Be steady* always in) the right course;
Tt	2	2	2 The older men should be ⌐reserved (lit. *temperate*), dignified,
1 P	1	13	Free your minds, then, of encumbrances; ⌐control them (lit. *be sober*), and put your trust in nothing but the grace
	4	7	to pray better, *keep a* calm and *sober mind*.
	5	8	*Be calm* but vigilant,

4. SELF-CONTROL, TEMPERANCE – INTEMPERANCE: *EN-KRATEIA*

2	*a-krasia*	2	1 *en-krateia* 4
4	*a-kratēs*	1	5 *en-kratēs* 1
			3 *en-krateuomai* 2

Mt	23	25	you hypocrites . . . clean the outside of cup and dish and 2 leave the inside full of extortion and *intemperance*.
Ac	24	25	[Paul] began to treat of righteousness, *self-control*
1 Co	7	5	then come together again in case Satan should take advantage 2 of your ⌐weakness (lit. *lack of self-control*) to tempt you.
		9	3 if they cannot *control* ⌐the sexual urges (lit. *themselves*), they should get married,

1 Co	9 25	3 All the fighters at the games *go into* strict *training*;
Ga	5 23	[the Spirit brings] gentleness and *self-control*.
2 Tm	3 3	4 [People will be] ⌐heartless (lit. *unrestrained*) and unappeasable;
Tt	1 8	5 [the president must be] moral, devout and *self-controlled*;
2 P	1 6	[add] *self-control* to your understanding, patience to your *self-control*,

---

WITH

---

1. With: *meta* + genitive
  1: (God, Jesus) With (a person)
  2: With (God, Jesus) – Companions (of Jesus)
  3: With (a person) – Companions, Followers
2. With: *syn*
  1: (Jesus, the Grace of God) With (a person)
  2: With (a person) – Companions, Supporters
3. Together

  1: Together: *homou*
  2: Together – Community: *epi to auto*
4. Without = Apart from, Separate from: *aneu* and *chōris*
5. With, In the sight of, Before (God, Jesus) – For – At the house of: *para* + dative
6. With = In the presence of: *pros* + accusative
  1: With, To the presence of (God, Jesus)
  2: With – Among (generally)

---

1. WITH: *META* + genitive

1 *meta* (+ genitive) (152)   2 *ho meta* (+ genitive) 12

1: (GOD, JESUS) WITH (A PERSON)

X = God is with Jesus

Mt	1 23	(Is 7 14) Immanuel, a name which means 'God-is-*with*-us'.
	2 11	[the magi] saw the child *with* his mother Mary,
	9 11	Why does your master eat *with* tax collectors and sinners?
	15	Surely the bridegroom's attendants would never think of mourning as long as the bridegroom is still *with* them?
	16 27	the Son of Man is going to come . . . *with* his angels,
	17 17	How much longer must I be *with* you?
	26 18	I am keeping the Passover *with* my disciples.
	20	[Jesus] was at table *with* the twelve disciples.
	29	until the day I drink the new wine *with* you
	36	Jesus came *with* them to . . . Gethsemane;
	28 20	I am *with* you always; yes, to the end of time.
Mk	1 13	He was *with* the wild beasts,
	29	he went *with* James and John straight to the house of Simon and Andrew.
	2 16	When the scribes . . . saw him eating *with* sinners and tax collectors, they said . . . 'Why does he eat *with* tax collectors and sinners?'
	19	[the attendants] would never think of fasting while the bridegroom is still *with* them? As long as they have the bridegroom *with* them, they could not think of fasting.
	3 7	Jesus withdrew *with* his disciples to the lakeside,
	5 24	Jesus went *with* [Jairus]
	8 10	getting into the boat *with* his disciples,
	38	the Son of Man . . . comes . . . *with* the holy angels.
	11 11	he went out to Bethany *with* the Twelve.
	14 14	Where is my dining room in which I can eat the passover *with* my disciples?
	17	When evening came he arrived *with* the Twelve.
Lk	1 28	Rejoice, so highly favoured! The Lord is *with* you.
	58	the Lord had shown ⌐[Elizabeth] so great a kindness (lit. so great a kindness *with* her),
	66	the hand of the Lord was *with* [John]
	72	Thus he shows mercy ⌐to (lit. *with*) our ancestors,
	2 51	He then went down *with* them . . . to Nazareth
	5 30	Why do you eat . . . *with* tax collectors and sinners?
	34	you cannot make the . . . attendants fast while the bridegroom is still *with* them?
	6 17	He then came down *with* them and stopped at a piece of level ground
	7 36	One of the Pharisees invited him to ⌐a meal (lit. dine *with* him)
	22 11	Where is the dining room in which I can eat the passover *with* my disciples?
	15	I have longed to eat this passover *with* you
	53	When I was ⌐among (lit. *with*) you in the Temple day after day
	24 29	they pressed him to stay *with* them. 'It is nearly evening' they said
	30	Now while he was *with* them at table,
Jn	3 2 X	no one could perform the signs . . . unless God were *with* him.
	22	Jesus . . . stayed *with* them and baptised

Jn	3 26	the man who was *with* you . . . the man to whom you bore witness,
	4 27	his disciples . . . were surprised to find him ˚speaking ⌐to (lit. *with*) a woman, though none of them asked . . . 'Why are you talking ⌐to (lit. *with*) her?'
	6 3	Jesus climbed the hillside, and sat down there *with* his disciples.
	7 33	I shall remain *with* you for only a short time now;
	8 29 X	he who sent me is *with* me,
	9 37	You are looking at him; he is speaking ⌐to (lit. *with*) you.
	11 54	Jesus . . . left the district for a town called Ephraim . . . and stayed there *with* his disciples.
	13 33	I shall not be *with* you much longer.
	14 9	Have I been *with* you all this time,
	16	he will give you another Advocate to be *with* you for ever,
	30	I shall not talk *with* you any longer,
	16 4	I did not tell you this from the outset, because I was *with* you;
	32 X	And yet I am not alone, because the Father is *with* me.
	17 12	While I was *with* them, I kept those you had given me
	18 2	Jesus had often ⌐met (lit. been *with*) his disciples in [Gethsemane],
Ac	7 9	God was *with* [Joseph]
	10 38 X	God was *with* [Jesus of Nazareth]
	11 21	⌐The Lord helped them (lit. the hand of the Lord was *with* them)
	14 27	they . . . gave an account of all that God had done *with* them.
	15 4	they . . . gave an account of all that God had done *with* them.
	18 10	[Paul, do not be afraid,] I am *with* you.
Rm	15 33	May the God of peace be *with* you all! Amen.
	16 20	The grace of our Lord Jesus Christ be *with* you.
	24	(ᵛ The grace of our Lord Jesus Christ be *with* you all! Amen.)
1 Co	16 23	The grace of the Lord Jesus be *with* you.
2 Co	13 11	the God of love and peace will be *with* you.
	13	The grace of the Lord Jesus Christ, the love of God and the fellowship of the Holy Spirit be *with* you all.
Ga	6 18	The grace of our Lord Jesus Christ be *with* your spirit,
Ep	6 24	May grace and eternal life be *with* all who love our Lord Jesus Christ.
Ph	4 9	Then the God of peace will be *with* you.
	23	May the grace of the Lord Jesus Christ be *with* your spirit.
Col	4 18	Grace be *with* you.
1 Th	3 13	when our Lord Jesus Christ comes *with* all his saints.
	5 28	The grace of our Lord Jesus Christ be *with* you.
2 Th	1 7	when the Lord Jesus appears . . . *with* the angels of his power.
	3 16	The Lord be *with* you all.
	18	May the grace of our Lord Jesus Christ be *with* you all.
1 Tm	6 21	Grace be *with* you.
2 Tm	4 22	The Lord be *with* your spirit. Grace be *with* you.
Tt	3 15	Grace be *with* you all.
Phm	25	May the grace of our Lord Jesus Christ be *with* your spirit.
Heb	13 25	Grace be *with* you all.
1 Jn	4 17	Love will come to its perfection ⌐in (lit. *with*) us
2 Jn	2	because of the truth that lives in us and will be *with* us for ever.
	3	⌐we shall have (lit. *with* us there will be) grace, mercy and peace from God . . . and from Jesus Christ,
Rv	1 12	I turned round to see who had spoken ⌐to (lit. *with*) me,
	2 16	or I shall soon come to you and attack these people *with* the sword out of my mouth.
	3 20	I will come in to share his meal, side by side *with* him.
	4 1	I . . . heard the same voice speaking ⌐to (lit. *with*) me,
	10 8	Then I heard the voice I had heard from heaven speaking ⌐to (lit. *with*) me again.
	21 3	Here God lives ⌐among (lit. *with*) men. He will make his home ⌐among (lit. *with*) them; they shall be his people, ⌐and he will be their God; his name is God-*with*-them, God *with* them, will be ᵛ their God) (G and God himself will be *with* them).
	22 21	May the grace of the Lord Jesus be *with* you all.

2: WITH (GOD, JESUS) – COMPANIONS (OF JESUS)

Mt	12 30	He who is not *with* me is against me, and he who does not gather *with* me scatters.
	17 3	Moses and Elijah . . . were talking *with* [Jesus].
	25 31	When the Son of Man comes in his glory, ⌐escorted by (lit. *with*) all the angels,
	26 23	Someone who has dipped his hand into the dish *with* me,
	38	Wait here and keep awake *with* me.
	40	So you had not the strength to keep awake *with* me one hour?
	51	2 one of ⌐the followers of (lit. *those with*) Jesus . . . struck out at the high priest's servant,
	69	You too were *with* Jesus the Galilean.
	71	This man was *with* Jesus the Nazarene.
Mk	3 14	[Jesus] appointed twelve; they were to be his *companions*
	4 36	there were other boats *with* him.
	5 18	the man . . . begged to be allowed to stay *with* him.
	37	And he allowed no one to go *with* him

Mk	14 18	one of you is about to betray me, one of you eating *with* me
	20	one who is dipping into the same dish *with* me.
	33	Then he took Peter and James and John *with* him.
	67	You too were *with* Jesus, the man from Nazareth.
	16 10	[Mary] then went to those who had been his *companions*
Lk	5 29	*with* them at table was a large gathering of tax collectors
	11 23	He who is not *with* me is against me; and he who does not gather *with* me scatters.
	22 21	here *with* me on the table is the hand of the man who betrays me.
	28	You are the men who have stood ᴿby me (lit. *with* me) faithfully in my trials;
	33	Lord . . . I would be ready to go to prison *with* you, and to death.
	59	This fellow was certainly *with* him.
	23 43	today you will be *with* me in paradise.
Jn	6 66	many of his disciples . . . stopped going *with* him.
	9 40	some Pharisees . . . were ᴿpresent (lit. there *with* him)
	11 16	Let us go too, and die *with* him.
	12 17	All who had been *with* him when he called Lazarus out of the tomb
	13 8	If I do not wash you, you can have nothing in common *with* me.
	18	Someone who ᴿshares my table (lit. eats (ᵛ bread) *with* me)
	15 27	because you have been *with* me from the outset.
	17 24	I want those you have given me to be *with* me where I am,
	18 26	Didn't I see you in the garden *with* him?
	19 18	they crucified him *with* two others,
Ac	2 28	you will fill me *with* gladness through your presence.
	7 38	it was only through Moses that our ancestors could communicate *with* the angel . . . on Mount Sinai.
1 Jn	1 3	we are in union *with* the Father and *with* his son Jesus Christ.
	6	If we say that we are in union *with* God
Rv	3 4	they are fit to come *with* me, dressed in white.
	20	I will come in to share his meal, ᴿside by side *with* him (lit. and he will share my meal *with* me)
	21	Those who prove victorious I will allow to ᴿshare (lit. sit *with* me on) my throne, just as I . . . took my place *with* my Father on his throne.
	14 1	a Lamb who had *with* him a hundred and forty-four thousand people,
	17 14	2 they will be defeated by ᴿhis followers (lit. those *with* him), the called, the chosen, the faithful.
	20 4	they . . . reigned *with* Christ for a thousand years.
	6	they will . . . reign *with* him for a thousand years.
	22 12	Very soon now, I shall be *with* you again,

3: WITH (A PERSON) – COMPANIONS, FOLLOWERS

Mt	5 25	while you are still on the way to the court *with* him,
	12 3	2 Have you not read what David did when he and his *followers* were hungry
	4	2 they ate the loaves . . . which neither he nor his *followers* were allowed to eat.
	27 54	Meanwhile the centurion, together *with* the others guarding Jesus,
Mk	1 36	2 Simon and his *companions* set out in search of him,
	2 25	2 David . . . when he and his *followers* were hungry
	5 40	[Jesus] taking with him the child's father and mother and his own *companions*,
Lk	6 3	2 you have not read what David did when he and his *followers* were hungry
	4	2 how he . . . took the loaves. . .and gave them to his *followers*,
Jn	11 31	2 the Jews *who were* in the house sympathising *with* Mary
	20 24	Thomas . . . was not *with* them when Jesus came.
	26	the disciples were in the house again and Thomas was *with* them.
Ac	9 19	After [Saul] had spent only a few days *with* the disciples in Damascus,
	39	clothes Dorcas had made when she was *with* them.
	20 34	the work I did earned enough to meet my needs and those of my *companions*.
Tt	3 15	2 All *those who are with* me send their greetings.

2. WITH: *SYN*

1   syn (53)   3 syn-eimi 2
2   ho syn   11

1: (JESUS, THE GRACE OF GOD) WITH (A PERSON)

Lk	7 6	So Jesus went *with* them,
	24 29	So he went in to stay *with* them.
	44	while I was still *with* you,
Jn	18 1	Jesus left *with* his disciples and crossed the Kedron valley.
1 Co	15 10	On the contrary, I, or rather the grace of God that is *with* me,

2: WITH (GOD, JESUS)

Mt	26 35	Even if I have to die *with* you,
	27 38	At the same time two robbers were crucified *with* him,
	44	Even the robbers who were crucified *with* him taunted him
Mk	15 27	And they crucified two robbers *with* him,
	32	Even those who were crucified *with* him taunted him.
Lk	8 1	he made his way through towns . . . *With* him went the Twelve,
	38	The man . . . asked to be allowed to stay *with* him,
	51	When he came to the house [of Jairus] he allowed no one to go in *with* him
	9 18	3 when he was praying alone *in the presence of* his disciples
	22 14	he took his place at table, and the apostles *with* him.
	56	This person was *with* him too,
	23 32	Now *with* him they were also leading out two other criminals to be executed.
Jn	12 2	Lazarus was among those at table (§ *with* him).
Ac	4 13	[the Sanhedrin] recognised [Peter and John] as *associates of* Jesus;
Rm	6 8	we believe that having died *with* Christ we shall return to life *with* him:
	8 32	Since God did not spare his own Son . . . we may be certain, after such a gift, that (§ *with* [the Son]) he will not refuse anything he can give.
2 Co	4 14	knowing that he who raised the Lord Jesus to life will raise us *with* Jesus . . . and put us by his side and you with us.
	13 4	we shall live *with* him.
Ph	1 23	I want to be gone and be *with* Christ,
Col	2 13	he has brought you to life *with* him,
	20	If you have really died *with* Christ
	3 3	the life you have is hidden *with* Christ in God.
	4	you too will be revealed in all your glory *with* him.
1 Th	4 14	God will bring [those who have died in Jesus] *with* him.
	17	So we shall stay *with* the Lord for ever.
	5 10	so that, alive or dead, we should still live ᴿunited to (lit. together *with*) him.
2 P	1 18	when we were *with* him on the holy mountain.

3: WITH (A PERSON) – COMPANIONS, SUPPORTERS

Mk	2 26	2 David . . . also gave some [loaves of offering] to *the men with* him?
Lk	2 13	And suddenly *with* the angel there was a great throng
	5 9	2 For [Simon Peter] and all his *companions* were completely overcome
	7 12	And a considerable number of the townspeople were *with* [the widow of Nain]
	8 45	2 Peter (ᵛ and his *companions*) said,
	9 32	2 Peter and his *companions* were heavy with sleep,
	24 10	2 Mary of Magdala, Joanna . . . The other women *with* them
	24	2 Some of our ᴿfriends (lit. *companions*) went to the tomb
	33	There they found the Eleven assembled together *with* their *companions*,
Ac	5 17	2 Then the high priest intervened with all his *supporters*
	21	2 When the high priest arrived, he and his *supporters* convened the Sanhedrin
	13 7	[Bar-jesus] was one of ᴿthe attendants of (lit. those *with*) the proconsul Sergius Paulus
	14 4 ○	some ᴿsupported (lit. were *with*) the Jews, others (§ *with*) the apostles
	22 9	2 *The people with* me saw the light
	11	3 my *companions* had to take me by the hand; so I came to Damascus.
	27 2	we had Aristarchus *with* us,
Rm	16 14	Asyncritus, Phlegon . . . and all the brothers who are *with* them;
	15	Philologus and Julia . . . and all the saints who are *with* them.
Ga	2 3	2 Titus who had come *with* me
Col	2 5	in spirit I am there ᴿamong (lit. *with*) you,

3. TOGETHER

1: TOGETHER: *HOMOU*
homou 4

Jn	4 36	thus sower and reaper rejoice *together*.
	20 4	They ran *together*,
	21 2	and two more of his disciples were *together*.
Ac	2 1	they had all ᴿmet (lit. come *together*) in one room,

2: TOGETHER – COMMUNITY: *EPI TO AUTO*
2 *kata to auto* 1   1 *epi to auto* (5)

Lk	17 35	two women will be grinding corn *together*:

Ac	1 15	there were about a hundred and twenty persons in the *congregation*
	2 44	The faithful all lived *together* and owned everything in common;
	47	Day by day the Lord added to their *community* those destined to be saved.
	14 1	[Paul and Barnabas] went to the Jewish synagogue ʳas they had (lit. in the same way; or: *together*) at Antioch,
	2	
1 Co	7 5 ○	Do not refuse each other except by mutual consent, and then only for an agreed time . . . then come *together* again.

4. WITHOUT = APART FROM, SEPARATE FROM: *ANEU* and *CHŌRIS*

2 *aneu* (1)   1 *chōris* (3)

Mt	10 29 2	And yet not one [sparrow] falls to the ground *without* your Father knowing.
Jn	1 3	Through [the Word] all things came to be, not one thing had its being *but through* him.
	15 5	for *cut off from* me you can do nothing.
Ep	2 12	there was a time when . . . you ʳhad no (lit. were *without*) Christ

5. WITH, IN THE SIGHT OF, BEFORE (GOD, JESUS) – FOR – AT THE HOUSE OF: *PARA* + dative

para (+ dative) (*34*)

Mt	6 1	by doing this you will lose all reward *from* your Father in heaven.
	19 26	*For* men . . . this is impossible; *for* God everything is possible.
Mk	10 27	*For* men . . . it is impossible, but not *for* God: because everything is possible *for* God.
Lk	1 30	you have won ʳGod's favour (lit. favour *with* God).
	2 52	And Jesus increased in wisdom . . . and in favour *with* God and men.
	9 47	[Jesus] took a little child and set him *by his side*.
	11 37	a Pharisee invited [Jesus] to dine *at his house*.
	18 27	Things that are impossible *for* men . . . are possible *for* God.
	19 7	He has gone to stay *at* a sinner's *house*
Jn	1 39	[the two disciples] stayed *with* him the rest of that day.
	4 40	the Samaritans . . . begged him to stay *with* them.
	8 38	What I . . . speak of is what I have seen *with* my Father;
	14 17	because [the Spirit of truth] is *with* you, he is in you.
	23	we shall . . . make our home *with* him.
	25	I have said these things to you while still *with* you;
	17 5	Now, Father, it is time for you to glorify me (§ *before* you) with that glory I had *with* you
Rm	2 11	ʳGod has no favourites (lit. there are no favourites *with* God).
	13	It is not listening to the Law but keeping it that will make people holy *in the sight of* God.
	9 14	Does it follow that ʳGod is unjust (lit. there can be injustice *before* God)?
1 Co	3 19	the wisdom of this world is foolishness *to* God.
	7 24	Each one of you, my brothers, should stay as he was *before* God at the time of his call.
Ga	3 11	The Law will not justify anyone *in the sight of* God,
Ep	6 9	ʳ[God] is not impressed by one person more than by another (lit. *with* God, no one person can make more of an impression than any other).
2 Th	1 6	God will very rightly (lit. It is very right *for* God to) repay with injury those who are injuring you,
Jm	1 17	the Father of all light; *with* him there is no such thing as alteration,
	27	Pure, unspoilt religion, *in the eyes of* God our Father
1 P	2 4	the living stone . . . precious *to* [God];
	20	The merit, *in the sight of* God, is in bearing [a beating] patiently when you are punished after doing your duty.
2 P	3 8	*with* the Lord, 'a day' can mean a thousand years,

6. WITH = IN THE PRESENCE OF: *PROS* + accusative

pros (+ accusative) (*16*)

1: WITH, TO THE PRESENCE OF (GOD, JESUS)

Jn	1 1	the Word was *with* God
	2	He was *with* God in the beginning.
	12 32	I shall draw all men *to* myself.
	14 3	I shall return to take you *with* me;
Rm	4 2	Abraham . . . would really have had something to boast about, though not *in God's sight*
	5 1	by faith we are judged righteous and at peace *with* God,
2 Co	5 8	we want to . . . make our home *with* the Lord.
1 Jn	1 2	the eternal life which was *with* the Father

1 Jn	2 1	we have our advocate *with* the Father, Jesus Christ, who is just;

2: WITH – AMONG (GENERALLY)

Mt	13 56	His sisters, too, are they not all here *with* us?
Mk	6 3	His sisters, too, are they not here *with* us?
	9 19	How much longer must I be *with* you?
	14 49	I was *among* you teaching in the Temple day after day
Lk	9 41	How much longer must I be *among* you
1 Th	3 4	when we were *with* you, we warned you
2 Th	3 10	We gave you a rule when we were *with* you:

WITNESS – TESTIFY

1: (Bear) Witness, Testify (to), Attest – Testimony, Evidence			2: Urge, Appeal – Put as a duty (to)		
1	*martyreō*	76	13	*epi-martyreō*	1
2	*martyria*	37	14	*syn-epi-martyreō*	1
4	*martyrion*	20	15	*pro-martyromai*	1
6	*martyromai*	5	7	(*pseudo-*)*martyreō*	5
3	*martys*	35	10	(*pseudo-*)*martyria*	2
12	*a-martyros*	1	11	(*pseudo-*)*martys*	2
8	*kata-martyreō*	3	9	*sym-martyreō*	3
5	*dia-martyromai*	15			

1: (BEAR) WITNESS, TESTIFY (TO), ATTEST – TESTIMONY, EVIDENCE

F = False witness   J = John the Baptist as witness

Mt	8 4		4	[Jesus said to the cured leper,] 'Make the offering prescribed by Moses, as *evidence* for them.'
	10 18		4	You will be dragged before . . . kings for my sake, to [bear] *witness* before them and the pagans.
	15 19	F	10	from the heart come . . . ʳperjury (lit. false *witness*), slander.
	18 16		3	(Dt 19 15) the evidence of two or three *witnesses* is required to sustain any charge.
	19 18	F	7	(Ex 20 16) You must not *bring* false *witness*.
	23 31			Your own *evidence* tells against you! You are the sons of those who murdered the prophets!
	24 14		4	This Good News of the kingdom will be proclaimed . . . as a *witness* to all the nations.
	26 59	F	10	The chief priests . . . were looking for (§ false) *evidence*
	60			against Jesus . . . 60 But they could not find any, though
		F	11	several lying *witnesses* came forward. Eventually two stepped
	62		8	forward . . . 62 The high priest . . . said to him, '. . . What is this *evidence* these men are *bringing against* you?'
	65		3	He has blasphemed. What need of *witnesses* have we now?
	27 13		8	Do you not hear how many *charges* they have *brought against* you?
Mk	1 44		4	make the offering for your healing prescribed by Moses as *evidence* of your recovery.
	6 11		4	shake off the dust from under your feet as ʳa sign to (lit. *testimony* against) them.
	10 19	F	7	(Ex 20 16) You must not *bring* false *witness*;
	13 9		4	you will stand before . . . kings for my sake, to [bear] *witness* before them,
	14 55			The chief priests and the whole Sanhedrin were looking for
	56	F	2/7	*evidence* against Jesus . . . 56 Several, indeed, *brought* false *evidence* against him, but their *evidence* was conflicting.
	57	F	7/2	57 Some stood up and *submitted* this false *evidence* against
	59			him . . . 59 But even on this point their *evidence* was con-
	60			flicting. 60 The high priest . . . put this question to Jesus,
			8	'. . . What is this *evidence* these men are *bringing against* you?'
	63		3	What need of *witnesses* have we now? . . . 64 You heard the blasphemy.
Lk	4 22			ʳ[Jesus] won the approval of all (lit. everyone *was witness* to [Jesus]),
	5 14		4	go and . . . make the offering for your healing as Moses prescribed it, as *evidence* for them.
	9 5		4	shake the dust from your feet as ʳa sign to (lit. *testimony* against) them.
	11 48		3	you both *witness* what your ancestors did and approve it;
	16 28		5	I have five brothers, [send Lazarus] to give them ʳwarning (lit. *evidence*) so that they do not come to this place of torment
	18 20	F	7	(Ex 20 16) You must not *bring* false *witness*;

Lk 21	13		[they will bring you before kings because of my name] – and that will be your opportunity to [bear] *witness*.
		4	
22	71	2	What need of *witnesses* have we now?
24	48		[It is written that the Christ would rise from the dead.] You are *witnesses* to this.
		3	
Jn 1	7 J	2/	[John] came as a *witness, as a witness to speak* for the light . . . ⁸ He was not the light, only *a witness to speak* for the light.
	8 J		
	15 J		John *appears as* his *witness*. He proclaims: . . . He who comes after me ranks before me because he existed before me.
	19 J	2	This is how John appeared as a *witness*.
	32 J		John also declared and *bore witness*, 'I saw the Spirit coming down on [Jesus] . . . ³⁴ Yes, I have seen and I *am the witness* that he is the ᵛ Chosen One (G Son) of God.
	34 J		
2	25		[Jesus] never needed *evidence* about any man;
3	11 X		we . . . *witness* only to what we have seen and yet you people reject our *evidence*.
	X	2	
	26		[John's disciples] went to John and said, 'Rabbi, . . . the man to whom you *bore witness*, is baptising now;
	J		
	28		You yourselves can *bear me out*: I said: I myself am not the Christ.
	32 X		[He who comes from heaven] *bears witness* to the things he has seen and heard, even if his *testimony* is not accepted;
	X	2	
	33 X	2	³³ though all who do accept his *testimony* are attesting the truthfulness of God.
	X		
4	39		Many Samaritans . . . believed in him on the strength of the woman's *testimony* when she said, 'He told me all I have ever done',
	44 X		[Jesus] himself has ʳdeclared (lit. *borne witness*) that there is no respect for a prophet in his own country.
5	31 X	/2	Were I to *testify* on my own behalf, my *testimony* would not be valid; ³² but there is another *witness* who can *speak* on my behalf, and . . . ʳhis *testimony* (lit. *witness* he *testifies* to) is valid. ³³ You sent messengers to John, and he *gave his testimony* to the truth; ³⁴ not that I depend on human *testimony* . . . ³⁶ But my *testimony* is greater than John's: the works my Father has given me to carry out . . . *testify* that the Father sent me. ³⁷ Besides, the Father . . . *bears witness* to me himself.
	32 Θ		
	33	2/	
	34 J		
	J	2/2	
	36		
	37		
	Θ		
	39		the scriptures . . . *testify* to me,
7	7 X		The world . . . does hate me, because I *give evidence* that its ways are evil.
8	13 X		the Pharisees said to [Jesus], 'You are *testifying* on your own behalf; your *testimony* is not valid'. ¹⁴ Jesus replied: It is true that I am *testifying* on my own behalf, but my *testimony* is still valid, because I know where I came from and where I am going;
	14 X	2	
	X		
	X	2	
	17	2	in your Law it is written (Dt 19 15) that the *testimony* of two [witnesses] is valid. ¹⁸ I may be *testifying* on my own behalf, but the Father who sent me *is my witness* too.
	18 X		
	Θ		
10	25		The works I do in my Father's name are my *witness*;
12	17		All who had been with [Jesus] when he called Lazarus out of the tomb . . . were *telling how they had witnessed* it;
13	21 X		Having ʳsaid (lit. *testified* to) this, Jesus . . . declared, 'I tell you solemnly, one of you will betray me'.
15	26 Ⓢ		the Spirit of truth . . . will *be my witness*. ²⁷And you too will *be witnesses*, because you have been with me from the outset.
	27		
18	23		If there is something wrong in what I said, *point it out*;
	37 X		I came into the world for this: to *bear witness* to the truth;
19	35	/2	This is the *evidence* of one who saw it – trustworthy *evidence*,
21	24		This disciple is the one who *vouches for* these things . . . and we know that his *testimony* is true.
		2	
Ac 1	8	3	you will be my *witnesses* not only in Jerusalem but . . . indeed to the ends of the earth.
	22		[We must choose] someone who was with us . . . until the day when [Jesus] was taken up from us – and he can act with us as a *witness* to his resurrection.
		3	
2	32	3	God raised this man Jesus to life, and all of us are *witnesses* to that.
3	15		God . . . raised him from the dead, and to that fact we are the *witnesses*;
		3	
4	33	4	The apostles continued to *testify* to the resurrection of the Lord Jesus with great power,
5	32	3	[God has now raised him up.] We are *witnesses* to all this, we and the Holy Spirit
	Ⓢ		
6	3		select from among yourselves seven men of good *reputation*, filled with the Spirit and with wisdom;
	13		[The Jews arrested Stephen and brought him before the Sanhedrin.] There they put up false *witnesses*
	F	3	
7	44 ○	4	in the desert our ancestors possessed the Tent of *Testimony*
	58	3	The *witnesses* (cf. Dt 17 7) put down their clothes at the feet of a young man called Saul.
8	25	5	Having *given* their *testimony* and proclaimed the word of the Lord, [Peter and John] went back to Jerusalem,
10	22		Cornelius . . . is . . . highly *regarded* by the entire Jewish people,

Ac 10	39	3	I, and those with me, can *witness* to everything [Jesus] did . . . ⁴⁰ . . . God raised him to life and allowed him to be seen ⁴¹ . . . by certain *witnesses* God had chosen beforehand . . . ⁴² and he has ordered us . . . to ʳtell (lit. *testify* to) [his people] that God has appointed him to judge everyone, alive or dead. ⁴³ It is to him that all the prophets *bear* [this] *witness*: that all who believe in Jesus will have their sins forgiven
	41	3	
	42	5	
	43	3	
13	22		[God] made David their king . . . whom he ʳapproved (lit. *testified* to) in these words (Ps 89 21), 'I have selected David . . . a man after my own heart,
	Θ		
	31		it is these same companions of [Jesus] who are now his *witnesses* before our people.
		3	
14	3 X		the Lord *supported* all [Paul and Barnabas] said about his gift of grace,
	17 Θ	12	[God] did not leave you *without evidence* of himself . . . he sends you rain from heaven, he makes your crops grow
15	8 Θ		God . . . ʳshowed his approval of (lit. *testified* to) [the pagans] by giving the Holy Spirit to them
16	2		The brothers at Lystra and Iconium *spoke* [well] *of* Timothy,
18	5	5	Paul . . . [was] ʳdeclaring (lit. *attesting*) to the Jews that Jesus was the Christ.
20	23 Ⓢ	5	the Holy Spirit . . . has *made it clear enough* that imprisonment and persecution await me.
	24	5	the mission the Lord Jesus gave me . . . was to *bear witness* to the Good News
	26	6	here and now I *swear* that my conscience is clear
22	5		[I persecuted this Way] as the high priest . . . can *testify*, Ananias, a devout follower of the Law and [highly] *thought of* by all the Jews living [at Damascus],
	12		
	15	3	you are to be *witness* before all mankind, [testifying] to what you have seen and heard.
	18	2	leave Jerusalem at once; they will not accept the *testimony* you are giving about me.
	20	3	[Lord,] when the blood of your *witness* Stephen was being shed, I was standing by
23	11	5	Courage [Paul]! You have *borne witness* for me in Jerusalem, now you must ʳdo the same (lit. *bear witness*) for me in Rome.
26	5		[The Jews] could *testify* . . . that I . . . lived as a Pharisee.
	16	3	I have appeared . . . to appoint you as my servant and as *witness* of this vision in which you have seen me,
	22	6	I have stood firm to this day, *testifying* to great and small alike,
28	23	5	[Paul] put his case to [the Jews in Rome], *testifying* to the kingdom of God
Rm 1	9 Θ	3	God . . . ʳknows (lit. is my *witness*) that I never fail to mention you in my prayers,
2	15	9	[Pagans] can point to the substance of the Law engraved on their hearts – they can call a *witness*, that is, their own conscience
3	21		God's justice . . . was made known and *testified* to through the Law and the prophets
8	16 Ⓢ	9	The Spirit himself and our spirit *bear united witness* that we are children of God.
9	1	9	it is the truth – my conscience *in union* with the Holy Spirit *assures* me of it
10	2		I can *swear* to [the Jews'] fervour for God,
1 Co 1	6	4	the *witness* to Christ has indeed been strong among you
2	1		I came to you . . . simply to tell you ʳwhat God had guaranteed (lit. the *testimony* of God).
	Θ	4	
15	15 F	11	[if Christ has not been raised] we are shown up as *witnesses* who have committed perjury before God, because we *swore in evidence* before God that he had raised Christ to life.
2 Co 1	12		There is one thing we are proud of, and our conscience *tells us it is true*:
		4	
	23 Θ	4	I call God to *witness* that the reason why I did not come to Corinth after all was to spare your feelings.
8	3		I can *swear* that [the Corinthians] gave not only as much as they could afford, but far more,
13	1	3	(Dt 19 15) The evidence of three, or at least two, *witnesses* is necessary to sustain the charge.
Ga 4	15		I *swear* that you would even have gone so far as to pluck out your eyes and give them to me.
5	3	6	ʳWith all solemnity I repeat my warning (lit. I will *testify* to it again): Everyone who accepts circumcision is obliged to keep the whole Law.
Ph 1	8 Θ	3	God ʳknows (lit. is my *witness*) how much I miss you all,
Col 4	13		I can *testify* for [Epaphras] that he works hard for you,
1 Th 2	5 Θ	3	ʳwe can swear it before God (lit. God is our *witness*), that never at any time have our speeches been simply flattery,
	10 Θ	3	You are *witnesses*, and so is God, that our treatment of you . . . has been impeccably right and fair.
4	6	5	the Lord always punishes sins of that sort, as we told you before and *assured* you,
2 Th 1	10	4	you are believers, through our *witness*.
1 Tm 2	6 X	4	[There is only one God. Christ] is the *evidence* of this, sent at the appointed time,
3	7	2	It is also necessary that people outside the Church should *speak* well *of* [the elder-in-charge],

1 Tm 5 10   [The widow] must be a woman *known* for her good works
    19   Never accept any accusation brought against an elder unless
       3   it is supported by two or three *witnesses*.
  6 12 3 you . . . spoke up for the truth in front of many *witnesses*.
   13 X   Jesus Christ . . . *spoke up as a witness* for the truth in front of Pontius Pilate.
2 Tm 1 8 4 you are never to be ashamed of *witnessing* to the Lord,
  2 2   You have heard everything that I teach ᵣin public (lit.
     3   through *witnesses*); hand it on to reliable people
Tt 1 13 2 [Cretans were never anything but liars:] that is a true *statement*.
Heb 2 4 14 God himself confirmed *their witness* with signs and marvels
   6   5 there is a passage that ᵣshows us this (lit. *testifies* to this for us). It runs: What is man that you should spare a thought for him,
  3 5   4 Moses was . . . *acting as witness* to the things which were to be divulged later;
  7 8   in the one case it is ordinary mortal men who receive the tithes, and in the other, someone who is ᵣdeclared (lit. *witnessed*) to be still alive.
   17 Θ   it was about [Christ] that the ᵣprophecy was made (lit. *testimony* was *given*): You are a priest . . . for ever.
 10 15 Ⓢ The Holy Spirit *assures* us of this: [I will put my laws into their hearts.]
   28   Anyone who disregards the Law of Moses is ruthlessly
     3   (Dt 17 6) put to death on the word of two *witnesses* or three;
 11 2   It was for faith that our ancestors were *commended*.
   4   It was because of his faith that Abel . . . was ᵣdeclared (lit.
    Θ   *attested*) to be righteous when God ᵣmade acknowledgement of (lit. *witnessed*) his offerings.
   5   it is *attested* that [Enoch] had pleased God.
   39   [Gideon, Barak . . .] are all ᵣheroes of (lit. [well] *attested* by their) faith, but they did not receive what was promised,
 12 1   3 With so many *witnesses* in a great cloud on every side of us, we too . . . should throw off everything that hinders us,
Jm 5 3   4 the same corrosion will ᵣbe your own sentence (lit. *testify* against you),
1 P 1 11 Ⓢ 15 The Spirit of Christ . . . *foretold* the sufferings of Christ and the glories that would come after them,
  5 1   3 I am an elder myself, and a *witness* to the sufferings of Christ,
   12 13 never . . . let go this true grace of God to which I *bear witness*.
1 Jn 1 2   That life was made visible: we saw it and we are *giving* our *testimony*,
  4 14   we *testify* that the Father sent his Son as saviour of the world.
  5 6 Ⓢ with the Spirit as another *witness* – since the Spirit is the
   7 Ⓢ truth – ⁷ so that there are three *witnesses*, ⁸ the Spirit, the water and the blood, and all three of them agree.
   9   2 We accept the *testimony* of human witnesses but God's
    Θ 2/2 *testimony* is much greater, and this is God's *testimony*,
   10   *given as evidence* for his Son. ¹⁰ Everybody who believes
    Θ 2 in the Son of God has this *testimony* inside him; and anyone who will not believe God is making God out to be a
    Θ 2 liar, because he has not trusted the *testimony* God has
   11 Θ /2 *given* about his Son. ¹¹ This is the *testimony*: God has given us eternal life and this life is in his Son;
3 Jn 3   [Gaius,] it was a great joy to me when some brothers . . . ᵣtold of (lit. *testified* to) your faithfulness to the truth,
  6   [These brothers] are a *proof* to the whole Church of your charity
  12   Demetrius has been ᵣapproved (lit. [well] *attested*) by everyone, and indeed by the truth itself. We too will *vouch for* him and you know that our *testimony* is true.
Rv 1 2   2 John . . . *swears* it is the word of God ᵣguaranteed (lit. *attested*) by Jesus Christ.
  5 X 3 Jesus Christ, the faithful *witness*,
  9   2 I was on the island of Patmos for having preached God's word and *witnessed* for Jesus;
  2 13 3 my faithful *witness*, Antipas, was killed in your own town,
  3 14 X Here is the message of the Amen, the faithful, the true
    3   *witness*,
  6 9   I saw underneath the altar the souls of all the people who had
    2   been killed on account of the word of God, for *witnessing* to it.
 11 3   3 I shall send my two *witnesses* to prophesy for those twelve hundred and sixty days,
  7   2 When they have completed their *witnessing*, the beast . . . is going to make war on them
 12 11   [Our brothers] have triumphed over [the dragon] by the
    2   blood of the Lamb and by the *witness* of their martyrdom,
  17   the dragon . . . went away to make war on . . . all who . . .
    2   [bear] *witness* for Jesus.
 15 5 ○ 4 the sanctuary, the Tent of the *Testimony*, opened in heaven,
 17 6   3 [the prostitute] was drunk with . . . the blood of the *martyrs* of Jesus;
 19 10   I am a servant . . . like you and all your brothers who are
    2/2   *witnesses* to Jesus . . . The *witness* Jesus gave is the same as the spirit of prophecy.

Rv 20 4   I saw the souls of all who had been beheaded for having
    2   *witnessed* for Jesus and for having preached God's word,
 22 16   I, Jesus, have sent my angel to ᵣmake (lit. *bear witness* to) these revelations to you
  18 X   This is my ᵣsolemn warning (lit. *testimony*) to all who hear the prophecies in this book:
  20 X   The one who ᵣguarantees (lit. *testifies* to) these revelations repeats his promise: I shall indeed be with you soon.

2: URGE, APPEAL – PUT AS A DUTY (TO)

Ac 2 40 5 [Peter] *spoke* to [the Jews] for a long time . . . and he urged them,
 20 21 5 [I have preached to you,] *urging* both Jews and Greeks to turn to God and to believe in our Lord Jesus.
Ep 4 17 6 I want to *urge* you in the name of the Lord, not to go on living the aimless kind of life that pagans live.
1 Th 2 12 6 [we are] *appealing* to you to live a life worthy of God,
1 Tm 5 21 5 Before God, and before Jesus Christ . . . I *put it* to you *as a duty* to keep these rules
2 Tm 2 14 5 *tell* them in the name of God that there is to be no wrangling about words:
  4 1   5 Before God and before Jesus Christ . . . I *put this duty* to you . . . proclaim the message

---

WORLD

---

1. the World, the Universe: *kosmos* | **2. the World, the Earth:** *oikoumenē*

1. THE WORLD, THE UNIVERSE: *KOSMOS*

   2 *kosmikos*   2   3 *kosmo(-kratōr)* 1
   1 *kosmos*   185/186

Mt 4 8   the devil showed him all the kingdoms of the *world*
  5 14   You are the light of the *world*.
 13 35   (cf. Ps 78 2) I will . . . expound things hidden since the foundation of the *world*.
   38   [The sower of the good seed is the Son of Man.] The field is the *world*.
 16 26   What . . . will a man gain if he wins the whole *world* and ruins his life?
 18 7   Alas for the *world* that there should be such obstacles!
 24 21   distress such as, until now, since the *world* began, there never has been,
 25 34   the kingdom prepared for you since the foundation of the *world*.
 26 13   wherever in all the *world* this Good News is proclaimed,
Mk 8 36   What gain . . . is it for a man to win the whole *world* . . .?
 14 9   wherever throughout all the *world* the Good News is proclaimed,
 16 15   Go out to the whole *world*; proclaim the Good News to all creation.
Lk 9 25   What gain . . . is it for a man to have won the whole *world* . . .?
 11 50   every prophet's blood that has been shed since the foundation of the *world*,
 12 30   It is the pagans of this *world* who set their hearts on these things.
Jn 1 9   The Word . . . was coming into the *world*.
  10   [The Word] was in the *world*, the *world* that had its being through him, and the *world* did not know him.
  29   the lamb of God that takes away the sin of the *world*.
 3 16   God loved the *world* so much that he gave his only Son,
  17   God sent his Son into the *world* not to condemn the *world*, but so that through him the *world* might be saved.
  19   the light has come into the *world*
 4 42   he really is the saviour of the *world*.
 6 14   This really is the prophet who is to come into the *world*.
  33   the bread of God is that which . . . gives life to the *world*,
  51   the bread that I shall give is my flesh, for the life of the *world*.
 7 4   since you are doing all this, you should let the whole *world* see.
  7   The *world* cannot hate you, but it does hate me,
 8 12   I am the light of the *world*;
  23   You are of this *world*; I am not of this *world*.
  26   what I have learnt from him I declare to the *world*.
 9 5   As long as I am in the *world* I am the light of the *world*.
  39   It is for judgement that I have come into this *world*.
 10 36   to someone the Father has consecrated and sent into the *world*.

Jn	11	9	a man can walk in the daytime without stumbling because he has the light of this *world* to see by;
		27	you are the *Christ*, . . . the one who was to come into this *world*.
	12	19	the whole *world* is running after him!
		25	anyone who hates his life in this *world* will keep it for the eternal life.
		31	Now sentence is being passed on this *world*; now the prince of this *world* is to be overthrown.
		46	I, the light, have come into the *world*,
		47	I have come not to condemn the *world*, but to save the *world*:
	13	1	Jesus knew that the hour had come for him to pass from this *world* to the Father.
	14	17	that Spirit of truth whom the *world* can never receive
		19	In a short time the *world* will no longer see me;
		22	Do you intend to show yourself to us and not to the *world*?
		27	my own peace I give you, a peace the *world* cannot give,
		30	because the prince of this *world* is on his way.
		31	the *world* must be brought to know that I love the Father
	15	18	If the *world* hates you, remember that it hated me before you.
		19	¹⁹ If you belonged to the *world*, the *world* would love you as its own; but because you do not belong to the *world*, because my choice withdrew you from the *world*, therefore the *world* hates you.
	16	8	when [the Advocate] comes, he will show the *world* how wrong it was, about sin, about who was in the right, and about judgement; . . . ¹¹ about judgement: proved by the prince of this *world* being already condemned.
		11	
		20	you will be weeping . . . while the *world* will rejoice;
		21	in her joy that a man has been born into the *world*.
		28	I came from the Father and have come into the *world* and now I leave the *world* to go to the Father.
		33	in the *world* you will have trouble, but be brave: I have conquered the *world*.
	17	5	that glory I had with you [the Father] before ever the *world* was.
		6	I have made your name known to the men you took from the *world* to give me.
		9	I am not praying for the *world* but for those you have given me,
		11	I am not in the *world* any longer, but they are in the *world*,
		13	while still in the *world* I say these things
		14	I passed your word on to them, and the *world* hated them, because they belong to the *world* no more than I belong to the *world*. ¹⁵ I am not asking you to remove them from the *world*, but to protect them from the evil one. ¹⁶ They do not belong to the *world* any more than I belong to the *world*.
		15	
		16	
		18	As you sent me into the *world*, I have sent them into the *world*,
		21	so that the *world* may believe it was you who sent me.
		23	that the *world* will realise that it was you who sent me
		24	you loved me before the foundation of the *world*.
		25	Father, Righteous One, the *world* has not known you,
	18	20	I have spoken openly for all the *world* to hear;
		36	Mine is not a kingdom of this *world*; if my kingdom were of this *world*, my men would have fought
		37	I came into the *world* for this: to bear witness to the truth;
	21	25	the *world* itself, I suppose, would not hold all the books that would have to be written.
Ac	17	24	God who made the *world* and everything in it
Rm	1	8	your faith is spoken of all over the *world*.
		20	Ever since God created the *world* his everlasting power and deity . . . have been there
	3	6	That would . . . mean God could never judge the *world*.
		19	to lay the whole *world* open to God's judgement;
	4	13	The promise of inheriting the *world* was not made to Abraham and his descendants on account of any law
	5	12	sin entered the *world* through one man,
		13	Sin existed in the *world* long before the Law was given.
	11	12	Think of the extent to which the *world* . . . has benefited from [the Jews'] fall
		15	[the Jews'] rejection meant the reconciliation of the *world*,
1 Co	1	20	Do you see now how God has shown up the foolishness of ʳhuman (lit. the *world's*) wisdom? ²¹ . . . it was God's wisdom that ʳhuman (lit. the *world's*) wisdom should not know God,
		21	
		27	it was to shame the wise that God chose what is foolish by ʳhuman (lit. the *world's*) reckoning, and to shame what is strong that he chose what is weak by ʳhuman (lit. the *world's*) reckoning; ²⁸ those whom the *world* thinks . . . contemptible are the ones that God had chosen.
		28	
	2	12	instead of the spirit of the *world*, we have received the Spirit that comes from God.
	3	19	the wisdom of this *world* is foolishness to God.
		22	Paul, . . . the *world*, life . . . all are your servants;
	4	9	we have been put on show in front of the whole *universe*,
		13	We are treated as the offal of the *world*,
	5	10	I was not meaning to include all the people in the *world* who are sexually immoral, . . . To [avoid associating with them], you would have to withdraw from the *world* altogether.
1 Co	6	2	As you know, it is the saints who are to 'judge the *world*';
	7	31	those who have to deal with the *world* should not become engrossed in it.
		33	a married man has to bother about the *world's* affairs
		34	The married woman . . . has to bother about the *world's* affairs
	8	4	we know that idols do not really exist in the *world*
	11	32	to . . . stop us being condemned with the *world*.
	14	10	There are any number of different languages in the *world*,
2 Co	1	12	we have always treated ʳeverybody (lit. the *world*), and especially you, with the . . . sincerity which comes from God,
	5	19	God in Christ was reconciling the *world* to himself.
	7	10	to suffer as the *world* knows suffering brings death.
Ga	4	3	we were as good as slaves to the elemental principles of this *world*,
	6	14	Jesus Christ, through whom the *world* is crucified to me, and I to the *world*.
Ep	1	4	Before the *world* was made, [God] chose us,
	2	2	[the sins] in which you used to live when you were following the ʳway of (lit. age which is) this *world*,
		12	you [pagans] were immersed in this *world*, without hope and without God,
	6	12	³ we have to struggle . . . against . . . the Powers who originate the darkness in this *world*,
Ph	2	15	you will shine in the *world* like bright stars
Col	1	6	[The Good News] which has reached you is spreading all over the *world*
	2	8	some . . . empty, rational philosophy based on the principles of this *world* instead of on Christ.
		20	If you have really died with Christ to the principles of this *world*, why do you still let rules dictate to you, as though you were still living in the *world*?
1 Tm	1	15	Christ Jesus came into the *world* to save sinners.
	3	16	He was made visible in the flesh, . . . believed in by the *world*,
	6	7	We brought nothing into the *world*, and we can take nothing out of it;
Tt	2	12	² what we have to do is to give up . . . all our *worldly* ambitions;
Heb	4	3	God's work was undoubtedly all finished at the beginning of the *world*;
	9	1	The first covenant also had . . . a ʳsanctuary on this earth ² (lit. *worldly* sanctuary).
		26	or else [Christ] would have had to suffer over and over again since the *world* began.
	10	5	this is what [Christ] said, on coming into the *world*: You who wanted no sacrifice
	11	7	By [Noah's] faith the *world* was convicted,
		38	[The prophets] were too good for the *world*
Jm	1	27	Pure, unspoilt religion . . . is this: . . . keeping oneself uncontaminated by the *world*.
	2	5	it was those who are poor according to the *world* that God chose,
	3	6	Among all the parts of the body, the tongue is a whole wicked *world* in itself:
	4	4	don't you realise that making the *world* your friend is making God your enemy? Anyone who chooses the *world* for his friend turns himself into God's enemy.
1 P	1	20	[Christ], though known since before the *world* was made, has been revealed only in our time,
	5	9	your brothers all over the *world* are suffering the same things.
2 P	1	4	you will be able to . . . escape corruption in a *world* that is sunk in vice.
	2	5	Nor did [God] spare the *world* in ancient times: . . . he sent the Flood over a disobedient *world*.
		20	anyone who has escaped the pollution of the *world* once
	3	6	the *world* of that time was destroyed by being flooded with water.
1 Jn	2	2	[Jesus Christ] is the sacrifice that takes our sins away, and . . . the whole *world's*.
		15	You must not love this passing *world* or anything that is in the *world*. The love of the Father cannot be in any man who loves the *world*, ¹⁶ because nothing the *world* has to offer . . . could ever come from the Father but only from the *world*; ¹⁷ and the *world*, with all it craves for, is coming to an end;
		16	
		17	
	3	1	Because the *world* refused to acknowledge [the Father], . . . it does not acknowledge us.
		13	You must not be surprised, brothers, when the *world* hates you;
		17	If a man who was rich enough in this *world's* goods
	4	1	there are many false prophets . . . in the *world*.
		3	now [the spirit of Antichrist] is here, in the *world*.
		4	you have in you one who is greater than anyone in this *world*;
		5	⁵ as for [the false prophets], they are of the *world*, and so they speak the language of the *world* and the *world* listens to them.
		9	God sent into the *world* his only Son
		14	we testify that the Father sent his Son as saviour of the *world*.

1 Jn   4 17   even in this *world* we have become as he is.
        5 4   anyone who has been begotten by God has already overcome
                the *world*; this is the victory over the *world* – our faith.
           5   [5] Who can overcome the *world*? Only the man who believes
                that Jesus is the Son of God:
          19   We know that . . . the whole *world* lies in the power of the
                Evil One.
2 Jn   7   There are many deceivers about in the *world*,
Rv   11 15   The kingdom of the *world* has become the kingdom of our
                Lord and his Christ,
     13 8   all the people of the world will worship [the beast], that is,
                everybody whose name has not been written down since
                the foundation of the *world* in the book of life
     17 8   And the people of the world, whose names have not been
                written since the beginning of the *world* in the book of life,

2. THE WORLD, THE EARTH: *OIKOUMENĒ*

oikoumenē 15

Mt   24 14   The Good News of the kingdom will be proclaimed to the
                whole *world*
Lk   2 1   Caesar Augustus issued a decree for a census of the whole
                world to be taken.
      4 5   the devil showed [Jesus] . . . all the kingdoms of the *world*,
     21 26   men dying of fear as they await what menaces the *world*,
Ac   11 28   Agabus . . . predicted that a famine would spread over the
                whole *world*.
     17 6   The people who have been turning the whole *world* upside
                down
        31   [God] has fixed a day when the whole *world* will be judged,
     19 27   a goddess venerated all over Asia, yes, and everywhere in the
                civilised *world*.
     24 5   [Paul] stirs up trouble among Jews the *world* over,
Rm   10 18   (Ps 19 4) their voice has gone out through all the earth, and
                their message to the ends of the *world*.
Heb   1 6   when [God] brings the First-born into the *world*,
      2 5   He did not appoint angels to be rulers of the *world* to come,
Rv   3 10   the time of trial which is going to come for the whole *world*,
     12 9   Satan, who had deceived all the *world*,
     16 14   demon spirits, . . . going out to all the kings of the *world*

WORSHIP

1. Worship – Service: *latreia*
   1: Worship (God) – Serve (ritually)
      – Holy duty
   2: Worship (another being) – Serve
2. Worship – Religion – Aussmed devo-
   tion: *thrēsekia*
3. Worship – Religious duty: *eu-sebeia*
   1: Worship (God) – Religion –
      Devout

   2: Worship, Make a god of –
      Venerate
   3: Duty to one's family
**4. Worship – Bow, Homage – Fall
   down before:** *pros-kyneō*
   1: God
   2: Jesus
   3: various

4. Kneel – Bow, Bend the knee: *gonu*

1. WORSHIP – SERVICE: *LATREIA*

2 latreia 5   1 latreuō 21

1: WORSHIP (GOD) – SERVE (RITUALLY) – HOLY DUTY

Mt   4 10   (Dt 6 13) You must worship the Lord your God, and *serve*
                him alone.
Lk   1 75   [God will grant us . . .] to *serve* him in holiness
      2 37   [Anna] never left the Temple, *serving* God night and day,
      4 8   (Dt 6 13) You must worship the Lord your God, and *serve*
                him alone.
Jn   16 2   [2] anyone who kills you will think he is doing a *holy duty* for God.
Ac   7 7   (Ex 3 12) they will . . . *worship* me in this place.
     24 14   I *worship* the God of my ancestors,
     26 7   our twelve tribes, constant in *worship* night and day,
     27 23   an angel of the God to whom I belong and whom I *serve*,
Rm   1 9   The God I *worship* spiritually . . . knows
      9 4   [2] the Law and the ⌐ritual (or: *worship*) were drawn up for [the
                Israelites], and the promises were made to them.
     12 1   [2] *worship* [God] . . . ⌐in a way that is worthy of thinking
                beings (or: in a spiritual way),
Ph   3 3   we who *worship* in accordance with the Spirit of God;
2 Tm   1 3   I thank God . . . remembering my *duty* to him
Heb   8 5   these only *maintain the service* of a model
      9 1   [2] The first covenant also had its laws *governing worship*, and
                its sanctuary,

Heb   9 6   priests are constantly going into the outer tent to carry out
          [2] their [acts *of*] *worship*,
         9   None of the . . . sacrifices . . . can possibly bring any
                worshipper to perfection
        14   so that we do our *service* to the living God.
     10 2   the *worshippers* . . . would have no awareness of sins.
     12 28   Let us . . . *worship* God in the way that he finds acceptable,
     13 10   We have our own altar from which *those who serve* the taber-
                nacle have no right to eat.
Rv   7 15   they now stand in front of God's throne and *serve* him day and
                night
     22 3   [God's] servants will *worship* him,

2: WORSHIP (ANOTHER BEING) – SERVE

Ac   7 42   God . . . abandoned [the Israelites] to the *worship* of the
                army of heaven,
Rm   1 25   [the pagans] have worshipped and *served* creatures instead of
                the creator,

2. WORSHIP – RELIGION – ASSUMED DEVOTION: *THRĒSKEIA*

1 thrēskeia 4   3 ethelo-thrēskia 1
2 thrēskos 1

Ac   26 5   I followed the strictest party in our *religion*
Col   2 18   people who like grovelling to angels and *worshipping* them;
        23   It may be argued that true wisdom is to be found in these
          [3] [regulations], with their *self-imposed devotions*, their
                self-abasement,
Jm   1 26   [2] Nobody must imagine that he is *religious* while he still goes
                on deceiving himself and not keeping control over his
                tongue; anyone who does this has the wrong idea of
                religion.
        27   Pure, unspoilt *religion*, in the eyes of God . . . is this:
                coming to the help of orphans

3. WORSHIP – RELIGIOUS DUTY: *EU-SEBEIA*

4	*sebasma*	2	3	*eu-sebēs*	3
7	*sebazomai*	1	6	*eu-sebōs*	2
2	*sebomai*	10	8	*(theo-)sebeia*	1
1	*eu-sebeia*	15	9	*(theo-)sebēs*	1
5	*eu-sebeō*	2			

1: WORSHIP (GOD) – RELIGION – DEVOUT

Mt   15 9   [2] (Is 29 13) The *worship* they offer me is worthless;
Mk   7 7   [2] (Is 29 13) The *worship* they offer me is worthless,
Jn   9 31   God does listen to men who are *devout* and do his will.
Ac   3 12   as though we had made this man walk by our . . . *holiness*
     10 2   [3] [Cornelius was] *devout* and God-fearing . . . and prayed
                constantly to God.
         7   [3] Cornelius called . . . a *devout* soldier
     13 43   [2] many . . . *devout* converts joined Paul and Barnabas,
        50   [2] the Jews worked upon some of the *devout* women of the upper
                classes
     16 14   [2] Lydia, a *devout* woman from the town of Thyatira
     17 4   Some . . . were convinced and joined Paul and Silas, and so
          [2] did a great many God-*fearing* (ᵛ people and) Greeks,
        17   [2] [Paul] held debates with the Jews and the God-*fearing*,
        23   the God whom I proclaim is in fact the one whom you already
          [5] *worship* without knowing it.
     18 7   [Paul] moved to the house next door that belonged to a
          [2] *worshipper* of God called Justus.
        13   [2] We accuse this man . . . of persuading people to *worship*
                God in a way that breaks the Law.
2 Th   2 4   the one who claims to be so much greater than all that men
          [4] call 'god', so much greater than anything that is *worshipped*,
1 Tm   2 2   so that we may be able to live *religious* and reverent lives in
                peace and quiet.
        10   good works that are proper for women who profess to be
          [8] *religious*.
      3 16   the mystery of our *religion* is very deep indeed: He was made
                visible in the flesh, attested by the Spirit . . . taken up in
                glory.
      4 7   Train yourself *spiritually*. [8] Physical exercises are useful
         8   enough, but the usefulness of *spirituality* is unlimited, since
                it holds out the reward of life
      6 3   Anyone who . . . does not keep to . . . the doctrine which is
                in accordance with true *religion*,
         5   people who . . . imagine that *religion* is a way of making a
         6   profit. [6] *Religion*, of course, does bring large profits, but
                only to those who are content with what they have.

1 Tm 6	11	You must aim to be saintly and *religious*, filled with faith and love,
2 Tm 3	5	They will keep up the outward appearance of *religion* but will have rejected the inner power of it.
	12	6 anybody who tries to live in *devotion* to Christ is certain to be attacked;
Tt 1	1	the knowledge of the truth that leads to true *religion*;
2	12	we have . . . to give up . . . our worldly ambitions; we must 6 . . . live good and *religious* lives
2 P 1	3	By his divine power, he has given us all the things that we need for life and for true *devotion*,
	6	[adding] true *devotion* to your patience, 7 kindness towards your fellow men to your *devotion*,
	7	
2	9	3 the Lord can rescue the *good* from the ordeal, and hold the wicked for their punishment
3	11	you should be living *holy* and saintly lives

2: WORSHIP, MAKE A GOD OF – VENERATE

Ac 17	23	4 [Men of Athens,] I strolled round admiring your ʳ*sacred monuments* (or: *objects of worship*),
	4	
19	27	2 Diana . . . a goddess *venerated* all over Asia, yes, and everywhere in the civilised world.
Rm 1	25	7 [the pagans] have *worshipped* and served creatures instead of the creator,

3: DUTY TO ONE'S FAMILY

1 Tm 5	4	5 [children] are to learn first of all to *do their duty to* their own families

4. WORSHIP – BOW, HOMAGE – FALL DOWN BEFORE: *PROS-KYNEŌ*

1 pros-kyneō 60   2 pros-kynētēs 1

1: GOD

Mt 4	10	(Dt 6 13 G ᵛ) You must *worship* the Lord your God,
Lk 4	8	(Dt 6 13 G ᵛ) You must *worship* the Lord your God,
Jn 4	20	[The Samaritan woman said:] Our fathers *worshipped* on this mountain, while you say that Jerusalem is the place where one ought to *worship*, ²¹ . . . the hour is coming when you will *worship* the Father neither on this mountain nor in Jerusalem. ²² You *worship* what you do not know; we
	21	
	22	
	23	2 *worship* what we do know . . . ²³ . . . true *worshippers* will *worship* the Father in spirit and truth: that is the kind of *worshipper* the Father wants. ²⁴ God is spirit, and those who *worship* must *worship* in spirit and truth.
	24	
12	20	Among those who went up to *worship* at the festival were some Greeks.
Ac 8	27	an Ethiopian had ʳbeen on pilgrimage to (lit. come to *worship* at) Jerusalem . . . ²⁸ He was now on his way home;
24	11	[Paul said to Felix:] I went up to Jerusalem ʳon pilgrimage (lit. to *worship*),
1 Co 14	25	and then [the unbeliever or uninitiated person] will fall on his face and *worship* God,
Rv 4	10	the twenty-four elders prostrated themselves . . . to *worship* the One who lives for ever and ever,
5	14	the elders prostrated themselves to *worship*.
7	11	all the angels . . . prostrated themselves before the throne, and touched the ground with their foreheads, *worshipping* God
11	1	Go and measure God's sanctuary . . . and the people who *worship* there;
	16	The twenty-four elders . . . prostrated themselves . . . *worshipping* God
14	7	Fear God . . . *worship* the maker of heaven and earth
15	4	(Ps 86 9) all the pagans will come and *adore* you
19	4	the twenty-four elders and the four animals prostrated themselves and *worshipped* God
	10	I am a servant just like you . . . It is God that you must *worship*.
22	9	I am a servant just like you . . . It is God that you must *worship*.

2: JESUS

Mt 2	2	Where is the infant king of the Jews? . . . We . . . have come to *do him homage*.
	8	let me know, so that I too may go and *do him homage*.
	11	[the Magi] saw the child . . . and falling to their knees they *did him homage*.
8	2	A leper came up and *bowed low* in front of him.
9	18	up came one of the officials, who *bowed low* in front of him
14	33	The men in the boat *bowed down* before him

Mt 15	25	the [Canaanite] woman . . . was *kneeling* at his feet.
20	20	the mother of Zebedee's sons came . . . to make a request of him, and *bowed low*;
28	9	the women . . . *falling down* before him, clasped his feet.
	17	When [the eleven disciples] saw him they *fell down* before him,
Mk 5	6	[the man with an unclean spirit] ran up and *fell at his feet*
15	19	[the soldiers] went down on their knees to *do him homage*
Lk 24	52	ᵛ [the eleven] *worshipped* him and then went back to Jerusalem
Jn 9	38	[the man born blind, cured] said, 'Lord, I believe', and *worshipped* him.
Heb 1	6	(Dt 32 43 G ᵛ; Ps 97 7 G ᵛ) when he brings the First-born into the world, [God] says: Let all the angels of God *worship* him.

3: VARIOUS

Mt 4	9 ⓓ	[The devil said to Jesus:] I will give you all these . . . if you fall at my feet and *worship* me.
18	26	the servant [who owed 10 000 talents] *threw himself down* at his master's feet.
Lk 4	7 ⓓ	[The devil said to Jesus:] *Worship* me, then, and [this power] shall all be yours.
Ac 7	43	Moloch . . . and . . . Rephan, those idols that you had made to *adore*
10	25	Cornelius . . . knelt at [Peter's] feet and *prostrated himself*.
Heb 11	21	Jacob . . . blessed each of Joseph's sons, leaning on the end of his stick as though *bowing to pray*.
Rv 3	9	the synagogue of Satan . . . I will make them come and *fall* at your feet
9	20 ⓓ	the rest of the human race . . . refused either to abandon . . . the idols . . . or to stop *worshipping* devils.
13	4 ⓓ	They *prostrated themselves* in front of the dragon because he had given the beast his authority; and they *prostrated themselves* in front of the beast,
8	ⓓ	and all people of the world will *worship* [the beast],
12		This second beast was servant to the first beast, and extended its authority everywhere, making the world and all its people *worship* the first beast,
15		the statue . . . was able . . . to have anyone who refused to *worship* the statue of the beast put to death.
14	9	All those who *worship* the beast and his statue,
11		There will be no respite . . . for those who *worshipped* the beast or its statue
16	2	on all the people who . . . had *worshipped* [the beast's] statue, there came disgusting and virulent sores.
19	10	I knelt at his feet to *worship* him, but he said to me, 'Don't do that: . . . It is God that you must worship.'
20		all who had been branded with the mark of the beast and *worshipped* his statue.
20	4	I saw . . . those who refused to *worship* the beast or his statue
22	8	I, John . . . knelt at the feet of the angel . . . to *worship* him;

5. KNEEL – BOW, BEND THE KNEE: *GONU*

1 gonu   10/12   4 kamptō 4   3 tithēmi 6/99
2 gony-peteō   4

Mt 17	14	2 a man came up to [Jesus] and *went down on his knees* . . . [take pity on my son]
27	29	2 To make fun of [Jesus, the soldiers] *knelt* to him
Mk 1	40	2 A leper came to [Jesus] and pleaded *on his knees*
10	17	2 a man ran up, *knelt before* [Jesus] and put this question to him,
15	19	3/ [the soldiers] *went down on their knees* to do [Jesus] homage.
Lk 22	41	3/ [Jesus] withdrew from them . . . *knelt down* and prayed.
Ac 7	60	3/ [Stephen] *knelt down* and said aloud, 'Lord . . .'
9	40	3/ Peter sent them all out of the room and *knelt down* and prayed.
20	36	3/ [Paul] *knelt down* with them all and prayed.
21	5	3/ When we reached the beach, we *knelt down* and prayed;
Rm 11	4	(1 K 19 18) I have kept for myself seven thousand men who 4/ have not *bent the knee* to Baal.
14	11	/4 (Is 45 23) every *knee shall bend* before me,
Ep 3	14	4/ This, then, is what I pray, *kneeling* before the Father,
Ph 2	10	4/ so that all beings . . . should *bend the knee* at the name of Jesus

WRITING – READ

1. Writing: *graphō*
   a) Scripture, Texts – Written, Wrote
   b) Letter of the Law – the Written Code
   c) the Scribes – Doctors of the law
   d) Letters = Learning – Educated, Uneducated
   e) the Town Clerk

f) Write to – Write (in) a letter
g) Write, Written (generally),
Letters – Register, Enrol,
Census – Record, Inscription
h) an Example
2. Passage (of Scripture): *peri-echō*
3. Put down in writing: *logos*
  a) Enrol – Put on a list
  b) Book – Treatise – Work
4. Book – Writ, Certificate: *biblion*
  1: Book – Scroll
    a) Book of the Scriptures – Scroll
    b) the Book of Life
    c) Book, Scroll (generally)

  2: Writ, Certificate (of dismissal, divorce)
5. Writing
  1: Scroll, Roll: *kephalis*
  2: Parchment(s): *membrana*
  3: (Writing-)Tablets, Tables: *plax* and *plinakidion*
  4: Notice – Title, Inscription: *titlos*
  5: Ink: *melan*
     Paper: *chartēs*
     Pen: *kalamos*
  6: Dot, Stroke: *keraia* and *iota*
6. Read: *ana-ginōskō*

1. WRITING: *GRAPHŌ*

4	*gramma*	15	13	*kata-graphō*	1
2	*grammateus*	63	14	*cheiro-graphon*	1
3	*graphē*	51	9	*en-graphō*	3
1	*graphō*	190	5	*epi-graphē*	5
11	*graptos*	1	6	*epi-graphō*	5
12	*a-grammatos*	1	15	*hypo-grammos*	1
10	*apo-graphē*	2	8	*pro-graphō*	4
7	*apo-graphō*	4			

a) Scripture, Texts – Written, Wrote

Mt 2 5 — for this is what the prophet *wrote* (Mi 5 1): And you, Bethlehem,
4 4 — *Scripture* says: (Dt 8 3): Man does not live on bread alone
6 — *scripture* says (Ps 91 11): He will put you in his angels' charge,
7 — *Scripture* also says (Dt 6 16); You must not put the Lord your God to the test.
10 — *scripture* says (Dt 6 13): You must worship the Lord your God,
11 10 — he is the one of whom *scripture* says (Ml 3 1): Look, I am going to send my messenger
21 13 — According to *scripture* (Is 56, 7; Jr 7 11) . . . my house will be called a house of prayer.
42 3 Have you never read in the *scriptures* (Ps 118 22–23): It was the stone rejected by the builders
22 29 3 you understand neither the *scriptures* (Ex 3 6) nor the power of God. . . . ³² I am the God of Abraham,
26 24 — The Son of Man is going to his fate, as the *scriptures* say he will,
31 — the *scripture* says (Zc 13 7): I shall strike the shepherd
54 3 how would the *scriptures* be fulfilled that say this is the way it must be?
56 3 all this happened to fulfil the prophecies in *scripture*.
Mk 1 2 — It is *written* (Ml 3 1; Is 40 3) . . . Look, I am going to send my messenger before you;
7 6 — It was of you hypocrites that Isaiah so rightly prophesied in this passage of *scripture* (Is 29 13): This people honours me only with lip-service,
9 12 — how is it that the *scriptures* say about the Son of Man that he is to suffer . . .?
13 — they have treated [Elijah] as they pleased, just as the *scriptures* say about him.
10 5 — [Moses] *wrote* this commandment (Dt 24 1) [about divorce] for you.
11 17 — Does not *scripture* say (Is 56 7; Jr 7 11): My house will be called a house of prayer . . .?
12 10 3 Have you not read this text of *scripture* (Ps 118 22–23): It was the stone rejected by the builders
19 — Master, we have it from Moses *in writing*, if a man's brother dies . . . the man must marry the widow
24 3 you understand neither the *scriptures* (Ex 3 6) nor the power of God
14 21 — the Son of Man is going to his fate, as the *scriptures* say he will,
27 — the *scripture* says (Zc 13 7): I shall strike the shepherd
49 3 this is to fulfil the *scriptures*.
15 28 3 (ᵛ So the *text of Scripture* came true that said, He was considered a criminal.)
Lk 2 23 — what stands *written* in the Law of the Lord (Ex 13 2): Every first-born male must be consecrated to the Lord
3 4 — as it is *written* in the book of . . . Isaiah (Is 40 3,5): A voice cries in the wilderness:
4 4 — *Scripture* says (Dt 8 3): Man does not live on bread alone.
8 — *Scripture* says (Dt 6 13): You must worship the Lord your God,
10 — *scripture* says (Ps 91 11): He will put his angels in charge of you
17 — [Jesus] found the place where it is *written* (Is 61 1–2): The spirit of the Lord has been given to me, . . . ²¹ . . .
21 3 This *text* is being fulfilled today
7 27 — he is the one of whom *scripture* says (Ml 3 1): See, I am going to send my messenger before you;
10 26 — What is *written* in the Law? What do you read there? (Dt 6 5; Lv 19 18) ²⁷ . . . You must love the Lord your God

Lk 18 31 — everything that is *written* by the prophets about the Son of Man is to come true.
19 46 — According to *scripture* (Is 56 7; Jr 7 11) . . . my house will be a house of prayer.
20 17 — what does this text in the *scriptures* (Ps 118 22) mean: It was the stone rejected by the builders . . .?
28 — Master, we have from Moses *in writing*, that if a man's married brother dies childless,
21 22 — this is the time of vengeance when all that *scripture* says must be fulfilled.
22 37 — these words of *scripture* (Is 53 12) have to be fulfilled in me: He let himself be taken for a criminal.
24 27 3 starting with Moses and going through all the prophets, [Jesus] explained to them the passages throughout the *scriptures* that were about himself.
32 3 Did not our hearts burn within us as he . . . explained the *scriptures* to us?
44 — everything *written* about me in the Law of Moses, in the Prophets and in the Psalms, has to be fulfilled.
45 3 [Jesus] then opened their minds to understand the *scriptures*,
46 — it is *written* that the Christ would suffer and on the third day rise from the dead,
Jn 1 45 — We have found the one Moses *wrote* about in the Law, the one about whom the prophets wrote: he is Jesus son of Joseph, from Nazareth.
2 17 — Then his disciples remembered the words of *scripture* (Ps 69 9): Zeal for your house will devour me.
22 3 when Jesus rose from the dead, his disciples . . . believed the *scripture* and the words he had said.
5 39 3 You study the *scriptures* . . .; [they] testify to me,
46 — it was I that [Moses] was *writing* about; ⁴⁷ but if you refuse
47 4 to believe what he *wrote*, how can you believe what I say?
6 31 — as *scripture* says (Ps 78 24): He gave them bread from heaven to eat.
45 — It is *written* in the prophets (Is 54 13): They will all be taught by God,
7 38 — As *scripture* says: From his breast shall flow fountains of living water.
42 3 Does not *scripture* (2 S 7 12) say that the Christ must be descended from David . . .?
8 17 — in your Law it is *written* (Dt 17 6) that the testimony of two witnesses is valid.
10 34 — Is it not *written* in your Law (Ps 82 6): I said, you are gods?
35 3 ³⁵ . . . and *scripture* cannot be rejected.
12 14 — as *scripture* says (Zc 9 9): Do not be afraid, daughter of Zion,
16 — later . . . [his disciples] remembered that this had been *written* about him
13 18 3 what *scripture* says (Ps 41 9) must be fulfilled: Someone who shares my table rebels against me.
15 25 — all this was only to fulfil the words *written* in their Law (Ps 35 19): They hated me for no reason.
17 12 3 not one is lost except the one who chose to be lost, and this was to fulfil the *scriptures* (Ps 41 9)
19 24 3 In this way the words of *scripture* were fulfilled (Ps 22 18): They shared out my clothing
28 3 to fulfil the *scripture* perfectly (Ps 69 21) [Jesus] said: I am thirsty.
36 3 all this happened to fulfil the words of *scripture* (Ex 12 46): Not one bone of his will be broken; ³⁷ and again . . .
37 3 *scripture* says (Zc 12 10): They will look on the one whom they have pierced.
20 9 3 the teaching of *scripture* (Ps 16 9–11), that he must rise from the dead.
Ac 1 16 3 brothers, the passage of *scripture* (Ps 41 9) had to be fulfilled in which the Holy Spirit . . . foretells the fate of Judas,
20 — in the Book of Psalms ⸢says (lit. is *written*) (Ps 69 25; 109 8): Let his camp be reduced to ruin, . . . and again: Let someone else take his office.
7 42 — God turned away from [the Israelites] . . . as *scripture* says in the book of the prophets (Am 5 25–27): Did you bring me victims . . .?
8 32 3 the passage of *scripture* [the Ethiopian] was reading was this (Is 53 7–8): Like a sheep that is led to the slaughter-house,
35 3 . . . ³⁵ Starting . . . with this text of *scripture* Philip started to explain the Good News
13 29 — When they had carried out everything that *scripture* foretells about him they took him down from the tree
33 — As *scripture* says in the ⸢first (ᵛ second) psalm (Ps 2 7): You are my son:
15 15 — This is entirely in harmony with the words of the prophets, since the *scriptures* say (Am 9 11–12): ¹⁶ . . . I shall . . . rebuild the fallen House of David;
17 2 3 Paul . . . developed the arguments from *scripture* for [the Jews of Thessalonika],
11 3 [the Jews of Beroea] studied the *scriptures* to check whether it was true.
18 24 3 Apollos . . . [had] a sound knowledge of the *scriptures*,
28 3 . . . ²⁸ . . . he refuted the Jews in public and demonstrated from the *scriptures* that Jesus was the Christ.

Ac 23 5   for *scripture* says (Ex 22 27): You must not curse a ruler of your people.

24 14   retaining my belief in all points of the Law and in what is *written* in the prophets;

Rm 1 2   [the Good News that God] promised long ago through his
3   prophets in the *scriptures.*

17   as *scripture* says (Hab 2 4): The upright man finds life through faith.

2 24   As *scripture* says (Is 52 5): It is your fault that the name of God is blasphemed among the pagans.

3 4   so *scripture* says (Ps 51 5): in all you say your justice shows,
10   As *scripture* says (Ps 14 1): There is not a good man left,

4 3   3 *scripture* says (Gn 15 6): Abraham put his faith in God,
17   As *scripture* says (Gn 17 4): I have made you the ancestor of many nations

23   *Scripture* . . . does not refer only to [Abraham] but to us as well when it says (Gn 15 6) that his faith was . . . considered [as justifying him]

8 36   As *scripture* (Ps 44 22) promised: For your sake we are being massacred daily,

9 13   as *scripture* says (Ml 1 2–3) . . .: I showed my love for Jacob and my hatred for Esau.

17   3 in *scripture* [God] says to Pharaoh (Ex 9 16): It was for this I raised you up,

33   [the stumbling-stone] mentioned in *scripture* (Is 28 16): See how I lay in Zion a stone to stumble over,

10 5   When Moses refers to being justified by the Law he *writes* (Lv 18 5): those who keep the Law will draw life from it.

11   3 *scripture* says (Is 28 16 G): those who believe in him will have no cause for shame,

15   as *scripture* says (Is 52 7): The footsteps of those who bring good news is a welcome sound.

11 2   3 Do you remember what *scripture* says of Elijah (1 K 19 10, 14) . . .? [3] Lord, they have killed your prophets

8   as *scripture* says (Is 29 10): God has given them a sluggish spirit,

26   As *scripture* says (Is 59 20): The liberator will come from Zion,

12 19   As *scripture* says (Dt 32 35; Pr 25 21–22): vengeance is mine

14 11   as *scripture* says (Is 45 23): . . . every knee shall bend before me,

15 3   the words of *scripture* (Ps 69 9) – the insults of those who insult you fall on me – apply to [Christ].

4   8/ everything that was *written long ago* in the *scriptures* was meant to teach us something about hope from the examples
3   *scripture* gives of . . . people who did not give up

9   as *scripture* says (Ps 18 49) . . .: For this I shall praise you among the pagans,

21   my chief concern has been to fulfil the *text* (Is 52 15 G): Those who have never been told about him will see him,

16 26   [a mystery] now so clear that it must be broadcast to pagans
3   everywhere . . . This is only what *scripture* has predicted,

1 Co 1 19   As *scripture* says (Is 29 14): I shall destroy the wisdom of the wise

31   As *scripture* says (Jr 9 23): if anyone wants to boast, let him boast about the Lord.

2 9   we teach what *scripture* calls (Is 64 3): the things that no eye has seen

3 19   As *scripture* says (Jb 5 13): The Lord knows wise men's thoughts:

9 9   It is *written* in the Law of Moses (Dt 25 4): You must not put a muzzle on the ox while it is treading out the corn.
10   . . . [10] . . . Clearly this was *written* for our sake

10 7   *scripture* says (Ex 32 6): After sitting down to eat and drink, the people got up to amuse themselves. . . . [11] All this
11   . . . was *written down* to be a lesson for us

14 21   in the *written* Law it says (Is 28 11–12): Through men speaking strange languages . . . I shall talk to the nation,

15 3   3 Christ died for our sins, in accordance with the *scriptures*;
4   he was raised to life on the third day, in accordance with the
3   *scriptures*;

45   The first man, Adam, as *scripture* says, became a living soul;
54   the words of *scripture* (Is 25 8; Ho 13 14) will come true: Death is swallowed up in victory.

2 Co 4 13   we have the same spirit of faith that is mentioned in *scripture* (Ps 116 10 G) – I believed, and therefore I spoke –

8 15   as *scripture* says (Ex 16 18): The man who gathered much had none too much,

9 9   As *scripture* says (Ps 112 9): He was free in almsgiving,

Ga 3 8   3 *Scripture* . . . proclaimed the Good News long ago when Abraham was told (Gn 12 3): In you all the pagans will be blessed.

10   *scripture* says (Dt 27 26): Cursed be everyone who does not persevere in observing . . . the Law.

13   *scripture* says (Dt 21 23): Cursed be everyone who is hanged on a tree.

22   3 *scripture* makes no exceptions when it says that sin is master everywhere (Ps 14 1–3).

4 22   [listen to what the Law says.] It [r]says (lit. is *written*) . . . that Abraham had two sons (Gn 21 2,9),

27   *scripture* says (Is 54 1): Shout for joy, you barren women

---

Ga 4 30   3 Does not *scripture* say (Gn 21 10): Drive away that slave-girl . . .?

1 Tm 5 18   3 As *scripture* says (Dt 25 4): You must not muzzle an ox when it is treading out the corn,

2 Tm 3 15   ever since you were a child, you have known the holy
4   *scriptures*,

16   3 All *scripture* is inspired by God and can profitably be used for teaching,

Heb 10 7   (Ps 40 7 G) then I said, just as [r]I was commanded (lit. it was *written*) in the scroll of the book, 'God, here I am!

Jm 2 8   3 the right thing to do is to keep the supreme law of *scripture* (Lv 19 18): you must love your neighbour as yourself,

23   3 This is what *scripture* really means when it says (Gn 15 6): Abraham put his faith in God,

4 5 Δ   3 Surely you don't think *scripture* is wrong when it says (cf. Ps 42 2): the spirit which he sent to live in us (cf. Gn 2 7) wants us for himself alone?

   scripture says (Lv 19 2): Be holy, for I am holy.

1 P 1 16

2 6   3 As scripture says (Is 28 16): See how I lay in Zion a precious cornerstone

2 P 1 20   2 the interpretation of *scriptural* prophecy is never a matter for the individual.

3 16   [there are] some points in [Paul's] letter that are hard to understand; these are the points that uneducated and unbalanced people distort, in the same way as they distort
3   the rest of *scripture*

b) Letter of the Law – the Written Code

Rm 2 27   you disobey the Law in spite of . . . having it all *written*
4   *down*.

29   4 the real circumcision is in the heart – something not of the *letter* but of the spirit.

7 6   now we are rid of the Law, . . . free to serve in the new spiritual
4   way and not in the old way of a *written law*.

2 Co 3 6   4 this new covenant . . . is not a covenant of *written letters*
4   but of the Spirit: the *written letters* bring death, but the Spirit gives life.

c) the Scribes – Doctors of the law

E = Elders + Scribes; P = Priests + Scribes

For Scribes + Pharisees *see* PHARISEE

Mt 2 4 P   2 [Herod] called together all the chief priests and the *scribes* of the people,

5 20   2 if your virtue goes no deeper than that of the *scribes* and Pharisees,

7 29   [Jesus] taught [the people] with authority, and not like their
2   own *scribes*.

8 19   2 One of the *scribes* then came up and said to him, 'Master, I will follow you wherever you go.'

9 3   2 some *scribes* said to themselves, 'This man is blaspheming.'

12 38   2 some of the *scribes* and Pharisees spoke up. 'Master, . . . we should like to see a sign from you.'

13 52   2 every *scribe* who becomes a disciple of the kingdom of heaven is like a householder

15 1   2 Pharisees and *scribes* from Jerusalem then came to Jesus and said, 'Why do your disciples break away from . . . tradition . . .?'

16 21   Jesus began to make it clear . . . that he was destined to . . .
E P   suffer grievously at the hands of the elders and chief priests
2   and *scribes*,

17 10   2 Why do the *scribes* say then that Elijah has to come first?

20 18   the Son of Man is about to be handed over to the chief
P   priests and *scribes*.

21 15 P   2 the chief priests and *scribes* were indignant.

23 2   2 The *scribes* and the Pharisees occupy the chair of Moses.

13   2 Alas for you, *scribes* and Pharisees, you hypocrites!
Repeated in 23 15, 23, 25, 27, 29

34   2 I am sending you prophets and wise men and *scribes*:

26 57   The men who had arrested Jesus led him off to Caiaphas the
E   2 high priest, where the *scribes* and the elders were assembled.

27 41 E   2 The chief priests with the *scribes* and elders mocked him.

Mk 1 22   2 unlike the *scribes*, [Jesus] taught [the people] with authority.

2 6   2 some *scribes* were sitting there, and they thought to themselves, [7] . . . 'Who can forgive sins but God?'

16   2 the *scribes* of the Pharisee party . . . said to his disciples, 'Why does he eat with tax collectors . . .?'

3 22   2 The *scribes* . . . were saying, 'Beelzebul is in him

7 1   2 The Pharisees and some of the *scribes* . . . gathered round
5   2 him . . . [5] So these Pharisees and *scribes* asked him, 'Why do your disciples . . . eat . . . with unclean hands?'

8 31 E   the Son of Man was destined . . . to be rejected by the elders
P   2 and the chief priests and the *scribes*,

9 11   2 Why do the *scribes* say that Elijah has to come first?

14   they saw a large crowd gathered round [the disciples] and
2   some *scribes* arguing with them.

10 33   the Son of Man is about to be handed over to the chief
P   2 priests and the *scribes*.

11 18 P   2 This came to the ears of the chief priests and the *scribes*,

Mk 11	27	P E 2	the chief priests and the elders and the *scribes* came to [Jesus],
12	28	2	One of the *scribes* . . . put a question to [Jesus], 'Which is the first of all the commandments?'
	32	2	The *scribe* said to him, 'Well spoken, Master;
	35	2	How can the *scribes* maintain that the Christ is the son of David?
	38	2	Beware of the *scribes* who like to walk about in long robes,
14	1	P 2	the chief priests and the *scribes* were looking for a way to arrest Jesus
	43	P E 2	Judas . . . came up with a number of men armed with . . . clubs, sent by the chief priests and the *scribes* and the elders.
	53	P E 2	the chief priests and the elders and the *scribes* assembled
15	1	P E 2	the chief priests together with the elders and *scribes*, in short the whole Sanhedrin
	31	P 2	the chief priests and the *scribes* mocked him . . . 'He saved others,
Lk 5	21	2	The *scribes* and the Pharisees began to think this over. . . . Who can forgive sins but God alone?
	30	2	The Pharisees and their *scribes* complained to his disciples and said, 'Why do you eat and drink with . . . sinners?'
6	7	2	The *scribes* and the Pharisees were watching him to see if he would cure a man on the sabbath,
9	22	E P 2	The Son of Man . . . is destined to . . . be rejected by the elders and chief priests and *scribes*
11	53	2	the *scribes* and the Pharisees began a furious attack on him
15	2	2	the Pharisees and the *scribes* complained. 'This man . . . welcomes sinners
19	47	P 2	The chief priests and the *scribes* . . . tried to do away with him,
20	1	P E	the chief priests and the *scribes* came up, together with the elders, and spoke to him,
	19	P 2	the *scribes* and the chief priests would have liked to lay hands on him
	39	2	Some *scribes* then spoke up, 'Well put, Master
	46	2	Beware of the *scribes* who like to walk about in long robes,
22	2	P 2	the chief priests and the *scribes* were looking for some way of doing away with him,
	66	E P 2	there was a meeting of the elders of the people, attended by the chief priests and *scribes*.
23	10	P 2	the chief priests and the *scribes* were there, violently pressing their accusations.
Jn 8	3	2	The *scribes* and Pharisees brought a woman along who had been caught committing adultery;
Ac 4	5	P E 2	the rulers, elders and *scribes* had a meeting in Jerusalem
6	12	E 2	Having in this way turned the people against him as well as the elders and *scribes*, they took Stephen by surprise,
23	9	2	some of the *scribes* from the Pharisees' party stood up and protested
1 Co 1	20	2	Where are the philosophers now? Where are the *scribes*?

d) Letters = Learning – Educated, Uneducated

Jn 7	15	4	How did [Jesus] ⌐learn to read (lit. get to know his *letters*)? He has not been taught.
Ac 4	13	12	Peter and John . . . were *uneducated* laymen;
26	24	4	Paul, . . . all that *learning* of yours is driving you mad.

e) the Town Clerk

Ac 19	35	2	the *town clerk* [of Ephesus] eventually succeeded in calming the crowd,

f) Write to – Write (in) a letter

Ac 15	23	[The apostles] gave [Barsabbas and Silas] this *letter* to take with them:
18	27	the brothers . . . *wrote* asking the disciples [in Achaia] to welcome [Apollos].
23	25	[The tribune] also *wrote* a letter [to the governor Felix]
25	26	I have nothing definite that I can *write* to [Caesar] about [Paul]; that is why I have produced him . . . before you, King Agrippa, so that after the examination I may have something to *write*.
28	21	4	We have received no *letters* from Judaea about you, [Paul]
Rm 15	15	The reason why I have *written* to you . . . is to refresh your memories,
16	22	I, Tertius, who *wrote* out this letter, greet you in the Lord.
1 Co 4	14	I am *saying* all this not just to make you ashamed
5	9	When I *wrote* my letter to you not to associate with people living immoral lives,
	11	What I *wrote* was that you should not associate with a brother Christian who is leading an immoral life,
7	1	Now for the questions about which you *wrote*.
9	15	I am not *writing* all this to secure this treatment for myself.
14	37	Anyone who claims to be a prophet . . . ought to recognise that what I am *writing* to you is a command from the Lord.
2 Co 1	13	⌐There are no hidden meanings in our letters (lit. We *write* you nothing) besides what you can read for yourselves and understand.

2Co 2	3		I *wrote* as I did to make sure that, when I came, I should not be distressed . . . ⁴ When I *wrote* to you, in deep distress, . . . it was not to make you feel hurt . . . ⁹ What I really *wrote* for . . . was to test you
	4		
	9		
3	2 ◯	9	you are yourselves our letter, *written* in our hearts . . .
3	3 ◯	9	³ . . . you are a letter from Christ, *written* not with ink but with the Spirit of the living God,
7	12		though I *wrote* the letter to you, it was not written for the sake . . . of the offender
9	1		There is really no need for me to *write* to you on the subject of offering your services to the saints,
13	10		[What we ask in our prayers is for you to be made perfect.] That is why I am *writing* this
Ga 1	20		I swear before God that what I have just *written* is the literal truth.
Ph 3	1		It is no trouble to me to repeat what I have already *written* to you,
1 Th 4	9		As for loving our brothers, there is no need for anyone to *write* to you about that,
5	1		You will not be expecting us to *write* anything to you, brothers about times and seasons,
1 Tm 3	14		At the moment of *writing* to you, I am hoping that I may be with you soon;
Phm	19		I am *writing* this in my own handwriting:
	21		I am *writing* with complete confidence in [your] compliance,
1 P 5	12		I *write* these few words to you through Silvanus,
2 P 3	1		My friends, this is ⌐my second letter (lit. the second letter I have *written*) to you,
	15		Paul . . . told you this when he *wrote* to you
1 Jn 1	4		We are *writing* this to you to make our own joy complete.
2	1		I am *writing* this . . . to stop you sinning;
	7		this is not a new commandment that I am *writing* to tell you . . . ⁸ Yet in another way, what I am *writing* to you is a new commandment; . . . ¹² I am *writing* to you, my own children, whose sins have already been forgiven . . . ¹³ I am *writing* to you, fathers, . . . I am *writing* to you, young men, . . . ¹⁴ I have *written* to you, children, . . . I have *written* to you, fathers, . . . I have *written* to you, young men,
	8		
	12		
	13		
	14		
	21		It is not because you do not know the truth that I am *writing* to you
	26		This is all that I am *writing* to you about the people who are trying to lead you astray.
5	13		I have *written* all this to you so that you . . . may be sure that you have eternal life.
2 Jn	5		I am *writing* now, . . . not to give you any new commandment,
	12		There are several things I have to ⌐tell (lit. *write* to) you, but I have thought it best not to trust them to paper and ink.
3 Jn	9		I have *written* a note for the members of the church,
	13		There were several things I had to ⌐tell (lit. *write* to) you but I would rather not ⌐trust them to (lit. *write* them in) pen and ink.
Jude	3		at a time when I was eagerly looking forward to *writing* to you about the salvation that we all share, I have been forced to *write* to you now and appeal to you
Rv 2	1		*Write* to the angel of the church in Ephesus
	8		*Write* to the angel of the church in Smyrna
	12		*Write* to the angel of the church in Pergamum
	18		*Write* to the angel of the church in Thyatira
3	1		*Write* to the angel of the church in Sardis
	7		*Write* to the angel of the church in Philadelphia
	14		*Write* to the angel of the church in Laodicea

g) Write, Written (generally), Letters – Register, Enrol, Census – Record, Inscription

R = Registration in a Census

Mt 22	20		5	Whose head is this? Whose ⌐name (or: *inscription*)?
27	37			Above his head was placed the charge against him; ⌐it read (lit. the *inscription* was): This is Jesus, the King of the Jews.
Mk 10	4			Moses allowed us . . . to ⌐draw up (or: *write*) a writ of dismissal
12	16		5	Whose head is this? Whose ⌐name (or: *inscription*)?
15	26		5	The *inscription* giving the charge against him ⌐read (lit. was *written*): The King of the Jews.
			6	
Lk 1	3			I . . . have decided to *write* an ordered account [of events]
	63			[Zechariah] asked for a writing tablet and *wrote*, His name is John.
2	1	R	7	Caesar Augustus issued a decree for a *census* of the whole world to be taken. ² This *census* . . . took place while Quirinius was governor of Syria,
	2	R	10	
	3	R	7	everyone went to his own town to be *registered*.
	5	R	7	[Joseph travelled up to Judaea] in order to be *registered* with Mary, his betrothed.
10	20		9	your names are *written* in heaven.
16	6		4/	'How much do you owe, . .?' 'A hundred measures of oil . . .' '. . . take your *bond*; sit down . . . and *write* fifty.
	7			⁷ '. . . And you, sir, how much do you owe?' 'A hundred measures of wheat . . .' '. . . take your *bond* and *write* fifty.
			4/	

Lk	20 24	5	Whose head and ˹name (or: inscription) are on it?
	23 38	5	Above him there was an inscription (ᵛ in Greek, Latin and
		4	Hebrew writing): This is the King of the Jews.
Jn	8 6	13	Jesus . . . started writing on the ground with his finger.
	8		Then he . . . wrote on the ground again.
	19 19		Pilate wrote out a notice . . . ˹it ran (lit. he had written): Jesus the Nazarene, King of the Jews.
	20		the writing was in Hebrew, Latin and Greek.
	21		You should not write King of the Jews, but This man said:
	22		Pilate answered, 'What I have written, I have written.'
	20 30		There were many other signs that Jesus worked . . . but they
	31		are not recorded in this book. ³¹ These are recorded so that you may believe
	21 24		This disciple is the one who vouches for these things and has
	25		written them down, . . . ²⁵ There were many other things that Jesus did; if all were written down, the world itself . . . would not hold all the books that would have to be written.
Ac	5 37	R 10	then there was Judas the Galilean, at the time of the census,
	17 23	6	an altar inscribed: To An Unknown God.
Rm	2 15	11	[Pagans] can point to the substance of the Law engraved on their hearts
			remember the maxim: Keep to what is written
1 Co	4 6		
2 Co	3 7	4	the administering of death, in the written letters engraved on stones,
Ga	3 1	8	in spite of the ˹plain explanation (lit. written account) you have had of the crucifixion of Jesus Christ.
	6 11	4	Take good note of what I am adding in my own handwriting and in large letters.
Ep	3 3	8	the mystery, as I have just described it
Col	2 14	14	[God] has . . . cancelled every record of the debt that we had to pay;
2 Th	3 17		From me, Paul, these greetings in my own handwriting,
Heb	8 10	6	(Jr 31 33) I will . . . write [my laws] on their hearts.
	10 16	6	(Jr 31 33) I will . . . write [my laws] on their minds.
	12 23		the whole Church in which everyone is a first-born son and
		7	˹a citizen of (lit. enrolled [as a citizen] in) heaven.
Jude	4	8	they are the [people] you had a warning about, in writing, long ago,
Rv	1 3		happy those who listen to [this prophecy], if they treasure all that ˹it says (lit. is written there),
	11		Write down all that you see in a book,
	19		write down all that you see
	2 17		a stone with a new name written on it,
	3 12		I will inscribe on [those who prove victorious] the name of my God
	5 1		a scroll that had writing on back and front
	10 4		I was preparing to write, when I heard a voice from heaven
	13 8		everybody whose name has not been written down since the foundation of the world in the book of life
	14 1		a hundred and forty-four thousand people, all with [the Lamb's] name and his Father's name written on their foreheads.
	13		Write down: Happy are those who die in the Lord!
	17 5		on [the woman's] forehead was written . . . a cryptic name: Babylon
	8		the people of the world, whose names have not been written since the beginning of the world in the book of life,
	19 9		Write this: Happy are those who are invited to the wedding feast of the Lamb,
	12		the name written on [the horseman] was known only to himself,
	16		On his cloak . . . there was a name written: The King of kings
	20 12		I saw the dead . . . standing in front of his throne, while . . . books [were] opened which were the record of what they had done in their lives,
	15		anybody whose name could not be found written in the book of life
	21 5		Write this: that what I am saying . . . will come true,
	12	6	over the [twelve] gates were written the names of the twelve tribes of Israel;
	27		only those who are listed in the Lamb's book of life.
	22 18		God will add to him every plague ˹mentioned (lit. described) in the book;
	19		the tree of life and . . . the holy city, which are described in the book.

h) an Example

1 P	2 21	15	Christ suffered for you and left an example for you to follow the way he took.

2. PASSAGE (OF SCRIPTURE): *PERI-ECHŌ*

1 *peri-echō* 1/2   2 *peri-ochē* 1

Ac	8 32	2	the passage of scripture he was reading was this:
1 P	2 6		As the passage of scripture (Is 28 16) says: See . .

3. PUT DOWN IN WRITING: *LOGOS*

1 *logos* 1/334   2 *kata-legō* 1

a) Enrol – Put on a list

1 Tm	5 9	2	Enrolment as a widow is permissible only for a woman at least sixty years old

b) Book – Treatise – Work

Ac	1 1		In my earlier work . . . I dealt with everything Jesus had done and taught

4. BOOK – WRIT, CERTIFICATE: *BIBLION*

3 *biblaridion* 3   2 *biblos* 10
1 *biblion*   34

1: BOOK – SCROLL

a) Book of the Scriptures – Scroll

Mk	12 26	2	have you never read in the Book of Moses,
Lk	3 4	2	as it is written in the book of the sayings of the prophet Isaiah:
	4 17		they handed [Jesus] the scroll of the prophet Isaiah. Unrolling
	20		the scroll he found the place where it is written: . . . ²⁰ He then rolled up the scroll,
	20 42	2	David himself says in the Book of Psalms:
Ac	1 20	2	in the Book of Psalms it says:
	7 42	2	as scripture says in the book of the prophets:
Ga	3 10		(Dt 27 26) Cursed be everyone who does not persevere in observing everything prescribed in the book of the Law.
Heb	9 19		Moses . . . sprinkled the book itself and all the people,
	10 7		then I said, just as I was commanded in the scroll of the book,

b) the Book of Life

Ph	4 3	2	[My helpers'] names are written in the book of life,
Rv	3 5		I shall not blot [the] names [of those who prove victorious]
		2	out of the book of life.
	13 8		everybody whose name has not been written down since the foundation of the world in the book of life of the sacrificial Lamb.
	17 8		the people of the world, whose names have not been written since the beginning of the world in the book of life,
	20 12		I saw the dead . . . standing in front of his throne, while the book of life was opened, and other books opened which were the record of what they had done in their lives, by which the dead were judged.
	15		anybody whose name could not be found written in the
		2	book of life was thrown into the burning lake.
	21 27		only those who are listed in the Lamb's book of life.

c) Book, Scroll (generally)

Mt	1 1	2	A ˹genealogy (lit. book of the genealogy) of Jesus Christ, son of David,
Jn	20 30		There were many other signs that Jesus worked . . . but they are not recorded in this book.
	21 25		if all [the things that Jesus did] were written down, the world . . . would not hold all the books that would have to be written.
Ac	19 19		a number of [believers] who had practised magic collected
		2	their books and made a bonfire of them
2 Tm	4 13		When you come, bring . . . the scrolls, especially the parchment ones.
Rv	1 11		Write down all that you see in a book,
	5 1		I saw that . . . there was a scroll that had writing on back and front and was sealed with seven seals. ² . . . 'Is there anyone
	2		worthy to open the scroll and break the seals of it?' ³ But
	3		there was no one . . . who was able to open the scroll and ˹read (lit. look at) it. ⁴ . . . there was nobody fit to open the
	4		scroll and ˹read (lit. look at) it.
	5		the Root of David . . . will open the scroll
	8		when [the Lamb] took the scroll, the four animals prostrated themselves . . . and the twenty-four elders . . . ⁹ . . .
	9		sang a new hymn: 'You are worthy to take the scroll and break the seals of it,
	6 14		the sky disappeared like a scroll rolling up
	10 2	3	[another angel] had a small scroll, unrolled; . . . ⁸ . . .
	8		'Go', [the voice from heaven] said, 'and take that open
	9		scroll out of the hand of the angel . . .' ⁹ I went to the angel
	10	3	and asked him to give me the small scroll . . . ¹⁰ . . . I
		3	took ˹it (lit. the small scroll) out of the angel's hand and swallowed it;
	20 12		I saw . . . other books opened ˹which were (lit. these books being) the record of what [the dead] had done
	22 7		Happy are those who treasure the prophetic message of this book.

Rv 22	9	those who treasure what you have written in this *book*.
	10	Do not keep the prophecies in this *book* a secret,
	18	This is my solemn warning to all who hear the prophecies in this *book*: if anyone adds anything to them, God will add to him every plague mentioned in the *book*; [19] if anyone cuts
	19	anything out of the prophecies in this *book*, God will cut off his share of the tree of life and of the holy city, which are described in the *book*.

2: WRIT, CERTIFICATE (OF DISMISSAL, DIVORCE)

Mt 19	7	(Dt 24 1) why did Moses command that a *writ* of dismissal should be given in cases of divorce?
Mk 10	4	Moses allowed us . . . to draw up a *writ* of dismissal and so to divorce.

5. WRITING

1: SCROLL, ROLL: *KEPHALIS*

kephalis 1

Heb 10	7	(Ps 40 8) then I said, just as ⌐I was commanded (lit. it was written) in the *scroll* of the book,

2: PARCHMENT(S): *MEMBRANA*

membrana 1

2 Tm 4	13	When you come, bring . . . the scrolls, especially the *parchment* ones.

3: (WRITING-)TABLETS, TABLES: *PLAX* and *PINAKIDION*

2 *pinakidion 1*   1 *plax 3*

Lk 1	63	2 [Zechariah] asked for a *writing-tablet* and wrote, His name is John.
2 Co 3	3	you are a letter from Christ, . . . written . . . not on stone *tablets* but on the *tablets* of your living hearts.
Heb 9	4	In [the ark of the covenant] were kept . . . the stone *tablets* of the covenant.

4: NOTICE – TITLE, INSCRIPTION: *TITLOS*

titlos 2

Jn 19	19	Pilate wrote out a *notice* and had it fixed to the cross;
	20	This *notice* was read by many of the Jews,

5: INK, PAPER, PEN: *MELAN, CHARTĒS, KALAMOS*

2 *kalamos 1/12*   3 *chartēs 1*   1 *melan 3*

2 Co 3	3	you are a letter from Christ, . . . written not with *ink* but with the Spirit of the living God,
2 Jn	12	There are several things I have to tell you, but I have thought [3/] it best not to trust them to *paper* and *ink*.
3 Jn	13	There were several things I had to tell you but I would [2/] rather not trust them to *pen* and *ink*.

6: DOT, STROKE: *KERAIA* and *IŌTA*

1 *keraia 2*   2 *iōta 1*

Mt 5	18	[2/] not one *dot*, not one little *stroke*, shall disappear from the Law
Lk 16	17	It is easier for heaven and earth to disappear than for one little *stroke* to drop out of the Law.

6. READ: *ANA-GINŌSKŌ*

1 *ana-ginōskō 32*   2 *ana-gnōsis 3*

Mt 12	3	Have you not *read* (cf. 1 S 21 1–7) what David did when he and his followers were hungry . . .?
	5	have you not *read* in the Law (Nb 28 9) that . . . the Temple priests break the sabbath without being blamed for it?
19	4	Have you not *read* (Gn 1 27) that the creator . . . made them male and female . . .?
21	16	have you never *read* this (Ps 8 2): By the mouths of children, babes in arms,
	42	Have you never *read* in the scriptures (Ps 118 22–23): It was the stone rejected by the builders
22	31	have you never *read* what God himself said to you (Ex 3 6): [32] I am the God of Abraham,
24	15	when you see the disastrous abomination, of which the prophet Daniel spoke (Dn 9 27) . . . (let the *reader* understand),
Mk 2	25	Did you never *read* (cf. 1 S 21 1–7) what David did in his time of need . . .?
12	10	Have you not *read* this text of scripture (Ps 118 22–23): It was the stone rejected by the builders
	26	have you never *read* in the Book of Moses (Ex 3 6) . . .: I am the God of Abraham,
13	14	When you see the disastrous abomination (Dn 9 27) . . . (let the *reader* understand),
Lk 4	16	[Jesus] stood up to *read*,
6	3	So you have not *read* (cf. 1 S 21 1–7) what David did when he and his followers were hungry
10	26	What is written in the Law? What do you *read* there? (Dt 6 5; Lv 19 18): . . . You must love the Lord your God . . . and your neighbour as yourself.
Jn 19	20	This notice was *read* by many of the Jews,
Ac 8	28	as [the Ethiopian] sat in his chariot he was *reading* the prophet Isaiah.
	30	Philip . . . heard [the Ethiopian] *reading* Isaiah . . . and asked, 'Do you understand what you are *reading*?'
	32	the passage of scripture he was *reading* was this (Is 53 7–8): like a sheep that is led to the slaughter-house,
13	15	After the lessons from the Law and the Prophets had been [2] *read*, . . . [Paul began to speak:]
	27	the prophecies *read* on every sabbath.
15	21	Moses . . . is *read* aloud in the synagogues every sabbath.
	31	The community [in Antioch] *read* [the apostles' letter] and were delighted
23	34	The governor *read* the [tribune's] letter
2 Co 1	13	There are no hidden meanings in our letters besides what you can *read* for yourselves and understand.
3	2 ○	you are yourselves our letter, written in our hearts, that anybody can see and *read*,
	14	that same veil is still there when the old covenant is being [2] *read*,
	15	whenever Moses is *read*, the veil is over their minds.
Ep 3	4	If you *read* my words, you will have some idea of the depths that I see in the mystery of Christ.
Col 4	16	After this letter has been *read* among you, send it on to be *read* in the church of the Laodiceans; and get the letter from Laodicea for you to *read* yourselves.
1 Th 5	27	this letter is to be *read* to all the brothers.
1 Tm 4	13	2 Make use of the time . . . by *reading* to the people, preaching and teaching.
Rv 1	3	Happy the man who *reads* this prophecy,

YEAR – MONTH – WEEK

1. Year
1: *en-iautos*
2: *etos*
2. Month: *mēn*
   a) Month

   b) (special) Month, (New)
      Moon (festival)
3. Week – Sabbath: *sabbaton*
   a) Week
   b) Sabbath

1. YEAR

1: YEAR: *EN-IAUTOS*
en-iautos 14

Lk	4 19	(Is 61 2) [The Lord has sent me] to proclaim the Lord's *year* of favour.
Jn	11 49	Caiaphas [was] the high priest that *year*,
	51	it was as high priest (§ for that *year*) that [Caiaphas] made this prophecy
	18 13	Caiaphas . . . was the high priest that *year*.
Ac	11 26	[Barnabas and Saul] were to live together in that church a whole *year*,
	18 11	Paul stayed [in Corinth] . . . for ⌜eighteen months (lit. one *year* and six months).
Ga	4 10 ○	You and your special days and months and seasons and *years*!
Heb	9 7	the second tent is entered only once a *year*, and then only by the high priest
	25	the high priest [goes] into the sanctuary every successive *year* with the blood that is not his own.
	10 1	the same sacrifices [are] repeatedly offered every *year*.
	3	the sins are recalled every successive *year* in the sacrifices.
Jm	4 13	Today or tomorrow we are off to this or that town; we are going to spend a *year* there,
	5 17	Elijah . . . prayed hard for it not to rain, and no rain fell for ⌜three-and-a-half years (lit. three *years* and six months);
Rv	9 15	These four angels had been put there ready for this hour of this day of this month of this *year*,

2: YEAR: *ETOS*

1		*etos 49*	3	(*tesserakonta-*)*etēs*	2
5		(*di-*)*etes*	1	7	(*tri-*)*etia*	1
2		(*di-*)*etia*	2	4	*per-ysi*	2
6		(*hekatonta-*)*etēs*	1			

A = (of) age, years old

Mt	2 16 A 5	Herod . . . had all the male children killed [in Bethlehem] who were two *years* [old] or under,
	9 20	Then . . . came a woman who had suffered from a haemorrhage for twelve *years*,
Mk	5 25	there was a woman who had suffered from a haemorrhage for twelve *years*;
	42 A	The little girl got up . . . and began to walk about, for she was twelve *years* [old].
Lk	2 36	[Anna] had been married for seven *years* [37] before becoming a widow. She was now eighty-four *years* [old] and never left the Temple,
	37 A	
	41	Every *year* [Jesus's] parents used to go to Jerusalem for the feast of Passover.
	42 A	When [Jesus] was twelve *years* [old], they went up for the feast
	3 1	In the fifteenth *year* of Tiberius Caesar's reign [the word of God came to John son of Zechariah]
	23 A	When he started to teach, Jesus was about thirty *years* [old],
	4 25	in Elijah's day . . . heaven remained shut for three *years* and six months
	8 42 A	[Jairus] had an only daughter about twelve *years* [old],
	43	there was a woman suffering from a haemorrhage for twelve *years*,
	12 19	My soul, you have plenty of good things laid by for many *years* to come;
	13 7	for three *years* now I have been coming to look for fruit on this fig tree
	8	Sir, . . . leave it one more *year*
	11	for eighteen *years* [the woman] had been possessed by a spirit that left her enfeebled;

Lk	13 16	Satan has held [this daughter of Abraham] bound these eighteen *years*
	15 29	Look at all these *years* that I have slaved for you
Jn	2 20	It has taken forty-six *years* to build this sanctuary:
	5 5	One man there had an illness which had lasted thirty-eight *years*,
	8 57 A	You are not fifty *years* [old] yet and you have seen Abraham!
Ac	4 22 A	The man who had been miraculously cured was over forty *years* old.
	7 6	(Gn 15 13) [Abraham's] descendants . . . would be slaves and oppressed for four hundred *years*.
	23 A 3	[Moses at] the age of forty *years* decided to visit his countrymen,
	30	Forty *years* later . . . an angel appeared to [Moses]
	36	It was Moses who, after performing miracles and signs . . . . . . led them . . . for forty *years*.
	42	Did you bring me victims and sacrifices in the wilderness for all those forty *years* . . .?
	9 33	Aeneas . . . had been bedridden for eight *years*.
	13 18 3	for about forty *years* [God] took care of them in the wilderness.
	20	[God put them in possession of their land] for about four hundred and fifty *years*.
	21	they demanded a king, and God gave them Saul . . . for forty *years*
	19 10	[Paul held daily discussions in the lecture room of Tyrannus.] This went on for two *years*,
	20 31 7	for three *years* I never failed to keep you right, . . . each one of you.
	24 10	[Paul said to Felix,] 'I know that you have administered justice over this nation for many *years*,
	17	After several *years* I came to bring alms to my nation
	27 2	When the two *years* came to an end, Felix was succeeded by Porcius Festus
	28 30 2	[In Rome] Paul spent the whole of the two *years* in his own rented lodging.
Rm	4 19 A 6	[Abraham became the father of nations;] he was about a hundred *years* old
	15 23	for many *years* I have been longing to pay you a visit.
2 Co	8 10 4	you were the first, a *year* ago, . . . in taking action
	9 2 4	Achaia has been ready since last *year*.
	12 2	I know a man . . . who, fourteen *years* ago, was caught up . . . right into the third heaven.
Ga	1 18	after three *years* I went up to Jerusalem to visit Cephas
	2 1	It was not till fourteen *years* had passed that I went up to Jerusalem again.
	3 17	once God had expressed his will . . ., no law that came four hundred and thirty *years* later could cancel that
1 Tm	5 9 A	Enrolment as a widow is permissible only for a woman at least sixty *years* [old]
Heb	1 12 Θ	(Ps 102 28) [Lord,] your *years* are unending.
	3 10	(Ps 95 10) [Your ancestors had seen what I could do] for forty *years*.
	17	those who made God angry for forty *years* were the ones who sinned
2 P	3 8	(Ps 90 4) with the Lord, 'a day' can mean a thousand *years*, and a thousand *years* is like a day.
Rv	20 2	[The angel] overpowered the dragon . . . and chained him up for a thousand *years*. [3] He threw him into the Abyss . . . until the thousand *years* had passed.
	3	
	4	the souls of all who had been beheaded . . . for Jesus . . . reigned with Christ for a thousand *years*. [5] . . . the rest of the dead did not come to life until the thousand *years* were over. [6] . . . those who share in the first resurrection will be priests of God and . . . reign with him for a thousand *years*. [7] When the thousand *years* are over, Satan will be released from his prison
	5	
	6	
	7	

2. MONTH: *MĒN*

1		*mēn 18*	3	(*tetra-*)*mēnos 1*
2	(*neo-*)*mēnia 1*		4	(*tri-*)*mēnos 1*

a) Month

Lk	1 24	for five *months* [Elizabeth] kept to herself.
	26	In the sixth *month* the angel Gabriel was sent by God to a town in Galilee called Nazareth,
	36	Elizabeth . . . is now in her sixth *month*,
	56	Mary stayed with Elizabeth about three *months*
	4 25	heaven remained shut for three years and six *months*

Jn	4	35	3 Four *months* and then the harvest.
Ac	7	20	[Moses] was looked after for three *months* in his father's house
	18	11	Paul stayed [in Corinth] . . . for eighteen *months*.
	19	8	[At Ephesus Paul] spoke out boldly . . . for three *months*,
	20	3	[Paul went to Greece] where he spent three *months*.
	28	11	At the end of three *months* [in Malta] we set sail
Heb	11	23	Moses, when he was born, was hidden by his parents for three *months*;

Jm	5	17	Elijah . . . prayed . . . and no rain fell for ⌜three-and-a-half years (lit. three years and six *months*);
Rv	9	5	[The locusts] were . . . to give [men without God's seal] pain for five *months*,
		10	[the locusts] were able to injure people for five *months*.
		15	These four angels had been put there ready for this hour of this day of this *month* of this year,
	11	2	pagans . . . will trample on the holy city for forty-two *months*.
	13	5	For forty-two *months* the beast was allowed to mouth its boasts
	22	2	the trees of life . . . bear twelve crops of fruit in a year, one in each *month*,

b) (special) Month, (New) Moon (festival)

Ga	4	10	You and your special days and *months* and seasons and years!
Col	2	16	never let anyone else decide . . . whether you are to observe
		2	annual festivals, New *Moons* or sabbaths.

3. WEEK – SABBATH: *SABBATON*

1 *sabbaton* 69   2 *pro-sabbaton* 1

a) Week

Mt	28	1	After the sabbath, and towards dawn on the first day of the *week*, Mary of Magdala . . . went to visit the sepulchre.
Mk	16	2	very early . . . on the first day of the *week* [the women] went to the tomb,
		9	Having risen in the morning on the first day of the *week*, [Christ] appeared first to Mary of Magdala
Lk	18	12	[The Pharisee prayed:] I fast twice a *week*;
	24	1	On the first day of the *week*, [the women] went to the tomb
Jn	20	1	very early on the first day of the *week* . . . Mary of Magdala came to the tomb.
		19	In the evening of that same day, the first day of the *week*, . . . Jesus came.
Ac	20	7	On the first day of the *week* we met to break bread.
1 Co	16	2	Every ⌜Sunday (lit. first day of the *week*), each one of you must put aside what he can afford,

b) Sabbath

Mt	12	1	Jesus took a walk one *sabbath day* through the cornfields.
		2	your disciples are doing something that is forbidden on the *sabbath*.
		5	on the *sabbath day* the Temple priests break the *sabbath* without being blamed for it.
		8 ●	the Son of Man is master of the *sabbath*.
		10	Is it against the law to cure a man on the *sabbath day*?
		11	If any one of you here had only one sheep and it fell down a hole on the *sabbath day*, would he not . . . lift it out?
		12	it is permitted to do good on the *sabbath day*.
	24	20	Pray that you will not have to escape in winter or on a *sabbath*.
	28	1	After the *sabbath*, and towards dawn on the first day of the week, Mary of Magdala . . . went to visit the sepulchre.
Mk	1	21	They went as far as Capernaum, and as soon as the *sabbath* came . . . [Jesus] began to teach.
	2	23	One *sabbath day* [Jesus] happened to be taking a walk through the cornfields,
		24	why are they doing something on the *sabbath day* that is forbidden?
		27 ●	The *sabbath* was made for man, not man for the *sabbath*;
		28 ●	the Son of Man is master even of the *sabbath*.
	3	2	they were watching him to see if he would cure him on the *sabbath day*,
		4	Is it against the law on the *sabbath day* to do good, or to do evil; to save life, or to kill?
	6	2	With the coming of the *sabbath* he began teaching in the synagogue
	15	42	2 it was Preparation Day (that is, the vigil of the *sabbath*),
	16	1	When the *sabbath* was over, Mary of Magdala . . . bought spices with which to go and anoint [the body of Jesus].
Lk	4	16	[at Nazara Jesus] went into the synagogue on the *sabbath day*
		31	[Jesus] went down to Capernaum . . . and taught them on the *sabbath*.
	6	1	one *sabbath* he happened to be taking a walk through the cornfields,
		2	Why are you doing something that is forbidden on the *sabbath day*?
		5 ●	The Son of Man is master of the *sabbath*.
		6	on another *sabbath* [Jesus] went into the synagogue

Lk	6	7	The scribes and the Pharisees were watching him to see if he would cure a man on the *sabbath*,
		9	is it against the law on the *sabbath* to do good, or to do evil . . .?
	13	10	One *sabbath day* [Jesus] was teaching in one of the synagogues,
		14	the synagogue official was indignant that Jesus had healed on the *sabbath*, and he addressed the people present. 'There are six [working] days . . . [do not] come . . . on the *sabbath*'.
		15	Is there one of you who does not untie his ox . . . from the manger on the *sabbath* and take it out for watering? [16] And
		16	this . . . daughter of Abraham whom Satan has held bound these eighteen years – was it not right to untie her bonds on the *sabbath day*?
	14	1	on a *sabbath day* [Jesus] had gone for a meal to the house of one of the leading Pharisees;
		3	Is it against the law . . . to cure a man on the *sabbath* . . .?
		5	Which of you here, if his son falls into a well . . . will not pull him out on a *sabbath day* . . .?
	23	54	It was Preparation Day and the *sabbath* was imminent.
		56	on the *sabbath day* they rested, as the Law required.
Jn	5	9	[The sick man was cured at once.] Now that day happened to be the *sabbath*,
		10	It is the *sabbath*; you are not allowed to carry your sleeping-mat.
		16	It was because he did things like this on the *sabbath* that the Jews began to persecute Jesus.
		18	not content with breaking the *sabbath*, he spoke of God as his own Father,
	6	59	He taught . . . at Capernaum, in the synagogue (ᵛ on the *sabbath*).
	7	22	you circumcise on the *sabbath*. [23] Now if a man can be circumcised on the *sabbath* . . . why are you angry with me for making a man whole and complete on a *sabbath*?
		23	
	9	14	It had been a *sabbath day* when Jesus made the paste and opened the man's eyes,
		16	This man cannot be from God: he does not keep the *sabbath*.
	19	31	to prevent the bodies remaining on the cross during the *sabbath* – since that *sabbath* was a day of special solemnity – the Jews asked Pilate to have . . . the bodies taken away.
Ac	1	12	they went back to Jerusalem, a short distance away, no more than a *sabbath* walk;
	13	14	[Paul and his friends] went to the synagogue on the *sabbath*
		27	[The people of Jerusalem fulfilled] the prophecies read on every *sabbath*.
		42	they were asked to preach on the same theme the following *sabbath*.
		44	The next *sabbath* almost the whole town assembled to hear the word of God.
	15	21	Moses has always had his preachers . . . and is read aloud in the synagogues every *sabbath*.
	16	13	[in Philippi] we went along the river . . . as it was the *sabbath* and this was a customary place for prayer.
	17	2	[In Thessalonika] Paul . . . for three consecutive *sabbaths* developed the arguments from scripture
	18	4	Every *sabbath* [Paul] used to hold debates in the synagogues,
Col	2	16	never let anyone else decide . . . whether you are to observe annual festivals, New Moons or *sabbaths*.

YEAST – LEAVEN – UNLEAVENED

1: Yeast, Leaven – Unleavened bread | 2: (The feast of) Unleavened Bread

1 *zymē* 13   2 *a-zymos* 9
3 *zymoō* 4

1: YEAST, LEAVEN – UNLEAVENED BREAD

Mt	13	33	The kingdom of heaven is like the *yeast* a woman . . . mixed
		3	in with three measures of flour till it was *leavened* all through.
	16	6 ○	be on your guard against the *yeast* of the Pharisees and Sadducees.
		11 ○	Beware of the *yeast* of the Pharisees and Sadducees.
		12	[Jesus] was telling them to be on their guard, not against the *yeast* for making bread, but against the teaching of the Pharisees
Mk	8	15 ○	be on your guard against the *yeast* of the Pharisees and the *yeast* of Herod.
Lk	12	1 ○	Be on your guard against the *yeast* of the Pharisees – that is, their hypocrisy.
	13	21	[The kingdom of God] is like the *yeast* a woman . . . mixed
		3	in with three measures of flour till it was *leavened* all through.

1 Co 5	6	/3 even a small amount of *yeast* is enough to *leaven* all the dough,
	7	[7] so get rid of all the old *yeast*, and make yourselves into a
	2	completely new batch of *bread unleavened* . . . Christ,
	8	our passover, has been sacrificed; [8] let us celebrate the feast, then, by getting rid of all the old *yeast* of evil and
	/2	the *yeast* of wickedness, having only the *unleavened bread* of sincerity and truth.
Ga 5	9	The *yeast* seems to be ⸢spreading through the whole batch of
	3	you (lit. *leavening* all the dough).

2: (THE FEAST OF) UNLEAVENED BREAD

Mt 26 17	2	on the first day of *Unleavened Bread* the disciples came to Jesus to say, 'Where do you want us to make the preparations . . .?'
Mk 14 1	2	It was two days before the Passover and the feast of *Unleavened Bread*,
12	2	On the first day of *Unleavened Bread* . . . the Passover lamb was sacrificed,
Lk 22 1	2	The feast of *Unleavened Bread*, called the Passover, was now drawing near,
7	2	The day of *Unleavened Bread* came round, the day on which the passover had to be sacrificed,
Ac 12 3	2	[Herod decided to arrest Peter] during the days of *Unleavened Bread*,
20 6	2	We ourselves left Philippi . . . after the days of *Unleavened Bread*

YES

1: Yes, I tell you | 2: Yes

nai 29

1: YES, I TELL YOU

nai legō hymin 4

Mt 11	9	To see a prophet? *Yes, I tell you*, and much more than a prophet:
Lk 7	26	A prophet? *Yes, I tell you*, and much more than a prophet:
11	51	*Yes, I tell you*, this generation will have to answer for it all.
12	5	*Yes, I tell you*, fear him.

2: YES

Mt 5	37	All you need say is ' *Yes* ' if you mean *yes*, 'No' if you mean no;
9	28	[Jesus] said to [the two blind men], 'Do you believe I can do this?' They, said, ⸢'Sir, we do (lit. *Yes*, sir)'.
11	26	*Yes*, Father, for that is what it pleased you to do.
13	51	'Have you understood all this?' They said, ' *Yes* '.
17	25	[Does your master not pay the half-shekel?] 'Oh *yes*' [Peter] replied.
21	16	'Do you hear what they are saying?' ' *Yes*,' Jesus answered
Lk 10	21	*Yes*, Father, for that is what it pleased you to do.
Jn 11	27	[I am the resurrection . . . Do you believe this?] ' *Yes*, Lord, . . . I believe that you are the Christ,'
21	15	'Simon . . ., do you love me more than these others do?' . . . ' *Yes*, Lord, you know I love you'.
16		'do you love me?' . . . ' *Yes*, Lord, you know I love you'.
Ac 5	8	'was this the price you sold the land for?' ' *Yes*, . . . that was the price,'
22	27	'are you a Roman citizen?' ⸢'I am (lit. *Yes*)'
2 Co 1	17	Do you really think . . . that I say *Yes*, yes, and No, no, at the same time? [18] . . . there is no *Yes* and No about what we say to you. [19] The Son of God, the Christ Jesus . . . was never *Yes* and No: with him it was always *Yes*, [20] and however many the promises God made, the *Yes* to them all was in him.
18		
19	X	
20	X	
Jm 5	12	If you mean 'yes', you must say 'yes'; if you mean 'no', say 'no'.
Rv 1	7	It is he who is coming . . . ⸢This is the truth (lit. *Yes*).
14	13	Happy are those who die in the Lord! ⸢Happy indeed (lit. *Yes*, happy), the Spirit says,
16	7	⸢Truly (lit. *Yes*), Lord God Almighty, the punishments you give are true and just.
22	20	⸢I shall indeed (lit. *Yes*, I shall) be with you soon.

Z

1. Zeal, Zealous – Jealous: *zēlos*
  1: Zeal, Zealous concern, Staunch upholder – Be Ambitious (to), Eager (to) – Aspire (to)
  2: Jealousy, Jealous Resentment – Stir to Jealousy, Rouse to Envy, Make anxious

2. Envy, Envious Jealous(y): *phthonos*
3. Greed, Avarice, Covetousness – Usurer(s): *pleon-exia*

1. ZEAL, ZEALOUS – JEALOUS: *ZĒLOS*

5	*zēleuō*	1	3	*zēlōtēs* 8	6 *kananaios* 2
2	*zēloō*	11	4	*para-zēloō* 4	
1	*zēlos*	16			

1: ZEAL, ZEALOUS CONCERN, STAUNCH UPHOLDER – BE AMBITIOUS (TO), EAGER (TO) – ASPIRE (TO)

Mt	10	4	[These are the names of the twelve apostles. . . . Thaddeus;]
		6	Simon the *Zealot*
Mk	3	18	[And so he appointed the Twelve: . . .] Thaddeus, Simon
		6	the *Zealot*
Lk	6	15	[he called them apostles:] . . . James son of Alphaeus,
		3	Simon called the *Zealot*,
Jn	2	17	3 (Ps 69 9) *Zeal* for your house will devour me.
Ac	1	13	[the apostles . . .] James son of Alphaeus and Simon the
		3	*Zealot*,
	21	20	thousands of Jews have now become believers, all of them
		3	*staunch upholders* of the Law,
	22	3	3 I was as *full of duty* towards God as you are today.
Rm	10	2	I can swear to [the Jews'] fervour for God, but their *zeal* is
			misguided.
	11	11	[the Jews'] fall . . . has saved the pagans in a way the Jews
		4	may now ʳwell emulate (lit. be *zealous* to emulate; or: be
			jealous of while emulating),
1 Co	12	31	2 *Be ambitious* for the higher gifts.
	14	1	2 *hope* for the spiritual gifts as well,
		12	3 since you *aspire* to spiritual gifts, concentrate on those which
			will grow
		39	2 by all means *be ambitious* to prophesy,
2 Co	7	7	[Titus] has told us . . . how *concerned* [you were] for me,
		11	Just look at what suffering in God's way has brought you:
			what . . . *concern* for me,
	9	2	I know how *anxious* you are to help;
Ga	1	14	3 [You must have heard] how ʳenthusiastic (lit. *zealous*) I was
			for the traditions of my ancestors.
Ph	3	6	as for ʳworking for religion (lit. religious *zeal*), I was a
			persecutor of the Church;
Tt	2	14	3 to purify a people so that it . . . would have no *ambition*
			except to do good.
Heb	10	27	the *raging* fire that is to burn rebels.
Jm	4	2	2 You ʳhave an ambition (or: have a [feeling of] jealous resent-
			ment) that you cannot satisfy;
1 P	3	13	3 No one can hurt you if you are ʳ*determined* to do (or: *zealous*
			for) only what is right;
Rv	3	19	5 [Laodicea,] repent *in real earnest*.

2: JEALOUSY, JEALOUS RESENTMENT – STIR TO JEALOUSY, ROUSE TO ENVY, MAKE ENVIOUS

Ac	5	17	Prompted by *jealousy*, [18] [the Sadducees] arrested the apostles
	7	9	2 The patriarchs *were jealous* of Joseph
	13	45	the Jews, prompted by *jealousy*, . . . contradicted everything
			Paul said.
	17	5	2 The Jews, *full of resentment*, enlisted the help of a gang
Rm	10	19	4 (Dt 32 21) I will *make* you *jealous* of people who are not even
			a nation; I will make you angry

Rm	11	11	[the Jews'] fall . . . has saved the pagans in a way the Jews
			may now ʳwell emulate (lit. be zealous to emulate, or: be
		4	*jealous* of while emulating).
		14	4 the purpose . . . is to *make* my own people *envious* of you,
	13	13	Let us live decently . . . no wrangling or *jealousy*.
1 Co	3	3	all the *jealousy* and wrangling that there is among you,
	10	22	ʳDo we want to make the Lord angry (lit. Could we think
		4	to *make* the Lord *jealous*) . . .?
	13	4	2 Love . . . *is* never *jealous*;
2 Co	11	2	2/ the *jealousy* that I *feel* for you is God's own *jealousy*:
	12	20	I am afraid . . . there will be wrangling, *jealousy*, and tempers
			roused,
Ga	4	17	2 they have ʳtried to win you over (lit. *been jealous* for you):
		2	. . . they ʳ*want to win you over* to (lit. *are jealous* for you
			for; or: want you to *be jealous* of) themselves. [18] It is
		18	2 always a good thing to ʳwin people over (lit. *be jealous* for
			people; or: have people *jealous* of you)
	5	20	[the results of self-indulgence:] feuds and wrangling, *jealousy*,
Jm	3	14	if at heart you have the bitterness of *jealousy*, . . . never
			make any claims for yourself
		16	Wherever you find *jealousy* and ambition, you find disharmony,
	4	2	2 You ʳhave an ambition (or: *have a* [feeling of] *jealous
			resentment*) that you cannot satisfy;

2. ENVY, ENVIOUS, JEALOUS(Y): *PHTHONOS*

2 *phthoneō* 1   1 *phthonos* 9

Mt	27	18	Pilate knew it was out of *jealousy* that they had handed
			[Jesus] over.
Mk	15	10	[Pilate] realised it was out of *jealousy* that the chief priests
			had handed Jesus over.
Rm	1	29	[pagans are] addicted to *envy*, murder, wrangling,
Ga	5	21	[the results of self-indulgence:] *envy*; drunkenness, orgies
		26	2 We must stop *being* conceited, provocative and *envious*.
Ph	1	15	some . . . are [announcing the Message] just out of ʳrivalry
			(or: *envy*) and competition.
1 Tm	6	4	All that can come of this is *jealousy*, contention, abuse
Tt	3	3	we lived then in wickedness and ʳill-will (or: *envy*),
Jm	4	5 △	the spirit which he sent to live in us ʳwants (lit. is *jealous* of)
			us for himself alone?
1 P	2	1	Be sure . . . you are never . . . *envious* and critical of each
			other.

3. GREED, AVARICE, COVETOUSNESS – USURER(S): *PLEON-EXIA*

2 *pleon-ektēs* 4   1 *pleon-exia* 10

Mk	7	22	[from men's hearts come] *avarice*, malice, deceit,
Lk	12	15	be on your guard against *avarice* of any kind,
Rm	1	29	[pagans are] steeped in all sorts of . . . *greed* and malice,
1 Co	5	10	2 I was not meaning . . . all *usurers* and swindlers . . . [but]
		11	2 [11] . . . a brother Christian who is . . . a *usurer*, or . . .
			dishonest;
	6	10	2 thieves, *usurers*, drunkards . . . will never inherit the kingdom
			of God.
2 Co	9	5	to . . . make sure . . . that it all comes as a gift out of your
			generosity and not by being ʳextorted from you (lit. prised
			from your *avarice*).
Ep	4	19	they . . . ʳeagerly (lit. *greedily*) pursue a career of indecency
			of every kind.
	5	3	Among you there must be not even a mention of fornication
		5	or . . . *greed*: . . . [5] . . . nobody who actually indulges
		2	in fornication or . . . *greed* . . . can inherit . . . the king-
			dom of God.
Col	3	5	fornication, impurity, . . . and especially *greed*, which is the
			same thing as worshipping a false god;
1 Th	2	5	never at any time have our speeches been simply . . . a cover
			for ʳ*trying to get money* (or: *greed*);
2 P	2	3	[False teachers] will ʳeagerly (lit. *greedily*) try to buy you for
			themselves
		14	*Greed* is the one lesson their minds have learnt.

INDEXES

English Index

Directly beneath each entry appears an exact reference to where the word, words, phrase or clause in question is to be found in the main body of the text, indicated by the (title of the) Theme under which it has been classified, and the Section number or numbers within that Theme. Very frequently there is more than one reference beneath an entry. To help the student or scholar, various simple typographic devices have been used to distinguish the relative importance of each reference.

Important references are printed in **bold type**; such a reference means that the word or words of the entry appear in the main heading of the Section indicated by the reference.

Slightly less important references appear in ordinary (medium) type, and mean that the word or words of the entry appear in the subheading or sub-subheading of the Section indicated by the reference.

References preceded by a + and printed in *italic type* show that the word or words of the entry do not appear in any heading or subheading but may nevertheless be of sufficient importance to be able to be looked up in the Section indicated.

When a reference includes two or more Sections from the same Theme, the title of the Theme is not repeated unless a later reference is of the third kind above.

A

Attend, Attend to, Attendant—(contd)
    SLAVE – SERVE – MINISTER 6.2:
        6.3:
        7.
        8.4:
    + *DO – MAKE – BEHAVE* 5.
    + *STAY – LIVE* 10.
    + *STAND* 1:
Attention, Give attention (to)
    SEE 8.
    HEAR – LISTEN – LEARN 4.1:
Attest
    WITNESS – TESTIFY 1:
Attract
    DRAG – DRAW 2.2:
Audience chamber
    HEAR – LISTEN – LEARN 3.
August, Eminent
    CAESAR
Austere, Austerity
    BITTER – SEVERE 2. b)
    SPARE 1:
Author
    + *RULE – AUTHORITY – LEADER* 3.1:
(In) Authority, Have authority (over)
    RULE – AUTHORITY – LEADER 4.
        5.
    GREAT – MANY – MORE 3.
    MASTER – LORD 2. d)
    + *RULE – AUTHORITY – LEADER* 3.4:
Autumn
    WIND – CLOUD – RAIN 5.4:
        7.1:
Auxiliary Spearmen
    WAR – ARMY – WEAPONS 5.
Avarice
    ZEAL – ENVY – GREED 3.
Avenge
    JUDGE – CONDEMN – PUNISH 4.
Avid (for), Itching (for)
    + *WEAKEN – SICKNESS* 3.8:
Avoid
    REJECT – AVOID – ESCAPE 7.1:
        8.
        9.
        10.
        11.1:
        12.
        13.2:
    KEEP – GUARD 1. c)
        2. d)
Await
    HOPE – EXPECT – WAIT FOR 2.1:b)
        2.2:
Awake
    SLEEP – WAKE 2.
        3.
Be) Aware, Awareness
    KNOW – UNDERSTAND 2.4:
        2.5:
    + *KNOW – UNDERSTAND* 1.2:
        1.8:
        2.2:
    + *SEE* 7.
Away (from)
    DISTANCE – AWAY – FROM 2.
        3.
"Away with (him)!"
    TAKE – BRING – LEAD 3.2:
Awe
    FEAR – AWE 3. a)
        1. a)
Awestruck
    ASTONISHED – WONDER 2.
Axe
    CUT – DIVISION 1.7:

B

Baal
    GOD 1.3:b)
Babe, Baby
    BEAR – BIRTH – CHILD 7.1:
        7.2:
        10.

Back
    ACCOMPANY – FOLLOW – AFTER 8.2:
Back (of the body)
    BODY 5.6:
Backbiting
    CURSE – ABUSE – SLANDER 2.4:
Bad
    EVIL – WRONG – HARM 2.3:
        8.
        10.
        11.
        1.1:
    + *EVIL – WRONG – HARM* 3.
Bad man, Bad men
    EVIL – WRONG – HARM 2.3:
Bad temper
    ANGER 2.2:
Bag
    VESSEL – BASKET – BAG 7.
Bag of gold
    + *MONEY* 9.1:
Bailiff
    STEWARD – GUARDIAN 2.
    CATCH – SEIZE – STEAL 9.2:
a Balance
    MEASURE 5.
(to) Balance
    SAME – LIKE – SUCH 2.
Ban
    CURSE – ABUSE – SLANDER 1.3:
Band of soldiers
    WAR – ARMY – WEAPONS 3.
Bandage
    ROPE – TIE – CHAIN 8. a)
Bandit
    CATCH – SEIZE – STEAL 11.
Bands, Linen strips
    CLOTH 2.3:
Banish
    KEEP – GUARD 11.
    TURN – RETURN 3.3:a)
(the) Bank, Bankers
    MONEY 13.
Banquet
    EAT – FOOD – DRINK 7.1:
        7.2:
Baptise, Baptism
    WATER – BAPTISE – WASH 2. a)
        2. b)
        1.1:a)
Barbarian
    FOREIGN – ALIEN 2.
Bare
    CLOTHING 5.2:c)
    SHOW – REVEAL – OPEN 7.1:
Barley
    FARM 3.4:
Barracks
    FORT – WALL – TOWER 1.1:
Barn
    FARM 6.1:
Barren
    BEAR – BIRTH – CHILD 11.
    FRUIT 2.1:
    + *IDLE – DELAY* 2.
Barrier
    FORT – WALL – TOWER 2.
Base, Foundation
    BUILDING 2. b)
Basin
    VESSEL – BASKET – BAG 4.1
Basket
    VESSEL – BASKET – BAG 6.
Bastard(s)
    SON – DAUGHTER 3.
Bath, Bathe
    WATER – BAPTISE – WASH 3.1:b)
Battalion
    + *WAR – ARMY – WEAPONS* 3.
Battered
    BEAT – STRIKE – WOUND 14.
Battle
    WAR – ARMY – WEAPONS 1.
        2. c)
    FIGHT – STRUGGLE 3.1:
    + *FIGHT – STRUGGLE* 1.
a Bay
    SEA – SHORE 5.

Be
    BE 1.
        2.1:
        2.2:
        4.
        5.
        6.
        7.2:
    PUT – SET – APPOINT 6.3:
    + *STAY – LIVE* 3.
        9.
Be a person's, Belong to
    BELONG TO
Beach
    SEA – SHORE 4.1:
Beacon
    + *SHINE – LIGHT* 1.1:
Beam, Plank
    TREE – WOOD 7.2:
Bear (= Carry)
    BEAR – BIRTH – CHILD 3.1:c)
        4.1:
    TAKE – BRING – LEAD 2.
        3.1:
        6.3:
        6.5:
Bear (fruit)
    FRUIT 1. a)
    GROW – SPROUT – BUD 4.
    GIVE 1.10:
    DO – MAKE – BEHAVE 3.2:
    TAKE – BRING – LEAD 6.6:
Bear (the animal)
    ANIMALS 2.1:
Bear with, Bear
    BEAR WITH – PATIENCE 1.
        2.
        3.
Bear witness
    WITNESS – TESTIFY 1:
Bearing, Behaviour
    DO – MAKE – BEHAVE 6.5:
Beast(s)
    ANIMALS 1.
        2.6:a)
Beat, Beaten, a Beating
    BEAT – STRIKE – WOUND 2.
        3.
        6.1:
        7.1:
        9.
        10.
    + *BEAT – STRIKE – WOUND* 8.
Beat one's breast
    MOURN – LAMENT 3.
Beat with rods
    ROD – STAFF – CLUB 1.4:
Beating
    BEAT – STRIKE – WOUND 9.
        6.1:
    + *BEAT – STRIKE – WOUND* 2.
Beautiful
    GOOD – BETTER 12.
Because of
    FOR 4.
Beckon
    + *SIGN* 2.
        3.
Become
    BE 2.3:
        2.4:
Become (= Be appropriate, well-suited)
    FITTING – WORTHY 1.2:
    + *FITTING – WORTHY* 2. a)
Become a believer
    BELIEVE – FAITH 1.1:a)
Bed
    SIT – LIE 3.3:
        6.
        4.2:
        4.3:
Bedridden
    SIT – LIE 8.
        4.2:
Bees
    BIRDS – INSECTS 3.2:
Befit
    FITTING – WORTHY 1.2:
    + *FITTING – WORTHY* 4.1:a)

Bunches (of grapes)
    FRUIT 3.1:
Bundle
    GREAT – MANY – MORE 6.2:
  + *ROPE – TIE – CHAIN* 8. a)
Burden, Be a burden (on)
    GREAT – MANY – MORE 13.
                  14.
    GATHERING 10.
    TAKE – BRING – LEAD 6.2:
Burglar, Burgle
    CATCH – SEIZE – STEAL 9.1:
                  13.
Burial, Buried: see Bury
Burn, Burning
    FIRE – BURN 1.1:
              1.2:
              1.5:
              4.
    DESTROY 3.
  + *FIRE – BURN* 7.
Burn incense
    SMELL – INCENSE – SPICE 2.1:
the Burning Bush
    TREE – WOOD 10.2:a)
Burst
    BREAK – GRIND – TEAR 3.1:
              3.4:
Burst into (tears)
    BEGINNING 2.
Bury, Burial, Buried
    BURY – TOMB 2.
              3.
Bush
    TREE – WOOD 10.1:
              10.2:a)
Business
    GAIN – PROFIT 5.
    GO – PASS 2.4:
  + *DO – MAKE – BEHAVE* 2.3:a)
  + *BUY – SELL – TRADE* 2.1:
Busy with
    CARE – CONCERN – DEVOTION 7.
Busybody
    CARE – CONCERN – DEVOTION 13.
Butcher's shop
  + *BUY – SELL – TRADE* 4.
Buy
    BUY – SELL – TRADE 1.
By
  + *THROUGH* 1:
Byroads
    STREET – PATH – WAY 2.3:b)
Bystander(s)
  + *STAND* 1:

C

Cables
    ROPE – TIE – CHAIN 3.
Caesar
    CAESAR
Cage
  + *KEEP – GUARD* 2. a)
Calf
    ANIMALS 2.7:c)
Call, Be called
    NAME – CALL 3.
              4.
              5.
              6.
  + *NAME – CALL* 1.3:
Call (to), Call for, Call upon
    NAME – CALL 5.3:
              5.5:
              5.6:
              6.2:
    ASK – PRAY 6.2:
    SAY – TELL – SPEAK 2.2:a)
  + *VOICE – SOUND* 3.1:c)
  + *DO – MAKE – BEHAVE* 3.5:b)
  + *ENCOURAGE – BOLD – PERSUADE* 8.1

Call (a person rude) names
  + *CURSE – ABUSE – SLANDER* 2.1:
  + *DO – MAKE – BEHAVE* 3.5:b)
Call together, Assemble
    GATHERING 5.
    NAME – CALL 5.6:
  + *GATHERING* 8.1:
(Be) Called: see Call
Calling, Vocation
  + *NAME – CALL* 5.5:
Calm, Keep calm
    QUIET – SILENCE 1.
              2.
    WISE – SOBER 3.
Calumny
  + *EVIL – WRONG – HARM* 2.3:
Came: see Come
Camel
    ANIMALS 2.4:
Camp
    FORT – WALL – TOWER 1.1:
    STAY –LIVE 13.2:
Can, Could
    POWER – ABLE TO 1.1:
              1.2:
              2.2:
              5.
              8.
  + *KNOW – UNDERSTAND* 2.4:a)
Canaanite
  + *TYRE AND SIDON*
  + *ZEAL – ENVY – GREED* 1.1:
Cancel (sins, debt)
    WIPE – WIPE OUT 2. b)
  + *COVER – VEIL* 2:
  + *MERCY – PITY* 5.
  + *DESTROY* 12.
Candle, Candle-stick
  + *SHINE – LIGHT* 3.
Cane
    TREE – WOOD 8.
Capable
  + *POWER – ABLE TO* 1.1:c)
Capital sum
  + *BUILDING* 2. b)
Captain
    RULE – AUTHORITY – LEADER 9. b)
                  10. a)
                  3.6:b)
Captive, Captivity
    KEEP – GUARD 6.
Capture
    CATCH – SEIZE – STEAL 12.2:
    TAKE – BRING – LEAD 1.2:
  + *CATCH – SEIZE – STEAL* 8.1:
  + *KEEP – GUARD* 6.
Care, Care for
    CARE – CONCERN – DEVOTION 1.
                  2.1:
                  4.
                  11.
                  7.
    HELP – SUPPORT 9.
  + *CARE – CONCERN – DEVOTION* 12.
Career, Life
    DO – MAKE – BEHAVE 6.3:
    RUN – QUICKLY 1.2:
  + *DO – MAKE – BEHAVE* 2.3:b)
(Be) Careful, Careful that, Ask carefully
    STEWARD – GUARDIAN 3.
    CAREFUL – ACCURATE – STRICT
    KEEP – GUARD 7.2:
    SEE 4.2:
(Be) Careful not to
    KEEP – GUARD 1. c)
              2. d)
              7.2:
Cargo
    FILL – FULL – FULFIL 1.2:
Carnelian
  + *STONE – JEWEL* 7.
Carousing
    EAT – FOOD – DRINK 13.
Carpenter
    DO – MAKE – BEHAVE 8.
Carriage
    CHARIOT 1.

Carry (in, off, away), (Be) Carried (back)
    TAKE – BRING – LEAD 2.
                  5.
                  6.1:
                  6.5:
                  3.1:
    HAVE – OWN – POSSESS 1.1:
  + *TAKE – BRING – LEAD* 1.4:
  + *CATCH – SEIZE – STEAL* 9.1:
Carry out
  + *DO – MAKE – BEHAVE* 2.1:
                  3.8:
                  3.10:
                  5.
  + *END – LAST* 1. a)
  + *FILL – FULL – FULFIL* 3.2:b)
Carry out for burial
    BURY – TOMB 2.
Carve(d)
    IMAGE – FORM – EXAMPLE 2.
  + *IMAGE – FORM – EXAMPLE* 4.1:
Case
    ACCUSE – CHARGE – DEFEND 4.
    MATTER – THING – AFFAIR 3.
                  1. b)
Cast, Cast down, Cast away
    THROW – DROP 1.
              2.
    REJECT – AVOID – ESCAPE 1.
  + *REJECT – AVOID – ESCAPE* 4.2:
Cast a vote
    TAKE – BRING – LEAD 6.4:
  + *AGREEMENT – CONSENT* 9.
Cast ashore
  + *SEA – SHORE* 6.4:
Cast lots
    CUT – DIVISION 3.3:
Cast out (devils)
    DRIVE – SEND OUT – PUSH 1. a)
Castle
  + *FORT – WALL – TOWER* 1.1:
  + *BUILDING* 4. a)
Catch, Catch hold of
    CATCH – SEIZE – STEAL 1.
                  2.
                  3.
                  7.2:
                  8.
    KEEP – GUARD 5.
  + *TAKE – BRING – LEAD* 1.2:
  + *CATCH – SEIZE – STEAL* 9.1:
Catch fire
    FIRE – BURN 1.2:a)
              1.3:
Catch out
    CATCH – SEIZE – STEAL 4.
    TAKE – BRING – LEAD 1.7:
Cattle
    ANIMALS 1.4:
              2.7:a)
              2.7:b)
              2.7:c)
Caught: see Catch
Cause
    GIVE 4.
    MATTER – THING – AFFAIR 1. b)
    DO – MAKE – BEHAVE 2.4:
                  3.10:
Cause for shame
  + *DISHONOUR – SHAME* 2.
Cause to sin
    STUMBLE – FALL 3.
Caution
    FEAR – AWE 1. b)
Caution (not to)
    BLAME – REBUKE – WARN NOT TO 8.
Cavalry
    ANIMALS 2.7:
Cave
    DIG – PIERCE – HOLE 5.
              3. b)
    ABYSS – HADES – HELL 2.2:
Cease
    END – LAST 7.1:
              7.2:
               8.
Celebrate, Celebration
    REJOICE – GLAD – HAPPY 4.

Celebrate (with) a feast
    FESTIVAL 1.
    DO – MAKE – BEHAVE 3.3:
the Celestial Angels
    BLESS – PRAISE – GLORY 2. c)
Celibate, Celibacy
    MARRY – UNMARRIED 6.
Cemetery
    + *BURY – TOMB* 3.
Censer
    SMELL – INCENSE – SPICE 2.2:b)
Census
    WRITING – READ 1. g)
Centurion
    RULE – AUTHORITY – LEADER 3.8:
(Be) Certain, Certainty
    FIRM – CONFIRM – GUARANTEE 3.
    ENCOURAGE – BOLD – PERSUADE 3.
                    10.1:
    + *KNOW – UNDERSTAND* 1.3:
Certainly
    BE 1.5:
    END – LAST 1. a)
    WHOLE – ALL – EACH 2.2:f)
Certainty: see Certain
Certificate
    WRITING – READ 3.2:
Chaff
    FARM 4.2:
Chain, Chain up
    ROPE – TIE – CHAIN 8.
                 9.
                 10.
Chair(s)
    + *SIT – LIE* 1.1:a)
Chair of judgement
    JUDGE – CONDEMN – PUNISH 6.3:
Chalcedony
    + *STONE – JEWEL* 7.
Challenge, Challenging
    SHAKE – STIR UP – PROVOKE 12.
    + *TEST* 1.1:
Chamberlain
    STEWARD – GUARDIAN 4.
Chance
    FIND – HAPPEN 3.
    PLACE – ROOM 1. d)
    TIME – DAY – HOUR 2.2:
    + *FIND – HAPPEN* 2.2:
Change
    CHANGE 1.
               2.
               3.
               4.
    REPENT
Change one's mind, Change of heart
    REPENT
Chant
    SING – PLAY MUSIC 1.2:a)
Charcoal fire
    FIRE – BURN 3.
Charge
    ACCUSE – CHARGE – DEFEND 1.1:a)
                       1.2:
                       4. a)
    MATTER – THING – AFFAIR 1. a)
    + *JUDGE – CONDEMN – PUNISH* 2.
Charge (at), Rush
    RUSH – SPRING – LEAP 1.
    RUN – QUICKLY 1.1:
Charge (a person) to
    ORDER – REGULATION – INSTRUCT 4.
    + *ORDER – REGULATION – INSTRUCT* 3.
    + *BLAME – REBUKE – WARN NOT TO* 9.
(In) Charge
    + *RULE – AUTHORITY – LEADER* 4. a)
Charger, Tray
    + *VESSEL – BASKET – BAG* 5.1:
Chariot
    CHARIOT
Charisma
    + *GRACE – THANKS* 1:
                      3:
Charity
    MERCY – PITY 1.4:
    + *LOVE* 1.3:d)
Charlatan
    DECEIVE – TRICK – PRETENCE 1.9:

Chaste
    PURE – INNOCENT – SIMPLE 4.
Chatter
    SAY – TELL – SPEAK 5.7:
Cheat
    CATCH – SEIZE – STEAL 15.1:
                      15.2:
    + *MOCK – LAUGH* 2.
Cheek
    HEAD – HAIR 2.2:
Cheer, Cheerful, Cheerfulness
    ENCOURAGE – BOLD – PERSUADE 2.
    REJOICE – GLAD – HAPPY 10.
    + *REJOICE – GLAD – HAPPY* 1.
                      4.
                      6.2:
Cherish
    CARE – CONCERN – DEVOTION 11.
Chest
    BODY 5.1:
            5.2:
            5.3:
Chicks
    BIRDS – INSECTS 2.3:
Chief
    END – LAST 4. a)
    RULE – AUTHORITY – LEADER 3.1:
    + *RULE – AUTHORITY – LEADER* 6.2:a)
    + *NUMBERS* 3.2:d)
Chief priest(s)
    PRIEST 1:
    + *PRIEST* 3:
Child, Children With child
    BEAR – BIRTH – CHILD 1.
                    2.
                    4.1:
                    4.4:
                    4.6:
                    5.
                    7.
    SON – DAUGHTER 1.3:
    + *BEAR – BIRTH – CHILD* 3.2:c)
Childless
    BEAR – BIRTH – CHILD 4.4:b)
    + *BEAR – BIRTH – CHILD* 11.
Choice: see Choose
Choke
    SPIRIT – SOUL – PERSON 1.4:
Choose, Chosen, Choice
    CHOOSE
    WILL – WANT 1.1:
                 3.
    REJOICE – GLAD – HAPPY 7.2:
    + *WILL – WANT* 2.4:
    + *CUT – DIVISION* 2.5:a)
Chose, Chosen: see Choose
Christ
    JESUS CHRIST
Christian(s)
    JESUS CHRIST
    + *HOLY* 1.6:
Chrysolite, Chrysoprase
    + *STONE – JEWEL* 7.
Church
    GATHERING 1.1:
Cinnamon
    SMELL – INCENSE – SPICE 3.4:
Circle
    ROUND – ROLL 2. a)
Circumcision
    CIRCUMCISION
Citizen(s), Citizenship
    CITY – TOWN – VILLAGE 1.2:
    MAN – PEOPLE – WOMAN 2.3:d)
                      3.3:c)
    + *FREE – SET FREE* 3.
Citizen of heaven
    + *WRITING – READ* 1. g)
City
    CITY – TOWN – VILLAGE 1.1:
Claim, Claim to be
    BOAST – PROUD – ARROGANT 6.
    TELL – PREACH – PROCLAIM 1.3:
    SAY – TELL – SPEAK 2.11:
    DO – MAKE – BEHAVE 3.5:a)
    + *BOAST – PROUD – ARROGANT* 1.
    + *TELL – PREACH – PROCLAIM* 2.1:
Claim to be great
    RISE – RAISE – HIGH 6.4:

Clanging, Clashing
    MOURN – LAMENT 9. b)
Clasp
    + *TAKE – BRING – LEAD* 1.2:
(to) Class
    SAME – LIKE – SUCH 6.
Class of the priesthood
    CUT – DIVISION 2.4:
Clay
    POTTERY – CLAY 3.
                    4.
Clean, Make clean
    PURE – INNOCENT – SIMPLE 2.
    + *PURE – INNOCENT – SIMPLE* 1.
Cleanse
    PURE – INNOCENT – SIMPLE 2.
    WATER – BAPTISE – WASH 3.1:a)
Clear, Clearly
    SHOW – REVEAL – OPEN 1.
                    2. a)
                    2. b)
                    3.1:
    SHINE – LIGHT 4.
    PURE – INNOCENT – SIMPLE 2.
(Steer, Stay) Clear of
    REJECT – AVOID – ESCAPE 8.
    + *REJECT – AVOID – ESCAPE* 9.
Clever
    KNOW – UNDERSTAND 4.
    + *WISE – SOBER* 1. a)
Cliff
    MOUNTAIN – HILL 4.
Climb
    RISE – RAISE – HIGH 4.4:
                    4.6:
                    5.
Cling to
    KEEP – GUARD 7:1
                    8.
    JOIN – ATTACH 5.
    ROUND – ROLL 4.
    CATCH – SEIZE – STEAL 7.2:
Cloak
    CLOTHING 2.1:
                2.2:
                2.3:
    DECEIVE – TRICK – PRETENCE 3.2:
Close (to), Close at hand, Closely
    NEAR – APPROACH – COME TO 6.
                      7.3:
Close inshore
    NEAR – APPROACH – COME TO 5.1:
(to) Close, Closed
    SHUT – CLOSED 1. b)
                    1. d)
                    2.
                    3. a)
    + *ROUND – ROLL* 9.3:
Closed (mind), Obstinacy
    HARDNESS – HARD HEART – SOFT 2.
    HEART 1:b)
    SHUT – CLOSED 1. d)
    + *HARDNESS – HARD HEART – SOFT* 1. a)
Cloth(s)
    CLOTH 1.7:
               2.2:b)
               2.4:
               2.5:
Clothe, Clothes, Clothing
    CLOTHING 1.1:
                 1.2:
                 1.3:
                 1.4:
                 1.5:
                 2.1:
    ROUND – ROLL 6.
    + *CLOTHING* 2.7:
                    5.
Clots (of blood)
    FLESH – BLOOD – BONE 2.2:
Cloud(s)
    WIND – CLOUD – RAIN 4.1:
                    4.2:
Club
    ROD – STAFF – CLUB 2.
Clusters (of grapes)
    FRUIT 3.
Coal(s)
    FIRE – BURN 3.

Conclude
    ENCOURAGE – BOLD – PERSUADE 11.
Condemn, Condemnation
    JUDGE – CONDEMN – PUNISH 1.2:
                                2.
                                3.1:c)
    CURSE – ABUSE – SLANDER 1.3:
Condole (with)
    + *ENCOURAGE – BOLD – PERSUADE* 9.
Conduct, Behaviour
    DO – MAKE – BEHAVE 6.1:
                                6.2:
    + *DO – MAKE – BEHAVE* 2.3:b)
                                3.7:
Conduct, Escort
    TAKE – BRING – LEAD 10.
Confer
    SAY – TELL – SPEAK 5.6:
                                5.10:
    + *GIVE* 1.4:
Confess, Confession
    TELL – PREACH – PROCLAIM 2.1:
                                2.2:
Confidence, Confident
    ENCOURAGE – BOLD – PERSUADE 1.
                                2.
                                3.
                                4.
                                10.
Confirm, Confirmation
    FIRM – CONFIRM – GUARANTEE 6.
    PUT – SET – APPOINT 2.2:
    + *FIRM – CONFIRM – GUARANTEE* 2.2:a)
                                5.
Conflict(s)
    + *WAR – ARMY – WEAPONS* 1.
    + *SAME – LIKE – SUCH* 2.
Conform, Conformity
    IMAGE – FORM – EXAMPLE 6.2:
    + *IMAGE – FORM – EXAMPLE* 5.1:
Confound
    CONFUSION – DISTURB 3.
Confront, to Face
    + *FACE – IN FRONT OF – BEFORE* 2.1:b)
Confusion
    CONFUSION – DISTURB 3.
                                4.
Confute
    + *BLAME – REBUKE – WARN NOT TO* 3.
Congratulate
    BLESS – PRAISE – GLORY 1.2:b)
Congregation
    GATHERING 1.1:
    + *GREAT – MANY – MORE* 6.1:
Conquer
    VICTORY – CONQUER 1.
    FIGHT – STRUGGLE 3.2:
Conscience
    KNOW – UNDERSTAND 2.5:
Consecrate, Consecrated to
    HOLY 1.2:
                                1.5:
    NAME – CALL 5.2:
    IDOL 2:
Consent (to)
    AGREEMENT – CONSENT 2.
                                3.
                                7.
    + *AGREEMENT – CONSENT* 6.
Consequence
    ACCUSE – CHARGE – DEFEND 4. b)
Consider, Consider as
    THINK – CONSIDER 10.
                                11.
                                12.
                                13.
                                8.2:
    KNOW – UNDERSTAND 5.
Considerable
    GREAT – MANY – MORE 4.
(Be) Considerate, Consideration
    HONOUR – RESPECT 1.1:
    + *SWEET – GENTLE – KINDLY* 2.2:
    + *MAN – PEOPLE – WOMAN* 2.6:
Consign to
    GIVE 1.8:
Console, Consolation
    ENCOURAGE – BOLD – PERSUADE 8.2:
                                9.

Conspicuous
    + *SHOW – REVEAL – OPEN* 3.1:
Conspiracy
    + *PROMISE – VOW – OATH* 6.2:
Constancy
    + *BEAR WITH – PATIENCE* 5.
Constant, Constantly
    OFTEN 1.
    STAY – LIVE 10.
    EVER – ETERNAL – AGE 3.
    END – LAST 7.1:
Constraint
    LITTLE 9.
    + *MUST – OUGHT TO* 5.
    + *SUFFER – ANGUISH* 4.
Construct
    MIX – ASSOCIATE 1. c)
Consult
    ASK – PRAY 9.
    SAY – TELL – SPEAK 5.10:
Consume
    EAT – FOOD – DRINK 2.2:c)
Consumed by fire
    DESTROY 3.
    FIRE – BURN 1.2:d)
Contain
    PLACE – ROOM 2.
Container
    VESSEL – BASKET – BAG 1.1:a)
                                1.2:
Contaminate
    DEFILE – FILTH 10.
Contemporary
    TIME – DAY – HOUR 3.
Contempt, Contemptible, Treat with contempt
    DISHONOUR – SHAME 1.
    DESPISE – DISREGARD 1.2:
    MOCK – LAUGH 3.
    + *DESPISE – DISREGARD* 1.1:
Contend, Contentions, Contention
    QUARREL – DISPUTE 2.
    + *QUARREL – DISPUTE* 1.
                                4.
    + *JUDGE – CONDEMN – PUNISH* 3.3:
(Be) Content (with, to)
    SATISFY – ENOUGH 2.
    AGREEMENT – CONSENT 3.
Continual(ly)
    EVER – ETERNAL – AGE 2.
                                3.
                                1.4:
    END – LAST 7.1:
Continue (to), Continuously
    STAY – LIVE 10.
                                3.3:
Continue a journey
    + *GO – PASS* 10.1:a)
Continue to spread, to grow
    GROW – SPROUT – BUD 1. c)
Continuously: see Continue
Contradict, Contradiction
    QUARREL – DISPUTE 5.
                                6.
Contrary (to)
    ENEMY – OPPOSE – AGAINST 3.
                                9.
    + *ENEMY – OPPOSE – AGAINST* 4.
    + *GREAT – MANY – MORE* 8.1:
Contribute (to)
    SHARE – PARTNER 1.1:
Control
    RULE – AUTHORITY – LEADER 12.
    ROPE – TIE – CHAIN 5.1:
    OBEY – SUBMIT – SUBJECT 8.
    TAKE – BRING – LEAD 8.2:
Controversy
    SAY – TELL – SPEAK 5.9:
Convene
    NAME – CALL 5.6:
Convenient, Timely
    TIME – DAY – HOUR 2.1:c)
(to) Convert, Be converted, Conversion
    TURN – RETURN 3.4:
    LEAVE 5.2:
    + *ENCOURAGE – BOLD – PERSUADE* 10.1:
(a) Convert
    NEAR – APPROACH – COME TO 7.4:
    + *FARM* 7.
Convey (between two parties)
    MID – AMONG 3:

Convict of
    BLAME – REBUKE – WARN NOT TO 3.
Conviction
    BELIEVE – FAITH 1.1:d)
    FILL – FULL – FULFIL 3.3:
    + *TEST* 3.2:
Convince, Be convinced
    ENCOURAGE – BOLD – PERSUADE 10.1:
                                11.
    FILL – FULL – FULFIL 3.3:
    + *KNOW – UNDERSTAND* 2.4:a)
    + *BLAME – REBUKE – WARN NOT TO* 3.
Convulsions, Convulse
    SHAKE – STIR UP – PROVOKE 4.
Cook(ed)
    FIRE – BURN 8.
Cool
    FERVENT – HOT – COLD 5.
Co-operate
    DO – MAKE – BEHAVE 2.5:
Copper, Coppersmith
    MONEY 8.1:
                                8.3:
                                9.8:
Copy
    IMAGE – FORM – EXAMPLE 7.
                                8.
    DO – MAKE – BEHAVE 3.9:
    + *IMAGE – FORM – EXAMPLE* 4.3:
Cord(s)
    ROPE – TIE – CHAIN 1.
Corn, Cornfields
    FARM 3.2:b)
                                3.3:
Corner
    CORNER – SQUARE 1.
    STRAIGHT – CROOKED 3. a)
    + *STREET – PATH – WAY* 1.2:
(Be) Cornered
    + *LITTLE* 9.
Cornerstone
    CORNER – SQUARE 1.2:
Coronet
    ADORN – CROWN 3.
Corpse
    BODY 2.
                                1. a)
    DIE – KILL 1.6:a)
Correct, Correction
    TEACHING 2.1:
    + *TEACHING* 3.
    + *BLAME – REBUKE – WARN NOT TO* 3.
                                4.
Corrode, Corrosion
    DESTROY 5.
                                6.
    + *EAT – FOOD – DRINK* 3.7:
Corrupt, Corruption
    DESTROY 8.
    DEFILE – FILTH 1.1:
    + *EVIL – WRONG – HARM* 10.
Cost, Costly
    PRECIOUS – EXPENSIVE 1.
                                2.
                                3.1:
Couch
    DISPERSE – SCATTER 5.3:
Could: see Can
Council
    PLAN – COUNCIL 2.
                                3.
    + *RULE – AUTHORITY – LEADER* 3.7:
Counsel
    PLAN – COUNCIL 2.
    + *WILL – WANT* 1.1:
Counsellor, Advocate
    ASK – PRAY 5.2:
    + *PLAN – COUNCIL* 2.
(to) Count, (Be) Counted
    NUMBERS 1.
                                2.
Count as
    THINK – CONSIDER 8.2:
                                10.
                                11.
to Count on (a person)
    + *REJOICE – GLAD – HAPPY* 7.
    + *GAIN – PROFIT* 8.
Counterfeit
    DECEIVE – TRICK – PRETENCE 2. b)

Countless
+ *NUMBERS* 1.
Country, Countryside
EARTH – LAND – COUNTRY 4. b)
                                    5. b)
                                    3. d)
+ *PLACE – ROOM* 1. a)
Countryman, Countrymen
BROTHER 3.
              1.5:
Countryside: see Country
Courage, Take courage
ENCOURAGE – BOLD – PERSUADE 1.
                                            2.
+ *ENCOURAGE – BOLD – PERSUADE* 4.
                                            9.
a Course
RUN – QUICKLY 1.
(Royal) Court
KING 6:
Court, Courtyard
BUILDING 4. a)
              4. b)
Court, Tribunal
JUDGE – CONDEMN – PUNISH 6.
Court official
KING 7:
Courteous, Courtesy
SWEET – GENTLE – KINDLY 2.1:a)
                                    2.2:
ADORN – CROWN 1.
Courtyard
BUILDING 4. a)
Cousin
BROTHER 2.
Covenant
COVENANT
Cover
COVER – VEIL
DECEIVE – TRICK – PRETENCE 3.2:
Cover with confusion
+ *DISHONOUR – SHAME* 2.
Cover with shadow
SHADOW 1:
Covet, Covetousness
ZEAL – ENVY – GREED 3.
DESIRE – LONGING 1.1:
Coward
FEAR – AWE 3. b)
Craft, Craftsmen
DO – MAKE – BEHAVE 8.
Crafty, Craftiness
DECEIVE – TRICK – PRETENCE 1.7:
Crave, Craving
+ *DESIRE – LONGING* 1.1:
                              4.
+ *WEAKEN – SICKNESS* 2.2:
Crawling animal, Reptile
SNAKE – DRAGON – SCORPION 1.1:
a Craze (for)
WEAKEN – SICKNESS 2.2:
Crazy
+ *FOOLISH – MAD* 6.
Create, Creator, Creature
DO – MAKE – BEHAVE 1.1:
                              3.1:
ANIMALS 1.2:a)
STAY – LIVE 2.4:
Create a place for
PUT – SET – APPOINT 2.4:
Creation
DO – MAKE – BEHAVE 1.1:
BEGINNING 1.2:
Creature: see Create
Credit
BLESS – PRAISE – GLORY 4.
GRACE – THANKS 3:b)
Creditor
BORROW – LEND 1.
Creeping thing, Reptile
+ *SNAKE – DRAGON – SCORPION* 1.1:
Cretan
ISLAND 3:
Crew
SHIP – SAIL 4. a)
Crime
EVIL – WRONG – HARM 2.3:
                                  3.
                                  14.
+ *EVIL – WRONG – HARM* 4.

Criminal
EVIL – WRONG – HARM 4.
                              1.2:
                              2.3:
Cripple, Crippled
LAME – CRIPPLED – PARALYSED
+ *WEAKEN – SICKNESS* 2.1:
Criticism, Criticise
BLAME – REBUKE – WARN NOT TO 1.
JUDGE – CONDEMN – PUNISH 3.3:
+ *BLAME – REBUKE – WARN NOT TO* 3.
+ *LABOUR – TROUBLE*
Crooked
STRAIGHT – CROOKED 3.
Crop, Crops
FARM 2.1:
              2.2:
FRUIT 2.1:
GROW – SPROUT – BUD 4.
Cross
CRUCIFY – HANG 1.
(to) Cross, Cross over
GO – PASS 11.2:
                          12.2:
                          10.1:a)
                          16.1:
Crossroads
STREET – PATH – WAY 2.3b:)
Crowd, Crowds
MAN – PEOPLE – WOMAN 6.
GREAT – MANY – MORE 6.1:
Crown, (Be) Crowned
ADORN – CROWN 4.1:
Crucify
CRUCIFY – HANG 1.1:
                            1.3:b)
Crumb(s)
EAT – FOOD – DRINK 3.5:b)
Crush
BREAK – GRIND – TEAR 1.
Cry, Cry out
VOICE – SOUND 3.
                        1.2:
Cry, Weep
MOURN – LAMENT 4.2:
Cryptic
+ *SECRET – MYSTERY* 3.
Crystal
STONE – JEWEL 8.1:
Cubit
MEASURE 2.4:
Cudgel
ROD – STAFF – CLUB 2.
Cultivate
FARM 1.1:
Cummin
GARDEN 2.2:
Cunning
DECEIVE – TRICK – PRETENCE 1.7:
+ *DECEIVE – TRICK – PRETENCE* 1.10:
Cup
EAT – FOOD – DRINK 10.
Cure, Be cured
SAVE – CURE 3. c)
                        4. a)
                        5.
                        6.
                        7. a)
+ *PURE – INNOCENT – SIMPLE* 2.
Current, Spate
RIVER – FLOW – FOUNTAIN 1.1:
Curry (favour)
GAIN – PROFIT 6.
Curse, Cursed
CURSE – ABUSE – SLANDER 1.
                                    2.1:
Curtain
CLOTH 2.1:
Cushion
SIT – LIE 9.
Custodian
KEEP – GUARD 3.3:
Custody
KEEP – GUARD 4.
                        1. a)
ROPE – TIE – CHAIN 8. c)
Custom, Customary
CUSTOM – PRACTICE 1. a)
                                  1. b)
                                  3.

Customs house
TAX 3.
Cut, Cut off
CUT – DIVISION 1.1:
                          1.2:
                          1.3:
TAKE – BRING – LEAD 4.1:
+ *TAKE – BRING – LEAD* 3.1:
+ *BREAK – GRIND – TEAR* 1.5:b)
Cut off from, Apart from
+ *WITH* 4.
Cut short
LITTLE 5.
TAKE – BRING – LEAD 3.3:
Cut the hair off
HEAD – HAIR 4.1:
Cut the head off
DIE – KILL 2.10:
Cut the throat (of)
DIE – KILL 2.5:
Cut to the heart, Pierce
DIG – PIERCE – HOLE 2.1:b)
Cut-throats, Assassins
DIE – KILL 2.6:
Cycle
ROUND – ROLL 7.
Cymbal
SING – PLAY MUSIC 2.2:
Cypriot
ISLAND 2:

D

Daily
TIME – DAY – HOUR 4.1:g)
                                4.2:
Dainty
+ *SHINE – LIGHT* 8.
Dais
RISE – RAISE – HIGH 4.8:
Damage
DESTROY 10.
CURSE – ABUSE – SLANDER 2.8:b)
Dance, Dancing
SING – PLAY MUSIC 3.
RUSH – SPRING – LEAP 4.
Danger, Dangerous
MISERY – DANGER 2.
+ *EVIL – WRONG – HARM* 13.
Dare, Daring
ENCOURAGE – BOLD – PERSUADE 5.
Dark, Darken(ed)
NIGHT – DARKNESS 2.
Darkness
NIGHT – DARKNESS 2.
Darnel
FARM 3.5:
Darts
WAR – ARMY – WEAPONS 6.8:
Dash (to pieces, to the ground)
DESTROY 19.
THROW – DROP 3.
BREAK – GRIND – TEAR 1.3:
Daub
ANOINT – OIL 1.2:
Daughter
SON – DAUGHTER 2.
+ *MARRY – UNMARRIED* 6.
Daughter of Zion (Sion) = Jerusalem
SON – DAUGHTER 2.2:
Daughter-in-law
MARRY – UNMARRIED 2.2:c)
Dawn
MORNING – EVENING 1.
SHINE – LIGHT 4.
                        1.1:
RISE – RAISE – HIGH 3.1:
Day, Daylight, Daily
TIME – DAY – HOUR 4.
                                5.2:
                                5.3:
NIGHT – DARKNESS 1. a)
the Day of Preparation
PREPARE – READY 2.2:

Distinct, Distinction—(contd)
+ *JUDGE – CONDEMN – PUNISH* 3.3:
Distinguish (between)
JUDGE – CONDEMN – PUNISH 3.3:
+ *SHOW – REVEAL – OPEN* 2. b)
Distinguished
HONOUR – RESPECT 1.1:
Distort
DESTROY 5.
TURN – RETURN 3.1:
(Be) Distracted, Distraction
DRAG – DRAW 3.4:
Distress, (Be) Distressed
SUFFER – ANGUISH 2.
3.
4.
5.
6.
7.
10.1:
MOURN – LAMENT 2.
+ *SUFFER – ANGUISH* 9.
Distribute
CUT – DIVISION 2.1:a)
PUT – SET – APPOINT 1.2:b)
+ *GIVE* 1.4:
District
EARTH – LAND – COUNTRY 5. b)
6.2:
CUT – DIVISION 3.1:d)
Disturb, Be disturbed, Disturbance
CONFUSION – DISTURB 5.
6.
7.
Ditch
DIG – PIERCE – HOLE 1.3:
Divide: see Division
Dividing wall
FORT – WALL – TOWER 2.
Divination
+ *MAGIC* 5.
Divine Justice
+ *JUDGE – CONDEMN – PUNISH* 4.
Divine majesty
+ *GREAT – MANY – MORE* 1. a)
Divine Retribution
ANGER 1.1:
+ *JUDGE – CONDEMN – PUNISH* 4.
Divine Revelation, the Divine Voice
SHOW – REVEAL – OPEN 6.
Divine Vengeance
+ *JUDGE – CONDEMN – PUNISH* 4.
Divinity
GOD 2.
+ *GOD* 1.1:
Division, Divide
CUT – DIVISION 2.1:a)
2.4:
3.1:a)
3.1:c)
LEAVE 3.2:
+ *QUARREL – DISPUTE* 7.
+ *GIVE* 1.4:
Division of opinion, Split
BREAK – GRIND – TEAR 3.2:b)
CUT – DIVISION 3.1:c)
Divorce
MARRY – UNMARRIED 3.
Do, Did, Done
DO – MAKE – BEHAVE 2.1:
2.2:
2.3:
2.4:
3.4:
3,6:
3.7:
3.8:
3.9:
3.10;
5.
7.
BE 2.2:b)
END – LAST 1. a)
+ *LABOUR – TROUBLE* 2.1:
+ *FILL – FULL – FULFIL* 3.2:b)
Do (= Suffice)
SATISFY – ENOUGH 5.
Do all one can to
CARE – CONCERN – DEVOTION 4.

Do away with
DESTROY 11.
12.
13. b)
DIE – KILL 2.2:
2.3:
TAKE – BRING – LEAD 3.2:
Do (one's) best to
CARE – CONCERN – DEVOTION 3.
+ *CARE – CONCERN – DEVOTION* 4.
Do business
GAIN – PROFIT 5.
Do evil, Do what is forbidden
EVIL – WRONG – HARM 1.2:
DO – MAKE – BEHAVE 3.7:
+ *EVIL – WRONG – HARM* 3.
Do good
GOOD – BETTER 9.
1. c)
4. a)
DO – MAKE – BEHAVE 3.6:
3.8:
+ *GOOD – BETTER* 2. b)
+ *RIGHTEOUS – JUSTIFY – VIRTUE*
Do harm
EVIL – WRONG – HARM 13.
1.2:
+ *EVIL – WRONG – HARM* 3.
Do homage
WORSHIP 4.2:
Do right
GOOD – BETTER 2. b)
DO – MAKE – BEHAVE 3.6:
3.8:
+ *GOOD – BETTER* 4. a)
Do well
GOOD – BETTER 2. b)
4. a)
+ *GOOD – BETTER* 1. c)
(Have to) Do with
MATTER – THING – AFFAIR 3.
Do without
LEAVE 10.3:
Do wrong
EVIL – WRONG – HARM 3.
7.
1.2:
15.1:
Doctor, Physician
SAVE – CURE 6.
Doctors (of the law, the Scribes)
WRITING – READ 1. c)
TEACHING 1.1:d)
Doctrine
TEACHING 1.1:c)
1.1:d)
Dog(s)
ANIMALS 2.11:
Dominate, Be dominated, Domination
EVIL – WRONG – HARM 11.
MASTER – LORD 2. f)
RULE – AUTHORITY – LEADER 4. a)
Dominion
MASTER – LORD 2. f)
+ *RULE – AUTHORITY – LEADER* 4. a)
+ *POWER – ABLE TO* 3.2:b)
Donkey
ANIMALS 2.6:
Door
BUILDING 6.1:a)
6.2:a)
6.2:b)
Doorkeeper
BUILDING 6.2:
(a) Dot
WRITING – READ 5.6:
Double, Doubly
NUMBERS 4.1:e)
Double-edged (sword)
CUT – DIVISION 1.4:
Double-minded
+ *NUMBERS* 4.1:d)
Double-talk
DECEIVE – TRICK – PRETENCE 1.5:b)
Doubt
BELIEVE – FAITH 2.
1.1:d)
Dough
EAT – FOOD – DRINK 4.2:

Dove
BIRDS – INSECTS 2.4:
Down
DOWN – BELOW – UNDER 1:
3:
Doze
SLEEP – WAKE 1.4:
Drachma
MONEY 9.4:
Drag
DRAG – DRAW 1.
2.1:
+ *TAKE – BRING – LEAD* 8.1:c)
Drag down
SEA – SHORE 3.2:
Dragnet
FISH 6.2:
Dragon
SNAKE – DRAGON – SCORPION 3.
(a) Drain
DEFILE – FILTH 8.
Draw (out, away, up, from)
DRAG – DRAW 2.2:
3.
RIVER – FLOW – FOUNTAIN 4.2:
DRIVE – SEND OUT – PUSH 1. c)
CATCH – SEIZE – STEAL 9.2:
+ *TAKE – BRING – LEAD* 1.4:
Draw aside
LEAVE 3.1:
Draw attention to
+ *SHOW – REVEAL – OPEN* 1.
Draw away
DRAG – DRAW 3.5:
LEAVE 5.2:
Draw back (from)
REJECT – AVOID – ESCAPE 11.2:
Draw lots
+ *GIVE* 1.11:
Draw near
NEAR – APPROACH – COME TO 6.
7.1:
Draw up (an account)
+ *GIVE* 1.11:
+ *ORDER – REGULATION – INSTRUCT* 9. a)
Dreadful
+ *FEAR – AWE* 1. a)
Drench
WATER – BAPTISE – WASH 2. d)
Dress, Dress up, Dressed
CLOTHING 1.1:
1.2:
1.3:
+ *ADORN – CROWN* 1.
+ *ROUND – ROLL* 6.
Drew: see Draw
Dried: see Dry
Drift away (metaphorically)
SHIP – SAIL 3.
+ *SHAKE – STIR UP – PROVOKE* 5. a)
Drink, Drinker
EAT – FOOD – DRINK 10.
Drive, Drive out
DRIVE – SEND OUT – PUSH 1.
2.
3.
4.1:
4.2:
WIND – CLOUD – RAIN 2.5:
DO – MAKE – BEHAVE 2.6:
+ *CUT – DIVISION* 2.6:a)
+ *TAKE – BRING – LEAD* 6.1:
Drive back
DRIVE – SEND OUT – PUSH 5.
Drive to resentment
SHAKE – STIR UP – PROVOKE 10.
Drooping
WEAKEN – SICKNESS 1.3:
Drop
THROW – DROP 1.
2.
STUMBLE – FALL 5.1:
(a wind) Drops
END – LAST 8.
Drops of blood
FLESH – BLOOD – BONE 2.2:
Dropsy
WEAKEN – SICKNESS 3.7:

(Be) Drowned
    SEA – SHORE 3.1:
    SPIRIT – SOUL – PERSON 1.4:
    EAT – FOOD – DRINK 10. f
Drowsy
    SLEEP – WAKE 1.1:
              1.4:
Drudge
    LABOUR – TROUBLE 1.1:
Drunk, Drunken(ness)
    EAT – FOOD – DRINK 12.4:
Drunkard
    EAT – FOOD – DRINK 12.4:
Dry, Dry up, Dried
    DRY – WITHER 1:
              2:
              3:
Due
    OWE 1.2:
Dull, Dulled (minds), Dullness
    HARDNESS – HARD HEART – SOFT 2.
                                    3.
                                    4.
    IDLE – DELAY 4.
    GREAT – MANY – MORE 13.
    HEART 1:b)
    + FOOLISH – MAD 2.
Dumb, Dumbness
    DEAF – DUMB – BLIND 1.
                       2.
    VOICE – SOUND 1.1:f)
(Be) Dumbfounded
    ASTONISHED – WONDER 3.1:
    + ASTONISHED – WONDER 1.
Dung-hill
    DEFILE – FILTH 7.
Dust
    EARTH – LAND – COUNTRY 2.
Duty
    MUST – OUGHT TO 2.
                    4.1:
    FITTING – WORTHY 1.1:
    WORSHIP 1.1:
              3.3:
    HONOUR – RESPECT 1.1:
    SLAVE – SERVE – MINISTER 9.1:
    + MUST – OUGHT TO 5.
Dwell
    STAY – LIVE 6.
               7.
               3.2:
    + STAY – LIVE 3.1:
                    3.3:
    + HOUSE 2. a)
a Dwelling
    HOUSE 2. a)
Dying: see Die
Dysentery
    WEAKEN – SICKNESS 3.6:

E

Each
    WHOLE – ALL – EACH 4.
Each other
    ONE – ANOTHER – EACH OTHER
Eager, Eagerness to
    CARE – CONCERN – DEVOTION 4.
                                     5.
    ZEAL – ENVY – GREED 1.1:
    + ZEAL – ENVY – GREED 3.
Eagle
    BIRDS – INSECTS 2.7:
Ear, Ears
    HEAR – LISTEN – LEARN 1.
                      2.1:
Ear(s) of corn
    FARM 3.2:b)
Earlier
    BEFORE 1.1:
    GO – PASS 9.1:b)
    + NUMBERS 3.2:d)
Early, Ancient
    NEW – OLD 2.4:a)

Early, Early in the morning
    MORNING – EVENING 1.
Earn
    FIND – HAPPEN 2.1:
    + HAVE – OWN – POSSESS 3.
    + FITTING – WORTHY 4.1:b)
Earn a living
    DO – MAKE – BEHAVE 2.3:a)
Earnest, Earnestly
    FERVENT – HOT – COLD 1.
    CARE – CONCERN – DEVOTION 4.
    GREAT – MANY – MORE 5.3:
    + ZEAL – ENVY – GREED 1.1:
Earth, Earthly, On earth
    EARTH – LAND – COUNTRY 1.2:b)
                                     2.2:
                                     3. a)
                                     3. b)
                                     3. c)
    WORLD 2.
    HEAVEN 1.2:
Earthen, Earthenware
    POTTERY – CLAY 1.1:
                     2.
Earthly: see Earth
Earthquake
    SHAKE – STIR UP – PROVOKE 7. a)
Ease
    + REST – RELIEVE – REFRESH 2,
                                  3,
Easier
    EASIER – DIFFICULT 1.
East
    EAST – WEST 1.
Eat, Ate
    EAT – FOOD – DRINK 2.
                         3.1:
                         5. b)
    + EAT – FOOD – DRINK 3.7:
    + SATISFY – ENOUGH 3.
Edge
    + MOUNTAIN – HILL 4.
    + CLOTHING 2.6:
Edge of a sword
    CUT – DIVISION 1.4:
Edict
    ORDER – REGULATION – INSTRUCT 7.
    + ORDER – REGULATION – INSTRUCT 2.
Edify
    BUILDING 1.1:c)
Educate(d)
    HEAR – LISTEN – LEARN 5.1:
    + TEACHING 2.1:
Effect, Effectual (in)
    DO – MAKE – BEHAVE 2.6:
    + DO – MAKE – BEHAVE 2.3:b)
    + FRUIT 2.1:
Effeminate
    HARDNESS – HARD HEART – SOFT 6.
Effort
    CARE – CONCERN – DEVOTION 4.
Egg
    EAT – FOOD – DRINK 4.6:
Eight, Eighth
    NUMBERS 10.
Eighteen, Eighty, Eighty-four
    NUMBERS 15.
(As far as) the Elbow
    HAND – ARM 4.
Elder
    NEW – OLD 2.3:
Eldest, First-born
    BEAR – BIRTH – CHILD 4.3:
    NEW – OLD 2.3:a)
Elect
    CHOOSE 1.
              2.
Element, Elemental, Elementary
    ELEMENT
Elemental principles, Elemental spirits
    ELEMENT 1:
Elementary principles
    ELEMENT 3:
Eleven, Eleventh
    NUMBERS 13.
Else
    + OTHER – DIFFERENT 1. a)
                          1. b)
                          2. a)

Elude
    + REJECT – AVOID – ESCAPE 13.2:
Embarrass(ment)
    DISHONOUR – SHAME 2.
Embody, Embodiment
    + IMAGE – FORM – EXAMPLE 5.1:
Embodying the soul
    SPIRIT – SOUL – PERSON 2.1:b)
Embrace
    KISS – EMBRACE 2.
Emerald
    + STONE – JEWEL 7.
Emerge
    RISE – RAISE – HIGH 4.6:
Emperor
    KING 3:
            5:b)
Employ, Employment
    + DO – MAKE – BEHAVE 2.3:a)
                              2.3:b)
                              3.8:
Employer
    + MASTER – LORD 2. h)
Empty, Empty out
    EMPTY – WORTHLESS – IN VAIN 1.
                                      2.
    FREE – SET FREE 7.
    RIVER – FLOW – FOUNTAIN 2.6:b)
Enable
    + GIVE 1.1:
Encampment
    STAY – LIVE 13.2:
Encircle, Encircling
    ROUND – ROLL 2. a)
                  2. b)
Encourage, Encouragement
    ENCOURAGE – BOLD – PERSUADE 6.
                                        8.1:
                                      9.
                                    11.
    BUILDING 1.1:c)
    DRIVE – SEND OUT – PUSH 4.4:
    + AGREEMENT – CONSENT 3.
Encumbrance
    PREVENT – HINDER – STRAIN 3.
End, Ends, Ending
    END – LAST 1. a)
                  3.
                  4. a)
                  5.
                  9. b)
                  9. c)
                  2. b)
                  7.1:
    DESTROY 3.
    + FILL – FULL – FULFIL 3.1:d)
    + STUMBLE – FALL 5.2:
End in (death)
    TAKE – BRING – LEAD 9.
End up (by), At the end
    END – LAST 9. b)
Endless
    END – LAST 5.
                  7.1:
Endorse
    FIRM – CONFIRM – GUARANTEE 4.
Endure, Endurance
    BEAR WITH – PATIENCE 1.
                              3.
                              5.
    + BEAR WITH – PATIENCE 2.
Endure, Last
    STAY – LIVE 3.4:
Enemy
    ENEMY – OPPOSE – AGAINST 1.
                                        2.
                                      3.
                                      4.
Energetic(ally)
    FERVENT – HOT – COLD 1.
Energy
    DO – MAKE – BEHAVE 2.6:
Engage in
    CARE – CONCERN – DEVOTION 10.
Engraved
    IMAGE – FORM – EXAMPLE 4.1:
Enjoin
    ORDER – REGULATION – INSTRUCT 4.

Feel, Felt
    THINK – CONSIDER 4.
    + *KNOW – UNDERSTAND* 1.2:
                            1.3:
    + *TOUCH* 1.
Feet: see Foot
Felicity
    + *REJOICE – GLAD – HAPPY* 5.
Fell: see Fall
Fellow-citizen
    CITY – TOWN – VILLAGE 1.2:
Fellow-prisoner
    KEEP – GUARD 6.
Fellow-servant
    + *SLAVE – SERVE – MINISTER* 3.1:
                            3.2:
Fellowship
    SHARE – PARTNER 1.2:
Fellow-soldier
    WAR – ARMY – WEAPONS 2. b)
Fellow-worker
    DO – MAKE – BEHAVE 2.5:
Felt: see Feel
Female
    MAN – PEOPLE – WOMAN 5.
Fence
    SHUT – CLOSED 3. b)
Fertilise
    + *DO – MAKE – BEHAVE* 2.6:
Fervent, Fervently
    FERVENT – HOT – COLD 1.
                           2.
Festal assembly, Festal gathering
    FESTIVAL 2.
Festival (time), Festivities
    FESTIVAL
Fetch
    TAKE – BRING – LEAD 3.1:
    SEND 2.4:
Fetter(s)
    ROPE – TIE – CHAIN 11.
    + *ROPE – TIE – CHAIN* 8. b)
Fever, Feverish attacks
    WEAKEN – SICKNESS 3.4:
Few, a Few
    LITTLE 3. a)
                3. c)
(Not) a few
    GREAT – MANY – MORE 7. a)
Fidelity
    BELIEVE – FAITH 1.2:
Field(s)
    EARTH – LAND – COUNTRY 4.
                       5. a)
    FARM 2.3:
Field (of activity)
    ORDER – REGULATION – INSTRUCT 8. b)
Fierce
    EASIER – DIFFICULT 2.3:
                        2.4:
    HARDNESS – HARD HEART – SOFT 1. b)
    ANGER 2.1:
    + *GREAT – MANY – MORE* 13.
Fiery
    + *FIRE – BURN* 1.1:
Fiery red
    BLACK – WHITE – RED 3.
Fifteen
    NUMBERS 15.
Fifth
    NUMBERS 7. a)
                    7. c)
Fifty, Fifty thousand
    NUMBERS 15.
Fig(s), Fig tree
    TREE – WOOD 9.1:
    FRUIT 4.
Fight, Fighting
    FIGHT – STRUGGLE 1.
                      2.
                      3.
    WAR – ARMY – WEAPONS 1.
                      2. c)
    QUARREL – DISPUTE 1.
                      2.
    + *FIGHT – STRUGGLE* 4.
    + *RISE – RAISE – HIGH* 1.5:
Figure
    IMAGE – FORM – EXAMPLE 4.1:

Figure of speech, Figuratively
    PARABLE – MYTH 2.
    + *PARABLE – MYTH* 1.
Fill, Filled (with)
    FILL – FULL – FULFIL 1.1:
                        3.1:
    + *SATISFY – ENOUGH* 3.
                        4.
Filth, Filthy
    DEFILE – FILTH 3. b)
                      4.
                      5.
    + *DISHONOUR – SHAME* 2.
Finally
    END – LAST 10.
                   1. a)
    LEAVE 8.5:
    + *END – LAST* 7. b)
Find, Found
    FIND – HAPPEN 1.
                   2.1:
Find fault with
    BLAME – REBUKE – WARN NOT TO 2.
    + *BLAME – REBUKE – WARN NOT TO* 1.
Find out
    KNOW – UNDERSTAND 1.8:
    ASK – PRAY 2.1:
Fine
    WIND – CLOUD – RAIN 6.2:
    GOOD – BETTER 12.1:
Fine (clothes)
    HARDNESS – HARD HEART – SOFT 6.
Fine linen
    CLOTH 1.1:
    + *CLOTH* 1.2:a)
Finely-cutting
    CUT – DIVISION 1.2:a)
Finger
    HAND – ARM 2.
Finish, Finished
    END – LAST 3.
                   6.
                   1. a)
                   7.2:
    BE 2.4:
    FILL – FULL – FULFIL 3.1:d)
Fire
    FIRE – BURN 1.
                   2.1:
                   3.
Firelight
    FIRE – BURN 1.6:
Firm, Firmly, Become firm
    FIRM – CONFIRM – GUARANTEE 1.
                   2.1:
                   2.2:a)
                   6.
    + *LEAN – BEND – BOW* 4.3:
First
    NUMBERS 3.
    BEFORE 1.1:
(from the) First
    BEGINNING 1.4:
First-born
    BEAR – BIRTH – CHILD 4.3:
    + *SHOW – REVEAL – OPEN* 8. f)
First-fruits
    BEGINNING 1.5:
First principles
    ELEMENT 3:
Fish
    FISH 1.
             2.
             3.
             5.
    + *EAT – FOOD – DRINK* 6.
Fisher, Fishermen
    FISH 5.
Fit (to, for), Fitting
    FITTING – WORTHY 1.
                   4.1:
                   4.3:
                   4.4:
    END – LAST 2. a)
Fit together
    JOIN – ATTACH 3.
Fitting: see Fit
Five
    NUMBERS 7.

Five hundred, Five thousand
    NUMBERS 15.
Fix, Fixed
    PUT – SET – APPOINT 2.2:
    FIRM – CONFIRM – GUARANTEE 2.2:b)
    + *ORDER – REGULATION – INSTRUCT* 2
Fix the limits of:
    + *CUT – DIVISION* 2.5:b)
to Flag
    IDLE – DELAY 3.1:
Flame, Flaming
    FIRE – BURN 1.1:
                     1.2:a)
                     1.3:
Flame colour
    BLACK – WHITE – RED 3.
Flash
    SHINE – LIGHT 6.
                   1.1:
Flask
    VESSEL – BASKET – BAG 1.2:
    + *VESSEL – BASKET – BAG* 4.1:
Flatter, Flattery
    BLESS – PRAISE – GLORY 1.1:c)
                    1.6:
    FAVOURITISM – PARTIALITY
Flax
    CLOTH 1.2:b)
Flee, Flight
    REJECT – AVOID – ESCAPE 12.
Flesh
    FLESH – BLOOD – BONE 1.1:
Flight
    ANIMALS 7.1:
    + *REJECT – AVOID – ESCAPE* 10.1:
Fling
    THROW – DROP 2.
                   1.1:
Fling out, Flung out
    + *DRIVE – SEND OUT – PUSH* 1. b)
Flippant
    + *MOCK – LAUGH* 6.
Flock
    SHEPHERD – FLOCK – HERD 1.
Flock to
    + *LEAVE* 2.1:
Flog
    BEAT – STRIKE – WOUND 2.
                   12.
                   13.
                   6.1:
    ROD – STAFF – CLUB 1.4:
Flood
    RIVER – FLOW – FOUNTAIN 1.1:
                   2.3:
                   2.4:
Flour
    EAT – FOOD – DRINK 4.3:
Flourish again
    GROW – SPROUT – BUD 8.
Flout
    REJECT – AVOID – ESCAPE 4.1:
Flow
    RIVER – FLOW – FOUNTAIN 2.1:
                   2.5:
Flower
    GARDEN 3.
Flung: see Fling
Flute
    SING – PLAY MUSIC 2.3:
Fly, Flying
    BIRDS – INSECTS 1.
Fly at, Hurl oneself at
    RUSH – SPRING – LEAP 3.1:
Fly from
    REJECT – AVOID – ESCAPE 13.2:
Foal
    SON – DAUGHTER 1.4:
    ANIMALS 2.6:c)
Foam, Foam at the mouth
    SPIT – FOAM – VOMIT 2.
Fog
    WIND – CLOUD – RAIN 4.3:
Fold, Sheepfold
    BUILDING 4. c)
Fold up
    ROUND – ROLL 8.2:
Follow, Following
    ACCOMPANY – FOLLOW – AFTER 2.
                      3.
                      4.
                      6.

Harvest
    FARM 10.1:a)
          10.3:
    FRUIT 1. b)
          2.1:
Has: see Have
Haste
    + *RUN – QUICKLY* 3.
Hate, Hateful
    HATE
Haughty
    BOAST – PROUD – ARROGANT 3.3:
    RISE – RAISE – HIGH 6.4:
          8.4:
Haul in (a net)
    DRAG – DRAW 2.1:
a Haunt
    + *KEEP – GUARD* 2. a)
    + *STAY – LIVE* 6.3:
Have, Had, Has
    HAVE – OWN – POSSESS 1.
    + *HAVE – OWN – POSSESS* 5.
          6.
    + *RECEIVE – ACCEPT* 1. d)
Have a child
    BEAR – BIRTH – CHILD 2.
          4.1:
    + *BEAR – BIRTH – CHILD* 3.1:c)
Have a right to
    MUST – OUGHT TO 4.2:
Have (a complaint) against
    BLAME – REBUKE – WARN NOT TO 6.
    + *ACCUSE – CHARGE – DEFEND* 1.
Have breakfast
    EAT – FOOD – DRINK 7.1:
Have compassion
    MERCY – PITY 3.
Have (something) done
    DO – MAKE – BEHAVE 3.5:b)
    + *ORDER – REGULATION – INSTRUCT* 1.
Have (an, no) idea (of)
    KNOW – UNDERSTAND 2.4:
Have mercy (on)
    MERCY – PITY 1.1:
          1.2:
    SPARE 1:
Have none of, Have nothing to do with
    REJECT – AVOID – ESCAPE 6.
          7.1:
          8.
          9.
Have on, Wear
    HAVE – OWN – POSSESS 1.1:
Have pity (on)
    MERCY – PITY 1.1:
          1.2:
    + *MERCY – PITY* 1.3:
Have time (to, for)
    TIME – DAY – HOUR 2.1:c)
Have to
    MUST – OUGHT TO 1.
          3.
          4.1:
          5.
Have to do with
    MATTER – THING – AFFAIR 3.
    MIX – ASSOCIATE 2. b)
          3.2:
Haven
    SEA – SHORE 6.1:
Haversack
    VESSEL – BASKET – BAG 7.
Havoc
    + *DESTROY* 9.
          10.
Hawk, Peddle
    BUY – SELL – TRADE 3.
Hay
    FARM 2.3:
Hazardous
    MISERY – DANGER 2.2:
Head
    HEAD – HAIR 1. a)
          1. b)
    + *IMAGE – FORM – EXAMPLE* 1.1:
Head of a household
    + *MASTER – LORD* 1.2:
Head wind
    + *HATE – ENEMY – AGAINST* 5.
Headlong
    STUMBLE – FALL 6.

Head-on
    SEE 3.4:
(Army) Headquarters
    + *FORT – WALL – TOWER* 1.1:
    + *HOUSE* 3.
Headstrong
    BOAST – PROUD – ARROGANT 3.1:
Heal, Healing
    SAVE – CURE 3. c)
          4. a)
          5.
          6.
Health, Healthy
    SAVE – CURE 4.
    POWER – ABLE TO 2.1:d)
    WHOLE – ALL – EACH 1.4:
Heap (up)
    GATHERING 10.
Hear, Hearing, Hear of
    HEAR – LISTEN – LEARN 2.
          3.
    TEACHING 1.3:
    KNOW – UNDERSTAND 1.8:
    + *HEAR – LISTEN – LEARN* 1.2:
    + *KNOW – UNDERSTAND* 2.4:b)
Heart
    HEART
    SPIRIT – SOUL – PERSON 1.1:b)
          2.1:a)
    BODY 6.3:c)
    + *BODY* 6.6:b)
Heart, Put new heart into
    + *REST – RELIEVE – REFRESH* 3.
    + *SPIRIT – SOUL – PERSON* 2.1:a)
    + *BODY* 6.6:b)
Heartless
    + *LOVE* 3.
Heat
    FERVENT – HOT – COLD 3.
    FIRE – BURN 1.2:c)
    + *FIRE – BURN* 1.2:a)
Heathen
    MAN – PEOPLE – WOMAN 9.3:
Heathen deities, Heathen temple
    IDOL 2:
         3:
Heaven
    HEAVEN
    ABOVE – OVER 1.1:
    RISE – RAISE – HIGH 8.2:
the Heavenly Host
    WAR – ARMY – WEAPONS 2. d)
Heavy
    GREAT – MANY – MORE 13.
Hebrew
    HEBREW
Hedge, Hedgerow
    SHUT – CLOSED 3. b)
Heed
    HEAR – LISTEN – LEARN 4.1:
    KEEP – GUARD 1. e)
          7.2:
Heel
    FOOT – LEG 1.3:
Heifer
    ANIMALS 2.7:d)
Height
    RISE – RAISE – HIGH 8.2:
          8.5:
Heir(s)
    INHERIT – HEIR – HERITAGE
    SON – DAUGHTER 1.3:
Held: see Hold
Hell
    ABYSS – HADES – HELL 3.
          4.
          2.2:
Hellenists
    GREECE 1.
Helm, Helmsman
    RULE – AUTHORITY – LEADER 11.
Helmet
    WAR – ARMY – WEAPONS 6.3:
Help
    HELP – SUPPORT 2.
          3.
          4.
          5.
          6.
          7.
          8.

Help—(contd)
    ENCOURAGE – BOLD – PERSUADE 8.2:
    DO – MAKE – BEHAVE 2.5:
    + *SLAVE – SERVE – MINISTER* 8.4:
    + *GOOD – BETTER* 9.
Help on (to) an animal
    RISE – RAISE – HIGH 4.5:
Help (a person) on his journey
    TAKE – BRING – LEAD 11.
Help to(wards), Go towards
    GO – PASS 8.3:
Help up, Help to stand
    RISE – RAISE – HIGH 1.1:
Helper
    SLAVE – SERVE – MINISTER 8.4:
(Be) Helpful
    GOOD – BETTER 6.
Helpless
    WEAKEN – SICKNESS 1.5:
    + *THROW – DROP* 2.
Hem
    + *CLOTHING* 2.6:
Hem in, Hemmed in
    PRESS – INSIST 2.
    + *LITTLE* 8.
Hen
    BIRDS – INSECTS 2.2:
Henceforth
    NOW – AT ONCE 1. b)
          2. b)
Herald
    TELL – PREACH – PROCLAIM 3.
Herbs
    GARDEN 2.
Herd
    SHEPHERD – FLOCK – HERD 2.
(Be) Here
    COME – ARRIVE 5. b)
    + *COME – ARRIVE* 4.
Hereafter
    + *NOW – AT ONCE* 1. b)
Heresy
    CUT – DIVISION 2.1:b)
Heritage
    INHERIT – HEIR – HERITAGE
the Herodians
    PHARISEE 3:
Hesitate
    BELIEVE – FAITH 2.
    REJECT – AVOID – ESCAPE 11.2:
Hew
    CUT – DIVISION 1.3:
Hidden purpose
    SECRET – MYSTERY 3.
Hidden truth
    SECRET – MYSTERY 3.
Hide, Hidden
    SECRET – MYSTERY 1.
          2.
          3.
    + *COVER – VEIL* 1:
    + *SHOW – REVEAL – OPEN* 2. d)
Hiding place, a Hidden place
    HOUSE 4.1:
High, Higher, Highly
    RISE – RAISE – HIGH 8.
          6.3:
    GREAT – MANY – MORE 11.
    ABOVE – OVER 1.2:
          1.4:
    + *GREAT – MANY – MORE* 1. f)
    + *ABOVE – OVER* 1.1:
(in, of) High Office
    GREAT – MANY – MORE 3.
    RISE – RAISE – HIGH 8.4:
High priest
    PRIEST 1:
         3:
High-flown (speech)
    BOAST – PROUD – ARROGANT 2.3:
Hill, Hillside
    MOUNTAIN – HILL 1. a)
          3.
Hinder
    PREVENT – HINDER – STRAIN 1.1:
          2.
          3.
Hire, Hired man
    PAY – REWARD – PRIZE 4.1:

Hit
  BEAT – STRIKE – WOUND 5.
                                        8.
                                        9.
  +   *BEAT – STRIKE – WOUND* 2.
                                        3.
                                        6.3:
Hoist up, aboard
  RISE – RAISE – HIGH 6.1:
Hold, Hold (fast, on) to, Hold firmly
  KEEP – GUARD 7.1:
                                        8.
                                        1. a)
                                        1. b)
  HEAR – LISTEN – LEARN 4.2:
  HAVE – OWN – POSSESS 1.1:
  JOIN – ATTACH 5. a)
Hold, Consider
  THINK – CONSIDER 11.
  +   *PUT – SET – APPOINT* 2 1:
Hold, Contain
  PLACE – ROOM 2.
Hold a banquet (feast) for
  DO – MAKE – BEHAVE 3.3:
Hold high
  RISE – RAISE – HIGH 6.3:
Hold (as) holy
  HOLY 1.1:
Hold in contempt
  +   *DESPISE – DISREGARD* 1.2:
Hold, Held, in great honour
  HONOUR – RESPECT 1.1:
  GREAT – MANY – MORE 1. b)
  +   *GREAT – MANY – MORE* 1. a)
Hold one's peace
  +   *QUIET – SILENCE* 4.
                                        5.
                                        6.
Hold up to contempt
  MOCK – LAUGH 3.
Hole
  DIG – PIERCE – HOLE 3. b)
                                        4.
                                        1.3:
  +   *IMAGE – FORM – EXAMPLE* 4.1:
Holiness: see Holy
Holocausts
  SACRIFICE – ALTAR 2.1:
Holy, Holy man, Holiness
  HOLY
  RIGHTEOUS – JUSTIFY – VIRTUE 1.
Holy duty
  WORSHIP 1.1:
  +   *WORSHIP* 3.1:
Holy fear, Reverence
  FEAR – AWE 2.
Holy of Holies
  HOLY 1.7:
the Holy One
  HOLY 1.2:
                                        2.1:
Holy Spirit, Holy Ghost
  SPIRIT – SOUL – PERSON 1.1:a)
Homage
  WORSHIP 4.
Home
  HOUSE 1. a)
                                        1. c)
                                        5.
  STAY – LIVE 8.
(Make a) Home (with, in)
  STAY – LIVE 8.
                                        3.2:
                                        6.2:
Home town
  FATHER – MOTHER 1.5:
Homeless
  HOUSE 5.
Homosexual
  +   *HARDNESS – HARD HEART – SOFT 6.*
Honest
  RIGHTEOUS – JUSTIFY – VIRTUE 1.
  +   *TRUE – AMEN* 2.1:
Honey, Honeycomb
  EAT – FOOD – DRINK 4.5:
Honour
  HONOUR – RESPECT 1.
  BLESS – PRAISE – GLORY 2. a)
                                        2. b)
  AGREEMENT – CONSENT 7. b)

Honourable
  GOOD – BETTER 2. a)
  FITTING – WORTHY 2.
  +   *FITTING – WORTHY* 4.2:
  +   *HONCUR – RESPECT* 1.1:
(fishing-)Hook
  FISH 6.3:
Hope
  HOPE – EXPECT – WAIT FOR 1.
  DESIRE – LONGING 6.
Horn(s)
  ANIMALS 3.1:
Horror, Horrified
  +   *FEAR – AWE* 1. b)
                                        5.
  +   *SUFFER – ANGUISH* 11.
Horse, Horsemen
  ANIMALS 2.5:
Hosanna
  SAVE – CURE 1.
Hospitable, Hospitably
  FOREIGN – ALIEN 1.2:
  +   *LOVE* 2.3:c)
Hospitality
  FOREIGN – ALIEN 1.2:
the Host (Army) of heaven
  WAR – ARMY – WEAPONS 2. d)
Hostile, Hostility
  ENEMY – OPPOSE – AGAINST 1.
Hot
  FERVENT – HOT – COLD 2.
  FIRE – BURN 1.2:c)
Hot temper
  ANGER 1.2:
Hour
  TIME – DAY – HOUR 6.
House
  HOUSE 1.
                                        2. a)
House (of God)
  TEMPLE – SANCTUARY 3.
(At the) House of
  WITH 5.
House-dogs
  +   *ANIMALS* 2.11:
Household
  HOUSE 1. b)
                                        1. d)
  SLAVE – SERVE – MINISTER 5.2:
Householder
  MASTER – LORD 1.2:
Housetops
  BUILDING 5.2:
How great
  GREAT – MANY – MORE 2.1:a)
How much, Whatever
  AS MANY AS – AS MUCH AS 2:
How often
  OFTEN 3.
Howl
  MOURN – LAMENT 8.
  +   *VOICE – SOUND* 3.1:c)
Huge
  GREAT – MANY – MORE 1. e)
                                        2.1:a)
  +   *GREAT – MANY – MORE* 5.2:b)
Human
  FLESH – BLOOD – BONE 1.1:
  MAN – PEOPLE – WOMAN 2.6:
  +   *WORLD* 1.
Human nature
  FLESH – BLOOD – BONE 1.1:
Humane, Humanity
  MAN – PEOPLE – WOMAN 2.6:
Humble, Humility
  POOR – HUMBLE – LOWLY 3.
  SWEET – GENTLE – KINDLY 2.1:a)
  +   *LITTLE* 4. a)
Humiliate, Humiliation
  POOR – HUMBLE – LOWLY 3.
  DISHONOUR – SHAME 1.
  CURSE – ABUSE – SLANDER 2.3:
  +   *DISHONOUR – SHAME* 2.
Humility: see Humble
a Hundred
  NUMBERS 15.
a Hundred and forty-four thousand
  NUMBERS 15.
a Hundred and twenty, Hundred and forty-four, Hundred
and fifty-three
  NUMBERS 15.

Hundredweight
  +   *MEASURE* 4.1:
Hunger, Hungry
  EAT – FOOD – DRINK 1.
Hurl abuse at
  +   *CURSE – ABUSE – SLANDER* 2.1:
                                        2.3:
Hurl oneself (at, against)
  RUSH – SPRING – LEAP 3.1:
  STUMBLE – FALL 5.5:
Hurl over, Hurl down
  THROW – DROP 4.
                                        1.1:
Hurricane
  WIND – CLOUD – RAIN 2.6:
Hurry
  RUN – QUICKLY 3.
                                        1.1:
  +   *RUN – QUICKLY* 4.
Hurt
  EVIL – WRONG – HARM 13.
  SUFFER – ANGUISH 1.2:
  +   *EVIL – WRONG – HARM* 1.2:
                                        3.
Husband
  MAN – PEOPLE – WOMAN 3.2:
  +   *MAN – PEOPLE – WOMAN* 2.2:
Husbandman
  +   *FARM* 1.1:
Husks, Pods
  FRUIT 5.
Hyacinth, Jacinth
  +   *STONE – JEWEL* 7.
Hymn(s)
  SING – PLAY MUSIC 1.
Hypocrisy, Hypocrite
  DECEIVE – TRICK – PRETENCE 3.1:
Hyssop
  GARDEN 2.4:

I

Idea(s)
  KNOW – UNDERSTAND 7.2:
Identical
  +   *SAME – LIKE – SUCH* 2.
Idle, Idler, Idleness
  IDLE – DELAY 1.
                                        2.
Idol
  IDOL
  +   *IMAGE – FORM – EXAMPLE* 4.1:
Idolater, Idolatry
  IDOL 1:
Ignoble
  +   *DISHONOUR – SHAME* 1.
Ignorance, Ignorant
  FOOLISH – MAD 5.
  KNOW – UNDERSTAND 1.4:
  TEACHING 2.2:
  +   *HEAR – LISTEN – LEARN* 5.1:
Ignore
  +   *CARE – CONCERN – DEVOTION* 1.
Ill, Illness
  WEAKEN – SICKNESS 2.4:
  +   *WEAKEN – SICKNESS* 2.1:
                                        2.2:
                                        2.5:
Ill repute, Ill spoken of
  +   *CURSE – ABUSE – SLANDER* 2.10:
Ill-treat, Ill-treatment
  EVIL – WRONG – HARM 1.3:
Illuminate(d)
  +   *SHINE – LIGHT* 1.1:
Illusory
  DECEIVE – TRICK – PRETENCE 1.3:
Ill-will
  +   *ZEAL – ENVY – GREED* 2.
Image
  IMAGE – FORM – EXAMPLE 1.
  +   *IMAGE – FORM – EXAMPLE* 4.1:
Imagine, Imagination
  THINK – CONSIDER 2.
                                        3.
                                        9.1:
                                        12.2:

Instrument
  VESSEL – BASKET – BAG 1.1:e)
Insult
  CURSE – ABUSE – SLANDER 2.1:
                        2.2:
                        2.3:
                        2.8:a)
Insurrection
  + CONFUSION – DISTURB 6.
Integrity
  + RIGHTEOUS – JUSTIFY – VIRTUE 1.
Intelligence, Intelligent
  KNOW – UNDERSTAND 4.
                    7.2:
  + WISE – SOBER 1. a)
Intemperance
  WISE – SOBER 4.
Intend, Intention
  WILL – WANT 1.1:
  THINK – CONSIDER 8.1:
                    12.2:
(Be) Intent on
  HONOUR – RESPECT 1.2:
Intention: see Intend
Intercede, Intercession
  ASK – PRAY 9.
Interest (commercial)
  GAIN – PROFIT 4.
(Be) Interested in
  THINK – CONSIDER 4.
  CARE – CONCERN – DEVOTION 12.
  + CARE – CONCERN – DEVOTION 1.
Interfere
  CARE – CONCERN – DEVOTION 13.
Intermediary
  MID – AMONG 4:
Interminable
  END – LAST 5.
Interpret, Interpretation
  INTERPRET – EXPLAIN 1.
                    2.
                    3.
  JUDGE – CONDEMN – PUNISH 3.3:
  + TEST 2.1:
Interrogate
  ASK – PRAY 3.
  + ASK – PRAY 4.2:
Interval
  DISTANCE – AWAY – FROM 4.
Intervene
  GO – PASS 10.1:a)
  RISE – RAISE – HIGH 2.3:
Intimidate, Intimidation
  ENCOURAGE – BOLD – PERSUADE 13.
Introduce
  TAKE – BRING – LEAD 8.3:b)
Invaders
  + FORT – WALL – TOWER 1.1:
Invest
  + GAIN – PROFIT 5.
Investigate
  KNOW – UNDERSTAND 1.5:
Invisible
  SEE 2.3:a)
  + SHOW – REVEAL – OPEN 2. d)
Invite, Invitation
  ASK – PRAY 4.3:
                5.1:
  NAME – CALL 5.6:
                6.2:
Invoke
  NAME – CALL 5.3:
Involve, Involved
  ROPE – TIE – CHAIN 6. c)
  DO – MAKE – BEHAVE 2.4:
Inward(ly)
  SPIRIT – SOUL – PERSON 1.1:b
Iron
  IRON
Irrational
  TEST 2.3:
  + KNOW – UNDERSTAND 8.
Irreligious
  HOLY 2.3:
  EVIL – WRONG – HARM 6.1:
Irreproachable
  PURE – INNOCENT – SIMPLE 9.
Irreverent
  EVIL – WRONG – HARM 6.2:

Irrevocable
  REPENT 1.
Is: see Be
Island
  ISLAND 1:
  + ISLAND 2:
              4:
              5:
Israel, Israelites
  ISRAEL
  SON – DAUGHTER 1.2:e)
Issue, Come out of
  LEAVE 1.4:
        2.2:
  + RIVER – FLOW – FOUNTAIN 2.1:b)
Issue, Descendants
  BEAR – BIRTH – CHILD 5.
Itching
  WEAKEN – SICKNESS 3.8:
Itinerant
  GO – PASS 1.2:
Ivory
  MOUTH – TONGUE 4.3:

J

Jail, Gaol
  KEEP – GUARD 1. a)
              2. a)
Jailer, Gaoler
  KEEP – GUARD 2. a)
Jar
  VESSEL – BASKET – BAG 2.
                    1.1:a)
Jasper
  + STONE – JEWEL 7.
Jealous, Jealousy
  ZEAL – ENVY – GREED 1.2:
                    2.
Jeer(ed) at
  MOCK – LAUGH 2.
  + CURSE – ABUSE – SLANDER 2.1:
Jerusalem
  JERUSALEM
Jesus
  JESUS CHRIST 1.
Jesus's Love
  LOVE 1.2:
       2.2:
Jew, Jewish
  JEW – JEWISH
Jewel(s)
  STONE – JEWEL 7.
  + STONE – JEWEL 3. a)
Join, Be joined (to)
  JOIN – ATTACH 1.
              2. b)
              3.
              5.
  GATHERING 4.
Join in, Help
  DO – MAKE – BEHAVE 2.5:
  SHARE – PARTNER 1.2:
Joint
  JOIN – ATTACH 3.
              4. b)
Joint heir
  + INHERIT – HEIR – HERITAGE
Jokes
  MOCK – LAUGH 6.
Journey
  GO – PASS 6.
          17.
          10.1:a)
  STREET – PATH – WAY 2.3:a)
Joy, Joyful
  REJOICE – GLAD – HAPPY 1.
                    2.
                    3.
Jubilant, Jubilation
  + REJOICE – GLAD – HAPPY 1.
                      2.
Judaean, of Judaea
  + JEW – JEWISH

Judge, Judgement
  JUDGE – CONDEMN – PUNISH 1.1:
                        3.1:a)
                        3.1:b)
                        3.3:
                        4.
  THINK – CONSIDER 6.
  ANGER 1.1:
  + THINK – CONSIDER 4.
Judge(d) Worthy
  FITTING – WORTHY 4.1:
Judgement: see Judge
Judgement seat
  JUDGE – CONDEMN – PUNISH 6.3:
Jug
  VESSEL – BASKET – BAG 2.5:
Jump
  + THROW – DROP 1.1:
              2.
Jump up
  RUSH – SPRING – LEAP 2.
                    3.1:
Jurisdiction
  RULE – AUTHORITY – LEADER 3.4:
  + RULE – AUTHORITY – LEADER 4. a)
Just, Fair
  RIGHTEOUS – JUSTIFY – VIRTUE 1.
Just, Merely
  ALONE – ONLY 1:d)
Just as
  AS MANY AS – AS MUCH AS 5:
  DO – MAKE – BEHAVE 6.6:b)
Justice
  JUDGE – CONDEMN – PUNISH 4.
                        3.1:b)
  + RIGHTEOUS – JUSTIFY – VIRTUE 1.
Justify, Justification
  RIGHTEOUS – JUSTIFY – VIRTUE 1.
  + DO – MAKE – BEHAVE 3.5:b)

K

(the ?) Kandake of Ethiopia
  KING 4:b)
Keen, Keenness
  CARE – CONCERN – DEVOTION 4.
Keep, Retain
  KEEP – GUARD 1. a)
              1. b)
              1. d)
              2. a)
              2. c)
              4.
              7.1:
Keep (= Observe)
  KEEP – GUARD 1. e)
              2. e)
              7.1:
              8.
  DO – MAKE – BEHAVE 3.3:
                    3.8:
                    [5.
  + DO – MAKE – BEHAVE 2.3:
  + FESTIVAL 1.
  + END – LAST 1. a)
Keep (= Board and lodging)
  + EAT – FOOD – DRINK 3.2:a)
Keep (on)
  STAY – LIVE 3.3:
Keep a place for
  PLACE – ROOM 2.
Keep awake
  SLEEP – WAKE 2.1:a)
Keep back (what is due)
  CATCH – SEIZE – STEAL 14.
Keep calm
  QUIET – SILENCE 2.
Keep faith
  AGREEMENT – CONSENT 7. b)
  + BELIEVE – FAITH 1.2:a)
Keep from
  PREVENT – HINDER – STRAIN 2.
  KEEP – GUARD 11.
              1. c)
              2. d)

Majesty
    GREAT – MANY – MORE 1. a)
    +   *MASTER – LORD* 2. h)
the Majority
    GREAT – MANY – MORE 5.2:a)
Make, Made
    DO – MAKE – BEHAVE 2.1:
                             2.3:b)
                             2.4:
                             3.1:
                             3.2:
                             3.3:
                             3.5:
                             3.10:
                             4.
    BE 2.2:b)
        2.3:
        2.4:
    PUT – SET – APPOINT 2.2:
    + *DO – MAKE – BEHAVE* 1.1:
    + *PUT – SET – APPOINT* 1.1:b)
                             1.4:
                             3.2:a)
Make (a person do something)
    MUST – OUGHT TO 5.
Make a bed
    DISPERSE – SCATTER 5.3:
Make a Covenant
    COVENANT – WILL 1:
Make a crossing
    GO – PASS 11.2:
Make a decision
    TEST 2.2:
Make a deep impression on
    ASTONISHED – WONDER 2.
    FEAR – AWE 1. a)
Make a fool of
    MOCK – LAUGH 1.
                  2.
Make a home (in, within)
    STAY – LIVE 8.
              3.2:
              6.2:
Make a mistake
    STUMBLE – FALL 4.
Make a move to
    RUSH – SPRING – LEAP 1.
Make a point of
    HONOUR – RESPECT 1.2:
Make a profit
    GAIN – PROFIT 2.
               5.
               1.
    DO – MAKE – BEHAVE 2.4:
                             3.2:
Make a promise
    PROMISE – VOW – OATH 1.
Make (it) a rule to
    HONOUR – RESPECT 1.2:
Make a run
    RUN – QUICKLY 1.1:
Make an accusation (against)
    ACCUSE – CHARGE – DEFEND 1.2:
Make an effort to
    CARE – CONCERN – DEVOTION 4.
    + *DO – MAKE – BEHAVE* 2.3:b)
Make an end (of, to)
    DESTROY 13. b)
Make as if to
    DECEIVE – TRICK – PRETENCE 4.
Make (one's) authority felt
    RULE – AUTHORITY – LEADER 4. a)
Make away with
    + *DESTROY* 13. b)
Make clear, Made clear
    SHOW – REVEAL – OPEN 1.
                        7.2:
    + *KNOW – UNDERSTAND* 1.8:
Make (it) difficult for
    LABOUR – TROUBLE 4.
Make envious, Make jealous
    ZEAL – ENVY – GREED 1.2:
Make excuses
    REJECT – AVOID – ESCAPE 7.2:
Make fast, Tie up
    SEA – SHORE 6.2:
Make for
    GO – PASS 2.1:a)
                 4.2:
    + *FACE* 1:b)

Make (a person) free
    FREE – SET FREE 3.
Make friends, disciples
    DO – MAKE – BEHAVE 3.5:a)
Make fun of
    MOCK – LAUGH 1.
Make great, Exalt
    RISE – RAISE – HIGH 8.4:
Make (to) grow, Increase
    GROW – SPROUT – BUD 1. c)
Make (a person) happy
    + *REJOICE – GLAD – HAPPY* 1.
Make haste
    RUN – QUICKLY 3.
Make holy, Made holy
    HOLY 1.9:
    + *HOLY* 1.5:
Make known, Made known
    SHOW – REVEAL – OPEN 2. a)
                           2. b)
                           7.2:
    DO – MAKE – BEHAVE 3.5:b)
    KNOW – UNDERSTAND 1.9:
    + *SHOW – REVEAL – OPEN* 1.
    + *KNOW – UNDERSTAND* 1.1:
                               1.6:
Make lower, Made lower
    LITTLE 4. a)
Make merry
    REJOICE – GLAD – HAPPY 4.
Make (one's) mind up: see Make up one's mind
Make money
    GAIN – PROFIT 1.
Make off
    GO – PASS 4.2:c)
Make off with
    + *CATCH – SEIZE – STEAL* 9.1:
Make (the) offering
    + *GIVE* 8.1:a)
Make (a person's) own
    HAVE – OWN – POSSESS 3.
Make peace
    PEACE – RECONCILE 1.
Make perfect
    + *END – LAST* 1. b)
Make (one's) power felt
    DO – MAKE – BEHAVE 2.6:
Make preparations (for)
    PREPARE – READY 1.2:
Make provision for
    CARE – CONCERN – DEVOTION 12.
Make ready
    PREPARE – READY 1.
Make rich, Enrich
    MONEY 1.
Make room (for)
    PLACE – ROOM 2.
Make signs (to)
    SIGN 2.
Make (a person, a thing) stand (in a place)
    PUT – SET – APPOINT 2.1:
Make straight
    STRAIGHT – CROOKED 1.2:
    + *DO – MAKE – BEHAVE* 3.5:b)
Make sure of
    END – LAST 2. b)
Make the most of, Make good use of
    GAIN – PROFIT 3.
Make trouble
    LABOUR – TROUBLE 4.
    CONFUSION – DISTURB 5.2:
Make unclean
    DEFILE – FILTH 2.
Make up, Complete
    FILL – FULL – FULFIL 3.1:d)
Make up (a quarrel)
    + *PEACE – RECONCILE* 2.
Make up one's mind
    JUDGE – CONDEMN – PUNISH 3.1:b)
Make void
    FIRM – CONFIRM – GUARANTEE 5.
    EMPTY – WORTHLESS – IN VAIN 1.3:
Make (one's) way to
    GO – PASS 17.
                2.1:a)
                11.1:
    + *LEAVE* 2.1:
    + *ENTER – GO IN – COME IN* 1.3:a)
    + *DO – MAKE – BEHAVE* 3.10:

Make welcome
    RECEIVE – ACCEPT 3.
Make whole
    + *SAVE – CURE* 3. c)
                        4. a)
Malachite
    + *STONE – JEWEL* 7.
Malcontents
    + *BLAME – REBUKE – WARN NOT TO* 2.
Male
    MAN – PEOPLE – WOMAN 5.
Malice, Malicious
    EVIL – WRONG – HARM 2.3:
                          1.1:
    + *ZEAL – ENVY – GREED* 2.
Malign
    CURSE – ABUSE – SLANDER 2.7:
Malignity
    + *EVIL – WRONG – HARM* 1.1:
Maltreat
    CURSE – ABUSE – SLANDER 2.8:a)
Mammon
    + *MONEY* 3.
Man, Men
    MAN – PEOPLE – WOMAN 2.
                             3.
                             5.
    SON – DAUGHTER 1 1:d)
                      1 3:
    + *NUMBERS* 3.1:b)
Manage
    RULE – AUTHORITY – LEADER 1.
Manager
    + *STEWARD – GUARDIAN* 1.
Manger
    EAT – FOOD – DRINK 8.
Manifest, Make manifest
    SHOW – REVEAL – OPEN 2. a)
                           2. b)
    + *SHOW – REVEAL – OPEN* 1
                             3.1:
Manifold
    OTHER – DIFFERENT 5.1:
Mankind
    FLESH – BLOOD – BONE 1.1:d)
    + *MAN – PEOPLE – WOMAN* 2.6:
Manna
    EAT – FOOD – DRINK 4.4:
Manner, Way
    DO – MAKE – BEHAVE 6.6:b)
    + *BE* 2.1:
Manner of life
    DO – MAKE – BEHAVE 6.1:
                             6.2:
Manners
    CUSTOM – PRACTICE 1. c)
Mantle
    CLOTHING 2.2:
Manure, Manure heap
    DEFILE – FILTH 7.
Many
    GREAT – MANY – MORE 4.
                           5.1:
                           5.2:
                           6.
Marble
    STONE – JEWEL 5.
Marjoram
    GARDEN 2.4:
Mark(s)
    IMAGE – FORM – EXAMPLE 2.
                             3.
                             4.1:
    SIGN 1.2:
Mark with a seal
    SEAL 1:
Market
    BUY – SELL – TRADE 2.
                      4.
Market place
    STREET – PATH – WAY 1.1:
Marriage
    MARRY – UNMARRIED 2.1:
Marriage-bed
    SIT – LIE 4.3:
Married: see Marry
Marrow
    FLESH – BLOOD – BONE 3.2:

N

Q

R

Reach
  COME – ARRIVE 7.
            8.
            9.
            10.
            1.3:
            1.4:c)
  ENTER – GO IN – COME IN 1.3:
                          1.4:
  BE 2.2:a)
  + *COME – ARRIVE* 1.4:d)
  + *FIND – HAPPEN* 2.1:
Read
  WRITING – READ 6.
Readiness, Readily
  CARE – CONCERN – DEVOTION 5.
Ready, Make ready
  PREPARE – READY 1.
                  2.1:
                  3.
  TEACHING 1.4:
  END – LAST 2. a)
  + *RISE – RAISE – HIGH* 2.5:
  + *STAY – LIVE* 10.
Reaffirm
  FIRM – CONFIRM – GUARANTEE 5.
Real, Really
  TRUE – AMEN 2.1:
  BE 1.5:
Realise
  KNOW – UNDERSTAND 2.4:
                      5.
                      1.8:
  + *KNOW – UNDERSTAND* 1.3:
                          1.4:
                          1.9:
Reality
  MATTER – THING – AFFAIR 2.
  BODY 1. b)
Really: see Real
Reap
  FARM 10.1:a)
Reason
  ACCUSE – CHARGE – DEFEND 4.
  KNOW – UNDERSTAND 7.2:
                      8.
  SAY – TELL – SPEAK 2.10:
  + *THINK – CONSIDER* 8.2:
Reasonable
  WISE – SOBER 2. b)
Reassure
  REST – RELIEVE – REFRESH 4.
  ENCOURAGE – BOLD – PERSUADE 8.2:
Rebel, Rebellious, Rebellion
  QUARREL – DISPUTE 9.
  OBEY – SUBMIT – SUBJECT 2.2:
  + *EVIL – WRONG – HARM* 4.
  + *FOOT – LEG* 1.3:
  + *LEAVE* 5.2:
  + *QUARREL – DISPUTE* 5.
  + *CONFUSION – DISTURB* 6.
Rebirth
  BE 2.4:
Rebuild
  BUILDING 1.1:a)
           1.1:c)
Rebuke
  BLAME – REBUKE – WARN NOT TO 3.
                                4.
  + *BLAME – REBUKE – WARN NOT TO* 5.
Recall
  REMEMBER – FORGET 1.1:
Receive
  RECEIVE – ACCEPT 1.
                   2.
                   4.
  PLACE – ROOM 2. b)
Receive information
  TEACHING 1.3:
Receive mercy
  MERCY – PITY 1.1:
Receive seed
  + *FARM* 3.2:a)
Receive strokes of the lash
  BEAT – STRIKE – WOUND 2.
  + *BEAT – STRIKE – WOUND* 6.1:
                              9.
Recently
  NEW – OLD 1.1:

Reception, Party
  RECEIVE – ACCEPT 2. d)
Reckless
  FOOLISH – MAD 8.
  + *IMMORALITY* 3.2:
Reckon, Reckon as, Reckoning
  THINK – CONSIDER 8.2:
                    9.2:
  + *NUMBERS* 2.
  + *GATHERING* 11.
Recline
  + *SIT – LIE* 4.1:
Recognise, Recognise as
  THINK – CONSIDER 9.2:
  KNOW – UNDERSTAND 1.3:
                      1.4:
                      1.6:
                      1.8:
                      2.3:
  JUDGE – CONDEMN – PUNISH 3.3:
  + *KNOW – UNDERSTAND* 2.4:
  + *TELL – PREACH – PROCLAIM* 2.1:
Recommend(ation)
  BLESS – PRAISE – GLORY 1.5:
Recompense
  + *PAY – REWARD – PRIZE* 4.2:
Reconcile, (Be) Reconciled
  PEACE – RECONCILE 2.
Record, Account
  WRITING – READ 1. g)
  + *WRITING – READ* 4. c)
Recover, Get back
  RECEIVE – ACCEPT 4.
Recover (from illness)
  SAVE – CURE 8.
  + *SAVE – CURE* 4. a)
Recover one's senses
  KNOW – UNDERSTAND 11.
Red
  BLACK – WHITE – RED 3.
the Red Sea
  SEA – SHORE 1.1:c)
Redeem, Redeemer
  FREE – SET FREE 1.3:
  BUY – SELL – TRADE 1.2:b)
Redemption
  FREE – SET FREE 1.3:
Red-hot
  FIRE – BURN 1.2:e)
  + *FIRE – BURN* 1.1:
                  1.3:
Reduce to ashes
  FIRE – BURN 4.
Reed
  TREE – WOOD 8.
Reef
  STRAIGHT – CROOKED 2.
Refined (by fire)
  FIRE – BURN 7.
Reflect, Reflection
  + *SHADOW* 2:
  + *THINK – CONSIDER* 8.2:
  + *SECRET – MYSTERY* 4.
Reform
  STRAIGHT – CROOKED 1.1:
  + *REPENT* 2.
Refractory
  QUARREL – DISPUTE 6.
Refrain from
  SPARE 2:
  KEEP – GUARD 1. c)
Refresh, Refreshment
  REST – RELIEVE – REFRESH 3.
                            4.
Refuge
  REJECT – AVOID – ESCAPE 13.1:
Refuse (to)
  REJECT – AVOID – ESCAPE 4.1:
                            7.1:
  PREVENT – HINDER – STRAIN 1.2:
  OBEY – SUBMIT – SUBJECT 2.2:
  HEAR – LISTEN – LEARN 2.7:
  CATCH – SEIZE – STEAL 15.2:
  + *WILL – WANT* 2.4:
Refuse, Rubbish
  DEFILE – FILTH 3. b)
Refute
  BLAME – REBUKE – WARN NOT TO 3.
  + *QUARREL – DISPUTE* 5.

Regalia
  + *BLESS – PRAISE – GLORY* 2. b)
Regard, Regard as
  THINK – CONSIDER 11.
                    9.2:
  + *HONOUR – RESPECT* 2.
Region(s)
  EARTH – LAND – COUNTRY 6.
  CUT – DIVISION 3.1:d)
  + *EARTH – LAND – COUNTRY* 5. b)
Register
  WRITING – READ 1. g)
Regret
  REPENT 1.
Regulation(s)
  ORDER – REGULATION – INSTRUCT 5. b)
                                   6.
                                   7.
Reign
  RULE – AUTHORITY – LEADER 2.
  KING 2:
       5:
  + *RULE – AUTHORITY – LEADER* 6.2:a)
  + *KING* 1:
Reject, Rejected, Rejection
  REJECT – AVOID – ESCAPE 1.
                          2.
                          3.
                          4.1:
                          5.
  DESPISE – DISREGARD 1.2:
  TEST 2.3:
  + *QUARREL – DISPUTE* 5.
Rejoice (in)
  REJOICE – GLAD – HAPPY 1.
                         2.
                         4.
  BOAST – PROUD – ARROGANT 1.
Rejoin
  GATHERING 4.
  COME – ARRIVE 1.3:b)
Relations, Relatives
  BROTHER 3.
Release
  FREE – SET FREE 1.1:b)
                  1.2:b)
                  1.3:
                  2.2:
  + *GRACE – THANKS* 2:c)
Reliable: see Rely (on)
Relieve, Relief
  REST – RELIEVE – REFRESH 2.
                           3.
                           4.
  SLAVE – SERVE – MINISTER 8.2:
Religion, Religious
  WORSHIP 2.
          3.
  FEAR – AWE 3. a)
  HOLY 3.1:
  TELL – PREACH – PROCLAIM 2.1:
Rely (on), Reliable
  ENCOURAGE – BOLD – PERSUADE 1.
                             10.2:
  BELIEVE – FAITH 1.2:b)
  + *FITTING – WORTHY* 4.3:
Remain
  STAY – LIVE 1.
              2.
              3.
  GREAT – MANY – MORE 10.
  LEAVE 8.3:
  + *STAY – LIVE* 8.
Remain quiet
  QUIET – SILENCE 4.
Remand (in custody)
  KEEP – GUARD 1. a)
Remarkable
  FIND – HAPPEN 2.2:
Remember
  REMEMBER – FORGET 1.
  KNOW – UNDERSTAND 2.4:
Remind, Reminder
  REMEMBER – FORGET 1.1:
Remnant
  LEAVE 8.3:
Remonstrate with
  BLAME – REBUKE – WARN NOT TO 4.
Remorse
  + *REPENT* 1.

Robe
      CLOTHING 2.1:
                2.2:
                2.4:
                2.5:
                1.2:
to Rock
      SHAKE – STIR UP – PROVOKE 6. a)
Rock, Rocky ground
      STONE – JEWEL 1.
Rocky
      STRAIGHT – CROOKED 2.
Rod
      ROD – STAFF – CLUB 1.
      TREE – WOOD 8.
Roll, Roll up
      ROUND – ROLL 8.
Roll, Scroll
      WRITING – READ 5.1:
Roman
      ROME – ROMAN – LATIN
Roof
      BUILDING 5.
Room, Room for
      PLACE – ROOM 1. c)
                2.
a Room
      HOUSE 4.1:
                4.2:
                4.3:
      +   STAY – LIVE 15.
Roost
      +   HOUSE 2. b)
Root
      TREE – WOOD 4.
      BEAR – BIRTH – CHILD 6.
Ropes
      ROPE – TIE – CHAIN 1.
                2.
Rose (= Got up): see Rise
Rostrum
      +   RISE - RAISE - HIGH 4.8:
Rotted. Rotting
      DESTROY 7.
Rotten, Bad
      EVIL – WRONG – HARM 10.
Rough
      STRAIGHT – CROOKED 2.
Rough water
      SEA – SHORE 2.3:
Roughly handled, Rough treatment
      BEAT – STRIKE – WOUND 9.
Round
      ROUND – ROLL 1.
                3.
                5.
                6.
                7.
                2. a)
                2. c)
Rouse
      RISE – RAISE – HIGH 1.2:
      SHAKE – STIR UP – PROVOKE 5. b)
      +   RISE – RAISE – HIGH 1.4:
Rout
      DISPERSE – SCATTER 2.1:
      BEAT – STRIKE – WOUND 7.2:
Row (a boat)
      DRIVE – SEND OUT – PUSH 4.1 b)
Rows, Ranks
      CORNER – SQUARE 2.
Royal
      KING 2:
                5:c)
                6:
Rub
      BREAK – GRIND – TEAR 2.4:
Rubbish
      DEFILE – FILTH 4.
Ruby
      +   STONE – JEWEL 7.
Rudder
      SHIP – SAIL 7.
(Be) Rude
      IMMORALITY 3.4:
Rue (the herb)
      GARDEN 2.2:
Rugged (topographically)
      STRAIGHT – CROOKED 2.

Ruin, Ruined,
      DESTROY 13. c)
                14.
                15.
                16.
                4. a)
      +   DESTROY 8.
      +   BREAK – GRIND – TEAR 1.2:
(to) Rule
      RULE – AUTHORITY – LEADER 1.
                2.
                3.1:
                3.4:
                12.
      +   SHEPHERD – FLOCK – HERD 1.
Rule(s)
      ORDER – REGULATION – INSTRUCT 7.
                8. a)
      +   ORDER – REGULATION – INSTRUCT 2.
                5. a)
      +   LAW 3:
Ruler
      RULE – AUTHORITY – LEADER 3.1:
                3.2:
                3.4:
                8.
      GATHERING 8.2:b)
      +   RULE – AUTHORITY – LEADER 6.2:a)
                12.
Run, Ran, Run away
      RUN – QUICKLY 1.
      REJECT – AVOID – ESCAPE 13.1:
      RIVER – FLOW – FOUNTAIN 2.6:a)
                2.6:e)
Run aground
      SEA – SHORE 6.3:
                6.4:
      DRIVE – SEND OUT – PUSH 4.2:
Rush
      RUSH – SPRING – LEAP 1.
                2.
      RIVER – FLOW – FOUNTAIN 2.6:e)
Rust
      DESTROY 6.

S

Sabaoth [= 'of hosts']
      +   MASTER – LORD 2. a)
Sabbath
      YEAR – MONTH – WEEK 3. b)
Sabbath rest
      REST – RELIEVE – REFRESH 1.
Sackcloth
      CLOTHING 4.2:
Sacred
      HOLY 1.9:
                3.1:
Sacrifice, Sacrifice for sin, Sacrificial
      SACRIFICE – ALTAR 1.
                2.1:
      DIE – KILL 2.5:b)
      GIVE 1.7:a)
Sacrilege, Sacrilegious
      HOLY 3.2:
                2.3:
      ABOMINATION 1:
Sad, Sadness
      MOURN – LAMENT 2.
                8.1:
the Sadducees
      PHARISEE 2:
Safe, Safety
      FIRM – CONFIRM – GUARANTEE 3.
      SAVE – CURE 3. b)
to Sail, a Sail
      SHIP – SAIL 1.
                2.
                9.
Sail along the coast
      GO – PASS 12.1:
Sail under the lee of
      +   SHIP – SAIL 1.

Sailors
      SHIP – SAIL 4. a)
Saint
      HOLY 1.6:
      +   RIGHTEOUS – JUSTIFY – VIRTUE 1.
Sale
      BUY – SELL – TRADE 3.
Salt, Salty, Salted
      EAT – FOOD – DRINK 3.7:
Salute, Salutation
      GREETINGS – FAREWELL 1.
Salvation
      SAVE – CURE 3. a)
Salve
      SAVE – CURE 8.
the Same, In the same way
      SAME – LIKE – SUCH 1.
                2.
                4.
                5.
Sanctify, Sanctification
      HOLY 1.2:
                1.3:
                1.5:
                1.9:
Sanctuary
      TEMPLE – SANCTUARY 2.1:
                1.2:
      HOLY 1.7:
      +   HOUSE 1. b)
Sand
      SEA – SHORE 4.4:
Sandals
      CLOTHING 3.
Sandalwood
      TREE – WOOD 6.1:
Sane
      WISE – SOBER 2. b)
Sanhedrin
      PLAN – COUNCIL 3.
Sap
      TREE – WOOD 5.
Sapphire
      +   STONE – JEWEL 7.
Sardonyx
      +   STONE – JEWEL 7.
Satan
      DEVIL 3.
Satisfy, (Be) Satisfied
      SATISFY – ENOUGH 1.
                2.
                3.
      +   DO – MAKE – BEHAVE 3.10:
      +   FILL – FULL – FULFIL 3.2:b)
Savage, a Savage
      FOREIGN – ALIEN 2.
      EASIER – DIFFICULT 2.4:
      +   GREAT – MANY – MORE 13.
Save, Save up
      SAVE – CURE 2.
                3.
      KEEP – GUARD 10.1:
      +   KEEP – GUARD 2. c)
Saviour
      SAVE – CURE 3. a)
Saw: see See
Saw, Sawn in half
      CUT – DIVISION 1.6:
Say
      SAY – TELL – SPEAK 1.
                2.
                3.
                4.
      TRUE – AMEN 3.1:
      +   MOUTH – TONGUE 1.1:b)
Say a blessing
      +   BLESS – PRAISE – GLORY 1.1:b)
Say goodbye to
      GREETINGS – FAREWELL 1.
      LEAVE 4.1:
Scales, Balance
      MEASURE 5.
Scales, Body-armour
      WAR – ARMY – WEAPONS 6.2:b)
Scales (covering the eyes)
      WEAKEN – SICKNESS 3.11:
Scarcely
      EASIER – DIFFICULT 2.2:
Scarlet
      CLOTH 1.6:

Vainglory
> BOAST – PROUD – ARROGANT 7.

Valid, Validate, Make valid
> FIRM – CONFIRM – GUARANTEE 5.
> > 6.
> TRUE – AMEN 2.1:

Valley
> MOUNTAIN – HILL 6.
> RIVER – FLOW – FOUNTAIN 2.1:c)

Value, Be of value
> PRECIOUS – EXPENSIVE 1.
> GREAT – MANY – MORE 11.
> + *GOOD – BETTER* 9.

Vanish, Vanish away
> REJECT – AVOID – ESCAPE 13.2:
> + *DESTROY* 3.
> > 13.
> + *SHOW – REVEAL – OPEN* 2. d)

Vanity
> BOAST – PROUD – ARROGANT 7.

Vapour
> WIND – CLOUD – RAIN 4.2:

(At) Variance (with)
> OTHER – DIFFERENT 3.

Variation, Variableness: see Vary
Varied, Various: see Vary

Variety
> CUT – DIVISION 2.1:a)

Vary, Varied, Various
> CHANGE 4.
> OFTEN 1.
> OTHER – DIFFERENT 4.
> > 5.1:

Vaunt oneself
> + *BOAST – PROUD – ARROGANT* 2.2:

Vegetables
> GARDEN 2.1:

Vegetation
> FARM 2.1:

Vehement
> + *FERVENT – HOT – COLD* 1.

Veil
> COVER – VEIL 1:
> CLOTH 2.1:

Venerate
> WORSHIP 3.2:

Vengeance
> JUDGE – CONDEMN – PUNISH 4.
> + *ANGER* 1.1:

Venom
> BITTER – SEVERE 1.2:d)

Venture, Risk oneself
> + *GIVE* 1.11:

Verdict
> + *JUDGE – CONDEMN – PUNISH* 3.1:b)
> > 3.2:

Very little, Very small
> LITTLE 4. b)

Vessel
> VESSEL – BASKET – BAG 1.1:a)
> > 1.1:b)
> > 1.2:
> SHIP – SAIL 4. a)
> + *SHIP – SAIL* 1.

Vial
> + *VESSEL – BASKET – BAG* 4.1:

Vice
> + *IMMORALITY* 3.1:

Victim
> DIE – KILL 2.5:b)

Victory, Victorious
> VICTORY – CONQUER 1.
> + *SAVE – CURE* 3. a)

View
> THINK – CONSIDER 4.

Vigilant
> SLEEP – WAKE 2.1:a)

Vigorous
> + *FERVENT – HOT – COLD* 1.

Vile, Vile people
> EVIL – WRONG – HARM 5.1:
> + *EVIL – WRONG – HARM* 8.

Village(s)
> CITY – TOWN – VILLAGE 2.

Villain
> EVIL – WRONG – HARM 14.
> indicate
> + *JUDGE – CONDEMN – PUNISH* 4.
> + *RIGHTEOUS – JUSTIFY – VIRTUE* 1.

Vine, Vinedresser, Vineyard
> FARM 1.2:
> > 1.3:

Vinegar
> BITTER – SEVERE 1.2:b)

Vintage
> + *FRUIT* 2.1:

Violence, Violent
> POWER – ABLE TO 7.
> EASIER – DIFFICULT 2.3:
> + *BEAT – STRIKE – WOUND* 6.1:
> + *GREAT – MANY – MORE* 1. f)

Viper
> SNAKE – DRAGON – SCORPION 2.1:
> > 2.2:

Virgin, Virginity
> MARRY – UNMARRIED 6.
> + *MAN – PEOPLE – WOMAN* 3.1:

Virtue, Virtuous
> RIGHTEOUS – JUSTIFY – VIRTUE

Visible
> + *SHOW – REVEAL – OPEN* 2. a)
> > 2. b)

Vision
> SEE 2.3:b)
> > 2.3:c)
> > 3.2:

Visit
> ENTER – GO IN – COME IN 4.
> COME – ARRIVE 1.4:c)
> GO – PASS 11.1:
> + *ENTER – GO IN – COME IN* 1.3:a)
> + *GO – PASS* 10.1:a)

Visitors
> FOREIGN – ALIEN 5.
> + *FOREIGN – ALIEN* 4.

Vocation
> NAME – CALL 5.5:

Voice
> VOICE – SOUND 1.
> > 2. a)

Void
> FIRM – CONFIRM – GUARANTEE 5.
> EMPTY – WORTHLESS – IN VAIN 1.3:

Vomit
> SPIT – FOAM – VOMIT 3.1:
> + *THROW – DROP* 1.1:

Vote
> AGREEMENT – CONSENT 9.

Votive offerings
> PROMISE – VOW – OATH 4.

Vow
> PROMISE – VOW – OATH 3.
> > 4.

Voyage
> + *SHIP – SAIL* 1.

Vulture
> BIRDS – INSECTS 2.7:

W

to Wag
> SHAKE – STIR UP – PROVOKE 5. a)

Wage(s)
> PAY – REWARD – PRIZE 4.
> > 5.
> + *MONEY* 9.5:

Wail, Wail over, Bewail
> MOURN – LAMENT 7.
> > 8.
> > 9. a)
> + *MOURN – LAMENT* 4.2:

Waist
> BODY 5.8:
> + *BODY* 5.1:
> > 5.2:

Wait
> STAY – LIVE 3.1:
> + *LEAVE* 10.2:

Wait for
> HOPE – EXPECT – WAIT FOR 2.

Wait upon, Wait on
> SLAVE – SERVE – MINISTER 7.
> > 8.4:

Wake, Wake up
> SLEEP – WAKE 3.
> > 2.1:a)
> RISE – RAISE – HIGH 1.2:
> + *RISE – RAISE – HIGH* 1.3:

Walk
> GO – PASS 1.1:
> > 1.5:
> > 11.1:
> + *GO – PASS* 2.3:
> > 10.1:
> + *LEAVE* 1.3:a)
> + *STREET – PATH – WAY* 2.3:a)

Walk onward, Walk uprightly
> STREET – PATH – WAY 2.4:
> GO – PASS 1.5:
> > 15.2:a)

Wall
> FORT – WALL – TOWER 2.
> + *SHUT – CLOSED* 3. b)

Wallow
> ROUND – ROLL 8.1:

Wander
> DECEIVE – TRICK – PRETENCE 1.1:
> + *GO – PASS* 10.1:a)

Want, Want to
> WILL – WANT 1.
> > 2.
> DESIRE – LONGING 2.
> > 4.
> SEEK – PURSUE 1.3:
> + *DESIRE – LONGING* 1.
> + *SATISFY – ENOUGH* 3.
> > 4.
> + *REJOICE – GLAD – HAPPY* 7.1:

Want, Need, Lack
> NEED 2.1:
> WEAKEN – SICKNESS 2.6:
> + *NEED* 1.

Wanton, Wantonness
> LUXURY – WANTONNESS 3.
> + *LUXURY – WANTONNESS* 2.

(Make, Wage) War, Warfare
> WAR – ARMY – WEAPONS 1.
> > 2. c)

Warden, Warder
> KEEP – GUARD 2. a)
> > 3.3:

Warm, Warm oneself
> FERVENT – HOT – COLD 3.

Warn, Warn not to
> BLAME – REBUKE – WARN NOT TO 8.
> > 9.
> TEACHING 3.
> ENCOURAGE – BOLD – PERSUADE 12.
> SHOW – REVEAL – OPEN 1.
> > 6.
> + *ORDER – REGULATION – INSTRUCT* 3.

Warning(s)
> IMAGE – FORM – EXAMPLE 4.2:
> + *IMAGE – FORM – EXAMPLE* 8.
> + *ORDER – REGULATION – INSTRUCT* 3.
> + *SHOW – REVEAL – OPEN* 6.

a Warrant
> + *RULE – AUTHORITY – LEADER* 4. a)

Warrior
> + *WAR – ARMY – WEAPONS* 1.

Was, Were: see Be

Wash
> WATER – BAPTISE – WASH 2. c)
> > 3.
> > 4.
> + *PURE – INNOCENT – SIMPLE* 2.
> + *REJECT – AVOID – ESCAPE* 4.2:

Waste, Wasted
> EMPTY – WORTHLESS – IN VAIN 4.
> DESTROY 4. a)
> > 13. d)

Waste time
> IDLE – DELAY 9.

Watch (out), Watch
> SEE 4.2:
> > 5.1:
> > 8.
> > 12.

Watch (over), Watchful
> SLEEP – WAKE 2.
> STEWARD – GUARDIAN 3.
> KEEP – GUARD 1. a)
> > 2. c)

Wipe, Wipe off, Wipe out
WIPE – WIPE OUT
Wise, Wisdom
WISE – SOBER 1. a)
2. a)
Wise men, Magi
MAGIC 3.
Wish, Hope
DESIRE – LONGING 6.
Witchcraft
MAGIC 4.
With
WITH
+ *STAY – LIVE 3.1:*
+ *ACCOMPANY – FOLLOW – AFTER 2.*
With child
BEAR – BIRTH – CHILD 1.
Withdraw
LEAVE 3.1:
5.1:
6.
DRAG – DRAW 3.5:
Wither, Withered, Wither away
DRY – WITHER 4:
5:
WEAKEN – SICKNESS 1.4:
+ *DESTROY 8.*
Withhold
PREVENT – HINDER – STRAIN 1.2:
Within
INSIDE – OUTSIDE 1.3:
Without, Separate from
WITH 4.
Without cause
EMPTY – WORTHLESS – IN VAIN 4.
5.
Without measure, Beyond measure
MEASURE 1.
Without (doing) something
NOT ANY – NO 1.2:
Without spot, Unstained
PURE – INNOCENT – SIMPLE 8.2:
8.3:
Withstand
ENEMY – OPPOSE – AGAINST 6.
Witness, Bear witness
WITNESS – TESTIFY 1:
Woe (to, betide)
MISERY – DANGER 1.1:
Woke(n): see Wake
Wolf
ANIMALS 2.3:
Woman, Women
MAN – PEOPLE – WOMAN 4.
5.
Womb
BODY 6.2:b)
6.3:b)
6.4:
Won: see Win
Wonder, Wonderful
ASTONISHED – WONDER 1.
5.
CONFUSION – DISTURB 2.
SIGN 1.1:a)
THINK – CONSIDER 8.1:
+ *ASTONISHED – WONDER 4.*
+ *GOOD – BETTER 2. c)*
Wood
TREE – WOOD 6.1:
+ *TREE – WOOD 2.*
Woodworm
BIRDS – INSECTS 3.4:
Wool
CLOTH 1.3:
Word, Words
SAY – TELL – SPEAK 2.1:
2.2:
2.3:
2.4:
Wore: see Wear
Work, Work hard
LABOUR – TROUBLE 2.1:
1.1:
DO – MAKE – BEHAVE 2.1:
2.2:
2.3:
3.1:
3.4:
3.10:

Work, Work hard—(contd)
BE 2.2:b)
+ *DO – MAKE – BEHAVE 5.*
7.
+ *END – LAST 1. a)*
+ *SLAVE – SERVE – MINISTER 3.1:*
Work (of authorship)
WRITING – READ 3. b)
Work of charity
GRACE – THANKS 1:c)
Work of mercy, of generosity
GRACE – THANKS 1:c)
Work out, Calculate
NUMBERS 2.
Work upon (a person's) feelings
SHAKE – STIR UP – PROVOKE 8.
Worker, Workman
DO – MAKE – BEHAVE 2.3:a)
the World
WORLD
EVER – ETERNAL – AGE 1.6:
+ *EARTH – LAND – COUNTRY 3. a)*
Worldly
+ *EVIL – WRONG – HARM 6.2:*
Worldly standards
FLESH – BLOOD – BONE 1.1:a)
Worm
BIRDS – INSECTS 3.5:
Worm one's way in(to)
ENTER – GO IN – COME IN 5.
Wormwood
BITTER – SEVERE 1.2:a)
Worn: see Wear
Worry, Be worried
SUFFER – ANGUISH 3.
5.
CARE – CONCERN – DEVOTION 2.
FEAR – AWE 5.
BEAT – STRIKE – WOUND 11.
CONFUSION – DISTURB 2.
7.
Worse
EVIL – WRONG – HARM 11.
12.
Worship, Worshipper
WORSHIP 1.
2.
3.1:
3.2:
4.
(Be) Worth, (of great) Worth
GREAT – MANY – MORE 11.
1. f)
Worthless
EMPTY – WORTHLESS – IN VAIN 2.
3.
TEST 2.3:
+ *EVIL – WRONG – HARM 10.*
16.
+ *GOOD – BETTER 10. b)*
Worthy, Worthy of
FITTING – WORTHY 4.
+ *BLESS – PRAISE – GLORY 1.4:*
Wound(s), Wounded
BEAT – STRIKE – WOUND 3.
5.
6.1:
6.2:
10.
14.
15.
Woven
CLOTH 3.2:
Wrangle, Wrangling
QUARREL – DISPUTE 2.
3.
Wrap
CLOTHING 1.5:
1.6:
1.7:
1.8:
Wrath
ANGER 1.1:
2.
Wreath
ADORN – CROWN 4.1:

Wreck, Shipwreck
SHIP – SAIL 3. b)
Wrench
TURN – RETURN 1.1:
Wrestle
FIGHT – STRUGGLE 1.
Wretch
+ *EVIL – WRONG – HARM 1.1:*
Wretched, Wretchedness
MISERY – DANGER 1.2:
WEAKEN – SICKNESS 2.5:
+ *EVIL – WRONG – HARM 1.1:*
Wrinkle
DEFILE – FILTH 12.
Writ, Certificate
WRITING – READ 4.2:
Writ of dismissal, of divorce
MARRY – UNMARRIED 3.1:
Write, Written, Writing
WRITING – READ 1.
3.
5.
SEND 1.4:
Writer(s)
DO – MAKE – BEHAVE 3.11:
Writhe
ROUND – ROLL 8.1:
Written Code of the Law
WRITING – READ 1. b)
Wrong
EVIL – WRONG – HARM 1.
3.
7.
8.
9.
15.1:
DECEIVE – TRICK – PRETENCE 1.1:
+ *EVIL – WRONG – HARM 16.*
+ *JUDGE – CONDEMN – PUNISH 2.*
+ *STUMBLE – FALL 4.*
5.3:
(Feel in the) Wrong
DISHONOUR – SHAME 3.
Wrongdoing
+ *EVIL – WRONG – HARM 3.*
Wrong-headed
EVIL – WRONG – HARM 9.

Y

Yardstick
ORDER – REGULATION – INSTRUCT 8. b
Year
YEAR – MONTH – WEEK 1.
Yearn for
DESIRE – LONGING 3.
+ *DESIRE – LONGING 2.*
Yeast
YEAST – LEAVEN – UNLEAVENED 1:
Yes, Yes I tell you
YES
Yesterday
TIME – DAY – HOUR 5.1:
Yet, Not yet
NOW – AT ONCE 4.
NOT YET – NEVER 1.
Yield, Yield up
FIGHT – STRUGGLE 5.
GIVE 1.10:
BEAR – BIRTH – CHILD 4.5:
LEAVE 10.4:
TAKE – BRING – LEAD 6.6:

Yield, Yield up—*(contd)*
    + *FRUIT* 1. b)
         2.1:
    + *DO – MAKE – BEHAVE* 3.2:
Yield dividends
    GAIN – PROFIT 2.
Yoke
    JOIN – ATTACH 2. a)
    NUMBERS 4.2:

Young, Younger
    NEW – OLD 1.3:b)
    LITTLE 1. a)
         4. a)
Young girl
    MARRY – UNMARRIED 6.
Youth
    NEW – OLD 1.3:b)

Z

Zeal, Zealous
    ZEAL – ENVY – GREED 1.1:
    CARE – CONCERN – DEVOTION 4.
Zealot, member of the Zealot party
    + *ZEAL – ENVY – GREED* 1.1:

Greek Index

To help those less familiar with Greek orthography, the words in this Index have been split where appropriate by hyphens into their respective derivative parts: prefixes and words comprising two or more root forms are thus clearly distinguishable. On the very few occasions that alternative Greek forms occur, both forms appear bracketed together or one after the other. Equally rare are Greek homonyms, the different meanings of which, as separate entries, are distinguished by means of a roman (upright, not italic) numeral to the left of each entry. Conjectural Greek forms are shown to be such by means of an asterisk immediately preceding them.

Immediately following almost every Greek form appears a number printed *in italics*, which represents the total number of times — the frequency with which — that form was used by the original writers of the New Testament. On the very few occasions when no number is given, it implies that the form is a preposition and that therefore only the most important proportion of the total number of instances within the New Testament has been included in this Concordance.

Finally, after the total frequency number, the capital letter *S*

may appear, indicating that the Greek form is also to be found in the Septuagint.

Directly beneath each entry appears an exact reference to where the Greek form is to be found translated into English in the main body of the text, shown by the (title of the) Theme under which it has been classified, and the Section number or numbers within that Theme.

Sometimes there is more than one reference beneath an entry, in which case the total number of instances found under each Theme referred to is shown to the left of each Theme title. (These frequency numbers may add up to more than the total frequency number given alongside the Greek form: this is because some texts may be read in two different ways and may thus be included under two different Themes.)

A frequency number in parentheses indicates that only a proportion of the total frequency has been included within the Concordance, and usually implies a preposition.

βαττα-λογέω *1*
  SAY 2.4:a)
βδέλυγμα *6 S*
  ABOMINATION
βδελυκτός *1 S*
  ABOMINATION 2:
βδελύσσω *2 S*
  ABOMINATION 2:
βέβαιος *9 S*
  FIRM 6.
βεβαιόω *8 S*
  FIRM 6.
βεβαίως *2 S*
  FIRM 6.
βέβηλος *5 S*
  EVIL 6.2:
βεβηλόω *2 S*
  EVIL 6.2:
βεεζεβούλ *7*
  DEVIL 1.
βελιάρ *1*
  DEVIL 4.
βελόνη *1*
  CLOTH 3.3:b)
βέλος *1 S*
  WAR 6.8:
βελτίων *1 S*
  GOOD 1. d)
βῆμα *12 S*
  1 FOOT 4.
  10 JUDGE 6.3:
  1 RISE 4.8:
βήρυλλος *1 S*
  STONE 7.
βία *4 S*
  POWER 7.
βιάζω *2 S*
  POWER 7.
βίαιος *1 S*
  POWER 7.
βιαστής *1*
  POWER 7.
βιβλαρίδιον *3*
  WRITE 4.1:c)
βιβλίον *34 S*
  WRITE 4.
βίβλος *10 S*
  WRITE 4.
βιβρώσκω *1 S*
  EAT 3.1:
βίος *10 S*
  STAY 5.
βιόω *1 S*
  STAY 5.1:
βίωσις *1 S*
  STAY 5.1:
βιωτικός *3*
  STAY 5.1:
βλαβερός *1 S*
  EVIL 13.
βλάπτω *2 S*
  EVIL 13.
βλαστάνω, -άω *4 S*
  GROW 4.
βλασ-φημέω *34 S*
  CURSE 2.1:
βλασ-φημία *18 S*
  CURSE 2.1:
βλάσ-φημος *4 S*
  CURSE 2.1:
βλέμμα *1*
  SEE 4.1:c)
βλέπω *133 S*
  2 FAVOURITISM
  131 SEE 4.
βλητέον *1*
  PUT 3.1:
βοάω *12 S*
  VOICE 3.2:
βοή *1 S*
  VOICE 3.2:
βοή-θεια *2 S*
  HELP 2.
βοη-θέω *8 S*
  HELP 2.
βοη-θός *1 S*
  HELP 2.
βόθυνος *3 S*
  DIG 1.3:

βολή *1 S*
  THROW 1.1:
βολίζω *2*
  THROW 1.1:
βόρβορος *1 S*
  DEFILE 6.
βορρᾶς *2 S*
  EAST 3.
βόσκω *9 S*
  EAT 3.6:
βοτάνη *1*
  FARM 2.1:
βότρυς *1 S*
  FRUIT 3.1:
βουλεύομαι *6 S*
  4 PLAN 2.
  2 WILL 1.2:
βουλευτής *2 S*
  PLAN 2.
βουλή *12 S*
  WILL 1.
βούλημα *3 S*
  WILL 1.
βούλομαι *37 S*
  WILL 1.
βουνός *2 S*
  MOUNTAIN 3.
βοῦς *8 S*
  ANIMALS 2.7:a)
βραβεῖον *2*
  PAY 7.1:
βραβεύω *1 S*
  RULE 2.
βραδύνω *2 S*
  IDLE 5.
βραδυ-πλοέω *1*
  1 IDLE 5.
  1 SHIP 1.
βραδύς *3*
  IDLE 5.
βραδύτης *1*
  IDLE 5.
βραχίων *3 S*
  HAND 3.2:
βραχύς *7 S*
  LITTLE 2.1:
βρέφος *8 S*
  BEAR 7.1:
βρέχω *7 S*
  2 WATER 4.
  5 WIND 5.1:
βροντή *12 S*
  VOICE 6.
βροχή *2 S*
  WIND 5.1:
βρόχος *1 S*
  ROPE 7.
βρυγμός *7 S*
  MOUTH 4.1:
βρύχω *1 S*
  MOUTH 4.1:
βρύω *1*
  RIVER 2.5:
βρῶμα *17 S*
  EAT 3.1:
βρώσιμος *1 S*
  EAT 3.1:
βρῶσις *11 S*
  2 BIRDS 3.4:
  2 DESTROY 6.1:
  9 EAT 3.1:
βυθίζω *2 S*
  SEA 3.2:
βυθός *1 S*
  ABYSS 2.1:a)
βυρσεύς *3*
  DO 9.
βύσσινος *5 S*
  CLOTH 1.1:
βύσσος *1 S*
  CLOTH 1.1:
βωμός *1 S*
  SACRIFICE 3.1:

γ

γαββαθά *1*
  STONE 3. b)

γάγγραινα *1*
  WEAKEN 3.3:
γάζα *1 S*
  KEEP 10.2:b)
γαζο-φυλακεῖον *5 S*
  KEEP 10.2:a)
γάλα *5 S*
  EAT 11.
γαλήνη *3*
  QUIET 1.
γαμέω *28 S*
  MARRY 2.1:
γαμίζω *7*
  MARRY 2.1:
γαμίσκομαι *1*
  MARRY 2.1:
γάμος *16 S*
  MARRY 2.1:
γαστήρ *9 S*
  7 BEAR 1.2:
  2 BODY 6.2:
γέεννα *12*
  ABYSS 4.
γεθσημανί *2*
  EARTH 5. a)
γείτων *4 S*
  NEAR 1.1:
γελάω *2 S*
  MOCK 5. b)
γέλως *1 S*
  MOCK 5. b)
γεμίζω *9 S*
  FILL 1.1:
γέμω *11 S*
  FILL 1.1:
γενεά *43 S*
  GENERATION
γενεα-λογέω *1 S*
  BEAR 3.5:
γενεα-λογία *2*
  BEAR 3.5:
γενέσιος *2*
  BEAR 3.2:c)
γένεσις *5 S*
  1 BE 2.4:
  4 BEAR 3.2:a), c), 5:
γενετή *1*
  BEAR 3.2:c)
γένημα *5 S*
  FRUIT 1.
γεννάω *99 S*
  BEAR 3.1:, 2:
γέννημα *4 S*
  BEAR 3.2:c)
γεννητός *2 S*
  BEAR 3.2:c)
γένος *21 S*
  15 BEAR 3.2:c)
  6 OTHER 5.2:
γερουσία *1 S*
  NEW 2.2:b)
γέρων *1 S*
  NEW 2.2:a)
γεύομαι *15 S*
  EAT 5.1:
γε-ωργέω *1 S*
  FARM 1.1:
γε-ώργιον *1 S*
  FARM 1.1:
γε-ωργός *19 S*
  FARM 1.1:
γῆ *252 S*
  174 EARTH 3.
  6 EGYPT
  70 HEAVEN 1.2:
  2 MESOPOTAMIA 1.
γῆρας *1 S*
  NEW 2.2:a)
γηράσκω *2 S*
  NEW 2.2:a)
γί(γ)νομαι *S*
  (234) BE 2.
  (4) BEAR 3.2:a), c)
  (7) BELONG TO 1.
  (2) FRUIT 1.
  (1) KNOW 11.
γι(γ)νώσκω *221 S*
  KNOW 1.1:, 2:, 3:, 7:, 8:
γλεῦκος *1 S*
  EAT 12.2:

γλυκύς *4 S*
  SWEET 1.
γλῶσσα *50 S*
  MOUTH 3.1:
γλωσσό-κομον *2 S*
  VESSEL 8.2:
γναφεύς *1 S*
  WATER 6.
γνήσιος *4 S*
  TRUE 1.
γνησίως *1 S*
  TRUE 1.
γνόφος *1 S*
  NIGHT 2.2:a)
γνώμη *9 S*
  THINK 6.
γνωρίζω *26 S*
  KNOW 1.1:, 6:, 8:, 9:
γνῶσις *29 S*
  KNOW 1.1:, 3:, 8:
γνώστης *1 S*
  KNOW 1.3:
γνωστός *15 S*
  KNOW 1.1:, 3:, 6:, 8:, 9:
γογγύζω *8 S*
  BLAME 7.
γογγυσμός *4 S*
  BLAME 7.
γογγυστής *1*
  BLAME 7.
γόης *1*
  DECEIVE 1.9:
γολγοθά *3*
  HEAD 2.1:
γόμος *3 S*
  FILL 1.2:
γονεῖς *20 S*
  FATHER 4.
γόνυ *12 S*
  2 FOOT 3.2:
  10 WORSHIP 5.
γονυ-πετέω *4*
  WORSHIP 5.
γράμμα *15 S*
  WRITE 1. a), b), d), f), g)
γραμματεύς *63 S*
  WRITE 1. c), e)
γραπτός *1 S*
  WRITE 1. g)
γραφή *51 S*
  WRITE 1. a)
γράφω *190 S*
  WRITE 1. a), f), g)
γραώδης *1*
  NEW 2.2:a)
γρηγορέω *23 S*
  SLEEP 2.1:
γυμνάζω *4 S*
  FIGHT 5.
γυμνασία *1*
  FIGHT 5.
γυμνιτεύω *1*
  CLOTHING 5.2:a)
γυμνός *15 S*
  CLOTHING 5.2:
γυμνότης *3 S*
  CLOTHING 5.2:a)
γυναικάριον *1*
  MAN 4.1:
γυναικεῖος *1 S*
  MAN 4.2:
γυνή *216 S*
  MAN 4.
γωνία *9 S*
  CORNER 1.1:

δ

δαιμονίζομαι *13*
  DEVIL 1.
δαιμόνιον *63 S*
  62 DEVIL 1.
  1 GOD 2.
δαιμονιώδης *1*
  DEVIL 1.
δαίμων *1 S*
  DEVIL 1.
δάκνω *1 S*
  MOUTH 4.2:a)

δάκρυ *10 S*
   MOURN 4.1:
δακρύω *1 S*
   MOURN 4.1:
δακτύλιος *1 S*
   ADORN 2.
δάκτυλος *8 S*
   HAND 2.
δαμάζω *4 S*
   OBEY 4.
δάμαλις *1 S*
   ANIMALS 2.7:d)
δανείζω *4 S*
   BORROW 1.
δάνειον *1 S*
   BORROW 1.
δανειστής *1 S*
   BORROW 1.
δαπανάω *5 S*
   PRECIOUS 3.1:
δαπάνη *1 S*
   PRECIOUS 3.1:
δέησις *18 S*
   ASK 7.1:
δεῖ *104 S*
   MUST 1.
δεῖγμα *1*
   IMAGE 7.
δειγματίζω *2*
   SHOW 1.
δείκνυμι, -ύω *33 S*
   SHOW 1.
δειλία *1 S*
   FEAR 3. b)
δειλιάω *1 S*
   FEAR 3. b)
δειλός *3 S*
   FEAR 3. b)
δεινῶς *2 S*
   FEAR 3. b)
δειπνέω *4 S*
   EAT 7.2:
δεῖπνον *16 S*
   EAT 7.2:
δεισι-δαιμονία *1*
   FEAR 3. a)
δεισι-δαίμων *1*
   FEAR 3. a)
δέκα *23 S*
   NUMBERS 12. a), b)
δεκάτη *4 S*
   NUMBERS 12. d)
δέκατος *3 S*
   NUMBERS 12. a), b), c)
δεκατόω *2 S*
   NUMBERS 12. d)
δεκτός *5 S*
   RECEIVE 2. a), c)
δελεάζω *3*
   DECEIVE 1.4:
δένδρον *25 S*
   TREE 1.1:
δεξιο-λάβος *1*
   WAR 5.
δεξιός *54 S*
   RIGHT
δέομαι *22 S*
   ASK 7.
δέος *1 S*
   FEAR 3. a)
δέρμα *1 S*
   CLOTHING 4.1:
δερμάτινος *2 S*
   CLOTHING 4.1:
δέρρις *1 S*
   CLOTHING 4.1:
δέρω *15 S*
   BEAT 2.
δεσμεύω *3 S*
   ROPE 8.
δέσμη *1*
   ROPE 8. a)
δέσμιος *16 S*
   ROPE 8. c)
δεσμός *18 S*
   ROPE 8.
δεσμο-φύλαξ *3*
   3 KEEP 2. a)
   3 ROPE 8. c)

δεσμωτήριον *4 S*
   ROPE 8. c)
δεσμώτης *2 S*
   ROPE 8. c)
δεσ-πότης *10 S*
   MASTER 1.1:
δεῦρο *9 S*
   8 COME 4.
   1 NOW 3.
δεῦτε *12 S*
   COME 4.
δευτεραῖος *1*
   NUMBERS 4:1:b)
δευτερό-πρωτος *1*
   NUMBERS 3.2:c), 4.1:b)
δεύτερος *44 S*
   NUMBERS 4.1:a), b), c), e)
δέχομαι *56 S*
   RECEIVE 2. b), c), e), f), g)
δέω *43 S*
   ROPE 8.
δῆλος *3 S*
   SHOW 3.1:
δηλόω *7 S*
   SHOW 3.1:
δημ-ηγορέω *1 S*
   1 MAN 8.
   1 SAY 5.3:
δημι-ουργός *1 S*
   DO 2.1:
δῆμος *4 S*
   MAN 8.
δημόσιος *4 S*
   MAN 8.
δηνάριον *16*
   MONEY 9.5:
δηποτοῦν *1*
   WHOLE 3.
διά *S*
   (10) EVER 3.
   (15) FOR 4.
   (78) THROUGH
   (1) WHOLE 1.3:
δια-βαίνω *3 S*
   GO 16.1:
δια-βάλλω *1 S*
   CURSE 2.5:
δια-βεβαιόομαι *2*
   FIRM 6.
δια-βλέπω *3*
   SEE 4.1:c), d)
διά-βολος *39 S*
   3 CURSE 2.5:
   36 DEVIL 2.
δι-αγγέλλω *3 S*
   TELL 1.1:, 2:
δια-γίνομαι *3 S*
   DISTANCE 5.
δια-γινώσκω *2 S*
   KNOW 1.5:
διά-γνωσις *1 S*
   KNOW 1.5:
δια-γογγύζω *2 S*
   BLAME 7.
δια-γρηγορέω *1*
   SLEEP 2.1:
δι-άγω *2 S*
   GO 15.1:
δια-δέχομαι *1 S*
   RECEIVE 2. f)
διά-δημα *3 S*
   ADORN 3.
δια-δίδωμι *4 S*
   GIVE 1.4:
διά-δοχος *1 S*
   ACCOMPANY 9.
δια-ζώννυμι *3*
   CLOTHING 2.8:
δια-θήκη *33 S*
   COVENANT
δι-αίρεσις *3 S*
   CUT 2.1:a)
δι-αιρέω *2 S*
   CUT 2.1:a)
δια-καθαίρω *1*
   PURE 2.
δια-καθαρίζω *1*
   PURE 2.
δια-κατ-ελέγχομαι *1*
   BLAME 3.

δια-κονέω *37*
   SLAVE 8.
δια-κονία *34 S*
   SLAVE 8.1:, 2:, 4:
διά-κονος *30 S*
   SLAVE 8.1:, 3:, 4:
δι-ακούω *1 S*
   HEAR 2.7:
δια-κρίνω *19 S*
   9 BELIEVE 2.2:
   10 JUDGE 3.3:
διά-κρισις *3 S*
   JUDGE 3.3:
δια-κωλύω *1 S*
   PREVENT 1.1:
δια-λαλέω *2*
   SAY 1.4:c)
δια-λέγομαι *13 S*
   SAY 2.9:
δια-λείπω *1 S*
   END 7.1:
διά-λεκτος *6 S*
   SAY 2.12:b)
δι-αλλάσσω *1 S*
   PEACE 2.
δια-λογίζομαι *16 S*
   9 SAY 9.
   14 THINK 8.1:
δια-λογισμός *14 S*
   4 SAY 9.
   11 THINK 8.1:
δια-λύω *1 S*
   DISPERSE 3.
δια-μαρτύρομαι *15 S*
   WITNESS
δια-μάχομαι *1 S*
   QUARREL 1.
δια-μένω *5 S*
   STAY 3.1:, 3:, 4:
δια-μερίζω *11 S*
   CUT 3.1:a), c)
δια-μερισμός *1 S*
   CUT 3.1:c)
δια-νέμω *1 S*
   DISPERSE 4.
δια-νεύω *1 S*
   SIGN 2.
δια-νόημα *1 S*
   THINK 12.2:
διά-νοια *12 S*
   KNOW 7.2:
δι-αν-οίγω *8 S*
   SHOW 8.1:b), c)
δια-νυκτερεύω *1 S*
   NIGHT 1. a)
δι-ανύω *1 S*
   END 3.
δια-παρα-τριβή *1*
   QUARREL 3.
δια-περάω *6 S*
   GO 11.2:
δια-πλέω *1*
   SHIP 1.
δια-πονέω *2 S*
   SUFFER 9.
δια-πορεύομαι *5 S*
   GO 11.1:
δι-α-πορέω *4*
   CONFUSION 2.
δια-πραγματεύομαι *1*
   GAIN 5.
δια-πρίω *2 S*
   ANGER 6.
δι-αρπάζω *3 S*
   CATCH 9.1:
δια-(ρ)ρήσσω *5 S*
   BREAK 3.1:a), b)
δια-σαφέω *2 S*
   INTERPRET 4.
δια-σείω *1*
   ENCOURAGE 13.
δια-σκορπίζω *9 S*
   DISPERSE 2.
δια-σπάω *2 S*
   BREAK 3.3:
δια-σπείρω *3 S*
   DISPERSE 1.
δια-σπορά *3 S*
   DISPERSE 1.

δια-στέλλομαι *8 S*
   ORDER 4.
διά-στημα *1 S*
   DISTANCE 4.
δια-στολή *3 S*
   CUT 2.7:
δια-στρέφω *7 S*
   TURN 3.1:, 3:b), 4:
δια-σῴζω *8 S*
   SAVE 3. b), c)
δια-ταγή *2 S*
   ORDER 2.
διά-ταγμα *1 S*
   ORDER 2.
δια-ταράσσω *1 S*
   CONFUSION 5.1:
δια-τάσσω *16 S*
   ORDER 2.
δια-τελέω *1 S*
   STAY 9.
δια-τηρέω *2 S*
   KEEP 1. b), c)
δια-τίθεμαι *7 S*
   COVENANT 1:, 3:
δια-τρίβω *10 S*
   STAY 11.
δια-τροφή *1 S*
   EAT 3.2:a)
δι-αυγάζω *1*
   SHINE 4.
δι-αυγής *1*
   SHINE 4.
δια-φέρω *13 S*
   8 GREAT 11.
   2 OTHER 4.
   3 TAKE 6.1:, 5:
δια-φεύγω *1 S*
   REJECT 13.1:
δια-φημίζω *3*
   SAY 3.5:
δια-φθείρω *6 S*
   DESTROY 8.
δια-φθορά *6 S*
   DESTROY 8.
διά-φορος *4 S*
   2 GREAT 11.
   2 OTHER 4.
δια-φυλάσσω *1 S*
   KEEP 2. c)
δια-χειρίζομαι *2*
   DIE 2.3:
δια-χλευάζω *1*
   MOCK 4.
δια-χωρίζω *1 S*
   LEAVE 3.1:
διδακτικός *2*
   TEACHING 1.1:c)
διδακτός *2*
   TEACHING 1.1:c), d)
διδασκαλία *21 S*
   TEACHING 1.1:c), d)
διδάσκαλος *59 S*
   TEACHING 1.1:a), c), d)
διδάσκω *97 S*
   TEACHING 1.1:b), c), d)
διδαχή *30 S*
   TEACHING 1.1:b), c), d)
δί-δραχμον *2 S*
   MONEY 9.4:
δίδωμι *415 S*
   4 DO 7.
   389 GIVE 1.
   12 PAY 3.1:
   11 PUT 4.
δι-εγείρω *6 S*
   RISE 1.2:, 4:
δι-εν-θυμέομαι *1*
   THINK 7.
δι-έξ-οδος *1 S*
   STREET 2.3:b)
δι-ερμηνευτής *1*
   INTERPRET 1.1:
δι-ερμηνεύω *6 S*
   INTERPRET 1.
δι-έρχομαι *41 S*
   GO 10.1:, 2:
δι-ερωτάω *1*
   ASK 4.1:

έμ-πτύω 6 S
  SPIT 1.
έμ-φανής 2 S
  SHOW 2. a)
έμ-φανίζω 10 S
  SHOW 2. a), b)
έμ-φοβος 5 S
  FEAR 1. a)
έμ-φυσάω 1 S
  SPIRIT 1.3:
έμ-φυτος 1 S
  FARM 7.
έν S
  (2) CARE 7.
  (70) INSIDE 1.4:, 5:
  (95) JESUS CHRIST (sign e) 1.2:
  (57) MASTER (sign e) 2. b), c)
  (40) NAME (sign a) 1.
  (35) SPIRIT (sign e) 1.1:a), c)
έν-αγκαλίζομαι 2 S
  KISS 2.
έν-άλιος 1
  FISH 3.
έν-αντι 2 S
  BEFORE 2.3:a)
έν-αντίον S
  (5) BEFORE 2.3:
έν-αντίος 8 S
  1 BEFORE 2.3:a)
  7 ENEMY 4.
έν-άρχομαι 2 S
  BEGINNING 1.1:
ένατος 10 S
  NUMBERS 11.
έν-δεής 1 S
  NEED 1.1:
έν-δειγμα 1
  SHOW 1.
έν-δείκνυμι 11 S
  SHOW 1.
έν-δειξις 4
  SHOW 1.
έν-δεκα 6 S
  NUMBERS 13. a)
έν-δέκατος 3 S
  NUMBERS 13. b)
έν-δέχομαι 1 S
  POWER 8.
έν-δημέω 3
  STAY 8.
έν-διδύσκω 2 S
  CLOTHING 1.1:a)
έν-δικος 2
  RIGHTEOUS 1.
έν-δοξάζω 2 S
  BLESS 2. a)
έν-δοξος 4 S
  1 ASTONISHED 5.
  3 BLESS 2. a), b)
έν-δυμα 8 S
  CLOTHING 1.1:
έν-δυναμόω 7 S
  POWER 1.1:e)
έν-δύνω 1
  ENTER 6.
έν-δυσις 1 S
  CLOTHING 1.1:a)
έν-δύω 28 S
  CLOTHING 1.1:
έν-δώμησις 1
  BUILDING 1.3:
έν-έδρα 2 S
  CATCH 6.
έν-εδρεύω 2 S
  CATCH 6.
έν-ειλέω 1 S
  CLOTHING 1.8:
έν-ειμι 1 S
  HAVE 5.
ένεκα, ένεκεν,
  είνεκεν S
  (15) FOR 5.
ένεός 1 S
  DEAF 3.
έν-έργεια 8 S
  DO 2.1:, 6:
έν-εργέω 21 S
  DO 2.1:, 3:b), 6:
έν-έργημα 2
  DO 2.6:

έν-εργής 3
  DO 2.1:, 3:a), 6:
έν-ευ-λογέω 2 S
  BLESS 1.1:a)
έν-έχω 3 S
  2 ANGER 7.
  1 OBEY 4.
έν-θυμέομαι 2 S
  THINK 7.
έν-θύμησις 4
  THINK 7.
ένι 6 S
  BE 1.3:
έν-ιαυτός 14 S
  YEAR 1.1:
έν-ίστημι 7 S
  NOW 5.
έν-ισχύω 2 S
  POWER 2.1:d)
έννέα 1 S
  NUMBERS 11.
έν-νεύω 1 S
  SIGN 2.
έν-νοια 2 S
  THINK 12.2:
έν-νομος 2 S
  LAW 3:
έν-νυχα 1
  NIGHT 1. b)
έν-οικέω 6 S
  STAY 6.2:, 3:
έν-ορκίζω 1
  PROMISE 5.4:
ένότης 2
  NUMBERS 3.1:e)
έν-οχλέω 2 S
  LABOUR 4.
έν-οχος 10 S
  9 ACCUSE 2.
  1 OBEY 4.
έν-ταλμα 3 S
  ORDER 5. b)
έν-ταφιάζω 2 S
  BURY 3.
έν-ταφιασμός 2
  BURY 3.
έν-τέλλομαι 16 S
  ORDER 5.
έν-τευξις 2 S
  ASK 9.1:
έν-τιμος 5 S
  3 HONOUR 1.1:
  3 PRECIOUS 1.
έν-τολή 67 S
  ORDER 5.
έν-τόπιος 1
  PLACE 1. a)
έντός 2 S
  INSIDE 1.3:, 4:
έν-τρέπω 9 S
  3 DISHONOUR 3.
  6 HONOUR 2.
έν-τρέφω 1
  EAT 3.2:a)
έν-τρομος 3 S
  FEAR 7.2:
έν-τροπή 2 S
  DISHONOUR 3.
έν-τρυφάω 1 S
  LUXURY 1.1:
έν-τυγχάνω 5 S
  ASK 9.
έν-τυλίσσω 3
  2 CLOTHING 1.7:
  1 ROUND 8.4:
έν-τυπόω 1
  IMAGE 4.1:
έν-υβρίζω 1
  CURSE 2.8:a)
έν-υπνιάζομαι 2 S
  SLEEP 1.7:
έν-ύπνιον 1 S
  SLEEP 1.7:
έν-ώπιον 94 S
  BEFORE 2.1:
έν-ωτίζομαι 1 S
  HEAR 1.2:
έξ 10 S
  NUMBERS 8.

έξ-αγγέλλω 1 S
  TELL 1.1:
έξ-αγοράζω 4 S
  3 BUY 1.2:b)
  2 GAIN 3.
έξ-άγω 12 S
  TAKE 8.1:a), b)
έξ-αιρέω 8 S
  6 SAVE 2.1:
  3 TAKE 4.1:
έξ-αίρω 1 S
  DRIVE 3.
έξ-αιτέω 1
  ASK 6.2:
έξ-αίφνης 5 S
  NOW 10.1:
έξ-ακολουθέω 3 S
  ACCOMPANY 4.3:
έξ-α-λείφω 5 S
  WIPE 2.
έξ-άλλομαι 1 S
  RUSH 3.1:
έξ-ανά-στασις 1
  RISE 2.2:
έξ-ανα-τέλλω 2 S
  GROW 6.
έξ-αν-ίστημι 3 S
  RISE 2.3:, 4:
έξ-απατάω 6 S
  DECEIVE 1.3:
έξάπινα 1
  NOW 10.3:
έξ-α-πορέω 2 S
  CONFUSION 2.
έξ-απο-στέλλω 13 S
  SEND 1.1:, 2:, 3:,
έξ-αρτίζω 2 S
  END 2.
έξ-αστράπτω 1 S
  SHINE 6.
έξ-αυτής 6
  NOW 8.
έξ-εγείρω 2 S
  RISE 1.3:, 4:
έξ-ειμι 4 S
  LEAVE 1.3:a)
έξ-έλκω 1 S
  DRAG 2.2:
έξ-έραμα 1
  SPIT 3.1:
έξ-ερευνάω 1 S
  SEEK 2.1:
έξ-έρχομαι 222 S
  LEAVE 1.
έξ-εστιν 32 S
  ALLOW 2.
έξ-ετάζω 3 S
  ASK 2.1:
έξ-ηγέομαι 6 S
  SAY 5.1:
έξης 5 S
  ACCOMPANY 6.
έξ-ηχέω 1 S
  VOICE 4.
έξις 1 S
  CUSTOM 2.
έξ-ίστημι 17 S
  15 ASTONISHED 3.1:
  2 FOOLISH 7.
έξ-ισχύω 1
  POWER 2.1:d)
έξ-οδος 3 S
  LEAVE 11.
έξ-ολεθρεύω 1 S
  DESTROY 13. d)
έξ-ομο-λογέω 10 S
  1 AGREEMENT 5.
  9 TELL 2.1:, 2:
έξ-ορκίζω 1
  PROMISE 5.4:
έξ-ορκιστής 1
  PROMISE 5.4:
έξ-ορύσσω 2 S
  1 BREAK 4.2:
  1 DIG 1.2:
έξ-ου-δ-ενέω 1 S
  DESPISE 1.2:
έξ-ου-θ-ενέω 11 S
  DESPISE 1.2:

έξ-ουσία 103 S
  13 ALLOW 2.
  93 RULE 4.
έξ-ουσιάζω 4 S
  RULE 4. a)
έξ-οχή 1 S
  GREAT 3.
έξ-υπνίζω 1 S
  SLEEP 3.
έξ-υπνος 1
  SLEEP 3.
έξω S
  (28) INSIDE 2.
έξωθεν 12 S
  INSIDE 2.
έξ-ωθέω 2 S
  DRIVE 4.2:
έξώτερος 3 S
  INSIDE 2.2:
έοικα 2 S
  IMAGE 1.3:
έορτάζω 1 S
  FESTIVAL 1.
έορτή 27 S
  FESTIVAL 1.
έπ-αγγελία 52 S
  PROMISE 1.
έπ-αγγέλλομαι 15 S
  13 PROMISE 1.
  2 TELL 1.3:
έπ-άγγελμα 2
  PROMISE 1.1:
έπ-άγω 3 S
  TAKE 8.1:d)
έπ-αγωνίζομαι 1
  FIGHT 3.1:
έπ-αθροίζομαι 1
  GATHERING 5.
έπ-αινέω 6 S
  BLESS 1.2:
έπ-αινος 11 S
  BLESS 1.2:
έπ-αίρω 19
  8 RISE 6.
  7 SEE 1.2:
  4 VOICE 1.1:e)
έπ-αισχύνομαι 11 S
  DISHONOUR 2.
έπ-αιτέω 2 S
  ASK 6.3:
έπ-ακολουθέω 4 S
  ACCOMPANY 4.1:, 3:
έπ-ακούω 1 S
  HEAR 2.2:
έπ-ακροάομαι 1
  HEAR 3.
έπ-άναγκες 1
  MUST 5.
έπ-αν-άγω 3 S
  2 SHIP 2.
  1 TURN 5.
έπ-ανα-μιμνήσκω 1
  REMEMBER 1.1:
έπ-ανα-παύω 2 S
  REST 3.
έπ-αν-έρχομαι 2 S
  COME 1.4:d)
έπ-αν-ίστημι 2 S
  RISE 2.4:
έπ-αν-όρθωσις 1 S
  STRAIGHT 1.1:
έπ-άνω S
  (5) ABOVE 1.3:, 4:
  (2) GREAT 9.2:
έπ-άρατος 1
  CURSE 1.1:
έπ-αρκέω 3 S
  HELP 7.
έπ-αρχεία 1
  RULE 3.7:
έπ-άρχειος 1
  RULE 3.7:
έπ-αυλις 1 S
  STAY 13.2:
έπ-αύριον 17 S
  TIME 5.2:
έπ-αφρίζω 1
  SPIT 2.
έπ-εγείρω 2 S
  RISE 1.4:

ἴχνος *3 S*
 STREET 2.2:a)
ἰῶτα *1*
 WRITE 5.6:

K

καθ-αίρεσις *3 S*
 DESTROY 2.
καθ-αιρέω *9 S*
 4 COME DOWN 3.
 4 DESTROY 2.
 1 TAKE 4.1:
καθαίρω *1 S*
 PURE 2.
καθ-άπερ *S*
 (3) SAME 4.
καθ-άπτω *1*
 JOIN 4. a)
καθαρίζω *31 S*
 PURE 2.
καθαρισμός *7 S*
 PURE 2.
καθαρός *27 S*
 PURE 2.
καθαρότης *1 S*
 PURE 2.
καθ-έδρα *3 S*
 SIT 1.1:a), 2:
καθ-έζομαι *7 S*
 SIT 1.1:a), 2:
καθ-εξῆς *5*
 ACCOMPANY 6.
καθ-εύδω *22 S*
 SLEEP 1.2:
καθ-ηγητής *2*
 RULE 6.2:a)
καθ-ήκω *2 S*
 FITTING 1.1:
κάθ-ημαι *91 S*
 89 SIT 2.
 5 STAY 7.
καθ-ημερινός *1 S*
 TIME 4.1:g)
καθ-ίζω *46 S*
 43 SIT 1.1:, 2:
 5 STAY 2.
καθ-ίημι *4 S*
 COME DOWN 4.1:
καθ-ίστημι *21 S*
 20 PUT 2.1:, 2:, 3:
 1 TAKE 10.
καθ-όλου *1 S*
 WHOLE 1.3:
καθ-οπλίζω *1 S*
 WAR 6.1:
καθ-οράω *1 S*
 SEE 2.3:a)
καθ-ώς *S*
 (22) SAME 4.
καθ-ώσπερ *1*
 SAME 4.
καινός *42 S*
 NEW 1.2:a)
καινότης *2 S*
 NEW 1.2:a)
καιρός *86 S*
 TIME 2.1:
καίω *12 S*
 FIRE 1.2:a), b), d)
κακία *11 S*
 EVIL 1.1:
κακο-ήθεια *1 S*
 EVIL 1.1:
κακο-λογέω *4 S*
 CURSE 1.2:
κακο-πάθεια *1 S*
 SUFFER 1.2:
κακο-παθέω *3 S*
 SUFFER 1.2:
κακο-ποιέω *4 S*
 EVIL 1.2:
κακο-ποιός *3 S*
 EVIL 1.2:
κακός *50 S*
 EVIL 1.1:, 2:
κακ-οῦργος *4 S*
 EVIL 1.2:

κακ-ουχέω *2 S*
 EVIL 1.3:
κακόω *6 S*
 EVIL 1.2:, 3:
κακῶς *16 S*
 1 CURSE 1.2:a)
 4 EVIL 1.1:
 11 WEAKEN 2.5:
κάκωσις *1 S*
 EVIL 1.3:
καλάμη *1 S*
 FARM 4.1:
κάλαμος *12 S*
 11 TREE 8.
 1 WRITE 5.5:
καλέω *146 S*
 NAME 5.1:, 5:, 6:
καλλι-έλαιος *1*
 FARM 5.
καλο-διδάσκαλος *1*
 1 GOOD 1. a)
 1 TEACHING 1.1:c)
καλο-ποιέω *1*
 GOOD 1. b)
καλός *102 S*
 101 GOOD 2.
 1 ISLAND 3:
κάλυμμα *4 S*
 COVER 1.1:
καλύπτω *8 S*
 COVER 1.1:, 2:
καλῶς *37 S*
 1 BLESS 1.3:
 35 GOOD 2.a), b), e)
 1 SAVE 8.1:
κάμηλος *6 S*
 ANIMALS 2.4:
κάμινος *4 S*
 FIRE 2.2:
καμ-μύω *2 S*
 SHUT 2.
κάμνω *2 S*
 WEAKEN 2.6:
κάμπτω *4 S*
 WORSHIP 5.
καναναῖος *2*
 ZEAL 1.1:
κανών *4 S*
 ORDER 8.
καπηλεύω *1*
 BUY 3.
καπνός *13 S*
 FIRE 5.1:
καρδία *157 S*
 HEART
καρδιο-γνώστης *2*
 2 HEART 1:a)
 2 KNOW 1.1:
καρπός *66 S*
 FRUIT 2.1:
καρπο-φορέω *8 S*
 8 FRUIT 2.1:
 8 TAKE 6.6:
καρπο-φόρος *1 S*
 1 FRUIT 2.1:
 1 TAKE 6.6:
καρτερέω *1 S*
 STAY 10.
κάρφος *6 S*
 TREE 7.2:
κατά *S*
 (2) ALONE 2:b)
 (5) BLAME 6.
 (1) CURSE 2.4:
 (20) ENEMY 8.
 (1) GREAT 3.
 (17) HAVE 2.3:
 (5) MATTER 3.
 (3) SAME 4.
 (6) SLEEP 1.6:
 (1) WITH 3.2:
κατα-βαίνω *82 S*
 COME DOWN 1.
κατα-βάλλω *2 S*
 1 PUT 3.1:
 1 THROW 1.1:
κατα-βαρέω *1*
 GREAT 13.
κατα-βαρύνω *1 S*
 GREAT 13.

κατά-βασις *1 S*
 COME DOWN 1. e)
κατα-βιβάζω *2 S*
 COME DOWN 1. b)
κατα-βολή *11 S*
 PUT 3.2:
κατα-βραβεύω *1*
 PAY 7.2:
κατ-αγγελεύς *1 S*
 TELL 1.1:
κατ-αγγέλλω *18*
 TELL 1.1:, 2:
κατα-γελάω *3 S*
 MOCK 5. a)
κατα-γινώσκω *3 S*
 JUDGE 2.
κατ-άγνυμι *4 S*
 BREAK 1.1:
κατα-γράφω *1 S*
 WRITE 1. g)
κατ-άγω *9 S*
 TAKE 8.1:a), c), e), 3:c)
κατ-αγωνίζομαι *1*
 FIGHT 3.2:
κατα-δέω *1 S*
 ROPE 8. a)
κατά-δηλος *1*
 SHOW 3.1:
κατα-δικάζω *5 S*
 JUDGE 1.2:
κατα-δίκη *1 S*
 JUDGE 1.2:
κατα-διώκω *1 S*
 SEEK 3.1:
κατα-δουλόω *2 S*
 SLAVE 3.3:
κατα-δυναστεύω *2 S*
 POWER 6.
κατά-θεμα *1*
 CURSE 1.3:
κατα-θεματίζω *1*
 CURSE 1.3:
κατ-αισχύνω *13 S*
 DISHONOUR 2.
κατα-καίω *13 S*
 FIRE 1.2:a)
κατα-καλύπτω *3 S*
 COVER 1.1:
κατα-καυχάομαι *4 S*
 BOAST 1.
κατά-κειμαι *12 S*
 SIT 4.1:, 2:
κατα-κλάω *2 S*
 BREAK 1.5:a)
κατα-κλείω *2 S*
 KEEP 5.
κατα-κληρο-νομέω *1 S*
 INHERIT
κατα-κλίνω *5 S*
 SIT 3.1:
κατα-κλύζω *1 S*
 RIVER 2.4:
κατα-κλυσμός *4 S*
 RIVER 2.4:
κατ-ακολουθέω *2 S*
 ACCOMPANY 4.2:
κατα-κόπτω *1 S*
 CUT 1.1:a)
κατα-κρημνίζω *1 S*
 THROW 4.
κατά-κριμα *3*
 JUDGE 3.2:
κατα-κρίνω *18 S*
 JUDGE 3.2:
κατά-κρισις *2 S*
 JUDGE 3.2:
κατα-κύπτω *1 S*
 LEAN 3.1:
κατα-κυριεύω *4 S*
 MASTER 2. h)
κατα-λαλέω *5 S*
 CURSE 2.4:
κατα-λαλιά *2 S*
 CURSE 2.4:
κατά-λαλος *1*
 CURSE 2.4:
κατα-λαμβάνω *15 S*
 5 KNOW 5.
 12 TAKE 1.2:, 5:, 7:

κατα-λέγω *1 S*
 WRITE 3. b)
κατα-λείπω *24 S*
 LEAVE 8.1:, 2:, 3:
κατα-λιθάζω *1*
 STONE 4.
κατ-αλλαγή *4 S*
 PEACE 2.
κατ-αλλάσσω *6 S*
 PEACE 2.
κατά-λοιπος *1 S*
 LEAVE 8.4:
κατά-λυμα *3 S*
 STAY 15.
κατα-λύω *17 S*
 15 DESTROY 1.
 2 STAY 15.
κατα-μανθάνω *1 S*
 THINK 13.
κατα-μαρτυρέω *3 S*
 WITNESS 1:
κατα-μένω *2 S*
 STAY 3.1:
κατ-αν-αλίσκω *1 S*
 DESTROY 3.
κατα-ναρκάω *3*
 GREAT 14.
κατα-νεύω *1*
 SIGN 2.
κατα-νοέω *14 S*
 9 SEE 7.
 7 THINK 12.1:
κατ-αντάω *13 S*
 COME 8.
κατά-νυξις *1 S*
 SLEEP 1.5:
κατα-νύσσω *1 S*
 DIG 2.1:b)
κατ-αξιόω *3 S*
 FITTING 4.1:b)
κατα-πατέω *5 S*
 FOOT 2. a)
κατά-παυσις *9 S*
 REST 3.
κατα-παύω *4 S*
 1 END 7.2:
 3 REST 3.
κατα-πέτασμα *6 S*
 CLOTH 2.1:
κατα-πίνω *7 S*
 EAT 10. f)
κατα-πίπτω *3 S*
 STUMBLE 5.1:, 4:
κατα-πλέω *1 S*
 SHIP 1.
κατα-πονέω *2 S*
 SUFFER 9.
κατα-ποντίζω *2 S*
 SEA 3.1:
κατ-άρα *6 S*
 CURSE 1.1:
κατ-αράομαι *5 S*
 CURSE 1.1:
κατ-αργέω *27 S*
 23 DESTROY 12.
 4 FREE 6.
κατ-αριθμέω *1 S*
 NUMBERS 1.
κατ-αρτίζω *13 S*
 END 2.
κατ-άρτισις *1*
 END 2. a)
κατ-αρτισμός *1*
 END 2. a)
κατα-σείω *4 S*
 SIGN 3.
κατα-σκάπτω *1 S*
 DESTROY 18.
κατα-σκευάζω *11 S*
 5 BUILDING 1.2:
 6 PREPARE 2.1:
κατα-σκηνόω *4 S*
 HOUSE 2.
κατα-σκήνωσις *2 S*
 HOUSE 2. b)
κατα-σκιάζω *1*
 SHADOW 1:
κατα-σκοπέω *1 S*
 SEE 13.1:

λόγχη *1 S*
　WAR 6.7:
λοιδορέω *4 S*
　CURSE 2.2:
λοιδορία *3 S*
　CURSE 2.2:
λοίδορος *2 S*
　CURSE 2.2:
λοιμός *2 S*
　WEAKEN 3.5:
λοιπός *55 S*
　LEAVE 8.3:, 4:, 5:
λουτρόν *2 S*
　WATER 3.1:a)
λούω *6 S*
　WATER 3.1:
λύκος *6 S*
　ANIMALS 2.3:
λυμαίνομαι *1 S*
　DESTROY 9.
λυπέω *26 S*
　MOURN 2.
λύπη *16 S*
　MOURN 2.
λύσις *1 S*
　FREE 1.1:c)
λυσι-τελέω *1 S*
　GOOD 7.
λύτρον *2 S*
　FREE 1.3:
λυτρόω *3 S*
　FREE 1.3:
λύτρωσις *3 S*
　FREE 1.3:
λυτρωτής *1 S*
　FREE 1.3:
λυχνία *12 S*
　SHINE 3.
λύχνος *14 S*
　SHINE 3.
λύω *42 S*
　13 DESTROY 1.
　30 FREE 1.1:

μ

μαγεία *1*
　MAGIC 3.
μαγεύω *1*
　MAGIC 3.
μάγος *6 S*
　MAGIC 3.
μαθητεύω *4*
　HEAR 5.2:a)
μαθητής *261*
　HEAR 5.2:
μαθήτρια *1*
　HEAR 5.2:a)
μαίνομαι *5 S*
　FOOLISH 6.
μακαρίζω *2 S*
　REJOICE 11.
μακάριος *50 S*
　REJOICE 11.
μακαρισμός *3*
　REJOICE 11.
μάκελλον *1*
　BUY 4.
μακράν *10 S*
　DISTANCE 1.1:
μακρόθεν *14 S*
　DISTANCE 1.1:
μακρο-θυμέω *10 S*
　BEAR WITH 6.
μακρο-θυμία *14 S*
　BEAR WITH 6.
μακρο-θύμως *1*
　BEAR WITH 6.2:
μακρός *4 S*
　2 DISTANCE 1.1:
　2 LONG 1.
μακρο-χρόνιος *1 S*
　1 LONG 1.
　1 TIME 1.
μαλακία *3 S*
　WEAKEN 2.2:
μαλακός *4 S*
　HARDNESS 6.

μάλιστα *12 S*
　GREAT 8.2:
μᾶλλον *81 S*
　GREAT 5.5:, 8.
μάμμη *1*
　FATHER 3.
μαμωνᾶς *4*
　MONEY 3.
μανθάνω *25 S*
　HEAR 5.1:
μανία *1*
　FOOLISH 6.
μάννα *4 S*
　EAT 4.4.
μαντεύομαι *2 S*
　MAGIC 5.
μαραίνομαι *1 S*
　WEAKEN 1.4:
μαράνα θά *1*
　1 COME 2.
　1 MASTER 2.1:b)
μαρὰν ἀθά *1*
　1 COME 2.
　1 MASTER 2.1:b)
μαργαρίτης *9*
　STONE 6.
μάρμαρος *1 S*
　STONE 5.
μαρτυρέω *76 S*
　WITNESS 1:
μαρτυρία *37 S*
　WITNESS 1:
μαρτύριον *20 S*
　WITNESS 1:
μαρτύρομαι *5 S*
　WITNESS
μάρτυς *35 S*
　WITNESS 1:
μασάομαι *1 S*
　MOUTH 4.2:b)
μαστιγόω *7 S*
　BEAT 12.
μαστίζω *1 S*
　BEAT 12.
μάστιξ *6 S*
　2 BEAT 12.
　4 WEAKEN 2.3:
μαστός *3 S*
　BODY 5.2:
ματαιο-λογία *1*
　1 EMPTY 2.
　1 SAY 2.4:c)
ματαιο-λόγος *1*
　1 EMPTY 2.
　1 SAY 2.4:c)
μάταιος *6 S*
　EMPTY 2.
ματαιότης *3 S*
　EMPTY 2.
ματαιόω *1 S*
　EMPTY 2.
μάτην *2 S*
　EMPTY 2.
μάχαιρα *29 S*
　WAR 6.5:
μάχη *4 S*
　QUARREL 1.
μάχομαι *4 S*
　QUARREL 1.
μεγαλεῖος *1 S*
　GREAT 1. a)
μεγαλειότης *3 S*
　GREAT 1. a), f)
μεγαλο-πρεπής *1 S*
　GREAT 1. a)
μεγαλύνω *8 S*
　GREAT 1. a), b), d), e)
μεγάλως *1 S*
　GREAT 1. f)
μεγαλωσύνη *3 S*
　GREAT 1. a)
μέγας *245 S*
　GREAT 1. a)
μέγεθος *1 S*
　GREAT 1. a)
μεγιστάν *3 S*
　GREAT 1. b)
μεθ-ερμηνεύω *8 S*
　INTERPRET 1.2:

μέθη *3 S*
　EAT 12.4:
μεθ-ίστημι *5 S*
　3 LEAVE 5.2:, 3:
　2 PUT 2.4:
μεθ-οδεία *2*
　DECEIVE 1.2:
μεθύσκω *5 S*
　EAT 12.4:
μέθυσος *2 S*
　EAT 12.4:
μεθύω *5 S*
　EAT 12.4:
μέλαν *2 S*
　WRITE 5.5:
μέλας *3 S*
　BLACK 2.
μελετάω *2 S*
　CARE 1.
μέλι *4 S*
　EAT 4.5:a)
μελίσσιος *1*
　BIRDS 3.2:
μέλλω *S*
　(1) IDLE 6.
　(19) NOW 6.
μέλος *35 S*
　BODY 4.
μέλω *10 S*
　CARE 1.
μεμβράνα *1*
　WRITE 5.2:
μέμφομαι *2 S*
　BLAME 2.
μεμψί-μοιρος *1*
　1 BLAME 2.
　1 CUT 3.1:a)
μένω *120 S*
　2 HOPE 2.2:
　118 STAY 3.
μερίζω *14 S*
　CUT 3.1:a), c)
μέριμνα *6 S*
　CARE 2.1:
μεριμνάω *19 S*
　CARE 2.1:
μερίς *5 S*
　CUT 3.1:a), d)
μερισμός *2 S*
　CUT 3.1:a), b)
μεριστής *1*
　CUT 3.1:a)
μέρος *41 S*
　CUT 3.1:
μεσ-ημβρία *2 S*
　1 EAST 4.2:
　2 MID 2:
　2 TIME 4.1:f)
μεσιτεύω *1*
　1 FIRM 8.
　1 MID 3:
μεσίτης *6 S*
　MID 4:
μεσο-νύκτιον *4 S*
　4 MID 2:
　4 NIGHT 1. c)
μέσος *59 S*
　MID 1:, 2:
μεσό-τοιχον *1*
　FORT 2.
μεσ-ουράνημα *3*
　3 HEAVEN 1.
　3 MID 1:b)
μεσόω *1 S*
　MID 1:b)
μεσσίας *2*
　JESUS CHRIST 1.1:
μεστός *9 S*
　FILL 2.
μεστόω *1*
　FILL 2.
μετά
　(2) STAY 6.4:
　(164) WITH 1.
μετα-βαίνω *12 S*
　LEAVE 13.1:
μετα-βάλλω *1 S*
　REPENT 3.
μετ-άγω *2 S*
　TAKE 8.2:

μετα-δίδωμι *5 S*
　GIVE 1.4:
μετά-θεσις *3 S*
　2 CHANGE 1.
　1 TAKE 5.
μετ-αίρω *2 S*
　LEAVE 12.
μετα-καλέω *4 S*
　NAME 5.6:
μετα-κινέω *1 S*
　SHAKE 5. a)
μετα-λαμβάνω *7 S*
　3 RECEIVE 1. d)
　4 TAKE 1.6:, 8:
μετά-λημψις *1*
　RECEIVE 1. d)
μετ-αλλάσσω *2 S*
　CHANGE 4.
μετα-μέλομαι *6 S*
　REPENT 1.
μετα-μορφόω *4*
　IMAGE 5.2:
μετα-νοέω *34 S*
　REPENT 2.
μετά-νοια *22 S*
　REPENT 2.
μεταξύ *S*
　(1) ACCOMPANY 3.
μετα-πέμπω *9 S*
　SEND 2.4:
μετα-στρέφω *2 S*
　CHANGE 2.
μετα-σχηματίζω *5*
　IMAGE 6.2:, 3:
μετα-τίθημι *6 S*
　2 CHANGE 1.
　1 REJECT 4.1:
　3 TAKE 5.
μετα-τρέπω *1*
　CHANGE 3.
μετ-έχω *8 S*
　SHARE 2.
μετ-εωρίζω *1 S*
　CARE 2.2:
μετ-οικεσία *4 S*
　FOREIGN 6.
μετ-οικίζω *2 S*
　FOREIGN 6.
μετ-οχή *1 S*
　SHARE 2.
μέτ-οχος *6 S*
　SHARE 2.
μετρέω *11 S*
　MEASURE 1.
μετρητής *1 S*
　MEASURE 3.3:
μετριο-παθέω *1*
　1 MEASURE 1.
　1 SUFFER 1.3:
μετρίως *1 S*
　MEASURE 1.
μέτρον *14 S*
　MEASURE 1.
μέτ-ωπον *8 S*
　FACE 2:
μη-δαμῶς *2 S*
　NOT ANY 1.2:
μη-δ-είς *89 S*
　NOT ANY 1.
μη-δέ-ποτε *1 S*
　NOT YET 2.
μη-δέ-πω *1 S*
　NOT YET 1.
μη-θ-είς *1 S*
　NOT ANY 1.2:
μῆκος *3 S*
　LONG 1.
μηκύνω *1 S*
　GROW 2.
μηλωτή *1 S*
　CLOTHING 4.1:
μήν *18 S*
　YEAR 2.
μηνύω *4 S*
　TELL 5.
μή-πω *2*
　NOT YET 1.
μηρός *1 S*
　FOOT 3.3:

πνέω 7 S
 WIND 2.4:
πνίγω 2 S
 SPIRIT 1.4:
πνικτός 3
 SPIRIT 1.4:
πνοή 2 S
 1 SPIRIT 1.1:f)
 1 WIND 2.4:
ποδ-ήρης 1 S
 CLOTHING 2.5:
πόθεν S
 (22) WHERE FROM
ποιέω 568 S
 520 DO 3.
 9 EVIL 1.2:
 25 GOOD 1. c), 2. b), 4. a)
 2 PEACE 1.
 5 REMEMBER 1.1:
 1 STAY 12.
 4 WAR 1.
ποίημα 2 S
 DO 3.1:
ποίησις 1 S
 DO 3.8:
ποιητής 6 S
 DO 3.8:, 11:
ποικίλος 10 S
 OTHER 5.1:
ποιμαίνω 11 S
 SHEPHERD 1.
ποιμήν 18 S
 SHEPHERD 1.
ποίμνη 5 S
 SHEPHERD 1.
ποίμνιον 5 S
 SHEPHERD 1.
πολεμέω 7 S
 WAR 1.
πόλεμος 18 S
 WAR 1.
πόλις 164 S
 12 ASIA 1.2:, 4., 6., 8., 12.
 3 CAESAREA
 47 CITY 1.1:
 2 DAMASCUS
 6 DECAPOLIS
 15 GALILEE 2., 3., 4.
 8 GREECE 2., 3., 4.
 1 ISLAND 3:
 44 JERUSALEM
 4 JUDAEA 1., 2., 4.
 10 MESOPOTAMIA 2.
 9 SAMARIA
 2 SODOM
 1 TYRE
πολιτ-άρχης 2
 RULE 3.7:
πολιτεία 2
 CITY 1.2:
πολίτευμα 1
 1 CITY 1.2:
 1 JERUSALEM 2.
πολιτεύομαι 2
 DO 6.2:
πολίτης 4 S
 CITY 1.2:
πολλάκις 18 S
 OFTEN 1.
πολλα-πλασίων 2
 GREAT 5.1:
πολυ-λογία 1 S
 1 GREAT 5.2:d)
 1 SAY 2.4:a)
πολυ-μερῶς 1
 1 CUT 3.1:g)
 1 GREAT 5.2:d)
πολυ-ποίκιλος 1
 OTHER 5.1:
πολύς 358 S
 GREAT 5.1:, 2:, 3:
πολύ-σπλαγχνος 1
 BODY 6.6:b)
πολυ-τελής 3 S
 PRECIOUS 2.
πολύ-τιμος 3
 PRECIOUS 1.
πολυ-τρόπως 1
 1 DO 6.6:b)
 1 GREAT 5.2:d)
 1 OFTEN 1.

πόμα 2 S
 EAT 10. a), b)
πονηρία 7 S
 EVIL 2.2:, 3:
πονηρός 78 S
 EVIL 2.
πόνος 4 S
 SUFFER 9.
πορεία 2 S
 GO 2.1:a), 4:
πορεύομαι 151 S
 GO 2.
πορθέω 3
 DESTROY 10.
πορισμός 2 S
 GAIN 2.
πορνεία 25 S
 IMMORALITY 1.
πορνεύω 8 S
 IMMORALITY 1.
πόρνη 12 S
 IMMORALITY 1.
πόρνος 10 S
 IMMORALITY 1.1:
πόρρω 4 S
 DISTANCE 1.2:
πόρρωθεν 2 S
 DISTANCE 1.2:
πορφύρα 4 S
 CLOTH 1.5:
πορφύρεος 4 S
 CLOTH 1.5:
πορφυρό-πωλις 1
 1 CLOTH 1.5:
 1 BUY 2.2:
ποσάκις 3 S
 OFTEN 3.
πόσις 2 S
 EAT 10. a), b)
ποταμός 17 S
 RIVER 1.
ποταμο-φόρητος 1
 1 RIVER 1.1:
 1 TAKE 6.1:
ποτέ S
 (18) BEFORE 1.5:
 (7) NOT YET 2.
ποτήριον 32 S
 EAT 10.
ποτίζω 15 S
 EAT 10. d), e)
πότος 1 S
 EAT 10. a)
πούς 94 S
 FOOT 1.1:a), b)
πρᾶγμα 11 S
 1 DO 5.
 11 MATTER 2.
πραγματεία 1 S
 MATTER 2.
πραγματεύομαι 1 S
 GAIN 5.
πραιτώριον 8
 HOUSE 3.
πράκτωρ 2 S
 CATCH 9.2:
πρᾶξις 6 S
 DO 5.
πρασιά 2 S
 CORNER 2.
πράσσω 39 S
 2 CATCH 9.2:
 36 DO 5.
 1 MATTER 2.
πραϋ-πάθια 1
 SWEET 2.1:a)
πραΰς 4 S
 SWEET 2.1:a)
πραΰτης 11 S
 SWEET 2.1:a)
πρέπω 7 S
 FITTING 1.2:
πρεσβεία 2 S
 SEND 3.
πρεσβεύω 2
 SEND 3.
πρεσβυτέριον 3
 NEW 2.3:d)

πρεσβύτερος 66 S
 NEW 2.3:
πρεσβύτης 3 S
 NEW 2.3:a)
πρεσβῦτις 1
 NEW 2.3:a)
πρ-ηνής 1 S
 STUMBLE 6.
πρίζω, πρίω 1 S
 CUT 1.6:
πρό S
 (3) BEFORE 1.1:
προ-άγω 20 S
 16 GO 9.1:, 14.5:
 4 TAKE 8.1:a), c)
προ-αιρέομαι 1 S
 CHOOSE 3.
προ-αιτιάομαι 1
 ACCUSE 4. a)
προ-ακούω 1
 HEAR 2.5:
προ-αμαρτάνω 2
 EVIL 7.1:
προ-αύλιον 1
 BUILDING 4. a)
προ-βαίνω 5 S
 GO 14.2:
προ-βάλλω 2 S
 1 DRIVE 4.3:
 1 GROW 7.
προ-βατικός 1 S
 ANIMALS 2.8:c)
προ-βάτιον 2 S
 ANIMALS 2.8:c)
πρό-βατον 37 S
 ANIMALS 2.8:c)
προ-βιβάζω 2 S
 DRIVE 4.4:
προ-βλέπω 1 S
 SEE 4.1:a)
προ-γίνομαι 1 S
 BE 2.2:b)
προ-γινώσκω 5 S
 KNOW 1.1:, 3:, 6:
πρό-γνωσις 2 S
 KNOW 1.1:
πρό-γονος 2 S
 FATHER 4.
προ-γράφω 4 S
 WRITE 1. a), g)
πρό-δηλος 3 S
 SHOW 3.1:
προ-δίδωμι 1 S
 GIVE 1.3:
προ-δότης 3 S
 GIVE 1.7:b), 8:
πρό-δρομος 1
 RUN 1.2:
προ-ελπίζω 1
 HOPE 1. a)
προ-εν-άρχομαι 1
 BEGINNING 1.1:
προ-επ-αγγέλλω 2
 PROMISE 1.
προ-έρχομαι 9 S
 GO 9.2:, 14.1:
προ-ετοιμάζω 2 S
 PREPARE 1.4:
προ-ευ-αγγελίζομαι 1
 TELL 1.1:
προ-έχομαι 1
 GOOD 8.
προ-ηγέομαι 1
 RULE 6.1:
πρό-θεσις 12 S
 4 GIVE 8.2:
 8 PLAN 1.
προ-θεσμία 1
 PUT 1.4:
προ-θυμία 5 S
 CARE 5.
πρό-θυμος 3 S
 CARE 5.
προ-θύμως 1
 CARE 5.
πρόϊμος 1 S
 WIND 5.4:
προ-ίστημι 8 S
 2 CARE 10.
 6 RULE 1.

προ-καλέω 1 S
 SHAKE 12.
προ-κατ-αγγέλλω 2
 TELL 1.1:
προ-κατ-αρτίζω 1
 END 2. b)
πρό-κειμαι 5 S
 PUT 6.3:
προ-κηρύσσω 1
 TELL 3.
προ-κοπή 3 S
 GO 14.4:
προ-κόπτω 6
 GO 14.4:
πρό-κριμα 1
 JUDGE 3.1:b)
προ-κυρόω 1
 FIRM 5.
προ-λαμβάνω 3 S
 1 BEFORE 1.3:
 2 TAKE 1.6:, 7:
προ-λέγω 15 S
 SAY 2.7:
προ-μαρτύρομαι 1
 WITNESS 1:
προ-μελετάω 1
 CARE 1.
προ-μεριμνάω 1
 CARE 2.1:
προ-νοέω 3 S
 CARE 12.
πρό-νοια 2 S
 CARE 12.
προ-οράω 4 S
 SEE 2.3:a), b), d)
προ-ορίζω 6
 CUT 2.5:b)
προ-πάσχω 1
 SUFFER 1.2:
προ-πάτωρ 1
 FATHER 1.3:d)
προ-πέμπω 9 S
 TAKE 11.
προ-πετής 2 S
 FOOLISH 8.
προ-πορεύομαι 2 S
 GO 9.3:
πρός S
 (2) BLAME 6.
 (6) MATTER 3.
 (5) TAKE 9.
 (16) WITH 6.
προ-σάββατον 1
 YEAR 3. b)
προσ-αγορεύω 1 S
 NAME 2.
προσ-άγω 5 S
 TAKE 8.1:a), c), d)
προσ-αγωγή 3
 NEAR 9.
προσ-αιτέω 1 S
 ASK 6.3:
προσ-αίτης 2
 ASK 6.3:
προσ-ανα-βαίνω 1
 RISE 4.7:
προσ-αν-αλίσκω 1
 PRECIOUS 5.
προσ-ανα-πληρόω 2 S
 FILL 3.1:d)
προσ-ανα-τίθεμαι 2
 1 ADD 1.1:
 1 SAY 5.10:
προσ-απ-ειλέω 1
 BLAME 8.
προσ-δαπανάω 1
 PRECIOUS 3.1:
προσ-δέομαι 1 S
 NEED 1.1:
προσ-δέχομαι 14 S
 8 HOPE 2.1:
 6 RECEIVE 2. b), c), e)
προσ-δοκάω 16 S
 HOPE 2.1:
προσ-δοκία 2 S
 HOPE 2.1:b)
προσ-εάω 1
 1 GO 14.3:
 1 NEAR 5.2:

προσ-εργάζομαι *1*
   DO 2.4:
προσ-έρχομαι *87 S*
   NEAR 7.1:, 2:, 3:
προσ-ευχή *37 S*
   ASK 8.
προσ-εύχομαι *87 S*
   ASK 8.
προσ-έχω *24 S*
   12 HEAR 4.1:
   12 KEEP 7.2:
προσ-ηλόω *1*
   CRUCIFY 1.3:a)
προσ-ήλυτος *4 S*
   NEAR 7.4:
πρόσ-καιρος *4*
   TIME 2.1:b)
προσ-καλέω *29 S*
   NAME 5.5:, 6:
προσ-καρτερέω *10 S*
   STAY 10.
προσ-καρτέρησις *1*
   STAY 10.
προσ-κεφάλαιον *1 S*
   SIT 9.
προσ-κληρόω *1*
   CUT 3.2:
προσ-κλίνω *1 S*
   LEAN 4.4:
πρόσ-κλισις *1*
   LEAN 4.5:
προσ-κολλάω *2 S*
   JOIN 5. b)
πρόσ-κομμα *6 S*
   STUMBLE 2.
προσ-κοπή *1*
   STUMBLE 2.
προσ-κόπτω *8 S*
   3 BEAT 7.1:
   5 STUMBLE 2.
προσ-κυλίω *2*
   ROUND 8.1:
προσ-κυνέω *60 S*
   WORSHIP 4.
προσ-κυνητής *1*
   WORSHIP 4.1:
προσ-λαλέω *2 S*
   SAY 1.4:b)
προσ-λαμβάνω *12 S*
   6 RECEIVE 1. c)
   6 TAKE 1.1:, 6:
πρόσ-λημψις *1*
   RECEIVE 1. c)
προσ-μένω *7 S*
   STAY 3.1:, 3:
προσ-ορμίζω *1*
   SEA 6.2:
προσ-οφείλω *1*
   MUST 4.2:
προσ-οχθίζω *2 S*
   ANGER 3.
πρόσ-πεινος *1*
   EAT 1.2:
προσ-πήγνυμι *1*
   CRUCIFY 1.3:b)
προσ-πίπτω *8 S*
   STUMBLE 5.4:, 5:
προσ-ποιέω *1 S*
   DECEIVE 4.
προσ-πορεύομαι *1 S*
   NEAR 8.
προσ-ρήγνυμι *2*
   BREAK 3.1:b)
προσ-τάσσω *7 S*
   ORDER 2.
προ-στάτις *1*
   HELP 6.
προσ-τίθημι *18 S*
   ADD 1.
προσ-τρέχω *3 S*
   RUN 1.1:
προσ-φάγιον *1*
   EAT 6. a)
πρόσ-φατος *1 S*
   NEW 1.1:
προσ-φάτως *1 S*
   NEW 1.1:

προσ-φέρω *46 S*
   1 DO 6.4:
   30 GIVE 8.1:
   17 TAKE 6.1:
προσ-φιλής *1 S*
   LOVE 2.3:d)
προσ-φορά *9 S*
   GIVE 8.1:a), b)
προσ-φωνέω *7 S*
   2 NAME 6.2:
   3 SAY 5.11:
   2 VOICE 1.2:
πρόσ-χυσις *1*
   RIVER 2.6:d)
προσ-ψαύω *1*
   TOUCH 3.
προσ-ωπο-λημπτέω *1*
   FAVOURITISM
προσ-ωπο-λήμπτης *1*
   FAVOURITISM
προσ-ωπο-λημψία *4*
   FAVOURITISM
πρόσ-ωπον *76 S*
   17 BEFORE 2.1:
   51 FACE 1:
   5 FAVOURITISM
   3 SEE 3.3:
   1 SPIRIT 2.2:b)
προ-τείνω *1 S*
   STRETCH OUT 2.2:
πρότερον *10 S*
   BEFORE 1.1:
πρότερος *1 S*
   BEFORE 1.1:
προ-τίθεμαι *3 S*
   3 PLAN 1.
   1 PUT 1.4:
προ-τρέπομαι *1 S*
   ENCOURAGE 6.
προ-τρέχω *2 S*
   RUN 1.1:
προ-ϋπ-άρχω *2 S*
   BEFORE 1.2:
πρό-φασις *6 S*
   1 ACCUSE 5.2:
   5 DECEIVE 3.2:
προ-φέρω *2 S*
   TAKE 6.5:
προ-φητεία *19 S*
   PROPHET 2:, 3:, 8:
προ-φητεύω *28 S*
   PROPHET 1:, 2:, 3:, 4:, 7:, 8:
προ-φήτης *144 S*
   PROPHET
προ-φητικός *2*
   PROPHET 2:
προ-φῆτις *2 S*
   PROPHET 4:, 9:
προ-φθάνω *1 S*
   BEFORE 1.4:
προ-χειρίζομαι *3 S*
   PUT 5.
προ-χειρο-τονέω *1*
   CHOOSE 2.
πρύμνα *3*
   SHIP 6.
πρωΐ *12 S*
   MORNING 1.2:
πρωΐα *2 S*
   MORNING 1.2:
πρωϊνός *2 S*
   MORNING 1.2:
πρῷρα *2*
   SHIP 6.
πρωτεύω *1*
   NUMBERS 3.2:a)
πρωτο-καθ-εδρία *4*
   4 NUMBERS 3.2:d)
   4 SIT 1.1:a)
πρωτο-κλισία *5*
   5 NUMBERS 3.2:d)
   5 SIT 3.1:
πρῶτον *61 S*
   NUMBERS 3.2:d)
πρῶτος *97 S*
   NUMBERS 3.2:a), b), c), d)
πρωτο-στάτης *1 S*
   RULE 1.
πρωτο-τόκια (τά) *1 S*
   BEAR 4.3:

πρωτό-τοκος *8 S*
   BEAR 4.3:
πρώτως *1*
   NUMBERS 3.2:e)
πταίω *5 S*
   STUMBLE 4.
πτέρνα *1*
   FOOT 1.3:
πτερύγιον *2 S*
   TEMPLE 4.
πτέρυξ *5 S*
   BIRDS 1.
πτηνός *1*
   BIRDS 2.1:
πτοέω *2 S*
   FEAR 5.
πτόησις *1 S*
   FEAR 5.
πτύον *2*
   FARM 11.1:
πτύρω *1*
   FEAR 5.
πτύσμα *1*
   SPIT 1.
πτύσσω *1*
   ROUND 8.3:
πτύω *3 S*
   SPIT 1.
πτῶμα *7 S*
   BODY 2.2:
πτῶσις *2 S*
   STUMBLE 5.1:, 2:
πτωχεία *3 S*
   POOR 2.
πτωχεύω *1 S*
   POOR 2.
πτωχός *34 S*
   POOR 2.
πυγμή *1 S*
   HAND 4.
πύθων *1*
   MAGIC 5.
πυκνός *3*
   OFTEN 2.
πυκτεύω *1*
   FIGHT 2.
πύλη *10 S*
   BUILDING 6.1:
πυλών *18 S*
   BUILDING 6.1:
πυνθάνομαι *11 S*
   ASK 3.
πῦρ *71 S*
   FIRE 1.1:
πυρά *2 S*
   FIRE 1.1:
πύργος *4 S*
   FORT 3.
πυρέσσω *2*
   WEAKEN 3.4:
πυρετός *6 S*
   WEAKEN 3.4:
πύρινος *1 S*
   1 BLACK 3.
   1 FIRE 1.1:
πυρόω *6 S*
   FIRE 1.1:, 7.
πυρράζω *2*
   BLACK 3.
πυρρός *2 S*
   BLACK 3.
πύρωσις *3 S*
   FIRE 1.1:
πωλέω *22 S*
   BUY 2.2:
πῶλος *12 S*
   ANIMALS 2.6:c)
πώ-ποτε *7 S*
   NOT YET 2.
πωρόω *5 S*
   HARDNESS 2.
πώρωσις *3*
   HARDNESS 2.

ρ

ῥαββί *15*
   TEACHING 1.2:
ῥαββουνί *2*
   TEACHING 1.2:a)

ῥαβδίζω *2 S*
   ROD 1.4:
ῥάβδος *12 S*
   ROD 1.
ῥαβδ-οῦχος *2*
   ROD 1.5:
ῥᾳδι-ούργημα *1*
   EVIL 14.
ῥᾳδι-ουργία *1*
   EVIL 14.
ῥακά *1*
   EMPTY 3.
ῥάκος *2 S*
   CLOTH 1.7:
ῥαντίζω *5 S*
   WATER 5.
ῥαντισμός *2 S*
   WATER 5.
ῥαπίζω *2 S*
   BEAT 8.
ῥάπισμα *3 S*
   BEAT 8.
ῥαφίς *2*
   CLOTH 3.3:a)
ῥέδη *1*
   CHARIOT 2.
ῥέω *1 S*
   RIVER 2.1:a)
ῥῆγμα *1 S*
   BREAK 3.1:b)
ῥήγνυμι, ῥήσσω *7 S*
   5 BREAK 3.1:b), c)
   2 THROW 3.
ῥῆμα *67 S*
   10 MATTER 1. a), c)
   58 SAY 2.1:, 2:a) 3:c), d) 4:a), b), c), 8:
ῥήτωρ *1*
   SAY 2.6:
ῥητῶς *1*
   SHOW 5.
ῥίζα *17 S*
   3 BEAR 6.
   14 TREE 4.
ῥιζόω *2 S*
   TREE 4.
ῥιπή *1*
   NOW 11.3:
ῥιπίζω *1 S*
   WIND 2.5:
ῥίπτω *8 S*
   THROW 2.
ῥοιζηδόν *1*
   VOICE 5.3:
ῥομφαία *7 S*
   WAR 6.6:
ῥύμη *4 S*
   STREET 1.3:
ῥύομαι *17 S*
   SAVE 2.2:
ῥυπαίνω *1*
   DEFILE 5.
ῥυπαρία *1*
   DEFILE 5.
ῥυπαρός *2 S*
   DEFILE 5.
ῥύπος *1 S*
   DEFILE 5.
ῥύσις *3 S*
   RIVER 2.1:b)
ῥυτίς *1*
   DEFILE 12.
ῥωμαϊκός *1*
   ROME
ῥωμαῖος *12 S*
   ROME
ῥωμαϊστί *1*
   ROME
ῥώννυμι *2 S*
   GREETINGS 3.

σ

σαβαχθάνι *2*
   LEAVE 8.1:
σαβαώθ *2 S*
   MASTER 2.1:a)
σαββατισμός *1*
   REST 1.

σάββατον *69 S*
    YEAR 3.
σαγήνη *1 S*
    FISH 6.2:
σαίνω *1*
    SHAKE 2.
σάκκος *4 S*
    CLOTHING 4.2:
σαλεύω *15 S*
    SHAKE 6.
σάλος *1 S*
    SEA 2.2:
σάλπιγξ *11 S*
    SING 2.5:
σαλπίζω *12 S*
    SING 2.5:
σαλπιστής *1*
    SING 2.5:
σανδάλιον *2 S*
    CLOTHING 3.
σανίς *1 S*
    TREE 7.1:
σαπρός *8*
    EVIL 10.
σάπφιρος *1 S*
    STONE 7.
σαργάνη *1*
    VESSEL 6.3:
σάρδιον *2 S*
    STONE 7.
σαρδ-όνυξ *1*
    STONE 7.
σαρκικός *7*
    FLESH 1.1:a), b)
σάρκινος *4 S*
    FLESH 1.1:b)
σάρξ *146 S*
    FLESH 1.1:
σαρόω *3*
    PURE 1.
σατανᾶς *36 S*
    DEVIL 3.
σάτον *2 S*
    MEASURE 3.4:
σβέννυμι *6 S*
    FIRE 6. a)
σεβάζομαι *1*
    WORSHIP 3.1:, 2:
σέβασμα *2 S*
    WORSHIP 3.1:, 2:
σεβαστός *3*
    CAESAR '
σέβομαι *10 S*
    WORSHIP 3.1:, 2:
σειρά *1 S*
    ROPE 9.
σεισμός *14 S*
    SHAKE 7. a)
σείω *5 S*
    SHAKE 7.
σελήνη *9 S*
    STAR 3.1:
σεληνιάζω *2*
    WEAKEN 3.10:
σεμίδαλις *1 S*
    EAT 4.3:b)
σεμνός *4 S*
    FITTING 4.2:
σεμνότης *3 S*
    FITTING 4.2:
σημαίνω *6 S*
    SIGN 1.2:
σημεῖον *77 S*
    SIGN 1.
σημειόομαι *1 S*
    SIGN 1.2:
σήμερον *41 S*
    TIME 4.1:e)
σήπω *1 S*
    DESTROY 7.
σηρικός *1*
    CLOTH 1.4:
σής *3 S*
    BIRDS 3.4:
σητό-βρωτος *1 S*
    1 BIRDS 3.4:
    1 EAT 3.1:
σθενόω *1*
    POWER 4.

σιαγών *2 S*
    HEAD 2.2:
σιγάω *10 S*
    QUIET 5.
σιγή *2 S*
    QUIET 5.
σιδήρεος *5 S*
    IRON
σίδηρος *1 S*
    IRON
σικάριος *1*
    DIE 2.6:
σίκερα *1 S*
    EAT 12.3:
σιμικίνθιον *1*
    CLOTH 2.7:
σίναπι *5*
    GARDEN 2.3:
σινδών *6 S*
    CLOTH 2.4:
σινιάζω *1*
    FARM 11.3:
σιρός *1*
    ABYSS 2.2:
σιτευτός *3 S*
    ANIMALS 2.7:c)
σιτίον *1 S*
    EAT 3.3:
σιτιστός *1*
    ANIMALS 2.7:b)
σιτο-μέτριον *1*
    1 FARM 3.3:
    1 MEASURE 1.
σῖτος *14 S*
    FARM 3.3:
σιωπάω *10 S*
    QUIET 6.
σκανδαλίζω *30 S*
    STUMBLE 3.
σκάνδαλον *15 S*
    STUMBLE 3.
σκάπτω *3 S*
    DIG 1.1:
σκάφη *3 S*
    SHIP 5.
σκέλος *3 S*
    FOOT 3.1:
σκέπασμα *1*
    CLOTHING 1.4:
σκευή *1*
    VESSEL 1.1:c)
σκεῦος *23 S*
    VESSEL 1.1:a), b), d), e)
σκηνή *20 S*
    HOUSE 2. a)
σκηνο-πηγία *1 S*
    HOUSE 2. a)
σκηνο-ποιός *1*
    1 DO 3.1:
    1 HOUSE 2. a)
σκῆνος *2 S*
    HOUSE 2. a)
σκηνόω *5 S*
    HOUSE 2. a)
σκήνωμα *3 S*
    HOUSE 2. a)
σκιά *7 S*
    SHADOW
σκιρτάω *3 S*
    RUSH 4.
σκληρο-καρδία *3 S*
    3 HARDNESS 1. a)
    3 HEART 1:b)
σκληρός *5 S*
    HARDNESS 1.
σκληρότης *1 S*
    HARDNESS 1. a)
σκληρο-τράχηλος *1 S*
    1 HARDNESS 1. a)
    1 HEAD 2.3:
σκληρύνω *6 S*
    HARDNESS 1. a)
σκολιός *4 S*
    STRAIGHT 3.
σκόλοψ *1 S*
    TREE 10.3:
σκοπέω *6 S*
    SEE 10.
σκοπός *1 S*
    END 6.

σκορπίζω *5 S*
    DISPERSE 2.1:, 2:
σκορπίος *5 S*
    SNAKE 4.1:
σκοτεινός *3 S*
    NIGHT 2.1:
σκοτία *17 S*
    NIGHT 2.1:
σκοτίζω *6 S*
    NIGHT 2.1:
σκότος *30 S*
    NIGHT 2.1:
σκοτόω *3 S*
    NIGHT 2.1:
σκύβαλον *1 S*
    DEFILE 4.
σκυθρ-ωπός *2 S*
    MOURN 10.1:
σκύλλω *4*
    LABOUR 3.
σκῦλον *1 S*
    CATCH 10.1:
σκωληκό-βρωτος *1*
    1 BIRDS 3.5:
    1 EAT 3.1:
σκώληξ *1 S*
    BIRDS 3.5:
σμαράγδινος *1*
    STONE 7.
σμάραγδος *1 S*
    STONE 7.
σμύρνα *2 S*
    SMELL 3.2:
σμυρνίζω *1*
    SMELL 3.2:
σορός *1 S*
    BURY 1.
σός *S*
    (10) BELONG TO 2.
σουδάριον *4*
    CLOTH 2.5:
σοφία *51 S*
    WISE 1.
σοφίζω *2 S*
    WISE 1. a)
σοφός *20 S*
    WISE 1.
σπαράσσω *3 S*
    SHAKE 4.
σπαργανόω *2 S*
    CLOTHING 1.6:
σπαταλάω *2 S*
    LUXURY 2.
σπάω *2 S*
    DRAG 3.1:
σπεῖρα *7 S*
    WAR 3.
σπείρω *52 S*
    FARM 3.2:a)
σπεκουλάτωρ *1*
    KEEP 3.2:
σπένδω *2 S*
    SACRIFICE 2.2:
σπέρμα *44 S*
    36 BEAR 5.
    9 FARM 3.2:a)
σπερμο-λόγος *1*
    1 FARM 3.2:a)
    1 GATHERING 9.
σπεύδω *6 S*
    2 CARE 4.
    4 RUN 3.
σπήλαιον *6 S*
    DIG 5.
σπιλάς *1*
    1 DEFILE 11.1:
    1 STUMBLE 1.
σπίλος *2*
    DEFILE 10.
σπιλόω *2 S*
    DEFILE 10.
σπλάγχνα (τά) *11 S*
    BODY 6.6:
σπλαγχνίζομαι *12 S*
    MERCY 3.
σπόγγος *3*
    SEA 7.
σποδός *3 S*
    FIRE 10.

σπορά *1 S*
    FARM 3.2:a)
σπόριμος *3 S*
    FARM 3.2:b)
σπόρος *3 S*
    FARM 3.2:a)
σπουδάζω *10 S*
    10 CARE 4.
    1 RUN 3.
σπουδαῖος *3 S*
    CARE 4.
σπουδαίως *4 S*
    4 CARE 4.
    1 RUN 3.
σπουδή *12 S*
    10 CARE 4.
    2 RUN 3.
σπυρίς *5*
    VESSEL 6.2:
στάδιον *7 S*
    6 MEASURE 2.2:
    1 RUN 2.
στάμνος *1 S*
    VESSEL 2.1:
στασιαστής *1*
    CONFUSION 6.
στάσις *9 S*
    8 CONFUSION 6.
    1 STAND 5:
στατήρ *1 S*
    MONEY 9.3:
σταυρός *27*
    CRUCIFY 1.1:
σταυρόω *46 S*
    CRUCIFY 1.1:
σταφυλή *3 S*
    FRUIT 3.2:
στάχυς *5 S*
    FARM 3.2:b)
στέγη *3 S*
    BUILDING 5.1:
στέγω *4 S*
    BEAR WITH 2.
στεῖρος *4 S*
    BEAR 11.
στέλλομαι *2 S*
    REJECT 11.1:
στέμμα *1*
    ADORN 4.2:
στεναγμός *2 S*
    MOURN 5.
στενάζω *6 S*
    MOURN 5.
στενός *3 S*
    LITTLE 9.
στενο-χωρέω *3 S*
    3 LITTLE 9.
    1 SUFFER 3.
στενο-χωρία *4 S*
    SUFFER 3.
στερεός *4 S*
    FIRM 2.1:
στερεόω *3 S*
    FIRM 2.1:
στερέωμα *1 S*
    FIRM 2.1:
στέφανος *18 S*
    ADORN 4.
στεφανόω *3 S*
    ADORN 4.1:
στῆθος *5 S*
    BODY 5.1:
στήκω *11 S*
    STAND 1:, 5:
στηριγμός *1*
    FIRM 2.2:a)
στηρίζω *14 S*
    FIRM 2.2:
στιβάς *1*
    TREE 3.3:
στίγμα *1*
    IMAGE 3.
στιγμή *1 S*
    NOW 11.2:
στίλβω *1 S*
    SHINE 7.
στοά *4 S*
    BUILDING 3.2:
στοιχεῖον *7 S*
    ELEMENT

Index to Proper Names

List of Greek Roots

α

ἀγάπη
ἄγγελος
ἅγιος
ἀγκών
ἄγνυμι
ἀγορά
ἀγρός
ἄγχω
ἄγω
ἄξιος
ᾄδω
αἶνος
αἱρέω
αἴρω
αἰτέω
ἄκρος
ἀλέω
ἁλίσκομαι
ἄλλος
ἀλοάω
ἅλς
ἁμαρτάνω
ἄμπελος
ἀμφί
ἀνάγκη
ἀνήρ
ἀντί
ἄνω
1. ἅπτω
2. ἅπτω
ἀραρίσκω
   ἀρέσκω
ἀριθμός
ἀριστερός
ἅρμα
ἄρτι
ἀρκέω
ἄρχω
ἀστήρ
αὐγή
αὐλή

autός (heading)

αὐτός
αὔω

β

βαίνω
βάλλω
βάπτω
βαρύς
βιβρώσκω
βίος
   ζάω
   ὑγιής
βοή
   βοη-θέω
βόσκω
βούλομαι
βραβεύω
βρέχω
βυθός

γ

γέλως
γῆ
γίνομαι
γινώσκω
γλυκύς
γλῶσσα-
γυμνός

δ

δαίμων
δάκτυλος
δαμάζω
δείκνυμι
   δίκη
δεξιός
δέομαι
δέρω
δέχομαι
   δοκέω
   δόξα
δέω
δῆμος
δίδωμι
δῖος

(δ continued)

δόμος
   δεσπότης
δράσσομαι
δύναμις
δύο
δύω

ε

ἕδος
ἔθω
1. εἴκω*
2. εἴκω
εἰλέω
εἰμί
εἶμι
εἷς
ἐκ
ἑκατόν
ἐκεῖνος
ἐλαία
ἐλαύνω
ἔλεγχος
ἐν
ἕννυμι
ἔργον
ἐρέω
ἔρημος
ἐρύω
ἔρχομαι
   εἶμι
   ἐλεύσομαι
ἐσθίω
   φάγος
εὐθύς
εὔχομαι
ἔχω

ζ

ζέω
ζυγός
ζώννυμι

η

ἡγέομαι
ἡδύς
ἥκω

(η continued)

ἡλίκος
ἡμέρα
ἥμισυς
ἦχος

θ

θεάομαι
θέλω
θεραπεύω
θέρος
θῆλυς
θήρ
θνήσκω
θροῦς
1. θύω
2. θύω
   θυμός

ι

ἴδιος
ἱερός
ἵημι
ἱκνέομαι
   ἱκανός
   ἱκέτης
ἱλάσκομαι
ἰός
ἵστημι
ἰσχύς

κ

καίω
κακός
κάλαμος
καλέω
καλός
κάμνω
κάμπτω
κατά
κεῖμαι
κείρω
κέλομαι
κενός
κεντέω

(κ continued)

κέραμος
κεράννυμι
κέρας
κεφαλή
κλάω
κλείω
κλίνω
κλύδων
κόκκος
κολάζω
κόμη
κονία
κόπτω
κορβᾶν
κόσμος
κράζω
κράτος
κρεμάζω
κρίνω
κτάομαι
κύπτω
κύριος
κύω

λ

λαλέω
λαμβάνω
λανθάνω
λαός
λατρεύω
1. λέγω
   ἐρῶ
   εἶπον
2. λέγω
3. λέγω
λεία
λείπω
λέπω
λευκός
λίβανος
λιμήν
λίπος
λύω

μ

μακρός
μαλακός
μάλα
μάστιξ
μεθύω
μέλας
μέλι
μέλω
μένος
   μανθάνω
   μιμνήσκομαι
   ? μάντις
μένω
μέσος
μετά
μέτρον
μήτηρ
μῦθος
μύω
μῶμος
μωρός

ν

νέμω
νέος
νεύω
νίπτω
νοῦς
νύσσω

ο

ὁδός
ὄζω
οἰκέω
οἷος
ὀλίγος
ὅλος
ὄμνυμι
ὁμός
ὀνίνημι
ὄνομα
ὀξύς
ὄπις*
ὁράω
   εἶδος
   ὄψ

ὀρέγομαι
ὀρθός
ὀρμή
ὄρος
ὀρφανός
ὅσος
ὀστέον
οὐ
  μή
ὀφείλω
ὄχλος
ὄψον

π

παῖς
πάλαι
πάλιν
πᾶς
πάσχω
πατέω
παύω
πείθω
πεῖρα
πείρω
  πόρνη
πέμπω
πένομαι
πέντε
πέρι
  περισσός

πετάννυμι
πέτομαι
πήγνυμι
πιέζω
πικρός
πίμπλημι
πίμπρημι
πίναξ
πίπτω
πλάξ
πλάσσω
πλατύς
πλέω
πλησίον
πλήσσω
-πλους
πνέω
ποιέω
πόλις
πολύς
ποτέ
πούς
πράσον
πράσσω
πρέπω
πρέσβυς
πρίζω
πρό
? πρύμνα

πρός
πρῶτος
πτοέω
πῦρ

ρ

ῥάβδος
ῥέω
ῥήγνυμι
ῥίπτω
ῥώννυμι

σ

σάββατον
σάλος
σέβομαι
σείω
σελήνη
σήπω
σθένος
σῖτος
σκάπτω
σκέπτομαι
σκεῦος
σκορπίος
σκῦλον
σοφός
σπάω

σπεῖρα
σπείρω
σπένδω
στέγω
στείχω
στέλλω
στερεός
στίζω
στόμα
στορέννυμι
στρέφω
στυγέω
σῦκον
συλάω
σφάλλω
σχολή
σῷος

τ

τάσσω
τείρω
τέλος
τέμνω
τέσσαρες
τηρέω
τίθημι
τίκτω
τιμή
τλάω

τόπος
τράχηλος
τρεῖς
τρέπω
τρέφω
τρέχω
  δρόμος
τυγχάνω
τύπτω
τύφω

υ

ὕδωρ
ὕλη
ὑπέρ
ὑπό
ὕπνος
ὕστερος

φ

φαίνω
φέρω
  ὄγκος
φημί
φίλος
φλύω
φόνος
φρήν
φύρομαι
φύλαξ

φυσάω
φύω
φωνή

χ

χαίρω
χαλκός
χάραξ
χεῖμα
χείρ
  χόρτος
χέω
χίλιοι
χλόη
χορός
χράομαι
χρίω
χρόνος
χρυσός
χώρα

ψ

ψάλλω
ψάω
ψῆφος
ψυχή

ω

ὠθέω
ὠνέομαι
ὥρα